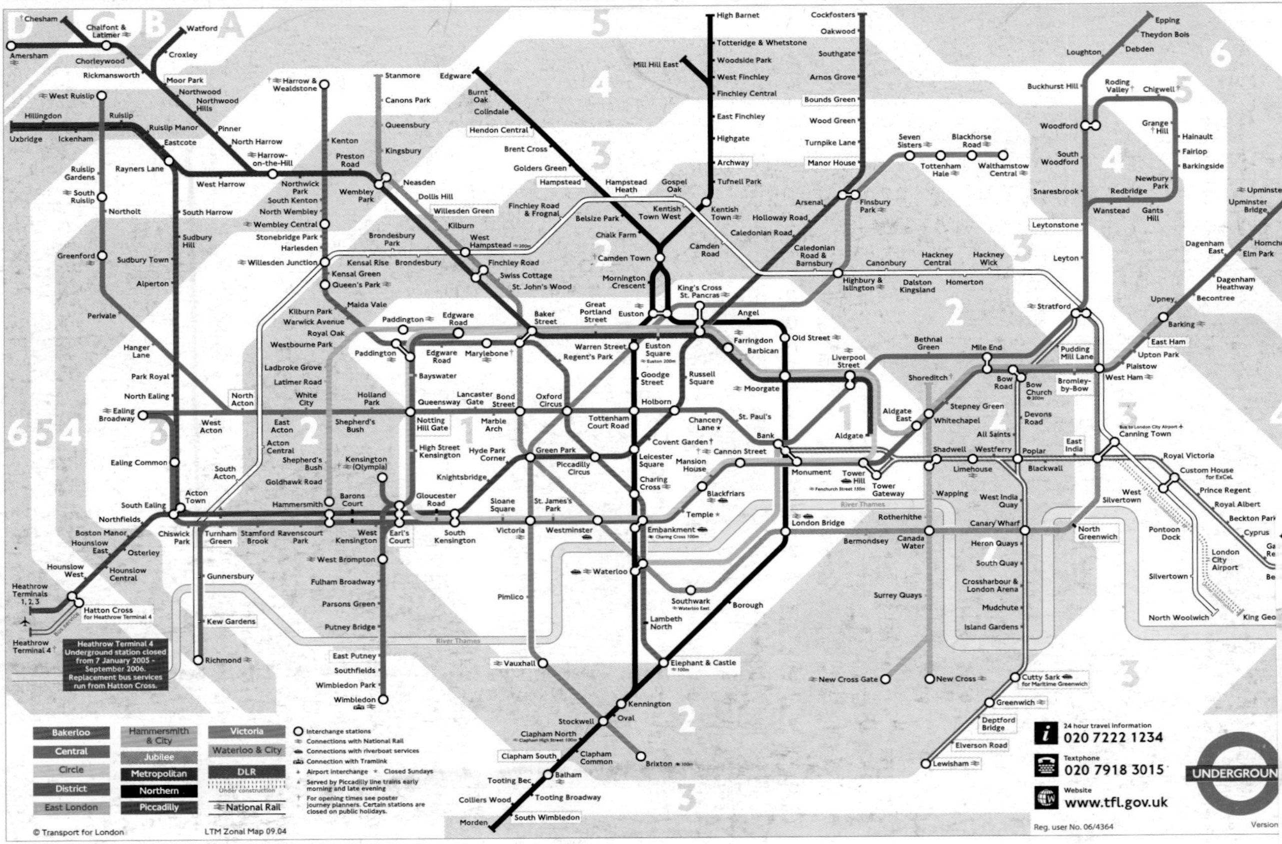

Chesham
Amersham
Chalfont & Latimer
Chorleywood
Rickmansworth
Watford
Croxley
Moor Park
Northwood
Northwood Hills
Pinner
North Harrow
Harrow-on-the-Hill
West Harrow
West Ruislip
Ruislip
Hillingdon
Uxbridge
Ickenham
Ruislip Manor
Eastcote
Rayners Lane
Ruislip Gardens
South Ruislip
Northolt
Greenford
Perivale
Hanger Lane
Park Royal
North Ealing
Ealing Broadway
West Acton
North Acton
Ealing Common
South Ealing
Northfields
Boston Manor
Hounslow East
Hounslow Central
Hounslow West
Osterley
Heathrow Terminals 1, 2, 3
Heathrow Terminal 4
Hatton Cross
for Heathrow Terminal 4
Bus service
Heathrow Terminal 4 Underground station closed from 7 January 2005 - September 2006. Replacement bus services run from Hatton Cross.
South Harrow
Sudbury Hill
Sudbury Town
Alperton
Harrow & Wealdstone
Kenton
South Kenton
North Wembley
Wembley Central
Stonebridge Park
Harlesden
Willesden Junction
Kensal Green
Queen's Park
Northwick Park
Preston Road
Wembley Park
Stanmore
Canons Park
Queensbury
Kingsbury
Neasden
Dollis Hill
Willesden Green
Kilburn
West Hampstead
Finchley Road
Swiss Cottage
St. John's Wood
Brondesbury Park
Kensal Rise
Brondesbury
Edgware
Burnt Oak
Colindale
Hendon Central
Brent Cross
Golders Green
Hampstead
Hampstead Heath
Finchley Road & Frognal
Belsize Park
Chalk Farm
Camden Town
Kentish Town West
Gospel Oak
Mill Hill East
High Barnet
Totteridge & Whetstone
Woodside Park
West Finchley
Finchley Central
East Finchley
Highgate
Archway
Tufnell Park
Kentish Town
Camden Road
Cockfosters
Oakwood
Southgate
Arnos Grove
Bounds Green
Wood Green
Turnpike Lane
Manor House
Arsenal
Holloway Road
Caledonian Road
Caledonian Road & Barnsbury
Finsbury Park
Seven Sisters
Tottenham Hale
Blackhorse Road
Walthamstow Central
Highbury & Islington
Canonbury
Dalston Kingsland
Hackney Central
Hackney Wick
Homerton
Kilburn Park
Maida Vale
Warwick Avenue
Royal Oak
Westbourne Park
Ladbroke Grove
Latimer Road
White City
East Acton
Shepherd's Bush
Holland Park
Acton Central
South Acton
Acton Town
Chiswick Park
Turnham Green
Stamford Brook
Ravenscourt Park
Goldhawk Road
Hammersmith
Barons Court
Kensington (Olympia)
West Kensington
Earl's Court
West Brompton
Fulham Broadway
Parsons Green
Putney Bridge
East Putney
Southfields
Wimbledon Park
Wimbledon
Gunnersbury
Kew Gardens
Richmond
Paddington
Edgware Road
Marylebone
Baker Street
Bayswater
Queensway
Notting Hill Gate
Lancaster Gate
Marble Arch
Bond Street
High Street Kensington
Gloucester Road
South Kensington
Knightsbridge
Hyde Park Corner
Sloane Square
Victoria
Pimlico
Vauxhall
St. James's Park
Westminster
Green Park
Piccadilly Circus
Oxford Circus
Tottenham Court Road
Great Portland Street
Regent's Park
Warren Street
Euston
Euston Square
Euston 200m
Mornington Crescent
King's Cross St. Pancras
Goodge Street
Russell Square
Holborn
Chancery Lane
Covent Garden
Leicester Square
Charing Cross
Embankment
Charing Cross 100m
Temple
Blackfriars
Mansion House
Cannon Street
St. Paul's
Farringdon
Barbican
Angel
Old Street
Moorgate
Liverpool Street
Bank
Monument
Tower Hill
Fenchurch Street 150m
Tower Gateway
Aldgate
Aldgate East
Waterloo
Lambeth North
Southwark
Waterloo East
Borough
London Bridge
Elephant & Castle
100m
Kennington
Oval
Stockwell
Brixton
Clapham North
Clapham High Street 100m
Clapham Common
Clapham South
Balham
Tooting Bec
Tooting Broadway
Colliers Wood
South Wimbledon
Morden
River Thames
Shoreditch
Whitechapel
Stepney Green
Bethnal Green
Mile End
Bow Road
Bow Church
200m
Bromley-by-Bow
Pudding Mill Lane
Stratford
Devons Road
All Saints
Shadwell
Limehouse
Westferry
Poplar
East India
Blackwall
Wapping
Rotherhithe
Canada Water
Bermondsey
Surrey Quays
New Cross Gate
New Cross
West India Quay
Canary Wharf
Heron Quays
South Quay
Crossharbour & London Arena
Mudchute
Island Gardens
Cutty Sark
for Maritime Greenwich
Greenwich
Deptford Bridge
Elverson Road
Lewisham
North Greenwich
Canning Town
Bus to London City Airport
West Silvertown
Royal Victoria
Custom House
for ExCeL
Prince Regent
Royal Albert
Beckton Park
Cyprus
Pontoon Dock
London City Airport
Silvertown
North Woolwich
King Geo
Ga
Re
Be
West Ham
Plaistow
Upton Park
East Ham
Barking
Upney
Becontree
Dagenham Heathway
Dagenham East
Elm Park
Hornchurch
Upminster Bridge
Upminster
Leyton
Leytonstone
Wanstead
Redbridge
Gants Hill
Newbury Park
Barkingside
Fairlop
Hainault
Grange Hill
Chigwell
Roding Valley
Woodford
South Woodford
Snaresbrook
Buckhurst Hill
Loughton
Debden
Theydon Bois
Epping
A
B
C
D
1
2
3
4
5
6
654
Bakerloo
Central
Circle
District
East London
Hammersmith & City
Jubilee
Metropolitan
Northern
Piccadilly
Victoria
Waterloo & City
DLR
Under construction
National Rail
Interchange stations
Connections with National Rail
Connections with riverboat services
Connection with Tramlink
Airport interchange
Closed Sundays
Served by Piccadilly line trains early morning and late evening
For opening times see poster journey planners. Certain stations are closed on public holidays.
© Transport for London
LTM Zonal Map 09.04
24 hour travel information
020 7222 1234
Textphone
020 7918 3015
Website
www.tfl.gov.uk
Reg. user No. 06/4364
UNDERGROUND
Version

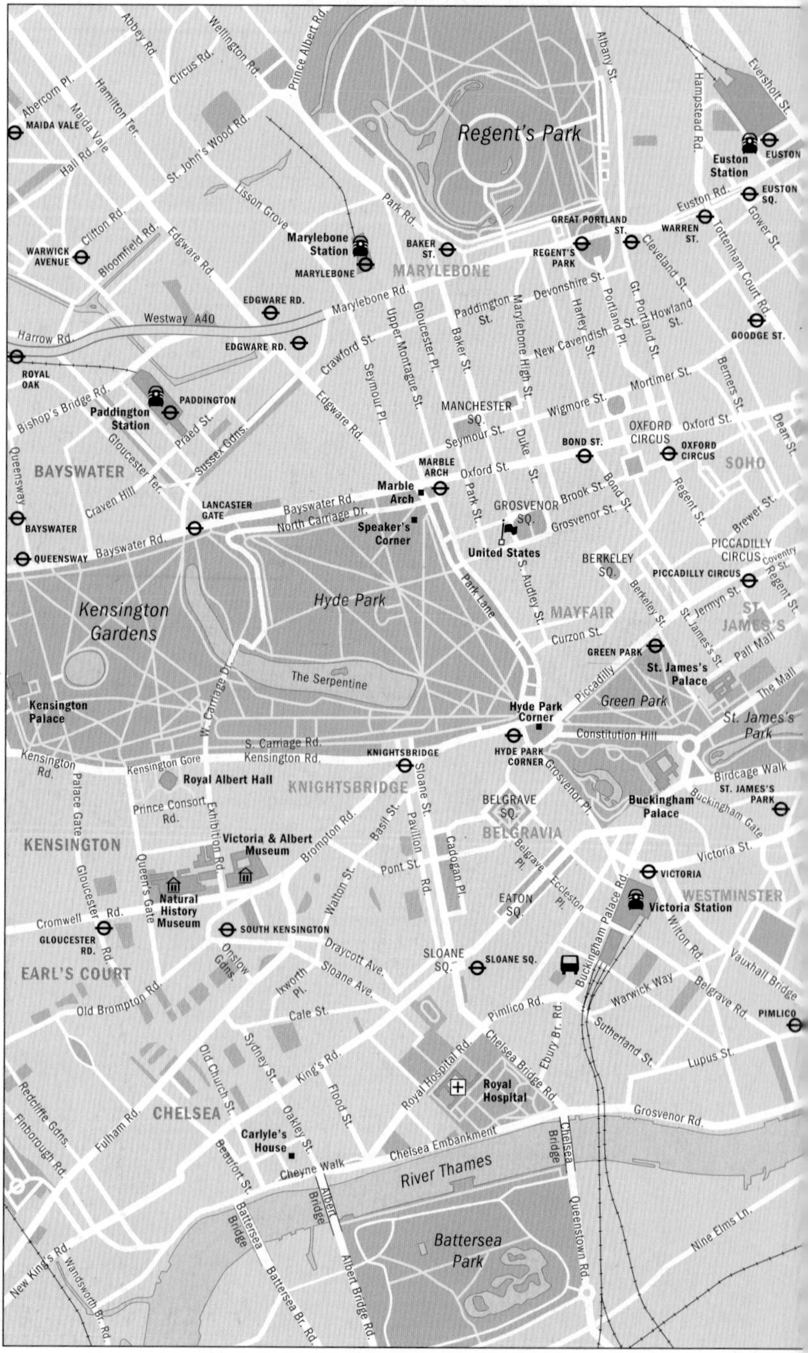
Regent's Park
Euston Station
EUSTON
EUSTON SQ.
WARREN ST.
GREAT PORTLAND ST.
REGENT'S PARK
BAKER ST.
Marylebone Station
MARYLEBONE
MARYLEBONE
MAIDA VALE
WARWICK AVENUE
EDGWARE RD.
EDGWARE RD.
ROYAL OAK
Paddington Station
PADDINGTON
BAYSWATER
BAYSWATER
QUEENSWAY
LANCASTER GATE
MARBLE ARCH
Marble Arch
Speaker's Corner
GROSVENOR SQ.
United States
MANCHESTER SQ.
BOND ST.
OXFORD CIRCUS
OXFORD CIRCUS
SOHO
PICCADILLY CIRCUS
PICCADILLY CIRCUS
BERKELEY SQ.
MAYFAIR
ST. JAMES'S
GREEN PARK
St. James's Palace
Green Park
St. James's Park
Hyde Park
Kensington Gardens
The Serpentine
Kensington Palace
Hyde Park Corner
HYDE PARK CORNER
KNIGHTSBRIDGE
KNIGHTSBRIDGE
Royal Albert Hall
Buckingham Palace
ST. JAMES'S PARK
BELGRAVE SQ.
BELGRAVIA
KENSINGTON
Victoria & Albert Museum
Natural History Museum
VICTORIA
Victoria Station
WESTMINSTER
EATON SQ.
GLOUCESTER RD.
SOUTH KENSINGTON
SLOANE SQ.
SLOANE SQ.
EARL'S COURT
PIMLICO
Royal Hospital
CHELSEA
Carlyle's House
River Thames
Battersea Park
Abbey Rd.
Wellington Rd.
Prince Albert Rd.
Circus Rd.
Abercorn Pl.
Hamilton Ter.
Maida Vale
Hall Rd.
St. John's Wood Rd.
Lisson Grove
Park Rd.
Albany St.
Hampstead Rd.
Eversholt St.
Euston Rd.
Gower St.
Tottenham Court Rd.
Cleveland St.
Clifton Rd.
Bloomfield Rd.
Edgware Rd.
Westway A40
Harrow Rd.
Marylebone Rd.
Upper Montague St.
Gloucester Pl.
Baker St.
Paddington St.
Devonshire St.
Marylebone High St.
Harley St.
Portland Pl.
Gt. Portland St.
Howland St.
New Cavendish St.
Crawford St.
Seymour Pl.
Montague St.
Berners St.
Mortimer St.
Wigmore St.
Seymour St.
Duke St.
Oxford St.
Dean St.
Bishop's Bridge Rd.
Praed St.
Gloucester Ter.
Sussex Gdns.
Queensway
Craven Hill
Park St.
Brook St.
Bond St.
Grosvenor St.
Regent St.
Brewer St.
Coventry St.
Bayswater Rd.
North Carriage Dr.
S. Audley St.
Park Lane
Berkeley St.
St. Jermyn St.
Regent St.
St. James's St.
Pall Mall
Curzon St.
Piccadilly
The Mall
Constitution Hill
W. Carriage Dr.
S. Carriage Rd.
Kensington Rd.
Kensington Gore
Kensington Rd.
Palace Gate
Sloane St.
Grosvenor Pl.
Birdcage Walk
Buckingham Gate
Prince Consort Rd.
Exhibition Rd.
Basil St.
Pavilion Rd.
Cadogan Pl.
Belgrave Pl.
Eccleston Pl.
Brompton Rd.
Victoria St.
Queen's Gate
Gloucester Rd.
Walton St.
Pont St.
Cromwell Rd.
Buckingham Palace Rd.
Wilton Rd.
Vauxhall Bridge
Onslow Gdns.
Draycott Ave.
Sloane Ave.
Ixworth Pl.
Warwick Way
Belgrave Rd.
Old Brompton Rd.
Cale St.
Pimlico Rd.
Sutherland St.
Ebury Br. Rd.
Chelsea Bridge Rd.
Royal Hospital Rd.
Lupus St.
Sydney St.
Old Church St.
King's Rd.
Flood St.
Redcliffe Gdns.
Finborough Rd.
Fulham Rd.
Oakley St.
Beaufort St.
Grosvenor Rd.
Chelsea Embankment
Chelsea Bridge
Cheyne Walk
Albert Bridge
Battersea Bridge
Queenstown Rd.
Nine Elms Ln.
New King's Rd.
Wandsworth Br. Rd.
Battersea Br. Rd.
Albert Bridge Rd.

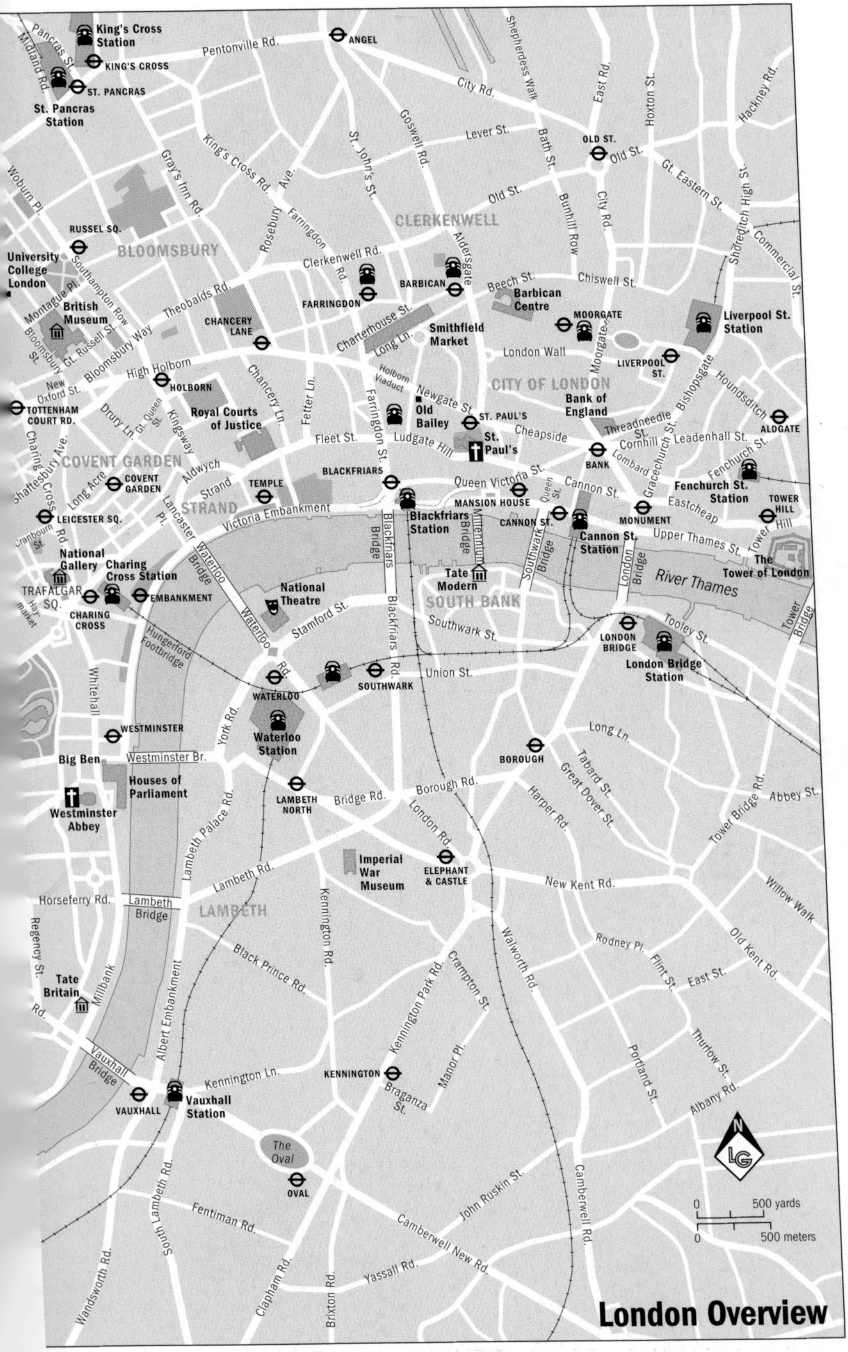

London Overview

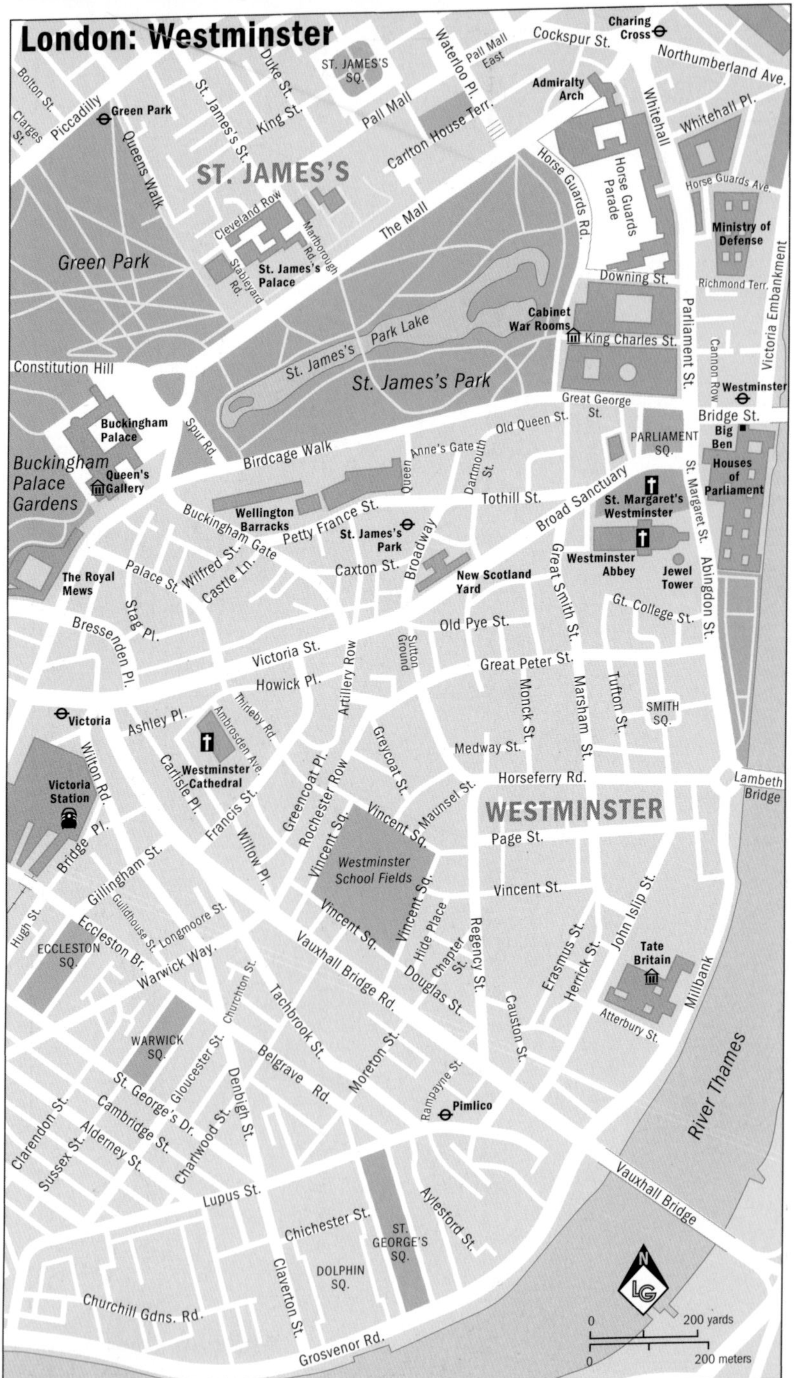
London: Westminster
ST. JAMES'S
WESTMINSTER
Green Park
St. James's Park
St. James's Park Lake
Buckingham Palace Gardens
River Thames
Charing Cross
Cockspur St.
Northumberland Ave.
Pall Mall East
Waterloo Pl.
ST. JAMES'S SQ.
Duke St.
Bolton St.
Clarges St.
Piccadilly
Green Park
Queens Walk
St. James's St.
King St.
Pall Mall
Carlton House Terr.
Admiralty Arch
Whitehall
Whitehall Pl.
Horse Guards Rd.
Horse Guards Parade
Horse Guards Ave.
Ministry of Defense
Cleveland Row
Marlborough Rd.
Stableyard Rd.
St. James's Palace
The Mall
Downing St.
Richmond Terr.
Victoria Embankment
Cabinet War Rooms
King Charles St.
Parliament St.
Cannon Row
Westminster
Constitution Hill
Great George St.
Bridge St.
Buckingham Palace
Spur Rd.
Old Queen St.
PARLIAMENT SQ.
Big Ben
Houses of Parliament
Birdcage Walk
Queen Anne's Gate
Dartmouth St.
Queen's Gallery
Tothill St.
Broad Sanctuary
St. Margaret's Westminster
St. Margaret St.
Wellington Barracks
Buckingham Gate
Petty France St.
St. James's Park
Broadway
Westminster Abbey
Jewel Tower
Abingdon St.
The Royal Mews
Palace St.
Wilfred St.
Castle Ln.
Caxton St.
New Scotland Yard
Great Smith St.
Gt. College St.
Stag Pl.
Bressenden Pl.
Old Pye St.
Sutton Ground
Victoria St.
Great Peter St.
Artillery Row
Howick Pl.
Tufton St.
Marsham St.
Monck St.
SMITH SQ.
Victoria
Ashley Pl.
Thirleby Rd.
Ambrosden Ave.
Westminster Cathedral
Greycoat St.
Medway St.
Wilton Rd.
Victoria Station
Carlisle Pl.
Francis St.
Greencoat Pl.
Rochester Row
Horseferry Rd.
Lambeth Bridge
Maunsel St.
Vincent Sq.
Page St.
Bridge Pl.
Willow Pl.
Westminster School Fields
Vincent St.
Gillingham St.
Guildhouse St.
Longmoore St.
Hugh St.
Eccleston Br.
ECCLESTON SQ.
Hide Place
Chapter St.
Regency St.
Erasmus St.
Herrick St.
John Islip St.
Tate Britain
Millbank
Warwick Way
Churchton St.
Vauxhall Bridge Rd.
Douglas St.
Causton St.
Atterbury St.
Tachbrook St.
WARWICK SQ.
Gloucester St.
Belgrave Rd.
Moreton St.
Rampayne St.
Pimlico
St. George's Dr.
Denbigh St.
Clarendon St.
Cambridge St.
Charlwood St.
Sussex St.
Alderney St.
Vauxhall Bridge
Lupus St.
Chichester St.
ST. GEORGE'S SQ.
Aylesford St.
DOLPHIN SQ.
Claverton St.
Churchill Gdns. Rd.
Grosvenor Rd.
N
0
200 yards
0
200 meters

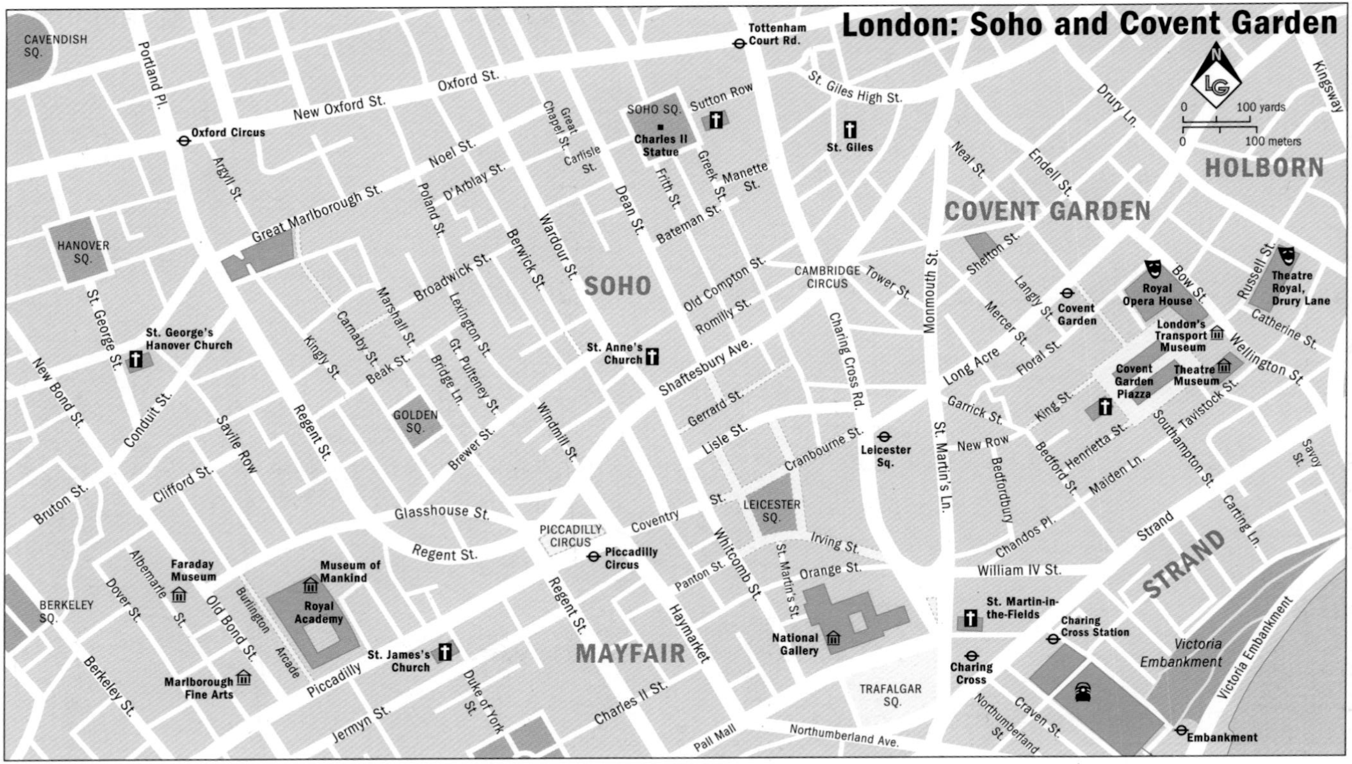

London: Soho and Covent Garden
0 100 yards
0 100 meters
HOLBORN
COVENT GARDEN
SOHO
MAYFAIR
STRAND
CAVENDISH SQ.
HANOVER SQ.
SOHO SQ.
GOLDEN SQ.
LEICESTER SQ.
BERKELEY SQ.
TRAFALGAR SQ.
PICCADILLY CIRCUS
CAMBRIDGE CIRCUS
Tottenham Court Rd.
Oxford Circus
Covent Garden
Leicester Sq.
Piccadilly Circus
Charing Cross
Charing Cross Station
Embankment
Charles II Statue
St. Giles
St. George's Hanover Church
St. Anne's Church
St. James's Church
St. Martin-in-the-Fields
Royal Opera House
Theatre Royal, Drury Lane
London's Transport Museum
Theatre Museum
Covent Garden Piazza
Museum of Mankind
Royal Academy
Faraday Museum
Marlborough Fine Arts
National Gallery
Victoria Embankment
Portland Pl.
Oxford St.
New Oxford St.
Sutton Row
St. Giles High St.
Kingsway
Drury Ln.
Neal St.
Endell St.
Argyll St.
Noel St.
Great Chapel St.
Carlisle St.
Frith St.
Greek St.
Manette St.
Great Marlborough St.
D'Arblay St.
Poland St.
Berwick St.
Wardour St.
Dean St.
Bateman St.
Old Compton St.
Romilly St.
Tower St.
Monmouth St.
Shelton St.
Langly St.
Mercer St.
Floral St.
Long Acre
Bow St.
Russell St.
Catherine St.
Wellington St.
Tavistock St.
Southampton St.
Savoy St.
Carting Ln.
Maiden Ln.
Henrietta St.
King St.
Bedford St.
Garrick St.
New Row
Bedfordbury
Chandos Pl.
Strand
William IV St.
Craven St.
Northumberland St.
Northumberland Ave.
St. Martin's Ln.
Charing Cross Rd.
Cranbourne St.
Lisle St.
Gerrard St.
Shaftesbury Ave.
Broadwick St.
Marshall St.
Lexington St.
Carnaby St.
Kingly St.
Beak St.
Bridge Ln.
Gt. Pulteney St.
Brewer St.
Windmill St.
Regent St.
Glasshouse St.
Coventry St.
Irving St.
Whitcomb St.
St. Martin's St.
Orange St.
Panton St.
Haymarket
Charles II St.
Pall Mall
Duke of York St.
Jermyn St.
Piccadilly
Burlington Arcade
Old Bond St.
Albemarle St.
Dover St.
Berkeley St.
Bruton St.
Clifford St.
Savile Row
Conduit St.
New Bond St.
St. George St.

London: West End

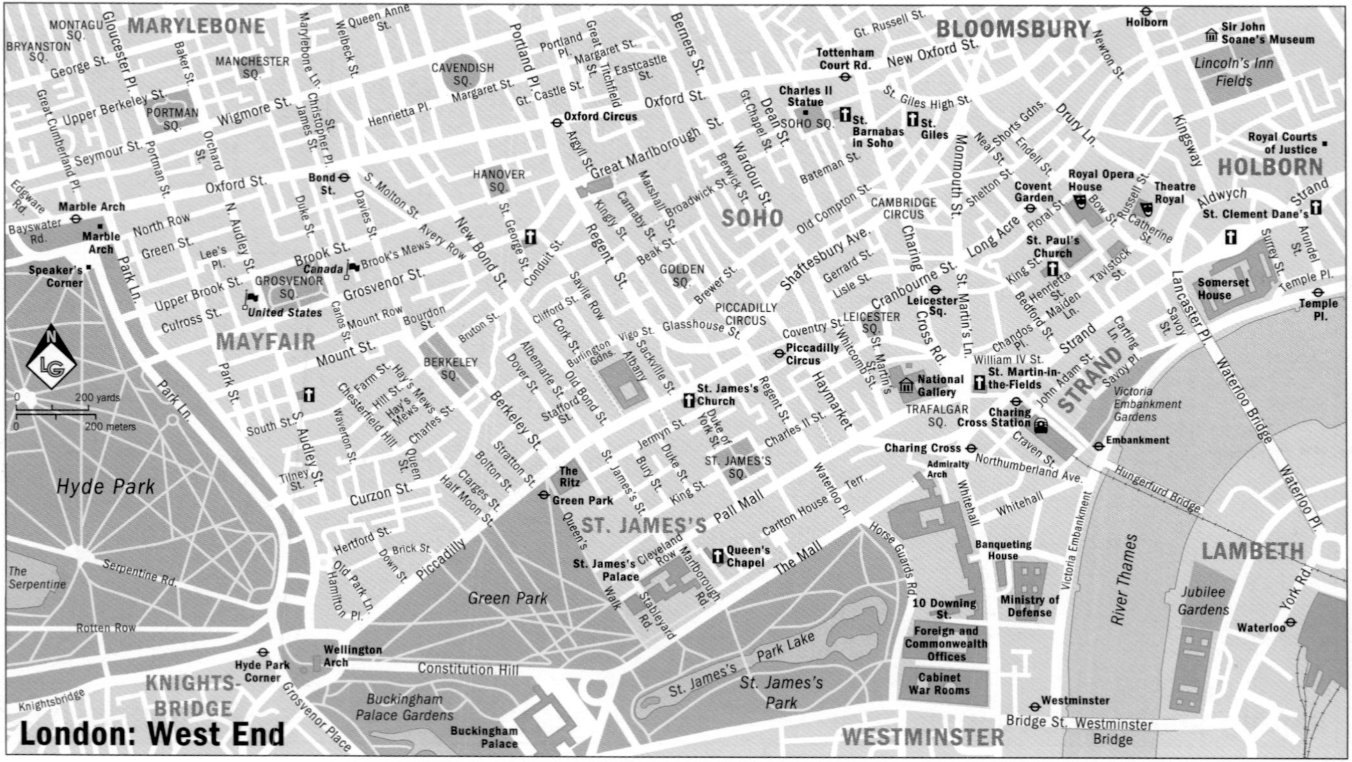

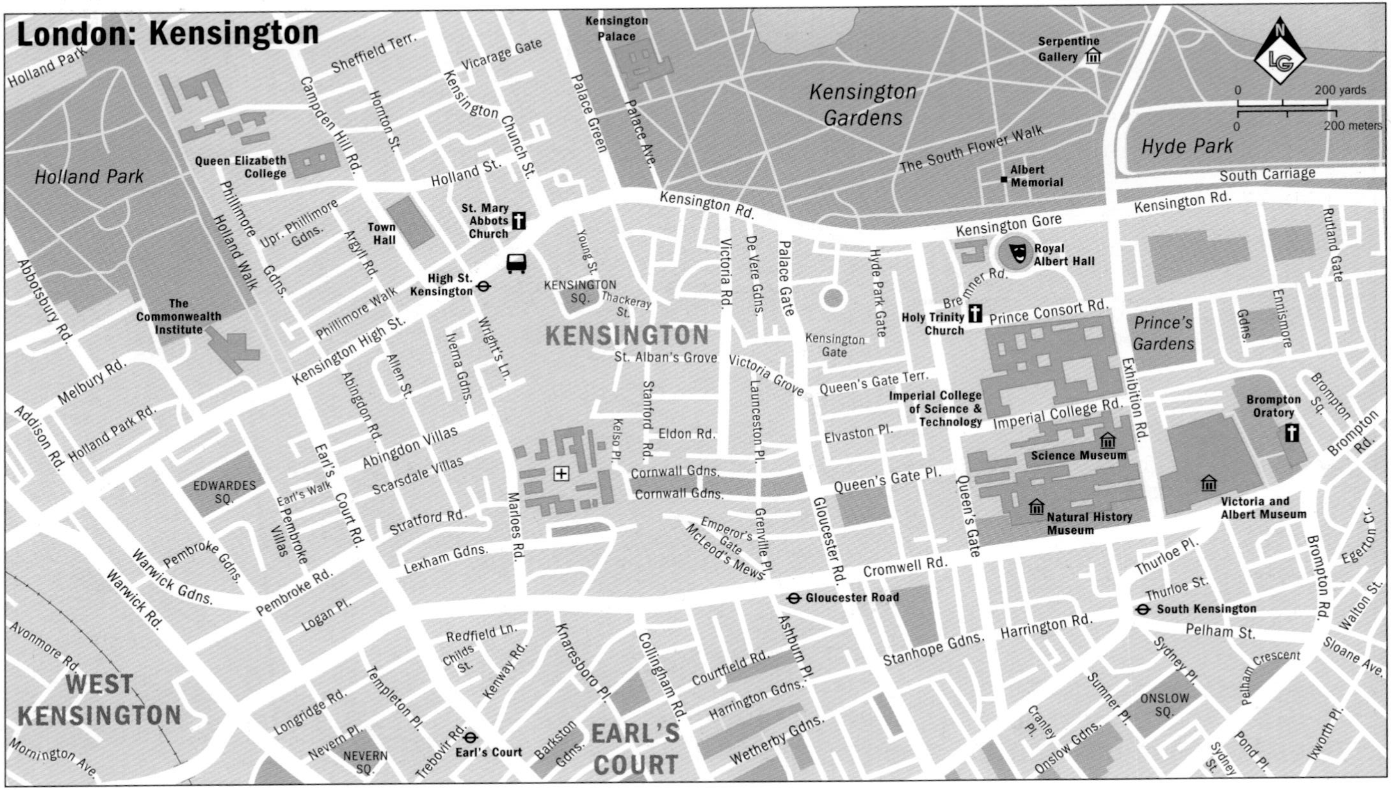
London: Kensington
Kensington Palace
Serpentine Gallery
Kensington Gardens
Hyde Park
Holland Park
0
200 yards
0
200 meters
The South Flower Walk
Albert Memorial
South Carriage
Kensington Rd.
Kensington Gore
Royal Albert Hall
Bremner Rd.
Holy Trinity Church
Prince Consort Rd.
Prince's Gardens
Exhibition Rd.
Rutland Gate
Ennismore Gdns.
Brompton Sq.
Brompton Rd.
Brompton Oratory
Imperial College of Science & Technology
Imperial College Rd.
Science Museum
Natural History Museum
Victoria and Albert Museum
Queen's Gate
Queen's Gate Terr.
Queen's Gate Pl.
Elvaston Pl.
Hyde Park Gate
Kensington Gate
Palace Gate
De Vere Gdns.
Victoria Rd.
Victoria Grove
Launceston Pl.
Gloucester Rd.
Grenville Pl.
Emperor's Gate
McLeod's Mews
Cromwell Rd.
Gloucester Road
Thurloe Pl.
Thurloe St.
South Kensington
Pelham St.
Pelham Crescent
Sloane Ave.
Walton St.
Egerton Cr.
Brompton Rd.
Harrington Rd.
Stanhope Gdns.
Sydney Pl.
Sumner Pl.
ONSLOW SQ.
Cranley Pl.
Onslow Gdns.
Sydney St.
Pond Pl.
Ixworth Pl.
Ashburn Pl.
Courtfield Rd.
Harrington Gdns.
Wetherby Gdns.
Collingham Rd.
Knaresboro Pl.
EARL'S COURT
Barkston Gdns.
Kenway Rd.
Redfield Ln.
Childs St.
Earl's Court
Trebovir Rd.
Templeton Pl.
Longridge Rd.
Nevern Pl.
NEVERN SQ.
KENSINGTON
St. Alban's Grove
Stanford Rd.
Eldon Rd.
Kelso Pl.
Cornwall Gdns.
Cornwall Gdns.
Marloes Rd.
Lexham Gdns.
Stratford Rd.
Scarsdale Villas
Abingdon Villas
Abingdon Rd.
Allen St.
Iverna Gdns.
Wright's Ln.
KENSINGTON SQ.
Thackeray St.
Young St.
Palace Green
Palace Ave.
Kensington Church St.
Vicarage Gate
Sheffield Terr.
Hornton St.
Campden Hill Rd.
Holland St.
St. Mary Abbots Church
Town Hall
High St. Kensington
Argyll Rd.
Upr. Phillimore Gdns.
Phillimore Walk
Kensington High St.
Phillimore Gdns.
Holland Walk
Queen Elizabeth College
The Commonwealth Institute
Holland Park
Abbotsbury Rd.
Melbury Rd.
Holland Park Rd.
Addison Rd.
EDWARDES SQ.
Earl's Walk
Earl's Court Rd.
Pembroke Villas
Pembroke Gdns.
Pembroke Rd.
Logan Pl.
Warwick Gdns.
Warwick Rd.
Avonmore Rd.
WEST KENSINGTON
Mornington Ave.

London: Notting Hill and Bayswater

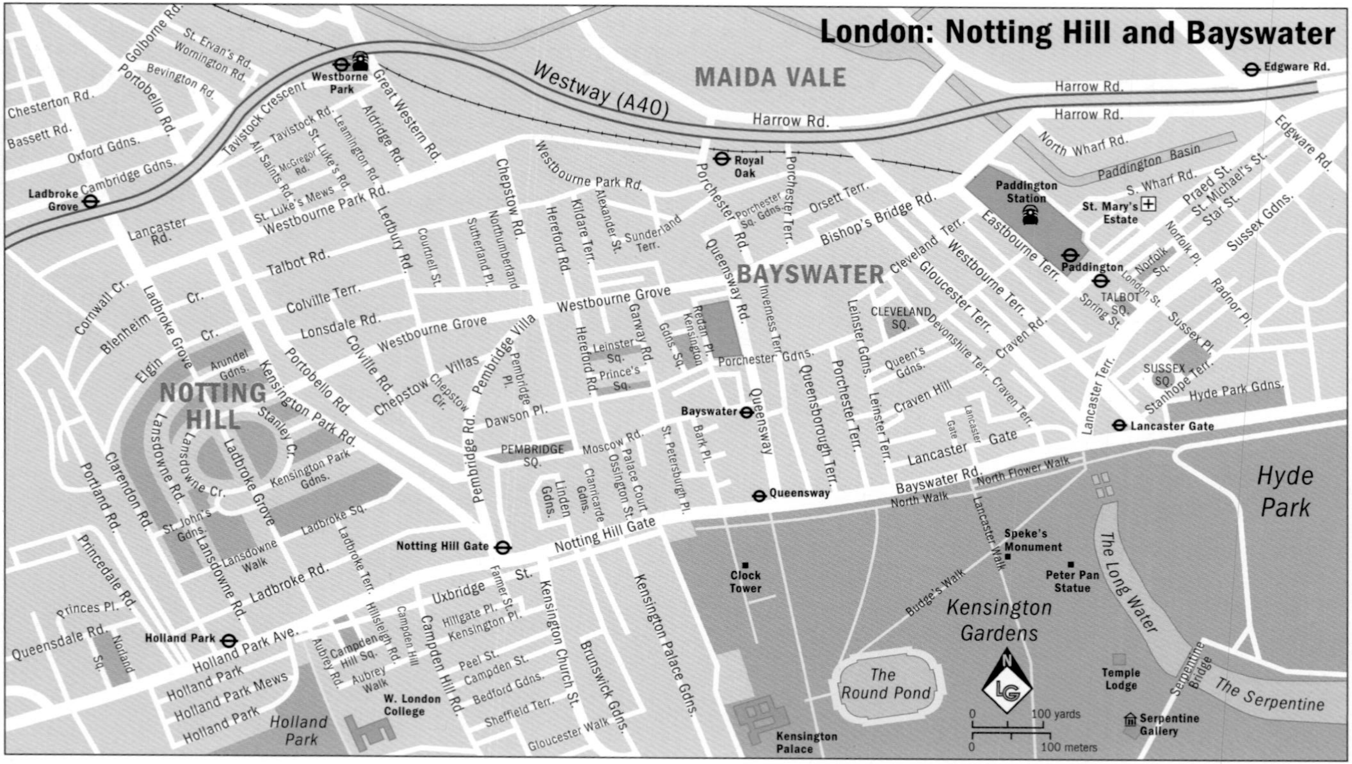

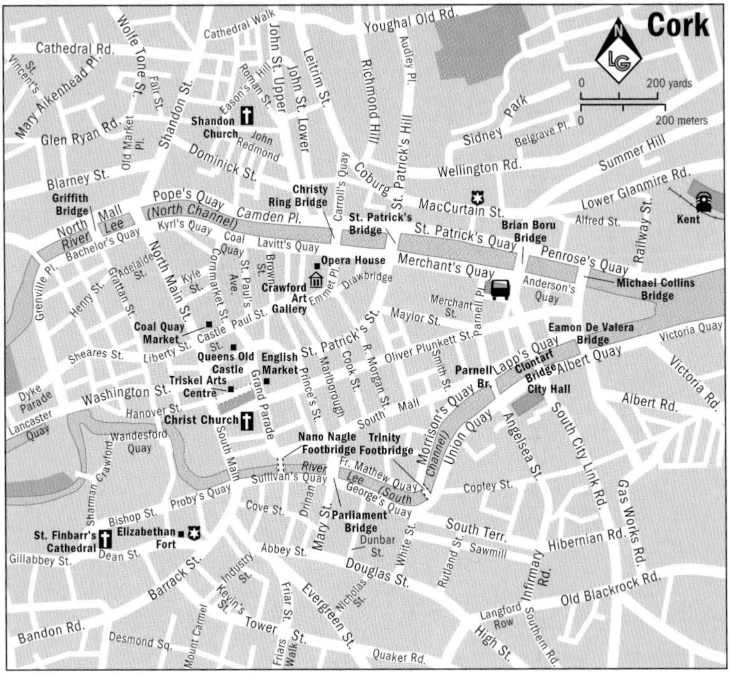
Cork
0
200 yards
0
200 meters
Cathedral Walk
Youghal Old Rd.
Cathedral Rd.
Wolfe Tone St.
St. Vincent's
Mary Aikenhead Pl.
Fair St.
Shandon St.
Eason's Hill
Roman St.
John St. Upper
John St. Lower
Leitrim St.
Richmond Hill
Audley Pl.
St. Patrick's Hill
Sidney Park
Belgrave Pl.
Summer Hill
Glen Ryan Rd.
Old Market Pl.
Shandon Church
John Redmond
Dominick St.
Carroll's Quay
Coburg St.
Wellington Rd.
Blarney St.
Griffith Bridge
North Mall
Pope's Quay
Christy Ring Bridge
MacCurtain St.
Lower Glanmire Rd.
North River Lee
(North Channel)
Camden Pl.
St. Patrick's Bridge
Brian Boru Bridge
Alfred St.
Railway St.
Kent
Bachelor's Quay
Kyrl's Quay
Coal Quay
Lavitt's Quay
St. Patrick's Quay
Penrose's Quay
Grenville Pl.
Adelaide St.
North Main St.
Commarket St.
St. Paul's Ave.
Brown St.
Opera House
Merchant's Quay
Anderson's Quay
Michael Collins Bridge
Henry St.
Grattan St.
Kyle St.
Crawford Art Gallery
Emmet Pl.
Drawbridge
Merchant St.
Parnell Pl.
Paul St.
Maylor St.
Coal Quay Market
Castle St.
Eamon De Valera Bridge
Victoria Quay
Sheares St.
Liberty St.
Queens Old Castle
English Market
St. Patrick's St.
R. Morgan St.
Oliver Plunkett St.
Lapp's Quay
Clontarf Bridge
Albert Quay
Victoria Rd.
Dyke Parade
Triskel Arts Centre
Grand Parade
Prince's St.
Marlborough
Cook St.
Smith St.
Parnell Br.
City Hall
Washington St.
South Mall
Albert Rd.
Lancaster Quay
Hanover St.
Christ Church
Morrison's Quay
Union Quay
Angelsea St.
South City Link Rd.
Wandesford Quay
South Main
Nano Nagle Footbridge
Trinity Footbridge
(South Channel)
Crawford
Sharman Crawford
River Lee (South)
Fr. Mathew Quay
George's Quay
Sullivan's Quay
Copley St.
Gas Works Rd.
Proby's Quay
Bishop St.
Cove St.
Drinan
Mary St.
Parliament Bridge
White St.
South Terr.
St. Finbarr's Cathedral
Elizabethan Fort
Dunbar St.
Rutland St.
Sawmill
Hibernian Rd.
Gillabbey St.
Dean St.
Abbey St.
Infirmary Rd.
Barrack St.
Industry St.
Douglas St.
Old Blackrock Rd.
Kevin's St.
Nicholas St.
Evergreen St.
Friar St.
Langford Row
Bandon Rd.
Tower St.
High St.
Desmond Sq.
Mount Carmel
Friars Walk
Quaker Rd.
Southern Rd.

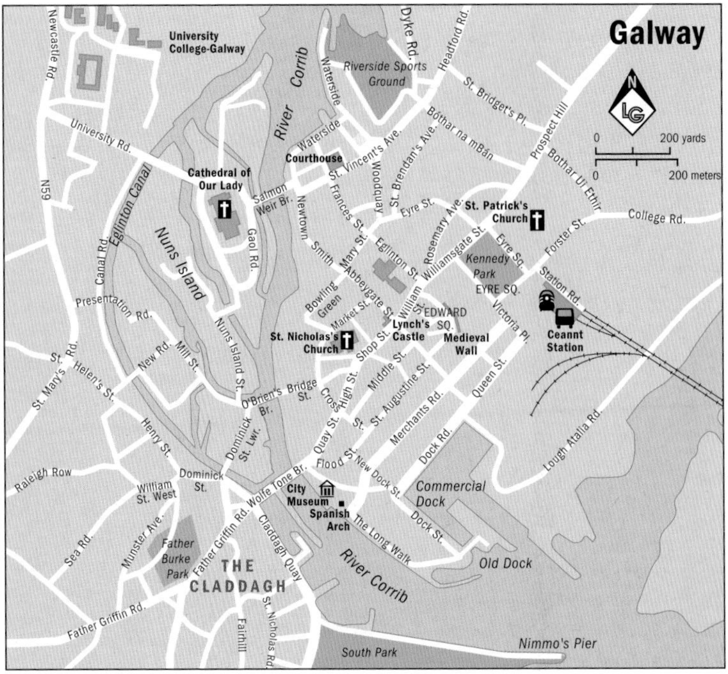
Galway
0
200 yards
0
200 meters
Newcastle Rd.
University College-Galway
Dyke Rd.
Headford Rd.
River Corrib
Waterside
Riverside Sports Ground
St. Bridget's Pl.
University Rd.
Bóthar na mBán
Prospect Hill
St. Vincent's Ave.
Woodquay
St. Brendan's Ave.
Courthouse
Bothar Ui Ethir
N59
Eglinton Canal
Cathedral of Our Lady
Salmon Weir Br.
Frances St.
Newtown Smith
Eyre St.
Rosemary Ave.
St. Patrick's Church
College Rd.
Nuns Island
Gaol Rd.
Mary St.
Eglinton St.
Williamsgate St.
Eyre Sq.
Forster St.
Canal Rd.
Kennedy Park
EYRE SQ.
Abbeygate St.
Station Rd.
Bowling Green
William St.
Presentation Rd.
Market St.
EDWARD SQ.
Victoria Pl.
Lynch's Castle
St. Nicholas's Church
Shop St.
Medieval Wall
Ceannt Station
New Rd.
Mill St.
Nuns Island St.
St. Mary's Rd.
St. Helen's St.
Middle St.
St. Augustine St.
Queen St.
O'Brien's Bridge St.
Cross St.
High St.
O'Brien's Br.
Henry St.
Merchants Rd.
Dominick St. Lwr.
Quay St.
Lough Atalia Rd.
Flood St.
New Dock St.
Dock Rd.
Raleigh Row
Dominick St.
William St. West
Wolfe Tone Br.
City Museum
Commercial Dock
Spanish Arch
Father Griffin Rd.
Claddagh Quay
The Long Walk
Dock St.
Sea Rd.
Munster Ave.
Father Burke Park
THE CLADDAGH
River Corrib
Old Dock
Father Griffin Rd.
St. Nicholas Rd.
Fairhill
Nimmo's Pier
South Park

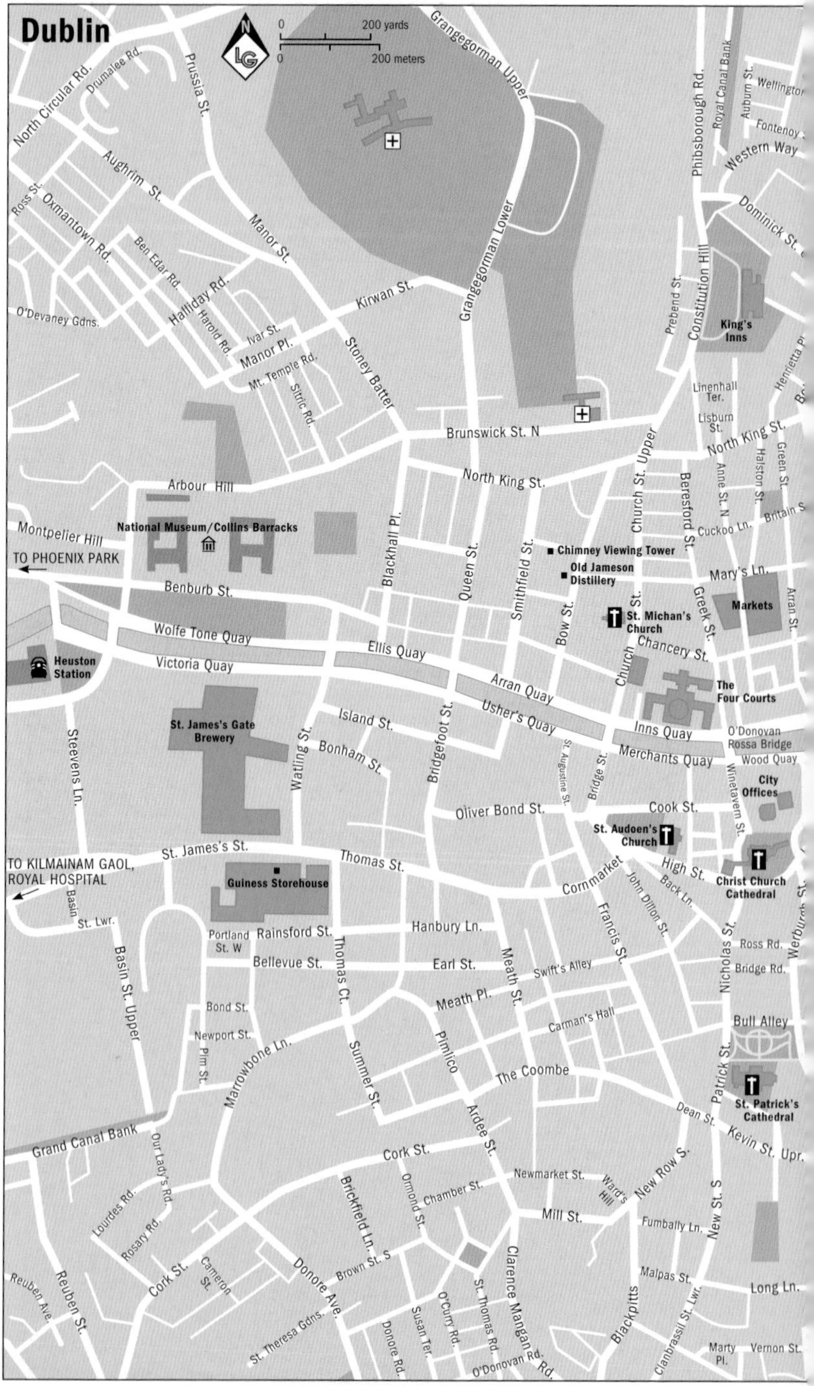
Dublin
0 200 yards
0 200 meters
Grangegorman Upper
Grangegorman Lower
Prussia St.
North Circular Rd.
Drumalee Rd.
Aughrim St.
Ross St.
Oxmantown Rd.
Ben Edar Rd.
Halliday Rd.
Harold Rd.
Manor St.
Kirwan St.
O'Devaney Gdns.
Ivar St.
Manor Pl.
Mt. Temple Rd.
Sitric Rd.
Stoney Batter
Brunswick St. N
North King St.
Arbour Hill
National Museum/Collins Barracks
Montpelier Hill
TO PHOENIX PARK
Benburb St.
Wolfe Tone Quay
Victoria Quay
Heuston Station
Ellis Quay
Arran Quay
Usher's Quay
Inns Quay
Merchants Quay
Blackhall Pl.
Queen St.
Smithfield St.
Bow St.
Chimney Viewing Tower
Old Jameson Distillery
St. Michan's Church
Church St.
Church St. Upper
Chancery St.
The Four Courts
Phibsborough Rd.
Royal Canal Bank
Auburn St.
Wellington
Fontenoy St.
Western Way
Dominick St.
Constitution Hill
Prebend St.
King's Inns
Linenhall Ter.
Lisburn St.
North King St.
Henrietta Pl.
Beresford St.
Anne St. N
Halston St.
Green St.
Cuckoo Ln.
Britain St.
Mary's Ln.
Greek St.
Markets
Arran St.
O'Donovan Rossa Bridge
Wood Quay
Winetavern St.
City Offices
St. James's Gate Brewery
Steevens Ln.
Island St.
Bonham St.
Watling St.
Bridgefoot St.
St. Augustine St.
Bridge St.
Oliver Bond St.
Cook St.
St. Audoen's Church
High St.
Back Ln.
Christ Church Cathedral
TO KILMAINAM GAOL, ROYAL HOSPITAL
St. James's St.
Thomas St.
Guiness Storehouse
Cornmarket
John Dillon St.
Francis St.
Basin St. Lwr.
Basin St. Upper
Portland St. W
Rainsford St.
Thomas Ct.
Hanbury Ln.
Bellevue St.
Earl St.
Meath St.
Swift's Alley
Nicholas St.
Ross Rd.
Bridge Rd.
Werburgh St.
Bond St.
Newport St.
Pim St.
Marrowbone Ln.
Summer St.
Meath Pl.
Pimlico
Carman's Hall
Bull Alley
The Coombe
Patrick St.
St. Patrick's Cathedral
Dean St.
Kevin St. Upr.
Grand Canal Bank
Our Lady's Rd.
Cork St.
Ardee St.
Lourdes Rd.
Rosary Rd.
Brickfield Ln.
Ormond St.
Chamber St.
Newmarket St.
Ward's Hill
New Row S.
Mill St.
Fumbally Ln.
New St. S
Cork St.
Cameron St.
Donore Ave.
Brown St. S
Clarence Mangan Rd.
Blackpitts
Malpas St.
Long Ln.
Reuben Ave.
Reuben St.
St. Theresa Gdns.
Donore Rd.
Susan Ter.
O'Curry Rd.
St. Thomas Rd.
O'Donovan Rd.
Clanbrassil St. Lwr.
Marty Pl.
Vernon St.

TO
St. George's
N. Circular Rd.
William St. N
Temple St. N
Blessington St.
Wellington St. Lwr.
Dorset St. Upper
Paradise Pl.
North
Mountjoy Sq.
East
West
South
Charles St. Great
Rutland St. Upr.
Summer St. N
Dunne St.
Portland Row
Gardiner Pl.
Denmark St.
Hill St.
Middle Gardiner St.
Gardiner Ln.
Summerhill Rd.
Rutland St. Lwr.
Upr. Buckingham St.
Empress Pl.
Killarney St.
Amiens St.
Dublin Writers Museum
Abbey Presbyterian
Hugh Lane Gallery
N. Great George's
Parnell Sq. N
Natl. Wax Museum
Garden of Remembrance
Parnell Sq. E
James Joyce Centre
Sean Mac Dermott St.
Lwr Buckingham St.
Parnell Sq.
Lower Gardiner St.
Railway St.
Connolly Station
Dominick St. Lower
Dominick Pl.
Parnell Sq. W
Gate Theatre
Marlborough St.
DART Trains
Rotunda Hospital
Parnell Sq. S
O'Connell St. Upper
Corporation St.
Foley St.
Main Entrance
Sheriff St. Lwr.
Moore Ln.
Moore St.
Tyrone House
Talbot Ln.
Amiens St.
Inner Dock
Parnell St.
Moore St. Market
Talbot St.
Earl St. N
Store St.
Busarus
Financial Services Center
Commons St.
Wolf Tone St.
Jervis St.
Central Library
Henry St.
Beresford Pl.
Memorial Rd.
George's Dock
Mary St.
Prince's St. N
O'Connell St. Lower
Lower Abbey St.
Custom House
Liffey St. Upr.
Abbey Theatre
Liberty Hall
St. Mary's Church
Middle Abbey St.
Eden Quay
Custom House Quay
North Wall
Upper Abbey St.
Liffey St. Lwr.
Lotts Row
O'Connell Monument
River Liffey
Bachelors Walk
O'Connell Bridge
Burgh Quay
George's Quay
City Quay
Strand St. Great
Poolbeg
Luke St.
Tara St.
Tara St. Station
Moss St.
Princes St.
Sir Rogerson's Quay
Ormond Quay
Ha'Penny Footbridge
Aston Quay
Westmoreland St.
D'Olier St.
Gloucester St.
Lombard St.
Creighton St.
Grattan Bridge
Millennium Bridge
Wellington Quay
Fleet St.
Garda
Townsend St.
Temple Bar
Stock Exchange
Pearse St.
Lombard St. E
Sandwith St. Lwr.
Parliament St.
Sycamore St.
Eustace St.
Temple Ln. S
Anglesea St.
Cope St.
Bank of Ireland
College Green
City Hall
Irish Film Centre
Dame St.
Pearse Station
Dublin Castle
Suffolk St.
Trinity College
Westland Row
Chester Beatty Library
Exchequer St.
American Express
Wicklow St.
Nassau St.
Boyne St.
Sandwith St. Upr.
S. Great Georges St.
Drury St.
William St. S
Clarendon St.
Grafton St.
Duke St.
Frederick St. S
Lincoln Pl.
Fenian St.
Stephen St. Upr.
Stephen St. Lwr.
Dublin Civic Museum
Chatham St.
Anne St. S
Frederick Ln.
National Library
National Gallery
Denzille Ln.
Longford St. Gt.
Molesworth St.
Mansion House
National Museums
National History
Leinster House
Holles St.
Adelaide Hospital
Aungier St.
Mercer St. Lwr.
St. Stephen's Green Shopping Centre
Dawson St.
Kildare St.
Archaeology and History Museum
Merrion Sq.
Peter Row
St. Stephen's Green N
Mount St. Lwr.
York St.
St Stephen's Green W
Merrion St. Upper
Bishop St.
Mercer St. Upr.
Merrion Row
Fitzwilliam Ln.
St. Stephen's Green
Hume St.
Ely Pl.
Mount St. Upr.
Kevin St. Lwr.
Wexford St.
St. Stephen's Green E
Baggot St. Lower
#29 Lower Fitzwilliam St.
Garda
St. Stephen's Green S
Fitzwilliam St. Lwr.
James's St. East
Bank of Ireland
Camden Row
Harcourt St.
Pembroke St. Lwr.
University College Dublin
Quinn's Ln.
Fitzwilliam St. Upr.
Lad Ln.
Pleasants St.
Camden St.
National Concert Hall
Earlsfort Ter.
Leeson St. Lwr.
Pembroke St. Upr.
Fitzwilliam Sq.

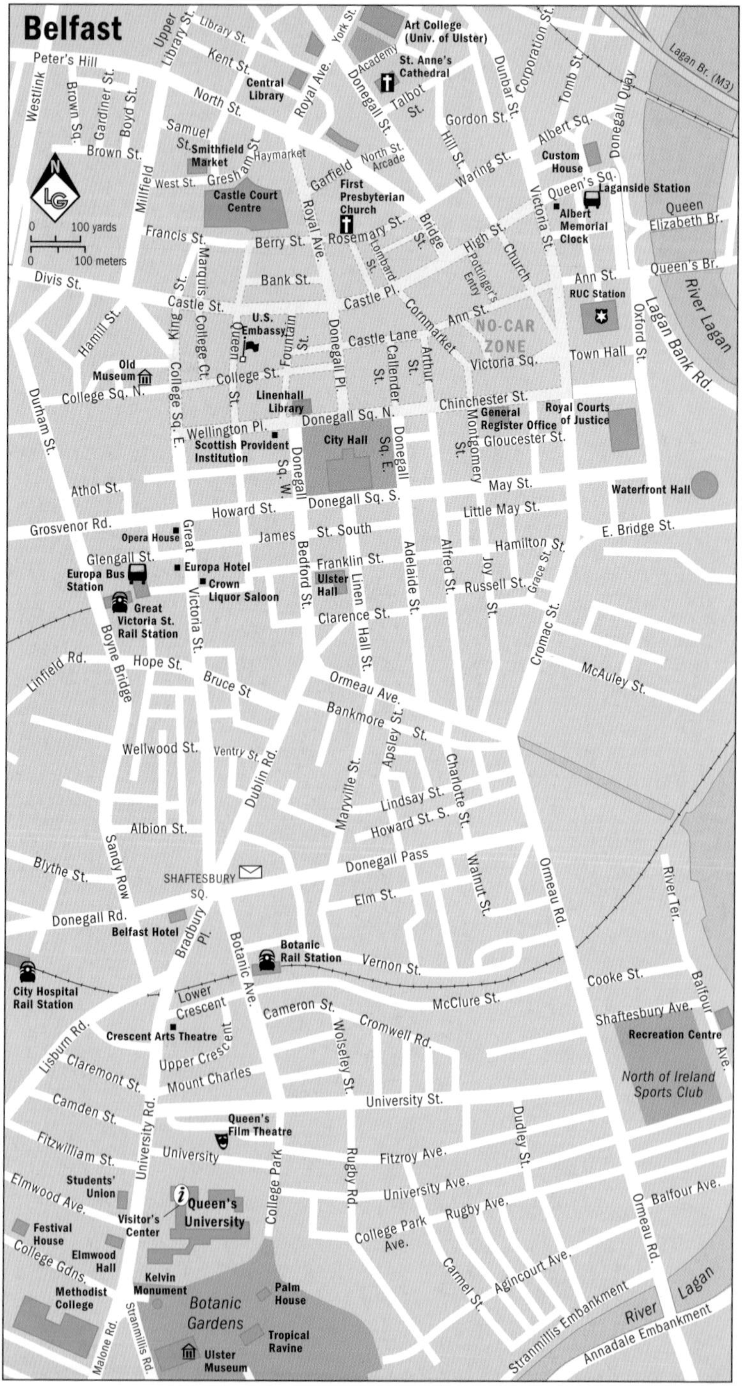

Belfast
Library St.
Upper Library St.
Kent St.
York St.
Art College (Univ. of Ulster)
Academy
St. Anne's Cathedral
Corporation St.
Lagan Br. (M3)
Peter's Hill
Central Library
Royal Ave.
Donegall St.
Talbot St.
Dunbar St.
Tomb St.
Westlink
Brown Sq.
Gardiner St.
Boyd St.
North St.
Gordon St.
Donegall Quay
Samuel St.
Smithfield Market
Gresham St.
Haymarket
North St. Arcade
Hill St.
Albert Sq.
Brown St.
Garfield
Waring St.
Custom House
West St.
Castle Court Centre
First Presbyterian Church
Victoria St.
Queen's Sq.
Laganside Station
Millfield
Albert Memorial Clock
Queen Elizabeth Br.
0 100 yards
0 100 meters
Francis St.
Berry St.
Rosemary St.
Bridge St.
High St.
Church
Lombard St.
Pottinger's Entry
Queen's Br.
Divis St.
Bank St.
Ann St.
River Lagan
Marquis St.
King St.
Castle St.
Castle Pl.
RUC Station
Lagan Bank Rd.
Hamill St.
U.S. Embassy
Cornmarket
Ann St.
Oxford St.
College Ct.
Queen St.
Fountain St.
Donegall Pl.
Castle Lane
NO-CAR ZONE
Old Museum
Callender St.
Arthur St.
Victoria Sq.
Town Hall
College Sq. N.
College St.
Linenhall Library
Chinchester St.
Durham St.
College Sq. E.
Donegall Sq. N.
General Register Office
Royal Courts of Justice
Wellington Pl.
Montgomery St.
Scottish Provident Institution
City Hall
Sq. E.
Donegall
Gloucester St.
Donegall Sq. W.
Athol St.
May St.
Waterfront Hall
Donegall Sq. S.
Howard St.
Little May St.
Grosvenor Rd.
Opera House
Great Victoria St.
James St. South
E. Bridge St.
Glengall St.
Bedford St.
Adelaide St.
Alfred St.
Hamilton St.
Europa Bus Station
Europa Hotel
Franklin St.
Joy St.
Grace St.
Crown Liquor Saloon
Ulster Hall
Linen Hall St.
Russell St.
Great Victoria St. Rail Station
Clarence St.
Cromac St.
Boyne Bridge
Linfield Rd.
Hope St.
McAuley St.
Bruce St
Ormeau Ave.
Bankmore St.
Apsley St.
Wellwood St.
Ventry St.
Dublin Rd.
Maryville St.
Charlotte St.
Lindsay St.
Albion St.
Howard St. S.
Sandy Row
Walnut St.
Ormeau Rd.
River Ter.
Blythe St.
Donegall Pass
SHAFTESBURY SQ.
Elm St.
Donegall Rd.
Belfast Hotel
Bradbury Pl.
Botanic Ave.
Botanic Rail Station
Vernon St.
Balfour Ave.
City Hospital Rail Station
Lower Crescent
Cameron St.
McClure St.
Cooke St.
Shaftesbury Ave.
Lisburn Rd.
Crescent Arts Theatre
Cromwell Rd.
Recreation Centre
Claremont St.
Upper Crescent
Mount Charles
Wolseley St.
North of Ireland Sports Club
Camden St.
University St.
University Rd.
Queen's Film Theatre
Dudley St.
Fitzwilliam St.
University
Rugby Rd.
Fitzroy Ave.
Students' Union
College Park
University Ave.
Elmwood Ave.
Queen's University
Balfour Ave.
Visitor's Center
Rugby Ave.
Festival House
College Park Ave.
College Gdns.
Elmwood Hall
Agincourt Ave.
Ormeau Rd.
Methodist College
Kelvin Monument
Palm House
Carmel St.
Botanic Gardens
Stranmillis Embankment
River Lagan
Tropical Ravine
Malone Rd.
Stranmillis Rd.
Ulster Museum
Annadale Embankment

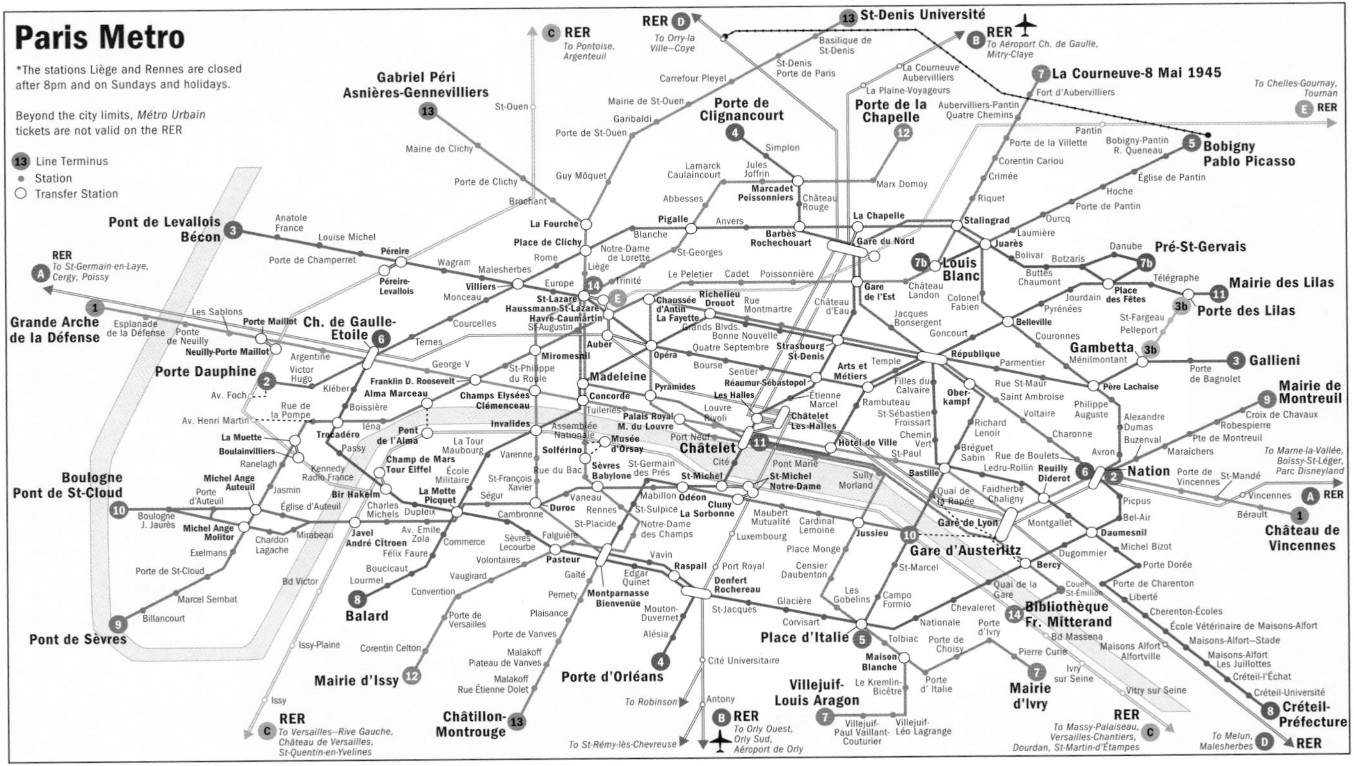
Paris Metro
*The stations Liège and Rennes are closed after 8pm and on Sundays and holidays.
Beyond the city limits, Métro Urbain tickets are not valid on the RER
13 Line Terminus
Station
Transfer Station
RER C To Pontoise, Argenteuil
RER D To Orry-la Ville–Coye
13 St-Denis Université
RER B To Aéroport Ch. de Gaulle, Mitry-Claye
7 La Courneuve-8 Mai 1945
To Chelles-Gournay, Tournan
E RER
Gabriel Péri Asnières-Gennevilliers
St-Ouen
Carrefour Pleyel
Basilique de St-Denis
St-Denis Porte de Paris
La Courneuve Aubervilliers
La Plaine-Voyageurs
Fort d'Aubervilliers
Mairie de St-Ouen
Garibaldi
Porte de St-Ouen
Porte de Clignancourt
Porte de la Chapelle
Aubervilliers-Pantin Quatre Chemins
Pantin
Bobigny-Pantin R. Queneau
5 Bobigny Pablo Picasso
Mairie de Clichy
Porte de Clichy
Guy Môquet
Lamarck Caulaincourt
Jules Joffrin
Simplon
Marcadet Poissonniers
Château Rouge
Marx Domoy
Porte de la Villette
Corentin Cariou
Crimée
Riquet
Église de Pantin
Hoche
Porte de Pantin
Brochant
Abbesses
Pont de Levallois Bécon
Anatole France
Louise Michel
Porte de Champerret
Pereire
Pereire-Levallois
Wagram
Malesherbes
Villiers
Monceau
La Fourche
Place de Clichy
Rome
Blanche
Notre-Dame de Lorette
Liège
Europe
Pigalle
Anvers
St-Georges
Trinité
Barbès Rochechouart
La Chapelle
Gare du Nord
Stalingrad
Jaurès
Ourcq
Laumière
Bolivar
Botzaris
Buttes Chaumont
Danube
Pré-St-Gervais
Télégraphe
Place des Fêtes
Mairie des Lilas
Porte des Lilas
Louis Blanc
Château Landon
Colonel Fabien
Jourdain
Pyrénées
Belleville
Couronnes
St-Fargeau
Pelleport
Gambetta
Ménilmontant
Gallieni
Porte de Bagnolet
RER A To St-Germain-en-Laye, Cergy, Poissy
Grande Arche de la Défense
Esplanade de la Défense
Les Sablons
Pont de Neuilly
Porte Maillot
Neuilly-Porte Maillot
Ch. de Gaulle-Etoile
Ternes
Courcelles
St-Lazare
Haussmann-St-Lazare
Havre-Caumartin
St-Augustin
Le Peletier
Cadet
Poissonnière
Chaussée d'Antin La Fayette
Richelieu Drouot
Rue Montmartre
Château d'Eau
Gare de l'Est
Jacques Bonsergent
Goncourt
Grands Blvds.
Bonne Nouvelle
Quatre Septembre
Strasbourg-St-Denis
Auber
Opéra
Porte Dauphine
Argentine
Victor Hugo
Kléber
George V
St-Philippe du Roule
Miromesnil
Madeleine
Bourse
Sentier
Réaumur-Sébastopol
Arts et Métiers
Temple
République
Parmentier
Rue St-Maur
Saint Ambroise
Père Lachaise
Philippe Auguste
Mairie de Montreuil
Croix de Chavaux
Robespierre
Pte de Montreuil
Maraîchers
Av. Foch
Av. Henri Martin
Rue de la Pompe
Boissière
Franklin D. Roosevelt
Alma Marceau
Champs Elysées Clémenceau
Concorde
Pyramides
Les Halles
Étienne Marcel
Rambuteau
Filles du Calvaire
Oberkampf
Alexandre Dumas
Buzenval
Avron
Trocadéro
Iéna
Pont de l'Alma
Invalides
Assemblée Nationale
Tuileries
Palais Royal M. du Louvre
Louvre Rivoli
Châtelet Les Halles
Châtelet
Pont Neuf
St-Sébastien Froissart
Chemin Vert
Richard Lenoir
Voltaire
Charonne
La Muette
Boulainvilliers
Ranelagh
Passy
Kennedy Radio France
Champ de Mars Tour Eiffel
La Tour Maubourg
École Militaire
Varenne
Solférino
Musée d'Orsay
Rue du Bac
Sèvres Babylone
St-Germain des Prés
Cité
Hôtel de Ville
St-Paul
Bréguet Sabin
Rue de Boulets
Ledru-Rollin
Reuilly Diderot
Nation
Porte de Vincennes
St-Mandé
To Marne-la-Vallée, Boissy-St-Léger, Parc Disneyland
Vincennes
Bérault
A RER
1 Château de Vincennes
Boulogne Pont de St-Cloud
Michel Ange Auteuil
Porte d'Auteuil
Jasmin
Bir Hakeim
La Motte Picquet
St-François Xavier
Ségur
Vaneau
Rennes
Mabillon
Odéon
St-Michel
St-Michel Notre-Dame
Cluny La Sorbonne
Pont Marie
Sully Morland
Bastille
Quai de la Rapée
Faidherbe Chaligny
Picpus
Bel-Air
Boulogne J. Jaurès
Michel Ange Molitor
Église d'Auteuil
Charles Michels
Dupleix
Cambronne
Duroc
St-Placide
St-Sulpice
Notre-Dame des Champs
Maubert Mutualité
Cardinal Lemoine
Jussieu
Gare de Lyon
Montgallet
Daumesnil
Michel Bizot
Porte Dorée
Exelmans
Chardon Lagache
Mirabeau
Javel André Citroen
Av. Emile Zola
Commerce
Sèvres Lecourbe
Falguière
Pasteur
Vavin
Raspail
Luxembourg
Place Monge
Gare d'Austerlitz
Dugommier
Bercy
Porte de St-Cloud
Marcel Sembat
Billancourt
Pont de Sèvres
Bd Victor
Félix Faure
Boucicaut
Lourmel
Balard
Convention
Vaugirard
Volontaires
Montparnasse Bienvenüe
Gaîté
Edgar Quinet
Port Royal
Denfert Rochereau
Censier Daubenton
St-Marcel
Quai de la Gare
Cour St-Émilion
Porte de Charenton
Liberté
Charenton-Écoles
École Vétérinaire de Maisons-Alfort
Maisons-Alfort–Stade
Maisons-Alfort Les Juillottes
Créteil-l'Échat
Créteil-Université
Créteil-Préfecture
Porte de Versailles
Pernety
Plaisance
Porte de Vanves
Malakoff Plateau de Vanves
Malakoff Rue Étienne Dolet
Mouton-Duvernet
Alésia
St-Jacques
Glacière
Corvisart
Les Gobelins
Campo Formio
Chevaleret
Nationale
Bibliothèque Fr. Mitterand
Bd Massena
Maisons Alfort Alfortville
Issy-Plaine
Corentin Celton
Mairie d'Issy
Issy
Châtillon-Montrouge
Porte d'Orléans
Cité Universitaire
Place d'Italie
Tolbiac
Porte de Choisy
Porte d'Ivry
Pierre Curie
Ivry sur Seine
Vitry sur Seine
Mairie d'Ivry
Maison Blanche
Porte d'Italie
Le Kremlin-Bicêtre
Villejuif-Louis Aragon
Villejuif-Paul Vaillant-Couturier
Villejuif-Léo Lagrange
RER C To Versailles–Rive Gauche, Château de Versailles, St-Quentin-en-Yvelines
To Robinson
Antony
To St-Rémy-lès-Chevreuse
RER B To Orly Ouest, Orly Sud, Aéroport de Orly
RER C To Massy-Palaiseau, Versailles-Chantiers, Dourdan, St-Martin-d'Étampes
To Melun, Malesherbes
D RER

Paris: Overview and Arrondissements

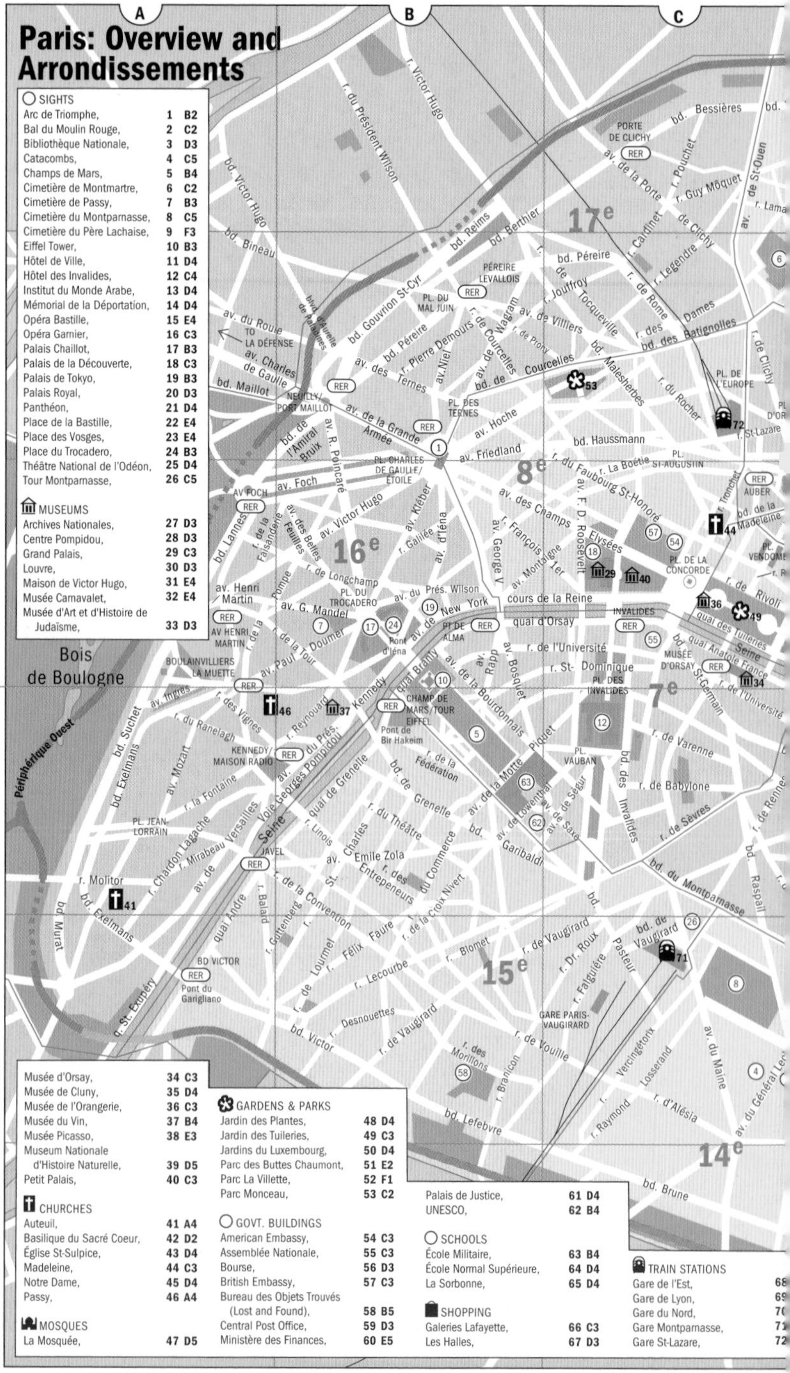

○ SIGHTS

Arc de Triomphe,	1	B2
Bal du Moulin Rouge,	2	C2
Bibliothèque Nationale,	3	D3
Catacombs,	4	C5
Champs de Mars,	5	B4
Cimetière de Montmartre,	6	C2
Cimetière de Passy,	7	B3
Cimetière du Montparnasse,	8	C5
Cimetière du Père Lachaise,	9	F3
Eiffel Tower,	10	B3
Hôtel de Ville,	11	D4
Hôtel des Invalides,	12	C4
Institut du Monde Arabe,	13	D4
Mémorial de la Déportation,	14	D4
Opéra Bastille,	15	E4
Opéra Garnier,	16	C3
Palais Chaillot,	17	B3
Palais de la Découverte,	18	C3
Palais de Tokyo,	19	B3
Palais Royal,	20	D3
Panthéon,	21	D4
Place de la Bastille,	22	E4
Place des Vosges,	23	E4
Place du Trocadero,	24	B3
Théâtre National de l'Odéon,	25	D4
Tour Montparnasse,	26	C5

MUSEUMS

Archives Nationales,	27	D3
Centre Pompidou,	28	D3
Grand Palais,	29	C3
Louvre,	30	D3
Maison de Victor Hugo,	31	E4
Musée Carnavalet,	32	E4
Musée d'Art et d'Histoire de Judaïsme,	33	D3
Musée d'Orsay,	34	C3
Musée de Cluny,	35	D4
Musée de l'Orangerie,	36	C3
Musée du Vin,	37	B4
Musée Picasso,	38	E3
Museum Nationale d'Histoire Naturelle,	39	D5
Petit Palais,	40	C3

CHURCHES

Auteuil,	41	A4
Basilique du Sacré Coeur,	42	D2
Église St-Sulpice,	43	D4
Madeleine,	44	C3
Notre Dame,	45	D4
Passy,	46	A4

MOSQUES

La Mosquée,	47	D5

GARDENS & PARKS

Jardin des Plantes,	48	D4
Jardin des Tuileries,	49	C3
Jardins du Luxembourg,	50	D4
Parc des Buttes Chaumont,	51	E2
Parc La Villette,	52	F1
Parc Monceau,	53	C2

○ GOVT. BUILDINGS

American Embassy,	54	C3
Assemblée Nationale,	55	C3
Bourse,	56	D3
British Embassy,	57	C3
Bureau des Objets Trouvés (Lost and Found),	58	B5
Central Post Office,	59	D3
Ministère des Finances,	60	E5
Palais de Justice,	61	D4
UNESCO,	62	B4

○ SCHOOLS

École Militaire,	63	B4
École Normal Supérieure,	64	D4
La Sorbonne,	65	D4

SHOPPING

Galeries Lafayette,	66	C3
Les Halles,	67	D3

TRAIN STATIONS

Gare de l'Est,	68
Gare de Lyon,	69
Gare du Nord,	70
Gare Montparnasse,	71
Gare St-Lazare,	72

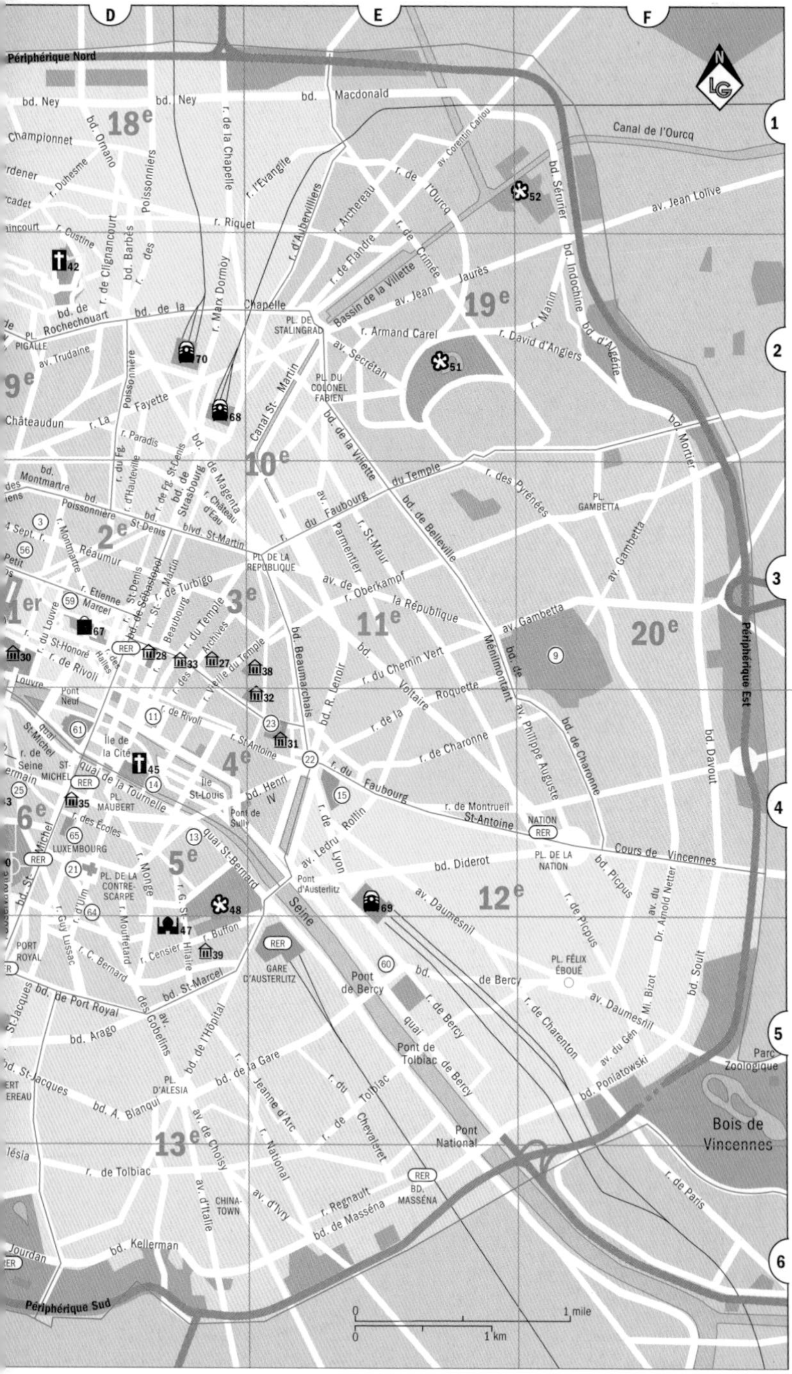

D
E
F
1
2
3
4
5
6
Périphérique Nord
Périphérique Est
Périphérique Sud
LG
bd. Ney
bd. Macdonald
18e
19e
20e
10e
11e
12e
13e
2e
3e
4e
5e
6e
9e
1er
bd. Ornano
Championnet
r. Duhesme
Poissonniers
r. de la Chapelle
r. l'Evangile
r. d'Aubervilliers
r. Archereau
r. de l'Ourcq
av. Corentin Cariou
Canal de l'Ourcq
bd. Sérurier
av. Jean Lolive
r. Riquet
r. Custine
r. de Clignancourt
bd. Barbès
r. Marx Dormoy
r. de Flandre
r. de Crimée
Bassin de la Villette
av. Jean Jaurès
bd. Indochine
bd. d'Algérie
r. Manin
bd. de Rochechouart
bd. de la Chapelle
PL. DE STALINGRAD
r. Armand Carel
r. David d'Angiers
PL. PIGALLE
av. Trudaine
av. Secrétan
PL. DU COLONEL FABIEN
r. Poissonnière
r. La Fayette
Canal St-Martin
bd. de la Villette
Châteaudun
r. Paradis
r. du Fg. Poissonnière
r. d'Hauteville
r. de Fg. St-Denis
bd. de Strasbourg
bd. de Magenta
r. Château d'Eau
r. du Faubourg du Temple
bd. de Belleville
r. des Pyrénées
PL. GAMBETTA
bd. Mortier
bd. Montmartre
bd. Poissonnière
bd. St-Denis
blvd. St-Martin
av. Parmentier
r. St-Maur
av. Gambetta
r. Réaumur
r. Montmartre
PL. DE LA RÉPUBLIQUE
r. Oberkampf
av. de la République
r. Etienne Marcel
r. de Turbigo
r. St-Denis
bd. de Sébastopol
r. St-Martin
r. Beaubourg
r. du Temple
r. des Archives
r. Vieille du Temple
bd. Beaumarchais
bd. Voltaire
r. du Chemin Vert
av. Gambetta
bd. de Ménilmontant
r. du Louvre
r. St-Honoré
r. de Rivoli
Les Halles
RER
Louvre
Pont Neuf
bd. R. Lenoir
r. de la Roquette
av. Philippe Auguste
bd. de Charonne
bd. Davout
quai St-Michel
r. de Seine
St-Germain
ST-MICHEL
Ile de la Cité
quai de la Tournelle
r. de Rivoli
r. St-Antoine
r. de Charonne
Ile St-Louis
bd. Henri IV
r. du Faubourg St-Antoine
r. de Montreuil
PL. MAUBERT
r. des Écoles
Pont de Sully
quai St-Bernard
r. de Lyon
r. Rollin
av. Ledru
NATION
PL. DE LA NATION
Cours de Vincennes
LUXEMBOURG
bd. St-Michel
r. Monge
PL. DE LA CONTRE-SCARPE
Pont d'Austerlitz
bd. Diderot
av. Daumesnil
bd. Picpus
r. de Picpus
av. du Dr. Arnold Netter
r. d'Ulm
r. Guy Lussac
r. Mouffetard
r. G. St. Hilaire
r. Buffon
r. Censier
Seine
PORT ROYAL
r. C. Bernard
GARE D'AUSTERLITZ
Pont de Bercy
bd. de Bercy
PL. FÉLIX ÉBOUÉ
Mi. Bizot
bd. Soult
bd. de Port Royal
bd. St-Marcel
av. des Gobelins
r. de Bercy
quai de Bercy
r. de Charenton
av. Daumesnil
av. du Gén.
bd. Arago
bd. de l'Hôpital
bd. de la Gare
Pont de Tolbiac
bd. Poniatowski
Parc Zoologique
bd. St-Jacques
PL. D'ALESIA
bd. A. Blanqui
r. Jeanne d'Arc
r. du Tolbiac
r. de Chevaleret
Bois de Vincennes
r. Nationale
Pont National
av. de Choisy
r. de Tolbiac
Alésia
r. Regnault
BD. MASSÉNA
av. d'Italie
CHINA-TOWN
av. d'Ivry
bd. de Masséna
r. de Paris
bd. Kellerman
bd. Jourdan
42
70
68
52
51
3
56
59
67
30
28
33
27
38
32
9
11
23
31
61
45
14
22
15
25
35
65
13
21
48
64
69
47
39
60
0
1 mile
1 km

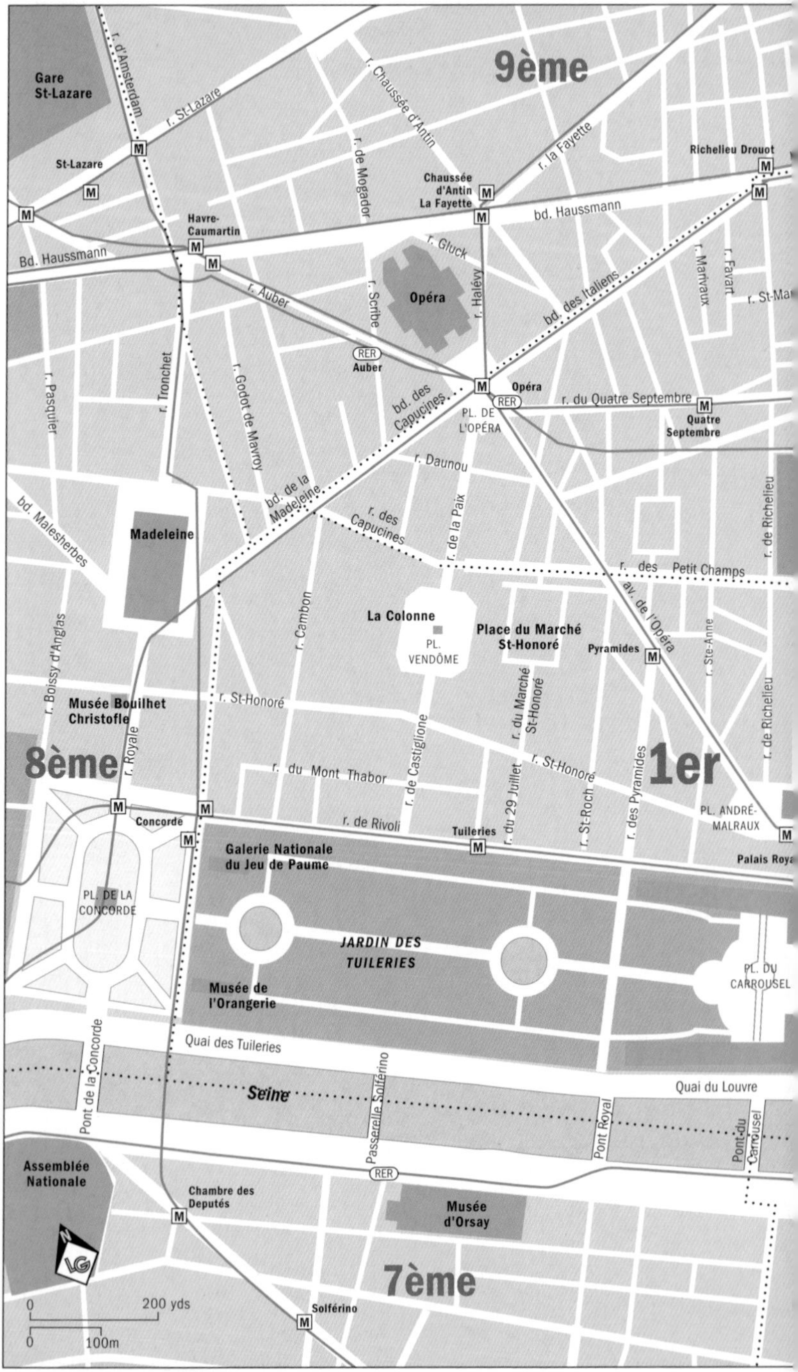

9ème
8ème
1er
7ème
Gare St-Lazare
St-Lazare
r. d'Amsterdam
r. St-Lazare
r. Chaussée d'Antin
r. de Mogador
r. la Fayette
Richelieu Drouot
Chaussée d'Antin La Fayette
bd. Haussmann
Bd. Haussmann
Havre-Caumartin
r. Gluck
r. Auber
r. Scribe
Opéra
r. Halévy
bd. des Italiens
r. Marivaux
r. Favart
RER
Auber
r. Pasquier
r. Tronchet
r. Godot de Mavroy
bd. des Capucines
PL. DE L'OPÉRA
r. du Quatre Septembre
Quatre Septembre
r. Daunou
bd. de la Madeleine
r. des Capucines
r. de la Paix
bd. Malesherbes
Madeleine
r. des Petit Champs
r. de Richelieu
La Colonne
PL. VENDÔME
Place du Marché St-Honoré
Pyramides
av. de l'Opéra
r. Cambon
r. Ste-Anne
r. Boissy d'Anglas
r. St-Honoré
Musée Bouilhet Christofle
r. du Marché St-Honoré
r. de Castiglione
r. Royale
r. du Mont Thabor
r. du 29 Juillet
r. St-Roch
r. des Pyramides
Concorde
r. de Rivoli
Tuileries
PL. ANDRÉ-MALRAUX
Palais Royal
Galerie Nationale du Jeu de Paume
PL. DE LA CONCORDE
JARDIN DES TUILERIES
PL. DU CARROUSEL
Musée de l'Orangerie
Quai des Tuileries
Pont de la Concorde
Passerelle Solférino
Seine
Quai du Louvre
Pont Royal
Pont du Carrousel
Assemblée Nationale
Chambre des Deputés
Musée d'Orsay
Solférino
0
200 yds
100m

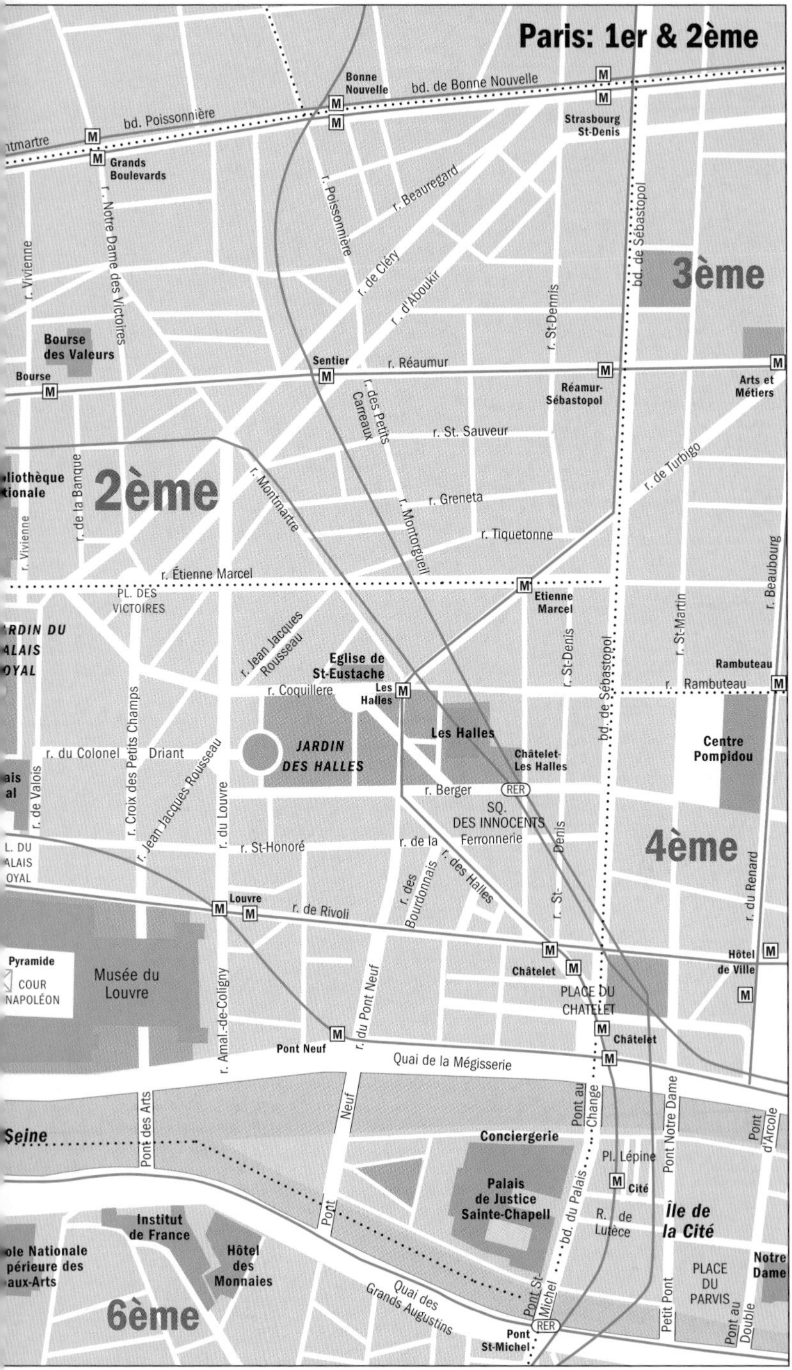

Paris: 1er & 2ème
bd. Poissonnière
bd. de Bonne Nouvelle
Bonne Nouvelle
Grands Boulevards
Strasbourg St-Denis
r. Notre Dame des Victoires
r. Poissonnière
r. Beauregard
r. de Cléry
r. d'Aboukir
bd. de Sébastopol
3ème
r. Vivienne
r. St-Denis
Bourse des Valeurs
Sentier
r. Réaumur
Bourse
Réaumur-Sébastopol
Arts et Métiers
r. des Petits Carreaux
r. St. Sauveur
r. de Turbigo
r. de la Banque
2ème
r. Montmartre
r. Greneta
r. Montorgueil
r. Tiquetonne
r. Étienne Marcel
PL. DES VICTOIRES
Etienne Marcel
r. Jean Jacques Rousseau
Eglise de St-Eustache
r. St-Martin
r. Beaubourg
Rambuteau
r. Rambuteau
r. Coquillere
Les Halles
r. Croix des Petits Champs
r. du Colonel Driant
JARDIN DES HALLES
Châtelet-Les Halles
Centre Pompidou
r. de Valois
r. du Louvre
r. Berger
RER
SQ. DES INNOCENTS
r. de la Ferronnerie
r. St-Honoré
4ème
r. des Bourdonnais
r. des Halles
r. du Renard
Louvre
r. de Rivoli
Pyramide
COUR NAPOLÉON
Musée du Louvre
r. Amal.-de-Coligny
r. du Pont Neuf
Châtelet
Hôtel de Ville
PLACE DU CHATELET
Pont Neuf
Quai de la Mégisserie
Pont des Arts
Pont Neuf
Pont au Change
Pont Notre Dame
Pont d'Arcole
Seine
Conciergerie
Pl. Lépine
Cité
Palais de Justice Sainte-Chapell
bd. du Palais
R. de Lutèce
Île de la Cité
Institut de France
Hôtel des Monnaies
PLACE DU PARVIS
Notre Dame
6ème
Quai des Grands Augustins
Pont St Michel
Pont St-Michel
Petit Pont
Pont au Double

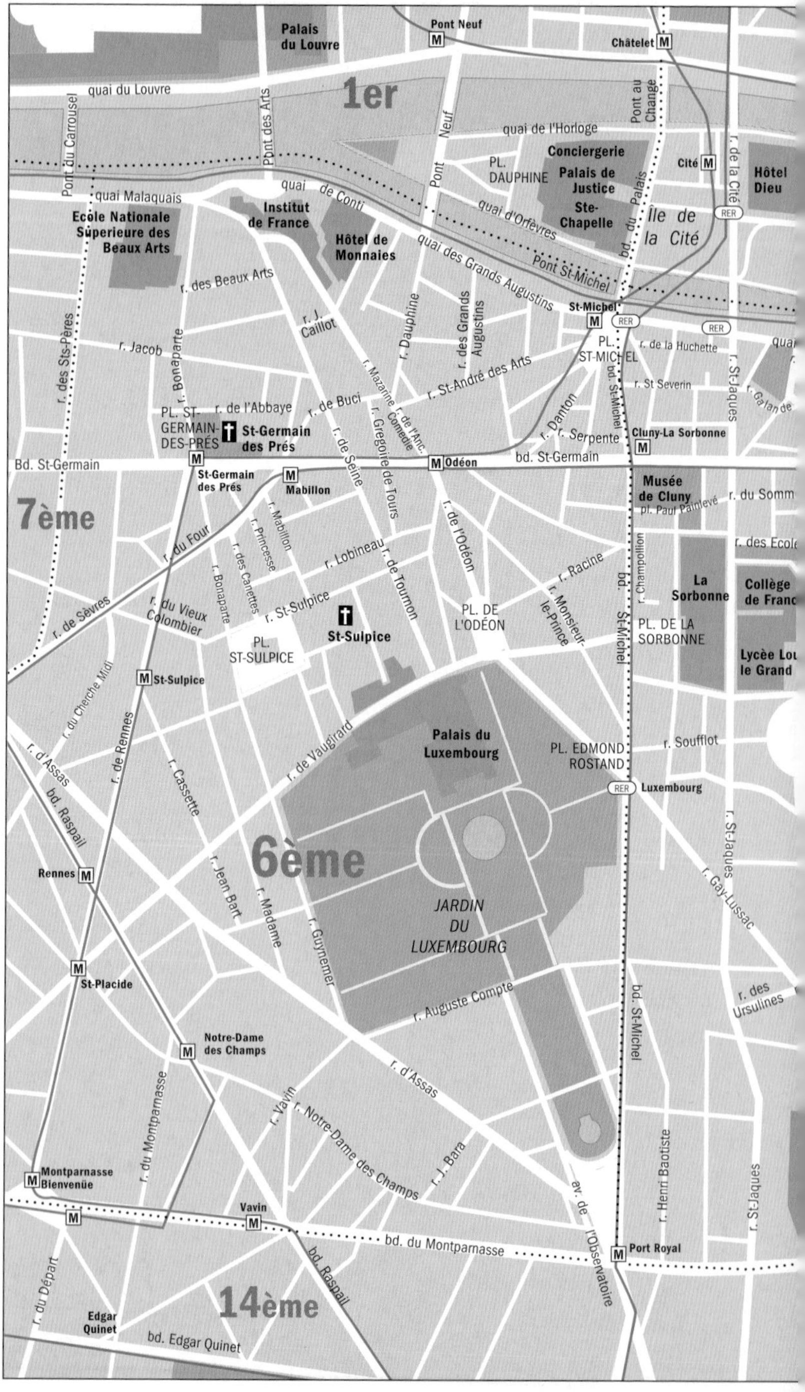
Palais du Louvre
Pont Neuf
Châtelet
1er
quai du Louvre
Pont du Carrousel
Pont des Arts
Pont Neuf
Pont au Change
quai de l'Horloge
Conciergerie
Palais de Justice
Ste-Chapelle
PL. DAUPHINE
Cité
r. de la Cité
Hôtel Dieu
quai Malaquais
quai de Conti
quai d'Orfèvres
Île de la Cité
bd. du Palais
RER
Ecole Nationale Superieure des Beaux Arts
Institut de France
Hôtel de Monnaies
quai des Grands Augustins
Pont St-Michel
r. des Beaux Arts
r. J. Caillot
r. Dauphine
r. des Grands Augustins
St-Michel
RER
RER
PL. ST-MICHEL
r. de la Huchette
quai
r. des Sts-Pères
r. Jacob
r. Bonaparte
r. Mazarine
r. St-André des Arts
r. St Severin
r. St-Jaques
r. Galande
bd. St-Michel
PL. ST-GERMAIN-DES-PRÉS
r. de l'Abbaye
r. de Buci
St-Germain des Prés
r. de l'Anc. Comédie
r. Danton
r. Serpente
Cluny-La Sorbonne
Bd. St-Germain
St-Germain des Prés
r. de Seine
r. Grégoire de Tours
Odéon
bd. St-Germain
Mabillon
Musée de Cluny
pl. Paul Painlevé
r. du Somm
7ème
r. Mabillon
r. Princesse
r. de l'Odéon
r. des Ecol
r. du Four
r. des Canettes
r. Lobineau
r. de Tournon
r. Racine
r. Champollion
La Sorbonne
Collège de Franc
r. Bonaparte
r. Monsieur-le-Prince
r. de Sèvres
r. du Vieux Colombier
r. St-Sulpice
St-Sulpice
PL. DE L'ODÉON
bd. St-Michel
PL. DE LA SORBONNE
PL. ST-SULPICE
Lycée Lou le Grand
St-Sulpice
r. du Cherche Midi
r. de Vaugirard
Palais du Luxembourg
PL. EDMOND ROSTAND
r. Soufflot
r. d'Assas
r. de Rennes
r. Cassette
RER
Luxembourg
bd. Raspail
r. St-Jaques
6ème
Rennes
r. Jean Bart
r. Madame
JARDIN DU LUXEMBOURG
r. Gay-Lussac
r. Guynemer
St-Placide
r. Auguste Compte
bd. St-Michel
r. des Ursulines
Notre-Dame des Champs
r. d'Assas
r. du Montparnasse
r. Vavin
r. Notre-Dame des Champs
r. J. Bara
r. Henri Baotiste
r. St-Jaques
Montparnasse Bienvenüe
av. de l'Observatoire
Vavin
bd. du Montparnasse
Port Royal
r. du Départ
bd. Raspail
14ème
Edgar Quinet
bd. Edgar Quinet

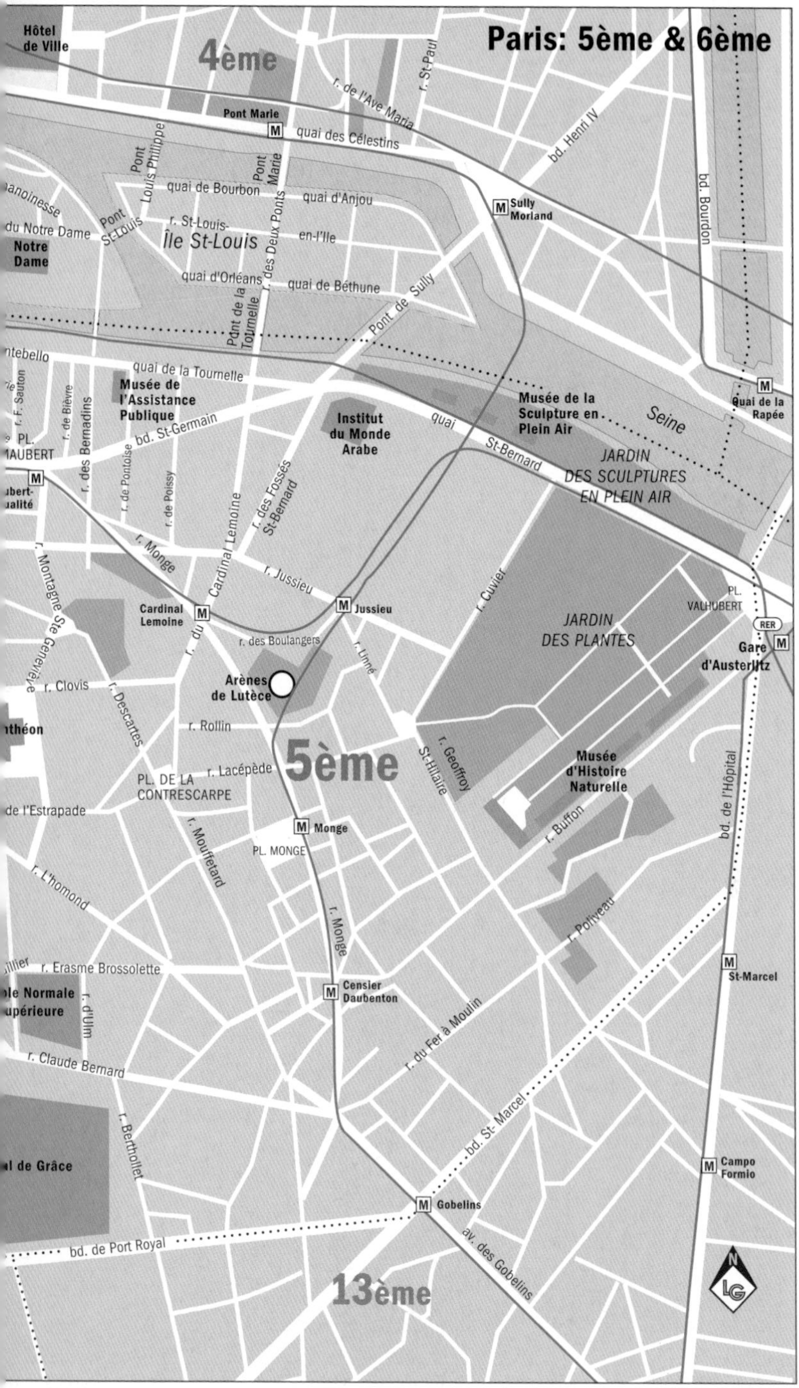

Paris: 5ème & 6ème
4ème
5ème
13ème
Hôtel de Ville
Notre Dame
Pont Marie
quai des Célestins
r. de l'Ave Maria
r. St-Paul
bd. Henri IV
bd. Bourdon
Pont Louis Philippe
Pont Marie
quai de Bourbon
quai d'Anjou
Pont St-Louis
r. St-Louis-en-l'Île
Île St-Louis
quai d'Orléans
quai de Béthune
r. des Deux Ponts
Pont de la Tournelle
Pont de Sully
Sully Morland
du Notre Dame
quai de la Tournelle
Musée de l'Assistance Publique
bd. St-Germain
Institut du Monde Arabe
quai St-Bernard
Musée de la Sculpture en Plein Air
Seine
JARDIN DES SCULPTURES EN PLEIN AIR
Quai de la Rapée
r. F. Sauton
r. de Bièvre
r. des Bernadins
PL. MAUBERT
r. de Pontoise
r. de Poissy
r. Cardinal Lemoine
r. des Fossés St-Bernard
r. Monge
r. Jussieu
Jussieu
Cardinal Lemoine
r. Montagne Ste Geneviève
r. des Boulangers
r. Linné
r. Cuvier
JARDIN DES PLANTES
PL. VALHUBERT
RER
Gare d'Austerlitz
Arènes de Lutèce
r. Clovis
r. Descartes
r. Rollin
r. Lacépède
PL. DE LA CONTRESCARPE
de l'Estrapade
r. Mouffetard
Monge
PL. MONGE
r. St-Hilaire
r. Geoffroy
Musée d'Histoire Naturelle
r. Buffon
bd. de l'Hôpital
r. L'homond
r. Poliveau
r. Erasme Brossolette
r. d'Ulm
Censier Daubenton
St-Marcel
r. du Fer à Moulin
r. Claude Bernard
r. Berthollet
bd. St- Marcel
Campo Formio
Gobelins
bd. de Port Royal
av. des Gobelins
LG
N

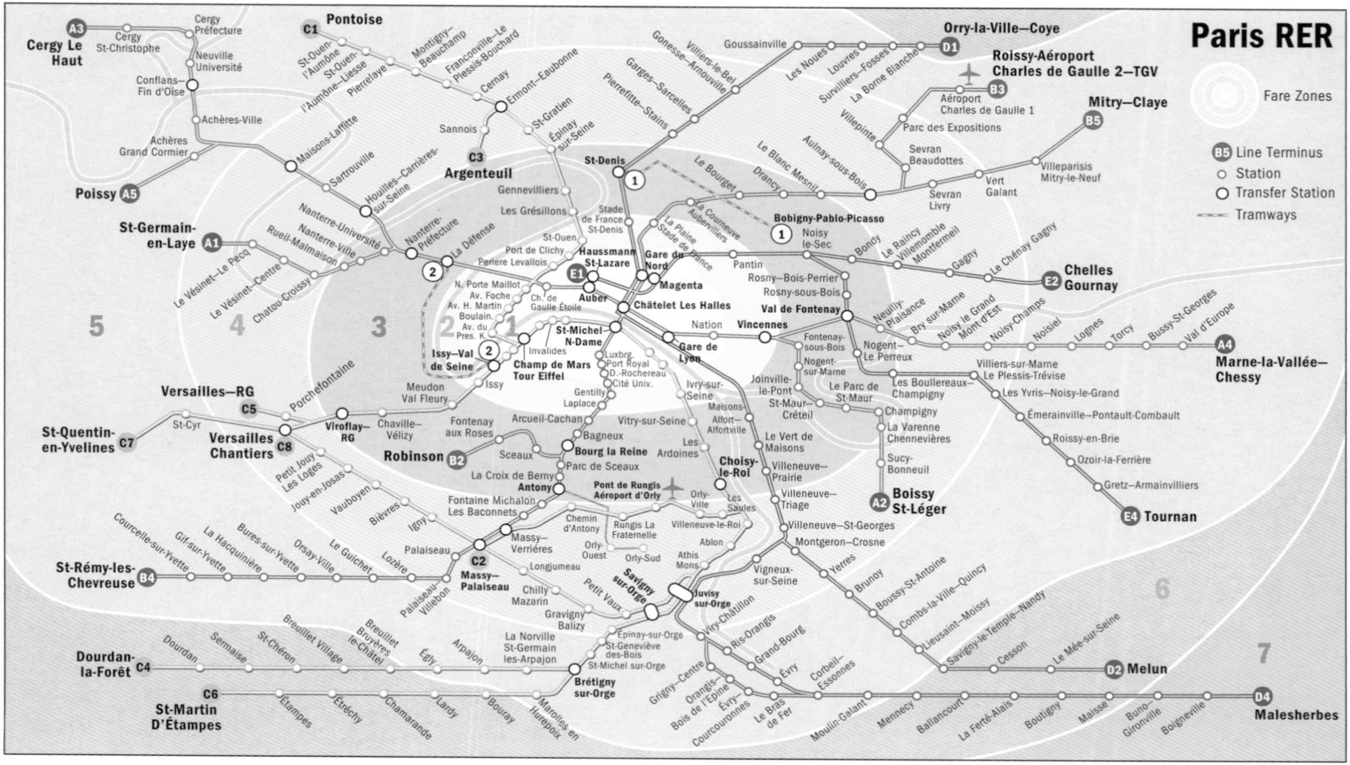

Paris RER
Fare Zones
B5 Line Terminus
Station
Transfer Station
Tramways
1
2
3
4
5
6
7
A1 St-Germain-en-Laye
Le Vésinet–Le Pecq
Le Vésinet–Centre
Chatou-Croissy
Rueil-Malmaison
Nanterre-Ville
Nanterre-Université
Nanterre-Préfecture
La Défense
Charles de Gaulle Étoile
Auber
Châtelet Les Halles
Gare de Lyon
Nation
Vincennes
Val de Fontenay
Fontenay-sous-Bois
Nogent-sur-Marne
Joinville-le-Pont
St-Maur–Créteil
Le Parc de St-Maur
Champigny
La Varenne Chennevières
Sucy-Bonneuil
A2 Boissy St-Léger
Neuilly-Plaisance
Bry sur-Marne
Noisy le Grand Mont d'Est
Noisy-Champs
Noisiel
Lognes
Torcy
Bussy-St-Georges
Val d'Europe
A4 Marne-la-Vallée–Chessy
A3 Cergy Le Haut
Cergy St-Christophe
Cergy Préfecture
Neuville Université
Conflans–Fin d'Oise
Achères-Ville
Achères Grand Cormier
A5 Poissy
Maisons-Laffitte
Sartrouville
Houilles–Carrières-sur-Seine
B3 Roissy-Aéroport Charles de Gaulle 2–TGV
Aéroport Charles de Gaulle 1
Parc des Expositions
Villepinte
Sevran Beaudottes
B5 Mitry–Claye
Villeparisis Mitry-le-Neuf
Vert Galant
Sevran Livry
Aulnay-sous-Bois
Le Blanc Mesnil
Drancy
Le Bourget
La Courneuve Aubervilliers
La Plaine Stade de France
Gare du Nord
St-Michel–N-Dame
Luxbrg.
Port Royal
D.-Rochereau
Cité Univ.
Gentilly
Laplace
Arcueil-Cachan
Bagneux
Bourg la Reine
Sceaux
Fontenay aux Roses
B2 Robinson
Parc de Sceaux
La Croix de Berny
Antony
Fontaine Michalon
Les Baconnets
Massy–Verrières
Massy–Palaiseau
Palaiseau
Palaiseau-Villebon
Lozère
Le Guichet
Orsay-Ville
Bures-sur-Yvette
La Hacquinière
Gif-sur-Yvette
Courcelle-sur-Yvette
B4 St-Rémy-les-Chevreuse
C1 Pontoise
St-Ouen-l'Aumône
St-Ouen-l'Aumône–Liesse
Pierrelaye
Montigny–Beauchamp
Franconville–Le Plessis-Bouchard
Cernay
Ermont–Eaubonne
St-Gratien
Épinay sur-Seine
Sannois
C3 Argenteuil
Gennevilliers
Les Grésillons
St-Ouen
Port de Clichy
Periere Levallois
N. Porte Maillot
Av. Foche
Av. H. Martin
Boulain.
Av. du Pres. K.
Issy–Val de Seine
Issy
Invalides
Champ de Mars Tour Eiffel
Meudon Val Fleury
Chaville–Vélizy
Viroflay–RG
Porchefontaine
C5 Versailles–RG
C8 Versailles Chantiers
St-Cyr
C7 St-Quentin-en-Yvelines
Petit Jouy Les Loges
Jouy-en-Josas
Vauboyen
Bièvres
Igny
Longjumeau
Chilly Mazarin
Gravigny Balizy
Petit Vaux
Savigny sur-Orge
Chemin d'Antony
Rungis La Fraternelle
Orly-Ouest
Orly-Sud
Pont de Rungis Aéroport d'Orly
Orly-Ville
Les Saules
Choisy-le-Roi
Les Ardoines
Vitry-sur-Seine
Ivry-sur-Seine
Villeneuve-le-Roi
Ablon
Athis Mons
Juvisy sur-Orge
Épinay-sur-Orge
St-Geneviève des-Bois
St-Michel sur-Orge
Brétigny sur-Orge
La Norville St-Germain les-Arpajon
Arpajon
Égly
Breuillet Bruyères le-Châtel
Breuillet Village
St-Chéron
Sermaise
Dourdan
C4 Dourdan-la-Forêt
Marolles en Hurepoix
Bouray
Lardy
Chamarande
Étréchy
Étampes
C6 St-Martin D'Étampes
Viry-Châtillon
Ris-Orangis
Grand-Bourg
Évry
Corbeil-Essonnes
Grigny–Centre
Orangis–Bois de l'Épine
Évry–Courcouronnes
Le Bras de Fer
Moulin-Galant
Mennecy
Ballancourt
La Ferté-Alais
Boutigny
Maisse
Buno–Gironville
Boigneville
D4 Malesherbes
D1 Orry-la-Ville–Coye
Goussainville
Les Noues
Louvres
Survilliers–Fosses
La Borne Blanche
Villiers-le-Bel
Gonesse–Arnouville
Garges–Sarcelles
Pierrefitte–Stains
St-Denis
Stade de France St-Denis
Haussmann St-Lazare
E1
Magenta
Pantin
Noisy le-Sec
Bondy
Le Raincy Villemomble Montfermeil
Gagny
Le Chénay Gagny
E2 Chelles Gournay
Rosny–Bois-Perrier
Rosny-sous-Bois
Nogent–Le Perreux
Les Boullereaux–Champigny
Villiers-sur-Marne Le Plessis-Trévise
Les Yvris–Noisy-le-Grand
Émerainville–Pontault-Combault
Roissy-en-Brie
Ozoir-la-Ferrière
Gretz–Armainvilliers
E4 Tournan
Bobigny-Pablo-Picasso
Maisons-Alfort–Alfortville
Le Vert de Maisons
Villeneuve–Prairie
Villeneuve–Triage
Villeneuve–St-Georges
Montgeron–Crosne
Vigneux-sur-Seine
Yerres
Brunoy
Boussy-St-Antoine
Combs-la-Ville–Quincy
Lieusaint–Moissy
Savigny-le-Temple–Nandy
Cesson
Le Mée-sur-Seine
D2 Melun

Berlin Transit

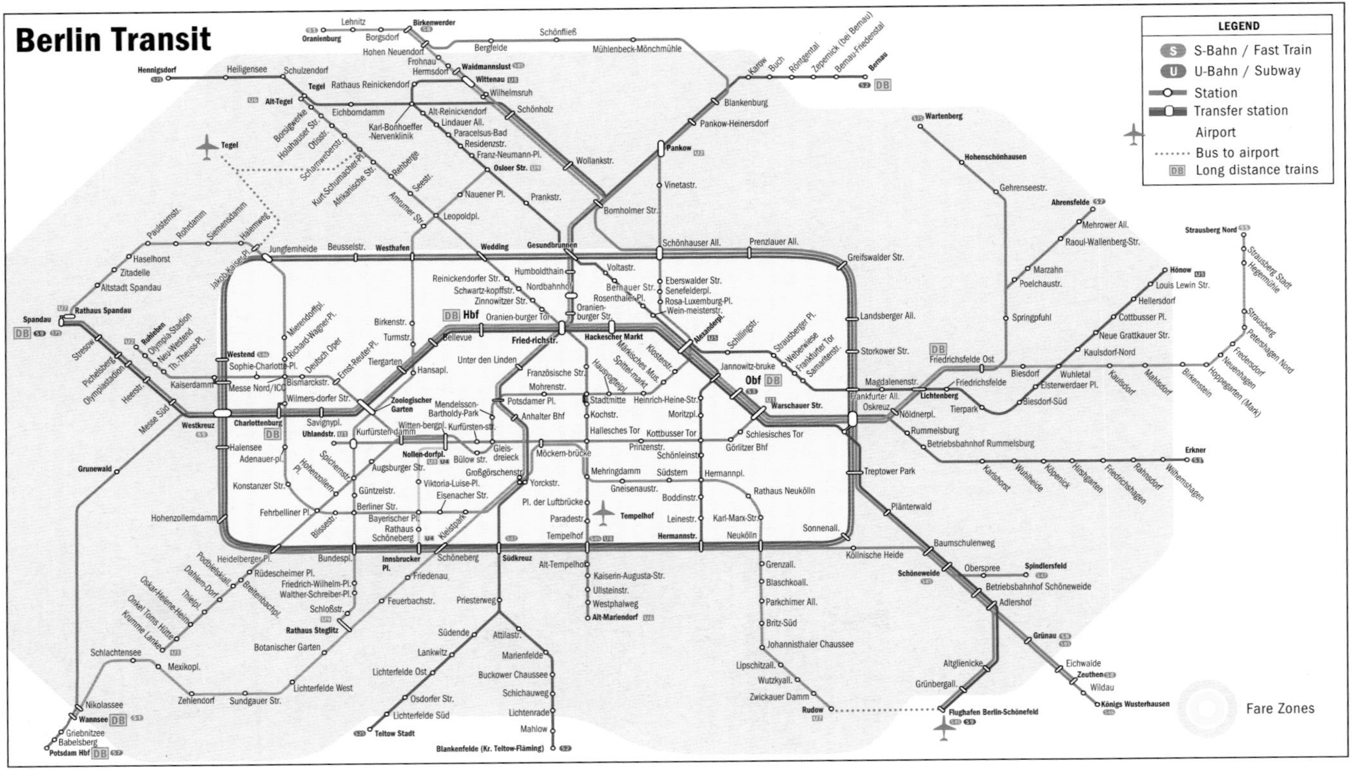

Berlin Overview

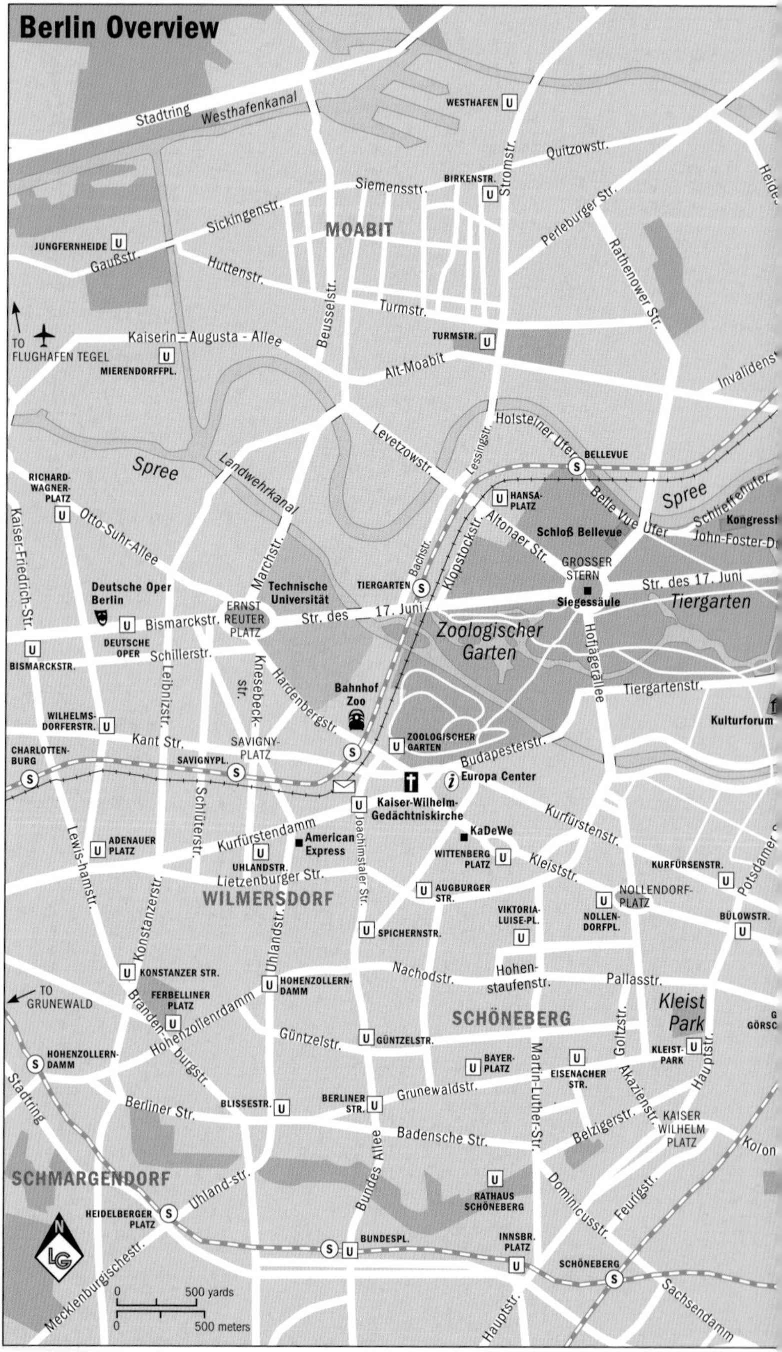

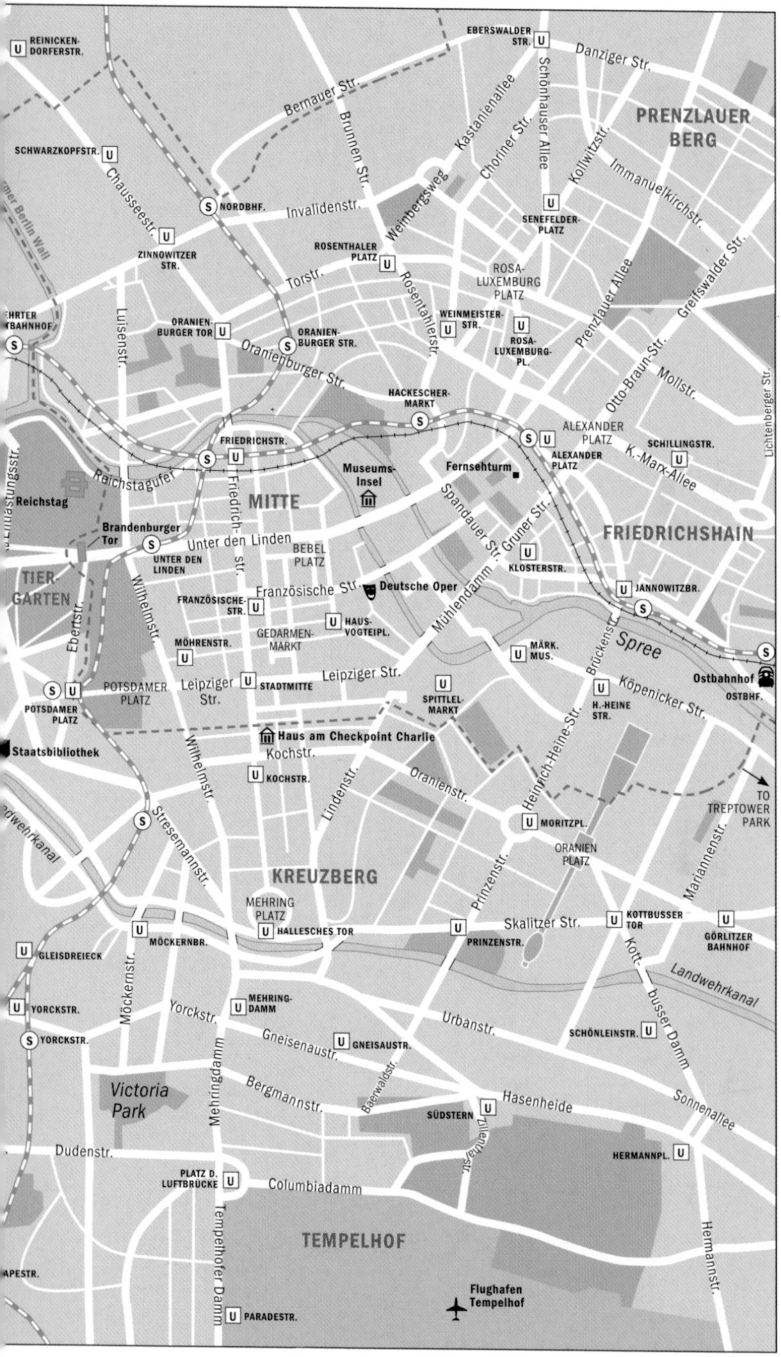
PRENZLAUER BERG
MITTE
FRIEDRICHSHAIN
TIERGARTEN
KREUZBERG
TEMPELHOF
REINICKENDORFERSTR.
EBERSWALDER STR.
SCHWARZKOPFSTR.
NORDBHF.
ZINNOWITZER STR.
ROSENTHALER PLATZ
SENEFELDER-PLATZ
ROSA-LUXEMBURG PLATZ
ORANIENBURGER TOR
ORANIENBURGER STR.
WEINMEISTERSTR.
ROSA-LUXEMBURG-PL.
HACKESCHER MARKT
FRIEDRICHSTR.
ALEXANDER PLATZ
SCHILLINGSTR.
Museums-Insel
Fernsehturm
Reichstag
Brandenburger Tor
UNTER DEN LINDEN
BEBEL PLATZ
KLOSTERSTR.
Deutsche Oper
FRANZÖSISCHE STR.
HAUSVOGTEIPL.
JANNOWITZBR.
MÖHRENSTR.
GEDARMENMARKT
MÄRK. MUS.
Spree
POTSDAMER PLATZ
STADTMITTE
SPITTELMARKT
H.-HEINE STR.
Ostbahnhof
OSTBHF.
Haus am Checkpoint Charlie
Staatsbibliothek
KOCHSTR.
TO TREPTOWER PARK
MORITZPL.
ORANIEN PLATZ
MEHRING PLATZ
HALLESCHES TOR
PRINZENSTR.
KOTTBUSSER TOR
GÖRLITZER BAHNHOF
MÖCKERNBR.
GLEISDREIECK
YORCKSTR.
MEHRINGDAMM
GNEISAUSTR.
SCHÖNLEINSTR.
Victoria Park
SÜDSTERN
HERMANNPL.
PLATZ D. LUFTBRÜCKE
Flughafen Tempelhof
PARADESTR.
Bernauer Str.
Danziger Str.
Brunnen Str.
Kastanienallee
Choriner Str.
Schönhauser Allee
Kollwitzstr.
Immanuelkirchstr.
Chausseestr.
Invalidenstr.
Weinbergsweg
Torstr.
Rosentahlerstr.
Greifswalder Str.
Prenzlauer Allee
Luisenstr.
Oranienburger Str.
Otto-Braun-Str.
Mollstr.
Lichtenberger Str.
Reichstagufer
Friedrich-str.
K.-Marx-Allee
Unter den Linden
Spandauer Str.
Gruner Str.
Wilhelmstr.
Französische Str.
Mühlendamm
Ebertstr.
Leipziger Str.
Brückenstr.
Köpenicker Str.
Heinrich-Heine-Str.
Kochstr.
Lindenstr.
Oranienstr.
Stresemannstr.
Landwehrkanal
Prinzenstr.
Mariannenstr.
Skalitzer Str.
Kottbusser Damm
Möckernstr.
Yorckstr.
Urbanstr.
Gneisenaustr.
Bergmannstr.
Baerwaldstr.
Hasenheide
Sonnenallee
Zillestr.
Mehringdamm
Dudenstr.
Columbiadamm
Tempelhofer Damm
Hermannstr.
Berlin Wall
APESTR.

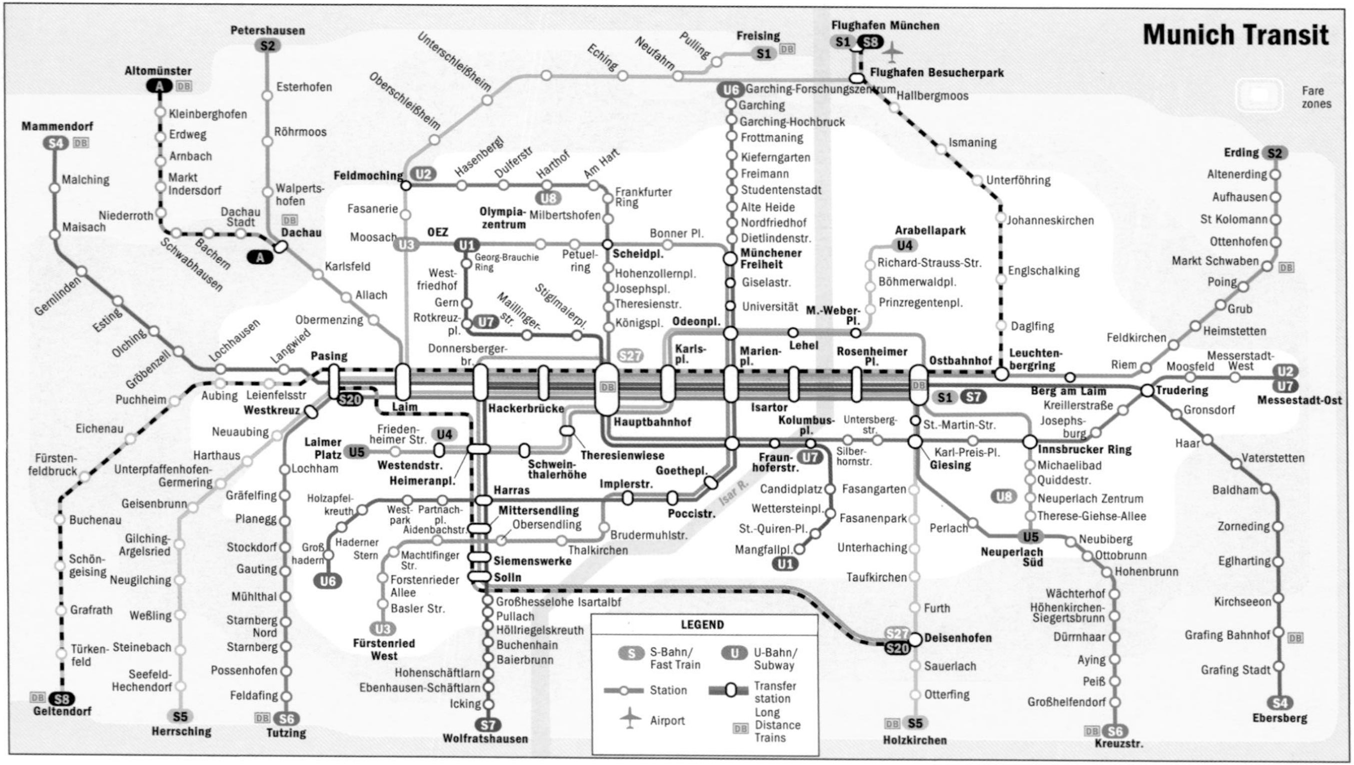
Munich Transit
Fare zones
LEGEND
S S-Bahn/ Fast Train
U U-Bahn/ Subway
Station
Transfer station
Airport
DB Long Distance Trains
Petershausen S2
Esterhofen
Röhrmoos
Walperts-hofen
Dachau
Altomünster A
Kleinberghofen
Erdweg
Arnbach
Markt Indersdorf
Niederroth
Dachau Stadt
Bachern
Schwabhausen
Mammendorf S4
Malching
Maisach
Gernlinden
Esting
Olching
Gröbenzell
Lochhausen
Langwied
Karlsfeld
Allach
Obermenzing
Pasing
Puchheim
Aubing
Leienfelsstr
Westkreuz
Eichenau
Fürsten-feldbruck
Buchenau
Schön-geising
Grafrath
Türken-feld
Geltendorf S8
Neuaubing
Harthaus
Unterpfaffenhofen-Germering
Geisenbrunn
Gilching-Argelsried
Neugilching
Weßling
Steinebach
Seefeld-Hechendorf
Herrsching S5
Lochham
Gräfelfing
Planegg
Stockdorf
Gauting
Mühlthal
Starnberg Nord
Starnberg
Possenhofen
Feldafing
Tutzing S6
Unterschleißheim
Oberschleißheim
Eching
Neufahrn
Pulling
Freising S1
Flughafen München S1 S8
Flughafen Besucherpark
Hallbergmoos
Ismaning
Unterföhring
Johanneskirchen
Englschalking
Daglfing
Leuchten-bergring
Feldmoching U2
Hasenbergl
Dülferstr
Harthof
Am Hart
Frankfurter Ring
U8
Milbertshofen
Olympia-zentrum
Fasanerie
Moosach
OEZ
U3 U1
Georg-Brauchle Ring
West-friedhof
Gern
Rotkreuz-pl.
U7
Maillinger-str.
Stiglmaierpl.
Petuel-ring
Scheidpl.
Bonner Pl.
Hohenzollernpl.
Josephspl.
Theresienstr.
Königspl.
U6 Garching-Forschungszentrum
Garching
Garching-Hochbruck
Frottmaning
Kieferngarten
Freimann
Studentenstadt
Alte Heide
Nordfriedhof
Dietlindenstr.
Münchener Freiheit
Giselastr.
Universität
Odeonpl.
Arabellapark U4
Richard-Strauss-Str.
Böhmerwaldpl.
Prinzregentenpl.
M.-Weber-Pl.
Lehel
Donnersberger-br.
S27
Karls-pl.
Marien-pl.
Rosenheimer Pl.
Ostbahnhof
Hackerbrücke
Hauptbahnhof
Laim
S20
Isartor
Kolumbus-pl.
Untersberg-str.
S1 S7
Berg am Laim
Trudering
Kreillerstraße
Josephs-burg
Innsbrucker Ring
St.-Martin-Str.
Karl-Preis-Pl.
Giesing
Frieden-heimer Str.
U4
Laimer Platz U5
Westendstr.
Heimeranpl.
Schwein-thalerhöhe
Theresienwiese
Goethepl.
Implerstr.
Poccistr.
Harras
Mittersendling
Obersendling
Aidenbachstr.
Holzapfel-kreuth
West-park
Partnach-pl.
Haderner Stern
Groß-hadern
U6
Machtlfinger Str.
Forstenrieder Allee
Basler Str.
U3
Fürstenried West
Siemenswerke
Solln
Thalkirchen
Brudermuhlstr.
Isar R.
Fraun-hoferstr.
U7
Silber-hornstr.
Candidplatz
Wettersteinpl.
St.-Quiren-Pl.
Mangfallpl.
U1
Großhesselohe Isartalbf
Pullach
Höllriegelskreuth
Buchenhain
Baierbrunn
Hohenschäftlarn
Ebenhausen-Schäftlarn
Icking
Wolfratshausen S7
Fasangarten
Fasanenpark
Unterhaching
Taufkirchen
Furth
S27 S20
Deisenhofen
Sauerlach
Otterfing
Holzkirchen S5
Perlach
U8
Michaelibad
Quiddestr.
Neuperlach Zentrum
Therese-Giehse-Allee
U5
Neuperlach Süd
Neubiberg
Ottobrunn
Hohenbrunn
Wächterhof
Höhenkirchen-Siegertsbrunn
Dürrnhaar
Aying
Peiß
Großhelfendorf
Kreuzstr. S6
Riem
Feldkirchen
Moosfeld
Messestadt-West
Messestadt-Ost U2 U7
Gronsdorf
Haar
Vaterstetten
Baldham
Zorneding
Eglharting
Kirchseeon
Grafing Bahnhof
Grafing Stadt
Ebersberg S4
Heimstetten
Grub
Poing
Markt Schwaben
Ottenhofen
St Kolomann
Aufhausen
Altenerding
Erding S2

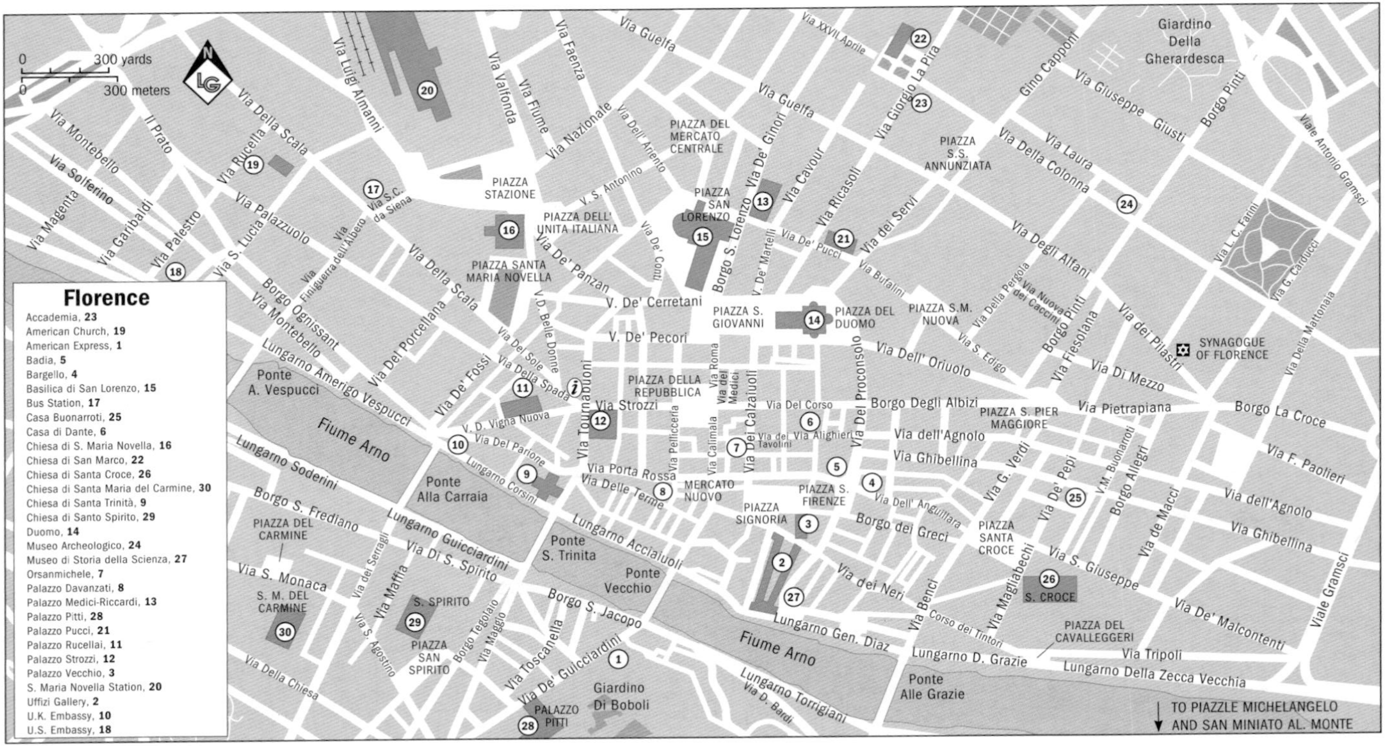
Florence
Accademia, 23
American Church, 19
American Express, 1
Badia, 5
Bargello, 4
Basilica di San Lorenzo, 15
Bus Station, 17
Casa Buonarroti, 25
Casa di Dante, 6
Chiesa di S. Maria Novella, 16
Chiesa di San Marco, 22
Chiesa di Santa Croce, 26
Chiesa di Santa Maria del Carmine, 30
Chiesa di Santa Trinità, 9
Chiesa di Santo Spirito, 29
Duomo, 14
Museo Archeologico, 24
Museo di Storia della Scienza, 27
Orsanmichele, 7
Palazzo Davanzati, 8
Palazzo Medici-Riccardi, 13
Palazzo Pitti, 28
Palazzo Pucci, 21
Palazzo Rucellai, 11
Palazzo Strozzi, 12
Palazzo Vecchio, 3
S. Maria Novella Station, 20
Uffizi Gallery, 2
U.K. Embassy, 10
U.S. Embassy, 18
0 300 yards
0 300 meters
N
LG
TO PIAZZLE MICHELANGELO AND SAN MINIATO AL. MONTE
Giardino Della Gherardesca
SYNAGOGUE OF FLORENCE
PIAZZA STAZIONE
PIAZZA DELL' UNITA ITALIANA
PIAZZA SANTA MARIA NOVELLA
PIAZZA DEL MERCATO CENTRALE
PIAZZA SAN LORENZO
PIAZZA S.S. ANNUNZIATA
PIAZZA S. GIOVANNI
PIAZZA DEL DUOMO
PIAZZA S.M. NUOVA
PIAZZA DELLA REPUBBLICA
PIAZZA S. PIER MAGGIORE
MERCATO NUOVO
PIAZZA S. FIRENZE
PIAZZA SIGNORIA
PIAZZA SANTA CROCE
S. CROCE
PIAZZA DEL CAVALLEGGERI
PIAZZA DEL CARMINE
S. M. DEL CARMINE
S. SPIRITO
PIAZZA SAN SPIRITO
PALAZZO PITTI
Giardino Di Boboli
Ponte A. Vespucci
Ponte Alla Carraia
Ponte S. Trinita
Ponte Vecchio
Ponte Alle Grazie
Fiume Arno
Via Luigi Almanni
Via Valfonda
Via Fiume
Via Faenza
Via Guelfa
Via Nazionale
Via Dell' Ariento
V. S. Antonino
Via De' Conti
Via XXVII Aprile
Via Giorgio La Pira
Gino Capponi
Via Giuseppe Giusti
Borgo Pinti
Viale Antonio Gramsci
Via Della Scala
Via Rucellai
Il Prato
Via Montebello
Via Solferino
Via Magenta
Via Garibaldi
Via Palestro
Via S. Lucia
Via Palazzuolo
Via S.C. da Siena
Via Finiguerra dell'Albero
Borgo Ognissant
Via Del Porcellana
Lungarno Amerigo Vespucci
Via De' Fossi
Via Del Sole
Via Della Spada
V.D. Belle Donne
Via De' Panzan
V. De' Cerretani
V. De' Pecori
Via De' Ginori
Borgo S. Lorenzo
V. De' Martelli
Via Cavour
Via Ricasoli
Via De' Pucci
Via dei Servi
Via Bufalini
Via Della Colonna
Via Laura
Via Degli Alfani
Via Della Pergola
Via Nuova dei Caccini
Via S. Edigo
Borgo Pinti
Via Fiesolana
Via dei Pilastri
Via Di Mezzo
Via L. C. Farini
Via G. Carducci
Via Della Mattonaia
Via Dell' Oriuolo
Via Tornabuoni
Via Strozzi
V. D. Vigna Nuova
Via Del Parione
Lungarno Corsini
Via Porta Rossa
Via Delle Terme
Via Pellicceria
Via Roma
Via Calimala
Via del Medici
Via Dei Calzaiuoli
Via del Tavolini
Via Alighieri
Via Del Corso
Via Del Proconsolo
Borgo Degli Albizi
Via Pietrapiana
Borgo La Croce
Via dell'Agnolo
Via Ghibellina
Via G. Verdi
Via De' Pepi
V.M. Buonarroti
Borgo Allegri
Via de Macci
Via F. Paolieri
Viale Gramsci
Via Dell' Anguillara
Borgo dei Greci
Via Magliabechi
Via S. Giuseppe
Via De' Malcontenti
Via dei Neri
Via Benci
Corso dei Tintori
Lungarno Gen. Diaz
Lungarno D. Grazie
Via Tripoli
Lungarno Della Zecca Vecchia
Lungarno Torrigiani
Via D. Bardi
Lungarno Acciaiuoli
Lungarno Soderini
Lungarno Guicciardini
Borgo S. Frediano
Via S. Monaca
Via dei Serragli
Via Maffia
Via S. Agostino
Via Di S. Spirito
Borgo Tegolaio
Via Maggio
Via Toscanella
Borgo S. Jacopo
Via De' Guicciardini
Via Della Chiesa

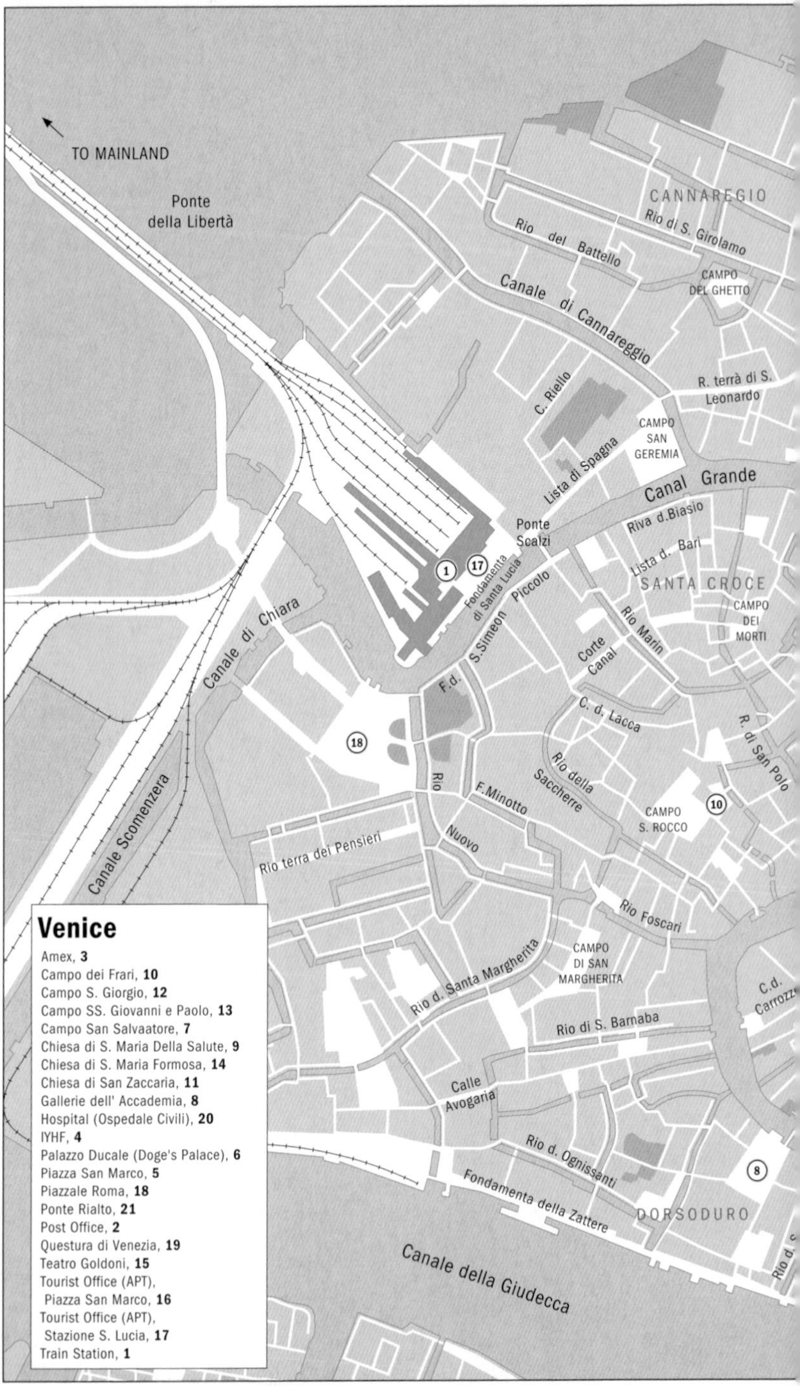

TO MAINLAND
Ponte della Libertà
CANNAREGIO
Rio di S. Girolamo
Rio del Battello
CAMPO DEL GHETTO
Canale di Cannareggio
R. terrà di S. Leonardo
C. Riello
CAMPO SAN GEREMIA
Lista di Spagna
Canal Grande
Ponte Scalzi
Riva d.Biasio
Lista d. Bari
SANTA CROCE
CAMPO DEI MORTI
Fondamenta di Santa Lucia
S.Simeon Piccolo
Rio Marin
Corte Canal
Canale di Chiara
F.d.
C. d. Lacca
R. di San Polo
Rio della Saccherre
Rio Nuovo
F.Minotto
CAMPO S. ROCCO
Canale Scomenzera
Rio terra dei Pensieri
Rio Foscari
CAMPO DI SAN MARGHERITA
Rio d. Santa Margherita
C.d. Carrozze
Rio di S. Barnaba
Calle Avogaria
Rio d. Ognissanti
Fondamenta della Zattere
DORSODURO
Canale della Giudecca
1
17
18
10
8
Venice
Amex, 3
Campo dei Frari, 10
Campo S. Giorgio, 12
Campo SS. Giovanni e Paolo, 13
Campo San Salvaatore, 7
Chiesa di S. Maria Della Salute, 9
Chiesa di S. Maria Formosa, 14
Chiesa di San Zaccaria, 11
Gallerie dell' Accademia, 8
Hospital (Ospedale Civili), 20
IYHF, 4
Palazzo Ducale (Doge's Palace), 6
Piazza San Marco, 5
Piazzale Roma, 18
Ponte Rialto, 21
Post Office, 2
Questura di Venezia, 19
Teatro Goldoni, 15
Tourist Office (APT), Piazza San Marco, 16
Tourist Office (APT), Stazione S. Lucia, 17
Train Station, 1

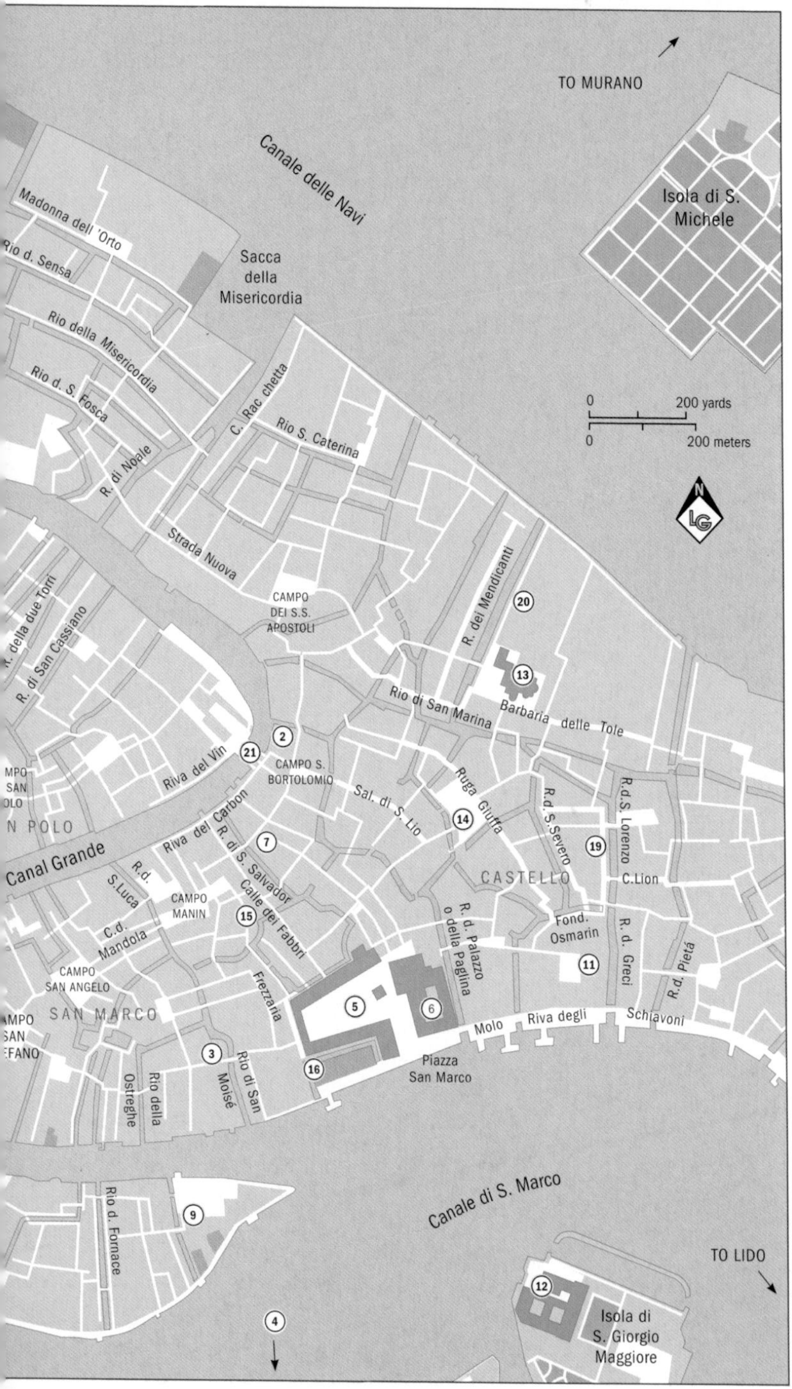

TO MURANO
Canale delle Navi
Isola di S. Michele
Madonna dell 'Orto
Rio d. Sensa
Sacca della Misericordia
Rio della Misericordia
Rio d. S. Fosca
C. Rac chetta
Rio S. Caterina
R. di Noale
0 200 yards
0 200 meters
Strada Nuova
R. della due Torri
R. di San Cassiano
CAMPO DEI S.S. APOSTOLI
R. dei Mendicanti
Rio di San Marina
Barbaria delle Tole
Riva del Vin
CAMPO S. BORTOLOMIO
Sal. di S. Lio
Ruga Giuffa
R.d.S.Severo
R.d.S. Lorenzo
SAN POLO
Canal Grande
Riva del Carbon
R. di S. Salvador
CASTELLO
C.Lion
R.d. S.Luca
CAMPO MANIN
Calle dei Fabbri
R. d. Palazzo o della Paglina
Fond. Osmarin
C.d. Mandola
R. d. Greci
R.d. Pietá
CAMPO SAN ANGELO
Frezzaria
SAN MARCO
Molo
Riva degli Schiavoni
Piazza San Marco
Rio di San Moisé
Rio della Ostreghe
Canale di S. Marco
Rio d. Fornace
TO LIDO
Isola di S. Giorgio Maggiore

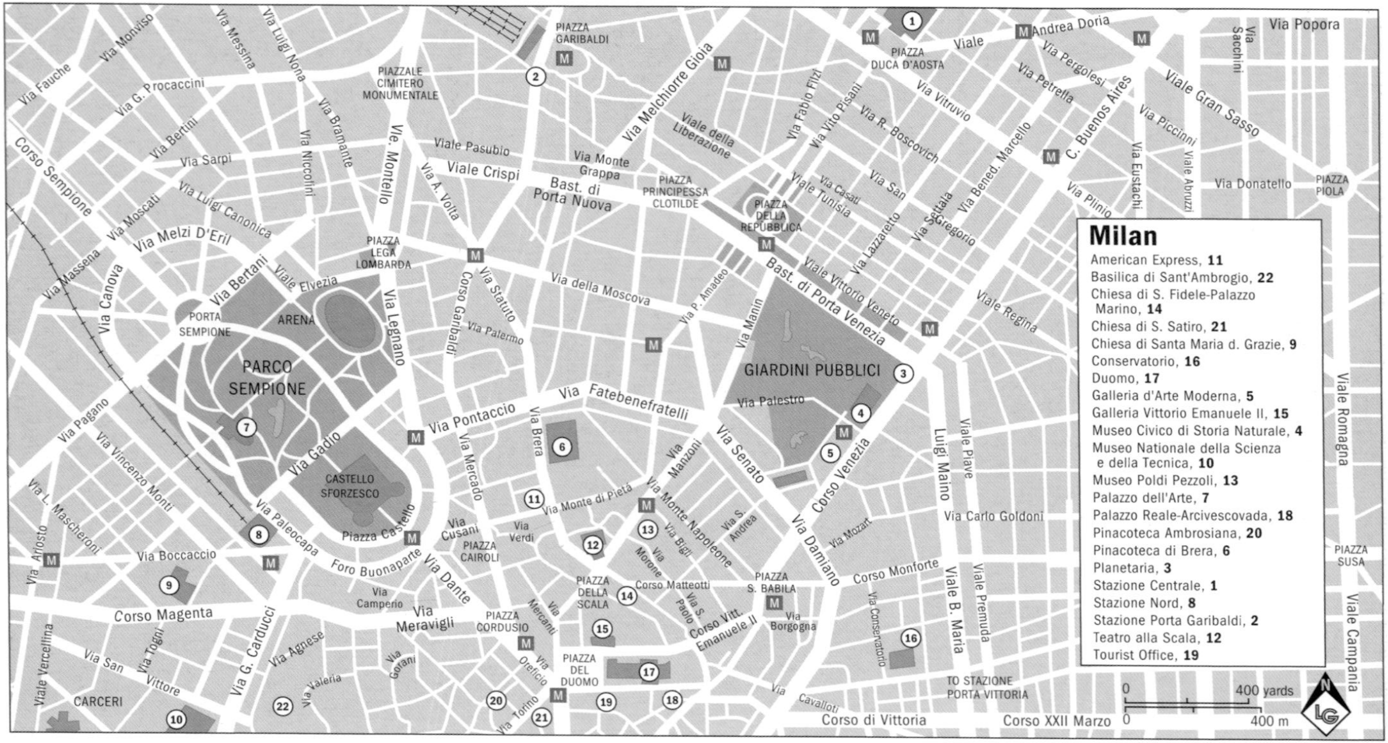
Milan
American Express, 11
Basilica di Sant'Ambrogio, 22
Chiesa di S. Fidele-Palazzo Marino, 14
Chiesa di S. Satiro, 21
Chiesa di Santa Maria d. Grazie, 9
Conservatorio, 16
Duomo, 17
Galleria d'Arte Moderna, 5
Galleria Vittorio Emanuele II, 15
Museo Civico di Storia Naturale, 4
Museo Nationale della Scienza e della Tecnica, 10
Museo Poldi Pezzoli, 13
Palazzo dell'Arte, 7
Palazzo Reale-Arcivescovada, 18
Pinacoteca Ambrosiana, 20
Pinacoteca di Brera, 6
Planetaria, 3
Stazione Centrale, 1
Stazione Nord, 8
Stazione Porta Garibaldi, 2
Teatro alla Scala, 12
Tourist Office, 19
0
400 yards
0
400 m
PARCO SEMPIONE
ARENA
PORTA SEMPIONE
CASTELLO SFORZESCO
GIARDINI PUBBLICI
PIAZZA GARIBALDI
PIAZZALE CIMITERO MONUMENTALE
PIAZZA LEGA LOMBARDA
PIAZZA PRINCIPESSA CLOTILDE
PIAZZA DELLA REPUBBLICA
PIAZZA DUCA D'AOSTA
PIAZZA PIOLA
PIAZZA SUSA
PIAZZA CAIROLI
PIAZZA CORDUSIO
PIAZZA DELLA SCALA
PIAZZA DEL DUOMO
PIAZZA S. BABILA
TO STAZIONE PORTA VITTORIA
CARCERI
Corso Sempione
Corso Magenta
Corso Garibaldi
Corso Venezia
Corso Monforte
Corso di Vittoria
Corso XXII Marzo
Corso Matteotti
Corso Vitt. Emanuele II
Foro Buonaparte
Piazza Castello
Bast. di Porta Nuova
Bast. di Porta Venezia
Viale Crispi
Viale Pasubio
Vle. Montello
Via Melchiorre Gioia
Viale della Liberazione
Via della Moscova
Via Fatebenefratelli
Via Pontaccio
Via Brera
Via Manzoni
Via Monte Napoleone
Via Senato
Via Damiano
Viale Romagna
Viale Campania
Viale Gran Sasso
Viale Abruzzi
Via Donatello
Via Popora
Viale Andrea Doria
Via Vitruvio
C. Buenos Aires
Luigi Maino
Viale B. Maria
Viale Piave
Viale Premuda
Via Carlo Goldoni
Via Dante
Via Meravigli
Via G. Carducci
Via Legnano
Via Bertani
Via Melzi D'Eril
Via Canova
Via Paleocapa
Via Gadio
Via Boccaccio
Via Vincenzo Monti
Via Sarpi
Via Bramante
Via Niccolini
Via Luigi Canonica
Via Moscati
Via Messina
Via Luigi Nona
Via Monviso
Via Fauche
Via G. Procaccini
Via Bertini
Via Massena
Via Pagano
Via L. Mascheroni
Via Ariosto
Viale Vercellina
Via San Vittore
Via Togni
Via Agnese
Via Valeria
Via Gorani
Via Torino
Via Orefico
Via Mercanti
Via Cusani
Via Verdi
Via Mercado
Via Monte di Pietá
Via Morone
Via Bigli
Via S. Andrea
Via S. Paolo
Via Borgogna
Via Conservatorio
Via Mozart
Via Cavallotti
Viale Regina
Via Palestro
Via Manin
Via P. Amadeo
Viale Vittorio Veneto
Via Lazzaretto
Via Settala
Via San Gregorio
Via Casati
Viale Tunisia
Via Fabio Filzi
Via Vito Pisani
Via R. Boscovich
Via Bened. Marcello
Via Petrella
Via Pergolesi
Via Piccinni
Via Eustachi
Via Plinio
Via Sacchini
Via Monte Grappa
Via A. Volta
Via Statuto
Via Palermo
Viale Elvezia
Via Campeiro

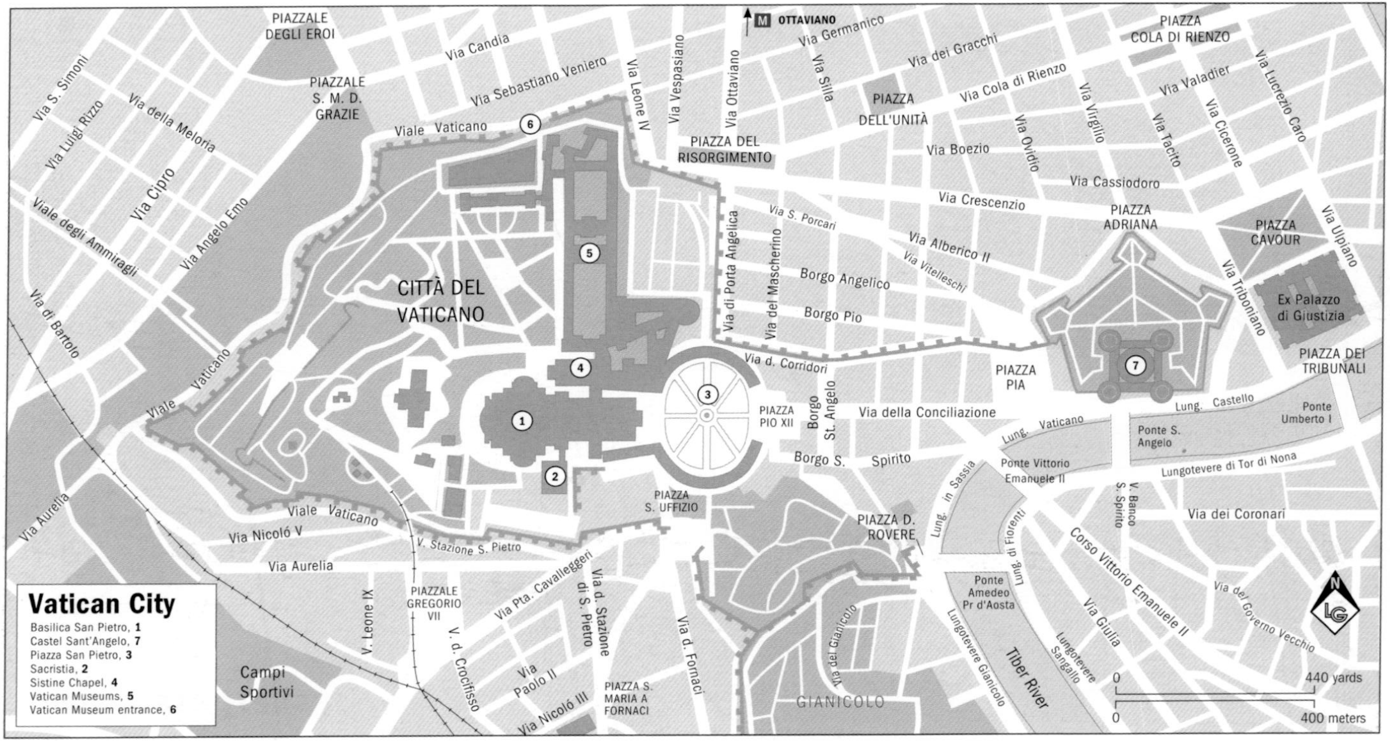
Vatican City
Basilica San Pietro, 1
Castel Sant'Angelo, 7
Piazza San Pietro, 3
Sacristia, 2
Sistine Chapel, 4
Vatican Museums, 5
Vatican Museum entrance, 6
CITTÀ DEL VATICANO
PIAZZALE DEGLI EROI
PIAZZALE S. M. D. GRAZIE
OTTAVIANO
PIAZZA DEL RISORGIMENTO
PIAZZA DELL'UNITÀ
PIAZZA COLA DI RIENZO
PIAZZA ADRIANA
PIAZZA CAVOUR
Ex Palazzo di Giustizia
PIAZZA DEI TRIBUNALI
PIAZZA PIA
PIAZZA PIO XII
PIAZZA S. UFFIZIO
PIAZZA D. ROVERE
PIAZZALE GREGORIO VII
PIAZZA S. MARIA A FORNACI
GIANICOLO
Campi Sportivi
Tiber River
Via S. Simoni
Via Luigi Rizzo
Via della Meloria
Via Cipro
Viale degli Ammiragli
Via Angelo Emo
Via di Bartolo
Via Aurelia
Via Candia
Via Sebastiano Veniero
Viale Vaticano
Via Leone IV
Via Vespasiano
Via Ottaviano
Via Germanico
Via Silla
Via dei Gracchi
Via Cola di Rienzo
Via Boezio
Via Ovidio
Via Virgilio
Via Tacito
Via Cicerone
Via Valadier
Via Lucrezio Caro
Via Cassiodoro
Via Crescenzio
Via Ulpiano
Via Tribononiano
Via S. Porcari
Via Alberico II
Via Vitelleschi
Via di Porta Angelica
Via del Mascherino
Borgo Angelico
Borgo Pio
Via d. Corridori
Borgo St. Angelo
Via della Conciliazione
Borgo S. Spirito
Lung. Castello
Lung. Vaticano
Ponte S. Angelo
Ponte Umberto I
Ponte Vittorio Emanuele II
Lungotevere di Tor di Nona
V. Banco S. Spirito
Via dei Coronari
Lung. in Sassia
Lung. di Fiorenti
Corso Vittorio Emanuele II
Via del Governo Vecchio
Via Giulia
Ponte Amedeo Pr d'Aosta
Lungotevere Gianicolo
Lungotevere Sangallo
Via del Gianicolo
Via d. Fornaci
Via d. Stazione di S. Pietro
Via Pta. Cavalleggeri
V. Stazione S. Pietro
Via Nicoló V
V. Leone IX
V. d. Crocifisso
Via Paolo II
Via Nicoló III
0 440 yards
0 400 meters

Rome Mass Transit

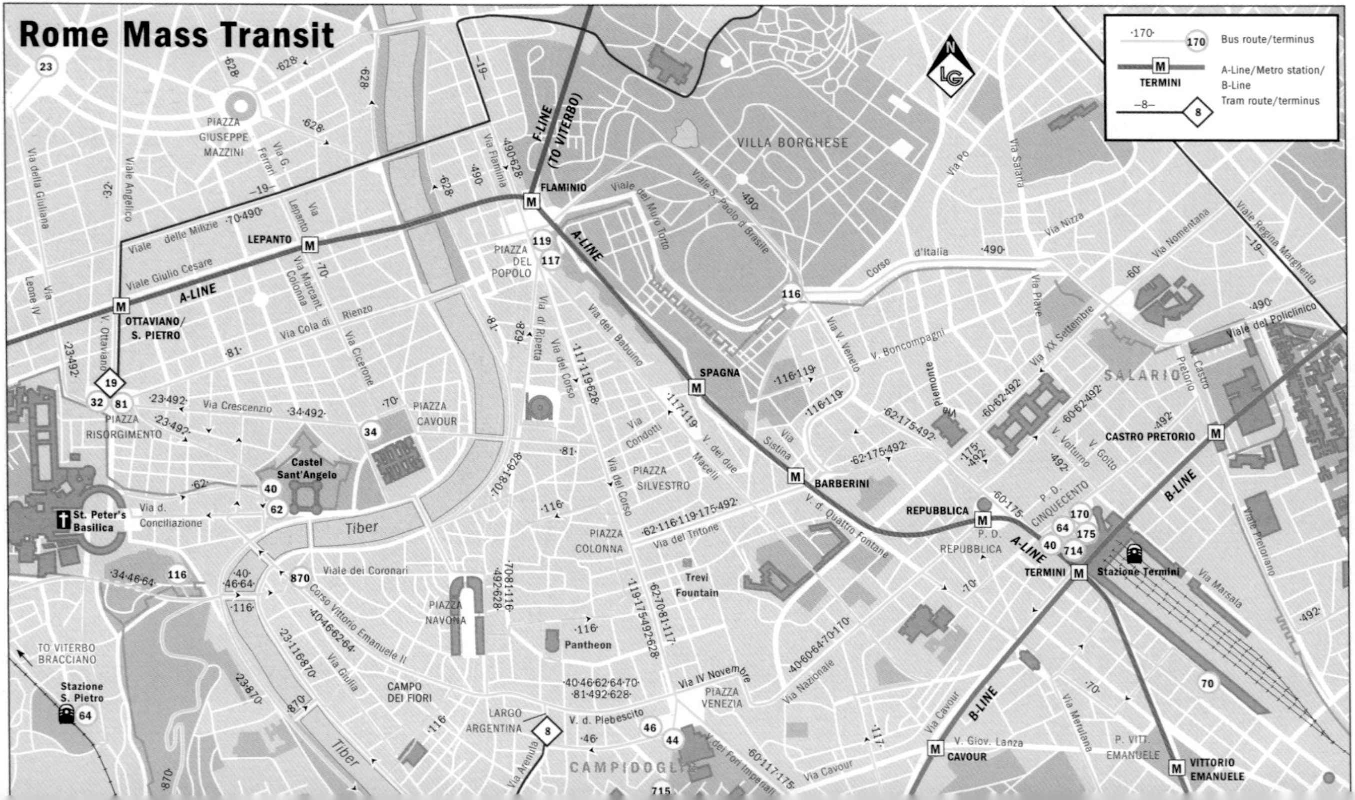

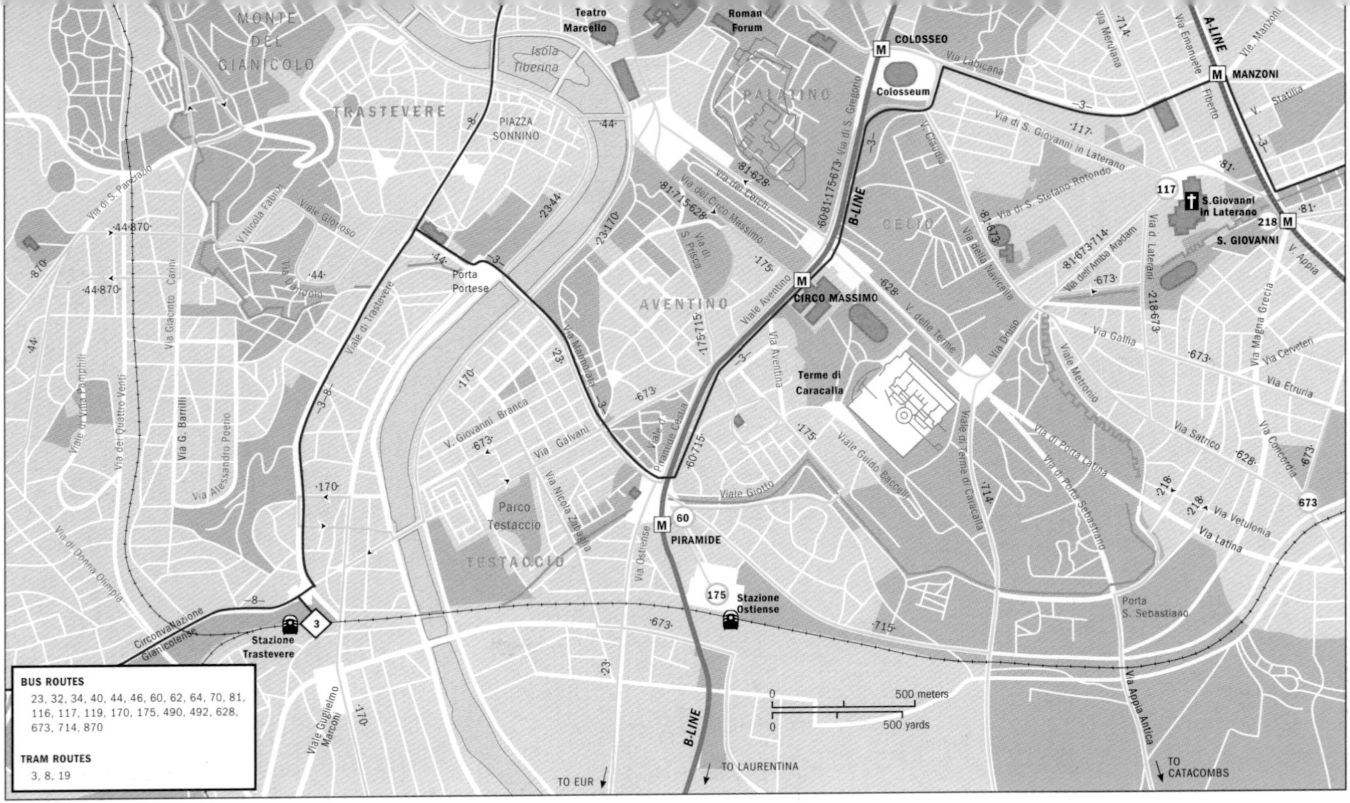

MONTE DEL GIANICOLO
TRASTEVERE
PIAZZA SONNINO
Isola Tiberina
Teatro Marcello
Roman Forum
PALATINO
COLOSSEO
Colosseum
MANZONI
A-LINE
B-LINE
CELIO
AVENTINO
TESTACCIO
CIRCO MASSIMO
Terme di Caracalla
S.Giovanni in Laterano
S. GIOVANNI
PIRAMIDE
Stazione Ostiense
Stazione Trastevere
Porta Portese
Parco Testaccio
Porta S. Sebastiano
Via Labicana
Via Merulana
Via Emanuele Fiberto
Vle. Manzoni
V. Statilia
Via di S. Giovanni in Laterano
Via di S. Stefano Rotondo
Via dell'Amba Aradam
Via d. Laterani
V. Appia
Via Magna Grecia
Via Cerveteri
Via Etruria
Via Gallia
Via Satrico
Via Concordia
Via Vetulonia
Via Latina
Viale Metronio
Via di Porta Latina
Via di Porta Sebastiano
Via Appia Antica
Viale di Terme di Caracalla
Via Druso
V. delle Terme
Via della Navicella
V. Claudia
Via di S. Gregorio
Via dei Cerchi
Via del Circo Massimo
Via di S. Prisca
Viale Aventino
Via Aventina
Viale Guido Baccelli
Viale Giotto
Viale d. Piramide Cestia
Via Ostiense
Via Marmorata
Via Galvani
V. Giovanni Branca
Via Nicola Zabaglia
Viale di Trastevere
Viale Glorioso
V.Nicola Fabrizi
Via Dandolo
Via di S. Pancrazio
Via Giacinto Carini
Via G. Barrilli
Via Alessandro Poerio
Via dei Quattro Venti
Viale di Villa Pamphili
Via di Donna Olimpia
Circonvallazione Gianicolense
Viale Guglielmo Marconi
TO EUR
TO LAURENTINA
TO CATACOMBS
0 500 meters
0 500 yards
BUS ROUTES
23, 32, 34, 40, 44, 46, 60, 62, 64, 70, 81, 116, 117, 119, 170, 175, 490, 492, 628, 673, 714, 870
TRAM ROUTES
3, 8, 19

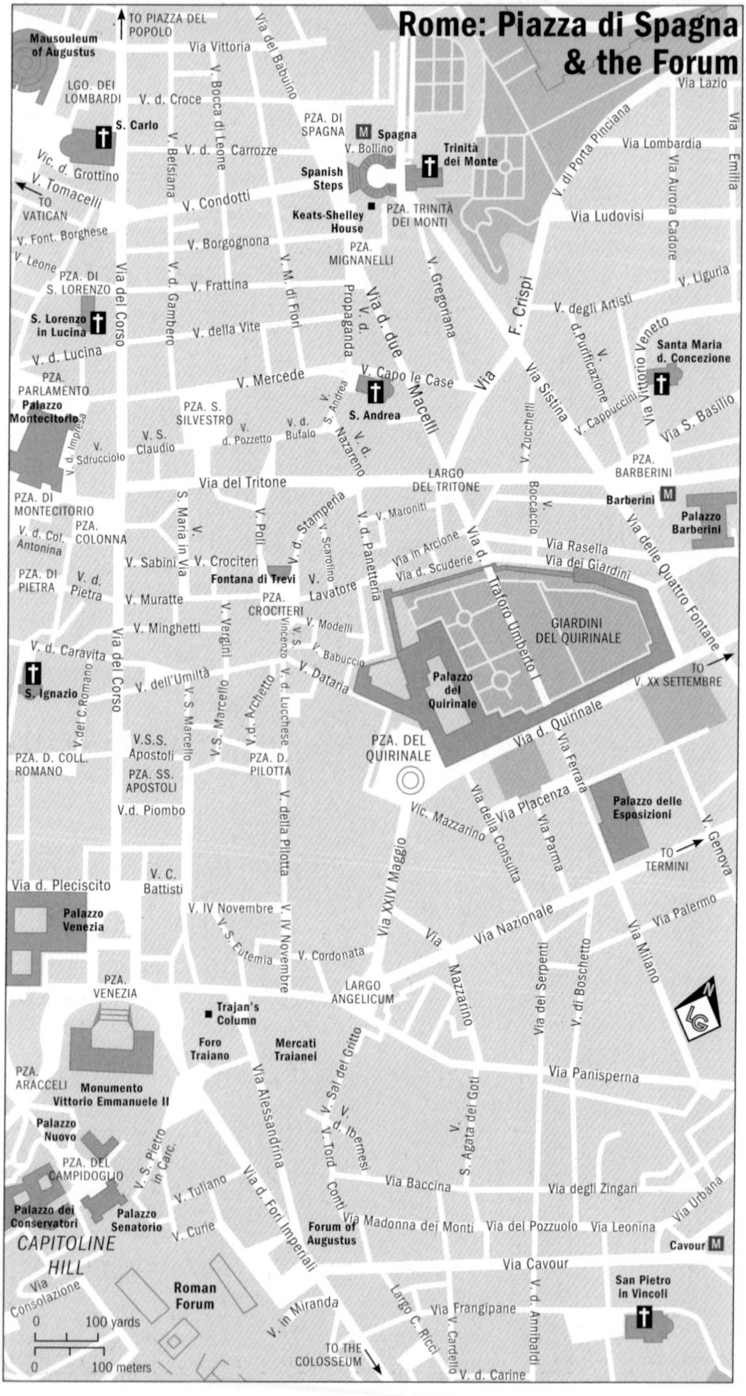

Rome: Piazza di Spagna & the Forum
TO PIAZZA DEL POPOLO
Mausoleum of Augustus
Via Vittoria
Via del Babuino
LGO. DEI LOMBARDI
V. d. Croce
V. Bocca di Leone
S. Carlo
V. Belsiana
V. d. Carrozze
PZA. DI SPAGNA
Spagna
V. Bollino
Trinità dei Monte
Via Lazio
Via Emilia
V. di Porta Pinciana
Via Lombardia
Vic. d. Grottino
V. Tomacelli
TO VATICAN
Spanish Steps
V. Condotti
Keats-Shelley House
PZA. TRINITÀ DEI MONTI
Via Ludovisi
Via Aurora Cadore
V. Font. Borghese
V. Borgognona
PZA. MIGNANELLI
V. Leone
PZA. DI S. LORENZO
V. d. Gambero
V. Frattina
V. M. di Fiori
V. d. Propaganda
Via d. due Macelli
V. Gregoriana
Via F. Crispi
V. degli Artisti
V. Liguria
S. Lorenzo in Lucina
Via del Corso
V. della Vite
V. d. Purificazione
Via Vittorio Veneto
Santa Maria d. Concezione
V. d. Lucina
V. Mercede
V. Capo le Case
Via Sistina
PZA. PARLAMENTO
Palazzo Montecitorio
PZA. S. SILVESTRO
V. d. Pozzetto
V. d. Bufalo
V. S. Andrea
S. Andrea
V. d. Nazareno
V. Cappuccini
Via S. Basilio
V. d. Impresa
V. Sdrucciolo
V. S. Claudio
V. Zucchelli
PZA. BARBERINI
Via del Tritone
LARGO DEL TRITONE
PZA. DI MONTECITORIO
V. S. Maria in Via
V. Poli
V. d. Stamperia
V. d. Panetteria
V. Maroniti
V. Boccaccio
Barberini
Palazzo Barberini
V. d. Col. Antonina
PZA. COLONNA
V. Scarolino
Via in Arcione
Via d. Traforo Umberto I
Via Rasella
Via delle Quattro Fontane
V. Sabini
V. Crociteri
Via d. Scuderie
Via dei Giardini
PZA. DI PIETRA
V. d. Pietra
Fontana di Trevi
V. Lavatore
V. Muratte
PZA. CROCITERI
GIARDINI DEL QUIRINALE
V. Minghetti
V. Vergini
V. Modelli
V. S. Vincenzo
V. d. Caravita
V. Babuccio
V. Dataria
TO V. XX SETTEMBRE
S. Ignazio
V. dell'Umiltà
V. d. Lucchese
V. d. Archetto
Palazzo del Quirinale
V. del C. Romano
V. S. Marcello
V. S. Marcello
Via d. Quirinale
V.S.S. Apostoli
PZA. DEL QUIRINALE
PZA. D. COLL. ROMANO
PZA. SS. APOSTOLI
PZA. D. PILOTTA
Via Ferrara
V.d. Piombo
V. della Pilotta
Via della Consulta
Via Placenza
Palazzo delle Esposizioni
Vic. Mazzarino
Via Parma
V. Genova
TO TERMINI
V. C. Battisti
Via XXIV Maggio
Via d. Pleciscito
Palazzo Venezia
V. IV Novembre
V. IV Novembre
V. S. Eutemia
Via Nazionale
Via Palermo
Via Mazzarino
V. Cordonata
Via Milano
PZA. VENEZIA
LARGO ANGELICUM
Via dei Serpenti
V. di Boschetto
Trajan's Column
Foro Traiano
Mercati Traianei
PZA. ARACCELI
Monumento Vittorio Emmanuele II
Via Alessandrina
V. Sal del Gritto
Via Panisperna
Palazzo Nuovo
V. S. Pietro in Carc.
V. d. Ibernesi
V. Tor d Conti
V. S. Agata dei Goti
PZA. DEL CAMPIDOGLIO
Via d. Fori Imperiali
V. Tuliano
Via Baccina
Via degli Zingari
Via Urbana
Palazzo dei Conservatori
Palazzo Senatorio
V. Curie
Forum of Augustus
Via Madonna dei Monti
Via del Pozzuolo
Via Leonina
Cavour
CAPITOLINE HILL
Via Cavour
Via Consolazione
Roman Forum
Largo C. Ricci
V. d. Annibaldi
San Pietro in Vincoli
0
100 yards
V. in Miranda
Via Frangipane
V. Cardello
0
100 meters
TO THE COLOSSEUM
V. d. Carine

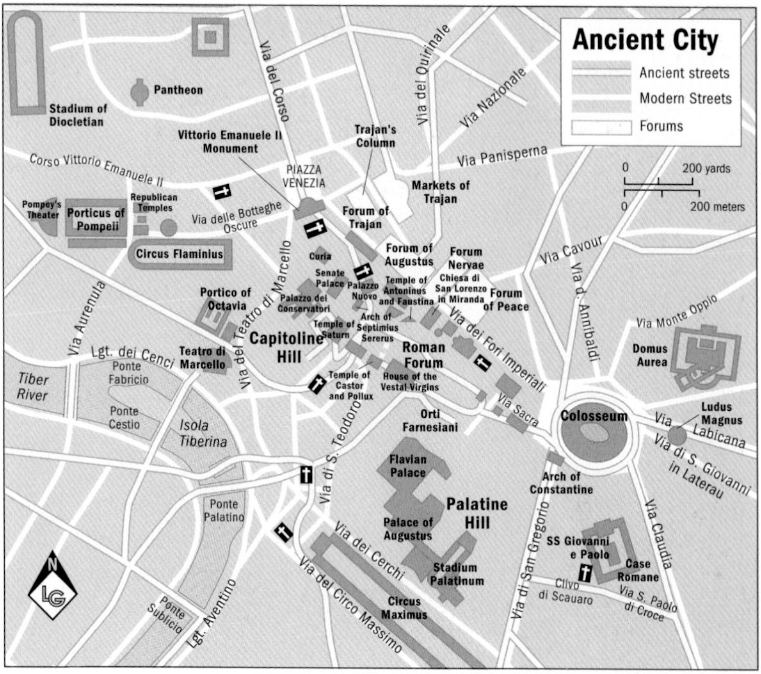

Ancient City
Ancient streets
Modern Streets
Forums
0
200 yards
0
200 meters
Pantheon
Stadium of Diocletian
Via del Corso
Via del Quirinale
Via Nazionale
Vittorio Emanuele II Monument
Trajan's Column
Via Panisperna
Corso Vittorio Emanuele II
PIAZZA VENEZIA
Markets of Trajan
Pompey's Theater
Porticus of Pompeii
Republican Temples
Via delle Botteghe Oscure
Forum of Trajan
Circus Flaminius
Curia
Senate Palace
Palazzo Nuovo
Forum of Augustus
Forum Nervae
Temple of Antoninus and Faustina
Chiesa di San Lorenzo in Miranda
Forum of Peace
Via Cavour
Via d. Annibaldi
Via Aurenula
Portico of Octavia
Via del Teatro di Marcello
Palazzo dei Conservatori
Arch of Septimius Sererus
Temple of Saturn
Via dei Fori Imperiali
Via Monte Oppio
Capitoline Hill
Roman Forum
Domus Aurea
Lgt. dei Cenci
Teatro di Marcello
Temple of Castor and Pollux
House of the Vestal Virgins
Tiber River
Ponte Fabricio
Ponte Cestio
Isola Tiberina
Orti Farnesiani
Via Sacra
Colosseum
Ludus Magnus
Via Labicana
Via di S. Giovanni in Laterau
Via di S. Teodoro
Flavian Palace
Arch of Constantine
Ponte Palatino
Palatine Hill
Palace of Augustus
Via dei Cerchi
Via di San Gregorio
Via Claudia
SS Giovanni e Paolo
Stadium Palatinum
Case Romane
Clivo di Scauaro
Via S. Paolo di Croce
Circus Maximus
Via del Circo Massimo
Ponte Sublicio
Lgt. Aventino
N
LG

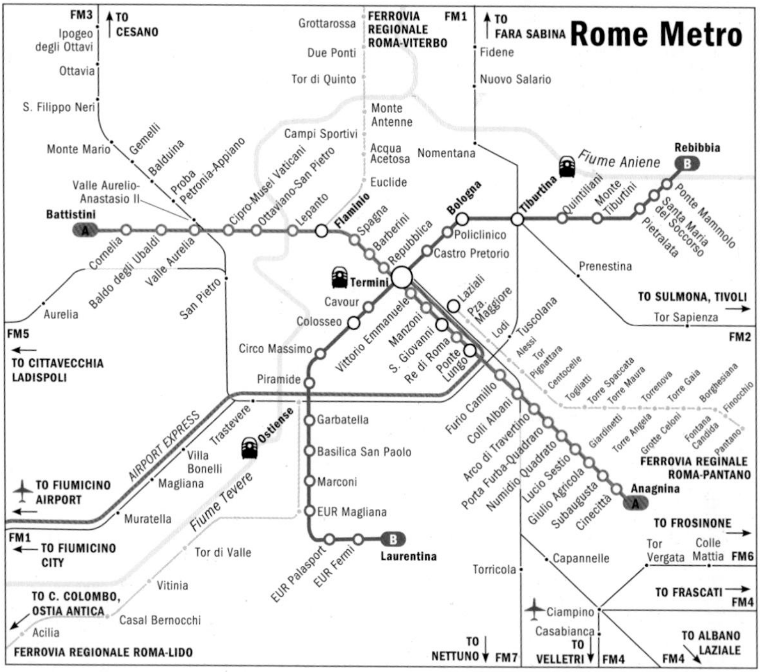

Rome Metro
FM3
TO CESANO
Ipogeo degli Ottavi
Ottavia
S. Filippo Neri
Monte Mario
Gemelli
Balduina
Proba Petronia-Appiano
Valle Aurelio-Anastasio II
Battistini
A
Cornelia
Baldo degli Ubaldi
Valle Aurelia
Cipro-Musei Vaticani
Ottaviano-San Pietro
Lepanto
Flaminio
Spagna
Barberini
Repubblica
Aurelia
San Pietro
Grottarossa
Due Ponti
Tor di Quinto
Campi Sportivi
FERROVIA REGIONALE ROMA-VITERBO
Monte Antenne
Acqua Acetosa
Euclide
FM1
TO FARA SABINA
Fidene
Nuovo Salario
Nomentana
Bologna
Policlinico
Castro Pretorio
Tiburtina
Fiume Aniene
Quintiliani
Monte Tiburtini
Rebibbia
B
Ponte Mammolo
Santa Maria del Soccorso
Pietralata
Prenestina
TO SULMONA, TIVOLI
Tor Sapienza
FM2
Termini
Cavour
Colosseo
Circo Massimo
Piramide
Vittorio Emanuele
Manzoni
S. Giovanni
Re di Roma
Ponte Lungo
Laziali
Pza. Maggiore
Lodi
Tuscolana
Alessi
Tor Pignattara
Centocelle
Togliatti
Torre Spaccata
Torre Maura
Torrenova
Torre Gaia
Borghesiana
Finocchio
FM5
TO CITTAVECCHIA LADISPOLI
AIRPORT EXPRESS
Trastevere
Ostiense
Villa Bonelli
Magliana
Muratella
Fiume Tevere
Garbatella
Basilica San Paolo
Marconi
EUR Magliana
EUR Palasport
EUR Fermi
Laurentina
Furio Camillo
Colli Albani
Arco di Travertino
Porta Furba-Quadraro
Numidio Quadrato
Lucio Sestio
Giulio Agricola
Subaugusta
Cinecittà
Anagnina
Giardinetti
Torre Angela
Grotte Celoni
Fontana Candida
Pantano
FERROVIA REGINALE ROMA-PANTANO
TO FIUMICINO AIRPORT
FM1
TO FIUMICINO CITY
Tor di Valle
Vitinia
TO C. COLOMBO, OSTIA ANTICA
Casal Bernocchi
Acilia
FERROVIA REGIONALE ROMA-LIDO
TO FROSINONE
Tor Vergata
Colle Mattia
FM6
Capannelle
Torricola
TO FRASCATI
FM4
Ciampino
Casabianca
TO NETTUNO
FM7
TO VELLETRI
FM4
FM4
TO ALBANO LAZIALE

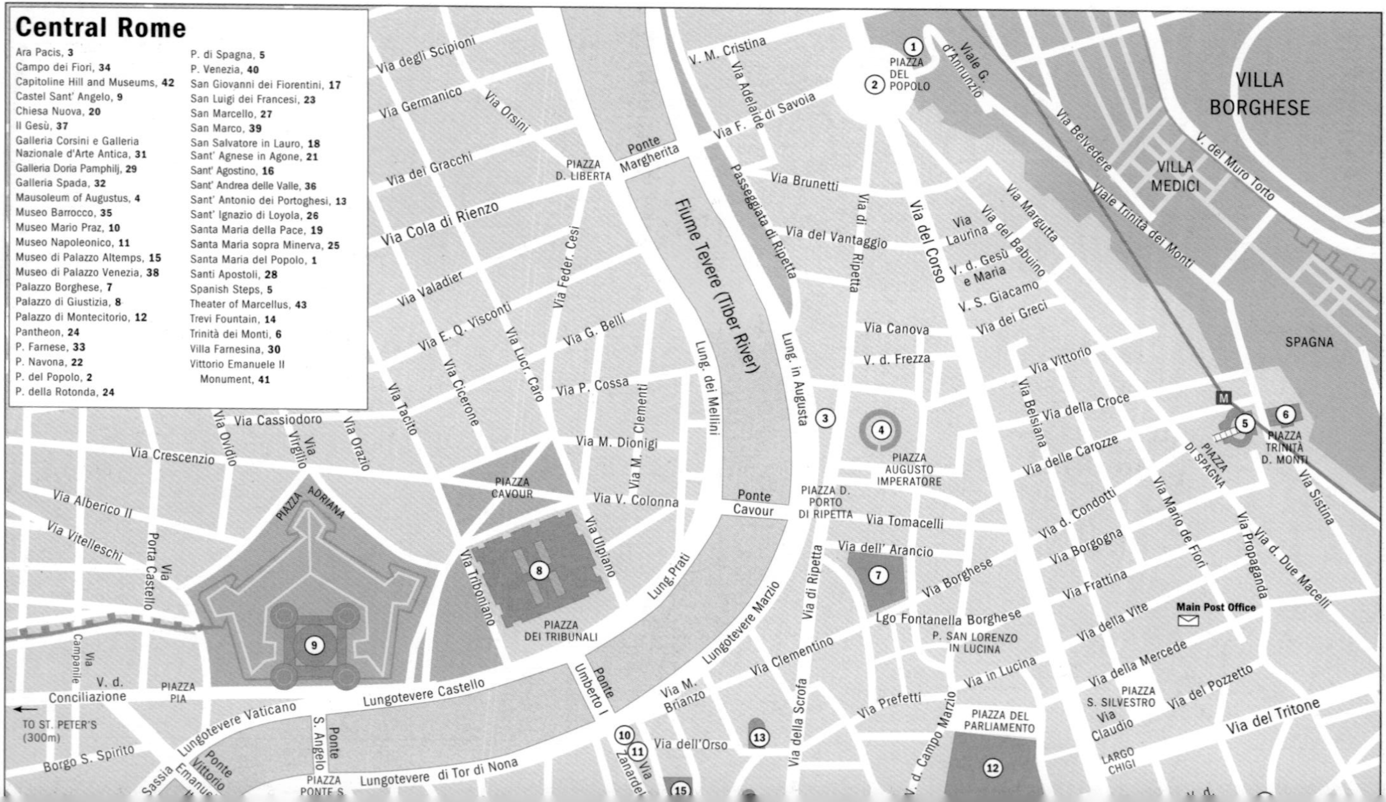
Central Rome
Ara Pacis, 3
Campo dei Fiori, 34
Capitoline Hill and Museums, 42
Castel Sant' Angelo, 9
Chiesa Nuova, 20
Il Gesù, 37
Galleria Corsini e Galleria Nazionale d'Arte Antica, 31
Galleria Doria Pamphilj, 29
Galleria Spada, 32
Mausoleum of Augustus, 4
Museo Barrocco, 35
Museo Mario Praz, 10
Museo Napoleonico, 11
Museo di Palazzo Altemps, 15
Museo di Palazzo Venezia, 38
Palazzo Borghese, 7
Palazzo di Giustizia, 8
Palazzo di Montecitorio, 12
Pantheon, 24
P. Farnese, 33
P. Navona, 22
P. del Popolo, 2
P. della Rotonda, 24
P. di Spagna, 5
P. Venezia, 40
San Giovanni dei Fiorentini, 17
San Luigi dei Francesi, 23
San Marcello, 27
San Marco, 39
San Salvatore in Lauro, 18
Sant' Agnese in Agone, 21
Sant' Agostino, 16
Sant' Andrea delle Valle, 36
Sant' Antonio dei Portoghesi, 13
Sant' Ignazio di Loyola, 26
Santa Maria della Pace, 19
Santa Maria sopra Minerva, 25
Santa Maria del Popolo, 1
Santi Apostoli, 28
Spanish Steps, 5
Theater of Marcellus, 43
Trevi Fountain, 14
Trinità dei Monti, 6
Villa Farnesina, 30
Vittorio Emanuele II Monument, 41
VILLA BORGHESE
VILLA MEDICI
SPAGNA
V. del Muro Torto
Viale Trinità dei Monti
Via Belvedere
Viale G. d'Annunzio
PIAZZA DEL POPOLO
Via Margutta
Via del Babuino
Via Laurina
V. d. Gesù e Maria
V. S. Giacamo
Via dei Greci
Via del Corso
Via di Ripetta
Via Brunetti
Via del Vantaggio
Passeggiata di Ripetta
Via Canova
V. d. Frezza
Via Vittorio
Via della Croce
Via Belsiana
Via delle Carozze
Via d. Condotti
Via Borgogna
Via Frattina
Via della Vite
Via della Mercede
Via del Pozzetto
Via del Tritone
Via Mario de Fiori
Via Propaganda
Via d. Due Macelli
Via Sistina
PIAZZA TRINITÀ D. MONTI
PIAZZA DI SPAGNA
Main Post Office
PIAZZA S. SILVESTRO
Via Claudio
LARGO CHIGI
PIAZZA AUGUSTO IMPERATORE
PIAZZA D. PORTO DI RIPETTA
Via Tomacelli
Via dell' Arancio
Via Borghese
Lgo Fontanella Borghese
P. SAN LORENZO IN LUCINA
Via in Lucina
Via Prefetti
V. d. Campo Marzio
PIAZZA DEL PARLIAMENTO
Via della Scrofa
Via Clementino
Lungotevere Marzio
Via M. Brianzo
Via dell'Orso
Via Zanardelli
Lung. in Augusta
Fiume Tevere (Tiber River)
Lung. dei Mellini
Ponte Cavour
Ponte Margherita
Ponte Umberto I
Ponte S. Angelo
Ponte Vittorio Emanuele
V. M. Cristina
Via Adelaide
Via F. di Savoia
PIAZZA D. LIBERTA
Via degli Scipioni
Via Germanico
Via Orsini
Via dei Gracchi
Via Cola di Rienzo
Via Valadier
Via E. Q. Visconti
Via Feder. Cesi
Via G. Belli
Via P. Cossa
Via M. Clementi
Via M. Dionigi
Via V. Colonna
Via Ulpiano
Via Lucr. Caro
Via Cicerone
Via Tacito
Via Orazio
Via Virgilio
Via Cassiodoro
Via Ovidio
Via Crescenzio
PIAZZA CAVOUR
Via Triboniano
PIAZZA DEI TRIBUNALI
Lung. Prati
PIAZZA ADRIANA
Lungotevere Castello
Lungotevere Vaticano
Lungotevere di Tor di Nona
PIAZZA PONTE S
Via Alberico II
Via Vitelleschi
Via Porta Castello
Via Campanile
V. d. Conciliazione
PIAZZA PIA
TO ST. PETER'S (300m)
Borgo S. Spirito
Sassia

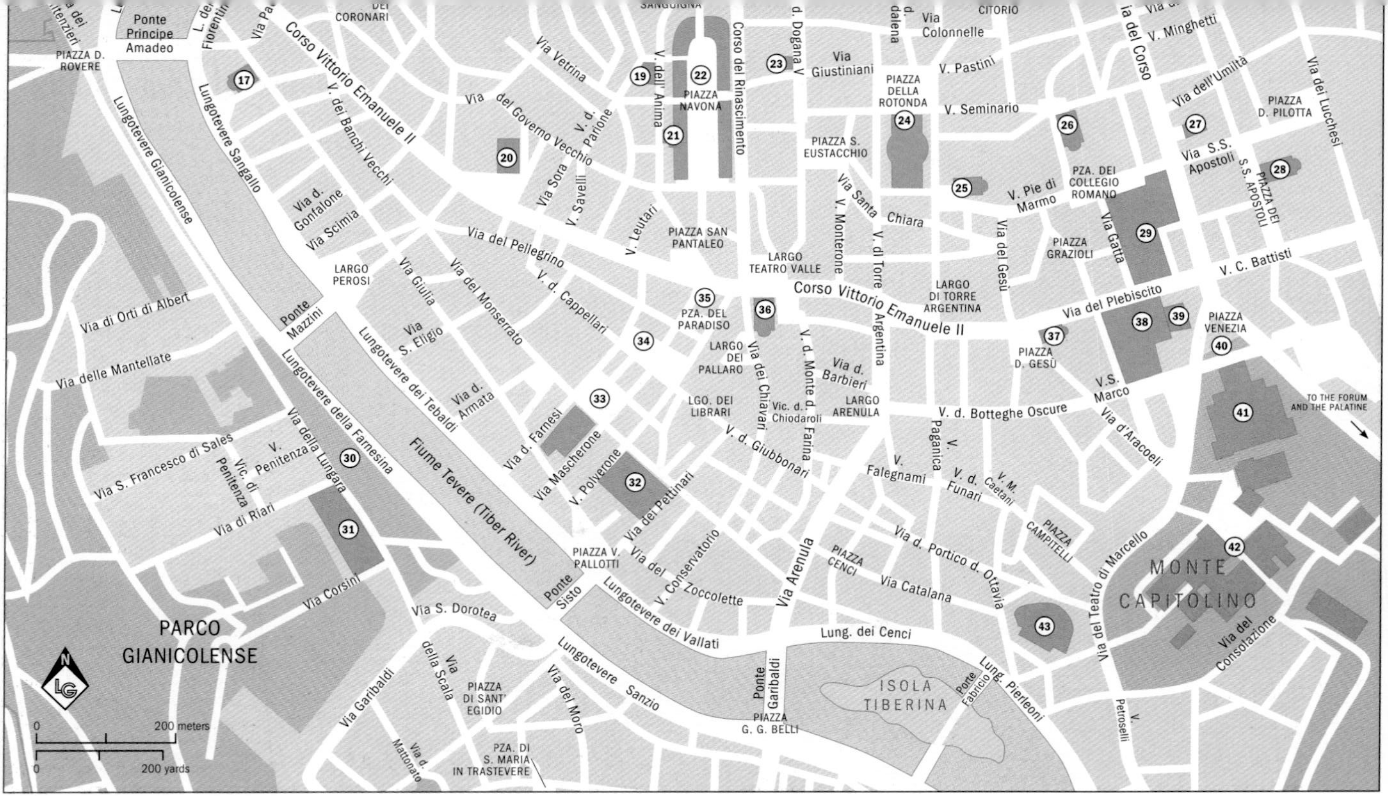
Ponte Principe Amadeo
PIAZZA D. ROVERE
Lungotevere Gianicolense
Lungotevere Sangallo
Corso Vittorio Emanuele II
V. dei Banchi Vecchi
Via d. Gonfalone
Via Scimia
LARGO PEROSI
Ponte Mazzini
Via di Orti di Albert
Via delle Mantellate
Lungotevere della Farnesina
Lungotevere dei Tebaldi
Via Giulia
Via S. Eligio
Via del Monserrato
Via d. Armata
Via del Pellegrino
V. d. Cappellari
Via Vetrina
Via del Governo Vecchio
V. d. Parione
Via Sora
V. Savelli
V. Leutari
V. dell' Anima
PIAZZA NAVONA
Corso del Rinascimento
PIAZZA SAN PANTALEO
PZA. DEL PARADISO
LARGO DEI PALLARO
LGO. DEI LIBRARI
Via dei Chiavari
V. d. Monte d. Farina
Vic. d. Chiodaroli
Via d. Barbieri
LARGO ARENULA
V. d. Giubbonari
LARGO TEATRO VALLE
V. Monterone
V. di Torre Argentina
Via Santa Chiara
PIAZZA S. EUSTACCHIO
d. Dogana V
Via Giustiniani
PIAZZA DELLA ROTONDA
V. Pastini
V. Seminario
Via Colonnelle
CITORIO
Via del Corso
V. Minghetti
Via dell'Umiltà
PIAZZA D. PILOTTA
Via dei Lucchesi
Via S.S. Apostoli
PIAZZA DEI S.S. APOSTOLI
PZA. DEI COLLEGIO ROMANO
V. Pie di Marmo
Via del Gesù
PIAZZA GRAZIOLI
Via Gatta
V. C. Battisti
LARGO DI TORRE ARGENTINA
Via del Plebiscito
PIAZZA VENEZIA
PIAZZA D. GESÙ
V.S. Marco
V. d. Botteghe Oscure
Via d'Aracoeli
TO THE FORUM AND THE PALATINE
V. Paganica
V. Falegnami
V. d. Funari
V. M. Caetani
PIAZZA CAMPITELLI
Via d. Portico d. Ottavia
PIAZZA CENCI
Via Catalana
Via Arenula
Via del Teatro di Marcello
MONTE CAPITOLINO
Via del Consolazione
V. Petroselli
Lung. dei Cenci
ISOLA TIBERINA
Ponte Fabricio
Lung. Pierleoni
Ponte Garibaldi
PIAZZA G. G. BELLI
Lungotevere dei Vallati
Via del Zoccolette
V. Conservatorio
Via dei Pettinari
V. Polverone
Via Mascherone
Via d. Farnesi
PIAZZA V. PALLOTTI
Ponte Sisto
Fiume Tevere (Tiber River)
Lungotevere Sanzio
Via del Moro
Via S. Dorotea
Via della Scala
PIAZZA DI SANT' EGIDIO
PZA. DI S. MARIA IN TRASTEVERE
Via d. Mattonato
Via Garibaldi
Via Corsini
Via della Lungara
V. Penitenza
Vic. di Penitenza
Via di Riari
Via S. Francesco di Sales
PARCO GIANICOLENSE
0
200 meters
0
200 yards
17
19
20
21
22
23
24
25
26
27
28
29
30
31
32
33
34
35
36
37
38
39
40
41
42
43

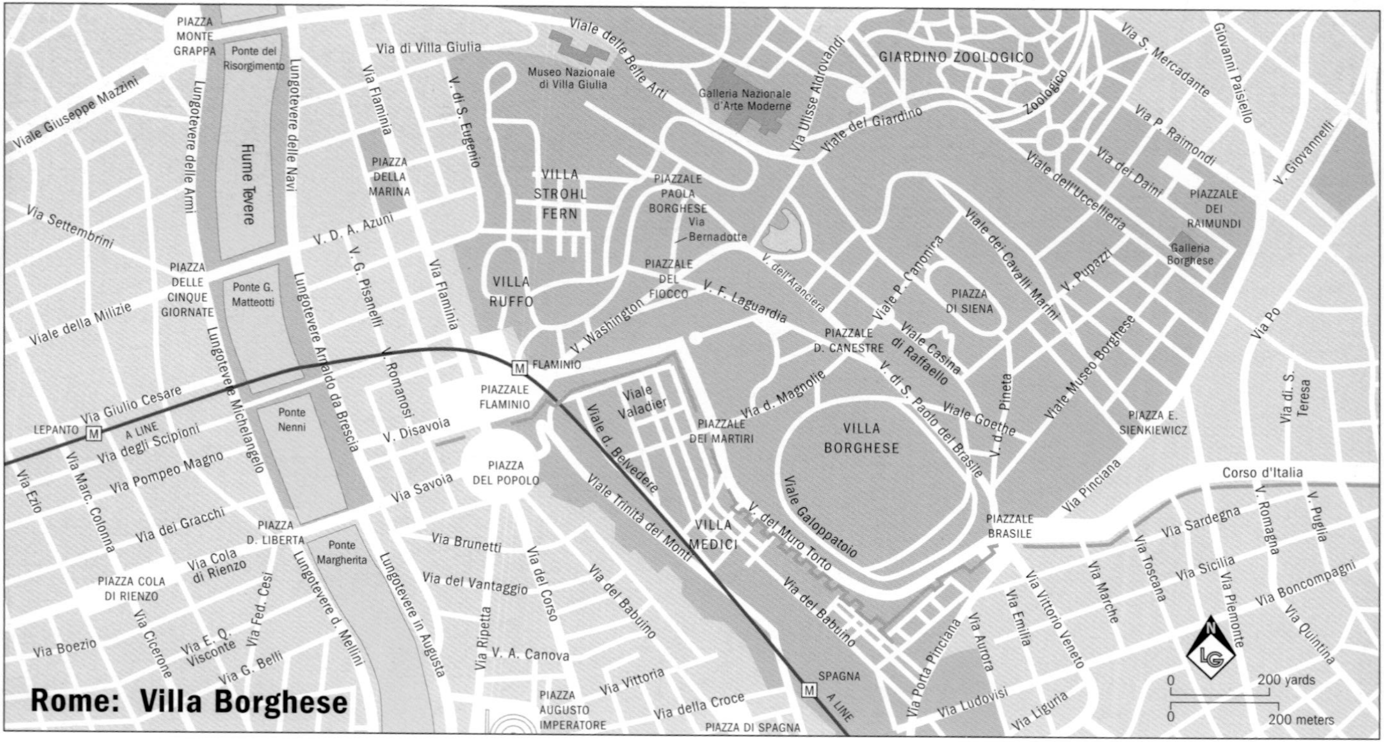

Rome: Villa Borghese

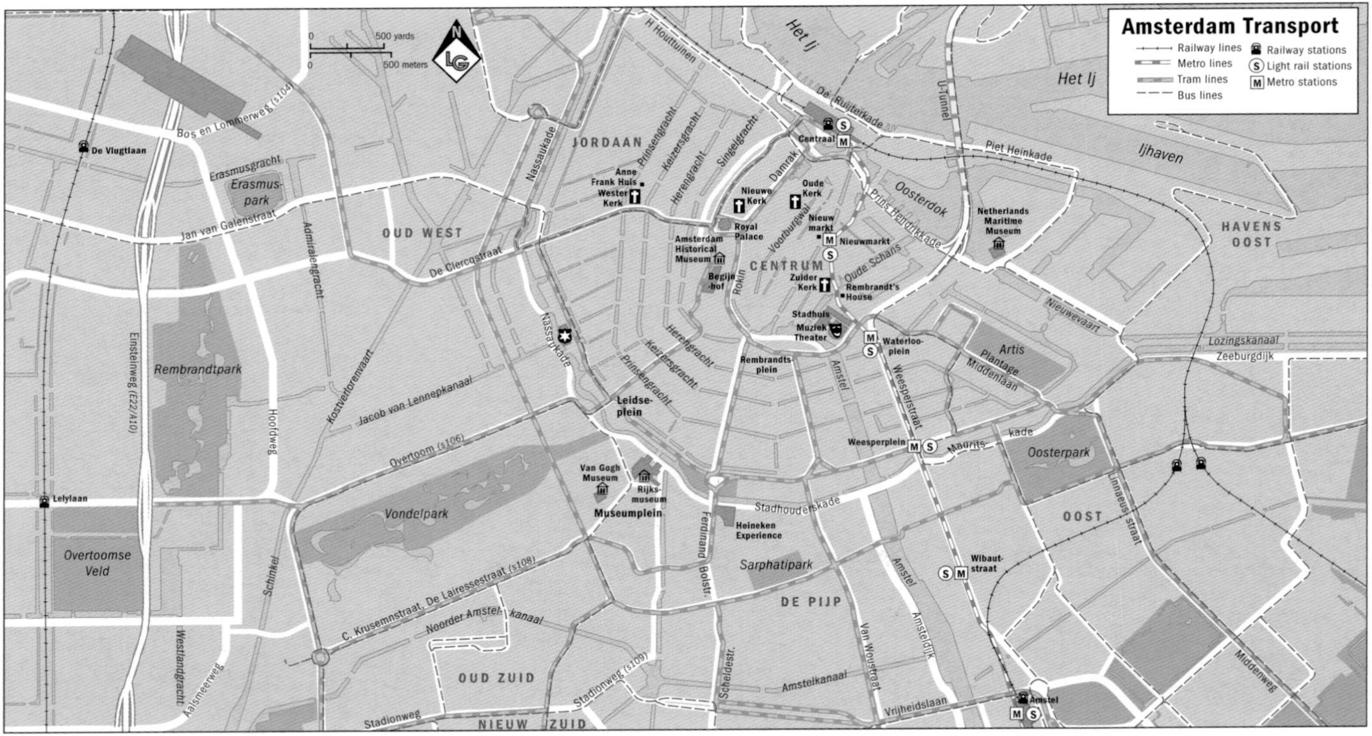

Amsterdam Transport
Railway lines
Metro lines
Tram lines
Bus lines
Railway stations
Light rail stations
Metro stations
0
500 yards
500 meters
Het Ij
Het Ij
Ijhaven
HAVENS OOST
U-Tunnel
Piet Heinkade
De Ruijterkade
Centraal
Oosterdok
Prins Hendrikkade
Netherlands Maritime Museum
Nieuwevaart
Lozingskanaal
Zeeburgdijk
Artis
Plantage Middenlaan
Oude Kerk
Nieuwe Kerk
Damrak
Voorburgwal
Nieuw markt
Nieuwmarkt
Oude Schans
Royal Palace
Amsterdam Historical Museum
Begijn -hof
CENTRUM
Rokin
Zuider Kerk
Rembrandt's House
Stadhuis Muziek Theater
Waterloo- plein
Rembrandts- plein
Amstel
Weesperstraat
Weesperplein
Maurits- kade
Oosterpark
Linnaeus straat
OOST
Wibaut- straat
Middenweg
Amstel
Amsteldijk
Van Woustraat
Vrijheidslaan
Amstelkanaal
Scheldestr.
DE PIJP
Sarphatipark
Heineken Experience
Stadhouderskade
Ferdinand Bolstr.
JORDAAN
H Houttuinen
Anne Frank Huis
Wester Kerk
Prinsengracht
Keizersgracht
Herengracht
Singelgracht
Nassaukade
Leidse- plein
Van Gogh Museum
Rijks- museum
Museumplein
Vondelpark
Overtoom (s106)
Jacob van Lennepkanaal
Kostverlorenvaart
De Clercqstraat
OUD WEST
Jan van Galenstraat
Erasmusgracht
Erasmus- park
Bos en Lommerweg (s104)
Admiralengracht
Hoofdweg
Rembrandtpark
Einsteinweg (E22/A10)
De Vlugtlaan
Lelylaan
Overtoomse Veld
Schinkel
Westlandgracht
Aalsmeerweg
C. Krusemnstraat, De Lairessestraat (s108)
Noorder Amstel- kanaal
OUD ZUID
Stadionweg (s109)
Stadionweg
NIEUW ZUID

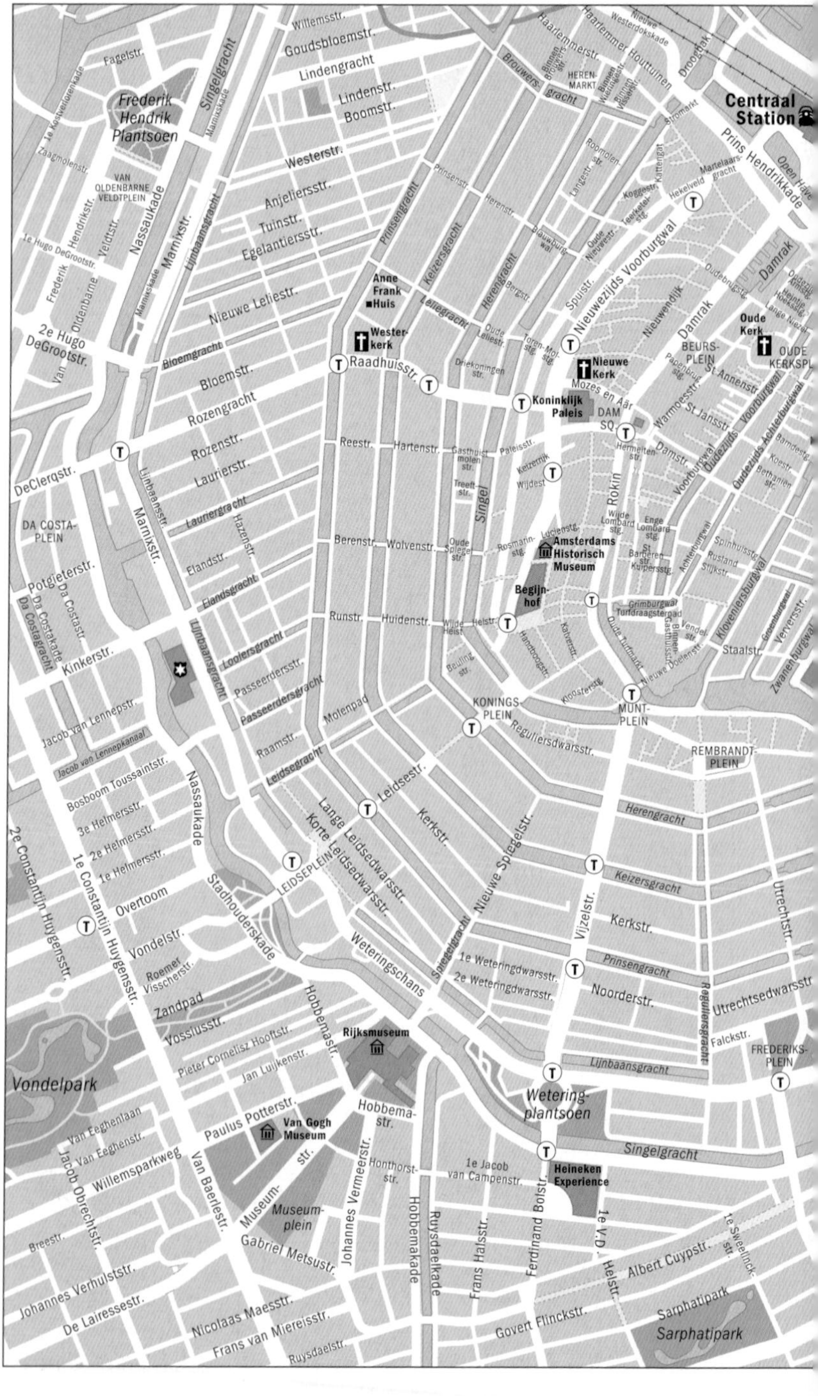

Centraal Station
Prins Hendrikkade
Willemsstr.
Goudsbloemstr.
Lindengracht
Lindenstr.
Boomstr.
Westerstr.
Anjeliersstr.
Tuinstr.
Egelantiersstr.
Nieuwe Leliestr.
Bloemgracht
Bloemstr.
Rozengracht
Rozenstr.
Laurierstr.
Lauriergracht
Hazenstr.
Elandstr.
Elandsgracht
Loolersgracht
Passeerdersstr.
Passeerdersgracht
Raamstr.
Leidsegracht
Fagelstr.
Frederik Hendrik Plantsoen
Singelgracht
Marnixkade
Zaagmolenstr.
1e Kostverlorenkade
VAN OLDENBARNEVELDTPLEIN
Nassaukade
Marnixstr.
Lijnbaansgracht
Hendrikstr.
Veldtstr.
1e Hugo DeGrootstr.
Frederik
Oldenbarne
2e Hugo DeGrootstr.
Van
DeClercqstr.
DA COSTA-PLEIN
Potgieterstr.
Da Costastr.
Da Costakade
Da Costagracht
Kinkerstr.
Lijnbaansstr.
Jacob van Lennepstr.
Jacob van Lennepkanaal
Bosboom Toussaintstr.
3e Helmersstr.
2e Helmersstr.
1e Helmersstr.
2e Constantijn Huygensstr.
1e Constantijn Huygensstr.
Overtoom
Vondelstr.
Roemer Visscherstr.
Zandpad
Vossiusstr.
Stadhouderskade
LEIDSEPLEIN
Pieter Cornelisz Hooftstr.
Jan Luijkenstr.
Hobbemastr.
Rijksmuseum
Vondelpark
Van Eeghenlaan
Van Eeghenstr.
Jacob Obrechtstr.
Willemsparkweg
Paulus Potterstr.
Van Gogh Museum
Van Baerlestr.
Museumstr.
Museumplein
Gabriel Metsustr.
Johannes Vermeerstr.
Honthorststr.
Hobbemakade
Ruysdaelkade
Breestr.
Johannes Verhulststr.
De Lairessestr.
Nicolaas Maesstr.
Frans van Mierisstr.
Ruysdaelstr.
Prinsengracht
Prinsenstr.
Keizersgracht
Anne Frank Huis
Westerkerk
Raadhuisstr.
Leliegracht
Herengracht
Herenstr.
Brouwersgracht
Haarlemmerstr.
Haarlemmer Houttuinen
Nieuwe Westerdokskade
HERENMARKT
Droogbak
Stromarkt
Roomolenstr.
Langestr.
Blauwburgwal
Bergstr.
Oude Leliestr.
Driekoningenstr.
Singel
Spuistr.
Nieuwezijds Voorburgwal
Nieuwendijk
Damrak
Martelaarsgracht
Hekelveld
Koggestr.
Teerketelstg.
Kattengat
Oude Nieuwstr.
Torensteeg
Molsteeg
Nieuwe Kerk
Koninklijk Paleis
Mozes en Aärstr.
DAM SQ.
BEURSPLEIN
Papenbrugstg.
St Annenstr.
Oude Kerk
OUDE KERKSPL
Oudebrugstg.
Lange Niezel
Warmoesstr.
St Jansstr.
Oudezijds Voorburgwal
Oudezijds Achterburgwal
Damstr.
Hermeltenstr.
Reestr.
Hartenstr.
Gasthuismolenstr.
Paleisstr.
Keizerrijk
Wijdesteeg
Treeftstr.
Berenstr.
Wolvenstr.
Oude Spiegelstr.
Rosmarijnsteeg
Amsterdams Historisch Museum
Begijnhof
Rokin
Wijde Lombardsteeg
Enge Lombardsteeg
St Barberenstr.
Kuipersstg.
Spinhuissteeg
Rusland
Slijkstr.
Grimburgwal
Turfdraagsterpad
Binnen Gasthuisstr.
Oude Turfmarkt
Vendelstr.
Staalstr.
Kloveniersburgwal
Groenburgwal
Verversstr.
Zwanenburgwal
Runstr.
Huidenstr.
Wijde Heisteeg
Heistr.
Handboogstr.
Kalverstr.
Beulingstr.
Kloosterstg.
Nieuwe Doelenstr.
KONINGSPLEIN
MUNTPLEIN
Reguliersdwarsstr.
REMBRANDTPLEIN
Molenpad
Leidsestr.
Kerkstr.
Lange Leidsedwarsstr.
Korte Leidsedwarsstr.
Nieuwe Spiegelstr.
Spiegelgracht
Weteringschans
1e Weteringdwarsstr.
2e Weteringdwarsstr.
Vijzelstr.
Noorderstr.
Reguliersgracht
Utrechtsestr.
Utrechtsedwarsstr.
Falckstr.
FREDERIKSPLEIN
Lijnbaansgracht
Weteringplantsoen
Singelgracht
Heineken Experience
1e Jacob van Campenstr.
Ferdinand Bolstr.
Frans Halsstr.
1e V.D. Helststr.
Albert Cuypstr.
1e Sweelinckstr.
Govert Flinckstr.
Sarphatipark

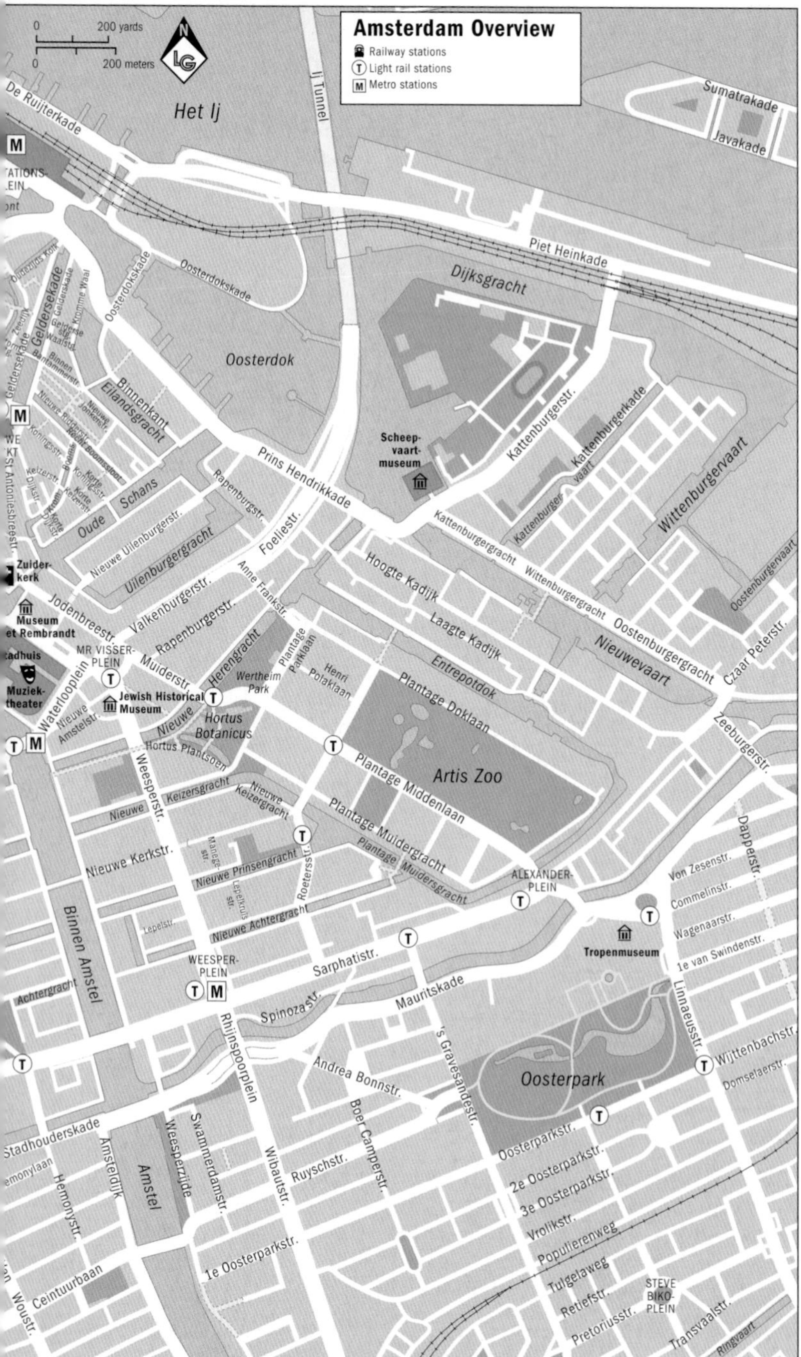
Amsterdam Overview
Railway stations
Light rail stations
Metro stations
0 200 yards
0 200 meters
Het Ij
Ij Tunnel
De Ruijterkade
Sumatrakade
Javakade
Piet Heinkade
Dijksgracht
Oosterdokskade
Oosterdok
Binnenkant
Eilandsgracht
Prins Hendrikkade
Scheepvaartmuseum
Kattenburgerstr.
Kattenburgerkade
Wittenburgervaart
Kattenburgergracht
Wittenburgergracht
Oostenburgergracht
Oostenburgervaart
Nieuwevaart
Czaar Peterstr.
Schans
Oude
Rapenburgstr.
Nieuwe Uilenburgerstr.
Uilenburgergracht
Foeliestr.
Hoogte Kadijk
Laagte Kadijk
Entrepotdok
Zuiderkerk
Museum het Rembrandt
Jodenbreestr.
Valkenburgerstr.
Rapenburgerstr.
Anne Frankstr.
MR VISSERPLEIN
Muiderstr.
Herengracht
Plantage Parklaan
Henri Polaklaan
Plantage Doklaan
Wertheim Park
Jewish Historical Museum
Muziektheater
Waterlooplein
Nieuwe Amstelstr.
Hortus Botanicus
Hortus Plantsoen
Artis Zoo
Plantage Middenlaan
Plantage Muidergracht
Zeeburgerstr.
Dapperstr.
Weesperstr.
Nieuwe Keizersgracht
Nieuwe Kerkstr.
Nieuwe Prinsengracht
Roetersstr.
ALEXANDERPLEIN
Von Zesenstr.
Commelinstr.
Wagenaarstr.
1e van Swindenstr.
Tropenmuseum
Binnen Amstel
Nieuwe Achtergracht
Sarphatistr.
WEESPERPLEIN
Achtergracht
Spinozastr.
Mauritskade
Linnaeusstr.
Rhijnspoorplein
Andrea Bonnstr.
's Gravesandestr.
Oosterpark
Wijttenbachstr.
Domselaerstr.
Stadhouderskade
Amsteldijk
Amstel
Weesperzijde
Swammerdamstr.
Wibautstr.
Ruyschstr.
Boer Camperstr.
Oosterparkstr.
2e Oosterparkstr.
3e Oosterparkstr.
Vrolikstr.
Populierenweg
Hemonystr.
1e Oosterparkstr.
Ceintuurbaan
Tulgelaweg
Retiefstr.
Pretoriusstr.
STEVE BIKO-PLEIN
Transvaalstr.
Ringvaart

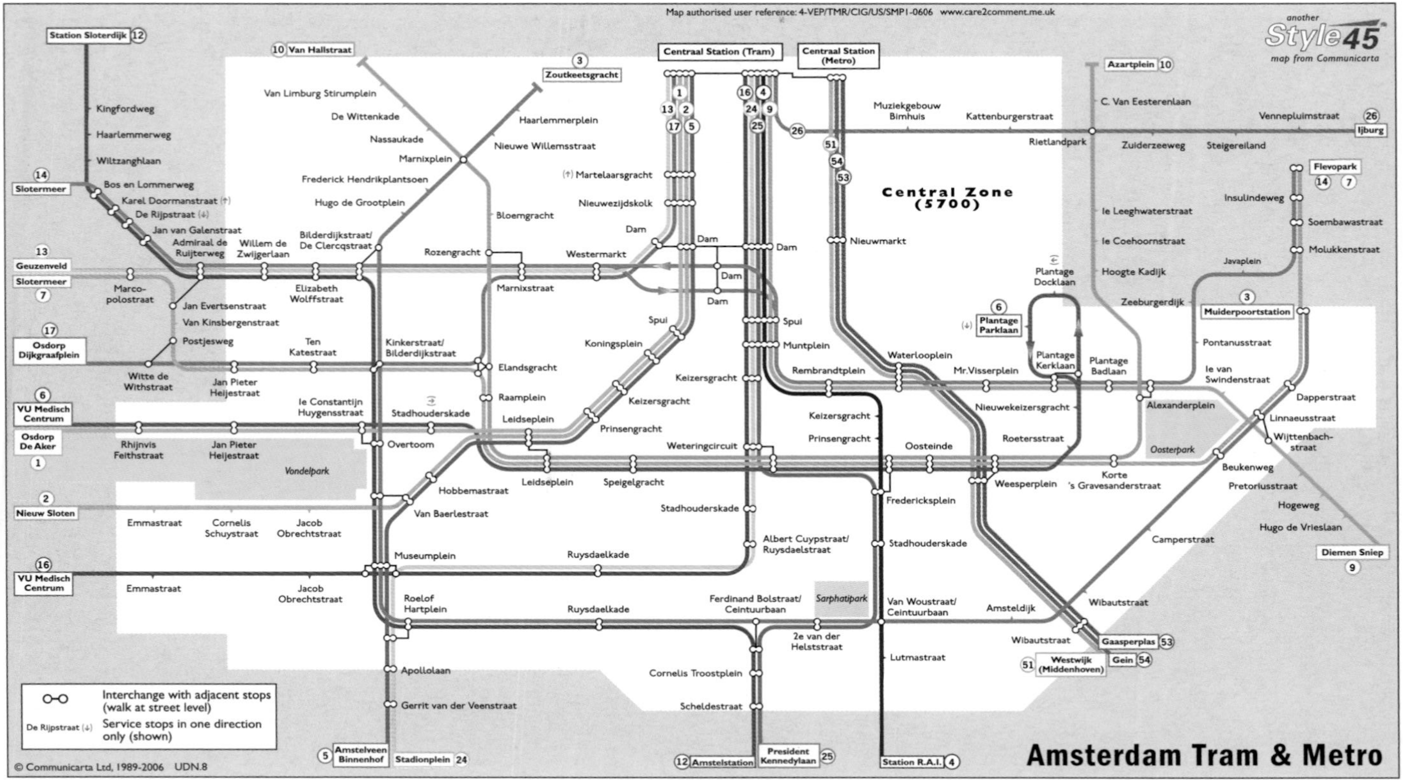
Amsterdam Tram & Metro
Map authorised user reference: 4-VEP/TMR/CIG/US/SMP1-0606 www.care2comment.me.uk
another Style45 map from Communicarta
Central Zone (5700)
Centraal Station (Tram)
Centraal Station (Metro)
Station Sloterdijk 12
10 Van Hallstraat
3 Zoutkeetsgracht
Azartplein 10
26 IJburg
Flevopark 14 7
14 Slotermeer
13 Geuzenveld
Slotermeer 7
17 Osdorp Dijkgraafplein
6 VU Medisch Centrum
Osdorp De Aker 1
2 Nieuw Sloten
16 VU Medisch Centrum
5 Amstelveen Binnenhof
Stadionplein 24
12 Amstelstation
President Kennedylaan 25
Station R.A.I. 4
Gaasperplas 53
Gein 54
51 Westwijk (Middenhoven)
Diemen Sniep 9
6 Plantage Parklaan
3 Muiderpoortstation
Kingfordweg
Haarlemmerweg
Wiltzanghlaan
Bos en Lommerweg
Karel Doormanstraat
De Rijpstraat
Jan van Galenstraat
Admiraal de Ruijterweg
Willem de Zwijgerlaan
Bilderdijkstraat/ De Clercqstraat
Marco-polostraat
Elizabeth Wolffstraat
Jan Evertsenstraat
Van Kinsbergenstraat
Postjesweg
Ten Katestraat
Kinkerstraat/ Bilderdijkstraat
Witte de Withstraat
Jan Pieter Heijestraat
Ie Constantijn Huygensstraat
Stadhouderskade
Overtoom
Rhijnvis Feithstraat
Jan Pieter Heijestraat
Vondelpark
Emmastraat
Cornelis Schuystraat
Jacob Obrechtstraat
Emmastraat
Jacob Obrechtstraat
Van Limburg Stirumplein
De Wittenkade
Nassaukade
Marnixplein
Frederick Hendrikplantsoen
Hugo de Grootplein
Haarlemmerplein
Nieuwe Willemsstraat
Martelaarsgracht
Nieuwezijdskolk
Bloemgracht
Rozengracht
Westermarkt
Marnixstraat
Dam
Elandsgracht
Raamplein
Leidseplein
Spui
Koningsplein
Keizersgracht
Prinsengracht
Leidseplein
Speigelgracht
Hobbemastraat
Van Baerlestraat
Museumplein
Roelof Hartplein
Ruysdaelkade
Apollolaan
Gerrit van der Veenstraat
Muntplein
Rembrandtplein
Keizersgracht
Weteringcircuit
Stadhouderskade
Albert Cuypstraat/ Ruysdaelstraat
Ferdinand Bolstraat/ Ceintuurbaan
Sarphatipark
2e van der Helststraat
Cornelis Troostplein
Scheldestraat
Keizersgracht
Prinsengracht
Fredericksplein
Stadhouderskade
Van Woustraat/ Ceintuurbaan
Lutmastraat
Nieuwmarkt
Waterlooplein
Mr.Visserplein
Nieuwekeizersgracht
Oosteinde
Roetersstraat
Weesperplein
Amsteldijk
Wibautstraat
Wibautstraat
Muziekgebouw Bimhuis
Kattenburgerstraat
Rietlandpark
C. Van Eesterenlaan
Zuiderzeeweg
Steigereiland
Vennepluimstraat
Ie Leeghwaterstraat
Ie Coehoornstraat
Hoogte Kadijk
Zeeburgerdijk
Javaplein
Insulindeweg
Soembawastraat
Molukkenstraat
Plantage Docklaan
Plantage Kerklaan
Plantage Badlaan
Pontanusstraat
Ie van Swindenstraat
Alexanderplein
Oosterpark
Dapperstraat
Linnaeusstraat
Wijttenbach-straat
Beukenweg
Korte 's Gravesanderstraat
Pretoriusstraat
Hogeweg
Hugo de Vrieslaan
Camperstraat
Interchange with adjacent stops (walk at street level)
De Rijpstraat Service stops in one direction only (shown)
© Communicarta Ltd, 1989-2006 UDN.8

Central Barcelona

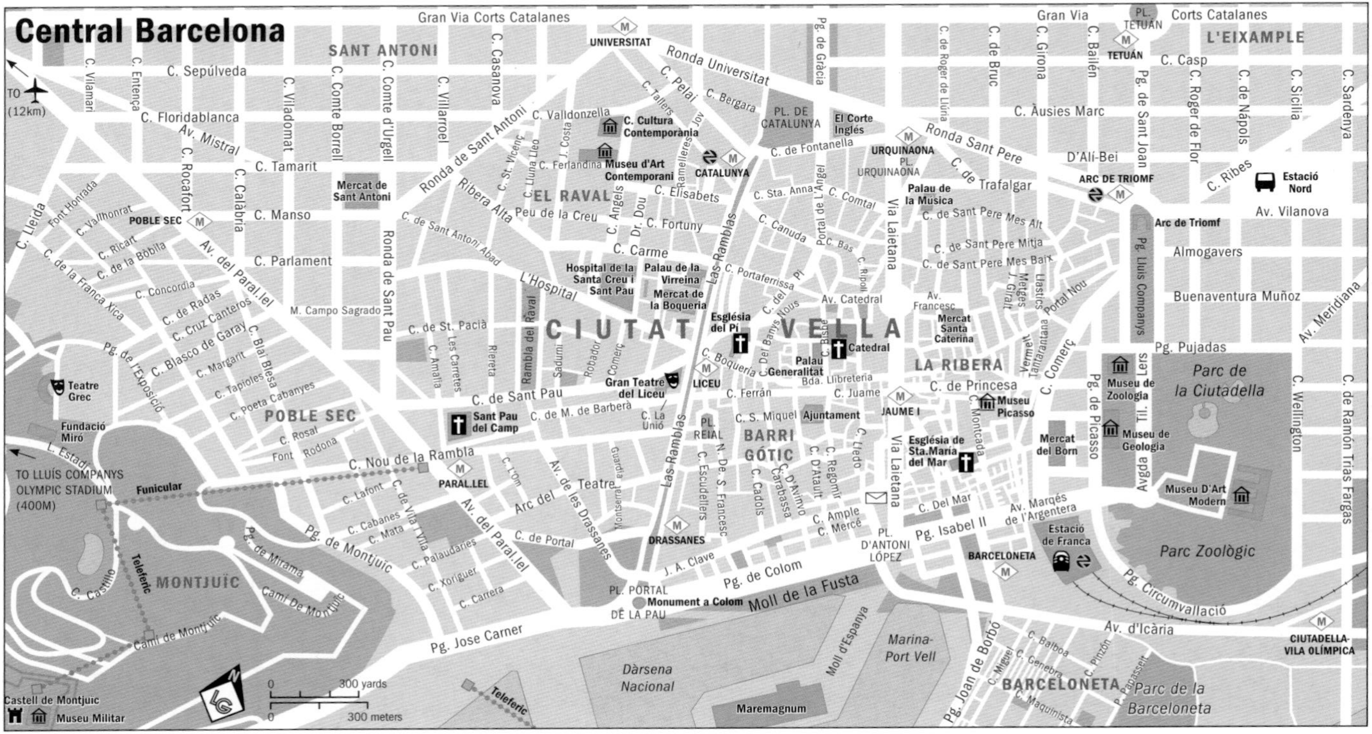

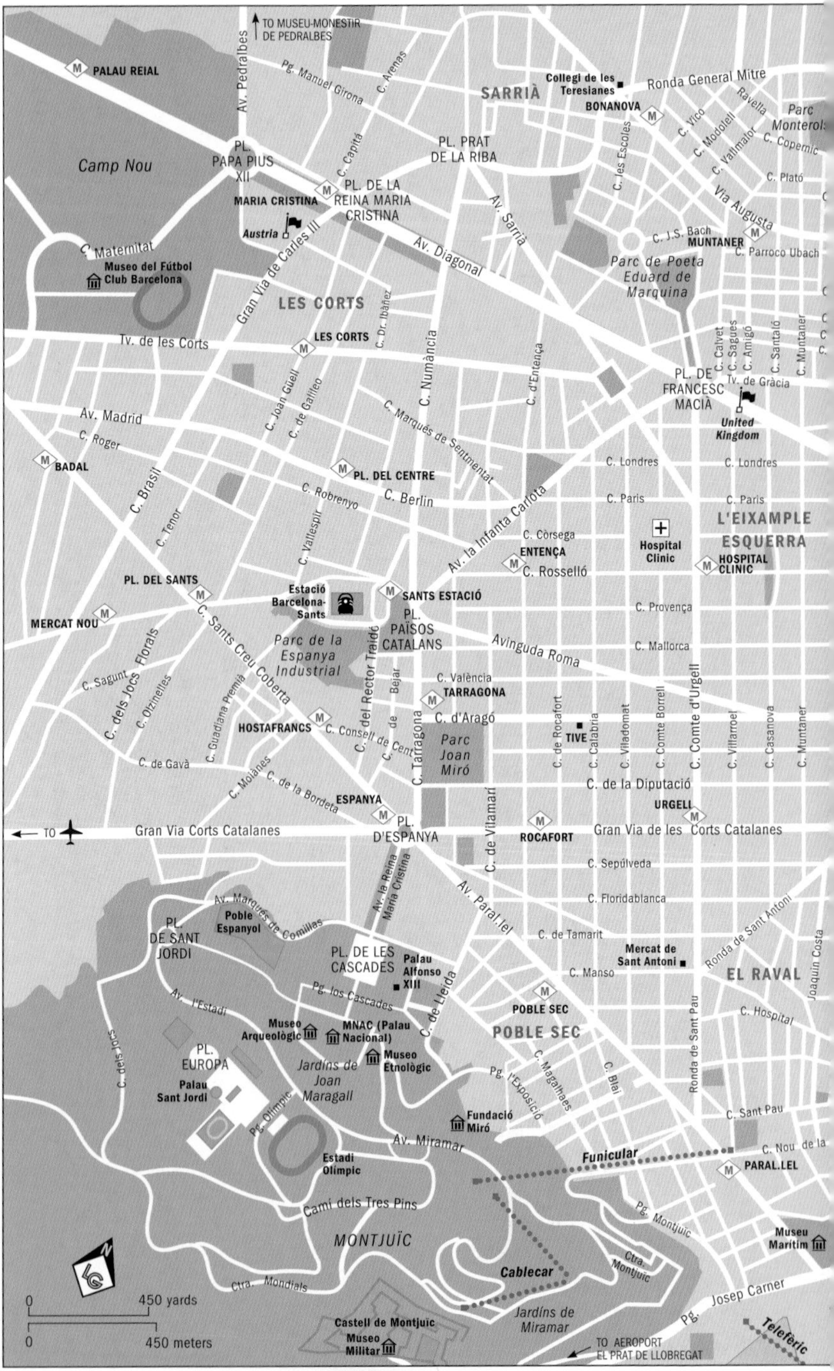
TO MUSEU-MONESTIR DE PEDRALBES
PALAU REIAL
Av. Pedralbes
Pg. Manuel Girona
C. Arenas
SARRIÀ
Collegi de les Teresianes
Ronda General Mitre
BONANOVA
Ravella
Parc Monterols
C. Vico
C. Modolell
C. Vallmajor
C. Copernic
C. Platò
C. les Escoles
Camp Nou
PL. PAPA PIUS XII
C. Capità
PL. PRAT DE LA RIBA
MARIA CRISTINA
PL. DE LA REINA MARIA CRISTINA
Av. Sarrià
Via Augusta
Austria
C. J.S. Bach
MUNTANER
C. Parroco Ubach
C. Maternitat
Museo del Fútbol Club Barcelona
Gran Via de Carles III
Av. Diagonal
Parc de Poeta Eduard de Marquina
LES CORTS
C. Dr. Ibáñez
Tv. de les Corts
LES CORTS
C. Numància
C. d'Entença
C. Calvet
C. Sagues
C. Amigó
C. Santaló
C. Muntaner
PL. DE FRANCESC MACIÀ
Tv. de Gràcia
United Kingdom
C. Joan Güell
C. de Galileo
Av. Madrid
C. Roger
C. Marqués de Sentmenat
BADAL
PL. DEL CENTRE
C. Londres
C. Londres
C. Brasil
C. Robrenyo
C. Berlin
C. Paris
C. Paris
Av. la Infanta Carlota
L'EIXAMPLE ESQUERRA
C. Tenor
C. Vallespir
C. Còrsega
Hospital Clinic
ENTENÇA
HOSPITAL CLINIC
C. Rosselló
PL. DEL SANTS
Estació Barcelona-Sants
SANTS ESTACIÓ
MERCAT NOU
C. Sants Creu Coberta
PL. PAÏSOS CATALANS
C. Provença
Avinguda Roma
Parc de la Espanya Industrial
C. Mallorca
C. dels Jocs Florals
C. Sagunt
C. Olzinelles
C. Guadiana Premià
C. del Rector Triadó
C. Bejar
C. València
TARRAGONA
C. de Rocafort
C. Calabria
C. Viladomat
C. Comte Borrell
C. Comte d'Urgell
C. Villarroel
C. Casanova
C. Muntaner
HOSTAFRANCS
C. Consell de Cent
C. d'Aragó
TIVE
C. Tarragona
Parc Joan Miró
C. de Gavà
C. Moianès
C. de la Bordeta
C. de la Diputació
ESPANYA
URGELL
TO
Gran Via Corts Catalanes
PL. D'ESPANYA
ROCAFORT
Gran Via de les Corts Catalanes
C. de Vilamarí
C. Sepúlveda
Av. la Reina Maria Cristina
Av. Paral.lel
C. Floridablanca
Av. Marqués de Comillas
Poble Espanyol
PL. DE SANT JORDI
C. de Tamarit
Ronda de Sant Antoni
Joaquín Costa
PL. DE LES CASCADES
Palau Alfonso XIII
Mercat de Sant Antoni
C. Manso
EL RAVAL
C. de Lleida
Pg. los Cascades
Av. l'Estadi
POBLE SEC
POBLE SEC
C. Hospital
Museo Arqueològic
MNAC (Palau Nacional)
Ronda de Sant Pau
PL. EUROPA
Museo Etnològic
C. dels Jocs
Jardíns de Joan Maragall
C. Magalhaes
C. Blai
Palau Sant Jordi
Pg. l'Exposició
Pg. Olímpic
Fundació Miró
C. Sant Pau
Av. Miramar
C. Nou de la
Estadi Olímpic
Funicular
PARAL.LEL
Camí dels Tres Pins
Pg. Montjuïc
MONTJUÏC
Museu Marítim
Cablecar
Ctra. Montjuïc
Ctra. Mondials
0
450 yards
0
450 meters
Jardíns de Miramar
Pg. Josep Carner
Castell de Montjuïc
Museo Militar
TO AEROPORT EL PRAT DE LLOBREGAT
Telefèric

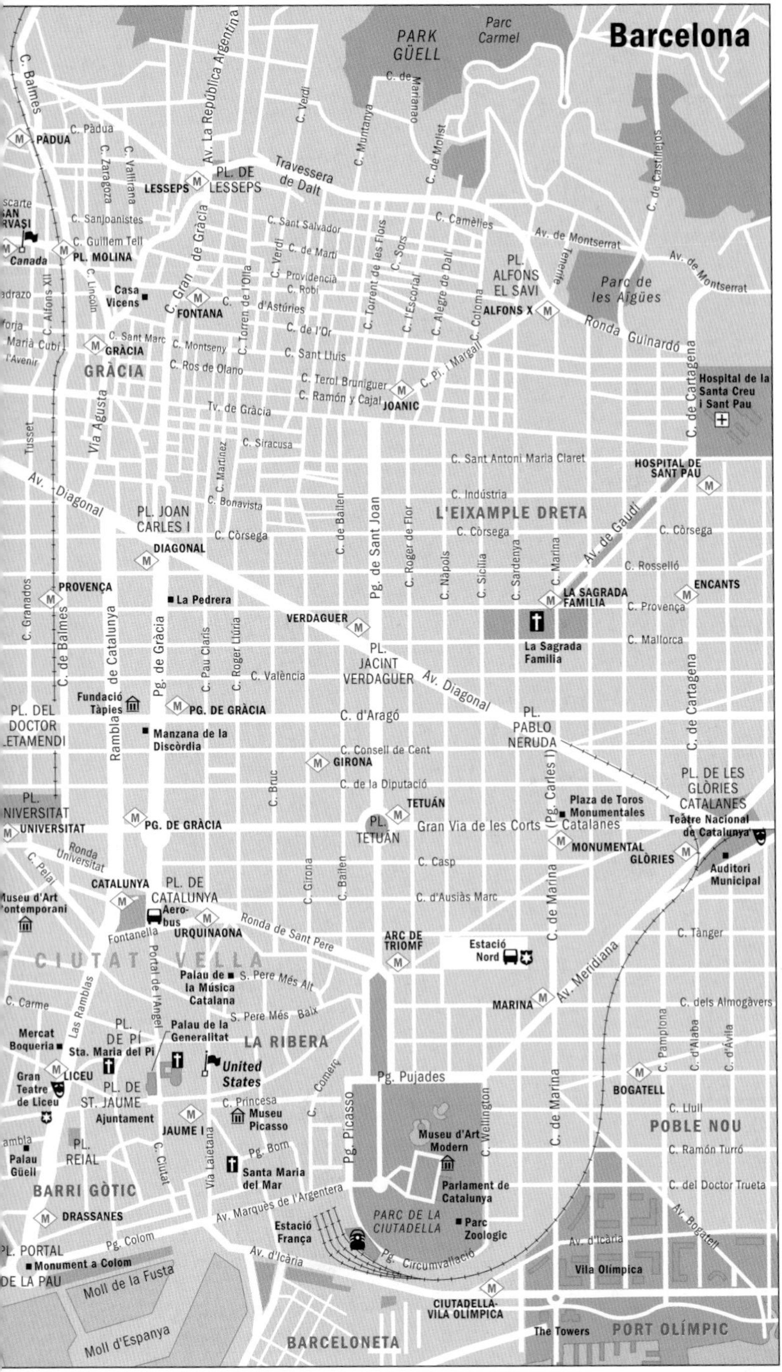

Barcelona
PARK GÜELL
Parc Carmel
C. Balmes
PÀDUA
C. Pàdua
C. Zaragoza
C. Vallirana
Av. La República Argentina
C. Verdi
C. Muntanya
C. de Mariano
C. de Mollist
C. de Castillejos
LESSEPS
PL. DE LESSEPS
Travessera de Dalt
C. Sanjoanistes
C. Guillem Tell
PL. MOLINA
Canada
C. Alfons XII
C. Lincoln
C. Gran de Gràcia
C. Torrent de l'Olla
C. Sant Salvador
C. de Martí
C. Providencia
C. Robí
C. d'Astúries
C. Torrent de les Flors
C. Sors
C. l'Escorial
C. Alegre de Dalt
C. Camèlies
Av. de Montserrat
PL. ALFONS EL SAVI
Tenerife
Parc de les Aigües
Casa Vicens
FONTANA
C. Sant Marc
C. Montseny
C. Ros de Olano
C. de l'Or
C. Sant Lluís
C. Coloma
ALFONS X
Ronda Guinardó
Marià Cubí
GRÀCIA
C. Terol Bruniguer
C. Ramón y Cajal
JOANIC
C. Pi. i Margall
C. de Cartagena
Hospital de la Santa Creu i Sant Pau
Tusset
Via Augusta
Tv. de Gràcia
C. Siracusa
C. Martínez
C. Sant Antoni Maria Claret
HOSPITAL DE SANT PAU
Av. Diagonal
C. Bonavista
C. Indústria
PL. JOAN CARLES I
C. Còrsega
L'EIXAMPLE DRETA
C. de Bailèn
Pg. de Sant Joan
C. Roger de Flor
C. Nàpols
C. Sicília
C. Sardenya
C. Marina
Av. de Gaudí
C. Rosselló
DIAGONAL
PROVENÇA
La Pedrera
LA SAGRADA FAMILIA
ENCANTS
C. Provença
C. Granados
C. de Balmes
Rambla de Catalunya
Pg. de Gràcia
C. Pau Claris
C. Roger Llúria
VERDAGUER
La Sagrada Familia
C. Mallorca
PL. JACINT VERDAGUER
C. València
Fundació Tàpies
PG. DE GRÀCIA
C. d'Aragó
PL. PABLO NERUDA
PL. DEL DOCTOR LETAMENDI
Manzana de la Discòrdia
C. Consell de Cent
GIRONA
C. de la Diputació
C. Bruc
(Pg. Carles I)
PL. DE LES GLÒRIES CATALANES
TETUÁN
Plaza de Toros Monumentales
Teatre Nacional de Catalunya
PL. UNIVERSITAT
UNIVERSITAT
PG. DE GRÀCIA
PL. TETUÁN
Gran Via de les Corts Catalanes
MONUMENTAL
GLÒRIES
Ronda Universitat
C. Pelai
C. Casp
Auditori Municipal
C. Girona
C. Bailèn
CATALUNYA
PL. DE CATALUNYA
C. d'Ausiàs Marc
Aero-bus
URQUINAONA
Ronda de Sant Pere
Fontanella
C. de Marina
C. Tànger
ARC DE TRIOMF
Estació Nord
CIUTAT VELLA
Portal de l'Àngel
Palau de la Música Catalana
S. Pere Més Alt
Las Ramblas
C. Carme
MARINA
Av. Meridiana
C. dels Almogàvers
S. Pere Més Baix
Mercat Boqueria
PL. DE PI
Sta. Maria del Pi
Palau de la Generalitat
LA RIBERA
United States
C. Pamplona
C. d'Alaba
C. d'Àvila
LICEU
Gran Teatre de Liceu
PL. DE ST. JAUME
C. Comerç
Pg. Pujades
BOGATELL
C. Princesa
Museu Picasso
Ajuntament
C. Wellington
C. Llull
POBLE NOU
JAUME I
Pg. Picasso
Museu d'Art Modern
C. Ramón Turró
Palau Güell
PL. REIAL
C. Ciutat
Pg. Born
Via Laietana
Santa Maria del Mar
Parlament de Catalunya
C. del Doctor Trueta
BARRI GÒTIC
Av. Marquès de l'Argentera
PARC DE LA CIUTADELLA
Parc Zoologic
Av. Bogatell
DRASSANES
Estació França
Av. d'Icària
Pg. Colom
Pg. Circumvallació
Vila Olímpica
Monument a Colom
Av. d'Icària
Moll de la Fusta
CIUTADELLA-VILA OLIMPICA
The Towers
PORT OLÍMPIC
Moll d'Espanya
BARCELONETA

Barcelona Metro

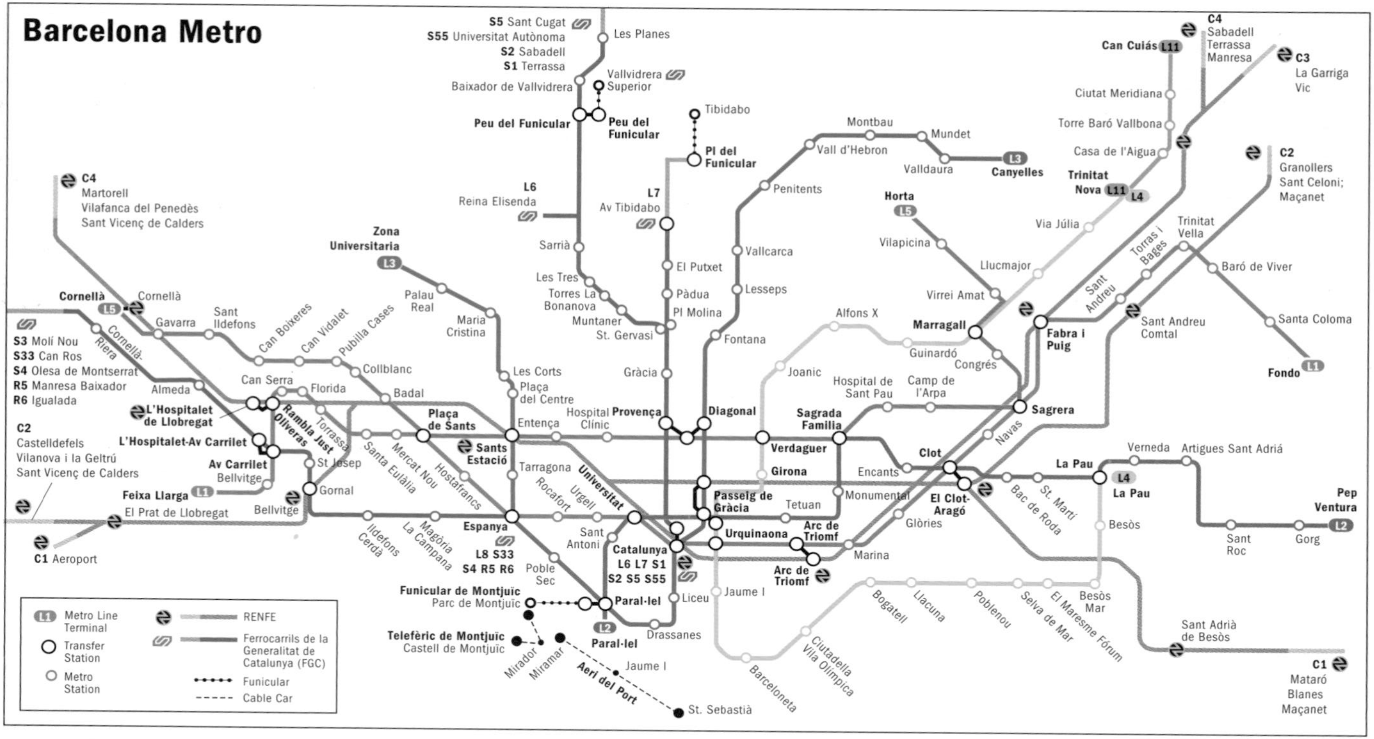

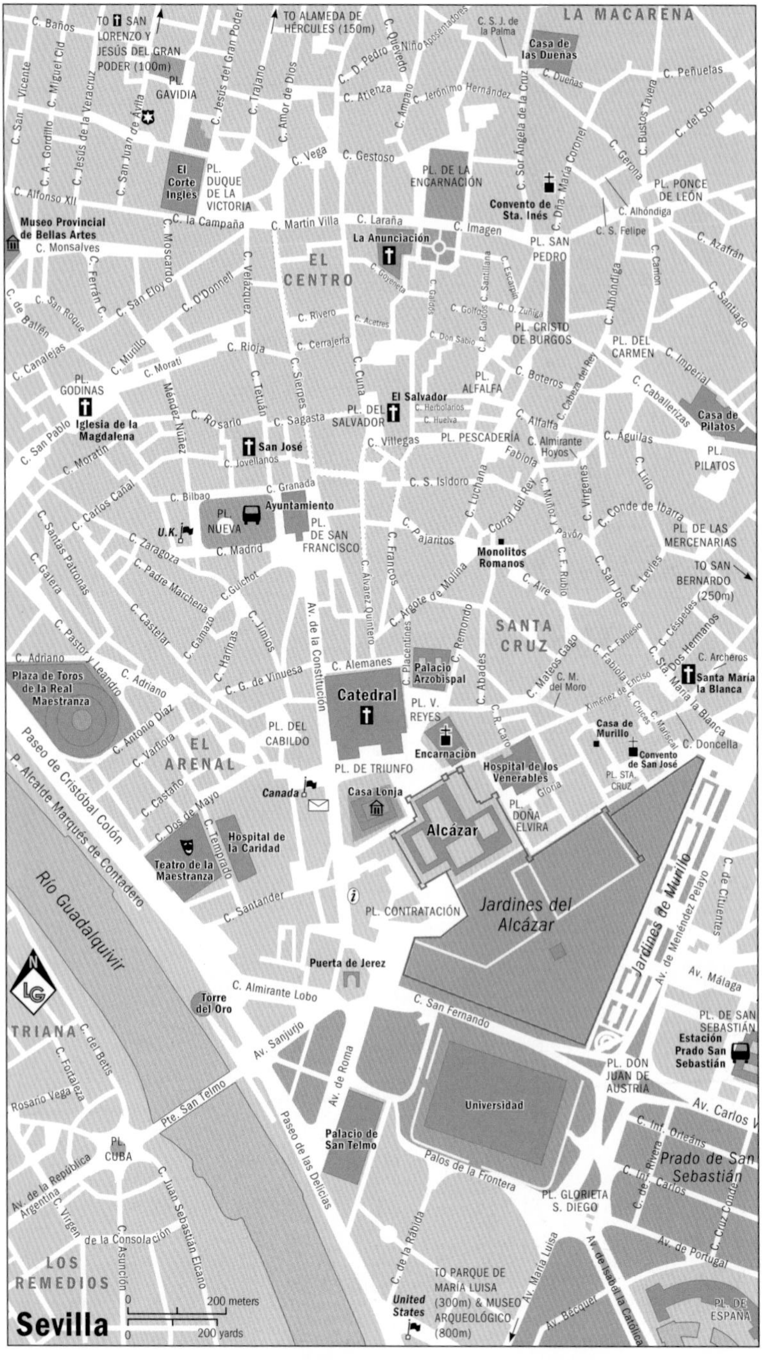
Sevilla
LA MACARENA
EL CENTRO
SANTA CRUZ
EL ARENAL
TRIANA
LOS REMEDIOS
TO SAN LORENZO Y JESÚS DEL GRAN PODER (100m)
TO ALAMEDA DE HÉRCULES (150m)
TO SAN BERNARDO (250m)
TO PARQUE DE MARÍA LUISA (300m) & MUSEO ARQUEOLÓGICO (800m)
Casa de las Dueñas
PL. GAVIDIA
El Corte Inglés
PL. DUQUE DE LA VICTORIA
PL. DE LA ENCARNACIÓN
Convento de Sta. Inés
PL. PONCE DE LEÓN
Museo Provincial de Bellas Artes
La Anunciación
PL. SAN PEDRO
PL. CRISTO DE BURGOS
PL. DEL CARMEN
PL. ALFALFA
El Salvador
PL. DEL SALVADOR
PL. GODINAS
Iglesia de la Magdalena
San José
Casa de Pilatos
PL. PILATOS
PL. PESCADERÍA
Ayuntamiento
PL. NUEVA
PL. DE SAN FRANCISCO
U.K.
Monolitos Romanos
PL. DE LAS MERCENARIAS
Plaza de Toros de la Real Maestranza
Palacio Arzobispal
Catedral
PL. V. REYES
PL. DEL CABILDO
Santa María la Blanca
Casa de Murillo
Convento de San José
Encarnación
Hospital de los Venerables
PL. STA. CRUZ
PL. DE TRIUNFO
Canada
Casa Lonja
Alcázar
PL. DOÑA ELVIRA
Teatro de la Maestranza
Hospital de la Caridad
PL. CONTRATACIÓN
Jardines del Alcázar
Jardines de Murillo
Puerta de Jerez
Torre del Oro
Río Guadalquivir
Paseo de Cristóbal Colón
P. Alcalde Marqués de Contadero
PL. DE SAN SEBASTIÁN
Estación Prado San Sebastián
PL. DON JUAN DE AUSTRIA
Universidad
Palacio de San Telmo
Prado de San Sebastián
PL. CUBA
PL. GLORIETA S. DIEGO
PL. DE ESPAÑA
United States
Av. de la Constitución
Av. de Roma
Paseo de las Delicias
Av. Sanjurjo
Pte. San Telmo
Av. de Menéndez Pelayo
Av. Carlos V
Av. de Portugal
Av. María Luisa
Av. de Isabel la Católica
Av. Becquer
Av. de la República Argentina
C. Juan Sebastián Elcano
C. San Fernando
Palos de la Frontera
C. Almirante Lobo
C. Sierpes
C. Tetuán
C. Imagen
C. Laraña
C. Martín Villa
C. la Campaña
C. Alfonso XII
C. Monsalves
C. Rioja
C. Sagasta
C. Villegas
C. S. Isidoro
C. Argote de Molina
C. Alemanes
C. G. de Vinuesa
C. Adriano
C. Dos de Mayo
C. Santander
C. Betis
C. Pureza
C. San Pablo
C. Reyes Católicos
C. Mateos Gago
C. Abades
C. Águilas
C. Caballerizas
C. Conde de Ibarra
C. San José
Rosario Vega
C. Virgen de la Consolación
C. Asunción
0
200 meters
0
200 yards

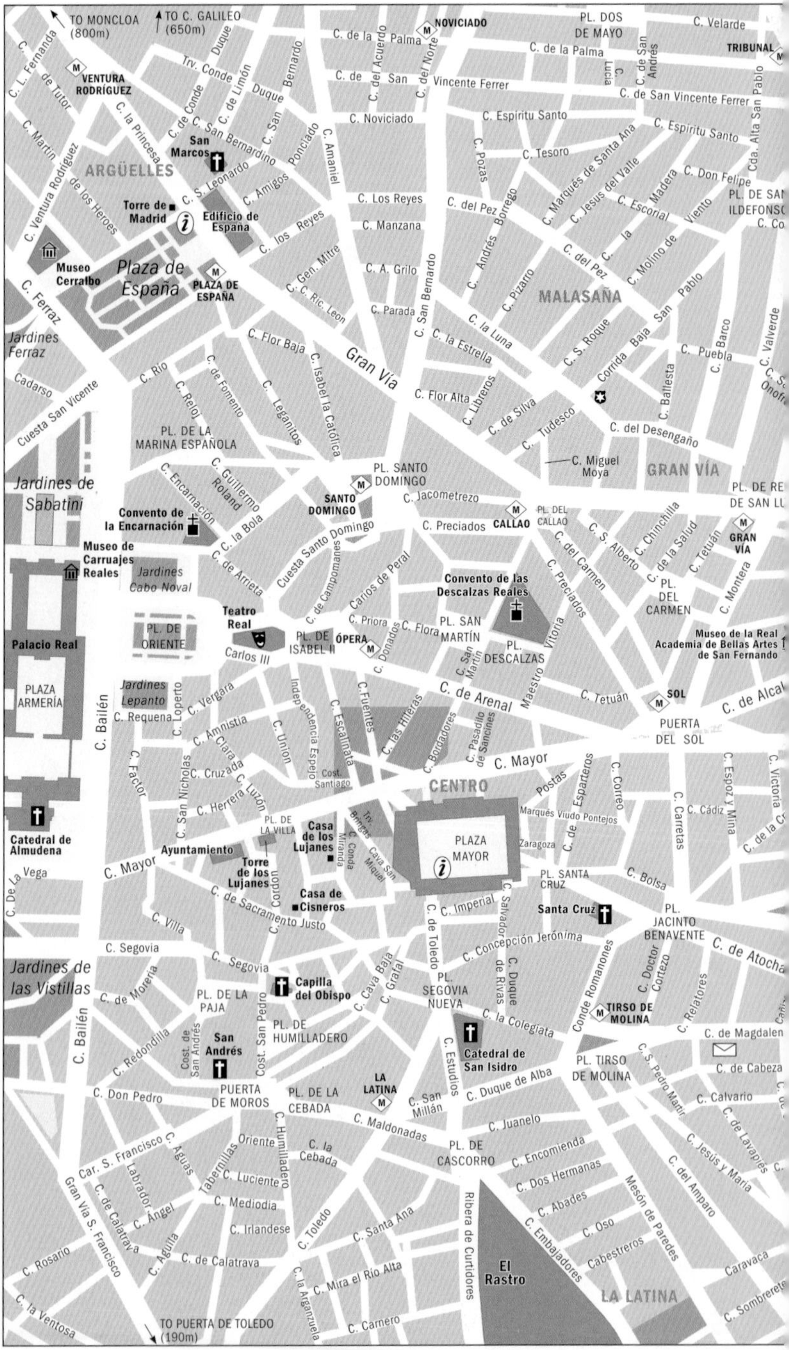
TO MONCLOA (800m)
TO C. GALILEO (650m)
NOVICIADO
PL. DOS DE MAYO
C. Velarde
TRIBUNAL
VENTURA RODRÍGUEZ
ARGÜELLES
San Marcos
Torre de Madrid
Edificio de España
Museo Cerralbo
Plaza de España
PLAZA DE ESPAÑA
Jardines Ferraz
MALASAÑA
Gran Vía
GRAN VÍA
PL. DE LA MARINA ESPAÑOLA
Jardines de Sabatini
Convento de la Encarnación
Museo de Carruajes Reales
Jardines Cabo Noval
PL. SANTO DOMINGO
SANTO DOMINGO
CALLAO
PL. DEL CALLAO
PL. DE SAN ILDEFONSO
PL. DE REY
PL. DEL CARMEN
Convento de las Descalzas Reales
PL. SAN MARTÍN
PL. DESCALZAS
Teatro Real
PL. DE ORIENTE
Palacio Real
PLAZA ARMERÍA
PL. DE ISABEL II
ÓPERA
Museo de la Real Academia de Bellas Artes de San Fernando
SOL
PUERTA DEL SOL
Jardines Lepanto
CENTRO
PLAZA MAYOR
Catedral de Almudena
Ayuntamiento
PL. DE LA VILLA
Casa de los Lujanes
Torre de los Lujanes
Casa de Cisneros
PL. SANTA CRUZ
Santa Cruz
PL. JACINTO BENAVENTE
Jardines de las Vistillas
Capilla del Obispo
PL. DE LA PAJA
San Andrés
PL. DE HUMILLADERO
PL. SEGOVIA NUEVA
Catedral de San Isidro
TIRSO DE MOLINA
PL. TIRSO DE MOLINA
PUERTA DE MOROS
PL. DE LA CEBADA
LA LATINA
PL. DE CASCORRO
El Rastro
LA LATINA
TO PUERTA DE TOLEDO (190m)
C. Bailén
C. Mayor
C. de Arenal
C. de Alcalá
C. de Atocha
C. de Toledo
C. Segovia
C. Princesa
C. San Bernardo
C. Preciados
C. Montera
C. Carretas
C. Duque de Alba
C. Maldonadas
C. Embajadores
Ribera de Curtidores
Mesón de Paredes
Gran Vía S. Francisco
C. de Calatrava
C. Mira el Río Alta
C. Carnero
C. la Ventosa

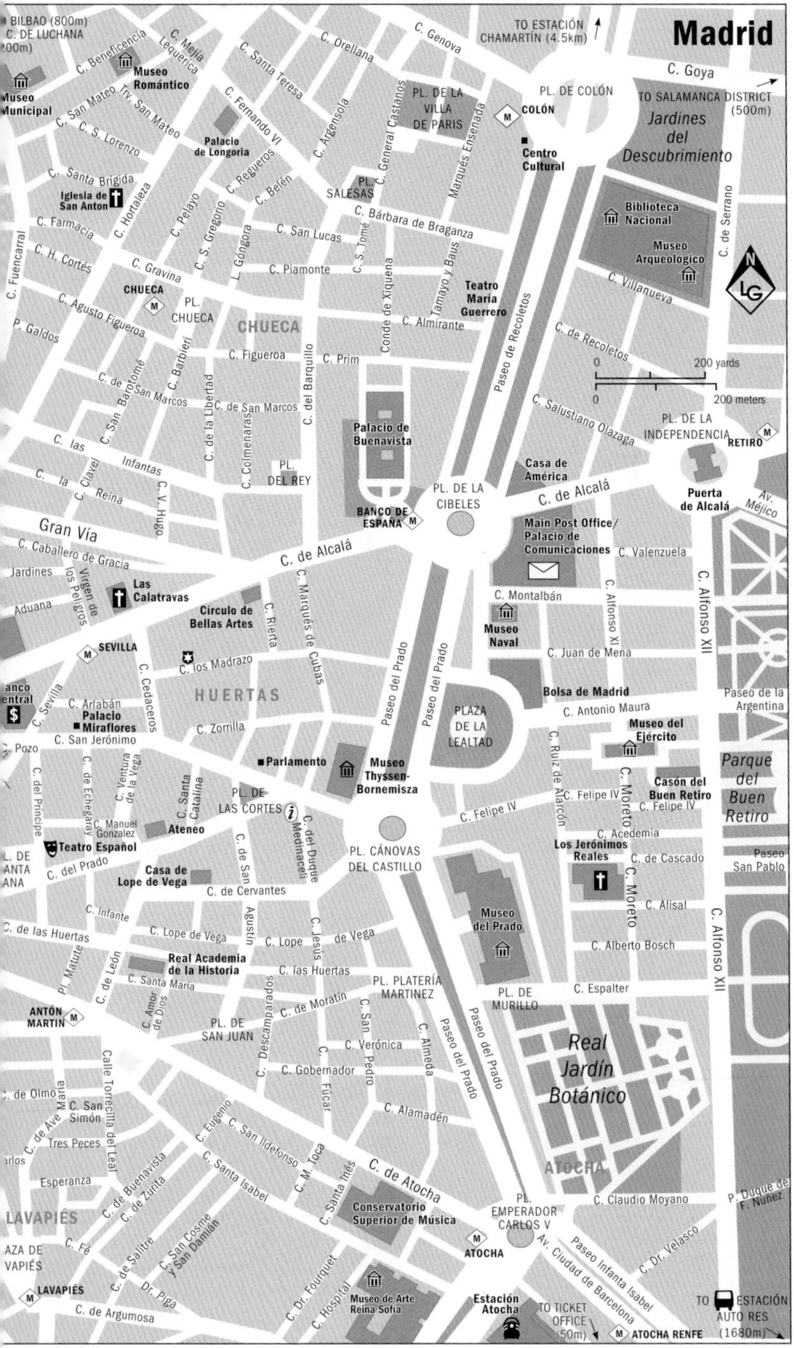

Madrid
TO ESTACIÓN CHAMARTÍN (4.5km)
BILBAO (800m)
C. DE LUCHANA
(200m)
Museo Municipal
Museo Romántico
C. Beneficencia
C. Mejía Lequerica
C. Santa Teresa
C. Orellana
C. Genova
C. Goya
PL. DE COLÓN
COLÓN
TO SALAMANCA DISTRICT (500m)
Jardines del Descubrimiento
PL. DE LA VILLA DE PARIS
Centro Cultural
C. San Mateo
Trv. San Mateo
C. S. Lorenzo
C. Fernando VI
Palacio de Longoria
C. Argensola
C. General Castaños
Marqués Ensenada
C. Santa Brígida
Iglesia de San Anton
C. Hortaleza
C. Regueros
C. Belén
PL. SALESAS
C. Bárbara de Braganza
Biblioteca Nacional
Museo Arqueológico
C. de Serrano
C. Farmacia
C. Pelayo
C. S. Gregorio
L. Góngora
C. San Lucas
C. S. Tomé
C. H. Cortés
C. Gravina
C. Piamonte
Tamayo y Baus
Teatro María Guerrero
C. Villanueva
C. Fuencarral
CHUECA
PL. CHUECA
C. Agusto Figueroa
C. Almirante
Conde de Xiquena
Paseo de Recoletos
C. de Recoletos
P. Galdos
C. Figueroa
C. Prim
C. Barbieri
C. del Barquillo
0
200 yards
200 meters
C. de San Marcos
C. San Barotomé
C. de la Libertad
C. Colmenares
Palacio de Buenavista
C. Salustiano Olazaga
PL. DE LA INDEPENDENCIA
RETIRO
C. las Infantas
C. Clavel
C. la Reina
C. V. Hugo
PL. DEL REY
PL. DE LA CIBELES
Casa de América
Puerta de Alcalá
Av. Méjico
C. de Alcalá
BANCO DE ESPAÑA
Main Post Office/ Palacio de Comunicaciones
C. Valenzuela
Gran Vía
C. Caballero de Gracia
Jardines
Virgen de los Peligros
Las Calatravas
Aduana
Círculo de Bellas Artes
C. Rierta
C. Marqués de Cubas
C. Montalbán
C. Alfonso XI
C. Alfonso XII
Museo Naval
SEVILLA
C. los Madrazo
Paseo del Prado
C. Juan de Mena
Banco Central
C. Cedaceros
HUERTAS
Bolsa de Madrid
Paseo de la Argentina
C. Sevilla
C. Arlabán
Palacio Miraflores
PLAZA DE LA LEALTAD
C. Antonio Maura
C. Zorrilla
Museo del Ejército
C. San Jerónimo
C. Pozo
C. Ruiz de Alarcón
C. Ventura de la Vega
Parlamento
Museo Thyssen-Bornemisza
Casón del Buen Retiro
Parque del Buen Retiro
C. del Príncipe
C. de Echegaray
C. Santa Catalina
PL. DE LAS CORTES
C. Felipe IV
C. Moreto
C. Manuel Gonzalez
Ateneo
C. del Duque Medinaceli
C. Acedemia
Teatro Español
PL. CÁNOVAS DEL CASTILLO
Los Jerónimos Reales
C. de Cascado
Paseo San Pablo
PL. DE SANTA ANA
C. del Prado
Casa de Lope de Vega
C. de San Agustín
C. de Cervantes
C. Alisal
C. Infante
Museo del Prado
C. de las Huertas
C. Lope de Vega
C. Jesús
C. Alberto Bosch
Pl. Matute
C. de León
Real Academia de la Historia
C. las Huertas
PL. PLATERÍA MARTINEZ
C. Santa María
C. Amor de Dios
C. Descamparados
PL. DE MURILLO
C. Espalter
ANTÓN MARTIN
PL. DE SAN JUAN
C. de Moratín
C. San Pedro
C. Almeda
Calle Torrecilla del Leal
C. Verónica
Real Jardín Botánico
C. de Olmo
C. Gobernador
C. Fúcar
C. de Ave María
C. San Simón
C. Alamadén
Tres Peces
C. Eugenio
C. San Ildefonso
C. M. Toca
Carlos
Esperanza
C. Santa Isabel
C. de Atocha
ATOCHA
C. de Buenavista
C. de Zurita
C. Santa Inés
Conservatorio Superior de Música
PL. EMPERADOR CARLOS V
C. Claudio Moyano
P. Duque de F. Nuñez
LAVAPIÉS
C. Fé
C. San Cosme y San Damián
Av. Ciudad de Barcelona
Paseo Infanta Isabel
C. Dr. Velasco
PLAZA DE LAVAPIÉS
C. de Salitre
Dr. Piga
C. Dr. Fourquet
C. Hospital
Museo de Arte Reina Sofía
Estación Atocha
TO TICKET OFFICE (50m)
ATOCHA RENFE
TO ESTACIÓN AUTO RES (1680m)
C. de Argumosa

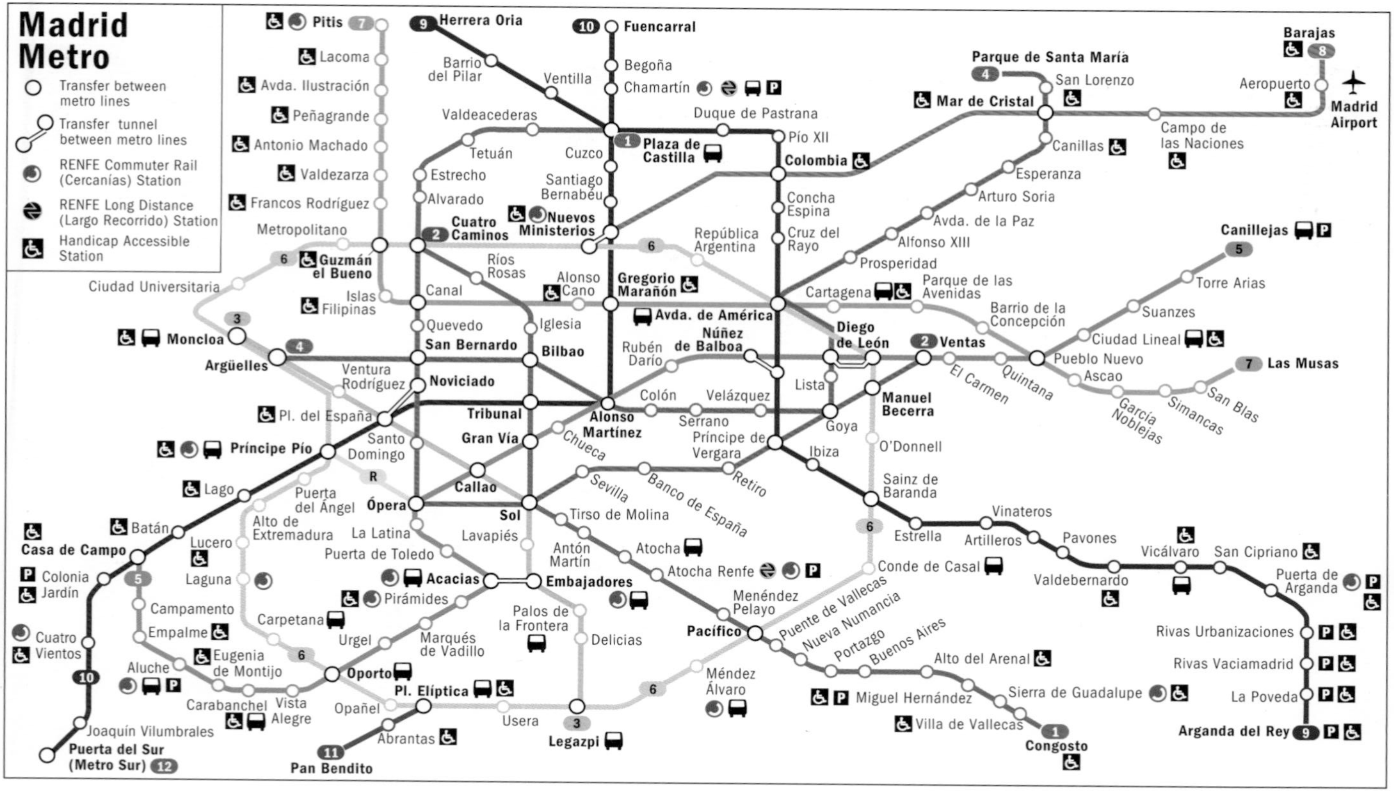

Madrid Metro
Transfer between metro lines
Transfer tunnel between metro lines
RENFE Commuter Rail (Cercanías) Station
RENFE Long Distance (Largo Recorrido) Station
Handicap Accessible Station
Pitis
Lacoma
Avda. Ilustración
Peñagrande
Antonio Machado
Valdezarza
Francos Rodríguez
Metropolitano
Guzmán el Bueno
Ciudad Universitaria
Islas Filipinas
Moncloa
Argüelles
Herrera Oria
Barrio del Pilar
Ventilla
Valdeacederas
Tetuán
Estrecho
Alvarado
Cuatro Caminos
Ríos Rosas
Canal
Quevedo
San Bernardo
Iglesia
Bilbao
Ventura Rodríguez
Noviciado
Pl. del España
Tribunal
Príncipe Pío
Santo Domingo
Gran Vía
Callao
R
Lago
Puerta del Ángel
Ópera
Sol
Batán
Alto de Extremadura
La Latina
Lavapiés
Casa de Campo
Lucero
Puerta de Toledo
Laguna
Colonia Jardín
Campamento
Carpetana
Acacias
Embajadores
Pirámides
Palos de la Frontera
Delicias
Cuatro Vientos
Empalme
Urgel
Marqués de Vadillo
Eugenia de Montijo
Aluche
Oporto
Pl. Elíptica
Carabanchel
Vista Alegre
Opañel
Usera
Legazpi
Joaquín Vilumbrales
Abrantas
Puerta del Sur (Metro Sur)
Pan Bendito
Fuencarral
Begoña
Chamartín
Duque de Pastrana
Plaza de Castilla
Pío XII
Cuzco
Santiago Bernabéu
Nuevos Ministerios
Colombia
Concha Espina
Cruz del Rayo
República Argentina
Gregorio Marañón
Alonso Cano
Avda. de América
Rubén Darío
Núñez de Balboa
Alonso Martínez
Colón
Velázquez
Serrano
Chueca
Príncipe de Vergara
Sevilla
Banco de España
Retiro
Tirso de Molina
Antón Martín
Atocha
Atocha Renfe
Menéndez Pelayo
Pacífico
Méndez Álvaro
Parque de Santa María
San Lorenzo
Mar de Cristal
Canillas
Esperanza
Arturo Soria
Avda. de la Paz
Alfonso XIII
Prosperidad
Cartagena
Parque de las Avenidas
Barrio de la Concepción
Diego de León
Lista
Goya
Manuel Becerra
Ventas
El Carmen
Quintana
Pueblo Nuevo
Ciudad Lineal
Suanzes
Torre Arias
Canillejas
Ascao
García Noblejas
Simancas
San Blas
Las Musas
O'Donnell
Ibiza
Sainz de Baranda
Estrella
Conde de Casal
Puente de Vallecas
Nueva Numancia
Portazgo
Buenos Aires
Alto del Arenal
Miguel Hernández
Sierra de Guadalupe
Villa de Vallecas
Congosto
Vinateros
Artilleros
Pavones
Valdebernardo
Vicálvaro
San Cipriano
Puerta de Arganda
Rivas Urbanizaciones
Rivas Vaciamadrid
La Poveda
Arganda del Rey
Barajas
Aeropuerto
Madrid Airport
Campo de las Naciones

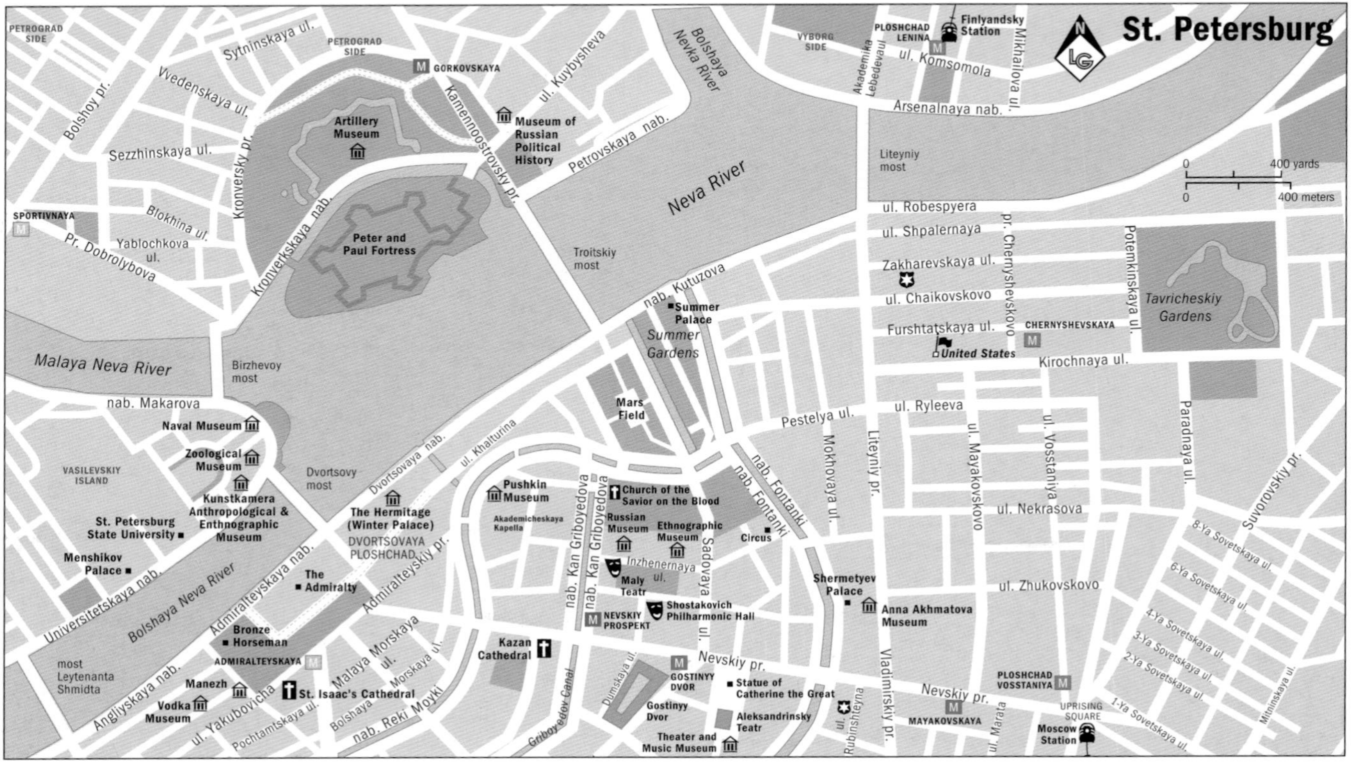
St. Petersburg
400 yards
400 meters
Petrograd Side
Sytninskaya ul.
Gorkovskaya
Vedenskaya ul.
Bolshoy pr.
Sezzhinskaya ul.
Kronversky pr.
Artillery Museum
Kamennoostrovsky pr.
Museum of Russian Political History
ul. Kuybysheva
Petrovskaya nab.
Bolshaya Nevka River
Vyborg Side
Ploshchad Lenina
Finlyandsky Station
Akademika Lebedeva ul.
ul. Komsomola
Mikhailova ul.
Arsenalnaya nab.
Liteyniy most
Sportivnaya
Blokhina ul.
Yablochkova ul.
Pr. Dobrolybova
Kronverkskaya nab.
Peter and Paul Fortress
Neva River
Troitskiy most
ul. Robespyera
ul. Shpalernaya
Zakharevskaya ul.
ul. Chaikovskovo
pr. Chernyshevskovo
Furshtatskaya ul.
Chernyshevskaya
United States
Kirochnaya ul.
Potemkinskaya ul.
Tavricheskiy Gardens
Paradnaya ul.
nab. Kutuzova
Summer Palace
Summer Gardens
Malaya Neva River
Birzhevoy most
nab. Makarova
Naval Museum
Zoological Museum
Kunstkamera Anthropological & Enthnographic Museum
Vasilevskiy Island
St. Petersburg State University
Menshikov Palace
Dvortsovy most
Dvortsovaya nab.
ul. Khalturina
The Hermitage (Winter Palace)
Dvortsovaya Ploshchad
Mars Field
Pushkin Museum
Akademicheskaya Kapella
nab. Kan Griboyedova
Church of the Savior on the Blood
Russian Museum
Ethnographic Museum
Inzhenernaya ul.
Maly Teatr
Sadovaya ul.
Circus
nab. Fontanki
Pestelya ul.
ul. Ryleeva
Mokhovaya ul.
Liteyniy pr.
ul. Mayakovskovo
ul. Vosstaniya
ul. Nekrasova
Suvorovskiy pr.
8-Ya Sovetskaya ul.
6-Ya Sovetskaya ul.
4-Ya Sovetskaya ul.
3-Ya Sovetskaya ul.
2-Ya Sovetskaya ul.
1-Ya Sovetskaya ul.
Mitninskaya ul.
ul. Zhukovskovo
Shermetyev Palace
Anna Akhmatova Museum
Universitetskaya nab.
Bolshaya Neva River
Admiralteyskaya nab.
The Admiralty
Admiralteyskiy pr.
Bronze Horseman
Admiralteyskaya
most Leytenanta Shmidta
Angliyskaya nab.
Manezh
Vodka Museum
ul. Yakubovicha
Pochtamtskaya ul.
St. Isaac's Cathedral
Malaya Morskaya ul.
Bolshaya Morskaya ul.
nab. Reki Moyki
Kazan Cathedral
Griboyedov Canal
Nevskiy Prospekt
Shostakovich Philharmonic Hall
Nevskiy pr.
Dumskaya ul.
Gostinyy Dvor
Statue of Catherine the Great
Aleksandrinsky Teatr
Theater and Music Museum
ul. Rubinshteyna
Vladimirskiy pr.
Mayakovskaya
ul. Marata
Ploshchad Vosstaniya
Uprising Square
Moscow Station

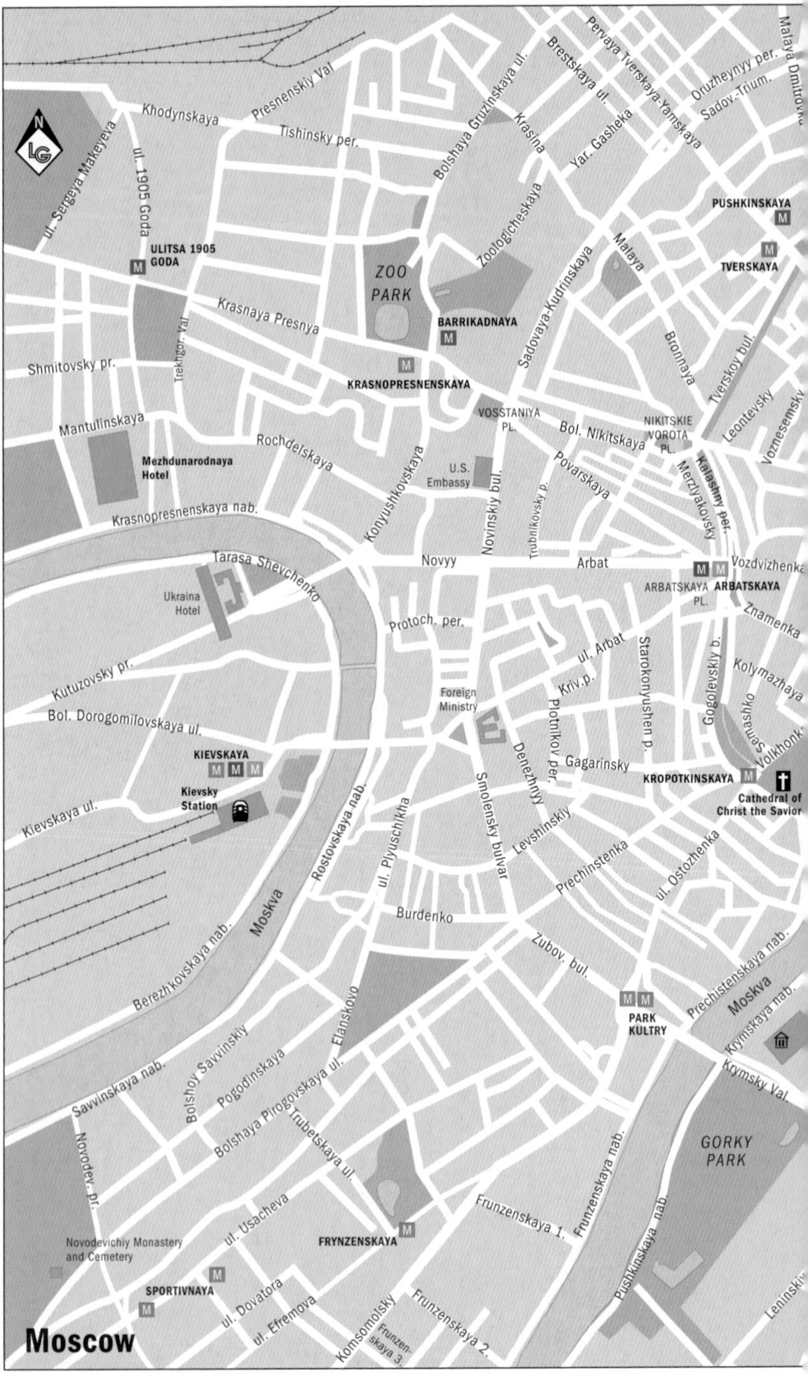
Moscow
ZOO PARK
GORKY PARK
ULITSA 1905 GODA
BARRIKADNAYA
KRASNOPRESNENSKAYA
PUSHKINSKAYA
TVERSKAYA
VOSSTANIYA PL.
NIKITSKIE VOROTA PL.
Mezhdunarodnaya Hotel
U.S. Embassy
Ukraina Hotel
Foreign Ministry
ARBATSKAYA PL.
ARBATSKAYA
KIEVSKAYA
Kievsky Station
KROPOTKINSKAYA
Cathedral of Christ the Savior
PARK KULTRY
FRYNZENSKAYA
SPORTIVNAYA
Novodevichiy Monastery and Cemetery
Khodynskaya
Presnenskiy Val
Tishinsky per.
ul. Sergeya Makeyeva
ul. 1905 Goda
Bolshaya Gruzinskaya ul.
Brestskaya ul.
Pervaya Tverskaya-Yamskaya
Oruzheynyy per.
Sadov.-Trium.
Malaya Dmitrovka
Krasina
Yar. Gasheka
Zoologicheskaya
Sadovaya-Kudrinskaya
Malaya
Bronnaya
Tverskoy bul.
Leontevsky
Voznesensky
Krasnaya Presnya
Shmitovsky pr.
Trekhgor. Val
Mantulinskaya
Rochdelskaya
Konyushkovskaya
Novinskiy bul.
Trubnikovsky p.
Bol. Nikitskaya
Povarskaya
Merzlyakovsky
Kalashny per.
Krasnopresnenskaya nab.
Tarasa Shevchenko
Novyy
Arbat
Vozdvizhenka
Znamenka
Kolymazhaya
Protoch. per.
Kutuzovsky pr.
Bol. Dorogomilovskaya ul.
ul. Arbat
Kriv.p.
Plotnikov per.
Starokonyushen p.
Gogolevskiy b.
Semashko
Volkhonka
Denezhnyy
Smolensky bulvar
Gagarinsky
Kievskaya ul.
Rostovskaya nab.
ul. Plyuschikha
Levshinskiy
Prechistenka
ul. Ostozhenka
Moskva
Burdenko
Berezhkovskaya nab.
Zubov. bul.
Prechistenskaya nab.
Krymskaya nab.
Krymsky Val.
Elanskovo
Bolshoy Savvinskiy
Pogodinskaya
Savvinskaya nab.
Bolshaya Pirogovskaya ul.
Trubetskaya ul.
Novodev. pr.
Frunzenskaya nab.
Frunzenskaya 1.
ul. Usacheva
Pushkinskaya nab.
Leninsky
ul. Dovatora
ul. Efremova
Komsomolsky
Frunzen-skaya 3.
Frunzenskaya 2.

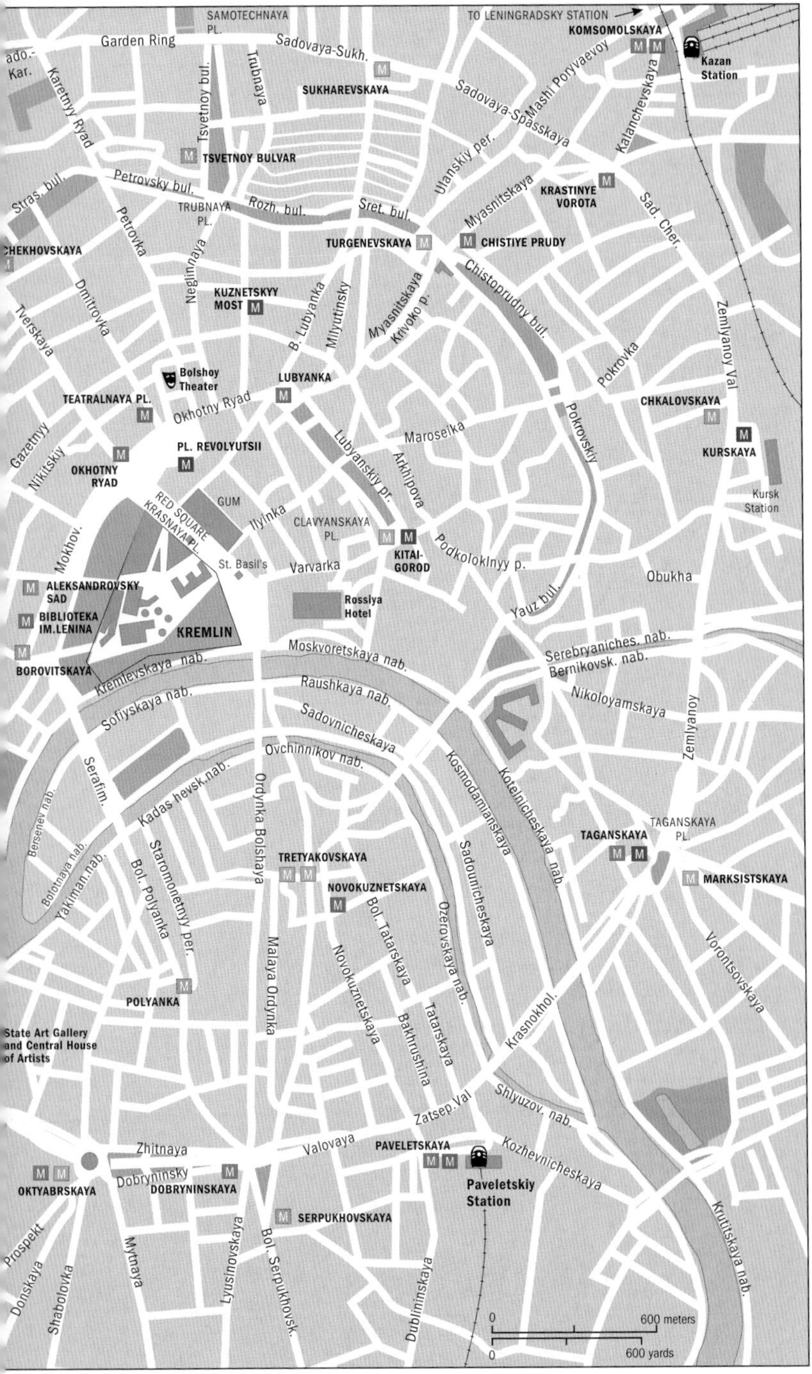

SAMOTECHNAYA PL.
TO LENINGRADSKY STATION
KOMSOMOLSKAYA
Kazan Station
Garden Ring
Sadovaya-Sukh.
SUKHAREVSKAYA
Sadovo-Kar.
Karetny Ryad
Tsvetnoy bul.
Trubnaya
Sadovaya-Spasskaya
Mashi Poryvaevoy
Kalanchevskaya
TSVETNOY BULVAR
Ulanskiy per.
Petrovsky bul.
Strast. bul.
TRUBNAYA PL.
Rozh. bul.
Sret. bul.
Myasnitskaya
KRASTINYE VOROTA
Sad. Cher.
Petrovka
TURGENEVSKAYA
CHISTIYE PRUDY
CHEKHOVSKAYA
Neglinnaya
Chistoprudny bul.
Dmitrovka
KUZNETSKYY MOST
B. Lubyanka
Milyutinsky
Myasnitskaya
Krivoko p.
Zemlyanoy Val
Tverskaya
Pokrovka
Bolshoy Theater
LUBYANKA
TEATRALNAYA PL.
Okhotny Ryad
CHKALOVSKAYA
Pokrovskiy
Maroseika
KURSKAYA
Gazetnyy
PL. REVOLYUTSII
Nikitskiy
OKHOTNY RYAD
Lubyanskiy pr.
Arkhipova
Kursk Station
GUM
RED SQUARE
KRASNAYA PL.
Ilyinka
CLAVYANSKAYA PL.
KITAI-GOROD
Podkoloklnyy p.
Mokhov.
St. Basil's
Varvarka
Obukha
ALEKSANDROVSKY SAD
Rossiya Hotel
Yauz bul.
BIBLIOTEKA IM.LENINA
KREMLIN
Moskvoretskaya nab.
Serebryaniches. nab.
Bernikovsk. nab.
BOROVITSKAYA
Kremlevskaya nab.
Raushkaya nab.
Nikoloyamskaya
Sofiyskaya nab.
Sadovnicheskaya
Zemlyanoy
Ovchinnikov nab.
Kosmodamianskaya
Kotelnicheskaya nab.
Serafim.
Kadashevsk.nab.
Ordynka Bolshaya
Bersenev nab.
TAGANSKAYA PL.
TAGANSKAYA
Sadounicheskaya
Staromonetnyy per.
TRETYAKOVSKAYA
MARKSISTSKAYA
Bolotnaya nab.
Yakiman.nab.
Bol. Polyanka
NOVOKUZNETSKAYA
Bol. Tatarskaya
Ozerovskaya nab.
Malaya Ordynka
Novokuznetskaya
Vorontsovskaya
POLYANKA
Krasnokhol.
Tatarskaya
Bakhrushina
State Art Gallery and Central House of Artists
Zatsep.Val
Shlyuzov. nab.
Zhitnaya
Valovaya
PAVELETSKAYA
Kozhevnicheskaya
OKTYABRSKAYA
Dobryninsky
DOBRYNINSKAYA
Paveletskiy Station
SERPUKHOVSKAYA
Krutitskaya nab.
Prospekt
Donskaya
Shabolovka
Mytnaya
Lysinovskaya
Bol. Serpukhovsk.
Dubininskaya
0
600 meters
0
600 yards

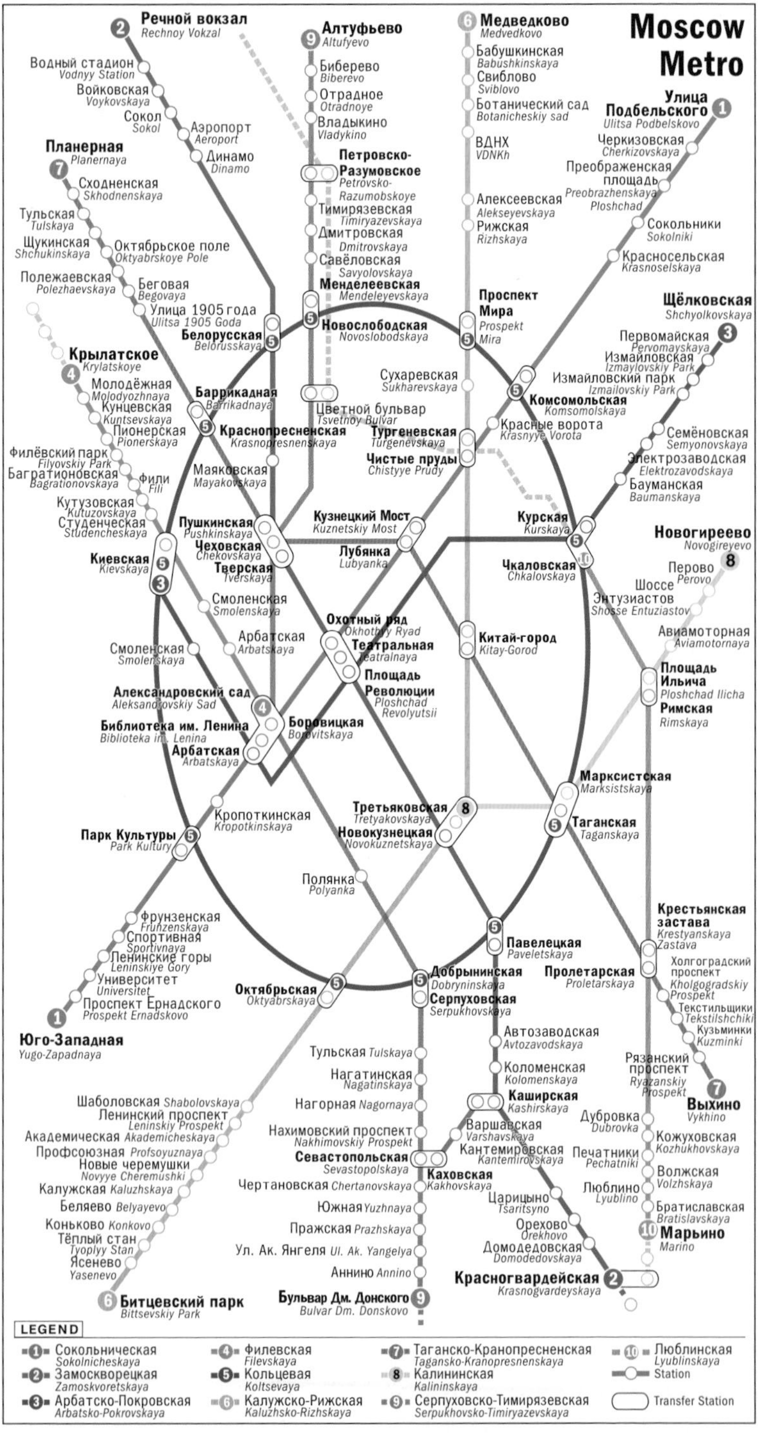

Moscow Metro
Речной вокзал Rechnoy Vokzal
Водный стадион Vodnyy Station
Войковская Voykovskaya
Сокол Sokol
Аэропорт Aeroport
Динамо Dinamo
Алтуфьево Altufyevo
Бибирево Biberevo
Отрадное Otradnoye
Владыкино Vladykino
Петровско-Разумовское Petrovsko-Razumobskoye
Тимирязевская Timiryazevskaya
Дмитровская Dmitrovskaya
Савёловская Savyolovskaya
Менделеевская Mendeleyevskaya
Новослободская Novoslobodskaya
Медведково Medvedkovo
Бабушкинская Babushkinskaya
Свиблово Sviblovo
Ботанический сад Botanicheskiy sad
ВДНХ VDNKh
Алексеевская Alekseyevskaya
Рижская Rizhskaya
Проспект Мира Prospekt Mira
Улица Подбельского Ulitsa Podbelskovo
Черкизовская Cherkizovskaya
Преображенская площадь Preobrazhenskaya Ploshchad
Сокольники Sokolniki
Красносельская Krasnoselskaya
Щёлковская Shchyolkovskaya
Первомайская Pervomayskaya
Измайловская Izmaylovskiy Park
Измайловский парк Izmailovskiy Park
Семёновская Semyonovskaya
Электрозаводская Elektrozavodskaya
Бауманская Baumanskaya
Планерная Planernaya
Сходненская Skhodnenskaya
Тульская Tulskaya
Щукинская Shchukinskaya
Октябрьское поле Oktyabrskoye Pole
Полежаевская Polezhaevskaya
Беговая Begovaya
Улица 1905 года Ulitsa 1905 Goda
Белорусская Belorusskaya
Крылатское Krylatskoye
Молодёжная Molodyozhnaya
Кунцевская Kuntsevskaya
Пионерская Pionerskaya
Филёвский парк Filyovskiy Park
Багратионовская Bagrationovskaya
Фили Fili
Кутузовская Kutuzovskaya
Студенческая Studencheskaya
Киевская Kievskaya
Баррикадная Barrikadnaya
Краснопресненская Krasnopresnenskaya
Маяковская Mayakovskaya
Сухаревская Sukharevskaya
Цветной бульвар Tsvetnoy Bulvar
Тургеневская Turgenevskaya
Чистые пруды Chistyye Prudy
Комсомольская Komsomolskaya
Красные ворота Krasnyye Vorota
Пушкинская Pushkinskaya
Чеховская Chekovskaya
Тверская Tverskaya
Кузнецкий Мост Kuznetskiy Most
Лубянка Lubyanka
Курская Kurskaya
Чкаловская Chkalovskaya
Новогиреево Novogireyevo
Перово Perovo
Шоссе Энтузиастов Shosse Entuziastov
Авиамоторная Aviamotornaya
Смоленская Smolenskaya
Охотный ряд Okhotnyy Ryad
Театральная Teatralnaya
Площадь Революции Ploshchad Revolyutsii
Китай-город Kitay-Gorod
Арбатская Arbatskaya
Смоленская Smolenskaya
Александровский сад Aleksandrovskiy Sad
Библиотека им. Ленина Biblioteka im. Lenina
Арбатская Arbatskaya
Боровицкая Borovitskaya
Площадь Ильича Ploshchad Ilicha
Римская Rimskaya
Марксистская Marksistskaya
Таганская Taganskaya
Кропоткинская Kropotkinskaya
Парк Культуры Park Kultury
Третьяковская Tretyakovskaya
Новокузнецкая Novokuznetskaya
Полянка Polyanka
Крестьянская застава Krestyanskaya Zastava
Пролетарская Proletarskaya
Холгоградский проспект Kholgogradskiy Prospekt
Текстильщики Tekstilshchiki
Кузьминки Kuzminki
Рязанский проспект Ryazanskiy Prospekt
Выхино Vykhino
Фрунзенская Frunzenskaya
Спортивная Sportivnaya
Ленинские горы Leninskiye Gory
Университет Universitet
Проспект Ернадского Prospekt Ernadskovo
Юго-Западная Yugo-Zapadnaya
Павелецкая Paveletskaya
Добрынинская Dobryninskaya
Серпуховская Serpukhovskaya
Октябрьская Oktyabrskaya
Автозаводская Avtozavodskaya
Коломенская Kolomenskaya
Каширская Kashirskaya
Варшавская Varshavskaya
Кантемировская Kantemirovskaya
Царицыно Tsaritsyno
Орехово Orekhovo
Домодедовская Domodedovskaya
Красногвардейская Krasnogvardeyskaya
Дубровка Dubrovka
Кожуховская Kozhukhovskaya
Печатники Pechatniki
Волжская Volzhskaya
Люблино Lyublino
Братиславская Bratislavskaya
Марьино Marino
Тульская Tulskaya
Нагатинская Nagatinskaya
Нагорная Nagornaya
Нахимовский проспект Nakhimovskiy Prospekt
Севастопольская Sevastopolskaya
Каховская Kakhovskaya
Чертановская Chertanovskaya
Южная Yuzhnaya
Пражская Prazhskaya
Ул. Ак. Янгеля Ul. Ak. Yangelya
Аннино Annino
Бульвар Дм. Донского Bulvar Dm. Donskovo
Шаболовская Shabolovskaya
Ленинский проспект Leninskiy Prospekt
Академическая Akademicheskaya
Профсоюзная Profsoyuznaya
Новые черемушки Novyye Cheremushki
Калужская Kaluzhskaya
Беляево Belyayevo
Коньково Konkovo
Тёплый стан Tyoplyy Stan
Ясенево Yasenevo
Битцевский парк Bittsevskiy Park
LEGEND
1 Сокольническая Sokolnicheskaya
2 Замоскворецкая Zamoskvoretskaya
3 Арбатско-Покровская Arbatsko-Pokrovskaya
4 Филевская Filevskaya
5 Кольцевая Koltsevaya
6 Калужско-Рижская Kaluzhsko-Rizhskaya
7 Таганско-Кранопресненская Tagansko-Kranopresnenskaya
8 Калининская Kalininskaya
9 Серпуховско-Тимирязевская Serpukhovsko-Timiryazevskaya
10 Люблинская Lyublinskaya
Station
Transfer Station

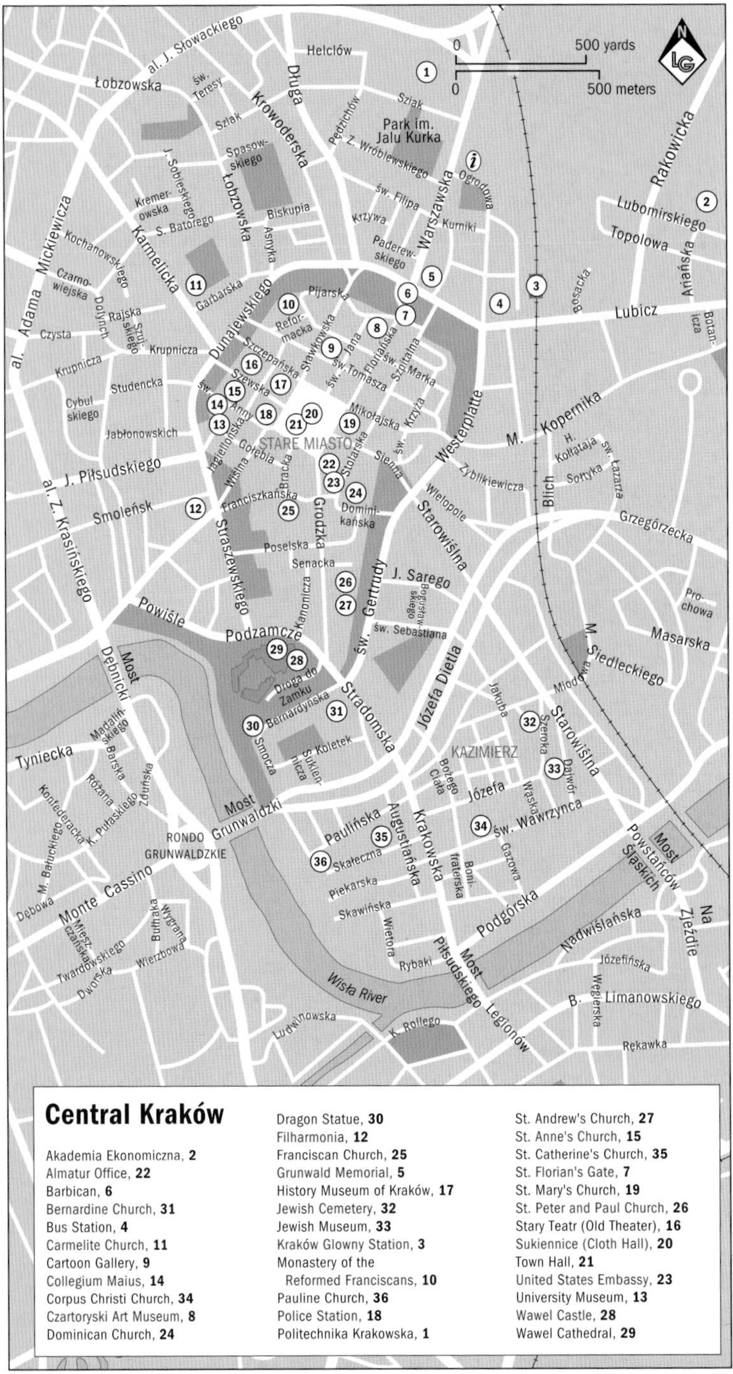

Central Kraków

Akademia Ekonomiczna, **2**
Almatur Office, **22**
Barbican, **6**
Bernardine Church, **31**
Bus Station, **4**
Carmelite Church, **11**
Cartoon Gallery, **9**
Collegium Maius, **14**
Corpus Christi Church, **34**
Czartoryski Art Museum, **8**
Dominican Church, **24**
Dragon Statue, **30**
Filharmonia, **12**
Franciscan Church, **25**
Grunwald Memorial, **5**
History Museum of Kraków, **17**
Jewish Cemetery, **32**
Jewish Museum, **33**
Kraków Glowny Station, **3**
Monastery of the Reformed Franciscans, **10**
Pauline Church, **36**
Police Station, **18**
Politechnika Krakowska, **1**
St. Andrew's Church, **27**
St. Anne's Church, **15**
St. Catherine's Church, **35**
St. Florian's Gate, **7**
St. Mary's Church, **19**
St. Peter and Paul Church, **26**
Stary Teatr (Old Theater), **16**
Sukiennice (Cloth Hall), **20**
Town Hall, **21**
United States Embassy, **23**
University Museum, **13**
Wawel Castle, **28**
Wawel Cathedral, **29**

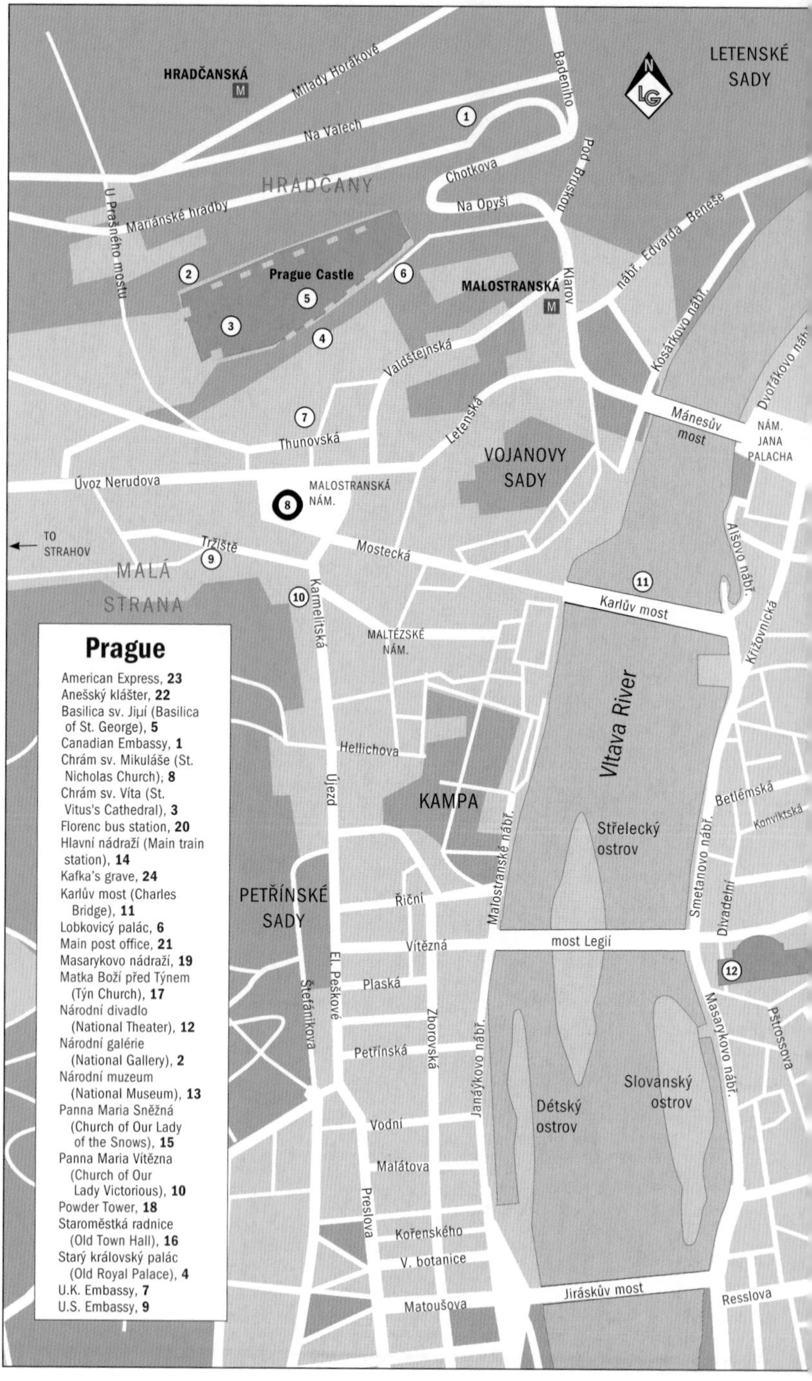

HRADČANSKÁ
M
Milady Horákové
Na Valech
Badeniho
LETENSKÉ SADY
N
LG
HRADČANY
Chotkova
Pod Bruskou
Na Opyší
Mariánské hradby
U Prašného mostu
nábř. Edvarda Beneše
Prague Castle
MALOSTRANSKÁ
M
Klárov
Kosárkovo nábř.
Dvořákovo nábř.
Valdštejnská
Letenská
Mánesův most
NÁM. JANA PALACHA
Thunovská
VOJANOVY SADY
Úvoz Nerudova
MALOSTRANSKÁ NÁM.
TO STRAHOV
Tržiště
Mostecká
MALÁ STRANA
Karmelitská
Alšovo nábř.
Karlův most
Křižovnická
MALTÉZSKÉ NÁM.
Vltava River
Hellichova
Újezd
KAMPA
Betlémská
Konviktská
Střelecký ostrov
Malostranské nábř.
Smetanovo nábř.
Divadelní
PETŘÍNSKÉ SADY
Říční
Vítězná
most Legií
Plaská
El. Peškové
Štefánikova
Zborovská
Masarykovo nábř.
Pštrossova
Petřínská
Janáčkovo nábř.
Slovanský ostrov
Dětský ostrov
Vodní
Malátova
Preslova
Kořenského
V. botanice
Jiráskův most
Matoušova
Resslova
Prague
American Express, 23
Anešský klášter, 22
Basilica sv. Jiuí (Basilica of St. George), 5
Canadian Embassy, 1
Chrám sv. Mikuláše (St. Nicholas Church), 8
Chrám sv. Víta (St. Vitus's Cathedral), 3
Florenc bus station, 20
Hlavní nádraží (Main train station), 14
Kafka's grave, 24
Karlův most (Charles Bridge), 11
Lobkovicý palác, 6
Main post office, 21
Masarykovo nádraží, 19
Matka Boží před Týnem (Týn Church), 17
Národní divadlo (National Theater), 12
Národní galérie (National Gallery), 2
Národní muzeum (National Museum), 13
Panna Maria Sněžná (Church of Our Lady of the Snows), 15
Panna Maria Vítězna (Church of Our Lady Victorious), 10
Powder Tower, 18
Staroměstká radnice (Old Town Hall), 16
Starý královský palác (Old Royal Palace), 4
U.K. Embassy, 7
U.S. Embassy, 9

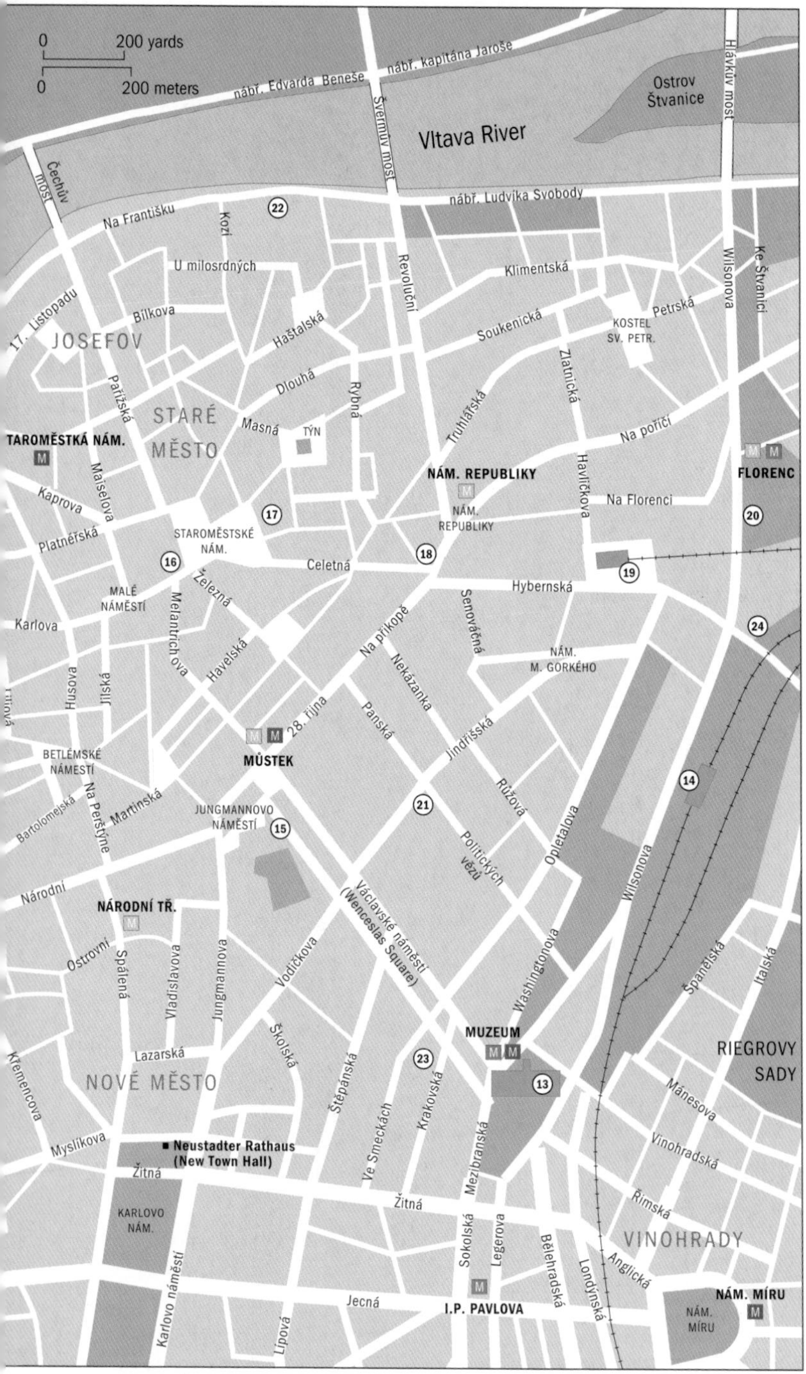
0 200 yards
0 200 meters
Vltava River
nábř. Edvarda Beneše
nábř. kapitána Jaroše
Ostrov Štvanice
Hlávkův most
Švermův most
Čechův most
nábř. Ludvíka Svobody
Na Františku
Kozí
U milosrdných
17. Listopadu
Bílkova
JOSEFOV
Haštalská
Revoluční
Klimentská
Soukenická
Petrská
KOSTEL SV. PETR.
Wilsonova
Ke Štvanici
Dlouhá
Rybná
Pařížská
STARÉ MĚSTO
Masná
TÝN
Zlatnická
Truhlářská
Na poříčí
TAROMĚSTKÁ NÁM.
Maiselova
NÁM. REPUBLIKY
Havlíčkova
FLORENC
Kaprova
Na Florenci
Platnéřská
STAROMĚSTSKÉ NÁM.
Celetná
Hybernská
MALÉ NÁMĚSTÍ
Železná
Melantrichova
Senovážná
Karlova
Na příkopě
NÁM. M. GORKÉHO
Havelská
Nekázanka
Husova
Jilská
28. října
Panská
Jindřišská
MŮSTEK
BETLÉMSKÉ NÁMĚSTÍ
Bartolomejská
Na Perštýně
Martinská
Růžová
JUNGMANNOVO NÁMĚSTÍ
Politických vězňů
Opletalova
Wilsonova
Národní
NÁRODNÍ TŘ.
Václavské náměstí (Wenceslas Square)
Vodičkova
Ostrovní
Spálená
Vladislavova
Jungmannova
Washingtonova
Španělská
Italská
Školská
MUZEUM
RIEGROVY SADY
Lazarská
Štěpánská
Krakovská
Křemencova
NOVÉ MĚSTO
Mánesova
Ve Smečkách
Myslíkova
Neustadter Rathaus (New Town Hall)
Mezibranská
Vinohradská
Žitná
KARLOVO NÁM.
Římská
Sokolská
Legerova
Bělehradská
VINOHRADY
Karlovo náměstí
Londýnská
Anglická
NÁM. MÍRU
Jecná
I.P. PAVLOVA
Lipová
13
14
15
16
17
18
19
20
21
22
23
24

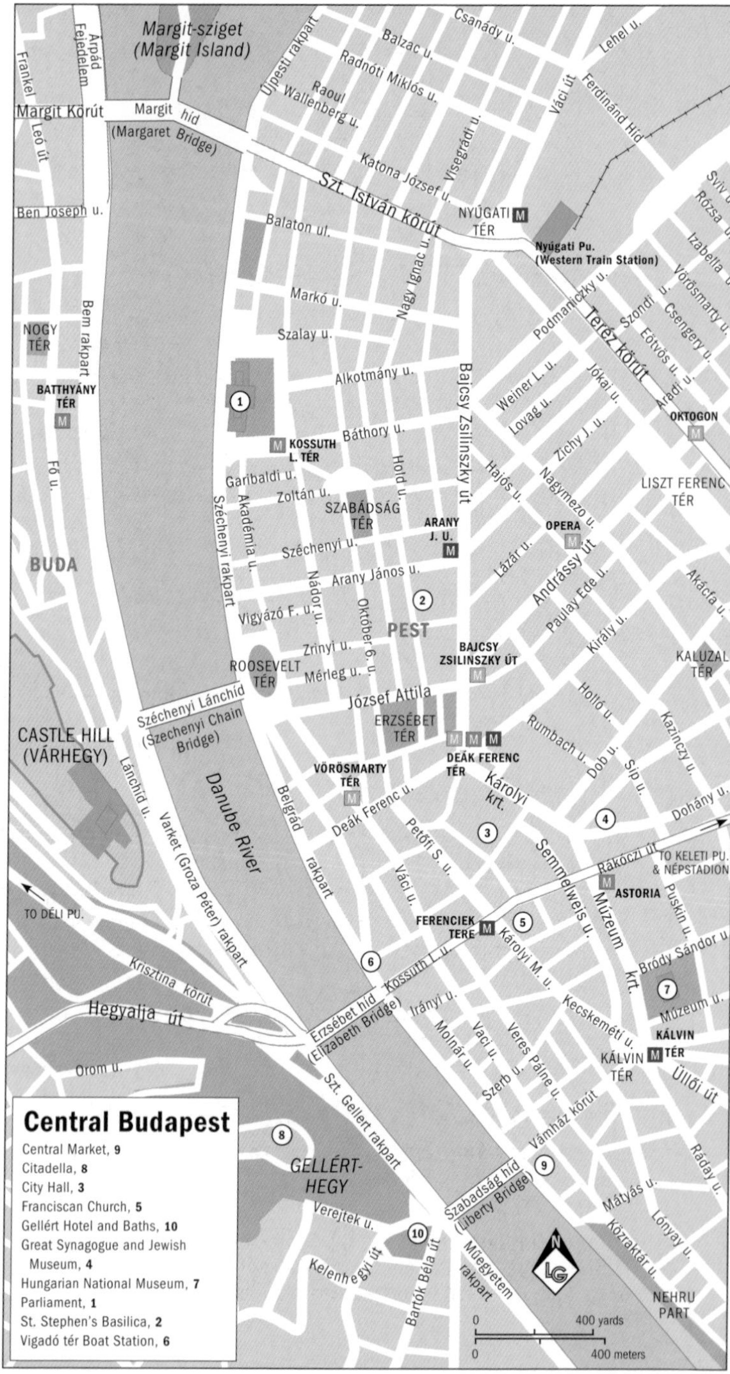
Central Budapest
Central Market, 9
Citadella, 8
City Hall, 3
Franciscan Church, 5
Gellért Hotel and Baths, 10
Great Synagogue and Jewish Museum, 4
Hungarian National Museum, 7
Parliament, 1
St. Stephen's Basilica, 2
Vigadó tér Boat Station, 6
Margit-sziget (Margit Island)
Margit híd (Margaret Bridge)
Margit Körút
Szt. István körút
NYÚGATI TÉR
Nyúgati Pu. (Western Train Station)
Teréz körút
OKTOGON
LISZT FERENC TÉR
OPERA
Andrássy út
KOSSUTH L. TÉR
SZABÁDSÁG TÉR
ARANY J. U.
PEST
BUDA
BAJCSY ZSILINSZKY ÚT
Bajcsy Zsilinszky út
ROOSEVELT TÉR
Széchenyi Lánchíd (Szechenyi Chain Bridge)
CASTLE HILL (VÁRHEGY)
Danube River
ERZSÉBET TÉR
VÖRÖSMARTY TÉR
DEÁK FERENC TÉR
KALUZAL TÉR
TO KELETI PU. & NÉPSTADION
ASTORIA
FERENCIEK TERE
TO DÉLI PU.
Erzsébet híd (Elizabeth Bridge)
Hegyalja út
Krisztina körút
GELLÉRT-HEGY
Szabadság híd (Liberty Bridge)
KÁLVIN TÉR
Üllői út
Múzeum krt.
Vámház körút
NEHRU PART
Bartók Béla út
400 yards
400 meters

LET'S GO

■ PAGES PACKED WITH ESSENTIAL INFORMATION

"Value-packed, unbeatable, accurate, and comprehensive."

—The Los Angeles Times

"The guides are aimed not only at young budget travelers but at the independent traveler; a sort of streetwise cookbook for traveling alone."

—The New York Times

"Unbeatable; good sight-seeing advice; up-to-date info on restaurants, hotels, and inns; a commitment to money-saving travel; and a wry style that brightens nearly every page."

—The Washington Post

■ THE BEST TRAVEL BARGAINS IN YOUR BUDGET

"All the dirt, dirt cheap."

—People

"Let's Go follows the creed that you don't have to toss your life's savings to the wind to travel—unless you want to."

—The Salt Lake Tribune

■ REAL ADVICE FOR REAL EXPERIENCES

"The writers seem to have experienced every rooster-packed bus and lunar-surfaced mattress about which they write."

—The New York Times

"[Let's Go's] devoted updaters really walk the walk (and thumb the ride, and trek the trail). Learn how to fish, haggle, find work—anywhere."

—Food & Wine

"A world-wise traveling companion—always ready with friendly advice and helpful hints, all sprinkled with a bit of wit."

—The Philadelphia Inquirer

■ A GUIDE WITH A SPIRIT AND A SOCIAL CONSCIENCE

"Lighthearted and sophisticated, informative and fun to read. [Let's Go] helps the novice traveler navigate like a knowledgeable old hand."

—Atlanta Journal-Constitution

"The serious mission at the book's core reveals itself in exhortations to respect the culture and the environment—and, if possible, to visit as a volunteer, a student, or a teacher rather than a tourist."

—San Francisco Chronicle

LET'S GO PUBLICATIONS

TRAVEL GUIDES

Australia 9th edition
Austria & Switzerland 12th edition
Brazil 1st edition
Britain 2007
California 10th edition
Central America 9th edition
Chile 2nd edition
China 5th edition
Costa Rica 3rd edition
Eastern Europe 12th edition
Ecuador 1st edition
Egypt 2nd edition
Europe 2007
France 2007
Germany 13th edition
Greece 8th edition
Hawaii 4th edition
India & Nepal 8th edition
Ireland 12th edition
Israel 4th edition
Italy 2007
Japan 1st edition
Mexico 21st edition
Middle East 4th edition
New Zealand 7th edition
Peru 1st edition
Puerto Rico 2nd edition
South Africa 5th edition
Southeast Asia 9th edition
Spain & Portugal 2007
Thailand 3rd edition
Turkey 5th edition
USA 23rd edition
Vietnam 2nd edition
Western Europe 2007

ROADTRIP GUIDE

Roadtripping USA 2nd edition

ADVENTURE GUIDES

Alaska 1st edition
Pacific Northwest 1st edition
Southwest USA 3rd edition

CITY GUIDES

Amsterdam 4th edition
Barcelona 3rd edition
Boston 4th edition
London 15th edition
New York City 16th edition
Paris 14th edition
Rome 12th edition
San Francisco 4th edition
Washington, D.C. 13th edition

POCKET CITY GUIDES

Amsterdam
Berlin
Boston
Chicago
London
New York City
Paris
San Francisco
Venice
Washington, D.C.

LET'S GO

EUROPE

2007

Lauren Truesdell Editor

Associate Editors

Calina A. Ciobanu
Cara B. Eisenpress
Mandy Gable
Inés Pacheco
Jessica R. Rubin-Wills
Kenneth G. Saathoff

Researcher-Writers

Ieva Chaleckyte
Jayme Herschkopf
Merrily E. McGugan
Adrian Mucalov
Danila Musante
Laura Cava Northrop
Paul Kirkpatrick Reardon
Alice Speri

Mariah S. Evarts Map Editor
Silvia Gonzalez Killingsworth Managing Editor

St. Martin's Press New York

HELPING LET'S GO. If you want to share your discoveries, suggestions, or corrections, please drop us a line. We read every piece of correspondence, whether a postcard, a 10-page email, or a coconut. **Address mail to:**

Let's Go: Europe
67 Mount Auburn St.
Cambridge, MA 02138
USA

Visit Let's Go at **http://www.letsgo.com,** or send email to:

feedback@letsgo.com
Subject: "Let's Go: Europe"

In addition to the invaluable travel advice our readers share with us, many are kind enough to offer their services as researchers or editors. Unfortunately, our charter enables us to employ only currently enrolled Harvard students.

Distributed outside the USA and Canada by Macmillan.

ISBN-13: 978-0-312-37018-3
ISBN-10: 0-312-37018-0
First edition
10 9 8 7 6 5 4 3 2 1

Let's Go: Europe is written by Let's Go Publications, 67 Mount Auburn St., Cambridge, MA 02138, USA.

ABOUT LET'S GO

NOT YOUR PARENTS' TRAVEL GUIDE

At Let's Go, we see every trip as the chance of a lifetime. If your dream is to grab a machete and forge through the jungles of Brazil, we can take you there. If you'd rather bask in the Riviera sun at a beachside cafe, we'll set you a table. We write for readers who know that there's more to travel than sharing double deckers with tourists and who believe that travel can change both themselves and the world—whether they plan to spend six days in London or six months in Latin America. We'll show you just how far your money can go, and prove that the greatest limitation on your adventures is not your wallet, but your imagination.

BEYOND THE TOURIST EXPERIENCE

To help you gain a deeper connection with the places you travel, our fearless researchers scour the globe to give you the heads-up on both world-renowned and off-the-beaten-track attractions, sights, and destinations. They engage with the local culture, only to emerge with the freshest insights on everything from local festivals to regional cuisine. We've also opened our pages to respected writers and scholars to hear their takes on the countries and regions we cover, and asked travelers who have worked, studied, or volunteered abroad to contribute first-person accounts of their experiences. In addition, we increased our coverage of responsible travel and expanded each guide's Beyond Tourism chapter to share more ideas about how to give back while on the road.

FORTY-SEVEN YEARS OF WISDOM

Let's Go got its start in 1960, when a group of creative and well-traveled students compiled their experience and advice into a 20-page mimeographed pamphlet, which they gave to travelers on charter flights to Europe. Four and a half decades later, we've expanded to cover six continents and all kinds of travel—while retaining our founders' adventurous attitude toward the world. Laced with witty prose and total candor, our guides are still researched and written entirely by students on shoestring budgets, experienced travelers who know that train strikes, stolen luggage, food poisoning, and marriage proposals are all part of a day's work.

THE LET'S GO COMMUNITY

More than just a travel guide company, Let's Go is a community. Our small staff comes together because of our shared passion for travel and our desire to help other travelers see the world the way it was meant to be seen. We love it when our readers become part of the Let's Go community as well—when you travel, drop us a postcard (67 Mt. Auburn St., Cambridge, MA 02138, USA), send us an e-mail (feedback@letsgo.com), or post on our forum (http://www.letsgo.com/connect/forum) to tell us about your adventures and discoveries.

For more information, visit us online: www.letsgo.com.

INTERLAKEN / SWITZERLAND - CENTRE OF EUROPE
LET'S GO TO
BALMER'S herberge
INTERLAKEN · SWITZERLAND
BALMER'S guesthouse
BALMER'S: WHERE THE FUN NEVER STOPS!
Looking for a cheap, clean and fun hostel? Look no further......
At the base of the Alps, (Eiger, Monch, Jungfrau), in Interlaken, we will strive to make your stay an unforgettable memory. With all it's outdoor activities, and breathtaking scenery, there is something for everyone.
BALMER'S with it's friendly service, warm atmosphere and over 60 years of experience makes it possible to enjoy the area, and all it has to offer, in comfort and as trouble-free as possible.
Don't miss one of our now legendary party at Balmer's Metro Bar.
Hauptstrasse 23-33 · CH-3800 Interlaken/Switzerland · phone +41 (0)33 822 19 61 · fax +41 (0)33 823 32 61 · mail@balmers.ch · www.balmers.com

CONTENTS

Europe: Chapters
Iceland pp. 532-549
Finland pp. 294-313
Sweden pp. 958-991
Norway pp. 736-770
Estonia pp. 284-293
Russia pp. 840-865
Latvia pp. 674-682
Britain pp. 116-201
Denmark pp. 259-283
Ireland pp. 550-579
Lithuania pp. 685-695
Netherlands pp. 705-736
Belgium pp. 97-115
Germany pp. 398-471
Poland pp. 771-801
Luxembourg pp. 696-704
Czech Rep. pp. 234-258
Ukraine pp. 1041-1051
Slovak Rep. pp. 866-877
Liechtenstein pp. 683-684
France pp. 314-397
Austria pp. 69-96
Hungary pp. 509-531
Switzerland pp. 992-1022
Romania pp. 824-839
Slovenia pp. 878-887
Croatia pp. 215-233
Portugal pp. 802-823
Spain pp. 888-957
Bulgaria pp. 202-214
Italy pp. 580-673
Turkey pp. 1023-1040
Greece pp. 472-508

PRICE RANGES>>EUROPE

Our researchers list establishments in order of value from best to worst; our favorites are denoted by the Let's Go thumbs-up (☒). Since the best value is not always the cheapest price, however, we have also incorporated a system of price ranges, based on a rough expectation of what you will spend. For **accommodations**, we base our range on the cheapest price for which a single traveler can stay for one night. For **restaurants** and other dining establishments, we estimate the average amount a traveler will spend. The table below tells you what you will *typically* find in Europe at the corresponding price range; keep in mind that no system can allow for every individual establishment's quirks.

ACCOMMODATIONS	WHAT YOU'RE *LIKELY* TO FIND
❶	Camping; most dorm rooms, such as HI or other hostels or university dorm rooms. Expect bunk beds and a communal bath; you may have to provide or rent towels and sheets.
❷	Upper-end hostels or small hotels. You may have a private bathroom, or there may be a sink in your room and communal shower in the hall.
❸	A small room with a private bath. Should have decent amenities, such as phone and TV. Breakfast may be included in the price of the room.
❹	Similar to 3, but may have more amenities or be in a more touristed area.
❺	Large hotels or upscale chains. If it's a 5 and it doesn't have the perks you want, you've paid too much.

FOOD	WHAT YOU'RE *LIKELY* TO FIND
❶	Mostly street-corner stands, falafel and Shawarma huts, or fast-food joints. Many snack foods, such as *tostis, broodjes,* and Belgian waffles. Desserts like *stropwafels* and *pannekoeken.* Soups and simple noodle dishes in minimalist surroundings. You may have the option of sitting down or getting takeout.
❷	Sandwiches, appetizers at a bar, or low-priced entrees and *tapas.* Ethnic eateries and pan-Asian noodle houses. Takeout is less frequent; generally a sit-down meal, sometimes with waiters, but only slightly more upscale decor.
❸	Mid-priced entrees, seafood, and complicated pasta dishes. More upscale ethnic eateries. Tip'll bump you up a couple euro, as you will have a waiter.
❹	A somewhat fancy restaurant or a steakhouse. Either way, you'll have a special knife. Few restaurants in this range have a dress code, but some may look down on T-shirt and jeans.
❺	Food with foreign names and a decent wine list. Slacks and dress shirts may be expected. Don't order PB&J.

ACKNOWLEDGEMENTS

TEAM EUROPE THANKS: Our RWs, for keeping us entertained and keeping us sane all summer. Silvia, because if you need a great editor, she is right upstairs. Mariah, for magnanimously making magnificent maps. Sammy, our favorite Mexican, we less-than-three you. Matthew, Anne, Stephanie, K-Fed, and Simon for making our lives easy. Richard and Chase, for fixing *everything*. Sergio, DJ extraordinaire and extraordinary person. Britain and Germany, for telling us their secrets through the wall. Matt Roller, we want you on our team. Jesse Bradford, Chamillionaire, Shakira feat. Wyclef, and Salt 'n' Pepa—you know what you did.

LT THANKS: Calina, for the totally unexpected rages; Cara, for the totally expected ones. Mandy, for going out to breakfast. Inés, the sweetest person in the world; Jess, who is hardly another person. That's really nice, Ken. Silvia, for the skills. Stevie, for elevating my game; Lemartin, for dealing when my game plummets. Uno's, for Su 8pm; Doyle's, for W 8pm. Raquel & Woody, for the past; J-train, for the future; the OBs, forever. SNK, who knows everything. Let's Go, for saying yes again. Mom, Dad, Lingo, and Billy—always.

CALINA THANKS: Adrian, for impeccable copy and coverage. LT, for leading the way with style. Cara, for culinary inspiration; Inés, for smiles that brighten my day and the caffeine that gets me through it; Jess, for being a great sport; Ken, for bringing back the ă; Mandy, for hilarity. Silvia, for contagious laughter. Sammy, for unrivaled sweetness. Sergio, for musical inspiration. Team Spain & Portugal for their help. Mom, Dad, and Cosmi—for everything.

CARA THANKS: LT for grown-up high-heels, Calina for killer legs, Inés for pretty (coffee-ringed) dresses, Jess for matching purple flip-flops and shirts, Ken for plaid shorts, Mandy for domestic aprons, and Silvia for dance-worthy leotards, who, together, compose my foolproof outfit; Danila for week-making phone updates; Team Italy and their RWs; the Square for its extensive ice cream options; TT; and Mom, Jill, and KK for making my g-chat ding and my office phone ring.

MANDY THANKS: Jayme for Finnish accents. "Everytime we touch..." LT. Inés for Hoosier love gangsta style. Calina for celebrity pets. Cara for picnics. Willis for our future trip to Scandinavia. Ken for mismatched shoes. Silvia for being CLF every day. Sammy for Human Sex, et al. Matthew and Melinda for Drunken Nessie. Court for lunch dates, Mel for bubble tea, Chenelle for wine. The fam for keeping me country. God for keeping me strong. Diolch yn fawr.

INÉS THANKS: LT for leading fearlessly. Calina for laughing fits. Cara for midnight Adams adventures. Jess for all the small things. Mandy for state fairs. Ken for quad cartwheels. 6eter for friendship. Lisha for Vegas. Serge, my comadre, for Embassy. Mag 8 for two great years. Anna for the Cape. Stephen, for vhs, apple pie, fyi, and some other elements too. La mama, Pops, and Belly for giving me the travel bug. Samantha for a truly breath-usurping summer.

JESSICA THANKS: Kirk, Laura, and Merrily, for stellar work and hilarious stories. LT, for really special times. Calina for the Goo Goo Dolls; Cara for rejecting the status quo; Inés for spirit and *Auflauf;* Ken for my nickname; Mandy for "Flowers for Algernon." Silvia, for using my nickname. Sammy, for arm-waving confusion. The Cabinet and friends, for doing what we want. Cambridge friends, who remember Cafe A. Mom, Dad, and Dan—I'd be lost without you.

KEN THANKS: Ieva, for Swiss rafter-climbing. LT, for opaque processes. Tell him he's a lucky guy. Călinaa, there are no words. Cara, for bobofying my world. Inés, for knocking it like a Hoosier. Mandy, for rugby cheers. Willis, I sweat your political stance on Tibet. Silvia, for the quesadilla quizzes. GER, for marzipan and secret loves. Sam, for symmetry. Prendi mi adesso. Asia/CORI/OZITA, for other homes. Laura, for virtue. FOP, for dinner and special chows.

MARIAH THANKS: Jess, Mandy, Cara, Ken, Inés, Calina, and LT for all the time and attention focused on maps; Cliff, Tom, Kevin, Shiyang, Richard, and Chase for a summer filled with laughter and fun; OZITA for beaches; and youtube.com for providing a productive mode of procrastination and for opening my eyes to the world of talking cats.

RESEARCHER-WRITERS

Ieva Chaleckyte *Austria, Liechtenstein, Slovenia, Switzerland*

Despite a painful and enduring leg injury, Ieva's sense of adventure never faltered, and she continually saw through touristy facades into gritty, glistening real life. An enthusiastic hiker and Let's Go veteran traveler who spent last summer researching in Scandinavia, Ieva, a native Lithuanian, used her multilingual flair to finesse situations from belligerent World Cup fans to rude Austrian waiters. No matter the obstacle, Ieva never let us down.

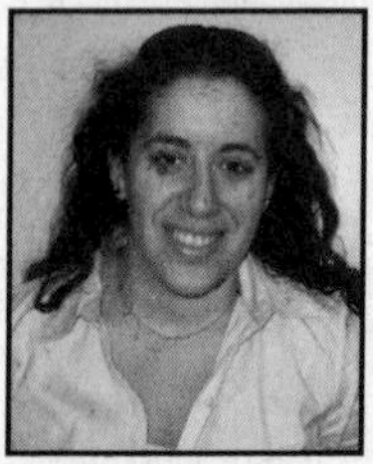

Jayme Herschkopf *Estonia, Finland, Latvia, Sweden*

Not many RWs catch an entire country on a 5-day bender, but then again, not many beg to be sent to the Arctic Circle either—Jayme did both. Heading to the Land of the Midnight Sun, Jayme schmoozed with the Sámi, hit up an Arctic ice bar, munched on Estonian pancakes (her new fave), and sat down one-on-one with Santa Claus. Her roll-with-the-punches attitude and experience working for *The Unofficial Guide to Life at Harvard* helped her produce flawlessly formatted copy every time.

Merrily E. McGugan *Ireland*

With unbridled enthusiasm, remarkable stamina, and a soundtrack of techno music, Merrily tackled her fast-paced itinerary through the Emerald Isle. Her thorough research included throwing back six shots of whiskey at the Old Jameson Distillery in Dublin, taking in a hurling match in Cork, and partying with attendees at the Letterkenny International Car Rally. Her editors loved her detailed copy, and Merrily loved the job, as her ear-to-ear grin made clear.

Adrian Mucalov *Bulgaria, Romania, Russia, Ukraine*

Also known as Adrian "Much-Love" to his doting editors, this rugged Canadian rugger took Eastern Europe by storm. A veteran traveler who has lived in Zambia and volunteered in the Canadian Arctic, Adrian blazed through his route in a mere 37 days—no small feat for one researching a sizable chunk of the former Soviet bloc. Following his penchant for cute vampires to Dracula's home base in Transylvania, Adrian left no stone unturned or castle unexplored.

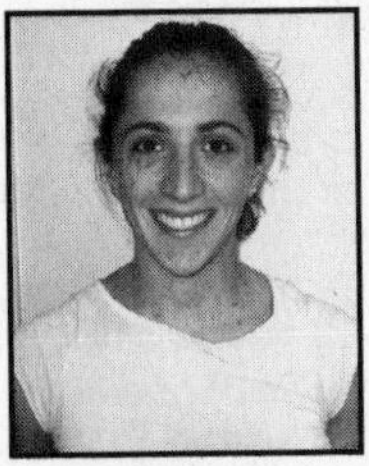

Danila Musante *Belgium, Luxembourg, the Netherlands*

Barely pausing to catch her breath, Danila sprinted, biked, chattered, and wrote her way through BeNeLux (an abbreviation she found most clever). This Californian track star sweetened her updates with odd facts, random anecdotes, and accounts of hilariously awkward exchanges. The cherry on top of the copy-sundae, though, was more chocolatey: her editors got their fix from rich confections sent from not one, but three candy-making countries.

Laura Cava Northrop *Czech Republic, Northern Hungary, Lithuania, Poland, Slovak Republic*

An observant and intrepid traveler, Laura first became acquainted with *Let's Go* as a reader, when she toted a copy along on a backpacking expedition through Southeast Asia. Moving to the other side of the editorial process, she displayed good humor and a keen ability to capture the essence of a place in prose—a skill that came in handy as she explored five different Eastern European countries.

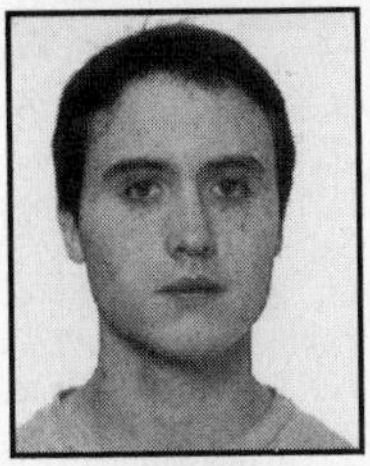

Paul Kirkpatrick Reardon *Denmark, Iceland, Norway*

Kirk made friends all along his journey, whether he was meeting a wizard in a record store in Reykjavík, chatting with a medieval reenactor in Denmark, or playing pool with fellow travelers at the world's northernmost pool table in Svalbard. Never daunted by transportation challenges, Kirk hiked through lava fields, biked up hills, and walked on glaciers. Thanks to his eye for detail and sharp wit, his editors eagerly awaited his copy and his tales from the road.

Alice Speri *Croatia, Greece, Southern Hungary, Turkey*

Undeterred by an impossible itinerary, Alice still found time to watch every Italian World Cup game, gaze off into each rosy sunset, and bask in the smoke of Turkish hookahs. Her traveler's know-how led her to the best bargains and beaches on the Dalmatian Coast and beyond. Cheerfully revamping coverage to emphasize the backpacker culture she loves, our wordly Italian RW continually amazed and amused us with her thorough and creative copy.

CONTRIBUTING WRITERS

Patrice M. Dabrowski *Celebrating the New Europe (p. 13)*
Dr. Patrice M. Dabrowski is a postdoctoral fellow at Brown University's Watson Institute for International Studies.

Derek Glanz *Maintaining the Borders in an Expanding EU (p. 14)*
Derek Glanz was the Editor of *Let's Go: Spain & Portugal 1998.*

Barbara Richter *Test Tubes and Teutons (p. 68)*
Barbara Richter was a Researcher-Writer for *Let's Go: Austria and Switzerland 2005.*

REGIONAL EDITORS AND RESEARCHER-WRITERS

LET'S GO: BRITAIN

Matthew E. Growdon *Editor*
Melinda Biocchi *Associate Editor*
Kristin Blagg *Researcher-Writer*
Kathleen E. Breeden *Researcher-Writer*
Amy Ru Chen *Researcher-Writer*
Cassandra Forsyth *Researcher-Writer*
Merrily E. McGugan *Researcher-Writer*
Ella Spottswood *Researcher-Writer*

LET'S GO: FRANCE

Anne Bensson *Editor*
Sandy Ullman *Associate Editor*
Andrew Sullivan *Associate Editor*
Vinnie Chiappini *Researcher-Writer*
Dominique Elie *Researcher-Writer*
Sara O'Rourke *Researcher-Writer*
Samantha Papadakis *Researcher-Writer*
Jack Pararas *Researcher-Writer*
Rachel Whitaker *Researcher-Writer*

LET'S GO: GERMANY

Stephanie O'Rourke *Editor*
Paul Katz *Associate Editor*
Amelia Atlas *Researcher-Writer*
Samuel Bjork *Researcher-Writer*
Nicholas Commins *Researcher-Writer*
Marion Guillaume *Researcher-Writer*
Catherine Jampel *Researcher-Writer*
Lisa Shu *Researcher-Writer*

LET'S GO: ITALY

Kathleen A. Fedornak *Editor*
Victoria Norelid *Associate Editor*

Beverly K. Chu *Associate Editor*
Lindsay Crouse *Researcher-Writer*
Mark Giangreco, Jr. *Researcher-Writer*
Lauren Holmes *Researcher-Writer*
Emma Millon *Researcher-Writer*
Felipe Tewes *Researcher-Writer*
Angela Wu *Researcher-Writer*

LET'S GO: PARIS

Mallory Hellman *Editor*
Olivia Brown *Researcher-Writer*
Kate Wang *Researcher-Writer*

LET'S GO: SPAIN AND PORTUGAL

Simon Nicholas *Editor*
Pilar Adams *Associate Editor*
Andrew Sullivan *Associate Editor*
Azzurra Cox *Researcher-Writer*
Laura Gordon *Researcher-Writer*
Olivia Jampol *Researcher-Writer*
Lucas Laursen *Researcher-Writer*
Saloni Malik *Researcher-Writer*
John Noss *Researcher-Writer*
Lauren Walker *Researcher-Writer*

Editor
Lauren Truesdell

Associate Editors
Calina A. Ciobanu
Cara B. Eisenpress
Mandy Gable
Inés Pacheco
Jessica R. Rubin-Wills
Kenneth G. Saathoff

Map Editor
Mariah S. Evarts

Managing Editor
Silvia Gonzalez Killingsworth

Typesetter
Ankur Ghosh

LET'S GO

Publishing Director
Alexandra C. Stanek
Editor-in-Chief
Laura E. Martin
Production Manager
Richard Chohaney Lonsdorf
Cartography Manager
Clifford S. Emmanuel
Editorial Managers
August Dietrich, Samantha Gelfand, Silvia Gonzalez Killingsworth
Financial Manager
Jenny Wong
Publicity Manager
Anna A. Mattson-DiCecca
Personnel Manager
Sergio Ibarra
Production Associate
Chase Mohney
IT Director
Patrick Carroll
Director of E-Commerce
Jana Lepon
Office Coordinators
Adrienne Taylor Gerken, Sarah Goodin

Director of Advertising Sales
Mohammed J. Herzallah
Senior Advertising Associates
Kedamai Fisseha, Roumiana Ivanova

President
Brian Feinstein
General Manager
Robert B. Rombauer

Europe
0
300 miles
0
300 kilometers
Reykjavík
ICELAND
Faroe Islands
Shetland Islands
Bergen
Orkney Islands
North Sea
NORTHERN IRELAND
SCOTLAND
Glasgow
Edinburgh
Belfast
IRELAND
DEN
GREAT BRITAIN
Dublin
WALES
ATLANTIC OCEAN
Cardiff
ENGLAND
NETHERLANDS
Amsterdam
London
Brussels
GER
BELGIUM
Frankfurt
LUXEMBOURG
Paris
Nantes
LIECHTENSTEIN
FRANCE
Zurich
Bay of Biscay
SWITZERLAND
Bern
Bordeaux
Lyon
Santiago de Campostela
Milan
Marseille
Nice
Florence
PORTUGAL
ANDORRA
MONACO
Madrid
Corsica (Fr.)
Barcelona
Lisbon
SPAIN
Valencia
Sardinia (It.)
Seville
Granada
Balearic Islands (Sp.)
Tangier
GIBRALTAR
Mediterranean Sea
Fez
Rabat
MOROCCO
ALGERIA
Algiers
TUNISIA

Rovaniemi
Gulf of Bothnia
Trondheim
FINLAND
NORWAY
Oslo
SWEDEN
Helsinki
Tallinn
St. Petersburg
Stockholm
ESTONIA
Gothenburg
Riga
Moscow
LATVIA
MARK
Baltic Sea
LITHUANIA
Copenhagen
Vilnius
RUSSIA
RUSSIA
Hamburg
Gdańsk
Minsk
Berlin
Warsaw
BELARUS
MANY
POLAND
Kiev
Prague
Kraków
Lviv
CZECH REPUBLIC
UKRAINE
SLOVAK REPUBLIC
Munich
Bratislava
Vienna
MOLDOVA
Budapest
Sea of Azov
AUSTRIA
Chișinău
Odessa
HUNGARY
Ljubljana
Venice
SLOVENIA
ROMANIA
Yalta
Zagreb
Bucharest
CROATIA
BOSNIA AND HERZEGOVINA
Belgrade
Black Sea
Sarajevo
SAN MARINO
BULGARIA
Dubrovnik
SERBIA AND MONTENEGRO
Adriatic Sea
Sofia
Rome
Istanbul
ITALY
F.Y.R. MACEDONIA
Tiranë
Ankara
Thessaloniki
Naples
ALBANIA
Tyrrhenian Sea
GREECE
Aegean Sea
TURKEY
Izmir
Ionian Sea
Sicily
Athens

HOW TO USE THIS BOOK

Hello, friend. This book was written with one goal in mind: to provide the most accurate and useful information possible to travelers who are preparing to tackle the infinitely rewarding adventure that is budget travel in Europe. This effort has—we hope you'll find—paid off handsomely; we're extremely proud of the tips our researchers have come up with on topics as varied as the best way to get from Bruges to Budapest and how to tell the good gelato from the bad. More to the point, we hope you'll find that the investment you've made in this book will be returned many times over, and not only through budget travel hints. This guide will not only keep you from busting your wallet; it will help you better navigate your European adventure, regardless of your budget, interests, or itinerary.

Things are changing in Europe. You can now travel among half the countries on the continent without so much as pulling out a passport, and you're more likely to come across an Internet terminal than a coin-operated pay phone. Whether you're a long-time expat or a first-time backpacker, the always-updated *Let's Go: Europe 2007* will keep you in good company.

ORGANIZATION. *Let's Go: Europe 2007* is arranged to make the info you need easy to find. The **Discover** chapter offers Europe-wide highlights, tips on when to travel (including a calendar of festivals), and suggested itineraries. The **Essentials** chapter details the nitty-gritty of money, communications, passports, and more—everything you'll need to plan your trip and stay safe on the road. The **Transportation** section will get you to and around Europe, while the **Beyond Tourism** chapter gives advice on how to work or volunteer your way across the continent. Next come 33 jam-packed **country chapters,** from Austria to Ukraine; each begins with essential information on traveling in that country. Don't overlook the **language phrasebook** (p. 1052), offering a crash course in the local tongues you'll encounter.

PRICE RANGES AND RANKINGS. Our 40 indefatigable researchers list establishments in order of value from best to worst; absolute favorites are denoted by the *Let's Go* thumbs-up (☒). Since the best value does not always mean the cheapest price, we have incorporated a system of **price ranges (❶❷❸❹❺)** into our coverage of accommodations and restaurants. At a glance, you can compare the cost of a night's stay in towns a mile apart or halfway across the country. The price ranges for each country can be found in the introductory sections of each chapter, and for more information on what to expect from each ranking, see p. xiv.

NEW FEATURES. Long-time readers will notice other changes in our series, most notably the sidebars that accompany much of our coverage. At the end of the Discover chapter, you'll also find a series of longer **Scholarly Articles** focused on issues affecting Europe as a whole. Whether read on a long train ride or in a quiet hostel, we hope these articles will inform and entertain. This year, we've also added a new chapter on Turkey, in recognition of the country's increasing popularity with budget travelers and its closer integration with Europe.

A NOTE TO OUR READERS. The information for this book was gathered by *Let's Go* researchers from May through August of 2006. Each listing is based on one researcher's opinion, formed during his or her visit at a particular time. Those traveling at other times may have different experiences since prices, dates, hours, and conditions are always subject to change. You are urged to check the facts presented in this book beforehand to avoid inconvenience and surprises.

DISCOVER EUROPE

Europe offers as many unique pathways as it has travelers to take them. For many, the continent's draw comes from familiar imagery. Aspiring writers still spin impassioned romances in Parisian garrets; a glass of sangria at twilight on the Plaza Mayor tastes as sweet as ever; and iconic treasures, from the onion domes of St. Basil's cathedral to the behemoth slabs of Stonehenge, inspire no small amount of awe. Yet against this ancient backdrop, a freshly costumed continent takes the stage. As the European Union has grown from a small clique of nations trading coal and steel to a 25-member commonwealth with a parliament and a central bank, Eastern and Western Europe find themselves more closely connected than ever before. Those lucky enough to be traveling in a continent that seems to be simultaneously shrinking and expanding can take advantage of the increased ease of travel to venture off the beaten path and determine on their own the must-see destinations of 21st-century Europe.

While Prague and Budapest may have been the hot spots a few years ago, emerging cities like Kraków and Stockholm are poised to inherit the lucrative tourist money train. Newly minted cultural meccas like Bilbao's Guggenheim and London's Tate Modern have breezily joined the ranks of timeless galleries like the Louvre and the Hermitage, while a constant influx of students and DJs keep Europe's nightlife dependably hot. Whether it's the pubs of Dublin, the upscale bistros of Lyon, the frozen north country of Sweden, or the dazzling beaches of Croatia's Dalmatian Coast that call to you, *Let's Go: Europe 2007* will help keep you informed and on-budget.

TACKLING EUROPE

Anyone who tells you that there exists any one "best way" to see Europe should be politely ignored. This book is designed to facilitate a variety of travel through Europe, from a few days in Prague to a continent-wide summer sprint. This chapter is made up of tools to help you make your own itinerary: **themed categories** let you know where to find your museums, your mountains, and your madhouses; **suggested itineraries** outline common paths across Europe. After getting a general impression of the continent, make sure to turn to the country-specific **Discover** section at the beginning of each chapter for more detailed information.

WHEN TO GO

While summer sees the most tourist traffic in Europe, the best mix of value and accessibility comes in early fall and late spring. To the delight of skiing and ice-climbing enthusiasts, the low season (mid-Sept. to June) brings cheaper airfares and accommodations, in addition to freeing you from the hordes of fanny-pack-toting tourists. On the flip side, many attractions, hostels, and tourist offices close in the winter, and in some rural areas local transportation dwindles or shuts down altogether. Most of Europe's best **festivals** (p. 5) also take place during the summer months. For more info on the best time to take your excursion, see each country's **Essentials** section and the weather chart on p. 1065.

WHAT TO DO

MUSEUMS

The vast majority of the breathtaking canon of Western art, from ancient Greece through the Renaissance to Impressionism and beyond, was created in Europe. Most of these masterworks have been kept close to home in artistic strongholds like the Louvre, the Prado, and the Vatican Museums. European museums do not merely house art, however. They also have exhibits on torture instruments, marijuana, puppets, erotica, marzipan, leprosy, secret police, and spirits both undead and delicious—in short, whatever can be classified and captioned. A trip across Europe qualifies as little more than a stopover without an afternoon spent among some of the paintings and artifacts listed below—whether they include pinnacles of Western culture or more risqué fare.

THE PICTURESQUE	AND THE OFTEN GROTESQUE
FRANCE: THE LOUVRE (p. 336). Along with troves of work by nearly every other master, Da Vinci's *Mona Lisa* smiles out from behind her glass case to crowds of enthusiastic tourists.	**RUSSIA: KGB MUSEUM** (p. 854). Quiz a current FSB agent and learn everything about Russia's secret police from Ivan the Terrible to the present. Everything, that is, except for its secrets.
RUSSIA: THE HERMITAGE (p. 861). In the palatial St. Petersburg home of the tsars resides the world's largest art collection. Only 5% of its 3 million pieces is on display at any one time.	**CZECH REPUBLIC: MUSEUM OF MEDIEVAL TORTURE INSTRUMENTS** (p. 249). Save lunch until after you've visited these meticulously detailed exhibits.
SPAIN: MUSEO DEL PRADO (p. 902). It's an art-lover's heaven to view the hell painted by Hieronymus Bosch. Also here are works by El Greco, Goya, Rubens, Titian, and Velázquez.	**THE NETHERLANDS: CANNABIS COLLEGE** (p. 721). Cannabis College is just like college, except there are no libraries, no lectures, no studying, no liquor, no dorms, and no full-time students.
ITALY: VATICAN MUSEUMS (p. 606). Look for the *School of Athens* here, in Rome; the painting crowns a mind-blowing amount of Renaissance and other art, including the incredible Raphael Rooms.	**GERMANY: EROTIC ART MUSEUM** (p. 439). Picasso's visual imagination is harnessed to add class to an otherwise naughty assortment of *Kama Sutra* poses and Victorian pornography.
BRITAIN: THE BRITISH MUSEUM (p. 138). Holding world artifacts like Egypt's Rosetta Stone and Iran's Oxus Treasure, the British Museum ironically contains almost nothing British at all.	**HUNGARY: SZABÓ MARZIPAN MUSEUM** (p. 525). Only one statuette on display at this museum is not composed of marzipan: an 80kg white chocolate effigy of Michael Jackson.
GREECE: NATIONAL ARCHAEOLOGICAL MUSEUM (p. 483). Athens itself may be museum enough for some, but this building collects what's too small to be seen with a placard on the street.	**LITHUANIA: DEVIL MUSEUM** (p. 694). Devil-worshippers can practice idolatry in 2000 different ways in this museum, which has amassed that many depictions of devils in various media.
BRITAIN: TATE GALLERIES (p. 138). While the Tate Modern collects Picassos, Duchamps, and others, the Tate Britain assembles the works of Blake, Hockney, Rosetti, and Turner.	**GERMANY: MUSEUM FÜR PUPPENTHEATER** (p. 440). Thousands of hand, string, shadow, and stick puppets from around the globe make up the largest private puppet collection in the world.
AUSTRIA: KUNSTHISTORISCHES MUSEUM (p. 83). Venetian paintings, an Egyptian burial chamber, and medieval arms in the world's 4th-largest art collection impress the history nerd in all of us.	**NORWAY: LEPROSY MUSEUM** (p. 755). Ancient treatments of this fabled disease are exhibited here in cells that housed as many as three patients at once, through the 1940s.
ITALY: GALLERIA BORGHESE (p. 606). Vivid paintings and graceful sculpture by Bernini, Caravaggio, Rubens, and Titian are a sight for sore eyes after staring at miles of Renaissance canvases.	**FRANCE: MUSÉE DU VIN** (p. 391). See the vats and winepresses housed in the 15th-century Hôtel des Ducs de Bourgogne for free before splurging on the age-ripened vintages themselves.
THE NETHERLANDS: RIJKSMUSEUM (p. 722). Renovations should not deter visitors who come to see the pinnacles of the Dutch Golden Age, including Rembrandts and Vermeers, that line the walls.	**SWITZERLAND: COLLECTION DE L'ART BRUT** (p. 1019). Inspiration and madness have never been harder to separate than in these artworks by institutionalized schizophrenics and criminals.

ARCHITECTURE

European history is legible not only in textbooks, but also in the architecture left behind by millennia of secular and religious tradition. Royal lines from the early Welsh dynasties and Polish kings to the Bourbons, Hapsburgs, and Romanovs have all been outlasted by the emblems of their magnificence—castles, palaces, and châteaux. Monarchs were careless of expense, and prodigiously jealous: Louis XIV's palace at Versailles, which has become a byword for opulence, whet the ambition of rival monarchs and spurred the construction of rival domiciles, among them Peter the Great's Peterhof, Charles III's Reggia, and Ludwig II's Herreninsel. No expense was spared for God, either, as the many splendid cathedrals, monasteries, synagogues, temples, and mosques that rise skyward from their low cityscapes attest. Córdoba's Mezquita mosque and Budapest's Great Synagogue are among the finest of their kind, while Chartres's Cathédrale de Notre Dame and Cologne's Dom are pinnacles—pun intended—of the Gothic style.

ROYAL REAL ESTATE	SACRED SITES
FRANCE: VERSAILLES PALACE (p. 343). Little can compare to Versailles, testimony to the extravagance of pre-Revolutionary France and the prototype for regal self-indulgence down the ages.	**ITALY: SISTINE CHAPEL** (p. 604). Since the 16th century, white smoke has risen from the chapel after the election of a new pope. Michelangelo's ceiling frescoes are also worth a glance.
GERMANY: NEUSCHWANSTEIN (p. 471). A waterfall, an artificial grotto, a byzantine throne room, and a Wagnerian opera hall deck out the inspiration for Disney's Cinderella Castle.	**SPAIN: MEZQUITA** (p. 912). Córdoba's Mezquita, one of the most important Islamic monuments in the West, is supported by 850 pink-and-blue marble and alabaster columns.
BRITAIN: BUCKINGHAM PALACE (p. 130). Queen Elizabeth still resides here, among the Throne Room, the Music Room, the opulent White Room, the gardens, and the galleries.	**FRANCE: CHARTRES CATHEDRAL** (p. 342). The world's finest example of early Gothic architecture has intact stained-glass windows from the 12th century and a crypt from the 9th.
RUSSIA: PETERHOF (p. 865). Nothing was too good for the tsars, or too holy to have been built by serf labor. Peter the Great's project stretches magnificently along the Gulf of Finland.	**BRITAIN: WESTMINSTER ABBEY** (p. 130). Royal weddings and coronations take place in the sanctuary; nearby, poets and politicians from the earliest kings to Winston Churchill rest in peace.
ITALY: PALAZZO PITTI (p. 654). The Medici family left this 15th-century *palazzo* slathered in artistic treasures and its adjacent Boboli gardens exquisitely landscaped.	**GREECE: THE PARTHENON** (p. 481). Keeping vigil over Athens from the Acropolis, the Parthenon, civilization's capital since the 5th century BC, is a required pilgrimage for any culture-worshipper.
AUSTRIA: SCHLOß SCHÖNBRUNN (p. 82). It's hard to tell which is more impressive, the palace or the classical gardens that stretch a full four times the length of the structure.	**RUSSIA: SERGIYEV POSAD** (p. 855). Under the trademark Orthodox onion domes, Russia's most celebrated pilgrimage site now thrives again after seven decades of state-propagated atheism.
POLAND: WAWEL CASTLE (p. 788). Kraków's hillside masterpiece includes a castle begun in the 900s, as well as a cathedral that was once the seat of the archbishopric of Pope John Paul II.	**HUNGARY: THE GREAT SYNAGOGUE** (p. 522). Europe's largest synagogue can hold 3,000 faithful. Inscribed leaves of a metal tree in the courtyard commemorate the victims of the Holocaust.
SPAIN: THE ALHAMBRA (p. 924). At an impressionistic distance, the Alhambra looks like a worn-out toy; zoom in, and its wood, stucco, and ceramics reveal exquisite beauty.	**GERMANY: KÖLNER DOM** (p. 446). With a 44m ceiling and 1350 sq. m of stained glass illuminating the interior with particolored sunlight, Cologne's cathedral is Germany's greatest.
FRANCE: CHENONCEAU (p. 353). A series of noblewomen crafted one of the most graceful châteaux in France. The mansion arches elegantly over the Cher River.	**ITALY: THE DUOMO** (p. 651). It is hard to know which to be more impressed by—the massive nave built by Arnolfo di Cambrio, or the dome built by Filippo Brunelleschi that crowns it.
BRITAIN: CAERNARFON CASTLE (p. 177). Edward I began this architectural feat in 1283 in order to maintain control over northern Wales, but left it unfinished when he ran out of money.	**AUSTRIA: STEPHANSDOM** (p. 82). Work on the north tower of Vienna's cathedral stopped, according to legend, after a pact with the devil went awry and the builder plunged to his death.

OUTDOORS

Granted, it may not be what you came for. Europe, as the seat of modern civilization, tends to draw people to its museums and ruins more than its mountains and rivers. But for any traveler, budget or otherwise, solo or companioned, expert or neophyte, an excursion to the outdoors can round off (or salvage, as the case may be) any journey. Fjords, volcanoes, valleys, gorges, and plateaus mark the spots where the Earth's plates collide. Waters of innumerable shades of blue wash up on uninhabited shores of black-, white-, and red-sand beaches. Mountains, whether sprawling with trees or culminating in ice, continue to challenge mankind and dwarf the man-made—just as they, and the rest of the European landscape, did when civilization began.

LANDSCAPES	SEAVIEWS
GERMANY: THE SCHWARZWALD (p. 460). The eerie darkness pervading this tangled expanse of evergreen, once the inspiration of the Brothers Grimm, continues to lure hikers and skiers alike.	**ITALY: THE AMALFI COAST** (p. 668). The azure waters that make up the coastline south of Naples are second only to the jagged, gravity-defying rocks that overlook them.
SWITZERLAND: INTERLAKEN (p. 999). Thanks to its mild climate and pristine landscape, Interlaken quenches the thirst for anything outdoors, whether it be bungee jumping, hiking, or skydiving.	**NORWAY: SOGNEFJORD** (p. 758). Thundering waterfalls give way to halcyon lakes, sweeping green meadows, and regal glaciers at the longest fjord in the world.
GREECE: MOUNT OLYMPUS (p. 494). Erupting out of the Thermaic Gulf, the 3000m height and formidable slopes of Olympus so awed the ancients that they believed it to be the divine dwelling of their immortal pantheon.	**FRANCE: D-DAY BEACHES** (p. 345). The heroism of the Allied forces is tastefully preserved on the beaches near Bayeux, where thousands of soldiers were killed in battle over 60 years ago.
ICELAND: ÞINGVELLIR NATIONAL PARK (p. 544). Few sights in the world allow visitors to straddle separating tectonic plates amid lava fields.	**DENMARK: ÆRØSKØBING** (p. 280). Economic stagnation and recent conservation efforts have successfully fossilized the 19th-century lifestyle and charm of this tiny island town.
BRITAIN: LAKE DISTRICT NATIONAL PARK (p. 170). Four million sheep have cast their votes for the loveliest park in England—an equal number of summertime tourists seem to agree.	**BRITAIN: NEWQUAY** (p. 153). Believe it or not, the best surfing in Europe may just be at this little city on the Cornish coast.
THE NETHERLANDS: HOGE VELUWE NATIONAL PARK (p. 733). Wild boars and red deer inhabit the 13,500 acres of forestry, while the park's museum houses works by Picasso and van Gogh.	**FRANCE: CANNES** (p. 372). Never mind the annual film festival; the essence of Cannes is on its stunning beaches and palm-lined boardwalks.
SLOVAKIA: SLOVENSKÝ RAJ NATIONAL PARK (p. 876). Hikers who tire of the views overlooking the Tatras can rest among the frozen columns, gigantic walls, and hardened waterfalls of the Dobăinksá Ice Caves, which date back to the last Ice Age.	**SWEDEN: SKÄRGÅRD ARCHIPELAGO** (p. 973). A popular daytrip from Stockholm, this archipelago has become a favorite of sailing enthusiasts, hikers, and picnickers.
ITALY: MT. VESUVIUS (p. 666). The only active volcano on the continent is overdue for another eruption. Scientists believe the next explosion will be more violent than the one that buried Pompeii in AD 79.	**SPAIN: IBIZA** (p. 955). One of the many destinations vying for the title "Jewel of the Mediterranean," Ibiza holds its own as a must-see beach island with prime tanning grounds and a nightlife almost as hot as the beaches.
AUSTRIA: HOHE TAUERN NATIONAL PARK (p. 91). Filled with glaciers, mountains, lakes, and endangered species, Europe's largest park offers mountain paths once trod by Celts and Romans.	**BRITAIN: LOCH LOMOND** (p. 191). While tales of monsters are generally reserved for another Loch, Lomond attracts travelers as the largest lake in Britain, dotted by 38 islands.
POLAND: WIELICZKA SALT MINES (p. 790). Miners and artists transformed the salt deposits into a maze full of sculptures and carvings.	**CROATIA: HVAR ISLAND** (p. 229). Hordes of sun-soaked and salt-licked revelers descend upon Hvar, internationally regarded as one of the 10 most beautiful beaches in the world.

FESTIVALS

COUNTRIES	APR. - JUNE	JULY - AUG.	SEPT. - MAR.
AUSTRIA AND SWITZERLAND	**Vienna Festwochen** (early May to mid-June)	**Salzburger Festspiele** (late July-Aug.)	**Escalade** (Geneva; early Dec.) **Fasnacht** (Basel; late Feb.)
BELGIUM	**Festival of Fairground Arts** (Wallonie; late May)	**Gentse Feesten** (Ghent; mid- to late July)	**International French Language Film Festival** (Namur; late Sept.)
BRITAIN AND IRELAND	**Bloomsday** (Dublin; June 16) **Wimbledon** (London; late June-early July)	**Fringe Festival** (Edinburgh; Aug.) **Edinburgh Int'l Festival** (mid-Aug. to early Sept.)	**Matchmaking Festival** (Lisdoonvarna; Sept.) **St. Patrick's Day** (Mar. 17)
CROATIA	**World Festival of Animated Film** (Zagreb; May)	**Int'l Folklore Festival** (July) **Summer Festival** (Dubrovnik; July-Aug.)	**International Puppet Festival** (Sept.) **Zagreb Fest** (Nov.)
CZECH REPUBLIC	**Prague Spring Festival** (May)	**Český Krumlov International Music Fest** (Aug.)	**International Organ Fest** (Olomouc; Sept.)
FRANCE	**Cannes Film Festival** (May)	**Tour de France** (July) **Festival d'Avignon** (July-Aug.)	**Carnevale** (Nice, Nantes; Feb.)
GERMANY	**May Day** (Berlin; May 1) **Christopher St. Day** (late June)	**Rhine in Flames Festival** (various locations in the Rhine Valley; throughout the summer)	**Oktoberfest** (Munich; late Sept.) **Fasching** (Munich; late Feb.- Mar.)
HUNGARY	**Golden Shell Folklore** (Siófok; June)	**Sziget Rock Fest** (Budapest; July) **Baroque Festival** (Eger; July)	**Eger Vintage Days** (Sept.) **Festival of Wine Songs** (Pécs; Sept.)
ITALY	**Maggio Musicale** (Florence; May to June)	**Il Palio** (Siena; July 2 and Aug. 16) **Umbria Jazz Festival** (July)	**Festa di San Gennaro** (Naples; Sept. 19) **Carnevale** (late Feb.) **Scoppio del Carro** (Florence; Easter Su)
THE NETHERLANDS	**Queen's Day** (Apr. 30) **Holland Festival** (June)	**Gay Pride Parade** (Aug.)	**Flower Parade** (Aalsmeer; early Sept.) **Cannabis Cup** (Nov.)
POLAND	**Int'l Short Film** (Kraków; May) **Festival of Jewish Culture** (Kraków; June)	**Street Theater** (Kraków; July) **Highlander Folklore** (Zakopane; Aug.)	**Kraków Jazz Fest** (Oct.) **Nat'l Blues Music** (Toruń; Nov.)
PORTUGAL	**Burning of the Ribbons** (Coimbra; early May)	**Lisbon Beer Festival** (July)	**Carnival** (early Mar.) **Semana Santa** (week before Easter Su)
SCANDINAVIA	**Midsummer** (late June) **Festspillene** (Bergen; late May-early June)	**Savonlinna Opera Festival** (July) **Quart Music Festival** (Kristiansand; early July)	**Helsinki Festival** (late Aug.-early Sept.) **Tromsø International Film Festival** (mid-Jan.)
SPAIN	**Feria de Abril** (Sevilla; mid-Apr.)	**San Fermines** (Pamplona; July)	**Las Fallas** (Valencia; Mar.) **Carnaval** (Mar.) **Semana Santa** (week before Easter Su)

SUGGESTED ITINERARIES

THE GRAND TOUR - EUROPE IN SIX (OR

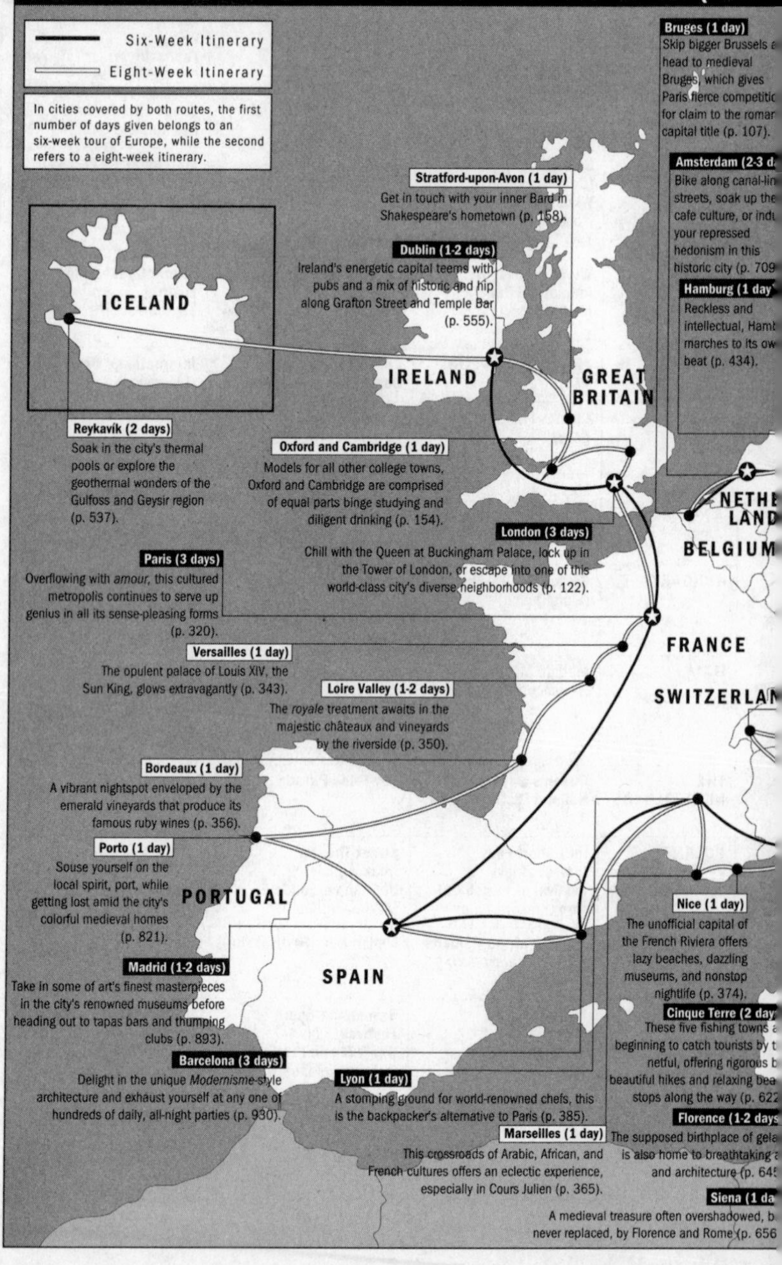

Six-Week Itinerary
Eight-Week Itinerary
In cities covered by both routes, the first number of days given belongs to an six-week tour of Europe, while the second refers to a eight-week itinerary.
ICELAND
IRELAND
GREAT BRITAIN
NETHE LAND
BELGIUM
FRANCE
SWITZERLA
PORTUGAL
SPAIN
Reykavík (2 days)
Soak in the city's thermal pools or explore the geothermal wonders of the Gulfoss and Geysir region (p. 537).
Stratford-upon-Avon (1 day)
Get in touch with your inner Bard in Shakespeare's hometown (p. 158).
Dublin (1-2 days)
Ireland's energetic capital teems with pubs and a mix of historic and hip along Grafton Street and Temple Bar (p. 555).
Oxford and Cambridge (1 day)
Models for all other college towns, Oxford and Cambridge are comprised of equal parts binge studying and diligent drinking (p. 154).
London (3 days)
Chill with the Queen at Buckingham Palace, lock up in the Tower of London, or escape into one of this world-class city's diverse neighborhoods (p. 122).
Bruges (1 day)
Skip bigger Brussels a head to medieval Bruges, which gives Paris fierce competitic for claim to the romar capital title (p. 107).
Amsterdam (2-3 d
Bike along canal-lin streets, soak up the cafe culture, or indu your repressed hedonism in this historic city (p. 709
Hamburg (1 day
Reckless and intellectual, Hamb marches to its ow beat (p. 434).
Paris (3 days)
Overflowing with amour, this cultured metropolis continues to serve up genius in all its sense-pleasing forms (p. 320).
Versailles (1 day)
The opulent palace of Louis XIV, the Sun King, glows extravagantly (p. 343).
Loire Valley (1-2 days)
The royale treatment awaits in the majestic châteaux and vineyards by the riverside (p. 350).
Bordeaux (1 day)
A vibrant nightspot enveloped by the emerald vineyards that produce its famous ruby wines (p. 356).
Porto (1 day)
Souse yourself on the local spirit, port, while getting lost amid the city's colorful medieval homes (p. 821).
Madrid (1-2 days)
Take in some of art's finest masterpieces in the city's renowned museums before heading out to tapas bars and thumping clubs (p. 893).
Barcelona (3 days)
Delight in the unique Modernisme-style architecture and exhaust yourself at any one of hundreds of daily, all-night parties (p. 930).
Lyon (1 day)
A stomping ground for world-renowned chefs, this is the backpacker's alternative to Paris (p. 385).
Marseilles (1 day)
This crossroads of Arabic, African, and French cultures offers an eclectic experience, especially in Cours Julien (p. 365).
Nice (1 day)
The unofficial capital of the French Riviera offers lazy beaches, dazzling museums, and nonstop nightlife (p. 374).
Cinque Terre (2 day
These five fishing towns a beginning to catch tourists by t netful, offering rigorous b beautiful hikes and relaxing bea stops along the way (p. 62
Florence (1-2 days
The supposed birthplace of gela is also home to breathtaking a and architecture (p. 64
Siena (1 da
A medieval treasure often overshadowed, b never replaced, by Florence and Rome (p. 656

EIGHT) WEEKS

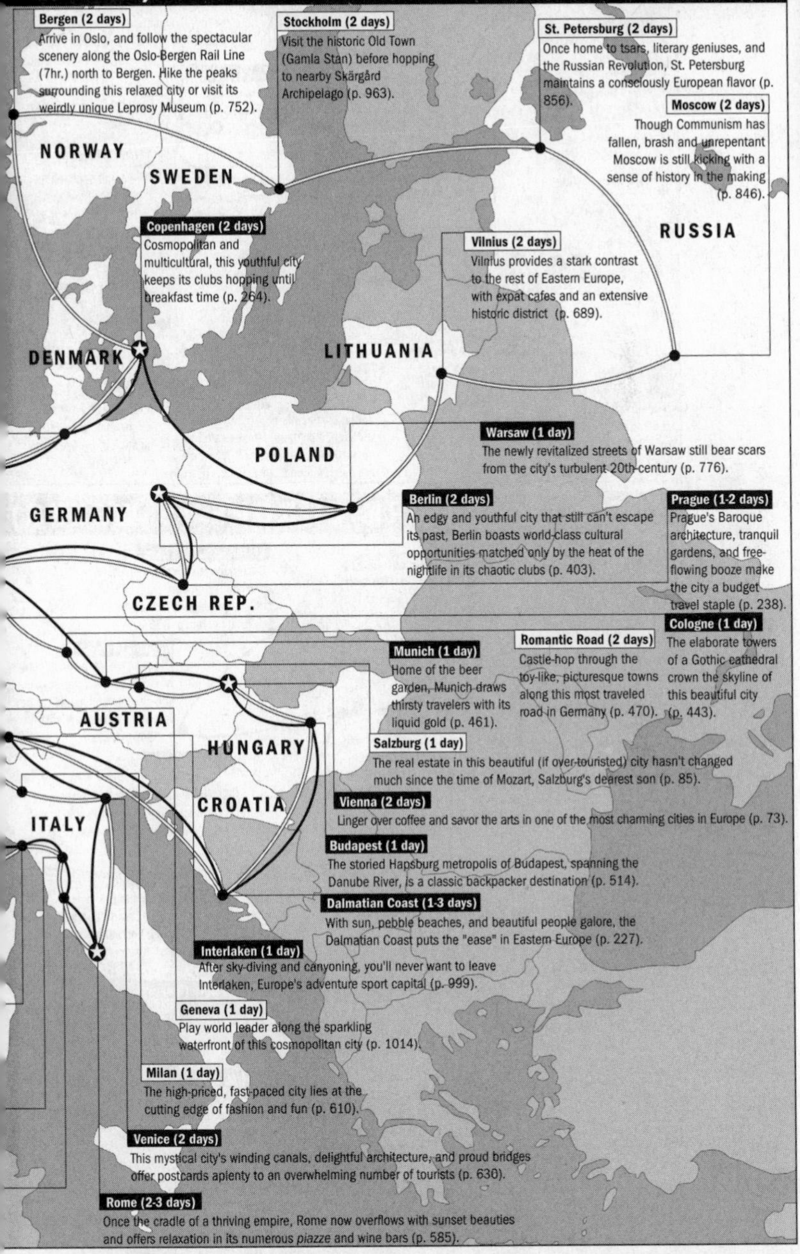
Bergen (2 days)
Arrive in Oslo, and follow the spectacular scenery along the Oslo-Bergen Rail Line (7hr.) north to Bergen. Hike the peaks surrounding this relaxed city or visit its weirdly unique Leprosy Museum (p. 752).
Stockholm (2 days)
Visit the historic Old Town (Gamla Stan) before hopping to nearby Skärgård Archipelago (p. 963).
St. Petersburg (2 days)
Once home to tsars, literary geniuses, and the Russian Revolution, St. Petersburg maintains a consciously European flavor (p. 856).
Moscow (2 days)
Though Communism has fallen, brash and unrepentant Moscow is still kicking with a sense of history in the making (p. 846).
NORWAY
SWEDEN
RUSSIA
Copenhagen (2 days)
Cosmopolitan and multicultural, this youthful city keeps its clubs hopping until breakfast time (p. 264).
Vilnius (2 days)
Vilnius provides a stark contrast to the rest of Eastern Europe, with expat cafes and an extensive historic district (p. 689).
DENMARK
LITHUANIA
Warsaw (1 day)
The newly revitalized streets of Warsaw still bear scars from the city's turbulent 20th-century (p. 776).
POLAND
Berlin (2 days)
An edgy and youthful city that still can't escape its past, Berlin boasts world-class cultural opportunities matched only by the heat of the nightlife in its chaotic clubs (p. 403).
Prague (1-2 days)
Prague's Baroque architecture, tranquil gardens, and free-flowing booze make the city a budget travel staple (p. 238).
GERMANY
CZECH REP.
Cologne (1 day)
The elaborate towers of a Gothic cathedral crown the skyline of this beautiful city (p. 443).
Romantic Road (2 days)
Castle-hop through the toy-like, picturesque towns along this most traveled road in Germany (p. 470).
Munich (1 day)
Home of the beer garden, Munich draws thirsty travelers with its liquid gold (p. 461).
AUSTRIA
HUNGARY
Salzburg (1 day)
The real estate in this beautiful (if over-touristed) city hasn't changed much since the time of Mozart, Salzburg's dearest son (p. 85).
CROATIA
ITALY
Vienna (2 days)
Linger over coffee and savor the arts in one of the most charming cities in Europe (p. 73).
Budapest (1 day)
The storied Hapsburg metropolis of Budapest, spanning the Danube River, is a classic backpacker destination (p. 514).
Dalmatian Coast (1-3 days)
With sun, pebble beaches, and beautiful people galore, the Dalmatian Coast puts the "ease" in Eastern Europe (p. 227).
Interlaken (1 day)
After sky-diving and canyoning, you'll never want to leave Interlaken, Europe's adventure sport capital (p. 999).
Geneva (1 day)
Play world leader along the sparkling waterfront of this cosmopolitan city (p. 1014).
Milan (1 day)
The high-priced, fast-paced city lies at the cutting edge of fashion and fun (p. 610).
Venice (2 days)
This mystical city's winding canals, delightful architecture, and proud bridges offer postcards aplenty to an overwhelming number of tourists (p. 630).
Rome (2-3 days)
Once the cradle of a thriving empire, Rome now overflows with sunset beauties and offers relaxation in its numerous piazze and wine bars (p. 585).

THE BEST OF THE MEDITERRANEAN

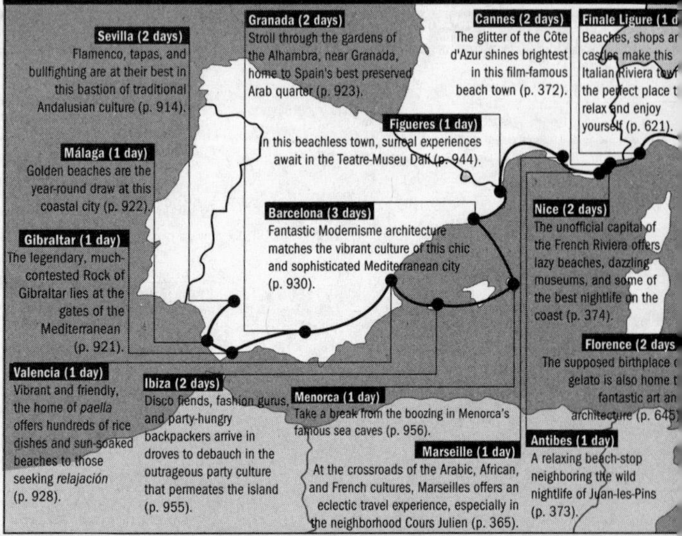
Sevilla (2 days)
Flamenco, tapas, and bullfighting are at their best in this bastion of traditional Andalusian culture (p. 914).
Granada (2 days)
Stroll through the gardens of the Alhambra, near Granada, home to Spain's best preserved Arab quarter (p. 923).
Cannes (2 days)
The glitter of the Côte d'Azur shines brightest in this film-famous beach town (p. 372).
Málaga (1 day)
Golden beaches are the year-round draw at this coastal city (p. 922).
Figueres (1 day)
In this beachless town, surreal experiences await in the Teatre-Museu Dalí (p. 944).
Gibraltar (1 day)
The legendary, much-contested Rock of Gibraltar lies at the gates of the Mediterranean (p. 921).
Barcelona (3 days)
Fantastic Modernisme architecture matches the vibrant culture of this chic and sophisticated Mediterranean city (p. 930).
Nice (2 days)
The unofficial capital of the French Riviera offers lazy beaches, dazzling museums, and some of the best nightlife on the coast (p. 374).
Valencia (1 day)
Vibrant and friendly, the home of paella offers hundreds of rice dishes and sun-soaked beaches to those seeking relajación (p. 928).
Ibiza (2 days)
Disco fiends, fashion gurus, and party-hungry backpackers arrive in droves to debauch in the outrageous party culture that permeates the island (p. 955).
Menorca (1 day)
Take a break from the boozing in Menorca's famous sea caves (p. 956).
Marseille (1 day)
At the crossroads of the Arabic, African, and French cultures, Marseilles offers an eclectic travel experience, especially in the neighborhood Cours Julien (p. 365).
Antibes (1 day)
A relaxing beach-stop neighboring the wild nightlife of Juan-les-Pins (p. 373).

BEST OF EASTERN EUROPE (6 WEEKS)

Rīga (3 days)
Rīga showcases architectural gems from the medieval to the Art Nouveau (p. 678).
St. Petersburg (3 days)
Once home to tsars, geniuses, and the Revolution, St. Petersburg remains Russia's cultural center (p. 856).
Vilnius (3 days)
Vilnius provides a stark contrast to the rest of Eastern Europe, with expat cafes and an extensive historic district (p. 689).
Moscow (4 days)
Moscow survived the Soviets, the city has ambitiously turned its eye to a new capitalist future (p. 846).
Warsaw (4 days)
The newly revitalized streets of Warsaw still bear scars from its turbulent 20th-century history (p. 776).
Kyiv (4 days)
On the site of the 2004 "Orange Revolution," promises of reform keep historic Kyiv looking forward (p. 1046).
Prague (5 days)
Prague's Baroque architecture, tranquil gardens, and free-flowing booze make the city a budget travel staple (p. 238).
Kraków (3 days)
Poland's cultural capital, Kraków is home to a lively student population and a rich Jewish history (p. 784).
Bratislava (2 days)
From castles to cafes, Bratislava is a surprisingly sophisticated example of the new Eastern Europe (p. 870).
Ljubljiana (2 days)
Stroll the relaxed, picturesque and untouristed streets of up-and-coming Ljubljana (p. 882).
Budapest (5 days)
The storied Hapsburg metropolis of Budapest, spanning the Danube River, is a classic backpacker destination (p. 514).
Dalmation Coast (5 days)
With sun, pebble beaches, and beautiful people galore, the Dalmation Coast puts the "ease" in Eastern Europe (p. 882).
Lake Balaton (2 days)
Enjoy a wide array of water sports, fresh seafood, and throbbing nightlife at Lake Balaton, a popular resort since Roman times (p. 530).

(6 WEEKS)

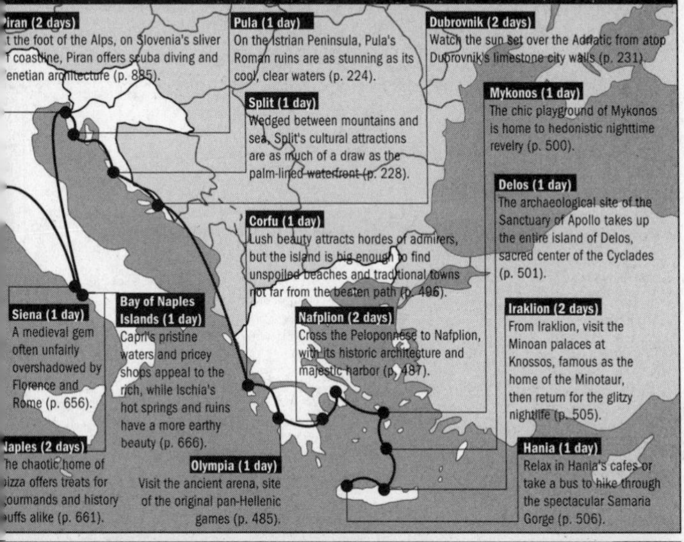

iran (2 days)
t the foot of the Alps, on Slovenia's sliver f coastline, Piran offers scuba diving and enetian architecture (p. 885).
Pula (1 day)
On the Istrian Peninsula, Pula's Roman ruins are as stunning as its cool, clear waters (p. 224).
Dubrovnik (2 days)
Watch the sun set over the Adriatic from atop Dubrovnik's limestone city walls (p. 231).
Split (1 day)
Wedged between mountains and sea, Split's cultural attractions are as much of a draw as the palm-lined waterfront (p. 228).
Mykonos (1 day)
The chic playground of Mykonos is home to hedonistic nighttime revelry (p. 500).
Delos (1 day)
The archaeological site of the Sanctuary of Apollo takes up the entire island of Delos, sacred center of the Cyclades (p. 501).
Corfu (1 day)
Lush beauty attracts hordes of admirers, but the island is big enough to find unspoiled beaches and traditional towns not far from the beaten path (p. 496).
Siena (1 day)
A medieval gem often unfairly overshadowed by Florence and Rome (p. 656).
Bay of Naples Islands (1 day)
Capri's pristine waters and pricey shops appeal to the rich, while Ischia's hot springs and ruins have a more earthy beauty (p. 666).
Nafplion (2 days)
Cross the Peloponnese to Nafplion, with its historic architecture and majestic harbor (p. 487).
Iraklion (2 days)
From Iraklion, visit the Minoan palaces at Knossos, famous as the home of the Minotaur, then return for the glitzy nightlife (p. 505).
Naples (2 days)
he chaotic home of pizza offers treats for gourmands and history buffs alike (p. 661).
Olympia (1 day)
Visit the ancient arena, site of the original pan-Hellenic games (p. 485).
Hania (1 day)
Relax in Hania's cafes or take a bus to hike through the spectacular Samaria Gorge (p. 506).

BEST OF SCANDINAVIA (4 WEEKS)

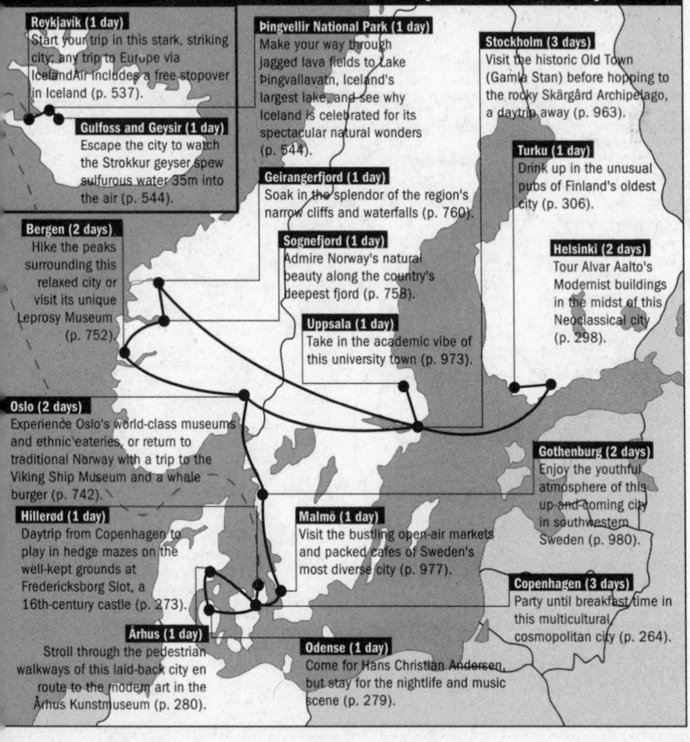

Reykjavík (1 day)
Start your trip in this stark, striking city; any trip to Europe via IcelandAir includes a free stopover in Iceland (p. 537).
Þingvellir National Park (1 day)
Make your way through jagged lava fields to Lake Þingvallavatn, Iceland's largest lake, and see why Iceland is celebrated for its spectacular natural wonders (p. 544).
Stockholm (3 days)
Visit the historic Old Town (Gamla Stan) before hopping to the rocky Skärgård Archipelago, a daytrip away (p. 963).
Gulfoss and Geysir (1 day)
Escape the city to watch the Strokkur geyser spew sulfurous water 35m into the air (p. 544).
Turku (1 day)
Drink up in the unusual pubs of Finland's oldest city (p. 306).
Geirangerfjord (1 day)
Soak in the splendor of the region's narrow cliffs and waterfalls (p. 760).
Bergen (2 days)
Hike the peaks surrounding this relaxed city or visit its unique Leprosy Museum (p. 752).
Sognefjord (1 day)
Admire Norway's natural beauty along the country's deepest fjord (p. 758).
Helsinki (2 days)
Tour Alvar Aalto's Modernist buildings in the midst of this Neoclassical city (p. 298).
Uppsala (1 day)
Take in the academic vibe of this university town (p. 973).
Oslo (2 days)
Experience Oslo's world-class museums and ethnic eateries, or return to traditional Norway with a trip to the Viking Ship Museum and a whale burger (p. 742).
Gothenburg (2 days)
Enjoy the youthful atmosphere of this up-and-coming city in southwestern Sweden (p. 980).
Hillerød (1 day)
Daytrip from Copenhagen to play in hedge mazes on the well-kept grounds at Fredericksborg Slot, a 16th-century castle (p. 273).
Malmö (1 day)
Visit the bustling open-air markets and packed cafes of Sweden's most diverse city (p. 977).
Copenhagen (3 days)
Party until breakfast time in this multicultural, cosmopolitan city (p. 264).
Århus (1 day)
Stroll through the pedestrian walkways of this laid-back city en route to the modern art in the Århus Kunstmuseum (p. 280).
Odense (1 day)
Come for Hans Christian Andersen, but stay for the nightlife and music scene (p. 279).

THE MIDDLE GROUND (1 MONTH)

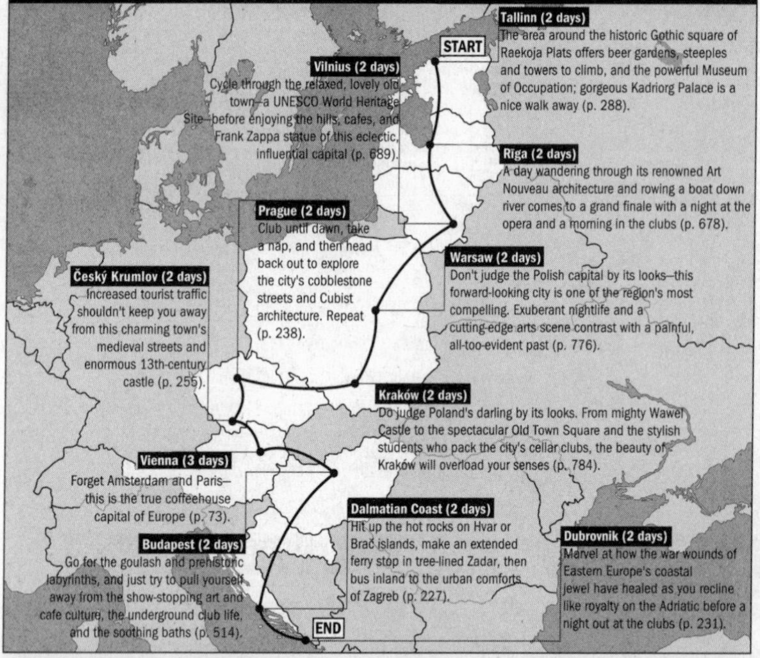

Once an industrial pit, a new, impressively cultural Liverpool has Beatles for sale in every form imaginable (p. 164).
Edinburgh (3 days)
Refashioned as cultural mecca by the Stuarts, the transformation stuck; Edinburgh shines on as the party-hearty jewel of Scotland (p. 179).
Manchester (1 day)
Excruciatingly hip, "Mad"chester has generated more pop hits than the concept of infidelity (p. 163).
Lake District (1 day)
Quite possibly the loveliest place in England (p. 170).
Catch your bearings, a black cab, a photo of Big Ben, and some of the best museums in the world for free (p. 122).
START
Think Shakespeare-upon-Shakespeare (p. 158).
Take a breather from all things modern amongst grazing sheep in villages unruffled by time's passage (p. 158).
Paris (5 days)
For a change of pace and attitude, head to Paris for wine, cheese, and some quality time with the Museé D'Orsay (p. 320).
Tallinn (2 days)
The area around the historic Gothic square of Raekoja Plats offers beer gardens, steeples and towers to climb, and the powerful Museum of Occupation; gorgeous Kadriorg Palace is a nice walk away (p. 288).
Vilnius (2 days)
Cycle through the relaxed, lovely old town—a UNESCO World Heritage Site—before enjoying the hills, cafes, and Frank Zappa statue of this eclectic, influential capital (p. 689).
Riga (2 days)
A day wandering through its renowned Art Nouveau architecture and rowing a boat down river comes to a grand finale with a night at the opera and a morning in the clubs (p. 678).
Prague (2 days)
Club until dawn, take a nap, and then head back out to explore the city's cobblestone streets and Cubist architecture. Repeat (p. 238).
Warsaw (2 days)
Don't judge the Polish capital by its looks—this forward-looking city is one of the region's most compelling. Exuberant nightlife and a cutting-edge arts scene contrast with a painful, all-too-evident past (p. 776).
Český Krumlov (2 days)
Increased tourist traffic shouldn't keep you away from this charming town's medieval streets and enormous 13th-century castle (p. 255).
Kraków (2 days)
Do judge Poland's darling by its looks. From mighty Wawel Castle to the spectacular Old Town Square and the stylish students who pack the city's cellar clubs, the beauty of Kraków will overload your senses (p. 784).
Vienna (3 days)
Forget Amsterdam and Paris—this is the true coffeehouse capital of Europe (p. 73).
Dalmatian Coast (2 days)
Hit up the hot rocks on Hvar or Brač islands, make an extended ferry stop in tree-lined Zadar, then bus inland to the urban comforts of Zagreb (p. 227).
Budapest (2 days)
Go for the goulash and prehistoric labyrinths, and just try to pull yourself away from the show-stopping art and cafe culture, the underground club life, and the soothing baths (p. 514).
Dubrovnik (2 days)
Marvel at how the war wounds of Eastern Europe's coastal jewel have healed as you recline like royalty on the Adriatic before a night out at the clubs (p. 231).
END

CHANNEL JUMPING (1 MONTH)

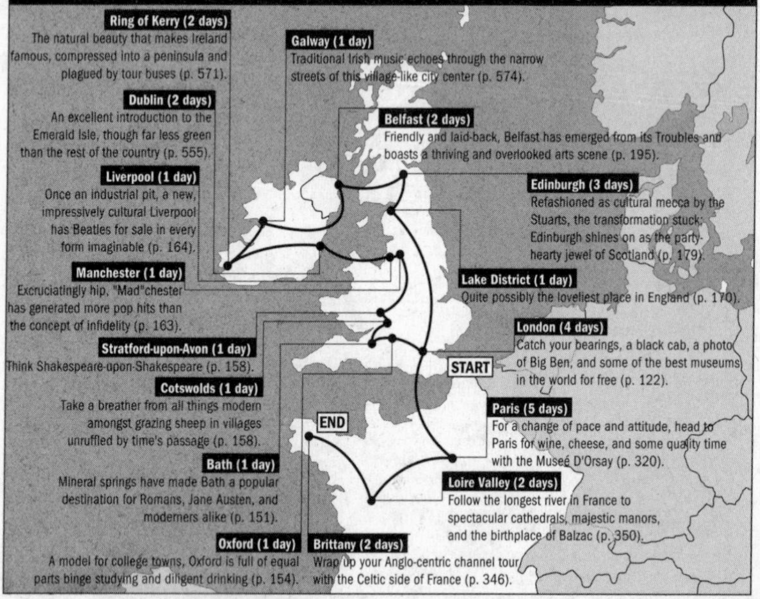

The natural beauty that makes Ireland famous, compressed into a peninsula and plagued by tour buses (p. 571).
Galway (1 day)
Traditional Irish music echoes through the narrow streets of this village-like city center (p. 574).
Dublin (2 days)
An excellent introduction to the Emerald Isle, though far less green than the rest of the country (p. 555).
Belfast (2 days)
Friendly and laid-back, Belfast has emerged from its Troubles and boasts a thriving and overlooked arts scene (p. 195).

Bath (1 day)
Mineral springs have made Bath a popular destination for Romans, Jane Austen, and moderners alike (p. 151).

Follow the longest river in France to spectacular cathedrals, majestic manors, and the birthplace of Balzac (p. 350).

A model for college towns, Oxford is full of equal parts binge studying and diligent drinking (p. 154).
Brittany (2 days)
Wrap up your Anglo-centric channel tour with the Celtic side of France (p. 346).

THE ULTIMATE PUB CRAWL

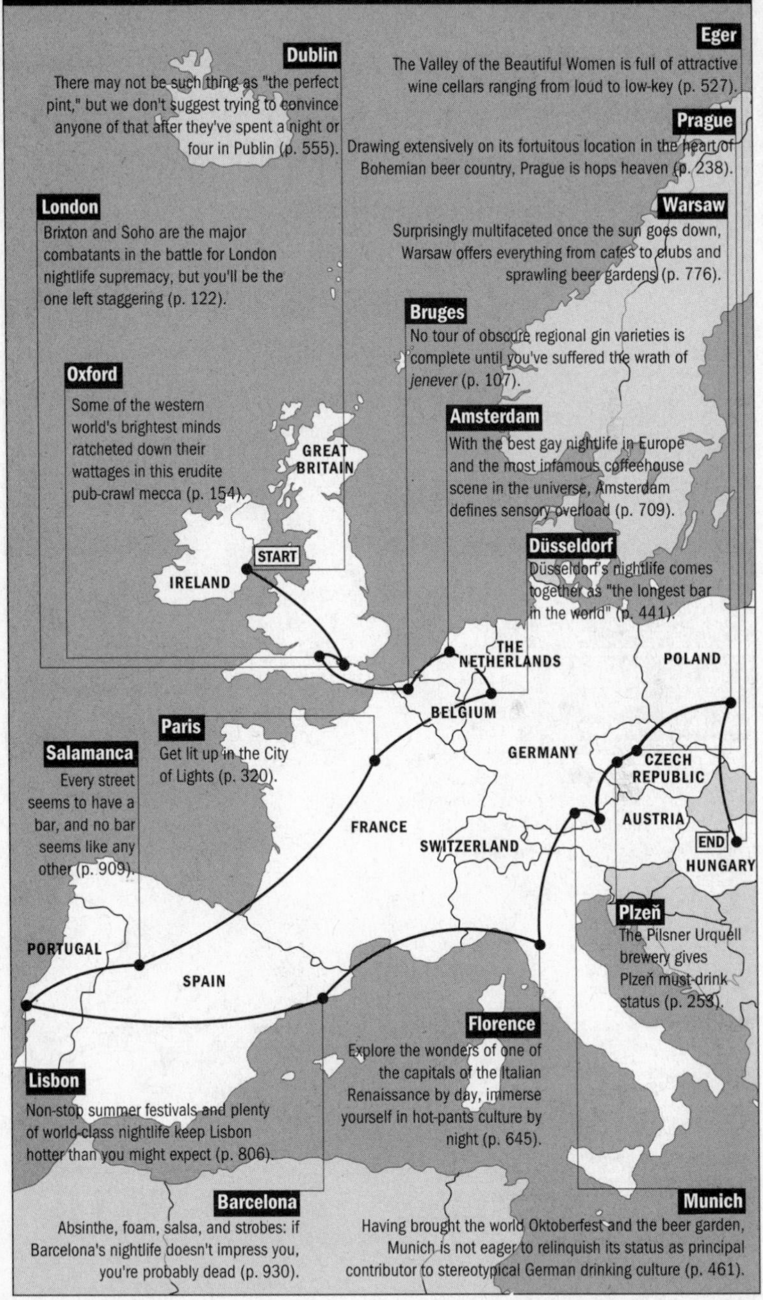
Dublin
There may not be such thing as "the perfect pint," but we don't suggest trying to convince anyone of that after they've spent a night or four in Publin (p. 555).
Eger
The Valley of the Beautiful Women is full of attractive wine cellars ranging from loud to low-key (p. 527).
Prague
Drawing extensively on its fortuitous location in the heart of Bohemian beer country, Prague is hops heaven (p. 238).
London
Brixton and Soho are the major combatants in the battle for London nightlife supremacy, but you'll be the one left staggering (p. 122).
Warsaw
Surprisingly multifaceted once the sun goes down, Warsaw offers everything from cafes to clubs and sprawling beer gardens (p. 776).
Bruges
No tour of obscure regional gin varieties is complete until you've suffered the wrath of *jenever* (p. 107).
Oxford
Some of the western world's brightest minds ratcheted down their wattages in this erudite pub-crawl mecca (p. 154).
Amsterdam
With the best gay nightlife in Europe and the most infamous coffeehouse scene in the universe, Amsterdam defines sensory overload (p. 709).
GREAT BRITAIN
Düsseldorf
Düsseldorf's nightlife comes together as "the longest bar in the world" (p. 441).
START
IRELAND
THE NETHERLANDS
POLAND
BELGIUM
Paris
Get lit up in the City of Lights (p. 320).
Salamanca
Every street seems to have a bar, and no bar seems like any other (p. 909).
GERMANY
CZECH REPUBLIC
FRANCE
AUSTRIA
SWITZERLAND
END
HUNGARY
Plzeň
The Pilsner Urquell brewery gives Plzeň must-drink status (p. 253).
PORTUGAL
SPAIN
Florence
Explore the wonders of one of the capitals of the Italian Renaissance by day, immerse yourself in hot-pants culture by night (p. 645).
Lisbon
Non-stop summer festivals and plenty of world-class nightlife keep Lisbon hotter than you might expect (p. 806).
Barcelona
Absinthe, foam, salsa, and strobes: if Barcelona's nightlife doesn't impress you, you're probably dead (p. 930).
Munich
Having brought the world Oktoberfest and the beer garden, Munich is not eager to relinquish its status as principal contributor to stereotypical German drinking culture (p. 461).

FESTIVALS

Bloomsday (July 16)
All of the action in James Joyce's *Ulysses* occurs on June 16, 1904, a date which is commemorated annually in Dublin, the setting of the novel (p. 555).

Stockholm Jazz Festival (Late July)
Held just outside Stockholm on the island of Skeppsholmen, this renowned festival has hosted jazz greats like Stan Getz and Dizzy Gillespie, and in recent years has branched out to include performers such as Bonnie Raitt, Bobby McFerrin, and Van Morrison (p. 963).

Amsterdam Gay Pride (Late August)
Over 250,000 spectators descend on Amsterdam to watch the annual parade that floats along the city's canals. The four-day celebration also features street parties, art shows, and sporting events (p. 709).

Quart (1st Week of July)
Kristiansand's annual rock and pop music festival; recent performers include Green Day, Foo Fighters, and Snoop Dogg (p. 750).

Edinburgh Fringe Festival (August)
Though it has grown to be the largest arts festival in the world, the Fringe stays true to its roots, allowing open access for all performers (p. 179).

Gentse Feesten (July 15-24)
Each summer Ghent commemorates the first vacation granted to laborers in 1860, largely by showing their predecessors up. Streets fill with performers, live music, carnival rides, great food, and rivers of beer (p. 112).

Bastille Day (July 14)
A national holiday of parades and fireworks commemorating the storming of the Bastille during the French Revolution (p. 320).

Spoleto Arts Festival (Early July)
In the beginning of July Spoleto hosts performances of dance, opera, drama, and film and visual arts exhibits (p. 585).

San Fermines (Early July)
Madness rules Pamplona for a week of bullfights, fireworks, and drunken partying, but the highlight is the Running of the Bulls, where adrenaline is the drug of choice (p. 946).

Sziget Festival (August)
This annual music festival welcomes young people from across Europe to stages playing rock, pop, dance, and a variety of other genres (p. 514).

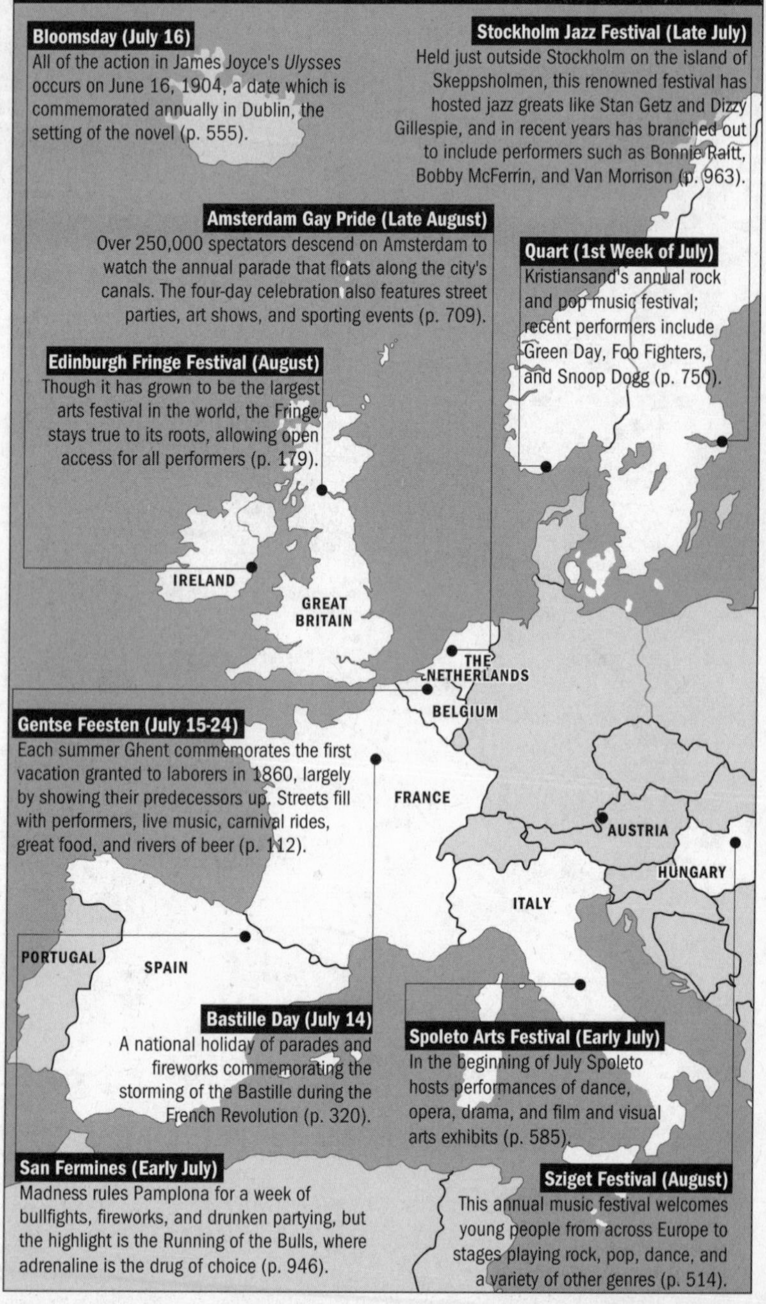

Manufacturing Continental Unity

As midnight approached on April 30th, 2004, corks could be heard popping across much of what used to be known as Eastern Europe. May 1st marked the beginning of a new era: ten new countries—Cyprus, the Czech Republic, Estonia, Hungary, Latvia, Lithuania, Malta, Poland, Slovakia, and Slovenia—were admitted into the European Union. The union, now 25 strong, set about commemorating its expansion across what had long been a divided continent. Concerts were held in Berlin and Warsaw, and all of Europe was able to watch televised broadcasts of the fireworks in Malta. All of this testified to the transformation of a Europe no longer divided into East and West.

Celebrations such as these can be enlightening. What and how we commemorate often tells more about who we are and what we claim to value than about the event or person being commemorated. May 1 had traditionally been a day to celebrate the working class (in the East) or labor more generally (in the West). This time, these themes were overshadowed by a different kind of internationalism: a sense on the part of the 10 inductees that they had finally become full-fledged members of "Europe." Examining this new Europe's celebrations tells us a good deal about just what the reinvented continent aspires to be.

What Europeans choose to remember or forget, how they recast their past and imagine the future, can all be gleaned from commemorations choreographed and spontaneous, solemn and joyous, permanent and ephemeral. Take, for example, the 60th anniversary of D-Day, celebrated in 2004. Those festivities brought not only aging war veterans and their families, but numerous international dignitaries to the coasts of Normandy for a week's worth of events. President George W. Bush underscored the contributions the United States had made to the security of Europe and the world as a whole, doubtless hoping that the luster of Normandy would rub off on his country's latest attempts at ridding the world of tyranny. Indeed, the American-led invasion of Normandy has long been a symbol of the larger *Pax Americana* that followed World War II, and although this vision has come under siege in recent years, it continues to be trumpeted in the public realm.

The festivities of 2004 brought changes to the D-Day anniversary, which had been celebrated regularly in previous decades. For the first time, the heads of Germany and Russia were present. The participation of both tells us much more about current alliances than about those that prevailed during the war. Recall that 20 years earlier, Ronald Reagan had been criticized for his visit to the Bitburg cemetery, where Nazi fighters lay buried. This time, the presence of Chancellor Gerhard Schröder at the festivities reflected the fact that a united Germany lies at the center of the new Europe. Russian participation in the D-Day festivities is even more interesting, since it signified recognition of one of the Allied Powers not often given its due. In the Cold War decades after the Axis Powers were vanquished, Soviet efforts in World War II were conveniently "forgotten" in the West. Given the improved relations between post-Communist Russia and the West, it had become acceptable to recall the Soviet Union's wartime sacrifices as well as those of Britain, France, and the United States.

Of course, not only battles are commemorated. A newly minted tradition, initiated by the European Union, is the designation of European Capitals of Culture. Each year, the designated city organizes festivities, exhibits, and events to showcase its cultural heritage. Cork, Ireland, enjoyed top billing in 2005, while Patras, Greece, held the honor in 2006. Such celebrations say much about the identity of these particular urban centers, and to some extent about how they situate themselves within European culture as a whole. The same is true of the European Heritage Days set aside each autumn, again celebrated in different ways in cities and towns across the continent. That the European Union promotes such local expressions of cultural inheritance suggests that it values the rich cultural mosaic that makes up Europe.

Thus, the second half of the European Union's slogan "unity in diversity" continues to receive attention. However, the first half of the slogan—unity—still lacks its own celebration. Is not European Unity Day—"E-Day"—equally worth celebrating in the aftermath of May 1, 2004? Perhaps Europeans will take it upon themselves to transform May Day into E-Day on a permanent basis. This might make up for the fact that the revolutions of 1989, which helped to initiate the reunification of Europe's two halves, received so little notice on their 15th anniversary. With the tearing down of the Berlin Wall, Europe lost one site for spontaneous celebrations such as those that took place on November 9, 1989. One fitting tribute to both 1989 and to the European reunification of 2004 might be fireworks over Budapest's Statue Park, with its collection of monuments to Karl Marx and V. I. Lenin. Here, perhaps, one could best appreciate the irony of Europe's slogan for the 21st century: "Europeans of the world, unite!"

Patrice M. Dabrowski is a postdoctoral fellow at Brown University's Watson Institute for International Studies. She is the author of Commemorations and the Shaping of Modern Poland, *published by Indiana University Press in 2004 and hailed by fellow scholars for its "tremendous erudition."*

The Struggle for a European Immigration Policy

In June of 2003, 200 would-be European immigrants believed to have embarked from Libya drowned in the rough waters south of Sicily; that same month, 2666 migrants from Africa survived the journey, landing on the isolated Italian island, Lampedusa, and creating a study in contrasts in the ongoing EU immigration debate. In the annals of European immigration, tragedies of this caliber are far from rare: The Sicily drowning occurred four years to the month after 58 Chinese refugees were asphyxiated in a container lorry at the English port of Dover. Even the illegal immigrants who beat the odds and the border control do not always escape tragic circumstances. Many are forced into black-market labor, such as prostitution, to pay back smugglers for their passage. While it is fairly clear that current EU immigration policies are harmful to refugees, liberalizing the policies on legal immigration is not only in the best interests of those seeking entrance—it now appears that the EU needs immigrants as desperately as immigrants need the EU.

Western European birthrates have crashed to an all-time low, averaging only 1.5 children per woman, and dipping as low as Spain's scant 1.1. At the other end of things, Europe's aging population has become a major strain on its pension systems. French Parliamentarian Elisabeth Guigou reports that, if present demographic trends continue, without relaxing immigration constraints, the mighty new 25-nation European Union will experience a net decline in population of 50 million people by 2050. Even now Europe is facing shortages in both its skilled and unskilled labor pools, making even more apparent its need for immigrants for economic prosperity to continue.

With so much at stake, the recent Europe-wide swing to the political right on immigration policy may be difficult to comprehend. Some of the most developed, prosperous nations, such as Germany and France, worry that an influx of immigrants will destabilize their economies and jeopardize publicly funded medical and social programs. Tensions have been primarily focused on African and Arab ghettos, commonly seen as drags on the welfare state and feared to be security threats in the wake of September 11. This explosive combination of fear and uncertainty has fueled the popularity of far-right populist political candidates running on anti-immigration platforms, spawning legislation severely restricting legal immigration.

Between June and July of 2003 at the Thessaloniki Summit, Britain, Germany, and Italy were the most vocal and influential players in the debate over how to manage illegal immigration while integrating legal immigrants. Some leaders, such as the former German Interior Minister Otto Schily, think agreements with countries of origin are the best way to curbing illegal immigration. Supporters of such efforts point to Italy's bilateral agreements with Libya, a hub for human trafficking from Africa to Europe, and Albania as models. In the former scenario, Italy will provide technical assistance to Libya, and the two countries will cooperate on offshore patrols. The 1997 Italian-Albanian cooperation deal contains a simplified repatriation scheme, quotas for seasonal workers, and joint patrols in Albanian waters of the Adriatic Sea that separate Italy and Europe's second-poorest nation.

The stage is set for what promises to be an ongoing debate, as Germany leads the fight to retain autonomous control of its border policies while nations like Britain and Italy attempt to institute centralized, EU-wide control of immigration policy and enforcement. For the moment, a stopgap EU program intended to "promote a tolerant and inclusive society by raising awareness of fundamental European values" and to project accurate information about immigrants' culture, traditions, and religion underscores the complexity of the situation. By educating immigrants in the cultural, social, and political characteristics of their adoptive state—and providing EU citizens with accurate information about immigrants' cultures—there is hope that some of the elements of mistrust and misunderstanding that have plagued the discussion thus far can be mitigated, and that the frustrated desperation that has cost the lives of so many refugees will give way to a peaceful, legal, and mutually beneficial solution.

Derek Glanz is a doctoral candidate in political science at the University of North Carolina at Chapel Hill. He was the Editor of Let's Go: Spain & Portugal 1998.

ESSENTIALS

PLANNING YOUR TRIP

BEFORE YOU GO

Passport (p. 15). Required for all non-EU citizens traveling in Europe.

Visa (p. 16). Not required for citizens of Australia, Canada, Ireland, New Zealand, the UK, and the US for stays shorter than 90 days in a 6-month period in most European countries.

Work Permit (p. 16). Required for all non-EU citizens planning to work in any European country.

Vaccinations (p. 25). Visitors to Europe should be up to date on vaccines, especially for diphtheria, hepatitis A, hepatitis B, and mumps. Visitors to Eastern Europe should also be vaccinated for measles, rabies, and typhoid.

EMBASSIES AND CONSULATES

CONSULAR SERVICES

Information about European consular services abroad and foreign consular services in Europe is located in individual country chapters; it can also be found at **www.embassiesabroad.com**, **www.embassyworld.com**, and **www.tyzo.com/planning/embassies.html**.

TOURIST OFFICES

Information about national tourist boards in Europe is located in individual country chapters; it can also be found at **www.towd.com**.

DOCUMENTS AND FORMALITIES

PASSPORTS

REQUIREMENTS. Citizens of Australia, Canada, Ireland, New Zealand, the UK, and the US need valid passports to enter European countries and to re-enter their home countries. Most countries do not allow entrance if the holder's passport expires within six months; returning home with an expired passport is illegal and may result in a fine.

NEW PASSPORTS. Citizens of Australia, Canada, Ireland, New Zealand, the UK, and the US can apply for a passport at any passport office and most post offices and courts of law. New passport or renewal applications must be filed at least two months before the departure date, though most passport offices offer rush services for a very steep fee. Be warned that even "rushed" passports can take up to two weeks to arrive. Citizens living abroad who need a passport or renewal should contact the nearest passport office or consulate of their home country.

PASSPORT MAINTENANCE. Photocopy the page of your passport with your photo, as well as your visas, traveler's check serial numbers, and any other important documents. Carry one set of copies in a safe place, apart from the originals,

ONE EUROPE. European unity has come a long way since 1958, when the European Economic Community (EEC) was created to promote European solidarity and cooperation. Since then, the EEC has become the European Union (EU), a mighty political, legal, and economic institution. On May 1, 2004, 10 Southern, Central, and Eastern European countries–Cyprus, the Czech Republic, Estonia, Hungary, Latvia, Lithuania, Malta, Poland, Slovakia, and Slovenia–were admitted to the EU, joining the 15 other member states: Austria, Belgium, Denmark, Finland, France, Germany, Greece, Ireland, Italy, Luxembourg, the Netherlands, Portugal, Spain, Sweden, and the UK. What does this mean for travelers to the EU? The EU's policy of **freedom of movement** means that border controls between the first 15 member states (minus Ireland and the UK, but plus Norway and Iceland) have been abolished, and visa policies harmonized. Under this treaty, formally known as the **Schengen Agreement,** travelers are still required to carry a passport (or government-issued ID card for EU citizens) when crossing an internal border, but once they have been admitted into one country, they are free to travel to other participating states. On June 5, 2005, Switzerland signed on, and it and Liechtenstein will become full participants by 2007. The 10 newest member states will implement the policy after 2007. Britain and Ireland have also formed a **common travel area,** abolishing passport controls between the UK and the Republic of Ireland. For more important consequences of the EU for travelers, see **The Euro** (p. 18) and **Customs in the EU** (p. 18).

and leave another set at home. Consulates also recommend that you carry an expired passport or an official copy of your birth certificate in a part of your baggage separate from other documents.

If you lose your passport, immediately notify the local police and the nearest embassy or consulate of your home government. To expedite its replacement, you must show ID and proof of citizenship; it also helps to know all information previously recorded in the passport. In some cases, a replacement may take weeks to process, and it may be valid only for a limited time. Any visas stamped in your old passport will be irretrievably lost. In an emergency, ask for immediate temporary traveling papers that will permit you to re-enter your home country.

VISAS, INVITATIONS, AND WORK PERMITS

VISAS. As of August 2006, citizens of Australia, Canada, Ireland, New Zealand, the UK, or the US did not need a visa to visit the following countries for fewer than 90 days: Austria, Belgium, Britain, Croatia, the Czech Republic, Denmark, Estonia, Finland, France, Germany, Greece, Hungary, Iceland, Ireland, Italy, Latvia, Liechtenstein, Luxembourg, the Netherlands, Norway, Poland, Portugal, the Slovak Republic, Slovenia, Spain, Sweden, and Switzerland. For travelers planning to spend more than 90 days in any European country, visas cost US$35-200 and typically allow you six months in that country. Visas can usually be purchased at a consulate or at www.itseasypassport.com/services/visas/visas.htm.

Double-check entrance requirements at the nearest embassy or consulate of your destination for up-to-date info before departure. US citizens can also consult http://travel.state.gov/foreignentryreqs.html.

WORK PERMITS. Admission as a visitor does not include the right to work, which is authorized only by a work permit. Entering a country in Europe to study typically requires a special study visa, though many study-abroad programs are able to subsidize it. For more information, see **Beyond Tourism,** p. 61.

IDENTIFICATION

When you travel, always carry at least two forms of identification on your person, including a photo ID; a passport and a driver's license or birth certificate is usually adequate. Never carry all of your IDs together; split them up in case of theft or loss, and keep photocopies of all of them in your luggage and at home.

STUDENT, TEACHER, AND YOUTH IDENTIFICATION. The **International Student Identity Card (ISIC),** the most widely accepted form of student ID, provides discounts on some sights, accommodations, food, and transportation; access to a 24hr. emergency helpline; and insurance benefits for US cardholders (see **Insurance,** p. 25). Applicants must be full-time secondary or post-secondary school students. Because of the proliferation of fake ISICs, some services (particularly airlines) require additional proof of student identity.

The **International Teacher Identity Card (ITIC)** offers teachers the same insurance coverage as the ISIC and similar but limited discounts. For travelers who are under 26 years old but are not students, the **International Youth Travel Card (IYTC)** also offers many of the same benefits as the ISIC.

Each of these identity cards costs US$22. ISICs and ITICs are valid until the new year unless purchased between September and December, in which case they are valid until the beginning of the following new year. IYTCs are valid for one year from the date of issue. To learn more about ISICs, ITICs, and IYTCs, try www.myisic.com. Many travel agencies issue the cards; for more information, see the **International Student Travel Confederation (ISTC)** website (www.istc.org).

The **International Student Exchange Card (ISE Card)** is a similar identification card available to students, faculty, and youths aged 12 to 26. The card provides discounts, medical benefits, access to a 24hr. emergency helpline, and the ability to purchase student airfares. An ISE Card costs US$25; for more info, call in the US ☎800-255-8000, or visit www.isecard.com.

CUSTOMS

When you enter a European country, you must declare certain items from abroad and pay a duty on the value of those articles if they exceed a set allowance. Note that goods purchased at **duty-free** shops are not exempt from duty or sales tax; "duty-free" merely means that you need not pay a tax in the country of purchase. Duty-free allowances were abolished for travel between EU member states, but still exist for those arriving from outside the EU. Upon returning home, you must likewise declare all articles acquired abroad and pay a duty on the value of articles in excess of your home country's allowance. In order to expedite your return, make a list of any valuables brought from home and register them with customs before traveling abroad, and be sure to keep receipts for all goods acquired abroad.

MONEY

CURRENCY AND EXCHANGE

The currency chart on the next page is based on August 2006 exchange rates between euros and Australian dollars (AUS$), Canadian dollars (CDN$), New Zealand dollars (NZ$), British pounds (UK£), and US dollars (US$). Check the currency converter on websites like www.xe.com or www.bloomberg.com, or a large newspaper, for the latest exchange rates.

As a general rule, it's cheaper to convert money in Europe than at home. While currency exchange will probably be available in your arrival airport, it's wise to bring enough currency to last for the first 24-72hr. of your trip.

CUSTOMS IN THE EU. In addition to the freedom of movement of people within the EU (p. 16), travelers in the older 15 EU member countries (Austria, Belgium, Denmark, Finland, France, Germany, Greece, Ireland, Italy, Luxembourg, the Netherlands, Portugal, Spain, Sweden, and the UK) can also take advantage of the freedom of movement of goods. This means that there are no customs controls at internal EU borders (i.e., you can take the blue customs channel at the airport), and travelers are free to transport whatever legal substances they like as long as they are for their own personal (non-commercial) use—up to 800 cigarettes, 10L of spirits, 90L of wine (including up to 60L of sparkling wine), and 110L of beer. Duty-free allowances have been abolished for travel between the older 15 EU member states; this now also applies to Cyprus and Malta. However, travelers between the EU and the rest of the world still get a duty-free allowance when passing through customs.

EURO (€)

AUS$1 = EUR€0.60	EUR€1 = AUS$1.68
CDN$1 = EUR€0.70	EUR€1 = CDN$1.42
NZ$1 = EUR€0.50	EUR€1 = NZ$2.00
UK£1 = EUR€1.48	EUR€1 = UK£0.68
US$1 = EUR€0.78	EUR€1 = US$1.28

When exchanging money abroad, try to go only to banks or official exchange establishments that have at most a 5% margin between their buy and sell prices. Because you lose money with every transaction, **convert large sums** (unless the currency is depreciating rapidly), but **no more than you'll need.**

If you use traveler's checks or bills, carry some in small denominations (the equivalent of US$50 or less) for times when you are forced to exchange money at disadvantageous rates, but bring a range of denominations, as charges may be levied per check cashed. Store your money in a variety of forms; ideally, at any given time you will be carrying some cash, some traveler's checks, and an ATM and/or credit card. All travelers should also consider carrying some US dollars (about US$50 worth), which are often preferred by local tellers.

TRAVELER'S CHECKS

Traveler's checks are one of the safest and least troublesome means of carrying funds. American Express and Visa are the most recognized brands. Many banks and agencies sell them for a small commission. Check issuers provide refunds if the checks are lost or stolen, and many provide additional services, such as toll-free refund hotlines abroad, emergency message services, and assistance with lost and stolen credit cards or passports. Ask about toll-free refund hotlines and the location of refund centers when purchasing checks; always carry emergency cash.

THE EURO. The official currency of 12 members of the European Union—Austria, Belgium, Finland, France, Germany, Greece, Ireland, Italy, Luxembourg, the Netherlands, Portugal, and Spain—is now the euro. Slovenia is set to join in 2007. The currency has some important—and positive—consequences for travelers hitting more than one euro-zone country. For one thing, money-changers across the euro-zone are obliged to exchange money at the official, fixed rate, and at no commission (though they may still charge a small service fee). Second, euro-denominated traveler's checks allow you to pay for goods and services across the euro-zone, again at the official rate and commission-free.

American Express: Cheques available with commission at select banks, at all AmEx offices, and online (www.americanexpress.com; US residents only). AmEx cardholders can also purchase checks by phone (☎800-528-4800). AmEx also offers the Travelers Cheque Card, a prepaid reloadable card. Cheques for Two can be signed by either of 2 people traveling together. For more information, contact AmEx's service centers: Australia ☎800 688 022, Canada and the US 800-221-7282, New Zealand 050 855 5358, UK 0800 587 6023; elsewhere, call US collect 801-964-6665.

Travelex: Thomas Cook MasterCard and Interpayment Visa traveler's checks available. For info about Thomas Cook MasterCard in Canada and the US call ☎800-223-7373, UK 0800 622 101; elsewhere, call UK collect 44 1733 318 950. For information about Interpayment Visa in Canada and the US ☎800-732-1322, in the UK 0800 515 884; elsewhere, call UK collect 44 1733 318 949. For more info, visit www.travelex.com.

Visa: Checks available (generally with commission) at banks worldwide. For the location of the nearest office, call the Visa Travelers Cheque Global Refund and Assistance Center: in the UK ☎0800 895 078, US 800-227-6811; elsewhere, call UK collect 44 2079 378 091. Visa also offers TravelMoney, a pre-paid debit card that can be reloaded online or by phone. For more information on Visa travel services, see http://usa.visa.com/personal/using_visa/travel_with_visa.html.

ESSENTIALS

CREDIT, ATM, AND DEBIT CARDS

Where they are accepted, credit cards often offer superior exchange rates—up to 5% better than the retail rate used by banks and other currency exchange establishments. Credit cards may also offer services such as insurance or emergency help, and are sometimes required when reserving hotel rooms or rental cars. **MasterCard** (a.k.a. **EuroCard** or **Access** in Europe) and **Visa** (a.k.a. **Carte Bleue** or **Barclaycard**) are the most widely accepted; **American Express** cards work at some ATMs and at AmEx offices and most major airports. A **debit card** can be used wherever its associated credit card company (usually MasterCard or Visa) is accepted, and the money is withdrawn directly from the holder's checking account. Debit cards also often function as ATM cards and can be used to withdraw cash from banks and ATMs throughout Europe. Ask your local bank about obtaining one.

The use of ATM cards is widespread in Europe. Depending on the system that your home bank uses, you can most likely access your personal bank account from abroad. ATMs get the same wholesale exchange rate as credit cards, but there is often a limit on the amount of money you can withdraw per day (usually around US$500). There is typically also a surcharge of US$1-5 per withdrawal.

The two major international money networks are **MasterCard/Maestro/Cirrus** (for ATM locations ☎800-424-7787; www.mastercard.com) and **Visa/PLUS** (for ATM locations ☎800-847-2911; www.visa.com).

PINS AND ATMS. To use a debit or credit card to withdraw money from a cash machine (ATM) in Europe, you must have a 4-digit **Personal Identification Number (PIN).** If your PIN is longer than 4 digits, ask your bank whether you can just use the first 4, or whether you'll need a new one. **Credit cards** don't usually come with PINs, so if you intend to hit up ATMs in Europe with a credit card to get cash advances, call your credit card company to request one before leaving.

Travelers with alphabetic, rather than numerical, PINs may also be thrown off by the lack of letters on European cash machines. The following are the corresponding numbers to use: QZ=1; ABC=2; DEF=3; GHI=4; JKL=5; MNO=6; PRS=7; TUV=8; and WXY=9. Note that if you mistakenly punch the wrong code into the machine 3 times, it will swallow your card for good.

GETTING MONEY FROM HOME

The easiest and cheapest solution for running out of money while traveling is to have someone back home make a deposit to the bank account linked to your credit card or ATM card. Failing that, consider one of the options below. The online **International Money Transfer Consumer Guide** (http://international-money-transfer-consumer-guide.info) may also be of help.

WIRING MONEY. It is possible to arrange a **bank money transfer,** which means asking a bank back home to wire money to a bank in Europe. This is the cheapest way to transfer cash, but it's also the slowest, usually taking several days or more. Note that some banks may only release your funds in local currency, potentially sticking you with a poor exchange rate; inquire about this in advance. Money transfer services like **Western Union** are faster and more convenient than bank transfers, but also much pricier. Western Union has many locations worldwide. To find one, visit www.westernunion.com, or call: Australia ☎800 173 833, Canada and US 800-325-6000, UK 0800 833 833. To wire money using a credit card, call in Canada and the US ☎800-225-5227, UK 0800 833 833. Money transfer services are also available to **American Express** cardholders and at selected **Thomas Cook** offices.

US STATE DEPARTMENT (US CITIZENS ONLY). In serious emergencies, the US State Department will forward money within hours to the nearest consular office, which will then disburse it according to instructions for a US$30 fee. To use this service, you must contact the Overseas Citizens Service division of the US State Department (☎202-647-5225, toll-free 888-877-8339).

COSTS

The cost of your trip will vary depending on where you go, how you travel, and where you stay. The most significant expenses will probably be your round-trip (return) **airfare** to Europe (see **Getting to Europe: By Plane,** p. 42) and a **railpass** or **bus pass** (see **Getting around Europe,** p. 46).

STAYING ON A BUDGET. Your daily budget will vary greatly from country to country. A bare-bones day in Europe would include camping or sleeping in hostels and buying food in supermarkets. A slightly more comfortable day would include sleeping in hostels or guesthouses and the occasional budget hotel, eating one meal per day at a restaurant, and going out at night. For a luxurious day, the sky's the limit. In any case, be sure to factor in emergency reserve funds (at least US$200) when planning how much money you'll need.

TIPS FOR SAVING MONEY. Some simple ways to save include searching out free entertainment, splitting accommodation and food costs with trustworthy fellow travelers, and buying food in grocery stores. Multi-day local transportation passes can also save you money. Bring a **sleepsack** (p. 22) to save at hostels that charge for linens, and do your **laundry** in the sink unless you're explicitly prohibited from doing so. Museums often have certain days when admission is free. If you are eligible, consider getting an ISIC or an IYTC; many sights and museums have reduced admission for cardholders. Renting a bike is cheaper than renting a moped or scooter. Purchasing drinks at bars quickly becomes expensive; it's cheaper to buy alcohol at a supermarket and drink before going out. Remember, though, that while staying within your budget is important, don't do so at the expense of your health or a great travel experience.

TIPPING AND BARGAINING

In most European countries, a 5-10% gratuity is included in the food service bill. Additional tipping is not expected, but an extra 5-10% for good service is not unusual. Where gratuity is not included, 10-15% tips are standard and rounding up to the next unit of currency is common. Many countries have their own unique tipping practices with which you should familiarize yourself before visiting. In general, tipping in bars and pubs is unnecessary and money left on the bar may not make it into the bartender's hands. For other services such as taxis or hairdressers, a 10-15% tip is usually recommended. Watch other customers to gauge what is appropriate. Bargaining is useful in Greece and in outdoor markets across Europe. See individual country chapters for more specific information.

TAXES

The EU imposes a **value added tax (VAT)** on goods and services, usually included in the sticker price. Non-EU citizens visiting Europe may obtain a refund for taxes paid on retail goods, but not for taxes paid on services. As the VAT is 15-25%, it might be worthwhile to file for a refund. To do so, you must obtain Tax-Free Shopping Cheques, available from shops sporting the Europe Tax-Free Shopping logo, and save your receipts. Upon leaving the EU, present your goods, invoices, and passport to customs and have your checks stamped. Then, go to an ETS cash refund office on site or file for a refund once back home. Keep in mind that goods must be taken out of the country within three months of purchase, and that most countries require minimum purchase amounts per store to become eligible for a refund. See www.globalrefund.org for more info and downloads of relevant forms.

PACKING

Pack lightly. Lay out what you absolutely need, then take half the clothes and twice the money. The Travelite FAQ (www.travelite.org) is a good resource for tips on traveling light. The **Universal Packing List** (http://upl.codeq.info) will generate a list of suggested items based on your trip length, the climate, your planned activities, and other factors. If you plan to do a lot of hiking, consult **The Great Outdoors,** p. 34.

Luggage: If you plan to cover most of your itinerary by foot, a sturdy **frame backpack** is unbeatable. (For backpack basics, see p. 36.) Toting a **suitcase** or **trunk** is fine if you plan to live in 1 or 2 cities, but not a great idea if you plan to move around frequently. In addition to your main piece of luggage, a **daypack** (a small backpack or courier bag) is useful.

Clothing: No matter when you're traveling, it's a good idea to bring a warm jacket, a rain jacket (Gore-Tex® is both waterproof and breathable), sturdy shoes, and thick socks. Waterproof sandals are a must-have for grubby hostel showers. You may also want one outfit for going out, and maybe a nicer pair of shoes. If you plan to visit religious or cultural sites, remember that you will need to dress modestly and respectfully.

Sleepsack: Some hostels require that you either provide your own linens or rent sheets from them. Save cash by making your own sleepsack: fold a full-size sheet in half the long way, then sew it closed along the long side and one of the short sides.

Adapters and Converters: In Europe, electricity is 230V AC, enough to fry any 120V North American appliance. Americans and Canadians should buy an adapter (changes the shape of the plug; US$10-30) and a converter (changes the voltage; US$10-30); don't use an adapter without a converter unless appliance instructions explicitly state otherwise. Australians and New Zealanders, who use 230V at home, won't need a converter, but will need a set of adapters. For more info, see http://kropla.com/electric.htm.

> TIP **DISPOSABLES.** If you're tight on space and plan to give your clothes a good workout, consider buying a pack of simple cotton undershirts. A pack of plain t-shirts is cheap and light, and you won't feel bad throwing them away when they get covered in backpacker grime.

Toiletries: Toothbrushes, towels, soap, deodorant, razors, tampons, and condoms are available, but it may be difficult to find your preferred brand, so bring extras. Also, be sure to bring enough contact lenses and solution for your entire trip. Also bring your glasses and a copy of your prescription in case you need an emergency replacement. If you use heat disinfection, either switch temporarily to chemical disinfection (check first to make sure it's safe with your brand of lenses), or buy a converter to 220/240V.

TIP **KEEP IT CLEAN.** Multi-purpose liquid soaps will save space and keep you from smelling like last night's fish and chips. Dr. Bronner's® and Campsuds® both make soap that you can use as toothpaste, shampoo, laundry detergent, dishwashing liquid, and more. Plus, they're biodegradable.

First Aid: For a basic first-aid kit, pack bandages, a pain reliever, antibiotic cream, a thermometer, a pocket knife, tweezers, moleskin, decongestant, motion-sickness remedy, diarrhea or upset-stomach medication (Pepto Bismol® or Imodium®), an antihistamine, sunscreen, insect repellent, and burn ointment. If you will be in remote regions of less-developed Eastern European countries, consider a syringe for emergencies (get an explanatory letter from your doctor). Leave all sharp objects in your checked luggage.

Film: Buying and developing film in Europe is expensive; bring enough for your entire trip and develop at home. If you don't want to bother with film, consider a digital camera. Bring a large enough memory card and extra batteries. For more on digital cameras, see www.shortcourses.com/choosing/contents.htm. Despite disclaimers, airport security X-rays can fog film, so buy a lead-lined pouch at a camera store or ask security to hand-inspect it. Always pack film in your carry-on luggage, as higher-intensity X-rays are used on checked luggage.

Other Useful Items: For safety, bring a **money belt** and a small **padlock.** Basic **outdoors equipment** (water bottle, compass, waterproof matches, pocketknife, sunglasses, sunscreen, hat) may also prove useful. To do laundry by hand, bring detergent, a small rubber ball to stop up the sink, and string for a makeshift clothesline. Extra **plastic bags** are crucial for storing food, dirty shoes, and wet clothes, and for keeping liquids from exploding all over your clothes. Other items include an umbrella, a battery-powered **alarm clock,** safety pins, a flashlight, a pocketknife, earplugs, and garbage bags. A **mobile phone** can be a lifesaver on the road; see p. 29 for more info.

Important Documents: Don't forget your passport, traveler's checks, ATM and/or credit cards, adequate ID, and photocopies of all of the aforementioned (p. 15). Other documents you may wish to have include: a hostelling membership card (p. 30); a driver's license (p. 17); travel insurance forms (p. 25); an ISIC (p. 17); a rail or bus pass(p. 50).

SAFETY AND HEALTH

GENERAL ADVICE

In any type of crisis, the most important thing to do is **stay calm.** Your country's embassy abroad is usually your best resource when things go wrong; registering with that embassy upon arrival in the country is often a good idea.

DRUGS AND ALCOHOL. Drug and alcohol laws vary widely throughout Europe. In the Netherlands "soft" drugs are available on the open market, while in much of Eastern Europe drug possession may lead to a heavy prison sentence. If you carry **prescription drugs,** carry both a copy of the prescriptions themselves and a note from a doctor, especially at border crossings. **Public drunkenness** is culturally unacceptable and against the law in many countries; it can also jeopardize your safety.

TERRORISM AND CIVIL UNREST. In the wake of September 11 and the war in Iraq, be vigilant near Western embassies and be wary of crowds and demonstrations. Keep an eye on the news, pay attention to travel warnings, and comply with security measures. Overall, risks of civil unrest tend to be localized and rarely directed toward tourists.

TRAVEL ADVISORIES. The following government offices provide travel information and advisories by telephone, by fax, or via the web:

Australian Department of Foreign Affairs and Trade: ☎1300 555 135; www.dfat.gov.au.

Canadian Department of Foreign Affairs and International Trade (DFAIT): ☎800-267-8376; www.dfait-maeci.gc.ca. Call for their free booklet, *Bon Voyage...But.*

New Zealand Ministry of Foreign Affairs and Trade: ☎044 398 000; www.mft.govt.nz/travel/index.html.

United Kingdom Foreign and Commonwealth Office: ☎020 7008 1500; www.fco.gov.uk.

US Department of State: ☎202-647-5225; http://travel.state.gov. Visit the website for the booklet *A Safe Trip Abroad.*

PERSONAL SAFETY

EXPLORING AND TRAVELING

To avoid unwanted attention, blend in as much as possible. Respecting local customs (in many cases, dressing more modestly than you would at home) may placate would-be hecklers. Take extra care in your dress and demeanor when visiting churches and culturally sensitive areas. Familiarize yourself with the area before setting out, and carry yourself with confidence. Check maps in shops rather than on the street. If you are traveling alone, be sure someone knows your itinerary, and never admit that you're by yourself. When walking at night, stick to busy streets. If you feel uncomfortable, leave the area as quickly as you can. There is no sure-fire way to avoid all the threatening situations you might encounter, but a **self-defense course** will give you concrete ways to react to unwanted advances. **Impact, Prepare,** and **Model Mugging** can refer you to self-defense courses in Australia, Canada, and the US. Visit www.modelmugging.org for a list of nearby chapters. Workshops (2-4hr.) start at US$50; full courses (20hr.) run US$350-500.

If you're using a **car,** learn local driving signals and study maps before you hit the road. For long drives, invest in a mobile phone and a roadside assistance program. Park in a garage or well-traveled area. **Sleeping in your car** is dangerous, and illegal in many countries. For info on the perils of **hitchhiking,** see p. 59.

POSSESSIONS AND VALUABLES

Be aware: crime occurs in even the most safe-looking hostels and hotels. Bring your own padlock for hostel lockers, and don't ever store valuable items in a locker. Be particularly careful on **buses** and **trains;** stories abound about determined thieves who wait for travelers to fall asleep. Carry your bag or purse in front of you where you can see it. When traveling with others, sleep in shifts. When alone, use good judgment in selecting a train compartment: never stay in an empty one, and lock your pack to the luggage rack. Use extra caution when traveling at night or on overnight trains. Try to sleep on the top bunk with your luggage stored above you (or in bed with you), and keep important documents on you at all times.

There are a few steps you can take to minimize the financial risk associated with traveling. First, **bring as little with you as possible.** Second, buy a few combination **padlocks** to secure your belongings either in your pack or in a hostel or train station locker. Third, **carry as little cash as possible.** Keep your traveler's checks and ATM/credit cards in a **money belt**—not a "fanny pack"—along with your passport and ID cards. Fourth, **keep a small cash reserve separate from your primary stash.** This should be about US$200 (US$ or euros are best) sewn into or stored in the depths of your pack, along with your traveler's check numbers and photocopies of your passport, your birth certificate, and other important documents.

In cities, **con artists** often work in groups and may employ children. Beware of the classics: sob stories that require money, rolls of bills "found" on the street, mustard spilled (or saliva spit) onto your shoulder to distract you while they snatch your bag. Be wary while using ATMs; notice who is behind you, stand in front of the display, and never turn your back on the machine when your card is inside. **Never let your passport and bags out of your sight.** Beware of **pickpockets,** especially on public transportation. Also, be alert in telephone booths: if you must say your calling card number, do so quietly; if you punch it in, be sure no one can see.

If you will be traveling with electronic devices, check whether your insurance covers theft or damage. If not, consider a low-cost property insurance policy. **Safeware** (☎800-800-1492; www.safeware.com) specializes in covering computers and charges US$90 for 90-day international travel coverage up to US$4000.

ESSENTIALS

PRE-DEPARTURE HEALTH

In your passport, write the names of any people you wish to be contacted in case of a medical emergency, and list any allergies or medical conditions you have. Matching a prescription to its foreign equivalent is not always possible, so if you take prescription drugs, bring legible prescriptions or a statement from your doctor stating the medication's trade name, manufacturer, chemical name, and dosage. While traveling, be sure to keep all medication with you in your carry-on luggage. For tips on packing a **first-aid kit** and other health essentials, see p. 23.

INSURANCE

Travel insurance covers four basic areas: medical/health problems, property loss, trip cancellation/interruption, and emergency evacuation. Though regular insurance policies may extend to travel-related accidents, consider purchasing separate travel insurance if the cost of potential trip cancellation, interruption, or emergency medical evacuation is greater than you can absorb. Prices for independent travel insurance run about US$50 per week for full coverage, while trip cancellation/interruption may be purchased separately at US$3-5 per day.

Medical insurance often covers costs incurred abroad; check with your provider. **Australians** traveling in Finland, Ireland, Italy, the Netherlands, Sweden, or the UK are entitled to many of the services that they would receive at home as part of the Reciprocal Health Care Agreement. **Homeowners' insurance** often covers theft during travel and loss of travel documents (passport, plane ticket, railpass, etc.) up to US$500. **ISIC** and **ITIC** (p. 17) provide basic insurance benefits to US cardholders (see www.isicus.com for details). Cardholders have access to a 24hr. helpline for all types of emergencies. **American Express** (☎800-338-1670) grants most cardholders collision and theft insurance on car rentals made with the card.

USEFUL ORGANIZATIONS AND PUBLICATIONS

The American **Centers for Disease Control and Prevention** (**CDC;** ☎877-FYI-TRIP/394-8747; www.cdc.gov/travel) maintains an international travelers' hotline and an informative website. Consult the appropriate government agency of your home country for consular information sheets on health, entry requirements, and other issues for various countries. For quick info on health warnings, call the **Overseas Citizens Services** (M-F 8am-8pm from US ☎888-407-4747, from overseas 202-501-4444), or contact a passport agency, embassy, or consulate abroad. For information on medical evacuation services and travel insurance firms, see the US government's website (http://travel.state.gov/travel/abroad_health.html) or the British Foreign and Commonwealth Office (www.fco.gov.uk). For general health info, contact the **American Red Cross** (☎202-303-4498; www.redcross.org).

STAYING HEALTHY

TIP **COMING IN HANDY.** A small bottle of liquid hand cleanser, a stash of moist towelettes, or even a package of baby wipes can keep your hands and face germ-free and refreshed on the road. The hand cleanser should have an alcohol content of at least 70% to be effective.

Common sense is the simplest prescription for good health. Drink water to prevent dehydration and constipation, and wear sturdy, broken-in shoes and clean socks.

For food- and water-borne diseases, prevention is the best cure: be sure your food is properly cooked and that the water you drink is clean. Tap water and fruits and vegetables with the peel on should be safe in most of Europe, especially in Western Europe. In some parts of Southern and Eastern Europe (in particular Moscow and St. Petersburg), avoid tap water and peel fruits and vegetables (including ice cubes and anything washed in tap water, like salad). Watch out for food from markets or street vendors. Buy bottled water, or purify your own water by bringing it to a rolling boil or treating it with **iodine tablets;** note, that some parasites such as *Giardia* have iodine-resistant exteriors, so boiling is more reliable.

Heat exhaustion and heatstroke: Heat exhaustion leads to nausea, excessive thirst, headaches, and dizziness. Avoid it by drinking plenty of fluids, eating salty foods (e.g., crackers), abstaining from dehydrating beverages (e.g., alcohol and caffeine), and wearing sunscreen. Victims should be cooled off with wet towels and taken to a doctor.

Sunburn: Always wear sunscreen (SPF 30 or higher) when spending excessive amounts of time outdoors. If you get sunburned, drink more fluids than usual and apply an aloe-based lotion. Severe sunburns can lead to sun poisoning, a condition that can cause fever, chills, nausea, and vomiting. Sun poisoning should always be treated by a doctor.

Hypothermia: A rapid drop in body temperature is the clearest sign of overexposure to cold. Victims may also shiver, feel exhausted, have poor coordination, slur their speech, hallucinate, or suffer amnesia. *Do not let hypothermia victims fall asleep*. To avoid hypothermia, keep dry, wear layers, and stay out of the wind.

High Altitude: Allow your body a couple of days to adjust to less oxygen before exerting yourself. Note that alcohol is more potent and UV rays are stronger at high elevations.

Tick-borne encephalitis: A viral infection of the central nervous system transmitted during the summer by tick bites (primarily in wooded areas) or by consumption of unpasteurized dairy products. Tick-borne encephalitis has been known to occur in Austria, the Czech Republic, Germany, Hungary, Poland, the former Soviet Union, Switzerland and less frequently in Bulgaria, Romania, and Scandinavia.

Giardiasis: Transmitted through parasites (microbes, tapeworms, etc. in contaminated water and food) and acquired by drinking untreated water from streams or lakes. Symptoms include diarrhea, abdominal cramps, bloating, fatigue, weight loss, and nausea. If untreated it can lead to severe dehydration. Occurs worldwide.

Traveler's diarrhea: Results from drinking fecally contaminated water or eating uncooked and contaminated foods. Symptoms include nausea, bloating, and urgency. Try quick-energy, non-sugary foods with protein and carbohydrates to keep your strength up. Over-the-counter anti-diarrheals (e.g., Imodium®) may counteract the problems. The most dangerous side effect is dehydration; drink 8 oz. of water with ½ tsp. of sugar or honey and a pinch of salt, try uncaffeinated soft drinks, or eat salted crackers. If you develop a fever or your symptoms don't go away after 4-5 days, consult a doctor.

Sexually transmitted infections (STIs): Gonorrhea, chlamydia, HPV, syphilis, herpes, HIV/AIDS, and other STIs are often very difficult to detect and can be extremely serious. If you think you may have contracted an STI, see a doctor immediately.

OTHER HEALTH CONCERNS

MEDICAL CARE ON THE ROAD. While health care systems in Western Europe tend to be quite accessible and of high quality, medical care varies greatly across Eastern and Southern Europe. Major cities such as Prague and Budapest have English-speaking medical centers or hospitals for foreigners. In general, medical service in these regions is not up to Western standards; though basic supplies are usually there, specialized treatment is not. Tourist offices may have names of local doctors who speak English. In a medical emergency, contact your embassy for aid and recommendations. All EU citizens can receive free or reduced-cost first aid and emergency services by presenting a **European Health Insurance Card.**

If you are concerned about obtaining medical assistance while traveling, you may wish to employ special support services. The MedPass from **GlobalCare, Inc.,** 6875 Shiloh Rd. E., Alpharetta, GA 30005, USA (☎800-860-1111; www.globalcare.net), provides 24hr. international medical assistance, support, and medical evacuation resources. The **International Association for Medical Assistance to Travelers (IAMAT;** Canada ☎519-836-0102, US 716-754-4883; www.iamat.org) lists English-speaking doctors worldwide, and offers detailed info on immunizations.

Those with medical conditions (such as diabetes, allergies to antibiotics, or epilepsy) may want to obtain a **MedicAlert** membership (first year US$35, annually thereafter US$20), which includes a stainless steel ID tag and a 24hr. collect-call number. Contact the MedicAlert Foundation, 2323 Colorado Ave., Turlock, CA 95382, USA (US ☎888-633-4298, elsewhere 209-668-3333; www.medicalert.org).

WOMEN'S HEALTH. Women traveling in unsanitary conditions are vulnerable to **urinary tract infections** (including bladder and kidneys). Over-the-counter medicines can alleviate symptoms, but if they persist, see a doctor. **Vaginal yeast infections** may flare up in hot and humid climates. Wearing loosely fitting trousers or a skirt and cotton underwear will help, as will over-the-counter remedies. **Tampons, pads,** and **contraceptive devices** are widely available in most of Western Europe, but they can be hard to find in areas of Eastern Europe—bring supplies with you. **Abortion** laws also vary from country to country. In most of Western Europe, abortion is legal during at least the first 10-12 weeks of pregnancy, but it remains illegal in Ireland, Monaco, Poland, and Portugal, except in extreme circumstances.

KEEPING IN TOUCH

BY EMAIL AND INTERNET

Email is easily accessible in most of Europe. **Internet cafes** and the occasional free Internet terminal at a public library or university are listed in the **Practical Information** sections of major cities, and hostels frequently offer Internet access. For additional cybercafes in Europe, check www.cybercaptive.com or www.world66.com/

netcafeguide. Increasingly, travelers find that taking their **laptops** on the road with them can be a convenient option for staying connected. Laptop users can use Internet cafes that allow them to connect to the Internet via DSL. Travelers with wireless-enabled computers may be able to take advantage of an increasing number of Internet "hot spots," where they can get online for free or for a small fee. Websites like www.jiwire.com, www.wi-fihotspotlist.com, and www.locfinder.net can help you find them.

BY TELEPHONE

PLACING INTERNATIONAL CALLS. All international dialing prefixes and country codes for Europe are shown in a chart inside the back cover of this book. To place international calls, dial:

1. The **international dialing prefix.** To call from **Australia,** dial 0011; **Canada** or the **US,** 011; **Ireland, New Zealand,** or the **UK,** 00.
2. The **country code** of the country you want to call. To call **Australia,** dial 61; **Canada** or the **US,** 1; **Ireland,** 353; **New Zealand,** 64; the **UK,** 44.
3. The **city/area code.** Let's Go lists the city/area codes for cities and towns in Europe opposite the city or town name, next to a ☎. If the 1st digit is a zero, omit it when calling from abroad.
4. The **local number.**

CALLING HOME FROM EUROPE

You can usually make **direct international calls** from pay phones, but if you aren't using a phone card, you may wind up spending more on your call than you will on a bed for the night. **Prepaid phone cards** are a common and relatively inexpensive means of calling abroad. Each one comes with a Personal Identification Number (PIN) and a toll-free access number. To use them, call the access number and then follow the directions for dialing your PIN. To purchase prepaid phone cards, check online for the best rates; www.callingcards.com is a good place to start. Online providers generally send your access number and PIN via email, with no actual "card" involved. Keep in mind that phone cards can be very specific and problematic in Russia, Slovenia, and Ukraine, so buying an international phone card once you arrive will probably save you headaches. You can also call home with prepaid phone cards purchased in Europe (see **Calling Within Europe,** p. 28).

Another option is to purchase a **calling card,** linked to a major national telecommunications service in your home country. Calls are billed collect or to your account. Companies that offer calling cards include: **AT&T Direct** (US ☎800-364-9292; www.att.com); **Canada Direct** (☎800-561-8868; www.infocanadadirect.com); **MCI WorldPhone** (US ☎800-777-5000; http://consumer.mci.com); **Telecom New Zealand Direct** (www.telecom.co.nz); **Telstra Australia** (☎13 22 00; www.telstra.com). To call home with a calling card, contact the local operator for your service provider by dialing the toll-free access number.

Placing a **collect call** through an international operator can be quite expensive, but may be necessary in an emergency. You can frequently call collect without even possessing a company's calling card just by calling its access number.

CALLING WITHIN EUROPE

Many travelers to Europe are opting to buy mobile phones for placing calls within the continent. (For more information on that option, see **Mobile Phones,** below.) Beyond that, perhaps the simplest way to call within a country is to use a public pay phone. Much of Europe has switched to a **prepaid phone card** system, and in some countries you may have a hard time finding any coin-operated phones. Prepaid phone cards, available at newspaper kiosks and tobacco stores, carry a certain amount of phone time depending on the card's denomination and usually save you time and money in the long run. A voice on the phone will tell you how much time you have left on your card. Another kind of prepaid phone card comes with a PIN and an access number. Instead of inserting the card into the phone, you call the access number and follow the directions on the card. These cards can be used to make international as well as domestic calls.

MOBILE PHONES

Mobile phones are an increasingly popular option for travelers calling within Europe. Virtually all of Western Europe has excellent coverage, and the use of the **Global System for Mobiles (GSM)** allows one phone to function in multiple countries. To make and receive calls in Europe, you need a GSM-compatible phone and a **subscriber identity module (SIM) card,** a chip that gives you a local phone number and plugs you into the local network. Buy SIM cards from carriers in any European country. Some companies lock their phones to prevent switches to competitor carriers, so inquire about using the phone in other countries. Phones in Europe cost US$30-80, and instead of requiring a service contract, they often run on prepaid minutes that are easily purchased in many locations. Incoming calls are frequently free. American cell phones usually do not work in Europe. For more information on GSM phones, check out www.telestial.com, www.vodafone.com, www.orange.co.uk, www.roadpost.com, www.t-mobile.com, or www.planetomni.com. Companies like **Cellular Abroad** (www.cellularabroad.com) and **Telestial** (www.telestial.com) rent phones that work in destinations around the world, providing a simpler option than picking up a phone in-country.

TIME DIFFERENCES

All of Europe falls within 3hr. of Greenwich Mean Time (GMT). For more info, consult the time zone chart on the inside back cover. GMT is 5hr. ahead of New York time, 8hr. ahead of San Francisco time, 10hr. behind Sydney time, and 12hr. behind Auckland time. Iceland is the only country in Europe to ignore Daylight Saving Time; fall and spring switchover times vary in countries that do observe Daylight Saving. A good source of information is www.worldtimeserver.com.

BY MAIL

SENDING MAIL HOME

Airmail is the best way to send mail home from Europe. From Western Europe to North America, delivery time averages about seven days; from Central or Eastern Europe, allow from seven days to three weeks. **Aerogrammes,** printed sheets that fold into envelopes and travel via airmail, are available at post offices and are the cheapest types of mail. Write "par avion" (or *por avión, mit Luftpost, via aerea,* etc.) on the front. **Surface mail** is the cheapest and slowest post option. It takes one to two months to cross the Atlantic and one to three to cross the Pacific. Check the beginning of each chapter for country-specific info.

RECEIVING MAIL IN EUROPE

To send mail abroad from home, mark envelopes "airmail" in both English and the local language; otherwise, your letter may never arrive. In addition to the standard postage systems, Federal Express (Australia ☎13 26 10, Canada and US 800-463-

3339, Ireland 1800 535 800, New Zealand 0800 733 339, UK 0800 123 800; www.fedex.com) handles express mail services from most countries to Europe.

There are several ways to arrange pick-up of letters sent to you by friends and relatives while you are abroad. Mail can be sent via **Poste Restante** (General Delivery; *Lista de Correos*, *Fermo Posta*, *Postlagernde Briefe*, etc.) to almost any city or town in Europe with a post office, though it can be unreliable in Eastern Europe. See individual country chapters to find out how to address *Poste Restante* letters. The mail will go to a desk in the central post office, unless you specify a post office by street address or Postal Code. It's best to use the largest post office, as mail may be sent there regardless. It is usually safer and quicker, though more expensive, to send mail express or registered. Bring your passport (or other photo ID) for pick-up; there may be a small fee. If the clerks insist that there is nothing for you, have them check under your first name as well. Let's Go lists post offices in the **Practical Information** section for most towns. **American Express's** offices throughout the world offer a free **Client Letter Service** (mail held up to 30 days and forwarded upon request) for cardholders who contact them in advance. Let's Go lists AmEx locations for large cities in **Practical Information** sections; for a complete list, call ☎800-528-4800 or visit www.americanexpress.com/travel.

ACCOMMODATIONS

HOSTELS

In the summer, Europe is overrun by young budget travelers drawn to hostels' low prices and communal spaces. Many hostels are dorm-style, with bunk beds in large single-sex or coed rooms, although smaller rooms are becoming more common. Some have kitchens, bike rentals, storage areas, transport to airports, breakfast and other meals, laundry facilities, and Internet access. There can be drawbacks: some hostels close for daytime "lockout" hours, have a curfew, don't accept reservations, or impose a maximum stay. In Western and Eastern Europe, a hostel bed will average around US$15-30 and US$5-20, respectively, and a private room around US$30 and US$20. Websites include www.hostels.com, www.hostelplanet.com, www.youth-hostels-in.com, and www.hostelseurope.com.

HOSTELLING INTERNATIONAL

Joining the youth hostel association in your own country (listed below) automatically grants you membership privileges in **Hostelling International (HI),** a federation of national hosteling associations. HI hostels are extremely common throughout Western Europe and in most major Eastern European cities. Non-HI members are often allowed to stay in HI hostels, but will have to pay extra to do so. When determining whether or not to purchase an HI membership, take into account how many nights you plan on staying in HI hostels, then factor in the typical 10-15% HI discount. Travelers planning to spend several weeks in Europe often find the initial investment pays off. HI's umbrella organization's website (www.hihostels.com) can be a great place to begin researching hosteling in a specific region.

Most HI hostels also honor **guest memberships**—you'll get a blank card with space for six stamps. Each night you'll pay a non-member supplement (one-sixth the membership fee) and earn one stamp; get six stamps, and you're a member. This system works well in most of Western Europe, but in some countries you may need to remind the hostel reception. A new membership benefit is the FreeNites program, which allows hostelers to gain points toward free rooms. Most travel agencies sell HI cards, as do all of the hosteling organizations listed below. All prices listed are valid for individual **one-year memberships.**

Australian Youth Hostels Association (AYHA), 422 Kent St., Sydney, NSW 200 (☎02 9261 1111; www.yha.com.au). AUS$52, under 18 AUS$19.

Hostelling International-Canada (HI-C), 205 Catherine St. #400, Ottawa, ON K2P 1C3 (☎613-237-7884; www.hihostels.ca). CAN$35, under 18 free.

An Óige (Irish Youth Hostel Association), 61 Mountjoy St., Dublin 7 (☎830 4555; www.irelandyha.org). EUR€20, under 18 EUR€10.

Hostelling International Northern Ireland (HINI), 22-32 Donegall Rd., Belfast BT12 5JN (☎02890 32 47 33; www.hini.org.uk). UK£13, under 18 UK£6.

Youth Hostels Association of New Zealand (YHANZ), Level 1, Moorhouse City, 166 Moorhouse Ave., P.O. Box 436, Christchurch (NZ ☎0800 278 299 or 03 379 9970; www.yha.org.nz). NZ$40, under 18 free.

Scottish Youth Hostels Association (SYHA), 7 Glebe Cres., Stirling FK8 2JA (☎01786 89 14 00; www.syha.org.uk). UK£6, under 17 £2.50.

Youth Hostels Association (England and Wales), Trevelyan House, Dimple Rd., Matlock, Derbyshire DE4 3YH (☎08707 708 868; www.yha.org.uk). UK£15.50, under 26 UK£10.

Hostelling International-USA, 8401 Colesville Rd., Ste. 600, Silver Spring, MD 20910 (☎301-495-1240; www.hiayh.org). US$28, under 18 free.

BOOKING HOSTELS ONLINE. One of the easiest ways to ensure you've got a bed for the night is by reserving online. Click to the **Hostelworld** booking engine through **www.letsgo.com,** and you'll have access to bargain accommodations from Argentina to Zimbabwe with no added commission.

OTHER TYPES OF ACCOMMODATIONS

HOTELS, GUESTHOUSES, AND PENSIONS

In Western Europe, **hotels** generally start at a hefty US$30 per person. For couples and larger groups, however, hotels can be a more reasonable option. You'll typically share a hall bathroom; private bathrooms cost extra, as may hot showers. Some hotels offer "full pension" (all meals) and "half pension" (no lunch). Smaller **guesthouses** and **pensions** are often cheaper than hotels. If you make **reservations** in writing, indicate your day of arrival and the length of your stay. The hotel will send you a confirmation and may request payment for the first night. Often it is easiest to make reservations over the phone with a credit card.

BED & BREAKFASTS (B&BS)

For a cozy alternative to impersonal hotel rooms, B&Bs (private homes with rooms available to travelers) range from acceptable to sublime. B&Bs are particularly popular in Britain and Ireland, where rooms average UK£20/€35 per person. For more information, check out **InnFinder** (www.inncrawler.com), **InnSite** (www.innsite.com), or **BedandBreakfast.com** (www.bedandbreakfast.com).

PRIVATE ROOMS

In much of Eastern Europe, due to a lack of budget travel infrastructure, the only accommodations in a backpacker's price range are rooms in private houses or apartments. Owners seek out tourists at the train or bus stations; tourist offices are also a source for finding a room. In larger towns and cities there are agencies that book private rooms. If renting directly from the owner, feel free to negotiate prices, and don't agree to anything before you see the room. This practice is illegal in some areas; check local laws before you rent a private room.

UNIVERSITY DORMS

Many **universities** open their residence halls to travelers when school is not in session. Getting a room may take a couple of phone calls and require advance planning, but rates tend to be low and many offer free Internet access. Where available, university dorms are listed in the **Accommodations** section of each city.

HOME EXCHANGES AND HOSPITALITY CLUBS

Home exchange offers accommodation in various types of homes (houses, apartments, condominiums, villas, and even castles in some cases), plus the opportunity to live like a native and save money. Contact Intervac International Home Exchange (http://intervac-online.com) or HomeExchange.com, P.O. Box 787, Hermosa Beach, CA 90254, USA (☎800-877-8723; www.homeexchange.com).

Hospitality clubs link their members with people abroad willing to host travelers for free or for a small fee to promote cultural exchange and general good karma. In exchange, members usually must be willing to host travelers in their own homes; a small membership fee may also be required. **The Hospitality Club** (www.hospitality-club.org) and **GlobalFreeloaders.com** (www.globalfreeloaders.com) are good places to start. **Servas** (www.servas.org) is an established, more formal organization that requires a fee and an interview. Similar organizations cater to special interests (e.g., women, GLBT travelers, members of certain professions). As always, use common sense when planning to stay with or host someone you do not know.

LONG-TERM ACCOMMODATIONS

Travelers planning to stay in Europe for extended periods of time may find it most cost-effective to rent an **apartment.** Rents vary widely by region, season, and quality. Generally, for stays shorter than three months, it is more feasible to **sublet** than lease your own apartment. Out of session, it may be possible to arrange to sublet rooms from university students on summer break. It is far easier to find an apartment once you have arrived at your destination than to attempt to use the Internet or phone from home, though www.craigslist.org can be helpful for major cities. By staying in a hostel for your first week or so, you can make local contacts and, more importantly, check out your new digs before you commit.

THE GREAT OUTDOORS

Camping can be a great way to see Europe on the cheap. There are organized **campgrounds** outside most cities. Showers, bathrooms, and a store are common; some sites have more elaborate facilities. Prices are low, usually US$5-15 per person plus additional charges for tents and cars. While camping is a cheaper option than hosteling, the cost of transportation to and from campgrounds can add up. Some parks and public grounds allow **free camping,** but check local laws. The **Great Outdoor Recreation Pages** (www.gorp.com) provides excellent general info.

USEFUL RESOURCES

A variety of publishing companies offer hiking guidebooks to meet the educational needs of the novice or the expert. For information about biking, camping, and hiking, write or call the publishers listed below to receive a free catalog. Campers heading to Europe should consider buying an **International Camping Carnet.** Similar to a hostel membership card, it's required at a few campgrounds and provides discounts at others. It is available in North America from the **Family Campers and RVers Association** (www.fcrv.org) and in the UK from **The Caravan Club** (see below).

LEAVE NO TRACE. Let's Go encourages travelers to embrace the "Leave No Trace" ethic, minimizing their impact on natural environments. Trekkers should set up camp on durable surfaces, use cookstoves instead of campfires, bury human waste away from water supplies, bag trash and carry it out with them, and respect wildlife and natural objects. For more detailed information, contact the **Leave No Trace Center for Outdoor Ethics,** P.O. Box 997, Boulder, CO 80306 (☎800-332-4100 or 303-442-8222; www.lnt.org).

Automobile Association, Contact Centre, Carr Ellison House, William Armstrong Dr., Newcastle-upon-Tyne NE4 7YA, UK (☎08706 000 371; www.theaa.com). Publishes *Caravan and Camping Europe* and *Britain & Ireland* (UK£10) as well as road atlases for Europe as a whole and for Britain, France, Germany, Ireland, Italy, and Spain.

The Caravan Club, East Grinstead House, East Grinstead, West Sussex RH19 1UA, UK (☎01342 326 944; www.caravanclub.co.uk). For UK£32, members get access to campgrounds, insurance services, equipment discounts, maps, and a magazine.

Sierra Club Books, 85 2nd St., 2nd fl., San Francisco, CA 94105, USA (☎415-977-5500; www.sierraclub.org). Publishes general resource books on hiking and camping.

The Mountaineers Books, 1001 SW Klickitat Way, Ste. 201, Seattle, WA 98134, USA (☎206-223-6303; www.mountaineersbooks.org). Over 600 titles on hiking, biking, mountaineering, natural history, and conservation.

WILDERNESS SAFETY

Staying **warm, dry,** and **well hydrated** are the keys to a happy and safe wilderness experience. Before any hike, prepare yourself for an emergency by packing a first-aid kit, a reflector, a whistle, high-energy food, extra water, raingear, a hat, mittens, and several **extra pairs of socks.** For warmth, wear wool or insulating synthetic materials designed for the outdoors. Cotton is a bad choice as it takes a ridiculously long time to dry and loses its insulating effect when wet.

Check **weather forecasts** often and pay attention to the skies when hiking, as weather patterns can change suddenly, especially in mountainous areas. Always let someone—a friend, your hostel staff, a park ranger, or a local hiking organization—know when and where you are going. Know your physical limits and do not attempt a hike beyond your ability.

CAMPING AND HIKING EQUIPMENT

WHAT TO BUY

Good camping equipment is both sturdy and light. North American suppliers tend to offer the most competitive prices.

Sleeping Bags: Most sleeping bags are rated by season; "summer" means 30-40°F (around 0°C) at night; "four-season" or "winter" often means below 0°F (-17°C). Bags are made of **down** (warm and light, but expensive, and miserable when wet) or of **synthetic** material (heavy, durable, and warm when wet). Prices range US$50-250 for a summer synthetic and US$200-300 for a good down winter bag.

Tents: The best tents are free-standing (with their own frames and suspension systems), set up quickly, and only require staking in high winds. Low-profile dome tents are the best all-around. 2-person tents start at US$100, 4-person tents US$160. Make sure your tent has a rain fly and seal its seams with waterproofer. Other useful accessories include a **battery-operated lantern,** a plastic **groundcloth,** and a nylon **tarp.**

Backpacks: Internal-frame packs mold to your back, keep a lower center of gravity, and flex to allow you to hike difficult trails, while **external-frame packs** are more comfortable for long hikes over even terrain, as they carry weight higher and distribute it more evenly. Make sure your pack has a hip-belt to transfer weight to your legs. Any serious backpacking requires a pack of at least 4000 cu. in. (16,000cc), plus 500 cu. in. for sleeping bags in internal-frame packs. Sturdy backpacks cost anywhere from US$125 to 420—your pack is an area where it doesn't pay to economize. On your hunt for the perfect pack, fill up each prospective model with something heavy, strap it on, and walk around the store to get a sense of how the model distributes weight. Either buy a **rain cover** (US$10-20) or store your belongings in plastic bags inside your pack.

Boots: Be sure to wear hiking boots with good **ankle support.** They should fit snugly and comfortably over 1-2 pairs of **wool socks** and a pair of thin **liner socks.** Break in boots over several weeks before you go to spare yourself from blisters.

Other Necessities: Synthetic layers, like those made of polypropylene or polyester, and a pile jacket will keep you warm even when wet. A **space blanket** (US$5-15) will help you to retain body heat, and doubles as a groundcloth. Plastic **water bottles** are vital; look for shatter- and leak-resistant models. Carry **water-purification tablets** for when you can't boil water. Virtually every organized campground in Europe forbids fires or the gathering of firewood, so you'll need a **camp stove** (the classic Coleman starts at US$50) and a propane-filled **fuel bottle** to operate it. Also bring a **first-aid kit, pocket-knife, insect repellent,** and **waterproof matches** or a **lighter.**

WHERE TO BUY IT

The online and mail-order companies listed below offer lower prices than many retail stores. A visit to a local camping or outdoors store will give you a good sense of the look and weight of certain items before you buy.

Campmor, 28 Parkway, P.O. Box 700, Upper Saddle River, NJ 07458, USA (☎800-525-4784; www.campmor.com).

Cotswold Outdoor, Unit 11 Kemble Business Park, Crudwell, Malmesbury Wiltshire SN16 9SH, UK (☎08704 427 755; www.cotswoldoutdoor.com).

Discount Camping, 880 Main North Rd., Pooraka, SA 5095, Australia (☎08 8262 3399; www.discountcamping.com.au).

Eastern Mountain Sports (EMS), 1 Vose Farm Rd., Peterborough, NH 03458, USA (☎888-463-6367; www.ems.com).

Gear-Zone, 8 Burnet Rd., Sweetbriar Rd. Industrial Estate, Norwich NR3 2BS, UK (☎1603 410 108; www.gear-zone.co.uk).

L.L. Bean, Freeport, ME 04033, USA (Canada and the US ☎800-441-5713, UK 0800 891 297; www.llbean.com).

Mountain Designs, 443A Nudgee Rd., Hendra, QLD 4011, Australia (☎07 3856 2344; www.mountaindesigns.com).

Recreational Equipment, Inc. (REI), Sumner, WA 98352, USA (Canada and the US ☎800-426-4840, elsewhere 253-891-2500; www.rei.com).

ORGANIZED ADVENTURE TRIPS

Organized adventure tours offer another way of exploring the wild. Activities include hiking, biking, skiing, canoeing, kayaking, rafting, climbing, photo safaris, and archaeological digs. Organizations that specialize in camping and outdoor equipment like REI and EMS (see above) are also a good source for info. **Specialty Travel Index** lists organized tour opportunities throughout Europe (from the US ☎888-624-4030, from elsewhere 415-455-1643; www.specialtytravel.com.)

SPECIFIC CONCERNS

SUSTAINABLE TRAVEL

As the number of travelers on the road continues to rise, the detrimental effect they can have on natural environments becomes an increasing concern. With this in mind, Let's Go promotes the philosophy of **sustainable travel.** Through a sensitivity to issues of ecology and sustainability, today's travelers can be a powerful force in preserving as well as restoring the places they visit.

Ecotourism focuses on conserving natural habitats and using them to build up the economy without exploitation or overdevelopment. Travelers can make a difference by doing advance research and by supporting organizations and establishments that pay attention to their impact on their natural surroundings and strive to be environmentally friendly. Delicate ecosystems like coastal and marine areas, riverbanks, islands, mountain ranges and watersheds receive the most attention from conservationists, and travelers should approach these areas with particular care. **International Friends of Nature** (www.nfi.at) has info about sustainable travel options in Europe. For more information, see **Beyond Tourism,** p. 61.

ECOTOURISM RESOURCES. For more information on environmentally responsible tourism, contact one of the organizations below:

Conservation International, 1919 M St., NW, Ste. 600, Washington, D.C. 20036, USA (☎800-406-2306 or 202-912-1000; www.conservation.org).

Green Globe 21 (☎61 2 6257 9102; www.greenglobe.com).

International Ecotourism Society, 733 15th St., NW, Ste. 1000, Washington, D.C. 20005, USA (☎202-347-9203; www.ecotourism.org).

United Nations Environment Program (UNEP), 39-43 Quai André Citroën, 75739 Paris 15, France (☎33 1 44 37 14 50; www.uneptie.org/pc/tourism).

RESPONSIBLE TRAVEL

The impact of tourist money on the destinations you visit should not be underestimated. The choices you make during your trip can have potent effects on local communities—for better or for worse. Travelers who care about the destinations they explore should become aware of the social, cultural, and political implications of the choices they make when they travel. **Community-based tourism** aims to channel tourist money into the local economy by emphasizing tours and cultural programs run by members of the host community and that often benefit disadvantaged groups. These tours often take travelers beyond the traditional attractions, benefiting the visitors as well as the locals. An excellent resource for general information on community-based travel is *The Ethical Travel Guide* (UK£13), a project of **Tourism Concern** (☎44 020 7133 3330; www.tourismconcern.org.uk).

TRAVELING ALONE

Benefits to traveling alone include independence and a greater opportunity to connect with locals. However, solo travelers are more vulnerable targets of harassment and street theft. If traveling alone, look confident, try not to stand out as a tourist, and be careful in deserted or crowded areas. Avoid poorly lit areas. If questioned, never admit that you are traveling alone. Maintain regular contact with someone at home who knows your itinerary, and always research your destination before traveling. For more tips, pick up *Traveling Solo* by Eleanor Berman

(Globe Pequot Press, US$18), visit www.travelaloneandloveit.com, or subscribe to **Connecting: Solo Travel Network,** 689 Park Rd., Unit 6, Gibsons, BC V0N 1V7, Canada (☎604-886-9099; www.cstn.org; membership US$30-48).

WOMEN TRAVELERS

Women traveling on their own face some additional safety concerns, but it's easy to be adventurous without taking undue risks. If you are concerned, consider staying in hostels that offer single rooms that lock from the inside or rooms for women only. Stick to centrally located accommodations and avoid solitary late-night treks or metro rides. Always carry extra money for a phone call, bus, or taxi. **Hitchhiking** is never safe for lone women, or even for two women traveling together. Look as if you know where you're going, and approach older women or couples for directions if you're lost or uncomfortable. Generally, the less you look like a tourist, the better off you'll be. Dress modestly, especially in rural areas. Wearing a conspicuous **wedding band** sometimes helps prevent unwanted advances.

Your best answer to verbal harassment is no answer at all; feigning deafness, pretending you don't understand the language, or staring straight ahead will usually do the trick. The extremely persistent can sometimes be dissuaded by a firm, loud "Go away!" in the appropriate language. Seek out a police officer or a passerby if you are being harassed. Memorize the emergency numbers in places you visit, and consider carrying a whistle on your keychain. A self-defense course will both prepare you for a potential attack and raise your level of awareness (see **Self Defense,** p. 25).

GLBT TRAVELERS

Attitudes toward gay, lesbian, bisexual, and transgendered (GLBT) travelers are particular to each region in Europe. On the whole, countries in Northern and Western Europe tend to be queer-friendly, while Eastern Europe harbors enclaves of tolerance in cities amid stretches of cultural conservatism. Countries like Romania that outlawed homosexuality as recently as 2002 are becoming more liberal today, and can be considered viable destinations for GLBT travelers. **Out and About** (www.planetout.com) has a newsletter and website addressing gay travel concerns. The online newspaper **365gay.com** (www.365gay.com/travel/travelchannel.htm) has a travel section, while the French-language site **netgai.com** (http://netgai.com/international/Europe) includes links to country-specific resources.

Gay's the Word, 66 Marchmont St., London WC1N 1AB, UK (☎020 7278 7654; http://freespace.virgin.net/gays.theword/). The largest gay and lesbian bookshop in the UK, with both fiction and non-fiction titles. Mail-order service available.

Giovanni's Room, 345 S. 12th St., Philadelphia, PA 19107, USA (☎215-923-2960; www.queerbooks.com). An international lesbian and gay bookstore with mail-order service (carries some of the publications listed below).

International Lesbian and Gay Association (ILGA), Avenue des Villas 34, 1060 Brussels, BEL (☎32 2 502 2471; www.ilga.org). Provides political information, such as homosexuality laws of individual countries.

TRAVELERS WITH DISABILITIES

European countries vary in accessibility to travelers with disabilities. Some tourist boards, particularly in Western and Northern Europe, provide directories on the accessibility of various accommodations and transportation services. If these services are not available, contact establishments directly. Be sure to inform airlines and hostels of any pertinent disabilities when making reservations; some time may

ADDITIONAL RESOURCES.

Spartacus International Gay Guide 2006. Bruno Gmunder Verlag and Briand Bedford (US$33).

The Damron Men's Travel Guide 2006. Gina M. Gatta, Damron Co. (US$20).

The Gay Vacation Guide: The Best Trips and How to Plan Them. Mark Chesnut, Kensington Books (US$15).

be needed to prepare special accommodations. **Guide dog owners** should inquire as to the quarantine policies of each destination country.

Rail is the most convenient form of travel for disabled travelers in Europe: many stations have ramps, and some trains have wheelchair lifts, special seating areas, and special toilets. All Eurostar, some InterCity (IC), and some EuroCity (EC) trains are wheelchair accessible. CityNightLine trains, French TGV (high speed), and Conrail trains feature special compartments. In general, the countries with the most **wheelchair-accessible rail networks** are: Denmark (IC and Lyn trains), France (TGVs and other long-distance trains), Germany (ICE, EC, IC, and IR trains), Ireland (most major trains), Italy (EC and IC trains), the Netherlands (most trains), Sweden (X2000s, most IC and IR trains), and Switzerland (all IC, most EC, and some regional trains). Austria, Poland, and the UK offer accessibility on selected routes. Bulgaria, the Czech Republic, Greece, Hungary, Slovakia, and Spain's rail systems have limited wheelchair accessibility. For those who wish to rent cars, some major **car rental** agencies (e.g., Hertz) offer hand-controlled vehicles.

USEFUL ORGANIZATIONS

Access Abroad, www.umabroad.umn.edu/access. A website devoted to making study abroad available to students with disabilities. The site is maintained by Disability Services, University of Minnesota, 230 Heller Hall, 271 19th Ave. S., Minneapolis, MN 55455, USA (☎612-626-7379).

Accessible Journeys, 35 W. Sellers Ave., Ridley Park, PA 19078, USA (☎800-846-4537; www.disabilitytravel.com). Designs tours for wheelchair users and slow walkers. The site has tips and forums for all travelers.

Flying Wheels, 143 W. Bridge St., P.O. Box 382, Owatonna, MN 55060, USA (☎507-451-5005; www.flyingwheelstravel.com). Specializes in escorted trips to Europe for people with physical disabilities; plans custom trips worldwide.

The Guided Tour, Inc., 7900 Old York Rd., Ste. 114B, Elkins Park, PA 19027, USA (☎800-783-5841; www.guidedtour.com). Organizes travel programs for persons with developmental and physical challenges in Ireland, Italy, Spain, and the UK.

Society for Accessible Travel and Hospitality (SATH), 347 5th Ave., Ste. 610, New York, NY 10016, USA (☎212-447-7284; www.sath.org). An advocacy group that publishes free online travel information and the travel magazine *Open World* (annual subscription US$13, free for members). Annual membership US$45, students and seniors US$30.

MINORITY TRAVELERS

In general, minority travelers will find a high level of tolerance in large cities; small towns and the countryside are less predictable. The increasingly mainstream reality of anti-immigrant sentiments means that travelers of African or Arab descent (regardless of their citizenship) may be the object of unwarranted assumptions and even hostility. The September 11 terrorist attacks on the United States and the July 7 attacks on the London Tube corresponded with an upsurge in anti-Muslim sentiments in Europe, while anti-Semitism also remains a very real problem in many countries, especially in France, Germany, and much of Eastern Europe. Jews, Muslims, and other minority travelers should keep an eye out for skinheads, who have been linked to racist violence in Central and Eastern Europe, and elsewhere. **The European Monitoring Centre on Racism and Xenophobia,** Rahlgasse 3, 1060 Vienna, AUT (☎43 15 80 30; http://eumc.eu.int), publishes a wealth of country-specific statistics and reports. Travelers can also consult **United for Intercultural Action,** Postbus 413, 1000 AK, Amsterdam, NTH (☎31 20 6834778; www.unitedagainstracism.org), for a list of over 500 country-specific organizations that work against racism and discrimination. For educational resources, contact **Youth United Against Racism in Europe,** P.O. Box 858, London, E11 1YG, UK (☎020 8558 7947).

DIETARY CONCERNS

Vegetarians will find no shortage of meat-free dining options throughout most of Northern and Western Europe, although **vegans** may have a trickier time away from urban centers, where eggs and dairy can dominate traditional cuisine. The cuisine of Eastern Europe still tends to be heavy on meat and gravy, although major cities often boast surprisingly inventive vegetarian and ethnic fare.

The travel section of The Vegetarian Resource Group's website, at www.vrg.org/travel, has a comprehensive list of organizations and websites that are geared toward helping vegetarians and vegans traveling abroad. The website for the **European Vegetarian Union (EVU),** at www.europeanvegetarian.org, includes links to organizations in 26 European countries. For more information, consult *The Vegetarian Traveler: Where to Stay if You're Vegetarian, Vegan, Environmentally Sensitive*, by Jed and Susan Civic (Larson Publications; US$16), *Vegetarian Europe*, by Alex Bourke (Vegetarian Guides; US$17), and the indispensably multilingual *Vegan Passport* (The Vegan Society; US$5), along with the websites www.vegdining.com, www.happycow.net, and www.vegetariansabroad.com.

Those looking to keep **kosher** will find abundant dining options across Europe; contact synagogues in larger cities for information, or consult www.kashrut.com/travel/Europe for country-specific resources. Hebrew College Online also offers a searchable database of kosher restaurants at www.shamash.org/kosher. Another good resource is the *Jewish Travel Guide*, edited by Michael Zaidner (Vallentine Mitchell; US$18). Travelers looking for **halal** groceries and restaurants will have the most success in France and Eastern European nations with substantial Muslim populations; consult www.zabihah.com for establishment reviews. Keep in mind that if you are strict in your observance, you may have to prepare your own food.

OTHER RESOURCES

USEFUL PUBLICATIONS

Let's Go tries to cover all aspects of budget travel, but we can't put *everything* in our guides. Listed below are books and websites that can serve as jumping-off points for your own research.

TRAVEL PUBLISHERS AND BOOKSTORES

The Globe Corner Bookstore, 90 Mt. Auburn St., Cambridge, MA 02138 (☎617-492-6277; www.globecorner.com). The Globe Corner sponsors an Adventure Travel Lecture Series and carries a vast selection of guides and maps to every imaginable destination. Online catalog also includes atlases and staff picks of outstanding travel writing.

Hippocrene Books, 171 Madison Ave., New York, NY 10016 (☎212-454-2366; www.hippocrenebooks.com), publishes foreign-language dictionaries and learning guides, along with ethnic cookbooks and a smattering of guidebooks.

Rand McNally, 8255 N. Central Park, Skokie, IL 60076 (☎800-275-7263, outside the US 847-329-6656; www.randmcnally.com), sells its own country maps (US$10), along with maps from well-respected companies including Michelin, PopOut, and StreetWise.

WORLD WIDE WEB

Almost every aspect of budget travel is accessible via the web. In 10min. at the keyboard, you can make a hostel reservation, get advice on travel hot spots from other intrepid travelers, or find out how much a train ride from Geneva to Nice costs. Listed here are some regional and travel-related sites to start off your surfing; other relevant websites are listed throughout the book. Because website turnover is high, use search engines (e.g., www.google.com) to strike out on your own.

WWW.LETSGO.COM. Let's Go's website features valuable information and advice, including excerpts from all our guides and monthly features on new hot spots in the most popular destinations. In addition to our online bookstore, we have great deals on everything from airfares to mobile phones. Our resources section is full of information you'll need before you hit the road, and our forums are buzzing with advice from other travelers. Check back often for frequent updates, exciting new tips, and prize giveaways. See you soon!

Backpacker's Ultimate Guide: www.bugeurope.com. Tips on packing, transportation, and where to go. Tons of country-specific travel information.

BootsnAll.com: www.bootsnall.com. Numerous resources for independent travelers, from planning your trip to reporting on it when you get back.

How to See the World: www.artoftravel.com. A compendium of great travel tips, from cheap flights to self defense to interacting with local culture.

Travel Intelligence: www.travelintelligence.net. A large collection of travel writing by distinguished travel writers.

Travel Library: www.travel-library.com. A fantastic set of links for general information and personal travelogues.

World Hum: www.worldhum.com. An independently produced collection of "travel dispatches from a shrinking planet."

INFORMATION ON EUROPE

BBC News: http://news.bbc.co.uk/europe. The latest coverage from one of Europe's most reputable sources for English-language news, for free.

CIA World Factbook: www.odci.gov/cia/publications/factbook. An indispensable source of hard info on countries' geography, governments, economies, and people.

EUROPA: http://europa.eu.int/index_en.htm. English-language gateway to the European Union, featuring news articles and a citizen's guide to EU institutions.

TRANSPORTATION

GETTING TO EUROPE

BY PLANE

When it comes to airfare, a little effort can save you a bundle. Courier fares are cheap, but they require flexibility to deal with the restrictions. Tickets bought from consolidators and standby seating are also good deals, but last-minute specials, airfare wars, and charter flights often beat these fares. The best strategy is to hunt around, be flexible, and ask persistently about discounts. Students and seniors should never pay full price for a ticket.

AIRFARES

Airfares to Europe peak between mid-June and early September; holidays are also expensive. The cheapest times to travel are November to mid-December and early January to March. Midweek (M-Th morning) round-trip flights run US$50-100 cheaper than weekend flights, but they are generally more crowded and less likely to permit frequent-flier upgrades. Not fixing a return date ("open return") or arriving in and departing from different cities ("open jaw") can be pricier than buying a round-trip flight. Flights between Europe's capitals or regional hubs (Amsterdam, London, Paris, Prague, Warsaw, Zürich) will tend to be cheaper.

If your European destinations are part of a more extensive globe-hop, consider a round-the-world (RTW) ticket. Tickets usually include at least five stops and are valid for about a year; prices range US$1200-5000. Try **Northwest Airlines/KLM** (☎800-225-2525; www.nwa.com) or **Star Alliance** (www.staralliance.com), a consortium of 16 airlines including United.

Fares for round-trip flights to European hubs from the Canadian or US east coast cost US$600-1000 in the high season and US$250-400 in the low season; from the west coast US$800-1000/400-500; from the UK to the continent, UK£50-100; from Australia AUS$2100-2400/1700-2300; from New Zealand NZ$1800-2200/1500-1800.

BUDGET AND STUDENT TRAVEL AGENCIES

While agents specializing in flights to Europe can make your life easy, they may not spend the time to find you the lowest possible fare—they get paid on commission. Travelers holding **ISICs** and **IYTCs** (p. 17) qualify for big discounts from student travel agencies. Most flights from budget agencies are on major airlines, but in peak season some may sell seats on less reliable chartered aircraft.

STA Travel, 5900 Wilshire Blvd., Ste. 900, Los Angeles, CA, 90036, USA (24hr. info and reservations ☎800-781-4040; www.sta-travel.com). A student and youth travel organization with over 150 offices worldwide (check their website for a listing of all their offices), including US offices in Boston, Chicago, L.A., New York, San Francisco, Seattle, and Washington, D.C. Ticket booking, travel insurance, railpasses, and more. Walk-in offices are located throughout Australia (☎03 9349 4344), New Zealand (☎09 309 9723), and the UK (☎08701 600 599).

Travel CUTS (Canadian Universities Travel Services Limited), 187 College St., Toronto, ON, M5T 1P7, CAN (☎800-592-2887; www.travelcuts.com). Offices across Canada and the US including Los Angeles, New York, San Francisco, and Seattle.

FLIGHT PLANNING ON THE INTERNET. The Internet may be the budget traveler's dream when it comes to finding and booking bargain fares, but the array of options can be overwhelming. Many airline sites offer special last-minute deals online, though some require membership logins or email subscriptions. Try www.airfrance.com, www.britishairways.com, www.icelandair.com, and www.lufthansa.de. For great links to practically every airline in every country, see www.travelpage.com. **STA** (www.sta-travel.com) and **StudentUniverse** (www.studentuniverse.com) provide quotes on student tickets, while **Expedia** (www.expedia.com), **Opodo** (www.opodo.com), **Orbitz** (www.orbitz.com), and **Travelocity** (www.travelocity.com) offer full travel services. **Priceline** (www.priceline.com) lets you specify a price, and obligates you to buy any ticket that meets or beats it; **Hotwire** (www.hotwire.com) offers bargain fares but won't reveal the airline or flight times until you buy. Other sites that compile deals include www.bestfares.com, www.flights.com, www.lowestfare.com, www.onetravel.com, and www.travelzoo.com. There are tools available to sift through multiple offers; **Booking Buddy** (www.bookingbuddy.com) and **SideStep** (www.sidestep.com) let you enter your trip information once and search multiple sites. An indispensable resource is the **Air Traveler's Handbook** (www.faqs.org/faqs/travel/air/handbook), a comprehensive listing of everything you should know before boarding a plane.

TRANSPORTATION

USIT, 19-21 Aston Quay, Dublin, 2, IRE (☎01 602 1904; www.usit.ie), Ireland's leading student/budget travel agency has 20 offices throughout Northern Ireland and the Republic of Ireland. Arranges work, study, and volunteer opportunities worldwide.

Wasteels, Skoubogade 6, 1158 Copenhagen K., DEN (☎3314 4633; www.wasteels.com). A huge chain with 180 locations across Europe. Sells Wasteels BIJ tickets discounted 30-45% off regular fare, 2nd-class international point-to-point train tickets with unlimited stopovers for those under 26 (sold only in Europe).

COMMERCIAL AIRLINES

Commercial airlines' lowest regular offer is the **APEX** (Advance Purchase Excursion) fare, which provides confirmed reservations and allows "open-jaw" tickets. Generally, reservations must be made seven to 21 days ahead of departure, with seven- to 14-day minimum stay and 90-day maximum stay restrictions. These fares carry hefty cancellation and change penalties (fees rise in summer). Reserve peak-season APEX fares early. Use **Expedia** or **Travelocity** to get an idea of the lowest published fares, then use the resources listed here to try to beat those fares.

TRAVELING FROM NORTH AMERICA

Basic round-trip fares to Europe range roughly US$200-750: to Frankfurt, US$350-750; London, US$250-550; Paris, US$300-700. Standard commercial carriers like **American** (☎800-433-7300; www.aa.com), **Northwest/KLM** (☎800-447-4747; www.nwa.com), and **United** (☎800-538-2929; www.ual.com) will probably offer the most convenient flights, but they may not be the cheapest. Check **Air France** (☎800-237-2747; www.airfrance.us), **Alitalia** (☎800-223-5730; www.alitaliausa.com), **British Airways** (☎800-247-9297; www.britishairways.com), and **Lufthansa** (☎800-399-5838; www.lufthansa.com) for cheap tickets from destinations throughout the US to all over Europe. You might find an even better deal on one of the following airlines, if any of their limited departure points are convenient for you.

Icelandair: ☎800-223-5500; www.icelandair.com. Stopovers in Iceland for no extra cost on most flights. New York to Frankfurt Apr.-Aug. US$700; Sept.-Oct. US$500; Dec.-Mar. US$400. For last-minute offers, subscribe to their "Lucky Fares" email list.

Finnair: ☎800-950-5000; www.finnair.com. Cheap round-trips from New York, San Francisco, and Toronto to Helsinki; connections throughout Europe. New York to Helsinki June-Sept. US$1050; Oct.-May US$670-770.

Martinair: ☎800-627-8462; www.martinairusa.com. Fly from Florida to Amsterdam mid-June to mid-Aug. US$880; mid-Aug. to mid-June US$770.

TRAVELING FROM THE UK AND IRELAND

Because of the many carriers flying from Britain and Ireland to the continent, we only include discount airlines or those with cheap specials here. **Lupus Travel** in London (☎870 737 0021; www.atab.co.uk) provides referrals to travel agencies and consolidators that offer discounted airfares out of the UK. **Cheapflights** (www.cheapflights.co.uk) publishes airfare bargains.

Aer Lingus: Ireland ☎0818 365 000; www.aerlingus.com. Round-trip tickets from Cork, Dublin, and Shannon to destinations across Europe (€4-244).

bmibaby: UK ☎0871 224 0224; www.bmibaby.com. Departures from throughout the UK to destinations across Europe. London to Amsterdam UK£60; Venice UK£90.

easyJet: UK ☎0871 244 2366; www.easyjet.com. London to Athens, Barcelona, Madrid, Nice, Palma, and Warsaw, among others. Average fare UK£42.

KLM: UK ☎08705 074 074; www.klmuk.com. Cheap round-trip tickets from 14 UK cities to destinations across Europe.

Ryanair: Ireland ☎0818 303 030, UK 0871 246 0000; www.ryanair.com. Rock-bottom fares (starting around €20, including taxes and fees) from Dublin, Glasgow, Liverpool, London, and Shannon to destinations throughout Western Europe and Poland.

TRAVELING FROM AUSTRALIA AND NEW ZEALAND

Air New Zealand: New Zealand ☎0800 73 70 00; www.airnz.co.nz. Auckland to London.

Qantas Air: Australia ☎13 13 13, New Zealand 0800 808 767; www.qantas.com.au. Flights from Australia and New Zealand to London for around AUS$2000.

Singapore Air: Australia ☎13 10 11, New Zealand 0800 808 909; www.singaporeair.com. Flies from Adelaide, Auckland, Brisbane, Christchurch, Melbourne, Perth, Sydney, and Wellington to Western Europe.

Thai Airways: Australia ☎1300 65 19 60, New Zealand 09 377 38 86; www.thaiair.com. Auckland, Melbourne, Perth, and Sydney to cities throughout Europe.

AIR COURIER FLIGHTS

Light packers should consider courier flights. Couriers transport cargo on international flights by using their checked luggage space for freight. Generally, couriers must travel with carry-ons only and deal with complex restrictions. Most flights are round-trip only, with short, fixed-length stays (usually one week) and a limit of one ticket per issue. Most of these operate only from major gateway cities, mostly in North America. Generally, you must be over 18 (in some cases 21). In summer, the most popular destinations require an advance reservation of about two weeks; otherwise, reserve up to two months ahead. Super-discounted fares are common for "last-minute" flights (three to 14 days ahead). Round-trip courier fares from the US to Western Europe run about US$200-500. Most flights leave from Los Angeles, Miami, New York, or San Francisco in the US; and from Montreal, Toronto, or Vancouver in Canada. The organizations below have members with lists of opportunities and courier brokers for an annual fee. Prices quoted are round-trip.

Air Courier Association, 1767A Denver West Blvd., Golden, CO 80401, USA (☎800-461-8556; www.aircourier.org). 10 departure cities throughout Canada and the US to major cities in Western Europe (high-season US$110-640). 1-year membership US$39.

International Association of Air Travel Couriers (IAATC; www.courier.org). From 7 North American cities to Western European cities, including London, Madrid, Paris, and Rome. 1-year membership US$45.

Courier Travel (www.couriertravel.org). Searchable online database. 6 departure points in the US to various European destinations.

STANDBY FLIGHTS

Traveling standby requires considerable flexibility in arrival and departure dates and cities. Companies dealing in standby flights sell vouchers rather than tickets, along with the promise to get you to your destination (or near your destination) within a certain window of time (typically 1-5 days). You call in before your specific window of time to hear your flight options and the probability that you will be able to board each flight. You can then decide which flights you want to try to make, show up at the right airport at the appropriate time, present your voucher, and board if space is available. Vouchers can usually be bought for both one-way and round-trip travel. You may receive a refund only if every available flight within your date range is full; if you opt not to take an available (but less convenient) flight, you can only get credit toward future travel. Read agreements carefully with any company offering standby flights, as tricky fine print abounds. To check on a company's service record in the US, contact the **Better Business Bureau** (☎703-276-0100; www.bbb.org). It is difficult to receive refunds, and clients' vouchers will not be honored when an airline fails to receive payment in time.

TICKET CONSOLIDATORS

Ticket consolidators, also known as **"bucket shops,"** buy unsold tickets in bulk from commercial airlines and sell them at discounted rates. Look for tiny ads in the Sunday travel section of any major newspaper; call quickly, as availability is almost always extremely limited. Not all bucket shops are reliable, so insist on a receipt that gives full details of flight restrictions, refund policies, and tickets, and pay by credit card (in spite of the 2-5% fee) so you can stop payment on your purchase if you don't receive your tickets. For more info, see www.travel-library.com/air-travel/consolidators.html.

TRAVELING FROM NORTH AMERICA

Consolidators worth trying are **Rebel** (☎800-732-3588; www.rebeltours.com), **Cheap Tickets** (www.cheaptickets.com), **Flights.com** (www.flights.com), and **TravelHUB** (www.travelhub.com). Keep in mind that these are only suggestions; Let's Go does not endorse any of these agencies. As always, be cautious, and research companies before you hand over your credit card number.

CHARTER FLIGHTS

Tour operators contract charter flights with airlines to fly extra loads of passengers during peak season. Charter flights fly less frequently than major airlines, make refunds particularly difficult, and are almost always fully booked. Schedules and itineraries may also change or be cancelled at the last moment (as late as 48hr. before the trip, and without a full refund). Check-in, boarding, and baggage claim are often much slower; however, charter flights can also be cheaper. Discount clubs and fare brokers offer members savings on last-minute charter and tour deals. Study contracts closely; you don't want to end up with an unwanted overnight layover. **Travelers Advantage** (☎800-835-8747; www.travelersadvantage.com; US$90 annual fee includes discounts and cheap flight directories) specializes in European travel and tour packages.

GETTING AROUND EUROPE

TIP **GOING MY WAY, SAILOR?** In Europe, fares are listed as either **single** (one-way) or **return** (round-trip). "Period returns" require you to return within a specific number of days; "day return" means you must return on the same day. Round-trip fares on trains and buses in Europe are simply twice the one-way fare. Unless stated otherwise, Let's Go always lists single fares.

BY PLANE

The emergence of no-frills airlines has made hopscotching around Europe by air increasingly affordable. Although these airlines often fly at inconvenient hours and serve less popular regional airports, it's never been cheaper to jet-set across the continent with one-way flights averaging about US$80. **Ryanair** is often the least expensive option, with fares starting around US$25, including taxes and fees. Ryanair serves 116 destinations throughout most of Europe. (Ireland ☎0818 303 030, UK 0871 246 0000; www.ryanair.com.) **EasyJet** serves 73 destinations and has an average fare of around US$70. (UK ☎0871 244 2366; www.easyjet.com.)

The **Star Alliance European Airpass** offers economy-class fares as low as US$65 for travel to more than 200 European destinations. The pass is available to non-European passengers on Star Alliance carriers, which include Air Canada, Air New Zealand, Austrian Airlines, BMI British Midland, LOT Polish Airlines, Lufthansa, SAS (Scandinavian Airlines), Singapore Airlines, SpanAir, Swissair, United, USAirways, and Varig, as well as certain partner airlines. See www.staralliance.com for more information. In addition, a number of European airlines offer discount coupon packets. Most are only available as tack-ons for transatlantic passengers, but some are stand-alone offers. Most must be purchased before departure, so research in advance. **Europe by Air's** *FlightPass* allows you to country-hop to over 150 European cities for US$99 per flight. (☎888-321-4737; www.europebyair.com.) **Iberia's** *Europass* allows Iberia passengers flying from the US to Spain to tack on a minimum of two additional destinations in Europe for discounted prices. (☎800-772-4642; www.iberia.com.)

BY TRAIN

Trains in Europe are generally comfortable, convenient, and reasonably fast, although quality varies by country. Second-class compartments, which seat two to six, are great places to meet fellow travelers. However, trains can be unsafe; for safety tips, see p. 24. For long trips, make sure you are on the correct car, as trains sometimes split at crossroads. Towns listed in parentheses on European train schedules require a switch at the town listed immediately before the parentheses.

You can either buy a **railpass,** which allows you unlimited travel within a particular region for a given period of time, or rely on buying individual **point-to-point** tickets as you go. Almost all countries give students or youths (usually defined as anyone under 26) direct discounts on regular domestic rail tickets, and many also sell a student or youth card that provides 20-50% off all fares for up to a year.

RESERVATIONS

Seat reservations (usually US$5-30) are required only for select trains (usually on major lines), you are not guaranteed a seat without one. Consider reserving ahead during peak holiday and tourist seasons (at the very latest, a few hours ahead). You will also have to purchase a **supplement** (US$10-50) or special fare for high-

TRANSPORTATION

Rail prices and times are subject to wide variation, and student or other discounts may be available. This map gives only a general picture of train travel in Europe. Consult *Thomas Cook's European Timetable* for accurate schedule info.
0
300 miles
0
300 kilometers
Shetland Islands
Orkney Islands
North Sea
SCOTLAND
NORTHERN IRELAND
Glasgow
$14-16 1hr.
Edinburgh
Belfast
$58 2hr.
IRELAND
Dublin
$69 3hr.
Cork
$145-156 4¾hr.
GREAT BRITAIN
ENGLAND
$159 5-6hr.
WALES
Cardiff
London
ATLANTIC OCEAN
NETHERLANDS
Amsterdam
$90 5hr.
$126 6¼hr.
$59 2¾hr.
$95-270 2¾hr.
$35-57 3½hr.
Brussels
Cologne
$11-13 20min
BELGIUM
Bonn
$32-46 2hr.
Frankfurt
$195-255 3hr.
$87 1½hr.
$105-145 4hr.
Paris
LUXEMBOURG
Nantes
$150 8-10hr.
$89 6hr.
Bay of Biscay
$76-89 3¼-6¼hr.
$104 2hr.
$87 3½hr.
Zurich
$87 4½hr.
$35 1¼hr.
Bern
SWITZERLAND
$35 2hr.
Santiago de Campostela
$116-137 12hr.
$49 2hr.
Geneva
$72 4hr.
$33-37 1½hr.
Bordeaux
Lyon
$119 5½hr.
Milan
FRANCE
$38-42 1½hr.
Turin
$52 2¾hr.
San Sebastián
$77 2hr.
Montpellier
$42 2hr.
Nice
$47 8hr.
$44 3hr.
$59 4½hr.
Marseille
$51 2¾hr.
Florence
PORTUGAL
ANDORRA
MONACO
Lisbon
$65 10hr.
Madrid
$42-113 4½-9hr.
Barcelona
Corsica (Fr.)
SPAIN
$46-54 3½hr.
$24-47 3½hr.
$55-60 1¾hr.
Valencia
Palma
Sardinia (It.)
Seville
$9-30 45min.
$37-41 6-7hr.
Córdoba
Balearic Islands (Sp.)
$20 2hr.
Málaga
Granada
GIBRALTAR
Mediterranean Sea

Rail Planner

TRANSPORTATION

speed or high-quality trains such as certain French TGVs, Finland's Pendolino, Germany's ICE, Italy's ETR500 and Pendolino, Spain's AVE, and Switzerland's Cisalpino. Inter Rail holders must also purchase supplements (US$3-20) for trains like EuroCity, InterCity, Sweden's X2000, and many French TGVs; supplements are often unnecessary for Eurailpass and Europass holders.

OVERNIGHT TRAINS

On night trains, you won't waste valuable daylight hours traveling and you can avoid the expense of staying in a hotel. However, the main drawbacks include discomfort, sleepless nights, and the lack of scenery. **Sleeping accommodations** on trains differ from country to country, but typically cost more than day fares; you can either sleep upright in your seat (supplement about $2-10) or pay for a separate space. **Couchettes** (berths) typically have four to six seats per compartment (supplement about US$10-50 per person); **sleepers** (beds) in private sleeping cars offer more privacy and comfort, but are considerably more expensive (supplement US$40-150). If you are using a railpass valid for a limited number of days, inspect train schedules to maximize the use of your pass: an overnight train or boat journey often uses up only one of your travel days if it departs after 7pm.

TRANSPORTATION

SHOULD YOU BUY A RAILPASS? Railpasses were conceived to allow you to jump on any train in Europe, go wherever you want whenever you want, and change your plans at will. In practice, it's not so simple. You still must stand in line to validate your pass, pay for supplements, and fork over cash for seat and couchette reservations. More importantly, railpasses don't always pay off. Consult our **railplanner** (at the front of this book) to estimate the point-to-point cost of each leg of your journey; add them up and compare the total with the cost of a railpass. If you are planning to spend a great deal time on trains, hopping between big cities, a railpass will probably be worth it. But in many cases, especially if you are under 26, point-to-point tickets may prove a cheaper option.

In Scandinavia, where distances are long and rail prices are high, a railpass is often your best bet. You may find it tough to make your railpass pay for itself in the Balkans, Belgium, Eastern Europe, Greece, Iceland, Ireland, Italy, Luxembourg, the Netherlands, Portugal, or Spain, where train fares are reasonable, distances short, or buses preferable. If, however, the total cost of your trips nears the price of the pass, the convenience of avoiding ticket lines may be worth the difference.

MULTINATIONAL RAILPASSES

EURAILPASSES. Eurail is **valid** in most of Western Europe: Austria, Belgium, Denmark, Finland, France, Germany, Greece, Hungary, Ireland, Italy, Luxembourg, the Netherlands, Norway, Portugal, Spain, Sweden, and Switzerland. It is **not valid** in the UK. Standard **Eurailpasses,** valid for a consecutive given number of days, are best for those planning on spending a large amount of time on trains every few days. **Eurailpass Flexi,** valid for any 10 or 15 (not necessarily consecutive) days within a two-month period, is more cost-effective for those traveling longer distances less frequently. **Eurailpass Saver** provides first-class travel for travelers in groups of two to five (prices are per person). **Eurailpass Youth** and **Eurailpass Youth Flexi** provide parallel second-class perks for those under 26. Passholders receive a timetable for major routes and a map with details on possible bike rental, car rental, hotel, and museum discounts. They often receive reduced fares or free passage on many boat, bus, and private railroad lines.

The **Eurail Selectpass** is a slimmed-down version of the Eurailpass: it allows five to 15 days of unlimited travel in any two-month period within three, four, or five bordering countries of 22 European countries; 15-day routes automatically include five countries. **Eurail Selectpasses** cost US$383-473 per person for a five-day pass and US$850 for 15 days. **Eurail Selectpass Savers,** for people traveling in groups of two to five, cost US$325-400 per person for a five-day pass and US$723 for 15 days. The **Eurail Selectpass Youth** (2nd-class), for those aged 12-25, costs US$249-306 per person for a five-day pass and US$553 for 15 days. You are entitled to the same **freebies** afforded by the Eurailpass, but only when they are within or between countries that you have purchased.

EURAILPASSES	15 DAYS	21 DAYS	1 MONTH	2 MONTHS	3 MONTHS
1st-class Eurailpass	US$605	US$785	US$975	US$1378	US$1703
Eurailpass Saver	US$513	US$668	US$828	US$1173	US$1450
Eurailpass Youth	US$394	US$510	US$634	US$896	US$1108
EURAILPASS FLEXI		**10 DAYS IN 2 MONTHS**		**15 DAYS IN 2 MONTHS**	
1st-class Eurailpass Flexi		US$715		US$940	
Eurailpass Saver Flexi		US$608		US$800	
Eurailpass Youth Flexi		US$465		US$611	

SHOPPING AROUND FOR A EURAIL. Eurailpasses can be bought only by non-Europeans, generally from non-European distributors. These passes must be sold at uniform prices determined by the EU. However, some travel agents tack on a US$10 handling fee, and others offer certain bonuses with purchase, so shop around. Also, keep in mind that pass prices usually go up each year, so if you're planning to travel early in the year, you can save cash by purchasing before January 1 (you have 3 months from the purchase date to validate your pass in Europe).

It is best to buy your Eurail before leaving; only a few places in major European cities sell them, and at a marked-up price. You can get a replacement for a lost pass only if you have purchased insurance on it under the Pass Security Plan (US$10-17). Eurailpasses are available through travel agents, student travel agencies like **STA** (p. 42), **Rail Europe** (Canada ☎800-361-7245, US 877-257-2887; www.raileurope.com), and **Flight Centre** (www.flightcentre.com). It is also possible to buy directly from Eurail's website, www.eurail.com. Reserve well ahead of your trip, however, as the company does not ship to Europe.

OTHER MULTINATIONAL PASSES. Regional passes are often good values for those whose travels will be limited to one area. Options available through Rail Europe include the **Balkan Flexipass,** which is valid for travel in Bulgaria, Greece, Macedonia, Montenegro, Romania, Serbia, and Turkey (1st-class travel 5 days in 1 month US$197, 10 days in 1 month US$344, 15 days in 1 month US$413); the **Benelux Tourrail Pass** for Belgium, the Netherlands, and Luxembourg (2nd-class travel 5 days in 1 month US$176; 25% discount for companion traveler); the **European East Pass** for Austria, the Czech Republic, Hungary, Poland, and Slovakia (1st-class travel 5 days in 1 month US$244, 2nd-class US$172); and the **Scanrail Pass** for Denmark, Finland, Norway, and Sweden (2nd-class travel 5 days in 2 months US$298, under 26 US$207; 10 days in 2 months US$400/278; 21 consecutive days US$463/323). Check www.raileurope.com and www.eurail.com for the regional passes most applicable to the countries you are visiting.

Inter Rail Passes are an economical option for those who have lived for at least six months in one of the European countries where they are valid. They allow travel within 30 European countries (excluding the passholder's country of residence), which are divided into eight **zones.** Passes may be purchased for one, two, or all eight zones. The one-zone pass (€286, under 26 €195) is good for 16 days of travel, the two-zone pass (€396/275) is good for 22 days of travel, and the global pass (8 zones; €546/385) is valid for one month. Passholders receive free admission to many museums, as well as **discounts** on accommodations, food, and many ferries to Ireland, Scandinavia, and the rest of Europe. Passes are available at www.interrailnet.com, as well as from travel agents, at major train stations throughout Europe, and through online vendors (www.railpassdirect.co.uk).

DOMESTIC RAILPASSES

For travelers planning to spend a significant amount of time within one country, a national pass—valid on all rail lines of a country's rail company—may be more cost-effective than a multinational pass. But many national passes are limited and don't provide the free or discounted travel on private railways and ferries that Eurail does. Some of these passes can be bought only in Europe, some only outside of Europe; check with a railpass agent or with national tourist offices.

NATIONAL RAILPASSES. The domestic analogs of the Eurailpass, national railpasses are valid either for a given number of consecutive days or for a specific number of days within a given time period. Usually, they must be purchased before you leave. Though they will usually save travelers some money, the passes may actually be a more expensive alternative to point-to-point tickets, particularly in Eastern Europe. For more information, check out www.raileurope.com/us/rail/passes/single_country_index.htm.

EURODOMINO. Like the Inter Rail Pass, the EuroDomino Pass is available to anyone who has lived in Europe for at least six months. However, it is only valid in one of the 28 European countries for which it is available, as designated at the time of purchase. Reservations must still be paid for separately. **Supplements** are included for many high-speed trains (e.g., ICE, TGV). The pass must be bought within your country of residence; each country has its own price. For more information, check www.raileurope.co.uk/railpasses/eurodomino.htm.

Free online service to make seat reservations and hostel bookings /// On-board-guides to answer all your travel querries /// Excellent activities organized in each city
EUROHOP!
FLEXIBLE TRANSPORTATION for INDEPENDENT TRAVELLERS
SANTIAGO DE COMPOSTELA
PICOS DE EUROPA
BILBAO
SEBASTIAN
PAMPLONA
PONTEVEDRA (Rias Bajas)
BURGOS
ZARAGOZA
SALAMANCA
MADRID
TOLEDO
BENIDORM
LISBON
CORDOBA
GRANADA
SEVILLE
MALAGA
TARIFA
The hop-on hop-off service, exclusively designed for independent travellers, offers you the possibility to design your own tour within the network.
CHOOSE THE EASIEST & CHEAPEST WAY TO DISCOVER SPAIN & PORTUGAL!
IBERIAN BACKPACKIN'
www.eurohop.eu

RAIL-AND-DRIVE PASSES. In addition to railpasses, many countries (as well as Eurail) offer rail-and-drive passes, which combine car rental with rail travel—a good option for travelers who wish both to visit cities accessible by rail and to travel in the surrounding areas. Prices range US$235-660, depending on the type of pass, type of car, and number of people included. Children under the age of 11 cost US$95-150, and adding more days costs US$39-215 per day (see **By Car,** p. 54).

RESOURCES ON TRAIN TRAVEL

Info on rail travel and railpasses: www.raileurope.com.

Point-to-point fares and schedules: www.raileurope.com/us/rail/fares_schedules/index.htm. Allows you to calculate whether buying a railpass would save you money. For a more portable resource, see our **railplanner** at the front of this book.

Railsaver: www.railpass.com/new. Uses your itinerary to calculate the best railpass for your trip.

European Railway Server: www.railfaneurope.net. Offers links to rail servers throughout Europe.

BY BUS

In some cases, buses prove a better option than train travel. In Britain and Hungary, the bus and train systems are on par; in the Baltics, Greece, Ireland, and Portugal, bus networks are more extensive, efficient, and often more comfortable; in Iceland and parts of northern Scandinavia, bus service is the only ground transportation available. In the rest of Europe, bus travel is more of a gamble; scattered offerings from private companies are often cheap, but sometimes unreliable. Amsterdam, Athens, London, Munich, and Oslo are centers for lines that offer long-distance rides across Europe. **International bus passes** allow unlimited travel on a hop-on, hop-off basis between major European cities, often at cheaper prices than railpasses.

Eurolines, The Colonnades, London, SW1, UK (☎1582 404 511; www.eurolines.co.uk or www.eurolines.com). The largest operator of Europe-wide coach services. Unlimited 15-day (high season UK£225, under 26 and over 60 UK£189; low season UK£135/115) or 30-day (high season UK£299/245; low season UK£205/159) travel passes that offer unlimited transit among 39 major European cities.

Busabout, 258 Vauxhall Bridge Rd., London, SW1V 1BS, UK (☎020 7950 1661; www.busabout.com). Offers 3 interconnecting bus circuits covering 60 cities and towns in Europe. 1 loop UK£275; 2 loops UK£450; 3 loops UK£575.

ADDITIONAL READING

Thomas Cook European Timetable, updated monthly, covers all major and most minor train routes in Europe. Buy directly from Thomas Cook (www.thomascooktimetables.com).

Independent Travellers Europe by Rail 2006: The Inter-railer's and Eurailer's Guide. Thomas Cook Publishing (US$23).

BY CAR

Cars offer speed, freedom, access to the countryside, and an escape from the town-to-town mentality of trains. Although a single traveler won't save by renting a car, four usually will. Some travelers may benefit from a combination of car and train travel; RailEurope and other railpass vendors offer rail-and-drive packages.

Fly-and-drive packages are also often available from travel agents and airline/rental agency partnerships.

Before setting off, know the laws of the countries in which you'll be driving (e.g., seat belts and headlights must be on at all times in Scandinavia, and driving is done on the left in Ireland and the UK). For an informal primer on European road signs and conventions, check out www.travlang.com/signs.

RENTING A CAR

Cars can be rented from a US-based firm (Alamo, Avis, Budget, or Hertz) with European offices, from a European-based company with local representatives (Europcar), or from a tour operator (Auto Europe, Europe By Car, and Kemwel Holiday Autos) that will arrange a rental for you from a European company. Multinationals offer greater flexibility, but tour operators often strike better deals. Ask airlines about special fly-and-drive packages; you may get up to a week of free or discounted rental. See **Costs and Insurance,** p. 56, for more info. Minimum age requirements vary but tend to fall in the range of 21-25, with some as low as 18; there may be an additional insurance fee for drivers under 25. At most agencies, all that's needed to rent a car is a driver's license from home and proof that you've had it for a year. Car rental in Europe is available through the following agencies:

Auto Europe (Canada and the US ☎888-223-5555; www.autoeurope.com).

Avis (Australia ☎136 333, Canada and the US 800-331-1212, New Zealand 0800 655 111, UK 0870 606 0100; www.avis.com).

Budget (Canada ☎800-268-8900, UK 8701 565 656, US 800-527-0700; www.budgetrentacar.com).

Europcar International, 3 Av. du Centre, 78 881 Saint Quentin en Yvelines, FRA (UK ☎1923 811 000, US 678-461-9880; www.europcar.com).

Europe by Car (US ☎800-223-1516 or 212-581-3040; www.europebycar.com).

Hertz (Australia ☎9698 2555, Canada and the US 800-654-3001, UK 08708 44 88 44; www.hertz.com).

Kemwel (US ☎877-820-0668; www.kemwel.com).

COSTS AND INSURANCE

Expect to pay US$100-500 per week, plus tax (5-25%), for a tiny car with a manual transmission; automatics can double or triple the price. Larger vehicles and 4WD will also raise prices. Reserve and pay in advance if at all possible. It is less expensive to reserve a car from the US than in Europe. Rates are generally lowest in Belgium, Germany, the Netherlands, and the UK, higher in Ireland and Italy, and highest in Scandinavia and Eastern Europe. Some companies charge fees for traveling into Eastern Europe. National chains often allow one-way rentals, with pick-up in one city and drop-off in another. There is usually a minimum hire period and sometimes an extra drop-off charge of several hundred dollars.

Many rental packages offer unlimited kilometers, while others offer a fixed distance per day with a per-kilometer surcharge after that. Be sure to ask whether the price includes **insurance** against theft and collision. Remember that if you are driving a conventional vehicle on an **unpaved road** in a rental car, you are almost never covered by insurance; ask about this before leaving the rental agency. Always check if prices quoted include tax and collision insurance; some credit card companies provide insurance, allowing their customers to decline the collision damage waiver. Ask about discounts and check the terms of insurance, particularly the size of the deductible. Beware that cars rented on an **American Express** or **Visa/Mastercard Gold or Platinum** credit cards in Europe might *not* carry the automatic insurance that they would in some other countries; check with your credit card company. Insurance plans almost always come with an **excess** (or deductible) for conventional vehicles; excess is usually higher for younger drivers and for 4WD. This provision means you pay for all damages up to the specified sum, unless they are the fault of another vehicle. The excess you will be quoted applies to collisions with other vehicles; other collisions ("single-vehicle collisions") will cost you even more. The excess can often be reduced or waived for an additional charge. Remember to return the car with a full tank of **gasoline** to avoid high fuel charges. Gas prices vary by country, and are generally highest in Scandinavia. Throughout Europe, fuel tends to be cheaper in cities than in outlying areas. Western Europeans and Scandinavians use unleaded gas almost exclusively, but it's not available in many gas stations in Eastern Europe.

LEASING A CAR

Leasing can be cheaper than renting, especially for more than 17 days. It is often the only option for those aged 18 to 21. The cheapest leases are agreements to buy the car and then sell it back to the manufacturer at a prearranged price. Leases generally include insurance coverage and are not taxed. The most affordable ones usually originate in Belgium, France, or Germany. Expect to pay US$1100-1800 for 60 days. Contact **Auto Europe, Europe by Car,** or **Kemwel** (p. 55) before you go.

BUYING A CAR

Buying a used car or van in Europe and selling it just before you leave can provide the cheapest wheels for longer trips. Check with consulates for import-export laws concerning used vehicles, registration, and safety and emission standards.

TRANSPORTATION

ON THE ROAD

Road conditions and **regional hazards** are variable throughout Europe. Steep, curvy mountain roads may be closed in the winter. Road conditions in Eastern Europe are often poor as a result of maintenance issues and inadequately enforced traffic laws; many travelers prefer public transportation. Western European roads are generally excellent, but keep in mind that each area has its own dangers. In Scandinavia, for example, drivers should be on the lookout for moose and elk; on the Autobahn, the threat may come from cars speeding by at 150kph. In this book, region-specific hazards are listed in country introductions. Carry emergency equipment with you (see box on **Driving Precautions,** below) and know what to do in case of a breakdown. Car rental companies will often have phone numbers for emergency services.

DRIVING PRECAUTIONS. When traveling in the summer, bring substantial amounts of water (a suggested 5L per person per day) for drinking and for the radiator. For long drives to unpopulated areas, register with police before beginning the trip, and again upon arrival at the destination. Check with the local automobile club for details. Make sure tires are in good repair and have enough air, and get good maps. A compass and a car manual can also be very useful. Always carry a spare tire and jack, jumper cables, extra oil, flares, a flashlight (torch), and heavy blankets (in case your car breaks down at night or in the winter). If you don't know how to change a tire, learn before heading out, especially if you are planning on traveling in deserted areas. Blowouts on dirt roads are exceedingly common. If you do have a breakdown, stay with your car.

TRANSPORTATION

DRIVING PERMITS AND CAR INSURANCE

INTERNATIONAL DRIVING PERMIT (IDP). To drive a car in Europe, you must be over 18 and have an International Driving Permit (IDP), though certain countries (such as the UK) allow travelers to drive with a valid American or Canadian license for a limited number of months. It may be a good idea to get an IDP anyway, in case you're in a situation (e.g., you get in an accident or become stranded in a small town) where the police do not know English; information on the IDP is printed in 11 languages, including French, German, Italian, Portuguese, Russian, Spanish, and Swedish.

Your IDP, valid for one year, must be issued in your home country before you depart. An application for an IDP usually requires one or two photos, a current local license, an additional form of identification, and a fee. To apply, contact your country's automobile association. Be careful when purchasing an IDP online or anywhere other than your home automobile association. Many vendors sell permits of questionable legitimacy for higher prices.

CAR INSURANCE. If you rent, lease, or borrow a car, you will need an International Insurance Certificate, or Green Card, to certify that you have liability insurance and that it applies abroad. Green Cards can be obtained at car rental agencies, car dealerships (for those leasing cars), some travel agents, and some border crossings. Rental agencies may require you to purchase theft insurance in countries they consider to have a high risk of auto theft.

BY CHUNNEL FROM THE UK

Traversing 43km under the sea, the Chunnel is undoubtedly the fastest, most convenient, and least scenic route from England to France.

BY TRAIN. **Eurostar,** Eurostar House, Waterloo Station, London, SE1 8SE (UK ☎08705 186 186; www.eurostar.com) runs frequent trains between London and the continent. Trains run to over 70 destinations, including Paris (4hr., 2nd class UK£70-80). Reserve online, at major rail stations in the UK, or at the office above.

BY BUS. **Eurolines** (p. 54) provides bus/ferry combinations.

BY CAR. **Eurotunnel,** P.O. Box 2000, Folkestone, Kent CT18 8XY (UK ☎08705 353 535; www.eurotunnel.co.uk) shuttles cars and passengers between Kent and Nord-Pas-de-Calais, FRA. Round-trip fares for one vehicle and all passengers range UK£100-200. Same-day round-trip costs UK£44-52. Reserve online or by phone. Travelers with cars can also look into sea crossings by ferry (see below).

BY BOAT

Most long-distance ferries are quite comfortable; the cheapest ticket typically includes a reclining chair or couchette. Fares jump sharply in July and August. Ask for discounts; ISIC holders can often get student fares, and Eurailpass holders get many reductions and free trips. You'll occasionally have to pay a port tax (under US$10). The fares below are **one-way** for **adult foot passengers** unless otherwise noted. Though standard round-trip fares are usually twice the one-way fare, **fixed-period returns** (usually within 5 days) may be cheaper. Ferries run **year-round** unless otherwise noted. Bringing a **bike** costs up to US$15 in high season.

FERRIES FROM BRITAIN AND IRELAND

Ferries are frequent and dependable. The main route across the English Channel from Britain to France is Dover-Calais. The main ferry port on England's southern coast is Portsmouth, with connections to France and Spain. Ferries also cross the Irish Sea, connecting Northern Ireland with Scotland and England, and the Republic of Ireland with Wales. See the directory at www.seaview.co.uk/ferries.html.

Brittany Ferries: France ☎08 25 82 88 28, UK 08703 665 333; www.brittany-ferries.com. Plymouth, BRI to **Roscoff, FRA** (6hr., summer 1-3 per day, UK£58), and **Santander, SPA** (18hr., 2 per week, UK£100); Poole, BRI to **Cherbourg, FRA** (4¼hr., 2-3 per day, UK£20); Portsmouth, BRI, to **St-Malo, FRA** (11hr., 1 per day, UK£29) and **Caen, FRA** (5¾hr., 2-4 per day, UK£45).

DFDS Seaways: UK ☎08705 444 333; www.dfdsseaways.co.uk. Harwich, BRI to **Esbjerg, DEN** (18hr., UK£29-49); Newcastle, BRI to **Amsterdam, NTH** (16hr., UK£19-39), **Gothenburg, SWE** (26hr., UK£19-59), and **Kristiansand, NOR** (18¼hr., UK£19-59).

Fjord Line: UK ☎08701 439 669; www.fjordline.no. Newcastle, BRI to **Stavanger, NOR** (19½hr., UK£30-40).

Hoverspeed: UK ☎0870 1642 114; www.hoverspeed.co.uk. Dover, BRI to **Dunkerque, FRA** (2hr., every 1-2hr., from UK£19).

Irish Ferries: Ireland ☎818 300 400; www.irishferries.ie. Holyhead, BRI to **Dublin, IRE** (2-3hr., UK£28-32); Rosslare Harbour, IRE, to **Cherbourg** and **Roscoff, FRA** (18hr., €78-108) and **Pembroke, BRI** (3¾hr., €27).

P&O Ferries: UK ☎08705 980 333; www.posl.com. Dover, BRI to **Calais, FRA** (1¼hr., 1 per hr., from UK£10). Daily ferries from Hull, BRI to **Bilbao, SPA, Rotterdam, NTH** (10hr.), and **Zeebrugge, BEL** (12½hr.); all 3 from UK£100.

SeaFrance: France ☎08 03 04 40 45, UK 08705 711 711; www.seafrance.com. Dover, BRI to **Calais, FRA** (1½hr., 1 per hr., UK£12).

Stena Line: UK ☎08705 707 070; www.stenaline.co.uk. Fishguard, BRI to **Rosslare Harbour, IRE** (1¾hr., €32); Harwich, BRI to **Hook of Holland, NTH** (4hr., UK£33); Holyhead, BRI to **Dublin** or **Dún Laoghaire, IRE** (1¾hr., €32).

FERRIES IN SCANDINAVIA

Ferries run to many North Sea destinations. Those content with deck passage rarely need to book ahead. Baltic Sea ferries sail between Poland and Scandinavia.

Color Line: Norway ☎0810 00 811; www.colorline.com. Ferries run from Norway to Denmark (€54-60) and Germany (€80).

Silja Line: Finland ☎09 18 041, Sweden 086 66 33 30, US 800-533-3755 ext. 114; www.silja.com. Helsinki, FIN to **Stockholm, SWE** (16hr., June-Dec., €52) and **Tallinn, EST** (3hr., June to mid-Sept., €34-46).

Viking Line: Sweden ☎0452 40 00, US 800-843-0602; www.vikingline.fi. Ferries run between Helsinki and Turku, FIN to destinations in Sweden and Estonia. Su-Th min. age 20; F-Sa 23. One-way €26-47. Eurail discounts available.

MEDITERRANEAN AND AEGEAN FERRIES

Mediterranean ferries may be the most glamorous, but they can also be the most turbulent. Ferries run from Spain to Morocco, from Italy to Tunisia, and from France to both Morocco and Tunisia. Reservations are recommended, especially in July and August. Schedules are erratic, with varying prices for similar routes. Shop around, and beware of small companies that don't take reservations.

Ferries traverse the Adriatic from Ancona, ITA to Split, CRO and from Bari, ITA to Dubrovnik, CRO. Ferries also cross the Aegean, from Ancona, ITA to Patras, GCE and from Bari, ITA to Igoumenitsa and Patras, GCE. **Eurail** is valid on certain ferries between Brindisi, ITA and Corfu, Igoumenitsa, and Patras, GCE. Countless ferry companies operate on these routes; see specific country chapters for more information.

BY MOPED AND MOTORCYCLE

Motorized bikes and mopeds don't use much gas, can be put on trains and ferries, and are a good compromise between costly car travel and the limited range of bicycles. However, they're uncomfortable for long distances, dangerous in the rain, and unpredictable on rough roads. Always wear a helmet, and never ride with a backpack. If you've never ridden a moped before, a twisting Alpine road is not the place to start. Expect to pay about US$20-35 per day for a moped; to find a cheap rental, try auto repair shops and remember to bargain. Motorcycles are more expensive and normally require a license, but are better for longer distances. Before renting, ask if the price includes tax and insurance, or you may be hit with an unexpected fee. Avoid handing your passport over as a deposit; if you have an accident or mechanical failure you may not get it back until you cover all repairs. Pay ahead of time instead.

BY THUMB

> **!** Let's Go strongly urges you to consider the risks before you choose to hitch. We do not recommend hitchhiking, and none of the information presented here is intended to do so.

No one should hitch without careful consideration of the risks involved. Hitching means entrusting your life to a unknown person and risking theft, assault, sexual harassment, and unsafe driving. However, some travelers report that hitchhiking in Europe allows them to meet locals and travel in areas where public transportation is sketchy.

Britain and **Ireland** are probably the easiest places in Western Europe to get a lift. Hitching in **Scandinavia** is slow but steady. Long-distance hitching in the developed countries of northwestern Europe demands close attention to expressway junctions, rest stop locations, and destination signs. Hitching in southern Europe is generally mediocre, and France is the worst. In some Eastern European countries, the line between hitching and taking a taxi is virtually nonexistent.

Hitchhiking at night can be particularly dangerous; experienced hitchers stand in well-lit places. For women traveling alone, hitching is simply too dangerous. A man and a woman are a safer combination, two men will have a harder time, and three will go nowhere. Experienced hitchers pick a spot outside of built-up areas, where drivers can stop, return to the road without causing an accident, and have time to look over potential passengers as they approach. Hitching (or even standing) on super-highways is usually illegal: one may only thumb at rest stops or at the entrance ramps to highways. Finally, success often depends on appearance.

Most Western European countries have ride services that pair drivers with riders; fees vary according to destination. **Eurostop** (www.taxistop.be/index_ils.htm), Taxistop's ride service, is one of the largest in Europe. Also try **Allostop** in France (French-language website www.allostop.net) and **Verband der Deutschen Mitfahrzentralen** in Germany (German-language website www.mitfahrzentrale.de). Not all organizations screen drivers and riders; ask ahead.

BEYOND TOURISM

A PHILOSOPHY FOR TRAVELERS

BEYOND TOURISM HIGHLIGHTS

NURTURE endangered griffon vultures on the Cres Island in **Croatia** (p. 220).

RESTORE castles in **France** (p. 62) and **Germany** (p. 403).

POLITICK as an intern at NATO in **Belgium** (p. 101).

IMMERSE yourself in Basque cuisine at a culinary institute in **San Sebastián** (p. 893).

As a tourist, you are always a foreigner. While hostel-hopping and sightseeing can be great fun, you may want to consider going *beyond* tourism. Connecting with a foreign place through studying, volunteering, or working can reduce that touristy stranger-in-a-strange-land feeling. Also, travelers can make a positive impact on the natural and cultural environments they visit. With this Beyond Tourism chapter, Let's Go hopes to promote a better understanding of Europe and to provide suggestions for those who want more than a photo album out of their travels.

As a **volunteer** in Europe, you can participate in projects from castle-cleaning in France to protecting the endangered turtles in Greece; such an expedition can be undertaken either on a short-term basis or as the main component of your trip. In this chapter, we recommend organizations that can help you find the opportunities that suit your interests, whether you're looking to pitch in for a day or a year.

Studying at a college or in a language program is another option. Those who choose to study abroad in Europe often find the immersion in the educational environment to be much more rewarding and genuine than the backpacker trail alone. With hundreds of programs from which to choose, students can select from a full spectrum of fields that cater to their individual interests.

Many travelers structure their trips by the **work** that they can do along the way—either odd jobs as they go, or full-time stints in cities where they plan to stay for some time. The availability and legality of temporary work vary across Europe. If you are interested in working your way across the continent, we recommend picking up Let's Go city and country guides for more specific information.

Start your search at **www.beyondtourism.com,** Let's Go's searchable database of alternatives to tourism, where you can find exciting feature articles and helpful program listings divided by country, continent, and program type.

VOLUNTEERING

Volunteering can be a personally fulfilling experience, especially if you combine it with the thrill of traveling in a new place. Whether your passion is for ecological, political, or social work, Europe can make use of your energies. Most people who volunteer in Europe do so on a short-term basis, at organizations that make use of

WHY PAY MONEY TO VOLUNTEER? Many volunteers are surprised to learn that some organizations require fees or "donations." Such fees often keep the organization afloat, in addition to covering airfare, room, board, and administrative expenses. (Other organizations rely on private donations and government subsidies.) If you're concerned about how a program spends its fees, request an annual report or finance account. Pay-to-volunteer programs are good for those looking for support and structure (e.g., pre-arranged transport and housing), or who would rather not deal with the uncertainty in creating a volunteer experience from scratch.

drop-in or once-a-week volunteers. The best way to find opportunities that match up with your interests and schedule may be to check with local or national volunteer centers. Those looking for longer, more intensive volunteer experiences usually choose to go through a parent organization that takes care of logistical details and often provides a group environment and support system, for a fee.

ONLINE DIRECTORIES: VOLUNTEERING

www.alliance-network.org. Umbrella website that brings together various international service organizations.

www.volunteerabroad.com. Searchable database of opportunities from many countries.

www.worldvolunteerweb.org. Lists organizations and events around the world.

COMMUNITY DEVELOPMENT

If working closely with locals, experiencing the "real" life of European countries, and helping in a very hands-on fashion appeal to you, check out the community development options. Many returning travelers report that working among locals in various projects was one of their most rewarding experiences.

Global Volunteers, 375 E. Little Canada Rd., St. Paul, MN 55117, USA (☎800-487-1074; www.globalvolunteers.org). A variety of 1- to 3-week volunteer programs throughout Europe. Fees range US$1945-2495, including room and board but not airfare.

Service Civil International Voluntary Service (SCI-IVS), 5505 Walnut Level Rd., Crozet, VA 22932, US (☎206-350-6585; www.sci-ivs.org). Arranges placement in 2- to 4-week outdoor service camps throughout Europe. 18+. Registration fee US$195, including room and board but not travel expenses.

CONSERVATION

Recently, conservation efforts have increased dramatically. As more people realize that long-cherished habitats and structures are in danger, diverse programs have stepped in to provide a way for citizens to lend a hand. Conservation programs are excellent for those who want to take ecotourism one step further.

Club du Vieux Manoir, Ancienne Abbaye du Moncel, 60700 Pontpoint, FRA (☎33 03 44 72 33 98; http://cvmclubduvieuxmanoir.free.fr). Offers year-long and summer programs restoring castles and churches throughout France. €14 annual membership and insurance fee. €12.50 per day, including food and tent. Website in French.

Earthwatch Institute, 3 Clock Tower Pl., Ste. 100, P.O. Box 75, Maynard, MA 01754, USA (☎800-776-0188; www.earthwatch.org). Arranges 10-day to 3-week programs to promote the conservation of natural resources. Fees vary based on program location and duration. Costs range US$700-4000, including room and board but not airfare.

The National Trust, Community, Learning and Volunteering, Heelis, Kemble Dr., Swindon, SN2 2NA, UK (☎44 0870 609 5383; www.nationaltrust.org.uk/volunteers). Arranges numerous volunteer opportunities, including Working Holidays. Working Holidays from £60 per week, including room and board but not travel expenses.

World-Wide Opportunities on Organic Farms (WWOOF), Main Office, P.O. Box 2675, Lewes, East Sussex BN7 1RB, UK (www.wwoof.org). Arranges volunteer work with organic and eco-conscious farms around the world. Must become a member of WWOOF in the country in which you plan to work; prices vary by country.

HUMANITARIAN AND SOCIAL SERVICES

Europe's complex and war-torn history has provided many opportunities for those looking to provide social aid. Peace programs are abundant and often prove to be very fulfilling for those interested in humanitarian work.

Brethren Volunteer Service (BVS), 1451 Dundee Ave., Elgin, IL 60120, USA (☎800-323-8039; www.brethrenvolunteerservice.org). Peace and social justice based programs in various Western European countries. Commitment of 1-2 years, must be 21 to serve overseas. US$500 fee for international volunteers.

Simon Wiesenthal Center, 1399 South Roxbury Dr., Los Angeles, CA 90035, USA (☎800-900-9036; www.wiesenthal.org). Fights anti-Semitism and Holocaust denial throughout Europe. Small, variable donation required for membership.

Volunteers for Peace, 1034 Tiffany Rd., Belmont, VT 05730, USA (☎802-259-2759; www.vfp.org). Arranges placement in camps throughout Europe. US$20 membership required for registration. Programs average US$250-500 for 2-3 weeks.

STUDYING

Study-abroad programs range from basic language and culture courses to college-level classes. In programs that have large groups of students who speak the same language, there is a trade-off. You may feel more comfortable, but you will not have the same opportunity to practice a foreign language or to befriend local students. For accommodations, dorm life provides an opportunity to meet fellow students, but there is less of a chance to experience the local scene. Living with a family offers the potential to build friendships with locals and experience day-to-day life; but conditions can vary greatly.

VISA INFORMATION. Different countries have different requirements for study-abroad students. Ask the local consulate for visa info. Generally, applicants must be able to provide a passport, proof of enrollment, insurance, and financial support before their visa can be issued.

UNIVERSITIES

Most university-level programs are language and culture enrichment opportunities and are conducted in the local language. Those relatively fluent in a foreign language may find it cheaper to enroll directly in a university abroad, although getting college credit may be more difficult.

ONLINE DIRECTORIES: STUDY-ABROAD

These websites are good resources for finding programs that cater to your particular interests. Each has links to various study-abroad programs broken down by a variety of criteria, including desired location and focus of study.

www.petersons.com/stdyabrd/sasector.html. Lists summer and term-time study abroad programs at accredited institutions that usually offer cross credits.

www.studyabroad.com. A great starting point for finding college- or high-school-level programs in foreign languages or specific academic subjects. Also includes information for teaching and volunteering opportunities.

www.westudyabroad.com. Lists language courses and college-level programs.

AMERICAN PROGRAMS

The following is a list of organizations that can either help place students in university programs abroad or that have their own branch in Europe.

American Institute for Foreign Study, College Division, River Plaza, 9 W. Broad St., Stamford, CT 06902, USA (☎800-727-2437; www.aifsabroad.com). Organizes programs for high-school and college study in universities in Austria, Britain, the Czech Republic, France, Ireland, Italy, Russia, and Spain. Summer programs: US$5000-6500; Semester long programs: US$12000-16000. Scholarships available.

American Field Service (AFS), 71 W. 23rd St., 17th fl., New York, NY, 10010 (☎212-807-8686; www.afs.org), has branches in over 50 countries. Summer-, semester-, and year-long homestay exchange programs for high-school students and graduating seniors. Some locations include the Czech Republic, Hungary, Latvia, Russia, and the Slovak Republic. Community service programs are also offered to those 18+.

American School of Classical Studies (ASCSA), 54 Souidias St., GR-106 76 Athens, GCE (☎30 210 72 36 313; www.ascsa.edu.gr). Offers archaeological and classical studies programs in Greece. Costs vary from summer to academic year. US$2950-16,000.

Association of Commonwealth Universities (ACU), John Foster House, 36 Gordon Sq., London WC1H OPF, UK (☎020 7380 6700; www.acu.ac.uk). Publishes information about Commonwealth Universities, including those in Cyprus and the UK.

Council on International Educational Exchange (CIEE), 7 Custom House St., 3rd fl., Portland, ME, 01401, USA (☎800-407-8839; www.ciee.org/study). Sponsors academic, internship, volunteer, and work programs in Belgium, Britain, the Czech Republic, France, Hungary, Ireland, Italy, the Netherlands, Poland, Russia, and Spain for around US$10,000 per semester. US$30 application fee. Scholarships available.

Cultural Experiences Abroad (CEA), 1400 E. Southern Ave., Ste. B-108, Tempe, AZ 85282 (☎800-266-4441; www.gowithcea.com). Operates programs in Britain, France, Hungary, Ireland, Italy, and Spain for undergraduates studying in Canada and the US. Costs range from US$3495 for a summer course to US$28,795 for the academic year.

Institute for the International Education of Students (IES), 33 N. LaSalle St., 15th fl., Chicago, IL 60602 (☎800-995-2300; www.iesabroad.org). Offers year-, semester-, and summer-long study abroad programs in Austria, Britain, France, Germany, Ireland, Italy, the Netherlands, and Spain, as well as a special European Union (EU) program based in Germany but including field study trips to several other European countries for college students. US$12,000-18,000 per semester. US$50 application fee.

International Association for the Exchange of Students for Technical Experience (IAESTE), 10400 Little Patuxent Pkwy., Ste. 250, Columbia, MD 21044, USA (☎410-997-2200). Offers 8- to 12-week internships throughout Europe for college students who have completed 2 years of technical study. US$50 application fee.

School for International Training (SIT), College Semester Abroad, Kipling Rd., P.O. Box 676, Brattleboro, VT 05302, USA (☎888-272-7881 or 802-257-7751; www.sit.edu/studyabroad). Each semester-long study-abroad program is planned around a theme, with a focus on social responsibility and intercultural understanding. Courses in Europe cost around US$17,000. Also runs the **Experiment in International Living** (☎800-345-2929; www.usexperiment.org), 3- to 5-week summer programs that offer high school students cross-cultural homestays in Britain, France, Germany, Ireland and N. Ireland, Italy, Poland, Spain, and Switzerland for around US$5000.

Youth for Understanding International Exchange (YFU), 6400 Goldsboro Rd., Ste. 100, Bethesda, MD 20817 (☎800-833-6243; www.yfu-usa.org). Places US high-school students with host families throughout Europe. Summer-, semester-, and year-long programs: US$5000-7000. US$75 application fee plus US$500 deposit.

LANGUAGE SCHOOLS

Language schools can be independently-run international or local organizations as well as divisions of foreign universities. They rarely offer college credit. They are a good alternative to university study for those who desire a deeper focus on the language or a slightly less rigorous courseload. Some worthwhile programs include:

Eurocentres, 1901 N. Fort Myer Dr. Suite 800, Arlington, VA, 22209, USA (☎703-243-7884; www.eurocentres.com), in Europe, Seestr. 247, CH-8038 Zürich, SWI (☎41 1 485 50 40; fax 481 61 24). Language programs for beginning to advanced students, with homestays in France, Germany, Italy, Russia, Spain, and Switzerland.

Language Immersion Institute, JFT 214, State University of New York at New Paltz, 75 S. Manheim Blvd., New Paltz, NY, 12561, USA (☎845-257-3500; www.newpaltz.edu/lii). 2-week summer language courses. Some courses in France, Italy, and Spain and a wide variety of stateside offerings. US$950 plus US$360-600 for accommodations.

Sprachcaffe Languages Plus, 413 Ontario St., Toronto, ON M5A 2V9, CAN (☎888-526-4758; www.sprachcaffe.com). Language classes in France, Germany, Italy, and Spain for US$200-600 per week. Price depends on course and accommodations. Homestays available. Also offers French and Spanish language and travel programs for teenagers.

WORKING

As with volunteering, work opportunities tend to fall into two categories: long- and short-term. Some travelers want long-term jobs that allow them to get to know another part of the world as a member of the community, while other travelers seek out short-term jobs to finance the next leg of their travels. In Europe, people who want to work long-term might find success where their language skills are in demand, such as in teaching or working with tourists. Employment opportunities for those who want short-term work may be more limited and are generally contingent upon the economic needs of the city or region. In addition to local papers, international English-language newspapers, such as the *International Herald Tribune* (www.iht.com), often list job opportunities in their classified sections.

LONG-TERM WORK

If you're planning on spending a substantial amount of time (more than three months) working in Europe, search for a job well in advance. International placement agencies are often the easiest way to find employment abroad, especially for those interested in teaching English. **Internships,** usually for college students, are a good way to segue into working abroad; although they are often unpaid or poorly paid, many say the experience is well worth it. Be wary of advertisements for companies claiming the ability to get you a job abroad for a fee—often the same listings are available online or in newspapers. Some reputable organizations include:

Escapeartist.com (http://jobs.escapeartist.com). International employers post directly to this website; various European jobs advertised.

International Cooperative Education, 15 Spiros Way, Menlo Park, CA, 94025, USA (☎650-323-4944; www.icemenlo.com). Finds summer jobs in Belgium, Britain, Germany, and Switzerland. Participants must be aged 18-30. US$200 application fee and a $600 placement fee.

ResortJobs.com (www.resortjobs.com). Searchable database of service and entertainment jobs at resorts in Germany and Greece.

StepStone (www.stepstone.com, branches across Europe listed at www.stepstone.com/offices.htm). Database covering international employment openings for most of Europe. Several search options and a constantly updated list of openings.

VISA INFORMATION

EU Citizens: The 2004 enlargement of the EU inspired fear in the 15 previous member states (EU-15) that waves of Eastern European immigrants would flood their labor markets. This fear caused some members of the union to institute a transition period of up to 7 years during which citizens of the new EU countries may still need a visa or permit to work. EU-15 citizens generally have the right to work in the pre-enlargement countries for up to 3 months without a visa; longer-term employment usually requires a work permit. By law, all EU-15 citizens are given equal consideration for jobs not directly related to national security.

Everyone else: For non-EU citizens, getting a work visa in Europe is difficult. Different countries have different laws for employing foreigners; ask at your local embassy for specific info. The process is invariably time-consuming and frustrating. Having a job lined up *before* braving the bureaucratic gauntlet can speed up the process, as employers can perform much of the administrative leg-work.

TEACHING ENGLISH

Teaching jobs abroad are rarely well-paid, although some private American schools offer competitive salaries. Volunteering as a teacher in lieu of getting paid is a popular option. In almost all cases, you must have a bachelor's degree to be a full-fledged teacher, although college undergraduates can often get summer positions tutoring. The difficulty of finding teaching jobs varies by country; EU countries are required to give EU applicants priority. Many schools require teachers to have a **Teaching English as a Foreign Language (TEFL)** certificate. Not having this certification does not necessarily exclude you from finding a teaching job, but certified teachers often find higher-paying jobs. Native English speakers working in private schools are most often hired for English-immersion classrooms where the local language is not spoken. Those teaching in poorer public schools are more likely to be working in both English and the native tongue. Placement agencies or university programs are the best resources for finding jobs. The alternative is to make contact directly with schools or just to try your luck once you get there. The best time to look for the latter is several weeks before the start of the school year. The following organizations are extremely helpful in placing teachers in Europe:

Central European Teaching Program (CETP), 3800 NE 72nd Ave., Portland, OR, 97213 (☎503-287-4977; www.ticon.net/~cetp). Provides college graduates with job placement as English teachers in Hungary. Semester US$1700, academic year US$2250.

International Schools Services (ISS), 15 Roszel Rd., P.O. Box 5910, Princeton, NJ, 08543, USA (☎609-452-0990; www.iss.edu). Hires teachers for more than 200 international and American schools around the world; candidates should have 2 years teaching experience and/or teacher certification. 2-year commitment expected.

Teaching English as a Foreign Language (TEFL), TEFL Professional Network Ltd., 72 Pentyla Baglan Rd., Port Talbot SA12 8AD, UK (www.tefl.com). Maintains the most extensive database of openings throughout Europe. Offers job training and certification.

AU PAIR WORK

Au pairs are typically women (although sometimes men), aged 18-27, who work as live-in nannies, caring for children and doing light housework in exchange for room, board, and a small stipend. Most former au pairs speak favorably of their experience. One perk of the job is that it allows you to really get to know the country without the high expenses of traveling. Drawbacks, however, often include mediocre pay and long hours of constantly being on duty. Au pairs in Europe typically work 25-40hr. per week and receive US$300-450 per month. Much of the au pair experience depends on the family with whom you're placed. The agencies below are a good starting point for looking for employment as an au pair.

Childcare International, Ltd., Trafalgar House, Grenville Pl., London NW7 3SA, UK, (☎020 8906 3116; www.childint.co.uk). Offers au pair and nanny placement in Britain, France, Germany, Italy, the Netherlands, and Spain.

InterExchange, 161 6th Ave., New York, NY 10013, USA (☎212-924-0446; www.interexchange.org). Au pair, internship, and short-term work placement in France, Germany, the Netherlands, Norway, and Spain. US$495-600 placement fee.

Sunny AuPairs (☎44 1722 415864; www.sunnyaupairs.com). Online, worldwide database connecting au pairs with families. Free registration. No placement fee.

SHORT-TERM WORK

Traveling for long periods of time can get expensive; therefore, many travelers try their hand at odd jobs for a few weeks at a time to help finance another month or two of touring around. Another popular option is to work several hours a day at a hostel in exchange for free or discounted room and/or board. Most often, these short-term jobs are found by word of mouth, or simply by talking to the owner of a hostel or restaurant. The legality of short-term work varies by country. Contact the embassy of the country you'll be traveling in for more information. Let's Go tries to list temporary jobs like these whenever possible; check out the list below for some of the available short-term jobs in popular destinations.

FURTHER READING ON BEYOND TOURISM

Alternatives to the Peace Corps: A Directory of Third World and U.S. Volunteer Opportunities, by Jennifer S. Willsea. Food First Books, 2003 (US$10).

How to Get a Job in Europe, by Sanborn and Matherly. Planning Communications, 2003 (US$22).

How to Live Your Dream of Volunteering Overseas, by Collins, DeZerega, and Heckscher. Penguin Books, 2002 (US$17).

International Directory of Voluntary Work, by Whetter and Pybus. Peterson's Guides and Vacation Work, 2000 (US$16).

International Job Finder: Where the Jobs Are Worldwide, by Daniel Lauber. Planning Communications, 2002 (US$20).

Live and Work Abroad: A Guide for Modern Nomads, by Francis and Callan. Vacation-Work Publications, 2001 (US$16).

Work Abroad: The Complete Guide to Finding a Job Overseas, by Hubbs, Griffith, and Nolting. Transitions Abroad Publishing, 2002 (US$16).

Research in Germany

During my time as a college student in the United States, I took an unforgettable semester off to work at the University of Ulm doing chemistry research. I was interested not only in learning about polypeptides and phenolphthalein, but also in discovering how Germans differ in their approaches to research, academics, and life. I wanted to get to know Germany (and Europe) more intimately than the average tourist, using the city of Ulm as the stronghold from which I would sally forth to other nations.

For centuries, Germany has been known for its rigorous intellectual tradition, especially in the physical sciences. After sitting in on a mind-blowing statistical mechanics lecture in Ulm, I learned that the professor was also deeply interested in history. In particular, he emphasized Einstein's variegate contributions to the field and the fact that Ulm was his birthplace. Germany may have lost some of its academic luster since the times of Boltzmann, Leibniz, and Hegel, but its academic research is still as vital as the flow of the mighty Rhine.

I began my search for a position in a German lab by talking to my academic advisor in the States about potential contacts in Germany. Finding professors who wanted an American protégé ended up being much easier than finding a reliable, sufficient, and legal method of financing my trip. I eventually was lucky enough to come upon a professor whose university could fund my studies, which meant I could stop trying to arrange my own funding through the **German Academic Exchange Program** (www.daad.de).

Undertaking academic research in Germany had several advantages over participating in a mere study-abroad program, the biggest being the financial backing. I also appreciated the interaction afforded by eating with students in their dining hall. During my time in Germany, I lived in university housing with visiting scholars from many different countries, all of whom had very different academic and personal backgrounds, and fascinating stories. The true highlight of my research experience, however, was the opportunity to get involved in intense, focused scholarship, which can be far more intellectually rewarding than the academic dabbling of broad overview classes.

To pursue academic research in Germany, you usually have to be a university student or graduate with a strong interest in pursuing a narrow research topic in a rigorous academic setting. In most fields, especially scientific ones, you do not need to speak any German at all, let alone know how to decline an unpreceded adjective in front of a feminine noun in the dative case. Everyone in my lab spoke some heartfelt variant of English, and I was actually required to give my presentations in English.

My six-month stay in Germany was one of the most rewarding experiences I've had abroad. Academically, my project succeeded beyond our wildest dreams. I worked hard, but received unending support from my labmates. I survived the student dining hall, sat in on classes, and went to a few raging university parties. But even as we climbed scientific mountains together, I saw first-hand the ways in which German students differed from Americans. One day I arrived at work to find that the students had gone on strike (by refusing to attend classes, a tough move for the industrious Germans) to protest an administrative fee that the university was planning to establish.

While based in Ulm, I also had the opportunities to explore Munich and Stuttgart and spend a strenuous but rewarding weekend biking at the glorious Chiemsee in Bavaria. Since I was a wage-earning chemist instead of a starving backpacker, my quick trips to Austria, England, and France had a more generous budget than they otherwise would have, and the superb European train system and new discount airlines helped make them relatively hassle-free. Academic research was a phenomenal way for me to get to know Germany, change the shape of my life for a while, see much of Europe, and even learn a little bit of science.

Barbara Richter was a Researcher-Writer for Let's Go: Austria & Switzerland. *A native Austrian, then New Jersian, she'll be continuing her studies in chemistry and physics as a graduate student.*

AUSTRIA (ÖSTERREICH)

With high culture in Vienna and high mountains in the Alps, Austria inclines toward very different extremes of beauty. It is home to the clear voices of the Vienna Boys Choir, jagged peaks that define the horizon, and fresh-fallen snow that awaits the imprint of skis. Although it is no longer the seat of the Hapsburg empire, Austria's capital city, Vienna, dazzles the senses with cosmopolitan flair. Follow any road away from the city, though, and you'll find golden onion-domed churches gracing small villages, green vines curling over half-timbered houses, and friendly people who smile and say *"Grüß Gott"* to passing strangers.

DISCOVER AUSTRIA: SUGGESTED ITINERARIES

THREE DAYS Spend all three days in **Vienna** (p. 73), the Imperial headquarters of passion. From the stately **Staatsoper** to the majestic **Hofburg,** Vienna's attractions will leave you with enough sensory stimulation to last until your next trip.

ONE WEEK Begin in **Innsbruck** (1 day; p. 92) to take advantage of its hiking and skiing opportunities. Stop in **Salzburg** (2 days; p. 85) to see the home of Mozart and the Salzburger Festspiele (p. 88). Move on to the Salzkammergut for the **Dachstein Ice Caves** (1 day; p. 90). End by basking in the glory of **Vienna** (3 days).

TWO WEEKS Start in **Innsbruck,** where museums and mountains meet (2 days), then swing by **Zell am See** and the Krimml Waterfalls (1 day; p. 91). Spend another two days wandering **Hohe Tauern National Park** (p. 91), visiting the Pasterze Glacier and the Großglockner Hochalpenstraße. Next, tour **Hallstatt** and its nearby ice caves (2 days; p. 89). Follow your ears to **Salzburg** (2 days), then head to **Graz** for its throbbing nightlife (1 day; p. 95). Finally, make your way to **Vienna** for a grand finale of romance, waltzes, and high coffeehouse culture (4 days).

ESSENTIALS

FACTS AND FIGURES

Official Name: Republic of Austria.
Capital: Vienna.
Major Cities: Graz, Innsbruck, Salzburg.
Population: 8,189,000.
Time Zone: GMT +1.
Language: German.
Religions: Roman Catholic (73%), Protestant (5%), Muslim (4%).

WHEN TO GO

Ski season reaches its peak between November and March, when prices in western Austria double and travelers need reservations months ahead. The situation reverses in the summer, when the eastern half of the country fills with tourists. Accommodations are cheaper and less crowded in the shoulder seasons (May-June and Sept.-Oct.). However, some Alpine resorts close in May and June—call ahead. Cultural opportunities also vary with the seasons: the Vienna State Opera, like many other theaters, has no shows in July or August, while the Vienna Boys' Choir only performs April-June and September-October.

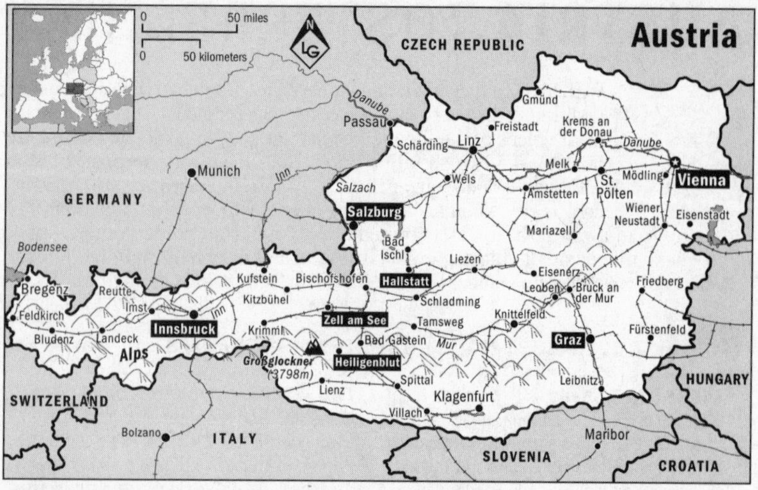

DOCUMENTS AND FORMALITIES

EMBASSIES. All foreign embassies in Austria are in Vienna (p. 73). Austrian embassies abroad include: **Australia,** 12 Talbot St., Forrest, Canberra, ACT, 2603 (☎02 6295 1533; www.austriaemb.org.au); **Canada,** 445 Wilbrod St., Ottawa, ON, K1N 6M7 (☎613-789-1444; www.austro.org); **Ireland,** 15 Ailesbury Ct., 93 Ailesbury Rd., Dublin, 4 (☎01 269 45 77); **New Zealand,** Level 2, Willbank House, 57 Willis St., Wellington, 6001 (☎04 499 63 93); **UK,** 18 Belgrave Mews West, London, SW1X 8HU (☎020 7344 3250; www.bmaa.gv.at/london); **US,** 3524 International Ct., NW, Washington, D.C., 20008 (☎202-895-6700; www.austria.org).

VISA AND ENTRY INFORMATION. EU citizens do not need a visa. Citizens of Australia, Canada, New Zealand, and the US do not need a visa for stays of up to 90 days, although this three-month period begins upon entry into any of the countries that belong to the EU's freedom-of-movement zone.

TOURIST SERVICES AND MONEY

EMERGENCY	Police: ☎133. Ambulance: ☎144. Fire: ☎122.

TOURIST OFFICES. Tourist offices are marked by signs with a green "i"; most brochures are available in English. Visit www.austria.info for further information.

MONEY. The unit of currency in Austria is the **euro (€).** As a general rule, it's cheaper to exchange money in Austria than at home. Railroad stations, airports, hotels, and most travel agencies offer exchange services, as do banks. If you stay in hostels and prepare most of your own food, expect to spend €30-60 per person per day. Accommodations start at about €12 and a basic sit-down meal usually costs around €8. Menus will say whether service is included *(Preise inklusive* or *Bedienung inklusiv);* if it is, a tip is not expected. If not, 10% will do. Austrian restaurants expect you to seat yourself, and servers will not bring the bill until you ask them to do so. Say *"Zahlen bitte"* (TSAHL-en BIT-uh) to settle your accounts, and don't leave tips on the table. Don't expect to bargain except at street markets. Austria has a 20% **value added tax (VAT),** which is applied to most purchased goods (p. 22). You can get refunds for one-time purchases of over €75 if you carry the goods out of Austria (and the EU) within three months of their purchase. Remember to keep your receipt or ask the customs office to endorse an invoice before you leave Austria. Contact the customs office to apply for your refund.

TRANSPORTATION

BY PLANE. The only major international airport is Vienna's Schwechat-Flughafen (VIE). Other airports are in Innsbruck, Graz, Linz, and Salzburg. From London-Stansted, **Ryanair** (☎3531 303 030; www.ryanair.com) flies to the latter three. For more information on flying to Austria, see p. 42.

BY TRAIN. The **Österreichische Bundesbahn** (**ÖBB;** www.oebb.at), Austria's state railroad, operates an efficient system with fast and comfortable trains. **Eurail** and **Inter Rail** are valid in Austria, but they do not guarantee a seat without a reservation. The **Austrian Railpass** allows three days of travel within any 15-day period on all rail lines. It also entitles holders to 40% off bike rentals at train stations (2nd-class US$107; each additional day US$15).

BY BUS. The Austrian bus system consists mainly of **PostBuses,** which cover areas inaccessible by train for comparably high prices. Buy tickets at the station or from the driver. For info, call ☎0222 711 01 7am-8pm.

BY CAR. Driving is a convenient way to see the more isolated parts of Austria, but gas is costly, an international license is required, and some small towns prohibit cars. The roads are well maintained and well marked, and Austrian drivers are quite careful. **Mitfahrzentralen** (ride-share services) in larger cities pair drivers with riders for a small fee. Riders then negotiate fares with the drivers. Be aware that not all organizations screen their drivers or riders; ask in advance.

BY BIKE. Bicycles are a great way to get around Austria, as roads in the country are generally smooth and safe. Many train stations rent bikes and allow you to return them to any participating station. Check tourist offices for bike routes and maps.

KEEPING IN TOUCH

PHONE CODES	**Country code:** 43. **International dialing prefix:** 00 (from Vienna, 900). For more information on how to place international calls, see inside back cover.

EMAIL AND THE INTERNET. It's not hard to find Internet cafes in Austria, especially in the larger cities. They cost about €2-6 per hour and sometimes lower their rates during slow times of the day or night.

TELEPHONES. Wherever possible, use a calling card for international phone calls, as long-distance rates for national phone services are often exorbitant. Prepaid phone cards and major credit cards can be used for direct international calls, but they are still less cost-efficient. For information on mobile phones, see p. 29. Direct-dial access numbers for calling out of Austria include **AT&T Direct** (☎0800 200 288), **British Telecom** (☎0800 200 209), **Canada Direct** (☎0800 200 217), **MCI WorldPhone** (☎0800 999 762), **Sprint** (☎0800 200 236), **Telecom New Zealand** (☎0800 200 222), and **Telstra Australia** (☎0800 261 202).

MAIL. Letters take one or two days within Austria. Airmail to North America takes four to seven days, and up to nine days to Australia and New Zealand. Mark all letters and packages *"mit Flugpost"* (airmail). Aerogrammes are the cheapest option. Let's Go lists the addresses for mail to be held *(Postlagernde Briefe)* in the **Practical Information** section of big cities.

LANGUAGE. German is the official language. English is the most common second language, but it's less common outside of cities and among older residents. For basic German words and phrases, see p. 1055.

ACCOMMODATIONS AND CAMPING

AUSTRIA	❶	❷	❸	❹	❺
ACCOMMODATIONS	under €16	€16-26	€26-34	€34-55	over €55

Always ask if your lodging provides a **guest card** *(Gästekarte)*, which grants discounts on activities, museums, and public transportation. The **Österreichischer Jugendherbergsverband-Hauptverband (ÖJH)** runs the over 80 HI **hostels** in Austria. Because of the rigorous standards of the national organization, these are usually very clean and orderly. Most charge €18-30 per night for dorms, with a €3-5 HI discount. **Independent hostels** vary in quality, but often have more personality and foster a lively backpacking culture. Slightly more expensive, **Pensionen** are similar to American and British B&Bs. In small to mid-sized towns, singles will cost about €20-30, but expect to pay twice as much in big cities. **Hotels** are expensive (singles over €35; doubles over €48). The cheapest ones generally have *"Gasthof," "Gästehaus,"* or *"Pension-Garni"* in the name. Renting a **Privatzimmer** (room in a family home) is an inexpensive and friendly option. Rooms range €16-30 per person; contact the local tourist office for a list. **Camping** in Austria is less about getting out into nature than having a cheap place to sleep; most sites are large plots glutted with RVs and are open in summer only. Prices run €10-12 per tent site and €5-7 per extra person. In the high Alps, hikers and mountaineers can retire to the famously well-maintained system of **mountain huts** *(Hütten)*, where traditional Austrian fare and a good night's rest await them—provided they reserve ahead.

HIKING AND SKIING. Nearly every town has hiking trails in its vicinity; consult the local tourist office. Trails are usually marked with either a red-white-red marker (only sturdy boots and hiking poles necessary) or a blue-white-blue marker (mountaineering equipment needed). Because of snow in high passes, most mountain hiking trails and mountain huts are open only from late June to early September. Western Austria is one of the world's best skiing regions; the areas around Innsbruck and Kitzbühel are saturated with lifts and runs. High season runs from November to March. Tourist offices provide information on regional skiing and can suggest budget travel agencies that offer ski packages.

FOOD AND DRINK

AUSTRIA	❶	❷	❸	❹	❺
FOOD	under €5	€5-10	€10-16	€16-25	over €25

Loaded with fat, salt, and cholesterol, traditional Austrian cuisine is bad for your skin, your heart, and your figure; enjoy! Austria's best known dish, *Wienerschnitzel,* is a breaded meat cutlet (usually veal or pork) fried in butter. Natives nurse their sweet tooth with *Kaffee und Kuchen* (coffee and cake), *Sacher Torte* (a rich chocolate cake layered with marmalade), and *Linzer Torte* (a light yellow cake with currant jam). Austrian beers are outstanding—try Stiegl, a Salzburg brew; Zipfer, from Upper Austria; and Styrian Gösser.

TIP **EAT YOUR VEGGIES.** Vegetarians should look on the menu for *Spätzle* (noodles), *Eierschwammerl* (yellow mushrooms), or anything with *"vegi"* in it.

AUSTRIA

HOLIDAYS AND FESTIVALS

Holidays: Just about everything closes on public holidays, so plan accordingly. In 2007, these holidays will be: New Year's Day (Jan. 1); Epiphany (Jan. 6); Good Friday (Apr. 6); Easter Monday (Apr. 9); Labor Day (May 1); Ascension (May 17); Corpus Christi (June 10); Assumption Day (Aug. 15); Austrian National Day (Oct. 26); All Saints' Day (Nov. 1); Immaculate Conception (Dec. 8); Christmas (Dec. 25); Boxing Day (Dec. 26).

Festivals: Vienna celebrates Fasching (Carnival) during the last two weeks of February. Austria's famous music festivals are the Wiener Festwochen (www.festwochen.at; early May to mid-June) and the Salzburger Festspiele (4th week in July to Aug. 31).

BEYOND TOURISM

Austria caters more to tourism than volunteerism; there are only limited opportunities to give back, so your best bet is to find them through a placement service. Opportunities for short-term work abound at hotels, ski resorts, and farms.

Actilingua Academy, Glorietteg. 8, A-1130 Vienna (☎431 877 6701; www.actilingua.com). Study German in Vienna.

Concordia, Heversham House, 2nd fl. 20-22 Boundary Rd., East Sussex, BN2 3HJ, UK (☎012 7342 2218). British volunteer organization that includes community projects in Austria, such as renovating historic buildings and parks, directing a youth drama project, and creating hiking paths.

VIENNA (WIEN) ☎01

Vienna (pop. 1,500,000) was transformed by war, marriage, and Hapsburg maneuvering from a Roman camp along the Danube into the political linchpin of the continent. Beethoven and Mozart made the city an arbiter of high culture—yet Vienna, as always, keeps to the beat of the younger generation. On any given afternoon, cafes turn the sidewalks into a sea of umbrellas, and on warm summer nights, bars and clubs pulse with experimental techno and indie rock until dawn.

INTERCITY TRANSPORTATION

Flights: The **Wien-Schwechat Flughafen (VIE;** ☎700 70), 18km from the city center, is home to **Austrian Airlines** (☎517 89; www.aua.com). The cheapest way to reach the city is the S-Bahn, which stops at **Wien Mitte** (☎65 17 17; 30min., every 20-30min. 5am-10pm, €3). The Vienna Airport Lines **bus** (☎93000 2300) takes 20min. to reach Südbahnhof and 40min. to Westbahnhof (every 30min. 6am-midnight; €6, round-trip €11). The **City Airport Train** (**CAT;** ☎25 250; www.cityairporttrain.com) takes only 16min. to reach **Wien Mitte** (every 30min. 6:05am-11:35pm) but is expensive (€10 when purchased on the train; €9, round-trip €16 from a ticket machine; €8, round-trip €15 online; Eurail not valid).

Trains: Vienna has 2 main train stations with international connections. Call ☎05 17 17 (24hr.) or check www.oebb.at for general train information.

Westbahnhof, XV, Mariahilferstr. 132. To: **Amsterdam, NTH** (12hr., 10 per day, €111); **Berlin, GER** (11hr., every 2hr., €80); **Budapest, HUN** (3hr., 10 per day, €36); **Hamburg, GER** (9hr., every 2hr., €80); **Innsbruck** (5-6hr., every 1½hr., €49); **Munich, GER** (5hr., 1 per hr., €68); **Paris, FRA** (14hr., 1 per hr. 7am-4pm, €110); **Salzburg** (3hr., 1 per hr., €37); **Zürich, SWI** (9hr., 8 per day, €165). Info counter open daily 7:30am-9pm.

Südbahnhof, X, Wiener Gürtel 1A. Trains go to: **Graz** (2½hr., every 2hr., €32); **Kraków, POL** (7-11hr., 5 per day, €48); **Prague, CZR** (4hr., 9-10 per day, €43); **Rome, ITA** (14hr., every 2hr., €100); **Venice, ITA** (9-10hr., 4 per day, €70). Info counter open daily 7am-8pm.

AUSTRIA

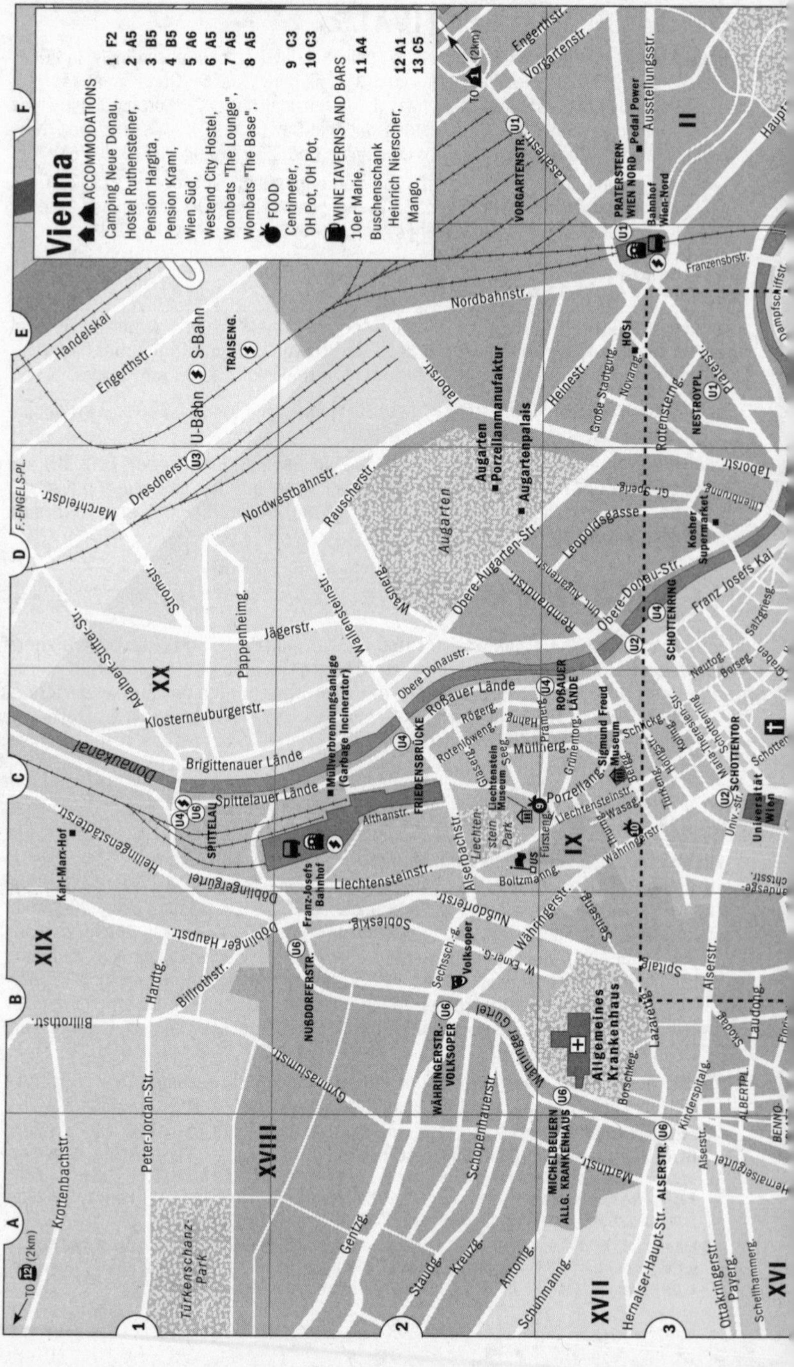
Vienna
ACCOMMODATIONS
Camping Neue Donau, 1 F2
Hostel Ruthensteiner, 2 A5
Pension Hargita, 3 B5
Pension Kraml, 4 B5
Wien Süd, 5 A6
Westend City Hostel, 6 A5
Wombats "The Lounge", 7 A5
Wombats "The Base", 8 A5
FOOD
Centimeter, 9 C3
OH Pot, OH Pot, 10 C3
WINE TAVERNS AND BARS
10er Marie, 11 A4
Buschenschank
Heinrich Nierscher, 12 A1
Mango, 13 C5
U-Bahn
S-Bahn
Donaukanal
Augarten
Augartenpalais
Porzellanmanufaktur
Allgemeines Krankenhaus
Universität Wien
Sigmund Freud Museum
Liechtenstein Museum
Franz-Josefs Bahnhof
Müllverbrennungsanlage (Garbage Incinerator)
Karl-Marx-Hof
Türkenschanz-Park
Volksoper
Kosher Supermarket
Pedal Power
HOSI
Bahnhof Wien-Nord
PRATERSTERN-WIEN NORD
SPITTELAU
FRIEDENSBRÜCKE
ROẞAUER LÄNDE
SCHOTTENRING
SCHOTTENTOR
NUẞDORFERSTR.
WÄHRINGERSTR.-VOLKSOPER
MICHELBEUERN ALLG. KRANKENHAUS
ALSERSTR.
VORGARTENSTR.
TRAISENG.
NESTROYPL.
XVI
XVII
XVIII
XIX
XX
IX
II

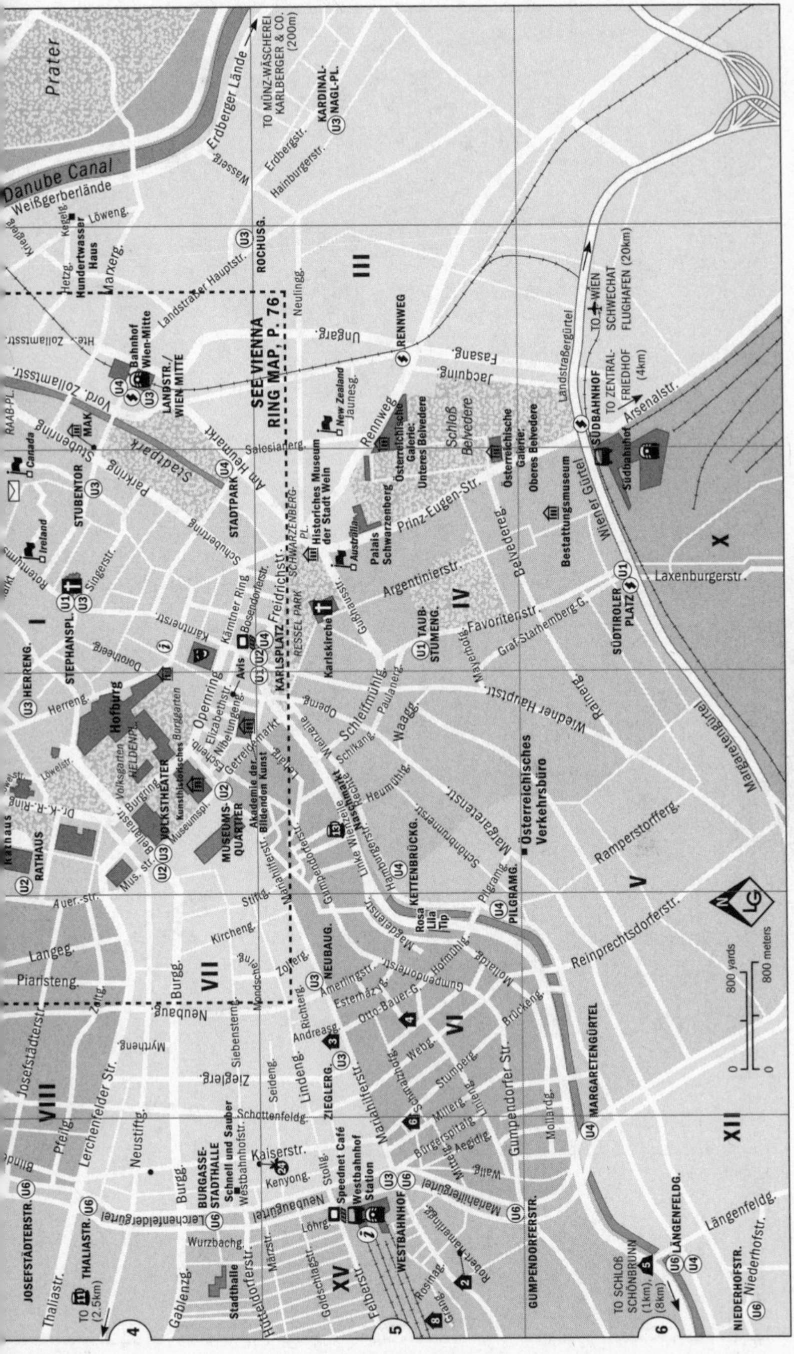
Prater
Danube Canal
Weißgerberlände
Erdberger Lände
TO MÜNZ-WÄSCHEREI KARLBERGER & CO. (200m)
KARDINAL-NAGL-PL.
Erdbergstr.
Hainburgerstr.
ROCHUSG.
Hundertwasser Haus
Löweng.
Marxerg.
Landstraßer Hauptstr.
Bahnhof Wien-Mitte
LANDSTR./WIEN MITTE
SEE VIENNA RING MAP, P. 76
Vord. Zollamtsstr.
MAK
Stubenring
Stadtpark
Am Heumarkt
STADTPARK
STUBENTOR
Canada
Ireland
Parkring
Schubertring
STEPHANSPL.
Singerstr.
Rotenturmstr.
I
HERRENG.
Herreng.
Hofburg
HELDENPL.
Volksgarten
Burggarten
Kunsthistorisches Museum
Dr.-K.-R.-Ring
RATHAUS
Rathaus
VOLKSTHEATER
MUSEUMS-QUARTIER
Akademie der Bildenden Künste
Opernring
Kärntner Ring
Kärntnerstr.
Dorotheerg.
Bosendorferstr.
Avis
KARLSPLATZ
Friedrichstr.
RESSEL PARK
SCHWARZENBERG-PL.
Historisches Museum der Stadt Wein
Karlskirche
Australia
Palais Schwarzenberg
New Zealand
Salesianerg.
Rennweg
Jauneg.
Ungarg.
RENNWEG
III
Neulingg.
Österreichische Galerie: Unteres Belvedere
Schloß Belvedere
Österreichische Galerie: Oberes Belvedere
Jacquing.
Fasang.
Prinz-Eugen-Str.
Argentinierstr.
Belvederег.
IV
TAUB-STUMENG.
Favoritenstr.
Graf-Starhemberg-G.
Bestattungsmuseum
SÜDTIROLER PLATZ
Laxenburgerstr.
X
Wiener Gürtel
SÜDBAHNHOF
Südbahnhof
Arsenalstr.
Landstraßergürtel
TO ZENTRAL-FRIEDHOF (4km)
TO WIEN SCHWECHAT FLUGHAFEN (20km)
Wiedner Hauptstr.
Schleifmühlg.
Operng.
Paulanerg.
Waagg.
Rainerg.
Margaretengürtel
Naschmarkt
Linke Wienzeile
Rechte Wienzeile
Heumühlg.
Schönbrunnerstr.
Margaretenstr.
Österreichisches Verkehrsbüro
KETTENBRÜCKG.
Rosa Lila Tip
PILGRAMG.
Ramperstorfferg.
V
Reinprechtsdorferstr.
NEUBAUG.
Mariahilferstr.
Gumpendorferstr.
VII
Kircheng.
Burgg.
Neubaug.
Langeg.
Piaristeng.
Josefstädterstr.
VIII
Lerchenfelder Str.
Zieglerg.
ZIEGLERG.
Siebensterng.
Mondscheing.
Lindeng.
Zollerg.
Amerlingstr.
Esterhazyg.
Otto-Bauer-G.
Andreasg.
VI
Hofmühlg.
Mollardg.
Brückeng.
Webg.
Stumperg.
Millerg.
Gumpendorfer Str.
MARGARETENGÜRTEL
Mollardg.
XII
Schottenfeldg.
Seideng.
Neustiftg.
Kaiserstr.
Kenyong.
Stollg.
BURGASSE-STADTHALLE
Schnell und Sauber
Westbahnhofstr.
Speednet Café
Westbahnhof Station
WESTBAHNHOF
Neubaugürtel
Lerchenfeldergürtel
Mariahilfergürtel
Wurzbachg.
Stadthalle
Gablenzg.
Hütteldorferstr.
Märzstr.
Goldschlagstr.
XV
Felberstr.
Rosinag.
Robert-Hamerling-G.
GUMPENDORFERSTR.
TO SCHLOẞ SCHÖNBRUNN (1km), (8km)
LÄNGENFELDG.
Längenfeldg.
NIEDERHOFSTR.
Niederhofstr.
JOSEFSTÄDTERSTR.
THALIASTR.
Thaliastr.
TO (2.5km)
4
5
6
800 yards
800 meters
0
0

AUSTRIA

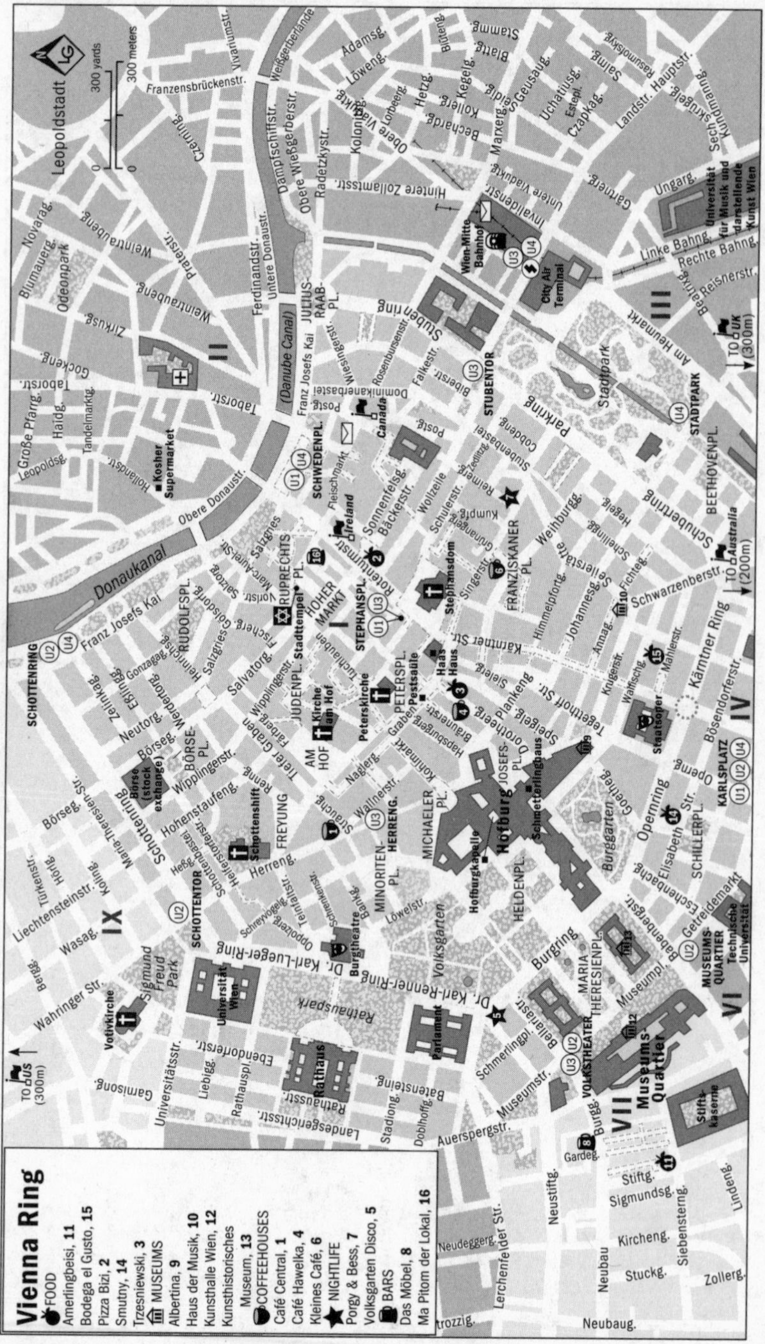
Vienna Ring
FOOD
Amerlingbeisi, 11
Bodega el Gusto, 15
Pizza Bizi, 2
Smutny, 14
Trzesniewski, 3
MUSEUMS
Albertina, 9
Haus der Musik, 10
Kunsthalle Wien, 12
Kunsthistorisches Museum, 13
COFFEEHOUSES
Café Central, 1
Café Hawelka, 4
Kleines Café, 6
NIGHTLIFE
Porgy & Bess, 7
Volksgarten Disco, 5
BARS
Das Möbel, 8
Ma Pitom der Lokal, 16
Leopoldstadt
300 yards
300 meters
Donaukanal
(Danube Canal)
Hofburg
Stephansdom
Stadtpark
Rathaus
Parlament
Universität Wien
Volksgarten
Burggarten
Rathauspark
Museums-Quartier
Staatsoper
Votivkirche
Burgtheatre
Peterskirche
Schottenring
Stubenring
Parkring
Schubertring
Kärntner Ring
Opernring
Burgring
Dr. Karl-Renner-Ring
Dr. Karl-Lueger-Ring

Buses: Buses in Austria are rarely cheaper than trains; compare prices before buying a ticket. **City bus terminals** at Wien Mitte/Landstr., Hütteldorf, Heiligenstadt, Floridsdorf, Kagran, Erdberg, and Reumannpl. Tickets sold onboard. Many international bus lines also have agencies in the stations. For info, call ☎711 01 between 7am-8pm.

ORIENTATION

Vienna is divided into 23 **districts** *(Bezirke)*. The first is **Innenstadt** (city center), defined by the **Ringstraße** (ring road) on three sides and the Danube Canal on the fourth. At the center of the Innenstadt lies **Stephansplatz** and much of the pedestrian district. The best way to reach Innenstadt is to take the U-bahn to **Stephanspl.** (U1, U3) or **Karlsplatz** (U1, U2, U4); **Schwedenplatz** (U1, U4) is close to the city's nightlife. Tram lines 1 and 2 circle the Innenstadt on the ring road, with line 2 heading clockwise and 1 counterclockwise.

The Ringstraße consists of different segments, each with its own name, such as Opernring or Kärntner Ring. Many of Vienna's major attractions are in District I and immediately around the Ringstr. Districts II-IX spread out from the city center following the clockwise traffic of the Ring. The remaining districts expand from yet another ring road, the **Gürtel** (Belt). Like the Ring, this major thoroughfare has numerous segments, including Margaretengürtel, Neubaugürtel, and Währinger Gürtel. Street signs indicate the district number in Roman or Arabic numerals before the street and number, as does *Let's Go*.

LOCAL TRANSPORTATION

Public Transportation: Wiener Linien (general info ☎790 91 00, www.wienerlinien.at.) The **subway** (U-Bahn), **tram** (Straßenbahn), **elevated train** (S-Bahn), and **bus** lines operate on a 1-ticket system, so you can transfer between types of transportation without having to buy a new ticket. Buy tickets at a machine, counter, tobacco shop, or onboard the trams and buses. A **single fare** (€2 onboard, €1.50 in advance) lets you travel to any destination in the city and switch from bus to U-Bahn to tram to S-Bahn in any order, as long as your travel is uninterrupted. Other ticket options include a **1-day pass** (€5), **1-day "shopping" pass** (M-Sa 8am-8pm, €4), **3-day rover ticket** (€12), **7-day pass** (€12.50; valid M 9am to the next M 9am), and an **8-day pass** (€24; valid any 8 days, not necessarily consecutive; can be split between several people travelling together, but must be validated for each person). To **validate a ticket,** punch it in the machine before entering the 1st vehicle, but don't stamp it again when you switch trains. Otherwise, plainclothes inspectors may fine you €60. Regular trams and subway cars stop running midnight-5am. **Night buses** run every 30min. along most routes; "N" signs designate night bus stops. A night bus schedule is available from information offices of the Wiener Linien (M-F 6:30am-6:30pm, Sa-Su 8:30am-4pm) in the Karlspl., Stepahnspl., Westbahnhof, and some other U-Bahn stations.

Taxis: ☎313 00, 401 00, 601 60, or 814 00. Stands are at Westbahnhof, Südbahnhof, Karlspl. in the city center, and by the Bermuda Dreieck for late-night revelers. Accredited taxis have yellow-and-black signs on the roof. Base rate €2.50, €0.20 per additional 0.2km; slightly more expensive holidays and 11pm-6am.

Car Rental: Avis, I, Opernring 3-5 (☎587 62 41 or 700 327 00). Open M-F 7am-6pm, Sa 8am-2pm, Su 8am-1pm. **Hertz** (☎70 07 32 661), at the airport. Open M-F 8am-11pm, Sa 8am-8pm, Su 7am-11pm.

Bike Rental: Pick up a *Vienna By Bike* brochure at the tourist office. **Pedal Power,** II, Ausstellungsstr. 3 (☎729 7234, www.pedalpower.at). Bike rental 5hr. (€24), day (€32), additional day (€22). 15 percent discount if you pick up the bike at their office. Open daily Apr.-Oct. 8am-7pm. Hostels (p. 79) are also a cheap and convenient option.

PRACTICAL INFORMATION

Main Tourist Office: I, Albertinapl. corner of Maysederg. (☎24 555). Follow Operng. up 1 block from the Opera House. The staff books rooms for a €2 fee and gives out free city maps, the pamphlet *Youth Scene*. Open daily 9am-7pm.

Embassies and Consulates: Australia, IV, Mattiellistr. 2-4 (☎506 740). Open M-F 8:30am-4:30pm. **Canada,** I, Laurenzerberg 2 (☎531 38 30 00) M-F 8:30am-12:30pm and 1:30-3:30pm. **Ireland,** I, Rotenturmstr. 16-18, 3rd fl. (☎71 54 24 6). Open M-F 9:30-11am and 1:30-4pm. **New Zealand,** III, Salesianerstr. 15 (☎318 85 05). **UK,** III, Jauresg. 10 (☎716 13 51 51, out of hours for UK nationals in emergencies only 0676 5694012). Open M-F 2-4pm. **US,** IX, Parkring 12 (☎313 390). Open M-F 8-11:30am, emergency services M-F 8am-5pm.

Currency Exchange: ATMs are your best bet. **Banks** and **airport exchanges** use the same official rates. Most open M-W and F 8am-12:30pm and 1:30-3pm, Th 8am-12:30pm and 1:30-5:30pm. **Train station** exchanges have long hours (daily 7am-10pm at the Westbahnhof) and a €6 min. fee for the 1st 3 checks (max. €300). Stay away from the 24hr. bill-exchange machines in Innenstadt, as they generally charge outrageous prices.

American Express Travel Agency: I, Kärntnerstr. 21-23 (☎515 40), near Stephanspl. Cashes AmEx and Thomas Cook checks (€7 min. commission for up to €250, €12 for €251-500) and sells event tickets. Open M-F 9am-5:30pm, Sa 9am-noon.

Luggage Storage: Lockers available at all train stations. €2-3.50 per 24hr.

Bookstores: The **British Bookshop,** I, Weihburgg. 24 (☎512 19 45), has an extensive travel section. Open M-F 9:30am-6:30pm, Sa 9:30am-5pm. AmEx/DC/MC/V.

GLBT Resources: Pick up the *Vienna Gay Guide* (www.gaynet.at/guide), *Extra Connect, Bussi,* or the tourism bureau's *Queer Guide* from any tourist office or gay bar, cafe, or club. **Rosa Lila Tip,** VI, Linke Wienzeile 102 (www.villa.at, lesbians ☎586 5150, gay men 585 4343), is a knowledgeable resource and social center. English spoken. Take the U4 to Pilgrimg. and look for the pink house on the left bank. Open M, W, F 5-8pm.

Laundromat: Schnell und Sauber, VII, Westbahnhofstr. 60. U6: Burgg./Stadthalle. Wash €4.50, dry €1 per 20min. Soap included. Open 24hr.

Emergency: Police: ☎133. **Ambulance:** ☎144. **Fire:** ☎122. **Emergency care:** ☎141.

Crisis Hotlines: All have English speakers. **Rape Crisis Hotline:** ☎523 22 22. Line staffed M, Th 1-6pm, Tu, F 10am-3pm. **24hr. immediate help for women:** ☎717 19.

24hr. Pharmacy Hotline: ☎15 50. Consulates have lists of English-speaking doctors.

Hospital: Allgemeines Krankenhaus, IX, Währinger Gürtel 18-20 (☎404 00 19 64).

Internet Access: bigNET.internet.cafe (☎533 29 39), I, Kärntnerstr. 61 or I, Hoher Markt 8-9. €3.70 per 30min. Open daily 9am-11pm.

Post Office: Hauptpostamt (☎0577 677 1010), I, Fleischmarkt 19. Open 24hr. Branches throughout the city and at the train stations; look for yellow signs with a trumpet logo. Address *Poste Restante* as in the following example: SURNAME, First name, *Postlagernde Briefe;* Hauptpostamt; Fleischmarkt 19, A-1010 Wien AUSTRIA. **Postal Codes:** A-1010 (1st district); A-1020 (2nd district); A-1030 (3rd district); continues to A-1230 (23rd district).

ACCOMMODATIONS AND CAMPING

Hunting for cheap rooms in Vienna during peak tourist season (June-Sept.) can be unpleasant; call for reservations at least five days ahead. Otherwise, plan on calling between 6 and 9am to put your name down for a reservation. For information on camping near Vienna, visit www.campingwien.at.

HOSTELS

Hostel Ruthensteiner, XV, Robert-Hamerlingg. 24 (☎893 4202; www.hostelruthensteiner.com). Exit Westbahnhof, turn right onto Mariahilferstr., then continue until Haidmannsg. Turn left before the Sato restaurant, then right on Robert-Hamerlingg. Knowledgeable staff, spotless rooms, kitchen, and a secluded courtyard. Bike rental €12 per day, half-day €8. Breakfast €2.50. Internet €2 per 40min. Reception 24hr. €10 key deposit. 32-bed summer dorm €12; 4- to 10-bed dorms €13-15; singles €28; doubles €45; quads €60. AmEx/MC/V; €0.40 per day surcharge. ❶

Wombats City Hostel, (☎897 2336, www.wombats-hostels.com) **"The Base"** (XV, Grang. 6). Exit Westbahnhof, turn right on Mariahilferstr., right on Rosinag., and left on Grang. Despite its proximity to train tracks, this wildly colorful hostel compensates with an in-house pub, English-language movie nights, and guided tours. **"The Lounge"** (XV, Mariahilferstr. 137) is the newer Wombats branch, closer to the train station, but farther from the tracks. The bright walls and leather couches add a modern touch to the college dorm atmosphere. Popular, loud bar in the basement vault. Breakfast €3.50. Internet €3 per hr. All rooms with bath. Dorms €18; singles €24; doubles €48. Cash only. ❷

Westend City Hostel, VI, Fügerg. 3 (☎597 6729, www.westendhostel.at), near Westbahnhof. Exit on Äussere Mariahilferstr., cross the large intersection diagonally, go right on Mullerg. and left on Fügerg. Plain dorms with bath. Breakfast included. Internet €2 per 20min. Reception 24hr. Check-out 10:30am. Lockout 10:30am-2pm. Mid-Mar. to Nov. dorms 18-20; singles €47-60; doubles €56-74. Cash only. ❷

PENSIONS

Pension Hargita, VII, Andreasg. 1 (☎526 1928; www.hargita.at). U3: Zieglerg. Hungarian decorations in the halls and immaculate hardwood floors. Breakfast €5. Reception 8am-8pm. Singles €38, with shower €45, with shower and toilet €52; doubles €52, with shower €58; triples with shower €73, with shower and toilet €80. MC/V. ❹

Pension Kraml, VI, Brauerg. 5 (☎587 85 88, www.pensionkraml.at). U3: Zierierg. Exit on Otto-Bauerg., take 1st left, then 1st right. Plush rooms in rich red, and a lounge with cable TV. Breakfast included. Reception 24hr. Singles €30; doubles €50, with shower €60, with shower and toilet €70; triples €70/80. 3- to 5-person apartment with bath €95-125. Cash only. ❸

CAMPING

Camping Neue Donau, XXII, Am Kleehäufel 119 (☎202 40 10). U1: Kaisermühlen. Take the Schüttaustr. exit, cross the street and then take bus #91A (every 30min.) to Kleehäufel. 4km from the city center and adjacent to Neue Donau beaches. Boat and bike rental. Supermarket and showers. Laundry €4.50. Reception 8am-12:30pm and 3-6:15pm. Open Easter-Sept. Tent sites €11-13, extra person €6-7. DC/MC/V. ❶

Wien Süd, XXIII, Breitenfurterstr. 269 (☎867 36 49). U6: Philadelphiabrücke, and bus #62A to Wien Süd. This former imperial park features a cafe, playground, supermarket, and kitchen. Laundry €4.50. Reception 7:45am-8pm. Open May-Sept. Tent sites €11-13, extra person €6-7. AmEx/DC/MC/V. ❶

FOOD

Restaurants that call themselves *Stüberl* or advertise *Schmankerl* serve Viennese fare. Innenstadt restaurants are expensive, but north of the university, where Universitätsstr. and Währingerstr. meet (U2: Schottentor), is more budget-friendly. Affordable cafes and restaurants line **Burggasse** in District VI and the area around the Rechte and Linke Wienzeile near Naschmarkt (U4: Kettenbrückeg). Supermarket chains include **Zielpunkt, Billa,** and **Spar.** The **kosher** market is at District II, Hollandstr. 10. (☎216 96 75. Open M-Th 8:30am-6:30pm, F 8am-3pm, Su 10am-noon.)

AUSTRIA

HOW DO YOU SOLVE A PROBLEM LIKE MARILLE?

..By baking a strudel 50m long, of course.

During the *Alles Marille* "Everything Apricot") festival in Krems, held the third Friday and Saturday in July, the fuzzy fruit appears in every form imaginable, rom apricot schnapps to apricot ce cream to apricot dumplings to apricot spritzer. The *pièce de ésistance*, however, is Café Hagmann's 50m long *Marillenstrudel*, which stretches down Taglisher Markt street. Everyone in town can literally get a piece of the action from this perpetual pastry, aden with fluffy apricot cream and sugared almonds (€3 per 30 min.). A folk band in traditional dress serenades the town with Austrian favorites from under an awning festooned with apricot balloons, while revelers sun themselves and imbibe all things apricot. All of Krems turns out for the un, including the mayor himself. Young and old alike stroll amid cafes and vendors, creating the closest thing to traffic Krems gets. To top it all off, Saturday ends with a huge party down by the *Schiffstation*, where the *Marillen* schnapps and punch flow like milk and honey. So as you bike, drive, or walk along the Danube and see the trees laden with their precious golden goods, drop into Krems and indulge with the locals n a truly lavish fruit fetish.

INSIDE THE RING

Trzesniewski, I, Dorotheerg. 1 (☎512 32 91), from Stephansdom, 3 blocks down on the left side of the Graben. Once Kafka's favorite place to eat; has been serving open-faced mini-sandwiches (€1) for over 100 years. Toppings include egg, cucumber, salmon, paprika, and herring. Open M-F 8:30am-7:30pm, Sa 9am-5pm. Cash only. ❶

Pizza Bizi, I, Rotenturmstr. 4 (☎513 37 05), 1 block up Rotenturmstr. from Stephanspl. One of the best deals in the city, this self-serve restaurant grills up meats with 2 sides for €5-6. Pizza slice €2.50. Pastas €5-6. Open daily 10:30am-11:30pm. Cash only. ❷

Smutny, I, Elisabethstr. 8 (☎587 13 56), U6: Karlspl. Traditional Viennese restaurant serving tasty *Schnitzel* (€14) and *Fiakergulash* (€11). M-F lunchtime *Menü* €7.80, Sa-Su €9.80. M-F daily special €5. Open daily 10am-midnight. AmEx/DC/MC/V. ❷

Bodega El Gusto, I, Mahlerstr. 7 (☎512 06 73). Walk toward Stephansdom on Kärntnerstr. and turn right on Mahlerstr. This cozy eatery serves tapas (€2-7; veggie options available), meat, and seafood Spanish dishes (€4-20). Open M-Sa 5pm-1am. MC/V. ❸

OUTSIDE THE RING

OH Pot, IX, Währingerstr. 22 (☎319 42 59; www.ohpot.at). U2: Schottentor. Serves filling "pots," stew-like veggie or meat concoctions with influences from Ethiopia to Bolivia (€7.20-8.20). Lunch special offers, soup or salad, any pot, and dessert for €6.20 (M-F 11am-3pm, Sa noon-3pm). Sunday buffet 11am-5pm (€11). Open daily 11am-midnight. Kitchen closes 9pm. AmEx/DC/MC/V. ❷

Centimeter, IX, Liechtensteinstr. 42 (☎470 06 06; www.centimeter.at). Tram D to Bauernfeldpl. This chain offers huge portions of greasy Austrian fare (€5.50-7) and an unbelievable selection of beers (€3-4 per L). Sandwiches €0.10-0.15 per cm. Open M-F 10am-midnight, Sa-Su 11am-midnight. AmEx/MC/V. ❶

Amerlingbeisl, VII, Stiftg. 8 (☎526 1660). U3: Neubaug. Soft lighting and a grapevine-covered courtyard are a perfect backdrop for Mediterranean-influenced entrees (€6-9). Vegetarian options (€6-7). Breakfast until 3pm (€4-8); Sa-Su brunch buffet €10. Open daily 9am-2am. Kitchen closes 1am. AmEx/MC/V. ❷

COFFEEHOUSES

Using Viennese coffeehouses for a midafternoon pick-me-up is like using the Magna Carta to clean up after a spill. These establishments have been havens for artists, writers, and thinkers. The most important dictate of coffeehouse etiquette is that you linger; the waiter *(Herr Ober)* will serve you, then leave you to sip, read, and cogitate. When you're ready to leave, ask to pay *("Zahlen bitte")*.

Kleines Café, I, Franziskanerpl. 3. Turn off Kärntnerstr. onto Weihburg. Escape from the busy pedestrian streets with a mélange (€3) and conversation on a leather couch. Sandwiches €3-5. Open daily 10am-2am. Cash only.

Café Central, I, Herreng. 14 (☎533 37 6424), at the corner of Strauchg. With green-gold arches and live music, this luxurious coffeehouse deserves its status as mecca of the cafe world. Open M-Sa 7:30am-10pm, Su 10am-6pm. AmEx/DC/MC/V.

Café Hawelka, I, Dorotheerg. 6 (☎512 82 30), off Graben. A Viennese institution since 1939, this legendary cafe has a long history as a meeting place for artists. Try the *Buchteln* (cake with plum marmalade); €3. *Mélange* €3.20. Open M and W-Sa 8am-2am, Su 4pm-2am. Cash only.

Demel, I, Kohlmarkt 14 (☎535 17 17). 5min. from the Stephansdom, down Graben. The most lavish *Konditorei,* or confectioner, in Vienna, Demel once served its creations to the imperial court. The chocolate is made fresh every morning, and the desserts are legendary. *Mélange* €3.80. Tortes €4. Open daily 10am-7pm. AmEx/MC/V.

WINE TAVERNS (HEURIGEN)

Marked by a hanging branch of evergreen, *Heurigen* serve wine and savory Austrian delicacies, often in a relaxed outdoors setting. Tourists head to the most famous region, **Grinzing,** in District XIX; you'll find better atmosphere in the hills of **Sievering** and **Neuwaldegg** (in XVII). To reach Perchtoldsdorf, take U4 to Hietzing and tram #6 to Rodaun. Walk down Ketzerg. until Hochstr. and continue on Hochstr. for several minutes. True *Heuriger* devotees make the trip to **Gumpoldskirchen.** Take the S-Bahn from the Südbahnhof.

AUSTRIA

Buschenschank Heinrich Nierscher, XIX, Strehlg. 21 (☎440 2146). U6: Währingerstr. Tram #41 to Plötzleinsdorf (the last stop); then take bus #41A to Plötzleinsfriedhof (the second stop) or walk up Pötzleing. which becomes Khevenhuller Str.; go right on Strehlg. Enjoy a white wine spritzer (.25L, €1.60) or *Heuriger* (€2.20) in the backyard overlooking the vineyards. Open M, Th-Su 3pm-midnight. Closed Nov. and Feb. Cash only.

10er Marie, XVI, Ottakringerstr. 222-224. U3: Ottakring, left on Thaliastr., then right onto Johannes-Krawarik-Gasse. Locals frequent the large garden behind the yellow house. 0.25L of wine €2. Cash only.

SIGHTS

INSIDE THE RING

A stroll in District I, the social and geographical center, is a feast for the senses. Cafe tables spill into the streets and musicians attract onlookers as Romanesque arches, *Jugendstil* apartments, and the modern **Haas Haus** overlook the action.

STEPHANSDOM, GRABEN, AND PETERSPLATZ. In the heart of the city, the massive **Stephansdom** is one of Vienna's most treasured symbols. For a view of the old city, take the elevator up the North Tower or climb the 343 steps of the South Tower. *(☎515 52 3526. North Tower open daily July-Aug. 9am-5pm; Apr.-June and Sept.-Oct. 8:30am-5:30pm; Nov.-Mar. 8:30am-5pm. South Tower open daily 9am-5:30pm. South Tower €3. North Tower €4.)* Downstairs, skeletons of plague victims fill the **catacombs.** The **Gruft** (vault) stores all of the Hapsburg innards. *(Tours M-Sa every 30min. 10-11:30am and 1:30-4:30pm, Su and holidays 1:30-4:30pm. €4.)* From Stephanspl., follow Graben for Jugendstil architecture, including the **Ankerhaus** (#10), Otto Wagner's red-marble

Grabenhof, and the underground public toilet complex designed by Adolf Loos. Graben leads to Peterspl. and the 1663 **Pestsaüle** (Plague Column), built to celebrate the passing of the Black Death *(U1 or 3: Stephanspl.).*

HOHER MARKT AND STADTTEMPEL. The biggest draw in Hoher Markt is the 1914 Jugendstil **Ankeruhr** (clock), whose figures—from Marcus Aurelius to Maria Theresa—rotate past the Viennese coat of arms accompanied by the tunes of their times. *(1 figure per hr. At noon all figures appear.)* Hidden on Ruprechtspl. is the **Stadttempel,** the only synagogue in Vienna to escape Kristallnacht. *(Seitenstetteng. 4. Required guided tours on M and Th at 11:30am, 2pm. Bring passport. €2, students €1.)*

AM HOF AND FREYUNG. Once a medieval jousting square, Am Hof now houses the **Kirche am Hof** and **Collalto Palace,** where Mozart gave his first public performance. *(From Stephanspl., walk down Graben until it ends, go right and continue on Bognerg.; Am Hof is on the right.)* Just west of Am Hof is Freyung, the square with the **Austriabrunnen** in the center. Medieval fugitives took asylum in the **Schottenstift** (Monastery of the Scots), giving rise to the name Freyung, or "sanctuary." Today, the annual **Christkindl market** fills the plaza with baked goods and holiday cheer.

OUTSIDE THE RING

Some of Vienna's most famous modern architecture is outside the Ring, where 20th-century designers found more space to build. This area is also home to a number of Baroque palaces and parks that were once beyond the city limits.

KARLSPLATZ. Karlsplatz is home to Vienna's most beautiful Baroque church, the **Karlskirche,** an eclectic masterpiece combining a Neoclassical portico with a Baroque dome and towers on either side. Under renovation until the end of 2006, the church may be best viewed from the outside; save your money unless you want to take an elevator to the top of the dome. *(Kreuzherreng. 1. U1, 2, or 4 to Karlspl. ☎504 61 87. Open M-F 7:30am-7pm, Sa 8:30am-7pm, Su 9am-7pm. €6, students €4.)*

SCHLOß BELVEDERE. The Schloß Belvedere was once the summer residence of Prince Eugène of Savoy, one of Austria's greatest military heroes. The grounds, stretching from Schwarzenberg Palace to the Südbahnhof, contain three excellent museums (p. 83) and an equal number of spectacular sphinx-filled gardens. *(Take tram D or #71 one stop past Schwarzenbergpl. Gardens open daily dawn to dusk. Free.)*

SCHLOß SCHÖNBRUNN. Schönbrunn began as a humble hunting lodge, but Maria Theresa's acquisitive instincts transformed it into the splendid palace it is today. The **Imperial Tour** passes through the **Great Gallery,** where the Congress of Vienna met, and the dazzling **Hall of Mirrors,** where six-year-old Mozart played. The longer **Grand Tour** also visits the exquisite rooms of Maria Theresa's time, including the ornate Millions Room. *(Schönbrunnerstr. 47. U4: Schönbrunn. Apartments open daily July-Aug. 8:30am-6pm; Apr.-June and Sept.-Oct. 8:30am-5pm; Nov.-Mar. 8:30am-4:30pm. Imperial Tour €9, students €8. Grand Tour €11.50/10.20. English-language audio tour included.)* As impressive as Schönbrunn itself, the **gardens** behind the palace contain a **labyrinth** and a profusion of manicured greenery, flowers, and statuettes. *(Park open daily 6am-dusk. Labyrinth open daily July-Aug. 9am-7pm; Apr.-June and Sept. 9am-6pm; Oct. 9am-5pm; also Nov. 9am-3:30pm. Park free. Labyrinth €2.60, students €2.20.)*

MUSEUMS

With a museum around almost every corner, Vienna could exhaust any zealous visitor. All museums run by the city are free every Friday before noon (except on public holidays), and some privately-held collections often have discounted or free days as well.

INSIDE THE RING

HAUS DER MUSIK. Science meets music in this interactive museum. Relax in the prenatal listening room, experience the physics of sound, learn about famous Viennese composers, and have a go at conducting an orchestra *(I, Seilerstätte 30, near the opera house. ☎516 480, www.hdm.at. Open daily 10am-10pm. €10, students €8.50.)*

ALBERTINA. First an Augustinian monastery and then the largest of the Hapsburg residences, the Albertina now houses the Collection of Graphic Arts. Past exhibits have featured Rembrandt and various Pop artists. The *Prunkräume*, or state rooms, exhibit some of Albrecht Dürer's finest prints, including the famous praying hands. *(Open M-Tu and Th-Su 10am-6pm, W 10am-9pm. €9, students €6.50.)*

JÜDISCHES MUSEUM (JEWISH MUSEUM). Jewish culture and history told through holograms and more traditional displays. Temporary exhibits focus on prominent Jewish figures and contemporary Jewish art. *(I, Dorotheerg. 11, near Stephanspl. ☎535 04 31. Open M-W, F, Su 10am-6pm, Th 10am-8pm. €5, students €3.)*

OUTSIDE THE RING

ÖSTERREICHISCHE GALERIE (AUSTRIAN GALLERY). The Österreichische Galerie's two museums are housed in the grounds of Schloß Belvedere. Home to *The Kiss* and other works by Klimt, the **Oberes Belvedere** supplements its permanent collection of 19th- and 20th-century art with rotating exhibits. The **Unteres Belvedere** contains the Austrian Museum of Baroque Art and of Medieval Art. *(Oberes Belvedere, III, Prinz-Eugen-Str. 27, in Schloß Belvedere behind Schwarzenbergpl. Walk up from the Südbahnhof, or take tram D to Schloß Belvedere. Unteres Belvedere, III, Rennweg 6. Tram #71 to Unteres Belvedere. ☎795 570. Both open Tu-Su 10am-6pm. €7.50, students €5.)*

KUNST HAUS WIEN. Artist-environmentalist Friedenreich Hundertwasser built this museum without straight lines—even the floor bends. Besides the comprehensive Hundertwasser exhibit, the Kunst Haus also hosts temporary contemporary art. *(III, Untere Weißgerberstr. 13. U1 or 4 to Schwedenpl., then tram N to Hetzg. ☎712 04 91; www.kunsthauswien.com. Open daily 10am-7pm. One exhibit €9, both €12; students €7/9. M €4.50/€6, except holidays.)*

ÖSTERREICHISCHES MUSEUM FÜR ANGEWANDTE KUNST (MAK). This intimate and eclectic museum is dedicated to design, from the smooth curves of Thonet bentwood chairs to the intricacies of Venetian glass to the steel heights of modern architecture. *(I, Stubenring 5. U3: Stubentor. ☎711 360; www.mak.at. Open Tu 10am-midnight, W-Su 10am-6pm. €8, students €5.50. Sa free.)*

KUNSTHISTORISCHES MUSEUM (MUSEUM OF FINE ARTS). One of the world's largest art collections features Venetian and Flemish paintings, Classical art, and an Egyptian burial chamber. The **Ephesos Museum** exhibits findings from excavations in Turkey, the **Hofjagd- und Rustkammer** is the second-largest collection of arms in the world, and the **Sammlung alter Musikinstrumente** includes Beethoven's harpsichord and Mozart's piano. *(U2: Museumsquartier. Across from the Burgring and Heldenpl. on Maria Theresa's right. ☎525 2441, www.khm.at. Open Tu-W, F-Su 10am-6pm, Th 10am-9pm. €10, students €7.50. English-language audio tour €2.)*

MUSEUMSQUARTIER. At 60 sq. km, it's one of the 10 biggest art districts in the world. Central Europe's largest collection of modern art, the **Museum Moderner Kunst (MUMOK),** highlights Classical Modernism, Pop Art, Photo Realism, Fluxus, and Viennese Actionism in a building made from basalt lava. *(Open Tu-Su 10am-6pm, Th 10am-9pm. €9, students €6.50.)* The **Leopold Museum** has the world's largest Schiele collection, plus works by Egger-Lienz, Gerstl, Klimt, and Kokoschka. *(Open M, W, F-Su 10am-7pm, Th 10am-9pm. €9, students €5.50.)* Themed exhibits of contemporary artists fill **Kunsthalle Wien.** *(U2: Museumsquartier. Open M-W, F-Su 10am-7pm, Th 10am-10pm. Exhibition Hall 1 €7.50, students €6. Exhibition Hall 2 €6/4.50; both €10.50/8.50. Students €2 on M. "Art" combination ticket admits visitors to all three museums; €21.50. "Duo" ticket admits to Leopold and MUMOK; €16, students €11.)*

FREUD MUSEUM. Freud's former home has bric-a-brac that includes his report cards and circumcision certificate. *(IX, Bergg. 19. U2: Schottentor; walk up Währingerstr. to Bergg. ☎319 15 96. Open daily July-Sept. 9am-6pm; Oct.-June 9am-5pm €8, students €5.)*

ENTERTAINMENT

All but a few of classical music's marquee names lived, composed, and performed in Vienna. Today, Vienna hosts many performances accessible to the budget traveler, although none of the venues listed below has performances in July or August. The **Bundestheaterkasse,** I, Hanuschg. 3, sells tickets for the Staatsoper, the Volksoper, and the Burgtheater. (☎514 44 78 80. Open June to mid-Aug. M-F 10am-2pm; mid-Aug. to June M-F 8am-6pm, Sa-Su 9am-noon; Sa during Advent 9am-5pm.)

Staatsoper, I, Opernring 2 (☎514 442 250; www.wiener-staatsoper.at). Vienna's premier opera performs nearly every night Sept.-June. No shorts. Seats €5-254. 500 standing-room tickets go on sale 80min. before every show (1 per person; €2-3.50); arrive 2hr. before curtain. Box office in the foyer open 9am until 1hr. before curtain, Sa 9am-noon; 1st Sa of each month and during Advent 9am-5pm.

Vienna Philharmonic Orchestra (Wiener Philharmoniker; www.wienerphilharmoniker.at) plays in the **Musikverein,** Austria's premiere concert hall. Even if you only want standing-room tickets, visit the box office (Bösendorferstr. 12) well ahead.

Vienna Boys' Choir (Wiener Sängerknaben; reservations ☎533 99 27) sings during mass every Su at 9:15am (mid-Sept. to late June) in the Hofburgkapelle (U3: Herreng.). Despite rumors to the contrary, standing room is free; arrive before 8am. Tickets €5-29.

AUSTRIA

NIGHTLIFE

With one of the highest bar-to-cobblestone ratios in the world, Vienna is the place to party. Take U1 or 4 to Schwedenpl., within blocks of the **Bermuda Dreieck** (Bermuda Triangle), packed with crowded clubs. If you make it out, head down **Rotenturmstraße** to Stephansdom or walk around the areas bounded by the synagogue and Ruprechtskirche. Outside the Ring, the streets off **Burggasse** and **Stiftgasse** in District VII and the **university quarter** in Districts XIII and IX have courtyards and hip bars. Viennese nightlife starts after 11pm. For listings, pick up *Falter* (€2).

Das Möbel, VII, Burgg. 10. U2 or 3: Volkstheater. (☎524 9497; www.das-moebel.net). An artsy crowd chats and reads amid metal couches and Swiss-army tables, all created by designers and available for sale. Don't leave without seeing the bathroom. Internet free for first 15min. Open daily 10am-1am. Cash only. MC/V accepted for furniture.

Ma Pitom der Lokal, I, Seitenstetteng. 5 (☎535 43 13). A cavernous space draws together a diverse crowd to chat over beer (.5L, €3.20) and pricey pub grub (€6-18). Beers €1.60 during daily 5-7pm happy hour. Open M-Th, Su 5pm-3am, F-Sa 5pm-4am.

Chelsea, VIII, Lerchenfeldergürtel U-Bahnbögen 29-32 (☎407 9309; www.chelsea.co.at), under the U-Bahn. Bands from all over Austria and the world rock this underground club twice a week, while DJs spin techno-pop on weekends. 0.5L beer €3.30. Open M-Th 6pm-4am, F-Sa 6pm-5am, Su 6pm-3am.

Volksgarten Disco, I, Burgring 1 (☎532 42 41; www.volksgarten.at). U2: Volkstheater. A fountain, palms, and a hot young crowd makes this one of the trendiest clubs in Vienna. M tango. Th alternative and house; F hip-hop; Sa house. Cover €5-10. Open M 8pm-2am, Th 8pm-4am, F 11pm-6am, Sa June-Aug. 9pm-6am; Sept.-May 11pm-6am.

Mango, VI, Laimgrubeng. 3 (☎587 44 48; www.mangobar.at). U2: Museumsquartier. With walls as golden as its namesake, Mango draws gay men with its pop music and casual atmosphere. Open daily 9pm-4am. AmEx/MC/V.

SALZBURGER LAND AND UPPER AUSTRIA

Salzburger Land's precious white gold, salt *(Salz)*, drew the first settlers over 3000 ago. Modern travelers prefer to seek instead the lakes and hills of the Salzkammergut, where Salzburg and Hallstatt are among the more enticing destinations.

SALZBURG ☎0662

Graced with Baroque wonders, Salzburg was the ecclesiastical center of Austria in the 17th and 18th centuries. The birthplace of Mozart, its rich musical culture lives on today, in everything from high concert halls to impromptu folk performances in the public squares.

TRANSPORTATION

Trains: Hauptbahnhof, in Südtirolerpl. (24hr. reservations ☎05 17 17). To: **Graz** (4hr., 1 per hr. 8am-6:30pm, €40); **Innsbruck** (2hr., 11 per day, €32); **Munich** (2hr., 30 per day, €26); **Vienna** (3½hr., 26 per day, €40); **Zurich** (6hr., 7 per day, €70).

Public Transportation: Buses depart from the depot in front of the train station. The information desk (☎44 80 61 66) at the bus depot can answer questions about local transportation. Open M-F 6am-6:45pm, Sa 7:30am-2:45pm. Single tickets (€1.60) available at automatic machines or from the drivers. 5-ticket books (€8), day passes (€4.20), and week passes (€11) are available at machines, the ticket office, or *Tabak* (newsstand/tobacco) shops. Punch your ticket when you board or risk a €36 fine. Buses usually make their last run 10:30-11:30pm.

ORIENTATION AND PRACTICAL INFORMATION

Three hills and the Salzach River define Salzburg, just a few kilometers from the German border. The Neustadt (new town) is north of the river, and the beautiful Altstadt (old town) squeezes between the southern bank and the Mönchsberg hill. The Hauptbahnhof is on the northern side of town beyond the Neustadt; buses #1, 3, 5, 6, 51, and 55 connect it to Hanuschplatz, the main public transportation hub in the Altstadt, by the river near Griesg. and the Staatsbrücke. Hubs in the Neustadt include Mirabellplatz and the Mozartsteg, the pedestrian bridge that leads across the Salzach to Mozartpl. To reach the Altstadt on foot, turn left out of the station onto Rainerstr. and follow it straight under the tunnel and on to Mirabellpl.

Tourist Office: is at Mozartpl. 5 (☎88 98 73 30). Open daily 9am-6pm.

Currency Exchange: Banks have better rates for cash than AmEx, but higher commissions. Hours M-F 8am-12:30pm and 2-4:30pm. Train station exchange open M-F 7am-9pm.

American Express: Mozartpl. 5 (☎80 80). Cashes AmEx cheques without commission and books tours. Open M-F 9am-5:30pm, Sa 9am-noon.

Luggage Storage: At the train station. 24hr. lockers €2-3.50.

GLBT Resources: Homosexual Initiative of Salzburg (HOSI), Müllner Hauptstr. 11 (☎43 59 27; www.hosi.or.at), hosts regular workshops and meetings and offers a free guide to Salzburg. Open M from 7pm, F-Sa from 8pm. Phone staffed F 7-9pm.

Emergency: Police: ☎133. **Ambulance:** ☎144. **Fire:** ☎122.

Pharmacies: Elisabeth-Apotheke, Elisabethstr. 1a (☎87 14 84). Pharmacies in the city center open M-F 8am-6pm, Sa 8am-noon. There are 3 pharmacies that rotate being open 24hr.; ask for an after-hours calendar at any pharmacy or check the list on the door if they're closed.

Internet Access: Internet Café, Mozartpl. 5 (☎84 48 22), near the tourist office. €0.15 per min. Open daily Sept.-June 10am-11pm; July-Aug. 9am-midnight. **Piterfun Internetc@fe,** Ferdinand-Porsche-Str. 7 (☎87 89 19), across from the train station. 10min. €1, 30min. €3, 1hr. €5. Open daily 10am-10pm.

Post Office: ☎88 30 30. At the train station. Open M-F 7am-8:30pm, counter closes 6pm; Sa 8am-2pm; Su 1-6pm. **Postal Code:** A-5020.

ACCOMMODATIONS

IN SALZBURG

Stadtalm, Mönchsberg 19c (☎84 17 29; www.diestadtalm.com). Take bus #1 (dir.: Maxglan) to Mönchsbergaufzug; go down the street and to the Mönchsberg lift (☎4480 6285; M-Tu, Th-Su 8am-7pm, W 8am-10pm; July-Aug. daily 8am-1am; €3). Follow signs at the top. One of the best views in Salzburg. Breakfast included. Reception 9am-10pm. Curfew 1am. Open Apr.-Sept. Dorms €15. Cash only. ❶

Eduard-Heinrich-Haus (HI), Eduard-Heinrich-Str. 2 (☎62 59 76; www.hostel-ehh.at). Take bus #3 (dir.: Salzburg-Süd) or 8 (dir.: Alpensiedlung) to Polizeidirektion. Cross over Alpenstr., turn right on Billrothstr., turn left on Robert-Stolz-Promenade footpath, walk 200m, and take the 1st right; it's the pink building. Spacious rooms look out into the garden and forest. Breakfast included. Internet €2.60 per 20min. Laundry €6. Key deposit of ID or €20. Reception 7-10am and 5pm-midnight. All rooms with bath except 4 dorms (€15-18). Other dorms €18-21; singles €27. MC/V. ❶

Institut St. Sebastian, Linzerg. 41 (☎87 13 86). From the station, bus #1, 3, 5, or 6 to Mirabellpl. Cross the street, continue in the same direction as the bus, turn left onto Bergstr., and left again onto Linzerg.; the hostel is through the arch. Clean rooms with fresh white walls. Breakfast included. Linen €2 for dorms. Wash €3, dry €3. Reception 8am-noon and 4-9pm. Dorms €16; singles €30, with shower €37; doubles €48/60; triples €68/73; quads €78/88. MC/V; €18 minimum charge. ❷

AUSTRIA

OUTSIDE SALZBURG

Haus Ballwein, Moosstr. 69a (☎82 40 29; www.haus-ballwein.at), south of the city. Colorful curtains, natural wood paneling, and braided rugs will rejuvenate any traveler. Bike rental €5 per half day. Breakfast included. Singles €23, with shower €33-35; doubles €44/48-52; triples with bath €65-70; apartment for 4 with kitchenette €80. Cash. ❷

Haus Lindner, Panoramaweg 5 (☎45 66 81; www.haus-lindner.at), north of the city. Some of the tastefully furnished rooms have balconies. Breakfast included. Call for pickup from the station. Doubles €32, triples €45, and quads €56. Cash only. ❷

Haus Christine, Panoramaweg 3 (☎45 67 73; haus.christine@gmx.at), Next to Haus Lindner. Spacious, clean triples and quads with a country motif. Breakfast served on a glass-enclosed patio overlooking the countryside—the best view on the block. 1st night €18, subsequent nights €17 per person. MC/V. ❶

FOOD

Indigo, Rudolfskai 8 (☎84 34 80), left of the Staatsbrücke when facing the Altstadt. Draws a local crowd with steaming Asian noodles, sushi, and set meals (€4.50-5). Salads €1.20 per 100g. Noodles €5. Sushi €0.55-1.65. Open M-Sa 10am-10pm. Cash only. ❶

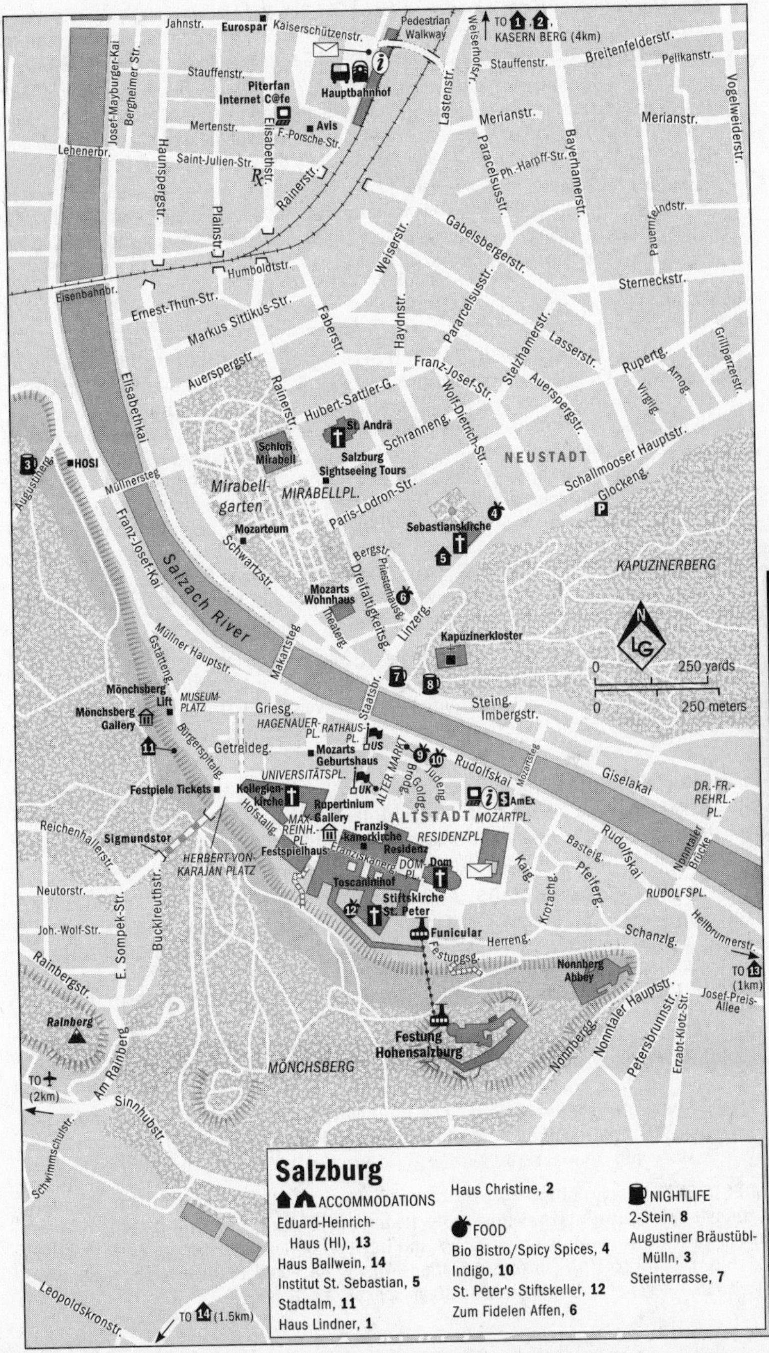
Salzburg
ACCOMMODATIONS
Eduard-Heinrich-Haus (HI), 13
Haus Ballwein, 14
Institut St. Sebastian, 5
Stadtalm, 11
Haus Lindner, 1
Haus Christine, 2
FOOD
Bio Bistro/Spicy Spices, 4
Indigo, 10
St. Peter's Stiftskeller, 12
Zum Fidelen Affen, 6
NIGHTLIFE
2-Stein, 8
Augustiner Bräustübl-Mülln, 3
Steinterrasse, 7
TO 1, 2, KASERN BERG (4km)
Pedestrian Walkway
Hauptbahnhof
Piterfan Internet C@fe
Avis
Eurospar
Jahnstr.
Kaiserschützenstr.
Stauffenstr.
Breitenfelderstr.
Pelikanstr.
Weiserhofstr.
Lastenstr.
Merianstr.
Vogelweiderstr.
Bayerhamerstr.
Paracelsusstr.
Ph.-Harpff-Str.
Josef-Mayburger-Kai
Bergheimer Str.
Mertenstr.
F.-Porsche-Str.
Elisabethstr.
Lehenerbr.
Saint-Julien-Str.
Haunspergstr.
Plainstr.
Rainerstr.
Gabelsbergerstr.
Pauernfeindstr.
Humboldtstr.
Weiserstr.
Sterneckstr.
Eisenbahnbr.
Ernest-Thun-Str.
Markus Sittikus-Str.
Faberstr.
Haydnstr.
Pararcelsusstr.
Stelzhamerstr.
Lasserstr.
Grillparzerstr.
Auerspergstr.
Franz-Josef-Str.
Rupertg.
Arnog.
Virgilg.
Elisabethkai
Hubert-Sattler-G.
Wolf-Dietrich-Str.
St. Andrä
Schranneng.
NEUSTADT
Schallmooser Hauptstr.
HOSI
Augustinerg.
Schloß Mirabell
Salzburg Sightseeing Tours
Müllnersteg
Mirabell-garten
MIRABELLPL.
Paris-Lodron-Str.
Glockeng.
Franz-Josef-Kai
Mozarteum
Sebastianskirche
Schwartzstr.
Salzach River
Bergstr.
Priesterhausg.
Dreifaltigkeitsg.
KAPUZINERBERG
Mozarts Wohnhaus
Theaterg.
Linzerg.
Kapuzinerkloster
Müllner Hauptstr.
Gstätteng.
Makartsteg
250 yards
250 meters
Mönchsberg Lift
MUSEUM-PLATZ
Mönchsberg Gallery
Griesg.
Staatsbr.
Steing.
Imbergstr.
HAGENAUER-PL.
RATHAUS-PL.
US
Getreideg.
Mozarts Geburtshaus
ALTER MARKT
Bürgerspitalg.
Rudolfskai
Mozartsteg
Giselakai
UNIVERSITÄTSPL.
Brodg.
Goldg.
Judeng.
AmEx
Festpiele Tickets
Kollegienkirche
UK
Rupertinium Gallery
ALTSTADT
MOZARTPL.
DR.-FR.-REHRL.-PL.
Reichenhallerstr.
MAX-REINH.-PL.
Hofstallg.
Franziskanerkirche
RESIDENZPL.
Nonntaler Brücke
Sigmundstor
Festspielhaus
Residenz
Basteig.
HERBERT-VON-KARAJAN PLATZ
Franziskanerg.
DOM-PL.
Dom
Kaig.
Pfeiferg.
Toscaninihof
Neutorstr.
Stiftskirche St. Peter
Krotachg.
RUDOLFSPL.
Joh.-Wolf-Str.
Funicular
Herreng.
Schanzlg.
Hellbrunnerstr.
Festungsg.
E. Sompek-Str.
Bucklreuthstr.
Rainbergstr.
Nonnberg Abbey
TO 13 (1km)
Josef-Preis-Allee
Rainberg
Nonntaler Hauptstr.
Petersbrunnstr.
Erzabt-Klotz-Str.
Festung Hohensalzburg
Nonnbergg.
MÖNCHSBERG
TO (2km)
Am Rainberg
Sinnhubstr.
Schwimmschulstr.
Leopoldskronstr.
TO 14 (1.5km)

AUSTRIA

Zum Fidelen Affen, Priesterhausg. 8 (☎87 73 61), off Linzerg. Hearty Austrian food keeps everyone coming back "To the Faithful Ape." Try the Monkey Steak, a roasted pork dish, for €10. Vegetarian options. Open M-Sa 5pm-midnight. DC/MC/V. ❷

Bio Bistro/Spicy Spices, Wolf-Dietrich-Str. 1 (☎87 07 12), at Linzerg. Spices from their own store ensure that each Indian dish is authentic and flavorful. Everything is vegetarian and certified organic, with many vegan options. Dish of the day, *chapati* bread, and lentils €5. Other entrees with 2 *naan* €6.50. Open daily 10am-10pm. Cash only. ❶

St. Peter's Stiftskeller, St.-Peter-Bezirk 1/4 (☎84 12 680). At the foot of the cliffs next to St. Peter's Monastery, this is the oldest restaurant in Central Europe, established in AD 803. Surprising options like quail. Entrees €10-23. Open M-F 11am-midnight, during the *Festspiele* until 1am. AmEx/DC/MC/V. ❸

SIGHTS

FESTUNG HOHENSALZBURG. Built up between 1077 and 1681 by the ruling archbishops, the imposing Hohensalzburg Fortress, which looms over Salzburg from atop Mönchsberg, is the largest completely preserved castle in all of Europe—partly because it was never successfully attacked. The castle contains formidable Gothic state rooms, an organ—nicknamed the "Bull of Salzburg" for its off-key snorting—and a watchtower that provides visitors with an unmatched panorama of the city. The **Burgmuseum** inside the fortress displays medieval instruments of torture and has side-by-side histories of Salzburg, the fortress, and the world. *(Take the trail or the Festungsbahn funicular up to the fortress from Festungsg. Funicular every 10min. 9am-10pm. Open daily July-Aug. 9am-7pm; Sept. and May-June 9am-6pm; Oct.-Apr. 9am-5:00pm. Funicular round-trip €9.80; includes fortress admission. If you walk, ticket including fortress and museums €8.60. Last entrance to the museum 30min. before closing.)*

MOZARTS GEBURTSHAUS. Overtouristed, Mozart's birthplace holds a collection of the child genius's belongings, including his first violin and a pair of keyboard instruments. Several rooms recreate his young years as a traveling virtuoso. Come before 11am to avoid the crowd. *(Getreideg. 9. Open daily 9am-6pm; July-Aug. 9am-7pm. Last entrance 30min. before closing. €6, students €5.)*

UNIVERSITÄTSKIRCHE. In Mozart's backyard stands the **University Church,** one of the largest Baroque chapels on the continent and designer Fischer von Erlach's masterpiece. Sculpted clouds coat the nave, while pudgy cherubim frolic all over the church's immense apse. *(Hours vary, generally open daily 9am-5pm. Free.)*

TOSCANINIHOF, CATACOMBS, AND THE DOM. Steps lead from Toscaninihof, the courtyard of **St. Peter's Monastery,** up the Mönchsberg cliffs. **Stiftskirche St. Peter,** a church within the monastery, features a marble portal from 1244. In the 18th century, the building was remodeled in Rococo style. *(☎844 5760. Open daily 9am-12:15pm and 2:30-6:30pm.)* In the cemetery, roses and ivy embellish the fanciful curls of wrought-iron crosses. The entrance to the Catacombs is near the far end of the cemetery, against the Mönchsberg. *(Open May-Sept. Tu-Su 10:30am-5pm; Oct.-Apr. W-Th 10:30am-3:30pm, F-Su 10:30am-4pm. €1, students €0.60.)* The exit at the other end of the cemetery leads to the immense Baroque *Dom* (cathedral), where Mozart was christened in 1756 and later worked as concertmaster and court organist. The square leading out of the cathedral, **Domplatz,** features a statue of the Virgin Mary and figures representing Wisdom, Faith, the Church, and the Devil.

RESIDENZ. The archbishops of Salzburg have resided in the magnificent Residenz since 1595. Stunning Baroque **State Rooms** have ornate ceiling frescoes, lavish gilded furniture, Flemish tapestries, and intricately detailed stucco work. A **gallery** exhibits 16th- to 19th-century art. *(State Rooms open daily 10am-5pm. €8, students €6. Audio tour included. Gallery open Tu-Su 10am-5pm.€6, students €4)*

MIRABELL PALACE AND GARDENS. Mirabellpl. holds the marvelous **Schloß Mirabell,** which the supposedly celibate Archbishop Wolf Dietrich built for his mistress and their 10 children in 1606. *(Open daily 7am-9pm. Free.)* Behind the palace is the **Mirabellgarten,** an ornate and well-maintained maze of flower beds that contains the moss-covered **Zauberflötenhäuschen,** where Mozart purportedly composed *The Magic Flute.*

ENTERTAINMENT

During the **Salzburger Festspiele** (July 24-Aug. 31, 2006), everyone from the Vienna Philharmonic to rising stars arrives in town for a month of performances, transforming Salzburg into a musical mecca. Operas, plays, films, concerts, and tourists overrun every available public space; expect room prices to rise accordingly and plan ahead. Info and tickets for *Festspiele* events are available through the ticket office *(Festspiele Kartenbüro)* and daily box office *(Direkt Verkauf)* at Karajanpl. 11, against the mountain, next to the tunnel. (☎804 5500; www.salzburgfestival.at. Tickets €15-360. Offices open mid-Mar. to June M-F 9:30am-3pm, July 1-24 M-Sa 9:30am-5pm, July 25 through the end of the *Festspiele* daily 9:30am-6pm.)

BARS AND BEER GARDENS

Augustinian Bräustübel-Mülln, Augustinerg. 4 (☎43 12 46). Even though the monks are no more, the *Bräukloster* they founded in 1621 continues to function. Follow the long halls to the end to reach the *Biergärten.* Beer €2.50-2.80. Open M-F 3-11pm, Sa-Su 2:30-11pm; last drink 10:30pm. Cash only.

2-Stein, Giselakai 9 (☎87 71 79). The place to come for Salzburg's gay and lesbian scene. Mixed drinks from €5. Open M-W 6pm-4am, Th-Su 6pm-5am. AmEx/DC/MC/V.

Steinterrasse, Giselakai 3-5 (☎88 20 70), on the 7th fl. of the Stein Hotel. This hip cafe-bar knows that a lofty rooftop panorama doesn't have to mean equally lofty prices. A young crowd comes to flirt and socialize while admiring the lights of the Altstadt (and each other). Beer €3-5. Mixed drinks €5-10. Open daily 9am-1am. AmEx/DC/MC/V.

HALLSTATT ☎06134

Teetering on the banks of the Hallstättersee, tiny Hallstatt (pop. 960) clings to the mountainside and crowds right up to the blue-green waters of the lake. Easily the most striking and touristed lakeside village in the Salzkammergut, Hallstatt also boasts salt-rich earth that has helped to preserve its archaeological treasures—so extensive that one era in Celtic studies (800-400 BC) is dubbed "the Hallstatt era."

TRANSPORTATION AND PRACTICAL INFORMATION. Buses are the cheapest way (€18) to get to Hallstatt from Salzburg but require layovers in both Bad Ischl and Gosaumühle. The bus station is in the neighboring town of Lahn; face away from the lake and head right for 10min. to reach the Hallstatt tourist office. The **train** station, across the lake, is not staffed. A boat runs between Hallstatt and the train station in accordance to the train schedule (€2). All trains come from Attnang-Puchheim in the north or Stainach-Irdning in the south. **Trains** run every hour 7am-6pm to Bad Ischl (30min., €3.50) and Salzburg (2½hr., €19.50) via Attnang-Puchheim. The **tourist office,** Seestr. 169, finds rooms and helps with the confusing system of street addresses. (☎82 08. Open July-Aug. M-F 9am-noon and 2-5pm; Nov.-May M-F 9am-noon.) There is an **ATM** at Volksbank, 114 Seestr. (☎48 13. Open M-Tu and Th-F 8am-noon and 2-5pm, W 8am-noon.) The **post office,** Seestr. 169, is below the tourist office and to the right of the bank. (Open M-Tu and Th-F 8am-4pm, W 8am-6pm.) **Postal Code:** A-4830.

ACCOMMODATIONS AND FOOD. To reach **Gästehaus Zur Mühle ❶**, Kirchenweg 36, from the tourist office, walk uphill and head for a short tunnel off the square; it's at the end of the tunnel by the waterfall. (☎48 13. €15 locker deposit. Linen €3. Reception 11am-2pm and 4-10pm. Closed Nov. Dorms €12. DC/MC/V.) Enjoy a glorious view of the lake from the beachside lawn at **Frühstückspension Sarstein ❷**, Gosamühlstr. 83, where the owners make guests feel at home. From the ferry, turn right on Seestr. and walk 10min. (☎82 17; pension.sarstein@aon.at. Breakfast included. Showers €1 per 10min. Singles €18-20, with bath €25-27; doubles €37-40, with shower €50-53, with bath €56-59; triples €58-62, with bath €76-78. Cash only.) **Camping Klausner-Höll ❶**, Lahnstr. 201, lies in the shadow of the mountains and at the trail head of hikes in the valley. To get there, turn right out of the tourist office and follow Seestr. for 10min.; from the bus stop, make a left down Lahnstr. (☎832 24. Kitchen available. Laundry €6. Reception 8am-noon and 4-8pm. Gate closed daily noon-3pm and 10pm-7:30am. Open May to mid-Sept. Tent sites €10.20, extra person €6.50. Discounts Apr. 15-June and Sept.-Oct. 15. AmEx/DC/MC/V.) The cheapest eats are at **Konsum** supermarket, Kernmagazinpl. 8, across from the bus stop, where the butcher prepares sandwiches on request. (☎8226. Open M-F 7:30am-noon and 3-6pm, Sa 7:30am-noon. Cash only.) The meat shop **Karl Forstinger ❶**, Seestr. 139, between the tourist office and the bus stop, grills up a wide variety of fresh regional *Vurst*. (☎0676 788 7299. *Wurst* and roll €2-3. Open M-F 10am-5pm, Sa 10am-4pm, Su 11am-4pm. Cash only.)

SIGHTS AND HIKING. Back when Rome was still a village, the "white gold" from the salt mines made Hallstatt a world-famous settlement. Above Hallstatt, the 2500-year-old **Salzbergwerk** is the oldest salt mine in the world. Take the 1hr. guided tour down a wooden mining slide to a lake deep inside the mountain. (☎200 2400; www.salzwelten.at. Open daily Apr. 24-Sept. 18 9:30am-4:30pm; Sept. 19-Oct. 26 9:30am-3pm. English-language tours every 15min. €15.50, students €9.30. Salzbergbahn cable car runs daily May-mid to mid-Sept. 9:30am-4:30pm, low season 9:30am-3pm. Up or down €5.10, students €3.10; round-trip €8.50/€5.10.)

The tourist office has an excellent English-language **hiking** guide (€6), which details 38 hikes in the area, as well as bike trail maps (€7). The easy **Waldbachstrub Waterfall hike** (1¾-2hr. round-trip) follows a glacial stream up to a waterfall. From the bus station, follow the brown Malerweg signs near the supermarket until you reach the Waldbachstrub sign (about 40min.). The waterfall is in the **Echental**, a valley blazed with trails leading deep into the valley. At the bridge before the waterfall, the path branches off to the left up to the Glacial Garden—a series of small glacial stream waterfalls and smoothly polished rocks. The **Gangsteig** (look off to the right just before the falls for a slippery stairway carved into a cliff), requires sturdy shoes and a strong will to climb and doesn't offer a great view.

DAYTRIP FROM HALLSTATT: DACHSTEIN ICE CAVES. Above Obertraun, across the lake from Hallstatt, the famed Rieseneishöhle (Giant Ice Cave) is part of the largest system of ice caves in the world. Frozen waterfalls and delicate curtains of ice transport visitors to a chilly wonderland. The Rieseneishöhle and mammoth Mammuthöhle rock cave are up on the mountain near the Schönbergalm cable car station. English-language tours are required; you'll be assigned to a group at Schönbergalm. Koppenbrüllerhöhle, a giant spring, is located in the valley below, an hour walk away from bottom cable car station. The cave temperatures are near freezing, so bring warm clothes. (☎84 00; www.dachsteinhoehlen.at. Buses to Dachstein leave every hr. 8:48am-4:52pm from the Lahn station; 10min., €1.60. The Koppenbrüller cave is a 15min. walk from the Koppenbrüllerhöhle train station one stop past Obertraun. Cable car runs every 15min. 8:40am-5:40pm from Obertraun to the ice caves at Schönbergalm, round-trip €14. Open daily May to

AUSTRIA

mid-Oct. 9am-5pm. Rieseneishöhle and Mammuthöhle €13.50. Each cave on its own €8.80. Koppenbrüllerhöhle open 10am-4pm. €7.50.)

ZELL AM SEE ☎06542

Surrounded by a ring of snow-capped mountains cradling a turquoise lake, Zell am See (pop. 9700) lures visitors craving the outdoors. The **Schmittenhöhebahn** cable car leads to many hikes. (Runs daily every 30min. Round-trip €19.60, up €15.50, down €11.50. Guest card discounts available.) PostBus #661 (every 30min., €1.80) goes to the lift. The moderate **Pinzgauer Spaziergang,** marked "Alpenvereinsweg" #19 or 719, begins at the top of the lift and levels off high in the Alps. Most devote an entire day to this trail, taking a side path to a town west of Zell am See and returning by bus. For those desiring a faster-paced experience, **Adventure Service,** Steinerg. 9 (☎0664 132 8552 or 735 25), leads a variety of trips.

Ask at your hostel for a free **guest card,** which provides discounts on activities throughout the city. **Haus der Jugend (HI) ❷,** Seespitzstr. 13, redefines "budget" with a terrace on the lake and spacious rooms with bath. From the station, take the exit facing the lake and turn right on the lakeside footpath; at the end, turn left on Seespitzstr. (☎571 85; www.jungehotels.at/seespitzstrasse. Breakfast included. Reception 7-9am and 4-10pm. Dorms €17-19; doubles €21. AmEx/DC/MC/V.) **Ristorante Pizzeria Giuseppe ❷,** Kircheng. 1, has an Italian ambience. From the station, walk up Bahnhofstr. past the church. (☎723 73. Pizza €6-10. Open Tu-Su 11:30am-11pm. DC/MC/V; €40 min. charge.) The **SPAR** is at Brucker-Bundesstr. 4. (☎700 19. Open M-Th 7:30am-6:30pm, F 7:30am-7pm, Sa 7:30am-5pm.)

The **train** station (☎7321 4357) is at Bahnhofstr. and Salzmannstr. Trains run to Innsbruck (1½-2hr., every 2hr., €22); Vienna (5hr., €43.50) via Salzburg (1½hr., 1-2 per hr., €12.40). The **bus station** is at Gartenstr. and Schulstr. Buy tickets onboard or at the kiosk. (☎54 44. Kiosk open M-F 7:45am-1:45pm.) Buses service: Franz-Josefs-Höhe (mid-June to mid-Sept.; 9:20am, 12:20pm; €10.40) and Salzburg (2hr., every 2hr. 6:40am-4:50pm, €10.20). The **tourist office** is at Brucker-Bundesstr. 1a. (☎770; www.europasportregion.info. Open July to mid-Sept. and mid-Dec. to Mar. M-F 9am-6pm, Sa 9am-noon and 2-6pm, Su 10am-noon; Apr.-June and Sept. to mid-Dec. closed Su.) The **post office** is at Postpl. 4. (☎73 79 10. Open M-F 7:30am-6pm, Sa 7-10am; July to mid-Sept. and Christmas-Easter Sa 7-11am.) **Postal Code:** A-5700.

AUSTRIA

HOHE TAUERN NATIONAL PARK

The enormous Hohe Tauern range, part of the Austrian Central Alps and forming the largest national park in central Europe, encompasses some 246 glaciers and 304 mountains over 3000m. Preservation is a primary goal in the park, so there are no large campgrounds or recreation areas. *An Experience in Nature*, available at park centers and most area tourist offices, plots and describes 84 different hikes, ranging from pleasant ambles to challenging mountain ascents. At the center of the park lies Franz-Josefs-Höhe, the most visited section, and the Pasterze Glacier, which hovers above the town of Heiligenblut.

TRANSPORTATION. Hohe Tauern National Park sits at the meeting point of the provinces of Salzburger Land, Tyrol, and Kärnten. The heart of the park is best reached by the highway **Großglockner Hochalpenstraße,** linked to Zell am See (p. 91) by Bundesstr. 311. As the zigzagging highway climbs high into the mountains, it passes mesmerizing vistas of jagged peaks and plunging valleys, high Alpine meadows and glacial waterfalls. **PostBus** #651 provides a scenic ride from Zell am See to Franz-Josefs-Höhe (1½-2½hr.; departs 9:20am, 12:20pm, returns 11:45am and 3pm; €10.40). The other parts of the park are criss-crossed by **bus** lines that operate on a complicated timetable.

FRANZ-JOSEFS-HÖHE. Tourist buses, cars and motorcycles climb the Großglockner Hochalpenstraße to this tourist mecca above the Pasterze Glacier. Once out of the parking area, the Panoramaweg affords a view of the Großglockner (3798m) on clear days. The elevator next to the info center leads to a path across the ridge to the **Swarovski Observation Center,** which provides free telescopes. (Open daily 10am-4pm. Free.) There is a Hohe Tauern **national park office** by the observation center. (☎04824 27 27. Open mid-May to mid-Oct. daily 10am-4pm.)

HIKING. Pick up a free hiking map from the National Park Office or tourist office; a detailed topographic map (€10) is recommended for prolonged hikes in the area. From the Franz-Josefs-Höhe parking lot, the initially steep **Pasterze Gletscherweg** (3hr.) descends to the edge of the retreating Pasterze Glacier and then continues through the valley and around the Stausee Margaritze to the **Glocknerhaus Alpine Center**; stay on the well marked path. A free shuttle bus runs between Franz-Josefs-Höhe and Glocknerhaus. Many hikes in the Großglockner area of the national park start at **Heiligenblut** from the Retschitzbrücke parking area outside of town via Gemeindestr. The easy **Gößnitzfall-Kachlmoor** trail (2hr.) leads through the Kachlmoor swamp to the Gößnitz Waterfalls at the head of the Gößnitz Valley. The rewarding but long **Gößnitztal-Langtalseen** hike (12hr.) continues through valleys and Alpine pastures. Spend the night in the Elberfelder Hütte before heading back to Heiligenblut via the Wirtsbauer Alm.

TYROL (TIROL)

Tyrol's soaring peaks challenge hikers with their celestial scale. Craggy summits in the northeast and south cradle the pristine Ötzal and Zillertal valleys while the mighty Hohe Tauern mountain range marches across eastern Tyrol.

INNSBRUCK ☎0512

The 1964 and 1976 winter Olympics were held in Innsbruck (pop. 128,000), bringing international recognition to this beautiful mountain city. The nearby Tyrolean Alps await skiers and hikers, and the tiny cobblestone streets of the Altstadt (old town) are peppered with fancy architecture and relics of the Hapsburg Empire.

TRANSPORTATION AND PRACTICAL INFORMATION

Trains: Hauptbahnhof, Südtirolerpl. (☎517 17). To **Munich, GER** (2hr., every two hours, €32), **Salzburg** (2½hr., every two hours, €32), and **Zürich, SWI** (4hr., 8 per day, €46).

Public Transportation: The **IVB** Office, Stainerstr. 2 (☎530 79, www.ivb.at), off Marktgraben, has bus schedules and route maps. Open M-F 7:30am-6pm. Single fare €1.60, 24hr. pass €3.50, week €11. Most buses stop around 11:30pm; 4 **Nachtbus** lines run hourly midnight-5am; most pass Maria-Theresien-Str., the train station, and Museumstr.

Bike Rental: Neuner Radsport, Maximilianstr. 23 (☎56 15 01). Mountain bikes and helmets €16 per half-day, €20 per day. Open M-F 9am-6pm, Sa 9am-noon.

Tourist Office: Innsbruck Tourist Office, Burggraben 3 (☎598 50), off the end of Museumstr. Sells maps (€1) and the **Innsbruck Card,** with unlimited public transport and admission to most sights. 1-day €23, 2-day €28, 3-day €33. Open daily 9am-6pm.

Police: ☎133. **Ambulance:** ☎144 or 142. **Fire:** ☎122. **Mountain Rescue:** ☎140.

Internet Access: International Telephone Discount, Südtirolerpl. 1 (☎282 3690). Go right from the Hauptbahnhof. €0.07 per min. Open daily 9am-11pm.

Post Office: Maximilianstr. 2 (☎500 7900). Open M-F 7am-9pm, Sa 7am-3pm, Su 10am-7:30pm. **Postal Code:** A-6010.

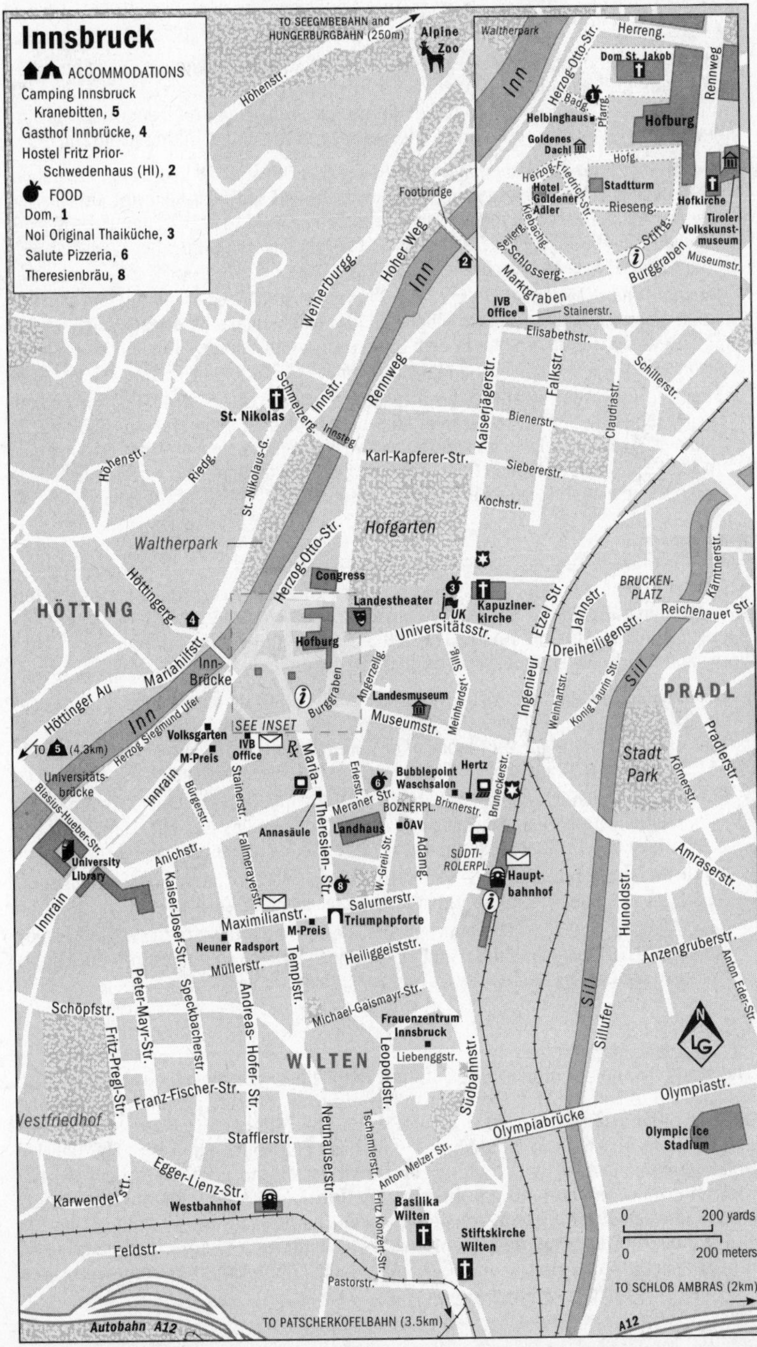
Innsbruck
ACCOMMODATIONS
Camping Innsbruck Kranebitten, 5
Gasthof Innbrücke, 4
Hostel Fritz Prior-Schwedenhaus (HI), 2
FOOD
Dom, 1
Noi Original Thaiküche, 3
Salute Pizzeria, 6
Theresienbräu, 8
TO SEEGMBEBAHN and HUNGERBURGBAHN (250m)
Alpine Zoo
Höhenstr.
Footbridge
Hoher Weg
Weiherburgg.
Inn
Rennweg
Schmelzerg.
Innstr.
St. Nikolas
Innsteg
Karl-Kapferer-Str.
Riedg.
St.-Nikolaus-G.
Waltherpark
Herzog-Otto-Str.
Hofgarten
Congress
Landestheater
UK
Kapuziner-kirche
HÖTTING
Höttingerg.
Mariahilfstr.
Inn-Brücke
Hofburg
Universitätsstr.
Burggraben
Angerzellg.
Landesmuseum
Meinhardstr.
Sillg.
Museumstr.
SEE INSET
Höttinger Au
TO 5 (4.3km)
Herzog Siegmund Ufer
Volksgarten
M-Preis
IVB Office
Universitäts-brücke
Blasius-Hueber-Str.
Innrain
Bürgerstr.
Stainerstr.
Maria-Theresien-Str.
Erlerstr.
Bubblepoint Waschsalon
Hertz
Meraner Str.
BOZNERPL.
Brixnerstr.
Bruneckerstr.
Annasäule
Landhaus
ÖAV
W.-Greil-Str.
Adamg.
SÜDTI-ROLERPL.
Hauptbahnhof
University Library
Anichstr.
Kaiser-Josef-Str.
Fallmerayerstr.
Salurnerstr.
Maximilianstr.
Triumphpforte
Neuner Radsport
Müllerstr.
Heiliggeiststr.
Templstr.
Speckbacherstr.
Andreas-Hofer-Str.
Peter-Mayr-Str.
Schöpfstr.
Fritz-Pregl-Str.
Michael-Gaismayr-Str.
Frauenzentrum Innsbruck
Liebenggstr.
WILTEN
Leopoldstr.
Südbahnstr.
Franz-Fischer-Str.
Westfriedhof
Stafflerstr.
Neuhauserstr.
Tschamlerstr.
Egger-Lienz-Str.
Anton Melzer Str.
Karwendelstr.
Westbahnhof
Fritz Konzert-Str.
Basilika Wilten
Stiftskirche Wilten
Feldstr.
Pastorstr.
TO PATSCHERKOFELBAHN (3.5km)
Autobahn A12
A12
TO SCHLOß AMBRAS (2km)
0 200 yards
0 200 meters
Olympiabrücke
Olympiastr.
Olympic Ice Stadium
Sillufer
Sill
Hunoldstr.
Anzengruberstr.
Anton Eder-Str.
Amraserstr.
Körnerstr.
Pradlerstr.
Stadt Park
PRADL
Weinhartstr.
König Laurin Str.
Ingenieur Etzel Str.
Dreiheiligenstr.
Jahnstr.
BRUCKEN-PLATZ
Reichenauer Str.
Kärntnerstr.
Kochstr.
Siebererstr.
Bienerstr.
Kaiserjägerstr.
Falkstr.
Claudiastr.
Schillerstr.
Elisabethstr.
Waltherpark
Herreng.
Dom St. Jakob
Rennweg
Badg.
Pfarrg.
Helbinghaus
Hofburg
Goldenes Dachl
Hofg.
Herzog-Friedrich-Str.
Hotel Goldener Adler
Stadtturm
Rieseng.
Hofkirche
Tiroler Volkskunst-museum
Kiebachg.
Seilerg.
Schlosserg.
Stiftg.
Burggraben
Museumstr.
Marktgraben
IVB Office
Stainerstr.
LG

AUSTRIA

ACCOMMODATIONS AND CAMPING

Budget accommodations are scarce in June, when some hostels close. The opening of student dorms to backpackers in July and August somewhat alleviates the crunch. Visitors can join the free **Club Innsbruck** at any Innsbruck accommodation; membership gives discounts on skiing, tours, and the club's hiking program.

Hostel Fritz Prior-Schwedenhaus (HI), Rennweg 17b (☎58 58 14). From the station, take bus #4 to Handelsakademie, continue to the end and cross Rennweg. By the river, this hostel has spacious rooms with private bath. Breakfast €5, 7-8am. Linen €1.50. Laundry €5.40. Reception 7-9am and 5-10:30pm. Lockout 9am-5pm. Open July-Aug. Dorms €11-16. Cash only. ❶

Gasthof Innbrücke, Innstr. 1 (☎28 19 34, www.gasthofinnbruecke.at). From the Altstadt, cross the Innbrücke. Comfy beds and fat pillows make for a restful night at this 581-year-old inn. Breakfast included. Singles €30, with shower €38; doubles €50/65; triples €63/93; quads €115; 5-person apartment €135; 6-person €160. DC/MC/V. ❸

Camping Innsbruck Kranebitten, Kranebitter Allee 214 (☎28 41 80, www.campinginnsbruck.at). Bus O to Technik, then bus LK (every 30min., last run 8:30pm) to Klammstr. Lush lawn in a mountain's shadow. Bike rental €5 per half day, €10 per day. Wash €3, dry €4. Reception 8am-noon and 2-9pm; after 9pm, find a site and check in the next morning. Tent sites €9.25, extra person €5.55. Tent rental €8. AmEx/MC/V. ❶

FOOD

The Altstadt cafes on Maria-Theresien-Str. are good but overpriced. Cross the Inn River to **Innstraße,** in the university district, for cheap pizzerias. There are **M-Preis** supermarkets at Maximilianstr. 3 (☎580 5110. Open M-F 7:30am-7pm, Sa 7:30am-5pm) and inside the train station. (☎58 07 30. Open daily 6am-9pm. MC/V.)

Theresienbräu, Maria-Theresien-Str. 51-53 (☎58 75 80), is built around giant copper brewing kettles. Try the dark house lager (*Pfiff;* 0.4L €2.70) alongside Tyrolean specialties (€6-7). Fondue for 2 or more after 6pm (chocolate €6.70 per person; cheese €12). Open M-W 10am-1am, Th-Sa 10am-2am, Su 10am-midnight. MC/V. ❷

Noi Original Thaiküche, Kaiserjägerstr. 1 (☎58 97 77). This tiny Thai kitchen packs a powerful punch with its spicy soups (€4.20-9) and noodles (€7-10). Lunch specials €8-9. Open M-F 11:30am-2:30pm and 6-11pm, Sa 6-11pm. Cash only. ❷

Salute Pizzeria, Innrainstr. 35 (☎585 818). Students flock to the cheapest pizza in town (€3.20-8.20). Salads €3.30-5. Open daily 11am-midnight. Cash only. ❶

Dom, Pfarrg. 3 (☎23 85 51). Atmospheric cafe-bar in the heart of the Altstadt. Enjoy soups (€3.30), salads (€4-8), and sandwiches (€4-6) with a glass of wine (€3-4) under vaulted ceilings. Open daily 11am-2am. AmEx/DC/MC/V. ❶

SIGHTS

The stony facades of Innsbruck's Altstadt repose beneath the even more majestic stony faces of Innsbruck's mountains. The old town centers around the **Goldenes Dachl** (Golden Roof), Herzog-Friedrich-Str. 15. The 16th-century gold-shingled balcony honors Maximilian I, Innsbruck's favorite Hapsburg emperor. The nearby **Helbinghaus** is graced with pale-green floral detail and intricate stucco work. Church domes and shopping boutiques line Innsbruck's most distinctive street, **Maria-Theresien-Straße,** which runs south from the edge of the Altstadt. At its far end stands the **Triumphpforte** (Triumphal Arch), built in 1765 after the betrothal of Emperor Leopold II. Up the street, the **Annasäule** (Anna Column) commemorates the Tyroleans' 1703 victory over the Bavarians. At **Dom St. Jakob,** 1 block behind the *Goldenes Dachl*, the unassuming gray facade conceals a riot of pink-and-white High Baroque ornamentation within. The cathedral's prized possession is the small altar painting of *Our Lady of Succor* by Lukas Cranach the Elder. (Open Apr.-Sept. M-Sa 8am-7:30pm, Su 12:30-7:30pm; Oct.-Mar. M-Sa 10am-6:30pm, Su 12:30-6:30pm. Mass M-Sa 9:30am, Su 10, 11:30am. Free.) Behind the Dom, **Hofburg,** the imperial palace, was built in 1460 but completely remodeled under Maria Theresa. Don't miss the gilded tableau in the Audience Room, depicting the whole Hapsburg gang in gold medallions. (☎58 71 86. Open daily 9am-5pm. Last admission 4:30pm. €5.45, students €3.63. English-language guidebook €1.80.) Bronze statues of the ancestors and heroes of Maximilian I line the nave at **Hofkirche,** in the Volkskunstmuseum building at Universitätsstr. 8, surrounding the massive tomb of the *Kaiser* himself. (☎58 43 02. Open July-Aug. M-Sa 9am-5:30pm, Su 12:30-5pm; Sept.-June M-Sa 9am-5pm, Su 12:30-5pm. €3, students €2.)

HIKING AND SKIING

A **Club Innsbruck** membership (free; see **Accommodations,** p. 94) lets you in on one of the best deals in Austria. The club's popular **hiking** program around Innsbruck and its surrounding villages provides free guides, transportation, and equipment. Moderate 3-5hr. group hikes from Innsbruck meet at the Congress Center (daily June-Sept. 9am), and return around 4 or 5pm. Free 1hr. nighttime lantern hikes to Heiligwasser near Igls leave Tuesday at 7:45pm and culminate in a hut party with traditional song and dance. To hike on your own, take the J bus to **Patscherkofel Seilbahnen** (20min.). The lift has access to moderate 1½-5hr. hikes near the summit of the Patscherkofel. (Open daily 9am-4:30pm, July-Aug. 9am-5pm. Round-trip €16.50, students €13.) For more challenging climbs, head to the lifts up to the **Nordkette** mountains. The first lift is a short hike from the river and the Schwedenhaus hostel. Skip to the second lift on the J bus to Hungerburgbahn, where the cable car ascends to the Seegrube, below the rocky peaks. A third lift leads to the top, at the Hafelekarspitze. From both the Seegrube and Hafelekarspitze, hikes lead up and along the jagged ridges of the Nordkette, but they are neither easy nor well marked. (☎29 33 44. Hungerburg to Seegrube €10, students €8.10; to Hafelekar €11.50/9.50; Seegrube to Hafelekar €3/2.40.) If you really want to fly, Innsbruck-Information has a €95 tandem **paragliding** package, including transport and equipment (bookings ☎37 84 88; www.tirol.com/mountainous).

For Club-led **ski excursions,** take the complimentary ski shuttle (schedules at the tourist office) to any cable car. The **Innsbruck Gletscher Ski Pass** (available at all cable cars) is valid for all 60 lifts in the region (with Club Innsbruck membership: 3-day €90, 6-day €155). Buy individual lift passes for Nordpark-Seegrube (€23.50), Patscherkofel (€25.50), and Glungezer (€21). The tourist office also rents **ski equipment** (€9-18 per day). One day of winter glacier skiing costs €32; summer ski packages (bus, lift, and rental) cost €49.

STYRIA (STEIERMARK)

Many of southern Austria's folk traditions live on in the emerald hills and sloping pastures of Styria, where even the largest city, Graz, remains calm and relatively untouristed. The Styrian vineyards are also essential to any wine tour of Europe.

GRAZ ☎0316

Graz may be Austria's second-largest city (pop. 226,000), but that seems to be a well-kept secret. The Altstadt (old town) has an unhurried Mediterranean feel, pic-

LOCAL LEGEND

HOW MANY GREEKS DOES IT TAKE TO KILL A RHINOCEROS?

Once upon a time, Klagenfurt, a town southwest of Graz, was harassed by a winged, virgin-consuming lizard, the *Lindwurm* (dragon). This awful monster terrorized the area, preventing settlers from draining the marshes. Even worse, the beast had a taste for beautiful Austrian women, decimating the eligible young maiden population.

Enter Hercules, who, strikingly out of his normal context, arrived all the way from Greece to quickly dispatch the beast and save the village. Centuries later, the skull of the slain beast was found, proving many an old wives' tale about the heroic defeat of the town's scaly scourge. The townspeople commissioned sculptor Ulrich Vogelsang to recreate the monster using the skull as his model. The bronze fountain-statue of the *Lindwurm* on Neuer Platz instantly became the town's symbol, despite the fact that, in 1840, scientists proved the skull belonged not to the beast, but to a prehistoric rhino.

Lindwurm or not, the skull now rests proudly in the *Landesmuseum*. Klagenfurt's collective heart broke in 1945 when an Allied soldier climbed onto the *Lindwurm*'s delicate tail, snapping it in two. However, in time the damage was completely repaired, and a fully-formed *Lindwurm* once again drools spitefully in Hercules's direction.

Landeszeughaus (Provincial Arsenal), Herreng. 16, has enough spears, muskets, and armor to outfit 28,000 mercenaries. (☎8017 9660; www.museum-joanneum.at. Open Apr.-Oct. daily 10am-6pm, Th 2hr. later; Nov.-Mar. Tu-Su 10am-3pm. English-language tours daily 10:30am, 3:30pm. €4.50, with tour €6, students €1.50/3.) North of Hauptpl., the **Schloßberg** (Castle Mountain) rises above Graz. Climb the steps of the **Schloßbergstiege,** built by Russian prisoners during WWI, for views of the Styrian plain. The newest addition to the riverscape, the shell-shaped **Murinsel,** houses a cafe, open-air theater, and playground. The **Opernhaus,** Franz-Josef-Pl. 10, at Opernring and Burgg., stages high-quality performances.

Most accommodations are pricey and far from the center, but efficient local transport at least provides an easy commute. To reach **Jugendgästehaus Graz (HI) ❷,** Idlhofg. 74, from the station, head right on Eggenberger Gürtel, left on Josef-Huber-G., then the first right; the complex is through the parking lot on the right. Buses #31, 32, and 33 run from Jakominipl. (☎70 83 50; www.jfgh.at). Breakfast included. Wash €2, dry €2. Internet €1.50 per 20min. Reception 7am-11pm. Dorms €25; singles €39; doubles €64. €1.50 HI discount. AmEx/DC/MC/V.) Concession stands sell sandwiches, *wurst* (€2-3), and other fast-food on **Hauptplatz.** Student hangouts line **Zinzendorfgasse** near the university. **Continuum ❶,** Sporg. 29, dishes up pizza (€1.50-7.50) in a space that transforms into a bar at night. (☎81 57 78. Weekend brunch buffet 10am-2pm €5. Open M-F 3pm-2am, Sa-Su 10am-2am. MC/V.) **SPAR** supermarket is in the train station. (Open daily 6am-9pm.) The hub of after-hours activity is the so-called **Bermuda Triangle,** behind Hauptpl., bordered by Mehlpl., Färberg., and Prokopig. At **Kulturhauskeller,** Elisabethstr. 30, music throbs all night. (19+. Cover €2. Open Tu-Sa 9pm-late.)

Trains run from the Hauptbahnhof to: Innsbruck (5-6hr., 7 per day, €45); Munich (6¼hr., 4 per day, €68); Salzburg (4¼hr., every 2hr., €40); Vienna Südbahnhof (2½hr., every hr., €28); Zurich (10hr., 5:40 and 9:40am, €79). From the train station, turn left onto Annenstr. and cross the bridge to **Hauptplatz,** the city center. Five minutes away is **Jakominiplatz,** the hub of the public transportation system. **Herrengasse,** a pedestrian street lined with cafes and boutiques, connects the two squares. The **tourist office,** Herreng. 16, has free maps, gives an English-language walking tour of the Altstadt (2hr.; Apr.-Oct. daily 2:30pm, Jan.-March Sa 2:30pm; €9.50), and books rooms for free. (☎80 750. July-Aug. M-F 10am-7pm, Sa 10am-6pm, Su 10am-4pm; Apr.-June, Oct.-Nov., and Dec. M-Sa 10am-6pm, Su 10am-4pm; Jan.-March and Nov. M-F 10am-5pm, Sa-Su 10am-4pm). **Postal Code:** A-8010.

BELGIUM (BELGIQUE, BELGIË)

Chocoholics, Europhiles, and art-lovers alike come together to worship in Belgium. Sweet-toothed foreigners flock to capital city Brussels to nibble chocolatey confections en route to European Union and NATO headquarters. In Flanders, Gothic towers overlook cobblestone squares, while visitors below admire Old Masters' canvases by day and guzzle monk-made ale by night. French-speaking Wallonie caters less to tourists, but the caves of the Lesse Valley and the forested trails of the Ardennes more than compensate with their natural beauty.

DISCOVER BELGIUM: SUGGESTED ITINERARY

Plan for at least two days in **Brussels** (p. 101), the capital whose **Grand-Place** Victor Hugo called "the most beautiful square in the world." Head north to see the elegant boulevards of **Antwerp** (p. 111) and the historic districts of **Ghent** (p. 112), then angle west to the winding streets and canals of romantic **Bruges** (p. 107). Connect to eastbound trains in the gritty university town of **Liège** (p. 114), or else take your time exploring the leafy Ardennes, using **Namur** (p. 115) as a base for hikes or bike rides into Belgium's rural south country.

ESSENTIALS

FACTS AND FIGURES

Official Name: Kingdom of Belgium.

Capital: Brussels.

Major Cities: Antwerp, Ghent, Liège.

Population: 10,400,000.

Time Zone: GMT +1.

Languages: Dutch (60%), French (40%), and German (less than 1%).

Religions: Roman Catholic (75%).

WHEN TO GO

May, June, and September are the best times to visit, with temperatures around 18-22°C (64-72°F) in Brussels and Antwerp, and about 6°C (10°F) higher in Liège and Ghent. July and August tend to be humid and rainy. Winters are cloudy and cool, with temperatures averaging 2-7°C (36-45°F), and a bit colder in the eastern Ardennes. Bring a sweater and rain gear whenever you go and a heavy jacket in the winter months.

DOCUMENTS AND FORMALITIES

EMBASSIES AND CONSULATES. All foreign embassies are in Brussels. For Belgian embassies in your home country: **Australia,** 19 Arkana St., Yarralumla, ACT 2600 (☎02 6273 2502; www.diplomatie.be/canberra); **Canada,** 360 Albert St., Ste. 820, Ottawa, ON, K1R 7X7 (☎613-236-7267; www.diplomatie.be/ottawa); **Ireland,** 2 Shrewsbury Rd., Ballsbridge, Dublin, 4 (☎01 205 71 00; www.diplomatie.be/dub-

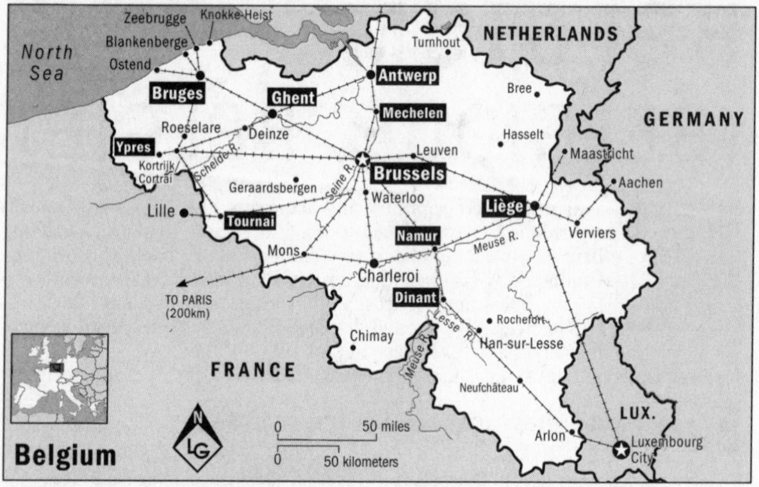

lin); **UK,** 17 Grosvenor Crescent, London, SW1X 7EE (☎020 7470 3700; www.diplobel.org/uk/uk.htm); **US,** 3330 Garfield St., NW, Washington, D.C., 20008; visit the website for state consulates (☎202-333-6900; www.diplobel.us). **New Zealanders** should contact the Belgian Honorary Consul for Auckland (☎05 75 62 02; ismackenzie@xtra.co.nz) or the Australian embassy.

VISA AND ENTRY INFORMATION. EU citizens do not need a visa. Citizens of Australia, Canada, New Zealand, and the US do not need a visa for stays of up to 90 days in any of the countries within EU's freedom-of-movement zone.

BELGIUM

TOURIST SERVICES AND MONEY

EMERGENCY	**Police:** ☎101. **Ambulance:** ☎100. **Fire:** ☎100.

TOURIST OFFICES. Bureaux de Tourisme, marked by green-and-white or blue signs labeled "i," are supplemented by **Infor Jeunes/Info-Jeugd,** information centers that help young people find work and secure accommodations in Wallonie and Flanders, respectively. The **Belgian Tourist Information Center (BBB),** Grasmarkt 63, Brussels (☎025 04 03 90), has national tourist info. The weekly English-language *Bulletin* (€2.70 at newsstands) includes movie listings, cultural events, and news.

MONEY. The **euro (€)** has replaced the franc as the unit of currency in Belgium. For exchange rates and more on the euro, see p. 18. ATMs generally offer the best rates, but checking accounts are often required to withdraw money. A bare-bones day in Belgium might cost €35, a more comfortable day €50-65. Restaurant bills usually include a service charge, although outstanding service warrants an extra 5-10% tip. EU member countries impose a **value added tax (VAT)** on goods and services purchased within the EU, included in the price; Belgium's stiff rate is 21%, although partial refunds are available for visitors who are not EU citizens (p. 22).

TRANSPORTATION

BY PLANE. Several major airlines fly into **Brussels International Airport (BRU)** from Europe, North America, and Australia. **SN Brussels Airlines** (Belgium ☎070 35 11 11, UK 0870 735 2345; www.flysn.com) flies into Brussels from most major European cities. Budget airline **Ryanair** (Ireland ☎353 1249 7700; www.ryanair.com) flies into **Brussels South Charleroi Airport (CRL),** 60km south of the city, from across Europe. Ryanair's rock-bottom fares, which start as low as €0.99 (excluding taxes and fees, generally €15-20), are the best deal for those willing to forgo convenience.

BY TRAIN AND BUS. The extensive and reliable **Belgian Rail** (www.b-rail.be) network traverses the country. **Eurail** passes are valid in Belgium. A **Benelux Tourrail Pass** (US$176, under 26 US$132) allows five days of unlimited train travel in a one-month period in Belgium, the Netherlands, and Luxembourg. Travelers who have time to explore the nooks and crannies of Belgium might consider the **Rail Pass** (€68) or **Go Pass** (under 26 only; €45), both of which allow 10 single trips within the country over a one-year period and can be transferred among travelers. Because trains are so widely available, **buses** are used primarily for local transport. Single tickets are €1.50, and cheaper when bought in packs.

BY FERRY. P&O Ferries (UK ☎087 0598 0333, Belgium 070 70 77 71; www.poferries.com) cross the Channel from **Hull, BRI** to **Zeebrugge,** north of Bruges (12½hr., 7pm, from €150).

BY CAR, BIKE, AND THUMB. Belgium honors most foreign drivers' licenses, including those from Australia, Canada, the EU, and the US. **New Zealanders** must contact the New Zealand Automobile Association (☎0800 822 422; www.aa.co.nz) for an International Driving Permit. **Speed limits** are 120kph on motorways, 90kph on main roads, and 50kph elsewhere. **Biking** is popular, and many roads in Flanders have bike lanes, while Wallonie has started to convert old railroad beds into paths for pedestrians and cyclists. **Hitchhiking** is illegal and uncommon, and Let's Go does not recommend it as a safe means of transport.

KEEPING IN TOUCH

PHONE CODES	**Country code:** 32. **International dialing prefix:** 00. For more information on how to place international calls, see inside back cover.

EMAIL AND THE INTERNET. There are cyber cafes in all of the larger towns and cities in Belgium. Expect to pay €2-3 per 30min. In smaller towns, Internet is generally available in hostels for €0.08-0.10 per min.

TELEPHONE. Most pay phones require a phone card (from €5), available at post offices, supermarkets, and newsstands. Calls are cheapest 6:30pm-8am and on weekends. Mobile phones see (p. 29) are increasingly popular and economical. For operator assistance, dial ☎12 07; international assistance ☎12 04 (€0.25). International direct dial numbers include: **AT&T** (☎0800 100 10); **British Telecom** (☎0800 89 0032); **Canada Direct** (☎0800 100 19); **MCI** (☎0800 100 12); **Sprint** (☎0800 100 14); **Telecom New Zealand** (☎0800 100 64); **Telstra Australia** (☎0800 100 61).

MAIL. A postcard or letter (up to 50g) sent within Belgium costs €0.46/0.52, within the EU €0.60/0.70, and to the rest of the world €0.65/0.80. Additional info is available at www.post.be.

LANGUAGE. Belgium's three official languages are each associated with a particular region and fierce regional sentiment. Flemish, a variant of Dutch, is spoken in Flanders, the northern half of the country; French is spoken in Wallonie, the southern region; German is spoken in a few districts east of Liège. Both Flemish and French are spoken in Brussels. In Flanders, many people speak some English; some knowledge of French is helpful in Wallonie. For basic French words and phrases, see p. 1055; for German, see p. 1055.

ACCOMMODATIONS AND CAMPING

BELGIUM	❶	❷	❸	❹	❺
ACCOMMODATIONS	under €10	€10-20	€20-30	€30-40	over €40

Hotels are fairly expensive, with rock-bottom singles from €30 and doubles from €40-45. Belgium's 31 **HI youth hostels** are run by the Flemish Youth Hostel Federation (☎03 232 72 18; www.vjh.be) in Flanders and Les Auberges de Jeunesses (☎02 219 56 76; www.laj.be) in Wallonie. Expect to pay around €18 per night, including linens, for modern, basic hostels. **Private hostels** often cost about the same but are usually nicer, although they may charge separately for linen. Most receptionists speak some English. Reservations are a good idea, particularly in the summer and on weekends. **Campgrounds** charge about €4 per night, and are common in Wallonie but not in Flanders. An **International Camping Card** is not required in Belgium.

FOOD AND DRINK

BELGIUM	❶	❷	❸	❹	❺
FOOD	under €5	€5-8	€8-12	€12-18	over €18

Belgian cuisine fuses French and German styles. It is acclaimed but expensive; an authentic evening meal may cost as much as a night's accommodations. Fresh seafood from the coast appears in *moules* or *mosselen* (steamed mussels) and *moules frites* (steamed mussels with french fries), the national dishes, which are often tasty and reasonably affordable (€14-20). *Frites* (french fries) are ubiquitous; Belgians eat them dipped in mayonnaise. Belgian **beer** is a source of national pride, its consumption a national pastime; more varieties—over 300, ranging from ordinary pilsners (€1) to Trappist ales (€3) brewed by monks—are produced here than in any other country. Leave room for chocolate **pralines** from Leonidas or Neuhaus and **waffles** *(gaufres)*, sold on the street and in cafes.

HOLIDAYS AND FESTIVALS

Holidays: Dates in 2007 are: Easter Sunday and Monday (Apr. 8-9); Labor Day (May 1); Feast of the Ascension (May 17); Whit Sunday and Monday (May 27-28); Flemish Community Day (July 11); National Day (July 21); Feast of the Assumption (Aug. 15); French Community Day (Sept. 27); All Saints' Day (Nov. 1); Armistice Day (Nov. 11).

Festivals: Ghent hosts the Gentse Feesten, celebrating culture (mid-July; www.gentsefeesten.be), plus the dance festival 10 Days Off (www.10daysoff.be). Bruges hosts the Cactus Festival music event (mid-July; www.cactusfestival.be) with alt-pop and hip-hop; eastern Belgium's Pukkelpop (late Aug.; www.pukkelpop.be) draws the alternative music set.

BEYOND TOURISM

Volunteer and work opportunities in Belgium center around its strong international offerings, especially in Brussels, which is home to both NATO and the EU. Private-sector short- and long-term employment is listed at www.jobs-in-europe.net. See p. 61 for Beyond Tourism opportunities throughout Europe.

Amnesty International, r. Berckmans 9, 1060 Brussels (☎02 538 81 77; www.amnestyinternational.be). One of the world's foremost human rights organizations has offices in Brussels. Paid positions and volunteer work *(bénévolat)* available.

The International School of Brussels, Kattenberg-Botisfort 19, Brussels (☎02 661 42 11; www.isb.be). The ISB hires teachers to positions lasting one year or more. Must have permission to work in Belgium.

North Atlantic Treaty Organization (NATO), bd. Leopold III, Brussels (www.nato.int). People under 30 who are fluent in at least 2 NATO languages can apply for six-month internships. Requirements and application details available at www.nato.int/structur/interns/index.html. Application deadlines are far ahead of start dates.

BRUSSELS (BRUXELLES, BRUSSEL) ☎02

The headquarters of both NATO and the EU, Brussels (pop. 1,200,000) is often identified by its population of terminally bland functionaries. Yet these civil servants aren't the only ones who speak for Belgium's capital; beneath the drone of parliamentary procedure bustles the witty clamor of local life. These voices echo throughout the city's intricate architecture, alternately Gothic and Art Nouveau, and jabber in both French and Flemish into the waning hours of Brussels nightlife.

TRANSPORTATION

Flights: Brussels Airport (**BRU;** ☎ 753 42 21, specific flight info 09007 0000, €0.45 per min.; www.brusselsairport.be) is 14km from the city and accessible by train. See www.flysn.be for info on **SN Brussels Airline,** the Belgian national carrier. **Brussels South Charleroi** (**CRL;** ☎71 25 12 11; www.charleroi-airport.com) is 46km outside the city, between Brussels and Charleroi, and services a number of European airlines, including Ryanair. Bus A runs from the airport to the Charleroi-SUDT train station where you can catch another train to Brussels. There is also a bus service which goes from the airport to Brussels' Gare du Midi (1hr., €10.50, buy tickets onboard).

Trains: (☎555 25 55; www.sncb.be). All international trains stop at **Gare du Midi;** most also stop at **Gare Centrale** (near Grand-Place) or **Gare du Nord** (near the Botanical Gardens). Trains run to: **Amsterdam, NTH** (3hr.; €32, under 26 €24); **Antwerp** (45min., €6); **Bruges** (45min., €12); **Cologne, GER** (2¾hr.; €39, under 26 €20); **Liège** (1hr. €13); **Luxembourg City, LUX** (1¾hr.; €28, under 26 €18); **Paris, FRA** (1½hr.; €72, under 26 €36). **Eurostar** goes to **London, BRI** (2¾hr.; €79-224), with Eurail or Benelux pass from €75, under 26 from €60).

Public Transportation: The **Métro (M), buses,** and **trams** run daily 5:30am-12:30am. 1hr. ticket €1.50, day pass €4, 5 trips €67, 10 trips €10.50. All 3 are run by the **Société des Transports Intercommunaux Bruxellois** (**STIB;** ☎0900 10 310, €0.45 per min.; www.stib.irisnet.be). STIB also offers the **Carte 3/5** (€9), which grants 3 days of unlimited intracity transport within 5 days' time; buy it in stations.

TIP **HOLD THAT STUB.** Always hold on to your receipt or ticket stub to avoid steep fines on public transportation, although enforcement appears rather lax.

BELGIUM

ORIENTATION AND PRACTICAL INFORMATION

Most major attractions are clustered around **Grand-Place,** between the **Bourse** (Stock Market) to the west and the **Parc de Bruxelles** to the east. One **Métro** line circles the city and another bisects it, while efficient **trams** run north-south. Signs list street names in both French and Flemish; Let's Go lists all addresses in French.

Tourist Offices: The **Brussels International Tourism and Congress** (**BITC;** ☎513 89 40 www.brusselsinternational.be). M: Bourse. On Grand-Place in the Town Hall, BITC is the city's official tourist office. It sells the **Brussels Card** (€30), which provides free public transportation and access to 30 museums in a 3-day period. Open daily 9am-6pm; Jan.-Easter closed Su. The **Flanders Tourist Office,** 63 r. des Marché aux Herbes (☎504 30 90; www.visitbelgium.com). M: Bourse. 1 block from Grand-Place. Ask for a free copy of the indispensable *What's On.* Open M-Th 9am-6pm, Sa-Su 9am-6pm.

Budget Travel: Infor-Jeunes Bruxelles, 155 r. Van Artevelde (☎514 41 11; www.inforjeunes-bxl.be). M: Bourse. Offers budget travel info for students over 18 and helps them to find jobs and apartments. Free Internet for students. Open M-F noon-5pm.

Embassies: Australia, 6-8 r. Guimard (☎286 05 00; www.austemb@dfat.gov.au). **Canada,** 2 av. Tervuren (☎741 06 11; www.ambassade.canada.be). **Ireland,** 50 r. Wiertz (☎235 66 76). **New Zealand,** 1 sq. de Meeus (☎512 10 40). **UK,** 85 r. d'Arlon (☎287 62 11; www.british-embassy.be). **US,** 27 bd. du Régent (☎508 21 11; www.usembassy.be).

Currency Exchange: Many exchange booths near Grand-Place are open until 11pm. Most charge a commission to cash checks. Try **Travelex,** 4 Grand-Place (☎513 21 11). Open M-F 9:15am-7:45pm, Sa 10:15am-7:45pm, Su 10:15am-4:45pm.

> **!** Women navigating Brussels on their own are often the target of unwanted advances from male admirers, ranging from playful requests for a kiss to cruder overtures. While sexual harassment is illegal in Belgium, isolated incidents are rarely prosecuted. See p. 38 for further tips specific to women travelers.

English-Language Bookstore: Sterling Books, 38 r. du Fossé aux Loups (☎223 62 23). M: De Brouckère. Open M-Sa 10am-9pm, Su noon-8:30pm. AmEx/MC/V.

GLBT Resources: The tourist office offers the *Safer Guide* to gay nightlife.

Laundromat: Wash Club, 68 r. du Marché au Charbon. M: Bourse. Wash €3.50 per 8kg, €7 per 18kg. Open daily 7am-10pm.

Emergencies: Police: ☎101. **Ambulance** and **Fire:** ☎100.

Pharmacy: Neos-Bourse Pharmacie, 61 bd. Anspach at r. du Marché aux Poulets (☎218 06 40). M: Bourse. Open M-Sa 8:30am-6:30pm. Pharmacies are prevalent and marked with neon crosses.

Medical Services: St. Luc's, 20 Hippokrateslaan (☎764 11 11), is convenient to Grand-Place. **Clinique St Etienne Kliniek,** 100 Meridien (☎ 225 9111), is close to the Centre van Gogh Hostel (see below).

Internet Access: Some Internet cafes with phone booths can be found on ch. de Wavre. M: Porte de Namur. They charge €1-1.50 per hr. **Axen,** 179 r. Royale, is located 1 block from the Centre van Gogh Hostel. Open daily 9am-midnight. €1.50 per hr.

Post Office: Corner of bl. Anspach and r. des Augustins (www.laposte.be). M: De Brouckère. Open M-F 8am-7pm, Sa 10:30am-6:30pm. Address mail to be held: First name LAST NAME, Poste Bruxelles de Brouckère, 1000 BXL, BELGIUM.

ACCOMMODATIONS

Accommodations can be difficult to find, especially on weekends in the summer. Overall, accommodations are well-kept and centrally located. The BITC (see **Practical Information,** p. 101) books rooms for free, sometimes at discounts up to 50%.

Sleep Well, 23 r. du Damier (☎218 50 50; www.sleepwell.be). M: Rogier. Choose hotel-like "Star" service or hostel-like "non-Star" service. Lockout for non-Star service 11am-3pm. Dorms €17-28; singles €28; doubles €50; triples €68; star singles €39; star doubles €57. €4 discount after 1st night for non-single, non-Star rooms. MC/V. ❷

Centre Vincent van Gogh (CHAB), 8 r. Traversière (☎217 01 58; www.chab.be). M: Botanique. Social, friendly common spaces recommend CHAB despite spartan rooms and inconveniently located bathrooms. Under 35 only. Reception 24hr. Lockout 10am-2pm. Dorms €14-17; singles €28; doubles €42; triples €63. AmEx/MC/V. ❷

Les Auberges de Jeunesse "Jacques Brel" (HI), 30 r. de la Sablonnière (☎219 56 76), on pl. des Barricades. M: Botanique. Spacious rooms surround a courtyard. Breakfast and linens included. Reception 8am-1am. Lockout noon-3pm. Dorms €19-21; singles €30; doubles €64; triples and quads €54-70. €3 HI discount. MC/V. ❷

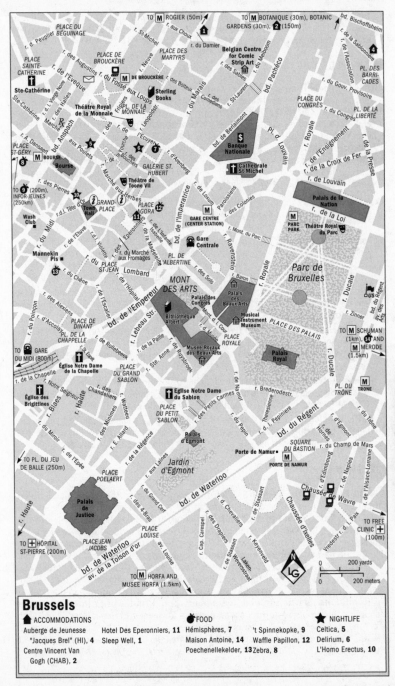

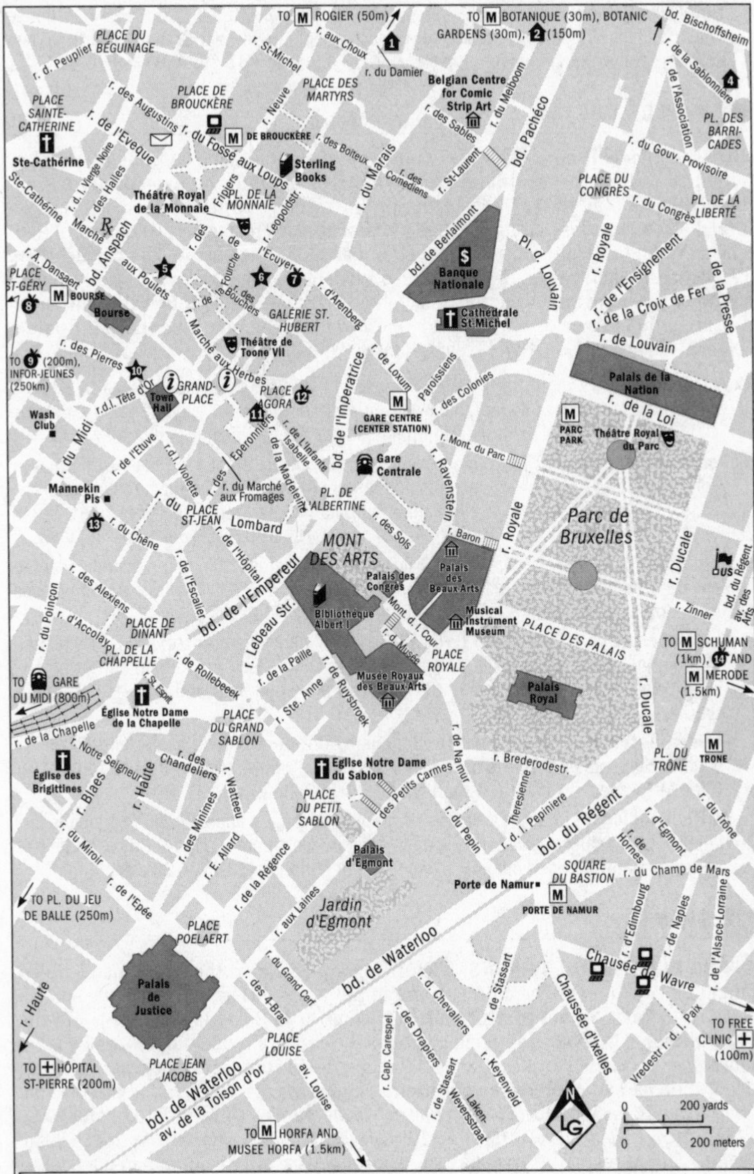

Brussels

ACCOMMODATIONS
Auberge de Jeunesse "Jacques Brel" (HI), **4**
Centre Vincent Van Gogh (CHAB), **2**
Hotel Des Eperonniers, **11**
Sleep Well, **1**

FOOD
Hémisphères, **7**
Maison Antoine, **14**
Poechenellekelder, **13**
't Spinnekopke, **9**
Waffle Papillon, **12**
Zebra, **8**

NIGHTLIFE
Celtica, **5**
Delirium, **6**
L'Homo Erectus, **10**

Hotel Des Eperonniers, 1 r. des Eperonniers (☎513 53 66). M: Gare Centrale. Choose basic singles or spacious studios for up to 6 people, right near Grand-Place. Breakfast €4. Reception 7am-midnight. Singles €30-57; doubles €45-73. AmEx/MC/V. ❹

FOOD

Brussels has earned its reputation as one of the culinary capitals of Europe, although the city's restaurants are often more suited to the five-star port-wine-reduction set than to the budget traveler. Inexpensive restaurants cluster outside **Grand-Place.** Vendors along the **Rue du Marché aux Fromages** to the south hawk cheap Middle Eastern food, while restaurants along the narrow **Rue des Bouchers** offer shellfish and paella. Seafood is also available at the small restaurants on **Quai aux Briques,** in the Ste-Catherine area behind pl. St-Géry. An **AD Delhaize** supermarket is on the corner of bd. Anspach and r. du Marché aux Poulets. (M: Bourse. Open M-Th and Sa 9am-8pm, F 9am-9pm, Su 9am-6pm. AmEx/DC/MC/V.)

't Spinnekopke, 1 pl. du Jardin aux Fleurs (☎511 86 95). M: Bourse. Locals "inside the spider's head" savor Belgian game and mussels in this cozy, elegant setting. Entrees €15-25. Open M-F 11am-3pm and 6pm-midnight, Sa 6-midnight. AmEx/MC/V. ❺

Poechenellekelder, 5 r. du Chêne (☎511 92 62). If the Manneken Pis's water makes you thirsty for a drink, head across the street for one here, amid hanging marionettes. A variety of beers (€3.20-4) is supplemented by a limited food menu of *tartines* (open-faced sandwiches; €3.50-7) and *pâté* (€7.20-8). Open Tu-Su 11am-1am. MC/V. ❸

Zebra, 3335 pl. St-Géry. M: Bourse. Known for its cocktails, this chic, centrally located cafe and bar also serves fruit juices and light sandwiches (€2.70-4.50). Kitchen closes at 11pm. Open M-Th and Su 11:45am-1am, F-Sa 11:45am-2am. MC/V. ❶

Hémisphères, 65 r. de l'Ecuyer (☎513 93 70; www.hemispheres-resto.be). This restaurant, art gallery, and "intercultural space" serves Middle Eastern, Indian, and Asian cuisine. Vegetarian options. Entrees €7-15. Open M-F noon-3pm and 6:30-10:30pm, Sa 6:30pm-midnight. MC/V. ❸

Maison Antoine, 1 pl. Jourdan. M: Schuman. The brown kiosk in the middle of the square. 58 years in business have perfected Maison's *frites* (french fries; €1.90-2.10). Open M-Th and Su 11:30am-1am, F-Sa 11:30am-2am. Cash only. ❶

Waffle Papillon, Pl. Agora. Of Brussels's abundant waffle stands, Waffle Papillion is distinctive. Gorge on waffles topped with homemade ice cream (€1.50-3.50) or choose to add chocolate, whipped cream, strawberries, or bananas (€1.50-4.20). ❶

SIGHTS

GRAND-PLACE AND ENVIRONS. Victor Hugo once called the statued and gilded Grand-Place "the most beautiful square in the world." During the day, be sure to see its buildings, former guilds, inside at La Maison du Roi (King's House), now the city museum whose most riveting exhibit is the collection of clothes worn by Mannekin Pis, or at the town hall where 40min. guided tours showcase over-the-top decoration and an impressive collection of paintings. *(La Maison du Roi ☎279 43 50. Open Tu-Su 10am-5pm. €2.50. Town Hall ☎548 04 45. French tours Tu, W 2:30pm, Su 11:30am; English tours Tu- W 3:15pm, Su 10:45am and 12:15pm; arrive early for tours. €3, students €2.50.)* At night, the town hall's tower-topped exterior is illuminated by colorful floodlights swirling to classical music. You'll find a brief introduction to Belgium's famed beers at the **Belgian Brewer's Museum.** *(10 Grand-Place. 2 buildings left of the town hall. ☎511 49 87; www.beerparadise.be. Open daily 10am-5pm. €5, includes 1 beer.)* Nearby, the **Museum of Cocoa and Chocolate** tells of Belgium's other renowned edible export. *(11 r. de la Tête d'Or. ☎514 20 48; www.mucc.be. Open July-Aug. and holidays* *daily 10am-4:30pm; Sept.-June Tu-Su 10am-4:30pm. €5, students €4.)* Three blocks behind the town hall, on the corner of r. de l'Etuve and r. du Chêne, is Brussels's beloved **Mannekin Pis,** a tiny fountain shaped like a boy who seems to be peeing continuously. Legend claims it commemorates a boy who defused a bomb destined for the Grand-Place, though it was in fact installed to supply drinking water during the reign of Archduke Albert and Archduchess Isabelle. Locals have created hundreds of outfits for him, each with a strategically placed hole. In order to even the gender gap, a statue of a squatting girl *(Jeanneken)* now pees down an ally off r. des Bouchers. Just north of Gare Centrale, the elaborate **Cathédrale St-Michel et Ste-Gudule** hosts royal affairs under its soaring ribbed vaults. At times, music—pipe organ or carillon—serenades visitors. *(Pl. Ste-Gudule. Open M-F 7am-6pm, Sa-Su 8:30am-6pm. Free.)*

MONT DES ARTS. The **Musées Royaux des Beaux-Arts** encompass the **Musée d'Art Ancien,** the **Musée d'Art Moderne,** several contemporary exhibits, and the **Musée Magritte,** opening in 2007. Together, the museums steward a huge collection of Belgian art organized by era, including Bruegel the Elder's famous *Landscape with the Fall of Icarus* and pieces by Rubens and Brussels native René Magritte. Other masterpieces on display include David's *Death of Marat* and paintings by Delacroix, Gauguin, Ingres, Seurat, and van Gogh. The great hall itself is a work of architectural beauty; the panoramic view of Brussels's cityscape from the fourth floor of the 19th-century wing alone justifies the admission fee. *(3 r. de la Régence. M: Parc. ☎508 32 11; www.fine-arts-museum.be. Open Tu-Su 10am-5pm. Some wings close noon-2pm. €9, students €3.50, special exhibits extra. 1st W of each month 1-5pm free. Audio tour €2.50.)* The **Musical Instrument Museum (MIM)** houses over 1500 instruments; stand in front of one and your headphones play a sample of its music. *(2 r. Montagne de la Cour. ☎545 01 30; www.mim.fgov.be. Open Tu-F 9:30am-4:45pm, Sa-Su 10am-5pm. €5, students €3.50; headphones included. 1st W of each month 1-5pm free.)*

BELGIAN CENTER FOR COMIC STRIP ART. Comic strips *(les BD)* are serious business in Belgium. Amusing displays document comic strip history, the museum library makes thousands of books available to scholarly researchers, and Tintin and the Smurfs make several appearances. *(☎214 01 40. r. des Sables. M: Rogier. From the station, take a right onto bd. du Jardin Botanique, a right onto r. du Marais, and turn left onto r. des Sables. Open Sa 10am-6pm, Su noon-6pm. €7.50, students with ISIC €6. Study library €1.20. €0.50 to enter the reading room without general museum ticket.)*

ON THE MENU

LETTIN' GO OF THE EGGO

At the base of the budget tourist's food pyramid in Belgium lies the auspicious dietary group, the waffle (*gaufre* in French, *wafel* in Dutch). There are two type of Belgian waffles, both made on such particular waffle irons that they can not be made well elsewhere.

Brussels waffles are flat and more or less rectangular. They're light and airy, and bear some resemblance ones eaten in the US (the kind served at diner brunches, not the ones that emerge from the freezer, pop out of the toaster, and beg to be drowned in Aunt Jemima's). Belgian recipes tend to use beaten egg whites and yeast as leavening agents, which give them their light, crisp texture. **De Lièges** waffles, ubiquitous on Belgian streets, are generally smaller, sweeter, and denser than their counterparts, and they have a crunchy caramelized-sugar crust.

Pause at a cafe for a Brussels waffle, and savor it with a knife and fork. Approach a street vendor for a hand-held Liège waffle and continue to wander (in search of your next waffle?) without missing a beat. Both can be topped with ice cream, fruit, or chocolate, or merely dusted with powdered sugar. Waffles generally cost about €1.50, though prices mount with the toppings.

Since you can't visit Belgium without sampling its waffles, you might as well indulge. Besides, vacation calories just don't count.

OTHER SIGHTS. The eerily illuminated Treasure Room and the Greco-Roman collection are the main attractions at the enormous **Musées Royaux d'Art et d'Histoire,** set in a beautiful park, while the Gothic Room and the Chinese draw-loom exhibits are quirkily enjoyable. *(10 Parc du Cinquantenaire. ☎741 72 11. M: Mérode. Open Tu-F 9:30am-5pm, Sa-Su 10am-5pm. Ticket office closes at 4pm. €4, students €3. 1st W of each month 1-5pm free.)* The out-of-the-way **Musée Horta,** home of 20th-century master architect Victor Horta, applies his Art Nouveau style to a domestic setting. *(25 r. Américaine. M: Horta. Go right, walk 7min. uphill on ch. de Waterloo and turn left onto ch. de Charleroi and right onto r. Américaine. ☎543 04 90. Open Tu-Su 2-5:30pm. €7, students €3.50.)*

ENTERTAINMENT AND NIGHTLIFE

The weekly *What's On*, part of the *Bulletin* newspaper and available free at the tourist office, contains extensive information on cultural events. The **Théâtre Royal de la Monnaie,** on pl. de la Monnaie, is renowned for its opera and ballet. (M: De Brouckère. ☎229 12 00, box office 70 23 39; www.lamonnaie.be. Tickets from €8.) The **Théâtre Royal de Toone VII,** 21 Petite r. des Bouchers, stages marionette performances. (☎513 54 86; www.toone.be for show times and prices. F-Sa 8:30pm, occasionally Tu-Th. €10, students €7.) **Nova,** 3 r. d'Arenberg, screens foreign and independent films. (☎511 24 77; www.nova-cinema.com. €5, students €3.50.)

On summer nights, performances and live concerts on **Grand-Place** and the **Bourse** bring the streets to life. The *All the Fun* pamphlet, available at the tourist office, lists the newest clubs and bars. On **Place St-Géry,** outdoor patios are jammed with a laid-back crowd of students and backpackers. **Zebra** (p. 104) and a host of other bars are lively until late. Choose from 2000 beers at **Delirium,** 4A impasse de la Fidélité. (☎251 44 34. Open daily 10am-4am.) **Celtica,** 55 r. aux Poulets, might have the world's longest Happy hour: throbbing techno accompanies €1 and €2 drafts 1pm-midnight. The bar downstairs is more relaxed, but a DJ spins at the upstairs disco. (☎514 32 53. Bar open daily 1pm-very late. Disco open Th-Sa 10pm.) **GBLT nightlife** centers around r. des Pierres and r. du Marché au Charbon, next to Grand-Place. **L'Homo Erectus,** 57 r. des Pierres, is extremely popular. (☎514 74 93; www.lhomoerectus.com. Open M-F noon-5am, Sa-Su 3pm-late.)

DAYTRIP FROM BRUSSELS: MECHELEN (MALINES)

The residents of Mechelen (pop. 78,000) are nicknamed the Moon Extinguishers *(Maneblussers)* for once a red moon for a fire in the tower of the local **St-Rombouts Tower and Cathedral.** Today, the cathedral's tower holds two 49-bell carillons and is home to the world's foremost bell-ringing school. (Free 1hr. carillon concerts June to mid-Sept. M 8:30pm.) You can hear 1hr. recitals from anywhere in Grote Markt on Monday and Saturday at 11:30am and Sunday at 3pm. To reach St-Rombouts from Centraal station, walk down Hendrick Consciencestr. to the pedestrian Grote Markt. (Cathedral open daily Easter-Oct. 8:30am-5:30pm; Nov.-Easter 8:30am-4:30pm. Tours daily Apr.-Sept. €5.) Nearby, the 15th-century **St. John's Church** boasts Rubens's *The Adoration of the Magi.* From the Grote Markt, walk down Fr. de Merodestr. and turn left onto St-Janstr. (Open Easter-Oct. Tu-Su 1:30-5:30pm; Nov.-Easter 1:30-4:30pm.) To reach the **Jewish Museum of Deportation and Resistance,** 153 Goswin de Stassartstr., follow Wollemarkt from behind St-Rombouts until it becomes Goswin de Stassart; it's on your left when the streets end at the canal, in 18th-century barracks used to hold Jews en route to Auschwitz-Birkenau. (☎29 06 60. Open Su-Th 10am-5pm, F 10am-1pm. Free.) **Trains** run to Antwerp (20min., 4 per hr., €3.20) and Brussels (20min., 4-5 per hr., €3.20). The **tourist office,** 2-4 Hallestr., is in the corner of the Grote Markt. (☎070 22 28 00; www.inenuitmechelen.be. Open Apr.-Sept. M 9:30am-7pm, Tu-F 9:30am-5:30pm, Sa-Su 10am-4:30pm; Oct.-Mar. M-F 9:30am-4:30pm, Sa-Su 10:30am-3:30pm.)

THE REAL DEAL. Skip the trip to Waterloo, the location of the famous battle. Hordes of tourists bear down on the site's unimaginatively displayed artifacts, ensuring that your trip to this historic battlefield will lack all meaning. If you really must go, take Bus W from the Gare du Midi (1hr., 2 per hr., €2.40-3). The tourist office is at 218 ch. de Bruxelles. (☎354 99 10; www.waterloo-tourisme.be. Open daily Apr.-Sept. 9:30am-6:30pm; Oct.-Mar. 10:30am-5pm.)

FLANDERS (VLAANDEREN)

Flanders, the moneyed, Flemish-speaking half of Belgium, spans quaint cities and a coastline firmly in the grip of the leisure industry. Ports once created great prosperity through trade in linen, wool, and diamonds; now tourism buoys the economy.

BRUGES (BRUGGE) ☎50

Famed for its relationship with Flemish painter Jan van Eyck, Bruges (pop. 116,000) is perhaps Belgium's most romantic city. Canals meander through rows of stone houses and cobblestone streets en route to the Gothic Markt. Despite the tourists that swarm it, a visit to Belgium shouldn't be without a visit to Bruges.

TRANSPORTATION

Trains leave from the Stationsplein, a 15min. walk south of the city. (Open daily 4:30am-11pm. Info desk open daily 8am-7pm.) Trains head to: Antwerp (1¼hr., 2 per hr., €13); Brussels (1hr., 1-3 per hr., €12); Ghent (20min., 3 per hr., €5.40); Knokke (20min., 2 per hr., €3); Ostend (15min., 3 per hr., €3.30).

ORIENTATION AND PRACTICAL INFORMATION

TIP **WATCH THAT BIKE!** In Bruges, as in many Flemish cities, bike lanes are marked in red. To escape cyclists' ire, pedestrians should avoid these areas.

Bruges is enclosed by a circular canal, with its main train station, **Stationsplein,** south of the canal. The historic district is walkable, while bikes are useful for countryside visits. The **Belfort** (Belfry) looms over the **Markt.** The windmill-lined **Kruisvestraat** and **Minnewater Park** are two of the most beautiful spots in Bruges.

Tourist Office: In and Uit, 't Zand 34 (☎44 46 46; www.brugge.be). From the train station, head left to 't Zand and walk for 10min.; the office is in the modern red concert hall. Books rooms for a €2.50 service fee and €20 deposit, and sells **maps** (€0.50) and **info guides** (€1). Also has free **Internet,** but not for email. (Open M-W and F-Su 10am-6pm, Th 10am-8am). Branch office at the train station.

Tours: The tourist office has maps for self-guided tours. 5 companies offer 30min. **boat tours** of the canals (Mar.-Nov., every 15-30min. 10am-5pm, €5.70); ask at the tourist office. **QuasiMundo Tours** offers 3 **bike tours** of Bruges and the countryside (3-4hr.). Tours depart daily at 10am and 7pm from Bruges, 1pm from the countryside. (☎33 07 75; www.quasimundo.com. Tours Mar.-Oct. €20, under 26 €18; includes free drink.)

Luggage Storage: At the train station. €2.60-3.60.

Laundromat: Belfort, Ezelstr. 51. Wash €3-6, dry €1. Open daily 7am-10pm.

Bike Rental: At the train station (☎30 23 28). €7 per ½-day, €12.50 per day. **Koffieboontje,** Hallestr. 4 (☎33 80 27; www.adventure-bike-renting.be), off the Markt to the right of the Belfort. €7 per 4hr.; €10 per day, students €7 per day. Also rents scooters.

Emergency: ☎ 100. **Police:** ☎ 44 89 30

Pharmacy: Apotheek Dryepondt, Wollestr. 7. Open M-Tu and Th-F 9am-12:30pm and 2-6:30pm, W 9am-12:30pm, Sa 9am-12:30pm and 2-6pm.

Hospitals: A. Z. St-Jan (☎ 45 21 11; not to be confused with Oud St-Janshospitaal, a museum). **St-Lucas** (☎ 36 91 11). **St-Franciscus Xaveriuskliniek** (☎ 47 04 70).

Internet Access: Coffee Link, Mariastr. 38 (☎ 34 99 73). €1.50 for 1st 15min., €0.10 per min. after. Open M-Tu, Th, and Sa-Su 11am-6pm, F 11am-3pm. Cash only.

Post Office: Markt 5. Open M and W-F 9am-6pm, Sa 9:30am-12:30pm. Address mail to be held: First name LAST NAME, *Poste Restante,* Markt 5, 8000 Brugge, BELGIUM.

ACCOMMODATIONS

Despite Bruges's popularity with tourists, reasonably priced accommodations are available just blocks from the city center. Reserve ahead for weekend stays.

Snuffel Backpacker Hostel, Ezelstr. 47-49 (☎ 33 31 33; www.snuffel.be). Take bus #3 or 13 (€1.30) from the station to the stop after Markt and take the 1st left. Staff lead free walking tours. The bar's Happy hour is so cheap, locals frequent it (9-10pm, beer €1). Bike rentals. Breakfast €3. Linens €2. Internet €1 per 30min. Key deposit €5. Reception 8am-midnight. Dorms €14; doubles €34; quads €60. AmEx/MC/V. ❷

Passage, Dweersstr. 26 (☎ 34 02 32; www.passagebruges.com). Ideal location nearly makes up for small rooms at this hostel-hotel-cafe combo. No locks on the doors, but there are safes. Breakfast €5. Internet €1 per 15min. Reception 9am-midnight. Dorms €14; singles €25-45; doubles €45-60; triples and quads €60. AmEx/DC/MC/V. ❷

Hotel Lybeer, Korte Vuldersstr. 31 (☎ 33 43 55; www.hostellybeer.com). Charming and well situated. Breakfast and linens included. Free Internet. Reception 7:30am-11pm. Dorms €16; singles €25-38; doubles €45-55; quads €90. AmEx/MC/V. ❸

Bauhaus International Youth Hostel and Hotel, Langestr. 133-137 (☎ 34 10 93; www.bauhaus.be). Take bus #6 or 16 from the station; ask to stop at the hostel. A giant candelabra and popular bar lead the way to airy rooms. Bike rental €9 per day. Breakfast and linens included. Lockers €1.50. Internet €3 per hr. Reception 8am-midnight. Dorms €15-17; singles €30-34; doubles €44-50; triples €62-72. AmEx/MC/V. ❷

Charlie Rockets, Hoogstr. 19 (☎ 330 660; www.charlierockets.com). You might even feel at home at the wannabe-American Charlie Rockets, in a converted movie theatre, now equipped with pool tables, darts, and, of course, 50s decor. Breakfast €3. Lockers €3. Linens included. Internet €2 per 20min. Dorms €16. MC/V. ❷

FOOD

Inexpensive restaurants can be hard to find in Bruges, but seafood lovers should splurge at least once on its famous mussels (*mosselen;* usually €15-22); they come from the **Vismarkt,** near the Burg. (Open Tu-Sa 8am-1pm.) Grab groceries at **Delhaize Proxy,** Noordzandstr. 4, near the Markt. (Open M-Sa 9am-7pm.)

Grand Kaffee de Passage, Dweersstr. 26-28 (☎ 34 02 32). Next to the Passage hostel. Traditional Belgian cuisine in a candlelit setting. Try the excellent Flemish stew (€11). Open daily 6am-midnight. AmEx/MC/V. ❸

Du Phare, Sasplein 2 (☎ 34 35 90; www.duphare.be). From the Burg, walk down Hoogstr. and turn left at the canal onto Verversdijk, crossing to the right side at the second bridge. Follow the canal for 20min. to Sasplein. Bus #4 stops right outside. This jazz and blues bistro serves international fare (€11-20). Open M-W 11:30am-2:30pm and 7pm-midnight, F-Sa 11:30am-2:30pm and 6:30pm-midnight, Su 11:30am-3pm and 6pm-midnight. Reservations recommended F-Sa. AmEx/DC/MC/V. ❸

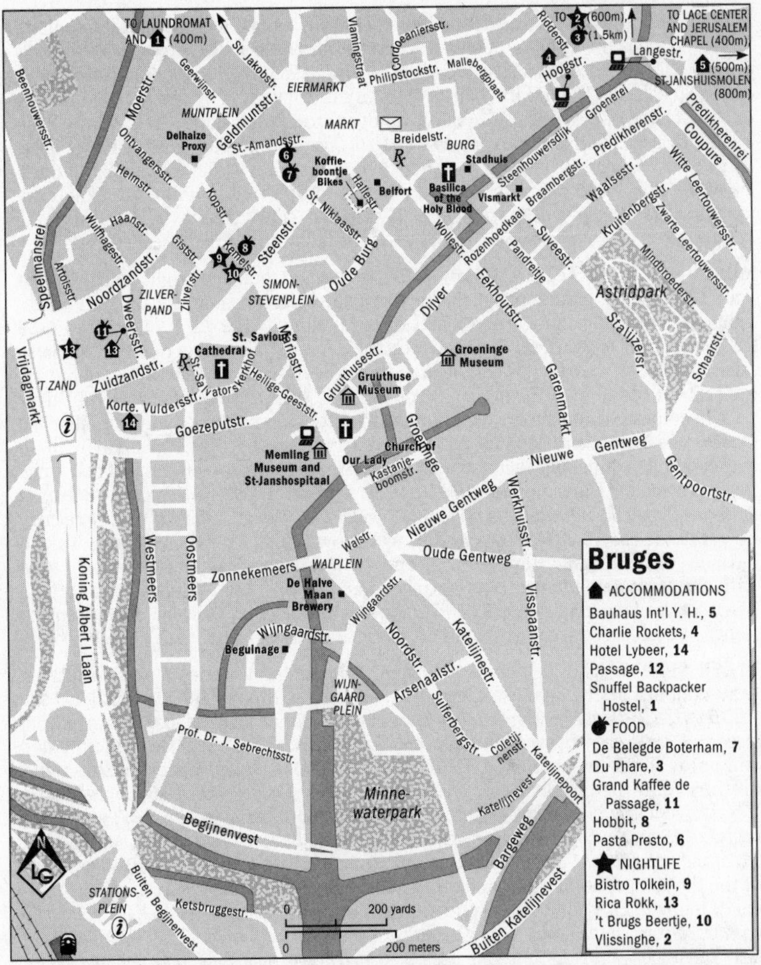

Hobbit, Kemelstr. 8-10 (☎33 55 20; www.hobbitgrill.be). Order filling meats and pastas from clever newsprint menus. Entrees €7-7.50. Open daily 6pm-1am. AmEx/MC/V. ❷

Pasta Presto, St-Amandsstr. 17 (☎34 55 36). Bargain-priced Italian fare, just off the Markt. Opt for pasta with choice of 9 sauces (€2.20 take out, €3-5 eat in), sandwiches, or salads. Open Su-M and W-Th 11:30am-8:30pm, F-Sa 11:30am-9pm. Cash only. ❷

De Belegde Boterham, Kleine St-Amandsstr. 5 (☎34 91 31). Health-conscious spot serves sandwiches (€6.50-7.50) and innovative salads (€9.50-10.50) in the chic interior or on lovingly mismatched tables outside. Open M-Sa noon-4pm. Cash only. ❷

SIGHTS

Filled with Gothic and neo-Gothic buildings, Bruges is best seen on foot. Avoid visiting on Mondays, when museums are closed. If you plan to visit many museums, buy a cost-saving combination ticket (€15, includes admission to 5 museums).

MARKT AND BURG. The medieval **Belfort** (Belfry) looms over the Markt; climb its 366 steep steps for a phenomenal view. *(Belfort open Tu-Su 9:30am-5pm. Tickets sold until 4:15pm. €5. Bell concerts mid-June to Sept. M, W, and Sa 9pm, Su 2:15pm; Oct. to mid-June W and Sa-Su 2:15pm.)* Behind the Markt, the Burg is dominated by the detailed facade of the **Stadhuis** (Town Hall). Inside, wander through the **Gothic Hall,** where residents of Bruges still get married. *(☎44 81 10. Open Tu-Su 9:30am-4:30pm. €2.50, under 26 €1.50. Audio tour included.)* In a corner of the Burg next to the Stadhuis, the **Basilica of the Holy Blood** supposedly holds the blood of Christ in an ornate sanctuary upstairs. *(Basilica open daily Apr.-Sept. 9:30-noon and 2-6pm; Oct.-Mar. 10am-noon and 2-4pm; closed W afternoon. Holy Relic can be viewed at 11am and 2-4pm. Museum €1.50.)*

MUSEUMS. From the Burg, follow Wollestr. left and then head right on Dijver and walk through the garden to reach the **Groeninge Museum;** small for its price, highlights are works by Jan van Eyck and Hans Memling. *(Dijver 12. ☎44 87. Open Tu-Su 9:30am-5pm. €8, under 26 €6. Audio tour included.)* Once a palace, the nearby **Gruuthuse Museum** houses a large collection of 16th- and 17th-century tapestries. *(Dijver 17. ☎44 87 62. Open Tu-Su 9:30am-5pm. €6, students €4. Audio tour included.)* Stay on Dijver as it becomes Gruuthusestr., walk under the stone archway to enter the **Memling Museum,** in **Oud St-Janshospitaal,** a pretty brick building that was a hospital in medieval times. The museum reconstructs life in the hospital and has several paintings by its namesake, Hans Memling. *(Mariastr. 38. ☎44 87 71. Open Tu-F 9:30am-4:30pm; Sa 9:30am-4:20pm; Su 1:30-4:50pm, tickets until 4:30pm. €8, under 26 €5. Audio tour included.)* To get to the **Lace Center,** Peperstr. 3A, walk down Hoogstr. from the Burg. Take a left onto Molenmeers after the canal and walk straight. The center shares a gate with the **Jerusalem Chapel.** Some afternoons a troop of wrinkled octogenarians demonstrate lace-making. *(☎33 00 72; www.kantcentrum.com. Open M-F 10am-noon and 2-6pm, Sa-Su 10am-noon and 2-5pm. €2.50, under 26 €1.50 for both Lace Center and Chapel.)*

OTHER SIGHTS. The 14th-century **Church of Our Lady,** at Mariastr. and Gruuthusestr., contains Michelangelo's *Madonna and Child. (Open M-F 9:30am-12:30pm and 1:30-5pm, Sa 9:30am-12:30pm and 1:30-4pm, Su 1:30-5pm. Church free. Tomb viewing €2.50, students €1.50. Ticket for the tomb included in Gruuthuse Museum ticket.)* Beer aficionados will enjoy the free samples at 150-year-old **De Halve Maan,** a beer museum and brewery renowned for its beer. *(Welplein 26. From the Church of Our Lady, turn left, follow Mariastr., turn right onto Wijngaardstr., and turn right onto Welplein. ☎33 26 97; www.halvemaan.be. 45min tours Apr.-Sept. every hr. M-F 11am-4pm, Sa-Su 11am-5pm; Oct.-Mar. tours at 11am and 3pm, Sa-Su 1 per hr. 11am-4pm. €4.50, includes free beer.)* Wander the grounds of the **Beguinage,** home to Benedictine nuns, and go inside to see furnishings typical of a medieval Flemish household. *(From Simon Stevinplein, follow Mariastr., turn right on Wijngaardstr.; at the canal, turn right and cross the footbridge. ☎33 00 11. Open Mar.-Nov. daily 10am-noon and 1:30-5pm; gate open 6:30am-6:30pm. Admission to garden free; house €2, under 26 €1.)* The 235-year-old windmill, **St-Janshuismolen,** still gives occasional flour-grinding demonstrations in summer when the wind is right. *(☎33 00 44. From the Burg, follow Hoogstr., which becomes Langestr.; turn left at the end on Kruisvestr. From bus #6 or 16, get off right before the bus crosses the canal and continue along the water to the 2nd windmill. Open May-Sept. daily 9:30am-12:30pm and 1:30-5pm. €2, under 26 €1.)*

ENTERTAINMENT AND NIGHTLIFE

Bruges plays host to the **Cactusfestival** (☎33 20 14; www.cactusfestival.be; €22-30 per day, €59-65 for 3 days), a series of alt-pop and hip-hop concerts the first full weekend in July. The city also sponsors **Klinkers,** an open-air music and film series that's free to the public during July and August (☎33 20 14; www.klinkers-brugge.be). At **'t Brugs Beertje,** Kemelstr. 5, off Steenstr., sample one of the 250 varieties of beer. (Open Su-M and Th 4pm-12:30am, F-Sa 4pm-1:30am.) Next door, the candlelit **Bistro Tolkien,** Kemelstr. 9, pours fruity *jenever* (€2), a flavored Dutch gin. (☎34 24 21. Open M and W-Sa noon-2pm and 6pm-11pm.) Try Bruges's oldest pub, the quieter **Vlissinghe,** Blekersstr. 2, established in 1515. From the Burg, take Hoogstr. and turn left onto Verversdijk immediately before the canal. Cross the second bridge onto Blekersstr. (☎34 37 37. Open W-Sa 11am-midnight, Su 11am-7pm.) Steer clear of the tourist clubs behind the Markt. Belgian students prefer the dance floor of **Rica Rokk,** 't Zand 6, where shots are €3 and a meter of beer starts at €19. (☎33 24 34; www.maricorokk.com. Open daily 9am-5am.) The tourist office has a list of **GLBT establishments.**

TIP **THE LONG ARM OF THE LAW.** If you're wobbling back to your hostel with a bellyful of beer, think twice before yielding to nature's call en route. Police will fine you up to €152 if they catch you urinating in public. Keep €0.30 handy for public toilets, although many of these stalls close at 8pm.

ANTWERP (ANTWERPEN, ANVERS) ☎03

While Antwerp (pop. 455,000) used to be known for its avant-garde fashions and jet-setting party hoppers, the hipster scene has since calmed. Antwerp's main promenades, **De Keyserlei** and the **Meir,** draw crowds to their elegant department stores and avant-garde boutiques. On the western edge of the shopping area, the **Cathedral of Our Lady,** Groenpl. 21, holds Rubens's *Descent from the Cross.* (☎213 99 51. Open M-F 10am-5pm, Sa 10am-3pm, Su 1-4pm. Included guided tours Sept. to mid-July M-Sa 11am and 2:15pm, Su 2:15pm; mid-July to Aug. M-F 11am, 2:15, 3:45pm, Sa 11am and 2:15pm, Su 1:15, 2:15, 3pm. €2.) Take in the busy exterior of the nearby **Stadhuis** (city hall), then hop on tram #11 (dir.:Eksterlaar) to see the wildly opulent mansions that line **Cogels Osylei.** A stroll by the Schelde River leads to the 13th-century **Steen Castle,** Steenplein 1, which houses the extensive collections of the **National Maritime Museum.** (☎201 93 40. Museum open Tu-Su 10am-5pm. €4, students €2.) The **Royal Museum of Fine Arts** (Museum Voor Schone Kunsten; KMSKA), Leopold De Waelpl. 1-9, possesses one of the world's finest collections of Old Flemish Master paintings. From Centraal, take tram #12 or 24 and get off at Verbondstr. (☎238 78 09; www.kmska.be. Open Tu-Sa 10am-5pm, Su 10am-6pm. €8, under 25 €6. Audio tour included.) The **Rubens Huis,** Wapper 9, off the Meir, was built by Antwerp's favorite son; its collection includes *The Annunciation.* (☎201 15 55. Open Tu-Su 10am-4:45pm. €6, under 26 €4. Audio tour included.) The **Diamant Museum,** Kon. Astridplein 19-23, chronicles Antwerp's role as diamond center through intriguingly weird audiovisual displays. (☎202 48 90. Open M-Tu and Th-Su 10am-5:30pm. €6, students €4. Audio tour included.)

The well-worn **New International Youth Hotel ❷,** Provinciestr. 256, is a 15min. walk from Centraal Station, on the corner of De Boeystr. and Provinciestr. Turn left out of the station onto Pelikaanstr., which becomes Simonsstr.; turn left on Plantin en Moretus, walk under the bridge, then turn right onto Provinciestr. (☎230 05 22; www.youthhotel.be. Breakfast included. Reception 8am-midnight. Dorms €19-20, under 26 €15; singles €32; doubles €48-60; triples €68-79. MC/V.) To reach **Guesthouse 26 ❺,** Pelgrimsstr. 26. M: Groenpl. Take Reyndersstr. from Groenpl. away from the Hilton and turn right onto Pelgrimsstr. (☎497 42 69. Breakfast included. Reserve ahead. Singles €55-75; doubles €65-85. AmEx/MC/V.) To reach **Camping Vogelzang ❶,** 2E Doodweg 17, from Groenpl., take tram #2 (dir.: Hoboken) to Bouwcentrum, then walk away from the fountain and take the first left. (☎58 47 014. Electricity €2.30. Reception open daily 9am-8pm. Open Apr.-Sept. Tent sites €1.25; €2.50 per person. 4-bed huts €32. €15 deposit. Cash only.) The **Grote Markt** and **Groenplaats** are surrounded by restaurants. **Suikerrui,** off Grote Markt, is the street for seafood lovers. At **Da Giovanni ❷,** Jan Blomstr. 8, just off

Groenpl., a flirtatious waitstaff serves up hearty pizzas (€4.50-13) along with faux marriage proposals. (☎226 74 50. Open daily 11am-midnight. 20% student discount. AmEx/MC/V.) More than 400 figurines accompany your meal at **'t Elfde Gebod ❹,** Torfburg 10, off Kaasrui. (☎289 34 66. Entrees €13-20. Open daily noon-2am. Kitchen closes 10:30pm. MC/V.) The **Super GB** supermarket is in the Grand Shopping Bazar; enter on the corner of Beddenstr. and Schoenmarkt. (Open M-Th and Sa 8:30am-8pm, F 8:30am-9pm. MC/V.) The palatial club **Café d'Anvers,** Verversrui 15, is north of Grote Markt in the red-light district. (☎226 38 70. Open F-Sa 11pm-7am.) Otherwise, **bars** are the place to be, either those behind the cathedral or in the trendy neighborhood around the Royal Museum of Fine Arts. For daily live jazz, hole up in the loft of **De Muze,** Melkmarkt 15. (Open daily 11am-4am.) Gay nightlife clusters around **Van Schoonhovenstraat,** just north of Centraal Station. Head to the **Gay and Lesbian Center,** Dambruggestr. 204, for more information.

Antwerp has two train stations: **Berchem,** which handles international traffic, and **Centraal,** the domestic station. Ornate Centraal's soaring arches make it a tourist destination in its own right. **Trains** go from Berchem to: Amsterdam, NTH (2hr., 1 per hr., €28); Brussels (45min., 4 per hr., €6); Rotterdam, NTH (1-2hr., 1 per hr., €18, students €13). Lockers are available in Centraal. The **tourist office** is downstairs in Centraal and has a branch at Grote Markt 15. To get to Grote Markt from Berchem, take tram #8 (€1.20, €1.50 on tram) to Groenpl. From Centraal take tram #2 (dir.: Linkeroever) or walk down the Meir, the pedestrian road, to Groenpl. ☎232 01 03. Open M-Sa 9am-5:45pm, Su 9am-4:45pm.) **Postal Code:** 2000.

GHENT (GENT) ☎09

Once the heart of Flanders's textile industry, modern Ghent (pop. 228,000) still celebrates the memory of its medieval greatness and its more recent industrial. The population is young, and the influx of tourists relatively low. The Gentse Feesten brings performers, carnival rides, and flowing *jenever* (flavored gin) to the city center. (July 12-23, 2007. www.gentsefeesten.be.) The **Leie canal** runs through the city and wraps around the **Gravensteen** (Castle of Counts), St-Veerlepl. 11, a partially restored medieval fortress. (☎225 93 06. Open daily Apr.-Sept. 9am-6pm; Oct.-Mar. 9am-5pm. €6, under 26 €1.20.) From Gravensteen, head down Geldmunt, make a right on Lange Steenst., and then a right into the historical **Partershol** quarter, a network of 16th- to 18th-century houses. Stroll down along the **Graslei,** a medieval street along the water, on the way to **St-Michielshelling,** which is lined with handsome guild houses. St-Michielshelling affords the best view of the Ghent's steepled skyline. Facing the bridge with Graslei behind you, find **St-Niklaaskerk,** where rich, medieval merchants worshipped. (☎225 37 00. Open M 2:30-5pm, Tu-Su 10am-5pm. Free.) On the left, on Limburgstr., **St-Baafskathedraal** holds Hubert and Jan van Eyck's many-paneled **Adoration of the Mystic Lamb** and Rubens's **St. Bavo's Entrance into the Monastery of Ghent.** (Cathedral and crypt open daily Apr.-Oct. 8:30am-6pm; Nov.-Mar. 8:30am-5pm. *Mystic Lamb* exhibit open Apr.-Oct. M-Sa 9:30am-5pm, Su 1-4:30pm; Nov.-Mar. M-Sa 10:30am-4pm, Su 1-3:30pm. Cathedral and crypt free. *Mystic Lamb* exhibit €3.) **Stedelijk Museum voor Actuele Kunst (SMAK),** in Citadel Park, a 30min. walk from the tourist office, rotates its collection of modern art. (☎221 17 03; www.smak.be. Open Tu-Su 10am-6pm. €5, students €3.80.)

To reach **De Draecke (HI) ❷,** St-Widostr. 11, from the station, take tram #1 (€1.20, €1.50 on tram) to Gravensteen (15min.). Facing the castle, go left over the canal, right on Gewad, and right on St-Widostr. (☎233 70 50; www.vjh.be. Breakfast and linens included. Internet €2 per 30min. Reception 7:30am-11pm. Dorms €20; singles €32; doubles €66. €3 HI discount. AmEx/MC/V.) To get to **Camping Blaarmeersen ❶,** Zuiderlaan 12, take bus #9 from St-Pietersstation toward Mariakerke and get off at Europaburg; cross the street and hop on bus #38 or 39 to

BELGIUM

Blaarmeersen. Take the first street on the left to its end. (☎266 81 60. Laundry and restaurant. Open Mar. to mid-Oct. Tent sites €4.50, low season €3.50; €4.50 per person, €3.50 low season.) **St-Pietersnieuwstraat,** by the university, has inexpensive kebab and pita joints. **Magazijn ❷,** Penitentenstr. 24, has filling fare (€8.50-16) and vegetarian options. (☎234 07 08. Kitchen open Tu-Sa 6-11pm. Bar open until late. Cash only.) For groceries, stop by the **Contact GB** at Hoogpoort 42. (☎225 05 92. Open M-Sa 8:30am-6pm. MC/V.)

Korenmarkt and **Vrijdagmarkt** are filled with restaurants, pubs, and music venues. The dimly lit **Charlatan,** Vlasmarkt 6, features a DJ every night. (www.charlatan.be. Open Tu-Su 7pm-7am.) For a quieter drink, go to **K27,** in the Vrijdag Markt at the corner of Baudelost. (Open M-F noon-last customer, Sa 2pm-last customer. Beer €1.60-3. Mixed drinks $4.50-5). For GLBT nightlife, consult Use-It's Ghent Gay Map or head to the **Foyer Casa Rosa,** Kammerstr. 22/Belfortstr. 39, an infocenter and bar. (☎269 28 12; www.casarosa.be. Open M-F 3pm-1am, Sa-Su 3pm-2am.)

Trains run from St-Pietersstation (accessible by tram #1) to Antwerp (50min., 2 per hr., €7.80), Bruges (25min., 3 per hr., €5.40), and Brussels (35min., 5 per hr., €7.40). The **tourist office,** Botermarkt 17A, in the crypt of the belfry, books rooms for free and leads walking tours. (☎266 52 32; www.visitgent.be. Open daily Apr.-Oct. 9:30am-6:30pm; Nov.-Mar. 9:30am-4:30pm. Tours Nov.-Apr. daily 2:30pm; buy tickets by 2pm. €7.) At the tourist office and most museums, you can buy a pass good for 15 museums and monuments in Ghent (€12.50). **Use-It,** St-Pietersnieuwstr. 21, has quirky maps and free **Internet.** (☎324 39 06; www.use-it.be. Open M-F 1-6pm.) **Postal Code:** 9000.

YPRES (IEPER) ☎57

Famous for its fields filled with poppies and lined with tombstones of fallen soldiers, Ypres (pop. 35,000) and its environs continue to bear witness to the city's significant role in WWI. Once a medieval textile center, Ypres was completely destroyed by four years of combat, but was impressively—and defiantly—rebuilt as a near-perfect replica of its former self. Today, the town is surrounded by over 150 **British cemeteries** and filled with memorial sites. The **In Flanders Field Museum,** Grote Markt 34, documents the gruesome history of the Great War. (☎239 220; www.inflandersfields.be. Open Apr.-Sept. daily 10am-6pm; Oct.-Mar. Tu-Su 10am-5pm. Last admission 1hr. before closing. €7.50. MC/V.) Behind the museum stands **St. Martin's Cathedral,** rebuilt using pre-war plans, and resplendent with a rose window, gift of the British Army. (☎20 80 04. Open daily 9am-noon and 2-6pm. Free.) Cross the street in front of St. Martin's and head right to reach **St. George's Memorial Church,** Elverdingsestr. 1 (☎21 56 85). Each brass plaque and kneeling pillow in the church commemorates a particular military group. (Open daily Apr.-Oct. 9:30am-8pm; Nov.-Mar. 9:30am-4pm. Free.) Across the Markt, the names of 54,896 missing British soldiers are inscribed on the somber **Menin Gate.** At 8pm each evening, the **Last Post** bugle ceremony honors those who defended Ypres (www.lastpost.be). At the nearby **Ramparts Cemetery,** white tombstones line the river in silent memorial. The battlefields are a long walk from town; **car tours,** though expensive, are the way to go. **Salient Tours,** Meenestr. 5 (☎21 46 57; www.salienttours.com; tours 10am and 2:30pm; €20-25), offers English tours. A thriftier option is to **bike** the 3-4km journey to the first cemetery.

B&Bs are the cheapest accommodations in Ypres, and though there are many of them, call ahead to ask about availability and arrival times. **B&B Zonneweelde ❸,** Masscheleinlann 18, has TVs in every room and is close to Grote Markt. From the tourist office, take a left out of Grote Markt onto Diksmuidsestr. and a left by the little river on Masscheleinlann. (☎20 27 23. Singles €25; doubles €48; triples €65.) The huts at **Camping Jeugdstadion ❶,** Bolwerkstraat 1, are less refined. (☎21 72 82; www.jeugdstadion.be. Showers included. Reception Mar. to mid-Nov. 8am-noon and 4-7:30pm. Tent sites €1.50 per night, €3 per person. 4-bed huts with kitchenette €32.) Restaurants line the Grote Markt, where free chocolate samples are handed out; they are especially rich at **Vandaele,** Grote Markt 9. (☎20 03 87. Open Tu-Su 9:30am-7pm.) Stock up on groceries at **Super GB,** Vandepeereboompl. 15. (☎20 29 35. Open M-Th and Sa 8:30am-7pm, F 8:30am-8pm.) **Trains** run to Bruges (2hr., 1 per hr., €11) and Brussels (1¾hr., 1 per hr., €15). The **tourist office,** Grote Markt 34, is inside the Cloth Hall. (☎239 220; www.ieper.be. Open Apr.-Sept. M-F 9am-6pm, Sa-Su 10am-6pm; Oct.-Mar. M-Sa 9am-5pm, Sa-Su 10am-5pm.)

WALLONIE

Wallonie, the French-speaking region of Belgium, has small towns and stunning grottoes that reveal a more relaxed side of the country. In the province of Namur, visitors sample local brews or head out to hiking trails and river expeditions in the nearby Ardennes. Nature-lovers will want to spend at least a night here, but for the less green-of-heart, there's art, history, and culture as well.

LIÈGE (LUIK) ☎041

Industrial Liège (pop. 200,000), the largest city in Wallonie, has a cutting-edge art scene and late-night student hangouts that color the city's nondescript utilitarianism. The **Coeur Historique** (Historic Heart) is a charming area knotted with narrow cobblestone streets. There, by the river, you'll find the solid **Musée de L'Art Wallon,** 86 Féronstrée, a collection of Belgian art dating back to the Renaissance, including a few works by Magritte. (☎221 92 31. Open Tu-Sa 1-6pm, Su 11am-4:30pm. €3.80, students €2.50.) To unwind post-museum, turn right onto Féronstrée and left at r. de. la Resistance at the Parc St-Léonard to reach the **Montagne de Bueren.** A 25min. hike up the steps leads to a view of the city. Or, with your back to La Meuse river, make a left on r. de la Cathédrale and visit the Gothic naves and sparkling gold treasure of the **Cathédrale de St-Paul.** (☎232 61 32. Cathedral open daily 8am-noon and 2-5pm. Treasure room open Tu-Su 2-5pm. Tour 3pm. Cathedral free. Treasure room €4, students €2.50, tour €2.50.) In between the banks of the river, a large island makes up the working-class neighborhood of **Outremeuse** and is home to the **Musée d'Art Moderne et d'Art Contemporain (MAMAC),** 3 Parc de la Boverie, which showcases minor works by Gauguin, Chagall, Rodin, and one piece each by Monet and Picasso. From the station, you can take bus #1 or 4 (€1.30) to le Parc d'Avroy and cross the Roi-Albert bridge. (☎343 04 03; www.mamac.org. Open Tu-Sa 1-6pm, Su 11am-4:30pm. €3.80, students €2.50.) To reach the convenient, modern **Auberge Georges Simenon de Jeunesse de Liège (HI) ❷,** 2 r. Georges Simenon, walk across the Pont des Arches from the Coeur Historique, or take bus #4 and get off at Auberge Simenon. (☎344 56 89. Breakfast and linens included. Internet €0.60 per 15min. Reception 7:30am-1am. Lockout 10am-3pm. Dorms €20; singles €32; doubles €48. €3 HI discount. MC/V.) Forgo expensive fare on r. Roture in favor of Outremeuse's pita joints. **Newave à la Passerelle ❷,** 13 bl. Saucy, serves panini (€3-4) and couscous (€6-14). (☎341 15 66. Open Tu-Su noon-10pm. Cash only.) Pick up groceries a block from the hostel at **Colruyt,** r. Gaston Grégoire. (Open M-F 9am-8pm, Sa 9am-7pm.) At night, students from the University of Liège pack the streets, of **Le Carré,** a pedestrian-only quadrant with narrow, bar-lined streets bisected by r. du Pot-d'Or. **Trains** run to Brussels (1hr., 2-5 per hr., €13). To get to the **tourist office,** 92 Féronstrée, take bus #1 or 4. (☎221 92 21; www.liege.be. Open M-F 9am-5pm.)

TOURNAI (DOORNIK) ☎069

The first city liberated from the Nazis by Allied forces, Tournai (pop. 68,000) has long been bounced between various empires; it was once a Roman trading post and later served as the capital of Gaul. The city has the world's only five-steepled cathedral, 800-year-old **Cathédrale Notre-Dame.** A 1999 tornado left the landmark in need of renovations, and half of the building is inaccessible. (Open daily June-Oct. 9:30am-noon and 2-5:30pm; Nov.-May 10am-noon and 2-4pm. Free.) Climb the 257 steps of the nearby **belfry,** the oldest in Belgium, for a stunning view. (Open Mar.-Oct. Tu-Sa 10am-1pm and 2-5:30pm, Su 11am-1pm and 2-6:30pm; Nov.-Feb. Tu-Sa 10am-noon and 2-5pm, Su 2-5pm. Last admission 45min. before close. €2, under 20 €1.) Two blocks away, next to the youth hostel, Victor Horta's sunlit **Musée des Beaux-Arts,** Enclos St-Martin, houses a small collection of Belgian and Dutch paintings. (Open Apr.-Oct. M and W-Su 9:30am-12:30pm and 2-5:30pm; Nov.-Mar. M and W-Sa 10am-noon and 2-5pm, Su 2-5pm. €3.) To reach the convenient **Auberge de Jeunesse (HI) ❷,** 64 r. St-Martin, continue up the hill from the tourist office or take bus #4, R, and W (€1.30) from the station. (☎21 61 36; www.laj.be. Breakfast and linens included. Reception 8am-noon and 5-10pm. Reserve ahead. Open Feb.-Nov. Dorms €18; singles €32; doubles €48. €3 HI discount. MC/V.) Head down r. des Chapeliers to riverside **Quai du Marché Poisson** for cheap food and drink. **Trains** run from pl. Crombez to Brussels (1hr., 1 per hr., €11). The **tourist office,** 14 Vieux Marché aux Poteries, is across from the belfry. (☎22 20 45; www.tournai.be. Open Apr.-Sept. M-F 8:30am-6pm, Sa 9:30am-noon and 2-5pm, Su 10am-noon and 2:30-6pm; Oct.-Mar. M-F 8:30am-5:30pm, Sa 10am-noon and 2-5pm, Su 2:30-6pm.)

NAMUR ☎081

Namur, capital of Wallonie (pop. 110,000), is a gateway for **hiking, biking, caving,** and **kayaking** in Belgium's mountainous regions. In September, Namur hosts a multicultural crowd at the **International French Language Film Festival** (☎24 12 36; www.fiff.be). The town's foreboding **citadel** (☎24 64 49; www.citadelle.namur.be) remained an active Belgian military base until 1978. To get there take bus #3 (1 per hr., dir.: Citadel). Take bus #3 or 4 (dir.: La Plante) from the train station to the homey **Auberge Félicien Rops (HI) ❷,** 8 av. Félicien Rops. (☎22 36 88; www.laj.be. Breakfast and linens included. Laundry €6.50. Free Internet. Reception 8am-11pm. Lockout 10am-4pm. Dorms €18-19. €3 HI discount.) To reach the **tourist office,** on the Sq. Léopold, turn left out of the station onto r. de la Gare. Pick up *Storming the Citadel!* with five walking tours. (☎24 64 49; www.namurtourism.be. Open daily 9:30am-6pm.) Rent bikes at **La Maison des Cyclistes,** 2 pl. de la Station. (☎81 38 48; www.velonamur.be. Open Tu-F 10am-noon and 1:30-4pm, Sa 10am-12:30pm and 1-5pm. €9 per day.) **Trains** link Namur to Brussels (1hr., 2 per hr., €7.40) and Dinant (30min., 1 per hr., €3.90).

DINANT ☎082

Razed by the German army in 1914, Dinant (pop. 13,000) has reinvented itself as a tourist destination. Descend into the beautiful depths of the **Grotte Merveilleuse,** 142 rte. de Phillipeville, 600m from the train station, for a witty 50min. tour of the cave's limestone formations. Bring a jacket to avoid underground chills. (☎22 22 10; www.dinantourism.com. Open daily July-Aug. 10am-6pm; Apr.-June and Sept.-Oct. 11am-5pm; Dec.-Mar. 1-4pm. Tours every hr., usually in English. €6.) Get set up to **kayak** at **Anseremme.** (☎22 43 97; www.lessekayaks.be. Kayaks €14-28.) To get to the **tourist office** from the train station, turn right, take the first left, and another immediate left by the river. (☎22 28 70; www.dinant-tourisme.be. Open M-F 8:30am-6pm, Sa 9:30am-5pm, Su 10am-4:30pm; low season reduced hours.) Rent bikes at **Raid Mountain-Bike,** 15 r. du Vélodrome (☎21 35 35. €16-20 per day). **Trains** run to Brussels (1½hr., 1 per hr., €11) and Namur (30min., 1 per hr., €3.90). On Sundays July 23-August 27, there's a one-way **river cruise** from Dinant to Namur (☎22 23 15 www.bateaux-meuse.be. 3½hr., €14).

BRITAIN

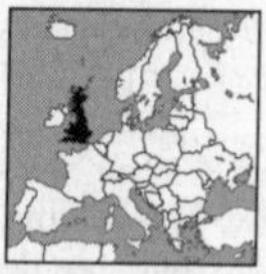

Having colonized two-fifths of the globe, spearheaded the Industrial Revolution, and won every foreign war in its history but two, Britain seems intent on making the world forget its tiny size. It's hard to believe that the rolling farms of the south and the rugged cliffs of the north are only a day's train ride apart, or that people as diverse as London clubbers, Cornish miners, Welsh students, and Gaelic monks all occupy a land area roughly the size of Mississippi. Beyond the stereotypical fairy-tale cottages and sheep farms of "Merry Olde England," today's Britain is a high- energy destination driven by international influence. Though the sun may have set on the British Empire, a colonial legacy survives in multicultural urban centers and a dynamic arts and theater scene. Brits now eat kebabs and curry as often as they do scones, and five-story dance clubs in post-industrial settings draw as much attention as elegant country inns.

DISCOVER BRITAIN: SUGGESTED ITINERARIES

THREE DAYS Spend it all in **London** (p. 122), the city of tea, royalty, and James Bond. After a stroll through **Hyde Park,** head to **Buckingham Palace** for the changing of the guard. Check out the renowned collections of the **British Museum** and the **Tate Modern.** Stop at famed **Westminster Abbey** and try to catch a play at Shakespeare's **Globe Theatre** before grabbing a drink in the **East End.**

ONE WEEK Begin in **London** (3 days), then immerse yourself in academia at the colleges of **Oxford** (1 day; p. 154). Travel north to Scotland for a day in the museums and galleries of **Glasgow** (p. 186) and finish off with pubs and parties in lively **Edinburgh** (2 days; p. 179).

THREE WEEKS Start off in **London** (4 days), where you'll explore the museums, theaters, and clubs. Tour the pleasant college greens in **Cambridge** (2 days; p. 160) and **Oxford** (2 days), then amble through the rolling hills of the **Cotswolds** (1 day; p. 158). Don't miss Shakespeare's hometown, **Stratford-upon-Avon** (1 day; p. 158), or that of The Beatles, **Liverpool** (1 day; p. 164). Head to **Manchester** for its nightlife (1 day; p. 163) before moving on to **Glasgow** (1 day) and nearby **Loch Lomond** (1 day; p. 191). Energetic **Edinburgh** (4 days) will keep you busy, especially during festival season. Finally, enjoy the beautiful **Lake District** (2 days; p. 170) and historic **York** (1 day; p. 167).

ESSENTIALS

WHEN TO GO

It may be wise to plan around the high season (June-Aug.). Spring and fall are more appealing times to visit; the weather is still reasonable and flights are cheaper, though there may be fewer services in rural areas. If you intend to visit the large cities and linger indoors at museums and theaters, the low season (Nov.-Mar.) is most economical. Keep in mind, however, that sights and accommodations often close or have reduced hours, especially in rural regions. Another factor to consider is hours of daylight. In Scotland, summer light lasts almost until midnight, but in winter, the sun may set as early as 3:45pm. Regardless of when you go, it will rain—have warm, waterproof clothing on hand.

FACTS AND FIGURES

Official Name: United Kingdom of Great Britain and Northern Ireland.

Capital: London.

Major Cities: Cardiff, Edinburgh, Glasgow, Liverpool, Manchester.

Population: 59,834,000.

Land Area: 244,800 sq. km.

Time Zone: GMT.

Language: English; also Welsh and Scottish Gaelic.

Religions: Christian: Protestant and Catholic (72%), Muslim (3%).

Total No. *Harry Potter* Books Sold: More than the populations of Britain, France, Germany, and Italy combined.

DOCUMENTS AND FORMALITIES

EMBASSIES AND CONSULATES. All foreign embassies in Britain are in London (p. 122). British embassies abroad include: **Australia,** Commonwealth Ave., Yarralumla, ACT 2600 (☎02 6270 6666; http://bhc.britaus.net); **Canada,** 80 Elgin St., Ottawa, ON K1P 5K7 (☎613 237 1530; www.britainincanada.org); **Ireland,** 29 Merrion Rd., Ballsbridge, Dublin 4 (☎01 205 3700; www.britishembassy.ie); **New Zealand,** 44 Hill St., Thorndon, Wellington (☎04 924 2888; www.britain.org.nz); **US,** 3100 Massachusetts Ave. NW, Washington, D.C. 20008 (☎900-255-6685; www.britainusa.com).

VISA AND ENTRY INFORMATION. EU citizens do not need a visa to enter Britain. Citizens of Australia, Canada, New Zealand, and the US do not need a visa for stays up to six months. Students planning to study in the UK for six months or more must obtain a student visa. For more information, call your local British embassy or complete an inquiry at www.ukvisas.gov.uk.

TOURIST SERVICES AND MONEY

EMERGENCY	**Police, Ambulance,** and **Fire:** ☎999.

TOURIST OFFICES. Formerly known as the British Tourist Authority, **Visit Britain** (☎020 8563 3000; www.visitbritain.com) is an umbrella organization for the separate tourist boards. Tourist offices in Britain, listed under **Practical Information** for each city and town, stock maps and provide info on sights and accommodations.

MONEY. The **pound sterling (£)** is the unit of currency in the United Kingdom. It is divided into 100 pence, with standard denominations of 1p, 2p, 5p, 10p, 20p, 50p, £1, and £2 in coins, and £5, £10, £20, and £50 in notes. The term *quid* is slang for pounds. Scotland has its own bank notes, which can be used interchangeably with English currency, though you may have difficulty using Scottish £1 notes outside Scotland. As a general rule, it's cheaper to exchange money in Britain than at home. ATMs offer the best exchange rates. Many British department stores, such as Marks & Spencer, also offer excellent exchange services. **Tips** in restaurants are often included in the bill, sometimes as a "service charge." If gratuity is not included, tip your server about 12.5%. Taxi drivers should receive a 10% tip, and bellhops and chambermaids usually expect £1-3. To the great relief of budget travelers from the US, tipping is not expected at pubs and bars in Britain. Aside from open-air markets, don't expect to bargain.

The UK has a 17.5% **value added tax (VAT),** a sales tax applied to everything but food, books, medicine, and children's clothing. The tax is **included** in the amount indicated on the price tag. Prices stated in Let's Go include VAT. In the airport, upon exiting the EU, non-EU citizens can claim a refund on the tax paid for purchases at participating stores. You can obtain refunds only for goods you take out of the country (i.e., not accommodations or meals). Participating shops display a "Tax Free Shopping" sign. They may have a purchase minimum of £50-100 before they offer refunds, and the complex procedure is probably only worthwhile for large purchases. To apply for a refund, fill out the form that you are given in the shop and present it with the goods and receipts at customs upon departure—look

BRITISH POUNDS (£)		
	AUS$1 = UK£0.42	UK£1 = AUS$2.38
	CDN$1 = UK£0.46	UK£1 = CDN$2.16
	EUR€1 = UK£0.68	UK£1 = EUR€1.47
	NZ$1 = UK£0.39	UK£1 = NZ$2.59
	US$1 = UK£0.55	UK£1 = US$1.80

for the Tax Free Refund desk at the airport. At peak times, this process can take up to an hour. You must leave the country within three months of your purchase in order to claim a refund, and you must apply for the refund before leaving the UK.

TRANSPORTATION

BY PLANE. For info on flying in from continental Europe, see p. 43. Most flights from outside Europe land at London's Heathrow (LHR; ☎0870 000 0123) or Gatwick (WSX; ☎012 9353 5353) airports, but some fly directly to regional airports like Manchester (MAN; ☎016 1489 3000) and Edinburgh (EDI; ☎0131 333 1000).

BY TRAIN. Trains run to Britain from the Continent through the **Chunnel** (p. 57). Britain's train network is extensive, criss-crossing the length and breadth of the island. Prices and schedules often change; find up-to-date information from **National Rail Enquiries** (☎08457 484 950; www.nationalrail.co.uk/planmyjourney) or **Network Rail** (www.networkrail.co.uk; schedules only). The **BritRail Pass,** sold only outside Britain, allows unlimited travel in England, Scotland, and Wales (www.britrail.net). In Canada and the US, contact **Rail Europe** (Canada ☎800-361-7245, US ☎877 257 2887; www.raileurope.com). **Eurailpasses are not valid in Britain.** Rail discount cards (£20), available at rail stations and through travel agents, grant 33% off most point-to-point fares and are available to those ages 16-25 or over 60, full-time students, and families. In general, traveling by train costs more than by bus.

BY BUS. The British distinguish between **buses,** which cover short local routes, and **coaches,** which cover long distances; Let's Go refers to both as buses. **National Express** (☎08705 808 080; www.nationalexpress.com) is the principal operator of long-distance bus service in Britain, although **Scottish Citylink** (☎08705 505 050; www.citylink.co.uk) has the most extensive coverage in Scotland. The **Brit Xplorer Pass** offers unlimited travel on National Express buses. (7-day £79, 14-day £139, 28-day £219.) **NX2** cards (£10), available online for those ages 16-26, reduce fares by up to 30%. For those who plan far ahead, the cheapest rides are National Express's **Fun Fares,** available only online. They offer a limited number of seats on buses out of London from £1.

BY CAR. To drive, you must be 18 and have a valid license from your home country; to rent, you must be over 21. Britain is covered by a high-speed system of **motorways** (M-roads) that connect London to other major cities. Visitors may not be accustomed to **driving on the left,** and automatic transmission is rare in rental cars. Roads are generally well maintained, but gasoline (petrol) gasoline prices are high. In London, driving is restricted during weekday working hours, with charges imposed in certain congestion zones; parking can be similarly nightmarish.

BY FERRY. Several ferry lines provide service between Britain and the Continent. Ask for discounts; ISIC holders can sometimes get student fares, and Eurail passholders are eligible for reductions and free trips. Seaview Ferries (www.seaview.co.uk/ferries.html) has a directory of UK ferries. In the summer, it's a good idea to book ahead. For more info on boats to Ireland and the Continent, see p. 58.

BY BIKE AND BY FOOT. Much of the British countryside is well suited for **biking.** Many cities and villages have bike rental shops and maps of local cycle routes. Large-scale Ordnance Survey maps, often available at tourist offices, detail the extensive system of long-distance **hiking** paths.

BY THUMB. Let's Go does not recommend hitchhiking. Hitchhiking is fairly common in Britain, especially in rural parts of Northern Ireland, Scotland, and Wales (England is tougher) where public transportation is unreliable. Hitchhiking or even standing on motorways (M-roads) in Britain is illegal.

KEEPING IN TOUCH

PHONE CODES	**Country code:** 44. **International dialing prefix:** 00. Within Britain, dial city code + local number, even when dialing inside the city. For more information on how to place international calls, see inside back cover.

EMAIL AND THE INTERNET. Internet access is ubiquitous in big cities, common in towns, and sparse in rural areas. **Cybercafes** or public terminals can be found almost everywhere; they usually cost £4-6 per hour, but you often pay only for the time used. For more info try www.cybercafes.com. Public **libraries** often have free or cheap Internet access, but you might have to wait or make an advance reservation. Many coffee shops, particularly chains like Starbucks, have wireless Internet.

TELEPHONE. For info on mobile phones, see p. 29. Most public pay phones in Britain are run by British Telecom (BT). Public phones charge a minimum of 30p and don't accept 1, 2, or 5p coins. A BT Chargecard will bill phone calls to your credit card, but most pay phones now have readers where you can swipe credit cards directly (generally AmEx/MC/V). The number for the operator in Britain is ☎100, and the international operator is ☎155. International direct dial numbers include: **AT&T Direct** ☎0800 89 0011; **British Telecom** ☎0800 14 41 44; **Canada Direct** ☎0800 096 0634 or 0800 559 3141; **MCI WorldPhone** ☎0800 279 5088; and **Sprint** ☎0800-890-877.

MAIL. Royal Mail has standardized their rates around the world. From Britain, it costs £0.23 to send a postcard domestically, £0.44 within Europe, and £0.50 to the rest of the world. Airmail letters up to 20g cost £0.21 domestically, £0.44 within Europe, and £0.72 elsewhere. Remember to write "Par Avión—Airmail" on the top left corner of your envelope or stop by any post office to get a free airmail label. Address mail to be held according to the following example: First name LAST NAME, *Poste Restante*, post office address, Post Office, Postal Code, UK.

ACCOMMODATIONS AND CAMPING

BRITAIN	❶	❷	❸	❹	❺
ACCOMMODATIONS	under £15	£15-20	£20-30	£30-40	over £40

Hostelling International (HI) hostels are prevalent throughout Britain. They are run by the **Youth Hostels Association of England and Wales** (**YHA;** ☎0870 770 8868; www.yha.org.uk), the **Scottish Youth Hostels Association** (**SYHA;** ☎01786 89 14 00; www.syha.org.uk), and the **Hostelling International Northern Ireland** (**HINI;** ☎28 9032 4733; www.hini.org.uk). Hostel dorms are around £11 in rural areas, £14 in larger cities, and £15-25 in London. Book **B&Bs** by calling directly, or by asking the local tourist office to help find accommodations. Tourist offices usually charge a flat fee of £1-5 plus a 10% deposit on the first night or the entire stay's price, deductible from the amount you pay the proprietor. **Grounds** tend to be privately owned and cost £3-10 per person per night. It is illegal to camp in national parks in Britain.

FOOD AND DRINK

BRITAIN	❶	❷	❸	❹	❺
FOOD	under £6	£6-10	£10-15	£15-20	over £20

A pillar of traditional British fare, the cholesterol-filled, meat-anchored **English breakfast** is still served in B&Bs across the country. **Beans on toast** or toast with **Marmite** (the most acquired of tastes—a salty, brown spread made from yeast) are breakfast staples. The best native dishes for lunch or dinner are **roasts**—

beef, lamb, and Wiltshire hams—and **Yorkshire pudding,** a type of popover drizzled with meat juices. Despite their intriguing names, **bangers and mash** and **bubble and squeak** are just sausages and potatoes and cabbage and potatoes, respectively. Pubs often serve savory meat pies like **Cornish pasties** (PASS-tees) or **ploughman's lunches** of bread, cheese, and pickles. **Fish and chips** (french fries) are traditionally drowned in malt vinegar and salt. **Crisps,** or potato chips, come in astonishing variety, with flavors like prawn cocktail. Britons make their **desserts** (often called "puddings" or "afters") exceedingly sweet and gloopy. Sponges, trifles, tarts, and the ill-named spotted dick (spongy currant cake) will satiate the sweetest tooth. British "tea" refers to both a drink, served strong and milky, and a social ritual. A **high tea** might include cooked meats, salad, sandwiches, and pastries, while the oft-stereotyped **afternoon tea** comes with finger sandwiches, scones with jam and clotted cream (a sinful cross between whipped cream and butter), and small cakes. **Cream tea,** a specialty of Cornwall and Devon, includes scones or crumpets, jam, and clotted cream.

HOLIDAYS AND FESTIVALS

Holidays: New Year's Day (Jan. 1); Good Friday (Apr. 6); Easter (Apr. 8); May Day (May 1); Bank Holidays (May 28 and Aug. 27); Christmas (Dec. 25); Boxing Day (Dec. 26).

Festivals: Scotland's New Year's Eve celebration, Hogmanay, takes over Edinburgh and Glasgow. The National Eisteddfod of Wales (Aug. 4-12) has brought Welsh writers, musicians, and artists together since 1176. One of the largest music and theater festivals in the world is the Edinburgh International Festival (Aug. 15-26); also highly recommended is the Fringe Festival (Aug. 1-31). Manchester's Gay Village hosts Manchester Pride (www.manchesterpride.com) in August, and London throws a huge street party at the Notting Hill Carnival (Aug. 26-27). Bonfires and fireworks abound at England's Guy Fawkes Day (Nov. 5), in celebration of a conspirator's failed attempt to destroy the Houses of Parliament in 1605.

BEYOND TOURISM

Opportunities for **volunteering, studying,** and **working** abound in Britain. As a volunteer, you can participate in everything, from archaeological digs to lobbying for social change. Explore your academic passions at the country's prestigious institutions or pursue an independent research project. To take an internship in Parliament or try your hand at teaching, Britain has plenty opportunities for paid work.

The National Trust, National Trust Central Volunteering Team, The National Trust, Heelis, Kemble Dr., Swindon SN2 2NA (☎0870 609 5383; www.nationaltrust.org.uk/volunteering). Arranges numerous volunteer opportunities, including working holidays.

The Teacher Recruitment Company, Pennineway Offices (1), 87-89 Saffron Hill, London EC1N 8QU (☎0845 833 1934; www.teachers.eu.com). International recruitment agency lists positions and provides information on jobs in the UK.

University of Oxford, College Admissions Office, Wellington Sq., Oxford OX1 2JD (☎0186 527 0000; www.ox.ac.uk). Large range of summer programs (£900-4000) and year-long courses (£8880-11,840).

ENGLAND

A land where the stately once prevailed, England is now a youthful, hip, and forward-looking nation on the cutting edge of art, music, and film. But traditionalists can rest easy; for all the moving and shaking in large cities, just around the corner scores of ancient towns, opulent castles, and comforting cups of tea still abound.

LONDON

☎020

London offers visitors a bewildering array of choices: Leonardo at the National Gallery or Hirst at the Tate Modern; Rossini at the Royal Opera or *Les Miséables* at the Queen's; Bond Street couture or Camden cutting-edge—you could spend your entire stay just deciding what to do. London is often described not as a unified city but rather a conglomeration of villages, whose heritage and traditions are still alive and evolving. Thanks to the feisty independence and diversity of each area, the London "buzz" is continually on the move.

INTERCITY TRANSPORTATION

Flights: Heathrow (**LON;** ☎08700 000 123) is London's main airport. The **Piccadilly Line** heads from the airport to central London (1hr., every 5min., £4-10). **Heathrow Connect** runs to Paddington (20min., every 30min., £10), as does the more expensive **Heathrow Express** (15min.; every 15min.; £14.50, round-trip £27). From **Gatwick Airport** (**LGW;** ☎08700 002 468), the **Gatwick Express** heads to Victoria (30min.; every 15min.; £14, round-trip £25).

Trains: London has 8 major train stations: **Charing Cross** (southern England); **Euston** (the northwest); **King's Cross** (the northeast); **Liverpool Street** (East Anglia); **Paddington** (the west and south Wales); **St. Pancras** (the Midlands and the northwest); **Victoria** (the south); **Waterloo** (the south, the southwest, and the Continent). All stations are linked by the subway, referred to as the Underground or Tube (⊖). Itineraries involving a change of stations in London usually include a cross-town transfer by Tube. Get information at the station ticket office or from the **National Rail Enquiries Line** (☎08457 484 950; www.britrail.com).

Buses: Long-distance buses (**coaches**) arrive in London at **Victoria Coach Station,** 164 Buckingham Palace Rd. ⊖Victoria. National Express (☎08705 808 080; www.nationalexpress.com) is the largest operator of intercity services.

ORIENTATION

The **West End,** stretching east from Park Lane to Kingsway and south from Oxford St. to the River Thames, is the heart of London. In this area you'll find aristocratic **Mayfair,** the shopping streets near **Oxford Circus,** the clubs of **Soho,** and the boutiques of **Covent Garden.** Heading east of the West End, you'll pass legalistic **Holborn** before hitting the ancient **City of London** ("the City"), the site of the original Roman settlement and home to Tower Bridge and the Tower of London. The City's eastern border jostles the ethnically diverse, working-class **East End.**

Westminster encompasses the grandeur of **Trafalgar Square** and extends south along the Thames; this is the location of both royal and political London, with the Houses of Parliament, Buckingham Palace, and Westminster Abbey. Farther west lies rich, snooty **Chelsea.** Across the river, the **South Bank** has an incredible variety of entertainment and museums. To the south, **Brixton** is one of the hottest nightlife spots in town, besides touristy Leicester Square and Piccadilly Circus. The huge expanse of **Hyde Park** lies west of the West End; along its southern border are chic **Knightsbridge** and posh **Kensington.** North of Hyde Park is the media-infested **Notting Hill** and the B&B- and hostel-filled **Bayswater.** Bayswater, Mayfair, and **Marylebone** meet at Marble Arch, on Hyde Park's northeast corner; from there, Marylebone stretches west to meet academic **Bloomsbury,** north of Soho and Holborn. **Camden Town, Islington, Hampstead,** and **Highgate** lie to the north of Bloomsbury and the City. A good street atlas is essential; **London A to Z** (£5) is available at newsstands and bookstores.

LOCAL TRANSPORTATION

Public Transportation: Run by **Transport for London** (TfL; 24hr. info ☎7222 1234; www.thetube.com). The **Underground** (a.k.a. the **Tube**) is divided into 6 concentric zones; fares depend on the number of zones crossed. Buy your ticket before you board and pass it through automatic gates at both ends of your journey. Runs 5:30am-12:30am, depending on the line. See this guide's color maps. **Buses** are divided into 4 zones. Zones 1-3 are identical to the Tube zones. Buses run 5:30am-midnight, after which a network of **Night Buses,** prefixed by "N," take over. Fares £1.50. **Travelcard** valid on all TfL services. 1-day Travelcard from £6.20 (Zones 1-2).

Licensed Taxicabs: An illuminated "taxi" sign on the roof of a black cab signals availability. Expensive but worth the price. Tip 10%. For pickup (min. £2 extra charge), call **Taxi One-Number** (☎08718 718 710).

Minicabs: Private cars. Cheaper but less reliable–stick to a reputable company. **London Radio Cars** (☎8905 0000; www.londonradiocars.com) offers 24hr. pickup.

PRACTICAL INFORMATION

Tourist Offices: Britain Visitor Centre, 1 Regent St. (www.visitbritain.com). ⊖Oxford Circus. Open M 9:30am-6:30pm, Tu-F 9am-6:30pm, Sa-Su 10am-4pm. **London Information Centre,** 1 Leicester Pl. (☎7292 2333; www.londoninformationcentre.com). ⊖Leicester Sq. Open daily 8am-midnight.

Tours: The **Big Bus Company,** 48 Buckingham Palace Rd. (☎7233 9533; www.bigbus.co.uk). ⊖Victoria. Has multiple routes and buses every 10-20min. 1hr. walking tours and mini Thames cruise. Buses start at central office and at hubs throughout the city. £20, purchased online £18. AmEx/MC/V. **Original London Walks** (☎7624 3978, recorded info 7624 9255; www.walks.com) runs themed walks, from "Haunted London" to "Slice of India." Most 2hr. £6, students £5, under 15 free.

Embassies: Australia, Australia House, Strand (☎7379 4334). ⊖Temple. Open M-F 9am-5pm. **Canada,** MacDonald House, 1 Grosvenor Sq. (☎7258 6600). ⊖Bond St. Open M-F 9am-5pm. **Ireland,** 17 Grosvenor Pl. (☎7235 2171). ⊖Hyde Park Corner. Open M-F 9:30am-1pm and 2:15-5pm. **New Zealand,** New Zealand House, 80 Haymarket (☎7930 8422). ⊖Piccadilly Circus. Open M-F 9am-5pm. **US,** 24 Grosvenor Sq. (☎7499 9000). ⊖Bond St. Open M-F 8:30am-5:30pm.

Currency Exchange: Banks, such as **Barclays, HSBC, Lloyd's,** and **National Westminster** (NatWest) have the best rates. **Branches** open M-F 9:30am-4:30pm. Call ☎7795 6703 for the nearest **American Express** location.

GLBT Resources: London Lesbian and Gay Switchboard (☎7837 7324; www.queery.org.uk). 24hr. helpline and information service.

Emergency: ☎999 from any landline, 122 from a mobile phone. Free.

Police: London is covered by 2 police forces: the **City of London Police** (☎7601 2222) for the City and the **Metropolitan Police** (☎7230 1212) for the rest. At least 1 station in each of the 32 boroughs is open 24hr. Call ☎7230 1212 to find the nearest station.

Pharmacies: Most pharmacies open M-Sa 9:30am-5:30pm; a "duty" chemist in each district opens Su; hours may be limited. Late-night and 24hr. chemists are rare. **Zafash Pharmacy,** 233-235 Old Brompton Rd. (☎7373 2798), ⊖Earl's Ct., is 24hr. **Bliss Chemist,** 5-6 Marble Arch (☎7723 6116), ⊖Marble Arch, is open daily 9am-midnight.

Hospitals: Charing Cross, Fulham Palace Rd. (☎8846 1799), entrance on St. Dunstan's Rd., ⊖Hammersmith. **Royal Free,** Pond St. (☎7794 0500), ⊖Belsize Park. **St. Thomas's,** Lambeth Palace Rd. (☎7188 7188), ⊖Waterloo. **University College London Hospital,** Grafton Way (☎0845 1555 000), ⊖Warren St.

Central London

● SIGHTS

Apsley House, **1**	**C4**
The Barbican, **2**	**E3**
Benjamin Franklin House, **3**	**D4**
British Library, **4**	**D2**
British Museum, **5**	**D3**
Buckingham Palace, **6**	**C4**
Cabinet War Rooms, **7**	**D4**
Chelsea Physic Garden, **8**	**C5**
Chinatown, **9**	**D4**
Courtauld Institute Galleries, **10**	**D4**
Design Museum, **11**	**F4**
The Gilbert Collection, **12**	**D4**
Guildhall Art Gallery, **13**	**E3**
The Houses of Parliament, **14**	**D4**
ICA, **15**	**D4**
Imperial War Museum, **16**	**E5**
Kensington Palace, **17**	**B4**
London Eye, **18**	**D4**
Madame Tussaud's, **19**	**C3**
Marble Arch, **20**	**C3**
Millennium Bridge, **21**	**E4**
Monument, **22**	**F4**
Museum of London, **23**	**E3**
National Gallery, **24**	**D4**
National Portrait Gallery, **25**	**D4**
Natural History Museum, **26**	**B5**
Royal Academy of Arts, **27**	**D4**
Royal Albert Hall, **28**	**B4**
Royal Courts of Justice, **29**	**E3**
The Royal Hospital, **30**	**C5**

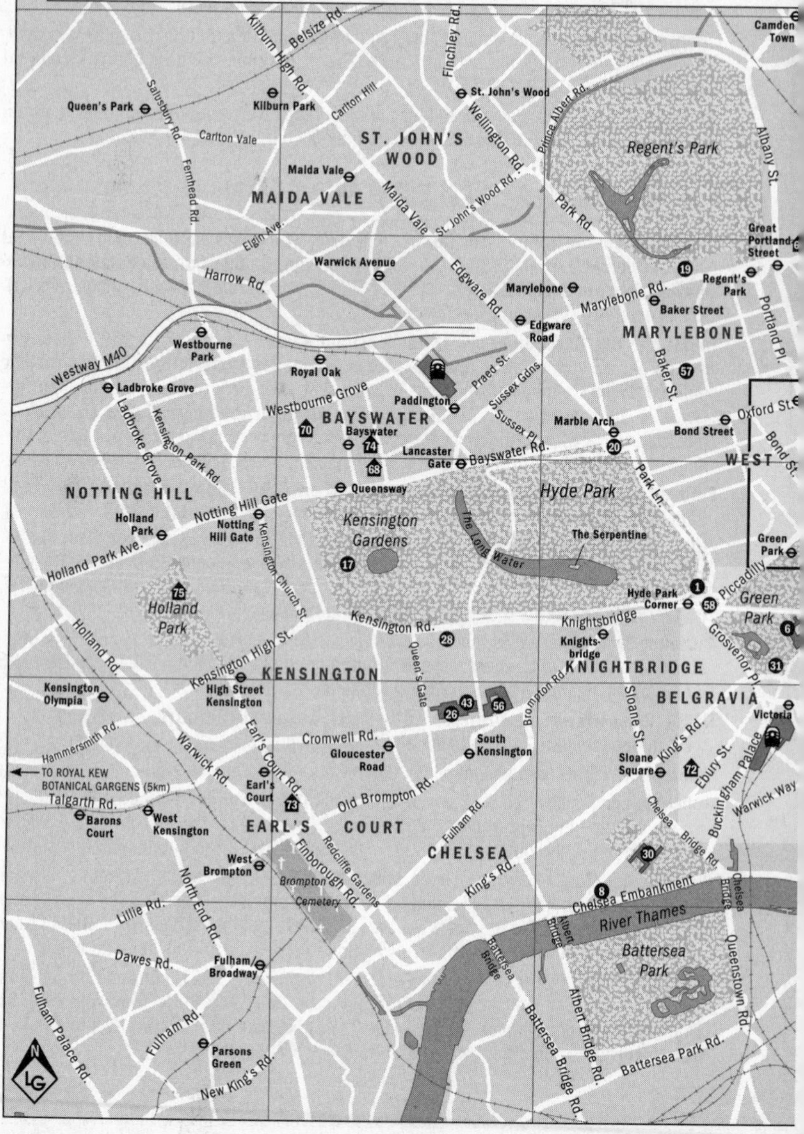

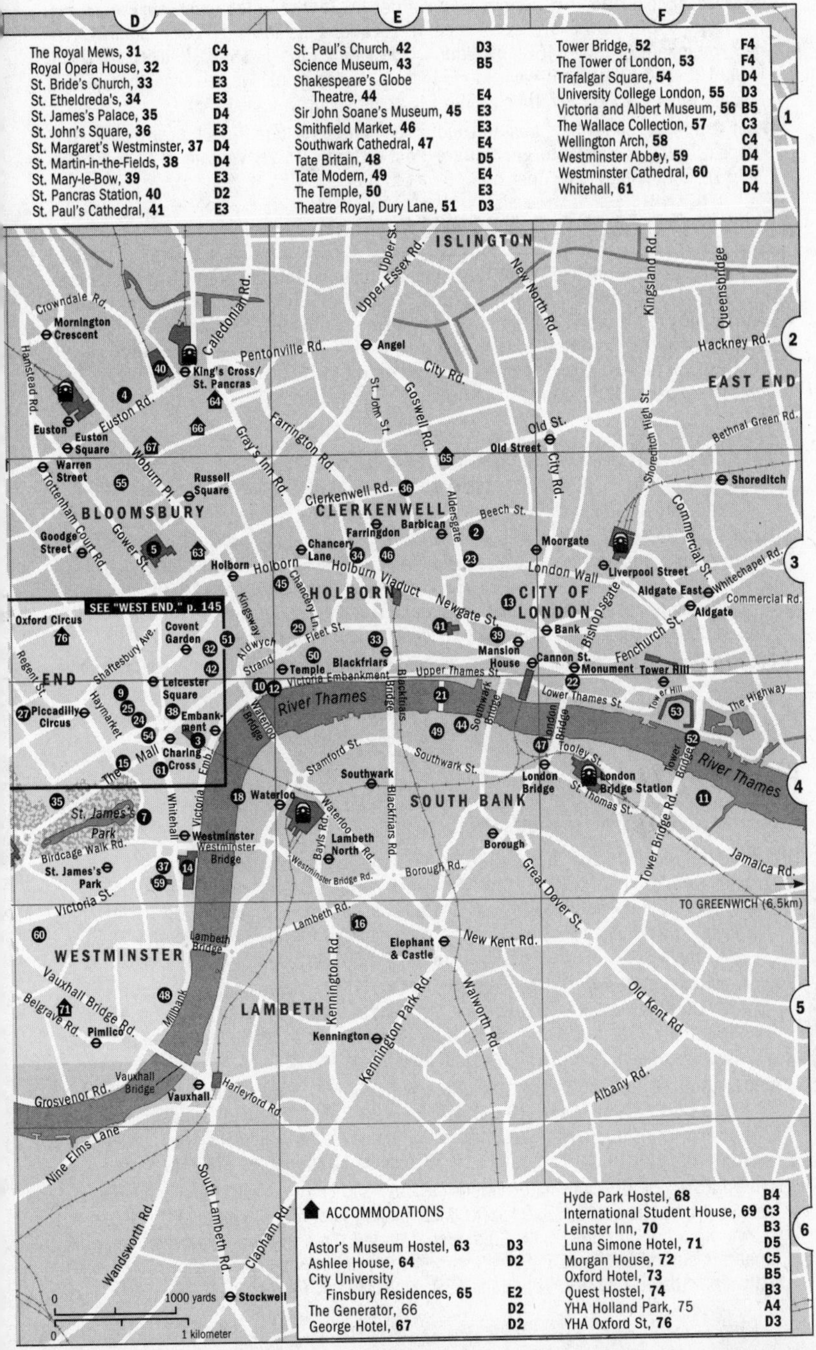

ACCOMMODATIONS

BRITAIN

Internet Access: Don't pay more than £2 per hr. Try the ubiquitous **easyEverything** (☎7241 9000; www.easyeverything.com). Locations include 9-16 Tottenham Ct. Rd. (⊖Tottenham Ct. Rd.); 456-459 Strand (⊖Charing Cross); 358 Oxford St. (⊖Bond St.); 160-166 Kensington High St. (⊖High St. Kensington). Prices vary with demand, usually around £1.60 per hr. Min. 50p-£1. Generally open until 11pm.

Post Office: When sending mail to London, be sure to include the full postal code. The largest office is the **Trafalgar Square Post Office,** 24-28 William IV St. (☎7484 9305), ⊖Charing Cross. Open M-Sa 8am-5:30pm.

ACCOMMODATIONS

The best deals in town are student residence halls, which rent out rooms over the summer and sometimes Easter vacations. "B&B" encompasses accommodations of wildly varying quality, personality, and price. Be aware that in-room showers are often prefabricated units jammed into a corner. Linens are included at all YHAs, but towels are not; buy one from reception (£3.50). YHAs also sell discount tickets to theaters and major attractions.

BAYSWATER

Quest Hostel, 45 Queensborough Terr. (☎7229 7782; www.astorhostels.com). ⊖Bayswater. Night Bus #N15, 94, N390. Cozy hostel with friendly staff. Continental breakfast included. Internet £1 per hr. Dorms £14-20; doubles £50. MC/V. ❶

Hyde Park Hostel, 2-6 Inverness Terr. (☎7229 5101; www.astorhostels.com). ⊖Bayswater. Night Bus #N15, 94, 148. Jungle-themed basement bar and dance space hosts DJs and parties (open W-Th and Su 7pm-2am, F-Sa 7pm-3am). Ages 18-35 only. Laundry, TV lounge, secure luggage room. Breakfast included. Reception 24hr. Reserve 2 weeks ahead in summer. Dorms £11-18; doubles £50. MC/V. ❶

Leinster Inn, 7-12 Leinster Sq. (☎7729 9641; www.astorhostels.com). ⊖Bayswater. Night Bus #N15, 94, 148. TV/pool room and small bar (open W-Th and Su 6pm-2am, F-Sa 6pm-5am). Kitchen, luggage room, and laundry. Breakfast included. Internet £1-1.60 per hr. Dorms £14-19; singles £40; doubles £51; triples £60. MC/V. ❷

BLOOMSBURY

Many B&Bs and hostels are on busy roads, so be wary of noise levels. The area becomes seedier closer to King's Cross.

The Generator, Compton Pl. (☎7388 7666; www.generatorhostels.com), off 37 Tavistock Pl. ⊖Russell Sq. or King's Cross St. Pancras. Night Bus #N19, 35, 38, 41, 55, 91, 243. The ultimate party hostel. 18+. Breakfast included. Internet 50p per 10min. Reserve 1 week ahead for Sa-Su. Credit card required for reservation. Dorms £12.50-17.50; singles £35/56; doubles £50/56; triples £60/69; quads £68/80. MC/V. ❶

Astor's Museum Hostel, 27 Montague St. (☎580 5360; www.astorhostels.com). ⊖Tottenham Ct. Rd., Russell Sq., or Goodge St. Night Bus #N19, 35, 38. Plain but friendly. Under-35 only. Free DVD rental. English breakfast and linens included. Towel purchase £5. Reserve ahead. Dorms £16-20; doubles £50. MC/V. ❷

Ashlee House, 261-265 Gray's Inn Rd. (☎7833 9400; www.ashleehouse.co.uk). ⊖King's Cross. Night Bus #N10, 63, 73, 91, 390. Laid-back hostel with small dorms. Private rooms include table, sink, and kettle. Breakfast and linens included; towels £1. Internet £1 per hr. Apr.-Oct. dorms £16-20; singles £37; doubles £50. MC/V. ❷

George Hotel, 58-60 Cartwright Gardens (☎7387 8777; www.georgehotel.com). ⊖Russell Sq. Night Bus #N10, 73, 91, 390. Meticulously kept rooms with satellite TV, kettle, alarm clock, phone, and sink. Breakfast included. Free Internet. Reserve 2 months ahead in summer. Singles £48, with shower £60; doubles £67, with shower £74, with bath £89; triples £79/89/99; quads £89. AmEx/MC/V. ❺

KENSINGTON AND EARL'S COURT

YHA Holland Park (HI), Holland Walk (☎7937 0748; www.yha.org.uk or www.hihostels.com). ⊖High St. Kensington or Holland Park. Night Bus #N9, 10, 27. 17th-century mansion with TV room, laundry, and kitchen. Breakfast included. Internet 50p per 7min. Reception 24hr. Reserve dorms ahead in summer. Dorms £25, under 18 £23; singles £33; doubles £53; triples £73; quads £93. £3 YHA/HI discount F-Sa. MC/V. ❷

Oxford Hotel, 24 Penywern Rd. (☎7370 1161; www.the-oxford-hotel.com). ⊖Earl's Court. Night Bus #N31, 74, 97. Mid-sized, bright rooms, all with shower and some with full bath. Rooms have comfortable beds, TV, kettle, and safe. Continental breakfast included. Reception 24hr., and books discounted tourist tickets/tours. In summer, reserve 2-3 weeks ahead. Singles with shower £40, with bath £55; doubles £60/70; triples with bath £82.50; quads £89/96; quints £120. Discount on stays over 7 days. £1 online booking discount. MC/V. ❹

OTHER NEIGHBORHOODS

City University Finsbury Residences, 15 Bastwick St. (☎7040 8811; www.city.ac.uk/ems/accomm/fins.html), in Clerkenwell. ⊖Barbican. Newly renovated rooms hide behind a 1970s tower-block facade. Night Bus #N35 and 55 stop at the corner of Old St. and Goswell Rd. Open early June to mid-Sept. Singles £21, doubles with bath £60. £1.50 per night discount on stays over 7 nights. MC/V. ❸

YHA Oxford Street (HI), 14 Noel St. (☎0870 770 5984), West End. ⊖Oxford Circus. Night Bus #N7, 74, 159. Stairwell murals poke fun at London institutions. Perfect location for Soho nightlife, though triple-decker bunk beds may feel cramped. Towels £3.50. Reserve 1 month ahead. Dorms £26, under 18 £22; doubles £53. £3 HI discount. ❷

Luna Simone Hotel, 47-49 Belgrave Rd. (☎7834 5897; www.lunasimonehotel.com), in Westminster. ⊖Victoria. Night Bus #N2, 24, 36. Overachieving staff and lovely rooms. Breakfast included. Free Internet. Reserve at least 3 weeks ahead. Singles £60; doubles £80; triples £100; quads £120. 10-20% low season discount. AmEx/MC/V. ❺

IES Chelsea Pointe, corner of Manresa Rd. and King's Rd. (☎7808 9200; www.iesreshall.com) in Chelsea. ⊖Sloane Sq., then bus #11, 19, 22, 319. Unheard-of prices in Soho. Rooms have bath, data ports, phone, kitchen, and laundry (£2.50). Wheelchair-accessible. Reserve ahead. Singles £47; doubles £53. MC/V. ❺

Morgan House, 120 Ebury St. (☎7730 2384; www.morganhouse.co.uk), in Knightsbridge and Belgravia. ⊖Victoria. A neighborhood standout: stylish rooms all have sink, TV, and kettle, and some have fireplaces. Breakfast included. Reserve 2-3 months ahead. Singles with sink £52; doubles with sink £72, with bath £92; triples £92/110; quad (1 double bed and bunk beds) with bath £130. MC/V. ❺

International Student House, 229 Great Portland St. (☎7631 8310, general switchboard 7631 8300; www.ish.org.uk), in Marylebone and Regent's Park. ⊖Great Portland St. Most rooms have sink and fridge; some have bath. Bar, cafeteria, and fitness center (£5 per day). Continental breakfast included with private rooms; English breakfast £2.30-4.50. Internet £2 per hr. Key deposit £10. Dorms £12; singles £34; doubles £51; triples £62; quads £74. 10% ISIC discount on private rooms. MC/V. ❶

FOOD

Any restaurant charging under £10 for a main course is relatively inexpensive; add drinks and service and you're nudging £15. It *is* possible to eat cheaply—and well—in London. For the best and cheapest **ethnic restaurants,** head to the source: **Whitechapel** for Bangladeshi *baltis*, **Chinatown** for dim sum, **South Kensington** for French pastries, **Edgware Road** for Shawarma. The cheapest places to get your own ingredients are **street markets** (see **Shopping,** p. 142). For all your food under one roof, try supermarket chains **Tesco, Safeway, Sainsbury's,** or **Marks & Spencer.**

BAYSWATER

Mr. Jerk, 19 Westbourne Grove (☎7221 4678; www.mrjerk.co.uk). ⊖Bayswater or Royal Oak. No-frills cafe with incredibly inexpensive food. Take-out available. Specialty jerk chicken £6.50. Open M-Sa 10am-11pm, Su noon-10pm. AmEx/MC/V. ❷

Levantine, 26 London St. (☎7262 1111; www.levant.co.uk). ⊖Paddington. Lebanese restaurant with loads of vegetarian options, nightly belly-dancing, and *shisha*. Lunch menu £5 noon-5:30pm. Open M-Sa noon-midnight, Su noon-11:30pm. AmEx/MC/V. ❷

BLOOMSBURY

ICCo (Italiano Coffee Company), 46 Goodge St. (☎7580 9688). ⊖Goodge St. To-die-for thin-crust 11 in. pizzas for an eye-popping £3. Pasta from £2. Sandwiches and baguettes ½-price after 4pm. Take-out available. Pizzas available from 11am. Open daily 7am-11pm. AmEx/MC/V. ❶

Navarro's Tapas Bar, 67 Charlotte St. (☎7637 7713; www.navarros.co.uk). ⊖Goodge St. Authenticity makes for superb food. Tapas £3.50-6.50; 2-3 per person is plenty. Min. £9.50 per person. Open M-F noon-3pm and 6-10pm, Sa 6-10pm. AmEx/MC/V. ❸

CHELSEA

Buona Sera, at the Jam, 289A King's Rd. (☎7352 8827). ⊖Sloane Sq., then bus #19 or 319. The "bunk" tables here are stacked high into the air. Pasta, fish, and steak entrees £7-13.50. Reserve ahead F-Sa. Open Tu-F noon-3pm and 6pm-midnight, Sa-Su noon-midnight. AmEx/MC/V. ❸

Chelsea Bun, 9A Limerston St. (☎7352 3635). ⊖Sloane Sq., then bus #11 or 22. Spirited and casual. Extensive vegetarian and vegan options. Pasta, salads, burgers, and omelettes £7-9. Early-bird specials M-F 7am-noon (£2.20-3.20). Sandwiches (£2.80-7) and breakfasts (from £4) served until 6pm. Min. £3.50 per person during lunch, £5.50 dinner. Open M-Sa 7am-11pm, Su 9am-7pm. MC/V. ❷

THE CITY OF LONDON

Café Spice Namaste, 16 Prescot St. (☎7488 9242; www.cafespice.co.uk). ⊖Tower Hill or DLR: Tower Gateway. The menu helpfully explains each Goan and Parsee specialty. Meat entrees are pricey (from £11.25), but vegetarian meals (from £7.75) are affordable. Open M-F noon-3pm and 6:15-10:30pm, Sa 6:30-10:30pm. AmEx/MC/V. ❸

Futures, 8 Botolph Alley (☎7623 4529; www1e.btwebworld.com/futures1/), between Botolph and Lovat Ln. ⊖Monument. Suits and their lackeys besiege this tiny take-out joint during the lunch hour. Vegetarian soups, salads, and entrees (from £2-4.40) change weekly. Open M-F 7:30-10am and 11:30am-3pm. ❶

CLERKENWELL AND HOLBORN

Anexo, 61 Turnmill St. (☎7250 3401; www.anexo.co.uk). ⊖Farringdon. This funky Spanish restaurant and bar serves up Iberian dishes, including authentic paella (£7.50-10). Live music Th 7pm. DJs F-Sa nights. Happy hour M-Sa 5-7pm. Open M-F 11am-11:30pm, Sa 5-11:30pm, Su 4:30-10pm. Bar open 11am-11:30pm. AmEx/MC/V. ❷

Bleeding Heart Tavern, corner of Greville St. and Bleeding Heart Yard (☎7242 2056; www.bleedingheart.co.uk). ⊖Farringdon. Highlights include the roast suckling pig with delicately spiced shards of apple (£12). Entrees £8-13. Open M-F noon-2:30pm and 6-10:30pm. Bar open M-F 7am-11pm. AmEx/MC/V. ❸

EAST LONDON

Café 1001, Dray Walk (☎7247 9679; www.cafe1001.co.uk). ⊖Aldgate East. Off Brick Ln. Twentysomethings lounge in the smoky, spacious upstairs. Fresh cakes (£2), pre-made salads, sandwiches (£2.20-3), and outdoor barbecue, weather permitting. Nightly DJs or bands 7pm-close. Open Su-W7am-11pm, Th-Sa 7pm-midnight. Cash only. ❶

Aladin, 132 Brick Ln. (☎7247 8210). ⊖Shoreditch. Pakistani, Bangladeshi, and Indian food. Plenty of vegetarian dishes. Entrees £4-8.50. 3-course lunch £6. Daily lunch special noon-4:30pm. Open Su-Th noon-11:30pm, F-Sa noon-1am. Cash only. ❷

KENSINGTON AND EARL'S COURT

Raison d'Être, 18 Bute St. (☎7584 5008). ⊖South Kensington. Huge range of filled baguettes and foccaccia (£3-6). Open M-F 8am-6pm, Sa 9:30am-4pm. Cash only. ❶

The Orangery, Kensington Palace (☎7376 0239; www.digbytrout.co.uk.) ⊖High St. Kensington. Built for Queen Anne's dinner parties and full of white, high-ceilinged stateliness. Light gourmet lunches £9-12. Afternoon tea from £8. Open daily 10am-noon for breakfast, noon-3pm for lunch, and 3-6pm for tea. MC/V. ❷

MARYLEBONE AND REGENT'S PARK

Mandalay, 444 Edgware Rd. (☎7258 3696). ⊖Edgware Rd. Burmese entrees with good vegetarian items (£4.50-7.50). Lunch specials offer great value. Take-out available. Open M-Sa noon-3pm and 6-11pm. Reserve ahead for dinner. AmEx/MC/V. ❶

Patogh, 8 Crawford Pl. (☎7262 4015). ⊖Edgware Rd. This tiny but charming Persian hole-in-the-wall serves large portions of sesame-seed flatbread (£2) and freshly prepared starters (£2.50-5). Take-out available. Open daily 12:30-11pm. Cash only. ❷

NORTH LONDON

Gallipoli, 102 Upper St. (☎7359 0630; www.gallipolicafe.com), **Gallipoli Again,** 120 Upper St. (☎7359 1578), **Gallipoli Bazaar,** 107 Upper St. (☎7226 5333). ⊖Angel. Lebanese, North African, and Turkish delights. 2-course lunch £6. Open M-Th 10:30am-11pm, F-Sa 10:30am-midnight. Reserve ahead F-Sa. AmEx/MC/V. ❷

La Crêperie de Hampstead, 77 Hampstead High St. (www.hampsteadcreperie.com), metal stand on the side of the King William IV. ⊖Hampstead. A fixture in the neighborhood. French-speaking cooks take your order and leave you to anticipate your crepe (£3.30). Open M-Th 11:45am-11pm, F-Su 11:45am-11:30pm. Cash only. ❶

THE WEST END

Rock and Sole Plaice, 47 Endell St. (☎7836 3785; www.rockandsoleplaice.com). ⊖Covent Garden. Self-proclaimed "master fryer" (qualifications unclear) delivers fish and chips for £8-11. Vegetarians can munch on samosas (£4.50). Take-out available, cheaper than eat-in. Open M-Sa 11:30am-10:30pm, Su noon-10:30 pm. MC/V. ❷

Masala Zone, 9 Marshall St. (☎7287 9966; www.realindianfood.com). ⊖Oxford Circus. South Indian favorites (£6-8), in addition to small bowls of "street food" (£3.40-5.50), and large *thali* (sampler platters; £7.50-11.50). Open M-F noon-3:30pm and 5:30-11pm, Sa 12:30-11pm, Su 12:30-3:30pm and 6-10:30pm. MC/V. ❷

OTHER NEIGHBORHOODS

Giraffe (☎7928 2004; www.giraffe.net), in the Royal Festival Hall in South Bank Centre. Music plays all day at this colorful eatery with outdoor seating and high-quality food for great prices. M-F 5-7pm 2-for-1 drinks, appetizer and main course £7; after 7 £9. Reserve ahead for dinner. Open daily 9am-11pm. AmEx/MC/V. ❷

George's Portobello Fish Bar, 329 Portobello Rd. (☎8969 7895), in Notting Hill. ⊖Ladbroke Grove. Fish like cod, rock, plaice, and skate come with a huge scoop of chunky chips (from £6.20). Burgers, kebabs, and falafel also available. Open M-F 11am-midnight, Sa 11am-9pm, Su noon-9:30pm. Cash only. ❷

Lazy Daisy Café, 59A Portobello Rd. (☎ 7221 8416), in Notting Hill. ⊖Notting Hill Gate. All-day breakfast during the week, including a lazy fry-up (£6) and eggs Florentine (£5). Lunches include niçoise salad (£6) and fish fingers (£5). Wheelchair-accessible. Open M-Sa 9am-5pm, Su noon-2:30pm. MC/V. ❶

SIGHTS

WESTMINSTER

The City of Westminster, now a borough of London, has been the seat of British power for over a thousand years. William the Conqueror was crowned in Westminster Abbey on Christmas Day, 1066, and his successors built the Palace of Westminster that today houses Parliament.

WESTMINSTER ABBEY. Founded as a Benedictine monastery, Westminster Abbey has evolved into a house of kings and queens both living and dead. Almost nothing remains of St. Edward's Abbey: Henry III's 13th-century Gothic reworking created most of the grand structure you see today. A door off the east cloister leads to the Chapter House, the original meeting place of the House of Commons. Next door to the Abbey (through the cloisters), the lackluster Abbey Museum is in the Norman undercroft. Just north of the Abbey, St. Margaret's Church enjoys a strange status: as a part of the Royal Peculiar, it is not under the jurisdiction of the diocese of England nor the archbishop of Canterbury. Since 1614, it's been the official worshipping place of the House of Commons. *(Parliament Sq., in Westminster. Access Old Monastery, Cloister, and Garden from Dean's Yard. ⊖Westminster. Abbey ☎7654 4900, Chapter Office 7222 5152, St. Margaret's 7654 4840; www.westminster-abbey.org. Abbey open M-Tu and Th-F 9:30am-3:45pm, W 9:30am-7pm, Sa 9:30am-1:45pm, Su for services only. Museum open daily 10:30am-4pm. Chapter Office open M-F 9am-5pm. Cloisters open daily 8am-6pm. Garden open Apr.-Sept. Tu-Th 10am-6pm; Oct.-Mar. daily 10am-4pm. St. Margaret's open M-F 9:30am-3:45pm, Sa 9:30am-1:45pm. Hours vary, call first. Abbey and museum £10, students £6, services free. Chapter Office, Gardens, and St. Margaret's free. Audio tour available in Abbey M-F 9:30am-3pm, Sa 9:30am-1pm; £3. 1½hr. tours in summer M-F 10, 10:30, 11am, 1:30pm, 2pm, 3:30pm; Sa 10, 10:30, 11am; winter M-F 10, 11am, 2, 3pm. £4. AmEx/MC/V.)*

BUCKINGHAM PALACE. Originally built for the Dukes of Buckingham, Buckingham House was acquired by George III in 1762 and converted into a full-scale palace by George IV. During the summer opening of the **State Rooms,** visitors have access to the **Throne Room,** the **Galleries,** and the **Music Room,** where Mendelssohn played for Queen Victoria. In the opulent **White Room,** the mirrored fireplace hides a door used by the Royal Family at formal dinners. Since 2001, Queen Elizabeth has also allowed visitors into the **gardens.** *(At the end of the Mall, between Westminster, Belgravia, and Mayfair. ⊖St. James's Park, Victoria, Green Park, or Hyde Park Corner. State room tickets available at ☎7766 7324. Reserve ahead.)* "God Save the Queen" is the rallying cry at the **Queens Gallery,** home to exhibitions of jaw-droppingly valuable items from the Royal Collection. *(☎7766 7301. Open daily 10am-5:30pm. £7.50, students £6.)* The **Royal Mews's** main attraction is the Queen's collection of coaches, including the four-ton Gold State Coach, which can be seen tooling around the streets in the early morning on practice runs for major events. *(☎7766 7302. Open late July-late Sept. daily 10am-5pm; Mar.-late July and late Sept.-late Oct. M-Th and Sa-Su 11am-4pm. £6.50, under 17 £4. AmEx/MC/V.)* To witness the spectacle of the Palace without the cost, attend a session of **Changing of the Guard.** Show up well before 11:30am and stand in front of the Palace in view of the guards, or use the steps of the Victoria Memorial as a vantage point. *((☎7766 7324. Apr.-July, daily, Aug.-Mar. every other day, provided the Queen is in residence, it's not raining hard, and there are no pressing state functions. Free.)*

THE HOUSES OF PARLIAMENT. The Palace of Westminster has been home to both the House of Lords and the House of Commons (together known as Parliament) since the 11th century, when Edward the Confessor established his court here. Standing guard on the northern side of the building is the Clock Tower, **Big Ben,** whose name actually refers to the 14-ton bell that hangs inside. **Victoria Tower,**

> **TIP** **PARLIAMENTARY PROCEDURE.** Arrive early in the afternoon to minimize waiting, which often exceeds 2hr. Keep in mind that the wait for Lords is generally shorter than for Commons. To sit in on Parliament's "question time" (40min.; M-W 2:30pm, Th-F 11am) apply for tickets several weeks in advance through your embassy in London.

at the south end of the Palace building, contains copies of every Act of Parliament since 1497. A flag flown from the top indicates that Parliament is in session. When the Queen is in the building a special royal banner is flown instead of the Union flag. Visitors with enough patience or luck to make it inside the chambers can hear the raucous debates between members of both the House of Lords and the House of Commons. *(Parliament Sq. ⊖Westminster. ☎08709 063 773, commons info office 7219 4272; www.parliament.uk/visiting/visiting.cfm. "Line of Route" tour includes both houses. Tours Aug.-Sept. Reserve online, by phone, or in person at Old Palace Yard ticket office (open summer) across from Palace of Westminster. Tours run Aug. M-Tu and F-Sa 9:15am-4:30pm, W-Th 1:15-4:30pm; Sept.-Oct. M and F-Sa 9:15am-4:30pm, Tu-Th 1:15-4:30pm. Tours depart every 15min. Tours £7 adults, £5 students. MC/V. Lords Chamber open Oct.-July M-W 2:30-10pm, Th 11am-7:30pm, and occasionally F from 11am. House of Commons open during session M-Th 9am-6pm, F 9am-4:30pm; during recess M-F 10am-5pm. Commons Chamber open Oct.-July M-Tu 2:30-10:30pm, W 11:30am-7:30pm, Th 10:30am-6:30pm, occasionally F 9:30am-3pm. Hours subject to change.)*

ST. JAMES'S PARK AND GREEN PARK. The streets leading up to Buckingham Palace are flanked by two sprawling expanses of greenery: St. James's Park and Green Park. In the middle of St. James's Park is the **St. James's Park Lake**—the lake and the grassy area surrounding it are an official waterfowl preserve. Across the Mall, the lush Green Park is the creation of Charles II, connecting Westminster and St. James. *(The Mall. ⊖St. James's Park or Green Park. Green Park open daily 5am-midnight; St. James's is always open. Lawn chairs ☎7486 8117; available June-Aug. 10am-10pm, Mar.-May and Sept.-Oct. 10am-6pm. £1.50 for 2hr. Last rental 2hr. before close.)*

WESTMINSTER CATHEDRAL. Following Henry VIII's divorce from the Catholic Church, London's Catholic community remained without a cathedral until 1884, when the Church purchased a derelict prison on a former monastery site. The Neo-Byzantine building looks somewhat like a fortress and is now one of London's great religious landmarks. An elevator, well worth the fee, carries visitors up the striped 273 ft. bell tower for a panoramic view of Westminster, the river, and Kensington. *(Cathedral Piazza, off Victoria St. ⊖Victoria. ☎7798 9055; www.westminstercathedral.org.uk. Open daily 7am-7pm. Suggested donation £2. Bell tower open daily Apr.-Nov. 9:30am-12:30pm and 1-5pm; Dec.-Mar. Th-Su 9am-12:30pm and 1-5pm. £3, students £1.50.)*

WHITEHALL. Whitehall refers to the stretch of road connecting Trafalgar Sq. with **Parliament Square** and is synonymous with the British civil service. Toward the north end of Whitehall, **Great Scotland Yard** marks the former headquarters of the Metropolitan Police. Nearer Parliament Sq., heavily guarded gates mark the entrance to **Downing Street.** The prime minister traditionally lives at #10, but Tony Blair's family is so big that he had to swap with the Chancellor, Gordon Brown at #11. The street is closed to visitors, but if you wait, you may see the PM going to or coming from work. *(Between Trafalgar Sq. and Parliament Sq. ⊖Westminster, Embankment, or Charing Cross.)*

THE CITY OF LONDON

ST. PAUL'S CATHEDRAL. Christopher Wren's masterpiece is the 5th cathedral to occupy the site. After three designs were rejected by the bishops, Wren, with Charles II's support, started building—sneakily, he had persuaded the king to let him make "necessary alterations" as work progressed, and the building that emerged in 1708 bore little resemblance to what Charles II had approved. The **Nave** can seat 2500 worshippers. The tombs, including those of Nelson, Wellington, and Florence Nightingale, are downstairs in the **crypt.** Christopher Wren lies beneath the epitaph *"Lector, si monumentum requiris circumspice"* ("Reader, if you seek his monument, look around"). To see the inside of the second-tallest freestanding **dome** in Europe (after St. Peter's in the Vatican), climb the 259 steps to the **Whispering Gallery.** From here, 119 more steps lead to the **Stone Gallery,** on the outer base of the dome, and it's another 152 to the summit's **Golden Gallery.** *(⊖St. Paul's. ☎7246 8348; www.stpauls.co.uk. Partially wheelchair-accessible. Open M-Sa 8:30am-4:30pm. Dome and galleries open M-Sa 9:30am-4pm. Open for worship daily 7:15am-6pm. Admission £9, students £8; worshippers free. Group of 10 or more £1 discount per ticket. Tours 90min. "Supertour" M-Sa 11, 11:30am, 1:30, 2pm; £3, students £2.50, children £1. "Triforium" tour M and Tu 11:30am and 2pm, F 2pm; £14 per person; reserve ahead. Audio tour daily 9am-3:30pm; £3.50, students £3. AmEx/MC/V.)*

ST. PAUL'S FOR POCKET CHANGE. To gain access to the cathedral's nave for free, attend an Evensong service (45min., M-Sa 5pm). Arrive at 4:50pm to be admitted to seats in the choir.

THE TOWER OF LONDON. The Tower of London, palace and prison of English monarchs for over 900 years, is steeped in blood and history. Conceived by William the Conqueror in 1067 to provide protection *from* rather than *for* his new subjects, the original wooden palisade was replaced by a stone structure that over the next 20 years would grow into the **White Tower.** From the western entrance near the **Middle Tower,** you pass over the old moat, now a garden. Beyond **Byward Tower** is a massive **bell tower;** the curfew bell has been rung nightly for over 500 years. **Traitor's Gate** was built by Edward I for his personal use, but is now associated with the prisoners who passed through it on their way to execution at **Tower Green.** Some victims are buried in the **Chapel Royal of St. Peter and Vincula,** including Henry VIII's wives Catherine Howard and Anne Boleyn. Across the green is the **Bloody Tower,** so named because Richard III allegedly imprisoned and murdered his nephews here before usurping the throne in 1483.

The most famous sights in the Tower are the **crown jewels;** moving walkways ensure that no awestruck gazers hold up the queue. While eyes are naturally drawn to the **Imperial State Crown,** featuring the Stuart Sapphire and 2876 diamonds, don't miss the **Sceptre with the Cross,** topped with the First Star of Africa, the largest quality-cut diamond in the world. Other famous gems include the **Koh-i-Noor,** set into the **Queen Mother's Crown;** legend claims the stone will bring luck only to women. *(⊖Tower Hill. ☎08707 566 060, ticket sales 0870 756 7070; www.hrp.org.uk or www.tower-of-london.org.uk. Open Mar.-Oct. Su-M 10am-6pm, Tu-Sa 9am-6pm; Nov.-Feb. Su-M 10am-5pm, Tu-Sa 9am-5pm. Last ticket sold 5pm and last entry 5:30pm. Tickets also sold at Tube stations; buy ahead to avoid queues.* ***"Yeoman Warder Tours"*** *meet near the entrance; 1hr., every 30min. M and Su 10am-5:30pm, Tu-Sa 9:30am-5:30pm. Audio tour £3.50, students £2.50. MC/V.)*

BRITAIN

ALL HALLOWS-BY-THE-TOWER. Nearly hidden by redevelopment projects and nearby office buildings, All Hallows bears its longevity proudly, incorporating a Saxon arch from AD 675. The undercroft is home to an array of archaeological finds, including Roman pavement and some stunning Celtic carvings. *(Byward St. ⊖Tower Hill. ☎7481 2928; www.ahbtt.org.uk. Church open M-F 8am-6pm, Sa-Su 10am-5pm. Crypt and museum open daily 10:30am-4pm. Free guided tours M, W, F 2:30pm. Free.)*

TOWER BRIDGE. Not to be mistaken for its plainer sibling, **London Bridge,** Tower Bridge is the one you know from all the London-based movies. Historians and technophiles will appreciate the **Tower Bridge Exhibition,** which combines scenic

140 ft. glass-enclosed walkways with videos of a bells-and-whistles history of the bridge. *(Entrance to the Tower Bridge Exhibition is through the west side (upriver) of the North Tower. ⊖Tower Hill or London Bridge. ☎7403 3761, for lift schedule 7940 3984; www.towerbridge.org.uk. Wheelchair-accessible. Open daily 10am-6pm. £5.50, students £4.25. MC/V.)*

THE SOUTH BANK

SHAKESPEARE'S GLOBE THEATRE. This incarnation of the Globe is faithful to the original, thatch roof and all. The first Globe burned down in 1613 after a 14-year run as the Bard's preferred playhouse. Today's reconstruction had its first full season in 1997 and now stands as the cornerstone of the International Shakespeare Globe Centre. For info on performances, see p. 142. *(Close to Bankside pier. ⊖London Bridge. ☎7902 1500; www.shakespeares-globe.org. Wheelchair-accessible. Open daily May-Oct. 9am-noon (exhibit and tours) and 12:30-5pm (exhibit only, plus a tour of the Rose Theatre archaeological site); Nov.-Apr. 10am-5pm. Tours daily every 30min. £9, students £7.50.)*

SOUTHWARK CATHEDRAL. A site of worship since AD 606, the cathedral has undergone numerous transformations in the last 1400 years. Shakespeare's brother Edmund is buried here. In the rear of the nave, there are four smaller chapels; the northernmost Chapel of St. Andrew is specifically dedicated to those living with and dying from HIV and AIDS. Near the center, the **archaeological gallery** is actually a small excavation of a first-century Roman road. *(Montague Close. ⊖London Bridge. ☎7367 6700; www.southwark.anglican.org/cathedral. Wheelchair-accessible. Open daily 9am-5pm. Suggested donation £4. Audio tour £5, students £4.)*

LONDON EYE. Also known as the Millennium Wheel, at 135m (430 ft.) the British Airways London Eye is the biggest observational wheel in the world. The ellipsoidal glass "pods" give uninterrupted views throughout each 30min. revolution. *(Jubilee Gardens, between County Hall and the Festival Hall. ⊖Waterloo. ☎0875 000 600; www.balondoneye.com. Wheelchair-accessible. Open June-Sept. 10am-9pm; Oct.-May 10am-8pm. Buy tickets from box office at the corner of County Hall; reserve ahead; check the weather. 10% online booking discount. £13, children £6.50. AmEx/MC/V.)*

> **THE REAL DEAL.** While the **London Eye** does offer magnificent views, it's overpriced and the queues are long. For equally impressive sights in a quieter atmosphere, head to the **Monument**, **Primrose Hill,** or **Hampstead Heath.**

BLOOMSBURY AND MARYLEBONE

Marylebone's most famous resident (and address) never existed. 221b Baker St. was the fictional home of Sherlock Holmes, but 221 Baker St. is actually the headquarters of the Abbey National Bank. Bloomsbury's intellectual reputation was bolstered in the early 20th century when Gordon Sq. resounded with the philosophizing and womanizing of the **Bloomsbury Group,** a set of intellectuals including John Maynard Keynes, Bertrand Russell, Lytton Strachey, and Virginia Woolf.

REGENT'S PARK. This is perhaps London's most attractive and most popular park, with landscapes ranging from football-scarred fields to Italian-style formal plantings. It's all very different from John Nash's vision of wealthy villas hidden among exclusive gardens; fortunately for us common folk, Parliament intervened in 1811 and guaranteed the space would remain open to all. *(⊖Baker St. 500 acres of gardens stretching north from Marylebone Rd. to Camden Town. Open daily 7am-dusk. Free.)*

BRITISH LIBRARY. Criticized during its long construction by traditionalists for being too modern and by modernists for being too traditional, the completed British Library building is unequivocally impressive. The heart of the library is underground, with 12 million books on 200 mi. of shelving. The brick building above-

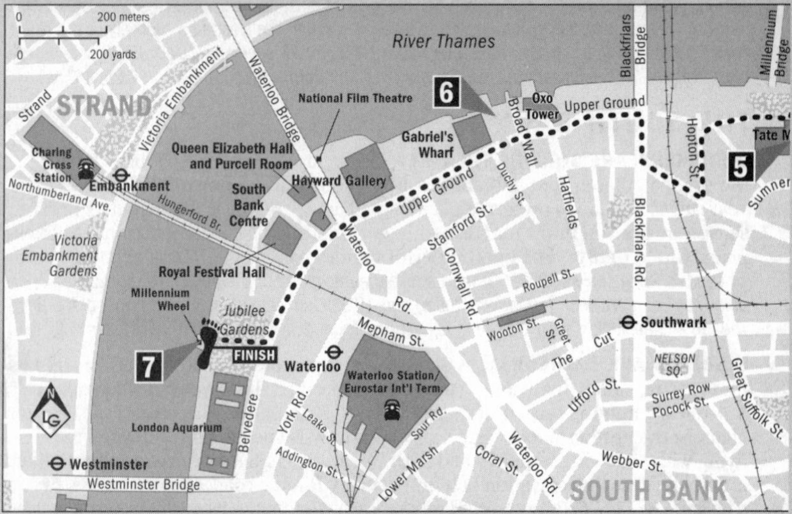

TIME: 8-9hr.

DISTANCE: 4km

WHEN TO GO: Start early morning

START: ⊖Tower Hill

FINISH: ⊖Westminster

A stroll along the South Bank is a trip through history. Across the river you will pass the timeless monuments of London's past, like the Tower of London and St. Paul's Cathedral, while next to you the round glass sphere of City Hall and the converted power facility that houses the Tate provide a stark, modern contrast. Whether you're searching for Shakespeare and Picasso or just hankering for a nice walk, no visit to the South Bank goes unrewarded.

1 TOWER OF LONDON. Begin your trek to the Tower early to avoid the crowds. Tours given by the Yeomen Warders meet every 1½hr. near the entrance. Listen as they expertly recount tales of royal conspiracy, treason, and murder. See the **White Tower,** once both fortress and residence of kings. Shiver at the executioner's stone on the Tower green and pay your respects at the Chapel of St. Peter ad Vinculum, which holds the remains of three queens. First get the dirt on the gemstones at **Martin Tower,** then wait in line to see the **Crown Jewels.** The jewels include such glittering lovelies as the First Star of Africa, the largest cut diamond in the world (p. 132). Time: 2hr.

2 TOWER BRIDGE. Tower Bridge is an engineering wonder that puts its plainer sibling, the London Bridge, to shame. Marvel at its beauty, but skip the overpriced Tower Bridge Exhibition. Or, better yet, call ahead to inquire what times the Tower drawbridge is lifted (p. 132). Time: no need to stop; take in the mechanics as you head to the next sight.

3 DESIGN MUSEUM. On Butler's Wharf, let the Design Museum introduce you to the latest innovations in contemporary design, from marketing to movements to haute couture. See what's to come in the forward-looking Review Gallery or hone in on individual designers and products in the Temporary Gallery, home to continually changing exhibitions. From the museum, walk along the Thames on the **Queen's Walk.** To your left you will find the **HMS Belfast,** which was launched in 1938 and led the landing for D-Day 1944. (☎0870 339 955. £7, students £5.) Time: 1hr.

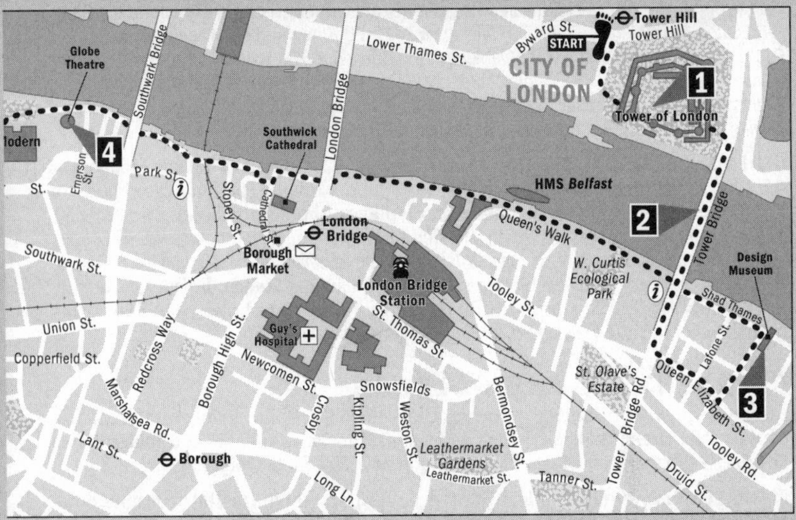

4 SHAKESPEARE'S GLOBE THEATRE. "I hope to see London once ere I die," says Shakespeare's Davy in *Henry IV.* In time, he may see it from the beautiful re-creation of Will's most famous theater. Excellent exhibits reveal the secrets of stage effects, re-create the costumes of Shakespearean actors, and tell of the painstaking process of rebuilding the theater almost 400 years after the original burned down (p. 133). You might be able to catch a matinee performance if you time your visit right. Call in advance for tour and show times during the summer. Time: 1hr. for tour and exhibit; 3hr. for performance.

5 TATE MODERN. It's hard to imagine anything casting a shadow over the Globe Theatre, but the massive former Bankside Power Station does just that. One of the world's premier Modern art museums, the Tate promises a new spin on well-known favorites and works by emerging British artists. Be sure to catch one of the informative docent tours, and don't forget to ogle the rotating installation in the Turbine Room (p. 138). Time: 2hr.

6 GABRIEL'S WHARF. Check out the cafes, bars, and boutiques of colorful **Gabriel's Wharf.** If you missed the top floor of the Tate Modern, go to the public viewing gallery on the 8th floor of the **OXO Tower.** On your way to the London Eye, stop by the **South Bank Centre.** Established as a primary cultural center in 1951, it now exhibits a range of music from philharmonic extravaganzas to jazz. You may even catch one of the free noon performances. Call in advance for dates and times (☎08703 800 400). Time: 1½hr. for schmoozing and dinner.

7 LONDON EYE. Once known as the Millennium Wheel, the "London Eye" has firmly established itself as one of London's top attractions, popular with locals and tourists. The Eye offers an amazing 360-degree view from its glass pods; you may be able to see all of London lit up at night. Reserve ahead to avoid long queues, but do check the weather (p. 133). Time: 1hr.

ground is home to cavernous reading rooms and an engrossing **exhibition gallery.** *(96 Euston Rd. ⊖King's Cross St. Pancras. ☎7412 7000; www.bl.uk. Wheelchair-accessible. Public spaces open M and W-F 9:30am-6pm, Tu 9:30am-8pm, Sa 9:30am-5pm, Su 11am-5pm. Free. To use reading rooms, bring 2 forms of ID, one with a signature and one with a home address. Tours of public areas Su-M, W, F, and Bank Holidays various times. M, W, F free tour of viewing gallery 11am. Reserve ahead. Audio tour £3.50, students £2.50.)*

OTHER BLOOMSBURY SIGHTS. Established in 1828, **University College London** was the first in Britain to admit Catholics, Jews, and women. The embalmed body of founder Jeremy Bentham has been on display in the South Cloister since 1850. *(Main entrance on Gower St. South Cloister entrance through the courtyard. ⊖Euston. www.ucl.ac.uk. Quadrangle gates open 24hr.; access to Bentham until 6:30pm. Free.)* Next to the British Library soar the Gothic spires of **St. Pancras Station.** Formerly the Midland Grand Hotel, Sir George Gilbert Scott's facade is a hollow shell awaiting rebirth as a Marriott. *(Euston Rd. ⊖King's Cross or St. Pancras.)*

CLERKENWELL AND HOLBORN

Although mostly off limits to tourists, Clerkenwell is full of lovely buildings. The **Clerkenwell Historic Trail** passes many of them. Maps are available at **3 Things Coffee Room.** (53 Clerkenwell Close. ⊖Farringdon. ☎7125 37438. Open daily 8am-8pm.)

THE TEMPLE. South of Fleet St., the land upon which this labyrinthine compound rests belonged to the crusading Knights Templar in the 13th century. The only remnant of that time is the round **Temple Church**. *(☎7353 3470. Hours vary and are posted outside the door of the church. Organ recitals W 1:15-1:45pm. No services Aug.-Sept. Free.)* According to Shakespeare's *Henry VI*, the red and white flowers that served as emblems in the Wars of the Roses were plucked in **Middle Temple Garden,** south of the hall. *(Open May-Sept. M-F noon-3pm. Free.)*

ROYAL COURTS OF JUSTICE. Straddling the official division between the City of Westminster and the City of London, this neo-Gothic structure encloses courtrooms and the Great Hall (home to Europe's largest mosaic floor) amid elaborate passageways. All courtrooms are open to the public during trials. *(Rear entrance on Carey St. ⊖Temple or Chancery Ln. ☎7947 6000. Wheelchair-accessible. Open M-F 9am-4:30pm; cases heard 10am-1pm and 2-3:30pm. Cameras not permitted; 50p to check them at the door. Free.)*

KENSINGTON AND EARL'S COURT

Nobody took much notice of Kensington before 1689, when the newly crowned William III and Mary II moved into Kensington Palace. In 1851, the Great Exhibition brought in enough money to finance museums and colleges. Now that the neighborhood is home to expensive stores like Harrods and Harvey Nichols, it's hard to imagine the days when the area was known for taverns and highwaymen.

HYDE PARK AND KENSINGTON GARDENS. Surrounded by London's wealthiest neighborhoods, Hyde Park has served as the model for city parks around the world. **Kensington Gardens,** adjacent to Hyde Park and originally part of the park proper, was created in the late 17th century when William and Mary set up house in Kensington Palace. In the middle of the park is **The Serpentine,** filled with dog-paddling tourists, rowers, and pedal boaters. The landlocked **Serpentine Gallery** has contemporary art. At the northeast corner of the park, near **Marble Arch,** you can see free speech in action as proselytizers, politicos, and flat-out crazies dispense their knowledge to bemused tourists at **Speaker's Corner** on Sundays, the only place in London where demonstrators may gather without a permit. *(⊖Queensway, or High St. Kensington. Park open daily 5am-midnight. Gardens open daily 6am-dusk. Both free.)*

KENSINGTON PALACE. Remodeled by Christopher Wren for William and Mary, parts of the palace are still a royal residence. Diana lived here until her death. The **Royal Ceremonial Dress Collection** features 19th-century court costumes along with the Queen's demure evening gowns and some of Diana's sexier numbers. *(Western edge of Kensington Gardens; enter through the park. ⊖High St. Kensington. Open daily Mar.-Oct. 10am-6pm; Nov.-Feb. 10am-5pm. £11.50, students £9.; £1 online booking discount. MC/V.)*

KNIGHTSBRIDGE AND BELGRAVIA

APSLEY HOUSE AND WELLINGTON ARCH. Apsley House, with the convenient address of "No. 1, London," was bought in 1817 by the Duke of Wellington. On display is his outstanding art collection, much of it given by grateful European royalty following the Battle of Waterloo. The majority of the paintings hang in the **Waterloo Gallery.** *(Hyde Park Corner. ⊖Hyde Park Corner. ☎7499 5676; www.english-heritage.org.uk/london. Open Apr.-Oct. Tu-Su 10am-5pm; Nov.-Mar. 10am-4pm. £5.10, students £3.80, ages 5-18 £2.60.)* Across from Apsley House, the **Wellington Arch** was dedicated to the Duke of Wellington in 1838. Later, to the horror of its architect, a huge statue of the Duke was placed on top. *(⊖Hyde Park Corner. Open W-Su 10am-5pm. £3.10, ISIC holders £2.30, ages 5-16 £1.60. Combo tickets with Apsley House: £6.50/4.90/3.30. MC/V.)*

THE WEST END

TRAFALGAR SQUARE. John Nash first suggested laying out this square in 1820, but it took almost 50 years for London's largest roundabout to take on its current appearance. The square is named in commemoration of the defeat of Napoleon's navy at Trafalgar, considered England's greatest naval victory. It has traditionally been a site for public rallies and protest movements. Towering over the square is the 51m granite **Nelson's Column,** which was one of the world's tallest displays of decades-old pigeon droppings. Now, thanks to a deep-clean sponsored by the mayor, this monument to hero Lord Nelson sparkles once again. *(⊖Charing Cross.)*

ST. MARTIN-IN-THE-FIELDS. The fourth church to stand here, James Gibbs's 1726 creation is instantly recognizable: the rectangular portico building supporting a soaring steeple made St. Martin-in-the-Fields the classic model for myriad Georgian churches in Ireland and America. Handel and Mozart both performed here, and the church hosts frequent concerts. To support church upkeep, a cafe, bookshop, and art gallery dwell in the crypt. *(St. Martin's Ln., northeast corner of Trafalgar Sq.; crypt entrance on Duncannon St. ØLeicester Sq. or Charing Cross. ☎7766 1100; www.smitf.org. Church open M-Sa 8am-6pm, Su 8am-7:30pm. Tours Th 11:30am. Free.)*

SOHO. Soho is one of London's most diverse areas. **Old Compton Street** is the center of London's GLBT culture. In the 1950s, Hong Kong immigrants began moving to the blocks just north of Leicester Sq., near **Gerrard Street** and grittier **Lisle Street:** now **Chinatown.** Gaudy, brash, and world-famous, **Piccadilly Circus** is made up of four of the West End's major arteries (Piccadilly, Regent St., Shaftesbury Ave., and the Haymarket). In the middle of all the glitz stands Gilbert's famous **Statue of Eros.** *(⊖Piccadilly Circus.)* Lined with tour buses, overpriced clubs, fast-food restaurants, and generic cafes, **Leicester Square** is one spot Londoners go out of their way to avoid. *(⊖Piccadilly Circus or Leicester Sq.)* A calm in the storm, **Soho Square** is a scruffy, green patch popular with picnickers. Its removed location makes it more hospitable than Leicester. *(⊖Tottenham Ct. Rd. Park open daily 10am-dusk.)*

MUSEUMS AND GALLERIES

Centuries spent as the capital of an empire, together with a decidedly English penchant for collecting, have given London a spectacular set of museums. Art lovers, history buffs, and amateur ethnologists won't know which way to turn. And there's even better news for museum lovers: since 2002, admission to all major collections is free indefinitely in celebration of the Queen's Golden Jubilee.

MAJOR COLLECTIONS

TATE MODERN. Since opening in May 2000, Tate Modern has been credited with single-handedly reversing the long-term decline in museum attendance in Britain. One of the largest modern art museums in the world, its most striking aspect is the building itself, formerly Bankside Power Station. The conversion to a gallery added a 7th floor with wraparound views, and turned the old **Turbine Hall** into an immense atrium that often overpowers the installations commissioned for it. The Tate groups works according to theme rather than period or artist. The divisions are **Still Life/Object/Real Life** and **Landscape/Matter/Environment** on Level 3, and **Nude/Action/Body** and **History/Memory/Society** on Level 5—even skeptics admit that this arrangement throws up interesting contrasts and forces visitors into contact with a wide range of art. It's now impossible to see the Tate's more famous pieces, such as Picasso's *Nude Woman with Necklace*, without also confronting challenging and invigorating works by less well-known contemporary artists. *(Bankside, on the South Bank. ⊖Southwark or Blackfriars. ☎7887 8000. Open Su-Th 10am-6pm, F-Sa 10am-10pm. Free tours meet on the gallery concourses. Audio tour £2.)*

NATIONAL GALLERY. The National Gallery was founded by an Act of Parliament in 1824, with 38 pictures displayed in a townhouse; it grew so rapidly in size and popularity that a new gallery was constructed in 1838. If you're pressed for time, head to **Art Start** in the Sainsbury Wing, where you can design and print out a personalized tour. Botticelli's *Venus and Mars*, and the *Leonardo Cartoon*, a detailed preparatory drawing by da Vinci for a never-executed painting both reside here. With paintings that date from 1510 to 1600, the **West Wing** is dominated by the Italian High Renaissance, German, and Flemish art. The **North Wing** spans the 17th century, with an exceptional display of Flemish and Spanish Renaissance works. The **East Wing,** home to paintings from 1700 to 1900, is the most crowded, with the most famous works and the Impressionist galleries. The focus is primarily on Room #45, which features one of van Gogh's *Sunflowers*. *(Main entrance on north side of Trafalgar Sq. ⊖Charing Cross or Leicester Sq. ☎7747 2885; www.nationalgallery.org.uk. Open M-Tu and Th-Su 10am-6pm, W 10am-9pm. Free 1hr. tours start at Sainsbury Wing information desk daily 11:30am and 2:30pm; plus W 6pm and 6:30pm; Sat. 11:30am, 12:30pm, 2:30pm, and 3:30pm. Free; some temporary exhibits £5-9, students £2-3. Audio tour free; £3 suggested donation. AmEx/MC/V.)*

NATIONAL PORTRAIT GALLERY. This artistic Who's Who in Britain began in 1856 and has grown to be the place to see Britain's freshest new artwork as well as centuries-old portraiture. New facilities include an IT Gallery, allowing you to print out a personalized tour, and a 3rd-floor restaurant with an aerial view of London. To see the paintings in historical order, take the escalator from the reception hall in the Ondaatje Wing to the top floor. *(St. Martin's Pl., Trafalgar Sq. ⊖Leicester Sq. or Charing Cross. ☎7306 0055; www.npg.org.uk. Open M-W and Sa-Su 10am-6pm, Th-F 10am-8:50pm. Lectures Tu, Th, Sa-Su 1:10 and 3pm; free but popular events require tickets on hand at the information desk. Special exhibits up to £6. Audio tour £2.)*

BRITISH MUSEUM. The funny thing about the British Museum is that there's almost nothing British in it. With 50,000 items, the magnificent collection is somewhat undermined by a chaotic layout and poor labeling, while staff shortages mean that even famous galleries are randomly closed. That said, the building itself is magnificent, especially the Great Court and the Reading Room, and a leisurely stroll through the less-frequented galleries is worth an afternoon visit. Most people don't even make it past the main floor, but they should—the galleries upstairs and downstairs are some of the best, if not the most famous. *(Great Russell St., in Bloomsbury. ⊖Tottenham Ct. Rd., Russell Sq., or Holborn. ☎7323 8000; www.thebritishmuseum.ac.uk. Great Court open in summer Su-W 9am-6pm, Th-Sa 9am-11pm; winter Su-W 9am-6pm, Th-Sa 9am-9pm; galleries open daily 10am-5:30pm, selected galleries open Th-F until 8:30pm. £3 suggested donation. Temporary exhibitions £5-10, students £3 and up. Free 40min. tours daily 12:30pm from the Enlightenment Desk. Audio tour £3.50. MC/V.)*

VICTORIA AND ALBERT MUSEUM. The Victoria and Albert is dedicated to displaying "the fine and applied arts of all countries, all styles, and all periods." The subject of a £31 million refit, the **British Galleries** hold a series of recreated rooms from every period between 1500 and 1900, mirrored by the vast **Dress Collection,** a dazzling array of the finest *haute couture* through the ages. If you only see one thing, make it the **Raphael Gallery,** hung with six massive paintings commissioned by Pope Leo X in 1515. The **Sculpture Gallery** and its works are not to be confused with the **Cast Courts,** a plaster-replica collection of the world's greatest sculptures, from Trajan's Column to Michelangelo's *David.* The V&A's **Asian** collections are particularly formidable. In contrast to the geographically laid-out ground floor, the **upper levels** are mostly arranged by material; here you'll find galleries devoted to everything from jewelry to musical instruments to stained glass. The six-level **Henry Cole wing** is home to British paintings, a display of Rodin bronzes and the "world's greatest collection" of miniature portraits. *(Main entrance on Cromwell Rd.; in Kensington and Earl's Court. ⊖South Kensington. ☎7942 2000; www.vam.ac.uk.. Open daily 10am-5:45pm, plus W and last F of month until 10pm. Tours meet at rear of main entrance. Call ahead for times. Gallery talks Th 1pm and Su 3pm; last F of month also draws a young, artistic crowd with live performances, guest DJs, late-night exhibition openings, bar, and food. Free.)*

TATE BRITAIN. The original Tate opened in 1897 as a showcase for modern British art. Before long, it had expanded to include contemporary art from all over the world, as well as British art from the Middle Ages to present. Despite expansions, it was clear that the dual role was too much; the problem was resolved with the relocation of almost all the contemporary art to the new Tate Modern at Bankside (p. 138). At the same time, the original Tate was rededicated to British art. The **Clore Gallery** continues to display the Turner Bequest of 282 oils and 19,000 watercolors; other painters featured are William Blake, John Constable, Lucien Freud, David Hockney, and Dante Gabriel Rossetti. Despite the Tate Modern's popularity, the annual **Turner Prize** for contemporary art is still held here. *(Millbank, near Vauxhall Bridge. ⊖Pimlico. ☎7887 8888; www.tate.org.uk. Open daily 10am-5:50pm. Special exhibits £7-10. Audio tour £3.50, students £3. MC/V.)*

OTHER MUSEUMS AND GALLERIES

Courtauld Institute, Somerset House, Strand, Clerkenwell and Holborn (☎7848 2526; www.courtauld.ac.uk). ⊖Charing Cross. Small, outstanding collection. 14th- to 20th-century abstractions, focusing on Impressionism. Cézanne's *The Card Players,* Manet's *A Bar at the Follies Bergères,* and van Gogh's *Self Portrait with Bandaged Ear.* Open daily 10am-6pm. £5, students £4. Free M 10am-2pm.

Cabinet War Rooms, Clive Steps, Westminster (☎7930 6961; www.iwm.org.uk). ⊖Westminster. Churchill and his strategists lived and worked underground here from 1939 to 1945. Highlights include the room with the top-secret transatlantic hotline—the official story was that it was Churchill's personal toilet. Open daily 9:30am-6pm. £11, students £8.50. MC/V.

British Library Galleries, 96 Euston Rd. (☎7412 7000; www.bl.uk). ⊖King's Cross. A stunning display of texts from the 2nd-century *Unknown Gospel* to The Beatles' handscrawled lyrics. Other highlights include a Gutenberg Bible, Joyce's handwritten *Finnegan's Wake,* and pages from da Vinci's notebooks. Open M and W-F 9:30am-6pm, Tu 9:30am-8pm, Sa 9:30am-5pm, Su 11am-5pm. Free. Audio tour £3.50, students £2.50.

Science Museum, Exhibition Rd., Kensington (☎08708 704 868; www.sciencemuseum.org.uk.). ⊖South Kensington. A mix of state-of-the-art interactive displays and priceless historical artifacts, encompassing all forms of technology. Daily demonstrations and workshops in the basement galleries and theater. Open daily 10am-6pm. Free.

Natural History Museum, on Cromwell Rd., Kensington (☎7942 5000; www.nhm.ac.uk). ⊖South Kensington. The Natural History Museum is home to an array of minerals and stuffed animals. Highlights include a frighteningly realistic *T. Rex* and the engrossing, interactive Human Biology gallery. Open M-Sa 10am-5:50pm, Su 11am-5:50pm. Free.

Museum of London, London Wall, The City of London (☎08704 443 851; www.museumoflondon.org.uk). ⊖Barbican. Enter through the Barbican. The collection traces the history of London from its foundations to the present day, cleverly incorporating adjacent ruins. Open M-Sa 10am-5:50pm, Su noon-5:50pm. Free.

Whitechapel Art Gallery, Whitechapel High St. (☎7522 7888; www.whitechapel.org). ⊖Aldgate East. At the forefront of the East End's art scene, Whitechapel hosts excellent, often controversial, shows of contemporary art. Th nights bring music, poetry readings, and film screenings. Open Tu-W and F-Su 11am-6pm, Th 11am-9pm. Gallery may close between installations; call ahead. Free.

ENTERTAINMENT

Although West End ticket prices are sky high and the quality of some shows questionable, the city that brought the world Shakespeare, the Sex Pistols, and Andrew Lloyd Webber still retains its originality and theatrical edge. London is a city of immense talent, full of student up-and-comers, experimental writers, and undergrounders who don't care about having their names flashed in neon lights.

CINEMA

The heart of the celluloid monster is Leicester Square, where releases premiere a day before hitting the city's chains. The dominant cinema chain is **Odeon** (☎0870 5050 007; www.odeon.co.uk). Tickets to West End cinemas cost £9-12.50; weekday matinees are cheaper. For less mainstream offerings, try the **Electric Cinema,** 191 Portobello Rd., for the combination of baroque stage splendor and the buzzing effects of a big screen. For an extra-special experience, choose a luxury armchair or two-seat sofa. (⊖Ladbroke Grove. ☎7908 9696; www.electriccinema.com. Tickets £5-£12.50; 2-seat sofa £20-£30. Double bills Su 2pm £5/7.50. Wheelchair-accessible. Box office open M-Sa 9am-8:30pm, Su 10am-8:30pm. MC/V.) **Riverside Studios,** Crisp Rd., shows a wide range of excellent foreign and classic films. (⊖Hammersmith. ☎8237 1111; www.riversidestudios.co.uk. £6.50, students £5.50.) The **National Film Theatre (NFT)** screens a mind-boggling array of films every evening starting around 6pm. (South Bank, underneath Waterloo Bridge. ⊖Waterloo or Embankment. ☎7928 3232; www.bfi.org.uk/nft. £8.60)

BRITAIN

COMEDY

Summertime visitors should note that London empties of comedians in **August,** when most head to Edinburgh for the annual festivals (p. 185). **July** brings comedians trying out material; check *TimeOut* or a newspaper. **Comedy Store,** 1A Oxendon St., is the UK's top comedy club and sower of the seeds that gave rise to *Ab Fab, Whose Line is it Anyway?*, and *Blackadder*. (⊖Piccadilly Circus. ☎7839 6642, tickets 0870 154 4040; www.thecomedystore.biz. Tu "Cutting Edge" (current events-based satire), W and Su Comedy Store Players improv, Th-Sa standup. Shows daily 8pm, plus F-Sa midnight. 18+. Tu "Cutting Edge," W and Su Comedy Store Players improv, Th-Sa standup. Shows Su-Th 8pm, F-Sa 8pm and midnight. 18+. Tu-W, F midnight, Su £13, students £8. Th-F early show and Sa £15. Box office open Tu-Th and Su 6:30-9:30pm, F-Sa 6:30pm-1:30am. M hrs. vary. AmEx/MC/V.) North London's **Canal Cafe Theatre,** Delamere Terr., above the Bridge House pub, is one of the few venues to specialize in sketch, as opposed to stand-up. (⊖Warwick Ave. ☎7289 6054; www.canalcafetheatre.com Shows W-Sa 7:30, 9:30pm; £5, students £4. Newsrevue £9, students £7. £1 membership included in price.)

MUSIC

CLASSICAL

Barbican Hall, Silk St. (☎0845 1216827; www.barbican.org.uk), in City of London. ⊖Barbican or Moorgate. A multi-function venue, the hall is home to a library, theater, and art gallery. The resident **London Symphony Orchestra** plays here frequently; the hall also hosts concerts by international orchestras, jazz artists, and world musicians. Call ahead for tickets, especially for popular events. The online and phone box office sometimes have good last-minute options. Orchestra tickets £8-29. AmEx/MC/V.

English National Opera, London Coliseum, St. Martin's Ln. (☎087 0145 0200; www.eno.org), Trafalgar Sq. ⊖Charing Cross or Leicester Sq. All performances in English. Box office open M-Sa 10am-8pm. Discounted tickets available 3hr. before show; balcony (£8-10), upper circle (£10), or dress circle (£20). Call to verify daily availability; however, tickets are usually available. Wheelchair-accessible. AmEx/MC/V.

Holland Park Theatre, Holland Park (box office ☎08452 309 769; www.operahollandpark.com), in Kensington and Earl's Court. ⊖High St. Kensington or Holland Park. Outdoor performance space in the ruins of Holland House. Performances June-early Aug. Tu-Sa 7:30pm. Box office in the Old Stable Block; open late Mar.-early Aug. M-Sa 1-6pm or 30min. after curtain. Tickets £21, £39 (£36 for students during select performances), and £43. Special allocation of tickets for wheelchair users. MC/V.

JAZZ

Spitz, 109 Commercial St. (☎7392 9032; www.spitz.co.uk), in East London. ⊖Liverpool St. Fresh range of live music, from klezmer and jazz to rap. Profits go to charity. Cover free to £15. Open M-W 7pm-midnight, Th-Sa 7pm-1am, Su 4-10:30pm. MC/V.

Jazz Café, 5 Parkway (☎7344 0044; www.jazzcafe.co.uk), in North London. ⊖Camden Town. Shows can be pricey, but a top roster of jazz, hip-hop, funk, and Latin performers (9pm, £15-30) explains the popularity. DJs spin F-Sa after shows to 2am. Wheelchair-accessible. Cover F-Sa after show £11, with flyer £6. Open M-Th 7pm-1am, F-Sa 7pm-2am, Su 7pm-midnight. Box office open M-Sa 10am-6pm, Su noon-6pm. AmEx/MC/V.

606 Club, 90 Lots Rd. (☎7352 5953; www.606club.co.uk), in Chelsea. ⊖Sloane Sq., then bus #11 or 22. Ring doorbell. The intrepid will be rewarded with British and European jazz, Latin, soul, and R&B in this basement venue. Reserve ahead. Cover (added to food bill) M-Th £8, F-Sa £10, Su £9. M-W doors open 7:30pm, music approx. 8pm-1am; Th-Sa doors open 8pm, music 9:30pm-1:30am; Su doors open 8pm, music 9pm-midnight. AmEx/MC/V.

POP AND ROCK

The Water Rats, 328 Grays Inn Rd., in Bloomsbury. (☎7837 7269; www.plummusic.com for the music gigs). ⊖King's Cross St. Pancras. Cafe by day, stomping ground for top new talent by night (from 8pm). Crowd varies with the music. Cover £5-6, with band flyer £4-5. Music M-Sa 8pm-late; headliner 9:45pm. AmEx/MC/V; min. £7.

Carling Academy, Brixton, 211 Stockwell Rd. (☎7771 3000, tickets 0870 771 2000; www.brixton-academy.co.uk), in South London. ⊖Brixton. Named *TimeOut*'s "Live Venue of the Year" in 2004, and was *NME*'s "Best Live Venue" in 2005. Order tickets online, by phone, or go to the Carling Academy, Islington box office. (16 Parkfield Street, Islington. Open M-Sa noon-4pm.) Tickets generally £5-30. AmEx/MC/V.

London Astoria (LA1), 157 Charing Cross Rd. (☎7434 9592, 24hr. ticket line 0870 060 3777; www.londonastoria.com), in Soho. ⊖Tottenham Ct. Rd. Formerly a pickle factory, strip club, and music hall, this varied venue now caters to rock fans and gay clubbers. The 2000-person venue is best known for its G-A-Y club nights M and Th-Sa (p. 146). Box office open M-F 10am-6pm, Sa 10am-5pm. MC/V.

THEATER

London's West End is dominated by musicals and plays that run for years, if not decades. For a list of shows and discount tickets, head to the **tkts** booth in Leicester Sq. (⊖Leicester Sq. www.tkts.co.uk. Most shows £20-30; up to £2.50 booking fee per ticket. Open M-Sa 10am-7pm, Su noon-3pm. MC/V.)

REPERTORY

Shakespeare's Globe Theatre, 21 New Globe Walk (☎7401 9919; www.shakespeares-globe.org), in the South Bank. ⊖London Bridge. Stages plays by Shakespeare and his contemporaries. Choose from 3 covered tiers of wooden benches or brave the elements as a "groundling." Wheelchair-accessible. Performances mid-May to early Oct. Tu-Sa 7:30pm, Su 6:30pm; June-Sept. also often Tu-Sa 2pm, Su 1pm. Box office open M-Sa 10am-6pm, 8pm on performance days. Seats from £15, students from £10; yard £5.

National Theatre, South Bank (info ☎7452 3400, box office 7452 3000; www.nationaltheatre.org.uk), in the South Bank. ⊖Waterloo. Laurence Olivier founded the National Theatre in 1976, and it has been at the forefront of British theater ever since. Wheelchair-accessible. Box office open M-Sa 10am-8pm. Complicated pricing scheme. Contact box office for details. Tickets typically start at £10. AmEx/MC/V.

Royal Court Theatre, Sloane Sq. (☎7565 5000; www.royalcourttheatre.com), in Chelsea. ⊖Sloane Sq. Recognized by *The New York Times* as a standout theater in Europe. Main auditorium £10-25, students £10. M all seats £10. Box office open M-Sa 10am-7:45pm, closes 6pm non-performance weeks. AmEx/MC/V.

"OFF-WEST END"

The Almeida, Almeida St. (☎7359 4404; www.almeida.co.uk), in North London. ⊖Angel or Highbury and Islington. Top fringe theater in London. Wheelchair-accessible. Shows M-F 7:30pm, Sa 3 and 7:30pm. Tickets £6-30. Student tickets available. MC/V.

Donmar Warehouse, 41 Earlham St. (☎08700 606 624; www.donmarwarehouse.com), in Covent Garden. ⊖Covent Garden. Artistic director Sam Mendes transformed this gritty space into one of the best theaters in England. Tickets £13-29; student standby 30min. before curtain, £12 (when available); £7.50 standing-room tickets available day of, once performance sells out. Box office open M-Sa 10am-7:30pm. AmEx/MC/V.

Royal Academy of Dramatic Arts (RADA), 62-64 Gower St. (☎7908 4800; www.rada.org), entrance on Malet St.; in Bloomsbury. ⊖Goodge St. Britain's most famous drama school has 3 on-site theaters. Wheelchair-accessible. £11, students £8. Regular Foyer events during the academic year including plays, music, and readings M-Th 7 or 7:30pm (free to £6). Box office open M-F 10am-6pm, until 7:30pm performance nights. AmEx/MC/V.

SHOPPING

London has long been considered one of the fashion capitals of the world. Unfortunately, the city features as many underwhelming chain stores as it does one-of-a-kind boutiques. The truly budget-conscious should forget buying altogether and stick to window-shopping in **Knightsbridge** and on **Regent Street.** Vintage shopping in **Notting Hill** is also a viable alternative; steer clear of **Oxford Street,** where so-called "vintage" clothing was probably made in 2002 and marked up 200%.

DEPARTMENT STORES

Harrods, 87-135 Brompton Rd. (☎7730 1234; www.harrods.com), in Knightsbridge and Belgravia. ⊖Knightsbridge. The only thing bigger than the store is the mark-up on the goods–no wonder only tourists and oil sheikhs actually shop here. Wheelchair-accessible. Open M-Sa 10am-8pm, Su noon-6pm. AmEx/MC/V.

Harvey Nichols, 109-125 Knightsbridge (☎7235 5000; www.harveynichols.com), in Knightsbridge. ⊖Knightsbridge. Rue St-Honoré and Fifth Ave. rolled into 5 fl. of fashion. Wheelchair-accessible. Open M-Sa 10am-8pm, Su noon-6pm. AmEx/MC/V.

Selfridges, 400 Oxford St. (☎0870 837 7377; www.selfridges.com), in the West End. ⊖Bond St. The total department store covers everything from traditional tweeds to space-age clubwear. Massive Jan. and July sales. Wheelchair-accessible. Open M-Sa 9:30am-8pm, Su 11:30am-6pm. AmEx/MC/V.

Liberty, 210-220 Regent St. (☎7734 1234; www.liberty.co.uk), in the West End. ⊖Oxford Circus. The focus on top-quality design and handcrafts makes it more like a giant boutique than a department store. Famous for custom fabric prints. Wheelchair-accessible. Open M-W and F-Sa 10am-7pm, Th 10am-8pm, Su noon-6pm. AmEx/MC/V.

Fortnum & Mason, 181 Piccadilly (☎7734 8040; www.fortnumandmason.co.uk), in the West End. ⊖Green Park or Piccadilly Circus. Gourmet department store provides quality foodstuffs fit for a queen. Wheelchair-accessible. Open M-Sa 10am-6:30pm, Su noon-6pm (food hall and patio restaurant only). AmEx/MC/V.

STREET MARKETS

Better for people-watching than hard-core shopping, street markets may not bring you the big goods, but they are a much better alternative to a day on Oxford St. **Portobello Road Markets** include food, antiques, and second-hand clothing. Come Friday or Saturday, when everything is sure to be open. (⊖Notting Hill Gate, Westbourne Park, or Ladbroke Grove. Stalls set their own times. General hours M-W and F-Sa 8am-6:30pm, Th 8am-1pm.) **Camden Passage Market** is more for looking than for buying—London's premier antique shops line these charming alleyways. (Islington High St., in North London. ⊖Angel. Stalls open W and Sa 7:30am-6pm; some stores open daily, but W is by far the best day to go.) **Brixton Market** has London's best selection of Afro-Caribbean fruits, vegetables, spices, and fish. (Along Electric Ave., Pope's Rd., and Brixton Station Rd., and inside markets in Granville Arcade and Market Row; in South London. ⊖Brixton. Open daily 7am-7pm; closes W 3:30pm.) Formerly a wholesale vegetable markets, **Spitalfields** has matured to be the best of the East End markets. On Sunday, the food shares space with rows of clothing by local independent designers. (Commercial St., in East London. ⊖Shoreditch, Liverpool St., or Aldgate East. Crafts market open M-F 10:30am-4:15pm, Su 10am-5pm. Antique market open Th 9am-5pm. Organic market open Su 10am-5pm.)

NIGHTLIFE

First-time visitors may initially head directly to the **West End,** drawn by the flashy lights and pumping music of Leicester Sq. Be warned, though, that like much of the West End, nightlife here is not the definitive voice of Londoners who like to rock out; for a more authentic experience, head to the **East End** or **Brixton.** Soho's **Old Compton Street** though, is still the center of GLBT nightlife. Before heading out for the evening, make sure to plan **Night Bus** travel. Listings open past 11pm include local Night Bus routes. Night Buses in the West End are ubiquitous—head to Trafalgar Sq., Oxford St., or Piccadilly Circus.

PUBS

Fitzroy Tavern, 16 Charlotte St. (☎7580 3714), in Bloomsbury. ⊖Goodge St. A perfect pub for sunny days and sipping beer on the street outside, this place attracts artists, writers, locals, and students in droves. Comedy W 8:30pm (£3-5). Open M-Sa 11am-11pm, Su noon-10:30pm. Min. £10. Debit cards min. £5. AmEx/MC/V.

The Jerusalem Tavern, 55 Britton St. (☎7490 4281; www.stpetersbrewery.co.uk), in Clerkenwell. ⊖Farringdon. Ideal for an evening of intense conversation. A broad selection of specialty ales (£2.40), including grapefruit, cinnamon, and apple, rewards the adventuresome. Open M-F 11am-11pm. AmEx/MC/V.

The Blue Anchor, Rolls Passage, off Chancery Ln. (☎7430 2205; www.theblueanchor.com). ⊖Chancery Lane. A beer garden in front and excellent food make this pub a pleasant place to come mid-week. Generally a business crowd. Food around £6-8. Open M-Th 11am-11pm, F 11am-11:30pm. Kitchen closes 9pm. AmEx/MC/V.

BARS

Bar Kick, 127 Shoreditch High St. (☎7739 8700; www.cafekick.co.uk); in East London. ⊖Old St. Night Bus hub at Liverpool St. Station, and #N55, 67, 243. The dozens of flags on the ceiling add even more international flavor to the European-style food and music. Wheelchair-accessible. Happy hour daily 4-7pm. Open M-W noon-11pm, Th-Sa noon-midnight, Su noon-7pm. Kitchen open M-W noon-3:30pm and 5-10pm, Th-F noon-3:30pm and 5-11pm, Sa noon-11pm, Su 10am-10:30pm. AmEx/MC/V; min. £5.

Lab, 12 Old Compton St. (☎7437 7820; www.lab-townhouse.com), in the West End. ⊖Leicester Sq. or Tottenham Ct. Rd. With restrooms for "bitches" and "bastards," the only thing this funky cocktail bar takes seriously is its stellar drink menu. DJs spin house and funk from 8pm nightly. Open M-Sa 4pm-midnight, Su 4pm-10:30pm. AmEx/MC/V.

Vibe Bar, 91-95 Brick Ln. (☎7247 3479; www.vibe-bar.co.uk), in East London. ⊖Aldgate East or Liverpool St. Night Bus: hub at Liverpool St. Station. Dance to hip-hop, soul, acoustic, and jazz. Pint £3. DJs spin M-Sa from 7pm, Su from 6pm. Cover F-Sa after 8pm £3.50. Open Su-Th 11am-11:30pm, F-Sa 11am-1am. Cash only; ATM in bar.

22 Below, 22 Great Marlborough St. (☎02074 374 106; www.22below.com), in the West End. ⊖Oxford Circus. In a basement next to Cafe Libre. Oversized fresh fruit martinis (£6-7), and a crowd mostly employed by the media industry. DJs Th-Sa from 8pm. Open M-F 5pm-midnight, Sa 8pm-midnight. AmEx/MC/V.

Filthy MacNasty's, 68 Amwell St. (☎7837 6067; www.filthymacnastys.com), in North London. ⊖Angel or King's Cross. Night Bus N63, N73, N205, or N214. This laid-back semi-Irish pub is known for having hosted jam sessions by Shane MacGowan, et. al. Open M-Sa noon-11pm, Su noon-10:30pm. MC/V min. £10; debit cards min. £5.

NIGHTCLUBS

Ministry of Sound, 103 Gaunt St. (☎7378 6528; www.ministryofsound.co.uk), in the South Bank. ⊖Elephant and Castle; take the exit for South Bank University. Night Bus #N35, 133, 343. Mecca for serious clubbers worldwide. Dress code casual, but famously unsmiling door staff make it prudent to err on the side of smartness. Cover F £12, Sa £15.

MO*VIDA, 7-8 Argyll St. (☎7734 5776), in Soho. Ultra-exclusive club is members- and guestlist-only–call ahead and put yourself on the list. Strict doorstaff; dress up and bring lots of cash. W house/techno music. Cover £15-20. Open W-Sa 8pm-3:30am.

The End, 16a West Central St. (☎7419 9199; www.endclub.com), in the West End. ⊖Tottenham Ct. Rd. Cutting edge clubbers' Eden; theme nights online. Wheelchair-accessible. Cover M £6; W £5-6; Th £6-£8; F £10-13; Sa £16. Open M 10pm-3am, W 10:30pm-3am, Th 10pm-4am, F 10pm-6am, Sa 10pm-7am. AmEx/MC/V; min. £10.

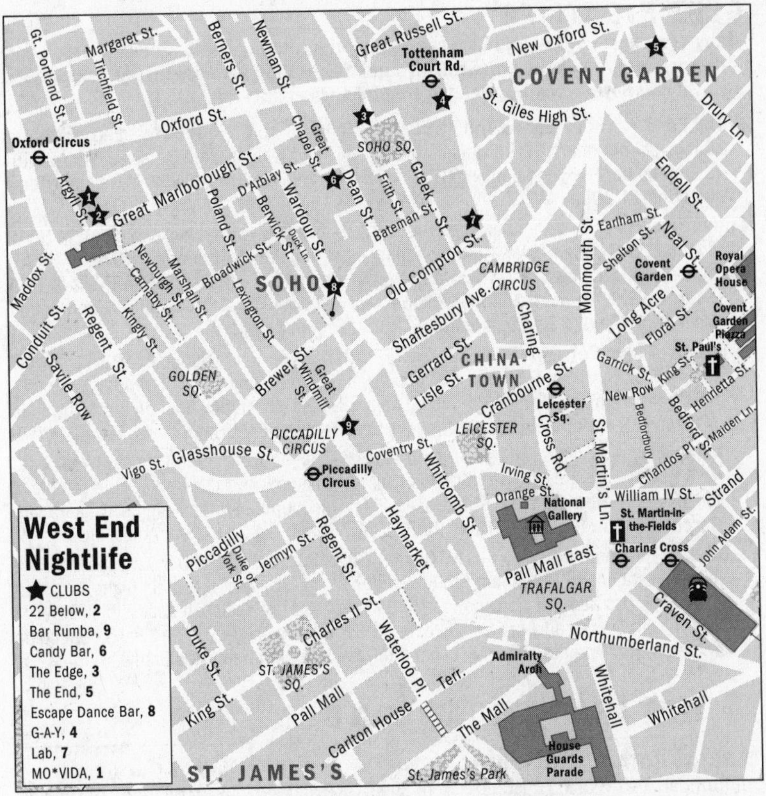

Fabric, 77A Charterhouse St. (☎7336 8898; www.fabriclondon.com), in Clerkenwell. ⊖Farringdon. Night Bus #N242. This club is deep underground with 5 bars, 3 rooms, and clubbers chugging down water, an assortment of pills, and other mind-altering substances. F "Fabriclive"; Su "DTPM Polysexual Night" (70/30 gay/straight split, playing house; www.dtpm.net). Wheelchair-accessible. Get there before 11pm on Saturday to avoid lines. Cover F £12; Sa after 11pm £15. Open F 9:30pm-5am, Sa 10pm-7am, Su 10pm-5am. AmEx/MC/V; min. £10. Cash only for admission.

Notting Hill Arts Club, 21 Notting Hill Gate (☎7460 4459; www.nottinghillartsclub.com), in Notting Hill. ⊖Notting Hill Gate. Night Bus #N94, N148, N207, N390. Unlabeled and unmarked (but right next to the Tex-Mex Tapas Bar). Not touristy and very chill. Later in the night 1-in, 1-out policy. Cover M after 8pm £5; Tu after 8pm £6; W after 8pm £7; Th £5; F-Sa after 8pm £6-8; Su after 6pm £6. Open M-Sa 6pm-2am, Su 6pm-1am. MC/V.

Bar Rumba, 36 Shaftesbury Ave. (☎7287 6933; www.barrumba.co.uk), in the West End. ⊖Piccadilly Circus. The Rumba crowd makes good use of the industrial-strength interior for dancing, mostly to R&B. Cover nightly £5-10; W women free before midnight, students £3 all night. Open M and W 9pm-3am, Tu 6pm-3am, Th 8pm-3:30am, F 6pm-3:30am, Sa 9pm-4am, Su 8:30pm-2:30am. MC/V; min. £10.

GLBT NIGHTLIFE

Many venues have Gay and Lesbian nights on a rotating basis. Check **TimeOut** and look for flyers/magazines floating around Soho: **The Pink Paper** (free from newsagents) and **Boyz** (www.boyz.co.uk; free from gay bars and clubs)

The Edge, 11 Soho Sq. (☎7439 1313; www.edge.uk.com), in the West End. ⊖Oxford Circus or Tottenham Ct. Rd. A chill, friendly gay and lesbian drinking spot. DJs spin Tu-Sa, piano bar Tu-F, and dancing F-Sa. Cover F-Sa after 11pm £2. Open M-Sa noon-1am, Su noon-11:30pm. MC/V.

The Black Cap, 171 Camden High St. (☎7428 2721; www.theblackcap.com), in North London. ⊖Camden Town. North London's most popular gay bar and cabaret is always buzzing. Mixed crowd. Food served daily noon-9pm. Downstairs cover Su-Th £2-3, F-Sa £4-5. Open M-Th noon-2am, F-Sa noon-3am, Su noon-1am. Downstairs cabaret open M-Th 10pm-2am, F-Sa 10pm-3am, Su 9pm-1am. AmEx/MC/V.

Escape Dance Bar, 10A Brewer St. (☎7731 2626; www.kudosgroup.com), in the West End. ⊖Leicester Sq. Dance to the latest pop hits in an enjoyably cramped space. DJs F-Sa from midnight. Cover Tu-Th after 11pm £3, F-Sa £5. Happy hour all day M-Th, F-Sa 5-10pm; £7 cocktail pitcher. Open M-Sa 5pm-3am. AmEx/MC/V.

Candy Bar, 4 Carlisle St. (☎7494 4041; www.thecandybar.co.uk), in the West End. ⊖Tottenham Ct. Rd. or Oxford Circus. This estrogen-packed drinking spot is the place for lesbian entertainment. Stripteases, DJs, and popular dance nights. W karaoke. Cover F-Sa after 9pm £5-6. Open Su-Th 5-11:30pm, F-Sa 5pm-2am. AmEx/MC/V.

G-A-Y, at the London Astoria at 157 Charing Cross Rd. (☎7434 9592; www.g-a-y.co.uk), in the West End. ⊖Tottenham Ct. Rd. London's biggest gay and lesbian night. Commercial-dance DJs and live pop shows rock Sa G-A-Y night. Wheelchair-accessible. Cover M and Th with flyer or ad £1; F with flyer or ad £2, after midnight £3; Sa £8-15 depending on performer. Open M and Th-F 11pm-4am, Sa 10:30pm-5am. Cash only.

DAYTRIP FROM LONDON

ROYAL BOTANICAL GARDENS, KEW. The Royal Botanical Gardens were announced as a World Heritage Site in 2003—a privilege shared by many of the historic sights in London. The 250-year-old Royal Botanical Gardens, about an hour's Tube ride outside of central London, extend 300-acres along the Thames. The three conservatories are at the center of the collection. The steamy Victorian **Palm House** boasts *Encephalartos altensteinii*, "The Oldest Pot Plant In The World," while the **Princess of Wales Conservatory** houses 10 different climate zones including two devoted entirely to orchids. Low-season visitors will not be disappointed—the **Woodland Glade** is renowned for displays of autumn color, and there is an annual orchid festival every spring. In the northern part of the gardens, the newly renovated **Kew Palace** is used by royalty on Garden visits, which is now open to the public for the first time in 200 years. On the hill behind and to the right of the palace, 17th-century medicinal plants flourish in the stunning **Queen's Garden;** small placards label one that cures back pain "caused by overmuch use of women." *(Kew, on the south bank of the Thames. The main entrance and visitors center is at Victoria Gate, nearest the Tube. Go up the white stairs that go above the station tracks, and walk straight down the road. ⊖Kew Gardens. ☎8332 5000 for 24hr. recorded information; www.kew.org. Open Apr.-Aug. M-F 9:30am-6:30pm, Sa-Su 9:30am-7:30pm; Sept.-Oct. daily 9:30am-6pm; Nov.-Jan. daily 9:30am-4:15pm; Feb.-Mar. daily 9:30am-5:30pm. Glass houses close Apr.-Oct. 5:30pm; Nov.-Jan. 3:45pm, Feb.-Mar. 5pm. Apr.-Sept. £11.75, students £8.75; after 4:45pm £4. Nov.-Mar. £9.50/£6.50. 1hr. walking tours daily 11am and 2pm from Victoria Gate Visitors Centre; free. 1hr. "Discovery Bus" tours for mobility-impaired M-F 11am and 2pm; booking required; free.)*

SOUTHERN ENGLAND

History and myth cloak Southern England as densely as the Atlantic fog. Cornwall, the alleged birthplace of King Arthur, was the last stronghold of the Celts in England, but traces of even older Neolithic communities linger in the massive stone circles they left behind. In WWII, German bombings uncovered long-buried evidence of an invasion by Caesar, whose Romans dotted the countryside with settlements, including the elaborate spas at Bath. William the Conqueror left his mark in the form of awe-inspiring castles and cathedrals. Apart from all this pomp and circumstance is another, less palpable, presence: the voices of such British literati as Jane Austen, Geoffrey Chaucer, Charles Dickens, and E. M. Forster still seem to echo above the sprawling pastures and seaside cliffs.

CANTERBURY ☎01227

Archbishop Thomas Becket met his demise at **Canterbury Cathedral** in 1170 after an irate Henry II asked, "Will no one rid me of this troublesome priest?" Later, in his famed *Canterbury Tales*, Chaucer caricatured the pilgrims who traveled the road from London to England's most famous execution site. (☎762 862; www.canterbury-cathedral.org. Cathedral open Easter-Sept. M-Sa 9am-6:30pm, Su 12:30-2:30pm and 4:30-5:30pm; Oct.-Easter M-Sa 9am-5pm, Su 12:30-2:30pm and 4:30-5:30pm. 1¼hr. tours available, 3 per day M-Sa; check nave or welcome center for times. Evensong M-F 5:30pm, Sa-Su 3:15pm. £6, students £4.50. Tours £4/3. 40min. audio tour £3.50/2.50.) The skeletons of soaring arches and crumbling walls are all that remain of **Saint Augustine's Abbey,** outside the city wall near the cathedral. St. Augustine himself is buried in a humble tomb under a pile of rocks. (☎767 345. Open Apr.-Sept. daily 10am-6pm; Oct.-Mar. W-Su 10am-4pm. £3.90, students £2.90.) England's first Franciscan friary, **Greyfriars,** 6A Stour St., has quiet riverside gardens. (☎462 395. Open Easter-Sept. M-Sa 2-4pm. Free.) **The Canterbury Tales,** on St. Margaret's St., plays abbreviated portions of Chaucer's masterpiece through headphones to herds of tourists browsing recreated scenes. (☎479 227; www.canterburytales.org.uk. Open daily July-Aug. 9:30am-5pm; Mar.-June and Sept.-Oct. 10am-5pm; Nov.-Feb. 10am-4:30pm. £7.25, students £6.25.)

B&Bs cluster around **High Street** and on **New Dover Road.** Try **Kipps Independent Hostel ❶**, 40 Nunnery Fields, for friendly management, a fully equipped kitchen, and a great movie selection. (☎786 121. Laundry £3. Internet £2 per hr. Key deposit £10. Dorms £14; singles £19; doubles £33. MC/V.) **Cafe des Amis du Mexique ❷**, St. Dunstan's St., serves Mexican-inspired dishes in a student-friendly atmosphere. (☎464 390. Entrees £5-10. Open M-Sa noon-10:30pm, Su noon-9:30pm. AmEx/MC/V.) Try **C'est la Vie ❶**, 17B Burgate, for sandwiches and baguettes from £2. (☎457 525. Open M-Sa 9:30am-3:30pm. 10% student discount. Cash only.) There's a **Safeway** supermarket on St. George's Pl. (☎769 335. Open M-F 8am-9pm, Sa 8am-8pm, Su 11am-5pm.) **Trains** from London Victoria arrive at Canterbury's East Station (1¾hr., 2 per hr., £20), while trains from London Charing Cross and Waterloo arrive at West Station (1½hr., every hr., £17). National Express **buses** (☎08705 808 080) arrive at St. George's Ln. from London (2hr., 2 per hr., £14). The **tourist office,** 12-13 Sun St., in the Buttermarket, books rooms for a £2.50 fee plus a 10% deposit. (☎378 100. Open Easter-Christmas M-Sa 9:30am-5pm, Su 10am-4pm; Christmas-Easter M-Sa 10am-4pm.) **Postal Code:** CT1 2BA.

BRIGHTON ☎01273

According to legend, heir to the throne George IV sidled into Brighton (pop. 180,000) for some decidedly common hanky-panky around 1784. Today, Brighton is still the unrivaled home of the "dirty weekend"—it sparkles with a tawdry luster all its own. Check out England's long-time obsession with the Far East at the excessively ornate **Royal Pavilion,** on Pavilion Parade, next to Old Steine. Rumor has it that King George IV wept tears of joy upon entering it, proving that wealth does not give you taste. (☎292 880. Open daily Apr.-Sept. 9:30am-5:45pm; Oct.-Mar. 10am-5:15pm. Tours daily 11:30am and 2:30pm; £1.55. Pavilion £6, students £4.30.) Around the corner on Church St. stands the **Brighton Museum and Art Gallery,** showcasing Art Nouveau and Art Deco pieces, English pottery, and a Brighton historical exhibit that thoroughly explains the phrase "dirty weekend." (☎292 882. Open Tu 10am-7pm, W-Sa 10am-5pm, Su 2-5pm. Free.) Before heading to the rocky **beach,** stroll the novelty shops and colorful cafes of the **North Laines,** off Trafalgar St.

West of West Pier along King's Rd. Arches, ☒**Baggies Backpackers ❶,** 33 Oriental Pl., boasts a super-social music room complemented by spontaneous parties on "Baggies Beach." Hanging with the mellow crowd beats a seedy club-hop any day. (☎733 740. Co-ed bathrooms. Dorms £13; one double £35. Cash only.) At **Bombay Aloo ❶,** 39 Ship St., loyal patrons return for blissfully cheap Indian vegetarian food and an unbeatable £5 all-you-can-eat special. (Open M-Th and Su noon-11pm; F-Sa noon-midnight. MC/V.) Buy groceries at **Somerfield,** 6 St. James's St. (☎570 363. Open M-Sa 8am-10pm, Su 11am-5pm.)

At ☒**Fortune of War,** 157 King's Rd. Arches, patrons can relax with a pint (£3.10) and watch the sun set over the Channel. (Open daily noon-manager's discretion. Bar open 24hr.) Most **clubs** are open Monday through Saturday 9pm-2am; after they close, the party moves to the waterfront. **The Beach,** 171-181 King's Rd. Arches, is a hopping shore-side club. (☎722 272. Cover £10, with student ID £8. Open M and W-Th 10pm-2am, F-Sa 10pm-3am.) **Casablanca Jazz Club,** 3 Middle St., offers live bands playing jazz, funk, and Latin music. (☎321 817; www.casablanca-jazzclub.com. Cover W £2 after 11pm, F-Sa £5-7. Students £1 discount. Open M and Th-Sa 9:30pm-3am, Tu-W 9:30pm-2am.) The gay and gay-friendly party hard at **Charles St.,** 8-9 Marine Parade, as live DJs spin current dance tracks. The anything-goes atmosphere is conducive to anything-goes dancing. (☎624 091. Cover M £1.50, Th £3, F £5, Sa £5-8. Open M 10:30pm-2am, Th-Sa 10:30pm-3am.) **Trains** (☎08457 484 950) leave from the northern end of Queen's Rd. for London Victoria (1hr., 2 per hr., £17) and Portsmouth (1½hr., 2 per hr., £14). National Express **buses** (☎08705 808 080) arrive at Pool Valley from London Victoria (2-2½hr., 1 per hr., £9.30). The **tourist office** is at 10 Bartholomew Sq. (☎0906 711 2255; www.visit-brighton.com. Open June-Sept. M-F 9am-5pm, Sa 10am-5pm, Su 10am-4pm; Oct.-May M-F 9:30am-5pm, Sa 10am-5pm.) **Postal Code:** BN1 1BA.

PORTSMOUTH ☎02392

Though its reputation has been tainted by a 900-year history of prostitutes, drunkards, and foul-mouthed sailors, Portsmouth (pop. 190,000) has recently come into its own as a respectable seaside vacation town. Stretching to the east, the half-hearted resort community of **Southsea** can feel like an entirely different city. War buffs and historians will want to plunge head-first into the ☒**Portsmouth Historic Dockyard,** in the Naval Yard, which houses a trio of Britain's most storied ships: Henry VIII's *Mary Rose,* Nelson's HMS *Victory,* and the HMS *Warrior.* The entrance is next to the tourist office on The Hard. (Ships open daily Apr.-Oct. 10am-5:30pm, last entry 4:30pm; Nov.-Mar. 10am-5pm, last entry 4pm. Each ship £10. Combination ticket £16.) The ☒**D-Day Museum,** on Clarence Esplanade in Southsea, leads visitors through life-size dioramas of the 1944 invasion. (☎9282 7261. Open daily Apr.-Sept. 10am-5:30pm; Oct.-Mar. 10am-5pm. £6, students £3.60.)

Moderately priced **B&Bs** (around £25) clutter **Southsea,** 2.5km southeast of The Hard, along the coast. Take any Southsea bus from Commercial Rd. and get off at the Strand to reach the **Portsmouth and Southsea Backpackers Lodge ❶,** 4 Florence Rd., where the amiable owners offer rooms to a pan-European crowd near the

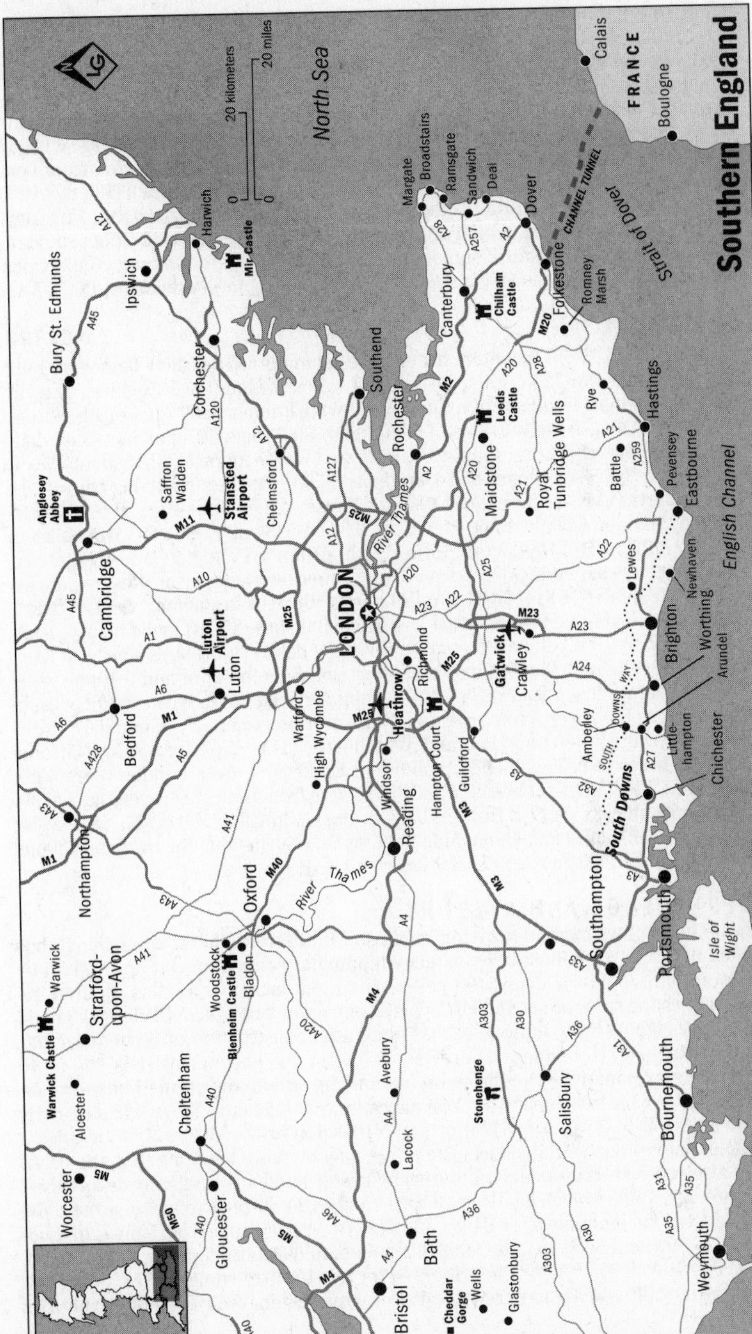
Southern England
North Sea
English Channel
Strait of Dover
CHANNEL TUNNEL
FRANCE
Calais
Boulogne
20 kilometers
20 miles
LONDON
River Thames
Heathrow
Gatwick
Luton Airport
Stansted Airport
Cambridge
Bury St. Edmunds
Ipswich
Harwich
Colchester
Chelmsford
Saffron Walden
Anglesey Abbey
Southend
Rochester
Canterbury
Margate
Broadstairs
Ramsgate
Sandwich
Deal
Dover
Folkestone
Romney Marsh
Chilham Castle
Leeds Castle
Maidstone
Royal Tunbridge Wells
Rye
Hastings
Battle
Pevensey
Eastbourne
Newhaven
Lewes
Brighton
Worthing
Arundel
Little-hampton
Amberley
Chichester
South Downs
SOUTH DOWNS WAY
Crawley
Guildford
Hampton Court
Richmond
Windsor
Reading
Watford
High Wycombe
Luton
Bedford
Northampton
Oxford
Woodstock
Blenheim Castle
Bladon
Stratford-upon-Avon
Warwick
Warwick Castle
Alcester
Cheltenham
Worcester
Gloucester
Bristol
Bath
Lacock
Avebury
Stonehenge
Salisbury
Southampton
Portsmouth
Isle of Wight
Bournemouth
Weymouth
Wells
Glastonbury
Cheddar Gorge
M1
M2
M3
M4
M5
M11
M20
M23
M25
M40
M50
A12
A45
A120
A127
A1
A6
A5
A10
A41
A43
A428
A20
A21
A22
A23
A24
A25
A27
A28
A32
A33
A36
A30
A303
A31
A35
A3
A4
A40
A46
A420
A257
A259
A2

BRITAIN

waterfront. (☎83 2495. Laundry £2. Internet £2 per hr. Dorms £13; doubles £30, with bath £34. Cash only.) **Britannia Guest House ❸,** 48 Granada Rd., has colorful rooms decorated with the friendly proprietor's own modern artwork. (☎814 234. Singles £25; doubles £45-50. MC/V.) There is a Tesco **supermarket** at 56-61 Elm Grove. (☎08456 269 090. Open daily 6am-midnight.) **Pubs** near The Hard provide galley fare and grog, while those on Albert Rd. cater to students. **Trains** (☎08457 484 950) run to Portsmouth and Southsea Station, on Commercial Rd., from London Waterloo (1¾hr., 4 per hr., £23). National Express **buses** (☎08705 808 080) arrive from London Victoria (2½hr., 1 per hr., £21) and Salisbury (1½hr., 1 per day, £8.30). The **tourist office,** which books rooms for a £2 fee and a 10% deposit, is on The Hard, near the historic ships. (☎82 6722; www.visitportsmouth.co.uk. Open daily Apr.-Sept. 9:30am-5:45pm; Oct.-Mar. 9:30am-5:15pm.) **Postal Code:** PO1 1AA.

SALISBURY

☎01722

Salisbury (pop. 37,000) centers around the mammoth **Salisbury Cathedral,** built between 1220 and 1258. Its spire was the tallest of medieval England, and the bases of its marble pillars actually bend inward under 6400 tons of limestone. (☎555 120. Open June-Aug. M-Sa 7:15am-8pm, Su 7:15am-6:15pm; Sept.-May daily 7:15am-6:15pm. Cathedral tours free. Roof and tower tours £4.50, students £3.50. Call ahead. Suggested donation £4, students £3.50.) The best surviving copy of the **Magna Carta** rests in the nearby **Chapter House.** (Open June-Aug. M-Sa 9:30am-5:30pm, Su noon-5:30pm; Sept.-May daily 9:30am-5:30pm. Free.) The **YHA Salisbury (HI) ❶,** Milford Hill House, on Milford Hill, offers a TV lounge and a cafeteria. (☎327 572. Breakfast included. Laundry £3. Internet £4.20 per hr. Reserve ahead. Dorms £18, under 18 £14. MC/V.) At **Harper's "Upstairs Restaurant" ❷,** 6-7 Ox Rd., Market Sq., inventive international and English dishes (£7-10) make hearty meals and the "Early Bird" dinner (2 courses for £9.50 before 8pm) buys a heap of food. (☎333 118. Open M-F noon-2pm and 6-9:30pm, Sa noon-2pm and 6-10pm, Su 6-9pm. Oct.-May closed Su. AmEx/MC/V.) **Trains** arrive at South Western Rd., west of town across the River Avon, from London Waterloo (1½hr., 2 per hr., £50), Portsmouth (1½hr., 2 per hr., £12), and Winchester (1hr., 2 per hr., £11). National Express **buses** (☎08705 808 080) pull into 8 Endless St. from London (3hr., 3 per day, £14); Wilts & Dorset buses (☎336 855) arrive from Bath (#X4; every hr., £4.20). The **tourist office** is on Fish Row, in back of the Guildhall in Market Sq. (☎334 956; www.visitsalisbury.com. Open June-Sept. M-Sa 9:30am-6pm, Su 10:30am-4:30pm; Oct.-May M-Sa 9:30am-5pm.) **Postal Code:** SP1 1AB.

STONEHENGE AND AVEBURY

A sunken colossus amid swaying grass and indifferent sheep, Stonehenge has been battered for millennia by winds whipping at 80km per hour and visited by legions of people for over 5000 years. The monument, which has retained its present shape since about 1500 BC, was at one point a complete circle of 6.5m tall stones weighing up to 45 tons each. Though the construction of Stonehenge has been attributed to builders as diverse as Merlin and extraterrestrials, the more plausible explanation—Neolithic builders using still-unknown methods—is perhaps the most astonishing of all. You may admire Stonehenge for free from nearby Amesbury Hill, 2.5km up A303, or pay admission at the site, which includes a 30min. audio tour with handset. The effect may be more haunting than the rocks themselves—a bizarre march of tourists who stop suddenly to silently devote their entire attention to black handsets. Ropes confine the throngs to a path around the outside of the monument. (☎01980 624 715. Open daily June-Aug. 9am-7pm; mid-Mar. to May and Sept. to mid-Oct. 9:30am-6pm; mid-Oct. to mid-Mar. 9:30am-4pm. £5.90, students £4.40.) For those looking for less touristy stone circles, the neighboring megaliths at **Avebury** are a good alternative. Dating from 2500 BC, Avebury's stones are older and larger than their favored cousins at Stonehenge. Wilts & Dorset **buses** (☎336 855) connect from Salisbury's center and train station, and run to both sites (#3, 5, and 6; 40min.-2hr., round-trip £4-7). An **Explorer** ticket (£6.50) allows travel all day on any bus. The closest lodgings are in **Salisbury** (see above).

BATH ☎01225

Bath (pop. 83,000) has been a must-see for travelers since AD 43, when the Romans built an elaborate complex to house the town's curative waters. Roman Bath flourished for 400 years, its hot (47°C) springs making the city a pilgrimage site for religious miracles, physical healing, and, later, social climbing. The **Roman Baths Museum,** Stall St., showcases the complexity of Roman engineering, which included central heating and internal plumbing. (☎447 785; www.romanbaths.co.uk. Open daily July-Aug. 9am-10pm; Mar.-June and Sept.-Oct. 9am-6pm; Nov.-Feb. 9:30am-5:30pm. Audio tour included. £10-11, students £8.50. Joint ticket with Museum of Costume £13/11.) The towering **Bath Abbey** fulfills masons George and William Vertue's oath to build "the goodliest vault in all England and France." (☎422 462. Open Apr.-Oct. M-Sa 9am-6pm, Su 1-2:30pm and 4:30-5:30pm; Nov.-Mar. M-Sa 9am-4pm, Su between services. Requested donation £2.50.) Walk up Gay St. to **The Circus,** a classic Georgian block where Thomas Gainsborough lived. Left of The Circus, the **Museum of Costume,** on Bennet St., hosts a dazzling parade of 400 years of catwalk fashions, from 17th-century silver tissue garments to J.Lo's racy Versace ensemble. (☎477 785; www.museumofcostume.co.uk. Open daily Mar.-Oct. 11am-5pm; Nov.-Feb. 11am-4pm. £6.50, students £5.50.) From The Circus, proceed up Brock St. to the **Royal Crescent,** a half-moon of stately 18th-century townhouses bordering **Royal Victoria Park.**

The extremely convenient **St. Christopher's Inn ❷**, 16 Green St., has clean beds and an ideal downstairs pub. (☎481 444; www.st-christophers.co.uk. Internet £3 per hr. Dorms £16-20. Discount for online booking. MC/V.) The **International Backpackers Hostel ❶,** 13 Pierrepont St., up the street from the train station and three blocks from the baths, is a laid-back backpackers' lair with music-themed rooms. (☎446 787. Luggage storage £1 per bag. Laundry £2.50. Internet £2 per hr. Reception 8am-midnight. Check-out 10:30am. Dorms Su-Th £13, F-Sa £14; doubles £35; triples £53. Room deposit £5. MC/V.) Find exotic vegetarian dishes at **Demuths Restaurant ❸,** 2 N. Parade Passage. (☎446 059; www.demuths.co.uk. Entrees £11-16. Open Su-F 10am-5pm and 6-10pm, Sa 9:30am-5:30pm and 6-11pm. Reserve ahead in summer. MC/V.) Next to Green Park Station there's a Sainsbury's **supermarket**. (☎444 737. Open M-F 8am-10pm, Sa 7am-10pm, Su 10am-4pm.)

Trains leave from Dorchester St. for: Birmingham (2hr., 1 per hr., £30); Bristol (15min., 3 per hr., £5); London Paddington (1½hr., 2 per hr., £36); London Waterloo (2-2½hr., 2 per day, £34). National Express **buses** (☎08705 808 080) run from Manvers St. to London (3½hr., every 1½hr., £15) and Oxford (2¼hr., 1 per day, £8.40). The train and bus stations are near the south end of Manvers St.; walk toward the town center and turn left on York St. to reach the **tourist office,** in Abbey Chambers. (☎08704 446 442; http://visitbath.co.uk. Open May-Sept. M-Sa 9:30am-6pm, Su 10am-4pm; Oct.-Apr. M-Sa 9:30am-5pm, Su 10am-4pm.) **Postal Code:** BA1 1AJ.

GLASTONBURY ☎01458

The reputed birthplace of Christianity in England, an Arthurian hot spot, and home to England's biggest summer music festival, Glastonbury (pop. 6900) is at a quirky intersection of mysticism and pop culture. Legend has it that Joseph of Arimathea founded the massive **Glastonbury Abbey,** on Magdalene St., in AD 63. Though the abbey was destroyed during the English Reformation, the colossal pile of ruins and its accompanying museum evoke the abbey's original grandeur. (☎832 267; www.glastonburyabbey.com. Open daily June-Aug. 9am-6pm; Sept.-May 10am-dusk. £4.50, students £4.) The 160m **Glastonbury Tor** is reputedly the site where King Arthur sleeps until his country needs him. To reach the Tor, turn right at the top of High St. onto Lambrook, which becomes Chilkwell St.; turn left onto Wellhouse Ln. and follow the path up the hill, looking out for cow dung. (Open year-round. Free.) The annual **Glastonbury Festival** is the biggest and best of Britain's summer music festivals. The week-long at the end of June has featured some of the world's biggest bands. (Tickets ☎834 596; www.glastonburyfestivals.co.uk.)

At **Glastonbury Backpackers ❷**, 4 Market Pl., in the center of town at the corner of Magdalene St. and High St., friendly staff and a lively cafe-bar complement the superb locale. (☎833 353; www.glastonburybackpackers.com. Internet £5 per hr. Check-in 4:30-11pm. Dorms £12; doubles £30, with bath £35. MC/V.) **Heritage Fine Foods,** 32-34 High St., has groceries. (☎831 003. Open M-W 7am-9pm, Th-Sa 9am-10pm, Su 8am-9pm.) National Express **buses** (☎08705 808 080) run from town hall to London (4¼hr., 1 per hr., £22) via Bristol. From the bus stop, turn right on High St. to find the **tourist office,** the Tribunal, 9 High St., which books rooms for a £3 fee plus a 10% deposit and sells an accommodation list for £1. (☎832 954; www.glastonburytic.co.uk. Open Apr.-Sept. Su-Th 10am-5pm, F-Sa 10am-5:30pm; Oct.-Mar. Su-Th 10am-4pm, F-Sa 10am-5:30pm.) **Postal Code:** BA6 9HG.

CHANNEL ISLANDS

The Channel Islands are composed of Jersey, Guernsey, and seven smaller islands. Situated in the waters 128km south of England and 64km west of France, the islands offer visitors a fusion of cultures and a touch of (expensive) elegance.

FERRIES TO THE CHANNEL ISLANDS. **Condor Ferries** (☎01202 207 216) runs one early and one late ferry per day from Poole and Weymouth, as well as St-Malo, FRA, docking at St. Peter Port, Guernsey, and Elizabeth Harbor at St. Helier, Jersey. Times, frequencies, and ticket prices are affected by the season and the tides. Call ☎0845 124 2003 or check www.condorferries.com for up-to-date schedules. ISIC holders are eligible for a 20% discount; ask before purchasing a ticket.

THE REAL DEAL. Though part of the UK, Jersey and Guernsey are essentially self-governing nations. The British pound is the official currency, but ATMs dish out Jersey or Guernsey pounds. These local pounds are on par with their British counterparts, but are not accepted outside the Channel Islands; you will have to exchange them upon returning to the mainland. Toward the end of your stay in the islands, make sure to ask local merchants to give you change in British pounds. Another quirk to keep in mind is that your mobile phone carrier may think you are in France (or not recognize you at all) and charge accordingly.

JERSEY. The largest of the Channel Islands, Jersey offers the teeming city center of St. Helier, gorgeous countryside, and rocky coastlines with extreme tides. Perhaps the most memorable of Jersey's sights is the gigantic **Mont Orgueil** castle on Gorey Pier. Climb to the top for a spectacular panorama. (☎01534 853 292. Open daily Apr.-Oct. 10am-6pm; Nov.-Mar. 10am-dusk. £6, students £5.20.) Across from Liberation Sq., by St. Helier Marina, the **Maritime Museum** features hands-on exhibits about the seas surrounding the island. (☎01534 811 043. Open daily Apr.-Oct. 10am-5pm; Nov.-Mar. 10am-4pm. £6, students £5.) In the fall, Jersey plays host to **Tennerfest,** challenging local restaurants to come up with the best £10 menu. Check out www.jersey.com for more on festivals throughout the year. The only hostel on the island is the beautiful **YHA Jersey (HI) ❷**, Pouclée et des Quatre, chemin St-Martin. Take bus #3A from St. Helier (20min., 1 per hr.); after 5:45pm take #1 to Gorey, walk up the hill, cross the road and turn left up the larger hill. 0870 770 6130. Breakfast included. Reception 7-10am and 5-11pm. Open Feb.-Nov. daily; Dec.-Jan. F-Sa. Dorms £18, under 18 £13. MC/V.) Chic furnishings and ample people-watching await at the **Beach House ❷,** on Gorey Pier. (☎01534 859 902. Wraps £6. Salmon £9. Open M 11am-6pm, Tu-Su 12:30-3:30pm and 6:30-9:30pm. MC/V.) An able **bus** system makes travel around Jersey painless. From Weighbridge terminal in St. Helier, **Connex** buses travel around the island. (☎01534 877 772; www.mybus.je. £0.90-1.60.) **Easylink** also offers a hop-on/hop-off tour service from the Terminal. (☎01534 876 418. Buses run Su-F. 1-day Explorer ticket £7.50, 3-day £18, 5-day £23.) Exit the harbor, head left, and follow signs to the Esplanade for the **tourist office,** Liberation Sq., St. Helier. (☎01534 500 700; www.jersey.com. Open in summer M-Sa 8:30am-7pm, Su 8:30am-2:15pm. Winter hours vary.)

GUERNSEY. Smaller in size but not in charm, Guernsey flaunts its French roots more than neighboring Jersey—cultural fusion is evident in the architecture, cuisine, and speech of the locals. **Hauteville House,** St. Peter Port, was Victor Hugo's home during his exile from France. It remains virtually unaltered from the days when he wrote *Les Misérables* here. The house is full of hidden inscriptions and mantles made by Hugo from recycled furniture. (☎01481 721 911. Open May-early Oct. M-Sa 10am-4pm; Apr. noon-4pm. £4, students £2, under 20 free.)

For lodgings near town with views of Sark and Herm, try **St. George's Hotel ❹,** St. George's Esplanade, St. Peter Port. (☎721 027. Breakfast included. £33 per person; Aug. £35. MC/V.) **Christies ❸,** Le Pollet, has an airy French bistro serving local seafood salads and sandwiches. (☎726 624. Entrees £4.50-15. Open daily noon-2:30pm and 6-10:30pm. MC/V.) Island Coachways (☎01481 720 210; www.buses.gg) **buses** operate all over the island and offer tours from May to September; call the office for fares and information. Routes #7 and 7a circle the coast every hour for £0.50. A **tourist office** is near the ferry at St. Peter Port; its larger office is located across the harbor on North Esplanade. The staff distributes maps and books rooms for a £2 fee plus a 10% deposit. *Naturally Guernsey* is a helpful guide to the island. (☎01481 723 552; www.guernseytouristboard.com. Open in summer M-Sa 9am-6pm, Su 9am-1pm; winter M-F 9am-5pm, Sa 9am-4pm.)

THE CORNISH COAST

With lush cliffsides stretching out into the Atlantic, Cornwall's terrain doesn't feel quite like England. Years ago, the Celts fled westward in the face of Saxon conquest; today, the migration to Cornwall continues in the form of artists, vacationers, and surfers. Though the Cornish language is no longer spoken, the area remains protective of its distinctive past and its ubiquitous pasties.

NEWQUAY. Known as "the new California," Newquay (NEW-key; pop. 20,000) is an incongruous slice of surfer culture in the middle of Cornwall. Atlantic winds descend with a vengeance on **Fistral Beach,** creating arguably the best surfing conditions in Europe. **Sunset Surf Shop,** 106 Fore St., rents equipment and books lessons. (☎877 624. Board rental £5-10 per day, £12-25 per 3 days, £25-40 per week. Wetsuits or bodyboards £4-5/10-12/20. Open Apr.-Oct. daily 9am-6pm.) For tamer waters, head to **Lusty Glaze** and **Tolcarne Beaches.** Enjoy sea views at **Original Backpackers ❷,** 16 Beachfield Ave. (☎874 668. Laundry £3. Dorms £11-17; low season £10. MC/V.) Newquay specializes in cheap take-out; sit-down food tends to be costly. For cheap eats, head to pubs or the Somerfield **supermarket** at the end of Fore St. (☎876 006. Open M-Th and Sa 8am-8pm, F 8am-9pm, Su 11am-4pm; July-Aug. closes 1hr. later.) At night, watch out for the stag and hen parties; head to the shore for more relaxed venues. Surfers and locals enjoy **The Koola,** 8-10 Beach Rd., one of Newquay's classiest clubs. (☎873 415; www.thekoola.com. Open daily.)

Trains (☎08457 484 950) from Newquay go to Penzance (1½hr., 12 per day, £11) and Plymouth (50min., 15 per day, £8.60). National Express **buses** (☎08705 808 080) leave Manor Rd. for London (7hr., 2-4 per day, £33). The **tourist office** is on Marcus Hill, a few blocks toward the city center from the train station. It has free maps and books accommodations for a £4 fee plus a 20% deposit. (☎854 020; www.newquay.co.uk. Open June-Sept. M-Sa 9:30am-5:30pm, Su 9:30am-12:30pm; Oct.-May reduced hours, closed Su.)

PENZANCE. Originally a sleepy resort village, Penzance now has a true penchant for pirates. A Benedictine monastery, **St. Michael's Mount,** marks the spot where the archangel St. Michael is said to have appeared in AD 495. The interior is modest, but the grounds are lovely and the views are well worth the 30-story climb. (☎710 507. Open Apr.-Oct. Su-F 10:30am-5:30pm; Nov.-Mar. by appointment only. £6, children £3.) During low tide, visitors can walk to the Mount; during high tide, take the ferry (£1.20). Penzance boasts an impressive number of art galleries; pick up the *Cornwall Galleries Guide* (£1) at the tourist office. Walk 30min. from the bus station, or take Sunset Coach #5 or 6 to the Pirate Pub and walk 10min. up Castle Horneck Rd. to reach the **YHA Penzance (HI)** ❶, Castle Horneck. Housed in an 18th-century mansion, the hostel has a friendly staff and clean rooms. (☎362 666. Internet £4.20 per hr. Lockout 10am-noon. Dorms £15.50, under 18 £13; doubles £35. Tent sites £7. MC/V.) **Admiral Benbow,** 46 Chapel St., is a pub decorated with paraphernalia from local shipwrecks. (☎363 448. Pints £2.20. Open M-Sa 11am-11pm, Su noon-10:30pm.) **Trains** leave Wharf Rd., at the head of Albert Pier, for London (5½hr., 7 per day, £68) and Newquay (3hr., 8 per day, £11). **Buses** also leave Wharf Rd. for London (8½hr., 7 per day, £34). The **tourist office** is between the train and bus stations on Station Rd. (☎362 207; www.visit-westcornwall.com. Open May-Sept. M-Sa 9am-5:30pm, Su 9am-1pm; Oct.-Apr. M-F 9am-5pm, Sa 10am-1pm.)

EAST ANGLIA AND THE MIDLANDS

The rich farmland and watery flats of East Anglia stretch northeast from London, cloaking the counties of Cambridgeshire, Norfolk, Suffolk, and parts of Essex. Mention of The Midlands inevitably evokes grim urban images, but there is a unique heritage and quiet grandeur to this smokestacked landscape. Even Birmingham, the region's much-maligned center, has its saving graces, among them lively nightlife and the Cadbury chocolate empire.

OXFORD ☎01865

Sprawling college grounds and 12th-century spires mark this Holy Grail of British academia. Nearly a millennium of scholarship at Oxford (pop. 145,000) has educated world leaders, including 25 British prime ministers. Despite the crowds of tourists, Oxford has an irrepressible grandeur and pockets of tranquility: the basement room of Blackwell's Bookshop, the impeccable galleries of the Ashmolean, and the perfectly maintained quadrangles of the university's 39 colleges.

TRANSPORTATION AND PRACTICAL INFORMATION. Trains (☎08457 484 950) run from Botley Rd., down Park End, to: Birmingham (1¼hr., 2 per hr., £19); Glasgow (7hr., 1 per hr., £70); London Paddington (1hr., 2-4 per hr., £9.50-19); Manchester (3hr., 1-2 per hr., £21-42). Stagecoach **buses** (☎772 250; www.stagecoachbus.com) run to Cambridge (3hr., 2 per hr., £6) and London (1¾hr.; 3-5 per hr.; £12, students £10). Oxford Bus Company (☎785 400; www.oxfordbus.co.uk)

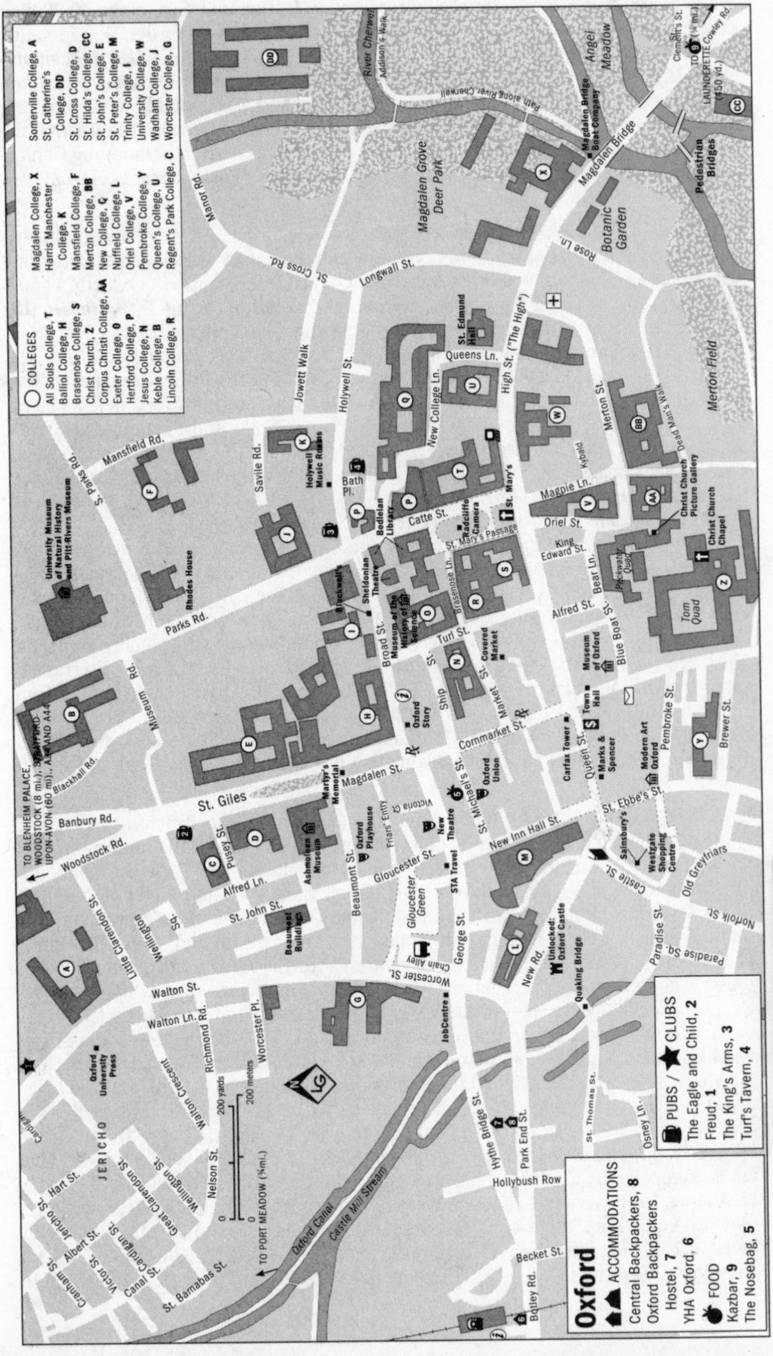
Oxford
ACCOMMODATIONS
Central Backpackers, 8
Oxford Backpackers Hostel, 7
YHA Oxford, 6
FOOD
Kazbar, 9
The Nosebag, 5
PUBS / CLUBS
The Eagle and Child, 2
Freud, 1
The King's Arms, 3
Turf's Tavern, 4
COLLEGES
All Souls College, T
Balliol College, H
Brasenose College, S
Christ Church, Z
Corpus Christi College, AA
Exeter College, O
Hertford College, P
Jesus College, N
Keble College, B
Lincoln College, R
Magdalen College, X
Harris Manchester College, K
Mansfield College, F
Merton College, BB
New College, Q
Nuffield College, L
Oriel College, V
Pembroke College, Y
Queen's College, U
Regent's Park College, C
Somerville College, A
St. Catherine's College, DD
St. Cross College, D
St. Hilda's College, CC
St. John's College, E
St. Peter's College, M
Trinity College, I
University College, W
Wadham College, J
Worcester College, G
TO BLENHEIM PALACE, WOODSTOCK (8 mi.), STRATFORD-UPON-AVON (60 mi.), A34 AND A44
TO PORT MEADOW (¾mi.)
TO 9 (¼ mi.) LAUNDERETTE (450 yd.)
200 yards
200 meters
University Museum of Natural History and Pitt-Rivers Museum
Rhodes House
Holywell Music Rooms
Sheldonian Theatre
Bodleian Library
Blackwell's
Museum of the History of Science
Radcliffe Camera
St. Mary's
St. Edmund Hall
Christ Church Picture Gallery
Christ Church Chapel
Tom Quad
Peckwater Quad
Covered Market
Museum of Oxford
Town Hall
Carfax Tower
Marks & Spencer
Modern Art Oxford
Sainsbury's
Westgate Shopping Centre
Oxford Story
Martyr's Memorial
Ashmolean Museum
Oxford Playhouse
New Theatre
Oxford Union
STA Travel
Beaumont Buildings
Gloucester Green
Unlocked: Oxford Castle
Quaking Bridge
JobCentre
Oxford University Press
JERICHO
Magdalen Grove Deer Park
Magdalen Bridge Boat Company
Magdalen Bridge
Pedestrian Bridges
Botanic Garden
Angel Meadow
Merton Field
River Cherwell
Path along River Cherwell
Addison's Walk
Oxford Canal
Castle Mill Stream
Woodstock Rd.
Banbury Rd.
St. Giles
Blackhall Rd.
Parks Rd.
S. Parks Rd.
Mansfield Rd.
Museum Rd.
Savile Rd.
Holywell St.
Jowett Walk
Longwall St.
St. Cross Rd.
Manor Rd.
Broad St.
Catte St.
New College Ln.
Queens Ln.
High St. ("The High")
Rose Ln.
Merton St.
Magpie Ln.
Oriel St.
King Edward St.
Kybald
Dead Man's Walk
Bear Ln.
Alfred St.
Blue Boar St.
St. Mary's Passage
Brasenose Ln.
Turl St.
Ship St.
Market St.
Cornmarket St.
Magdalen St.
St. Michael's St.
New Inn Hall St.
Queen St.
St. Ebbe's St.
Pembroke St.
Brewer St.
Castle St.
Old Greyfriars
Norfolk St.
Paradise St.
Paradise Sq.
New Rd.
George St.
Gloucester St.
Friars' Entry
Victoria Ct.
Beaumont St.
Pusey St.
Alfred Ln.
St. John St.
Wellington Sq.
Little Clarendon St.
Walton St.
Walton Ln.
Richmond Rd.
Worcester Pl.
Worcester St.
Chain Alley
Walton Crescent
Nelson St.
Wellington St.
Great Clarendon St.
Cardigan St.
Canal St.
St. Barnabas St.
Victor St.
Albert St.
Jericho St.
Hart St.
Cranham St.
Hythe Bridge St.
Park End St.
Hollybush Row
St. Thomas St.
Osney Ln.
Becket St.
Botley Rd.
Bath Pl.
St. Clement's St.
Cowley Rd.

BRITAIN

sends **buses** from Gloucester Green to: London Gatwick (1¾hr.; every 15-20min.; £11, students £9); stops along the way include Victoria, High Street, St. Clements. The **tourist office,** 15-16 Broad St., books rooms for a £4 fee plus a 10% deposit and offers 2hr. walking tours for £6.50. (☎726 871; www.visitoxford.org. Open June-July M-Sa 9:30am-5pm, Su 10am-4pm, Easter-May and Aug.-Oct. M-Sa 9:30am-5pm, Su 10am-3:30pm; Nov.-Easter M-Sa 9:30am-5pm.) You can access the **Internet** for free at the **Oxford Central Library,** on Queen St. near the Westgate Shopping Center. (☎815 549. Open M-Th 9:15am-7pm, F-Sa 9:15am-5pm.) **Postal Code:** OX1 1ZZ.

ACCOMMODATIONS AND FOOD. Reserve at least a week ahead June to September. If it's late and you're homeless, call the **Oxford Association of Hotels and Guest Houses** (East Oxford ☎721 561, West Oxford 862 138, North Oxford 244 691, South Oxford 244 268). Turn right from the train station for the **YHA Oxford (HI) ❷,** 2A Botley Rd., which features quiet rooms and a kitchen. (☎727 275. Breakfast included. Lockers £1. Towels 50p. Laundry £3. Internet £4.20 per hr. Dorms £21, under 18 £16; doubles £46. £3 student discount. MC/V.) The **Oxford Backpackers Hostel ❶,** 9A Hythe Bridge St., between the bus and train stations, fosters a social air with a cheap bar, pool table, and music. (☎721 761. Passport required. Laundry £2.50. Internet £2 per hr. Dorms £14; quads £16. MC/V.) The newest hostel in town, **Central Backpackers ❷,** 13 Park End St., has bright rooms and a rooftop terrace. (☎242 288. Internet available. Reception 8am-11pm. Check-out 11am. 4-bed dorms £18; 6-bed female or 8-bed co-ed dorms £16; 12-bed dorms £14. MC/V.)

Students fed up with bland college food and tourists on the go are easily seduced by a bevy of budget options. If cooking for yourself, try **Gloucester Green Market,** behind the bus station, for cheap treats. (Open W 8am-3:30pm.) The **Covered Market** between Market St. and Carfax has fresh produce and bread. (Open M-Sa 7am-8pm, Su 11am-5pm.) Look for after-hours **kebab vans,** usually at Broad, High, Queen, and St. Aldate's St. **Kazbar ❶,** 25-27 Cowley Rd., is a Mediterranean tapas bar with Spanish-style decor. (☎202 920. Tapas £2.20-4.75. Open M-F 4-11pm, Sa-Su noon-midnight. AmEx/MC/V.) Great vegetarian and vegan options can be found at **The Nosebag ❷,** 6-8 St. Michael's St., an eclectic cafeteria. (☎721 033. Open M-Th 9:30am-10pm, F-Sa 9:30am-10:30pm, Su 9:30am-9pm. AmEx/MC/V.)

SIGHTS. The tourist office sells a map (£1.25) and the *Welcome to Oxford* guide (£1), which lists the visiting hours of Oxford's **colleges.** Don't bother trying to sneak in after hours; even after hiding your pack and copy of *Let's Go,* bouncers, affectionately known as "bulldogs," will squint their eyes and kick you out. Just down St. Aldate's St. from Carfax, **Christ Church College** has Oxford's grandest quad and most distinguished alumni, including 13 former prime ministers. The dining hall and Tom Quad are also shooting locations for the *Harry Potter* movies. The **Christ Church Chapel** functions as the university's cathedral. It was here that the Rev. Charles Dodgson (better known as Lewis Carroll) first met Alice Liddell, the dean's daughter; the White Rabbit is immortalized in the hall's stained glass. **Tom Quad** takes its name from Great Tom, the seven-ton bell in Tom Tower that has faithfully rung 101 (the original number of students) strokes at 9:05pm (the original undergraduate curfew) every evening since 1682. (☎286 573; www.chch.ox.ac.uk. Open M-Sa 9am-5:30 pm, Su 1-5:30pm. Chapel services M-F 6pm; Su 8, 10, 11:15am, 6pm. £4.70, students £3.70.) J. R. R. Tolkien lectured at **Merton College,** Merton St., whose library houses the first printed Welsh Bible. Nearby **St. Alban's Quad** has some of the university's best gargoyles. (☎276 310; www.merton.ox.ac.uk. Open M-F 2-4pm, Sa-Su 10am-4pm. Free.) Soot-blackened **University College,** High St., was built in 1249 and vies with Merton for the title of oldest, claiming Alfred the Great as its founder. (☎276 602; www.univ.ox.ac.uk. Open to tours only.) South of Oriel, **Corpus Christi College** surrounds a sundialed quad. The garden gate here was built for visits between Charles I and his queen, who lived nearby during the Civil Wars. (☎276 700; www.ccc.ox.ac.uk. Open daily 1:30-4:30pm.) The prestigious **All Souls College,** at the corner of High and Cattle St., admits only the best—and stores only the best in its wine cellar. (☎279 379; www.allsouls.ox.ac.uk. Open M-F 2-4:30pm.) At **The Queen's College,** High St., a boar's head graces the table at Christmas to commemorate a student who, attacked by a boar on the outskirts of town, choked the animal to death with a volume of Aristotle. (☎279 120; www.queens.ox.ac.uk. Open to tours only.) With extensive grounds, flower-edged quads, and a deer park, **Magdalen College** (MAUD-lin), on High St. near the Cherwell, is considered Oxford's handsomest. Oscar Wilde is one of the college's alumni. (☎276 000; www.magd.ox.ac.uk. Open daily July-Sept. noon-6pm; Oct.-Mar. 1pm-dusk; Apr.-June 1-6pm. £3, students £2.)

The grand **Ashmolean Museum,** on Beaumont St., houses works by van Gogh, Matisse, Michelangelo, Monet, and da Vinci. Opened in 1683, the Ashmolean was Britain's first public museum and still possesses one of the country's finest collections. (☎278 000. Open in summer Tu-W and F-Sa 10am-5pm, Th 10am-7pm, Su noon-5pm; winter Tu-Sa 10am-5pm, Su noon-5pm. Free. Tours £2.) **Bodleian Library,** on Broad St., is Oxford's main reading and research library with over five million books and 50,000 manuscripts. It receives a copy of every book printed in Great Britain, but no one has ever been allowed to check one out. (☎277 000; www.bodley.ox.ac.uk. Tours leave from the Divinity School in the main quadrangle; in summer M-Sa 4 per day, winter 2 per day. Open in summer M-F 9am-7pm, Sa 9am-1pm; winter M-F 9am-10pm, Sa 9am-1pm; Tours £4, audio tours £2.) Next door on Broad St. is the **Sheldonian Theatre,** an auditorium designed by a teenage Christopher Wren. Graduation ceremonies, conducted in Latin, take place in the Sheldonian, as do world-class opera performances. (☎277 299. Open July-Aug. M-Sa 10am-12:30pm and 2-4:30pm, Su 11am-4pm; June and Sept.-Oct. 10am-12:30pm and 2-4:30pm; Nov.-May M-Sa 10am-12:30pm and 2-3:30pm. £2, students £1.) You could browse the 10km of bookshelves for days at **Blackwell's Bookstore,** 53 Broad St., a local favorite. (☎792 792. Open M and W-Sa 9am-6pm, Tu 9:30am-6pm, Su 11am-5pm.)

ENTERTAINMENT AND NIGHTLIFE. **Punting** on the River Thames or on the River Cherwell (CHAR-wul) is a traditional Oxford pastime. **Magdalen Bridge Boat Company,** just under Magdalen Bridge, rents boats. (☎202 643. Open Mar.-Oct. daily 10am-dusk. £12 per hr.; £30 deposit and ID required. Cash and checks only.) Bring along your own wine or champagne for a floating toast.

Music and drama at Oxford are cherished arts. *This Month in Oxford* and *Daily Information* (www.dailyinfo.co.uk), both available at the tourist office for free, list upcoming events. **Pubs** far outnumber colleges in Oxford. Many are so small that a single band of students will squeeze out other patrons—luckily, there's usually another place just around the corner, so be ready to crawl. Known to students as "the Turf," **Turf's Tavern,** 4 Bath Pl., off Holywell St., is a wildly popular 13th-century pub tucked in the alley of an alley, against the ruins of the city wall. (☎243 235. Open M-Sa 11am-11pm, Su noon-10:30pm. Kitchen closes 7:30pm. AmEx/MC/V.) Merry masses head to back rooms at **The King's Arms,** 40 Holywell St., Oxford's unofficial student union. (☎242 369. Open M-Sa 10:30am-11pm, Su 10:30-10:30pm. MC/V.) **The Eagle and Child,** 49 St. Giles soothed the parched throats of C. S. Lewis and J. R. R. Tolkien for 25 years. *The Chronicles of Narnia* and *The Hobbit* were first read aloud here. (☎302 925. Open M-Sa 11am-11pm, Su noon-10:30pm. Kitchen closes M-F 10pm, Sa-Su 9pm. AmEx/MC/V.) After happy hour at the pubs, head to the clubs at **Walton Street** or **Cowley Road.** In a former church, **Freud,** 119 Walton St., is a cafe by day and cocktail bar by night. (☎311 171. Open M-Tu and Su 11am-midnight, W 11am-1am, Th-Sa 11am-2am. MC/V.)

STRATFORD-UPON-AVON ☎ 01789

William Shakespeare is the area's industry, and proprietors tout a dozen-odd properties linked, however remotely, to the Bard. Stratford's Will-centered sights are best seen before the daytrippers arrive at 11am, or after 4pm when the crowds disperse. Diehard fans can buy the **All Five Houses** ticket for admission to the official Shakespeare properties: Anne Hathaway's Cottage, Mary Arden's House and Countryside Museum, Hall's Croft, New Place and Nash's House, and Shakespeare's Birthplace. (Tickets available from any house. £14, students £12.) The **Three In-Town Houses** pass covers the latter three. (£11, students £9.) **Shakespeare's Birthplace,** on Henley St., is part period re-creation and part exhibit of Shakespeare's life and works. (☎ 201 822. Open in summer M-Sa 9am-5pm, Su 9:30am-5pm; mid-season daily 10am-5pm; winter M-Sa 10am-4pm, Su 10:30am-4pm. £7, students £5.50.) **New Place,** on High St., was Stratford's finest home when Shakespeare bought it in 1597; now only the foundation remains. View it from **Nash's House,** on Chapel St., which belonged to the first husband of Shakespeare's granddaughter. Pay homage to the Bard's **grave** in the **Holy Trinity Church,** on Trinity St. (☎ 266 316. Open Apr.-Sept. M-Sa 8:30am-6pm, Su noon-5pm; low season reduced hours. Requested donation £1.) The world-famous ■**Royal Shakespeare Company** sells over one million tickets each year. Tickets for the **Royal Shakespeare Theatre,** the **Swan Theatre,** and **The Courtyard Theatre** are sold through the box office in the Royal Shakespeare Theatre, on the Waterside; beginning in early 2007, the main-stage and the box office for the RSC will move to The Courtyard Theatre. £5 student standing-room-only tickets offer spectacular views. (Info ☎ 403 444, tickets 0870 609 1110; www.rsc.org.uk. Open M-Sa 9:30am-8pm. Tickets £5-40. Students and under 25 eligible for advance half-price tickets for M-W performances, same-day tickets for Th-Su. Standbys £12-15.)

B&Bs line **Evesham Place, Evesham Road, Grove Road,** and **Shipston Road,** but reservations are a must. ■**Carlton Guest House ❸,** 22 Evesham Pl., has spacious rooms and friendly service. (☎ 293 548. £20-26 per person. Cash only.) Classy yet cozy, **The Oppo ❸,** 13 Sheep St., gets rave reviews for its varied cuisine. (☎ 269 980. Transcendent lasagna £9. Open M-Th noon-2pm and 5:30-9:30pm, F-Sa noon-2pm and 5-11pm, Su noon-2pm and 6-9:30pm. MC/V.) A Somerfield **supermarket** is in Town Sq. (☎ 292 604. Open M-W 8am-7pm, Th-Sa 8am-8pm, Su 10am-4pm.) RSC actors make almost nightly appearances at ■**Dirty Duck Pub,** 66 Waterside. (☎ 297 312. Open M-Sa 11am-11pm, Su noon-10:30pm.) **Trains** (☎ 08457 484 950) arrive at Station Rd., off Alcester Rd., from Birmingham (50min., 1 per hr., £5.20) and London Paddington (2¼hr., every 2hr., £37). National Express (☎ 08705 808 080) runs **buses** to London (3hr., 3 per day, £14). Local Stratford Blue bus #X20 stops at Wood and Bridge St., and goes to Birmingham (1¼hr., 1 per hr., £4). The **tourist office,** Bridgefoot, across Warwick Rd., books rooms for a £3 charge and a 10% deposit. (☎ 08701 607 930. Open Apr.-Sept. M-Sa 9am-5:30pm, Su 10:30am-4:30pm; Oct.-Mar. M-Sa 9am-5pm.) Surf the **Internet** at **Cyber Junction,** 28 Greenhill St. (☎ 263 400. £4 per hr., students £3.50. Open M-F 10am-6pm, Sa 10:30am-5:30pm, Su 11am-5pm.) **Postal Code:** CV37 6PU.

THE COTSWOLDS

"Cotswolds" means "sheep enclosure in rolling hillsides," and that pretty much covers it. Grazing sheep and cattle roam 2000 sq. km of postcard-ready hillsides linking heavily touristed towns.

■ ? **TRANSPORTATION AND PRACTICAL INFORMATION.** Public transportation to and in the Cotswolds is scarce; planning ahead is a must, as some locations may be impossible to reach by public transport. Useful gateway cities are Bath, Bristol, Cheltenham, Oxford, and Stratford-upon-Avon. **Moreton-in-Marsh,** one of the bigger villages, runs **trains** to London (1½hr., every 1-2hr., £22) via Oxford (30min., £8.20). It's far easier to reach the Cotswolds by **bus.** The Cheltenham tourist office's free *Getting There* pamphlet has detailed bus information. *Explore the Cotswolds by Public Transport*, available for free at village tourist offices, has bus frequency and routes; get timetables from the tourist office at your starting point. Pulham's Coaches (☎01451 820 369) run from Cheltenham to Moreton-in-Marsh (#801; 1hr., M-Sa 7 per day, £1.75) via Stow-on-the-Wold (50min., £1.70).

Local roads are perfect for **biking.** Rent bikes at **The Toy Shop** on High St. in Moreton-in-Marsh. (☎01608 650 756. £12 per ½-day, £14 per day. Open M and W-Sa 9am-1pm and 2-5pm.) Visitors can also experience the Cotswolds as the English have for centuries, by treading the well-worn footpaths from village to village. The **Cotswold Way,** spanning over 160km from Bath to Chipping Camden, offers lovely vistas of hills and dales. Contact the **National Trails Office** (☎01865 810 224) for details on this and other trails. The free *Cotswold Events* booklet lists everything from music festivals and antique markets to cheese-rolling and wool-sack races. The **Cotswold Discovery Tour** is a full-day bus tour that starts in Bath and visits five of the most scenic and touristed villages. (☎09067 112 000; www.madmax.abel.co.uk. Apr.-Oct. Tu, Th, Su 9am-5:15pm. £25.)

WINCHCOMBE, MORETON-IN-MARSH, AND STOW-ON-THE-WOLD. Ten kilometers north of Cheltenham on A46, **Sudeley Castle,** once the manor of King Ethelred the Unready, crowns the town of **Winchcombe.** (☎01242 602 308; www.sudeleycastle.co.uk. 10:30am-5pm. £7.20, students £6.20.) The Winchcombe **tourist office** is on High St., next to Town Hall. (☎01242 602 925. Open Apr.-Oct. M-Sa 10am-5pm, Su 10am-4pm; Nov.-Mar. Sa-Su 10am-4pm.) With a train station, relatively frequent bus service, and a bike shop, **Moreton-in-Marsh** is a convenient base for exploring the Cotswolds. Its **tourist office** is in the District Council Building on High St. (☎01608 650 881. Open M 8:45am-4pm, Tu-Th 8:45am-5:15pm, F 8:45am-4:45pm, Sa 10am-1pm.) **Warwick House B&B ❸,** on London Rd., has an energetic owner and a bevy of perks. Follow A44 east out of town toward Oxford for 10min; the hostel is on the left. (☎01608 650 733; www.snoozeandsizzle.com. Free pickup from train station. £30-35 per person. Cash only.) **Stow-on-the-Wold,** the self-proclaimed "Heart of the Cotswolds," sits atop a hill, offering visitors fine views and a sense of the Cotswold pace of life. The **tourist office** (☎01451 831 082) is in Hollis House on The Square. The **YHA (HI) ❷,** beside the tourist office, has bright rooms in a beautiful building. (☎01451 830 497. Laundry £3. Reception 8-10am and 5-10pm. Lockout 10am-5pm. Curfew 11pm. Reserve 1 month ahead. Open mid-Feb. to Oct. daily; Nov.-Dec. F-Sa. Dorms £15, under 18 £11. AmEx/MC/V.) A Tesco **supermarket** is on Fosse Way. (Open M-F 6am-midnight, Sa 6am-10pm, Su 10am-4pm.)

BIRMINGHAM ☎0121

Birmingham (pop. 1,000,000), second only to London in population, has a long-standing reputation as a grim, industrial metropolis. To counter this bleak stereotype, the city has revitalized its central district with a sure-fire visitor magnet: **shopping**—and lots of it. The massive Bullring, Europe's largest retail establishment, is the foundation of Birmingham's material-world makeover. Recognizable by the wavy, scaled Selfridges, the shopping center has more than 150 stores. (☎632 1500; www.bullring.co.uk. Open M-F 9:30am-8pm, Sa 9am-8pm, Su 11am-5pm.) Twelve minutes south of town by rail or bus lies **Cadbury World,** a cavity-inducing celebration of the famed chocolate empire. Take a train from New St. to Bournville, or bus #84 from the city center. (☎451 4159. Open Mar.-Oct. daily 10am-3pm; Nov.-Feb. Tu-Th and Sa-Su 10am-3pm. Reserve ahead. £12.50, students £10.) The **Birmingham International Jazz Festival** brings over 200 performers to town during the first two weeks of July. (☎454 7020; www.birminghamjazzfestival.com.)

Despite its size, Birmingham has no hostels, and inexpensive B&Bs are rare. Busy **Hagley Road** is your best bet. **Fountain Court Hotel ❹,** 339-343 Hagley Rd., offers rooms with bath and lounges. (☎429 1754; www.fountain-court.co.uk. Singles £49; doubles £75. AmEx/MC/V.) Get groceries from **Sainsbury's,** Martineau Pl., 17 Union St. (☎236 6496. Open M-Sa 7am-8pm, Su 11am-5pm.) **Broad Street** is teeming with trendy cafe-bars and clubs, and gets very rowdy on the weekends; as always, exercise caution at night. Pick up the bimonthly *What's On* to discover the latest hot spots. **Rococo Lounge,** 260 Broad St., has a large outdoor patio and retro-modern furnishings. (☎207 0283. Open Su-W 9am-1am, Th-Sa 9am-2am.) A thriving gay-friendly scene centers around **Lower Essex Street.**

Trains arrive at New St. Station (☎08457 484 950) from: Liverpool Lime St. (1½hr., 1 per hr., £20); London Euston (2hr., 2 per hr., £28); Piccadilly (2hr., 1 per hr., £21); Oxford (1¼hr., 2 per hr., £19). National Express **buses** (☎08705 808 080) arrive at Digbeth Station from: Cardiff (2½hr., 3 per day, £20); Liverpool (3hr., 4 per day, £13); London (3hr., 1 per hr., £14); Manchester (2½hr., every 2hr., £11). The **tourist office,** across from New St. Station, books rooms for a 10% deposit. (☎202 5099; www.beinbirmingham.com. Open M-Sa 9:30am-5:30pm, Su 10:30am-4:30pm.) **Postal Code:** B2 4TU.

CAMBRIDGE ☎01223

In contrast to museum-oriented, metropolitan Oxford, Cambridge is determined to retain its pastoral academic roots; the city manages, rather than encourages, visitors. Once the exclusive preserve of sons of privilege, the university now welcomes women and state-school pupils. During May Week (cleverly named to disguise the fact that the party occurs over two weeks in June), which marks term's end, Cambridge shakes off its reserve with Pimm's-soaked glee.

TRANSPORTATION AND PRACTICAL INFORMATION. **Trains** (☎08457 484 950) run from Station Rd. to London King's Cross (45min., 3 per hr., £18) and London Liverpool St. (1¼hr., 5 per hr., £18). From Drummer St., National Express **buses** (☎08705 808 080) go to London Victoria (3hr., 1 per hr., £10). Stagecoach Express buses (☎01604 676 060) go to Oxford (3hr., 1 per hr., from £6.50). Bicycles are the primary mode of transportation in Cambridge. Rent bikes at **Mike's Bikes,** 28 Mill Rd. (☎312 591. £10 per day plus £35 deposit. Open M-Sa 9am-6pm, Su 10am-4pm. MC/V.) The **tourist office,** south of Market Sq. on Wheeler St., books rooms for £3 plus a 10% deposit. (☎09065 862 526; www.visitcambridge.org. Open Easter-Oct. M-F 10am-5:30pm, Sa 10-5pm, Su 11am-4pm; Nov.-Easter M-F 10am-5:30pm, Sa 10am-5pm.) **Postal Code:** CB2 3AA.

ACCOMMODATIONS AND FOOD. Rooms are scarce in Cambridge, which makes prices high and quality low. Most **B&Bs** aren't in the town center, but those around **Portugal Street** and **Tenison Road** are close to the train station. Check the guide to accommodations (£0.50) at the tourist office. **YHA Cambridge (HI) ❷,** 97 Tenison Rd., has a popular TV lounge and a welcoming atmosphere close to the train station. (☎354 601. Breakfast included. Lockers £1. Laundry £3. Internet £4 per hr. Reception 24hr. Reserve ahead. Dorms £19, under 18 £15. MC/V.) Two blocks from the train station, **Tenison Towers Guest House ❸,** 148 Tenison Rd., has impeccably clean, airy rooms with fresh flowers, and a free breakfast including homemade muffins. (☎363 924; www.cambridgecitytenisontowers.com. Singles £35; doubles £55. Cash only.) **Market Square** has pyramids of fruit and vegetables. (Open M-Sa 9:30am-4:30pm.) Students buy their Pimm's and baguettes at **Sainsbury's,** 44 Sidney St. (☎366 891. Open M-F 8am-9pm, Sa 7:30am-9pm, Su 11am-5pm.) South of town, **Hills Road** and **Mill Road** have good budget options. **Dojo's**

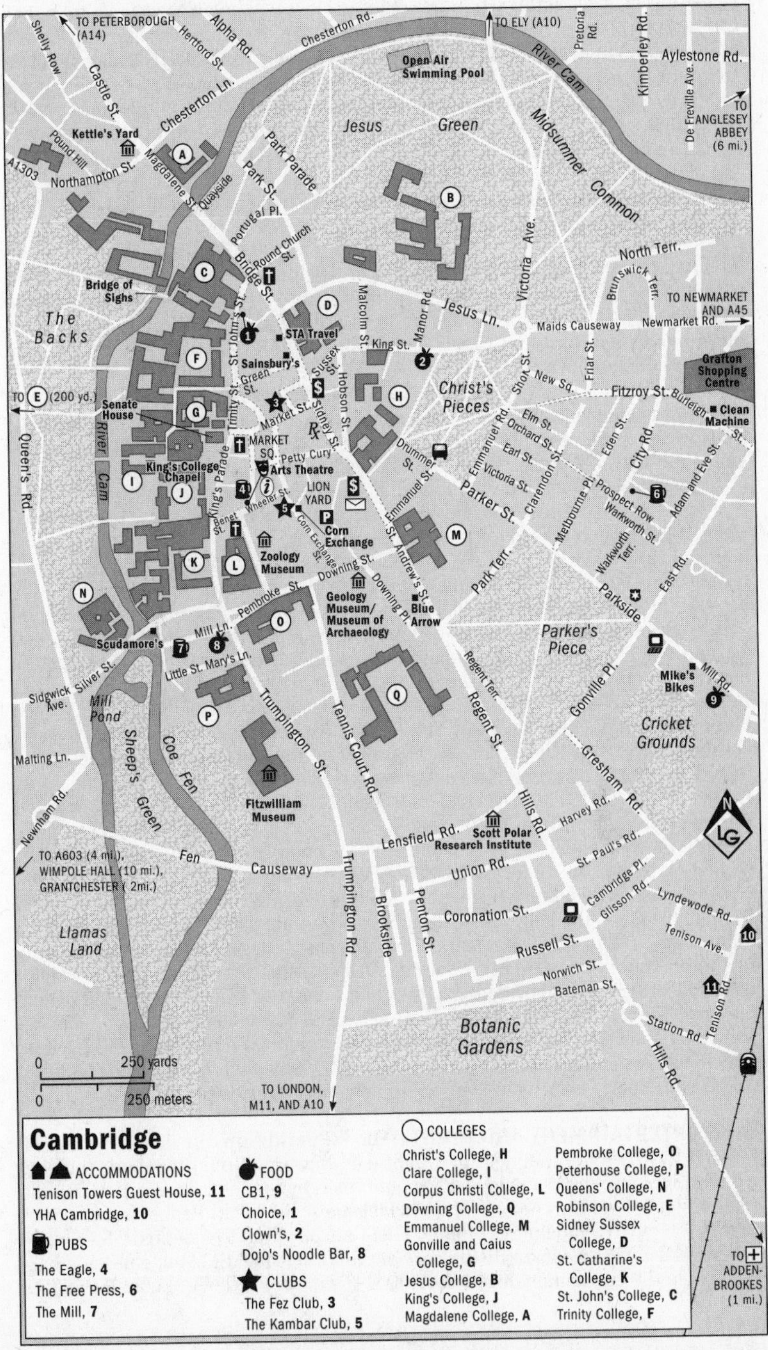

Cambridge

ACCOMMODATIONS
Tenison Towers Guest House, **11**
YHA Cambridge, **10**

PUBS
The Eagle, **4**
The Free Press, **6**
The Mill, **7**

FOOD
CB1, **9**
Choice, **1**
Clown's, **2**
Dojo's Noodle Bar, **8**

CLUBS
The Fez Club, **3**
The Kambar Club, **5**

COLLEGES
Christ's College, **H**
Clare College, **I**
Corpus Christi College, **L**
Downing College, **Q**
Emmanuel College, **M**
Gonville and Caius College, **G**
Jesus College, **B**
King's College, **J**
Magdalene College, **A**
Pembroke College, **O**
Peterhouse College, **P**
Queens' College, **N**
Robinson College, **E**
Sidney Sussex College, **D**
St. Catharine's College, **K**
St. John's College, **C**
Trinity College, **F**

BRITAIN

Noodle Bar ❶, 1-2 Mill Rd., whips up enormous plates of Asian noodles for less than £7. (☎363 471; www.dojonoodlebar.co.uk. Open M-Th noon-2:30pm and 5:30-11pm, F noon-4pm and 5:30-11pm, Sa-Su noon-11pm. Cash only.) **Choice ❶,** 11 St. John's St., lures in plenty of students with filling sandwiches (£2-2.60) and divine smells. (☎568 336. Open daily 8am-5pm. Cash only.) Children's drawings plaster the orange walls at **Clown's ❶,** 54 King St., which serves a variety of homemade pastas and Italian desserts. (☎355 711. Entrees £3-7. Open M-Sa 8am-midnight, Su 8am-11pm. Cash only.) Students sip coffee at **CB1 ❶,** 32 Mill Rd. surrounded by walls crammed with books. (☎576 306. Internet £2.40 per hr. Coffee £1-1.50. Open M-F 8am-8pm, Sa-Su 10am-8pm. Cash only.)

SIGHTS. Cambridge is an architect's dream, packing some of England's most breathtaking monuments into less than three square kilometers. Soaring **King's College Chapel** and St. John's **Bridge of Sighs** are sightseeing staples, while more obscure college courts veil largely undiscovered gardens and courtyards. The **University of Cambridge** has three eight-week terms: Michaelmas (Oct.-Dec.), Lent (Jan.-Mar.), and Easter (Apr.-June). Many of its colleges close to sightseers during Easter term, and virtually all are closed during exams (mid-May to mid-June); your best bet is to call ahead for hours. Porters (bowler-wearing former servicemen) guard the gates. Travelers that look like undergrads (no backpack, camera, or Cambridge sweatshirt) can often wander freely through the grounds after hours. The fastest way to blow your cover is to trample the sacred grass of the courtyards, a privilege reserved for the elite.

If you only have time for a few colleges, try Trinity, King's, St. John's, and Queens'. Sir Isaac Newton originally measured the speed of sound by timing the echo in the cloisters along the north side of the Great Court at **Trinity College,** on Trinity St. Also the alma mater of Vladimir Nabokov, Ernest Rutherford, and Alfred Lord Tennyson, Trinity houses the stunning **Wren Library,** with A. A. Milne's handwritten manuscript of *Winnie the Pooh* and the original copy of Newton's *Principia.* (☎338 400. Chapel and courtyard open daily 10am-5pm. Library open M-F noon-2pm. Easter-Oct. £2.20, students £1.30. Nov.-Easter free.) **King's College,** south of Trinity on King's Parade, is E. M. Forster and Salman Rushdie's alma mater. Reubens's arresting *Adoration of the Magi* hangs behind the altar of its Gothic chapel. (☎331 100. Open M-Sa 9:30am-5pm, Su 10am-5pm. Tours arranged through the tourist office. £4.50, students £3.) Established in 1511 by Henry VIII's mother, **St. John's College,** on St. John's St., is one of seven colleges founded by women. It boasts the 12th-century School of Pythagoras, thought to be the oldest complete building in Cambridge, a replica of the Bridge of Sighs, and the longest room in the city—the Fellows' Room in Second Court spans 28m. (☎338 600. Open daily 10am-5:30pm. £2.50, students £1.50.) **Queens' College,** Silver St., has the only unaltered Tudor courtyard in Cambridge. Despite rumors to the contrary, its Mathematical Bridge is supported by screws and bolts, not just mathematical principles. (☎335 511. Open Mar.-Oct. M-F 10am-5pm, Sa-Su 9:30am-5pm. £1.30.) A break from academia, the **Fitzwilliam Museum,** on Trumpington St., displays Egyptian, Greek, and Asian treasures as well as works by Brueghel, Monet, and Reubens. (☎332 900. Open Tu-Sa 10am-5pm, Su noon-5pm. Suggested donation £3.)

ENTERTAINMENT AND NIGHTLIFE. **Punting** on the River Cam is a favored form of entertainment in Cambridge. Beware of punt-bombers; jumping from bridges into the river alongside a punt, thereby tipping its occupants into the Cam, has evolved into an art form. **Scudamore's,** Silver St. Bridge, rents boats. (☎359 750; www.scudamores.com. M-F £14 per hr. plus £70 deposit, Sa-Su £16 per hr. MC/V.) **Pubs** constitute the core of Cambridge nightlife, but clubs and bars are also in the curriculum. **King Street** has a diverse collection of pubs. **The Mill,** 14

Mill Ln., off Silver St. Bridge, sits beside a riverside park that's perfect for punt- and people-watching. (Open M-Th noon-11pm, F noon-midnight, Sa 11am-midnight, Su 11am-11pm.) When Watson and Crick ran into **The Eagle,** 8 Benet St., to announce their discovery of DNA, the barmaid insisted they settle their 4-shilling tab before she'd serve them. Cambridge's oldest pub also boasts a RAF room, where British and American WWII pilots stood on each other's shoulders to burn their initials into the ceiling. (☎505 020 Open M-Sa 11am-11pm, Su noon-10:30pm.) Locals haunt **The Free Press,** Prospect Row, named after an abolitionist newspaper. (No smoking or mobile phones. Open M-F noon-2:30pm and 6-11pm, Sa noon-3pm and 6-11pm, Su noon-3pm and 7-10:30pm.) **The Kambar Club,** 1 Wheeler St., has weekly nights for indie rock, garage, goth, electronica, and drum 'n' bass music. (Cover £5, students £3. Open M-Sa 10pm-2:30am.) **The Fez Club,** 15 Market Passage, boasts lush, Moroccan-themed decor. (Cover £2-8. Open daily 9pm-3am.)

NORTHERN ENGLAND

The north's major cities grew out of the wool and coal industries, and bear the 19th-century scars to prove it, but their reinvigorated city centers have embraced post-industrial hipness with fresh youth culture. The region's innovative music and arts scenes are world-famous: Liverpool and Manchester alone have produced four of *Q Magazine*'s 10 biggest rock stars of the 20th century. When you need a break from frenetic urbanity, find respite in the Peak District's green hills or the Lake District's crags and waters.

MANCHESTER ☎0161

Teeming with electronic beats and post-industrial glitz, Manchester (pop. 430,000) has risen from factory soot to savor a reputation as one of England's hippest spots. "Madchester" played an instrumental role in the evolution of pop and punk, especially during the New Wave of the 80s. The city is a hive of activity, from its booming shopping and museums to its wild nightlife and controversial soccer team.

TRANSPORTATION AND PRACTICAL INFORMATION. Flights arrive at **Manchester International Airport** (**MAN;** ☎489 3000). **Trains** leave Piccadilly Station on London Rd. and Victoria Station on Victoria St., for: Birmingham (1¾hr., 1 per hr., £21); Edinburgh (4hr., 5 per day, £49); Liverpool (50min., 2 per hr., £8); London Euston (2½-3hr., 1 per hr., £54); York (40min., 2 per hr., £17). National Express **buses** (☎08705 808 080) go from Chorlton St. to Liverpool (55min., 1 per hr., £5.50) and London (4-6hr., 7-12 per day, £20). Nearly 50 local bus routes stop at Piccadilly Gardens; pick up a route map at the tourist office. (Bus day pass £3.30.) **Manchester Visitor Centre,** in the Town Hall Extension on Lloyd St., books rooms for £2.50 and a 10% deposit. (☎234 3157; www.visitmanchester.com. Open M-Sa 10am-5:30pm, Su 10:30am-4:30pm.) Free **Internet** is available at **Central Library,** St. Peter's Sq. (☎234 1982. Open M-Th 9am-8pm, F-Sa 9am-5pm.) **Postal Code:** M2 1BB.

BRITAIN

ACCOMMODATIONS AND FOOD. Cheap stays in the city center are hard to find. The highest concentration of budget lodgings is 3-5km south, in the suburbs of **Didsbury, Fallowfield,** and **Withington;** take bus #40, 42, or 157. Browse *Where to Stay* (free at tourist office) for listings. Take the metro to G-Mex Station or bus #33 (dir.: Wigan) from Piccadilly Gardens to Deansgate to reach the clean and spacious **YHA Manchester (HI)** ❷, Potato Wharf, Castlefield. (☎0870 770 5950; www.yhamanchester.org.uk. Breakfast included. Laundry £1.50. Internet 7p per min. Reception 24hr. Dorms £21; doubles £45. MC/V.) In a renovated hat factory in the Northern Quarter, **The Hatters Tourist Hostel ❷**, 50 Newton St., has clean but crowded rooms and incredibly friendly service. (☎236 9500; www.hatters-group.com. Breakfast included. Laundry £1.50. Reception 24hr. Dorms £14-18; doubles £45; triples £60. MC/V.)

Restaurants in **Chinatown** can be pricey, but most offer a reasonable, multi-course "Businessman's Lunch" (M-F noon-2pm; £4-8). Better yet, visit **Curry Mile,** a stretch of Asian restaurants on Wilmslow Rd. **Tampopo Noodle House ❷**, 16 Albert Sq., is one of Manchester's favorites, serving noodles from Indonesia, Japan, Malaysia, Thailand, and Vietnam. (☎819 1966; www.tampopo.co.uk. Noodles £6-11. Open daily noon-11pm. AmEx/MC/V.) At **Eden ❸**, 3 Brazil St., a canalside restaurant in the Gay Village, Adams and Eves enjoy the pizza special (2 pizzas and 2 bottles of beer £12; M-Sa noon-5pm) from "the barge." (☎237 9852. Open M-F 11am-11pm, Sa-Su 11am-2am.) Find a Tesco **supermarket** at 58-66 Market St. (☎911 9400. Open M-F 6am-midnight, Sa 7am-10pm, Su 11am-5pm.)

SIGHTS AND ENTERTAINMENT. Don't miss the fantastic **Urbis** museum, Cathedral Gardens, which explores modern urban culture and art. The awe-inspiring museum is itself a sculpture, covered in 2200 handmade plates of glass beneath a "ski-slope" copper roof. (☎605 8200; www.urbis.org.uk. Open Tu-Su 10am-6pm. Free.) Be sure to take a peek at the **Central Library,** behind the Town Hall Extension. One of the largest municipal libraries in Europe, the domed building has a music and theater library, a language and literature library, and the UK's second-largest Judaica collection. (☎234 1900. Call for hours.) The **Manchester Art Gallery,** Nicholas St., holds Rossetti's stunning *Astarte Syriaca* in its gigantic collection. (☎235 8888. Open Tu-Su and bank holidays 10am-5pm. Free.)

Loved and reviled in equal proportion, Manchester United is England's reigning soccer team. From the Old Trafford Metrolink stop, follow the signs up Warwick Rd. to reach the **Manchester United Museum and Tour Centre,** Sir Matt Busby Way, at the Old Trafford soccer stadium. Memorabilia from the club's inception in 1878 to its recent trophy-hogging success may just convert you. (☎0870 442 1994. Open daily 9:30am-5pm. Tours every 10min. except on match days. Reserve ahead. £9.)

> **!** At night, streets in the Northern Quarter are dimly lit. If crossing from Piccadilly to Swan St. or Great Ancoats St., use Oldham St., where the neon-lit clubs provide reassurance. There's no shame in short taxi trips at night in this town.

NIGHTLIFE. At **Thirsty Scholar,** off Oxford St., the student crowd descends beneath a railroad bridge. On weekend nights, the thud of overhead trains is drowned out by the music of local DJs. (☎236 6071. M and Th acoustic nights. F-Su DJ. Open M-Th 11am-2am, F-Sa 11am-2:30am, Su 11am-1am.) Centered around **Oldham Street,** the **Northern Quarter** is the city's youthful outlet for live music. Partiers flock to **Oxford Street** for late-night clubbing. At **Cord,** 8 Dorsey St., corduroy meets chic. The small venue makes for a subdued, exclusive spot to drink. (Open Su-Th noon-10:30pm, F-Sa noon-1am.) GLBT clubbers will want to check out the **Gay Village,** northeast of Princess St. Evening crowds fill the bars lining **Canal Street,** in the heart of the area, which is also lively during the day. Huge booths and flat-screen TVs at the new bar **Queer,** 4 Canal St., create a great atmosphere. (☎228 1360; www.queer-manchester.com. Open M-Sa 11am-2am, Su 11am-12:30am.)

LIVERPOOL ☎0151

Many Brits still scoff at once-industrial Liverpool, but Scousers—as Liverpudlians are colloquially known—have watched their metropolis undergo a cultural face-lift, trading in working-class grit for offbeat vitality. Several free museums, two deified football squads, and top-notch nightlife helped earn the city the title of European Capital of Culture 2008. Oh, yeah—some fuss is made over The Beatles.

TICKET TO RIDE. Trains (☎08457 484 950) leave Lime St. Station for: Birmingham (1¾hr., M-Sa 1 per hr., £20.80); London Euston (3hr., 1 per hr., £56.20); and Manchester Piccadilly (1hr., 2-4 per hr., £8.10). National Express **buses** (☎08705 808 080) run from Norton St. Station to: Birmingham (3hr., 5 per day, £10.50); London (4½-5½hr., 5-6 per day, £22); and Manchester (1hr., 1-3 per hr., £6). The Isle of Man Steam Packet Company (☎08705 523 523; www.steam-packet.com) runs **ferries** from Princess Dock to the Isle of Man and Dublin. The **tourist office,** 08 Pl., gives away the handy brochure *Visitor Guide to Liverpool, Merseyside, and England's Northwest* and books rooms for a 10% fee. (☎233 2008; www.visitliverpool.com. Open M and W-Sa 9am-5:30pm, Tu 10am-5:30pm, Su 10:30am-4:30pm.) Expert guide Phil Hughes runs personalized 3-4hr. Beatles tours leaving from Strawberry Fields and Eleanor Rigby's grave (☎228 4565; £12). Surf the **Internet** for free at the Central **Library** on William Brown St. (☎233 5835. Open M-F 9am-6pm, Sa 9am-5pm, Su noon-4pm.) **Postal Code:** L1 1AA.

A HARD DAY'S NIGHT. Most budget hotels are located around **Lord Nelson Street,** next to the train station, and **Mount Pleasant,** one block from Brownlow Hill. **Embassie Backpackers ❷,** is a first-rate hostel with a friendly staff. (☎707 1089; www.embassie.com. Laundry. Reception 24hr. Dorms £14.50. Cash only.) Housed in a former Victorian warehouse, **International Inn ❷,** 4 South Hunter St., is clean and fun, with an adjoining Internet cafe. (☎709 8135; www.internationalinn.co.uk. Free coffee, tea, and toast. Linens included. Internet £2 per hr. Dorms Su-Th £15, F-Sa £18; doubles £36/40. AmEx/MC/V.) Trendy cafes and kebab stands line **Bold** and **Hardman Streets.** Many of the fast-food joints on **Berry** and **Leece Streets** stay open late. There's a Tesco Metro **supermarket** in Clayton Sq., across from St. John's Shopping Centre. (Open M-F 6am-midnight, Sa 6am-10pm, Su 11am-5pm.) At **Tabac ❶,** 126 Bold St., sleek, trendy decor belies surprisingly affordable food. Sandwiches (from £3.50) on freshly baked foccaccia are served all day. (☎709 9502. Breakfast from £2. Dinner specials £6.50-9.50. Open M-F and Su 8:30am-11pm, Sa 8:30am-midnight. MC/V.) The **Country Basket Sandwich Bar ❶** has outrageously low prices. (☎236 0509. Open 7:30am-2:30pm. Cash only.)

MAGICAL MYSTERY TOUR. The tourist office's **Beatles Map** (£3) leads visitors through the city's myriad Beatles-themed sights, including **Strawberry Fields** and **Penny Lane.** At Albert Dock, **The Beatles Story** traces the rise and fall of the band through Hamburg, the Cavern Club, and a pseudo-shrine to John's legacy of love. (☎709 1963; www.beatlesstory.com. Open daily 10am-6pm. £9, students £6.) The Liverpool branch of the **Tate Gallery,** also on Albert Dock, contains a select collection of 20th-century art. (☎702 7400; www.tate.org.uk/liverpool. Open Tu-Su 10am-5:50pm. Suggested donation £2. Special exhibits £5, students £4.) Completed in 1978, the Anglican **Liverpool Cathedral,** on Upper Duke St., boasts the highest Gothic arches and the heaviest bells in the world. Climb the tower for a view that extends to Wales. (☎709 6271; www.liverpoolcathedral.org.uk. Cathedral open daily 8am-6pm. Tower open daily Mar.-Sept. 11am-5pm; Oct.-Feb. 11am-4pm. Cathedral free. Tower £3.25.) Neon-blue stained glass casts a glow over the controversial modern interior of the **Metropolitan Cathedral of Christ the King,** on Mt. Pleasant. (☎709 9222. Open in summer M-Sa 8am-6pm, Su 8am-5pm; closes earlier in winter. Free.) The **Liverpool** and **Everton football clubs**—intense rivals—offer tours of their grounds. Bus #26 runs from the city center to Anfield; bus #19 runs from the city center to Goodison Park. (Everton ☎330 2277; tour £9, students £5. Liverpool ☎260 6677; tour £9, students £5.50. Reserve ahead.)

TWIST AND SHOUT. Consult the *Liverpool Echo* (£0.35), sold daily by street vendors, for the most up-to-date information on nightlife in the city. The downtown **Ropewalks** area—especially **Matthew Street, Church Street,** and **Bold Street**—overflows with clubbers on weekends. Fabulous **Society,** 47 Fleet St., draws decadent crowds and posh VIPs to its steamy dance floor. (☎707 3575. Cover F £7, Sa £10, Su £5. Open F 10:30pm-2am, Sa 10:30pm-4am, Su 10:30pm-1am.) **The Cavern Club,** 10 Matthew St., where the Fab Four gained prominence, draws live bands hoping history will repeat itself. (☎236 9091. Cover £2-4 after 9pm. Pub open M-Sa from 11am, Su noon-11:30pm. Club open M-W 6pm-midnight, Th-Sa 6pm-2:30am.) **BaaBar,** 43-45 Fleet St., offers 35 varieties of shooters with nearly nightly specials. (☎708 8673. Open M-Sa 11-2am, Su 4pm-midnight. MC/V.)

PEAK DISTRICT NATIONAL PARK

Though the Peak District has no true mountains, its 1400 sq. km offer almost everything else: deep gullies, green pastures, rocky hillsides, and soft peat moorland. The natural beauty of the area may come as a surprise situated near industrial giants Manchester, Nottingham, and Sheffield. Transportation is easiest in the south and near cities, but hikers should head north for a more isolated escape.

TRANSPORTATION AND PRACTICAL INFORMATION. The *Peak District Timetables* (£0.60), available at tourist offices, has accommodation and bike rental information, transport routes, and maps. Two **train** lines (☎08457 484 950) originate in Manchester and enter the park at New Mills. One stops at Buxton, near the park's edge (1hr., 1 per hr., £6.35). The other crosses the park (11-16 per day) via Edale (55min., £7.40), Hope, and Hathersage (both 1hr., £7.50), ending in Sheffield (1½hr., £12.20). **Buses** make a noble effort to connect the scattered Peak towns, and **Traveline** (☎0870 608 2608; www.traveline.org.uk) is a vital resource. "Transpeak" makes the 3hr. journey between Buxton, Bakewell, and Matlock, stopping at towns in between (6 per day). Bus #173 runs from Bakewell to Castleton (50min., 3-5 per day). Bus #200 runs from Castleton to Edale (20min., M-F 3-7 per day). The **Derbyshire Wayfarer** ticket, available at Manchester train stations and NPICs, allows one day of train and bus travel through the Peak District as far north as Sheffield and as far south as Derby. (£8, students £4.)

The **NPICs** at Bakewell, Buxton, Castleton, and Edale carry walking guides. **YHA** operates 20 **hostels** ❶ in the park (reserve ahead; dorms £9-16). For Bakewell, Buxton, Castleton, and Edale, see below. For the park's 11 **YHA Camping Barns (HI)** ❶ (£6 per person), book at the **Camping Barns Reservation Office,** 6 King St., Clitheroe, Lancashire BB7 2EP (☎0870 770 8868). The park has seven **Cycle Hire Centres** (£13 per day); the free brochure *Cycle Derbyshire*, available at NPICs, includes phone numbers, hours, locations, and a map with on- and off-road tracks.

BAKEWELL AND EDALE. The town of **Bakewell,** 50km southeast of Manchester, is the best base from which to explore the region. Several scenic walks through the **White Peaks** begin nearby. Bakewell's **NPIC** is in Old Market Hall, on Bridge St. (☎0870 444 7275. Open daily Mar.-Oct. 9:30am-5:30pm; Nov.-Feb. 10am-5pm.) The cozy **YHA Bakewell (HI)** ❶, on Fly Hill, is 5min. from the town center. (☎0870 770 5682. Dorms £12, under 18 £9. Cash only.) A **Midlands Co-op** sells groceries at the corner of Granby Rd. and Market St. (Open M-Sa 8am-10pm, Su 10am-4pm.)

The northern Dark Peak area has some of the wildest, most rugged hill country in England, including spectacular peat marshes around **Edale.** For details on shorter **trails** nearby, check the National Park Authority's publication *8 Walks Around Edale* (£1.40). The town of Edale itself offers little more than a church, cafe, pub, school, and the nearby **YHA Edale (HI)** ❶, Rowland Cote. (☎0870 770 5808. Dorms £13, under 18 £9. Cash only.)

CASTLETON. Castleton's (pop. 1200) main attraction is the **Treak Cliff Cavern,** which hides purple seams of Blue John, a semi-precious mineral found only in these hills. (☎620 571. Open daily Mar.-Oct. 10am-4:20pm; Nov.-Feb. 10am-3:20pm. 40min. tours every 20-30min. £6.50, students and YHA members £5.50.) Castleton's **NPIC** is on Buxton Rd. (☎0870 444 7275. Open daily Apr.-Oct. 9:30am-5:30pm; Nov.-Mar. 10am-5pm.) **YHA Castleton (HI)** ❷ is in the heart of town; it may be unavailable in July and August, when it hosts children's camps. (☎0870 770 5758. Kitchen. Internet £5 per hr. Reserve 2-3 weeks ahead. Open Feb.-Dec. Dorms £14, under 18 £10. Members only. Cash only.)

BUXTON. A main hub for Peak travel, the spa town of Buxton, highly reminiscent of Bath, is a picture of Georgian elegance. Outside of town in the Buxton Country Park is **Poole's Cavern,** a cave that has drawn tourists for centuries; legend has it that Mary, Queen of Scots once visited. (☎01298 269 78. Open daily Mar-Oct., 10am-5pm. Tours leave every 30min. and last 45min. £6.20, students £5. Dress warmly.) The **tourist office** is in The Crescent. (☎01298 25 106; www.visitbuxton.com. Open daily Mar.-Sept. 9:30am-5pm; Oct.-Feb. 10am-4pm.) **Roseleigh Hotel** ❸, on Broad Walk overlooking the Pavilion Gardens, has a reading parlor with shelves of travel and adventure books. (☎249 04; www.roseleighhotel.co.uk. £30-32 per person. MC/V.) A Co-op, on Spring Gardens, sells **groceries** (☎278 44; open daily 8am-11pm). **The Slopes Bar** ❶, on Spring Gardens, offers a "world menu" of light meals, plus cafe fare. (☎238 04. Open 9:30am-midnight; hot food served noon-8pm. MC/V.)

YORK ☎01904

Once impenetrable to outsiders, the crumbling medieval walls of York (pop. 137,000) are now defenseless against hordes of tourists. Brandishing cameras in place of swords, the invaders come to ogle Britain's largest Gothic cathedral and roam through the tiny medieval alleyways of "the most haunted city in the world."

TRANSPORTATION AND PRACTICAL INFORMATION. Trains (☎08457 484 950) leave Station Rd. for: Edinburgh (2½hr., 2 per hr., £65); London King's Cross (2hr., 2 per hr., £71); Manchester Piccadilly (1½hr., 3 per hr., £17); Newcastle (1hr., 4 per hr., £20). National Express **buses** (☎08705 808 080) depart from 20 Rougier St., Exhibition Sq., the train station, Piccadilly, and The Stonebow for: Edinburgh (6hr., 1 per day, £31); London (5½hr., 15 per day, £23); Manchester (3hr., 15 per day, £12). Take Station Rd. to Museum St., cross the bridge, and go left on St. Leonard's Pl. for the **tourist office,** Exhibition Sq. (☎621 756; www.visityork.org. Open Apr.-Oct. M-Sa 9am-6pm, Su 10am-5pm; Nov.-May M-Sa 9am-5pm, Su 10am-4pm.) **Cafe of the Evil Eye,** 42 Stonegate, has **Internet.** (☎640 002. £2 per hr.) **Postal Code:** YO1 8DA.

ACCOMMODATIONS AND FOOD. B&Bs (from £22) are on the side streets along **Bootham** and **Clifton,** in the Mount area down **Blossom Street,** and on **Bishopthorpe Road,** south of town. Reserve weeks ahead in the summer, when competition is fierce; the tourist office can help. **York Backpackers** ❷, 88-90 Micklegate, is a Georgian mansion with a kitchen, TV lounge, and "dungeon bar" with 24hr. liquor license. (☎627 720; www.yorkbackpackers.co.uk. Continental breakfast included. Laundry £3. Dorms £15; doubles £38. Ask about working in exchange for accommodation. MC/V; 50p surcharge.) At **Foss Bank Guest House** ❸, 16 Huntington Rd., the friendly owner offers elegant rooms and an inviting guest lounge. (☎635 548. Singles £28; doubles £50, with bath £58. Cash only.) The **York Youth Hotel** ❷, 11-13 Bishophill Senior, is a conveniently located, no-frills hostel catering primarily to groups. (☎625 904; www.yorkyouthhotel.com. Laundry and Internet. Key deposit £3. Reception 24hr. Dorms £12; singles £25; doubles £38. AmEx/MC/V.)

Greengrocers peddle at **Newgate Market** between Parliament St. and the Shambles. (Open Apr.-Dec. M-Sa 9am-5pm, Su 9am-4:30pm; Jan.-Mar. M-Sa 9am-5pm.) Find cheap eats at the many Indian restaurants outside the city gates. Buy groceries at **Sainsbury's,** at the intersection of Foss Bank and Heworth Green. (☎643 801. Open M-Sa 8am-8pm, Su 11am-5pm.) At **El Piano ❷,** 15 Grape Ln., Mexican flavors infuse veggie dishes. Meals are served in 3 sizes: *chica* (£2.45), tapas (£4), and *ración* (£6), in this laid-back eatery. (☎610 676. Breakfast £6. Cheap chow M-F 5-6pm, £5. Open M-Sa 10am-midnight, Su noon-5pm. MC/V.) At **The Fudge Kitchen ❶,** 58 Low Petergate, over 20 flavors of gooey fudge, from Vintage Vanilla to Banoffee, are made right before your eyes. (☎645 596. Free samples. Slices £2.25 for 100g. Open M-Sa 10am-6pm, Su 10am-5:30pm. MC/V.) Huge sandwiches and burgers (£5-6) await at **Victor J's Artbar ❷,** 1 Finkle St., a casual, colorful, and convenient bistro. (☎541 771. Open M-Sa 10am-11pm, Su 11am-7pm. MC/V.)

SIGHTS. The best introduction to York is the 4km walk along its **medieval walls.** Beware the tourist stampede, which wanes only in the early morning and just before the walls and gates close at dusk. The **Association of Voluntary Guides** (☎621 756) offers free 2hr. **walking tours,** which leave at 10:15am, 2:15, and 6:45pm in summer and 10:15am in winter. Tourists, priests, and worshippers alike converge at **York Minster,** the largest Gothic cathedral this side of Italy. Inside, throwing stones isn't recommended—it's estimated that half of all the medieval stained glass in England lines the walls. The Great East Window depicts the beginning and end of the world in over 100 scenes. Nearby, see if you can spot the statue of Archbishop Thomas Lamplugh. Evensong is magical. (☎557 216 639 347; www.yorkminster.org. Open daily 7am-6:30pm. Evensong M-Sa 5pm, Su 4pm. Free 1hr. tours every 30min., daily Apr.-Sept. 9:30am-3:30pm, Oct.-Mar. 10am-2pm. £5 Combined ticket with Undercroft, Treasury, and Crypt £7; students £4/5.) The **Chapter House** is home to grotesque medieval carvings of everything from roguish demons to a three-faced woman. Look for the tiny Virgin Mary on the right upon entering, a carving so small that it went unnoticed by Cromwell's idol-smashing thugs. (Open daily 9am-6pm. Free.) Climb up to **Central Tower** for a view of York's rooftops, but be sure to plan accordingly since ascents are only allowed during a 5min. period every 30min. because the narrow staircase won't allow passing traffic. (Open daily Apr.-Sept. 9:30am-6pm, Oct.-Mar. 10am-4pm. £2.50.) After you make your way down from the heights of the Minster, venture into its depths. The **Undercroft, Treasury,** and **Crypt** are filled with interesting sights, including the spot where Constantine the Great was proclaimed Emperor and the 12th-century **Doomstone** upon which the cathedral was built. (Open daily Apr.-Sept. 9:30am-5pm; Oct.-Mar. 10am-5pm, 45min. audio tour included. £4, students £3.)

The **York Castle Museum,** between Tower St. and Piccadilly, is arguably Britain's premier museum of everyday life, with a fascinating and extensive collection of household items. Rooms include Kirkgate, a reconstructed Victorian shopping street, and Half Moon Court, its Edwardian counterpart. (☎650 335; www.yorkcastlemuseum.org.uk. Open daily 9:30am-5pm. £6.50, students £5.) **Clifford's Tower,** Tower St., is one of the last remaining pieces of **York Castle** and a chilling reminder of the worst outbreak of anti-Jewish violence in English history. In 1190, Christian merchants tried to erase their debts to Jewish bankers by annihilating York's Jewish community. About 150 Jews took refuge in the tower where, faced with the prospect of starvation or butchery, they committed mass suicide. (☎646 940. Open daily Apr.-Sept. 10am-6pm; Oct. 10am-5pm; Nov.-Mar. 10am-4pm. £3, students £2.30.) The **Jorvik Viking Centre,** on Coppergate, is one of the busiest attractions in York; arrive early or late to avoid lines, or reserve at least a day ahead. Visitors float in "time cars" through the York of AD 948, past authentic artifacts, life-like mannequins, and painfully accurate smells. (☎643 211, reservations 543 403;

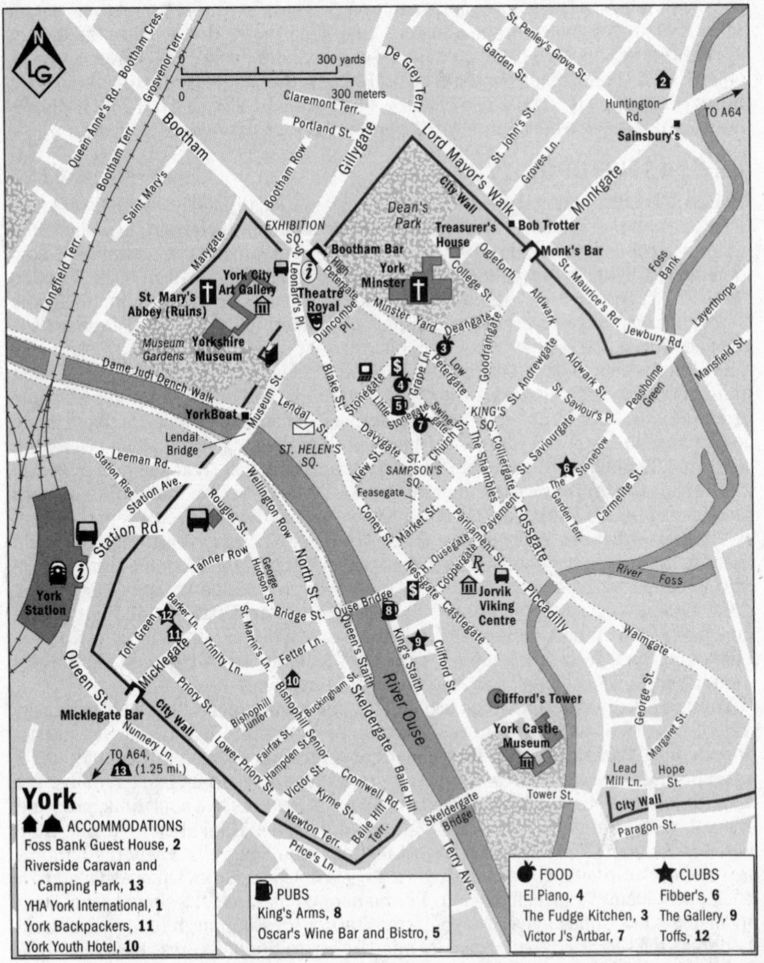

www.vikingjorvik.com. Open daily 10am-5pm. £7.75, students £6.60.) Hidden in the 10 gorgeous acres of the **Museum Gardens,** the **Yorkshire Museum** houses Roman, Anglo-Saxon, and Viking artifacts, as well as the priceless **Middleham Jewel** (c. 1450), an opulent sapphire set in gold. The haunting ruins of **St. Mary's Abbey,** once the most influential Benedictine monastery in northern England, are also there. (Enter from Museum St. or Marygate. ☎687 687; www.yorkshiremuseum.org.uk. Open daily 10am-5pm. Museum £5.50, students £4.50. Gardens and ruins free.)

ENTERTAINMENT AND NIGHTLIFE. The Minster and local churches host a series of **summer concerts,** including the **York Early Music Festival.** (☎658 338; www.ncem.co.uk. July 6-14, 2007.) The *What's On* and *Artscene* guides, available at the tourist office, publish info on live music, theater, cinema, and exhibits. In the evenings, barbershop quartets share the pavement of **King's Square** and **Stone-**

gate with jugglers, magicians, and soapboxers. There are more pubs in the center of York than gargoyles on the Minster's east wall. York's dressy club, **The Gallery,** 12 Clifford St., has two hot dance floors and six bars. (☎647 947. Cover £3.50-10. Open Su-Th 10pm-2am, F-Sa 10pm-3am.) **Fibber's,** Stonebow House, the Stonebow, hosts live music nightly. DJ and dancing starts after 10:30pm. (☎651 250; www.fibbers.co.uk. Check website or *What's On* for events. Cover varies with act.)

NEWCASTLE-UPON-TYNE ☎0191

The largest city in the northeast, Newcastle (pop. 278,000) all but shed its image as a faded capital of industry. The **BALTIC Centre for Contemporary Art,** in a renovated grain warehouse, is Britain's largest center for contemporary art outside of London. (☎478 1810; www.balticmill.com. Open M-Tu and Th-Su 10am-6pm, W 10am-8pm. Free.) The Centre is part of a trio of new structures on the river, including the steel-and-glass **Sage Gateshead,** a complex of concert halls, and the **Gateshead Millennium Bridge,** the only rotating bridge in the world, which opens like a giant eyelid to allow ships to pass. **Castle Garth Keep,** at the foot of St. Nicholas St., is all that remains of the 12th-century New Castle complex. The city did not get its name from the New Castle; rather, it actually derives its name from a castle that existed over 100 years earlier. (☎232 7938. Open daily Apr.-Sept. 9:30am-5:30pm; Oct.-Mar. 9:30am-4:30pm. £1.50, students £0.50.) Theater buffs can treat themselves to an evening at the gilt-and-velvet **Theatre Royal,** 100 Grey St., undoubtedly northern England's premier stage. (☎0870 905 5060; www.theatreroyal.co.uk.)

The new **Albatross Backpackers ❷,** 51 Grainger St., has everything you could want in an inner city hostel: secure, modern facilities 2min. from the train station and adjacent to major nightlife areas. (233 1330; www.albatrossnewcastle.com. 24hr. reception. 2- to 10-bed dorms £17-23. MC/V.) **Pani's Cafe ❷,** 61 High Bridge St., has £5-10 Italian dishes and a boisterous vibe.(☎232 4366; www.paniscafe.com. Open M-Sa 10am-10pm. Cash only.) **Safeway** is on Clayton St., in the city center. (☎261 2805. Open M-Sa 8am-7pm, Su 11am-5pm.)

Home of the nectar known as brown ale, Newcastle's party scene is legendary. *The Crack* (free at record stores) has the best nightlife listings in Newcastle. Rowdy **Bigg Market** features the highest concentration of pubs in England, while neighboring **Quayside** attracts herds of twentysomethings to its packed clubs. **The Head of Steam,** 2 Neville St., near the train station, features live soul, funk, jazz, and reggae, with packed shows most nights and occasional local DJs. (☎230 4236. Open M-Sa noon-1am, Su noon-12am.) **Digital,** Time Square, attracts the nation's top DJs to Saturday night's "Shindig." (☎261 9755. Cover £3-12. Open M-Tu and Th 10:30pm-2:30am, F-Sa 10:30pm-4am.) For a happening gay and lesbian scene, head to **Time Square. Trains** leave from Central Station for Edinburgh (1½hr., £40) and London King's Cross (3½hr., every 30 min., £108). National Express **buses** (☎08705 808 080) leave St. James Blvd. for Edinburgh (3hr., 4 per day, £15) and London (7hr., 4 per day, £27). The **tourist office** is at 27 Market St. in the Central Arcade. (☎277 8000. Open M-F 9:30am-5:30pm, Sa 9am-5:30pm.) **Postal Code:** NE1 7AB.

LAKE DISTRICT NATIONAL PARK

Blessed with some of the most stunning scenery in England, the Lake District owes its beauty to a thorough glacier-gouging during the Ice Age. The district's jagged peaks and glassy lakes form a giant playground for hikers, bikers, and boaters, who in the summer nearly equal sheep in number—and with four million sheep, that's quite a feat. Yet there's always some lonely hill or quiet cove where you will seem the sole visitor. Use the villages of Windermere, Ambleside, Grasmere, and Keswick as bases from which to ascend into the region's hills—the farther west you go from the A591, the more countryside you'll have to yourself.

TRANSPORTATION AND PRACTICAL INFORMATION. **Trains** (☎08457 484 950) run to Oxenholme, the primary gateway to the lakes, from: Birmingham (2hr., 1 per hr., £45); Edinburgh (2hr.; M-F 10 per day, Sa-Su 5 per day; £33); London Euston (3½hr., 9 per day, £107); Manchester Piccadilly (1½hr., 9-10 per day, £20). Trains also run from Oxenholme to Windermere (20min., 1 per hr., £3.50), and from Manchester Piccadilly to Windermere (1¾hr.; M-Sa 5 per day, Su 1 per day; £20). National Express **buses** (☎08705 808 080) arrive in Windermere from Birmingham (4½hr., 1 per day, £31) and London (8hr., 1 per day, £29), continuing north through Ambleside and Grasmere to Keswick. **Stagecoach in Cumbria** (☎0870 608 2608) is the primary bus service in the region; a complete timetable, *The Lakesrider*, is available for free at tourist offices and onboard each bus. An **Explorer ticket** offers unlimited travel on all area Stagecoach buses (1-day £8.50; 4-day £19). YHA Ambleside offers a convenient **minibus** service (☎01539 432 304) between hostels (2 per day, £2.50) as well as service from the Windermere train station to the hostels in Windermere and Ambleside (first ride free, £2 thereafter).

The **National Park Visitor Centre** is in **Brockhole,** halfway between Windermere and Ambleside. (☎01539 446 601; www.lake-district.gov.uk. Open Apr.-Oct. daily 10am-5pm.) **National Park Information Centres (NPICs)** book accommodations and dispense free information and maps. Though B&Bs line every street in every town and there's a hostel around every bend, lodgings fill up in summer; reserve ahead.

WINDERMERE AND BOWNESS. **Windermere** and its sidekick **Bowness-on-Windermere** fill to the gills with vacationers in summer, when sailboats and waterskiers swarm the lake. The short, steep climb to **Orrest Head** (2.5km round-trip) is moderately difficult, but affords one of the best views in the Lake District. It begins opposite the TIC on the other side of A591. To get to the spacious **YHA Windermere (HI)** ❶, Bridge Ln., 3.2km north of Windermere off A591, catch the YHA shuttle from the train station. (☎01539 443 543. Breakfast, packed lunch, and dinner available with advance notice for £3.50-5.50 per meal. Internet £5 per hr. Open Feb.-Nov. daily; early Dec. F-Sa only. Dorms £13-16, under 18 £9-11.) To camp at **Park Cliffe** ❷, Birks Rd., 7km south of Bowness, take bus #618 from Windermere. (☎01539 531 344. Tent sites £11-12. MC/V.) **Windermere Lake Cruises** (☎01539 443 360), at the northern end of Bowness Pier, sends boats to Waterhead Pier in Ambleside (30min., round-trip £7.30) and south to Lakeside (40min., round-trip £7.60). The Lakeland Experience **bus** #599 (3 per hr., £1) leaves for Bowness pier from the train station in Windermere. The **tourist office** is near the train station. (☎01539 446 499. Open Easter-Aug. M-Sa 9am-5:30pm, Su 10am-5pm.) The local **NPIC,** on Glebe Rd., is beside Bowness Pier. (☎01539 442 895. Open daily Apr.-Oct. 9.30am-5.30am; Nov.-Mar. 10am-4pm.)

AMBLESIDE. Set in a valley 1.5km north of Lake Windermere, Ambleside is an attractive village with convenient access to the southern lakes. **Hiking** trails extend in all directions. The top of **Loughrigg,** a moderately difficult climb (11km round-trip), has splendid views of high fells. The lovely **Stockghyll Force** waterfall is an easy 1.5km from town. The tourist office has guides to these and other walks. Bus #555 stops in front of **YHA Ambleside (HI)** ❶, 1.5km south of Ambleside and 5km north of Windermere, a magnificent former hotel with refurbished rooms, great food, and swimming off the pier. (☎01539 432 304. Bike rental £1.50 per hr. Internet £5 per hr. Dorms £20, under 18 £15.) Pick up organic fruits and veggies at **Granny Smith's,** Market Pl. (☎01539 433 145. Open M-F 8am-5pm, Sa 8am-6pm, Su 9am-4pm. Cash only.) Lakeslink **bus** #555 (☎01539 432 231) leaves from Kelsick Rd. for Grasmere, Keswick, and Windermere (1 per hr., £2-6.50). The **tourist office** is in the Central Building on Market Cross. (☎01539 432 582. Open daily 9am-5pm.)

GRASMERE. The peace that William Wordsworth felt in the village of Grasmere is still palpable on quiet mornings. Guides provide 30min. tours of the early 17th-century **Dove Cottage,** where the poet lived from 1799 to 1808; the cottage is almost exactly as he left it. Next door is the superb Wordsworth Museum. (☎01539 435 544. Both open daily mid-Feb. to mid-Jan. 9:30am-5pm. Cottage and museum £6.20, students and HI members £4.90. Museum only £4.90.) The 10km **Wordsworth Walk** circles the two lakes of the Rothay River, passing the cottage, the poet's grave in St. Oswald's churchyard, and **Rydal Mount,** where he died in 1850. (Rydal ☎01539 433 002. Open Mar.-Oct. daily 9:30am-5pm; Nov. and Feb. M and W-Su 10am-4pm. £5, students £3.75.) A steep, strenuous scramble leads to the top of Helm Cragg (6km round-trip). **YHA Butharlyp Howe (HI) ❷,** on Easedale Rd., is a large Victorian house with Internet. (☎01539 435 316. Dorms £16, under 18 £11. MC/V.) A staple since 1854, the famous gingerbread at **Sarah Nelson's Grasmere Gingerbread Shop ❶,** in Church Cottage, outside St. Oswald's Church, is a bargain at £0.33 per piece. (☎01593 435 428; www.grasmeregingerbread.co.uk. Open Easter-Sept. M-Sa 9:15am-5:30pm, Su 12:30-5:30pm; Oct.-Easter M-Sa 9:30am-4:30pm, Su 12.30-5:30pm.) **Bus** #555 stops in Grasmere every hour on its way south to Ambleside or north to Keswick.

KESWICK. Between towering Skiddaw peak and the northern edge of Lake Derwentwater, Keswick (KEZ-ick) rivals Windermere as the Lake District's tourist capital. A standout 6km day-hike from Keswick culminates with the eerily striking **Castlerigg Stone Circle,** a 5000-year-old Neolithic henge. Another short walk leads to the beautiful **Friar's Crag,** on the shore of Derwentwater, and **Castlehead,** a viewpoint encompassing the town, the lakes, and the peaks beyond. Both of these walks are fairly easy, with only a few strenuous moments. **YHA Derwentwater (HI) ❶,** Barrow House, Borrowdale, is a 200-year-old house with its own waterfall. Take bus #79 (1 per hr.) 3km south out of Keswick. (☎01768 777 246. Open Mar.-Oct. daily; Nov.-Feb. F-Sa only. Dorms £14, under 18 £10. MC/V.) Maps and information on area walks are available at the **NPIC,** in Moot Hall, Market Sq. (☎01768 772 645. Open Apr.-Oct. daily 9:30am-5:30pm.)

WALES (CYMRU)

If many of the nearly three million Welsh people had their druthers, they would be floating miles away from the English. Ever since England solidified its control over Wales with the murder of Prince Llywelyn ap Gruffydd in 1282, relations between the two countries have been marked by a powerful unease. Wales clings steadfastly to its Celtic heritage, and the Welsh language endures in conversation, commerce, and literature. As mines faltered in the mid-20th century, Wales turned its economic eye from heavy industry to tourism. Travelers today come for the dramatic beaches, cliffs, mountains, and brooding castles.

CARDIFF (CAERDYDD) ☎029

Formerly the main port of call for Welsh coal, Cardiff (pop. 306,000) is now the port of arrival for a distinctive international population. "Europe's youngest capital" stakes its reputation on its progressive attitudes, yet tradition, evidenced by the red dragons emblazoned on every flag and store window, remains strong.

TRANSPORTATION AND PRACTICAL INFORMATION. Trains (☎08457 484 950) leave Central Station, Central Sq., for: Bath (1-1½hr., 1-3 per hr., £13); Birmingham (2hr., 2 per hr., £22); Edinburgh (7-7½hr., 3 per day, £96); London

Paddington (2hr., 2 per hr., £46). National Express **buses** (☎08705 808 080) leave from Wood St. for Birmingham (2¼hr., 8 per day, £21), London (3½hr., 9 per day, £19), Manchester (6hr., 8 per day, £21). Pick up a free *Wales Bus, Rail, and Tourist Map and Guide* at the tourist office. Cardiff Bus (Bws Caerdydd), St. David's House, Wood St. (☎2066 6444), runs green and orange city buses in Cardiff and surrounding areas. (Service ends M-Sa 11:20pm, Su 11pm. £0.65-1.55, week pass £12.) The **tourist office,** the Old Library, The Hayes, books rooms for a £2 fee and a 10% deposit. (☎2022 7281; www.visitcardiff.info. Open M-Sa 10am-6pm, Su 10am-4pm.) The public **library,** at Frederick St. and Bridge St., offers free **Internet** in 30min. slots. (☎2038 2116. Open M-W and F 9am-6pm, Th 9am-7pm, Sa 9am-5:30pm.) **Postal Code:** CF10 2SJ.

ACCOMMODATIONS AND FOOD. Budget rooms are hard to find; the cheapest B&Bs (from £20) are on the city outskirts. **Cardiff International Backpacker ❷,** 98 Neville St., is a dream, with a Happy hour (Su-Th 7-9pm) and a roof patio with hammocks. (☎2034 5577; www.cardiffbackpacker.com. Light breakfast. Internet £2 per hr. Curfew Su-Th 2:30am. Dorms £17; doubles £38; triples £48. Credit card required for advance booking. MC/V.) **Acorn Camping and Caravaning ❶,** near Rosedew Farm, Ham Ln. South, Llantwit Major, is 1hr. by bus #X91 from Central Station and a 15min. walk from the Ham Ln. stop. (☎01446 794 024. Electricity £3. Tent sites £6.) **Celtic Cauldron Wholefoods ❶,** 47-49 Castle Arcade, is the place for Glamorganshire sausage, seaweed-based laverbread, and Welsh rarebit. (☎2238 7185. Entrees £5. Open M-Sa 8:30am-5pm, Su 11am-4pm. MC/V.) Find budget food at the **Central Market,** between St. Mary St. and Trinity St., with produce, bread, and raw meat. (Open daily 10am-4pm.) **Caroline Street** is a post-club hot spot, with curried or fried goodies at shops that stay open until 3 or 4am.

SIGHTS AND ENTERTAINMENT. After 2000 years, the peacocks that strut around the green of **Cardiff Castle** still wear crowns (of sorts) suited for the royalty that inspired the castle's Norman keep, Victorian mansion, and other extravagant buildings. (☎2087 8100. Open daily Mar.-Oct. 9:30am-6pm; Nov.-Feb. 9:30am-5pm. £6.50, students £5.) The **Civic Centre,** in Cathays Park, includes Alexandra Gardens, City Hall, and the **National Museum and Gallery.** The museum's exhibits range from a room full of carved Celtic crosses to a walk-through display of Wales's indigenous flora and fauna. (☎2039 7951. Open Tu-Su 10am-5pm. Free.)

VICTORIAN VICTUALS

A step into Cardiff's bustling Central Market is a step into a past century. Vendors at Victorian-style stalls call out to shoppers, urging them to buy fresh fruit, honeyed rolls, veal cuts, and flowers. Elderly country women shuffle past with their satchels, arguing over lamb prices. But you won't find the market a complete anachronism. Next to traditional food sellers (and in the same antique-style stalls), other vendors offer watch straps, mobile phone cards, and cuff links to the passing crowds. Vendors and people of all walks of life are crammed into this pleasant space, lit by 19-century skylights far above.

Central Market, in addition to serving as an intriguing cultural lesson, has dirt-cheap pricing on most food goods. The bakery near the center of the ground floor stalls, sells heaping chunks of bread pudding for 40p, while scones and cakes start at 50p. The rolls, when paired with cheeses (try local ones—like the mild, semi-crumbly cheese from Caerphilly) and meats from other sellers, provide great picnic fare. Locals rave about the seafood.

Take a bag of market plunder to the Cardiff Castle grounds (admission free) and watch the glossy peacocks strut around the green as you eat.

Cardiff's Central Market is located on The Hayes in the city center. Open 8am-5:30pm, but opening times of individual stalls may vary.

After 11pm the majority of Cardiff's popular downtown pubs stop serving alcohol, and the action migrates to an array of nearby clubs, most located on or around **St. Mary Street.** For up-to-date nightlife info, check the free *Buzz* guide or the *Itchy Cardiff Guide* (£3.50). Locals love **Clwb Ifor Bach,** 11 Womanby St. Three worlds collide in the eclectic Clwb: the ground floor plays cheesy pop and oldies; the bar on the middle floor lets clubbers unwind to softer music; the top, with low ceilings, rocks out to live bands or hardcore trance. There are drink specials every night, but the cover can be hefty (£3-8) for popular bands. Be sure to check the listing beforehand—the Clwb's atmosphere varies radically depending on the night. (☎232 199; www.clwb.net. Open M-Th until 2am, F-Sa until 3am.) Trendy clubbers of every persuasion gyrate at **Club X,** 35 Charles St., on weekends after other clubs close. (Cover €3-7. Open W 9pm-2am, F-Sa 10pm-6am.)

DAYTRIP FROM CARDIFF: CAERPHILLY CASTLE. Visitors to **Caerphilly Castle,** 13km north of Cardiff, may find the 30-acre castle easy to navigate today, but 13th-century warriors had to contend with pivoting drawbridges, trebuchets, crossbows, and catapults (now unloaded and on display) when attacking this stronghold, the most technologically advanced fortification of its time. Take the train (20min., M-Sa 2 per hr., £3.30) or bus #26 from Central Station. (☎2088 3143. Open June-Sept. daily 9:30am-6pm; Apr.-May daily 9:30am-5pm; Oct.-Mar. M-Sa 9:30am-4pm, Su 11am-4pm. £3.50, students £3.)

WYE VALLEY

It's no wonder that William Wordsworth mused on the tranquility and pastoral majesty that suffuse the once-troubled Welsh-English border territory of Wye Valley. As the Wye River (Afon Gwy) meanders through the tranquil valley riddled with sheep farms, trails, abbeys, and castles, much of the landscape still seems utterly untouched by human encroachment and the passage of time.

TRANSPORTATION. Chepstow is the best entrance to the valley. Trains (☎08457 484 950; www.nationalrail.com) run to Chepstow from Cardiff (45min., 1-2 per hr., £5.40). National Express buses (☎08705 808 080; www.nationalexpress.com) arrive from Cardiff (50min., 13 per day, £4.30) and London (2½hr., 7 per day, £17). For info on walking trails accessible by local bus, pick up *Discover the Wye Valley on Foot and by Bus* (£0.50). Hiking is a great way to explore. The 220km Wye Valley Walk treks north from Chepstow, through Hay-on-Wye, and on to Prestatyn. Offa's Dyke Path has 285km of hiking and biking paths along the Welsh-English border. For info, ask the Offa's Dyke Association (☎01547 528 753).

CHEPSTOW AND TINTERN ☎01291

Flowers spring from the cliffside ruins of **Castell Casgwent,** Britain's oldest datable stone castle (c. 1070), which offers stunning views of the Wye. (☎624 065. Open daily 9:30am-6pm. £3.50, students £3.) The **First Hurdle Guest House ❸,** 9-10 Upper Church St., has comfy rooms near the castle. (☎622 189. Singles £35; doubles £55. AmEx/MC/V.) Find groceries at **Tesco** on Station Rd. (Open M 8am-midnight, Tu-F 24hr., Sa midnight-10pm, Su 10am-4pm.) **Trains** arrive on Station Rd.; **buses** stop in front of Somerfield supermarket. Buy tickets at **The Travel House,** 9 Moor St. (☎623 031. Open M-Sa 9am-5:30pm.) The **tourist office** is on Bridge St. (☎623 772; www.chepstow.co.uk. Open daily Apr.-Oct. 10am-5:30pm; Nov.-Mar. 10am-3:30pm.) **Postal Code:** NP16 5DA.

Eight kilometers north of Chepstow on A466, the Gothic arches of **Tintern Abbey** "connect the landscape with the quiet of the sky"—as described in Wordsworth's famous poem, written just a few kilometers away. (☎689 251. Open June-

Sept. daily 9:30am-6pm; Apr.-May and Oct. daily 9:30am-5pm; Nov.-Mar. M-Sa 9:30am-4pm, Su 11am-4pm. £3.50, students £3. 45min. audio tour £1.) A 3km hike along **Monk's Trail** leads to **Devil's Pulpit,** from which Satan is said to have tempted the monks as they worked in the fields. **YHA St. Briavel's Castle (HI) ❶,** 6km north-east of Tintern across the English border, occupies a 13th-century fortress. While a unique experience—it was formerly King John's hunting lodge—it's somewhat remote, and should only be booked by those prepared for a 3km uphill hike. From A466 (bus #69 from Chepstow; ask to be let off at Bigsweir Bridge) or Offa's Dyke, follow signs from the edge of the bridge. (☎01594 530 272. Lockout 10am-5pm. Curfew 11:30pm. Dorms £18. MC/V.) Campers can use the **field ❶** next to the old train station (£2). Try **The Moon and Sixpence ❷,** on High St., for classic pub grub. (☎689 284. Kitchen open noon-2:30pm and 6:30-9:30pm. Open daily noon-11pm.)

BRECON BEACONS NATIONAL PARK

The Parc Cenedlaethol Bannau Brycheiniog encompasses 1340 sq. km of red sandstone crags, shaded forests, and breathtaking waterfalls. The park is divided into four main regions: Brecon Beacons, where King Arthur's fortress is thought to have stood; Fforest Fawr, with the spectacular waterfalls of Ystradfellte; the eastern, Tolkien-esque Black Mountains; and the remote, western, and confusingly named Black Mountain. Brecon, on the park's edge, is the best base for touring.

TRANSPORTATION. Trains (☎08457 484 950) run from London Paddington via Cardiff to Abergavenny, at the park's southeastern corner, and to Merthyr Tydfil, on the southern edge. National Express (☎08705 808 080) **bus** #509 runs to Brecon once per day from Cardiff (1¼hr., £3.50) and London (5hr., £23). Stagecoach Red and White bus #21 arrives in Brecon from Abergavenny (50min., 7 per day, £5.80). The free *Brecon Beacons: A Visitor's Guide*, available at NPICs, details bus coverage and lists walks accessible by public transportation.

BRECON (ABERHONDDU). Hikers start at the northern edge of the mountains in Brecon. Rooms fill up well in advance during the mid-August **Jazz Festival**—remember to reserve ahead. Camp at **Pencelli Castle Caravan and Camping Park ❶,** about 5km from Brecon on the Taff Trail. (☎665 451. £7.50-8.50 per person, varies by season.) **Buses** arrive at the **Bulwark** in the central square from Cardiff (1¼hr., 1 per

THE BIG SPLURG

CRAZY, OR COASTEERING?

St. David's may be the birthplac of the Welsh patron saint, but i recent years it's witnessed a dif ferent kind of *naissance:* the ris of a unique adventure sport (o insanity) called coasteering.

Picture it—you swim throug churning waves to a rocky out cropping at the base of a cliff. Yo clamber out of the sea, then scal the rock face until you reach ledge 30 ft. above. You paus and peer into the water far below The crashing surf obscures th surface, but you know what to do you draw in a deep breath, stee yourself, and take the plunge.

Inspired by Pembrokeshire' dramatic shoreline, coasteering i a thrilling combination of roc scrambling, cliff diving, and ope water swimming. You'll spend a least 3hr. navigating up and dow the coast, so some level of fitnes is required. Still, the beginning level trips are far from grueling, s coasteering is a surprisingl accessible sport.

TYF Adventure in St. David' specializes in coasteering an offers courses in three levels from novice to advanced. A hal day of coasteering is £45. TY also offers weekend packages including meals, two nights' sta in the TYF-run B&B, and multipl sessions of coasteering (£200).

Booking office on High St. in S David's. ☎01347 721 611 www.tyf.com. Open daily 9an 5:30pm, longer in summer.

day, £3.30). The **tourist office** is in the Cattle Market parking lot; walk through Bethel Square off Lion St. (☎01874 622 485. Open M-F 9:30am-5:30pm.)

THE BRECON BEACONS. These peaks at the center of the park lure hikers with grassy slopes and impressive vistas, provided the day is clear. The most convenient (and most overcrowded) route to the top begins at **Storey Arms** (a parking lot and bus stop on the A470) and offers views of **Llyn Cwm Llwch** (HLIN koom hlooch), a 600m deep glacial pool. Consult guides at the NPICs in Brecon or Abergavenny for recommendations on alternate trails.

FFOREST FAWR. Forests abound with moss and ferns and funnel water over spectacular falls near **Ystradfellte** (uh-strahd-FELTH-tuh), about 11km southwest of the Beacons. Sixteen kilometers of trails pass Fforest Fawr, the headlands of the waterfall district, on their way to the somewhat touristy **Dan-yr-Ogof Showcaves.** (☎01639 730 284. Open Apr.-Oct. daily 10am-3pm. £9, children £6.) Stagecoach Red and White **bus** #63 (1½hr., 2-3 per day, £3-4) stops at the caves en route to Brecon.

THE BLACK MOUNTAINS. Located in the easternmost section of the park, the Black Mountains are a group of long, lofty ridges offering 200 sq. km of solitude and unsurpassed ridge-walks. Begin forays from **Crickhowell,** on the A40, or travel the eastern boundary along **Offa's Dyke Path,** which is dotted with impressive ruins. The **YHA Capel-y-ffin (HI)** ❶ (kap-EL-uh-fin), along Offa's Dyke Path, is 13km from Hay-on-Wye. Take Stagecoach Red and White **bus** #39 from Hereford to Brecon, stop before Hay-on-Wye, and walk uphill. (☎01873 890 650. Lockout 10am-5pm. Curfew 11pm. Open all year, but call 48hr. ahead. Camping £5 per tent. Dorms £11, under 18 £8. MC/V. YHA plans to close Capel-y-Ffin in October 2007.)

SNOWDONIA NATIONAL PARK

Amid Edward I's impressive man-made battlements in Northern Wales lies the 2175 sq. km natural fortress of Snowdonia National Park. Snowdonia's craggy peaks, the highest in England and Wales, yield diverse terrain—pristine, glittering blue lakes dot rolling grasslands, while slate cliffs slope into wooded hills.

TRANSPORTATION AND PRACTICAL INFORMATION. Trains (☎08457 484 950) stop at larger towns on the park's outskirts, including Conwy (p. 178). The Conwy Valley Line runs across the park from Llandudno through Betws-y-Coed to Blaenau Ffestiniog (1hr., 2-7 per day). There it connects with the narrow-gauge Ffestiniog Railway (p. 177), which runs through the mountains to Porthmadog, meeting the Cambrian Coaster line to Llanberis and Aberystwyth. **Buses** run to the interior of the park from Conwy and Caernarfon; consult the *Gwynedd Public Transport Maps and Timetables* and *Conwy Public Transport Information,* free in all regional tourist offices. The **Snowdonia National Park Information Headquarters (NPIC)** is in Penrhyndeudraeth, Gwynedd (☎01766 770 274; www.eryri-npa.gov.uk or www.gwynedd.gov.uk).

HIKING. The highest peak in England and Wales at 1085m, **Mount Snowdon** is the park's most popular destination. Its Welsh name is *Yr Wyddfa* (the burial place)—local lore holds that Rhita Gawr, a giant cloaked with the beards of the kings he slaughtered, is buried here. Six paths of varying difficulty wind their way up Snowdon; pick up *Ordnance Survey Landranger Map #115* (£6.50) and *Outdoor Leisure Map #17* (£7.50), as well as individual trail guides, at tourist offices and NPICs. No matter how beautiful the weather is below, it will be cold, wet, and unpredictable high up—dress accordingly. Contact **Mountaincall Snowdonia** (☎09068 500 449) for local forecasts and ground conditions or visit an NPIC.

LLANBERIS ☎01286

Llanberis owes its outdoorsy bustle to the appeal of Mt. Snowdon, just south of town. The popular and pricey **Snowdon Mountain Railway** has been helping visitors "climb" to Snowdon's summit since 1896. (☎0870 458 0033; www.snowdonrailway.co.uk. Open daily Mar.-early Nov. 9am-5pm. Mar.-May trains stop halfway to the summit. £14, round-trip £20.) From the bus station, walk up the hill past the railway station and the Victoria Hotel, and round the bend to the left to reach the lovely **Snowdon Cottage ❸**, offering a garden with a castle view, welcoming hearth, and gracious hostess. (☎872 015. £22 per person. Discount for multiple nights. Cash only.) KMP (☎870 880) **bus** #88 runs from Caernarfon (25min.; 1-2 per hr.; £1.50, round-trip £2). The **tourist office** is at 41B High St. (☎870 765. Open Easter-Oct. daily 9:30am-5pm; Nov.-Easter M and F-Su 11am-4pm.)

HARLECH ☎01766

Harlech Castle is part of the "iron ring" of fortresses built by Edward I to keep an eye on Welsh troublemakers, but it later served as the insurrection headquarters of Welsh rebel Owain Glyndŵr. (☎780 552. Open June-Sept. daily 9:30am-6pm; Apr.-May and Oct. daily 9:30am-5pm; Nov.-Mar. M-Sa 9:30am-4pm, Su 11am-4pm. £3, students £2.50.) Enjoy spacious rooms and breakfast overlooking the ocean and castle at **Arundel ❷**, Stryd Fawr. Energetic Mrs. Stein (pronounced "Steen") will pick you up if the steep climb from the train station isn't appealing. (☎780 637. £16 per person. Cash only.) **The Weary Walker's Cafe ❶**, on Stryd Fawr near the bus stop, has sandwich and baguette options. Most are £2-3. (☎780 751. Open in summer daily 9:30am-5pm; low season 10:30am-4pm. Cash only.) Harlech lies midway on the Cambrian Coaster line; Arriva Cymru **train** T5 arrives from Porthmadog (20min., 3-7 per day, £6.40) and connects to other towns on the Llyn Peninsula. The **Day Ranger** pass allows unlimited travel on the Coaster line for one day (£7, children £3.50). The **tourist office,** on Stryd Fawr, doubles as an NPIC. (☎780 658. Open daily Easter-Oct. 9:30am-12:30pm and 1:30-5:30pm.) **Postal Code:** LL46 2YA.

LLŶN PENINSULA ☎01766

The seclusion and sublime tranquility of the Llŷn Peninsula have humbled visitors since the Middle Ages, when pilgrims traversed it on their way to Bardsey Island. Today, sun worshippers make the pilgrimage to the beaches that line the southern coast. **Porthmadog,** on the southeastern part of the peninsula, is the main gateway. This travel hub's main attraction is the **Ffestiniog Railway,** which offers a bumpy, scenic ride from Harbour Station, High St., into the hills of Snowdonia. (☎516 000; www.festrail.co.uk. 3hr. round-trip; 2-10 per day; £17, students £14.) The birthplace of Lawrence of Arabia, **Snowdon Lodge ❶**, is a great option in nearby Tremadog, 15min. down High St. from the centre of Porthmadog. (☎515 354; www.snowdonlodge.co.uk. Breakfast included. Laundry £2. Dorms £12.50-13.50; doubles £29-33; triples £44-50. AmEx/MC/V.) The northern end of the Cambrian Coaster **train** (☎08457 489 450) runs from Aberystwyth or Birmingham to Porthmadog (2hr., 3-7 per day) via Machynlleth. Express Motors (☎01286 881 108) **bus** #1 stops in Porthmadog on its way from Blaenau Ffestiniog to Caernarfon (1hr., 1 per hr., £2.60). The **tourist office** is on High St. by the harbor. (☎512 981. Open daily Easter-Oct. 9:30am-5:30pm; Nov.-Easter 10am-5pm.) **Postal Code:** LL9 9AD.

BRITAIN

CAERNARFON ☎01286

Majestic and fervently Welsh, the walled city of Caernarfon (car-NAR-von) has a world-famous castle at its prow and mountains in its wake. Edward I began building **Caernarfon Castle** in 1283 to contain and intimidate the rebellious Welsh, but it was left unfinished when he ran out of money. The castle is nonetheless an architectural feat; its walls withstood a rebel siege in 1404 with only 28 defenders. (☎677 617. Open June-Sept. daily 9:30am-6pm; Apr.-May and Oct. daily 9:30am-5pm; Nov.-Mar. M-Sa 9:30am-4pm, Su 11am-4pm. £4.90, students £4.50.) **☒Totter's Hostel ❶,** 2 High St., has spacious rooms, a comfortable living room, and terrific owners. (☎672 963. Dorms £13. Cash only.) Charming **Hole-in-the-Wall Street** offers a tremendous collection of bistros, cafes, and restaurants from which to choose. Arriva Cymru (☎08706 082 608) **buses** #5 and 5X leave the city center at Penllyn for Conwy (1¾hr., 1-3 per hr.). National Express (☎08705 808 080) runs to London (9hr., 1 per day, £26). The **tourist office** is on Castle St. (☎672 232. Open Apr.-Oct. daily 9:30am-5:30pm; Nov.-Mar. M-Sa 10am-4:30pm.) **Postal Code:** LL55 2ND.

CONWY
☎01492

The central attraction of this tourist mecca is the imposing, 13th-century ☒**Conwy Castle.** Try to get on "celebrity" guide Neville Hortop's tour; his ferocious approach to history is very entertaining. (☎592 358. Open June-Sept. daily 9:30am-6pm; Apr.-May and Oct. daily 9:30am-5pm; Nov.-Mar. M-Sa 9:30am-4pm, Su 11am-4pm. £4, students £3.50. Tours £1.) Enjoy comfy rooms at **Swan Cottage ❷,** 18 Berry St., a renovated 16th-century building. (☎596 840; myweb.tiscali.co.uk/swancottage. £20 per person. Cash only.) **Pen-y-Bryn Tea Rooms ❶,** on High St., caters to those with a fondness for good tea (high tea £4.50). (☎596 445. Sandwiches from £3.50. Open M-F 10am-5pm, Sa-Su 10am-5:30pm. Cash only.) Arriva Cymru **buses** (☎08706 082 608) #5 and 5X stop in Conwy on their way to Caernarfon from Llandudno (1-1¼hr., 1-2 per hr., £5). The **tourist office,** at the castle entrance, books beds for £2 plus a 10% deposit. (☎592 248. Open daily June-Sept. 9:30am-6pm; May and Oct.-Nov. 9:30am-5pm; Dec.-Apr. 9:30am-4pm.) **Postal Code:** LL32 8H7.

SCOTLAND

A little over half the size of England but with only one-tenth of its population, Scotland possesses the open spaces and natural splendor its southern neighbor cannot hope to rival. The craggy, heathered Highlands and the luminescent mists of the Hebrides will elicit awe, while farmlands and fishing villages harbor a gentler beauty. Scotland at its best is a world apart from the rest of the UK, and its people revel in a culture all their own. The Scots defended their independence for hundreds of years before reluctantly joining with England in 1707. While the kilts, bagpipes, and souvenir clan paraphernalia of the big cities may grow tiresome, a visit to the less touristed regions of Scotland will allow you to rub elbows with the inheritors of many cherished ancient traditions: a B&B owner speaking Gaelic to her children, a crofter cutting peat, or a fisherman setting out in his skiff at dawn.

✈ ▐ TRANSPORTATION

Bus travel from London is generally cheaper than **train** fares. **British Airways** (☎0870 8509 850; www.ba.com) sells round-trip England-to-Scotland tickets starting at £80. **British Midland** (☎08706 070 555; www.flybmi.com) offers saver fares from London to Glasgow (from £78 round-trip). Some of the cheapest fares available are through **easyJet** (☎08706 000 000; www.easyjet.com), which flies to Edinburgh and Glasgow from London (Online fares only; prices vary).

In the **Lowlands** (south of Stirling and north of the Borders), train and bus connections are frequent. In the **Highlands,** trains snake slowly along a few restricted routes, bypassing the northwest almost entirely; buy tickets onboard. A great money-saver is the **Freedom of Scotland Travelpass,** which allows unlimited train travel, transport on most Caledonian MacBrayne ferries, and discounts on other lines. Purchase it *before* traveling to Britain from any BritRail distributor. **Buses** are the best way to travel; Scottish Citylink (☎08705 505 050) provides most inter-city service. **Postbuses** (Royal Mail customer service ☎08457 740 740) are red mail vans that pick up passengers and mail once or twice a day in more remote locales, charging 40p-£5 (often nothing). They're a reliable way to get around the Highlands. HAGGiS (☎01315 579 393; www.haggisadventures.com) and MacBackpackers (☎01315 589 900; www.macbackpackers.com) cater to the young, adventurous set with witty pre-packaged or hop-on/hop-off tours.

EDINBURGH ☎0131

A city of elegant stone amid rolling hills and ancient volcanoes, Edinburgh (ED-in-bur-ra; pop. 500,000) is Scotland's jewel. Since David I granted it burgh (town) status in 1130, it has been a hotbed for forward-thinking artists and intellectuals.That tradition lives on today as new clubs emerge beneath its medieval spires. In August, Edinburgh becomes a mecca for the arts, drawing talent and crowds from around the world to its International and Fringe Festivals.

TRANSPORTATION

Flights: Edinburgh International Airport (☎0870 040 0007), 7 mi. west of the city. Lothian **Airlink** (☎555 6363) shuttles between the airport and Waverley Bridge (25min.; every 10-15min., 1 per hr. after midnight; £3, children £2. Round-trip £5/3).

Trains: Waverley Station (☎08457 484 950), between Princes St., Market St., and Waverley Bridge. Trains to: **Aberdeen** (2½hr.; M-Sa 1 per hr., Su 8 per day; £35); **Glasgow** (1hr., 4 per hr., £9.90); **Inverness** (3½hr., every 2hr., £32); **London King's Cross** (4¾hr., 1 per hr., £111); **Stirling** (50min., 2 per hr., £5.90).

Buses: Edinburgh Bus Station, on the east side of St. Andrew Sq. Open daily 6am-midnight. National Express (☎08705 808 080) to **London** (10hr., 4 per day, £31). Scottish Citylink (☎08705 505 050) to: **Aberdeen** (4hr., 1 per hr., £18); **Glasgow** (1hr., M-Sa 4 per hr., Su 2 per hr., £4); **Inverness** (4½hr., 8-10 per day, £17). A combination bus-ferry route goes to **Belfast** (2 per day, £20) and **Dublin, IRE** (1 per day, £28).

Public Transportation: Lothian buses (☎555 6363; www.lothianbuses.com) provide most services. Exact change required (£1 flat fare, children 60p). **Daysaver** ticket (£2.30, children £2) available from any driver. **Night buses** cover selected routes after midnight (£2). **First Edinburgh** (☎0870 872 7271) also operates locally. **Traveline** (☎0870 6082 608) has information on all area public transport.

ORIENTATION AND PRACTICAL INFORMATION

Edinburgh is a glorious city for walking. **Princes Street** is the main thoroughfare in **New Town,** the northern section of the city. From there you can view the impressive stone facade of the towering **Old Town** to the south. The **Royal Mile** (Castle Hill, Lawnmarket, High St., and Canongate) is the major road in the Old Town and connects Edinburgh Castle in the west to the Palace of Holyroodhouse in the east. **North Bridge, Waverley Bridge,** and **The Mound** connect Old and New Town. Two kilometers northeast, **Leith** is the city's seaport on the Firth of Forth.

Tourist Office: Waverley Market, 3 Princes St. (☎0845 22 55 121), on the north side of Waverley Station. Books rooms for £3 plus 10% deposit; sells bus, museum, tour, and theater tickets. Open July-Aug. M-Sa 9am-8pm, Su 10am-8pm; May-June and Sept. M-Sa 9am-7pm, Su 10am-7pm; Apr. and Oct. M-Sa 9am-6pm, Su 10am-6pm; Nov.-Mar. M-Sa 9am-5pm, Su 10am-5pm.

GLBT Resources: Pick up *ScotsGay* at the tourist office, or drop by **Edinburgh Lesbian, Gay, and Bisexual Centre,** 58A-60 Broughton St. (☎478 7069), inside Sala Cafe-Bar.

Emergency: ☎999 or 112, free from any payphone.

Police: Headquarters at Fettes Ave. (☎311 3901; www.lbp.police.uk).

Hospital: Royal Infirmary of Edinburgh, 51 Little France Cr. (☎536 1000, emergencies 536 6000).

Internet Access: Free at the **Central Library** (☎242 8000) on George IV Bridge. Open M-Th 10am-8pm, F 10am-5pm, Sa 9am-1pm. **easyInternet Cafe,** 58 Rose St. (☎220 3577), inside Caffe Nero. £2 per hr. Open M-Sa 7am-10pm, Su 9am-10pm.

Post Office: (☎556 9546.) In the St. James Centre beside the bus station. Open M-Sa 9am-5:30pm. **Postal Code:** EH1 3SR.

ACCOMMODATIONS

Edinburgh accommodations cater to every kind of traveler. Hostels and hotels are the only city-center options, while B&Bs and guesthouses begin on the periphery. It's a good idea to reserve ahead in summer, and essential to be well ahead of the game at New Year's and during festival season (late July-early Sept.).

Budget Backpackers, 37-39 Cowgate (☎226 2351; www.budgetbackpackers.co.uk). The cleanest, brightest, and most modern of the inner city hostels. Spacious 2- to 12-bed rooms; female dorms available. Free city tour daily, pub crawl M-Sa. Continental breakfast £2. Free lockers. Reception 24hr. Dorms £9-24. MC/V. ❶

Globetrotter Inn, 46 Marine Dr. (☎336 1030; www.globetrotterinns.com). Only 15min. from both Waverley train station and Edinburgh International Airport, this hostel feels like a world of its own on large grounds next to the Firth of Forth. Hourly shuttle, 24hr. bar, shop, movie and TV rooms, gym, and hot tub. Curtained bunks offer maximum privacy. Light breakfast included. Free lockers. Dorms £15-18. Doubles £23. ❷

Castle Rock Hostel, 15 Johnston Terr. (☎225 9666; www.scotlands-top-hostels.com). Just steps from the castle, this friendly hostel has a party atmosphere. Nightly movies. 220 beds in 8- to 16-bed dorms. Continental breakfast £1.90. Laundry £2.50. Internet access 80p per 30min. Dorms £13-15; doubles and triples £15-17. AmEx/MC/V. ❷

Royal Mile Backpackers, 105 High St. (☎557 6120; www.scotlands-top-hostels.com). A well-kept wee hostel with community feel. Guests can use amenities at nearby High St. Hostel. 38 beds in 8-bed dorms. Continental breakfast £1.90. No lockable dorms. Laundry £2.50. Internet access 80p per 30min. Dorms £13-15. AmEx/MC/V. ❶

FOOD

Edinburgh features an exceptionally wide range of cuisines and restaurants. For a traditional taste of Scotland, the capital offers everything from haggis to creative "modern Scottish." Many pubs offer student and hosteler discounts in the early evening. Takeout shops on **South Clerk Street, Leith Street,** and **Lothian Road** have reasonably priced Chinese and Indian food. Buy groceries at **Sainsbury's,** 9-10 St. Andrew Sq. (☎225 8400. Open M-Sa 7am-10pm, Su 10am-8pm.)

The City Cafe, 19 Blair St. (☎220 0125), off the Royal Mile behind Tron Kirk. Relaxed cafe by day, flashy pre-club spot by night. Wraps for £6 and great shakes. Happy hour daily 5-8pm. Open daily 11am-1am. Kitchen closes M-Th 11pm, F-Su 10pm. MC/V. ❷

The Mosque Kitchen, 50 Potterrow. Tucked away in the courtyard of Edinburgh's modern central mosque, a jumble of mismatched chairs and long tables make this outdoor cafeteria popular with students from the university. £3.50 heaped plates of curry are hard to beat. Open M-Th and Sa-Su noon-7pm, F noon-1pm and 1:45-7pm. Cash only. ❶

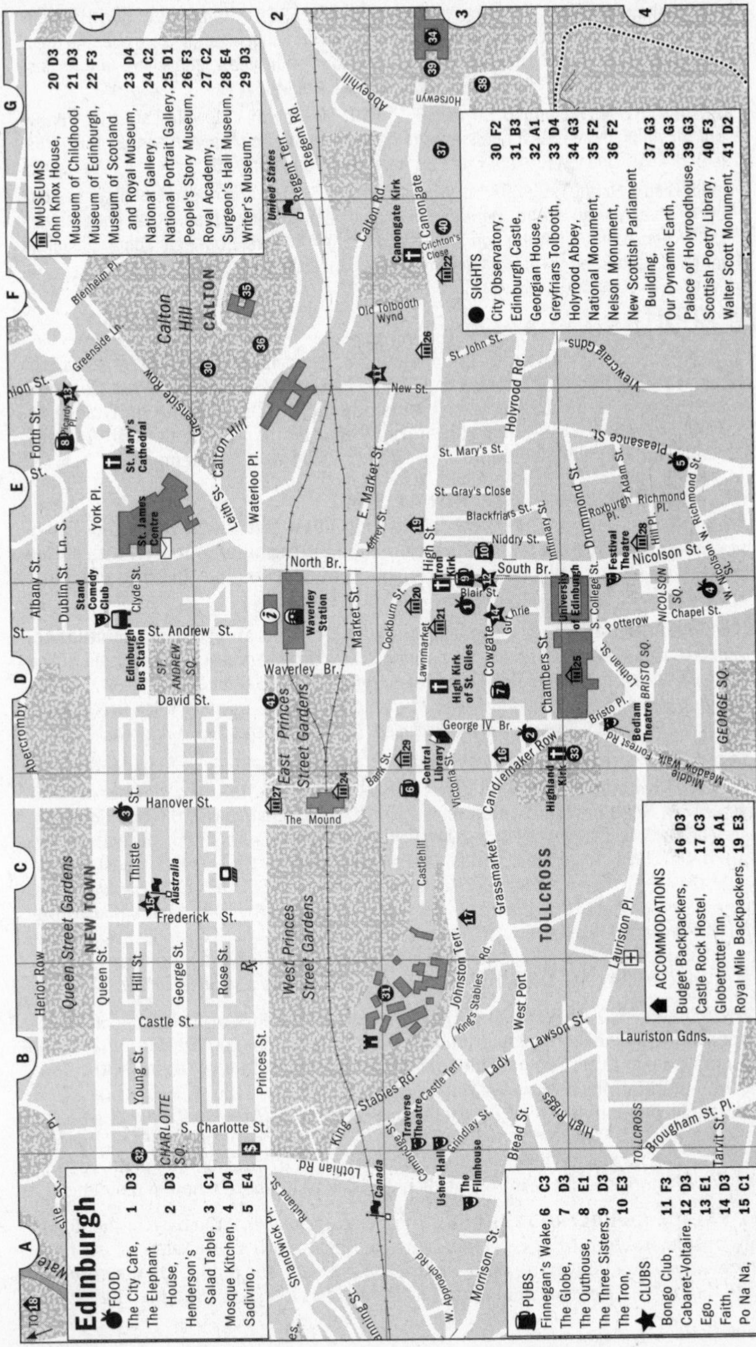
Edinburgh
FOOD
The City Cafe, 1 D3
The Elephant House, 2 D3
Henderson's Salad Table, 3 C1
Mosque Kitchen, 4 D4
Sadivino, 5 E4
PUBS
Finnegan's Wake, 6 C3
The Globe, 7 D3
The Outhouse, 8 E1
The Three Sisters, 9 D3
The Tron, 10 E3
CLUBS
Bongo Club, 11 F3
Cabaret-Voltaire, 12 D3
Ego, 13 E1
Faith, 14 D3
Po Na Na, 15 C1
ACCOMMODATIONS
Budget Backpackers, 16 D3
Castle Rock Hostel, 17 C3
Globetrotter Inn, 18 A1
Royal Mile Backpackers, 19 E3
MUSEUMS
John Knox House, 20 D3
Museum of Childhood, 21 D3
Museum of Edinburgh, 22 F3
Museum of Scotland and Royal Museum, 23 D4
National Gallery, 24 C2
National Portrait Gallery, 25 D1
People's Story Museum, 26 F3
Royal Academy, 27 C2
Surgeon's Hall Museum, 28 E4
Writer's Museum, 29 D3
SIGHTS
City Observatory, 30 F2
Edinburgh Castle, 31 B3
Georgian House, 32 A1
Greyfriars Tolbooth, 33 D4
Holyrood Abbey, 34 G3
National Monument, 35 F2
Nelson Monument, 36 F2
New Scottish Parliament Building, 37 G3
Our Dynamic Earth, 38 G3
Palace of Holyroodhouse, 39 G3
Scottish Poetry Library, 40 F3
Walter Scott Monument, 41 D2

BRITAIN

The Elephant House, 21 George IV Bridge (☎220 5355). Harry Potter and Hogwarts were born here as hasty scribblings. A perfect place to chill, chat, or pore over the stack of newspapers. Exotic teas and coffees, delicious shortbread, and filling fare for less than £7. Live music Th 8pm. Open daily 8am-11pm. MC/V. ❶

Sadivino, 52 W. Richmond St. (☎667 7719). A friendly sidewalk cafe that fills up quickly at lunchtime. Best of all, everything from paninis to more substantial Italian fare is under £4. Open M-F 11am-6pm, Sa noon-6pm. Cash only. ❶

Henderson's Salad Table, 94 Hanover St. (☎225 2131). The original member of Edinburgh's vegetarian scene, Henderson's have been dishing up seriously good salads (£4) for as long as anyone can remember. At night the wine bar gets going, offering a range of vegan and organic choices. Open M-Sa 7:30am-10:30pm. MC/V. ❶

SIGHTS

A boggling array of tours tout themselves as "the original," but the most worthwhile is the Edinburgh Literary Pub Tour. Led by professional actors, this 2hr. crash course in Scottish literature meets outside the Beehive Inn on Grassmarket. (☎226 6665; www.edinburghliterarypubtour.co.uk. June-Sept. daily 7:30pm; Mar.-May and Oct. Th-Su 7:30pm; Nov.-Feb. F 7:30pm. £7, students £6.)

THE OLD TOWN AND THE ROYAL MILE

Edinburgh's medieval center, the fascinating **Royal Mile,** defines the Old Town. Once lined with narrow shopfronts and slums towering to a dozen stories, this famous strip is now a playground for hostelers and locals alike, buzzing with bars, attractions, and the inevitable cheesy souvenir shops.

EDINBURGH CASTLE. Dominating the skyline from atop an extinct volcano, the castle is a testament to the city's past strategic importance. The castle is the result of centuries of renovation and rebuilding. The **One O'Clock Gun** fires Monday through Saturday. *(☎225 9846; www.historic-scotland.gov.uk. Open daily Apr.-Oct. 9:30am-6pm; Nov.-Mar. 9:30am-5pm. Guided tour included. £10.30, students £8.50. Audio tours £3/2.)*

CASTLE HILL AND LAWNMARKET AREA. The Scotch Whisky Experience at the **Scotch Whisky Heritage Centre** provides a Disney-style tour through the "history and mystery" of Scotland's most famous export. *(354 Castle Hill. ☎220 0441. Open daily June-Sept. 9:45am-5:30pm; Oct.-May 10am-5pm. Tours every 15min. £8.95, students £6.95.)* Staffed with knowledgeable guides, **Gladstone's Land** (c. 1617) is the oldest surviving house on the Royal Mile. *(477B Lawnmarket. ☎226 5856. Open daily July-Aug. 10am-7pm; Apr.-June and Sept.-Oct. 10am-5pm. £5, students £4.)* Nearby, **Lady Stair's House** contains the **Writer's Museum,** featuring memorabilia of three of Scotland's greatest literary figures: Robert Burns, Sir Walter Scott, and Robert Louis Stevenson. *(Lawnmarket. ☎529 4901. Open M-Sa 10am-5pm; during Festival also Su 2-5pm. Free.)*

BRITAIN

HIGH STREET AND CANONGATE AREA. At the **High Kirk of St. Giles** (St. Giles Cathedral), Scotland's principal church, John Knox delivered the fiery Presbyterian sermons that drove Mary, Queen of Scots, into exile. Most of today's structure was built in the 15th century, but parts date as far back as 1126. The Kirk hosts free concerts throughout the year. *(Where Lawnmarket becomes High St. ☎225 9442; www.stgilescathedral.org.uk. Open daily M-Sa 9am-5pm, Su 1-5pm. Suggested donation £1.; Canongate same hrs.)* The **Canongate Kirk,** on the hill at the end of the Royal Mile, is the resting place of economist Adam Smith; royals used to worship here when in residence.

THE PALACE OF HOLYROODHOUSE. This Stewart palace, at the base of the Royal Mile beside Holyrood Park, remains Queen Elizabeth II's official Scottish residence. As a result, only parts of the interior are open to the public. On the grounds stand the ruins of **Holyrood Abbey,** built by David I in 1128 and ransacked during the

Reformation. Only a single doorway remains from the original construction; most of the ruins date from the 13th century. in a recently renovated 17th-century schoolhouse near the entrance, the **Queen's Gallery** displays exhibits from the royal art collection. *(☎556 5100. Open Apr.-Oct. daily 9:30am-6pm; Nov.-Mar. M-Sa 9:30am-4:30pm. Closed to visitors while royals are in residence often June-July. £8.80, students £7.80. Queen's Gallery £5/4.50. Combo ticket £12.50/11. Audio tour free.)*

OTHER SIGHTS IN THE OLD TOWN. The **Museum of Scotland** and the **Royal Museum,** on Chambers St., south of the George IV Bridge, are not to be missed. The former houses a collection of Scottish artifacts. Don't miss the working **Corliss Steam Engine** and the **Maiden,** Edinburgh's pre-French-Revolution guillotine. The Royal Museum has European art and ancient Roman and Egyptian artifacts. *(☎247 4422; www.nms.ac.uk. Both open daily 10am-5pm. Free.)* Across the street, a statue of Greyfriar's pooch marks the entrance to the 17th-century **Highland Kirk,** ringed by an supposedly haunted churchyard. *(Off Candlemaker Row. ☎225 1900. Open Apr.-Oct. M-F 10:30am-4:30pm, Sa 10:30am-2:30pm; Nov.-Mar. Th 1:30-3:30pm. Free.)*

THE NEW TOWN

Edinburgh's new town is a masterpiece of Georgian design. James Craig, a 23-year-old architect, won the city-planning contest in 1767; his rectangular grid of three parallel streets (**Queen, George,** and **Princes**) linking two large squares (**Charlotte** and **St. Andrew**) reflects the Scottish Enlightenment's love of order.

ROYAL YACHT BRITANNIA. Northeast of the city center floats one of Edinburgh's top tourist attractions, the Royal Yacht *Britannia*. Used by the royals from 1953 to 1997, *Britannia* sailed around the world on state visits and royal holidays before settling here in Edinburgh for permanent retirement. Visitors can follow a free audio tour. *(Entrance on the Ocean Terminal's 3rd fl. Take bus #22 from Princes St. or #35 from the Royal Mile to Ocean Terminal; £1. ☎555 5566; www.royalyachtbritannia.co.uk. Open daily Mar.-Oct. 9:30am-4pm; Nov.-Feb. 10am-4:30pm. £9, students £7.)*

GEORGIAN HOUSE AND SCOTT MONUMENT. Georgian House gives a fair picture of how Edinburgh's elite lived 200 years ago. *(7 Charlotte Sq. ☎226 3318. Open daily July-Aug. 10am-7pm; Apr.-June and Sept.-Oct. 10am-5pm; Mar. and Nov. 11am-3pm. £5, students £4.)* The **Walter Scott Monument** is a "steeple without a church"; climb to the top for views stretching out to Princes St., the castle, and the surrounding city. *(Princes St. between The Mound and Waverley Bridge. ☎529 4068. Open Apr.-Sept. M-Sa 9am-6pm, Su 10am-6pm; Oct - Mar. M-Sa 9am-3pm, Su 10am-3pm. £2.50.)*

LOCAL LEGEND

GREYFRIARS BOBBY

Undoubtedly the most famous resident of the Greyfriars Tollbooth and Highland Kirk's ancient cemetery is a certain John Gray. The night after Gray's burial in 1858, his scruffy Skye terrier, Bobby, laid down on his master's grave. The next night, Bobby returned and again held vigil, as he would every night for the next 14 years. As word spread of this extraordinary display of loyalty, the legend of Greyfriars Bobby became a permanent part of Edinburgh lore; in 1867, the Lord Provost even paid for a renewal of Bobby's license.

After living to the age of 16, Greyfriars Bobby finally passed away, having spent all but two of his years guarding the tombstone. To honor his loyalty, the city erected a statue of the dog and buried him near his beloved master in the very same kirk.

Over the years this sweet story has found its way into numerous books and even a Disney film. The likeness, which sits at the intersection of George IV Bridge and Candlemaker Row, is the most photographed statue in Scotland. Still, there are those who have their doubts about this touching saga. Some claim that the grave that Bobby watched over belonged to another John Gray and not to his master. Others claim that the dog's real affection was for a nearby bakery. Such spoilsports, however, have been unsuccessful in tarnishing the legend of (dead) man's best friend.

THE NATIONAL GALLERIES. The National Galleries of Scotland in Edinburgh form an elite group, with excellent collections housed in stately buildings, all connected by a free shuttle that runs every 45min. The flagship is the **National Gallery of Scotland,** on The Mound, which has a superb collection of works by Renaissance, Romantic, and Impressionist masters. Don't miss the octagonal room which displays Poussin's entire *Seven Sacraments.* The basement houses a fine spread of Scottish art. The **Scottish National Portrait Gallery,** 1 Queen St., north of St. Andrew Sq., features the faces of famous men and women who have shaped Scotland's history. The gallery also hosts excellent visiting exhibits of contemporary artists. Take the free bus #13 from George St., or walk to the **Scottish National Gallery of Modern Art,** 75 Belford Rd., west of town, to see works by Braque, Matisse, and Picasso. The landscaping out front represents the concept of chaos theory using dirt and greenery. Part of the Gallery of Modern Art, the **Dean Gallery,** 73 Belford Rd., is dedicated to Dadaist and Surrealist art. *(☎624 6200; www.nationalgalleries.org. All open daily 10am-5pm; during Festival 10am-6pm. All free.)*

GARDENS AND PARKS

Off the eastern end of the Royal Mile, the oasis of **Holyrood Park** is a natural wilderness. **Arthur's Seat** is the park's highest point; the walk to the summit takes about 45min. Located in the city center and offering great views of the Old Town and the castle, the **Princes Street Gardens** are on the site of the drained Nor'Loch, where Edinburghers used to drown their accused witches. On summer days all of Edinburgh eats lunch here. The **Royal Botanic Gardens** are north of the city center. Tours wander across the grounds and through greenhouses. *(Inverleith Row. Take bus #23 or 27 from Hanover St. ☎552 7171. Open daily Apr.-Sept. 10am-7pm; Mar. and Oct. 10am-6pm; Nov.-Feb. 10am-4pm. Free. Glasshouses £3.50, students £3, children £1, families £8.)*

ENTERTAINMENT AND NIGHTLIFE

The summer sees an especially joyful string of events—music in the gardens, plays and films, and *ceilidhs* (KAY-lee; traditional Scottish dances). In winter, shorter days and the crush of students promote a flourishing nightlife. For the most up-to-date info on what's going on, check out *The List* (£2.50), available from any local newsstand. The **Festival Theatre,** 13-29 Nicholson St., stages ballet and opera, while the affiliated **King's Theatre,** 2 Leven St., hosts comedy, drama, musicals, and opera. (☎529 6000. Box office open M-Sa 10am-6pm. Tickets £5-55.) **The Stand Comedy Club,** 5 York Pl., has nightly acts. (☎558 7272. Tickets £1-8.) The **Filmhouse,** 88 Lothian Rd., shows quality European, arthouse, and Hollywood cinema. (☎228 2688. Tickets £3.50-5.50.) Edinburgh's live music scene is particularly vibrant. Enjoy live jazz at **Henry's Jazz Cellar,** 8 Morrison St. (☎538 7385. Tickets £5. Open daily 8pm-3am.) **Whistle Binkie's,** 4-6 South Bridge, off High St., is a subterranean pub with at least two live bands per night. (☎557 5114. Open daily until 3am.)

PUBS

Students and backpackers gather each night in the Old Town. Pubs on the **Royal Mile** attract a mixed crowd. Casual pub-goers move to live music on **Grassmarket, Candlemaker Row,** and **Victoria Street.** Historical pubs in the New Town cluster on **Rose Street,** parallel to Princes St. Depending on where you are, you'll hear last call sometime between 11pm and 1am, 3am during Festival season.

The Tron, 9 Hunter Sq., behind the Tron Kirk. Wildly popular for its great deals. 3 floors frequently host live music. Students and hostelers get £1 drinks on W nights. A mix of alcoves and pool tables downstairs. Open M-Sa 11:30am-1am, Su 12:30pm-1am.

The Outhouse, 12A Broughton St. (☎557 6668). Hidden up an alley off Broughton St., this bar is well worth seeking out. More stylish than your average pub but just as friendly, with one of the best beer gardens in the city. Open 11am-1am.

The Globe, 13 Niddry St. Backpackers recommend this hole-in-the-wall up and down the Royal Mile. Airs international sports, hosts DJs, and holds karaoke and quiz nights. Open M-F 4pm-1am, Sa noon-1am, Su 12:30pm-1am; during Festival until 3am.

The Three Sisters, 139 Cowgate. Loads of space for dancing, drinking, and chilling. Attracts a young crowd to its 3 bars (Irish, Gothic, and American). Close to 1000 people pass through the beer garden and barbecue on Sa nights. Open daily 9am-1am.

Finnegan's Wake, 9B Victoria St. Drink Ireland-style with several stouts on tap, road signs from Cork, and live Irish music every night. Open daily 1pm-1am.

CLUBS

Club venues are constantly closing down and reopening under new management; consult *The List* for updated info. Clubs cluster around the historically disreputable **Cowgate,** just downhill from and parallel to the Royal Mile. Most close at 3am, 5am during the Festival. The Broughton St. area of the New Town (better known as the **Broughton Triangle**) is the center of Edinburgh's gay community.

Cabaret-Voltaire, 36-38 Blair St. (☎220 6176; www.thecabaretvoltaire.com). With a wide range of live music, dance, and art, this club throws a great party. M cheap drinks. W huge 'We Are Electric' party. Cover up to £12. Open daily10pm-3am.

Bongo Club, 14 New St. (☎558 7604). Students and backpackers flock to the long-running and immensely popular Messenger (reggae) and Headspin (funk and dance) nights, each 1 Sa per month. Cover up to £7.

Faith, 207 Cowgate (☎225 9764). Inside an old church, this purple-hued club specializes in R&B. Very popular Su Chocolate. Occasional cover up to £7.

Po Na Na, 43B Frederick St. (☎226 2224), beneath Cafe Rouge. Moroccan-themed with parachute ceilings, red velvet couches, and an eclectic mix of music. Cover £2.50-6. Open Su-M and Th 11pm-3am, F-Sa 10pm-3am.

Ego, 14 Picardy Pl. (☎478 7434). Not strictly a gay club, Ego hosts gay nights, including the Vibe (Tu) and Blaze (3 F per month). Cover £3-10.

FESTIVALS

In August, Edinburgh is *the* place to be in Europe. What's commonly referred to as "the Festival" actually encompasses serveral independent events. For more info, check out www.edinburghfestivals.co.uk. The **Edinburgh International Festival** (www.eif.co.uk; Aug. 13-Sept. 2, 2007), the largest of them all, features a kaleidoscopic program of music, drama, dance, and art. Tickets (£7-58; 50% discount for students) are sold beginning in April, but a limited number of £5 tickets are available 1hr. before every event. Bookings can be made by mail, phone, fax, web, or in person at **The HUB** (☎473 2000), Edinburgh's Festival center, on Castle hill.

A less formal **Fringe Festival** (www.edfringe.com; Aug. 5-27, 2007) has grown around the established festival. Anyone who can afford the small registration fee can perform, guaranteeing a multitude of great to not-so-good independent acts and an absolutely wild month. The **Edinburgh Jazz and Blues Festival** is in late July. (www.jazzmusic.co.uk. Tickets on sale in June.) The excellent **Edinburgh International Film Festival** occurs during the second and third weeks of August at The Filmhouse. (www.edfilmfest.org.uk. Tickets on sale starting late July.) The fun doesn't stop for winter: **Hogmanay,** the traditional New Year's Eve festival, is a serious street party with a week of associated events (www.edinburghshogmanay.org).

DAYTRIP FROM EDINBURGH: ST. ANDREWS

Golf overruns the small city of St. Andrews, where the rules of the sport were formally established. Today, a mix of golfers and college students converge on its three medieval streets. Mary, Queen of Scots supposedly played at the **Old Course** just days after her husband was murdered. Non-members must present a handicap certificate or letter of introduction from a golf club. Reserve at least a year ahead, enter your name into a near-impossible lottery by 2pm the day before you hope to play, or get in line before dawn by the caddie master's hut as a single. (☎01334 466 666. Apr.-Oct. £80-120 per round; Nov.-Mar. £56.) The lovely budget option is the nine-hole **Balgove Course** (£10). If you need a break from the green, visit the **British Golf Museum,** next to the Old Course on Bruce Embankment, which details the ancient origins of the game. (☎01334 460 046. Open Mar.-Oct. M-Sa 9:30am-5:30pm, Su 10am-5pm; Nov.-Mar. daily 10am-4pm. £5, students £4.) **St. Andrews Castle** hides medieval siege tunnels and bottle-shaped dungeons. (☎01334 477 196. Open daily Apr.-Sept. 9:30am-6:30pm; Oct.-Mar. 9:30am-4:30pm. £4.) **Trains** (☎08457 484 950) stop 8km away in Leuchars, where buses #94 and 96 depart for St. Andrews (£1.85). **Buses** (☎01383 621 249) pull into City Rd. from Edinburgh (#X60; 2hr., M-Sa 1-2 per hr., £6.50) and Glasgow (#X24; 2½hr., M-Sa 1 per hr., £6.50). To get from the bus station to the **tourist office,** 70 Market St., turn right on City Rd. and take the first left. Ask for the free *St. Andrews Town Map and Guide.* (☎01334 472 021. Open July-Sept. M-Sa 9:30am-7pm, Su 9:30am-5pm; Apr.-June M-Sa 9:30am-5:30pm, Su 11am-4pm; Oct.-Mar. M-Sa 9:30am-5pm.)

GLASGOW ☎0141

Glasgow (pop. 630,000), Scotland's largest city, has reinvented itself many times and retains the mark of each transformation. Stately architecture recalls Queen Victoria's reign, while cranes littering the River Clyde bear witness to its sooty past as a major industrial hub. By day, world-class art museums and collections give Glasgow a thriving creative energy, but the city truly comes alive at night, fueled by its soccer-crazed locals.

TRANSPORTATION AND PRACTICAL INFORMATION. Flights land at **Glasgow International Airport (GLA;** ☎08700 400 0008; www.baa.co.uk/glasgow). Citylink bus #905 connects to Buchanan Station (25min., 6 per hr., £3.30). From **Glasgow Prestwick International Airport** (**PIK;** ☎0871 223 0700; www.gpia.co.uk), 52km away, express bus #X99 runs to Buchanan Station (50min., £3.40) and trains leave for Central Station every hour (30min.; £5.20, with Ryanair flight printout £2.60). **Trains** pull into Central Station, on Gordon St. (U: St. Enoch), from London King's Cross (6hr., 1 per hr., £91) and Manchester (4hr., 1 per hr., £40). From Queen St. Station, on George Sq. (U: Buchanan St.), trains go to: Aberdeen (2½hr., 7-11 per day, £34); Edinburgh (50min., 4 per hr., £8.20); Inverness (3¼hr., 4-7 per day, £34). Bus #88 (£0.50) connects the two stations, but it's only a 5-10min. walk. Scottish Citylink (☎08705 505 050) **buses** leave Buchanan Station, on Killermont St., for: Aberdeen (4hr., M-Sa 1 per hr., £17); Edinburgh (50min., 4 per hr., £4); Inverness (3½hr., M-Sa 7 per day, £34). National Express (☎08705 808 080) goes to London (8½hr., 3 per day, £30). Local transportation includes the **Underground (U)** subway line (M-Sa 6:30am-11pm, Su 11am-5:30pm; £1, all-day Discovery Ticket £1.70). The **tourist office,** 11 George Sq., books rooms for a £3 fee plus 10% deposit. (☎204 4400; www.seeglasgow.com. U: Buchanan St. Open July-Aug. M-Sa 9am-8pm, Su 10am-6pm; Sept.-June M-Sa 9am-7pm, Su 10am-6pm.) Connect to the **Internet** at **Hub,** 8 Renfield St. (☎222 2227. £1.80 per hr. Day pass or wireless connection £3.50. Open M-Th 7:30am-10pm, F-Sa 7:30am-9pm, Su 10am-9pm.) **Postal Code:** G2 5QX.

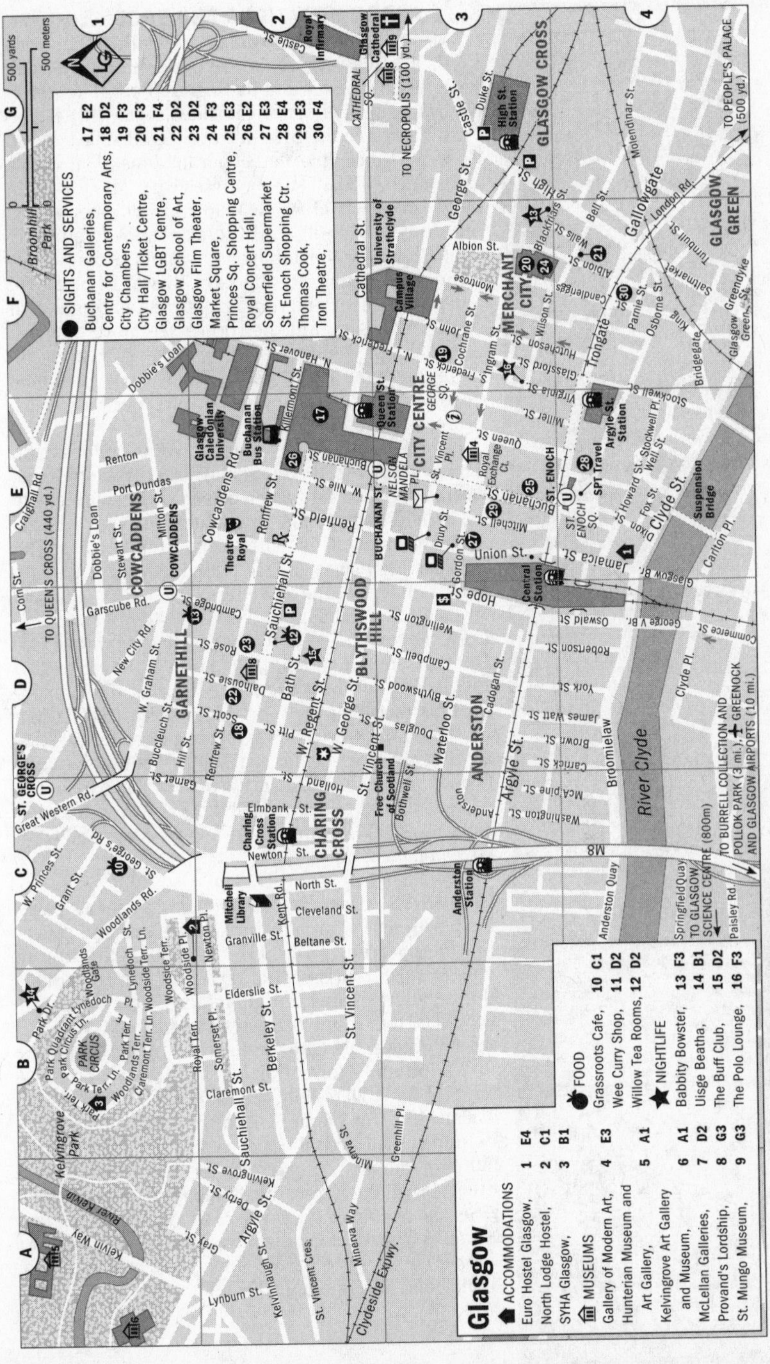
Glasgow
ACCOMMODATIONS
Euro Hostel Glasgow, 1 E4
North Lodge Hostel, 2 C1
SYHA Glasgow, 3 B1
MUSEUMS
Gallery of Modern Art, 4 E3
Hunterian Museum and Art Gallery, 5 A1
Kelvingrove Art Gallery and Museum, 6 A1
McLellan Galleries, 7 D2
Provand's Lordship, 8 G3
St. Mungo Museum, 9 G3
FOOD
Grassroots Cafe, 10 C1
Wee Curry Shop, 11 D2
Willow Tea Rooms, 12 D2
NIGHTLIFE
Babbity Bowster, 13 F3
Uisge Beatha, 14 B1
The Buff Club, 15 D2
The Polo Lounge, 16 F3
SIGHTS AND SERVICES
Buchanan Galleries, 17 E2
Centre for Contemporary Arts, 18 D2
City Chambers, 19 F3
City Hall/Ticket Centre, 20 F3
Glasgow LGBT Centre, 21 F4
Glasgow School of Art, 22 D2
Glasgow Film Theater, 23 D2
Market Square, 24 F3
Princes Sq. Shopping Centre, 25 E3
Royal Concert Hall, 26 E2
Somerfield Supermarket 27 E3
St. Enoch Shopping Ctr. 28 E4
Thomas Cook, 29 E3
Tron Theatre, 30 F4
500 yards
500 meters
TO QUEEN'S CROSS (440 yd.)
TO NECROPOLIS (100 yd.)
TO PEOPLE'S PALACE (500 yd.)
TO GLASGOW SCIENCE CENTRE (800m)
TO BURRELL COLLECTION AND POLLOK PARK (3 mi.), GREENOCK AND GLASGOW AIRPORTS (10 mi.)
GARNETHILL
COWCADDENS
BLYTHSWOOD HILL
CHARING CROSS
ANDERSTON
CITY CENTRE
MERCHANT CITY
GLASGOW CROSS
GLASGOW GREEN
River Clyde
Kelvingrove Park
PARK CIRCUS
Central Station
Queen St. Station
Buchanan Bus Station
Charing Cross Station
Anderston Station
Argyle St. Station
High St. Station
University of Strathclyde
Glasgow Caledonian University
Royal Infirmary
Glasgow Cathedral
Mitchell Library
Theatre Royal
Free Church of Scotland
Campus Village
SPT Travel
Suspension Bridge
Sauchiehall St.
Argyle St.
Buchanan St.
St. Vincent St.
W. George St.
George St.
Hope St.
Clyde St.
Trongate
Gallowgate
High St.
Clydeside Expwy.
M8

BRITAIN

IT'S COMING UP CEILIDHS

A ceilidh *(KAY-lee) is a traditional Scottish dance party, with a live band (usually including fiddle, accordion, and pipes) and a caller who reminds the crowd how to do the dances. In the hands of a certain subset of Glasgow's cutting-edge underground music scene,* ceilidh *music is being reborn in a brilliant fusion of pop and culture.* Let's Go *snagged an interview with 24-year-old John Somerville, accordion player for the popular modern* ceilidh *band Croft Number Five, during a break from his jam session at a local club.*

On his introduction to *ceilidh* music: I grew up going to *ceilidhs* in town halls in the rural area where I lived. When that music is all around you, you get inspired by it. I started learning the accordion from a local crofter (farmer) who would come down from the mountains to play at the *ceilidhs*. We also used to go see the big bands perform, like the Battlefield Band, Boys of the Lough, and Wolf Stone—at least, we thought they were big because they toured abroad, in the US and Canada.

On the future of *ceilidh* music: We add new instruments all the time—tonight we've got the drum set and the bass [guitar]—and it's like, Scottish music remixed. We come play at clubs like this to try and get younger people inter-

ACCOMMODATIONS AND FOOD. Reserve ahead for B&Bs and hostels, especially in summer. B&Bs are scattered on either side of **Argyle Street,** near the university and **Kelvingrove Park.** The newly renovated rooms of the **SYHA Glasgow (HI) ❶**, 7-8 Park Terr., are the best in town. (☎332 3004. U: St. George's Cross. Internet £3 per hr. June-Sept. dorms £16, under 18 £12. Oct.-May rates vary. MC/V.) At the **North Lodge Hostel ❶**, 19 Woodside Pl., the staff is hilariously friendly and the atmosphere soundly Scottish (www.northlodgehostel.com or www.hostelbookers.com). At the **Euro Hostel Glasgow ❶**, recently redecorated, the bright pink entrance hall might be jarring, but the rooms are more tasteful, and they are well-insulated from the parties in the large common areas. (☎222 2828; www.euro-hostels.com. Breakfast included. Internet £4 per hr. Dorms £13-16. MC/V.)

The area bordered by **Otago Street** to the west, **St. George's Road** to the east, and **Great Western Road, Woodlands Road,** and **Eldon Street,** brims with cheap kebab-and-curry joints. **Byres Road** and tiny, parallel **Ashton Lane** overflow with cheap, trendy cafes. The **Willow Tea Rooms ❷**, 217 Sauchiehall St., upstairs from Henderson the Jewellers, are a cozy Glasgow landmark. (☎332 0521; www.willowtearooms.co.uk. U: Buchanan St. Tea £1.95 per pot. Afternoon tea £11. Open M-Sa 9am-4:30pm, Su 11am-4:15pm. MC/V.) Find Glasgow's best vegetarian food at the happening **Grassroots Cafe ❷**, 97 St. George's Rd. (☎333 0534. U: St. George's Cross. Handmade pastas from £6.80. Open daily 10am-10pm. AmEx/MC/V.) **The Wee Curry Shop ❶**, 7 Buccleuch St., is the best deal in a town full of pakora and poori. (☎353 0777. U: Cowcaddens. Entrees £5.80-10. Open M-Sa noon-2:30pm and 5:30-10:30pm. Cash only.)

SIGHTS. Glasgow is a budget sightseer's paradise, with period architecture, museums, and galleries, many free; *The List* (£2.50), available at newsstands, is an essential review of current exhibitions, galleries, music, and nightlife. Your first stop should be the Gothic **Glasgow Cathedral,** on Castle St., the only full-scale cathedral spared by the 16th-century Scottish Reformation. (☎552 6891. Open Apr.-Sept. M-Sa 9:30am-6pm, Su 1-5pm; Oct.-Mar. M-Sa 9:30am-4pm, Su 1-4pm. Ask for free personal tours.) Behind the cathedral is the **necropolis,** a terrifying hilltop cemetery. Be careful after dark. (Open 24hr. Free.) Down the street, the **St. Mungo Museum of Religious Life and Art,** 2 Castle St., surveys religions from Islam to Yoruba, and displays Dalí's *Christ of St. John's Cross.* (☎553 2557. Open M-Th and Sa 10am-5pm, F and Su 11am-5pm. Free.)

In the West End, wooded **Kelvingrove Park** lies on the banks of the River Kelvin. In the southwestern corner of the park, at Argyle and Sauchiehall St., the magnificent **Kelvingrove Art Gallery and Museum** shelters works by van Gogh, Monet, and Rembrandt. (☎87 2699. Argyle St. U: Kelvinhall. Open M-Th and Sa 10am-5pm, F and Su 11am-5pm. Free.) Farther west rise the Gothic edifices of the **University of Glasgow.** The main building is on University Ave., which runs into Byres Rd. While walking through campus, stop by the **Hunterian Museum,** home to the Blackstone chair, in which all students originally sat their oral examinations while timed by an hourglass. You can also see 19th-century Scottish art at the **Hunterian Art Gallery,** across the street. (U: Hillhead. Both open M-Sa 9:30am-5pm. Free.)

Take bus #45, 47, 48, or 57 from Jamaica St. (15min., £1.20) to reach the famous **Burrell Collection,** in the Pollok Country Park. Once the private stash of ship magnate William Burrell, the collection includes paintings by Cézanne and Degas, medieval armor, and fine china. (☎287 2550. Open M-Th and Sa 10am-5pm, F and Su 11am-5pm. Tours daily 11am and 2pm. Free.) Also in the park is the **Pollok House,** a Victorian mansion with a small collection of paintings, some by El Greco and Goya. (☎616 6410. Open daily 10am-5pm. £5, students £3.75. Nov.-Mar. free.)

ENTERTAINMENT AND NIGHTLIFE. The infamous **Byres Road** pub crawl slithers past the University area, starts at Tennant's Bar and proceeds toward the River Clyde. For traditional Scottish grub, you can't beat **Babbity Bowster,** 16-18 Blackfriars St. (☎ 552 5055. Entrees £4-8. Open M-Sa 11am-midnight, Su 10am-midnight.) With 100 varieties, **Uisge Beatha** *(ISH-ker VAH)*, 232 Woodlands Rd., reminds you that in Scotland, it's spelled "whisky." (☎564 1596. U: Kelvinbridge. Whisky from £2. Open M-Sa noon-midnight, Su 12:30pm-midnight.) **The Buff Club,** 142 Bath Ln., is *the* after-hours club scene in Glasgow. 2 dance floors combine friendly comfort with an edgy hipness. (☎248 1777. Cover £3-6, free with receipt from local bar; ask at the door for details. Open Su-Th 11pm-3am, F-Sa 10:30pm-3am.) Labyrinthine dance club **The Polo Lounge,** 58 Wilson St., has Glasgow's most popular gay scene. (☎553 1221. Open M-Th 5pm-1am, F-Sa 5pm-3am. Cover £5.)

STIRLING ☎01786

It was once said that "he who controls Stirling controls Scotland." The third point of a strategic triangle completed by Glasgow and Edinburgh, Stirling has historically presided over north-south travel in the region. At the 1297 Battle of Stirling Bridge, William

ested, but we don't advertise or anything yet; we want it to be more organic, more underground. There are a lot of us [*ceilidh* players] in Glasgow. The scene is here and it's happening and it's a really vibrant thing to be a part of.

On the difference between Scottish and Irish music: People often confuse Scottish music with Irish music, but it's different. Irish music is often more minor and flowing, really sweet. Scottish music is more rhythmic and major, and uses the pipes. Nobody realizes there's a difference—it's subtle, but it's there.

On the band: This band tonight isn't really a set group of musicians—we're just jamming at the moment, doing a lot of improv. Right now it's whoever wants to show up and play; the *ceilidh* music scene here is really close. I'd say the guys here tonight have been playing together for about 5-6 years, but next week it might be a totally different group of blokes, with a different history of playing together.

Let's Go found John at ***The Walkabout,*** *where he plays most Thursday nights (128 Renfield St., ☎0141 332 8209). Shots are distributed as prizes for the best dancers each round. He can also be found at www.croftmusic.net, or jamming at other local pubs and other venues including* ***North Lodge Hostel*** *(see left), almost any night.*

Wallace (of *Braveheart* fame) overpowered the English army, enabling Robert the Bruce to finally overthrow the English at **Bannockburn,** 3km south of town. Take bus #51 or 52 from Murray Pl. in Stirling. (Visitors Centre open Mar.-Oct. daily 10am-5:30pm. Battlefield open year-round.) **Stirling Castle** is decorated with prim gardens that belie its turbulent history. (☎450 000. ☎450 000. Open daily Apr.-Oct. 9:30am-6pm; Nov.-Mar. 9:30am-5pm. Free 30min. guided tours. Castle £8.50, students £6.50.) **Argyll's Lodging,** a 17th-century mansion below the castle, has been impressively restored. (Open daily Apr.-Oct. 9:30am-6pm; Nov.-Mar. 9:30am-5pm. £4, students £3, with castle admission free.)

At colorful **Willy Wallace Hostel ❶,** 77 Murray Pl., near the train station, the warm staff and hostel dog foster a fun atmosphere. (☎446 773. Internet £1 per hr. Dorms £10-14. MC/V.) Find a variety of sandwiches (£1.35-4) at **Cisco's ❶,** 70 Port St., (☎445 900. Open M-Sa 10am-5pm. MC/V) **The Greengrocer,** 81 Port St., has fresh produce. (☎479 159. Open M-Sa 9am-5:30pm.) **Trains** (☎08457 484 950) run from Goosecroft Rd. to: Aberdeen (2hr., M-Sa 1 per hr., £34); Edinburgh (50min., 2 per hr., £5.90); Glasgow (40min., 2-3 per hr., £6.10); Inverness (3hr., 3-4 per day, £35); London King's Cross (5½hr., 1 per day, £118). Scottish Citylink **buses** (☎0870 50 50 50) also leave from Goosecroft Rd. for: Edinburgh (1¼hr., every 2 hr., £4.20); Fort William (2¾hr., 1 per day, £16); Glasgow (40min., 1 per hr., £4.20); Inverness via Perth (3¾hr., 4-6 per day, £14).The **tourist office** is at 41 Dumbarton Rd. (☎475 019. Open M-Sa 9am-7pm, low season reduced hours.) **Postal Code:** FK8 2BP.

THE TROSSACHS ☎01877

The most accessible tract of Scotland's wilderness, the mountains and misty lochs of the Trossachs (from Gaelic for "bristly country") are popular for their moderate hikes and unbeatable beauty. The Trossachs and Loch Lomond form Scotland's first national park, where the highlands meet the lowlands.

TRANSPORTATION. Access to the Trossachs is easiest from Stirling. First **buses** (☎01324 613 777) connect to the region's two main towns, running from Stirling to Aberfoyle (#11; 45min., 4 per day, £2.50) and Callander (#59; 45min., 12 per day, £3). Scottish Citylink also runs a bus from Edinburgh to Callander (1¾hr., 1 per day, £9.60) via Stirling. In summer, the useful **Trossachs Trundler** (☎01786 442 707) ferries between Callander, Aberfoyle, and the Trossachs Pier at Loch Katrine; one daily trip begins and ends in Stirling. (June-Sept. M-Tu and Th-Su 4 per day; Day Rover £5, students £4.)

CALLANDER. Beside the quiet River Teith, the town of Callander is a good base for exploring the Trossachs. Dominating the horizon, **Ben Ledi** (880m) provides a strenuous but not overly challenging trek. A trail up the mountain (9km) begins just north of town along A84. A number of walks depart from Callander itself. **The Crags** (10km) heads up through the woods to the ridge above town, while the popular walk to **Bracklinn Falls** (8km) wanders through a picturesque glen. **Cyclists** can join a lovely stretch of the **Lowland Highland Trail,** which runs north to Strathyre along an old railway line. Callander's **Rob Roy and Trossachs Visitor Centre,** Main St., is a combination **tourist office** and exhibit on the 17th-century hero. (☎330 342. Open daily June-Sept. 10am-6pm; Mar.-May and Oct. 10am-5pm; Nov.-Feb. 11am-4pm. Exhibit £3.60, students £2.40.) Walkers should grab the *Callander Walks and Fort Trails* pamphlet; cyclists can consult *Rides around the Trossachs* (both £2). Rent bikes at **Cycle Hire Callander,** Ancaster Sq., beside the tourist office. (☎331 052. 331 052. £7 ½-half day, £10 per day. Open daily 9am-6pm. MC/V.) The hidden gem of the region's lodgings is **Trossachs Backpackers ❷,** Invertrossachs Rd., 0.8km south of Callander. This hostel's forest-clearing location makes it an ideal base. Friendly owners Janet and Mark Shimitzu often pick up guests from Callander. (☎331 200 for hostel, 331 100 for bike rental. Bike £13 per day. Breakfast included. Laundry. Dorms £15. MC/V.)

ABERFOYLE. Aberfoyle, another springboard into the wilderness, is at the heart of the **Queen Elizabeth Forest Park,** which covers territory from the shore of Loch Lomond to the Strathyre Mountains. For more information on **trails,** visit the **Trossachs Discovery Centre,** in town. (☎382 352. Open July-Aug. daily 9:30am-6pm; Apr.-June and Sept.-Oct. daily 10am-5pm; Nov.-Mar. Sa-Su 10am-5pm.) Keep an eye out for visiting deer and foxes at **Corrie Glen B&B ❺,** Manse Rd. (☎382 427. Open Mar.-Nov. Singles £35, doubles £50. Cash only.)

LOCH KATRINE. The A821 winds through the heart of the Trossachs between Aberfoyle and Callander. Named the **Trossachs Trail,** this scenic drive passes near the majestic Loch Katrine, the Trossachs' original attraction and the setting of Sir Walter Scott's "The Lady of the Lake." The popular **Steamship Sir Walter Scott** cruises from Trossachs Pier and tours the loch, stopping at Stronachlachar, on the northwestern bank. (☎376 316. Apr.-Oct. M-Tu and Th-Su 11am, 1:45, 3:15pm; W 1:45 and 3:15pm. £5.50-6.50) At the pier, rent bikes from **Katrinewheelz.** (☎376 284. £14 per day.) For a daytrip, take the ferry to Stronachlachar and then walk or ride back along the 22km wooded shore road to the pier. Above the loch hulks **Ben A'an** (460m), a reasonable 3km ascent that begins from a parking lot 1.5km along A821.

LOCH LOMOND ☎01389

Immortalized by the famous ballad, the pristine wilderness surrounding Loch Lomond continues to awe visitors. Britain's largest loch is dotted by some 38 islands, but given their proximity to Glasgow, parts of these bonnie banks can get crowded, especially in summer. Hikers adore the **West Highland Way,** which snakes along the entire eastern side of the loch and stretches north to Fort William. The *West Highland Way* official guide (£15) includes maps for each section of the route. Attractions and services at the **Loch Lomond Shores** visitor complex and shopping mall in Balloch include a big-screen film about the loch, a National Park Information Centre, a **tourist office,** and bike and canoe rentals. (☎722 406. Open daily June-Sept. 10am-6pm; Oct.-May 10am-5pm.) Departing from Loch Lomond Shores and the Balloch tourist office on the River Leven, **Sweeney's Cruises** provide top-notch 1hr. intros to the area. (☎752 376; www.sweeneyscruises.com. 1 per hr. 10:30am-4:30pm. £5.50.) The **SYHA Loch Lomond (HI) ❷,** 3km north of town, is a stunning 19th-century mansion. From the train station, follow the main road for 1km, turn right at the roundabout, continue 2.5km, and follow signs to the hostel. Citylink buses to Oban and Campbelltown stop right outside, as do buses #305 and 306 from Balloch. (☎01389 850 226. Internet £5 per hr. Open Mar.-Oct. Dorms £15-16, under 18 £11. MC/V.) **Trains** (☎08457 484 950) leave Balloch Rd. for Glasgow (45min., 2 per hr., £3.70). Scottish Citylink (☎08705 505 050) **buses** also serve Glasgow (45min., 7 per day, £4.30). The **tourist office,** Balloch Rd., is in the Old Station Building. (☎753 533. Open daily July-Aug. 9:30am-6pm; June 9:30am-5:30pm; Sept. 10am-5:30pm; May 10am-5pm.)

INVERNESS AND LOCH NESS ☎01463

Inverness, the "hub of the Highlands," is a traveler's town, worth a stop before exploring the hills, lochs, and castles of the nearby Highland region. Every year, thousands of tourists descend upon **Loch Ness,** 8km south of Inverness, drawn by fantastic tales of its legendary inhabitant. In AD 565, St. Columba repelled a savage sea beast as it attacked a monk; the monster has captivated the world's imagination ever since. The loch is 700 ft. deep just 70 ft. from its shore; no one has determined how vast it really is, or what life exists at the bottom. The easiest

BRITAIN

way to see the loch is with a tour group, departing from the Inverness tourist office. **Jacobite Cruises,** Tomnahurich Bridge, Glenurquhart Rd., whisks you around on coach or boat trips. (☎233 999; www.jacobite.co.uk. £9-20, includes admission to Urquhart Castle. Student discounts available.) South on A82 sits **Urquhart Castle** *(URK-hart)*, one of the largest in Scotland before it was blown up in 1692 to prevent Jacobite occupation. (☎450 551. Open Apr.-Sept. daily 9:30am-6:30pm; Oct.-Mar. M-Sa 9:30am-4:30pm. £6.50, students £5.) **Cawdor Castle,** complete with drawbridge and garden maze, also has humorous placards describing the castle sights; take the Highland Country bus #7 (30min., 1 per hr., £5), leaving from the Inverness post office at 14-16 Queensgate. (☎01667 4404 401; www.cawdorcastle.com. Open May-Oct. daily 10am-5pm. £7, students £6.)

In an ideal location for travelers arriving by bus or by train, the **Inverness Tourist Hostel ❶** features swank leather couches and a flat-screen TV. (☎241 962. Dorms £11-14. MC/V). A few blocks from Inverness Castle, the friendly staff at the **Inverness Student Hotel ❶,** has no comparison. (☎236 556. Breakfast £1.90. Laundry £2.50. Internet access £1 per hr. Dorms £12-13.50.) Try the **Lemon Tree ❶,** 18 Inglis St., for filling all-day breakfast fare (£3.55), sweet orange lemonade (£1.25), and soup for £2.25. (☎241 114. Open M-Sa 8:30am-5:45pm.) Afterward, hit up **Hootananny,** 67 Church St., where you can stamp your feet to *ceilidh* bands on the first floor or groove to live bands upstairs. (Open daily noon-1am. MC/V.) **Trains** (☎08457 484 950) run from Academy St. in Inverness's Station Sq., to: Edinburgh (3½hr., 8 per day, £34); Glasgow (3½hr., 8 per day, £34); Kyle of Lochalsh (2½hr., 4 per day, £16); London (8-11hr., 1 per day, £104). **Buses** run from Farraline Park to: Edinburgh (4½hr., 1 per hr., £17); Glasgow (4hr., 1 per hr., £17); Kyle of Lochalsh (2hr., 2 per day, £12); London (13hr., 1 per day, £39). Find the **tourist office** at Castle Wynd; from the stations, turn left on Academy St., and then right onto Union St. (☎234 353. Internet £3 per hr. Open mid-June to Aug. M-Sa 9am-6pm, Su 9:30am-4pm; Sept. to mid-June M-Sa 9am-5pm, Su 10am-4pm.)

FORT WILLIAM AND BEN NEVIS ☎01397

In 1654, General Monck founded the town of Fort William among Britain's highest peaks in order to keep out "savage clans and roving barbarians." His scheme backfired: today, thousands of Highlands-bound hikers invade Fort William, an ideal base for exploring some of Scotland's most impressive wilderness. Just outside of town, beautiful **Glen Nevis** runs southeast into Britain's tallest mountain. The breathtaking peak of **Ben Nevis** (1343m), the region's biggest draw, offers a challenging but manageable hike. One trail originates from the **Glen Nevis Visitor Centre,** where hikers stock up on maps and useful advice. (☎705 922. Open Easter-Oct. daily 9am-5pm.) The ascent (13km; 6-8hr. round-trip) is difficult more for its length than for its terrain, but harsh conditions near the summit can be treacherous for the unprepared. Bring plenty of water and warm, waterproof clothes, and be sure to inform someone of your route. The **West Coast Railway's** Jacobite steam train rose to stardom as the Hogwarts Express in the *Harry Potter* films. The rail line, connecting Fort William and Mallaig, traverses some of Scotland's finest scenery. (☎0124 732 100; www.westcoastrailway.co.uk. 2hr.; June to mid-Oct. M-F departs Fort William 10:20am, departs Mallaig 2:10pm; £20, round-trip £27.)

Fort William's accommodations fill up quickly in summer. From the train station, turn left onto Belford Rd. and right onto Alma Rd., bear left at the fork, and vault into a top bunk at **Fort William Backpackers ❶,** 6 Alma Rd., a fun, welcoming hostel. (☎700 711; www.scotlandstophostels.com. Breakfast £1.90. Laundry £2.50. Internet access £1.90 per hr. Reception closed 1:30-4pm. Curfew 2am. Dorms £12.50-13.50. AmEx/MC/V.) Before heading to the hills, pick up a packed lunch (£3) or a sweet at the **Nevis Bakery ❶,** 49 High St., across from the tourist office. (☎704 101. Open M-F 8am-5pm, Sa 8am-4pm. Cash only.) **Trains** (☎08457 484 950) leave from the station beyond the north end of High St. for Glasgow Queen St. (3¾hr., 2-3 per day, £20). The Caledonian overnight sleeper train runs to London Euston (12hr., 1 per day, £99). **Buses** arrive next to Morrison's grocery store by the train station. Scottish Citylink (☎08705 505 050) runs to: Edinburgh (4hr., 3 per day, £21); Glasgow (3hr., 4 per day, £14); Inverness (2hr., 7-8 per day, £8.80); Kyle of Lochalsh (2hr., 3 per day, £14). The **tourist office,** Cameron Sq., in the center of High St., books rooms for a £3 fee plus a 10% deposit. (Open July-Aug. M-Sa 9am-7pm, Su 9:30am-5pm; Sept.-June reduced hours.) Free **Internet** at the **Fort William Library,** High St. (Open M and Th 10am-8pm, Tu and F 10am-6pm, W and Sa 10am-1pm.) **Postal Code:** PH33 6AR.

ISLE OF SKYE

From the serrated peaks of the Cuillin Hills to the commanding cliffs of the Trotternish Peninsula, the Isle of Skye possesses unparalleled natural beauty. The island's charms are no secret; Skye has been fought over for centuries. Today, the victors are the tourists who invade each summer to take part in the Isle's year-round celebration of Scottish heritage.

TRANSPORTATION. The **Skye Bridge** links the island to the mainland's Kyle of Lochalsh. Pedestrians can take the bridge's 2.5km **footpath** or the **shuttle bus** (1 per hr., £0.70). **Trains** (☎08457 484 950) run to Kyle from Inverness (2½hr., 2-3 per day, £16). Scottish Citylink **buses** arrive daily from: Fort William (2hr., 3 per day, £14), Glasgow (6hr., 3 per day, £22), and Inverness (2hr., 2 per day, £12). Buses on Skye are infrequent and expensive; grab the *Public Transport Map: The Highlands, Orkney, Shetland and Western Isles* at any tourist office.

KYLE OF LOCHALSH AND KYLEAKIN. Kyle of Lochalsh ("Kyle" for short) and Kyleakin (Ky-LOCK-in) bookend the Skye Bridge. Kyle is most often used en route to Skye. Though Kyleakin is short on conveniences, three hostels and countless tours are based there, making it a boisterous backpacker's hub. **MacBackpackers Skye Trekker Tour,** departing from the Skye Backpackers hostel in Kyleakin, offers a one-day tour emphasizing the mystical history and legends of the island and a two-day eco-conscious hike into the Cuillin Hills, with all necessary gear provided. (☎01599 534 510. Reserve ahead. Departure Sa 7:30am. 1-day £18, 2-day £30.) Located between Kyle of Lochalsh and Inverness, **Eilean Donan Castle** is the restored 13th-century seat of the MacKenzie family, and the most photographed monument in Scotland. It offers one of the country's best castle tours. (☎01599 555 202; www.eileandonancastle.com. Open Apr.-Oct. daily 10am-5:30pm. £4.50, students £3.60.)The friendly owners of **Dun-Caan Hostel ❶,** in Kyleakin, have masterfully renovated a 200-year-old cottage. (☎01599 534 087; www.skyerover.co.uk. Reserve ahead. Bikes £10 per day. Dorms £12. MC/V.)The amiable staff of **Harry's ❶,** on the pier in Kyleakin, serves steaming pots of tea (£0.95) with tasty sandwiches and hot entrees (£4-7) to backpackers and seafarers alike. (☎01599 534 641. Open M-Tu and Th-Sa 9am-5:30pm, Su 10am-3pm. Cash only.)

SLIGACHAN. Renowned for their cloud and mist formations as well as their hiking trails, the **Cuillin Hills** *(COO-leen)*, the highest peaks in the Hebrides, are visible from nearly every part of Skye. Legend says the warrior Cúchulainn was the lover of the Amazon ruler of Skye, who named the hills for him after he returned to Ireland to die. The Cuillins are great for experienced hikers, but may be risky for beginners. Tourist offices, campsites, and hostels have many maps and books for walks in the region. West of Kyleakin, the smooth Red Cuillins and the craggy Black Cuillin Hills meet in Sligachan, little more than a bunkhouse, hotel, pub, and campground in a jaw-dropping setting. A handy base for hiking, **Sligachan Bunk-**

house ❶, is a classic mountain lodge. (☎650 204. Linens £2. Dorms £10. MC/V.) To get to the stunning **Glenbrittle Campsite** ❶, at the foot of the Black Cuillin Hills, take bus #53 (M-Sa 2 per day) from Portree or Sligachan to Glenbrittle. (☎01478 640 404. Open Apr.-Oct. £4.50 per person, £2.50 per child. AmEx/MC/V.)

PORTREE. The island's cheerful harbor capital is a festive hub for music, arts, crafts, and transportation. **Dunvegan Castle,** the seat of the MacLeod clan, holds the record for the longest-inhabited Scottish castle, with continuous residence since the 13th century. Highland Country bus #56 (☎01478 612 622; M-Sa 3 per day) runs from Portree to the castle. (☎01478 521 206; www.dunvegancastle.com. Open daily mid-Mar. to Oct. 10am-5:30pm; Nov. to mid-Mar. 11am-4pm. £7, students £6.) The **Portree Independent Hostel** ❶, The Green, has a prime location and enthusiastic staff. (☎01478 613 737. Dorms £12-13. MC/V.) **Buses** to Portree from Kyle of Lochalsh and Kyleakin stop at Somerled Sq. (5-10 per day, £8). The **tourist office,** on Bayfield Rd., books accommodations and helps explain bus routes. (☎01478 612 137. Open July-Aug. M-Sa 9am-6pm, Su 10am-4pm; Sept.-June reduced hours.)

TROTTERNISH PENINSULA. The east side of Trotternish is a geological masterpiece of rock punctuated by thundering waterfalls, while the western side has a softer landscape of rolling hills. Northeast of Portree, the A855 snakes along the the east coast past the black stone **Old Man of Storr** and the **Quirang** rock pinnacles. Geologists may enjoy the science behind these formations, but others just stare dumbfoundedly at one of Mother Nature's most spectacular playgrounds. The Old Man of Storr is accessible by a steep **hike**. Take Highland Country bus #57 on the Portree-Staffin route (June-Sept. M-Sa 4-6 per day, Su 3 per day; Oct.-May M-Sa 4 per day; Day Rover pass £5); ask the driver to drop you at the parking lot.

ISLE OF LEWIS (LEODHAS) ☎01851

Fantastic hiking, biking, surfing, and archaeological sites attract adventurers and historians alike to Lewis, the most populous of the Outer Hebridean Islands. The small city of **Stornoway** is a splash of urban life in the untouched moorland and half-cut fields of peat. Second only to Stonehenge in grandeur, the **Callanish Stones,** 22km west of Stornoway on the A858, are considerably less overrun with tourists. (Open 24hr. Free.) Most of Lewis's biggest attractions, including the Callanish Stones and other archaeological sites, line the west coast and can be reached via the W2 bus, which operates on a circuit beginning at the Stornoway bus station (M-Sa 4-6 per day in either direction). Galson Motors offers a day pass on this route (£6), or a round-trip ticket to see one, two, or three of the sights (May-Oct., £4-5). Alternatively, travel with **Out and About Tours** (☎612 288; personalized group tours from £67 per ½-day, £102 per day) or **Albannach Guided Tours** (☎830 433; from £10 per hr.); both depart from the tourist office. Lewis is also home to "the most consistent surf in Europe." Warm currents and long daylight hours draw **surfers** to spots like the popular **Dalmor Beach,** near the village of Dalbeg, which has hosted several competitions (take the W2 bus from Stornoway).

Mr. and Mrs. Hill ❷, Robertson Rd., is a better pick than the hostels in town. Head north up Church St. from the tourist office, turn left on Matheson Rd., and take the first right onto Robertson. (☎705 553. £25 per person. Cash only.) Buy groceries at the **Co-op** on Cromwell St. (☎702 703. Open M-Sa 8am-8pm.) Stornoway's only affordable sit-down restaurant is **Thai Cafe** ❷, 27 Church St. (☎701 811. Entrees £4-6. Open M-Sa noon-2:30pm and 5-11pm. Cash only.) CalMac **ferries** sail to Stornoway from Ullapool (2¾hr., 2-3 per day, £15, with car £70/120). Western Isles **buses** leave from Stornoway's Beach St. station; pick up a free *Lewis and Harris Bus Timetable* for destinations. Be aware that the only things running on Sundays are planes and churchgoers late for services. The **tourist office** is at 26 Cromwell St.

From the ferry terminal, turn left onto South Beach, then right on Cromwell St. (☎703 088. Open Apr.-Oct. daily 9am-6pm and 8-9pm; Nov.-Mar. M-F 9am-5pm.) Rent bikes at **Alex Dan's Cycle Centre,** 67 Kenneth St. (☎704 025. £12 per day; £38 per week. Open M-Sa 9am-6pm.) **Internet** is free at the Stornoway Library. (☎708 631. Open M-W and Sa 10am-5pm, Th-F 10am-6pm.) **Postal Code:** HS1 2AA.

NORTHERN IRELAND

In Northern Ireland, hillside castles coexist with fishing villages and the city of Belfast. The calm tenor of everyday life has long been overshadowed by headlines screaming about riots and bombs. Negotiations continue to help make the region as peaceful as it is beautiful. Beyond its cities, Northern Ireland still holds fast to its old-world welcome.

BELFAST (BÉAL FEIRSTE) ☎028

The second-largest city on the island of Ireland, Belfast (pop. 270,000) is the focus of Northern Ireland's cultural, commercial, and political activity. While Belfast has suffered from the stigma of its violent past, it has rebuilt itself and now surprises most visitors with its neighborly, urbane feel. The Belfast pub scene ranks among the best in the world, combining the historical appeal of old-fashioned watering holes with more modern bars and clubs.

TRANSPORTATION

Flights: Belfast International Airport (☎9448 4848; www.belfastairport.com) in Aldergrove, serves Aer Lingus (☎08708 765000; www.aerlingus.com), British Airways (☎0870850 9850; www.ba.com), easyJet (☎087124 42366; www.easyjet.com), and many other airlines arrive from London and other European cities. **Airbus** (☎9066 6630) runs to the Laganside and Europa bus stations in the city center (40min.; M-Sa every 10min. 6:20am-9:40pm, Su every 30min. 6:20am-9:40pm; £4 single). **Taxis** do the same for £25 (☎9448 4353). **Belfast City Airport** (☎9093 9093; www.belfastcityairport.com), at the harbor, has arrivals from regional carriers. Trains run to **Central Station** (M-Sa every 20min., Su 12 per day; £1.30).

Trains: For info on trains and buses, contact **Translink** (☎9066 6630; www.translink.co.uk; open daily 7am-8pm). Trains arrive at Belfast's **Central Station,** E. Bridge St., from **Derry/Londonderry** (2hr.; M-Sa 9-10 per day, Su 4 per day; £9.80) and **Dublin, IRE** (2hr.; M-Sa 8-9 per day, Su 5 per day; £24). **Metro** buses are free with rail tickets.

Buses: Europa Bus Terminal (☎9066 6630), off Great Victoria St. Ticket office open M-Sa 7:35am-8:05pm, Su 9:25am-6pm. Buses from **Derry/Londonderry** (1¾hr.; M-F 24 per day, Sa 19 per day, Su 11 per day; £9.40) and **Dublin, IRE** (3hr., 16 per day, £8.30). The Centrelink bus connects the station with the city center.

Ferries: Norfolk Line Ferries (☎087 0600 4321; www.norfolkline-ferries.co.uk), go to Liverpool twice a day from Belfast. Pedestrian fee varies £20-30. **Stena Line** (☎08705 707 070; www.stenaline.com) has service to **Stranraer, Scotland** (1¾hr., £19).

Public Transportation: Belfast has 2 bus services. Many local bus routes connect through Laganside Bus Station, Queen's Sq. **Metro buses** (☎9066 6630; www.translink.co.uk) gather in Donegall Sq. 12 main routes cover Belfast. Ulsterbus "blue buses" cover the suburbs. Travel within the city center £1.30, under 16 65p; Travelink 10-journey passes £10; day passes after 10am £2.50. **Nightlink Buses** shuttle the tipsy from Donegall Sq. W to various towns outside of Belfast. F-Sa 1 and 2am. £3.

> Visitors should avoid West Belfast during Marching Season, around July 12; the parades can inflame sectarian violence. At all times, do not wander across the Peace Line. Rather, return to the city center between visits to Shankill and the Falls to prevent misunderstandings.

Taxis: 24hr. metered cabs abound. **Value Cabs** (☎9080 9080); **Fon a Cab** (☎9033 3333). For most destinations within the city proper, fares will be under £5.50.

ORIENTATION AND PRACTICAL INFORMATION

Buses arrive at the Europa Bus Station on **Great Victoria Street.** To the northeast is **City Hall** in **Donegall Square.** Donegall Pl. turns into **Royal Avenue** and runs from Donegall Sq. through the shopping area. To the east, in **Cornmarket,** pubs in narrow entries (small alleyways) offer an escape. The stretch of Great Victoria St. that runs between the bus station and Shaftesbury Sq. is known as the **Golden Mile** for its highbrow establishments and Victorian architecture. **Botanic Avenue** and **Bradbury Place** (which becomes **University Road**) extend south from Shaftesbury Sq. into **Queen's University's** turf. The city center, Golden Mile, and the university are relatively safe areas. Though locals advise caution in the east and west, central Belfast is safer than most European cities. **Westlink Motorway** divides working-class **West Belfast,** historically more politically volatile than the center, from the rest of Belfast. The Protestant district stretches along **Shankill Road,** just north of the Catholic neighborhood, centered around the **Falls Road.** The **River Lagan** splits industrial **East Belfast** from Belfast proper. The shipyards and docks extend north on both sides of the river as it grows into **Belfast Lough.** During the week, the area north of City Hall is essentially deserted after 6pm. Though muggings are rare in Belfast, it's wise for travelers to use taxis to get around after dark, particularly near clubs and pubs in the northeast.

Tourist Office: Belfast Welcome Centre, 47 Donegall Pl. (☎9024 6609; www.gotobelfast.com). Has a comprehensive free booklet on Belfast and info on surrounding areas. Books accommodations in Northern Ireland and the Republic for £2. Open June-Sept. M-Sa 9am-7pm, Su noon-5pm; Oct.-May M-Sa 9am-5pm.

Banks: 24hr. ATMs at **Bank of Ireland,** 54 Donegall Pl. (☎9043 3000); **First Trust,** 11-15 Donegall Sq. (☎084 5600 5925). Banks open M-F 9am-4:30pm, Sa 10am-noon.

Police: 6-18 Donegall Pass, Musgrave St., or 65 Knock Rd. (both ☎9065 0222). Lost property, extension ☎26049.

Hospital: Belfast City Hospital, 91 Lisburn Rd. (☎9032 9241). From Shaftesbury Sq., follow Bradbury Pl. and take a right at the fork. **The Royal Victoria Hospital,** 274 Grosvenor Rd. (☎9024 0503).

Internet Access: Belfast Central Library, 122 Royal Ave. (☎9050 9150). £1.50 per 30min. Wheelchair-accessible. Open M and W-Th 9am-8pm, Tu 9am-5:30pm, Sa 9am-4:30pm. **Belfast Welcome Centre,** 47 Donegall Pl. £1 per 15min.; £2.50 per hr., students £1. Open M-Sa 9:30am-7pm, Su noon-5pm.

Post Office: Central Post Office, on the corner of High St. and Bridge St. (☎08457 223 344). Open M-Sa 10am-5:30pm. **Postal Code:** BT2 7FD.

ACCOMMODATIONS

Nearly all budget accommodations are near Queen's University. If hindered by baggage, catch **Metro bus** #8, 9, or 93 from Donegall Sq. to areas in the south. Reserve ahead in summer.

Paddy's Palace, 68 Lisburn Rd. (☎9033 3367; www.paddyspalace.com), at the corner of Fitzwilliam St. Satellite TV and kitchen. Pleasant back garden is popular in nice weather. Breakfast included. Laundry £5. Free Internet. Reception Su-Th 8am-8pm, F-Sa 8am-10pm. Dorms from £9.50. MC/V. ❶

Belfast Hostel (HINI), 22 Donegall Rd. (☎9031 5435; www.hini.org.uk), off Shaftesbury Sq. A clean, inviting interior with a cafe (open daily 8-11am) and modern rooms. Pool table and TV lounge. Wheelchair-accessible. Full breakfast £4.45. Laundry £3.50. Internet £1 per 20min. Reception 24hr. 4- to 6-bed dorms Su-Th £7.50-11.75, F-Sa £10.50-12.75; singles £19; doubles and triples £32-34. MC/V. ❶

Avenue Guest House, 23 Eglantine Ave. (☎9066 5904; www.avenueguesthouse.com). Four airy rooms equipped with TV, phone, and wireless Internet. Full Irish breakfast included. Singles £45; doubles £50-60. Cash only. ❸

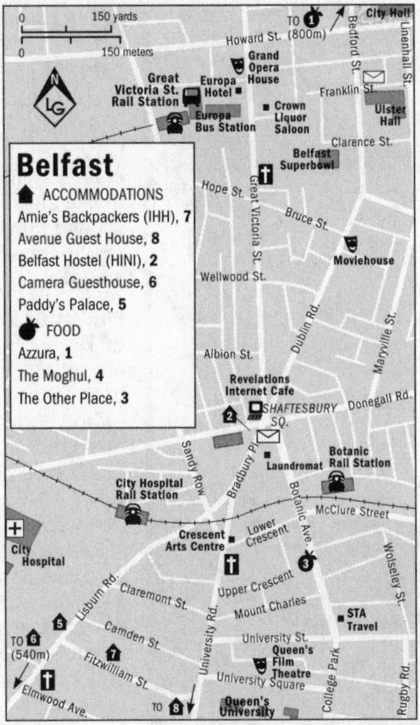

Arnie's Backpackers (IHH), 63 Fitzwilliam St. (☎9024 2867; www.arniesbackpackers.co.uk). From Europa Bus Station, take a right on Great Victoria St. and go through Shaftsbury Sq. to Bradbury Pl., which becomes University Rd.; then take a right on Fitzwilliam, across from Queen's University. Relaxed and friendly, although a bit cramped. Kitchen available. Internet £1 per 30min. Laundry £4. 8-bed dorms £9; 4-bed dorms £11. Cash only. ❶

Camera Guesthouse, 44 Wellington Park (☎9066 0026). This pristine Victorian house offers full Irish organic breakfasts along with white silk sofas in the parlor. Singles £34-50; doubles £56-62. AmEx/MC/V; 3% surcharge. ❹

FOOD

The huge Tesco **supermarket,** 2 Royal Ave., has better prices than convenience stores and is a good bet for cheap eats. (☎9032 3270. Open M-W and Sa 7am-7pm, Th 8am-9pm, F 8am-8pm, Su 1-5pm.)

Azzura, 8 Church Ln. (☎9024 2444). Tiny cafe with excellent meat and vegetarian dishes. Gourmet pizzas, pastas, soups, and sandwiches arrive warm from the oven for £2.40-5. Peppers grown fresh by the owners. Open M-W 11am-3:30pm, Th 11am-midnight, F-Sa 11am-2am. Cash only. ❷

The Other Place, 79 Botanic Ave. (☎9020 7200). Decadent fried breakfasts until 5pm (£3-6). Entrees £8-8.50. Open daily 8am-10pm. MC/V; min. £10. ❷

The Moghul, 62A Botanic Ave. (☎9032 6677). Sit overlooking the street from 2nd fl. corner windows. Outstanding Indian lunch M-Th £3. Lunch buffet F £6. Takeaway options. Open Su-Th noon-2pm and 5-11:30pm, F-Sa noon-2pm and 5pm-midnight. MC/V. ❷

THE CATHOLIC MURALS

The murals of West Belfast are a powerful testament to the volatile past and fierce loyalties of the divided neighborhoods. Many of the most famous Catholic murals are on the Falls Rd., which saw some of the worst of the Troubles.

1. Mural illustrating protestors during the **Hunger Strikes of 1981,** in which they fasted for the right to be considered political prisoners.
2. Portrayal of **Bobby Sands,** the first hunger-striker to die, is located on the side of the Sinn Féin Office, Sevastopol St. Sands was elected as a member of the British Parliament under a "political prisoner" ticket during this time and is the North's most famous martyr.
3. Formerly operating as Northern Ireland's National RUC Headquarters, the most bombed of any police station in England. Its fortified, barbed-wire facade is on Springfield St.

SIGHTS

DONEGALL SQUARE. The most impressive piece of architecture in Belfast also its administrative and geographic center. Dominating the grassy square that serves as the locus of downtown, **City Hall's** green copper dome (52m) is visible from nearly any point in the city. Inside, a grand staircase ascends to the second floor, where portraits of the city's Lord Mayors line the halls. *(☎9027 0456. 1hr. tours M-F 11am, 2, and 3pm; Sa 2 and 3pm. Tour times subject to change. Free.)*

THE DOCKS AND EAST BELFAST. The poster child of Belfast's riverfront revival, **Odyssey** packs big attractions into one huge entertainment center. The best feature is the **W5 Discovery Centre** (short for "whowhatwherewhywhen?"), a playground for curious minds and hyperactive schoolchildren. *(2 Queen's Quay. ☎9045 1055; www.theodyssey.co.uk. Box office ☎9073 9074; www.odysseyarena.com. W5 ☎9046 7700; www.w5online.co.uk. Wheelchair-accessible. Box office open M-Sa 10am-7pm. W5 open M-Sa 10am-6pm, Su noon-6pm. W5 £6.50, students and seniors £5, children £4.50, families £19.)* For nautical enthusiasts, **Sinclair Seamen's Church** is sure to please. The minister delivers his sermons from a pulpit carved in the shape of a prow, collections are taken in miniature lifeboats, and an organ from a Guinness barge—with port and starboard lights—carries the tune. *(Corporation St. ☎9071 5997. Su services at 11:30am and 7pm. Open W 2-5pm.)*

CORNMARKET AND ST. ANNE'S. North of the city center, this shopping district envelops eight blocks around **Castle Street** and **Royal Avenue.** Relics of the old city remain in **entries,** or tiny alleys. Construction on St. Anne's Cathedral, also known as the **Belfast Cathedral,** was begun in 1899, but to keep from disturbing regular worship, it was built around a smaller church already on the site; upon completion of the new exterior, builders extracted the earlier church brick by brick. *(☎9032 8332. Donegall St. Open M-Sa 10am-4pm, Su before and after services at 10, 11am, 3:30pm.)*

THE GOLDEN MILE. This strip along Great Victoria St. contains many of Belfast's historical jewels. Of these, the **Grand Opera House** is city's pride and joy, sadly making it a repeated bombing target for the IRA. *(☎9024 1919; www.goh.co.uk. Office open M-F 8:30am-6pm. Tours Sa 11am. £4, students £3.)* If opera is not your thing, visit the popular **Crown Liquor Saloon,** 46 Great Victoria St., a showcase of carved wood and stained glass, recently restored by the National Trust. Finally, check out the **Europa Hotel,** which has the dubious distinction of being "Europe's most-bombed hotel," having survived 31 blasts.

WEST BELFAST. West Belfast is not a tourist "sight" in the traditional sense. The buildings display political **murals.** Visitors should definitely take a **black cab tour** of the murals, easily booked at most hostels. **Black Taxi Tours** (☎08000 523 914; www.belfast-tours.com) offer witty, objective presentations. The Catholic neighborhood is centered on the **Falls Road,** where the **Sinn Féin** office is easily spotted: one side of it is covered with an enormous portrait of Bobby Sands and an advertisement for the *Sinn Féin* newspaper, *An Phoblacht.* On **Divis Street,** Divis Tower is formerly an IRA stronghold, now occupied by the British army. Farther north is the **Shankill Road** and the Protestant neighborhood. Between the Falls and Shankill is the **Peace Line.** The side streets on the right guide you to the **Shankill Estate** and more murals. **Crumlin Road,** through the estate, is the site of the oldest Loyalist murals.

ENTERTAINMENT AND NIGHTLIFE

Belfast's cultural events and performances are covered in the *Arts Council Artslink*, free at the tourist office, while the bi-monthly *Arts Listings* covers entertainment throughout Northern Ireland. **Fenderesky Gallery,** 2 University Rd., in the Crescent Arts building, hosts shows and sells local work. (☎9023 5245. Open Tu-Sa 11:30am-5pm.) The **Old Museum Arts Centre,** 7 College Sq. N, is the largest venue for contemporary work. (☎9023 5053; www.oldmuseumartscentre.org. Open M-Sa 9:30am-5:30pm.) The city center becomes deserted late at night. Many begin a night out downtown, move to Cornmarket's historic entries, and then party late near the university. For extra suggestions, check *Belfast In Your Pocket*, available at the TIC. After pubs and clubs close, catch a taxi home; Belfast is spread out.

The Duke of York, 7-11 Commercial Ct. (☎9024 1062). From City Hall, go up Donegall Pl., turn right on Castle Pl., left on Waring, and left on Donegall St. Small entry marked "Duke of York." Boxing venue turned communist printing press, rebuilt after IRA bombing in the 60s; now home to the city's largest selection of Irish whiskeys. Th traditional Irish music 10pm. Sa disco £5. Open M-Tu 11:30am-11pm, W 11:30am-midnight, Th-F 11:30am-1am, Sa 11:30am-2am. Cash only.

Thompson's Nightclub (☎9032 3762; www.clubthompsons.com), next to City Hall, off Donegall Sq. E. The club to go to for late-night R&B on W or pounding dance music on F. Wait until after midnight to hit up this 2-level, fog-machine-filled club. Cocktails £4. Cover Su-Tu and Th £5, W £4, F £7, Sa £10. Open daily 10pm-3am.

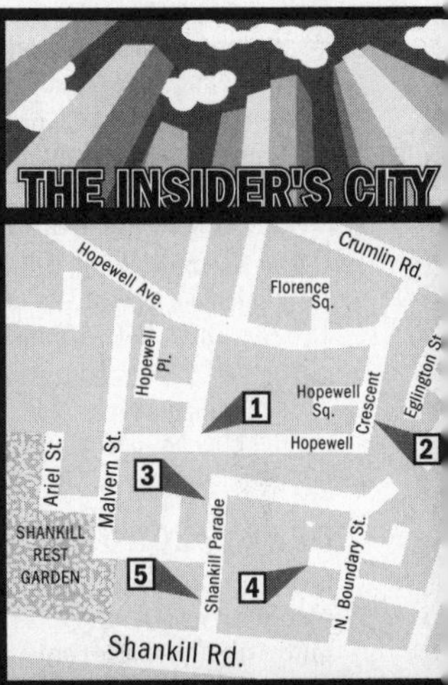

THE PROTESTANT MURALS

The Protestant murals, in the Shankill area of West Belfast, tend to be overtly militant. Most are found near Hopewell St. and Hopewell Cres., to the north of the Shankill Rd., or down Shankill Parade, and are accessed by traveling south from Crumlin Rd.

1. Painting of a Loyalist martyr, killed in prison in 1997.
2. A collage of Loyalist militant groups including the **Ulster Volunteer Force (UVF),** the **Ulster Defense Union (UDU),** and the **Ulster Defense Association (UDA).** Presiding over the whole mural is the portrait of a menacing **Ulster Freedom Fighter (UFF).**
3. Mural of the Battle of the Boyne, commemorating William of Orange's 1690 victory over James II.
4. The **Marksman's** gun seems to follow you as you pass by.
5. Portrait of the infamous **Top Gun,** a man responsible for the deaths of many high-ranking Republicans.

Katy Daly's Pub, 17 Ormeau Ave. (☎9032 5942), behind City Hall. With high ceilings and wood paneling, this pub is a true stalwart of the Belfast music scene. Pint £2.50. M live music; Tu student night; W live music or DJs; F-Sa DJs.

McHugh's, 29-31 Queen's Sq. (☎9050 9999), opposite the Custom House, sells native Belfast ale. Wrought-iron banisters and a chess set with caricatures of political figures add to the allure of this pub, open since 1711. Mixed crowd, but often touristy. Pint £2.50. F-Sa live music £5. Open Su-Tu noon-midnight, W-Sa noon-1am.

The Northern Whig, 2 Bridge St. (☎9050 9888). Occupying the building of its demised namesake's press, the Whig boasts a full list of cocktails (£3.95). Pint £2.60. Th-Sa DJ. 21+. Open M-Tu 10am-11pm, W-Sa 10am-1am, Su 1-11pm.

The Fly, 5-6 Lower Crescent (☎9050 9750; www.theflybar.com), is home to a crowd of students and young professionals. 1st fl. bar for pints (£2.70), 2nd for dancing, 3rd for the cocktail bar. M music quiz night with £100 prize. Open M-Th 7pm-2am, F-Sa 5pm-2am, Su 8pm-12:30am.

DERRY/LONDONDERRY ☎028

Modern Derry/Londonderry is trying to cast off the legacy of its political Troubles with much success. Although the landscape was razed by years of bombings and violence still erupts occasionally, recent years have been relatively peaceful. Today's rebuilt city is beautiful and intimate.

> **!** **WHAT'S IN A NAME?** Originally christened *Diore,* or "oak grove," the city's name was anglicized to Derry and finally Londonderry. The label remains a source of contention, as the minority Protestant population uses the official title while many Republican Northerners and informal Protestants refer to it as Derry.

TRANSPORTATION AND PRACTICAL INFORMATION. Trains (☎7134 2228) arrive on Duke St., Waterside, from Belfast (2hr., 4-9 per day, £9.60). A free Rail-Link bus connects the **train station** and the **bus station,** on Foyle St., between the walled city and the river; it leaves the bus station 15min. before each train is due to depart. Ulsterbus **buses** (☎7126 2261) go to Belfast (1½-3hr.; 28-36 per day; £9.40, students £6) and Dublin, IRE (4¼hr., 6-8 per day, £14/11). The **tourist office,** 44 Foyle St., has free maps and copies of the *Visitor's Guide to Derry.* (☎7126 7284; www.derryvisitor.com. Open July-Sept. M-F 9am-7pm, Sa 10am-6pm, Su 10am-5pm; low season reduced hours.) The **police** station is on Strand Rd. (☎7136 7337), and **Internet** access is available at the central **library,** 35 Foyle St. (☎7127 2310. £1.50 per 30min. Open M and Th 8:30am-8pm, Tu-W and F 8:30am-5:30pm, Sa 9:15am-5pm.) **Postal Code:** BT48 6AT.

BRITAIN

ACCOMMODATIONS AND FOOD. Go down Strand Rd. and turn left up Great James St. to reach the friendly and social **Derry City Independent Hostel ❶,** 44 Great James St. (☎7128 0542; www.derryhostel.com. Light breakfast included. Free Internet. Dorms £11; doubles £32. MC/V.) **The Saddler's House (No. 36) ❸,** 36 Great James St., offers elegant rooms in a lovely Victorian home. (☎7126 9691; www.thesaddlershouse.com. TV and tea/coffee facilities in all rooms. Large breakfast included. Singles £35; doubles £50. MC/V.) **The Ice Wharf/Lloyd's No. 1 Bar ❶,** on Strand Rd., has every type of food imaginable at incredibly low prices. Get two meals for the price of one all day long, or a burger with a drink and chips for only £4. (☎7127 6610; www.lloydsno1.co.uk. Open M-Th 10am-midnight, F-Sa 10am-1am, Su noon-midnight.) **The Sandwich Co. ❶,** The Diamond, is perfect for cheap sandwiches. (☎7137 2500. Sandwiches £2.25-3.15. Open M-Sa 8am-5pm.) The **Tesco** supermarket is in the Quayside Shopping Centre, a short walk from the walled city along Strand Rd. (Open M-Th 9am-9pm, F 8:30am-9pm, Sa 8:30am-8pm, Su 1-6pm.)

SIGHTS AND NIGHTLIFE. The **city walls,** 5.5m high and 6m thick, erected between 1614 and 1619, have never been breached—hence Derry's nickname "the Maiden City." The walls separate the commercial center from the surrounding neighborhoods and bar-lined streets. The tower topping Derry's southeast wall past New Gate was built to protect **St. Columb's Cathedral,** on London St., the symbolic focus of the city's Protestant defenders. (☎7126 7313. Open M-Sa Easter-Oct. 9am-5pm; Nov.-Easter 9am-1pm and 2-4pm. Tours £1.50.) At Union Hall Pl., just inside Magazine Gate, the **Tower Museum's** exhibits recount Derry's history. (☎7137 2411; www.derrycity.gov/uk/museums. Open Tu-Sa 9am-5pm. £3, students £2.) West of the city walls, Derry's residential neighborhoods—both the Protestant **Waterside** and **Fountain Estate,** as well as the Catholic **Bogside**—display murals.

After dark, check out **The Gweedore** or **Peadar O'Donnell's,** 53-60 Waterloo St., where Celtic and Orangeman paraphernalia hang and rock bands bang at night. Peadar O'Donnell's has trad every night at 11pm, while The Gweedore has younger rock bands; both pubs are connected and owned by the same person, although they cater to different crowds. (☎7137 2318; www.peaderodonnells.com. Open daily 11am-1am.) **The Metro,** 6 Bank Pl., is a good option any night of the week for live music, DJs, or just plain old craic. (☎7128 7401. Pint £2.20. M-Tu and Th live music 10pm-12:30am, 12:30-1:30am DJs. W and F-Su DJs. Open M-Th 11:30am-1:30am, F-Sa 11:30am-2:30am.) **Bound For Boston,** 27-31 Waterloo St., is a place for a younger crowd to chill out and yell above the live music that goes down Tuesday and Thursday to Sunday. (☎7127 1315; www.boundforboston.com. Pint £2.45. Open M-Sa 11:30am-1am, Su 1pm-1am.)

DAYTRIP FROM DERRY: THE GIANT'S CAUSEWAY

Take the free shuttle from the Derry bus station across the river to the train station (it leaves 15min. before the train departs), and catch a train to Coleraine. From Coleraine, catch bus #172 or 252 to the Causeway. Ulsterbuses #172, 252 (the Antrim Coaster), the Causeway Rambler, and the Bushmills Bus (you must catch the last 2 from Bushmills Distillery) drop visitors at the Giant's Causeway Visitors Centre. From the Centre, there is a minibus that runs to the most popular part of the Giant's Causeway; it's 1km or a 2min. ride, every 15min. Round-trip £1.80. ☎2073 1855; www.giantscauseway.com. Centre open daily May-June 10am-5pm; July-Aug. 10am-6pm; Sept.-Oct. 10am-4:30pm. The Causeway is free and always open.

The Giant's Causeway is a profoundly awesome sight to behold. Comprising over 38,000 symmetrical, hexagonal basalt columns, it resembles a large descending staircase leading from the cliffs to the ocean's edge. Geologists believe the unique rock formations were created some 60 million years ago by ancient lava outpourings that left curiously shaped cracks in their wake. Several other rock formations stand within the Great Causeway: the **Giant's Organ,** the **Wishing Chair,** the **Granny,** the **Camel,** and the **Giant's Boot.** Advertised as the eighth natural wonder of the world, the Giant's Causeway is Northern Ireland's most famous sight, so don't be surprised if 2000 other travelers pick the same exact day to visit. Visit early in the morning or after the Centre closes to avoid crowds. Do be aware, however, that the Causeway is outside and on the coast; bring adequate layers and rain gear.

The informative **Giant's Causeway Visitors Centre** is inland from the Causeway. From the Centre there are two routes to the coast. The low road is a well-marked 20min. walk. The high road, which rambles 7km up a sea cliff to the romantic Iron-Age ruins of **Dunseverick Castle,** is a longer but very beautiful option. Buses #172 and 252 (the Antrim Coaster) stop in front of the castle. A free map of the area is available at the Visitors Centre, which also offers a 12min. film (every 15min.; £1, children 50p) about the legend of Finn MacCool and the geological explanation for the rock formations.

BULGARIA (БЪЛГАРИЯ)

Barely through the latest saga in its turbulent history, Bulgaria is currently attempting to get back to its golden days. Once the most powerful state in the Balkans, Bulgaria fell to the Turks in the 14th century. In their 500 years of rule, the conquerors obliterated Bulgaria's nobility and enserfed its peasants. Underground monasteries preserved Bulgarian culture, enabling the construction of much of Bulgaria's stately architecture during the National Revival of the 1870s. Today, still reeling from the recent Balkan wars, the country struggles to increase its economic output and join the EU. Travelers to the region will be rewarded by journeys to cosmopolitan Sofia, the lush countryside, or the beautiful Black Sea Coast.

DISCOVER BULGARIA: SUGGESTED ITINERARIES

THREE DAYS Two days is probably enough to take in **Sofia's** (p. 207) museums, cathedrals, and cafes. Going to the **Rila Monastery** (1 day; p. 211) is easier said than done, but the gorgeous atmosphere and environs are worth it.

ONE WEEK If two days exploring the stunning ruins of **Veliko Târnovo** (p. 212) isn't enough, bus down to **Plovdiv** (p. 212) for even more Roman remains before heading to the **Rila Monastery** and then ending up in bustling **Sofia.**

ESSENTIALS

FACTS AND FIGURES

Official Name: Republic of Bulgaria.

Capital: Sofia.

Major Cities: Burgas, Plovdiv, Varna.

Population: 7,717,000.

Land Area: 110,550 sq. km.

Time Zone: GMT +2.

Language: Bulgarian.

Religions: Bulgarian Orthodox (83%), Muslim (13%).

WHEN TO GO

Bulgaria's temperate climate makes it easy to catch good weather. Spring (Apr.-May) is pleasant, offering a bevy of festivals and cultural events. Mild summers (June-Sept.) are perfect for hiking and beachgoing. Beware of the crowds that gravitate toward the coast. Skiing season runs from December until April.

DOCUMENTS AND FORMALITIES

EMBASSIES. Foreign embassies for Bulgaria are in Sofia (p. 207). For Bulgarian embassies abroad, contact: **Australia,** 4 Carlotta Rd., Double Bay, NSW 2028 (☎293 27 75 81); **Canada,** 325 Stewart St., Ottawa, ON K1N 6K5 (☎613-789-3215); **Ireland,** 22 Bulington Rd., 4 Dublin (☎1 660 3293); **UK,** 186-188 Queensgate, London SW7 5HL (☎207 584 9400; www.bulgarianembassy.org.uk/); **US,** 1621 22nd St. NW, Washington, D.C. 20008 (☎202-387-0174; www.bulgaria-embassy.org).

VISA AND ENTRY INFORMATION. Citizens of European Union countries, Ireland, the UK, and the US do not need visas for stays of up to 30 days. Nationals of Australia, Canada, and New Zealand can enter Bulgaria without a visa if they have made pre-arranged plans with an authorized Bulgarian travel agency to stay for a minimum of three days. Those planning to stay more than 30 days must obtain a 90-day visa from their local embassy. Visas are free for US citizens. For non-US citizens, single-entry visas are US$63-82; US$120 for multiple-entry visas. Prices include a border tax of approximately US$20; those not needing visas must pay the tax upon entering the country. A passport valid for six months after departing from Bulgaria is require. If staying in a private residence, register your visa with police within 48hr. of entering Bulgaria; hostels and hotels will do this for you.

TOURIST SERVICES AND MONEY

TOURIST OFFICES. Tourist offices and local travel agencies throughout Bulgaria are generally knowledgeable and good at reserving private rooms; some mostly plan itineraries. Staff are helpful and sometimes speak English, German, and/or Russian. Big hotels often have an English-speaking receptionist and maps and make good resources.

ENTRANCE REQUIREMENTS

Passport: Required for all travelers; must be valid for 6 months beyond stay.

Visa: Not required for citizens of EU countries, Ireland, the UK, or the US for stays up to 30 days.

Letter of Invitation: Not required for those who do not need a visa.

Inoculations: Not required. Recommended up-to-date on DTaP (diphtheria, tetanus, and pertussis), hepatitis A, hepatitis B, MMR (measles, mumps, and rubella), polio booster, and typhoid.

Work Permit: Required for all foreigners planning to work in Bulgaria.

International Driving Permit: Required for all those planning to drive.

MONEY. The unit of currency is the **lev (lv),** plural leva. One lev is equal to 100 stotinki. Sometimes US dollars or euros are accepted. Private banks and exchange bureaus exchange money, but bank rates are more reliable. The four largest **banks** are Bulbank, Biochim, DSK, and Hebros. **Traveler's checks** can only be cashed at banks (with the exception of a few exchange bureaus). Many banks also give Visa **cash advances. Credit cards** are rarely accepted. **ATMs** give the best exchange rates and usually accept MasterCard, Visa, Plus, and Cirrus. It is illegal to exchange currency on the street. Also beware of officially sanctioned overcharging; some museums and theaters will charge foreigners double. **Businesses** usually open at 8 or 9am and take a 1hr. lunch break sometime between 11am and 2pm. Banks are usually open 8:30am to 4pm, but some close at 2pm. Tourist offices, post offices, and shops stay open until 6 or 8pm; in big cities, shops may close as late as 10pm.

LEVA (LV)		
	AUS$1 = 1.15LV	1LV = AUS$0.88
	CDN$1 = 1.38LV	1LV = CDN$0.72
	EUR€1 = 1.95LV	1LV = EUR€0.51
	NZ$1 = 0.96LV	1LV = NZ$1.04
	UK£1 = 2.85LV	1LV = UK£0.35
	US$1 = 1.53LV	1LV = US$0.66

HEALTH AND SAFETY

While basic medical supplies are available in hospitals, specialized treatment is not. Emergency care is better in Sofia than elsewhere, but it's best to avoid hospitals entirely. Travelers must carry proof of insurance; most doctors expect cash payment. In the case of extreme emergency, air evacuation runs about US$50,000.

The sign "Apteka" marks a **pharmacy.** There is always a night-duty pharmacy in larger towns. *Analgin* is headache medicine; *sitoplast* are bandages. Foreign brands of condoms *(prezervatifs)* are the most reliable. Prescription drugs are difficult to obtain—bring enough of your own. Public **bathrooms** ("Ж" for women, "M" for men) are often holes in the ground; pack toilet paper and hand sanitizer, and expect to pay 0.05-0.20lv. **Tampons** are widely available. Don't buy bottles of **alcohol** from street vendors, and be careful with homemade liquor. Asthmatics, beware: Bulgaria's restaurants, taverns, and public transportation are often smoke-filled; the exception is the bus system. 2005 legislation supposedly ensures properly-ventilated non-smoking sections in all bars, cafes, and restaurants.

Watch out for petty **street crime,** especially pickpocketing and purse-snatching. Also be wary of people posing as government officials; always ask for ID. Take only marked taxis and ascertain that the meter is on for the entire ride. Nightclubs in large cities are often associated with organized crime; beware of fights.

It's generally fine for **women** to travel alone, but it's always safer to have at least one travel companion. Wear long skirts and blouses to avoid unwanted attention; only young girls wear sneakers, tank tops, or shorts outside of big cities. Although wheelchair accessibility is slowly improving, visitors with physical **disabilities** will confront many challenges in Bulgaria. **Discrimination** is focused on Roma (gypsies). Dark-skinned minorities are occasionally confused for Roma and discriminated against accordingly. While hate crimes are rare, persons of foreign ethnicities may receive stares. Though the Bulgarian government has recently officially recognized **homosexuality,** acceptance is slow in coming. It is prudent to avoid public displays of affection. For more information about GLBT clubs and resources in areas you plan to visit, check out www.queer-bulgaria.org or www.bulgayria.com.

EMERGENCY **Police:** ☎166. **Ambulance:** ☎150. **Fire:** ☎160.

TRANSPORTATION

BY PLANE. All flights to Sofia (SOF) connect through London, BRI or Western Europe. Though tickets to the capital may run over US$2500 in the summer, budget airline **WizzAir** offers cheap flights from Frankfurt, London, and Paris. Budget travelers might also fly into a nearby capital—Athens, Bucharest, or İstanbul—and take a bus to Sofia. Bulgarian airports are on par with international standards.

BY TRAIN. Bulgarian trains run to Greece, Hungary, Romania, and Turkey and are the best form of transportation in the north. The train system is comprehensive but slow, crowded, and smoke-filled. Purse-slashing, pickpocketing, and theft have been reported on more crowded lines. Buy tickets at the Ticket Center *(Bileti Tsentur)* in stations. There are three types of trains: express *(ekspres)*, fast *(burz)*, and slow *(putnicheski)*. Avoid *putnicheski*—they stop at anything that looks inhabited, even if only by goats. Arrive well in advance if you want a seat. Because stations are poorly marked and often only in Cyrillic, know when you're reaching your destination, bring a map, and ask for help. First class *(purva klasa)* is identical to second *(vtora klasa)*, and therefore not worth the extra money. Store luggage at the *garderob*.

BY BUS. Buses are better for travel in eastern and western Bulgaria and are often faster than trains, though they are less frequent and less comfortable. Buses head north from Ruse, to İstanbul, TUR from anywhere on the Black Sea Coast, and to Greece from Blagoevgrad. For long distances, **Group Travel** and **Etap** have modern buses with A/C and bathrooms. Some buses have set departure times; others leave when full.

BY BOAT. Ferries from Varna make trips to İstanbul, TUR and Odessa, UKR.

BY TAXI AND BY CAR. Yellow taxis are everywhere in cities. Refuse to pay in US dollars and insist on a ride *sus apparata* (with meter); ask the distance and price per kilometer. Don't try to bargain. Some taxi drivers rig the meters to charge more. Tipping taxi drivers usually means rounding up to the nearest lev or half-lev. Some Black Sea towns can only be reached by car. Renting is cheapest from a local agent, who will charge less than the €15-60 that larger companies do. While urban roads are generally in fair condition, rural roads are often in disrepair; rocks and landslides pose a threat in mountainous areas. Seat belts are mandatory when driving in Bulgaria.

BY BIKE AND BY THUMB. **Motoroads** (www.motoroads.com) and travel agencies offer bike tours. Stay alert when biking in urban areas, as Bulgarian drivers disregard traffic signals. Hitchhiking is rare because drivers rarely stop. While those who hitchhike say it is generally safe, Let's Go does not recommend it.

KEEPING IN TOUCH

PHONE CODES	**Country code:** 359. **International dialing prefix:** 00. For more information on how to place international calls, see inside back cover.

EMAIL AND THE INTERNET. Internet cafes can be found throughout urban centers, cost approximately 0.60-3lv per hr., and are often open 24hr.

TELEPHONE. Making **international phone calls** from Bulgaria can be a challenge. Pay phones are ludicrously expensive; opt for phone offices instead. If you must make an international call from a pay phone with a card, purchase the 400-unit,

YES AND NO. In rural areas, Bulgarians shake their heads from side to side to indicate "yes" and up and down to indicate "no," the opposite of Brits and Yanks. It may be easier to just hold your head still and say *"da"* or *"neh."*

22lv card. Units run out quickly on international calls, so speak rapidly or have multiple cards ready. There are two brands: **BulFon** (orange) and **Mobika** (blue), which work only at telephones of the same brand; BulFon is more prevalent. One minute costs 0.40lv to Australia and New Zealand, 0.20lv to Europe and the US. To **call collect,** dial ☎0123 for an international operator. The Bulgarian phrase for collect call is *"za tyahna smetka."* For **local calls,** pay phones seldom accept coins, so it's best to buy a phonecard (see above). You can also call from the post office, where a clerk assigns you a booth, a meter records your bill, and you pay when finished. International access codes include: **AT&T Direct** (☎00 800 0010); **BT Payphones** (☎00 800 99 44); and **MCI** (☎00 800 0001).

MAIL. "Свъздушна поща" on letters indicates **airmail.** Though far more reliable than ground transport mail, it is sometimes difficult to convince postal workers to let you pay extra to have your mail sent airmail. Sending a letter abroad costs 0.60lv to Europe, 0.90lv to the US, and 0.80-1lv to Australia and New Zealand; a Bulgarian return address is required. Packages must be unwrapped for inspection. Register important packages, and allow two weeks for them to arrive. Mail can be received general delivery through **Poste Restante,** though the service is unreliable. Address envelope as follows: First name, LAST NAME, POSTE RESTANTE, писма до поискване централна поща, (post office address, optional), City, Postal Code, България (Bulgaria).

LANGUAGE. Bulgarian is a South Slavic language written in the Cyrillic alphabet. A few words are borrowed from Turkish and Greek, but most vocabulary is similar to Russian and its related languages. **English** is most commonly spoken by young people in cities and in tourist areas. **German** and **Russian** are often understood by locals. Street names are in the process of changing; you may need both old and new names to navigate. The Bulgarian alphabet is much the same as Russian (see **Cyrillic Alphabet,** p. 1052) except that "щ" is pronounced "sht" and "ъ" is "ŭ" (like the "u" in bug).

ACCOMMODATIONS AND CAMPING

BULGARIA	❶	❷	❸	❹	❺
ACCOMMODATIONS	under 20lv	20-35lv	35-50lv	50-70lv	over 70lv

Bulgarian **hotels** are classed on a star system and licensed by the Government Committee on Tourism; rooms in one-star hotels are nearly identical to rooms in two- and three-star hotels; the only difference is that one-star hotels have no private bathrooms. All accommodations provide linens and towels. Expect to pay US$25-35. Beware that foreigners are often charged double or more of what locals pay. **Hostels** can be found in most major cities and run US$10-18 per bed. Almost all include free breakfast and many offer Internet and laundry services. For a complete list of hostels in Bulgaria, see www.hostels.com/en/bg.html. **Private rooms,** which can be found in any small town, are cheap (US$6-12) and usually have all the amenities of a good hotel.

Outside major towns, most **campgrounds** provide spartan bungalows and tent space. Call ahead in the summer to reserve bungalows. Some are poorly maintained or unpredictable, so check before it is too late to stay elsewhere.

FOOD AND DRINK

BULGARIA	❶	❷	❸	❹	❺
FOOD	under 4lv	4-9lv	9-14lv	14-20lv	over 20lv

Food from **kiosks** is cheap (0.60-2.50lv); **restaurants** average 6lv per meal. Kiosks sell *kebabcheta* (sausage burgers), sandwiches, pizzas, and *banitsa sus sirene* (feta-cheese-filled pastries). Try *shopska salata*, a mix of tomatoes, peppers, and cucumbers with feta cheese. *Kavarma*, meat with onions, spices, and egg, is slightly more expensive than *skara* (grills). **Vegetarians** should request their food *iastia bez meso* (iahs-tea-ah bez meh-so). **Kosher** diners would also be wise to order vegetarian meals, as pork often sneaks into Bulgarian main dishes. *Ayran* (yogurt with water and ice) and *boza* (similar to beer, but sweet, thicker, and less alcoholic) are popular drinks that complement breakfast. Bulgaria exports mineral water and locals swear by its healing qualities.

Tap water is generally safe to drink, though home-brewed alcohols should be avoided. Melnik produces famous red **wine,** while the northeast is known for its excellent white wines. On the Black Sea Coast, *Albenu* is a good sparkling wine. Bulgarians begin meals with *rakiya* (grape or plum brandy). Good Bulgarian **beers** include *Kamenitza* and *Zagorka.*

HOLIDAYS AND FESTIVALS

Holidays: Liberation Day (Mar. 3); Orthodox Easter (Apr. 23); Labor Day (May 1); St. George's Day (May 6); Education and Culture Day, also known as the Day of Slavic Heritage (May 24); Kazanlŭk (Festival of the Roses; June 3); Day of Union (Sept. 6); Independence Day (Sept. 22).

Festivals: On Christmas, it is traditional in Bulgaria for groups of people to go from house to house and perform *koledouvane,* or caroling, while holding beautiful oak sticks called *koledarkas.* On New Year's, a group of *sourvakari* wish their neighbors well while holding decorated cornel rods called *sourvachka*. Baba Marta (Spring Festival; Mar. 1) celebrates the beginning of spring. Bulgarians traditionally give each other *martenitzas,* small red-and-white charms. The Festival of Roses is celebrated in Kazanlŭk and Karlovo on the 1st Sunday in June.

BEYOND TOURISM

American University in Bulgaria, Blagoevgrad 2700, Bulgaria (☎73 888 235; www.aubg.bg). University in Bulgaria based on the American liberal arts model. Accepts international students.

Peace Corps, Office of Volunteer Recruitment and Selection, 1111 20th St. NW, Washington, D.C., 20526, US (☎800-424-8580; www.peacecorps.gov). Sends volunteers to developing nations such as Bulgaria. Must be US citizen age 18+ willing to make a 2-year commitment. Bachelor's degree usually required.

SOFIA (СОФИЯ) ☎02

A history of assimilation has left much of Bulgaria unsure of its identity. Nevertheless, 7000-year-old Sofia (pop. 1,139,000) is now leading the country into the era of EU integration. Europe's highest capital dominates modern Bulgaria's commercial enterprise as well as its bustling nightlife. Often overlooked because it lacks the tourist attractions of other capitals, Sofia offers some of its nation's best churches, food, music, and shopping—of both the traditional and modern varieties.

TRANSPORTATION

Flights: Airport Sofia (International departures ☎937 22 11). Bus #84 (0.50lv) runs from the airport to Orlov Most (Орлов Мост; Eagle Bridge), a 10min. walk from the city center. If you take **OK Taxi** downtown (20-30min.), your ride should cost about 8lv.

Trains: Tsentralna Gara (Централна Гара; Central Train Station; ☎932 33 33; www.bdz.bg), bul. Knyaginya Mariya Luiza (Княгиня Мария Луиза), 1.6km north of pl. Sv. Nedelya. Information booth and ticket counter are on 1st fl. Trains run to **Plovdiv** (2½-3½hr., 9 per day, 8-10lv), **Varna** (7-9hr., 6 per day, 20lv), and **Veliko Tŭrnovo** (5-7hr., 4 per day, 10lv). Buy all international tickets at **Rila Travel Bureau** (Рила; ☎932 33 46; www.bdz-rila.com), left of the main entrance. International destinations include: **Belgrade, SER** (2 per day, 28lv); **Bucharest, ROM** (2 per day, 36lv to Romania); **Budapest, HUN** (via Belgrade or Bucharest, 3 per day, 77-111lv); **İstanbul, TUR** (1 per day, 60lv); **Thessaloniki, GCE** (3 per day, 25lv). Open daily 7am-11pm.

Buses: Private buses, which leave from the parking lot across from the train station, are a bit pricier than trains but are faster and more comfortable. Schedules available online at www.centralnaavtogara.bg. **Grup Travel** sends buses to: **Plovdiv** (2hr., 9-10lv), **Varna** (7hr., 20 per day, 22-24lv), and **Veliko Tŭrnovo** (3hr., 20 per day, 11-13lv). Buses go to **Belgrade, SER** (7hr., 1-2 per day, 98lv); **İstanbul, TUR** (9-10hr., 8 per day, 40lv); and **Thessaloniki, GCE** (7-8hr., 8 per day, 43lv). Ticket office open daily 7am-7pm.

Local Transportation: Trams, trolleybuses, and buses cost 0.50lv per ride, 2lv for 5 rides, 1-day pass 2.20lv, 5-day pass 10lv. Buy tickets at kiosks labeled Билети (*bileti;* tickets) or from the driver. Validate them onboard to avoid a 5lv fine. If you put your backpack on a seat, you may be fined 5lv. Public transportation runs 5am-11pm. Sofia has a subway line that starts at the TSUM shopping center and goes west for 7 stops.

Taxis: Some travelers have terrible tales. **OK Taxi** (☎973 21 21) is reliable and affordable. Always make sure that the company's name and phone number are on the side of the car and insist that the driver turn on the meter. Drivers frequently don't speak English, so bring Bulgarian directions. Fares 0.45-0.5lv per km, higher 10pm-6am.

ORIENTATION AND PRACTICAL INFORMATION

The city center of Sofia, **ploshtad Sveta Nedelya** (Света Неделя), is a triangle formed by the church Tsurkva Sv. Nedelya, the wide building housing the Sheraton Hotel, and the large department store Tsentralen Universalen Magazin ("TSUM"). **Bulevard Knyaginya Mariya Luiza** (Княгиня Мария Луиза) connects pl. Sv. Nedelya to the train station. Bul. Vitosha, one of the main shopping and nightlife thoroughfares, links pl. Sv. Nedelya to **ploshtad Bŭlgaria** and the huge, concrete **Natsionalen Dvorets na Kultura** (Национален Дворец на Култура; NDK, National Palace of Culture). On your right as you go down bul. Mariya Luiza, historic **Bulevard Tsar Osvoboditel** (Цар Освободител; Tsar the Liberator) leads to **Sofia University.** The *Inside & Out Guide* (free at the Sheraton Hotel and at tourist centers) has tourist info in English.

Tourist Office: Odysseia-In/Zig Zag Holidays, bul. Stamboliyski 20B (Стамболийски; ☎980 51 02; www.zigzagbg.com). From pl. Sv. Nedelya, head down Stamboliyski and turn right on Lavele. 30min. consultation 5lv, first 5min. free. Train and bus schedules available. Open daily 8:30am-7:30pm; low season open M-F 8:30am-7:30pm. MC/V.

Embassies: Australia, ul. Trakiya 37 (☎946 13 34; www.embassy.gov.au/bg). **Canada,** Moskovska 9 (Московска; ☎969 97 10). **UK,** ul. Moskovska 9 (☎933 92 22). Open M-Th 9am-noon and 2-4pm, F 9am-noon. **US,** ul. Kozyak 16 (☎937 5100, emergency 937 51 01; fax 937 5122). Open M-F 9am-noon and 2-4pm. Citizens of **Ireland** and **New Zealand** should contact the UK embassy.

Luggage Storage: Downstairs at Tsentralna Gara. 2lv per piece. Claim bags 30min. before departure. Open daily 6am-11pm.

Emergency: Police: ☎166. **Ambulance:** ☎150. **Fire:** ☎160.

24hr. Pharmacies: Apteka Sv. Nedelya, pl. Sv. Nedelya 5 (☎950 50 26). **Apteka Vasil Levski,** bul. Vasil Levski 70 (☎986 17 55).

Medical Services: State-owned hospitals offer free 24hr. emergency aid to all; note that staff may not all speak English. **Pirogov Emergency Hospital,** bul. Gen. Totleben 21 (Ген. Тотлебен; ☎51 531; www.pirogov.net), opposite Hotel Rodina. Take tram #5 or 19 from the city center. Open 24hr.

Telephones: Telephone Center, ul. General Gurko 4. Offers fax and photocopy services. International calls 0.36lv per min. Internet 0.50lv per 30min. Open 24hr.

Internet Access: Stargate, Pozitano 20 (Позитано), 30m on the left if facing Hostel Sofia. 1lv per hr. Open 24hr.

Post Office: ul. General Gurko 6 (Гурко; ☎949 64 46). Send international mail at windows #6-8; *Poste Restante* at window #12. Open M and Sa 7am-7pm, Tu-F 7am-8:30pm, Su 8am-1pm. Limited services available Su. **Postal Code:** 1000.

ACCOMMODATIONS AND FOOD

Big hotels are rarely worth the exorbitant prices; hostels or private rooms are the best option. **Hostel Mostel ❶,** 2 Ivan Denkoglu Str., earns high acclaim. Its location is excellent, and its free beer and pasta are always a hit. Walking tours €3-4.50 are available. (☎0889 22 32 96; www.hostelmostel.com. Kitchen facilities and lockers. Breakfast included. Common room with TV and DVD. Laundry 4-6lv. Free Internet. Reception 24hr. Free pickup if arranged ahead. Dorms 20lv; doubles 60lv. 10% discount on stays of more than 2 nights. Cash only.) **Hostel Sofia ❶,** Pozitano 16 (Позитано), has a great location and a homey feel. From pl. Sv. Nedelya, walk down bul. Vitosha and turn right on Pozitano. (☎989 85 82; www.hostelsofia.com. Common room with TV and DVD. Breakfast included. Laundry 5lv. Free Internet. Reception 24hr. Dorms 20lv, low season 18lv. Cash only.)

Cheap meals are easy to find. Across bul. Mariya Luiza from TSUM are two large **markets,** the Women's Bazaar and Central Hall. Facing McDonald's in pl. Slaveikov, take the left side-street and continue right at the fork to **Divaka ❷,** ul. William Gladstone 54, for huge salads and sizzling veggie and meat dishes served up on iron plates. (☎989 95 43. Branch at 6th September 41A, ☎986 69 71. English menu available. Beer 1.50-2.50lv. Appetizers 1-4lv. Entrees 3-10lv. Open 24hr.) **Murphy's Irish Pub ❷,** Kŭrnigradska 6 (Кърниградска), is a haven for homesick English-speakers. (☎980 28 70. Beer 3-4.50lv. Entrees from 7.50lv. F live music. Open Su-Th noon-12:30am, F-Sa noon-1:30am. Cash only.)

SIGHTS

PLOSHTAD ALEXANDER NEVSKY. With the tsar-liberator as its patron saint, the golden-domed **St. Alexander Nevsky Cathedral** (Св. Александр Невски; Sv. Aleksandr Nevski) was erected as a memorial to the 200,000 Russians and Bulgarians who died in the 1877-1878 Russo-Turkish War. Accessible through a separate entrance left of the main church, the **crypt** houses all manner of painted icons and religious artifacts collected over the past 1500 years. A craft market is located just outside of the cathedral. *(☎988 17 04. Cathedral open daily 7am-7pm. Daily liturgy 9am and 5pm. Crypt open Tu-Su 10am-6pm. Cathedral free. Silence requested in church. Crypt 4lv, students 2lv. Guided tours of the crypt are 25lv per person for groups of 5 or more, 20lv for groups of fewer than 5.)*

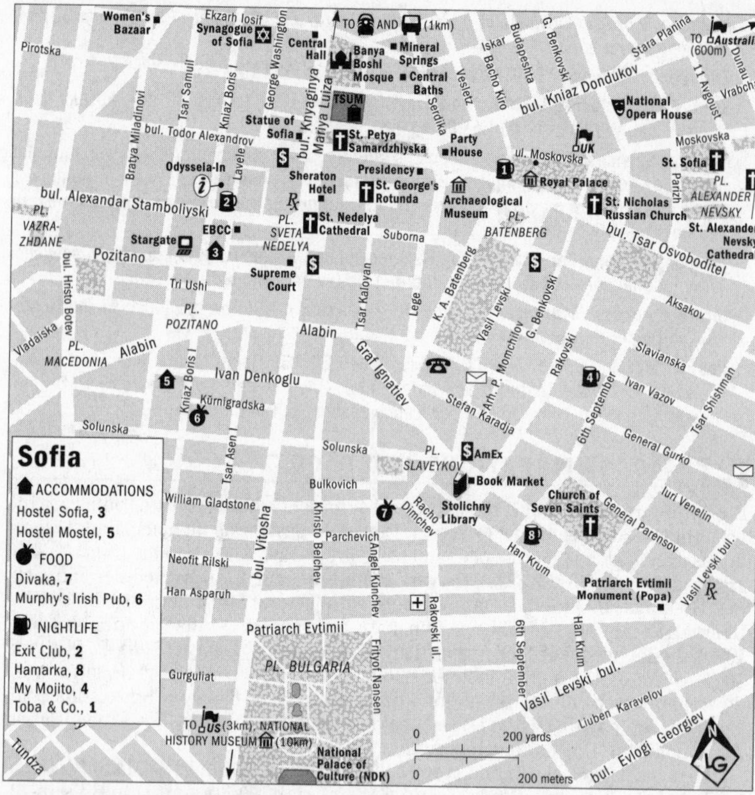

AROUND PLOSHTAD SVETA NEDELYA. The focal point of pl. Sv. Nedelya, the domed **Cathedral of St. Nedelya** (Катедрален Храм Св. Неделя; Katedralen Hram Sv. Nedelya) is a reconstruction of a 19th-century original that was blown up by communists attempting to assassinate Tsar Boris III in 1925. The liturgy shows off the church's great acoustics. *(Open daily 7am-6:30pm. Liturgy daily 9am and 5pm. Free.)* In the courtyard behind the Sheraton Hotel stands the 4th-century **St. George's Rotunda** (Св. Георги; Sv. Georgi), adorned inside with beautiful 11th- to 14th-century murals. The rotunda lies on the site of former Roman baths; massive WWII-era bunkers are also hidden underground. *(Open daily 8am-6pm. Services daily 9am and 5pm. Free.)* Walk up bul. Mariya Luiza and turn left on Ekzarh Iosif to reach the **Sofia Synagogue** (Софийска Синагога; Sofiyska Sinagoga), the city's only synagogue. *(☎983 12 73. Open M-Sa 8am-4pm. Services daily 8am, Sa also 10am. Admission €1.)*

ALONG BULEVARD TSAR OSVOBODITEL. Sofia's very first paved street, bul. Tsar Osvoboditel, runs the distance between the **House of Parliament** and the **Royal Palace.** The **Party House,** pl. Nezavisimost, isn't nearly as fun as it sounds; formerly the headquarters of the Communist Party Central Committee, it now serves as office space for parliamentarians. The **St. Nicholas Russian Church** (Св. Николай; Sv. Nikolay), bul. Tsar Osvoboditel 3, contains icons from the Novgorod school. *(☎986 27 15. Open M-Sa 8am-6:30pm, Su 8am-5:30pm. Liturgy W 9am and 5pm, Th-F and Su 9am, Sa 9am and 5:30pm. Free.)*

MUSEUMS. The Royal Palace houses the **National Museum of Ethnography** (Национален Етнографски Музей; Natsionalen Etnografski Muzey), devoted to four centuries of Bulgarian folk history, and the **Center of Folk Arts and Crafts** souvenir shop. *(Pl. Batenberg 1. ☎987 41 91, gift shop 989 64 16; www.bulgariancrafts.hit.bg. Open Tu-Su 10am-6pm. 3lv. Guided tours 10lv.)* In the same building, the **National Art Gallery** (Национална Художествена Галериа; Natsionalna Hudozhestvena Galeriya) displays Bulgaria's most prized traditional and contemporary art. *(Pl. Batenberg. ☎980 00 93. Open Tu-W and F-Su 10am-6pm, Th 10am-7:30pm. 4lv, students 2lv; Tu free. English-language tours 20lv.)* The **National History Museum,** Residence Boyana, Palace 1 (Национален Исторически Музей; Natsionalen Istoricheski Muzey), showcases archaeological and cultural artifacts from prehistory to the present. *(Bul. Tsar Osvoboditel 1. ☎955 42 80. Open daily 9:30am-5:30pm. 10lv, students 5lv. Guided tour 10lv.)*

ENTERTAINMENT AND NIGHTLIFE

Half a dozen theaters line **Rakovski.** From the town center, a left on Rakovski leads to the columns of the **National Opera House,** Rakovski 59. (☎987 13 66. Performances most days 6 or 7pm. Box office open M-Tu 9:30am-2pm and 2:30-7:30pm, W-F 8:30am-7pm, Sa 10:30am-7pm, Su 10am-6pm. Tickets 6-30lv.)

At night, smartly dressed Sofians roam the main streets, filling the outdoor bars along **bulevard Vitosha** and the cafes around the **National Palace of Culture.** For the younger set, nightlife centers around **Sofia University** at the intersection of bul. Vasil Levski and bul. Tsar Osvoboditel. At **My Mojito,** Ivan Vazov 12, students mix with young professionals. (☎986 32 70. Cover F-Sa men 5lv. Open daily 9pm-5am.) Hidden away at 6th September 22, **Hamarka** (The Barn) is a former Communist newspaper office turned tavern. (Open daily 8pm-last customer.) Party like a tsar at regal **Toba & Co,** ul. Moskovska 6, behind the Royal Palace. (☎989 46 96. Open daily 10pm-last customer.) **Exit Club,** str. Lavele 16, is a gay-friendly club. (☎0887 965 026; www.exit-club.com. Open daily 8am-2am.)

DAYTRIPS FROM SOFIA

RILA MONASTERY. Holy Ivan of Rila built the 10th-century Rila Monastery (Рилски Манастир; Rilski Manastir), the largest and most famous in Bulgaria, as a refuge from worldly temptation. The **Nativity Church** is decorated with 1200 brilliantly colored frescoes. Modest clothing is necessary, especially for women. (Monastery open daily approximately 7:30am-8:30pm.) The **museum** in the monastery houses the intricate **wooden cross** that took 12 years to carve (with a needle) and left its creator, the monk Rafail, blind. (Open daily 8:30am-4:30pm. 5lv, students 3lv. English lecture 15lv.) Signs throughout the monastery show hiking routes in nearby **Rila National Park;** Cyrillic maps of the paths (7lv) are sold in the **Manastirski Padarŭtsi** (Манастирски Падаръци) shop.

Inquire at room #170 in the monastery about staying in a spartan but heated **monastic cell** ❷. (☎070 54 22 08 until 5pm. 2-3 beds per room, single-sex. Doors lock at 10pm; ring the bell after that. Rooms 20lv, with bath 25lv.) Behind the monastery are restaurants, cafes, and a mini-market. To get to the monastery, take **tram** #5 from pl. Sv. Nedelya to Ovcha Kŭpel Station (Овча Къпел) and take the **bus** to Rila Town (2hr., 10:20am, 5lv). From there, catch the bus to the monastery (30min., 3 per day, 1.50lv). A direct bus goes back from Rila to Sofia at 3pm (7lv).

KOPRIVSHTITSA. Todor Kableshkov's 1876 "letter of blood," urging rebellion against Ottoman rule, incited the **April Uprising** and ultimately the **War of Liberation** in this little village in the Sredna Gora mountains. Today, Koprivshtitsa (Копри-

BULGARIA

вщица; pop. 2,600), is a charming village of stone cottages and winding streets. Many homes have verandas and famously delicate woodwork, and six have been turned into **museums;** buy tickets at the tourist office. (Most open 9:30am-5:30pm, all open W-Su, some closed M or Tu. 5lv each, combined ticket 10lv.)

Trains run to Plovdiv (3-4hr., 4 per day, 5-7lv) and Sofia (2-2½hr., 5 per day, 4-5lv). Private **buses** also run to Plovdiv (2½hr., 1 per day, 6lv) and Sofia (2hr., 2 per day, 6lv). Backtrack along the river to the main square to reach the **tourist office.** (☎071 84 21 91; www.koprivshtitsa.info. Open daily 10am-7pm.)

PLOVDIV (ПЛОВДИВ) ☎032

Picturesque Plovdiv (pop. 341,000) abounds with 19th-century National Revival structures (houses of prominent Revolution-era Bulgarians that are now museums), galleries, and churches. Roman ruins also remain from the city's ancient days under Roman rule. Its historical and cultural treasures are concentrated among the **Trimondium** (three hills) of **Stariya Grad** (Стария Град; Old Town). To reach the 2nd-century **Roman amphitheater** (Античен Театър; Antichen Teatŭr) from pl. Tsentralen (Централен), take a right off Knyaz Alexander (Княз Александр) onto Sŭborna (Съборна), then go right up the steps along Mitropolit Paisii. Dating from the early Roman occupation of the Balkans, this marble masterpiece now hosts concerts and shows, such as the **Verdi Opera Festival** in June (☎632 348; tickets 20lv for foreigners) and the **Festival of the Arts** in late summer (Amphitheater open daily 9am-7pm. 3lv.) Follow Knyaz Alexander to pl. Dzhumaya (Джумая), home to the 15th-century **Dzhumaya Mosque** (under renovation at press time) and the remains of an ancient Roman **stadium.** (Both free.) At the end of ul. Suborna on Dr. Chomakov 2, the **Museum of Ethnography** (Етнографски Музей; Etnografski Muzey) exhibits artifacts such as *kukerski maski*, masks used to scare away evil spirits. (☎62 56 54. Open Tu, Th, Sa-Su 9am-noon and 2-5pm, W and F 9am-noon. 4lv, students 2lv.)

Hiker's Hostel ❶, ul. Sŭborna 53, offers free Internet and big breakfasts; the staff also organizes daytrips. (☎359 885 194 553; www.hikers-hostel.org/pd. Free pickup. Kitchen available. Laundry 4lv. Reserve ahead. Reception 24hr. Dorms €10, private room €24. Cash only.) **Trains** run to Burgas (5hr., 4 per day, 10lv), Sofia (2½-5hr., 15 per day, 5-9.50lv), and Varna (6-7hr., 3 per day, 14-17lv). Buy international tickets at **Rila,** bul. Hristo Botev 31A. (☎64 31 20. Open M-F 8am-7:30pm, Sa 8am-2pm. Cash only.) **Buses** to Sofia (2hr., 1-3 per hr. 7am-8pm, 9-10lv) leave from Yug (Юг) station, bul. Hristo Botev 47 (☎62 69 37), opposite the train station. Vendors sell maps in Cyrillic or English (3lv). Check email at **Speed,** Knyaz Alexander 12. (1lv per hr. Open 24hr.) **Postal Code:** 4000.

BACHKOVO MONASTERY

In the Rodopi mountains, 28km south of Plovdiv, is Bulgaria's second-largest monastery, **Bachkovo Monastery** (Бачковски Манастир; Bachkovski Manastir; ☎03 32 72 77), built in 1083. The main church holds the **Icon of the Virgin Mary and Child** (Икона Света Богородица; Ikona Sveta Bogoroditsa), which is said to have miraculous healing powers. (Open daily 8am-8pm. Free.) Hiking paths lie uphill from the monastery. The Smolyan **bus** (30min., 1-2 per hr. 6am-8pm, 2.70lv) leaves from platform #1 at the Rodolpi station in Plovdiv; ask to go to Bachkovo. (*Kassa* open 5:30am-8pm.)

VELIKO TŬRNOVO (ВЕЛИКО ТЪРНОВО) ☎062

Veliko Tŭrnovo (pop. 66,000), on the steep hills above the Yantra River, has watched over Bulgaria for more than 5000 years. The city's residents led the national uprising against Byzantine rule in 1185; its revolutionaries wrote the country's first constitution here in 1879. The ruins of the ■Tsarevets (Царевец), a fortress that was the main citadel and center of power of the Second Bulgarian Kingdom (1185-1393), span a hillside outside the city. (Open daily 8am-7pm, *kassa* closes 6pm. 4lv, students 2lv. Guided tours in English sometimes available.) Once inside, climb uphill to the **Church of the Ascension** (Църква Възнесениегосподне; Tsŭrkva Vŭzneseniegospodne), which was restored in honor of the country's 1300th anniversary in 1981. A great place to browse traditional Bulgarian crafts is the cobblestone street **Rakovski** (Раковски). For a foray into modern Bulgarian history, go down Nezavisimost, and turn right at ul. Ivan Vazov (Иван Вазов) to reach the **National Revival Museum** (Музей на Възраждането; Muzey na Vŭzrazhdaneto). The museum building housed Bulgaria's first parliament and now contains a copy of its first constitution. (☎629 821. Open M and W-Su 9am-6pm. 4lv.) On summer evenings when there is sufficient tourist demand, there is a ■**sound and light show** above Tsarevets Hill. (Begins between 9:45 and 10pm and lasts 20min. 15lv.) The **International Folklore Festival**, which takes place in late July or early August, showcases folk dance and music.

■**Hiker's Hostel ❶** is at Rezervoarska 91 (Резервоарска). From Stambolov, turn left on Rakovski, left into the small square, go straight, and take the small street uphill. (☎0889 69 16 61; www.hikers-hostel.org/vt. Breakfast included. Free Internet. Dorms 20lv; doubles 26lv. Cash only.) **Trains** stop at Gorna Oryakhovitsa (Горна Оряховица). **Buses** are run by private companies from several stations. ETAP sends buses to Sofia (3hr., 13 per day, 13lv) and Varna (3hr., 10 per day, 13lv). Ask at the tourist office for other departures. Bus #10 leaves from the main square in Veliko Tŭrnovo for Gorna (1lv). Destinations include Burgas (6hr., 6 per day, 11lv), Sofia (5hr., 9 per day, 12lv), and Varna (4hr., 5 per day, 11lv). Minibuses and bus #10 go from the station to pl. Mayka Bŭlgaria (Майка България), the town center. The **tourist office** is at bul. Hristo Botev 5. (☎622 148. Open M-F 9am-6pm.) Check email at **Matrix Internet Club,** Nezavisimost 32 (Независимост); under renovation at press time. (☎605 959. Before 10pm 0.98lv per hr., after 10pm 0.68lv per hr. Open 24hr.) **Postal Code:** 5000.

BLACK SEA COAST (ЧЕРНО МОРЕ)

Bulgaria's premier vacation spot, the Black Sea Coast is laden with secluded bays and pricey resorts. Still, ancient fishing villages are just a step off the beaten path.

VARNA (ВАРНА) ☎052

Visitors are drawn to Varna (pop. 312,000) by its expansive beaches, Mediterranean-like climate, open-air nightlife, and frequent summer festivals. From the train station, go right on bul. Primorski (Приморски) to reach ■**beaches** and **seaside gardens.** The ■**Archaeological Museum** (Археологически Музей; Arheologicheski Muzey), bul. Maria Luiza 41, in the park on Mariya Luiza, has the world's oldest (over 6000 years old) gold artifacts. (☎681 030. Open in high season Tu-Su 10am-5pm; low season Tu-Sa 10am-5pm. 10lv, students 2lv.) On San Stefano in the city's old quarter, **Grŭtska Mahala** (Гръцка Махала), visit the well-preserved ruins of the **Roman Thermal Baths** (Римски Терми; Rimski Termi. ☎600 059. Open Tu-Su 10am-5pm. 4lv, students 2lv.) The **Ethnographic Museum,** str. Panagjurishte 22, portrays the traditional Bulgarian lifestyle. (☎630 588. Open in high season Tu-Su 10am-5pm; in low season M-F 10am-5pm.) Varna's cultural events include the **International Jazz Festival** in August (☎659 167; www.vsjf.com) and the **Varna Summer Festival** (www.varnasummerfest.org), a music (☎603 504), theater (☎603 504), and folk (☎659 159) festival that takes place June-July. For schedules and tickets, check the **Festival and Congress Center,** bul. Primorski, which is also the location of **Love is Folly,** a film festival in September. (☎608 445. Box office open 10am-9pm.)

Nightlife is centered on the beach in Primorski Park, which features a strip of **outdoor discos** along Krabrezhna Aleya. **Gregory's Backpackers Hostel ❶**, str. Fenix 82, in Zvezditsa village 10km from Varna, includes a swimming pool and a great lounge/bar. (☎379 909; www.hostelvarna.com. Free pickup. Breakfast included. Laundry 8lv. Internet 1.80lv per hr. Reserve ahead. Open Apr.-Oct. Dorms €10. Cash only.) **Trains** depart from near the commercial harbor for Plovdiv (6-7hr., 3 per day, 14-17lv) and Sofia (7½-9½hr., 6 per day, 19-22lv). **Buses,** ul. Vladislav Varenchik (Владислав Варенчик), are operated by different companies; ETAP goes to Sofia (6hr., 11 per day, 24lv) via Veliko Tŭrnovo (3hr., 13lv). The Victory bus company goes to Burgas (2½hr., 2 per day, 8lv). The **tourist office** is on bul. Knyaz Boris I, near the Masala Palace Hotel. **Astra Tour,** near track #6 at the train station, finds private singles for 25-30lv and doubles for 30-40lv. (☎60 58 61; astratur@yahoo.com. Open in summer daily 7am-9pm.) Access the Internet at **Bitex.com,** str. Zamenhof 1, 3rd fl., off pl. Nezavisimost. (☎63 17 65. 1lv per hr., 2lv for all of 9am-2pm, 3lv for all of midnight-8am. Open 24hr.) **Postal Code:** 9000.

CROATIA (HRVATSKA)

Croatia is a land of preternatural beauty, blessed with dense forests, barren mountains, and crystal-clear waters. At the convergence of the Adriatic, the Alps, and the Pannonian Plain, Croatia has also been situated along dangerous political boundaries—of the Frankish and Byzantine empires in the 9th century, of the Catholic and Orthodox churches since the 11th century, and of Christian Europe and the Islamic Ottoman Empire from the 15th to 19th centuries. In the past few decade, the political conflict has extended to its own fractious ethnic groups. After the devastating 1991-1995 war, however, the country achieved full independence for the first time in 800 years.

DISCOVER CROATIA: SUGGESTED ITINERARIES

THREE DAYS. Spend a day poking around the bizarre architecture of **Split** (p. 228) before ferrying down the coast to the beach paradise that awaits at either **Hvar** or **Brač** islands (1 day; p. 229) and the city some would consider the most beautiful in Eastern Europe—**Dubrovnik** (1 day; p. 231).

BEST OF CROATIA, ONE WEEK. Enjoy the East-meets-West feel of **Zagreb** (1 day; p. 220), then make your way on to **Zadar** (p. 227) on Croatia's gorgeous Dalmatian Coast. Next, take the ferry to tree-lined **Korčula** (1 day; p. 230) before **Hvar** and **Brac** (2 days). End your journey in **Dubrovnik** (2 days).

ESSENTIALS

FACTS AND FIGURES

Official Name: Republic of Croatia.

Capital: Zagreb.

Major Cities: Dubrovnik, Ploce, Split.

Population: 4,496,000.

Land Area: 56,414 sq. km.

Time Zone: GMT +1.

Language: Croatian.

Religions: Roman Catholic (88%).

WHEN TO GO

Croatia's best weather lasts from May to September, though the crowds typically show up in July and August along the Adriatic coast. If you go in late August or September, you'll find fewer crowds, lower prices, and an abundance of figs and grapes. Come later in the fall for wine season. While April and October may be too cool for camping, the weather is usually nice along the coast and private rooms are plentiful. It's warm enough to swim in the sea from mid-June to late September.

DOCUMENTS AND FORMALITIES

EMBASSIES AND CONSULATES. Embassies of other countries in Croatia are all in Zagreb (p. 220). Croatia's embassies and consulates abroad include: **Australia,** 14

Jindalee Cres., O'Malley, ACT, 2606, Canberra (☎2 6286 6988; croemb@dynamite.com.au); **Canada,** 229 Chapel St., Ottawa, ON, K1N 7Y6 (☎613-562-7820; www.croatiaemb.net); **New Zealand** Consulate, 291 Lincoln Rd., Henderson, Auckland (☎9 836 5581); **UK,** 21 Conway St., London, W1P 5HL (☎20 7387 2022; amboffice@croatianembassy.co.uk); **US,** 2343 Massachusetts Ave., NW, Washington, D.C., 20008 (☎202-588-5899; www.croatiaemb.org).

VISA AND ENTRY INFORMATION. Citizens of Australia, Canada, Ireland, New Zealand, the UK, and the US do not need visas for stays of up to 90 days. All visitors must register with the police within 48hr. of arrival—hotels, campgrounds, and accommodation agencies should automatically register you, but those staying with friends or in private rooms must do so themselves to avoid fines or expulsion. To register, go to room #103 on the second floor of the central police station in Zagreb at Petrinjska 30. Bring your passport and use form #14. (☎456 36 23, after hours 456 31 11. Open M-F 8am-4pm.) Police may check foreigners' passports anywhere and at any time, so be sure to always carry it on your person. The best value for entering or exiting Croatia is by bus or train between Zagreb and neighboring capitals, such as Ljubljana or Budapest.

ENTRANCE REQUIREMENTS

Passport: Required for all travelers.
Visa: Not required for stays under 90 days for citizens of Australia, Canada, Ireland, New Zealand, the UK, and the US.
Letter of Invitation: Not required.
Inoculations: Not required. Recommended up-to-date on DTaP (diphtheria, tetanus, and pertussis), hepatitis A, hepatitis B, MMR (measles, mumps, and rubella), polio booster, and typhoid.
Work Permit: Required for all foreigners planning to work in Croatia.
Driving Permit: Required for all those planning to drive.

TOURIST SERVICES AND MONEY

TOURIST OFFICES. Even small towns have a branch of the excellent **state-run tourist board** *(turistička zajednica)*. Staff speak English, almost always Italian, and often German and French, and give out free maps and booklets. You can also seek help with booking accommodations through private agencies *(turistička/putnička agencija)*. The largest is **Atlas,** but local outfits are generally cheaper.

MONEY. Croatia's monetary unit, the **kuna** (kn), which is divided into 100 lipa, is extremely difficult to exchange abroad, except in Bosnia, Hungary, and Slovenia. **Inflation** hovers around 2.5%. Most tourist offices, hotels, and transportation stations **exchange currency** and traveler's checks, but banks generally have the best rates. Most banks give MasterCard and Visa cash advances, and credit cards are accepted. ATMs are everywhere. Banks are open Monday through Friday 8am-7pm, Saturday 7am-noon. Travel in Croatia is becoming more costly, so expect to spend anywhere from 300kn to 470kn per day. **Tipping** is not expected, although it

KUNA (KN)

AUS$1 = 4.34KN	1KN = AUS$0.23
CDN$1 = 5.12KN	1KN = CDN$0.20
EUR€1 = 7.29KN	1KN = EUR€0.14
NZ$1 = 3.63KN	1KN = NZ$0.28
UK£1 = 10.78KN	1KN = UK£0.09
US$1 = 5.69KN	1KN = US$0.18

is appropriate to round up when paying; in some cases, the establishment will do it for you—check your change. Fancy restaurants often add a service charge. **Bargaining** is only for informal transactions, such as hiring a boat for a day or renting a private room directly from an owner. **Value added tax (VAT)** is significant at 22%.

SAFETY AND HEALTH

Travel to the former conflict area of the **Slavonia** and **Krajina** regions remains dangerous due to **unexploded landmines,** which are not expected to be cleared until at least 2010. In July 2005, a tourist was badly injured by a mine on the island of Vis, which inspectors had previously declared safe. If you choose to visit these or other affected regions, do not stray from areas expressly permitted for travel, and consult the Croatian Mine Action Center website at www.hcr.hr. **Pharmacies** are well stocked with Western products, including tampons, sanitary napkins *(sanitami ulosci)*, and condoms *(prezervativ)*. UK citizens receive free medical care with a valid passport. Tap **water** is normally chlorinated, and while relatively safe, may cause mild digestive difficulties. Bottled water is readily available. Croatians are sometimes a little too friendly to **females;** go out in public with a companion to ward off unwanted displays of machismo. **Disabled travelers** should contact Savez Organizacija Invalida Hrvatske (☎1 369 4502), and be aware that Zagreb's cobblestones and lack of ramps make getting around difficult. Though Croatians are slowly beginning to accept **homosexuality,** it's still best to be discreet in public.

EMERGENCY	**Police, Ambulance,** and **Fire:** ☎112.

TRANSPORTATION

BY PLANE AND TRAIN. Croatia Airlines flies from many cities, including Chicago, Frankfurt, London, and Paris to Dubrovnik, Split, and Zagreb, Zadar, and sometimes Pula. Trains (www.hznet.hr) run to Zagreb from Budapest, HUN, Ljubljana, SLV, Venice, ITA, and Vienna, AUT, and continue to other Croatian destinations. Due to destruction from the 1991-1995 war, trains are very slow, and nonexistent south of Split. *Odlazak* means departures, *dolazak* arrivals.

BY BUS. Buses (www.akz.hr) are the best option for domestic travel, running faster and farther than trains at comparable prices. Tickets are cheaper if you buy them onboard, bypassing the 2kn service charge at station kiosks. In theory, luggage must be stowed (3kn), but this is only enforced on the most crowded lines.

BY CAR AND BIKE. Anyone over 18 can rent a car in larger cities (350-400kn per day), but downtown parking and gas are expensive. Rural roads are in bad condition, and those traveling through the Krajina region and other conflict areas should be cautious of off-road **landmines.** Traveling by car can get especially expensive when island-hopping—Jadrolinija ferries charge a bundle for decking your wheels. Moped and bicycle rentals (50-80kn per day) are good and cheap options in resort or urban areas. Let's Go does not recommend **hitchhiking.**

BY FERRY. Jadrolinija ferries (www.jadrolinija.hr) sail the Rijeka-Split-Dubrovnik route, stopping at islands on the way. Ferries also go to Ancona, ITA from Split and Zadar and to Bari, ITA from Dubrovnik and Split. Ferries are frequently overnight and cheap beds sell out fast, so buy tickets ahead. A basic ticket provides only a place on the deck.

KEEPING IN TOUCH

PHONE CODES	**Country code:** 385. **International dialing prefix:** 00. For more information on how to place international calls, see inside back cover.

EMAIL AND THE INTERNET. Most towns, no matter how small, have at least one Internet cafe. Connections on the islands are slower and less reliable than those on the mainland.

TELEPHONE. Post offices usually have pay phones; pay after you talk. All phones on the street require a phone card *(telekarta)*, sold at newsstands and post offices. Fifty "impulses" cost 23kn (1 impulse equals 3min. domestic, 36sec. international; 50% discount M-Sa 10pm-7am, Su, and holidays). Voicecom and Telnet cards offer the least expensive rates for calls abroad. Direct access numbers include: **AT&T** (☎0800 22 00 11); **British Telecom** (☎0800 22 01 13); **Canada Direct** (☎0800 22 01 01); **MCI WorldPhone** (☎0800 22 01 12); **Telecom New Zealand** (☎0800 22 01 64). For the international operator, dial ☎901. Elaborate **mobile phone** ringtones can be heard virtually everywhere in Croatia, where there are two networks, T-Mobile and VIP. If you bring or buy a phone compatible with the GSM 900/1800 network, SIM cards are widely available and cost around 400kn.

MAIL. The **Croatian Post** is generally quite reliable. Mail from the US should arrive within one week. Mail addressed to **Poste Restante** will be held for 30 days at the main post office. Address envelope as follows: First name LAST NAME, *POSTE*

RESTANTE, post office address, Postal Code, city, CROATIA. *Avionski* and *zrakoplovom* both mean "airmail."

LANGUAGE. Croats speak **Croatian,** a South Slavic language written in the Latin alphabet. The language fairly recently became distinguished from Serbo-Croatian. **German** and **Italian** are common second languages among older adults. Most Croatians under 30 speak some **English.** For a phrasebook, see **Glossary: Croatian,** p. 1053.

ACCOMMODATIONS AND CAMPING

CROATIA	❶	❷	❸	❹	❺
ACCOMMODATIONS	under 100kn	100-150kn	150-210kn	210-360kn	over 360kn

For info on the country's seven youth **hostels** (in Dubrovnik, Krk, Pula, Punat, Veli Losinj, Zadar, and Zagreb), contact the Croatian Youth Hostel Association, Savska 5, 10000 Zagreb (☎1 482 92 94; www.hfhs.hr.). **Hotels** in Croatia can be wildly expensive—a cheap overnight stay in a Zagreb hotel will run at least US$80. If you opt for a hotel, call a few days ahead, especially in summer along the coast. Apart from hostels, **private rooms** are the only budget accommodations. To find one, look for *sobe* signs, especially near transportation stations. Be aware, though, English is rarely spoken by owners. Agencies generally charge 30-50% more if you stay fewer than three nights. All accommodations are subject to a tourist tax of 5-10kn (one reason the police require foreigners to register). Croatia is one of the top **camping** destinations in Europe—33% of travelers choose to sleep in Croatia's beautiful outdoors. Facilities usually meet Western standards for space and utilities, and prices are among the cheapest along the Mediterranean. Camping outside of designated areas is illegal. For more info, contact the **Croatian Camping Union,** HR-52440 Pionirska 1, Poreč. (☎52 451 324; www.camping.hr.)

FOOD AND DRINK

CROATIA	❶	❷	❸	❹	❺
FOOD	under 40kn	40-70kn	70-110kn	110-190kn	over 190kn

In continental Croatia near and east of Zagreb, heavy meals featuring meat and creamy sauces dominate. *Purica s mlincima* (turkey with pasta) is popular near Zagreb. Also popular are *burek*, a layered pie made with meat or cheese, and the spicy Slavonian *kulen*, considered one of the world's best **sausages** by a panel of German men who decide such things. *Pašticada* (slow-cooked meat) is another excellent option. On the coast, textures and flavors change with the presence of **seafood** and Italian influence. Don't miss on *lignje* (squid) or *Dalmatinski pršut* (smoked ham). The **oysters** from Ston Bay have received many awards at international competitions. If your budget does not allow for such treats, *slane sardele* (salted sardines) are a tasty substitute. **Vegetarian** and **kosher** eating are difficult in Croatia, but not impossible if you're willing to live off pizza and baked goods. Croatia offers excellent **wines,** though the upper tier can get quite expensive. Mix red wine with tap water to concoct the popular *bevanda*, and white wine with carbonated water to make *gemišt*. *Šljivovica* is a hard-hitting plum brandy found in many small towns. *Karlovačko* and *Ožujsko* are the two most popular beers.

HOLIDAYS

Holidays: New Year's Day (Jan. 1); Epiphany (Jan. 6); Old Christmas (Jan. 7); Easter Sunday and Monday (Apr. 8 and 9); May Day (May 1); Anti-Fascist Struggle Day (June 22); National Thanksgiving Day (Aug. 5); Assumption of the Blessed Virgin Mary (Aug. 15); Independence Day (Oct. 8); All Saints' Day (Nov. 1).

BEYOND TOURISM

Coalition for Psychotrauma and Peace, Gunduliceva 18, 32000 Vukovar, Croatia (☎385 32 444 662; www.cwwpp.org). Work for 1½-2 years in education and health care concerns related to long-term conflict in Croatia.

Firefly UK/Bosnia, 3 Bristo Pl., Edinburgh, Midlothian, EH1 1 EY, UK (☎79 56 98 38 85; www.fireflybosnia.org). Scottish organization that arranges summer camps in Croatia for refugees from Bosnian youth centers.

Learning Enterprises, 2227 20th St. #304, NW, Washington, D.C., 20009, USA (☎202-309-3453; www.learningenterprises.org). 6-week summer programs place first-time English teachers in rural Croatia, Hungary, Romania, and Slovakia, with the option to switch countries half-way.

Eco-Centre Caput Insulae-Beli, Beli 4, 51559 Beli, Cres Island, CRO (☎385 51 840 525; www.caput-insulae.com). Volunteers protect the endangered griffon vultures, the environment, and the cultural heritage of Cres Island. 2 weeks €122-271.

ZAGREB

☎01

Zagreb (pop. 780,000) possesses all the grand architecture, wide boulevards, and sprawling parks of a major European city, but is only just starting to be discovered by the tourists. Those who take a chance to enjoy this young, laid-back capital, rather than rushing through en route to the Croatian coast, will be rewarded.

TRANSPORTATION AND PRACTICAL INFORMATION. Trains leave the Glavni Kolodvor (main station) on Trg Kralja Tomislava 12 (☎060 333 444, international info 378 25 32; www.hznet.hr) for: Ljubljana, SLV (2¼hr., 8 per day, 89kn) where they continue to Munich, GER, Venice, ITA, and Zurich, SWI; Rijeka (4½hr., 7 per day, 64kn); Sarajevo, BOS (9hr., 1 per day, 172kn); Split (6½-8½hr., 5 per day, 107kn); Varaždin (2½hr., 16 per day, 50kn). To reach the main square, Trg b. Josipa Jelačića, from the station, cross the street, walk along the left side of the park to the end, then follow the Praska. Buses (☎060 313 333; www.akz.hr) leave the mall-like Autobusni Kolodvor (bus station), Držićeva bb, to: Dubrovnik (11hr., 8 per day, 180kn); Ljubljana, SLV (2½hr., 2 per day, 90kn); Pula (5hr., 4 per day, 125kn); Split (7-9hr., 27 per day, 120kn); Varaždin (1¾hr., 28 per day, 56kn); Vienna, AUT (5-7hr., 2 per day, 227kn); and the airport. Luggage storage is available at the bus station (small bags 1.20kn per hr., above 15kg 2.30kn per hr.), as are toilets (3kn) and currency exchange. To reach Trg b. Josipa Jelačića, exit the station on the right onto Držićeva, cross the street, pass the fruit and vegetable market, go up Visrdlsvova, past Trg Žrtava Fašizma and Rackoga, and make a left onto Jurišićeva.

The main **tourist office,** Trg b. Josipa Jelačića 11, is efficient and provides free maps and several informative brochures. (☎481 40 51; www.zagreb-touristinfo.hr. Open M-F 9am-9pm, Sa 9am-5pm, Su 9am-2pm.) **Mediaturist,** Zrinjevac 17, exchanges currency and finds accommodations for a 15% commission. (☎080 136 376; www.media-turist.hr. Rooms from 100kn. Open M-F 8.30am-8pm, Sa 9am-2pm. AmEx/MC/V.) Find **laundry service** at Draskoviceva 31 (☎461 2990. Open M-F 7am-7pm, Sa 8am-noon. 1 load usually 29kn.) Get online at **A1 Internet Cafe,** Zrinskog 14. Walk into the inner courtyard and downstairs. (Internet 0.25kn per min., Internet phone 0.5kn per min. Open M-Sa 10am-8pm.) **Postal Code:** 10000.

ACCOMMODATIONS AND FOOD. It can be hard to find a cheap room in downtown Zagreb, and as a result, most budget options are usually packed. The incredibly social, laid-back **Hostel Fulir ❶,** Radiceva 3A, gets its name from the

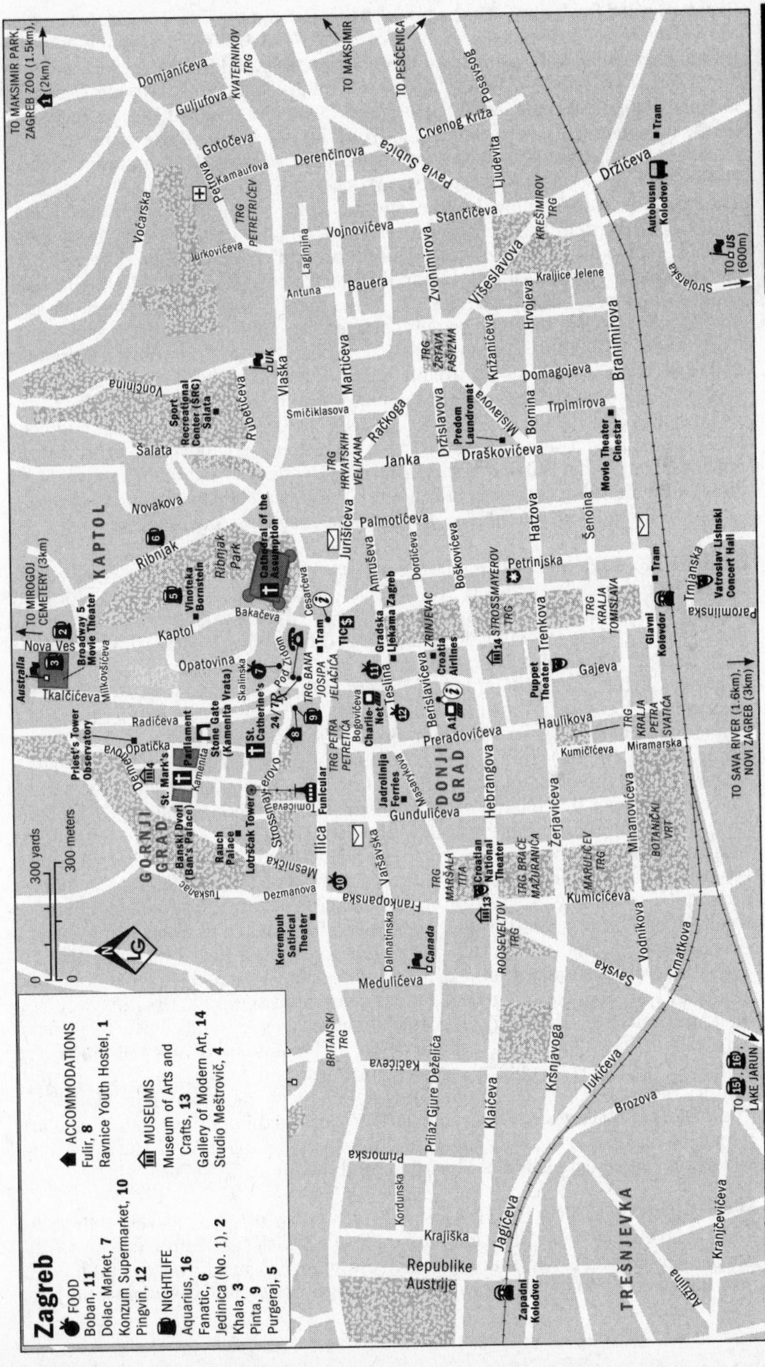

Zagreb
FOOD
Boban, 11
Dolac Market, 7
Konzum Supermarket, 10
Pingvin, 12
NIGHTLIFE
Aquarius, 16
Fanatic, 6
Jedinica (No. 1), 2
Khala, 3
Pinta, 9
Purgeraj, 5
ACCOMMODATIONS
Fulir, 8
Ravnice Youth Hostel, 1
MUSEUMS
Museum of Arts and Crafts, 13
Gallery of Modern Art, 14
Studio Meštrović, 4
300 yards
300 meters
TO MAKSIMIR PARK, ZAGREB ZOO (1.5km), (2km)
TO MAKSIMIR
TO PEŠĆENICA
TO MIROGOJ CEMETERY (3km)
TO SAVA RIVER (1.6km), NOVI ZAGREB (3km)
TO LAKE JARUN
TO US (600m)
KAPTOL
GORNJI GRAD
DONJI GRAD
TREŠNJEVKA
Cathedral of the Assumption
St. Mark's
Parliament
Stone Gate (Kamenita Vrata)
St. Catherine's
Priest's Tower Observatory
Banski Dvori (Ban's Palace)
Rauch Palace
Lotrščak Tower
Funicular
Kerempuh Satirical Theater
Croatian National Theater
Puppet Theater
Movie Theater Cinestar
Broadway 5 Movie Theater
Vinoteka Bornstein
Sport Recreational Center (SRC) Šalata
Predom Laundromat
Gradska Ljekarna Zagreb
Jadrolinija Ferries
Croatia Airlines
Charlie-Net
Vatroslav Lisinski Concert Hall
Glavni Kolodvor
Autobusni Kolodvor
Zapadni Kolodvor
Australia
Canada
UK
TIC
Tram
24/7
Ilica
Vlaška
Jurišićeva
Draškovićeva
Branimirova
Savska
Vukovarska

Croatian word for "pimp," after a popular movie from the 70s. The English-speaking owners often take guests to explore Zagreb's nightlife. Themed, co-ed dorm rooms have clean bathrooms, and there's a communal kitchen. Linens, lockers, and Internet are included. (☎483 0882; www.fulir-hostel.com. Reservations recommended. 145kn per night. MC/V.) The immaculate and cheerful **Ravnice Youth Hostel ❶**, 1 Ravnice 38D, is a 20min. ride from the city center. Take tram #11 or 12 from Trg b. Jelačića, #4 from the train station, or #7 from the bus station toward Dubrava or Dubec. Get off at Ravnice, two stops past the Dinamo football stadium. The hostel is in two yellow houses, and has cozy, simple rooms and bathrooms and a lovely garden. The friendly owner, Vera, and her daughter, Lea, both speak English. (☎233 23 25; www.ravnice-youth-hostel.hr. Laundry 40kn. Internet 16kn per hr. Reserve ahead. Dorms 112kn; doubles 224kn. Cash only.) Near the main square, the kiosk **Pingvin ❶**, Teslina 7, is a local favorite, with a friendly staff and speedy service, that serves delicious, design-your-own grilled sandwiches. (Sandwiches 15-20kn. Open M-Sa 24hr., Su 5am-noon. Cash only.) **Restaurant Boban ❷**, Gajeva 9, serves affordable pastas (spaghetti 30-40kn) and salads in a vaulted brick dining room and garden patio. A pub is at the street level, and the restaurant is downstairs. (☎481 15 49. Entrees 40-80kn. Open daily 10am-midnight. MC/V.) Shop for a healthful meal (or just walk around and take in the action) at the colorful, traditional **Dolac Market** Zagreb. (Upstairs in the main square. Open daily in the morning and early afternoon.) There is a **Konzum** supermarket on the corner of Preradoviceva and Ilica. (Open M-Sa 7am-9pm. AmEx/MC/V.)

SIGHTS. Zagreb is best seen on foot. From Trg b. Josipa Jelačića, take Ilica, then turn right on Tomiceva to the funicular (3kn), which gives access to many sights on the hills of Gornji Grad (Upper Town). **Lotrscak Tower** hosts free and interesting exhibits by young, local artists and has a spectacular view of the city from the top. (Open Mar.-Nov. daily 11am-7pm. 10kn, students 5kn.) Visible anywhere in Zagreb, the neo-Gothic bell towers of the 11th-century **Cathedral of the Assumption** (Katedrala Marijina Uznesenja) loom over Kaptol Hill. (Open daily 10am-5pm. Services M-Sa 7, 8, 9am, Su 7, 8, 9, 10, 11:30am. Free.) Take a bus (8min., every 15min.) from Kaptol to the beautiful **Mirogoj Cemetery,** Croatia's largest, with 12 green-and-cream-colored towers, a garden with cypress trees and touching epitaphs that tell the troubled history of the region. (Open M-F 6am-8pm, Su 7:30am-6pm. Free.) Walk through the intricate streets of the wonderful and tranquil old town, passing by the country's main administrative buildings and then returning to its bustling center through the **Stone Gate** (Kamenita Vrata), a corner arch under which passersby stop to pray. Zagreb's many museums would merit weeks of exploration. Start by getting a **Zagreb Card,** available at most travel agencies and tourist offices; it grants you discounts at all of the city's museums (70-80kn). **Studio Mestrovič,** Mletačka 8, behind St. Mark's, is in the former home and studio of Ivan Mestrovič, Croatia's most celebrated sculptor. His intensely dramatic portraits are displayed in a beautiful building. (☎485 1123. Open Tu-F 10am-6pm, Sa-Su 10am-2pm. 20kn, students 10kn.) The **Museum of Arts and Crafts,** Trg Maršala Tita 10, has timepieces, antique furniture, and decorations from the 15th century onward. (Open Tu-F 10am-7pm, Sa-Su 10am-2pm. 20kn, students 10kn.) The **Gallery of Modern Art,** Herbrangova 1, features exhibits of Croatia's best art. (Open Tu-Sa 10am-6pm, Su 10am-1pm. Prices vary by exhibit.) If you have time, check out **Zagreb University's** old buildings and the futuristic **National Library.**

NIGHTLIFE AND FESTIVALS. With a variety of clubs at **Lake Jarun** and many relaxed sidewalk cafes and bars on lovely **Tkalcićeva,** Zagreb has an exceptional nightlife scene, which intensifies in the summer when the city's youth pours into the streets. Dance and swim at the lakeside cafe-club, **Aquarius,** on Lake

Jarun. Take tram #17 to Srednjaci, the third unmarked stop after Studenski dom S. Radić (15min.). Cross the street, and when you reach the lake (15min.), turn left and continue along the boardwalk; Aquarius is the last building. (☎364 02 31. Cafe open daily 9am-9pm. Club cover 30kn. Club open Tu-Su 10pm-4am.) The cheapest beer in town can be found at **Pinta,** a pub just downstairs from Hostel Fulir, and understandably popular with locals and travelers alike. (Beer 0.5L 10kn. Open daily until 11pm.) **Khala,** Nova Ves 17, is a surprisingly affordable, ethno-chic lounge and wine bar, with smart music and waiters clad in black. The old city's club scene is perpetually in transformation, but some popular places at the moment are **Jedinica** (also called N.1) for house music, and **Fanatic** and **Purgeraj** for alternative rock, blues, and jazz, all within walking distance from the main square.

In late June, the city echoes with music from **Cest is d'Best** (The Streets are the Best) and the **Eurokaz Avant-Garde Theaters Festival.** Zagreb will play host in mid-July 2007 to the 41st **International Folklore Festival,** known as the premier gathering of European folk singers and dancers. September brings the **International Puppet Festival,** and October the **International Jazz Days.** Zagreb's **Christmas Fair** sets mid-December aglow. Check online at www.zagreb-touristinfo.hr for updated schedules.

DAYTRIP FROM ZAGREB: TRAKOŠĆAN CASTLE. The white walls of fairy-tale Trakošćan rise high above the surrounding forests and green hills. While Trakošćan is quite rightly known as Croatia's most beautiful castle, you might not be terribly impressed if you've seen your share of castles. Inside, there is castle paraphernalia from the 15th through 19th centuries. The sumptuousness of the apartments on closer inspection proves fake: some of the marble is painted on. The castle is not for the impatient; the visiting pace is slowed by large groups of schoolchildren. To escape the crowds and the overpriced restaurant at the bottom of the hill, bring a picnic and meander through the quiet grounds, then find the lake, Trakošćan's most romantic spot. (☎42 79 62 81. www.mdc.hr/trakoscan. Open daily Apr.-Oct. 9am-6pm; Nov.-Mar. 9am-4pm. 20kn, students 10kn. Cash only.) **Buses** run from the Zagreb bus station to Varaždin (1¾hr., 30 per day, 56 kn), where a local bus continues to Trakošćan (1½hr., 8-12 per day, 30kn). From noon to 2pm, local buses are crowded with schoolchildren. Leave Zagreb early (7:15am) in order to make the connection (9:30am) and still have plenty of time at the castle before the last bus to Varaždin.

CROATIA COMES OUT

In October 2005, Croatians opened several of the country's major newspapers to read, under the heading "We don't want to hide anymore," the names of over 1200 countrymen and women going public with their homosexuality. Though no last names were published, the names were folllowed by age, specific sexual orientation, and the invitation to "Reconsider your prejudice."

In a country where 88% of the population declares itself Roman Catholic, homosexuality continues to be a major taboo, and despite the 2003 law recognizing gay civil unions, discrimination and severe intolerance remain common. The first 200-person Gay Pride of the Balkans march was held in Zagreb in 2002, and was not received well. After police left the parade, many of the marchers were badly beaten by angry religious protesters. Still, gay rights groups like *Iskorak* (Step Forward) have been challenging the nation's conservatism one step at a time in spite of violent anti-gay protests. The group Queer Zagreb sponsors an annual GLBT festival, featuring movies, visual art, dance, and discussions about being gay in Croatia (www.queerzagreb.com).

Because of lingering homophobia, Croatia's recent government-sponsored coming out is more than symbolic: it is truly an act of courage.

PLITVICE LAKES NATIONAL PARK

Though it's a trek from either Zagreb or Zadar, Plitvice Lakes National Park (Nacionalni Park Plitvička Jezera) is definitely worth the transportation hassle. Some 30,000 sq. km of forested hills, dappled with 16 lakes and hundreds of waterfalls, make this pocket of paradise one of Croatia's most spectacular sights. Declared a national park in 1949, Plitvice was added to the UNESCO World Heritage list in 1979 for the unique evolution of its lakes and waterfalls, which formed through the interaction of water and petrified vegetation. There are eight main trails, lettered A-K, around the lake, all of different lengths and difficulties; none is particularly demanding. A system of wooden paths hovering just above the iridescent blue surface of the lakes winds around the many waterfalls.

> **!** The takeover of Plitvice Lakes National Park by the Serbs in 1991 marked the beginning of Croatia's bloody war for independence. Throughout the conflict (1991-95), the Serbs holding the area planted landmines in the ground; though both the park's premises and surrounding area have been officially cleared of mines, the last mine-related accident dates back to 2002. Don't let this warning stop you from visiting the natural wonder of the Plitvice Lakes, but never wander into the woods or stray from the trail for any reason.

Free shuttles drive around the lakes every 20min. and a boat goes across Jezero Kozjak, the largest of the lakes, every 20-30min. (9:30am-6:30pm). At the entrance, local women sell delicious **strudels:** bread-cakes stuffed with cheese, apples, or cherries (15kn). The nature-paradise aura may be sullied when committees of septuagenarians cover up the gorgeous views by snapping pictures with their cellphones. If you want to enjoy the peace of the lakes by yourself, go early in the morning or late in the afternoon and keep away from the shortest trails. Most tourists circulate around the four lower lakes (Donja Jezera) to get a shot of Plitvice's famous 78m waterfall, **Veliki Slap.** The hidden falls of the 12 upper lakes, **Gornja Jezera,** make for a more relaxed walk. A private accommodation service across from tourist center #1 helps find rooms. (☎751 280. Open daily June-Sept. 7am-8pm. Singles 150kn; doubles 200-300kn.)

Buses run to and from: Karlobag (1hr., 50kn); Rijeka (3 hr., 1 per day, 120kn); Split (3½hr., 9 per day, 150kn); Zadar (2½hr., every 45min., 80kn); Zagreb (2½hr., 2 per hr., 80kn). Most bus drivers let passengers off at the park's main entrance. There are tourist offices at each of the three entrances, which offer maps and change currency for a 1.5% commission (☎75 20 15; www.np-plitvicka-jezera.hr. Park open daily July-Aug. 7am-8pm, May-June 7am-7pm. Call to check the opening times. July-Aug. 100kn, students 60kn; May-June and July-Oct. 80kn/50kn; Nov.-Apr. 40kn/20kn. MC/V.) To get to the info center, walk toward the pedestrian overpass; crossing the road can be dangerous. Though no luggage storage is officially provided, they may let you keep your bags at the info center.

NORTHERN COAST

The coast is surrounded by cold, crystal-clear waters, covered in wild forests, and inhabited by sun, wind, and wild griffon vultures. Part of Italy until WWII, this region mixes Italian culture with Croatian sensibilities.

PULA (POLA) ☎052

If it weren't for its history-filled center, which is home to some of the best-preserved ruins of its Roman origin, Pula (pop. 62,000), the largest city on the Istrian Peninsula, would be merely a densely populated and chaotic major transportation

> **TIP** **THE NAKED TRUTH.** Wondering what those FKK signs along the beach mean? FKK is a German acronym for Freikörperkultu, or "free body culture" and indicate that there's a nude beach nearby. Before dropping trou, check for the sign—skinny dipping on non-nude beach is generally not accepted.

hub. Its relatively unimpressive beaches don't quite make up for the ever-expanding residential complexes that cover the city. Known as "the capital of Istria," Pula has a trendy and intense social scene. Pula is best savored around sunset, when it's not so hot and the chaos has calmed a bit. Its white-stone **Amphitheater,** the second-largest in the world, is often used as a concert venue. To get there from the bus station, take a left on Istarska. (Open daily 8am-9pm. 20kn, students 10kn.) From there, walk down to the water and along the port to reach the **Forum** and **Temple of Augustus** (Augustov hram), finished in AD 1, and then climb up the narrow streets of the old town to the peaceful **Franciscan Monastery,** the **Fort** (hosting the **Historical Museum of Istria;** 10kn, students 5kn), the ancient **Roman Theater,** and the **Arch of the Sergians** (Slavoluk obitelji Sergii), a stone dating from 29 BC. To reach the private coves of Pula's **beaches,** buy a bus ticket (10kn) from any newsstand and take bus #1 to the Stója campground.

To reach the **Omladinski Hostel (HI)** ❶, Zaljev Valsaline 4, take bus #2A (dir.: Veruda, 10kn) from the station. Get off at the first stop on Veruda and follow the HI sign; take a left off the road and walk 5min. down the hill. (☎39 11 33; www.hfhs.hr. Breakfast included. Reservations recommended. Camping €5-9; dorms €10-15. €1.50 HI discount. MC/V.) **Biska** ❶, Sisplac 15, has superb seafood and pasta in a cheerful bistro setting, and for a third of Old Town prices. Walking back toward Pula, take the street on the left opposite the football stadium. After 100m, turn to your left again. (☎38 73 33. Entrees 40-60kn. Open M-Sa 8am-11pm, Su 2-11pm.) **Trains** (☎54 19 82) run from Kolodvorska 5 to Ljubljana, SLV (7½hr., 2 per day, 127kn), and Zagreb (7hr., 3 per day, 112-125kn). **Buses** (☎50 29 97), a much more convenient option, run from Trg Istarske Brigade to Dubrovnik (12hr., 1 per day, 458kn); Trieste, ITA (3hr., 5 per day, 112kn); Zagreb (5-6hr., 15 per day, 155kn). To reach the islands, go to Rijeka or take a bus to Brestova (on the Rijeka line, 40kn), and walk the 4km down to the ferry departure dock. The **tourist office** is at Forum 3. (☎21 29 87; www.pulainfo.hr. Singles 350-450kn; doubles 550-650kn. Open M-Sa 8am-midnight, Su 10am-6pm.) **Postal Code:** 52100.

ROVINJ ☎052

Purported to be one of the healthiest places in the world because of its mild climate and cool waters, Rovinj (ro-VEEN; pop. 14,000) was the favorite summer resort of Austro-Hungarian emperors. Today's vacationers still bask in this Mediterranean jewel's unspoiled beauty. Rovinj is the most Italian of Istria's towns: everybody here either is or speaks Italian and all streets have names and signs in both language. 18th-century **Saint Euphemia's Church** (Crkva Sv. Eufemije) houses the remains of St. Euphemia, the 15-year-old martyr who was killed by the circus lions in AD 800. Inside, stairs lead to the **bell tower** (61m), with views of the city and coast. In summer, there are classical music performances on the lawn. (Open M-Sa 10am-6pm. Services M-Sa 7pm, Su 10:30am and 7pm. Free. Bell tower 10kn.)

Rovinj's best beaches are on **Sv. Katarina Island** and **Red Island** (Crveni Otok), two small islands right in front of town. The first has a huge resort and crowds, while the second is a haven for snorkelers and nude sunbathers. To get there, take the ferry from the dock at the center of town to Sv. Katarina (15kn) and Crveni Otok (40kn.) At night, head through the arch in the main square and follow the signs up Grisia toward the church at the top of the hill, where members of an artist colony display their work. Near the church, **Valentino Bar,** Santa Croce 28, has elegant white tables right on the water. (☎830 683. Mixed drinks 50kn. Open daily June-Sept. 6pm-2am; Oct.-May noon-midnight.) Across the street from the bus station is **Natale,** Carducci 4, which arranges private rooms in and around the center commission-free. (☎81 33 65; www.rovinj.com. Reserve ahead in summer. Doubles €40-46; 8-person apartments €120. Fishing permits 60kn per day, 300kn per week. Open June-Sept. daily 7:30am-10pm.) **Camping Polari ❶,** 2.5km east of town, has a supermarket and several bars. To get there, take a bus (6min., 9kn) from the station. (☎80 15 01. July-Aug. 100kn per person; June 85kn per person.) Bustling **Stella di Mare ❷,** Santa Croce 4, offers great deals on huge pizzas. (☎528 88 83. Pizzas 40-70kn. Seafood 50-200kn. Open daily 10am-midnight. AmEx/MC/V.)

To reach the **tourist office,** walk along the water past the main square, to Pino Budičin 12. (☎81 15 66; www.tzgrovinj.hr. Open daily mid-June to Sept. 8am-9pm; Oct. to mid-June 8am-4pm.) Rovinj and its surroundings are best explored on bike trails that veer in every direction. Bike rental (60kn per day) is available at **Bike Planet,** Trg na Lokvi 3, which also has maps. (☎81 33 96. Day rental 60kn. Open M-F 7:30am-12:30pm and 5-8pm, Sa 8:30am-1pm.) Boats, tied along the dock, offer slightly overpriced 1½hr. panoramic **excursions** (€10) and one-day boat trips to Venice, ITA (380-480kn). With no train station, Rovinj sends **buses** to Ljubljana, SLV (5hr., 8am, 146kn); Pula (1hr., 20 per day, 28kn); Zagreb (5-6hr., 9 per day, 150-160kn). Bus companies charge 7kn to store luggage under the bus. The bus station has luggage storage. (☎811 453. 10kn per day.) **Postal Code:** 52210.

CRES ☎051

Though most visitors spend the entire duration of their stay in Cres Town and on the beaches nearby, Cres island (pop. 3300) has a wealth of magnificent undiscovered beauties, from tiny villages with less than a dozen inhabitants to idyllic beaches made all the more beautiful by their isolation. Explore the island by car, rent a bike and try out the numerous nature trails, or discover the intricate coast by boat. Smaller towns, like the magical **Lubenice,** on one of the highest peaks of the island, are worth exploring. A 1hr. hike down from town leads to a pristine beach—on clear mornings, you can see the Italian coast across the Adriatic. In July, classical concerts are held in the town's old chapel. For those arriving in late July or August, it's becoming necessary to reserve a couple months ahead. The beachfront **Camp Kovacine ❶,** 1km north of Cres Town, hosts most of the island's visitors. Besides the usual amenities, the camp also has a nudist section (indicated by the yellow FKK sign), as does the nearby beach. (☎573 150; www.camp-kovacine.com. Tent sites €4-8, €5-10 per person; 4-person bungalow €40-110. AmEx/MC/V.) Next to the camp, **Hotel Kimen ❷,** Varozina 25, is an old-fashioned hotel in a tranquil park. (☎571 161. Breakfast included. €20-35 per person.) Getting to Cres can be complicated. **Ferries** run from Rijeka (1hr., 1 per day, 30kn) to Cres Town and from Brestova, Istria, to Porozina, at the northern tip of the island (30min.; 12 per day; 13kn per person, 60kn per car). **Buses** go from Cres Town to Losinj, the next island, stopping in several smaller towns along the way (1¼hr., 6-8 per day, 40kn). The **tourist office** is in Cres Town, Cons 10 (☎571 535; www.tzg-cres.hr). **Currency exchange, Internet** (1kn per min.), and **bike rentals** (20kn per hr., 80kn per day) are available at the **Agencija Croatia,** Melin II/33. (☎573 053; www.cres-travel.com. Open M-Sa 8am-8pm. AmEx/MC/V.) **Postal Code:** 51557.

RAB ☎051

Despite centuries of Byzantine, Venetian, and Hungarian rule, Rab still has Roman ruins dating from the time of its construction during the reign of Augustus. Stroll along **Gornja Ulica** from the remains of **St. John's Church** (Crkva sv. Jvana), a Roman basilica, to **St. Justine's Church** (Crkva sv. Justine), which houses a museum of Christian art. (Open daily 10am-12:30pm and 7:30-10pm. 5kn.) Atop the bell tower of the 13th-century **St. Mary's Church** (Crkva sv. Marije), behold the sunset on the horizon or the nuns' lush garden below. (Open daily 10am-1pm and 7:30-10pm. 5kn.) **Beaches** dot the perimeter of the island; most of the island's sand beaches, among the few in Croatia, are in the north, while rocky beaches lie on the western edge and pebble beaches to the east. **Katurbo,** M. de Dominisa 5, between the bus station and the town center, arranges private rooms and rents bicycles. (☎724 495; www.katurbo.hr. Open daily July-Aug. 8am-9pm; Sept.-June 8am-1pm and 4-9pm. Bikes 20kn per hr. Singles €15-20; doubles €26-40. Tourist tax 7kn.) Walk 2km east along the bay from the bus station to reach **Camping Padova III ❶** and its lovely beaches. (☎72 43 55; www.imperial.hr. Tent sites 62-93kn; 24-39kn per person.) **St. Maria ❸,** Dinka Dokule 6, serves Hungarian specialties in a beautiful medieval courtyard. (Entrees 60-105kn. Open daily 10am-2pm and 5pm-midnight.) A **supermarket** neighbors the post office at Dalit 88. (Open daily 6am-10pm.) **Buses** arrive from Zagreb (5½hr., M-Sa 3 per day, 157kn). The **tourist office,** Trg. Municipium Arba 8, is behind the bus station. (☎771 111; www.tzg-rab.hr. Open daily 8am-10pm.) **Postal Code:** 51280.

DALMATIAN COAST

Touted as the new French Rivera, the Dalmatian Coast offers a stunning seascape of unfathomable beauty set against a backdrop of dramatic mountains. With more than 1100 islands, Dalmatia is not only Croatia's largest archipelago, but also has the cleanest and clearest waters in the Mediterranean.

ZADAR ☎023

Zadar (pop. 77,000), crushed in both WWII and the recent Balkan war, is now beautifully rejuvenated, and though its modern neighborhoods might not impress those entering the city, the Old Town (Stari Grad) is a peaceful island, where time seems to have stopped long before both conflicts. With the extraordinary Kornati Islands just a boat ride away, a history so well preserved that Roman ruins serve as city benches, and plenty of boutiques and cafes, Zadar is the quintessential Dalmatian city. On the southern dock of the Old Town, concrete steps into the water are actually part of a 70m long **Sea Organ,** which plays notes at random as the seawater rushes in, resulting in continual melody. In the ancient Forum in the center of the peninsula, the Byzantine **St. Donat's Church** (Crkva Sv. Donata; open daily 9am-7:30pm, 8kn) sits atop the ruins of an ancient Roman temple.

At the entrance to the Old Town, coming from Obala Kralja Tomislava, **Miatours,** on Vrata Sv. Krševana, books private rooms and transportation to nearby islands. (☎254 400; www.miatours.hr. Open July-Aug. 8am-8pm; Sept.-June 8am-2:30pm. Singles 100-150kn; doubles 200-300kn. AmEx/DC/MC/V.) **Trattoria Canzona,** Stomorica 8, is always packed with young Zadarians, as are many of the similar restaurants in this lively corner of town. (☎212 081. Entrees 30-70kn. Open M-Sa 10am-11pm, Su noon-11pm. Cash only.) There is also a small **supermarket** between Borelli and Madijevaca (open M-Sa 6:30am-9pm, Su 7am-noon).

Buses (☎211 555) run from Ante Starevica 1 to: Dubrovnik (8hr., 8 per day, 148-202kn); Podgorica, MON (11hr., 1 per day, 290kn); Pula (7hr., 3 per day, 187kn); Rijeka (4½hr., 12 per day, 112kn); Šibenik (1½hr., 2 per hr., 30kn); Split (3¼hr., 2 per hr., 77kn); Trieste, ITA (7hr., 2 per day, 150kn); Zagreb (3½hr., 20 per day, 120kn). **Luggage storage** is available (1.20kn per hr. Open 6am-10pm). Both the train and bus stations are a 20min. walk from town, but trains are generally much less convenient. To get to the Old Town, go through the pedestrian underpass and continue to Zrinsko-Frankopanska. Follow this to the water, turn left, and at the **Kopnena Vrata** (Main Gate) of the Old Town, turn on Široka, the main street. **Daytrips** to the Kornati Islands leave twice a week. (☎09 15 63 43 61. 270kn.) The **tourist office,** M. Klaića bb, in the far corner of Narodni trg, has free maps and a young, English-speaking staff. (☎31 61 66; tzg-zadar@zd.tel.hr. Open daily 8am-midnight; low season 8am-8pm.) There is an **Internet Center** on Varoska 3. (☎311 265. Open daily 10am-11pm. 30kn per hr.) **Postal Code:** 23000.

SPLIT ☎021

With many activities and nightlife, this city by the sea is more a cultural center than a beach resort. The Old Town (Stari Grad), wedged between a mountain range and a palm-lined waterfront, sprawls inside and around a luxurious open-air **palace** where the Roman emperor Diocletian used to summer when not persecuting Christians. Here, centuries of history have left their trace, making the city a fascinating labyrinth of perfectly preserved Roman monuments, medieval streets with laundry hanging from the windows, and modern bars with huge screens showing soccer matches. The city's **cellars** are near the palace entrance, at the beginning of pedestrian **Obala hrvatskog narodnog preporoda** when coming from the bus and ferry station. Turn to either entrance to lose your way in this haunting maze of imperial statues, modern art exhibits, and the cool relief of underground Split. (Open M-F 9am-9pm, Sa-Su 9am-6pm. 12kn, students 6kn.)

Through the cellars and up the stairs is the open-air **peristyle,** a roofless, round building that leads to the Catholic **cathedral,** the world's oldest; which, ironically, was once Diocletian's mausoleum, and is now opulently decorated in a questionable combination of styles. The view from the adjoining **Bell Tower of St. Dominus** (Zvonik sv. Duje, 60m) is incredible, but watch your head when climbing up. (Cathedral and tower open 7am-noon and 5-7pm. 5kn each.) A 25min. walk along the waterfront, in a gorgeous villa facing the sea, the **Mestrović Gallery** (Galerija Ivana Meštrovića), Šetaliste Ivana Meštrovića 46, houses the splendid bronze, stone, and wood works of Croatia's most celebrated sculptor. To get there from the center of town, walk right facing the water, pass the marina, and follow the road up the hill; the gallery is right after the modern Archaeological Museum. (☎340 800. Open May-Sept. Tu-Sa 9am-9pm, Su noon-9pm; Oct.-Apr. Tu-Sa 9am-4pm, Su 10am-3pm. 20kn, students 10kn. Illustrated guides 20-80kn.) At night, locals skinny-dip at the hip **Bacvice beach,** near a strip of waterfront bars.

The small **Daluma Travel Agency,** Obala kneza domagoja 1, near the train station, books private rooms, changes currency, and organizes excursions. (☎33 84 84; www.daluma.hr. Open July-Aug. M-F 8am-9pm, Sa 8am-8pm, Su 8am-1pm; Sept.-June M-F 8am-8pm, Sa 8am-1pm.) **Al's Place ❷,** Kruziceva 10, is the first hostel in Split, outside the right corner of the palace. There are only 12 beds, which are usually full; reserve ahead. (☎098 918 29 23; www.hostelsplit.com. June-Aug. 120kn; Sept.-May 100kn. Cash only.) In the Old Town there are plenty of snack bars and restaurants, as well as kiosks with filling **pizzas** (slices 6-8kn) and **bureks** (10kn); you can also stock up on fruit and vegetables at the crowded **market** on the road between Obala Riva and the bus and ferry terminal. The best cafes are lined up on palm-lined Obala Riva, and at night they turn into popular bars. **St.Riva**, right in the center, has side-street swing-couches and a narrow balcony packed with partying youth. Hidden on a narrow line of steps, **Puls** is a great bar with low tables, cushions directly on the pavement, and occasional live jazz. To get there from Obala Riva, enter Trg brace Radic, turn right at the corner snack bar, and continue straight. (Open M-F 7am-midnight, Sa 7am-1am, Su 4pm-midnight.)

Buses (☎32 73 27; www.ak-split.hr) run to: Dubrovnik (4¼hr., 20 per day, 122kn); Ljubljana, SLV (11hr., 1 per day, 169kn); Rijeka (7½hr., 13 per day, 249kn); Zadar (3¼hr., 26 per day, 93kn); Zagreb (5hr., every 30min., 144kn).

Ferries (☎33 83 33) depart from the dock right across from the bus station to: Supetar, Brač Island (45min., 10-14 per day, 28kn), Stari Grad, Hvar Island (1hr., 3 per day, 38kn). Ferries also leave the international harbor to Ancona, ITA (10hr., M-Th and Sa-Su, 274kn). Deciphering the ferry schedules distributed at the **Jadrolinija** office can be a bit nerve-wracking, so ask for help from the busy assistants. (Open daily 4:15am-8:30pm and 12:45-1:30am.) Find the **tourist office** at Obala HNP 12. (☎34 72 71; www.turistbiro-split.hr. Open July-Aug. M-F 8am-9pm, Sa 8am-10pm, Su 8am-1pm; Sept.-June M-F 8am-9pm, Sa 8am-10pm.) Those who stay in town for more than three days are entitled to a free **SplitCard** that gets big discounts for sightseeing, shopping, and sleeping. Bring a hostel receipt to any tourist office to prove your stay; otherwise you can purchase the card for €5. **Postal Code:** 21000.

HVAR ISLAND ☎021

One of the most glorious isles in Europe, the thin, 88km Hvar Island (pop. 11,000) grants its visitors breathtaking views of mainland mountains and nearby islands from its own high, rugged hills. Hvar is today a prime destination for classy tourists, with an increasing number of wealthy Americans and a consequent rise in prices. Hvar Town maintains its easy-going village feel, even as the latest American pop hits play from buses' radios and souvenir shops. Many other destinations on this long island remain virtually untouched by tourists, and with a car or a rented boat you could turn Hvar into your private paradise. The island is packed in July and August. From mid-May to mid-October, the **Hvar Summer Festival** brings outdoor classical music and drama performances to the island's Franciscan monastery. **Trg Sv. Stjepana,** directly below the bus station by the waterfront, is the main square. From there, facing the sea, take a left to reach the **tourist office** and ferry terminal. To the right, stairs lead to the 13th-century **Fortica** (Venetian fortress). The climb up is short (20min.) but steep; avoid climbing in the heat and bring water. Once there, you can relax at the restaurant, and count the islands in front of Hvar. Legend has it that fairies dance here at night. Nearby, the **Hellish Islands** (Pakleni Otoci) include **Palmižana** beach, with sparse sand, and **Jerolim,** with nude sunbathers. (Taxi boats 2 per hr. 10am-6:30pm, 20-40kn.)

Lodging rates are not backpacker-friendly in Hvar; for the cheapest rooms try haggling with the owners of the *sobe* (private room) signs. **Luna ❷,** on a side street up the steps to the fortress, has a gorgeous "moon" terrace. The staff is friendly and the fettuccine with salmon (60kn) is fantastic. (☎741 400. Entrees 60-75kn. Open daily noon-11pm.) At the end of Riva past the Jadrolinija office, waterfront **Carpe Diem** has dark wood floors and low sofas, a hip crowd, and live DJs, as well as creative drinks and a young staff. (☎742 369; www.carpe-diem-hvar.com. Juices and shakes 28-38kn. Sandwiches 48kn. Mixed drinks 55-68kn. Open daily 8am-3am.)

Ferries run to Split (2hr., 3-7 per day, 38kn) and Vela Luka, Korčula (3hr., 1 per day, 22kn). Private—and faster—**catamarans** go directly to Korčula Town (2hr., 1 per day, 33kn). **Buses** connect Old Town to Hvar Town (25min., 5 per day, 20kn). To reach the bus station from the marina, walk through Trg Sv. Stjepana, bearing left of the church. **Jadrolinija,** Riva bb, on the left tip of the waterfront, sells ferry tickets. (☎74 11 32. Open M-Sa 5:30am-1pm and 3-8pm; Su 8-9am, noon-1pm, and 3-4pm.) The **tourist office,** Trg Sv. Stjepana 16, has island maps (20kn) and bus schedules. (☎74 10 59; www.tzhvar.hr. Open July-Aug. 8am-2pm and 3-10pm; Sept.-June M-Sa 8am-2pm and 3-8:30pm, Su 8am-1pm.) **Postal Code:** 21450.

BRAČ ISLAND: BOL ☎021

Central Dalmatia's largest island, Brač (pop. 13,000) is an ocean-lover's paradise. Most visitors come here for **Zlatni rat,** a beautiful and crowded peninsula of white-pebble beach surrounded by emerald waters, big waves, and a few too many strict rules. If you prefer the "deserted island" environment, head for the less explored, calmer beaches that are situated to the east of town. Bol town is also pleasant, small enough to cross in 10min., and equipped with its fair share of ice-cream parlors, exchange offices, and plenty of tiny chapels. The 1475 **Dominican Monastery,** on the eastern tip of Bol, displays Tintoretto's altar painting *Madonna with Child.* (Open daily 10am-noon and 5-7pm. 10kn.) There are eight **campsites** around Bol; most of them lie on the road into the western part of town, on the side of the Zlatni rat and main hotels. The largest is **Kito ❶,** Bračka cesta bb.(☎63 55 51. Open May-Sept. Tent sites 44kn.)

The **ferry** from Split docks at Supetar (1hr., 14 per day, 28kn), the island's largest town. (Open daily 4:15am-8:30pm and 12:45-1:30am. AmEx/MC/V.) From there, take a **bus** to Bol (1hr., 7-13 per day, last bus M-Sa 7pm, Su 6pm, 25kn). The hourly buses don't always coordinate with the ferries' arrivals; if you don't want to wait, you can take a slightly overpriced **taxi van** to Bol. (35min., 400kn, max. 7 people) Otherwise, kill the wait at the beach across the street. With your back to the water from the bus station in Bol, walk right to reach the **tourist office,** Porad bolskich pomorca bb, on the far side of the marina. (☎63 56 38; www.bol.hr. Open daily 8:30am-10pm; low season 8:30am-2pm and 4:30-9pm.) **Postal Code:** 21420

KORČULA ☎020

Within sight of the mainland, the slender cypresses of the town of Korčula mark Marco Polo's birthplace. Sacred monuments here date back to the time of the Apostles. **Marko Polo's house** is in the Old Town, in a tower with views of the sea. (Open daily 9:30am-1:30pm and 4:30-8pm. 10kn.) Though now turned into a biweekly tourist attraction, the **Festival of Sword Dances** is a millennia-old tradition in which local dancers come to reproduce the story of the White Prince and Black Prince fighting over a kidnapped princess. The sword fight is spectacular; go on July 29th for the real (not touristy) thing. (www.moreska.hr. 90kn; tickets available at travel agencies.)

Marko Polo, Biline 5, is a helpful travel agency, with a knowledgeable owner that seems to know every secret spot on the island. (☎71 54 00; www.korcula.com. Reserve ahead. Singles 120-200kn; doubles 170-2800kn. Open daily 8am-9pm.) **The Happy House (Korčula Backpacker) ❶,** Hrvatske Bratske Zajednice 6, is a colorful hostel run by a party-loving, South-Africa-raised Korčulan. The clean and comfortable rooms are co-ed and there is an Indian-inspired hang out space that turns into pub at night, with music, cheap beer, and international snacks for 20kn. (☎098 997 6353; booking@korculabackpacker.com. Shuttle service to Dubrovnik 90kn. Mountain biking and fishing daytrips 300kn. Ages 18-35 only. Dorms 90kn. Cash only.) **Fresh ❶,** right next to the bus station, specializes in healthy wraps (22-25kn) and smoothies. Try the self-explanatory Strawberry Fields Forever (20kn), or find some beach reading from their English-language book exchange (☎091 896 7509; www.igotfresh.com. Open daily 9am-2am. Cash only.) The eatery **Adio Mare ❷,** Marka Pola 2, serves authentic local fare. (☎711 253. Entrees 30-90kn. Open M-Sa 5:30pm-midnight, Su 6pm-midnight.)

Buses (Obala Korčulanskih Brodograditelja) board ferries to the mainland and head to Dubrovnik (3½hr., 1 per day, 85kn) and Zagreb (11-13hr., 1 per day, 210kn). On the island, they run to Lumbarda (9 per day, 13kn), Pupnat (8 per day, 40kn), and Vela Luka (7 per day, 30kn). Ticket and info office is open Monday through Saturday 6am-8pm and Sunday 2-8pm. The **Jadrolinija** office sells ferry tickets. (Open M-F 8am-8pm, Sa 8am-1pm and 6-10pm, Su 6am-1pm. AmEx/MC/V.) Ferries leave from both sides of town; ask where yours leaves from upon buying a ticket. **Postal Code:** 20260.

DUBROVNIK ☎020

George Bernard Shaw once wrote: "Those who seek Paradise on earth should come to Dubrovnik." Though such praise is a bit exaggerated and Dubrovnik's surroundings tend to be overrated, a stroll through the torch-lit winding lanes of the Old Town (Stari Grad) or a sunset into the sea from the city walls certainly justify Dubrovnik's reputation as one of Croatia's best destinations.

TRANSPORTATION AND PRACTICAL INFORMATION. Jadrolinija **ferries** (☎41 80 00; www.jadrolinija.hr) depart opposite Obala S. Radića 40 for Bari, ITA (9hr., 5 per week, 274kn), Korčula (3½hr., 5 per week, 67kn), and Split (8hr., 3 per week, 97kn). The **Jadrolinija** office is right across the dock (open M and W 7:30am-11pm, Tu 8am-11pm, Th-F 8am-8pm, Sa 7:30am-8pm, Su 8am-3pm and 7:30-8:30pm). **Buses** (☎35 70 88) run from Vukovarska, behind the new port, to: Ljubljana, SLV (14hr., 1 per day, 380kn); Split (4½hr., 16 per day, 125kn); Trieste, ITA (15hr., 1 per day, 340kn); Zagreb (11hr., 8 per day, 180kn). **Luggage storage** is available at the station (open daily 4:30am-10pm; 10kn per bag) and there's a gigantic **Konzum** supermarket as well. (Open M-Sa 8am-9pm, Su 8am-2pm.) To reach the Old Town, face away from the station and turn left on Ante Starčevića; follow it 25min. uphill to the Pile Gate. All local buses except #5, 7, and 8 go to the Pile Gate (8kn at kiosks, 10kn onboard).

Walk 50m away from the Old Town's entrance to reach the **tourist office,** Ante Starčevića 7, for free maps and cheap Internet. (☎42 75 91. Internet 5kn per 15min. Office open daily 8am-8pm. Internet available 8am-10pm.)The **post office,** Široka 8, in the Stari Grad, has a number of public telephones, and ATMs; it also offers Western Union services. (☎32 34 27. Open M-F 7:30am-9pm, Sa 10am-5pm.) **Postal Code:** 20108.

ACCOMMODATIONS AND FOOD. A private room tends to be the cheapest and most comfortable option for two; arrange one through any of the indistinguishable agencies. Take bus #6 from the Stari Grad or #7 from the ferry and bus

> **!** Make sure to ask for a receipt when you pay for a private room. No receipt means that your stay won't be registered and that the accommodation is illegal.

terminal, get off two stops past the Lapad post office, cross the street, climb the steps uphill on Mostarska, and turn left at Dubravkina to reach **Apartmani Burum** ❷, Dubravkina 16, in Babin Kuk. This popular guesthouse is comfortable, and Nikola is known to drive guests around town for a small fee. (☎435 467; www.burum-accommodation.com. Kitchen available. Pick-up available. 100-150kn per person. Cash only.) **Begović Boarding House** ❷, Primorska 17, offers spacious doubles and apartments in a cozy villa with satellite TVs, a social terrace shaded by fig trees, and a pleasant family feel. Call ahead and Sado, the owner, will pick you up. (☎43 51 91; bega_dbk@yahoo.com. Reserve ahead in July-Aug. Singles 150-200kn; doubles 200-240kn; triples 180-300kn. Cash only.) **Lokarda Peskarija** ❶, Na Ponti bb, has excellent seafood. From the bell tower, take a right out on Pred Dvorum and the first left out of the city walls. (☎32 47 50. Seafood 20-60kn. Open daily 8am-midnight.) Exchange books, savor smoothies, and nosh on wraps at **Fresh** ❶, on Vetranićeva. (Wraps 25kn. Smoothies 20kn. Open daily 8am-2am.)

SIGHTS. The Old Town is packed with churches, museums, monasteries, palaces, and fortresses. The entrance to the 2km limestone **city wall** *(gradske zidine)* lies just inside the Pile Gate, on the left, and there is a second entrance at

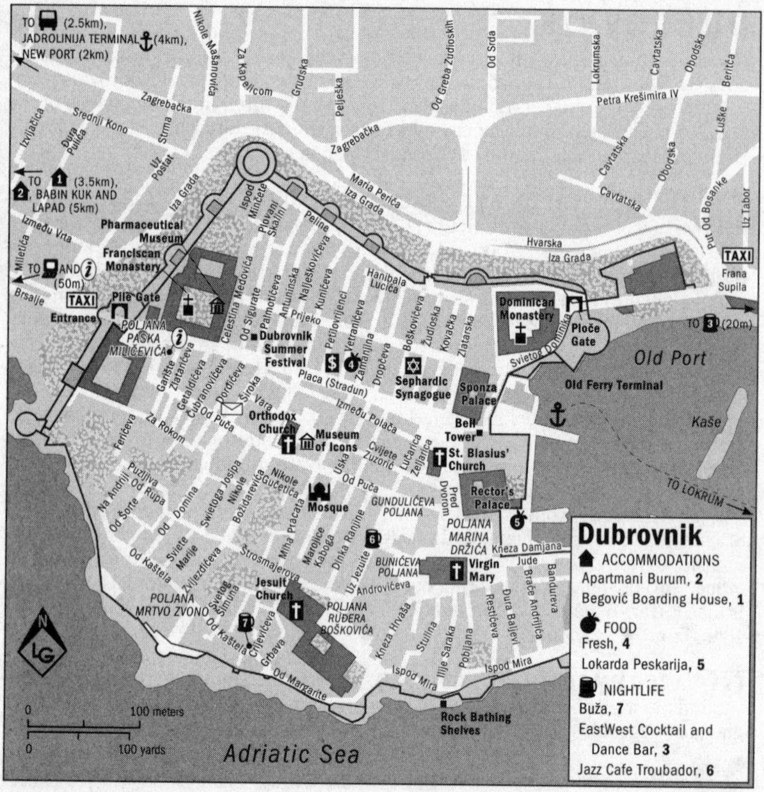

the other end town. Go at dusk to be dazzled by the sunset. (Open daily 8am-7:30pm. 50kn, students 20kn.) The 14th-century **Franciscan Monastery** *(Franjevački samostan)*, next to the city-wall entrance on Placa, houses the oldest pharmacy (est. 1317) in Europe. (Open daily 9am-6pm. 20kn, students 10kn.) The **Cathedral of the Assumption of the Virgin Mary** *(Riznica Katedrale)*, Kneza Damjana Jude 1, is built on the site of a Romanesque cathedral and a 7th-century Byzantine cathedral. Its treasury houses the "Diapers of Jesus." (Cathedral open daily 7:30am-6pm; treasury open daily 8am-8pm. Cathedral free, treasury 10kn.) The 19th-century **Serbian Orthodox Church** *(Pravoslavna Crkva)* and its **Museum of Icons** *(Muzej Ikona)*, Od Puča 8, stand as a symbol of Dubrovnik's tolerance together with the small **synagogue** and **mosque.** Classical performances are held throughout the summer in many of the Old Town's churches.

BEACHES. Outside the fortifications of the Old Town are a number of **rock shelves** for sunning and swimming. To reach a pristine but overcrowded **pebble beach** from the Placa's end, turn left on Svetog Dominika, bear right after the footbridge, and continue on Frana Supila. Descend the stairs by the post office. For a surreal seaside swim, take a dip in the cove at the foot of the old **Hotel Libertas.** Once Dubrovnik's most luxurious hotel, the building was damaged during WWII and then abandoned; now it looks like a post-apocalyptic movie set, though new construction may start soon. Walk 10min. along Starčevića away from Old

As tempting as it may be to stroll through the hills above Dubrovnik or wander the unpaved paths on Lopud, both may still be laced with **landmines.** Stick to paved paths and beaches.

Town, then take a left after having passed the hotel's hill. Local kids carelessly dive into the sea from 6 ft. rocks, but this isn't the smartest idea: the water is much shallower than it looks. Ferries run daily from the Old Port (20min., 4 per hr., 35kn) to the nearby island of **Lokrum,** which has a nude beach. More modest travelers can stroll (fully clothed) through the **nature preserve.**

FESTIVALS AND NIGHTLIFE. Dubrovnik becomes a party scene and cultural mecca from mid-July to mid-August during the **Dubrovnik Summer Festival** (Dubrovački Ljetni Festival). The **festival office** on Placa has schedules and tickets. (☎42 88 64; www.dubrovnik-festival.hr. Open daily during the festival 8:30am-9pm, tickets 9am-2pm and 3-7pm. 50-300kn.) By night Dubrovnik's crowds gravitate to bars in Stari Grad and cafes on Buničeva Poljana, where live bands and street performers turn up in summer. From the open-air market, climb the stairs toward the monastery, veer left, and follow the signs marked "Cool Drinks and (truly) the Most Beautiful View" along Od Margarite to **Buža,** Crijevićeva 9. Perched above the bright blue Adriatic, this laid-back watering hold is the best place to enjoy spectacular sunsets. (Beer 17-22kn. Mixed drinks 30kn. Open daily 9am-2am.) Enjoy live jazz and occasional belly dancing at the classy but unpretentious **Jazz Cafe Troubador,** Bunićeva 2. (Beer 18-40kn. Wine 20-40kn. Open daily 9am-2am.) At **EastWest Cocktail and Dance Bar,** Frana Supila bb, dressed-to-impress clientele recline on leather sofas on the beach. (Beer 12-30kn. Mixed drinks 40-100kn. Thai massage 200kn for 30min., 300kn for 1hr. Open daily 8am-3am.)

DAYTRIP FROM DUBROVNIK: LOPUD ISLAND. Less than an hour from Dubrovnik is enchanting Lopud. A short walk along the shore leads to an abandoned **monastery,** which can be explored—beware of crumbling floors. The island's highlight is its beach, **Plaža Šunj.** Arguably the best beach in Croatia, this cove has one thing that most of the Dalmatian Coast lacks: sand. Facing the water, walk turn left on the road between the high wall and the palm park; look for the Konoba Barbara sign and continue over the hill; keep right when the path forks.

CZECH REPUBLIC (ČESKÁ REPUBLIKA)

From the rise of the Holy Roman Empire to the fall of the USSR, the Czechs have long stood at a crossroads of international affairs. Unlike many of their neighbors, the citizens of this small, landlocked country have rarely resisted as armies marched across their borders, often choosing to fight with words instead of weapons. The Czech Republic has a long history of trying to implement democracy and human rights, though long-term democracy wasn't achieved until late in 1989. As a result of their few domestic conflicts, as well as their peaceful divide from Slovakia, Czech towns and cities are among the best-preserved and most beautiful in Europe.

DISCOVER CZECH REPUBLIC: SUGGESTED ITINERARIES

THREE DAYS. You know where to go: **Prague** (p. 238). Stroll across the **Charles Bridge** to see **Prague Castle,** leave the beaten tourist path to explore areas like **Josefov,** and have some beer.

ONE WEEK. Keep exploring Prague (5 days); there's more to see. Once you need a break from the big city, head to **Český Krumlov** (2 days; p. 255) for hiking, biking, and another ancient castle.

BEST OF CZECH REPUBLIC, THREE WEEKS. Start with 2 weeks in Prague, including a trip to the Terezín concentration camp (p. 251). Then spend 4 days in UNESCO-protected Český Krumlov getting to know the bike trails and floating down the Vltava River in an inner tube. Check out the curious Revolving Theater while you're at it. Wrap things up with 3 days in Olomouc (p. 257).

ESSENTIALS

FACTS AND FIGURES

Official Name: Czech Republic.

Capital: Prague.

Major Cities: Brno, České Budějovice, Ostrava, Plzen.

Population: 10,250,000.

Time Zone: GMT +1.

Language: Czech.

Religions: Unaffiliated (68%), Roman Catholic (27%), Protestant (2%).

WHEN TO GO

The Czech Republic is the most touristed country in Eastern Europe. It may be wise to avoid the high season (July-Aug.), despite the pleasant weather. Reserve ahead for travel to any area during festivals and holidays. The best mix of good weather and minimal crowds will probably be in late spring or early fall.

DOCUMENTS AND FORMALITIES

EMBASSIES AND CONSULATES. Foreign embassies for the Czech Republic are in Prague (p. 238). Czech embassies abroad include: **Australia,** 8 Culgoa Circuit, O'Malley, Canberra, ACT, 2606 (☎612 6290 1386; www.mfa.cz/canberra); **Canada,** 251 Cooper St., Ottawa, ON, K2P OG2 (☎613-562-3875; www.mfa.cz/ottawa); **Ire-**

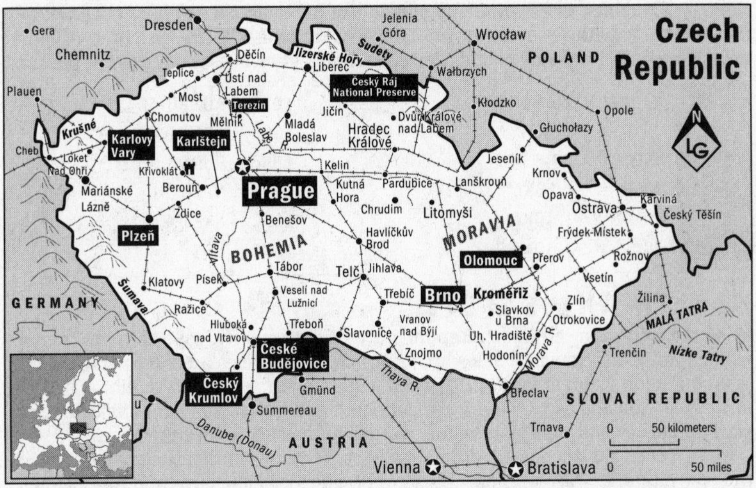

land, 57 Northumberland Rd., Ballsbridge, Dublin (☎1 668 1135; www.mzv.cz/dublin); **UK,** 26 Kensington Palace Gardens, London, W8 4QY (☎20 7243 7913; www.czechembassy.org.uk); **US,** 3900 Spring of Freedom St., NW, Washington, D.C., 20008 (☎202-274-9123; www.mzv.cz/washington). Citizens of **New Zealand** should consult the embassy in Canberra, AUS.

VISA AND ENTRY INFORMATION. Citizens of Australia, Canada, Ireland, New Zealand, the US, and the EU may stay in the Czech Republic for up to 90 days without a visa. Citizens of the UK may stay for up to 180 days visa-free. Check with your embassy for specific information. Visas are not available at the border.

ENTRANCE REQUIREMENTS

Passport: Required for all travelers.

Visa: Not required for stays under 90 days for citizens of Australia, Canada, Ireland, New Zealand, the US, and the EU. Citizens of the UK may remain in the country for up to 180 days without a visa.

Letter of Invitation: Not required for citizens.

Inoculations: None required. Recommended up-to-date on DTaP (diphtheria, tetanus, and pertussis), hepatitis A, hepatitis B, MMR (measles, mumps, and rubella), polio booster, and typhoid.

TOURIST SERVICES AND MONEY

TOURIST OFFICES. Municipal tourist offices in major cities provide info on sights and events, distribute lists of hostels and hotels, and often book rooms. In Prague, these offices may be crowded and staffed by cranky employees. **CKM,** Zitna 12, Prague (☎2491 5767), a national student tourist agency, is helpful for young travelers, booking hostel beds and issuing ISICs and HI cards. Most bookstores sell a national hiking map, *Soubor turistických map*, with an English-language key.

MONEY. The Czech unit of currency is the **koruna (Kč),** plural koruny. One koruna is equal to 100 haléř. The country plans to adopt the euro by 2009. **Inflation** is around 2.8%. **Banks** offer good exchange rates. **Komerční banka** is a common bank chain. **ATMs** are everywhere—look for the abundant *"Bankomat"* signs—and offer the best exchange rates. **Traveler's checks** can be exchanged almost everywhere, though rarely without commission. MasterCard and Visa are accepted at most establishments, but many hostels and other budget businesses are wary of plastic.

KORUNY (Kč)		
	AUS$1 = 16.81Kč	10Kč = AUS$0.60
	CDN$1 = 20.44Kč	10Kč = CDN$0.49
	EUR€1 = 28.33Kč	10Kč = EUR€0.35
	NZ$1 = 14.16Kč	10Kč = NZ$0.71
	UK£1 = 41.46Kč	10Kč = UK£0.24
	US$1 = 22.50Kč	10Kč = US$0.44

HEALTH AND SAFETY

Medical facilities in the Czech Republic are of high quality, especially in Prague. Major foreign insurance policies are accepted. Pharmacies are *Lékárna*, and the most common chain is **Droxies;** they and supermarkets carry international brands of *náplast* (bandages), *kondomy* (condoms), and *tampóny* (tampons). For prescription drugs and aspirin, look for pharmacies marked with a green cross.

Petty **crime** has increased dramatically in recent years, especially on public transportation; beware of pickpockets in Prague's main squares and tourist sites. **Women** traveling alone generally experience few problems in the Czech Republic. However, caution should be exercised while riding public transportation, especially after dark. **Minorities** generally do not encounter any trouble, though travelers with darker skin might be mistaken for Roma (gypsies) and be discriminated against. Gay nightlife is taking off in the Czech Republic, but open displays of homosexuality may not be accepted; **GLBT** travelers may receive stares and are advised to remain cautious in public situations, especially outside Prague.

EMERGENCY	**Police:** ☎158. **Ambulance:** ☎155. **Fire:** ☎150.

TRANSPORTATION

BY PLANE. Many major European and North American carriers, including **Air Canada, Air France, American Airlines, British Airways, ČSA, Delta, KLM, Lufthansa,** and **SAS** fly into Prague International Airport (PRG).

BY TRAIN. The easiest and cheapest way to travel between cities is by train. **Eastrail** is accepted in the Czech Republic, but **Eurail** is not. The fastest international trains are *EuroCity* and *InterCity* (*expresní;* marked in blue on schedules). *Rychlík* trains are fast domestic trains (*zrychlený vlak;* marked in red). Avoid slow *osobní* trains, marked in white. Departures *(odjezdy)* are printed on yellow posters, arrivals *(příjezdy)* on white. Seat reservations (*místenka;* 10Kč) are recommended on express and international trains and for first-class seating.

BY BUS. Czech buses are efficient, but schedules can be confusing. For travel in the countryside, they're quicker and cheaper than trains. **ČSAD** runs national and international bus lines, and many European companies operate international service. Consult the timetables or buy your own bus schedule (25Kč) from kiosks.

BY CAR. Roads are well kept and **roadside assistance** is usually available. In addition to a US **driver's license,** US citizens must have an International Driving Permit. **Taxis** are safe, though many overcharge tourists, especially in Prague. Negotiate the fare beforehand and make sure the meter is running, as exorbitant rates often result when cabbies "estimate" the fare. Calling a taxi service is often cheaper than flagging a cab. Let's Go does not recommend hitchhiking, though it is common.

KEEPING IN TOUCH

PHONE CODES	**Country code:** 420. **International dialing prefix:** 00. For more information on how to place international calls, see inside back cover.

EMAIL AND THE INTERNET. Internet access is readily available throughout the Czech Republic. Internet cafes offer fast connections for about 1-2Kč per minute.

TELEPHONE. Card-operated phones (200Kč per 50 units) are simpler to use than coin phones and easier to find. You can purchase **phone cards** *(telefonní karta)* at most tobacco stores *(tábaks)* and convenience stores *(trafika)*. To make domestic calls, simply dial the entire number. City codes no longer exist in the Czech Republic and dialing zero is not necessary. To make an international call from the Czech Republic, dial the country code followed by the phone number. Calls cost 8Kč per minute to Australia, Canada, Ireland, the UK, and the US; 12Kč per minute to New Zealand. Dial ☎1181 for English-language info, 0800 12 34 56 for the international operator. International access codes include: **AT&T Direct** (☎00 800 222 55288); **British Telecom** (☎00 420); **Canada Direct** (☎800 001 115); **MCI WorldPhone** (☎800 001 112); **Sprint** (☎004 208 7187).

MAIL. The postal system is reliable and efficient, though few postal employees speak English. A postcard to Europe costs 9Kč, to the US 12Kč. To send **airmail,** stress that you want your package to go on a plane *(letecky)*. Go to the customs office to send packages heavier than 2kg abroad. **Poste Restante** is generally available. Address envelopes as follows: First Name LAST NAME, *POSTE RESTANTE*, post office street address, Postal Code, city, CZECH REPUBLIC.

LANGUAGE. **Czech** is a West Slavic language, closely related to Slovak and Polish. **English** is widely understood among young people, and **German** can be useful, especially in South Bohemia because of its proximity to the German and Austrian borders. You're more likely to encounter **Polish** in eastern regions. **Russian** was taught to all schoolchildren under Communism, but use it carefully, as the language is not always welcome. For a few choice expressions, see **Phrasebook: Czech,** p. 1053.

ACCOMMODATIONS AND CAMPING

CZECH REPUBLIC	❶	❷	❸	❹	❺
ACCOMMODATIONS	under 320Kč	320-500Kč	500-800Kč	800-1200Kč	over 1200Kč

University dorms are the cheapest options in July and August; two- to four-bed dorms cost 250-400Kč. **Hostels** (300-500Kč) are clean and safe, though scarce in areas with few students. **Pensions** are the next most affordable option at 600-800Kč, including breakfast. **Hotels,** from 1000Kč, tend to be more luxurious and more expensive than hostels or pensions. From June to September, reserve at least one week ahead in Prague, Český Krumlov, and Brno. Private homes are not nearly as popular (or cheap) as in the rest of Eastern Europe; to find them, scan train stations for "*Zimmer frei*" signs. Quality varies; do not pay in advance. There are **campgrounds** across the country; most are open only mid-May to September.

FOOD AND DRINK

CZECH REPUBLIC	❶	❷	❸	❹	❺
FOOD	under 80Kč	80-110Kč	110-150Kč	150-200Kč	over 200Kč

Loving Czech cuisine starts with learning to pronounce *knedlíky* (KNED-lee-kee). These thick lumps of dough, feebly known in English as dumplings, are a staple of

Czech cuisine. Meat lies at the heart of almost all main dishes; the **national meal** (known as *vepřo-knedlo-zelo*) is *vepřové* (roast pork), *knedlíky*, and *zelí* (sauerkraut). If you're in a hurry, grab *párky* (frankfurters) or *sýr* (cheese) at a food stand. **Vegetarian** restaurants serving meatless *(bez masa)* specialties are uncommon outside Prague; traditional restaurants serve few options beyond *smaženy sýr* (fried cheese) and *saláty* (salads), which may or may not contain meat products. Keeping **kosher** is feasible, but beware of pork, which often finds its way into Czech cuisine. Coffee-lovers should ask for *káva espresso* rather than just *káva:* the Czech brew may be unappealing to Western palates. *Jablkový závin* (apple strudel) and *ovocné knedlíky* (fruit dumplings) are favorite sweets, but the most beloved is *koláč*—a tart filled with poppy seeds or sweet cheese. Moravian **wines** are of high quality. They're typically drunk at a *vinárna* (wine bar), which serves a variety of spirits, including *slivovice* (plum brandy) and *becherovka* (herbal bitter), the national drink. Local brews like *Plzeňský Prazdroj* (Pilsner Urquell), *Budvar*, and *Krusovice* dominate the drinking scene.

HOLIDAYS AND FESTIVALS

Holidays: New Year's Day (Jan. 1); Easter Holiday (Apr. 8-9); May Day/Labor Day (May 1); Liberation Day (May 8); St. Cyril and Methodius Day (July 5); Jan Hus Day (July 6); Czech Statehood Day (Sept. 28); Independence Day (Oct. 28); Struggle for Freedom and Democracy Day (Nov. 17).

Festivals: The Czech Republic hosts a number of internationally renowned festivals; make sure to reserve tickets and a room well in advance. Classical musicians and world-class orchestras descend on Prague (p. 238) for the Spring Festival, held from mid-May to early June. In June, the Five-Petaled Rose Festival, a boisterous medieval festival in Český Krumlov (p. 255), features music, dance, and a jousting tournament. Villages celebrate Masopust, the Moravian version of Mardi Gras, from Epiphany to Ash Wednesday (Jan.-Mar.). Revelers dressed in animal masks feast, dance, and sing until Lent.

BEYOND TOURISM

INEX—Association of Voluntary Service, Senovážné nám. 24, 116 47 Prague 1, CZR (☎234 621 527; www.inexsda.cz/eng). Ecological and historical preservation efforts, as well as construction projects, in the Czech Republic.

The Prague Center for Further Education and Professional Development, Pštrossova 19, 110 00 Prague 1, CZR (☎257 534 013; www.prague-center.cz). Teaches courses on art, filmmaking, and design in Prague.

The Prague Post (www.praguepost.com). English-language newspaper with job ads.

University of West Bohemia, Univerzitní 8, 306 14 Plzeň, CZR (☎377 631 111; www.zcu.cz). An international university centrally located in a student-friendly Czech brewery city.

World-Wide Opportunities on Organic Farms (WWOOF), Main Office, P.O. Box 2675, Lewes, BN7 1RB, England, BRI (www.wwoof.org). Arranges volunteer work on organic and eco-conscious farms in the Czech Republic and around the world.

PRAGUE (PRAHA)

According to legend, Countess Libuše stood above the Vltava River around AD 800 and declared, "I see a grand city whose glory will touch the stars." Medieval kings, benefactors, and architects fulfilled her prophecy with cathedrals and palaces that reflected the status of Prague (pop. 1,166,000) as capital of the Holy Roman Empire. Prague's maze of alleys spawned legends of demons and occult forces,

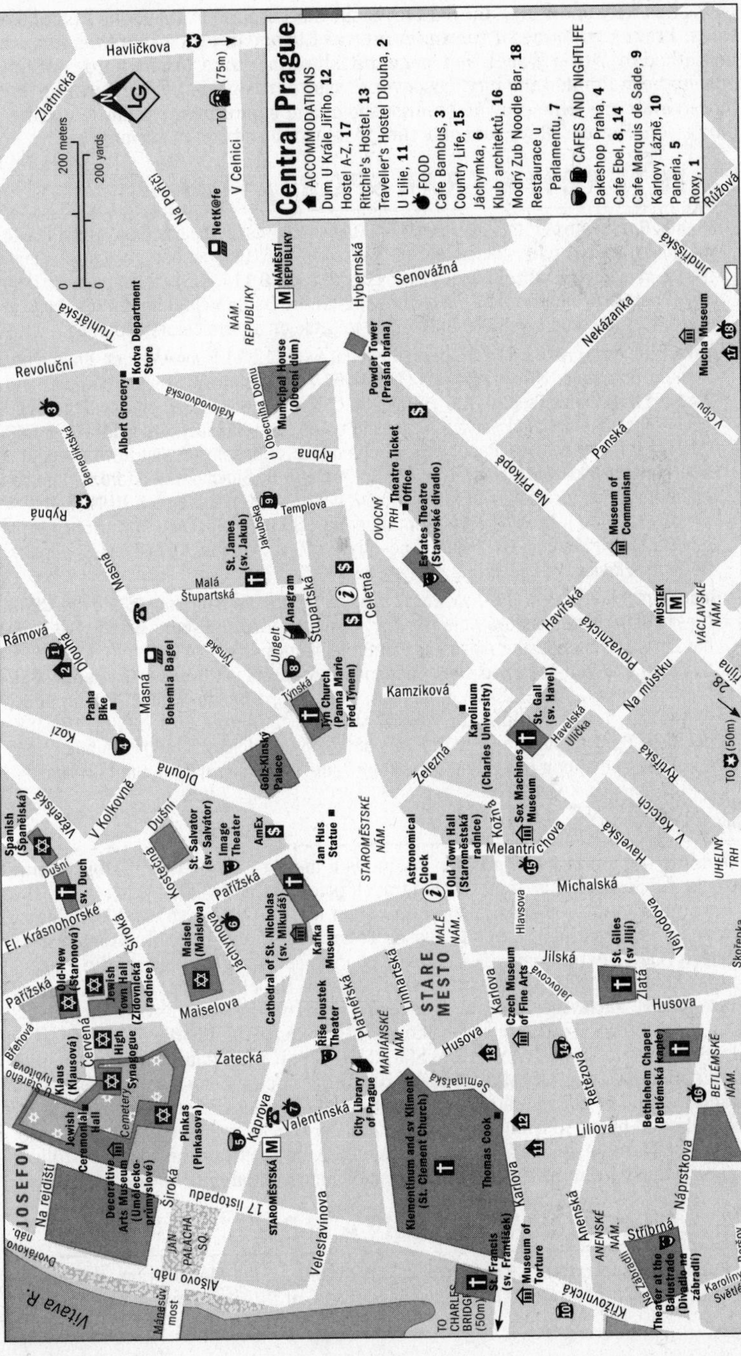
Central Prague
ACCOMMODATIONS
Dum U Krále Jiřího, 12
Hostel A-Z, 17
Ritchie's Hostel, 13
Traveller's Hostel Dlouha, 2
U Lilie, 11
FOOD
Cafe Bambus, 3
Country Life, 15
Jáchymka, 6
Klub architektů, 16
Modrý Zub Noodle Bar, 18
Restaurace u Parlamentu, 7
CAFES AND NIGHTLIFE
Bakeshop Praha, 4
Cafe Ebel, 8, 14
Cafe Marquis de Sade, 9
Karlovy Lázně, 10
Paneria, 5
Roxy, 1
200 meters
200 yards
TO (75m)
TO (50m)
TO CHARLES BRIDGE (50m)
JOSEFOV
STARE MESTO
Vltava R.
Old Town Hall (Staroměstská radnice)
Astronomical Clock
Týn Church (Panna Marie před Týnem)
Golz-Kinský Palace
Jan Hus Statue
Cathedral of St. Nicholas (sv. Mikuláš)
Kafka Museum
Municipal House (Obecní dům)
Powder Tower (Prašná brána)
Estates Theatre (Stavovské divadlo)
Theatre Ticket Office
Karolinum (Charles University)
Museum of Communism
Mucha Museum
Klementinum and sv Kliment (St. Clement Church)
Thomas Cook
City Library of Prague
Museum of Torture
St. Francis (sv. František)
Czech Museum of Fine Arts
Bethlehem Chapel (Betlémská kaple)
Theater at the Balustrade (Divadlo na zábradlí)
St. Giles (sv Jiljí)
St. Gall (sv. Havel)
Sex Machines Museum
St. James (sv. Jakub)
Anagram
Bohemia Bagel
Praha Bike
Albert Grocery
Kotva Department Store
NetK@fe
Old-New (Staronová)
Jewish Town Hall (Židovnická radnice)
High Synagogue
Klaus (Klausová)
Jewish Ceremonial Hall
Cemetery
Pinkas (Pinkasova)
Maisel (Maislova)
Spanish (Španělská)
sv. Duch
St. Salvator (sv. Salvátor)
Image Theater
AmEx
Decorative Arts Museum (Uměleckoprůmyslové)
Říše loustek Theater
NÁMĚSTÍ REPUBLIKY
STAROMĚSTSKÁ
MŮSTEK
STAROMĚSTSKÉ NÁM.
MALÉ NÁM.
MARIÁNSKÉ NÁM.
BETLÉMSKÉ NÁM.
ANENSKÉ NÁM.
VÁCLAVSKÉ NÁM.
UHELNÝ TRH
OVOCNÝ TRH
NÁM. REPUBLIKY
JAN PALACHA SQ.
Havlíčkova
Zlatnická
Na Poříčí
V Celnici
Truhlářská
Revoluční
Hybernská
Senovážná
Jindřišská
Růžová
Nekázanka
Panská
V Cípu
Na Příkopě
Králodvorská
U Obecního Domu
Rybná
Benediktská
Templová
Jakubská
Masná
Malá Štupartská
Štupartská
Celetná
Ungelt
Týnská
Rámová
Dlouhá
Kozí
Kamzíková
Železná
Havířská
Provaznická
Na můstku
Rytířská
28. října
Havelská
Havelská Ulička
V. Kotcích
Melantrichova
Kožná
Michalská
Vejvodova
Skořepka
Jilská
Jalovcova
Zlatá
Husova
Hlavsova
Řetězová
Liliová
Náprstkova
Stříbrná
Boršov
Karoliny Světlé
Na Zábradlí
Křižovnická
Anenská
Karlova
Seminářská
Linhartská
Platnéřská
Valentinská
Kaprova
Žatecká
Maiselova
Jáchymova
Pařížská
El. Krásnohorské
Široká
Červená
Břehová
U Starého hřbitova
Vězeňská
Dušní
V Kolkovně
Kostečná
17 listopadu
Veleslavínova
Alšovo nábř.
Na rejdišti
Dvořákovo nábř.
Mánesův most

giving this "city of dreams" the dark mystique that inspired Franz Kafka's paranoid tales. Prague was one of the only Central European cities that was largely unscathed by World War II, and since the fall of the Iron Curtain, hordes of foreigners have flooded the city. Discover Prague's true gems by wandering a few blocks away from the crowded tourist sights and exploring the numerous cafes, parks, cobblestone alleys, and churches that lend the city its magic appeal.

INTERCITY TRANSPORTATION

Flights: Ruzyně Airport (☎220 113 313), 20km northwest of the city. Take bus #119 to Metro A: Dejvická (daily 5am-midnight; 14Kč, luggage 10Kč per bag); buy tickets from kiosks or machines. **Airport buses** run by **Cedaz** (☎220 114 296) collect travelers from nám. Republiky and Dejvická Metro stops (2 per hr. 5:30am-9:30pm, 90Kč). **Taxis** to the airport are expensive (500-800Kč); try to settle on a price before departing.

Trains: Domestic ☎221 111 122, international 840 112 113; www.vlak.cz. Prague has 4 main terminals. **Hlavní nádraží** (☎224 615 249; Metro C: Hlavní nádraží) and **Nádraží Holešovice** (☎224 806 793; Metro C: Nádraží Holešovice) are the largest and cover most international service. Domestic trains leave **Masarykovo nádraží** (☎840 112 113; Metro B: nám. Republiky), on the corner of Hybernská and Havlíčkova, and from **Smíchovské nádraží** (☎972 226 150; Metro B: Smíchovské nádraží). International trains run to: **Berlin, GER** (5hr., 7 per day, 1347Kč); **Budapest, HUN** (7-9hr., 4 per day, 1260Kč); **Kraków, POL** (8hr., 4 per day, 833Kč); **Moscow, RUS** (35hr., 1 per day, 1720Kč); **Munich, GER** (6hr., 4 per day, 1450Kč); **Vienna, AUT** (4½hr., 5 per day, 840Kč); **Warsaw, POL** (10hr., 2 per day, 1150Kč).

Buses: Info ☎900 144 444; www.vlak-bus.cz. Open daily 6am-9pm. State-run **ČSAD** (Česká státní automobilová doprava; Czech National Bus Transport; ☎257 319 016) has several terminals. The biggest is **Florenc**, Křižíkova 4 (☎224 219 680; Metro B or C: Florenc). Info office open daily 6am-9pm. Buy tickets in advance. To: **Berlin, GER** (7hr., 4 per day, 500-1000Kč); **Budapest, HUN** (8hr., 1 per day, 700-1260Kč); **Paris, FRA** (14hr., 1 per day, 2080Kč); **Vienna, AUT** (5hr., 2 per day, 550-750Kč). 10% ISIC discount. The **Tourbus** office (☎224 218 680; www.eurolines.cz), at the terminal, sells **Eurolines** and airport bus tickets. Open M-F 7am-7pm, Sa 8am-7pm, Su 9am-7pm.

ORIENTATION

Spanning the **Vltava River**, greater Prague is a mess of suburbs and labyrinthine streets. All destinations of interest to travelers are in the compact downtown. The Vltava runs south-northeast, separating **Staré Město** (Old Town) and **Nové Město** (New Town) from **Malá Strana** (Lesser Town). On the right bank, **Staroměstské náměstí** (Old Town Square) is the heart of Prague. From the square, the elegant **Pařížská ulice** (Paris Street) leads north to **Josefov**, the old Jewish ghetto. South of Staré Město, **Václavské náměstí** (Wenceslas Square), the commercial core, leads into Nové Město. To the west of Staroměstské nám., the **Charles Bridge** (Karlův Most) spans the Vltava, connecting Staré Město with **Malostranské náměstí** (Lesser Town Square). **Prague Castle** (Pražský Hrad) overlooks Malostranské nám. from **Hradčany** hill. The Hlavní nádraží train station and Florenc bus station lie northeast of Václavské nám. All train and bus terminals are on or near the excellent Metro. To reach Staroměstské nám., take the Metro A line to Staroměstská and follow Kaprova away from the river. Bookstores sell an essential *plán města* (map).

LOCAL TRANSPORTATION

Public Transportation: Buy interchangeable tickets for the **Metro, tram,** and **bus** at newsstands, *tabák* kiosks, machines in stations, or DP (Dopravní podnik; transport authority) kiosks. Validate tickets in machines above escalators to avoid fines issued by plainclothes inspectors who roam transport lines. 3 **Metro** lines run daily 5am-midnight: A is green on maps, B yellow, C red. **Night trams** #51-58 and **buses** #502-514 and 601 run after the last Metro and cover the same areas as day trams and buses (every 30min. midnight-5am); look for dark blue signs with white letters at bus stops. 14Kč tickets are good for a 20min. ride or 4 stops. 20Kč tickets are valid for 75min., with transfers, for all travel in the same direction. Large bags and bikes 10Kč. The DP office (☎296 191 817; www.dpp.cz; open daily 7am-9pm), in the Muzeum stop on Metro A and C lines, sells **multi-day passes** (1-day 80Kč, 3-day 220Kč, 1-week 270Kč).

Taxis: Radiotaxi (☎272 731 848) and **AAA** (☎140 14) are particularly reliable. 34Kč flat rate plus 25Kč per km and 5Kč per min. waiting.

TIP **GOING THE DISTANCE.** To avoid taxi scams, always ask in advance for a receipt *(Prosím, dejte mi paragon)* with distance traveled and price paid.

PRACTICAL INFORMATION

Tourist Offices: Green "i"s mark tourist offices, which book rooms and sell maps. **Pražská Informační Služba** (PIS; Prague Information Service; ☎12 444, from outside Prague 224 223 613; www.pis.cz) is in the Staroměstské Radnice (Old Town Hall). Open Apr.-Oct. M-F 9am-7pm, Sa-Su 9am-6pm; Nov.-Mar. M-F 9am-6pm, Sa-Su 9am-5pm. Branches at Na příkopě 20 and Hlavní nádraží. Open in summer M-F 9am-7pm, Sa-Su 9am-6pm; low season M-F 9am-6pm, Sa-Su 9am-5pm. Branch in the tower by the Malá Strana side of the Charles Bridge. Open Apr.-Oct. daily 9am-7pm.

Budget Travel: Arctic, Václavské nám. 56 (☎222 721 595). Metro A: Můstek. Offers discounted airfare to those under 26. Open M-Th 10am-6pm, F 10am-4pm. **BIJ Wasteels** (☎224 641 954; www.wasteels.cz), on the 2nd fl. of Hlavní nádraží, sells discounted international train tickets to those under 26, and books couchettes and bus tickets. Open M-F 8am-6pm, Sa 9am-4pm.

Passport Office: Foreigner Police Headquarters, Olšanská 2 (☎974 841 356). Metro A: Flora. From the Metro, turn right on Jičínská and go right again on Olšanská. Or, take tram #9 from Václavské nám. toward Spojovací and get off at Olšanská. Little English spoken. Open M-Th 7:30-11:30am, noon-4:30pm, and 5-7pm.

Embassies and Consulates: Canada, Muchova 6 (☎272 101 800; www.canada.cz). Metro A: Hradčanská. Open M-F 8:30am-12:30pm and 1:30-4:30pm. **Ireland,** Tržiště 13 (☎257 530 061). Metro A: Malostranská. Open M-F 9:30am-12:30pm and 2:30-4:30pm. **UK,** Thunovská 14 (☎257 402 111; www.britain.cz). Metro A: Malostranská. Open M-Th 8:30am-5pm, F 8:30am-4pm. **US,** Tržiště 15 (☎257 022 000; www.usembassy.cz). Metro A: Malostranská. Open M-F 8am-4:30pm. **Australia,** Klimentská 10, 6th fl. (☎296 578 350; www.embassy.gov.au/cz.html), has a consulate open M-Th 8:30am-5pm, F 8:30am-2pm; citizens should contact the UK embassy in an emergency. Citizens of **New Zealand** should contact the embassy in Berlin.

Currency Exchange: Exchange counters are everywhere, but their rates vary wildly. The counters in the train station have high rates. Never change money on the street. **Chequepoints** are convenient and open late, but usually charge a large commission or fee. **Komerční banka,** Na příkopě 33 (☎222 411 111), buys notes and checks for a 2% commission. 24hr. **ATMs** *(Bankomats)* abound and can offer the best rates, but often charge large fees.

American Express/Interchange: Václavské nám. 56 (☎222 211 089). Metro A or C: Muzeum. AmEx **ATM** outside. Grants MC/V cash advances for a 3% commission. Western Union services available. Open daily 9am-10pm.

Luggage Storage: Lockers in all train and bus stations take 2 5Kč coins. If the lockers are full or if you need to store your cargo longer than 24hr., use the luggage offices to the left in the basement of **Hlavní nádraží** (15-30Kč per day; open 24hr.) or halfway up the stairs at **Florenc** (30Kč per day; open daily 5am-11pm).

English-Language Bookstore: The Globe Bookstore, Pštrossova 6 (☎224 934 203; www.globebookstore.cz). Metro B: Národní třída. Exit Metro left on Spálená, take the first right on Ostrovní, then take the 3rd left on Pštrossova. Wide variety of new and used books and periodicals. Internet 1.50Kč per min. Open daily 10am-midnight.

Laundromat: Famos Laundromat, Karolíny Světlé 10 (☎224 222 957). Metro B: Národní třída. Head west on Národní, turn right on Voršilská, and bear left onto Karolíny Světlé. Wash and dry 200Kč per 5kg. Open M-F 7:30am-7pm, Su 10am-5pm.

Emergency: Police: ☎158. **Ambulance:** ☎0155. **Fire:** ☎150.

Medical Services: Na Homolce (Hospital for Foreigners), Roentgenova 2 (☎257 272 146, after hours 257 211 111; www.homolka.cz). Bus #167. Open M-F 7am-5pm. 24hr. emergency services. **Canadian Medical Center,** Velesavínská 1 (☎235 360 133, after hours 724 300 301; www.cmc.praha.cz). Open M-F 8am-6pm.

24hr. Pharmacy: U Lékárna Anděla, Štefánikova 6 (☎257 320 918, after hours 224 431 112). Metro B: Anděl. With your back to the train station, turn left and follow Nádražní until it becomes Štefánikova. For after-hours service, press the button marked "Pohotovost" to the left of the main door.

Telephones: Phone cards cost 200Kč per 50 units at kiosks and post offices. Don't let kiosks rip you off. Pay phones also take coins (local calls from 10Kč per min.).

Internet Access: Bohemia Bagel, Masná 2 (www.bohemiabagel.cz), has a friendly atmosphere and delicious food. Metro A: Staroměstská. 2Kč per min. Open M-F 7am-midnight, Sa-Su 8am-midnight. Branch at Újezd 16. Open daily 9am-midnight.

Post Office: Jindřišská 14 (☎221 131 445). Metro A: Můstek. Airmail to the US takes 7-10 days. For *Poste Restante,* address mail as follows: First name LAST NAME, Poste Restante, Jindřišská 14, Praha 1 110 00, CZECH REPUBLIC. Open daily 2am-midnight. Tellers close 8pm. **Postal Code:** 1 110 00.

ACCOMMODATIONS AND CAMPING

Hotel prices are through the roof in Prague, and hostel rates are also increasing. Reservations are a must at hotels and a good idea at the hostels that accept them. A growing number of Prague residents rent affordable rooms.

HOSTELS

If you tote a backpack in Hlavní nádraží or Holešovice stations, you will likely be approached by hostel runners offering cheap beds. Many of these are university dorms vacated June to August, and they often provide free transportation, convenient for late-night arrivals. It's a good idea to call ahead, especially in the summer. Staff at hostels typically speak English.

STARÉ MĚSTO

Travellers' Hostel, Dlouhá 33 (☎224 826 662; www.travellers.cz). Metro B: nám. Republiky. Seasonal branches at Husova 3, Josefská, Střelecký Ostrov, and U Lanové Dráhy 3. Social atmosphere. Same building as the Roxy (p. 251). Breakfast and linens included. Laundry 150Kč. Internet 1Kč per min. Reserve ahead in summer. Dorms 380-550Kč; singles 1120Kč, with bath 1300Kč; doubles 1200/1300Kč. ISIC discount. ❷

Ritchie's Hostel, Karlova 9 (☎222 221 229; www.ritchieshostel.cz). Metro A: Staroměstská. From the Charles Bridge, head down Karlova past the small square.

Basic, clean accommodations in the thick of the tourist district. Breakfast 25Kč. Dorms 390-500Kč, low season 350-500Kč; doubles 1890-2000Kč. MC/V. ❷

NOVÉ MĚSTO AND VINOHRADY

Czech Inn, Francouzská 76 (☎267 267 600; www.czech-inn.com). Metro A: nám. Míru. From the Metro, take tram #4, 22, or 23 to Krymská and walk uphill. This ultra-modern, fashionable hostel sets sky-high standards for budget accommodations. Breakfast 120Kč. Internet 50Kč per hr. Reserve far ahead. Dorms 390-450Kč; singles 1200Kč; doubles 1400Kč. Private room prices increase 200Kč on weekends. AmEx/DC/MC/V. ❷

Hostel Advantage (HI), Sokolská 11-13 (☎224 914 062; www.advantagehostel.cz). Metro C: I.P. Pavlova. Take the stairs on the left leading to Ječná and turn left on Sokolská. This well-kept hostel has simple, comfortable rooms. Breakfast included. Free Internet. Dorms 400Kč; singles 600Kč; doubles 1000Kč. 10% ISIC discount. MC/V. ❷

Hostel Elf, Husitská 11 (☎222 540 963; www.hostelelf.com). Metro B: Florenc. From the Metro, take bus #207 to U Památníku; the hostel is through the wooden gate. Despite noisy train tracks nearby, this graffiti-covered hostel is always packed. Don't be surprised to find the party continuing past dawn. Breakfast included. Free Internet. Dorms 320Kč; singles 800Kč, with bath 1000Kč; doubles 900/1200Kč. ❷

Hostel AZ, Jindřišská 5 (☎224 241 664; www.hostel-az.com). Metro A: Můstek. Across from the post office. Superb location; bright geometric murals add pizzazz to tidy, plain rooms. Dorms 400-450Kč; singles 1000Kč; doubles 1260Kč. MC/V. ❷

Pension Unitas Art Prison Hostel, Bartolomějská 9 (☎224 221 802; www.unitas.cz). Metro B: Národní třída. Cross Národní třída, head up Na Perštýně, and turn left on Bartolomějská. This former Communist prison is now a clean and colorful hostel, though the small rooms still feel like cells. Breakfast included. Reception 24hr. Dorms 350-440Kč; singles 1050Kč; doubles 1200Kč. 7th night free. MC/V. ❷

Hostel U Melounu, Ke Karlovu 7 (☎224 918 322; www.hostelumelounu.cz). Metro C: I.P. Pavlova. Follow Sokolská and go right on Na Bojišt, then left onto Ke Karlovu. A historic building with great facilities. Bar and private garden. Breakfast included. Check-out 10am. Dorms 390Kč; singles 700Kč; doubles 1000Kč. ISIC discount. AmEx/MC/V. ❷

OUTSIDE THE CENTER

Sir Toby's, Dělnická 24 (☎283 870 635; www.sirtobys.com). Metro C: Nádraží Holešovice. From the Metro, take the tram to Dělnická, walk to the corner of Dělnická, and turn left. Beautiful, classy hostel with a huge, fully equipped kitchen. Free wireless Internet. Dorms 340-400Kč; singles 1000Kč; doubles 1350Kč. MC/V. ❷

Hostel Boathouse, Lodnická 1 (☎241 770 051; www.hostelboathouse.com). Take tram #14 from Národní třída south toward Sídliště. Get off at Černý Kůň (20min.), go down the ramp to the left, and follow the yellow signs. Social atmosphere, caring staff, and home-cooked meals. Breakfast included. Dorms from 350Kč. ❷

Hostel Sinkule, Zíkova 13 (☎224 320 202; www.bed.cz). Metro A: Dejvická. Cheap, tidy university dorm far from the city center, but near the airport shuttle stop. Check-in 2pm. Check-out 9:30am. Singles 550Kč; doubles 1000Kč. DC/MC/V. ❸

HOTELS AND PENSIONS

Budget hotels are scarce in Prague, and generally the better hostel options offer more bang for the buck. Lower rates at hotels are often available if you call ahead.

Dům U Krále Jiřího (Hotel King George), Liliová 10 (☎222 220 925; www.kinggeorge.cz). Metro A: Staroměstská. Luxurious rooms with private bath. Buffet breakfast included. Reception open daily 7am-11pm. Singles 2100Kč; doubles 3100Kč; triples 3750Kč; apartments 3100-6050Kč. Dec.-Feb. 300Kč discount. ❺

U Lilie, Liliová 15 (☎222 220 432; www.pensionulilie.cz). Metro A: Staroměstská. A lovely courtyard, satellite TV, and a minibar in every room. Breakfast included. Singles with shower 2000Kč; doubles 3050Kč, with bath 3600Kč. Cash only. ❺

CAMPING

Campgrounds can be found on the Vltava Islands as well as on the outskirts of Prague. Bungalows must be reserved ahead, but tent space is generally available without prior notice. Tourist offices sell a guide to sites near the city (15Kč).

Camp Sokol Troja, Trojská 171 (☎233 542 908), north of the center in the Troja district. From Metro C: Nádraží Holešovice, take bus #112 and ask for Kazanka. Similar places line the road. Clean facilities. July-Aug. and Dec. tent sites 90-150Kč, extra person 120Kč; singles 330Kč; doubles 660Kč. Low season reduced rates. ❶

FOOD

The nearer you are to the city center, the more you'll pay. You will be charged for everything the waiter brings to the table; check your bill carefully. **Tesco,** Národní třída 26, has groceries. (Open M-F 7am-10pm, Sa 8am-8pm, Su 9am-8pm.) Look for the **daily market** in Staré Město. After a night out, grab a *párek v rohlíku* (hot dog) or a *smažený sýr* (fried cheese sandwich) from a Václavské nám. vendor.

RESTAURANTS

STARÉ MĚSTO

Klub architektů, Betlémské nám. 169/5A (☎224 401 214). Metro B: Národní třída. A 12th-century cellar with 21st-century ambience. Veggie options 70-150Kč. Meat entrees 160-320Kč. Open daily 11:30am-midnight. AmEx/MC/V. ❸

Jáchymka, Jáchymova 4 (☎224 819 621). Metro A: Staroměstská. A local favorite, Jáchymka serves gigantic, affordable cuts of meat. Salads from 30Kč. Entrees 150-335Kč. Open daily 11am-11pm. MC/V. ❸

Country Life, Melantrichova 15 (☎224 213 366; www.countrylife.cz). Metro A: Staroměstská. 3 fresh vegetarian buffets—hot, cold, and salad bar—are a welcome respite from meat-heavy Czech cuisine. Buffet 20-50Kč per 100g. Soup 20Kč. Juices from 20Kč. Open M-Th 9am-8:30pm, F 8:30am-5pm, Su 11am-8:30pm. Cash only. ❷

Restaurace u Parlamentu, Valentinská 8 (☎721 415 74). Metro A: Staroměstská. Serves Czech specialties (60-118Kč) and cold glasses of Pilsner Urquell. Popular with local business-lunchers. Open M-F 9:30am-11pm, Sa-Su 11am-11pm. MC/V. ❷

Cafe Bambus, Benediktská 12 (☎224 828 110; www.cafebambus.com). Metro B: nám. Republiky. Patrons nosh on Thai and Indian dishes (pad thai and curry each 130Kč) and Czech *palančinky* (crepes; 55-75Kč). Beer from 42Kč. Open M-F 9am-2am, Sa 11am-2am, Su 11am-midnight. AmEx/MC/V. ❷

NOVÉ MĚSTO

Radost FX, Bělehradská 120 (☎224 254 776; www.radostfx.cz). Metro C: I.P. Pavlova. A stylish dance club and late-night cafe with an imaginative menu and great vegetarian food. Entrees 120-195Kč. Brunch Sa-Su 95-140Kč. Open daily 9am-last customer. ❸

Universal, V jirchářích 6 (☎224 934 416). Metro B: Národní třída. Asian, French, and Mediterranean cuisines served in a spacious dining room reminiscent of a Parisian cafe. Huge, fresh salads 131-195Kč. Entrees 149-299Kč. Su brunch buffet 185-205Kč. Open M-Sa 11:30am-1am, Su 11am-midnight. MC/V; 500Kč min. charge. ❹

Ultramarin Grill, Ostrovní 32 (☎224 932 249; www.ultramarin.cz). Metro B: Národní třída. With your back to the Metro, turn left and then immediately right on narrow Ostrovní. International clientele, but the portion sizes and most of the menu are purely American. Thai-inspired steak, duck, and lamb entrees 130-350Kč. Salads 100-180Kč. Open daily 10am-4am. AmEx/MC/V. ❸

Modrý Zub Noodle Bar, Jindřišská 5 (☎222 212 622). Metro A: Můstek. Across from the post office. Dishes out heaping portions of pad thai and various types of tasty noodles (120-145Kč). Open M-F 10am-11pm, Sa-Su 11am-10pm. Cash only. ❸

Govinda Vegetarian Club, Soukenická 27 (☎224 816 631; www.govinda.cz). Metro B: nám. Republiky. Go down Revoluční away from the Municipal House (Obecní Dum) and turn right on Soukenická. Tiny lunch counter has a set menu of stew, rice, salad, and chutney. Small portions 80Kč, large 90Kč. A la carte 21-40Kč. Open M-F 11am-5pm. ❶

Velryba (The Whale), Opatovická 24. Metro B: Národní třída. Cross the tram tracks and follow Ostrovní, then go left onto Opatovická. Relaxed Italian/Czech restaurant with art gallery downstairs. Entrees 77-145Kč. Open daily 11am-midnight. MC/V. ❷

MALÁ STRANA

Bar bar, Všehrdova 17 (☎257 313 246; www.barbar.cz). Metro A: Malostranská. From Malostranské nám., go down Karmelitská and left on Všehrdova. Reggae-inspired basement cafe with surprisingly affordable menu. Lunch noon-2pm 100Kč. Entrees 98-175Kč. Beer from 28Kč. Open Su-Th noon-midnight, F-Sa noon-2am. MC/V. ❷

U Tří Černých Ruží, Zámecká 5 (☎257 530 019; www.u3cr.com). Metro A: Malostranská. At the foot of the New Castle steps. A small, quirky restaurant and bar that serves up large portions and pours endless pints at low prices. Entrees 80-200Kč. Beer 18Kč. Open daily 11am-midnight. ❷

CAFES AND TEAHOUSES

Cafe Rybka, Opatovická 7. Metro B: Národní třída. Congenial corner cafe with a sea motif, fantastic coffee, and a tiny book store. Espresso 25Kč. Tea 22Kč. Open daily 9:15am-10pm. Cash only.

Cafe Ebel, Řetězová 9 (☎603 441 434; www.ebelcoffee.cz). Metro A or B: Staroměstská. Ebel's espresso (40-50Kč) is blended in-house by people who clearly know what they're doing. English spoken. Branch at Týnská 2. Both open M-F 8am-8pm, Sa-Su 8:30am-8pm. AmEx/MC/V.

Kavárna Medúza, Belgická 17. Metro A: nám. Míru. Walk down Rumunská and turn left at Belgická. Local clientele by day, hipsters by night. Coffee 19-30Kč. Crepes 52-70Kč. Open M-F 10am-1am, Sa-Su noon-1am. MC/V.

U zeleného čaje, Nerudova 19 (☎225 730 027). Metro A: Malostranská. From Malostranské nám., go down Nerudova. This adorable shop at the foot of Prague Castle takes tea to new heights. Tea 35-75Kč. Open daily 11am-10pm. Cash only.

Bakeshop Praha, Kozí 1. Metro A: Staroměstská. From Staroměstské nám., follow Dlouhá to the intersection with Kozí. Mouthwatering pastries, salads, sandwiches, and quiches. Branch at Lázenska 19. 10% extra to eat in. Open daily 7am-7pm.

Paneria, Kaprova 7, on the corner of Kaprova and Valentinská. Metro A: Staroměstská. Affordable, reliable, and convenient, with 3Kč rolls, 8Kč croissants, and espresso from 32Kč. Open M-F 7am-2am, Sa-Su 7am-8pm.

SIGHTS

Escape the crowds that flock to Prague's downtown sights by venturing away from **Staroměstské náměstí,** the **Charles Bridge,** and **Václavské náměstí.** There are plenty of attractions for visitors hidden in the old Jewish quarter of **Josefov,** the hills of **Vyšehrad,** and the streets of **Malá Strana.**

CZECH REPUBLIC

STARÉ MĚSTO (OLD TOWN)

Getting lost among the narrow roads and cobblestone alleys of Staré Město is probably the best way to appreciate the 1000-year-old neighborhood's charm.

CHARLES BRIDGE. Thronged with tourists and the hawkers who feed on them, the Charles Bridge (Karlův Most) is Prague's most recognizable landmark. The defense towers on each side offer splendid views. Five stars and a cross mark the spot where, according to legend, St. Jan Nepomucký was tossed over the side of the bridge for guarding the queen's extramarital secrets from a suspicious King Wenceslas IV in the 14th century. *(Metro A: Malostranská or Staroměstská.)*

OLD TOWN SQUARE. Staroměstské náměstí (Old Town Square) is the heart of Staré Město, surrounded by eight magnificent towers. *(Metro A: Staroměstská; Metro A or B: Můstek.)* The **Staroměstské Radnice** (Old Town Hall) has been missing a piece of its front facade since the Nazis partially demolished it in the final days of WWII. Crowds gather on the hour to watch the **astronomical clock** chime as the skeletal Death empties his hourglass and a procession of apostles marches by. *(Open M 11am-6pm, Tu-Su 9am-7pm. Clock tower open M-F 2-7pm, Sa-Su 10am-7pm; enter through 3rd fl. Exhibition hall 20Kč, students 10Kč. Clock tower 50/40Kč.)* The spires of **Týn Church** (Chrám Matka Boží před Týnem) rise above a mass of medieval homes. Buried inside is famous astronomer Tycho Brahe, whose overindulgence at Emperor Rudolf's lavish dinner party in 1601 may have cost him his life. Since it was deemed improper to leave the table unless the emperor himself did so, Tycho had to remain in his chair until his bladder burst. He died 11 days later, though scholars believe mercury poisoning may have been the culprit. *(Open M-F 9am-noon and 1-2pm. Mass W-F 6pm, Sa 8am, Su 11am and 9pm. Free.)* The bronze statue of 15th-century theologian **Jan Hus,** the country's most famous martyr, stands in the middle of the square. The nearby **Golz-Kinský Palace** is the finest of Prague's Rococo buildings. *(Open Tu-F 10am-6pm; closes early in summer for daily concerts.)* While smaller and less impressive than its counterpart on the other side of the Vltava, **St. Nicholas's Cathedral** has a stunning crystal chandelier and beautiful ceiling frescoes. *(Next to the Kafka Museum. Open daily 8am-5pm. Mass Su 10:30am. Free.)*

NOVÉ MĚSTO (NEW TOWN)

Established in 1348 by Charles IV, Nové Město has become the commercial center of Prague, complete with American chain stores. The Franciscan Gardens offer visitors an oasis of natural calm amid the bustle of business.

WENCESLAS SQUARE. More a boulevard than a square, Václavské náměstí (Wenceslas Square) owes its name to the equestrian statue of Czech ruler and patron **St. Wenceslas** (Václav) that stands in front of the National Museum. Wenceslas has presided over a century of turmoil and triumph, witnessing five momentous events from his pedestal: the 1918 declaration of the new Czechoslovak state, the 1939 invasion by Hitler's troops, the 1968 arrival of Soviet tanks, the 1969 immolation of Jan Palach in protest of the Soviet invasion, and the 1989 Velvet Revolution. The square stretches from the statue past department stores, thumping discos, posh hotels, and glitzy casinos. **Radio Free Europe,** which provides global news updates and advocates peace, has been headquartered in a glass building behind the National Museum since 1995. *(Metro A or C: Muzeum.)*

FRANCISCAN GARDEN AND VELVET REVOLUTION MEMORIAL. Monks somehow manage to preserve this serene **rose garden** in the heart of Prague's commercial district. *(Metro A or B: Můstek. Enter through the arch to the left of Jungmannova and Národní, behind the statue. Open daily mid-Apr. to mid-Sept. 7am-10pm; mid-Sept. to mid-Oct. 7am-8pm; mid-Oct. to mid-Apr. 8am-7pm. Free.)* Down the street on Národní, a **plaque**

under the arcades and across from the Black Theatre memorializes the hundreds of citizens beaten by police on November 17, 1989. A subsequent wave of protests led to the collapse of communism in Czechoslovakia during the Velvet Revolution.

DANCING HOUSE. American architect Frank Gehry (of Spain's Guggenheim-Bilbao fame) built the gently swaying Dancing House (Tančící dům) at the corner of Resslova and Rašínovo nábřeží. Since its 1996 unveiling, it has been called an eyesore by some and a shining example of postmodern design by others. *(Metro B: Karlovo nám. As you walk down Resslova toward the river, the building is on the left.)*

JOSEFOV

Josefov, Central Europe's oldest Jewish settlement, lies north of Staroměstské nám., along Maiselova. In 1180, Prague's citizens built a 4m wall around the area. The closed neighborhood bred exotic tales, many of which centered around Rabbi Loew ben Bezalel (1512-1609) and his legendary *golem*—a mud creature that supposedly came to life to protect Prague's Jews. The city's Jews remained clustered in Josefov until WWII, when the Nazis sent the residents to death camps. Ironically, Hitler's wish to create a "museum of an extinct race" sparked the preservation of Josefov's cemetery and synagogues. Though only a fraction of its former size, Prague still has an active Jewish community.

SYNAGOGUES. The **Maisel Synagogue** (Maiselova synagoga) displays artifacts from the Jewish Museum's collections, only returned to the community in 1994. *(On Maiselova, between Široká and Jáchymova.)* Turn left on Široká to reach the **Pinkas Synagogue** (Pinkasova). Drawings by children interred at the Terezín camp are upstairs. Some 80,000 names line the walls downstairs, a sobering requiem for Czech Jews persecuted in the Holocaust. Backtrack along Široká and go left on Maiselova for the oldest operating synagogue in Europe, the 700-year-old **Old-New Synagogue** (Staronová), still the religious center of Prague's Jewish community. Up Široká at Dušní, the **Spanish Synagogue** (Španělská) has an ornate Moorish interior modeled after Granada's Alhambra. *(Metro A: Staroměstská. Men must cover their heads; kippot 5Kč. Synagogues open Apr.-Oct. Su-F 9am-6pm; Nov.-Mar. Su-F 9am-4:30pm. Closed Jewish holidays. Admission to all 6 of the area's synagogues except Staronová 300Kč, students 200Kč. Staronová 200/140Kč.)*

OLD JEWISH CEMETERY. The Old Jewish Cemetery (Starý židovský hřbitov) is Josefov's most visited

BONE-CHILLING CHAPEL

In and around Prague, you'll find churches made of stone, brick, iron, glass—and one of bones. Kutná Hora, a small, picturesque village 1hr. from Prague, is infamous for its ossuary, a chapel filled with artistic and religious creations made entirely from parts of human skeletons. The village earned its fame from silver mining in the 14th century; its morbid side only came out when its graveyard gained a reputation as a sacred place to bury plague victims. Since the cemetery was overflowing with corpses, the Cistercian Order built a chapel to house the extra remains. In a fit of creativity (or possibly insanity), one monk began designing flowers from pelvises and crania. He never finished the ossuary, but the artist František Rint eventually completed the project in 1870, decorating the chapel from floor to ceiling with the bones of over 40,000 people.

Trains run from Hlavní nádraží in Prague to Kutná Hora (1½hr., 1 per hr., round-trip 196Kč). The ossuary is a 1km walk from the station. Turn right out of the station, then take a left, and go left again on the highway. Continue for 500m and go right at the church; the ossuary is at the end of the road. Open daily Apr.-Sept. 8am-6pm; Oct. 9am-noon and 1-5pm; Nov.-Mar. 9am-noon and 1-4pm. 40Kč, students 20Kč. Cameras 30Kč, video cameras 60Kč.

sight. Between the 14th and 18th centuries, 20,000 graves were laid in 12 layers. The striking clusters of tombstones visible today were formed as older stones rose from the lower layers. Rabbi Loew is buried by the wall opposite the entrance. *(At the corner of Široká and Žatecká. Open Apr.-Oct. Su-F 9am-6pm; Nov.-Mar. Su-F 9am-4:30pm. Closed Jewish holidays.)*

MALÁ STRANA

A seedy hangout for criminals and counter-revolutionaries for nearly a century, the cobblestone streets of Malá Strana have become prized real estate. In **Malostranské Náměstí,** the towering dome of the Baroque **St. Nicholas's Cathedral** (Chrám sv. Mikuláše) is one of Prague's most prominent landmarks. Mozart played the organ here when he visited Prague, and the cathedral now hosts nightly classical music concerts. *(Metro A: Malostranská. Follow Letenská to Malostranské nám. Open daily 9am-4:30pm. 50Kč, students 25Kč.)* Along Letenská, a wooden gate opens into the **Wallenstein Garden** (Valdštejnská zahrada). With a beautifully tended stretch of green and a bronze Venus fountain, this is one of the city's best-kept secrets. *(Letenská 10. Open Apr.-Oct. daily 10am-6pm. Free.)* The **Church of Our Lady Victorious** (Kostel Panna Marie Vítězné) is known for its famous wax statue of the **Infant Jesus of Prague,** said to bestow miracles on the faithful. *(Follow Letecká through Malostranské nám. and continue onto Karmelitská. Church open M-Sa 8:30am-6pm, Su 9:30am-8pm. Museum open M-Sa 9:40am-5:30pm, Su 1-6pm. Free.)* **Petřín Gardens and View Tower,** on the hill beside Malá Strana, provides a tranquil retreat with spectacular views. Climb the steep, serene footpath, or take the funicular from just above the intersection of Vítězná and Újezd. *(Look for Lanovka Dráha signs. Funicular 4-6 per hr., 9am-11:20pm, 20Kč. Tower open May-Aug. daily 10am-10pm.)*

PRAGUE CASTLE (PRAŽSKÝ HRAD)

Prague Castle, one of the biggest castles in the world, has been the seat of Czech government for over 1000 years. The first Bohemian royal family established their residence here in the 9th century; since then, the castle has housed Holy Roman Emperors, the Communist Czechoslovak government, and now the Czech Republic's president. The main entrance is at the end of the lush **Royal Gardens** (Královská zahrada), where the Singing Fountain spouts its watery, harp-like tune in front of the **Royal Summer Palace.** *(From Metro A: Malostranská, take trams #22 or 23 to Pražský Hrad and go down U Prašného Mostu. Open daily Apr.-Oct. 9am-5pm; Nov.-Mar. 9am-4pm. Royal Gardens open Apr.-Sept. 10am-6pm. Buy tickets opposite St. Vitus's Cathedral inside the castle walls. Tickets valid for 2 days at Royal Crypt, Cathedral and Powder Tower, Old Royal Palace, and the Basilica. 350Kč, students 175Kč.)*

ST. VITUS'S CATHEDRAL. Inside the castle walls stands the beautiful Gothic St. Vitus's Cathedral (Katedrála sv. Víta), which was not completed until 1929, 600 years after construction began. To the right of the high altar stands the silver **Tomb of St. Jan Nepomucký.** In the main church, the walls of **St. Wenceslas's Chapel** (Svatováclavská kaple) are lined with a painting cycle depicting the legend of Wenceslas. Climb the 287 steps of the **Great South Tower** for an excellent view, or descend underground to the **Royal Crypt,** which holds the tomb of Charles IV.

OLD ROYAL PALACE. The Old Royal Palace (Starý Královský Palác) is to the right of the cathedral, behind the Old Provost's House and the statue of St. George. The lengthy **Vladislav Hall** once hosted jousting competitions. Upstairs is the **Chancellery of Bohemia,** where the Second Defenestration of Prague took place in 1618. A Protestant assembly found two Catholic governors guilty of religious persecution and threw them out the window. They landed in a pile of manure and survived, but the event contributed to the beginning of the Thirty Years' War.

ST. GEORGE'S BASILICA AND ENVIRONS. Across the courtyard from the Old Royal Palace stands St. George's Basilica (Bazilika sv. Jiří), where the skeleton of St. Ludmila is on display. The St. Agnes convent next door houses the **National Gallery of Bohemian Art,** which displays pieces ranging from Gothic to Baroque. *(Open Tu-Su 10am-6pm. 100Kč, students 50Kč.)* To the right of the Basilica, follow Jiřská halfway down and take a right on tiny **Golden Lane** (Zlatá ulička). Alchemists once worked here attempting to create gold, and Kafka later lived at #22.

OUTER PRAGUE

In the beautiful neighborhood of Troja, French architect J. B. Mathey's **château** overlooks the Vltava. The building has a terraced garden, oval staircase, and magnificent collection of 19th-century Czech artwork. *(From Metro C: Nádraží Holešovice, take bus #112 to Zoologická Zahrada. Open Apr.-Oct. Tu-Su 10am-6pm; Nov.-Mar. Sa-Su 10am-5pm. 100Kč, students 50Kč.)* **Břevnov Monastery,** the oldest monastery in Bohemia, was founded in AD 993 by King Boleslav II and St. Adalbert, who were guided by a divine dream to build a monastery atop a bubbling stream. To the right of **St. Margaret's Church** (Bazilika sv. Markéty), the stream leads to a pond. *(From Metro A: Malostranská, take tram #22 uphill to Břevnovský klášter. Church open only for mass, M-Sa 7am and 6pm, Su 7:30, 9am, 6pm. Tours Sa-Su 10am, 2, 4pm. 50Kč, students 30Kč.)* The **Prague Market** (Pražskátrznice) has acres of stalls selling all kinds of wares. *(Take tram #3 or 14 from nám. Republiky to Vozovna Kobylisy and get off at Pražskátrznice. Open M-F 7am-5pm, Sa 7am-2pm.)* Giant bronze babies, fixed in mid-crawl, climb up and down the **Prague Radio/TV Tower,** creating one of Europe's most bizarre outdoor art installations. Schedule a nighttime visit, when the babies are silhouetted against the brightly lit tower. *(Metro A: Jiřího z Poděbrad. Turn right on Slavikova, then right on Ondřičkova. The tower is in the park at the intersection with ul. Fibichova.)*

MUSEUMS

MUCHA MUSEUM. The museum is devoted to the work of Alfons Mucha, the Czech Republic's most celebrated artist. Mucha, the pioneer of the Art Nouveau movement, gained fame for his poster series of "la divine" Sarah Bernhardt. *(Panská 7. Metro A or B: Můstek. Walk up Václavské nám. toward the St. Wenceslas statue. Go left on Jindřišská and left again on Panská. Open daily 10am-6pm. 140Kč, students 70Kč.)*

FRANZ KAFKA MUSEUM. This fantastic, newly opened multimedia exhibit of Kafka memorabilia uses photographs and original scribbles to bring visitors back to 19th-century Prague, as experienced by the renowned author. *(Cihelná 2. Metro A: Staroměstská. Head west on Kaprova, cross Mánesýv bridge, and turn left on Klarov, which becomes Cihelná. www.kafkamuseum.cz. Open daily 10am-6pm. 120Kč, students 60Kč.)*

NATIONAL GALLERY. The collection of the National Gallery (Národní Galerie) is spread among nine locations throughout Prague; the notable Šternberg Palace and Klášter sv. Jiří are in **Prague Castle** (p. 248). The **Trade Fair Palace and the Gallery of Modern Art** (Veletržní palác a Galerie moderního umwní) exhibit an impressive collection of 20th-century Czech and European art. *(Dukelských hrdinů 47. Metro C: Nádraží Holešovice. All locations open Tu-Su 10am-6pm. 150Kč, students 70Kč.)*

MUSEUM OF COMMUNISM. This gallery is committed to exposing the flaws of the Communist system that oppressed the Czech people from 1948 to 1989. A model factory and interrogation office send visitors behind the Iron Curtain. *(Na Příkopě 10. Metro A: Můstek. Open daily 8am-9pm. 170Kč, students 150Kč.)*

MUSEUM OF MEDIEVAL TORTURE INSTRUMENTS. The collection and highly detailed explanations are sure to nauseate. In the same building, the **Exhibition of Spiders and Scorpions** shows live venomous creatures in their natural habitats.

(Mostécka 21. Metro A: Malostranská. Follow Letenská from the Metro and turn left. Open daily 10am-10pm. Torture museum 140Kč. Spiders exhibition 100Kč, children 80Kč.)

SEX MACHINES MUSEUM. Three prurient floors house over 200 mechanical sexual appliances, ranging from antique lingerie to fetishist whips, chains, and leather. Erotic cinema plays vintage Spanish pornographic films. This museum is a favorite among groups of giggling teenagers. *(Melantrichova 18. Metro A: Staroměstská. www.sexmachinesmuseum.com. Open daily 10am-11pm. Students 150Kč.)*

ENTERTAINMENT

To find info on Prague's concerts and performances, consult *Threshold, Do města-Downtown, The Pill* (all free at many cafes and restaurants), or *The Prague Post.* Most performances start at 7pm and offer standby tickets 30min. before curtain. Between mid-May and early June, the **Prague Spring Festival** draws musicians from around the world. June brings all things avant-garde with the **Prague Fringe Festival** (☎224 935 183; www.praguefringe.com), featuring dancers, comedians, performance artists, and—everyone's favorite—mimes. For tickets to the city's shows, try **Bohemia Ticket International,** Malé nám. 13, next to Čedok. (☎224 227 832; www.ticketsbti.cz. Open M-F 9am-5pm, Sa 9am-1pm.)

The majority of Prague's theaters close in July and August, but the selection is extensive during the rest of the year. The **National Theater** (Národní divadlo), Národní 2/4, stages drama, opera, and ballet. (☎224 901 487; www.narodni-divadlo.cz. Metro B: Národní třída. Box office open Sept.-June daily 10am-8pm and 45min. before performances. Tickets 30-1000Kč.) Every performance at the **Image Theater,** Pařížská 4, is silent, conveying the message through dance, pantomime, and creative use of black light. (☎222 314 448; www.blacktheatreprague.cz. Performances daily 8pm. Box office open daily 9am-8pm.) The **Marionette Theater** (Říše loutek), Žatecká 1, stages a hilarious version of *Don Giovanni,* now in its 15th season. (☎224 819 322. Metro A: Staroměstská. Performances June-July M-Tu and Th-Su 8pm. Box office open daily 10am-8pm. 490-600Kč, students 390-590Kč.)

TIP **HIGH CULTURE, LOW BUDGET.** Prague's state-run theaters will often hold a group of seats in the higher balconies until the day of the performance before selling them off at reduced prices. By visiting your venue of choice the morning of a performance, you can often score tickets for as little as 50Kč.

NIGHTLIFE

With some of the world's best beer on tap, it's no surprise that pubs and beer halls are Prague's most popular nighttime hangouts. Tourists have overrun the city center, so authentic pub experiences are largely restricted to the suburbs and outlying Metro stops. Although clubs abound, Prague is not a prime dancing town—locals prefer the many jazz and rock hangouts scattered throughout the city.

BARS

Vinárna U Sudu, Vodičkova 10 (☎222 237 207). Metro A or B: Můstek. Cross Václavské nám. to Vodičkova and follow the curve left. An infinite labyrinth of cavernous cellars. Red wine 125Kč per 1L. Open M-Th 8am-3am, F-Sa 8am-4am, Su 8am-2am. MC/V.

Duende, Karolíny Světlé 30 (☎775 186 077), near the Charles Bridge. A diverse, laid-back crowd packs in even on those rare nights when Staroměstské nám. is dead. Beer from 19Kč. Shots 75Kč. Open daily 11am-1am.

Vinárna Vinečko, Lodynská 135/2 (☎222 511 035). Metro A: Nám. Miru. Head west on Rumunská and turn left on Lodynská. A wine bar in the heart of the Vinohrady district brimming with thirsty locals and expats. Wine 26-34Kč per 0.2L, 64-92Kč per bottle. Open M-F 11am-midnight, Sa-Su 2pm-midnight. MC/V.

Cafe Marquis de Sade, Templova 5. Metro B: nám. Republiky. Roomy microbrewery and bar decorated in red velvet. Beer from 35Kč. Shots 80Kč. Open daily 2pm-2am.

Jo's Bar and Garáž, Malostranské nám. 7. Metro A: Malostranská. For those homesick for Anybar, USA. Foosball, darts, card games, and a dance floor downstairs. American bar food—nachos, burgers, burritos, and steaks (60-295Kč). Beer from 31Kč. Long Island Iced Tea 115Kč. Open M-Th 11am-8pm, Sa-Su 11am-2am. AmEx/MC/V.

CLUBS AND DISCOS

Karlovy Lázně, Novotného lávka 1, next to the Charles Bridge. Popularly known as "Five Floors," this tourist magnet boasts 5 levels of themed dance floors. Cover 120Kč, 50Kč before 10pm and after 4am. Open daily 9pm-5am.

Palác Akropolis, Kubelíkova 27 (☎296 330 911). Metro A: Jiřího z Poděbrad. Head down Slavíkova and turn right onto Kubelíkova. 2 music rooms with separate DJs; live Czech bands several times a week. Beer from 25Kč. Open daily 8pm-5am.

Cross Club, Plynámi 23 (www.crossclub.cz). Metro C: Nádraží Holešovice. Plastered with mechanical oddities, including cogs, springs, and black lights, the rooms in this underground maze are mesmerizing. Beer from 28Kč. Open Su-Th 2pm-late, F-Sa 4pm-late.

Roxy, Dlouhá 33. Metro B: nám. Republiky. Same building as the Travellers' Hostel (p. 242). Artsy studio and club with experimental DJs and theme nights. Beer 35Kč. Cover Tu and Th-Sa 100-350Kč. Open daily 10pm-late.

U Malého Glena II, Karmelitská 23 (☎257 531 717; www.malyglen.cz), near Prague Castle. Basement bar with nightly live music including blues, salsa, and jazz. Call ahead for weekend tables. Beer 35Kč. Entrees 95-130Kč. Shows at 9:30pm, F-Sa 10pm-1:30am. Cover 100-150Kč. Open daily 8pm-2am. AmEx/MC/V.

GLBT NIGHTLIFE

All of the places below distribute *Amigo* (90Kč; www.amigo.cz), the most thorough English-language guide to gay life in the Czech Republic. Check www.praguegayguide.net or www.praguesaints.cz for a list of attractions and resources.

The Saints, Polksá 32 (☎332 250 326; www.praguesaints.cz). Metro A: Jiřího z Poděbrad. This small, comfy club welcomes GLBT visitors and organizes the GLBT community. Mixed crowd and free wireless Internet. Beer from 22Kč. Open daily 7pm-4am.

Friends, Bartolomejská 11 (☎224 236 272; www.friends-prague.cz). Metro B: Národní třída. From the station, turn right, head down Na Perštýně, and take a left on Bartolomejská. Rotating schedule features music videos, house, parties, and theme nights. Women and straight customers welcome. Beer from 30Kč. Open daily 6pm-5am.

Tingl Tangl, Karolíny Světlé 12 (☎777 322 121; www.tingltangl.cz). Metro B: Národní třída. Draws a diverse crowd for its transvestite cabarets. Women welcome. Entrees (110-165Kč) served 11am-11pm. Cover 150Kč. Open W 9:30pm-5am, F-Sa 9pm-5am.

DAYTRIPS FROM PRAGUE

TEREZÍN (THERESIENSTADT). In 1941, when the Nazis opened a concentration camp at Terezín, their propaganda films touted the area as a resort. In reality, over 30,000 Jews died there, while another 85,000 were transported to camps farther east. The **Ghetto Museum,** left of the bus stop, places Terezín in the wider context of WWII. Across the river, the **Small Fortress** was used as a Gestapo prison. *(Bus from*

Prague's Florenc station to the Terezín LT stop. 1hr., 70Kč. Museum and barracks open daily Apr.-Oct. 9am-6pm; Nov.-Mar. 9am-5:30pm. Fortress open daily Apr.-Sept. 8am-6pm; Oct.-Mar. 8am-4:30pm. Tour included in admission price for groups larger than 10; reserve ahead. Museum, barracks, and fortress 180Kč, students 140Kč.) Outside the walls lie the **cemetery** and **crematorium.** Men should cover their heads before entering. *(Open Su-F Apr.-Sept. 10am-5pm; Nov.-Mar. 10am-4pm. Free.)* Since WWII, Terezín has been repopulated to about half its former size. Families live in the former barracks, and supermarkets occupy former Nazi offices. The **tourist office,** Nám. ČSA 179, is located near the bus stop. *(☎416 782 616; www.terezin.cz. Open M-Th 8am-5pm, F 8am-1:30pm, Su 9am-3pm.)*

CZECH REPUBLIC

KARLŠTEJN. Charles IV built this **castle** in the 14th century as a depository for the royal treasures. To reach Karlštejn, turn right from the train station and go left over the bridge; turn right and walk through the village for 25min. *(Train from Prague's Hlavní station. 55min., 2 per hr., 46Kč. www.hradkarlstejn.cz. Open Tu-Su July-Aug. 9am-6pm; May-June and Sept. 9am-noon and 12:30-5pm; Apr. and Oct. 9am-noon and 1-4pm; Nov.-Mar. 9am-3pm. 220Kč, students 120Kč.)* The **Chapel of the Holy Cross** is inlaid with precious stones and 132 apocalyptic paintings by medieval artist Master Theodorik. *(☎02 74 00 81 54; reservace@stc.npu.cz. Open June-Oct. Tu-Su 9am-5pm. Tours by reservation only. Reservation fee 30Kč. Chapel and fortress tour 300Kč, students 100Kč.)*

ČESKÝ RÁJ NATIONAL PRESERVE. The sandstone pillars and gorges of **Prachovské skály** (Prachovské rocks) offer climbs and hikes with stunning views. Highlights include the **Pelíšek** rock pond and the ruins of the 14th-century **Pařez** castle. A network of **trails** cross the 588 acres of the park; green, blue, and yellow signs guide hikers to sights, while triangles indicate scenic vistas. Red signs mark the "Golden Trail," which connects Prachovské skály to **Hrubá Skála** (Rough Rock), a rock town surrounding a castle. From the castle, the trail leads up to the remains of **Valdštejnský Hrad** (Wallenstein Castle). The red and blue trails are open to cyclists, but only the blue trail is suited for biking. *(Buses run from Prague's Florenc station to Jičín. 1½hr., 8 per day, 86Kč. From there, buses go to Prachovské skály and other spots in Český Ráj. Buses can be unpredictable; you can also walk along a 6km trail beginning at Motel Rumcajs, Konwva 331.)*

WEST AND SOUTH BOHEMIA

West Bohemia overflows with curative springs; over the centuries, emperors and intellectuals alike have soaked in the waters of Karlovy Vary (also known as Carlsbad). Visitors seeking good beer head to the Pilsner Urquell brewery in Plzeň or the Budvar brewery in České Budějovice. South Bohemia is more rustic than West Bohemia, with a landscape marked by brooks, forests, and ruins.

KARLOVY VARY ☎353

The hot springs and enormous spas of Karlovy Vary (pop. 55,000) have drawn legendary Europeans including J. S. Bach, Sigmund Freud, Karl Marx, and Peter the Great. Today, the most frequent visitors are elderly Germans and Russians who sip from jugs filled with the springs' therapeutic waters. Movie stars and fans also journey to the town for its International Film Festival each July.

TRANSPORTATION AND PRACTICAL INFORMATION. Buses, much more convenient than trains, run from Dolní nádraží, on Západní (☎505 353), to Plzeň (1¾hr., 10 per day, 92Kč) and Prague (2¼hr., 20 per day, 120Kč). To reach the town center from the station, turn left and take the left fork of the pedestrian underpass toward Lázně. Turn right at the next fork, follow the sign for the supermarket, and go up the stairs to reach T. G. Masaryka, which runs parallel to the main thoroughfare, Dr. Davida Bechera. **Centrum Taxi,** Zeyerova 9 (☎223 000), offers 24hr. service. **Infocentrum,** Lázeňská 1, next to the Mill Colonnade, has free Internet access, sells maps (up to 55Kč) and theater tickets (250-500Kč), and books rooms from 450Kč. (☎224 097; www.karlovyvary.cz. Open Jan.-Oct. M-F 9am-7pm, Sa-Su 10am-6pm; Nov.-Dec. M-F 9am-5pm, Sa-Su 10am-5pm.) Another branch is in the bus station (☎232 838). The **post office,** T. G. Masaryka 1, has **Western Union** and **Poste Restante.** (Open M-F 7:30am-7pm, Sa 8am-1pm, Su 8am-noon.) **Postal Code:** 36001.

ACCOMMODATIONS AND FOOD. The name may be scary, but **Titty Twister Hostel & Music Bar ❷,** Moravská 4442, offers apartment-like rooms with spacious bathrooms and kitchens. Guests get a 10% discount at the bar. Take bus #2, 8, 11, or 13 four stops to Na Vyhlídce. Walk straight on Na Vyhlídce, veer right at the fork past the market, go downhill, then continue straight ahead uphill on Moravská. (☎239 071; www.hosteltt.cz. Breakfast 80Kč. 4- to 6-bed dorms 359Kč; doubles 459Kč.) Next to the post office, **Pension Romania ❹,** Zahradní 49, has rooms overlooking the Teplá River. (☎222 822. Breakfast included. Singles 900Kč, students 715Kč; doubles 1480-1630Kč; triples 1900Kč. Oct.-Mar. reduced rates.) Karlovy Vary is known for its sweet *oplatky* (spa wafers; from 5Kč). In a town geared mainly to the old and the monied, **E&T Bar ❷,** Zeyerova 3, is a haven of quality Czech food at reasonable prices, with pleasant terrace seating. (☎226 022. Salads and entrees 60-210Kč. Open M-Sa 9am-2am, Su 10am-2am.) Travelers looking for variety can spice up their meal at **Mañana ❷,** Na Vyhlídce 52, next to the bus stop, which serves heaping plates of Mexican cuisine in a welcoming atmosphere. (☎226 407. Salads and entrees 70-220Kč. Open daily 10am-10pm. MC/V.) **Albert supermarket,** Horova 1, is in the building marked "Městská tržnice," behind the bus station. (Open M-F 6am-7pm, Sa 7am-5pm, Su 9am-8pm. MC/V.)

SIGHTS AND ENTERTAINMENT. The **spa district,** with springs, baths, and colonnades, starts at **Elizabeth Bath 5** (Alžbětiny Lázně 5), Smetanovy Sady 1, across from the post office. The spa offers water-based treatments including thermal baths (355Kč), massages (360-600Kč), and lymph drainage (180Kč). Reserve a few days ahead. (☎222 536; www.spa5.cz. Pool and sauna open M-F 7:30am-6pm, Sa-Su 8:30am-6pm. Treatments M-F 7am-3pm. Pool 90Kč. MC/V.) Follow the Teplá River to **Bath 3,** Mlýnské nábř 5, which offers massages for 550Kč. (☎225 641. Treatments daily 7-11:30am and noon-3pm. Pool 100Kč.) Next door, the **Mill Colonnade** (Mlýnská kolonáda) hosts free concerts in the summer. Farther down is **Zawojski House,** Tržiště 9, an ornate Art Nouveau building that now houses Živnostenská Banka. Two doors down, **Sprudel Spring** (Vřídlo pramen), inside **Sprudel Colonnade** (Vřídelní kolonáda), is Karlovy Vary's hottest and highest-shooting spring, spouting 30L of water each second. (Open daily 6am-7pm.)

Follow Stará Louka to find signs for the **funicular,** which takes passengers up 127m to the **Diana Observatory** and its panoramic view of the city. (Funicular every 15min. June-Sept. 9am-7pm; Apr.-May and Oct. 9am-6pm; Feb.-Mar. and Nov.-Dec. 9am-4pm. Tower open daily 9am-7pm. Funicular 36Kč, round-trip 60Kč. Tower 10Kč.) *Promenáda*, a monthly booklet with schedules and other info, is available for free at kiosks around town. It includes details on the popular **International Film Festival,** which screens independent films in early July. **Rotes Berlin,** Jaltská 7, off Dr. Davida Bechera, attracts Karlovy Vary's youth with cheap beer and live music. (Beer from 20Kč. Open M-F noon-midnight, Sa-Su 3pm-2am.)

DAYTRIP FROM KARLOVY VARY: PLZEŇ. Recent attempts to clean up Plzeň (pop. 175,000) have left its buildings and gardens looking fresh. But it's the world-famous beer, not the architecture, that lures so many visitors. A beer-lover's perfect day begins at legendary **Pilsner Urquell Brewery** (Měšťanský Pivovar Plzeňský Prazdroj), where knowledgeable guides lead groups to the cellars for samples. The on-site beerhouse **Na Spilce,** the largest pub in the Czech Republic, pours Pilsner for 25Kč per pint. The entrance to the complex is across the Radbuza River from Staré Město, where Pražská becomes Prazdroje u. Cross the street and take the overpass. (☎377 062 888. Brewery open daily 8am-4pm. 70min. tours daily June-Aug. 12:30, 2pm; Sept.-May 12:30pm. Tours 120Kč, students 60Kč. Na Spilce open M-Th and Sa 11am-10pm, F 11am-11pm, Su 11am-9pm.) Plzeň is also home to the world's third-largest **synagogue,** built in the Neoclassical style but with onion domes. Closed from 1973 to 1988, the synagogue is now a museum; the marble halls house photography exhibits. From the southern end of nám. Republiky, go down Prešovská to Sady Pětatřicátníků and turn left; the synagogue is on the right. (Open Su-F Apr.-Sept. 10am-6pm; Oct. 10am-5pm; Nov. 10am-4pm. 45Kč, students 30Kč.) **Restaurace Bulvár ❷,** ul. B. Smetany 10, just off the main square on a road perpendicular to nám. Republiky, offers various delights including fresh salads and luscious desserts. (☎777 223 067. Salads and entrees 79-290Kč. Open M-Th 8:30am-midnight, F 8:30am-1am, Sa 10am-1am, Su 11am-8pm. Cash only.)

Buses leave from Husova 58 for Karlovy Vary (1¾hr., 16 per day, 70-80Kč) and Prague (2½hr., 16 per day, 65-80Kč). To reach nám. Republiky, the main square, turn left on Husova, which becomes Smetanovy Sady, and turn left on Bedřicha Smetany, or take tram #2 (12Kč). The **tourist office,** nám. Republiky 41, books rooms (from 190Kč), sells phone cards (150-350Kč), and offers free maps. (☎378 035 330; www.icpilsen.cz. Open Apr.-Sept. daily 9am-7pm; Oct.-Mar. M-F 10am-5pm, Sa-Su 10am-3:30pm.) **Postal Code:** 30101.

ČESKÉ BUDĚJOVICE ☎38

České Budějovice (pop. 100,000), also known as Budweis, inspired the name for Budweiser, but the pale American brew bears little resemblance to the thoroughly enjoyable, malty local Budvar. Rivalry lingers between Anheuser-Busch and the **Budvar Brewery,** Karoliny Světlé 4. From the center, take bus #2 toward Borek, Točna. (Tours for groups of 8+ by reservation M-F 9am-6pm, Sa 9am-5pm, Su 9am-4pm. 100Kč, students 50Kč.) **Staré Město** (Old Town) centers on the main square, **Náměstí Přemysla Otakara II,** which is surrounded by colorful Renaissance and Baroque buildings. **Jihočeskě Motocylově Museum,** Piaristická nám., houses the antique private collection of a motorcycle fanatic. (40Kč, students 20Kč.) To reach **AT Penzion ❸,** Dukelská 15, from Nám. Otakara II, turn right on Dr. Stejskala. At the first intersection, turn left and follow Široká, veering right on Dukelská; AT Penzion is on the left. The rooms have private bath, TV, and fridge. (☎7312 529. Breakfast 50Kč. Reception 24hr. Singles 550Kč; doubles 850Kč.) **Fresh Restaurant ❷,** Piaristická nám. 21, is a chic pizzeria and salad bar located in an idyllic courtyard next to the motorcycle museum. (☎721 672 341. Salads 45-80Kč. Pizza 59-170Kč. Open daily 9am-9pm.) At the **Motorcycles Legend Pub,** Radniční 9, visitors can join the locals in their intense love of the iron horse. (Beer 27Kč. Open M-Sa 5pm-3am, Su 5pm-midnight.)

Trains (☎7854 361) leave from Nádražní 12, opposite the bus station, for: Brno (4½hr., 5 per day, 168-274Kč); Český Krumlov (50min., 8 per day, 46Kč); Plzeň (2hr., 10 per day, 100-162Kč); Prague (2½hr., 12 per day, 204Kč). **Buses** (☎386 354 444) run to Brno (4½hr., 6 per day, 184Kč), Český Krumlov (50min., 25 per day, 28Kč), and Prague (2½hr., 10 per day, 120-144Kč). To reach the town center from the train station, turn right on Nádražní, take a left at the first crosswalk, and follow Lannova třída, which becomes Kanovnická. The **tourist office** is at Nám. Otakara II 2. (☎6801 413; www.c-budejovice.cz. Open M-F 9am-6pm, Sa 9am-5pm, Su 9am-noon and 12:30-4pm.) **Postal Code:** 37001.

ČESKÝ KRUMLOV

This once-hidden gem of the Czech Republic has been discovered—some might say besieged—by tourists escaping Prague's overcrowded attractions. Yet Český Krumlov won't disappoint visitors who wander the medieval streets, raft down the meandering Vltava, and explore the enormous castle that looms over the city.

TRANSPORTATION AND PRACTICAL INFORMATION. **Buses** (☎420 337 3415) run from Kaplická 439 to České Budějovice (30min., M-F 37 per day, Sa-Su 14 per day; 28Kč) and Prague (3hr., M-F 9 per day, Sa-Su 6 per day; 130-145Kč). To get to the main square, **Náměstí Svornosti,** take the path from the back of the terminal, to the right of stops #20-25. Go downhill at Kaplická, cross the highway, and head to Horní, to the square. The **tourist office,** Nám. Svornosti 2, books rooms (from 300Kč) and provides info for visitors. (☎380 704 622; www.ckrumlov.cz/infocentrum. Open Apr.-Oct. M-Sa 9am-1pm and 2-7pm.) **Postal Code:** 38101.

ACCOMMODATIONS AND FOOD. The laid-back **Krumlov House ❶,** Rooseveltova 68, is run by an American expat couple. To get there from the bus station, walk out of the square on Horní. Turn left on Rooseveltova after the lights, then follow the signs. (☎380 711 935; www.krumlovhostel.com. Dorms 300Kč; doubles 700Kč; suites 800Kč.) **Hostel 99 ❷,** Věžní 99, has a free keg every Wednesday night, endearing itself to the fun-loving, rowdy crowd. From Nám. Svornosti, take Radniční, which becomes Latrán; at the red-and-yellow gate turn right on Věžní. (☎380 712 812; www.hostel99.com. Dorms 300-390Kč; doubles 700Kč.) Tiny **Hostel Merlin ❶,** Kájovská 59, on the right before the bridge, has cheerful yellow rooms but no space for partying. (☎606 256 145; www.hostelmerlin.com. Free Internet. Reception 11am-8pm. 5-bed dorms 250Kč; doubles 500Kč; triples 750Kč.) Just off Radniční, **Laibon ❶,** Parkán 105, serves excellent vegetarian cuisine on its terrace. (Entrees 30-150Kč. Open daily 11am-11pm. Cash only.) Next door, the riverfront **U dwau Maryi ❷,** Parkán 104, specializes in medieval fare, served by an English-speaking waitstaff in period costume. (Entrees 54-220Kč. Open Apr.-Oct. daily 11am-11pm. Cash only.) Get groceries at **Jednota Potraviny,** Latrán 55. (Open M-F 7am-6pm, Sa 7am-noon, Su 7am-3pm.)

SIGHTS AND NIGHTLIFE. The majestic **Zamek** (Castle) has been home to a succession of Bohemian and Bavarian nobles since the 1200s. Follow Radniční across the river to the entrance on Latrán. Two tours cover different parts of the interior, which includes a frescoed ballroom and a Baroque theater. Climb the 162 steps of the tower for a fabulous view. (☎380 704 721. Castle open June-Aug. Tu-Su 9am-noon and 1-6pm; Apr.-May and Sept.-Oct. 9am-noon and 1-5pm. Last tour 1hr. before closing. Tower open daily June-Aug. 9am-5:30pm; Apr.-May and Sept.-Oct. 9am-4:30pm. Castle tour 160Kč, students 80Kč. Tower 35Kč.) The castle gardens host the popular **Revolving South Bohemia Theater,** where operas and plays are performed in summer. (Gardens open daily May-Sept. 8am-7pm; Apr. and Oct. 8am-5pm. Free. Shows begin 8:30-9:30pm. Tickets 200-900Kč; available at the tourist office. Reserve ahead.) Egon Schiele (1890-1918) lived in Český Krumlov until residents ran him out for painting the burghers' daughters in the nude. The **Egon Schiele Art Center,** Široká 70-72, displays his works alongside those of other 20th-century Central European artists. (☎380 704 011; www.schieleartcentrum.cz. Open daily 10am-6pm. 180Kč, students 145Kč.) The busy nighttime spot **Cikánská Jizba** (Gypsy Bar), Dlouhá 31, offers Roma cuisine (80-180Kč), cheap beer (18Kč), and live music. (☎380 717 585. Open daily 3-11pm.) Get global with the internationally themed decor at the brand-new **Boom Bar,** Na Fortně 22, off Latrán. (Beer 30Kč. Mixed drinks 50-90Kč. Open daily 6pm-1am.)

OUTDOOR ACTIVITIES. Most hostels provide free **inner tubes** so guests can ride down the Vltava River and admire the views of the castle. **VLTAVA,** Kájovská 62, rents equipment for **rafting** down the river or **biking** in the countryside. (☎380 711 978; www.ckvltava.cz. Bike rental 320Kč per day. Open daily 9am-5pm.) Go horseback riding at **Jezdecký klub Slupenec,** Slupenec 1. Follow Horní to the highway, take the second left on Křížová, and follow the red trail to Slupenec. (☎380 711 052; www.jk-slupenec.cz. 250Kč per hr. Open Tu-Su 9am-6pm.)

MORAVIA

The valleys and peaks of Moravia make up the easternmost third of the Czech Republic. Home to the country's two leading universities, the region is the birthplace of Tomáš G. Masaryk, first president of the former Czechoslovakia, psychoanalyst Sigmund Freud, and geneticist Johann Gregor Mendel. In addition to producing famous names, Moravia is renowned for producing the nation's finest wines and the Moravian Spice Cookie, the world's thinnest dessert.

BRNO

The two thin spires of St. Peter's Cathedral dominate the skyline of Brno (pop. 370,000), the second-largest city in the Czech Republic and an international marketplace since the 13th century. Today, global corporations compete with family-owned produce stands, and ancient churches soften the glare of casinos and clubs.

TRANSPORTATION AND PRACTICAL INFORMATION. **Trains** (☎542 214 803) go to: Bratislava, SLK (2hr., 12 per day, 196Kč); Budapest, HUN (4hr., 5 per day, 969Kč); Prague (3-4hr., 22 per day, 354Kč); Vienna, AUT (1½hr., 5 per day, 537Kč). **Buses** (☎543 217 733) leave from the corner of Zvonařka and Plotní for Prague (2½hr., 36 per day, 140Kč) and Vienna, AUT (2½hr., 2 per day, 200Kč). Student Agency buses (☎542 42 42) also run to Prague (40 per day, 99-145Kč) from the stop down the road to the right of the train station. From the station, cross the tram tracks, walk left, then head right on Masarykova to reach **Náměstí Svobody** (Freedom Square), the center of the city. The **tourist office,** Radnická 8, is inside the town hall. To get there from Nám. Svobody, take Masarykova and turn right on Průchodní. (☎542 211 090; www.ticbrno.cz. Open M-F 8:30am-6pm, Sa-Su 9am-5:30pm.) **Veřejny Internet Center,** Masarykova 24, through the courtyard, has free Internet access. (Open daily 9am-noon and 12:30-5pm.) **Postal Code:** 60100.

ACCOMMODATIONS AND FOOD. From the train station, cross the tram tracks, turn right, then take a left up the stairs. At the top, turn right and follow Novobranská to the centrally located **Hotel Astorka ❸,** Novobranská 3. (☎542 592 111. Open July-Sept. Singles 580Kč; doubles 1160Kč; triples 1740Kč. 50% student discount. AmEx/MC/V.) **Travellers' Hostel ❶,** Jánská 22, sets up dorm beds in the classrooms of a secondary school during the summer. Follow the directions to Hotel Astorka, continue down Novobranská, and bear left on Jánská. (☎542 213 573. Breakfast 15Kč. Beer 15Kč. Free Internet. Dorm beds 290Kč. DC/MC/V.) From Masarykova, turn left and walk down Orlí to reach the delicious, all-organic vegetarian buffet at **Rebio ❶,** Orlí 26. (☎542 211 130. Entrees 18.90Kč per 100g. Open M-F 8am-7pm, Sa 10am-3pm. Cash only.) A suit of armor guards the door and the kitchen prepares Czech feasts at **Dávně Časy ❸,** Starobrněnská 20, off Zelný trh. (Entrees 70-400Kč. Open daily 11am-11pm. AmEx/V.) At the glamorous **Caffetteria Top Shop ❶,** Jakubské nám. 4, tea lights sparkle and a well-dressed crowd sips coffee. From Nám. Svobody, take Rašínova and turn right. (Espresso from 29Kč. Beer

35Kč. Open M-Th 8am-10pm, F 8am-midnight, Sa 10am-midnight, Su 10am-10pm.) An **Interspar** supermarket and laundromat is located between the bus and train stations, in the Vaňkovka Galerie shopping center. (Open daily 7am-10pm.)

SIGHTS AND NIGHTLIFE. **Špilberk Castle** (Hrad Špilberk) earned a reputation as the cruelest prison in Hapsburg Europe. Today the castle is a museum, and its former solitary cells house Baroque art. From Nám. Svobody, take Zámečnická and go right on Panenská; after Husova, head uphill. (www.spilberk.cz. Open July-Aug. daily 9am-6pm; May-June and Sept. Tu-Su 9am-6pm; Apr. and Oct. Tu-Su 9am-5pm; Nov.-Mar. W-Su 10am-5pm. 100Kč, students 50Kč; castle only 60/30Kč.) From the station, turn left off Masarykova onto Basty and climb the path to reach the peaceful **Denisovy Šady** park, which offers sweeping views of Brno. Down Masarykova on the left is the **Capuchin Monastery Crypt** (Hrobka Kapucínského kláštera), where 18th-century monks developed a burial technique in which air ducts allowed bodies to dry naturally. One hundred bodies of 18th-century monks and nobles attest to its effectiveness. (Open June-Aug. daily 9am-5pm; Sept.-Oct. Sa-Su 9am-4pm; Apr.-May Tu-Su 9am-4pm. 40Kč, students 20Kč.) The **Mendelianum,** Mendlovo nám. 1A, documents the life and work of Johann Gregor Mendel, who discovered inherited genotypes while raising peas in a Brno monastery and founded the science of genetics. (Open May-Oct. daily 10am-6pm; Nov.-Apr. W-Su 10am-6pm. 80Kč, students 40Kč.)

In the summer, posters in Brno announce upcoming **raves.** After performances in the attached Merry Goose Theater, artsy crowds gather at **Divadelní hospoda Veselá husa,** Zelný trh. 9. (Open M-F 11am-1am, Sa-Su 3pm-1am.) Brno's largest nightclub, **Klub Flëda,** Štefánikova 24, hosts concerts and live DJs. Take tram #26 up Štefánikova to Hrncirska; Flëda is on the right. (www.fleda.cz. Open daily 2pm-midnight.) The free guide *Metropolis* lists upcoming events.

OLOMOUC

Formerly the capital of Moravia, the inviting university town of Olomouc (pop. 103,000) resembles Prague as it was before the city was totally overwhelmed by tourists. Baroque architecture lines the paths in the town center, locals stroll outdoors during the day, and students keep the clubs thumping all night and until dawn. Every year in May, the town plays host to the second-largest Oktoberfest celebration in all of Europe.

ALL OVER OLOMOUC

At the Poet's Corner Hostel in Olomouc, owners Francie and Greg act as an unofficial tourist welcoming committee, steering guests to the city's best attractions. They provided a list of their top recommendations:

1. Watch the **astronomical clock** on the town hall strike noon. Stay for the surprise at the end.

2. Enjoy a refreshing summer beer in one of the main square's **beer gardens;** in the winter, opt for mulled wine.

3. Savor a slice of decadent **chocolate pie** at Café 87, Denisova 47.

4. For a bit of dodgy novelty, pop into the **Aeroplane Bar,** in a Communist-era Russian plane that's now on Legionářská in front of the stadium. Drinks in the aircraft seats or dance in the cockpit.

5. Peruse the exhibits at the new **Archdiocese Museum,** Václavské nám. 3, which displays art collected by Olomouc's bishops since the 16th century.

6. Rent a bike and ride out to **Poděbrady,** one of the surrounding lakes, for a swim.

7. At night, head to one of Olomouc's **student bars** for cheap drinks and fun-loving company.

8. Explore the old city walls in shady **Bezruč Park.**

9. Make a daytrip to Helfštýn or Bouzov **castles.**

10. Join locals at the **Olomouc Beer Festival** each May.

TRANSPORTATION AND PRACTICAL INFORMATION. **Trains** (☎584 722 175) leave from Jeremenkova 23 for Brno (1½hr., 5 per day, 120Kč) and Prague (3½hr., 19 per day, 294Kč). **Buses** (☎585 313 917) leave from Rolsberská 66 for Brno (1½hr., 10 per day, 75-85Kč) and Prague (4½hr., 4 per day, 240-275Kč). From the stations, take the pedestrian way under Jeremenkova, then tram #4 or 5 to the center. The **tourist office,** Horní nám., in the town hall, has maps and books rooms. (☎685 513 385; www.olomoucko.cz. Open daily Mar.-Nov. 9am-7pm; Dec.-Feb. 9am-5pm.) **Internet u Dominika,** Slovenská 12, has plenty of terminals. (☎777 181 857. 60Kč per hr. Open M-F 9am-9pm, Sa-Su 10am-9pm.) **Postal Code:** 77127.

ACCOMMODATIONS AND FOOD. The small **Poet's Corner Hostel ❶,** Sokolská 1, feels more like home than a hostel, with owners who cheerfully offer guidance on the town's attractions. From the train station, take tram #4, 5, 6, or 7 to Nám. Hridinů and walk north toward the Red Dome. Turn right on Sokolská; the hostel is on the 4th floor through the door on the left. (☎777 570 730; www.hostelolomouc.com. Laundry 100Kč. 7-person dorms July-Aug. 300Kč; doubles 800Kč; triples 1100Kč.) To reach **Pension na Hradbách ❸,** Hrnčírská 3, from Horní nám., head down Školní, straight on Purkrabská, then right on Hrnčírská. This small pension is on one of the quietest streets in the town center and has clean singles with TV and bath. (☎585 233 243; nahradbach@quick.cz. Reserve ahead. Singles 600Kč; doubles 800Kč; triples 900Kč.) **Hanácká Hospoda ❶,** Dolní nám. 38, is packed with locals devouring excellent Czech fare. (☎777 721 171. Entrees 45-199Kč. Open daily 10am-midnight. AmEx/MC/V.) **Supermarket Delvita,** 8 května 24, is in the basement of Prior department store at the corner of 28 října. (☎685 535 135. Open M-F 7am-8pm, Sa 7am-2pm.)

SIGHTS AND NIGHTLIFE. The 1378 **town hall** *(radnice)* and its clock tower dominate the town center. The tourist office arranges trips up the tower (daily 11am, 3pm; 15Kč). An amusing **astronomical clock** is set in the town hall's north side. In 1955, Communist clockmakers replaced the attractive mechanical saints with archetypes of "the people"; today the masses still strike noon with their hammers and sickles. The 35m black-and-gold **Trinity Column** (Sloup Nejsvětější Trojice), in the middle of the square, soars higher than any other Baroque sculpture in the country. Also in the square, the **Arion Fountain** pays homage to the constellation Orion; rubbing the marble dolphin is thought to ensure a return visit to Olomouc. To reach **St. Wenceslas Cathedral** (Metropolitní Kostel sv. Václava), follow the spires. The interior is in impeccable condition, having been reworked virtually every century since it was damaged by fire in 1265. (Open Tu and Th-Sa 9am-5pm, W 9am-4pm, Su 11am-5pm. Donations requested.) Next to the cathedral, the walls of the **Přemyslid Palace** (Přemyslovský palác) are covered in beautiful frescoes. (Open Apr.-Sept. Tu-Su 10am-6pm. 15Kč, students 5Kč. W free.) Kick back with a bottle of the cheapest beer in Old Town at **Vertigo,** Universitni 6, Olomouc's most popular student club. (Beer from 15Kč. Open daily 5pm-2am.) Expert DJs keep a well-boozed crowd shimmying into the wee hours on the dance floor at **Belmondo,** Mlynská 4. (☎585 220 425. Cover F-Sa 50Kč. Open W-Su 9pm-5am.)

DENMARK (DANMARK)

Straddling the border between Scandinavia and continental Europe, Denmark packs majestic castles, thriving nightlife, and pristine beaches onto the compact Jutland peninsula and its network of islands. Fairy-tale lovers can tour Hans Christian Andersen's home in rural Odense, while vibrant Copenhagen boasts the busy pedestrian thoroughfare of Strøget and the world's tallest carousel in Tivoli Gardens. The nation's Viking past has given way to a dynamic multicultural society that draws in visitors as it turns out Legos and Skagen watches.

DISCOVER DENMARK: SUGGESTED ITINERARIES

THREE DAYS Start off in the cosmopolitan capital, **Copenhagen** (p. 264), soaking up some sunshine on a **bike tour** (p. 270) of the central city or waiting out showers in the medieval ruins beneath **Christianborg Slot.** Channel the Bard at Kronborg Slot in **Helsingør** (p. 273), where the real-life Hamlet slept.

BEST OF DENMARK, 12 DAYS Begin your journey in **Copenhagen** (3 days), then castle-hop to Frederiksborg Slot in nearby **Hillerød** (1 day; p. 273). The best way to explore the beautiful farmlands, forests, and beaches of **Bornholm** (2 days; p. 275) to take a **bike tour** (p. 276) around the island. After returning to the mainland, head west to **Odense** (1 day; p. 279) for celebrations of Hans Christian Andersen's birth. Discover the superb museums and lively nightlife of little-known **Århus** (2 days; p. 280) before indulging your inner child at Legoland in **Billund** (1 day; p. 281). Finish your journey at the northern tip of Jutland, where the quaint yellow houses of **Skagen** (2 days; p. 283) look out on the tumultuous Baltic Sea.

ESSENTIALS

FACTS AND FIGURES

Official Name: Kingdom of Denmark.

Capital: Copenhagen.

Major Cities: Aalborg, Århus, Odense.

Population: 5,451,000.

Land Area: 42,394 sq. km.

Time Zone: GMT +1.

Languages: Danish. Pockets of Faroese, Greenlandic, and German. English is nearly universal as a second language.

Religion: Evangelical Lutheran (95%).

WHEN TO GO

Denmark is best visited between May and September, when the days are usually sunny and temperatures average 10-16°C (50-61°F). Winter temperatures average 0°C (32°F). Although temperate for its northern location, Denmark can turn rainy or cool at a moment's notice; pack a sweater and an umbrella, even in the summer.

DOCUMENTS AND FORMALITIES

EMBASSIES AND CONSULATES. All foreign embassies are in Copenhagen (p. 265). Danish embassies abroad include: **Australia** (Consulate General), Gold Fields House, Level 21, 1 Alfred St., Circular Quay, Sydney, NSW, 2000 (☎02 92 47 22 24; www.gksydney.um.dk/en); **Canada**, 47 Clarence St., Ste. 450, Ottawa, ON, K1N 9K1 (☎613-562-1811; www.ambottawa.um.dk/en); **Ireland,** 121-122 St. Stephen's Green,

Dublin, 2 (☎01 475 64 04; www.ambdublin.um.dk/en); **New Zealand** (Consulate General), Level 7, Forsyth Barr House, 45 Johnston Street, Wellington, 6001 or P.O. Box 10874, Wellington, 6036 (☎04 471 05 20; www.danishconsulatesnz.org/nz); **UK**, 55 Sloane St., London, SW1X 9SR (☎020 7333 0200; www.amblondon.um.dk/en); **US**, 3200 Whitehaven St., NW, Washington, D.C., 20008 (☎202-234-4300; www.denmarkemb.org).

VISA AND ENTRY INFORMATION. EU citizens do not need a visa. Citizens of Australia, Canada, New Zealand, and the US do not need a visa for stays of up to 90 days, beginning upon entry into any of the countries belonging to the EU's freedom-of-movement zone. For more information, see p. 18.

TOURIST SERVICES AND MONEY

EMERGENCY	**Police, Ambulance,** and **Fire:** ☎112.

TOURIST OFFICES. The Danish Tourist Board has an office in Copenhagen at Islands Brygge 43 (☎32 88 99 00; www.visitdenmark.dt.dk).

MONEY. The Danish unit of currency is the **krone** (plural kroner), divided into 100 *øre*. The easiest way to get cash is from **ATMs;** cash cards are widely accepted, and many machines give advances on credit cards. Expect to pay a 30kr fee to exchange money or traveler's checks. Denmark has a high cost of living, which it passes along to visitors; expect to pay 100-130kr for a hostel bed, 450-800kr for a hotel room, 80-130kr for a day's groceries, and 50-90kr for a cheap restaurant meal. A bare-bones day in Denmark might cost 250-350kr; a more comfortable day might cost 400-600kr. There are no hard and fast rules for **tipping.** In general, service at restaurants is included in the bill, but it's polite to round up to the nearest 10kr in restaurants and for taxis and to leave an additional 10-20kr for good service. The European Union imposes a **value added tax (VAT)** on goods and services purchased within the EU (p. 22), which is included in the price. Denmark's 25% VAT is one of the highest in Europe. Non-EU citizens can get a partial VAT refund upon leaving the EU for purchases in any one store that total over 300kr.

KRONER (KR)		
	AUS$1 = 4.42KR	10KR = AUS$2.26
	CDN$1 = 5.27KR	10KR = CDN$1.90
	EUR€1 = 7.46KR	10KR = EUR€1.34
	NZ$1 = 3.71KR	10KR = NZ$2.69
	UK£1 = 10.92KR	10KR = UK£0.92
	US$1 = 5.79KR	10KR = US$1.73

TRANSPORTATION

BY PLANE. International flights arrive at **Kastrup Airport** in Copenhagen (**CPH;** ☎3231 3231; www.cph.dk). Flights from Europe also arrive at **Billund Airport,** outside Århus (**BLL;** ☎7650 5050; www.billund-airport.dk). Smaller airports in Århus and Esbjerg serve as hubs for budget airline **Ryanair** (☎353 1249 7791; www.ryanair.com), which flies from London. **SAS** (Scandinavian Airlines; Denmark ☎7010 2000, UK 0870 6072 7727, US 800-221-2350; www.scandinavian.net), the national airline company, offers youth discounts to some destinations.

BY TRAIN AND BY BUS. The state-run rail line in Denmark is **DSB;** their helpful **route planner** is online at www.rejseplanen.dk. **Eurail** is valid on all state-run routes. The **Scanrail pass** (p. 52) is good for rail travel through Denmark, Finland, Norway,

and Sweden, as well as many discounted ferry and bus rides. Remote towns are typically served by buses from the nearest train station. **Buses** are reliable and can be less expensive than trains. You can take buses or trains over the **Øresund bridge** from Copenhagen to Malmö, Sweden.

BY FERRY. Several companies run ferries to and from Denmark. **Scandlines** (☎3315 1515; www.scandlines.dk) arrives from Germany and Sweden and has domestic routes. **Color Line** (Norway ☎47 810 00 811; www.colorline.com) runs between Denmark and Norway. **DFDS Seaways** (UK ☎08702 520 524; www.dfdsseaways.co.uk) sails from Harwich, BRI to Esbjerg and from Copenhagen to Oslo, NOR. For additional info, check www.aferry.to/ferry-to-denmark-ferries.htm. Tourist offices can help you sort out the dozens of smaller ferries that serve Denmark's outlying islands. For more info on connections from Bornholm to Sweden, see p. 275; for connections from Jutland to Norway and Sweden, see p. 283.

TIP **RAIL SAVINGS.** Scanrail passes purchased outside Scandinavia may be cheaper, depending on the exchange rate, and they are also more flexible. Travelers who purchase passes within Scandinavia can only use three travel days in the country of purchase. Check www.scanrail.com for more information on where to purchase passes at home.

BY CAR. Denmark's only toll roads are the **Storebæltsbro** (Great Belt Bridge; 200kr) and the **Øresund bridge** (235kr). Speed limits are 50kph (30 mph) in urban areas, 80kph (50 mph) on highways, and 110-130kph (65-80 mph) on motorways. **Gas** averages 9-11kr per liter. Watch out for bikes, which have the right-of-way. High parking prices and numerous one-way streets make driving something of a nightmare in cities. For more info on driving, contact the **Forenede Danske Motorejere (FDM),** Firskovvej 32, Box 500, 2800 Kgs. Lyngby (☎7013 3040; www.fdm.dk).

BY BIKE AND BY THUMB. With its flat terrain and well-marked bike routes, Denmark is a cyclist's dream. You can rent bikes (50-80kr per day) from some tourist offices, rental shops, and a few train stations. The **Dansk Cyklist Forbund** (☎3332 3121; www.dcf.dk) provides info about cycling in Denmark and investing in long-term rentals. Pick up *Bikes and Trains* at any train station for info on bringing your bike on a train (which costs 50kr or less). **Hitchhiking** on motorways is illegal and uncommon. Let's Go does not recommend hitchhiking.

KEEPING IN TOUCH

PHONE CODES	**Country code:** 45. **International dialing prefix:** 00. For more information on how to place international calls, see inside back cover.

EMAIL AND THE INTERNET. In Copenhagen and other cities, you can generally find at least one cybercafe; expect to pay 20-40kr per hr. DSB, the national railroad, maintains cybercafes in some stations as well. In smaller towns, access at public libraries is free, although you typically have to reserve a slot in advance.

TELEPHONES. Pay phones accept both coins and phone cards, available at post offices or kiosks in 100kr denominations. Mobile phones (p. 29) are a popular and economical alternative. For domestic directory info, dial ☎118; for international info, dial ☎113. International direct dial numbers include: **AT&T Direct** (☎8001 0010); **Canada Direct** (☎8001 0011); **MCI WorldPhone** (☎8001 0022); **Sprint** (☎8001 0877); **Telecom New Zealand** (☎8001 0064); **Telstra Australia** (☎8001 0061).

MAIL. Mailing a postcard or letter to Australia, Canada, New Zealand, or the US costs 7.50kr; to elsewhere in Europe costs 6.50kr. Domestic mail costs 4.50kr.

LANGUAGE. Danish is the official language of Denmark, although natives of Greenland and the Faroe Islands still speak local dialects. The Danish add *æ* (pronounced like the "e" in egg), *ø* (pronounced "euh"), and å (sometimes written *aa;* pronounced "oh" with tightly pursed lips) to the end of the alphabet; thus Århus would follow Skagen in an alphabetical listing of cities. *Let's Go* indexes these under "ae," "o," and "a." Nearly all Danes speak flawless English.

ACCOMMODATIONS AND CAMPING

DENMARK	❶	❷	❸	❹	❺
ACCOMMODATIONS	under 100kr	100-160kr	160-220kr	220-350kr	over 350kr

Denmark's hotels are uniformly expensive, so **youth hostels** *(vandrehjem)* tend to be mobbed by budget travelers of all ages. HI-affiliated **Danhostels** are the most common, and are often the only option in smaller towns. Facilities are clean, spacious, and comfortable, often attracting families as well as backpackers. Eco-conscious tourists can choose from one of the 13 Danhostels that have earned a **Green Key** (www.green-key.org) for their environmentally friendly practices. Dorms run about 155kr per night, with a 35kr HI discount. Linens cost 40kr; sleeping bags are not permitted. Reserve ahead, especially in summer and near beaches. Danhostel check-in times are usually a non-negotiable 3-4hr. window. For more info, contact the Danish Youth Hostel Association (☎3331 3612; www.danhostel.dk). **Independent hostels,** found mostly in cities and larger towns, draw a younger crowd and tend to be more sociable, although their facilities are rarely as nice as those in Danhostels. Most tourist offices book rooms in private homes (150-250kr).

Denmark's 510 **campgrounds** (about 60kr per person) range from one star (toilets and drinking water) to three stars (showers and laundry) to five stars (swimming, restaurants, and stoves). Info is available at **DK-Camp** (☎7571 2962; www.dk-camp.dk). You'll need a **Camping Card Scandinavia** (1-year 80kr; available for purchase at www.camping.se; allow at least 3 weeks for delivery), valid across Scandinavia and sold at campgrounds as well as through the Danish Youth Hostel Association. Campsites affiliated with hostels generally do not require a card. If you plan to camp for only a night, you can buy a 24hr. pass (20kr). The **Danish Camping Council** *(Campingradet)*, Mosedalv. 15, 2500 Valby (☎3927 8844; www.campingraadet.dk) sells passes and the *Camping Denmark* handbook (95kr). Sleeping in train stations, in parks, or on public property is illegal.

DENMARK

FOOD AND DRINK

DENMARK	❶	❷	❸	❹	❺
FOOD	under 40kr	40-70kr	70-100kr	100-150kr	over 150kr

A "danish" in Denmark is a *wienerbrød* (Viennese bread), found in bakeries alongside other flaky treats. Traditionally, Danes have favored open-faced sandwiches called *smørrebrød* for a more substantial meal, although today they have become more of a rarefied delicacy. Herring is served in various forms, usually pickled or raw with onions or a curry mayonnaise. For cheap eats, look for lunch specials *(dagens ret)* and all-you-can-eat buffets. National beers include Carlsberg and Tuborg; bottled brews tend to be cheaper. A popular alcohol is *snaps* (or *aquavit*), a clear distilled liquor flavored with fiery spices, usually served chilled and unmixed. Many vegetarian *(vegetarret)* options are the result of Indian and Mediterranean influences, and both salads and veggies *(grønsager)* can be found on most menus. Expect to pay around 120kr for a sit-down meal at a restaurant, although cheaper eats can be found in cafes and ethnic takeaways for 40-80kr.

HOLIDAYS AND FESTIVALS

Holidays: New Year's Day (Jan. 1); Easter (Apr. 5-9); Queen's Birthday (Apr. 16); Worker's Day (May 1); Whit Sunday/Monday (May 27-28); Constitution Day (June 5); Valdemar's Day (June 15); Midsummer's Eve (June 23), Christmas (Dec. 24-26).

Festivals: In February, Danish children assault candy-filled barrels with birch branches on *Fastelavn* (Shrovetide), while adults take to the streets for carnivals. Guitar solos ring out over Roskilde during the open-air Roskilde Festival in early July, just before Copenhagen and Århus kick off their annual jazz festivals.

BEYOND TOURISM

For short-term employment in Denmark, check www.jobs-in-europe.net.

The American-Scandinavian Foundation (AMSCAN), 58 Park Ave., New York, NY, 10016, USA (☎212-879-9779; www.amscan.org/jobs/index.html). Volunteer and job opportunities throughout Scandinavia. Fellowships for Americans to study in Denmark.

Vi Hjælper Hinanden (VHH), Aasenv. 35, 9881 Bindslev, DEN, c/o Inga Nielsen (☎45 9893 8607; www.wwoof.dk). For 50kr, Danish branch of World-Wide Opportunities on Organic Farms (WWOOF) provides a list of farmers currently accepting volunteers.

COPENHAGEN (KØBENHAVN) ☎33, 35

The center of Europe's oldest monarchy, Copenhagen (pop. 1,800,000) embodies a laid-back spirit. The Strøget, the city's famed pedestrian thoroughfare, now bustles with Middle Eastern restaurants and cybercafes, and neon signs glimmer next to angels in the architecture. The up-and-coming districts of Vesterbro and Nørrebro reverberate with some of Europe's wildest nightlife, while the hippie paradise of Christiania swings to a more downbeat vibe.

TRANSPORTATION

Flights: Kastrup Airport (**CPH;** ☎3231 3231; www.cph.dk). **Trains** connect the airport to København H (13min., 6 per hr., 27kr or 2 clips). Ryanair flies into nearby **Sturup Airport** in Malmö, SWE (**MMX;** ☎40 613 1000; www.sturup.com) at low rates.

Trains: København H (Hovedbanegården or Central Station; domestic travel ☎7013 1415, international 7013 1416; www.dsb.dk). Trains run to: **Berlin, GER** (8hr., 9 per day, 803kr); **Hamburg, GER** (5hr., 5 per day, 537kr); **Malmö, SWE** (25min., every 20min., 71kr), **Oslo, NOR** (8hr., 2 per day, 821kr); **Stockholm, SWE** (5hr., every 1-2hr., 1040kr). For international trips, fares depend on seat availability and can drop as low as 50% of the quotes listed above; **book at least 14 days in advance.**

> TIP **TAKE A RIDE.** Tickets on the S-togs are covered by Eurail, Scanrail, and Inter Rail passes. So ride away!

Public Transportation: Copenhagen has an extensive public transportation system. **Buses** (☎3613 1415; www.hur.dk) run daily 5:30am-12:30am; maps are available on any bus. **S-togs** (subways and suburban trains; ☎3314 1701) run M-Sa 5am-12:30am, Su 6am-12:30am. The **metro** (☎7015 1615; www.m.dk) is small but efficient. All 3 types of public transportation operate on a zone system. To travel any distance, a 2-zone **ticket** is required (17kr; additional zones 8.50kr), which covers most of Copenhagen. For extended stays, the best deal is the **rabatkort** (rebate card; 110kr), available from supermarkets, corner stores, and kiosks, which offers 10 2-zone tickets at a discount. The **24hr. pass** (100kr), available at train stations, grants unlimited bus and train transport in the Northern Zealand region, as does the **Copenhagen Card** (see **Orientation and Practical Information,** p. 265). **Night buses,** marked with an "N," run 12:30-5:30am on limited routes and charge double fare; they accept the 24hr. pass.

Taxis: Københavns Taxa (☎3535 3535) and **Hovedstadens Taxi** (☎3877 7777) charge a base fare of 32kr for arranged pickups and 19kr otherwise, plus 10kr per km during the day and 13kr at night. From København H to Kastrup Airport costs around 200kr.

Bike Rental: City Bike (www.bycyklen.dk/engelsk) lends bikes mid-Apr. to Nov. from 110 racks all over the city for a 20kr deposit. Anyone can return your bike and claim your deposit, so keep an eye on it. **Københavns Cyklebørs,** Gothersg. 157 (☎3314 0717; www.cykelborsen.dk) rents bikes for 60kr per day, 270kr per wk.; 200kr deposit. Open M-F 8:30am-5:30pm, Sa 10am-1:30pm. MC/V.

ORIENTATION AND PRACTICAL INFORMATION

Copenhagen lies on the east coast of the island of **Zealand** (Sjælland), across the Øresund Sound from Malmö, Sweden. The 28km **Øresund bridge and tunnel,** which opened July 1, 2000, established the first "fixed link" between the two countries. Copenhagen's main train station, København H, lies near the city center. Just north of the station, **Vesterbrogade** passes **Tivoli** and **Rådhuspladsen,** the main square, then cuts through the city center as **Strøget** (STROY-yet), the world's longest pedestrian thoroughfare. As it heads east, Strøget goes through a series of names: **Frederiksberggade, Nygade, Vimmelskaftet, Amagertorv,** and **Østergade.** The city center is ringed to the west by five **lakes;** on the outside of the lakes are the less touristed communities of **Vesterbro, Nørrebro,** and **Østerbro.** Vesterbro and Nørrebro are home to many of the region's immigrants, while some of Copenhagen's highest-income residents live on the wide streets of Østerbro.

Tourist Offices: Copenhagen Right Now, Vesterbrog. 4A (☎7022 2442; www.visit-copenhagen.com). From København H, cross Vesterbrog. toward the Axelrod building. Open July-Aug. M-Sa 9am-8pm, Su 10am-6pm; May-June M-Sa 9am-6pm; Sept.-Apr. M-F 9am-4pm, Sa 9am-2pm. Sells the **Copenhagen Card** (1-day 199kr; 3-day 429kr), which grants free or discounted admission to most sights and unlimited travel throughout Northern Zealand; however, cardholders will need to keep up an almost manic pace to justify the cost. ☒**Use It,** Rådhusstr. 13 (☎3373 0620; www.useit.dk), has indispensable info and services for budget travelers. Offers *Playtime,* a comprehensive budget guide to the city. Provides daytime luggage storage, has free **Internet** (max. 20min.), holds mail, and finds lodgings for no charge. Open daily mid-June to mid-Sept. 9am-7pm; mid-Sept. to mid-June M-W 11am-4pm, Th 11am-6pm, F 11am-2pm.

Budget Travel: STA Travel, Fiolstr. 18 (☎3314 1501). Open M-Th 9:30am-5:30pm, F 10am-5:30pm. **Kilroy Travels,** Skinderg. 28 (☎7015 4015). Open M-F 10am-5:30pm, Sa 10am-2pm. **Wasteels Rejser,** Skoubog. 6 (☎3314 4633). Open M-F 9am-5pm.

Embassies and Consulates: Australia, Dampfærgev. 26, 2nd fl. (☎7026 3676). **Canada,** Kristen Bernikowsg. 1 (☎3348 3200). **Ireland,** Østbaneg. 21 (☎3542 3233). **New Zealand,** Store Strandst. 21, 2nd fl. (☎3337 7702). **UK,** Kastelsv. 36-40 (☎3544 5200). **US,** Dag Hammarskjölds Allé 24 (☎3341 7100).

Currency Exchange: Forex, in København H. 20kr commission for cash exchanges, 10kr per traveler's check. Open daily 8am-9pm.

Luggage Storage: Free at **Use It** (see above) and most hostels.

Laundromats: Look for **Vascomat** and **Møntvask** chains. Locations at Borgerg. 2, Vendersg. 13, and Istedg. 45. Wash and dry each 40-50kr. Most open daily 7am-9pm. At the ☒**Laundromat Café,** Elmeg. 15 (☎3535 2672), bus 3A or 80N, you can pick up a used book, check email on the free wireless **Internet,** or enjoy a meal while you wait for your laundry. Salads 65kr. Entrees 95kr. Wash 32kr, dry 1kr per min. Open M-Th 8am-midnight, F-Sa 8am-2am, Su 10am-midnight. MC/V.

GLBT Resources: Landsforeningen for Bøsser og Lesbiske (LBL), Teglgårdstr. 13 (☎3313 1948; www.lbl.dk). Open M-F 11am-5pm. The monthly *Out and About,* which lists nightlife options, is available at gay clubs and the tourist office. Other resources include www.copenhagen-gay-life.dk and www.gayguide.dk.

Emergency: ☎112.

Police: ☎3325 1448. Headquarters at Halmtorvet 20.

24hr. Pharmacy: Steno Apotek, Vesterbrog. 6C (☎3314 8266), across from the Banegårdspl. exit of København H. Ring the bell at night. Cash only.

Medical Services: Doctors on Call (☎7027 5757). Emergency rooms at **Amager Hospital,** Italiensv. 1 (☎3234 3234), **Frederiksberg Hospital,** Nordre Fasanv. 57 (☎3816 3816), and **Bispebjerg Hospital,** Bispebjerg Bakke 23 (☎3531 3531).

Internet Access: Free at **Use It** and **Copenhagen Hovedbibliotek** (Central Library), Krystalg. 15 (☎3373 6060). Coffee shop on 1st fl. Open M-F 10am-7pm, Sa 10am-2pm. **Boomtown,** Axeltorv. 1-3 (☎3332 1032; www.boomtown.net), across from the Tivoli entrance. 30kr per hr. Open 24hr.

English-Language Bookstore: Arnold Busck International Boghandel, Købmagerg. 49 (☎3373 3500; www.arnoldbusck.dk). Open M 10am-6pm, Tu-Th 9:30am-6pm, F 9:30am-7pm, Sa 10am-4pm. AmEx/DC/MC/V.

Post Office: In København H. Open M-F 8am-9pm, Sa-Su 10am-4pm. Address mail to be held as follows: LAST NAME First name, Post Denmark, Hovedbanegårdens Posthus, Hovedbanegården, 1570 Copenhagen V, DENMARK. **Use It** (p. 265) also holds mail for 2 months. Address mail to be held as follows: First name LAST NAME, *Poste Restante*, Use It, Rådhusstr. 13, 1466 Copenhagen K, DENMARK.

ACCOMMODATIONS AND CAMPING

Comfortable and inexpensive accommodations can be hard to find near the city center, but pedestrian-friendly streets and the great public transportation system ensure that travelers are never far from the action. Many hostels are also dynamic social worlds unto themselves. Reserve well in advance in summer.

Sleep-In Heaven, Struenseeg. 7 (☎3535 4648; www.sleepinheaven.com), in Nørrebro. M: Forum. From København H, take bus #250S 2 stops (dir.: Buddinge; every 10-20min.) to H.C. Ørsteds V. Take your 1st right on Kapelvej, then take a left into the alley just after Kapelvej 44. Guests chat around the pool table or on the outdoor patio before heading to the packed dorms. Breakfast 40kr. Linens 30kr. Free wireless Internet. Reception 24hr. Under 35 only. Dorms 130-150kr; doubles 500kr. AmEx/MC/V. ❷

City Public Hostel, Absalonsg. 8 (☎2425 6639; www.city-public-hostel.dk), in Vesterbro. Popular hostel with large, single-sex dorms, close to sights and nightlife. Breakfast 25kr. Linens 35kr, towel 5kr, pillow 10kr. Internet 10kr per 20min.; free wireless. Reception 24hr. Check-out 10am. Open May to mid-Aug. Dorms 140kr. Cash only. ❷

Sleep-In Green, Ravnsborgg. 18, Baghuset (☎3537 7777). M: Nørreport. Eco-friendly hostel with colorful rooms. Guests are less likely to congregate in common spaces. Organic breakfast 40kr. Sheet included; pillow and blanket 30kr. Free Internet. Reception 24hr. Lockout noon-4pm. Open June-Oct. 8- to 30-bed dorms 100kr. Cash only. ❶

Jørgensen's Hostel/Hotel Jørgensen, Rømersg. 11 (☎3313 8186; www.hoteljoergensen.dk). M: Nørreport. The hostel is in the basement of the hotel and offers cozy rooms in a convenient location. Breakfast included. Linens 30kr. Max. stay 5 nights. Dorm lockout 11am-3pm. Dorms under 35 only. No reservations for dorms. 6- to 14-bed dorms 140kr; singles 475-575kr; doubles 575-700kr; triples 775-900kr. Cash only for dorms; AmEx/DC/MC/V for private rooms. ❷

København Vandrerhjem Copenhagen City (HI), H.C. Andersens Bvd. 50 (☎3311 8585; www.danhostel.dk/copenhagencity). This 15-story "designer hostel" provides sleek accommodations just 5min. from the city center. Bike rental 100kr per day. Breakfast 50kr. Linens 60kr. Internet 39kr per hr. Reception 24hr. Check-in 2-5pm. Reserve ahead. Dorms 155kr; private rooms 515kr. 35kr HI discount. AmEx/MC/V. ❷

Sleep-In-Fact, Valdemarsg. 14 (☎3379 6779; www.sleep-in-fact.dk), in Vesterbro. Spacious, modern factory-turned-hostel. Bike rental 50kr per day. Breakfast included. Linens 30kr. Internet 20kr per 30min. Reception 7am-noon and 3pm-3am. Lockout noon-3pm. Curfew 3am. Open July-Aug. 10- to 30-bed dorms 100-120kr. Cash only. ❷

Bellahøj Camping, Hvidkildev. 66 (☎3331 2070; www.bellahoj-camping.dk). Take bus #2A from København H (dir.: Tingbjerg; 15min., every 5-10min.) all the way to Hulgårdsv. Backtrack from there and turn left on Hulgårdsv., stay left of the church, and then make another left. Basic campground 5km from the city center. Showers included. Electricity 25kr. Reception 24hr. Open June-Aug. Tent sites 63kr. Cash only. ❶

FOOD

Good, inexpensive food is plentiful in central Copenhagen. Strøget is lined with all-you-can-eat pizza, pasta, and Indian buffets. Around **Kongens Nytorv,** elegant cafes serve filling *smørrebrød* (open-faced sandwiches) and herring meals. **Open-air markets** provide fresh fruits and veggies; a popular one is at **Israel Plads** near

DENMARK

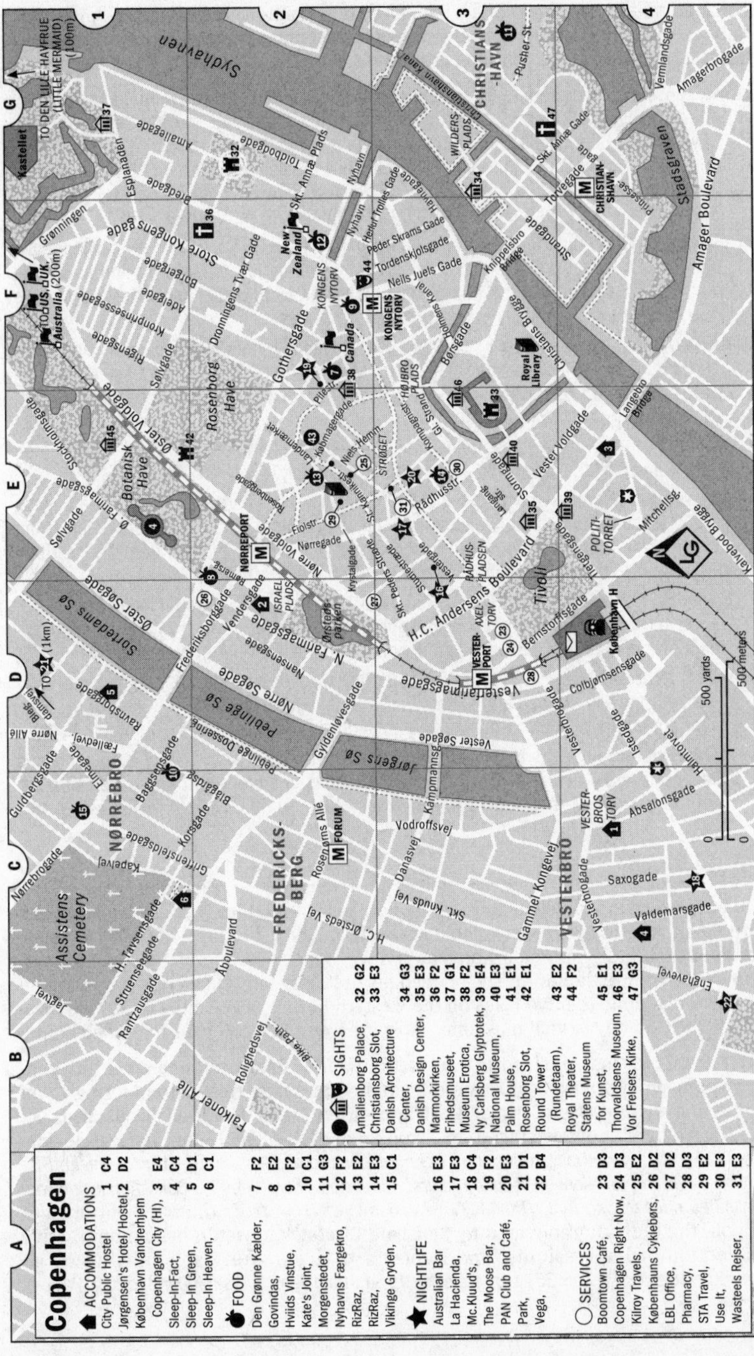
Copenhagen
ACCOMMODATIONS
City Public Hostel 1 C4
Jørgensen's Hotel/Hostel,2 D2
København Vandrerhjem Copenhagen City (HI), 3 E4
Sleep-In-Fact, 4 C4
Sleep-In Green, 5 D1
Sleep-In Heaven, 6 C1
FOOD
Den Grønne Kælder, 7 F2
Govindas, 8 E2
Hviids Vinstue, 9 F2
Kate's Joint, 10 C1
Morgenstedet, 11 G3
Nyhavns Færgekro, 12 F2
RizRaz, 13 E2
RizRaz, 14 E3
Vikinge Gryden, 15 C1
NIGHTLIFE
Australian Bar 16 E3
La Hacienda, 17 E3
Mc.Kluud's, 18 C4
The Moose Bar, 19 F2
PAN Club and Café, 20 E3
Park, 21 D1
Vega, 22 B4
SERVICES
Boomtown Café, 23 D3
Copenhagen Right Now, 24 D3
Kilroy Travels, 25 E2
Københauns Cyklebørs, 26 D2
LBL Office, 27 D2
Pharmacy, 28 D3
STA Travel, 29 E2
Use It, 30 E3
Wasteels Rejser, 31 E3
SIGHTS
Amalienborg Palace, 32 G2
Christiansborg Slot, 33 E3
Danish Architecture Center, 34 G3
Danish Design Center, 35 E3
Marmorkirken, 36 F2
Frihedsmuseet, 37 G1
Museum Erotica, 38 F2
Ny Carlsberg Glyptotek, 39 E4
National Museum, 40 E3
Palm House, 41 E1
Rosenborg Slot, 42 E1
Round Tower (Rundetaarn), 43 E2
Royal Theater, 44 F2
Statens Museum for Kunst, 45 E1
Thorvaldsens Museum, 46 E3
Vor Frelsers Kirke, 47 G3
NØRREBRO
FREDERICKSBERG
VESTERBRO
CHRISTIANSHAVN
Assistens Cemetery
Botanisk Have
Rosenborg Have
Tivoli
Sydhavnen
Kastellet
TO DEN LILLE HAVFRUE (LITTLE MERMAID) (100m)
Sortedams Sø
Peblinge Sø
Sankt Jørgens Sø
Stadsgraven
Royal Library
København H
NØRREPORT
KONGENS NYTORV
VESTERPORT
FORUM
CHRISTIANSHAVN
STRØGET
500 yards
500 meters

Nørreport Station. (Open M-Th 9am-5:30pm, F 9am-6:30pm, Sa 9am-3pm. Cash only.) Greengrocers line the main streets in **Vesterbro** and **Nørrebro,** and **Fakta** and **Netto** supermarkets are common around Nørrebro (M: Nørreport).

Morgenstedet, Langgaden, Bådsmandsstr. 43 (☎3295 7770; www.morgenstedet.dk), in Christiania. Walk down Pusher St. and take a left at the end, leaving Cafe Nemoland to your right. Then take a right up the concrete ramp at the bike shop and left before the bathrooms; it will be on your right. Filling organic meals are served on the cheap in this welcoming restaurant, where complete strangers chat at long wooden tables. Soup 39kr. Entrees 52kr, with salad 55kr. Open Tu-Su noon-9pm. Cash only. ❷

Vikinge Gryden (Viking Cauldron), Nørrebrog. 46 (☎3535 2564; www.vikingegryden.dk). M: Nørreport. Basic local eatery is legendary for its large portion sizes. The food is meant for takeout; a nearby park makes an ideal picnic spot. Massive burgers 45kr, fries 26kr. Open daily noon-10pm. Cash only. ❷

RizRaz, Kompagnistr. 20 (☎3315 0575). M: Kongens Nytorv. Also at Store Kannikestr. 19 (☎3332 3345). Vegetarian buffet with Mediterranean and Middle Eastern specialties. Lunch buffet 59kr. Dinner 69kr. Open daily 11:30am-11pm. AmEx/DC/MC/V. ❷

Den Grønne Kælder, Pilestr. 48 (☎3393 0140). M: Kongens Nytorv. Vegetarian and vegan dining in a cozy basement cafe. Takeout available. Sandwiches 40kr. Lunch 65kr. Dinner 85kr. Open M-Sa 11am-10pm. Cash only. ❷

Nyhavns Færgekro, Nyhavn 5 (☎3315 1588; www.nyhavnsfaergekro.dk). M: Kongens Nytorv. Upscale cafe along the canal with lunch bargains. Try 10 styles of herring at the all-you-can-eat lunch buffet (109kr) or pick just one (45kr). Dinners from 169kr. Open Tu-Su 9am-11:30pm. Lunch served 11:30am-5pm. DC/MC/V. ❹

Govindas, Nørre Farimagsg. 82 (☎3333 7444). M: Nørreport. Hare Krishnas serve vegetarian and vegan fare. Not much atmosphere, but great deals. All-you-can-eat lunch buffet 55kr, dinner buffet 75kr. Open M-F noon-9pm, Sa 1pm-6pm. Cash only. ❷

Kate's Joint, Blågårdsg. 12 (☎3537 4496), in Nørrebro. Bus: 5A. Rotating menu of pan-Asian cuisine with African and Middle Eastern influences. Entrees 70-90kr. Stir-fry, tofu, other appetizers 50-69kr. Open daily 6pm-midnight. Kitchen closes 10pm. MC/V. ❸

Hviids Vinstue, Kongens Nytorv 19 (☎3315 1064). M: Kongens Nytorv. Copenhagen's oldest pub. 55kr lunch special includes 3 varieties of *smørrebrød* and a Danish beer. Beer 38kr. Open M-Th 10am-1am, F-Sa 10am-2am, Su 10am-10pm. AmEx/MC/V. ❷

SIGHTS

Compact, flat Copenhagen lends itself to exploration by **bike** (p. 271). **Walking tours** are detailed in *Playtime* (available at **Use It,** p. 265). Window-shop down pedestrian **Strøget** until you reach Kongens Nytorv; opposite is the picturesque **Nyhavn,** where Hans Christian Andersen penned his first fairy tale. On a clear day, take the 6.4km walk along the five **lakes** on the western border of the city center. Wednesday is the best day to visit museums; most are free and some have extended hours.

CITY CENTER. Just outside the train station, **Tivoli Gardens,** the famous 19th-century amusement park, features old-fashioned and new rides, shimmering fountains, and a world-class **Commedia dell'arte** variety show. The **Tivoli Illuminations,** an evocative light show, is staged on Tivoli Lake each night 15min. before closing. *(☎3315 1001; www.tivoligardens.com. Open mid-June to mid-Aug. Su-Th 11am-midnight, F-Sa 11am-12:30am; low season reduced hours. Admission 75kr. Rides 15-60kr. Admission with unlimited rides 275kr. AmEx/DC/MC/V.)* Across the street from the back entrance of Tivoli, the recently renovated **Ny Carlsberg Glyptotek** museum has an impressive collection of Impressionist and Danish art. Tickets for free guided tours go quickly. *(Dantes Pl. 7. ☎3341 8141. Open Tu-Su 10am-4pm. Tours mid-June to Aug. W 2pm.*

40kr, free with ISIC. W and Su free. MC/V.) Nearby, the **Danish Design Center** showcases trends in Danish fashion and lifestyles. The Flow Market exhibition downstairs lets visitors buy items to take home. *(H.C. Andersens Bvd. 27. ☎3369 3369; www.ddc.dk. Open M-Tu and Th-F 10am-5pm, W 10am-9pm, Sa-Su 11am-4pm. 40kr, students 20kr. W after 5pm free. AmEx/DC/MC/V.)* To reach the **National Museum** from H.C. Andersens Bvd., turn onto Stormg., take a right on Vester Volg., and go left on Ny Vesterg. Its vast collections include several large rune stones, examples of ancient Viking art, and the fabulous permanent ethnographic exhibit, "People of the Earth." *(Ny Vesterg. 10. ☎3313 4411; www.natmus.dk. Open Tu-Su 10am-5pm. Free.)*

Christiansborg Slot, the home of Parliament *(Folketing)* and the royal reception rooms, displays vivid modernist tapestries that were designed by Bjørn Nørgård and presented to the Queen on her 50th birthday. Visitors can tour the subterranean ruins underneath the Slot. *(Prins Jørgens Gård 1. ☎3392 6492; www.ses.dk/christrainsborg. Ruins open May-Sept. daily 10am-4pm; Oct.-Apr. Tu-Su 10am-4pm. Call ☎3392 6494 for English-language castle tours, May-Sept. daily 11am, 1, 3pm; Oct.-Apr. Tu, Th, and Sa-Su 3pm. Ruins 40kr, students 30kr. Castle tour 60/50kr.)* Nearby, the **Thorvaldsens Museum** has colorfully painted rooms with works by Danish sculptor Bertel Thorvaldsen, including some original plaster models. Head upstairs to see the collection of Etruscan and Egyptian artifacts. *(Bertel Thorvaldsens Pl. 2. ☎3332 1532; www.thorvaldsensmuseum.dk. Open Tu-Su 10am-5pm. 20kr. W free.)* Astronomer Tycho Brahe once observed the stars from the top of the **Round Tower** (Rundetaarn), which provides a sweeping view of the city. *(Købmagerg. 52A. ☎3373 0373; www.rundetaarn.dk. Open June-Aug. M-Sa 10am-8pm, Su noon-8pm; Sept. to mid-Oct. and Apr.-May M-Sa 10am-5pm, Su noon-5pm; mid-Oct. to Mar. M and Th-Sa 10am-5pm, Tu-W 10am-5pm and 7-10pm, Su noon-5pm. 25kr. AmEx/DC/MC/V.)* Down the street, the **Museum Erotica** celebrates all things carnal; the videos from the Porn Room can be purchased at the front desk. *(Købmagerg. 24. ☎3312 0311; www.museumerotica.dk. Open June-Sept. daily 10am-11pm; Oct.-May Su-Th 11am-8pm, F-Sa 11am-10pm. 109kr with guidebook. AmEx/MC/V.)*

DENMARK

CHRISTIANSHAVN. In 1971, a few dozen flower children established the "free city" of **Christiania** in an abandoned Christianshavn fort. Today, the thousand-odd residents continue the tradition of artistic expression and unconventionality. Vendors sell clothing and jewelry, while spots like **Woodstock Cafe** and **Cafe Nemoland** have cheap beer and the most diverse crowds in town. Recent government crackdowns have driven **Pusher Street's** once-open drug trade underground, and arrests for possession have become commonplace. A large sign warns passersby not to take pictures on Pusher St. *(Main entrance on Prinsesseg. Take bus #66 from København H.)* Planned renovations have been slow at the landmark **Vor Frelsers Kirke** (Our Savior's Church); check to see whether the gold-accented interior and 90m spire are open to the public. *(Sankt Annæg. 9. M: Christianshavn or bus #66. Turn left onto Prinsesseg. ☎3257 2798; www.vorfrelserskirke.dk. Spire ☎3254 1573. Church free. Spire 20kr. Cash only.)* The **Danish Architecture Center** hosts elegantly presented exhibits. *(Strandg. 27B. ☎3257 1930; www.dac.dk. Open daily 10am-5pm. 40kr, students 25kr. DC/MC/V.)*

FREDERIKSTADEN. Northeast of the city center, Edvard Eriksen's tiny **Little Mermaid** (Lille Havfrue) statue at the mouth of the harbor honors Hans Christian Andersen's beloved tale. *(S-tog: Østerport. Turn left out of the station, go left on Folke Bernadottes Allé, bear right on the path bordering the canal, go left up the stairs, and then head right along the street.)* Head back along the canal and turn left across the moat to reach **Kastellet,** a rampart-enclosed 17th-century fortress that's now a park. *(Open daily 6am-10pm.)* On the other side of Kastellet, the fascinating **Frihedsmuseet** (Museum of Danish Resistance) documents the German occupation of 1940-1945, when the Danes helped over 7000 Jews escape to Sweden. *(At Churchillparken. ☎3313 7714. Open May-Sept. Tu-Sa 10am-4pm, Su 10am-5pm; Oct.-Apr. Tu-Sa 10am-3pm, Su 10am-4pm. English-language tours Tu, Th, Su 2pm. Free.)* Walk south down Amalieng. to reach

The *Copenhagen Post* estimates that there may be more bikes than Danes in Denmark, and the city of Copenhagen leads the way as one of most bike-friendly capitals in Europe this side of Amsterdam. Rentals from **City Bike** (p. 264) are the most convenient way to go in Copenhagen, although the company's rules require that you only ride the bikes in the city center. The eastern banks of the five western lakes are fair game under these regulations, but if you cross over to the other side of the lakes, you'll face a 1000kr fine.

A tour of the parks, monuments, and canals just outside the central city.

TIME: 4hr. With visits to Rosenborg Slot and Christiansborg Slot, 6hr.

DISTANCE: About 6km.

SEASON: Year-round, although Rosenborg Slot has reduced hours Nov.-Apr.

When biking through the city, avoid pedestrian thoroughfares like Strøget, unless you're in the mood for slaloming around strolling couples and scampering children. If you want to ride out into the countryside, ask your hostel about rental bikes. You can take your bike onto an S-tog for 10kr. In Denmark you are legally required to use lights when riding at night, and police are not shy about handing out 400kr fines to enforce this law. Helmets are strongly recommended, but are not mandatory.

This tour starts and ends at the **Rådhus.** Begin by carefully making your way down busy Hans Christian Andersens Boulevard.

1 BOTANISK HAVE. Take a right onto Nørre Voldg. and follow it until you see the gates leading into the University of Copenhagen's lush **Botanical Gardens** (p. 269). Wander along paths lined with more than 13,000 species of plants, or hone in on the **Palm House** to view its extravagant orchids, cycads, and other tropical rarities.

2 STATENS MUSEUM FOR KUNST AND ROSENBORG SLOT. Turn left out of the gardens onto Øster Voldg. At the intersection with Sølvg., you'll see the gates of the **Statens Museum for Kunst** (State Museum of Fine Arts; p. 269) to the north and the spires of **Rosenborg Slot** (p. 269) to the south. The latter served as the 16th-century summer house of King Christian IV, and the royal family took refuge here in 1801 when the British navy was shelling Copenhagen. Lock up your bike and pop inside for a look at the Sculpture Street in the museum or Denmark's crown jewels in the Slot's treasury.

3 ROUND TOWER. Backtrack down Øster Voldg. and turn left onto Gothersg. Make a right onto Landemærket and then hop off again to scale the heights of the **Round Tower** (p. 268), a onetime royal observatory that still affords a sweeping view of the city.

4 AMALIENBORG PALACE. Head back up to Gothersg. and then turn right. Pass by **Kongens Nytorv,** the 1670 "new square" that turns into a skating rink each winter, and take a left onto Bredg. Keep your eyes peeled for the gilded dome of the **Marmorkirken** (Marble Church; p. 269) on your left, and then turn right to enter the octagonal plaza of **Amalienborg Palace** (p. 269), a set of four dazzling Rococo mansions that the queen and her family call home.

5 NYHAVN. Continue on through the plaza, turn right on Toldbodg., and then right before the bridge onto Nyhavn. Part of the city of Copenhagen's old waterfront, Nyhavn was known for centuries as a seedy strip for sailors to find grog, women, and a tattoo artist sober enough to wield a firm needle. Over the past 30 years, Copenhagen has embarked on a clean-up campaign, and today you're more likely to find an upscale deli serving *smørrebrod* than a tumbledown soup kitchen. Whenever a scrap of sunshine can be found, the good people of Copenhagen are soaking it up along the wharf, joined by Swedes from Malmö in search of cheap Danish beer.

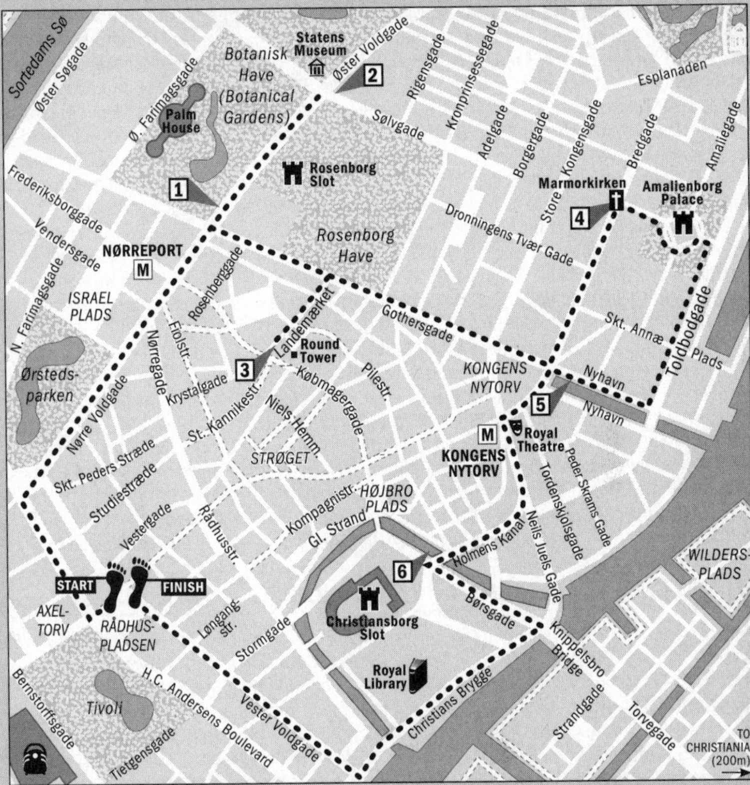

6 CHRISTIANBORG SLOT. Walk your bike through Kongens Nytorv, and then thread your way between the **Royal Theater** (p. 272) and the metro station down Neils Juels G. Turn right onto Holmens Kanal and cross the bridge to reach **Christiansborg Slot** (p. 268), seat of the Danish Parliament. Look for the building's 103m tower; it's difficult to miss. If you arrive before 3:30pm, try to catch a tour of the Royal Reception Rooms, or head down into the ruins of the four previous castles underneath the present-day building. The first castle was demolished to make way for a larger one, the next two burned down in spectacular fires, and the Hanseatic League dismantled the fourth castle stone by stone after they captured the city in 1369.

7 SLIDING INTO HOME. You're in the home stretch. Head east toward the Knippelsbro Bridge and **Christiania** (p. 269), taking in the industrial skyline before lugging your bike down the steps to Christians Brygge below. Turn right and bike along the canal. Keep watch for the Black Diamond annex of the **Royal Library,** built in 1996 from black marble imported from Zimbabwe. Make a quick stop to check your email at one of the two free terminals inside. Make a right onto Vester Voldg. and coast back up to the Rådhus. You've earned the right to call it a day.

Amalienborg Palace, a complex of four enormous mansions that serve as the winter residences of the royal family. Several apartments are open to the public, including the studies of 19th-century Danish kings. The changing of the guard takes place at noon on the vast plaza. *(☎3312 0808; www.rosenborgslot.dk. Open May-Oct. daily 10am-4pm; Nov.-Apr. Tu-Su 11am-4pm. 50kr, students 30kr. Combined ticket with Rosenborg Slot 80kr. Photography 20kr. MC/V.)* The imposing 19th-century **Marmorkirken** (Marble Church), opposite the palace, features an ornate interior under Europe's third-largest dome. *(Fredriksg. 4. ☎3315 0144; www.marmorkirken.dk. Open M-Tu and Th 10am-5pm, W 10am-6pm, F-Sa noon-5pm. English-language tours to the top of the dome mid-June to Aug. daily 1 and 3pm; Oct. to mid-June Sa-Su 1 and 3pm. Free. Tours 25kr. Cash only.)*

The **Statens Museum for Kunst** (State Museum of Fine Arts) displays an eclectic collection of Danish and international art in two buildings linked by a long, glass-roof gallery. *(Sølvg. 48-50. S-tog: Nørreport. Walk up Øster Voldg. ☎3374 8494; www.smk.dk. Open Tu and Th-Su 10am-5pm, W 10am-8pm. English-language tours July-Aug. Sa-Su 2pm. Permanent collection free. Special exhibits 70kr, students 50kr. W free. AmEx/MC/V.)* Opposite the museum, the Baroque **Rosenborg Slot,** built by King Christian IV in the early 17th century as a summer residence, shows off the crown jewels and the opulent Unicorn Throne, which legend holds is constructed from unicorn horns. *(Øster Voldg. 4A. M: Nørreport. ☎3315 3286; www.rosenborgslot.dk. Open June-Aug. daily 11am-5pm; May and Sept. daily 10am-4pm; Oct. daily 11am-3pm; Nov.-Apr. Tu-Su 11am-2pm. 60kr, students 40kr. AmEx/DC/MC/V.)* About 13,000 plant species thrive in the nearby **Botanisk Have** (Botanical Gardens); tropical and subtropical plants mingle happily in the iron-and-glass **Palm House.** *(Gardens open June-Aug. daily 8:30am-6pm; Sept.-May Tu-Su 8:30am-4pm. Palm House open June-Aug. daily 10am-3pm; Sept.-May Tu-Su 10am-3pm. Free.)*

DENMARK

ENTERTAINMENT AND FESTIVALS

For info on events, consult *Copenhagen This Week* or ask at Use It. The **Royal Theater** is home to the world-famous Royal Danish Ballet. The box office at Tordenskjoldsg. 7 sells same-day half-price tickets. (☎3369 6969. Open M-Sa 10am-6pm.) The **Tivoli ticket office,** Vesterbrog. 3, has half-price tickets for the city's other theaters. (☎3315 1012. Open daily mid-Apr. to mid-Sept. 11am-8pm; mid-Sept. to mid-Apr. 9am-5pm.) Tickets are also available online at www.billetnet.dk. Relaxed **Kul-Kaféen,** Teglgårdsstr. 5, is a great place to see live performers and listen to stand-up comedy. (☎3332 1777. Cover up to 50kr. Open M 11am-midnight, Tu-Sa 11am-2am. MC/V.) In late March and early April, international and domestic releases compete for Danish distribution deals at the **NatFilm Festival** (☎3312 0005; www.natfilm.dk). During the world-class **Copenhagen Jazz Festival** (July 6-15, 2007; ☎3393 2013; http://festival.jazz.dk), the city teems with free outdoor concerts. Throughout July and August, **Zulu Sommerbio** (Summer Cinema; www.zulu.dk) holds free screenings in parks and squares across the city. Movies are shown in their original languages with Danish subtitles.

NIGHTLIFE

> **!** The areas behind København H, the central train station, can be unsafe, especially at night. Explore with caution, and bring a friend.

In Copenhagen, weekends often begin on Wednesday, and clubs pulse with activity late enough to serve breakfast with their martinis. On Thursdays, many bars and clubs have cheaper drinks and reduced covers. The streets of the city center, as well as those of **Nørrebro** and **Vesterbro,** are lined with hip, crowded bars. Fancier options abound along Nyhavn, where laid-back Danes frequently bring their own beer and sit on the pier; open containers are legal within the city limits. Unless otherwise noted, all bars and clubs are 18+. Copenhagen has a thriving gay and lesbian scene; check out *Playtime* or *Out and About* for listings.

Vega, Enghavev. 40 (☎3326 0954; www.vega.dk), in Vesterbro. Bus: 80N, 84N. Copenhagen's largest nightclub, 2 concert venues, and a popular bar. Come before 1am to avoid paying cover and party all night with the glitterati. Bar 18+; club 20+. Club cover 60kr after 1am. Club open F-Sa 11pm-5am. Bar open F-Sa 7pm-5am. MC/V.

The Moose Bar, Sværtev. 5 (☎3391 4291). M: Kongens Nytorv. Rowdy local spirit dominates in this popular bar, famous for its cheap beer and its jukebox playing classic rock hits. Beer 24kr, 2 pints 30kr. 2 mixed drinks 30-35kr. Reduced prices Tu, Th, and Sa 9pm-close. Open M-W 1pm-5am, Th-Sa 1pm-7am, Su 1pm-3am. AmEx/MC/V.

The Australian Bar, Vesterg. 10 (☎2024 1411). M: Nørreport. With cheap drinks, a hyperactive smoke machine, and a dance-club playlist, this bar caters to students. Beer 20kr. Mixed drinks 30kr. Cover 40kr. Open Su-W 4pm-2am, Th-Sa 4pm-5am. MC/V.

Park, Østerbrog. 79 (☎3525 1661; www.park.dk). Bus 85N. Far from the center, this club has a live music hall, lavish lounges, and a rooftop patio. Beer 45kr. Dress to impress. F 20+, Sa 22+. Cover Th-Sa 50-70kr. Restaurant open Tu-Sa 11am-10pm. Club open Su-Tu 11am-midnight, W 11am-2am, Th-Sa 11am-5am. AmEx/DC/MC/V.

PAN Club and Café, Knabrostr. 3 (☎3311 1950; www.pan-cph.dk). M: Nørreport. Gay cafe, bar, and multiple dance floors sprawl out around an endless series of staircases. W hip-hop. Th theme night. Beer 35kr. Mixed drinks 60kr. Cover F-Sa 50kr. Cafe open W-Sa 10pm-last customer. Disco open 11pm-last customer. AmEx/DC/MC/V.

Mc.Kluud's, Istedg. 126 (☎3331 6383; www.mckluud.dk), in Vesterbro. Bus 10 or 84N. Artists and students come to sample the cheap beer at this Wild West bar inspired by the American TV show McCloud. Beer 15-17kr. Open daily 1pm-2am. Cash only.

La Hacienda/The Dance Floor, Nørreg. 1 (☎3311 7478; www.la-hacienda.dk). M: Nørreport. Choose between **La Hacienda,** a laid-back lounge playing soul and hip-hop, and **The Dance Floor,** a 2-story trance-driven club. Cover for men 150kr, women 130kr; includes 1 champagne and 1 beer. Open F 11pm-8am, Sa 11pm-10am. AmEx/MC/V.

DENMARK

DAYTRIPS FROM COPENHAGEN

Copenhagen's **S-togs** and other regional lines can whisk travelers away from the urban din to museums, castles, countryside scenery, and well-trodden beaches. It's significantly cheaper and more flexible for travelers to buy cards and stamp them with clips rather than purchasing one-way tickets.

HILLERØD. Hillerød is home to **Frederiksborg Slot,** one of Denmark's most impressive castles. Close to 90 rooms are open to the public, including the Chapel, the Rose Room, the Great Hall, and the Baroque gardens. From the train station, cross the street onto Vibekev. and continue straight along the path until you can follow the signs; at the Torvet (main plaza), walk to the pond and bear left, following its perimeter to reach the castle entrance. *(Hillerød is at the end of S-tog lines A and E. 40min., every 10min., 63kr or 4 clips. ☎4826 0439; www.frederiksborgmuseet.dk. Gardens open May-Aug. daily 10am-9pm; low season reduced hours. Castle open daily Apr.-Oct. 10am-5pm; Nov.-Mar. 11am-3pm. Gardens free. Castle 60kr, students 50kr. AmEx/MC/V.)*

HELSINGØR. Helsingør sits at a strategic entrance to the Baltic Sea, just 5km from the coast of Sweden. Originally built to levy taxes on passing ships, the majestic 16th-century **Kronborg Slot** is better known as **Elsinore,** the setting for Shakespeare's *Hamlet.* A statue of Viking chief Holger Danske sleeps in the dank, forbidding **dungeon;** legend holds that he will awake to defend Denmark in its darkest hour. *(☎4921 3078; www.kronborg.dk. Book tours in advance. Open May-Sept. daily 10:30am-*

> **STOP THAT TRAIN!** In much of Denmark, especially rural areas, trains do not stop at every station on the line. Be sure to check at the ticket counter to find out which train to take, and ask whether you need to sit in a particular car.

5pm; Apr. and Oct. Tu-Su 11am-4pm; Nov.-Mar. Tu-Su 11am-3pm. 75kr. AmEx/MC/V.) In early August, the **Hamlet Sommer** festival *(www.hamletsommer.dk)* brings Hamlet's ghost back to life in a series of avant-garde performances in the castle's commons. The **tourist office,** Havnepl. 3, is in the Kulturhus, across from the station. *(☎4921 1333; www.visithelsingor.dk. Open mid-June to Aug. M-Th 9am-5pm, F 9am-6pm, Sa 10am-3pm; Sept. to mid-June M-F 9am-4pm, Sa 10am-1pm. Helsingør is at the end of the northern train line from Malmö, SWE via Copenhagen. 1hr., every 20min., 63kr or 4 clips.)*

HUMLEBÆK AND RUNGSTED. The spectacular **Louisiana Museum of Modern Art,** 13 Gl. Strandv., in Humlebæk, honors the three wives (all named Louisa) of the estate's original owner. The museum rounds out its permanent collection—including works by Warhol, Lichtenstein, and Picasso—with several major exhibits each year. Landscape architects have lavished attention on the seaside sculpture garden and the sloping lake garden. From the Humlebæk station, follow signs for 10min. or catch bus #388. *(From Copenhagen, take a Helsingør-bound train. 45min., every 20min., 63kr or 4 clips. ☎4919 0719; www.louisiana.dk. Open M-Tu and Th-Su 10am-5pm, W 10am-10pm. 80kr, students 70kr. AmEx/DC/MC/V.)* Near the water in Rungsted stands the house where Karen Blixen wrote her autobiographical 1937 novel *Out of Africa* under the pseudonym Isak Dinesen. The **Karen Blixen Museum,** Rungsted Strandv. 111, provides a candid chronicle of the author's life. The grounds are home to 40 species of birds. Follow the street leading out of the train station and turn right on Rungstedv., then right again on Rungsted Strandv., or take bus #388. *(From Copenhagen, take a Nivå-bound train. 30min., every 20min., 63kr or 4 clips. ☎4557 1057. Open May-Sept. Tu-Su 10am-5pm; Oct.-Apr. W-F 1-4pm, Sa-Su 11am-4pm. 40kr. AmEx/MC/V.)*

MØN

Hans Christian Andersen once called the isle of Møn the most beautiful spot in Denmark. The sheer white **Møns Klint** (Chalk Cliffs), which plunge straight into calm blue waters, can be appreciated from the rocky beaches below or the densely forested hiking trails above. The **Liselund Slot** (Doll Castle) looks more like a big country house than a castle. The main attraction is the surrounding park, with peacocks and thatched-roof farmhouses. (☎5581 2178. English-language castle tours daily May-Sept. 10:30, 11am, 1:30, 2pm. Tour 20kr.) Walking away from the castle and parking lot, you'll reach a path that becomes a **hiking trail,** which snakes 3km through a lush forest before arriving at the cliffs. Buses to Møn arrive in **Stege,** the island's largest town, located across the island from the castle and cliffs. From Stege, take bus #52 to Busene (every 1-2hr., 13kr) and walk 10min. to the cliffs. Between mid-June and late August, bus #632 runs from Stege to the parking lots at the cliffs (30min.; 9:15, 11:45am, and 1:50pm; 13kr). Another way to see Møn is by renting a **bike** in Klintholm Havn, the last stop on bus #52. Across the street from the bus stop is a **Kwik Spar** grocery store (open M-Sa 8am-8pm) that doubles as the town's unofficial tourist information center. Store your luggage here for free before renting a bike (70kr per day). From the store, it's a beautiful 6km bike ride uphill to Liselund Slot and Møns Klint; the downhill ride back to town is a blast.

Orchids line the trail of the 143m **Aborrebjerg** (Bass Mountain) near the island's youth hostel, the lakeside **Møns Klint Vandrerhjem (HI) ❷,** Langebjergv. 1. Between late June and mid-August, take bus #632 from Stege to the campground stop, then continue in the direction of the bus and take the first right. In low season, take bus #52 to Magleby and walk left 2.5km down the road. (☎5581 2030. Breakfast 50kr. Linens 45kr. Laundry 30kr. Reception 8-10:30am and 4-7pm. Open May-Sept.

Dorms 185kr; singles and doubles 335-370kr. 35kr HI discount. MC/V; 5% surcharge.) **Stege Camping ❶,** Flacksvej 5, is just a 5min. walk from the Stege bus stop. (☎5581 8404. Hot water 20kr. Reception 24hr. Open May to mid-Oct. Tent site 50kr. Cash only.) To get to Møn, take the **train** from Copenhagen to Vordingborg (1½hr., 120kr), then bus #62 to Stege (45min., 39kr). The info center, **Feriepartner Møn,** Storeg. 2, is right next to the Stege bus stop and sells maps. (☎5586 0400; www.visitmoen.com. Open July-Aug. M-F 9:30am-5pm, Sa 9am-12:30pm; Sept.-June M-F 9:30am-4:30pm, Sa 9am-noon.)

ROSKILDE ☎46

Once the capital of the Danish Empire, Roskilde (pop. 53,000) is an easy daytrip from Denmark's modern-day capital. Each summer, music fans arrive in droves to hear performances by artists such as Kanye West and Bob Dylan at the **Roskilde Music Festival** (July 5-8, 2007; www.roskilde-festival.dk), northern Europe's largest outdoor concert. The red-brick **Roskilde Domkirke,** off the Stændertorvet, is a large church where stunning sarcophagi hold the remains of generations of Danish royalty. Head left out of the train station, go right on Herseg., and left onto Alg. (☎35 16 24; www.roskildedomkirke.dk. Open Apr.-Sept. M-F 9am-4:45pm, Sa 9am-noon, Su 12:30-4:45pm; Oct.-Mar. Tu-Sa 10am-3:45pm, Su 12:30-3:45pm. English-language tours mid-June to mid-Aug. M-F 11am and 2pm, Sa-Su 2pm depending on church services. Domkirke 25kr, students 15kr. Tours 20kr.) On the harbor next to the hostel, the **Viking Ship Museum,** Vindeboder 12, displays five ships unearthed from the Roskilde Fjord. The museum includes a shipyard where volunteers build vessels using Viking methods. Some of the ships are available for sailing. (☎30 02 00; www.vikingeskibsmuseet.dk. Open daily 10am-5pm. English-language tours mid-June to Aug. 3pm. 80kr, students 70kr. AmEx/MC/V.) The **Roskilde Vandrerhjem (HI) ❸,** Vindeboder 7, has bright rooms in a harborside location near the town center. (☎35 21 84; www.danhostel.dk/roskilde. Breakfast 45kr. Linens 45kr. Reception 7am-10pm. Dorms 185kr. 35kr HI discount. AmEx/DC/MC/V.) Restaurants line **Algade** and **Skomagergade** in the town center. **Trains** depart for Copenhagen (25-30min., every 15min., 63kr) and Odense (1¼hr., 3 per hr., 178kr). The **tourist office,** Gullandsstr. 15, books rooms for a 25kr fee and 10-15% deposit. Walk through the Stændertorvet turn left on Allehelgensgade, and follow the signs. (☎31 65 65. Open late June to late Aug. M-F 9am-5pm, Sa 10am-1pm; low season reduced hours.)

BORNHOLM

Residents of the island of Bornholm like to say that when Scandinavia was created, God saved the best piece for last and dropped it into the Baltic Sea. After a day or two in Bornholm, you might be inclined to agree. The undulating farmlands of the south are ideal for bikers, while nature lovers will favor the dramatic, rocky landscape of the north. The central forest is one of the largest in Denmark, and the sandiest beaches are at Dueodde, on the island's southern tip.

TRANSPORTATION. The cheapest way to get to Bornholm from Copenhagen is by a **bus** and **ferry** combination. Bornholmerbussen #866 leaves from København H for Ystad, SWE, where passengers can transfer to the ferry. (☎4468 4400. 3hr., 5 per day, 220kr.) A **train** and **ferry** combo runs from Copenhagen to Rønne by way of Ystad. (Train ☎7013 1415; www.dsb.dk; 1¼hr., 5-6 per day. Ferry ☎5695 1866; www.bornholmferries.dk; 80min. Combination round-trip 448kr.) A discount "red ticket" (224kr, low season 150kr) for the ferry is available online a week in advance, but the combo ticket is cheaper for travelers coming from Copenhagen. Overnight ferries from Køge (S-tog: A+, E, Ex), south of Copenhagen, leave at 11:30pm and arrive in Rønne at 6:30am (240kr, 473kr for a dorm bed).

DENMARK

One of the best ways to enjoy a scenic day on Bornholm is to bike through the island's rolling hills and peaceful villages. The reliable bus service allows you to bring your bike onboard for a mere 20kr extra, making it easy to get around.

A tour of the island's round church, museums, and natural attractions.

TIME: Set aside a day to complete the tour and enjoy the sights along the way.

DISTANCE: About 12km on bike.

SEASON: Year-round, although Østerlars Rundkirke is only open Apr.-Oct.

This tour starts and ends in the southwestern port of Rønne, Bornholm's biggest town. You can rent bikes at **Bornholms Cykeludlejning,** Ndr. Kystv. 4, next to the tourist office. (☎5695 0604. Reserve ahead in July. 60kr per day. Open daily mid-Apr. to Sept. 9am-6pm. AmEx/MC/V.) You can also pick up bus schedules and tourist info there before setting out on your trip. For more details on the island's sights, check www.bornholm.info.

1 Rent a bike in Rønne and take it with you on bus #3 to investigate the **Østerlars Rundkirke,** the largest and most enigmatic of Bornholm's four round churches. Scholars believe the Knights Templar built these unusual churches between 1120 and 1250. Drawing lines between the four churches reveals several geometric patterns, one of which can be seen as part of a pentacle, an ancient pagan symbol. These findings have drawn theorists and treasure hunters to the island looking for clues to the brotherhood's occult rituals.

The Østerlars Rundkirke has windows positioned to face sunrise at the winter solstice, a central fresco depicting the life of Jesus, and a large rune stone that was discovered in the walls of the belfry. The well-tended churchyard in the back has a beautiful view of the valley and several of Denmark's new windmills churning in the distance. (☎5649 8264. Open July M-Sa 9am-5pm, Su 1-5pm; Apr.-June and Aug.-Oct. M-Sa 9am-5pm. 10kr.)

2 From the church, it's a quick 500m downhill bike ride to the **Medieval Center of Bornholm** (Bornholms Middelaldercenter), Strangevej 1. Spread over 14 hectares of land, including woods and rocky pastures, this outdoor museum and tourist attraction recreates life in a medieval town, with actors in period attire inhabiting the peasants' dwellings and nobleman's farm. The hands-on workshops show you how to make medieval crafts and let you take away your handiwork free of charge. Make your own coins at the mint, or try your hand at shaping your own arrows and lances. Depending on the date of your visit, you may also see ballad singers or fire eaters. On Thursdays, food is served at the farm, and the actors demonstrate a rune hunt. (☎5649 8319; www.bornholmsmiddelaldercenter.dk. 85kr, low season 65kr. MC/V.)

3 After testing your arrows at the Medieval Center's archery range, continue biking north along the car road for about 3km until you come to **Gudhjem,** a small hillside fishing town. Head down to the harbor, carefully controlling your speed on the steep descent.

At the waterfront, you'll find some of Bornholm's most famous fish smokehouses; stop at one for a quick *smørrebrød* (open-faced sandwich), an essential experience for any visitor to the island. **Røgeri,** Eoner Mikkelsensvej 9, serves smoked herring that is legendary across Denmark, as well as the popular *smørrebrød* that the eatery invented: Sunrise over Gudhjem (Sild Sol over Gudhjem), with two pieces of smoked herring, herbs, and egg yolk on a single slice of bread. To get to Røgeri, head to the the Christiansø ferry terminal by the harbor, and continue walking with the sea to your right for 5min. (☎5648 5708. Lunch buffet 87kr. Sandwiches 28-32kr. Beer 23kr. Open daily high season 10am-midnight; low season 10am-5pm. MC/V.)

4 Get back on your bike and head west along Bornholm's rocky northern coast. Although the ride is hilly, the views of the fields and coastline are worth the effort. You can rest up at the beautiful **Bornholm Museum of Art** (Bornholms Kunst Museum), on Helligdommen near Rø, about 3km from Gudhjem. This striking museum, which opened in 1993, was

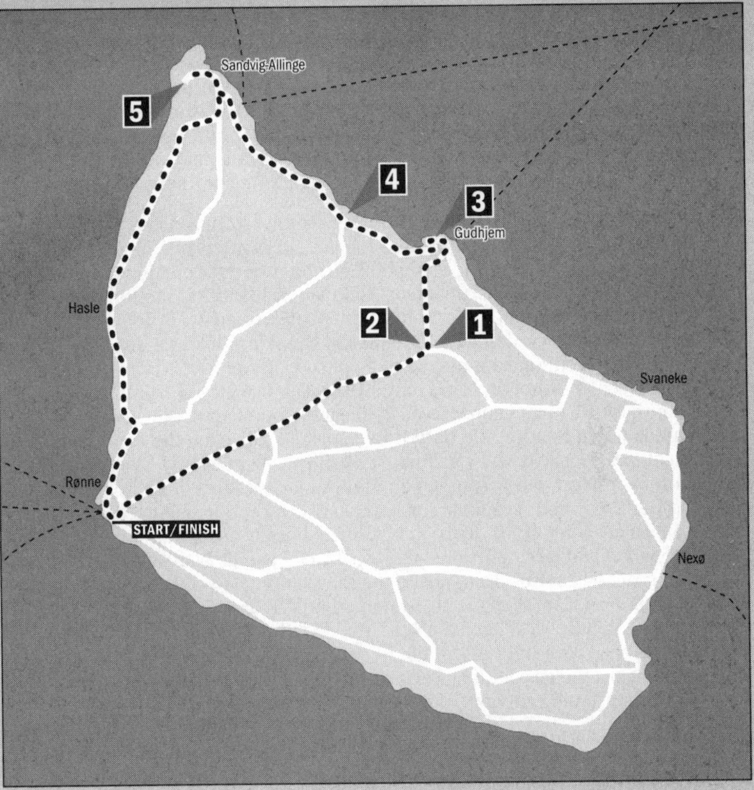

designed by two Danish architects to complement the surrounding landscape. It displays an extensive collection of paintings by members of the Bornholm School, a group of artists who lived and worked on the island at the turn of the 20th century. Their paintings depict some of the same majestic landscapes of Bornholm that you'll see in living glory on your bike tour. In addition to biking, you can also get to the museum from Rønne by taking bus #3 to Gudhjem and switching to bus #9. (☎5648 4386; www.bornholms-kunstmuseum.dk. Open July-Aug. daily 10am-5pm; Apr.-May and Sept.-Oct. Tu-Su 10am-5pm; Nov.-Mar. Tu and Th 1-5pm. 50kr, students 40kr. AmEx/MC/V.)

Just a 5min. walk from the museum lies the former holy spring Rø Kjila, at the foot of **Helligdomsklippen,** a sheer granite cliff overlooking the ocean. The site of religious pilgrimages in the Middle Ages, the "sacred cliffs" of northern Bornholm are connected to each other by a well-maintained hiking trail that is remarkably untouristed. Wooden stairways lead from the cliffs to the water's edge.

5 Hammershus, the largest medieval fortification in northern Europe, is less than 6km from the museum, at the northermost tip of Bornholm. The hilltop fortress was built in the 12th century by Denmark's Catholic leaders, conquered by the king's army several times in the Middle Ages, and partially destroyed in the mid-18th century. After touring the restored ruins and admiring the view of the surrounding forest and sea, head to the nearby villages of Allinge or Sandvig to catch bus #1 or 2 back to Rønne.

Bornholm has an efficient local BAT **bus** service, although buses run less frequently on weekends. (☎5695 2121. 36-45kr, bikes 20kr; 24hr. pass 130kr.) Bus #7 makes a circuit of the coastline, heading from Rønne to Hammershus and stopping at most of the island's towns and attractions along the way. Bus #3 from Rønne passes by Østerlars Church on its way to Gudhejm, where the ferry departs for Christiansø, a small island to the north of Bornholm. There are well-marked **bike** paths between all the major towns; pick up a guide (40kr) at Rønne's tourist office. The ride from Rønne to either Sandvig in the north or Dueodde in the southeast is about 30km. For one suggested bike route through the island, see p. 276.

RØNNE. Rønne (pop. 14,000), on Bornholm's southwestern coast, is the principal port of entry. **Rønne Vandrerhjem (HI) ❷,** Arsenalv. 12, is in a peaceful wooded area. From the ferry, head toward the tourist office and turn right on Munch Petersens V. Bear left up the hill on Zahrtmannsv., follow it to the left at the top of the hill, and turn right at the roundabout onto Søndre Allé; Arsenalv. is 100m up on the right. (☎5695 1340; www.danhostel-roenne.dk. Breakfast 45kr. Linens 50kr. Wash 30kr, dry 50kr. Reception 8am-noon and 4-5pm. Open Apr.-Oct. Dorms 150kr; singles 300kr. 35kr HI discount. Cash only.) **Galløkken Camping ❶,** Strandvejen 4, is 15min. south of the town center, near the beach. Follow directions to the hostel, but continue down Søndre Allé until it becomes Strandvejen; the campground is on the right. (☎5695 2320; www.gallokken.dk. Bikes 60kr per day. Electricity 25kr. Reception 8am-noon and 5-7pm. Open May-Aug. Tent sites 60kr. Scandinavian Camping Card required; available for purchase at reception, 80kr. MC/V; 5% surcharge.) **Sam's Corner ❷,** St. Torv 2, is a basic burger and pizza joint with low prices (45-60kr) and large portions. (☎5695 1523. Open daily 10:30am-9pm. Cash only.) Get groceries at **Kvickly,** opposite the tourist office. (☎5695 1777. Open mid-June to Aug. daily 9am-8pm; Sept. to mid-June M-F 9am-8pm, Sa 9am-5pm, Su 10am-4pm. Cash only.) The **tourist office,** Ndr. Kystv. 3, books private rooms (160-215kr) for no fee. Turn right out of the ferry terminal, pass the BAT bus terminal, and cross toward the gas station; look for the green flag. (☎5695 9500. Open mid-June to mid-Aug. daily 9am-5pm; low season reduced hours. MC/V.)

DENMARK

ALLINGE AND SANDVIG. These seaside villages, 1km apart, are excellent starting points for hikes and bike rides through Bornholm's northern coast. Many trails originate in Sandvig; the rocky area around **Hammeren,** northwest of the town, is a beautiful 2hr. walk that can only be covered on foot. Just outside Sandvig is the lakeside **Sandvig Vandrerhjem (HI) ❷,** Hammershusv. 94. Get off the bus one stop past Sandvig Gl. Station, continue up the road, and follow the signs. (☎5648 0362. Breakfast 45kr. Linens 50kr. Laundry 40kr. Reception 9-10am and 4-6pm. Open May-Sept. Dorms 150kr; singles 275kr; doubles 400kr. 35kr HI discount. Cash only.) **Riccos ❷,** Strandg. 8, in Sandvig, is a pleasant cafe in a private home near the sea and has free **Internet.** (☎5648 0314. Open daily 7am-10pm. MC/V.) The **tourist office** is at Kirkeg. 4 in Allinge. (☎5648 0001. Open mid-June to mid-Aug. M-F 10am-5pm, Sa 10am-3pm; mid-Aug. to mid-June M-F 10am-5pm, Sa 10am-noon.) Rent **bikes** at the **Sandvig Cykeludlejning,** Strandvejen 121. (☎2145 6013. Open May-Sept. M-F 9am-3:30pm, Sa 9am-1pm, Su 10am-1pm. 60kr per day. Cash only.)

FUNEN (FYN)

Nestled between Zealand to the east and the Jutland Peninsula to the west, the island of Funen attracts fairy-tale fans and cyclists alike. Isolated in the time of golden son Hans Christian Andersen, this once-remote breadbasket has since been connected to Zealand by the magnificent Storebæltsbro bridge and tunnel. Bike maps (75kr) are available at tourist offices.

ODENSE ☎63, 65, 66

The legacy of Hans Christian Andersen draws most tourists to Odense (OHN-suh; pop. 200,000), Denmark's third-largest city. While fairy tales still reign supreme in the writer's hometown, a thriving nightlife and music scene also make Odense a destination for the young and trendy.

TRANSPORTATION AND PRACTICAL INFORMATION. **Trains** run from Odense to Copenhagen (1½hr., 3 per hr., 214kr). **Buses** depart from behind the train station. The **tourist office,** in the Rådhuset, offers free **Internet** and bike maps and books rooms for a 35kr fee. Turn left out of the train station, make a right on Thomas Thriges G. at the second light, then go right on Vesterg. (☎6612 7520; www.visitodense.com. Open mid-June to Aug. M-F 9:30am-6pm, Sa-Su 10am-3pm; Sept. to mid-June M-F 9:30am-4:30pm, Sa 10am-1pm.) The library in the station has free **Internet.** (☎6551 4421. Open Apr.-Sept. M-Th 10am-7pm, F 10am-4pm, Sa 10am-2pm; low season extended hours.) Rent **bikes** at **City Cykler,** Vesterbro 27. Continue down Vesterg. from the tourist office for 10min.; it will be on the right. (☎6613 9783. 99kr per day, with 750kr deposit. Open M-F 10am-5:30pm, Sa 10am-1pm.) **Postal Code:** 5000.

ACCOMMODATIONS AND FOOD. **Danhostel Odense City (HI) ❸**, next to the train station, has excellent facilities. (☎6311 0425; www.cityhostel.dk. Breakfast 50kr. Linens 60kr. Laundry 45kr. Internet 10kr per 15min. Reception 8am-noon and 4-8pm. Dorms 185kr; singles 400kr; doubles 550kr; triples 585kr; quads 617kr. 35kr HI discount. MC/V; 4% surcharge.) To reach **DCU-Camping Odense ❷,** Odensev. 102, 4km from town, take bus #21, 22, 23, or 24 (dir.: Højby; 14kr) and ask the driver to drop you off. (☎6611 4702. Reception mid-June to mid-Aug. 7:30am-noon and 2-10pm; low season 7:30am-noon and 4-10pm. Tent sites 106kr; low season 86kr. Electricity 25kr. 4-person cabin with stove 390kr. AmEx/MC/V.) **Vestergade,** a long pedestrian street, has ethnic restaurants and cafes. Don't overlook the alleys off Vesterg., including **Brandts Passage,** filled with hip cafes, and the more low-key **Vintapperstræde.** Get groceries at **Aktiv Super,** Nørreg. 63, at the corner of Nørreg. and Skulkenborgg. (☎6612 8559. Open M-F 9am-7pm, Sa 9am-4pm. Cash only.)

SIGHTS AND NIGHTLIFE. At **Hans Christian Andersen Hus,** Bangs Boder 29, visitors can learn about the author's eccentricities and see the home where he grew up and worked. Enjoy free performances of his timeless stories in a mix of Danish, English, and German on the museum's lawn in the summer. From the tourist office, walk right on Vesterg., turn left on Thomas Thriges G., and go right on Hans Jensens Str. (☎6551 4601; www.museum.odense.dk. Open June-Aug. daily 9am-6pm; Sept.-May Tu-Su 10am-4pm. Summer performances 11am, 1, 3pm.) Music wafts through the halls of the **Carl Nielsen Museum,** Claus Bergs G. 11, which depicts the life of the famous Danish composer. (Open Th-F 4-8pm, Su noon-4pm. 25kr.) Down Vesterg., near the tourist office, **St. Knud's Cathedral** has a magnificent triptych by Claus Berg. Inside, view the skeleton of St. Knud, murdered at the altar of the church that previously stood on the site. (☎6612 0392. Open Apr.-Oct. M-Sa 10am-5pm, Su noon-5pm; low season M-Sa 10am-4pm, Su noon-5pm.)

On weekend evenings, the area around Vesterg. is packed with people of all ages drinking and listening to live bands. After 11pm, the club and bar scene takes over. *What's On?*, available at the tourist office, provides nightlife info. **Crazy Daisy,** Klingenberg 14, Skt. Knuds Kirkestr. just past Radhuspl., has six bars on three floors. (☎6614 6788. Cover 50kr. Open F-Sa 11pm-6am.) A young crowd moves to the beats of Odense's best DJs at **Boogie Dance Cafe,** Norreg. 21. (☎6614 0039. Cover Th 20kr, F-Sa 40kr after midnight. Open Tu-Sa 10:30pm-5:30am. MC/V.)

DAYTRIP FROM ODENSE: KVÆRNDRUP. **Egeskov Slot,** 25min. south of Odense in Kværndrup, is a magnificent castle that appears to float on the lake. The grounds include imaginative gardens, hedge mazes, and small museums. (☎6227 1016. Castle open July M-Tu and Th-Su 10am-7pm, W 10am-11pm; May-June and Aug.-Sept. daily 10am-5pm. Grounds open daily July 10am-8pm; June and Aug. 10am-6pm; Apr.-May and Sept. 10am-5pm. Grounds, mazes, and museums 95kr, with castle 150kr. MC/V.) Take the Svendborg-bound **train** (25min., 50kr) that leaves 38min. past the hour from Odense. In Kværndrup, turn right out of the station and walk up to Bøjdenv., where you can catch bus #920 (1 per hr., 16kr), or turn right and walk 20min. to the castle. From mid-June to mid-August, you can take FynBus #801 from Odense directly to the castle (1hr., 3-8 per day, 44kr).

ÆRØ

☎62

The wheat fields, harbors, and hamlets of Ærø (EH-ruh), a small island off the southern coast of Funen, use modern technology to preserve an earlier era of Danish history. Almost 80% of the island is powered by renewable energy sources, keeping the air pristine. The town of **Ærøskøbing** (pop. 3900) serves as a gateway to the island. Hollyhocks and half-timbered houses line the cobblestone streets, and one-lane roads, rolling fields, and picturesque windmills lure vacationing Danes into exploring the rest of the island by bicycle. Several **trains** running from Odense to Svendborg are timed to meet the ferry to Ærøskøbing. (☎52 40 00. 1¼hr.; 5-6 per day; 132kr, round-trip 264kr. Cash only.) On the island, bus #990 travels among the towns of Ærøskøbing, Marstal, and Søby (23kr, day pass 75kr). Ærøskøbing's **tourist office,** Vesterg. 1, has **Internet** for 25kr per 15min. (☎52 13 00; www.arre.dk. Open M and W-F 10am-3:30pm, Sa-Su 10am-1:30pm.) **Postal Code:** 5970.

DENMARK

JUTLAND (JYLLAND)

Jutland's sandy beaches and historic houses complement its sleek wind turbines and contemporary art. Vikings used to journey to the trading centers on the western half of the peninsula, but now the coast attracts windsurfers in search of prime waves. Cyclers and canoers enjoy the vast open spaces of the central lakes region, and the cities of Århus and Aalborg have emerged as cultural havens in the east.

ÅRHUS

☎86-89

Pedestrian walkways wind through the impressive museums, crowded nightclubs, and well-developed art scene of Århus (OR-hoos; pop. 280,000), Denmark's second-largest city. Copenhagen may draw more tourists, but Århus takes some of the capital's urban sophistication and tempers it with a dose of Jutland practicality.

TRANSPORTATION AND PRACTICAL INFORMATION. Trains run from Århus to Aalborg (1½hr., 2 per hr., 150kr), Copenhagen (3hr., 2 per hr., 297kr), and Frederikshavn (2¾hr., 1 per hr., 195kr). **Buses** leave from outside the train station. From May to October, **free bikes** are available to borrow from stands across the city with a 20kr deposit. **MM Cykler Værksted,** Mejlg. 41, rents bikes for 85kr per day. (☎8619 2927. Open M-F 9am-5pm.) To get to the **tourist office,** Banegårdspl. 20, head left after exiting the train station and cross the street. The office books private rooms (200-500kr) for free and sells the **24hr. Tourist Ticket** (55kr), which offers unlimited use of the city's extensive bus system. The **Århus pass** (1-day 119kr, 2-day 149kr, 1-week 206kr) includes admission to most museums and sights as well as unlimited public transit. (☎8731 5010; www.visitaarhus.com. Open mid-June to early Sept. M-F 9:30am-6pm, Sa 9:30am-5pm, Su 9:30am-1pm; low season reduced hours.) The main **library,** Mølleg. 1 in Mølleparken, offers free **Internet.** (☎8940 9255. Open May-Sept. M-Th 10am-7pm, F 10am-5pm, Sa 10am-2pm; Oct.-Apr. M-Th 10am-8pm, F 10am-6pm, Sa-Su 10am-3pm.) **Postal Code:** 8000.

ACCOMMODATIONS AND FOOD. The popular, social **Århus City Sleep-In ❷,** Havneg. 20, is near the city's nightlife. From the train station, turn right and follow Ny Banegårdsg., passing Europalads, then turn left onto Havneg. when the street forks in front of the train tracks. Walk up Havneg., leaving the harbor to your right. (☎8619 2055; www.citysleep-in.dk. Breakfast 45kr. Linens 45kr, deposit 30kr. Laundry 30kr. Key deposit 50kr. Reception 24hr. Dorms 115kr; doubles 360kr. MC/V; 4.75% surcharge.) The quieter **Århus Vanderhjem (HI) ❷,** Marienlundsv. 10, is 5min. north of the city, in a public park near one of Århus's nicest beaches. Take bus #1, 6, 9, or 16 to Marienlunds. (☎8616 7298; www.aarhus-danhostel.dk. Breakfast 50kr. Linens 45kr. Free wireless Internet. Reception Apr.-Oct. 8am-noon and 4-8pm, Nov.-Mar. 8am-noon and 4-7pm. Dorms 120kr; private rooms 475kr. 35kr HI discount. MC/V; 2.3% surcharge.) Ethnic restaurants and pizzerias line **Skolegade,** which becomes Mejlg. **Det Grønne Hjorne ❷,** Fredricksg. 60, has a delicious buffet of Mediterranean and Middle Eastern dishes, with vegetarian options. (☎8613 5247. Lunch buffet 59kr. Dinner buffet 99kr. Open M-Sa 11:30am-9pm, Su 4:30pm-9pm. MC/V.) Pick up groceries at **Netto,** in St. Knuds Torv; take Ryeseg. from the station and turn right into the square across from the church. (☎8612 3112. Open M-Th 5-10pm, F-Sa noon-10pm. Cash only.)

DENMARK

SIGHTS AND ENTERTAINMENT. The exceptional **Århus Kunstmuseum (ARoS),** Aros Allé 2, off Vester Allé, features eight winding levels of galleries that hold multimedia exhibits and a huge collection of modern art. Highlights include Ron Mueck's *Boy*, a colossal 5m statue of a crouching boy. (☎8730 6600; www.aros.dk. Open Tu and Th 10am-5pm, W 10am-10pm. 70kr, students 55kr.) The nation's tallest cathedral, **Århus Domkirke,** Skoleg. 17, is near the harbor. (☎8620 5400; www.aarhus-domkirke.dk. Open May-Sept. M-Sa 9:30am-4pm, Oct.-Apr. M-Sa 10am-3pm. Free.) At **Den Gamle By,** Viborgvej 2, actors recreate life in a colorful medieval village with authentic houses transported from all over Denmark. The shoemaker's wife serves coffee brewed on an old-fashioned stove; more adventurous visitors try flirting with the minister's daughter up the street. (☎8612 3188; www.dengamleby.dk. Open mid-June to mid-Sept. 9am-6pm. 80kr. MC/V.) The **Moesgård Museum of Prehistory,** Moesgård Allé 20, 15min. south of town, features the eerie, mummified **Grauballe Man.** Take bus #6 from the train station to the end. (☎8942 1100; www.moesmus.dk. Open Apr.-Sept. daily 10am-5pm; Oct.-Mar. Tu-Su 10am-4pm. 45kr, students 35kr. AmEx/DC/MC/V.) The 3km **Prehistoric Trail** behind the museum reconstructs Danish forests from different ages and leads to a popular **beach.** In summer, bus #19 returns from the beach to the train station.

Every year in mid-July, Århus hosts its acclaimed **International Jazz Festival** (www.jazzfest.dk). The **Århus Festuge** (☎8940 9191; www.aarhusfestuge.dk), a rollicking celebration of theater, dance, and music, is held from late August through early September. **The Social Club,** Klosterg. 34, has three bars and two levels of loud music. (☎8519 4250; www.socialclub.dk. Beer and liquor 20kr. Cover after 2am Th 20kr, F-Sa 40kr. 11pm-midnight entrance only with student ID; free beer and no cover. Open Th-Sa 11pm-6am.) Gay nightlife in Århus centers around the **Pan Club,** Jægergårdsg. 42 (☎8613 1343), a late-night disco.

DAYTRIP FROM ÅRHUS: LEGOLAND. Billund is the home of **Legoland,** an amusement park with sprawling Lego sculptures made from over 50 million of the candy-colored blocks. The **Power Builder** ride will make a convert of any adult skeptic. (☎7533 1333; www.legoland.com. Open daily July to mid-Aug. 10am-

9pm; June and late Aug. 10am-8pm; Apr.-May and Sept.-Oct. reduced hours. Day pass 225kr. Free entrance 30min. before rides close.) Take the **train** from Århus to Vejle (45min., 1 per hr., 85kr), then take **bus** #244 (dir.: Grinsted; 46kr).

RIBE ☎75, 76

Denmark's oldest settlement, Ribe (pop. 18,000) is a well-preserved medieval town near Jutland's west coast. The tower of the 12th-century **Domkirke** (Cathedral) offers a sweeping view of the town's red-shingled roofs. (☎7542 0619. Open July to mid-Aug. M-Sa 10am-5:30pm, Su noon-5:30pm; May-June and mid-Aug. to Sept. M-Sa 10am-5pm, Su noon-5pm; low season reduced hours. 12kr.) Near the Torvet (Main Square), the **Old Town Hall,** on Von Støckens Pl., houses a former debtors' prison where artifacts of Ribe's medieval "justice" system are displayed. (☎7688 1122. Open June-Aug. daily 1-3pm; May and Sept. M-F 1-3pm. 15kr.) A singing **night watchman** leads entertaining walking tours, beginning in the Torvet. (40min. June-Aug. 8 and 10pm; May and Sept. 10pm. Free.) The **Ribe Vandrerhjem (HI) ❷,** Sct. Pedersg. 16, has a knowledgeable staff that relates tidbits of Ribe's history. From the station, cross the parking lot, bear right, walk to the end of Sct. Nicolajg., then turn right on Saltg. and immediately left. (☎7542 0620; www.danhostel-ribe.dk. Breakfast 50kr. Linens 44kr. Wash 30kr, dry 15kr. Internet 20kr per 30min. Reception 8am-noon and 4-6pm. Check-in 4-6pm. Open Feb.-Nov. Dorms 135-185kr; singles 285-500kr; doubles 315-500kr. 35kr HI discount. AmEx/MC/V.) **Overdammen,** which begins at the Torvet, has inexpensive cafes and pizzerias. **Trains** go to Århus (3½hr., every 1-2hr., 214kr) via Fredricia. The **tourist office,** Torvet 3, books rooms for a 25kr fee. From the train station, walk down Dagmarsg.; the office is in the main square. (☎7542 1500; www.visitribe.dk. Open July-Aug. M-F 9am-6pm, Sa 10am-5pm, Su 10am-2pm; June and Sept. M-F 9am-5pm, Sa 10am-1pm; Jan.-May and Oct.-Dec. M-F 9:30am-4:30pm, Sa 10am-1pm.)

AALBORG ☎96, 98, 99

A laid-back student haven by day, Aalborg (OLE-borg; pop. 162,000) heats up after nightfall. At the corner of Alg. and Molleg., an elevator descends from outside the Salling Department Store to the half-excavated ruins of a **Franciscan friary.** (☎9631 0410. Open Tu-Su 10am-5pm; elevator closes at 4:30pm. Elevator 20kr per 2-3 people, up to 250kg.) North of town, the solemn grounds of **Lindholm Høje,** Vendilav. 11, hold 700 ancient Viking graves and a museum of artifacts. Take bus #2C, which departs near the tourist office. (☎9931 7400; www.nordjyllandshistoriskemuseum.dk. Grounds open 24hr. Museum open Apr.-Oct. daily 10am-5pm; Nov.-Mar. Tu 10am-4pm, Su 11am-4pm. English-language tours in July W 2pm. Grounds free. Museum 30kr, students 15kr. MC/V.) At night, **Jomfru Ane Gade,** a pedestrian strip of bars and clubs, is packed with students and partygoers. For a wilder time, visit the last weekend in May for **Karneval i Aalborg** (May 24-26, 2007; www.karnevaliaalborg.dk), when the city celebrates spring with Northern Europe's largest carnival.

Cozy private cabins double as dorms at **Aalborg Vandrerhjem and Camping (HI) ❸,** Skydebanev. 50. Take bus #13 (dir.: Fjordparken, 2 per hr.) to the end of the line. (☎9811 6044. Breakfast 48kr. Linens 35kr. Laundry 35kr. Free Internet. Reception mid-June to mid-Aug. 8am-11pm; low season 8am-noon and 4-9pm. Dorms 185kr; singles 285-475kr; doubles 410-570kr. 35kr HI discount. Camping electricity 28kr. Tent sites 70-82kr. MC/V; 4% surcharge.) The **Føtex supermarket,** Slotsg. 8-14, is past Boomtown on Nytorv. (☎9932 9000. Open M-F 9am-8pm, Sa 8am-5pm. Cash only.) **Trains** run to Århus (1½hr., 1 per hr., 150kr) and Copenhagen (5hr., 2 per hr., 331kr). To find the **tourist office,** Østeråg. 8, head out of the station, cross JFK Pl., and turn left on Boulevarden, which becomes Østeråg. (☎9930 6090; www.visitaalborg.com. Open July M-F 9am-5:30pm, Sa 10am-4pm; late June and Aug. M-F 9am-5:30pm, Sa 10am-1pm; Sept. to mid-June M-F 9am-4:30pm, Sa 10am-1pm.)

FREDERIKSHAVN ☎96, 98, 99

Once a fishing village and naval base, Frederikshavn (fred-riks-HOW-n; pop. 35,000) is now a transport hub for ferry lines. **Stena Line** (☎9620 0200; www.stenaline.com) leaves for Gothenburg, SWE (3¼hr.; 210-280kr, 30% Scanrail discount) and Oslo, NOR (8½hr.; 310kr, 50% Scanrail discount). **Color Line** (☎9956 1977; www.colorline.com) sails to Larvik, NOR (6¼hr., 420kr). To get from the station to **Frederikshavn Vandrerhjem (HI) ❷**, Buhlsv. 6, walk right on Skipperg., turn left onto Nørreg., and take a right on Buhlsv. (☎9842 1475; www.danhostel.dk/frederikshavn. Breakfast 50kr. Linens 45kr. Laundry 40kr. Reception 8am-noon and 4-8pm. Dorms 120kr; singles 285kr; doubles 440kr. 35kr HI discount. Cash only.) Restaurants and shops line **Søndergade** and **Havnegade;** Rådhus Allé has grocery stores. To get to the commercial area from the train station, turn left and cross Skipperg. A church, the Frederikshavn Kirke, with a huge anchor on its front lawn, will be on the left. Walk up one block to Danmarksg., the main pedestrian thoroughfare, and turn left. Danmarksg. becomes Sønderg. and intersects with Havneg.

SKAGEN ☎98

Perched on Denmark's northernmost tip, spectacular Skagen (SKAY-en; pop. 10,000) is bordered by white sand dunes that descend to ice-blue water. Bright "Skagen yellow" houses with red roofs welcome fishermen home. Danish tourists discovered Skagen's colorful, idyllic charms long ago, but international visitors are just beginning to venture here. The **Skagens Museum,** Brøndumsv. 4, features 19th- and 20th-century work by Skagen-based artists. From the train station, walk left down Sct. Laurentii V. and right on Brøndumsv. (☎44 64 44; www.skagensmuseum.dk. Open May-Sept. daily 10am-5pm; Oct.-Apr. W-Su 10am-3pm. 60kr. AmEx/MC/V.) At nearby **Grenen,** the currents of the North and Baltic Seas collide in striking rhythm. Unlike the 60km of beach in other areas of Skagen, Grenen is strictly off-limits for swimming due to its life-threatening currents. Take the bus from the Skagen station (15kr) or walk 2km down Fyrv. About 13km south of Skagen is the enormous **Råberg Mile** (ROH-bayrg MEE-leh), a sand dune formed by a 16th-century storm. The dune resembles a moonscape and migrates 15m east each year. Take bus #99 or the train from Skagen to Hulsig, then walk 4km down Kandestedv. Each July, Skagen welcomes Irish fiddlers and Scandinavian troubadours for the **Skagen Folk Music Festival** (☎9844 4094; www.skagenfestival.dk; July 5-8, 2007).

Reserve ahead at the popular **Skagen Ny Vandrerhjem ❸,** Rolighedsv. 2. From the station, turn right on Chr. X's V., then go left on Rolighedsv. (☎44 22 00; www.danhostelnord.dk/skagen. Breakfast 50kr. Linens 50kr. Reception 9am-noon and 4-6pm. Open Feb.-Dec. Dorms 185kr; singles 515-535kr; doubles 615-635kr. 35kr HI discount. Cash only.) To reach the campgrounds at **Poul Egg Camping ❶,** Batterivej 21, turn left out of the train station, walk 3km down Sct. Laurentii V., and left on Batterivej. (☎9844 1470. Bike rental 60kr per day. Tent sites 75kr. Cash only.) Turn right out of the station onto Sct. Laurentii V. to get to restaurants near **Havnevej.** In the center, **Orchid Thai Restaurant ❶,** Sct. Laurentii V., offers authentic, cheap, filling lunches for 35kr. (☎9844 6044. Open daily 11am-10pm. MC/V.) Pick up picnic supplies at **Super Brugsen,** Sct. Laurentii V. 28. (☎44 17 00. Open daily 9am-10pm.)

Trains run from Skagen to Frederikshavn (40min., 1 per hr., 45kr). Despite the wind, **biking** is the best way to experience Skagen. Rent bikes at **Cykelhandler,** Kappelborgv. 23; from the station, turn right onto Sct. Laurentii V., right onto Havnev., and right again. (☎44 25 28. 20kr per hr., 60kr per day. Open M-F 8am-5:30pm, Sa 9:30am-noon. Cash only.) The **tourist office** is in the station. (☎44 13 77; www.skagen-tourist.dk. Open July M-Sa 9am-6pm, Su 10am-4pm; June and Aug. M-Sa 9am-5pm, Su 10am-2pm; low season reduced hours.) The **library,** Sct. Laurentii V. 23, has free **Internet.** (☎44 28 22; www.skagen.dk/skagbib. Open M and Th 10am-6pm; Tu-W and F 1-6pm, Sa 10am-1pm.)

ESTONIA (EESTI)

Cheap and fresh, Estonia has become a vacation destination for fun-seeking Europeans. Though Estonians have been enthusiastically patriotic since the 19th century, their emotion was smothered for nearly as long by a constant stream of Russian, Swedish, and Danish invaders. Between the World Wars, Estonia briefly enjoyed independence, but the U.S.S.R. intruded in 1939. It was not until 1994 that the Soviets reestablished the Republic of Estonia. A decade later, still bounding with post-bloc euphoria, Estonia reached a milestone joining both NATO and the European Union (EU) in 2004. Though Soviet housing units and sub-par living standards outside cities remain as reminders of its turbulent past, Estonia continues to gain footing in the world arena.

DISCOVER ESTONIA: SUGGESTED ITINERARIES

THREE DAYS. Spend a day exploring the streets and sights of Old Town **Tallinn** (p. 288)—don't miss the Museum of Occupations. On your second day, head outside the old city walls to **Kumu** (p. 290), Estonia's main art museum, before heading down to **Pärnu** (p. 291). Spend your third day in there lying on the beaches and exploring the town by bike.

ONE WEEK. Begin in the south by enjoying the uniqueness of **Tartu** (2 days; p. 292). Then move west to **Pärnu** (1 day), and its Museum of New Art. Next, head out to the island of **Saaremaa** (2 days; p. 292). Rent a bicycle and take in the unspoiled beauty of the region, including meteorite craters and far-flung peninsulas. Spend your last 2 days in **Tallinn.**

ESSENTIALS

FACTS AND FIGURES

Official Name: Republic of Estonia.
Capital: Tallinn.
Major Cities: Pärnu, Tartu.
Population: 1,324,000.
Time Zone: GMT +2.
Languages: Estonian (official), Russian.
Religions: Evangelical Lutheran (14%), Eastern Orthodox (13%).

WHEN TO GO

The best time to visit Estonia is in the late spring (Apr.-May) and summer (June to early Sept.) The temperature reaches 30°C (86°F) in July and August, and days are long (up to 19 hours of light). Winters are cold and dark but have ideal conditions for skiing, skating, and ice fishing. The fall is frequently damp.

DOCUMENTS AND FORMALITIES

EMBASSIES AND CONSULATES. Embassies of other countries in Estonia are in Tallinn (p. 288). Estonia's embassies and consulates abroad include: **Australia,** 86 Louisa Rd., Birchgrove, NSW, 2041 (☎298 10 74 68; eestikon@ozemail.com.au); **Canada,** 260 Dalhousie St., Ste. 210, Ottawa, ON, K1N 7E4 (☎613-789-4222; www.estemb.ca); **UK,** 16 Hyde Park Gate, London, SW7 5DG (☎20 7589 3428; www.estonia.gov.uk); **US,** 2131 Massachusetts Ave., NW, Washington, D.C., 20008 (☎202-588-0101; www.estemb.org).

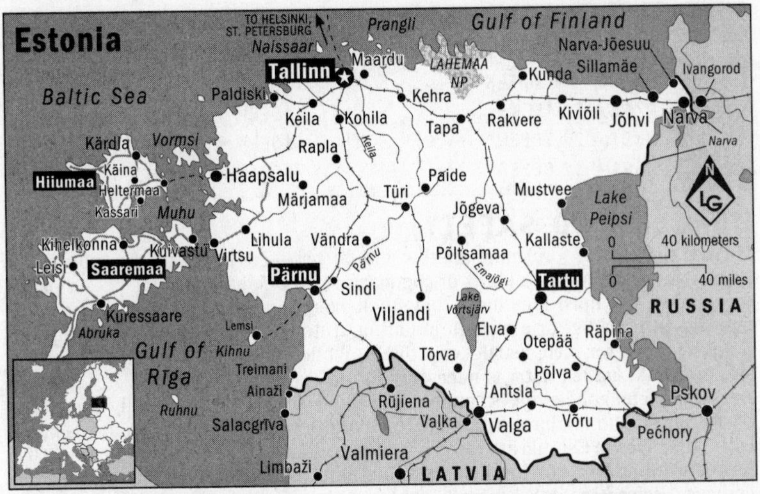

VISA AND ENTRY INFORMATION. Citizens Australia, Canada, EU countries, New Zealand, and the US can visit Estonia for up to 90 days in a six-month period without a visa. Visa extensions are not granted. For more specific info, consult www.vm.ee/eng. Arriving by land is easiest from Moscow or St. Petersburg (RUS), or Rīga (LAT). Visas are not granted at the border.

ENTRANCE REQUIREMENTS

Passport: Required for all travelers; EU citizens may use personal ID.

Visa: Not required for citizens of EU countries; not required for citizens of Australia, Canada, New Zealand, and the US, and assorted other countries for stays under 90 days in a 6-month period.

Letter of Invitation: Not required.

Inoculations: Not required. Recommended up-to-date on DTaP (diphtheria, tetanus, and pertussis), hepatitis A, hepatitis B, MMR (measles, mumps, and rubella), polio booster, and typhoid.

Work Permit: Required for all foreigners planning to work.

International Driving Permit: Required for all those planning to drive.

TOURIST SERVICES AND MONEY

TOURIST OFFICES. Tourist offices, marked with a small white "i" on a green background, are present in most towns; they sell maps and offer helpful advice. Offices generally keep extended hours during the summer months. Tourist office locations and other information can be found at www.visitestonia.com.

MONEY. The Estonian unit of currency is the **kroon (EEK)**, plural kroons or krooni. One kroon is equal to 100 senti. The kroon is pegged to the euro at €1=15.6466EEK as a preliminary measure for changeover to the **euro (€)**, expected in 2008. **Inflation** hovers between 3 and 4%. Though this keeps the economy steady, it is high enough to be a hindrance in the process of adopting the euro. Many restaurants and shops accept **MasterCard** and **Visa,** and **ATMs** are available everywhere. When purchasing an item, cash is not usually passed between hands, but is placed instead in a small tray. **Tipping** is becoming more common; 10% is generally expected in restaurants.

KROONI (EEK)		
	AUS$1 = 9.08EEK	10EEK = AUS$1.10
	CDN$1 = 10.98EEK	10EEK = CDN$0.91
	EUR€1 = 15.65EEK	10EEK = EUR€0.64
	NZ$1 = 7.64EEK	10EEK = NZ$1.31
	UK£1 = 22.75EEK	10EEK = UK£0.44
	US$1 = 12.06EEK	10EEK = US$0.83

HEALTH AND SAFETY

Medical services for foreigners are few and far between, and usually require cash payments. There are two kinds of **pharmacies** *(apteek)*; some stock prescription medication, but most are chains that stock everything. Public **toilets** *(tasuline)*, marked with an "N" or a triangle pointing up for women and "M" or a triangle pointing down for men, usually cost 3EEK. While Tallinn's tap water is generally safe to drink, **bottled water** is necessary in the rest of the country. Petty **crime** is rare, though pickpocketing is common in Tallinn's Old Town, especially along Viru St. **Women** should not have a problem traveling alone, but may want to dress modestly. **Minorities** in Estonia are rare; they receive stares but generally experience little discrimination. For English-speaking help in an emergency, contact your embassy. **Homosexuality** is generally treated with curiosity rather than suspicion.

EMERGENCY	**Police:** ☎110. **Ambulance** and **Fire:** ☎112.

TRANSPORTATION

BY PLANE, TRAIN, AND FERRY. Several international airlines fly to Tallinn; try **SAS** (www.scandinavian.net) or **AirBaltic** (www.airbaltic.com), which crosslists flights with **Estonian Air** (www.estonian-air.ee). Ferries connect Tallinn to Scandinavia and Germany; Tallinn's port website (www.ts.ee) has ferry info and schedules. A **helicopter** service (www.copterline.com) flies between Helsinki, FIN and Tallinn. Local **train** lines are **Edelaraudtee, EVR Ekspress,** and **Elektriraudtee** (www.elektriraudtee.ee, in Estonian, but timetables are decipherable).

BY BUS. Euroline (www.eurolines.ee) and Ecoline (www.ecoline.net) **buses** run to Estonia from international cities. Domestic buses (www.bussireisid.ee) are cheaper and more efficient than trains, though service can be infrequent between smaller cities. Taking buses on the islands can be especially frustrating. From September to late June, students receive half-price bus tickets.

BY CAR, BIKE, AND THUMB. If entering Estonia by car, avoid routes through Kaliningrad and Belarus: both require visas. Although road conditions are steadily improving, the availability of **roadside assistance** remains poor. Check out the Estonian National Road Administration (www.mnt.ee). **Taxis** (about 7EEK per km) are generally a safe. Bicycling is common in Estonia. Those who want to **hitchhike** just stretch out an open hand. Let's Go does not recommend hitchhiking.

KEEPING IN TOUCH

PHONE CODES	**Country code:** 372. **International dialing prefix:** 800. For more on placing international calls, see inside back cover.

EMAIL AND THE INTERNET. Though Internet cafes are not as common as you might expect, wireless Internet is ubiquitous. Free wireless for those with laptops can be found at www.wifi.ee, or at establishments with the **wifi.ee** sign.

TELEPHONE. Pay phones are common and require magnetic cards, available at kiosks. Calls to the Baltic states cost 5EEK per minute, to Russia 10EEK. **Prepaid phonecards** can get you rates of US$0.30-0.50 per minute to phone the US; otherwise, expect to pay US$1-4 per minute International access codes include: **AT&T Direct** (☎0 800 12 001); **Canada Direct** (☎0 800 12 011); **MCI WorldPhone** (☎0 800 12 122). Internet access, which is common, usually costs 30-60EEK per hour.

PHONE MAYHEM. Tallinn numbers all begin with the number 6 and have 7 digits. Numbers in smaller towns often have only 5 digits. Tallinn has no city code; to call Tallinn from outside Estonia on the digital system, dial Estonia's country code (☎372) and then the number. To call any city besides Tallinn from outside the country, dial the country code, city code, and number. The 0 listed before each city code only needs to be dialed when placing calls within Estonia.

MAIL. Post offices are generally Monday through Friday 9am-6pm and Saturday 9:30am-3pm. Sending letters costs 6EEK to Britain and 6.50EEK to the US, Canada, and Australia; postcards are an extra *kroon* apiece. Mail can be received through **Poste Restante.** Address envelopes as follows: First name LAST NAME, POSTE RESTANTE, Post Office address, Postal Code, city, ESTONIA.

LANGUAGE. **Estonian** is a **Finno-Ugric** language, closely related to **Finnish.** Estonians speak the best **English** in the Baltic states; most young people know at least a few phrases. Many also know **Finnish** or **Swedish,** but **German** is more common among the older set and in the resort towns. **Russian** used to be mandatory, but Estonians in remote areas have often forgotten it, with time or by choice.

ACCOMMODATIONS AND CAMPING

ESTONIA	❶	❷	❸	❹	❺
ACCOMMODATIONS	under 200EEK	200-400EEK	400-550EEK	550-600EEK	over 600EEK

Each tourist office has accommodations listings for its town. There is little distinction between **hotels, hostels,** and **guesthouses;** some upscale hotels still have hall toilets and showers. The word *võõrastemaja* (guesthouse) usually implies that a place is less expensive. Some hostels are wings or floors of larger hotels, so be sure to ask for the cheaper rooms. For info on HI hostels around Estonia, contact the **Estonian Youth Hostel Association,** Narva Mantee 16-25, 10121, Tallinn (☎372 6461 455; www.balticbookings.com/eyha). **Camping** is the best way to experience Estonia's islands, but doing so outside of designated areas is illegal and dangerous for wildlife. **Farm stays** are becoming popular. For more info visit **Rural Tourism** (www.maaturism.ee), or search accommodations at www.visitestonia.com.

FOOD AND DRINK

ESTONIA	❶	❷	❸	❹	❺
FOOD	under 50EEK	50-80EEK	80-100EEK	100-140EEK	over 140EEK

Verivorst (blood sausage) is eaten at Christmas while *sült* (jellied, mixed pork parts) is served yearround. Bread is prized, and *schnitzel* (breaded and fried pork filet) appears on nearly every menu. Most cheap Estonian cuisine is fried and doused with sour cream. More palatable Estonian specialties include *seljanka* (meat stew) and *pelmenid* (dumplings), as well as smoked salmon and trout. Pancakes with *kohupiim* (cheese curd) and berries are a delicious, common dessert. The national brew *Saku* and the darker *Saku Tume* are excellent, but local beers, such as Kuressaare's *Saaremaa*, are less consistent.

HOLIDAYS AND FESTIVALS

Holidays: New Year's Day (Jan. 1); Independence Day (Feb. 24); Good Friday (Apr. 6); Easter (Apr. 8); Labor Day (May 1); Pentecost (May 27); Victory Day (June 23); *Jaanipäev* (Midsummer's Day; June 24); Restoration of Independence (Aug. 20); Boxing Day (Dec. 26).

Festivals: In June, Memme-taadi Days, a celebration of Estonian folk culture, culminate on the 24th with *Jaanipäev*, or Midsummer's Day. Haapsalu's White Lady Festival, held around the August full moon, celebrates Estonia's most famous ghost. Check www.culture.ee for festival listings.

BEYOND TOURISM

Earthwatch, 3 Clocktower Pl., Ste. 100, P.O. Box 75, Maynard, MA, 01754 (☎800-776-0188; www.earthwatch.org). Arranges 1- to 3-week environmental conservation programs in Eastern Europe, such as grassland restoration in Estonia. €1790 for 11 days, including simple accommodations and authentic meals.

Youth For Understanding (YFU), 6400 Goldsboro Rd., Ste. 100, Bethesda, MD, 20817 (☎716-592-4090; www.yfu.org). Runs summer and year-long programs for high-school students and recent graduates. Participants live with host families and attend local schools at locations around the world. Summer program fee US$4995, full year US$7195. Sponsored scholarships listed on website.

ESTONIA

TALLINN ☎0

Crisp sea air gusts over the medieval buildings and spires of Tallinn (pop. 401,000), the self-proclaimed "Heart of Northern Europe." Unfortunately, wall-to-wall tourists and vendors in "historical dress" often give the cobblestone streets of Old Town a theme-park feel. Visitors willing to venture beyond the compact center will be delighted by quirky cafes, lush parks, and the glorious seaside promenade.

TRANSPORTATION

Trains: Toompuiestee 35 (☎615 86 10; www.evr.ee). Trams #1 and 5 run between the station and the town center. To **Moscow, RUS** (14½hr.; 1 per day; 600EEK, sleeper car 898EEK), **Pärnu** (2½hr., 2 per day, 60EEK), and **Tartu** (3-4hr., 4 per day, 80-130EEK).

Buses: Lastekodu 46 (☎680 09 00), 1.5km southeast of Vanalinn. Trams #2 and 4 run between Hotel Viru and the station. Buy tickets at the station or from the driver. **Eurolines** (www.eurolines.ee) runs to **Rīga, LAT** (5-6hr., 5 per day, 200-230EEK), **St. Petersburg, RUS** (8-10½hr., 6-7 per day, 270-350EEK), and **Vilnius, LIT** (10½hr., 2 per day, 430EEK). 10% ISIC discount.

Ferries: (☎631 85 50). At the end of Sadama. Ferries cross to **Helsinki, FIN** (1½-3½hr., 47 per day, 350-755EEK). **Mainedd** travel agency, Raekoja pl. 18 (☎644 47 44; mainedd@hot.ee), books ferry tickets with no commission. Ask for student rates. Open M-F 9:30am-5:30pm. MC/V.

Public Transportation: Buses, trams, minibuses, and **trolleys** run 6am-midnight. Buy tickets *(talong)* from kiosks (10EEK) or from drivers (15EEK). 10-ticket booklet 85EEK. Validate tickets in the metal boxes onboard or face a 600EEK fine. 1hr., 2hr., and 1-day tickets are also available from kiosks (15/20/45EEK). Cash only.

Taxi: Rate per km should be posted on your taxi's window. Call ahead and order a car to avoid a "waiting fee." **Klubi Takso** (☎142 00), 5.50-7EEK per km, min. 35EEK. **Kiisu Takso** (☎655 07 77), 5.50EEK per km. **Linnatakso** (☎644 24 42), 7EEK per km, can provide taxis for disabled passengers. A quirky option Mar.-Oct. is to order a bicycle taxi (Velotaxi; ☎50 88 810), which operates in Vanalinn and costs 35EEK per passenger.

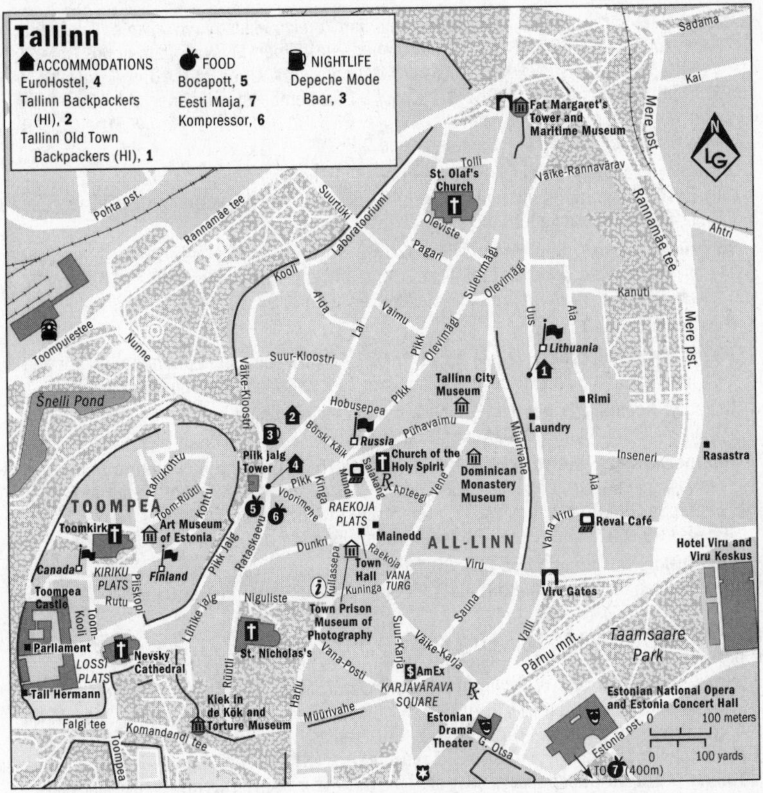

ORIENTATION AND PRACTICAL INFORMATION

Even locals lose their way along the winding medieval streets of Tallinn's **Vanalinn** (Old Town), an egg-shaped maze ringed by five main streets: **Rannamäe tee, Mere puistee, Pärnu mantee, Kaarli puistee,** and **Toompuiestee.** Vanalinn has two sections: **All-linn** (Lower Town) and **Toompea,** a rocky, fortified hill west of All-linn. Only about 50% of the wall that once encircled Vanalinn is intact, but the best entrance is still through the 15th-century **Viru Gate,** across from Hotel Viru, Tallinn's central landmark (unless you come from the ferry terminal, in which case it's best to go through the Great Coastal Gate, **Surr Rannavärav,** to the north). **Viru,** the main thoroughfare, leads directly to **Raekoja plats** (Town Hall Square), the center of town. **Pikk** and **Vene** run northeast of Raekoja pl. **Uus,** the first street on your right after entering the Vanalinn gates, runs north toward the ferry ports. South of Raekoja pl., a number of smaller streets run into each other and eventually cross **Müürivahe,** which borders the southern and eastern edges of Vanalinn.

Tourist Office: Kullassepa 4/Niguliste 2 (☎645 77 77; www.tourism.tallinn.ee). Sells *Tallinn In Your Pocket* (35EEK). Open July-Aug. M-F 9am-8pm, Sa-Su 10am-6pm; May-June M-F 9am-7pm, Sa-Su 10am-5pm; Sept. M-F 9am-6pm, Sa-Su 10am-5pm; Oct.-Apr. M-F 9am-5pm, Sa 10am-3pm. For travelers under 26, **Taninfo,** Pärnu mnt. 6 (www.taninfo.ee.), has info on activities and events, as well as work and volunteer opportunities throughout Estonia. Open M-F June-Aug. 10am-4pm, Sept.-May 10am-6pm.

Embassies: For more info, contact the Estonian Foreign Ministry (www.vm.ee). **Canada,** Toom-kooli 13 (☎627 33 11; tallinn@canada.ee). Open M, W, F 9am-noon. **Ireland,** Vene 2 (☎681 18 88; embassytallinn@eircom.net). Open M-F 10am-1pm and 2-3:30pm. **UK,** Wismari 6 (☎667 47 00; www.britishembassy.ee). Open M-F 10am-noon and 2-4:30pm. **US,** Kentmanni 20 (☎668 81 00, emergency 509 21 29; www.usemb.ee). Open M-F 9am-noon and 2-5pm.

Currency Exchange: Banks have better rates than hotels and private exchange bureaus. Try **Eesti Uhispank,** Pärnu mnt. 12 (☎640 36 14). Open M-F 9am-6pm, Sa 10am-3pm. There are **ATMs** throughout the city.

American Express: Suur-Karja 15 (☎626 63 35; www.estravel.ee). Books hotels and tours, sells airline, ferry, and rail tickets, and provides visa services. Open June-Aug. M-F 9am-6pm, Sa 10am-5pm; Sept.-May M-F 9am-6pm, Sa 10am-3pm.

Emergency: ☎112.

Pharmacy: Raeapteek, Raekoja pl. 11 (☎631 48 30). The oldest pharmacy still operating in Europe, in business since 1422. Open Tu-F 9am-7pm, Sa 9am-5pm. MC/V.

Laundry: Keemilin Pubastus, Uus 9, will wash your clothing for you for 20EEK per kg. Open M-F 9am-6pm, Sa 10am-4pm. Cash only.

Internet Access: Metro, Viru valjak 4 (☎610 15 19), in the bus station below Viru keskus. 15EEK per 15min.; 35EEK per hr., students 15EEK per hr. Open M-F 7am-11pm, Sa-Su 10am-11pm. MC/V; min. 50EEK. **Central Library,** Estonia pst. 8, 2nd fl. (☎683 09 02). 15min. free with reservation. Open M-F 11am-7pm, Sa 10am-5pm.

Post Office: Narva mnt. 1 (☎661 66 16), opposite Hotel Viru. **Poste Restante** in basement. Open Tu-F 7:30am-8pm, Sa 8am-6pm, Su 9am-3pm. **Postal Code:** 10101.

ESTONIA

ACCOMMODATIONS AND FOOD

Hostels fill up fast, so reserve ahead. **Rasastra,** Mere pst. 4, 2nd fl., finds private rooms in Tallinn, Rīga, and Vilnius. (☎661 62 91; www.bedbreakfast.ee. Open M-Sa 9:30am-6pm, Su 9:30am-5pm. Singles 330-350EEK; doubles 550-600EEK; triples 700-750EEK. Cash only.) **Tallinn Backpackers (HI) ❷,** Lai 10, and the smaller **Tallinn Old Town Backpackers (HI) ❷,** Uus 14, offer some the city's most sociable settings. (Backpackers ☎539 576 88. Old Town www.balticbackpackers.com. Linens 25EEK. Free Internet and wireless. Dorms from 225EEK. 25EEK HI discount. MC/V.) Modern, clean **Eurohostel ❷,** Nunne 2, is right in the midst of Vanalinn's nightlife. (☎644 77 88; www.eurohostel.ee. Luggage storage 15EEK. Free wireless. Dorms 280EEK; doubles 650EEK. Sept.-May reduced rates. Cash only.)

The secret is out about **Kompressor ❶,** Rataskaevu 3; this is the best place in town for Estonian pancakes, offering giant portions with meat, fish, and veggie fillings. The waits are worth it. (Pancakes 35-50EEK. Kitchen open daily noon-10pm, longer on weekends; bar open late. Cash only.) **Eesti Maja ❷,** A. Lauteri 1, has favorites like *sült* (jellied pig legs; 80EEK), and its own history magazine. (www.eestimaja.ee. M-F 11am-3pm all-you-can-eat buffet 95EEK. Entrees 45-195EEK. Open daily 11am-11pm. MC/V.) **Bocapott ❶,** Pikk Jalg 9, serves soup, sausages, sandwiches, and savory pies on dishes made in the adjoining ceramics studio. (www.bogapott.ee. Soups 5-30EEK, sausages 15-35EEK, sandwiches 22EEK, pies 10EEK. Open daily June-Sept. 10am-7pm; Oct.-May 10am-6pm. MC/V.)

SIGHTS

ALL-LINN (LOWER TOWN). Head up Viru to reach **Raekoja plats,** where beer flows and local troupes perform throughout the summer. Tallinn's **town hall,** Europe's oldest, is right on the square. The museum inside details daily life in medieval Tallinn. Next door is a tower with one of the world's tallest toilets (77m), built so guards could relieve themselves without descending. *(Town hall open July-Aug. M-Sa 10am-4pm. Tower open June-Aug. daily 11am-6pm. Town hall 35EEK, students 20EEK. Tower 25/15EEK. Cash only.)* Take Mündi from the square, turn right on Pühavaimu, and then right on Vene to reach **Katariinan Käytävä,** one of the town's most pleasant alleys, lined with galleries and cafes. At the north end of All-linn, the tower of **St. Olaf's Church** offers such a great view of the Old Town that the KGB used it as an observation post. *(Lai 50. Open daily Apr.-Oct. 10am-6pm. Services M and F 6:30pm, Su 10am and noon. Church free. Tower 30EEK, students 15EEK. Cash only.)*

TOOMPEA. Toompea's **Lossi plats** (Castle Sq.) is dominated by the onion domes of the Russian Orthodox **Alexander Nevsky Cathedral.** *(From Raekoja pl., head down Kullassepa, right on Niguliste, and uphill on Lühike jalg. Open daily 8am-6:30pm. Services 9am.)* Directly behind **Toompea Castle,** the seat of the Estonian Parliament (closed to the public), lies the impressive medieval fortification of **Tall Hermann** (Pikk Hermann). Walk south on Toompea from Lossi pl. to the **Museum of Occupation and of the Fight for Freedom,** which documents Estonia's repression by the Germans and Soviets. *(Open Tu-Sa 11am-6pm. 10EEK, students 5EEK. Cash only.)*

KADRIORG. In Kadriorg Park is Peter the Great's **Kadriorg Palace,** which houses a lovely collection art, and whose sumptuous grand hall is a stunning example of Baroque architecture. The grounds also house the **Mikkel Museum,** with similar work, and the **Peter the Great House Museum** in his former temporary residence which holds many of the tsar's original furnishings, as well as an imprint of his extremely large hand. *(Mäekalda 2. Palace open May-Sept. Tu-W and F-Su 10am-5pm, Th 10am-9pm; Oct.-Apr. W-Su 10am-5pm. Mikkel Museum open May-Sept. W and F-Su 10am-9pm; Oct.-Apr. W-Su 10am-5pm. House Museum open mid-May to Sept. W-Su 10:30am-5pm. Palace 45EEK, students 25EEK. Mikkel Museum 15/5EEK. House Museum 10/5EEK. MC/V.)* At the opposite end of the park from the tram stop is **Kumu,** the main branch of the Art Museum of Estonia. *(Weizenbergi 34. www.ekm.ee. Open May-Sept. Tu-W and F-Su 11am-6pm, Th 11am-9pm; Oct.-Apr. Tu-Su 11am-6pm. 75EEK, students 40EEK. MC/V.)*

ENTERTAINMENT AND NIGHTLIFE

Pick up a free copy of *Tallinn This Week* at the tourist office. The **Estonia Concert Hall** and the **Estonian National Opera** (Rahvusooper Estonia) are both at Estonia pst. 4. (Concert hall ☎614 77 60; www.concert.ee. Opera ☎683 12 60; www.opera.ee. Concert hall box office open M-F noon-7pm, Sa noon-5pm, Su 1hr. before curtain. Opera box office open daily 11am-7pm. Tickets 30-400EEK. MC/V.) Celebrate the power of barley early July at **Beersummer** (www.ollesummer.ee). **Depeche Mode Baar,** Nomme 4, plays all Depeche Mode, all day long and serves drinks named after their songs. (www.edmfk.ee/dmbaar. Beer 45EEK per 0.5L. Open daily noon-4am. MC/V min. 50EEK.)

PÄRNU ☎44

Famous for its mud baths, beaches, and festivals, Pärnu (pop. 45,000) is the summer capital of Estonia. Soak up some culture at Pärnu's **Museum of New Art,** Esplanaadi 10, which features a statue of Lenin with an amputated right hand. (☎30 772. Open daily 9am-9pm. 25EEK, students 15EEK. MC/V.)

It is wise to make restaurant reservations ahead in summer. **Georg ❶,** Rüütli 43, is a cafeteria-style eatery packed with locals enjoying fried fish, schnitzel, and open-faced sandwiches. (☎31 110. Sandwiches 7-15EEK. Entrees 30-50EEK. Open in summer M-F 7:30am-10pm, Sa-Su 9am-10pm; winter M-F 7:30am-7:30pm, Sa-Su

9am-5pm. MC/V.) Head to **Veerev Olu** (The Rolling Beer), Uus 3A, for live rock and folk Saturday 9:30pm-1am. (☎534 03 149. Beer 20EEK 0.5L. Food 17-35EEK. Open M-Sa 11am-1am, Su 1pm-1am. MC/V.) Eurolines **buses** (☎442 78 41) go from Ringi 3 to Rīga, LAT (3½hr., 6-8 per day, 110EEK), Tallinn (2hr., 42 per day, 80-120EEK), and Tartu (2½hr., 21 per day, 90-120EEK.) Cash only. **City Bike,** based in the beachside Rannahotell, will deliver a bicycle to you anywhere in Pärnu. (☎566 080 90; www.citybike.ee. 100EEK for 6hr., 150EEK per day. MC/V.) The **tourist office,** Rüütli 16, books rooms for a fee. (☎73 000; www.parnu.ee. Open mid-May to mid-Sept. M-F 9am-6pm, Sa 9am-4pm, Su 10am-3pm; mid-Sept. to mid-May M-F 9am-5pm. Cash only.) **Postal Code:** 80010.

TARTU ☎7

Tartu (pop. 100,000) is home to **Tartu University** (Tartu Ülikool). In **Raekoja plats** (Town Hall Square), the building that has the **Tartu Art Museum** (Tartu Kunstimuuseum) leans a little to the left—just like the student population. (Open W-Su 11am-6pm. 25EEK, students 10EEK. Ground floor 12/5EEK. F free. Cash only.) In the attic of the university's main building is the **student lock-up** *(kartser)*, which was used to detain rule-breaking students; their drawings and inscriptions are still visible. (Open M-F 11am-5pm. 5EEK, students 4EEK. Cash only.) The ruins of the **Cathedral of St. Peter and St. Paul,** Lossi 25, are undergoing a renovation, and now house the **Tartu University History Museum,** which showcases the scariest dentist chair you've ever seen. (Museum open W-Su 11am-5pm. 20EEK, students 5EEK. Towers open June-Aug. daily 10am-7pm; May and Sept. daily 11am-5pm; Oct.-Apr. reduced hours. 15/10EEK. Combo ticket 25/10EEK. Cash only.)

ESTONIA

The university dorms at **Hostel Pepleri ❷,** Pepleri 14, are more luxurious than many hotels. (☎27 608; www.kyla.ee. Free Internet for laptops. Singles 300EEK; doubles 500EEK. MC/V.) At attic lounge **Maailm,** Rüütli 12, you can enjoy drinks or ice-cream shakes. (☎742 90 99; www.klubimaailm.ee. 21+ after 9pm. Open M-Sa noon-1am, Su noon-10pm. MC/V.) **Wilde Irish Pub,** Vallikraavi 4, blends the Irish and Estonian traditions of its two namesakes, Oscar and Eduard Wilde. (Entrees 49-195EEK. Open Su-Tu noon-midnight, W-Th noon-1am, F-Sa noon-3am. MC/V.)

Buses (☎477 227) leave from Turu 2, 300m southeast of Raekoja pl., for: Pärnu (4hr., 20 per day, 100-125EEK); Tallinn (2-3hr., 46 per day, 80-165EEK); Rīga, LAT (5hr., 2 per day, 150EEK); St. Petersburg, RUS (9hr., 1 per day, 270EEK). **Trains** (☎615 68 51), generally less reliable than buses, go from the intersection of Kuperjanovi and Vaksali to Tallinn (2½-3½hr., 3 per day, 85EEK). The **tourist office,** Raekoja pl. 14, offers free Internet. (☎442 111; www.visittartu.com. Open mid-Sept. to mid-May M-F 9am-6pm, Sa 10am-5pm, Su 10am-3pm; late Sept. to early May M-F 9am-5pm, Sa-Su 10am-3pm.) Many cafes in Raekoja pl. have wireless. **Postal Code:** 51001.

ESTONIAN ISLANDS

SAAREMAA ☎(0)45

Kuressaare (pop. 16,000), the largest town on Saaremaa, is making a comeback with tourists but remains tranquil. Head south from Raekoja pl. (Town Hall Sq.) along Lossi to reach **Bishopric Castle** (Piiskopilinnus). Inside, hidden staircases and shafts with roaring lions share space with the **Saaremaa Museum,** which chronicles the island's history. (Open May-Aug. daily 10am-7pm; Sept.-Apr. W-Su 11am-6pm. 30EEK, students 15EEK. Cash only.)

Sug Hostel ❶, Kingu 6, is your best bet for budget rooms. (☎45 543 88. Breakfast 40EEK. Free Internet. Reception 24hr. Open June-Aug. Dorms 110-130EEK; singles

210-250EEK; doubles 300-350EEK; quads 480-580EEK. MC/V.) Grab traditional Estonian pancakes (16-33EEK) or nontraditional Estonian pizza (35-85EEK) at **Pannkoogikohvik ❶**, Kohtu 1. (☎45 335 75. Open M-Th 9am-midnight, F-Sa 9am-2am, Su 10am-midnight. MC/V.) Direct **buses** (☎45 316 61) leave from Pihtla tee 2, at the corner with Tallinna, for Pärnu (3hr., 5 per day, 155EEK) and Tallinn (4-5hr., 9-11 per day, 190-200EEK.) The **tourist office,** Tallinna 2, in the town hall, offers free **Internet** and arranges private rooms. (☎45 331 20; www.saaremaa.ee. Open May to mid-Sept. M-F 9am-7pm, Sa 9am-5pm, Su 10am-3pm; mid-Sept. to Apr. M-F 9am-5pm.)

HIIUMAA ☎46

By restricting access to Hiiumaa (pop. 11,000) for 50 years, the Soviets unwittingly preserved the island's rare plant and animal species. Creek-laced **Kärdla** (pop. 4000) is Hiiumaa's biggest town. To explore the sights along the coast, rent a **bike** (100EEK per day) from **Priit Tikka,** which will deliver anywhere on the island (☎5660 6377; www.hot.ee/jalgrattalaenutus. Cash only.) Bike west from Kärdla toward Kõrgessaare to the chilling **Hill of Crosses** (Ristimägi; 6km). About 2km past that, a right turn leads to the cast-iron **Tahkuna Lighthouse** (11km). Back on the main road, turn right again toward Kõrgessaare; continue 20km past the town to reach the impressive 16th-century **Kõpu Lighthouse.** (20EEK, students 10EEK. Cash only.) The island of **Kassari,** attached to Hiiumaa by a land bridge, can be reached from Kärdla by infrequent local buses (you'll still have at least a 4km trek ahead of you) or a 22km bike ride south. On Kassari's southern tip, is the **Sääretirp** peninsula, where pine and juniper bushes give way to a windswept rocky promontory.

Eesti Posti Hostel ❶, Posti 13, has comfy beds and clean baths. (☎533 118 60. Call for check-in. May-Sept. 200EEK per person; Oct.-Apr. 150EEK. Cash only.) In the town square, **Arteesia Kohvik ❶**, Keskväljak 5, serves home-cooked meat and seafood. (Entrees 20-85EEK. Open M-Th 11am-11pm, F-Sa 11am-midnight, Su 11am-10pm. MC/V.) Direct **buses** run from Sadama 13 (☎46 320 77), north of Kärdla's main square, Keskväljak, to Tallinn (4½hr.; 2-3 per day; 160EEK, students 145EEK. Cash only). Once you're on Hiiumaa, you can get to Saaremaa via public transportation, but it's difficult to find transportation in the opposite direction, or from the ferry terminal on Saaremaa to town. The **tourist office,** Hiiu 1, in Keskväljak, sells **The Lighthouse Tour** (25EEK), a guide to sights with local legends. (☎462 22 32; www.hiiumaa.ee. Open May to mid-Sept. M-F 9am-6pm, Sa-Su 10am-3pm; mid-Sept. to Apr. M-F 9am-5pm. Cash only.) The town center has free wireless.

FINLAND (SUOMI)

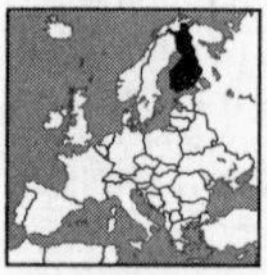

After seven centuries in the crossfire of warring Sweden and Russia, Finland gained autonomy in 1917 and never looked back. Seaside towns balance bustling Helsinki, where Aalto's Modernist constructions rise in contrast to the historic city center. With thousands of lakes and 68% of its land area carpeted in rich boreal forest, the country's geography reels in serious hikers, and southern cities draw architecture students and art gurus. Budget travelers will find Finland—outside of its stylish capital—more affordable than its Scandinavian neighbors.

DISCOVER FINLAND: SUGGESTED ITINERARY

Start things off in the lakeside capital of **Helsinki** (p. 298) by ambling along the tree-lined *Esplanadi* and checking out some of the city's grade-A museums. Leave time to bike down the Pellinge archipelago south of **Porvoo** (p. 305). Out west, the venerable city of **Turku** (p. 306) is worth a look, but today **Tampere** (p. 308) is the rising star of Finnish urbanity, with a lively music scene and factories-turned-museum. Picnic on the islands of **Savonlinna** (p. 310), and daytrip out to the transcendent Retretti Art Center. From here, decide between heading back to Helsinki or embarking on the trek north to **Rovaniemi** (p. 312), where you can launch a foray into the wilds of the Arctic Circle.

ESSENTIALS

FACTS AND FIGURES

Official Name: Republic of Finland.
Capital: Helsinki.
Major Cities: Oulu, Tampere, Turku.
Population: 5,256,000.
Land Area: 338,000 sq. km.
Time Zone: GMT +2.
Languages: Finnish, Swedish.
Religions: Evangelical Lutheran (89%).

WHEN TO GO

The long days of Finnish summers make for a tourist's dream, but the two-month polar night *(kaamos)* found during winter in Finland's northernmost regions is difficult to handle. The whole country shuts down for a Midsummer festivities (June 23-24). In early February, winter-sport fanatics start hitting the slopes; the skiing continues well into March and April. Temperatures average about 20-25°C (68-77°F) in summer, and dip as low as -20°C (-5°F) in winter.

DOCUMENTS AND FORMALITIES

EMBASSIES AND CONSULATES. All foreign embassies are in Helsinki. Finnish embassies abroad include: Australia, 12 Darwin Ave., Yarralumla, ACT, 2600 (☎26 273 38 00; www.finland.org.au); Canada, 55 Metcalfe St., Ste. 850, Ottawa, ON, K1P 6L5 (☎613-288-2233; www.finland.ca/en); Ireland, Russell House, Stokes Pl., St. Stephen's Green, Dublin 2 (☎01 478 1344); UK, 38 Chesham Pl., London, SW1X 8HW (☎020 7838 6200; www.finemb.org.uk); US, 3301 Massachusetts Ave., NW, Washington, D.C., 20008 (☎202-298-5800; www.finland.org). New Zealanders should contact the Australian embassy.

VISA AND ENTRY INFORMATION. EU citizens do not need a visa. Citizens of Australia, Canada, New Zealand, and the US do not need a visa for stays of up to 90 days, although this three-month period begins upon entry into any of the countries that belong to the EU's freedom-of-movement zone. For more info, see p. 15.

TOURIST SERVICES AND MONEY

EMERGENCY	**Police, Ambulance,** and **Fire:** ☎112.

TOURIST OFFICES. The Finnish Tourist Board (☎212 885 9700; www.visitfinland.com) maintains an official online travel guide, which customizes its travel information and advice by your home country.

MONEY. The **euro (€)** has replaced the Finnish markka as the unit of currency in Finland. For exchange rates and more info on the euro, see p. 18. Banks exchange currency for a €2-5 commission, though **Forex** offices and **ATMs** offer the best exchange rates. Food from grocery stores runs €10-17 per day; meals cost somewhere around €8 for lunch and €12 for dinner. Restaurant bills include a service charge, although an extra 5-10% **tip** is appreciated for particularly good service. For other services, tips are not expected. All EU countries impose a **value added tax (VAT)** on goods and services purchased within the Union. Prices in Finland include the country's 22% VAT rate, although partial refunds up to 16% are available for visitors who are not EU citizens. For additional information on the VAT, see p. 22.

TRANSPORTATION

BY PLANE. Several major airlines fly into Helsinki from Australia, Europe, and North America. **Finnair** (Finland ☎0600 140 140, UK 087 0241 4411, US 800-950-5000; www.finnair.com) flies from 50 international cities and also covers the domestic market. Finnair offers special youth rates—inquire before purchasing your tickets. **Ryanair** (www.ryanair.com) flies to Tampere.

BY TRAIN. The national rail company is **VR Ltd., Finnish Railways** (☎0600 41 902; www.vr.fi). Travelers pay high prices for efficient trains; seat reservations (€1.20-30) are required on InterCity and Pendolino trains. **Eurail** is valid in Finland. A **Finnrail pass,** available only outside Finland, gives three (€121), five (€162), or 10 travel days (€218) in a one-month period. The **Scanrail pass,** purchased abroad, is good for rail travel through Denmark, Finland, Norway, and Sweden, as well as discounted ferry and bus rides. See p. 52 for more info. Finnrail or Scanrail pass is often your best bet for longer trips, since Finnish trains only offer student discounts to those with Finnish IDs.

> **TIP** **RAIL SAVINGS.** Scanrail passes purchased outside Scandinavia are much more flexible than Scanrail passes purchased once you arrive, and may be less expensive depending on the exchange rate. Check www.scanrail.com for more information on where to purchase passes at home.

BY BUS. Buses are the only way to reach some smaller towns and to travel past the Arctic Circle. **Oy Matkahuolto Ab** (☎9 682 701; www.matkahuolto.fi) coordinates bus service across Finland. ISIC holders can buy a **student card** (€5.40) at bus stations, which grants a 50% discount on one-way tickets for routes longer than 80km. **Railpasses** are valid on buses when trains are not in service. Travelers should note that some town names take a modified form on train and bus schedules. "To Helsinki" is written *Helsinkiin*, while "from Helsinki" is *Helsingistä.*

BY FERRY. Viking Line (Finland ☎09 123 51, Sweden 08 452 4000; www.vikingline.fi) runs from Stockholm to Helsinki, Mariehamn, and Turku. **Silja Line** (Finland ☎09 180 41, Sweden 08 666 33 30; www.silja.fi) sails from Stockholm to Helsinki, Mariehamn, and Turku. On Viking ferries, **Scanrail** holders get 50% off and a **Eurailpass** plus train ticket entitles holders to a free passenger fare (mention this discount when booking). Viking offers "early bird" discounts of 15-50% for those who book at least 30 days in advance within either Finland or Sweden. On Silja, both Scan- and Eurailers ride either for free or at reduced rates, depending on the route and type of ticket.

BY CAR. Finland honors foreign driver's licenses for up to one year for drivers aged 18 years or older. **Speed limits** are 120kph on expressways, 50kph in densely populated areas, and 80-100kph elsewhere. Headlights must be used at all times. Driving conditions are good, but take extra care in winter weather and be wary of reindeer. For more info on car rental and driving in Europe, see p. 54.

BY BIKE AND BY THUMB. Finland has a well-developed network of **cycling** paths. **Fillari GT** route maps are available at bookstores (€10-16). Check www.visitfinland.com/cycling for pre-trip route planning. Let's Go does not recommend **hitchhiking.** It is uncommon in Finland and illegal on highways, although www.cs.helsinki.fi/u/kjokisal/liftaus does give suggestions for hitchhiking routes.

KEEPING IN TOUCH

PHONE CODES	**Country code:** 358. **International dialing prefix:** 00. For more information on how to place international calls, see inside back cover.

EMAIL AND THE INTERNET. Cybercafes in Helsinki are relatively scarce compared to other European capitals, and in smaller towns they are virtually nonexistent. However, many tourist offices and public libraries offer short (15-30min.) time slots of free Internet, and there is some free wireless access in Helsinki.

TELEPHONE. To make a long-distance call within Finland, dial 0 and then the number. Pay phones are nearly nonexistent, however **mobile phones** are extremely popular in the nation that gave the world Nokia, and prepaid mobile phone cards can be used to make international calls (never cheap, but cheapest 5pm-8am). For more info on mobile phones, see p. 29. For operator assistance, dial ☎118; for help with international calls, dial ☎020 208. International direct dial numbers include: **AT&T Direct** (☎0800 1100 15); **Canada Direct** (☎0800 1100 11); **MCI WorldPhone** (☎0800 1102 80); **Sprint** (☎0800 1102 84); **Telecom New Zealand** (☎0800 1106 40).

MAIL. Mail service in Finland is fast and efficient. Postcards and letters under 50g cost €0.65 within Finland, €0.90 to the EU, and €1.20 to anywhere outside Europe. International letters weighing under 20g cost €0.65.

LANGUAGES. Finnish is spoken by most of the population, although children learn both Swedish and Finnish from the seventh grade. Three dialects of Sámi are also spoken by an ethnic minority of roughly 2000 in northern Finland. English is also widely spoken, with two-thirds of Finns reporting that they can speak at least some English; city-dwellers and those under 35 are generally the most proficient. For basic Finnish words and phrases, see **Phrasebook: Finnish,** p. 1054.

ACCOMMODATIONS AND CAMPING

FINLAND	❶	❷	❸	❹	❺
ACCOMMODATIONS	under €15	€15-28	€28-50	€50-75	over €75

Finland has over 100 **youth hostels** (*retkeilymaja;* RET-kay-loo-MAH-yah), although only half of them are open year-round. The **Finnish Youth Hostel Association** (Suomen Retkeilymajajärjestö; ☎09 565 71 50; www.srmnet.org) is Finland's HI affiliate. Prices are generally around €23 per person for a dorm room, with an HI discount of €2.50. Most have laundry facilities and a kitchen; some have saunas and rent bicycles or skis. **Hotels** are generally expensive (over €50 per night); *kesähotelli* (summer hotels) are usually student lodgings vacated from June to August, and cost about €25 per night. **Camping** is common; more than 350 campgrounds pepper the countryside. Seventy of them are open year-round (tent sites €10-25 per night; small cottages from €30). The **Camping Card Scandinavia** (€6) qualifies cardholders for discounts and includes limited accident insurance. For a campground guide or to purchase the Camping Card, contact the **Finnish Camping Site Association.** (☎09 477 407 40; www.camping.fi. Allow 3 weeks for delivery of the card.) Finland's *jokamiehenoikeudet* (right to public access) means that travelers can temporarily camp for free in the countryside, as long as they stay a reasonable distance from private homes.

FOOD AND DRINK

FINLAND	❶	❷	❸	❹	❺
FOOD	under €8	€8-15	€15-20	€20-30	over €30

Kebab and pizza joints are cheap and popular, but the local **Kauppatori** markets and **Kauppahalli** food courts are more likely to serve fresh, recognizably Finnish fare. Finland's traditional diet slants toward breads and sausages. In season, however, menus feature freshly caught trout, perch, pike, and herring; a new wave of five-star chefs in Helsinki are starting to pair French and Mediterranean ingredients with the bounty of Finland's fisheries. Bowls of reindeer stew are a staple of Lapland, while Kuopio is known for its pillowy rye pastries. Don't bypass strawberries in summer; Finland is the top European producer. A surprising number of adults drink milk with meals, followed by interminable pots of coffee. You must be 18 to purchase beer and wine, 20 for liquor; the minimum age in bars is usually 18, but can go up to 25. Alcohol stronger than light beer must be bought at state-run **Alko** liquor stores, open weekdays until at least 6pm and Saturdays until at least 4pm.

HOLIDAYS AND FESTIVALS

Holidays: New Year's Day (Jan. 1); Epiphany (Jan. 6); Good Friday (Apr. 16); Easter (Apr. 8-9); May Day (May 1); Ascension Day (May 17); Whit Sunday (May 27); Midsummer (June 23-24); All Saints' Day (Nov. 1); Independence Day (Dec. 6); Christmas Day (Dec. 25); Boxing Day (Dec. 26).

Festivals: Flags fly high and *kokko* (bonfires) blaze on Midsummer's Eve (June 23), when the Finnish desert their cities for seaside cabins. July is the festival high season in Finland, with gays and lesbians celebrating Helsinki Pride, Turku's youth taking to the mosh pits of Ruisrock, and Pori's residents launching their eclectic Jazz Festival. Savonlinna's Opera Festival continues into early August, while the Helsinki Festival, Oulu's Music Video Festival, and Lahti's Sibelius Festival close out the summer. Check out www.festivals.fi for more info and 2007 dates.

BEYOND TOURISM

It is relatively difficult for foreigners to secure full-time employment in Finland, but travelers may be able to obtain summer work. Check the **CIMO** website (see below) or www.jobs-in-europe.net for information on work placement. The organizations below coordinate limited work and volunteer opportunities. See p. 61 for Beyond Tourism opportunities throughout Europe.

The American-Scandinavian Foundation (AMSCAN), 58 Park Ave., New York, NY 10016, USA (☎212-879-9779; www.amscan.org/jobs/index.html). Volunteer and job opportunities throughout Scandinavia. Limited number of fellowships for study in Finland available to Americans.

Centre for International Mobility (CIMO), Hakaniemenkatu 2, Helsinki (☎1080 6767; http://finland.cimo.fi). Provides information on youth exchange programs, technical and agricultural internships, and study abroad in Finland. CIMO also organizes **European Voluntary Service** programs (http://europa.eu.int/comm/youth/program/guide/action2_en.html) for citizens of the EU, who can spend a fully funded year doing service in another EU country. In Finland, EVS opportunities are largely in social work.

Council of International Fellowship (**CIF;** www.ciffinland.org). Cultural exchange programs for human service professionals, including homestays in various Finnish cities. Must have 2 years of work experience.

HELSINKI (HELSINGFORS) ☎09

With all the appeal of a big city but none of the grime, Helsinki's (pop. 560,000) broad avenues, grand architecture, and green parks make it a showcase of both eastern and western Europe. A hub of the design world, the city also distinguishes itself with a multicultural flair: Lutheran and Russian Orthodox cathedrals stand almost face-to-face, and youthful energy mingles with old-world charm.

TRANSPORTATION

Flights: Helsinki-Vantaa Airport (**HEL;** ☎020 01 46 36; www.ilmailulaitos.fi). **Bus** #615 runs from airport Platform 1B and the train station. (40min.; from the airport M-F 6am-11pm 3-4 per hr., 11pm-1am 1-2 per hr., Sa-Su 6am-1am 1-2 per hr.; to the airport 5am-midnight; €3.60. Cash only.) A **Finnair bus** runs from airport Platform 1A and the Finnair building next to the train station (☎0600 14 01 40. 25min., 4-5 per hr. To the airport 5am-midnight, from the airport 6am-1am. €5.20. AmEx/DC/MC/V.)

Trains: (☎030 072 09 00, English-language info 231 999 02; www.vr.fi.) To: **Moscow, RUS** (14hr., 5:40pm, €96); **Rovaniemi** (10-13hr., 5-8 per day, €72-75); **St. Petersburg, RUS** (5½hr., 2 per day, €56); **Tampere** (2hr., 8-12 per day, €21-23); **Turku** (2hr., 12 per day, €23-34). See p. 840 for **entrance requirements** to Russia.

Buses: Narinkka 3 (☎020 040 00; www.matkahuolti.fi) is inside the Kamppi shopping center. From the train station, take Postik. past the statue of Mannerheim. Cross Mannerheimintie onto Salomonk. Station will be on your left. To **Lahti** (1½hr., 2 per hr., €19), **Tampere** (2½hr., 1 per hr., €21), and **Turku** (2½hr., 2 per hr., €24.10).

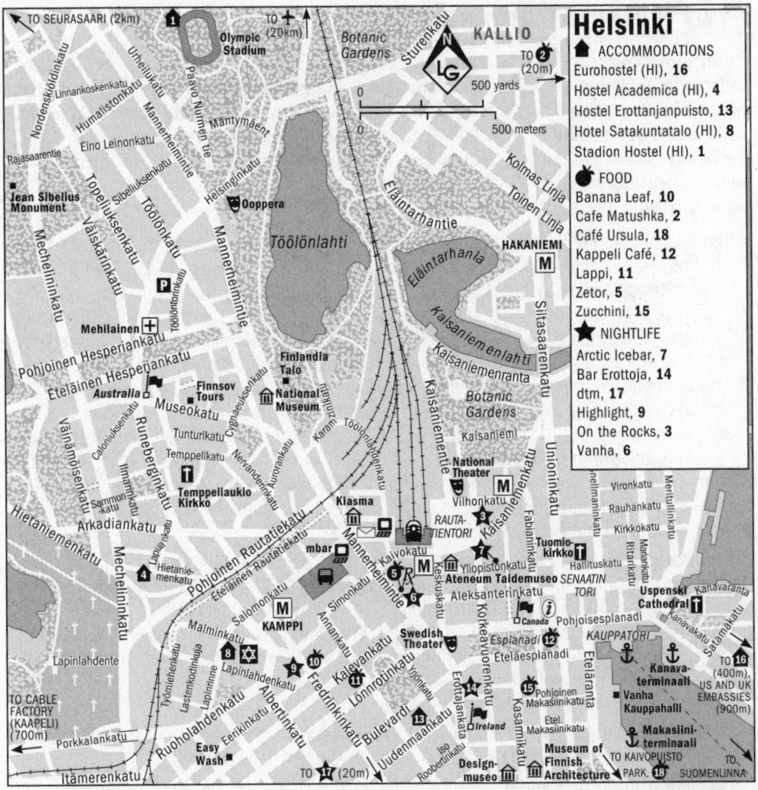

Ferries: Viking Line, Lönnrotink. 2 (☎12 35 77; www.vikingline.fi), sails to **Stockholm, SWE** (17hr., 5:30pm, from €46) and **Tallinn, EST** (3hr., 12:30and 9pm, €12-17). AmEx/DC/MC/V. Tram #2 or bus #13 to Katajanokka terminal. **Tallink,** Erottajank. 19 (☎22 83 11), sails to **Tallinn, EST** (3¼hr.; May to mid-Aug. 8-12 per day, mid-Aug. to Apr. 2-3 per day; from €20). AmEx/MC/V. Take bus #15 to West terminal.

Local Transportation: (☎472 3454; www.hkl.fi/english.html). **Buses, trams,** and the **metro** run 5:30am-11pm; major bus and tram lines, including tram #3T, run until 1:30am. **Night buses,** marked with "N," run F-Sa after 2am (€3). Single-fare tram €1.80; with 1hr. of transfers to buses, trams, and the metro €2. **City Transport Office** *(HKL Palvelupiste)* is in the Rautatientori metro, below the train station. Open mid-June to July M-Th 7:30am-6pm, F 7:30am-5pm, Sa 10am-3pm; low season M-Th 7:30am-7pm, F 7:30am-5pm, Sa 10am-3pm. Sells the **tourist ticket** (as does the tourist office), a good investment for unlimited access to buses, trams, the metro, and trains. 1-day €6, 3-day €12, 5-day €18. AmEx/DC/MC/V.

Taxis: Taxi Centre Helsinki (☎0100 07 00). Special airport prices with **Yellow Line** (☎0600 55 55 55). Reserve 1 day ahead, before 6pm. 20min., €25. AmEx/DC/MC/V.

Bike Rental: From mid-June to Aug., the city provides over 300 free, lime-green bikes at major destinations throughout the city; it can be tricky to track one down, but when you do, deposit a €2 coin in the lock and then retrieve your deposit upon "returning" the bike to any location. Free cycling maps of the city are available at the tourist office.

ORIENTATION AND PRACTICAL INFORMATION

Water surrounds Helsinki in every direction and facilitates relaxing city beaches and gorgeous lakeside parks. Its main street, **Mannerheimintie,** passes between the bus and train stations on its way south to the city center, coming to an end at the **Esplanadi.** This tree-lined promenade leads east to **Kauppatori** (Market Square) and the beautiful South Harbor. Northeast of the city center lies **Kallio,** the bohemian district. Both Finnish and Swedish are used on all street signs and maps; *Let's Go* uses the Finnish names.

Tourist Offices: Pohjoisesplanadi 19 (☎169 37 57; www.visithelsinki.fi). From the train station, walk 2 blocks down Keskusk. and turn left on Pohjoisesplanadi. Free Internet and wireless access. Open May-Sept. M-F 9am-8pm, Sa-Su 9am-6pm; Oct.-Apr. M-F 9am-6pm, Sa-Su 10am-4pm. Representatives in green vests patrol the city center in summer to distribute maps and answer questions. The **Helsinki Card,** sold at the **Tour Shop** in the tourist office, provides unlimited local transportation, free or discounted guided tours, and free or discounted admission to most museums, although cardholders have to keep up a blistering pace to make their purchase worthwhile. 1-day €29, 2-day €42, 3-day €53. The shop also books various amenities for a fee. (☎2288 1200; www.helsinkiexpert.fi. Open June-Aug. M-F 9am-7pm, Sa-Su 9am-5pm; Sept.-May M-F 9am-5pm, Sa 10am-4pm. AmEx/DC/MC/V.) **Finnsov Tours,** Museok. 15 (☎436 69 61; www.finnsov.info) arranges trips to Russia and expedites the visa process. Open M-F 8:30am-5pm. AmEx/DC/MC/V.

Embassies: Canada, Pohjoisesplanadi 25B (☎22 85 30; www.canada.fi). Open June-Aug. M-Th 8:30am-noon and 1-4:30pm, F 8:30am-1:30pm; Sept.-May M-F 8:30am-noon and 1-4:30pm. **Ireland,** Erottajank. 7A (☎64 60 06; helsinki@dfa.ie). Open M-F 9am-5pm. **UK,** Itäinen Puistotie 17 (☎22 86 51 00; www.ukembassy.fi). Citizens of **Australia** and **New Zealand** should contact the UK embassy. Open June-Aug. M-F 8:30am-3:30pm; Sept.-May M-F 9am-5pm. **US,** Itäinen Puistotie 14A (☎61 62 50; www.usembassy.fi). Open M-F 8:30am-5pm.

Currency Exchange: Forex (☎020 7512 510) has 4 locations and the best rates in the city. Hours vary; the branch in the train station is open daily 8am-9pm.

Luggage Storage: Lockers in the train station €2-3 per day. The Kiasma museum (p. 304) will provide free storage during the day, even if you don't pay admission.

GBLT Resources: Seta Ry, Mannerheimintie 170A 4, 5th fl. (☎681 2580; www.seta.fi) Tram #10. A national organization with info on gay services in the country and a trans support center. Copies of *Gay Guide Helsinki* are at the tourist office.

Laundromat: Café Tin Tin Tango, Töölöntorink. 7 (☎27 09 09 72; www.tintintango.info), a combination bar, cafe, laundromat, and sauna. Wash €3.50, dry €1.80, detergent €1. Sandwiches €5-8. Open M-Th 7am-midnight, F 7am-2am, Sa 9am-2am, Su 10am-2am. MC/V. For a more traditional laundromat, try **Easy Wash,** Kalevank. 45 (☎67 97 89). Wash €4 per 5kg, dry €3 per 5kg, detergent €1. Open M-Th 10am-8pm, F 10am-6pm, Sa 10am-4pm. MC/V.

Emergency: ☎112. **Police:** ☎100 22. **24hr. Medical Hotline:** ☎100 23

24hr. Pharmacy: Yliopiston Apteekki, Mannerheimintie 5 (☎ 0203 20200).

Hospital: 24hr. medical clinic **Mehilainen,** Runeberginк. 47A (☎010 414 44 44).

Telephone: Telecenter Worldwide, Vuorik. 8 (☎670 612; www.woodgong.com), offers reasonable rates to call most countries. Open M-F 9am-9pm, Sa 11am-9pm, Su noon-9pm. Australia €0.30 per min., UK €0.20, US €0.25. MC/V.

Internet Access: Library 10, Elielinaukio 2G, upstairs in the main post office building. Free wireless, free 30min. slots, up to 3hr. with reservation. Open M-Th 10am-10pm, F 10am-6pm, Sa-Su noon-6pm. **mbar,** Mannerheimintie 22-24 (☎6124 5420;

www.mbar.fi), offers free wireless access and 13 terminals. €5 per hr. Open M-Tu 9am-midnight, W-Th 9am-2am, F-Sa 9am-3am, Su noon-midnight. MC/V. Many cafes in the city center provide free Internet and wireless access. Go to the tourist office for a complete list, or log onto www.hel.fi/en/wlan.

Post Office: Elielinaukio 2F (☎20 07 10 00). Open M-F 7am-9pm, Sa-Su 10am-6pm. Address mail to be held in the following format: First name LAST NAME, *Poste Restante*, post office address, Helsinki, FINLAND.

ACCOMMODATIONS AND CAMPING

Helsinki's budget hostels are often quite nice. Reserve ahead in June and July.

Hostel Erottajanpuisto (HI), Uudenmaank. 9 (☎64 21 69; www.erottajanpuisto.com). Friendly staff tends well-kept rooms in a central location. Breakfast €5. Lockers €1. Laundry €7. Internet €1 per 10min. Reception 24hr. Summer dorms €23; singles €46; doubles €63. Low season singles €44; doubles €61. €2.50 HI discount. AmEx/MC/V. ❷

Hostel Satakuntatalo (HI), Lapinrinne 1A (☎69 58 52 32; www.sodexho.fi/satakunta). M: Kamppi. Spacious, well-equipped rooms close to the city center. Breakfast and sauna included. Lockers €2. Linens €5. Laundry €5.50. Internet €6 per hr. Reception 24hr. Open June-Aug. Dorms €20; singles from €36; doubles from €54; triples from €75; quads from €86. €2.50 HI discount. AmEx/DC/MC/V. ❷

Hostel Academica (HI), Hietaniemenk. 14 (☎1311 4334; www.hostelacademica.fi). M: Kamppi. Turn right onto Runebergink., and go left after crossing the bridge. University housing changes into a hostel in summer. Morning sauna and swim included. Breakfast and linens included for singles and doubles. Breakfast €6.50. Linens €5.50, towel €1. Internet €4 per hr.; wireless €2 per hr., €5 per day. Reception 24hr. Open June-Aug. Dorms €18; singles €40-57; doubles €60-75. €2.50 HI discount. AmEx/DC/MC/V. ❷

Eurohostel (HI), Linnank. 9 (☎622 04 70; www.eurohostel.fi), 200m from the Katajanokka ferry terminal. Bright rooms, cafe, and free morning sauna. Evening sauna €5. Breakfast €6.30. Laundry €2.50. Internet €6 per hr., wireless €5 per day. Reception 24hr. Singles €39-42; doubles €47-52; triples €70-78. €2.50 HI discount. MC/V. ❸

Stadion Hostel (HI), Pohj. Stadiontie 3B (☎477 84 80; www.stadionhostel.com). Take tram #3 or 7A to Auroran Sairaala and walk down Pohj. This hostel might look like a high-school locker room, but it boasts a much healthier social life. Breakfast €5.60. Linens €5. Laundry €2.50. Free Internet and wireless. Reception June to mid-Sept. 7am-3am; mid-Sept. to May 7am-2am. Lockout noon-4pm. Curfew 3am. Dorms €16; singles €32; doubles €44. €2.50 HI discount. MC/V. ❷

Rastila Camping, Karavaanik. 4 (☎321 65 51; www.hel.fi/rastila). M: Rastila. Change trains at Itäkeskus. A large campground 12km from the city next to a public beach. Kitchen, showers, and electricity each €4.50-7. Reception mid-May to mid-Sept. 24hr; mid-Sept. to mid-May daily 8am-10pm. Tent sites in summer €10, winter €6, up to 5 extra people €5. Cabins €38-64. Hostel open June-July. Dorms €19. MC/V. ❶

FOOD

Restaurants and cafes are easy to find on **Esplanadi** and the streets branching off from **Mannerheimintie** and **Uudenmaankatu.** Cheaper options surround the **Hietalahti** flea market at the southern end of Bulevardi. A large **supermarket** is under the train station. (Open M-F 7:30am-10pm, Sa 9am-10pm, Su 10am-10pm.) Helsinki has many budget restaurants that serve all manner of ethnic food. Get lunch at the open-air market of **Kauppatori** where stalls sell a variety of freshly cooked fish and local produce; a meal from one of the cafes will cost about €8. (Open June-Aug. M-Sa 6:30am-5pm; Sept.-May M-F 7am-2pm.)

Zetor, Mannerheimintie 3-5 (☎66 69 66; www.zetor.net), in the mall opposite train station. Cheeky menu, cheekier farm-inspired decor, a trademark tractor, and ridiculously good Finnish food. Homemade beer €5. Entrees €10-27. Attached bar 22+. Open Su-M 3pm-2am, Tu 3pm-3am, W-F 3pm-4am, Sa 11am-4am. AmEx/DC/MC/V. ❷

Kappeli Café, Eteläesplanadi 1 (☎681 24 40; www.kappeli.fi). Since 1867, this cafe has served the bohemian and the elite. Salads and sandwiches €6-9. Open May-Aug. M-Sa 9am-2am, Su 9am-midnight; Sept.-Apr. daily 10am-midnight. Kitchen closes 1hr. before closing. AmEx/DC/MC/V. ❶

Café Ursula (☎65 28 17; www.ursula.fi), Ehrenströmintie 3. This upscale cafe also has delicious budget options and an idyllic setting on the edge of the Baltic Sea. Sandwiches €5-6. Salad bar €11. Entrees €9-13. Open daily in summer 9am-midnight; spring and fall 9am-10pm; winter 9am-8pm. AmEx/DC/MC/V. ❷

Zucchini, Fabianink. 4 (☎622 29 07), south of the tourist office. Popular vegetarian eatery with organic produce and vegan fare. Open M-F 11am-4pm. AmEx/DC/MC/V. ❷

Banana Leaf, Fredrink. 49 (☎605 167; www.malesia.net/bananaleaf). Tasty Malaysian and Thai food served in a serene setting. Ask the server to add some spice to your dish—Finns take their Asian food bland. Entrees €8-17. Lunch buffet €8. Open 10:30am-3pm. AmEx/DC/MC/V. ❷

Lappi, Annank. 22 (☎64 55 50; www.lappires.com). Tourists splurge on specialties like reindeer, lingonberries, and Arctic char amid smoky smells, wood, and fur. Entrees from €16. Reserve ahead. Open in summer M-F 5-10:30pm, Sa-Su 1-10:30pm; winter M-F noon-10:30pm, Sa-Su 1-10:30pm. AmEx/DC/MC/V. ❸

Cafe Matushka, Flemingink. 5. This slightly seedy, but decidedly untouristed restaurant/bar serves some of the cheapest, most authentic Russian food in the city with an atmosphere that captures the spirit of the mother country. €7 buys the day's selection. Beer €3. Happy hour daily 11am-8pm; beer €2.40. Open daily 11am-2am. MC/V. ❶

FINLAND

SIGHTS

Helsinki's Neoclassical buildings and bold new forms reflect Finnish architect Alvar Aalto's joke: "Architecture is our form of expression because our language is so impossible." Helsinki's Art Nouveau *(Jugendstil)* and Modernist structures are home to a dynamic design community. Much of the layout and architecture of the old center, however, is the brainchild of a German, Carl Engel, who designed a city modeled after St. Petersburg. Older buildings are often adorned with humorous statues, so keep an eye out. Most of the major sights are crammed into the city's compact center, making it ideal for walking tours; pick up *See Helsinki on Foot* from the tourist office for suggested routes. Trams #3B and 3T loop around the major sights in roughly 1hr., providing a cheap alternative to sightseeing buses. Helsinki is dotted with parks, including **Kaivopuisto** in the south, **Töölönlahti** in the north, and **Esplanadi** and **Tähtitorninvuori** in the center of town.

SUOMENLINNA. Five interconnected islands are home to this 18th-century Swedish military fortification. The old fortress's dark passageways are an adventure to explore. The **Suomenlinna Museum** and the **Coastal Artillery Museum,** located within one of the ramparts, offer military aficionados an informative approach to history. *(☎684 1880; www.suomenlinna.fi. Museums open daily May-Aug. 10am-6pm; Sept.-Apr. 11am-4pm. €5, students €4. AmEx/DC/MC/V.)* The islands also feature the world's only combination church and **lighthouse,** which contains the country's largest bell, as well as Finland's only remaining WWII **submarine,** the *Vesikko*. *(Church ☎684 7471. Usually open W-F noon-4pm. Submarine ☎1814 5295. Open mid-May to Aug. 11am-6pm. €4, students €2.)* The young and young at heart flock to the **Toy Museum,** on the main island. *(☎668 417. Open July daily 11am-6pm; May-June and Aug. daily 11am-5pm; Apr. and*

Sept. Sa-Su 11am-4pm. €5, students €4. MC/V. Tours leave from the museum June-Aug. daily 11am and 2pm, winter Sa-Su 1:30pm. €6, including admission to the Ehrensvard Museum. AmEx/DC/MC/V.) Southern island's smooth rocks are popular with sunbathers and swimmers. *(City Transport ferries depart from Market St.; 15min., every 20min. 8am-11pm, round-trip €3.60. Combo ticket for museums and submarine €6, students €3. Cash only.)*

SENAATIN TORI (SENATE SQUARE). The square and its gleaming white **Tuomiokirkko** (Dome Church) showcase Engel's work and exemplify the splendor of Finland's 19th-century Russian period. The church's stunning marble reliefs house an interior so elegantly simple that every gilded detail becomes magnified. *(At Aleksanterink. and Unionink. in the city center. ☎2340 6120. Free organ recitals W at noon in July. Church open June-Aug. M-Sa 9am-midnight, Su noon-8pm; Sept.-May M-Sa 9am-6pm, Su noon-6pm.)* Around the corner from Tuomiokirkko, at the Hallitusk. stop of trams #7A and 7B, is the **Bank of Finland Museum.** *(Snellmanink. 2. ☎010 831 2981. Open Tu-F noon-6pm, Sa-Su 11am-4pm. Free.)* Just south of Senate Sq., on a small street running between Unionink. and Snellmanink., the **Helsinki City Museum** chronicles the city's 450-year history. The City Museum also has exhibits throughout Helsinki; pick up a list at the museum or at the tourist office. *(Sofiank. 4. ☎169 3933. Open M-F 9am-5pm, Sa-Su 11am-5pm. Each exhibit €4, students €2. Free Th. DC/MC/V.)* The red-brick **Uspenski Orthodox Cathedral** (Uspenskinkatedraadi), the largest Orthodox church in Western Europe, evokes images of Russia with its ornate interior and onion domes. *(☎634 267. Open M and W-Sa 9:30am-4pm, Tu 9:30am-6pm, Su noon-3pm. Closed M in winter.)*

ESPLANADI AND MANNERHEIMINTIE. A lush boulevard dotted with statues and fountains, Esplanadi is a great place to people-watch. The **Designmuseo,** which presents the work of established designers like Aalto and Eliel Saarinen alongside creations by young artists and first-rate temporary exhibits. *(Korkeavuorenk. 23. ☎622 0540; www.designmuseum.fi. Open June-Aug. daily 11am-6pm; Sept.-May Tu 11am-8pm, W-Su 11am-6pm. €7, students €3. AmEx/DC/MC/V.)* One block away, the tiny **Museum of Finnish Architecture** has temporary exhibits on the significance of architecture in the last century. *(Kasarmik. 24. ☎8567 5100; www.mfa.fi. Open Tu-Su 10am-4pm, W 10am-8pm. €3, students €1.70. AmEx/MC/V.)* At the end of Esplanadi, turn right onto Mannerheimintie and right again onto Kaivok. past the train station to reach the **Ateneum Art Museum** (Ateneum Taidemuseo), Finland's largest, with comprehensive exhibits on Finnish art. *(Kaivok. 2, opposite the train station. ☎17 33 64 01; www.ate-*

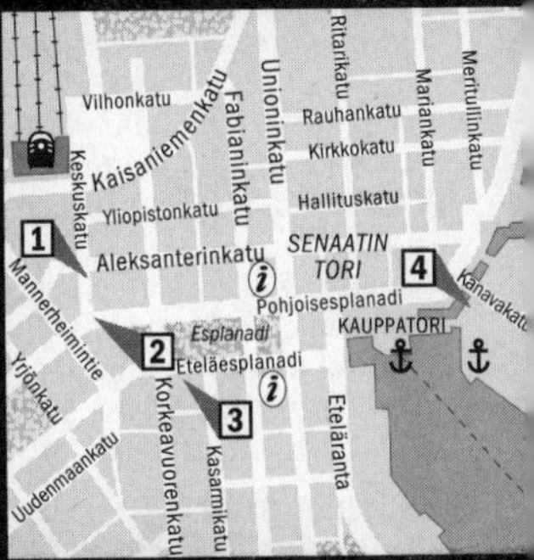

AALTO'S HELSINKI

Finlandia Hall may be architect Alvar Aalto's most recognizable gift to Helsinki, but a number of his other Modernist creations give a sense of his aesthetic breadth.

1. **Rautatalo** (Iron House), Keskusk. 3. The stark facade conceals an airy atrium meant to recall an Italian *piazza,* one of Aalto's favorite motifs.

2. **Academic Bookstore,** Pohjoisesplanadi 39. The country's largest bookstore named its upstairs cafe after the architect who designed the copper and marble building in 1969.

3. **Savoy Restaurant,** Eteläesplanadi 14. The €40 entrees are too pricey for the budget traveler, but the decor is all Aalto's work—right down to the trademark vases.

4. **Stora Enso Headquarters,** Kanavak. 1. This ultramodern "sugar cube" overlooks the South Harbor and provides a provocative contrast to the two churches that flank it.

neum.fi. Open Tu and F 9am-6pm, W-Th 9am-8pm, Sa-Su 11am-5pm. €6, students €4; €8/6.50 during temporary exhibits. Free W 5-8pm. AmEx/DC/MC/V.) Continue on Mannerheimintie to **Kiasma** (Museum of Contemporary Art), a warehouse that features top-flight modern art and calibrates the width of its doors to Fibonacci's golden ratio. When the first floor and outside host exhibits, they are often free. *(Mannerheiminaukio 2. ☎17 33 65 01; www.kiasma.fi. Open Tu 9am-5pm, W-Su 10am-8:30pm. €6, students €4. Free F 5-8:30pm. AmEx/DC/MC/V.)* After passing the grandiose Parliament building, you'll find yourself between two of Helsinki's most stunning buildings. On the left is Saarinen's **National Museum of Finland** (Suomen Kansallismuseo), featuring a ceiling fresco by Gallen-Kallela. *(Mannerheimintie 34. ☎40 501; www.kansallismuseo.fi. Open June-Aug. Tu-W 11am-8pm, Th-Su 11am-6pm; Sept.-May M-F 9am-4pm, Sa-Su noon-4pm. €6, students €4. Free Tu 5:30-8pm. AmEx/DC/MC/V.)* Head back down Mannerheimintie, turn right on Arkadiank., and right again on Fredrikink. to reach the stunning **Temppeliaukio Kirkko.** Hewn out of a hill of rock with only the roof visible from the outside, the huge domed ceiling recalls both the beauty which humanity is capable of creating along with its insignificance in the face of nature's grandeur. *(Lutherink. 3. ☎2340 5920. English services Su 2pm. Usually open M-Tu and Th-F 10am-8pm, W 10am-6:45pm, Sa 10am-noon, Su noon-1:45pm and 3:30-5:45pm.)*

OTHER SIGHTS. North of Senate Sq. along Unionink. lies the University of Helsinki's **Botanic Garden.** *(Unionink. 44. Take trams #3B/3T or 6 to Kaisaniemi. ☎191 24455. Garden open daily 9am-8pm. Free. Glass houses open Apr.-Sept. Tu-Su 10am-5pm; Oct.-Mar. 10am-3pm. €4.20, students €2.20. MC/V.)* In an industrial area west of the city center, the **Cable Factory** (Kaapeli) houses three museums, dozens of studios and galleries, and various performance areas. The **Finnish Museum of Photography** *(www.fmp.fi)* has provocative displays of photo from the past century. The **Hotel and Restaurant Museum** *(www.hotellijaravintolamuseo.fi)* offers a history of menus and minibars, and the **Theater Museum** *(www.teatterimuseo.fi)* contains set models and costume designs from the national theater. *(Tallbergink. 1. M: Ruoholahti. After exiting, walk 5 blocks down Itämerenk. Museums are in the G entrance. ☎68 50 9121; www.kaapelitehdas.fi. Open Tu-Su 11am-6pm. Theater Museum closed in July. Photography Museum €6, students €4; Hotel and Restaurant Museum €2/1; Theater Museum €5.50/2.50. MC/V.)* Near the Western Harbor, the well-touristed **Jean Sibelius Monument** pays homage to one of the 20th century's greatest composers. *(On Mechelinink. in Sibelius Park. Take bus #24, dir.: Seurasaari, from Mannerheimintie and get off at Rasjasaarentie; the monument is behind you.)*

ENTERTAINMENT

Helsinki's parks are always animated. A **concert series** enlivens the **Esplanadi** park all summer Monday through Friday at 4pm. Highlights of the program are **Jazz Espa** in July, and **Ethno Espa** showcasing international music (www.kulttuuri.hel.fi/espanlava). The **Helsinki Festival** (www.helsinkifestival.fi), toward the end of August, wraps up the summer with cultural events ranging from music and theater to film and visual arts. At the end of September, **Helsinki Design Week** (www.helsinkidesignweek.fi) reinforces Helsinki's image as a city of design, while the **Love and Anarchy Film Festival** (www.hiff.fi) features works from across the globe. Throughout summer, concerts rock **Kaivopuisto** (on the corner of Puistok. and Ehrenstromintie, in the southern part of town) and **Hietaniemi Beach** (down Hesperiank. on the western shore). The free English-language papers *Helsinki This Week*, *Helsinki Your Way*, and *City* list popular cafes, nightspots, and events; get it at the tourist office or your hostel. Also check out the *Nordic Oddity* pamphlet series, with insider advice on sights, bars, and activities. For high culture, try the Helsinki Philharmonic and Radio Symphony Orchestra, the National Opera, or the National Theater. **Lippupiste,** Aleksanterink. 52 (☎0600 90 09 00), in the Stockmann department store, sells tickets for most big venues (AmEx/DC/MC/V).

NIGHTLIFE

Bars and beer terraces fill up in late afternoon; most clubs don't get going until midnight and stay crazy until 4am. Bars and clubs line **Mannerheimintie, Uudenmaankatu,** and **Iso Roobertinkatu.** East of the train station, nightlife centers around **Yliopistonkatu** and **Kaisaniemenkatu,** while in bohemian Kallio, the bars around **Fleminginkatu** have some of the cheapest beer in the city. A popular night activity is heavy-metal karaoke; check out Wednesday and Sunday at **Hevimesta,** Hallitusk. 3.

On the Rocks, Mikonk. 15 (☎612 20 30; www.ontherocks.fi). The legendary rock bar and club offers solid Finnish bands at rock-bottom prices. Beer €4.50. Tu-Th live music. 23+. Cover Tu-Th €6-12; F-Sa €7. Open daily 8pm-4am. AmEx/D/MC/V.

Bar Erottaja, Erottajank. 13-17 (☎61 11 96). This art-student hangout is packed with people engaged in conversation over hip-hop music. Beer €4. F-Sa DJ. 22+ after 6pm. Open Su-M 2pm-1am, Tu 2pm-2am, W-Sa 2pm-3am. AmEx/D/MC/V.

Vanha, Mannerheimintie 3 (☎13 11 43 68; www.vanha.fi). A student crowd gathers here for club nights every other weekend; check website for details. Beer €4.50. Cover F-Sa €2-4. Open M-Th 11am-1am, F 11am-midnight, Sa 11am-4am. AmEx/DC/MC/V.

Highlight, Fredrinkink. 42 (☎050 409 00 79). A dance club for the young and fit—and those who want to hold onto adolescence for a few more years. Beer €4. 19+. Cover F-Sa 11pm-3am €5. Open W and F-Sa 10pm-4am. AmEx/D/MC/V.

dtm, Iso Roobertink. 28 (☎67 63 14; www.dtm.fi). This huge, popular gay club draws a mixed crowd to 2 stories of everything from foam parties to drag bingo; check website for full schedule. May 2007 will see a month-long Eurovision party. Beer €4. Lesbian nights on occasional Sa. 22+ after 10pm. Cover Sa €5, special events €5-10. Happy hour M-Sa 9am-4pm. Open M-Sa 9am-4am, Su noon-4am. AmEx/DC/MC/V.

Arctic Icebar, Yliopistonk. 5 (www.uniq.fi). Not affiliated with the other Icebars around the globe, this one sets itself apart by being the smallest (with a capacity of 12) and coldest (-10°C). The €10 cover gets you a thermal parka, gloves, booties, and a vodka-based drink—the only kind that won't crack the glasses. Additional drinks €10 each. 18+. Open W-Sa 5pm-4am. AmEx/DC/MC/V.

OUTDOOR ACTIVITIES

Just north of the train station lie the two city lakes; take an afternoon walk on the winding paths around them. Northwest of the Sibelius Monument across a bridge, the island of **Seurasaari** offers retreat from the city. It is also home to an **open-air museum** of farmsteads and churches transplanted from around Finland. On Midsummer's Eve, drunken revelers light tall bonfires *(kokko)*. *(Take bus #24 from Erottaja, to the last stop. The island is always open for hiking. Museum open June-Aug. daily 11am-5pm; Sept.-May Sa-Su 9am-3pm. Tours June 15-Aug. 15 daily 3pm. €5, students €4. MC/V.)* Many islands south of the city feature **public beaches** that are accessible by ferry, including a nude beach on Pihlajasaari Island. Beyond Espoo, lies the **Nuuksio National Park** where flying squirrels are more common than anywhere else in Finland. *(☎0205 64 4790; www.outdoors.fi. Take the train to Espoo railway station and bus #85 from there to Nuuksionpää.)*

DAYTRIPS FROM HELSINKI

PORVOO. Porvoo (pop. 46,000) lies along **Old King Road.** In 1809, Tsar Alexander I granted Finland autonomy at the whitewashed **cathedral** in Porvoo's Old Town. Unfortunately, the cathedral was a victim of arson in May 2006; all that can be seen now is the spire above the scaffolding. Pick up a walking tour map from the tourist office, or join the guide that leaves from Town Hall Sq. from late June to August on weekdays at 2pm. *(€6.)* The house of Finland's national poet **Johan Ludvig Runeberg,** looks just as it did when he called it home in the mid-1800s; the works of his son, sculptor Walter Runeberg, are on display across the street. *(Aleksanterink. 3. Open May-Aug. daily 10am-4pm; Sept.-Apr. W-Su 10am-4pm. For both €5, students €2. Cash only.)* The **Historical Museum,** in the 1764 Town Hall in Old Market Sq., features local artists like Impressionist painter Albert Edelfelt and has an eccentric array of artifacts. *(☎019 574 7500. Open May-Aug. M-Sa 10am-4pm, Su 11am-4pm; Sept.-Apr. W-Su noon-4pm. €5. MC/V.)* Charming (if slightly overpriced) cafes line the streets of Old Town. Many sell Runeberg cakes, which the poet enjoyed, for about €3. Recipes vary, but essentially it is a small round cake with almonds and cinnamon topped off with raspberry jam and a squeeze of icing. **Porvoo Pyörätalo,** Mannerheimink. 12 (☎019 58 51 04), rents **bikes** to visitors heading as far south as Pellinki (30km). **Buses** run from Helsinki (1hr., every 15min., €12). The **tourist office,** Rihkamak. 4, offers free Internet and helps book rooms. *(☎019 520 23 16; www.porvoo.fi. Open mid-June to Aug. M-F 9am-6pm, Sa-Su 10am-4pm; low season reduced hours.)*

LAHTI. World-class winter sports facilities make Lahti (pop. 100,000) a popular destination for the snow-bunny set. Year-round, the **Ski Museum** has ski-jump and biathlon simulators. (☎038 14 45 23. Open M-F 10am-5pm, Sa-Su 11am-5pm. €5, students €3. MC/V.) Towering 200m above the museum, the tallest of three **ski jumps** is accessible by a chairlift/elevator combo. (Open in summer daily 10am-5pm. €4; with Ski Museum €7, students €4.) The cross-country **ski trails** (100km) from the sports complex are great for hiking; the tourist office has hiking **maps** (€1), plus info on the **Ilvesvaellus Trail,** a 30min. bus ride to the northwest. At the city's northern part, in Kariniemi Park, the **Musical Fountains** combine water and music daily at 1 and 6pm in the summer, 7pm in the spring and fall. At the harbor, Sibelius Hall holds the **Sibelius Festival** in September, with performances of many of the composer's works. **Trains** head to Helsinki (1½-2hr., 1 per hr., from €18), Savonlinna (3-3½hr., 5 per day, from €36), and Tampere (2hr., every 1-2hr., from €24). The **tourist office,** Rautatienk. 22, has free **Internet** and rents bikes for €15 per day. (☎0207 281 750; www.lahtitravel.fi. Open M-Th 9am-5pm, F 9am-4pm; also open mid-July to mid-Aug. Sa 10am-2pm. AmEx/DC/MC/V.) The city center, from just north of the train station, has free wireless **Internet** access. **Postal Code:** 15110.

TURKU (ÅBO) ☎02

Finland's oldest city, Turku (pop. 175,000), has grown weatherbeaten with the passing of 775 years. It was the focal point of Swedish and Russian power struggles, the seat of Finnish governance until 1812, and then the victim of the worst fire in Scandinavian history in 1827. Despite its difficult past, Turku has rebuilt itself into a cultural and academic center that continues to endure.

TRANSPORTATION AND PRACTICAL INFORMATION. **Trains** run to Helsinki (2hr., 1 per hr., €23-30) and Tampere (2hr., every 1-2hr., €21-23). Viking Line **ferries** sail to Stockholm, SWE (10hr., 2 per day, €14-30; AmEx/MC/V), as do Silja Line ferries (12hr., daily 6:30pm, from €20; MC/V). To get to the ferry terminal, catch bus #1 from the Kauppatori (€2) or walk to the end of Linnank. A bus day pass costs €4.50. The **tourist office,** Aurak. 4, rents bikes (€10), offers 15min. of free **Internet** access, and sells the TurkuCard (24hr. €21; 48hr. €28), which provides free entry to the city's museums and buses, as well as other discounts. (☎262 74 44; www.turkutouring.fi. Open Apr.-Sept. M-F 8:30am-6pm, Sa-Su 9am-4pm; Oct.-Mar. M-F 8:30am-6pm, Sa-Su 10am-3pm. AmEx/MC/V.) There are unstaffed—and usually crowded—**cybercafes** at Hämeenk. 12 and Mariank. 2. (Open M-F 9am-9pm, Sa-Su 10am-9pm. €0.04 per min. Coins only.) Many cafes in the city center offer free wireless access, as does the university campus to the east.

ACCOMMODATIONS AND FOOD. To get to the spacious, riverside **Hostel Turku (HI) ❷**, Linnank. 39, from the station, walk west on Ratapihank., turn left on Puistok., and go right at the river. Reserve one month ahead in high season. (☎262 76 80; www.turku.fi/hostelturku. Bike rental €5 per 4hr., €10 per day, with €10 deposit. Breakfast €4.50. Linens €4.70. Laundry €2. Internet €2.40 per hr. Reception 6-10am and 3pm-midnight. Check-in 3pm. Curfew 2am for dorm residents. Dorms €14; singles €35; doubles €40; quads €58. €2.50 HI discount. MC/V.) **Interpoint Hostel ❶**, Vähä Hämeenk. 12A, offers what may well be the cheapest beds in Finland. (☎231 4011. Open July to mid-Aug. Breakfast €2.50. No lockers. Linens €0.50. Laundry €1.50. Reception 8-11am and 5-10pm. Lockout 11am-5pm. Dorms €8.50; singles €20; doubles €30; quads €40. Cash only.) For peaceful, well-kept rooms try the nun-run **Bridgettine Convent Guesthouse ❸**, Ursinink. 15A, at Puutarhak. (☎250 19 10; www.kolumbus.fi/birgitta/turku. Breakfast included. Reception 8am-9pm. Singles €42; doubles €62; triples €80. Cash only.) Take bus #8 from Eerikink. to **Ruissalo Camping ❷**, on the tip of Ruissalo Island. (☎262 51 00. Electricity €3.50. Showers included. Reception July 7am-11pm; May-June and Aug. 7am-10pm. Open May-Aug. Tent sites €14, extra person €4. MC/V.)

Produce fills the outdoor **Kauppatori** (open M-Sa 7am-2pm) and indoor **Kauppahalli** (open M-F 8am-5:30pm, Sa 8am-3pm) on Eerikink. There is a **supermarket** inside Sokos, next to the Kauppatori. (Open M-F 9am-9pm, Sa 9am-6pm. MC/V.) Cheap eateries line **Humalistonkatu.** Locals pack **Kerttu ❷**, Läntinen Pitkäk. 35, where they feast on Jallupulla meatballs (€9; veggie or meat) and other fare while surfing the free wireless or doing laundry (€2.50 per 2hr.). By night, Kerttu transforms into a bar. (☎250 69 90; www.kerttu.fi. Open M-F 10:30am-2pm.) The boat-restaurant **Kasvisravintola Kaida ❷**, Itäinen Rantak. 61, serves vegetarian food for €8. Walk 20min. along the river, or take bus #3, 14, 15, or 55 from the Kauppatori. (☎535 3018; www.kasviskaidas.com. Open M-F 11am-5pm. MC/V.)

SIGHTS AND ENTERTAINMENT. Over a decade ago, when a tobacco magnate's riverside mansion was being renovated into a museum, workers discovered a medieval city block 7m beneath the house, and dug it out. Today, the **Aboa Vetus and Ars Nova Museums,** Itäinen Rantak. 4-6, house a modern art collection in juxtaposition to the extensive dig beneath it. The building is a sight in itself, and houses the excellent Aula Cafe. (☎250 05 52; www.aboavetusarsnova.fi. Open Apr. to mid-Sept. daily 11am-7pm; late Sept.-Mar. Tu-Su 11am-7pm. Tours July-Aug. 11:30am. €8, students €7. AmEx/DC/MC/V.) The medieval **Turku Cathedral,** Tuomiokirkkotori 20, serves as the spiritual center of Finland's Lutheran Church. Finnish public radio has broadcast the cathedral's noontime chiming of the bells since 1944. (☎261 7100; www.turunseurakunnat.fi. Open daily mid-Apr. to mid-Sept. 9am-8pm; mid- Sept. to mid Apr. 9am-7pm. Evening concerts June-Aug. Tu 8pm. English services Su 4pm. Cathedral free. Cash only.) Around the corner, the **Sibelius Museum,** Piispank. 17, houses memorabilia, as well as over 300 instruments, from antique organs to African whistles. (☎215 44 94; www.sibeliusmuseum.abo.fi. Open Tu and Th-Su 11am-4pm, W 11am-4pm and 6-8pm. Concerts in fall and spring W 7pm. Museum €3, students €1. Concerts €7/3. MC/V.) The 700-year-old **Turun Linna** (Turku Castle), Linnank. 80, 3km from the town center, contains a historical museum with dark passageways and medieval artifacts. Catch bus #1 (€2) from Market Sq. or walk to the end of Linnank. (☎262 03 00. Open mid-Apr. to mid-Sept. daily 10am-6pm; mid-Sept. to mid-Apr. Tu-Su 10am-3pm. Guided tours in summer 12:10, 2:10, 4:10pm; €2. €6, students €3.50. MC/V.)

The end of June brings the **Medieval Market** to town, while power chords rock Ruissalo Island at July's **Ruisrock** festival (www.ruisrock.fi). In August, the annual

Turku Music Festival (www.turkumusicfestival.fi) brings a range of artists to non-traditional venues throughout the city. Turku is known throughout Finland for its laid-back pubs and breweries. In summer, Turku's nightlife centers around the river, where both Finns and tourists crowd the boats docked by the banks to dance and drink. Pull up a stool at the medicine counter of an old apothecary, **Pub Uusi Apteekki,** Kaskenk. 1, across the Auran bridge from the center. (☎250 25 95; www.kolumbus.fi/uusi.apteekki. 20+. Open daily 10am-3am. DC/MC/V.) A 19th-century girls' school, **Brewery Restaurant Koulu,** Eerikink. 18, offers its own brews, as well as wine, whiskey, and wildly popular blueberry cider. (☎274 57 57; www.panimoravintolakoulu.fi. Beer €3.80-5. Cider €3.60-4. F-Sa 22+. Open Su-Th 11am-2am, F-Sa 11am-3am. AmEx/DC/MC/V.) An upscale crowd dances and drinks cocktails at **Zanzibar,** Humalistonk. 7B. (☎240 4102; www.zanzibar.fi. Beer €5. Mixed drinks from €6.40. 20+. Open M-Th 2pm-3am, F 2pm-4am, Sa 10am-4am, Su 6pm-3am. MC/V.)

DAYTRIPS FROM TURKU: RAUMA AND PORI. Farther north on the Baltic Coast, **Rauma** (pop. 37,000) is known for the well-preserved wooden buildings that make up the **old town.** Pick up maps at the tourist office; tours begin at the frescoed **Church of the Holy Cross,** which shed its past as a Franciscan monastery to become a Lutheran chapel, making it a poster child for the Reformation. The old town features four **museums,** all of which can be seen with a combo ticket (€4, students €2). Many islands in Rauma's **archipelago** are great for hiking; try the trails on **Kuuskajaskari,** a former fortress. (Ferries 30min., in summer 2-3 per day, €8. MC/V.) The **Finnish Rock Festival** (www.rmj.fi) throws the biggest midsummer party in Finland. Late August brings the **Blue Sea Film Festival** (www.blueseafilmfestival.com), which shows the best domestic films of the year. **Buses** head to Turku (1½-2hr., 1 per hr., €11). To reach the **tourist office,** Valtak. 2, follow the street by the supermarket. (☎8378 7731; www.visitrauma.fi. Open June-Aug. M-F 8am-6pm, Sa 10am-3pm, Su 11am-2pm; Sept.-May M-F 8am-4pm.)

Each July, elegant **Pori** (pop. 76,000) is mobbed by crowds attending the **Pori Jazz Festival,** an event that has fuddled jazz traditionalists by hosting Macy Gray and Ladysmith Black Mambazo alongside the usual suspects. (☎626 22 00; www.porijazz.fi. July 14-22, 2007. Tickets from €7; some concerts free. AmEx/MC/V.) For modern art, head to the **Pori Art Museum,** on the corner of Eteläranta k. and Raatihuonek. (☎621 10 80; www.poriartmuseum.fi. Open Tu and Th-Su 11am-6pm, W 11am-8pm. €5, students €2.50. AmEx/MC/V.) In a graveyard west of the town center, on Maantiek., the **Juselius Mausoleum** is adorned with frescoes painted by Jorma Gallen-Kallela using sketches drawn by his father. (☎623 87 46. Open May-Aug. daily noon-3pm. Free.) Bus #2 (30min., €4.20) leads northwest to **Yyteri Beach,** home to windsurfers in summer and cross-country skiers in winter. Loll in the sand with a Karhu beer, brewed in Pori. **Trains** go to Helsinki (3½-4hr., 5-8 per day, €32). **Buses** head for Tampere (2hr., 4 per day, €14) and Turku (2hr., 6-7 per day, €18). The **tourist office,** Yrjönk. 17, offers 15min. of free Internet access and finds rooms. (☎621 12 73; www.pori.fi. Open June-Aug. M-F 8am-6pm, Sa 10am-3pm; Sept.-May M-F 8am-4pm.)

FINLAND

TAMPERE

☎03

A striking example of successful urban renewal, the city of Tampere (pop. 200,000) has converted its old brick factories into innovative museums and planted trees along waterways where paddle wheels and turbines once whirred. As telecommunications and information technology edged out textile and metal plants, an attractive city has emerged to give Turku a run for its money as Finland's second capital.

TRANSPORTATION AND PRACTICAL INFORMATION. Trains head to: Helsinki (2hr., 2 per hr., €25-31); Oulu (4-5hr., 8 per day, €53-60); Turku (2hr., every 1-2hr., €21). **City buses** cost €2, and most pass through the main square on Hämeenk. The **tourist office,** Verkatehtaank. 2, offers 15min. of free **Internet.** Its staff members offer help around town. From the train station, walk up Hämeenk. four blocks and turn left before the bridge. (☎020 716 6800; www.tampere.fi/tourism. Open June-Aug. M-F 9am-8pm, Sa-Su 10am-5pm; Sept. M-F 9am-5pm, Sa-Su 10am-5pm; Oct.-May M-F 9am-5pm.) The city library, Pirkank. 2, offers 1-2hr. slots of free **Internet.** (☎020 716 4020. Open June to mid-Aug. M-F 9:30am-7pm, Sa 9:30am-3pm; late Aug.-May M-F 9:30am-8pm, Sa 9:30am-3pm.) **Postal Code:** 33100.

ACCOMMODATIONS AND FOOD. Tampeeren NNKY (HI) ❷, Tuomiokirkonk. 12A, has bunks in casual quarters. (☎254 40 20. Breakfast M-F €5. Linens €4.50, towel €2. Reception 8-10am and 4-11pm. Open June-Aug. Dorms €14-16; singles €34; doubles €46. €2.50 HI discount. Cash only.) **Hostel Tampere (HI) ❷**, Pirkank. 10, has larger rooms but less socializing. (☎222 94 60; www.hosteltampere.com. Breakfast €4.50. No lockers. Reception May-Aug. M-Th 6:30am-11:30pm, F-Sa 24hr., Su midnight-9:30pm; Sept.-Apr. M-Sa 6:30am-10:30pm, Su 6:30am-2:30pm. Dorms €20; singles €39-42; doubles €54; triples €69. €2.50 HI discount. Cash only.) Bus #1 (€2) goes to **Camping Härmälä ❶**, Leirintäk. 8, where tightly packed cabins sit on the shore of Lake Pyhäjärvi. (☎265 13 55; www.lomaliitto.fi. Electricity €4. Open May-late Aug. Tent sites €10. Cabins €32-66. MC/V.)

Restaurants line **Hämeenkatu** and **Aleksanterinkatu.** The city's oldest pizzeria, **Napoli ❶**, Aleksanterink. 31, serves 100 different varieties in a casual yet classy setting. (☎223 88 87. Pizza €7-12. Open M-Th 11am-11pm, F 11am-midnight, Sa noon-midnight, Su 1-11pm. DC/MC/V.) Next to the Finlayson food court **Plevna Panimoravintola ❷**, Itäinenk. 8, serves microbrews and heavy local specialties in a converted weaving mill. (☎260 12 00; www.plevna.fi. Entrees €8-16. Beer €4-6. Open M 11am-11pm, Tu-Th 11am-1am, F-Sa 11am-2am, Su noon-3am. MC/V.) The gastronomically bold can also try *mustamakkara*, a black blood sausage, available from €1 at Tampere's vast **Kauppahalli,** Hämeenk. 19, the largest market hall in Scandinavia. (Open M-F 8am-6pm, Sa 8am-3pm.) There is a **Lindi Supermarket** at Rautatienk. 21. (Open M-F 7am-9pm, Sa 7am-6pm, Su noon-9pm. MC/V.)

SIGHTS. The delightfully haphazard **Vapriikki Museum Center,** Veturiaukio 4, has collections that run the gamut from local history to ice hockey. (☎314 66 966. Open Tu and Th-Su 10am-6pm, W 11am-8pm. €5, students €1. Special exhibitions €6-9/4, including museum admission. AmEx/DC/MC/V.) Scottish cotton magnate James Finlayson gave his name to the **Finlayson Complex,** which includes the **Media Museum Rupriikki.** (☎260 4180. Open Tu-Su 10am-6pm. €4, students €1; Temporary exhibits €4/1; combo ticket €5/2. AmEx/DC/MC/V.) The complex also houses the **Central Museum of Labor,** with the country's largest steam engine (☎253 8800; www.tkm.fi; open Tu-Su 11am-6pm; €4), and the world's oldest **Spy Museum,** Satakunnank. 18, which lets you find out how you'd measure up in espionage. (☎212 30 07; www.vakoilumuseo.fi. Open May-Aug. M-Sa 10am-6pm, Su 10am-4pm; Sept.-Apr. M-F noon-6pm, Sa-Su 11am-5pm. Agent test €4. Museum €7, students €5.50. Cash only.) In December 1905, a conference in the Tampere Workers' Hall was the occasion of Lenin and Stalin's first meeting; a century later, the **Lenin Museum,** Hämeenpuisto 28, occupies the same room. (☎276 81 00; www.lenin.fi. Open M-F 9am-6pm, Sa-Su 11am-4pm. €4, students €2. MC/V.) The frescoes of the **Tuomiokirkko,** Tuomiokirkkonk. 3 (open daily 9am-6pm), are matched in beauty only by the vaulted wooden ceiling of the **Aleksanterinkirkko,** on Pyynikin kirkkopuisto; ask the guide nicely, and she may let you see the views from the church's belltower. (Open daily June-Aug. 10am-5pm; Sept.-May 11am-3pm.)

At the western edge of the city, the **Pyynikki Observation Tower** offers views of the nature conservation area. Enjoy a traditional *munkki*, a doughnut-like pastry dipped in sugar (€1.40), at the downstairs cafe. (☎212 32 47. Open daily 9am-8pm. €1. Cash only.) The city's northern lakefront is home to **Särkänniemi,** a theme park. Rides, a planetarium, an aquarium, and a dolphinarium round out the attractions. (☎0207 130 212; www.sarkanniemi.fi. The Adventure Key grants admission to all attractions, including rides, for €29. Otherwise, admission to each attraction or ride €5. Hours vary; check website. MC/V.)

ENTERTAINMENT AND NIGHTLIFE. Tampere's internationally recognized **Short Film Festival** draws entries from around the globe (www.tamperefilmfestival.fi; Mar. 7-11, 2007). Mid-July's **Tammerfest** (www.tammerfest.net) fills the city with music, while August's **International Theater Festival** takes over city parks for performances of Finnish works (www.teatterikesa.fi). **Hämeenkatu, Aleksanterinkatu, Itsenäisyydenkatu,** and the surrounding streets are energetic at night, and many hotels host discos. **Cafe Europa,** Aleksanterink. 29, serves drinks in a bohemian lounge. (☎223 55 26; www.cafeeuropa.net. Beer €4. Cider €4.30. ISIC discounts. Open Su-Th noon-2am, F-Sa noon-3am. Dancing at upstairs **Club Apple** F-Sa 10pm-3am. Live piano Su. 20+. Club free 10-11pm, then €3; club Happy hour 10pm-midnight. AmEx/DC/MC/V.) **Telakka,** Tullikamarinaukio 3, houses a bar, restaurant, club, and theater. (☎225 07 00. Live music F-Sa. Cover up to €5. Open M-Th 11am-2am, F 11am-3am, Sa noon-3am, Su noon-midnight. MC/V.) Finland's oldest gay bar, **Mixei,** Itsenäisyydenk. 7-9, fills up late with a crowd of all ages. (☎222 0364; www.mixei.com. Beer €4. Karaoke Th 9pm. 18+. Happy hour 8-10pm. Cover F-Sa €5-7 after 10pm. Open Tu-Th 8pm-2am, F-Sa 8pm-4am. MC/V.)

SAVONLINNA ☎015

Each summer, vacationers descend upon Savonlinna, an island region in the heart of Finland's lake country. Built on three of these islands is the captivating town of Savonlinna (pop. 28,000), the region's epicenter. The **Olavinlinna Castle** was built in 1475 to reinforce the eastern border against the tsars. The free English-language tour will take you into rooms closed to general visitors. There are also two small museums which feature treasures and ecclesiastical artifacts. (☎531 164. Open daily June to mid-Aug. 10am-5pm; mid-Aug. to May 10am-3pm. Tour departs on the hour. €5, students €3.50. MC/V.) Near the castle, on Riihisaari, the **Provincial Museum** details the history of the region, focusing on the shipping industry. While you're there, creep around the eerily preserved museum ships moored at the island. (☎571 47 12. Museum open July daily 11am-5pm; Aug.-June Tu-Su 11am-5pm. Ships open mid-May to mid-Sept. €5, students €3. Cash only.) The secluded northern island **Sulosaari** is a retreat with several walking trails. From the Kauppatori, go under the train tracks, cross the footbridge, go through the parking lot, and cross the next footbridge; look for the "no cars" sign to the right of the building.

Make time for a daytrip out to the **Retretti Art Center,** where caves have dreamlike installations whose illumination and shadows are as much on display as the works. (☎775 22 00; www.retretti.fi. Open daily July 10am-6pm; June and Aug. 10am-5pm. €15, students €9. AmEx/DC/MC/V.) Buses (7 per day, €5.20) make the 30min. trip from Savonlinna. Walk along the breathtaking **Punkaharju Ridge** to reach **Lusto** (Finnish Forest Museum), which details the environmental history of the area. (☎345 10 00; www.lusto.fi. Open daily June-Aug. 10am-7pm; low season reduced hours. 1hr. tour departs July-Aug. daily 3pm. €7, students €6. MC/V.)

Summer Hotel Vuorilinna (HI) ❸, on Kylpylaitoksentie near the casino, has well-equipped student apartments. From the Kauppatori, walk under the tracks and cross the bridge. (☎739 54 95; www.spahotelcasino.fi. Reception 7am-11pm. Open June-Aug., but call ahead for specific dates. Linens, laundry, Internet, pool, and sauna all included. Dorms €27; singles €55-65; doubles €65-75. €2.50 HI discount. DC/MC/V.) Bus #3 (€2.50) runs to **Vuohimäki Camping ❶**, a site on the Lake Pihlajavesi shore. (☎537 353. Bike rental €9 per day. Showers €1-2. Electricity €4. Laundry €1-2. Reception and cafe open M-Th 8am-11pm, F-Sa 8am-midnight, Su 8am-10pm. Open June to mid-Aug. Tent sites €10-12. Cabins with bath €74-82; June and Aug. 14-28 €56-69. MC/V.) The **Kauppatori** market sells local produce and pastries (open June M-F 6am-4pm, Sa 6am-5pm; July M-F 6am-8pm, Sa 6am-4pm, Su 9am-4pm; Aug.-May M-F 7am-3pm, Sa 7am-2pm). Bars and cafes line **Olavinkatu** and the marketplace area. **Huvila,** Puisok. 4, offers six types of beer brewed on site and beer garden. It also has a B&B that's one of the better budget options in low season. (☎555 0555. Beer €3.30-5.50. 18+, concerts 20+. Open June-Aug. M-Sa noon-2am, Su noon-midnight; low season reduced hours. B&B doubles June to mid-Aug. €120; late-Aug. to May €65. AmEx/DC/MC/V.)

Trains run from Savonlinna to Helsinki (5-6hr., 3-5 per day, from €44). The **Savonlinna-Kauppatori** stop is in the center of town; **Savonlinna Station** is closer to the bus station and campground. Neither station is staffed. To get to town from the main station, walk straight out, cross the street, and continue on Olavink. The **tourist office,** Puistok. 1, across the bridge from the market, offers Internet, room and tour bookings, and luggage storage—all for free. (☎517 510; www.savonlinnatravel.com. Open June-Aug. daily 9am-8pm; Sept.-May M-F 9am-5pm. AmEx/MC/V.) **Postal Code:** 57100.

KUOPIO ☎017

Eastern Finland's largest city, Kuopio (pop. 91,000) lies in the midst of the beautiful Saimaa lake district. The archbishop of the Finnish Orthodox Church resides here, and the **Orthodox Church Museum,** 10min. from town on Karjalank. 1, shows a collection of stunning textiles and icons. (☎287 22 44. Open May-Aug. Tu-Su 10am-4pm; Sept.-Apr. M-F noon-3pm, Sa-Su noon-5pm. €5, students €3. Cash only.) The **Kuopio Museum,** Kauppak. 23, which holds both the Natural and Cultural History Museums, delights with its life-size mammoth reconstruction. In summer 2007, the museum will hold an exhibition on its own history in celebration of its hundredth anniversary. (☎182 603; www.kulttuuri.kuopio.fi/museo. Open Tu and Th-F 10am-5pm, W 10am-7pm, Sa-Su 11am-5pm. €5, students €3. Cash only.) The **VB Photographic Center,** Kuninkaank. 14-16, brings temporary exhibits of world-class photography to Kuopio. Check the website for latest exhibit info. (☎261 55 99; www.vb.kuopio.fi. Open June-Aug. M-F 10am-7pm, Sa-Su 11am-4pm; winter reduced hours and rates. €5, students €4. Cash only.) The 2km hike uphill to the **Puijo Tower** culminates in a view of Lake Kallavesi and the coniferous forests beyond. From the Kauppatori, walk toward the train station on Puijonk., cross the tracks and the highway on your left, and continue up the hill, following signs for "Puijon Torni." (☎255 5253; www.puijo.com. Open daily June 9am-9pm; July-Aug. 9am-11pm; Sept.-May M-Sa 11am-10pm, Su noon-5pm. €3.50. MC/V.) In mid-June, the **Kuopio Dance Festival** (www.kuopiodancefestival.fi) draws crowds to its performances, and lures wannabe Baryshnikovs with dance lessons for all. (Adult classes from €60. MC/V.) Happy drunkards toast to a different country every year at the **Wine Festival** (www.kuopiowinefestival.fi), in early July.

Embrace your inner schoolmarm at the **Virkkula Youth Hostel ❷**, Asemak. 3, which offers bare-bones rooms in an old-fashioned schoolhouse. (☎040 418 21 78. Linens and towels €6. Internet €1 for 1st 30min., €0.50 per 30min. thereafter. Reception 24hr. Open June-July. Dorms €15. Cash only.) All rooms at the **Rautatie Guest House ❸**, Asemak. 1, have their own TVs; more costly rooms have private baths. Reception is in the Asemagrilli restaurant in the train station. (☎580 05 69. Breakfast included. Reception Su-F 7:30am-8pm, Sa 7:30am-6pm. Singles €40-50; doubles €60-80; triples €100; quads €125. MC/V.) Affordable eateries pepper the

FINLAND

town center. **Muikkuravintola Sampo ❷,** Kauppak. 13, draws praise for its take on vendace *(muikku)*, a small local whitefish. (☎261 46 77. Entrees €9-12. Open M-Sa 11am-midnight, Su noon-midnight. AmEx/DC/MC/V.) There's fresh produce at the **Kauppatori** market in the center of town and inside the comely **Kauppahalli** market hall, where you can also get a taste *("mualiman pienimmat")* of the local specialty, *kalakukko* fish-and-pork pie, for €2 in the first shop on your left. (www.kuopionkauppahalli.net. Kauppatori open M-Sa 8am-4pm. Kauppahalli open M-F 8am-5pm, Sa 8am-3pm.) **Trains** run to Helsinki (5½hr., 5-10 per day, from €51) and Oulu (4½hr., 3-6 per day, from €40). To get to the **tourist office,** Haapaniemenk. 17, from the station, go right on Asemak. and turn left on Haapaniemenk. They will book rooms for €5. Ask about the Kuopio Card (€12, students €6), which will pay for itself after you visit at least 2 to 3 sights. (☎18 25 84; www.kuopioinfo.fi. Open July M-F 9:30am-5pm, Sa 9:30am-3pm; June and Aug. M-F 9:30am-5pm; Sept.-May M-F 9:30am-4:30pm. AmEx/DC/MC/V.) **Internet** is available for free (30min. drop-in or 1hr. reserved slots) at all branches of Kuopio library. (☎182 219; www.kuopio.fi/kirjasto. Open M-F 10am-7pm, Sa 10am-3pm.) **Postal Code:** 70100.

OULU

☎08

Most travelers just pass through Oulu (pop. 128,000), a relaxed university town. Unless you are in for late August's **Oulu Music Video Festival** (www.omvf.net) or the associated **Air Guitar World Championships,** there is little reason for a long stay. For a brief diversion between trains, stroll through **Ainola Park,** the north corner of which borders a 750m salmon ladder. From the train station, walk down Asemak., turn right on Kirkkok., and walk to its end. Down Nahkurinpl., the **Science Center Tietomaa,** Nahkatehtaank. 6, attracts crowds with its interactive exhibits, IMAX theater, and observation tower. (☎55 84 13 40; www.tietomaa.fi. Open July daily 10am-8pm; May-June daily 10am-6pm; Aug.-Apr. M-F 10am-4pm, Sa-Su 10am-6pm. €12.50, students €10. MC/V.) The nearby island of **Pikisaari** draws picnickers with bright cottages and boutiques; take the footbridge at the end of Kaarlenväylä.

Cheap rooms are hard to come by in Oulu. The **Oppimestari Summer Hotel (HI) ❸,** Nahkatehtaank. 3, provides generously furnished rooms with kitchenettes. (☎884 85 27; www.merikoski.fi/oppimestari. Breakfast included. Laundry €3. Open mid-June to July. Reception 24hr. Singles €40; doubles €58. €2.50 HI discount. AmEx/MC/V.) Bus #17 (€2.60) goes to **Nallikari Camping ❶,** Hietasaari, located right on the water. (☎55 86 13 50; www.nallikaricamping.fi. Electricity €3.50-5. Showers included. Open year round. Tent sites €5-8, extra person €4. 4-person cabins €30-34. MC/V.) Cheap food, on the other hand, is easy to find; it's hard to walk 10m without passing a pizzeria or kebab joint. The **Kauppatori,** at the end of Kauppurienk. by the harbor, sells produce and is flanked by old warehouses turned into yuppie cafes. (Open daily approx. 8am-7pm.) Nightlife spills out of the pavilion on **Kirkkokatu** and the terraces lining **Otto Karhin Park** and **Kappurienkatu.**

Trains pass through Oulu, heading south to Helsinki (6-7hr., 5-6 per day, €64-70) and north to Rovaniemi (2½hr., 4 per day, from €28). To reach the **tourist office,** Uusik. 26, take Hallitusk. and then turn left at the park. (☎55 84 13 30; www.oulutourism.fi. Open mid-June to Aug. M-F 9am-6pm, Sa-Su 11am-3pm; Sept. to mid-June M-F 9am-4pm.) **Taitonetti Ky,** Rautatienkatu 16, offers **Internet** two blocks left of the train station. (☎530 2000. €1 per 15min. Open M-Th 1-8pm, F-Sa noon-9pm, Su 3-8pm. MC/V.) In addition, Oulu has free wireless access in many of its public areas; check http://www.panoulu.net. **Postal Code:** 90100.

ROVANIEMI

☎016

Just south of the Arctic Circle, Rovaniemi (pop. 35,000) is the capital of Finnish Lapland and a gateway to the northern wilderness. After retreating German troops burned the city to the ground in October 1944, architect Alvar Aalto stepped in with the Reindeer Antler Plan, a reconstruction scheme using rivers and existing highways to rebuild the settlement in the shape of a reindeer's head. Not all of Aalto's plan was executed, but you can look at a modern map of Rovaniemi with east facing up and see the resemblance. The **Arktikum,** housed in a beautiful glass corridor at Pohjoisranta 4, has a cache of info on Arctic peoples and landscapes. (☎322 3260; www.arktikum.fi. Open mid-June to mid-Aug. daily 9am-7pm; low season reduced hours. €8, students €7. AmEx/MC/V.) To dash your childhood dreams of Christmas once and for all, head to the **Santa Claus Village,** 8km north of Rovaniemi, where Father Christmas holds office hours. Kids may find it difficult to understand why Santa lives in a gift shop. For a diversion from the gift store trinkets, cross the Arctic Circle line, which runs through the center of the village. Take bus #8 (30min.; €3.10, round-trip €5.60) from the train station or the city center to Arctic Circle. (☎356 20 96; www.santaclausvillage.info. Open daily May-Aug. 9am-6pm; Sept.-Nov. and Jan.-Apr. 9am-5pm; Dec. 9am-7pm. "Santa naptime" 11am-noon and 3-4pm.)

Hostel Rudolf (HI) ❸, Koskik. 41, has well-furnished rooms with private baths. (☎321 321. Reception 24hr. at the Quality Hotel Santa Claus, Korkalonk. 29. Turn left out of the tourist office, walk two blocks, then go left on Koskik. for the hostel, right for reception. Breakfast €8 at the hotel. Dorms Apr. to mid-Nov. €25, mid-Nov. to Mar. €37; singles €37/48. €2.50 HI discount. AmEx/DC/MC/V.) **Koskikatu** is lined with cafes, bars, and a **K** supermarket. (Open M-F 8am-9pm, Sa 8am-6pm. MC/V.) **Trains** travel south to Helsinki (10hr., 4-5 per day, €78) via Oulu (2½hr., €30) and Kuopio (8hr., 3-4 per day, from €70). **Buses** run to destinations throughout northern Finland, and to Nordkapp, NOR (11hr., 1 per day, €101). The **tourist office,** Rovak. 21, offers free same-day luggage storage and books northern wilderness safaris for €20-120; turn right out of the train station or walk straight from the bus station toward the yellow building marked "Posti." Walk under the highway, then bear left to reach the sidewalk. Follow it two blocks to Rovak., then turn left and walk three blocks. (☎34 62 70; www.rovaniemi.fi. Internet €2 per 15min. Open June-Aug. M-F 8am-6pm, Sa-Su 10am-6pm; Sept.-Nov. and Jan.-May M-F 8am-5pm; Dec. M-F 8am-5pm, Sa-Su 10am-2pm. MC/V.) The **library,** Jorma Eton tie 6, one of Aalto's signature designs, offers free **Internet.** Drop in for 20min., or reserve for 1hr. Expect lines in the afternoon. (Open in summer M-Th 11am-7pm, F 11am-5pm, Sa 11am-3pm; in winter M-Th 11am-8pm, F 11am-5pm, Sa 11am-4pm.) **Postal Code:** 96200.

IN RECENT NEWS

MONSTER MANIA

With its infamously difficult language and tiny population, it's no wonder that Finland takes perceived slights to its public image rather seriously. The latest controversy in Finnish entertainment involves the "monster band" Lordi, who was the country's representative at 2006's Eurovision song contest, an international pop-music competition.

With band members like "Amen the unstoppable mummy" and "Kita the manbeast with the combined strengths of all the beasts known to man," Lordi's inclusion raised concerns for Finns about the image they were presenting to the rest of the world. According to the *New York Times*, some even called on President Tarja Halonen to veto the band and replace it with a more traditional one.

Considering that Finland placed last in the contest eight times, however, many citizens welcomed the change. Ilkka Mattila, the music editor for Finnish newspaper *Helsingin Sanomat*, stated simply, "we have nothing to lose anymore." And indeed, they didn't.

Lordi rocked Finland, and the rest of the world, when they performed "Hard Rock Hallelujah" for the contest. The instant hit propelled the monster band to a landslide win, ending the 40-year Finnish losing streak and proving to the world that nightmares don't always end badly.

FRANCE

With its lavish châteaux, fields of lavender, medieval streets, and sidewalk cafes, France can conjure up any number of postcard-ready scenes. To the proud French, it is only natural that outsiders should flock to their history-steeped and art-rich homeland. Even though France may no longer control the course of world events, the vineyards of Bordeaux, the museums of Paris, and the beaches of the Riviera draw more tourists than any other nation worldwide. Centuries-old farms and churches share the landscape with modern architecture, street posters advertise jazz festivals as well as Baroque concerts, and the country's rich culinary tradition rounds out a culture that simply cannot be sent home on a four-by-six.

DISCOVER FRANCE: SUGGESTED ITINERARIES

THREE DAYS. Don't even think of leaving **Paris,** the City of Light (p. 320). Explore the shops and cafes of the **Latin Quarter,** then cross the Seine to reach **Île de la Cité** to admire **Sainte Chapelle.** Visit the wacky **Centre National d'Art et de Culture Georges Pompidou** before seeing the hot spot of 1789, the **Bastille.** Swing through **Marais** for food and fun. The next day, stroll down the **Champs-Elysées,** starting at the **Arc de Triomphe,** meander through the **Jardin des Tuileries,** and over to the **Musée d'Orsay.** See part of the **Louvre** the next morning, then spend the afternoon at **Versailles.**

ONE WEEK. After three days in **Paris,** go to **Tours** (1 day; p. 352), a great base for exploring the châteaux of the **Loire Valley** (1 day; p. 350). Head to **Rennes** for medieval sights and modern nightlife (1 day; p. 346), then to the dazzling island of **Mont-St-Michel** (1 day; p. 346).

BEST OF FRANCE, THREE WEEKS. Begin with three days in **Paris,** with a daytrip to the royal residences at **Versailles.** Whirl through the **Loire Valley** (2 days) before traveling to the wine country of **Bordeaux** (1 day; p. 356). Check out the rose-colored architecture of **Toulouse** (1 day; p. 359) and the medieval walls of **Carcassonne** (1 day; p. 360) before sailing through **Avignon** (p. 363), **Aix-en-Provence** (p. 364), and **Nîmes** (p. 362) in sunny **Provence** (3 days). Let loose in **Marseille** (2 days; p. 365), and bask in the glitter of the Riviera in **Nice** (2 days; p. 374). Then show off your tan in the Alps as you travel to **Lyon** (2 days; p. 385) and **Chamonix** (1 day; p. 384). Eat your fill in **Dijon** (1 day; p. 390), and finish your trip with a little German flavor in **Strasbourg** (1 day; p. 391), where trains will whisk you away to your next European adventure.

ESSENTIALS

WHEN TO GO

In July, Paris starts to shrink; by August it is devoid of Parisians and animated only by tourists and the pickpockets who love them. The French Riviera fills with Anglophones from June to September. French natives flee to other parts of the country during these months, especially the Atlantic coast. Early summer and fall are the best times to visit Paris—the city has warmed up but not completely emptied out. The north and west have cool winters and mild summers, while the less-crowded center and east have a more temperate climate. From December to February, the Alps provide some of the best skiing in the world, while the Pyrenees offer a calmer, if less climatically dependable, alternative.

DOCUMENTS AND FORMALITIES

FACTS AND FIGURES	
Official Name: French Republic.	**Time Zone:** GMT +1.
Capital: Paris.	**Land Area:** 534,965 sq. km.
Major Cities: Lyon, Marseille, Nice.	**Language:** French.
Population: 60,880,000.	**Religion:** Roman Catholic (90%).

EMBASSIES. Foreign embassies in France are in Paris (p. 321). French embassies abroad include: **Australia,** 6 Perth Ave., Yarralumla, Canberra, ACT 2600 (☎02 62 16 01 00; www.ambafrance-au.org); **Canada,** 42 Sussex Dr., Ottawa, ON K1M 2C9 (☎613-789-1795; www.ambafrance-ca.org); **Ireland,** 36 Ailesbury Rd., Ballsbridge, Dublin 4 (☎00 353 1 227 5000; www.ambafrance.ie); **New Zealand,** 34-42 Manners St., Wellington (☎64 384 25 55; www.ambafrance-nz.org); **UK,** 58 Knightsbridge, London SW1X 7JT (☎44 207 073 1000; www.ambafrance-uk.org); **US,** 4101 Reservoir Rd., NW, Washington, D.C. 20007 (☎202-944-6195; www.ambafrance-us.org).

VISA AND ENTRY INFORMATION. EU citizens do not need a visa. Citizens of Australia, Canada, New Zealand, and the US do not need a visa for stays of up to 90 days. For stays longer than 90 days, all non-EU citizens need visas, available at French consulates.

TOURIST SERVICES AND MONEY

EMERGENCY	**Police:** ☎17. **Ambulance:** ☎15. **Fire:** ☎18. **General Emergency:** ☎112.

TOURIST OFFICES. The official **French Government Tourist Office** (FGTO; www.franceguide.com), also known as **Maison de la France,** runs tourist offices in France and offers tourist services to travelers abroad. Tourist offices are called *syndicats d'initiative* or *offices de tourisme;* in the smallest towns, the *mairie* (town hall) may also distribute maps and pamphlets, help travelers find accommodations, and suggest sights and excursions.

MONEY. The **euro (€)** has replaced the franc as the unit of currency in France. For more information, see p. 18. As a general rule, it's cheaper to exchange money in France than at home. Be prepared to spend at least €20-40 per day, and considerably more in Paris. **Tips** are generally included in meal prices at restaurants and cafes, as well as in drink prices at bars and clubs; look for the phrase *service compris* on the menu or ask. If service is not included, tip 15-20%. Even when service is included, it is polite to leave a *pourboire* of up to 5% at a cafe, bistro, restaurant, or bar. Workers such as concierges may expect at least a €1.50 tip for services beyond the call of duty; taxi drivers won't expect more than €1. A **value added tax (VAT; TVA** in French) of up to 19.6% is included in the price of a wide range of goods and services (p. 22). Non-EU citizens bringing purchased goods home with them can usually be refunded this tax for purchases over €175 per store. Ask for VAT forms at the time of purchase and present them at the *détaxe* booth at the airport. You must carry these goods with you at all times (at the airport and on the airplane) and you must claim your refund within six months.

FEATURED ITINERARY: WINE-TASTING IN FRANCE

Start your tour in **Paris** (p. 320), and preview some of France's most distinctive vintages at **La Belle Hortense,** an egghead wine bar in the Marais. Then set out for **Reims** (p. 395), where the folks at **Champagne Pommery** offer tours of cellars that hold magnums of the bubbly stuff. Spend a night in **Epernay** (p. 396), and saunter down the avenue de Champagne for wine-tastings at blue-blood **Moët & Chandon** and the more populist **Mercier.** Then head for **Strasbourg** (p. 391), the northernmost point on Alsace's legendary **Route du Vin** (p. 392). Frequent trains will whisk you south to touristy **Colmar** (p. 394), while buses are a better bet as you head to Riquewihr and quaint Kaysersberg. Catch a train to Dijon—just to the south lies **Beaune** (p. 391), surrounded by the storied Côte de Beaune vineyards. Don't pass up a visit to **Patriarche Père et Fils,** where a tour of the byzantine cellars includes mouthfuls of 13 regional wines. Then dart back to Paris, or extend your itinerary to explore the Médoc region around **Bordeaux** (p. 356) and the vineyards at **Sélestat** (p. 393).

TRANSPORTATION

BY PLANE. Most transatlantic flights to Paris land at **Roissy-Charles de Gaulle (CDG;** ☎01 48 62 22 80). Many continental and charter flights use **Orly (ORY;** ☎01 49 75 15 15). **Aéroports de Paris** (www.aeroportsdeparis.fr) has information about both airports. For more info on flying to France, see p. 42. Once in France, you shouldn't need to take a plane unless you're headed to Corsica (p. 380).

BY TRAIN. The French national railway company, **SNCF** (☎08 92 30 83 08; www.sncf.fr), manages one of Europe's most efficient rail networks. **TGV** trains (high-speed, or *train à grande vitesse*), among the fastest in the world, now link many major cities in France, as well as some other European destinations, including Brussels, Geneva, Lausanne, and Zürich. **Rapide** trains are slower; local **Express** trains are, strangely enough, the slowest option. French trains offer discounts of 25-50% on tickets for travelers under 26 with the **Carte 12-25** (€49; good for 1 year). Locate the ticket counters *(guichets)*, the platforms *(quais)*, and the tracks *(voies)*, and you will be ready to roll. Terminals can be divided into suburb *(banlieue)* and the bigger intercity trains *(grandes lignes)*. Yellow ticket machines *(billetteries)* sell tickets for credit cards with PINs. While reservations are required only for select trains, you are not guaranteed a seat without one (usually US$5-30). Reserve ahead during peak holiday and tourist seasons. Some railpasses require a **supplement** (US$10-50) or special fare for high-speed trains such as TGVs.

> TIP **VALIDATE = GREAT.** Be sure to validate *(composter)* your ticket before boarding. Orange validation boxes can be found in every train station.

If you are planning to spend a great deal of time on trains, a railpass might be worth it, but in many cases, especially if you are under 26, point-to-point tickets may be cheaper. **Eurail** is valid in France. Standard **Eurailpasses,** valid for a given number of consecutive days, are best for those spending long periods of time on trains every few days. **Flexipasses,** valid for any 10 or 15 (not necessarily consecutive) days within a two-month period, are more cost-effective for those traveling longer distances less frequently. **Youth passes** and **Youth Flexipasses** provide the same second-class perks for those under 26. It is best to purchase a pass before going to France. For prices and more info, contact student travel agencies, **Rail Europe** (Canada ☎800-361-7245, UK 08 705 848 848, US 877-257-2887; www.raileurope.com), or **DER Travel Services** (☎888-213-7245; www.der.com).

BY BUS. Within France, long-distance buses are a secondary transportation choice, as service is relatively infrequent. However, in some regions buses are indispensable for reaching out-of-the-way towns. Bus services operated by SNCF accept railpasses. *Gare routière* is French for "bus station."

BY FERRY. Ferries across the English Channel *(La Manche)* link France to England and Ireland. The shortest and most popular route is between Dover, BRI and Calais (1-1½hr.), and is run by P&O Stena Line, SeaFrance, and Hoverspeed. Hoverspeed also travels from Newhaven, BRI to Dieppe (2¼-4¼hr.). Brittany Ferries travels from Portsmouth, BRI to Caen (6hr.) and St-Malo (9hr.). For more info on English Channel ferries, see p. 57. For info on ferries to Corsica, see p. 380.

BY CAR. Drivers in France should have either an **International Driving Permit (IDP)** or a valid EU-issued driving license. Seat belts are mandatory for both drivers and passengers. Unless traveling in a group of three or more, you won't save money going by car instead of by train, thanks to tolls, high gas costs, and rental charges. Some agencies require renters to be 25 and most charge those aged 21-24 an additional insurance fee (around €25 per day). If you don't know how to drive stick, you'll need to pay a hefty premium for a car with automatic transmission. With the exception of Corsica and the Alps, French roads are usually in great condition.

BY BIKE AND BY THUMB. Of all Europeans, the French may be alone in loving cycling more than soccer. Drivers usually accommodate bikers on wide country roads, and many cities banish cars from select streets each Sunday to make way for cyclists. Renting a bike (€8-19 per day) beats bringing your own if you're only touring one or two regions. Hitchhiking is illegal on French highways, and many people consider France to be the hardest country in Europe for hitchhikers. Let's Go does not recommend hitchhiking.

KEEPING IN TOUCH

PHONE CODES	**Country code:** 33. **International dialing prefix:** 00. For more information on how to place international calls, see inside back cover. When calling within a city, dial 0 + city code + local number.

EMAIL AND THE INTERNET. Most major **post offices** offer Internet access at special *cyberposte* terminals, where rechargeable cards provide 1hr. of access for €7 (€4 each additional hr.). A large town in France will usually have at least one **cybercafe**; check www.cybercafes.com for locations.

TELEPHONE. Publicly owned **France Télécom** pay phones charge less than their privately owned counterparts. They accept stylish *Télécartes* (phonecards), available in 50-unit (€7.50) and 120-unit (€15) denominations at *tabacs*, post offices, and train stations. Most pay phones now also accept credit cards such as MasterCard (or EuroCard) and Visa. An expensive alternative is to call collect *(faire un appel en PCV)*; an English-speaking operator can be reached by dialing the appropriate service provider listed below. *Décrochez* means pick up; you'll then be asked to *patientez* (wait) to insert your card; at *numérotez* or *composez*, you can dial. The number for general information is ☎12; for an international operator, call ☎00 33 11. For information on purchasing **mobile phones,** see p. 29. International direct dial numbers include: **AT&T Direct** ☎0 800 99 00 11; **Canada Direct** ☎0 800 99 00 16 or 99 02 16; **MCI WorldPhone** ☎0 800 99 00 19; **Sprint** ☎0 800 99 00 87; **Telecom New Zealand** ☎0 800 99 00 64; **Telstra Australia** ☎0 800 99 00 61.

MAIL. Airmail between France and North America takes five to 10 days; writing "*prioritaire*" on the envelope should ensure delivery in four to five days at no extra charge. To send a 20g airmail letter or postcard within France or from France to another EU destination costs around €0.50, to a non-EU European country €0.75, and to Australia, Canada, New Zealand, or the US €0.90. Mail can be held for pickup through **Poste Restante** at almost any city or town with a post office. Address letters to be held according to the following example: Last name First name, *Poste Restante*, city, France. It's best to use the largest post office in a given town. Bring your passport (or other photo ID) for pickup; there may be a small fee.

LANGUAGE AND POLITESSE. Even if your French is near-perfect, waiters and salespeople who detect the slightest accent will often immediately respond in English. If your language skills are good, continue to speak in French; more often than not, the person will revert to French. The French put a premium on pleasantries. Always say "*bonjour Madame/Monsieur*" when you enter a business, restaurant, or hotel, and "*au revoir*" when you leave. If you knock into someone on the street, always say "*pardon.*" When meeting someone for the first time, a handshake is appropriate. However, friends and acquaintances greet each other with a kiss on each cheek. For some useful French, see **Phrasebook: French** p. 1055.

ACCOMMODATIONS AND CAMPING

FRANCE	❶	❷	❸	❹	❺
ACCOMMODATIONS	under €15	€15-26	€26-37	€37-55	over €55

The French Hostelling International (HI) affiliate, **Fédération Unie des Auberges de Jeunesse** (**FUAJ;** ☎01 44 89 87 27; www.fuaj.org), operates 160 hostels within France. A bed in a hostel averages €10-15. Some hostels accept reservations through the International Booking Network (www.hostelbooking.com). Two or more people traveling together will often save money by staying in cheap hotels rather than hostels. The French government has a four-star hotel rating system. *Gîtes d'étapes* are rural accommodations for cyclists, hikers, and other amblers in less-populated areas; they provide beds, a kitchen, and a resident caretaker. After 3000 years of settlement, true wilderness in France is hard to find. It's illegal to camp in most public spaces, including national parks. Look forward to organized *campings* (campgrounds), full of vacationing families and programmed fun. Most camps have toilets, showers, and outlets, though such luxuries cost €1.50-6 extra; you often pay a car fee, too (€3-8). In total, expect to pay €8-15 per site.

FOOD AND DRINK

FRANCE	❶	❷	❸	❹	❺
FOOD	under €7	€7-12	€12-18	€18-33	over €33

French chefs cook for one of the most finicky clientele in the world. The largest meal of the day is lunch *(le déjeuner)*. A complete French meal includes a drink *(apéritif)*, an appetizer *(entrée)*, a main course *(plat)*, salad, cheese, dessert, fruit, coffee, and an after-dinner drink *(digestif)*. The French drink wine with virtually every meal; *boisson comprise* entitles you to a free drink (usually wine) with your food. Most restaurants offer a *menu à prix fixe* (fixed-price meal) that costs less than ordering *à la carte*. The *formule* is a cheaper, two-course version. Odd-hour cravings between lunch and dinner can be satisfied at *brasseries*, the middle ground between casual cafes and structured restaurants. *Service compris* means the tip is included *(l'addition)*. It's easy to get a satisfying dinner for under €10 with cheese, pâté, wine, bread, and chocolate. For a picnic, get fresh produce at an outdoor market *(marché)*, then hop between specialty shops. Start with a bakery *(boulangerie)* for bread, proceed to a butcher *(charcuterie)* for meats, and finally to pastry shops *(pâtisseries)* and candy shops *(confiseries)* to satisfy a sweet tooth. When choosing a cafe, remember that those on a major boulevard are more expensive than smaller places a few steps down a side street. Prices are also cheaper at the counter *(comptoir)* than in the seating area *(salle)*. For supermarket shopping, look for the chains Carrefour, Casino, Monoprix, and Prisunic.

HOLIDAYS AND FESTIVALS

Holidays: New Year's Day (Jan. 1); Easter (Apr. 8); Labor Day (May 1); Victory Day (May 8); Ascension Day (May 20); Whit Monday (June 4); Bastille Day (July 14); Feast of the Assumption (Aug. 15); All Saints' Day (Nov. 1); Armistice Day (Nov. 11); Christmas (Dec. 25).

Festivals: Many cities celebrate Carnaval—Nice (Feb. 16-Mar. 4) has the most over-the-top festivities. The Cannes Film Festival (May 16-27; www.festival-cannes.com) caters to the rich and famous. For the first time in history, the Tour de France will begin in London before heading to its neighbor across *La Manche* (starting July 6; www.letour.fr). The Festival d'Avignon (July-Aug.; www.festival-avignon.com) is famous for its theater. The biggest national holiday, Bastille Day (July 14), is marked nationwide by parades and fireworks.

BEYOND TOURISM

Care France, CAP 19, 13 r. Georges Auric, 75019 Paris (☎01 53 19 89 89; www.carefrance.org). An international organization providing volunteer opportunities in 6000 locations throughout France, from combating AIDS to promoting education.

Jeunesse et Reconstruction, 8 et 10 r. de Trevise, 75009 Paris (☎01 47 70 15 88; www.volontariat.org). A database of volunteer opportunities in preservation and historical reconstruction. Open June-Sept. M-Sa 9:30am-1pm and 2-6pm.

Trade Art Abroad, Boîte No. 45, Maison des Associations du 20ème, 1-3 r. Frederick Lematire, 75020 Paris. Brings local art to the communities of Paris and beyond.

PARIS

☎01

Anglophones have long seen Paris (pop. 2,150,000) as the way life should be, idolizing the lifestyle of its inhabitants, fast-paced, yet marked by fashion, food, and *flâneurs.* In the 19th century, Haussmann revamped the city's Right Bank, creating wide, straight avenues that frame monumental sights like the Baroque Louvre and the modern Centre Pompidou; the medieval streets of the Left Bank are as winding as ever. Paris is everything you expect—and much more that you don't.

INTERCITY TRANSPORTATION

Flights: Aéroport Roissy-Charles de Gaulle (CDG, Roissy;☎48 62 22 80; www.adp.fr), 23km northeast of Paris, serves most transatlantic flights. 24hr. English-speaking information center. **Aéroport d'Orly (ORY;** ☎49 75 15 15), 18km south of Paris, is used by charters and many continental flights. The cheapest and fastest ways to get into the city are by **RER** (trains) or **bus,** especially AirFrance buses (www.cars-airfrance.com).

Trains: Paris has 6 major train stations: **Gare d'Austerlitz** (to the Loire Valley, southwestern France, Spain, and Portugal); **Gare de l'Est** (to Austria, the Czech Republic, eastern France, southern Germany, Hungary, Luxembourg, and Switzerland); **Gare de Lyon** (to southern France, Greece, Italy, and Switzerland); **Gare du Nord** (to Belgium, Britain, eastern Europe, the Netherlands, northern France, northern Germany, and Scandinavia); **Gare Montparnasse** (to Brittany and southwestern France on the TGV); **Gare St-Lazare** (to Normandy). All are accessible by Métro.

Buses: Gare Routière Internationale du Paris-Gallieni, 28 av. du Général de Gaulle, just outside Paris in Bagnolet. Ⓜ Gallieni. **Eurolines** (☎49 72 57 80; www.eurolines.fr) sells tickets to most destinations in France and neighboring countries.

ORIENTATION

FRANCE

The **Île de la Cité** and **Île St-Louis** sit at the center of the city, while the **Seine,** flowing east to west, splits Paris into two sections: the **Left Bank (Rive Gauche)** to the south and the **Right Bank (Rive Droite)** to the north. Paris is divided into 20 **arrondissements** (districts) that spiral clockwise around the Louvre. Each *arrondissement* is referred to by its number (e.g., the Third). In French, "Third" is said *troisième* (TWAZ-yem) and abbreviated "*3ème.*" The same goes for every *arrondissement* except the First, which is said *premier* (PREUM-yay) and abbreviated 1*er.*

The Left Bank encompasses the **Latin Quarter, St-Germain-des-Prés, Les Invalides, Tour Eiffel** (Eiffel Tower), and **place d'Italie.** The Right Bank has the **Louvre, Montorgeuil, Marais, place de la Concorde, Champs-Elysées, Place Charles de Gaulle-Étoile.** South of the Étoile, old and new money fill the exclusive 16*ème*, bordered to the west by the **Bois de Boulogne** park and to the east by the Seine and the **Trocadéro,** the place from which to view the Eiffel Tower. The Opéra, Grand Boulevards, and department stores are in the 9*ème*, while the red-light district, **Pigalle,** is to the north. The 10*ème* is known primarily as home to the **Gare du Nord** and **Gare de l'Est.** East of the **Bastille** area, the 11*ème* and 12*ème* claims the newest hip nightlife scene in Paris. The 17*ème*, in the northwest, is a mix of affluent and working class neighborhoods and, like the 19*ème* and 20*ème*, offers some of the best deals to those who venture out. The 18*ème* is home to the heavily touristed **Montmartre.**

LOCAL TRANSPORTATION

Public Transportation: The efficient **Métro** (Ⓜ) runs 5:30am-12:15am. Lines are numbered and are generally referred to by their number and final destinations; connections are called *correspondances*. Single-fare tickets within the city cost €1.30; carnet of 10 €9.60. Buy extras for when ticket booths are closed (after 10pm) and hold onto your ticket until you exit. The **RER (Réseau Express Régional),** the commuter train to the suburbs, goes outside the city periphery and serves as an express subway within central Paris; changing to and getting off the RER requires sticking your validated ticket into a turnstile. Watch the signboards next to the RER tracks and check that your stop is lit up before riding. **Buses** use the same €1.30 tickets (validate in the machine by the driver); transfers require a new ticket. Buses run 7am-8:30pm, *Autobus de Nuit* (€2.50) until 1:30am, and *Noctambus* 1 per hr. 1-6am at stops marked with the bug-eyed moon between the Châtelet stop and the *portes* (city exits). The **Mobilis** pass covers the Métro, RER, and buses (€5.20 for a 1-day pass in Zones 1 and 2). A **Carte Orange** weekly pass *(carte orange hebdomadaire)* costs €14.50 and expires on Su; photo ID required. Refer to the front of the book for **color maps** of Paris's transit network.

Taxis: Alpha Taxis (☎45 85 85 85). **Taxis Bleus** (☎49 36 10 10). Taxis take 3 passengers (fourth passenger €2-3 surcharge). *Tarif A,* M-Sa 7am-7pm (€0.62 per km). *Tarif B,* M-Sa 7pm-7am, Su 24hr., and from the airports and immediate suburbs (€1.06 per km). *Tarif C,* from the airports 7pm-7am (€1.24 per km). Meter starts running when you phone. Taxi stands are indicated by a blue light.

Bike Rental: Paris-Vélo, 2 r. de Fer-à-Moulin, 5*ème* (☎43 37 59 22). €14 per day.

PRACTICAL INFORMATION

Tourist Office: Bureau Gare d'Austerlitz, 13*ème* (☎45 84 91 70). Ⓜ Gare d'Austerlitz. Open M-Sa 8am-6pm. Open daily 10am-7pm. **Bureau Tour Eiffel,** Champs de Mars, 7*ème* (☎08 92 68 31 12). Ⓜ Bir-Hakeim. Open daily May-Sept. 11am-6:40pm.

Embassies: Australia, 4 r. Jean-Rey, 15*ème* (☎40 59 33 00; www.france.embassy.gov.au). Ⓜ Bir-Hakeim. Open M-F 9am-5pm. **Canada,** 35 av. Montaigne, 8*ème* (☎44 43 29 00; www.international.gc.ca/canada-europa/france). Ⓜ Franklin D. Roosevelt. Open daily 9am-noon and 2-5pm. **Ireland,** 4 r. Rude, 16*ème* (☎44 17 67 00; www.embassyofirelandparis.com). Ⓜ Trocadéro. Open M-F 9:30am-noon. **New Zealand,** 7ter r. Léonard de Vinci, 16*ème* (☎45 01 43 43; www.nzembassy.com/france). Ⓜ Victor-Hugo. Open July-Aug. M-Th 9am-1pm and 2-4:30pm, F 9am-2pm; Sept.-June M-Th 9am-1pm and 2-5:30pm, F 9am-1pm and 2-4pm. **UK,** 18bis r. d'Anjou, 8*ème* (☎44 51 31 02; www.amb-grandebretagne.fr). Ⓜ St-Augustin. Open M and W-F 9:30am-12:30pm and 2:30-5pm, Tu 9:30am-4:30pm. **US,** 2 r. St-Florentin, 1*er* (☎43 12 22 22; www.amb-usa.fr). Ⓜ Concorde.

FRANCE

Currency Exchange: Most **ATMs** accept MasterCard and Visa. Crédit Lyonnais ATMs take AmEx; Crédit Mutuel and Crédit Agricole ATMs are on the **Cirrus** network; and most Visa ATMs accept **PLUS**-network cards. Hotels, train stations, and airports offer poor rates; Gare de Lyon, Gare du Nord, and both airports have booths open 6:30am-10:30pm.

American Express: 11 r. Scribe, 9*ème* (☎47 77 79 28). Ⓜ Opéra or Auber. Open M-Sa 9am-6:30pm; exchange counters also open Su 10am-5pm.

GLBT Resources: Centre Gai et Lesbien, 3 r. Keller, 11*ème* (☎43 57 27 93). Ⓜ Ledru Rollin or Bastille. Information hub for all gay services and associations in Paris. English spoken. Open M-F 4-8pm.

Laundromats: Laundromats are everywhere, especially in the 5*ème* and 6*ème*. **Marass,** 21 r. Debelleyme, 3*ème* (☎48 03 71 40).

Emergency: Police: ☎17. **Ambulance:** ☎15. **Fire:** ☎18.

Crisis Lines: Rape, SOS Viol (☎08 00 05 95 95). Call free anywhere in France for medical and legal counseling. Open M-F 10am-7pm.

Pharmacies: Every *arrondissement* in Paris has a designated **pharmacie de garde,** which is open 24hr. Names are posted on every pharmacy's door.

Hospitals: American Hospital of Paris, 63 bd. Hugo, Neuilly (☎46 41 25 25). Ⓜ Port Maillot, then bus #82 to the end of the line. **Hôpital Franco-Britannique de Paris,** 3 r. Barbès, in the suburb of Levallois-Perret (☎46 39 22 22). Ⓜ Anatole France.

Internet Access: Cyber Cube, 5 r. Mignon, 6*ème* (☎53 10 30 50). Ⓜ St-Michel or Odéon. Branch at 12 r. Daval, 11*ème* (☎49 29 67 67). Ⓜ Bastille. Both locations €0.15 per min., €30 per 5hr., €40 per 10hr. Open M-Sa 10am-10pm.

Post Office: Poste du Louvre, 52 r. du Louvre, 1*er* (☎40 28 20 40). Ⓜ Louvre. Open 24hr. Address mail to be held: LAST NAME First name, *Poste Restante,* 52 r. du Louvre, 75001 Paris, FRANCE. **Postal Codes:** 750xx, where "xx" is the *arrondissement* (e.g., 75003 for any address in the 3*ème*).

ACCOMMODATIONS

Due to the massive influx of travelers during the summer months, the already high prices climb even more. In a hotel, expect to pay at least €30 for a single and €40 for a double. Hostels are a better option for single travelers, whereas staying in a hotel is more economical for groups. Paris's hostels skip many standard restrictions (e.g., curfews) and tend to have flexible maximum stays. In cheaper hotels, few rooms have private baths; hall showers cost about €2.50 per use. Rooms fill quickly after morning check-out; arrive early or reserve ahead. Most hostels and *foyers* include the **taxe de séjour** (€0.10-2 per person, per day) in listed prices.

ÎLE DE LA CITÉ, 1ER, AND 2ÈME ARRONDISSEMENTS

Near the Louvre, the Tuileries, the Seine, and the ritzy pl. Vendôme, this area still has a few budget hotels.

Hôtel Henri IV, 25 pl. Dauphine, Île de la Cité (☎43 54 44 53). Ⓜ Pont Neuf. One of Paris's most central and least expensive hotels. Spacious rooms have sturdy, mismatched furnishings and clean baths. Breakfast included. Showers €2.50. Reserve 1 month ahead. Singles €29-34, with shower €48; doubles €38-48, with shower and toilet €58; triples €72. MC/V. ❷

Centre International de Paris (BVJ): Paris Louvre, 20 r. Jean-Jacques Rousseau, 1*er* (☎53 00 90 90). Ⓜ Louvre or Palais-Royal. Bright, dorm-style rooms with 2-10 beds per room. English spoken. Breakfast and showers included. Lockers €2. Internet €1 per 10min. Reception 24hr. Reserve ahead. Dorms €26; doubles €29. ❷

Hôtel Tiquetonne, 6 r. Tiquetonne (☎42 36 94 58). Ⓜ Etienne-Marcel. Small, simple rooms only a stone's throw from the sex shops on r. St-Denis and the market on r. Montorgueil. Breakfast €6. Showers €6. Reserve ahead. Singles €30, with shower €36; doubles with shower €50. AmEx/MC/V. ❸

FRANCE

3ÈME AND 4ÈME ARRONDISSEMENTS

Some of the Marais's 17th-century mansions now house budget hotels close to the **Centre Pompidou** and the **Île St-Louis;** the area is also convenient for sampling nightlife, as Paris's night buses converge nearby at Ⓜ Châtelet.

Hôtel du Séjour, 36 r. du Grenier St-Lazare (☎48 87 40 36). Ⓜ Etienne-Marcel. Follow traffic on r. Etienne-Marcel, which becomes rue du Grenier St-Lazare. You'll feel like part of the family at this newly renovated hotel. Showers €4. Reception 7am-10:30pm. Singles €35; doubles €47, with bath €58. Extra person €22. Cash only. ❸

Hôtel des Jeunes (MIJE; ☎42 74 23 45; www.mije.com). Le Fourcy, Le Fauconnier, and Maubuisson are 3 small hostels in Marais's medieval mansions. English spoken. Ages 18-30 only. Breakfast, in-room shower, and linens included. Internet €1 per 10min. Max. stay 7 days. Reception 7am-1am. Lockout noon-3pm. Curfew 1am. Check-in before noon. Reserve 1 month ahead. MIJE membership required (€2.50). 4- to 9-bed dorms €28; singles €43; doubles €66; triples €87; quads €110. ❸

Le Fourcy, 6 r. de Fourcy. From Ⓜ St-Paul, walk opposite the traffic on r. St-Antoine and turn left on r. de Fourcy. Large courtyard ideal for meeting travelers or picnicking.

Le Fauconnier, 11 r. du Fauconnier. From Ⓜ St-Paul, take r. du Prevôt, turn left on r. Charlemagne, and right on r. du Fauconnier. Ivy-covered building steps away from the Seine and Île St-Louis.

Maubuisson, 12 r. des Barres. From Ⓜ Pont Marie, walk against traffic on r. de l'Hôtel-de-Ville and turn right on r. des Barres. A former convent on a silent street by the St-Gervais monastery.

5ÈME AND 6ÈME ARRONDISSEMENTS

The Latin Quarter and St-Germain-des-Prés are near **Notre-Dame,** the **Panthéon,** and the **Jardin du Luxembourg,** which all have an energetic student cafe culture.

Hôtel Stella, 41 r. Monsieur-le-Prince (☎40 51 00 25). Ⓜ Odéon. Family-owned and operated for years. Reserve ahead. Singles €30, with bath €35; doubles €35/55; triples €75; quads €85. Cash and traveler's checks only. ❷

Young and Happy (Y&H) Hostel, 80 r. Mouffetard (☎47 07 47 07; www.youngandhappy.fr). Ⓜ Monge. A backpacker's home away from home. The lively atmosphere, clean rooms, and relaxed staff make for an enjoyable stay. English spoken. Breakfast included. Internet €2 per 30min. Lockout 11am-4pm. Curfew 2am. Apr.-Dec. dorms €23; doubles €52. Jan.-Mar. €21/50. ❷

Hôtel St-Jacques, 35 r. des Écoles (☎44 07 45 45; www.paris-hotel-stjacques.com). Ⓜ Maubert-Mutualité. Rooms with balcony, bath, and TV. Breakfast €8.50-10. Internet available. Singles €55-84; doubles €95-124; triples €152. AmEx/MC/V. ❹

7ÈME AND 8ÈME ARRONDISSEMENTS

Hôtel Montebello, 18 r. Pierre Leroux (☎47 34 41 18; hmontebello@aol.com). Ⓜ Vaneau. A bit far from the *7ème*'s sights, but rates are unbeatable for this upscale neighborhood. Clean, cheery rooms. Breakfast €4. Reserve 2 weeks ahead. Singles €35-42; doubles €40-49. Extra bed €10. ❸

Hôtel Eiffel Rive Gauche, 6 r. du Gros Caillou (☎45 51 24 56; www.hotel-eiffel.com). Ⓜ École Militaire. Hôtel Eiffel's bright courtyard is a cozy yellow and is as welcoming as the cheerful staff. Rooms have cable TV, phone, Internet, and full bath; some have Eiffel Tower views. Breakfast €9. Safe deposit box €3. Singles €75; doubles €85; triples €105; quads €125. Extra bed €10. MC/V. ❺

9ÈME AND 10ÈME ARRONDISSEMENTS

Woodstock Hostel, 48 r. Rodier (☎48 78 87 76; www.woodstock.fr). Ⓜ Anvers. With reggae music and tie-dyed paraphernalia, this hostel tries to channel the 60s. Breakfast included. Linens €2.50, towels €1. Internet access €2 per 30min. Lockout 11am-3pm. Curfew 2am. Reserve ahead. 4- or 6-person dorms €21; doubles €24. ❷

Perfect Hôtel, 39 r. Rodier (☎42 81 18 86 or 42 81 26 19; www.paris-hostel.biz). Ⓜ Anvers. This hotel lives up to its name with hotel-quality rooms at hostel prices. Fun atmosphere. English-speaking staff. Breakfast included for *Let's Go* users. Phones, refrigerator and kitchen access, free coffee, and beer vending machine (€1.50). Reserve ahead. Singles €38, with toilet €58; doubles €50/58. MC/V. ❷

Hôtel Palace, 9 r. Bouchardon (☎40 40 09 45). Ⓜ Strasbourg-St-Denis. A sparkling hotel with the rates of a hostel. Breakfast €3.50. Shower €3.50. Reserve ahead. Singles €19-33; doubles €25-38; triples €51; quads €61-71. AmEx/MC/V. ❷

11ÈME AND 12ÈME ARRONDISSEMENTS

These hotels are close to hopping bars and clubs, but be careful at night.

Hôtel Beaumarchais, 3 r. Oberkampf (☎53 36 86 86; www.hotelbeaumarchais.com). Ⓜ Oberkampf. Elegantly decorated with colorful, modern furniture, clean baths, and cable TV. Each room is decorated in the style of artists like Kandinsky. A/C. Breakfast €10. Reserve ahead. Singles €75-90; doubles €110; suites €150. AmEx/MC/V. ❺

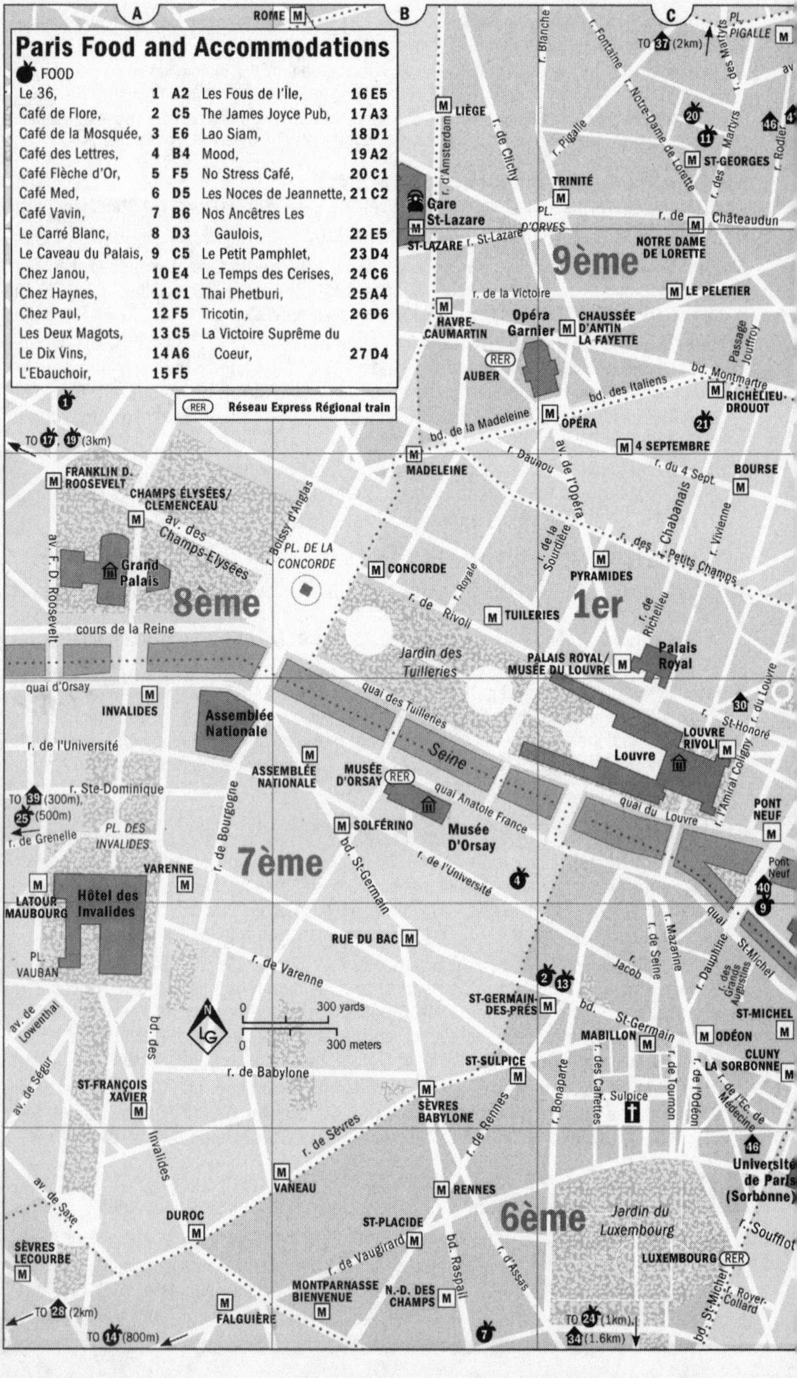

Paris Food and Accommodations

FOOD

Le 36,	1	A2
Café de Flore,	2	C5
Café de la Mosquée,	3	E6
Café des Lettres,	4	B4
Café Flèche d'Or,	5	F5
Café Med,	6	D5
Café Vavin,	7	B6
Le Carré Blanc,	8	D3
Le Caveau du Palais,	9	C5
Chez Janou,	10	E4
Chez Haynes,	11	C1
Chez Paul,	12	F5
Les Deux Magots,	13	C5
Le Dix Vins,	14	A6
L'Ebauchoir,	15	F5
Les Fous de l'Île,	16	E5
The James Joyce Pub,	17	A3
Lao Siam,	18	D1
Mood,	19	A2
No Stress Café,	20	C1
Les Noces de Jeannette,	21	C2
Nos Ancêtres Les Gaulois,	22	E5
Le Petit Pamphlet,	23	D4
Le Temps des Cerises,	24	C6
Thai Phetburi,	25	A4
Tricotin,	26	D6
La Victoire Suprême du Coeur,	27	D4

RER Réseau Express Régional train

FRANCE

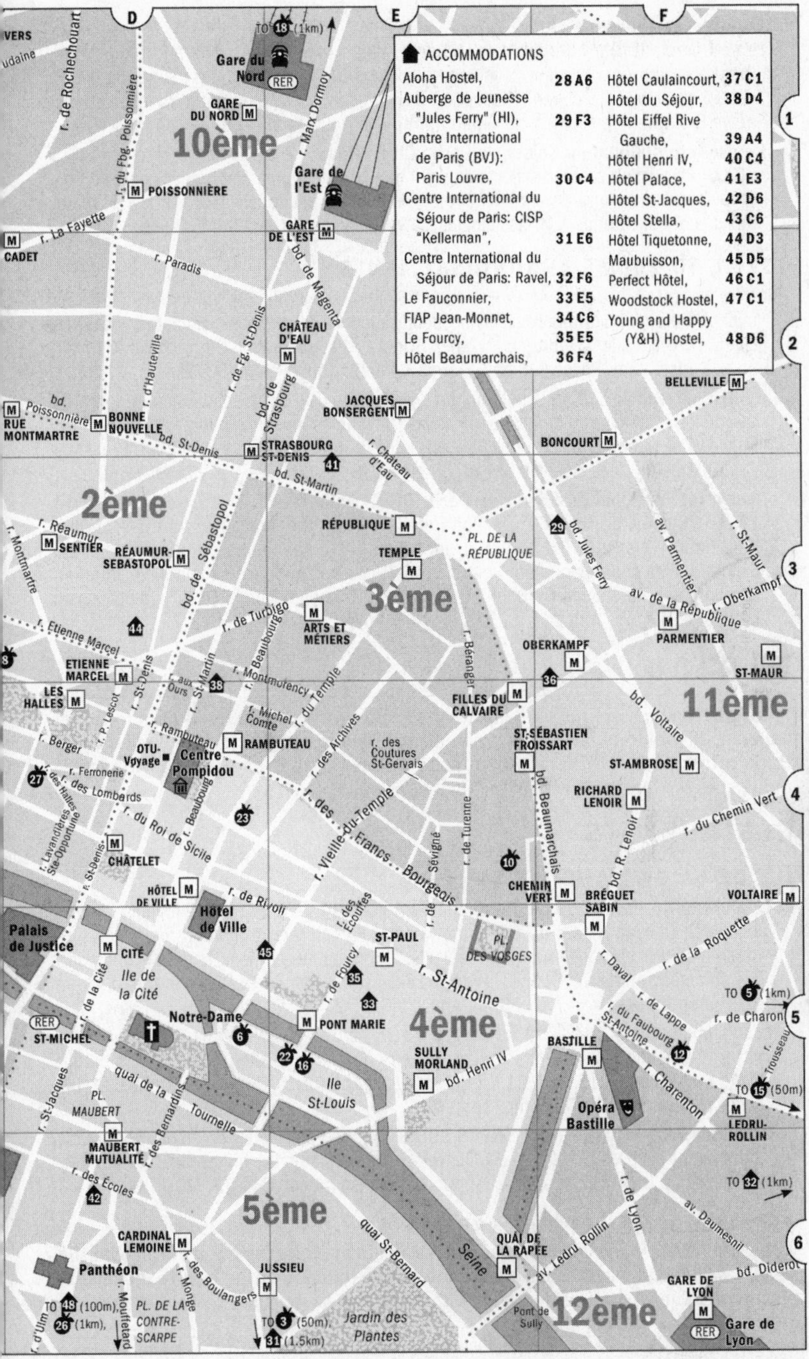
ACCOMMODATIONS
Aloha Hostel, 28 A6
Auberge de Jeunesse "Jules Ferry" (HI), 29 F3
Centre International de Paris (BVJ): Paris Louvre, 30 C4
Centre International du Séjour de Paris: CISP "Kellerman", 31 E6
Centre International du Séjour de Paris: Ravel, 32 F6
Le Fauconnier, 33 E5
FIAP Jean-Monnet, 34 C6
Le Fourcy, 35 E5
Hôtel Beaumarchais, 36 F4
Hôtel Caulaincourt, 37 C1
Hôtel du Séjour, 38 D4
Hôtel Eiffel Rive Gauche, 39 A4
Hôtel Henri IV, 40 C4
Hôtel Palace, 41 E3
Hôtel St-Jacques, 42 D6
Hôtel Stella, 43 C6
Hôtel Tiquetonne, 44 D3
Maubuisson, 45 D5
Perfect Hôtel, 46 C1
Woodstock Hostel, 47 C1
Young and Happy (Y&H) Hostel, 48 D6
D
E
F
1
2
3
4
5
6
10ème
2ème
3ème
11ème
4ème
5ème
12ème
Gare du Nord
GARE DU NORD
Gare de l'Est
GARE DE L'EST
TO 18 (1km)
RER
POISSONNIÈRE
CADET
r. de Rochechouart
r. du Fbg. Poissonnière
r. La Fayette
r. Paradis
r. Max Dormoy
bd. de Magenta
CHÂTEAU D'EAU
r. de Fg. St-Denis
bd. de Strasbourg
r. d'Hauteville
JACQUES BONSERGENT
BONNE NOUVELLE
RUE MONTMARTRE
bd. Poissonnière
bd. St-Denis
STRASBOURG ST-DENIS
r. Château d'Eau
bd. St-Martin
BELLEVILLE
BONCOURT
RÉPUBLIQUE
PL. DE LA RÉPUBLIQUE
TEMPLE
bd. Jules Ferry
av. Parmentier
r. St-Maur
r. Oberkampf
av. de la République
PARMENTIER
ST-MAUR
OBERKAMPF
r. Réaumur
SENTIER
RÉAUMUR-SEBASTOPOL
r. Montmartre
bd. de Sébastopol
r. de Turbigo
ARTS ET MÉTIERS
r. Etienne Marcel
ETIENNE MARCEL
LES HALLES
r. St-Denis
r. St-Martin
r. aux Ours
r. Beaubourg
r. Montmorency
r. du Temple
r. Béranger
FILLES DU CALVAIRE
bd. Voltaire
r. P. Lescot
r. Rambuteau
RAMBUTEAU
r. Michel le Comte
r. des Archives
r. des Coutures St-Gervais
ST-SÉBASTIEN FROISSART
ST-AMBROSE
RICHARD LENOIR
r. Berger
OTU-Voyage
Centre Pompidou
r. Ferronerie
r. des Lombards
r. des Halles
r. Lavandières Ste-Opportune
r. du Roi de Sicile
r. Vieille-du-Temple
r. des Francs Bourgeois
r. de Sévigné
r. de Turenne
bd. Beaumarchais
bd. R. Lenoir
r. du Chemin Vert
CHÂTELET
HÔTEL DE VILLE
r. de Rivoli
Hôtel de Ville
r. des Écouffes
CHEMIN VERT
BRÉGUET SABIN
VOLTAIRE
Palais de Justice
CITÉ
Ile de la Cité
ST-PAUL
PL. DES VOSGES
r. de la Roquette
r. Daval
r. de Fourcy
r. St-Antoine
TO 5 (1km)
r. de Lappe
r. de Charonne
r. du Faubourg St-Antoine
r. de la Cité
RER
ST-MICHEL
Notre-Dame
PONT MARIE
SULLY MORLAND
bd. Henri IV
BASTILLE
r. Charenton
r. Trousseau
TO 15 (50m)
Ile St-Louis
quai de la Tournelle
r. St-Jacques
PL. MAUBERT
MAUBERT MUTUALITÉ
r. des Bernardins
Opéra Bastille
LEDRU-ROLLIN
r. des Écoles
r. de Lyon
TO 32 (1km)
av. Daumesnil
CARDINAL LEMOINE
quai St-Bernard
Seine
QUAI DE LA RAPÉE
av. Ledru Rollin
bd. Diderot
Panthéon
JUSSIEU
r. Monge
r. des Boulangers
GARE DE LYON
TO 48 (100m), 26 (1km),
PL. DE LA CONTRE-SCARPE
r. Mouffetard
r. d'Ulm
TO 3 (50m), 31 (1.5km)
Jardin des Plantes
Pont de Sully
Gare de Lyon

FRANCE

Auberge de Jeunesse "Jules Ferry" (HI), 8 bd. Jules Ferry (☎43 57 55 60; auberge@micronet.fr). Ⓜ République. Modern, clean rooms with sinks and tiled floors. Breakfast, showers, and linens included. Lockers €2. Laundry €3, dry €2. Internet €1 per 10min. Max. stay 1 week. Reception 24hr. Lockout 10:30am-2pm. No reservations; arrive 8-11am for a room. 4- to 6-bed dorms and doubles €21 per person. MC/V. ❷

Centre International du Séjour de Paris: CISP "Ravel," 6 av. Maurice Ravel (☎44 75 60 00; www.cisp.asso.fr). Ⓜ Porte de Vincennes. Large rooms and outdoor pool (€3-4). Breakfast, linens, and towels included. Free Internet. Reception 24hr. Curfew 1:30am. Reserve ahead. Dorms €19-23; singles €30; doubles €48. AmEx/MC/V. ❷

13ÈME TO 20ÈME ARRONDISSEMENTS

Aloha Hostel, 1 r. Borromée (☎42 73 03 03; www.aloha.fr). Ⓜ Volontaires. A mix of backpackers inhabits this hostel. No outside alcohol on premises. Breakfast included. Linens €3, towels €3. Internet €2 per 30min. Reception 8am-2am. Lockout 11am-5pm. Curfew 2am. Reserve ahead. Dorms €17-22; doubles €46-50. ❷

Hôtel Caulaincourt, 2 sq. Caulaincourt (☎46 06 46 06; www.caulaincourt.com). Ⓜ Lamarck-Caulaincourt. Formerly used as artists' studios, the simple rooms have wonderful views of Montmartre and the Paris skyline. TV and phone in every room. Breakfast €5.50. Free Internet. Reserve ahead. Singles €38-68; doubles €52-86. MC/V. ❸

Centre International du Séjour de Paris: CISP "Kellerman," 17 bd. Kellerman (☎44 16 37 38; www.cisp.asso.fr). Ⓜ Porte d'Italie. Cross the street and turn right on bd. Kellerman. This 396-bed hostel resembles a retro spaceship on stilts. Breakfast included. Free showers on floors with dorms. TV room, laundry, meeting rooms, Internet, and cafeteria. Reception 6:30am-1:30am. Reserve ahead. Dorms €19-23; singles with bath €34; doubles with bath €25. AmEx/MC/V. ❷

FOOD

Splurging on a delicious French meal should not be considered an additional expense; it should be like paying an entrance fee to see a world-renowned sight. Paris offers some of the most exquisite culinary experiences in the world, so indulge. However, be aware that chic doesn't equal expensive.

RESTAURANTS

ÎLE DE LA CITÉ AND ÎLE ST-LOUIS

Le Caveau du Palais, 19 pl. Dauphine (☎43 26 04 28). Ⓜ Cité. A favorite among locals, Le Caveau serves up traditional, hearty French fare in a warm room with timbered ceilings and rough-hewn stone walls. The meat-heavy menu is pricey, but worth the splurge. Appetizers €10-15. *Plats* €18-28. Desserts €8-9. Reserve ahead. Open daily noon-2:30pm and 7-10:30pm. AmEx/MC/V. ❸

Les Fous de l'Île, 33 r. des Deux Ponts (☎43 25 76 67). Ⓜ Pont Marie. A mellow, dimly lit bistro with friendly servers. Evening concerts (jazz, pop, piano, rock) every Th except in Aug. Delicious €15 and €19 lunch *menus*. Appetizers €6.50-10. *Plats* €11-14. Open W noon-3pm, Th-Sa noon-11pm. ❸

Café Med, 79 r. St-Louis-en-l'Île (☎43 29 73 17). Ⓜ Pont Marie. Cross the Pont Marie and make a right on r. St-Louis-en-l'Île; the restaurant is on the left. Small, bustling bistro serves up both French and Italian food. 3-course *menus* €10-13. MC/V. ❷

1ER AND 2ÈME ARRONDISSEMENTS

The 1*er* and 2*ème* are small but packed with culinary experiences from all over the world. While expensive, touristy eateries can be found near the Louvre, Asian cuisine is near the Opéra Garnier, and bistros line the streets near r. Montorgueil.

FRANCE

Le Carré Blanc, 62 r. Jean-Jacques Rousseau (☎40 28 99 04). Ⓜ Les Halles. Dishes include lamb skewers flavored with oregano and coriander and roasted eggplant *mille-feuille.* This small restaurant has a great ambience and simple but classy decor. Lunch *menus* €7-15. Open M-F noon-2:30pm and 7:45-10:30pm, Sa noon-2:30pm and 7:45-11pm. AmEx/MC/V. ❸

Les Noces de Jeannette, 14 r. Favart and 9 r. d'Amboise (☎42 96 36 89). Ⓜ Richelieu-Drouot. Exit onto bd. des Italiens, then turn left on r. Favart. *Menu du Jeanette* (€27) includes salad, grilled meat, roasted fish or duck *plats,* and fabulous desserts. *Kir* included with meal. *Menu Bistro* is €3 more and includes a half-bottle of Bordeaux. Reserve ahead. Open daily noon-1:30pm and 7-9:30pm. ❹

La Victoire Suprême du Coeur, 41 r. des Bourdonnais (☎01 40 41 93 95). Ⓜ Châtelet. Walk down r. de Rivoli and turn right on r. des Bourdonnais. Tasty vegetarian dishes. 2-course *menu* €16. Open M-F 11:45am-10pm, Sa noon-10pm. AmEx/MC/V. ❸

3ÈME AND 4ÈME ARRONDISSEMENTS

The Marais offers chic bistros, kosher delis, and couple-friendly cafes.

Le Petit Pamphlet, 15 r. St-Gilles (☎42 71 22 21). Ⓜ Chemin-Vert. This casually elegant and cozy new bistro is hard to beat for inexpensive, excellent cuisine. The menu uses only fresh ingredients and changes weekly, but the service is always attentive. Meals begin with a delightful, complimentary *amuse-bouche.* Appetizers €9. *Plats* €12-15. Desserts €7. Open daily noon-2pm and 7-10:30pm. Reserve ahead. MC/V. ❸

Chez Janou, 2 r. Roger Verlomme (☎42 72 28 41). Ⓜ Chemin-Vert. On the corner of r. Roger Verlomme. Inexpensive gourmet food is not on menus; the dishes are listed on blackboards scattered throughout the restaurant. The *ratatouille* and goat cheese (€9) is delicious. *Plat du jour* €14. Reserve ahead. Open M-F noon-3pm and 7:45pm-midnight, Sa-Su noon-4pm and 7:45pm-midnight. ❸

5ÈME AND 6ÈME ARRONDISSEMENTS

Enjoy the buzzing cafe culture that earned the Latin Quarter its contemporary fame. Tiny, low-priced restaurants and cafes pack the quadrangle bounded by bd. St-Germain, bd. St-Michel, r. de Seine, and the Seine River.

Café de la Mosquée, 39 r. Geoffrey St-Hilaire (☎43 31 38 20). Ⓜ Censier-Daubenton. In the Mosquée de Paris. With fountains, white marble floors, and an exquisite multi-level terrace, this cafe deserves a visit whether or not a trip to the Mosquée is on your itinerary. Couscous €9-25. Open daily 9am-11pm. MC/V. ❷

Café Vavin, 18 r. Vavin (☎43 26 67 47). Ⓜ Vavin. The elusive creature: a cafe with personality, location, and delicious food. Funky tiling adds to its bohemian look. *Entrecôte* and fries €13. Salads €9.50-12. Open daily 8am-1am, Su 8am-8:30pm. MC/V. ❷

Café de Flore, 172 bd. St-Germain (☎45 48 55 26). Ⓜ St-Germain-des-Prés. Walk against traffic on bd. St-Germain. A literary landmark: Jean-Paul Sartre composed *Being and Nothingness* here. Check out Sartre and Simone de Beauvoir's booth in the Art Deco seating upstairs. Coffee €5.50. Pastries €5-10. *Salade flore* €13. Open daily 7:30am-1:30am. AmEx/MC/V. ❸

Les Deux Magots, 6 pl. St-Germain-des-Prés (☎45 48 55 25). Ⓜ St-Germain-des-Prés. The cafe has been home to literati from Mallarmé to Hemingway since 1885. Sandwiches €6.80-13. Pastries from €8.50. Coffee €4. Hot chocolate €6.50. Breakfast *menu* €18. Open daily 7:30am-1am. AmEx/MC/V. ❹

7ÈME AND 8ÈME ARRONDISSEMENTS

Mood, 114 av. des Champs-Elysées and 1 r. Washington (☎42 89 98 89). Ⓜ George V. Japanese fusion cuisine. Nightly live music and DJ. *Plats* €16-22. Mixed drinks €10. Open daily 10am-4am. Reserve ahead. MC/V. ❸

Le 36, 36 r. du Colisée (☎45 62 94 00). Ⓜ Franklin D. Roosevelt. Delicious family-style cuisine. Try the house specialties, such as the *feuilleté de canard* (€18) and *cassoulet* (€20). Vegetarian dishes upon request. Open M-Sa 11am-3pm and 7-11pm. MC/V. ❸

Café des Lettres, 53 r. de Verneuil (☎42 22 52 17). Ⓜ Solférino. This Scandinavian cafe touts fresh, healthy fare. Enjoy platters of smoked salmon and *blinis* (€21) and other Danish seafood dishes (€11-24). Coffee €2.50. Beer €5. Reserve ahead. Open M noon-3pm, Tu-F noon-11pm, Sa noon-7pm. ❹

9ÈME TO 11ÈME ARRONDISSEMENTS

Restaurants close to the Opéra cater to the after-theater and movie crowd and can be quite expensive. **Rue Faubourg-Montmartre** is packed with cheap eateries.

No Stress Café, 2 pl. Gustave Toudouze (☎48 78 00 27). Ⓜ St-Georges. Walk uphill on r. Notre Dame de Lorette and turn right on r. H. Monnier. A funky place with a holistic approach to dining: massages are available after 9pm (W-Sa). Vegetarian options abound. Su brunch noon-3:30pm. Open Tu-Su 11am-2am. MC/V. ❸

Chez Paul, 13 r. de Charonne (☎47 00 34 57). Ⓜ Bastille. Go east on r. du Faubourg St-Antoine and turn left on r. de Charonne. St. Antoine's Temptation (€18) is a dish of pig ear, foot, tail, and groin. Reserve ahead for dinner. Open daily noon-2:30pm and 7pm-2am. Kitchen closes 12:30am. AmEx/MC/V. ❸

Chez Haynes, 3 r. Clauzel (☎48 78 40 63). Ⓜ St-Georges. Opened in 1949, Paris's first African-American-owned restaurant is now run by a Portuguese and Brazilian couple. F-Sa nights live music; cover €5. Soul food menu Tu-Sa, Brazilian food Su. Open Tu-Su 7pm-midnight. AmEx/MC/V. ❸

12ÈME TO 14ÈME ARRONDISSEMENTS

The 13*ème* is a budget gourmet's dream, with scores of Asian restaurants packing Paris's **Chinatown,** south of pl. d'Italie on av. de Choisy, and numerous affordable French restaurants in the **Butte-aux-Cailles** area. The 14*ème* is bordered at the top by the busy **boulevard du Montparnasse,** which is lined with a diverse array of restaurants. **Rue du Montparnasse** has Breton creperies; **rue Daguerre** is lined with vegetarian-friendly restaurants; and inexpensive eateries cluster on **rue Didot, rue du Commerce, rue de Vaugirard,** and **boulevard de Grenelle.**

Tricotin, 15 av. de Choisy (☎45 84 74 44). Ⓜ Porte de Choisy. 6 chefs prepare delicious food from Cambodia, Thailand, and Vietnam, which is served in 2 large, cafeteria-style rooms. Cambodian fried rice with beef €7. Open daily 9:30am-11:30pm. MC/V. ❶

L'Ebauchoir, 45 r. de Citeaux (☎43 42 49 31). Ⓜ Faidherbe-Chaligny. Walk down r. du Faubourg St-Antoine and turn left on r. de Citeaux. L'Ebauchoir feels something like a funky, dressed-up diner. €14 lunch *menu* includes a drink. *Plats* from €15. Open M 8-11pm, Tu-Sa noon-11pm. Kitchen open noon-2:30pm and 8-11pm. MC/V. ❹

Le Temps des Cerises, 18 r. de la Butte-aux-Cailles (☎45 89 69 48). Ⓜ Place d'Italie. Take rue Bobillot and turn right on r. de la Butte-aux-Cailles. Le Temps has been in shared ownership by its workers since 1976. French dishes like *andouillette* (€14) are house specialties. Lunch *menu* €9.50; dinner *menus* €15-23. Open M-F 11:45am-2:15pm and 7:30-11:45pm, Sa 11:45am-2:15pm. Reserve ahead. AmEx/MC/V. ❹

15ÈME AND 16ÈME ARRONDISSEMENTS

Thai Phetburi, 31 bd. de Grenelle (☎40 58 14 88; www.phetburi-paris.com). Ⓜ Bir-Hakeim. The *tom yam koung* (shrimp soup flavored with lemongrass; €7.30) is a favorite. Vegetarian options. Open M-Sa noon-2:30pm and 7-10:30pm. AmEx/MC/V. ❷

Le Dix Vins, 57 r. Falguière (☎43 20 91 77; www.le-dix-vins.com). Ⓜ Pasteur. Follow Pasteur away from the rails and make a left onto r. Falguière. This outstanding bistro has a *menu* (€24) that, while not exactly cheap, offers diners a classic meal with a *nouvelle cuisine* twist. Open M-F noon-2:30pm and 7:30-11pm. MC/V. ❹

17ÈME TO 20ÈME ARRONDISSEMENTS

The 17*ème*'s **Village des Batignolles** is a great place to dine on a budget, far from the tourist traffic of the city. In the 18*ème*, bistros and cafes line **rue des Abbesses** and **rue Lepic.** Ethnic enclaves in the 19*ème* and 20*ème* offer cheap, funky eats.

The James Joyce Pub, 71 bd. Gouvion St-Cyr (☎44 09 70 32; www.kittyosheas.com). Ⓜ Porte Maillot (exit at Palais de Congrès). Take bd. Gouvion St-Cyr past Palais de Congrès. Upstairs is a welcoming restaurant with stained-glass windows depicting scenes from Joyce's novels. Downstairs, the pub pulls pints of Guinness. F live Irish rock from 9:30pm, except in summer. Open daily 11am-2am. AmEx/MC/V. ❷

Lao Siam, 49 r. de Belleville (☎40 40 09 68). Ⓜ Belleville. This Chinese and Thai favorite serves a unique Thai dried-calamari salad (€6.30) that makes for a light preamble to the *poulet royal au curry* (€8.40). Open daily noon-3pm and 7-11:30pm. MC/V. ❶

Café Flèche d'Or, 102bis r. de Bagnolet (☎44 64 01 02; www.flechedor.fr). Ⓜ Alexandre Dumas. Near Porte de la Réunion at Père Lachaise. In a defunct train station, this bar/cafe/performance space serves internationally inspired dishes. Dinner *menus* €12-15. Bar and cafe open daily 10am-2am. Dinner served 8pm-1am. MC/V. ❸

SALONS DE THÉ (TEA ROOMS)

Mariage Frères, 30 r. du Bourg-Tibourg, 4*ème* (☎01 42 72 28 11). Ⓜ Hôtel-de-Ville. Tea *menu* includes sandwiches, pastries, and tea (€25). Brunch *menu* €25. Branches at 13 r. des Grands Augustins, 6*ème* (☎40 51 82 50) and 260 r. du Faubourg St-Honoré, 8*ème* (☎46 22 18 54). Open daily 10:30am-7:30pm. AmEx/MC/V.

Ladurée, 16 r. Royale (☎42 60 21 79) and 75 av. des Champs-Elysées, 8*ème* (☎40 75 08 75). Ⓜ Concorde. Famous for the many-flavored mini macaroons stacked in the window (€3). Pastry counter for takeout. Specialty tea *Ladurée mélange* €6.50. Su brunch *menu* €29. Open daily 8:30am-7pm. AmEx/MC/V.

SPECIALTY SHOPS

Food shops, particularly *boulangeries* (bakeries) and *pâtisseries* (pastry shops), are on virtually every street in Paris, or at least it seems like it. Your gustatory experiences, particularly when buying breads or pastries, will vary depending on how recently your food has left the oven.

Berthillon, 31 r. St-Louis-en-l'Île (☎43 54 31 61). Ⓜ Cité or Pont Marie. Choose from dozens of ice cream *parfums* (flavors) ranging from gingerbread to the house specialty, *nougat miel* (honey nougat). 1 scoop €2; 2 scoops €3; 3 scoops €4. Open Sept. to mid-July. Open W-Su 10am-8pm. Closed 2 weeks in Feb. and Apr.

Amorino, 47 r. St-Louis-en-l'Île (☎44 07 48 08). Ⓜ Pont Marie. Cross the Pont Marie and turn right on r. St-Louis-en-l'Île. With a selection of 20 *gelati* and *sorbetti* flavors, Amorino's amazing concoctions come in generous servings. Cone €4. Branches at 4 r. de Buci, 6*ème*; 4 r. de Vavin, 6*ème*; 31 r. Vieille du Temple, 4*ème*.

Julien, 75 r. St-Honoré, 1*er* (☎42 36 24 83). Ⓜ Tuileries. The best of everything: breads, sandwiches, pastries, cakes. For an indulgent breakfast, try the *pain au chocolat* (a flaky, buttery chocolate croissant; €1) or the very different but equally delicious *pain chocolat* (a small loaf of bread with chocolate chips; €1.50). Lunch lines are long.

Barthélémy, 51 r. de Grenelle, 7*ème* (☎45 48 56 75). Ⓜ Rue du Bac. A cluttered, old-fashioned store with the finest cheese in Paris. President Chirac has been known to stop in. Open Tu-F 8am-1pm and 4-7:15pm, Sa 8am-1:30pm and 3:30-7:15pm.

MARKETS

Marché Monge, Ⓜ Monge. In pl. Monge at the Métro exit. A bustling, friendly, and easy-to-navigate market. You'll find everything from cheese to shoes to jewelry and flowers in these stalls. Look for the very popular prepared foods (perfect for a lunch picnic at the Arènes de Lutèce). Open W, F, and Su 8am-1pm.

Marché Montorgueil, *2ème.* Ⓜ Etienne Marcel. Walk along r. Etienne Marcel away from the Seine, then take the 2nd right. A center of gastronomy since the 13th century, this market offers home-grown cheese, meat, and produce. Open Tu-Su 8am-7:30pm.

SIGHTS

While it would take weeks to see all of Paris's monuments, museums, and gardens, the city's small size makes sightseeing easy and enjoyable. In a few hours, you can walk from the heart of the Marais in the east to the Eiffel Tower in the west, passing most major monuments along the way. A solid day of wandering will show you how close the medieval Notre Dame is to the modern Centre Pompidou and the funky Latin Quarter to the royal Louvre—the Paris diversity is all the more amazing for the compact area in which it unfolds.

ÎLE DE LA CITÉ AND ÎLE ST-LOUIS

If any one place is the heart of Paris, it is the small island of Île de la Cité in the Seine. In the 3rd century BC, when it was inhabited by the *Parisii*, a Gallic tribe of merchants and fishermen, the Île was all there was to Paris. Today, all distances in France are measured from *kilomètre zéro*, a sundial in front of Notre Dame.

CATHÉDRALE DE NOTRE DAME DE PARIS. This 12th- to 14th-century cathedral, begun under Bishop Maurice de Sully, is one of the world's most famous and beautiful examples of medieval architecture. After the Revolution, the building fell into disrepair—it was even used to shelter livestock—until Victor Hugo's 1831 novel *Notre Dame de Paris* (a.k.a. *The Hunchback of Notre Dame*) inspired citizens to lobby for the cathedral's restoration. The apocalyptic facade and soaring, apparently weightless walls are effects produced by brilliant Gothic engineering and optical illusions. The cathedral's biggest draws are the enormous stained-glass **rose windows** that dominate the northern and southern ends of the transept. A staircase inside the towers leads to a perch from which gargoyles survey the city. *(Ⓜ Cité. ☎42 34 56 10, crypt 55 42 50 10. Cathedral open daily 7:45am-7pm. Towers open July-Aug. M-F 10am-6:30pm, Sa-Su 10am-11pm; Apr.-June and Sept. daily 10am-6:30pm; Oct.-Mar. daily 10am-5:30pm. Treasury open M-F 9:30am-6pm, Sa 9:30am-5pm, Su 1-1:30pm and 6-6:30pm. Crypt open Tu-Su 10am-6pm. English-language tours W-Th noon, Sa 2:30pm; in French M-F noon, Sa 2:30pm; free. Cathedral and towers €7.50, ages 18-25 €5, under 18 free. Treasury €3, under 26 €2. Crypt €3.50, over 60 €2.50, under 27 €1.50.)*

FRANCE

STE-CHAPELLE, PALAIS DE JUSTICE, AND CONCIERGERIE. The **Palais de la Cité** contains three vastly different buildings. The opulent, Gothic **Ste-Chapelle** was built by St-Louis (Louis IX) to house his most precious possession, Christ's crown of thorns, now in Notre Dame. On sunny days, light pours through the **Upper Chapel's** medieval stained glass, illuminating frescoes of saints and martyrs. Around the corner is the **Conciergerie,** one of Paris's most famous prisons; Marie-Antoinette and Robespierre were incarcerated here during the Revolution. *(6 bd. du Palais. Ⓜ Cité. ☎53 73 78 50. Open daily Mar.-Oct. 9:30am-6pm; Nov.-Feb. 9am-5pm. €6.50, ages 18-25 €4.50, under 18 free. Combo ticket with Conciergerie €9.50, seniors and ages 18-25 €7, under 18 free if accompanied by parent.)* Built after the great fire of 1776, the Palais de Justice houses France's district courts. *(☎44 32 51 51. Courtrooms open M-F 9am-noon and 1:30-end of last trial. Free.)*

Otel.com
Are you aiming for a budget vacation?
DO NOT DISTURB
US & CANADA
1-800-820-4171 OR 1-212-594-8045
EUROPE
00-800-468-35482 OR 44-207-099-2035

CellularAbroad
With Cellular Abroad,
talk is not only cheap,
it's free.
Unlimited FREE
incoming calls
and no bills
or contracts
for overseas use!
1-800-287-5072
www.cellularabroad.com

ÎLE ST-LOUIS. The Île St-Louis has been home to some of Paris's most privileged elite, from Pompidou to Voltaire, Baudelaire to Marie Curie. The city's best ice cream is at ☒**Berthillon.** *(31 r. St-Louis-en-l'Île, p. 329.)* **Rue Saint-Louis-en-l'Île** rolls down the center of the island. This charming street is a welcome distraction from busy Parisian life. Ambling shoppers enjoy a wealth of specialty shops and quaint bistros with a small-village feel. Visit the **Église St-Louis-en-Île** to see Louis Le Vau's 17th-century Rococo interior. *(19bis r. St-Louis-en-l'Île.)*

LOUVRE AND OPÉRA: 1ER, 2ÈME, AND 9ÈME ARRONDISSEMENTS

World-famous art museum and former residence of kings, the **Louvre** (p. 336) occupies about one-seventh of the 1*er arrondissement.* The **Jardin des Tuileries,** at the western end of the Louvre, celebrates the victory of geometry over nature. It was commissioned by Catherine de Médici in 1564 and improved by André Le Nôtre (designer of Versailles's gardens) in 1649. *(Ⓜ Tuileries. ☎ 40 20 90 43. Garden open daily Apr.-Sept. 7am-11pm; Oct.-Mar. 7:30am-7:30pm. English-language tours from the Arc de Triomphe du Carrousel.)* North of the Tuileries along r. de Castiglione, ☒**place Vendôme** was built to house embassies, but bankers instead created lavish private homes behind the elegant facades. Today, the smell of money is still in the air: designer shops, perfumers, and jewelers line the square.

LES HALLES. A sprawling market since 1135, Les Halles received a much-needed face-lift in the 1850s with the construction of large iron-and-glass pavilions to shelter the vendors' stalls. In 1970, the medieval market was torn down and replaced with an extensive underground shopping mall and cinema called **Forum des Halles,** with its own Métro station. The area has seen a recent influx of younger locals.

OPÉRA GARNIER. The exterior of the Opéra Garnier, with its newly restored multi-colored marble facade, sculpted golden goddesses, and ornate columns and friezes is as impressive as it is kitschy. Designed by Charles Garnier under Napoleon III, the lavish interior decor transports visitors back to a time when the Opéra was haunted by the famous phantom. *(Ⓜ Opéra. ☎ 08 92 89 90 90; www.operadeparis.fr. See p. 337 for ticket info. Concert hall and museum open daily mid-July to Aug. 10am-5:30pm; Sept. to mid-July 10am-4:30pm. Concert hall closed during rehearsals; call ahead. English tours daily 10am and 2:30pm. Admission €7, students €4.)*

PIGALLE. Farther north, on the border of the 18*ème,* is the salacious Pigalle district. Stretching along bd. de Clichy from pl. Pigalle to pl. Blanche, this is home to famous old cabarets (Folies Bergère, Moulin Rouge, Folies Pigalle) and overtly raunchy newcomers like Le Coq Hardy and Dirty Dick. Visitors traveling alone should exercise caution. *(Ⓜ Pigalle.)*

MARAIS: 3ÈME AND 4ÈME ARRONDISSEMENTS

☒ **PLACE DES VOSGES.** At the end of r. des Francs-Bourgeois sits the magnificent pl. des Vosges, Paris's oldest public square. The manicured central park is surrounded by 17th-century Renaissance townhouses. The *place* is one of Paris's most idyllic spots for a picnic or an afternoon siesta. Victor Hugo lived at no. 6, which is now a museum of his life and work. *(Ⓜ Chemin Vert or St-Paul.)*

RUE DES ROSIERS. In the heart of the Jewish community of the Marais, r. des Rosiers is packed with kosher shops and falafel stands. When Philippe-Auguste expelled the Jews from Paris in the 13th century, many families moved to this area, just outside the city walls. Since then, the quarter has been repopulated by an influx of Russian Jews in the 19th century and North African Sephardim fleeing Algeria in the 1960s. *(Ⓜ St-Paul.)*

HÔTEL DE VILLE. Paris's grandiose city hall dominates a large square scattered with fountains and *Belle Époque* lampposts. The present edifice is a 19th-century replica of the original medieval structure, a meeting hall for the cartel that controlled traffic on the Seine. *(29 r. de Rivoli. Ⓜ Hôtel-de-Ville. ☎42 76 43 43. Open M-F 9am-7pm when there is an exhibit, 9am-6pm otherwise.)*

LATIN QUARTER AND ST-GERMAIN-DES-PRÉS: 5ÈME AND 6ÈME ARRONDISSEMENTS

The Latin Quarter, named for the prestigious universities that taught here in Latin until 1798, has its soul in the ever-vibrant student population. Since the student riots in May 1968, many artists and intellectuals have migrated to the cheaper outer *arrondissements*, and the *haute bourgeoisie* have moved in. The *5ème* still presents the most diverse array of bookstores, cinemas, and jazz clubs in the city. Designer shops and edgy art galleries are found around St-Germain-des-Prés.

JARDIN DU LUXEMBOURG. Parisians flock to these formal gardens to sunbathe or read. A residential area of Roman Paris, the site of a medieval monastery, and later the home of 17th-century French royalty, the gardens were liberated during the Revolution and are now free to all. *(Ⓜ Odéon or RER: Luxembourg. Main entrance on bd. St-Michel. Open daily dawn-dusk.)*

MOSQUÉE DE PARIS. The *Institut Musulman* houses the beautiful Persian gardens, elaborate minaret, and shady porticoes of the Mosquée de Paris, a mosque constructed in 1920 by French architects to honor the role of North African countries in WWI. Travelers can relax in the Turkish baths at the exquisite *hammam* or sip mint tea in the soothing cafe. *(Ⓜ Censier Daubenton. Walk down r. Daubenton and turn left on r. Georges Desplas; the mosque is on the right. ☎43 31 38 20; www.la-mosquee.com. Open daily 10am-noon and 2-5:30pm. Guided tour €3, students €2.* Hammam *open for men Tu 2-9pm, Su 10am-9pm; women M, W-Th, Sa 10am-9pm, F 2-9pm. €15.)*

RUE MOUFFETARD. South of pl. de la Contrescarpe, r. Mouffetard plays host to one of the liveliest street markets in Paris, which draws a mix of Parisians and visitors. The stretch of r. Mouffetard past pl. de la Contrescarpe, and onto r. Descartes and r. de la Montagne Ste-Geneviève, is the quintessential Latin Quarter stroll. *(Ⓜ Cardinal Lemoine or Pl. Monge.)*

FRANCE

PLACE ST-MICHEL AND ENVIRONS. At the center of the Latin Quarter, bd. St-Michel, which divides the *5ème* and *6ème*, is filled with cafes, restaurants, bookstores, and clothing boutiques. Place St-Michel, to the north, is packed with students and tourists. Visitors should check out the many traditional bistros on nearby r. Soufflot and r. des Fossés St-Jacques. *(Ⓜ St-Michel.)*

LA SORBONNE. The Sorbonne is one of Europe's oldest universities, founded in 1253 by Robert de Sorbon as a dormitory for 16 theology students. Nearby **place de la Sorbonne,** off bd. St-Michel, is flooded with cafes, bookstores, and, during termtime, students. Visitors can stroll through the **Chapelle de la Sorbonne** (entrance off pl. de la Sorbonne), which houses temporary exhibits on arts and letters. *(45-47 r. des Ecoles. Ⓜ Cluny-La Sorbonne or RER: Luxembourg.)*

PANTHÉON. The **crypt** of the Panthéon, which occupies the highest point on the Left Bank, houses the tombs of Louis Braille, Victor Hugo, Jean Jaurès, Jean-Jacques Rousseau, Voltaire, and Émile Zola. The building's other attraction is **Foucault's Pendulum,** which proves the rotation of the earth. *(Pl. du Panthéon. Ⓜ Cardinal Lemoine. Walk down r. Cardinal Lemoine, turn right on r. Clovis, and walk around to the front of the building. ☎44 32 18 04. Open daily 10am-6:30pm. €7.50, students €5, under 18 free. Oct.-Mar. 1st Su of each month free.)*

JARDIN DES PLANTES. Opened in 1640 to grow medicinal plants for King Louis XIII, the garden now features science museums, rosaries, and a zoo, which Parisians raided for food during the Prussian siege of 1871. *(Ⓜ Gare d'Austerlitz or Jussieu. ☎40 79 37 94. Open daily in summer 7:30am-8pm; winter 8am-5:30pm.)*

7ÈME ARRONDISSEMENT

EIFFEL TOWER. Gustave Eiffel wrote of his creation: "France is the only country in the world with a 300m flagpole." Designed in 1889 as the tallest structure in the world, the Eiffel Tower was conceived as a modern monument to engineering that would surpass the Egyptian pyramids in size and notoriety. Critics dubbed it a "metal asparagus" and a "Parisian tower of Babel," but when it was inaugurated in March 1889 as the centerpiece of the World's Fair, the tower earned the love of Paris. *(Ⓜ Bir-Hakeim or Trocadéro. ☎44 11 23 23; www.tour-eiffel.fr. Open daily mid-June to Aug. 9am-midnight; Sept. to mid-June 9:30am-11pm. Stairs open 9:30am-6pm. Elevator to 1st fl. €4, to 2nd fl. €7.30, to 3rd fl. €10.40. Stairs to 1st and 2nd fl. €3.50.)*

INVALIDES. The gold-leaf dome of the Hôtel des Invalides shines at the center of the *7ème*. The grassy **Esplanade des Invalides** runs from the *hôtel* to the **Pont Alexandre III,** a bridge with gilded lampposts from which you can catch a great view of the Invalides and the Seine. The **Musée de l'Armée, Musée des Plans-Reliefs,** and **Musée de l'Ordre de la Libération** are housed in the Invalides complex, as is **Napoleon's tomb,** in the **Église St-Louis.** Enter from either pl. des Invalides or pl. Vauban and av. de Tourville. *(127 r. de Grenelle. Ⓜ Invalides.)*

CHAMPS-ELYSÉES AND NEARBY: 8ÈME AND 16ÈME ARRONDISSEMENTS

PARC MONCEAU. The signs say *pelouse interdite* (keep off the lawn), but on a sunny day, no one follows the rules. This lush urban enclave is encircled by gold-tipped iron gates and borders the elegant bd. de Courcelles. A number of architectural oddities—covered bridges, Dutch windmills, Roman ruins, and roller rinks—make this a kids' romping ground as well as a formal garden. *(Ⓜ Monceau or Courcelles. Open daily Apr.-Oct. 7am-10pm; Nov.-Mar. 7am-8pm.)*

ARC DE TRIOMPHE. Napoleon commissioned the Arc, at the western end of the Champs-Elysées, in 1806 to honor his Grande Armée. In 1940, Parisians were brought to tears by the sight of Nazis goose-stepping through the Arc. The terrace at the top has a fabulous view. The **Tomb of the Unknown Soldier** has been under the Arc since November 11, 1920. An eternal flame has been burning strong since 1921. *(Pl. Charles de Gaulle. Ⓜ Charles-de-Gaulle-Éoile. Open daily Apr.-Sept. 10am-11pm; Oct.-Mar. 10am-10:30pm. €8, ages 18-25 €5, under 17 free.)*

PLACE DE LA CONCORDE. Paris's most famous public square lies at the eastern end of the Champs-Elysées and the Jardin des Tuileries. Built between 1757 and 1777 as a monument to Louis X, the area soon became the **place de la Révolution,** site of the guillotine that severed 1343 aristocratic heads. After the Reign of Terror, the square was renamed *concorde* (peace). The huge 13th-century BC **Obélisque de Luxor** depicts the deeds of Egyptian pharaoh Ramses II. Given to Charles X by the Viceroy of Egypt, it is Paris's oldest monument. *(Ⓜ Concorde.)*

AVENUE DES CHAMPS-ELYSÉES. Extending from the Louvre, this wide thoroughfare was a piecemeal project begun under the reign of Louis XIV. By the first half of the 20th century, opulence reigned—ornate mansions towered above exclusive cafes. *(Ⓜ Charles de Gaulle-Étoile. Runs from the pl. Charles de Gaulle-Étoile southeast to the pl. de la Concorde.)*

TROCADÉRO. In the 1820s, the Duc d'Angoulême built a memorial to his victory in Spain at Trocadéro. Jacques Carlu designed the **Palais de Chaillot** for the 1937 World's Fair. The terrace offers brilliant views of the Eiffel Tower and Champs de Mars. Be aware of pickpockets and traffic as you gaze upward. *(Ⓜ Trocadéro.)*

BASTILLE: 10ÈME, 11ÈME, AND 12ÈME ARRONDISSEMENTS

CANAL ST-MARTIN. The most pleasant area of the 10*ème* is the tree-lined Canal St-Martin. In recent years, the city has made efforts to improve water quality in the canal and clean up its banks, resulting in a local renaissance. Children line up along the quays to watch the working locks lift barges and boats. *(Ⓜ République or Goncourt will take you to the more beautiful end of the canal.)*

PLACE DE LA BASTILLE. This busy intersection was once the home of the famous Bastille Prison, which was stormed on July 14, 1789, sparking the French Revolution. Two days later, the National Assembly ordered the prison demolished, but the ground plan of the prison's grand turrets remains embedded in the road near r. du Faubourg St-Antoine. *(Ⓜ Bastille.)*

OPÉRA DE LA BASTILLE. One of Mitterrand's *Grands Projets*, the Opéra opened in 1989 to loud protests over its unattractive design. It has been described as a huge toilet because of its resemblance to the city's coin-operated *pissoirs*. The opera has not struck a completely sour note, though, as it has helped renew local interest in the arts. The guided tour offers a behind-the-scenes view of the largest theater in the world. *(130 r. de Lyon. Ⓜ Bastille. Look for the words "Billeterie" on the building. ☎40 01 19 70; www.opera-de-paris.fr. 1hr. tours almost every day, usually at 1 or 5pm; call ahead. Tours in French, but groups of 10 or more can arrange for English. €11, students and over 60 €9.)*

EASTERN LEFT BANK: 13ÈME ARRONDISSEMENT

QUARTIER DE LA BUTTE-AUX-CAILLES. Historically a working-class neighborhood, the old-fashioned Butte-aux-Cailles Quarter has a long-standing tradition of defiance. The area was one of the first to fight during the Revolution of 1848. Later, it was the unofficial headquarters of the *soixante-huitards*, the student and intellectual activists behind the 1968 Paris riots. Funky new restaurants and galleries have cropped up in recent years. *(Ⓜ Corvisart. Exit onto bd. Blanqui and turn onto r. Barrault, which will meet r. de la Butte-aux-Cailles.)*

MONTPARNASSE: 14ÈME AND 15ÈME ARRONDISSEMENTS

PARC ANDRÉ CITROËN. This futuristic park was created by landscapers Alain Provost and Gilles Clément in the 1970s. The hot-air balloon ride that launches from the central garden offers spectacular aerial views. *(2 r. de la Montagne de la Fage. Ⓜ Javelor Balard. ☎44 26 20 00; www.aeroparis.com. Open M-F 7:30am-9:30pm, Sa-Su 9am-9:30pm. Balloon rides Sa-Su and holidays €12, ages 12-17 €10, ages 3-11 €6; M-F €10/9/5.)*

THE CATACOMBS. Almost 2km of tunnels 20m below the streets were originally excavated to provide stone for building the city. By the 1770s, much of the Left Bank was in danger of caving in and digging was promptly halted. The former quarry was then used as a mass grave, relieving Paris's foul and overcrowded cemeteries. During WWII, the Resistance set up underground headquarters among the departed. *(1 av. du Colonel Henri Rol-Tanguy. Ⓜ Denfert-Rochereau. Exit to pl. Denfert-Rochereau and cross av. du Général Leclerc. ☎43 22 47 63; www.catacombs.paris.fr. 45min. tour. Open Tu-Su 10am-4pm. €5, ages 14-26 €2.50, under 14 free.)*

MONTMARTRE AND PÈRE-LACHAISE: 18ÈME, 19ÈME, AND 20ÈME ARRONDISSEMENTS

BASILIQUE DU SACRÉ-COEUR. The Basilique du Sacré-Coeur crowns the *butte* Montmartre like an enormous white meringue. Its onion dome is visible from almost anywhere in the city, and its 112m bell tower is the highest point in Paris. Nearby, pl. du Tertre is full of touristy cafes and amateur artists. *(35 r. du Chevalier-de-la-Barre. Ⓜ Anvers or Abbesses. ☎53 41 89 00. Church open daily 6am-11pm. Wheelchair-accessible. Dome open daily 9am-6pm. Church free. Dome €5.)*

PARC DE LA VILLETTE. Inaugurated by President Mitterrand in 1985 as "the place of intelligent leisure," this park has museums, libraries, and concert halls in the Cité des Sciences and the Cité de la Musique. The **Promenade des Jardins** links several thematic gardens. Every July and August, La Villette holds a free open-air **film festival.** The **Zénith** concert hall hosts major rock bands, and the **Trabendo** jazz and modern music club holds an extraordinarily popular annual jazz festival. *(Ⓜ Porte de Pantin. General info ☎40 03 75 03. Promenade des Jardins open 24hr. Free.)*

CIMETIÈRE PÈRE LACHAISE. This cemetery holds the remains of such famous Frenchmen as Balzac, Sarah Bernhardt, Colette, Danton, David, Delacroix, La Fontaine, Haussmann, Molière, Proust, and Seurat within its peaceful paths and elaborate sarcophagi. Foreigners buried here include Modigliani, Gertrude Stein, and Oscar Wilde; the most frequently visited grave is that of Jim Morrison. French Leftists make a ceremonial pilgrimage to the **Mur des Fédérés** (Wall of the Federals), where 147 *communards* were executed. *(16 r. du Repos. Ⓜ Père Lachaise. Open Mar.-Oct. M-F 8am-6pm, Sa 8:30am-6pm, Su and holidays 9am-6pm; Nov.-Feb. M-F 8am-5:30pm, Sa 8:30am-5:30pm, Su and holidays 9am-5:30pm. Free.)*

PARC DES BUTTES-CHAUMONT. In the south of the *19ème*, Parc des Buttes-Chaumont is a mix of man-made topography and transplanted vegetation; Napoleon III commissioned it in 1860 out of a longing for London's Hyde Park, where he spent much of his exile. Today's visitors walk the winding paths, sunbathe in the summer, and enjoy a great view of the *quartier* from the cave-filled cliffs topped with a Roman temple. *(Ⓜ Buttes-Chaumont or Botzaris. Open daily 7am-10:30pm.)*

BAL DU MOULIN ROUGE. Along the bd. de Clichy and bd. de Rochechouart, you'll find many Belle Époque cabarets and nightclubs, including the infamous cabaret Bal du Moulin Rouge, immortalized by the paintings of Toulouse-Lautrec, the music of Offenbach, and Baz Luhrmann's Hollywood blockbuster. The crowd is tourists out for an evening of sequins, tassels, and skin. The revues are still risqué, but the price of admission is the real shock. *(82 bd. de Clichy. Ⓜ Blanche. ☎53 09 82 82; www.moulin-rouge.com. Shows 7, 9, 11pm. Dinner and show €140-170, 11pm show €87.)*

PERIPHERY SIGHTS

LA DÉFENSE. Outside the city limits, west of the *16ème*, the skyscrapers and modern architecture of La Défense are Paris's newest (unofficial) *arrondissement*, home to 14 of France's top 20 corporations. The **Grande Arche** completes the *axe historique* running through the Louvre, pl. de la Concorde, and the Arc de Triomphe. There's yet another stunning view from the top. Trees, shops, and sculptures by Calder and Miró line the esplanade. *(Ⓜ or RER: La Défense. Arche open daily 10am-8pm. €7.50, students and under 18 €5.50.)*

BOIS DE BOULOGNE. By day, this 2000-acre park, with numerous gardens, several stadiums, and two lakes, is a popular spot for picnics, jogging, and bike-riding. The *bois* is notorious for drugs, violent crime, and prostitution by night. *(On the western edge of the 16ème. Ⓜ Porte Maillot, Sablons, Pont de Neuilly, or Porte Dauphine.)*

MUSEUMS

The **Carte Musées et Monuments** grants immediate entry to 65 Paris museums (no waiting in line) and will save you money if you plan to visit three or more museums and major sights per day. It's available at major museums and Métro stations. (1-day €15; 3-day €30; 5-day €45.)

MUSÉE D'ORSAY. If only the *Académiciens* who turned the Impressionists away from the Louvre could see the Musée d'Orsay. Now considered masterpieces, these "rejects" are well worth the pilgrimage to this mecca of modernity. The collection, installed in a former railway station, includes painting, sculpture, decorative arts, and photography from 1848 until WWI. On the ground floor, Classical and Proto-Impressionist works are on display, including Manet's *Olympia*, a painting that caused a scandal when it was unveiled in 1865. Other highlights include Monet's *La Gare St-Lazare* and *Cathédrale de Rouen* series, Renoir's *Le bal du Moulin de la Galette*, Edgar Dégas's *La classe de danse*, Rodin's *Gates of Hell*, and paintings by Cézanne, Morisot, Pissarro, Sisley, and Seurat. Over a dozen works by van Gogh are also featured. The top floor offers one of the most comprehensive collections of Impressionist and Post-Impressionist art in the world. In addition, the exterior and interior balconies offer supreme views of the Seine and the jungle of sculptures below. *(62 r. de Lille, 7ème. Ⓜ Solférino, RER: Musée d'Orsay. ☎ 40 49 48 14; www.musee-orsay.fr. Open June 20-Sept. 20 Tu-W and F-Sa 9:30am-6pm, Th 10am-9:45pm, Su 9am-6pm; Sept. 21-June 19 Tu-W and F-Sa 9:30am-6pm, Th 10am-9:45pm. Th-Sa €7, Su €5.50, students €5, under 18 free.)*

MUSÉE DU LOUVRE. No visitor has ever allotted enough time to ponder every display at the Louvre, as it would take weeks to peruse the over 30,000 items on display. Masterpieces include Hammurabi's Code, David's *The Oath of the Horatii* and *The Coronation of Napoleon*, Delacroix's *Liberty Leading the People*, Vermeer's *Lacemaker*, da Vinci's *Mona Lisa*, the *Winged Victory of Samothrace*, and the *Venus de Milo*. Enter through I. M. Pei's stunning glass **Pyramid** in the Cour Napoléon, or skip the line by entering directly from the Métro. The Louvre is organized into three different wings: Denon, Richelieu, and Sully, each divided according to the artwork's date, national origin, and medium. *(1er. Ⓜ Palais-Royal/Musée du Louvre. ☎ 40 20 53 17; www.louvre.fr. Open M, Th, Sa 9am-6pm, W and F 9am-10pm. €8.50, W and F after 6pm €6. Under 26 F after 6pm and 1st Su of each month free.)*

FRANCE

CENTRE POMPIDOU. This inside-out building has inspired debate since its opening in 1977. Whatever its aesthetic merits, the exterior's chaotic colored piping provides an appropriate shell for the Fauvist, Cubist, Pop, and Conceptual works inside. *(Pl. Georges-Pompidou, r. Beaubourg, 4ème. Ⓜ Rambuteau or Hôtel-de-Ville. ☎ 44 78 12 33; www.centrepompidou.fr. Centre open M and W-Su 11am-10pm. Museum open M and W-Su 11am-9pm. €10, under 26 €8, under 18 and 1st Su of each month free.)*

MUSÉE RODIN. The 18th-century Hôtel Biron holds hundreds of sculptures by Auguste Rodin (and by his student and lover, Camille Claudel), including the *The Thinker*, *The Hand of God*, and *The Kiss*. Bring a book and repose in the fertile gardens amid bending flowers and flexing sculptures. *(77 r. de Varenne, 7ème. Ⓜ Varenne. ☎ 44 18 61 10; www.musee-rodin.fr. Open Tu-Su Apr.-Sept. 9:30am-5:45pm; Oct.-Mar. 9:30am-4:45pm. €6, ages 18-25 €4, under 18 and 1st Su of each month free.)*

MUSÉE PICASSO. When Picasso died in 1973, his family paid the French inheritance tax in artwork. The French government put this collection, which includes work from his Cubist, Surrealist, and Neoclassical years, on display in 1985 in the 17th-century Hôtel Salé. *(5 r. de Thorigny, 3ème. Ⓜ Chemin Vert. ☎ 42 71 25 21. Open M and W-Su Apr.-Sept. 9:30am-6pm; Oct.-Mar. 9:30am-5:30pm. Last entry 45min. before closing. €6.50, ages 18-25 and Su €4.50, under 18 and 1st Su of each month free.)*

MUSÉE JACQUEMART-ANDRÉ. The 19th-century mansion of Nélie Jacquemart and her husband has a a world-class collection of Renaissance art, including *Madonna and Child* by Botticelli. *(158 bd. Haussmann, 8ème. Ⓜ Miromesnil. ☎45 62 11 59. Open daily 10am-6pm. €9.50, students and ages 7-17 €7.50.)*

MUSÉE DE CLUNY. One of the world's finest collections of medieval art, the Musée de Cluny is housed in a medieval monastery built atop Roman baths. Works include **La Dame et La Licorne** (The Lady and the Unicorn), a striking medieval tapestry series. *(6 pl. Paul Painlevé, 5ème. Ⓜ Cluny-La Sorbonne. ☎53 73 78 00. Open M and W-Sa 9:15am-5:45pm. €6.50, ages 18-25 and 1st Su of each month €4.50, under 18 free.)*

INSTITUT DU MONDE ARABE. Featuring Arabesque art from the 3rd to 18th centuries, the IMA building itself was designed to look like the ships that carried North African immigrants to France. The southern face comprises 240 mechanized portals, which automatically open and close. *(1 r. des Fossés St-Bernard, 5ème. Ⓜ Jussieu. ☎40 51 38 38; www.imarabe.org. Museum open Tu-Su 10am-6pm. €4, under 26 €3, under 12 free. Library open July-Aug. 1-6pm; Sept.-June Tu-Sa 1-8pm. Free. Cinema €4, under 26 €3.)*

FONDATION CARTIER POUR L'ART CONTEMPORAINE. This gallery of contemporary art looks like a synthetic indoor forest, with a stunning glass facade surrounding the grounds' natural greenery. *(261 bd. Raspail, 14ème. Ⓜ Raspail. ☎42 18 56 50; www.fondation.cartier.fr. Open Tu-Sa noon-8pm. €6, students and seniors €4.50.)*

MAISON DE BALZAC. In this three-story hillside *maison*, home of Honoré de Balzac from 1840 to 1847, visitors can view some of the author's original manuscripts. The picturesque garden is filled with flowers in the summertime. *(47 r. Raynouard, 16ème. Ⓜ Passy. Walk up the hill and turn left onto r. Raynouard. ☎55 74 41 80. Open Tu-Su 10am-6pm. Free.)*

PALAIS DE TOKYO. Recently refurbished, this large warehouse space is known as the **site création contemporaine** and is outfitted to host prominent avant-garde sculptures, video displays, and multimedia installations. Be on the lookout for each exhibit's *vernissage* (private viewing) for free entrance and refreshments. *(13 av. du Président-Wilson, 16ème. Ⓜ Iéna. Follow av. du Président-Wilson with the Seine on your right. ☎47 23 54 01; www.palaisdetokyo.com. Wheelchair-accessible. Open Tu-Su noon-midnight. €6, students under 26 €4.50.)*

FRANCE

ENTERTAINMENT

Pick up one of the weekly bibles of Parisian entertainment: *Pariscope* (€0.40) and *Figaroscope* (€1), on sale at any newsstand or *tabac*. *Pariscope* includes an English-language section. For concert listings, check the free *Paris Selection*, available at tourist offices. Free concerts are often held in churches and parks, especially during summer festivals. FNAC sells concert tickets.

Opéra Garnier, pl. de l'Opéra, 9*ème* (☎08 92 89 90 90; www.operadeparis.fr). Ⓜ Opéra. Beautiful building (see p. 331) hosts symphonies, music, and ballet. Tickets usually available 2 weeks before shows. Box office open M-Sa 10am-6:30pm. Last-minute discount tickets on sale 1hr. before showtime. Ticket prices vary. AmEx/MC/V.

Au Duc des Lombards, 42 r. des Lombards, 1*er* (☎42 33 22 88; www.ducdeslombards.com). Ⓜ Châtelet. The best French jazz, with occasional American soloists and hot items in world music. 3 sets per night. Beer €7-10. Mixed drinks €10. Cover €19-23, students €12 if reserved ahead. Music 10pm-1:30am. Open M-Sa 5pm-2am. MC/V.

Opéra Comique, 5 r. Favart, 2*ème* (☎42 44 45 46; www.opera-comique.com). Ⓜ Richelieu-Drouot. Operas on a lighter scale. The building has been recently renovated, and upcoming shows include *Carmen 2: Le Retour*. Box office open M-Sa 9am-9pm. Tickets €7-100. Cheapest tickets usually available until just before the show starts.

Aux Trois Mailletz, 56 r. Galande, 5*ème* (☎43 54 00 79; before 5pm 43 25 96 86). Ⓜ St-Michel. Walk along the Seine on the Quai St-Michel; turn right on r. du Petit Pont and left on r. Galande. Basement cafe features world music and jazz vocals. Grog €9. Mixed drinks €13. Cover Sa-Su for club €13-19. Bar open daily 5pm-dawn; cafe 10pm-dawn.

SHOPPING

Shopping in Paris is as diverse as the city itself, from the wild club wear sold near r. Etienne-Marcel to the unique boutiques of the Marais to the upscale designer shops of St-Germain-des-Prés. The great *soldes* (sales) of the year begin after New Year's and at the very end of June. **Au Bon Marché,** 22 r. de Sèvres, 7*ème*, was the first to offer *prêt à porter* fashion but now is known for its high prices. (Ⓜ Sèvres-Babylone. ☎44 39 80 00. Open M-W and F 9:30am-7pm, Th 10am-9pm, Sa 9:30am-8pm. AmEx/MC/V.) With 18 floors of stores in three buildings, **Galeries Lafayette,** 40 bd. Haussmann, 9*ème*, is a shopping vacuum that will suck you in and never let you out. Its food market, **Lafayette Gourmet,** has everything from a sushi counter to a mini-*boulangerie*. (Ⓜ Chaussée d'Antin. ☎42 82 34 56. Open M-W and F-Sa 9:30am-7:30pm, Th 9:30am-9pm. AmEx/MC/V.)

Around **rue Tiquetonne,** fabrics are trendier and cheaper than in other parts of the city. **Le Shop,** 3 r. d'Argout, 2*ème*, has 1200 sq. m of sleek club wear plus a live DJ. (Ⓜ Etienne-Marcel. Open M 1-7pm, Tu-Sa 11am-7pm. AmEx/MC/V.) From Ⓜ Etienne-Marcel, walk against traffic on r. de Turbigo and go left on r. Tiquetonne to reach **Espace Kiliwatch,** 64 r. Tiquetonne, 2*ème*. This is one of Paris's most popular shops, with funky new and pre-owned clothes, books, and furnishings. (Open Tu-Sa 11am-7pm, Su 2-7pm. MC/V.) What the Marais does best is independent designer shops. Vintage stores line **rue Vieille-du-Temple, rue de Sévigné, rue Roi de Sicile,** and **rue des Rosiers. Alternatives,** 18 r. de Roi de Sicile, 4*ème*, sells an eclectic collection of quality secondhand clothes. (Ⓜ St-Paul. Open M-Sa 1-7pm. MC/V.)

The **Champs-Elysées** area, in the 8*ème*, is perfect for a day of window shopping. Take a break and walk along **avenue Montaigne** to admire the great *couture* houses; their collections change every season but are invariably innovative, gorgeous, and jaw-droppingly expensive. The **Bastille** area (11*ème* and 12*ème*) boasts some of the newest names in Paris fashion. Trendsetters hit the boutiques on **rue de Charonne** and **rue Keller.** Meanwhile, the 18*ème*, around **Montmartre,** has some of the city's most eclectic shops. Explore near **rue de Lavieuville** for funky independent designer

FROLICSOME FIREMEN

You know Bastille Day is approaching when two things occur: French flags go up around the city, and all Parisians leave town. The weekend is the most extravagant and fun of the year, but expats in Paris will find themselves enjoying the festivities with a large proportion of other tourists, as many French locals prefer to escape to the countryside for the long weekend. Despite the prevalence of the English language, Bastille "Day" provides an action-packed weekend of fun.

For a truly unusual patriotic experience, be sure not to miss *Les Saupeurs Pompiers*. Paris celebrates the night of July 13th with huge parties in fire stations called "Fireman's Balls." Makes sense, right? *Les Saupeurs Pompiers* open the courtyards of their stations to the public for a night of flowing alcohol, loud music, and, yes, firemen. Those less than smitten with the idea of partying in a sea of beefy *pompiers* should not be put off—these balls are fun for everyone. Doors open at around 9pm, depending on the station, and lines can be very long. Show up early or late for shorter queues. The parties go on until 4am, but time flies as you dance, drink, and are entertained by shows put on by the *pompiers*. Entrance is free and drinks are cheap, usually €2-5.

wear. Across the river in the **Latin Quarter,** you'll find plenty of chain clothing and shoe stores around **boulevard St-Michel** and numerous little boutiques selling chic scarves and jewelry, but bookstores of all kinds are where the *5ème* really stands out. St-Germain-des-Prés, particularly the triangle bordered by **boulevard St-Germain, rue St-Sulpice,** and **rue des Sts-Pères,** is saturated with high-budget names.

NIGHTLIFE

CAFES AND BARS

LES HALLES AND MARAIS (1ER, 2ÈME, 3ÈME, 4ÈME)

Le Champmeslé, 4 r. Chabanais (☎42 96 85 20). Ⓜ Pyramides. This lesbian bar is Paris's oldest and most famous; everyone is welcome. Beer €4-5. Mixed drinks €8. Th cabaret show 10pm. Open M-Sa 3pm-dawn.

Chez Richard, 37 r. Vieille du Temple (☎42 74 31 65). Ⓜ St-Paul or Hôtel de Ville. Ideal for chilling on weekdays, with suave bartenders and mellow beats. Mixed drinks €5. Happy hour 6-8pm. Open daily 6pm-2am. AmEx/MC/V.

Banana Café, 13 r. de la Ferronerie (☎42 33 35 31; www.bananacafeparis.com). Ⓜ Châtelet. Take r. Pierre Lescot to r. de la Ferronerie. This *très branché* (way cool) evening arena is the most popular GLBT bar in the *1er.* Beer €5.50. Mixed drinks €8.50. Cover F-Sa €10; includes 1 drink. Open daily 5:30pm-6am. AmEx/MC/V.

Amnésia Café, 42 r. Vieille du Temple (☎42 72 16 94). Ⓜ St-Paul or Hôtel de Ville. A largely queer crowd comes to lounge on plush sofas in Amnésia's classy interior. 1st fl. cafe, 2nd fl. lounge, and basement club with music beginning 9pm. *Kir* €4. Mixed drinks €7.50-8.50. Open M and F-Sa 11am-3am, Tu-Th and Su 11am-2am. MC/V.

LATIN QUARTER AND ST-GERMAIN (5ÈME, 6ÈME, 7ÈME)

Le Caveau des Oubliettes, 52 r. Galande (☎46 34 23 09). Ⓜ St-Michel. Head away from pl. St-Michel on quai de Montebello and turn right on r. Petit Pont, then left onto r. Galande. 2 scenes in 1, both with a mellow, funky vibe: the upstairs bar (La Guillotine) has sod carpeting, ferns, and a real guillotine. The downstairs cellar is an outstanding jazz club. Free *soirée boeuf* (jam session) Su-Th 10pm-1:30am; F-Sa concerts free. Drinks from €5. Happy hour daily 5-9pm. Open daily 5pm-2am.

Le Club des Poètes, 30 r. de Bourgogne (☎47 05 06 03; www.poesie.net). Ⓜ Varenne. A restaurant by day, Le Club des Poètes is transformed at 10pm each night when a troupe of readers and comedians, including Rosnay's family, bewitches the audience with poetry from Baudelaire, Rimbaud, Villon, and others. Drinks €7.50. Open Tu-Sa noon-3pm and 8pm-1am. Kitchen closes 10pm. Closed Aug. MC/V.

Le 10 Bar, 10 r. de l'Odéon (☎43 26 66 83). Ⓜ Odéon. Walk against traffic on bd. St-Germain and make a left on rue de l'Odéon. Le 10 Bar is a classic student hangout, where Parisian youth indulge in philosophical and political discussion. After several glasses of their famous spiced sangria (€3.50), you might feel inspired to join in. Jukebox plays everything from Édith Piaf to Aretha Franklin. Open daily 6pm-2am.

Bob Cool, 15 r. des Grands Augustins (☎46 33 33 77). Ⓜ Odéon. Bob Cool's music is at the discretion of the bartender and veers all over the spectrum, from salsa to The Corrs. Happy hour 5-9pm. Pints €4.50. Mixed drinks €5-6. Open daily 5pm-2am.

CHAMPS-ELYSÉES (8ÈME)

buddha-bar, 8 r. Boissy d'Anglas (☎53 05 90 00; www.buddha-bar.com). Ⓜ Madeleine or Concorde. The legendary buddha-bar has to be the most glamorous watering-hole in the world (Madonna drops by when she's in town). Beer €8-10. Wine €10-12 per glass. Open M-F noon-3pm and 6pm-2am, Sa-Su 6pm-2am.

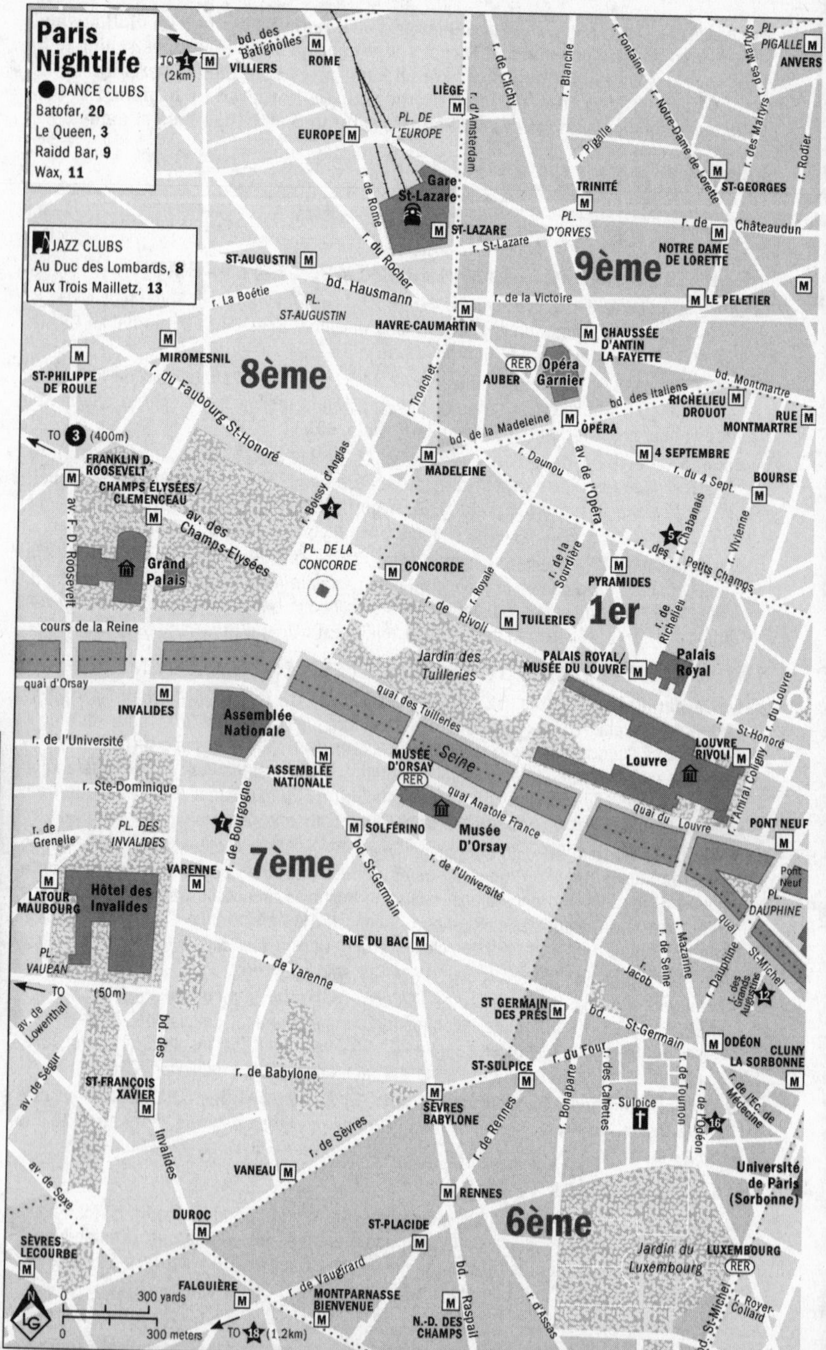
Paris Nightlife
DANCE CLUBS
Batofar, 20
Le Queen, 3
Raidd Bar, 9
Wax, 11
JAZZ CLUBS
Au Duc des Lombards, 8
Aux Trois Mailletz, 13
TO 1 (2km)
TO 3 (400m)
TO (50m)
TO 18 (1.2km)
bd. des Batignolles
VILLIERS
ROME
LIÈGE
EUROPE
PL. DE L'EUROPE
r. d'Amsterdam
r. de Clichy
r. Blanche
r. Fontaine
r. Notre-Dame de Lorette
r. des Martyrs
PL. PIGALLE
ANVERS
r. Rodier
r. Pigalle
TRINITÉ
ST-GEORGES
r. de Châteaudun
PL. D'ORVES
NOTRE DAME DE LORETTE
9ème
LE PELETIER
r. de Rome
Gare St-Lazare
ST-LAZARE
r. St-Lazare
r. du Rocher
ST-AUGUSTIN
bd. Hausmann
r. La Boétie
PL. ST-AUGUSTIN
r. de la Victoire
HAVRE-CAUMARTIN
CHAUSSÉE D'ANTIN LA FAYETTE
MIROMESNIL
8ème
ST-PHILIPPE DE ROULE
r. du Faubourg St-Honoré
RER
AUBER
Opéra Garnier
bd. Montmartre
bd. des Italiens
RICHELIEU DROUOT
RUE MONTMARTRE
r. Tronchet
bd. de la Madeleine
OPÉRA
MADELEINE
r. Daunou
av. de l'Opéra
4 SEPTEMBRE
r. du 4 Sept.
BOURSE
FRANKLIN D. ROOSEVELT
CHAMPS ÉLYSÉES/ CLEMENCEAU
av. des Champs-Elysées
r. Boissy d'Anglas
r. Chabanais
r. Vivienne
r. des Petits Champs
PL. DE LA CONCORDE
CONCORDE
r. Royale
r. de la Sourdière
PYRAMIDES
av. F. D. Roosevelt
Grand Palais
r. de Rivoli
TUILERIES
1er
r. de Richelieu
cours de la Reine
Jardin des Tuileries
PALAIS ROYAL/ MUSÉE DU LOUVRE
Palais Royal
quai d'Orsay
quai des Tuilleries
r. St-Honoré
r. du Louvre
INVALIDES
Assemblée Nationale
r. de l'Université
Seine
MUSÉE D'ORSAY
Louvre
LOUVRE RIVOLI
ASSEMBLÉE NATIONALE
r. de l'Amiral Coligny
r. Ste-Dominique
quai Anatole France
quai du Louvre
PONT NEUF
r. de Grenelle
PL. DES INVALIDES
SOLFÉRINO
Musée D'Orsay
r. de Bourgogne
bd. St-Germain
VARENNE
7ème
r. de l'Université
Pont Neuf
PL. DAUPHINE
LATOUR MAUBOURG
Hôtel des Invalides
RUE DU BAC
r. Mazarine
r. de Seine
quai St-Michel
PL. VAUBAN
r. de Varenne
r. Jacob
r. Dauphine
r. des Grands Augustins
av. de Lowenthal
bd. des Invalides
ST GERMAIN DES PRÉS
bd. St-Germain
ODÉON
CLUNY LA SORBONNE
ST-SULPICE
r. du Four
r. des Canettes
r. de Tournon
r. Bonaparte
av. de Ségur
r. de Babylone
ST-FRANÇOIS XAVIER
SÈVRES BABYLONE
Sulpice
r. de l'Odéon
r. de l'Ec. de Médecine
r. de Sèvres
r. de Rennes
VANEAU
Université de Paris (Sorbonne)
av. de Saxe
RENNES
DUROC
ST-PLACIDE
6ème
SÈVRES LECOURBE
Jardin du Luxembourg
LUXEMBOURG
r. de Vaugirard
bd. Raspail
FALGUIÈRE
MONTPARNASSE BIENVENUE
N.-D. DES CHAMPS
r. d'Assas
bd. St-Michel
r. Royer-Collard
0 300 yards
0 300 meters
N
LG

FRANCE

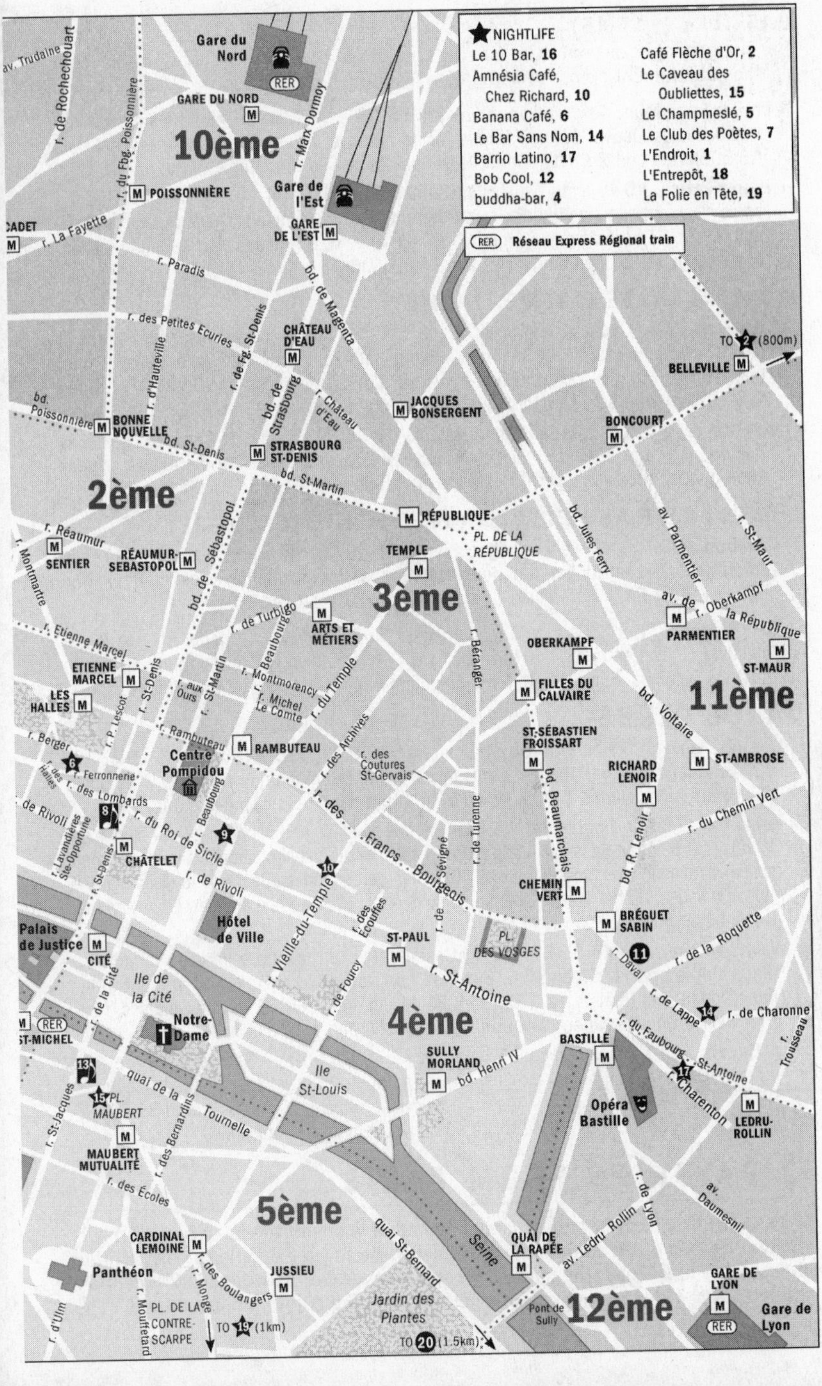
NIGHTLIFE
Le 10 Bar, 16
Amnésia Café, Chez Richard, 10
Banana Café, 6
Le Bar Sans Nom, 14
Barrio Latino, 17
Bob Cool, 12
buddha-bar, 4
Café Flèche d'Or, 2
Le Caveau des Oubliettes, 15
Le Champmeslé, 5
Le Club des Poètes, 7
L'Endroit, 1
L'Entrepôt, 18
La Folie en Tête, 19
RER Réseau Express Régional train
10ème
2ème
3ème
11ème
4ème
5ème
12ème
Gare du Nord
GARE DU NORD
Gare de l'Est
GARE DE L'EST
POISSONNIÈRE
CADET
CHÂTEAU D'EAU
JACQUES BONSERGENT
BELLEVILLE
TO 2 (800m)
BONCOURT
BONNE NOUVELLE
STRASBOURG ST-DENIS
RÉPUBLIQUE
PL. DE LA RÉPUBLIQUE
TEMPLE
SENTIER
RÉAUMUR-SEBASTOPOL
ARTS ET MÉTIERS
OBERKAMPF
PARMENTIER
ST-MAUR
ETIENNE MARCEL
LES HALLES
FILLES DU CALVAIRE
ST-SÉBASTIEN FROISSART
RAMBUTEAU
Centre Pompidou
RICHARD LENOIR
ST-AMBROSE
CHÂTELET
CHEMIN VERT
BRÉGUET SABIN
Hôtel de Ville
Palais de Justice
CITÉ
ST-PAUL
PL. DES VOSGES
Ile de la Cité
Notre-Dame
ST-MICHEL
SULLY MORLAND
Ile St-Louis
BASTILLE
Opéra Bastille
PL. MAUBERT
MAUBERT MUTUALITÉ
LEDRU-ROLLIN
CARDINAL LEMOINE
Panthéon
JUSSIEU
QUAI DE LA RAPÉE
GARE DE LYON
Gare de Lyon
Jardin des Plantes
Pont de Sully
Seine
PL. DE LA CONTRE-SCARPE
TO 19 (1km)
TO 20 (1.5km)
av. Trudaine
r. de Rochechouart
r. du Fbg. Poissonnière
r. Marx Dormoy
r. La Fayette
r. Paradis
r. des Petites Ecuries
r. de Fg. St-Denis
r. d'Hauteville
bd. de Magenta
bd. de Strasbourg
r. Château d'Eau
bd. Poissonnière
bd. St-Denis
bd. St-Martin
bd. de Sébastopol
r. Réaumur
r. Montmartre
r. de Turbigo
r. Etienne Marcel
r. Montmorency
r. Beaubourg
r. aux Ours
r. St-Martin
r. St-Denis
r. Michel Le Comte
r. du Temple
r. P. Lescot
r. Berger
r. Rambuteau
r. des Archives
r. des Coutures St-Gervais
r. Ferronnerie
r. des Halles
r. des Lombards
r. de Rivoli
r. du Roi de Sicile
r. Lavandières Ste-Opportune
r. des Francs Bourgeois
r. Vieille-du-Temple
r. des Ecouffes
r. de Sévigné
r. de Turenne
r. Béranger
bd. Beaumarchais
bd. Jules Ferry
av. Parmentier
r. St-Maur
av. de la République
r. Oberkampf
bd. Voltaire
r. du Chemin Vert
bd. R. Lenoir
r. de la Roquette
r. Daval
r. de Lappe
r. de Charonne
r. Trousseau
r. du Faubourg St-Antoine
r. Charenton
r. St-Antoine
r. de Fourcy
bd. Henri IV
r. de la Cité
quai de la Tournelle
r. St-Jacques
r. des Bernardins
r. des Écoles
quai St-Bernard
r. de Lyon
av. Daumesnil
av. Ledru Rollin
r. Monge
r. des Boulangers
r. Mouffetard
r. d'Ulm

FRANCE

BASTILLE (11ÈME)

Bar-hoppers spill out onto the narrow lane of **rue de Lappe** as catchy tunes from each establishment compete with beats from the bar next door.

Le Bar Sans Nom, 49 r. de Lappe (☎48 05 59 36). Ⓜ Bastille. The No-Name Bar is a laid-back, seductive lounge famous for its creative mixed drinks. Beer €5-7. Shots €6.50. Mixed drinks €8-10. Open Tu-Th 6pm-2am, F-Sa 6pm-4am. MC/V; min. €12.

Barrio Latino, 46-48 r. du Faubourg St-Antoine (☎55 78 84 75). Ⓜ Bastille. Has the same swanky owners as buddha-bar. Potent mixed drinks include the strawberry margarita (€12). DJ from 10pm. Su brunch (noon-4pm, €28) includes a free salsa lesson. Dress to impress. Open daily noon-2am. AmEx/MC/V.

MONTPARNASSE (13ÈME, 14ÈME)

L'Entrepôt, 7-9 r. Francis de Pressensé (☎45 40 07 50, restaurant reservations 45 40 07 50; www.lentrepot.fr). Ⓜ Pernety. Cinema, restaurant, art gallery, and bar all in one. Beer €3.50. World music concerts F-Sa; cover €5-7. Su brunch noon-3pm (€22). Open M-Sa 11am-1am, Su 11am-midnight. Kitchen open daily noon-3pm and 8-11pm.

La Folie en Tête, 33 r. de la Butte-aux-Cailles (☎45 80 65 99). Ⓜ Corvisart. The artsy *axis mundi* of the 13*ème*. Beer €3. Punch €5. Concerts Sept.-June Sa nights, usually Afro-Caribbean music (cover €8). Happy hour 6-8pm. Open M-Sa 6pm-2am. MC/V.

MONTMARTRE AND BEYOND (17ÈME, 18ÈME, 20ÈME)

L'Endroit, 67 pl. du Dr. Félix Lobligeois (☎42 29 50 00). Ⓜ Rome. Hip, young 17*ème*-ers come for the snazzy bar and ideal location. Classics include the apple martini. Wine €3.50-4. Beer €4. Mixed drinks €8-9. Open daily 10am-2am. MC/V.

Café Flèche d'Or, 102bis r. de Bagnolet (☎44 64 01 02; www.flechedor.fr). Live music nightly, from reggae to hip-hop to Celtic rock. Concerts: beer €3, mixed drinks €7. Club: beer €4-5, mixed drinks €8. Th-Sa DJ midnight-6am. Happy hour 7-9pm. MC/V.

DANCE CLUBS

Batofar, facing 11 quai François-Mauriac (☎53 60 17 42). Ⓜ Quai de la Gare. This 520-ton barge is in with the electronic music crowd but maintains a friendly vibe. Cover €8-15; usually includes 1 drink. Open M-Th 11pm-6am, F-Su 11pm-late. MC/V.

Raidd Bar, 23 r. du Temple. Ⓜ Hôtel de Ville. The most hip and happening GLBT club in the Marais and perhaps Paris. Spinning disco globes cast undulating shadows in the intimate space, illuminating the muscular torsos of the topless bartenders. Beer €4. Tu disco night, W 80s and house, Su house mix. Notoriously strict door policy–women are allowed in with men Su-Th, but might not be so lucky F-Sa.

Wax, 15 r. Daval (☎48 05 88 33). Ⓜ Bastille. One of those rare Parisian miracles: a place that is always free and fun. This mod bar/club gets very crowded at night with a mix of locals and tourists. Beer €5.50-6.50. Mixed drinks €9.50. W and Su disco/funk, Th R&B, F-Sa house. Open daily 9pm-dawn. MC/V; min. €15 min.

Le Queen, 102 av. des Champs-Elysées (☎53 89 08 90). Ⓜ George V. Where drag queens, superstars, models, moguls, and go-go boys get down to mainstream rhythms. Drinks €10. M disco, W ladies' night, Th-Sa house, Su 80s. Cover M-Th and Su €15, F-Sa €20; includes 1 drink. Bring ID. Open daily 11pm-dawn. AmEx/MC/V.

DAYTRIPS FROM PARIS

CHARTRES. Chartres's phenomenal cathedral is one of the most beautiful surviving creations of the Middle Ages. Arguably the finest example of early Gothic architecture in Europe, the cathedral retains several of its original 12th-century stained-glass windows, many featuring the stunning color, "Chartres blue." The rest of the windows and the sculptures on the main portals date from the 13th century, as does the carved floor in the rear of the nave. You can enter the 9th-century **crypt** only from opposite the cathedral's south entrance. *(☎02 37 21 75 02; www.cathedrale-chartres.com. Open daily Easter-Oct. 8am-8pm; Nov.-Easter 8:30am-7pm. Closed to tourists during Mass. North Tower open May-Aug. M-Sa 9:30am-noon and 2-5:30pm, Su 2-5:30pm; Sept.-Apr. M-Sa 9:30am-noon and 2-4:30pm, Su 2-4:30pm. Cathedral free. Tower €4.10, Sept.-Apr. 1st Su of month free.)* **Trains** run from Paris's Gare Montparnasse (1¼hr.; 10 per day; round-trip €25, under 26 €19). From the station, go straight, turn left into the pl. de Châtelet, right on r. Ste-Même, and left on r. Jean Moulin.

VERSAILLES. Louis XIV, the Sun King, built and held court at Versailles's extraordinary palace, 12km west of Paris. The château embodies the extravagance of the Old Regime, especially in the **Hall of Mirrors** (under renovation until 2007; only portions are open to visitors), the antique-furnished **Queen's Bedchamber,** and the fountain-filled **gardens.** Most visitors enter at **Entrance A,** on the right-hand side in the north wing, or **Entrance C,** in the archway to the left, where you can pick up an audio tour. *(Info ☎30 83 78 00. Château open Tu-Su Apr.-Oct. 9am-6:30pm; Nov.-Mar. 9am-5:30pm. Gardens open daily dawn-dusk. Château €8, after 3:30pm €6, under 18 free. Gardens €3, under 18 and after 6pm free. Tour €4-20, depending on type. Audio tour €4.50.)* A **shuttle** (round-trip €5.80, ages 11-18 €4) runs behind the palace to Louis's hideaways, the **Grand** and **Petit Trianons,** and to Marie Antoinette's pastoral fantasy, the **Hameau.** *(Both Trianons open Tu-Sa Apr.-Oct. noon-6:30pm; Nov.-Mar. noon-5:30pm. €5, Sa-Su after 3:30pm €3.)* Take any RER C5 **train** beginning with a "V" from Ⓜ Invalides to the Versailles Rive Gauche station (30-40min., every 15min., round-trip €5.20). Buy your RER ticket before getting to the platform.

NORMANDY (NORMANDIE)

Fertile Normandy is a land of fields, fishing villages, and cathedrals. Invasions have twice secured the region's place in military history: in 1066, William of Normandy conquered England; on D-Day, June 6, 1944, Allied armies began the liberation of France on Normandy's beaches.

ROUEN ☎02 35

Madame Bovary, literature's most famous desperate housewife, may have criticized Rouen (pop. 106,000), but Flaubert's hometown is no provincial hamlet. Though commonly remembered as the site of Joan of Arc's 1431 execution, Rouen is most memorable for its splendid Gothic cathedrals, buzzing urban energy, and *vieille ville.* The most famous of Rouen's "hundred spires" belong to the **Cathédrale de Notre-Dame,** in pl. de la Cathédrale; one of them, standing at 151m, is the tallest in France. Art lovers may also recognize the cathedral's facade from Monet's celebrated studies of light. (Open M 2-7pm, Tu-Sa 7:30am-7pm, Su 8am-6pm.) Combining the disparate themes of Flaubert, who was raised on the premises, and the history of medicine, the **Musée Flaubert et d'Histoire de la Médicine,** 51 r. de Lecat, down r. de Crosne from pl. de Vieux-Marché, houses a large collection of bizarre paraphernalia on both subjects. (☎15 59 95; www.chu-rouen.fr. Open Tu 10am-6pm, W-Sa 10am-noon and 2-6pm. €3, ages 18-25 €1.50.)

Hotel des Arcades ❷, 52 r. de Carmes, is down the street from Notre Dame. (☎70 10 30; www.hotel-des-arcades.fr. Breakfast €6.50. Singles €29, with shower €40; doubles €30/41. AmEx/MC/V.) Cheap eateries surround **place du Vieux-Marché** and the **Gros Horloge** area. A popular on-the-go lunch option for locals, **Estival Eric ❶,** 23 allée Eugène Delacroix, between the Musée des Beaux-Arts and the Palais de Justice, serves 32 different types of fresh bread. (☎98 28 58. Open M-Sa 7am-7pm. MC/V.) A **Monoprix** supermarket is at 73 r. du Gros Horloge. (Open M-Sa 8:30am-9pm.)

LOCAL LEGEND

A SAINTLY GIFT

Every year since 1156, on the morning of Ascension Day, a prisoner has been brought before Rouen's parliament. Without a judge, without a jury, without even a trial, he is set free. The most perplexing part of this strange practice is the reason behind it: St-Romain's defeat of a dragon.

While serving as Bishop of Rouen in the 7th century, St-Romain practiced a life of quiet piety, but it was not until well after his death in 641 that Romain's fame as a dragon-slayer began to spread. When the saint's remains were moved within Rouen's walls in the 10th century, they were interred in a flood-prone part of town that subsequently ceased to flood. It was then that the legend of Romain's run-in with a dragon began to capture popular imagination.

As the story goes, one day a dragon emerged from the Seine and sent a flood over Rouen. St-Romain tried to recruit villagers to stop the beast, but only a prisoner answered his plea. The two entered the dragon's cave, St-Romain made the sign of the cross, and the beast collapsed.

In order to honor their legendary patron saint and the lone convict who aided him, the people of Rouen began to annually pardon a prisoner. Improbable as it may seem, this tradition has continued for close to a millennium, and every year a prisoner is offered the gift of a saint.

Trains leave r. Jeanne d'Arc, on pl. Bernard Tissot, for Lille (3hr., 3 per day, €27) and Paris (1½hr., 1 per hr., €19). From the station, walk down r. Jeanne d'Arc and turn left on r. du Gros Horloge to reach the **tourist office,** 25 pl. de la Cathédrale. (☎02 32 08 32 40. Open May-Sept. M-Sa 9am-7pm, Su 9:30am-12:30pm and 2-6:30pm; Oct.-Apr. M-Sa 9am-6pm, Su 10am-1pm.) **Postal Code:** 76000.

CAEN ☎02 31

Although Allied bombing leveled three-quarters of its buildings during WWII, Caen (pop. 113,000) has skillfully rebuilt itself into an active university town.

TRANSPORTATION AND PRACTICAL INFORMATION. Trains run to: Paris (2¼hr., 13 per day, €28); Rennes (3hr., 7 per day, €29); Rouen (2hr., 8 per day, €21); Tours (3½hr., 3 per day, €30). Bus Verts (☎08 10 21 42 14) **buses** cover the beaches and the rest of Normandy. Twisto operates local buses and **trams** and has schedules at its office on 15 r. de Gêole. (15 55 55; €1.20, *carnet* of 10 €9.30.) The **tourist office** is in pl. St-Pierre. (☎27 14 14; www.caen.fr/tourisme. Open July-Aug. M-Sa 9am-7pm, Su 10am-1pm and 2-5pm; Apr.-June and Sept. M-Sa 9:30am-6:30pm, Su 10am-1pm; Oct.-Mar. M-Sa 9:30am-1pm and 2-6pm, Su 10am-1pm.) **Postal Code:** 14000.

ACCOMMODATIONS AND FOOD. In a great spot, **Hôtel de la Paix ❷**, 14 r. Neuve-St-Jean, off av. du 6 Juin, is a stone's throw from the château. Rooms come with a TV and firm beds, but the decor is a bit worn. (☎86 18 99; fax 38 20 74. Breakfast €5. Reception 24hr. Singles €26, with shower €29, with toilet €32; doubles €29/35/37; triples €37/43/45; quads with shower €53. Extra bed €8. MC/V.) Ethnic restaurants, creperies, and *brasseries* are near the château and between **Place Courtonne, Église St-Pierre,** and **Église St-Jean.** Get groceries at **Monoprix,** 45 bd. du Maréchal Leclerc. (Open M-Sa 8:30am-8:30pm.)

SIGHTS AND NIGHTLIFE. Caen's biggest draw is the **Mémorial de Caen,** which immerses visitors in a powerful, tasteful, and creative exploration of WWII, from the "failure of peace" to the modern prospects for global harmony. Take bus #2 to Mémorial. (☎06 06 44; www.memorial-caen.fr. Open daily mid-July to late Aug. 9am-8pm; early Feb. to mid-July and late Aug. to Oct. 9am-7pm; mid-Jan. to early Feb. and Nov.-Dec. 9am-6pm. Closed first 2 weeks in Jan. €17-18; students, seniors, and ages 10-18 €14-16. Prices vary by season.) The ruins of William the Conqueror's enormous **château** sprawl above the center of town.

The **Musée de Normandie,** within the château grounds on the left, traces the cultural evolution of people living on Norman soil from the beginning of civilization to the present. (☎30 47 60; www.musee-de-normandie.caen.fr. Open M and W-Su 9:30am-6pm. Free.) The **Musée des Beaux-Arts de Caen,** inside the château to the right, is an immense, labyrinthine complex housing a collection of 600 works from the 17th-century Classical and Baroque periods. (☎30 47 70; www.ville-caen.fr/mba. Open daily 9:30am-6pm. Free.) At night Caen's already busy streets turn boisterous; well-attended bars and clubs populate **rue de Bras, rue des Croisiers, quai Vendeuvre,** and **rue St-Pierre.** Check out the medieval decor of **Vertigo,** 14 r. Ecuyère, just past the intersection with r. St-Pierre. (☎02 31 85 43 12. Beer €2.20-2.70. Mixed drinks €2.70-3). Also, visit **Farniente Factory,** 13 r. Paul Doumer, an modern lounge with movie seats that screams "underground chic." (☎86 30 00. Beer €3-5. Mixed drinks €7. DJ nightly. Cover €2; can be put toward a drink. Open Tu-W 7pm-1am, Th-Sa 7pm-4am. AmEx/MC/V.)

BAYEUX ☎02 31

Relatively unharmed by WWII, beautiful Bayeux (pop. 15,000) is an ideal base for exploring the nearby D-Day beaches. Visitors should not miss the 900-year-old **Tapisserie de Bayeux,** 70m of embroidery depicting William the Conqueror's invasion of England. The tapestry is displayed in the **Centre Guillaume le Conquérant,** on r. de Nesmond. (Open daily May-Aug. 9am-7pm; mid-Mar. to Apr. and Sept.-Oct. 9am-6:30pm; Nov. to mid-Mar. 9:30am-12:30pm and 2-6pm. €7.60, students €3.) The nearby **Cathédrale Notre-Dame** is the original home of the tapestry. (Open daily July-Sept. 8:30am-7pm; Oct.-Dec. 8:30am-6pm; Jan.-Mar. 9am-5pm; Apr.-June 8am-6pm. French-language tours of the old city, including access to the labyrinth and treasury, daily June-Aug. €4.) The **Musée de la Bataille de Normandie,** bd. Fabian Ware, recounts the D-Day landing. (☎51 46 90. Open daily May to mid-Sept. 9:30am-6:30pm; mid-Sept. to Apr. 10am-12:30pm and 2-6pm. Closed last 2 weeks in Jan. €6, students €4.)

From the tourist office, turn right onto r. St-Martin, follow it through several name changes, and turn left onto r. Général de Dais for the **Family Home/Auberge de Jeunesse (HI) ❷,** 39 r. Général de Dais. (☎92 15 22; www.fuaj.org. Dorms €20. HI discount €1. Cash only.) Get groceries at **Marché Plus,** just up the pedestrian walkway from the tourist office on r. St-Jean. (Open M-Sa 7am-9pm, Su 8:30am-12:30pm.) **Trains** (☎92 80 50) leave pl. de la Gare for Caen (20min., 15 per day, €8) and Paris (2½hr., 12 per day, €30). To reach the **tourist office,** pont St-Jean, turn left onto bd. Sadi-Carnot, go right at the roundabout, bear right up r. Larcher toward the cathedral, then turn right on r. St-Martin. (☎51 28 28; www.bayeux-bessin-tourism.com. Open July-Aug. M-Sa 9am-7pm, Su 9am-1pm and 2-6pm; Sept-June reduced hours.) **Postal Code:** 14400.

FRANCE

D-DAY BEACHES

On June 6, 1944, hundreds of thousands of Allied soldiers invaded the beaches of Normandy, leading to the liberation of France and the downfall of Nazi Europe. Today, reminders of that first devastating battle can be seen in the somber gravestones, remnants of German bunkers, and pockmarked landscape. The First US Infantry Division scaled 30m cliffs at the **Pointe du Hoc,** between **Utah** and **Omaha Beaches,** to capture the supposedly heavily fortified strategic stronghold of the Germans—only to find nothing there. Of the 225 men in the division, only 90 survived. The Pointe is considered a military cemetery because so many casualties remain there, crushed beneath collapsed sections of the 5m thick concrete bunkers. Often referred to as "bloody Omaha," **Omaha Beach,** next to Colleville-sur-Mer and east of the Pointe du Hoc, is the most famous of the beaches. Nothing went right at this beach on D-Day—scouts failed to detect a German presence and bombardment of the fortifications was entirely ineffective due to fog. The rows of 9387 graves of the **American Cemetery** stretch throughout the expansive grounds overlooking the beach. (Open daily 9am-5pm.) Ten kilometers north of Bayeux and just east of Omaha is **Arromanches,** a small town just west of **Gold Beach,** where the British built Port Winston in six days to provide shelter while the Allies unloaded their supplies. The **Arromanches 360° Cinéma** combines images of modern Normandy with those of D-Day. To get there, turn left on r. de la Batterie from the museum and climb the steps. (Open daily June-Aug. 9:40am-6:40pm; Sept.-May reduced hours. €4, students €3.50.)

Reaching the beaches can be difficult without a car. Some sites are accessible by **bus** from Caen and Bayeux with Bus Verts on lines #1, 3, 4 (Caen), 70, and 74 (Bayeux), and the special summer D-Day line from Bayeux and Caen to Omaha Beach. (☎08 10 21 42 14; www.busverts14.fr. Mid-June to Aug. only. All buses leave 9:20-9:40am. Tickets €1.50-17.20, depending on distance and how many times you get off.) **Normandy Sightseeing Tours,** r. des Cuisiniers in Bayeux, runs private half-day and full-day guided tours with fluent English-speaking guides. (☎02 31 51 70 52; www.normandywebguide.com. 4hr. tour €35, students €25; 8hr. tour €75/65. Pick-up at train station or pl. du Québec at 8:30am and 1:30pm. MC/V.) **Vélos Location** rents bikes, 5 r. Larcher, across from the tourist office. (☎92 89 16. €10 per ½-day, €15 per day, €105 per week. Passport used as deposit.)

MONT-ST-MICHEL ☎02 33

Regarded as a paradise in the Middle Ages, the fortified island of Mont-St-Michel is a maze of stone arches, spires, and stairways that lead up to the **abbey.** Adjacent to the abbey church, **La Merveille** (the Marvel), a 13th-century Gothic monastery, encloses a seemingly endless web of corridors and chambers. (Open daily May-Aug. 9am-7pm; Sept.-Apr. 9:30am-6pm. €8, ages 18-25 €5.) Hotels on Mont-St-Michel are expensive, starting at €50 per night. The cheapest beds are at the **Centre Duguesclin (HI) ❶,** r. du Général Patton, Pontorson. (☎/fax 60 18 65. Dorms €14, HI members €11.50. Cash only.) The Mont is most stunning at night, but plan ahead; there's no late-night public transportation off the island. Consider Mont-St-Michel as a daytrip via bus. Courriers Bretons, 104 r. Couesnon in Pontorson (☎02 99 19 70 70), runs **buses** from Rennes (1½hr., 1-6 per day, €3) and St-Malo (1¼min., 2-4 per day, €2.50). **Biking** from Pontorson takes about 1hr. on terrain that is flat but not always bike-friendly. The path next to the Couesnon River may be the best route. The Pontorson **tourist office** is in pl. de l'Église. (☎60 20 65; www.mont-saint-michel-baie.com. Open July-Aug. M-F 9am-noon and 2-6pm, Sa 10am-noon and 3-6pm, Su 10am-noon; Sept.-June reduced hours.) **Postal Code:** 50170.

BRITTANY (BRETAGNE)

Brittany fiercely maintains its Celtic heritage. Bretons fled from Anglo-Saxon invaders to this beautiful peninsula between the 5th and 7th centuries; over the following 800 years, they defended their independence from the Franks, Normans, French, and English. Even today, traditional headdresses appear at folk festivals, and lilting *Breizh* (Breton) is spoken at pubs and ports in the west of the province.

RENNES ☎02 99

The cultural capital of Brittany, Rennes (pop 206,000) has a well-deserved reputation as the party mecca of northwestern France. Ethnic eateries, colorful night-spots, and crowds of university students lend interest to the picturesque cobblestones and half-timbered houses of the *vieille ville*.

TRANSPORTATION AND PRACTICAL INFORMATION. **Trains** leave pl. de la Gare for: Caen (3hr., 8 per day, €30); Paris (3hr., 1 per hr., €50-64); St-Malo (1hr., 15 per day, €14); Tours (2½-3hr., 4 per day, €34) via Le Mans. **Buses** go from 16 pl. de la Gare to Angers (2½-3hr., 2 per day, €13) and Mont-St-Michel (1½hr., 4 per day, €10). Local buses run Monday through Saturday 5:15am-12:30am and Sunday 7:25am-12:30am. The **metro** line uses the same ticket (€1.10, day pass €3.20, *carnet* of 10 €10). To get from the train station to the **tourist office,** 11 r. St-Yves, follow av. Jean Janvier all the way to quai Chateaubriand. From there, turn left and walk along the river and through pl. de la République, turn right on r. George Dottin, then turn right again on r. St-Yves. (☎67 11 11; www.tourisme-rennes.com. Open July-Aug. M-Sa 9am-7pm, Su 11am-1pm and 2-6pm; Sept.-June M 1-6pm, Tu-Sa 10am-6pm, Su 11am-1pm and 2-6pm.) Access the **Internet** at **Neurogame,** 2 r. de Dinan. (☎65 53 85. €3 per hr. Open July-Aug. M-F 10am-1am, Sa noon-3am, Su 2-10pm; Sept.-June daily 10am-1am.) **Postal Code:** 35000.

ACCOMMODATIONS AND FOOD. The **Auberge de Jeunesse (HI) ❶**, 10-12 Canal St-Martin, has simple dorms, a TV room, and a cafeteria. Take the metro (dir.: Kennedy) to Ste-Anne. Follow r. de St-Malo downhill on r. St. Martin; the hostel will be on the right after the bridge. (☎33 22 33; rennes@fuaj.org. Breakfast included. Reception 7am-11pm. Dorms €16. AmEx/MC/V.) **Hôtel Maréchal Joffre ❷**, 6 r. Maréchal Joffre, has small, cheerful, and quiet rooms above a tiny lunch counter on a busy street. (☎79 37 74. Breakfast €5. Reception 24hr. Singles €25-34; doubles €38; triples €44. MC/V.) **Rue St-Malo** has many ethnic restaurants, while the *vieille ville* contains more traditional *brasseries* and cheap kebab stands. In general, the best food is found on the outskirts, north and east of the city center, around **rue St-Georges** and the **place de Lices.** Organic vegetarian *plats* (€10-11) and *menus* (€13-18) attract tree-huggers to **Le St-Germain des Champs (Restaurant Végétarien-Biologique) ❸**, 12 r. du Vau St-Germain. (☎79 25 52. Open Tu-Th noon-2:30pm, F-Sa noon-2:30pm and 7-10pm. MC/V.) **Crêperie des Portes Mordelaises ❶**, 6 r. des Portes Mordelaises, is one of the best in the city. (Salads €2-8. *Galettes* and crepes €3-11. Open daily 11:45am-2pm and 6:45-11pm. MC/V.) A **Champion** supermarket is in the mall on r. d'Isly. (Open M-Sa 9:30am-8pm. MC/V.)

SIGHTS AND ENTERTAINMENT. Rennes's *vieille ville* is peppered with medieval architecture, particularly on **rue de la Psalette** and **rue St-Guillaume.**

LOCAL LEGEND

ROMANCE! TRAGEDY! CASTRATION!

Pierre Abélard, born of a noble family near Nantes, was a professor of rhetoric and philosophy in Paris in the early 12th century. After years of chastity, he fixed his gaze upon the beautiful and intelligent Héloïse, more than 20 years his junior. He convinced her uncle, Canon Fulbert, to hire him as a live-in tutor to the precocious girl. A strong attraction developed, and soon they bypassed academics and spent their time studying one another. Héloïse soon found herself pregnant, and the two secretly wed. To avoid Fulbert's wrath, Abélard spirited Héloïse away to Brittany, where she gave birth to their son, Astrolabe.

Despite their efforts, news of Astrolabe's birth reached Héloïse's uncle. One night, the furious Canon Fulbert dispatched servants to Abélard's home, who broke in and cruelly castrated him. A stricken Abélard wrote to Héloïse of his dismay that "one wretched stroke of fortune" had robbed him of his love. Retreating to a monastery, he encouraged Héloïse to take the veil and become a nun. For the rest of their lives, the two lovers fervently exchanged spiritually intense letters, cementing their place among history's most famous couples. Upon their deaths, the two were re-united in Père-Lachaise Cemetery (see p. 335). Today, their tomb is among the most popular in the cemetery.

At the end of r. St-Guillaume, turn left onto r. de la Monnaie to visit the **Cathédrale St-Pierre,** founded in 1787 on a site previously occupied by a pagan temple, a Roman church, and a Gothic cathedral. The center of attention is the intricately carved altarpiece depicting the life of the Virgin. (Open daily 9:30am-noon and 3-6pm.) he **Musée des Beaux-Arts,** 20 quai Émile Zola, houses a small collection, including works by Picasso and Gauguin. (☎28 55 85 40. Open Tu-Su 10am-noon and 2-6pm. €4.10, students €2.10, under 18 free.) Across the river and up r. Gambetta is the **Jardin du Thabor,** ranked among the most beautiful gardens in France. Concerts are often held here and a gallery on the northern side exhibits local artwork. (☎38 05 99. Open daily June-Aug. 7:15am-9:30pm; Sept.-June 7:30am-6pm.) With enough bars for a city twice its size and clubs that draw students from Paris and beyond, Rennes is a partygoer's weekend mecca, more so during the school year. Look for action in **place Ste-Anne, place St-Michel, place de Lices,** and the surrounding streets. **Le Zing,** 5 pl. des Lices, packs two floors and four bars with the young and beautiful. (☎79 64 60. Mixed drinks €8. Open daily from 3pm, busy midnight-2am. AmEx/MC/V.) **Delicatessen,** 7 allée Rallier du Baty, around the corner from pl. St-Michel in a former prison, has swapped jailhouse bars for dance cages to become one of Rennes's hottest clubs. (Cover €5-14. Open Tu-Sa midnight-5am.)

ST-MALO ☎02 99

St-Malo (pop. 52,000) merges all the best of northern France, with miles of sandy beaches, imposing ramparts guarding a walled *vieille ville*, and a worldliness that livens days of sun worship with international festivals, rock concerts, and an active art scene. East of the walled city is **Grande Plage de Sillon,** the town's largest and longest beach. The slightly more secluded **Plage de Bon Secours** lies to the west and features the curious (and free) **Piscine de Bon Secours,** three cement walls that hold in a pool's worth of warm salt water even when the tide recedes. The best view of St-Malo is from its **ramparts,** the high walls around the city, which once kept out invaders but now attract tourists in droves. All entrances to the city have stairs leading up to the old walls; the view from the north side reveals a sea speckled with islands, including the **Fort National,** the **Grand Bé,** and the **Petit Bé,** all of which can be reached on foot at low tide. **Auberge de Jeunesse (HI) ❶,** 37 av. du Révérend Père Umbricht, has 248 beds near the beach. From the train station, take bus #5 (dir.: Paramé, Davier, or Rothéneuf; last bus 7:30pm) to Auberge de Jeunesse or bus #11 (July-late Aug. 1 per hr. 8am-11:30pm) from St-Vincent or the tourist office. (☎40 29 80. Reception M-F 8:30am-noon, 1:30-7pm and 8-10pm, Sa-Su 8:45am-10pm. Dorms €14-17.) The best eateries lie close to the center of the *vieille ville.* Try country-casual **La Brigantine ❶,** 13 r. de Dinan. (☎56 82 82. *Galettes* €2-9. Crepes €1.50-6. Open M and Th-F July-Aug. noon-11pm, Sept.-June noon-3pm and 7-11pm. MC/V.) **Trains** run from Sean Coquelin to Dinan (1hr., 4 per day, €8), Paris (5hr., 10 per day, €57-72), and Rennes (1hr., 7-15 per day, €12). From the station, cross bd. de la République and follow av. Louis Martin to esplanade St-Vincent for the **tourist office.** (☎56 64 48. Open July-Aug. M-Sa 9am-7:30pm, Su 10am-6pm; low season reduced hours.) **Postal Code:** 35400.

FRANCE

DINAN ☎02 96

Perhaps the best-preserved medieval town in Brittany, Dinan (pop. 10,000) has cobblestone streets lined with 15th-century houses inhabited by traditional sculptors and painters. On the ramparts, the 13th-century **Porte du Guichet** is the entrance to the **Château de Dinan,** also known as the **Tour de la Duchesse Anne,** which has served as a military stronghold, residence, and prison. (Open June-Sept. daily 10am-6:30pm; low season reduced hours. €4.20, ages 12-18 €1.65.) On the ramparts behind the château are the **Jardins "des Petits Diables" du Val Cocherel,** which hold huge bird cages, a zoo of peacocks and roosters, and a minigolf course.

(Open Apr.-Oct. daily 8am-7:30pm; Nov.-Mar. M-Sa 8am-7:30pm, Su noon-7:30pm.) A long, picturesque walk down the steep r. du Petit Fort and left along the river will lead you to the **Maison d'Artiste de la Grande Vigne,** 103 r. du Quai. This former home of painter Yvonne Jean-Haffen (1895-1993) is a work of art, with exhibitions of her work, murals adorning the walls, and a hillside garden. (☎87 90 80. Open daily July-Aug. 10:30am-6pm; Sept.-June reduced hours. €2.75, students €1.75.)

To reach the **Auberge de Jeunesse (HI) ❷,** in Vallée de la Fontaine-des-Eaux, turn left from the station, cross the tracks, then turn right and follow the tracks downhill for 1km before turning right again. (☎39 10 83. Reception July-Aug. 8am-noon and 5-9pm; low season reduced hours. Dorms €12. MC/V.) **Rue de la Cordonnerie** and **place des Merciers** have inexpensive *brasseries.* A **Monoprix** supermarket is at 7 pl. du Marchix. (Open M-Sa 9am-7:30pm.) **Trains** run from pl. du 11 Novembre 1918 to Paris (3hr., 8 per day, €57-63) and Rennes (1hr., 8 per day, €13). To get to the **tourist office,** 9 r. du Château, from the station, bear left across pl. du 11 Novembre 1918 onto r. Carnot, turn right on r. Thiers, then left into the *vieille ville,* and bear right onto r. du Marchix, which becomes r. de la Ferronnerie; it will be on your right. (☎87 69 76. Open July-Aug. M-Sa 9am-7pm, Su 10am-12:30pm and 2:30-6pm; Sept.-June M-Sa 9am-12:30pm and 2-6pm.) **Postal Code:** 22100.

QUIMPER ☎02 98

With a central waterway crisscrossed by flower-adorned pedestrian footbridges, Quimper (*kam-PAIR;* pop. 63,000) has irrepressible charm to fuel its fierce Breton pride. At **Faïenceries de Quimper HB-Henriot,** r. Haute, guides lead visitors through the studios of the town's renowned earthenware. (☎90 09 36; www.hb-henriot.com. Open July-Aug. M-Sa 9am-noon and 2-5pm; Sept.-June M-F 9am-noon and 2-5pm. French- or English-language tours 35min., €3.50.) The dual spires of the **Cathédrale St-Corentin,** built between the 13th and 15th centuries, mark the entrance to the old quarter from quai St-Corentin. Inside, the choir is curved to mimic the angle of Jesus's drooping head during the crucifixion. (Open May-Oct. M-Sa 8:30am-noon and 1:30-6:30pm, Su 8:30am-noon and 2-6:30pm; Nov.-Apr. M-Sa 9am-noon and 1:30-6pm, Su 1:30-6pm.)

To reach the comfortable **Centre Hébergement de Quimper (HI) ❶,** 6 av. des Oiseaux, take bus #1 (dir.: Kermoysan; last bus 7:30pm) from pl. de la Résistance to Chaptal; the hostel will be up the street on your left. (☎64 97 97; quimper@fuaj.org. Breakfast €3.40. Linens included. Dorms €14, under 26 €12. Non-HI members pay extra. Cash only.) The **Les Halles market,** off r. Kéréon on r. St-François, has produce, seafood, meat, and cheese. (Open daily Apr.-Oct. 8am-8pm; Nov.-Mar. 9am-7pm, but hours vary.) At night, head to the cafes near the cathedral, or to **The Pointín Still,** 2 av. de la Liberation, where live Irish music plays every Friday night at 10pm. (Beer €2-5. Open M-Sa 3pm-1am, Su 5pm-1am. MC/V.) **Trains** go from av. de la Gare to Brest (1½hr., 4 per day, €10) and Rennes (2¼hr., 10 per day, €29-31). From the train station, go right onto av. de la Gare and follow it, with the river on your right, until it becomes bd. Dupleix and leads to pl. de la Résistance. The **tourist office,** 7 r. de la Déesse, is on your left. (☎53 04 05; www.quimper-tourisme.com. Open July-Aug. M-Sa 9am-7pm, Su 10am-1pm and 3-5:45pm; Sept.-June reduced hours.) **Postal Code:** 29000.

NANTES ☎02 40

Successfully shrugging off its violent past, modern Nantes (pop. 270,000) blends high-tech industry and a professional population with a large university crowd. Make sure to see the **Passage Pommeraye,** off pl. du Commerce, an unusual 19th-century shopping arcade—still full of unique boutiques—built on three levels around a monumental staircase. (Guided visits available at the tourist office.) Gothic vaults soar 38m in the remarkably bright **Cathédrale St-Pierre.** A complete restoration of the interior has undone the ravages of time, though it could not salvage the stained glass that shattered during WWII. Only one piece, the largest in France, remains 25m above the tomb of King François II. (Open daily 10am-7pm.) Reopened in 2005, the **Musée Jules Verne,** 3 r. de l'Hermitage, showcases beautiful first editions, paraphernalia from the author's life, and amazingly detailed sketches of his ideas. (Take bus #81, dir.: Indre, from pl. du Commerce to Salorges. Bear right at the fork; the museum is at the top of the hill on the left. Open M and W-Sa 10am-noon and 2-6pm, Su 2-6pm. €3, students €1.50.)

Some of the clean rooms at **Hôtel St-Daniel ❸,** 4 r. du Bouffay, off pl. du Bouffay, overlook a garden. (☎47 41 25; www.hotel-saintdaniel.com. Breakfast €3. Reception M-Sa 7:30am-10pm, Su 7:30am-2pm and 7-10pm. Singles and doubles with shower €32, with toilet €35, with both €40, with bath €45; triples and quads with shower and toilet €50. AmEx/MC/V.) The alleys off **place du Pilori** are full of eateries. The creperies behind **place du Bouffay** are also especially good. **La Cigale ❸,** 4 pl. Graslin, is one of the most beautiful bistros in France, filled with painted tiles, huge mirrors, and wall sculptures. The food deserves equal acclaim. (☎02 51 84 94 94; www.lacigale.com. *Plats* €12-19. *Menus* €17-27. Brunch daily 10am-4pm €20. Open daily 7:30am-12:30am. MC/V.) **Monoprix** supermarket, 2 r. de Calvaire, is off cours des 50 Otages. (Open M-Sa 9am-9pm.) **Quartier St-Croix,** near pl. du Bouffay, has countless bars and cafes. **Trains** leave from 27 bd. de Stalingrad for Bordeaux (4hr., 5 per day, €40), Paris (2-4hr., 1 per hr., €52-67), and Rennes (2hr., 1-8 per day, €20). The **tourist office** is at 3 cours Olivier de Clisson. (☎08 92 46 40 44; www.nantes-tourisme.com. Open M-Sa 10am-6pm.) **Postal Code:** 44038.

LOIRE VALLEY (VAL DE LOIRE)

The Loire, France's longest and most celebrated river, meanders toward the Atlantic through a valley containing the fertile soil of vineyards that produce some of France's best wines. It's hardly surprising that a string of French (and English) kings chose to station themselves in opulent châteaux by these waters rather than in the commotion of their capital cities.

TRANSPORTATION

Faced with such widespread grandeur, many travelers plan overly ambitious itineraries—two châteaux per day is a reasonable goal. The city of Tours is the region's best **rail** hub. However, train schedules are often inconvenient and many châteaux aren't accessible by train. **Biking** is the best way to explore the region. Many stations distribute the invaluable *Châteaux pour Train et Vélo* booklet with train schedules and bike and **car** rental information.

ORLÉANS

☎02 38

A gateway from Paris into the Loire, Orléans (pop. 117,000) cherishes its historical connection to Joan of Arc, who marched triumphantly down **rue de Bourgogne** in 1429 after liberating the city from a seven-month British siege. Most of Orléans's highlights are near **place Sainte-Croix.** With towering buttresses and stained-glass windows that depict Joan's story, the **Cathédrale Sainte-Croix,** pl. Ste-Croix, is Orléans's crown jewel. (Open daily July-Aug. 9:15am-7pm; Sept.-June reduced hours.) The **Musée de Beaux Arts,** 1 r. Ferdinand Rabier, has a collection of French, Italian, and Flemish works. (☎79 21 55; www.ville-orleans.fr. Open Tu-Sa 9:30am-12:15pm and 1:30-5:45pm, Su 2-6:30pm. €3, students €1.50, under 16 free; temporary exhibits €4/2.50.) One block from the train station, **Hôtel de L'Abeille ❹,** 64 r. Alsace-Lorraine, celebrated its 100th anniversary in 2003 and has been owned by the same family since 1919. Thirty-one luxurious rooms with antique furniture and fireplaces are worth the price for the amenities they offer. (☎53 54 87; www.hoteldelabeille.com. Breakfast €7, in bed €8. Singles with shower €42-52, with bath €59; doubles €45-58/73; triples €59/73; quads with bath €76. AmEx/MC/V.) Rue de Bourgogne and **rue Sainte-Catherine** have a variety of cheap eateries and a loud bar scene at night. At **Mijana ❸**, 175 r. de Bourgogne, a charming Lebanese couple prepares gourmet cuisine, including vegetarian options, with pride. (☎62 02 02; www.mijanaresto.com. Sandwiches €4-6. Falafels €7. Lunch *menus* €14-26. *Plats* from €12. Open M-Sa noon-1:30pm and 7-10pm. AmEx/MC/V.) Find groceries at **Carrefour,** in the mall at pl. d'Arc. (Open M-Sa 8:30am-9pm. AmEx/MC/V.)

Trains from the Gare d'Orléans on pl. Albert I for Blois (30min., 15 per day, €9), Paris (1¼hr., 2-4 per hr., €17), and Tours (1½hr., 2 per hr., €16). To reach the **tourist office,** 2 pl. de l'Étape, exit the train station onto r. de la République and continue straight until pl. du Martroi. Turn left onto r. d'Escures to pl. de l'Étape. (☎24 05 05; www.tourisme-orleans.com. Open May-Sept. Tu-Sa 9am-1pm and 2-7pm; Oct.-Apr. reduced hours.) **Postal Code:** 45000.

BLOIS ☎02 54

Awash in a rich regal history, Blois (pop. 50,000) is one of the Loire's most charming and popular cities. Once home to monarchs Louis XII and François I, Blois's gold-trimmed **château** was the Versailles of the late 15th and early 16th centuries. Housed within are impressive collections and excellent museums. Royal apartments showcase extravagant and elegant pieces, the **Musée des Beaux-Arts** features a gallery of 16th- to 19th-century portraits, and the **Musée Lapidaire** exhibits sculpted pieces from nearby châteaux. (☎90 33 33. Open daily Apr.-Sept. 9am-6:30pm; Jan.-Mar. and Oct.-Dec. 9am-12:30pm and 2-5:30pm. €6.50, students under 25 €5.) The most enjoyable attractions in Blois might be its hilly streets and ancient staircases. Bars and bakeries on r. St-Lubin and r. des Trois Marchands tempt those en route to the 12th-century **Abbaye St-Laumer,** now the **Église St-Nicolas.** (Open daily 9am-6:30pm. Sunday Mass 9:30am.) The winding streets east of r. Denis Papin are especially beautiful. Five hundred years of expansions to **Cathédrale St-Louis,** one of Blois's architectural jewels, endowed it with a beautiful mix of styles. (Open daily 7:30am-6pm; crypt open June-Aug.) A spectacular view from the **Jardin de l'Evêché,** behind the cathedral, spans past the rooftops and winding alleys of the old quarter, stretching along the brilliant Loire. At sunset, cross the Loire and turn right onto quai Villebois Mareuil to see the château rising above the roofs of the town. **Hôtel du Bellay ❷,** 12 r. des Minimes, is at the top of porte Chartraine, 2min. above the city center. It offers comfortable rooms with colorful decor. (☎78 23 62; http://hoteldubellay.free.fr. Breakfast €5. Singles and doubles with sink €24-26, with toilet €27, with shower €28, with bath €37; triples €54; quads €62. MC/V.) Fragrant *pâtisseries* entice visitors on **rue Denis Papin,** while **rue. St-Lubin, place Poids du Roi,** and **place de la Résistance** have more dining options. An **Intermarché** supermarket is at 16 av. Gambetta. (Open M-Sa 9am-7pm.) At night, Blois lights up. Move from the cafes of pl. de la Résistance to the hip combination *discothèque* and lounge bar, **Z 64,** 6 r. Mal. de Tassigny. (☎74 27 76. Mixed drinks €5-8. Min. consumption €6. Open Sept.-July Th-Sa 10pm-5am.)

Trains leave pl. de la Gare for Orléans (30-50min., 14 per day, €9), Paris (1¾hr., 8 per day, €23), and Tours (1hr., 8-13 per day, €8.75). Transports Loir-et-Cher (TLC; ☎58 55 44; www.TLCinfo.net) sends **buses** from the station to nearby châteaux (45min.; May 15-Sept. 2 per day; €11, students €8.60). Or, rent a **bike** from Bike in Blois, 8 r. Henri Drussy near pl. de la Résistance. (☎56 07 73; www.locationdevelos.com. 1st day €13, tandem €38; discount thereafter. Open M-Sa 9:15am-12:30pm and 2-6:30pm, Su 10am-1pm and 4-6:30pm. Cash only.) The **tourist office** is in pl. du Château. (☎90 41 41; www.loiredeschateaux.com. Open Apr.-Sept. M-Sa 9am-7pm, Su 10am-7pm; Oct.-Mar. reduced hours.) **Postal Code:** 41000.

CHAMBORD AND CHEVERNY ☎02 54

Built between 1519 and 1545 to satisfy François I's egomania, Chambord is the largest and most extravagant of the Loire châteaux. With 440 rooms, 365 chimneys, and 83 staircases, the castle could accommodate the entire royal court—up to 10,000 people. To cement his claim, François stamped 200 of his trademark stone salamanders throughout this "hunting lodge," which also boasts a spectacular double-helix staircase designed by Leonardo da Vinci. (☎50 40 00. Open daily Apr.-Sept. 9am-6:15pm; Oct.-Mar. reduced hours. €9.50, ages 18-25 €6, under 18 free.) Take the TLC **bus** from Blois (45min.; 32 per day; €11, students €8.60) or **bike** south from Blois on D956 for 2-3km, and then turn left on D33 (1hr.).

Cheverny has been privately owned since 1634 by the Hurault family, whose members have served as financiers and officers to the kings of France. The château's magnificent furnishings include elegant tapestries and delicate Delft vases. Fans of Hergé's *Tintin* books may recognize Cheverny's Renaissance facade as the inspiration for Marlinspike, Captain Haddock's mansion. The **kennels** hold nearly 90 mixed English-Poitevin hounds who stalk stags on hunting expeditions. (☎79 96 29. Open daily July-Aug. 9:15am-6:45pm; Apr.-June and Sept. 9:15am-6:15pm; Oct.-Mar. reduced hours. €6.50, students €4.50.) Cheverny is 45min. south of Blois by bike and is on the TLC bus route. Travelers to Chambord or Cheverny should plan to stay in **Blois.**

AMBOISE ☎02 47

Amboise (pop. 12,000) is guarded by the parapets of the 15th-century château that six cautious French kings called home. In the **Logis du Roi,** intricate 16th-century Gothic chairs stand over 2m tall to prevent attacks from behind. The jewel of the grounds is the **Chapelle St-Hubert,** the final resting place of **Leonardo da Vinci.** (☎57 00 98. Open daily July-Aug. 9am-6:30pm; Sept.-June reduced hours. €8, students €6.80.) Four hundred meters farther is **Clos Lucé,** where da Vinci spent his last three years. The manor's main attraction is a collection of 40 machines realized from da Vinci's visionary designs and built with the materials of his time. (☎57 62 88. Open daily July-Aug. 9am-8pm; Apr.-June and Sept.-Oct. 9am-7pm; Nov.-Dec. 9am-6pm; Jan. 10am-5pm. €12, students €9.50. Low season €9/7.) The **Centre International de Séjour Charles Péguy (HI) ❶,** on Île d'Or, sits on an island in the Loire. Follow r. Jules Ferry from the station, cross the first bridge on your left, and head downhill to the right immediately after the bridge. (☎30 60 90; www.ucrif.asso.fr. Breakfast €3. Linens €3.40. Reception M-F 10-noon and 2-8pm. Dorms €11. Cash only.) Try the local favorite **Chez Hippeau ❸,** 1 r. François 1er, for delicious regional treats in an unbeatable location between the château and the Loire. The owner will be happy to guide you through the menu options. (☎57 26 30. *Menu* €10-28. Salads €6-14. Open daily noon-3pm and 7-10:30pm. MC/V.) **Trains** leave 1 r. Jules-Ferry for: Blois (20min., 14 per day, €5.60); Orléans (1hr., 8 per day, €27); Paris (2¼hr., 5 per day, €25); Tours (20min., 27 per day, €4.80). To reach the **tourist office,** take a left from the station and follow r. Jules-Ferry, crossing the first bridge to your left and passing the residential Île d'Or. After crossing the second bridge, turn right immediately; the office is 30m down in a circular building on quai du Général de Gaulle. (☎57 09 28; www.amboise-valdeloire.com. Open July-Aug. M-Sa 9am-8pm, Su 10am-6pm; Sept.-June reduced hours.) **Postal Code:** 35400.

TOURS ☎02 47

Home to 30,000 students, abundant restaurants, and a booming nightlife, Balzac's birthplace is a comfortable base for château-hopping. The **Cathédrale St-Gatien,** r. Jules Simon, first erected in the 4th century, combines solid Romanesque columns, delicate Gothic carvings, two Renaissance spires, and an intricate facade. (Cathedral open daily 9am-7pm. Cloister open Easter-Sept. daily 9:30am-12:30pm and 2-6pm; Oct.-Easter W-Su 9:30am-12:30pm and 2-5pm. Cathedral free. Cloister €2.50.) Jutting up from modern commercial streets, the imposing **Tours du Basilique St-Martin,** on r. Descartes, include the **Tour de l'Horloge** and **Tour de Charlemagne,** which can only be viewed from the outside. The **Nouvelle Basilique St-Martin** is an ornate church designed by Victor Laloux, architect of the Tours railway station and of the Musée d'Orsay in Paris. (Open Apr.-Nov. Su-M 8am-7pm, Tu-Sa 7:40am-9pm; Dec.-Mar. Su-M 8am-7pm, Tu-Sa 7:40am-7pm. Mass daily 11am.) The **Musée du Gemmail,** 7 r. du Murier, showcases colored glass mosaics unique to Tours. (Open Mar.-Oct. Tu-Su 2-6:30pm. €5.40, students €4, ages 13-18 €3.10, under 12 €2.)

Hôtel Foch ❸, 20 r. du Maréchal Foch, is a warm hotel with spacious rooms, pleasant decor, and clean baths. (☎05 70 59; hotel-foch.tours@wanadoo.fr. All but 1 room with shower. Breakfast €5. Parking €5. Reserve ahead in high season. Singles €20-34; doubles €23-46; triples €37-58; quads €51-58. MC/V.) Try **place Plumereau** and **rue Colbert** for great restaurants, cafes, and bars. Cheese-lovers converge for the delicious selection at **La Souris Gourmande ❷,** 100 r. Colbert, where the food is almost overshadowed by the bovine-obsessed decor. (☎47 04 80. Fondue €12-14. Crepes and omelets €7-8. Open Tu-Sa noon-2pm and 7-10:30pm. AmEx/MC/V.) At night, the elegant **place Plumereau** is the place to be. The prime location and quirky decor at **Au Temps des Rois,** 3 pl. Plumereau, make this bar a long-time popular spot. (☎05 04 51. Beer €2.50-3. Open daily 9am-2am. MC/V.) **Trains** leave pl. du Général Leclerc for Bordeaux (2½hr., 9 per day, €41) and Paris (2¼hr., 14 per day, €37; TGV 1hr., 28 per day, €49). To reach the **tourist office,** 78-82 r. Bernard Palissy, from the station, walk through pl. du Général Leclerc, cross bd. Heurteloup, and veer to the right. (☎70 37 37; www.ligeris.com. Open mid-Apr. to mid-Oct. M-Sa 8:30am-7pm, Su 10am-12:30pm and 2:30-5pm; mid-Oct. to mid-Apr. M-Sa 9am-12:30pm and 1:30-6pm, Su 10am-1pm.) **Postal Code:** 37000.

CHENONCEAU AND LOCHES ☎02 47

Chenonceau, sometimes called the *château des dames* (castle of the ladies), owes its beauty to the series of women who designed it: first a 16th-century tax collector's wife; then Henri II's lover, Diane de Poitiers; and finally Henri's widowed wife, Catherine de Médici. The part of the château bridging the Cher River marked the border between occupied and Vichy France during WWII. (☎23 90 07. Open daily mid-Mar. to mid-Sept. 9am-7pm; low season reduced hours. €9, students €7.50.) **Trains** from Tours roll into the station in front of the castle (30min., 8 per day, €5.70). Fil Vert **buses** also run from Amboise (25min., M-Sa 2 per day, €1.30) and Tours (1¼hr., M-Sa 2 per day, €2.30).

The château of Loches is surrounded by a walled medieval town that merits a visit in itself. The oldest structures are the 11th-century keep and watchtowers to the north, converted into a state prison under Louis XI. The three-story **tower,** whose floors have fallen out, offers fantastic panoramic views of the village below. The extravagant **Logis Royal** (Royal Lodge) honors the famous ladies who held court here, including Charles VII's lover Agnès Sorel, the first officially-declared Mistress of the King of France. (☎59 01 32. Open daily Apr.-Sept. 9am-7pm; Oct.-Mar. 9:30am-5pm. Dungeon or Logis Royal €5, students €3.50.) **Trains** run from Tours to Loches (1hr.; M-F 2 per day, Sa-Su 1 per day). **Buses** also go to Loches (M-F 11 per day, Sa 9 per day, Su 5 per day; €7.50). Plan to find accommodations in **Tours.**

ANGERS ☎02 41

Angers (pop. 151,000) has grown into a sophisticated city, building on its illustrious aristocratic origins. From behind the stone walls of the **Château d'Angers,** pl.

FRANCE

Kennedy, the medieval Dukes of Anjou ruled the surrounding area, including the Anglo-Saxon island across the Channel. Inside the château is the 14th-century **Tapisserie de l'Apocalypse,** the world's largest tapestry. (Open daily May-Aug. 9:30am-6:30pm; Sept.-Apr. 10am-5:30pm. €7.50, students €4.80.) Maker of the famous liqueur since 1849, the **Musée Cointreau** offers tours of the factory and free tastings. Take bus #7 from the train station to Cointreau. (Open daily July-Aug. 10:30am-6:30pm; low season reduced hours. €5.50.) **Royal Hôtel ❸,** 8bis pl. de la Visitation, offers spacious rooms with double beds, big windows, and cable TV. (☎88 30 25; fax 81 05 75. Breakfast €5. Free Internet in lobby. Reception 6:45am-midnight, reduced hours Sa-Su. Singles €28-40; doubles €30, with private shower or bath €50; triples €52; quads €62. AmEx/DC/MC/V.) Cheap food is abundant along **rue St-Laud** and **rue St-Aubin.** Grab groceries in **Galeries Lafayette,** at r. d'Alsace and pl. du Ralliement. (Open M-Sa 9am-8pm.)

From r. de la Gare, **trains** leave for Paris (1-2hr., 15 per day, €42-58) and Tours (1hr., 10 per day, €15-18). **Buses** run from the Esplanade de la Gare, in front of the train station, to Rennes (3hr., 2 per day, €14). To get from the station to the **tourist office,** pl. Kennedy, exit straight onto r. de la Gare, turn right at pl. de la Visitation on r. Targot, and turn left on bd. du Roi-René; the office sits on the right, across from the château. (☎23 50 00; www.angers-tourisme.com. Open May-Sept. M-Sa 9am-7pm, Su 10am-6pm; low season reduced hours.) **Postal Code:** 49052.

PÉRIGORD AND AQUITAINE

Périgord's green countryside is splashed with yellow sunflowers, white chalk cliffs, and plates of black truffles. First settled 150,000 years ago, the area around Les Eyzies-de-Tayac has seen the excavation of more Stone-Age artifacts than anywhere else on earth, and the prehistoric painted caves of Lascaux are the most extensive in the world. Farther south, Aquitaine grows its grapes in the world-famous vineyards of the Médoc that surround Bordeaux.

PÉRIGUEUX ☎05 53

Rich with tradition and gourmet cuisine, the lovely old quarters of Périgueux (pop. 65,000) preserve architecture from medieval and Gallo-Roman times. The towering steeple and five massive Byzantine cupolas of the **Cathédrale St-Front** dominate the city from above the Isle River. Fifteen-hundred years of rebuilding and restoration have produced the largest cathedral in southwestern France. (Open daily 8am-7pm.) Just down r. St-Front, the **Musée du Périgord,** 22 cours Tourny, houses one of France's most important collections of prehistoric artifacts, including a set of 2m mammoth tusks. (☎06 40 70. Open Apr.-Sept. M and W-F 10:30am-5:30pm, Sa-Su 1-6pm; Oct.-Mar. M and W-F 10am-5pm. €4, students €2.) The **Musée Gallo-Romain,** r. Claude Bertrand, has an intricate walkway over the excavated ruins of the Domus de Vésone, once the home of a wealthy Roman merchant. (☎05 65 65. Open July-Sept. daily 10am-7pm; Apr.-June daily 10am-12:30pm and 2-6pm; mid-Nov. to Dec. and Feb.-Mar. Tu-Sa 10am-12:30pm and 2-5:30pm. Closed Jan. €5.50. Tours in French July-Aug. €1. English-language audio tour €1.) Across from the train station, the owners of the welcoming **Les Charentes ❷,** 16 r. Denis Papin, offer clean rooms and plenty of information about the region. (☎53 37 13. Breakfast €5. Reception 7am-10pm. Closed late Dec. to early Jan. Reserve ahead in summer. Singles with shower €23, with TV €28, with toilet €33; doubles €28/33/38. Extra person €5. AmEx/MC/V.) The more affordable **Foyer des Jeunes Travailleurs Residence Lakanal (HI) ❶,** r. des Thermes, offers small four-bunk dorms, a busy TV room, cafeteria, and bar. (☎06 81 40. Reception closed M-F noon-1:30pm and 6-8:30pm, Sa-Su closed 2:30-6:30pm. Dorms with linens and breakfast €12.20, with dinner €19.10. MC/V; min. €15.) **Au Bien Bon ❷**, 15 r. de l'Aubergerie, serves *magret* (duck steak; €14) and other regional specialties. (☎09 69 91. *Plats* €9-14. Lunch *menus* €10-14. Open M noon-2pm, Tu-F noon-2pm and 7:30-9:30pm, Sa 7:30-9:30pm.) **Monoprix** supermarket is on pl. Bugeaud. (Open M-Sa 8:30am-8pm.) Trains leave r. Denis Papin for: Bordeaux (1½hr., 12 per day, €17.70); Lyon (6-8hr., 1 per day, €50.60); Paris (4-6hr., 12 per day, €45.90); Toulouse (4hr., 8 per day, €37). The **tourist office** is on 26 pl. Francheville. From the station, turn right on r. Denis Papin, bear left on r. des Mobiles-de-Coulmierts, which becomes r. du Président Wilson, and take the next right after the Monoprix; the tourist office will be on your left. (☎53 10 63; www.ville-perigueux.fr. Open June-Sept. M-Sa 9am-6pm, Su 10am-1pm and 2-6pm; Oct.-May M-Sa 9am-1pm and 2-6pm.) **Postal Code:** 24000.

SARLAT ☎05 53

The medieval *vieille ville* of Sarlat (pop. 11,000) is the best base for exploring the **Caves of Lascaux** and the **Dordogne Valley,** but it also merits attention for its medieval *centre ville*. Sarlat's accommodations have become expensive since the town's only hostel closed; the best option is to book a room at one of the nearby *chambres d'hôtes* (rooms €25-50; the tourist office has a complete list). For the true deal, the campground **Maisonneuve ❶**, 11km from Sarlat and down the river from Castelnaud on the D57, offers a cafe, minigolf, ping-pong, a riverside swimming hole, a three-bedroom *gîte*, and a base for exploring Castelnaud, Domme, La Roque Gageac, and the Dordogne Valley. (☎29 51 29; www.camping-maisonneuve.com. Cafe open 8am-11pm. Electricity €3.50. Reception 9am-10pm. Reserve ahead July-Aug. Open Mar.-Oct. €5-7 per tent site; €5-7 per extra person; *gîte* €10.) A **Champion** supermarket sells lots of cheap alcohol (beer from €0.50) and is a 15min. walk from the *vielle ville* on av. de Selves. (Open M-Sa 9am-7:30pm. MC/V.) **Chez le Gaulois ❷**, 1 r. Tourny, near the tourist office, provides excellent and meaty meals in a friendly atmosphere. (☎59 50 64. *Plats* €9.50-11. Open July-Aug. daily noon-2:30pm; Sept.-Oct. and Dec.-June Tu-Sa noon-2:30pm and 7-10pm. V.) **Trains** go from av. de la Gare to Bordeaux (2½hr., 3-5 per day, €21) and Périgueux (3hr., 3 per day, €13). **Buses** run from pl. Pasteur to Périgueux (1½hr., 1 per day, €9). To reach the **tourist office,** off r. Tourny in the *centre ville*, turn left out of the train station onto av. de la Gare and take a right at the bottom of the hill onto av. Thiers, which becomes av. Général Leclerc, then r. de la

YOUR DAILY BREAD

Bread is one of those Frenc icons that, like the sidewalk cafe is as present on the its streets a in the imagination. Though the average Parisian consumes onl around 160g of bread per day down from around 1kg in 1900, i is still eaten with almost ever meal, and is as much of a Frencl cultural icon as the Eiffel Tower.

But with 1300 *boulangeries* i Paris alone, how do you separat the wheat from the chaff? Star with the definition. According t the craft, a baguette must weig 250-300g, measuring abou 70cm in length and 6cm in diam eter. The crust must be smoot and golden, ready to crackl under moderate finger-pressur (ask for it *"bien cuit"*). The under side, or "sole," should never b charred; beware a honeycom imprint, which indicates acceler ated cooking in a rotating oven- the taste will be cut short. Th inside *(mie)* should be light, wit large air holes. The bread shoul have a full, salty taste and a sub tly doughy texture.

Each February, Paris's city hal holds a cut-throat competition the Grand Prix de la Baguette. Th winner becomes the officia baguette of the Elysée Palace fo the next year. Current residen Jacques Chirac takes his brea seriously: he has dismisse supermarket baguettes as "no even a Christian food."

République. Bear right on r. Lakanal; the office is on the left. (☎31 45 42; www.ot-sarlat-perigord.fr. Open July-Aug. M-Sa 9am-7pm, Su 10am-noon and 2-6pm; Sept.-Oct. and Apr.-May M-Sa 9am-noon and 2-7pm, Su 10am-noon and 2-6pm; Nov.-Mar. M-Sa 9am-noon and 2-6pm.) **Postal Code:** 24200.

CAVES OF THE VÉZÈRES VALLEY ☎05 53

The most spectacular cave paintings ever found line the **Caves of Lascaux,** "the Sistine Chapel of prehistory," near the town of **Montignac,** 25km north of Sarlat. Discovered in 1940 by teenagers, the caves were closed to the public in 1963—the breath of millions of visitors had fostered algae and micro-stalactites that ravaged the paintings. **Lascaux II** replicates the original cave in the same pigments used 17,000 years ago. Although they may lack ancient mystery, the new caves—filled with 5m paintings of bulls, horses, and bison—still manage to inspire. The ticket office (☎51 96 23) shares a building with Montignac's **tourist office** (☎51 82 60), on pl. Bertrand-de-Born. (Ticket office open 9am until sold out. Reserve tickets 1 week ahead. €8.) The **train** station is at Le Lardin, 10km away; you can then call a **taxi** (☎50 86 61). During the academic year, CFTA (☎05 55 86 07 07) runs **buses** from Périgueux and Sarlat. Numerous **campgrounds** dot the Vézères Valley near Montignac; the tourist office has a complete list. At the **Grotte de Font-de-Gaume,** 1km east of **Les Eyzies-de-Tayac** on D47, 15,000-year-old friezes are still open for viewing. (☎06 86 00; www.leseyzies.com/grottes-ornees. Open mid-May to mid-Sept. M-F and Su 9:30am-5:30pm; mid-Sept. to mid-May daily 9:30am-12:30pm and 2-5:30pm. English-language tours 1hr. Reserve 2-4 weeks in advance. €6.10, ages 18-25 €4.10.) From Les Eyzies, **trains** go to Paris (6-8hr., 3 per day, €49), Périgueux (30min., 5 per day, €6.30), and Sarlat (1hr., 3 per day, €7.50). Rooms tend to be expensive—consider staying in **Périgueux.** Pleasant and well-located **Chambre d'Hôte ❷,** rte. de Sarlat, is 3min. outside of Les Eyzies From the train station, follow signs to Sarlat; the house is past the laundromat on the right. (☎06 91 43. Breakfast €5. Singles and doubles €25-36; triples and quads €48.)

FRANCE

BORDEAUX ☎05 56

Though its name is synonymous with wine, the city of Bordeaux (pop. 215,000) holds more than the intoxicating drink. In the city center, punk rockers, tourists, and everyone in between gather to relax in the streets. Filled with history, high culture, and urban nightlife, Bordeaux holds more than most tourists expect.

TRANSPORTATION AND PRACTICAL INFORMATION. Trains leave Gare St-Jean, r. Charles Domercq, for: Lyon (8-10hr., 1 per day, €57); Marseille (5-6hr., 5 per day, €62); Nice (9-10hr., 2 per day, €75); Paris (3hr., 15-25 per day, €61); Toulouse (2-3hr., 11 per day, €28.40). From the train station, take tramway line B to pl. Gambetta (€1.30) and walk toward the Monument aux Girondins to reach the **tourist office,** 12 cours du 30 juillet. (☎00 66 00; www.bordeaux-tourisme.com. Open July-Aug. M-Sa 9am-7:30pm, Su 9:30am-6:30pm; May-June and Sept.-Oct. M-Sa 9am-7pm, Su 9:30am-6:30pm; Nov.-Apr. M-Sa 9am-6:30pm, Su 9:45am-4:30pm.) **Postal Code:** 33000.

ACCOMMODATIONS AND FOOD. A favorite among backpackers, **Hôtel Studio ❷,** 26 r. Huguerie, has clean, newly remodeled rooms with phone, bathroom, and TV. (☎48 00 14; www.hotel-bordeaux.com. Breakfast €4. Reserve ahead. Singles €18-27; doubles €27-32. AmEx/MC/V.) Run by the same family, **Hôtel de la Boétie ❷,** 4 r. de la Boétie, offers similar amenities. Check in around the corner at Hôtel Bristol, 4 r. Bouffard. (☎81 76 68; fax 81 24 72. Breakfast €5. Singles and doubles €23-27; triples €39. AmEx/MC/V.)

The Bordelais possess a flair for food that rivals their vineyard expertise. Hunt around **rue St-Remi** and **place St-Pierre** for regional specialties: oysters, *foie gras*, and beef braised in wine sauce. Busy **L'Ombrière ❷**, 13 pl. du Parlement, serves country-style cuisine in one of Bordeaux's most beautiful squares. (Meal-sized salads €14. *Menu* €12 or €19. Open daily 11:45am-2pm and 7:30-10:45pm. MC/V.) Delicious dessert crepes (€3-8) at **La Crêperie ❶**, 20 r. Georges Bonnac, take the French staple to a whole new level. (☎51 02 33. *Galettes* €5-10. Salads €2-7. Open daily noon-midnight. MC/V.) **Cassolette Café ❷**, 20 pl. de la Victoire, cultivates its amicable atmosphere with unique style, offering *tartiflette* (€2.50-7) among over 30 staples. (☎92 94 96; www.cassolettecafe.com. *Menu* €10-12. Open daily noon-midnight. MC/V.) **Auchan** supermarket is at the Centre Meriadeck on r. Claude Bonnier. (Open M-Sa 8:30am-10pm.)

SIGHTS AND ENTERTAINMENT. Nearly nine centuries after its consecration, the **Cathédrale St-André,** in pl. Pey-Berland, sits at the heart of Gothic Bordeaux. Its bell tower, the **Tour Pey-Berland,** rises 50m into the sky. (Cathedral open M 2-7pm, Tu-F 7:30am-6pm, Sa 9am-7pm, Su 9am-6pm. Tower open June-Sept. daily 10am-12:45pm and 2-6pm; Oct.-May Tu-Su 10am-12:30pm and 2-5:30pm. €5, ages 18-25 and seniors €3.50, under 18 free.) Nearby, the **Musée des Beaux Arts,** 20 cours d'Albret, contains works by masters such as Caravaggio, Matisse, and Picasso. The permanent collection is held in the two buildings that frame the Hôtel de Ville; the temporary exhibits are across the street. (Open M and W-Su 11am-6pm. Permanent collection free. Temporary collection €5, students €2.50. EU students, under 18, and 1st Su of every month free.) For the best cityscape of Bordeaux, look down from the 114m tower of the **Église St-Michel.** Although students, immigrants, and bohemian types mingle in the local markets and cafes surrounding the church, travelers may feel uncomfortable visiting this area alone or at night. (Tower open June-Sept. daily 2-7pm. €2.50, under 12 free.) On pl. de Quinconces, the elaborate **Monument aux Girondins** commemorates Revolutionary leaders from towns bordering the Gironde who were guillotined in 1797. Bordeaux's opera house, the **Grand Théâtre,** conceals a breathtakingly intricate interior behind an austere Neoclassical facade, and houses operas, concerts, and plays. (☎00 85 95; www.opera-bordeaux.com. Open for tours M-Sa 11am-6pm. Concerts €8. Operas up to €70. 50% discount for students and ages 25 and under.)

Check out the free *Clubs and Concerts* brochure at the tourist office. Students and visitors pack the bars in year-round hot spots **Place de la Victoire** and **Place Gambetta. St-Michel,** where locals gather at cafe tables from 6pm until midnight, has a more mellow atmosphere. **El Bodegon,** on pl. de la Victoire, draws students with theme nights and weekend giveaways. (Beer €2.50. Open M-Sa 7am-2am, Su 2pm-2am.) Covered in lights and mirrors, the gay bar **BHV,** 4 r. de l'Hôtel de Ville, is almost always full. (Beer €3.50. W theme night. Open daily 6pm-2am.)

THE PAYS BASQUE AND GASCONY

While the Gascons have long considered themselves French, the Basques still struggle to maintain their identity; some separatists see themselves as an independent people rather than a part of France or Spain. Today, people come to Gascony to be healed: millions of believers descend on Lourdes in search of miracles, while thousands undergo natural treatments in the hot springs of the Pyrenees.

BAYONNE ☎05 59

The pace of life in Bayonne (pop. 42,000) has not changed for centuries. Locals rise early to set up lively markets on the banks of the Nive and shop in the *vieille ville.* In the afternoon, they retreat indoors behind exposed wooden beams and colorful shutters. The **Musée Bonnat,** 5 r. Jacques Laffitte, showcases works by Bayonnais painter Léon Bonnat alongside others by Degas, van Dyck, Goya, Rembrandt, and Reubens. (Open May-Oct. M and W-Su 10am-6:30pm; July-Aug. M and Th-Su 10am-6:30pm, W 10am-9:30pm; Nov.-Apr. daily 10am-12:30pm and 2-6pm. €5.50, students €3.) Starting the first Wednesday in August, locals let loose for five days during the **Fêtes Traditionnelles** (www.fetes-de-bayonne.com).

The **Hôtel Paris-Madrid ❷**, pl. de la Gare, has large rooms and knowledgeable, English-speaking proprietors. (☎55 13 98. Breakfast €4. Reception Sept.-June 6:30am-1am; July-Aug. 24hr. Singles €18, with toilet €27, with shower and toilet €33-48; doubles €24/27/33-48; triples and quads with bath €42-48. MC/V.) A **Monoprix** supermarket is at 8 r. Orbe. (Open M-Sa 8:30am-7:30pm.) **Trains** depart from pl. de la Gare for: Biarritz (20min., 18 per day, €3.90); Bordeaux (2hr., 12 per day, €25.70); Paris (5hr., 8 TGV per day, €77.20); San Sebastian, SPA via Hendaye (30min., 15 per day, €7.80); Toulouse (4hr., 5 per day, €35.50). Local STAB **buses** (☎59 04 61) depart from the Hôtel de Ville for Biarritz (buses #1, 2, and 6 run M-Sa 6:30am-8pm, Su 6:30am-7pm. €1.20). From the train station, take the middle fork onto pl. de la République, veer right over pont St-Esprit, pass through pl. Réduit, cross pont Mayou, and turn right on r. Bernède, which becomes av. Bonnat. The **tourist office,** pl. des Basques, is on the left. (☎46 01 46; www.bayonne-tourisme.com. Open July-Aug. M-Sa 9am-7pm, Su 10am-1pm; Sept.-June M-F 9am-6:30pm, Sa 10am-6pm.) **Postal Code:** 64100.

LOURDES ☎05 62

In 1858, 14-year-old Bernadette Soubirous saw the first of 18 visions of the Virgin Mary in the **Grotte de Massabielle** in Lourdes (pop. 16, 300). Today, five million people make the pilgrimage each year. Follow av. de la Gare, turn left on bd. de la Grotte, and follow it to the right and across the River Gave to reach the Grotte de Massabielle. There, visitors whisper prayers, receive blessings, and carry home water from the spring where Bernadette washed her face. (No shorts or tank tops. Open 24hr., Grotto open for touching daily 11:15am-3:30pm.) The **Rosaire Basilica** and the **Upper Basilica** were built double-decker style above the grotto. The **Basilique St-Pius X,** a huge concrete echo chamber designed to resemble an overturned ship, is hidden underground. (Basilicas open daily Easter-Oct. 6am-7pm; Nov.-Easter 8am-6pm.) **Processions** depart from the grotto at 5pm.

Hôtel Lutétia ❷, 19 av. de la Gare, is in an Art-Nouveau building to the right of the train station. Upon mention, the owner gives reduced rates to students. Rooms fill quickly in the summer, so reserve ahead. (☎94 22 85; info@lutetialourdes.com. Elevator and free parking. Singles €17.50, with toilet €24.50, with shower €31.50, students €28.50, with bath €40; doubles €24.50-64, depending on room type and season. MC/V.) The cheapest eateries are near the tourist office and on bd. de la Grotte. Stock up at the **market** at Les Halles, pl. du Champ Commun. (Open June-Sept. daily 8am-1pm and 4-7pm; Oct.-May M-Sa 9am-1pm and 4-7pm, Su 8am-1pm.) **Trains** leave 33 av. de la Gare for: Bayonne (2hr., 5 per day, €18.40); Bordeaux (3hr., 7 per day, €29.50); Paris (7-9hr., 5 TGV per day, €88.40); Toulouse (2½hr., 8 per day, €21.50). To reach the **tourist office,** pl. Peyramale, turn right onto av. de la Gare, bear left onto av. Maransin, cross the bridge above bd. du Lapacca, and continue straight. (☎42 77 40; www.lourdes-infotourisme.com. Open May-Oct. M-Sa 9am-7pm, Su 10am-6pm; early to mid-Nov. and mid-Mar. to Apr. M-Sa 9am-noon and 2-7pm; mid-Nov. to mid-Mar. 9am-noon and 2-6pm.) **Postal Code:** 65100.

THE PYRENEES ☎05 62

The **Parc National des Pyrénées Occidentales** shelters hundreds of endangered species in its snow-capped mountains and lush valleys. Touch base with the friendly **Parc National Office,** Maison du Parc, pl. de la Gare, in Cauterets, before braving the wilderness. The staff has maps (€7-9) and info on the park, the 14 **hiking** trails that begin and end in Cauterets, and various **ski** paths. (☎92 52 56; www.parc-pyrenees.com. Open June to mid-Sept. daily 9:30am-noon and 3-7pm; mid-Sept. to May M-Tu and F-Sa 9:30am-noon and 3-6pm, Th 3-6pm.) The park's trails are appropriate for a wide range of skill levels. From Cauterets, the **GR10,** which intersects most other hikes in the area, winds through Luz-St-Saveur, over the mountain, and then on to Gavarnie, another day's trek up the valley (a.k.a. **circuit de Gavarnie**). One of the most spectacular trails follows the GR10 to the turquoise **Lac de Gaube** and then to the end of the glacial valley (2hr. past the *lac*), where you can spend the night at the **Refuge des Oulettes ❶.** (☎92 62 97. Open June-Sept. Reserve 2 days ahead. Dorms €16.) Other *gîtes* (shelters) in the park, usually located in towns along the GR10, cost about €11 per night.

CAUTERETS ☎05 62

Nestled in a narrow valley on the edge of the **Parc National des Pyrénées Occidentales** is tiny, sleepy Cauterets (pop. 1300). Cauterets's sulfuric hot springs (*thermes*) have long been instruments of healing; for more info, contact **Thermes de César,** av. du Docteur Domer. (☎92 51 60. Open June-Sept. M-Sa 5-8pm; Sept.-June M-Sa 4-8pm and some Su.) Today, most visitors come to ski and hike. **Hotel le Chantilly ❸,** 10 r. de la Raillère, just one street away from the center of town, is owned by a charming Irish couple. (☎92 52 77. Closed Oct. to mid-Dec. Reception 7:30am-10:30pm. Breakfast €6. Singles and doubles €30, with shower €35; triples from €38. Prices higher July-Sept. MC/V.) **Buses** run from pl. de la Gare to Lourdes (1hr., 8 per day, €6.20). Rent **bikes** at Le Grenier, 4 av. du Mamelon Vert. (☎92 55 71. Full day €22-53, half-day €16-39. 8:30am-12:30pm and 3-7:30pm.) The **tourist office** is in pl. Foch. (☎92 50 50; www.cauterets.com. Open July-Aug. M-Sa 9am-12:30pm and 2-7pm, Su 9am-12:30pm and 3-6pm; Sept.-June reduced hours.) **Postal Code:** 55110.

LANGUEDOC-ROUSSILLON

Occitania was once a region independent of both France and Spain, stretching from the Rhône Valley to the foothills of the Pyrenees. When it was eventually integrated into France, its Cathar religion was persecuted and its language, *langue d'oc*, faded. Regional pride was never lost, and Languedoc's citizens today display it with impromptu street performances, festivals, and protests calling for national attention. Roussillon, in the far southwest corner of France, was historically part of Cataluña and today its locals still identify more with Barcelona than with Paris. Architecture, food, and nightlife all bear the marks of Spanish neighbors.

FRANCE

TOULOUSE ☎05 61

Vibrant and zany Toulouse (pop. 390,000) is known as *la ville en rose* (the pink city); it's the place to visit when all French towns begin to look alike. An abundance of museums and concert halls makes France's fourth largest city the Southwest's cultural capital. Family-owned art galleries, independent theaters, and a diverse music scene continue the city's free-thinking tradition.

TRANSPORTATION AND PRACTICAL INFORMATION. **Trains** leave Gare Matabiau, 64 bd. Pierre Sémard, for: Bordeaux (2-3hr., 14 per day, €28); Lyon (6½hr., 3-4 per day, €60); Marseille (4½hr., 8 per day, €50); Paris (6hr., 4 per day, €78). Eurolines, 68-70 bd. Pierre Sémard, sends **buses.** (☎26 40 04; www.eurolines.fr. Open M-F 9:30am-6:30pm, Sa 9:30am-5pm.) To get from the station to the **tourist office,** r. Lafayette, in pl. Charles de Gaulle, head straight down r. de Bayard.

Veer left around pl. Jeanne d'Arc and continue on r. d'Alsace-Lorraine; the office is on the right. (☎11 02 22; www.ot-toulouse.fr. Open May-Sept. M-Sa 9am-7pm, Su 10:30am-5:15pm; Oct.-Apr. M-Sa 9am-6pm, Su 9am-5pm.) Surf the **Internet** at **Feeling Copies,** 3 r. Valade. (€1 per hr. Open M-F 9am-7pm.) **Postal Code:** 31000.

ACCOMMODATIONS AND FOOD. While it lacks a youth hostel, Toulouse has a number of well-located budget hotels. To reach the spacious and charming **Hôtel des Arts ❷,** 1 bis r. Cantegril, off r. des Arts, take the metro (dir.: Basso Cambo) to pl. Esquirol. Walk down r. de Metz away from the river; r. des Arts is on the left. (☎23 36 21; fax 12 22 37. Breakfast €5. Singles €26-29, with shower €31.50; doubles €33/34.50. MC/V.) Take bus #59 (dir.: Camping) from pl. Jeanne d'Arc to camp at **Pont de Rupé ❶,** 21 ch. du Pont de Rupé, at av. des États-Unis along N20 north. (☎70 07 35; fax 70 00 71. €13.50 for 1-2 people, a tent, and a caravan; €2.80 per additional person.) Cheap eateries on **rue du Taur,** in the student quarter, serve meals for €5.50-10. Markets (open Tu-Su 6am-1pm) line **place des Carmes, place Victor Hugo,** and **boulevard de Strasbourg.** Neighborhood favorite **Jour de Fête ❶,** 43 r. du Taur, is a relaxed *brasserie* with tastes as creative as the local art on its walls. (☎23 36 48. *Plat du jour* €6.70. Open daily 11am-midnight. Cash only.) **La Faim des Haricots ❸,** r. du Puits Vert, between pl. du Capitole and the student quarter, is a vegetarian's dream. (☎22 49 25. Open M-Sa noon-2:30, Th-Sa noon-2:30pm and 7-10:30pm. MC/V.)

SIGHTS AND NIGHTLIFE. The **Capitole,** the brick palace next door to the tourist office, is Toulouse's most prominent monument. The building was once home to the bourgeois *capitouls*, who unofficially ruled the city in the 12th century. (Open daily 9am-7pm. Free.) R. du Taur leads to the **Basilique St-Sernin,** the longest Romanesque structure in the world. Its **crypt** houses holy relics from the time of Charlemagne. (Church open July-Sept. M-Sa 8:30am-6:15pm, Su 8:30am-7:30pm; Oct.-June reduced hours. Crypt open July-Sept. M-Sa 10am-6pm, Su noon-6pm; Oct.-June 10-11:30am and 2:30-5pm, Su 11:30am-6pm. Church free. Crypt €2.) From pl. du Capitole, take a right on r. Romiguières, and turn left on r. Lakanal to get to the 13th-century southern Gothic **Jacobin church,** where the remains of St. Thomas Aquinas are housed in an elevated tomb. (Open daily 9am-7pm. Cloister €3.) Just across the St-Pierre bridge, **Les Abbatoirs,** 76 allées Charles-de-Fitte, houses intermittent exhibits by up-and-coming contemporary artists in old slaughterhouses converted into a vast art space. (☎51 10 60. Open Tu-Su 11am-7pm. €6.10, students €3.05.) The restored **Hôtel d'Assézat,** at pl. d'Assézat on r. de Metz, houses the **Fondation Bemberg,** a modest collection of Bonnards, Gauguins, and Pissarros. (☎12 06 89. Open Tu, W, and F-Su 10am-12:30pm and 1:30-6pm, Th 10am-12:30pm and 1:30-9pm. €4.60, students €2.75.) Toulouse has something to please almost any nocturnal whim, although nightlife is best when students are in town. Numerous cafes flank **place St-Georges, place St-Pierre,** and **place du Capitole,** and late-night bars line **rue de la Colombette** and **rue des Filatiers.** For cheap drinks and a rambunctious atmosphere, try **Café Populaire,** 9 r. de la Colombette, where you can polish off 13 glasses of beer for only €20, €13 on Mondays. Happy hour is daily 7:30-8:30pm, and every 13th of the month beer is only €1. (☎63 07 00. Open M-F 11am-2am, Sa 2pm-4am.) The best dancing is at the spacious, and wildly touristy, two-story **Bodega-Bodega,** 1 r. Gabriel Péri, just off bd. Lazare Carnot. (Cover €6 Th-Sa. Open M-F and Su 7pm-2am, Sa 7pm-6am. MC/V.)

CARCASSONNE ☎04 68

Walking over the drawbridge and through the stone portals into Carcassonne's *La Cité* (pop. 46,000) is like stepping into a fairy tale; the first-century ramparts still seem to resound with the clang of armor. It's almost enough to make you forget that the only battles raging today are between camera-wielding visitors vying for space on the narrow streets. Built as a palace in the 12th century, the **Château Comtal,** 1 r. Viollet-le-Duc, became a citadel after the royal takeover in 1226. (Open daily Apr.-Sept. 10:15am-6:15pm; Oct.-Mar. 9:30am-5pm. €6.50, under 25 €4.50.) Agglo'Bus runs **shuttles** from the bus stop across the canal from the train station to the citadel gates (mid-June to mid-Sept. 9:30am-noon and 1:30-7:30pm 4 per hr., round-trip €1.50). Converted into a fortress after the city was razed during the Hundred Years' War, the Gothic **Cathédrale St-Michel,** r. Voltaire, in the bastide St-Louis, still has fortifications on its southern side. (Open M-Sa 7:30am-noon and 2-7pm, Su 9:30am-noon.) The evening is the best time to experience *La Cité.* Nestled in an alley in the heart of *La Cité,* the **Auberge de Jeunesse (HI) ❷,** r. de Vicomte Trencavel, offers affordable comfort. (☎25 23 16; carcassonne@fuaj.org. Internet €3 per hr. Reception 24hr. Lockout 10am-3pm. Dorms €16. HI nonmembers €2.90 extra. MC/V.) Restaurants in *La Cité* are on the expensive side. For somewhat better deals, head to the lower city. The traditional French cuisine at **Les Fontaines du Soleil ❸,** 32 r. du Plô, is best savored as part of a €13 lunch *formule.* (☎47 87 06. Salads €9-21. Dinner *menu* €18-49. Open daily noon-3pm and 7-10pm. MC/V.) Save room for crepes and other desserts around **pl. Marcou.** While Carcassonne has effervescent nightlife during the year, the city quickly falls asleep in summer when most of the regulars go to the beach. Nonetheless, several bars and cafes along **boulevard Omer Sarraut** and **place Verdun,** both in the lower city, stay open past midnight. **Le Bar à Vins,** 6 r. du Plô, remains popular and full throughout the summer. (☎47 38 38. Beer €2.80-5. Wine €2 per glass. Open Feb.-Nov. daily 9am-2am. MC/V.) Down a pint of Guinness (€6) at **O'Sheridans,** 13 r. Victor Hugo, off pl. Carnot, a convivial Irish pub filled with French and Anglo crowds. (☎72 06 58. Live music Sept.-June every other Th 10pm. Happy hour 6-8pm; whiskey ½ price. Open daily 5pm-2am. MC/V.)

Trains (☎71 79 14) depart behind Jardin A. Chenier for: Marseille (3-4hr., 3 per day, €42); Nice (6hr., 5 per day, €57); Nîmes (2-3hr., 9 per day, €28); Toulouse (1hr., 5 per day, €15). Shops, hotels, the cathedral, and the train station are in the **Bastide St-Louis,** once known as the *basse ville* (lower city). From the station, walk down av. de Maréchal Joffre, which becomes r. Clemençeau; after pl. Carnot, turn left on r. de Verdun to reach the **tourist office,** 28 r. de Verdun. (☎10 24 30; www.carcassonne-tourisme.com. Open July-Aug. daily 9am-7pm; Sept.-June M-Sa 9am-6pm, Su 9am-noon.) **Postal Code:** 11000.

MONTPELLIER ☎04 67

Live music brings every street corner to life in Montpellier (pop. 230,000), the most lighthearted city in southern France. The gigantic **Musée Fabre,** 39 bd. Bonne Nouvelle, is undergoing renovations until February 2007; it normally displays one of the largest collections of 17th- to 19th-century paintings outside of Paris, with works by Delacroix, Ingres, and Poussin. Temporary exhibits are on display at the **pavilion** on the opposite side of Esplanade Charles de Gaulle. (☎66 13 46. Hours and prices vary; call in advance.) Bd. Henri IV leads to the **Jardin des Plantes,** France's first botanical garden. (☎63 43 22. Open Tu-Su June-Sept. noon-8pm; Oct.-Mar. noon-6pm. Free.) The friendly owner of **Hôtel des Etuves ❷,** 24 r. des Etuves, keeps 13 plain, comfortable rooms, all with toilet and shower. (☎/fax 60 78 19; www.hoteldesetuves.fr. Breakfast €5. Reception M-Sa 7am-11pm, Su 7am-noon and 6-11pm. Reserve 1 wk. ahead. Singles €23, with TV €33-42; doubles €37-42. Cash only.) Standard French cuisine dominates Montpellier's *vieille ville,* while a number of Indian and Lebanese restaurants have taken hold on **rue des Ecoles Laïques.** Behind the Crédit Lyonnaise on pl. de la Comédie, **Crêperie le Kreisker ❶,**

3 passage Bruyas, serves 80 kinds of delicious crepes (€3.20-6.60) topped with everything from buttered bananas to snails. (☎60 82 50. Open M-Sa 11:30am-3pm and 6:30-11pm. MC/V.) Get groceries at **INNO,** in the basement of the Polygone commercial center, just past the tourist office. (Open M-Sa 9am-8:30pm. MC/V.) At dusk, **rue de la Loge** fills with vendors, musicians, and stilt-walkers. The liveliest bars are in **place Jean-Jaurès.** Popular with 20-somethings, **Cubanito Cafe,** 13 r. de Verdun, just off pl. de la Comédie, starts early and parties late. (☎92 65 82. Mixed drinks €5. Open daily noon-2am; low season noon-1am. MC/V.) Prominent gay nightlife is centered around **place du Marché aux Fleurs.**

Trains leave pl. Auguste Gibert (☎08 92 35 35 35) for: Avignon (1hr., 12 per day, €14); Marseille (1¾hr., 12 per day, €17); Nice (4hr., 3 per day, €48); Paris (3½hr., 12 per day, €91); Toulouse (2½hr., 13 per day, €32). From the train station, r. Maguelone leads to **place de la Comédie,** Montpellier's modern center. The **tourist office,** 30 allée Jean de Lattre de Tassigny, is a block to the right. (☎60 60 60; www.ot-montpellier.fr. Open July-Aug. M-F 9am-7:30pm, Sa 10am-6pm, Su 9:30am-1pm and 2:30-6pm; Sept.-June reduced hours.) Access the **Internet** at **Cybercafé www,** 12bis r. Jules Ferry, across from the train station. (€1.50 per hr. Open M-Sa 10am-10pm.) **Postal Code:** 34000.

PROVENCE

Olive groves and vineyards carpet hills dusted with sunflowers and mimosas, while the fierce winds of the *mistral* carry the scents of lavender, rosemary, and sage. From the Roman arena and cobblestone elegance of Arles to Cézanne's lingering footsteps in Aix-en-Provence, life along the region's shaded paths tastes as good as a bottomless glass of *pastis*.

NÎMES ☎04 66

Southern France flocks to Nîmes (pop. 132,000) for the *férias*, celebrations featuring bullfights, flamenco dancing, and other hot-blooded fanfare (mid-Sept., mid-Feb., and May 27). The city lights up every Thursday night in summer, when the old town fills with art and music. Outside of festival season, Nîmes attracts few visitors, and most who come don't stay long. **Les Arènes** is a well-preserved, first-century **Roman amphitheater** that still has bullfights and concerts. (☎21 82 56. Open July-Aug. daily 9am-7pm; Apr.-May and Sept. 9am-6pm; Mar. and Oct. 9am-5:30pm; Nov.-Feb. 9:30am-4:30pm. €7.70, students €5.60.) North of the arena stands the **Maison Carrée,** a rectangular temple built in the first century BC. (Open same hours as Les Arènes. Film shows every 30min. €4.50, students €3.60.) Across the square, the **Carrée d'Art** displays traveling exhibits of contemporary art. (Open Tu-Su 10am-6pm. €4.80, students €3.60.) Near the mouth of the canals are the spacious grounds, *boule* courts, and luscious woods of the **Jardins de la Fontaine.** A hike through the park reveals the Roman ruins of the **Tour Magne.** (Garden open daily mid.-Mar. to mid-Oct. 7:30am-10pm; mid-Oct. to mid-Mar. reduced hours. Tower open same hours as Les Arènes. Garden free. Tower €2.70, students €2.30.)

To get to the newly renovated **Auberge de Jeunesse (HI) ❶,** 257 ch. de l'Auberge de Jeunesse, take bus I (dir.: Alès) from the train station to Stade, rte. d'Alès and follow the signs uphill. With jovial staff, this comfortable hostel is worth the 45min. trek from the train station. (☎68 03 20. Breakfast €3.40. Internet €1 per 15min. Reception 24hr. Open Mar.-Sept. Dorms €12. Camping €5.85. HI members only. MC/V.) For groceries, head to the **Monoprix,** 3 bd. Admiral Courbet, near Esplanade Charles de Gaulle. (Open M-Sa 8:30am-8pm, Su 9am-noon. MC/V.) **Trains** go from bd. Talabot to: Arles (25min., 8 per day, €7); Marseille (1¼hr., 9 per day, €18); Montpellier (30min., 31-46 per day, €8); Toulouse (3hr., 3-4 per day,

€38). **Buses** (☎29 52 00) depart from behind the train station for Avignon (1½hr., M-Sa 3-4 per day, €8). The **tourist office** is at 6 r. Auguste. (☎58 38 00; www.ot-nimes.fr. Open July-Aug. M-W and F 8:30am-8pm, Th 8:30am-9pm, Sa 9am-7pm, Su 10am-6pm; Sept.-June reduced hours.) **Postal Codes:** 30000; 30900.

PONT DU GARD ☎04 66

In 19 BC, Augustus's friend and advisor Agrippa built an **aqueduct** to channel water 50km to Nîmes from the Eure springs near Uzès. The fruit of this 15-year project is the Pont du Gard, spanning the gorge of the Gardon River and towering over sunbathers and swimmers. An amazing way to experience Pont du Gard is to kayak from Collias, 6km from the aqueduct. **Kayak Vert,** in Collias, rents canoes, kayaks, and bikes. (☎22 80 76. Canoes and kayaks €19 per day, bikes €16 per day. 10% discount for students and guests at the Nîmes youth hostel. Call a day ahead to make reservations and arrange for pickup at Pont du Gard.) More accommodations are in Nîmes. STDG **buses** (☎29 27 29) run to the Pont du Gard from Avignon (45min., 6 per day, €6.60) and Nîmes (40min.; 7 per day; €6.20, round-trip €11).

AVIGNON ☎04 90

Immortalized by the French children's song about its bridge, Avignon (pop. 89,500) also hosts Europe's most prestigious theater festival. For three weeks in July, the **Festival d'Avignon** holds theatrical performances in at least 30 venues, from factories to cloisters to palaces. (☎14 14 14; www.festival-avignon.com. Tickets free-€36. Reservations accepted from mid-June. Standby tickets available 45min. before shows; under 25 €12.) The **Festival OFF,** also in July, is more experimental and almost as well established. (☎25 24 30; www.avignon-off.org. Tickets under €16. €10 Carte OFF grants holders a 30% discount on all tickets.) The golden **Palais des Papes,** the largest Gothic palace in Europe, is a reminder of the city's brief stint as the center of the Catholic Church. Although revolutionary looting stripped the interior of its lavish furnishings, and fires erased its medieval murals, the vast chambers and few remaining frescoes are still remarkable. (☎27 50 00. Open daily July 9am-9pm; Aug.-Sept. 9am-8pm; Oct. and Apr.-June 9am-7pm; Nov.-Mar. 9:30am-5:45pm. €9.50.)

Avignon's accommodations fill up three to four months before festival season; reserve ahead or stay in Arles or Nîmes. At **Hôtel du Parc ❸,** 18 r. Perdiguier, bright rooms have a view of a quiet courtyard. (☎82 71 55. Breakfast €7. Hallway shower €2. Reception daily 6am-10pm. Reserve ahead. Singles €27, July €45; with shower €32, high season €36, July €58; doubles with bath and toilet €44/48/62; triples with shower and toilet €58/65/80. €1.50 discount with *Let's Go* mid-Nov. to mid-Mar. MC/V.) Sleep for cheap at **Camping du Pont d'Avignon ❶,** 10 chemin de la Barthelasse. (☎80 63 50; www.camping-avignon.com. Open Mar.-Oct. High season 1-person tent site €16; 2 people €22; extra person €5.10. Low-season prices 60% lower. MC/V.) A regular crowd enjoys delicious *tartines* (€5.30) and occasional guitar serenades at **La Cuisine des Méchantes ❶,** 68 r. de la Bonneterie. (☎86 14 81. Open M noon-2pm, W-F noon-2pm and 7-11pm, Sa 7-11pm. Cash only.) During festivals, free performances spill into the streets at night, and many eateries stay open until 2 or 3am. **Place des Corps Saints** has bars that remain busy year-round.

Trains (☎27 81 89) run from bd. St-Roch to: Arles (20min., 19 per day, €7.40); Lyon (2hr., 5-7 per day, €34); Marseille (1¼hr., 18-22 per day, €17); Nîmes (30min., 13-15 per day, €8); Paris (TGV 3½hr., 2 per day, €78). **Buses** leave to the right of the train station for Arles (1½hr., 5 per day, €7.10) and Marseille (2hr., 2 per day, €18). From the train station, walk straight through porte de la République to reach the **tourist office,** 41 cours Jean Jaurès. (☎04 32 74 32 74; www.avignon-tourisme.com. Open July M-Sa 9am-7pm, Su 10am-5pm; Apr.-June and Aug.-Oct. M-Sa 9am-6pm, Su 10am-5pm; Nov.-Mar. reduced hours.) **Postal Code:** 84000.

ARLES ☎04 90

All roads in Arles (pop. 35,000), once the capital of Roman Gaul, seem to meet at the great Roman arena. Built in the AD first century to seat 20,000 spectators, **Les Arènes** is still used for bullfights. (Open daily May-Sept. 9am-6pm; Oct.-Apr. reduced hours. €5.50, students €4.) Provençal daily life and folklore are showcased at the **Muséon Arlatan,** 29 r. de la République. (Open June-Aug. daily 9:30am-1pm and 2-6:30pm; Apr.-May and Sept. Tu-Su 9:30am-12:30pm and 2-6pm; Oct.-Mar. Tu-Su 9:30am-12:30pm and 2-5pm. €4, students €3.) The excellent **Musée de l'Arles Antique,** on av. de la 1*er* D. F. L., revives the city's Roman past. (Open daily Apr.-Oct. 9am-7pm; Nov.-Mar. 10am-5pm. €5.50, students €4.) The contemporary **Musée Réattu,** 10 r. du Grand Prieuré, houses 57 Picasso drawings inspired by the city. (Open daily July-Sept. 10am-7pm; Mar.-June and Oct. 10am-12:30pm and 2-6pm; Nov.-Feb. 1-6pm. €6, students €4.50.) The annual three-week-long **Fête d'Arles** brings traditional costumes, Provençal dancing, and bullfights to town beginning on the summer solstice. Every three years, the city elects the Queen of Arles and her six ladies, who represent the city's language, customs, and history at local events and international exchanges. The next election will occur in 2008.

To get from the station to the **Auberge de Jeunesse (HI) ❶,** 20 av. Maréchal Foch, follow directions to the tourist office. Then, make a right onto bd. Émile Zola, behind tourist office, and a left on av. du Maréchal Foch; the hostel will be on your left 50m down the street. Simple single-sex dorms await. (☎96 18 25. English-speaking staff. Breakfast and linens included. Reception 7-10am and 5-11pm. Lockout 10am-5pm. Curfew midnight, in winter 11pm. Dorms €15. MC/V.) The *brasseries* on **place du Forum** are pricey but popular, while those on **place Voltaire** have cheaper, though not as elegant, cafes. A **Monoprix** supermarket is in pl. Lamartine. (Open M-Th 8:30am-7:30pm, F-Sa 8:30am-8pm. MC/V.)

Trains leave av. P. Talabot for: Avignon (20min., 12-20 per day, €6.10); Marseille (50min., 18-27 per day, €13); Montpellier (1hr., 5-8 per day, €14); Nîmes (20min., 8-11 per day, €7). **Buses** depart from next to the station and from bd. Georges Clemenceau for Nîmes (55min., M-Sa 4 per day, €5.50). To get to the **tourist office,** esplanade Charles de Gaulle on bd. des Lices, turn left outside the station and walk to the roundabout. Veer clockwise, turning left after the Monoprix onto bd. Émile Courbes. At the end of the city walls, take a right on bd. des Lices. (☎18 41 20; www.arlestourisme.com. Open daily June-Sept. 9am-6:45pm; Oct.-Apr. reduced hours.) **Postal Code:** 13200.

AIX-EN-PROVENCE ☎04 42

Famous for festivals, fountains, and former residents Paul Cézanne and Émile Zola, Aix-en-Provence (*"X;"* pop. 134,000) caters to tourists without being ruined by them. The **chemin de Cézanne,** 9 av. Paul Cézanne, features a 2hr. self-guided walking tour that leads visitors to the artist's birthplace, his favorite cafes, and his studio. (Open daily July-Aug. 10am-6pm; Sept.-June 10am-noon and 2-6pm. €5.50, students €2.) The **Fondation Vasarely,** av. Marcel-Pagnol, in Jas-de-Bouffan, is a must-see for modern art fans. (Open M-Sa May-Sept. 10am-6pm; Oct.-Apr. 10am-5pm. €7, students €4.) An eclectic mix of Romanesque, Gothic, and Baroque, the **Cathédrale St-Saveur,** r. Gaston de Saporta, fell victim to misplaced violence during the Revolution; angry *Aixois* mistook the statues of the apostles for statues of royalty and defiantly chopped off their heads. The statues were recapitated in the 19th century, but remain *sans* neck. (Open daily 8am-noon and 2-6pm.) In June and July, famous performers and rising stars descend on Aix for the **Festival d'Aix-en-Provence,** a series of opera and orchestral performances. (☎16 11 70; www.festival-aix.com. Tickets from €8.) Aix also hosts **Danse à Aix,** a two-week dance festival starting in late July. (☎23 41 24; www.danse-a-aix.com. Tickets €7-33.)

Aix has few cheap hotels; travelers should reserve in March for festival season (July). The rooms at the excellent **Hôtel du Globe ❸,** 74 cours Sextius, are spacious and well lit. (☎26 03 58; www.hotelduglobe.com. Singles €36, with shower €39; doubles €52/59; triples €89; quads €95. AmEx/MC/V.) To camp at **Arc-en-Ciel ❶,** on rte. de Nice, take bus #3 from La Rotonde to Trois Sautets. (☎26 14 28. €6 per person, €5.70 per tent.) The roads north of **cours Mirabeau** are packed with reasonably priced restaurants, as is **rue Verrerie.** You'll find tasty Provençal *tartines* (grilled bread with cheese and toppings; €10-13) at **Le P'tit Bistrot ❷,** 38 r. Lieutaud. (☎27 52 20. Open Tu-Sa 9am-3pm and 6pm-1am. MC/V.) There's a **Petit Casino** supermarket at 3 cours d'Orbitelle. (Open M-Sa 8am-1pm and 4-7:30pm.) **Rue Verrerie,** off r. des Cordiliers, is lined with bars and clubs. **Bistro Aixois,** 37 cours Sextius, packs in international students. (Open daily 7pm-2am.)

Trains, at the end of av. Victor Hugo, run to Cannes (3½hr., 25 per day, €26-30), Marseille (45min., 27 per day, €6), and Nice (3-4hr., 25 per day, €30). **TGV** trains leave for Paris CDG (3½hr., 5 per day, €89) from the TGV station, accessible via a shuttle (20min., 4 per hr., €4) from the bus station. **Buses** (☎08 91 02 40 25) from av. de l'Europe run to Marseille (30min., 6 per hr., €4.40). From the train station, follow av. Victor Hugo, bearing left at the fork, until it feeds into La Rotonde. On the left is the **tourist office,** 2 pl. du Général de Gaulle. (☎16 11 61; www.aixenprovencetourism.com. Open July-Aug. M-Sa 8:30am-9pm, Su 10am-1pm and 2-7pm; Sept.-June M-Sa 8:30am-8pm, Su 8:30am-1pm and 2-6pm.) **Postal Code:** 13100.

MARSEILLE ☎04 91

Dubbed "the meeting place of the entire world" by Alexandre Dumas, Marseille (pop. 800,000) is a jumble of color and commotion. A walk through its side streets is punctuated by the vibrant hues of West African fabrics, the sounds of Arabic music, and the smells of North African cuisine. A true immigrant city, Marseille offers a taste of both the ancient and modern cultures of the entire Mediterranean.

FRANCE

TRANSPORTATION

Flights: Aéroport Marseille-Provence (MRS; ☎04 42 14 14 14; www.marseille.aeroport.fr). Flights to **Corsica, Lyon,** and **Paris.** Buses connect the airport to Gare St-Charles (3 per hr. 5:30am-9:50pm, €8.50).

Trains: Gare St-Charles, pl. Victor Hugo (☎08 92 35 35 35). To: **Lyon** (1½hr., 21 per day, €42), **Nice** (2¾hr., 21 per day, €26, and **Paris** (3hr., 18 per day, €72-80).

Buses: Gare Routière, pl. Victor Hugo (☎08 16 40), near the train station. To **Avignon** (2hr., 5 per day, €15), **Cannes** (2¼-3hr., 4 per day, €21), and **Nice** (2¾hr., 1 per day, €24). Ticket windows open M-F 6:15am-7:30pm, Sa 6:30am-6:30pm, Su 7:30am-12:30pm and 1:30-6:30pm.

Ferries: SNCM, 61 bd. des Dames (☎08 25 88 80 88; www.sncm.fr). To: **Corsica** (12hr.; €35-53, students €20-40) and **Sardinia** (14½hr., €59-69/50-65). Open M-F 8am-6pm, Sa 8am-noon and 2-5:30pm. Prices higher June-Sept.

Local Transportation: RTM, 6 r. des Fabres (☎91 92 10; www.rtm.fr). Tickets sold at bus and metro stations (€1.70, day pass €4.50, 5- to 10-ride **Carte Liberté** €6-12). **Metro** runs M-Th 5am-9pm, F-Su 5am-12:30am.

Taxis: (☎02 20 20). 24hr. €20-30 to hostels from Gare St-Charles.

ORIENTATION AND PRACTICAL INFORMATION

Although the city is divided into 16 *arrondissements,* Marseille is understood by *quartier* (neighborhood) names and major streets. **La Canebière** is the main artery,

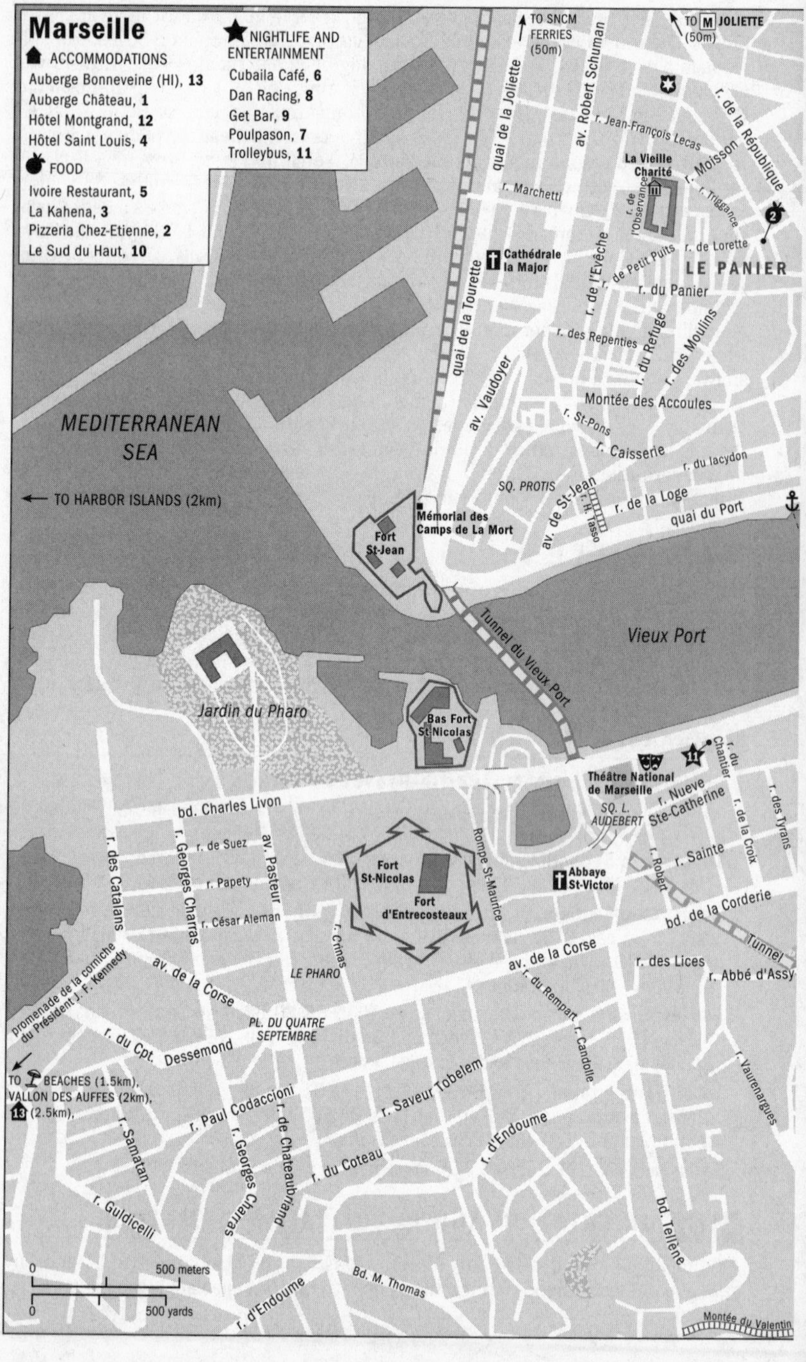
Marseille
ACCOMMODATIONS
Auberge Bonneveine (HI), 13
Auberge Château, 1
Hôtel Montgrand, 12
Hôtel Saint Louis, 4
FOOD
Ivoire Restaurant, 5
La Kahena, 3
Pizzeria Chez-Etienne, 2
Le Sud du Haut, 10
NIGHTLIFE AND ENTERTAINMENT
Cubaila Café, 6
Dan Racing, 8
Get Bar, 9
Poulpason, 7
Trolleybus, 11
TO SNCM FERRIES (50m)
TO M JOLIETTE (50m)
MEDITERRANEAN SEA
TO HARBOR ISLANDS (2km)
Vieux Port
LE PANIER
Jardin du Pharo
Fort St-Jean
Mémorial des Camps de La Mort
Bas Fort St-Nicolas
Fort St-Nicolas
Fort d'Entrecosteaux
Cathédrale la Major
La Vieille Charité
Théâtre National de Marseille
Abbaye St-Victor
Tunnel du Vieux Port
bd. Charles Livon
av. de la Corse
TO BEACHES (1.5km), VALLON DES AUFFES (2km), 13 (2.5km),
0 500 meters
0 500 yards

FRANCE

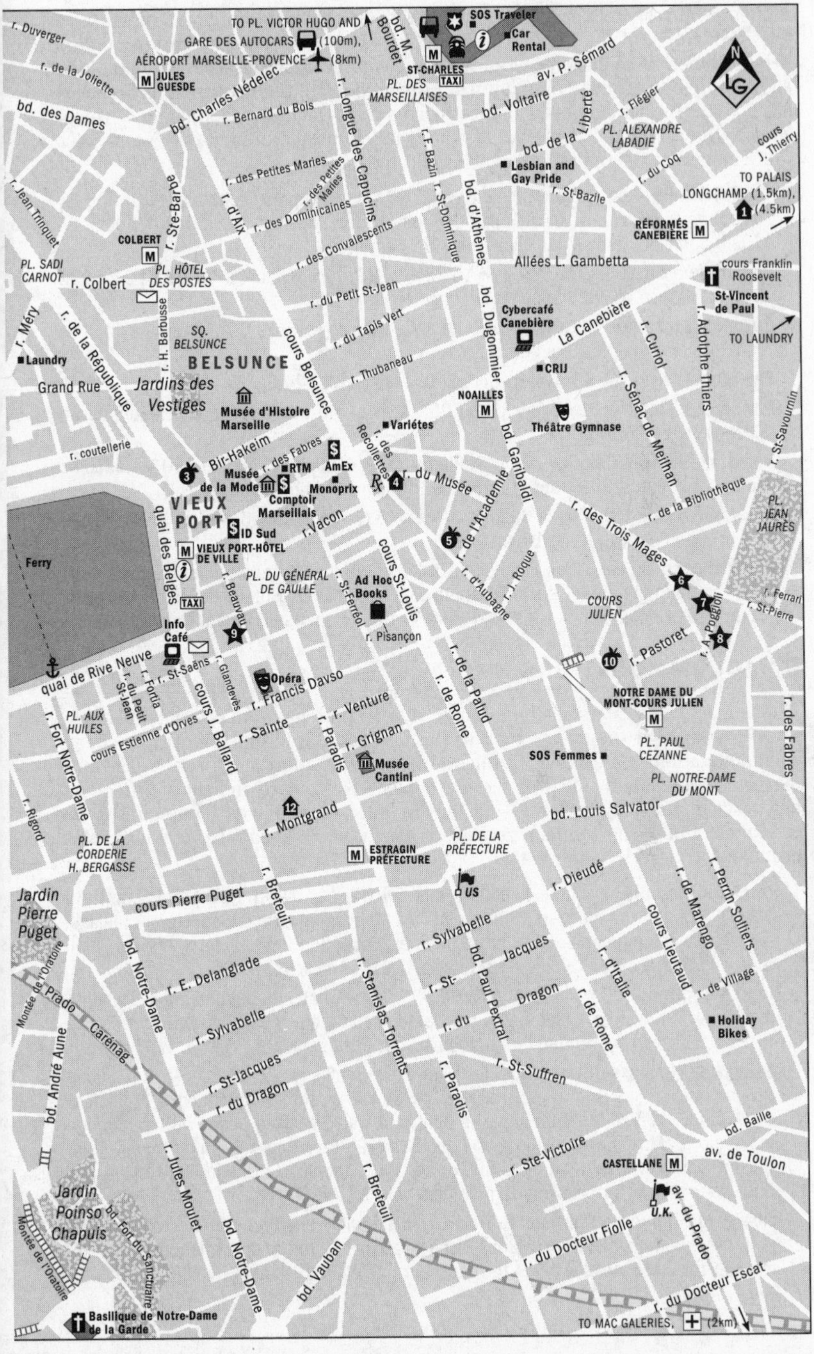
TO PL. VICTOR HUGO AND
GARE DES AUTOCARS (100m),
AÉROPORT MARSEILLE-PROVENCE (8km)
SOS Traveler
Car Rental
ST-CHARLES
TAXI
PL. DES MARSEILLAISES
JULES GUESDE
r. Duverger
r. de la Joliette
bd. des Dames
bd. Charles Nédelec
r. Bernard du Bois
bd. M. Bourdet
r. Longue des Capucins
av. P. Sémard
bd. Voltaire
r. F. Bazin
bd. de la Liberté
r. Flégier
PL. ALEXANDRE LABADIE
cours J. Thierry
r. du Coq
Lesbian and Gay Pride
r. St-Bazile
TO PALAIS LONGCHAMP (1.5km), (4.5km)
RÉFORMÉS CANEBIÈRE
r. des Petites Maries
r. des Petites Maries
r. des Dominicaines
r. St-Dominique
bd. d'Athènes
r. Jean Trinquet
r. Ste-Barbe
r. d'Aix
COLBERT
r. des Convalescents
Allées L. Gambetta
PL. SADI CARNOT
r. Colbert
PL. HÔTEL DES POSTES
r. du Petit St-Jean
cours Franklin Roosevelt
St-Vincent de Paul
TO LAUNDRY
r. Méry
r. de la République
r. H. Barbusse
SQ. BELSUNCE
BELSUNCE
r. du Tapis Vert
bd. Dugommier
Cybercafé Canebière
La Canebière
r. Curiol
r. Adolphe Thiers
Laundry
Grand Rue
Jardins des Vestiges
Musée d'Histoire Marseille
cours Belsunce
r. Thubaneau
CRIJ
NOAILLES
r. Sénac de Meilhan
r. St-Savournin
Variétes
Théâtre Gymnase
r. coutellerie
Bir-Hakeim
r. des Fabres
RTM
AmEx
r. des Recolettes
bd. Garibaldi
Musée de la Mode
Comptoir Marseillais
Monoprix
r. du Musée
VIEUX PORT
quai des Belges
ID Sud
r. Vacon
r. de l'Academie
r. de la Bibliothèque
PL. JEAN JAURÈS
r. des Trois Mages
VIEUX PORT-HÔTEL DE VILLE
cours St-Louis
Ferry
PL. DU GÉNÉRAL DE GAULLE
r. Beauvau
r. St-Ferréol
Ad Hoc Books
r. d'Aubagne
r. J. Roque
COURS JULIEN
r. Ferrari
r. St-Pierre
TAXI
Info Café
r. Pisançon
r. A. Poggioli
r. de la Palud
r. Pastoret
quai de Rive Neuve
r. St-Saëns
r. Glandevès
r. Fortia
r. du Petit St-Jean
Opéra
r. Francis Davso
r. de Rome
NOTRE DAME DU MONT-COURS JULIEN
r. des Fabres
PL. AUX HUILES
cours Estienne d'Orves
cours J. Ballard
r. Sainte
r. Venture
r. Paradis
r. Grignan
Musée Cantini
SOS Femmes
PL. PAUL CEZANNE
PL. NOTRE-DAME DU MONT
r. Fort Notre-Dame
r. Rigord
r. Montgrand
bd. Louis Salvator
PL. DE LA CORDERIE H. BERGASSE
ESTRAGIN PRÉFECTURE
PL. DE LA PRÉFECTURE
Jardin Pierre Puget
cours Pierre Puget
r. Breteuil
US
r. Dieudé
r. de Marengo
r. Perrin Solliers
r. Sylvabelle
r. Stanislas Torrents
bd. Paul Pextral
r. St-Jacques
cours Lieutaud
r. d'Italie
r. de Village
Montée de l'Oratoire
bd. Notre-Dame
r. E. Delanglade
Prado Carénag
r. Sylvabelle
r. du Dragon
r. de Rome
Holiday Bikes
bd. André Aune
r. St-Jacques
r. du Dragon
r. St-Suffren
r. Paradis
bd. Baille
r. Ste-Victoire
CASTELLANE
av. de Toulon
r. Jules Moulet
Jardin Poinso Chapuis
bd. Fort du Sanctuaire
r. Breteuil
U.K.
av. du Prado
Montée de l'Oratoire
bd. Notre-Dame
bd. Vauban
r. du Docteur Fiolle
r. du Docteur Escat
Basilique de Notre-Dame de la Garde
TO MAC GALERIES, (2km)

funneling into the **vieux port** (old port), with its upscale restaurants and nightlife, to the west. North of the *vieux port*, working-class residents pile into the hilltop neighborhood of **Le Panier,** east of which lies the **Quartier Belsunce,** the hub of the city's Arab and African communities. A few blocks to the southeast, **cours Julien** has a young, bohemian feel. Both **metro** lines go to the train station; line #1 (blue) goes to the *vieux port.* The **bus** system is much more thorough but complex—a route map from the tourist office helps enormously.

Tourist Office: 4 bd. de la Canebière (☎13 89 00; www.marseille-tourisme.com). Daily city tours (€16 by bus, €5 by open-car train). Open July-Sept. M-Sa 9am-7:30pm, Su 10am-6pm; Oct.-June M-Sa 9am-7pm, Su 10am-5pm.

Consulates: UK, 24 av. du Prado (☎15 72 10). **US,** 12 bd. Paul Peytral (☎04 91 54 92 00). Both open by appointment M-F 9am-noon and 2-5pm.

Currency Exchange: ID SUD, 3 pl. Général de Gaulle (☎13 09 00). Good rates and no commission. Open M-F 9am-6pm, Sa 9am-5pm.

Emergency: ☎17. **SOS Traveler,** Gare St-Charles (☎62 12 80).

Police: 2 r. Antoine Becker (☎39 80 00). Also in the train station on esplanade St-Charles (☎14 29 97).

Hospital: Hôpital Timone, 246 r. St-Pierre (☎38 60 00). M: Timone. **SOS Médecins** (☎52 91 52) and **SOS Dentist** (☎85 39 39) connect to on-call doctors.

Internet Access: Cyber Café de la Canebière, 87 r. de la Canebière (☎05 94 24). €2 per hr. Open daily 8:30am-10pm.

Post Office: 1 pl. Hôtel des Postes (☎15 47 00). Follow r. de la Canebière toward the sea and turn right onto r. Reine Elisabeth as it becomes pl. Hôtel des Postes. **Currency exchange** at main branch. Open M-F 8am-7pm, Sa 8am-noon. **Postal Code:** 13001.

ACCOMMODATIONS

Like any large city, Marseille has a range of hotel options, from pricey hotels scattered throughout the *vieux port* to the less reputable but temptingly cheap accommodations in Belsunce. Listings here prioritize safety and location. The hostels are inconveniently far from the city center—particularly in light of infrequent bus service and early curfews—but they're quiet. Most places fill up quickly on weekends and in the summer; reserve at least a week ahead. Large white signs provide directions to major hotels.

Hôtel Saint-Louis, 2 r. des Recollettes (☎54 02 74; www.hotel-st-louis.com). M: Noailles. Brightly painted, spacious rooms just off bustling r. de la Canebière. Breakfast €6. Free but temperamental wireless Internet. Reception 24hr. Singles €38-47; doubles with bath €49-54; triples €58. Extra bed €10. AmEx/MC/V. ❸

Hôtel Montgrand, 50 r. Montgrand (☎00 35 20; www.hotel-montgrand-marseille.com). M: Estragin-Préfecture. Quiet, newly renovated, clean rooms near the *vieux port.* Breakfast €5. Singles €41-49; family-size rooms €59, extra person €5. MC/V. ❸

Auberge de Jeunesse Bonneveine (HI), impasse Bonfils (☎17 63 30). M: Rond-Point du Prado. Take bus #44 to pl. Bonnefon, backtrack toward the roundabout, turn left at av. J. Vidal, then go left onto impasse Bonfils. A well-organized hostel with an international crowd. Max. stay 6 nights. Reception 9am-12:45pm and 1:30-6pm. Curfew 1am. Closed mid-Dec. to mid-Jan. Apr.-Aug. dorms €17; doubles €20. Mid-Jan. to Mar. and Sept. to mid-Dec. €1 discount. HI members only. MC/V. ❷

Auberge de Jeunesse Château de Bois-Luzy (HI), allée des Primevères (☎49 06 18). M: Chartreux. Take bus #6 to Marius Richard, go right onto bd. de l'Amandière, and follow the road around the fields to reach the hostel. A 19th-century château east of

Marseille. Breakfast €4. Reception 7:30am-noon and 5-10:30pm. Lockout noon-5pm. Curfew 10:30pm; in summer 11:30pm. Dorms 1st night €12, thereafter €9.50; singles €17/14; doubles €14/12. HI members only. Cash only. ❶

FOOD

Marseille's restaurants are as diverse its inhabitants. African eateries and kebab stands line **cours St-Louis,** and the streets surrounding the **vieux port** are packed with outdoor cafes. Buy groceries on the second floor of the **Monoprix** supermarket across from the AmEx office on bd. de la Canebière. (Open M-Sa 8:30am-8:30pm.)

Pizzeria Chez Etienne, 43 r. Lorette. From r. de la République, turn right through "Passage de Lorette;" Chez Etienne is on the left, just beyond the stairs. Customers at this crowded pizzeria needn't look beyond their own tables to meet the friendly owner; Etienne can be found filling open seats and conversing with his guests. Though there's a selection of grilled meats and salads, regulars opt for pizza. €7 for 1 person, €12 for 2, €16 for 3, €18.50 for 4. Cash only. ❶

Ivoire Restaurant, 57 r. d'Aubagne (☎33 75 33). M: Noailles. Loyal patrons come to this no-frills restaurant for authentic West African cuisine and helpful advice from Mama Africa, the exuberant owner. The Côte d'Ivoire specialties include *maffé* (€8), a meat dish with peanut sauce, and *gingembre* (€3.50), a refreshingly spicy ginger drink and a natural West African aphrodisiac. Open daily 11am-2am. Cash only. ❷

Le Sud du Haut, 80 cours Julien (☎92 66 64). M: Cours Julien. Inviting decor, spacious outdoor seating, and traditional *provençal* cuisine make this the ideal place for a leisurely meal along the cours Julien. Funky bathrooms supply markers and paper so patrons can add to the glowing reviews on the walls. Entrees €9-13. *Plats* €14-25. Open M-Sa noon-2:30pm and 8pm-12:30am. AmEx/MC/V. ❸

La Kahena, 2 r. de la République (☎90 61 93). M: Vieux Port. Tasty couscous dishes (€8.50-15), with various additions including fresh fish and traditional African ingredients, served on hand-painted plates. Speedy service makes for a scrumptious, quick meal. Entrees €4.50-5.50. Open daily noon-2:30pm and 7-10:30pm. MC/V. ❸

SIGHTS

A walk through the **city streets** of Marseille tops any other sights-oriented itinerary, providing glimpses of active African and Arabic communities amid ancient Roman ruins and 17th-century forts. Check www.museum-paca.org for the latest info on the region's museums. Unless otherwise noted, all museums listed below have the same opening hours (Tu-Sa June-Sept. 11am-6pm; Oct.-May 10am-5pm).

BASILIQUE DE NOTRE DAME DE LA GARDE. A hilltop location has made this church strategically important for centuries, and today it offers visitors a stunning view of the city, surrounding mountains, and stone-studded bay. During the WWII liberation of Marseille, the French Resistance fought to regain the basilica, which remains pocked with bullet holes and shrapnel scars. Towering nearly 230m above the city, the golden statue of the Madonna cradling the infant Christ, known as *la bonne mère*, is often regarded as the symbol of Marseille. *(☎13 40 80. Open daily in summer 7am-8pm; low season 7am-7pm. Free.)*

HARBOR ISLANDS. Resembling an elaborate version of a child's sand castle, the **Château d'If** guards the city from its rocky perch outside the harbor. Its dungeon, immortalized in Dumas's *Count of Monte Cristo*, once held a number of hapless Huguenots. Nearby, the **Île Frioul** was only marginally successful in isolating plague victims when an outbreak in 1720 killed half of the city's citizens. A handful of

FRANCE

small shops and restaurants, combined with inlets popular for swimming, make the islands a convenient escape from the city. *(Boats depart from quai des Belges for both islands. Round-trip 1hr.; €10 per island, both €15. Château €4.60, ages 18-25 €3.10.)*

LA VIEILLE CHARITÉ. A formidable example of the 17th-century work of local architect Pierre Puget, La Charité was originally constructed to house the hundreds of beggars congesting the entrances to Marseille's churches. Now a national historical monument, it houses several museums, including the anthropological collections of the **Musée des Arts Africains, Océaniens et Amérindiens.** *(2 r. de la Charité. ☎14 59 30. €2, students €1. Temporary exhibits €5/2.)*

MUSÉE CANTINI. This memorable museum chronicles the region's 20th-century artistic successes, with major Fauvist and Surrealist collections, including works by Henri Matisse and Paul Signac. *(19 r. Grignan. ☎54 77 75. €2, students €1.)*

MÉMORIAL DES CAMPS DE LA MORT. This small museum is located in a blockhouse built by the Germans during their occupation of Marseille. A collection of photos and news articles recalls the death camps of WWII and the deportation of 20,000 Jews from the *vieux port* in 1943. Sobering quotes by Primo Levi, Louis Serre, and Elie Wiesel and an unsettling collection of ashes are on display. *(Quai de la Tourette. ☎90 73 15. Open Tu-Su June-Aug. 11am-6pm; Sept.-May 10am-5pm. Free.)*

ABBAYE ST-VICTOR. St-Victor, an abbey fortified against pirates and Saracen invaders, is one of the oldest Christian sites in Europe. The eerie 5th-century crypt and basilica contain pagan and Christian relics, including the remains of two 3rd-century martyrs. The abbey hosts a concert festival each year from September to December. *(On r. Sainte at the end of quai de Rive Neuve. Open daily 9am-7pm. Crypt €2.)*

OTHER SIGHTS. The rotating exhibits at the **Musée de la Mode** pay homage to the fashion world, featuring designers from around the globe. *(Espace Mode Méditerranée, 11 bd. de la Canebière. €1.50, students €1.)* The remains of Marseille's original port rest peacefully in the quiet **Jardin des Vestiges.** Millennia-old artifacts, including pottery pieces and the skeleton of a 6th-century fishing boat, are displayed in the adjacent **Musée d'Histoire de Marseille.** *(Enter through the lowest level of the Centre Bourse mall. ☎90 42 22. Open M-Sa noon-7pm. €2, students €1.)* Bus #83 (dir.: Rond-Point du Prado) takes you from the *vieux port* to Marseille's main **public beaches.** Get off the bus just after it rounds the statue of David (20-30min.). Both the north and south **plages du Prado** offer views of Marseille's surrounding cliffs.

ENTERTAINMENT AND NIGHTLIFE

Late-night restaurants and a few nightclubs center around **place Thiers,** near the *vieux port.* On weekends, tables from the bars along the **quai de Rive Neuve** spill out into the sidewalk. A more creative, counter-cultural crowd unwinds along the **cours Julien.** Tourists should exercise caution at night, particularly in Panier and Belsunce, and near the Opera on the *vieux port.* Night buses are scarce, taxis are expensive, and the metro closes early (Su-Th 9pm, F-Sa 12:30am).

Trolleybus, 24 quai de Rive Neuve. M: Vieux Port. A mega-club in an 18th-century warehouse with 3 separate cave-like rooms for pop-rock, techno, and soul-funk-salsa. Prize-winning French and international DJs have been spinning here for 14 years. Beer from €5. Mixed drinks €5-9. Cover Sa €10, includes 1 drink. Open July-Aug. Tu-Sa 11pm-6am; low season Th-Sa 11pm-6am. MC/V.

Dan Racing, 17 r. André Poggioli. M: Cours Julien. Let your inner rock star run wild at this fun, casual bar, where drunken revelers can hop on stage to jam on 15 guitars, 2 drum sets, and countless other instruments. Auto- and bike-racing decor adds to the atmosphere. Drinks €2-4.50. Open M-Sa 9pm-2am.

Cubaila Café, 40 r. des Trois Rois (☎48 97 48). M: Cours Julien. Take your mójito from the striped couches of the 1st fl. down to the basement, where you'll find a perfect replica of the *Malécon* (boardwalk) in Havana, complete with miniature house facades and a view of the "ocean." Drinks €3-9. Open Tu-Sa 8:30pm-4am.

Poulpason, 2 r. André Poggioli. M: Cours Julien. DJs spin hip-hop, funk, jazz, reggae, and electro-house. A giant octopus reaching out from the wall, wave and vortex mosaics, and a black-lit aquarium make for a surreal atmosphere. Drinks €3-5. Cover on specially featured DJ nights €3-10. Open M-Sa 10pm-2am. MC/V.

Get Bar, 10 r. Beauvau (☎33 64 79; www.get-bar.com). M: Vieux Port-Hôtel de Ville. Men and women relax on soft benches with plush pillows at this gay bar, formerly called MP Lounge. Pink runner lights, subtle rainbow patterns, and elaborate metal sconces add class to this new hot spot. Try the specialty "surprise" drink, La Bombe (€3). Beer €2.50-3. Mixed drinks €6.50. W theme nights, Su scantily clad servers (male and female). Open daily 6:30pm-4am. MC/V.

FRENCH RIVIERA (CÔTE D'AZUR)

Between Marseille and the Italian border, the sun-drenched beaches and warm waters of the Mediterranean form the backdrop for this fabled playground of the rich and famous. Chagall, F. Scott Fitzgerald, Matisse, Picasso, and Renoir are among those who flocked to the coast in its heyday. Now, the Riviera is a curious combination of high-rolling millionaires and low-budget tourists. High society steps out every May for the Cannes Film Festival and the Monte-Carlo Grand Prix. Less exclusive are Nice's summer jazz festivals and uproarious *Carnaval*.

ST-TROPEZ ☎04 94

Hollywood stars, corporate giants, and curious backpackers congregate on the spotless streets of St-Tropez (pop. 5400), where the glitz and glamor of the Riviera shines brightest. The young, beautiful, and restless flock to this "Jewel of the Riviera" to flaunt their tans on its infamous **beaches** and their designer clothing in its posh nightclubs. The best beaches can be difficult to reach without a car, but a **shuttle** *(navette municipale)* leaves pl. des Lices for **Les Salins,** a secluded sunspot, and **plage Tahiti** (Capon-Pinet stop), the first of the famous **plages des Pampelonne.** (M-Sa 5 per day, €1. Ask for schedule at the tourist office.) Take a break from the sun at the **Musée de l'Annonciade,** pl. Grammont, which showcases Fauvist and neo-Impressionist paintings. (Open M and W-Su June-Sept. 10am-noon and 2-6pm; Oct.-May 10am-1pm and 4-7pm. €4.60, students €2.30.)

Budget hotels do not exist in St-Tropez, and the closest youth hostel is in Fréjus (p. 372). **Camping** is the cheapest option; **Kon Tiki ❷** has a choice location near the northern stretch of the Pampelonne beaches. In July and August, Sodetrav sends daily buses (4 per day, €1.60) from the station to the campground. Or, take the municipal shuttle from pl. des Lices to Capon-Pinet and follow the signs downhill to plage Tahiti; walk 30-40min. down the beach to reach the site. Campers can soak up sun by day and wild parties by night at Kon Tiki's in-house bar. (☎55 96 96; www.campazur.com. Open Apr. to mid-Oct. July-Aug. 2 people, tent, and car €50; Apr.-June and Sept. to mid-Oct. €20-27.) The *vieux port* and the streets behind the waterfront are lined with incredibly pricey restaurants, so create your own meal at **Monoprix** supermarket, 9 av. du Général Leclerc (open daily July-Aug. 8am-10pm, Sept.-June 8am-8:20pm), or stop by the snack stands and cafes near **place des Lices,** also the center of St-Tropez's wild nightlife. Shell out €25,000 for a bottle of Cristal at **Les Caves du Roy,** av. Paul Signac, in the Hotel Byblos, or if things look shaky on the trust-fund front, settle for the €25 gin and tonic. (☎56 68 00. Open July-Aug.

daily 11pm-5am; June and Sept. F-Sa 11:30pm-4am. AmEx/MC/V.) The **tourist office** is on quai Jean Jaurès. (☎97 45 21;www.saint-tropez.st. Open daily July-Sept. 9:30am-8pm; Sept.-Oct. and mid-Mar. to June 9:30am-12:30pm and 2-7pm; early Nov. to mid-Mar. 9:30am-12:30pm and 2-6pm.) **Postal Code:** 83990.

ST-RAPHAËL AND FRÉJUS ☎04

With affordable accommodations, convenient transportation, and proximity to the sea, the twin cities of St-Raphaël (pop. 32,000) and Fréjus (pop. 48,000) provide a good base for exploring the Riviera. In St-Raphaël, golden beaches stretch along the coast and the boardwalk turns into a carnival on summer evenings, while Fréjus trades sandy shores for Roman ruins. Take av. du 15ème Corps d'Armée from the Fréjus tourist office and turn left on chemin de Counillier after the second roundabout to reach the **Auberge de Jeunesse de St-Raphaël-Fréjus (HI) ❶**, a friendly hostel located in a secluded 170-acre forest. (☎94 53 18 75; frejus-st-raphael@fuaj.org. Linens €2.80. Reception 8-11am and 5:30-10pm. Lockout 11am-5:30pm. Curfew June-Aug. 11pm; Sept.-Nov. and Feb.-Mar. 10pm. Closed Dec.-Jan. Dorms €15-17. Camping €10 per person with tent. Cash only.) In St-Raphaël, the **Hôtel les Pyramides ❸**, 77 av. Paul Doumer, offers rooms near the waterfront. To get to the hotel, turn left out of the station, make a right onto r. Henri Vadon, and take the first left onto av. Paul Doumer. (☎98 11 10 10; www.saint-raphael.com/pyramides. Breakfast €7. Reception 7am-9pm. Open mid-Mar. to mid-Nov. Singles €28; doubles €39-58; triples €59; quads €69. MC/V.) (Open M-Sa 8:30am-7:30pm.) St-Raphaël sends **trains** every 30min. from pl. de la Gare to Cannes (25min., €5.90) and Nice (1hr., €9.80). **Buses** leave from behind the train station in St-Raphaël for Fréjus (25min., 1 per hr., €1.10) and St-Tropez (1½hr., 11 per day, €9.50). The **St-Raphaël tourist office,** on r. Waldeck Rousseau, is opposite the train station. (☎94 19 52 52; www.saint-raphael.com. Open July-Aug. daily 9am-7pm; Sept.-June M-Sa 9am-12:30pm and 2-6:30pm.) Take bus #6 from St-Raphaël to pl. Paul Vernet to reach the Fréjus **tourist office,** 325 r. Jean Jaurès. (☎94 51 83 83. Open July-Aug. M-Sa 10am-noon and 2:30-6:30pm, Su 10am-noon and 3-6pm; Sept.-June M-Sa 10am-noon and 2-6pm.) **Postal Codes:** 83700 (St-Raphaël); 83600 (Fréjus).

CANNES ☎04 93

Cannes conjures images of its annual film festival, where countless stars compete for camera time. During the rest of the year, Cannes (pop. 67,000) rolls up the red carpet and becomes the most accessible of all the Riviera's glam towns. A palm-lined boardwalk, gorgeous sandy beaches, and innumerable boutiques draw the wealthy as well as the young and friendly. The world-famous **Festival International du Film** (May 16-27, 2007) is invite-only, though celebrity-spotting is always free. Of the town's three **casinos,** the least exclusive is **Le Casino Croisette,** 1 espace Lucien Barrière, next to the Palais des Festivals. (No shorts, jeans, or t-shirts. Jackets required for men. 18+. Cover €10. Open daily 10am-4am; tables games 8pm-4am.) Hostels are 10-20min. farther from the beach than other lodgings, but are the cheapest options in town. **Hotel Mimont ❸,** 39 r. de Mimont, is the best budget hotel in Cannes. English-speaking owners maintain basic but clean rooms two streets behind the train station, off bd. de la République. (☎39 51 64; canneshotelmimont65@wanadoo.fr. Singles €29; doubles €38; triples €55. AmEx/MC/V.) Run by a young, English-speaking couple, **Hostel Les Iris ❷,** 77 bd. Carnot, was converted from an old hotel into a clean, bright hostel with sturdy bunks, a Mexican-themed terrace restaurant, and small cafe. (☎68 30 20; www.iris-solola.com. Dorms €20. AmEx/MC/V.) The pedestrian zone around **rue Meynadier** has inexpensive restaurants. Stock up at **Champion** supermarket, 6 r. Meynadier. (Open M-Sa 8:30am-7:30pm. MC/V.) Cafes and bars near the waterfront stay open all night and are a great alternative to the expense of gambling and the glitz of posh clubs. Nightlife thrives around **rue Dr. G. Monod.** Try **Morrison's,** 10 r. Teisseire, for casual company in a literary-themed pub. (☎04 92 98 16 17. Beer from €5. Happy hour 5-8pm. Open daily 5pm-2am. MC/V.) **Trains** depart 1 r. Jean Jaurès for: Antibes (15min., €2.30); Marseille (2hr., €24); Monaco (1hr., €7.50); Nice (40min., €5.20); St-Raphaël (25min., €5.70). The **tourist office** is at 1 bd. de la Croisette. (☎39 24 53; www.cannes.fr. Open July-Aug. daily 9am-8pm; Sept.-June M-F 9am-7pm.) Get on the **Internet** at **Cap Cyber,** 12 r. 24 Août. (€3 per hr. Open 10am-11pm; low season 10am-10pm.) **Postal Code:** 06400.

ANTIBES ☎04 93

Blessed with beautiful beaches and a charming *vieille ville*, Antibes (pop. 72,000) is less touristy than Nice and more relaxed than St-Tropez; with access to top-notch nightlife in neighboring **Juan-les-Pins,** it provides a much needed middle ground on the glitterati-controlled coast. The **Musée Picasso,** in the Château Grimaldi on pl. Mariejol, which displays works by the former Antibes resident and his contemporaries, is closed for renovations until August 2007. The two main public beaches in Antibes, **plage du Ponteil** and neighboring **plage de la Salis,** are crowded all summer. Cleaner and more secluded, the rocky beach on **Cap d'Antibes** has a pretty landscape of white cliffs and blue water perfect for snorkeling.

For the cheapest accommodations in Antibes, grab a bunk with a rowdy crowd of yacht-hands in the basic rooms at **The Crew House ❷,** 1 av. St-Roch. From the train station, walk down av. de la Libération; just after the roundabout, make a right onto av. St-Roch. (☎04 92 90 49 39; workstation_fr@yahoo.com. Internet €4.80 per hr. Reception M-F 9am-7pm, Sa-Su 10am-6pm. Dorms Apr.-Oct. €20; Nov.-Mar. €15. MC/V.) A variety of restaurants set up outdoor tables along **boulevard d'Aguillon,** behind the *vieux port*. For cheaper eats, you're better off at **place Nationale,** a few blocks away. The **Marché Provençal,** on cours Masséna, is considered one of the best fresh produce markets on the Côte d'Azur. (Open Tu-Su 6am-1pm.) Come summer, the young and hip Juan-les-Pins is synonymous with wild nightlife. Frequent **buses** and **trains** run from Antibes, although walking between the two towns along bd. Wilson is also an option. Boutiques generally remain open until midnight, cafes until 2am, *discothèques* until 5am, and bars past dawn. In Juan-Les-Pins, **Pam Pam Rhumerie,** 137 bd. Wilson, is a hot Brazilian sit-down bar that turns wild when bikinied showgirls take the stage at 9:30pm to dance around and down flaming drinks. (☎61 11 05. Open daily mid-Mar. to early Nov. 2pm-5am.) In psychedelic **Whisky à Gogo,** 5 r. Jacques

JUST TRYING TO GET SOME BOOTY

In the past five years, Antibes has changed dramatically. Always a Riviera vacation spot, Antibes has seen a recent influx of work-seeking, English-speaking youths who have altered the town's once leisurely atmosphere.

A small town with a large private Mediterranean marina, Antibes has become the best place to find work for self-proclaimed "yachties," young, mainly Anglophone workers hoping to score a ride (and a job) on the world's largest boats. Once on board, yachties can be expected to do a variety of jobs, from cleaning the ship to serving dinner; the job's major perks include free travel to exotic destinations and large paychecks. Each yachtie has his own story, from the young man trying to make money seeing the world, to the recent nuclear astrophysics graduate looking to try something new before being shut up in a lab all day.

While waiting for the call that could put them on a boat to Istanbul, Ft. Lauderdale, or beyond, yachties have plenty of opportunities to blow their cash in Antibes. In between yacht jobs, newcomers and old hands work together as day laborers on the docks, scrubbing decks and engine rooms. Friendships ignite after a day of working or a night of drinking—who knows who could turn up in the bunk next to you (on shore or off) tomorrow evening?

Leonetti, water-filled columns lit with blacklights frame a young crowd on the intimate dance floor. (Cover €16, students €8; includes 1 drink. Open July-Aug. daily midnight-5am; Apr.-June and Sept.-Oct. Th-Sa midnight-5am.)

Trains leave pl. Pierre Semard, off av. Robert Soleau, for Cannes (15min., 23 per day, €2.30), Marseille (2¼hr., 12 per day, €25), and Nice (15min., 25 per day, €3.60). RCA **buses** leave pl. de Gaulle for Cannes (20min.) and Nice (45min.). All buses depart every 20min. and cost €1.30. From the train station, turn right on av. Robert Soleau and follow the signs to the **tourist office,** 11 pl. de Gaulle. (☎04 97 23 11 11; www.antibesjuanlespins.com. Open July-Aug. daily 9am-7pm; Sept.-June M-F 9am-12:30pm and 1:30-5pm.) **Postal Code:** 06600.

NICE

☎04 93

Sophisticated and spicy, Nice ("niece"; pop. 340,000) is the unofficial capital of the Riviera. Its non-stop nightlife, top-notch museums, and bustling beaches are unerring tourist magnets. During the three-week *Carnaval* in February, visitors and *Niçois* alike ring in the spring with grotesque costumes and wild revelry. No matter when you visit Nice, prepare to have more fun than you'll remember.

TRANSPORTATION

Flights: Aéroport Nice-Côte d'Azur (**NCE;** ☎08 20 42 33 33). **Air France,** 10 av. de Verdun (☎08 02 80 28 02), serves **Bastia, Corsica** (€116; under 25, over 60, and couples €59) and **Paris** (€93/50).

Trains: Gare SNCF Nice-Ville, av. Thiers (☎14 82 12). Open daily 5am-12:30am. To: **Cannes** (40min., 3 per hr., €5.60); **Marseille** (2½hr., 16 per day, €27); **Monaco** (15min., 2-6 per hr., €3.10); **Paris** (5½hr., 9 per day, €94).

Buses: 5 bd. Jean Jaurès (☎85 61 81). Info booth open M-F 8:30am-5:30pm, Sa 9am-4pm. To **Cannes** (1½hr., 2-3 per hr., €5.90) and **Monaco** (45min., 4-6 per hr., €4).

Ferries: Corsica Ferries, Port du Commerce (☎04 92 00 42 93; www.corsicaferries.com). Take bus #1 or 2 (dir.: Port) from pl. Masséna. To **Corsica** (€40, bikes €10).

Public Transportation: Ligne d'Azur, 10 av. Félix Faure (☎13 53 13; www.sunbus.com), near pl. Leclerc and pl. Masséna. Buses run daily 7am-8pm. Tickets €1.30, 1-day pass €4, 8-ticket *carnet* €8.29, 5-day pass €13, 1-week pass €16.77. Purchase tickets and day passes onboard the bus; *carnet,* 5-day, and 1-week passes from the office. **Noctambus** (night service) runs 4 routes daily 9:10pm-1:10am.

Bike and Scooter Rental: Holiday Bikes, 34 av. Auber (☎16 01 62), a few doors down from the train station. Bikes €5 per hr., €18-20 per day, €70-88 per week; €250 deposit. Also rents in-line skates. 5-10% student discount, 10% if you reserve by email. Open daily Feb.-Nov. 9am-6pm. AmEx/DC/MC/V.

ORIENTATION AND PRACTICAL INFORMATION

Avenue Jean-Médecin, on the left as you exit the train station, and **boulevard Gambetta,** on the right, run to the beach. **Place Masséna** is 10min. down av. Jean-Médecin. Along the coast, **promenade des Anglais** is a people-watcher's paradise. To the southeast, past av. Jean-Médecin and toward the bus station, is **Vieux Nice.** Women should not walk alone after sundown, and everyone should exercise caution at night around the train station, in *Vieux Nice*, and on promenade des Anglais.

Tourist Office: av. Thiers (☎08 92 70 74 07; www.nicetourisme.com), next to the train station. Ask for *Nice: A Practical Guide.* The free *Le Pitchoun* has tips from students on restaurants, entertainment, and nightlife. Open June-Sept. M-Sa 8am-8pm, Sun 10am-5pm; Oct.-May M-Sa 8am-7pm, Su 9am-6pm.

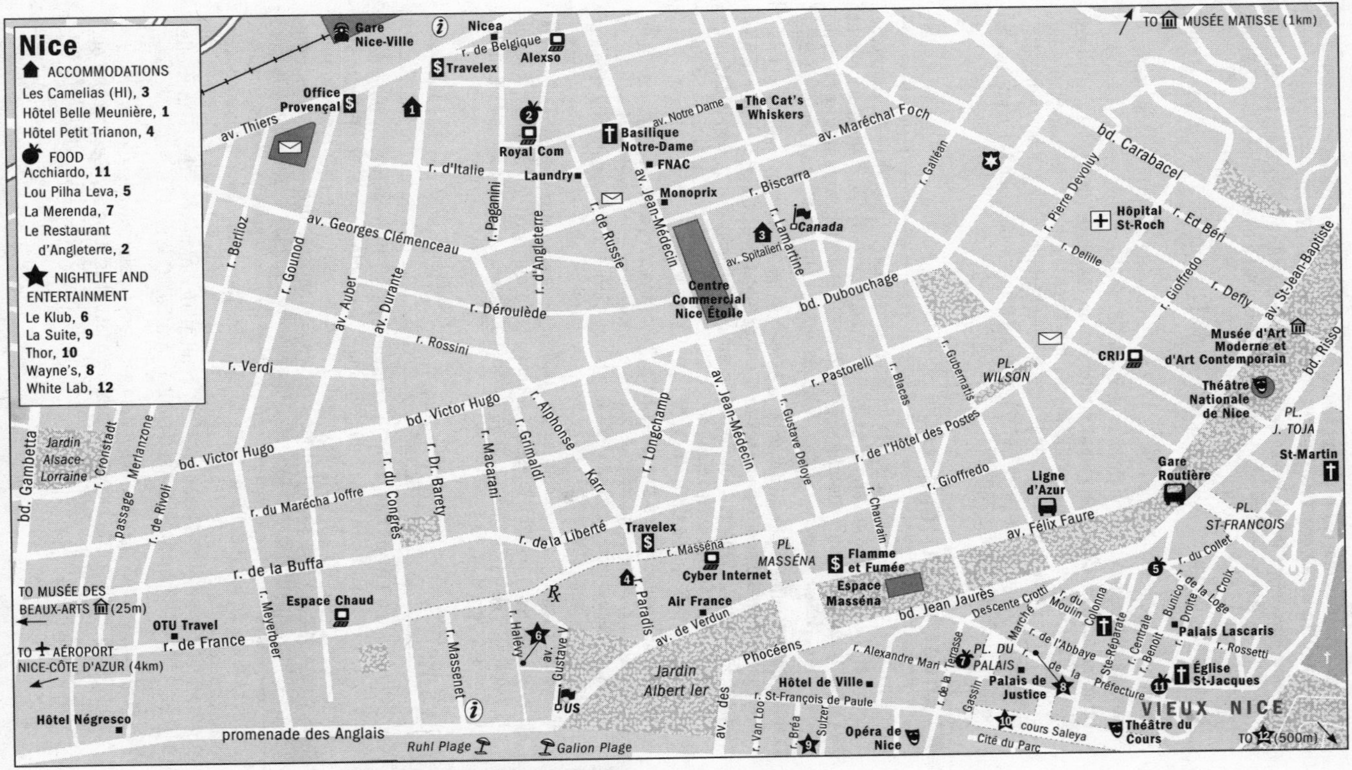
Nice
ACCOMMODATIONS
Les Camelias (HI), 3
Hôtel Belle Meunière, 1
Hôtel Petit Trianon, 4
FOOD
Acchiardo, 11
Lou Pilha Leva, 5
La Merenda, 7
Le Restaurant d'Angleterre, 2
NIGHTLIFE AND ENTERTAINMENT
Le Klub, 6
La Suite, 9
Thor, 10
Wayne's, 8
White Lab, 12
TO MUSÉE MATISSE (1km)
TO MUSÉE DES BEAUX-ARTS (25m)
TO AÉROPORT NICE-CÔTE D'AZUR (4km)
TO 12 (500m)
Gare Nice-Ville
Nicea
Alexso
Travelex
Office Provençal
Royal Com
Laundry
Basilique Notre-Dame
FNAC
Monoprix
The Cat's Whiskers
Canada
Centre Commercial Nice Étoile
Hôpital St-Roch
CRIJ
Musée d'Art Moderne et d'Art Contemporain
Théâtre Nationale de Nice
St-Martin
Gare Routière
Ligne d'Azur
Flamme et Fumée
Espace Masséna
Cyber Internet
Air France
Espace Chaud
OTU Travel
Hôtel Négresco
US
Jardin Albert Ier
Jardin Alsace-Lorraine
Hôtel de Ville
Opéra de Nice
Palais de Justice
Palais Lascaris
Église St-Jacques
Théâtre du Cours
VIEUX NICE
Ruhl Plage
Galion Plage
promenade des Anglais
av. Thiers
av. Georges Clémenceau
av. Jean-Médecin
av. Maréchal Foch
av. Notre Dame
bd. Carabacel
bd. Dubouchage
bd. Victor Hugo
bd. Gambetta
bd. Jean Jaurès
bd. Risso
av. St-Jean-Baptiste
av. Félix Faure
av. de Verdun
av. des Phocéens
av. Gustave V
av. Durante
av. Auber
av. Spitalieri
r. de Belgique
r. d'Italie
r. Paganini
r. d'Angleterre
r. de Russie
r. Biscarra
r. Lamartine
r. Galléan
r. Pierre Devoluy
r. Ed Béri
r. Delille
r. Gioffredo
r. Defly
r. Berlioz
r. Gounod
r. Déroulède
r. Rossini
r. Verdi
r. Pastorelli
r. Blacas
r. Gubernatis
r. Alphonse Karr
r. Grimaldi
r. Macarani
r. Dr. Barety
r. du Congrès
r. Longchamp
r. Gustave Deloye
r. de l'Hôtel des Postes
r. Chauvain
r. du Maréchal Joffre
r. de la Liberté
r. Masséna
r. Paradis
r. de la Buffa
r. Meyerbeer
r. de France
r. Halévy
r. Massenet
r. Cronstadt
passage Merlanzone
r. de Rivoli
r. Van Loo
r. Bréa
r. Sulzer
r. St-François de Paule
r. Alexandre Mari
r. de la Terrasse
r. Gassin
Cité du Parc
cours Saleya
r. de la Préfecture
r. de l'Abbaye
r. du Moulin
Descente Crotti
Marché
r. Colonna
r. Ste-Réparate
r. Centrale
r. Benoit
r. Bunico
r. Droite
r. de la Loge
r. Croix
r. du Collet
r. Rossetti
PL. WILSON
PL. MASSÉNA
PL. ST-FRANCOIS
PL. J. TOJA
PL. DU PALAIS

Consulates: Canada, 10 r. Lamartine (☎92 93 22). Open M-F 9am-noon. **US,** 7 av. Gustave V (☎88 89 55). Open M-F 9-11:30am and 1:30-4:30pm.

Currency Exchange: Office Provençal, 17 av. Thiers (☎88 56 80), opposite the train station. 4% commission on euro-denominated traveler's checks. Open M-F 7:30am-8pm, Sa-Su 7:30am-7:30pm.

Laundromat: Lavomatique, 7 r. d'Italie (☎85 88 14). Wash €3.50, dry €1 per 18min. Open daily 7am-9pm.

Police: 1 av. Maréchal Foch (☎04 92 17 22 22), opposite end from av. Jean-Médecin.

Hospital: St-Roch, 5 r. Pierre Dévoluy (☎04 92 03 33 75).

Internet Access: Centre Régional d'Information Jeunesse (CRIJ), 19 r. Gioffredo (☎80 93 93). Free with student ID; 30min. limit. Open M-F in summer 9am-6pm; winter 10am-7pm. **Royal Com,** 23 r. d'Angleterre. €2 per hr. Open daily 7:30am-midnight.

Post Office: 23 av. Thiers (☎82 65 22), near the train station. Open M-F 8am-7pm, Sa 8am-noon. **Postal Code:** 06033.

ACCOMMODATIONS

Come to Nice with reservations. The city has two clusters of budget accommodations: near the train station and near *Vieux Nice*. Those by the station are newer but more remote; the surrounding neighborhood has a rough reputation, so exercise caution. Hotels closer to *Vieux Nice* are more convenient but less modern.

Hôtel Belle Meunière, 21 av. Durante (☎88 66 15; fax 82 51 76), opposite the train station. A relaxed crowd of backpackers fills 4- to 5-bed co-ed dorms in a former mansion. Showers €2. Laundry from €5.50. Reception 7:30am-midnight. Dorms €15, with shower in room €20; doubles with shower €50; 2-person apartment min. stay 3 days. €36; triples €60; quads €80. MC/V. ❷

Auberge de Jeunesse Les Camélias (HI), 3 r. Spitalieri (☎62 15 54; nice-camelias@fuaj.org), behind the Centre Commercial Nice Étoile. A new hostel with clean rooms. Breakfast included. Laundry €6. Internet €5 per hr. Reception 24hr. Lockout 11am-3pm. Dorms €20. MC/V. ❷

Hôtel Petit Trianon, 11 r. Paradis (☎87 50 46; hotel.nice.lepetittrianon@wanadoo.fr). A motherly owner looks after guests in 8 comfortable rooms off pl. Masséna. Reserve ahead via email. Singles €30, with bath €35; doubles €40-42/50-53; triples €60-75; quads €76-96. MC/V. ❸

FOOD

Niçois cuisine is flavored with Mediterranean spices. Try crusty *pan bagnat,* a round loaf of bread topped with tuna, sardines, vegetables, and olive oil, or *socca,* a thin, olive-oil-flavored chickpea bread. The famous *salade niçoise* combines tuna, olives, eggs, potatoes, tomatoes, and a spicy mustard dressing. The eateries along promenade des Anglais and av. Masséna are expensive and unremarkable. Save your euros for olives, cheese, and produce from the **markets** at cours Saleya and av. Maché de la Libération (both open Tu-Su 7am-1pm). **Avenue Jean-Médecin** features reasonable *brasseries, panini* vendors, and kebab stands. Load up on groceries at fan-favorite **Monoprix,** av. Jean-Médecin, next to the Nice Étoile. (☎04 92 47 72 62. Open M-Sa 8:30am-8:50pm. AmEx/MC/V.)

La Merenda, 4 r. de la Terrasse. Behind stained-glass exterior and a beaded curtain, this intimate restaurant offers some of the best regional dishes in the city. Seatings at 7 and 9pm only; reserve in the morning in person for dinner. *Plats* €11-16. Open M-F noon-1:30pm and 7-9pm. Cash only. ❷

FRANCE

Lou Pilha Leva, 10-13 r. du Collet (☎13 99 08), in *Vieux Nice*. At lunch and dinnertime, a line of locals and tourists hungry for cheap *Niçois* fare extends around the corner. Open daily 8am-midnight. Cash only. ❶

Acchiardo, 38 r. Droite (☎85 51 16), in *Vieux Nice*. Long, crowded family-style tables fill with simple but appetizing French and Italian dishes served up by a quick, dedicated staff. Open M-F July 7-10pm; Sept.-June noon-1:30pm and 7-10pm. ❶

Le Restaurant d'Angleterre, 25 r. d'Angleterre (☎88 64 49), near the train station. Frequented by a loyal crowd of locals who come for traditional French favorites. The €14 *menu* includes salad, *plat*, side dish, dessert, and *digestif*. Open Tu-Sa 11:45am-2pm and 6:45-9:55pm, Su 11:45am-2pm. AmEx/MC/V. ❸

SIGHTS

Many visitors to Nice head straight for the beaches and don't retreat until the day is done. However, despite dreams you've had about Nice's beaches, the hard reality is an endless stretch of pebbles; bring a beach mat if you plan to soak up the sun in comfort. Perfecting your tan has its merits, but don't forget that blue waves and topless sunbathers aren't Nice's only attractions.

MUSÉE NATIONAL MESSAGE BIBLIQUE MARC CHAGALL. Chagall founded this extraordinary concrete-and-glass museum in 1966 to showcase his 17 *Message Biblique* paintings. Twelve of these strikingly colorful canvases illustrate the first two books of the Old Testament, and the remaining five, done entirely in shades of red, illustrate the Song of Songs. Other works include a huge reflecting pool, and a small auditorium with stained-glass panels illustrating the creation of the world. The museum stages concerts and lectures. *(Av. du Dr. Ménard. Walk 15min. north of the station, or take bus #15, dir.: Rimiez, to Musée Chagall. ☎53 87 20; www.chagall.fr. Open M and W-Su July-Sept. 10am-6pm; Oct.-June 10am-5pm. €6.70, students 18-25 €5.20, under 18 free. 3rd Su of each month free.)*

MUSÉE MATISSE. Henri Matisse visited the city of Nice in 1916 and ended up never leaving its shores. Originally a 17th-century Genoese villa, this museum contains a small collection of paintings and a dazzling exhibit of Matisse's 3D work, including bronze reliefs and cut paper tableaux. *(164 av. des Arènes de Cimiez. Take bus #15, 17, 20, 22, or 25 to Arènes. Free bus between Musée Chagall and Musée Matisse; ask at either ticket counter. ☎81 08 08. Open M and W-Su 10am-6pm. €4, students €2.50. 1st and 3rd Su of each month free.)*

MUSÉE D'ART MODERNE ET D'ART CONTEMPORAIN. An impressive glass facade welcomes visitors to this museum, which houses the work of French New Realists and American Pop artists, including Lichtenstein and Warhol. Minimalist galleries enshrine the avant-garde pieces. The fantastic statues of Niki de St. Phalle and "color-field" pieces by Yves Klein are standouts. *(Promenade des Arts, at the intersection of av. St-Jean Baptiste and Traverse Garibaldi. Take bus #5, dir.: St-Charles, to Musée Promenade des Arts. ☎62 61 62; www.mamac-nice.org. Open Tu-Su 10am-6pm. €4, students €2.50, under 18 and 1st and 3rd Su of each month free. English-language tours €7.)*

LE CHÂTEAU. At the eastern end of promenade des Anglais, Le Château—the formal name for the ruins of an 11th-century fort—marks the site of the city's birthplace. The château itself was destroyed by Louis XIV, but it still provides a spectacular view of Nice and the sparkling Baie des Anges. In the summer, an outdoor theater hosts orchestral and vocal concerts. The vista can be reached by climbing 400 steps or catching the elevator at the Tour Bellanda. *(Park open daily June-Aug. 9am-8pm; Sept. 10am-7pm; Oct.-Mar. 8am-6pm; Apr.-May 8am-7pm. Elevator runs daily June-Aug. 9am-8pm; Sept.-Mar. 10am-6pm; Apr.-May 10am-7pm. €0.70, round-trip €1.)*

FRANCE

MUSÉE DES BEAUX-ARTS JULES CHARET. The former villa of Ukraine's Princess Kotschoubey has been converted into a celebration of French and Italian academic painting. Raoul Dufy, a *Niçois* Fauvist painter, celebrated the spontaneity of his city with sensational pictures of the town at rest and at play. *(33 av. Baumettes. Take bus #38 to Chéret or #12 to Grosso. ☎04 92 15 28 28. Open Tu-Su 10am-6pm. €4, students €2.50, under 18 free. 1st and 3rd Su of each month free.)*

CATHÉDRALE ORTHODOXE RUSSE ST-NICOLAS. Also known as the **Église Russe,** this cathedral was commissioned by Russian Empress Maria Feodorovna in memory of her husband, Tsar Nicholas I, who died in Nice in 1865. Built to imitate Moscow's 16th-century churches, the onion-domed structure quickly became a spiritual home for exiled Russian nobles. Its color scheme, however, is straight from the Riviera, dominated by Mediterranean light-blue and yellow rather than dark-blue and gray. *(17 bd. du Tsarevitch, off bd. Gambetta. ☎96 88 02. Open M-Sa 9am-noon and 2:30-5:30pm, Su 2:30-5:30pm. €2.50, students €2.)*

JARDIN ALBERT I. The city's oldest park, Jardin Albert I, has plenty of palm trees, benches, and fountains. Its outdoor **Théâtre de Verdun** presents jazz and drama in summer. Contact the tourist office for a schedule. Unfortunately, the park is one of the most dangerous spots in Nice after dark; women especially should avoid walking here at night. *(Between av. Verdun and bd. Jean Jaurès, off promenade des Anglais. Box office open daily 10:30am-noon and 3:30-6:30pm.)*

OTHER SIGHTS. Named by the rich English community that commissioned it, the **promenade des Anglais,** a posh, palm-lined seaside boulevard, is Nice's answer to the great pedestrian thoroughfares of Paris, London, and New York. Today, the promenade is lined by luxury hotels like the stately **Négresco** (toward the western end), where the staff still dons top hats and 19th-century uniforms. Just east of the Négresco, the **Espace Masséna** provides a lovely, shady area where romantic picnickers can flirt beside the fountains. The seashore between bd. Gambetta and the Opéra alternates private **beaches** with crowded public strands, but a large section west of bd. Gambetta is reserved entirely for public use.

FRANCE

ENTERTAINMENT AND NIGHTLIFE

Nice's **Jazz Festival,** in mid-July at the Parc et Arènes de Cimiez near the Musée Matisse, attracts world-famous performers. (☎08 20 80 04 00; www.nicejazzfest.com. Tickets €33.) The **Carnaval,** in late February, gives Rio a run for its money with three weeks of parades, floral processions, confetti, fireworks, and parties.

Bars and nightclubs around r. Masséna and *Vieux Nice* pulsate with dance and jazz. Most will turn you away if you are wearing shorts, sandals, or a baseball cap. To experience Nice's nightlife without spending a euro, head down to the **promenade des Anglais,** where street performers, musicians, and pedestrians fill the beach and boardwalk. The free brochure *La Côte d'Azur en Fêtes*, available at the tourist office, provides info on nightlife and festivals. Exercise caution after dark; men have a reputation for harassing lone women on the promenade, near the train station, and in the Jardin Albert I, while the beach becomes a gathering place for prostitutes and thugs. Travelers should walk in groups if possible, and only take main, well-lit avenues to get back to their accommodations.

Thor, 32 cours Saleya (☎62 49 90). Svelte bartenders pour pints for a youthful clientele amid war shields, long wooden oars, and glasses shaped like Viking horns in this raucous faux-Scandinavian pub. Daily live bands blare rock starting at 10pm. Happy hour 6-9pm; pints €4.50. Open daily 6pm-2:30am. MC/V.

White Lab, 26 quai Lunel (☎26 54 79). Young fashionistas posture against a backdrop of white vinyl stools and blank tile walls. Cover €15. Open Th-Sa midnight-5am.

Wayne's, 15 r. de la Prefecture (☎13 46 99, www.waynes.fr). A laid-back crowd drinks at tables by the bar; the rowdier crew finds its way downstairs to the noticeably darker dance floor. Patrons dance on tables and each other. Pints €6.10. Mixed drinks €6.50. Su karaoke. Other nights live music or DJ. Happy hour noon-9pm; all drinks €3.50. Open daily noon-2am.

La Suite, 2 r. Brea (☎92 92 91). With velvet theater curtains and tall white candles, this swanky *boite* attracts a well-dressed set. Go-go girls help make parties sizzle F-Sa. Cover €13. Open Tu-Sa 11pm-2:30am. MC/V.

Le Klub, 6 r. Halévy (☎16 87 26). Nice's most popular gay "klub" attracts a large "krew" of men and women to the sleek lounge and active dance floor. Mixed drinks €6-10. Cover €11-14, includes 1 drink. Open W-Su midnight-5am. AmEx/MC/V.

DAYTRIP FROM NICE: EZE AND THE CORNICHES

Rocky shores and luxurious villas line the coast between hectic Nice and high-rolling Monaco. More relaxed than their glamorous neighbors, these tiny towns have interesting museums, ruins, and pleasant countryside. The train offers a glimpse of the coast up close, while bus rides on the high roads allow bird's-eye views of the steep cliffs and crashing sea below. Bus #100 leaves Nice every 15min., stopping in **Villefranche-sur-Mer** (10min.), **Beaulieu-sur-Mer** (20min.), **Monaco-Ville** (40min.), and **Monte-Carlo** (45min.). **Eze-le-Village** can be reached by bus #82 (20min.; M-Sa 14 per day; Su 8:30, 10, 11:30am, 1:30, 3, 5pm), while #81 serves **St-Jean-Cap-Ferrat** from Nice (25min., M-Sa 9:10am and 12:15pm). All tickets cost €1.30.

EZE. Three-tiered hilltop Eze owes its fame to the Roman village-turned-medieval citadel overlooking the Corniches. The **Porte des Maures** was the Moors' golden ticket into Eze during a 10th-century surprise attack; they ended up controlling the village for the next 70 years. The 18th-century **Église Paroissial** is adorned with *trompe l'oeil* frescoes and sleek Phoenician crosses. (Open daily July-Aug. 9:30am-7:30pm; Sept.-June 9:30am-6pm.) To get to these historic landmarks, take the 40min. hike up the **Sentier Friedrich Nietzsche,** named for the philosopher who found inspiration there; the path begins in Eze Bord-du-Mer, 100m east of the tourist office, and ends at the base of the medieval city. Or, take the bus from the train station to the village. **Trains** run to Eze from Nice (12min., €2.20).

FRANCE

MONACO AND MONTE-CARLO

In 1297, François Grimaldi of Genoa established his family as Monaco's rulers, staging a coup with a few henchmen disguised as monks. The tiny principality has since jealously guarded its independence and exclusivity. Monaco (pop. 7100) proves its wealth with ubiquitous surveillance cameras, high-speed luxury cars, multi-million-dollar yachts, and the famous casino in Monte-Carlo.

CALLING TO AND FROM MONACO

Monaco's country code is 377. To call Monaco from France, dial 00377, then the eight-digit number. To call France from Monaco, dial 0033 and drop the first zero of the French number.

TRANSPORTATION AND PRACTICAL INFORMATION. Trains run from the new **Gare SNCF,** pl. Ste-Dêvote, to Antibes (1hr., 2 per hr., €6.10), Cannes (1¼hr., 2 per hr., €7.70), and Nice (25min., 2 per hr., €3.10). **Buses** (☎04 93 85 64 44) leave bd. des Moulins and av. Princesse Alice for Nice (45min., 4 per hr., €1.30). The enormous **Rocher de Monaco** (Rock of Monaco) looms over the harbor, with **Monaco-Ville** clustered at the top. **La Condamine** quarter, Monaco's port, sits below Monaco-Ville, with a morning market, spirited bars, and lots of traffic.

Monaco's famous glitz is concentrated in **Monte-Carlo,** home to the casino. Bus #4 links the Ste-Dêvote train station entrance to the casino; buy tickets onboard (€1.50, *carnet* of 4 €3.60). The **tourist office is** at 2A bd. des Moulins. (☎92 16 61 16. Open M-Sa 9am-7pm, Su and holidays 10am-noon.) **FNAC,** Le Métropole Shopping Center, 17 av. des Spélugues, offers 20min. of free **Internet.** (☎93 10 81 81. Open M-Sa 10am-5:30pm.) **Postal Code:** MC 98000 Monaco.

ACCOMMODATIONS AND FOOD. There's no need to stay in Monaco itself; the nearby town of **Beausoleil,** in France, has several options and is only a 10min. walk from the casino. The rooms at **Hôtel Diana ❸,** 17 bd. du Général Leclerc, are modest, but come with A/C and TV. (☎04 93 78 47 58; www.monte-carlo.mc/hotel-diana-beausoleil. Singles €40-48; doubles €35-65; triples €67-70. AmEx/MC/V.) Not surprisingly, Monaco has little in the way of budget fare. Try the narrow streets behind the **place du Palais** for affordable sit-down meals, or fill a picnic basket at the **market** on pl. d'Armes at the end of av. Prince Pierre. (Open daily 6am-1pm.) The bright, merry **Café Costa Rica ❷,** 40 bd. des Moulins, serves up *bruschetta*, salads, and other flavorful Italian staples at lunchtime, and tea and crepes after 3pm. (☎93 25 44 45. Pasta €8-11. Open July-Aug. M-F 8am-7:30pm, Sa-Su 8am-3pm; Sept.-June daily 8am-7pm. Closed Aug. 1-15. V.)

SIGHTS AND ENTERTAINMENT. At the notorious **Monte-Carlo Casino,** pl. du Casino, Richard Burton wooed Elizabeth Taylor, and Mata Hari shot a Russian spy. Optimists tempt fate at **slot machines** (July-Aug. daily from noon; Sept.-June M-F from 2pm, Sa-Su from noon), **blackjack,** and **roulette** (daily from noon). The exclusive *salons privés*, where French games such as *chemin de fer* and *trente et quarante* begin at noon, have a €10 cover. Next door, the more relaxed **Café de Paris** opens at 10am and has no cover. All casinos have **dress codes** (no shorts, sneakers, sandals, or jeans), and the *salons privés* require a coat and tie. Guards are strict about the **age requirement** (18+); bring a passport as proof. Perched above the casino is the **Palais Princier,** the occasional home of Monaco's tabloid-darling royal family. Visitors curious for a glimpse of royal life can tour the small but lavishly decorated palace. (Open daily June-Sept. 9:30am-6pm; Oct. 10am-5pm. €6, students €3.) Next door, the **Cathédrale de Monaco,** at pl. St-Martin, was the venue for Prince Rainier and Grace Kelly's 1956 wedding. Princess Grace lies behind the altar in a tomb marked with her Latinized name, "Patritia Gracia." Prince Rainier is buried to the right of her tomb. (Open daily Mar.-Oct. 8am-7pm; Nov.-Feb. 8am-6pm. Mass Sa 6pm, Su 10:30am. Free.) The **Private Collection of Antique Cars of His Serene Highness Prince Rainier III,** on les Terraces de Fontvieille, showcases 100 of the sexiest cars ever made. (Open daily 10am-6pm. €6, students €3.)

Monaco's nightlife offers fashionistas a chance to see and be seen. **La Condamine,** near the port, is a cheaper area and caters to a younger clientele. Pricier spots near the casino are frequented by glitzy trust-funders. **Stars N' Bars,** 6 quai Antoine 1er, draws international masses with its vintage decor, video games, and the latest pop and techno beats. (Open daily 11am-3am.)

CORSICA (LA CORSE)

Napoleon claimed that the smell of herbs on Corsica's hillsides was so distinctive that he could identify his home island with his eyes shut. Even if your senses aren't that acute, there's no confusing Corsica with the French mainland. Despite centuries of invasions, the island has preserved their unique culture. Natives remain divided over the issue of allegiance to France, and often reject the French language in favor of Corse. Most of Corsica's visitors come for the endless possibilities offered by its unspoiled landscapes, which are easily accessible from major towns. Nearly one-third of the island is a protected nature reserve, with over 100 summits, far-reaching networks of hiking and ski trails, and unbroken coastlines that beckon to kayakers, windsurfers, sailors, and sunbathers alike.

TRANSPORTATION

Air France and its subsidiary Compagnie Corse Méditerranée (CCM) send **flights** to Ajaccio and Bastia from Marseille (€88, students €71), Nice (€85/68), and Paris (€112/109). In Ajaccio, the Air France/CCM office is at 3 bd. du Roi Jérôme (☎08 20 82 08 20). **Ferries** between the mainland and Corsica can be a rough trip, and aren't always much cheaper. High-speed ferries (3½hr.) run from Nice, while overnight ferries from Marseille take at least 10hr. The Société National Maritime Corse Méditerranée (☎08 91 70 18 01; www.sncm.fr) sends ferries from Marseille (€40-58, under 25 €25-45) and Nice (€35-47/20-35) to Ajaccio and Bastia. **Corsica Ferries** (☎08 25 09 50 95; www.corsicaferries.com) has similar destinations and prices. SAREMAR (☎04 95 73 00 96) and Moby Lines (☎04 95 73 00 29) go from Santa Teresa, Sardinia to Bonifacio. (€15, cars €26-52). Rumor has it that the Marquis de Sade and Machiavelli collaborated on the design of Corsica's transportation system. **Train** service is slow, limited to destinations north of Ajaccio, and doesn't accept railpasses. **Buses** (☎04 95 21 06 30) provide more comprehensive service, but twisting roads often induce motion sickness. **Hiking** is the best way to explore the island's mountainous interior. The **GR20** is an extremely difficult 180km trail that takes hikers across the island from Calenzana to Conca. The **Parc Naturel Régional de la Corse,** 2 Sargent Casalonga, in Ajaccio, has a guide to *gîtes d'étape* (hostels) and maps. (☎04 95 51 79 00; www.parc-naturel-corse.com.)

AJACCIO (AIACCIU) ☎04 95

Napoleon must have insisted on the best from the very beginning: the little dictator couldn't have picked a better place to call home. Brimming with more energy than most Corsican towns, Ajaccio (pop. 60,000) has excellent museums and nightlife to complement its palm-lined boulevards, yellow sunlit buildings, and white-sand beaches. Inside the **Musée Fesch,** 50-52 r. Cardinal Fesch, cavernous rooms hold an impressive collection of 14th- to 19th-century Italian paintings gathered by Napoleon's art-collecting uncle. Also within the complex is the **Chapelle Impériale,** the final resting place of most of the Bonaparte family, though Napoleon himself is buried in Paris. (Open July-Aug. M 2-6pm, Tu-Th 10:30am-6pm, F 2-9:30pm, Sa-Su 10:30am-6pm; Sept.-June reduced hours. Museum €5.35, students €3.80. Chapel €1.50/0.75.) Ajaccio has many hotels, but from June through August, rates soar and vacancies plummet. The welcoming **Pension de Famille Tina Morelli ❹,** 1 r. Major Lambroschini, fills up quickly; reserve ahead. (☎/fax 21 16 97. Singles with breakfast and 4-course meal €50, with breakfast and 2 full meals €72; doubles €70/122. Cash only.) Though Ajaccio has no shortage of restaurants, your best option is the **morning market** on pl. du Marché. (Open Tu-Su 8am-1pm.) Pizzerias, bakeries, and one-stop *panini* shops can be found on **rue Cardinal Fesch;** at night, patios on the festive dock offer affordable seafood and pizza. Get groceries at **Monoprix,** 31 cours Napoléon. (Open July-Sept. M-Sa 8:30am-8pm; Oct.-June 8:30am-7:20pm.) **Boulevard Pascal Rossini,** near the casino, is home to Ajaccio's busiest strip of bars.

TCA bus #8 (€4.50) shuttles from the bus station at quai l'Herminier to **Aéroport Campo dell'Oro (AJA;** ☎23 56 56). **Trains** (☎23 11 03) leave pl. de la Gare for Bastia (3-4hr., 4 per day, €24) and Corte (2½hr., 4 per day, €13). **Buses**

(☎21 06 30) go to Bastia (3hr., 2 per day, €18) and Bonifacio (3hr., 2 per day, €21). The local **tourist office** is at 3 bd. du Roi Jérôme. (☎51 53 03. Open July-Aug. M-Sa 8am-8:30pm, Su 9am-1pm and 4-7pm; Sept.-June reduced hours.) **Postal Code:** 20000.

BONIFACIO (BONIFAZIU) ☎04 95

At the southern tip of Corsica, the stone ramparts of Bonifacio (pop. 3000), perched on 70m limestone cliffs, present an imposing visage to miles of empty turquoise sea. Bonifacio's fantastic **boat tours** reveal multicolored cliffs, coves, and stalactite-filled grottoes. Ferries also run to the pristine sands of **Îles Lavezzi,** a nature reserve with beautiful reefs perfect for **scuba diving. Les Vedettes Thalassa** offers tours (☎06 86 34 00 49. Grottes-Falaises-Calanques tour every 30min. 9am-6:30pm; €15. Îles Lavezzi 5 per day, last return 5:30pm; €25. Cash only.) To explore the *haute ville*, head up the steep, broad steps of the **montée Rastello,** located halfway down the port, where excellent views of the hazy cliffs to the east await. Continue up montée St-Roch to the lookout at **Porte des Gênes,** a drawbridge built by invaders, then walk to the **place du Marché** to see Bonifacio's famous cliffs and the **Grain de Sable,** an enormous limestone formation that serves as a perch for daring cliff-divers. **Camping** is the best option when prices soar in August. **L'Araguina ❶**, av. Sylvère Bohn, is near the port. (☎73 02 96. Open Apr. to mid-Oct. Laundry €6. Electricity €3. €6.10 per person, €2.40 per tent or car. Cash only.) The **tourist office** is at the corner of av. de Gaulle and r. F. Scamaroni. (☎73 11 88. Open July-Aug. daily 9am-8pm; May-June and Sept. daily 10am-7pm; Oct.-Apr. M-F 9am-noon and 2-6pm.) **Postal Code:** 20169.

BASTIA ☎04 95

Bastia (pop. 40,000), the second-largest city in Corsica, is one of the island's most trampled gateways, with countless connections to the French mainland as well as to more removed villages and vacation spots. Its enormous 14th-century **citadel,** also called Terra Nova, has remained almost perfectly intact, with ramparts reaching down the hill toward the *vieux port*, dwarfing nearby shops and bakeries. The tiny **Eco-Musée,** in the citadel's old powder magazine, contains a detailed replica of a traditional Corsican village, complete with miniature houses and authentic vegetation. (Open Apr.-Oct. M-Sa 9am-noon and 2-6pm. €3.50, students €3.) On the other side of the *vieux port*, the 17th-century **Église St-Jean Baptiste,** pl. de l'Hôtel de Ville, towers over the city. The immense interior of the largest church in Corsica has gilded walls and ornate altars constructed with funds raised by local fishermen. While there are no true budget hotels in Bastia, the **Hôtel Central ❺**, 3 r. Miot, is a good value, complete with antique furniture in large, well-kept rooms. (☎31 71 12; www.centralhotel.fr. Breakfast €6. May-Oct. singles €55-60; doubles €60-80. Nov.-June €10 less. AmEx/MC/V.) To reach **Camping Les Orangiers ❶**, take bus #4 (€1.15) from the tourist office to Licciola-Miomo. (☎33 24 09. Electricity €3.50. Open May to mid-Oct. Tent sites €7.30, extra person €4.60.) Inexpensive cafes crowd **place St-Nicolas.** Though nightlife is almost nonexistent in Bastia, young people find their way to **Port de Plaisance de Toga.**

Shuttle buses (30min., €8) leave from the *préfecture*, across from the train station, for the **Bastia-Poretta Airport** (**BIA;** ☎54 54 54), where flights go to Marseille, Nice, and Paris. **Trains** (☎32 80 61) run from pl. de la Gare to Ajaccio (4hr., 4 per day, €24) and Calvi (3hr., 4 per day, €19). Eurocorse **buses** (☎21 06 31) leave from rte. du Nouveau Port for Ajaccio (3hr., 1-2 per day, €20). The **tourist office** is in pl. St-Nicolas. (☎54 20 40. Open daily July-Aug. 8am-8pm; Sept.-June 8:30am-noon and 2-6pm.) **Postal Code:** 20200.

THE ALPS (LES ALPES)

Nature's architecture is the real attraction of the Alps. The curves of the Chartreuse Valley rise to rugged crags in the Vercors range and crescendo at Europe's highest peak, Mont Blanc. From bases like Chamonix, winter skiers enjoy some of the world's most challenging slopes. In the summer, hikers take over the mountains, seeking endless vistas and clear air. As a rule, the farther into the mountains you want to go, the harder it is to get there, especially outside ski season.

GRENOBLE ☎04 76

Young scholars from all corners of the globe and sizable North and West African populations collide in Grenoble (pop. 168,000), a dynamic city whose surrounding snow-capped peaks are cherished by both athletes and aesthetes.

TRANSPORTATION AND PRACTICAL INFORMATION. **Trains** leave pl. de la Gare for: Lyon (1½hr., 30 per day, €18); Marseille (2½-4½hr., 15 per day, €44); Nice (5-6½hr., 5 per day, €58); Paris (3hr., 9 per day, €80). **Buses** leave from left of the train station for Geneva, SWI (3hr., 1 per day, €26). From the station, turn right into pl. de la Gare, take the third left on av. Alsace-Lorraine, and follow the tram tracks on r. Félix Poulat and r. Blanchard to reach the **tourist office,** 14 r. de la République. (☎42 41 41; www.grenoble-isere.info. Open M-Sa 9am-6:30pm, Su 10am-1pm and 2-5pm.) **Postal Code:** 38000.

ACCOMMODATIONS AND FOOD. From the tourist office, follow pl. Ste-Claire to pl. Notre-Dame and take r. du Vieux Temple on the far right to reach **Le Foyer de l'Etudiante ❶**, 4 r. Ste-Ursule. This stately building serves as a dorm during most of the year, but opens its large, modern rooms to travelers from June to August. (☎42 00 84; www.multimania.com/foyeretudiante. Laundry €2.20. Free Internet. Min stay 3 nights. Singles €15; doubles €24.) Regional restaurants cater to locals around **pl. de Gordes,** while Italian eateries and cheap pizzerias line **quai Perrière** across the river. *Pâtisseries* and North African joints lie around **rue Chenoise** and **rue Lionne,** between the pedestrian area and the river. Cafes and smaller bistros cluster around **place Notre-Dame** and **place St-André,** in the heart of the *vieille ville.* The seven-table gem **Tête à l'Envers ❸,** 12 r. Chenoise, serves a melange of international cuisine. (☎51 13 42. *Plat du jour* €11. Mention *Let's Go* for a free coffee or *digestif.* Open Tu-F noon-3pm and 7:30pm-1am, Sa 7:30pm-1am. MC/V.)

SIGHTS AND ENTERTAINMENT. **Téléphériques** (cable cars) depart from quai Stéphane-Jay every 10min. for the 16th-century **Bastille,** a fort perched 475m above the city. (Open July-Aug. M 11am-12:15am, Tu-Su 9:15am-12:15am; Sept.-June reduced hours. €3.95, round-trip €5.80; students €3.25/4.65.) After enjoying the views from the top, you can walk down via the **Parc Guy Pape,** through the other end of the fortress, to the **Jardin des Dauphins** (1hr.). Cross the Pont St-Laurent and go up Montée Chalemont for the **Musée Dauphinois,** 30 r. Maurice Gignoux, which displays well-produced exhibits on the people of the Alps and the history of skiing. (Open M and W-Su June-Sept. 10am-7pm; Oct.-May 10am-6pm. Free.) The **Musée de Grenoble,** 5 pl. de Lavelette, houses one of France's most prestigious art collections. (☎63 44 44; www.museedegrenoble.fr. Open M and W-Su 10am-6:15pm. €5, students €2.) Another attractive aspect of Grenoble is its proximity to the slopes. The biggest and most developed **ski areas** are to the east in **Oisans;** the **Alpe d'Huez** has 220km of trails. (Tourist office ☎11 44 44, ski area 80 30

30.) The **Belledonne** region, northeast of Grenoble, has both a lower elevation and lower prices; its most popular ski area is **Chamrousse.** (Tourist office ☎89 92 65. Lift tickets €24 per day.) Grenoble's funky night scene can be found between **place St-André** and **place Notre-Dame.** A twenty-something crowd relaxes at graffiti-covered **Le Couche-Tard,** 1 r. du Palais. (Open M-Sa 7pm-2am. AmEx/MC/V.)

CHAMONIX

☎04 50

The site of the first Winter Olympics in 1924, Chamonix (pop. 10,000) combines the dignity of **Mont Blanc,** Europe's highest peak (4807m), with the spirit of its energetic visitors. Whether you've come to climb up the mountains or ski down them, be cautious—steep grades and potential avalanches make the slopes as challenging as they are beautiful. The **Aiguille du Midi téléphérique** (cable car) offers a pricey, knuckle-whitening ascent over forests and snowy cliffs to a needlepoint peak at the top, revealing a fantastic panorama from 3842m. (☎08 92 68 00 67. Round-trip €35.) Bring your passport to continue by gondola to **Helbronner, ITA** for views of three countries and of the **Matterhorn** and Mont Blanc peaks. (May-Sept., round-trip with Aiguille du Midi €54.) The mountains surrounding Chamonix are ideal for **skiing.** To the south, **Le Tour-Col de Balme** (☎54 00 58; day pass €32), above the village of **Le Tour,** draws beginners and intermediates, while **Les Grands Montets** (☎54 00 71; day pass €36), to the north, is the *grande dame* of Chamonix skiing, with advanced terrain and **snowboarding** facilities. Chamonix has 350km of **hiking;** the tourist office has a map with the departure points and estimated durations of all trails (€4), though some are accessible only by cable car.

From the train station, walk down av. Michel Croz and take a right onto r. Joseph Vallot for the **Red Mountain Lodge ❷,** 435 r. Joseph Vallot, with social co-ed dorms, tidy doubles, and a homey living room. (☎53 94 97. Breakfast included. Reception 8am-noon and 5-7pm. Dorms €16; doubles €35. Cash only.) Restaurants, nightclubs, and bars in Chamonix center around the town center on **Rue du Docteur Paccard** and **Rue des Moulins.** Get groceries at **Super U,** 117 r. Joseph Vallot. (Open M-Sa 8:15am-7:30pm, Su 8:30am-noon.) **Trains** leave av. de la Gare (☎53 12 98) for: Annecy (2½hr., 6 per day, €20); Geneva, SWI (2½hr., 7 per day, €45); Lyon (3½hr., 7 per day, €35); Paris (6-7hr., 6 per day, €70-90). Société Alpes Transports **buses** (☎53 01 15) leave the train station for Geneva, SWI (1½hr., 1-5 per day, €33). Local buses (€1.50) connect to ski slopes and hiking trails. From the station, follow av. Michel Croz, turn left on r. du Dr. Paccard, and take the first right to reach pl. de l'Église and the **tourist office,** 85 pl. du Triangle de l'Amitié. (☎53 00 24; www.chamonix.com. Open daily July-Sept. and mid-Dec. to Apr. 8:30am-12:30pm and 2-7pm; May-June and Oct. to mid-Dec. 9am-12:30pm and 2-6:30pm.)

ANNECY

☎04 50

With narrow cobblestone streets, romantic canals, and a turreted castle, Annecy (pop. 53,000) appears more like a fairy tale than a modern city. The **Palais de l'Isle,** in the beautiful *vieille ville,* is a 13th-century château that served as a prison for Resistance fighters during WWII. (☎33 87 30. Open June-Sept. daily 10:30am-6pm; Oct.-May M and W-Su 10am-noon and 2-5pm. €3.20, students €1.) The shaded **Jardin de l'Europe** is Annecy's pride and joy. In summer, the crystalline **lake** is a popular spot for windsurfing and kayaking, particularly along the **plage d'Albigny.** Annecy's Alpine forests has excellent hiking and biking trails. One of the best hikes begins at the **Basilique de la Visitation,** near the hostel, a scenic 25km *piste cyclable* (bike route) hugs the eastern shore of the lake.

In summer, you can reach the clean, beautifully located **Auberge de Jeunesse "La Grande Jeanne" (HI) ❷,** rte. de Semnoz, via the *ligne d'été* bus (dir.: Semnoz; €1) from the train station. Or, take bus #6 (dir.: Marquisats) from the station to

Hôtel de Police, turn right on av. du Tresum, and follow signs to Semnoz. (☎45 33 19; annecy@fuaj.org. Breakfast included. Reception 8am-10pm. 4- and 5-bed dorms with showers €17. MC/V.) **Place Ste-Claire** has morning **markets** (Tu, F, Su 8am-noon) and some of the most charming restaurants in the city. A €12.50 *menu* at **Quoi de n'Oeuf ❸,** 19 Faubourg Ste-Claire, includes generous portions of *tartiflette*, salad, and dessert. (☎45 75 42. Open M-F noon-2pm and 7-9:45pm, Sa noon-2pm. MC/V.) **Trains** run from pl. de la Gare to: Chamonix (2½hr., 6 per day, €19); Grenoble (2hr., 9 per day, €17); Lyon (2hr., 9 per day, €21); Nice (7-9hr., 7 per day, €75); Paris (4hr., 6 per day, €64). Autocars Frossard **buses** (☎45 73 90) leave from next to the station for Geneva, SWI (1¼hr., 2-3 per day, €10). From the train station, take the underground passage to r. Sommelier, go left onto r. Vaugelas for four blocks, and enter the Bonlieu shopping mall to reach the **tourist office,** 1 r. Jean Jaurès, in pl. de la Libération. (☎45 00 33; www.lac-annecy.com. Open daily July-Aug. 9am-6:30pm; Sept.-June reduced hours.) **Postal Code:** 74000.

LYON ☎04 78

Ultra-modern, friendly, and undeniably gourmet, the city of Lyon (pop. 515,000) elicits cries of "forget Paris" from backpackers. Foreign merchants settled in Lyon during the Renaissance; in the 15th century, Lyon became Europe's printing house. In the 16th century, silk cemented the city's economic power. The ornate facades and courtyards of the 16th-century townhouses in *vieux Lyon* attest to its former glory. If the way to your heart is through your stomach, Lyon will have you at *"bon appetit."*

TRANSPORTATION

Flights: Aéroport Lyon-Saint-Exupéry (☎08 26 80 08 26). **Satobuses/Navette Aéroport** (☎04 72 68 72 17) has **shuttles** to Gare de la Part-Dieu, Gare de Perrache, and subway stops Grange-Blanche, Jean Mace, and Mermoz Pinel (every 20min., €8.40). **Air France,** 5 rue Jessieu, 2*ème* (☎08 20 82 08 20), has 12 flights per day to Paris's Charles de Gaulle and Orly airports (€101-215). Open M-Sa 9am-6pm.

Trains: The TGV, which stops at the airport, is cheaper and much more convenient than flights to Paris. Trains passing through Lyon stop only at **Gare de la Part-Dieu,** bd. Marius Vivier-Merle (M: Part-Dieu), on the Rhône's east bank. Info desk open M-F 9am-7pm, Sa 9am-6:30pm. Trains terminating in Lyon continue to **Gare de Perrache,** pl. Carnot (M: Perrache). Ticket windows open M-Sa 5am-8pm, Su 6:10am-10:20pm. **SNCF** trains go from both stations to: **Dijon** (2hr., 22 per day, €24); **Grenoble** (1¼hr., 23 per day, €17.30); **Marseille** (3½hr., 13 per day, €38); **Nice** (6hr., 12 per day, €58); **Paris** (2hr., 30 per day, €59); **Strasbourg** (5½hr., 6 per day, €46). The **SNCF Boutique,** 2 pl. Bellecour, is near the tourist office. Open M-F 9am-6:45pm, Sa 10am-6:30pm.

Buses: On the lowest level of the Gare de Perrache and at Gorge de Loup in the 9ème (☎04 72 61 72 61 for both). Domestic companies include **Philibert** (☎04 78 98 56 00) and **Transport Verney** (☎04 78 70 21 01), but it's almost always cheaper and faster to take the train. **Eurolines** (☎04 72 56 95 30; www.eurolines.fr) travels out of France; office on the main floor of Perrache open 9am-9pm.

Local Transportation: TCL (☎08 20 42 70 00; www.tcl.fr), has information offices at both train stations and at many major metro stops. Pocket maps are also available from any TCL branch. The efficient **métro** system runs 5am-12:20am, as do **buses** and **trams.** Tickets are valid for all mass transport. 1hr. single-fare ticket €1.50; 10-ride *carnet* €12.20, students €10.50. The *Ticket Liberté* day pass (€4.30) allows for unlimited use of mass transit.

ORIENTATION AND PRACTICAL INFORMATION

Lyon is divided into nine **arrondissements** (districts). The *1er*, *2ème*, and *4ème* lie on the **presqu'île** (peninsula), which juts south toward the **Saône** River to the west and the **Rhône** to the east. Starting in the south, the *2ème* (the *centre ville*) includes the **Gare de Perrache** and **place Bellecour.** The nocturnal **Terreaux** neighborhood, with its popular cafes and student-packed bars, makes up the *1er*. Farther north are the *4ème* and the **Croix-Rousse.** The main pedestrian roads on the *presqu'île* are **rue de la République** and **rue Victor Hugo.**

Tourist Office: In the **Pavilion** at pl. Bellecour, *2ème* (☎04 72 77 69 69; www.lyon-france.com). M: Bellecour. The **Lyon City Card** authorizes unlimited public transport along with admission to 14 museums and various tours. 1-day pass €18; 2-day €28; 3-day €38. Open May-Oct. M-Sa 9am-7pm, Su 10am-6pm; Nov.-Apr. reduced hours.

Police: 47 r. de la Charité (☎42 26 56). M: Perrache.

Hospital: Hôpital Hôtel-Dieu, 1 pl. de l'Hôpital, *2ème,* near quai du Rhône, is the most central. City hospital line ☎08 20 69.

Internet Access: Raconte Moi la Terre (☎92 60 23), at of r. Grolee and r. Thomassin, *2ème*. €4 per hr. Open M-Sa 10am-7:30pm. Free wireless at **McDonald's.**

Post Office: 2 pl. Antonin Poncet, *2ème* (☎04 72 40 65 22), near pl. Bellecour. **Postal Codes:** 69001-69009; last digit indicates *arrondissement.*

ACCOMMODATIONS

France's second-largest financial center (after Paris, *bien sûr*) is filled on most weekday nights with businessmen, who often leave town on the weekends. Fall is the busiest season in Lyon; it's easier to find a place in the summer. A room less than €30 is rare, but low-end hotels lie east of **pl. Carnot,** and other less expensive options are north of **pl. des Terreaux.** Prices are high close to **pl. Bellecour.**

Auberge de Jeunesse (HI), 41-45 montée du Chemin Neuf, *5ème* (☎15 05 50; fax 15 05 51). M: Vieux Lyon. Spectacular views from the grassy terrace and a jumping bar. It's a hike up the hill and the bathrooms may be less than spotless, but the prime location makes up for any discomfort. Staff speaks English. Breakfast and linens included. Laundry €4. Internet €4.90 per hr. Reception 24hr. Dorms €16. MC/V. HI members only. ❶

Hôtel Iris, 36 r. de l'Arbre Sec (☎39 93 80; www.hoteliris.freesurf.fr). M: Hôtel de Ville. This convent-turned-hotel has creatively decorated rooms. Breakfast €5. Reception 8am-8:30pm. Reserve 2 weeks ahead. Singles and doubles with sink €39, with toilet and shower €45-50; triples €61. MC/V. ❸

Hôtel St-Vincent, 9 r. Pareille, *1er* (☎27 22 56; www.hotel-saintvincent.com), just off quai St-Vincent. M: Hôtel de Ville. Modern wood-paneled rooms with lots of floor space and sparkling clean bathrooms. Breakfast €5.50. Reception 24hr. Reserve ahead. Singles €45-55; doubles €55; triples €65-75. MC/V. ❸

FOOD

The galaxy of Michelin stars adorning Lyon's restaurants confirms its status as the gastronomic capital of the Western world. It's difficult to go wrong when it comes to cuisine here: while most *menus* don't dip below €16, cheaper, but equally appealing alternatives can be found on **rue St-Jean, rue des Marronniers,** and **rue Mercière.** Ethnic restaurants center near **rue de la République.** There are **markets** on the quais of the Rhône and Saône (Tu-Su 8am-1pm).

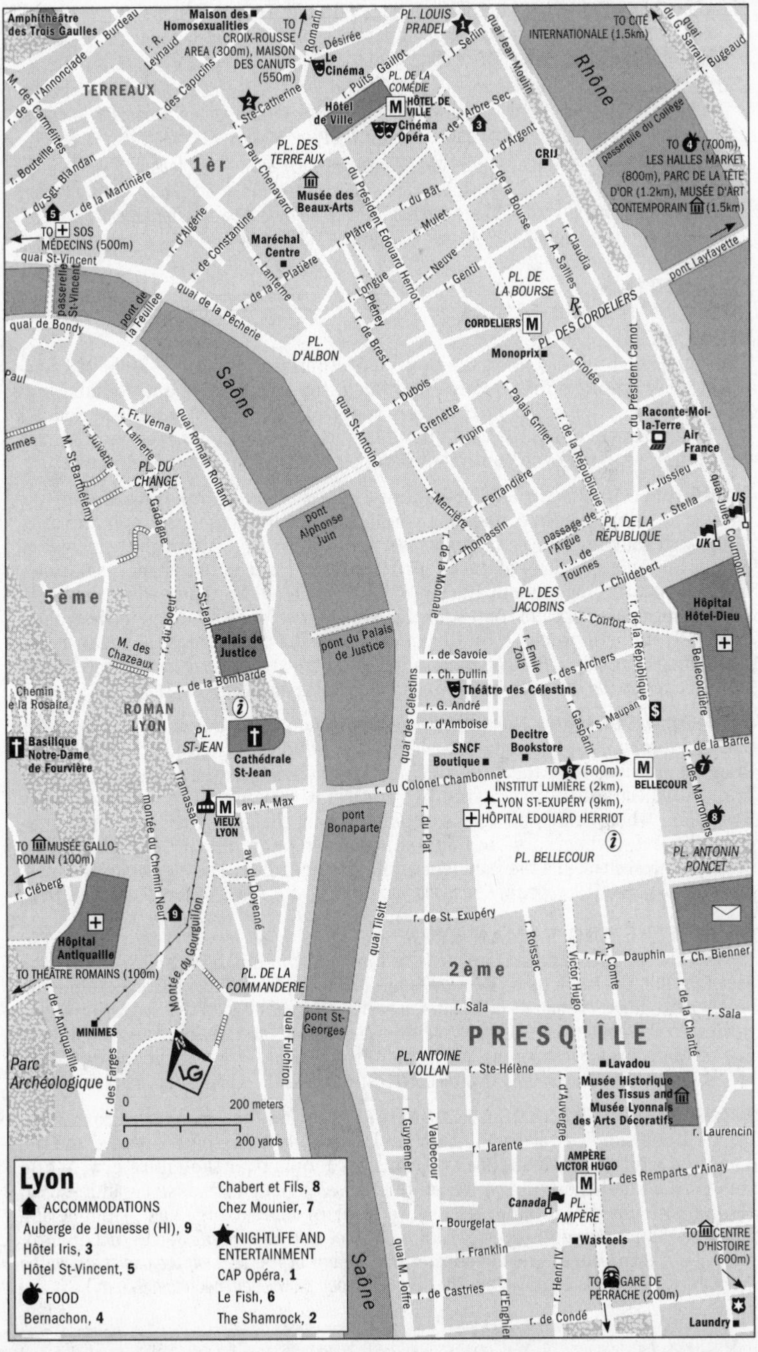
Lyon
ACCOMMODATIONS
Auberge de Jeunesse (HI), 9
Hôtel Iris, 3
Hôtel St-Vincent, 5
FOOD
Bernachon, 4
Chabert et Fils, 8
Chez Mounier, 7
NIGHTLIFE AND ENTERTAINMENT
CAP Opéra, 1
Le Fish, 6
The Shamrock, 2
Amphithéâtre des Trois Gaulles
Maison des Homosexualities
TO CROIX-ROUSSE AREA (300m), MAISON DES CANUTS (550m)
PL. LOUIS PRADEL
TO CITÉ INTERNATIONALE (1.5km)
Rhône
Le Cinéma
TERREAUX
PL. DE LA COMÉDIE
Hôtel de Ville
HÔTEL DE VILLE
Cinéma Opéra
PL. DES TERREAUX
1èr
Musée des Beaux-Arts
CRIJ
TO (700m), LES HALLES MARKET (800m), PARC DE LA TÊTE D'OR (1.2km), MUSÉE D'ART CONTEMPORAIN (1.5km)
TO SOS MÉDECINS (500m)
Maréchal Centre
PL. DE LA BOURSE
CORDELIERS
PL. DES CORDELIERS
Monoprix
PL. D'ALBON
Saône
Raconte-Moi-la-Terre
Air France
PL. DU CHANGE
pont Alphonse Juin
PL. DE LA RÉPUBLIQUE
US
UK
5ème
PL. DES JACOBINS
Hôpital Hôtel-Dieu
Palais de Justice
pont du Palais de Justice
Théâtre des Célestins
ROMAN LYON
PL. ST-JEAN
Cathédrale St-Jean
Basilique Notre-Dame de Fourvière
SNCF Boutique
Decitre Bookstore
TO (500m), INSTITUT LUMIÈRE (2km), LYON ST-EXUPÉRY (9km), HÔPITAL EDOUARD HERRIOT
BELLECOUR
VIEUX LYON
pont Bonaparte
PL. BELLECOUR
PL. ANTONIN PONCET
TO MUSÉE GALLO-ROMAIN (100m)
Hôpital Antiquaille
TO THÉÂTRE ROMAINS (100m)
PL. DE LA COMMANDERIE
2ème
MINIMES
pont St-Georges
PRESQU'ÎLE
Parc Archéologique
PL. ANTOINE VOLLAN
Lavadou
Musée Historique des Tissus and Musée Lyonnais des Arts Décoratifs
0
200 meters
200 yards
AMPÈRE VICTOR HUGO
Canada
PL. AMPÈRE
Wasteels
TO CENTRE D'HISTOIRE (600m)
TO GARE DE PERRACHE (200m)
Laundry

FRANCE

Bernachon, 42 cours F. Roosevelt (☎52 23 65). M: Foch. Don't come to this grand *patisserie* for a cheap snack. Serves up expensive but delicious desserts (from €5.80). Open Tu-Sa 9am-6:30pm. MC/V. ❷

Chez Mounier, 3 r. des Marronniers, 2*ème* (☎37 79 26). M: Bellecour. Exceptional value and top-notch cuisine in a welcoming restaurant. Afternoon *menu* €8. 4-course *menus* €11-20. Open Tu-Sa noon-2pm and 7-11pm, Su noon-1:30pm. MC/V. ❸

Chabert et Fils, 11 r. des Marronniers, 2*ème* (☎37 01 94). M: Bellecour. A well-known, well-loved *bouchon,* 1 of 4 such *bouchons* on r. des Marronniers run by the same family. The lunch *menus* (€8-13) are the best way to enjoy Chabert. Dinner *menus* €17-33. Open Su-Th noon-2pm and 7-11pm, F-Sa until 11:30pm. MC/V. ❸

SIGHTS

VIEUX LYON

Stacked against the Saône at the bottom of Fourvière Hill, the streets of *Vieux Lyon* wind among spirited cafes and magnificent medieval and Renaissance houses. The striking *hôtels particuliers* (once-private homes), with their delicate carvings, shaded courtyards, and ornate turrets, were built between the 15th and 18th centuries when Lyon controlled Europe's silk and publishing industries.

TRABOULES. The distinguishing features of *Vieux Lyon* townhouses are the *traboules,* indoor passages connecting parallel streets through mazes of courtyards, often with vaulted ceilings and exquisite spiral staircases. Although their original purpose is debated, many of the later *traboules* were used to transport silk safely from looms to storage rooms. During WWII, the passageways proved invaluable as info-gathering and escape routes for the Resistance. Many are open to the public, especially in the morning. A tour beginning near the cathedral is the ideal way to see them; the tourist office also has a list of addresses. *(Consult tourist office. English-language tours in summer every few days at 2:30pm; winter hours vary. €9, students €5.)*

CATHÉDRALE ST-JEAN. The cathedral's soaring columns dominate the southern end of *Vieux Lyon.* Paris might have been worth a Mass, but Lyon got the wedding cake; it was here that Henri IV met and married Maria de Médici in 1600. Some of the stained-glass windows are relatively new; the originals were destroyed when Lyon's bridges exploded during the 1944 Nazi retreat. Inside, every hour between noon and 4pm, automatons pop out of the 14th-century **astronomical clock** in a reenactment of the Annunciation. The clock can calculate feast days until 2019. *(Open M-F 8am-noon and 2-7:30pm, Sa-Su 8am-noon and 2-5pm. Free.)*

FRANCE

FOURVIÈRE AND ROMAN LYON

From r. du Bœuf at r. de la Bombarde in *Vieux Lyon,* climb the stairs up to reach **Fourvière Hill,** the nucleus of Roman Lyon. From the top of the stairs, continue up via the rose-lined **chemin de la Rosaire,** a series of switchbacks that leads through a garden to the **esplanade Fourvière,** where a model of the city indicates local landmarks. Many prefer to take the less strenuous **funicular** *(la ficelle)* to the top of the hill. It leaves from the *Vieux Lyon* metro station, at the head of av. A. Max.

BASILIQUE NOTRE-DAME DE FOURVIÈRE. During the Franco-Prussian War, Lyon's archbishop vowed to build a church if the city were spared. It was, and the basilica's white, meringue-like exterior now looms over the entire city. While some locals feel the building resembles an *éléphant renversé* (upside-down elephant) from the outside, its ornate interior is amazing. Vast, shimmering mosaics depict religious scenes, Joan of Arc, and the naval battle of Lepanto. Architect Pierre Bossan designed the low, heavy crypt. *(Behind the esplanade at the top of the hill. Chapel open daily 7am-7pm. Basilica open daily 10am-noon and 2-5pm.)*

LA PRESQU'ÎLE AND LES TERREAUX

At the heart of the *presqu'île* is **place Bellecour,** which links Lyon's two main pedestrian arteries. **Rue Victor Hugo** heads south. To the north, crowded **rue de la République,** or "la Ré," is the urban aorta of Lyon. It runs through **place de la République** and ends at **place Louis Pradel** in the 1*er*, at the tip of the Terreaux. Once a marshy wasteland, this area was filled with soil to create terraces *(terreaux)* and established the neighborhood as the place to be for chic locals.

MUSÉE DES BEAUX-ARTS. This excellent museum takes visitors on a whirlwind tour through diverse exhibits: an archaeological wing displays Egyptian sarcophagi and Roman busts; distinguished French, Dutch, and Spanish paintings including works by Monet, Renoir, and Picasso line the third-floor walls; and a tranquil sculpture garden graces the inner courtyard. Beyond the all-star Impressionist collections, the museum's assortment of local works will impress any aesthete. Highlights are a fascinating Islamic art display and an unbelievably large coin collection. *(20 pl. des Terreaux. www.mairie-lyon.fr. Open M 10am-2pm, W-Su 10am-6pm. Sculpture galleries closed noon-2:15pm; painting galleries closed 1-2:15pm. €6, under 26 €4, students free. MC/V.)*

LA CROIX-ROUSSE AND THE SILK INDUSTRY

Though mass silk manufacturing is based elsewhere today, Lyon is proud of its historical dominance of the industry in Europe. The city's Croix-Rousse district, a steep, uphill walk from pl. des Terreaux, houses the vestiges of its silk-weaving days; Lyon's few remaining silk workers still create delicate handiwork, reconstructing and replicating rare patterns for museum and château displays.

LA MAISON DES CANUTS. Aiming to bring Lyon's glorious silk-weaving past to life, the back room of this tiny museum contains a small collection of ancient silk looms. Tours demonstrate the weaving techniques of the *canuts* (silk weavers). The shop sells silk made by its own *canuts*. A scarf costs €32 or more, but silk enthusiasts can take home a handkerchief for €8.50. *(10-12 r. d'Ivry, 4ème. Open M-F 9am-noon and 2-6:30pm, Sa 9am-noon and 2-6pm. Closed M in Aug. €5, students €2.50.)*

MUSÉE HISTORIQUE DES TISSUS. The museum's exhibits about Lyon's history in the silk trade may be interesting, but everyone comes here for the clothes. In dark rooms, rows of costumes recall skirt-flaunting, bosom-baring characters of the past. The collection includes examples of Marie-Antoinette's Versailles winter wardrobe as well as ornate silk wall-hangings resembling stained-glass windows. Included with admission is the neighboring **Musée des Arts Décoratifs,** in a fully furnished 18th-century *hôtel*, which displays an array of clocks, painted plates, silverware, and furniture dating from the Renaissance to the present. *(34 r. de la Charité, 2ème.* Tissus *open Tu-Su 10am-5:30pm.* Arts Décoratifs *open Tu-Su 10am-noon and 2-5:30pm. €5, students €3, under 18 free.)*

EAST OF THE RHÔNE AND MODERN LYON

Lyon's newest train station and monstrous space-age mall form the core of the ultra-modern Part-Dieu district. Locals call the commercial **Tour du Crédit Lyonnais** *"le Crayon"* for its unintentional resemblance to a giant pencil standing on end. Next to it, the shell-shaped **Auditorium Maurice Ravel** hosts major cultural events.

CENTRE D'HISTOIRE DE LA RÉSISTANCE ET DE LA DÉPORTATION. Housed in a building where Nazis tortured detainees during the Occupation, this museum presents a sobering collection of documents, photos, and films of the Resistance based in Lyon. An audio tour lead visitors past heartbreaking letters and inspiring autobiographies. *(14 av. Bertholet, 7ème. M: Jean Macé. Open W-F 9am-5:30pm, Sa-Su 9:30am-6pm. €3.80, students €2, under 18 free; includes audio tour in 3 languages.)*

FRANCE

MUSÉE D'ART CONTEMPORAIN. This extensive, entertaining mecca of modern art, video, and high-tech installations resides in the futuristic **Cité International de Lyon,** a super-modern complex with shops, theaters, and Interpol's world headquarters. All of its exhibits are temporary; even the walls are rebuilt for each installation. *(Quai Charles de Gaulle, next to Parc de la Tête d'Or,* 6ème. *Take bus #4 from M: Foch. Open W-Su noon-7pm. €5, students €3.50, under 18 free.)*

NIGHTLIFE

Nightlife in Lyon is fast and furious; the city teems with bars and nightclubs. The best late-night spots are a strip of **riverboat dance clubs** docked by the east bank of the Rhône. The intimate bars along **r. Ste-Catherine** (*1er*) are popular among students until 1am, before they head to the clubs. *Lyon Libertin* (€2) lists hot nightlife venues. For superb tips about gay nightlife, pick up *Le Petit Paumé*.

The Shamrock, 15 r. Ste-Catherine (☎04 72 07 64 96). M: Hôtel de Ville. At this happening Irish pub, a young crowd knocks back €4 pints to the beat of W night jam sessions and live concerts 1 Th per month. Open daily 6pm-1am. AmEx/MC/V.

Le Fish, across from 21 quai Augagneur (☎04 72 84 98 98). M: Guillotière. Plays hip-hop, jungle, disco, and house on a swanky boat with a boisterous top-floor deck. Dress well; admission is competitive. Cover (€12) includes 1 drink. Open Th 10pm-5am, F-Sa 10pm-6am. AmEx/MC/V.

CAP Opéra, 2 pl. Louis Pradel, 1*er*. A popular gay pub, with red lights to match the Opéra next door. A more mellow crowd early in the evening spills out on to the stairs outside as night descends. Occasional theme nights. Open daily 9am-3am. Cash only.

BERRY-LIMOUSIN AND BURGUNDY

Too often passed over for beaches and big cities, Berry-Limousin offers undisturbed countryside and fascinating towns. To the east, Burgundy declined such secular ornaments in favor of abbeys and cathedrals that bear witness to the religious fervor of the Middle Ages. Today, Burgundy draws epicureans worldwide for its fine wines and delectable dishes like *coq au vin* and *bœuf bourguignon.*

DIJON ☎03 80

Dijon (pop. 150,000) isn't just about the mustard. The capital of Burgundy, once home to dukes who wielded a power unmatched by the puny French monarchy, counters the signs of its historic grandeur with an irreverent lifestyle. The diverse **Musée des Beaux-Arts** occupies the east wing of the colossal **Palais des Ducs de Bourgogne,** on pl. de la Libération at the center of the *vieille ville.* (☎74 52 70. Open M and W-Su May-Oct. 9:30am-6pm; Nov.-Apr. 10am-5pm. Free. Temporary exhibits €2, students €1.) Built in only 20 years, the **Église Notre-Dame,** pl. Notre Dame, is one of France's most famous churches. Its 11th-century cult statue of the Black Virgin is credited with having liberated the city on two desperate occasions: in 1513 from a Swiss siege and in 1944 from the German occupation. The brightly tiled towers of **Cathédrale St-Bénigne,** in pl. St-Bénigne, are noticeable from anywhere in town; inside, the church features a spooky circular crypt. (☎30 39 33. Church open daily 9am-7pm. Crypt €1.) Dijon's **Estivade** (☎74 53 33; tickets under €8) brings dance, music, and theater to the streets and indoor venues throughout July. In late summer, the week-long **Fêtes de la Vigne** and **Folkloriades Internationales** (☎30 37 95; www.fetesdelavigne.com; tickets €10-46) celebrate the grape harvest with dance and music from around the world.

Hotel Victor Hugo ❸, 23 r. des Fleurs, is run by friendly proprietors and features antique touches, armchairs, and tiled bathrooms. (☎43 63 45. Breakfast €5.50. Reception 24hr. Singles €30-39; doubles €38-46. AmEx/MC/V.) **Rue Amiral Boussin** has charming cafes, while reasonably priced restaurants line **rue Berbisey, rue Monge, rue Musette,** and **place Émile Zola.** Fend for yourself at the **supermarket** in the basement of the Galeries Lafayette department store, 41 r. de la Liberté. (Open M-Sa 9:15am-8pm.) From the station at cours de la Gare, **trains** run to Lyon (2hr., 14 per day, €25-28), Nice (6-8hr., 6-8 per day, €70-85), and Paris (1¾-3hr., 15-19 per day, €36-51). The **tourist office,** in pl. Darcy, is straight down av. Maréchal Foch from the station. (☎08 92 70 05 58; www.dijon-tourism.com. Open daily May to mid-Oct. 9am-7pm; mid-Oct. to Apr. 10am-6pm.) **Postal Code:** 21000.

BEAUNE ☎03 80

Wine has poured out of the well-touristed town of Beaune (pop. 23,000), just south of Dijon, for centuries. Surrounded by the famous Côte de Beaune vineyards, the town itself is packed with wineries offering free *dégustations* (tastings). The largest of the *caves* (cellars), a 5km labyrinth of corridors with over four million bottles, belongs to **Patriarche Père et Fils,** 5-7 r. du Collège. (☎24 53 78. Open daily 9:30-11:30am and 2-5:30pm. €10; all proceeds to charity.) Oenophiles thirsting for knowledge can learn more about wine-making on the Côte at the **Musée du Vin,** r. d'Enfer, off pl. Général Leclerc. (☎22 08 19. Open Apr.-Nov. daily 9:30am-6pm; Dec.-Mar. W-Su 9:30am-5pm. €5.40, students €3.50.) Beaune is also home to the **Hôtel-Dieu,** 2 r. de l'Hôtel-Dieu, one of France's architectural icons. Originally a hospital, built in 1443 to help the city's poor recover from the famine following the Hundred Years' War, the building is now a museum. (☎24 45 00. Open daily late Mar. to mid-Nov. 9am-7:30pm; mid-Nov. to late-Mar. 9-11:30am and 2-6:30pm. €5.60, students €4.80.) **Hôtel le Foch ❷**, 24 bd. Foch, has colorful but cramped rooms on the other side of the ramparts from the train station. (☎24 05 65. Singles and doubles €25, with shower €33-38; triples €45; quads €48. MC/V.) Cheap accommodations are hard to come by in Beaune; staying in Dijon may be a better option. **Trains** run from Dijon (20-35min., 26 per day, €6.40-8.10). The **tourist office** is at 1 r. de l'Hôtel-Dieu. (☎26 21 30; www.ot-beaune.fr. Open late June-late Sept. M-Sa 9am-7pm, Su 9am-6pm; late Sept.-late June reduced hours.) To escape the wine tourists, rent a bike at **Bourgogne Randonées,** 7 av. du 8 septembre, near the station, and follow their suggested route to the *caves.* (☎22 06 03. Bikes €3 per hr., €15 per day, €28 per 2 days, €80 per week. Credit card deposit required. Open M-Sa 9am-noon and 1:30-7pm, Su 10am-noon and 2-7pm. MC/V.) **Postal Code:** 21200.

ALSACE-LORRAINE AND FRANCHE-COMTÉ

As first prize in the endless Franco-German border wars, France's northeastern frontier has a long and bloody history. Influenced by its tumultuous past, the entire region maintains a fascinating blend of French and German in the local dialects, cuisine, and architecture. Alsatian towns display half-timbered Bavarian houses and canals, while Lorraine's wheat fields are interspersed with elegant cities.

STRASBOURG ☎03 88

On the Franco-German border, Strasbourg (pop. 450,000) is a city with true international character. The tower of the ornate Gothic **Cathédrale de Strasbourg** stretches 142m skyward; young Goethe scaled its 332 steps regularly to cure his fear of heights. Inside the cathedral, the **Horloge Astronomique** demonstrates the wizardry of 16th-century Swiss clockmakers daily at 12:30pm, and the **Pilier des Anges** (Angels' Pillar) depicts the Last Judgment. (Cathedral open M-Sa 7-11:40am and 12:40-7pm, Su 12:45-6pm. Tower open daily July-Aug. 8:30am-7pm; Apr.-June and Sept. 9am-6pm; Mar. and Oct. 9am-5:30pm; Nov.-Feb. 9am-4:30pm. Clock tickets for sale inside cathedral or at southern entrance; €1. Tower €4.40, students €2.20.) **Palais Rohan,** 2 pl. du Château, houses three small but excellent museums: the **Musée des Beaux-Arts,** the **Musée des Arts Décoratifs,** and the **Musée Archéologique.** (All open M and W-Su 10am-6pm. €4 each, students €2. Free 1st Su of every month.)

High-quality, inexpensive hotels abound, especially around the train station. Wherever you stay, make reservations early, particularly in the summer. The **Centre International d'Accueil de Strasbourg (CIARUS) ❷,** 7 r. Finkmatt, has rooms complete with shower and toilet. From the train station, take r. du Maire-Kuss to the canal, turn left, and follow quai St-Jean through various name changes; turn left on r. Finkmatt and the hostel will be on your left. (☎15 27 88; www.ciarus.com. Breakfast included. Dorms €20-24; singles €42; doubles €53. MC/V.) The **La Petite France** neighborhood, especially along r. des Dentelles, is full of informal *winstubs* with Alsatian specialties such as *choucroute garnie* (spiced sauerkraut with meats).For groceries, swing by **ATAC,** 47 r. des Grandes Arcades, off pl. Kléber. (Open M-Sa 8:30am-8:30pm.) **Bar Exils,** 28 r. de l'Ail, offers over 40 beers and comfy leather couches. (Beer from €2. Open M-F noon-4am, Sa-Su 2pm-4am. MC/V; min. €6.) **Trains** (☎08 92 35 35 35) go to: Frankfurt, GER (3hr., 10 per day, €48); Luxembourg (2½hr., 14 per day, €33); Paris (4hr., 16 per day, €45); Zürich, SWI (3hr., 3-4 per day, €40). The **tourist office** is at 17 pl. de la Cathédrale. (☎52 28 28; www.ot-strasbourg.fr. Open daily 9am-7pm.) **Postal Code:** 67000.

LA ROUTE DU VIN

The vineyards of Alsace flourish along the foothills of the Vosges from Strasbourg to Mulhouse—a region known as the Route du Vin. The Romans were the first to ferment Alsatian grapes, and today Alsatians sell over 150 million bottles annually. Consider staying in **Colmar** (p. 394) or **Sélestat** (p. 393), and daytripping to the smaller (and pricier) towns. The best source of info on regional *caves* is the **Centre d'Information du Vin d'Alsace,** 12 av. de la Foire aux Vins, at the Maison du Vin d'Alsace in Colmar. (☎03 89 20 16 20. Open M-F 9am-noon and 2-5pm.)

FROM THE ROAD

FRENCH 101: A CRASH COURSE

Traveling through France, you will undoubtedly encounter familiar words on signs and menus. Though these cognates will appear to help in your struggle to comprehend *le monde francophone,* beware! Some can also lead you astray. Here are some *faux amis* (false cognates; literarlly, "false friends") to watch out for:

Blesser has nothing to do with spirituality. It means **to hurt,** not to bless.

Pain is anything but misery for French people: it is their word for **bread.**

Bras is not a supportive undergarment, it is an **arm.**

Rage is not just regular anger, it is **rabies.**

Rabais, it follows, is not the disease you can catch from a dog, but a **discount.**

A *sale* is not an event with a lot of *rabais;* it means **dirty.**

Draguer means **to hit on,** not to drag, unless you encounter an overly aggressive flirt.

Balancer is **to swing,** not to steady oneself.

A *peste* is slightly more serious than a bothersome creature. It is a **plague.**

Preservatif is not something found in packaged food, but it can be found in other packages, so to speak. This is the French word for **condom.**

TRANSPORTATION

Buses run frequently from Colmar to surrounding towns, but the smaller northern towns are more difficult to get to. **Car** rental from Strasbourg or Colmar smooths out transportation problems but drains any wallet. **Biking,** especially from Colmar, is only for those with the stamina to gut out lengthy journeys, but trails and turn-offs are well marked. **Trains** connect Sélestat, Molsheim, Barr, Colmar, and Mulhouse. Country roads are difficult to walk along as they have minimal sidewalks.

SÉLESTAT ☎03 88

Sélestat (pop. 17,500), between Colmar and Strasbourg, is a calm haven of good wines often overlooked by tourists on their way to more "authentic" Route cities. Founded in 1452, the **Bibliothèque Humaniste,** 1 r. de la Bibliothèque, contains a collection of illuminated manuscripts and handwritten books produced during Sélestat's 15th-century Humanistic boom. (Open July-Aug. M and W-F 9am-noon and 2-6pm, Sa 9am-noon and 2-5pm, Su 2-5pm; Sept.-June M and W-F 9am-noon and 2-6pm, Sa 9am-noon. €3.70, students €2.15.) The **Maison du Pain,** r. du Sel, reveals the history of breadmaking from 12,500 BC to the present. A workshop in the ground-floor *pâtisserie* allows visitors to twist their own pretzels. (Open Jan. and Mar.-Nov. Tu-F 9:30am-12:30pm and 2-6pm, Sa 9am-12:30pm and 2-6pm, Su 9am-12:30pm and 2:30-6pm; Dec. daily 10am-7pm. Closed 2 weeks after Christmas and Jan. 15 through Feb. €4.60, students €2.30.)

Hôtel de l'Ill ❸, 13 r. des Bateliers, has 15 cheerfully colored rooms with shower and TV. (☎92 91 09. Breakfast €5. Reception 7am-9pm. Singles €30; doubles €40; triples €50. AmEx/MC/V.) A local favorite, **JP Kamm ❶,** 15 r. des Clefs, has a dazzling selection of desserts. (☎92 11 04. Pizzas and quiches €3.50-4.70; cheaper if ordered to go. Open Tu and Th-F 8am-7pm, W 8:30am-7pm, Sa 8am-6pm, Su 8am-1pm. Terrace service Tu-F until 6:30pm, Sa until 5:30pm. MC/V; min. €8.) From pl. de la Gare, **trains** run to Colmar (15min., 38 per day, €4) and Strasbourg (30min., 54 per day, €7). The **tourist office,** bd. Général Leclerc, in the Commanderie St-Jean, rents **bikes** (€12.50 per day). From the train station, go straight on av. de la Gare, pass pl. du Général de Gaulle, to av. de la Liberté. Turn left onto bd. du Maréchal Foch, which becomes bd. Général Leclerc. (☎58 87 20; www.selestat-tourisme.com. Open July-Aug. M-Sa 9:30am-12:30pm and 1:30-6:45pm, Su 10:30am-3pm; Sept.-June reduced hours.) **Postal Code:** 67600.

Crayon means **pencil,** not crayon, and *gomme* is not for chewing, unless you like the taste of rubber–it is an **eraser.**

An *extincteur* is not some sort of bazooka. It is a **fire extinguisher.**

Fesses is not a colloquial term for "coming clean;" it means **buttocks.**

As is not another way to say *fesses* or even an insult. This is a French compliment, meaning **ace** or **champion.**

Ranger is neither a woodsman nor a mighty morpher. This means **to tidy up.**

A *smoking* has little to do with tobacco (or any other substance). It is a **tuxedo** or **dinner suit.**

Raisins are juicy **grapes,** not the dried-up snack food. Try *raisins-secs* instead.

Prunes are plums. *Pruneaus* are the dried fruit.

Tampons are stamps (for documents), not the feminine care item. If you are looking for those, ask for a *tampon hygenique* or *napkins.* To wipe your mouth, you would do better with a *serviette.*

The *patron* is the **boss,** not the customer.

A *glacier* is a glacier, but you are more likely to see it around town meaning **ice cream vendor,** as the word *glace* does not mean the panes in the window, but a frozen summer treat.

If the French language seems full of deception, think again. *Déception* in French actually means disappointment.

COLMAR ☎03 89

Best used as a base for exploring smaller Route towns, Colmar (pop. 68,000) is defined by its diverse pastel facades and crowds of tourists. The collection of the **Musée Unterlinden,** 1 r. d'Unterlinden, ranges from Romanesque to Renaissance, including Grünewald's *Issenheim Altarpiece.* (Open May.-Oct. daily 9am-6pm; Nov.-Apr. M and W-Su 9am-noon and 2-5pm. €7, students €5.) The **Église des Dominicains,** pl. des Dominicains, is a bare-bones showroom for Colmar's other masterpiece, Schongauer's ornate *Virgin in the Rose Bower.* (Open June-Oct. Su-Th 10am-1pm and 3-6pm, F-Sa 10am-6pm; Apr.-May and Nov.-Dec. daily 10am-1pm and 3-6pm. €1.30, students €1.) The 10-day **Foire aux Vins d'Alsace** in mid-August is the region's largest wine fair, with concerts and free tastings. (☎03 90 50 50 50; www.foire-colmar.com. €1-5. Concerts €23-33.)

To reach the **Auberge de Jeunesse (HI) ❶,** 2 r. Pasteur, take bus #4 (dir.: Europe) to Pont Rouge. (☎80 57 39. Breakfast included. Linens €4. Reception Apr.-Sept. 7-10am and 5pm-midnight; Nov. to mid-Dec. and mid-Jan. to Feb. 7-10am and 5-11pm. Closed mid-Dec. to mid-Jan. Lockout 10am-5pm. Curfew midnight, 11pm in winter. Dorms €12.50; singles €17.50; doubles €30. Non-members €2.90 extra. MC/V.) **La Pergola et sa Taverne ❷,** 28 r. des Marchands, offers great regional cuisine in a quiet restaurant full of toy pigs and puppets. (☎41 36 79. *Tartes flambées* and potato-and-cheese *roestis* €8.50-13. Open M-W and F-Su noon-2:30pm and 6-10pm. MC/V.) **Trains** depart pl. de la Gare for Lyon (4½-5½hr., 9 per day, €42), Paris (5¼hr., 2 per day, €52), and Strasbourg (30min., 12 per day, €10). To get to the **tourist office,** 4 r. d'Unterlinden, from the train station, turn left on av. de la République, which becomes r. Kléber, and follow it to the right to pl. Unterlinden. (☎20 68 92; www.ot-colmar.fr. Open July-Aug. M-Sa 9am-7pm, Su 10am-1pm; Sept.-June reduced hours.) **Postal Code:** 68000.

BESANÇON ☎03 81

Bounded by the River Doubs on three sides and a steep bluff on the fourth, Besançon (pop. 123,000) baffled Julius Caesar and was later made completely impenetrable with Vauban's enormous **citadel,** at the end of r. des Fusilles de la Résistance. Though its mountaintop fortifications are more daunting than pretty, Besançon hosts a slew of world-class museums and an active student population. Within the citadel, the deeply moving **Musée de la Résistance et de la Déportation** chronicles the Nazi rise to power and the events of WWII from a French perspective. (Citadel ☎87 83 33; www.citadelle.com. Open daily July-Aug. 9am-7pm, Sept.-June reduced hours; Oct.-Mar. closed Tu. All citadel museums in summer €7.80, students €6.50; in winter €7.20/6.) The ticking **Musée du Temps,** 96 Grand Rue, presents clocks from Galileo's era to today. (☎87 81 50. Open Tu-Sa 9:15am-noon and 2-6pm, Su 10am-6pm. €5, Sa €2.50, Su free, students free.)

To reach the **Foyer Mixte de Jeunes Travailleurs (HI) ❷,** 48 r. des Cras, take a left from the train station onto r. de la Viotte, the first right onto r. de l'Industrie, then a right on r. de Belfort to pl. de la Liberté. Take bus #5 or night line A (both dir.: Orchamps, 3-5 per hr., €1.05) to the hostel, at Les Oiseaux stop. The hostel has clean rooms with private baths. (☎40 32 00. Open Apr.-Sept. Singles €23, 2nd night €18. AmEx/MC/V.) **La Boîte à Sandwiches ❶,** 21 r. du Lycée, offers enormous portions. (☎81 63 23. Entrees €3-7.50. Open M-F 11:30am-2pm and 7-10pm, Sa 11:30am-2pm. AmEx/MC/V.) Buy groceries at **Monoprix,** 12 Grande R. (☎65 36 36. Open M-Sa 8:30am-8pm. AmEx/MC/V.)

Trains (☎08 36 35 35 35) leave av. de la Paix for Dijon (1hr., 34 per day, €13), Paris (2½hr., 9 per day, €49), and Strasbourg (3hr., 9 per day, €30). Monts Jura **buses** (☎08 25 00 22 44), with an office in the train station, go to Pontarlier (1hr., 8 per day, €7.50). From the station, walk downhill; follow av. de la Paix as it turns into av. Maréchal Foch and continue left as it becomes av. de l'Helvétie before the river. Once you reach pl. de la 1ère Armée Française, the *vieille ville* is across pont de la République; the **tourist office,** 2 pl. de la 1ère Armée Française, is on the right. (☎80 92 55; www.besancon-tourisme.com. Open June-Sept. M 10am-7pm, Tu-Sa 9:30am-7pm, Su 10am-5pm; Oct.-May reduced hours.) **Postal Code:** 25000.

NANCY ☎03 83

Nancy (pop. 106,000), the city that spawned the Art Nouveau "Nancy School," is today the artistic and intellectual heart of modern Lorraine. The stunning works on display at the **Musée de L'École de Nancy,** 36-38 r. du Sergent Blandan, reject the straight lines of previous art and architecture, and instead use organic forms to recreate aspects of the natural landscape. Take bus #122 (dir.: Villers Clairlieu) or 123 (dir.: Vandoeuvre Cheminots) to Painlevé. (☎40 14 86; www.ecole-de-nancy.com. Open W-Su 10:30am-6pm. €6, students €4. W students free. €8 pass buys entry to all of Nancy's museums.) The dazzling, recently renovated **place Stanislas** houses three Neoclassical pavilions, including **place de la Carrière,** a former jousting ground that Stanislas refurbished with Baroque architecture, golden angel sculptures, and wrought-iron ornaments. The collection in the **Musée des Beaux-Arts,** 3 pl. Stanislas, features works from the 14th century to the present, including gems by Monet, Picasso, and Rodin. (☎85 30 72. Open M and W-Su 10am-6pm. €6, students €4. W students free.)

Hôtel de L'Académie ❷, 7 r. des Michottes, may seem slightly shabby at first glance, but its large rooms and convenient location come at a great price. (☎35 52 31. Breakfast €3.50. Reception 7am-11pm. Singles €20-28; doubles €28-39. AmEx/MC/V.) Restaurants line **rue des Maréchaux, place Lafayette,** and **place St-Epvre.** A Shopi **supermarket** sits at 26 r. St-Georges. (Open M-F 9am-8pm, Sa 9am-7:30pm. MC/V.) Nancy has a dynamic arts and nightlife scene. **Rue Stanislas** and **Grand Rue** are great places to grab a drink. **Blitz,** 76 r. St-Julien, is smoky red-velvet suave at its best. (Beer from €2.50. Mixed drinks from €5. Open M-Sa 11:30am-2am. AmEx/MC/V; min. €7.) **Trains** depart from the station at 3 pl. Thiers for Paris (3½hr., 27 per day, €42) and Strasbourg (1¼hr., 20 per day, €23). To reach pl. Stanislas, head through pl. Thiers, turn left on r. Mazagran, and pass through a stone archway on the right; continue straight on to the place and the **tourist office.** (☎35 22 41; www.ot-nancy.fr. Open Apr.-Oct. M-Sa 9am-7pm, Su 10am-5pm; Nov.-Mar. M-Sa 9am-6pm, Su 10am-1pm.) **Postal Code:** 54000.

CHAMPAGNE AND THE NORTH

Legend has it that when Dom Perignon first tasted champagne, he exclaimed, "Come quickly! I am drinking stars!" Few modern-day visitors need further convincing as they flock to the wine cellars in Reims and Epernay, where champagne is produced from regional grapes according to a rigorous, time-honored method. As you head north to the ferry ports, don't overlook the intriguing Flemish culture in Arras or the world-class art collections in Lille.

REIMS ☎03 26

From the 26 monarchs crowned in its cathedral to the bubbling champagne of its famed *caves*, everything Reims (pop. 191,000) touches turns to gold. The **Cathédrale de Notre-Dame,** built with golden limestone taken from the medieval city walls, features sea-blue stained-glass windows by Marc Chagall. (☎47 55 34. Open daily 7:30am-7:30pm. Free. Tours in French €5.50. English-language audio tour €5.) The adjacent **Palais du Tau,** 2 pl. du Cardinal Luçon, houses original statues from the cathedral's facade alongside majestic 16th-century tapestries. (☎47 81 79. Open May-Aug. Tu-Su 9:30am-6:30pm; Sept.-Apr. reduced hours. €6.50, ages

18-25 €4.50.) **Champagne Pommery,** 5 pl. du Général Gouraud, gives the best tours of Reims's champagne *caves.* Its 75,000L vat *(tonneau)* is the one of the largest in the world. (☎61 62 56; www.pommery.com. Tours by reservation; various tasting options €8-15, students €6.) The schoolroom where Germany surrendered to the Allies during WWII is now the **Museé de la Reddition,** 12 r. Franklin Roosevelt, a potent time capsule for the momentous event it witnessed. (☎47 84 19. Open M and W-Su 10am-noon and 2-6pm, Tu 2-6pm only. €3 pass includes Musée-Abbaye St-Rémi, Foujita Chapel, Musée de Beaux-Arts, and the planetarium, students free.) In July, Reims kicks off the **Flâneries Musicales d'Eté,** with over 80 concerts in six weeks. (☎77 45 12. Many concerts free. Paid concerts €10-12, students €8-10.)

The **Centre International de Séjour/Auberge de Jeunesse (HI) ❶,** ch. Bocquaine, has clean rooms park-side. (☎40 52 60; fax 47 35 70. Breakfast €3.40. Reception 24hr. Dorms €12-18; singles €20, with shower €32; doubles €13.10/17.80 per person. Non-members €3 extra. MC/V.) A **Monoprix** supermarket is at 21 r. Chativesle. (Open M-Sa 9am-8pm.) Cafes, restaurants and bars crowd **place Drouet d'Erlon. Trains** leave bd. Joffre for Epernay (20min., 11 per day, €4.80) and Paris (1½hr., 11 per day, €21). To get to the **tourist office** from the train station, 2 r. Guillaume de Machault, follow the right curve of the roundabout to pl. Drouet d'Erlon, turn left onto r. de Vesle, and right on r. du Trésor; the office is on the left before the cathedral. (☎77 45 00; www.reims-tourisme.com. Open mid-Apr. to mid-Oct. M-Sa 9am-7pm, Su 10am-6pm; mid-Oct. to mid-Apr. reduced hours.) **Postal Code:** 51100.

EPERNAY ☎03 26

The showcase town of the Champagne region, Epernay (pop. 26,000), is appropriately lavish and seductive. The aptly named **avenue de Champagne** is distinguished by its palatial mansions, lush gardens, and swanky champagne companies. **Moët & Chandon,** 20 av. de Champagne, produces the king of all champagnes: **Dom Perignon.** (☎51 20 20; www.moet.com. Open Apr. to mid-Nov. daily 9:30-11:30am and 2-4:30pm; mid-Nov. to Mar. M-F 9:30am-11:30am and 2-4:30pm. Tours with several tasting options €8-21.) Ten minutes away is **Mercier,** 70 av. de Champagne, the self-proclaimed "most popular champagne in France," which gives tours in roller-coaster-style cars. (☎51 22 22. Open mid-Mar. to mid-Nov. daily 9:30-11:30am and 2-4:30pm; mid-Nov. to mid-Dec. and mid-Feb. to mid-Mar. M and Th-Su 9:30-11:30am and 2-4:30pm. 30min. tour €6.50-14.)

Epernay caters to the champagne set—budget hotels are rare. **Hôtel St-Pierre ❷,** 1 r. Jeanne d'Arc, is your best bet with spacious, antique-furnished rooms. (☎54 40 80; fax 57 88 68. Breakfast €6. Reception 7am-10pm. Singles €21, with shower €30; doubles €24/36. MC/V.) Ethnic food options line **rue Gambetta.** The area around **place des Arcades** and **place Hugues Plomb** is dotted with delis and bakeries.

Trains leave Cours de la Gare for Paris (1¼hr., 18 per day, €19) and Strasbourg (3½hr., 3 per day, €40). From the station, walk straight ahead through pl. Mendès France, go one block up r. Gambetta to pl. de la République, and turn left on av. de Champagne to reach the **tourist office,** 7 av. de Champagne. (☎53 33 00; www.ot-epernay.fr. Open Easter to mid-Oct. M-Sa 9:30am-12:30pm and 1:30-7pm, Su 11am-4pm; mid-Oct. to Easter reduced hours.) **Postal Code:** 51200.

TROYES ☎03 25

Although the city plan resembles a champagne cork, little else links Troyes (pop. 60,000) with its grape-crazy northern neighbors. Troyes has Gothic churches, 16th-century mansions, and an abundance of museums complementing an energetic and social scene. The enormous **Cathédrale St-Pierre et St-Paul,** pl. St-Pierre, down r. Clemençeau past the town hall, is a flamboyant Gothic church. Its stunning stained glass, in the unique Troyes style, has survived several fires, bombings, and other disasters. (Open daily 10am-7pm. Free.) The **Musée d'Art Moderne,** next door on pl. St-Pierre, houses over 2000 works by French artists. (☎76 26 80. Open Tu-Su 10am-1pm and 2-6pm. €5, students and 1st Su of each month free.) The freshwater **Grands Lacs** dot the Forêt d'Orient region around Troyes. The **Comité Départemental du Tourisme de l'Aube,** 34 quai Dampierre has info on outdoor activities. (☎42 50 00. Open M-F 9:30am-12:30pm and 1:30-6pm.)

Les Comtes de Champagne ❸, 56 r. de la Monnaie, is in a 16th-century mansion with lace-curtained windows and large, airy rooms. (☎73 11 70; www.comtesdechampagne.com. Reception 7am-10pm. Singles from €30; doubles from €35; triples from €57; quads from €63. AmEx/MC/V.)Creperies and inexpensive eateries lie near **rue Champeaux,** in *quartier* St-Jean, and on **rue Général Saussier,** in *quartier* Vauluisant. **Aux Crieurs de Vin ❷,** 4-6 pl. Jean Jaurès, compensates for a tiny menu of delicious *plats* with an elaborate selection of wines. A meal with a glass of wine runs about €13. (☎40 01 01. Open Tu-Sa noon-2pm and 7:30-10pm. MC/V.) Cinemas and pool halls rub elbows with chic boutiques on **rue Émile Zola.** On warm nights, locals fill the cafes and taverns of **rue Champeaux** and **rue Molé** near **place Alexandre Israël. Trains** run from av. Maréchal Joffre to Paris (1½hr., 16 per day, €22). The **tourist office,** 16 bd. Carnot, is one block from the station. (☎82 62 70; www.ot-troyes.fr. Open Apr.-Oct. M-Sa 9am-12:30pm and 2-6:30pm; Nov.-Mar. M-Sa 9am-12:30pm and 2-6:30pm, Su 10am-1pm.) **Postal Code:** 10000.

LILLE ☎03 20

A long-time international hub with rich Flemish ancestry and the best nightlife in the north, Lille (pop. 220,000) has abandoned its industrial days to become a stylish and diverse metropolis. The **Palais des Beaux-Arts,** on pl. de la République (M: République), has the second-largest art collection in France, with a comprehensive display of 15th- to 20th-century French and Flemish masterpieces. (Open M 2-6pm, W-Su 10am-6pm. €5, students €3.50.) With artwork displayed around a renovated indoor pool, the aptly named **La Piscine,** 23 r. de L'Espérance (M: Gare Jean Lebas), has a collection that includes works from the 19th and early 20th centuries. (Open Tu-Th 11am-6pm, F 11am-8pm, Sa-Su 1-6pm. €3, F students free.) Dating from the 15th century, the **Vieille Bourse** (Old Stock Exchange), pl. Général de Gaulle, is now home to regular book markets. (Open Tu-Su 9:30am-7:30pm.)

To reach the friendly **Auberge de Jeunesse (HI) ❶,** 12 r. Malpart (M: Mairie de Lille), from Gare Lille Flandres, circle left around the station, then turn right onto r. du Molinel, left onto r. de Paris, and right onto r. Malpart. (☎57 08 94; lille@fuaj.org. Breakfast and linens included. Reception 24hr. Lockout 11am-3pm. Open late Jan. to mid-Dec. Dorms €16. HI discount. MC/V.) In *vieux* Lille, **La Pâte Brisée ❷,** 65 r. de la Monnaie, has seating along the quiet, cobblestone street. (☎74 29 00. *Menus* €8, €12, and €18. Open M-F noon-10:30pm, Sa-Su noon-11pm. MC/V.) At night, students flock to the pubs along **rue Solférino** and **rue Masséna,** while *vieux* Lille has a trendier bar scene.

Trains leave from Gare Lille Flandres, on pl. de la Gare, for Brussels, BEL (1¾hr., 1-3 per day, €20-23) and Paris (1hr., 20 per day, €36-50). Gare Lille Europe, on r. Le Corbusier (M: Gare Lille Europe), sends **Eurostar** trains to Brussels, BEL (40min., 15 per day, €24) and London, BRI (1¾hr., 15 per day, 1¾hr., €188), and **TGVs** to Paris (1¼hr., 6 per day, €36-50). Eurolines **buses** (☎78 18 88) run from Gare Lille Europe to: Amsterdam, NTH (5hr., 2 per day, round-trip €47), Brussels, BEL (1½hr., 3 per day, round-trip €21), and London, BRI (5½hr., 2 per day, round-trip €52). From Gare Lille Flandres, walk straight down r. Faidherbe and turn left through pl. du Théâtre and pl. Général de Gaulle; turn right at the Théâtre du Nord. The **tourist office,** pl. Rihour, is inside the Palais Rihour. (☎21 94 21. Open M-Sa 9:30am-6:30pm, Su 10am-noon and 2-5pm.) **Postal Code:** 59000.

GERMANY (DEUTSCHLAND)

Whether glittering skyscrapers or the burnished roofs of medieval towns greet you as you enter Germany, this land will be sure to enchant. World-class music rings out of every concert hall in the glitzy big cities, where museums and parks vie for travelers' attention during the day and clubs light up the streets at night. Near these circles of urban sophistication, charming towns crop up from rolling hills while castles beckon from cliffsides. Although the rise of the Nazi regime marked a bitter break in Germany's humanistic tradition and the Cold War divided the nation, Germans today are fashioning a new, united identity.

DISCOVER GERMANY: SUGGESTED ITINERARIES

THREE DAYS. Enjoy two days in **Berlin** (p. 403): stroll along **Unter den Linden** and the **Ku'damm,** gape at the **Brandenburger Tor** and the **Reichstag,** and explore the **Tiergarten.** Walk along the **East Side Gallery** and visit **Checkpoint Charlie** for a history of the Berlin Wall, then pass an afternoon at **Schloß Sanssouci** (p. 425). Overnight it to **Munich** (p. 461) for a stein-themed last day.

ONE WEEK. After scrambling through **Berlin** (3 days), head north to racy **Hamburg** (1 day; p. 434). Take in the cathedral of **Cologne** (1 day; p. 443) before slowing down in the bucolic **Lorelei Cliffs** (1 day; p. 455). End your trip Bavarian-style with the castles, cathedrals, and beer gardens of **Munich** (1 day).

THREE WEEKS. Start in **Berlin** (3 days). Party in **Hamburg** (2 days), then zip to **Cologne** (1 day) and the former West German capital, **Bonn** (1 day; p. 448). Contrast the Roman ruins at **Trier** (1 day, p. 452) with glitzy **Frankfurt** (1 day; p. 449), then visit Germany's oldest university in **Heidelberg** (2 days; p. 456). Lose your way in the fairy-tale **Black Forest** (2 days; p. 460), before finding it again in **Munich** (2 days). Marvel at **Neuschwanstein** (1 day; p. 471) and tour the wineries of the **Romantic Road** (2 days; p. 470). Get cultured in Goethe's **Weimar** (1 day; p. 432)—then dramatize your learnings in Faust's cellar in **Leipzig** (1 day; p. 430). End your trip in the reconstructed splendor of **Dresden** (1 day; p. 426).

ESSENTIALS

FACTS AND FIGURES

Official Name: Federal Republic of Germany.

Capital: Berlin.

Major Cities: Cologne, Frankfurt, Hamburg, Munich.

Population: 82,431,390.

Land Area: 357,021 sq. km.

Time Zone: GMT +1.

Language: German.

Religions: Protestant (38%), Roman Catholic (34%), Muslim (2%).

WHEN TO GO

Germany's climate is temperate, with rain year-round (especially in summer). The cloudy, mild months of May, June, and September are the best time to go, as there are fewer tourists and the weather is pleasant. In July, Germans head to summer spots en masse with the advent of school vacations. Winter sports gear up from November to April; the ski season takes place from mid-December to March.

DOCUMENTS AND FORMALITIES

EMBASSIES. All foreign embassies are in Berlin (p. 403). German embassies abroad include: **Australia,** 119 Empire Circuit, Yarralumla, Canberra, ACT 2600 (☎02 6270 1911; www.germanembassy.org.au); **Canada,** 1 Waverly St., Ottawa, ON K2P OT8 (☎613-232-1101; www.ottawa.diplo.de); **Ireland,** 31 Trimleston Ave.,

Booterstown, Blackrock, Co. Dublin (☎01 269 3011; www.germanembassy.ie); **New Zealand,** 90-92 Hobson St., Thorndon, Wellington 6001 (☎04 473 6063; www.wellington.diplo.de); **UK,** 23 Belgrave Sq., London SW1X 8PZ (☎020 7824 1300; www.german-embassy.org.uk); **US,** 4645 Reservoir Rd. NW, Washington, D.C. 20007 (☎202-298-4000; www.germany-info.org).

VISA AND ENTRY INFORMATION. Citizens of Australia, Canada, the EU, New Zealand, and the US do not need visas for stays of up to 90 days, although this three-month period begins upon entry into any of the countries that belong to the EU's freedom-of-movement zone. Residence and work permits can be obtained after entering the country (see www.germany-info.org for more information).

TOURIST SERVICES AND MONEY

EMERGENCY	**Police:** ☎110. **Ambulance** and **Fire:** ☎112.

TOURIST OFFICES. Every city in Germany has a tourist office, usually near the Hauptbahnhof (main train station) or *Marktplatz* (central square). All are marked by a sign with a thick lowercase "*i*," and many book rooms for a small fee. Also consult the website of the **National Tourist Board** (www.germany-tourism.de).

MONEY. On January 1, 2002, the **euro (€)** replaced the **Deutschmark (DM)** as the unit of currency in Germany. For more info, see p. 17. As a general rule, it's cheaper to exchange money in Germany than at home. Costs for those who stay in hostels and prepare their own food may range anywhere from €20-40 per person per day. **Tipping** is not practiced as liberally in Germany as elsewhere—most natives just round up €1. Tips are handed directly to the server with payment of the bill—if you don't want any change, say "*Das stimmt so*" (das SHTIMMT zo). Germans rarely bargain except at flea markets. As in other EU nations, most goods and services bought in Germany automatically include a **value added tax (VAT);** see p. 22. You can get VAT refunds for one-time purchases if you carry the goods out of Germany within three months of their purchase. To apply for a refund, notify the retailer at the time of purchase, who will give you either an export invoice or a Tax Free Shopping Check. Submit these to customs with your passport on your way out of the country. The invoice will be sent to the retailer, who will send a check to the address you specify.

TRANSPORTATION

BY PLANE. Most flights land in Frankfurt; Berlin, Munich, and Hamburg also have international airports. **Lufthansa,** the national airline, is not always the best-priced option. Often it is cheaper to travel domestically by plane than by train; check out **Air Berlin** (www.airberlin.com), among other options.

BY TRAIN. The **Deutsche Bahn (DB;** www.bahn.de) network (www.bahn.de) is Europe's best—and one of its most expensive. Luckily, all trains have clean and comfy second-class compartments, and there are a wide variety of train lines to choose from. **RegionalExpress (RE)** and the slightly slower **RegionalBahn (RB)** trains include rail networks between neighboring cities. **InterRegio (IR)** trains, covering larger networks between cities, are speedy and comfortable. **D** trains are foreign trains that serve international routes. **EuroCity (EC)** and **InterCity (IC)** trains zoom between major cities every hour from 6am-10pm. You must purchase a supplement *(Zuschlag)* for IC or EC trains. **InterCityExpress (ICE)** trains approach the luxury and kinetics of airplanes, barreling along the tracks at speeds up to 280kph.

Eurail is valid in Germany. The **German Railpass** allows unlimited travel for four to 10 days within a one-month period. Non-EU citizens can purchase German Railpasses in their home countries and, with a passport, in major German train stations (2nd class 4-day pass €160, 10-day €324; under 26 €142/220). A **Schönes-Wochenende-Ticket** (€33) gives up to five people unlimited travel on any of the slower trains (RE or RB) from 12:01am Saturday or Sunday until 3am the next day; single travelers often find larger groups who will share their ticket.

BY BUS. Bus service runs from the local **ZOB** *(Zentralomnibusbahnhof)*, usually close to the main train station. Buses are usually slightly more expensive than trains. Railpasses are not valid on buses except for a few run by Deutsche Bahn.

BY CAR AND BY BIKE. German road conditions are generally excellent. The rumors are true: there is no speed limit on the *Autobahn*, only a recommendation of 130kph (80 mph). Germans drive fast. Watch for signs indicating the right-of-way (usually designated by a yellow triangle). The *Autobahn* is marked by an "A" on signs; secondary highways, where the speed limit is usually 100kph (60 mph), are accompanied by signs bearing a "B." In cities and towns, speed limits hover around 30-60kph (20-35 mph). **Mitfahrzentralen** are agencies that pair up drivers and riders for a small fee; riders then negotiate payment for the trip with the driver. Seat belts are mandatory. Police strictly enforce driving laws. Germany has designated lanes for **bicycles.** *Germany by Bike*, by Nadine Slavinski (Mountaineers Books, 1994; US$15), details 20 tours throughout Germany.

KEEPING IN TOUCH

PHONE CODES	**Country code:** 49. **International dialing prefix:** 00. For more information on how to place international calls, see inside back cover.

EMAIL AND THE INTERNET. Almost all German cities, as well as a surprising number of smaller towns, have at least one Internet cafe with web access for about €2-10 per hour. Wireless Internet is often available in bigger cities; in Berlin's new Sony Center (p. 414), the wireless is completely, blissfully free. Some German universities have banks of available computers hooked up to the Internet in their libraries, intended for student use.

TELEPHONE. Most public phones will accept only a phone card *(Telefonkarte)*, available at post offices, kiosks, and some Deutsche Bahn counters. **Mobile phones** are a popular and economical alternative (p. 29). Phone numbers have no standard length. International access numbers include **AT&T USADirect** (☎0800 225 5288), **Canada Direct** (☎0800 888 0014), **MCI WorldPhone** (☎0800 888 8000), **Telecom New Zealand** (☎0800 080 0064), and **Telstra Australia** (☎0800 080 0061).

MAIL. Airmail (*Luftpost* or *par avion*) usually takes three to six days to Ireland and the UK, four to 10 days to Australia and North America. *Let's Go* lists addresses for mail to be held *(Postlagernde Briefe)* in the **Practical Information** sections of big cities. Mail will go to the main post office unless you specify a subsidiary by street address. Address mail to be held according to the following example: First name Last name, *Postlagernde Briefe*, Postal Code city, GERMANY.

LANGUAGE. Younger Germans often speak at least some English, and residents of Western Germany are usually proficient as well. Recent spelling reforms did not eliminate the letter **ß** (the *ess-tset*); it is equivalent to a double "s" in English. German basics are listed on p. 1055.

ACCOMMODATIONS AND CAMPING

GERMANY	❶	❷	❸	❹	❺
ACCOMMODATIONS	under €15	€15-25	€25-33	€33-50	over €50

Germany currently has about 600 **hostels**—more than any other nation on the planet. Official hostels in Germany are overseen by **DJH** *(Deutsches Jugendherbergswerk)*, Bismarckstr. 8, 32756 Detmold, Germany (☎05231 740 10; www.jugendherberge.de). A growing number of **Jugendgästehäuser** (youth guesthouses) have more facilities than hostels and attract slightly older guests. DJH publishes *Jugendherbergen in Deutschland*, a guide to all federated German hostels. Most hostels charge €15-25 for dorms. The cheapest **hotel-style** accommodations are places with *Pension*, *Gasthof*, *Gästehaus*, or *Hotel-Garni* in the name. Hotel rooms start at €20 for singles and €45 for doubles; in large cities, expect to pay nearly twice as much. Breakfast *(Frühstück)* is almost always available, if not included. The best bet for a cheap bed is often a **Privatzimmer** (a room in a family home), where a rudimentary knowledge of German is very helpful. Prices can be as low as €15 per person. Reservations are made through the local tourist office or through a private-room booking office *(Zimmervermittlung)*, sometimes for a small fee. Germans love **camping;** over 2600 campsites dot the landscape. Facilities are well maintained and usually provide showers, bathrooms, and a restaurant or store. Camping costs €7-12 per tent site and €4-6 per extra person, with additional charges for tent and vehicle rental. Blue signs with a black tent on a white background indicate official sites.

FOOD AND DRINK

GERMANY	❶	❷	❸	❹	❺
FOOD	under €4	€4-8	€8-12	€12-20	over €20

A typical breakfast *(Frühstück)* consists of coffee or tea with rolls *(Brötchen)*, cold sausage *(Wurst)*, and cheese *(Käse)*. Germans' main meal, lunch *(Mittagessen)*, includes soup, broiled sausage or roasted meat, potatoes or dumplings, and a salad or vegetable side dish. Dinner (*Abendessen* or *Abendbrot*) is a reprise of breakfast, with beer in place of coffee and a wider selection of meats and cheeses. Many older Germans indulge in a daily ritual of coffee and cake *(Kaffee und Kuchen)* at 3 or 4pm. To eat cheaply, stick to a restaurant's daily menu *(Tagesmenü)*, buy food in supermarkets, or, if you have a student ID, head to a university *Mensa* (cafeteria). Fast-food stands *(Imbiß)* also offer cheap eats; the ubiquitous Turkish *Döner* resembles a gyro. The average German beer is maltier and more "bread-like" than Czech, Dutch, or American beers; a common nickname for German brew is *flüßige Brot* (liquid bread).

HOLIDAYS AND FESTIVALS

Holidays: New Year's Day (Jan. 1); Epiphany (Jan. 6); Good Friday (Apr. 6); Easter (Apr. 8-9); Labor Day (May 1); Ascension (May 17); Pentecost (May 27); Corpus Christi (June 7); Assumption (Aug. 15); Day of German Unity (Oct. 3); Reformation Day (Oct. 31); All Saints' Day (Nov. 1); Repentance Day (Nov. 22); Christmas (Dec. 25-26).

Festivals: Check out the pre-Lenten bacchanalia during *Fasching* in Munich (Feb. 20-24) and *Karneval* in Cologne (Feb. 19; p. 447); international film in the Berlinale Film Festival (Feb. 9-19; p. 421); parades on Christopher Street Day in major cities (late June; p. 424); vanishing kegs during Oktoberfest in Munich (Sept. 16-Oct. 1; p. 461); and the Christmas Market in Nuremberg (Dec.).

BEYOND TOURISM

Volunteer opportunities often involve environmental preservation—working on farms or in forests and educating on environmental protection—though civil service and community building opportunities exist, especially in eastern Germany.

World-Wide Opportunities on Organic Farms (WWOOF), Postfach 210259, 01263 Dresden, Germany (www.wwoof.de). €18 membership in WWOOF gives you room and board at a variety of organic farms in Germany in exchange for chores.

Open Houses Network, Goethepl. 9B, D-99423 Weimar (☎03643 502390; www.open-houses.de). A group dedicated to restoring and sharing public space (mostly in the former DDR), providing lodging for anyone who arrives, in return for work.

BERLIN ☎030

Berlin is bigger than Paris, up later than New York, and wilder than Amsterdam. Dizzying, electric, and dynamic, this city of 3.4 million has an increasingly diverse population, and it can be hard to keep track of which neighborhood *(Bezirk)* is currently deemed the trendiest. Yet even as Berlin surges ahead as one of Europe's most vibrant cities, memories of the past century's Nazi and Communist regimes remain etched in residents' minds. Psychological division between East and West Germany—the problem dubbed "wall in the head" *(Mauer im Kopf)*—is still felt nearly two decades after the fall of the physical Berlin Wall.

INTERCITY TRANSPORTATION

Flights: For info on all 3 of Berlin's airports, call ☎0180 500 01 86. The city is now transitioning from 3 airports to 1, but at least until 2011, **Flughafen Tegel** will remain West Berlin's main international airport. Take express bus #X9 from Bahnhof Zoo, bus #109 from Jakob-Kaiser-Pl. on U7, bus #128 from Kurt-Schumacher-Pl. on U6, or bus TXL from Potsdamer Pl. or Bahnhof Zoo. **Flughafen Schönefeld,** southeast of Berlin, is used for intercontinental flights and travel to developing countries. Take S9 or 45 to Flughafen Berlin Schönefeld, or ride the Schönefeld Express train, which runs every 30min. through most major S-Bahn stations. **Flughafen Tempelhof** was slated to close in 2003 but remains open for flights within Europe. Take U6 to Pl. der Luftbrücke.

Train Stations: Berlin's massive new **Hauptbahnhof** is the city's major transit hub, with some international and domestic trains continuing to **Ostbahnhof** in the East. **Bahnhof Zoologischer Garten** (almost always called **Bahnhof Zoo**), formerly the West's main station, now connects only to regional destinations. Many trains also connect to **Schönefeld** airport. A number of U- and S-Bahn lines make stops at **Oranienburg, Potsdam,** and **Spandau.** Trains in the Brandenburg regional transit system tend to stop at all major stations, as well as Friedrichstr. and Alexanderpl.

Buses: ZOB (☎301 03 80), the central bus station, is by the Funkturm near Kaiserdamm. U2 to Kaiserdamm or S4, 45, or 46 to Witzleben. Open M-F 6am-9pm, Sa-Su 6am-3pm. Check the magazines *Zitty* and *Tip* for deals on long-distance buses, which are slower and cheaper than trains. **Gullivers,** at ZOB (☎311 02 11; www.gullivers.de) and Hardenbergpl. 14 (☎0800 48 55 48 37), often has good deals on bus fares. Call ahead for promotions. Open daily 8am-9:30pm; in winter reduced hours. To **Paris, FRA** (13hr.; €73, students €58) and **Vienna, AUT** (10½hr.; €57/51).

Mitfahrzentralen (Ride Share): Citynetz, Joachimstaler Str. 17 (☎194 44), has a computerized ride share database. U9 or 15 to Kurfürstendamm. To **Hamburg** or **Hanover** (€18) and **Frankfurt** (€31). Open M-F 9am-8pm, Sa-Su 10am-6pm. Check *Zitty, Tip,* and *030* for addresses and phone numbers.

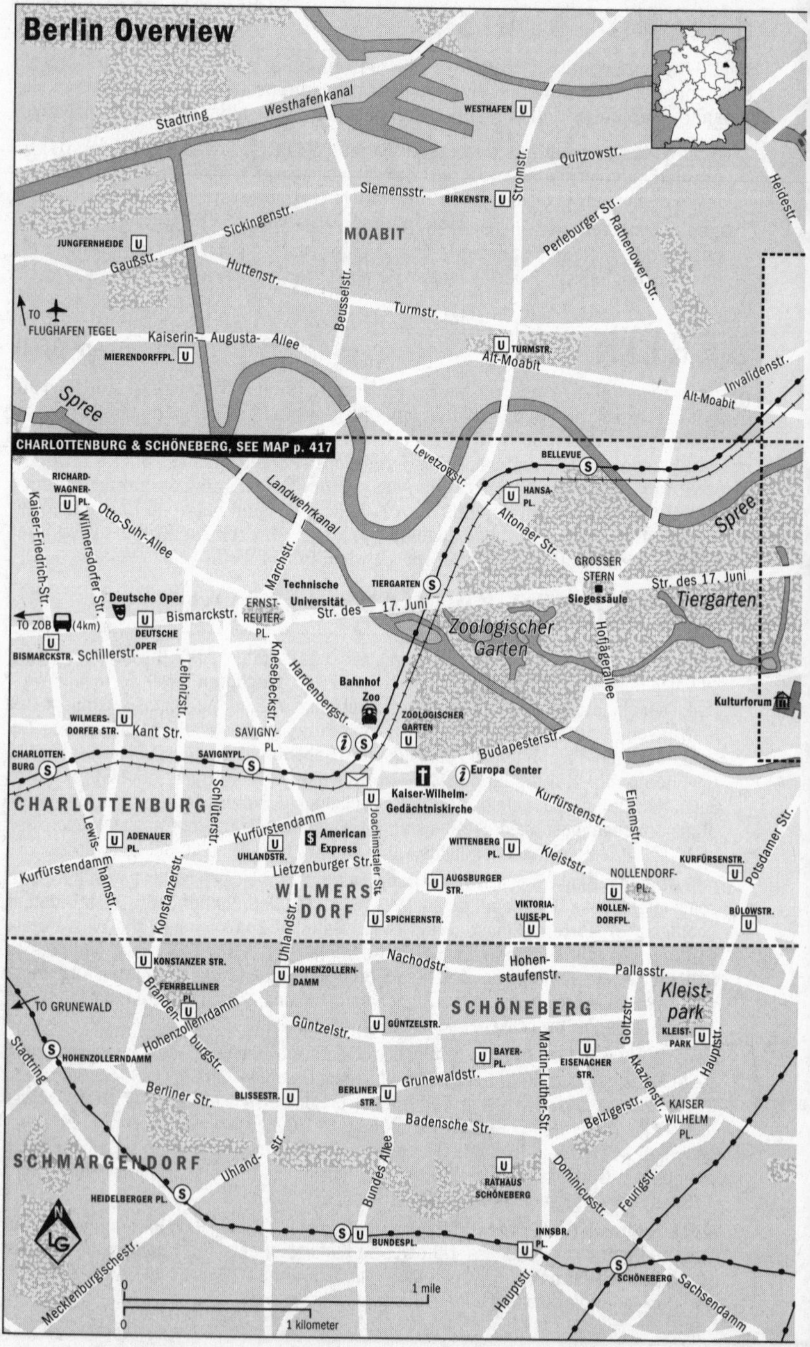
Berlin Overview
Stadtring
Westhafenkanal
WESTHAFEN
Quitzowstr.
Siemensstr.
BIRKENSTR.
Stromstr.
Heidestr.
Sickingenstr.
MOABIT
Perleburger Str.
Rathenower Str.
JUNGFERNHEIDE
Gaußstr.
Huttenstr.
Beusselstr.
Turmstr.
TO FLUGHAFEN TEGEL
Kaiserin-Augusta-Allee
MIERENDORFFPL.
TURMSTR.
Alt-Moabit
Invalidenstr.
Alt-Moabit
Spree
CHARLOTTENBURG & SCHÖNEBERG, SEE MAP p. 417
Levetzowstr.
BELLEVUE
HANSA-PL.
RICHARD-WAGNER-PL.
Otto-Suhr-Allee
Landwehrkanal
Altonaer Str.
Spree
Kaiser-Friedrich-Str.
Wilmersdorfer Str.
Marchstr.
GROSSER STERN
Str. des 17. Juni
Technische Universität
TIERGARTEN
Siegessäule
Tiergarten
Deutsche Oper
ERNST-REUTER-PL.
Str. des 17. Juni
Zoologischer Garten
TO ZOB (4km)
Bismarckstr.
DEUTSCHE OPER
Hofjägerallee
BISMARCKSTR.
Schillerstr.
Leibnizstr.
Knesebeckstr.
Hardenbergstr.
Bahnhof Zoo
Kulturforum
WILMERSDORFER STR.
Kant Str.
SAVIGNY-PL.
ZOOLOGISCHER GARTEN
Budapesterstr.
CHARLOTTENBURG
SAVIGNYPL.
Europa Center
Kaiser-Wilhelm-Gedächtniskirche
CHARLOTTENBURG
Schlüterstr.
Joachimstaler Str.
Kurfürstenstr.
Einemstr.
Lewis-hamstr.
ADENAUER PL.
Kurfürstendamm
American Express
UHLANDSTR.
WITTENBERG PL.
Kleiststr.
Potsdamer Str.
Kurfürstendamm
Lietzenburger Str.
NOLLENDORF-PL.
KURFÜRSENSTR.
AUGSBURGER STR.
Konstanzerstr.
WILMERSDORF
Uhlandstr.
SPICHERNSTR.
VIKTORIA-LUISE-PL.
NOLLEN-DORFPL.
BÜLOWSTR.
KONSTANZER STR.
Nachodstr.
Hohenstaufenstr.
Pallasstr.
HOHENZOLLERN-DAMM
FEHRBELLINER PL.
Kleistpark
TO GRUNEWALD
Brandenburgstr.
Hohenzollerndamm
SCHÖNEBERG
Güntzelstr.
GÜNTZELSTR.
Goltzstr.
KLEIST-PARK
HOHENZOLLERNDAMM
BAYER-PL.
EISENACHER STR.
Martin-Luther-Str.
Stadtring
Hauptstr.
Akazienstr.
Grunewaldstr.
Berliner Str.
BLISSESTR.
BERLINER STR.
Belzigerstr.
KAISER WILHELM PL.
Badensche Str.
SCHMARGENDORF
Uhlandstr.
Bundes Allee
RATHAUS SCHÖNEBERG
Dominicusstr.
Feurigstr.
HEIDELBERGER PL.
BUNDESPL.
INNSBR. PL.
Mecklenburgischestr.
SCHÖNEBERG
Sachsendamm
Hauptstr.
0
1 mile
0
1 kilometer

GERMANY

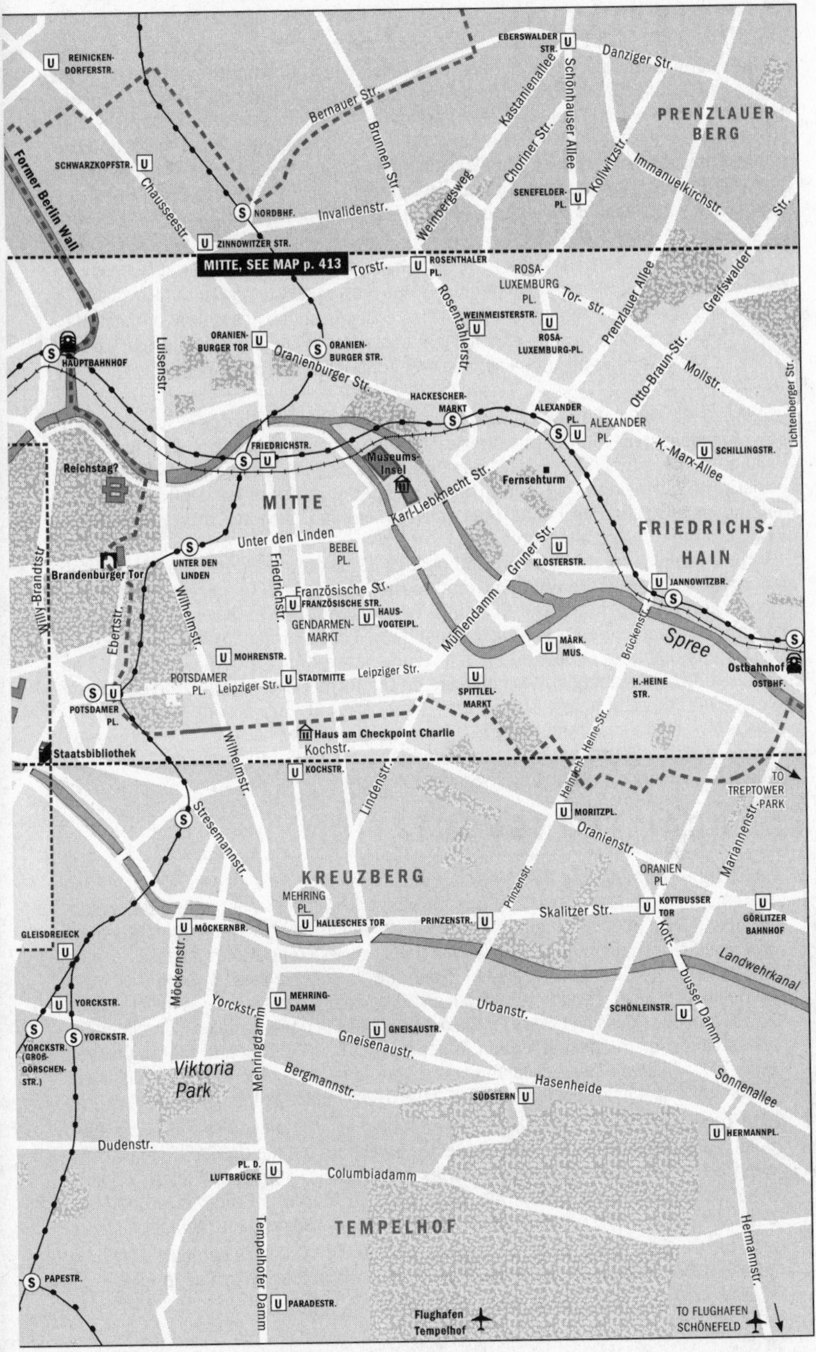
REINICKENDORFERSTR.
SCHWARZKOPFSTR.
Former Berlin Wall
Chausseestr.
NORDBHF.
ZINNOWITZER STR.
MITTE, SEE MAP p. 413
Bernauer Str.
Brunnen Str.
Invalidenstr.
Weinbergsweg
Kastanienallee
Choriner Str.
EBERSWALDER STR.
Schönhauser Allee
Danziger Str.
PRENZLAUER BERG
SENEFELDER-PL.
Kollwitzstr.
Immanuelkirchstr.
Greifswalder Str.
ROSENTHALER PL.
Torstr.
ROSA-LUXEMBURG PL.
Tor- str.
Prenzlauer Allee
WEINMEISTERSTR.
ROSA-LUXEMBURG-PL.
Rosenthalerstr.
ORANIENBURGER TOR
ORANIENBURGER STR.
Oranienburger Str.
Luisenstr.
HAUPTBAHNHOF
HACKESCHER-MARKT
ALEXANDER PL.
ALEXANDER PL.
Otto-Braun-Str.
Mollstr.
Lichtenberger Str.
K.-Marx-Allee
SCHILLINGSTR.
FRIEDRICHSTR.
Reichstag?
Museums-insel
Fernsehturm
Karl-Liebknecht Str.
MITTE
FRIEDRICHS-HAIN
Unter den Linden
UNTER DEN LINDEN
BEBEL PL.
Brandenburger Tor
Friedrichstr.
Gruner Str.
KLOSTERSTR.
JANNOWITZBR.
Französische Str.
FRANZÖSISCHE STR.
HAUS-VOGTEIPL.
GENDARMEN-MARKT
Mühlendamm
Willy-Brandtstr.
Ebertstr.
Wilhelmstr.
MÄRK. MUS.
Brückenstr.
Spree
Ostbahnhof
OSTBHF.
MOHRENSTR.
POTSDAMER PL.
Leipziger Str.
STADTMITTE
Leipziger Str.
SPITTEL-MARKT
H.-HEINE STR.
Heinrich-Heine-Str.
POTSDAMER PL.
Haus am Checkpoint Charlie
Staatsbibliothek
Kochstr.
KOCHSTR.
Wilhelmstr.
Lindenstr.
TO TREPTOWER PARK
Stresemannstr.
MORITZPL.
Oranienstr.
Mariannenstr.
KREUZBERG
ORANIEN PL.
MEHRING PL.
Prinzenstr.
Skalitzer Str.
KOTTBUSSER TOR
GÖRLITZER BAHNHOF
GLEISDREIECK
MÖCKERNBR.
HALLESCHES TOR
PRINZENSTR.
Kottbusser Damm
Landwehrkanal
Möckernstr.
YORCKSTR.
MEHRING-DAMM
Yorckstr.
Urbanstr.
SCHÖNLEINSTR.
YORCKSTR. (GROẞGÖRSCHENSTR.)
YORCKSTR.
GNEISAUSTR.
Gneisenaustr.
Viktoria Park
Mehringdamm
Bergmannstr.
Hasenheide
SÜDSTERN
Sonnenallee
HERMANNPL.
Dudenstr.
PL. D. LUFTBRÜCKE
Columbiadamm
TEMPELHOF
Tempelhofer Damm
Hermannstr.
PAPESTR.
PARADESTR.
Flughafen Tempelhof
TO FLUGHAFEN SCHÖNEFELD

GERMANY

ORIENTATION

Berlin's main landmarks include the **Spree River,** which flows through the city from west to east, and the narrower **Landwehrkanal River** that flows into the Spree from the south. The vast central park, the **Tiergarten,** stretches between the waterways. Two radio towers loom above the park: the pointed **Funkturm,** in the west, and the globed **Fernsehturm,** rising above **Alexanderplatz** in the east. In the west, the major thoroughfare **Kurfürstendamm** (a.k.a. Ku'damm) is lined with department stores and leads to the **Bahnhof Zoologischer Garten,** the transportation hub of West Berlin.

SAFETY PRECAUTION. Berlin is by far the most tolerant city in Germany, with thriving minority communities. However, minorities, gays, and lesbians should exercise caution in the outlying eastern suburbs, especially at night. If you see people wearing dark combat boots (especially with white laces), exercise caution but do not panic, and avoid drawing attention to yourself.

Grand, tree-lined **Straße des 17. Juni** runs east-west through the Tiergarten, ending at the **Brandenburger Tor,** the gate marking the park's eastern border. The **Reichstag** (Parliament) is north of the gate; several blocks south, **Potsdamer Platz** bustles beneath the glittering Sony Center and the headquarters of the Deutsche Bahn. Heading east, Straße des 17. Juni becomes **Unter den Linden** and travels past most of Berlin's imperial architecture.

Berlin's streets tend to be short and change names often; addresses often climb higher and higher and then wrap around to the other side of the street, placing the highest- and lowest-numbered buildings across from one another. Well-indexed maps are invaluable. Berlin is rightly considered a collection of towns, not a homogeneous city; each neighborhood has a strong sense of its individual history. The districts of **Charlottenburg** and **Schöneberg,** in the former West Berlin, have become the city's commercial heart. Also in the former West Berlin, despite its geographical location in the east, **Kreuzberg** is a bastion of counter-culture. The happening districts of **Mitte, Prenzlauer Berg,** and **Friedrichshain,** in the former East, are home to much of the city's chaotic and legendary nightlife.

LOCAL TRANSPORTATION

Public Transportation: The **BVG** (www.bvg.de) is one of the most efficient transportation systems in the world; the extensive **Bus, Straßenbahn** (streetcar or tram), **U-Bahn** (subway), and **S-Bahn** (surface rail) networks will get you to your destination safely and relatively quickly. The city is divided into 3 transit zones. **Zone A** encompasses central Berlin, including Flughafen Tempelhof. The rest of Berlin is in **Zone B; Zone C** consists of the outlying areas, including Potsdam and Oranienburg. An AB ticket is the best deal, as you can buy extension tickets for the outlying areas. A **one-way ticket** (Einzelfahrausweis) is good for 2hr. after validation. Zones AB €2.10, BC €2.30, ABC €2.60. Children under 6 free with an adult; children under 14 pay a reduced fare. Within the validation period, the ticket may be used on any S-Bahn, U-Bahn, bus, or tram.

Night Transport: U- and S-Bahn lines generally stop running M-F 1-4am. On F-Sa nights, S-Bahn and U-Bahn lines run less frequently. Exceptions are the U4, S45, and S85. An extensive system of about 70 **night buses** runs every 20-30min. and tends to follow major transit lines; pick up the free *Nachtliniennetz* map at a Fahrscheine und Mehr office. The letter N precedes night bus numbers. Trams also continue to run at night.

Taxis: ☎26 10 26 or 21 02 02 or, for free, 080 02 63 00 00. Call at least 15min. in advance. Women can request female drivers. Trips within the city cost up to €21.

Car Rental: Most companies have counters at the airports and around Bahnhof Zoo, Ostbahnhof, and Friedrichstr. stations. Offices are also in EuropaCenter, with entrances at Budapester Str. 39-41. Rates average around €65 for a small car. Must be 19. **Hertz** (☎261 10 53), open M-F 7am-8pm, Sa 8am-4pm, Su 9am-1pm; **Avis** (☎230 93 70), open 24hr.; **4 Rent** (☎355 3003), open M-F 9am-7pm, Sa 9am-4pm.

Bike Rental: Fahrradstation, Dorotheenstr. 30 (☎20 45 45 00; www.fahrradstation.de), near the Friedrichstr. S-Bahn station. Turn in at the parking lot next to STA. €15 per day. Open in summer daily 8am-8pm; winter M-F 8am-7pm, Sa 10am-3pm. **Prenzelberger Orangebikes,** Kollwitz Pl. 37 (☎0163 89 12 64 27). U2 to Senefelderpl. €5 per day. Open M-F noon-6pm, Sa noon-4pm. **Deutsche Bahn Call-A-Bike** (☎0700 522 55 22; www.callabike.de) operates all over the city. After signing up (€5), call to unlock a bike. €0.07 per min. (up to €15 per day), or €60 per week.

PRACTICAL INFORMATION

Tourist Offices: Euraide (www.euraide.com), is in the Hauptbahnhof, across from McDonald's. Open June-Oct. daily 8am-noon and 1-6pm; Nov.-May M-F 8am-noon and 1-4:45pm. **EuropaCenter,** on Budapester Str. in Charlottenburg. Walk 2 blocks from Bahnhof Zoo. English-speaking staff reserves rooms for €3. City maps €1. Open M-Sa 10am-7pm, Su 10am-6pm.

City Tours: The guides at **Terry Brewer's Best of Berlin** (www.brewersberlin.com) are legendary for their vast knowledge and engaging personalities. 8hr. tours (€12) leave daily at 10:30am from in front of the Australian Ice Cream shop on Friedrichstr. (S5, 7, 9, or 75 or U6 to Friedrichstr.) and at 11am from the Neue Synagoge on Oranienburger Str., near the intersection with Tucholskystr. (S1, 2, or 25 to Oranienburger Str.). **New Berlin Tours** (☎973 03 97; www.newberlintours.com) offers free walking and bike tours of the city; bring cash to tip the guides. 3½hr. walking tours leave daily at 10:30am and 12:30pm from Zoologischer Garten in front of Dunkin' Donuts and at 11am, 1, 4pm at Brandenburger Tor in front of Starbucks (S1, 2, or 25 to Unter den Linden).

Embassies and Consulates: Australia, Mitte, Wallstr. 76-79 (☎880 08 80; www.australian-embassy.de). U2 to Märkisches Museum. Open M-Th 8:30am-5pm, F 8:30am-4:15pm. **Canada,** Mitte, Leipziger Pl. 27 (☎20 31 20; www.canada.de). S1, 2 or U2 to Potsdamer Pl. Open M-F 8:30am-12:30pm and 1:30-5pm. **Ireland,** Mitte, Friedrichstr. 200 (☎22 07 20; www.botschaft-irland.de). U2 or 6 to Stadtmitte. Open M-F 9:30am-12:30pm and 2:30-4:45pm. **New Zealand,** Mitte, Friedrichstr. 60 (☎20 62 10; www.nzembassy.com). U2 or 6 to Stadtmitte. Open M-Th 9am-1pm and 2-5:30pm, F 9am-1pm and 2-4:30pm. **UK,** Mitte, Wilhelmstr. 70-71 (☎20 42 70; www.britischebotschaft.de). S1-3, 5, 7, 9, 25, or 75, or U6 to Friedrichstr. Open M-F 9am-4pm. **US,** Clayallee 170 (☎832 92 33; fax 83 05 12 15). U1 to Oskar-Helene-Heim. After a long debate over the security of proposed locations, the US Embassy will move to a spot next to the Brandenburg Gate by 2008. Open M-F 8:30am-noon. Telephone advice available M-F 2-4pm; after hours, call ☎830 50 for emergency advice.

Currency Exchange: The best rates are usually found at exchange offices with **Wechselstube** signs outside, at most major train stations, and in large squares. **ReiseBank,** at the Hauptbahnhof (open M-Sa 8am-10pm), at Bahnhof Zoo (☎881 71 17; open daily 7:30am-10pm) and at Ostbahnhof (☎296 43 93; open M-F 7am-10pm, Sa 8am-8pm, Su 8am-noon and 12:30-4pm), is conveniently located, but has poor rates.

American Express: Main Office, Bayreuther Str. 37-38 (☎21 47 62 92). U1 or 2 to Wittenbergpl. Holds mail and offers banking services. No commission for cashing American Express Travelers Cheques. Expect out-the-door lines F-Sa. Open M-F 9am-7pm, Sa 10am-2pm. Branch at Friedrichstr. 172 (☎204 55 72). U6 to Französische Str.

Luggage Storage: In the **Hauptbahnhof,** in DB Gepack Center. €3 for up to 3 bags. In **Bahnhof Zoo.** Lockers €3-5 per day, depending on size. Max 72hr. Open daily 6:15am-10:30pm. Lockers, accessible 24hr., are also at **Ostbahnhof** and **Alexanderpl.**

Bookstores: Marga Schöler Bücherstube, Knesebeckstr. 33 (☎881 11 12), at Mommsenstr., between Savignypl. and the Ku'damm. S5, 7, 9, or 75 to Savignypl. Contemporary English reading material. Open M-W 9:30am-7pm, Th-F 9:30am-8pm, Sa 9:30am-4pm. **Dussman,** Friedrichstr. 90 (☎20 25 11 11). S1-3, 5, 7, 9, 25, or 75, or U6 to Friedrichstr. English books on the 2nd fl. Open M-Sa 10am-10pm.

Emergency: Police: ☎110. **Ambulance** and **Fire:** ☎112.

Crisis Lines: American Hotline (☎0177 814 15 10) is a crisis and referral service. **Berliner Behindertenverband,** Jägerstr. 63D (☎204 3847), has advice for the disabled. Open M-F 8am-4pm. **Frauenkrisentelefon** (☎611 0333) is a women's crisis line. Open M and W noon-2pm, Th 2-4pm.

Pharmacies: Pharmacies *(Apotheken)* are everywhere. **DominoApotheke,** Tauentzienstr. 13 (☎261 41 42), near Bahnhof Zoo. Open M-F 6am-8pm, Sa 9am-4pm. Pharmacies list a rotating schedule of 24hr. service.

Medical Services: The American and British embassies list English-speaking doctors. **Emergency doctor:** ☎31 00 31. **Emergency dentist:** ☎89 00 43 33. Both 24hr.

Internet Access: Admission to the **Deutsche Staatsbibliothek** allows free Internet access. **Netlounge,** Auguststr. 89 (☎24 34 25 97; www.netlounge-berlin.de). U-Bahn to Oranienburger Str. €2.50 per hr. Open noon-midnight. **Easy Internet:** Karl-Marx-Str. 78, Kurfürstendamm 224, Schloßstr. 102, Sony Center, Rathausstr. 5. Wireless **Internet** access is available throughout Berlin, including free and charge-based services.

Post Offices: Joachimstaler Str. 7 (☎88 70 86 11), down Joachimstaler Str. from Bahnhof Zoo and near the intersection with Kantstr. Open M-Sa 9am-8pm. Branches: **Tegel Airport,** open M-F 8am-6pm, Sa 8am-noon; **Ostbahnhof,** open M-F 8am-8pm, Sa-Su 10am-6pm. Most branches are open M-F 9am-7pm, Sa 9am-1pm. **Postal Code:** 10706.

ACCOMMODATIONS

Longer stays are most conveniently arranged through one of Berlin's **Mitwohnzentrale,** which set up house-sitting gigs or sublets (from €250 per month). **Home Company Mitwohnzentrale,** Joachimstaler Str. 17, has a useful placement website. (☎194 45; www.homecompany.de. U9 or 15 to Kurfürstendamm. Open M-Th 9am-6pm, F 9am-5pm, Sa 11am-2pm. MC/V.)

GERMANY

MITTE

Mitte's Backpacker Hostel, Chausseestr. 102 (☎28 39 09 65). U6 to Zinnowitzer Str. Up Chausseestr. on the left. The apex of hostel hipness, with an outgoing English-speaking staff and themed rooms, from "Aztec" to the more scandalous "Temptation." Large lounge area with big-screen TV and bar. Bike rental €10 per day. Linens €2.50. Laundry €5. Internet €6 per hr. Reception 24hr. Dorms €13-18; singles €29-30; doubles €43-56; triples €60-63; quads €76-80. Low season reduced rates. AmEx/DC/MC/V. ❷

BaxPax Downtown Hostel/Hotel, Ziegelstr. 28 (☎251 52 02; www.baxpax-downtown.de). S1, 2, or 25 to Oranienburger Str. or U6 to Oranienburger Tor. This gleaming new hostel is the sleeker sibling of the Kreuzberg branch. The outdoor lounge and rooftop bar make it an ideal hangout spot. Breakfast €4.50. Laundry €5. Internet €3 per hr. Dorms €16-21; singles €30-45; doubles €48-88; triples €66; quads €88. MC/V. ❸

Circus, Weinbergsweg 1A (☎28 39 14 33). U8 to Rosenthaler Pl. Clean, modern, and well-run. Wheelchair-accessible. Breakfast €2-5. Internet €0.60 per 10min. Reception and bar 24hr. Dorms €17-19; singles €33, with shower €45; doubles €50; triples €63; apartments with kitchen and balcony €77. Low season reduced rates. MC/V. ❷

TIERGARTEN

Jugendherberge Berlin International (HI), Kluckstr. 3 (☎257 99 808; www.jh-berlin-international.de). U1 to Kurfürstenstr. Walk up Potsdamer Str., go left on Pohlstr., and take a right on Kluckstr. Feels like sleeping in your elementary school—cafeteria breakfast and kids included—but features a big-screen TV, table tennis, and large common room. Grill €3. Bike rental €10 per day. Internet €3 per hr. Reception and cafe 24hr. Dorms €24, under 27 €21; doubles €28/24. Backyard camping €16. MC/V. ❷

CHARLOTTENBURG

Berolina Backpacker, Stuttgarder Pl. 17 (☎32 70 90 72; www.berolinabackpacker.de). S3, 5, 7, 9, or 75 to Charlottenburg. Quiet hostel with an ivy-laced facade keeps things elegant with print art in the bunk-free dorms and daisies on the breakfast table. The delightful surrounding cafes and proximity to the S-Bahn make up for its removal from the rush of the city. Breakfast €6. Reception 24hr. Check-out 11am. Dorms €13-14; singles €33; doubles €44; triples €48. €4 discount Nov.-Apr. AmEx/MC/V.

A&O Hostel, Joachimstaler Str. 1-3 (☎0800 222 57 22; www.aohostels.com), 30m from Bahnhof Zoo. Turn right at the Hardenbergpl. exit and cross the street, then climb the stairs just past the *Wurst* stand. Reliably cheap dorms in a prime location. Lobby, bar, and rooftop terrace are packed at night. Breakfast €5, included for private rooms. Linens €3. Internet access €2.50 per hr. Reception 24hr. 16-bed dorm from €14; smaller dorms €15-17, with showers €20-24; singles €43-76; doubles €44-86. Low season reduced rates. MC/V. Branches in Mitte and Friedrichshain. ❷

Jugendgästehaus am Zoo, Hardenbergstr. 9A (☎312 94 10; www.jgh-zoo.de), opposite the Technical University Mensa. Take bus #245 to Steinpl., or walk from Bahnhof Zoo down Hardenbergstr. (not Hardenbergpl.). Tucked away in a quiet, late-19th-century building; contains 85 beds in simple rooms. The prices and location are hard to beat. Reception 24hr. Check-out 10am. Lockout 10am-2pm. 4- to 8-bed dorms €20, under 27 €17; singles €28/25; doubles €47/44. Cash only. ❸

SCHÖNEBERG AND WILMERSDORF

Jugendhotel Berlincity, Crellestr. 22 (☎78 70 21 30; www.jugendhotel-berlin.de). U7 to Kleistpark. Swanky lounge and helpful staff make this small hotel fill up fast; reserve ahead. Breakfast included. Singles €38, with bath €55; doubles €60/79; triples €84/99; quads €108/118. Discounted rates for extended stays. AmEx/MC/V. ❸

Meininger City Hostel, Meininger Str. 10 (from abroad ☎666 36 100, in Germany 0800 634 6464; www.meininger-hostels.de). U4 or bus #146 to Rathaus Schöneberg. Walk toward the Rathaus tower on Freiherr-vom-Stein-Str., turn left onto Martin-Luther-Str., and go right on Meininger Str. The best value in town, with a bar and beer garden. Linen deposit €5. Internet €3 per hr. Reception 24hr. Dorms €14-16; singles €25; doubles €40; quads €68. 10% *Let's Go* discount on 1st night stay. See website for additional specials. Branches at Hallesches Ufer and Tempelhofer Ufer with same rates. MC/V. ❶

KREUZBERG

Bax Pax, Skalitzer Str. 104 (☎69 51 83 22; www.baxpax.de). U1 or 15 to Görlitzer Bahnhof. At the start of Oranienstr., with a pool table and a bed inside a VW Bug (ask for room #3). Linens €2.50. Internet €3 per hr. Reception 24hr. Dorms €16; singles €30; doubles €46; triples €60. €1-2 discount Nov.-Feb. AmEx/MC/V. ❷

Hostel X Berger, Schlesische Str. 22 (☎695 1863; www.hostelxberger.com). U1 or 15 to Schlesisches Tor or night bus #N65 to Taborstr. Newly opened in 2006, this hostel provides access to one of the most up-and-coming areas in Kreuzberg. Spacious, bare-bones dorms. Women-only dorms available. Linens €2. Free Internet. Reception 24hr. Dorms €11-13; singles €25; doubles €36; triples €48; quads €56. Cash only. ❶

FRIEDRICHSHAIN

Sunflower Hostel, Helsingforser Str. 17 (☎44 04 42 50; www.sunflower-hostel.de). U1 to Warschauer Str. Lounge adorned with bright sunflowers and a fountain. Some rooms with balconies. Locker deposit €3. Laundry €4.50. Internet €0.50 per 20min. Reception 24hr. Dorms €13-15; singles €35; doubles €45; triples €57; quads €68. Low season reduced rates. 7th night free. 5% ISIC discount. MC/V. ❶

Globetrotter Hostel Odyssee, Grünberger Str. 23 (☎29 00 00 81; www.globetrotterhostel.de). U1 to Warschauer Str. or U5 to Frankfurter Tor. Gothic statues and candlelit tables greet you as you enter, but rooms are modern and spotless. Bar open until dawn. Breakfast €3. Linen deposit €3. Internet €0.50 per 20min. Reception 24hr. Check-in 4pm. Check-out noon. Reserve ahead. Dorms €13; doubles €45-52; triples €57; quads €68. Low season reduced rates. 7th, 13th, and 14th nights free. MC/V. ❶

PRENZLAUER BERG

East Seven, Schwedter Str. 7 (☎93 62 22 40; www.eastseven.de). U2 to Senefelderpl. New hostel on a quiet street in trendy Prenzlauer Berg. The orange facade and classy paint job will make you feel as sunny as the light-filled, bunkless dorms. Kitchen facilities. Linens €3. Laundry €4. Internet €0.50 per 20min. Dorms €15-17; singles €32; doubles €46; triples €60; quads €72. Low season reduced rates. Cash only. ❶

Lette'm Sleep Hostel, Lettestr. 7 (☎44 73 36 23; www.backpackers.de). U2 to Eberswalder Str. The big kitchen with comfy couches is the social nexus of this 48-bed hostel. Wheelchair-accessible. Linens €2. Free Internet. Dorms €17-20; doubles €49. Low season reduced rates. 10% discount for stays over 3 nights. AmEx/MC/V. ❷

FOOD

Berlin's cuisine is more diverse than traditional German fare, thanks to the city's Indian, Italian, Thai, and Turkish populations. In early summer, expect an onslaught of Germans' beloved asparagus *(Spargel)*. An even dearer culinary tradition is breakfast, which street-side cafes extend well into the afternoon. For quick bites grab a *Bratwurst* or hit the Turkish *Döner* stands.

MITTE

Monsieur Vuong, Alte Schönhauser Allee 46 (☎30 87 26 43; www.monsieurvuong.de). U2 to Rosa-Luxemburg-Pl. Serves a limited but delicious menu of Vietnamese food—1 chicken and rice dish and 1 meat and noodle dish each day. Outdoor seating available. All entrees €6.40. Open M-Sa noon-midnight, Su 2pm-midnight. Cash only. ❷

Dada Falafel, Linienstr. 132 (☎27 59 69 27), just off Oranienburgerstr. S1 or 2 to Oranienburger Tor. Caters to executives during the day and rowdy club-goers at night. Falafel and Shawarma €3. Open daily 10am-2am, F-Sa 10am-4am. Cash only. ❶

Bagels & Bialys, Rosenthalerstr. 46 (☎283 65 46). U8 to Rosenthaler Pl. Because even Dada closes sometimes. An array of sandwiches with international flair. The selection and prices (€2.50-4) are hard to beat. Open 24hr. Cash only. ❶

GERMANY

CHARLOTTENBURG

Schwarzes Café, Kantstr. 148 (☎313 8038). S3, 5, 7, 9, or 75 to Savignypl. Popular, bohemian cafe has candlelit tables, a patio full of colorful places to sit, and a handy 24hr. breakfast menu (€4.90-8). Open 24hr. except Tu 3-11am. Cash only. ❸

Orchidee, Stuttgarter Pl. 13 (☎31 99 74 67; www.restaurantorchidee.de). *Won ton, phở,* and *maki* all under one roof; the Vietnamese offerings on the menu stand out. Lunch special 11am-5pm, half-price sushi or free appetizer with any €5-11 entree. Open M-Sa 11am-midnight, Su 3pm-midnight. Cash only. ❸

Mario Pasta Bar, Leibnizstr. 43 (☎324 3516). S 5, 7, 9, or 75 to Savignypl. A warm, personable place where a menu is rarely offered—instead, the cook greets guests and helps them select their meals. Delicious handmade pasta €6.50-9.50. Meat (€17) on a rotating weekly menu. Open M-Sa noon-midnight. Cash only. ❹

SCHÖNEBERG

Café Bilderbuch, Akazienstr. 28 (☎78 70 60 57; www.cafe-bilderbuch.de). U7 to Eisenacher Str. Relax in the Venetian library or the airy courtyard. Customers can choose what CDs to play. Known for daily breakfasts named after fairy tales (€7-8). Open M-Th 9am-1am, F-Sa 9am-2am, Su 10am-1am. Kitchen closes 11pm. Cash only. ❸

Cafe Berio, Maaßenstr. 7 (☎216 1946; www.cafe-berio.de). U1, 2, 3, or 4 to Nollendorfpl. Always jam-packed with locals, this 2-fl. Viennese-style cafe tempts passersby off the street with its unbeatable breakfast menu (€3.50-8.50) and perfect location for people-watching. Open daily 8am-1am. Cash only. ❷

Die Feinbäckerei, Vorbergstr. 2 (☎8149 4240; www.feinbaeck.de). U7 to Kleistpark or Eisenacher Str. Swabian cuisine as unassuming as the restaurant's tasteful interior. Unbeatable *Spätzle* (noodles; €6.50). Lunch special M-F 10am-5pm €4.90. Open daily noon-midnight. Cash only. ❷

KREUZBERG

Wirtshaus Henne, Leuschnerdamm 25 (☎614 7730; www.henne-berlin.de). U1 or 15 to Kottbusser Tor. The fried chicken (*Brathänchen;* €6) is arguably Berlin's best. Reserve ahead; the place is packed. Open Tu-Su 7pm-late. Cash only. ❷

Café V, Lausitzer Pl. 12 (☎612 4505). U1 or 15 to Görlitzer Bahnhof. Vegan and fish entrees are served in the romantic interior of Berlin's oldest vegetarian cafe. Top-of-the-line entrees from the bottom of the food chain include spinach balls in cream sauce (€8.80) and an array of specials (€6-8). Open daily 10am-2am. Cash only. ❸

FRIEDRICHSHAIN AND PRENZLAUER BERG

Nosh, Pappelallee 77 (☎44 04 03 97; www.nosh-berlin.de). U2 to Eberswalder Str. "Borderless cooking" means bagels with pesto-olive spread (€3), pad thai (€7.50), and the "Brighton Breakfast" (eggs, baked beans, grilled tomatoes, bacon, and toast; €6.50). Open daily 10am-late. Kitchen closes M-Sa midnight, Su 11pm. Cash only. ❸

Massai, Lychener Str. 12 (☎48 62 55 95; www.massai-berlin.de). U2 to Eberswalder Str. African art and carved wooden chairs complement savory entrees (€8-10) and delicious vegetarian options (€7-9). Open daily noon-2am. AmEx/MC/V. ❸

Cappuccino, Simon-Dach-Str. 7 (☎292 6457). U5 to Frankfurter Tor. A frantically popular eatery serving pastas and pizzas (€3-4.50). A flaming sambuca shot might come free with entrees if you're lucky. Open M-F 10am-1am, Sa-Su noon-1am. Cash only. ❷

Prater Biergarten, Kastanienallee 7-9 (☎448 5688; www.pratergarten.de). U2 to Eberswalder Str. Sit with locals at the picnic tables at Berlin's oldest beer garden. Outdoor theater and big-screen TV for watching sports. Bratwurst €2. Beer €2.20-3.10. Open in good weather Apr.-Sept. M-Sa 6pm-late, Su noon-late. Cash only. ❶

SIGHTS

Most of central Berlin's major sights lie along the route of **bus #100,** which runs every 5min. from Bahnhof Zoo to Prenzlauer Berg and passes by the **Siegessäule, Brandenburger Tor,** other sights along **Unter den Linden,** the **Berliner Dom,** and **Alexanderplatz.** Remnants of the **Berlin Wall** survive in only a few places: in **Potsdamer Platz;** near the **Haus Am Checkpoint Charlie;** in Prenzlauer Berg, next to the sobering **Documentation Center;** and, memorably, at the **East Side Gallery** in Friedrichshain.

MITTE

Mitte was once the heart of Berlin, but the wall split it down the middle, and much of it languished in disrepair under the GDR. The wave of revitalization that swept Berlin after the collapse of Communism came to Mitte first. Even though the area received a final coat of polish, you can still find war wrecks squeezed in among the grandiose Prussian palaces, glittering modern buildings, swank galleries, and stores so hyper-hip that they only sell one thing, like messenger bags, acid-tone sweaters, or rugs with words on them.

UNTER DEN LINDEN

One of Europe's best-known boulevards, Unter den Linden was the spine of imperial Berlin. During the Cold War it was known as the "Idiot's Mile" because it was often all that visitors to the East saw, and it gave them little idea of what the city was like. Beginning in Pariser Pl. in front of Brandenburger Tor, the street extends east through Bebelpl. and the Lustgarten, punctuated by dramatic squares. *(S1, 2, or 25 to Unter den Linden. Bus #100 runs the length of the boulevard every 4-6min.)*

BRANDENBURGER TOR. Built as a tribute to peace in the 18th century, this gate later came to symbolize the city's division: facing the Berlin Wall, it became a barricaded gateway to nowhere. After serving as the iconic backdrop for the fall of the Berlin Wall, the gate is now the most powerful emblem of reunited Germany. Visitors can reflect in the **Room of Silence** at the northern end.

RUSSIAN EMBASSY. Rebuilding the edifices of the rich wasn't a priority in the workers' state of the GDR. One exception was Berlin's largest embassy, which covers almost an entire city block. Although the *Palais* lost its special status after the end of the Cold War, visitors still marvel at its imposing architecture from behind a cast-iron fence. *(Unter den Linden 55.)*

BEBELPLATZ. In this square on May 10, 1933, Nazi students burned nearly 20,000 books by "subversive" authors such as Heinrich Heine and Sigmund Freud, both of Jewish descent. In the center today, a small glass window in the ground reveals empty bookcases beneath and a plaque that translates to, "Wherever they burn books, eventually they will burn people too." On the western side of Bebelpl., the building with a curved facade is the **Alte Bibliothek;** once the royal library, it's now

Berlin Mitte map legend

ACCOMMODATIONS
- Circus, **2** & **11**
- BaxPax Downtown Hostel, **6**
- Mitte's Backpacker Hostel, **1**

FOOD & DRINK
- Bagels & Bialys, **9**
- Dada Falafel, **4**
- Monsieur Vuong, **10**

BARS & NIGHTLIFE
- 2BE-Club, **7**
- Kaffee Burger, **5**
- Week-End, **f**
- Café Moskau, **20**

ENTERTAINMENT
- Deutsche Staatsoper, **22**
- Konzerthaus, **23**
- Philharmonie, **24**

SIGHTS
- Fernsehturm, **19**
- Neue Synagoge, **8**
- Russian Embassy, **21**

MUSEUMS
- Alte Nationalgalerie, **15**
- Bodemuseum, **13**
- Gemäldegalerie, **25**
- Hamburger Bahnhof, **3**
- Neues Museum, **16**
- Pergamonmuseum, **14**

CHURCHES
- Berliner Dom, **17**
- Marienkirche, **18**

See map p. 413

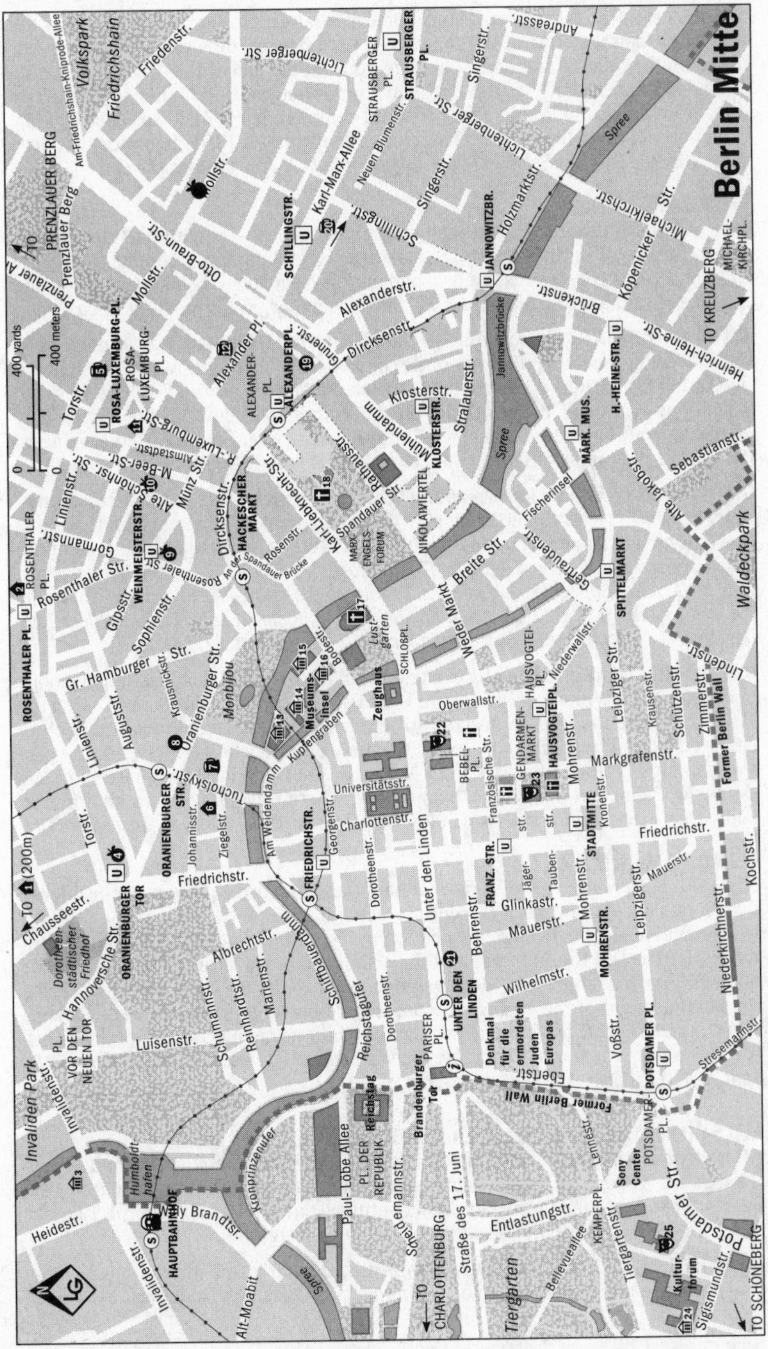
Berlin Mitte
0 400 yards
0 400 meters
TO PRENZLAUER BERG
TO KREUZBERG
TO SCHÖNEBERG
TO CHARLOTTENBURG
TO (200m)
Volkspark Friedrichshain
Invaliden Park
Tiergarten
Waldeckpark
Monbijou
Lustgarten
Museumsinsel
Zeughaus
Reichstag
Brandenburger Tor
PARISER PL.
PL. DER REPUBLIK
Denkmal für die ermordeten Juden Europas
Former Berlin Wall
Sony Center
Kulturforum
Humboldthafen
Spree
Dorotheenstädtischer Friedhof
MARX-ENGELS-FORUM
NIKOLAIVIERTEL
GENDARMENMARKT
HAUPTBAHNHOF
ORANIENBURGER TOR
ORANIENBURGER STR.
ROSENTHALER PL.
WEINMEISTERSTR.
ROSA-LUXEMBURG-PL.
HACKESCHER MARKT
ALEXANDERPL.
SCHILLINGSTR.
STRAUSBERGER PL.
JANNOWITZBR.
KLOSTERSTR.
MÄRK. MUS.
H.-HEINE-STR.
SPITTELMARKT
HAUSVOGTEIPL.
STADTMITTE
MOHRENSTR.
FRANZ. STR.
FRIEDRICHSTR.
UNTER DEN LINDEN
POTSDAMER PL.
MICHAELKIRCHPL.
KEMPERPL.
Unter den Linden
Straße des 17. Juni
Karl-Marx-Allee
Friedrichstr.
Leipziger Str.
Potsdamer Str.
Alexanderstr.
Invalidenstr.
Chausseestr.
Torstr.
Oranienburger Str.
Rosenthaler Str.
Karl-Liebknecht-Str.
Spandauer Str.
Breite Str.
Mühlendamm
Holzmarktstr.
Köpenicker Str.
Heinrich-Heine-Str.
Wilhelmstr.
Behrenstr.
Ebertstr.
Entlastungstr.
Lindenstr.
Kochstr.
Stresemannstr.

home to the law faculty of Humboldt-Universität. On the eastern side is the **Deutsche Staatsoper,** one of Berlin's three opera houses, fully rebuilt after the war based on the original sketches. The blue dome at the end of the square belongs to **St.-Hedwigs-Kathedrale,** the first Catholic church built in Berlin after the Reformation. Modeled on the Roman Pantheon and completed in 1773, it was destroyed by Allied bombers in 1943. The church was rebuilt in the 1950s in a more modern style. *(Open M-Sa 10am-5pm, Su 1-5pm. Organ concerts W 3pm. Cathedral free.)*

TIERGARTEN

Once a hunting ground for Prussian monarchs, the lush Tiergarten (Animal Park) is now the eye of Berlin's metropolitan storm. Stretching from Bahnhof Zoo to the Brandenburger Tor, the vast landscaped park is frequented by bikers, joggers, and families out for a stroll. **Straße des 17. Juni** bisects the park from west to east.

THE REICHSTAG. Today home to the *Bundestag*, Germany's governing body, the Reichstag was central to one of the most critical moments in history. When it mysteriously burned down in 1933, Hitler declared a state of emergency and seized power. Today, a glass dome offers visitors 360° views of the city as they climb the spiral staircase inside. Go before 8am or after 8pm to avoid long lines. *(☎22 73 21 52; www.bundestag.de. Open daily 8am-midnight; last entrance 10pm. Free.)*

SIEGESSÄULE. Fondly known as the "chick-on-a-stick," this column commemorates Prussia's victory over France in 1870. The goddess of victory on the top is made of melted French cannons. Climb the 285 steps for a panoramic look at the city. *(Großer Stern. Take bus #100 or 187 to Großer Stern or S5, 7, or 9 to Tiergarten and walk 5min. down Straße des 17. Juni. Accessible via the stairs at the West corners around the traffic circle. ☎391 29 61. Open Apr.-Nov. M-F 9:30am-6:30pm, Sa-Su 9:30am-7pm; Dec.-Mar. M-F 10am-5pm, Sa-Su 10am-5:30pm. €2.20, students €1.50.)*

POTSDAMER PLATZ. Originally designed to allow the rapid mobilization of troops under Friedrich Wilhelm I, Potsdamer Pl. is Berlin's commercial center. During the 1990s, it formed the city's largest construction site; now, its ambitious architecture never fails to impress visitors. Most of the new office space is empty, but the central complex includes Berlin's Film Museum, the towering headquarters of the Deutsche Bahn, and the glitzy **Sony Center,** where travelers can watch a movie, enjoy free wireless Internet, or window-shop. *(U2, or S1, 2, or 25 to Potsdamer Pl.)*

GENDARMENMARKT

Several blocks south of Unter den Linden, this gorgeous square was considered the French Quarter in the 18th century, when it became the main settlement for Protestant Huguenots fleeing persecution by "Sun King" Louis XIV. During the last week of June and the first week of July, the square transforms into a stage for open-air classical concerts. *(U6 to Französische Str. or U2 or 6 to Stadtmitte.)* Gracing the southern end of the square, the **Deutscher Dom** houses **Wege Irrwege Umwege** ("Milestones, Setbacks, Sidetracks"), an exhibition tracing German political history from despotism to democracy. *(Gendarmenmarkt 1. ☎22 73 04 31. Open Tu-Su Sept.-May 10am-6pm; June-Aug. 10am-7pm. Free.)*

MUSEUMSINSEL AND ALEXANDERPLATZ

After crossing the Spree, Unter den Linden becomes Karl-Liebknecht-Str. and cuts through the Museumsinsel (Museum Island), home to five major museums and the **Berliner Dom.** Karl-Liebknecht-Str. then continues onward to Alexanderpl. Take S3, 5, 7, 9, or 75 to Hackescher Markt, or bus #100 to Lustgarten.

BERLINER DOM. Berlin's most recognizable landmark, this multi-domed cathedral proves that Protestants can be as dramatic as Catholics. Built during the reign of Kaiser Wilhelm II, the Dom suffered damage in a 1944 air raid and only recently emerged from two decades of restoration. Inside, keep an eye out for the likenesses of Protestant luminaries Calvin and Luther *(Open M-Sa 9am-8pm, Su noon-8pm, closed during services 6:30-7:30pm. Free organ recitals W-F 3pm. Combined admission to Dom, crypt, tower, and galleries €5, students €3.)*

MARIENKIRCHE. The church is Gothic, the altar and pulpit Rococo, and the tower Neo-Romantic after several centuries of additions to the original structure. Relatively undamaged during the war, this little church still holds relics from nearby churches that used it as a shelter. Knowledgeable guides explain the artifacts, as well as the painting collection, mainly including works from the Dürer and Cranach schools. *(☎242 44 67. Open daily in summer 10am-6pm, winter 10am-4pm.)*

FERNSEHTURM. Berlin's tallest structure at 368m, this bizarre TV tower was built to prove East Germany's technological capabilities—even though Swedish engineers helped construct it. The Swedes left a controversial *"Papsts Rache"* (Pope's Revenge): a crucifix appears when the sun hits the dome, defying the GDR's anti-religious agenda. An elevator-accessible view from the node 203m above the city. *(☎242 33 33. Open daily Mar.-Oct. 9am-11pm; Nov.-Feb. 10am-midnight. €8.)*

SCHEUNENVIERTEL AND ORANIENBURGER STRAßE

Northwest of Alexanderpl., near Oranienburger Str. and Große Hamburger Str., is the Scheunenviertel, once the center of Berlin's Orthodox Jewish community. Prior to WWII, Berlin did not have ghettos; the city's assimilated Jews lived in Western Berlin, while Orthodox Jews from Eastern Europe settled here. The district shows traces of Jewish life back to the 13th century but is now known mainly for its outdoor cafes. *(S1, 2, or 25 to Oranienburger Str. or U6 to Oranienburger Tor.)*

NEUE SYNAGOGE. This synagogue was used for worship until 1940, when the Nazis occupied it and used it for storage. Amazingly, the building survived *Kristallnacht.* The striking building no longer holds services; instead, it houses small exhibits on the history of Berlin's Jews. *(Oranienburger Str. 29. ☎88 02 83 00. Open May-Aug. Su-M 10am-8pm, Tu-Th 10am-6pm, F 10am-5pm; Sept.-Apr. M-Th and Su 10am-6pm, F 10am-2pm. A series of security checks is required to enter. €3, students €2. Dome €1.50/1.)*

CHARLOTTENBURG

Charlottenburg was originally a separate town huddled around Friedrich I's imperial palace. Now the neighborhood is home to Berlin's main shopping drag, the Ku'damm (p. 422), full of uppity boutiques. The area's sights can be expensive; budget travelers come mostly to explore the attractions near Bahnhof Zoo.

AROUND BAHNHOF ZOO. The former West Berlin centered around Bahnhof Zoo, the station that inspired U2's "Zoo TV" tour. In the surrounding area, a jumble of peepshows mingle with department stores, souvenir shops, and other G-rated attractions. Many of the animals at the renowned **Zoologischer Garten** live in open-air habitats; the flamingos have no confines. *(Budapester Str. 34. Open daily May-Sept. 9am-6:30pm; Oct.-Feb. 9am-5pm; Mar.-Apr. 9am-5:30pm. €11, students €8.)*

KAISER-WILHELM-GEDÄCHTNISKIRCHE. Nicknamed "the hollow tooth" *(Hohler Zahn)*, this shattered church has been left in its jagged state as a reminder of WWII. Its colorful mosaics are mostly intact, and the church houses an exhibit of photos showing the church both before and after the Allied bombings. *(☎218 5023. Church open daily 9am-7pm. Exhibit open M-Sa 10am-4pm.)*

SCHLOß CHARLOTTENBURG. This monumental Baroque palace occupies a park in northern Charlottenburg and contains more 18th-century French paintings than any other location outside of France. The pristine grounds include the beautifully furnished **Altes Schloß,** the marbled receiving rooms of the **Neuer Flugel,** the **Neuer Pavillon,** and the palace **Mausoleum.** The **Belvedere,** which houses the royal family's porcelain collection, is also on the grounds. Leave time to stroll the **Schloßgarten** behind the main buildings, a paradise of small lakes, fountains, and footbridges. *(Take bus #145 from Bahnhof Zoo to Luisenpl./Schloß Charlottenburg or U2 to Sophie-Charlotte Pl. and walk 10-15min. up Schloßstr. ☎320 9275.* ***Altes Schloß*** *open Tu-F 9am-5pm, Sa-Su 10am-5pm. Mandatory tour (in German, with written translations available in English and French). €8, students €5. Upper floor €2/1.50.* ***Neuer Flügel*** *open Tu-F 10am-6pm, Sa-Su 11am-6pm. €5/4.* ***Neuer Pavillon*** *open Tu-Su 10am-5pm. €2/1.50.* ***Mausoleum*** *open Apr.-Oct. Tu-Su 10am-noon and 1-5pm. €1.* ***Belvedere*** *open Apr.-Oct. Tu-Su 10am-5pm; Nov.-Mar. Tu-F noon-4pm, Sa-Su noon-5pm. €2/1.50.* ***Schloßgarten*** *open Tu-Su 6am-10pm. Free.* ***Combination ticket*** *includes admission to everything except the Altes Schloß €9/7.)*

SCHÖNEBERG

South of the Ku'damm, Schöneberg is a pleasant residential district notable for its shopping streets, tasty restaurants, and laid-back cafes where locals lounge for hours. In busy **Nollendorfplatz,** the nexus of Berlin's gay and lesbian community, even the military store is draped with rainbow flags.

GRUNEWALD. In summer, this 745-acre birch forest, the dog-walking turf of many a Berliner, provides a retreat from the chaos of the city. About 1km into the forest, the **Jagdschloß,** a restored royal hunting lodge, houses paintings by Cranach, Graff, and other German artists as well as a one-room hunting museum. *(Am Grunewaldsee 29. U3 or 7 to Fehrbelliner Pl., or S45 or 46 to Hohenzollerndamm, then bus #115 (dir.: Neuruppiner Str.) to Pücklerstr. Walk west 5min. on Pücklerstr. and continue straight into the forest to reach the lodge. ☎813 35 97. Open May 15-Oct. 15 Tu-Su 10am-5pm; Oct. 16-May 14 Sa-Su tours only at 11am, 1, 3pm. €2, students €1.50; with tour €3/2.50.)*

KREUZBERG

In what was once West Germany, Kreuzberg today is counter-culture central. Much of the area was occupied by squatters *(Hausbesetzer)* in the 60s and 70s, but the city government evicted most of them in the early 80s. Protests are still frequent and intense; the most prominent is an annual demonstration on Labor Day. Home to a large portion of the city's immigrant population, the district has recently seen an influx of hipsters amid a wider wave of gentrification.

Charlottenburg and Schöneberg map legend

ACCOMMODATIONS

A&O Hostel, **7**

Berolina Backpacker, **1**

Jugendgästehaus am Zoo, **3**

Jugendherberge Berlin International (HI), **8**

Jugendhotel Berlincity, **13**

Meininger City Hostel, **11**

FOOD & DRINK

Cafe Berio, **10**

Café Bilderbuch, **14**

Die Feinbeckerei, **16**

Mario Pasta Bar, **4**

Orchidee, **2**

Schwarzes Café, **5**

BARS & NIGHTLIFE

Hafen, **9**

Heile Welt, **17**

Mister Hu, **15**

Quasimodo, **6**

Slumberland, **12**

See map p. 417

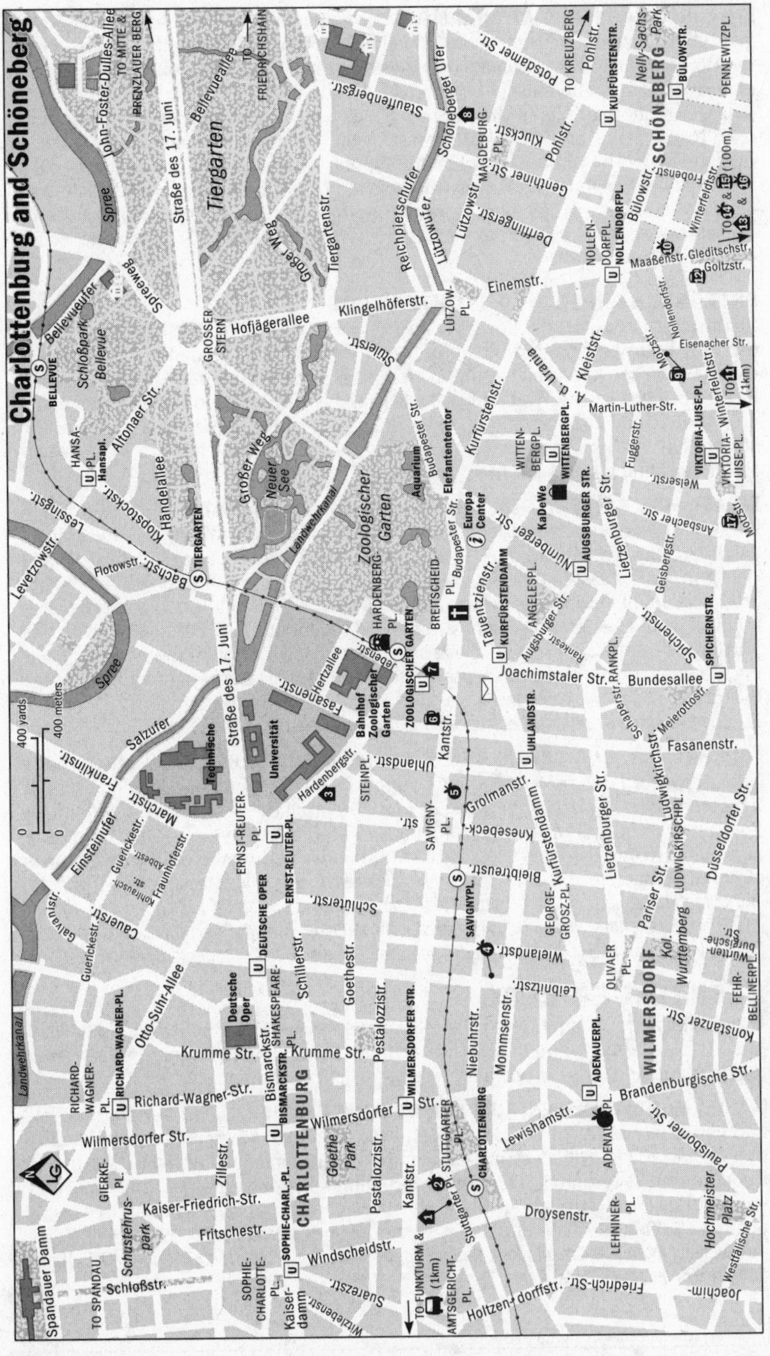
Charlottenburg and Schöneberg
400 yards
400 meters
Tiergarten
Zoologischer Garten
CHARLOTTENBURG
WILMERSDORF
SCHÖNEBERG
Straße des 17. Juni
Bahnhof Zoologischer Garten
Universität
Technische
Deutsche Oper
KaDeWe
Europa Center
Elefantentor
Aquarium
Neuer See
Landwehrkanal
Spree
Schloßpark Bellevue
GROSSER STERN
Goethe Park
Schustehrus-park
TO MITTE & PRENZLAUER BERG
TO FRIEDRICHSHAIN
TO KREUZBERG
TO SPANDAU
TO FUNKTURM & (1km)
Kurfürstendamm
Kantstr.
Hardenbergstr.
Tauentzienstr.
Bismarckstr.
Otto-Suhr-Allee
Kaiser-Friedrich-Str.
Wilmersdorfer Str.
Potsdamer Str.
Bundesallee
Hohenzollerndamm

HAUS AM CHECKPOINT CHARLIE. A strange mix of earnest eastern sincerity and glossy western salesmanship, Checkpoint Charlie documents the history of the Berlin Wall and the dramatic escapes that once centered around its wire-and-concrete barrier. The museum showcases all manner of artwork, newspaper clippings, and photographs of the Berlin Wall, as well as a collection of contraptions used to get over, under, or through it. Out on the street, the checkpoint itself is overshadowed by photos of two soldiers, one American and one Russian, each symbolically keeping watch over what used to be the other's territory. *(Friedrichstr. 43-45. U6 to Kochstr. ☎253 72 50; www.mauer-museum.de. Museum open daily 9am-10pm. German-language films with English subtitles every 2hr. from 9:30am. €9.50, students €5.50. Audio tour €3.)*

FRIEDRICHSHAIN AND LICHTENBERG

As the alternative scene follows the low rents eastward, **Friedrichshain** is becoming the new hallowed ground of the unpretentiously hip. The district hasn't been extensively renovated since reunification, so it retains old pre-fab apartments and large stretches of the Wall. **Simon-Dach-Straße** is filled with outdoor cafes and a crowd of 20-somethings. The grungier area surrounding **Rigärstraße** is one of the strongholds of Berlin's legendary alternative scene, home to squatter bars, makeshift clubs, and lounging grounds for punks.

EAST SIDE GALLERY. The longest remaining portion of the Wall, this 1.3km stretch of cement slabs and asbestos also serves as the world's largest open-air art gallery, unsupervised and open at all hours. The murals are not remnants of Cold War graffiti, but instead the efforts of an international group of artists who gathered here in 1989 to celebrate the end of the city's division. It was expected that the wall would be destroyed soon after and the paintings lost, but in 2000, with this portion still standing, many of the artists reconvened to repaint their work, covering others' scrawlings. Unfortunately, the new paintings are being rapidly eclipsed by graffiti. *(Along Mühlenstr. Take U1 or 15 or S3, 5-7, 9, or 75 to Warschauer Str. or S5, 7, 9, or 75 to Ostbahnhof and walk back toward the river. www.eastsidegallery.com.)*

FORSCHUNGS- UND GEDENKSTÄTTE NORMANNENSTRAßE. The Lichtenberg suburb harbors the most feared building of the GDR regime: the headquarters of the **secret police** (*Staatssicherheit*, or *Stasi*). During the Cold War, the *Stasi* kept dossiers on six million East Germans. An exhibit displays a collection of tiny microphones and cameras used by the *Stasi* and a bizarre shrine filled with busts of Lenin. *(Ruschestr. 103, Haus 1. U5 to Magdalenenstr. From the station, walk up Ruschestr. and take the first right into the complex of buildings. Haus #1 is straight ahead; a sign on Ruschestr. marks the turn. ☎553 68 54; www.stasimuseum.de. Exhibits in German. Recommended English info booklet €3. Open M-F 11am-6pm, Sa-Su 2-6pm. €3.50, students €2.50.)*

GERMANY

PRENZLAUER BERG

Everything in Prenzlauer Berg used to be something else. Brunches unfold in what once were butcher shops, furniture exhibits bring domestic grace to a former power plant, and kids cavort in breweries-turned-nightclubs.

DOKUMENTATIONSZENTRUM DER BERLINER MAUER. A museum, chapel, and entire city block of the Berlin Wall—two concrete barriers separated by the open *Todesstreife* (death strip)—make up a controversial memorial to "victims of the communist tyranny." The Center assembles historic photos, film clips, and sound bites from throughout the Wall's history. Ascend the spiral staircases to achieve the full, desolate effect of visiting the spot. *(Bernauer Str. 111. ☎464 10 30; www.berliner-mauer-dokumentationszentrum.de. U8 to Bernauer Str. Open Tu-Su Apr.-Oct. 10am-6pm; Nov.-Mar. 10am-5pm. Free.)*

MUSEUMS

Berlin is one of the world's great museum cities, with over 170 museums that include collections from every epoch in world history. The *Berlin Programm* (€1.60) lists museums and galleries.

SMB MUSEUMS

Staatliche Museen zu Berlin (SMB) runs over 20 museums in four major areas of Berlin—the **Museumsinsel, Tiergarten-Kulturforum, Charlottenburg,** and **Dahlem**—and elsewhere in Mitte and the Tiergarten. All museums sell single-admission tickets (€6, students €3) and the three-day card (*Drei-Tage-Karte;* €12, students €6). Admission is free the first Sunday of every month and on Thursdays after 6pm. Unless otherwise noted, all SMB museums are open Tuesday through Sunday 10am-6pm and Thursday 10am-10pm. All offer free English-language audio tours.

MUSEUMSINSEL (MUSEUM ISLAND)

Germany's greatest cultural treasures reside in five separate museums, separated from the rest of Mitte by two arms of the Spree. Two museums are undergoing renovations: the **Bodemuseum** should reopen in 2006, the **Neues Museum** in 2008. *(S3, 5, 7, 9, or 75 to Hackescher Markt or bus #100 to Lustgarten. ☎20 90 55 55.)*

PERGAMONMUSEUM. One of the world's great ancient history museums, Pergamonmuseum is named for the Turkish city from which the enormous **Altar of Zeus** (180 BC) was taken. The collection of artifacts from the ancient Near East includes the colossal blue **Ishtar Gate of Babylon** (575 BC) and the Roman **Market Gate of Miletus.** *(Bodestr. 1-3. ☎20 90 55 77. €10, students €5.)*

ALTE NATIONALGALERIE (OLD NATIONAL GALLERY). After extensive renovations, this museum is now reopened to lovers of 19th-century art. The gallery presents everything from German Realism to French Impressionism; Camille Pisarro is but one name in an all-star cast. Enjoy a drink at the outdoor Sage Bar under the columns overlooking the water. *(Lustgarten. ☎20 90 58 01.)*

TIERGARTEN-KULTURFORUM

The Tiergarten-Kulturforum, a complex of museums at the eastern end of the Tiergarten near the Staatsbibliothek and Potsdamer Pl., is a good place to find fine arts students and local aficionados. *(Take S1, 2, or 25, or U2 to Potsdamer Pl. and walk down Potsdamer Str.; look for Matthäikirchpl. on the right. ☎20 90 55 55.)*

GEMÄLDEGALERIE. One of Germany's best-known museums, the Gemäldegalerie beautifully displays nearly 3000 masterpieces by Dutch, Flemish, German, and Italian masters from the 13th to 18th centuries, including works by Botticelli, Dürer, Raphael, Rembrandt, Titian, and Vermeer. *(Stauffenbergstr. 40. ☎266 29 51.)*

HAMBURGER BAHNHOF/MUSEUM FÜR GEGENWART. North of the Tiergarten, Berlin's foremost modern art collection occupies a full 10,000 sq. m of this former train station. Its artist roster includes Beuys, Kiefer, and Warhol, and the museum also hosts outrageous sculptures and temporary exhibits. *(Invalidenstr. 50-51. S3, 5, 7, 9, or 75 to Hauptbahnhof, or U6 to Zinnowitzer Str. ☎39 78 34 11. Open Tu-F 10am-6pm, Sa 11am-8pm, Su 11am-6pm. €8, students €4; Th 2-6pm free.)*

CHARLOTTENBURG

Many excellent museums surround **Schloß Charlottenburg.** Take bus #145 from Bahnhof Zoo to Luisenpl./Schloß Charlottenburg, or take U2 to Sophie-Charlotte-Pl. and walk 10-15min. up the tree-lined Schloßstr.

ÄGYPTISCHES MUSEUM. This Neoclassical building displays ancient Egyptian art complemented by dramatic lighting. The most famous work is the limestone bust of **Queen Nefertiti** (1340 BC), but the sarcophagi and mummified cats are also worth seeing. *(Schloßstr. 70. ☎34 35 73 11. Open daily 10am-6pm. Th 2-6pm free.)*

MUSEUM BERGGRUEN. Subtitled "Picasso and His Time," this three-story museum explores the work of the groundbreaking 20th-century artist and the movements that sprung up around him. Picasso's influences, which include African masks and late paintings by Matisse, occupy the bottom floor. On the top floor are the elongated sculptures of Giacometti and paintings by Klee. *(Schloßstr. 1, across from the Ägyptisches Museum. ☎32 69 58 11. Open Tu-Su 10am-6pm.)*

DAHLEM

ETHNOLOGISCHES MUSEUM. It's worth the trek to suburban Dahlem to see the Ethnology Museum's ancient Central American stonework, African elephant tusks, and boats from the South Pacific. In the same building, the smaller **Museum für Indisches Kunst** (Museum for Indian Art) features ornate shrines and bright murals. The **Museum für Ostasiatisches Kunst** (Museum for East Asian Art) houses extremely long tapestries. *(U1 to Dahlem-Dorf; follow the "Museen" signs to get to the main building. ☎830 14 38. Open Tu-F 10am-6pm, Sa-Su 11am-6pm. Th 2-6pm free.)*

INDEPENDENT (NON-SMB) MUSEUMS

DEUTSCHE GUGGENHEIM BERLIN. Located in a renovated building across the street from the Deutsche Staatsbibliothek, this joint venture of the Deutsche Bank and the Guggenheim Foundation features new exhibits of modern and contemporary art every few months. *(Unter den Linden 13-15. ☎202 09 30; www.deutsche-guggenheim.de. Open M-W and F-Su 11am-8pm, Th 11am-10pm. €4, students €3; M free.)*

KUNST-WERKE BERLIN. Under the direction of Mitte art luminary Klaus Biesenbach, this former margarine factory now houses artists' studios, rotating modern exhibits, and a garden cafe. *(Auguststr. 69. U6 to Oranienburger Tor. ☎243 45 90; www.kw-berlin.de. Exhibitions open Tu-W and F-Su noon-7pm, Th noon-9pm. €6, students €4.)*

FILMMUSEUM BERLIN. This new museum chronicles the development of German film, with a focus on older films like *Metropolis* and rooms devoted to superstars including Leni Riefenstahl and Marlene Dietrich. *(Potsdamer Str. 2; 3rd and 4th fl. of the Sony Center. S1, 2, 25 or U2 to Potsdamer Pl. ☎300 90 30; www.filmmuseum-berlin.de. Open Tu-W and F-Su 10am-6pm, Th 10am-8pm. €6, students €4, children €2.50.)*

JÜDISCHES MUSEUM BERLIN. Daniel Libeskind designed this museum in such a way that no facing walls run parallel. Jagged hallways end in windows overlooking "the void." Wander through the labyrinthine Garden of Exile or shut yourself in the Holocaust Tower, a room virtually devoid of light and sound. *(Lindenstr. 9-14. U6 to Kochstr., or U1, 6, or 15 to Hallesches Tor. ☎308 78 56 81; www.jmberlin.de. Open M 10am-10pm, Tu-Su 10am-8pm. €5, students €2.50. Special exhibits €4.)*

ENTERTAINMENT

Berlin has one of the world's most vibrant cultural scenes, with countless exhibitions, concerts, plays, and dance performances. The city generously subsidizes its art scene despite recent cutbacks, and tickets are usually reasonably priced. Most theaters and concert halls offer up to 50% off for students who buy at the *Abendkasse* (evening box office), which generally opens 1hr. before shows. Other ticket outlets charge 15-18% commissions and do not offer student discounts. The

KaDeWe (p. 422) has a ticket counter. (☎217 77 54. Open M-F 10am-8pm, Sa 10am-4pm.) Theaters generally accept credit cards, but many ticket outlets do not. Most theaters and operas close from mid-July to late August.

CONCERTS, OPERA, AND DANCE

Berlin reaches its musical zenith in September during the fabulous **Berliner Festwochen,** which draws the world's best orchestras and soloists. The **Berliner Jazztage** in November features top jazz musicians. For tickets (which sell out months in advance) and more information for both festivals, call or write to Berliner Festspiele (☎25 48 90; www.berlinerfestspiele.de). In mid-July, the **Bachtage** feature an intense week of classical music, while every Saturday night in August the **Sommer Festspiele** turns the Ku'damm into a multifaceted concert hall with punk, steel-drum, and folk groups competing for attention.

The monthly pamphlets *Konzerte und Theater in Berlin und Brandenburg* (free) and *Berlin Programm* (€1.75) list concerts, as do the biweekly *Zitty* and *Tip*. The programs for many theaters and opera houses are also listed on huge posters in U-Bahn stations. Tickets for the *Philharmonie* and the *Oper* are nearly impossible to get without writing months in advance; you can try standing outside before performances with a small sign saying *"Suche Karte"* (seeking ticket).

Berliner Philharmonisches Orchester, Herbert Von Karajanstr. 1 (☎25 48 81 32; www.berlin-philharmonic.com). Take S1, 2, or 25 or U2 to Potsdamer Pl. and walk up Potsdamer Str. It may look bizarre, but this yellow building, designed by Scharoun in 1963, is acoustically perfect: every audience member hears the music exactly as it is meant to sound. The Berliner Philharmoniker, led by Sir Simon Rattle, is one of the world's finest orchestras. It is practically impossible to get a seat; check 1hr. before concert time or write at least 8 weeks in advance. Closed late June-early Sept. Box office open M-F 3-6pm, Sa-Su 11am-2pm. Tickets start at €7 for standing room, €13 for seats.

THEATER

Theater listings can be found on the yellow and blue posters in most U-Bahn stations and in the monthly pamphlets *Kultur!news* and *Berlin Programm*, as well as in *030*, *Zitty*, and *Tip*. In addition to the world's best German-language theater, Berlin also has a strong English-language scene; look for listings in *Zitty* or *Tip* that say *"in englischer Sprache"* (in English). A number of privately run companies called *Off-Theaters* also occasionally feature English-language plays.

Deutsches Theater, Schumannstr. 13A (☎28 44 12 25; www.deutsches-theater.berlin.net). U6 or S1, 2, 5, 7, 9, 25, or 75 to Friedrichstr. Go north on Friedrichstr., turn left on Reinhardtstr., and then go right on Albrechtstr., which curves into Schumannstr. Even western Berlin admits it: this is the best theater in Germany, producing innovative takes on classics and newer works from Büchner to Ibsen. Box office open M-Sa 11am-6:30pm, Su 3-6:30pm. Tickets €5-43, students €8.

FILM

O.F. next to a movie listing means original version (i.e., not dubbed in German); *O.m.U.* means original version with German subtitles. Check *Tip* or *Zitty* for theater schedules. Mondays through Wednesdays are *Kinotage* at most theaters, with reduced prices and further discounts for those with a student ID. The city also hosts the international **Berlinale** film festival (Feb. 8-18, 2007).

Arsenal, in the Filmhaus at Potsdamer Pl. (☎26 95 51 00). U2 or S1, 2, or 25 to Potsdamer Pl. Run by the founders of the *Berlinale,* Arsenal showcases indie films and some classics (€4.50, students €3.50). Frequent appearances by guest directors make the theater a popular meeting place for Berlin's filmmakers.

SHOPPING

The high temple of consumerism is the seven-story **KaDeWe department store** on Wittenbergpl. at Tauentzienstr. 21-24, the largest department store on the continent. The name is a German abbreviation of *Kaufhaus des Westens* (Department Store of the West). (☎212 10. Open M-F 10am-8pm, Sa 9:30am-8pm.) The sidewalks of the 2-mile-long **Kurfürstendamm,** near Bahnhof Zoo, have at least one big store from every mega-chain you can name. Near Hackescher Markt and Alte Schönhauser Str., the art galleries of Mitte give way to clothing galleries with similar price tags. The flea market on **Str. des 17. Juni** probably has the best selection, but the prices are higher than those at other markets. Take S5, 7, 9, or 75 to Tiergarten. (Open Sa-Su 11am-5pm.) **Winterfeldtplatz,** near Nollendorfpl., overflows with food, flowers, and people crooning Dylan tunes over acoustic guitars. (Open W and Sa 8am-1pm.)

NIGHTLIFE

Berlin's nightlife is absolute madness. Bars typically open around 6pm and get going around midnight, just as clubs begin to open their doors. The bar scene winds down anywhere between 1 and 6am; meanwhile, clubs fill up and don't empty until dawn, when they pass the baton to after-parties and 24hr. cafes. Between 1 and 4am, take advantage of the **night buses** and **U-Bahn** 9 and 12, which run all night on Friday and Saturday. Info about bands and dance venues can be found in the pamphlets *Tip* (€2.50) and *Zitty* (€2.30), available at newsstands, or in *030* (free), distributed in hostels, cafes, and bars.

Berlin's largest bar scene sprawls down pricey **Oranienburger Straße** in Mitte, but areas around **Schönhauser Allee** and **Danziger Straße,** such as the **"LSD" zone** (named for Lychener Str., Schliemannstr., and Dunckerstr.), still harbor an alternative edge. Bars can also be found on **Simon-Dach-Straße** and **Gabriel-Max-Straße** in Friedrichshain, and dance venues for younger crowds are scattered between the car dealerships and empty lots of **Mühlenstraße.** Gay and lesbian nightlife centers on **Nollendorfplatz,** in the west.

BARS AND CLUBS

MITTE

Weekend, Alexanderpl. 5 (www.week-end-berlin.de), 12th fl. of the building with the neon "Sharp" sign. A rising staple of the Berlin scene, with house devotees rocking out as the sun rises over East Berlin. Cover €6-8. Open Th-Sa 11pm-4am. Cash only.

FROM THE ROAD

I EAT BEATS FOR BREAKFAST

So proclaims the T-shirt of the boy bopping arhythmically in front of me at Maria am Bahnhof, a hot spot in the Friedrichshain club scene. Yes, I am at a techno concert—my first—and am trying to learn the particularities of dancing to something that has neither lyrics nor a recognizable melody (not that I can dance under any circumstances, to be fair).

More difficult than learning the nuances of moving to electronic music is knowing what its various sub-categories even mean. As I researched Berlin, I would frequently learn that a club played, say, "drum 'n' bass" on Fridays and "electro" on Saturdays. I would give a confident nod and record this information while secretly having no idea what these terms meant, my own taste being generally confined to faux-obscure indie pop. So for those who are looking to test the waters of Berlin nightlife but are equally clueless about its fiendish electronic music culture, I can offer some information, if not some dance moves:

Drum 'n' Bass—Also called "dnb," this form is mostly a product of British rave culture. The quick drum beats and complex bass lines are the most prominent sonic elements. Influenced by hip-hop, it is usually mid-tempo and can involve samples or synthesized bass lines.

Cafe Moskau, Karl-Marx-Allee 34. U5 to Schillingstr. Moves often; check www.wmfclub.de. Hip-hop fanatics and electro-junkies fill the floor of this former cabaret. Beer €3. Su gay night. Cover €7-13. Open Sa and sometimes F 11pm-6am, Su 10pm-5am. Cash only.

2BE-Club, Ziegelstr. 23 (☎89 06 84 10; www.2be-club.de). U6 to Oranienburger Tor. Reggae and hip-hop in a huge space with 2 dance floors and a tented courtyard. Cover €7.50-8; women free until midnight. Open F-Sa and sometimes W 11pm-late. Cash only.

Kaffee Burger, Torstr. 60 (☎28 04 64 95; www.kaffee-burger.de). U2 to Rosa-Luxemburg-Pl. This awesomely oblivious retro bar feels a bit GDR-era. An eclectic crowd and nightly parties. Don't miss bimonthly "Russian Disco" night. Th live bands 10pm. Cover Su-Th €1, F-Sa €5-6. Open Su-Th 7pm-late, F 8pm-late, Sa 9pm-late. Cash only.

CHARLOTTENBURG (SAVIGNYPLATZ)

Quasimodo, Kantstr. 12A (www.quasimodo.de). U2 or S5, 7, 9, or 75 to Zoologischer Garten. Beneath a huge cafe, this cozy venue showcases soul, R&B, and jazz. Concert tickets available from 5pm at the cafe upstairs or through the Kant-Kasse ticket service (☎313 45 54). Concerts 11pm; cover €8-20. Call or check the website for schedules; tickets are cheaper if reserved ahead. Open daily noon-late. Cash only.

SCHÖNEBERG

Slumberland, Goltzstr. 24 (☎216 53 49). U1, 2, 3, or 4, to Nollendorfpl. Palm trees, African art, a sand floor, and tantalizing mixed drinks encourage kicking back and jamming to the reggae music. Open Su-F 6pm-late, Sa 11am-late. Cash only.

Mister Hu, Goltzstr. 39 (☎217 21 11; www.misterhu-berlin.de). U1, 2, 3, or 4 to Nollendorfpl. This bar made of rocky tiles serves up creative drinks that the relaxed crowd enjoys outdoors on the sidewalk patio. Happy hour M-Sa 5-8pm, Su all day; mixed drinks €4.50. Open Su-Th 6pm-2am, F-Sa 6pm-4am. Cash only.

KREUZBERG

Club der Visionaere, Am Flutgraben 1 (☎695 18 944; www.clubdervisionaere.de). U1 or 15 to Schlesisches Tor or night bus #N65 to Heckmannufer. From the multiple languages drifting through the air to the people settled on ground-cushions, Club der Visionaere has a decidedly backpacker vibe. For the best view of the water, take in the torch-light from a raft attached to the terrace. DJ spins house inside. Beer €3. Open M-F 3pm-late, Sa-Su noon-late. Cash only.

SO36, Oranienstr. 190 (☎61 40 13 06; www.SO36.de). U1 to Görlitzer Bahnhof or night bus #N29 to

Electro - Shorthand for "electro funk." This brand of electronic hip-hop, sometimes traced all the way back to German stalwarts Kraftwerk, relies heavily on drum machines, synthetic bass lines, and elaborate sonic reverberations. It often takes on futuristic themes. Lyrics are digitially remastered in order to make the voices sound mechanical.

House - A form of electronic dance music in which the 4/4 beat is heavily accentuated by the drum. It tends to have a Latin influence and often tries to approximate the experience of live music, sampling everything from pop to jazz. Although the drum accents vary in their placement, the uptempo beat structure stays relatively consistent.

Techno - Techno employs computerized sequences that layer different rhythms and syncopations. Generally more melodic than its counterparts, it tends to use exclusively inorganic sounds.

Trance - Using the high degree of repetition common to melodic song structures, trance often builds up a steady crescendo using recurring synthesizer phrases. A bass drum catches the down beats while minor scales add variety. Occasionally, though not often, vocal layers are added to the mix.

— Amelia Atlas

Heinrichpl. One of Berlin's best mixed clubs. Named for the local postal code, the club holds a massive, dark dance floor and a stage for occasional concerts (€7-25). Diverse array of music. Cover €4-8. Cash only.

Heinz Minki, Vor dem Schlesischen Tor 3 (☎695 33 766; www.heinzminki.de). U1 or 15 to Schlesisches Tor or night bus #N65 to Heckmannufer. A beer garden that, shockingly, is actually a garden. Patrons pound down beers (0.5L, €3.10) at long tables under hanging colored lights, surrounded by trees and shrubbery. Gourmet pizza €2.60. Open daily noon-late; shorter hours in winter. Cash only.

Freischwimmer, vor dem Schlesischen Tor 2 (☎61 07 43 09; www.freischwimmer-berlin.de). U1 or 15 to Schlesisches Tor or night bus #N65 to Heckmannufer. Relax by the water amid roses, chill inside on a comfy sofa, or lounge on the floating dock. Seems to stretch out infinitely along the bank. Su brunch 11am-4pm, €8.20; reserve ahead. Open M-F noon-late, Sa-Su 11am-late. Cash only.

FRIEDRICHSHAIN

Maria am Ostbahnhof, Am der Schillingbrücke (☎21 23 81 90; www.clubmaria.de). S3, 5, 7, 9, or 75 to Ostbahnhof. From the Stralauer Pl. exit, take Str. der Pariser Kommune to Stralauer Pl. and follow it right along the wall. Turn left at the bridge and look for the red lights by the water. Tucked away by the river in an old factory, this club embraces Friedrichshain's industrial past. Grey-toned murals line the wall, and converted speakers serve as seating. Mostly electronic music, occasional punk and reggae. Beer €2.50. Cover €10. Open F-Sa 11pm-late, Su-Th for concerts and events only. Cash only.

PRENZLAUER BERG

Intersoup, Schliemannstr. 31 (☎23 27 30 45; www.intersoup.de). U2 to Eberswalder Str. This bar eschews big-name drink brands and popular music in favor of worn 70s furniture, soup specials (€4.50-5), and retro floral wallpaper. Downstairs, the small club **Undersoup** has live music (most W and Sa), Th karaoke, films, and even puppet theater (M-Tu). DJs most nights. Club cover max. €3. Open daily 4pm-late. Cash only.

KulturBrauerei, Knaackstr. 97 (☎441 92 69; www.kulturbrauerei.de). U2 to Eberswalder Str. A dauntingly massive party space in an old East German brewery, housing the popular clubs **Soda** (www.soda-berlin.de), **Kesselhaus** (www.kesselhaus-berlin.de), and **nbi,** along with upscale cafes, a cinema, a beer garden, and much more. Cover and hours vary between venues.

TREPTOW

Insel, Alt-Treptow 6 (☎20 91 49 90; www.insel-berlin.net). S4, 6, 8, or 9 to Treptower Park, then bus #265 or N65 from Puschkinallee to Rathaus Treptow. Enter through the park at the corner of Alt-Treptow. Located on an island in the Spree River, the club is a winding 3-story tower crammed with gyrating bodies, multiple bars, riverside beach chairs, and an open-air movie theater. Depending on the night, the top 2 floors spin reggae, hip-hop, ska, and house—sometimes all at once—while a techno scene dominates the basement. Cover Th-Sa €4-6. Open F-Sa 10 or 11pm-late, some W 7pm-late. Cafe open in summer daily 2pm-late; low season Th 2-7pm, Sa-Su 2pm-late. Cash only.

GLBT NIGHTLIFE

Berlin is one of the most gay-friendly cities in Europe. **Goltzstraße, Akazienstraße,** and **Winterfeldtstraße** have mixed bars and cafes, while the **"Bermuda Triangle"** of Motzstr., Fuggerstr., and Eisenacherstr. is more exclusively gay.

Siegessäule, *Sergej*, and *Gay-yellowpages* have GLBT entertainment listings. The **Christopher Street Day (CSD)** parade (June 23, 2007), a 6hr.-long street party with ecstatic, champagne-soaked floats, draws over 250,000 participants. Nollendorfpl. hosts the **Lesbisch-schwules Stadtfest** (Lesbian-Gay City Fair) the weekend prior to the parade.

Hafen, Motzstr. 19 (www.hafen-berlin.de), in Schöneberg. U1, 2, 3, or 4 to Nollendorfpl. The artist owners created the nautical decor for "Harbor." The mostly gay male, but not restricted, crowd jams the sidewalk in summer. Open daily 8pm-late. Cash only.

Rose's, Oranienstr. 187 (☎615 6570), in Kreuzberg. U1 or U8 to Kottbusser Tor or U1 to Görlitzer Bahnhof. Marked only by a sign over the door that reads "Bar." A friendly, mixed clientele packs this claustrophobic party spot at all hours. The voluptuous dark-red interior is adorned with hearts, glowing lips, furry ceilings, feathers, and glitter. Vodka tonic €5 and absolutely "no fucking cocktails." Open daily 10pm-6am. Cash only.

Die Busche, Warschauer Pl. 18 (☎296 08 00; www.diebusche.de), in Friedrichshain. U1 or S3, 5-7, 9, or 75 to Warschauer Str. East Berlin's most famous disco is a color-saturated haven for dancers, spinning techno, Top 40, and German Schlager to a mixed crowd. Cover €2-6. Open W 10pm-5am, F-Sa 10pm-7am, Su 10pm-4am. Cash only.

Heile Welt, Motzstr. 5 (☎21 91 75 07), in Schöneberg. U1, 2, 3, or 4 to Nollendorfpl. Sitting rooms in the back offer a quieter ambience. Mostly gay male crowd during "prime time," mixed in the early evening. Open daily 6pm-4am. Cash only.

DAYTRIPS FROM BERLIN

KZ SACHENHAUSEN. Located just north of Berlin, the small town of Oranienburg was the setting for the Nazi concentration camp Sachsenhausen, where over 100,000 Jews, communists, intellectuals, Roma (gypsies), and homosexuals were killed between 1936 and 1945. **Gedenkstätte Sachsenhausen,** Str. der Nationen 22, a memorial preserving the camp remains, includes some of the original barracks, the cell block where "dangerous" prisoners were tortured, and a pathology wing where Nazis experimented on inmates. A stone monolith commemorating the camp's victims stands guard over the grounds and museums. To get there, take S1 (dir.: Oranienburg) to the end (40min.), then either use the infrequent bus service on lines #804 and 821 to Gedenkstätte or take a 15-20min. walk from the station. Follow the signs, turn right on Bernauer Str., left on Str. der Einheit, and right on Str. der Nationen. (☎03301 20 00; www.stiftung-bg.de. Open daily Mar. 15-Oct. 14 8:30am-6pm; Oct. 15-Mar. 14 8:30am-4:30pm. Museums closed M. Free. Audio tour €3.)

POTSDAM. Satisfy cravings for imperial splendor in nearby Potsdam, the glittering city of Friedrich II (the Great). Potsdam is best seen by bike or by tour, since the attractions are spread out. On the S-Bahn platform at the station, **Potsdam Per Pedales** rents bikes and provides maps of the sights. (☎74 80 057; www.pedales.de. Open May-Sept. daily 9:30am-7pm.) The **tourist office** is at Brandenburger Str. 3. (☎508 88 38. Open Apr.-Oct. M-F 9am-6pm, Sa-Su 9:30am-4pm; Nov.-Mar. M-F 10am-6pm, Sa-Su 10am-2pm.) Spread over 600 acres, **Park Sanssouci** is testimony to the size of Friedrich's treasury and the diversity of his aesthetic. (Open daily May-Oct. 8am-5pm; Nov.-Feb. 9am-4pm.) **Schloß Sanssouci,** the park's main attraction, was Friedrich's answer to Versailles. German-language tours leave every 20min.; the final tour at 5pm usually sells out hours earlier. Also in the park, the **Bildergalerie** displays works by Caravaggio, van Dyck, and Rubens. (☎0331 96 94 181. Open mid-May to mid-Oct. Tu-Su 10am-5pm. €2, students €1.50. Tours €1.) The stunning **Sizilianischer Garten** is at the opposite end of the park from the largest of the four castles, the 200-chambered **Neues Palais.** (Open M-Th and Sa-Su Apr.-Oct. 9am-5pm; Nov.-Mar. 9am-4pm. €6, students €5. Summer tours €1.) Potsdam's second park, the **Neuer Garten,** contains several royal residences.

EASTERN GERMANY

Saxony *(Sachsen)* and Thuringia *(Thüringen)*, the most interesting regions in eastern Germany outside of Berlin, encompass Dresden, Leipzig, and Weimar. The architecture of the area is defined by contrasts: castles attest to Saxony's one-time decadence, while boxy GDR-era buildings recall the socialist aesthetic.

DRESDEN ☎0351

The buildings that form the skyline of Dresden's magnificent Altstadt look ancient, but most of them are newly reconstructed—the Allied firebombings in February 1945 that claimed over 40,000 lives also destroyed 75% of the city center. Long-delayed healing has accompanied the city's reconstruction, and today, its Baroque architecture, dazzling views of the Elbe River, world-class museums, and thriving Neustadt nightlife give Dresden (pop. 479,000) a dynamic edge.

TRANSPORTATION

Flights: Dresden's **airport** (☎881 33 60; www.dresden-airport.de) is 9km from the city. S2 runs there from both train stations (20min. from the Hauptbahnhof, 25min. from Neustadt; 2 per hr. 4am-11:30pm; €1.70).

Trains: Nearly all trains stop at both the **Hauptbahnhof** in the Altstadt and **Bahnhof Dresden Neustadt** across the Elbe. Trains run to: **Berlin** (3hr., 1 per hr., €32); **Budapest, HUN** (11hr., 2 per day, €81); **Frankfurt am Main** (4½hr., 1 per hr., €76); **Leipzig** (1½hr., 1-2 per hr., €19); **Munich** (7hr., 1-2 per hr., €108); **Prague, CZR** (2½hr., 7 per day, €26); **Warsaw, POL** (8½hr., 2 per day, €71). Tickets are available from the machines in the station main hall, but are cheaper at the *Reisezentrum* desk.

Public Transportation: Much of Dresden is accessible on foot, but **streetcars** cover the whole city. 1hr. ticket €1.70. Day pass €4.50. The €5.50 Family Card, good for 2 passengers until 4am, is probably the best deal. Weekly pass €16.50. Tickets are available from *Fahrkarte* dispensers at major stops and on streetcars. For info and maps, go to one of the **Service Punkt** info stands in front of the Hauptbahnhof or at Postpl. Open M-F 8am-7pm, Sa 8am-6pm, Su 9am-6pm. Most major lines run hourly after midnight—look for the moon sign marked **Gute-Nacht-Linie.**

Taxis: ☎211 211 and 888 88 88.

Bike Rental: In the Hauptbahnhof (☎461 32 62). €7 per day. Open M-F 6am-8pm, Sa-Su 8am-8pm. Also available at many hostels.

Ride-Share: Mitfahrzentrale, Dr.-Friedrich-Wolf-Str. 2 (☎194 40; www.mf24.de). On Slesischen Pl., across from Bahnhof Neustadt. Open M-F 9am-8pm, Sa-Su 10am-4pm.

Hitchhiking: Let's Go does not recommend hitchhiking. Hitchhikers stand by *Autobahn* signs at on-ramps. To **Berlin:** streetcar #3 or 13 to Liststr., then bus #81 to Am Olter. To **Frankfurt** or **Prague:** bus #72 or 88 to Luga, or bus #76, 85, or 96 to Lockwitz.

ORIENTATION AND PRACTICAL INFORMATION

The **Elbe** River bisects Dresden 60km northwest of the Czech border, dividing the city into the **Altstadt** in the south (where the Hauptbahnhof is located) and the **Neustadt** in the north. Many of Dresden's attractions lie in the Altstadt between the **Altmarkt** and the Elbe. Nightlife centers in the Neustadt to the north by **Albertplatz.**

Tourist Office: 2 main branches: Prager Str. 2A, near the Hauptbahnhof (open M-F 10am-6pm, Sa 10am-4pm), and Theaterpl. in the Schinkelwache, a small building directly in front of the Semper-Oper (☎49 19 20; open M-F 10am-6pm, Sa-Su 10am-

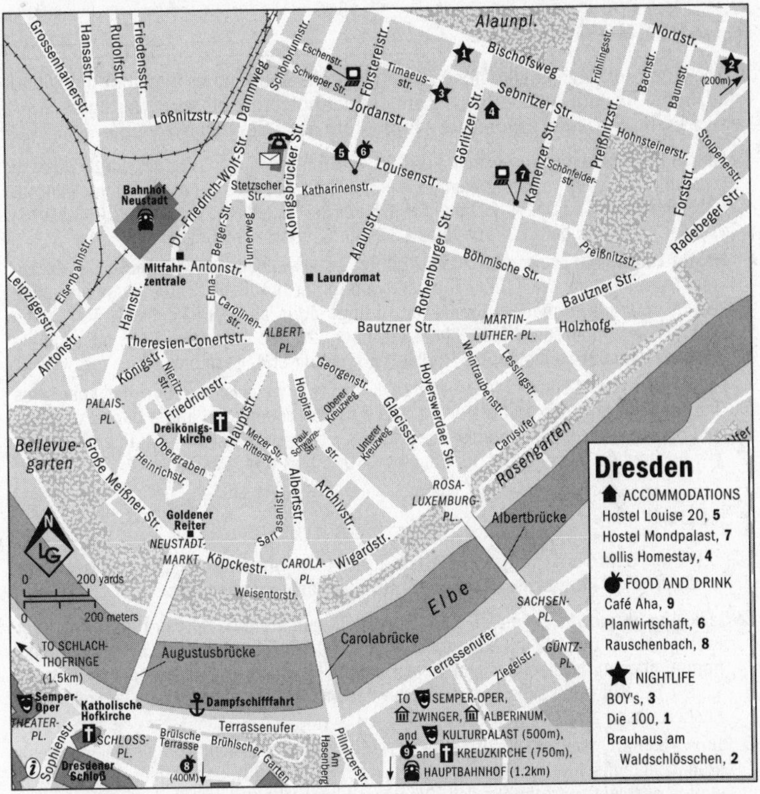

4pm). Call the city hotlines for general information (☎49 19 21 00), room reservations (☎49 19 22 22), tours (☎49 19 21 40), and advance tickets (☎49 19 22 33).

Currency Exchange: ReiseBank (☎471 21 77), main hall of the Hauptbahnhof. €5 commission for exchanges; 1-1.5% commission to cash **traveler's checks** (none for AmEx Cheques). Open M-F 8am-7:30pm, Sa 9am-noon and 12:30-4pm, Su 9am-1pm.

ATMs: The **Deutsche Bank** at the corner of Königsbrücker Str. and Stetzscherstr. has a 24hr. ATM, as do many other central banks.

Luggage Storage: At both train stations. Lockers €1-2 for 24hr.

Laundromat: Eco-Express, Königsbrücker Str. 2. Wash €1.50 6-11am, €2 11am-11pm. Dry €0.50 per 10min. Open M-Sa 6am-11pm. Also try "Crazy" Waschsalon, 6 Louisenstr. (Wash €2.50. Dry €0.50 per 10min. Open M-Sa 7am-11pm.)

Emergency: Police: ☎110. **Ambulance** and **Fire:** ☎112.

Pharmacy: Apotheke Prager Straße, Prager Str. 3 (☎490 30 14). Open M-F 8:30am-7pm, Sa 8:30am-4pm. The Notdienst sign outside lists 24hr. pharmacies.

Internet Access: Groove Station, Katharinenstr. 11-13. €3 per hr. Open M-Sa 7pm-late, Su 4pm-late. There are also several Internet cafes along Königsbrücker Str.

Post Office: The **Hauptpostamt,** Königsbrücker Str. 21/29 (☎819 13 73). In the Neustadt. Open M-F 9am-7pm, Sa 10am-1pm. Branch in the Altstadt on Weberg. at the Altmarkt Galerie. Open daily 9:30am-8pm. **Postal Code:** 01099.

ACCOMMODATIONS

In the Neustadt, high-quality hostels with late check-out times neighbor clubs and bars. In the Altstadt, quieter hostels and pricier hotels are closer to the sights. Anywhere in the city, reservations are a must from April through November.

Hostel Mondpalast, Louisenstr. 77 (☎563 40 50; www.mondpalast.de). Settle down in a comfy bed after a night hanging out in the lively bar downstairs. Bike rental €4 per 3hr. Breakfast €5. Linens €2. Internet €3 per hr. Reception 24hr. Dorms €13.50-16; singles €29, with bath €39; doubles €37/50; quads €74. MC/V. ❶

Hostel Louise 20, Louisenstr. 20 (☎889 48 94; www.louise20.de). Above the restaurant Planwirtschaft. Walk through a courtyard for this luxurious hostel, where a winding staircase leads to modern rooms and a huge dorm attic. Breakfast €4.50. Linens €2.50. Reception 7am-11pm. Check-out noon. 20-bed attic dorm €10; other dorms €15; singles €26; doubles €37; triples €48; quads €64. Cash only. ❶

Lollis Homestay, Görlitzer Str. 34 (☎81 08 45 58; www.lollishome.de). This hostel has the relaxed atmosphere of a student flat, with free coffee, tea, and a book exchange. Old bikes are available to borrow. Breakfast €3. Linens €2. Laundry €3. Internet €2.50 per hr. Dorms €13; singles €30; doubles €40; triples €54. Cash only. ❶

FOOD

It's difficult to find anything in the Altstadt not targeting tourists; the cheapest eats are at the *Imbiß* stands along **Prager Straße** and around **Postplatz.**

Café Aha, Kreuzstr. 7 (☎496 06 73; www.ladencafe.de), across the street from Kreuzkirche in the Altstadt. Often exotic, always delicious, Café Aha introduces food from a different developing country each month. Abundant vegetarian options. Entrees €3.90-11. Fair trade shop located in the basement. Cafe open daily 10am-midnight. Kitchen closes 10:30pm. Cash only. ❶

Planwirtschaft, Louisenstr. 20 (☎801 31 87). German dishes with ingredients fresh from local farms. Inventive soups, crisp salads (€3.50-6.90), and entrees (€7-13) from stuffed eggplant to fresh lake fish. Breakfast buffet (€8.60) until 3pm. Outdoor courtyard seating. Open Su-Th 9am-1am, F-Sa 9am-2am. MC/V. ❸

Rauschenbach, Weisseg. 2 (☎821 27 60; www.rauschenbach-deli.de). Chandelier crystals dangle from soft, red fluorescent lights in this cafe servings tapas and sandwiches (€2.50-4.20) to hordes of young locals. Reserve ahead F-Sa. Open Su-Th 9am-1am, F-Sa 9am-3am. AmEx/MC/V/DC. ❷

SIGHTS

Saxony's electors once ruled nearly all of central Europe from the banks of the majestic Elbe River. Despite the Altstadt's demolition in WWII and only partial reconstruction during Communist times, this area of Dresden remains a formidable cultural center.

SEMPER-OPER. Dresden's opera house echoes the splendor of the Zwinger's north wing. Painstaking restoration has returned the building to its pre-war state. *(Theaterpl. 2. ☎491 14 96. Tours usually M-Sa every 30min. 11am-3pm, but times vary each week; check at the entrance. €5, students €3.)*

DRESDENER SCHLOß. Once the home of August the Strong, the Polish king who built most of the Dresden area's castles, this palace is home to the **Grünes Gewölbe** (Green Vault). From the mindblowing collection of rare medieval chalices to the lavish Baroque jewels, the vault dazzles with some of the finest metal and gem work in all of Europe. *(☎49 14 20 00. Open M, W-Su 10am-6pm. €6, students €3.50. English audio tour €2.)*

FRAUENKIRCHE. The product of a 10-year reconstruction, the Frauenkirche re-opened on Oct. 31, 2005, completing Dresden's skyline with its regal silhouette Floods of tourists gaze at the circular ascending balconies, golden altar, and glorious cupola. *(Neumarkt. ☎498 11 31. Open M-F 10am-noon and 1-6pm, Sa-Su hours vary, check the small, white information center on Neumarkt for details. English audio tour €2.50.)*

MUSEUMS

After several years of renovations, Dresden's museums are once again ready to compete with the best in Europe. If you plan on visiting more than one in a day, consider a **Tageskarte** (€10, students €6), which grants one-day admission to the Albertinum museums, the Schloß, most of the Zwinger, and more. The **Dresden City-Card** and **Dresden Regio-Card** (see **Practical Information,** p. 426) also include admission to museums in their prices. Information about all the museums can be found at www.skd-dresden.de. Most museums are closed on Monday.

ZWINGER. Through the archway from the Semper-Oper, **Gemäldegalerie Alte Meister** has a first-rate collection of Italian and Dutch paintings from 1400 to 1800, including Cranach the Elder's luminous *Adam and Eve*, Rubens's *Leda and the Swan*, and Raphael's enchanting *Sistine Madonna*. *(☎491 46 19. Open Tu-Su 10am-6pm. €6, students €3.50. Tickets include admission to the Rüstkammer.)* The **Rüstkammer** shows shiny but deadly toys from the court of the Wettin princes: ivory-inlaid guns, chain mail, and the armor of the Wettin toddlers. *(☎491 46 82. Open Tu-Su 10am-6pm. €3, students €2.)*

ALBERTINUM. The **Gemäldegalerie Neue Meister** picks up in the 19th century where the Alte Meister gallery leaves off, with exhibits by hometown Romantic painter Caspar David Friedrich and by the Impressionists Degas, Monet, and Renoir. Check out Otto Dix's renowned *War* triptych and the Expressionist works. *(Open M and W-Su 10am-6pm. €6, students €3.50.)*

ENTERTAINMENT

Most theaters break from mid-July to early September, but open-air festivals bridge the gap. Outdoor movies screen along the Elbe during **Filmnächte am Elbufer** in July and August. (Office at Alaunstr. 62. ☎89 93 20. Movies show 9pm. Tickets €6.) The **Zwinger** has classical concerts on summer evenings; shows start 6:30pm.

Sächsische Staatsoper (Semper-Oper), Theaterpl. 2 (☎491 10). Some of the finest opera in the world. Tickets can sell out; call ahead. Tickets €3-80. Box office at Schinkelwache open M-F 10am-6pm, Sa 10am-1pm, and 1hr. before performances.

Kulturpalast, Schloßstr. 2, in Altmarkt (☎486 66 66; www.kulturpalast-dresden.de). Home to the **Dresdner Philharmonie** (☎486 63 06; www.dresdnerphilharmonie.de) as well as a variety of performances. Open M-F 10am-7pm, Sa 10am-2pm.

NIGHTLIFE

It's as if the entire Neustadt spends the day anticipating nightfall. Little over ten years ago, the area north of Albertpl. was a maze of gray streets lined with crumbling buildings; since then, an alternative community has sprung up in bars on Louisenstr., Königsbrücker Str., Bischofsweg, Kamenzerstr., and Albertpl. The German-language *Kneipen Surfer*, free at Neustadt hostels, describes every bar.

Brauhaus am Waldschlösschen, Am Brauhaus 8B (☎652 3900; www.waldschloesschen.de). Take tram #11 to Waldschlösschen or walk 25min. up Baunitzerstr. Beautiful views overlooking the Elbe complement beer by the liter (€4.80) and classic German entrees. Order from the garden cafeteria downstairs or be served by barmaids in the touristy restaurant above. Open daily 11am-1am. AmEx/MC/V.

Wash Room, Hermann-Mende-Str. 1 (☎441 57 08). Take bus #7 or #8 to Industriegelände and follow the crowds. Despite the waterfalls and popular full-size indoor beach volleyball court, the main attraction is still the frenetic dance floor. Open F-Sa 10:22pm-5am. Cover F €5, Sa €4-8. Cash only.

Die 100, Alaunstr. 100 (☎801 39 57). The candlelit interior and intimate stone courtyard of this well-stocked wine cellar provide an escape from the social flurry elsewhere. Open daily 5pm-3am. Cash only.

BOY's, Alaunstr. 80, just beyond the Kunsthof Passage. A half-clad devil mannequin guards one of Dresden's popular gay-friendly bars. Drinks €1.90-6. Open Tu-Th 8pm-3am, F-Su 8pm-5am. MC/V.

DAYTRIP FROM DRESDEN: MEIßEN

In 1710, the Saxon elector turned the city's defunct castle into Europe's first porcelain factory. Tour the **Staatliche Porzellan-Manufaktur Meißen,** Talstr. 9, and observe the craftsmen in action. You can peruse finished products in the *Schauhall*, but the real fun is in the *Schauwerkstatt* (show workshop), where you can watch porcelain artists paint petal-perfect flowers before your disbelieving eyes. (☎46 82 08. Open daily May-Oct. 9am-6pm; Nov.-Apr. 9am-5pm. English-language audio tour €3. €8, students €4.) Narrow, romantic alleyways lead up to the **Albrechtsburg** Castle and Cathedral (www.albrechtsburg-meissen.de). To get there from the train station, walk straight onto Bahnhofstr. and follow it over the Elbbrücke. Cross the bridge, continue to the Markt, and turn right onto Burgstr. Follow the signs to Albrechtsburg up the hill, then look for a staircase to your right that hugs the alleyway; this will lead you to the castle. (Open daily Mar.-Oct. 10am-6pm; Nov.-Feb. 10am-5pm. €3.50, students €2.50. English-language audio tour €2.) Next door is the **Meißener Dom,** a Gothic cathedral featuring four 13th-century statues by the Naumburg Master and a triptych by Cranach the Elder. (Open daily Apr.-Oct. 9am-6pm; Nov.-Mar. 10am-4pm. €2.50, students €1.50.) **Trains** run to Meißen from Dresden (40min., €5.10). The **tourist office** is at Markt 3. (☎0352 419 40. Open Apr.-Oct. M-F 10am-6pm, Sa-Su 10am-4pm; Nov.-Mar. M-F 10am-5pm, Sa 10am-3pm.) **Postal Code:** 01662.

GERMANY

LEIPZIG

☎0341

Leipzig (pop. 493,000) is known as the city of music, and indeed, it's hard to walk more than a few blocks in town without being serenaded by a classical quartet, wooed by a Spanish guitar, or riveted by the sound of choir music. Large enough to have a life outside the university, but small enough to feel the influence of its students, Leipzig has both world-class museums and corners packed with cabarets and second-hand stores.

TRANSPORTATION AND PRACTICAL INFORMATION. Leipzig lies on the Berlin-Munich line. **Trains** run to: Berlin (1½hr., 2 per hr., €33); Dresden (2hr., 2 per hr., €25); Frankfurt (3½hr., 1 per hr., €61); Munich (5hr., every 2hr., €74). The **tourist office** is at Richard-Wagner-Str. 1. The **Leipzig Card** is good for free public transport and discounted museums (1-day, until 4am, €7.90; 3-day €16.50. ☎710 4265. Open M-F 10am-7pm, Sa 10am-4pm, Su 10am-2pm.) **Postal Code:** 04109.

ACCOMMODATIONS AND FOOD. To reach **Hostel Sleepy Lion ❶**, Käthe-Kollwitz-Str. 3, take streetcar #1 (dir.: Lausen) to Gottschedstr. Run by young locals, it draws an international crowd with its spacious lounge area, foosball table, and separate non-smoking area. (☎993 94 80; www.hostel-leipzig.de. All rooms with bath. Bike rental €5 per day. Breakfast €3. Linens €2. Internet €2 per hr. Reception 24hr. Dorms €14-15; singles €28; doubles €40; quads €64. Winter reduced rates. AmEx/MC/V.) Less than 5min. from the train station, **Central Globetrotter ❶**, Kurt-Schumacher-Str. 41, fills its wildly spray-painted rooms with all types. Take the west exit and turn right onto Kurt-Schumacher-Str. (☎149 89 60; www.globetrotter-leipzig.de. Group showers. Breakfast €4. Linens €2. Internet €2 per hr. Dorms €13-14; singles €24; doubles €36; quads €60. AmEx/MC/V.)

Outside the city center, **Karl-Liebknecht-Straße** (streetcar #10 or 11 to Südpl.) is packed with cafes and bars. A favorite with many locals, **Aladin Döner ❷**, Burgstr. 12 (☎0170 976 67 07), tops off pitas and falafel with a free cup of tea after every meal. (Open daily 9-2am. Cash only.) The hip cafe **Bellini's ❷**, Barfußgäßchen 3-5 (☎961 76 81), serves baguettes, salads, and pasta in the heart of the Markt. (Open daily noon-late. MC/V.) **100-Wasser Cafe ❷**, Barfussg. 15 (☎215 79 27). Designed in the whimsical style of Friederich Hundertwasser, this cafe serves generous pastas in the middle of town. (Entrees €5.50-13. Open M-Sa 8-2am, Su 9-2am. AmEx.)

SIGHTS AND NIGHTLIFE. The heart of Leipzig is the **Marktplatz,** guarded by the slanted 16th-century **Altes Rathaus.** Head to the Rathaus and follow Thomasg. to the **Thomaskirche.** Bach spent his last 27 years here as cantor; his grave is by the altar. (☎960 2855. Open daily 9am-6pm. Free.) Behind the church is the **Johann-Sebastian-Bach-Museum,** Thomaskirchof 16, with exhibits on the composer's life, an annual Bach festival (June 7-17, 2007), and fall concerts. (Open daily 10am-5pm. €4, students €2. English audio tour free.) Head back to Thomasg., turn left, then turn right on Dittrichring to reach the **Museum in der Runden Ecke,** Dittrichring 24, with stunningly blunt exhibits on the GDR-era *Stasi* (secret police). Ask in the office for an English-language brochure. (☎961 2443; www.runde-ecke-leipzig.de. Open daily 10am-6pm. Free.) Leipzig's **Gewandhaus-Orchester,** Augustuspl. 8, has been a major orchestra since 1843. (☎127 0280. Open M-F 10am-6pm, Sa 10am-2pm, and 1hr. before performances. Tickets €12-50. Th 20% student discount.) The free magazines *Fritz* and *Blitz* have nightlife info, as does *Kreuzer* (€1.50 at newsstands). **Barfußgäßchen,** a street just off the Markt, is the place to see and be seen for the student and young professional crowd. Leipzig university students spent eight years excavating a series of medieval tunnels so they could party in the **Moritzbastei,** Universitätsstr. 9, with multi-level dance floors under vaulted brick ceilings. (☎70 25 90. Cover €4, students with ID €2.50. Cafe open M-F 11:30am-midnight, Sa-Su 2pm-midnight. Disco open W and Sa until 6am. Cash only.)

WITTENBERG ☎03491

Martin Luther inaugurated the Protestant Reformation here in 1517 when he nailed his 95 Theses to the door of the Schloßkirche; Wittenberg (pop. 48,000) has been fanatical about its native heretic ever since. The **Lutherhalle,** Collegienstr. 54, chronicles the Reformation through letters, texts, art, and artifacts. (☎420 30. Open Apr.-Oct. daily 9am-6pm; Nov.-Mar. Tu-Su 10am-5pm. €5, students €3.) Down Schloßstr., the **Schloßkirche** allegedly holds Luther's body and a copy of the Theses. (Tower ☎40 25 85. Church open daily 10am-6pm. Tower open Easter-Oct. M-F noon-3:30pm, Sa-Su 10am-4:30pm. Church free. Tower €2, students €1.) The **Jugendherberge (HI) ❷** is in a castle tower. Follow signs for the Schloßkeller Restaurant just before the tourist office on your left. Enter the courtyard and look to your right for the entrance. (☎40 32 55. Breakfast and linens included. Reception

6:30am-10pm. Check-out 9:30am. Curfew 10pm, but keys are available for a €5 deposit. Dorms €19, under 27 €16. HI members only. MC/V.) People, potatoes, and a very quirky ceiling converge at the **Wittenberger Kartoffelhaus**, Schloßstr. 2. (☎41 12 00. Entrees €3.50-13. Open daily 11am-1am. V.) **Trains** leave for Berlin (45min., 1 per hr., €22) and Leipzig (1hr., 1 per hr., €10). The **tourist office** is at Schloßpl. 2. (☎49 86 10. Open Mar.-Oct. M-F 9am-6pm, Sa 10am-3pm, Su 11am-4pm; Nov.-Feb. M-F 10am-4pm, Sa 10am-2pm, Su 11am-3pm.) **Postal Code:** 06886.

WEIMAR

☎03643

The writer Goethe once said of Weimar (pop. 62,000), "Where else can you find so much that is good in a place that is so small?" Indeed, Weimar's diverse cultural attractions, lustrous parks, and rich history make it a worthwhile destination. The **Goethehaus** and **Goethe-Nationalmuseum,** Frauenplan 1, preserve the chambers where the poet wrote, entertained guests, and, after a half-century in Weimar, died. (Open Apr.-Sept. Tu-F and Su 9am-6pm, Sa 9am-7pm; Oct. Tu-Su 9am-6pm; Nov.-Mar. 9am-4pm. €6.50, students €5. Museum €2.50/2.) The multi-talented Goethe landscaped the **Park an der Ilm,** Corona-Schöfer-Str., which contains his first Weimar residence, the **Gartenhaus.** (Open daily Apr.-Oct. 10am-6pm; Nov.-Mar. 10am-4pm. €3.50, students €2.50.) South of the town center is the **Historischer Friedhof** cemetery, where Goethe and Schiller both rest. (Cemetery open daily Mar.-Sept. 8am-9pm; Oct.-Feb. 8am-6pm. Tomb open daily Apr.-Oct. 10am-6pm; Nov.-Mar. 10am-4pm. Tomb €2.50, students €2.)

Relax in front of the piano at the **Hababusch Hostel ❶,** Geleitstr. 4, run by art students in the heart of Weimar. To get there, follow Geleitstr. from Goethepl. After a sharp right, you'll come to a statue on your left; the entrance is behind it. (☎85 07 37; www.hababusch.de. Linens €2.50. Key deposit €10. Reception 24hr. Dorms €10; singles €15; doubles €24. Cash only.) **Jugendherberge Germania (HI) ❷,** Carl-August-Allee 13, is close to the train station but a 15min. walk from the city center. (☎85 04 90; www.djh-thueringen.de. Breakfast included. Free Internet. 1st night €24, under 27 €21; each night thereafter €22/19. Cash only.) Enjoy one of the crepes at **Crêperie du Palais ❷,** Am Palais 1, near Theaterpl. (Open daily 9:30am-midnight. Cash only.) Both a cafe and a gallery, **ACC ❷,** Burgpl. 1-2, serves food (€5-6.50), screens art films, and has free Internet for its clientele. (Open daily May-Sept. 10am-1am, Oct.-Apr. 11am-1am. AmEx/MC/V.)

Trains run to Dresden (2hr., 1 per hr., €39), Frankfurt (3hr., 1 per hr., €49), and Leipzig (1hr., 1 per hr., €22). To reach **Goetheplatz,** a bus hub at the center of the Altstadt, from the station, follow Carl-August-Allee downhill to Karl-Liebknecht-Str., which leads into Goethepl. (15min.). The **tourist office** is at Markt 10. (☎74 50. Open M-F 9:30am-6pm, Sa-Su 9:30am-3pm.)

BUCHENWALD

☎03643

During WWII, the Buchenwald camp interred 250,000 prisoners, including Jews, gypsies, homosexuals, and communists. Although Buchenwald was not built as an extermination camp, over 50,000 died here from medical experimentation, or abominably harsh treatment by the SS. The **Buchenwald National Monument and Memorial** has two principal sites. The **KZ-Lager** is what remains of the camp; a large storehouse documents the history of Buchenwald (1937-1945) and of Nazism. Camp **archives** are open to anyone searching for records of family and friends between 1937 and 1945; schedule an appointment with the curator. (Archives ☎43 01 54, library 43 01 60. Outdoor camp area open daily sunrise-sunset.) Sadly, the suffering at Buchenwald did not end with liberation. Soviet authorities later used the site as an internment camp, **Special Camp No. 2.** The best way to reach the camp is by **bus** #6 from Weimar's train station or from Goethepl. Check the schedule carefully; some #6 buses go to Ettersburg rather than Gedenkstätte Buchenwald. (20min.; M-Sa 1 per hr., Su every 2hr.). The hourly bus picks up at the KZ-Lager parking lot and at the road by the *Glockenturm* (bell tower). Be sure to watch the info center's 30min. video, which plays every hour. (☎43 00; www.buchenwald.de. Limited English info. Open daily Apr.-Oct. 10am-6pm; Nov.-Mar. 10am-4pm.)

EISENACH ☎03691

Eisenach (pop. 44,000) is best known as home to **Wartburg Fortress,** which protected Martin Luther in 1521 after his excommunication. It was here, disguised as a bearded noble named *Junker* (Squire) Jörg, that Luther famously fought an apparition of the devil with an inkwell. The view from its southern tower is spectacular. (Open daily Mar.-Oct. 8:30am-5pm; Nov.-Feb. 9am-3:30pm. Accessible only through tours, except July 7-Nov. 19, 2007, when anyone may walk through. Tour in German every 10min. Tour in English 1:30pm. €6.50, students €3.50.) Eisenach is also the birthplace of composer **Johann Sebastian Bach.** Local legend holds that Bach was born in 1685 in the **Bachhaus,** Frauenplan 21. Roughly every hour, a guide plays one of the museum's period instruments and provides historical context in German. (Open daily 10am-6pm. €4, students €3. English translations available.) Up the street is the latticed **Lutherhaus,** Lutherpl. 8, where Luther lived during his school days. (Open daily 10am-5pm. €3, students €1.50.)

The **Residenz Haus ❷,** Auf der Esplanade, has spacious rooms in an 18th-century tower. (☎21 41 33. Shared bathrooms. Breakfast €5. Singles and doubles €20 per person, €15 for students with ID. Cash only.) **La Fontana ❶,** Georgenstr. 22, serves pasta in the center of town—look for the fountain in front. Most dishes are €3. (☎74 35 39. Open Su-Th 11:30am-2:30pm and 5-11pm, F-Sa 11:30am-2:30pm and 5-11:30pm. Cash only.) **Trains** run to Weimar (1hr., 1 per hr., €12). The **tourist office** is at Markt 9. (☎792 30. Open Apr.-Oct. M-F 10am-6pm, Sa 10am-4pm, Su 11am-1pm; Nov.-Mar. M-F 10am-6pm, Sa 10am-4pm.) **Postal Code:** 99817.

NORTHERN GERMANY

Schleswig-Holstein bases its livelihood on the trade generated at its port towns. Between the North Sea and the Baltic, the velvety plains are populated primarily by sheep and bales of hay. Farther south, the huge, less idyllic Hamburg is notoriously rich and radical, and the small city of Hanover charms visitors with its orderly English gardens and flourishing culture.

HANOVER (HANNOVER) ☎0511

Despite its relatively small size, the city of Hanover (pop. 515,000) has the art, culture, and landscape to rival any European city. Hanover's highlights are the three bountiful **Herrenhausen gardens.** The largest, **Großer Garten,** features geometrically pruned shrubbery and is also home to the **Große Fontäne,** one of Europe's highest-shooting fountains. To get there from the train station, walk to the far end of the lower shop level and take the U4 or 5 to Herrenhauser Garten. (Garden open daily Apr. to mid-Oct. 9am-8pm; mid-Oct. to Mar. 8am-dusk. Entrance €4, including admission to Berggarten. Performances June-Aug.; ☎16 84 12 22 for schedule.) On the outskirts of the Altstadt stands the **Neues Rathaus;** take the elevator up the tower for a lovely view year-round or ascend to the dome on a summer evening. (Open May-Sept. M-F 9am-6:30pm, Sa-Su 10am-6:30pm. Elevator runs M-F 9:30am-6:30pm, Sa-Su 10am-6:30pm, ticket sales until 6pm. €2, students €1.50.) Nearby, the **Sprengel Museum,** Kurt-Schwitters-Pl., hosts some of the 20th century's greatest art, including works by Dalí and Picasso. (Open Tu 10am-8pm, W-Su 10am-6pm. €7, students €4.) **Kestner-Museum,** Trammpl. 3, showcases decorative arts, with a focus on chairs from every era. (☎16 84 21 20; www.kestner-museum.de. Open Tu and Th-Su 11am-6pm, W 11am-8pm. €3; students €1.50. F free.)

Hotel Flora ❸, Heinrichstr. 36 (☎38 39 10; www.hotel-flora-hannover.de), is located in the center of town 10 min. from the station. Take the back exit and turn right onto Berliner Allee, then left onto Henrichstr. Carpeting, framed Monet paintings, TVs in every room, ample desk space, and attentive breakfast included makes you feel at home for short or long stays. Reception 8am-8pm. Singles €32-42, doubles €55-75, triples €67-84, dogs €7.50. AmEx/MC/V.For German fare and some great house brews, head to **Uwe's Hannenfaß Hannover ❷,** Knochenhauerstr. 36, in the center of the Altstadt. The house-brewed Hannen Alt (€3.65 for 0.5L), accompanies perfectly the steaming potato casserole Niedersachsenschmaus (€5). (Entrees €5-7. Open M-Th, Su 4pm-2am, F 4pm-4am, Sa noon-4am. AmEx/MC/V; €25 minimum charge.) **Jalda ❷,** Limmerstr. 97, serves Greek and Middle Eastern dishes for €4-8. Take U10 to Ungerstr. (Open M-Th, Su 11:30am-midnight, F-Sa 11:30am-1am. Cash only.)

Trains leave at least every hour for: Amsterdam (4½-5hr., €58-63); Berlin (2½hr., €51-65); Frankfurt (3hr., €70); Hamburg (1½hr., €35); Munich (4½hr., €98). The **tourist office** is at Ernst-August-Pl. 8. (☎12 34 51 11. Open M-F 9am-6pm, Sa 9am-2pm; Su during the summer.) The office also sells the Hannover Card (1 day €9; 3 days €15), makes transportation in Hanover free and reduces. Postal Code: 30159.

HAMBURG ☎040

The largest port city in Germany, Hamburg (pop. 1,700,000) radiates an inimitable recklessness. Riots and restorations defined the post-WWII landscape; today, Hamburg is a haven for contemporary artists, intellectuals, and partygoers who live it up in Germany's self-declared "capital of lust."

TRANSPORTATION

Trains: The **Hauptbahnhof** has hourly connections to: **Berlin** (1½hr., €47); **Copenhagen, DEN** (5hr., €76); **Frankfurt** (3½hr., €93); **Hanover** (1½hr., €36); **Munich** (6hr., €115). **DB Reisezentrum** ticket office open M-F 5:30am-10pm, Sa-Su 7am-10pm. The **Dammtor** train station is near the university; **Harburg** station is south of the Elbe; **Altona** station is to the west of the city; and **Bergedorf** is to the southeast. 24hr. **lockers** (€1-6 per day) are available at stations.

Buses: The **ZOB** is on Steintorpl. across from the Hauptbahnhof, just past the Museum für Kunst und Gewerbe. Open Su-Th 5am-10pm, F-Sa 5am-midnight. **Autokraft** (☎280 86 60) runs to **Berlin** (3¼hr., 10-12 per day, €24). **Gulliver's** (☎253 28 978) runs to **Amsterdam, NTH** (5½hr., 1 per day, €36) and **Paris, FRA** (12hr., 1 per day, €55). Student discounts available.

Public Transportation: HVV operates an efficient U-Bahn, S-Bahn, and bus network. One-way tickets within the downtown area cost €1.55; prices vary with distance and network. 1-day pass €5.80, after 9am or Sa-Su €4.90; 3-day pass €14.40. Buy tickets at *Automaten* (machines).

Bike Rental: Fahrradstation Dammtor/Rothebaum, Schlüterstr. 11 (☎41 46 82 77), rents bikes in Hamburg for just €3 per day. Open M-F 9am-6pm. **Fahrradladen St. Georg,** Schmilinskystr. 6 (☎24 39 08), is off Lange Reihe toward the Außenalster. €8 per day, €56 per week with €50 deposit. Open M-F 10am-7pm, Sa 10am-1pm.

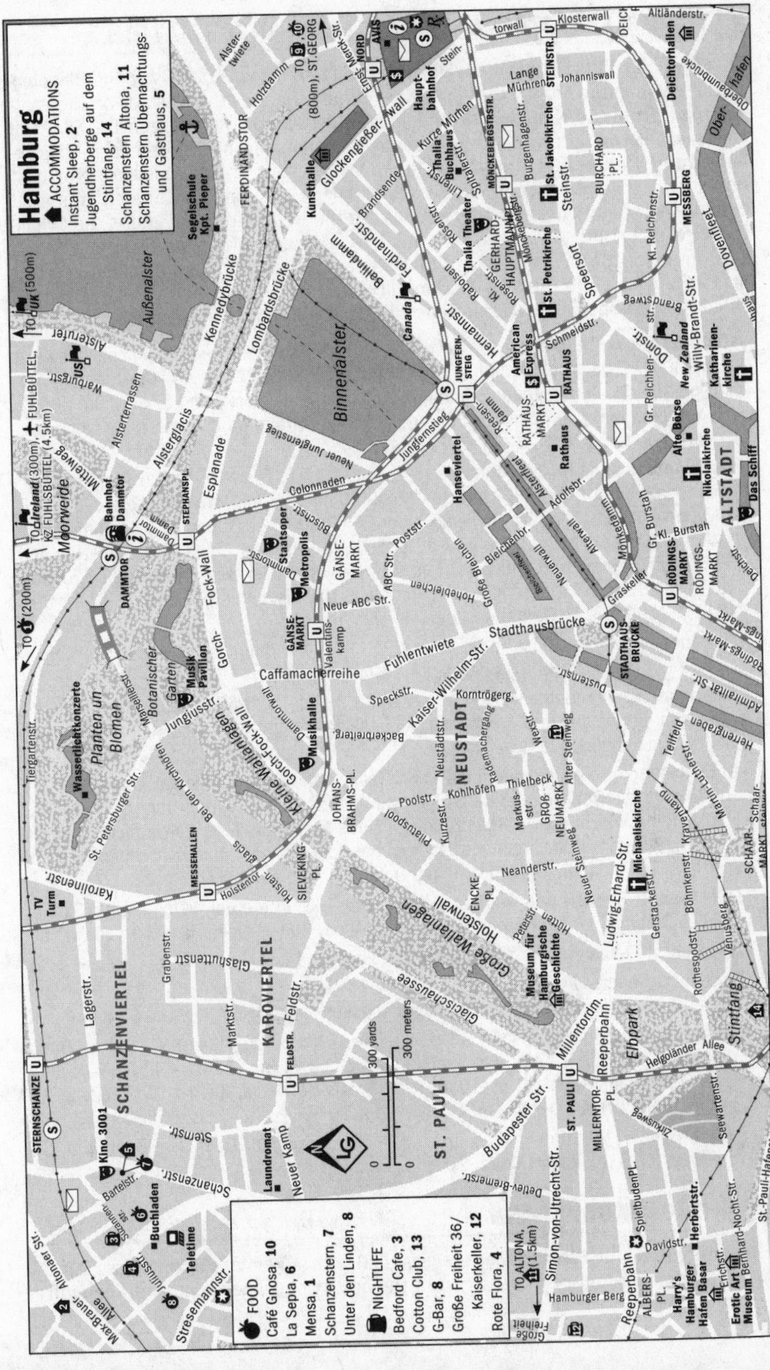
Hamburg
ACCOMMODATIONS
Instant Sleep, 2
Jugendherberge auf dem Stintfang, 14
Schanzenstern Altona, 11
Schanzenstern Übernachtungs- und Gasthaus, 5
FOOD
Café Gnosa, 10
La Sepia, 6
Mensa, 1
Schanzenstern, 7
Unter den Linden, 8
NIGHTLIFE
Bedford Cafe, 3
Cotton Club, 13
G-Bar, 8
Große Freiheit 36/ Kaiserkeller, 12
Rote Flora, 4
ALTSTADT
NEUSTADT
ST. PAULI
SCHANZENVIERTEL
KAROVIERTEL
Binnenalster
Außenalster
Planten un Blomen
Elbpark
300 yards
300 meters

GERMANY

ORIENTATION AND PRACTICAL INFORMATION

The city center sits between the **Elbe River** and two lakes, **Außenalster** and **Binnenalster.** Bisecting downtown, the Alsterfleet canal separates the Altstadt on the eastern bank from the Neustadt on the west. Most sights are between the **St. Pauli Landungsbrücken** port area in the west and the **Hauptbahnhof** in the east. **Mönckebergstraße,** Hamburg's famous shopping street, runs to **Rathausmarkt.** North of downtown, the **university** dominates the **Dammtor** area and sustains an animated community of students and intellectuals. To the west of the university, the **Schanzenviertel** is a politically active area home to artists, squatters, and a sizable Turkish population. At the south end of town, an entirely different atmosphere reigns in St. Pauli, where the raucous **Fischmarkt** (fish market) is surpassed only by the wilder **Reeperbahn,** home to Hamburg's best discos and its infamous sex trade.

Tourist Offices: The **Hauptbahnhof** office, in the Wandelhalle near the Kirchenallee exit (☎300 51 201; www.hamburg-tourism.de), books rooms for €4. Open daily 7am-10pm. The **St. Pauli Landungsbrücken** office, between piers 4 and 5 (☎30 05 12 03), is less crowded. 1-day card €7.30, 3-day €15. The **Group Card** provides the same benefits for up to 5 people. 1-day €14, 3-day €24.

Consulates: Canada, Ballindamm 35 (☎460 0270). S- or U-Bahn to Jungfernstieg; between Alstertor and Bergstr. Open M-F 9:30am-12:30pm. **Ireland,** Feldbrunnenstr. 43 (☎44 18 61 13). U1 to Hallerstr. Open M-F 9:30am-12:30pm. **New Zealand,** Domstr. 19, Zürich-Haus 3rd fl. (☎442 55 50). U1 to Messberg. Open M-Th 9am-1pm and 2-5:30pm, F 9am-1pm and 2-4:30pm. **UK,** Harvestehuder Weg 8A (☎448 0320). U1 to Hallerstr. Open M-Th 9am-4pm, F 9am-3pm. **US,** Alsterufer 26-28 (☎41 17 11 00). S11, S21, or S31 to Dammtor. Open M-F 9am-noon.

Currency Exchange: ReiseBank, on the 2nd fl. of the Hauptbahnhof near the Kirchenallee exit (☎32 34 83), is open daily 7:30am-10pm.

American Express: Rathausmarkt 10 (☎30 39 38 11). U3 to Rathaus. Across from the bus stop, on the corner of Hermanstr. All banking services available. Mail (letters only) held for members up to 5 weeks. Open M-F 9:30am-1pm and 2-6pm, Sa 10am-3pm.

GLBT Resources: The neighborhood of St. Georg is the center of the gay community. Try picking up the free *Hinnerk* magazine and *Friends: The Gay Map* from **Café Gnosa,** Lange Reihe 93 (p. 438). Organizations include **Hein und Fiete,** Pulverteich 21 (☎24 03 33). Walk down Steindamm away from the Hauptbahnhof, turn right on Pulverteich, and look for a rainbow-striped building. Open M-F 4-9pm, Sa 4-7pm.

Laundromat: Schnell und Sauber, Grindelallee 158, in the university district. S21 or S31 to Dammtor. Wash €4 per 6kg. Dry €0.50 per 10min. Open daily 7am-10:30pm.

Emergency: Police: ☎110. **Ambulance** and **Fire:** ☎112.

Pharmacy: Senator-Apotheke, Hachmannpl. 14 (☎32 75 27 or 33 92 92). Turn right from the station's Kirchenallee exit. English spoken. Open M-F 7am-8pm, Sa 8am-4pm.

Internet Access: Internet Cafe, Adenauerallee 10 (☎28 00 38 98). €1 per hr. Open daily 10am-11:55pm. **Teletime,** Schulterblatt 39 (☎41 30 47 30). €0.50 per 15min. Open M-F 10am-10pm, Sa-Su 10am-7pm. **Spiele-Netzwerk,** Kleiner Schäferkamp 24 (☎45 03 82 10). €3 per hr. Open daily 10am-2am.

Post Office: At the Kirchenallee exit of the Hauptbahnhof. Open M-F 8am-6pm, Sa 8:30am-12:30pm. **Postal Code:** 20099.

ACCOMMODATIONS

Hamburg's dynamic **Schanzenviertel** area, filled with students, working-class Turks, and left-wing dissenters, houses two of the best backpacker hostels in the entire city. Small, relatively cheap pensions line **Steindamm** and the area around the **Hauptbahnhof,** although the area's prostitutes and wannabe mafiosi detract from its charm. **Lange Reihe** has equivalent lodging options in a cleaner neighborhood. More expensive accommodations line the **Binnenalster** and eastern **Außenalster.**

Schanzenstern Übernachtungs- und Gasthaus, Bartelsstr. 12 (☎439 84 41; www.schanzenstern.de). S21 or 31, or U3 to "Sternschanze." Left onto Schanzenstr., right on Susannenstr., and left on Bartelsstr. Bright, hotel-like rooms in a renovated pen factory. Near St. Pauli. Wheelchair-accessible. Breakfast €4-6. Reception 6:30am-2am. Reserve ahead in summer. Dorms €18; singles €36; doubles €51; triples €61; quads €74; quints €92. Cash only. ❷

Instant Sleep, Max-Brauer-Allee 277 (☎43 18 23 10; www.instantsleep.de). S21 or 31 or U3 to "Sternschanze." From the station, take a right onto Schanzenstr., turn left on Altonaer Str., and follow it until it becomes Max-Brauer-Allee. Helpful, bilingual staff contributes to a family feel at this backpacker hostel. Guests lounge while they wait for laundry, read books from the improvised library, or cook dinner in the communal kitchen. Lockers €5 deposit. Linens €2. Internet €1 per 30min. Reception 8am-2am. Check-out 11am. Dorms €15-18; singles €28; doubles €44; triples €60. Cash only. ❷

Schanzenstern Altona, Kleiner Rainstr. 24-26 (☎39 91 91 91; www.schanzenstern-altona.de). From Altona station, take the Offenser Hauptstr. exit. After 2 blocks, turn right on Bahrneldstr., then immediately left on Kleine Rainstr. Just as nice as its counterpart in the Schanzenviertel. Close to the Altona station with frequent S-Bahn service. Dorms €18; singles €40; doubles €55-65; triples €70; quads €80. Cash only. ❸

Jugendherberge auf dem Stintfang (HI), Alfred-Wegener-Weg 5 (☎31 34 88). S1, S3, or U3 to Landungsbrücke. The hostel is above the Landungsbrücke station—look for stairs that lead up the hill to reveal a view of the harbor. Entrance around the left side. Bunk beds, checkered curtains, and views of the nearby woods contribute to a camp-style feel. Breakfast and linens included. Lunch and dinner €5. Reception 12:30pm-12:30am. Check-out 9:30am. Curfew 2am. Dorms €22-24, under 27 €19-21. HI members only, although membership can be purchased at the hostel. DC/MC/V. ❸

FOOD

Seafood abounds in the port city of Hamburg. In **Schanzenviertel,** avant-garde cafes and Turkish falafel stands entice hungry passersby. **Schulterblatt, Susannenstraße,** and **Schanzenstraße** are home to funky cafes and restaurants, while slightly cheaper establishments abound in the **university** area, especially along **Rentzelstraße, Grindelhof,** and **Grindelallee.** In **Altona,** the pedestrian zone near the train station is packed with food stands and produce shops.

La Sepia, Schulterblatt 36 (☎432 24 84). This Portuguese-Spanish restaurant serves some of the city's most reasonably priced seafood. For your pocketbook's sake, come for lunch (11am-5pm), when €5 gets you a big plate of grilled tuna with sauteed and scalloped carrots and potatoes, a basket of fresh bread, and a bowl of soup. Lunch €4-6. Dinner €7.50-22. Open daily noon-3am. AmEx/MC/V. ❷

Schanzenstern, Bartelsstr. 12 (☎43 29 04 09; www.schanzenstern.de). Delicious (although a little overpriced) organic masterpieces are served in the Schanzenviertel hostel. Lunch €6.50. Dinner €8-12.50. Open M 4pm-1am, Tu-Sa 10:30am-1am, Su 11am-1am. Cash only. ❷

Unter den Linden, Juliusstr. 16 (☎43 81 40). Read complimentary German papers over *Milchkaffee* (coffee with foamed milk; €3.30), breakfast (€4.30-7), or salad (€3.50-6.80) in a relaxed atmosphere underneath, as the name suggests, the linden trees. Open daily 10am-1am. Cash only. ❷

Mensa, Von-Melle-Park 5. S21 or 31 to Dammtor, then bus #4 or 5 to Staatsbibliothek (1 stop). Lots of cafeteria food and a bulletin board of university events. Meals €1.55-2 with student ID. Open M-Th 11am-4pm, F 11am-3:30pm. Cash only. ❶

Café Gnosa, Lange Reihe 93 (☎24 30 34; www.gnosa.de). A mixed crowd flocks to Gnosa. Drinks €2-5. Open Su-Th 10am-1am, F-Sa 10am-2am. Cash only. ❶

SIGHTS

ALTSTADT

GROßE MICHAELSKIRCHE. The 18th-century Michaelskirche is the symbol of Hamburg, and with good reason. Destroyed successively by lightning, accidents, and Allied bombs and finally rebuilt after the Cold War, its fate has kept in tandem with the city's. Restored in 1996, the scalloped walls of the interior recall the space of a concert hall. A panoramic view of Hamburg awaits those who climb the 462 stairs of the spire—or those who opt for the elevator. In the crypt, a multimedia presentation on the history of the church screens on weekends. *(U-Bahn to Baumwall, S-Bahn to Stadthausbrücke. ☎37 67 81 00. Church open daily May-Oct. 9am-8pm; Nov.-Apr. 10am-5pm. Crypt open June-Oct. daily 11am-4:30pm; Nov.-May Sa-Su 11am-4:30pm. Screenings M-Sa 1 per hr. 12:30-3:30pm, Su every 30min 11:30am-3:30pm. Church suggested donation €2. Crypt €1.50. Screenings €2.50. Tower €2.50.)*

RATHAUS. The city and state governments convene amid the mahogany carvings and two-ton chandeliers of the most richly ornamented building in Hamburg. In front, the **Rathausmarkt** hosts political demonstrations and medieval fairs. *(☎428 31 24 70. English-language tours every 30min. M-Th 10:15am-3:15pm, F-Su 10:15am-1:15pm. €1.50, under 14 €0.50.)*

NIKOLAIKIRCHE. The spire of this neo-Gothic ruin, bombed in 1943, has been preserved as a memorial for victims of war and persecution. *(U3 to Rödingsmarkt. Exhibition open M-F 10:30am-5:30pm. €2, students €1.50, children €1.)* The buildings along nearby **Trostbrücke** sport huge copper models of clipper ships on their spires in testimony to Hamburg's sea-trade wealth. *(Just south of the Rathaus, off Ost-West-Str.)*

MÖNCKEBERGSTRAßE. Two spires punctuate Hamburg's shopping zone, which stretches from the Rathaus to the Hauptbahnhof. The one closest to the Rathaus is **St. Petrikirche,** the oldest church in Hamburg. *(☎32 57 400. Open M-Sa 10am-5pm, Su 11:30am-4pm. Frequent free concerts.)* The other, **St. Jakobikirche,** is known for its 14th-century Arp-Schnittger organ. *(☎30 37 370. Open M-Sa 10am-6pm.)*

BEYOND THE ALTSTADT

PLANTEN UN BLOMEN. West of the Außenalster, this huge expanse of manicured flower beds and trees includes the largest Japanese garden in all of Europe. *(S21 or 31 to Dammtor. Open daily 7am-11pm. Free.)* In summer, performers in the outdoor **Musikpavillon** range from Irish step-dancers to Hamburg's police choir. *(May-Sept. daily 3pm.)* At night, opt for the **Wasserlichtkonzerte,** with a choreographed play of fountains and underwater lights. *(May-Aug. daily 10pm; Sept. 9pm.)* To the north, the tree-lined paths bordering the two **Alster lakes** provide refuge from the crush of the city's crowds.

ST. PAULI LANDUNGSBRÜCKEN. The harbor lights up at night with ships from all over the world. Look for the 1200m **Elbtunnel,** completed in 1911 and still active behind Pier 6 in the building with the copper cupola. At the **Fischmarkt,** vendors hawk fish, produce, and other goods. *(S1, S3, or U3 to Landungsbrücken or S1 or S3 to Königstr. or Reeperbahn. Open Su Apr.-Oct. 5-10am; Nov.-Mar. 7-10am.)*

BEYOND THE CENTER

Two different testaments to the atrocities of the Nazi regime are a short trip away from Hamburg's city center.

KZ NEUENGAMME. An idyllic agricultural village east of Hamburg provided the backdrop for the Neuengamme concentration camp, where Nazis killed 55,000 prisoners through slave labor. In 1989, the Hamburg Senate built a memorial on the site. A mile-long path begins at the **Haus des Gedenkens,** a memorial building containing banners inscribed with the names and death dates of the victims; the path eventually leads to the former **Walther-Werke** factory, where visitors can listen to the recorded testimony of survivors. Exhibits are in English. *(Jean-Doldier-Weg 39. S21 to Bergedorf, then bus #227, about 1½hr. from city. Bus runs from Bergedorf M-Sa 1 per hr., Su every 2hr. ☎428 96 03. Museum and memorial open May-Sept. M-F 9:30am-4pm, Sa-Su noon-7pm; Oct.-Mar. daily noon-5pm. Path open 24hr. Tours Su noon and 2pm.)*

GEDENKSTÄTTE BULLENHUSER DAMM UND ROSENGARTEN. Surrounded by warehouses, this schoolhouse is a memorial to 20 Jewish children brought here for "testing" and murdered by the SS only hours before Allied troops arrived. Visitors are invited to plant a rose for the children in the flower garden behind the school. *(Bullenhuser Damm 92. S21 to Rothenburgsort. Follow the signs to Bullenhuser Damm along Ausschläger Bildeich to the intersection with Grossmannstr.; the garden is on the far left side, the school 200m farther. ☎428 13 10; www.kz-gedenkstaette-neuengamme.de. Rose garden open 24hr. Exhibit open Su 10am-5pm, Th 2-8pm. Free.)*

MUSEUMS

The **Hamburg Card** provides free access to all museums except the Deichtorhallen, the Hafen Basar, and the Erotic Art Museum. *Museumswelt Hamburg,* a free newspaper, lists exhibits and events and can be picked up at tourist offices. Most museums are closed on Mondays.

HAMBURGER KUNSTHALLE. This sprawling, first-rate fine-arts museum would require many days to appreciate fully. The lower level presents the Old Masters and extensive special exhibits. In the connected four-level **Galerie der Gegenwart,** contemporary art takes a stand, and a loud one at that—check out the pneumatic dancing legs on the top floor. *(Glockengießerwall 1. Turn right from the Spitalerstr./City exit of the Hauptbahnhof and cross the street. ☎428 13 12 00; www.hamburger.kunsthalle.de. Open Tu-W and F-Su 10am-6pm, Th 10am-9pm. €8.50, students €5, families €14.)*

MUSEUM FÜR KUNST UND GEWERBE. Handicrafts, china, photographs, and furnishings from all corners of the earth fill the applied arts museum. A huge exhibit chronicles the evolution of the modern piano with dozens of the world's oldest harpsichords, clavichords, and hammerklaviers. *(Steintorpl. 1., 1 block south of the Hauptbahnhof. ☎428 134; www.mkg-hamburg.de. Open Tu-W and F-Su 10am-6pm, Th 10am-9pm. €8, students, Hamburg Card holders, and seniors €5, under 18 free.)*

EROTIC ART MUSEUM. This four-story museum hosts everything from Victorian pornography to gigantic Russian dolls in varying degrees of undress. Drawings by Picasso add fame—and a dose of propriety—to an otherwise shocking display. *(Bernhard-Nocht-Str. 69. S1 or S3 to Reeperbahn. ☎317 47 57; www.erotic-art-museum.de. Open Su-Th noon-10pm, F-Sa noon-1am. €8, students €5. Under 16 not admitted.)*

ENTERTAINMENT AND NIGHTLIFE

The **Staatsoper,** Große Theaterstr. 36, houses one of the best **opera** companies in Germany; the associated **ballet** is the nation's best. (U2 to Gänsemarkt. ☎35 68 68.

Open M-Sa 10am-6:30pm and 1½hr. before performances.) **Orchestras** include the Philharmonie, the Norddeutscher Rundfunk Symphony, and Hamburg Symphonia, which all perform at the **Musikhalle** on Johannes-Brahms-Pl. (U2 to Gänsemarkt. ☎34 69 20; www.musikhalle-hamburg.de.) Live music also prospers in Hamburg. Superb traditional jazz swings at the **Cotton Club** and **Indra.** Early on Sundays, musicians talented and otherwise play at the **Fischmarkt.** The **West Port Jazz Festival,** Germany's largest, runs in mid-July; for info, call the *Konzertkasse* (ticket office; ☎32 87 38 54).

Hamburg's unrestrained nightlife scene heats up in the **Schanzenviertel** and **St. Pauli** areas. The infamous **Reeperbahn** runs through the heart of St. Pauli; lined with sex shops, strip joints, and peep shows, it's also home to the city's best bars and clubs. Though the Reeperbahn is generally safe, women especially may want to avoid adjacent streets. Parallel to the Reeperbahn lies **Herbertstraße,** Hamburg's official prostitution strip, where licensed prostitutes flaunt their flesh. Herbertstr. is open only to men over the age of 18; potential patrons should be warned that engaging with streetwalkers in the city involves playing a game of venereal Russian roulette. Students head north to the streets of the Schanzenviertel, where cafes create an atmosphere more leftist than lustful. The **St. Georg** district, near Berliner Tor and along Lange Reihe, is the center of Hamburg's **gay scene.** In general, clubs open and close late, with some techno and trance clubs remaining open all night. *Szene* (€3), available at newsstands, lists events.

Große Freiheit 36/Kaiserkeller, Große Freiheit 36 (☎317 7780). Everyone from Ziggy Marley to Matchbox 20 has performed on the big stage and dance floor upstairs. Live music or DJs usually 10pm-4am. Cover €5-6. Concerts €10-30, with higher prices for bigger names. Entry often free until 11pm.

Rote Flora, Schulterblatt 71 (www.roteflora.de). Spray-paint and posters seem to hold together this looming mansion of graffiti in the heart of the Schanzenviertel scene. Entrance hidden on the side; crowds come at midnight. Beer €1.50 F-Sa. Cover F-Sa €3-5. Cafe open M-F 6-10pm. Music starts around 10pm. Cash only.

Bedford Cafe, on the corner of Schulterblatt and Suzannensstr. One of the most crowded bars in the Schanzenviertel, it's known to locals as the "no-name bar" and is a prime place to see and be seen. Look for the "Pascucci" sign outside. Beer €2-3.40. Mixed drinks €5-6. Open daily 10am-late. Cash only.

G-Bar, Lange Reihe 81 (☎28 00 46 90). Young male waiters could be models at this clean-cut gay bar. Beer €2-3. Mixed drinks €6-7. Open daily 7pm-2am. Cash only.

Cotton Club, Alter Steinweg 10 (☎34 38 78; www.cotton-club.de). U3 to Rödingsmarkt. New Orleans, dixie, swing, and Big Band jazz in a warmly lit setting. Cover €5 for Hamburg bands, around €10 for guest bands. Shows 8:30pm. Open M-Th 8pm-midnight, F-Sa 8pm-1am; Sept.-Apr. also open Su 11pm-3am. AmEx/MC/V.

LÜBECK

☎0451

Lübeck (pop. 215,000) is easily Schleswig-Holstein's most beautiful city—you'd never guess that it was mostly razed in WWII. In its heyday, it controlled trade across all of Northern Europe. No longer a center of commercial or political influence, today Lübeck is a merchant of delicious marzipan and red-blond Dückstein beer, as well as a gateway to the Baltics. Between the station and the Altstadt stands the massive **Holstentor,** one of Lübeck's four 15th-century defensive gates and the city's symbol. The museum inside deals equally in trade and torture. (Open Apr.-Sept. daily 10am-5pm; Oct.-Mar. Tu-Su 10am-5pm. €4, students and seniors €2, families €8.) The skyline is dominated by the twin brick towers of the **Marienkirche,** a gigantic church housing the largest mechanical organ in the world. (☎39 77 01 80. Open daily in summer 10am-6pm; winter 10am-4pm. Suggested donation

€1. Tours June-Sept. W and Sa 3:15pm; Apr.-May and Oct. Sa 3:15pm. €3.50, students €2.50.) For a sweeping view of the spire-studded Altstadt, take the elevator to the top of **Petrikirche.** (☎39 77 30. Church open Tu-Su 11am-4pm. Tower open daily Apr.-Oct. 9am-7pm, Mar. and Nov. 11am-5pm, Dec. 9am-7pm. Church suggested donation €2. Tower €2.50, students €1.50.) The **Theaterfigurenmuseum,** Kolk 14, holds the world's largest private puppet collection. (☎786 26. Open daily Apr.-Sept. 10am-6pm; Oct. 10am-4pm; Nov.-Mar. 10am-3pm. €3, students €2.50, children €1.50.)

To reach **Rucksack Hotel ❷,** Kanalstr. 70, take bus #1, 11, 21, or 31 to Katharineum and turn right at the church onto Glockengießerstr. This popular hostel is a member of a collective of communalist, eco-friendly shops in a former glass factory. (☎70 68 92; www.rucksackhotel-luebeck.de. Breakfast €3. Linens €3. Reception 10am-1pm and 5-9pm. 6- to 10-bed dorms €13; doubles with bath €40; quads €60, with bath €68.) Stop by the famous confectionery **I.G. Niederegger Marzipan Café ❶,** Breitestr. 89, for marzipan (€1.95), Lübeck's specialty, in the shape of pigs, jellyfish, and even the town gate. (☎530 11 26. Open M-F 9am-7pm, Sa 9am-6pm, Su 10am-4pm. AmEx/MC/V.) **Trains** run to Berlin (3½hr., 1 per hr., €36-66) and Hamburg (45min., 1 per hr., €11). Lübeck's **tourist office,** Holstentorpl. 1, books rooms for free. Lübeck's **Happy Day Card** provides unlimited access to public transportation and museum discounts. (☎88 22 33. Open June-Sept. M-F 9am-7pm, Sa 10am-3pm; Jan.-May and Oct.-Nov. M-F 9:30am-6pm, Sa 10am-3pm; Dec. M-F 9:30am-6pm, Sa 10am-2pm.) **Postal Code:** 23552.

CENTRAL AND WESTERN GERMANY

Lower Saxony *(Niedersachsen)*, stretching from the North Sea to the hills rolling through central Germany, comprises agricultural plains and foggy marshland. Just south, North Rhine-Westphalia is the most economically powerful area in Germany, and is equally densely populated.

DÜSSELDORF ☎0211

As Germany's fashion hub and multinational corporation base, the rich city of Düsseldorf (pop. 571,000) crawls with would-be aristocrats. The nation's "Hautstadt"—a pun on the German *"Hauptstadt"* (capital) and the French *"haute couture"*—is a stately metropolis with an Altstadt featuring shopping and nightlife.

TRANSPORTATION AND PRACTICAL INFORMATION. Trains run to: Amsterdam, NTH (3hr., 2-3 per hr., €32-42); Berlin (4½hr., 2 per hr., €72-88); Frankfurt (2hr., 3 per hr., €41-64); Hamburg (4hr., 2 per hr., €60-72); Munich (5-6hr., 2-3 per hr., €92-112). Düsseldorf's S-Bahn is integrated into the regional **VRR** *(Verkehrsverbund Rhein-Ruhr)* system, which links most nearby cities and is the cheapest way to get to Aachen and Cologne. Call ☎582 28 for a schedule. On the **public transportation** system, single tickets cost €1.10-8. *Tagestickets* (€5-20) allow up to five people travel for 24hr. on any line. To reach the **tourist office,** Immermannstr. 65, head straight out of the train station and to the right; look for the Immermannhof building. It books rooms for free on your day of arrival, except during trade fairs, and has numerous city maps. (☎172 02 22. Open M-F 9:30am-6:30pm, Sa 9am-2pm.) The **post office,** on Konrad-Adenauer-Pl., is to the right of the tourist office. (Open M-F 8am-6pm, Sa 9am-2pm.) **Postal Code:** 40210.

ACCOMMODATIONS AND FOOD. Trade fairs from April to August cause prices to rise. Fairly close to the center of town, **Backpackers Düsseldorf ❷,**

Fürstenwall 180, has lime-green beds and a common room equipped with a TV and DVD player. Take bus #725 (dir.: Lausward/Franziusstr.) from the station, and get off at Kirchpl. (☎302 08 48; www.backpackers-duesseldorf.de. Kitchen available. Breakfast, lockers, linens, and towels included. Free Internet. Reception 8am-9pm. Check-out noon. Reserve 1-2 weeks ahead in summer F-Sa. Dorms €22. MC/V.) **Jugendgästehaus Düsseldorf (HI) ❷,** Düsseldorfer Str. 1, is just over the Rheinkniebrücke. Take U70, 74, 75, 76, or 77 to Luegpl.; then walk 500m down Kaiser-Wilhelm-Ring, or get off at Belsenpl., and take bus #835 or 836 to Jugendherberge. (☎55 73 10; jh-duesseldorf@djh-rheinland.de. Breakfast included. Reception 7am-1am. Curfew 1am. Dorms €24; singles €36; doubles €59. €3.10 HI discount. Cash only.) **Hotel Weidenhof ❹,** Oststr. 87, is a convenient hotel with huge bathtubs and moderate prices. From the station, walk down Immermannstr., and turn left onto Oststr. (☎130 64 60; www.hotelweidenhof.de. Breakfast included. Reserve ahead. Singles €40; doubles €60; apartments from €25 per person. AmEx/MC/V.) To camp at **Kleiner Torfbruch ❶,** take any S-Bahn to Düsseldorf Geresheim, then bus #735 (dir.: Stamesberg) to Seeweg. (☎899 20 38. Open Apr.-Oct. Tent sites €10, extra person €5. Cash only.) The Altstadt has cheap food. **A Tavola ❸,** Wallstr. 11, has meticulous pastas (€7.50-14) and bottomless bread. (☎13 29 23. Open daily noon-3pm and 6-11pm. MC/V.) **Pilsner Urquell ❷,** Grabenstr. 6, specializes in Eastern European fare. (☎868 14 11. Entrees €4-11. Open M-Sa 10am-1am, Su 4pm-midnight. MC/V.) There is a **supermarket** in Carlsplatz. (Open M-Sa 8am-8pm.)

SIGHTS. Glitzy **Königsallee** (the "Kö"), just outside the Altstadt, embodies the vitality and glamor of wealthy Düsseldorf. To reach the Kö from the train station, walk 10min. down Graf-Adolf-Str. Midway up the street is the marble-and-copper **Kö-Galerie.** Better deals in non-designer stores can be found along Flingerstr. in the Altstadt. To get to the Baroque **Schloß Benrath,** Benrather Schloßallee 104, in the suburbs of Düsseldorf, take S6 (dir.: Köln) to Schloß Benrath. The Schloß was originally built as a pleasure palace and hunting grounds for Elector Karl Theodor. Strategically placed mirrors and false exterior windows make the castle appear larger than it is, but the enormous French gardens still dwarf it. (☎899 38 32; www.schloss-benrath.de. Open Tu-Su mid-Apr. to Oct. 10am-6pm; Nov. to mid-Apr. 11am-5pm. Tours every hr. €4, students €2.) The **Heinrich-Heine-Institut,** Bilker Str. 12-14, is the official shrine of Düsseldorf's melancholic son. (☎899 55 71. Open Tu-F and Su 11am-5pm, Sa 1-5pm. €3, students €1.50.) At the upper end of the Kö is the **Hofgarten,** the oldest public park in Germany. At its eastern end, the 18th-century **Schloß Jägerhof,** Jakobistr. 2, houses the **Goethe Museum.** Take streetcar #707 or bus #752 to Schloß Jägerhof. (☎899 62 62. Open Tu-F and Su 11am-5pm, Sa 2-5pm. €2, students €1.) The **Kunstsammlung am Grabbeplatz,** Grabbepl. 5, houses works by Expressionists, Surrealists, Picasso, and former Düsseldorf resident Paul Klee. (U70, 75, 76, 78, or 79 to Heinrich-Heine-Allee, and walk two blocks north. ☎838 11 30. Open Tu-F 10am-6pm, Sa-Su 11am-6pm. Tours W 3:30pm, Su 11:30am. €3, students €1.50.)

NIGHTLIFE. It is said that Düsseldorf's 500 pubs make up the longest bar in the world *(die längste Theke der Welt)*—by nightfall it's nearly impossible to see where one pub ends and the next begins in the packed Altstadt. **Bolkerstraße** is jam-packed with street performers. The newsletter *Prinz* (€3) gives tips on the entertainment scene; it can often be found for free at the city's youth hostels. **Unique,** Bolkerstr. 30, lives up to its name, drawing a young, trendy crowd to its red-walled interior. (www.uniqueclub.de. Cover €5-10. Open W-Sa 10pm-late. MC/V.) **Nachtresidenz,** Bahnstr. 13-15, is half-lounge, half-disco, and caters to a slightly older crowd. (☎136 57 55; www.nachtresidenz.de. 21+. Open F-Sa 10pm-5am. Cash only.) **GLBT nightlife** clusters along Bismarckstr., at the intersection with Charlottenstr. *Facolte* (€2), a gay and lesbian nightlife magazine, is available at most newsstands in the city. **Parkhouse,** Charlottenstr. 62, is a popular gay and lesbian club. (☎160 94 94; www.club-parkhouse.de. Open F-Sa 10pm-5am.)

AACHEN ☎0241

The capital of Charlemagne's Frankish empire in the 8th century, Aachen (pop. 246,000) is a trove of historical treasures and a forum for up-and-coming European artists. The natural springs that run through the area scared off early settlers who believed the water came from hell. The Romans realized the advantage of hell-water, however, and constructed the city's first **mineral baths.** These baths are now the luxurious **Carolus Thermen,** Passstr. 79, with eight pools and numerous themed saunas. Take bus #51 to Carolus Thermen. (☎18 27 40; www.carolus-thermen.de. 2½hr. soak €9.50, with sauna €19; day-long €14/28. Open daily 9am-11pm.) The three-tiered dome and blue-gold mosaics of the **Dom,** in the city center, look down on the reliquary behind the altar that houses Charlemagne's remains. (Open M-Sa 7am-7pm, Su 1-7pm, except during services.) Around the corner is the **Schatzkammer,** Klosterpl. 2, a treasury that holds a silver bust of Charlemagne that holds the emperor's skull, among other treasures. (Open M 10am-1pm, Tu-Su 10am-5pm. €4, students €3.)

Hotel Cortis ❸, Krefelderstr. 52, near the Stadtgarten, is a comfortable B&B with cable TV in each room. Take bus #51 to Rolandstr., and turn left on Krefelderstr. (☎977 4110; webmaster@hotel-cortis.de. Breakfast included. Singles €28; doubles €50-55, with bath €60. MC/V.) **Euroregionales Jugendgästehaus (HI) ❷,** Maria-Theresia-Allee 260, has clean, bright rooms about a 20min. bus ride from the city center. From the station, walk left on Lagerhausstr. to the Finanzamt bus stop and take bus #2 (dir.: Preusswald) to Ronheide. (☎71 10 10; www.jugendherberge.de/jh/aachen. Breakfast included. Curfew 1am. Dorms €22; singles €37; doubles €55. Cash only.) **Sausalitos ❸,** Markt 47, is a popular Mexican restaurant with a huge cocktail bar. (☎234 9200. Entrees €7-13. Open Su-Thu noon-1am, F-Sa noon-2am. Cash only.) **Pontstraße,** off Marktpl., also hosts affordable restaurants.

Trains run to Brussels, BEL (2hr., 1 per hr., €22-28) and Cologne (1hr., 2-3 per hr., €12). The tourist office, on Friedrich-Wilhelm-Pl. in the Atrium Elisenbrunnen, provides free maps and books rooms for free. From the station, head up Bahnhofstr., turn left onto Theaterstr., which becomes Theaterpl., and then turn right onto Kapuzinergraben, which becomes Friedrich-Wilhelm-Pl. (☎180 29 60. Open Easter-Christmas M-F 9am-6pm, Sa 9am-2pm, Su 10am-2pm; Christmas-Easter M-F 9am-6pm, Sa 9am-2pm.) Postal Code: 52062.

COLOGNE (KÖLN) ☎0221

Although 90% of inner Cologne (pop. 968,000) crumbled in WWII, the magnificent Gothic *Dom* amazingly survived 14 bombings and remains Cologne's main attraction. Today, the city is the largest in North Rhine-Westphalia and is its most important cultural center, with a full range of first-rate museums and theaters.

TRANSPORTATION

Flights: Flights depart from **Köln-Bonn Flughafen.** Flight information ☎018 03 80 38 03; www.koeln-bonn-airport.de. S13 leaves the train station M-F every 20min., Sa-Su every 30min. Shuttle to **Berlin** 24 times per day 6:30am-8:30pm.

Trains: Amsterdam, NTH (2½-3½hr., every 2hr., €37-47); **Berlin** (4½hr., 1 per hr., €75-90); **Düsseldorf** (30min.-1hr., 5-7 per hr., €9-17); **Frankfurt** (1¼-2hr., 2 per hr., €35-55); **Hamburg** (4hr., 2-3 per hr., €63-78); **Munich** (4½-5hr., 1-2 per hr., €85-110); **Paris, FRA** (4hr., €87-120).

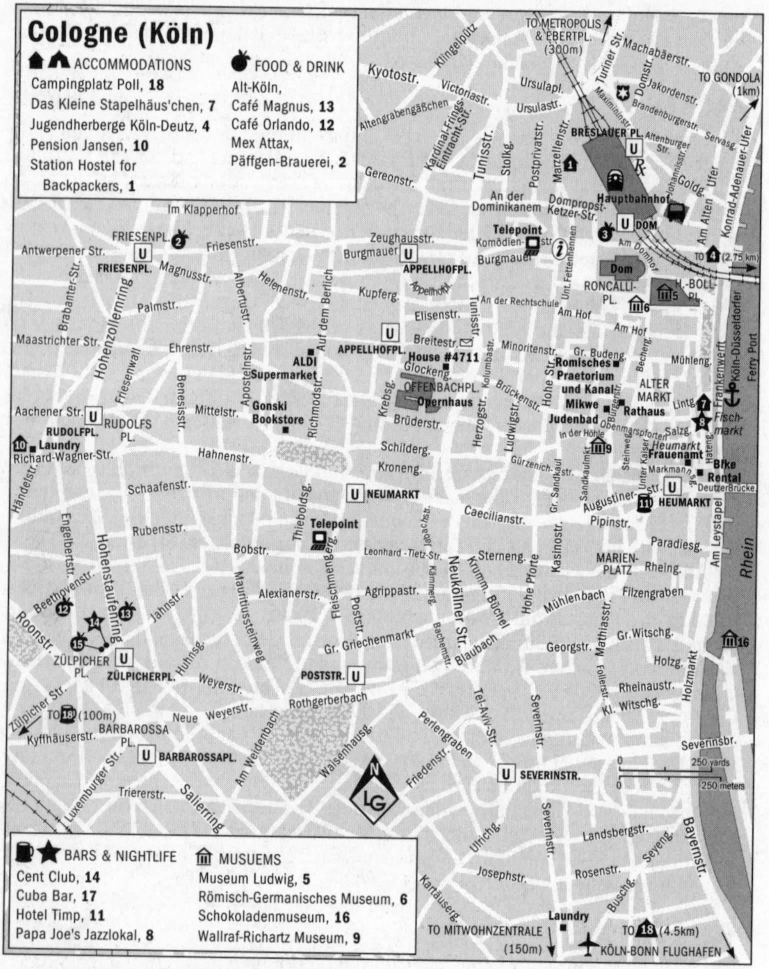

Ride Share: Citynetz Mitfahrzentrale, Maximilianstr. 2 (☎194 40). Turn left from the back of the train station. Open daily 9am-7pm.

Ferries: Köln-Düsseldorfer (☎208 8318; www.k-d.com) runs popular Rhine cruises to **Koblenz** (€34) or **Mainz** (€48). Ships to **Bonn** (€11). Eurail valid on most trips.

Public Transportation: VRS offices have free maps of the S- and U-Bahn, bus, and streetcar lines; Branch downstairs in the Hauptbahnhof. Single ride tickets €1.20-8, depending on distance. Day pass €5.50. The *Minigruppen-Ticket* (from €7.50) allows up to 5 people to ride M-F 9am-midnight and all day Sa-Su. Week tickets €12-20.

Bike Rental: Kölner Fahrradverleih, Markmannsg. (☎0171 629 87 96), in the Altstadt. €2 per hr., €10 per day, €40 per week; €25 deposit. Open daily 10am-6pm.

ORIENTATION AND PRACTICAL INFORMATION

Cologne extends across the Rhine, but the city center and nearly all sights are located on the western side. The Altstadt splits into **Altstadt-Nord,** near the **Hauptbahnhof,** and **Altstadt-Süd,** just south of the **Severinsbrücke** bridge.

Tourist Office: KölnTourismus, Unter Fettenhennen 19 (☎22 13 04 10; www.koelntourismus.de), across from the main entrance to the Dom, books rooms for a €3 fee. The €1 booklet called "*Köln im* [current month]" gives city information and event schedules. Open July-Sept. M-Sa 9am-10pm, Su 10am-6pm; Oct.-June M-Sa 9am-9pm.

Currency Exchange: Reisebank, in the train station. Open daily 7am-10pm.

Emergency: Police: ☎110. **Ambulance** and **Fire:** ☎112.

Pharmacy: Apotheke im Hauptbahnhof (☎139 11 12), at the back of the train station, near platform 11. Open M-F 6am-8pm, Sa 9am-8pm.

Internet: Telepoint Callshop & Internet C@fe, Komödenstr. 19 (☎250 99 30), by the Dom. €1.50 per hr. Open M-F 8:30am-midnight, Sa-Su 9am-midnight. **Branch** at Fleischmengerg. 33 (☎397 52 46), near Neumarkt. €1 per hr. Open M-F 8:30am-midnight, Sa-Su 10am-midnight.

Post Office: At the corner of Breite Str. and Tunisstr. in the *WDR-Arkaden* shopping gallery. Open M-F 9am-7pm, Sa 9am-2pm. **Postal Code:** 50667.

ACCOMMODATIONS

Conventions fill hotels in spring and fall, and Cologne's hostels often sell out in summer. If you're staying over a weekend in the summer, book at least two weeks in advance. **Mitwohnzentrale,** Maximinenstr. 2, behind the train station, arranges apartments for longer stays. (☎194 40. Open daily 8am-8pm.)

Station Hostel for Backpackers, Marzellenstr. 44-56 (☎912 5301; www.hostel-cologne.de). From the station, walk down Dompropst-Ketzer-Str., and take the 1st right on Marzellenstr. Abuzz with backpackers in a college dorm atmosphere. Breakfast €3. Free Internet. Reception 24hr. Check-in 2pm. Check-out noon. 4- to 6-bed dorms €17-21; singles €27-30; doubles €45-52; triples €72. Cash only. ❷

Pension Jansen, Richard-Wagner-Str. 18 (☎25 18 75; www.pensionjansen.de). U1, 6, 7, 15, 17, or 19 to Rudolfpl. Family-run, with beautiful, high-ceilinged rooms and colorful walls. Breakfast included. Singles €30-42; doubles €62. Cash only. ❸

Das Kleine Stapelhäus'chen, Fischmarkt 1-3 (☎272 7777; www.koeln-altstadt.de/stapelhaeuschen). To get there from the Rathaus, cross the Altenmarkt, and take Lintg. all the way to the Fischmarkt. An old-fashioned inn overlooking the Rhine in the Altstadt. Breakfast included. Singles €39-51, with shower or full bath €52-81; doubles €64-85/90-141. MC/V. ❹

Jugendherberge Köln-Deutz (HI), Siegesstr. 5A (☎814 711; www.koeln-deutz.jugendherberge.de), just over the Hohenzollernbrücke. Take U1 or 7-9 to Deutzer Freiheit; then walk under the pedestrian walkway, and turn right on Siegesstr. 7-story, 520-bed hostel with minishop boasts immaculate rooms, all with shower and toilet. Breakfast included. Internet €4 per hr. Reception 24hr. Reserve ahead. Dorms €24; singles €40; doubles €60. €3.10 HI discount. MC/V. ❸

Campingplatz Poll, Weidenweg (☎83 19 66), southeast of the Altstadt on the Rhine. U16 to Heinrich-Lübke-Ufer, across the Rodenkirchener Brücke. Reception 8am-noon and 5-8pm. Open mid-Apr. to Oct. Tent sites €8, extra person €5. MC/V. ❶

FOOD

The *Kölner* diet includes *Rievekoochen*, or fried potato dunked in applesauce, and the city's trademark smooth *Kölsch* beer. Cheap restaurants gather on **Zülpicherstraße** and **Weidengasse** in the Turkish district. Mid-range ethnic restaurants line the perimeter of the Altstadt, particularly from **Hohenzollernring** to **Hohenstaufenring.** German eateries surround **Domplatz.** Mornings, an **open-air market** on Wilhelmspl. takes over the Nippes neighborhood. (Open M-Sa 8am-1pm.)

Päffgen-Brauerei, Friesenstr. 64. Take U3-6, 12, or 15 to Friesenpl. A local favorite since 1883. *Kölsch* (€1.30) is brewed on the premises, consumed in cavernous halls and in the 600-seat beer garden, and refilled until you put your coaster on top of your glass. Entrees €2-19. Open daily 10am-midnight. Cash only. ❸

Cafe Orlando, Engelbertstr. 7 (☎23 75 23; www.cafeorlando.de). U8 or 9 to "Zülpicher Pl." Free wireless Internet, tapestry-covered wooden benches, marble tabletops, stained-glass lamps, and an assortment of newspapers create a Sunday morning atmosphere any time of day. Complete breakfasts (from €3.10), omelettes and salads (€5.50-6.80), and cocktails (€3.50-4.80) draw a devoted following of students who squeeze into the benches at all hours. Open daily 9am-midnight. Cash only. ❷

Alt Köln, Trankg. 7-9 (☎13 74 71). Regional meat and fish specialties with a seasonal menu (€4-18) and cheap *Kölsch* (€1.45). Open daily 8am-midnight. AmEx/MC/V. ❷

Mex Attax, Hohenstaufenring 23. Take U8 or 9 to Zülpicher Pl. Mouth-watering wraps (€3-5), quesadillas (€2-4), and sweet-potato soup (€3). At night, grab a mixed drink to go (€3.50). Open M-Th 11am-11pm, F-Sa 11am-1am. Cash only. ❶

Café Magnus, Zülpicherstr. 48 (☎24 14 69). Take U8 or 9 to Zülpicher Pl. Locals flock to this crowded cafe for funky tunes, artfully prepared meals from €4, and many vegetarian options (€5-7). Open M-Th 8am-3am, F-Sa 8am-5am, Su 8am-1am. Cash only. ❷

SIGHTS

DOM. Germany's greatest cathedral, the *Dom*, is the perfect realization of High Gothic style. Built over the course of six centuries, it was finished in 1880 and miraculously escaped destruction during WWII. Today, its colossal spires define the skyline of Cologne, eclipsing the sun for those standing below. A chapel on the inside right houses a 15th-century **triptych** depicting the city's five patron saints. Behind the altar in the center of the choir is the **Shrine of the Magi,** the cathedral's most sacred compartment, which allegedly holds the remains of the Three Kings. Before exiting the choir, stop in the **Chapel of the Cross** to admire the 10th-century **Gero crucifix,** the oldest intact sculpture of a crucified Christ with his eyes shut. It takes 15min. to scale the 509 steps of the **Südturm** tower. *(Cathedral open daily 6am-7:30pm. 45min. English-language tours M-Sa 10:30am and 2:30pm, Su 2:30pm. Tower open daily May-Sept. 9am-6pm; Nov.-Feb. 9am-4pm; Mar.-Apr. and Oct. 9am-5pm. Cathedral free. Tours €4, children €2. Tower €2, students €1.)*

MUSEUMS. Four words about the **Schokoladenmuseum:** Willy Wonka made real. It presents every step of chocolate production, from the rain forests to the gold fountain that spurts streams of silky free samples. *(Rheinauhafen 1A, near the Severinsbrücke. ☎931 88 80; www.schokoladenmuseum.de. From the train station, head for the Rhine, and walk to the right along the river; go under the Deutzer Brücke, and take the 1st footbridge. Open Tu-F 10am-6pm, Sa-Su 11am-7pm. €5.50, students €3.)* Heinrich-Böll-Pl. houses the **Museum Ludwig,** whose collection includes everything from Impressionism to Pop Art. *(Bischofsgartenstr. 1, behind the Römisch-Germanisches Museum. ☎22 12 61 65. Open Tu-Su 10am-6pm, 1st F of each month 10am-10pm. €7.50, students €5.50.)* Masterpieces from the Middle Ages to the Post-Impressionist period are gathered in the **Wallraf-**

Richartz Museum. *(Martinstr. 39. From the Heumarkt, take Gürzenichtstr. 1 block to Martinstr. ☎276 94; www.museenkoeln.de/wrm. Open Tu 10am-8pm, W-F 10am-6pm, Sa-Su 11am-6pm. €5.80, students €3.30.)* The **Römisch-Germanisches Museum** displays a large array of artifacts documenting the daily lives of Romans. *(Roncallipl. 4. Open Tu and F-Su 10am-5pm, W 10am-8pm. €4.50, students €2.70.)*

HOUSE #4711. The fabled **Eau de Cologne,** once prescribed as a drinkable curative, earned the town worldwide recognition. Today, the house of its origin, labeled #4711 by a Napoleonic system that abolished street names, is a boutique where a fountain flows with the scented water. Visit the gallery upstairs for a history of the fragrance. *(On Glockeng. near the intersection with Tunisstr. From Hohe Str., turn right on Brückenstr., which becomes Glockeng. Open M-F 9am-7pm, Sa 9am-6pm. Free.)*

ENTERTAINMENT AND NIGHTLIFE

Cologne explodes in celebration during **Karneval** (mid- to late Feb. 2007), a week-long pre-Lenten festival made up of 50 neighborhood processions. **Weiberfastnacht** (Feb. 15, 2007) is the first major to-do: the mayor mounts the platform at Alter Markt and abdicates leadership to the city's women, who then hunt down their husbands at work and chop off their ties. The weekend builds to the out-of-control parade on **Rosenmontag** (Rose Monday; Feb. 19, 2007), when thousands of merry participants sing and dance their way through the city center while exchanging *bützchen* (kisses on the cheek). While most revelers nurse their hangovers on Shrove Tuesday, pubs and restaurants set fire to the straw scarecrows hanging out their windows. For more info, pick up the Karneval booklet at the tourist office.

Roman mosaics dating back to the third century record the wild excesses of the city's early residents; they've toned it down only a bit since. The best way to know what you'll get is to pick up the monthly magazine *Kölner* (€1) from newsstands. The closer to the Rhine or *Dom* you venture, the faster your wallet will empty. After dark in **Hohenzollernring,** crowds move from theaters to clubs and finally to cafes in the early morning. Students gather around Zülpicherstr. and Zülpicher Pl., as well as along the Hohenstaufenring. Radiating westward from Friesenpl., the **Belgisches Viertel** (Belgian Quarter) has slightly more expensive bars and cafes.

Papa Joe's Jazzlokal, Buttermarkt 37 (☎257 7931). Papa Joe has a legendary reputation for providing good jazz and good times. Add your business card or expired ID to the informal collage that adorns the perimeter of the bar. *Kölsch* (€3.60) in 0.4L glasses, not the usual 0.2L. Live jazz M-Sa 10:30pm-12:30am; linger afterward and buy the band a round. Open daily 7pm-1am, F-Sa 7pm-3am. Cash only.

Cent Club, Hohenstaufenring 25-27 (www.centclub.de). Near Zülpicher Pl. Take U8 or 9 to Zülpicher Pl. Rivaling Das Ding across the street, this student disco features more dance (R 'n' B, pop, dance classics) and less talk, with the appeal of dirt-cheap drinks (shooters €0.50, mixed drinks €1, beer €1.50). Cover W-Sa €5. Open M-Sa 9pm-late.

Cuba Bar, Zülpicherstr. 25 (☎21 60 280). Take U8 or 9 to Zülpicher Pl. This cocktail lounge and bar with an extensive Latin American drink list and alternating reggaetón and salsa playlist has curious blown-up portraits of Che Guevara plastered on its walls and awning. Rotating drink specials (€3.50-4.50) like the Mother's Finest (84-proof rum, fresh cream, apple, and cinnamon) at all hours give patrons reason to stray from the traditional but excellent mojitos and caipirinhas. Open daily 5pm-3am.

Hotel Timp, Heumarkt 25 (☎258 1409; www.timp.de). Across from the U-Bahn stop. This club and hotel has become a virtual institution in Cologne for gaudy, glittery travesty theater. Gay and straight crowds come here for the gaudy and glitter-filled cabarets. Drag shows daily 1-4am. No cover, but 1st drink Su-Th €8, F-Sa €13. Open daily 11pm-late. AmEx/MC/V.

BONN ☎0228

Bonn's Rhine-side setting, popular concert scene, and diverse museums attract just enough visitors nowadays to keep the city (pop. 305,000) well touristed, but not overly so. Once housed in Bonn, the *Bundestag* moved to Berlin in 1999 and returned Bonn to its low profile.

TRANSPORTATION AND PRACTICAL INFORMATION. **Trains** run to Cologne (20min., 5 per hr., €5-8), Frankfurt (2hr., 3 per hr., €25-32), and Koblenz (45min., 3 per hr., €8-13). The **tourist office** is at Windeckstr. 1, off Münsterpl. Follow Poststr. from the station. They have free maps and book rooms via phone for €2 or online for free. (☎77 50 00; www.bonn.de. Open M-F 9am-6:30pm, Sa 9am-4pm, Su 10am-2pm.) The **post office** is at Münsterpl. 17. (Open M-F 9am-8pm, Sa 9am-4pm.) **Postal Code:** 53111.

ACCOMMODATIONS AND FOOD. **Deutsches Haus ❸**, Kasernenstr. 19-21, is on a quiet residential street connecting Münsterpl. and Berlinerpl. The best part is the decadent included breakfast, served in a tulip-filled room. (☎63 37 77; info@hotel-deutscheshaus.net. Reception 6am-11pm. Singles €34-39, with bath €35-41; doubles €60-77; triples €66-99. MC/V.) For the super-modern **Jugendgästehaus Bonn-Venusberg (HI) ❷**, Haager Weg 42, take bus #621 (dir.: Ippendorf Altenheim) to Jugendgästehaus. (☎28 99 70; jgh-bonn@t-online.de. Wheelchair-accessible. Breakfast and linens included. Laundry €4. Curfew 1am. Dorms €22; singles €36; doubles €52. MC/V.) The Münsterpl. **market** teems with haggling vendors and determined customers. (Open M-Sa 8am-6pm.) Take a break from meaty German specialties at **Cassius-Garten ❷**, Maximilianstr. 28D. This sunny veggie bar serves 50 kinds of salads, pasta, and whole-grain baked goods, all for €1.50 per 100g. (☎65 24 29; www.cassiusgarten.de. Open M-F 9am-10pm, Sa 9am-6pm.)

SIGHTS AND NIGHTLIFE. Bonn's lively pedestrian zone has many historic nooks. **Beethovenhaus,** Bonng. 20, Beethoven's birthplace, houses a collection of the composer's personal effects, from his first violin to primitive hearing aids. (☎981 75 25. Open Apr.-Oct. M-Sa 10am-6pm, Su 11am-6pm; Nov.-Mar. M-Sa 10am-5pm, Su 11am-5pm. €4, students €3.) In its heyday as parliament, the **Bundeshaus** earned the title of "least prepossessing parliament building" in the world. Its transparent walls were meant to symbolize transparency in government. (Take bus #610 to Bundeshaus. Inside open by tour only, Sa-Su 2 and 3pm; request free tickets at tourist office.) Forty thousand students study in the **Kurfürstliches Schloß,** the huge 18th-century palace now serving as the center of Friedrich-Wilhelms-Universität. To reach Bonn's "other" palace, stroll down Poppelsdorfer Allee to **Poppelsdorfer Schloß,** which has a French facade, an Italian courtyard, and beautifully manicured botanical gardens. (Gardens open Apr.-Sept. M-F 9am-6pm, Su 9am-1pm; Oct.-Mar. M-F 9am-4pm.) Interactive exhibits at the **Haus der Geschichte,** Willy-Brandt-Allee 14, examine post-WWII Germany. (☎916 50. Open Tu-Su 9am-7pm. Free.) One block away, the immense **Kunstmuseum Bonn,** Friedrich-Ebert-Allee 2, houses a superb collection of 20th-century German art. (☎77 62 60. Open Tu and Th-Su 10am-6pm, W 10am-9pm. €5, students €2.50.)

Schnüss (€1), sold at newsstands, has club and concert listings. **The Jazz Galerie,** Oxfordstr. 24, is a jazz-less disco popular with swanky youths. (☎65 06 62. Cover Th €5, F-Sa €7.50; includes 1 drink. Open Tu and Th 9pm-3am, F-Sa 10pm-5am. Cash only.) **Balustrade,** Heerstr. 52, has a huge TV and theme nights like beach, snowball, and jungle. (Open M-Th 7pm-1am, F-Sa 7pm-late. Cash only.) **Pantheon,** Bundeskanzlerpl. 2-10, hosts concerts, stand-up comedy, and art exhibits. (☎21 25 21; www.pantheon.de. Cover €6.50. Disco open 11pm-late. MC/V.)

KASSEL ☎0561

The curious monuments and sweeping green vistas that surround Kassel (pop. 194,000) make it well worth visiting; both can be found at the antiquated hillside park, **Wilhelmshöhe.** Inside, **Schloß Wilhelmshöhe** is a dressed-down but more authentically furnished version of the Residenz in Würzburg. Just uphill, **Schloß Löwenburg** was built by Wilhelm in the 18th century with stones deliberately missing so it would resemble a crumbling medieval castle—he was obsessed with the year 1495 and quixotically imagined himself a knight. To reach the castles, take streetcar #1 from Bahnhof Wilhelmshöhe. (Both castles open Mar.-Oct. Tu-Su 10am-5pm; Nov.-Feb. 10am-4pm. Required tours every hr. Each castle €3.50, students €2.50.) Park paths lead to the statue of **Herkules,** Kassel's emblem, where visitors can climb onto the pedestal and, if they're brave enough, into a club. (Pedestal and club open daily mid-Mar. to mid-Nov. 10am-5pm. €2, students €1.25. Access to the base of the statue free.) The **Brüder-Grimm-Museum,** Schöne Aussicht 2, displays a handwritten copy of The Brothers Grimm's *Children's and Household Tales.* (Open daily 10am-5pm. €1.)

To reach **Jugendherberge und Bildungsstätte Kassel (HI) ❷,** Schenkendorfstr. 18, take streetcar #4 from the Wilhelmshöhe station to Annastr., backtrack on Friedrich-Ebert-Str., and turn right on Querallee, which becomes Schenkendorfstr. (☎77 64 55; www.djh-hessen.de/jh/kassel. Breakfast included. Internet €2 per hr., €15 per day. Reception 11am-11:30pm. Curfew 12:30am. Dorms €20; singles 28; doubles €51. HI members only. Cash only.) **Hotel Kö78 ❸,** Kölnische Str. 78, has a lovely garden in back, as well as cable TV and phones. (☎716 14; www.koe78.de. Breakfast included. Reception 7am-10pm. Singles €32, with toilet €41-51; doubles €51/61-75. MC/V.) **Friedrich-Ebert-Straße,** the upper part of **Wilhelmshöher Allee,** and the area around **Königsplatz** all have supermarkets, take-out stands, and cafes sprinkled among clothing stores. **Limerick ❷,** Wilhelmshöher Allee 116, has a pan-European menu boasting 237 entrees and appetizers. The pizza list alone (60 total, €2.60-6.70) is broken down by meat, vegetarian, poultry, and seafood categories. A large variety of fixed four-course lunches (€4.90-7.90) and 25 beers on tap attract loyal crowds that consistently fill its spacious dining room and even larger garden. (☎77 66 49; www.restaurant-limerick.de. Open M-Th 11am-1am, F-Sa 11am-2am, Su 11am-midnight. Cash only.) Kassel has two **train** stations, Bahnhof Wilhelmshöhe and the Hauptbahnhof, but most trains stop only at Wilhelmshöhe. Trains run to: Berlin (3hr., 2 per hr., €74); Düsseldorf (3½hr., 1 per hr., €38-45); Frankfurt (2hr., 2 per hr., €41-49); Hamburg (2½hr., 2 per hr., €57-65); Munich (4hr., 1 per hr., €78-87). The **tourist office,** in Bahnhof Wilhelmshöhe, has free maps and books rooms for a €2.50 fee. (☎70 77 07; www.kassel-tourist.de. Open M-F 9am-6pm, Sa 9am-2pm.) **Postal Code:** 34117.

FRANKFURT AM MAIN ☎069

International offices, shiny skyscrapers, and expensive cars are everywhere in Frankfurt (pop. 660,000), lovingly nicknamed "Mainhattan" for its spot on the Main River and its glitzy vitality. Both people and money are constantly in motion in this major transport hub, which is also home to the central bank of the EU.

TRANSPORTATION

Flights: The busy **Flughafen Rhein-Main** (☎01805 372 46 36) is connected to the Hauptbahnhof by S-Bahn trains S8 and 9 (every 15min.). Buy tickets (€3) from the green machines marked *Fahrkarten* before boarding. Taxis to the city center (around €20) can be found outside any terminal.

Trains: Trains run from the **Hauptbahnhof** to: **Amsterdam, NTH** (4hr., every 2hr., €97); **Berlin** (5-6hr., 2 per hr., €98); **Cologne** (2½hr., 1 per hr., €75); **Hamburg** (3½-5hr., 2 per hr., €93); **Munich** (3½-4½hr., 3 per hr., €55); **Paris, FRA** (6-8hr., 4 per day, €83). Call ☎01805 19 41 95 for schedules, reservations, and info.

Public Transportation: Frankfurt's public transportation system runs daily 4am-1:30am. Single-ride tickets (€1.70; 6-9am and after 4pm €2) are valid for 1hr. in 1 direction, transfers permitted. **Eurail** is valid only on S-Bahn trains. The **day pass** (*Tageskarte;* valid until midnight of the purchase date) provides unlimited transportation on the S-Bahn, U-Bahn, streetcars, and buses. Day passes can be purchased from machines in any station (€4.70, children €2.80). Ticketless passengers face €40 fines.

Ride-share: Stuttgarter Str. 12 (☎23 64 44). Take a right on Baseler Str. at the side exit of the Hauptbahnhof (track 1) and walk 2 blocks. Arranges rides to **Berlin** (€30), **Munich** (€89), and elsewhere. Open M-F 8am-6:30pm, Sa 8am-4pm, Su 10am-4pm.

Taxis: ☎23 00 01, 23 00 33, or 25 00 01. €1.38-1.53 per km.

Bike Rental: Deutsche Bahn (DB) runs the citywide service **Call a Bike** (☎0700 05 22 55 22; www.callabike.de). Bikes marked with the red DB logo can be found throughout the city. To rent one, call the service hotline. €0.07 per min., €15 per day.

ORIENTATION AND PRACTICAL INFORMATION

Frankfurt's Hauptbahnhof opens into its red light district; from the station, the Altstadt is a 20min. walk down Kaiserstr. or Münchener Str. The well-touristed **Römerberg** square is north of the Main, while the commercial center lies farther north along **Zeil.** Cafes and services cluster near the university in **Bockenheim** (U6 or 7 to Bockenheimer Warte). Across the river, the **Sachsenhausen** area draws pub-crawlers and museum-goers (U1, 2, or 3 to Schweizer Pl.).

Tourist Office: in the Hauptbahnhof (☎21 23 88 00; www.frankfurt-tourismus.de). Books rooms for a €3 fee; free if you call ahead. Sells maps (€0.50) and the **Frankfurt Card** (1-day €8, 2-day €12), which allows unlimited use of public transportation and provides discounts on many sights. Open M-F 8am-9pm, Sa-Su and holidays 9am-6pm.

Currency Exchange: at banks. Locations in the airport and station have higher rates.

Laundromat: Waschsalon, Wallstr. 8, near the hostel in Sachsenhausen. Wash €3, dry €0.50 per 15min. Soap included. Open daily 6am-11pm.

Emergency: Police: ☎110. **Ambulance** and **Fire:** ☎112.

Pharmacy: Abstexpress, in the train station's **Einkaufspassage** (☎271 14 20). Open M-F 6am-midnight, Sa 7am-midnight, Su 8am-midnight. Call ☎192 92 for emergencies.

Internet Access: Alpha, in the Hauptbahnhof's gambling salon, past track #24. €2.50 per hr. Open 24hr.

Post Office: Goethe Pl. Walk 10min. down Taunusstr. from the Hauptbahnhof, or take the U- or S-Bahn to Hauptwache and walk south to the square. Open M-F 9:30am-7pm, Sa 9am-2pm. **Postal Code:** 60313.

ACCOMMODATIONS

Deals are rare and trade fairs make rooms scarce; reserve at least 2-3 weeks ahead. The **Westend/University** area has a few cheap options.

Haus der Jugend (HI), Deutschherrnufer 12 (☎610 0150; www.jugendherberge-frankfurt.de). Bus #46 from the station to "Frankensteiner Pl." Turn right along the river; the hostel is at the end of the block. Its location along the Main and in front of Sachsenhausen's pubs and cafes makes it popular with students. Some private bathrooms.

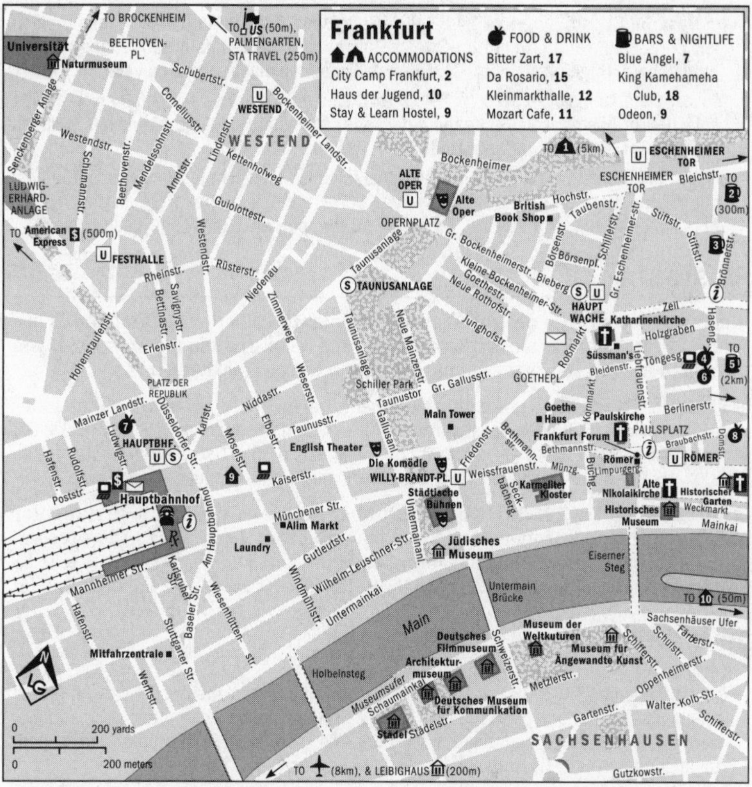

Breakfast (7-9am) and linens included. Locks available with €5 deposit. Check-in 1pm. Check-out 9:30am. Curfew 2am. Dorms from €20, under 27 from €15. MC/V. ❷

Stay & Learn Hostel, Kaiserstr. 74 (☎247 5130; info@room-frankfurt.de). In the heart of the action—and the red-light district—this airy hostel is a convenient option. Luggage storage and laundry included. Internet €1 per hr. Dorms €17-20; singles €40; doubles €50; triples €75. Higher rates during trade fairs. MC/V. ❷

City Camp Frankfurt, An der Sandelmühle 35B (☎57 03 32; www.city-camp-frankfurt.de). U1-3: Heddernheim. Take a left at the Kleingartnerverein sign and continue until you reach the Sandelmühle sign. Cross the stream, turn left, and follow signs to the campground. Showers €1 per 4min. Reception Mar.-Oct. 9am-1pm and 4-8pm; Nov.-Feb. 4-8pm. €5.50 per person, €2.30 per child; €3.50 per tent. Cash only. ❶

FOOD

The cheapest meals are near the university in **Bockenheim. Sachsenhausen** pubs also serve food at decent prices. Blocks from the HI hostel is an **HL Markt,** Dreieichstr. 56. (Open M-F 8am-8pm, Sa 8am-4pm.) **Alim Markt,** Münchener Str. 37, is near the Hauptbahnhof. (Open M-F 8:30am-7:30pm, Su 8am-2pm.) **Kleinmarkthalle,** on Haseng. between Berlinerstr. and Töngesg., is a three-story warehouse with bakeries, butchers, and produce stands. (Open M-F 8am-6pm, Sa 8am-4pm.)

Da Rosario, Ottostr. 17 (☎24 24 81 82). Go left out of the Hauptbahnhof, take the first left on Poststr., and go right on Ottostr. This small pizzeria has an endearingly hectic atmosphere. Huge pizzas from €4. Open daily noon-midnight. Cash only. ❷

Mozart Cafe, Töngesg. 23-25 (☎29 19 54). Lauded by locals, this cafe serves a wide selection of pastas, salads, heaping desserts, and famously huge breakfasts. Entrees €4.90-6.80. Open M-Sa 8am-10pm, Su 9am-10pm. MC. ❷

Bitter Zart, Domstr. 5 (☎94 94 28 46). This famous sweets shop sells some of the best chocolates (from €3 per 100g) and *gelee früdde* (from €2.50 per 100g) in the city. The hot chocolate suits any season. Open M-F 10am-7pm, Sa 10am-4pm. Cash only. ❷

SIGHTS

Allied bombing in 1944 destroyed everything but the cathedral, so Frankfurt's historic splendor survives mostly in memories and reconstructed monuments. If you plan on touring the city's museums, consider buying a **Frankfurt Card** (p. 450).

STÄDEL. The Städel's collection represents seven centuries of art and includes notable works by Old Masters, Impressionists, and Modernists. *(Schaumainkai 63, between Dürerstr. and Holbeinstr. ☎605 09 80. Open Tu and F-Su 10am-5pm, W-Th 10am-9pm. €8, students €6, under 12 and last Sa of each month free. English-language audio tour €2.)*

MUSEUM FÜR MODERNE KUNST. Dubbed "slice of cake," this triangular building displays European and American art from the 1960s to the present, including works by Lichtenstein, Johns, and emerging talents. *(Domstr. 10. ☎21 23 04 47; www.mmk-frankfurt.de. Open Tu and Th-Su 10am-5pm, W 10am-8pm. €6, students €3.)*

NIGHTLIFE

Odeon, Seilerstr. 34 (☎28 50 55). Look for the whitewashed medieval villa with ornate pillars and cut-out octopi on the door. This 2 fl. club vibrates with house, soul, and hip-hop. M hip-hop, Th student night, F 27+, Sa Wild Card. M and Th-F drinks ½-price until midnight. Cover €5, Th students €3. Open M-Sa 10pm-late. Cash only.

King Kamehameha Club, Hanauer Landstr. 192 (☎48 00 370; www.king-kamehameha.de). With an indoor stream and a raging dance floor, this club lures young party goers. Open Th 9pm-3am, F-Sa 10pm-4am. Cash only.

Blue Angel, Brönnerstr. 17 (☎28 27 72). Techno music and flashing lights rock the interior of the liveliest gay club around, a Frankfurt institution for 30 years. Ring the bell to be let in. Crowd doesn't begin to arrive until after 1am. Cover €5. Usually open daily 11pm-late, 24hr. straight from 2am Sa. Cash only.

SOUTHWESTERN GERMANY

There is much to be seen in the Rhine and Mosel River Valleys in the southwest of Germany, and much to be drunk. Vineyards upon vineyards produce the best German wines. Nearby, the Mosel River curls downstream along the Rhine Gorge to a shore of castle-studded hills. Farther south, modern cities fade slowly into the beautiful hinterlands of the Black Forest.

TRIER ☎0651

The oldest town in Germany, Trier (pop. 100,000) has weathered more than two millennia in the western end of the Mosel Valley. An inscription at Trier's Hauptmarkt (Main Market) reads: "Trier stood one thousand and three hundred years before Rome." Founded by the Gallo-Celtic Treveri tribe, but seized by the Romans under Augustus, Trier reached its zenith in the early 4th century when it served as the capital of the Western Roman Empire and was a major center of Christianity in Europe. This rich historical legacy, coupled with the tiered vineyards of the surrounding valley, attracts throngs of tourists who crowd the streets day and night. Today's Trier is at its core a university city catering to a large and highly visible student population.

To reach **Jugendgästehaus Trier (HI) ❷**, An der Jugendherberge 4, take buses #2, 8, 12, or 87 to Zurlaubenerufer. (Bus #2 leaves from the train station.) The hostel is a 10min. walk downstream from the bus stop. (☎292 92; www.diejugendherbergen.de. Breakfast included. Laundry €5. Dorms €21; singles €27; doubles €53. €3.10 HI discount. MC/V.) In the city center are the rooms of **Jugendgästehaus im Kolpinghaus Warsberger Hof ❶**, Dietrichstr. 42. (☎97 52 50; www.warsberger-hof.de. Reception 8am-11pm. Reserve ahead. Dorms €16; singles €25; doubles €42. MC/V.) Moderately priced restaurants line the pedestrian path along the river between the youth hostel and the Kaiser-Wilhelm-Brücke. Two blocks from Viehmarkt-Pl., **Astarix ❷**, Karl-Marx-Str. 11, dishes out large portions of pasta and pizza from €4. Squeezed in a passageway, Astarix can be reached from the Trier Theater area or by walking down Brückenstr. toward the river. It serves excellent, cheap food in a mellow environment. (Salads €2.60-5.40; baguettes €2.60-5.40; pasta and pizza €3.50-5.40. Open daily 11am-11:30pm.) **Plus** supermarket, Brotstr. 54, is near the Hauptmarkt. (Open M-F 8:30am-8pm, Sa 8:30am-6pm.)

The Roman ruins decorating the heart of the city will keep history buffs occupied for hours, and the greenery of the riverside promenade offers an escape for walkers, bikers, or those just looking to relax. A one-day **combination ticket** (€6.20, students €3.10) provides access to all the city's Roman monuments. The most impressive is the massive and well-preserved 2nd-century **Porta Nigra** (Black Gate), which travelers can climb for a view of Trier. (Open daily Apr.-Sept. 9am-6pm; Oct. and Mar. 9am-5pm. Nov.-Feb. 9am-4pm. €2.10, students €1.60.) The nearby **Dom** shelters the *Tunica Christi* (Holy Robe of Christ) and the tombs of many archbishops. (Open daily Apr.-Oct. 6:30am-6pm; Nov.-Mar. 6:30am-5:30pm. Free.) The enormous **Basilika** was originally the location of Emperor Constantine's throne room. (Open Apr.-Oct. M-Sa 10am-6pm, Su noon-6pm; Nov.-Mar. Tu-Sa 11am-noon and 3-4pm, Su noon-1pm. Free.) Near the southeast corner of the city walls are the 4th-century **Kaiserthermen** (Emperor's baths),

THE BEST *WURST*

So you're finally in Germany and itching to sink your teeth into your first authentic *Wurst*. With over 1500 varieties, you'll have plenty of choices. All have one thing in common: German law mandates that sausages can only be made of meat and spices. If it has cereal filling, it's not *Wurst*.

Bockwurst: This tasty sausage is common roasted or grilled at street stands, and is served dripping with ketchup and mustard in a *Brötchen* (roll). Although *Bock* means billy-goat, this *Wurst* is made of ground veal with parsley and chives. Complement your *Bockwurst* with some *Bock* beer.

Thüringer Bratwurst: Similar to the *Bockwurst*, the *Bratwurst* also has pork, plus ginger and nutmeg.

Frankfurter: Unlike the American variety, the German *Frankfurter* can only have this name if it is made in Frankfurt. It's made of lean pork ground into a paste and then cold smoked, which gives it its orange-yellow coloring.

Knockwurst: Shorter and plumper, this sausage is served with *sauerkraut*. It's made of lean pork and beef, with a healthy dose of garlic.

Weißwurst: Cream and eggs give this "white sausage" its pale coloring. *Weißwurst* goes with rye bread and mustard.

Currywurst: A great late-night snack, this pork *Bratwurst* is smothered in tomato sauce and sprinkled with paprika and curry.

with underground passages that once served as Roman sewers. (Open daily Apr.-Sept. 9am-6pm; Oct.-Mar. 9am-5pm. €2.10, students €1.60.) From there, a 10min. walk uphill along Olewiger Str. leads to the **amphitheater.** Once a gladiatorial arena, it's now a stage for city productions. (Amphitheater open daily Apr.-Sept. 9am-6pm; Oct. and Mar. 9am-5pm; Nov.-Feb. 9am-4pm. €2.10, students €1.60.)

Trains run to Koblenz (1½hr., 2 per hr., €16) and Luxembourg City (45min., 1 per hr., €10-14). From the station, walk straight down Theodor-Haus-Allee and turn left under the Porta Nigra to reach the **tourist office.** (☎97 80 80; www.trier.de. Open May-Sept. M-Sa 9am-7pm, Su 10am-5pm; Oct.-Dec. and Mar.-Apr. M-Sa 9am-6pm, Su 10am-3pm; Jan.-Feb. M-Sa 10am-5pm, Sa 10am-1pm. 2hr. English-language city tour Sa 1:30pm; 1hr. German- and English-language coach tour daily 1pm. Each €6, students €5.) A **Trier Card,** available at the tourist office, offers free intra-city bus fare and discounts on museums and Roman sites over a three-day period (€9, family card €15). **Postal Code:** 54292.

RHINE VALLEY (RHEINTAL)

Castles tower above tiny villages and green hillsides as the Rhine River carves its way through the 80km stretch of the Rhine Valley, flowing north from Mainz through Bacharach and Koblenz to charming Bonn.

TRANSPORTATION

Two different **train** lines traverse the Rhine Valley, one on each bank; the line on the western side stays closer to the water and has superior views. It's often tricky to switch banks, as train and ferry schedules don't always match up, so plan your trip in advance. Although full of tourists, **boats** are probably the best way to see the sights; the **Köln-Düsseldorfer (KD) Line** and **Bingen Rüdesheim Line** cover the Mainz-Koblenz stretch three to four times per day in summer.

MAINZ ☎06131

Pastel-colored buildings decorate the Altstadt of Mainz (pop. 190,000), which proudly honors its connection to famed printer Johannes Gutenberg. The **Martinsdom,** a colossal sandstone cathedral, stands as a memorial to the city's former status as the greatest Catholic diocese north of the Alps. (☎25 34 12. Open Mar.-Oct. Tu-F 9am-6pm, Sa 9am-2pm, Su 1-2:45pm and 4-6:30pm; Nov.-Feb. M-F 9am-5pm, Sa 9am-4pm, Su 12:45-3pm and 4-5pm. Free.) On a hill south of the Dom, the Gothic **Stephanskirche** on Stephansberg is inlaid with stunning stained-glass windows by Russian exile Marc Chagall. (Open M-F 10am-noon and 2-5pm, Sa 2-5pm. Free.) The 1455 advent of movable type is immortalized at the **Gutenberg-Museum,** Liebfrauenpl. 5, across from the Dom, which has a replica of Gutenberg's original press. (Open Tu-Sa 9am-5pm, Su 11am-3pm. €3.50, students €2.)

To reach the clean rooms of **Jugendgästehaus (HI) ❷,** Otto-Brunfels-Schneise 4, take bus #62 (dir.: Weisenau) or 63 (dir.: Laubenheim) to Viktorstift/Jugendherberge, and follow the signs. (☎853 32; www.diejugendherbergen.de. Breakfast included. Reception 6:30am-10pm. 4- to 6-bed dorms €18; singles €27; doubles €48. MC/V.) **Der Eisgrub-Bräu ❷,** Weißlilieng. 1A, on the edge of the Altstadt, serves breakfast and lunch buffets (€2.90/5.10) and its own house beer. (Open Su-Th 9am-1pm, F-Sa 9am-2pm. MC/V.) **Trains** run to Frankfurt (30min., €9), Heidelberg (1½hr., €15), and Koblenz (1hr., €15). KD **ferries** (☎23 28 00; www.k-d.com) depart from the wharfs on the other side of the Rathaus. The **tourist office,** in Brückenturm by the river in the Altstadt, conducts English-language tours, gives out free maps, and reserves rooms for a €2.50 fee. From the station, walk straight down Schottstr., turn right onto Kaiserstr., and continue straight until you reach Ludwigstr.; turn left, and follow the green signs. (☎28 62 10; www.info-mainz.de/tourist. Open M-F 9am-6pm, Sa 10am-3pm. 2hr. English-language tours May-Oct. W and F-Sa 2pm; Nov.-Apr. Sa 2pm. €5.) **Postal Code:** 55001.

BACHARACH ☎06473

Bacharach (Altar of Bacchus) lives up to its name, with wine cellars *(Weinkeller)* tucked between every other half-timbered house along the village's cobblestoned main street. Try some of the Rhine's best wines (from €2) and cheeses (€3.10-6.50) at **Die Weinstube,** Oberstr. 63. (Open M-F from 1pm, Sa-Su from noon. Cash only.) Nearby, up the path to the hostel, is the 14th-century **Wernerkapelle,** the remains of a red sandstone chapel that took 140 years to build but only hours to destroy during the Palatinate War of Succession in 1689. At the height of hostel greatness, **Jugendherberg Stahleck (HI) ❷** is a converted 12th-century castle with a panoramic view. The steep 15min. hike to the hostel is worth every step. Make a right out of the station, turn left at the stairs between the tourist office and the Peterskirche, and follow any of the marked paths up the hill. (☎12 66; www.diejugendherbergen.de. Breakfast included. Reception 7:30am-7:30pm. Curfew 10pm. Reserve ahead. Dorms €17. MC/V.) At **Café Restaurant Rusticana ❷,** Oberstr. 40, a lovely German couple serves three-course meals of regional fare for €6-11. (☎17 41. Open May-Oct. M-W and F-Su noon-9:30pm. Cash only.) The **tourist office,** Oberstr. 45, near the town center, offers **Internet** access (€0.50 per 5min.) and books rooms for free. (☎91 93 03. Open Apr.-Oct. M-F 9am-5pm, Sa-Su 10am-1pm; Nov.-Mar. M-F 9am-noon.) **Postal Code:** 55422.

LORELEI CLIFFS AND CASTLES

Sailors were once lured to these cliffs by the infamous Lorelei maiden, but her hypnotic song seems to be superfluous today, as hordes of travelers are seduced by the area's romantic villages, slanting vineyards, and restored medieval castles. **St. Goarshausen** and **St. Goar,** towns on either side of the Rhine, host the spectacular **Rhein in Flammen** (Rhine Ablaze) fireworks celebration in mid-September. St. Goarshausen, on the east bank, provides access by foot to the Lorelei statue and the cliffs. Above the town, **Burg Katz** (Cat Castle) eternally stalks its prey, the smaller **Burg Maus** (Mouse Castle). To get there, face the river, head right, and follow the signs. Burg Maus offers daily falconry demonstrations at 11am and 2:30pm from May to early October. (☎06771 76 69. €6.50, children €5.50.)

To reach the cliffside **Jugendheim Loreley ❶,** on the St. Goarshausen side of the Rhine, follow the signs from Rheinstr. (☎06771 26 19; tuhe@loreley-herberge.de. Breakfast included. Linens €3.50. Curfew 10pm. Dorms €8.50. Cash only.) **Trains** run from St. Goarshausen to Cologne (1½hr., €23) and Mainz (1½hr., €16) and from St. Goar to Cologne (1½hr., €22) and Mainz (1hr., €9.70). The *Lorelei VI* **ferry** connects St. Goarshausen and St. Goar (M-F 6am-11pm, Sa-Su 7am-11pm; €1.30). For St. Goarhausen's **tourist office,** Bahnhofstr. 8, turn left from the train station, and follow the signs. (☎06771 91 00; www.loreley-touristik.de. Open M 9:30am-noon and 2-4:30pm, Th 2-4:30pm, F 2-5:50pm, Sa-Su 9:30am-noon.) St. Goar's **tourist office,** Heerstr. 86, is a 5min. walk from the ferry dock. (☎06741 383; www.st-goar.de. Open M-F 8am-12:30pm and 2-5pm, Sa 10am-noon.) **Postal Code:** 56329.

KOBLENZ ☎0261

A menacing fortress perched high above the city of Koblenz (pop. 107,000) overlooks the confluence two of Germany's major rivers, the Rhine and the Mosel, which corner the Altstadt far below. Koblenz has long been a strategic hot spot. In the two millennia since its birth, the city has hosted every empire seeking to conquer Europe. It centers around the **Deutsches Eck** (German Corner) at the intersection of the rivers, which purportedly witnessed the birth of the German nation in 1216. To the right, the **Mahnmal der Deutschen Einheit** (Monument to German Unity) is a tribute to Kaiser Wilhelm I. The **Museum Ludwig im Deutschherrenhaus,** Danziger Freiheit 1, behind the *Mahnmal*, features contemporary French art. (☎30 40 40; www.ludwigmuseum.org. Open Tu-Sa 10:30am-5pm, Su 11am-6pm. €2.50, students €1.50.) Head across the river to the **Festung Ehrenbreitstein,** a fortress at the highest point in the city. Today, it contains a youth hostel, numerous museums, and rotating historical exhibits. (Non-hostel guests €1.10, students €0.60. See below for hostel information.)

Jugendherberge Koblenz (HI) ❷, in the fortress, has breathtaking views of the Rhine and Mosel. Take bus #9 or 8 from the bus station to Ehrenbreitstein. From there, walk left along the main road for 100m and take the paved path to your right. (☎97 28 70; www.diejugendherbergen.de. Breakfast included. Reception 7:15am-10pm. Curfew midnight. Dorms €17; doubles €44. €3.10 HI discount. MC/V.) With soft carpets and white curtains, the family-run **Hotel Jan von Werth ❷,** Von-Werth-Str. 9, is near the center of town. From the station, walk up Bahnhofstr. to the market district and take a right on Von-Werth-Str. (☎365 00. Breakfast included. Reception 6:30am-10pm. Singles from €28, with bath €41; doubles from €53/62; triples €60. MC/V.) Ferries (€0.80) cross the Mosel to **Campingplatz Rhein-Mosel ❶,** Am Neuendorfer Eck. (☎827 19. Reception 8am-10pm. Open Apr.-Oct. 15. €4.50 per person, €2.50 per site.) **Kaffeewirtschaft ❷,** Münzpl. 14, serves light meals (€8-14) and mouth-watering desserts (€1.50-5) amid crimson walls and fresh roses. (Open M-Th 9am-midnight, F-Sa 9am-2am, Su 10am-midnight. MC/V.)

Trains run to: Bonn (30min., 3 per hr., €4.20-8.40); Cologne (1½hr., 4 per hr., €11-14); Frankfurt (2hr., 2-3 per hr., €13-26); Mainz (1hr., 3 per hr., €9); Trier (2hr., 2-3 per hr., €16). Across from the station is the **tourist office,** Bahnhofpl. 17, which gives out maps and book rooms at no charge. (☎100 43 99. Open May-Oct. M-F 9am-7pm, Sa-Su 10am-7pm; Nov.-Apr. M-F daily 9am-6pm.) **Postal Code:** 65068.

HEIDELBERG ☎06221

Sun-drenched Heidelberg (pop. 142,000) and its crumbling castle have lured scores of writers and artists over the years, from Goethe to Twain. Today, legions of visitors fill the length of Hauptstraße, where postcards and T-shirts sell like hotcakes and every sign is posted in four languages. Fortunately, the buzz of tourism doesn't detract from this university town's beautiful hillside setting above the Neckar River and its student-driven nightlife.

TRANSPORTATION AND PRACTICAL INFORMATION

Trains run to Frankfurt (50min., 2 per hr., €18-22), Mannheim (20min., 2 per hr., €6), and Stuttgart (40min., 1 per hr., €21-28). Within Heidelberg, single-ride **bus** tickets cost around €2; day passes (€5) are available on the bus. **Rhein-Neckar-Fahrgastschifffahrt** (☎201 81; www.rnf-schifffahrt.de), in front of the Kongresshaus, runs **ferries** all over Germany and cruises up the Neckar to Neckarsteinach (3hr., Easter-late Oct. every 1½hr. 9:30am-4:50pm, €9.50). Heidelberg's attractions are mostly in the eastern part of the city, along the south bank of the Neckar. From the train station, take any bus or streetcar to Bismarckpl., then walk east down **Hauptstraße,** the city's main thoroughfare, to the Altstadt. The **tourist office,** in front of the station, sells maps with a city guide (€1) and books rooms for a €3 fee and a small deposit. (☎138 8121. Open Apr.-Oct. M-Sa 9am-7pm, Su 10am-6pm; Nov.-Mar. M-Sa 9am-6pm.) The **Heidelberg Card** includes unlimited public transit and admission to most sights. (2-day card €14, 4-day €21.) The **post office** is at Sofienstr. 8-10. (Open M-F 9:30am-6pm, Sa 9:30am-1pm.) **Postal Code:** 69115.

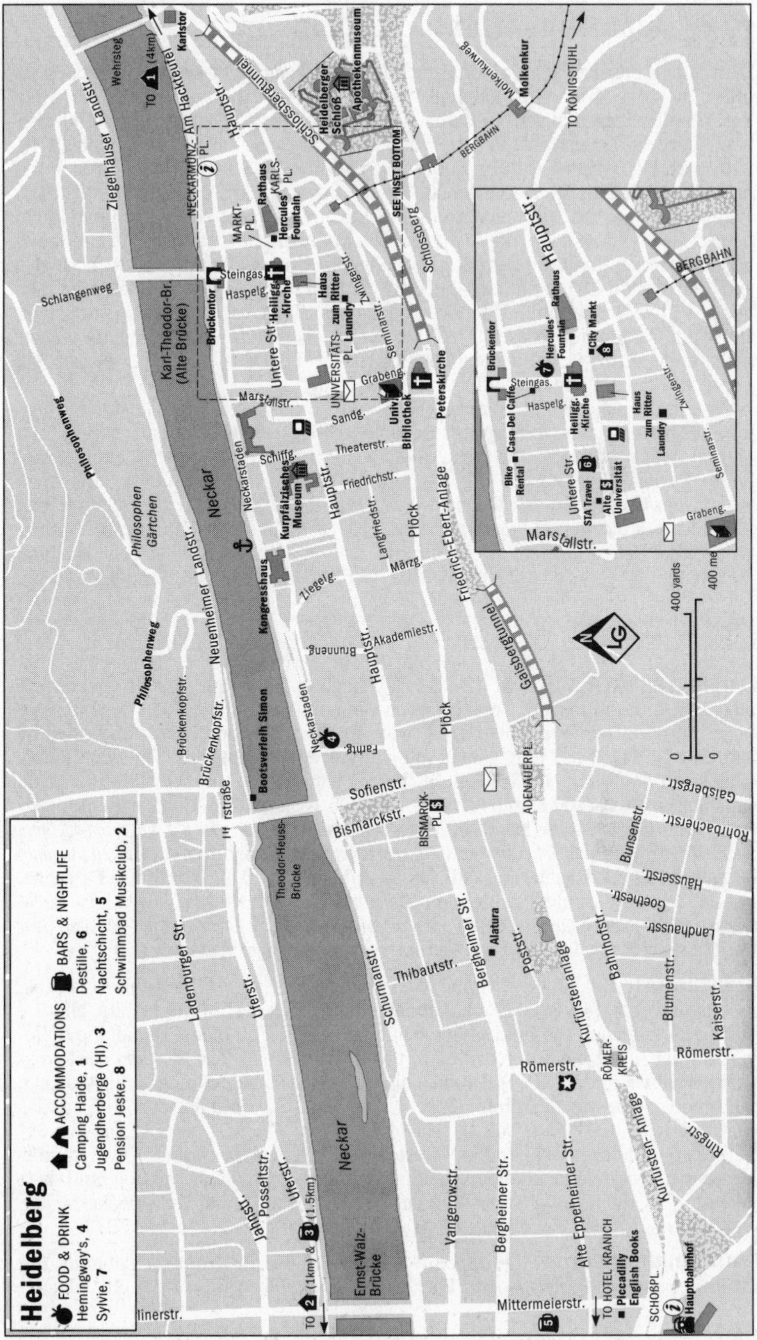
Heidelberg
FOOD & DRINK
Hemingway's, 4
Sylvie, 7
ACCOMMODATIONS
Camping Haide, 1
Jugendherberge (HI), 3
Pension Jeske, 8
BARS & NIGHTLIFE
Destille, 6
Nachtschicht, 5
Schwimmbad Musikclub, 2
Neckar
Karl-Theodor-Br. (Alte Brücke)
Theodor-Heuss-Brücke
Ernst-Walz-Brücke
Philosophenweg
Philosophen Gärtchen
Schlangenweg
Ziegelhäuser Landstr.
Neuenheimer Landstr.
Brückenkopfstr.
Ladenburger Str.
Uferstr.
Jahnstr.
Posseltstr.
Wehrsteg
Karlstor
Brückentor
Heiliggeist-Kirche
Rathaus
Hercules' Fountain
MARKT-PL.
KARLS-PL.
Heidelberger Schloß
Apothekenmuseum
Molkenkur
Molkenkurweg
BERGBAHN
TO KÖNIGSTUHL
Schlossbergtunnel
Schlossberg
Haus zum Ritter
Laundry
UNIVERSITÄTS-PL.
Univ. Bibliothek
Peterskirche
Kurpfälzisches Museum
Kongresshaus
Bootsverleih Simon
Hauptstr.
Untere Str.
Steingas.
Haspelg.
Marstallstr.
Neckarstaden
Sandg.
Theaterstr.
Friedrichstr.
Grabeng.
Seminarstr.
Zwingerstr.
Plöck
Friedrich-Ebert-Anlage
Gaisbergtunnel
Akademiestr.
Brunneng.
Ziegelg.
Märzg.
Langfriedstr.
Fahrtg.
Sofienstr.
Bismarckstr.
BISMARCK-PL.
ADENAUERPL.
Gaisbergstr.
Rohrbacherstr.
Bunsenstr.
Häusserstr.
Goethestr.
Landhausstr.
Bahnhofstr.
Blumenstr.
Kaiserstr.
Römerstr.
RÖMER-KREIS
Ringstr.
Kurfürstenanlage
Kurfürsten-Anlage
Poststr.
Alatura
Bergheimer Str.
Thibautstr.
Schurmanstr.
Vangerowstr.
Alte Eppelheimer Str.
Mittermeierstr.
TO HOTEL KRANICH
Piccadilly English Books
SCHOßPL.
Hauptbahnhof
SEE INSET BOTTOM
NECKARMÜNZ-PL.
Am Hackteufel
TO 1 (4km)
TO 2 (1km) & 3 (1.5km)
400 yards
400 meters
Bike Rental
Casa Del Caffe
City Markt
STA Travel
Alte Universität

ACCOMMODATIONS AND FOOD

In summer, reserve accommodations ahead. **Pension Jeske ❸,** Mittelbadg. 2, offers the area's friendliest lodgings, with a perfect location in the Altstadt. Take bus #33 (dir.: Ziegelhausen) to Rathaus/Kornmarkt. (☎237 33; www.pension-jeske-heidelberg.de. Reception 11am-1pm and 5-7pm. Reserve far ahead. Doubles €40, with bath €60; triples €60/75; quints with bath €100. Cash only.) To reach the **Jugendherberge (HI) ❷,** Tiergartenstr. 5, take bus #33 (dir.: Zoo-Sportzentrum) to Jugendherberge. Located next to one of Europe's largest zoos, this hostel also teems with wild species like *Schoolchildus germanius.* (☎65 11 90. Breakfast included. Reception until 2am. Reserve ahead. Dorms €24, under 27 €21; singles and doubles add €5 per person. AmEx/MC/V.) For camping, head to **Haide ❶.** Take bus #35 (dir.: Neckargmünd) to Orthopädisches Klinik, cross the river, turn right, and walk for 20min. (☎06223 21 11. Showers €0.50 per 5min. Electricity €2 per night. Reception 8-11:30am and 4-8pm. Open Apr. 11-Oct. 31. €4.70 per person, €3 per tent or RV, €1 per car. Cabins €13. Cash only.)

Restaurants near Hauptstr. are expensive; historic student pubs outside the center offer better values. **Hemingway's Bar-Café-Meeting Point ❷,** Fahrtg. 1, serves food on a crowded, shaded patio along the Neckar. (☎16 50 331; www.hemingways-hd.de. Lunch entrees from €4.10. Open Su-Th 9am-1am, F-Sa 9am-3am. Cash only.) Near Untere Str. and the river, **Sylvie ❷,** Steing. 11, serves affordable Italian specialties and regional salads for €5.50-10. (☎65 90 90. Open daily 10am-1am. Cash only.) Grocery stores are in Marktpl. and on adjoining side streets; **Alnatura,** Bergheimer 59-63, is a health-food store. (☎61 86 34. Open daily 9am-8pm.)

SIGHTS

HEIDELBERGER SCHLOß. Tourists lay siege to Heidelberg Castle every summer, and for good reason. Construction began on the castle early in the 14th century; though it has been destroyed twice by war (1622 and 1693) and once by lightning (1764), it has only gained in beauty over the centuries. The cool, musty wine cellar houses the **Großes Faß,** the largest wine cask ever used with a 221,726L capacity; the **Kleines Faß** holds a mere 125,000L. *(☎53 84 21. Grounds open daily 8am-6pm. English-language audio tour €3.50. English-language tours every hr. M-F 11:15am-4:15pm, Sa-Su 10:15am-4:15pm; €4, students €2. Schloß, Großes Faß, and Pharmaceutical Museum €3, students €1.50.)* Reach the castle by the uphill path (10min.) or by the **Bergbahn,** one of Germany's oldest cable cars. *(Take bus #11, dir.: Karlstor, or #33, dir.: Ziegelhausen, to Bergbahn/Rathaus. Cable cars leave from the parking lot next to the bus stop daily Mar.-Oct. every 10min. 9am-8pm; Nov.-Feb. every 20min. 9am-6pm. Round-trip €5.)*

UNIVERSITÄT. Heidelberg is home to Germany's oldest (est. 1386) and most prestigious university. Over 20 Nobel laureates have been part of the faculty, and the university launched the field of academic sociology. The oldest remaining buildings border the stone lion fountain of the Universitätspl. The **Museum der Universität Heidelberg** traces the institution's history; in the same building is the **Alte Aula,** the school's oldest auditorium. *(Grabeng. 1. ☎54 21 52. Open Apr.-Sept. Tu-Su 10am-6pm; Oct. Tu-Su 10am-4pm; Nov.-Mar. Tu-Sa 10am-4pm. €2.50, students €2; includes Studentenkarzer.)* Before 1914, students were exempt from prosecution by civil authorities due to a code of academic freedom, so crimes from plagiarism to grand theft were tried by the faculty. Guilty students were punished in the **Studentenkarzer** jail, and their colorful graffiti adorns the walls today. *(Augustinerg. 2. ☎54 35 54.)*

PHILOSOPHENWEG. On the opposite side of the Neckar from the Altstadt, the Philosophenweg (Philosopher's Path) has unbeatable views of the city. Famed thinkers Goethe, Ludwig Feuerbach, and Ernst Jünger once strolled here. On the top of **Heiligenberg** (Holy Mountain) lie the ruins of the 9th-century **St. Michael Basilika,** the 13th-century **Stefanskloster,** and an **amphitheater** built on the site of an ancient Celtic gathering place. *(To get to the path, take tram #1 or 3 to Tiefburg, or use the steep, stone-walled footpath 10m west of the Karl-Theodor-Brücke.)*

MARKTPLATZ. At the center of the Altstadt is the cobblestoned Marktpl., where accused witches and heretics were burned at the stake in the 15th century. Two of Heidelberg's oldest structures border the square. The 14th-century **Heiliggeistkirche** (Church of the Holy Spirit) is now used for Protestant worship; its tower offers great views of the city and mountains. The 16th-century inn **Haus Zum Ritter** is opposite the church. *(Church open M-Sa 11am-5pm, Su 1-5pm. Church free. Tower €1.)*

NIGHTLIFE

Most popular nightspots fan out from the **Marktplatz.** On the Neckar side of the Heiliggeistkirche, **Untere Straße** has the densest collection of bars in the city, and drunken revelers fill the narrow way until 2am in pleasant weather. **Steingasse,** off the Marktpl. toward the Neckar, also attracts crowds, and **Hauptstraße** harbors a fair number of higher-end venues. At **Nachtschicht,** in the Landfried-Komplex near the train station, university students dance to mixed beats in a basement resembling an old factory. (☎43 85 50; www.nachtschicht.com. Cover €3.50; M and F students €1.50. Open M and Th-Sa 10pm-4am, W 10pm-3am. Cash only.) A giant, life-like tree grows out of the forest-themed bar **Destille,** Unterstr. 16, where students drink themselves silly with quirky shots. (☎228 08. Open Su-Th noon-2am, F-Sa noon-3am. Cash only.) **Schwimmbad Musikclub,** Tiergartenstr. 13, near the youth hostel, attracts a sizable crowd with four levels of live music, dancing, and movies. (☎47 02 01. Open W-Th 8pm-3am, F-Sa 9pm-4am. Cash only.)

STUTTGART ☎0711

Porsche, Daimler-Benz, and a host of other corporate thoroughbreds keep Stuttgart (pop. 591,000) speeding along in the fast lane, but the main streets are never far from manicured gardens and ornate fountains. The city's amazing **mineral baths** *(Mineralbäder)*, fueled by Western Europe's most active mineral springs, draw young and old to their healing waters. The health-care facility **Mineralbad Leuze,** Am Leuzebad 2-6, has indoor and outdoor thermal pools. Take U1 or tram #2 to Mineralbäder. (☎216 42 10. Open daily 6am-9pm. Day card €14, students €10. 2hr. soak €5.50, ages 3-18 €3.80; 4hr. €7/5.40.) The superb **Staatsgalerie Stuttgart,** Konrad-Adenauer-Str. 30-32, displays Dalí, Kandinsky, and Picasso in its new wing, as well as paintings from the Middle Ages to the 19th century in its old wing. (☎47 04 00; www.staatsgalerie.de. Open Tu-W and F-Su 10am-8pm, Th 10am-9pm; 1st Sa of every month 10am-midnight. €8, students €6; W free.) The **Mercedes-Benz Museum,** Mercedesstr. 100, is a must for car-lovers. Take S1 (dir.: Ploschingen) to Gottlieb-Daimler-Stadion and look for signs. (☎173 00 00; www.mercedes-benz.com/museum. Open Tu-Su 9am-6pm. €8, students €4. Factory tour free.)

An international clientele crashes in bright, hip rooms with funky walls at **Alex 30 Hostel ❷,** Alexanderstr. 30. Take tram #15 (dir.: Ruhbank) to Eugenspl. (☎838 89 50; www.alex30-hostel.de. Breakfast €6. Linens €3. Dorms €19; singles €20-29; doubles €50. MC/V.) The comfortable rooms at the **Jugendgästehaus Stuttgart (HI) ❷,** Richard-Wagner-Str. 2, have views of the city. Take tram #15 (dir.: Ruhbank) or night bus #N8 to Bubenbad and take the next right. (☎24 11 32; jgh-stuttgart@internationaler-bund.de. Breakfast and linens included. Reception 24hr. Dorms €18, with bath €24; singles €21/26; doubles €37/42. 1-night stays add €2.50. AmEx/MC/V.) Look for mid-range restaurants in the pedestrian zone between Pfarrstr. and

Charlottenstr. **San's Sandwich Bar ❷,** Eberhardstr. 47, serves fresh sandwiches (€2.70-3.50) with plenty of vegetarian options; the homemade brownies are heavenly. (☎236 57 60; www.sans-stuttgart.de. Open M-F 8:30am-10pm, Sa 10am-7pm. Cash only.) The basement of the **Kaufhof Galeria,** Königstr. 6, has a **supermarket** (open M-F 9:30am-8pm, Sa 9am-8pm). Stuttgart's club scene doesn't pick up until after midnight, but when it does, **Theodor-Heuss-Straße, Rotebühlplatz,** and **Eberhardstraße** are the most popular areas. **Suite 212,** Theodor-Heuss-Str. 15, is a popular bar and lounge featuring DJs and video-mixing on weekends. (☎253 61 13; www.suite212.org. Beer €2.50-3. Mixed drinks €6.50-8. Open M-W 11am-2am, Th 11am-3am, F-Sa 11am-5am, Su 2pm-2am. Cash only.) The monthly magazine *Schwulst* (www.schwulst.de) has info on gay and lesbian nightlife.

Trains run to: Basel, SWI (3½hr., 2-4 per hr., €48-60); Berlin (6hr., 2 per hr., €112); Frankfurt (1-2hr., 2 per hr., €34-49); Munich (2½-3½hr., 2 per hr., €31-46); Paris, FRA (8hr., 4 per day, €82-97). The **tourist office,** Königstr. 1A, is across from the train station. (☎22 280. Open Apr.-Oct. M-F 9am-8pm, Sa 9am-6pm, Su 11am-6pm; Nov.-Mar. daily 1-6pm.) The **post office,** Arnulf-Klett-Pl. 2, is in the train station. (Open M-F 8:30am-6pm, Sa 8:30am-12:30pm.) **Postal Code:** 70173.

BLACK FOREST (SCHWARZWALD)

The eerie darkness of the Black Forest inspired German fairy tales including *Hansel and Gretel;* today, it lures hikers and skiers with its natural beauty and castle ruins. The gateway to the forest is Freiburg, accessible by train from Basel and Stuttgart. Visitors tend to favor exploring the area by bike or by car, as public transportation is sparse. Rail lines encircle the forest, but only two cut through. Bus service is more thorough, but slow and infrequent.

CONSTANCE (KONSTANZ) ☎07531

Located on the **Bodensee** (Lake Constance) and ranking among Germany's most popular vacation spots, Constance (pop. 29,000) has river promenades and narrow streets that wind around beautiful Baroque and Renaissance facades. Constance emerged unscathed from WWII, since part of the city extends into Switzerland and the Allies were leery of striking neutral territory. The **Münster** cathedral in the town center displays ancient religious relics beneath its soaring 76m Gothic spire. (Open M-F 10am-5pm, Sa-Su 12:30-5pm.) Wander down **Seestraße,** near the yacht harbor on the lake, or **Rheinsteig,** along the Rhine, for picturesque promenades. Constance boasts a number of **public beaches;** all are free and open from May to September. Take bus #5 to **Freibad Horn,** which is the largest and most crowded beach and has a nude sunbathing section enclosed by hedges.

Reserve accommodations a few weeks ahead in summer. The **Jugendherberge Otto-Möricke-Turm (HI) ❷,** Zur Allmannshöhe 18, has a terrific view, though it isn't within walking distance. Take bus #4 from the train station to Jugendherberge; turn back and head uphill on Zur Allmannshöhe. (☎322 62; www.jugendherberge-konstanz.de. Breakfast included. Dinner €4.50, compulsory for stays over 1 night. Linens €3.10. Reception Apr.-Oct. 8am-noon and 3-10pm; Nov.-Mar. 8am-noon and 5-10pm. Lockout 9:30am-noon. Curfew 10pm, house key for €20 deposit. Reserve 2 months ahead. Dorms €27, under 27 €24; additional nights €23/20. AmEx/MC/V.) In the center of town, **Pension Gretel ❸,** Zollernstr. 6-8, offers bright rooms at surprisingly low prices. (☎45 58 25; www.hotel-gretel.de. Breakfast included. Reserve at least a month ahead in summer. Singles €45; doubles €60-78; triples €94; quads €102; extra bed €18. Nov.-Mar. around €10 discount per person. Cash only.) Fall asleep to lapping waves at **DKV-Campingplatz Brudehofer ❶,** Fohrenbühlweg 50. Take bus #1 to Staad and walk for 10min. with the lake to your left. The campground is on the waterfront. (☎313 88; www.campingkonstanz.de. Warm showers €1. Reception closed noon-2:30pm. €3.50 per person, €2 per child, €3.10-4.50 per tent, €7 per RV, €0.50 per bike, €2.60 per car. Cash only.) **Café Zeitlos ❷**, St.-Stephans-Pl. 25, cooks all meals (€5.10-7.70) with local ingredients. (☎18 93 84. All-you-can-eat brunch Su 10am, €12.50. Open daily 10am-1am, kitchen open 10am-3pm and 6-10pm. Cash only.) **Groceries** are in the basement of the Karstadt department store on Augustinerpl. and Blätzlepl. (☎12 31 58. Open M-F 9:30am-8pm, Sa 9:30am-7pm.)

Trains run from Constance to most cities in southern Germany. BSB **ferries** leave hourly for ports around the lake. Buy tickets on board or at Hafenstr. 6, in the building behind the train station. (☎364 03 89; www.bsb-online.com. Open Apr.-Oct. M-Th 8am-noon and 1-4pm, F 8am-noon and 1-5pm.) The friendly **tourist office,** Bahnhofspl. 13, to the right of the train station, finds private rooms (€21-30) for a €2.50 fee. (☎13 30 30; www.konstanz.de. Open Apr.-Oct. M-F 9am-6:30pm, Sa 9am-4pm, Su 10am-1pm; Nov.-Mar. M-F 9:30am-12:30pm and 2-6pm.) **Postal Code:** 78462.

BAVARIA (BAYERN)

Bavaria is the Germany of Teutonic myth and Wagnerian opera. From the Baroque cities along the Danube to mad King Ludwig's castles high in the Alps, the region attracts more tourists than any other part of the country.

MUNICH (MÜNCHEN) ☎089

The capital and cultural center of Bavaria, Munich (pop. 1.3 million) is a sprawling, liberal metropolis where world-class museums, handsome parks, architecture, and a genial population create a city of astonishing vitality. *Müncheners* party zealously during *Fasching*, or Mardi Gras (Jan. 7-Feb. 20, 2007), shop with abandon during the Christ Child Market (Dec. 1-23, 2006), and chug unfathomable quantities of beer during the legendary Oktoberfest (Sept. 22-Oct. 7, 2007).

TRANSPORTATION

Flights: Flughafen München (☎97 52 13 13). S1 and 8 run from the airport to the Hauptbahnhof and Marienpl. (40min., every 20min. 3:57am-12:57am, €8 or 8 strips on the *Streifenkarte*); buy a *Tageskarte* that covers all zones (*Gesamtnetz;* €9). The **Lufthansa** shuttle bus makes the same trip (40min., every 20min., €9.50).

Trains: Munich's **Hauptbahnhof** (☎118 61) is the hub of southern Germany, with connections to: **Amsterdam, NTH** (7-9hr., 15 per day, €136); **Berlin** (6½hr., 2 per hr., €96); **Cologne** (6hr., 2-4 per hr., €112); **Frankfurt** (4hr., 2 per hr., €75); **Füssen** (2hr., 1 per hr. 6am-9pm); **Hamburg** (6hr., 1-2 per hr., €115); **Paris, FRA** (8-10hr., 6 per day, €125); **Prague, CZR** (6-7hr., 7 per day, €50); **Salzburg, AUT** (2hr., 2 per hr., €26); **Vienna, AUT** (5hr., 1 per hr., €50); **Zürich, SWI** (5hr., 5 per day, €60). Purchase a **Bayern-Ticket** (single €18, 2-5 people €25) for unlimited train transit in Bavaria and to Salzburg M-F 9am-3am. **EurAide,** in the station, provides free train info and sells tickets. **Reisezentrum** info counters at the station are open daily 7am-9:30pm.

Ride Share: Mitfahrzentrale, Lämmerstr. 6 (☎194 40). Arranges intercity transportation with drivers going the same way. Around €30. Open M-Sa 8am-8pm.

Public Transportation: MVV (☎41 42 43 44) is the public transport system. The U-Bahn (U; subway) runs Su-Th 5am-12:30am, F-Sa 5am-2am. S-Bahn (S) trains run from 3:30am until 2 or 3am. Night buses and trams serve Munich's dedicated clubbers (route number prefixed by "N"). Eurail, Inter Rail, and German railpasses are valid on the S-Bahn but *not* on the U-Bahn, streetcars, or buses.

Tickets: Buy tickets at the blue vending machines and validate them in the blue boxes marked with an "E" before entering the platform. If you jump the fare *(Schwarzfahren),* you risk a €40 fine.

Prices: Single-ride tickets €2.20 (valid 3hr.). **Short-trip** *(Kurzstrecke)* tickets €1.10 (1hr. or 2 stops on the U- or S-Bahn, 4 stops on a streetcar or bus). A **10-strip ticket** *(Streifenkarte)* costs €10 and can be used by more than 1 person. Cancel 2 strips per person for a normal ride, or 1 strip for a short trip; for rides beyond the city center, cancel 2 strips per zone. A **single-day ticket** *(Single-Tageskarte)* is valid until 6am the next day (€4.50). **3-day pass** €11. The **Munich Welcome Card,** at the tourist office (p. 462), also has transport discounts. The **XXL Ticket** gives daylong transit on all transport in Munich and surroundings (single €13; up to 5 people €23).

Taxis: Taxi-München-Zentrale (☎216 10 or 194 10). Women can ask for female drivers.

Bike Rental: Radius Bikes (☎59 61 13), in the Hauptbahnhof, behind the lockers opposite tracks 30-36. €3 per hr., €14 per day. €50 or passport deposit. Open daily May to mid-Oct. 10am-6pm. 10% student or Eurailpass discount.

ORIENTATION

Downtown Munich is split into quadrants by thoroughfares running east-west and north-south. These intersect at Munich's central square, **Marienplatz,** and link the traffic rings at Karlsplatz (called Stachus by locals) in the west, Isartorplatz in the east, Odeonsplatz in the north, and Sendlinger Tor in the south. In the east beyond the Isartor, the Isar River flows north-south. The **Hauptbahnhof** is just beyond Karlspl. to the west of the ring. To get to Marienpl. from the station, use the main exit and make a right on Bahnhofpl., then a left on Bayerstr. heading east through Karlspl., and continue straight. Or, take any S-Bahn to Marienpl. The **university** is to the north amid the budget restaurants of the **Schwabing** district; to the east of Schwabing is the **English Garden,** to the west, the **Olympiapark.** South of downtown is the **Glockenbachviertel,** filled with nightlife hot spots and gay bars. A seedy area with hotels and sex shops surrounds the Hauptbahnhof. Oktoberfest takes place on the large and open **Theresienwiese,** southeast of the train station on the U4 and 5 lines.

PRACTICAL INFORMATION

The most comprehensive list of services, events, and museums can be found in the English-language monthly *Munich Found* (€3), available at newsstands.

Tourist Offices: Main office (☎23 39 65 55), on the front side of the Hauptbahnhof, next to the SB-Markt on Bahnhofpl. Books rooms for free with a 10-15% deposit, sells English-language city maps (€0.30), and sells the **Munich Welcome Card** for transportation and sights discounts (1-day €7.50, 3-day €18). Open M-Sa 9am-8pm, Su 10am-6pm. **Branch office** on Marienpl. at the entrance to the Neues Rathaus tower. Books tickets for concerts and other events. MC/V. **EurAide** (☎59 38 89), room #2 along track 11 of the Hauptbahnhof. Books train tickets for free, explains public transportation, sells maps (€0.50), and books English-language city tours. Pick up the free brochure *Inside Track.* Open June-Sept. M-Sa 7:45am-12:45pm and 2-6pm, Su 7:45am-12:45pm; Oct. daily 7:45am-12:45pm and 2-4pm; Nov.-Apr. daily 8am-noon and 1-4pm; May daily 7:45am-12:45pm and 2-4:30pm.

Tours: Mike's Bike Tours, Bräuhausstr. 10 (☎25 54 39 88; www.mikesbiketours.com). If you only have 1 day in Munich, take this tour. Starting from the Altes Rathaus on Marienpl., the 4hr., 6.5km city tour includes a *Biergarten* break. Tours leave daily mid-Apr. to Aug. 11:30am and 4pm; Sept. to mid-Nov. and Mar. to mid-Apr. 2:30pm. Look for coupons at youth hostels. €24.

Consulates: Canada, Tal 29 (☎219 95 70). Open M-F 9am-noon; 2-4pm by appointment only. **Ireland,** Dennigerstr. 15 (☎20 80 59 90). Open M-F 9am-noon. **UK,** Bürkleinstr. 10, 4th fl. (☎21 10 90). Open M-F 8:45-11:30am and 1-3:15pm. **US,** Königinstr. 5 (☎288 80). Open M-F 1-4pm.

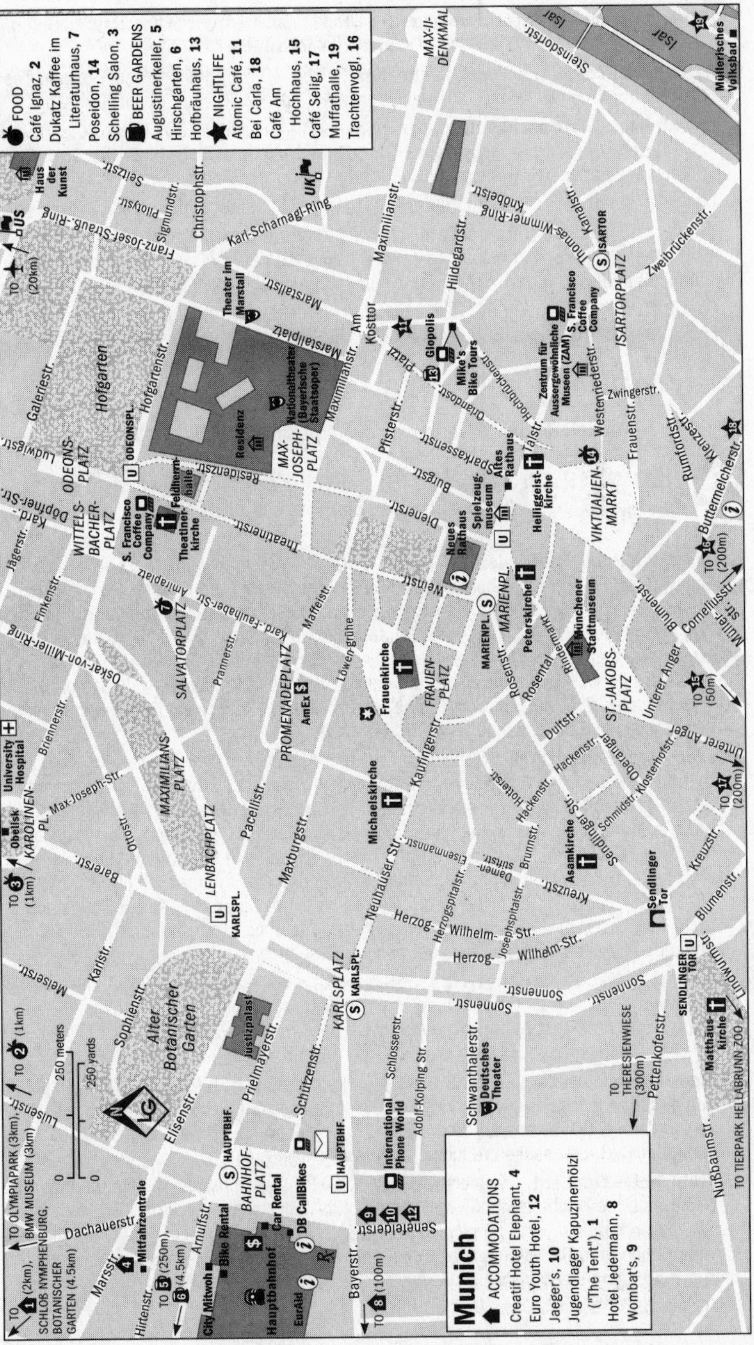
Munich
ACCOMMODATIONS
Creatif Hotel Elephant, 4
Euro Youth Hotel, 12
Jaeger's, 10
Jugendlager Kapuzinerhölzl ("The Tent"), 1
Hotel Jedermann, 8
Wombat's, 9
FOOD
Café Ignaz, 2
Dukatz Kaffee im Literaturhaus, 7
Poseidon, 14
Schelling Salon, 3
BEER GARDENS
Augustinerkeller, 5
Hirschgarten, 6
Hofbräuhaus, 13
NIGHTLIFE
Atomic Café, 11
Bei Carla, 18
Café Am Hochhaus, 15
Café Selig, 17
Muffathalle, 19
Trachtenvogl, 16

Currency Exchange: ReiseBank (☎551 08 13), at the front of the Hauptbahnhof. Slightly cheaper than other banks. Open daily 7am-10pm.

GLBT Resources: Gay services information (☎260 30 56), hotline open 7-10pm. **Lesbian information** (☎725 42 72), hotline open M and W 2:30-5pm, Tu 11:30am-1pm.

Laundromat: SB Waschcenter, Lindwurmstr. 124. Wash €3.50 (soap €0.30), dry €0.60 per 10min. Open daily 7am-11pm. **Branch** at Untersbergstr. 8. U2, 7, or 8 to Untersbergstraße. Free wireless Internet. Same prices and hours.

Emergency: Police: ☎110. **Ambulance** and **Fire:** ☎112. **Medical:** ☎192 22.

Internet Access: easyInternetCafé, on Bahnhofpl. next to the post office. Over 400 PCs. Prices depend on demand (around €2.20-2.40 per hr.); rates are cheapest after midnight and can go down to €1.70. Unlimited pass for 24hr. €5. Open 24hr.

Post Office: Bahnhofpl. In the yellow building opposite the Hauptbahnhof exit. Open M-F 7:30am-8pm, Sa 9am-4pm. **Postal Code:** 80335.

ACCOMMODATIONS AND CAMPING

Lodgings in Munich tend to be either seedy, expensive, or booked solid.

> **REMINDER.** HI-affiliated hostels in Bavaria generally do not admit guests over age 26, except families or groups of adults with young children.

Euro Youth Hotel, Senefelderstr. 5 (☎59 90 88 11; www.euro-youth-hotel.de). From the Bayerstr. exit of the Hauptbahnhof, turn left on Bayerstr., then right on Senefelderstr.; the hostel is on the left. The fun and noisy travelers' bar serves *Augustinerbräu* (€2.80) daily 6pm-4am, lending the hostel a frat-house atmosphere. Breakfast buffet €3.90. Internet access €1 per 20min., wireless €3 per 4hr. Wash €2.80. Dry €1.30. Reception 24hr. Dorms €18.50; beds in 3- to 5-person rooms €22; singles without bathroom €39; doubles €50, with shower, phone, and breakfast €60; quads €84. Rates vary; in winter, cheapest beds available online. MC/V. ❷

Jugendlager Kapuzinerhölzl (The Tent), In den Kirschen 30 (☎141 43 00; www.the-tent.de). Streetcar #17 from the Hauptbahnhof (dir.: Amalienburgstr.) to Botanischer Garten (15min.). Follow the signs straight on Franz-Schrank-Str. and turn left onto In den Kirschen; The Tent is on the right. Join 250 international "campers" under a gigantic tent on a wooden floor. Evening campfires. Free city tours in German and English on W mornings. Kitchen and laundry available. Free lockers. Internet access €0.50 per 15min. Key deposit €25 or passport. Reception 24hr. Open June-Aug. €9 gets you a foam pad, wool blankets, bathrooms, shower facilities, and breakfast. Beds €12. Camping tent sites €5.50, €5.50 per person. Cash only. ❶

Wombat's, Senefelderstr. 1 (☎59 98 91 80; www.wombats.at/munich-hostel/index.php). Unusual touches include a glass-enclosed "winter garden" and a free welcome drink. Breakfast buffet €4. Internet €1 per 20min., wireless €3 per 4hr. Reception 24hr. Dorms €22; private rooms €62 per person. Cash only. ❷

Jaegers, Senefelderstr. 3 (☎55 52 81; www.jaegershotel.de). Modern, colorful hostel with a mellow lounge and welcoming English-speaking staff. Reception 24hr. Bed in 40-person dorm €19.50; smaller dorms €21-25; singles with bathroom €45; doubles with bathroom €78. Low season reduced rates. AmEx/MC/V. ❷

Creatif Hotel Elephant, Lämmerstr. 6 (☎55 57 85; www.creatif-hotel-elephant.com), 300m from the Hauptbahnhof. From the Arnulfstr. exit, take a quick right on Pfefferstr., turn left on Hirtenstr., and go right on Lämmerstr. All rooms have colorful decor, private bath, phone, and TV. Breakfast included. Free Internet access. Reception 24hr. Singles from €39; doubles from €59. Extra beds €15. Best rates online. AmEx/MC/V. ❹

Hotel Jedermann, Bayerstr. 95 (☎54 32 40; www.hotel-jedermann.de). Exit the Hauptbhanhof at Bayerstr., make a right, and walk for 5-10min.; the hotel is on your left. Or take tram #18 or 19 (dir.: Freiham Süd) to Hermann-Lingg-Str. Beautiful rooms, inviting common areas, and welcoming staff at this family-owned hotel and pension. Satellite TV and phones available. Large breakfast buffet included. Free Internet access. Singles from €34; doubles from €49. Extra bed €15. MC/V. ❸

FOOD

For an authentic Bavarian lunch, spread a *Brez'n* (pretzel) with *Leberwurst* (liverwurst) or cheese. *Weißwürste* (white veal sausages) are a regional specialty; don't eat the skin, just slice them open for their tender meat. The tasty *Leberkäse* is a pinkish loaf of ground beef and bacon; *Leberknödel* are liver dumplings.

Off **Ludwigstraße,** the university district supplies students with inexpensive, filling meals. Many reasonably priced restaurants and cafes cluster on **Schellingstraße, Amalienstraße,** and **Türkenstraße** (U3 or 6 to Universität). Munich is also the place where someone first connected the "beer" concept to the "garden" concept to create the **beer garden.** Now they're all over the city (see **Nightlife,** p. 467).

Dukatz Kaffee im Literaturhaus, Salvatorpl. 1 (☎291 96 00; www.dukatzmunich.de). The center of literary events in Munich since 1997. Gourmet food (€7-9) complements creative drink options (€2-4). Sip a cup of coffee and people-watch—you'll be observing the city's trendiest writers. Open M-Sa 10am-1am, Su 10am-7pm. Cash only. ❸

Café Ignaz, Georgenstr. 67 (☎271 60 93). U2 to Josephspl., then take Adelheidstr. 1 block north and turn right on Georgenstr. Dinners range from crepes to stir-fry dishes (€5-9) at this eco-friendly cafe. Breakfast buffet M and W-F 8-11:30am (€7); lunch buffet M-F noon-2pm (€6.50); brunch buffet Sa-Su 9am-1:30pm (€8). Open M and W-F 8am-10pm, Tu 11am-10pm, Sa-Su 9am-10pm. AmEx. ❷

Schelling Salon, Schellingstr. 54 (☎272 07 88). U3 or U6 to Universität. Bavarian *Knödel* and billiards since 1872. Rack up at tables where Lenin, Rilke, and Hitler once played (€7 per hr.). Breakfast €3-5.10. German entrees €4-11. Open M and Th-Su 6:30am-1am. Kitchen closes midnight. A free **billiard museum** covers the history of pool dating back to the Pharaohs; open by advance request. Cash only. ❸

Augustiner Beerhall and Restaurant, Neuhauser Str. 27 (☎23 18 32 57). This restaurant, between Marienpl. and the train station, offers Bavarian specialties and Augustiner brew (*Maß* €6). English menu. Entrees €4-13.50. Open daily 10am-midnight. ❸

Poseidon, Westenriederstr. 13 (☎29 92 96), off the Viktualienmarkt. Bowls of *bouillabaisse* with bread (€10) in a bustling fish-market atmosphere. Join Müncheners in the know for the special sushi menu on Th (€20). Other seafood dishes €4-13. Open M-W 8am-6:30pm, Th-F 8am-7pm, Sa 8am-4pm. Cash only. ❸

SIGHTS

RESIDENZ. Down the pedestrian zone from Odeonspl., the ornate rooms of the Residenz (Palace) celebrate the wealth left behind by the Wittelsbach dynasty. The **Schatzkammer** (treasury) contains crowns, swords, precious stones, and ivory. The **Residenzmuseum** is comprised of the Wittelsbach apartments and State Rooms, a collection of European porcelain, and a 17th-century court chapel. *(Max-Joseph-Pl. 3. U3-6 to Odeonspl. ☎29 06 71. Open daily Apr. to mid-Oct. 9am-6pm, Th 9am-8pm; mid-Oct. to Mar. 10am-4pm. German-language tours meet outside museum entrance Su 11am. Schatzkammer and Residenzmusuem each €6, students €5. Combo ticket €9/8.)* Behind the Residenz, the manicured **Hofgarten** shelters the lovely temple of Diana. *(Free.)*

> **!** Be wary when passing through Marienpl. With all the tourists looking upward at the Glockenspiel, pickpockets have a field day.

MARIENPLATZ. The **Mariensäule,** an ornate 1683 monument to the Virgin Mary, commemorates the city's survival of the Thirty Years' War. At the **Neues Rathaus,** the **Glockenspiel** chimes and pleases tourists with a display of jousting knights and dancing coopers. Look, but watch out for pickpockets! At 9pm, a mechanical watchman marches out and the Guardian Angel escorts the *Münchner Kindl* (Munich Child) to bed. *(Daily at 11am, noon, 3pm; in summer also 5pm.)* A sweeping view of the plaza makes the neo-Gothic **tower** of the Neues Rathaus worth a visit. *(Open daily 10am-7pm. €2, under 19 €1.)* Adorning the **Altes Rathaus** tower, at the far end of Marienpl., are all of Munich's coats of arms but one: the swastika emblem of the Nazi era.

PETERSKIRCHE AND FRAUENKIRCHE. Across from the Neues Rathaus, the 12th-century Peterskirche is the city's oldest parish church. Scale over 300 steps for a spectacular view of Munich. *(Open M-Tu and Th-Su 7:30am-7pm. Tower €1.50, students €1.)* From Marienpl., take Kaufingerstr. one block toward the Hauptbahnhof to the onion-domed towers of the 15th-century Frauenkirche—one of Munich's most notable landmarks and an emblem of the city. *(Frauenpl. 1 Tower open daily 7am-7pm. €3.50, students €1.50, under 6 free.)*

ENGLISCHER GARTEN. More expansive than New York's Central Park and London's Hyde Park, the Englischer Garten is the largest metropolitan public park in Europe. On sunny days, the city turns out to bike, play badminton, or ride horseback. The garden includes a Japanese tea house, a Chinese pagoda, a Greek temple, and German beer gardens. Nude sunbathing areas are designated FKK (*Frei-Körper-Kultur;* free body culture) on signs and park maps. Daring *Münchener*s surf the rapids of the Eisbach, which flows through the park.

SCHLOß NYMPHENBURG. After a decade spent trying for an heir, Ludwig I celebrated the birth of his son in 1662 by erecting an elaborate summer playground northwest of the city. Today, the swans of Schloß Nymphenburg have become camera fodder for the hundreds of tourists flocking for the perfect shot. In the **Marstallmuseum** (Carriage Museum), learn about the means of 17th-century royal travel. *(Streetcar #17, dir.: Amalienburgstr., to Schloß Nymphenburg. ☎17 90 86 68. All attractions open Apr. to mid-Oct. M-W and F-Su 9am-6pm, Th 9am-8pm; mid-Oct. to Mar. daily 10am-4pm. Schloß €5, students €4. Marstallmuseum €4/3. Entire complex €10/8. Park grounds free. English-language audio tour free.)*

MUSEUMS

Getting the most out of Munich's museums requires days of exhaustive perusal. The *Münchner Volkshochschule* (☎48 00 62 29) gives €6 exhibit tours. You can buy a **day pass** to state-owned museums at the tourist office (€15). These state-owned museums are all **€1 on Sunday.**

DEUTSCHES MUSEUM. Even if you don't know (or care) how engines power a Boeing 747, the Deutsches Museum's more than 50 departments on science and technology will still keep you entertained and educated. Exhibits include one of the first telephones and a recreated subterranean labyrinth of mining tunnels, as well as realistic models of medieval alchemist laboratories and musical instruments from all over the world. *(Museuminsel 1. S1-8 to Isartor or streetcar #18 to Deutsches Museum. ☎217 91; www.deutsches-museum.de. Open daily 9am-5pm. €8.50, students €3. English-language guidebook €4.)*

BMW MUSEUM. This sleek driving museum, housed in a silver globe, displays past, present, and future BMW products. The main building is closed for renovation until summer 2007; in the meantime, the foot of the Olympiaturm houses a temporary exhibit. *(Main building at Petuelring 130. U3 to Olympiazentrum. ☎38 22 56 52; www.bmw-museum.de. Check website for post-renovation prices and hours.)*

ENTERTAINMENT

Monatsprogramm (€1.50) and *Munich Found* (€3) list schedules for Munich's stages, museums, and festivals. In July, a magnificent **opera festival** arrives at the **Bayerische Staatsoper** (Bavarian National Opera), Max-Joseph-Pl. 2. (Tickets ☎21 85 01, info 21 85 19 19; www.bayerische.staatsoper.de. U3-6 to Odeonspl. or streetcar #19 to Nationaltheater. Standing-room and student tickets €8, sold 1hr. before performances; find out which shows have these available 2 weeks in advance. Box office for standing-room and student tickets at the theater. Regular box office at Marstallpl. 5; call ☎2185 1920; open M-F 10am-6pm, Sa 10am-1pm. No performances Aug. to mid-Sept.)

NIGHTLIFE

BEER GARDENS (BIERGÄRTEN)

Augustinerkeller, Arnulfstr. 52 (☎59 43 93), at Zirkus-Krone-Str. S1-8 to Hackerbrücke. From the station, make a right on Arnulfstr. Founded in 1824, Augustiner is viewed by many as the finest *Biergarten* in town, with enormous *Brez'n* and dim lighting beneath 100-year-old chestnut trees. Don't miss the delicious, sharp *Augustiner* beer (*Maß* €6.50). Food €3-15. Open daily 10am-1am. Kitchen closes 10:30pm. AmEx/MC/V.

Hirschgarten, Hirschgarten 1 (☎17 25 91). Streetcar #17 (dir.: Amalienburgstr.) to Romanpl. Walk south to the end of Guntherstr. Europe's largest *Biergarten* (seating 9000) is boisterous and crowded. Check out the carousel and deer. Entrees €5-15. *Maß* €5.50. Open daily 9am-midnight. Kitchen closes 10pm. Cash only.

Hofbräuhaus, Platzl 9 (☎290 13 60), 2 blocks from Marienpl. Come here for the full *Biergarten* experience: this is as jolly, as festive, and as loud as it gets. Go in the early afternoon to avoid tourists. *Maß* €6.20. *Weißwürste* €4.20. Open daily 9am-midnight.

BARS

Tractenvogl, Reichenbachstr. 47 (☎201 51 60). U1-2 or 7-8 to Frauenhofer. Enjoy one of their 32 types of hot chocolate (some with alcohol, of course) in a cozy

THE LOCAL STORY

THE PROPER *PROST!*

It is a truth universally acknowl edged that a European traveler i possession of a dry throat mus be in want of a German *Bier* Careless drinkers be warned: Ger man drinking protocol is simple but strictly enforced. Bavarian custom requires each drinker t wait until everyone has receive his or her beverage before an glass is touched. Once the whol party has been served, everyon greets each other with a heart *"Prost"* (cheers). Failure to mak eye contact with the perso whose glass you're clinking i invidious at best, and at worst i supposed to result in seven year of bad sex. (*Let's Go,* however believes that readers are respon sible for the quality of their ow sex lives.) After glasses hav been tapped all the away aroun the group, everyone hits his or he *stein* to the table before takin the first sip.

This final tap is said to dat back to King Ludwig I, who sen the political and social pressure of ruling Munich and Bavari straight to his belly, growing quit fat in his old age. When he woul *Prost* his companions at the di ner table, he would be s exhausted from holding up hi *Maß* that he had to set down hi beer again before he could mus ter up the energy to drink.

So channel the spirit of Lud wig, get ready for some eye con tact, and *Prost* with heartfel drunken pride.

living room with chic lamps. F live bands. Su chocolate fondue (reservations required). Happy hour daily 6-7pm; Astra beer €1.50. Open Su-Th 10am-1am, F-Sa 10am-3am. Cash only.

Café Am Hochhaus, Blumenstr. 29 (☎89 05 81 52). U1-3 or 6 to Sendlinger Tor. Sometimes a dance party, sometimes a relaxed cafe, the mood at the popular Café Am Hochhaus changes with the nightly crowd. Open M-Sa 8pm-3am or later. Cash only.

CLUBS

Muffathalle, Zellstr. 4 (☎45 87 50 10; www.muffathalle.de), in Haidhausen. Take S1-8 to Rosenheimerpl. and walk toward the river on Rosenheimer Str. for 2 blocks, or take streetcar #18 (dir.: St. Emmeram) to Deutsches Museum. This former power plant generates hip-hop, spoken word, jazz, and dance performances. Cover from €5. Open M-Sa 7pm-4am, Su 4pm-1am. Buy tickets online or through München Ticket.

Atomic Café, Neuturmstr. 5 (☎228 30 52), around the corner from the Hofbräuhaus, is the Bavarian take on late-60s glory. Sticks to 60s and 70s beats, avoiding disco. Live Britpop, R&B, ska, and reggae. Beer €3.70 per 0.5L. Cover €3-7. Happy hour 9-10pm; mixed drinks €6. Open Tu-Th 10pm-3am, F-Sa 10pm-5am. Cash only.

Café Selig, Hans-Sachs Str. 3 (☎23 88 88 78; www.einfachselig.de). U1 or 2 to Frauenhofer Str. Join the diverse crowd (mixed by day, mostly gay Sa-Su and at night) at this unpretentious cafe and bar with international coffees, homemade cakes, and strudel (€5-7). Open M and W 9pm-1am, F 9am-3am, Sa-Su 9am-late. AmEx/MC/V.

Bei Carla, Buttermelcherstr. 9 (☎22 79 01). S1-8 to Isartor, then walk 1 block south on Zweibrückenstr., take a right on Rumfordstr., turn left on Klenzestr., and take another left onto Buttermelcherstr. This friendly lesbian bar is a real find. Women flock here for conversation, cocktails, and darts. Open M-Sa 4pm-1am, Su 6pm-1am. Cash only.

DAYTRIP FROM MUNICH: DACHAU

Arbeit Macht Frei (Work Will Set You Free) was the first message prisoners saw as they passed through the iron gate of the **Jourhaus** on the way into Dachau, where over 206,000 "undesirables" were interned between 1933 and 1945. The Third Reich's first concentration camp, Dachau was primarily a work camp rather than a death camp like Auschwitz; knowing the Allies would not bomb prisoners, the SS reserved it for the construction of armaments. The walls, gates, and crematorium were restored in 1962 and now form a **memorial** to the victims. (Open Tu-Su 9am-5pm.) Located in the former administrative buildings, the **museum** examines pre-1930s anti-Semitism, the rise of Nazism, the establishment of the concentration camp system, and the lives of prisoners through a gathering of photographs, newspapers, documents, and other artifacts. A **short film** (22min.) screens in English at 11:30am, 2, and 3:30pm. Displays in the **Bunker,** the prison and torture chamber, chronicle prisoners' lives and the barbarism of SS guards. Two English-language **tours** depart from the museum: 30min. tours of the museum (June-Aug. M-F 12:30pm, Sa-Su 11am and 12:30pm; Sept.-May Sa-Su 12:30pm; €1.50) and 2½hr. tours of the memorial site. (June-Aug. M-F 1:30pm, Sa-Su noon and 1:30pm; Sept.-May Sa-Su 1:30pm; €3.) Or, purchase the worthwhile audio tour (€3) for a self-

THE REAL DEAL. As a 50th birthday gift, the Nazi party built Adolf Hitler a mountain retreat near Berchtesgaden. Afraid of heights, Hitler rarely visited the **Eagle's Nest.** The resort no longer exists, but the site remains a draw. While this region has excellent hiking and the views are hard to beat, the Eagle's Nest is probably best skipped by those looking for insight into the man it was built for.

guided walk around the camp. Food and beverages are not available at Dachau; pack your own. Take the S2 (dir.: Petershausen) to Dachau (20min.; €4 or 4 strips on the *Streifenkarte*). Then take bus #724 (dir.: Kräutergarte) or 726 (dir.: Saubachsiedlung) to KZ-Gedenkstätte (10min.; €1 or 1 strip on the *Streifenkarte*).

PASSAU ☎0851

Baroque arches cast long shadows across the cobblestone alleys of Passau (pop. 51,000), a two-millennium-old city situated at the confluence of the Danube, the Inn, and the Ilz rivers. Passau's crowning attraction is the Baroque **Stephansdom,** Dompl., where the world's largest church organ looms above the choir. Its 17,774 pipes and multiple keyboards can fit five organists. (Open daily in summer 6:30am-7pm; in winter 6:30am-6pm. Church free. Tours €3, students €1.50. Organ concerts May 2-Oct. and Dec. 27-31 M-F noon; €3, students €1. May-Oct. Th 7:30pm. €5-8, students €3-4.) Behind the cathedral is the **Residenz,** home to the **Domschatz,** an extravagant collection of tapestries and gold. Enter through the back of the Stephansdom, to the right of the altar. (☎39 33 74. Open Easter-Oct. M-Sa 10am-4pm. €2.50, students €1.50.) Various floods have left their high-water marks on the outer wall of the 13th-century Gothic **Rathaus.** (Open daily Apr.-Dec. 10am-4pm. €1.50, students €1.) Over the Luitpoldbrücke is the former palace of the bishopric, **Veste Oberhaus,** now home to the **Cultural History Museum.**

Fahrrad Pension ❶, Bahnhofstr. 33, has cheap beds over a bakery. (☎34784; www.fahrrad-pension.com. 4-bed dorms €10. Cash only.) Possibly the most oddly shaped hotel you'll ever stay in, the **Rotel Inn ❸,** Hauptbahnhof/Donauufer, is built like a sleeping man, with tiny rooms just wide enough to fit a bed. (☎951 60. Breakfast €5. Reception 24hr. Singles €25; doubles €30. Cash only.) Cheap places to eat fill the student district around **Innstraße,** parallel to the Inn River. Get fresh meat, baked goods, sandwiches, and salads at the supermarket **Schmankerl Passage,** Ludwigstr. 6. (Open M-F 7am-6pm, Sa 7am-4pm.) There is an **open-air market** in Dompl. Tuesday and Friday mornings. Nightlife centers around the university and across the footbridge in the **Innenstadt.** Get a hold of the free German-language magazine *Pasta*, which lists the hottest venues.

Trains depart every 2hr. for: Frankfurt (4½hr., €67); Munich (2hr., 1-2 per hr., €26); Nuremberg (2hr., €36); Vienna, AUT (3½hr., €38). The **tourist office** is at Rathauspl. 3. (☎95 59 80. Open Easter to mid-Oct. M-F 8:30am-6pm, Sa-Su 9am-4pm; mid-Oct. to Easter M-Th 8:30am-5pm, F 8:30am-4pm.) A branch is at Bahnhofstr. 36. **Postal Code:** 94032.

NUREMBERG (NÜRNBERG) ☎0911

Before it witnessed the fanaticism of Hitler's massive Nazi rallies, Nuremberg (pop. 491,000) hosted Imperial Diets in the first *Reich*. Today, the remnants of both regimes draw visitors to the city, which new generations have rechristened *Stadt der Menschenrechte* (City of Human Rights). Locally, the city is known more for its Christmas market, toy fairs, sausages, and gingerbread than for its politics.

Jugendgästehaus (HI) ❷, Burg 2, sits in a castle above the city. From the tourist office, follow Königstr. through Lorenzerpl. and over the bridge to the Hauptmarkt, head toward the fountain on the left, and go right on Burgstr. (☎230 93 60. Reception 7am-1am. Curfew 1am. Dorms €19-21. MC/V.) If you must pass up the magnificence of the HI hostel, then the quirkily named rooms of Lette'm Sleep ❷, Frauentormauer 42, are only a short walk away from the train station. Take the first left immediately after entering the Altstadt through Königpl. (☎992 81 28. Linens €3. Free Internet. Reception 24hr. 8-bed women-only dorms €16; 5- to 6-bed co-ed dorms €18; doubles €48-52. MC/V.) In the southwestern corner of the Altstadt, Zum Gulden Stern ❷, Zirkelschmiedg. 26, is the world's oldest bratwurst kitchen. (☎205 92 98. 6 for €6. Other Frankish entrees €5-10. Open daily 11am-10pm. AmEx/MC/V.) Cheaper fare is at the Bratwursthäusle ❶, Rathauspl. 1. Goods to go include three *Rostbratwurst* in a *Weckla* (roll) for €1.80, six *Würste* with *Kraut* for €3.70, and *Spargel* (white asparagus) for €4. (☎22 76 95. Eat-in entrees €3-8. Open daily 10am-11pm. Cash only.) Super Markt Straub, Hauptmarkt 12, is near the Frauenkirche. (Open M-F 8am-6pm, Sa 8am-6pm.) The Hauptmarkt fills with produce vendors in the mornings and afternoons.

Allied bombing left little of old Nuremberg untouched, but its castle and some other buildings have been reconstructed. The walled-in **Handwerkerhof** near the station is a tourist trap disguised as a history lesson; head up Königstr. for the real sights. Go left for the pillared **Straße der Menschenrechte** (Avenue of Human Rights) as well as the gleaming glass **Germanisches Nationalmuseum,** Kartäuserg. 1, which chronicles German art since prehistoric times. (☎133 10. Open Tu-Su 10am-6pm, W 10am-9pm. €5, students €4. W 6-9pm free.) Across the river is the **Hauptmarktplatz,** site of the annual **Christmas market.** Hidden in the fence of the **Schöner Brunnen** (Beautiful Fountain) in the Hauptmarkt is a seamless golden ring; spinning it is said to bring good luck. The **Kaiserburg** (Fortress of the Holy Roman Emperor) looms over Nuremberg as a symbol of the city. Climb the **Sinwellturm** for the best view of the city. (Open daily Apr.-Sept. 9am-6pm; Oct.-Mar. 10am-4pm. Mandatory tours in German every hr. €6, students €5.)

The **Reichsparteitagsgelände,** the ruined site of Nazi rallies, reminds visitors of Nuremberg's darker history. On the far side of the lake is the **Tribüne,** the platform from which Hitler spoke to the masses. The exhibit in the **Kongresshalle** covers the Nazi era. (☎231 56 66. Open M-F 9am-6pm, Sa-Su 10am-6pm. €5, students €2.50.) Tram #9 from the train station stops by Kongresshalle (Dokumentationszentrum stop). To reach the Tribüne (or Zeppelinwiese), walk around the lake from the Kongresshalle or take S2 (dir.: Feucht/Altdorf) to Dutzendteich, then take the middle of three exits, go down the stairs, and turn left.

Nuremberg's nightspots are often by the river. Cine Città, Gewerbemuseumspl. 3 (U-Bahn to Wöhrder Wiese), has 16 bars and cafes, myriad theaters, and a disco. (☎20 66 60. Open Su-Th until 2am, F-Sa until 3am.) Wies'n Biergarten is on Johann Sörgel Weg. (☎240 66 68. *Maß* €4.10. Open May-Sept. daily 10am-10pm.) Hirsch, Vogelweiherstr. 66, has multiple bars and a *Biergarten* out front. (www.der-hirsch.de. Mixed drinks €5.50. M-Th frequent concerts. Cover €3-15. Open F-Sa 10pm-5am. Cash only.) Cartoon, An der Sparkasse 6, is a popular gay bar near Lorenzpl. (☎22 71 70. 0.4L beer €3. Open W 6pm-3am, F-Sa 8pm-3am or later.) **Trains** go to: Berlin (5hr., 1 per hr., €77); Frankfurt (2-3hr., 2 per hr., €32); Munich (1½hr., 2 per hr., €28); Stuttgart (2hr., 1 per hr., €27). A *Nürnberg Card* (€18), available at the tourist office, covers two days of public transport and entrance to most museums. The **tourist office** is at Königstr. 93. (☎233 6131. Open M-Sa 9am-7pm.) **Postal Code:** 90402.

ROMANTIC ROAD

Groomed fields of sunflowers, vineyards, and green hills checker the landscape between Würzburg and Füssen. It was christened the Romantic Road *(Romantische Straße)* in 1950, helping to make it the most traveled route in Germany.

TRANSPORTATION

Train travel is the most flexible and economical way to see the Romantic Road. **Europabus** also has a variety of routes; up-to-date reservations and schedule info can be found at www.touring.de or www.romantischestrasse.de. There is a 10% student and under-26 discount, and a 60% Eurail and German Railpass discount.

ROTHENBURG OB DER TAUBER ☎09861

Possibly the only walled medieval city without a single modern building, Rothenburg (pop. 12,000) is *the* Romantic Road stop. After the Thirty Years' War, the town had no money to modernize and didn't change for 250 years. Tourism brought economic stability and more reasons to keep the medieval Altstadt. The English tour led by the **night watchman** gives a fast-paced and entertaining introduction to Rothenburg history. (Starts at the Rathaus on Marktpl. Easter-Christmas daily 8pm. €6, students €4.) A long climb up the stairs of the 60m **Rathaus Tower** leads to a panoramic view of the town and valley. (Open Apr.-Oct. daily 9:30am-12:30pm and 1:30-5pm; Nov. and Jan.-Mar. Sa-Su noon-3pm; Dec. daily noon-3pm. €1.) During the Thirty Years' War, the conquering general Johann Tilly offered to spare the town if any local could chug a keg containing 3.25L (almost a gallon) of wine. Mayor Nusch successfully met the challenge, passed out for several days, then lived to a ripe old age. His *Meistertrunk* (Master Draught) is reenacted with great fanfare each year (May 25-28, Sept. 2, Oct. 6 and 10, 2007).

For unregistered private rooms, look for *Zimmer frei* (free room) signs in restaurants and stores. The 500-year-old half-timbered **Pension Raidel ❷,** Wengg. 3, will make you feel like you're sleeping in the past. (☎31 15. Breakfast included. Singles €19, with bath €39; doubles €39/49. Cash only.) **Pension Pöschel ❷,** Wengg. 22, has standard rooms. (☎34 30; pension.poeschel@t-online.de. Breakfast included. Singles €20; doubles €35-45; triples €45-55. Cash only.) **Trains** run to Steinach (15min., 1 per hr., €1.80), with transfers to Munich and Würzburg. The **tourist office** is at Marktpl. 2. (☎404 800. Open May-Oct. M-F 9am-noon and 1-6pm, Sa-Su 10am-3pm; Nov.-Apr. M-F 9am-noon and 1-5pm, Sa 10am-1pm.) **Postal Code:** 91541.

KÖNIGSSCHLÖßER (ROYAL CASTLES)

King Ludwig II, a frenzied visionary, used his cash to build fantastic castles soaring into the Alpine skies. In 1886, a band of nobles and bureaucrats deposed Ludwig, declared him insane, and imprisoned him; three days later, the king was mysteriously discovered dead in a lake. The glitzy Schloß Neuschwanstein inspired Disney's Cinderella Castle and is one of Germany's iconic attractions. Its chambers include an artificial grotto and an immense Wagnerian opera hall. Hike to the Marienbrücke, a bridge that spans the gorge behind the castle. Climb the mountain on the other side of the bridge for enchantment minus the crowds. Ludwig summered in the yellow Schloß Hohenschwangau across the valley. Tickets for both castles are sold at the Ticket-Service Center, Alpseestr. 12, about 100m uphill from the Hohenschwangau bus stop. (☎08362 93 08 30. Both castles open daily Apr.-Sept. 9am-6pm, ticket sales 8am-5pm; Oct.-Mar. castles 10am-4pm, tickets 9am-3pm. Obligatory tours of each castle €9; English available. Combination ticket €17/15.) From the Füssen train station, take bus #73 or 78, marked "Königsschlößer" (10min.; 2 per hr.; one-way €1.60, round-trip €3.10). The bus stops at the info booth. (☎81 97 65. Open daily 9am-6pm.) Separate paths lead uphill to the castles. A *Tagesticket* (€7.60) is good for a day's worth of regonal bus use.

GREECE Έλλας

Greece's treasures are impossibly varied. This is a land where sacred monasteries are mountainside fixtures, 3hr. seaside siestas are standard issue, and circle dancing and drinking until daybreak is a summer rite. Renaissance men long before the Renaissance, the ancient Greeks sprung to prominence with their intellectual and athletic mastery. The Greek lifestyle is a frustratingly delicious mix of high speed and sun-inspired lounging.

DISCOVER GREECE: SUGGESTED ITINERARIES

THREE DAYS. Spend it all in **Athens** (p. 476). Roam the **Acropolis,** gaze at the treasures of the **National Archaeological Museum,** and pay homage at the **Parthenon.** Visit the ancient **Agora,** then take a trip down to **Poseidon's Temple** at Cape Sounion.

ONE WEEK. Begin your week with a sojourn in **Athens** (3 days). Scope out sea turtles in sunny **Zakynthos** (1 day; p. 499). Sprint to **Olympia** (1 day; p. 485) to see where the games began. Take the ferry to **Corfu** (1 day; p. 496) then soak up Byzantine history in **Thessaloniki** (1 day; p. 489).

BEST OF GREECE, THREE WEEKS. Explore **Athens** (4 days) before visiting the mansions of **Nafplion** (1 day; p. 487). Race west to **Olympia** (1 day), then take a ferry from **Patras** to the beaches of **Corfu** (2 days). Back on the mainland, wander through **Thessaloniki** (2 days), then climb to the cliffside monasteries of **Meteora** (1 day; p. 495). Consult the gods at **Mount Olympus** (1 day; p. 494) and the Oracle of **Delphi** (1 day). On **Crete** (3 days; p. 505), hike Europe's largest gorge. Seek rest on **Santorini** (1 day; p. 504), debauchery on **Ios** (1 day; p. 503), and sun on **Mykonos** (1 day; p. 500).

ESSENTIALS

FACTS AND FIGURES

Official Name: Hellenic Republic.
Capital: Athens.
Major Cities: Thessaloniki, Patras.
Population: 10,688,000.
Land Area: 131,940 sq. km.
Time: GMT +2.
Language: Greek.
Religion: Eastern Orthodox (98%).

WHEN TO GO

June through August is high season; it is best to visit in May, early June, or September, when smaller crowds enjoy the gorgeous weather. Visiting during low season means cheaper lodging and food prices, but many sights and accommodations have shorter hours or close altogether.

DOCUMENTS AND FORMALITIES

EMBASSIES. Foreign embassies in Greece are in Athens (p. 476). Greek embassies abroad include: **Australia,** 9 Turrana St., Yarralumla, Canberra, ACT, 2600 (☎6273 3011); **Canada,** 80 MacLaren St., Ottawa, ON, K2P 0K6 (☎613-238-6271;

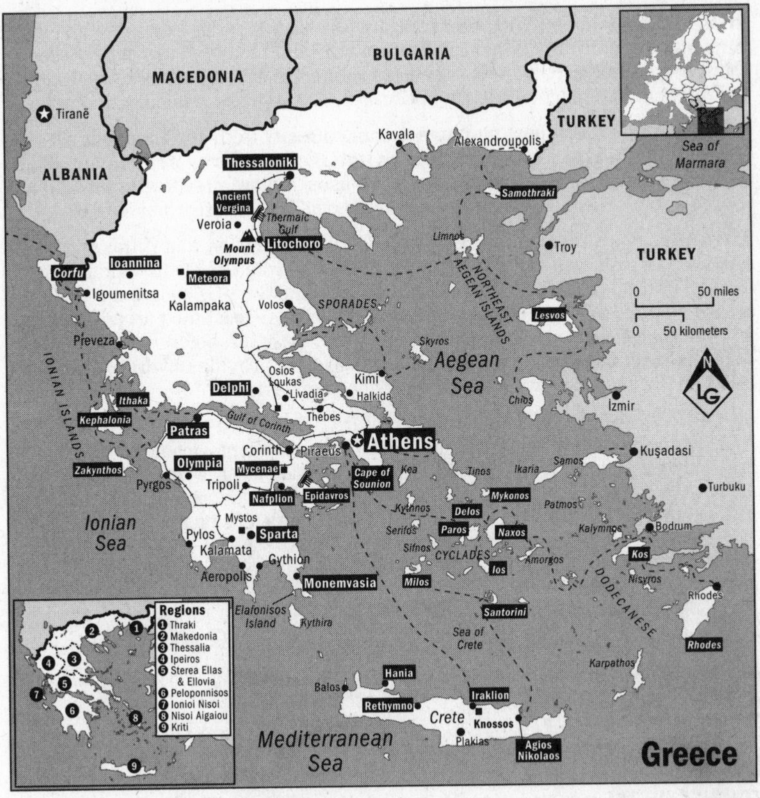

www.greekembassy.ca); **Ireland,** 1 Upper Pembroke St., Dublin, 2 (☎31 676 72 54, ext. 5); **New Zealand,** 5-7 Willeston St., 10th fl., P.O. Box 24066, Wellington (☎44 473 7775, ext. 6); **UK,** 1a Holland Park, London W11 3TP (☎020 7221 6467; www.greekembassy.org.uk); and **US,** 2221 Massachusetts Ave., NW, Washington, D.C., 20008 (☎202-939-1300; www.greekembassy.org).

VISA AND ENTRY INFORMATION. EU citizens do not need a visa. Citizens of **Australia, Canada, New Zealand,** and the **US** don't need one for stays of up to 90 days, beginning upon entry into any of the countries in the EU's freedom-of-movement zone. Contact your Greek embassy to apply for a visa to work or study in Greece.

TRANSPORTATION

BY PLANE. Most international flights land in Athens (ATH; ☎21035 30 000; www.aia.gr), though some airlines also serve Corfu (CFU), Iraklion (HER), Kos (KSG), and Thessaloniki (SKG). **Olympic Airways,** Syngrou 96-100, Athens, 11741 (☎21092 69 111; www.olympicairlines.com), offers extensive domestic service. A 1hr. flight from Athens (€60-90) can get you to almost any island in Greece.

BY TRAIN. Greece is served by a number of international train routes that connect Athens, Larisa, and Thessaloniki to European cities. Train service within Greece is limited and sometimes uncomfortable; no lines go to the western coast. The new air-conditioned, intercity express trains, while slightly more expensive and less frequent, are worth the price. **Eurailpasses** are valid on all Greek trains. **Hellenic Railways Organization** (OSE; www.osenet.gr) connects Athens to major Greek cities and offers a 25% student discount; in Greece, call ☎1110 for schedules and prices.

BY BUS. There are almost no buses running directly from any European city to Greece. Domestic bus service is extensive and fares are cheap. **KTEL** (www.ktel.org) operates most domestic buses; always check with an official source about scheduled departures, as posted schedules are often outdated.

BY FERRY. Boats travel from Bari, ITA to Corfu, Kephalonia, and Patras and from Ancona, ITA, to Corfu and Patras. Ferries also run from Greece to various points on the Turkish coast. There is frequent service to the Greek islands, but schedules are irregular. Check schedules posted at the tourist office, at the port police, or at www.ferries.gr. Make reservations and arrive at least 1hr. before your departure time. **Hellenic Seaways** (www.hellenicseaways.gr) provides hydrofoil service between the islands at twice the cost and speed of ferries.

BY CAR AND MOPED. You must be 18 to drive in Greece and 21 to rent a car; some agencies require renters to be at least 23 or 25. Rental agencies may quote low daily rates that exclude the 18% tax and **collision damage waiver (CDW)** insurance; expect to pay €30-60 per day for a rental. Foreign drivers must have an **International Driving Permit** and an **International Insurance Certificate** to drive in Greece. The **Automobile and Touring Club of Greece (ELPA),** Messogion 395, Athens, 15343, provides assistance and offers reciprocal membership to members of foreign auto clubs like AAA. (☎21060 68 800, 24hr. emergency roadside assistance 104, Athens infoline 174, elsewhere 21060 68 838; www.elpa.gr; open M-F 7am-3pm.) Mopeds can be great for exploring, but they are extremely dangerous; wear a helmet.

TOURIST SERVICES AND MONEY

EMERGENCY	**Police:** ☎100. **Ambulance:** ☎166. **Fire:** ☎106. **Emergency:** ☎112.

TOURIST OFFICES. Two national organizations oversee tourism in Greece: **Greek National Tourist Organization (GNTO;** known as the **EOT** in Greece**)** and the **tourist police** *(touristiki astinomia)*. The GNTO, Tsoha 7, Athens (☎2108 70 7000; www.gnto.gr; open M-F 8am-3pm), known as the **EOT** in Greece, can supply general information about sights and accommodations throughout the country. The tourist police deal with local and immediate problems with bus schedules, accommodations, and lost passports. Offices are open long hours and are willing to help, but English may be limited.

MONEY. The official currency of Greece is the **euro (€).** For exchange rates and more information on the euro, see p. 17. If you're carrying more than €1000 in cash when you enter Greece, you must declare it upon entry. It's generally cheaper to change money in Greece than at home. When changing money in Greece, try to go to a bank (τράπεζα; TRAH-peh-za) with at most a 5% margin between its buy and sell prices. A bare-bones day in Greece costs €40-50. A day with more comforts runs €50-65. There is a 15% **gratuity** included in all restaurant prices; tipping is unnecessary. **Taxi** drivers do not expect tips. Generally, **bargaining** is expected for street wares and in other informal venues, but when in doubt, wait and watch to avoid offending merchants. Bargaining is also common in *domatia* (rooms to let) and small hotels, as well as for unmetered taxi rides. There is a **value added tax (VAT)** of 19% on goods and services sold in mainland Greece and 13% in the Aegean islands, included in the listed price. Travelers from non-EU countries who spend more than €120 in one shop on one day may be entitled to a VAT refund. Claiming your refund involves complicated paperwork; ask about the VAT when making large purchases and save your receipts. For more info, see p. 17.

KEEPING IN TOUCH

PHONE CODES	**Country code:** 30. **International dialing prefix:** 00. For more information on how to place international calls, see inside back cover.

EMAIL AND THE INTERNET. The availability of the Internet in Greece is rapidly expanding. In all big cities, most small cities and large towns, and on most islands, you'll be able to find Internet cafes. Expect to pay €3-6 per hour.

TELEPHONE. Pay phones in Greece use prepaid phone cards, sold at streetside kiosks *(peripteros)* in denominations of €3, €12, and €25. Time is measured in minutes or talk units (100 units=30min. domestic). A calling card is the cheapest way to make international phone calls; contact your service provider's Greek operator. Mobile phones are increasingly popular; for more info, see p. 29.

MAIL. To send a letter (up to 20g) anywhere from Greece costs €0.65. Mail sent to Greece from elsewhere in Europe takes at least three days to arrive; from Australia, New Zealand, and the US, airmail takes up to two weeks. Address mail to be held for you at a Greek post office according to the following example: First name LAST NAME, Town Post Office, Island, Greece, Postal Code, POSTE RESTANTE.

LANGUAGE. To the non-Greek speaker, the intricate levels of idiom, irony, and poetry in the language can present a seemingly impenetrable wall to understanding. Greek (Ελληνικά, eh-lee-nee-KAH) is one of the most difficult languages for English speakers to learn fluently, but learning enough to order a meal, send a postcard, or get to the airport is surprisingly easy. Greek is obsessively phonetic; though a cursory knowledge of the Greek alphabet (p. 1053) does not always help with the double consonants and double vowels, all multisyllabic words come with a handy accent called a *tonos*, which marks the emphasized syllable. Greeks are famously welcoming of foreigners who try their hand at the language, but many Greeks will understand English. For useful phrases, see **Phrasebook: Greek,** p. 1053.

ACCOMMODATIONS AND CAMPING

GREECE	❶	❷	❸	❹	❺
ACCOMMODATIONS	under €17	€17-28	€28-40	€40-60	above €60

Local tourist offices usually maintain lists of inexpensive accommodations. A bed in a **hostel** averages €15-25. Those not endorsed by HI are in most cases still safe and reputable. In many areas, **domatia** (rooms to let) are a good option; you may be approached by locals offering cheap lodging—a practice that is common but illegal. Prices vary; expect to pay €20-30 for a single and €25-45 for a double. Always see the room and negotiate with *domatia* owners before settling on a price; never pay more than you would for a hotel room. When in doubt, ask the tourist police; they may set you up with a room and conduct negotiations themselves. **Hotel** prices are regulated, but proprietors may push you to take the most expensive room. Check your bill carefully, and threaten to contact the tourist police if you think you are being cheated. Greece has plenty of official **campgrounds,** which cost €2-3 per tent plus €4-8 per person. Camping on public beaches—sometimes illegal—is common in summer but may not be the safest option.

FOOD AND DRINK

GREECE	❶	❷	❸	❹	❺
FOOD	under €4	€4-9	€10-16	€17-25	above €25

Penny-pinching carnivores will thank Zeus for lamb, chicken, or pork *souvlaki*, stuffed into a pita to make *gyros* (YEE-ros). Vegetarians can also eat their fill on the cheap: options include *horiatiki* (Greek salad) and savory pastries like *tiropita* (cheese pie) and *spanakopita* (spinach and feta pie). Frothy iced coffee milkshakes take the edge off the summer heat. *Ouzo* (a powerful, licorice-flavored spirit) is served with *mezedes* (snacks of octopus, cheese, and sausage). Breakfast, served only in the early morning, is generally very simple: a piece of toast with *marmelada* or a pastry. Lunch, a hearty and leisurely meal, can begin as early as noon but is more likely eaten sometime between 2 and 5pm. Dinner is a drawn-out, relaxed affair served late. Greek restaurants are known as *tavernas* or *estiatorios;* a grill is a *psistaria*. Many restaurants don't offer printed menus.

HOLIDAYS AND FESTIVALS

Holidays: Feast of St. Basil/New Year's Day (Jan. 1); Epiphany (Jan. 6); Clean Monday (Feb. 19); Greek Independence Day (Mar. 25); Easter (Apr. 8); St. George's Day (Apr. 23); Labor Day (May 1); Ascension (May 17); Pentecost (May 27); Feast of the Assumption of the Virgin Mary (Aug. 15); The Virgin Mary's Birthday (Sept. 8); Feast of St. Demetrius (Oct. 26); Okhi Day (Oct. 28).

Festivals: Three weeks of Carnival feasting and dancing (starting Jan. 28) precede Lenten fasting. April 23 is St. George's Day, when Greece honors the dragon-slaying knight with horse races, wrestling matches, and dances. The Feast of St. Demetrius (Oct. 26) is celebrated with particular enthusiasm in Thessaloniki. Aq3na

BEYOND TOURISM

Anglo-Hellenic Teacher Recruitment (☎27410 53 511; www.anglo-hellenic.com) provides employment, training, and support for English teachers in Greece.

Conservation Volunteers Greece (☎21038 25 506; www.cvgpeep.gr) offers summer programs in environmental and cultural conservation, as well as social outreach.

ATHENS Αθήνα ☎210

Athens is haunted by its illustrious past. The ghosts of antiquity peer down from every hilltop and lurk in each dark alley. But with 6 million people—half of Greece's population—Athens is also a daring and modern place; its fiercely patriotic citizens pushed their capital into the 21st century with massive clean-up and building projects before the 2004 Olympic Games. Creative international menus, hipster bars, and large warehouse performance spaces crowd among Byzantine churches, traditional *tavernas*, and toppled columns. Don't miss the chance to explore a city that is now more energetic and exciting than ever.

TRANSPORTATION

Flights: Eleftherios Venizelou (ATH; ☎353 0000; www.aia.gr). Greece's new international airport operates as one massive yet navigable terminal. Arrivals are on the ground floor, departures are on the 2nd. The new **suburban rail** services the airport from the city center in 30min. 4 bus lines run to Athens, Piraeus, and Rafina.

Trains: Hellenic Railways (OSE), Sina 6 (☎362 4402; www.ose.gr). **Larisis Train Station** (☎210 529 8837) serves northern Greece. Ticket office open daily 5am-midnight. Take trolley #1 from El. Venizelou in Pl. Syndagma (every 10min. 5am-midnight, €0.50) or the metro to Sepolia. Trains depart for **Thessaloniki** (7hr., 5 per day, €14; express 5½hr., 6 per day, €28). No luggage storage available.

Buses: Terminal A, Kifissou 100 (☎512 4910). Take blue bus #051 from the corner of Zinonos and Menandrou near Pl. Omonia (every 15min. 5am-11:30pm, €0.50). Buses to: **Corfu** (10hr., 4 per day, €30); **Corinth** (1½hr., every 30min., €5); **Patras** (3hr., every 30min., €13); **Thessaloniki** (6hr., 11 per day, €30) and other destinations. **Terminal B,** Liossion 260 (M-F ☎831 7153). Take blue bus #024 from Amalias, outside the National Gardens (45min., every 20min., €0.50). Buses to **Delphi** (3hr., 6 per day, €13) and other destinations.

Public Transportation: KTEL (ΚΤΕΛ) **buses** travel all around Attica from orange bus stops around the city. Other buses around Athens and its suburbs are blue and designated by 3-digit numbers. **Trolleys** sport 1- or 2-digit numbers. There are 2 **tram** lines. **Line 1** runs from Pl. Syndagma to the coast and Helliniko. **Line 2** runs from Neo Faliro along the Apollo Coast to Glyfada. Buy bus and trolley tickets at any street kiosk. Hold on to your ticket or face a €18-30 fine. A standard bus/trolley ticket costs €0.50. The modern Athens **metro** consists of 3 lines running 5am-midnight. **M1** runs from northern Kifisia to Piraeus, **M2** from Sepolia to Ag. Dimitrios, **M3** from Ethniki Amyna to Monastiraki in central Athens. Buy tickets (€0.80) in any station. A 24hr. ticket costs €3.

Car Rental: Try the places on **Syngrou.** €40-60 per day for a small car with 100km mileage (including tax and insurance); higher rates in summer. Up to 50% student discount.

Taxis: Companies include **Ermis** (☎411 5200); **Ikaros** (☎515 2800); **Kosmos** (☎1300). Base fare €0.85; plus €0.30 per km, midnight-5am €0.53 per km. €3 surcharge from the airport and a €0.80 surcharge for trips from bus and railway terminals, plus €0.29 for each piece of luggage over 10kg. Call for pick-up (€1.50-2.50 extra).

PIRAEUS PORT FERRIES. Most ferries from Athens leave from the Piraeus port. Unfortunately, the ferry schedule changes on a daily basis; the following information is only approximate. Check *Athens News* and the back of the *Kathimerini* English-language edition for updated schedules. Ferries sail directly to nearly all major Greek islands except for the Sporades and Ionians. Ferries to Crete: **Hania** (11hr., 1-2 per day); **Iraklion** (11hr., 1-3 per day); **Rethymno** (11hr., 3 per week). Additional ferries to: **Chios** (9hr., 1-2 per day); **Ios** (7½hr., 3 per day); **Kos** (13½ hr., 1-2 per day); **Lesvos** (12hr., daily); **Limnos** (18hr., 3 per week); **Milos** (7hr., 1-2 per day); **Mykonos** (6hr., 2-4 per day); **Naxos** (6hr., 5-7 per day); **Paros** (5hr., 4-7 per day); **Patmos** (8hr., daily); **Rhodes** (14hr., 2-5 per day); **Samos** (10hr., daily); **Santorini** (9hr., 3-5 per day). International ferries (2 per day) head to destinations in **Turkey.**

ORIENTATION AND PRACTICAL INFORMATION

Athens's crowded streets and winding alleys are large enough to intimidate any newcomer, but after diving into the bustling neighborhoods for a few days, the city's geography will start to make sense. Most travelers hang around the **Acropolis** and the **Agoras** down the hill, and the central **Plaka** is packed with guide-bearing foreigners. **Adrianou** and **Mitropoleos** are the most crowded streets in Plaka. **Monastiraki** is a hectic and exciting neighborhood packed with travelers, gypsies, and gyros stands. At the heart of the city, lively **Syndagma** square is the center of all transportation. On the opposite side of Stadiou, **Omonia** square is the insane, eternally traffic-jammed junction of the city. A short walk north on **Em. Benaki** leads to

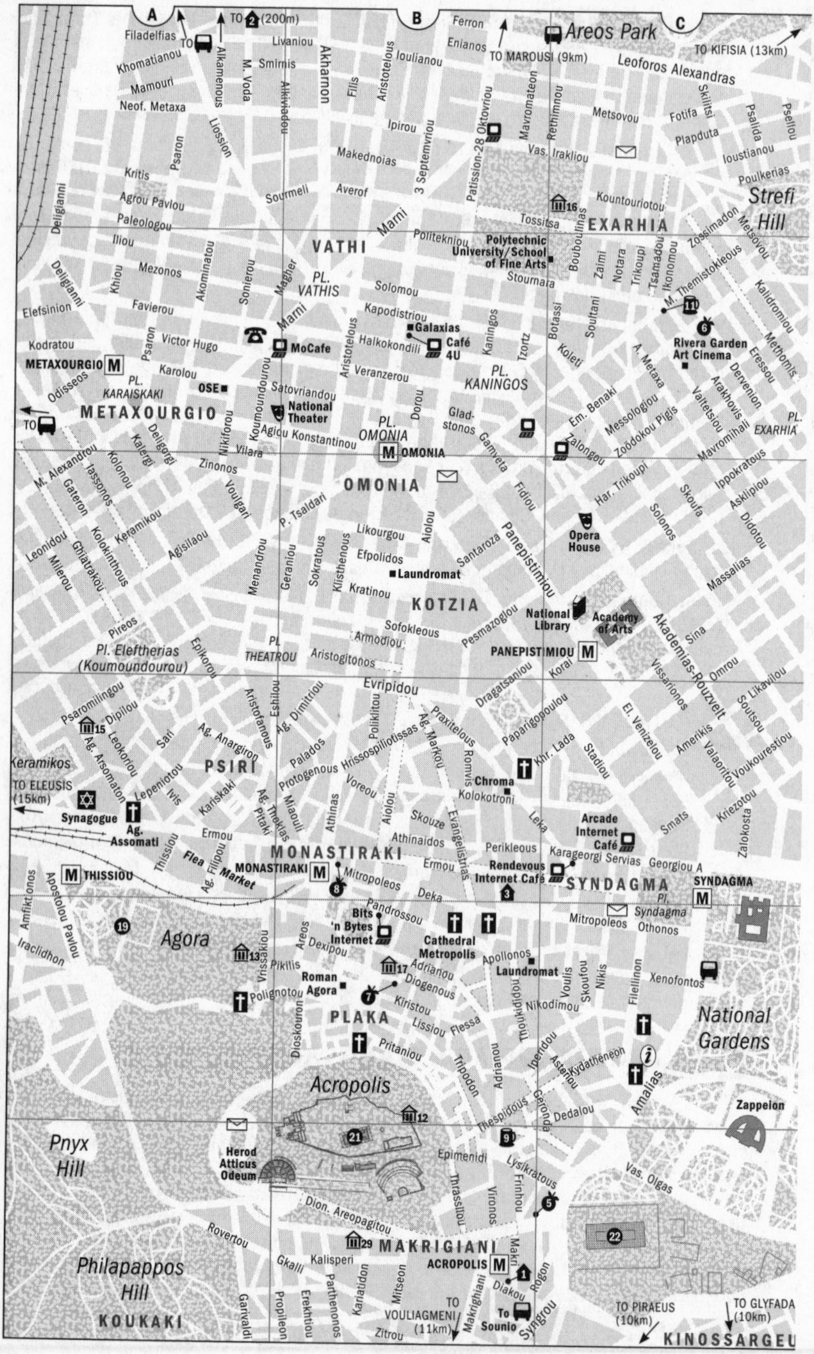
A
B
C
TO 2 (200m)
Filadelfias
TO
Ferron
Enianos
Areos Park
TO MAROUSI (9km)
TO KIFISIA (13km)
Livaniou
Khomatianou
Alkamenous
M. Voda
Smirnis
Akharnon
Ioulianou
Aristotelous
Filis
Leoforos Alexandras
Mamouri
Neof. Metaxa
Liossion
Alkiviadou
Ipirou
Patission-28 Oktovriou
Mavromateon
Rethimnou
Metsovou
Fotifa
Skiltsi
Psalida
Pselou
Plapduta
Ioustianou
Psaron
Makednoias
3 Septemvriou
Vas. Irakliou
Poulkerias
Kritis
Agrou Pavlou
Sourmeli
Averof
16
Kountouriotou
Strefi Hill
Deligianni
Paleologou
Tossitsa
EXARHIA
Metsovou
Zossimadou
Marni
Politekniou
Iliou
VATHI
Polytechnic University/School of Fine Arts
Boubouliinas
Zaimi
Notara
Trikoupi
Tsamadou
Ikonomou
M. Themistokleous
Mezonos
Akominatou
Sonierou
Magher
PL. VATHIS
Stournara
Deligianni
Khiou
Solomou
Kalidromiou
Elefsinion
Favierou
Marni
Kapodistriou
Botassi
Soultani
11
Galaxias
Café 4U
6
Methonis
Kodratou
Psaron
Victor Hugo
MoCafe
Halkokondili
Kaningos
Tzortz
Koleti
A. Metaxa
Rivera Garden Art Cinema
Eressou
METAXOURGIO M
Karolou
Aristotelous
Veranzerou
PL. KANINGOS
Dervenion
Odisseos
PL. KARAISKAKI
OSE
Satovriandou
Kaumoundourou
Em. Benaki
Messologiou
Valtetsiou
Arakhovis
METAXOURGIO
Nikiforou
National Theater
Dorou
Gladstonos
Zoödokou Pigis
Mavromihali
PL. EXARHIA
TO
Deligiorgi
Agiou Konstantinou
PL. OMONIA
Kalergi
Vilara
M OMONIA
Gamveta
Zalongou
M. Alexandrou
Kolonou
Zinonos
Ippokratous
Iassonos
Gateron
OMONIA
Fidiou
Har. Trikoupi
Skoufa
Asklipiou
Voulgari
P. Tsaldari
Keramikou
Likourgou
Aiolou
Panepistimiou
Solonos
Didotou
Leonidou
Kolokinthous
Agisilaou
Efpolidos
Santaroza
Opera House
Milerou
Ghiatrakou
Menandrou
Geraniou
Sokratous
Klisthenous
Laundromat
Massalias
Kratinou
KOTZIA
Pireos
National Library
Academy of Arts
Pesmazoglou
Sofokleous
Akademias-Rouzvelt
Epikorou
PL. THEATROU
Armodiou
Sina
Pl. Eleftherias (Koumoundourou)
Aristogitonos
PANEPISTIMIOU M
Koral
Vissarionos
Omrou
Evripidou
Dragatsaniou
Likavitou
Psaromilingou
Dipilou
Aristofanous
Eshilou
Ag. Dimitriou
Praxitelous
Soutsou
15
Sarri
Ag. Anargiron
Ag. Markou
Papagopoulou
El. Venizelou
Amerikis
Ag. Arsomaton
Leokoriou
Palados
Hrissospiliotissas
Polikitou
Romvis
Khr. Lada
Stadiou
Valaoritou
Voukourestiou
Keramikos
PSIRI
Protogenous
Chroma
TO ELEUSIS (15km)
Lepeniotou
Kariskaki
Ag. Pitaki
Ag. Thoklas
Miaouli
Voreou
Kolokotroni
Synagogue
Ivis
Athinas
Aiolou
Skouze
Evangelistrias
Leka
Arcade Internet Café
Kriezotou
Ag. Assomati
Smats
Zalokosta
Ermou
Athinaidos
MONASTIRAKI
Perikleous
Thissiou
Flea Market
Karageorgi Servias
Georgiou A
Ag. Filipou
MONASTIRAKI M
Mitropoleos
Ermou
Rendevous Internet Café
M THISSIOU
SYNDAGMA
SYNDAGMA M
Amfiktionos
Apostolou Pavlou
8
Deka
3
Pl. Syndagma
Pandrossou
Mitropoleos
Othonos
19
Bits 'n Bytes Internet
Cathedral Metropolis
Agora
Areos
Iraclidhon
Dexipou
Apollonos
13
Pikilis
17
Adrianou
Laundromat
Xenofontos
Vrissakiou
Roman Agora
Diogenous
Thoukididou
Voulis
Skoufou
Nikis
Filellinon
Polignotou
Nikodimou
7
Kiristou
National Gardens
PLAKA
Dioskouron
Lissiou
Flessa
Pritaniou
Adrianou
Ipendou
Asteriou
Kydatheneon
Tripodon
Amalias
Acropolis
Dedalou
Thespidous
Geronda
Zappeion
12
Pnyx Hill
21
9
Herod Atticus Odeum
Epimenidi
Lysikratous
Vas. Olgas
Thrassilou
Vironos
Frinhou
5
Dion. Areopagitou
Rovertou
22
29
MAKRIGIANI
Makri
Kalisperi
ACROPOLIS M
1
Philapappos Hill
Gkalli
Diakou
Rogon
Garivaldi
Propileon
Erekhtiou
Parthenonos
Kariatidon
Mitseon
Makrighiani
TO VOULIAGMENI (11km)
To Sounio
Syngrou
TO PIRAEUS (10km)
TO GLYFADA (10km)
KOUKAKI
Zitrou
KINOSSARGEU

GREECE

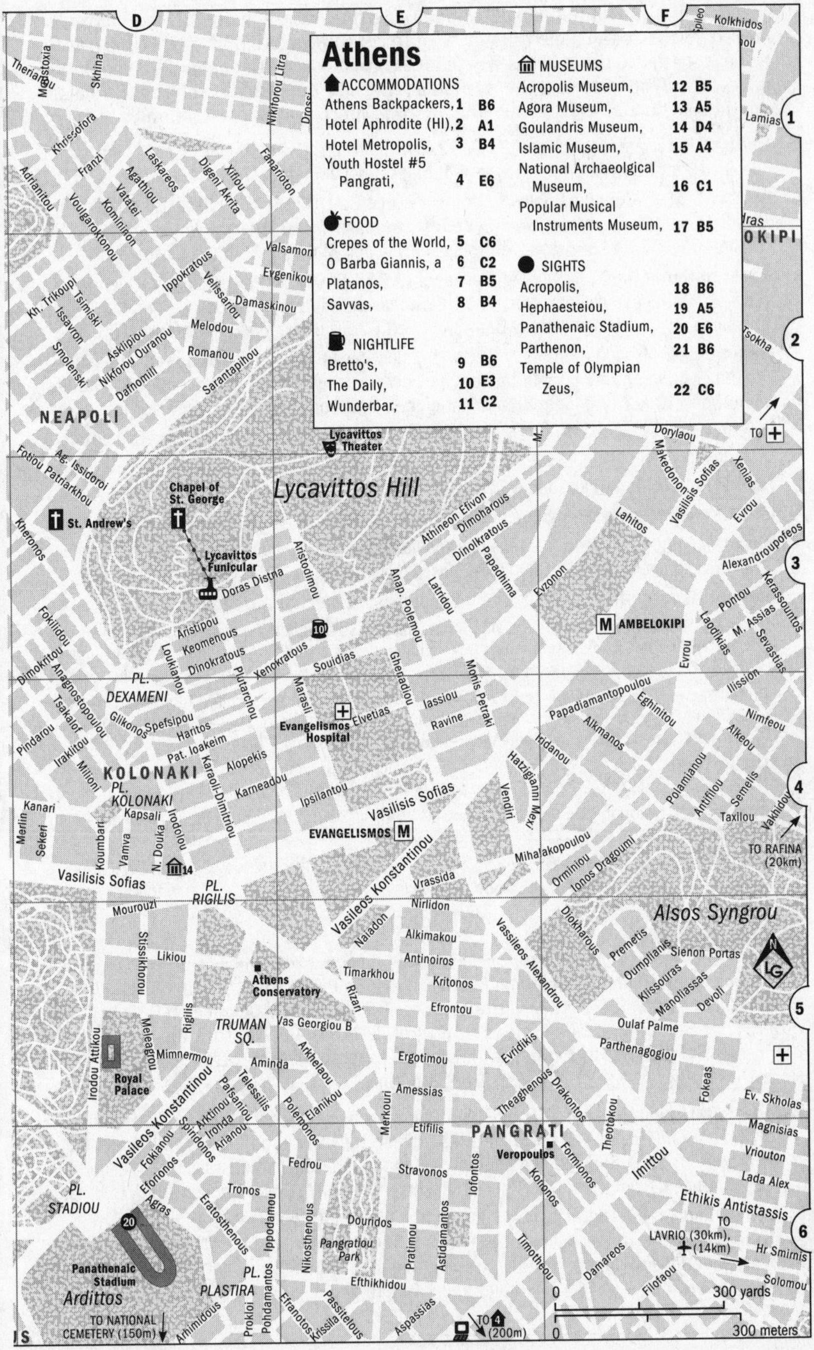
Athens
ACCOMMODATIONS
Athens Backpackers, 1 B6
Hotel Aphrodite (HI), 2 A1
Hotel Metropolis, 3 B4
Youth Hostel #5 Pangrati, 4 E6
FOOD
Crepes of the World, 5 C6
O Barba Giannis, a 6 C2
Platanos, 7 B5
Savvas, 8 B4
NIGHTLIFE
Bretto's, 9 B6
The Daily, 10 E3
Wunderbar, 11 C2
MUSEUMS
Acropolis Museum, 12 B5
Agora Museum, 13 A5
Goulandris Museum, 14 D4
Islamic Museum, 15 A4
National Archaeolgical Museum, 16 C1
Popular Musical Instruments Museum, 17 B5
SIGHTS
Acropolis, 18 B6
Hephaesteiou, 19 A5
Panathenaic Stadium, 20 E6
Parthenon, 21 B6
Temple of Olympian Zeus, 22 C6
D
E
F
1
2
3
4
5
6
NEAPOLI
Lycavittos Hill
Lycavittos Theater
Chapel of St. George
St. Andrew's
Lycavittos Funicular
PL. DEXAMENI
KOLONAKI
PL. KOLONAKI
Evangelismos Hospital
EVANGELISMOS
AMBELOKIPI
PL. RIGILIS
Athens Conservatory
TRUMAN SQ.
Royal Palace
PANGRATI
Veropoulos
PL. STADIOU
Panathenaic Stadium
Ardittos
PL. PLASTIRA
Pangratiou Park
Alsos Syngrou
Vasilisis Sofias
Vasileos Konstantinou
Vasileos Alexandrou
Mihalakopoulou
Ethikis Antistassis
Imittou
TO RAFINA (20km)
TO LAVRIO (30km), (14km)
TO NATIONAL CEMETERY (150m)
TO 4 (200m)
0 300 yards
0 300 meters

GREECE

the quiet and pleasant hill neighborhood of **Exarhia,** where many travelers haven't ventured yet. Take the metro 30min. west to get to Athens's port city, **Piraeus,** and to the east to get to the **beaches** where locals go to escape the heat. If you get lost, just look for Syndagma and the Acropolis; they are the clearest reference points. From those, you can walk or take the metro to most central destinations.

Tourist Office, Amalias 26 (☎331 0392; www.gnto.gr). Open May-Sept. M-F 9am-8pm, Sa-Su 10am-6pm; Oct.-Apr. M-F 9am-4pm, Sa-Su 10am-4pm.

Budget Travel: Consolas Travel, Aiolou 100 (☎321 9228; consolas@hol.gr), 9th fl. Open M and Sa 9am-2pm, Tu-F 9am-5pm. **Robissa Travel Agency,** Voulis 43, is STA-affiliated (☎321 1188; statravel@robissa.gr). Open M-F 9am-5pm, Sa 10am-2pm.

Bank: National Bank, Karageorgi Servias 2 (☎334 0500), in Pl. Syndagma. Open M-Th 8am-2:30pm, F 8am-2pm. Next door, **Eurochange** offers currency exchange, but commissions are steep. Open daily 9am-8pm. Fee €2.50 under €50, €8 under €100.

Laundromat: Most laundromats *(plintirias)* post signs in English. **National,** Apollonos 17, in Syndagma, offers both laundry and dry cleaning. €4.50 per kg. Open M and W 8am-5pm, Tu and Th-F 8am-8pm. Most hostels and hotels offer the same service.

Emergency: Police: ☎100 or 103. **Ambulance:** ☎166. **Medical:** Athens ☎105, or 646 7811; line available 2pm-7am. **AIDS Help Line:** ☎722 2222.

Tourist Police: Dimitrakopoulou 77 (☎171). English spoken. Open 24hr.

Pharmacies: Marked by a green cross hanging over the street. Many are open 24hr.

Hospitals: *Athens News* lists emergency hospitals. Free emergency care for tourists. **Aeginitio,** Vas. Sofias 72 (☎722 0811) and Vas. Sofias 80 (☎777 0501), close to the center.

Internet Access: Athens teems with Internet cafes. Expect to pay around €3 per hr.

Arcade Internet Cafe, Stadiou 5 (☎ 321 0701), just up Stadiou from Pl. Syndagma, set in a shopping center about 15m from the main thoroughfare. Laptop connection available. Complimentary coffee. €3 per hr., €0.50 per additional 10min.; min. €1. Open M-Sa 9am-10pm, Su noon-8pm.

Rendez-Vous Cafe, Voulis 18 (☎322 3158), in Syndagma. Sip on a coffee frappe (€1.50) or snack on freshly made sweets like white chocolate chip cookies (€1) in this small, cozy cafe. Internet €3 per hr., min. €1. Open M, W, Sa 8am-6pm, Tu and Th-F 8am-9pm.

Calling Center, Victor Hugo 2 (☎522 0804), in Omonia. One of the cheapest in Athens. Internet €2.50 per hr. Calls to Canada, Europe, and US €0.25 per min. Open daily 9am-11pm.

Bits 'n Bytes Internet, Kapnikareas 19 (☎382 2545 or 330 6590), in Plaka, or Akademias 78 (☎522 7717), in Exarhia. €3 per hr. Open 24hr.

Post Office: Syndagma (☎622 6253), on the corner of Mitropoleos. Open M-F 7:30am-8pm, Sa 7:30am-2pm. **Postal Code:** 10300.

ACCOMMODATIONS

The **Greek Youth Hostel Association,** Damareos 75, in Pangrati, lists other cheap hostels in Greece (☎751 9530; www.grhotels.com). The **Hellenic Chamber of Hotels,** Stadiou 24, in Syndagma, has listings of all hotels in Greece, but no longer makes reservations. Call for information in several languages. The office is on the 7th floor to the left. (☎323 7193. Open M-F 8am-2pm.)

Athens Backpackers, Makri 12 (☎922 4044; www.backpackers.gr). By far the best hostel in Athens. This popular place has an awesome staff and a rooftop bar right under the Acropolis. Trips to Sounion, Delphi, and Nafplion €45-50. Breakfast included. Laundry €5. Internet €1 per 15min., €3 per hr. Reserve far ahead. Co-ed dorms €25. MC/V. ❷

Youth Hostel #5 Pangrati, Damareos 75 (☎751 9530; y-hostels@ote.net). From Pl. Syndagma, take trolley #2 or 11 to Filolaou. Though far from the city center, this hostel is friendly and cheap. Bring a sleeping bag to stay on the roof (€10). Hot showers €0.50 per 7min. Laundry €4. Quiet hours 2-5pm and 11pm-7am. Dorms €10-12. ❶

Hostel Aphrodite (HI), Einardou 12 (☎881 0589; www.hostelaphrodite.com), by the Larissa train station. Basic rooms with A/C. Low prices, friendly atmosphere, and proximity to the station make this a backpackers' favorite. Free Internet. Reception 24hr. Dorms €16; doubles €46; triples €57; quads €60. ❷

Hotel Metropolis, Mitropoleos 46 (☎321 7469; www.hotelmetropolis.gr), in Syndagma. Enjoy comfortable rooms and views of the cathedral and the Acropolis. Elevator and A/C. Laundry €10. Singles €40, with bath €50; doubles €45/60; triples €75. ❹

FOOD

Athens offers a mix of fast-food stands, open-air cafes, side-street *tavernas*, and intriguing restaurants. On the streets, vendors sell dried fruits and nuts or fresh coconut (€1-2), and you can find the usual spinach and cheese pies at any local bakery (€1.50-2). Cheap food abounds around **Syndagma.** Places in **Plaka** tend to serve "authentic Greek for tourists." If you really want to eat like a local, head to the simple *tavernas* uphill on **Em. Benaki** and in **Kolonaki.**

Crepes of the World, Areopagitou 3, in Plaka. On the corner with Amalias, right under the Acropolis. This colorful place serves the best crepes in town, all internationally themed. More expensive to sit on the Acropolis promenade. Open daily 7am-3am. ❶

Savvas, Mitropoleos 86, right off of Pl. Monastiraki, across from the flea market. Cab drivers and kiosk vendors alike recommend this always-busy joint for the best souvlaki in town. Save money by eating on the fly; restaurant prices for gyros plates (€8) shrink to €1.50-1.80 for take-out wraps. Open daily 8:30am-3am. Cash only. ❶

O Barba Giannis, Em. Benaki 94 (☎382 4138). From Syndagma, walk down Stadiou, make a right on Em. Benaki, and walk uphill for 10min. Order one of the satisfying specials, on display in front. Entrees €3.50-7. Open M-Sa noon-1:30am. Cash only. ❷

Platanos, Diogenous 4 (☎322 0666). Near the hustle of touristy Adrianou and Kydatheon, Platanos offers authentic fare—the menu hasn't changed since 1932. Several veggie options from €5.50. Open July-Aug. M-Sa noon-4:30pm and 7:30pm-midnight; Sept.-June M-Sa noon-4:30pm and 7:30pm-midnight, Su noon-4:30pm. Cash only. ❷

SIGHTS

ACROPOLIS

Looming over the city, the Acropolis has been the heart of Athens since the 5th century BC. Although each Greek *polis* had an *acropolis* (high point of the city), the buildings atop Athens's peak outshone their imitators and continue to awe visitors. Visit as early in the day as possible to avoid crowds and the broiling midday sun. *(Entrance on Dionissou Areopagitou or Theorias. ☎321 0219. Open daily 8am- 7:30pm; low season 8am-2:30pm. Admission includes access to all of the sights below the Acropolis, including Hadrian's Arch, the Temple of Olympian Zeus, and the Agora, within a 48hr. period; tickets can be purchased at any of the sights. €12, students €6, under 19 free. Cash only.)*

PARTHENON. The **Temple of Athena Parthenos** (Athena the Virgin), more commonly known as the Parthenon, watches over Athens. Ancient Athenians saw their city as the capital of civilization; the **metopes** (scenes in the spaces above the columns) on the sides of the temple celebrate Athens's rise. The architect Iktinos integrated the Golden Mean, a four-to-nine ratio, in every aspect of the temple.

ACROPOLIS MUSEUM. The museum, which neighbors the Parthenon, houses a superb collection of sculptures, including five of the original **Caryatids** that supported the southern side of the Erechtheion. The statues initially seem to be identical, but a close look at the folds of their drapery reveals delicately individualized detail. Compare the stylized face and frozen pose of the Archaic period **Moschophoros** (calf-bearer) sculpture to the idealized Classical period **Kritios Boy.** The museum is perhaps one of the most interesting stops in a visit to the Acropolis. *(Open M 11am-7pm, Tu-Su 8am-7:30pm; low season M 11am-2pm, Tu-Su 8am-2pm.)*

TEMPLE OF ATHENA NIKE. This tiny temple was raised during the Peace of Nikias (421-415 BC), a respite from the Peloponnesian War. The temple, known as the "jewel of Greek architecture," is ringed by eight miniature Ionic columns and houses a statue of Nike, the winged goddess of victory. The Athenians, afraid Nike might abandon them, amputated her wings. The remains of the 5m-thick **Cyclopean wall,** which once circled the Acropolis, are visible below the temple.

ERECHTHEION. Completed in 406 BC, just before Sparta defeated Athens in the Peloponnesian War, the Erechtheion lies to the left of the Parthenon and is supported by copies of the famous Caryatids in the museum. The building is named after the snake-bodied hero Erechtheus, speared during a battle between Athena and Poseidon over the city's patronage. The goddess won the battle and offered the Athenians a better gift—an olive tree—than the horse her rival donated. The eastern half of the Erechtheion, where the symbolic olive tree stands, is devoted to the goddess of wisdom, and the western half to the god of the sea.

ELSEWHERE ON THE ACROPOLIS. The southwestern corner of the Acropolis looks down over the **Odeon of Herodes Atticus,** a reconstructed theater dating from AD 160. See the *Athens News* for a performance schedule. You'll also see nearby ruins of the **Classical Theater of Dionysus,** the **Asclepion,** and the **Stoa of Eumenes II.**

OTHER SIGHTS

AGORA. The Agora served as the city's marketplace, administrative center, and hub of daily life from the 6th century BC to the AD 6th century. Here, the debates of Athenian democracy raged; Socrates, Aristotle, Demosthenes, Xenophon, and St. Paul all instructed. The 415 BC **Hephaesteion,** on a hill in the northwest corner of the Agora, is the best-preserved Classical temple in Greece, boasting **friezes** depicting Hercules's labors and Theseus's adventures. The **Stoa of Attalos** was an ancient shopping mall and home to informal philosophers' gatherings. Reconstructed in the 1950s, it now houses the **Agora Museum.** According to Plato, Socrates's first trial was held at the **Royal Stoa,** left of the Adrianou exit. *(Enter the Agora off Pl. Thission, from Adrianou, or as you descend from the Acropolis. ☎321 0185. Agora open daily 8am-7:30pm; low season 8am-2:30pm. Museum open Tu-Su 8am-7:30pm; low season 8am-2:30pm. €4, students and EU seniors €2, under 18 and EU students free.)*

ROMAN AGORA. The Roman Agora was a large rectangular structure built between 19 and 11 BC with donations from Julius and Augustus Caesar. The ruined columns of the two surviving **prophylae,** a nearly intact entrance gate, and the **gate of Athena Archgetis** stand as testaments to what was once a lively meeting place. Also nearby are the **vespasianae,** or public toilets, constructed in the AD first century, as well as a 1456 mosque. By far the most intriguing structure in the site is the well-preserved (and restored) **Tower of the Winds,** with reliefs of the eight winds on each side of the clock tower. This octagonal stone tower, originally built in the first century BC by the astronomer Andronikos, was initially crowned by a weathervane. Etched onto the walls are markings that allowed it to be used as a sundial from the outside and a water-clock from the inside. *(☎324 5220. Open daily 8am-7:30pm. €2, students €1, under 19 and EU students free.)*

KERAMIKOS. This geometrically designed site includes a large-scale cemetery built around the **Sacred Way,** the road to Eleusis, where illustrious Athenians were buried in ancient times. A wide boulevard from the site ran to the sanctuary of **Aka-**

demes, where Plato founded his school. The **Oberlaender Museum** displays moving funerary stones and highly detailed pottery and sculpture. *(Northwest of the Agora. From Syndagma, walk 1km toward Monastiraki on Ermou. ☎346 3552. Open Tu-Su 8:30am-7:30pm. €2, students €1, under 19 and EU students free.)*

TEMPLE OF OLYMPIAN ZEUS AND HADRIAN'S ARCH. On the edge of the National Gardens in Plaka, you can spot traces of the Temple of Olympian Zeus, the largest temple ever built in Greece. Started in the 6th century BC, it was completed 600 years later by Roman emperor Hadrian, who added an arch to mark the boundary between the ancient city of Theseus and his new city. *(Vas. Olgas at Amalias. Open daily 8am-7:30pm. Temple €2, students and EU seniors €1, under 19 free. Arch free.)*

PANATHENAIC STADIUM. The impressive Panathenaic Olympic Stadium, also known as the Kallimarmaro, is carved into a hillside between the National Gardens and Pangrati, and its white steps are easily spotted from any of Athens's hills. The site of the first modern Olympic Games in 1896, the stadium seats 70,000 and served as the finish line of the marathon and the venue for archery during the 2004 Summer Olympic Games. A new Olympic stadium sits in the northern suburb of Marousi. *(On Vas. Konstantinou. From Syndagma, walk up Amalias for 15min. to Vas. Olgas, then follow it left. Or take trolley #2, 4, or 11 from Syndagma. Open daily 8am-8:30pm. Free.)*

MUSEUMS

NATIONAL ARCHAEOLOGICAL MUSEUM. Almost every artifact in this collection is a masterpiece. The museum's highlights include the so-called **Mask of Agamemnon,** excavated from the tomb of a king who lived at least three centuries earlier than Agamemnon himself, as well as the perfect, bronze **Poseidon of Artemision,** believed to represent Zeus. The museum also has a comprehensive timeline of the development of Greek sculpture. *(Patission 44. Take trolley #2, 4, 5, 9, 11, 15, or 18 from the uphill side of Syndagma, or trolley #3 or 13 from the northern side of Vas. Sofias. ☎821 7717. Open M 1-7:30pm, Tu-Su 8am-7:30pm, holidays 8:30am-3pm. €7, students and EU seniors €3, under 19 and EU students free. No flash photography.)*

MUSEUM OF ISLAMIC ART. Built on the ruins of ancient Athenian fortifications, the building's large glass windows, spotless marble staircases, and sparkling white walls showcase a collection of brilliant tiles, metalwork, and tapestries documenting the history of the Islamic world from the 12th to 18th centuries. The exhibit includes an inlaid marble reception room transported from a 17th-century Cairo mansion and a plaque with the footprints of the Prophet. *(Ag. Asomaton 22, in Psiri. M: Thissou. ☎367 1000; www.benaki.gr. Open Tu and Th-Su 9am-3pm, W 9am-9pm. €5, students and seniors €2.50, EU students free. W free.)*

MUSEUM OF GREEK POPULAR MUSICAL INSTRUMENTS. A three-floor building just off the bustle of Plaka, this fascinating little museum displays all kinds of traditional instruments, from flutes in all pitches and shapes, to bells, mandolins, bag pipes, and violins, accompanied by photographs and by headphones for listening to each sound in local folk melodies. *(1-2 Diogenous, in Plaka. ☎325 0198. Open Tu and Th-Su 10am-2pm, W noon-6pm. Free.)*

GOULANDRIS MUSEUM OF CYCLADIC AND ANCIENT GREEK ART. Established by the Goulandris shipping family, this museum displays a stunning collection of Cycladic figurines—sleek, abstract marble works, some almost 5000 years old—as well as bronze jewelry from Skyros, a collection of vases, and Corinthian helmets. Past the cafe, follow the hallway to the extension of the museum, located in a gorgeously renovated 1895 **mansion** on the corner of Vas. Sofias and Herodotou. This wing hosts temporary exhibits of works by world-renowned painters. *(Neophy-*

tou Douka 4. Walk 20min. toward Kolonaki from Syndagma on Vas. Sofias; turn left on Neophytou Douka. Accessible by trolleys #3 and 13. ☎722 8321. No photography. Open M and W-F 10am-4pm, Sa 10am-3pm. €5, seniors, students, and Sa €2.50.)

ENTERTAINMENT AND NIGHTLIFE

The weekly *Athens News* (€1) lists events, as well as news and ferry information. Summer performances are staged in **Lycavittos Theater** as part of the **Athens Festival.** Chic Athenians head to the seaside clubs of **Glyfada,** where Balux, Prime, Envy, and Plus Soda are perfect places to enjoy the breezy night air. (Drinks €4-10. Cover €10-15. Dress well; no shorts.) Take the A2, A3, or B3 bus from Vas. Amalias to Glyfada (€0.75), then catch a cab from there to your club. Taxis to Glyfada run about €8; the return trip typically costs €10-15. **Psiri** is the bar district, just across the main square in Monastiraki. Get started on **Miaouli,** where young crowds gather after dark. For an alternative to spending money in a bar, follow the guitar-playing local teens and couples that pack **Pavlou** at night.

Bretto's, Kydatheneon 41, between Farmaki and Afroditis in Plaka. This historical establishment with walls covered in dusty bottles serves almost exclusively home-brewed alcohol. €5 per bottle of red wine; €2 per sizable glass. Open daily 10am-midnight.

Daily, Xenokratous 47. Kolonaki's friendly student population converges here to drink, listen to reggae and Italian pop, and watch sports on TV. Great outdoor seating. Mixed drinks €3-6. Open daily 9am-2am.

Wunderbar, Themistokleous 80, on Pl. Exarhia, plays pop to relaxed cocktail-sippers. Late-night revelers lounge outside under large umbrellas. Beer €5-6. Mixed drinks €8-9. Open Su-Th 9am-3am, F-Sa 9am-5am. Cash only.

THE PELOPONNESE Πελοπόννεσος

Stretching its fingers into the Mediterranean, the Peloponnese transports its visitors to another time and place through its rich history and folklore. The achievements of ancient civilizations dot the stunning landscape of the peninsula. Here rest the majority of Greece's most significant archaeological sites, including Corinth, Epidavros, Messini, Mycenae, Mystras, and Olympia. Away from large, urban transportation hubs, serene villages welcome visitors to traditional Greece.

FERRIES TO ITALY

Boats sail from Patras to Ancona, Bari, Brindisi, and Venice, all on the Adriatic coast of Italy. Several ferry lines make the trip; they all have different prices, so check the travel offices along Othonas Amalias and make sure to shop around for cheaper deals. Railpasses won't work for domestic ferries, but for international ferries, **Superfast Ferries,** Oth. Amalias 12 (☎2610 622 500; open daily 9am-9pm), accepts Eurailpasses. Questions about departures from Patras should be directed to the Port Authority (☎2610 341 002).

PATRAS Πάτρας ☎2610

Patras (pop. 350,000) suffers from the consequences of charter tourism that skips the city to head directly to the nearby islands. Its location on the northwestern tip of the Peloponnese continues to make it one of the fundamental transportation hubs in the region. The crazy **Carnival** (Jan. 17-Feb. 21; info ☎222 157; www.carnivalpatras.gr) revives ancient celebrations in honor of Dionysus—god of debauchery—and becomes one gigantic dance floor of costumed and inebriated people, consumed by pre-Lenten madness. Follow the waterfront with the town to your left to reach **Agios Andreas,** the largest Orthodox cathedral in Greece; it is entirely covered in colorful frescoes. (Open daily 7am-9pm.) Sweet black grapes are made into Mavrodaphne wine at the **Achaïa Clauss Winery,** Greece's most famous vineyard. Take bus #7 (30min., €1.20) toward Seravali from the intersection of Kanakari and Gerokostopoulou. (☎368 100. Open daily 10am-6pm. Hourly tours in English 10am-3pm. Free.) Built on the ruins of an ancient acropolis and continuously in use from the 6th century through WWII, Patras's **Castle** is up the steps from the central Nikolaou. (☎990 691. Open Tu-Su 8:30am-7pm. Free.) **Patras Youth Hostel ❶,** Polytechniou 62, has basic bunk-bed dorms in an old villa surrounded by a eucalyptus garden, right across the street from the sea. (☎42 72 78; www.patrasrooms.gr. Free safes. Linens €0.50. Reception 24hr. Check-out 10:30am. Dorms €10.) The laid-back, cafeteria-style **Europa Center ❶,** on Amalias next to the tourist office, is run by enthusiastic, Boston-raised Greeks, serves large portions (entrees €3-7), and offers Internet (€1.50 per 30min.), free luggage storage, and a book exchange. (Open daily 7am-midnight. MC/V.) The hippest bar on the Ag. Nikolaou strip, **Cibo Cibo ❷,** on the left coming from the port, serves fresh and fancy Italian food during the day (salads €6; entrees €5-12), and mixed drinks (€8) late into the evening. (☎620 761. Open daily 7am-3am.)

Trains (☎639 108) leave from the central Amalias 47, right across the port, for Athens (4¼hr., 8 per day, €5.30-10) and Kalamata (5½hr., 3 per day, €5-10) via Pirgos (2hr., €2.80-5.40), where you can catch a bus to Olympia. KTEL **buses** (☎623 886; www.ktel.org) leave from farther down on Oth. Amalias for: Athens (3hr., 2 per hr., €15); Ioannina (4hr., 2 per day, €18); Kalamata (3½hr., 2 per day, €18); Thessaloniki (7½hr., 4 per day, €35). **Ferries** go to: Corfu (7hr., 2 per day, €26-30); Ithaka (2-3½hr., 2 per day, €13); Kephalonia (2½hr., 2 per day, €13); Zakynthos (1½hr., 6 per day, €6). Six major ferry lines have international connections to Italy: Ancona (21hr., 4 per day); Bari (16hr., 2 per day); Brindisi (14hr., 1 per day); Venice (30hr., 2 per day). The **tourist office** is 50m pas the bus station on Amalias. (☎461 740. Open daily 8am-10pm.) **Postal Code:** 26001.

OLYMPIA Ολυμπία ☎26240

Every four years in ancient times, city-states would call a sacred truce and travel to Olympia for a pan-Hellenic assembly that showcased athletic ability and fostered peace and diplomacy. Modern Olympia,

THE IDIOT'S GUIDE TO DRINKING OUZO

When you go out for your first meal in Greece, don't be surprised or flattered if your waiter rushes out before your entree arrives to present you with a shot glass full of liquor, a glass of water, and the simple command, "Drink!" He's just assuming that you, like almost every Greek, want to cleanse your palate and ease your mind with some ouzo.

The art to enjoying the anise-flavored national drink is important to know if you don't want to expose yourself as a neophyte. First, don't take that shot like a frat boy. Good ouzo is around 40% alcohol by volume and just isn't made to be chugged. It's invariably served with a glass of water for the purpose of mixing; that's what turns it milky-white. The key is to keep adding water as you drink to avoid dehydration and other ill effects. Second, snack on some *mezedes* while you take your ouzo. Munching on a salad, some cheese, or vegetables will temper the alcohol and prolong the experience. That's the point, after all: Greece's obsession with ouzo has nothing to do with getting plastered on something that tastes like licorice. Instead, it's about drinking lazily, relaxing in a *kafeneion,* and chatting with friends until the sun sets and dinner begins.

set among meadows and shaded by cypress and olive trees, is recognized for its pristine natural beauty as much as for its illustrious past. The ancient **Olympic arena,** whose central sanctuary was called the **Altis,** draws hordes of tourists. In **Ancient Olympia,** to the north of the Bouleuterion (toward the entrance), lie the ruins of the **Temple of Zeus.** Once home to master sculptor Phidias's awe-inspiring **Statue of Zeus,** one of the Seven Wonders of the Ancient World, the 27m sanctuary was the largest temple completed on the Greek mainland before the Parthenon. The ruins of the **Temple of Hera,** dating from the 7th century BC, are better preserved than those of Zeus's Temple; they sit to the left, facing the hill, past the temples of Metroön and the Nymphaeum. Today, the **Olympic Flame** lighting ceremony takes place here before the symbol travels around the world to announce the opening of the games. (Open June-Sept. daily 8:30am-7:30pm.) The **Archaeological Museum** has an impressive sculpture collection. (Open M noon-7:30pm, Tu-Su 8am-7:30pm. Temple and museum each €6, students €3. Site and museum together €9/5.) Many of the museums are air-conditioned, including the interesting **Museum of the History of the Olympic Games** and the small **Museum of the History of Excavations,** with photographs documenting the site's recovery. (Open M 12:30-7:30pm, Tu-Su 8am-7:30pm. Free.)

The centrally located **Youth Hostel ❶,** Kondili 18, across from the main square, is a cheap place to get to know international backpackers and has bright, airy rooms and narrow balconies. (☎22 580. Linens €1. Curfew 11pm. Check-out 10am. Closed Jan. Dorms €10; doubles €25. Cash only.) Mini-markets, bakeries, and fast-food establishments line **Kondili,** while a walk toward the railroad station or up the hill leads to inexpensive *tavernas*. A filling meal is as Greek as it gets at **Vasilakis Restaurant ❷,** on the corner of Karamanli and Spiliopoulou. Take a right off Kohili before the Youth Hostel, or just follow your nose; the delicious meat dishes can be smelled from a block away. (☎22 104. Entrees €5-10. Open daily 11:30am-4pm and 6pm-1am.) **Trains** leave the station in the lower part of town to Pyrgos (30min., 5 per day), as do **buses** (45min., 15 per day, €1.70). The Town Hall **information center,** at the right end of Kondili, before the turn to the sites, acts as a tourist office. (☎22 549; aolympia@otenet.gr. Open M-F 8am-2pm.) **Postal Code:** 27065.

SPARTA Σπάρτη AND MYSTRAS Μυστράς ☎27310

Though the fierce Spartans of antiquity were known to throw babies off cliffs, today's Spartans make olive oil, not war. The meager ruins at **Ancient Sparta** are actually a couple of stones and a field of olive trees, a 1km walk north along Paleologou from the center of town. Coming from the bus station, two blocks before the central *plateia* on Lykourgou lies perhaps the most interesting sight in town, Sparta's **Archaeological Museum.** In a romantic garden of orange trees and headless statues, this old museum displays the usual vases and stones as well as some fascinating votive masks, mosaics, and lead figurines that look like a toy army. (Open Tu-Sa 8:30am-3pm, Su 9:30am-2:30pm. €2, students €1, EU students free.) Accommodations in Sparta rarely come cheap, and there is nothing about the place that makes it a terribly tempting place to stay. **Hotel Cecil ❸,** Paleologou 125, on the corner with Thermopylon, has ordinary, spotless rooms with TV, A/C, phone, and private baths in a freshly renovated building. (☎24 980. Reservations required. Singles €40; doubles €60; triples €75. V.) **Buses** from Sparta go to: Areopolis (1½hr., 2 per day, €5.40); Athens (3½hr., 10 per day, €16) via Tripoli (1hr., €4.20); Corinth (2½hr., €10); Monemvasia (2½hr., 3 per day, €8). To reach the town center from the bus station, walk about 10 blocks slightly uphill on Lykourgou; the **tourist office** is on the third floor of the glass building in the *plateia*. (☎24 852. Open M-F 8am-2pm.) Buses to Mystras leave from the station and from the corner of Lykourgou and Leonidou in Sparta for the ruins, and they return 15min. later (20min., 4-9 per day, €1).Taxis go to Mystras from the corner of Paleologou and Lykourgou (€5).

Sparta makes a good base for visiting **Mystras,** 6km away. Once the religious center of all of Byzantium and the locus of Constantinople's rule over the Peloponnese, this medieval town on a hill is perhaps one of the best preserved of its kind; a walk up its narrow footpaths has the power to take you back to the past in an unusually realistic way. Its extraordinary ruins comprise a city of Byzantine churches, chapels, and monasteries, alongside frescoed walls, olive trees, and wildflowers. Although churches like **Agia Sophia** and **Agios Theodoros** are the highlights, a visit to the **Palace** is a must, where pointed arches and stone walls tell a history of the region. Modest dress is required to visit the functioning nunnery and its beautifully decorated **Pantanassa Church. Postal Code:** 23100.

MONEMVASIA Μονεμβασία ☎27320

Perched on a monolithic rock that seems to spring from the sea like a gigantic iceberg, the island of Monemvasia is a jewel. No cars or bikes are allowed within the walls of the tiny Old Town, so wandering around the flowered balconies and picturesque corners gives the feeling that time stopped in the Middle Ages. At the edge of town is **Agia Sofia,** a 12th-century basilica. (Open daily 8:30am-3pm and 6:30-8:30pm. Free.) Across the street is the **Archaeological Museum** (Open M noon-5pm, Tu-Su 8am-5pm. Free.) To get to the Old Town, cross the bridge from New Monemvasia and follow the road as it curves up the hill. It's an easy 20min. walk, but the heat and crowd both increase as the day goes on. It's better to go in the early morning or late evening, when the setting sun gives the panorama breathtaking shades. There is also a white van that shuttles people up and down the road that leaves from the bridge at the foot of the hill and stops at the entrance to the Old Town (2min., every 15min. 8am-midnight, free). Past the Old Town, it's also possible to walk all the way to the top of the rock to the castle. Follow the 30min. paths on either end of town and wear sturdy shoes.

It is much less expensive to stay in **New Town Monemvasia,** across the bridge from old Monemvasia. The waterfront *domatia* along the harbor are the best option for budget travelers. The rock walls and elegant interior of **Hotel Belissis ❸,** with beautiful rooms, A/C, TV, fridge, and private baths, feel like they belong in the Old Town. From the bus station, walk along the main road, Spartis, away from the bridge for less than 5min. It will be on the left, right across the street from the beach. (☎61 217 or 61 610. Singles €30; doubles €45; 4-person apartment with kitchenette €50-60. Cash only.) With a unique ambience, dining in the Old Town is beautiful and very expensive. On the main road on the right, just before the Archaeological Museum, is **Restaurant Matoula ❸,** which offers terrace seating, and the unobstructed views of the clear waters below almost justify a €7 moussaka. (☎61 660. Entrees €8-15. Open daily noon-midnight. MC/V.) For those on a tighter budget, there are many cheap Greek fast-food eateries and bakeries. Backpackers often picnic on the beach in the New Town, soaking in the same views for free.

Buses leave from Spartis for: Athens, either express (1 per day, 5:15am, €23) or via Skala (40min., €23); Ithsmos (4hr., €23); Sparta (2hr.); Tripoli (3hr.). **Malvasia Travel Agency,** by the bus stop, provides **currency exchange** (3% commission), and tickets for **ferries** that leave Monemvasia to Athens and Kithira island. (☎61 752; fax 61 432. Open daily in high season 7am-3:30pm and 5-8pm; low season 7am-3:30pm.) **Postal Code:** 23070.

NAFPLION Ναύφπλιο ☎27520

A tiny Venetian town surrounded on three sides by sky-blue waters, Nafplion is one of the Peloponnese's most beautiful—and most touristed—destinations. In July and August, the town plays host to more Americans and Italians than locals. After passing from the Venetians to the Ottomans and back again, Nafplion became Greece's first capital in 1821. The town's crown jewel is the 18th-century

Palamidi fortress, with spectacular views of the town and gulf. Walk up the 999 steps from across the central *plateia*, right across from the bus station, or if that's too grueling, take a taxi up the 3km road. (Open 8am-7pm. €4, non-EU students €2, EU students and under 18 free.) A small, pebbly beach, **Arvanitia,** is farther along Polizoidhou, past the Palamidi steps; if it's too crowded, follow the footpath to lovely private coves, or take a taxi (€5) to sandy **Karathona** beach.

To reach **Bouboulinas,** the waterfront promenade, go left from the bus station and follow Syngrou to the harbor; the **Old Town** is on your left. If you are coming from Arvanitia, you can also walk the short **path** around the promontory, keeping the sea to your left and the town's walls to your right. Accommodations in Old Town are often expensive, but **Dimitris Beka Domatia ❷** is an excellent budget option. The simple rooms are clean and have A/C. There is a fantastic roof terrace overlooking the Old Town, and the owner is a friendly collector of American baseball memorabilia. From the bus station, walk right onto Fotomara until you reach the small Catholic church, then turn right onto Zygomala, and left up the first set of stairs. (☎24 594. Reserve ahead July-Aug. Singles €19; doubles from €25; triples €33. All prices negotiable. Cash only.) **Ellas ❷,** in pl. Syndagma, serves refreshingly inexpensive Greek and Italian food, and is a great spot for people-watching on the central *plateia*. (☎27 278. Veal with potatoes €6.50. Pasta dishes €4. V.) **Buses** (☎27 323 28 555) leave from Syngrou for: Athens (3hr., 1 per hr.) via Argos (1hr.) and Corinth (2hr.); Epidavros (45min., 4 per day, €2.30); and Mycenae (45min., 3 per day, €2.30). English-language schedules are posted outside the station; buy tickets on the bus. The **tourist office** is at 25 Martio. (☎24 444. Open daily 9am-1pm and 4-8pm.) **Postal Code:** 21100.

EPIDAVROS Επίδαυρος ☎27530

Like Olympia and Delphi, Epidavros was once both a town and a sanctuary—first to the ancient deity Maleatas and then to Apollo. Eventually the energies of the sanctuary were directed toward the demigod **Asclepius,** the son of Apollo who caught Zeus's wrath (and even worse, his fatal thunderbolt) when the good doctor got a little overzealous and began to raise people from the dead. Under the patronage of Asclepius, Epidavros became famous across the ancient world as a center of medicine. Today, visitors can explore the **sanctuary** and visit an overcrowded and non-air-conditioned **museum** of ancient medical equipment and other artifacts. (☎22 009. Sanctuary open daily June-Sept. 8am-7pm; Oct.-May 8am-5pm. Museum open June-Sept. M noon-7pm, Tu-Su 8am-7pm; Oct.-May M noon-5pm, Tu-Su 8am-5pm. Both open during festival F-Sa 8am-8pm. €6, non-EU students €3, EU students and under 19 free.) The best-known structure at the site, however, is the splendidly preserved **theater,** built in AD 2 and renowned for its extraordinary acoustics. When the theater is silent, you can hear a piece of paper being ripped on stage from any seat in the house, but the place is usually too packed with loud visitors to test it out. Epidavros is best visited as a daytrip from Nafplion (returns at noon, 1, 4, 6pm). There are also buses to Athens (2hr., 6:30am and noon, €7). The helpful **tourist office** is located near the theater. (☎22 026. Open June-Aug. M-Th 9am-7pm, F-Su 9am-10pm.)

MYCENAE Μυκήνες ☎27330

The head of the Greek world from 1600 to 1100 BC, Mycenae was ruled by the legendary Agamemnon, leader of the Greek forces in the Trojan War. Excavations of ancient Mycenae have continued since 1876, turning the hillside ruins into one of the most visited sites in Greece. The imposing **Lion's Gate** into the ancient city has two lions carved in relief above the lintel and is estimated to weigh 20 tons. On top, a line of stones marks the perimeter of what used to be one of the ancient world's most illustrious palaces. At the far end of the city, between the palace and the **postern gate,** is the **underground cistern,** which guaranteed water during sieges. Across from the entrance, a **museum** details the history of the town and its excavations. Characteristic of Mycenaean Greece, a *tholos* is a beehive-shaped tomb generally built into the side of a hill. The most famous *tholos* in Mycenae is the **Tomb of Agamemnon** (a.k.a. the Treasury of Atreus), 400m downhill toward the town, a large and impressive *tholos* that children love to climb. (Sites open daily June-Oct. 8am-7:30pm; Nov.-May 8am-3pm. €8, students €4, EU students and children free. Keep your ticket for the museum and *tholos* or pay twice.) **Buses** from Mycenae go to Nafplion (45min.; 11am, 1, 3pm; €2.30) via Argos (30min., €2), or you can walk the 3km downhill to nearby Fihtio, where you can catch connections to Athens and Corinth.

NORTHERN AND CENTRAL GREECE

For travelers seeking to distance themselves from hectic Athens and the tourist-packed islands, northern and central Greece offer an idyllic escape. Ripe with fantastic hiking and Byzantine and Hellenistic heritage, the Greek heartland also boasts several major cities, including Thessaloniki and Ioannina. A region connected both ethnically and historically to its Balkan neighbors, the north is where the multicultural Greek state surfaces.

THESSALONIKI Θεσσαλονίκη ☎2310

Thessaloniki (a.k.a. Salonica; pop. 1,083,000), the Balkans' trade center, has historically been one of the most diverse cities in Greece, second in size only to Athens. The city is an energetic bazaar of cheap clothing shops and fashionable cafes, while its harbor, churches, and mosques provide a material timeline of the region's restless past. Romans, Venetians, Turks, Jews, Greeks, and Albanians have all had influence here, giving the city both an intriguing Middle Eastern feel and the lively rhythm of a southern European port, bathed in golden mosaics, gleaming frescoes, and the floating domes of the many Byzantine churches. Most travelers spend a couple of days in Thessaloniki checking out the sights, visiting the world-class museums, clubbing, and touring the nearby archaeological sites at Pella and Vergina, but the city is also an important transportation hub.

TRANSPORTATION

Flights: The **airport** (**SKG;** ☎985 000), 16km east of town, can be reached by bus #78 from the KTEL bus station on Pl. Aristotelous, or by taxi (€15). **Olympic Airways,** Kountouriotou 3, (☎368 311, general info 801 114 4444, from abroad 0030 10 966 6666; www.olympicairlines.com) and **Aegean Airlines,** Nikis and Av. Venizelos 1, (reservations ☎476 470, general info 801 112 0000, from abroad 0030 21 06 26 10 00; www.aegeanair.com), the two domestic carriers, have offices at the departure terminal and in the city center, on the street across from the port.

Trains: To reach the **main terminal** (☎599 421 or 517 513); Monastiriou 28, in the western part of the city, take any bus to Egnatia (€0.50). Facing the street, the train station is 20m to the left. Trains go to: **Athens** (4½-6½hr., 11 per day, €15-49); **İstanbul, TUR** (11½-14hr., 2 per day, €40-48); **Sofia, BUL** (7hr., 3 per day, €15); **Skopje, MAC** (3hr., 2 per day, €11); **Xanthi** (3½-4½hr., 7 per day, €7-13.50). The **travel office** (☎11 10) has schedules, English-language assistance, and maps.

Buses: Most **KTEL** buses leave from the dome-shaped **Macedonia Bus Station,** west of the city center (☎595 411 or 595 421). Local buses leave and arrive outside of the dome. Bus #1 is a shuttle service between the train and bus stations (every 15min.,

€0.50), but any bus going to Egnatia will stop at the station (#8 and 12 are among the most frequent). Intercity buses leave and arrive under the dome. To: **Athens** (6hr., 11 per day, €33); **Corinth** (7½hr., 11:30pm, €37); **Ioannina** (6½hr., 5 per day, €25); **Patras** (7½hr., 4 per day, €35). **Go,** the Macedonia Station's timetable booklet, is distributed for free at the station and has the complete list of times and destinations, but schedules are still subject to change. The station has **luggage storage** (☎595 505. Open M-F 9am-7:30pm, Sa 9am-2:30pm. 4hr. €1.50, 8 hr. €2, 1 day €3, 10 days €14).

Ferries: Buy tickets at **Karacharisis Travel and Shipping Agency,** Kountouriotou 8 (☎513 005 or 524 544; fax 532 289), next to the post office by the port. Open M-F 8:30am-8:30pm, Sa 8:30am-2:30pm. Mid-June to early Sept., ferries travel to: **Chios** (21hr.) via **Limnos** (8hr.) and **Lesvos** (14 hr.); **Kos** (21hr.) via **Samos** (16hr.).

Local Transportation: Local buses run frequently throughout the city. Buy tickets for €0.50 at *periptera* or newsstand booths or for €0.60 on the bus. The automatic machines don't give change. A €2 ticket allows unlimited rides for 24hr. There are 5 main **taxi** operators in the city (Thessaloniki ☎551 525; Macedonia 550 500); they gather at stands on Ag. Sophia, Mitropoleos/Aristotelou, and at the train and bus stations.

ORIENTATION AND PRACTICAL INFORMATION

Though large and chaotic, Thessaloniki is not difficult to navigate, made up of broad walkways running parallel or perpendicular to the water. **Egnatia,** a Roman highway, starts at **Demokratias Square** and runs east-west through town. Most sights, like the Rotunda and the Kamara Arch, are around the northeast side of the town center, above Egnatia, while on the opposite side, Egnatia becomes **Monastiriou** and signals the beginning of the industrial area and the road to the bus and train stations. The street is home to most budget hotels, and most buses stop along it. Between Egnatia and the water, **Ermou, Tsimiski, Mitropoleos,** and **Nikis** are also lined with shops, banks, and services. Cutting perpendicularly through all of them, right in the center of the city, the pedestrian walkway **Aristotelou** runs the ruins of the **Roman Agora,** right below **Agios Dimitrios.** The port is at the left end of the waterfront, while at the opposite end, the **White Tower** (Levkos Pyrgos) marks the limit of the town's center and the beginning of the broad **theatres** and **museums** district, and of the **international fairgrounds** to the north. There is no clearly marked separation between the new and the **old city,** and no such distinction seems to have ever existed, as modern complexes spring from Byzantine ruins, and wherever you walk you will stumble across the remains of churches and ancient baths.

Tourist Offices: EOT, Tsimiski 136, in a new glass building in the Eastern part of the center, (☎221 100; www.eot.gr; open M-F 8am-2:45pm, Sa 8:30am-2pm) has a 24hr. **ATM.** Info centers are also at the arrivals floor at the airport and at the passenger terminal of the port, but there is no information at the Macedonia Bus Station.

Banks: Banks with currency exchange and 24hr. **ATMs** line Tsimiski, including **Citibank,** Tsimiski 21 (☎373 300). Open M-Th 8am-2:30pm, F 8am-2pm.

Tourist Police: Dodekanissou 4, 3rd fl. (☎554 871). Open daily 7:30am-10pm.

Telephones: OTE, Karolou Diehl 33 (☎134), at the corner of Ermou with Karolou, 1 block east of Aristotelous. Open M, W, and Sa 7:30am-3pm, T and Th-F 7:30am-9pm.

Internet Access: There is no shortage of Internet cafes in Thessaloniki. Behind the shopping complex that houses the American Consulate, **E-Global,** Vasileos Irakliou 40 (☎252 780), is 1 block to the right. Midnight-noon €1.50 per hr., noon-6pm €1.90 per hr., 6pm-midnight €2.40 per hr. Discount for members, membership €0.50. They also have a second branch on Egnatia 117, 50m left of the Arch of Galerius. **Meganet,** Pl. Navarinou 5 (☎250 331; www.meganet.gr), in the little square by the ruins of Galerius's palace. €1 per 30min.; noon-midnight €1.80 per hr. Laptop access. Open 24hr.

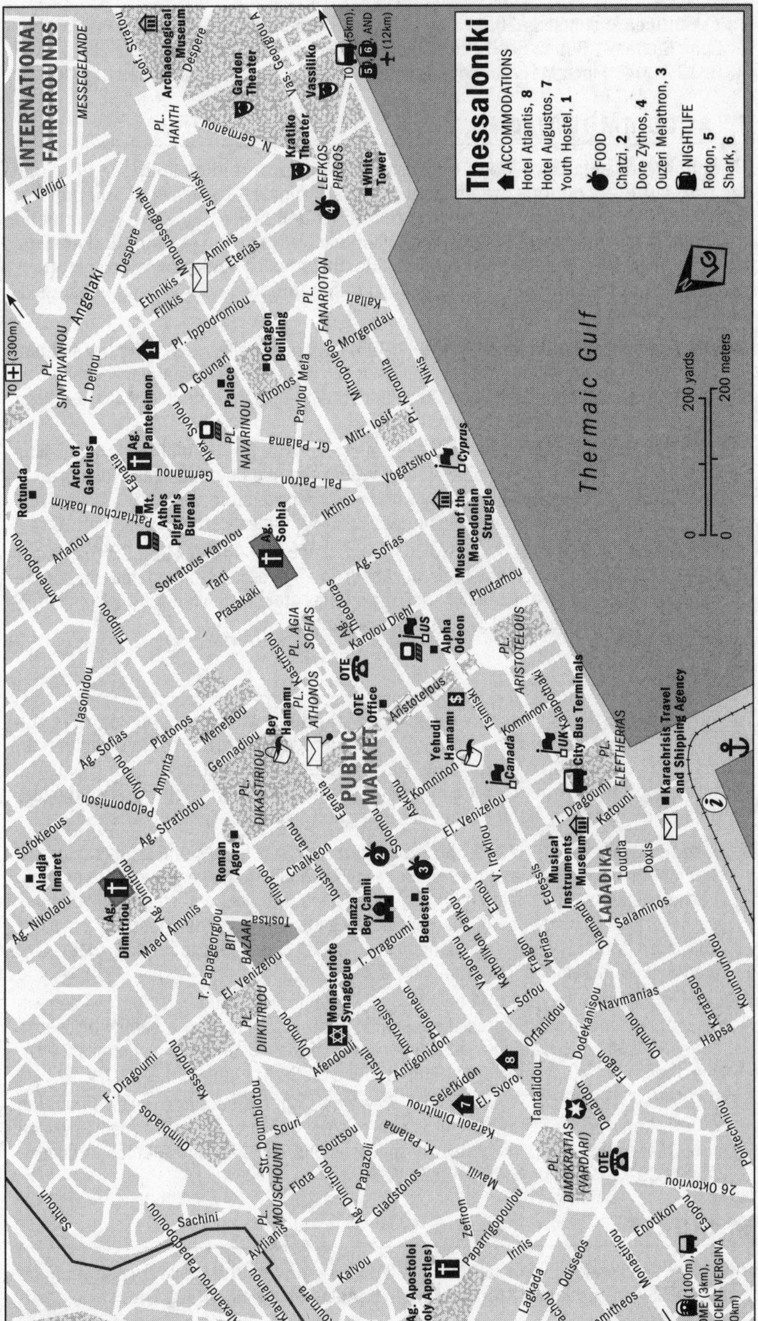
Thessaloniki
ACCOMMODATIONS
Hotel Atlantis, 8
Hotel Augustos, 7
Youth Hostel, 1
FOOD
Chatzi, 2
Dore Zythos, 4
Ouzeri Melathron, 3
NIGHTLIFE
Rodon, 5
Shark, 6
Thermaic Gulf
200 yards
200 meters
INTERNATIONAL FAIRGROUNDS
MESSEGELANDE
Archaeological Museum
Garden Theater
Kratiko Theater
Vassiliko
White Tower
LEFKOS PIRGOS
PL. HANTH
PL. SINTRIVANIOU
PL. NAVARINOU
PL. FANARIOTON
Rotunda
Arch of Galerius
Ag. Panteleimon
Palace
Octagon Building
Mt. Athos Pilgrim's Bureau
Ag. Sophia
PL. AGIA SOFIAS
Museum of the Macedonian Struggle
Cyprus
US
Alpha Odeon
PL. ARISTOTELOUS
OTE
OTE Office
PUBLIC MARKET
Bey Hamami
Yehudi Hamami
Canada
UK
City Bus Terminals
PL. ELEFTHERIAS
Karachrisis Travel and Shipping Agency
Musical Instruments Museum
LADADIKA
PL. DIKASTIRIOU
Roman Agora
Aladja Imaret
Ag. Dimitriou
BIT BAZAAR
Hamza Bey Camii
Bedesten
Monasteriote Synagogue
PL. DIIKITIRIOU
PL. DIMOKRATIAS (VARDARI)
PL. MOUSCHOUNTI
Ag. Apostoloi (Holy Apostles)
TO (300m)
TO (5km), 5, 6, AND (12km)
TO (100m), DOME (3km), ANCIENT VERGINA (30km)
Egnatia
Tsimiski
Mitropoleos
Nikis
Ag. Sofias
El. Venizelou
Aristotelous
Angelaki
N. Germanou
Vas. Georgiou A
Lagkada
Monastiriou
26 Oktovriou
Filippou
Olympou
Kassandrou
Ag. Dimitriou

Post Office: Aristotelous 26, just below Egnatia. Open M-F 7:30am-8pm, Sa 7:30am-2pm, Su 9am-1:30pm. Send parcels at the branch on Eth. Aminis near the White Tower (☎227 604). Open M-F 7am-8pm. Both offer *Poste Restante.* **Postal Code:** 54101.

ACCOMMODATIONS

Welcome to the big city—don't expect to find comfort and cleanliness all at one low price. Budget options are available, but be prepared to get what you pay for. Thessaloniki's less expensive, slightly run-down hotels are along the western end of **Egnatia** between **Plateia Dimokratias** (500m east of the train station) and **Aristotelous.** Most face the chaotic road on one side and squalid backstreets on the other, but they are right in the city's center. April to September is fair season in Thessaloniki and hostels fill up quickly.

Hotel Augoustos, El. Svoronou 4 (☎522 955; augustos@hellasnet.gr). Prettier and better kept than most in the same price range, it has comfortable rooms with frescoed ceilings and wooden floors. Singles €20, with bath and A/C €30; doubles €25/38; huge triples €50. Cash only. ❷

Hotel Atlantis, Egnatia 14 (☎540 131; atlalej@otenet.gr). Helpful English-speaking management offers standard budget rooms with sinks and tiny balconies. Nothing exciting, with decent hallway bathrooms. Some newly renovated rooms with A/C are available. Singles €20, with bath €35; doubles €25/40; triples €30/45. Cash only. ❷

Thessaloniki Youth Hostel, Alex. Svolou 44 3rd. fl., (☎225 946; fax 262 208). In a run-down building, this hostel has basic bunkbeds in an unexciting old apartment, but the narrow terrace is a great hang-out spot. Max. 5-day stay. Reception 9:30-11am and 7-11pm. No curfew. Dorms €13. 10% ISIC discount. ❶

FOOD

The old city overflows with *tavernas* and restaurants with sweeping views of the gulf, while in and around the lovely Bit Bazaar, you will find the characteristic *ouzeries.* Thessaloniki's restaurants have a delightful custom of giving patrons free watermelon or sweets after a meal, but if you crave anything from dried fruits to apple-sized cherries, head to the bustling public **market,** right off Aristotelou.

Chatzi, El. Venizelou 50 (☎279 058; www.chatzis.gr), has been satiating Thessaloniki's sweet tooth since 1908, and their photo-menu is enough to make you want to try it all. Greek sweets are pure sugar and honey, often filled with nuts and creams; if you think you can't take that, try one of the delicious yogurts. The *kourkoumpinia* are orgasmic (€12 per kg, but 100g has enough sugar to satisfy any sweet tooth). Pastries €2-4. Open Su-F 7am-3am, Sa 7am-4am. MC/V. ❶

Ouzeri Melathron, Karypi 21-34 (☎275 016 www.ouzoumelathron.gr). The long and wittily subtitled menu features chicken, snails, lamb, octopus, and a variety of cheese tapas. The great prices and pub atmosphere make this a student favorite. Entrees €4-14. Free drink with ISIC. Open M-F 1:30pm-1:30am, Sa-Su 1:30pm-2am. D/MC/V. ❷

Dore Zythos, Tsiroyianni 7 (☎279 010; www.zithos.gr), by the garden across from the White Tower, specializes in Mediterranean cuisine. Sea breezes and a Mediterranean menu make this a local favorite. Try the delicious Tunisian and Moroccan dishes. Entrees €5-12. Open daily 10am-2am. V. ❷

SIGHTS

The streets of modern Thessaloniki are graced with reminders of its significance during the Byzantine and Ottoman Empires. **Agios Dimitrios,** on Ag. Dimitriou north of Aristotelous, is the city's oldest and most famous church. Although most of the interior was gutted in a 1917 fire, some lovely mosaics remain. (Open daily 7:30am-10pm. Dress modestly. Free.) Originally part of a grand palace designed for Roman Caesar Galerius when he made Thessaloniki his capital, the impressive ■**Rotunda** became a church in late Roman times, then a mosque under the Ottomans. Its walls were once plastered with brilliant mosaics of saints and New Testament stories; unfortunately, almost all is lost. (☎968 860. Open Tu-F 8am-5pm, Sa-Su 8:30am-3pm. Free.) To its left, past the yellow chairs of the alternative Classics Cafe, **Agios Georgiou** is one of the many lush-gardened Byzantine beauties that seem to have been forgotten in the middle of the city's traffic. At the intersection of D. Gounari and Egnatia stands the striking ■**Arch of Galerius,** known to locals simply as Kamara (Arch). It was erected to commemorate Galerius's victory over the Persians, and is now an interrupted bridge joining ancient and modern in Thessaloniki's unique way. Towards the center, on the homonymous street, **Agia Sophia** is the largest Byzantine Church, and walking around it in virtually any direction you will find the ruins of palaces and *domatiae*, now only inhabited by stray cats and children playing soccer. Farther west down Egnatia, ■**Bey Hamami** is a perfectly preserved 15th-century bath house, the oldest in Thessaloniki, while a few hundred meters west, **Yehudi Hamami** is the largest one. Formerly host to the Ottoman governor and his retinue, it now houses art exhibits. (Open M-F 8:30am-3pm. Free.) Its gruesome executions earned the **White Tower** the nickname "Bloody Tower," and it is all that remains of a 15th-century Venetian seawall. Today it is Thessaloniki's most recognizable landmark, presiding over the waterfront like a giant chess piece.

◪ NIGHTLIFE

Thessaloniki is a city that lives outside, and cafes, bars, and boardwalks are the locals' second home. The **Ladadika** district, a two-by-three-block rectangle of *tavernas* right behind the port, was the city's red-light strip until the 80s, but has transformed into a sea of dance clubs. The heart of the city's social life during the winter, it shuts down almost entirely in the summer, when everyone moves to the dance-till-you-drop open-air discos around the **airport,** popular with tourists as well. **Rodon** and **Shark** are the city's most expensive clubs, but their popularity rises and falls frequently. At the moment popular clubs include **Lido, Back to Base,** and **Mamounia Live,** but ask the locals for an update. The bustling **waterfront** cafes and the elegant Aristotelou promenade are always packed, as is the student-territory ■**Bit Bazaar,** a cobblestoned square of *ouzeries* and wine and tapas bars.

◪ DAYTRIP FROM THESSALONIKI

■**ANCIENT VERGINA.** The tombs of Vergina (Βέργινα), final homes of ancient Macedonian royalty, lie only 30km from Thessaloniki. The principal sight is the ■ **Great Tumulus,** a man-made mound 12m tall and 110m wide. Visitors enter this dimly-lit "Cave of Wonders" to see its magnificent burial treasures, intricate gold work, and brilliant frescoes. The unparalleled magnificence of these tombs has convinced archaeologists that they hold the bones of **Philip II** and **Alexander IV,** the murdered father and son of Alexander the Great, respectively. Walking underground to the tombs' intact doors might just send shivers down your spine. (Open in summer M noon-7:30pm, Tu-Su 8am-7:30pm; in winter Tu-Su 8:30am-3pm. €8, non-EU students €4, EU students free.) **Buses** run from Thessaloniki to Veria (1hr., 1 per hr., €5.30), from which you can take the bus to Vergina's *plateia* (25-30min., 1 per hr., €1); follow the signs to the sites.

MOUNT OLYMPUS Ολύμπος Όρος ☎23520

Erupting out of the Thermaic Gulf, the formidable slopes of Mt. Olympus, Greece's highest peak, so mesmerized the ancients that they believed it to be the divine dwelling place of their pantheon. Today, a network of well-maintained **hiking** trails makes the summit accessible to anyone with sturdy legs. Mt. Olympus has eight peaks: Ag. Andonios (2817m), Kalogeros (2701m), Mytikas (2918m), Profitis Ilias (2803m), Skala (2866m), Skolio (2911m), Stefani (the Throne of Zeus; 2907m), and Toumba (2801m). The region became Greece's first national park in 1938. There are several ways to take on Olympus; all originate from the town of **Litochoro** (pop. 6,000, elev. 500m). The first and most popular trail begins at **Prionia** (elev. 1100m), 18km from the village, and ascends 4km through a sheltered, forested ravine to **Kostas Zolotas** refuge, also known as Refuge A, but there are four more trails in different locations on the mountain. There you'll find reliable resources for all aspects of hiking—updates on weather and trail conditions, advice on routes, and reservations for any of the **Greek Alpine Club (EOS)** refuges. The staff has years of experience and dispenses info over the phone in English. (☎81 800. Curfew 10pm. Open mid-May to Oct. Camping €5; dorms €10.) After spending the night at Zolotas, you can ascend to the summit the next day. Hikers can spend another night in a mountaintop refuge and walk down the next day to Diastavrosi (3-4hr.), or make the whole trip in one day. All of the trails are easy to follow, and most are marked with red and yellow blazes. Unless you're handy with crampons and an ice axe, make your ascent between May and October. Mytikas, the tallest peak, is inaccessible without special equipment before June.

Litochoro Town, at the foot of the mountain, is a relaxed village, and the sea is only a 5min. bus ride down the hill. In June, the **Olympus Marathon** (www.olympus-marathon.com) gathers athletes and fans for a 44km run with the gods. The night before your hike, head to **Hotel Park ❷,** Ag. Nikolaou 23, at the bottom of the hill, before the park. This simple, recently renovated hostel has mosaic floors and large rooms with A/C, bath, TV, fridge, phone, and balconies with views of snow-covered peaks on one side and the blue sea on the other. (☎81 252. hotelpark_litochoro@yahoo.gr. Singles July-Aug. €24, Sept.-June €20; doubles €30; triples €35. Cash only.) KTEL **buses** (☎81 271) go from Litochoro to Athens (5hr., 3 per day, €25) and Thessaloniki (1½hr., 1 per hr., €7). Buses running to Litochoro from Larisa and other towns on the mainland will drop you off on the highway; from there, walk 10min. to the exit and wait for the hourly bus from Katerini up to town. The **tourist office** is on Ag. Nikolaou by the park. (☎83 100. Open daily 7:30am-2:30pm.) **Postal Code:** 60200.

IOANNINA Ιωάννινα ☎26510

The capital of Epirus and the eighth-largest city in Greece, Ioannina is full of trendy boutiques and chic cafes. The city serves as the main transportation hub for the Epirus region of northern Greece. The city reached its peak after it was captured in 1788 by **Ali Pasha,** an Albanian-born leader and womanizer. Legend has it that when Ali Pasha wasn't able to get a girl he had wanted, he strangled all of his other lovers and threw their bodies into this lake. This is also the site of the **Frourio,** a monumental fortress built in the 14th century, and still home to many of Ioannina's residents. To reach the **Itş Kale** (inner citadel) from the main entrance of the Frourio, veer left, and follow the signs. To the immediate right along the wall are the remnants of Ali Pasha's **hamam** (baths). Catch a ferry from the waterfront (10min., €1) for **Nisi** ("the Island") to explore various Byzantine monasteries as well as the **Ali Pasha Museum** (open daily 8am-10pm; €2). A hike through the **Vikos Gorge,** the world's steepest canyon just north of Ioannina, will rejuvenate anyone tired of city life.

Hotel Tourist ❸, Kolleti 18, on the right a few blocks up G. Averof from the *kastro*, offers baths, phones, and A/C. (☎25 070. Singles €30; doubles €40; triples €55.) **Buses,** Zosimadon 4, depart from the main terminal to: Athens (6½hr., 9 per day, €31); Igoumenitsa (2hr., 8 per day, €8); Kalambaka (2hr., 2 per day, €11); Thessaloniki (5hr., 4 per day, €25). For info, call 4am-3pm ☎26 344, 3pm-midnight 26 286. To reach the **tourist office,** walk 500m down Dodonis; the office is on the left, after the playground. (☎46 662. Open M-F 7:30am-2:30pm.) **Postal Code:** 45110.

METEORA Μετέωρα ☎24320

Atop a series of awe-inspiring pinnacles, which seem to ascend upward into the sky, is the monastic community of Meteora. Believed to be inhabited by hermits as early as the 11th century, these summits were picked as the location of a series of 21 gravity-defying, frescoed Byzantine monasteries in the 14th century. Six monasteries are still in use and open to the public. However, don't expect a hidden treasure—tour buses and sweaty faces are as common in Meteora as Byzantine icons, and the traditionally dressed monks drive Jeeps and clip cell phones to their belts. For breathtaking sunset views of the valley and monastic silence, drive or walk up the complex after visiting hours. Though the museums are closed, you'll get a real sense of the place's peace, impossible during the day. The **Grand Meteora Monastery** is the oldest, largest, and most popular. It houses a **folk museum** and the 16th-century **Church of the Transfiguration,** as well as a collection of early printed secular books by Aristotle and Plato, and dozens of monks' skulls. Two minutes down the road is **Varlaam.** If you take the right fork, you'll reach **Roussanou,** visible from most of the valley, and one of the most spectacularly situated monasteries in the area. Accessible only by rope ladder until 1897, there are now two wooden bridges that lead to the entrance. (Modest dress is required; women should wear their own skirt if they don't want one of the nylon ones handed out at the entrance. Hours vary. Apr.-Sept. Grand Meteora open M and W-Su 9am-5pm; Varlaam open M-W and F-Su 9am-2pm and 3:15-5pm; Roussanous open M-Tu and Th-Su 9am-6pm. Each monastery €2.)

Kalampaka and Meteora's rocky landscapes are also a **climbing** paradise; for info, lessons, excursions and equipment rental, contact the local Climbing Association. (☎6972 567 582; kliolios@kalampaka.com.) In the Old Town, at the base of Meteora, **Alsos House ❸,** Kanari 5, has rooms with private bath, A/C, and balcony. It's an 8min. walk from the central *plateia;* follow Vlachava until it ends, then follow the signs. (☎24 097; www.alsoshouse.gr. Reserve ahead. Laundry €5. Singles €25; doubles €35-40; triples €50; 2-room apartment with kitchen €60. Free internet, parking and kitchen. 10% Let's Go and student discount. AmEx/MC/V.) The owner sometimes hires students willing to help out in summer in exchange for room and board. Room owners approach travelers at the bus station offering low prices, but picking up people from the station here is illegal. On the road up to Meteora, **Camping Vrachos Kastraki** has all the usual amenities. (☎23 134. www.campingmeteora.gr. €6; cars €1. MC/V.) Right in the center of town, **Taverna Paramithy ❶** (Fairytale), Dimitriou 14, has cheap and delicious traditional cuisine. (☎24 441. Entrees €2.50-5. Open M-Su 11am-midnight. Cash only.) Meteora is accessible from the central bus station (15min., 9am and 1pm, €1); otherwise, you can walk the easy 45min. path that heads up to the hill from the end of Vlachava. **Trains** leave Kalambaka for Athens (5hr., 4 per day, €20). **Buses** depart Kalambaka for: Athens (5hr., 7 per day, €23); Ioannina (3hr., 2 per day, €10); Patras (5hr.; Tu 10am, F 5pm, Su 3pm; €24); Thessaloniki (3½hr., 6 per day, €10). The closest thing to a tourist office, the **Office of Public Services**, at the beginning of Vlachava, has an English-speaking staff and provides bus timetables, free maps of town and the monastery hours (☎77 900. Open M-F 8am-8pm, Sa 8am-2pm). **Postal Code:** 42200.

DELPHI Δέλφοι ☎22650

Troubled denizens of the ancient world journeyed to the stunning mountaintop of the Oracle of Delphi, where the priestess of Apollo related cryptic prophecies of the gods. As you walk your way up the hillside **Sacred Way,** you will find the remains of the legendary **Temple of Apollo,** followed by a perfectly preserved **theater** and a **stadium,** behind the sanctuary's perimeter, that once hosted the holy **Delphic Games.** At the entrance to the site, the **museum** exhibits several artifacts found near the Temple, including the **Sphinxes,** guards to the oracle. Head east from the town of Delphi to reach the Temple, but go early in the morning or go armed with patience to skirt the nonstop flow of guided groups. (Temple open daily 7:30am-7:30pm. Museum open M noon-6:30pm, Tu-Su 7:30am-7:30pm. €6 each, both sites €9; students €3/5; EU students free.) If you spend the night, stay at the recently renovated **Hotel Sibylla ❷,** Pavlou 9, with wonderful views and private baths at the best prices in town. The hotel also has commission-free **currency exchange.** (☎82 335; sibydel@otenet.gr. Singles €20; doubles €26; triples €34. €2 discount for Let's Go readers.) In July, Delphi springs to life with a series of musical and theatrical **performances** at its modern Cultural Center (☎210 331 2781; www.eccd.gr). **Buses** leave Athens for Delphi from Terminal B, Liossion 260. From Delphi, they leave at the opposite end of town from the ruins (3hr., 6 per day 7:30am-8pm, last return 6pm, €13). Delphi's **tourist office,** Pavlou 12 or Friderikis 11, is right up the stairs next to the town hall. (☎82 900. Open M-F 8am-2:30pm.) **Postal Code:** 33054.

IONIAN ISLANDS Νησιά Του Ιόνιου

West of mainland Greece, the Ionian Islands entice travelers with their lush vegetation and shimmering turquoise waters. Never conquered by the Ottomans, the islands show traces of Venetian, British, French, and Russian occupants. Today, they are a favorite among Western Europeans and ferry-hopping backpackers.

FERRIES TO ITALY

To catch a ferry from Corfu to Italy, buy your ticket at least a day ahead and ask if the port tax is included. **International Tours** (☎26610 39 007) and **Ionian Cruises** (☎26610 31 649), both across the street from the port on El. Venizelou, can help with scheduling. Destinations include: Bari (10hr., M-F 1 per day), Brindisi (8hr., 1-2 per day), and Venice (24hr., 1 per day). Schedules vary; call ahead.

CORFU Κέρκυρα ☎26610

Ever since Homer's Odysseus washed ashore and raved about Corfu's lush beauty, the surrounding seas have brought a constant stream of conquerors, colonists, and tourists to the verdant island. The modern part of **Corfu Town** (pop. 10,000) is a jumbled labyrinth of clotheslines stretching from ornate iron balconies. Discover the pleasures of colonialism at the English-built **Mon Repos Estate,** which features lovely gardens and an exhibit of archaeological treasures from the island. (Estate open daily 8am-7pm. Museum open Tu-Su 8:30am-3pm. Estate free. Museum €3, EU students €2.) **Paleokastritsa** beach, where Odysseus washed ashore, is west of Corfu Town; take a KTEL bus to Paleokastritsa (45min., 2-7 per day, €1.80).

Finding cheap accommodation in Corfu Town is virtually impossible. Plan to stay in a nearby village or reserve months ahead. The **Corfu Owners of Tourist Villas and Apartments Federation,** Polilas 2A, is more of a local service for hostel owners than an tourist office, but can be helpful in a crunch. (☎26 133; oitkcrf@otenet.gr.

Open M-F 9am-3pm and 5-8pm.) KTEL **buses** run from Corfu Town to Ag. Gordios (45min., 2-6 per day, €1.80), home to impressive rock formations, but more importantly to the backpacker's legend **Pink Palace Hotel ❷.** More famous among travelers than the Acropolis, this 700-bed hostel hosts hordes of Americans and Canadians. Travelers enjoy a 24/7 bacchanalia: among the many excuses to drink and get debaucherous at this quintessential party hostel are toga parties, cross-dressing competitions, the daily Booze Cruise (€20), and cliff diving. (☎53 103; www.thepinkpalace.com. Laundry €9. Internet €2 per 35min. Bar open 24hr. Dorms from €18; private rooms €22-30.) For more mellow digs, take bus #11 to nearby Pelekas (20min., 7 per day 7am-8:30pm, €0.95), where the friendly owners of the **Pension Martini ❷** offer rooms with superb views. (☎94 326; martini@pelekas.com. Singles €18; doubles €25-30.)The **Disco Strip,** on Eth. Antistaseos, 2km west of the new port, is the center of Corfu's nightlife. **Ferries** run from Corfu Town to Igoumenitsa (1½hr.), Patras (7-9hr.), and Paxos (4hr.). There are international connections to Albania (2hr., 1 per day), Bari and Brindisi, ITA (9 hr., 6 per week), and Venice, ITA (24hr., 6 per week). KTEL intercity **buses** depart from between I. Theotaki and the New Fortress to Athens (3 per day, €35) and Thessaloniki (1 per day, €33). On the mainland, Igoumenitsa (☎30 627) has more frequent buses and better connections. Blue municipal buses leave from Pl. San Rocco (€0.70-1). The **tourist office** is in Pl. San Rocco. (☎20 733. Open M-Sa 8am-8pm, Su 8am-4pm.) **Postal Code:** 49100.

KEPHALONIA Κεφαλόνια ☎26710

With soaring mountains, subterranean lakes and rivers, caves, and forests, Captain Corelli's island is a nature lover's paradise and deservedly popular. The bus schedules are erratic and the taxis very expensive, but armed with your own transportation, you can uncover picturesque villages on lush hillsides and never-ending beaches. **Argostoli,** the capital of Kephalonia, is a pastel-colored city that offers easy access to other points on the island; taxis from the nearby airport to town cost approximately €10. **Hotel King Agamemnon ❷,** I. Metaxa 36, on the waterfront five blocks north of the tourist office, has sparkling rooms with TV, A/C, fridge, and spotless baths, at half the price of its competitors. Ask for one of the rooms with a balcony on the bay. (☎24 260; agamemnon_std@yahoo.gr. Singles €20-30; doubles €25-50. Cash only.) Next door, **Taverna Patsouras ❶,** Metaxa 32, has excellent food, the best prices in town, and large portions in a simple veranda with a

FROM THE ROAD

FERRY TALES

It took Odysseus ten years of shipwrecks, monsters, and wrong turns to find his way back to Ithaca after setting Troy aflame. Today's travelers may find that the modern Mediterranean isn't any less treacherous than it was for Homer's hero, as island-hopping inevitably comes with its share of experiences, frustrations, and wrong turns. Navigating ferry companies, however, can be an equally headache-inducing ordeal: it's not easy to distinguish between Minoans, Aquas, Flying Cats, and Dolphins.

The fundamental difference is among fast boats (the Cats and Dolphins above) and slow boats. Cats are taking over the Greek seas with their bold Ferrari-like colors, plane-like cabins, and stomach-churning speeds.

Unfortunately, Cats' prices are quickly rising, and budget-friendly slow boats are almost extinct. These slow ferries are the backpackers' favorite: sitting under the stars instead of being cooped up in a cabin makes freezing on a cheap dock seat romantic. They run infrequently on amorphous schedules no travel agent seems to know. And because Greeks fear the wind as much as Odysseus's companions should have, they use inopportune breezes as the main reason for cancelling ferries. For good luck, pray to Aeolus, god of the winds, before heading out.

—Alice Speri

leafy roof. (☎22 779. Entrees €3-8. Open daily 11am-midnight. MC/V). The **tourist office,** near the ferry docks, is not open too regularly. (☎23 364. Open daily 7am-2:30pm.) **Internet** is available at **Daccapo Cafe Bar,** Rizospaston 12, parallel to the waterfront. (☎23 557. Internet €3 per hr. Open daily 8:30am-3:30am.)

On the eastern coast, 24km from Argostoli, is the hushed town of **Sami,** a major port and a great base from which to explore the many nearby beaches. 1.5 and 2.5km west, the striking **Melissani Lake** and **Drogarati Cave,** are respectively an underground pool of cold crystalline water and a large cavern filled with stalactites and stalagmites. (Lake ☎26740 22 997; cave 26740 23 302. Lake open daily July-Aug. 9:30am-10pm; Easter-June and Sept.-Oct. 9:30am-7:30pm. €5, under 12 €2.50. Cave 8:30am-8pm. €3/1.50.) For a more adventurous tour of the island, try Sami's **Horse Riding Stables,** which has 1-5hr., day-long, or three-to-seven-day horseback-riding trips around the island's canyons and olive groves, as well as lessons for beginners. (☎6977 533 203; www.kefaloniathewaytogo.com.)

Fiskardo, at the northern tip of the island, is one of Kephalonia's most beautiful towns, home to upscale tourists and very expensive cafes. Its Venetian architecture escaped the 1953 earthquake that devastated most of the island. The few buses to and from Fiskardo stop at the turn-off for the breathtaking **Myrtos Beach,** possibly the single best spot on the island, with brilliant white pebbles and clear, blue water lapping against sheer cliffs. (Beach 4km from turn-off.) This popular beach offers wonderful swims, but beware of the strong underwater currents. Fatal accidents happen far too regularly, so keep close to the shore.

ITHAKA Ιθάκη ☎26740

Discovering Ithaka means uncovering 6000 years of history, traversing the homeland of legendary Odysseus, and exploring in solitude. Surprisingly not as touristy as its neighboring islands, Ithaka is the ultimate Greek experience, relaxed beyond imagination and truly suspended in time. **Vathy,** Ithaka's alluring capital, wraps around a circular bay filled with garish fishing boats and luxurious yachts, with precipitous green hillsides nudging up against the water. Small enough for streets to not have names, Vathy is basically a few flower-covered houses around a pleasant *plateia*, and makes for an ideal base from which to navigate the nearly deserted island. Taxis are available but expensive; it's best to hire a car or a scooter. **Sholi Omirou** (Homer's School) is one of three sites contending for recognition as **Odysseus's Palace.** From the village of **Stavros,** follow the yellow signs to the footpath; the ruins are about 250m down. Downhill from Stavros's central square, **Polis Bay** is the stunning beach where Odysseus is thought to have hidden huge treasures on his return to Ithaka. (Taxi from Vathy €25 one-way.) The **Cave of the Nymphs** is 2km outside Vathy on the road uphill to Stavros. The enchanting **Monastery of Panagia Katharon** perches on Ithaka's highest mountain, Mt. Neritos, and has views of the surrounding islands and sea; take a moped or taxi (€30 round-trip) toward the town of Anoghi and follow the signs up the curvy road for about 20min. The monks ask visitors to close the front door to keep goats from wandering in, and expect women to cover their legs in the church. (Open sunrise-sunset. Free.) On the stunning white pebble beaches of **Filiatro** and **Sarakiniko,** the water glows in the sun and trees droop into the sea. From Vathy, walk to the end of town with the water on your left and turn uphill before the last houses. The beaches are 3.5 and 2.5km out, respectively. Another beautiful beach is by the tiny **Piso Aetos** port. From there, the ferry leaves twice a day, but otherwise you'll have the place to yourself. For a light snack, stop by **Drakouli ❶,** an old white mansion-turned-cafe, with an artificial lake in the palm garden and a pool table inside. Try the cooling *giaourti me meli* (yogurt with honey; €4.50), a Greek specialty. As you face inland, it is on the left end of the waterfront. (☎33 435. Coffee €2-3. Fruit salads €6. Mixed drinks €7-10. Open daily 9am-midnight.) **Postal Code:** 28300.

ZAKYNTHOS Ζάκυνθος ☎26950

Known as the greenest of the Ionian Islands, Zakynthos is home to thousands of plant and flower species and a large population of *Caretta caretta*, or loggerhead sea turtles. Bustling **Zakynthos Town** maintains a romantic, nostalgic air. Boats from Zakynthos Town go to many of the island's most spectacular sights, including the glowing, stalactite-filled **Blue Caves** on the northeastern shore past Skinari. Southwest of the Blue Caves is **Smuggler's Wreck,** a large boat skeleton that has made the beach one of the most photographed in the world. Farther south are **Keri Caves** and **Marathonissi.** Agencies advertise along Lombardou; most excursions leave around 9:30am, return at 5:30pm, and charge about €20. For a more intimate travel experience, skip the huge cruise ships from Zakynthos Town and hire a small fishing boat from the docks in nearby villages. A 10min. walk down the beach (with the water on your right) will take you to the long and beautifully deserted sands of **Kalamaki,** a turtle nesting site and protected **National Marine Park** (☎29 870; www.nmp-zak.org). Some of the most picturesque beaches, like the beautiful **Gerakas,** on the southeastern tip of the island, are inhabited at night by the turtles. (Open daily 7am-7pm.)

> **!** The loggerhead turtles that share Zakynthos' shores with beachgoers are an **endangered species,** and their nesting ground should be respected. Let's Go encourages readers to embrace the "Leave No Trace" ethic when visiting the island's more secluded beaches.

Athina Marouda Rooms for Rent ❶, on Tzoulati and Koutouzi, has simple but clean rooms with fans and large windows, communal baths, and backpacker-friendly prices. (☎45 194. June-Sept. singles €15; doubles €30. Oct.-May €10/20. Cash only.) Dining in the *plateias* and by the waterfront in Zakynthos Town is a treat. On the beaches, vendors sell delicious cups of fresh fruit salad (€2). Getting around the island can be frustrating—taxis tend to be terribly overpriced and tour operators can seem like glorified tourist babysitters. Dozens of places rent **scooters** (€15 per day), but driver's license requirements are strictly enforced. **Buses** go to Laganas and Kalamaki (20min., 12 per day, €1.20). Buses also board ferries to the mainland and continue to Athens (4 per day, €21), Patras (4 per day, €6), and Thessaloniki (1 per day, €39). The bus station, located two blocks away from the water, provides timetables in English. **Postal Code:** 29100.

CYCLADES Κυκλάδες

Sun-drenched, winding stone streets, trellis-covered *tavernas*, and nonstop winds characterize all of the Cycladic islands, but subtle quirks make each distinct. Bright white windmills and black pebble beaches coat the shores of beautiful Santorini, rocky cliffs shape the terrain of arid Sifnos, and celebrated archaeological sites distinguish sacred Delos. Naxos and Paros offer travelers peaceful mountains and villages, Milos's coast has unusual, cavernous rocks, and notorious party spots Ios and Mykonos uncork some of wildest nightlife on earth. Whether choosing a beach for a two-week vacation or embarking on some legendary island-hopping, tourists on any island will find plenty of natural beauty and local flavor.

TRANSPORTATION

Ferries run from Athens to: Ios (7½hr., 3 per day); Milos (7hr., 1-2 per day); Mykonos (6hr., 2-4 per day); Naxos (6hr., 5-7 per day); Paros (5hr., 4-7 per day);

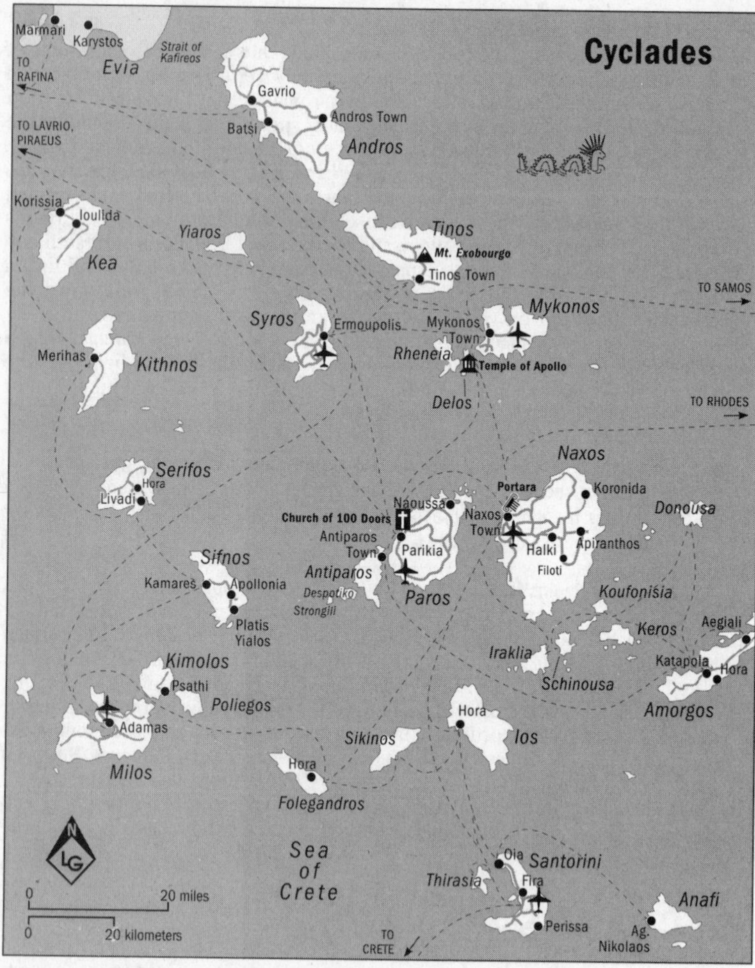

Santorini (9hr., 3-5 per day). From Iraklion, Crete to: Mykonos (8½hr., 2 per week); Naxos (8hr., 1 per week); Paros (7hr., 2 per week); Santorini (4hr., 3 per week). Ferries run frequently among the islands in the Cyclades, and biweekly connections link them to the Dodecanese and Northeast Aegean islands, and continue to the Turkish coast. See p. 58 for more information. High-speed ferries cover the same routes at twice the cost and speed, and have become increasingly more convenient than traditional ferries.

GREECE

MYKONOS Μύκονος ☎22890

Coveted by pirates in the 18th century, Mykonos is still lusted after by those seeking revelry and excess. Nightlife options, both gay and straight, abound in **Mykonos Town** and on the beaches, the expensive playground of chic sophisticates. Ambling down colorful alleyways at dawn or dusk, among the **pink pelicans,** is the cheapest and most exhilarating way to experience the island, especially Mykonos Town. In general, though, there isn't much to do here other than drink and sunbathe. All of Mykonos's beaches are nude, but the degree of bareness varies and in most places, people prefer to show off their designer bathing suits rather than their bare bodies. **Platis Yialos** and **Super Paradise** beach are the most daring; **Elia** is a bit tamer. The super-famous **Paradise** beach is actually so crowded with hungover Italians and overpriced sunbeds that you can barely see the water. Buses run south from Mykonos Town to Platis Yialos and Paradise (20min., 2 per hr., 8:10am-10:10pm €1.10; 10:40pm-7:40am €1.50) and to Elia (30min., 8 per day 11am-7:30pm, €1.10). **Caprice Bar,** on the water, is a popular post-beach hangout for its breathtaking sunsets, funky music, and lively company. (Beer €7. Mixed drinks €10. Open daily 6:30pm-4am.) The **Skandinavian Bar,** on the waterfront, is a two-building party complex. (☎22 669. Beer and shots €5-8. Mixed drinks from €9. Open daily 9pm-5am.) **Cavo Paradiso,** on Paradise beach, is considered one of the world's top dance clubs; it hosts internationally renowned DJs and inebriated crowds of thousands. (☎27 205. Drinks €10. Cover €25, after 2am €40, includes one drink. Free bus to and from Mykonos Town. Open daily midnight-11am.)

Like everything else on the island, accommodation is prohibitively expensive and the only budget option is camping. In town, **Hotel Philippi ❹,** Kalogera 25, provides fully equipped rooms with bath, fridge, and A/C, around a garden of tulips so bright they seem fake. (☎22 294; chriko@otenet.gr. Open Apr.-Oct. Singles €50-80; doubles €65-100; triples €75-120. AmEx/MC/V.). The popular **Paradise Beach Camping ❶,** 6km from the village, is always packed. It has decent facilities and plenty of services. (☎22 129; www.paradisemykonos.com. Free pickup at port or airport. Free safes. Internet €1 per 15min., €4.50 per 1½hr. Tent sites €4, €8 per person; 2-person beach cabin €18-30 per person; rooms €30-50 per person.) **Appaloosa ❸,** Mavrogeneous 11, one block from Taxi Sq., serves salads, pastas, and Mexican food. (☎27 086. Pastas €9-15. Burritos €9.50-15. Salads €9.50-13. Cover €2, includes bread and olive pâté. Open daily 7:30pm-1am.) Under sprays of pink flowers, **Pelican Restaurant ❸,** just past Appaloosa in a small *plateia*, complements seafood and Greek dishes. (☎26 226. Entrees €8-14. Open daily noon-1:30am. AmEx/MC/V.) **Ferries** run from the New Port, west of town, to: Iraklion, Crete (6 per week, €48); Naxos (1 per day, €20); Paros (hydrofoil 1 per day, €17; traditional 1 every 2 weeks, €9); Piraeus (6hr., 2-3 per day, €26); Santorini (2 per day, €28) via Ios (€27). The helpful, English-speaking **tourist police** are located at the ferry landing. (☎22 482. Open daily 8am-9pm.) **Windmills Travel,** on Xenias, around the corner from South Station, books lodgings, and provides free maps, as well as GLBT resources (☎26 555; www.windmillstravel.com). Mykonos is a very GLBT-friendly island. For more specific information, contact the **Gay Tourism Department** of Windmills (☎69367 09 105). **Postal Code:** 84600.

DELOS Δήλος ☎22890

Delos is the sacred center of the Cyclades. The island-wide **archaeological site** is expansive, but its highlights can be seen in about 3hr., and is best visited as a daytrip from Mykonos. From the dock, head straight to the **Agora of the Competaliasts;** continue in the same direction and turn left onto the wide **Sacred Road** to reach the **Sanctuary of Apollo,** a group of temples that date from Mycenaean times to the 4th century BC. On the right is the biggest and most famous, the **Temple of Apollo.** Continue 50m past the end of the Sacred Road to the beautiful **Terrace of the Lions.** The **museum,** next to the cafeteria, contains an assortment of archaeological finds. (Open Tu-Su 8:30am-3pm. €5, students and seniors €3.) From the museum, a path leads to the summit of **Mt. Kythnos** (112m), from which Zeus supposedly watched Apollo's birth. Temples dedicated to Egyptian gods, including the **Temple of Isis,** line the descent. Excursion **boats** leave for Delos from the Old Port of Mykonos Town, just past Little Venice. Buy tickets at all travel agencies. (35min.; Tu-Su 9am-3pm; round-trip €10, with guided tour €32.)

PAROS Πάρος ☎22840

Now a central transportation hub, Paros was once famed for its slabs of pure white marble, used for many of the great statues and buildings of the ancient world. It's a far cry from the luxurious debauchery of Mykonos and the youth-filled streets of Ios. Behind the commercial surface of **Parikia,** Paros's port and largest city, flower-lined streets wind through archways to one of the most treasured Orthodox basilicas, the **Panagia Ekatontapiliani** (Church of Our Lady of 100 Doors). This white three-building complex is dedicated to St. Helen, mother of the Emperor Constantine, who reportedly had a vision of the True Cross at the site while traveling to the Holy Land. (Dress modestly. Open daily 7am-11pm. Mass daily 7pm, Free.) About 8km north of town, **Naoussa** beach is the most popular and crowded destination on the island. On the opposite coast, **Aliki** beach is much quieter, but often windy. Turn left at the dock and take a right after the cemetery ruins to reach the well-kept, cottage-like **Rena Rooms.** (☎22 220. Free pickup and luggage storage. Reserve ahead. Doubles €20-40; triples €30-55. 20% discount for Let's Go readers; discount if paid in cash. MC/V.) The funky **Happy Green Cow ❸,** a block off the plateia behind the National Bank, serves tasty vegetarian dinners. (☎24 691. Entrees €12-15. Open daily Apr.-Nov. 7pm-midnight.) Paros's nightlife centers at the far end of the Old Town's waterfront, 5min. past the port and bus station. A central courtyard connects themed bar areas of **The Dubliner,** an Irish pub, **Down Under,** the Aussie bar, and the **Paros Rock Cafe,** with bright colors and the appropriate flags. Across the street, **Sex Bar** specifies it is a dance club only. Follow the spotlight and crowds to the end of the harbor. (Beer €3-5. Mixed drinks €5-8. Cover €3-5, includes 1 drink.)

Ferry schedules and prices change regularly. The busy **Kontostavlos A.S Travel Agents** (☎21 353), on the left corner across from the port's windmill, sells tickets for all companies. Ferries go to: Crete (4hr.); Ios (2hr.); Mykonos (hydrofoil 40min.); Naxos (1hr.); Santorini (3hr.). The **tourist police** are on the *plateia* behind the telephone office. (☎21 673. Open daily 7am-2:30pm.) **Postal Code:** 84400.

NAXOS Νάξος ☎22850

The ancients believed Naxos, the largest of the Cyclades, was home to Dionysus, god of wine and

LOCAL LEGEND

PETROS: PELICAN OF MYSTERY

very summer, tourist-paparazzi warm around Mykonos Town, ttempting to get a photo of the rea's biggest celebrity taking a troll by the windmills, perhaps, or njoying a seafood dinner in Little enice, compliments of a generous *taverna*-keeper.

The town superstar isn't what ou would call typical, though. In act, he's a pelican named Petros. n his standard pose, the white-nd-pink bird can be hard to spot n the midst of the town's white uildings—at least until he blinks is beady black eyes and extends is heavy wings and long, slender eck. Though he is constantly surounded by admirers, Petros's main concern is scoring free fish; f you feed him, be prepared to be ollowed and "asked" for more.

But Petros's obsessive fish abit, typical of most pelicans, nay be hiding the fact that he's ot really Petros after all. The first elican known as "Petros" lived ere for over 30 years after being tranded by a storm in the 1950s nd adopted by locals. Since his eath, however, any pelican in lykonos gets the royal treatment; here are currently 2-3 regulars.

Petros (or possibly Petroses) as been sighted all over the orthwestern city. To catch a limpse, wander around the whitewashed churches of the Paraporiani and the surrounding *avernas.* Just look for a crowd of ourists wielding cameras.

revelry. Olive groves and wineries, small villages and white ruins, silent monasteries and unexplored hikes fill its interior, and sandy beaches line its shores. **Naxos Town,** the capital, is a dense collection of labyrinthine streets, bustling *tavernas*, and museums, crowned by the **Kastro,** an inhabited Venetian fortress atop town, tranquil despite the tourists. At the Kastro's entrance, the **Domus Della Rocca-Barozzi,** also called the **Venetian Museum,** exhibits photographs, books, and furniture belonging to a local aristocratic family. (☎22 387; www.naxosisland.gr/VenetianMuseum. Open daily in high season 10am-3pm and 7-11pm; low season 10am-3pm and 7-10pm. €5, students €3. Concerts nightly in the summer 9:15pm. €10; reserve ahead at the museum reception.) The **Archaeological Museum** occupies the former Collège Français, where Nikos Kazantzakis, author of *Zorba the Greek*, studied. (Open Tu-Su 8am-5pm. €3, students €2.) In Naxos Town, **Anna's Studios** are centrally located. (☎23 782. Singles €20-50; doubles €30-55. Cash only.) **Ferries** go from Naxos Town to: Crete (7hr.); Ios (1hr.); Kos (7hr.); Mykonos (3hr.); Paros (1hr.); Piraeus (6hr.); Rhodes (13hr.); Santorini (3hr.). A bus goes from the port to the beaches of Ag. Giorgios, Ag. Prokopios, Ag. Anna, and Plaka (7:30am-2am, 2 per hr., €1.20). **Buses** (☎22 291) also run from Naxos Town to the village of **Apiranthos.** (1hr., 6 per day, €2.30). To get to the Tragea highland valley, an enormous olive grove, take a bus to Halki (30min., 7 per day, €1.20). The **tourist office** is by the bus station. (☎22 993. Open daily 8am-11pm.) **Postal Code:** 84300.

IOS Ίος ☎22860

Despite the recent and concerted effort to tone down its party-animal reputation, Ios remains the Greek debauchery heaven—or hell, depending on the view—it's always been famous for being. The island's life seems, in fact, to revolve around its insane nightlife: breakfast is served at 2pm, people don't go out before midnight, and partiers dance madly in the streets. The **port** of Gialos is at one end of the island's sole paved road. The town of Hora sits above it on a hill, but most visitors spend their days at **Mylopotas beach,** a 15min. walk downhill from Hora or a bus ride from the port or town (every 20min. 7:20am-midnight, €1.10). Establishments on the beach offer windsurfing, water-skiing, and snorkeling during the day (€14-40), and the afternoon bars and dance floors are no less crowded than the nighttime ones. Sunning is typically followed by drinking. Head up from the *plateia* to reach the **Slammer Bar** for tequila slammers (€3), then stop by **Disco 69** for some dirty dancing. (Drinks €5. Cover €6 after midnight.) Get lost in the streetside **Voodoo** or **Red Bull,** dance on the tables at **Sweet Irish Dream** (cover after 2:30am), or grind to techno at **Scorpion Disco,** the island's largest club (cover after 2am). All bars serve Ios's legendary **Flaming Lamborghini,** a next-to-fatal cocktail of every liquid left at the bar. Most clubs close between 5 and 7am, when the drunkenness spills onto the streets. A few hours later, crowds begin to re-gather at the beach.

Everyone knows **Francesco's ❶,** where you'll find harbor views and a terrace bar serving afternoon breakfast to hungover backpackers (breakfast €4; "morning cure" Bloody Mary €4). Take the steps up the hill to the left in the *plateia* and then the first left at the Diesel shop. (☎91 223; www.francescos.net. Internet €1 per 15min. Dorms €10-15; private rooms with A/C and bath €20-50.) **Ali Baba's ❷,** next to Ios Gym, serves Thai food in a funky setting. (☎91 558. Greek snacks or tempura €4-5. Entrees €6-12. Mixed drinks €5-6. Open Mar.-Oct. daily 6pm-midnight.) Off the main church's *plateia*, **Old Byron's ❸** is a wine bar and restaurant with creative renditions of Greek staples. (☎69 78 19 22 12. Entrees €9-15. Reserve ahead. Open daily 6pm-midnight. MC/V.) **Ferries** go to: Naxos (1¾hr., 3 per day, €9); Paros (3hr., 3 per day, €13); Piraeus (8hr., 2-3 per day, €26); Santorini (1¼hr., 3 per day, €8). **Acteon Travel,** by the central *plateia*, sells tickets. (☎91 343. Open daily 8am-11pm.) **Postal Code:** 84001.

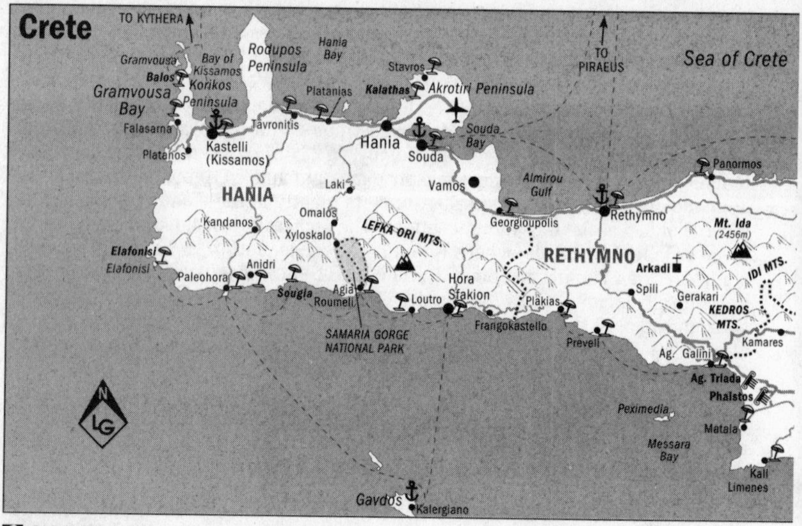

SANTORINI Σαντορίνη ☎22860

Whitewashed towns balanced delicately on cliffs, black-sand beaches, and deeply scarred hills make Santorini's landscape nearly as dramatic as the volcanic cataclysm that created it. Despite the abundant kitsch in touristy **Fira,** the island's capital, nothing can ruin the pleasure of wandering the town's cobbled streets or browsing its craft shops. Head away from the center and wander the virtually streetless hillside towards silent **Firostefani** to find tiny, blinding-white chapels and views of the volcano. At the northern tip of the island, the town of **Oia** (pronounced *Eea*) is the best place in Greece to watch the sunset, though its fame draws crowds hours in advance. To get to Oia, catch a bus from Fira (25min., 23 per day, €1). Although every establishment in Oia is shockingly overpriced, it is a spectacular setting not to be missed.

Red Beach, and the impressive archaeological excavation site of the Minoan city **Akrotiri,** entirely preserved by lava, lie on the southwestern edge of the island, but the site is currently closed for repairs. Buses run to Akrotiri from Fira (30min., 14 per day, €1.60). Buses also leave Fira for the black-sand beaches of **Kamari** (20min., 32 per day, €1) and **Perissa** (30min., 21 per day, €1.50). The bus stops before Perissa in Pyrgos; from there, you can hike (2¼hr.) to the ruins of **Ancient Thira.** Stop after 40min. at **Profitis Ilias Monastery,** whose lofty location provides an island panorama. (Open Tu-Su 8am-3pm. Free.) Close to Perissa beach, **Youth Hostel Anna ❶** has colorful rooms. (☎82 182. Port pick-up and drop-off included. Reception 9am-5pm and 7-10pm. Check-out 11:30am. Reserve ahead. June-Aug. 10-person dorms €12; 4-person dorms €15; doubles €50; triples €60. Sept.-May €6/8/22/30. MC/V.) At night, head to **Murphy's** in Fira, which claims to be the first Irish pub in Greece. (Beer €5. Mixed drinks €6.50. Cover €5. Open Mar.-Oct. daily noon-late.) **Ferries** from Fira run to: Crete (2hr.); Ios (1hr.); Mykonos (2-3 hr.); Naxos (3hr., 3-4 per day, €15-20); Paros (4hr.); Piraeus (10hr.). Most ferries depart from Athinios Harbor; frequent **buses** (25min., €1.50) connect to Fira, but most hostels and hotels offer shuttle service. Ferry schedules and prices are extremely variable. Check at any travel agency, and be aware that the self-proclaimed tourist offices at the port are for-profit agencies. **Postal Codes:** 84700 (Fira); 84702 (Oia).

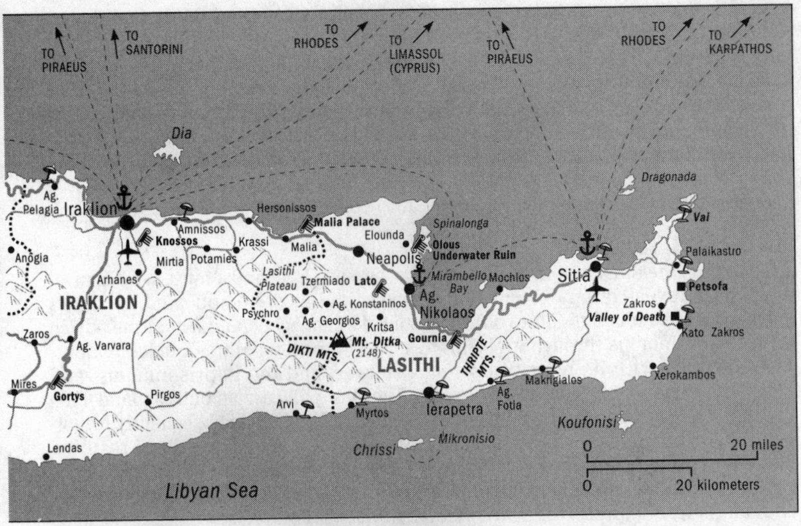

CRETE Κρήτη

According to a Greek saying, a Cretan's first loyalty is to his island, his second to his country. Since 3000 BC, when Minoan civilization flourished on the island, Crete has maintained an identity distinct from the rest of Greece; pride in the island proves well-founded. Travelers will be drawn to the island's warm hospitality, mosques, monasteries, mountain villages, gorges, grottoes, and beaches.

GETTING THERE

Olympic Airways (☎21096 66 666) and **Aegean/Cronus Airlines** (☎21099 88 300) fly from Athens to Hania (1hr., 4-5 per day) in the west, Iraklion (50min., 4-5 per day) in the center, and Sitia (1hr., 2-3 per week) in the east.

IRAKLION Ηράκλειο ☎2810

Iraklion is Crete's capital and primary port, and though it's not particularly pretty, its importance as a transportation hub makes it a necessary stop on the way to Crete's more scenic destinations. The chic locals live life in the fast lane, which translates into an urban brusqueness unique in Crete, but also the most diverse nightlife on the island. Iraklion's main attraction after nearby **Knossos** is the superb **Archaeological Museum,** off Pl. Eleftherias. By appropriating major finds from all over the island, the museum has amassed a comprehensive record of the Neolithic and Minoan stages of Cretan history. (Open M 1-7:30pm, Tu-Su 8:30am-7:30pm. €6; students and seniors €3; "classicists," fine arts students, under 18, and EU students free.) The **Tomb of Nikos Kazantzakis,** on top of the city walls, offers the best view of the city and is a necessary stop for fans of the author or his creation, Zorba. With planes flying overhead seemingly every 10min., it can be difficult to get a good night's sleep at Iraklion's **Youth Hostel ❶,** Vironos 5. Central and cheap, the hostel has basic dorms in a slightly run down building. From the port or bus station, walk up 25 Augustou and take the second right. (☎286 281. Reception 8am-10pm. Dorms €10; doubles €25. Cash only.) The **open-air market** on 1866, near Pl. Venizelou, sells produce, cheese, and meat. (Open M-Sa 8am-8pm.) **Ouzeri Tou Terzaki ❷,** Loch. Marineli 17, serves meals with complimentary fruit and *raki*. (☎221 444. Entrees €4-6. Open M-Sa noon-midnight. MC/V.)

From Terminal A, between the old city walls and the harbor, **buses** leave for Agios Nikolaos (1½hr., 20 per day, €5.30) and Hania (3hr., 17 per day, €12) via Rethymno (1½hr., €6.50), as well as for Knossos. Buses leave across from Terminal B for Phaistos (1½hr., 9 per day, €4.80). The **tourist office** is at Xandthoudidou 1. (☎246 299. Open M-F 8am-2:30pm.) Use the Internet at **Netc@fé,** 1878 4. (€1.50 per hr. Open M-Sa 10am-2am, Su noon-2am.) **Postal Code:** 71001.

KNOSSOS Κνωσός

Knossos is the most famous archaeological site on Crete and a must-see. Excavations have revealed the remains of the largest and most complicated of Crete's **Minoan palaces.** It is difficult to differentiate between legend and fact at the palace of Knossos, famous throughout history as the site of King Minos's machinations, the labyrinth with its monstrous son Minotaur, and the imprisonment—and winged escape—of Daedalus and Icarus. The first palace was built around 1700 BC, but was partially destroyed by a fire around 1450 BC and subsequently forgotten. Sir Arthur Evans, who financed and supervised the excavations, restored large parts of the palace. His work often crossed the line from preservation to artistic interpretation, giving the palace a bit of a Disneyland feel, though the site is nonetheless impressive. Don't miss the **Queen's Bathroom,** where, over 3000 years ago, she took milk baths while gazing up at elaborate dolphin frescoes. Walking north from the royal quarters, you'll stumble across the grand **pithoi**—jars so big that, according to legend, Minos's son met a Pooh Bear-esque fate by drowning in one filled with honey. (Open daily 8am-7:30pm. €6, students €3.) To reach Knossos from Iraklion, take **bus** #2 from Terminal A (20min., 2 per hr., €1.10).

HANIA Χάνια ☎28210

Crete's second largest city, Hania (pop. 60,000), is covered in an avalanche of tourists, yet somehow manages to be low-key. A day in Old Hania is easily spent people-watching from cafes, window-shopping, or wandering along the waterfront. The **Venetian lighthouse** marks the entrance to the city's stunning architectural relic, the Venetian Inner Harbor, built by Venetian conquerors in the 13th century. The ruins of the fortress have sunset views over the open sea. The inlet has retained its original breakwater and Venetian arsenal, though much was destroyed by the Nazis during WWII. Nestled away on the northwestern tip of Crete, the heavenly **blue lagoon** of **Balos** offers bright white sand and warm, shallow waters to visitors who make the trek out. The most popular excursion from Hania and Iraklion is the 4-5hr. hike down **Samaria Gorge** (Φράγγι της Σαμαριάς), a spectacular 16km ravine extending through the White Mountains. Sculpted by 14 million years of rainwater, the gorge is the longest in Europe. (Open daily May to mid-Oct. 6am-3pm. €5, under 15 free.) The trail starts at **Xyloskalo;** take an early bus from Hania to Xyloskalo (1½hr., €5.60) for a day's worth of hiking.

The only backpacker-friendly accommodation in Hania is the central **Pension Fidias ❶,** 6 Kal. Sarpaki. From the bus station walk toward the harbor on Halidon and turn right onto Athenagora, which becomes Sarpaki. (☎52 494. Check-out noon. Dorms with bath €10; doubles €20. Cash only.) Hania's nightlife happens along the old harbor. **Ferries** arrive in the port of Souda, near Hania; buses connect from the port to Hania's municipal market on Zymvrakakidon (25min., €1). **Buses** (☎93 052) leave from the station on the corner of Kidonias and Kelaidi for the airport (25min.), Iraklion (2½hr.), and Rethymno (1hr.). **Taxis** charge €16-18. The **tourist office** is next to the city hall. (☎36 155; www.chania.gr. Open M-F 9am-8pm, Sa 9am-2pm.) **Postal Code:** 73100.

EASTERN AEGEAN ISLANDS

Scattered along Turkey's coast, the islands of the **Dodecanese** are marked by a history of persistence in the face of myriad invasions. The more isolated islands of the **Northeast Aegean** remain sheltered from creeping globalization. Cultural authenticity here is palpable—a traveler's welcome and reward.

RHODES Ρόδος ☎22410

The undisputed tourism capital of the Dodecanese, the island of Rhodes has retained its sense of serenity in the sandy beaches along its eastern coast, the jagged cliffs skirting its western coast, and the green mountains dotted with villages in its interior. Beautiful ancient artifacts, remnants from a rich past, carpet the island. Rhodes is best known for a sight that no longer exists—the 33m **Colossus,** which was once one of the Seven Wonders of the Ancient World. The pebbled streets of the Old Town, constructed by the Knights of St. John, lend **Rhodes Town** a medieval flair. At the top of the hill, a tall, square tower marks the entrance to the **Palace of the Grand Master,** which contains 300 rooms filled with intricate mosaics and medieval artwork. (☎25 500. €6, students €3.) The beautiful halls and courtyards of the **Archaeological Museum,** which dominates the **Plateia Argiokastrou,** shelter the exquisite statue of *Aphrodite Bathing*, which dates from the first century BC. (Open Tu-Su 8:30am-2:30pm. €3, students €2.) With whitewashed houses clustered at the foot of a castle-capped acropolis, **Lindos,** south of Rhodes Town, is far less touristy and is perhaps the most picturesque town on the island. The vine-enclosed garden-bar of **Hotel Anastasia ❷**, 28 Oktovriou 46, complements bright pastel rooms. (☎28 007. Breakfast €4. Singles €25-30; doubles €30-40; triples €35-50; quads €40-55. V.) Nightlife in Rhodes's Old Town focuses around the street of **Militadou,** off Apelou. **Orfanidou,** in the New Town, is popularly known as Bar Street. There is a **tourist office** in Rhodes Town at the intersection of Makariou and Papagou. (☎44 335; www.ando.gr/eot. Open M-F 8am-3pm.) **Postal Code:** 85100.

KOS Κως ☎22420

Antiquity knew Kos as the sacred land of Asclepius, the god of healing, and the birthplace of Hippocrates, the father of modern medicine. Today, **Kos Town** attracts a young, loud, and inebriated crowd more interested in sexual healing. The more sedate can escape to serene mountain villages or the sanctuary of **Asclepeion,** 4km southwest of Kos Town, the location of Hippocrates's medical school, which opened in the 5th century BC. In the summer, mini-trains run there from Kos Town. (Open Tu-Su 8am-2:30pm. €4, students €2.) For a steamy daytrip, hop a ferry to the neighboring island of **Nisyros** (1½hr.) to take a peek into the craters of the active **Mandraki Volcano,** which emit sulfur crystals and steam. The island's best beaches stretch along southern Kos to Kardamena and are all accessible by bus; stops are by request. Take the first right off Megalou Alexandrou to get to **Pension Alexis ❷**, Irodotou 9, a beloved travel institution. (☎28 798. Doubles €25-35; triples €39-45.) Heaping portions characterize **Taverna Hellas ❷**, Psaron 7, down the street from Pension Alexis at the corner with Amerikis. (☎22 609. Vegetarian options. Open daily noon-late.) **Nafklirou** has many bars. **Ferries** run to Patmos (4hr., 2 per day), Piraeus (11-15hr., 3 per day), and Rhodes (4hr., 3 per day). The **tourist office** is at Vas. Georgiou B 1. (☎24 460; www.hippocrates.gr. Open M-F 8am-2pm and 5-8pm, Sa 8am-2pm.) **Postal Code:** 85300.

LESVOS Λέσβος ☎22510

Olive groves, remote monasteries, art colonies, and a petrified forest harmonize on Lesvos in an irresistible siren song. Most travelers pass through modern

Mytilini, the capital and central port city. At the **Archaeological Museum,** on 8 Noemvriou, visitors can walk on preserved mosaic floors dating from Lesvos's Neolithic past. (Open Tu-Su 8am-7:30pm. €3, students €2, EU students and under 18 free.) Only 4km south of Mytilini along El. Venizelou, the village of **Varia** is home to two excellent museums. **Theophilos Museum** features the work of the neo-Primitivist painter Theophilos Hadzimichali. (Open Tu-Su 9am-2:30pm and 6-8pm. €2, students free.) **Musée Tériade** displays lithographs by Chagall, Matisse, Miró, and Picasso. (Open daily 9am-2pm and 5-8pm. €2, students free.) Local buses (20min.) to Varia leave Mytilini every hour. Tell the driver you're going to the museums. **Molyvos** is a quintessential artists' colony; though frequented by tourists, its atmosphere remains serene. It can be reached by bus from Mytilini (2hr., 4 per day, €4.70). **Eftalou** has beautiful black-pebble beaches, accessible by bus from Molyvos. A 20-million-year-old **petrified forest,** 4km from Sigri, is one of only two such forests in the world. (Open daily July-Aug. 8am-7pm; Sept.-June 8am-3pm. €2.) Mytilini *domatia* are plentiful and well advertised. Doubles run €20-25 before July 15, and start at €35 during the high season. **Ferries** go from Mytilini to Chios (3hr.), Limnos (5hr.), and Thessaloniki (13hr.). Reserve tickets at **NEL Lines,** Pavlou Koudourioti 67 (☎46 595). **Postal Code:** 81100.

SAMOTHRAKI Σαμοθράκη ☎22510

Samothraki (also called Samothrace) was once a pilgrimage site for Thracians who worshipped the great Anatolian gods. When those first colonists arrived in the 10th century BC, they saw the same vista seen today at the ferry dock: dry, grassy fields at the base of the Aegean's tallest peak, 1670m Fengari. **Kamariotissa,** the port town, is the island's unattractive transportation hub. From there it is easy to get to the **Sanctuary of the Great Gods at Paleopolis,** where the famous *Winged Victory of Samothrace*, now a centerpiece in the Louvre, was found in 1863. (Open daily 8:30am-8:30pm. €3, students €2, EU students free.) Above the sanctuary are the remains of the ancient Samothraki. **Therma,** a charming one-road village, has natural hot springs and is the starting point for the 4hr. climb up Fengari. The easy 2km hike from Therma to Fonias meanders along a gurgling stream and beneath gnarled trees. The trail ends at a sheer cliff face by a cascading waterfall. **Brisko Rooms ❸**, set back from the road across from the dock in Kamariotissa, has quiet rooms with A/C and private baths off of its flower-lined terrace. Some of the rooms have a view of the Aegean. (☎41 328. Singles €27; doubles €35; triples €47.) **Klimataria ❷**, on the north end of the waterfront, has enticing homemade dishes. (☎41 535. Open daily noon-5pm and 7pm-1am.) **Ferries** dock on the southern edge of Kamariotissa and run to: Alexandroupoli (2½hr.); Kavala (3½hr.); Lavrio via Psara (13hr.); Lesvos (7hr.); Limnos (3½hr.). **Postal Code:** 68002.

HUNGARY (MAGYARORSZÁG)

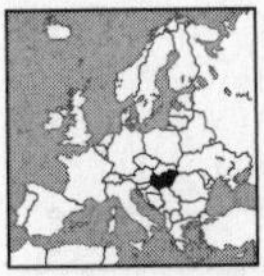

Today considered off the beaten track—if only just—Hungary was central to Europe's development for centuries. Steadily ruled with Austria under the Hapsburgs, Hungary's more recent history has been peppered with revolutions and changes in political regimes. After World War II, Communism dismembered the economy, but since 1968, leaders have worked to put it back together, and an economically liberal Hungary joined the European Union in 2004. Teeming Budapest may still be the country's socioeconomic keystone, but those who pass over the countryside for the capital risk mistaking Hungary's heart for its soul. Travelers will be rewarded by visits to Hungary's varied landscapes: by sunny plains, beach resorts, and wine valleys—all immortalized in Hungary's rich folk tradition.

DISCOVER HUNGARY: SUGGESTED ITINERARIES

THREE DAYS. Three days is hardly enough time for **Budapest** (p. 514). Spend a day at the churches and museums of **Castle Hill** and an afternoon in the waters of the **Széchenyi Baths** before exploring the **City Park.** Get a lesson in Hungarian history at the **Parliament** before taking in the **Opera House.**

ONE WEEK. After four days in the capital, head up the Danube Bend to see the rustic side of Hungary in **Szentendre** (1 day; p. 525). Farther down the river, **Visegrad's** citadel looms over the town (1 day; p. 525). Next, explore **Eger** (1 day; p. 527) and sample the wines of the **Valley of the Beautiful Women.**

ESSENTIALS

WHEN TO GO

Spring is the best time to visit Hungary, as flowers are in bloom throughout the countryside and the tourists have yet to arrive. July through August is Hungary's high season, and in rural areas the weather is pleasant even when summer temperatures peak at 26°C (79°F). Cities, however, can be sweltering. Autumn's mild weather lasts through October. December, January, and February see temperatures slightly below freezing, and tourist spots may close or reduce their hours during the winter.

FACTS AND FIGURES

Official Name: Hungary.

Capital: Budapest.

Major Cities: Debrecen, Eger, Pécs.

Population: 9,981,000.

Land Area: 93,030 sq. km.

Time Zone: GMT +1.

Language: Hungarian.

Religions: Roman Catholic (60%), Protestant (20%).

DOCUMENTS AND FORMALITIES

EMBASSIES AND CONSULATES. Foreign embassies to Hungary are in Budapest (p. 514). Hungary's embassies and consulates abroad include: Australia, Ste. 405, Edgecliff Center, 203-233 New South Head Rd., Edgecliff, NSW, 2027 (☎9328 7857;

www.hunconsydney.com); Canada, 299 Waverley St., Ottawa, ON, K2P 0V9 (☎613-230-2717); Ireland, 2 Fitzwilliam Pl., Dublin 2 (☎661 2902; www.kum.hu/dublin); New Zealand, 37 Abbott St., Ngaio, Wellington 6004 (☎04 973 7507; www.hungarianconsulate.co.nz); UK, 35 Eaton Pl., London, SW1X 8BY (☎020 7235 5218; www.huemblon.org.uk); US, 3910 Shoemaker St., NW, Washington, D.C., 20008 (☎202-362-6730; www.hungaryemb.org.

VISA AND ENTRY INFORMATION. Citizens of Australia, Canada, Ireland, New Zealand, the UK, and the US can visit Hungary without a visa for up to 90 days if they do not intend to work; EU citizens need only a national identity card to enter. Passports must be valid for six months after you plan to depart Hungary. There is no fee for crossing a Hungarian border. In general, plan on 30min. crossing time.

ENTRANCE REQUIREMENTS

Passport: Required for all non-EU citizens.
Visa: Not required for stays under 90 days for citizens of Australia, Canada, Ireland, New Zealand, the UK, and the US.
Letter of Invitation: Not required.
Inoculations: Not required. Recommended up-to-date on DTaP (diphtheria, tetanus, and pertussis), hepatitis A, hepatitis B, MMR (measles, mumps, and rubella), polio booster, and typhoid.
Work Permit: Required for all foreigners planning to work in Hungary.
Driving Permit: International Driving Permits are recognized in Hungary, as are US and European driver's licenses with Hungarian translations attached.

TOURIST SERVICES AND MONEY

TOURIST OFFICES. Tourinform (☎06 80 630 800; http://www.tourinform.hu) has 140 branches and is a useful first stop for finding vacancies in university dorms and private pensions *(panzió)*. Many employees speak English and German. Most **IBUSZ** (www.ibusz.hu) offices book private rooms, exchange money, and sell train tickets; they are generally better at assisting in travel plans than at providing info. *Tourist Information: Hungary*, *Budapest in Your Pocket*, and the monthly entertainment guide *Programme in Hungary* are both free and in English.

FORINTS (FT)

AUS$1 = 158.49FT	1000FT = AUS$6.31
CDN$1 = 192.19FT	1000FT = CDN$5.20
EUR€1 = 270.26FT	1000FT = EUR€3.70
NZ$1 = 133.64FT	1000FT = NZ$7.48
UK£1 = 395.34FT	1000FT = UK£2.53
US$1 = 213.97FT	1000FT = US$4.67

MONEY. The national currency is the **forint (Ft)**; coins and bills each come in seven denominations. Hungary has a **value added tax (VAT)** rate of 20%. **Inflation** hovers around 4%, though its general trend has been downward. Currency exchange machines are slow but offer good rates, and banks like **OTP Bank** and **Postabank** offer the best rates for changing traveler's checks. Never change money on the street or in extended-hour exchange offices. Watch for scams: the maximum legal commission for cash-to-cash exchange is 1%. **ATMs** are common; major **credit cards** are accepted in some establishments. A bare-bones day in Hungary—dorm accommodation, transport, and food—costs 4500-5500Ft. For less ascetic living, expect to spend 5500-7000Ft. **Tips** are not usually included, and it is routine to tip around 10%. Don't bother bargaining with cabbies; set a price before getting in.

HEALTH AND SAFETY. It is not difficult to obtain **medical services** in Budapest. Embassies have lists of Anglophone doctors, and most hospitals have some on staff. Outside Budapest, try to bring a Hungarian speaker to the hospital with you. **Tourist insurance** is valid—and necessary—for many medical services. **Tap water** is usually clean, except in Tokaj; **bottled water** is available at most food stores. Public bathrooms vary in cleanliness: pack soap, a towel, and 30Ft for the attendant. Carry **toilet paper,** as many hostels do not provide it, and you only get a single square in public restrooms. Women should look for *Női* signs, men for *Férfi*. Many **pharmacies** *(gyógyszertár)* stock Western brands, tampons, and condoms.

Violent **crime** is low, but in Budapest and other large cities, foreign tourists are targets for petty thieves, pickpockets, and scams. In an emergency, your embassy will likely be more helpful than the police. **Minorities** are generally accepted, though dark-skinned travelers may be mistaken for Roma (gypsies) and encounter prejudice. Though Hungary is growing more tolerant, **GLBT** travelers may face serious discrimination, especially outside Budapest.

EMERGENCY	**Police:** ☎107. **Ambulance:** ☎104 **Fire:** ☎105. **General Emergency:** ☎112.

TRANSPORTATION

BY PLANE. Many international airlines arrive in Budapest. The cheapest options are **Sky Europe** (www.skyeurope.com) and **WizzAir** (www.wizzair.com), two Eastern European budget airlines. Standbys **Air Berlin** (www.airberlin.com) and **easyJet** (www.easyjet.com) both offer service between Budapest and Geneva, London, Paris, and several German cities. The national airline, **Malév** (www.malev.hu), flies from Budapest to major European cities.

BY TRAIN. Many **trains** *(vonat)*, both international and domestic, pass through Budapest and tend to be reliable and inexpensive. Several types of **Eurailpasses** are valid in Hungary. Check schedules and fares at **www.elvira.hu.** *Személyvonat* trains have many local stops and are excruciatingly slow; *gyorsvonat* trains, listed in red on schedules, move much faster for the same price. Large towns are connected by blue express lines; these InterCity trains are fast and air-conditioned. A *pótjegy* (seat reservation) is required on trains labeled "R;" if you don't reserve, you'll face a hefty fine. *Érkezés* means arrival, *indulás* departure, *vágány* is track, and *állomás* and *pályaudvar* (abbreviated *pu*) mean station. The *peron* (platform) is rarely named before the train nears a stop, so pay attention. Many stations are not marked; ask the conductor or gesticulate to find out arrival times.

BY BUS AND FERRY. Buses, which are clean but crowded, and often slightly more expensive than trains, are best for travel between outer provincial centers. **Volánbusz** (www.volanbusz.hu) runs coaches domestically and internationally; **Eurolines** (www.eurolines.com) also coordinates bus service among European cities. Within larger cities, buy your ticket at the kiosk and get it punched on board. There's a fine if you're caught without a ticket. A ferry runs down the Danube from Vienna, AUT or Bratislava, SLK to Budapest; schedules for ferry company **Mahart Passnave** are online at www.mahartpassnave.hu.

BY CAR AND BIKE. Taxi prices should not exceed the following: 6am-10pm base fare 200Ft, 240Ft per km, 60Ft per min. waiting; 10pm-6am are 300/280/70Ft. Beware of taxi scams. Before getting in, check that the meter is working and ask how much the ride will cost. Taxis ordered by phone cost less. European and US driver's licenses are respected for up to one year; you may also drive in Hungary with an International Driving Permit (IDP). There is a zero-tolerance policy for drunk driving, meaning that blood alcohol levels must be at 0.00 at all times when behind the wheel. To travel on some motorways, drivers must purchase stickers, which are good for nine days, one month, or one year, at tollbooths, post offices, or the **Magyar Autoklub (MAK).** For info on road conditions, contact ☎322 2238 (24hr.) or 443 5651. There are emergency phones every 2km on motorways. For 24hr. English-language assistance, contact MAK (in Budapest ☎345 1800). Biking terrain varies; the northeast is hilly while the south is generally flat. Roads are usually well paved. Though it is common, Let's Go does not recommend **hitchhiking.**

KEEPING IN TOUCH

PHONE CODES	**Country code:** 36. **International dialing prefix:** 00. For more information on how to place international calls, see inside back cover.

EMAIL AND THE INTERNET. The Internet is accessible in major cities. The Hungarian keyboard differs significantly from English-language keyboards; click the "Hu" icon at the bottom right of the screen and switch the setting to "Angol" to shift to an English keyboard. Most Internet cafes charge 150-300Ft per hour.

TELEPHONE. For **intercity calls,** wait for the tone and dial slowly; "06" goes before the phone code. Use red phones for **international calls.** Phones often require *telefonkártya* (phonecards). The best cards for international calls are **Neophone,** available at the post office, and **Micronet,** available at Fotex stores. Calls to Australia, Canada, and Ireland cost 45-50Ft per minute, to the UK 39Ft per minute, to the US 35Ft per minute. Make direct calls from Budapest's phone office. A 20Ft coin is required to start most calls. International access numbers include: **AT&T Direct** (☎06 800 01111); **Canada Direct** (☎06 800 01211); **MCI WorldPhone** (☎06 800 01411); **Sprint** (☎06 800 01877); **Telecom New Zealand** (☎06 800 06411). **Mobile phones** are common; service can be purchased from Pannon GSM, T-Mobile, or Vodafone.

MAIL. Magyar Posta (www.posta.hu), the Hungarian post office, delivers mail reliably; airmail *(légiposta)* takes seven to 10 days to reach Europe and the US. Rates for a letter (up to 20g) to Europe are 170Ft, for a postcard 120Ft; to anywhere else,

140Ft/190Ft. Mail can be received Post Restante in Hungary by having envelopes addressed: First name LAST NAME, POSTE RESTANTE, post office address, Postal Code, city, Hungary.

LANGUAGE. Hungarian, a Finno-Ugric language, is unrelated to most modern European languages and is closer to Finnish and Estonian. After German, English is Hungary's most common second language. Most young people know some English. "Hello" is used as an informal greeting. "Szia!" (sounds like "see ya!") is another greeting. See **Phrasebook: Hungarian,** p. 1057.

ACCOMMODATIONS AND CAMPING

HUNGARY	❶	❷	❸	❹	❺
ACCOMMODATIONS	under 2000Ft	2000-3000Ft	3000-6000Ft	6000-10,000Ft	over 10,000Ft

Tourism is developing rapidly, and rising prices elsewhere make **hostels** attractive; **Hostelling International (HI)** cards are useful for the best rates. Many hostels can be booked through a student travel agency or through local tourist offices. Try www.hostelhungary.com to book. In smaller towns, university dormitory-turned-hostels are the cheapest options in summer; hostels appear more rarely outside Budapest. Locations change annually, so inquire at Tourinform and call ahead. Year-round, **guesthouses** and **pensions** *(panzió)*, more common than hotels in small towns, and **private rooms** are also viable options. Singles in guesthouses are scarce; finding a roommate can be worthwhile, as solo travelers must often pay for doubles. Check prices ahead if you can, as agencies may try to rent you the most expensive rooms. Outside Budapest, it pays to plan as you go, as the best booking offices are region-specific; after staying a few nights, make arrangements directly with the owner to save the 20-30% commission. There are over 300 **campgrounds** in Hungary. Most are open from May to September. For more information, consult *Camping Hungary* at tourist offices, or contact Tourinform in Budapest (p. 515).

FOOD AND DRINK

HUNGARY	❶	❷	❸	❹	❺
FOOD	under 400Ft	400-800Ft	800-1300Ft	1300-2800Ft	over 2800Ft

Hungarian food, laced with spices and laden with meats, is more flavorful than that of many of its Eastern European neighbors. **Paprika,** Hungary's chief agricultural export, lends spice as it colors dishes red. In Hungarian restaurants (*vendéglő* or *étterem*), *halászlé*, a spicy fish stew, and *gyümölesleves*, a cold fruit soup with whipped cream, are traditional choices. The Hungarian national dish is *bográcsgulyás*, a beef and pepper stew. Sour cream often tops soups and stews. **Vegetarians** can fill up on tasty *rántott sajt* (fried cheese) and *gombapörkölt* (mushroom stew); in some small-town restaurants, *salata* (salad) and *sajt* (cheese) may be the only vegetarian options. Delicious Hungarian fruits and vegetables abound in summer. Desserts include *túrós rétes*, strudel-like pastries filled with sweet cheese, fruit, or nuts, and *somlói galuska*, a rich, rum-soaked sponge cake of chocolate, nuts, and cream. Hungary produces an array of fine **wines.** The northeastern towns of Eger and Tokaj produce famous red and white wines, respectively. Hungarian **beer** *(sör)* ranges from first-rate to acceptable. Lighter beers include *Dreher Pils*, *Szalon Sör*, *Steffl*, *Gold Fassl*, and *Gösser*. Hungary also produces *pálinka*, a drink similar to brandy; the tastiest variations are *barackpálinka* (apricot) and *körtepálinka* (pear). *Unicum*, advertised as the national drink, is an herbal liqueur the Hapsburgs used to cure digestive ailments.

HOLIDAYS AND FESTIVALS

Holidays: New Year's Day (Jan. 1); National Day (Mar. 15); Easter Sunday and Monday (Apr. 8-9); Labor Day (May 1); Pentecost (May 27); Constitution Day (Aug. 20); Republic Day (Oct. 23); All Saints' Day (Nov. 1); Christmas (Dec. 25-26).

Festivals: Central Europe's largest rock festival, **Sziget Festival** (www.sziget.hu), hits Budapest for a week at the end of July or the beginning of August and features rollicking crowds and international superstars. During Pécs's fabulous **World Festival of Wine Songs** (www.winesongfestival.hu; Sept. 28-30), choruses and world-famous vintages converge on the city.

BEYOND TOURISM

Central European University, Nador u. 9, 1051 Budapest, Hungary (☎1 327 30 34; www.bard.edu/ceu). University affiliated with the Open Society Institute-Budapest offers English-language program for international students. Tuition US$12,000 per semester. Financial aid available.

Hungarian Dance Academy, Columbus u. 87-89, Budapest, Hungary (☎361 273 34 34; www.mtf.hu). Summer dance programs for international students ages 11-24.

Central European Teaching Program, 3800 NE 72nd Ave., Portland, OR 97213, USA (☎503-287-4977; www.ticon.net/~cetp). Places English teachers in state schools in Hungary and Romania for 1 semester (US$1700) or 10 months (US$2250); additional training fees apply.

BUDAPEST ☎01

A spicy goulash of East and West, medieval and modern, Budapest (pop. 1.9 million) is rapidly earning a reputation as "Queen of the Danube," thanks to its unique brand of urban chic. Unlike the toyland center of Prague, Budapest's sights and famous thermal baths are spread throughout the energetic city. Once two separate cities, Buda and Pest were joined in 1872 to become the Hapsburg Empire's number-two city. Proud Hungarians rebuilt Budapest from rubble after WWII and weathered 40 years of Communist rule. These triumphs resonate today as Budapest finally resumes its place as a major European capital.

TRANSPORTATION

Flights: Ferihegy Airport (BUD; ☎296 9696). Malév (Hungarian Airlines; reservations ☎235 3888) flies to major cities. From the airport, the cheapest way to reach the city center is by bus #93 (20min., 4 per hr. 4:55am-11:20pm, 100Ft), and then by the M3 to Kőbánya-Kispest (15min. to Deák tér in downtown Pest).

Trains: Major stations are **Keleti Pályaudvar, Nyugati Pályaudvar,** and **Déli Pályaudvar.** (International info ☎461 5500, domestic 461 5400; www.mav.hu.) Most international trains arrive at Keleti pu., but some from Prague go to Nyugati pu. For schedules, check www.elvira.hu. To: **Berlin, GER** (12-15hr.; 2 per day; 42,465Ft, 1500Ft reservation fee); **Bucharest, ROM** (14hr., 5 per day, 21,147Ft); **Prague, CZR** (8hr., 4 per day, 12,939Ft); **Vienna, AUT** (3hr.; 17 per day; 8835Ft, 700FT reservation fee); **Warsaw, POL** (11hr.; 2 per day; 17,385Ft, 2000Ft reservation fee). Purchase tickets at an **International Ticket Office** (Keleti pu. open daily 8am-7pm; Nyugati pu. open M-Sa 5am-9pm). Or try **MÁV Hungarian Railways,** VI, Andrássy út 35, with branches at all stations. (☎461 5500. Open M-F 9am-5pm. Say *"diák"* for student or under 26 discounts.) The HÉV **commuter railway** station is at Batthyány tér, opposite Parliament. Trains head to **Szentendre** (45min., 4 per hr. 5am-9pm, 320Ft). Purchase tickets at the station for transport beyond the city limits.

Buses: Buses to international and some domestic destinations arrive at and depart from the **Népliget** station, X, Ulloi u. 131. (M3: Népliget. ☎219 8080. Ticket window open M-F 6am-6pm, Sa-Su 6am-4pm.) To **Berlin, GER** (14½hr., 6 per week, 16,900Ft), **Prague, CZR** (8hr., 6 per week, 7700Ft), and **Vienna, AUT** (3-3½hr., 4 per day, 6390Ft). Catch buses to destinations east of Budapest at the **Népstadion** station, XIV, Hungária körút 46-48. (M2: Népstadion. ☎252 1896. Open M-F 6am-6pm, Sa-Su 6am-4pm.) Buses to the Danube Bend and parts of northern Hungary depart outside **Árpád híd** metro station on the M3 line. (☎329 1450. Cashier open 6am-8pm.) Check www.volanbusz.hu for schedules.

Public Transportation: Subways, buses, and **trams** are cheap and convenient. The **metro** has 3 lines: M1 (yellow), M2 (red), and M3 (blue). Night transit (É) buses run 11pm-5am along major routes: #7É and 78É follow the M2 route; #6É follows the 4/6 tram line; #14É and 50É follow the M3 route. **Single-fare tickets** for all public transport (one-way on 1 line; 185Ft) are sold in metro stations, in *Trafik* shops, and by sidewalk vendors. Punch them in the orange boxes at the gate of the metro or on buses and trams; punch a new ticket when you change lines, or face fines. One-way tickets are cheaper in blocks of 10 or 20. Passes: 1-day 1150Ft, 3-day 2500Ft, 1-week 3400Ft.

Taxis: Beware of scams; check for a yellow license plate and running meter. **Budataxi** (☎233 3333) charges less for rides requested by phone. Also reliable are **Főtaxi** (☎222 2222), **6x6 Taxi** (☎266 6666), and **Tele 5 Taxi** (☎355 5555). Maximum fares by law: 6am-10pm 200Ft base fare plus 200Ft per km and 60Ft per min. waiting; 10pm-6am 280Ft base fare plus 280Ft per km and 70Ft per min. waiting.

ORIENTATION

Buda and Pest are separated by the **Danube River** (Duna), and the modern city preserves the distinctive character of each side. On the west bank, **Buda** has winding streets, beautiful vistas, a hilltop citadel, and the Castle District. Down the north slope of **Várhegy** (Castle Hill) is **Moszkva tér,** Buda's tram and local bus hub. On the east bank, **Pest,** the commercial center, is home to shopping boulevards, theaters, Parliament (Országház), and the Opera House. Metro lines converge in Pest at **Deák tér,** next to the main international bus terminal at **Erzsébet tér.** Two blocks west toward the river lies **Vörösmarty tér** and the pedestrian shopping zone **Váci utca.** Three main bridges join Budapest's halves: **Széchenyi Lánchíd** (Chain Bridge), **Erzsébet híd** (Elizabeth Bridge), and **Szabadság híd** (Freedom Bridge).

Budapest addresses begin with a Roman numeral representing one of the city's 23 **districts.** Central Buda is I; central Pest is V. A **map** is essential for navigating Budapest's confusing streets; pick one up at any tourist office or hostel.

PRACTICAL INFORMATION

Tourist Offices: All offices sell the **Budapest Card** (Budapest Kártya), which provides discounts, unlimited public transportation, and admission to most museums (2-day card 5200Ft, 3-day 6500Ft). The card is a great deal, except on Mondays when museums are closed. An excellent first stop in the city is **Tourinform,** V, Sütő u. 2 (☎438 8080; www.hungary.com). M1, 2, or 3: Deák tér. Off Deák tér behind McDonald's. Open daily 8am-8pm. **STA Travel,** Erkel 13 (☎299 0404; www.statravel.hu), arranges tours and accommodations. Open M-F 9am-6pm, Sa 10am-4:30pm. **Budapest in Your Pocket** (www.inyourpocket.com) is an up-to-date city guide.

Embassies: Australia, XII, Királyhágo tér 8/9 (☎457 9777; www.australia.hu). M2: Déli pu., then bus #21 or tram #59 to Királyhágo tér. Open M-F 8:30am-11am. **Canada,** XII, Ganz út 12-14 (☎392 3360; www.canada.hu). Open M-Th 8:30-10:30am and 2-3:30pm. **Ireland,** V, Szabadság tér 7 (☎301 4960), in Bank Center. M3: Arany J. u.

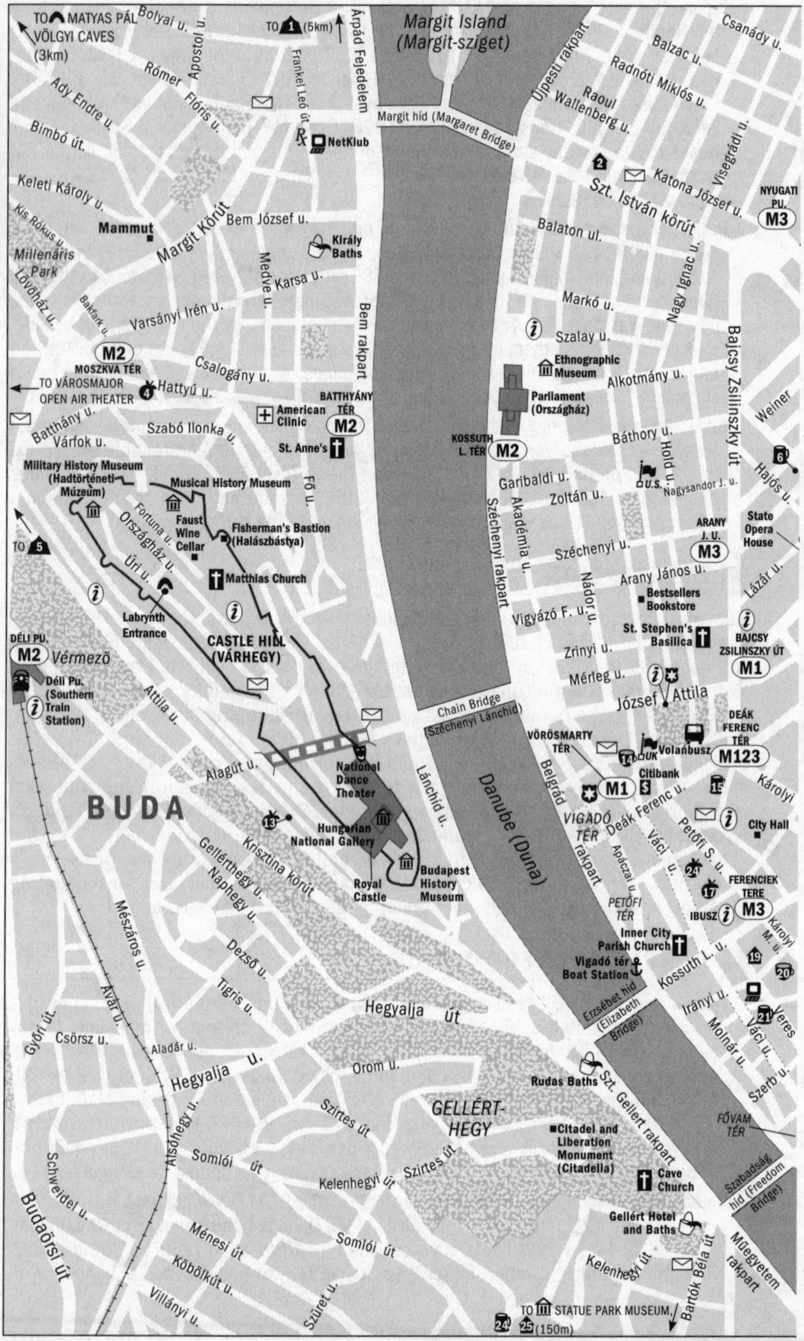

TO MATYAS PÁL VÖLGYI CAVES (3km)
TO 1 (5km)
Margit Island (Margit-sziget)
Margit híd (Margaret Bridge)
NetKlub
Mammut
Millenáris Park
Király Baths
M2 MOSZKVA TÉR
TO VÁROSMAJOR OPEN AIR THEATER
BATTHYÁNY TÉR M2
American Clinic
St. Anne's
Military History Museum (Hadtörténeti Múzeum)
Musical History Museum
Faust Wine Cellar
Fisherman's Bastion (Halászbástya)
Matthias Church
Labrynth Entrance
CASTLE HILL (VÁRHEGY)
TO 5
DÉLI PU. M2
Vérmező
Déli Pu. (Southern Train Station)
Chain Bridge (Széchenyi Lánchíd)
National Dance Theater
Hungarian National Gallery
Royal Castle
Budapest History Museum
BUDA
Danube (Duna)
Ethnographic Museum
Parliament (Országház)
KOSSUTH L. TÉR M2
NYUGATI PU. M3
U.S.
ARANY J. U. M3
State Opera House
Bestsellers Bookstore
St. Stephen's Basilica
BAJCSY ZSILINSZKY ÚT M1
VÖRÖSMARTY TÉR M1
UK
Volanbusz
DEÁK FERENC TÉR M123
Citibank
VIGADÓ TÉR
PETŐFI TÉR
City Hall
FERENCIEK TERE M3
IBUSZ
Inner City Parish Church
Vigadó tér Boat Station
Erzsébet híd (Elizabeth Bridge)
Rudas Baths
GELLÉRT-HEGY
Citadel and Liberation Monument (Citadella)
Cave Church
Gellért Hotel and Baths
FŐVAM TÉR
Szabadság híd (Freedom Bridge)
TO STATUE PARK MUSEUM, 25 (150m)

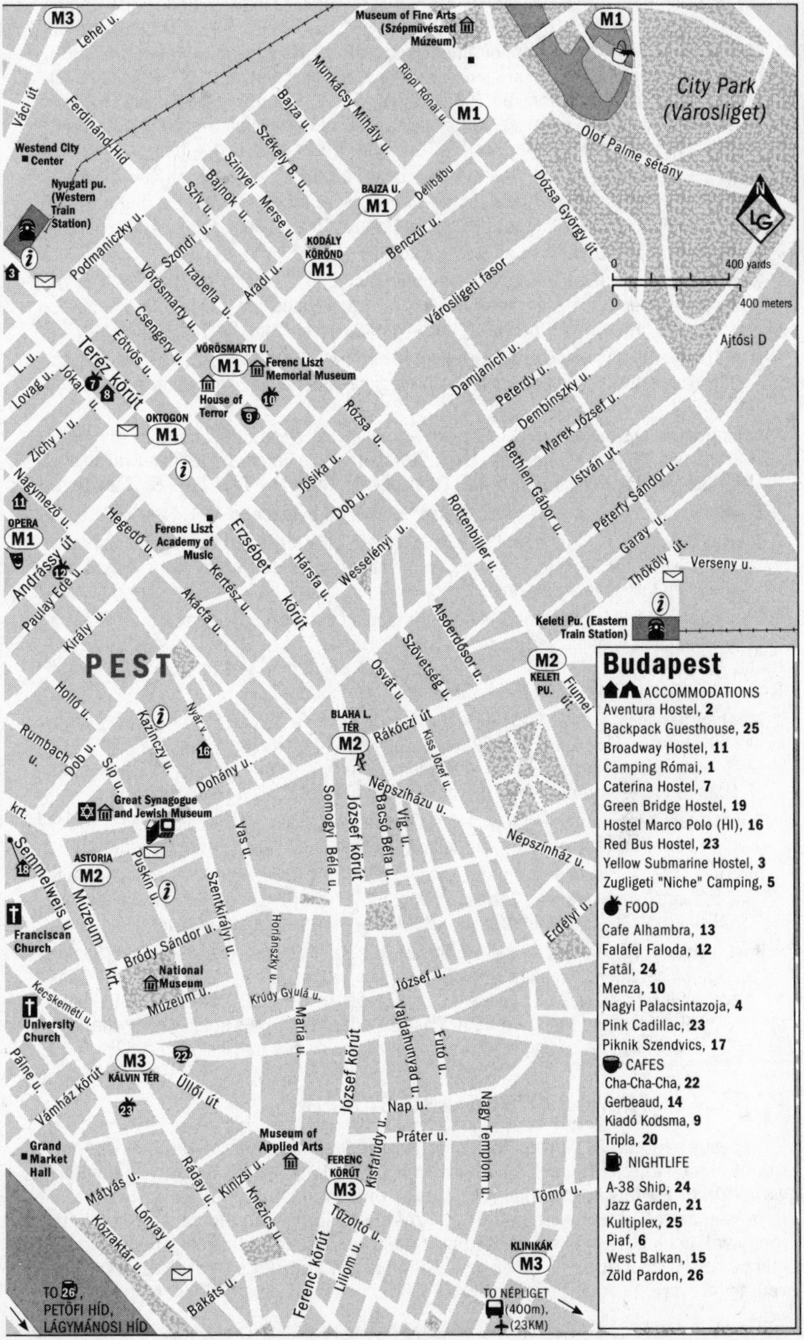
City Park
(Városliget)
PEST
Museum of Fine Arts
(Szépmüvészeti
Múzeum)
Westend City
Center
Nyugati pu.
(Western
Train
Station)
Ferenc Liszt
Memorial Museum
House of
Terror
Ferenc Liszt
Academy of
Music
Great Synagogue
and Jewish Museum
Franciscan
Church
National
Museum
University
Church
Grand
Market
Hall
Museum of
Applied Arts
Keleti Pu. (Eastern
Train Station)
VÖRÖSMARTY U.
OKTOGON
OPERA
BAJZA U.
KODÁLY
KÖRÖND
ASTORIA
BLAHA L.
TÉR
KELETI
PU.
KÁLVIN TÉR
FERENC
KÖRÚT
KLINIKÁK
M1
M2
M3
Lehel u.
Váci út
Ferdinánd híd
Podmaniczky u.
Munkácsy Mihály u.
Rippl Rónai u.
Bajza u.
Székely B. u.
Szinyei Merse u.
Bajnok u.
Szív u.
Szondi u.
Délibábu
Benczúr u.
Aradi u.
Izabella u.
Vörösmarty u.
Csengery u.
Eötvös u.
Teréz körút
Jókai u.
Lovag u.
L. u.
Zichy J. u.
Nagymező u.
Andrássy út
Paulay Ede u.
Király u.
Hegedű u.
Kertész u.
Akácfa u.
Erzsébet körút
Hársfa u.
Wesselényi u.
Dob u.
Jósika u.
Rózsa u.
Damjanich u.
Városligeti fasor
Dózsa György út
Olof Palme sétány
Ajtósi D
Peterdy u.
Dembinszky u.
Marek József u.
Bethlen Gábor u.
István út.
Péterfy Sándor u.
Garay u.
Thököly út.
Verseny u.
Rottenbiller u.
Alsóerdősor u.
Szövetség u.
Osvát u.
Rákóczi út
Kiss József u.
Fiumei út
Népszínház u.
Holló u.
Rumbach u.
Dob u.
Síp u.
Kazinczy u.
Nyár u.
Dohány u.
Somogyi Béla u.
József körút
Bacsó Béla u.
Víg u.
Vas u.
Szentkirályi u.
Puskin u.
Semmelweis u.
Múzeum krt.
Bródy Sándor u.
Múzeum u.
Horánszky u.
Krúdy Gyula u.
Mária u.
József u.
Vajdahunyad u.
Futó u.
Erdélyi u.
Nagy Templom u.
Kecskeméti u.
Pálffy u.
Vámház körút
Üllői út
Nap u.
Práter u.
Kisfaludy u.
Mátyás u.
Ráday u.
Kinizsi u.
Knézics u.
Tűzoltó u.
Tömő u.
Közraktár u.
Lónyay u.
Liliom u.
Ferenc körút
Bakáts u.
krt.
TO 26,
PETŐFI HÍD,
LÁGYMÁNOSI HÍD
TO NÉPLIGET
(400m),
(23KM)
0
400 yards
0
400 meters
Budapest
ACCOMMODATIONS
Aventura Hostel, 2
Backpack Guesthouse, 25
Broadway Hostel, 11
Camping Római, 1
Caterina Hostel, 7
Green Bridge Hostel, 19
Hostel Marco Polo (HI), 16
Red Bus Hostel, 23
Yellow Submarine Hostel, 3
Zugligeti "Niche" Camping, 5
FOOD
Cafe Alhambra, 13
Falafel Faloda, 12
Fatâl, 24
Menza, 10
Nagyi Palacsintazoja, 4
Pink Cadillac, 23
Piknik Szendvics, 17
CAFES
Cha-Cha-Cha, 22
Gerbeaud, 14
Kiadó Kodsma, 9
Tripla, 20
NIGHTLIFE
A-38 Ship, 24
Jazz Garden, 21
Kultiplex, 25
Piaf, 6
West Balkan, 15
Zöld Pardon, 26

Walk down Bank u. toward the river. Open M-F 9:30am-12:30pm and 2:30-4:30pm. **New Zealand,** VI, Nagymezo u. 50 (☎302 2484; sardi@axelero.hu). M3: Nyugati pu. Open M-F 11am-4pm by appointment only. **UK,** V, Harmincad u. 6 (☎266 2888; www.britishembassy.hu), near the intersection with Vörösmarty tér. M1: Vörösmarty tér. Open M-F 9:30am-12:30pm and 2:30-4:30pm. **US,** V, Szabadság tér 12 (☎475 4400, after hours 475 4703; www.usembassy.hu). M2: Kossuth tér. Walk 2 blocks down Akadémia and turn on Zoltán. Open M-Th 1-4pm, F 9am-noon and 1-4pm.

Currency Exchange: Banks have the best rates. **Citibank,** V, Vörösmarty tér 4 (☎374 5000). M1: Vörösmarty tér. Cashes traveler's checks for no commission and provides MC/V cash advances. Bring your passport. Open M-Th 9am-5pm, F 9am-4pm.

Luggage Storage: Lockers at all 3 train stations. 150-600Ft.

English-Language Bookstore: **Treehugger Dan's,** VI, Csengery u. 48 (☎332 0774; www.treehugger.hu). M2: Oktogon. Organic fair-trade coffee and a wide selection of secondhand English books. Open M-F 10am-7pm, Sa 10am-5pm, Su 10am-4pm. MC/V.

GLBT Resources: GayGuide.net Budapest (☎0630 932 3334; www.budapest.gayguide.net). Volunteers post an online guide and run a hotline (daily 4-8pm) with info about gay-friendly lodgings.

Laundromat: Mosómata, VI, Ó u. 24-26. M1: Oktogon. Wash 600Ft per 9kg, dry 400Ft per 20min. Open M-F 9am-7pm, Sa-Su 10am-4pm. Commercial facilities available at **Irisz Szalon,** V, Városház u. 3-5. M3: Ferenciek tér. Open M-F 7am-7pm, Sa 7am-1pm.

Emergency: ☎112 connects to all. **Police:** ☎107. **Ambulance:** ☎104. **Fire:** ☎105.

Tourist Police: V, Sütő u. 2 (☎438 8080). M1, 2, or 3: Deák tér. Inside the Tourinform office. Open 24hr. Beware of people on the street pretending to be Tourist Police and demanding to see your passport.

Pharmacies: Look for green-and-white signs labeled *Apotheke, Gyógyszertár,* or *Pharmacie.* Minimal after-hours service fees apply. **II,** Frankel Leó út 22 (☎212 4311). AmEx/MC/V. **VI,** Teréz krt. 41 (☎311 4439). Open M-F 8am-8pm, Sa 8am-2pm. **VII,** Rákóczi út 39 (☎314 3694). Open M-F 7:30am-9pm, Sa 7:30am-2pm.

Medical Services: Falck (SOS) KFT, II, Kapy út 49/B (☎200 0100) offers emergency ambulance services. **American Clinic,** I, Hattyú u. 14 (24hr. emergency ☎224 9090; www.firstmedcenters.com). Open M 8:30am-7pm, Tu-W 10am-6pm, Th 11:30am-6pm, F 10am-6pm. The US embassy (see above) has a list of English-speaking doctors.

Telephones: Phone cards are sold at kiosks and metro stations. 50-unit card 800Ft, 120-unit card 1800Ft. Domestic operator and info ☎198; international operator 190, info 199.

Internet Access: Cybercafes are everywhere, but they can be expensive and long waits are common. **Ami Internet Coffee,** V, Váci u. 40 (☎267 1644; www.amicoffee.hu). M3: Ferenciek tér. 200Ft per 10min., 1050Ft per hr. Open daily 9am-2am.

Post Office: V, Városház u. 18 (☎485 9012). M3: Ferenciek tér. *Poste Restante (Postán Mar)* in office around the right side of the building. Open M-F 8am-8pm, Sa 8am-2pm. Branches include: Keleti pu.; Nyugati pu.; VI, Teréz krt. 105/107; VIII, Baross tér 11/C (☎322 9013). Open M-F 7am-9pm. **Postal Code:** Varies by district, taking the form 1XX2, where XX is the 2-digit district number (e.g., district V translates to 1052).

ACCOMMODATIONS AND CAMPING

Budapest's hostels are centers for the backpacker social scene, and their common rooms can be as exciting as expat bars and clubs. Many hostels are run by the **Hungarian Youth Hostels Association (HI),** which operates from an office in Keleti pu. Representatives wearing Hostelling International shirts—and legions of competitors—will accost travelers as they get off the train. Be aware that they may provide inaccurate descriptions of other accommodations in order to sell their own. Private rooms are more expensive than hostels, but they do offer peace, quiet, and private showers. Arrive early, bring cash, and haggle. **Best Hotel Service,** V, Sütő u. 2, arranges hotel, apartment, and hostel reservations (6000Ft and up). Take M1, 2, or 3 to Deák tér. (☎318 4848; www.besthotelservice.hu. Open daily 8am-8pm.)

Backpack Guesthouse, XI, Takács Menyhért u. 33 (☎209 8406; www.backpackbudapest.hu), in Buda, 12min. from central Pest. From Keleti pu., take bus #7 or 7A toward Buda; get off at Tétenyi u., backtrack, take a left under the railway bridge, another left on Hamzsabégi út, and then the 3rd right. Hostel life doesn't get much better than this laid-back place, which has themed dorms, genuinely helpful owners, and a common room with movies, music, and cheap beer. Free Internet. Reception 24hr. Reserve ahead. Dorms 3000Ft; doubles 9000Ft. Cash only. ❷

Aventura Hostel, XIII, Visegrádi u. 12 (☎70 310 2003; www.aventurahostel.com), in Pest. M3: Nyugati tér. Eclectic decor and shining clean facilities. Breakfast included. Laundry 1200Ft. Free Internet. Reception 24hr. Dorms 3360Ft. ❸

Green Bridge Hostel, V, Molnár u. 22-24 (☎266 6922; greenbridge@freemail.hu), in Pest's central district. The unbeatable location, friendly staff, and free snacks earn rave reviews. Free Internet. Reception 24hr. Flexible check-out. Dorms 4480Ft. Cash only. ❸

Museum Guest House, VIII, Mikszáth Kálmán tér 4, 1st fl. (☎318 9508; museumgh@freemail.c3.hu), in Pest. M3: Kálvin tér. Convenient location, colorful rooms, and loft beds. English spoken. Free Internet. Reception 24hr. Check-out 11am. Reserve ahead. Dorms 3200Ft. Cash only. ❸

Broadway Hostel, VI, Ó u. 24-26 (☎688 1662; www.broadwayhostel.hu), in Pest's theater district. M1: Opera. A new, luxurious alternative to the backpacking scene, with curtained partitions and fluffy comforters. Free wireless Internet. Reception 24hr. Dorms 3800-4200Ft; singles 16,000Ft; doubles 32,000Ft. ❸

Red Bus Hostel, V, Semmelweis u. 14 (☎266 0136; www.redbusbudapest.hu). Spacious dorms in downtown Pest. Breakfast included. Laundry 1200Ft. Internet 12Ft per min. Reception 24hr. Check-out 10am. 10-bed dorms 2800-3200Ft; singles 8300Ft; doubles 16,900Ft. AmEx/MC/V. ❷

Caterina Hostel, III, Teréz krt. 30, apt. #28, ring code 48 (☎269 5990; www.caterinahostel.hu), in Pest. M1: Oktogon, or trams #4 and 6. Clean, recently renovated rooms. Internet 400Ft per hr. Reception 24hr. Check-out 10am. Reserve online. Dorms 2500-3200Ft; doubles 6800Ft; triples 10,200Ft. Low season 2000-3000/6000/9000Ft. Cash only. ❷

Yellow Submarine Hostel, VI, Teréz krt. 56, 3rd fl. (☎331 9896; www.yellowsubmarinehostel.com), in Pest across from Nyugati pu. Known as a party hostel; facilities include a kitchen and bar. Doubles and triples located in nearby apartments. Breakfast included. Internet 10Ft per min. Check-out 9am. Dorms 2900Ft; singles 7500Ft; doubles 9000Ft; triples 10,500Ft; quads 14,000Ft. 10% HI discount. MC/V. ❷

Hostel Marco Polo (HI), VII, Nyár u. 6 (☎413 2555; www.marcopolohostel.com), in Pest. M2: Astoria or M2: Blaha Lujza tér. Dorm bunks are in compartments separated by curtains. Breakfast included. Reception 24hr. Reserve ahead in summer. Dorms 4200Ft; singles 13,000Ft; doubles 17,600Ft. 10% HI and ISIC discount. MC/V. ❸

Camping Római, III, Szentendrei út 189 (☎388 7167). M2: Batthyány tér. Take HÉV to Római fürdő; walk 100m toward river. Huge complex with swimming pool, shady park, and nearby grocery store and restaurants. Electricity 600Ft. Breakfast 880Ft. Laundry 800Ft. Tent sites 3100Ft per person; bungalows 17,600-21,100Ft, 1160Ft per extra person, children 590Ft. Cars 3400Ft. 3% tourist tax. 10% HI discount. ❸

Zugligeti "Niche" Camping, XII, Zugligeti út 101 (☎200 8346; www.campingniche.hu). Take bus #158 from above Moszkva tér to Laszállóhely, the last stop. On-site restaurant. Communal showers. Electricity 1200Ft. Tent sites 880Ft; large tents 1300Ft. 1200Ft per person. Cars 990Ft, caravans 2400Ft. ❶

FOOD

Cafeterias with *"Önkiszolgáló Étterem"* signs serve cheap food (entrees 300-500Ft), and a neighborhood *kifőzés* (kiosk) or *vendéglő* (vendor) offers a real taste of Hungary. Corner markets, many with 24hr. windows, stock the basics. The **Grand Market Hall,** IX, Fövam tér 1/3, next to Szabadság híd (M3: Kálvin tér), was built in 1897; it now has 2½ acres of stalls, making it a tourist attraction in itself. Ethnic restaurants inhabit the upper floors of **Mammut Plaza,** just outside the Moszkva tér metro in Buda, and **West End Plaza,** near the Nyugati metro in Pest.

RESTAURANTS

Fatál, V, Vací u. 67 (☎266 2607), in Pest. M3: Ferenciek tér. Hands-down the best place in Budapest for enormous portions of down-home, delicious Hungarian cuisine. Entrees 590-2500Ft. Open daily 11:30am-2am. MC/V. ❷

Nagyi Palacsintazoja, II, Hattyu u. 16 (☎201 5321), in Buda. M2: Moszkva tér. Tiny, mirror-covered eatery dishes out sweet and savory crepes (118-298Ft) piled with toppings like cheese, fruit, or chocolate sauce. Seating is limited. Open 24hr. ❶

Cafe Alhambra, VI, Jókai tér 3 (☎354 1068), in Pest. M1: Oktogon. Relax outdoors on the terrace or admire the treasures inside this peaceful Moroccan eatery. Tapas 260-1890Ft. Entrees 600-2490Ft. Open M-Sa noon-midnight, Su 6pm-midnight. MC/V. ❷

Pink Cadillac, IX, Ráday u. 22 (☎216 1412; www.pinkcadillac.hu), in Pest. M3: Kálvin tér. Choose from inventive offerings and dine *al fresco* at this wildly popular gourmet pizzeria. Pizzas 750-1690Ft. Open M-F 11am-midnight, Sa-Su noon-midnight. MC/V. ❷

Falafel Faloda, VI. Paulay Ede u. 53 (☎351 1243), in Pest. M1: Opera. Vegetarians come in droves for on-the-go falafel (620Ft) and the city's best salad bar. Salads 320-660Ft. Open M-F 10am-8pm, Sa 10am-6pm. Cash only. ❷

Menza, Liszt Ferenc tér 2 (☎413 1482; www.menza.co.hu). Reminiscent of Communist-era *"menza,"* or canteens, this elegant eatery's decor offers the perfect balance of 70s camp and modern chic. Menu boards tacked to the wall list all manner of excellent Hungarian and international dishes on offer. Entrees 650-1790Ft. Open daily 10am-1am. AmEx/MC/V. ❷

Piknik Szendvics, V, Haris Köz 1 (☎318 3334; www.piknik-szendvics.hu), in Pest. M3: Ferenciek tér. Even the most cash-strapped traveler can create a meal from the hors d'oeuvre-sized open-faced sandwiches served here (119-199Ft). Open M-F 9am-6pm, Sa 9am-2pm. Cash only. ❶

CAFES

Once the haunts of the literary, intellectual, and cultural elite—as well as political dissidents—Budapest's cafes boast histories as rich as the pastries they serve.

Cha-Cha-Cha, IX, Kálvin tér underground (☎215 0545; www.chachacha.hu), in Pest. Improbably located beneath the Kálvin tér metro station, this wonderfully weird bar and cafe has free wireless Internet. Coffee 290Ft. Beer 450Ft. Open M-Sa 9am-10pm.

Tripla, V, Király Pál u. 6 (☎06 20 264 1404). This quiry cafe features an unusual ambience and eclectic artwork. Espresso 180Ft. Tea 250Ft. Mixed drinks 700-900Ft. Open daily 6pm-midnight.

Kiadó Kocsma, VI, Jókai tér 3 (☎331 1955), in Pest, next to Cafe Alhambra. M1: Oktogon. Irresistibly playful atmosphere and tranquil, shady terrace, perfect for coffee (250Ft), tea (200Ft), or spirits (550-700Ft). Open daily 9am-midnight.

Gerbeaud, V, Vörösmarty tér 7 (☎429 9020; www.gerbeaud.hu). M1: Vörösmarty tér. This Budapest institution has been serving its layer cakes (620Ft) and homemade ice cream (250Ft) since 1858. Open daily 9am-9pm. AmEx/MC/V.

SIGHTS

In 1896, Hungary's millennial birthday bash prompted the construction of what are today Budapest's most prominent sights. Among the works commissioned by the Hapsburgs were **Hősök tér** (Heroes' Square), **Szabadság híd** (Liberty Bridge), **Vajdahunyad Vár** (Vajdahunyad Castle), and continental Europe's first **metro** system. Slightly grayer for wear, war, and occupation, these monuments attest to the optimism of a capital on the verge of its Golden Age. See the sights, find your way around, and meet other travelers with **Absolute Walking and Biking Tours.** (☎211 8861; www.absolutetours.com. 3½hr. tours 4000Ft, students 3500ft. Specialized tours 4000-6000Ft.) **Boat tours** leave from Vigadó tér piers 6-7, near Elizabeth Bridge in Pest. The evening *Danube Legend* costs 4200Ft; its daytime counterpart, the *Duna Bella*, costs 2600Ft for 1hr. and 3600Ft for 2hr.

BUDA

On the east bank of the Danube, Buda sprawls between the base of **Várhegy** (Castle Hill) and southern **Gellérthegy** and leads into the city's main residential areas. Older and more peaceful than Pest, Buda is filled with parks and lush hills.

CASTLE DISTRICT. Towering above the Danube on Várhegy, the Castle District has been razed three times in its 800-year history, most recently in 1945. With its winding, statue-filled streets, impressive views, and hodgepodge of architectural styles, the UNESCO-protected district now appears much as it did under the Hapsburg reign. The reconstructed **Buda Castle** (Vár) houses fine museums (p. 523). Bullet holes in the palace facade recall the 1956 Uprising. *(M1, 2, or 3: Deák tér. From the metro, take bus #16 across the Danube. Or, from M2: Moszkva tér, walk up to the hill on Várfok u. "Becsi kapu" marks the castle entrance.)* Beneath Buda Castle, the **Castle Labyrinths** (Budvári Labirinths) provide a spooky glimpse of the subterranean world of the city. *(Úri u. 9. ☎489 3281. Open daily 9:30am-7:30pm. 1400Ft, students 1100Ft.)*

MATTHIAS CHURCH. The colorful roof of Matthias Church (Mátyás templom) on Castle Hill is one of Budapest's most photographed sights. The church was converted into a mosque in 1541, then renovated again 145 years later when the Hapsburgs defeated the Turks. Ascend the spiral steps to view the exhibits of the **Museum of Ecclesiastical Art.** *(Open M-F 9am-5pm, Sa 1-5pm. High Mass daily 7, 8:30am, 6pm; Su and holidays also 10am and noon. Church and museum 600Ft, students 400Ft.)*

IN RECENT NEWS

REVISITING THE GYPSY FOLKTALE

Eastern Europe is home to an estimated 7-9 million Gypsies, or Roma, making them the region's largest minority group. In Hungary, they account for 9-11% of the population. The Roma are believed to have migrated from India, and they have been living in Europe for centuries, particularly in the Balkans. The scarf-clad Gypsies have long been a staple character in Eastern European folk tales, stereotypically cast as colorful roving musician-types.

In reality, the Roma story is not so rosy—they have long been victims of extreme discrimination, with inadequate access to housing, jobs, public education, and health care. At its most extreme, this discrimination has taken the form of forced sterilization or racially motivated murders.

The plight of the Roma is now beginning to generate a worldwide outcry. The first large-scale conference to address the Roma's situation was held in Budapest in 2003. Delegates from eight Eastern European countries as well as international NGOs joined forces to launch the "Decade of Roma Inclusion," beginning in 2005. This initiative aims to "change the lives of Roma" across the region and reduce rates of poverty and illiteracy. Recent news updates suggest that the Roma are finally, albeit slowly, on the path to an improved socioeconomic status. For more information, check out www.romadecade.com.

GELLÉRT HILL. After the coronation of King Stephen, the first Christian Hungarian monarch, in AD 1001, the Pope sent Bishop Gellért to convert the Magyars. After those unconvinced by the bishop's message hurled him to his death from the summit of Budapest's principal hill, it was named Gellérthegy in his honor. The **Liberation Monument** (Szabadság Szobor), on the hilltop, honors Soviet soldiers who died ridding Hungary of Nazis. The adjoining **Citadel** was built as a symbol of Hapsburg power after the foiled 1848 revolution; the view from there is especially stunning at night. At the base of the hill is **Gellért** (p. 524), Budapest's most famous Turkish bath. *(XI. Take tram #18 or 19 or bus #7 to Hotel Gellért; follow Szabó Verjték u. to Jubileumi Park, continuing on marked paths to the summit. Citadel 300Ft.)*

PEST

Constructed in the 19th century, the winding streets of Pest now link cafes, corporations, and monuments. The crowded **Belváros** (Inner City) is based around **Vörösmarty tér** and the swarming pedestrian boulevard **Váci utca.**

PARLIAMENT. The palatial Gothic Parliament (Országház) stands 96m tall, a number that symbolizes the date of Hungary's millennial anniversary. The building was modeled after the UK's, right down to the facade and the riverside location. The **crown jewels** were moved from Hungary's National Museum to the Cupola Room here in 1999. *(M2: Kossuth tér. ☎441 4000. English-language tours M-F 10am, noon, 2, 2:30, 5, and 6pm; Sa-Su 10am; arrive early. Min. 5 people. Ticket office at Gate X opens at 8am. Entrance with mandatory tour 2300Ft, students 1150Ft. Free with EU passport.)*

GREAT SYNAGOGUE. The largest synagogue in Europe and the second-largest in the world, Pest's Great Synagogue (Zsinagóga) was designed to hold 3000 worshippers. The enormous metal **Tree of Life,** a Holocaust memorial, sits in the garden above a mass grave for thousands of Jews killed near the end of the war. The Hebrew inscription reads: "Whose pain can be greater than mine?" and the Hungarian beneath pledges: "Let us remember." Each leaf bears the name of a family that perished. Next door, the **Jewish Museum** (Zsidó Múzeum) documents the storied past of Hungary's Jews. *(VII. At the corner of Dohány u. and Wesselényi u. M2: Astoria. Open May-Oct. M-Th 10am-5pm, F and Su 10am-2pm; Nov.-Apr. M-Th 10am-3pm, F and Su 10am-1pm. Services F 6pm. Admissions often start at 10:30am. Covered shoulders required. Tours M-Th 10:30am-3:30pm on the half-hour, F and Su 10:30, 11:30am, 12:30pm. Admission to Synagogue and Museum 600Ft, students 400Ft. Tours 2000/1600Ft.)*

ST. STEPHEN'S BASILICA (SZ. ISTVÁN BAZILIKA). Though seriously damaged in WWII, the neo-Renaissance facade of the city's largest church has been mostly restored. The **Panorama Tower** offers an amazing 360° view of the city. A curious attraction is St. Stephen's mummified right hand, one of Hungary's most revered religious relics; a 100Ft donation dropped in the box will illuminate it for 2min. *(V. M1, 2, or 3: Deák tér. Open June-Aug. M-Sa 9am-6pm; Sept.-May M-Sa 9:30am-5pm. Mass M-Sa 7, 8am, 6pm, Su 8:30, 10am, noon, 6pm. Tower open daily June-Aug. 9:30am-6pm; Sept.-Oct. 10am-5:30pm; Apr.-May 10am-4:30pm. Church free. Tower 500Ft, students 400Ft.)*

ANDRÁSSY ÚT AND HEROES' SQUARE. Hungary's grandest boulevard, Andrássy út extends from Erzsébet tér northeast to Heroes' Square (Hősök tér). The **State Opera House** (Magyar Állami Operaház) is a vivid reminder of Budapest's Golden Age; its gilded interior glows on performance nights. Take a tour if you can't see an opera. *(Andrássy út 22. M1: Opera. ☎332 8197. 1hr. English-language tours daily 3 and 4pm. 2500Ft, students 1300Ft.)* At the Heroes' Sq. end of Andrássy út, the **Millennium Monument** (Millenniumi emlékmű) commemorates the nation's most prominent leaders.

CITY PARK (VÁROSLIGET). Budapest's park, located northeast of Heroes' Sq., is home to a zoo, a circus, an aging amusement park, and the lakeside **Vajdahunyad Castle.** The castle's collage of Baroque, Gothic, and Romanesque styles chronicles the history of Hungarian design. Outside the castle is the hooded statue of King Béla IV's **anonymous scribe,** who left the major record of medieval Hungary. Rent a **rowboat** or **ice skates** on the lake next to the castle. The park's main road is closed to automobiles on weekends. *(XIV. M1: Széchenyi Fürdő. Park ☎363 8310. Open July-Aug. daily 10am-8pm; May-June M-F 11am-7pm, Sa-Su 10am-8pm. Zoo ☎343 3710. Open May-Aug. M-Th 9am-6:30pm, F-Su 9am-7pm; Mar. and Oct. M-Th 9am-5pm, F-Su 9am-5:30pm; Apr. and Sept. M-Th 9am-5:30pm, F-Su 9am-6pm; Nov.-Jan. daily 9am-4pm. 1300Ft, students 1000Ft.)*

MUSEUMS

MUSEUM OF FINE ARTS (SZÉPMŰVÉSZETI MÚZEUM). A spectacular collection of European art is housed in this museum near Heroes' Sq. The El Greco room is not to be missed. *(M1: Hősök tér. ☎069 036 9300. Open Tu-W and F-Su 10am-5:30pm, Th 10am-10pm. English-language tours Tu-F 11am. Free. Special exhibits 800-1800Ft.)*

HOUSE OF TERROR. Both the Nazi and Soviet regimes housed prisoners in the basement of this building near Heroes' Sq. An acclaimed museum opened here in 2002 to document life under the two reigns of terror and memorialize the victims who were tortured and killed. *(Andrássy út 60. M1: Vörösmarty tér. ☎374 2600; www.terrorhaza.hu. Open Tu-F 10am-6pm, Sa-Su 10am-7:30pm. 1500Ft, students 750Ft.)*

LUDWIG MUSEUM (LUDVIG MÚZEUM). Located on the outskirts of the city, the Ludwig Museum ("LuMu") displays cutting-edge Hungarian painting and sculpture. *(IX. Komor Marcell u. 1. Take tram #4 or 6 to Boráros tér, then take the HÉV commuter rail 1 stop to Lagymanyosi híd. ☎555 3444; www.ludwigmuseum.hu. Open Tu, F, Su 10am-6pm, W noon-6pm, Th noon-8pm, Sa 10am-8pm. Free. Special exhibits 1000Ft, students 500Ft.)*

NATIONAL MUSEUM (NEMZETI MÚZEUM). An extensive exhibit on the second floor chronicles the history of Hungary from the founding of the state through the 20th century; the first floor is reserved for temporary exhibits. *(VIII. Múzeum krt. 14/16. M3: Kálvin tér. ☎338 2122; www.mng.hu. Open Tu-Su 10am-6pm. 600Ft.)*

STATUE PARK MUSEUM. After the collapse of Soviet rule, the open-air Statue Park Museum (Szoborpark Múzeum) was created in Buda, south of Gellérthegy, to display Soviet statues removed from Budapest's parks and squares. The indispensable English-language guidebook (1000Ft) explains the statues' histories. *(XXII. On the corner of Balatoni út and Szabadkai út. Take express bus #7 from Keleti pu. to Étele tér, then take the Volán bus from terminal #2 bound for Diósd (15min., every 15min.) and get off at the Szoborpark stop. Or, take tram 49 to Deák tér and take the bus to Szoborpark. ☎424 7500; www.szoborpark.hu. Open daily 10am-dusk. 600Ft, students 400Ft.)*

MUSEUM OF APPLIED ARTS (IPARMŰVÉSZETI MÚZEUM). Hungary's 1896 millennium celebration prompted the construction of this Art Nouveau building. Inside is an eclectic collection of handcrafted objects, including furniture and Tiffany glass, and excellent temporary exhibits. *(IX. Üllői út 33-37. M3: Ferenc körút. ☎456 5100. Open Tu-Su 10am-6pm. 1-2hr. guided tours. Fewer than 6 people 2500Ft total; 6-25 people 200Ft each. English-language pamphlet 100Ft. Museum 600Ft, students 300Ft.)*

BUDA CASTLE. Buda Castle (p. 521) houses several museums. **Wings B-D** hold the huge **Hungarian National Gallery** (Magyar Nemzeti Galéria), a definitive collection of Hungarian painting and sculpture. Its treasures include works by Realist Mihály Munkácsy and Impressionist Paál Lászlo, medieval gold altarpieces, and many depictions of national tragedies. *(☎801 9082. Open Tu-Su 10am-6pm. Free. Special exhibits 1500Ft, students 750Ft.)* In **Wing E,** the **Budapest History Museum** (Budapesti Történéti Múzeum) displays a collection of recently unearthed medieval artifacts, including weapons, tombstones, and glassware. *(I. Szent György tér 2. ☎225 7815. Open daily May-Sept. 10am-6pm; Nov.-Feb. 10am-4pm. 900Ft, students 450Ft.)*

ENTERTAINMENT

The **Budapest Spring Festival** (www.fesztivalvaros.hu), in late March, showcases Hungary's premier musicians and actors. In August, Óbudai Island hosts the week-long **Sziget Festival** (www.sziget.hu), an open-air rock festival. *Budapest Program, Budapest Panorama, Pesti Est,* and *Budapest in Your Pocket* are the best English-language entertainment guides, available at tourist offices and hotels. The "Style" section of the *Budapest Sun* (www.budapestsun.com; 300Ft) has film reviews and a 10-day calendar. Prices are reasonable; check **Ticket Express Hungary,** Andrássy u. 18. (☎312 0000; www.tex.hu. Open M-F 9:30am-6:30pm.)

The **State Opera House** (Magyar Állami Operaház), VI, Andrássy út 22 (p. 522), is one of Europe's leading performance centers. (M1: Opera. Box office ☎353 0170; www.opera.hu. Tickets 800-8700Ft. Box office open M-Sa 11am-7pm, Su 11am-1pm and 4-7pm. Closes at 5pm on non-performance days.) The **National Dance Theater** (Nemzetí Táncszínház), Szinház u. 1-3, on Castle Hill, hosts a variety of shows, but Hungarian folklore is the most popular. (☎201 4407, box office 375 8649; www.nemzetitancszinhaz.hu. Most shows 7pm. Tickets 1200-4000Ft. Box office open M-Th 10am-6pm, F 10am-5pm.) The lovely **Városmajor Open-Air Theater,** XII, Városmajor, in Buda, hosts musicals, operas, and ballets. (M1: Moszkva tér. ☎375 5922; www.szabadter.hu. Open June 27-Aug. 18. Box office open daily 2-6pm.)

Both travelers and locals head to Budapest's thermal baths to soak away the urban grime. Operating since 1565, the baths offer services from mud baths to massages. **Széchenyi,** XIV, Állatkerti u. 11/14, is one of Europe's largest bath complexes. (M1: Hősök tér. ☎363 3210. Open May-Sept. daily 6am-7pm; Oct.-Apr. M-F 6am-7pm, Sa-Su 6am-5pm. 2000Ft; 800Ft returned if you leave within 2hr., 500Ft within 3hr., 200Ft within 4hr.; **keep your receipt.** 15min. massage 2000Ft. Cash only.) The elegant **Gellért,** XI, Kelenhegyi út 4/6, has a rooftop sundeck and an outdoor wave pool. Take bus #7 or tram #47 or 49 to Hotel Gellért, at the base of Gellérthegy. (Open May-Sept. daily 6am-7pm; Oct.-Apr. M-F 6am-7pm, Sa-Su 6am-5pm. 3000Ft, with scaled refund. 15min. massage 2400Ft. Pedicure 1300Ft. MC/V.)

NIGHTLIFE

Outdoor parties, elegant after-hours clubs, nightly bump-and-grind—Budapest has it all. Pubs and bars stay busy until 4am, though the streets can be poorly lit. Upscale cafes near Pest's **Ferencz Liszt tér** (M2: Oktogon) attract Budapest's hip youth, while other neighborhoods have more eclectic late-night attractions.

West Balkan, VIII, Kisfaludy u. 36 (☎371 1807; www.westbalkan.com), in Pest. M3: Ferenc körút. From Ferenc körút, turn right onto Corvin u. and walk past the cinema to the red door on the opposite side of the street. 3 bars and a whimsical outdoor garden keep Budapest's alternative scene grooving. Beer 390Ft. Open daily 2pm-4am.

Kultiplex, IX, Knizsi u. 28 (☎219 0706), in Pest. M3: Kálvin tér. With a concert hall, courtyard, 2 bars, and a cinema, this cavernous hang-out promises something different for each visit. Beer 250Ft. Movies 250-500Ft. Cover 200Ft. Open daily 10am-5am.

A-38 Ship, XI (☎464 3940; www.a38.hu), anchored on the Buda side of the Danube, south of Petőfi Bridge. DJs spin on the decks of this revamped Ukrainian freighter. Beer 300Ft. Cover varies. Restaurant open daily 11am-midnight. DJ nights open 11am-4am.

Zöld Pardon, XI (www.zp.hu), on the Buda side of Petőfi Bridge. This giant open-air summer festival features a pool and 5 bars; 3 large screens project the crowd on the dance floor. Beer 250-400Ft. Cover 100Ft. Open Apr. 20-Sept. 16 daily 9am-6am.

Jazz Garden, V, Veres Pálné u. 44A (☎266 7264; www.jazzgarden.hu), in Pest. M3: Ferenciek tér. Low-hanging vines and branches create a laid-back atmosphere. Beer 350Ft. Live jazz daily 9pm. Open M-Th 6pm-1am, F-Sa 6pm-2am.

NIGHTLIFE SCAM. There have been reports of a scam involving English-speaking Hungarian women who ask foreign men to buy them drinks. When the bill comes, accompanied by imposing men, it can be US$1000 per round. If victims claim to have no money, they are directed to an ATM in the bar. For a list of questionable establishments, check the US Embassy website at http://budapest.usembassy.gov/tourist_advisory.html. If you are taken in, call the police. You'll probably still have to pay, but get a receipt to file a complaint.

Piaf, VI, Nagymező u. 25, in Pest. M1: Opera. Knock on the inconspicuous door at this popular lounge near the bus station. Cover 800Ft, includes 1 beer. Open Su-Th 10pm-6am, F-Sa 10pm-7am.

DAYTRIPS FROM BUDAPEST: THE DANUBE BEND

North of Budapest, the Danube sweeps in a dramatic arc called the Danube Bend *(Dunakanyar)*, deservedly one of Hungary's most popular tourist attractions.

SZENTENDRE. The cobblestone streets of Szentendre (pop. 23,000) brim with upscale galleries and restaurants. Head up **Church Hill** (Templomdomb) in Fő tér for an amazing view from the 13th-century church. The **Czóbel Museum,** Templom tér 1, exhibits the work of post-Impressionist artist Béla Czóbel, including his bikini-clad *Venus of Szentendre.* (Open Tu-Su 10am-6pm. 400Ft, students 200Ft.) The popular **Kovács Margit Museum,** Vastagh György u. 1, off Görög u., displays whimsical ceramics by the 20th-century Hungarian artist. (Open daily Oct.-Feb. 9am-7pm; Mar.-Sept. 9am-5pm. 600Ft, students 300Ft.) The real "thriller" at the **Szamos Marzipan Museum and Confectionery,** Dumtsa Jenő u. 12, is an 80kg white-chocolate statue of Michael Jackson. (www.szamosmarcipan.hu. Open daily May-Oct. 10am-7pm; Nov.-Apr. 10am-6pm. 350Ft.) The **National Wine Museum** (Nemzeti Bormúzeum), Bogdányi u. 10, exhibits wines from across Hungary. (www.borkor.hu. Open daily 10am-10pm. Exhibit 100Ft, tasting and English tour 1800Ft.)

HÉV **trains** travel to Szentendre from Budapest's Batthyány tér station (45min., every 20min., 320Ft). **Buses** run from Szentendre to Budapest's Árpád híd metro station (30min., every 20-40min., 184Ft), Esztergom (1½hr., 1 per hr., 572Ft), and Visegrád (45min., 1 per hr., 318Ft). The train and bus stations are 10min. from Fő tér; descend the stairs past the end of the HÉV tracks and head through the underpass up Kossuth u. At the fork, bear right onto Dumtsa Jenő u., which leads to the center. **Tourinform,** Dumtsa Jenő u. 22, between the center and the stations, has maps. (☎026 317 965. Open mid-Mar. to Oct. daily 9:30am-1pm and 1:30-4:30pm; Nov. to mid-Mar. M-F 9:30am-1pm and 1:30-4:30pm.)

VISEGRÁD. Host to the royal court in medieval times, Visegrád was devastated in 1702 when the Hapsburgs destroyed its 13th-century **citadel** in a struggle against freedom fighters. The citadel, a former Roman outpost, provides a dramatic view of the Danube and surrounding hills. To reach it, head north on Fő út, go right on Salamontorony u., and follow the path. In the foothills above Fő út are the ruins of King Matthias's **Royal Palace** (Királyi Palota), considered a myth until archaeologists unearthed its remains. Exhibits include a computerized reconstruction of the original palace. At the end of Salamontorony u., the **King Matthias Museum** inside Solomon's Tower (Alsóvár Salamon Torony) exhibits artifacts from the ruins. (Palace open Tu-Su 9am-5pm. Museum open May-Oct. Tu-Su 9am-5pm. Free. 50min. English-language tours of palace and museum 8000Ft.) The palace grounds relive their glory days with parades, jousting, and music during the mid-July **Viségrad Palace Games.** (☎30 933 7749; www.palotajatekok.hu. 1800Ft, students

800Ft.) **Buses** run to Visegrád from Budapest's Árpád híd metro station (1½hr., 30 per day, 504Ft). The **tourist office,** Rév út 15, sells maps for 300Ft. (☎026 39 81 60; www.visegradtours.hu. Open Apr.-Oct. daily 8am-6pm; Nov.-Mar. M-F 10am-4pm.)

ESZTERGOM. A millennium of religious history revolves around the **Basilica of Esztergom,** a hilltop cathedral that is now the seat of the Catholic Church in Hungary. Pilgrims travel to Esztergom to see the basilica and the relics of saints inside. The **cupola** has a stunning view of the Danube Bend. (Open Mar.-Oct. Tu-Su 9am-4:30pm; Nov.-Dec. Tu-F 9am-4:30pm, Sa-Su 10am-3:30pm. Cupola 200Ft. Treasury 450Ft, students 220Ft.) The red marble **Bakócz Chapel,** to the left of the nave, is a Renaissance masterwork. (Open daily Mar.-Oct. 6:30am-6pm; Nov.-Dec. 7am-4pm. Free.) **Trains** go to Budapest (1½hr., 22 per day, 544Ft). To reach the main square from the train station, turn left on Baross Gábor út and make a right onto Kiss János Altábornagy út, which becomes Kossuth Lajos u. **Buses** run to Szentendre (1½hr., 1 per hr., 635Ft) and Visegrád (45min., 1 per hr., 381Ft). MAHART **boats** (☎484 4013; www.mahartpassnave.hu) depart from the pier at Gőzhajó u. on Primas Sziget Island for Budapest (4hr., 3 per day, 1490Ft) and Visegrád (1½hr., 2 per day, 790Ft). **Grantours,** Széchenyi tér 25, at the edge of Rákóczi tér, sells maps (300-500Ft) and books rooms. (☎033 41 70 52; grantour@mail.holop.hu. Open July-Aug. M-F 8am-6pm, Sa 9am-noon; Sept.-June M-F 8am-4pm.)

PÉCS ☎072

Pécs (PAYCH; pop. 180,000), at the foot of the Mecsek mountains, is an animated university town, rich in all that makes an intellectual center: plenty of museums, bookstores, and sidewalk cafes.

TRANSPORTATION AND PRACTICAL INFORMATION. Trains run to: Budapest (3hr., 4 per day, 2880Ft). To reach the train station, just south of the historic district, take bus #30, 32, or 33 from town, or walk for about 20min. down Szabadsag or Irganasok; be very cautious on Irgalmasok, which can feel unsafe at night. **Buses** go to: Budapest (4½hr., 5 per day, 2680Ft); Siófok (3hr., 3 per day, 220Ft). The bus station is 15min. away from the old city; from the center take Irgalmasok and turn right onto Nagy Lajos Kiraly (☎520 155). Local **bus** tickets cost 180Ft, but most places in the city are walkable. **Tourinform,** Széchenyi tér 9, sells maps and phone cards, which are also available at the many news kiosks around Széchenyi tér. (☎211 134 or 212 034. Open May-Oct. Sa-Su 9am-2pm; Nov.-Apr. M-F 8am-4pm.) **ATMs** and **currency exchange** are available at several locations along Irgalmasok. There are **pharmacies** at Széchenyi tér, near the pink-and-white St. Sebastiano Church. At the corner of Jokai and Ferencesek, **Corvina** bookstore sells English language books (open M-F 9am-6pm, Sa 9am-1pm). Down the road at Ferencesek 32, **Internet Cafe Cávézó** offers speedy connections (10Ft per min.). It is relatively easy to find English-speakers here; students are generally eager to help visitors. **Postal Code:** 7621.

ACCOMMODATIONS AND FOOD. Private rooms close to the town center are the best budget option in this student town. Right in the center of town, **Pollack Mihály Students' Hostel ❷,** Jokai u. 8, has small but comfortable dorm-like singles with clean shared baths. (☎513 650. Singles 2700Ft.) Take bus #21 from the main bus terminal or #43 from the train station and get off at 48-as tér, or walk 30min. up the hill to Rákóczi út. and turn right to reach **Szent Mór Kollégium ❶,** 48-as tér 4, in a gorgeous old university wing by a small park, where local students will be your hallway-mates. The rooms are pretty, though worn, and have shared baths. (☎503 610. Reception 24hr. No visitors after 11pm. Ring the bell if the door is closed. Reserve ahead. Dorms 1700Ft. Cash only.) Pécs' restaurants, cafes, and bars are among the city's biggest attractions. Sink your sweet tooth into pastries (from 150Ft) and hypercaloric cakes (250Ft) amid the antique chandeliers, marble cafe tables, and velvet chairs at **Caflisch Cukrászda ❶**, Király u. 32. (☎310 391. Open daily 10am-10pm.) Chill with the artists and students at **Dante Cafe ❶**, Janus Pannonis u. 11, in an inner courtyard of the Csontváry Museum building. (Beer 350-420Ft. Live jazz Sa-Su. Open May-Oct. Th-Su 10am-6pm.) **Afiúm ❷**, downstairs at Irgalmasok u. 2, is an intimate restaurant with dim lights, elegant tablecloths, and a delicious Italian and Hungarian menu with vegetarian options. (☎511 434. Entrees 1100-2500Ft. Open M-F 11am-1am, Su 11am-midnight.) In the old town's center, **Ferences ❷**, Ferencesek 24, is a quiet place for a simple meal consisting of excellent fresh salads (300-500Ft) and Hungarian entrees (1000-1500Ft). **Interspar,** Bajcsy-Zsilinszky u. 11, inside Árkád Shopping Mall, is a fully stocked grocery store with a salad bar, deli, and bakery. (Open M-Th and Sa 7am-9pm, F 7am-10pm, Su 8am-7pm.)

SIGHTS. The atelier at the **Zsolnay Museum,** Káptalan u. 4, exhibits the world-famous porcelains of the Zsolnay family, who have been crafting it since the 19th century. There is also a reconstruction of the family's elegant residence, including their porcelain violin. To get there, walk up Szepessy I. u. and turn left on Káptalan u. (☎514 040. Open daily 10am-6pm. 600Ft, students 300Ft; photography 400Ft.) Next door, the **Vasarely Museum,** Káptalan u. 3, displays the works of Viktor Vasarely, a pioneer of Op-Art and geometric abstraction, along with those of other 20th-century artists of the same ilk. (☎514 040, ext. 21. Open Apr.-Oct. Tu-Sa 10am-6pm, Su 10am-4pm. 500Ft, students 250Ft; photography 400Ft, video 800Ft.) In the same yard, the unusual **Mecksek Museum** reproduces a traditional mine in a 400m cellar. The museum also shows mineral samples, and photographs. Staffed by actual mine workers, it impressively reproduces a mine's claustrophobic feel. (400Ft, students 200Ft.) At central Széchenyi tér stands the **Mosque of Ghazi Kassim** (Gázi Khasim Pasa Dzsámija). The church was once a Turkish mosque built on the site of an even earlier church. Its modern fusion of Christian and Muslim traditions has made it an emblem of the city. (Open mid-Apr. to mid-Oct. M-Sa 10am-4pm, Su 12:30-4pm; mid-Oct. to mid-Apr. M-Sa 10am-noon, Su open for Mass only 9:30, 10:30, and 11:30am. Free.) Walk downhill from Széchenyi tér on Irgalmasok u. to Kossuth tér to find the 1869 **Synagogue.** Its intricate ceiling frescoes and stunning Ark of the Covenant gives it a magical atmosphere. At the entrance is the history of the Holocaust, touchingly presented in photographs, poems, and the names of the 112 local children killed in concentration camps. (Yarmulkes provided; mandatory for men. Open Mar.-Oct. M-F and Su 10-11:30am and noon-1pm. 300Ft, students 200Ft.) Atop Pécs' hill on Dóm tér, the 4th-century Romanesque **Cathedral,** whose four towers are visible from any point in the city, reverberates with organ music and has a painted ceiling supported by patterned columns. (☎513 030. Open M-Sa 9am-5pm, Su 1-5pm. Mass M-Sa 6pm; Su 8, 9:30, 11am, and 6pm. 1000Ft, students 500Ft.) Check out the catacombs and the **Dom Muzeum** for displays of carved stones from the 12th century. (Open M-Sa 9am-5pm. 300Ft, students 150Ft.)

EGER ☎036

In the 16th century, Eger (EGG-air; pop. 57,000) was the site of Captain István Dobó's legendary struggles against Ottoman conquest. In addition to its proud history, the town's claim to fame is its homemade wine. The spirited cellars of the Valley of the Beautiful Women lure travelers from Budapest who seek the alleged strengthening powers of Egri Bikavér (Bull's Blood) wine.

TRANSPORTATION AND PRACTICAL INFORMATION. **Trains** leave from the station on Vasút u. (☎314 264) for Budapest (2hr.; 21 per day, 4 direct; 1420Ft). Indirect trains run to Budapest via Füzesabony. Trains also go to: Aggtelek (3hr., 8 per day, 1420Ft); Debrecen (3hr., 12 per day, 1212Ft); Szeged (4½hr., 12 per day, 2670Ft); Szilvásvárad (1hr., 6 per day., 342Ft). **Buses** (☎517 777; www.agria-volan.hu) head from the station on Barkóczy u. to Budapest (2hr., 25-30 per day, 1520Ft). **City Taxi** (☎555 555) runs cabs in Eger. **Dobó tér,** the main square, is a 15min. walk from the train station. Head straight and take a right on Deák Ferenc út, a right on Kossuth Lajos u., and a left on Tokaj u. To get to the center from the bus station, turn right on Barkóczy u. from terminal #10 and right again at Bródy u. Follow the stairs to the end of the street, turn right on Széchenyi u., and go left down Érsek u. Most sights are within a 10min. walk of the square. Find free maps at **TourInform,** Bajcsy-Zsilinszky u. 9. (☎517 715; www.ektf.hu/eger. Open M-F 9am-5pm, Sa 9am-1pm.) **Postal Code:** 3300.

ACCOMMODATIONS AND FOOD. **Private rooms** are the best budget option; look for *"Zimmer frei"* or *"szòba eladò"* signs, particularly on Almagyar u. and Mekcsey István u. near the castle. **Eger Tourist ❷,** Bajcsy-Zsilinszky u. 9, next to TourInform, arranges private rooms that cost about 3000Ft. (☎517 000. Open M-F 9am-5pm.) Family-run **Lukács Vendégház ❸,** Bárány u. 10, next to Eger Castle, has a lush garden, an outdoor patio, and large, comfortable rooms. (☎/fax 411 567. Singles 3500Ft; doubles 5000Ft; quads 7200Ft. Tourist tax 310Ft. Cash only.) Centrally located **Hotel Minaret ❹,** Knézich K. u. 4, features a swimming pool, restaurant, and gym. (☎410 233; www.hotelminaret.hu. All rooms with satellite TV. Singles 8400Ft; doubles 14,600Ft; triples 19,200Ft; quads 22,900Ft. Nov.-Mar. 1000Ft less. AmEx/MC/V.) From the Valley of the Beautiful Women, follow signs to **Tulipan Camping ❶,** Szépasszonyvölgy. (☎410 530. Open mid-Apr. to mid-Oct. 24hr. Office open daily 8-10am and 7-8pm. Tent sites 500Ft, 600Ft per person. Cash only.) **Széchenyi utca** is lined with restaurants. In the Valley of the Beautiful Women, crowds fill the courtyard of **Kulacs Csárda Panzió ❸.** (☎311 375; www.kulacscsarda.hu. Entrees 950-2000Ft. Open daily noon-10pm. AmEx/MC/V.) Near Eger Castle, **Palacsintavár Étterem ❷,** Dobó u. 9, lures a steady stream of crepe-craving customers. (☎413 390. Crepes 640-1490Ft. Open daily noon-11pm. MC/V.) **Dobos Cukrászola ❶,** Széchenyi u. 6, serves mouth-watering desserts. (Ice cream 100Ft. Confections 350-600Ft. Open daily 9:30am-10pm.)

SIGHTS AND FESTIVALS. To sample Eger's renowned vintage, wander through the web of wine cellars at the **Valley of the Beautiful Women** (Szépasszonyvölgy). Walk down Széchenyi u. with Eger Cathedral to your right, turn right on Kossuth Lajos u., and left when it dead-ends into Vörösmarty u. Take a right on Király u. and keep walking (25min.). Built into the hillside, the valley contains 25 different cellars. Most consist only of a few tables with benches, but each has its own personality: some are hushed while others burst with Hungarian and Gypsy sing-alongs. (Open from 9am, closing times vary; July-Aug. some open until midnight. 0.1L taste 50-150Ft, 1L 350Ft.) In the summer, **open-air baths** offer a break from the sweltering heat. (www.egertermal.hu. Open May-Sept. M-F 6am-7pm, Sa-Su 8am-7pm; Oct.-Apr. daily 9am-7pm. 950Ft, students 800Ft.) From late July to mid-August, Eger resonates with opera and early court music at the **Baroque Festival.**

BARADLA CAVES

On the Slovak-Hungarian border, **Aggtelek National Park** is home to the fantastic Baradla Caves. Formed 200 million years ago and spanning over 25km, the limestone caves are filled with imposing stone formations. Tours range from 1hr. basic and Bat Branch tours (daily 10am, noon, 1, 3, 5pm; low season no 5pm tour;

4000Ft, students 2400Ft) to 5hr. guided hikes (6000/2400Ft). Arrange longer tours with **TourInform** (☎503 000). The temperature is 10°C year-round, so bring a jacket. The caves can be visited as a daytrip from Eger, but you'll miss the return bus if you take a longer hike. The **bus** leaves Eger daily at 8:45am and arrives in Aggtelek at 11:25am, returning from the stop across the street at 3pm. From the bus, cross the street and go down the path to the caves; the park entrance is on the right. (☎503 002; www.anp.hu. Open daily Apr.-Sept. 8am-6pm; Oct.-Mar. 8am-4pm.)

GYŐR ☎096

In the unspoiled western region of Őrség, Győr (DYUR; pop. 130,000) overflows with monuments, museums, and 17th- and 18th-century architecture. Turn right out of the train station, take a left before the underpass, and cross the street to reach the pedestrian-only **Baross Gábor utca.** Walk uphill on Czuczor Gergely u., one street to the right of Baross Gábor u., and turn left at Gutenberg tér to reach the **Ark of the Covenant** statue (Frigylada szobov) and **Chapter Hill** (Káptalandomb). At the top of the hill is the **Episcopal Cathedral** (Székesegyház) with its **Weeping Madonna of Győr;** according to legend, the icon wept blood for persecuted Irish Catholics on St. Patrick's Day in 1697. The **Diocesan Library and Treasury** (Egyházmegyei Kincstár), Káptalandomb 26, in an alley off the cathedral square, displays 14th-century gold and silver. (Open Mar.-Oct. Tu-Su 10am-4pm. 700Ft, students 450Ft.) The **Imre Patkó collection,** Széchenyi tér 4, presents contemporary art; buy tickets in the Xántus Janos Museum next door and enter at Stelczera u. (Open Tu-Su 10am-6pm. 400Ft, students 200Ft.) Across the river is the huge **Rába Quelle water park,** Fürdő tér 1, supplied by thermal springs. From Bécsi Kapu tér, take the bridge over the small island and make the first right on the other side, then go right again onto Cziráky tér. (www.gyortermal.hu. Open daily 9am-10pm. 3hr. ticket 1350Ft, students 850Ft; full-day ticket 1700/1100Ft.)

In an alley off Bécsi Kapu tér, **Katalin Kert ❹,** Sarkantyú köz 3, has huge, beautiful rooms with private baths. (☎54 20 88; katalinkert@axelero.hu. Singles 7100Ft; doubles 9100Ft; triples 12,500Ft. Tax 300Ft per person. Cash only.) **Matróz Restaurant ❷,** Dunakapu tér 3, off Jedlik Ányos u., serves succulent fish, turkey, and pork dishes. (Entrees 460-1390Ft. Open Su-Th 9am-10pm, F-Sa 9am-11pm.) **John Bull Pub ❸,** Aradi u. 3, offers a break from the Hungarian diet with Italian dishes, grilled meat, and salads. (Salads 360-580Ft. Entrees 1200-2905Ft. Open daily 10am-midnight. MC/V.) **Kaiser's** supermarket is at the corner of Arany János u. and Aradi vértanúk. (Open M 7:30am-7pm, Tu-F 6:30am-7pm, Sa 6:30am-3pm. MC/V.) At night, Győr's sophisticates head to **The 20th Century,** Schweidel u. 25. (Beer 195-400Ft. Mixed drinks 520-1250Ft. Open M-F 9am-midnight, Sa-Su 5pm-1am.) Zone out with waterpipes and an endless selection of tea at the soothing **Mandala Tea House,** Sarkantyú köz 7. (www.mandalateahaz.hu. Tea 250-550Ft. Shisha 1000Ft. Open M-Th 10am-10pm, F-Sa 10am-11pm, Su 2-9pm. Cash only.)

Trains run from Budapest (2½hr., 34 per day, 1420Ft) and Vienna, AUT (2hr., 13 per day, 5073Ft). **Buses** run to Budapest (2½hr., 1 per hr., 1530Ft). The train station is 3min. from the city center. An underpass linking the platforms also leads to the bus station, heading in the opposite direction from the town. The **TourInform kiosk,** Árpád u. 32, at the intersection with Baross Gábor u., arranges lodgings. (☎31 17 71. Open June-Aug. M-F 8am-8pm, Sa-Su 9am-6pm.) **Postal Code:** 9021.

ARCHABBEY OF PANNONHALMA. Visible on a clear day from Győr, the hilltop Archabbey of Pannonhalma (Pannonhalmi Főapátság) has seen a millennium of destruction and rebuilding since its establishment by the Benedictine order in AD 996. It now houses a 360,000-volume library and a 13th-century basilica, and it also hosts organ concerts (1500Ft, students 700Ft). **TriCollis Tourist Office,** to the left of the entrance, leads tours (1½hr.) and provides concert info. (☎57 01 91; www.bences.hu. Hungarian-language tour of abbey with English text every hr. English-language tours June-Sept. daily 11:20am, 1:20, 3:20pm; Oct.-May Tu-Su 11:20am and 1:20pm. Hungarian tours 1500Ft, students 700Ft. English tours 2100/1300Ft.) Tours of the on-site **winery** provide insight into traditional monastic viticulture. (Daily June-Sept. 12:30, 2:30, 4:30pm; Oct.-Nov. and Apr.-May 11:30am, 1:30, 3:30pm; Dec.-Mar. 11:30am and 1:30pm. 450Ft, with wine tasting 1200Ft.) From Győr, take the **bus** from platform #11 (45min., 7 per day, 318Ft). Ask for Pannonhalma vár and get off at the huge gates.

LAKE BALATON

A retreat since Roman times, warm Lake Balaton drew European elite in the 19th century, but is now a budget paradise for German and Austrian students. Be aware that storms roll in quickly—when the yellow lights on harbor buildings speed up to one revolution per second, one's approaching. Don't worry, though; most storms last less than half an hour.

SIÓFOK. The density of tourist offices reflects Siófok's popularity with summer vacationers. The **Strand** is a series of lawns running to the shore; entry is free to some sections, 200-400Ft to others. The largest private **beach** lies to the right of town as you face the water. (700Ft, children 350Ft. Open M-F 8am-3am.) Bars and clubs line the lakefront, and **disco boats** (☎310 050) push off nightly. **☒Renegade Pub,** Petőfi sétány 3, is a crowded bar and dance club. (Open June-Aug. daily 8pm-4am.) Up-and-coming **Big Shot's Pub,** Fő út. 43, doubles as a restaurant and Internet cafe. (Pizzas 890-1200Ft. Beer 0.25L 300Ft, 0.4L 500Ft. Internet 290Ft per 15min. Open daily 11am-2am. MC/V.)

Take a 25min. bus or train ride to Balatonszéplak felsö for **☒Villa Benjamin Youth Hostel ❷,** Siófoki u. 9, which has a helpful owner and rooms surrounding a garden. (☎084 350 704. Free Internet. Singles 2500-3000Ft; doubles 5000Ft; triples 7500Ft; 4- to 6-person apartments 14,000-21,000Ft; 8- to 10-person house 28,000-35,000Ft. Tax 300Ft. 10% HI discount. Cash only.) **Balaton Véndegló és Panzió ❷,** Kinizsi u. 3, is a conveniently located hotel and restaurant. (☎084 311 313. Shared doubles 5000-7600Ft. MC/V.) **Trains** run to Budapest (2hr., 7 per day, 1212Ft). **Buses** head to Budapest (1½hr., 9 per day, 1320Ft) and Pécs (3hr., 4 per day, 1650Ft). **Tourinform,** Fő út. at Szabadság tér, in the water tower opposite the train station, helps find rooms. (☎061 438 8080; www.tourinform.hu. Open mid-June to mid-Sept. M-Sa 8am-8pm, Sa-Su 9am-6pm; mid-Sept. to mid-June M-F 9am-4pm.)

TIHANY. Scenic hikes, charming cottages, and panoramic views grace the Tihany peninsula. Though slightly creepy, the fascinating **Dolls' Museum,** Visszhang u. 4, packs an impressive collection of 19th-century toys into two rooms. (Open daily 10am-6pm. 400Ft, students 300Ft.) The **Benedictine Abbey** (Bencés Apátság) draws over a million visitors annually with its luminous frescoes and gilded Baroque altars. (Open daily Mar.-Oct. 9am-6pm; last entrance 5:30pm. 500Ft, students 250Ft.) The well-marked **☒green line trail** runs past the Hermit's Place (Barátlakások), where the cells and chapel hollowed by 11th-century hermits are still visible. MAHART **ferries** go to Tihany from Siófok (1-1¼hr.; 6-9 per day; 1020Ft, students 765Ft). To reach the town from the ferry pier and neighboring **Strand,** walk underneath the elevated road and follow the Apátság signs up the steep hill to the abbey.

KESZTHELY. At the lake's western tip, Keszthely (KEST-hay), once the playground of the powerful Austro-Hungarian Festetics family, is home to year-round thermal springs. The **☒Helikon Palace Museum** (Helikon Kastélymúzeum) in the

Festetics Palace (Kastély) is a storybook Baroque palace with a 90,000-volume library, extravagantly furnished chambers, an exotic arms collection, and a porcelain exhibit. From Fő tér, follow Kossuth Lajos u. toward Tourinform until it becomes Kastély u. (Open July-Aug. daily 9am-6pm., June Tu-Su 9am-5pm, Sept.-May Tu-Su 10am-5pm. 1300Ft, students 700Ft.) The **Strand,** on the coast to the right as you exit the train station, draws crowds with its giant slide, paddle boats, and volleyball nets. From the center, walk down Erzsébet Királyné u. as it curves right into Vörösmarty u., then cut through the park, crossing the train tracks on the other side to get to the beach. (Open mid-May to mid-Sept. daily 9:30am-7pm. Before 4pm 440Ft, children 300Ft; 4-6:30pm 380/260Ft; 6:30-7pm free.)

Central **Kiss&Máté Panzió ❸,** Katona J u. 27, has spacious rooms. (☎83 319 072. Free laundry. Singles 5000Ft; doubles 6000Ft; triples 9000Ft.) **Castrum Camping ❶,** Móra Ferenc u. 48, has large sites and tennis courts. (☎83 31 21 20. 900Ft per person. July-Aug. tent sites 600Ft; Sept.-June 480Ft.) **Corso Restaurant ❸,** Erzsébet Királyné u. 23, in the Abbázia Club Hotel, serves fish from Balaton. (Entrees 800-2800Ft. Open M-Sa 7am-10pm. AmEx/MC/V.) **Donatello ❷,** Balaton u. 1/A, serves pizza and pasta in an open courtyard. Though the restaurant is named after the Teenage Mutant Ninja Turtle, the chefs are genuine Italian masters. (☎83 31 59 89. Pasta 410-880Ft. Pizza 440-1080Ft. Open daily noon-11pm.) InterCity **trains** run to Budapest (3hr.; 13 per day; 1926Ft, reservations 400Ft). **Buses** run from near the train station to Pécs (4hr., 5 per day, 1926Ft). From the station, take Mártirok u., which ends in Kossuth Lajos u., and turn left to reach the main square, Fő tér. **Tourinform,** Kossuth Lajos u. 28, on the palace side of Fő tér, has free maps and checks room availability. (☎83 31 41 44. Open July-Aug. M-F 9am-8pm, Sa-Su 9am-6pm; Sept.-June M-F 9am-5pm, Sa 9am-1pm.)

ICELAND (ÍSLAND)

Conceived when the European and North American continents collided, Iceland's landscape is uniquely warped and contorted, marked by still-active volcanoes and the tortoise-like crawl of advancing and retreating glaciers. Nature is the country's greatest attraction, as demonstrated by its thriving ecotourism industry. Visitors can pick their way through sunken ice kettles (holes left by glaciers), bathe in natural hot springs, and bike among fishing villages with no one but seabirds for company. An emphasis on natural farming has made Icelandic produce and meat sought-after exports and Icelandic dining a pleasure.

ESSENTIALS

FACTS AND FIGURES

Official Name: Republic of Iceland.

Capital: Reykjavík.

Major Cities: Akureyri, Ísafjörður, Kópavogur, Hafnarfjörður.

Population: 300,000.

Time Zone: GMT.

Language: Icelandic.

Religions: Evangelical Lutheran (87%), Lutheran Free Church (4%), Roman Catholic (2%).

WHEN TO GO

Visitors should brave high-season crowds to enjoy all Iceland has to offer; June through August have the most accommodation and transportation options, and the longest days by far. The sky never gets quite dark in summer months, though the sun dips below the horizon for a few hours each night. July temperatures average 11°C (52°F). In December and January, sunlight lasts only four hours, but the nights are illuminated by *aurora borealis*. Winter in Reykjavík averages 0°C (32°F), making travel feasible, though slow, as transportation is unreliable.

TIP **BURNING THE MIDNIGHT OIL.** The midnight sun pops its head out June through August. While the near-24hr. sunlight makes for easy all-night partying, it can take its toll on visitors. Bring a sleeping mask and over-the-counter, non-habit-forming sleep aids, such as melatonin, to avoid sleepless nights.

DOCUMENTS AND FORMALITIES

EMBASSIES. Foreign embassies in Iceland are in Reykjavík. Icelandic embassies and consulates abroad include: **Australia,** 16 Hann St., Griffith, Canberra (☎262 95 68 19; benefitfarm@bigpond.com.au); **Canada,** 360 Albert St., Ste. 710, Ottawa, ON, K1R 7X7 (☎613-482-1944; www.iceland.org/ca); **Ireland,** Cavendish House, Smithfield, Dublin (☎1 872 9299; jgg@goregrimes.ie); **New Zealand,** Sanford Ltd., 22 Jellicoe St., Auckland (☎9 379 4720); **UK,** 2A Hans St., London, SW1X 0JE (☎020 7259 3999; www.iceland.org/uk); **US,** 1156 15th St., NW, Ste. 1200, Washington, D.C., 20005 (☎202-265-6653; www.iceland.org/us).

VISA AND ENTRY INFORMATION. EU citizens do not need a visa to travel to Iceland and may enter with passports or national identity cards. Citizens of Australia, Canada, New Zealand, and the US do not need a visa for stays of up to 90 days. For more information, see p. 16.

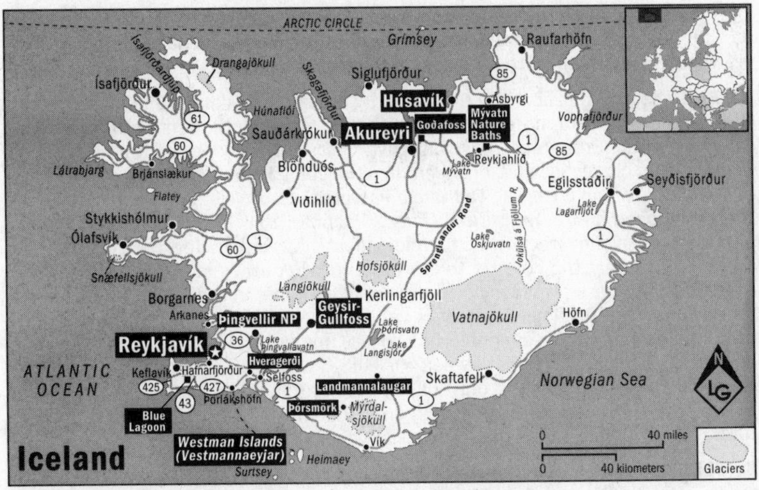

TOURIST SERVICES AND MONEY

EMERGENCY	**Police, Ambulance,** and **Fire:** ☎112.

TOURIST OFFICES. Tourist offices in large towns have maps, brochures, and the all-important BSÍ bus schedule; check at hotel reception desks in smaller towns for local info. The **Icelandic Tourist Board** website is www.icetourist.is. **Destination Iceland** (☎585 42 70; www.dice.is), which has offices in the Reykjavík bus terminal, has a helpful planning website.

MONEY. Iceland's unit of currency is the **króna (ISK),** plural krónur. One króna is equal to 100 aurars. There's no way around it; costs are high. On average, a night in a hostel will cost 1700ISK, a guesthouse 3000-4000ISK, and a meal's worth of groceries 700-1200ISK. Restaurants include a service charge on the bill; **tipping** further is unnecessary and even discouraged. Iceland imposes a **value added tax (VAT)** of 24.5% on goods and services purchased within the European Economic Area (EEA: the EU plus Iceland, Liechtenstein, and Norway). Prices in Iceland include the VAT, but partial refunds are available for non-EEA citizens (p. 22).

ICELANDIC KRÓNUR (ISK)		
	AUS$1 = 55.21ISK	100ISK = AUS$1.80
	CDN$1 = 67.29ISK	100ISK = CDN$1.48
	EUR€1 = 93.10ISK	100ISK = EUR€1.07
	NZ$1 = 46.62ISK	100ISK = NZ$2.14
	UK£1 = 136.30ISK	100ISK = UK£0.73
	US$1 = 73.92ISK	100ISK = US$1.35

TRANSPORTATION

BY PLANE. Icelandair (Iceland ☎505 01 00, UK 0207 874 1000, US 800-223-5500; www.icelandair.net) flies to Reykjavík year-round from Europe and the US. Icelandair provides free stopovers of up to seven days on flights to European cities, and runs a Lucky Fares email list with discounted flights. No-frills **Iceland Express** (Iceland ☎550 06 00, UK 0870 240 5600; www.icelandexpress.com) flies from

Copenhagen, Frankfurt, and London from April through late October. Fares start at €98 one-way. Icelandair's domestic counterpart **Air Iceland** (☎570 30 30; www.airiceland.is) flies from Reykjavík to most major towns in Iceland.

BY BUS. Several bus lines are organized by **Bifreiðastöð Íslands** (**BSÍ**; www.bsi.is); they are cheaper and more scenic than flights, although they run infrequently in the low season. From mid-June to August, buses run daily on the Ring Road, the highway that circles Iceland, but even then the going is slow, since some stretches in the east are unpaved. The **Full Circle Passport** lets travelers circle the island at their own pace on the Ring Road (May 20-Sept. 5; 23,900ISK). However, it only allows travel in one direction, so travelers must move either clockwise or counter-clockwise around the country to get back to where they started. For an extra 12,000ISK, the pass provides access to the Westfjords in the extreme northwest (Jun.-Aug.). The **Omnibus Passport** is valid for periods of up to three weeks for unlimited travel on all scheduled bus routes, including non-Ring roads (1-week 26,900ISK, 2-week 42,000ISK, 3-week 50,000ISK; valid May 15-Sept. 15). Travelers, especially those arriving in groups of two or more, should note that the inflexibility of the Full Circle pass and the high cost of the Omnibus Passport make it wise for those heading to rural areas to rent cars. Iceland has no intercity train service.

BY FERRY. The best way to see Iceland's gorgeous shoreline is on the **Norröna** ferry (☎570 86 00; www.smyril-line.fo, website in Icelandic) that crosses the North Atlantic to Hanstholm, DEN; Tórshavn in the Faroe Islands; and Seyðisfjörður, ICE (7 days; May 28-Sept. 2. One-way sleeper cabin €336; low season €240; students under 26 with ID 25% less). From Tórshavn, you can either continue on to Bergen, NOR, or return to Seyðisfjörður. An **Eimskip Transport** liner leaves Reykjavík at weekly between March and October and takes five days to get to continental ports at Århus, DEN, Gothenburg, SWE; Hamburg, GER; and Rotterdam, NTH. (Reservations ☎585 43 00; travel@dice.is. Fares from 33,030ISK. Bikes 3150ISK.)

BY CAR. Rental cars provide the most freedom to travelers and may even be the cheapest option for those who want to visit rural areas. Car rental *(bílaleiga)* companies charge 4000-8000ISK per day for a small car, and 20,000-25,000ISK for the **four-wheel-drive vehicles** that are imperative outside of settled areas. On these routes, drivers should bring a container of extra fuel, since some roads continue for 300km without a single refueling station and strong headwinds can significantly affect the rate of fuel consumption. It is not uncommon for local drivers to **ford streams** in their vehicles; do not attempt this in a compact car, and cross in a convoy if possible. (24hr. reports on road conditions ☎800 63 16, June-Aug. in English.) Drivers are required to wear seat belts and to keep their headlights on at all times. Iceland recognizes foreign driver's licenses, but you may need to purchase insurance for the rental vehicle (1500-3500ISK).

BY BIKE AND BY THUMB. Ferocious winds, driving rain, and gravel roads make long-distance cycling difficult. Hug the Ring Road if you prefer company; for less-traveled paths, branch out to the coastal roads that snake their way through the Eastfjords, or check **Cycling in Iceland** (http://home.wanadoo.nl/erens/icecycle.htm). Pedal in the country's rugged interior on a mountain bike; get in touch with the **Icelandic Mountainbike Club** (☎562 00 99; www.mmedia.is/~ifhk) or drop by their clubhouse in Reykjavík, at Brekkustíg. 2, the first Thursday night of each month after 8pm for some friendly advice. Buses will carry bikes for a 500-900ISK fee, depending on the route. Hitchhikers sometimes try the roads in summer, but sparse traffic and harsh weather exacerbate the risks. Still, rides can be found with relative ease between Reykjavík and Akureyri; flagging down a ride is harder in the east and the south. Let's Go does not recommend hitchhiking.

KEEPING IN TOUCH

PHONE CODES	**Country code:** 354. **International dialing prefix:** 00. There are no city codes in Iceland. For more information on how to place international calls, see inside back cover.

EMAIL AND THE INTERNET. Internet access is widespread in Iceland. In small towns get it for free in libraries; at cafes, Internet costs 200-300ISK per hour.

TELEPHONE. Síminn, the state-owned telephone company, usually has offices in the same buildings as post offices, where you can buy phone cards and get the best rates on international calls. Pay phones accept prepaid phone cards, credit cards (cheapest for calls to mobile phones), as well as 10ISK, 50ISK, and 100ISK coins. Iceland uses two different mobile phone networks: digital GSM phones service 98% of the country's population, but only a small fraction of its land area, so hikers, fishermen, and others who travel outside of settled areas rely on analog NMT phones, which reach into rural regions. Prepaid GSM phone cards are available at gas stations and at convenience stores. OG Vodafone generally offers the best prepaid rates. For operator assistance within Iceland, dial ☎118; for international assistance, dial ☎1811. International direct dial numbers include: **AT&T Direct** (☎800 222 55 288); **British Telecom** (☎800 89 0354); **Canada Direct** (☎800 90 10); **MCI WorldPhone** (☎800 90 02); **Telecom New Zealand** (☎800 90 64).

MAIL. Mailing a letter or postcard (up to 20g) from Iceland costs from 55ISK within Iceland, from 65ISK to Europe, and from 70ISK outside of Europe. Post offices *(póstur)* are generally open Monday to Friday 9am-4:30pm and for several hours on Saturdays. Check www.postur.is for additional info.

LANGUAGE. Icelandic is a Nordic language which developed in ninth-century Norway and was enriched to its present form in 12th-century Iceland. Most Icelanders, especially those under 35, speak at least some English.

ACCOMMODATIONS AND CAMPING

ICELAND	❶	❷	❸	❹	❺
ACCOMMODATIONS	under 2000ISK	2000-3000ISK	3000-5000ISK	5000-10,000ISK	over 10,000ISK

Iceland's 26 **HI youth hostels** are clean and reasonably priced at approximately 1800-2200ISK for nonmembers. HI members receive a 150-400ISK discount. Visit **Hostelling International Iceland,** Sundlaugarveg. 34, 105 Reykjavík (☎553 81 10; www.hostel.is), for locations and pricing and for information on Iceland's seven eco-friendly **Green Hostels.** Expect to pay around 2000ISK for **sleeping-bag accommodations** (*svefnpokapláss;* beds with no linens or blankets included). Guesthouses and **farmhouses** (☎570 27 00; www.farmholidays.is) are a cheap, homey option outside of cities. Many remote lodgings will pick up tourists in the nearest town for a small fee. Campers can choose among Iceland's 125 designated **campsites** or rough it on uncultivated land. Squatters need to get permission if they set up camp in a nature reserve or near houses, if more than three people are sleeping in a tent, or if the anticipated stay is longer than three nights; they should also bring a camp stove, as open fires are frowned upon. Official campsites range from grassy areas with cold-water taps to sumptuous facilities around Reykjavík; listings can be found at www.camping.is (in Icelandic). Visit www.infoiceland.is/infoiceland/accommodation/camping for general accommodation tips.

FOOD AND DRINK

ICELAND	❶	❷	❸	❹	❺
FOOD	under 500ISK	500-1000ISK	1000-1400ISK	1400-2000ISK	over 2000ISK

Fresh fish and gamey free-range lamb are staples of Icelandic cuisine, though vitamin-rich vegetables grown in greenhouse towns such as Hveragerði (p. 544) and a range of cheeses have infiltrated the diet. A history of shortage has made preserved food prized—pickled, salted, dried, smoked, and rotted dishes abound, especially in winter. More exotic methods and flavorings have been introduced by a trickle of Asian immigrants in the past decade; now, not everything is simply boiled and salted. Still, tradition is strong: *skyr*, a dairy product between yogurt and fresh cheese, is more popular than ever. Food in Iceland is very expensive, and a cheap restaurant meal will cost at least 800ISK. Grocery stores, which can be found in virtually every town, are the way to go. Alcohol presents the same quandary; beer costs 500-600ISK for a large glass (0.5L, approx. 17 oz.) at pubs and cafes, while the price of hard liquor is even steeper. The country's national drink is *brennivín*, a schnapps made from potato and usually seasoned with caraway. For a cheaper buzz, bootleggers in the countryside cook up batches of *landi*, a potent homemade moonshine. Let's Go does not recommend moonshine.

HOLIDAYS AND FESTIVALS

Holidays: New Year's Day (Jan. 1); Maundy Thursday (Apr. 5); Good Friday (Apr. 6); Easter (Apr. 8-9); *Sumardagurinn Fyrsti* (first day of summer; Apr. 19); Labor Day (May 1); Ascension Day (May 17); Whit Sunday and Monday (May 27-28); National Day (June 17); Tradesman's Day (Aug. 6); Christmas (Dec. 24-25); Boxing Day (Dec. 26); New Year's Eve (Dec. 31).

Festivals: The month-long Thorrablót festival (Feb.-Mar. 2006) celebrates *Thorramatur,* the diet of past centuries: Icelanders eat *svið* (singed and boiled sheep's head), *hrútspungur* (pickled ram's testicles), and *hákarl* (shark meat that has been allowed to rot underground) in celebration of their heritage. *Sumardagurinn Fyrsti* marks the first day of summer with a carnival. The Reykjanes Peninsula celebrates *Sjomannadagur* (Seamen's Day) on June 4 with boat races and tug-of-war. In August, Icelanders head to the country for *Verslunarmannahelgi,* a weekend of barbecues, camping, and drinking.

BEYOND TOURISM

Travelers hoping to stay in Iceland may be able to secure summer work. Check www.jobs-in-europe.net for information on work placement. Ecotourism opportunities abound; organizations run tours on horseback, to hot springs, and up mountains. See p. 61 for Beyond Tourism opportunities throughout Europe.

Earthwatch Institute, 3 Clock Tower Pl., Ste. 100, Box 75, Maynard, MA, 01754 (Canada and the US ☎1-800-776-0188, the UK 44 1865 318838, Australia 03 9682 6828; www.earthwatch.org). For a hefty fee ($2500+), Earthwatch organizes volunteers, guided by scientists, to conduct geological fieldwork in the Icelandic glaciers. They also help coordinate fundraising efforts to curtail the fee.

International Cultural Youth Exchange, Große Hamburger Str. 30, Berlin, GER (☎49 30 2839 0550; www.icye.org). ICYE brings together volunteers and host organizations on a variety of projects worldwide, including several in Iceland. ICYE also organizes European Voluntary Service programs (http://europa.eu.int/comm/youth/program/guide/action2_en.html) for EU citizens to serve for a fully funded year in another EU country.

Volunteers for Peace (☎802-259-2759; www.vfp.org). Runs 2800 "workcamps" throughout the world, including several in Iceland. $250 per 2- to 3-week workcamp, including room and board, plus $20 VFP membership fee.

REYKJAVÍK

Home to three out of every five Icelanders, Reykjavík (pop. 180,000) is a modestly sized capital with an international clubbing reputation. Bold, modern architecture juts out above the searingly blue waters of the Faxaflói Bay, and the city's refreshingly clear air complements the clean streets and well-kept gardens. The frequent rain in the spring and the perpetual night in the winter force social life indoors, where many locals start bands or sip espresso while arguing over environmental policy. As the Seattle of Scandinavia, Reykjavík has energy to spare.

TRANSPORTATION

Flights: International flights arrive at **Keflavík Airport (KEF),** 55km from Reykjavík. From the main exit, catch a **Flybus** (☎562 1011; www.flybus.is) to BSÍ Bus Terminal (40-50min.; 1100ISK, round-trip 1900ISK). Flybus offers free minivan transport from the bus terminal to most hostels and hotels; check online for a list of locations. Catch public buses to the city center at the Gamla-Hringbraut stop across the street from the bus terminal (M-F 7am-midnight, Sa-Su 10am-midnight; 250ISK). Flybus service to the airport departs from the bus terminal; most hostels and hotels can arrange free pick-ups. The smaller **Reykjavík Airport** is the departure point for domestic flights; take bus #15.

Buses: Umferðarmiðstöð BSÍ (BSÍ Bus Terminal), Vatnsmýrarveg. 10 (☎562 1011; www.bsi.is), off Gamla-Hringbraut near Reykjavík Airport. Walk 15-20min. south along Tjörnin from the city center or take bus #14, 15, S1, or S3-S6 (every 20min., 250ISK). Open May-Oct. 24hr., Nov.-Apr. daily 5am-10pm.

Public Transportation: Bus service can be infrequent and roundabout; walking is often a speedier option. **Strætó** (☎540 2700; www.bus.is) operates yellow city buses (250ISK). **Hlemmur,** the major terminal, is located about 1km east of Lækjartorg where Hverfisg. meets Laugavegur (open M-Sa 7am-11:30pm, Su 10am-11:30pm). Pick up a schedule at the terminal. Don't feel bad asking for navigational help at hostels and information desks—recent changes in the bus routes have confused even the drivers. Buy packages of 10 adult fares (2000ISK) or pay fare with coins; drivers do not give change. Ticket packages are sold at the terminal as well as at swimming pools. If you need to change buses, ask the driver for a free transfer ticket *(skiptimiði)* when you get on the first bus, valid for 45min. after fare has been paid. Most buses run every 20-30min. M-Sa 7am-midnight, Su and holidays 10am-midnight.

Taxis: BSR (☎561 0000). 24hr. service. **Hreyfill** (☎588 5522; www.hreyfill.is/english). Also offers private tours for groups of 1-8, 7900-44,000ISK.

Car Rental: Berg, Bíldshöfða 10 (☎577 6050; www.bergcar.is). Under 100km from 4800ISK per day, unlimited km from 8850ISK per day; low season reduced rates. Pick-up available at Keflavík and Reykjavík Airports 2000ISK. **Hertz** (☎505 0600; www.hertz.is), at the Reykjavík Airport. From 6110ISK per day. Pick-up available at Keflavík Airport 2300ISK. **Avis** (☎591 4000; www.avis.is), **Budget** (☎562 6060; www.budget.is), and **Hasso** (☎464 1030; http://hasso.co.is) also rent cars from locations in Reykjavík.

Bike Rental: At the **Reykjavík Youth Hostel** campground (p. 540). 6hr. 1200ISK, 24hr. 1700ISK. Helmet included.

Hitchhiking: Hitchhiking is more common outside the capital than around Reykjavík, but it is never completely safe. Let's Go does not recommend hitchhiking.

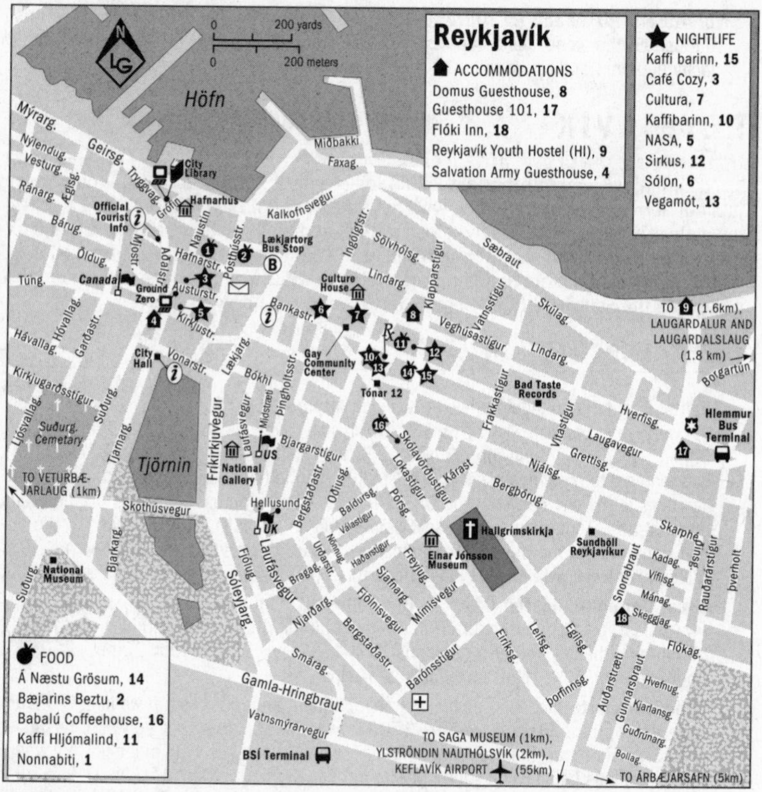

ORIENTATION AND PRACTICAL INFORMATION

Lækjartorg is Reykjavík's main square and a good base for navigation. **Lækjargata,** a main street, leads southwest from Lækjartorg to **Lake Tjörnin** (the Pond), the southern limit of the city center. Reykjavík's most prominent thoroughfare extends eastward from Lækjartorg, changing names from **Austurstræti** to **Bankastræti** and then to **Laugavegur,** as it is most commonly known. Helpful publications, including *What's On in Reykjavík*, *Reykjavík City Guide*, and *The Reykjavík Grapevine*, are available for free at tourist offices. The *Grapevine*, published by American expatriates, includes opinionated local news coverage and comprehensive listings of current music and arts events.

Tourist Offices: Upplýsingamiðstöð Ferðamanna í Reykjavík, Aðalstr. 2 (☎590 1550; www.visitreykjavik.is). Open June-Aug. daily 8:30am-7pm; Sept.-May M-Sa 9am-6pm, Su 10am-2pm. Sells the **Reykjavík Card** (1-day 1200ISK, 2-day 1700ISK, 3-day 2200ISK), which allows unlimited public transportation, free entry to some sights and thermal pools (p. 542), and limited Internet access at the tourist center. The **Discount Guide** (www.coupons.is) offers deals on a variety of services. **Kleif Tourist Information Center,** Bankastræti 2 (☎510 5700; www.kleif.is). Open daily May-Aug. 8am-10pm; Sept.-Apr. 10am-6pm. **City Hall Information Center,** Vonarstræti 3 (☎563 2005), in the lobby of City Hall. Open M-F 8:20am-6:15pm, Sa-Su noon-4pm.

Embassies: Canada, Túng. 14 (☎533 5500). Open M-F 9am-noon. **UK,** Laufásveg. 31 (☎550 5100). Open M-F 9am-noon. **US,** Laufásveg. 21 (☎562 9100). Open M-F 8am-5pm.

Currency Exchange: Most banks are open M-F 9:15am-4pm. There are **ATMs** throughout the city. Avoid the **Exchange Group** in the tourist office, which has steep commissions.

Luggage Storage: At BSÍ Bus Terminal (☎580 5462), next to the ticket window. 400ISK for the first day, 200ISK per subsequent day. Open daily 7:30am-7pm.

GLBT Resources: Gay Community Center, Laugavegur 3, 4th fl. (☎552 7878; www.samtokin78.is). Office open M and Th 1-5pm and 8-11pm, Tu-W and F 1-5pm; cafe open M and Th 8-11:30pm; library open M and Th 8-11pm. More info available at www.gayice.is.

Emergency: ☎112. **Police:** Hverfisg. 113 (☎444 1000).

Pharmacies: Lyfja Laugavegi, Laugavegur 16 (☎552 4045). Open M-F 10am-7pm, Sa 10am-4pm. **Lyfja Lágmúla,** Lágmúla 5 (☎533 2300). Open 24hr.

Hospital: National Hospital at Fossvogur, on Hringbraut (☎543 1000), has a 24hr. emergency ward. Take bus #14, S1, or S3-S6 southeast from the city center.

Internet Access: ☒ **Reykjavík Public Library,** Tryggvag. 15 (☎563 1705). Extensive comic book collection on the 2nd fl. 200ISK per hr. Open M 10am-9pm, Tu-Th 10am-8pm, F 11am-7pm, Sa-Su 1-5pm. **Snarrót,** Laugavegur 21 (☎551 8927). Located in the basement of Kaffi Hljómalind (p. 540), Snarrót is also a hub for local student activism. 300ISK per hr. Open M-F 9am-11pm, Sa-Su 10am-11pm. MC/V. **Ground Zero,** Vallarstr. 4 (☎562 7776). 300ISK per 30min., 450ISK per hr. Open M-F 11am-1am, Sa-Su noon-1am. AmEx/MC/V.

Post Office: Íslandspóstur, Pósthússtr. 5 (☎580 1121), at the intersection with Austurstr. Open M-F 9am-4:30pm. Address mail to be held in the following format: First name LAST NAME, *Poste Restante,* ÍSLANDSPÓSTUR, Pósthússtr. 5, 101 Reykjavík, ICELAND.

ACCOMMODATIONS AND CAMPING

Gistiheimili (guesthouses) offer "sleeping-bag accommodations" starting from 2500ISK (bed and pillow in a small room; add 300-600ISK for a blanket). Hotels cost at least 5500ISK. Call ahead for reservations, especially in the summer.

☒ **Reykjavík Youth Hostel (HI),** Sundlaugarveg. 34 (☎553 8110). Bus #14 from Lækjarg. This popular, eco-friendly hostel is well east of the city center, but it's adjacent to Reykjavík's largest thermal pool and has excellent facilities. The friendly and candid staff of international students and young locals give tips for exploring the city's less touristy sights. Breakfast 800ISK. Luggage storage 300ISK per night. Linens 600ISK. Laundry 300ISK. Internet 200ISK per 20min. Reception 8am-11pm; ring bell after hours. Dorms 2050ISK, with HI discount 1700ISK; doubles 4000ISK/3500ISK. ❷

Salvation Army Guesthouse, Kirkjustr. 2 (☎561 3203; www.guesthouse.is). Located near City Hall in the heart of Reykjavík, this bright yellow hostel is cozy, if slightly worn in. Its prime location makes it ideal for exploring the nightlife. Breakfast included with singles and doubles. Laundry 800ISK. Sleeping-bag accommodations 2500ISK; singles 5500ISK; doubles 8000ISK. AmEx/MC/V. ❷

Domus Guesthouse, Hverfisgt. 45 (☎561 1200). Take bus #13, S1, or S3-S6 and get off across from the Regnboginn movie theatre on Hverfisgötu. Close to the city center, the guesthouse offers spacious rooms with TVs and leather couches. All sleeping-bag accommodations are located across the street in a large, dark room partitioned by curtains. Breakfast included with singles and doubles. Sleeping-bag accommodations 2900ISK; singles 9500ISK; doubles 11,300ISK. Reduced prices Oct.-Apr. MC/V. ❷

Flóki Inn, Flókag. 1 (☎552 1155; www.innsoficeland.is). Relax in this intimate guesthouse and let the exceptional, worldly staff take care of the rest. Kettle, fridge, and TV in every room. Breakfast included. Reception 24hr. Check-in 2pm. Check-out noon. Sleeping-bag accommodations 5500ISK; singles 7500ISK; doubles 9900ISK. Extra bed 3700ISK. Reduced prices Sept.-May. AmEx/MC/V. ❹

Guesthouse 101, Laugavegur 101 (☎562 6101; www.iceland101.com), off Snorrabraut. Converted office building east of the city center has small, bright rooms with great views. Wheelchair-accessible. Breakfast included. Singles 6500ISK; doubles 8900ISK; triples 11,500ISK. 10% off with cash payment. Reduced prices in winter. MC/V. ❹

Reykjavík Youth Hostel Campsite (☎568 6944), next to the hostel. Friendly staff and lively campers make this a good alternative to indoor facilities. Outdoor showers included. Electricity 350ISK. Luggage storage 300ISK. Reception 24hr. Open June to mid-Sept. Tent sites 800ISK. 4-person cabins 4000ISK. MC/V. ❶

FOOD

An authentic Icelandic meal featuring seafood, lamb, or puffin costs upwards of 1500ISK, but it's worth the splurge at least once. For days on a leaner budget, the stands west of Lækjartorg hawk *pylsur* (hot dogs made of lamb meat) for around 200ISK. Ask for "the works," including *remoulade* (a spicy mayonnaise-based sauce). **Groceries** are available on Austurstræti, Hverfisgata, and Laugavegur.

Kaffi Hljómalind, Laugavegur 21 (☎517 1980), east of the city center. Organic and vegetarian-friendly cafe serves big portions of soup (650ISK) and lasagna (1090ISK). Free wireless, vocal patrons, a box of toys, and large windows make this a great place for people-watching or passing the time before the nightlife kicks into high gear. Live music or poetry reading W-F 8pm. Open M-F 9am-11pm, Sa-Su 10am-11pm. MC/V. ❷

Á Næstu Grösum, Laugavegur 20B (☎552 8410), entrance off Klapparstígur. The first all-vegetarian restaurant in Iceland uses only fresh, seasonal ingredients. The decoration space is used as a gallery to highlight the work of up-and-coming local artists. Soup (750ISK) comes with free refill and bread. Small plate 900ISK. Lunch special 1350ISK. Dinner 1750ISK. Open M-F 11:30am-10pm, Sa noon-10pm, Su 5-10pm. MC/V. ❸

Babalú Coffeehouse, Skólavörðustigur 22A (☎552 2278). 2nd fl. cafe has large savory crepes for 730ISK and smaller sweet crepes for 330ISK. Head to the patio to enjoy dinner under the midnight sun. Free wireless. Open daily 11am-11:30pm. AmEx/MC/V. ❷

Nonnabiti, Hafnarstr. 11 (☎551 2312), west of Lækjartorg. toward the main tourist office. No-frills sandwich shop is good for cheap, satisfying meals. Burgers 390ISK. Hot sandwiches 790ISK. Open M-F 9:30am-2am, Sa-Su 9:30am-5:30am. MC/V. ❶

Bæjarins Beztu, corner of Tryggvag. and Pósthússtr. This tiny stand on the harbor serves the Icelandic hot dog (210ISK) by which all others are measured. Weekend crowds head here to satisfy late-night cravings, often singing while they wait. Open until 12:30am, or as late as there is a crowd—sometimes past 6am. MC/V. ❶

SIGHTS

CITY CENTER. Reykjavík's **City Hall,** located on the northern shore of **Lake Tjörnin** in the heart of the city center, houses an impressive three-dimensional model of Iceland that vividly renders the country's striking topography. *(Open M-F 8am-7pm, Sa-Su noon-6pm. Free.)* Just beyond City Hall lies **Aðalstræti,** the oldest street in the city. The **Hafnarhús** (Harbor House) is the most eclectic of the three wings of the Reykjavík Art Museum. In the byzantine corridors of a renovated warehouse, the museum holds an extensive collection of paintings by Erro, Iceland's pre-eminent contemporary artist. To get to the museum from Aðalstr., walk past the tourist office and turn onto Grófin. *(Tryggvag. 17, off Aðalstr. ☎590 1201; www.listasafnreykjavikur.is. Open daily high season 10am-5pm; low season 1-4pm. 500ISK for all 3 wings. M free.)* Follow Tryggvag. to the intersection of Lækjarg. and Hverfisg. to see the **statue of Ingólfur Arnason,** Iceland's first settler, and revel in the view of the mountains to the north. The **Culture House** has a detailed exhibit on Iceland's ancient history, including carefully preserved vellum manuscripts of the Eddas and Sagas. In the cafe on the first floor, the chef cooks meals for state functions; framed menus with diplomats' names decorate the wall. *(Hverfisg. 15. ☎545 1400. Open daily 11am-5pm. 300ISK, students 200ISK. W free.)*

East of Lake Tjörnin, the **National Gallery of Iceland** presents highlights of contemporary Icelandic art. The toys and cushions on the bottom floor aren't part of an ultramodern exhibit; they're for the restless children of patrons. *(Fríkirkjuveg. 7. ☎515 9600. Open Tu-Su 11am-5pm. Free.)* Continue eastward to the landmark **Hallgrímskirkja** church on Skólavörðustígur, with a tower that provides a panoramic view from the city's highest point. *(☎510 1000. Open daily 9am-5pm. Elevator to the top 350ISK.)* Across from the church, the **Einar Jónsson Museum** on Njarðarg. exhibits 300 of the sculptor's imposing, allegorical works inspired by Iceland's Christian and pagan heritage. Don't miss the free sculpture garden in the back. *(☎561 3797; www.skulptur.is. Open June to mid-Sept. Tu-Su 2-5pm; mid-Sept.-May Sa-Su 2-5pm. 400ISK.)*

ART FOR POCKET CHANGE. If you don't want to pay to see art, visit any of Reykjavík's many free galleries on Laugavegur and Skólavörðustígur.

LAUGARDALUR. Additional sights cluster around Laugardalur, a large park well east of the city center. Orient yourself around **Áskirkja** church, which looks like a ship's prow and stands on a hill at the east side of Laugardalur. The white dome of the **Ásmundarsafn** (Ásmundur Sveinsson Sculpture Museum) on Sigtún houses works spanning Sveinsson's career in a building the artist designed and lived in. The free sculpture garden surrounding the museum features larger works, some of which have been designed as interactive pieces ideal for climbing. *(Take bus #15 to the stop outside the museum. ☎553 2155. Open daily May-Sept. 10am-4pm; Oct.-Apr. 1-4pm. 500ISK. M free.)* From the same bus stop, follow Engjaveg. to the entrance of the **Reykjavík Botanic Garden** and stroll through one of the few forested areas in Iceland. *(Skúlatún 2. ☎553 8870. Garden open 24hr. Greenhouse and pavilion open daily Apr.-Sept. 10am-10pm; Oct.-Mar. 10am-5pm. Free.)* Just outside the garden, opposite the pavilion and greenhouse, a free outdoor exhibit outlines the history of the **Washing Springs,** Reykjavík's geothermal square, where the women of the city once came to do their cooking and laundry. The city's largest thermal swimming pool, **Laugardalslaug** (see **Thermal Pools,** below), is also located in this area.

OTHER SIGHTS. The **Saga Museum** uses costumed staff and life-size plastic dolls to depict Icelandic history. One doll shows a woman exposing her breast, an event that supposedly caused the entire army of Norway to retreat. *(Bus #18 south to Perlan. ☎511 1517; www.sagamuseum.is. Open Mar.-Oct. 10am-6pm; Nov.-Feb. noon-5pm. 800ISK, students 600ISK.)* The renovated **National Museum** has a more comprehensive overview of Iceland's past. *(Suðurgt. 41. Bus #14, S1, or S3-S6 from Hlemmur station. ☎530 2200; www.natmus.is. Open high season daily 10am-5pm; low season Tu-Su 11am-5pm. 600ISK, students 300ISK. W free.)* From the National Museum, take bus #12 to **Árbæjarsafn,** an open-air museum chronicling the lives and architecture of past generations of Icelanders. Check www.reykjavikmuseum.is for special events such as folk dances and Viking games. *(☎411 6300. Open June-Aug. daily 10am-5pm. 600ISK.)*

THERMAL POOLS

Reykjavík's thermal pools are all equipped with a hot pot (naturally occurring hot tub) and steam room or sauna, although each pool maintains a distinct character. Freeloaders should seek out the city beach and its free hot pot at Nauthólsvik. All pools listed below charge 280ISK admission, with 10 visits for 2000ISK.

Laugardalslaug, Laugardalslaug-Sundlaugarveg. (☎411 5100). Take bus #14 from the city center; entrance is on the right, facing the parking lot. The city's largest thermal pool features a water slide, a children's slide, 4 hot pots, and a sauna. Swimsuit or towel 300ISK. Swimsuit, towel, and admission 600ISK. Open Apr.-Sept. M-F 6:30am-10:30pm, Sa-Su 8am-10pm; Oct.-Mar. M-F 6:30am-10:30pm, Sa-Su 8am-8pm. MC/V.

Sundhöll Reykjavíkur, Barónsstígur 45 (☎551 4059). This centrally located pool has a much smaller outdoor area than the other pools, but is the only one equipped with diving boards. Open M-F 6:30am-9:30pm, Sa-Su 8am-7pm. AmEx/MC/V.

Sundlaug Seltjarness, Iþróttamiðstöð (☎561 1551). Take bus #11 from Hlemmur station to Sundlaug bus stop and follow the signs. Recently renovated, this is the only city pool that offers salt-water hot pots. Facilities include a water slide, 2 hot pots, and a sauna. Swimsuit or towel 300ISK. Open M-F 7am-9pm, Sa-Su 8am-7pm. AmEx/MC/V.

Ylströndin Nauthólsvík. Take bus #16 south until the last stop, or take bus #18 to Perlan and hike down Öskuhlíð. This remote city beach is hard to reach using public transportation, but it's worth the trek to soak in the hot pot in the midst of sea water and take in the view of Reykjavík's smaller fjords. Locker 200ISK. Swimming free. Open May-Sept. daily 10am-8pm. Closed in rainy weather.

HIKING

Reykjavík features a range of hikes for different experience levels. For easier hikes, take bus #18 to the Perlan stop to reach trails on the forested hill around Perlan, one of which features a working model of the Strókur geyser. At the southwest corner of the park is **Nauthólsvík** beach (see above) and a beautiful trail around the airport that leads back to the city. If you get tired, catch bus #12 on Skeljanes back to the center. Pick up maps at the tourist office. To bask in the midnight sun on a black lava beach, visit the bird reserve **Grótta** on the western tip of the peninsula. Take bus #11 out to Hofgarður and walk about 15min. along the sea on Byggarðstangi. Although the Grótta itself is closed during nesting season (May-June), the bird-filled sky is still an amazing sight. Check out the lighthouse at the edge of the peninsula: high tides separate it from Reykjavík, making it a temporary island. South of the city lies the **Heiðmörk Reserve,** a large park with picnic spots and beginner to intermediate hiking trails. Take bus #S1 or S2 from Hlemmur to Hamraborg and transfer to bus #28. Ask the driver to let you off at Lake Elliðavatn; from there, you can walk or bike 3-4km south to the reserve.

Secluded and slow-paced **Viðey Island,** home to Reykjavík's oldest house and Iceland's second-oldest church, has been inhabited since the 10th century. The island features several sculpture exhibitions and the new, playfully postmodern "Blind Pavilion." Take the ferry from the Reykjavík harbor Miðbakki or take bus #16 east from Lækjartorg or Hlemmur to Sundahöftn. (☎892 0098; www.ferja.is. Ferry departs daily at 1, 2, 3, 7, and 9pm; June 10-Aug. 12 also at 8:30am. Round-trip 750ISK.) Across the bay from Reykjavík looms **Mt. Esja,** which you can ascend via a well-maintained trail (2-3hr.). The trail is not difficult, but hikers should be prepared for rain, hail, or even a brief but powerful snow squall. Take bus #15 to Háholt and transfer to bus #27, exiting at Mógilsá. (Bus #27 runs once every 1-2hr.; consult SVR city bus schedule.)

TIP **DOOR-TO-DOOR.** Do your legs ache after a long hike? The friendly drivers on BSÍ buses will generally let you off anywhere along the route upon request. Also, you can flag buses down like taxis and they will often stop to pick you up even if you're not at the stop.

NIGHTLIFE

Despite being unnervingly quiet on weeknights, Reykjavík asserts its status as a wild party town each weekend. The city's thriving independent music scene centers on **12 Tónar,** Skólavörðustígur 12, and **Bad Taste Records,** Laugavegur 59, in the basement of the Bonus supermarket. After taking in the concerts, Icelanders hit the bars and clubs until the wee hours. Most bars do not have cover charges, but bouncers tend to regulate who enters after 2am. Clubs have steep drink prices, so many locals drink at home before going out. Don't bother showing up before 12:30am, and plan to be out until 4 or 5am. Boisterous crowds tend to bar-hop around **Austurstræti, Tryggvagata,** and **Laugavegur.** The establishments listed below are 20+, unless otherwise noted.

! The shipyards along the harbor can be unsafe, especially at night. Travel with a friend if possible, and make sure to bring a reliable map.

Barinn, Laugavegur 22 (☎868 8655). With 3 floors, each with its own distinct personality and clientele, this newly opened bar/club has a DJ every night. Skip the well-dressed clubbers on the first floor and head upstairs, where a younger crowd gets funky to an eclectic mix of 80s, classic R&B, and contemporary dance music. The top floor is the conversation room for those who are literally above it all. Beer 500ISK. Mixed drinks 700ISK. Open Su-Th 10am-1am, F-Sa 10am-6am. AmEx/MC/V.

Sirkus, Klapparstíg. 30 (☎551 1999). A tropical patio and intimate upstairs bungalow room contribute to a deliciously out-of-place atmosphere at this venue frequented by local underground artists. Beer 500ISK. Open Su-Th 2pm-1am, F-Sa 2pm-5am.

Sólon, Bankastr. 7A (☎562 3232). This trendy cafe morphs at night into a posh club bouncing with grade-A hip-hop and electronica. Cafe downstairs, large dance floor and bar upstairs. Famous for Svali (700ISK), a fruity, energy-drink-based concoction. Beer 600ISK. Th live music. Open M-Th and Su 11am-1am, F-Sa 11am-5:30am.

Café Cozy, Austurstræti 3 (☎511 1033; cafecozy@simnet.is), near the tourist center. This quiet cafe serves traditional Icelandic fare during the day, but at night it's one of the wildest clubs in Reykjavík. Gay-friendly; attracts a mixed crowd. Expect to see dancing on the tables by 3am. Beer 500ISK. Mixed drinks 800ISK. F-Sa live DJ. Open Su-Th 1:30pm-2am, F-Sa 1:30pm-5am. AmEx/MC/V.

Kaffibarinn, Bergstaðastr. 1 (☎551 1588), off Laugavegur. This atmospheric lounge is a chill alternative to the whirling dervish of dancing elsewhere. Beer 550ISK, after 1am 600ISK. Mixed drinks 750ISK. Th-Sa live DJ. W white wine 500ISK. 22+. Open M-Th 10:30am-1am, F 10:30am-5am, Sa 11:30am-5am, Su 2pm-1am. MC/V.

Vegamót, Vegamótarstíg. 4 (☎511 3040), off Laugavegur. Students and well-dressed urban professionals head to this posh bar to flaunt it and see others do the same. Beer 600ISK. Th-Sa live DJ. Open M-Th 11pm-1am, F-Sa 11pm-5am. MC/V.

Cultura, Hverfisg. 18 (☎530 9314), across from the National Theater. Cafe by day and smoky bar by night, Cultura radiates a multicultural, laid-back feel. Converse over round mosaic tables before dancing in the room next door. Beer 600ISK. W tango night. F-Sa live house DJ. Open Su-Th 11:30am-1am, F-Sa 11:30am-4am. MC/V.

NASA, Thorraldssenstr. 2 (☎511 1313; www.nasa.is), at Austurvollur Square. The large dance floor in the center draws a varied crowd, depending on the evening's band. Beer 700ISK. F-Sa live bands. Cover 500-1500ISK. Open F-Sa 11pm-late. MC/V.

DAYTRIPS FROM REYKJAVÍK

Iceland's main attractions are its mesmerizing natural wonders. **Iceland Excursions** runs the popular "Golden Circle" tour, which stops at Hveragerði, Kerið, Skálholt, Geysir, Gullfoss, and Þingvellir National Park. (☎562 1011; www.icelandexcursions.is. 9-10hr., 6200ISK.) **Highlanders** offers exciting, if pricey, off-road tours in "super jeeps" that can traverse rivers, crags, and even glaciers. (☎568 3030; www.hl.is. 10,600-17,500ISK.)

GULLFOSS AND GEYSIR. The glacial river Hvita plunges down 32m to create **Gullfoss** (Golden Falls). A gravel walkway passes through the mist rising from the bottom of the waterfall. Climb the stairs up the adjacent hill for a stunning view of the surrounding mountains, plains, and cliffs. On the horizon you can see the tip of Longjökull, a glacier the size of Hong Kong. The **Geysir** area, 10km down the road, is a rugged tundra with steaming pools of hot water scattered across the landscape. The **Strokkur Geyser** (the Churn) erupts every 5-10min., spewing sulfurous water at heights up to 35m. Watch your footing; more than one tourist has fallen into the nearby **Blesi pool** and been badly scalded. The excellent **museum** at the visitors center offers a multimedia show on the science behind these natural phenomena. *(Museum 450ISK, students 350ISK. BSÍ runs a round-trip bus to Gulfoss and Geysir, departing from the BSÍ Terminal in Reykjavík June-Aug. daily 8:30am. 2½hr., round-trip 4000ISK.)*

ÞINGVELLIR NATIONAL PARK. Þingvellir National Park straddles the divide between the European and North American tectonic plates. Stand in the chasm between the continents, but don't linger too long—the plates are moving apart at a rate of 2cm per year. Train your eyes on the dark lines in the sloping hills of the valley; these fault lines mirror the slow movement of the plates. The Öxará River, slicing through lava fields and jagged fissures, leads to the **Drekkingarhylur** (Drowning Pool), where adulterous women were once drowned, and to **Lake Þingvallavatn,** Iceland's largest lake. Not far from the Drekkingarhylur lies the site of the **Alþing** (ancient parliament), where for almost nine centuries Icelanders gathered in the shadow of the **Lögberg** (Law Rock) to discuss matters of blood, money, and justice. Grab maps at the **Þingvellir Information Center.** *(Info Center ☎482 2660. Open June-Aug. daily 9am-7pm; Apr.-May and Sept.-Oct. daily 9am-5pm; Nov.-Mar. Sa-Su 9am-5pm. BSÍ does not run buses to Þingvellir; the site can only be reached by taking a tour bus or driving.)*

BLUE LAGOON. The southwest corner of the Reykjanes peninsula harbors a primordial paradise: a vast pool of geothermally heated water hidden in the middle of a lava field. The lagoon has become a tourist magnet, but it's worth braving the crowds. The cloudy blue waters are rich in silica, minerals, and algae and are famous for their healing powers. Bathers who have their fill of wading through the 36-39°C (97-102°F) waters can indulge in a steam bath, a skin-soothing silica facial, or an in-water massage (1300ISK per 10min.). Stand under the waterfall for a free, all-natural shoulder massage. *(Buses run from BSÍ Bus Terminal in Reykjavík. 1hr.; 6 per day 10am-8pm; round-trip 3400ISK, includes Blue Lagoon admission. ☎420 8800; www.bluelagoon.com. Open daily mid-May to Aug. 9am-9pm; Sept. to mid-May 10am-8pm. Towel rental 300ISK. Bathing suit rental 350ISK. Admission and locker 1300ISK. AmEx/MC/V.)*

HVERAGERÐI. Hveragerði (pop. 2000) sits on a geothermal hotbed so volatile that geysers have burst through the floors of local houses. Geothermal energy also powers the town's numerous **greenhouses,** where locals grow peppers, bananas, and other produce that would not otherwise survive in Iceland's unpredictable climate. Most of the greenhouses do not run organized tours, but many owners will be happy to show you around upon request. **The Garden of Eden,** Austurmörk 25, which boasts a nursery and an ice cream parlor, is one of the few that caters to tourists. *(Located across the street from the gas station where the bus stops. ☎483 49 00; www.eden.smart.is. Open daily high season 9am-11pm; low season 9am-7pm.)* The **tourist office,** Sunnumörk 2, has info on guesthouses, campgrounds, and hiking routes in the surrounding area. *(Buses run from the BSÍ terminal in Reykjavík. 40min.; 5-6 times per day in high season. ☎483 46 01. Open high season M-F 9am-5pm, Sa-Su noon-4pm; low season M-F 9am-4:30pm.)*

WESTMAN ISLANDS (VESTMANNAEYJAR)

Jutting from the depths of the North Atlantic, the black cliffs off the **Westman Islands** are the most recent offerings of the volcanic fury that created the Icelandic mainland. As recently as 1973, the fiery **Eldfell** volcano tore through the northern section of **Heimaey,** the only inhabited island, spewing lava and ash and forcing the population to flee overnight. When the eruption tapered off five months later, one-third of the town's houses had been destroyed, and the island itself had grown by the same amount. Visitors can still feel the heat of the cooling lava. The **Volcanic Film Show** on Heiðarveg. runs a documentary about the eruption. (☎481 1045. 55min. shows daily mid-June to mid-Aug. 11am, 2, 3:30, 9pm; mid-Aug. to mid-Sept. 11am and 3:30pm. 600ISK, students 500ISK.) Across the street, the **aquarium,** Heiðarveg. 12, displays some of the island's sea creatures. The **Natural History Museum** downstairs has exhibits on the island's unique birds and geology. Only basic info is available in English. A combination ticket (750ISK) also grants admission to the **Folkmuseum,** on the second floor of the Cultural Center on Ráðhúströ, which recreates the eruption of Eldfell. (Aquarium ☎481 1997 or 899 2540. Folkmuseum ☎481 1194. Aquarium and museums open May-Aug. daily 11am-5pm; Sept.-Apr. Sa-Su 3-5pm. 400ISK each. AmEx/DC/MC/V.) Next to the harbor, **Landlyst,** the city's second-oldest house, is on the site of **Skansinn,** where an ancient fortress used to guard against pirates. Only the foundations remain, but the spot is now home to a medieval wooden church, recently donated by the Norwegian government in commemoration of 1000 years of Christianity in Iceland.

Though less than 15 sq. km in area, the island of Heimaey has spectacular hikes. **Cafe Cró,** Suðurgerdi 4, provides detailed hiking advice, Internet access, and caffeine to fuel the journey. (☎488 4884. Coffee

IN RECENT NEWS

THE NEXT BIG THING?

Silvía Night is Iceland's latest eccentric pop culture export. Like Björk before her, Silvía has grabbed the spotlight for her quirky personality as much as for her art. The host of her own reality TV show "See ya—with Silvía Night," she has attracted attention for her good looks and her stated ambition to become the world's greatest superstar. With the recent release of her hit song "Congratulations," nothing seems to be standing in Silvía's way, except for one problem—she's not a real person.

Silvía Night, the creation of two Reykjavík artists, is played by a formerly unknown actress named Ágústa Eva Erlendsdóttir. Her character mocks the crasser elements of pop culture. With lyrics such as, "Hello, is it God?/It's your favorite person in the world, Silvía Night," her hit song rejects any pretense of modesty or good taste. Still, the act gained such a following that, in 2006, fans voted Silvía as Iceland's representative to Eurovision, the largest European pop song competition.

Silvía's rude outbursts at Eurovision drew criticism from journalists and audience members who weren't in on the joke. She was booed during her performance in the May semi-finals and failed to make it to the finals. Still, even if Silvía may not attain world's-greatest-superstar status, she's got the title of Iceland's greatest fictional superstar in the bag.

250ISK. Internet 500ISK per 30min. Open daily 10am-5pm.) On the western side of the island, the cliff's edge at Há is a scenic spot. A longer hike (2hr. round-trip) along Ofanleitishamar on the western coast leads from the campsite to **Stórhöf,** passing two puffin colonies and a beach overlooking **Surtsey,** the world's youngest island. After a steep climb, the best view awaits on the top of **Heimaklettur,** the island's highest point. The neighboring volcanic peaks of Eldfell and Helgafell can be scaled, although strong gusts often make for rough going. Hidden in the north-east corner of the lava bed is **Gaujulundur,** a small garden and elf village, complete with a miniature windmill. This spot is quiet and remote; some consider it sacred and have built a miniature fence to protect the elves. Don't forget to sign the guestbook. To get there, walk east along Strandvegur into the lava bed. Stay on the side of the road to leave room for passing cars and continue until you hit a fork in the road. Take the left fork and walk until you see a sign for the garden. The three-day **People's Feast** (Þjóðhátíð) draws thousands of young people to the island during the first weekend in August for bonfires, drinking, and related revelry. Reserve transportation well ahead.

The centrally located, welcoming **Guesthouse Hreiðrið ❷,** Faxastíg. 33, is just past the Volcanic Film Show theater on Heiðarveg. (☎481 1045; http://tourist.eyjar.is. Reception 24hr. in summer. Sleeping-bag accommodations 1800ISK; singles 3500ISK; doubles 5800ISK. Low season reduced rates. 10% ISIC discount. AmEx/MC/V.) **Guesthouse Sunnuhóll (HI) ❷,** Vestmannabraut 28B, has bright, newly renovated rooms with space to stretch out after a long hike. The reception desk is located in Hotel Þórshamar, Vestaunrabraut 28, near the center of town, so solo travelers may have the entire guesthouse to themselves. (☎481 2900; http://hotel.eyjar.is. Breakfast 600ISK. Linens 600ISK. Free wireless Internet in the hotel. Sleeping-bag accommodations 2100ISK, with HI discount 1750ISK; singles 3400ISK. Low season reduced rates. AmEx/MC/V.) **Herjólfsdal Camping ❶,** 10min. west of town on Dalveg., is at the bottom of one of the oldest craters on the island. Next door is the site of the island's first settlement, marked by a life-size model of the original settler's wooden hut. (Campground ☎692 6952 or 861 4347. Showers free. Tent sites 700ISK. MC/V.) Pick up groceries at **Krónan** on Strandaveg. (Open daily 11am-7pm.) Air Iceland runs **flights** to the Westman Islands from Reykjavík Airport. (☎481 3255; www.airiceland.is. 30min., from 4500ISK.) The Herjólfur **ferry** departing from Þorlákshöfn is slower but cheaper. (☎481 2800. 2¾-3hr.; departs daily noon and 7:30pm; returns daily 8:15am and 4pm. 1800ISK, with ISIC 900ISK; Internet tickets 10% discount.) **Buses** go from BSÍ Station to the ferry 1hr. before departure (1000ISK). The **tourist office** is on Ráðhúströ, on the first floor of the Cultural Center. (☎481 3535; www.vestmannaeyjar.is. Open mid-May to mid-Sept. M-F 9am-5pm, Sa-Su 11am-4pm; mid-Sept. to mid-May M-F 9am-5pm.)

LANDMANNALAUGAR AND ÞÓRSMÖRK

Wedged between southern Iceland's glaciers, lava fields, and mountains made of colorful volcanic rock, Landmannalaugar and Þórsmörk are popular jumping-off points for **hikers.** The demanding four-day, 54km trek between the two areas poses a number of challenges, including uncertain weather conditions. Other trails go through gentler terrain, like the 2hr. loop through Landmannalaugar's volcanoes and bubbling hot springs and the walk from Þórsmörk to the peak of **Valahnjukur,** overlooking rivers and ash fields. **Ferðafélag Íslands** (Iceland Touring Association) offers guided hikes (☎568 25 33; www.fi.is). Footsore travelers can soak away their aches and pains in Landmannalaugar's soothing **thermal brook.** Landmannalaugar has a **campsite ❶** and **lodge ❷** run by Ferðafélag Íslands; reserve online. (Open July-Sept. Camping 800ISK; mountain huts 2200ISK.) In Þórsmörk, **Húsadalur Þórsmörk ❶** provides hiking tips and simple accommodations. (☎580 5400;

www.thorsmork.is. Breakfast 850ISK. Open mid-Apr. to mid-Oct. Camping 500ISK; sleeping-bag accommodations 1600ISK; 5-person cabin with kitchen 6000ISK.) **Buses** run from the BSÍ terminal in Reykjavík to Landmannalaugar (4½hr.; mid-June to mid-Sept. daily 8:30am, return 2:45pm; round-trip 9000ISK) and Þorsmork (3½hr.; June to mid-Sept. daily 8:30am, return 3:30pm; round-trip 7400ISK).

AKUREYRI

Although Akureyri (ah-KOO-rare-ee) has only 16,000 inhabitants, it is still Iceland's second-largest city. In addition to being a college town with trendy hangouts, Akureyri serves an outpost for exploring the region's breathtaking highlands.

TRANSPORTATION AND PRACTICAL INFORMATION. **Flights** arrive from Reykjavík daily at Akureyri Airport, 3km south of the city center along Drottningarbraut, the seaside road. Reserving ahead or flying standby may snag you rates that are cheaper than bus fares. For flight information, contact Air Iceland (☎460 7000; www.airiceland.is). **Buses** run from the Trex bus station, Kaldbaksgata 1, to Reykjavík (6hr., 8:30am and 5pm, 6600ISK). To get to the Trex station, walk down Strandgata away from the city center until you reach Kaldbaksgata. **Car rental** agencies are located at the airport. Most of the agencies have 24hr. service, but not necessarily on site: **Avis** (☎461 2428; www.avis.is); **Budget** (☎462 3400); **Hasso** (☎464 1030; hasso.co.is); **Hertz** (☎461 1005; www.hertz.is). For **taxis,** try **BSÓ,** on Strandgata across from Götu Grillð. (☎461 1010. Open M-F 7am-2am, Sa-Su 24hr. Also runs private tours starting from 20,000ISK. AmEx/MC/V.)

Mountains and the harbor border Akureyri to the west, while the imposing Eyjafjörður fjord abuts the town on the east. Within the city limits, follow **Hafnarstræti** to its end to reach Akureyri's main square, **Ráðhústorg.** The **tourist office,** Hafnarstr. 82, books tours, accommodations, and car rentals. (☎550 0720; www.nordurland.is. Open late June-Aug. M-F 8:30am-7pm, Sa-Su 8am-7pm; low season M-F 8:30am-5pm. MC/V.) Most major services, including **banks,** can be found around Ráðhústorg. **KB Banki** and **Landsbanki** banks (open M-F 9:15am-4pm) are just off the square. The **police** station is at Þorunnarstræti 138 (☎464 7700). The **hospital,** Eyrarlandsvegur (☎463 0100), on the south side of the botanical gardens, has a 24hr. emergency ward. For **Internet** access, walk from Ráðhústorg up Brekkugata to the **library,** Brekkugata 17, on the corner of Oddeyarargata. (☎460 1250. Open mid-June to mid-Sept. M-F 10am-7pm, Sa noon-5pm; low season M-W and F 10am-7pm, Th 10am-10pm. 200ISK per hr.)

ACCOMMODATIONS AND FOOD. Akureyri's only hostel, **Stórholt ❶,** Stórholt 1, draws an adventurous crowd of Arctic travelers who relax in quiet, comfy common spaces. Ask about discounted whale-watching tickets. (☎462 3657; storholt@simnet.is. Linens 600ISK. Laundry 600ISK. Dorms 1800ISK; singles 3300ISK; doubles 5400ISK. HI discount 400-600ISK.) In a peaceful neighborhood near the city center, the cottages at **Gula Villan ❷,** Brekkugt. 8 and Þingvallastr. 14, have bright and tidy rooms. (☎896-8464; gulavillan@nett.is. Free laundry. Sleeping-bag accommodations from 2200ISK; singles 3300ISK; doubles 4800ISK; triples 6600ISK. AmEx/DC/MC/V.) The **Central Campsite ❶,** on a hill in the city center, is next to a thermal pool and overlooks the fjord. (☎462 3379. Tent sites 800ISK.)

The incredible **Götu Grillð ❷,** Strandgt. 11, flavors Icelandic fish with Indian spices. The chefs from India craft dishes with healthy portions, strong curry, and extra-buttery naan. Burgers start from 550ISK, and the lunch buffet with at least one vegetarian option fills you up for 1195ISK. (☎462 1800. Open mid-June to Sept. daily 11am-11pm; Oct. to mid-June M-F noon-2pm and 5-10pm, Sa-Su 5-10pm. AmEx/MC/V.) Travelers staying at Stórholt hostel enjoy a 10% discount at

Café Konditori ❶, Langholt (☎460 5920), which offers cheap pastries (150ISK), pizza (295ISK), and coffee to go (170ISK). **Brynja ❶**, Aðalstræti 3 has the definitive Icelandic treat: frozen yogurt smothered in chocolate or caramel. (☎462 4478. Cones from 190ISK. Open M-F 9am-11:30pm, Sa-Su 10am-11:30pm. MC/V.) Get groceries at the **Bonus** on Hörgárbraut, near the hostel. (☎466 3500. Open M-Th noon-6:30pm, F 10am-7:30pm, Sa 10am-6pm, Su noon-6pm. MC/V.)

SIGHTS AND NIGHTLIFE. For a glimpse of late 19th-century life in Akureyri, visit **Nonnahús,** Aðalstr. 54. The museum focuses on Icelandic author Jón Sveinsson, whose children's book *Nonni and Manni* has been translated into over 30 languages. (☎462 3555. Open June-Sept. daily 10am-5pm; call ahead in low season. 350ISK. MC/V.) Tropical and subtropical plants fight off the sub-Arctic climate at the northernmost **botanical gardens** in the world, at Hrafnagilsstr. and Eyrarlandsveg. (Open M-F 8am-10pm, Sa-Su 9am-10pm. Free.) Travelers can hike to **Mount Súlur** (1144m) along a trail that starts 4km out of town. More challenging hikes that require specialized gear for glaciers include **Strýta** (1456m) and **Kerling** (1536m). The tourist office has hiking maps (200-300ISK). Culture lovers arrive for the annual **Summer Arts Festival** (late June-late Aug.), which includes theater, poetry readings, and history walks. Check www.listagil.is for details.

Many streets in Akureyri are deserted at night, but lines of cars slowly circle one building in the town square in a tradition known as **Rúnturinn.** High schoolers often meet their first significant others through an exchange of furtive glances from one windshield to another. Inside this central building, a well-dressed crowd spends hours people-watching at **Café Amour.** The popular cocktail Mr. Big (1000ISK) is a vanilla vodka concoction. Beer starts at 600ISK (try the locally brewed Thule), but look for deals on five bottles (1500ISK) during occasional Happy hours. (☎461 3030; www.cafeamour.is. Open Su-Th 10am-1am, F-Sa 10am-4am. MC/V.) **Kaffi Akureyri,** Strandgt. 7, is a no-frills bar, with a crowd ranging from 20- to 60-year-olds. Knock down Opal licorice shots with the locals for 400ISK. (☎461 3999; kaffiakureyri.is. 20+. Open Su-Th 3pm-1am, F-Sa 3pm-4am. AmEx/DC/MC/V.)

DAYTRIPS FROM AKUREYRI: MÝVATN NATURE BATHS AND GOÐAFOSS. Tourists fleeing the hordes at the Blue Lagoon (p. 544) head to the freshwater **Mývatn Nature Baths,** 90km east of Akureyri. **Buses** run round-trip from Akureyri to Reynihlíð (June-Aug. daily 8am, returning 3:30pm; round-trip 4400ISK). From Reynihlíð, it is a 4km hike to the baths. Take the first right past the Verslun Supermarket, and enjoy the view of the lake, lava fields, and craters. Follow the road and take the first right, in sight of two power stations. The baths are a 5min. walk down this road. (☎464 4411; www.naturebaths.com. Open daily June-Aug. 9am-midnight; Sept.-May noon-10pm. 1100ISK. Towel or swimsuit rental 350ISK. MC/V.)

According to legend, Þorgeir flung statues of pagan gods into a waterfall in AD 1000 to celebrate Iceland's conversion to Christianity. **Goðafoss** (Waterfall of the Gods) stands 12m high, but is set against a beautiful backdrop, making it an ideal rest stop on the road to Akureyri. The waterfall is 50km from both Akureyri and Húsavík off Rte. 1, and difficult to reach without a **car.** A **bus** departs Akureyri daily at 8am between June and August, but returns only at 4:05pm (40min., 1200ISK).

HÚSAVÍK

The premier whale-watching destination in Europe, Húsavík (WHO-saah-veek; pop. 2500) boasts a diverse set of attractions ranging from the natural to the bizarre. For a unique mix of science, art, and humor, head to **The Icelandic Phallological Museum** at Héðinsbraut 3A. The giant erect phallus that greets passersby makes the museum hard to miss. Inside, the collection includes the reproductive organs of over 86 species, from the hamster specimen that measures less than

2mm to the sperm whale's organ that weighs 70kg. Don't miss the folklore section, which displays a merman penis and two different types of ghost's penises. (☎561 6663; www.phallus.is. Open daily mid-May to mid-Sept. noon-6pm. 500ISK.) Farther down Héðinsbraut, the **Húsavík Whale Museum,** next to the harbor, houses several complete skeletons of different whale species. Visitors can stand inside the lower jaw bone of a humpback whale or learn about Keiko, the star of the film *Free Willy*, who was captured near Iceland in 1979. The museum's volunteer program draws students from abroad. (☎464 2520; www.icewhale.is. Open daily June-Aug. 9am-9pm, May and Sept. 10am-5pm. 600ISK, students 500ISK. MC/V.) To go whale-watching, book a 3hr. tour with **Gentle Giants** or **North Sailing.** (Gentle Giants ☎464 1500. Tours May-Sept., call for times. 3700ISK. MC/V. North Sailing ☎464 2350; www.northsailing.is. Tours May-Sept., call for times. 3800ISK. MC/V.)

Two **guesthouse** options are available along Baldursbrekka (the second street on the right when heading north from the bus stop). The welcoming **Aðalbjörg Birgisdóttir Guesthouse ❷,** Baldursbrekka 20, has small rooms above ground and at basement level. (☎464 1005; onad@simnet.is. Breakfast 1000ISK. Sleeping-bag accommodations 2000ISK; singles 3500ISK; doubles 5000ISK. Cash only.) Across the street, **Emhild K. Olsen ❶,** Baldursbrekka 17, caters to the sleeping-bag crowd with large rooms in the basement of a family's home. (☎464 1618. Breakfast 700ISK; included for singles and doubles. Sleeping-bag accommodations 1800ISK. Singles 3600ISK; doubles 6000ISK. Cash only.) **Salka Restaurant ❷,** on the harbor, is famous for its shrimp and salmon dishes (850ISK-2050ISK). Relax with a beer upstairs on leather couches and take in a beautiful view of the harbor. (☎464 2551. Entrees from 850ISK. Pizzas from 1600ISK. Kitchen open daily 11:30am-10pm. Bar open June-Aug. M-Th until 11pm, year-round F-Sa until 3am. MC/V.) During the day, **Heimabakarí konditori,** Garðarsbraut 15, features *kleina* (63ISK), an Icelandic donut-like treat. (☎464 2901. Open M-F 9am-6pm, Sa 10am-4pm. MC/V.)

Trex (☎587 6000; www.trex.is) has bus service to Akureyri (1hr., 4 per day, 2100ISK). **Buses** leave from Esso gas station at Héðinsbraut 2, on the main street north of the harbor. SBA (☎550 0771; www.sba.is) has bus tours of the area. Buses leave the Shell at Héðinsbraut 6 for Reynihilð on Lake Mývatn (45min., late June-Aug. 2-3 per day, 1600ISK). The **tourist office** is inside Kasko supermarket, Garðarsbraut 5. (☎464 4300; www.markthing.is. Open June-Aug. M-Th 10am-6:30pm, F 10am-7pm, Sa 10am-6pm, Su noon-6pm.) **Internet** access is at the Húsavík Public Library, Stórigarður 17. (☎464 1173. Open June-Aug. M-Th 10am-7pm, F 10am-5pm; Sept.-May M-Th 10am-7pm, F 10am-5pm, Sa 11am-3pm. 5ISK per min.)

JÖKULSÁRGLJÚFUR NATIONAL PARK

The Jökulsa á Fjöllum River flows into Jökulsárgljúfur National Park from the Vatnajökull glacier in the south, creating astounding waterfalls throughout the region. Jökulsárgljúfur is a trek from any transport hub, but the park's magnificent **Dettifoss** waterfall rewards travelers who sit through a long bus ride, book a pricey tour, or rent a car for the occasion. Dettifoss is the most powerful waterfall in Europe, and its horseshoe-shaped torrent fertilizes the surrounding area. Walk 1.4km upstream, past river beaches covered with dark lava sand, to reach **Sellfoss,** a smaller but still imposing waterfall. Jökulsárgljúfur's third major waterfall, **Hafragilsfoss,** is 2km downstream from Dettifoss. The Hafragilsfoss parking area has a majestic view of both the waterfall and the canyon below. Round-trip **buses** run mid-June to August from Akureyri (5hr., daily 8:15am, 8700ISK). **Nonni Travels,** Brekkugata 5, in Akureyri, books bus and Jeep tours to Dettifoss from Húsavík and Akureyri. Groups of four can book the Super Jeep tour from Mývatn for 10,500ISK; an optional bus from Akureyri is an additional fee. (☎461 1841; www.nonnitravel.is. Open M-F 9am-5pm. MC/V.) A rental car (p. 547), preferably four-wheel-drive, is often the cheapest and easiest way to reach Jökulsárgljúfur.

REPUBLIC OF IRELAND

The green, rolling hills of Ireland, dotted with Celtic crosses, medieval monasteries, and Norman castles, have long inspired poets and artists. Yet visitors today who admire the Emerald Isle's jagged coastal cliffs and untouched mountain chains are also drawn to the thriving urban centers. Dublin pays tribute to the virtues of fine brews and to the legacy of resisting British rule, while Galway boasts a vibrant arts scene. The recent growth of the computing and tourism industries have raised Ireland out of its economic doldrums, and its living standards are now among the highest in Europe. The homeland of Joyce and Yeats also claims the world-famous rock band U2 as its own. Despite fearful murmurs about the decline of traditional culture, the Irish language lives on in secluded areas known as the *gaeltacht*, and dark village pubs still echo with reels and jigs.

DISCOVER IRELAND: SUGGESTED ITINERARIES

THREE DAYS. Spend it all in **Dublin** (p. 555). Wander through **Trinity College,** admire the ancient **Book of Kells,** and sample the whiskey at the **Old Jameson Distillery.** Take a day to visit the **National Museums,** stopping to relax on **St. Stephen's Green,** and get smart at the **James Joyce Cultural Centre.** Work your pubbing potential by night in **Temple Bar** and on **Grafton Street.**

ONE WEEK. After visiting the sights and pubs of **Dublin** (3 days), enjoy the natural wonders of **Killarney** (1 day; p. 570) and the **Ring of Kerry** (1 day; p. 571). Return to the urban scene in the cultural center of **Galway** (2 days; p. 574).

BEST OF IRELAND, THREE WEEKS. The first stop is to explore **Dublin** (4 days), then head to **Sligo** (3 days; p. 578) and visit the surrounding lakes and mountains. Continue on to **Galway** (3 days) and the **Aran Islands** (1 day; p. 576). After taking in the views from the **Cliffs of Moher** (1 day; p. 574), tour the scenic **Ring of Kerry** (2 days). Spend time in beautiful **Killarney** (2 days; p. 570) and the southernmost **Schull Peninsula** (1 day; p. 569) before hitting the big city of **Cork** (2 days; p. 566). On the way back to Dublin, stop by the beaches and crystal factory in Ireland's oldest city, **Waterford** (1 day, p. 565).

ESSENTIALS

FACTS AND FIGURES

Official Name: Éire.
Capital: Dublin.
Major Cities: Cork, Galway, Limerick.
Population: 4,062,000.
Time Zone: GMT.
Languages: English, Irish.
Religion: Roman Catholic (88%), Anglican Church of Ireland (3%).

WHEN TO GO

Ireland has a consistently cool, wet climate, with temperatures ranging from around 4°C (39°F) in the winter to 16°C (61°F) in the summer. Bring raingear in any season, but take heart when you wake to cloudy, foggy mornings—it usually clears by noon. The southeastern coast is the driest and sunniest, while western Ireland is considerably wetter and cloudier. May and June are the sunniest months, July and August the warmest. December and January have short, wet days, but temperatures rarely drop below freezing.

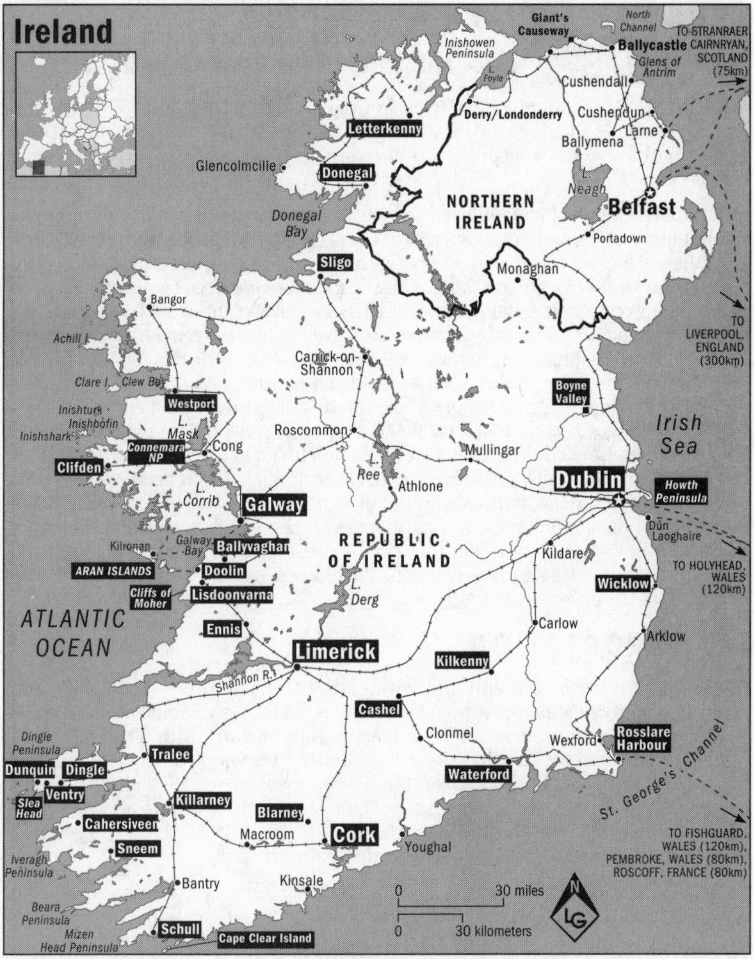

DOCUMENTS AND FORMALITIES

EMBASSIES. Embassies for Ireland are in Dublin (p. 555). Irish embassies abroad include: **Australia,** 20 Arkana St., Yarralumla, Canberra, ACT 2600 (☎06 273 3022; irishemb@cyberone.com.au); **Canada,** Ste. 1105, 130 Albert St., Ottawa, ON K1P 5G4 (☎613-233-6281; embassyofireland@rogers.com); **New Zealand,** Level 7, 23 Customs Street E., Auckland (☎09 977 2252; www.ireland.co.nz); **UK,** 17 Grosvenor Pl., London SW1X 7HR (☎020 7235 2171); **US,** 2234 Massachusetts Ave., NW, Washington, D.C. 20008 (☎202-462-3939; www.irelandemb.org).

VISA AND ENTRY INFORMATION. Citizens of Australia, Canada, the EU, New Zealand, the UK, and the US do not need a visa for stays of up to 90 days. For longer stays, non-EU citizens should register for free with the **Garda National Immigration Bureau,** 13-14 Burgh Quay, Dublin 2 (☎01 666 9100).

TOURIST SERVICES AND MONEY

EMERGENCY	**Police, Ambulance,** and **Fire:** ☎999. **Emergency:** ☎112.

TOURIST OFFICES. Bord Fáilte (Irish Tourist Board; ☎1850 230 330; www.ireland.ie) operates a nationwide network of offices. Most tourist offices book rooms for a small fee and a 10% deposit, but many hostels and B&Bs are not on the board's central list.

MONEY. The **euro (€)** has replaced the Irish pound (£) as the unit of currency in the Republic of Ireland. As a general rule, it is cheaper to exchange money in Ireland than at home. If you stay in hostels and prepare your own food, expect to spend about €30 per person per day; a slightly more comfortable day (sleeping in B&Bs, eating one meal per day at a restaurant, going out at night) would cost €50. Most people working in restaurants do not expect a tip, unless the restaurant is targeted exclusively toward tourists. In that case, consider leaving 10-15%. Tipping is very uncommon for other services, such as taxis and hairdressers. In most cases, people are usually happy if you simply round up the bill to the nearest euro.

Ireland charges a **value added tax (VAT),** a national sales tax on most goods and some services. The 21% VAT is almost always included in listed prices, and it does not apply to food, health services, or children's clothing. **VAT refunds** are available to citizens of non-EU countries who fill out a form at the time of purchase. Look for the "Cashback" sticker on tourist-oriented stores, which means that the establishment will give you a voucher that can be presented for a refund at Cashback service desks located in the airports. Purchases greater than €250 must be approved at the customs desk first.

TRANSPORTATION

BY PLANE. Flying to London and connecting to Ireland is often easier and cheaper than flying directly. A popular carrier to Ireland is national airline **Aer Lingus** (☎081 836 5000, US 800-474-7424; www.aerlingus.com), with direct flights to London, Paris, and the US. **Ryanair** (☎081 830 3030; www.ryanair.com) offers low fares from Dublin and Shannon to destinations across Europe. Web-based phenom **easyJet** (UK ☎0871 244 2366; www.easyjet.com) offers cheap flights between Cork and London. **British Airways** (Ireland ☎890 626 747, UK 0870 850 9850, US 800-247-9297; www.ba.com) flies into most major Irish airports daily.

BY TRAIN. Iarnród Éireann (Irish Rail; ☎01 850 366 222; www.irishrail.ie) is useful only for travel to urban areas. The **Eurailpass** is accepted in the Republic but not in Northern Ireland. The **BritRail** pass does not cover travel in the Republic or in Northern Ireland, but the month-long **BritRail+Ireland** pass (€345-550) does, and includes rail options and round-trip ferry service between Britain and Ireland.

BY BUS. Bus Éireann (☎01 836 6111; www.buseireann.ie), Ireland's national bus company, operates long-distance Expressway buses that link larger cities and local buses that serve the countryside and smaller towns. One-way fares between cities generally range €5-25; student discounts are available. Bus Éireann offers the **Irish Rover** pass, which also covers the Ulsterbus service in Northern Ireland (3 of 8 consecutive days €70, under 16 €40; 8 of 15 days €158/87; 15 of 30 days €235/128). The **Emerald Card,** also available through Bus Éireann, offers unlimited travel on Expressway and other buses, Ulsterbus, Northern Ireland Railways, and local services (8 of 15 consecutive days €228, under 16 €114; 15 of 30 days €393/196).

Bus Éireann works in conjunction with ferry services and the bus company **Eurolines** (www.eurolines.com) to connect Ireland with Britain and the continent. Eurolines passes for unlimited travel between major cities range €199-439. Discounts are available in the low season and for people under 26 or over 60. A major route runs between Dublin and Victoria Station in London; other stops include Birmingham, Bristol, Cardiff, Glasgow, and Liverpool, with services to Cork, Derry/Londonderry, Galway, Limerick, Tralee, and Waterford, among others.

BY FERRY. Ferries run between Britain and Ireland several times per day. Fares for adult foot travelers generally range €15-30. **Irish Ferries** (www.irishferries.com) and **Stena Line** (www.stenaline.com) typically offer discounts to students, seniors, families, and youth traveling alone. Ferries run from Dublin to Holyhead, BRI; from Cork to South Wales and Roscoff, FRA (p. 564); and from Rosslare Harbour to Pembroke, Wales, Cherbourg, FRA, and Roscoff, FRA (p. 564).

BY CAR. Drivers in Ireland use the left side of the road. Gasoline (petrol) prices are high. Be particularly cautious at roundabouts—give way to traffic from the right. **Dan Dooley** (☎062 53103, UK 0800 282 189, US 800-331-9301; www.dan-dooley.com) and **Enterprise** (☎1 800 227 800, UK 0870 350 3000, US 800-261-7331; www.enterprise.com) will rent to drivers between 21 and 24, though such drivers must pay an additional daily surcharge. Fares are €85-200 per week (plus VAT), including insurance and unlimited mileage. If you plan to drive a car in Ireland for longer than 90 days, you must have an **International Driving Permit (IDP).** If you rent, lease, or borrow a car, you will need a **green card** or **International Insurance Certificate** to certify that you have liability insurance that applies abroad. It is always significantly less expensive to reserve a car from the US than from within Europe.

BY BIKE, FOOT, AND THUMB. Ireland's countryside is well suited for **biking,** as many roads are not heavily traveled. Single-digit "N" roads are more trafficked; try to avoid these. Ireland's mountains, fields, and hills make **walking** and **hiking** arduous joys. The **Wicklow Way,** a hiking trail in the mountains southeast of Dublin, has hostels within a day's walk of each other. Some locals caution against **hitchhiking** in County Dublin and the Midlands. Let's Go does not recommend hitchhiking.

KEEPING IN TOUCH

PHONE CODES	**Country code:** 353. **International dialing prefix:** 00. For more information on how to place international calls, see inside back cover. From inside the Republic, dial the city code only when calling from outside the city.

EMAIL AND THE INTERNET. Internet access is available in cafes, hostels, and most libraries. One hour of web time costs about €3-6; an ISIC often earns you a discount. Find listings of cybercafes in Ireland at www.cybercafes.com.

TELEPHONE. Ireland's public phones accept coins and phone cards (€0.50 for local calls, €1 for short international calls). Many towns have call centers attached to Internet cafes, with rates around €0.10-0.20 per minute for local and international calls. Dial ☎114 for an international operator, 10 for a national operator, or 11811 for directory assistance. International direct dial numbers in Ireland include: **AT&T Direct** (☎800 550 000); **British Telecom** (☎800 550 144); **Canada Direct** (☎800 555 001); **MCI WorldPhone** (☎800 55 1001); **Telstra Australia** (☎800 55 00 61).

MAIL. Postcards and letters up to 50g cost €0.48 within Ireland and €0.75 to Europe and other international destinations. Airmail parcels take five to nine days between Ireland and North America. Dublin is the only place in the Republic with Postal Codes (p. 558). Address *Poste Restante* as follows: First name LAST NAME, *Poste Restante*, City, Ireland. The mail will go to a desk in the central post office unless you specify otherwise.

ACCOMMODATIONS AND CAMPING

IRELAND	❶	❷	❸	❹	❺
ACCOMMODATIONS	under €17	€17-26	€26-40	€40-56	over €56

A **hostel** bed will average €13-20. **An Óige** ("an OYJ"), the **HI** affiliate, operates 24 hostels countrywide (☎01 830 4555; www.irelandyha.org. One-year membership €20, under 18 €10). Many An Óige hostels are in remote areas or small villages and are designed primarily for nature-seekers, and so do not offer the social environment typical of other European hostels. Over 100 hostels in Ireland belong to **Independent Holiday Hostels (IHH;** ☎01 836 4700; www.hostels-ireland.com). Most IHH hostels have no lockout or curfew, accept all ages, require no membership, and have a less institutional feel than An Óige; all are Bord Fáilte-approved. In virtually every Irish town, **B&Bs** can provide a quiet, luxurious break from hostelling; expect €30-35 for singles and €45-60 for doubles. "Full Irish breakfasts" are often filling enough to last until dinner. **Camping** in Irish State Forests and National Parks is not allowed; camping on public land is permissible if there is no official campsite nearby. Sites cost €5-13. For more info, see www.camping-ireland.ie.

FOOD AND DRINK

IRELAND	❶	❷	❸	❹	❺
FOOD	under €6	€6-10	€10-15	€15-20	over €20

Food in Ireland can be expensive, but the basics are simple and filling. Find quick and greasy staples at chippers (fish and chips shops) and takeaways (takeout joints). Most pubs serve Irish stew, burgers, soup, and sandwiches. Cafes and restaurants have begun to offer more vegetarian options to complement the typical meat-based entrees. Soda bread is delicious, and Irish cheeses are addictive. Guinness, a rich, dark stout, is revered with a zeal usually reserved for the Holy Trinity. Known as "the dark stuff" or "the blonde in the black skirt," its head is so thick it's rumored that you can stand a match in it. Irish whiskey (p. 561), which Queen Elizabeth once claimed was her only true Irish friend, is sweeter than its Scotch counterpart. Ordering at an Irish **pub** is not to be done willy-nilly. In a small group, one individual will usually approach the bar and buy a round of drinks for everyone. Once those drinks are downed, another individual will buy the next round. It's considered poor form to refuse someone's offer to buy you a drink.

HOLIDAYS AND FESTIVALS

Holidays: Holidays for the Republic of Ireland in 2007 include: New Year's Day (Jan. 1); St. Patrick's Day (Mar. 17); Good Friday and Easter Monday (Apr. 6 and Apr. 9); and Christmas (Dec. 25). There are bank holidays in the Republic and Northern Ireland during the summer months; check tourist offices for dates. Northern Ireland has the same national holidays as the Republic; it also observes Orangemen's Day (July 12).

Festivals: All of Ireland goes green for St. Patrick's Day (Mar. 17). On Bloomsday (June 16), Dublin celebrates James Joyce's *Ulysses*. In mid-July, the Galway Arts Festival offers theater, trad, rock, and film. Tralee crowns a lucky young lady as "Rose of Tralee" at a festival in late August, and many return happy from the Lisdoonvarna Matchmaking Festival in the Burren in early September.

BEYOND TOURISM

To find opportunities that match up with your interests and schedule, check with national agencies such as **Volunteering Ireland** (www.volunteeringireland.com).

L'Arche Ireland, "Seolta," Warrenhouse Rd., Baldoyle, Dublin, 13 (☎01 839 4356; www.larche.ie). Assistants can join residential communities in Cork, Dublin, or Kilkenny to live with, work with, and teach people with learning disabilities. Room, board, and small stipend provided. Commitment of 1-2 years expected.

Sustainable Landuse Company, Doorian, Glenties, Co. Donegal (☎074 955 1286; www.donegalorganic.ie). Offers opportunities to assist with organic farming, forestry, habitat maintenance, and wildlife in the northern county of Donegal.

Focus Ireland, 9-12 High St., Dublin, 8 (☎01 881 5900; www.focusireland.ie). Advocacy and fundraising for the homeless in Dublin, Limerick, and Waterford.

DUBLIN ☎01

In a country known for its rural landscapes, the international flavor and frenetic pace of the city of Dublin stand out. Ireland's capital since the Middle Ages, Dublin offers all the amenities of other world-class cities on a more manageable scale, with all buildings topping off at five stories. Prestigious Trinity College holds treasures of Ireland's past, while Temple Bar has become one of Europe's hottest nightspots. While Dublin is not immune to the crime and poverty that afflict any metropolitan area, it still retains much of its traditional charm. The city's musical, cultural, and drinkable attractions continue to draw droves of visitors.

TRANSPORTATION

Flights: Dublin Airport (**DUB;** ☎814 1111; www.dublinairport.com). Dublin **buses** #41, 41B, and 41C run from the airport to Eden Quay in the city center (40-45min., every 10min., €1.75). **Airlink shuttle** (☎703 3139) runs nonstop to Busáras Central Bus Station and O'Connell St. (30-35min., every 15min. 5:45am-11:30pm, €5), and to Heuston Station (50min., €5). A **taxi** to the city center costs roughly €20-25.

Trains: The **Iarnród Éireann** travel center, 35 Lower Abbey St. (www.irishrail.ie), sells train tickets. Open M-F 8:30am-5pm. Info ☎836 6222 M-Sa 9am-6pm, Su 10am-6pm.

Pearse Station, Pearse St. (☎703 3592), is a departure point for **Dublin Area Rapid Transit (DART)** trains serving the suburbs and coast (every 10-15min. 6am-11:30pm, €2-6.70).

Connolly Station, Amiens St. (☎703 2359), north of the Liffey and close to Busáras. Bus #20B heads south of the river, and the DART runs to Tara Station on the south quay. Trains to **Belfast** (2hr.; M-Sa 8 per day, Su 5 per day; €50), **Sligo** (3hr., 3-4 per day, €35), and **Wexford** (3hr., 3 per day, €24).

Heuston Station (☎703 3299), south of Victoria Quay and west of the city center (a 25min. walk from Trinity College). Buses #26, 78, and 79 run to the city center. Trains to: **Cork** (3hr., 9 per day, €59); **Galway** (2¾hr., 8 per day, €42); **Limerick** (2½hr., 9 per day, €47); **Waterford** (2½hr., 4-5 per day, €29).

Buses: Intercity buses to Dublin arrive at **Busáras Central Bus Station,** Store St. (☎836 6111), next to Connolly Station. Info available at the **Dublin Bus Office,** 59 Upper O'Connell St. (☎873 4222; www.dublinbus.ie). The Bus Éireann (www.buseireann.ie) window is open daily 7am-8:30pm. Buses run to: **Belfast** (3hr., 6-7 per day, €12); **Derry/Londonderry** (4¼hr., 4-5 per day, €19); **Donegal** (4¼hr., 4-5 per day, €17); **Galway** (3½hr., 15 per day, €14); **Limerick** (3½hr., 13 per day, €12); **Rosslare** (3hr., 13 per day, €17); **Sligo** (4hr., 4-6 per day, €17); **Tralee** (6hr., 6 per day, €22); **Wexford** (2¾hr., 10-13 per day, €13). ISIC discount.

Ferries: Ferries depart for Holyhead, BRI at the **Dublin Port** (☎855 2296). Bus #20B runs from the port every hr. to Busáras station (€1.05). **Stena Line** ferries leave for Holyhead at the **Dún Laoghaire** ferry terminal (☎204 7777; www.stenaline.ie); from there DART trains run to the city center. Dublin Bus runs buses timed to fit the ferry schedules (€2.50).

Public Transportation: Info on local bus service available at **Dublin Bus Office,** 59 Upper O'Connell St. (☎873 4222; www.dublinbus.ie). Open M 8:30am-5:30pm, Tu-F 9am-5:30pm, Sa 9am-2pm, Su 9:30am-2pm. **Rambler** passes offer unlimited rides for a day (€5) or a week (€20). Dublin Bus runs the **NiteLink** service to the suburbs (M-W 12:30 and 2am, Th-Sa every 20min. 12:30-4:30am; €4-6; passes not valid).

Taxis: Blue Cabs (☎802 2222) and **ABC** (☎285 5444) have wheelchair-accessible cabs (call in advance). Available 24hr.

Car Rental: Budget, 151 Lower Drumcondra Rd. (☎837 9611; www.budget.ie), and at the airport. From €40 per day. 23+.

Bike Rental: Cycleways, 185-6 Parnell St. (☎873 4748; www.cycleways.com). Open M-W and F-Sa 10am-6pm, Th 10am-8pm. €20 per day, €80 per week.

ORIENTATION AND PRACTICAL INFORMATION

Dublin is refreshingly compact. Street names are posted high up on the sides of buildings at most intersections. The essential *Dublin Visitor Map* is free at the Dublin Bus Office. The **Liffey River** divides the city's North and South Sides. Heuston Station, famous sights, posh stores, and upscale restaurants are on the **South Side,** while Connolly Station, most hostels, and the bus station are on the **North Side.** The North Side is less expensive than the more touristed South Side, but it also has the reputation of being rougher. The streets along the Liffey are called **quays** ("keys"); the quay name changes with every bridge. **O'Connell Street,** three blocks west of Busáras Central Bus Station, is the link between northern and southern Dublin. On the North Side, **Henry** and **Mary Streets** are a pedestrian shopping zone, intersecting with O'Connell St. two blocks from the Liffey at the **General Post Office.** On the South Side, a block from the river, **Fleet Street** becomes **Temple Bar,** an area full of music centers and galleries. **Dame Street** runs parallel to Temple Bar and leads east to **Trinity College,** the nerve center of Dublin's cultural activity.

Tourist Office: Main Office, Suffolk St. (☎605 7700, international 0800 039 7000; www.visitdublin.com). Near Trinity College in a converted church. Open M-Sa 9am-5:30pm, Su 10:30am-3pm. July-Aug. open until 7pm. Reservation desks for buses and tour bookings close 30min. earlier.

Embassies: Australia, Fitzwilton House, Wilton Terr., 7th fl. (☎664 5300; www.australianembassy.ie); **Canada,** 65-68 St. Stephen's Green (☎417 4100); **UK,** 29 Merrion Rd. (☎205 3700; www.britishembassy.ie); **US,** 42 Elgin Rd. (☎668 8777; http://dublin.usembassy.gov). Citizens of **New Zealand** should contact their embassy in London.

Banks: Bank branches with **currency exchange** and 24hr. **ATMs** cluster on Lower O'Connell St. on the North Side of the river and on Grafton, Suffolk, and Dame St. on the South Side. Most open M-W and F 10am-4pm, Th 10am-5pm.

Luggage Storage: Connolly Station. First-come, first-serve lockers €4-7. Open daily 7am-10pm. **Busáras.** Lockers €6-10. Open 24hr.

Laundromat: Laundry Shop, 191 Parnell St. (☎872 3541). Wash and dry €9. Open M-F 9am-7pm, Sa 9am-6pm.

Emergency: ☎999.

Police (Garda): Dublin Metro Headquarters, Harcourt St. (☎666 6666; www.garda.ie); Store St. Station (☎666 8000); Fitzgibbon St. Station (☎666 8400); Pearse Station (☎666 9000).

Pharmacy: Hickey's, 56 Lower O'Connell St. (☎873 0427). Open M-F 7am-10pm, Sa 7:30am-10pm, Su 10am-10pm. Other branches on Grafton St. and Westmoreland St.

Hospitals: St. James's Hospital, James's St. (☎410 3000; www.stjames.ie). Take bus #123. **Mater Misericordiae Hospital,** Eccles St. (☎803 2000; www.mater.ie), off Lower Dorset St. Buses #3, 10, 11, 16, 22, and 121.

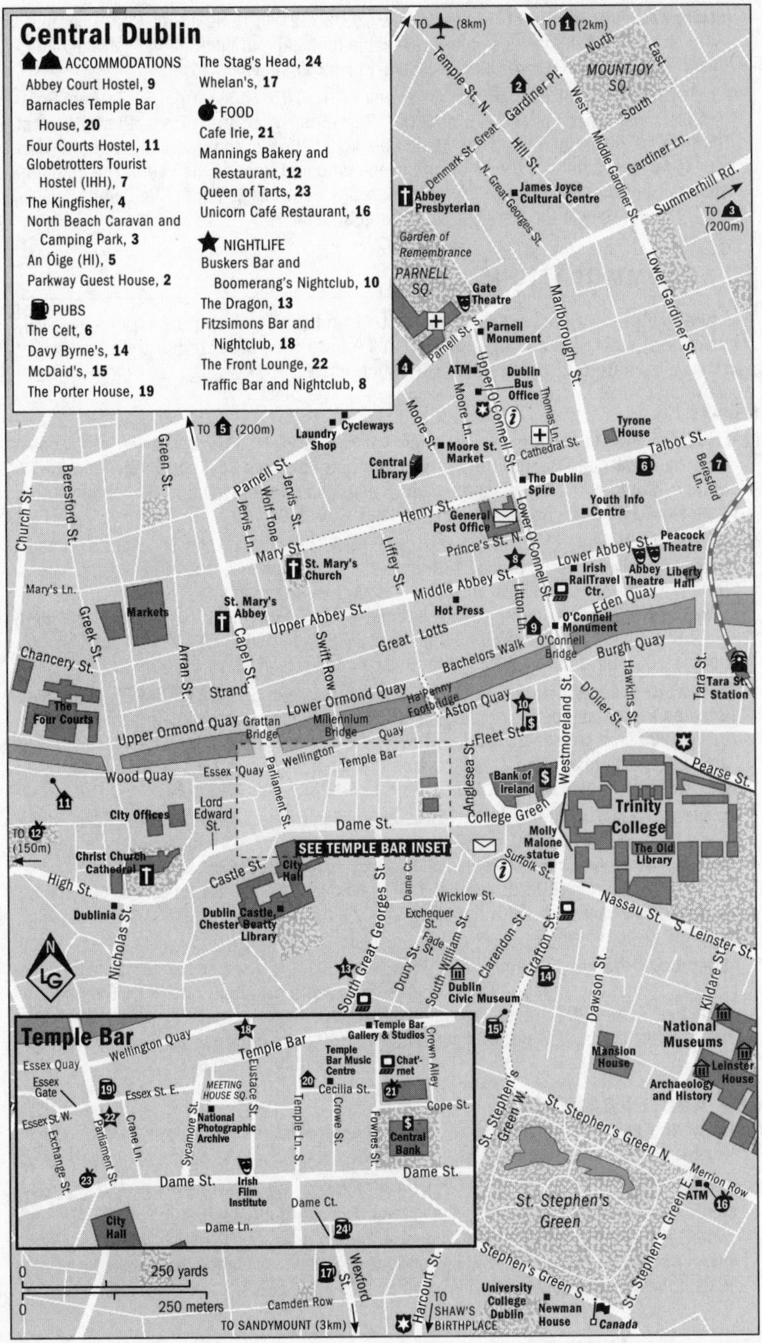
Central Dublin
ACCOMMODATIONS
Abbey Court Hostel, 9
Barnacles Temple Bar House, 20
Four Courts Hostel, 11
Globetrotters Tourist Hostel (IHH), 7
The Kingfisher, 4
North Beach Caravan and Camping Park, 3
An Óige (HI), 5
Parkway Guest House, 2
PUBS
The Celt, 6
Davy Byrne's, 14
McDaid's, 15
The Porter House, 19
The Stag's Head, 24
Whelan's, 17
FOOD
Cafe Irie, 21
Mannings Bakery and Restaurant, 12
Queen of Tarts, 23
Unicorn Café Restaurant, 16
NIGHTLIFE
Buskers Bar and Boomerang's Nightclub, 10
The Dragon, 13
Fitzsimons Bar and Nightclub, 18
The Front Lounge, 22
Traffic Bar and Nightclub, 8
TO (8km)
TO 1 (2km)
TO 3 (200m)
TO 5 (200m)
TO 12 (150m)
TO SANDYMOUNT (3km)
TO SHAW'S BIRTHPLACE
Temple St. N.
Gardiner Pl.
MOUNTJOY SQ.
North
East
West
South
Denmark St. Great
Hill St.
N. Great Georges St.
James Joyce Cultural Centre
Middle Gardiner St.
Gardiner Ln.
Summerhill Rd.
Abbey Presbyterian
Garden of Remembrance
PARNELL SQ.
Gate Theatre
Parnell St.
Parnell Monument
Lower Gardiner St.
Marlborough St.
Upper O'Connell St.
ATM
Dublin Bus Office
Moore St.
Moore Ln.
Thomas Ln.
Laundry Shop
Cycleways
Moore St. Market
Cathedral St.
Tyrone House
Talbot St.
Beresford Ln.
Central Library
The Dublin Spire
Youth Info Centre
Green St.
Beresford St.
Church St.
Jervis Ln.
Wolf Tone
Jervis St.
Henry St.
General Post Office
Liffey St.
Mary St.
Prince's St. N.
Lower O'Connell St.
Lower Abbey St.
Peacock Theatre
Abbey Theatre
Liberty Hall
St. Mary's Church
Irish RailTravel Ctr.
Middle Abbey St.
Mary's Ln.
Markets
St. Mary's Abbey
Upper Abbey St.
Hot Press
Litton Ln.
Eden Quay
O'Connell Monument
Greek St.
Capel St.
Swift Row
Great Lotts
Bachelors Walk
O'Connell Bridge
Burgh Quay
Chancery St.
Arran St.
Strand
Westmoreland St.
Hawkins St.
Tara St.
Tara St. Station
The Four Courts
Lower Ormond Quay
Ha'Penny Footbridge
Aston Quay
D'Olier St.
Upper Ormond Quay
Grattan Bridge
Millennium Bridge
Quay
Fleet St.
Wood Quay
Essex Quay
Wellington
Temple Bar
Parliament St.
Anglesea St.
Bank of Ireland
Pearse St.
Trinity College
The Old Library
City Offices
Lord Edward St.
Dame St.
College Green
Molly Malone statue
SEE TEMPLE BAR INSET
Christ Church Cathedral
Castle St.
City Hall
Suffolk St.
High St.
Dublinia
Nicholas St.
Dublin Castle, Chester Beatty Library
South Great Georges St.
Dame Ct.
Exchequer St.
Wicklow St.
Nassau St.
S. Leinster St.
Fade St.
Drury St.
South William St.
Clarendon St.
Grafton St.
Dawson St.
Kildare St.
Dublin Civic Museum
National Museums
Mansion House
Leinster House
Archaeology and History
St. Stephen's Green W.
St. Stephen's Green N.
Merrion Row
ATM
St. Stephen's Green
St. Stephen's Green E.
Stephen's Green S.
Harcourt St.
University College Dublin
Newman House
Canada
Wexford St.
Camden Row
Temple Bar
Wellington Quay
Temple Bar Gallery & Studios
Crown Alley
Essex Quay
Essex Gate
Essex St. E.
MEETING HOUSE SQ.
Eustace St.
Temple Bar Music Centre
Chat'-rnet
Cecilia St.
Cope St.
Essex St. W.
Exchange St.
Parliament St.
Crane Ln.
Sycamore St.
National Photographic Archive
Temple Ln. S.
Crowe St.
Fownes St.
Central Bank
Dame St.
Irish Film Institute
Dame Ct.
City Hall
Dame Ln.
0
250 yards
250 meters

IRELAND

Internet Access: Chat'rnet, Fownes St. (☎633 6582), in Temple Bar. €0.05 per min., min. charge €0.50. Also has phones available for local and international calls at cheap rates. Free coffee and tea. Open M-F 8am-11pm, Sa-Su 10am-11pm.

Post Office: General Post Office, O'Connell St. (☎705 7000). Open M-Sa 8am-8pm. Smaller post offices open M-Tu and Th-F 9am-6pm, W 9:30am-6pm. **Postal Codes:** The city is organized into regions numbered 1-18, 20, 22, and 24, with odd-numbered codes for areas north of the Liffey and even-numbered ones to the south. The numbers radiate out from the center of the city: North City Centre is 1, South City Centre 2. Dublin is the only city in the Republic with Postal Codes.

ACCOMMODATIONS

The beds south of the river fill up the fastest and tend to be more expensive. Still, for travelers who plan to stay out late in Temple Bar, picking a lodging close by will make the late-night stumble home much easier.

HOSTELS

Barnacles Temple Bar House, 19 Temple Ln. (☎671 6277; www.barnacles.ie). Unbeatable location near Temple Bar. Very clean; gets loud on weekends. Kitchen and TV lounge. Continental breakfast included. Luggage storage available. Reception 24hr. Check-out 10:30am. Dorms €18-27; doubles €39. MC/V. ❷

Four Courts Hostel, 15-17 Merchants Quay (☎672 5839), on the South Side, directly across from Four Courts. Bus #748 from the airport stops next door. Spacious, spotless rooms. Continental breakfast included. Luggage storage included. Security boxes and towels €1.50 each. Laundry €7.50. Internet €1 per 15min., €2 per 40min. Long-term stays available. Check-in 3:30pm. Check-out 10:30am. Dorms €17-27; singles €45-50; doubles €60-66; triples €90. In winter, discounted weekly stays €99. MC/V. ❷

Globetrotters Tourist Hostel (IHH), 46-7 Lower Gardiner St. (☎873 5893). Right near Busáras station and perfect for late-night arrivals. Huge dorms with bathrooms and high bunks. Full Irish breakfast included. Towels €1 with €5 deposit. Free Internet, parking, and luggage storage. Book at least a month in advance in summer. Dorms €20-23; singles €60-66; doubles €104-110; triples €114-126; quads €127. ❷

An Óige (HI), 61 Mountjoy St. (☎830 1766; www.anoige.ie). To get there, take either bus 16A or bus 41 from the airport to the Dorset St. stop. All rooms are large, bright, and single-sex. Continental breakfast included; Irish breakfast €4. Lockers €1.25 (bring a padlock). Laundry €2.50. Internet €1 per 15min. Check-in 11am. Check-out 10am. Dorms €20-21; singles €30; doubles €52; triples €75; quads €92-100. HI discount €2. AmEx/MC/V. ❷

Abbey Court Hostel, 29 Bachelor's Walk (☎878 0700; www.abbey-court.com), right near O'Connell St. Clean, narrow, smoke-free rooms overlook the Liffey. Continental breakfast 7:30-9:30am. Free luggage storage; safe deposit box €1. Laundry €8. Internet €1 per 15min., €2 per 40min. Check-in 2:30pm. Check-out 10:30am. For weekends, book 3 weeks in advance. Dorms €18-29; doubles €76-88. MC/V. ❷

BED AND BREAKFASTS

B&Bs with a green shamrock sign out front are registered and approved by Bord Fáilte. All prices include a full Irish breakfast.

Parkway Guest House, 5 Gardiner Pl. (☎874 0469; www.parkway-guesthouse.com), 5min. walk from O'Connell St. High-ceilinged, beautifully decorated rooms. Ask the owner, a cheerful and chatty former hurling star, for advice on the city's restaurants and pubs. Check-in 12:30pm. Check-out noon. Book well in advance, especially for weekends. Singles €38; doubles €55-80; triples €75-120; quads €100-140. MC/V. ❸

The Kingfisher, 166 Parnell St. (☎872 8732; www.kingfisherdublin.com). Clean, modern rooms, with traditional dishes served in attached restaurant. Check-in 1pm. Check-out noon. Rooms €35-60. 10% discount for stays longer than 5 days. AmEx/MC/V. ❸

CAMPING

Most official campsites are far away from the city center. While it may seem convenient, camping in **Phoenix Park** is both illegal and unsafe.

North Beach Caravan and Camping Park (☎843 7131; www.northbeach.ie), in Rush. Accessible by bus #33 from Eden Quay (45min., 25 per day), and by suburban rail. Open Apr.-Sept. Electricity €2. Showers €1. €9 per person, children €4.50. ❶

FOOD

Fresh, cheap fixings are available at Dublin's many **open-air markets,** including the fun, cozy market held on Sundays in Market Sq. in the heart of Temple Bar. On the North Side, Henry St., off O'Connell St., hosts a large market with fruit and flowers from Monday to Saturday 7:30am-6pm. The cheapest **supermarket** is the **Dunnes Stores** chain; there is one at St. Stephen's Green (☎478 0188; open M and F 8:30am-8pm, Tu-W and Sa 8:30am-7pm, Th 8:30am-9pm, Su 10am-7pm). **SPAR** grocery stores are also ubiquitous in Dublin (open M-Sa 7am-11pm, Su 9am-6pm).

Queen of Tarts, Dame St. (☎670 7499), across from Dublin Castle. This little red shop offers scrumptious homemade pastries, cakes, soups, and coffee. Go early to try the apple crumble before it sells out. Breakfast €4-8. Savory flaky scones with fresh cream €3. Open M-F 7:30am-6pm, Sa 9am-6pm, Su 9:30am-6pm. ❷

Cafe Irie, 11 Fownes St., off Temple Bar, on the left above the clothing store Sé Sí Progressive. Small, hidden eatery has bright Jamaican decorations and an impressive selection of heaping sandwiches (€5-6). Vegan- and vegetarian-friendly. Tomato, pesto, and mozzarella panini is especially good. Open daily 9am-9pm. Cash only. ❶

Mannings Bakery and Restaurant, 39-40 Thomas St. (☎454 2114), past Christ Church Cathedral on the way to the Guinness Storehouse. A constant stream of customers comes for sandwiches and panini (€5), hot food, and pastries (under €2) at this self-service eatery. Open M-F 7:30am-5:30pm, Sa 7:30am-6pm. ❶

Unicorn Café Restaurant, 12B Merrion Ct. (☎676 2182), near St. Stephen's Green. Legendary upscale Italian restaurant. Small bar inside; outdoor seating available. Entrees from €13. Lunch antipasti buffet of 40-50 items is extremely popular: €9.50 starter, €16.50 main course. Open M-Th 12:30-4pm and 6-11pm, F-Sa 12:30-4pm and 6-11:30pm. AmEx/MC/V. ❹

Unicorn Food Store and Café, Merrion Row (☎678 8588). Offers food from the Unicorn Café Restaurant kitchen for a fraction of the price. Open daily 8am-6pm. ❷

SIGHTS

Most of Dublin's sights lie near O'Connell Bridge. The 2hr. **Historical Walking Tour,** led by Trinity College graduates, stops at many of them. Meet at Trinity College's main gate. (Information/group bookings 17 St. Mary's Pl., ☎878 0227, 087 668 9412, or 087 830 3523; www.historicalinsights.ie. Tour May-Sept. daily 11am and 3pm; Apr. and Oct. daily 11am; Nov.-Mar. F-Su 11am. €12, students €10.)

TRINITY COLLEGE AND GRAFTON STREET. The British built **Trinity College** in 1592 as a Protestant seminary that would "civilize the Irish and cure them of Popery"; the Catholic Church still deemed it a cardinal sin to attend Trinity until the 1960s. Today, Trinity is one of Ireland's most prestigious universities and a not-to-be-missed stop on a tour of Dublin. *(Between Westmoreland and Grafton St., on the South Side. The main* *entrance fronts the block-long roundabout now called College Green. ☎608 1000; www.tcd.ie. Grounds always open. Free.)* Trinity's **Old Library** holds a collection of ancient manuscripts including the renowned and beautiful Book of Kells. Upstairs, the awe-inspiring **Long Room** contains Ireland's oldest harp—the **Brian Ború Harp,** pictured on Irish coins—and one of the few remaining copies of the original **1916 Proclamation** of the Republic of Ireland. *(On the south side of Library Sq. Kells ticket desk ☎608 2308, library 608 2320; www.tcd.ie/library. Open June-Sept. M-Sa 9:30am-5pm, Su 9:30am-4:30pm; Oct.-May M-Sa 9:30am-5pm, Su noon-4:30pm. €8, students €7.)* The blocks south of College Green are off-limits to cars, making the area a pedestrian playground. Performers on Grafton St. keep crowds entertained.

KILDARE STREET. Southeast of Trinity College, the museums on Kildare St. offer scientific and artistic wonders. The **Natural History Museum** displays fascinating examples of taxidermy, including enormous Irish deer skeletons. *(Upper Merrion St. Open Tu-Sa 10am-5pm, Su 2-5pm. Free.)* The **National Gallery's** extensive collection includes canvases by Brueghel, Caravaggio, Goya, Rembrandt, and Vermeer. *(Merrion Sq. W. Open M-W and F-Sa 10am-5:30pm, Th 10am-8:30pm, Su noon-5pm. Free.)* **Leinster House,** the former home of the Duke of Leinster, today provides chambers for the **Irish Parliament.** The **National Museum of Archaeology and History,** Dublin's largest museum, has artifacts spanning the last two millennia, including the **Tara Brooch** and the bloody vest of nationalist **James Connolly.** *(Kildare St., next to Leinster House. ☎677 7444; www.museum.ie. Open Tu-Sa 10am-5pm, Su 2-5pm. Free.)*

TEMPLE BAR. West of Trinity College, between Dame St. and the Liffey, the cobblestone streets and central square of Temple Bar contain cafes, hotels, and some of Dublin's best pubs and clubs. The government-sponsored Temple Bar Properties spent over €40 million to build a fleet of arts-related attractions. **The Irish Film Institute** screens specialty and art-house films. *(6 Eustace St. ☎679 5744; www.irishfilm.ie. Open daily 2-10pm. €8; before 6pm M-F and before 4pm Sa-Su €7.50.)* The **Temple Bar Music Centre** hosts shows by local and international performers. *(Curved St., between Eustace St. and S. Temple Ln. ☎670 9202; www.tbmc.ie.)*

DAME STREET AND THE CATHEDRALS. King John built **Dublin Castle** in 1204, and for the next 700 years it would be the seat of British rule in Ireland. Since 1938, each president of Ireland has been inaugurated here. *(Dame St., at the intersection of Parliament and Castle St. Open M-F 10am-4:45pm, Sa-Su 2-4:45pm. €4.50, students €3.50. Grounds free.)* At the **Chester Beatty Library,** behind Dublin Castle, visitors can see the treasures bequeathed to Ireland by American mining magnate Alfred Chester Beatty. *(☎407 0750; www.cbl.ie. Open May-Sept. M-F 10am-5pm, Sa 11am-5pm, Su 1-5pm; Oct.-Apr. closed M. Free.)* Across from the castle sits the historic **Christ Church Cathedral.** Sitric Silkenbeard, King of the Dublin Norsemen, built a wooden church on the site around 1038; Strongbow rebuilt it in stone in 1169. Fragments of the ancient pillars are now scattered about like bleached bones. *(At the end of Dame St. Take bus #50 from Eden Quay or 78A from Aston Quay. www.cccdub.ie. M-F 9:45am-5pm, except during services. €5, students €2.50.)* Deriving its name from an ancient Latin term for Dublin, **Dublinia** is an engaging three-story interactive exhibit recounting the city's history. *(Across from Christ Church Cathedral. ☎679 4611; www.dublinia.ie. Open daily Apr.-Sept. 10am-5pm; Oct.-Mar. 11am-4pm. Last admission 45min. before closing. €6, students €5.)* **St. Patrick's Cathedral,** Ireland's largest, dates to the 12th century. Jonathan

THE REAL DEAL. The Guinness Storehouse is worth the trek, if only to work up a thirst in preparation for the free pint you'll receive after the tour. The Old Jameson Distillery tour is very similar; it's best to pick whiskey or beer and only visit one of the factories. In the pub, however, there is no need to limit yourself!

Swift spent his last years as Dean of St. Patrick's; his grave is marked discreetly on the floor of the south nave. *(Patrick St. ☎453 9472; www.stpatrickscathedral.ie. Open Mar.-Oct. daily 9am-5pm; Nov.-Feb. Sa 9am-5pm, Su 10am-3pm. €5, students €4.)*

GUINNESS BREWERY AND KILMAINHAM. Guinness brews its black magic at the St. James's Gate Brewery, next to the **Guinness Storehouse.** Walk through the quirky seven-story atrium containing Arthur Guinness's 9000-year lease on the original brewery. Then drink, thirsty traveler, drink. *(St. James's Gate. From Christ Church Cathedral, follow High St. west through its name changes: Cornmarket, Thomas, and St. James. Or, take bus #51B or 78A from Aston Quay or #123 from O'Connell St. Open daily July-Aug. 9:30am-8pm; Sept.-June 9:30am-5pm. €14, students over 18 €9.50.)* Almost all the rebels who fought in Ireland's struggle for independence from 1792 to 1921 spent time at **Kilmainham Gaol,** 600m west of the Guinness Storehouse. Guided tours of the jail wind through the limestone corridors. *(Inchicore Rd. Take bus #51B, 51C, 78A, or 79 from Aston Quay. ☎453 5984. Tours approx. every 30min. Open Apr.-Sept. daily 9:30am-6pm; Oct.-Mar. M-F 9:30am-5:30pm, Su 10am-6pm. €5.30, seniors €3.70, students €2.10.)*

O'CONNELL STREET AND PARNELL SQUARE. Once Europe's widest street, O'Connell St. on the North Side now holds the less prestigious distinction of being Dublin's biggest shopping thoroughfare. Statues of Irish leaders **Daniel O'Connell, Charles Parnell,** and **James Larkin** adorn the traffic islands. The **General Post Office** on O'Connell St. was the center of the 1916 Easter Rising. *(☎705 7000. Open M-Sa 8am-8pm.)* The city's rich literary heritage comes to life at the **Dublin Writers' Museum,** which displays rare editions, manuscripts, and memorabilia of Beckett, Joyce, Wilde, Yeats, and other famous Irish writers. *(18 Parnell Sq. N. ☎872 2077; www.writersmuseum.com. Open June-Aug. M-F 10am-6pm, Sa 10am-5pm, Su 11am-5pm; Sept.-May M-Sa 10am-5pm, Su 11am-5pm. €6.70, students and seniors €5.70. Price includes audio tour.)* The **James Joyce Cultural Centre** features a wide range of Joyceana, including portraits of the individuals who inspired his characters. Call for info on lectures, Bloomsday events, and walking tours. *(35 N. Great Georges St. ☎878 8547; www.jamesjoyce.ie. Open July-Aug. Tu-Sa 10am-5pm. €5, students and seniors €4.)*

OTHER SIGHTS. Once a private estate, **St. Stephen's Green** was later bequeathed to the city by the Guinness clan. The beautiful 27-acre park on the South Side, at the end of Grafton St., hosts musical and theatrical productions in the summer. *(Open M-Sa 8am-dusk, Su 10am-dusk.)* **Four Courts,** on Inn's Quay, was

FROM THE ROAD

WATER OF LIFE

Guinness is synonymous with Ireland the world over, but Irish whiskey comes in a close second as the unofficial national drink of the Emerald Isle. Being rather partial to this potent beverage, I went straight to the source: the Old Jameson Distillery in Dublin, where the most famous Irish whiskey is produced.

The Irish name for whiskey, *uisce beatha*, translates into "water of life." But after my tour of the distillery involved six shots of whiskey downed in rapid succession, my life depended more on the regular water that I gulped down from a pitcher. Four lucky visitors on each tour sit at the bar in front of the rest of the group and throw back five shots (three Irish whiskeys, one American, and one Scotch) before selecting their favorite and downing one last shot of the firewater they prefer.

As I learned when the tour guide selected me, it's quite an experience to drink in front of 60 tourists laughing as you cough and try to get each shot down—especially if, like me, you happen to be on a tour at 4pm.

Despite the potential for making a fool of yourself, though, the Old Jameson Distillery is well worth a visit. Unlike the Guinness Brewery, the distillery offers guided tours, and in place of a dark pint you end up with a sparkling glass of amber whiskey. Drink up! I sure did.

—Merrily McGugan

once seized by members of the IRA, sparking the Irish Civil War when members of the Free State Government attacked the garrison. The building now houses Ireland's highest national court. *(☎872 6785. Open M-F 9:30am-4:30pm. Free.)* The dry air in the nave of **St. Michan's Church** has preserved the corpses in the vaults; it was these seemingly living bodies that inspired Bram Stoker to write about the living deadman in *Dracula*. The church, near Four Courts on Church St., boasts Dublin's earliest altar plates and an incredible organ from 1723. *(☎872 4154. Open Mar. 17-Oct. M-F 10am-12:45pm and 2-4:30pm, Sa 10am-12:45pm; Nov.-Mar. 16 M-F 12:30-3:30pm, Sa 10am-12:45pm. Church of Ireland services Su 10am. Crypt tours €3.50, students and seniors €3.)* At the **Old Jameson Distillery,** learn how science, grain, and tradition come together to create world-famous Irish whiskey (p. 561). Everyone gets a free glass of the "water of life" at the end of the 30min. tour. *(Bow St. From O'Connell Bridge, at the foot of O'Connell St., walk down the quays to Four Courts and take a right on Church St. Follow the signs to the Distillery, which is down a cobblestone street on the left. Or take the Luas Tram bound for Tallaght from Abbey St. to the Smithfield stop. ☎807 2355; www.jamesonwhiskey.com. Tours daily every 45min. 10am-5:15pm. Come early; tours fill up quickly. €8.75, students €7.)*

ENTERTAINMENT AND NIGHTLIFE

The free *Event Guide*, available at the tourist office and Temple Bar restaurants, offers comprehensive entertainment listings.

THEATER

Dublin's curtains rise on a range of mainstream and experimental theater. Smaller theater companies thrive off Dame St. and Temple Bar. Call ahead for tickets.

Abbey Theatre, 23-26 Lower Abbey St. (☎878 7222). Ireland's national theater was founded in 1904 by Yeats and Lady Gregory. Tickets €15-30; Sa 2:30pm matinee €15, students and seniors with ID €12. Box office open M-Sa 10:30am-7pm.

Peacock Theatre, 26 Lower Abbey St. (☎878 7222). The Abbey's experimental studio theater downstairs offers evening shows in addition to occasional lunchtime plays, concerts, and poetry. Tickets €20. Sa 2:30pm matinee €12.

PUBLIN

James Joyce once proposed that a "good puzzle would be to cross Dublin without passing a pub." A radio station later offered €125 to the first person to meet the challenge. The winner explained that you could take any route—you'd just have to visit them all on the way. Decades later, pubs still dominate Dublin's scene. They normally close at 11:30pm Sunday through Wednesday and 12:30am Thursday through Saturday, but an increasing number of establishments are closing later. Some of the best pubs in Temple Bar serve their brews until 2:30am. Begin your journey at the gates of Trinity College, stumble onto Grafton St., teeter down Camden St., stagger onto South Great Georges St., and finally, crawl triumphantly into the Temple Bar area. Don't expect to do any early sightseeing the next morning.

The Stag's Head, 1 Dame Ct. (☎679 3701), in Temple Bar. Gorgeously atmospheric Victorian pub with stained-glass windows, marble-topped round tables, and a gigantic moose head suspended above the bar. Excellent pub grub. Pint €4.10. Entrees €5-11. Live music W-Sa 9:30pm-midnight. Open M-Th 10:30am-11:30pm, F-Sa 10:30am-12:30am, Su 11:30am-11pm. Kitchen open M-Sa until 4pm.

The Porter House, 16-18 Parliament St. (☎679 8847), in Temple Bar. A huge selection of beer including 10 home brews—but you won't find Guinness here. Live music every night. Pint €3.90. Open M-W 11:30am-11:30pm, Th-F 11:30am-2am, Sa 11:30am-2:30am, Su 11:30am-11pm. Irish pub grub until 9:30pm.

Whelan's, 25 Wexford St. (☎478 0766), south of Temple Bar near St. Stephen's Green. Dark, busy pub hosts big-name acts. Carvery lunch (starter, entree, dessert, and tea; €10) and entrees (€6-12) served noon-2pm. Live music nightly from 8:30pm (doors open 8pm). Cover €8-21. Open Su-W 10am-1:30am, Th-Sa 10:30am-2:30am.

The Celt, 81-82 Talbot St. (☎878 8665), north of Trinity College. Step out of the city and into Olde Ireland at this touristy spot. Small, comfortably worn, and truly welcoming with low tables and stools. Pint €3.90. Trad M-Sa 9pm-close, Su 5-7pm and 9-11pm. Open M-Th 10:30am-11:30pm, F-Sa 10:30am-12:30am, Su 12:30-11pm.

McDaid's, 3 Harry St. (☎679 4395), off Grafton St. across from S. Anne St. Old books on high shelves recall McDaid's status as the center of the 1950s Irish literary scene. The din of the after-work, older crowd fills the pub. Pint €4.30. Open M-Th 10:30am-11:30pm, F-Sa 10:30am-12:30am, Su 12:30-11:30pm.

Davy Byrne's, 21 Duke St. (☎677 5217), off Grafton St. Lively, middle-aged crowd fills the pub where Joyce set the Cyclops chapter in *Ulysses*. Outdoor cafe; traditional Irish food (€8-11) served until 8:45pm. Pint €4.30. Trad Su-Tu 9-11pm. Open M-Th 11am-11:30pm, F-Sa 9am-12:30am, Su 12:30-11pm.

CLUBS

Clubs open at 10:30 or 11pm, but things don't heat up until at least midnight, after pubs start closing. Clubbing is an expensive way to end the night; covers run €7-20 and mixed drinks cost €7-10. Some of the best clubs are run by their attached upstairs bars in the Temple Bar district. Prominent gay nightlife spots are in the "pink triangle" zone of Parliament and S. Great Georges St. Check out the queer pages of *In Dublin* for gay-friendly pubs, restaurants, and clubs, or try **Gay Switchboard Dublin** for event info. (☎872 1055. Available M-F 7:30-9:30pm, Sa 3:30-6pm.)

Fitzsimons Bar and Nightclub, 21-22 Wellington Quay (☎677 9315; www.fitzsimonshotel.com), in Temple Bar. Their motto is "4 Floors, 4 Bars, & 4 DJs–All 4U!" Free nightclub in the basement, live acts and bands on the first floor, and Dublin's only rooftop terrace bar. Open daily 11:30am-2:30am.

Buskers Bar and Boomerang's Nightclub, Fleet St. (☎612 9246), in Temple Bar. 3 bars, modern decor, and sizzling music attract a student crowd. Pint €4.65. 21+. Cover W-Th €5, F €10, Sa €15. Bar open M-Sa 11:30am-2am, Su noon-1am. Downstairs nightclub open W-Sa 9pm-2:30am.

The Dragon, 64-65 S. Great Georges St. (☎478 1590), south of Temple Bar, a few doors down from The George. Largest gay club in Dublin packs a happening crowd on weekends. Huge bar, lounge, dance floor, and high blue-lit ceilings with fuzzy lamps. Pints from €4.70. 18+. Open M and Th-Sa 5pm-2:30am, Tu-W 5-11:30pm, Su 5-11pm.

The Front Lounge, 33-34 Parliament St. (☎670 4112). The red velvet seats of this gay-friendly bar are filled nightly by a young, trendy, and mixed crowd. Pint €4.40. Mixed drinks €8.50. Open M-Th noon-midnight, F-Sa 3pm-3am, Su 3pm-midnight.

Traffic Bar and Nightclub, 54 Middle Abbey St. (☎873 4800), off O'Connell St. DJ spins hip-hop, house, or techno as a 20-something crowd gets down. Su gay night. 21+. Occasional cover €6-10. Open M-W noon-11:30pm, Th and Sa noon-2:30am, F 3pm-2:30am, Su noon-1:30am. Downstairs nightclub open Th-Sa 11pm-2:30am.

DAYTRIP FROM DUBLIN

BOYNE VALLEY. Ireland's greatest archaeological treasures are in Boyne Valley, 50km from Dublin. Between Slane and Drogheda lie 40 Neolithic tombs from the fourth millennium BC. **Newgrange** is the most spectacular; a roof box over the entrance allows a solitary beam of sunlight to shine directly into the tomb for 17min. on the winter solstice, a breathtaking sight that is simulated on the tour.

Newgrange can only be entered with admission to **Brú na Bóinne Visitors Centre,** near Donore on the south side of the River Boyne, across from the tombs. *(By car, take the M1 motorway, exit at Donore, and continue 3km to the Visitor's Centre. By bus, take bus to Drogheda and another to Brú na Bóinne (1hr.). ☎041 988 0300. Open daily May 9am-6:30pm; June-Sept. 9am-7pm; Mar.-Apr. and Oct. 9:30am-5:30pm; Nov.-Feb. 9:30am-5pm. Arrive early; tours sell out 2-3hr. in advance. Centre and Newgrange tour €5.70, students €2.90.)* A group of well-preserved Norman castles—including **Trim Castle,** conquered by Mel Gibson in *Braveheart*—overlooks **Trim** proper on the River Boyne. *(By car, drive 40min. down Trim Rd. Buses run direct every 15min. from Busáras Central Bus Station to Trim. ☎046 943 8619. Open Easter-Sept. daily 10am-6pm; Oct. daily 10am-5:30pm; Nov.-Easter Sa-Su 10am-5pm. Tours every 45min. Grounds €1.60, students €1. Tour and grounds €7/1.30.)*

IRELAND

SOUTHEASTERN IRELAND

Ireland's southeastern region is famous for its strawberries and oysters, and their aphrodisiacal powers may account for the gaggles of children playing on the beaches. Roundtowers, built by monks to defend against Viking attacks, litter the countryside from the medieval city of Kilkenny to the Rock of Cashel. The lush green fields and stunning mountain views provide a vibrant contrast to the trad and rock pumping through the pubs of Waterford, Kilkenny, and Wexford.

FERRIES TO FRANCE AND BRITAIN

Stena Line (☎053 61560; www.stenaline.ie) and **Irish Ferries** (☎053 33158) run from Rosslare Harbour to Pembroke and Fishguard, Wales (2-6 per day) and to Roscoff and Cherbourg, FRA (1 every other day). **Eurail** passes are valid on ferries to France.

THE WICKLOW MOUNTAINS ☎0404

Over 600m tall, carpeted in fragrant heather, dotted with ubiquitous yellow flowers, and pleated by sparkling rivers, the Wicklow summits provide a tranquil stop just outside Dublin. The **Wicklow Way,** a 125km hiking trail, winds past grazing sheep, scattered villages, and monastic ruins. The **National Park Information Office,** between the two lakes, is the best source for hiking advice (☎45425. Open May-Aug. daily 10am-6pm, closed for lunch; Sept.-Apr. Sa-Su 10am-dusk.) When the office is closed, call the **ranger office** (☎45800) in nearby Trooperstown Wood. The valley of **Glendalough** is home to St. Kevin's 6th-century monastery. At the secluded **Glendalough International Hostel (HI) ❷,** 5min. up the road from the Glendalough Visitor Centre, guests won't hear rambunctious travelers, just chirping birds. (☎45342; www.anoige.ie. Breakfast €4-6.50; request it the night before. Towels €1.50. Laundry €5. Internet €1 per 15min., €2 per 40min. Dorms June-Oct. €23, Nov.-May €18; quads €100. €2 HI discount. MC/V.) Just 1.5km up the road, **Laragh** has food options and plenty of B&Bs. **St. Kevin's Bus Service** (☎01 281 8119; www.glendaloughbus.com) arrives at the Glendalough Visitor's Centre from the end of Dawson St. nearest to St. Stephen's Green in Dublin. (Buses run M-Sa 11:30am and 6pm, Su 11:30am and 7pm; €11.) Public transportation in the mountains is extremely limited; the bus service or taxis are your best bet. **Glendalough Cabs** (☎087 972 9452; www.glendaloughcabs.com) offers 24hr. service.

ROSSLARE HARBOUR ☎053

Rosslare Harbour is a useful departure point for ferries to Wales or France. **Trains** run from the port to Dublin and Limerick via Waterford. **Buses** run from the port to: Dublin (3hr., 10-12 per day); Galway via Waterford (6 hr., 4 per day); Limerick (M-Sa 5 per day, Su 3 per day); Tralee (M-Sa 4 per day, Su 2 per day). Contact Wexford Tourism (☎912 3111) for **tourist information.**

KILKENNY ☎056

Eight churches share the streets with 80 pubs in Kilkenny (pop. 30,000), Ireland's best-preserved medieval town, which pairs relics from the past with thoroughly modern nightlife. **Tynan Walking Tours** explore Kilkenny's history and architecture. (☎087 265 1745; www.tynantours.com. 1hr. tours depart from tourist office. €6, students €5.50.) The 13th-century **Kilkenny Castle** housed the Earls of Ormonde until 1932. (☎772 1450. Open daily June-Aug. 9:30am-7pm; Sept. 10am-6:30pm; Oct.-Mar. 10:30am-12:45pm and 2-5pm; Apr.-May 10:30am-5pm. Required tour €5, students €2.) Climb the 30m tower of **St. Canice's Cathedral,** up the hill off Dean St., for a panoramic view. (☎776 4971. Open June-Aug. M-Sa 9am-6pm, Su 2-6pm; Apr.-May and Sept. M-Sa 10am-1pm and 2-5pm, Su 2-5pm; Oct.-Mar. M-Sa 10am-1pm and 2-4pm, Su 2-4pm. €3, students €2. Tower €2/1.50.) Conveniently located near the pubs on High St., the **Kilkenny Tourist Hostel ❶**, 35 Parliament St., offers clean, spacious rooms. (☎776 3541. Check-in 9am-11pm. Check-out 10am. Dorms €17; doubles €42; quads €76. Cash only.) **La Creperie ❶**, 80 John St., serves hot, satisfying, and fresh food, including crepes (€3-7) and sandwiches (€3.50-5), at affordable prices. (Open M-Sa 10am-6pm, Su 10am-4pm.) A **Dunnes** supermarket is on Kieran St. (☎776 1655. Open daily 24hr.) Start your pub crawl at the end of **Parliament Street,** then work your way to the wilder bars on **John Street,** which are open later. **Trains** (☎772 2024) arrive at the station on Dublin Rd. from Dublin (2hr., €22) and Waterford (45min., €10). **Buses** (☎77 879 000) also arrive at the Dublin Rd. station and the city center from: Cork (3hr., 5 per day, €16); Dublin (2hr., 6 per day, €11); Galway (5hr., 5 per day, €20); Limerick (2½hr., 4 per day, €16); Rosslare Harbour (2hr., 2 per day, €14); Waterford (1½hr., 2 per day, €9). The **tourist office** is on Rose Inn St. (☎775 1500; www.southeastireland.com. Open May-Sept. M-F 9am-6pm, Sa 10am-6pm; Oct.-Apr. M-Sa 9am-5pm.)

WATERFORD ☎051

Waterford is Ireland's oldest city, founded in AD 914 by the grandson of Viking Ivor the Boneless. The small city, situated on a beautiful river, attracts travelers looking to shop, club, and then relax on the beaches a mere 11km away. At the fully operational ■**Waterford Crystal Factory**, 3km away on N25, tours allow you to watch experienced cutters and engravers transform grains of sand into molten glass and finally into sparkling crystal. The showroom is free and contains the largest collection of Waterford crystal in the world. Catch the **City Imp** minibus outside Dunnes on Michael St. (10-15min., every 15-20min., €1.30) and request a stop at the factory. (☎332 500; www.waterfordvisitorcentre.com. Open daily Mar.-Oct. 8:30am-6pm; Nov.-Feb. 9am-5pm. 1hr. tours every 15-20min. during high season. €9, students €6.) **Waterford Treasures** at the granary has Viking artifacts and the only remaining item of Henry VIII's clothing, a velvet hat. (☎304 500; www.waterfordtreasures.com. Open Apr.-Sept. daily 9:30am-6pm, Oct.-Mar. M-F 10am-5pm, Sa-Su 11am-5pm. €7, students €5.) Jack Burtchaell keeps audiences entertained on his ■**Walking Tour of Historic Waterford.** (☎873 711. 1hr. tours depart from Waterford Treasures Mar.-Oct. daily 11:45am and 1:45pm. €5.)

Jane and Robert Hovenden provide clean, quiet accommodations at **Mayor's Walk B&B ❸**. From the bus station, walk down the quay to the clock tower and turn right. Head up the main street and turn right at the traffic lights. Mayor's Walk is the second road on the left up the hill. (☎855 427; mayorswalkbandb@eircom.net. Breakfast included. Singles €27; doubles €50. Cash only.) ■**Haricot's Wholefood Restaurant ❸**, 11 O'Connell St., serves hearty portions of healthful food with special consideration for dietary restrictions. The owners' parents grow all of the vegetables themselves, as reflected in the freshness, color, and incredible taste of the dishes. (☎841 299. Entrees €9.80. Open daily 10am-6pm.) The quay is crowded with pubs; **T&H Doolan's,** 31-32 George's St., has been serving drinks in its dark wooden interior for 300 years. (Pub food €14-19. Trad nightly at 9:30pm. Open M-Th 10am-11:30pm, F-Sa 10am-12:30am, Su 12:30pm-11pm.) A younger set flocks to the "Golden Mile" of bars at the intersection of **John, Manor,** and **Parnell Streets.** Try **Ruby's Nightclub** (☎858 130) on the corner, or **Oxygen** (☎873 693) across the street.

Trains (☎317 886; www.irishrail.ie) leave from the quay across the bridge for: Dublin (2½hr., M-F 8 per day); Kilkenny (50min., 6 per day); Limerick; Rosslare Harbour. **Buses** depart for: Cork (2½hr.); Dublin (2¾hr.); Galway (4¾hr.); Limerick (2½hr.). The **tourist office** is on the Quay across from the bus station. (☎875 823; www.southeastireland.com. Open M-F 9:15am-6pm, Sa 10am-6pm.)

CASHEL

☎062

Cashel sits at the foot of the 90m **Rock of Cashel** (also called **St. Patrick's Rock** or **Cashel of the Kings**), a limestone outcropping topped by medieval buildings. (☎61437. Open daily mid-June to mid-Sept. 9am-7pm; mid-Mar. to mid-June and mid-Sept. to mid-Oct. 9am-5:30pm; mid.-Oct. to mid-Mar. 9am-4:30pm. €5.30, students €2.10.) The internationally acclaimed **Brú Ború Heritage Centre,** at the base of the Rock, stages traditional music and dance performances. (☎61122; www.comhaltas.com. Mid-June to mid-Sept. Tu-Sa 9pm.) Head down the cow path from the Rock to see the ruins of **Hore Abbey,** built by Cistercian monks and currently inhabited by sheep. The **Bolton Library,** on John St., houses ecclesiastical texts and rare manuscripts. (☎61944. Open M-F 10am-4:30pm; inquire at the tourist office about tours.) Enjoy a view of the Rock from the homey **O'Brien's Holiday Lodge ❷**, a 10min. walk out of town on Dundrum Rd. To get there from the tourist office, walk down Main St. and turn right at the end; continue until you see the lodge on the left. (☎61003; www.cashel-lodge.com. Laundry €10-12. Camping available separately, €10 per person including showers. Dorms €18-20; doubles €55-65; triples €75; quads €80. Cash only.)

Buses (☎061 313 333) leave from Main St. near the tourist office for Cork (1½hr., 6 per day, €10) and Dublin (3hr., 6 per day, €10). Buy tickets in the SPAR grocery store at the counter. The **tourist office** is in City Hall on Main St. (☎62511; www.casheltouristoffice.com. Open Mar.-Oct. daily 9:30am-5:30pm; Nov.-Feb. M-F 9:30am-5:30pm.)

SOUTHWESTERN IRELAND

The dramatic landscape of Southwestern Ireland ranges from lakes and mountains to stark, ocean-battered cliffs. Outlaws and rebels once hid among the coves and glens, but the region is now dominated by tourists taking in the stunning scenery of the Ring of Kerry and Cork's southern coast.

FERRIES TO BRITAIN AND FRANCE

Swansea-Cork Ferries, 52 S. Mall, runs passengers between Cork and Swansea, BRI. (☎021 427 1166. 10hr., 1 per day, from €42.) **Brittany Ferries,** 42 Grand Parade, sails from Cork to Roscoff, FRA. (☎021 427 7801. 12hr., Sa only, from €83.)

CORK

☎021

Cork (pop. 150,000) hosts most of the cultural activities in the southwest. The county gained the nickname "Rebel Cork" from its residents' early opposition to the British Crown and 20th-century support for Irish independence. Today, Cork's river quays and pub-lined streets reveal architecture both grand and grimy, evidence of the city's legacy of resistance and reconstruction.

TRANSPORTATION

Trains: Kent Station, Lower Glanmire Rd. (☎450 6766; www.irishrail.ie), across the North Channel from the city center. Open M-Sa 6:30am-8pm, Su 7:50am-8pm. To: **Dublin** (3hr., 9 per day, €55); **Killarney** (2hr.; M-Sa 7 per day, Su 4 per day; €22); **Limerick** (1½hr., 8 per day, €22); **Tralee** (2½hr., 3 per day, €28).

Buses: Parnell Pl. (☎450 8188), 2 blocks east of St. Patrick's Bridge on Merchant's Quay. Info desk open daily 9am-5:30pm. **Bus Éireann** travels to: **Dublin** (4½hr.; M-Sa 6 per day, Su 5 per day; €10); **Galway** (4hr., 12 per day, €19); **Killarney** (2hr.; M-Sa 13 per day, Su 11 per day; €15); **Limerick** (2hr., 14 per day, €15); **Rosslare Harbour** (4hr., 2 per day, €21); **Sligo** (7hr., 5 per day, €25); **Tralee** (2½hr., 12 per day, €16); **Waterford** (2¼hr., M-Sa 13 per day, €16).

Public Transportation: Downtown **buses** run every 10-30min. M-Sa 7:30am-11:15pm, with reduced service Su 10am-11:15pm. Fares from €1.30. Catch buses and pick up schedules along St. Patrick's St., across from the Father Matthew statue.

ORIENTATION AND PRACTICAL INFORMATION

The center of Cork is compact and pedestrian-friendly, framed by the North and South Channels of the River Lee. From the bus station along the North Channel, **Merchant's Quay** leads west to **St. Patrick's Street,** which curves through the center of the city and becomes **Grand Parade.** On the other side of the North Channel, across St. Patrick's Bridge, **MacCurtain Street** runs east to **Lower Glanmire Road** and passes the train station before becoming the N8 to Dublin. Downtown shopping and nightlife concentrates on **Washington, Oliver Plunkett,** and St. Patrick's Streets.

Tourist Office: Tourist House, Grand Parade (☎425 5100; www.corkkerry.ie), near the corner of South Mall, books accommodations (€4). Open June-Sept. M-F 9am-6pm, Sa 9am-5pm, Su (July only) 10am-5pm; Sept.-May M-Sa 9:15am-5pm.

Banks: Ulster Bank Limited, 88 St. Patrick's St. (☎427 0618; www.ulsterbank.ie). Open M 10am-5pm, Tu-F 10am-4pm. **Bank of Ireland,** 70 St. Patrick's St. (☎427 7177). Open M 10am-5pm, Tu-F 10am-4pm. Most banks in Cork have 24hr. **ATMs.**

Police (Garda): Anglesea St. (☎452 2000).

Pharmacies: Regional Late-Night Pharmacy, Wilton Rd. (☎434 4575), opposite the hospital. Bus #8. Open M-F 9am-10pm, Sa-Su 10am-10pm. **Phelan's Late Night,** 9 St. Patrick's St. (☎427 2511). Open M-F 8:30am-10pm, Sa 9am-10pm, Su 10am-10pm.

Hospital: Cork University Hospital, Wilton Rd. (☎454 6400). Bus#8.

Internet Access: **Wired To The World Internet Cafe,** 6 Thompson House, MacCurtain St. (www.wiredtotheworld.ie). Gaming, phone booths, and wireless. Internet €0.05 per min. Open daily 8am-midnight.

Post Office: Oliver Plunkett St. (☎485 1032). Open M-Sa 9am-5:30pm.

ACCOMMODATIONS

B&Bs cluster north of the river on **St. Patrick's Hill, Glanmire Road,** and **Wellington Road,** as well as on **Western Road** near University College. Cork is a popular destination, so call ahead June through August.

Brú Bar and Hostel, 57 MacCurtain St. (☎455 9667; www.bruhostel.com), located just north of the river. A lively place to stay up late and hit the attached bar with other guests (open 4pm-4am for guests). Continental breakfast included. Towels €2. Laundry €5. Free Internet. Check-in 1pm. Check-out 10:30am. 6-bed dorms €17; 4-bed dorms €21; doubles €50. MC/V. ❶

Sheila's Budget Accommodation Centre (IHH), 4 Belgrave Pl. (☎450 5562; www.sheilashostel.ie), off Wellington Rd. at the top of York St. Hill. Sauna €2 for 40min. Breakfast €3. Internet €1 per 20min., €2.50 per hr. Reception 24hr. Check-in 2pm. Check-out 10:30am. Dorms €14-18; singles €40; doubles €52. ❶

Roman House, 3 St. John's Terr. (☎450 3606; www.romanhouse.info), on Upper John St. opposite Kinlay House. This colorful spot markets itself as a welcoming place for GLBT travelers. Full Irish breakfast included. Singles from €45; doubles from €65. ❹

Cork International Hostel (An Óige/HI), 1-2 Redclyffe, Western Rd. (☎454 3289), a 20min. walk from Grand Parade. A globe-trotting clientele, as the name implies. Continental breakfast €4, Irish breakfast €6.50. Internet €1 per 15min. Luggage storage available. Reception 8am-midnight. Check-in after 1pm. Check-out 10:30am. Dorms €17-19; doubles €42. €2 HI discount. ❶

FOOD

Inside the Shopping Centre on Paul St., **Tesco** is the biggest grocery store in town. (☎427 0791. Open M-Sa 8am-10pm, Su 10am-8pm.)

Tribes, 8 Tuckey St. (☎427 4446), off Oliver Plunkett St. Eclectic menu and global spectrum of coffee keeps the young crowd buzzing. Food served until 30min. before closing. Open M-Th 10:30am-midnight, F-Sa 10:30am-4am, Su 1-9:30pm. ❶

Quay Co-op, 24 Sullivan's Quay (☎317 7026), next to the South Channel. Vegetarian and vegan meals. Open M-F 9am-8pm, Sa 9am-6:15pm. ❷

Café Paradiso, 16 Lancaster Quay (☎427 7939), near the university campus. Award-winning vegetarian meals served in a Mediterranean setting. Menu changes often. Lunch €6-16. Dinner €11-23. Open Tu-Sa noon-3pm and 6:30-10:30pm. ❸

SIGHTS

Cork's sights are concentrated in the old city, the Shandon neighborhood to the north, and the university to the west. Reach all sights by foot; pick up the *Cork Area City Guide* (€1.50) at the tourist office to help you find your way around. In the old city, looming over Proby's Quay, **St. Finbarr's Cathedral** is a testament to the Victorian obsession with the neo-Gothic. The cathedral houses art exhibits in the summer. *(Bishop St. ☎963 387. Open M-F 10am-12:45pm and 2-5pm. €3, students €1.50.)* In Shandon, the steeple of **St. Anne's Church** houses the famous "Bells of Shandon," which you can ring before climbing to the top. Its four clock faces are notoriously out of sync, earning the church its nickname, "the four-faced liar." *(Walk up John Redmond St. and take a right at the Craft Centre; St. Anne's is on the right. ☎450 5906. Open M-Sa 10am-5:30pm. €6, students and seniors €5.)* In Western Cork, **University College Cork's** campus, built in 1845, has brooding Gothic buildings, manicured lawns, and sculpture-studded grounds. *(Main gate on Western Rd. ☎427 6871; www.ucc.ie.)* **Fitzgerald Park** has rose gardens, a pond, and art exhibits courtesy of the **Cork Public Museum.** *(From the front gate of UCC, follow the signposted walkway across the street. ☎427 0679. Open M-F 11am-1pm and 2:15-5pm, Su 3-5pm. Free.)* Don't miss the **Cork City Gaol** across the river from the park. Furnished cells, sound effects, and videos illustrate the experience of inmates at the 19th-century prison. *(☎430 5022; www.corkcitygaol.com. 1hr. audio tour. Open daily Mar.-Oct. 9:30am-6pm; Nov.-Feb. 10am-5pm. €6, students €5.)*

NIGHTLIFE

Try **Oliver Plunkett Street, Union Quay, Washington Street,** and **South Main Street** for pubs, clubs, and live music. Check out the *WhazOn? Cork* pamphlet, free at local shops, or the Thursday "Downtown" section in the *Evening Echo* newspaper. The busiest bar is **Reardens,** 26 Washington St. (☎427 1969; www.reardens.com. Live music W, F, Su. 23+. Open M-F 8am-2am, Sa-Su noon-2am.) **The Old Oak,** 113 Oliver Plunkett St., is huge, packed, and great for the 20s-30s crowd. (☎427 6165. Pint €4. Open M-Sa noon-1:45am, Su noon-1am.) **Court House Tavern,** 3 Cross St., off Washington St., attracts a younger crowd. (Open M-Sa 3pm-12:30am, Su 3pm-midnight.)

DAYTRIP FROM CORK

BLARNEY. Tourists eager for quintessential Irish scenery and a cold kiss head northwest from Cork to see **Blarney Castle** and its legendary Blarney Stone. Legend holds that those who kiss the stone will acquire the "gift of Irish gab." Visitors can explore the castle's many rooms; the top offers a beautiful view. *(Buses run from Cork to Blarney. 10-16 per day, round-trip €4.50. Open May-Aug. M-Sa 9am-7pm, Su 9:30am-5:30pm; Sept. M-Sa 9am-6:30pm, Su 9:30am-sunset; Oct.-Apr. M-Sa 9am-6pm, Su 9:30am-5:30pm. Last admission 30min. before closing. Castle and grounds €7, students €5.)*

SCHULL AND THE MIZEN HEAD PENINSULA ☎028

The peaceful seaside hamlet of Schull is an ideal base for exploring Ireland's craggy southwest tip. Although Schull has only 700 residents in the winter, its population swells to over 3000 in the summer. A calm harbor and numerous shipwrecks make it a diver's paradise; the **Schull Watersport Centre Ltd.** rents gear. (☎28554. Open June-Oct. M-F 9:30am-1pm and 2-6pm, Sa 10am-1pm and 2-6pm.) The coastal road winds past **Barley Coast Beach** and continues on to **Mizen Head.** The Mizen becomes more scenic and less populated to the west of Schull, but it's mobbed during July and August, when sun-loving vacationers pack the sandy beaches. **Betty Johnson's Bus Hire** offers tours of the area. (☎28410, mobile 086 265 6078. Call ahead. Open M-F 9:30am-6pm. €15-30.) In summer, **ferries** (☎28278) depart from Schull for Cape Clear Island (June-Sept. 2-3 per day, round-trip €13). At **Stanley House B&B ❹,** Colla Road, the friendly owners provide beautifully decorated lodgings with incredible views. From Colla Rd. at the end of Main St., take a right opposite the church ruins and follow the signs to the B&B. (☎28425; www.stanley-house.net. Reserve ahead. Singles €42; doubles €68; quads €90-100. MC/V.) **The Courtyard Bar and Restaurant ❷,** Main St., has fresh seafood options and an array of beers. (☎087 262 9778. Panini €5.50. Crab claws €10. Live music F-Su at 9:30pm. Open M-Th 10:30am-11:30pm, F-Sa 10:30am-12:30am, Su 10:30am-11pm. Kitchen open M-Th noon-5pm, F-Su noon-7pm.) **Buses** (☎021 450 8188; www.buseireann.ie) arrive in Schull from Cork (2-3 per day, €15) and Goleen (1-2 per day, €3.80). There is no other public transportation on the peninsula. Confident **bicyclists** can daytrip to Mizen Head (29km from Schull).

CAPE CLEAR ISLAND ☎028

A mere 125 people live year-round on the beautiful island of Cape Clear (Oileán Chléire), the historic seat of the O'Driscoll clan. The island provides asylum for gulls, petrels, and their attendant flocks of ornithologists at the **Cape Clear Bird Observatory** (☎39181) on North Harbour. The **Cape Clear Heritage Centre** has everything from a family tree of the ubiquitous O'Driscolls to a chair from the *Lusitania.* (Open June-Aug. M-Sa noon-5pm, Su 2-5pm. €4, students €2.) On the road to the Heritage Centre, **Cléire Goats** (☎39126) claims that its **goat's milk ice cream** is creamier than the generic bovine variety. **Cape Clear Island Youth Hostel (HI) ❶** has simple but clean rooms and a fantastic location on the secluded South Harbour. It's a 10min. walk from the pier; turn right onto the main road past the pottery shop and stay to the left. (☎41968; www.anoige.fenlon.net. Internet €2 per 15min.

Dorms €15.) To reach **Cuas an Uisce Campsite ❶,** follow the directions to the hostel but bear right before Ciarán Danny Mike's; it's 400m up on the left. (☎39119. Open June-Sept. Tent sites €7 per person.) **Ciarán Danny Mike's Pub ❸** (☎39153) serves pub grub (noon-6pm, €3-10) and dinner (7-10pm, €11-20). Groceries and hot food (€6-16) are available at pier-side **An Siopa Beag.** (☎39099. Open June-Aug. daily 10am-8pm; Sept.-May M-Sa 11am-4pm.) **Ferries** (☎28138) go to Schull (45min., 3-4 per day, round-trip €14). There is an **information office** in the pottery shop at the end of the pier. (☎39100. Open June-Sept. daily 11am-1pm and 3-6pm.)

KILLARNEY AND KILLARNEY NATIONAL PARK ☎064

The town of Killarney is just minutes from some of Ireland's most glorious natural scenery. Outside of town, forested mountains rise from the famous three **Lakes of Killarney** in the 95 sq. km national park. It could take an entire day to explore **Muckross House,** 5km south of Killarney on Kenmare Rd., a 19th-century manor and garden. A path leads to the 20m **Torc Waterfall,** the starting point for several short trails along beautiful **Torc Mountain.** It's a 3.5km stroll in the opposite direction to the **Meeting of the Waters,** a quiet spot where channels come together. Away from the paved path, the more secluded dirt trail through the **Yew Woods** is inaccessible to bikes.To get to the 14th-century **Ross Castle,** the last stronghold in Munster to fall to Cromwell's army, take a right on Ross Rd. off Muckross Rd. when leaving town. The castle is 3km from Killarney. For a more scenic route, take the footpaths from Knockreer, outside of town along New St. (☎35851. Open daily June-Aug. 9am-6:30pm; May and Sept. 10am-6pm; mid-Mar. to Apr. and Oct. 10am-5pm. €5.30, students €2.10) The nicest outdoor activity in the area is to bike around the **Gap of Dunloe,** which borders **Macgillycuddy's Reeks,** Ireland's highest mountain range. Or hop on a boat from Ross Castle to the head of the Gap (1½hr., €8; book at the tourist office). From **Lord Brandon's Cottage,** on the Gap trail, head left over the stone bridge, continue 3km to the church, and then turn right onto a winding road. Climb 2km and enjoy an 11km stroll downhill with breathtaking views. The 13km trip back to Killarney passes the ruins of **Dunloe Castle** (bear right after Kate Kearney's Cottage, turn left on the road to Fossa, and turn right on Killorglin Rd.).

Neptune's Hostel (IHH) ❶, on Bishop's Ln. off of New St., has a central location, clean dorms, and common spaces for meeting other travelers. (☎35255; www.neptuneshostel.com. Breakfast €2.50. Laundry €7. Free Internet. Free bike lockup. Check-in 1-3pm. Check-out 10am. Curfew 3am. Dorms €14-18; doubles €37-42. 10% 1st night discount with student ID. MC/V.) For delectable meat, seafood, and vegetarian dishes, try **The Stonechat ❸,** 8 Fleming's Ln., the best restaurant in Killarney. (☎34295. Lunch €7-10. Dinner €13-20. Early-bird dinner special 6-7:30pm, 3 courses for €20. Open M-Sa noon-4pm and 6-10pm.) Live music wafts down Killarney's streets on summer nights. A trendy 20-something crowd gets down in the lounge-like **McSorley's,** College St., which offers a change from the usual trad session. (☎39770. Pint €4. Open M-Sa noon-2:30am, Su noon-1:30am. Nightclub upstairs open 11:30pm-2:30am. Cover Sa €10.) The popular **Grand Bar and Nightclub,** Main St., hosts nightly trad (9:30-11pm) and live rock (11:30pm-1:30am) performances. (☎31159. Pint €4. Open M-Sa 7:30pm-2:30am, Su 7:30pm-1:30am. Disco in back open 11pm-3am. Cover €5 after 11pm, Sa €8.) **Trains** (☎31067) leave from Killarney station, off E. Avenue Rd., to Cork (2hr., 7 per day, €22), Dublin (3½hr., 7 per day, €57), and Limerick (3hr., 7 per day, €25). **Buses** (☎30011) leave from Park Rd. for Belfast (4 per day, €33), Cork (2hr., 10 per day, €15), and Dublin (6hr., 6 per day, €22). **O'Sullivan's,** on Lower New St., rents **bikes.** (☎31282. Open daily 8:30am-6:30pm. €12 per day, €70 per week.) The **tourist office** is on Beech Rd. (☎31633; www.corkkerry.ie. Open July-Aug. M-Sa 9am-8pm, Su 10am-1pm and 2:15-6pm; June and Sept. M-Sa 9am-6pm, Su 10am-1pm and 2:15-6pm; Oct.-May M-Sa 9:15am-1pm and 2:15-5pm.)

RING OF KERRY ☎066

The Southwest's most celebrated peninsula offers picturesque villages, ancient forts, and rugged mountains. You'll have to brave congested roads hogged by tour buses, but rewards await those who take the time to explore on foot or by bike.

TRANSPORTATION

The term "Ring of Kerry" usually describes the entire **Iveragh Peninsula,** though it technically refers to the ring of roads circumnavigating it. Hop on the circuit run by **Bus Éireann** (☎064 30011), based in Killarney (mid-June to Aug., 1 per day, departs 1:15pm, returns approx. 5:30pm; entire ring in 1 day €21). Stops include Cahersiveen (from Killarney 2½hr., €11.60) and Caherdaniel (from Cahersiveen 1hr., €7.50). Or, book a bus tour with a private company; offices are scattered across the town, and many accommodations can book a tour for you.

CAHERSIVEEN ☎066

Although best known as the birthplace of patriot Daniel O'Connell, Cahersiveen (CAR-sah-veen) also serves as a useful base for jaunts to Valentia Island, the Skelligs, and local archaeological sites. To see the ruins of **Ballycarbery Castle,** head past the barracks on Bridge St., left over the bridge, and left off the main road. About 200m past the castle turn-off stands a pair of Ireland's best-preserved stone forts, **Cahergall** and **Leacanabuaile Fort.** Enjoy scenic views of the countryside and castle from the second-floor balcony at **Sive Hostel (IHH) ❶,** 15 East End, Church St. (☎947 2717. Laundry €8. Dorms €14; doubles €33-36. Camping €7 per person.) The pubs on **Main Street** still retain the authentic feel of their former proprietors' main business, including a general store, a blacksmithy, and a leather shop. The Ring of Kerry **bus** stops in front of Banks Store on Main St. (mid-June to Aug., 2 per day) and continues on to Killarney (2½hr., €12) and Caherdaniel (1hr., €7.50). The **tourist office** is across from the bus stop. (☎947 2589. Open June to mid-Sept. M, W, F 9:15am-1pm and 2-5:15pm, Tu and Th 9:15am-1pm.)

SNEEN ☎064

Sneen is usually a quick stop for tour buses on the Ring of Kerry, but this tiny locale is worth more than just a short 20min. visit; in years past, it has won awards for being the tidiest and prettiest town in all of Ireland. The two sides of town are connected by a stone bridge. The cheerful **Bank House B&B ❸,** in North Sq., has delicious breakfast options. (☎45226; the_bank_house@yahoo.ie. €30 per person sharing.) **The Village Kitchen ❷,** in the very center of town, serves fresh seafood and sandwiches made on homemade traditional brown bread. (☎45281. Entrees €8-10. Open daily 9:30am-8:30pm.)

DINGLE PENINSULA

For decades, the Ring of Kerry's undertouristed counterpart, the Dingle Peninsula, has maintained a healthy ancient-site-to-tour-bus ratio. Only recently has the Ring's tourist blitz begun to encroach upon the spectacular cliffs and sweeping beaches of this Irish-speaking peninsula.

TRANSPORTATION

Dingle Town is most easily reached by **Bus Éireann** from Tralee (1¼hr.; M-Sa 4-6 per day, Su 2-5 per day; €10). There is no public transportation on the peninsula; many visitors explore the area by **bike.**

IRELAND

DINGLE TOWN

☎915

Lively Dingle Town is the adopted home of **Fungi the Dolphin,** who has lived in the harbor for over two decades and is now a focus of the tourism industry. Visitors can swim with Fungi daily 9-11am by booking a boat trip from the tourist office. **Sciúird Archaeology Tours** leave from the Dingle pier for bus tours of the area's ancient spots. (☎1606. 2½hr., 2 per day, €15.) **Moran's Tours** runs trips to Slea Head, passing through majestic scenery and stopping at historic sites. (☎1155. 2 per day, €15.) **Ballintaggart Hostel (IHH) ❶,** a 25min. walk east of town on Tralee Rd. (N86), is supposedly haunted by the murdered wife of the Earl of Cork. According to local legend, the Earl tried to kill her with poisoned mushrooms, but when that failed, he resorted to strangling her instead. The hostel has a quiet policy after 11pm. (☎1454; info@dingleaccomodation.com. Towels €1.50. Laundry €8. Open Apr.-Oct. Dorms €14-19; doubles €52-70. Tent sites €8. MC/V.) The busy **Homely House Cafe ❷,** Green St., has a varied menu, including fish, sandwiches, and salads. (☎2431; www.homelyhouse.com. Entrees €4-10. Open July-Aug. M-Tu 11am-5pm, W-Sa 11am-5pm and 6-10pm; Sept.-June M-Sa 11am-5pm.) The **tourist office** is on Strand St. (☎1188. Open mid-June to mid-Sept. M-Sa 9am-7pm, Su 10am-1pm and 2:15-5pm; mid-Sept. to mid-June daily 9am-1pm and 2:15-5pm.)

SLEA HEAD, VENTRY, AND DUNQUIN

☎915

The most rewarding way to see the cliffs and crashing waves of Dunquin and Slea Head is to **bike** along the predominantly flat **Slea Head Drive.** Past Dingle Town toward Slea Head, the village of Ventry (Ceann Trá) is home to a sandy **beach** and the **Celtic and Prehistoric Museum,** a massive collection that includes a 50,000-year-old woolly mammoth. (☎9191; www.celticmuseum.com. Open Mar.-Nov. daily 10am-5:30pm; call ahead Dec.-Feb. €5, students €4.) The **Ballybeag Hostel ❶** in Ventry is out of the way but offers low rates. (☎9876; www.iol.ie/~balybeag. Laundry €3. Dorms €15; doubles €44. Cash only.)

North of Slea Head and Ventry, the scattered settlement of Dunquin (Dún Chaoin) consists of stone houses, a pub, and little else. Past Dunquin on the road to Ballyferriter, the **Great Blasket Centre** has excellent exhibits about the isolated Blasket Islands. (☎6444. Open daily July-Aug. 10am-7pm; Easter-June and Sept.-Oct. 10am-6pm. Last admission 45min. before closing. €3.70, students €1.30.) At the **Dun Chaoin An Óige Hostel (HI) ❶** in Ballyferriter, on the Dingle Way across from the turn-off to the Blasket Centre, each bunk has a panoramic ocean view. (☎6121; mailbox@anoige.ie. Breakfast €4. Reception 9-10am and 5-10pm. Lockout 10am-5pm. Open Feb.-Nov. Dorms €15-17; doubles €34. €2 HI discount. MC/V.) **Kruger's,** the westernmost pub in Europe, has music sessions and great views. (☎6127. Live music Tu, Th, Sa 9:30pm, Su 7:30pm. Open M-Th 11am-11:30pm, F-Sa 11am-12:30pm, Su 11am-11pm.)

TRALEE

☎066

The economic and residential capital of County Kerry, Tralee (pop. 20,000) is a good departure point for excursions to the Ring of Kerry or the Dingle Peninsula. The **Kerry County Museum,** in Ashe Memorial Hall on Denny St., uses advanced technology to present the history of Ireland. (☎712 7777; www.kerrymuseum.ie. Open June-Aug. daily 9:30am-5:30pm; Sept.-Dec. Tu-Sa 9:30am-5pm; Jan.-Mar. Tu-F 10am-4:30pm; Apr.-May Tu-Sa 9:30am-5:30pm. €8, students €6.50.) During the last week of August, Tralee hosts the nationally known **Rose of Tralee Festival,** at which lovely Irish lasses compete for the title of "Rose of Tralee." Though lodging rates in Tralee are slightly higher than average, the clean rooms, hardwood floors, TVs, and excellent showers make the **Whitehouse Budget Accommodation and B&B ❸,** in Boherbee across from the bus station, a great choice. (☎712 9174; www.whitehousetralee.com. Wheelchair-accessible. Continental breakfast included. Dorms €20; singles €40; doubles €50-60.) **The Allegro Restaurant ❷**, 7 Castle St., serves tasty pizza, pasta, and steaks at affordable prices. (☎712 2704. Entrees €9-18. Open daily 10am-11pm.) **Trains** depart from the station on Oakpark Rd. for: Cork (2½hr., 3-5 per day, €29); Dublin (4hr., 3-6 per day, €57); Galway (5-6hr., 3 per day, €57); Killarney (40min., 4 per day, €8). **Buses** leave from the train station for: Cork (2½hr., 8 per day, €16); Galway (9 per day, €20); Killarney (40min., 10-14 per day, €7.30); Limerick (2¼hr., 10 per day, €15). To get from the station to the **tourist office** in Ashe Memorial Hall, head down Edward St., turn right on Castle St., and then left on Denny St. The well-informed staff provides free maps. (☎712 1288. Open July-Aug. M-Sa 9am-7pm, Su 10am-6pm; Sept.-May M-Sa 9am-6pm.)

WESTERN IRELAND

Even Dubliners will say that the west is the "most Irish" part of Ireland; in remote areas you may hear Gaelic being spoken almost as often as English. The potato famine was most devastating in the west—entire villages emigrated or died—and the current population is still less than half of what it was in 1841. The mountainous landscapes from Connemara north to Ballina are great for hiking and cycling.

LIMERICK ☎061

Although its 18th-century Georgian streets and parks are regal and elegant, 20th-century industrial and commercial development cursed Limerick (pop. 80,000) with a featureless urban feel. The city gained a reputation for violence, and Frank McCourt's celebrated memoir *Angela's Ashes* revealed its squalor. But now, with help from the EU and a strong student scene, Limerick is a city on the rise. It is a fine place to stay en route to points west, but perhaps best seen in a single day. The **Hunt Museum,** in the Custom House on Rutland St., holds a gold crucifix that Mary, Queen of Scots gave to her executioner, as well as a coin reputed to be one of the infamous 30 pieces of silver paid to Judas by the Romans. (☎312 833; www.huntmuseum.com. Open M-Sa 10am-5pm, Su 2-5pm. €7.20, students €5.80.)

Limerick suffered from a series of hostel closures in 2002 and another smaller wave in 2005, but a number of B&Bs can be found on O'Connell St. or Ennis Rd. **Mount Gerard B&B ❸,** O'Connell Ave., has rooms in a Victorian house. Walk down O'Connell St. away from the center of town for about 15min. until the name changes to O'Connell Ave. The B&B is across from the Model School. (☎314 981. Breakfast included. €35 per person. MC/V.) **O'Grady's Cellar Restaurant ❷,** 118 O'Connell St., serves traditional favorites in a cozy underground atmosphere. (☎418 286; www.ogradyscellarrestaurant.com. Entrees €8.50-14. 4-course lunch special M-F until 4pm, €10. Open daily 9am-10:30pm.) Limerick's student population adds spice to the nightlife scene during term time. The area where **Denmark Street** and **Cornmarket Row** intersect is a good place to quench your thirst or listen to live music. **Dolan's,** 3-4 Dock Rd., hosts rambunctious local patrons and nightly trad in its dark interior. (☎314 483. Entrees €6-10. Lunch menu €3.50-8; served noon-7pm. Music nightly 9:30pm-close. Pub open M 7:30am-11:30pm, Tu-Th 9am-11:30pm, F-Sa 8am-2am, Su 10am-11pm.)

Trains (☎315 555) leave for Cork (2½hr., 5-6 per day, €22) and Dublin (2½hr., 8-9 per day, €42). **Buses** (☎313 333; www.buseireann.ie) leave Colbert Station, off Parnell St., for Cork (2hr., 14 per day, €15), Dublin (3½hr., 13 per day, €12), and Galway (2½hr., 1 per hr., €15). The **tourist office** is on Arthurs Quay. From the station, walk down Davis St., turn right on O'Connell St., and take a left at Arthurs Quay Mall; the office is on the corner of the park. (☎317 522. Open July-Aug. M-F 9am-6pm, Sa-Su 9:30am-5:30pm; Sept.-June reduced hours.)

ENNIS AND DOOLIN ☎065

Ennis's proximity to Shannon Airport and the Burren makes it a common stopover for tourists, though there is little to do in the town itself. **Abbey Tourist Hostel ❶**, Harmony Row, welcomes guests with flowers. (☎682 2620. Continental breakfast included. Towels €1. Dorms €16-18; singles €27; doubles €44. MC/V.) Overfilled sandwiches bring locals to **Henry's ❶**, in the Abbey St. parking lot by the river. (☎682 2848. Open M-W 10:30am-6pm, Th-Sa 10:30am-6pm and 7-11pm.) At **Cruises Pub**, on Abbey St., local musicians appear nightly for cozy trad sessions in one of the oldest buildings (ca. 1658) in Co. Clare. (☎684 1800. Open M-Th 4pm-12:30am, F-Sa 4pm-2am, Su noon-12:30am.) **Glor**, a state-of-the-art performance center, features eclectic music, theater, and dance shows. (☎684 3103; www.glor.ie. Box office open M-Sa 10am-5pm. Tickets €12-25.) **Trains** (☎684 0444; www.irishrail.ie) leave from Station Rd. for Dublin (7 per day, €42). **Buses** (☎682 4177) also leave from Station Rd. every hour for: Cork (3hr., €17); Dublin (4hr., €16); Galway (1hr., €12); Limerick (40min., €9); Shannon Airport (40min., €6). The **tourist office** is on Arthur's Row, off O'Connell Square. (☎28366; www.shannonregiontourism.ie. Open June-Sept. M-Sa 9:30am-5:30pm; Oct.-Dec. Tu-Sa 9:30am-1pm and 2-5:30pm; Jan.-May M-F 9:30am-1pm and 2-5:30pm.)

As a shrine to Irish music, the little village of **Doolin** draws thousands every year to its three pubs: **McDermott's** and **McGann's** in the Upper Village and **O'Connor's** in the Lower Village. **Buses** go to Dublin via Ennis and Limerick (#15; 5¼hr., 2 per day) and Galway (#50; 1½hr., 2 per day).

THE CLIFFS OF MOHER AND THE BURREN ☎065

Plunging 213m straight down to the open sea, the **Cliffs of Moher** provide incredible views of the Kerry Mountains, the Twelve Bens mountain range, and the Aran Islands. Be careful of extremely strong winds; they blow a few tourists off every year. Let's Go strongly discourages straying from the established paths. The shop and cafe have basic tourist information and a schedule of bus service to the cliffs. (☎708 1171. Open daily mid-July to mid-Aug. 9am-7:30pm; mid-Aug. to mid-July 9:30am-5:30pm.) To reach the cliffs, head 5km south of Doolin on R478, or hop on the Galway-Cork **bus** (in summer 2-3 per day). From Liscannor, **Cliffs of Moher Cruises** (☎708 6060; www.mohercruises.com) sails directly under the cliffs (1¾hr., 1 per day, €20). **Ferries** also run to the cliffs from Doolin (1hr., 2-3 per day, €20.)

The 260 sq. km landscape of the nearby **Burren** resembles an enchanted fairyland, with secluded coves, bright wildflowers, and 28 species of butterflies fluttering in the air. The old stone forts and isolated trees sprinkled around the countryside are supposedly home to leprechauns. The Burren town of **Lisdoonvarna** is synonymous with its **Matchmaking Festival**, a six-week long craic-and-snogging celebration that attracts over 10,000 singles each September. The **Hydro Hotel ❹** has festival information and nightly music. (☎707 4005; www.whites-hotelsireland.com. Full Irish breakfast included. Open Mar.-Oct. €45 per person; during festival €60. MC/V.) In the town of Ballyvaughan, guests at **O'Brien B&B ❸**, on Main St., enjoy the huge rooms and the fireplaces in the adjacent pub. The bus from Galway arrives in front of the B&B. (☎707 7003. Doubles from €30. MC/V.) There are **no ATMs** in Ballyvaughan. A **bus** (☎091 562 000) connects Galway to towns in the Burren a few times a day in summer but infrequently in winter.

GALWAY ☎091

As the cultural capital of Ireland and one of the fastest-growing cities in Europe, Galway (pop. 70,000) has a youthful, exuberant spirit. Performers dazzle crowds on the appropriately named Shop St., locals and tourists lounge in outdoor cafes, and hip crowds pack the pubs and clubs at night. In addition to its peaceful quay-side walks, Galway is only a short drive away from beautiful Connemara.

TRANSPORTATION AND PRACTICAL INFORMATION. **Trains** leave the station by Eyre Sq. (☎561 444; open daily 9am-6pm) for Dublin (3hr., 5-6 per day, €29) via Portarlington (€23-34); transfer at Portarlington for all other lines. **Buses** also leave from Eyre Sq. (☎562 000) for Belfast (7½hr., 3 per day, €30), Donegal (4hr., 5 per day, €18), and Dublin (4hr., every hr. on the ½hr., €14). The **tourist office,** on Forster St. near the train and bus stations, provides info on the Aran Islands, exchanges currency, and books accommodations. (☎537 700. Open daily 9am-5:45pm.) To access the Internet or make a cheap international phone call, head to **e-2008 Internet Cafe,** on Forster St. next to the tourist office. (☎532 652. Open daily 9am-midnight. €1.40 per 20min., €2.10 per 30min., €4 per hr.) The **post office** is at 3 Eglinton St. (☎534 727. Open M-Sa 9am-5:30pm.)

ACCOMMODATIONS AND FOOD. Most of the B&Bs in town are in the Salthill area or on College Rd. **Barnacle's Quay Street House (IHH) ❶,** 10 Quay St., is the most conveniently located hostel in Galway. Its bright, spacious rooms are perfect for crashing after a night on the town. (☎568 644; www.barnacles.ie. Light breakfast included. Towels €1. Laundry €8. Internet €1 per 15min. Check-in 2pm. Check-out 10:30am. All-female dorms available. 4- to 12-bed dorms €16-23; doubles €56. Low season reduced rates. MC/V.) At **St. Martin's B&B ❸,** 2 Nun's Island Rd., on the west bank of the river at the end of O'Brien's Bridge, the gorgeous back garden features a waterfall cascading into the river. This friendly B&B caters to young travelers, and owner Mary Sexton greets every guest with homemade brown bread. (☎568 286; stmartins@gmail.com. Singles €35; doubles €70; large family room €30 per person. Cash only.)

The cafes and pubs around **Quay, High,** and **Shop Streets** are good options for budget dining. On Saturdays, an **open-air market** on Market St. sells fruit and ethnic foods. (Open 8am-4pm.) **Riordan's ❷,** on Quay St., has huge portions of tasty Irish food at low prices. Their specials (lunch €6, dinner €14) are a steal. (☎567 810; www.riordans.2ya.com. Open M-Sa 9am-10:30pm, Su 11am-10pm.) At **The Home Plate ❷,** on Mary St., diners enjoy large sandwiches (€6-10) on tiny wooden tables. (☎561 475. Open Su-W noon-8pm, Th-Sa noon-9pm.)

SIGHTS AND ENTERTAINMENT. The **Nora Barnacle House,** 8 Bowling Green off Market St., has

LOCAL LEGEND

A NICE RING TO IT

Galway is now one of Europe's fastest-growing cities, but in the 17th century it was a small town. It was in Galway Bay's Claddagh, a fishing village cut off from the main part of town by the River Corrib, that Ireland's most famous piece of jewelry got its start.

According to tradition, Richard Joyce was en route to the West Indies when he was captured by slave-trading pirates and sold to a Moorish goldsmith. Joyce missed his wedding to a woman back home, but he learned the goldsmith's craft and made a ring for her. When he finally returned to Galway in 1689, he gave the ring to his true love, married her, and set up his own goldsmith shop, where he produced his ring.

The Claddagh ring features two hands clasping a heart with a crown on top, and it symbolizes "letting love and friendship reign." The rings served as wedding bands in the Claddagh for 300 years. Since the mid-19th century, they have become popular throughout Ireland, often passed down from mothers to daughters.

The Claddagh ring is no longer used only to denote married status; if the ring is worn on the right hand with the heart facing outward, the wearer's heart remains unattached. But if the heart is turned inward, the wearer, like Richard Joyce during his captivity, is in love and waiting to enter a state of wedded bliss, when the ring is moved to the left hand.

hardly changed since James Joyce's future wife Nora lived there with her family at the turn of the 20th century. Check out Joyce's love letters to his life-long companion. (www.norabarnacle.com. Open mid-May to mid-Sept. M-Sa 10am-1pm and 2-5pm, or by appointment. €2.50, students €2.) At the **Church of St. Nicholas** on Market St., a stone marks the spot where Columbus supposedly stopped to pray to the patron saint of travelers before sailing the ocean blue. (Open May-Sept. daily 8:30am-6:30pm. Free.) On Shop St., **Lynch's Castle** is a well-preserved 16th-century merchant's residence that now houses a bank. From Quay St., head across Wolfe Tone Bridge to the **Claddagh,** an area that was an Irish-speaking, thatch-roofed fishing village until the 1930s. The famous Claddagh rings are today's mass-produced reminders of yesteryear (p. 575). Satiate your aquatic cravings at the **National Aquarium of Ireland,** on the Salt Hill Promenade. (☎585 100; www.nationalaquarium.ie. Open daily 10am-6pm. €8, students €6.)

Event listings are published in the free *Galway Advertiser* and *Galway Xposed* (www.irelandxposed.com). In mid-July, the **Galway Arts Festival** (☎566 577) attracts droves of trad musicians, rock groups, theater troupes, and filmmakers. At ■**The Living Room,** Bridge St., weekend DJs keep the young crowd drinking and dancing at the far side of the red-lit bar. (☎563 804. Open M-W 10:30am-11:30pm, Th-Su 10:30am-2am. Kitchen closes at 6pm.) **The King's Head,** High St., has three floors and a huge stage devoted to nightly rock. (☎566 630. Pint €3.60. Open M-W 10:30am-11:30pm, Th-Su 10:30am-2am. Bar food served 10:30am-5pm. Pizza menu 5-8pm.) Between 11:30pm and 12:30am, the pubs drain out and the young and tireless go dancing. The crowd usually ends up at ■**Central Park,** on Upper Abbeygate St. With five bars and a huge, packed dance floor, this is the place to be in Galway. (☎565 976; www.centralparkclub.com. Pint €4. Cover M-Tu €5, W and Su €6, Th €7, F €8, Sa €10. Open Su-W 11pm-2am, Th-Sa 11pm-2:30am.) **Cuba,** on Prospect Hill, right past Eyre Sq., features danceable live music on two floors. (☎565 991; www.cuba.ie. Su stand-up comedy 8:30pm; free admission to club afterward. Cover €6-10. Many hostels give out 50% discount cards. Open daily 11pm-2:30am.)

ARAN ISLANDS (OILEÁIN ÁRANN) ☎099

The spectacular Aran Islands (Oileáin Árann) lie on the westernmost edge of Co. Galway, isolated by 32km of the swelling Atlantic Ocean. Ruins, forts, churches, and holy wells rise from the stony terrain of **Inishmore** (Inis Mór; pop. 900), the largest of the three islands. At the **Dún Aengus** ring fort, stones circle a sheer 100m drop. The **Inis Mór Way** is a mostly paved route that passes the majority of the island's sights. There are similar paths on **Inisheer** (Inis Oírr; pop. 260), the smallest island, and windswept **Inishmaan** (Inis Meáin; pop. 200). On Inishmore, the **Kilronan Hostel ❷** next to the pier has gorgeous views. (☎61255. Light breakfast included. Bike rental €10. All-female dorms available. Dorms €16-18.) The **Spar** supermarket in Kilronan (☎61203) functions as an unofficial community center. **Island Ferries** (☎091 561 767) go from Rossaveal, west of Galway, to Inishmore (45min., 2-4 per day, round-trip €25) and Inisheer (2 per day). **Clan Eagle II** (☎566 535), based in the islands, also leaves from Rossaveal for Inishmore (45min.; 10:30am, 1, and 6pm; round-trip €25). Both companies run **buses** to Rossaveal (€5), which leave from Kinlay House, on Merchant St. in Galway, 1½hr. before ferry departure. The **tourist office** on Inishmore stores luggage (€1) and helps find accommodations. (☎61263. Open daily June-Aug. 10am-7pm; Sept.-May 10am-5pm.)

CONNEMARA

Connemara, a largely Irish-speaking region in northwest Co. Galway, is comprised of a lacy net of inlets and islands that provide stunning views of two major mountain ranges: the Twelve Bens and the Maamturks.

CLIFDEN (AN CLOCHÁN) ☎095

English-speaking Clifden attracts crowds of tourists. For the best scenery, bike along the **Sky Road,** a 20km loop that overlooks the coastline, castles, and fields. **Bike** rentals are available at **Mannion's,** on Bridge St. (☎21160. July-Aug. €15 per day, €70 per week; Sept.-June €10 per day. €10 deposit. Open daily 9:30am-7pm.) **The White Heather House B&B ❸,** on the Square, offers panoramic views. (☎21655. Singles €35; doubles €60. MC/V.) Near the pubs, **Clifden Town Hostel (IHH) ❶,** Market St., has a helpful owner and a quiet atmosphere. (☎21076 or 21642; www.clifdentownhostel.com. Open year-round, but call ahead Nov.-Feb. Dorms €15-16; doubles €34-36; triples €51; quads €64. AmEx.) The family-run **Cullen's Bistro and Coffee Shop ❹,** Market St., cooks up hearty meals and delicious desserts. (☎21983. Irish stew €16. Open Apr.-Nov. daily noon-10pm.) **O'Connor's SuperValu,** on the Square, sells **groceries.** (☎21182. Open M-Sa 8:30am-10pm, Su 9am-7pm.) Bus Éireann runs **buses** from the library on Market St. to Galway via Oughterard (1½hr., 2-6 per day, €10) and to Westport via Leenane (1½hr., late June-Aug. M-Sa 1 per day). Michael Nee buses (☎34682; michaelnee@eircom.net) leave across the street from the tourist office for Galway (1½hr.; 2 per day; €11, round-trip €14). The **tourist office** is on Galway Rd. (☎21163; www.irelandwest.ie. Open July-Aug. daily 10am-6pm; Mar.-June and Sept.-Oct. M-Sa 10am-5pm.)

CONNEMARA NATIONAL PARK ☎095

The park occupies 12.5 sq. km of mountainous countryside. Bogs, often deceptively covered by a screen of grass and flowers, constitute much of the park's terrain. The **Srufanboy Nature** and **Ellis Wood** trails are easy 20min. hikes. The new pathway up **■Diamond Hill** offers a more difficult hike, but rewards with views of bog, harbor, and forest (or impenetrable mist). Experienced hikers head for the **Twelve Bens** (Na Beanna Beola; also called the Twelve Pins), a rugged mountain range that reaches up to 2200m. A tour of six peaks takes a full day. **Biking** the 65km circle through Clifden, Letterfrack, and the Inagh Valley is truly captivating, but only appropriate for fit bikers. The **Visitors Centre** will help in planning hikes. (☎41054. Open daily June-Aug. 9:30am-6:30pm; Mar.-May and Sept. 10am-5:30pm. €2.90, students €1.30.) Turn off from N59, 13km east of Clifden, to reach the park.

WESTPORT ☎098

Natural attractions await just outside of Westport's busy streets. Rising 650m over Clew Bay, **Croagh Patrick** has been revered as a holy site for thousands of years. According to legend, St. Patrick prayed on the mountain for 40 days and nights in AD 441 to banish the snakes from Ireland. Climbers start their journey up Croagh Patrick from the 15th-century **Murrisk Abbey,** west of Westport on R335 toward Louisburgh. **Buses** go to Murrisk via Louisburgh (2-3 per day); ask to be dropped off in Murrisk. Sheep calmly rule **Clare Island,** a beautiful speck of land in the Atlantic. Hop on a bus to Roonagh Pier, 29km from Westport, and then take a ferry to the island. (Bus departs from Westport's tourist office July-Aug. 10am, returns by 6pm; €25 for bus and ferry combined.) B&Bs in Westport cluster on **Altamont Road** and **The Quay.** The extensive breakfast options and warm hospitality at **■The Altamont B&B ❸,** Altamont St., have kept travelers coming back for 44 years. (☎25226. Rooms €30-33.) Most restaurants are on **Bridge Street.** The **SuperValu** supermarket is on Shop St. (☎27000. Open M-Sa 8am-10pm, Su 9am-9pm.) **Matt Molloy's,** on Bridge St., is owned by the flautist of the Chieftains and has nightly trad at 9:30pm. (☎26655. Pint €3.40. Open Su-Th 1pm-1am, F-Sa 1pm-2am.) **Trains** leave from the Altamont St. Station (☎25253), a 10min. walk up the North Mall, to Dublin (3-4 per day, €29) via Athlone. **Buses** (☎096 71800) leave from Mill St. to Galway (2hr., 8 per day, €14). The **tourist office** is on James St. (☎25711. Open daily 9am-5:45pm.)

SLIGO ☎071 91

Since the early 20th century, William Butler Yeats devotees have made a literary pilgrimage to Sligo; the poet spent summers in town as a child and set many of his works around Sligo Bay. The former Dominican friary, **Sligo Abbey,** is on Abbey St. (Open Apr.-Dec. daily 10am-6pm, last admission 5:15pm; Jan.-Mar. reduced hours. €2.10, students €1.10.) **Model Arts and Niland Gallery,** on the Mall, houses one of the country's finest collections of modern Irish art. (☎41405; www.modelart.ie. Open June-Oct. Tu-Sa 10am-5:30pm, Su 11am-4pm. Free.) Yeats is buried in **Drumcliffe Churchyard,** on the N15, 6.5km northwest of Sligo. Catch a bus from Sligo to the Derry stop at Drumcliffe (15min., 7 per day, round-trip €5.10).

Eden Hill Holiday Hostel (IHH) ❶, off Pearse Rd., has Victorian decor and a friendly staff. Follow Pearse Rd., turn right at the Marymount sign, and take another right after one block. (☎43204; www.edenhillhostel.com. Laundry €8. Bike rental €15 per day. Dorms €15; doubles €40. 2-person tents €9 per person. MC/V.) A **Tesco** supermarket is on O'Connell St. (☎62788. Open 24hr.) **The Left Bank,** 15-16 Stephen's St., across the river, is a popular weekend destination for live music and dancing. (☎40100; www.leftbank.ie. Cover after 11pm W €5, F-Sa €6. Open M and W-Su noon-2:30am, Tu noon-12:30am.) **McLaughlin's Bar,** 9 Market St., is a true musician's pub, with pick-up jam sessions in the back room. (☎44209. Pint €3.60. Open M-Th 5-11:30pm, F-Sa 5pm-12:30am, Su 5-11pm.)

Trains (☎1 850 836 6222; www.irishrail.ie) leave from Lord Edward St. to Dublin (3hr., 6 per day, €25 round-trip) via Carrick-on-Shannon and Mullingar. From the same station, **buses** (☎60066; www.buseireann.ie) head to: Belfast (4hr.; 3-4 per day; €23, students €19); Derry/Londonderry (3hr., 8-10 per day, €16/13); Donegal (1hr., 7-9 per day, €12/10); Dublin (3-4hr., 7 per day, €17/14); Galway (2½hr., 7 per day, €14/11). Turn left on Lord Edward St., then follow the signs right onto Adelaide St. and around the corner to Temple St. to find the **tourist office.** (☎61201; www.irelandnorthwest.ie. Open July-Aug. M-F 9am-5pm, Sa 11am-3pm.)

NORTHWESTERN IRELAND

A sliver of land connects the mountains, lakes, and ancient monuments of Co. Sligo to Co. Donegal. Among Ireland's counties, Donegal (DUN-ee-gahl) is second only to Cork in size and second to none in glorious wilderness. Its *gaeltacht* is the largest sanctuary of the living Irish language in Ireland, and its geographic isolation and natural beauty embrace travelers sick of the tourist hordes farther south.

DONEGAL TOWN (DÚN NA NGALL) ☎074 97

A gateway for travelers heading to more isolated destinations in the north and northwest, the compact, sometimes sleepy Donegal Town erupts with live music in pubs on weekends. The center of town is called **the Diamond,** a triangle bordered by the main shopping streets. Six craftsmen open their studios to the public around the pleasant courtyard of the **Donegal Craft Village,** 1.6km south of town on the Ballyshannon Rd. (☎22225. Open July-Aug. M-Sa 10am-6pm, Su noon-6pm; Sept.-June Tu-Sa 10am-5:30pm.) The **Waterbus** shuttle provides aquatic tours of Donegal Bay, departing from the quay next to the tourist office. (Departure times depend on tides; call ahead. €15.) For two weeks in July, the **Earagail Arts Festival** celebrates the county's art scene. (☎074 916 8800, tickets 074 912 1986; www.eaf.ie. Prices range from free to €25.) From late September to early October, the **Donegal Blue Stack Festival** (☎21986; www.donegalculture.com) features theater, arts, and music.

A 10min. walk from town, the family-run **Donegal Town Independent Hostel (IHH/IHO) ❶,** Killybegs Rd., welcomes road-weary backpackers. (☎22805. Dorms

€15-16; doubles €36-40. Tent sites €8 per person. MC/V.) **The Blueberry Tea Room ❷,** Castle St., buzzes with patrons enjoying daily specials for €10. (☎22933. Internet €2 for 30min. Open M-Sa 9am-7:30pm.) For groceries, head to **SuperValu,** 2min. from the Diamond down Ballyshannon Rd. (☎22977. Open M-Sa 8:30am-9pm, Su 10am-6pm.) **The Reveller,** in the Diamond, caters to a younger crowd that likes pool, loud music, and late drinks. (☎21201. Th-Su live music 10:30pm-close. Open M-Th 10:30am-11:30pm, F-Sa 10:30am-12:30am, Su noon-11pm.) The lantern-lit **Schooner Bar and B&B** (☎21671), Upper Main St., draws a mix of hostelers and locals for the best trad sessions in town. (Trad 8:30pm F-Sa, June-Aug. also M-Tu.) **Buses** (☎21101) leave from the Abbey Hotel on the Diamond for Derry/Londonderry (7-9 per day, €13) via Letterkenny (€8.20), Dublin (3½hr., 6 per day, €17), and Galway (4hr., 4 per day, €15). To reach the **tourist office,** face away from the Abbey Hotel and turn right; the office is outside the Diamond on the Ballyshannon/Sligo Rd. (☎21148; www.irelandnorthwest.ie. Open July-Aug. M-Sa 9am-6pm, Su 11am-3pm; Sept.-Oct. and Easter-June M-Sa 9:30am-5:30pm.)

LETTERKENNY ☎074 91

Letterkenny is difficult to navigate, but it is lively at night and is a useful stop for making bus connections to the rest of Ireland and to Northern Ireland. **The Townview B&B ❸,** on Leck Rd., 30min. uphill from the bus station, has a fabulous view and award-winning breakfasts. Call for pickup from town or take a taxi; the walk can be daunting. (☎21570; www.townviewhouse.com. Singles €35; doubles €60-66; triples €75. MC/V.) The town's only hostel is **The International Port Hostel (IHO) ❶,** Covehill Port Rd., behind the theater. (☎25315; www.porthostel.ie. Laundry €5. Free wireless Internet. Dorms €15-25; doubles €50; triples €60. Camping €7 per person. Reduced rates online and in winter. MC/V.) A **Tesco** supermarket is in the shopping center behind the bus station. (Open 24hr.) **Buses** leave from the station at the junction of Port (Derry) and Pearse Rd., in front of the shopping center. Bus Éireann (☎21309) runs to Derry/Londonderry (30min.; 8 per day; €7.30, students €5.70), Dublin (4½hr., 6 per day, €17/15), and Galway (4¾hr., 4 per day, €16/12) via Donegal Town (50min., €9/7). Lough Swilly (☎22863) buses run to Derry/Londonderry (M-Sa 12 per day, €7.50) and the Inishowen Peninsula (M-F 2-3 per day, €7.50). The **tourist office** (☎21160) is off the second roundabout at the intersection of Port (Derry) and Blaney Rd., 1.2km from town past the bus station.

ITALY (ITALIA)

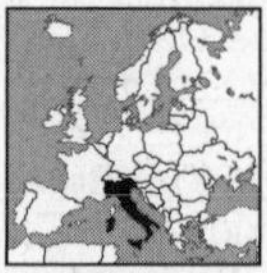

Innovation, elegance, and culture distinguish Italy and its beloved art, fashion, and food. Its breathtaking vistas range from steep Alpine peaks in the north to the hills of the interior, lush with olive trees, to the aquamarine waters of the south. Civilizations evolved piecemeal throughout the country, bequeathing a culture whose people and traditions retain distinct regional characteristics. Ruins of the Roman empire contextualize the imposing sculptures and paintings of Renaissance masters and the couture creations of today's fashion designers. And the Italians seem to possess a knowledge of the life's pleasures: indulging in daily siestas and hosting leisurely feasts on a regular basis. The openness of the Italian people lets travelers ease into this country's relaxed and admired way of life.

DISCOVER ITALY: SUGGESTED ITINERARIES

THREE DAYS. Spend it all in the Eternal City of **Rome** (p. 585). Go back in time at the **Ancient City:** be a gladiator in the **Colosseum,** explore the **Roman Forum,** and stand in the well-preserved **Pantheon.** Spend the next day admiring the fine art in the **Capitoline Museums** and the **Galleria Borghese,** then satiate your other senses in a disco. The next morning, redeem your debauched soul in **Vatican City,** gazing at the ceiling of the **Sistine Chapel,** gaping at **St. Peter's Cathedral,** and enjoying the **Vatican Museums.**

ONE WEEK. Spend 3 days taking in the sights in **Rome** before heading north to **Florence** (2 days; p. 645) to immerse yourself in Italy's amazing Renaissance art at the Uffizi Gallery. Move to **Venice** (2 days; p. 630) to float through the canals.

BEST OF ITALY, 3 WEEKS. Begin by immersing yourself in the sights and history of **Rome** (3 days), seek out the medieval houses of **Siena** (1 day; p. 656), then move to **Florence** (3 days). Head up the coast to **Finale Ligure** (1 day; p. 621), and the beautiful **Cinque Terre** (2 days; p. 622). Visit cosmopolitan **Milan** (2 days; p. 610) for shopping and **Lake Como** for hiking (1 day; p. 617). Find your Romeo or Juliet in **Verona** (1 day; p. 641). Be paddled through the winding canals in **Venice** (2 days) before flying south to **Naples** (2 days; p. 661), being sure to visit preserved, ancient **Pompeii** (1 day; p. 666). Then hike and swim along the **Amalfi Coast** (1 day; p. 668), and see the Grotto Azzura on the island of **Capri** (1 day; p. 667).

ESSENTIALS

WHEN TO GO

Traveling in late May or early September, which average 77°F (25°C), is a good bet, though weather differences from north and south are substantial. Tourism goes into overdrive in June, July, and August: hotels are booked solid and prices know no limits. In August, many Italians flock to the coast for vacations.

DOCUMENTS AND FORMALITIES

EMBASSIES AND CONSULATES. Foreign embassies are in Rome (p. 585). Italian embassies abroad include: **Australia,** 12 Grey St., Deakin, Canberra ACT 2600 (☎612 62 73 33 33; www.ambitalia.org.au); **Canada,** 275 Slater St., 21st fl., Ottawa, ON K1P 5H9 (☎613-232-2401; www.italyincanada.com); **Ireland,** 63/65 Northum-

berland Rd., Dublin (☎353 166 017 44); **New Zealand,** 34 Grant Rd., Wellington (☎644 44 73 53 39; www.italy-embassy.org.nz); **UK,** 14 Three Kings Yard, London W1K 4EH (☎020 73 12 22 00; www.embitaly.org.uk); **US,** 3000 Whitehaven St., Washington, D.C. 20008 (☎202-612-4400; www.ambwashingtondc.esteri.it).

FACTS AND FIGURES

Official Name: Italian Republic.

Capital: Rome.

Major Cities: Florence, Milan, Naples, Venice.

Population: 58,134,000.

Time Zone: GMT +1.

Language: Italian; some German, French, and Slovene.

Religion: Roman Catholic (90%).

Longest Salami: Made by Rino Parenti in Zibello, displayed on Nov. 23, 2003; 486.8m in length.

ITALY

VISA AND ENTRY INFORMATION. EU citizens do not need a visa. Citizens of Australia, Canada, New Zealand, and the US do not need a visa for stays of up to 90 days, beginning upon entry into any of the countries within the EU's freedom-of-movement zone.

TOURIST SERVICES AND MONEY

EMERGENCY	**Police:** ☎112. **Ambulance:** ☎118. **Fire:** ☎115. **Emergency:** ☎113.

TOURIST OFFICES. The **Italian State Tourist Board (ENIT)** has useful information about the country, including the arts, nature, history, and leisure activities. Visit their website, www.enit.it, for information in seven languages. The office in Rome (☎06 49 7111; sedecentrale@cert.enit.it) can locate branches not listed online.

MONEY. The **euro (€)** has replaced the lira as the unit of currency in Italy. For more information, see p. 18. The **value added tax** (**VAT,** or **IVA** in Italy) is a sales tax levied in the EU; in Italy the VAT rate is 20%. Foreigners making any purchase over €335 may be refunded this percentage. At most stores, you can fill out a tax refund form, then have it stamped upon leaving the country. Not all storefront "Tax-Free" stickers imply an immediate, on-site refund; ask before making a purchase.

BUSINESS HOURS. Nearly everything closes from 1 to 3 or 4pm for siesta. Most museums are open 9am-1pm and 3-6pm; some open through lunch, however. Monday is often a *giorno di chiusura* (day of closure).

TRANSPORTATION

BY PLANE. Rome's international airport (FCO), known as both Fiumicino and Leonardo da Vinci, is served by most major airlines. Other hubs are Florence's Amerigo Vespucci airport and Milan's Malpensa and Linate airports. **Alitalia** (☎800-223-5730; www.alitalia.com) is Italy's national airline.

BY TRAIN. The Italian State Railway **Ferrovie dello Stato,** or **FS** (national information line ☎848 88 80 88; www.trenitalia.com), has inexpensive, efficient service. Trenitalia passes are the domestic equivalent of Eurailpasses. A *Locale* train stops at every station on a particular line; the *diretto* makes fewer stops than the *locale;* and the *espresso* stops only at major stations. The air-conditioned *rapido*, an **InterCity (IC)** train, zips along but costs more. Reserve tickets ahead for the fast, pricey **Eurostar** trains. **Eurailpasses** are valid without a supplement on all trains except Eurostar. Those under 26 who plan to travel extensively in Italy should be sure to buy a Carta Verde (€26) to get year-long 20% discounts.

> TIP **VALIDATE = GREAT.** Always **validate** your train ticket **before boarding.** Validation machines are located all over train stations. Insert and remove your ticket from the slot and check to see if the machine stamped it. Failure to validate may result in steep fines (€120 or more), and train operators do not accept ignorance as an excuse. The same goes for bus tickets, which should be validated immediately after boarding the bus using the machines onboard.

BY BUS. Intercity buses serve points inaccessible by train. For city buses, buy tickets in *tabaccherie* or kiosks. Validate your ticket immediately on boarding to avoid a €120 fine. Check websites www.bus.it and www.italybus.it for schedules.

BY FERRY. Sicily, Sardinia, Corsica, and smaller islands along the coast are connected to the mainland by **ferries** *(traghetti)* and **hydrofoils** *(aliscafi)*. Italy's largest private ferry service, **Tirrenia** (www.gruppotirrenia.it), runs ferries to Sardinia, Sicily, and Tunisia. Other lines, such as the **SNAV** (www.snavali.com), have hydrofoil services from major ports such as Ancona, Bari, Brindisi, Genoa, La Spezia, Livorno, Naples, and Trapani. Ferry service is also prevalent in the Lake Country. Reserve well ahead, especially in July and August.

BY CAR. There are four kinds of roads: *autostrada* (superhighways; mostly tollroads; usually 130km per hr. speed limit); *strade statali* (state roads); *strade provinciali* (provincial); and *strade communali* (local). Driving is frightening; congested traffic is common in large cities and in the north. On three-lane roads, the center lane is for passing. **Mopeds** (€30-40 per day) can be a great way to see the islands and more scenic areas but can be disastrous in the rain and on rough roads. Always exercise caution; practice in empty streets and learn to keep with the flow of traffic. Drivers in Italy—especially in the south—are notorious for ignoring traffic laws. Call the **Automobile Club Italiano** (**ACI;** ☎116; www.aci.it) for help on the road. If you plan to drive a car while in Italy, you must be 18 or older and have an **International Driving Permit** (IDP) or an EU driver's license.

BY BIKE AND BY THUMB. Bicycling is a popular sport, but bike trails are rare. Rent bikes where you see a *noleggio* sign. Except in the Po Valley, the terrain is challenging. Let's Go does not recommend hitchhiking, which can be particularly unsafe in Italy, especially in areas south of Rome or Naples.

KEEPING IN TOUCH

PHONE CODES	**Country code:** 39. **International dialing prefix:** 00. When calling within a city, dial 0 + city code + local number. All 10-digit numbers listed in this chapter are mobile phones and do not require a city code. For more information on how to place international calls, see inside back cover.

EMAIL AND THE INTERNET. Internet cafes are very popular in large cities, and rural areas and cities in the south are catching up. Rates range €1.50-6 per hr. For has recently improved, although easy laptop hook-ups in Internet cafes are rare.

TELEPHONE. As coin-operated public phones are being phased out, the most common phone requires a prepaid card *(scheda)*, sold by phone card vendors, *tabaccherie*, Internet cafes, and post offices. Italy has no area codes, only regional prefixes that are incorporated into the number. Mobile phones are widely used in Italy; buying a prepaid SIM card for a GSM phone can be a good option. Of the service providers, TIM and Vodafone-Omnitel have the best networks. International direct dial numbers include: **AT&T Direct** (☎800 172 444); **British Telecom** (☎0800 89 0039); **Canada Direct** (☎800 172 213); **MCI WorldPhone** (☎800 90 5825); **Sprint** (☎800 172 405).

MAIL. Airmail letters sent from Australia, North America, or the UK to Italy take anywhere from four to 15 days to arrive. Since Italian mail is notoriously unreliable, it is usually safer and quicker to send mail priority *(prioritaria)* or registered *(raccomandata)*. It costs €0.60 to send a letter worldwide. *Fermo Posta* is Italian for **Poste Restante** and should be addressed: First name LAST NAME, Fermo Posta, Postal Code, city, ITALY.

LANGUAGE. The Italian language has evolved from Latin. As a result of Italy's fragmented history, variations in dialects are notable. The throaty **Neapolitan** is actually its own language, a different grammar making it difficult for a northerner to understand; **Ligurians** use a mix of Italian, Catalán, and French; **Sardo,** spoken in

Sardinia, bears little resemblance to standard Italian; and many **Tuscan** dialects differ from Italian in pronunciation. Some in the northern border regions don't speak Italian at all: the population of Valle d'Aosta speaks mainly French, and Trentino-Alto Adige harbors a German-speaking minority. In the southern regions of Puglia, Calabria, and Sicily, entire villages speak a form of Albanian called **Arbresh.** To facilitate conversation, locals do their best to employ standard Italian when speaking with foreigners, although some may be shy or hesitant to do so at first. Many Italians, especially older people or those who live in rural towns, do not speak English, although many young people do.

ACCOMMODATIONS AND CAMPING

ITALY	❶	❷	❸	❹	❺
ACCOMMODATIONS	under €16	€16-25	€25-40	€40-60	over €60

Associazione Italiana Alberghi per la Gioventù (AIG), the Italian hostel federation, is a **Hostelling International (HI)** affiliate. A full list of AIG hostels is available at www.ostellionline.org. Prices in Italy start at about €8 per night for **dorms.** Hostels are the best option for solo travelers (single rooms are relatively scarce in hotels in the country), but curfews, lockouts, distant locations, and less-than-perfect security can detract from their appeal for many. Italian **hotel** rates are set by the state. Hotel singles *(camera singola)* usually start at around €25-50 per night, and doubles *(camera doppia)* start at €40-82 per room. A room with a private bath *(con bagno)* usually costs 30-50% more. Smaller **pensioni** are often cheaper than hotels. Be sure to confirm charges before checking in; Italian hotels are notorious for tacking on additional costs at check-out time. The **Azienda di Promozione Turismo (APT)** provides lists of hotels that have paid to be listed; some of the hotels *Let's Go* recommends may not be on the list. **Affittacamere** (rooms for rent in private houses) are another inexpensive option. There are over 1700 **campgrounds** in Italy; tent sites average €4.20. The **Federazione Italiana del Campeggio e del Caravaning** (www.federcampeggio.it) has a complete list of sites. The **Touring Club Italiano** (www.touringclub.it) publishes books and pamphlets on the outdoors.

ITALY

FOOD AND DRINK

ITALY	❶	❷	❸	❹	❺
FOOD	under €7	€7-15	€15-20	€20-25	over €25

Breakfast is the least elaborate meal in Italy; at most, *la colazione* consists of coffee and a *cornetto* (croissant). For *il pranzo* (lunch), people rush to grab a *panino* (sandwich) or salad at a bar, or dine more calmly at an inexpensive *tavola calda* (cafeteria-style snack bar), *rosticceria* (grill), or *gastronomia* (prepares hot dishes for takeout). *La cena* (dinner) usually begins at 8pm or later; in Naples, it's not unusual to go for a midnight pizza. Traditionally, Italian dinner is the longest meal of the day, usually lasting much of the evening and consisting of an *antipasto* (appetizer), a *primo piatto* (starch-based first course like pasta or risotto), a *secondo piatto* (meat or fish), and a *contorno* (vegetable side dish). It is important to note, however, that lunch is usually the most important meal of the day in rural regions where daily work comes in two shifts and is separated by a long lunch and siesta. Finally comes the *dolce* (dessert or fruit), then *caffè* (espresso), and often an after-dinner liqueur. Many restaurants offer a fixed-price *menù turistico* including *primo*, *secondo*, bread, water, and wine. While food varies regionally—seafood in the South and the coast, heartier selections in the North; mascarpone cheese in Lombardy, truffles in Piemonte, herbs and olive oil in Liguria, gnocchi in Trentino-Alto Adige, parmesan and balsamic vinegar in Emilia-Romagna, and rustic stews in Tuscany—the importance of relaxing and having an extended meal does not. *La bella figura* (a good figure) is another social imperative, and the after-dinner *passeggiata* (promenade) is as much an institution as the meal itself. The ubiquitous gelato is an extremely popular snack and dessert. Coffee and wine are their own institutions, each with their own devoted followers.

TIP **THE UGLY DUCKLING.** Before shelling out the euros for a *piccolo cono* (small cone), assess quality by looking at the banana gelato: if it's bright yellow, it's been made from a mix. If it's slightly gray, real bananas were used. *Gelati* in metal bins also tend to be homemade, whereas that in plastic tubs is not.

HOLIDAYS AND FESTIVALS

Holidays: New Year's Day (Jan. 1); Epiphany (Jan. 6); Easter Sunday and Monday (Apr. 8-9); Liberation Day (Apr. 25); Labor Day (May 1); Ascension Day (May 20); Feast of the Assumption (Aug. 15); All Saints' Day (Nov. 1); Immaculate Conception (Dec. 8); Christmas Day (Dec. 25); Santo Stefano (Dec. 26).

Festivals: Carnevale, a country-wide celebration, is the 10 days leading up to Lent. In Venice, costumed revelers fill the streets and canals. During **Scoppio del Carro,** in Florence's P. del Duomo on Easter Sunday, Florentines set off a cart of explosives, remembering Pazziano dei Pazzi, who returned from the Crusades with a few splinters from the holy sepulcher, used to light a simple fireworks display. Each June and July, the **Spoleto Festival** (known as the Festival dei Due Mondi, or Festival of Two Worlds) features concerts, operas, ballets, film screenings, and modern art shows (www.spoletofestival.it).

BEYOND TOURISM

One of the most satisfying ways to develop a deeper understanding of Italian culture is through personal interaction with the people and landscape. From harvesting grapes on vineyards in Siena to restoring and protecting marine life in the Mediterranean, opportunities abound. Those in search of something more lucrative might work as an intern for the Italian press or teaching English. For more on Beyond Tourism opportunities throughout Europe, see **Beyond Tourism,** p. 61.

Abruzzo National Park, PNALM, V. Roma s.n.c., 67030 Villetta Barrea, AQ Italy (☎0864 89 102; www.parcoabruzzo.it), hosts 1000 summer volunteers for 1 week or more. Opportunities range from maintenance to nature education. Program fee €110-170.

Gruppi Archeologici d'Italia, V. Baldo degli Ubaldi 168, 00165 Rome (☎06 63 85 256; www.gruppiarcheologici.org). Organizes 2-week-long volunteer programs at archaeological digs throughout Italy. Offers links to various programs hoping to promote cultural awareness about archaeological preservation. Program fee €195-400.

Carmelita's Cook Italy (☎39 34 90 07 82 98; www.cookitaly.com). Region- or dish-specific cooking classes. Venues in Bologna, Cortona, Lucca, and Sicily, among others. Courses run 3 days to 2 weeks. Program fee from €990 (includes housing and meals).

ROME (ROMA) ☎06

Rome (pop. 2.5 million) is a city of superlatives: Michelangelo's *David*, the most perfect specimen; the most beautiful art; the most spirited people; and the most impressive ruins. Follow the winding, medieval streets to the majestic vistas on the Via del Corso and the Via dei Fori Imperiali, but balance your tours with glimpses of tucked-away side streets on strolls through the *centro storico*. Augustus once boasted that he found Rome a city of brick and left it one of marble. However you find it, you may leave Rome as you see fit—if you can, in fact, depart.

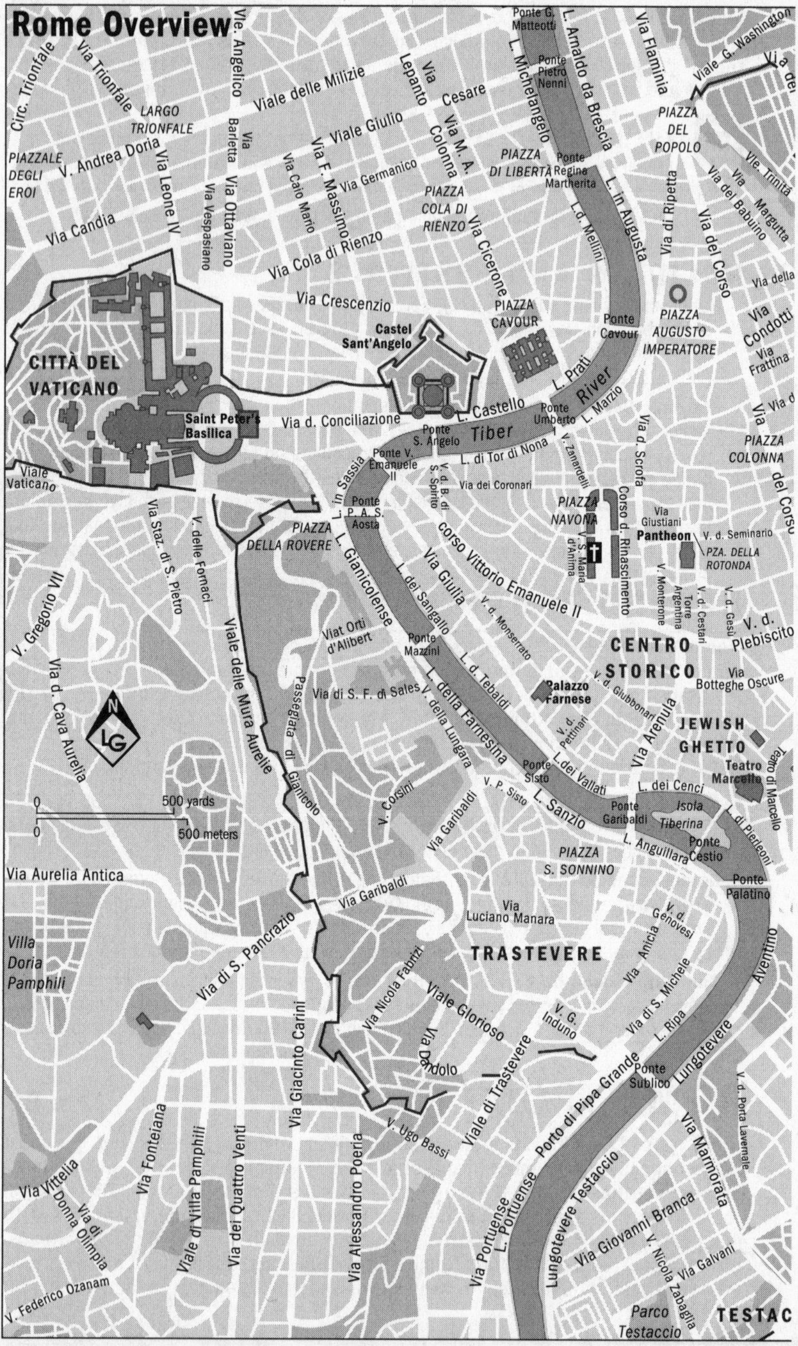
Rome Overview
CITTÀ DEL VATICANO
Saint Peter's Basilica
Castel Sant'Angelo
Tiber River
PIAZZA CAVOUR
PIAZZA DEL POPOLO
PIAZZA AUGUSTO IMPERATORE
PIAZZA NAVONA
Pantheon
PZA. DELLA ROTONDA
PIAZZA COLONNA
CENTRO STORICO
JEWISH GHETTO
Teatro Marcello
Palazzo Farnese
Isola Tiberina
PIAZZA S. SONNINO
TRASTEVERE
TESTAC
Villa Doria Pamphili
Parco Testaccio
PIAZZA DELLA ROVERE
PIAZZA COLA DI RIENZO
PIAZZA DI LIBERTÀ
PIAZZALE DEGLI EROI
LARGO TRIONFALE
500 yards
500 meters
Via Cola di Rienzo
Via Crescenzio
Via d. Conciliazione
Viale delle Milizie
Viale Giulio Cesare
Via Candia
Via Ottaviano
Via Leone IV
V. Andrea Doria
Viale Vaticano
Viale delle Mura Aurelie
Via Gianicolense
Corso Vittorio Emanuele II
Via Giulia
Via Aurelia Antica
Via di S. Pancrazio
Via Garibaldi
Viale di Trastevere
Via Portuense
Lungotevere Testaccio
Via Marmorata
Via Flaminia
Via del Corso
Via di Ripetta
Via del Babuino
Via Condotti
Via Arenula
Via Giacinto Carini
Via dei Quattro Venti
Viale di Villa Pamphili
Via Alessandro Poeria
Via Fonteiana
Via Vitellia
V. Federico Ozanam
Ponte Sisto
Ponte Garibaldi
Ponte Cestio
Ponte Palatino
Ponte Sublicio
Ponte Mazzini
Ponte Cavour
Ponte Umberto
Ponte S. Angelo
Ponte Regina Martherita
Ponte Pietro Nenni
Ponte G. Matteotti

ITALY

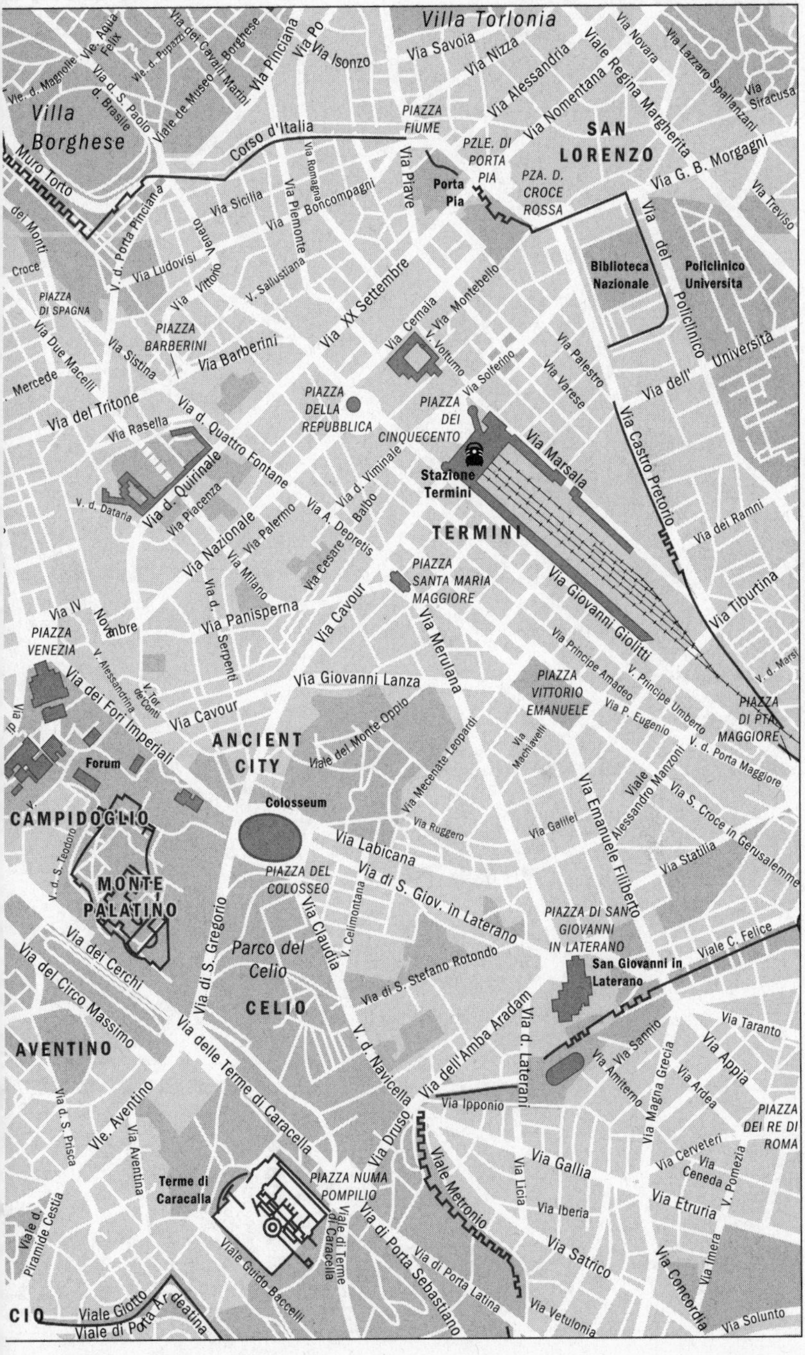
Villa Torlonia
Villa Borghese
Vle. d. Magnolie
Vle. Aqua Felix
Via d. S. Paolo d. Brasile
Vle. d. Pupazzi
Via dei Cavalli Marini
Viale de Museo Borghese
Via Pinciana
Via Po
Via Isonzo
Via Savoia
Via Nizza
Via Alessandria
Viale Regina Margherita
Via Novara
Via Lazzaro Spallanzani
Via Siracusa
Corso d'Italia
PIAZZA FIUME
Via Nomentana
SAN LORENZO
Via G. B. Morgagni
Muro Torto
Via Romagna
Via Piave
PZLE. DI PORTA PIA
Porta Pia
PZA. D. CROCE ROSSA
Via Treviso
dei Monti
V. d. Porta Pinciana
Via Sicilia
Via Boncompagni
Via Piemonte
Veneto
Via Ludovisi
Vittorio
V. Sallustiana
Biblioteca Nazionale
Policlinico Universita
Via del Policlinico
Croce
PIAZZA DI SPAGNA
Via XX Settembre
Via Cernaia
V. Via Montebello
V. Volturno
Via Palestro
Via Varese
Via Due Macelli
Via Sistina
PIAZZA BARBERINI
Via Barberini
Via dell' Università
Mercede
Via del Tritone
PIAZZA DELLA REPUBBLICA
PIAZZA DEI CINQUECENTO
Via Solferino
Via Rasella
Via d. Quattro Fontane
Via Marsala
Via Castro Pretorio
Via d. Quirinale
Stazione Termini
Via d. Viminale
V. d. Dataria
Via Piacenza
Via A. Depretis
Balbo
Via dei Ramni
TERMINI
Via Nazionale
Via Palermo
Via Cesare
Via Milano
PIAZZA SANTA MARIA MAGGIORE
Via Giovanni Giolitti
Via Tiburtina
Via IV Novembre
PIAZZA VENEZIA
Via Panisperna
Via d. Serpenti
Via Cavour
Via Merulana
Via Principe Amadeo
V. Principe Umberto
V. d. Marsi
V. Alessandrina
V. Tor de Conti
Via dei Fori Imperiali
Via Giovanni Lanza
PIAZZA VITTORIO EMANUELE
Via P. Eugenio
PIAZZA DI PTA. MAGGIORE
ANCIENT CITY
Viale del Monte Oppio
Via Machiavelli
V. d. Porta Maggiore
Forum
Via Mecenate Leopardi
Viale Alessandro Manzoni
Via S. Croce in Gerusalemme
CAMPIDOGLIO
Colosseum
Via Ruggero
Via Galilei
Via Emanuele Filiberto
V. d. S. Teodoro
Via Labicana
Via Statilia
MONTE PALATINO
PIAZZA DEL COLOSSEO
Via di S. Giov. in Laterano
Via Claudia
V. Celimontana
Via di S. Gregorio
PIAZZA DI SAN GIOVANNI IN LATERANO
Viale C. Felice
Via dei Cerchi
Parco del Celio
Via di S. Stefano Rotondo
San Giovanni in Laterano
Via del Circo Massimo
CELIO
Via dell' Amba Aradam
Via d. Laterani
Via Taranto
AVENTINO
Via delle Terme di Caracalla
V. d. Navicella
Via Sannio
Via Amiterno
Via Magna Grecia
Via Appia
Via Ardea
V. d. S. Prisca
Vle. Aventino
Via Aventina
Via Ipponio
PIAZZA DEI RE DI ROMA
Via Druso
Viale Metronio
Via Gallia
Via Licia
Via Cerveteri
Via Ceneda
V. Pomezia
Terme di Caracalla
PIAZZA NUMA POMPILIO
Viale di Terme di Caracella
Via Iberia
Via Etruria
Viale d. Piramide Cestia
Via di Porta Sebastiano
Via di Porta Latina
Via Satrico
Via Imera
Viale Guido Baccelli
Via Concordia
CIO
Viale Giotto
Viale di Porta Ardeatina
Via Vetulonia
Via Solunto

ITALY

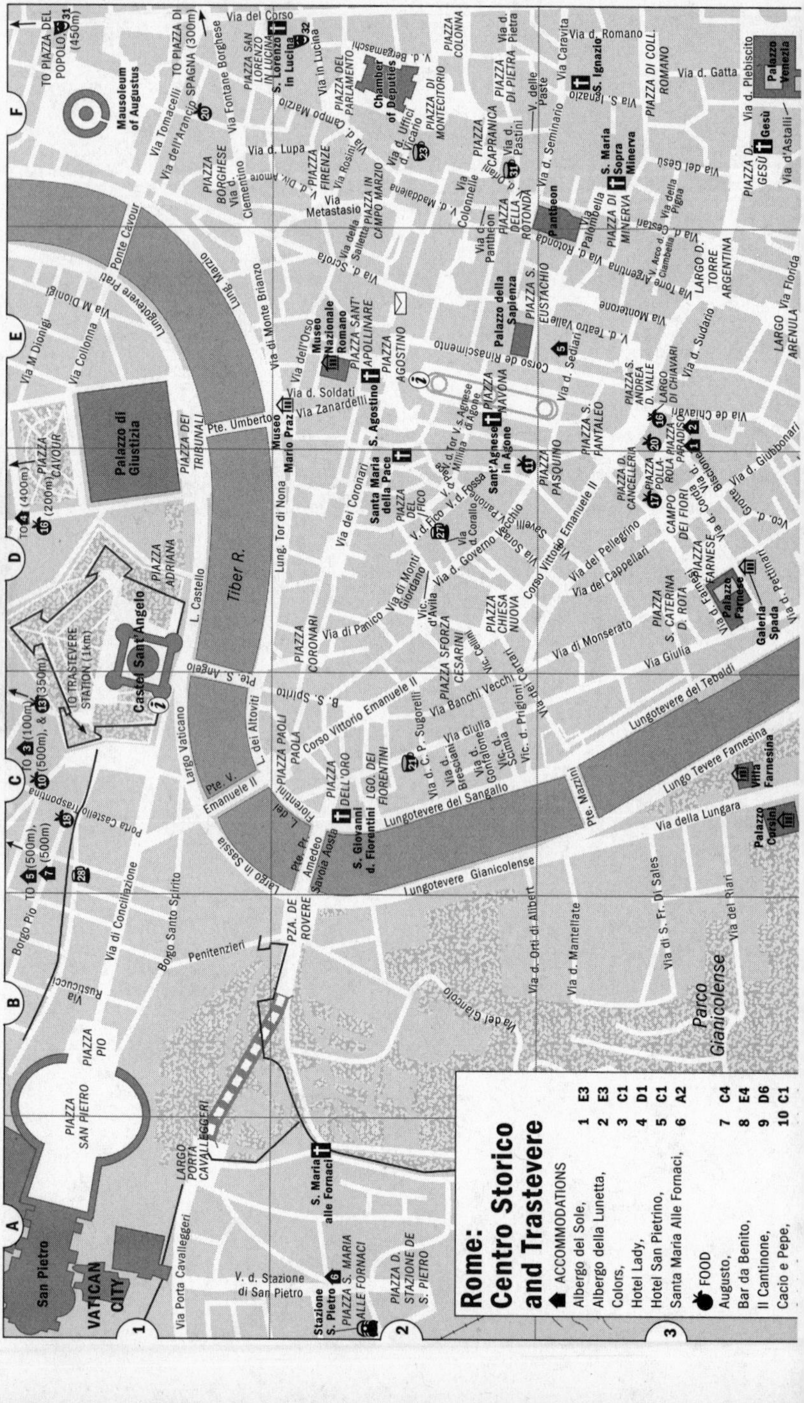
Rome:
Centro Storico
and Trastevere
ACCOMMODATIONS
Albergo del Sole, 1 E3
Albergo della Lunetta, 2 E3
Colors, 3 C1
Hotel Lady, 4 D1
Hotel San Pietrino, 5 C1
Santa Maria Alle Fornaci, 6 A2
FOOD
Augusto, 7 C4
Bar da Benito, 8 E4
Il Cantinone, 9 D6
Cacio e Pepe, 10 C1
A
B
C
D
E
F
1
2
3
San Pietro
VATICAN CITY
PIAZZA SAN PIETRO
PIAZZA PIO
Castel Sant'Angelo
Palazzo di Giustizia
Tiber R.
Mausoleum of Augustus
Chamber of Deputies
Pantheon
Palazzo della Sapienza
PIAZZA NAVONA
Sant'Agnese in Agone
Santa Maria della Pace
S. Agostino
Museo Nazionale Romano
Museo Mario Praz
S. Maria Sopra Minerva
S. Ignazio
S. Lorenzo in Lucina
Gesù
Palazzo Venezia
CAMPO DEI FIORI
Palazzo Farnese
Galleria Spada
Villa Farnesina
Palazzo Corsini
S. Giovanni d. Fiorentini
S. Maria alle Fornaci
Stazione S. Pietro
Parco Gianicolense
Corso Vittorio Emanuele II
Corso de Rinascimento
Lungotevere Gianicolense
Lungotevere del Sangallo
Lungotevere dei Tebaldi
Via Giulia
Via della Lungara
Via di Conciliazione
Borgo Santo Spirito
Borgo Pio
Via del Corso
TO PIAZZA DEL POPOLO (450m)
TO PIAZZA DI SPAGNA (300m)
TO TRASTEVERE STATION (1km)

Cul de Sac,	11 D2
Enoteca Trastevere,	12 D4
Franchi,	13 C1
Pizza Art,	14 E4
Pizzeria San Callisto,	15 C4
Pizzeria San Marco,	16 D1
Ristorante Grappolo d'Oro Zampanò,	17 D3
"Lo Spuntino" da Guido e Patrizia,	18 C1
Trattoria da Giggetto,	19 E4
Trattoria da Settimio all'Arancio,	20 F1
CAFES	
Bar Giulia,	21 C2
Biscottificio Artigianale Innocenti,	22 D5
Giolitti,	23 F2
Pasticceria Ebraico Boccione,	24 E4
NIGHTLIFE	
Artu Café,	25 C4
Caffè della Scala,	26 C4
Il Fico,	27 D2
The Proud Lion Pub,	28 C1
THEATERS	
Cinema Reale,	29 D5
Cinema Roma,	30 D5
Metropolitan,	31 F1
Nuovo Olimpia,	32 F2
Nuovo Sacher	33 D6

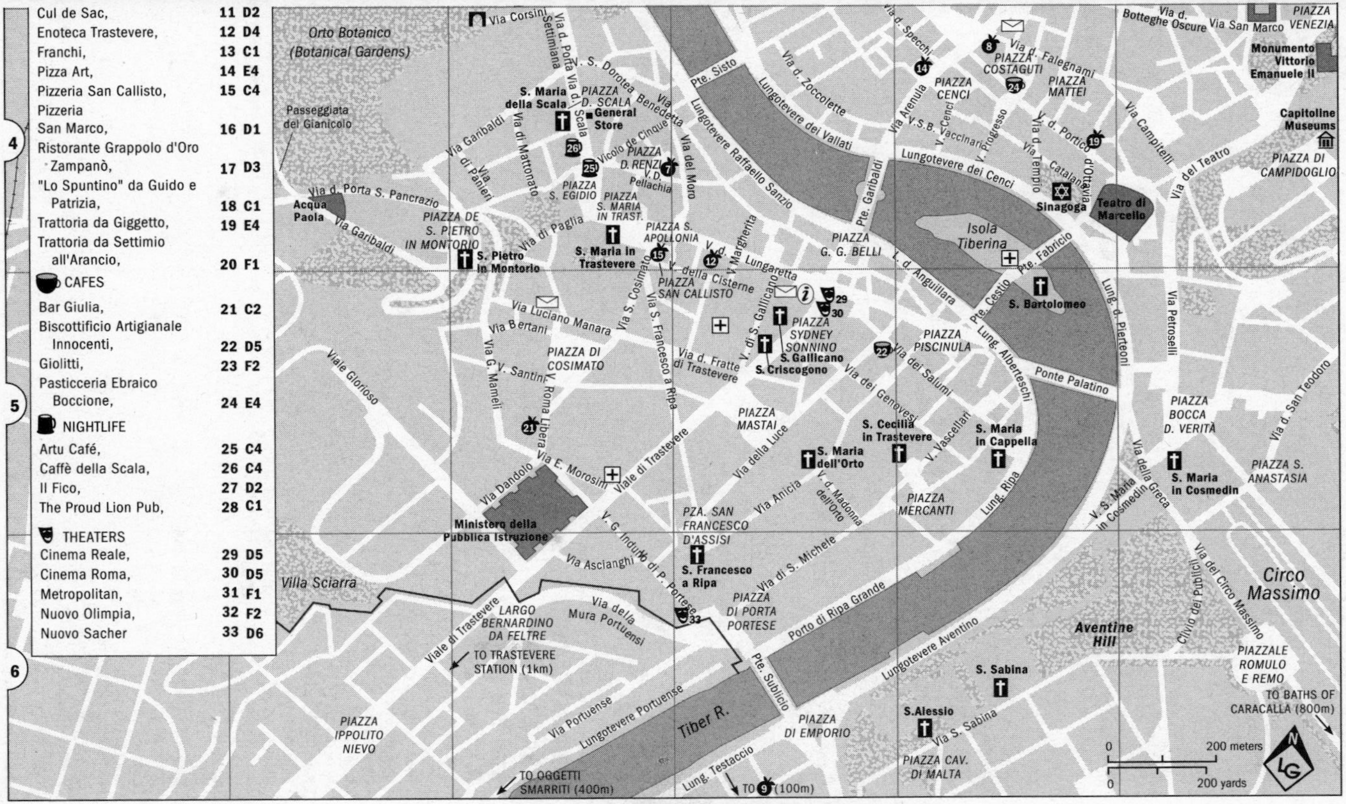

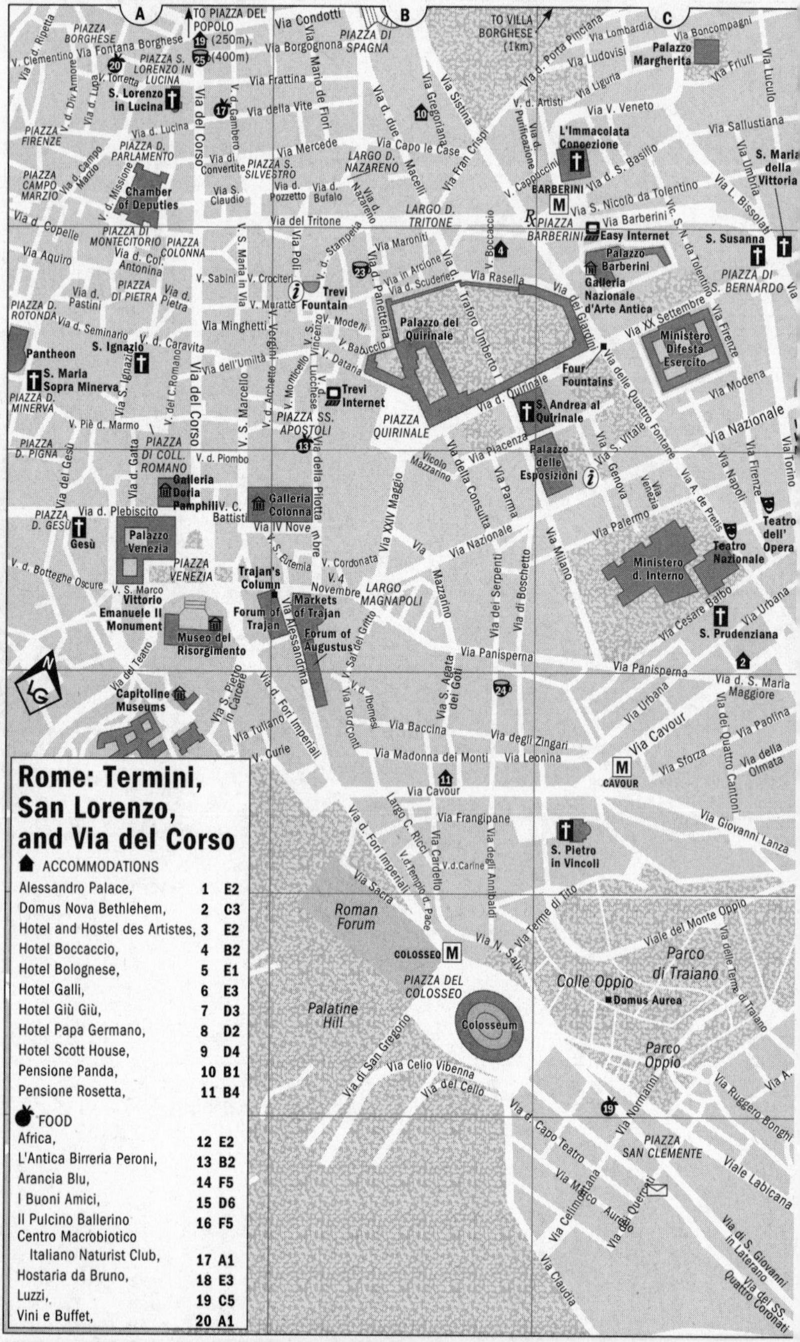
Rome: Termini, San Lorenzo, and Via del Corso
ACCOMMODATIONS
Alessandro Palace, 1 E2
Domus Nova Bethlehem, 2 C3
Hotel and Hostel des Artistes, 3 E2
Hotel Boccaccio, 4 B2
Hotel Bolognese, 5 E1
Hotel Galli, 6 E3
Hotel Giù Giù, 7 D3
Hotel Papa Germano, 8 D2
Hotel Scott House, 9 D4
Pensione Panda, 10 B1
Pensione Rosetta, 11 B4
FOOD
Africa, 12 E2
L'Antica Birreria Peroni, 13 B2
Arancia Blu, 14 F5
I Buoni Amici, 15 D6
Il Pulcino Ballerino 16 F5
Centro Macrobiotico Italiano Naturist Club, 17 A1
Hostaria da Bruno, 18 E3
Luzzi, 19 C5
Vini e Buffet, 20 A1
A
B
C
TO PIAZZA DEL POPOLO 19 (250m), 25 (400m)
TO VILLA BORGHESE (1km)
PIAZZA BORGHESE
Via Fontana Borghese
PIAZZA S. LORENZO IN LUCINA
S. Lorenzo in Lucina
Via Condotti
Via Borgognona
PIAZZA DI SPAGNA
Via Frattina
Via della Vite
Via del Corso
Via Mario de Fiori
Via Sistina
Via Gregoriana
Via Capo le Case
Via Mercede
LARGO D. NAZARENO
PIAZZA S. SILVESTRO
Via del Tritone
LARGO D. TRITONE
Via d. Porta Pinciana
Via Lombardia
Via Boncompagni
Palazzo Margherita
Via Ludovisi
Via V. Veneto
Via Sallustiana
L'Immacolata Concezione
BARBERINI
PIAZZA BARBERINI
Via Barberini
Easy Internet
Palazzo Barberini
Galleria Nazionale d'Arte Antica
S. Maria della Vittoria
S. Susanna
PIAZZA DI S. BERNARDO
Via XX Settembre
Ministero Difesa Esercito
PIAZZA FIRENZE
PIAZZA CAMPO MARZIO
PIAZZA D. PARLAMENTO
Chamber of Deputies
PIAZZA DI MONTECITORIO
PIAZZA COLONNA
PIAZZA DI PIETRA
PIAZZA D. ROTONDA
Pantheon
S. Ignazio
S. Maria Sopra Minerva
PIAZZA D. MINERVA
Trevi Fountain
Trevi Internet
Via Rasella
Palazzo dei Quirinale
Four Fountains
S. Andrea al Quirinale
PIAZZA QUIRINALE
PIAZZA SS. APOSTOLI
Via Nazionale
Palazzo delle Esposizioni
Via Torino
Teatro dell' Opera
Teatro Nazionale
Ministero d. Interno
PIAZZA D. PIGNA
PIAZZA DI COLL. ROMANO
Galleria Doria Pamphili
Galleria Colonna
PIAZZA D. GESÙ
Gesù
Via d. Plebiscito
Palazzo Venezia
PIAZZA VENEZIA
Vittorio Emanuele II Monument
Museo del Risorgimento
Trajan's Column
Markets of Trajan
Forum of Trajan
Forum of Augustus
LARGO MAGNAPOLI
Via Milano
Via Cesare Balbo
S. Prudenziana
Via Panisperna
Capitoline Museums
Via d. Fori Imperiali
Via Baccina
Via degli Zingari
Via Madonna dei Monti
Via Leonina
Via Cavour
CAVOUR
Via Giovanni Lanza
S. Pietro in Vincoli
Via Frangipane
Roman Forum
Via Sacra
COLOSSEO
PIAZZA DEL COLOSSEO
Colosseum
Palatine Hill
Colle Oppio
Parco di Traiano
Domus Aurea
Parco Oppio
Viale del Monte Oppio
Via di San Gregorio
Via Celio Vibenna
Via del Celio
Via d. Capo Teatro
PIAZZA SAN CLEMENTE
Viale Labicana
Via Claudia
Via di S. Giovanni in Laterano
Via dei SS. Quattro Coronati

ITALY

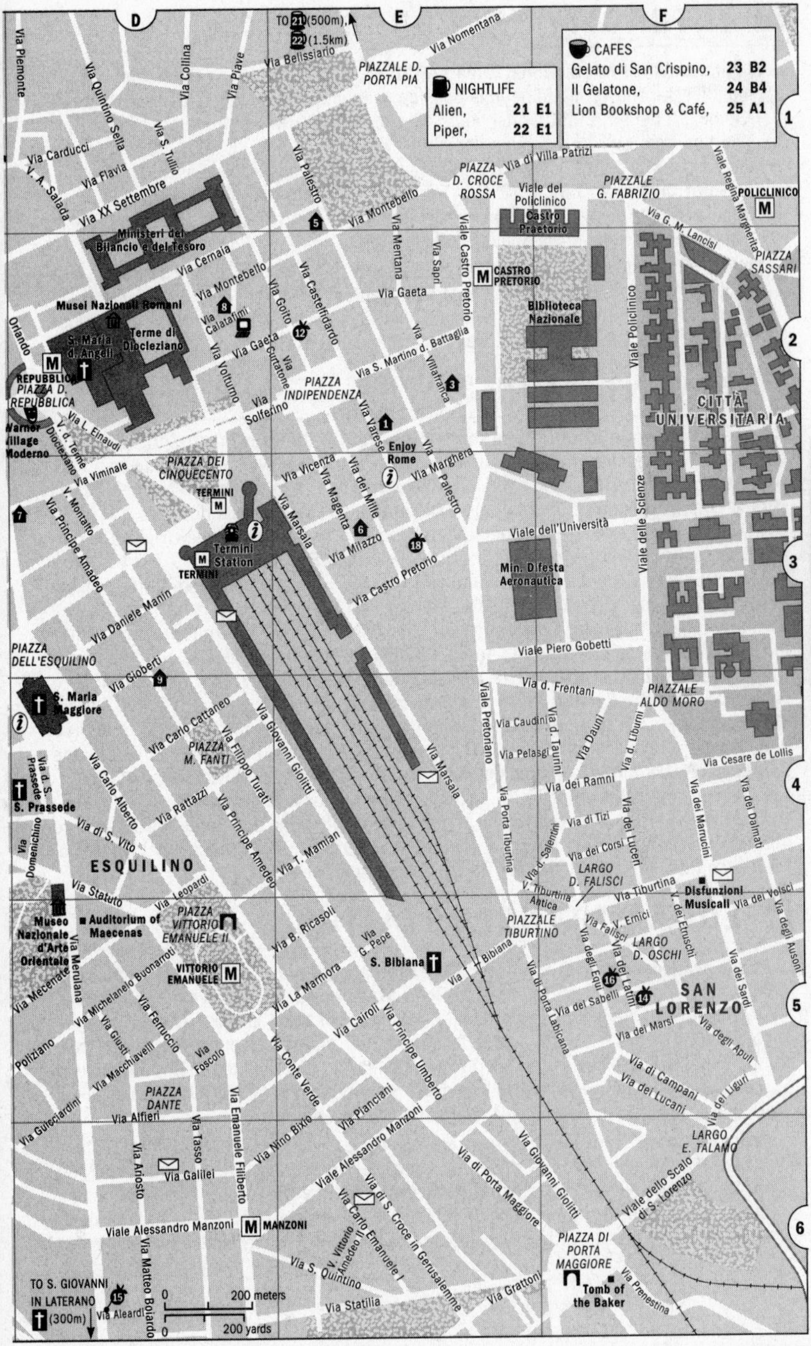
NIGHTLIFE
Alien, 21 E1
Piper, 22 E1
CAFES
Gelato di San Crispino, 23 B2
Il Gelatone, 24 B4
Lion Bookshop & Café, 25 A1
D
E
F
1
2
3
4
5
6
TO 21 (500m), 22 (1.5km)
Via Nomentana
Via Piemonte
Via Quintino Sella
Via Collina
Via Piave
Via Belissario
PIAZZALE D. PORTA PIA
Via Carducci
V. A. Salada
Via S. Tullio
Via Flavia
Via XX Settembre
Via Palestro
Via Montebello
PIAZZA D. CROCE ROSSA
Via di Villa Patrizi
Viale del Policlinico
PIAZZALE G. FABRIZIO
Viale Regina Margherita
POLICLINICO
Via G. M. Lancisi
PIAZZA SASSARI
Castro Pretorio
Ministeri del Bilancio e del Tesoro
Via Cernaia
Via Mentana
Via Sapri
Viale Castro Pretorio
CASTRO PRETORIO
Via Gaeta
Via Castelfidardo
Via Goito
Musei Nazionali Romani
Via Calatafimi
Terme di Diocleziano
S. Maria d. Angeli
Orlando
REPUBBLICA
PIAZZA D. REPUBBLICA
Via Gaeta
Via Cuttatone
Via Volturno
Via S. Martino d. Battaglia
Via Villafranca
Biblioteca Nazionale
Viale Policlinico
PIAZZA INDIPENDENZA
Via Solferino
Via Varese
Warner Village Moderno
Via L. Einaudi
V. d. Terme Diocleziano
CITTÀ UNIVERSITARIA
Enjoy Rome
Via Vicenza
Via Marghera
Via Magenta
Via dei Mille
Via Palestro
Via Viminale
PIAZZA DEI CINQUECENTO
TERMINI
V. Montalto
Via Principe Amedeo
Via Marsala
Via Milazzo
Viale dell'Università
Viale delle Scienze
Termini Station
Via Castro Pretorio
Min. Difesa Aeronautica
Via Daniele Manin
PIAZZA DELL'ESQUILINO
Viale Piero Gobetti
Via Gioberti
S. Maria Maggiore
Via d. Frentani
PIAZZALE ALDO MORO
Viale Pretoriano
Via Caudini
Via d. Taurini
Via Dauni
Via d. Liburni
Via Carlo Cattaneo
Via Giovanni Giolitti
PIAZZA M. FANTI
Via Filippo Turati
Via Pelasgi
Via Cesare de Lollis
Via d. S. Prassede
S. Prassede
Via Carlo Alberto
Via Rattazzi
Via Marsala
Via dei Ramni
Via dei Marrucini
Via dei Dalmati
Via di S. Vito
Via Principe Amedeo
Via Porta Tiburtina
Via di Tizi
Via dei Luceri
Via Domenichino
ESQUILINO
Via T. Mamiani
Via d. Salentini
Via dei Corsi
LARGO D. FALISCI
Via Statuto
Via Leopardi
V. Tiburtina Antica
Via Tiburtina
Disfunzioni Musicali
Via dei Volsci
Museo Nazionale d'Arte Orientale
Auditorium of Maecenas
PIAZZA VITTORIO EMANUELE II
Via B. Ricasoli
Via G. Pepe
PIAZZALE TIBURTINO
Via Falisci
V. Emici
V. dei Etruschi
Via degli Ausoni
Via Merulana
Via Michelangelo Buonarroti
VITTORIO EMANUELE
S. Bibiana
Via Bibiana
Via degli Equi
Via dei Latini
LARGO D. OSCHI
Via dei Sardi
Via Mecenate
Via La Marmora
Via di Porta Labicana
Via del Sabelli
SAN LORENZO
Via Giusti
Via Ferruccio
Via Cairoli
Via Principe Umberto
Via dei Marsi
Via degli Apuli
Poliziano
Via Macchiavelli
Via Foscolo
Via Conte Verde
Via di Campani
Via dei Lucani
Via dei Liguri
PIAZZA DANTE
Via Alfieri
Via Emanuele Filiberto
Via Tasso
Via Nino Bixio
Via Pianciani
Via Guicciardini
Viale Alessandro Manzoni
LARGO E. TALAMO
Via Ariosto
Via Galilei
Via di Porta Maggiore
Via Giovanni Giolitti
Viale dello Scalo di S. Lorenzo
Via di S. Croce in Gerusalemme
Via Carlo Emanuele I
V. Vittorio Amedeo II
Viale Alessandro Manzoni
MANZONI
Via Matteo Bolardo
PIAZZA DI PORTA MAGGIORE
Via S. Quintino
Tomb of the Baker
Via Prenestina
TO S. GIOVANNI IN LATERANO (300m)
Via Aleardi
Via Statilia
Via Grattoni
0 200 meters
0 200 yards

ITALY

INTERCITY TRANSPORTATION

Flights: Da Vinci International Airport (**FCO;** ☎65 951), known as **Fiumicino,** handles most flights. The **Termini** line runs nonstop to Rome's main station, **Stazione Termini** (30min., 2 per hr., €9.50). After hours, take the blue COTRAL **bus** (☎800 15 00 08) to Tiburtina from outside the main doors after customs (4 per day, €5). From Tiburtina, take bus #175 or 492, or metro B to Termini. A few domestic flights, including Ryanair, arrive at **Ciampino** (**CIA;** ☎79 49 41). To get to Rome, take the COTRAL bus (every 30min., €1) to Anagnina station, or the **Terravision Shuttle** (www.terravision.it) to V. Marsala at the Hotel Royal Santina (40min., €9).

Trains: rains leave Stazione Termini for: **Bologna** (2½-3½hr., €26-37); **Florence** (1½-3¾hr., €15-30); **Milan** (4½-8hr., €31-47); **Naples** (1¾-2½hr., €11-23); **Venice** (4½-5½hr., €36-58). Trains arriving in Rome between midnight and 5am arrive at **Stazione Tiburtina** or **Stazione Ostiense,** which are connected to Termini by the #175 bus.

ORIENTATION

Because navigating Rome's winding streets can be difficult, it's helpful to orient yourself by major landmarks, main arteries, or the **Tiber River,** which snakes north-south through the city. Most trains arrive in **Stazione Termini,** east of Rome's **centro storico** (historic center). **Termini** and **San Lorenzo** to the east are home to the city's largest university and most budget accommodations. **Via Nazionale** originates two blocks northwest of Termini Station in **Piazza della Repubblica** and leads to **Piazza Venezia,** the city's focal point, recognizable by the wedding-cake-like **Vittorio Emanuele II monument.** From P. Venezia, **Via dei Fori Imperiali** runs southeast to the Ancient city, where the **Colosseum** and the **Roman Forum** commemorate former glory. **Via del Corso** stretches from P. Venezia to **Piazza del Popolo,** centered on a black obelisk, in the north. The **Trevi fountain, Piazza Barberini,** and fashionable streets around the **Spanish Steps** in **Piazza di Spagna** lie to the east of V. del Corso. **Villa Borghese,** with its impressive gardens and museums, is northeast of P. di Spagna. To the west of V. del Corso is the *centro storico,* with its tangle of sights: **the Pantheon, Piazza Navona, Campo dei Fiori,** and the old **Jewish Ghetto.** West of P. Venezia, **Largo Argentina,** marks the start of **Corso Vittorio Emanuele II,** which runs through the *centro storico* to the river. **Vatican City** and the **Borgo-Prati** area are across the river. To the south of the Vatican is **Trastevere** and residential **Testaccio.** Pick up a free, necessary map at Enjoy Rome (see below).

LOCAL TRANSPORTATION

Public Transportation: The A and B **Metropolitana** subway lines (www.metroroma.it) meet at Termini and run 5:30am-11:30pm. **ATAC Buses** (www.atac.roma.it) run 5am-midnight (with limited late-night routes); validate your ticket in the machine when you board. Buy tickets (€1) at *tabaccherie,* newsstands, and station machines; they're valid for 1 metro ride or unlimited bus travel within 1¼hr. of validation. **BIG daily tickets** (€4), 3-day tourist passes (€11), and **CIS weekly tickets** (€16) allow for unlimited public transport. Pickpocketing is rampant on buses and trains.

Taxis: Radiotaxi (☎06 35 70). Taxis are expensive. Find them at stands or flag them down. Ride only in yellow or white taxis, and make sure your taxi has a meter (if not, negotiate the price before riding). **Surcharges** apply at night (€2.60), on Su (€1), and when heading to or from Fiumicino (€7.25) or Ciampino (€5.50). Fares run about €7.75 from Termini to Vatican City, around €35 between the city center and Fiumicino.

PRACTICAL INFORMATION

Tourist Office: Enjoy Rome, V. Marghera 8/A (☎44 56 68 90; www.enjoyrome.com). From the middle concourse of Termini, exit right; cross V. Marsala and follow V. Marghera for 3 blocks. Staff makes reservations at museums, shows, and accommodations, and leads tours (€24, under 26 €18). Good map and *When in Rome* booklet. Open Apr.-Oct. M-F 8:30am-7pm, Sa 8:30am-2pm; Nov.-Mar. M-F 9am-6pm, Sa 9am-2pm.

Embassies: Australia, V. Antonio Bosio 5 (☎85 2721; www.italy.embassy.gov.au). Open M-F 8:30am-5pm. **Canada,** V. Zara 30 (☎85 44 41; www.canada.it). Open M-F 9am-5pm. **Ireland,** P. di Campitelli 3 (☎697 91 21). **New Zealand,** V. Zara 28 (☎441 71 71). Open M-F 8:30am-12:45pm and 1:45-5pm. **UK,** V. XX Settembre 80 (☎42 20 00 01). Consular section open M-F 9:15am-1:30pm. **US,** V. Vittorio Veneto 119/A (☎467 41; www.usembassy.it/mission). Open M-F 8:30am-5:30pm.

Currency Exchange: Banca di Roma and **Banca Nazionale del Lavoro** have good rates, but near-ubiquitous **ATMs** have the best. Open M-F 8:30-1:30pm.

American Express: P. di Spagna 38 (☎67 641, lost cards 72 282). Open Sept.-July M-F 9am-7:30pm, Sa 9am-3pm; Aug. M-F 9am-6pm, Sa 9am-12:30pm.

Luggage Storage: In Termini, underneath track #24.

Lost Property: Oggetti Smarriti (☎58 16 040). On buses (☎58 16 040); Metro A (☎48 74 309), call M, W, F 9am-12:30pm; Metro B (☎57 53 22 65), call M, W, F-Sa 7-9am.

GLBT Resources: ARCI-GAY, V. Goito 35/B (☎64 50 11 02; www.arcigayroma.it). Open M-F 3-6pm. **Circolo Mario Mieli di Cultura Omosessuale,** V. Efeso 2/A (☎54 13 985); www.mariomieli.org). M: B-San Paolo. Open daily 10am-7pm.

Laundromat: BollaBlu, V. Milazzo 20/B. (☎44 70 30 96). Laundry about €8. Open daily 8am-midnight. **OndaBlu** (info ☎800 86 13 46). 17 locations throughout the city.

Emergency: ☎113. **Police:** ☎112. **Ambulance:** ☎118. **Fire:** ☎115.

Pharmacies: Farmacia Internazionale, P. Barberini 49 (☎487 11 95). Open 9am-12:30pm and 3-9pm. MC/V. **Farmacia Piram,** V. Nazionale 228 (☎488 07 54). Open 24hr. MC/V.

Hospitals: International Medical Center, V. Firenze 47 (☎48 82 371; www.imc84.com). Call ahead. Referral service to English-speaking doctors. General visit €100. Open M-Sa 9am-8pm; on-call 24hr. **Rome-American Hospital,** V.E. Longoni 69 (24hr. service ☎225 51, appointments 22 55 290; www.rah.it). Visits average €100-200.

Internet Access: A new Italian law requires a passport or driver's license to use an Internet cafe. **Splashnet,** V. Varese 33 (☎49 38 20 73), near Termini. €1.50 per hr. Open daily in summer 8:30am-1am; in winter 8:30am-11pm. **Easy Internet,** V. Barberini 2/16. Copying, scanning, laptop connection. About €2 per hr. Open daily 8am-1am.

Post Office: Main Post Office (Posta Centrale), P. San Silvestro 19. Open M-F 8am-7pm, Sa 8am-1:15pm. Branch at V. d. Terme di Diocleziano 30, near Termini.

ACCOMMODATIONS

Rome swells with tourists around Easter, May through July, and in September. Prices vary widely with the seasons, and a proprietor's willingness to negotiate depends on length of stays and group size. Termini swarms with hotel scouts. Many are legitimate and have IDs issued by tourist offices; however, some impostors with fake badges direct travelers to run-down locations charging exorbitant rates. The three **Hostels Alessandro** (www.hotstelsalessandro.com) around the Termini station offer great prices and a fun, social atmosphere.

ITALY

HOTELS AND HOSTELS

CENTRO STORICO AND ANCIENT CITY

If being a bit closer to the sights is important to you, then choosing Rome's medieval center over the area near Termini may be worth the higher prices.

Pensione Rosetta, V. Cavour 295 (☎47 82 30 69; www.rosettahotel.com). Buzz to open doors. 9 renovated ones have bigger bathrooms and showers, plus A/C (€10). Reserve 2 months ahead. Singles €60; doubles €85; triples €95; quads €110. AmEx/MC/V. ❹

Albergo della Lunetta, P. del Paradiso 68 (☎68 61 080; www.albergodellalunetta.it). Bus #64 to S. Andrea della Valle. From Piazza Navona, take the 1st right off V. Chiavari, behind Sant'Andrea della Valle. Clean well-lit rooms, some facing a small courtyard. Luggage storage and lockers. Reserve ahead. Singles €60, with bath €70; doubles €90/120; triples €120/150; quads €180. MC/V. ❹

Albergo del Sole, V. d. Biscione 76 (☎68 80 68 73; www.solealbiscione.it), off Campo dei Fiori. Comfortable, modern rooms with phone and TV. Luggage storage and safe. Reception 24hr. Check-in and check-out 11am. Reserve 2 months ahead. Singles €65-85; doubles €95-150; triples €175; quads €212. Cash or checks only. ❺

PIAZZA DI SPAGNA AND ENVIRONS

Though prices near P. di Spagna can be very steep, accommodations are often newer than in the *centro storico* and closer to the metro.

Pensione Panda, V. della Croce 35 (☎67 80 179; www.hotelpanda.it). M: A-Spagna. Between P. di Spagna and V. del Corso. 28 renovated rooms with faux marble statues and frescoed ceilings. English spoken. A/C €6. Free Internet connection. Reserve ahead. Singles €48, with bath €68; doubles €68/98; triples €130; quads €170. Jan.-Feb. 5% *Let's Go* discount when paying with cash. AmEx/MC/V. ❹

Hotel Boccaccio, V. del Boccaccio 25 (☎48 85 962; www.hotelboccaccio.com). M: A-Barberini. Near P. Barberini. Cozy and worn-in, with 8 simply furnished rooms and a terrace. Singles €43; doubles €73, with bath €93; triples €94/126. AmEx/MC/V. ❹

BORGO AND PRATI (NEAR VATICAN CITY)

Pensioni near the Vatican offer some of the best deals in Rome and the sobriety one would expect from a neighborhood with this kind of nun-to-tourist ratio.

Colors, V. Boezio 31 (☎68 74 030; www.colorshotel.com). M: A-Ottaviano. With a design scheme Mondrian would have applauded, this 3-fl. complex is part hostel, part hotel. Communal terraces and kitchens open 7:30am-10pm. Internet €2 per hr. Call by 9pm the night before to reserve dorms. Hostel: dorms €23; singles €60-65; doubles €90-110; triples €110-130. Hotel: singles €90; doubles €120; triples €140; quads €150. Free breakfast with hotel rooms. Cash only. ❷

Hotel San Pietrino, V. G. Bettolo 43, 3rd fl. (☎37 00 132; www.sanpietrino.it). M: A-Ottaviano. Spacious rooms are simple, clean, and have free A/C, TV, DVD, and DSL Internet connection. Terrace with communal fridge. Bikes €5 per day. Laundry €6-8. Reserve 1 month ahead in high season. Singles €30-45; doubles €70-98; triples €90-125; family suite €112-155. 10% *Let's Go* discount. AmEx/MC/V. ❸

Hotel Lady, V. Germanico 198, 4th fl. (☎32 42 112; www.hoteladyroma.it). Rooms have antique furniture and handmade linens in addition to sinks, desks, phones, and fans, but no A/C. Breakfast €10. Free Internet. High season singles €80; doubles €110, with bath €150; triples €135. Low-season rates vary. AmEx/MC/V. ❺

Ostello Per La Gioventù Foro Italico (HI), V. delle Olimpiadi 61 (☎32 36 267; bookingrome@tiscali.it). M: A-Ottaviano, then bus #32 from P. di Risorgimento to the second "LGT Cadorna Ostello Gioventù" stop (15min.). Hostel is next to a Carabinieri station on your left. If you feel nostalgic for dorm life, this hostel is for you. A barrack-style building holds giant dorm rooms, bathrooms, cafeteria, and common room. Breakfast, showers, and linens included. Luggage storage €1 per day. Laundry and Internet. Reception 7am-11pm. Curfew 1-1:30am. Dorms €21. €3 HI discount. AmEx/MC/V. ❷

SAN LORENZO AND EAST OF TERMINI

Welcome to budget traveler and backpacker central. While Termini is chock-full of traveler's services, use caution when walking in the area, especially at night, and keep close watch on your pockets and/or purse.

Hotel and Hostel Des Artistes, V. Villafranca 20, 5th fl. (☎44 54 365; www.hoteldesartistes.com). Des Artistes houses a hotel and a renovated hostel with large, sunny rooms, communal bathrooms, and free Internet. Hostel towels €1, plus €10 deposit. Reception 24hr. Check-out 11am. Dorms €20-26. Hostel cash only. Hotel AmEx/MC/V. ❷

Hotel Galli, V. Milazzo 20 (☎44 56 859, fax44 68 501; www.albergogalli.com). Reception on 2nd fl. 12 rooms have bath, minifridge, phone, TV, and safe. A/C €5. Check-in noon. Check-out 10am. Reserve by fax or email. Singles €70; doubles €100; triples €120; quads €160. AmEx/MC/V. ❹

VIA XX SETTEMBRE AND NORTH OF TERMINI

Dominated by government ministries and private apartments, this area is less noisy and touristy than nearby Termini.

Hotel Papa Germano, V. Calatafimi 14/A (☎48 69 19; www.hotelpapagermano.com). Clean rooms with TV, hair dryer, and mini-fridge. A/C €5. Breakfast, linens, and towels included. Internet €2 per hr. Check-out 11am. Dorms €23-28; singles €50; doubles €80-95; triples €100; quads €120. AmEx/MC/V. ❷

Hotel Bolognese, V. Palestro 15, 2nd fl. (☎/fax 49 00 45; hbolognese@tiscali.it). The artist-owner's paintings distinguish this otherwise standard hotel. Check-out 11am. Singles €30-60; doubles €40-80; triples €90. Extra bed for €20. AmEx/MC/V. ❸

ESQUILINO AND WEST OF TERMINI

Esquilino, south of Termini, has tons of cheap hotels close to major sights. The area west of Termini is more inviting than Esquilino, with busy, shop-lined streets.

Alessandro Palace, V. Vicenza 42 (☎446 19 58; www.hostelalessandropalace.com). Exit Termini at track #1. Turn left on V. Marsala, right on V. Vicenza. Renovated dorms, all with bath and A/C. Bar. Breakfast included. Linens included. Towels €2 in dorms. Internet €2 per hr. Dorms €23-25; doubles €80; quads €120. AmEx/MC/V. ❷

Alessandro Downtown, V. C. Cattaneo 23 (☎443 40 147; www.hostelalessandrodowntown.com). Exit Termini by track #22, make a left on V. Giolitti, then a right onto V. C. Cattaneo. Slightly quieter than the Palace, guests can go to its bar. Kitchen, TV, fans, but no A/C. Breakfast included. Lockers available. Towels €2. Dorms €22-25; doubles €70, with bath €90; quads €108/120. AmEx/MC/V. ❷

Hotel Scott House, V. Gioberti 30 (☎446 53 79; www.scotthouse.com). Colorful, modern rooms have full private baths, A/C, phones, and satellite TV. Breakfast included. Free Internet. Check-out 11am. Dorms €22-25; singles €68; doubles €98; triples €114; quads €129. AmEx/MC/V. €5 discount per night if paying in cash. ❸

Hotel Giù Giù, V. d. Viminale 8 (☎482 77 34; www.hotelgiugiu.com). This elegant *palazzo* filled with knick-knacks makes guests feel like they're spending time at grandma's. Rooms with A/C; all but singles have private baths. Breakfast €8. Check-out 10am. Singles €40; doubles €70; triples €90; quads €120. Prices quoted are for *Let's Go* users. Cash only. ❸

ITALY

RELIGIOUS HOUSING

Don't automatically think "Catholic" or even "cheap;" most are open to people of all religions, and single rooms can run to €155. Don't expect quaint rooms in cloisters; the rooms in religious housing have amenities similar to hotel rooms. Do, however, think sober: early curfews and/or chores are standard.

Domus Nova Bethlehem, V. Cavour 85/A (☎47 82 44 14). Take V. Cavour from Termini, past P. d. Esquilino. Modern religious icons abound. Rooms with A/C, bath, and TV. Breakfast included. Internet with phonecard. Summer curfew 2:30am, winter 1am. Singles €78; doubles €114; triples €140; quads €150. AmEx/MC/V. ❺

Santa Maria Alle Fornaci, P. S. Maria alle Fornaci 27 (☎393 676 32; www.trinitaridematha.it). Facing St. Peter's, turn left through a gate in the basilica onto V. d. Fornace. Take 3rd right onto V. d. Gasperi, which leads to P. S. Maria alle Fornaci. Go down the steps just to the church's left. Rooms have bath and phone. Common room. Breakfast included. Reception 24hr. Singles €55; doubles €85; triples €120. AmEx/MC/V. ❹

FOOD

Traditional Roman cuisine includes *spaghetti alla carbonara* (egg and cream sauce with bacon), *spaghetti all'amatriciana* (spicy, with thin tomato sauce, chiles, and bacon), *carciofi alla giudeia* (deep-fried artichokes, common in the Jewish Ghetto), and *fiori di zucca* (stuffed, fried zucchini flowers). Pizza is often good, and like elsewhere in Italy is always eaten with a fork and a knife. Instead of the usually bland bread, try *pizza romana*, which is more like foccaccia: a flat bread rubbed with olive oil, sea salt, and rosemary, and sometimes covered with a few more toppings. Lunch is typically the main meal of the day, although some Romans now munch *panini* on the go during the week. Restaurants tend to close between 3 and 7:30pm.

RESTAURANTS

ANCIENT CITY AND CENTRO STORICO

The area around the Forum and the Colosseum is home to some of Italy's finest tourist traps. The restaurants in the *centro storico* can be frightfully expensive and generic, especially those near famous landmarks. Head to **Via del Governo Vecchio** and its tiny cross streets for more authentic fare. The **Campo dei Fiori,** a daily food and clothing market, is surrounded by a labyrinth of crooked streets that can be frustrating, but almost invariably worthwhile, to navigate.

I Buoni Amici, V. Aleardi 4 (☎70 49 19 93). M: B-Colosseo. The owner's exceptional service complements the popular *linguine alle vongole* (with clams; €7) and the self-serve *antipasto* bar. *Primi* €7-8, *secondi* €7-12. Wine €7-18. Cover €1. Open M-Sa 12:30-3pm and 7:30-11:30pm. AmEx/DC/MC/V. ❷

Luzzi, V. S. Giovanni in Laterano 88 (☎70 96 332), 3 blocks past the Colosseum coming from V. dei Fori Imperiali, yet always packed with locals. Cheap, no-fuss, traditional fare and house wine. *Antipasto* €4. Cheeses €3-4. Omelettes from €4. *Primi* €3.50-6, *Secondi* €4-10. Open M-Tu and Th-Su noon-3pm and 7pm-midnight. AmEx/MC/V. ❷

L'Antica Birreria Peroni, V. San Marcello 19 (☎67 95 310). Ask for the *rosso,* 1 of 4 well-priced beers on tap. Fantastic *fiori di zucca* (€2). *Primi* €6. Cover €1.50 Open M-Sa noon-midnight. AmEx/MC/V. ❷

Pizza Art, V. Arenula 76 (☎68 73 160). This place looks like a typical pizzeria but in fact serves thick slices of foccaccia, priced per kg. Toppings include tomato, mozzarella, and goat cheese. Average slice €2.40. Open daily 12:30-around 11 pm. Cash only. ❶

Ristorante Grappolo d'Oro Zampanò, P. della Cancelleria 80/83 (☎68 97 080). This slightly upscale *hostaria's* pastas are homemade. Decor is sleeker than that of the average *trattoria*. *Antipasti* €7.50-8.50. *Primi* €9-10. *Secondi* €14-15. Open M and W-Su noon-2:30pm and 7:30-11pm, Tu 7:30-11pm, Sa 7:30-11:30pm. AmEx/MC/V. ❸

JEWISH GHETTO

A 10min. walk south of the Campo, restaurants here serve Roman specialties alongside traditional Jewish and kosher dishes. Many close on Saturdays.

Bar Da Benito, V. d. Falegnami 14 (☎68 61 508). A rare combination—*secondi* for less than €5 and a place to sit and enjoy your food. 2 *primi* prepared daily (€4.50). *Secondi* €3.50-6.50. *Dolci* €2-3.50. Open Sept.-July M-Sa 6:30am-7:30pm. Cash only. ❷

Trattoria da Giggetto, V. d. Portico d'Ottavia 21-22 (☎68 61 105). No animal parts go to waste here. In the Roman tradition, *fritto di cervello d'abbacchino* (brains with vegetables; €12) are served alongside delicacies like fried artichokes (€5). *Primi* €7.50-12. *Secondi* €8-18. Cover €1.50. Open Tu-Su 12:15-3pm and 7:30-11pm. Closed the last 2 weeks of July. Reserve ahead for dinner. AmEx/MC/V. ❸

PIAZZA DI SPAGNA

The P. di Spagna and Trevi Fountain area, though busy at night and closer to tourist destinations, is on the disappointing side of the quality-for-money spectrum. Head off the main drags (V. del Corso and V. dei Condotti) for worthy eateries.

Trattoria da Settimio all'Arancio, V. dell'Arancio 50-52 (☎68 76 119). Not to be confused with pizzeria. Portions are generous. *Primi* from €7.50, *secondi* from €8.50. Open M-Sa 12:30-3pm and 7:30-11:30pm. Reserve ahead. AmEx/MC/V. ❹

Vini e Buffet, V. Torretta 60 (☎06 68 71 445), near P. d. Spagna. A favorite of Romans with a penchant for regional wine, chic neighborhoods, *pâtés* (€3.50-4), *crostini*, or *scarmorze* (smoked mozzarella; €6.50-8.50). Variety of salads €7.50-9. Wine €10-24. Open M-Sa 12:30-3pm and 7-11pm. Reservations recommended. Cash only. ❷

Centro Macrobiotico Italiano Naturist Club, V. della Vite 14, 4th fl. (☎67 92 509). This veggie haven has tuned traditional Roman cuisine to the pitch of organic vegan-vegetarian. Lunch *menù* €14, dinner *menù* €20-25. "Natural snacks" €8-10. Open M-Sa 12:30-3pm and 7:30-11pm. Dinner reservation required. AmEx/MC/V. ❹

BORGO AND PRATI (NEAR VATICAN CITY)

The streets near the Vatican are paved with bars and pizzerias that serve mediocre sandwiches at inflated prices. For better, much cheaper food, venture down **Via Cola di Rienzo** several blocks toward P. Cavour and explore the side streets.

Franchi, V. Cola di Rienzo 204 (☎68 74 651; www.franchi.it). Benedetto Franchi ("Frankie") has been providing the citizens of Prati with luxurious picnic supplies for a half-century. Especially delicious is the *fritti misti* (deep-fried vegetables). Be careful to look at each price before you buy. Open M-Sa 8:15am-9pm. AmEx/MC/V. ❷

Cacio e Pepe, V. Giuseppe Avezzana 11 (☎32 17 268). From P. Mazzini, turn right on V. Settembrini, at P. dei Martiri di Belfiore, and again on V. G. Avezzana (a 20min. walk from P. di Risorgimento). The namesake is pasta piled high with olive oil, grated cheese, and freshly ground pepper and carried to outdoor tables. Full lunch €5-10. Open M-F 12:30-3pm and 7pm-12:30am, Sa 12:30-3pm. Cash only. ❷

"Lo Spuntino" da Guido e Patrizia, Borgo Pio 13 (☎68 75 491), near Castel Sant'Angelo. Casual atmosphere and homey decor make Lo Spuntino popular with lunching locals, and Guido holds court behind a well-stocked *tavola calda*. Full meal (*primo, secondo,* and wine) runs less than €8. Open M-Sa 8am-8pm. Cash only. ❷

TRASTEVERE

The waits are long and the street-side tables are cramped, but you can't get more Roman than Trastevere. The tiny cobblestone side streets winding in and out of the *piazze* are crowded with locals sitting at the cafes, stands, and restaurants.

Pizzeria San Callisto, P. S. Callisto 9/A (☎581 82 56), off P. S. Maria. Simply the best pizza (€4.20-7.80) in Rome. Thin-crust pizzas so large they hang off the plates. Order to go to avoid waits. Open Tu-Su 7pm-midnight. AmEx/DC/MC/V. ❷

Pizzeria San Marco, V. Plinio 2 (☎323 53 98), off V. Cola d. Rienzo. 2nd best thin-crust pies. Topping-heavy pizzas (€8.50) are crispy with dough bubbles. AmEx/MC/V. ❷

Augusto, P. de' Renzi 15 (☎58 03 798). Pastas (approx. €5) appear almost immediately. Open Sept.-July M-F 12:30-3pm and 8-11pm, Sa 12:30-3pm. Cash only. ❶

SAN LORENZO AND TERMINI

Again, tourist traps proliferate in the Termini area. There is a well-stocked **CONAD** supermarket on the lower floor of the Termini Station, just inside the V. Marsala entrance. (☎87 40 60 55. Open daily 8am-midnight.) An abundance of budget-conscious students with discriminating palates in San Lorenzo makes for inexpensive food with local character. At night, map a route and avoid walking alone.

Africa, V. Gaeta 26-28 (☎494 10 77), near P. Indipendenza. Decked out in yellow and black, Africa has been making Eritrean and Ethiopian food for 20 years. The meat-filled *sambusas* (€3) are a flavorful starter. Vegetarian *secondi* €8-10. 0.75L wine €9-14. Cover €1. Open Tu-Su 8am-1:30am. DC/MC/V. ❷

Arancia Blu, V. d. Latini 65 (☎445 41 05), off V. Tiburtina. This elegant and popular vegetarian restaurant has an inspired menu, affordable in spite of its fine ingredients and upscale style. English menus available. Extensive wine list €12-130 per bottle. Chocolate-tasting *menù* (€14). Open daily 8:30pm-midnight. Cash only. ❷

Hostaria da Bruno, V. Varese 29 (☎49 04 03). From V. Marsala, take V. Milazzo and turn right on V. Varese. Italians who work in Termini lunch at this oasis amid tourist traps. Chocolate crepe €4. Open M-Sa noon-3pm and 7-10pm. AmEx/MC/V. ❷

TESTACCIO

Il Cantinone, P. Testaccio 31/32 (☎06 57 46 253). M: B-Piramide. A down-to-earth restaurant with massive portions of pasta (*pappardelle* with boar sauce €7.50), hearty meat dishes (approx. €9), and a terrific house white. Long tables make it group-friendly. Open M and W-Su noon-3pm and 7pm-midnight. AmEx/MC/V. ❸

Il Volpetti Più, V. Alessandro Volta 8 (☎06 57 44 306). Pick out large portions of food cafeteria-style, and then battle the lunching locals for a seat. Fresh salad, pasta, and pizza from €4. Open M-Sa 10:30am-3:30pm and 5:30-9:30pm. AmEx. ❶

DESSERT AND COFFEE

While gelato is everywhere in Rome, good gelato is not. Look for the signs of quality (See **The Ugly Duckling,** p. 585). Bakeries sell all kinds of cookies, pastries, and cakes, all priced by the *etto* (100g). Coffee is taken either standing up at the bar or sitting down at a table, with higher prices for table service.

Gelato di San Crispino, V. della Panetteria 42 (☎67 93 924). 2nd left off V. del Lavatore. A scoop, especially of the honey flavor, from San Crispino's is worth wishing for at the Trevi fountain. Open Su-M and W-Th noon-12:30am, F-Sa noon-1:30am. Cash only.

Biscottificio Artigiano Innocenti, V. della Luce 21, Trastevere (☎570 39 26), off V. dei Salumi. The shop sells divine cookies and biscuits at a counter in its no-nonsense stockroom. Stock up on hazelnut, chocolate, and jam cookies (€1.50 for 7 cookies).

The Lion Bookshop and Café, V. dei Greci, 33/36, P. di Spagna (☎06 326 54 007). This English-language bookstore has a cafe for thumbing through books while you sip espresso (€1.50-2.50) and listen to music from the conservatory across the street. Open M 3:30-7:30pm, Tu-Su 10am-7:30pm. AmEx/MC/V.

Pasticceria Ebraico Boccione, V. del Portico d'Ottavia 1, Jewish Ghetto (☎687 86 37), on the corner of P. Costaguti. This family-run bakery only makes about 8 items, including delicious challah twisted into croissants and filled with custard (€0.60), and *ciambelle.* Su-Th 8am-7:30pm, F 8am-3:30pm. In summer closed Su 2-4pm.

Bar Giulia (a.k.a. Cafe Peru), V. Giulia 84, Ancient City (☎06 68 61 310), near P. V. Emanuele II. Serves what may be the cheapest (and most delicious) coffee in Rome (€0.60, at table €0.70) and adds your favorite liqueur free. You may have to crowd surf to get your fresh-squeezed Orange juice. Open M-Sa 5am-9:30pm. Cash only.

Il Gelatone, V. dei Serpenti 28, Ancient City (☎48 20 187). Try *Gelatone* (*nocciola* and vanilla with chocolate chips). Cones €1.50-3. Open daily 11am-1am. Cash only.

ENOTECHE (WINE BARS)

Wine bars range from laid-back and local to chic and international, acting both as simple afternoon cafes and urban nightclub-lounges. *Enoteche* usually serve small dishes and plates, like cheese selections, smoked meats, *antipasti*, and salads, which make light, budget meals. Romans eat dinner around 9pm, so they either go to *enoteche* before dinner or sip and nibble their way through the entire night.

Enoteca Trastevere, V. della Lungaretta 86, Trastevere (☎58 85 659). A block off P. S. Maria. This casual *enoteca* attracts couples and jovial groups. Staff helps pick a bottle from the high-caliber wine list. Arrive late, as things pick up around midnight. Wine €3.50-5 per glass. Meat and cheese (€9-13). Open M-Sa 6pm-2:30am, Su 6pm-1am.

Cul de Sac, P. Pasquino 73 (☎68 80 10 94), off P. Navona. One of Rome's first wine bars, Cul de Sac has an extensive wine list (from €2 per glass). Specialty homemade pâtés such as boar and chocolate or pheasant with truffle (€6.20) are exquisite. Cheeses and meats €5-8. Open daily noon-4pm and 6pm-12:30am. MC/V.

SIGHTS

From ancient temples, medieval churches, and Renaissance basilicas to Baroque fountains and contemporary museums, *La Città Eterna* is a city bursting with masterpieces from every era of Western Civilization. Remember to dress modestly when visiting churches or the Vatican.

ANCIENT CITY

THE COLOSSEUM. This enduring symbol of the Eternal City—a hollowed-out marble ghost that dwarfs every other ruin in Rome—once held as many as 50,000 spectators. Within 100 days of its AD 80 opening, some 5000 wild beasts perished in the arena. The floor once covered a labyrinth of brick cells, ramps, and elevators used to transport wild animals from cages up to arena level. *(M: B-Colosseo. Open daily late Mar.-Aug. 9am-7:30pm; Sept. 9am-7pm; Oct. 9am-6:30pm; Nov. to mid-Feb. 9am-4:30pm; mid-Feb. to Mar. 9am-5pm. Combined ticket with Palatine Hill €11. English tours with archaeologist daily every 30-45min. 9:45am-1:45pm and 3-5pm. €3.50.)*

PALATINE HILL. Legend has it that the Palantine Hill was home to the she-wolf who suckled Romulus, mythical founder of Rome, and his brother Remus. The best way to attack the Palatine is from the stairs near the Forum's **Arch of Titus** (where ticket lines are shorter than at the Colosseum), which lead to gardens and lookouts. On the southwest side of the hill is an ancient village with the **Casa di Romulo,** alleged home of Romulus. The stairs to the left lead to the **Casa**

di Livia, home of Augustus's wife, which used to connect to the **Casa Augusto** next door. Around the corner, the spooky **Cryptoporticus** tunnel ties Tiberius's palace to nearby buildings. Solemn **Domus Augustana** was once the emperors' private space; sprawling **Domus Flavia,** to its right, once held a gigantic octagonal fountain. Between them stands the **Stadium Palatinum,** a sunken space once used as a riding school and now a museum with excavated artifacts. *(South of the Forum. Same hours and prices as Colosseum. Guided English tour daily 12:15pm. €3.50.)*

ROMAN FORUM. Etruscans and Greeks used the Forum as a marketplace, then early Romans founded a thatched-hut shanty town here in 753 BC. Enter by **Via Sacra,** Rome's oldest street, which leads to the **Arch of Titus.** In front of the **Curia** (Senate House), off V. Sacra to the right, was the **Comitium,** where male citizens came to vote and representatives gathered for public discussion. Bordering the Comitium is the large brick **Rostra** (speaker's platform), erected by Julius Caesar in 44 BC. The **market square** holds a number of shrines and sacred precincts, including the *Lapis Niger* (Black Stone), where Romulus was supposedly murdered by Republican senators; below that are the underground ruins of a 6th-century BC altar and the oldest known Latin inscription in Rome. In the square, the **Three Sacred Trees of Rome**—olive, fig, and grape—have been replanted. The **Lower Forum** holds the eight-columned, 5th-century BC **Temple of Saturn,** next to the *Rostra,* which achieved mythological status during Rome's Golden Age, when it hosted Saturnalia, a raucous, anything-goes Roman winter party. At the end of Vicus Tuscus stands the **Temple of Castor and Pollux,** built to celebrate the 499 BC Roman defeat of the Etruscans. The **Temple of Vesta,** where Vestal Virgins kept the city's sacred fire lit for more than 1000 years, is next to the **House of the Vestal Virgins,** where they lived for 30 secluded years beginning at the ripe old age of seven. V. Sacra continues out of the Forum proper to the Velia and the gargantuan **Basilica of Maxentius,** which once contained a gigantic bronze and marble statue of Constantine. *(M: B-Colosseo, or bus to P. Venezia. Main entrance is on V. dei Fori Imperiali, at Largo C. Ricci. Open daily in summer 8:30am-7:15pm, last entry 6:15pm; in winter 9am-4:15pm. English guided tour 11am. Audio tour €4.)*

ITALY

FORI IMPERIALI. Closed indefinitely for excavations, the **Fori Imperiali,** across the street from the Ancient Forum, is a complex of temples, basilicas, and public squares constructed in the first and second centuries, still visible from the railing at V. dei Fori Imperiali. Built between AD 107 and 113, the **Forum of Trajan** included a colossal equestrian statue of Trajan and an immense triumphal arch. At one end of the now-destroyed Forum, 2500 carved legionnaires march their way up the almost perfectly preserved **Trajan's Column,** one of the greatest specimens of Roman relief-sculpture. The crowning statue is St. Peter, who replaced Trajan in 1588. The gray rock wall of the **Forum of Augustus** commemorates Augustus's victory over Caesar's murderers in 42 BC. The only remnant of **Vespasian's Forum** is the mosaic-filled **Chiesa della Santi Cosma e Damiano** across V. Cavour, near the Roman Forum. *(Visitor's center open daily 9am-7:30pm. Free.)*

CAPITOLINE HILL. Home to the original capitol, the **Monte Capitolino** still serves as the seat of the city government. Michelangelo designed its **Piazza di Campidoglio,** now home to the **Capitoline Museums** (p. 606). Stairs lead up to the rear of the 7th-century **Chiesa di Santa Maria in Aracoeli.** *(Santa Maria open daily 9am-12:30pm and 2:30-6:30pm. Donation requested.)* The gloomy **Mamertine Prison,** consecrated as the **Chiesa di San Pietro in Carcere,** lies down the hill from the back stairs of the Aracoeli. *(Prison open daily in summer 9am-12:30pm and 2:30-6:30pm; in winter 9am-12:30pm and 2-5pm. Donation requested.)* At the far end of the *piazza,* opposite the stairs, lies the turreted **Palazzo dei Senatori,** the home of Rome's mayor. *(Take any bus to P. Venezia. From P. Venezia, walk around to P. d'Aracoeli, and take the stairs up the hill.)*

VELABRUM. The Velabrum area is in a Tiber flood plain, south of the Jewish Ghetto. At the bend of V. del Portico d'Ottavia, a shattered pediment and a few ivy-covered columns are all that remain of the once magnificent **Portico d'Ottavia.** The **Teatro di Marcello** next door was the model for the Colosseum's facade. One block south along V. Luigi Petroselli and undergoing renovations, the **Chiesa di Santa Maria in Cosmedin** harbors the **Bocca della Verità,** a drain cover made famous by the film *Roman Holiday.* The river god's face on it will supposedly chomp any liar's hand. *(Chiesa open daily 10am-1pm and 3-4pm.)*

DOMUS AUREA. The Domus Aurea is closed for renovations over the next two years. This park houses a portion of Nero's "Golden House," which once covered a huge chunk of Rome. After deciding that he was a god, Nero had architects build a house worthy of his divinity. The Forum was reduced to a vestibule of the palace; Nero crowned it with the 35m *Colossus*, a huge statue of himself as the sun. *(Starting Dec. 2006, the Domus Aurea will close until further notice, most likely until 2008.)*

CENTRO STORICO

VIA DEL CORSO AND PIAZZA VENEZIA. Shopping street **Via del Corso,** between P. del Popolo and busy P. Venezia, takes its name from its days as Rome's premier race course. **Palazzo Venezia** was one of the first Renaissance *palazzi* in the city; Mussolini used it as an office and delivered orations from its balcony, but today it's little more than a glorified roundabout dominated by the **Vittorio Emanuele II monument.**

ITALY

THE PANTHEON. Architects still wonder how this 2000-year-old temple was erected; its dome—a perfect half-sphere made of poured concrete without the support of vaults, arches, or ribs—is the largest of its kind. The light that enters the roof was used as a sundial and as indication of the dates of equinoxes and solstices. In AD 606, it was consecrated as the **Chiesa di Santa Maria ad Martyres.** *(In P. della Rotonda. Open M-Sa 8:30am-7:30pm, Su 9am-6pm. Closed Jan. 1, May 1, Dec. 25. Free.)*

PIAZZA NAVONA. Originally a first-century stadium, the *piazza* hosted wrestling matches, track and field events, and mock naval battles in which the stadium was flooded and filled with fleets skippered by convicts. Each of the river god statues in Bernini's **Fountain of the Four Rivers** represents one of the four continents of the globe (as known then): Ganges for Asia, Danube for Europe, Nile for Africa, and Río de la Plata for the Americas. *(Open daily 9am-noon and 4-7pm.)*

CAMPO DEI FIORI. Across C. Vittorio Emanuele II from P. Navona, Campo dei Fiori is one of the last authentically Roman areas of the *centro storico.* Home to a bustling market Monday through Saturday mornings (see p. 608), it morphs into a hot spot at night. The Renaissance **Palazzo Farnese,** built by Alessandro Farnese, the first Counter-Reformation pope, dominates P. Farnese, south of the Campo.

THE JEWISH GHETTO

Rome's Jewish community is the oldest in Europe—Israelites came in 161 BC as ambassadors from Judas Maccabei, asking for help against invaders. The Ghetto, the tiny area to which Pope Paul IV confined the Jews in 1555, was dissolved in 1870 but is still the center of Rome's Jewish population. In the center are **Piazza Mattei** and the 16th-century **Fontana delle Tartarughe.** Nearby is the **Chiesa di Sant'Angelo in Pescheria** where Jews, forced to attend mass, resisted by stuffing wax in their ears. *(V. de Funari, after P. Campitelli. Both fountain and church under restoration indefinitely.)* The **Sinagoga Ashkenazita,** on the Tiber near the Theater of Marcellus, was bombed in 1982; guards now search all visitors. Inside is the **Jewish Museum,** which has ancient Torahs and Holocaust artifacts. *(Synagogue open for services only. Museum open June-Sept. Su-Th 9am-7pm, F 9am-4pm; Oct.-May Su-Th 9am-5pm, F 9am-4pm. €7.50, students €3.)*

PIAZZA DI SPAGNA AND ENVIRONS

FONTANA DI TREVI. The bombastic **Fontana di Trevi** has enough presence and grace to turn even the most skeptical, jaded visitor into a sighing, romantic mush. Legend says that a traveler who throws a coin into the fountain is ensured a speedy return to Rome; one who tosses two will fall in love there. Opposite is the Baroque **Chiesa dei Santi Vincenzo e Anastasio.** The crypt preserves the hearts and lungs of popes from 1590 to 1903. *(Open daily 7:30am-12:30pm and 4-7pm.)*

THE SPANISH STEPS. Designed by an Italian, funded by the French, named for the Spaniards, occupied by the British, and now under the sway of American ambassador-at-large Ronald McDonald, the **Scalinata di Spagna** exude internationalism. The pink house to the right is where John Keats died; it's now the **Keats-Shelley Memorial Museum.** *(Open M-F 9am-1pm and 3-6pm, Su 11am-2pm and 3-6pm. €3.)*

PIAZZA DEL POPOLO. In the center of the "people's square," once the venue for the execution of heretics, is the 3200-year-old **Obelisk of Pharaoh Ramses II** that Augustus brought back from Egypt in AD 10. The **Church of Santa Maria del Popolo** contains Renaissance and Baroque masterpieces. *(Open M-Sa 7am-noon and 4-7pm, Su 7:30am-1:30pm and 4:30-7:30pm.)* Two exquisite Caravaggios, *The Conversion of St. Paul* and *Crucifixion of St. Peter*, are found in the **Cappella Cerasi,** which Raphael designed. *(Open M-Sa 7am-noon and 4-7pm, Su 7:30am-1:30pm and 4:30-7:30pm.)*

VILLA BORGHESE. To celebrate his purchase of a cardinalship, Scipione Borghese built the **Villa Borghese** north of P. di Spagna and V. V. Veneto. Its huge park houses three art museums: world-renowned **Galleria Borghese,** stark **Galleria Nazionale d'Arte Moderna,** and intriguing **Museo Nazionale Etrusco di Villa Giulia.** North are the **Santa Priscilla catacombs** and the **Villa Ada** gardens. *(M: A-Spagna and follow the signs. Open M-F 9:30am-6pm, Sa-Su 9:30am-7pm. €8.50.)*

VATICAN CITY

Reduced to 108½ autonomous acres within the borders of Rome lies the foothold of the Roman Catholic Church, once the mightiest power in Europe. The Vatican has symbolically preserved its independence by minting coins (euros with the Pope's face), running a separate press and postal system, maintaining an army of Swiss Guards, and hoarding art in the **Musei Vaticani.** *(M: A-Ottaviano. Or, catch bus #64, 271, or 492 from Termini or Largo Argentina, #62 from P. Barberini, or #23 from Testaccio.)*

THE INSIDER'S CITY

UNKNOWN BERNINI

Multi-talented Gianlorenzo Bernini (1598-1680) worked under every pope in his lifetime, and practically defined 17th-century Roman sculpture. Although his most famous works are hard to miss, take an afternoon to explore the lesser-known masterpieces.

1. P. Barberini has the Triton-crowned **Fontana del Tritone** for its centerpiece, while the **Fontana dei Api** (Fountain of the Bees) on the corner of V. V. Veneto spectacularly displays the Bernini family coat of arms.
2. Bernini's **Four Fountains** representing the four seasons are built into each corner of this busy intersection.
3. The sculpture **Ecstasy of St. Theresa** in S. Maria della Vittoria is controversial for its depiction of the saint pierced by an angel's dart in a pose resembling sexual climax.
4. Bernini only asked for bread from the Jesuit novitiate for the construction of the beloved oval **San Andrea al Quirinal.**

BASILICA DI SAN PIETRO (ST. PETER'S). A Bernini colonnade leads from **Piazza San Pietro** to the church. The **obelisk** in the *piazza*'s center is framed by two fountains; stand on the discs in the pavement and the quadruple rows of the colonnade will visually resolve into one perfectly aligned row. Above the colonnade are 140 statues; those on the basilica represent Christ, John the Baptist, and the Apostles (except for Peter). The pope opens the **Porta Sancta** (Holy Door) every 25 years by knocking on the bricks with a silver hammer; on warm Wednesday mornings, he holds audiences on a platform in the *piazza.* The basilica itself rests on the reputed site of St. Peter's tomb. Inside, metal lines mark the lengths of other major world churches. To the right, Michelangelo's *Pietà* has been protected by bullet-proof glass since 1972, when an axe-wielding fiend smashed Christ's nose and broke Mary's hand. The climb to the top of the **dome** might very well be worth the heart attack it could cause. An elevator will take you up about 300 of the 350 stairs. *(Dress modestly. Multilingual confession available. Church: Open daily Apr.-Sept. 7am-7pm; Oct.-Mar. 7am-6pm. Mass M-Sa 8:30, 10, 11am, noon, 5pm; Su 9, 10:30, 11:30am, 12:10, 1, 4, 5:30pm. Free. Dome: From inside the basilica, exit the building, and re-enter the door to the far left. Open daily Apr.-Sept. 8am-5:45pm; Oct.-Mar. 7am-4:45pm. Dome €4, elevator €7.)*

TIP **SISTINE SIGHTSEEING.** The Sistine Chapel is at the end of the standard route through the Vatican Museums (p. 606), and it's extremely crowded. You may want to go straight to the Sistine Chapel to enjoy Michelangelo's masterpiece. It's relatively empty early in the morning.

SISTINE CHAPEL. Since its completion in the 16th century, the **Sistine Chapel** (named for its founder, Pope Sixtus IV) has served as the chamber in which the College of Cardinals elects new popes. Michelangelo's ceiling, at the pinnacle of artistic creation, gleams post-restoration. The meticulous compositions hover above, each section depicting a story from Genesis, each scene framed by *ignudi* (young nude males). Michelangelo did not in fact paint flat on his back, but standing up craning backward, a position that irreparably strained his neck and eyes. *The Last Judgment* fills the altar wall; the figure of Christ, as judge, sits in the upper center surrounded by saints and Mary. Michelangelo painted himself as a flayed human skin hanging symbolically between heaven and hell. The cycle was completed by 1483 by artists under Perugino, including Botticelli, Ghirlandaio, Roselli, Pinturicchio, Signorelli, and della Gatta. The frescoes on the side walls predate Michelangelo's ceiling; on the right, scenes from the life of Moses parallel scenes of Christ's life on the left. *(Admission included with Vatican Museums, p. 606.)*

CASTEL SANT'ANGELO. Built by Hadrian (AD 117-138) as a mausoleum for himself and his family, this mass of brick and stone has been a fortress, prison, and palace. When the plague struck Rome, Pope Gregory the Great saw an angel at its top; the plague soon abated, and the edifice was rededicated to the angel. The fortress offers an incomparable view of Rome. *(Walk along the river from St. Peter's toward Trastevere. Open daily in summer Tu-Su 9am-8pm; in winter 9am-7pm. €5. Audio tour €4.)*

TRASTEVERE

On V. di Santa Cecilia, through the gate and the courtyard is the **Basilica di Santa Cecilia in Trastevere;** Carlo Maderno's statue of Santa Cecilia is under the altar. *(Open daily 9:30am-1pm and 4:30-7pm. Donation requested. Cloisters open M-F 10:15am-12:15pm, Sa-Su 11:15am-12:15pm. Cloisters €2.50. Crypt €2.50.)* From P. Sonnino, V. della Lungaretta leads west to P. S. Maria in Trastevere, home to the 4th-century **Chiesa di Santa Maria in Trastevere.** *(Open M-Sa 9am-5:30pm, Su 8:30-10:30am and noon-5:30pm.)* North of the *piazza* are the Rococo **Galleria Corsini,** V. della Lungara 10, and the **Villa Farnesina** (see p. 607), once home to Europe's wealthiest man. *(V. della*

Lungara 230. Open Mar. 15-June M 9am-4pm, Tu-Su 9am-1pm; July-Mar. 14 M-Sa 9am-1pm.) Atop the Gianicolo Hill is the **Chiesa di San Pietro in Montorio,** built on the spot believed to be that of St. Peter's upside-down crucifixion. Inside is del Piombo's *Flagellation*, which uses Michelangelo's designs. Next door is Bramante's ■**Tempietto,** which commemorates Peter's martyrdom. Rome's **botanical gardens** have a rose garden with the bush from which all the world's roses are said to descend. *(Church and Tempietto open Tu-Su May-Oct. 9:30am-12:30pm and 4-6pm; Nov.-Apr. 9:30am-12:30pm and 2-4pm. Gardens open M-Sa Apr.-Oct. 9:30am-6:30pm; Nov.-Mar. 9:30am-5:30pm.)*

NEAR TERMINI

■**PIAZZA DEL QUIRINALE.** At the southeast end of V. del Quirinale, this *piazza* occupies the summit of one of Ancient Rome's seven hills. In its center, statues of Castor and Pollux stand on either side of an obelisk from the Mausoleum of Augustus. The President of the Republic resides in the **Palazzo del Quirinale,** its Baroque architecture by Bernini, Maderno, and Fontana. Bernini's ■**Four Fountains** are built into the intersection of V. delle Quattro Fontane and V. del Quirinale. *(Palazzo closed to the public. San Carlo open M-F 10am-1pm and 3-7pm, Sa-Su 10am-1pm.)*

■**BASILICA OF SANTA MARIA MAGGIORE.** Crowning the Esquiline Hill, this is officially part of Vatican City. To the right of the altar, a marble slab marks **Bernini's tomb.** The 14th-century mosaics in the **loggia** depict the August snowfall that showed the pope where to build the church; the snowstorm is re-enacted each August with white flower petals. *(Modest dress required. Open daily 7am-7pm. Loggia open daily 9:30am-12:30pm. Tickets in souvenir shop €3. Audio tour €4.)*

SOUTHERN ROME

The area south of the center is home to the city's best nightlife as well as some of its grandest churches. Residential area EUR has strangely square architecture and a beautiful, artificial lake. Take bus #714 or M: B-EUR Palasport.

■**APPIAN WAY.** The Appian Way was the most important thoroughfare of Ancient Rome. Sundays, when the street is closed to traffic, take a break from the city to bike through the countryside. *(M: B-S. Giovanni to P. Appio; take bus #218 from P. di S. Giovanni to V. Appia Antica; get off at the info office.)* **San Callisto** is the largest catacomb in Rome. Its four levels once held 16 popes, St. Cecilia, and 500,000 other Christians. *(V. Appia Antica 110, entrance on road parallel to V. Appia. Open Dec.-Jan. M-Tu and Th-Su 8:30am-noon and 2:30-5pm. €5.)* Catacomb **Santa Domitilla** houses an intact 3rd-century portrait of Christ and the Apostles. *(V. delle Sette Chiese 283. Facing V. Ardeatina from San Callisto exit, cross street, and walk right up V. Sette Chiese. Open Feb.-Dec. M and W-Su 8:30am-noon and 2:30-5pm. €5. Cash only.)*

CAELIAN HILL. Southeast of the Colosseum, the Caelian was the hill where elite Romans made their home in ancient times. The ■**Chiesa di San Giovanni in Laterano** was the seat of the papacy until the 14th century; founded by Constantine in AD 314, it is Rome's oldest Christian basilica. The two golden reliquaries over the altar contain the skulls of St. Peter and St. Paul. Outside to the left, **Scala Santa,** has what are believed to be the 28 steps used by Jesus outside Pontius Pilate's home. *(Dress code enforced. M: A-S. Giovanni or bus #16. Through the archway of the wall. Open daily 9am-6pm. €2, students €1.)* The **Chiesa di San Clemente** is split into three levels, each from a different era. A fresco cycle by Masolino dating from the 1420s graces its **Chapel of Santa Caterina.** *(M: B-Colosseo. Turn left down V. Labicana away from the Forum. Open M-Sa 9am-12:30pm and 3-6pm, Su 10am-12:30pm and 3-6pm. €3.)*

AVENTINE HILL. The **Roseto Comunale,** a public rose garden, is host to the annual Premio Roma, the worldwide competition for the best blossom. *(V. d. Valle Murcia,* *across the Circus Maximus from the Palatine Hill. Open May-June daily 8am-7:30pm.)* The top left-hand panel of the wooden front doors at nearby **Chiesa di Santa Sabina** is one of the earliest-known representations of the Crucifixion. V. S. Sabina runs along the crest of the hill to **Piazza dei Cavalieri di Malta,** home of the crusading order of the Knights of Malta. Through the **keyhole** in the cream-colored, arched gate is a perfectly framed view of the dome of St. Peter's Cathedral.

MUSEUMS

Etruscans, emperors, popes, and *condottiere* have been busily stuffing Rome full of artwork for several millennia, leaving behind a city teeming with collections. Museums are generally closed on Mondays, Sunday afternoons, and holidays.

GALLERIA BORGHESE. Upon entering, don't miss Mark Antonio's **ceiling,** depicting the Roman conquest of Gaul. **Room I,** on the right, houses Canova's sexy statue of **Paolina Borghese** portrayed as Venus triumphant with Paris's golden apple. The next rooms display the most famous sculptures by Bernini: a striking **David,** crouching with his slingshot; **Apollo and Daphne;** the weightless body in **Rape of Proserpina;** and weary-looking Aeneas in **Eneo e Anchise.** Paintings in the **Caravaggio Room** include *Self Portrait as Bacchus* and *David and Goliath.* The collection continues in the *pinacoteca* upstairs, accessible from the gardens around the back by a winding staircase. **Room IX** holds Raphael's **Deposition** while Sodoma's *Pietà* graces **Room XII.** Look for Bernini's self portraits, del Conte's *Cleopatra and Lucrezia*, Rubens's *Pianto sul Cristo Morto*, and Titian's *Amor Sacro e Amor Profano*. *(Vle. del Museo Borghese. M: A-Spagna; take the Villa Borghese exit. Open Tu-Su 9am-7:30pm. Entrance every 2hr. Reserve ahead. Tickets €8.50. Audio tour €5.)*

ITALY

VATICAN MUSEUMS. The Vatican Museums constitute one of the world's greatest art collections. Ancient, Renaissance, and modern statues and paintings are rounded out with papal odds and ends. The **Museo Pio-Clementino** has the world's greatest collection of antique sculpture. Two Molossian hounds guard the **Stanza degli Animali,** a marble menagerie. Among other gems is the **Apollo Belvedere.** From the last room, the Simonetti Stairway climbs to the **Museo Etrusco,** filled with artifacts from Tuscany and northern Lazio. Its landing is where the long trudge to the Sistine Chapel begins, passing through the **Galleria degli Arazzi** (tapestries), the **Galleria delle Mappe** (maps), the **Apartamento di Pio V** (where there is a sneaky shortcut to *la Sistina*), the **Stanza Sobieski,** and the **Stanza della Immaculata Concezione.** A door leads into the first of the four **Stanze di Rafaele,** apartments built for Pope Julius II. One *stanza* features Raphael's **School of Athens,** painted as a trial piece for Julius, who fired his other painters and commissioned Raphael to decorate the entire suite. From here, take a staircase to either the frescoed Borgia Apartments, which house the **Museum of Modern Religious Art,** or go to the Sistine Chapel (p. 604). On the way out of the Sistine Chapel, take a look at the **Room of the Aldobrandini Marriage,** which contains rare, ancient Roman frescoes. Finally, the Vatican's painting collection, the **Pinacoteca,** spans eight centuries and is one of the best in Rome. *(Walk north from P.S. Pietro along the wall of Vatican City for 10 blocks. ☎698 849 47; www.vatican.va. Open Mar.-Oct. M-F 8:45am-3:20pm, Sa 8:45am-1:20pm; Nov.-Feb. M-Sa 8:45am-12:20pm. Last entrance 1hr. before closing. €12, with ISIC €8. Open last Su of the month 8:45am-12:20pm, free.)*

MUSEI CAPITOLINI. This collection of ancient sculpture is the world's first public museum of ancient art. The Palazzo Nuovo contains the *piazza*'s original statue of **Marcus Aurelius.** The collections continue across the *piazza* in the Palazzo dei Conservatori. See fragments of the **Colossus of Constantine** and the famous **Capitoline Wolf,** an Etruscan statue that has symbolized the city of Rome since antiquity.

At the top of the stairs, the **pinacoteca's** masterpieces include Bellini's *Portrait of a Young Man*, Caravaggio's *St. John the Baptist*, and Rubens's *Romulus and Remus Fed by the Wolf*. *(On Capitoline Hill behind the Vittorio Emanuele II monument. ☎67 10 24 75. Open Tu-Su 9am-8pm. €6.50-8, with ISIC €4.50-6.)*

OTHER COLLECTIONS. The **Villa Farnesina** was the sumptuous home of the one-time wealthiest man in Europe, Agostino "il Magnifico" Chigi, and now displays decadent artwork. The **Stanza delle Nozze** (Marriage Room), is particularly noteworthy. *(V. della Lungara 230. Across from Palazzo Corsini on Lungotevere della Farnesina. Open July-Mar. 14. M-Sa 9am-1pm; Mar. 15-June, M 9am-4pm, Tu-Su 9am-1pm. €5.)* The **Museo Nazionale D'Arte Antica's** collection of 12th- through 18th-century art is split between Palazzo Barberini and Palazzo Corsini, in different parts of the city. **Palazzo Barberini** contains paintings from the medieval through Baroque periods, while the **Galleria Corsini** holds works by 17th- and 18th-century painters from Rubens to Caravaggio. *(Palazzo: V. Barberini 18. Open Tu-Su 8:30am-7pm. €5. Galleria Corsini: V. della Lungara 10. Opposite Villa Farnesina in Trastevere. Open July-Aug. daily 8:30am-2pm; Sept.-June Tu-Su 8:30am-7:30pm. €4.)* The fascinating **Museo Nazionale Romano Palazzo Massimo alle Terme** covers the art of the Roman Empire, including the *Lancellotti Discus Thrower*. *(Largo di V. Peretti 1, in P. dei Cinquecento. Open Tu-Su 9am-7:45pm. €6.)* Differently themed *Museo Nazionale* are located around the city.

ENTERTAINMENT

The weekly *Roma C'è* (with a section in English) and *Time Out*, both available at newsstands, have comprehensive and up-to-date club, movie, and event listings.

ITALY

THEATER

The **Festival Roma-Europa** (www.romaeuropa.net) in late summer brings a number of world-class acts to Rome. For year-round performances of classic Italian theater, **Teatro Argentina,** Largo di Torre Argentina 52, is the matriarch of all Italian venues. (☎684 000 345. Box office open M-F 10am-2pm and 3-7pm, Sa 10am-2pm. Tickets €14-26, students €10-13. AmEx/D/MC/V.) **Teatro Colosseo,** V. Capo d'Africa 5/A, usually features work by foreign playwrights translated into Italian, but it also hosts an English-language theater night. (☎700 49 32. M: B-Colosseo. Box office open Sept.-Apr. Tu-Sa 6-9:30pm. Tickets €10-20, students €8.)

CINEMA

Most English-language films are dubbed into Italian; for films in their original languages, check newspapers or *Roma C'è* for listings with a **v.o.** or **l.o. Il Pasquino,** P. San Egidio 10, off P. S. Maria in Trastevere, has a program of English-language films that changes daily. (☎580 36 22. €6.20, students €4.20.) **Nuovo Sacher,** Largo Ascianghi 1 (☎581 81 16), the theater of famed Italian director Nanni Moretti, shows independent films. (In original language M-Tu. €7, matinee and W €4.50.)

MUSIC

Founded by Palestrina in the 16th century, the **Accademia Nazionale di Santa Cecilia,** V. Vittoria 6, off V. del Corso (☎06 36 11 064; www.santacecilia.it) remains the best in classical music performance. Concerts are held at the Parco della Musica, V. Pietro di Coubertin 30. (www.musicaperroma.it. Tickets at Parco della Musica; season runs Sept.-June. €15, students €8.) **Alexanderplatz Jazz Club,** V. Ostia 9, is known as one of Europe's best jazz clubs; it moves outside to the Villa Celimontana in summer. (☎397 421 71; www.alexanderplatz.it. M: A-Ottaviano. Required membership €7. Open daily Sept.-May 9pm-2am. Shows start at 10pm.) The **Cornetto Free Music Festival Roma Live** (www.cornettoalgida.it.) has attracted the likes of Pink Floyd and the Backstreet Boys; it takes place throughout the summer.

SPECTATOR SPORTS

Though May brings tennis and equestrian events, sports revolve around *calcio*, or soccer. Rome has two teams in *Serie A*, Italy's prestigious league: **S.S. Lazio** and the 2000 European champion **A.S. Roma.** Matches are held at the **Stadio Olimpico,** in Foro Italico, almost every Sunday from September to June. If possible, check out the two Roma-Lazio games, which often prove decisive in the race for the championship. Single-game tickets (from €15.50) can be bought at team stores like **A.S. Roma,** P. Colonna 360 (☎678 65 14; www.asroma.it; tickets sold daily 10am-6:30pm; AmEx/MC/V); and **Lazio Point,** V. Farini 34/36, near Termini. (☎482 66 88. Open daily 10am-6:30pm. AmEx/MC/V.) Tickets can also be obtained at the stadium before games, but beware of long lines and the possibility of tickets running out; if you're buying last minute, watch out for overpriced or fake tickets.

SHOPPING

No trip to Italy would be complete without a bit of shopping. There are four kinds of clothing shops in Rome. Chain stores like **Motivi, Mango, Stefanel, Intimissimi, Zara,** and the ubiquitous **United Colors of Benetton,** are supplemented by techno-blasting teen stores in central thoroughfares, tiny boutiques like **Ethic** and **Havana** in the *centro storico* and throughout the city, and designer shrines like **Cavalli, Dolce & Gabbana,** and **Prada,** with their cardiac-arrest-inducing prices.

Via del Corso, the main street connecting P. del Popolo and P. Venezia, offers a mix of high- and low-end, Euro-chic **leather goods, men's suits,** and **silk ties,** but beware of high-priced tourist traps. Across the river from V. d. Corso, **Via Cola di Rienzo** offers a more leisurely shopping approach—minus the tourists—with stores like **Mandarina Duck, Mango, Stefanel,** and Benetton. **COIN** department store, V. Cola d. Rienzo 171/173, won't leave you penniless. Unique boutiques and haute-couture designer stores cluster around the Spanish Steps and V. dei Condotti. Purchases of over €155 at a single store are eligible for a tax refund for non-EU residents. Most of the fancy-schmancy stores—**Armani, Bruno Magli, Dolce & Gabbana, Gianni Versace, Gucci, Prada, Salvatore Ferragamo**—can be found on **V. dei Condotti.** Italian favorite **Fendi** breaks the rule and can be found on Largo Goldini, right off V. del Corso. The **General Store,** V. della Scala 62a (☎06 58 17 675), sells discounted Diesel, Adidas, and Nike. Authentic, Euro-chic clothing stores on **Via dei Giubbonari,** off Campo dei Fiori, will have you dressed to the nines before eight.

OUTDOOR MARKETS

Porta Portese, in Trastevere. Tram #8 from Largo d. Torre Argentina. This gigantic flea market is a surreal experience, with booths selling hordes of other items you never knew you needed. Keep your friends close and your money closer. Open Su 5am-1:30pm.

Campo dei Fiori, in the *centro storico*. Tram #8 or bus #64. Transformed daily by stalls of fruits and vegetables, meat, poultry, and fish. Also find dried fruit, nuts, spices, fresh flowers, and the usual basic cotton tops, skirts, socks, and knock-off designer bags. Open M-Sa 7am until vendors decide their wares have run out (usually 1:30pm).

NIGHTLIFE

Though *enoteche* tend to be the primary destination for many locals, pubs are still a fun way to knock a few back without covers. Many are of the Irish variety, and the best are in Campo dei Fiori. Italian discos are flashy and fun, and may have spoken or unspoken dress codes. Clubs in many areas of the city close in the summer in favor areas such as Fregene or Frascati, where clubs stay open until 5am and club-goers party on the beach until the first trains depart for Rome.

Caffé della Scala, P. della Scala 4 (☎58 03 610), on V. della Scala before P. San Egidio. In nice weather the filled tables at this casual cafe-bar line the neighboring street of V. della Scala day and night. Drinks have unusual ingredients, like lime, cinnamon, juniper, and hot pepper in the "Capoeira." Open daily 5:30pm-2am. Cash only.

The Proud Lion Pub, Borgo Pio 36 (☎68 32 841). A tiny pub in the Vatican area whose Roman location belies its Scottish atmosphere. Beer €4. Open daily 8:30pm-2am.

Il Fico, P. del Fico 26/28 (☎68 65 205). Take V. d. Tor Millina off P. Navona, past V. del Pace. P. del Fico is on the right. The patio is shaded by fig trees; live jazz plays within. Aperitifs €4. Mixed drinks €7. Open daily noon-3pm and 6pm-2:30am. D/DC/MC/V.

Artu Café, Largo Fumasoni Biondi 5 (☎06 58 80 398), in P. San Egidio, behind Santa Maria. Patrons swear this bar/lounge is the best in Trastevere. Beer €4.50. Wine €3-5.50 per glass. Cocktails €6-7. Free snack buffet 7-9pm. Open Tu-Su 6pm-2am. MC/V.

Distillerie Clandestine, V. Libetta 13 (☎573 051 02). Speakeasy-like club hosts a restaurant with live music and DJ. Cover F-Sa €20. Open W-Sa 8:30pm-3am.

Jungle, V. di Monte Testaccio 95 (☎33 37 20 86 94; www.jungleclubroma.com). A rock feel pervades on F; it becomes a smoky bar full of Italian goths on Sa. Extravagant yet disorienting light effects. Cover €10. Open F-Sa 10:30pm-5am.

Gilda-Alien-Piper, (www.gildabar.it). With steep covers and exclusive guest lists, this nightclub empire caters to the hipsters of Roman nightlife. In the summer, Piper and Alien move to Gilda on the Beach, located in Fregene near Fiumicino, 30km from Rome.

Alien, V. Velletri 13-19 (☎841 22 12). One of the biggest discos in Rome attracts a well-dressed crowd. Cover about €15, includes 1 drink; Sa €20. Open Tu-Su 11pm-5:30am.

Piper, V. Tagliamento 9 (☎855 53 98). North of Termini. From V. XX Settembre, take V. Piave (V. Salaria). Turn right on V. Po (V. Tagliamento). Or take bus #319 from Termini to Tagliamento. Caters to a more exclusive crowd, with international DJs spinning 70s, rock, disco, house, and underground. Cover €15-20, includes 1 drink. Open F-Sa 11pm-4:30am.

Gilda on the Beach, Lungomare di Ponente 11 (☎665 606 49). Ultra-cool clientele make the pilgrimage to Gilda for 4 dance floors, a private beach, a pool, and a restaurant. Cover €20. Disco open daily 11pm-4am. Dinner served from 8:30pm. Open May-Sept. AmEx/MC/V.

ITALY

DAYTRIP FROM ROME: TIVOLI

From M: B-Rebibbia, exit the station and follow signs for Tivoli through an underpass to reach the other side of V. Tiburtina. Take the blue COTRAL bus to Tivoli. Tickets (€1.60) are sold in the metro station or in the bar next door. Once the bus reaches Tivoli (30-40min.), get off at Ple. delle Nazioni Unite. The return bus to Rome will stop at the tourist office across the street. This tourist office offers info on villas, maps, and bus schedules. (☎07 74 31 12 49. Open M and W 9am-1pm, Tu and Th-Sa 9am-3pm and 4-7pm, although hours are unreliable.) There is also an information kiosk in Ple. delle Nazioni Unite, with free maps.

Tivoli is a beautifully preserved medieval town whose villas, once owned by Latin poets Horace, Catullus, and Propertius, are the major attraction. The tourist office provides a fantastic **map** with walking tours to temple ruins, a 15th-century castle, and Gothic-style houses. **Villa d'Este,** a castle-garden, was intended to recreate an ancient Roman *nymphaea* and pleasure palace. (☎0774 31 20 70; www.villadestetivoli.com. Open Tu-Su May-Aug. 9am-6:45pm; Sept.-Apr. 9am-4pm. €9.) **Villa Gregoriana,** at the other end of town, is a park with hiking trails and lookout points over Tivoli's **Temple of Vesta,** better preserved than Rome's. (€4. Audio tour €4.)

LOMBARDY (LOMBARDIA)

Part of the industrial triangle that drives Italy's economy, home to fashion mecca Milan, and rearer of rice fields as lush as China's, Lombardy is one of the most prosperous regions not just of Italy but of the European Union. The Lombards who ruled the area after the fall of the Romans had close relations with the Franks and the Bavarians, and the region's culture today has much in common with the refined traditions of its northern neighbors. Medieval *piazze* grace its small towns and snow falls on regions in the foothills of the Alps.

MILAN (MILANO) ☎02

Unlike Rome, Venice, or Florence, which wrap themselves in veils of historic allure, Milan (pop. 1,400,000), though once the capital of the western half of the Roman Empire, presents itself simply as it is: rushed, refined, and cosmopolitan. Home to Da Vinci's *Last Supper*, Milan owes much of its artistic heritage to the medieval Visconti and Sforza families, and its culture to French, Spanish, and Austrian occupiers. Now that Italians run the show, the city flourishes as the country's producer of cutting-edge style, hearty risotto, and die-hard soccer fans.

TRANSPORTATION

Flights: Malpensa Airport (MXP), 48km from the city, handles intercontinental flights. **Malpensa Express** leaves Cadorna Metro station and Stazione Nord for the airport (40min., €4.50). **Linate Airport (LIN),** 7km away, covers domestic and European flights. From there, take **Starfly buses** (20min., €2.50) to Stazione Centrale, quicker than bus #73 (€1) to San Babila Metro Station. Ryanair flies to **Orio al Serio Airport (BGY),** from which a shuttle runs to Stazione Centrale (1hr., €6.70).

Trains: Stazione Centrale (☎848 888 088), in P. Duca d'Aosta on MM2. Trains run to: **Bergamo** (1hr., 1 per hr., €3.45); **Florence** (3½hr., 5 per day, €22-29); **Rome** (7hr., 1 per hr., €42-47); **Turin** (2hr., 1 per hr., €7.90); **Venice** (3hr., 1 per hr., €25).

Buses: Stazione Centrale. Intercity buses tend to be less convenient and more expensive than trains. **SAL, SIA, Autostradale,** and other carriers leave from P. Castello (MM1: Cairoli) and Porta Garibaldi for **Bergamo,** the **Lake Country, Trieste,** and **Turin.**

Public Transportation: The **Metro** (Metropolitana Milanese, or **MM**) runs 6am-midnight. Line #1 (red) stretches from the east of Stazione Centrale to west to the youth hostel. Line #2 (green) connects Milan's 3 train stations. Use **buses** for trips outside the city. Metro tickets can be purchased at *tabaccherie* (ticket booths) and station machines. Keep a few extra tickets, as *tabaccherie* close at 8pm. Single-fare tickets €1, 1-day pass €3, 2-day €5.50, 10-ticket pass €9.20. White **taxis** are omnipresent in the city.

ORIENTATION AND PRACTICAL INFORMATION

Milan resembles a bull's-eye, defined by ancient concentric city walls. The outer rings were built in the 50s to house southern immigrants. The inner circle has four squares: **Piazza del Duomo,** where **Via Orefici, Via Mazzini,** and **Corso Vittorio Emanuele II** meet; **Piazza Castello** and the attached **Largo Cairoli,** near the Castello Sforzesco; **Piazza Cordusio,** connected to Largo Cairoli by **Via Dante;** and **Piazza San Babila,** entrance to the business and fashion district. The **duomo** and **Galleria Vittorio Emanuele** are at the center of the circles. The **Giardini Pubblici** and the **Parco Sempione** radiate out. From the **Stazione Centrale,** to the northeast, take MM3 to the *duomo.*

Tourist Office: IAT, V.G. Marconi 1 (☎725 24 301; www.milanoinfotourist.com), in P. del Duomo. Open M-Sa 8:45am-1pm and 2-6pm, Su 9am-1pm and 2-5pm. **Branch** in Stazione Centrale on 2nd fl. Open M-Sa 9am-6pm, Su 9am-1pm and 2-5pm.

American Express: V. Larga 4 (☎721 04 010), on the corner of V. Larga and S. Clemente. Handles wire transfers and holds mail for up to 1 month for AmEx cardholders. Also exchanges currency. Open M-F 9am-5:30pm.

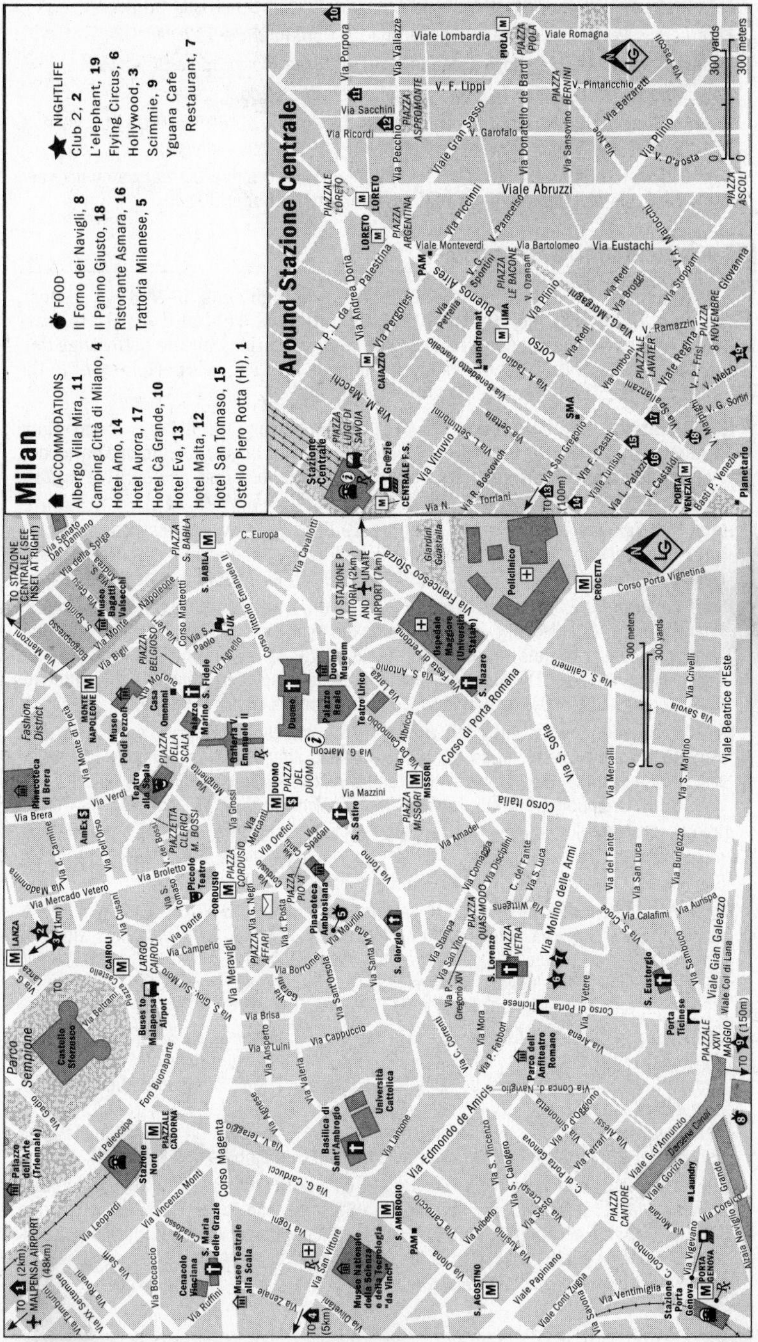
Milan
ACCOMMODATIONS
Albergo Villa Mira, 11
Camping Città di Milano, 4
Hotel Arno, 14
Hotel Aurora, 17
Hotel Cà Grande, 10
Hotel Eva, 13
Hotel Malta, 12
Hotel San Tomaso, 15
Ostello Piero Rotta (HI), 1
FOOD
Il Forno dei Navigli, 8
Il Panino Giusto, 18
Ristorante Asmara, 16
Trattoria Milanese, 5
NIGHTLIFE
Club 2, 2
L'elephant, 19
Flying Circus, 6
Hollywood, 3
Scimmie, 9
Yguana Cafe Restaurant, 7
Around Stazione Centrale
300 yards
300 meters

Lost Property: Ufficio Oggetti Smarriti Comune, V. Fruili 30 (☎884 53 900).

Emergency: Police: ☎113. **Ambulance:** ☎118. **Caribinieri:** ☎112.

Hospital: Ospedale Maggiore di Milano, V. Francesco Sforza 35 (☎550 31).

24hr. Pharmacy: (☎669 07 35). In Stazione Centrale's 2nd fl. galleria.

Internet Access: Internet Enjoy, Vle. Tunisia 11 (☎365 55 805). MM1: Pta. Venezia. €1.30-1.60 per 30min. Open M-Sa 9am-midnight, Su 2pm-midnight.

Post Office: P. Cordusio 4 (☎724 82 126), near P. del Duomo. Currency exchange and an ATM. Open M-F 8am-7pm, Sa 8:30am-2pm. **Postal Code:** 20100.

ACCOMMODATIONS

Every season in expensive, fashionable Milan is high season—except August, when many hotels close. September, November, March, and April are busy because of theater season and business conventions; prices hit the high range during these times. For the best deals, try the hostels on the city's periphery or in the areas east of Stazione Centrale. Reserve well ahead.

Hotel Malta, V. Ricordi 20 (☎20 49 615; www.hotelmalta.it). MM1/2: Loreto. Floral decorations offer a respite from busy Milan days. The 15 bright, quiet rooms have bath, TV, fan, and hair dryer; some have balconies over the lush rose garden. Free luggage storage. Reserve ahead. Singles €35-65; doubles €50-95. MC/V. ❹

Hotel San Tomaso, Vle. Tunisia 6, 3rd fl. (☎29 51 47 47; www.hotelsantomaso.com). MM1: Pta. Venezia. Sparkling rooms with TV, fan, phone, and showers. Singles €35-60; doubles €45-85, with bath €65-110; triples €69-90/75-145. AmEx/MC/V. ❸

Hotel Cà Grande, V. Porpora 87 (☎/fax 26 14 40 01; www.hotelcagrande.it). 7 blocks from P. Loreto, in a pleasant yellow house on the right. Tram #33 stops 50m from hotel. English-speaking owners will have you feeling right at home, and A/C will cool you down. All rooms have TV, sink, and phone. Breakfast included. Singles €40, with bath €45; doubles €60/70. Mention *Let's Go* for a discount. AmEx/D/MC/V. ❹

Hotel Aurora, C. Buenos Aires 18 (☎20 47 960; www.hotelaurorasrl.com). MM1: Pta. Venezia. On the right side of hectic C. Buenos Aires after V. F. Casati, Aurora offers simple, spotless rooms with phone, TV, fan, and serenity. Reserve ahead. Singles €40, with bath €50-70; doubles €60-95; triples €80-130. AmEx/MC/V. ❹

Albergo Villa Mira, V. Sacchini 19 (☎29 52 56 18). MM1/2: Loreto. The 10 bright pink rooms in this family-run hostel are simple and impeccably clean. All have bathrooms. Singles €30; doubles €50; triples €70. Cash only. ❸

Hotel Eva and Hotel Arno, both at V. Lazzaretto 17, 4th fl. (☎67 06 093; www.hotelevamilano.com and www.hotelarno.com). MM1: Pta. Venezia. 20 large rooms with lace curtains, TV, and phone. Ring bell to enter building. Clean shared bathroom. Wheelchair-accessible. Free luggage storage. 30min. free Internet. Singles €30-45; doubles €45-75; triples €65-90. AmEx/MC/V. ❸

Ostello per la Gioventù AIG Piero Rotta (HI), V. M. Bassi 2 (www.ostellionline.org), northwest of the city. MM1: QT8. Facing the white church, turn right on V. Salmoiraghi and walk 300m. Institutional building. Breakfast and linens included. Laundry €5.50. Phone-card Internet. Max. stay 3 nights. Reception 7-9am and 3:30pm-1am. Check-out 9am. Lockout 9am-3:30pm. Closed Dec. 24-Jan. 12. Reserve on website only. 6-bed dorms €19-20; family rooms €22 per person. Non-HI members add €3. MC/V. ❷

Campeggio Città di Milano, V. G. Airaghi 61 (☎48 20 01 34; www.parcoaquatica.com). MM1: De Angeli, then bus #72 to S. Romanello Togni. Backtrack 10m, turn right on V. Tongi, and walk 10min. Enter at Aquatica waterpark. Modern facilities. Laundry €5. Reserve ahead. Closed Dec.-Jan. €6.50-8.50 per tent, €7.50 per person. 2- to 6-person cabins €37-88; bungalows with bath and A/C €80-120. MC/V. ❶

ITALY

FOOD

Trattorie still adhere to Milanese traditions by preparing *risotto alla Milanese* (rice with saffron), *cotoletta alla Milanese* (breaded veal cutlet with lemon), and *osso buco* (shank of lamb, beef, or veal). Especially in the Navigli district, home to all manner of cheap grub, local bars include Happy hour buffets of foccaccia, pasta, and risotto with drink purchases. Near the Giardini Pubblici, try the cuisine of the neighborhood's immigrant population. A **PAM** supermarket is at Vle. Olona 1/3, outside the MM2: S. Ambrogio stop (open M-Sa 8am-9pm, Su 9am-7:30pm).

Il Forno dei Navigli, V. A. Naviglio Pavese 2. At the corner of Ripa di Porta Ticinese. Out of "the oven of Navigli" come the most moist and decadent pastries in the city. Pastries and breads €0.50-6. Open M-Sa 7am-2pm and 4pm-2am, Su 6pm-1am. Cash only. ❶

Ristorante Asmara, V. L. Palazzi 5 (☎89 07 37 98). MM1: Pta. Venezia. Spicy Eritrean food includes a *zighini* platter (€10.50) with meat and veggie pieces served on *ingera,* a typical flatbread. Vegetarian options available. *Antipasti* €4-5.50. Entrees €8-12.50. Cover €1.50. Open M-Tu and Th-Su 10am-4pm and 6pm-midnight. AmEx/MC/V. ❸

Trattoria Milanese, V. S. Marta 11 (☎86 45 19 91). MM1/3: Duomo. From P. del Duomo, take V. Torino; turn right on V. Maurilio and on V. S. Marta. Serves up *mondeghili milanesi* (breaded meatballs; €12). *Primi* €6-9. *Secondi* €7-22. Cover €2. Open M and W-Su 10am-3pm and 7pm-1am. Closed last 2 weeks of July. AmEx/MC/V. ❸

Big Pizza: Da Noi 2, V. G. Borsi 1 (☎83 96 77), takes its name seriously. Epic pizzas (€4-8.50) emerge from the stone oven, and beer flows liberally. The house pizza has a pasta on top (€8.50). Cover €1. Open daily 10am-3:30pm and 5:30pm-2am. Branches: Ple. XXIV Maggio 7 (MM2: Pta. Genova) and V. Buonarroti 16 (MM1: Buonarroti). ❷

Il Panino Giusto, V. Malpighi 3. MM1: Pta. Venezia. If you believe sandwiches should contain goat cheese, truffled olive oil and veal *pâté,* welcome home. *Panini* €4.50-8. Open daily 11:30am-1am. Branch on P. Beccaria near P. del Duomo. AmEx/MC/V. ❷

SIGHTS

DUOMO. The geographical and spiritual center of Milan and a good starting point for any walking tour of the city, the *duomo*, the third-largest church in the world was begun in 1386 by **Gian Galeazzo Visconti,** who hoped to persuade the Virgin Mary to grant him a male heir. Work proceeded over the next centuries and was completed in 1809 at Napoleon's command. Climb (or ride) to the **roof walkway** for prime views of the Alps. The **Museo del Duomo** archives the cathedral's construction. *(MM1/3: Duomo. Cathedral open daily 7am-7pm. Modest dress required. Free. Roof open daily mid-Feb. to mid-Nov. 9am-5:45pm; mid-Nov. to mid-Feb. 9am-4:15pm. €4, elevator €6. Museum open daily 10am-1:15pm and 3-6pm. €5, students €3.)*

PINACOTECA AMBROSIANA. The 23 palatial rooms of the Ambrosiana display exquisite works from the 14th through 19th centuries, including Botticelli's circular *Madonna of the Canopy*, Caravaggio's *Basket of Fruit* (the first Italian still-life), Raphael's wall-sized *School of Athens*, Titian's *Adoration of the Magi*, and da Vinci's *Portrait of a Musician*. The statue-filled courtyard is enchanting. *(P. Pio XI 2. MM1/3: Duomo. Open Tu-Su 10am-5:30pm. €7.50.)*

CASTELLO SFORZESCO. The Castello Sforzesco was constructed in 1368 as a defense against Venice. Later, it was used as an army barrack, a horse stall, and a storage house before da Vinci converted it into a studio. Restored after WWII bomb damage, the complex houses 10 **Musei Civici** (Civic Museums). The **Museum of Ancient Art** contains Michelangelo's unfinished *Pietà Rondanini* (1564), his last work, and the **Museum of Decorative Art** showcases ornate household furnishings and Murano glass. The underground level has jeweled mummy cases in its small Egyptian collection. *(MM1: Cairoli or MM2: Lanza. Open Tu-Su 9am-5:30pm. Combined admission €3, students €1.50. Free F 2-5:30pm.)*

TEATRO ALLA SCALA. Founded in 1778, La Scala has established Milan as the opera capital of the world. Its understated Neoclassical facade and lavish interior set the stage for premieres of works by Mascagni, Puccini, Rossini, and Verdi, performed by virtuosos like Maria Callas and Enrico Caruso. Visitors can soak up La Scala's historical glow at the **Museo Teatrale alla Scala.** *(Access through the Galleria Vittorio Emanuele from P. del Duomo. www.teatroallascala.org. Museum on left side of building. Open daily 9am-12:30pm and 1:30-5:30pm. €5, students €2.50.)*

BASILICA DI SANT'AMBROGIO. A prototype for the Lombard-Romanesque churches found throughout Italy, Sant'Ambrogio is the most influential medieval building in all of Milan. St. Ambrose presided over this very church from AD 379 to 386, and his skeletal remains rest inside, beside martyr St. Protasio. The 4th-century **Cappella di San Vittore in Ciel D'oro,** with exquisite mosaics adorning its cupola, lies through the seventh chapel on the right. *(MM2: S. Ambrogio. Walk up V. G. Carducci, and the church is on the right. Church open M-Sa 7:15am-noon and 2:30-7pm, Su 7:15am-1pm and 3-8pm. Free. Chapel open Tu-Su 9:30-11:45am and 2:30-6pm. €2, students €1.)*

ITALY

CHIESA DI SANTA MARIA DELLA GRAZIE. The church's Gothic nave is dark and patterned with frescoes, in contrast to the Renaissance tribune by Bramante. To the left of the church entrance is the **Cenacolo Vinciano** (Vinciano Refectory), with one of the most important art pieces in the world: da Vinci's **Last Supper.** Reserve ahead or risk missing it. *(P. di S. Maria della Grazie 2. MM1: Conciliazione. From P. Conciliazione, take V. Boccaccio and then go right onto V. Ruffini for about 2 blocks. Church open M-Sa 7am-noon and 3-7pm, Su 7:30am-12:15pm and 3:30-9pm. Modest dress required. Refectory open Tu-Su 8:15am-6:45pm. €6.50. Reservations ☎89 42 11 46. Reservation fee €1.50.)*

BASILICA DI SANT'EUSTORGIO. Founded in the 4th century to house the bones of the Magi, the church lost its function when the relics were spirited to Cologne in 1164. A great masterpiece of early Renaissance art is the **Portinari Chapel** (1468), to the left of the entrance. Frescoes within illustrate the life of St. Peter. Pagan and early Christian tombs are down the steps before the chapel entrance. *(P. S. Eustorgio 3. MM2: S. Ambrogio. Basilica open M and W-Su 8:30am-noon and 3:30-6pm. Cappella open Tu-Su 10am-6:30pm. Basilica free. Cappella €6, students and seniors €3.)*

GALLERIA VITTORIO EMANUELE II. Light pours through a glass-and-metal cupola (48m) and into a five-story arcade of cafes, shops, and offices. Elegant mosaics on the floors and walls represent the continents besieged by the Romans. Spin on the mosaic bull three times for good luck. *(North of the duomo. Free.)*

GALLERIA D'ARTE MODERNA. Napoleon lived here with Josephine when Milan was the capital of the Napoleonic Kingdom of Italy (1805-1814). The gallery displays modern Lombardian art and Impressionist works. Of note are Klee's *Wald Bau*, Modigliani's *Beatrice Hastings*, Morandi's *Natura Morta con Bottiglia*, and Picasso's *Testa*. *(V. Palestro 16, in the Villa Reale. MM1/2: Palestro. Open Tu-Su 9:30am-1pm and 2-5:30pm. Free.)* The adjacent **Padiglione D'Arte Contemporanea (PAC)** is an extravaganza of photographs, multimedia, and painting. *(Open Tu-W and F 9:30am-5:30pm, Th 9:30am-9pm, Sa-Su 9:30am-7:30pm. €5.20, students €2.60.)*

PINACOTECA DI BRERA. The Brera Art Gallery presents a collection of 14th- to 20th-century paintings, with an emphasis on the Lombard School. Works include Bellini's *Pietà*, Mantegna's brilliant *Dead Christ*, and Raphael's *Marriage of the Virgin*. *(V. Brera 28. MM2: Lanza. Wheelchair-accessible. Open Tu-Su 8:30am-7:15pm. €5.)*

SHOPPING AND ENTERTAINMENT

In a city where clothes really do make the man (or woman), fashionistas arrive in spring and summer to watch the newest styles take their first sashaying steps down the runway. When the music has faded and the designers have bowed, world-famous **saldi** (sales) in July and January usher the garb into the real world.

For window shopping, take the Metro to MM1: S. Babila and stroll around the **Golden Triangle,** especially **Via Monte Napoleone** and **Via Sant'Andrea.** Designer creations are available to mere mortals at the trendy boutiques along **Corso di Porta Ticinese.** Small shops and affordable staples from brand names can be found on **Via Torino** near the *duomo* and on **Corso Buenos Aires** near MM1: Pta.Venezia. Fashionistas who can tolerate the stigma of being a season behind can purchase famous designer wear from *blochisti* (stocks or wholesale clothing outlets), such as the well-known **Il Salvagente,** V. Bronzetti 16, off C. XXII Marzo (MM1: S. Babila), or **Gruppo Italia Grandi Firme,** V. Montegani #7/A (MM2: Famagosta). True bargain hunters cull the bazaars on **Via Faucé** (MM2: Garibaldi; Tu and Sa) and **Viale Papinian** (MM2: Agnostino; Sa mornings). Milan's famed tradition and unparalleled audience enthusiasm make **La Scala** one of the best places in the world to see an opera. La Scala also sponsors a **ballet** season run primarily out of the **Teatro degli Arcimboldi** north of the city. (Infotel Scala ☎720 037 44; www.teatroallascala.org. Opera season runs Jan.-July and Sept.-Nov. Central box office located in the Metro station beneath P. del Duomo. Open daily noon-6pm. Tickets €10-105.) The La Verdi season of the **Milan Symphony Orchestra** runs from September to May at the **Auditorium di Milano.** The soccer clubs **Inter Milan** and **AC Milan** face off at their shared three-tiered stadium. **Ticket One,** in FNAC stores, sells tickets for both teams and for concerts and other events (☎39 22 61; www.ticketone.it). Milan's increasingly popular **Carnevale,** in the days preceding Ash Wednesday, is the longest-lasting in Italy. One night each June, **La Notte Bianca** (White Night) keeps the Metro, theater, shops, and restaurants open all night (3pm-6am). The **Serate al Museo** stages free concerts (classical and contemporary) throughout Milan; the schedule is at the tourist office (☎88 46 23 45; www.comune.milano.it/museiemostre).

ITALY

NIGHTLIFE

The nightlife in **Navigli** is popular with students. Simply stroll down V. Sforza for all desired nightlife options. The **Brera** district invites tourists and Milanese to test their vocal skills while sipping mixed drinks at one of its piano bars. **Corso di Porta Ticinese** is the sleek land of the all-night Happy-hour buffet, where the price of an enormous mixed drink (€6-8) also buys dinner. A single block of **Corso Como** near **Stazione Garibaldi** is home to the most exclusive clubs. Bars and clubs cluster around **Largo Cairoli,** where the summer brings Milan's hottest outdoor dance venues, and southeast of **Stazione Centrale,** where there is an eclectic mix of bars and much of Milan's gay and lesbian scene. Guard the invaluable **Nightlife Map,** free at the tourist office, as vigilantly as your cocktail.

Scimmie, V. A. Sforza 49 (☎89 40 28 74; www.scimmie.it). A legendary nightclub in 3-part harmony: pub on a river barge, *ristorante,* and cool bar with nightly performances. Talented underground musicians play fusion, jazz, blues, Italian swing, and reggae. Concerts 10:30pm. Schedule online. Bar: drinks €5-9. Open daily 7pm-2am. MC/V.

Flying Circus, P. Vetra 21 (☎58 31 35 77). Walk down V. E. de Amicis and V. M. d. Armi to P. Vetra; the bar is on the right. Mixed drinks and wine €6-8. Weekly themed summer calendar includes Tu "Re-Wine" (2nd wine free), W "Kill Beer" (€3 beer), Th "Chupa Chupitos" (€1 shots), and Sa "Try Flying" (3 cocktails for €15). Happy-hour buffet daily 6:30-9:30pm with drink. Open M-F 10am-2am, Sa 6:30pm-2am. AmEx/MC/V.

Yguana Café Restaurant, V. P. Gregorio XIV 16 (☎89 40 41 95), off P. Vetra. Lounge outside or on a couch upstairs, or groove to the nightly DJs spinning house and hip-hop downstairs. Mixed drinks €8-10. Happy-hour buffet M-Sa 5:30-9:30pm, Su 5:30-10pm. Open Su-Th 5:30pm-2am, F-Sa 5:30pm-3am. Sister location, **Cheese Café,** next door on the *piazza*. Only at night, same hours and prices. AmEx/MC/V.

L'elephant, V. Melzo 22 (☎29 51 87 68). MM2: Pta. Venezia. From C. Buenos Aires, go right on V. Melzo and continue about 5 blocks. A sultry atmosphere makes the party liable to overflow outside. Mixed drinks €6. Gay and lesbian friendly, though Happy hour food draws all types 6:30-9:30pm. Open Tu-Su 6:30pm-2am. Cash only.

Hollywood, C. Como 15 (☎65 98 996). Slip into something stunning and pout for the bouncer: this disco selects its revelers with the utmost care. Tu hip-hop, W house, Th-Sa music by resident DJs. Su tends to be invite-only for celebrities. Cocktails from €10. Cover €20. Student discount with ID. Open Tu-Su 11pm-5am. MC/V.

Club 2, V. Formentini 2 (☎86 46 48 07), down V. Madonnina from V. F. Chiari. Piano bar with restaurant upstairs, karaoke disco-pub downstairs. *Primi* and *secondi* €7-16. Beer €8. Mixed drinks €10. Open M-F 8:30pm-3am, Sa-Su 8pm-3am. AmEx/MC/V.

MANTUA (MANTOVA) ☎0376

Mantua (pop. 47,000) owes its literary fame to its celebrated son, the poet Virgil; two millennia later, the international **Festivaletteratura** brings writers from John Grisham to Salman Rushdie to the city in September. Mantua's grand *palazzi*, including the opulent **Palazzo Ducale,** P. Sordello 40, were built by the powerful Gonzaga family, who ascended to power in 1328, ruled for 400 years, and brought well-known artists to leave their marks on the town's mansions and churches. See the array of facades, gardens, and frescoes, including Mantegna's painted **Bridal Chamber,** with the entire Gonzaga clan, in the Castello di San Giorgio wing. (Open Tu-Su 8:45am-7:15pm. €6.50, EU students €3.25.) Music lovers first filled the **Teatro Bibiena,** V. Accademia 4, when 14-year-old Mozart inaugurated the building in 1769. The inside looks like a fairy-tale castle. (Open Tu-Su 9:30am-12:30pm and 3-6pm. €2.50, students €1.20.) In the south of the city, down V. P. Amedeo, which becomes V. Acrebi, through P. Veneto, and down Largo Parri, lies the **Palazzo del Te,** built by Giulio Romano in 1534 as a retreat for Federico II Gonzaga. It is widely considered the finest Mannerist building. The frescoed **Room of Giants** depicts the demise of the titans at the hands of Jupiter. The hidden garden and grotto at the end are often overlooked. (Open M 1-6pm, Tu-Su 9am-6pm. €8, students €2.50.) South of P. Sordello is the 11th-century Romanesque **Piazza dell'Erbe.** Opposite the *piazza* is Leon Alberti's **Chiesa di Sant'Andrea,** Mantua's greatest contribution to the Renaissance. (Open daily 8am-noon and 3-7pm. Free.)

Hotel ABC ❷, P. D. Leoni 25, across from the train station, is a modern hotel with comfortable rooms and an outdoor patio. (www.hotelabcmantova.it. Breakfast included. Prices vary according to payment method and skyrocket during Festivaletteratura. Reserve ahead online. Singles €44-88; doubles €66-121; triples €77-160; quads €88-180.) **Ostello del Mincio ❷,** V. Porto 23/25, 15km from Mantua, is the only youth hostel in the area. (☎65 43 08; www.cortemincio.org. Inquire at hostel for bus directions. Dorms €15-20, with breakfast €17-22.) A friendly proprietor serves exquisite regional dishes at **Antica Osteria ai Ranari ❸,** V. Trieste 11, south of the town canal on V. Trieste. (☎32 84 31. *Primi* €6-7. *Secondi* €9-13. Wide variety of *salumi* €6-10. Cover €1. Open Tu-Su noon-3pm and 8pm-2am. Closed for 3 weeks during summer; call ahead. AmEx/MC/V.) A **market** is held every Thursday morning in P. dell'Erbe. Head to **CompraBene Supermercati,** V. Porto 31/A, for groceries. (Open M-Sa 8am-7:30pm.) A **market** is held every Thursday morning in P. dell'Erbe. **Trains** go from P. D. Leoni to Milan (2¼hr., 9 per day, €8.35) and Verona (40min., 20 per day, €2.25). From the train station, turn left on V. Solferino, then right on Via Bonomi to the main street, **Corso Vittorio Emanuele II.** Follow it to P. Cavallotti to C. Umberto I, which leads to P. Marconi, P. Mantegna, and **Piazza dell'Erbe** and **Piazza Sordello.** The **tourist office** is at P. Mantegna 6; follow V. Solferino until it becomes V. Fratelli Bandiera, then go right on V. Verdi. (☎32 82 53; www.aptmantova.it. Open daily 9am-7pm.) **Postal Code:** 46100.

BERGAMO ☎035

Bergamo (pop. 120,000) features two distinct neighborhoods that reflect its colorful history. The *città bassa* (lower city) is a modern commercial metropolis packed with Neoclassical buildings, while the *città alta* (upper city), a compact medieval town accessible by funicular, was born as a Venetian outpost. Though tourism in Bergamo is growing, it's still delightfully invisible. Opera season lasts from September to November and accentuates the work of native composer Donizetti. In the *città bassa*, V. S. Tomaso leads to the **Galleria dell'Accademia Carrara,** which shows works by locals Botticelli and Lotto, plus Brueghel, van Dyck, Rubens, and Titian. (Open Tu-Su 10am-1pm and 2:30-5:30pm. €2.85.) From the Galleria, the cobbled pathway **Via Noca** ascends to the *città alta*. Stroll down V. Porta Dipinta to the main thoroughfare **Via Gambito,** which ends at **Piazza Vecchia,** a mix of medieval and Renaissance buildings. Behind it lies the magnificent **Basilica di Santa Maria Maggiore,** with a bright Baroque interior. (Open Apr.-Oct. M-Sa 9am-12:30pm and 2:30-6pm, Su 9am-1pm and 3-6pm; Nov.-Mar. reduced hours. Free.)

The train station, bus station, and many budget hotels are in the *città bassa*, though the best food and atmosphere is in the *città alta*. To get from the train station to **Ostello Città di Bergamo (HI) ❷,** V. G. Ferraris 1, head to Porta Nuova up V. Giovanni and take bus #6 (every 15min.), connecting to bus #3, which will leave you at the door. (☎36 17 24; www.ostellodibergamo.it. All rooms with bath and balcony. 4- to 8-bed dorms €18; singles €26; doubles €43; 3-6 person rooms €21 per person. €3 HI discount.) Many of Bergamo's best eateries and bars are on the main tourist drag, V. Bartolomeo and its branches, V. B. Colleoni and V. Gombito. Pick up staples at **Pellicano** supermarket, Vle. V. Emanuele II 17, straight from the station past Ple. Repubblica. (Open M 8:30am-1:30pm, Tu-F 8:30am-1:30pm and 3:30-8pm, Sa 8:30am-8pm. MC/V.) **Trains** (☎24 79 50) run from Ple. Marconi to Milan (1hr., 1 per hr., €3.45) and Venice (3hr., 1 per day, €20). **Buses** run from the left of the train station to Como (6 per day, €4.40) and Milan (2 per hr., €4.40). The **airport bus** (€1.55) runs between the train station and Bergamo's airport. ATB runs buses in Bergamo. To get to the *città alta* from the train station, take bus #1 to the *funicolare di città alta*, which ascends from **Via Vittorio Emanuele** to the Mercato delle Scarpe. The **tourist office** in the *città alta* is at V. Gombito 13, in the tower. (☎24 22 26; www.provincia.bergamo.it.) In the *città bassa*, it is in the center of P. Marconi, in front of the station. **Postal Code:** 24122.

THE LAKE COUNTRY

When Italy's monuments start blurring together, escape to the clear waters and mountains of the northern Lake Country, partly in Piedmont, partly in Lombardy. Artistic visionaries like Liszt, Longfellow, and Wordsworth sought rest among the serene shores of the northern lakes. A young crowd descends upon Lake Garda for its watersports and bars; the mansion-spotted coast of Lake Como is home to a thriving silk industry; palatial hotels dot Lake Maggiore's sleepy shores.

LAKE COMO (LAGO DI COMO)

As the numerous luxurious villas on the lake's shores attest, the well-to-do have been using Lake Como as a refuge since before the Roman Empire. Three lakes form the forked Lake Como, joined at the three central lake towns: Bellagio, Menaggio, and Varenna. Be sure to leave Como; hop onto a bus or ferry, and step off whenever a villa, castle, vineyard, or small town beckons.

TRANSPORTATION. The only town on the lake accessible by **train** is Como. Trains go from Stazione San Giovanni (☎031 89 20 21) to Milan (1hr., 26 per day, €4.85) and Zürich, SWI (4hr., 5 per day, €43). **Bus** C46 leaves P. Matteotti for Bergamo (2hr., 4 per day, €4.40), and C10 goes from near Ferrovia Nord to Menaggio (1hr., 1 per hr., €3). Spend the day zipping between the stores, gardens, villas, and wineries of the lake by **ferry** (day pass €4-18), leaving from the piers at P. Cavour.

COMO. Situated on the southwestern tip of the lake, at the end of the Milan rail line, semi-industrial Como (pop. 86,000) is the lake's largest town. **Ostello Villa Olmo (HI)** ❷, V. Bellinzona 2, offers cramped but clean rooms in a familial atmosphere. From the train station, walk 20min. down V. Borgo Vico to V. Bellinzona. (☎031 57 38 00; ostellocomo@tin.it. Bike rentals. Breakfast included. Reception 7-10am and 4-11:30pm. Lockout 10am-4pm. Strict curfew 11:30pm. Open Mar.-Nov. Reserve ahead. Dorms €18. €3 HI discount. Cash only.) A **Gran Mercato** supermarket is at P. Matteotti 3. (Open Su-M 8:30am-1pm, Tu-F 8:30am-1:30pm and 3:30-7:30pm.) The **tourist office** is at P. Cavour 17. From the station, go left on V. Fratelli Ricchi and right on Vle. Fratelli Rosselli, which turns into Lungo Lario Trento and leads to the *piazza*. (☎031 26 97 12. Open Mar.-Sept. M-Sa 9am-1pm and 2:30-6pm, Su 9:30am-1pm; Oct.-Apr. M-Sa 9am-1pm and 2:30-6pm.) **Postal Code:** 22100.

ITALY

MENAGGIO. Halfway up Lake Como's western shore, Menaggio's beauty and excellent ferry connections make it the perfect base for exploring any part of the lake. Daytrips by ferry to the gardens and villas of **Bellagio** and **Varenna** (both 10-15min., 1-2 per hr., €2.90-4.60) are extremely popular. Closer to home, hikers can make trips to the 1736m **Monte Grona** and the 1623m **Chiesa di Sant'Amate** (1hr. each way) from the top of the **Rifugio Menaggio** mountain station, 1400m above the lake. A 2hr. hike (one-way) leads through outlying villages and farms to the **Sass Corbee Gorge waterfall.** To get to the laid-back **Ostello La Prinula (HI)** ❶, V. IV Novembre 86, head uphill from the ferry and turn left onto the main thoroughfare. (☎034 43 23 56. Breakfast included. Reception 8-10am and 4pm-midnight. Lockout 10am-4pm. Reserve ahead. Open Mar.-Nov. Dorms €17; 4- to 6-bed suites with private bath €18 per person. €3 HI discount. Cash only.) Just up the street from the ferry dock, **Super Cappa Market,** V. IV Novembre 107, stocks groceries and hiking supplies. (Open M 3:30-7pm, Tu-Sa 8am-12:30pm and 3:30-7pm.) In the *centro* at P. Garibaldi 4, the helpful **tourist office** has info on excursions. **Postal Code:** 22017.

LAKE MAGGIORE (LAGO MAGGIORE)

A translation of Stendhal reads: "If it should befall that you possess a heart and shirt, then sell the shirt and visit the shores of Lake Maggiore." Though writers and authors have always been seduced by the lake's beauty, today Lake Maggiore is less touristed than its neighbors. Stay at the **Albergo Luina** ❸, V. Garibaldi 21, to the right past the ferry dock. (☎0323 30 285. Breakfast €3.50. Reserve ahead in summer. Singles €35-52; doubles €55-80; triples €56-80. MC/V.) To reach the *centro* and the **IAT Tourist Office,** P. Marconi 16, on the ferry dock, exit the train station, turn right on V. P. d. Piemonte, take a left on Vle. D. d. Genova, and walk toward the water. **Trains** run from Stresa to Milan (1¼hr., every 30min., €4.23). **Stresa** is a perfect stepping-stone to the gorgeous **Borromean Islands.** On **Isola Bella,** the rooms of opulent **Palazzo e Giardini Borromeo** are meticulously designed. (Open Mar. 25-Oct. 22 daily 9am-6pm. €10.) From Isola Bella, ferries go to **Isola Superiore dei Pescatori,** which has a quaint fishing village with a rocky beach, though the water's freezing. **Isola Madre** is the greenest island. Its 16th-century villa contains several room-sized puppet theaters, and its gardens hold exotic flowers. Daily excursion tickets allow you to hop back and forth between Stresa and the islands.

LAKE GARDA (LAGO DI GARDA)

Garda has staggering mountains and breezy summers. **Desenzano,** the lake's southern transport hub, is only 1hr. from Milan and 2hr. from Venice. **Sirmione** and **Gardone Riviera** are best explored as daytrips. **Riva del Garda,** at the lake's northern tip, has an affordable hostel to use as a base. Exploring Sirmione's 13th-century castle and Roman ruins can fill a leisurely day or a busy afternoon. Gardone village, formerly the playground of the rich and famous, is home to Lake Garda's most famous sight: the villa of 20th-century poet, nationalist, and latter-day Casanova, Gabriele d'Annunzio. His quirky mansion, **Il Vittoriale,** with a battleship installed in the garden, sprawls above Gardone. (Villa open Apr.-Sept. Tu-Su 9:30am-7pm; Oct.-Mar. Tu-Su 9am-1pm and 2-5pm. Gardens open daily Apr.-Sept. 8:30am-8pm; Oct.-Mar. 9am-5pm. €7 each, combined €11.) Riva del Garde's calm and beautiful pebble beaches are Lake Garda's restitution for the budget traveler put off by steep local prices. Visitors **swim, windsurf, hike,** and **climb.** Sleep at backpacker hotspot **Ostello Benacus (HI)** ❶, P. Cavour 10. (☎0464 55 49 11. Breakfast included. Laundry €4. Internet €2 per hr. Reception 7-9am and 3-11pm. Reserve ahead. Dorms €14; rooms €17 per person. AmEx/MC/V.) Exploring Sirmione's 13th-century castle and Roman ruins can fill a leisurely day or a busy afternoon. Sirmione's **tourist office,** V. Guglilmo Marconi 6, is in the circular building. (☎030 91 61 14; www.commune.sirmione.bs.it. Open Apr.-Oct. daily 9am-8pm; Nov.-Mar. M-F 9am-12:30pm and 3-6pm, Sa 9am-12:30pm.) Gardone's **tourist office,** V. Repubblica 8, is in the center of Gardone Sotto. (☎/fax 0365 20 347. Open daily June-Sept. 9am-12:30pm and 3-6pm; Oct.-May 9am-12:30pm and 2:30-6pm.) Riva del Garde's **tourist office** is at Giardini di Porta Orientale 8. (☎0464 55 44 44; www.gardatrentino.it. Open M-Sa 9am-noon and 3-6:30pm, Su 9am-noon and 3:30-6:30pm.) **Buses** run from Sirmione and Riva del Garde to Verona (1-2hr., 1 per hr., €3.85-5.20); from Gardone Riviera to Desenzano (30min., 6 per day 6:52am-6:22pm, €2.40.) Tickets are sold at Giornale di Brescia, C. Zanardelli 22 in Gardone Riviera. (Open 6:30am-7pm, closed Su afternoons), or on the bus for €1 extra. **Ferries** run until 8pm from Sirmione to Gardone Riviera (1¼-2hr., €5.70-8.40) and Riva del Garda (2-4hr., €8.10-12); from P. Catena in Riva del Garda to Gardone (1-3hr., 5 per day, €7-10). **Posta.l Code:** 25019 (Sirmione), 25083 (Gardone Riviera), 38066 (Riva del Garda).

ITALIAN RIVIERA (LIGURIA)

The Italian Riviera stretches 350km along the Mediterranean between France and Tuscany, forming the most touristed area of the Italian coastline. Genoa anchors the luminescent Ligurian coastal strip between the **Riviera di Levante** (rising sun) to the east and the **Riviera di Ponente** (setting sun) to the west. The elegant coast is where Riviera glamor mixes with seaside relaxation. Especially lovely is the **Cinque Terre** area (p. 622), just west of **La Spezia.**

GENOA (GENOVA) ☎010

Genoa (pop. 640,000), city of grit and grandeur, has little in common with its resort neighbors. As a Ligurian will tell you, *"si deve conoscerla per amarla"* (you have to know her to love her). Once home to Liguria's most noble families, Genoa's main streets are lined with *palazzi* and *piazze;* medieval churches and maze-like pathways scented with its famous pesto complete the picture.

TRANSPORTATION. Colombo Internazionale **Airport (GOA),** in Sesti Ponente, services European destinations. Volabus #100 runs to Stazione Brignole from the airport (every 20min. 5:30am-10:30pm, €3). Most visitors arrive at one of Genoa's two train stations: **Stazione Principe,** in P. Acquaverde, or **Stazione Brignole,** in P. Verdi. **Trains** go to Rome (5-6hr., 12 per day, €33), Turin (2hr., 2-3 per hr., €8-12), and points along the Italian Riviera. AMT **buses** (☎558 24 14) run through the city (€1; all-day pass €3). **Ferries** to Olbia, Sardinia, and Palermo, Sicily depart from the Ponte Assereto section of the port; buy tickets at the Stazione Marittima.

ORIENTATION AND PRACTICAL INFORMATION. From Stazione Principe, take V. Balbi to V. Cairoli, which becomes V. Garibaldi. Turn right on V. XXV Aprile at P. delle Fontane Marose to get to **Piazza de Ferrari** in the center of town. From Stazione Brignole, turn right out of the station, then left on V. Fiume and right onto V. XX Settembre. Or, take bus #18, 19, or 30 from Stazione Principe, or bus #19 or 40 from Stazione Brignole. Travelers should avoid walking on **Via di Prè** and be cautious by **Via della Maddalena** and in the *centro* at night. The **tourist office,** GenovaInforma, Palazzo Ducale, is near the aquarium on Portico Antico. (☎86 87 452. Open daily 9am-1pm and 2-6pm.) Use **Internet** at **Number One Bar/Cafe,** P. Verdi 21R. (☎54 18 85. €4 per hr. Open daily 7:30am-11:30pm.) **Postal Code:** 16121.

ITALY

ACCOMMODATIONS AND FOOD. Delight in views of the city below at **Ostello per la Gioventù (HI) ❶,** V. Costanzi 120. From Stazione Principe, take bus #35 to V. Napoli and transfer to #40, which runs to the hostel until 12:50am. (☎242 24 57; www.geocities.com/hostelge. Breakfast included. Dorms €15. HI members only.) The rooms at **Albergo Carola ❸,** V. Gropallo 4/12, are carefully decorated. (☎839 13 40; albergocarola@libero.it. Singles €28; doubles €46, with bath €56; triples €62; quads €82. Cash only.) **Camp** at **Genova Est ❶,** on V. Marcon Loc Cassa. Take the train from Stazione Brignole to the suburb of Bogliasco (10min., 6 per day, €1); a free van (5min., every 2hr. 8am-6pm) runs from there to the cliffside campground. (☎347 20 53; www.camping-genova-est.it. Tent sites €15. €5.90 per person, €5.10-7.80 per tent.) **Trattoria da Maria ❷,** V. Testa d'Oro 14R, off V. XXV Aprile, has authentic Genovese daily specials. (☎58 10 80. 3-course *menù* €10.50. Open M-Sa 11:45am-3pm. MC/V.) To sample Genoa's famous salami or pesto, stop by **Salvi Salumeria,** V. S. Lorenzo 2, near Porto Antico (MC/V).

SIGHTS AND NIGHTLIFE. Genoa's multitude of *palazzi* were built by its famous merchant families. Follow V. Balbi through P. della Nunziata and continue to L. Zecca, where V. Cairoli leads to **Via Garibaldi,** called "Via Aurea" (Golden Street) after the wealthy families who inhabited it. The 17th-century **Palazzo Reale,** V. Balbi 10, west of V. Garibaldi, is filled with Rococo rooms bathed in gold and upholstered in red velvet. (Open Tu-W 9am-1:30pm, Th-Su 9am-7pm. €4, ages 18-25 €2.) The **Galleria di Palazzo Bianco,** V. Garibaldi 11, exhibits Dutch, Flemish, and Ligurian paintings. Across the street, the 17th-century **Galleria Palazzo Rosso,** V. Garibaldi 18, has magnificent furnishings in a lavishly frescoed interior. (Both open Tu-F 9am-7pm, Sa-Su 10am-7pm. One gallery €5, both €7.) The **Villetta Di Negro,** on the hill farther down V. Garibaldi, contains waterfalls, grottoes, and terraced gardens. From P. delle Fontane Marose, take Salita di S. Caterina to P. Corvetto. (Open daily 8am-dusk.) From P. de Ferrari, take V. Boetto to P. Matteotti for a glimpse of the ornate interior and Rubens paintings in **Chiesa di Gesù.** (Church open daily 7:15am-12:30pm and 4-7:30pm. Closed to tourists during Su mass. Free.) **Centro storico,** the eerie and beautiful historical center, is bordered by Porto Antico, V. Garibaldi, and P. Ferrari, is a mass of winding and confusing streets that contain some of Genoa's most memorable sights, including the asymmetrical **San Lorenzo Duomo,** down V. S. Lorenzo from P. Matteotti. (Open daily 9am-noon and 3-

6pm. Free.) Go down V. S. Lorenzo toward the water, turn left on V. Chiabrera, and left on V. di Mascherona to reach the **Chiesa Santa Maria di Castello,** in P. Caricamento, a labyrinth of chapels, courtyards, cloisters, and crucifixes. (Open daily 9am-noon and 3:30-6:30pm. Closed during Su Mass. Free.) The **aquarium** on Porto Antico is the town's concession to the over-the-top. (Open July-Aug. daily 9am-11pm; Mar.-June and Sept.-Oct. M-W and F 9am-7:30pm, Th 9am-10pm, Sa-Su 9am-8:30pm; Nov.-Feb. daily 9:30am-7:30pm. Last entrance 1½hr. before close. €14.)

Corso Italia is an upscale road home to much of Genoa's nightlife. Most use cars, however, as clubs are difficult to reach on foot and the city streets can be dangerous at night. Students flock to bars in **Piazza Erbe** and along **Via San Bernardo.** It is easy and fairly safe to reach **Al Parador,** P. della Vittoria 49R, from Stazione Brignole. It's in the northeast corner of P. Vittoria, near the intersection of V. Cadorna and V. B. Liguria. (☎58 17 71. Mixed drinks €4.50. Open M-Sa 24hr. Cash only.)

RIVIERA DI PONENTE

FINALE LIGURE ☎019

A beachside plaque proclaims the town of Finale Ligure (pop. 12,000) the place for *"il riposo del popolo"* (the people's rest). In Finale, *riposo* may be bodysurfing in choppy waves, browsing through chic boutiques, or scaling the 15th-century ruins of **Castello di San Giovanni.** Climb the tough trail starting at Finalborgo's post office to the ruins of **Castel Govone** for an amazing view. Explore nearby medieval towns **Borgio** and **Verezzi**. Walk east along V. Aurelia through the first tunnel to find a free **beach,** less populated than those closer to town. **Finalborgo,** Finale Ligure's historic quarter, is a 1km walk or 2min. ACTS bus ride up V. Bruneghi from the station.

Its immaculate rooms and views make **Castello Wuillerman (HI) ❶,** V. Generale Caviglia well worth the hike. From the train station, cross the street and turn left onto V. Raimondo Pertica. After passing a church, turn left onto V. Alonzo. (☎69 05 15; www.hostelfinaleligure.com. Breakfast included. Reception 7-10am and 5-10pm. Curfew midnight. Dorms €13.50. HI members only. Cash only.) **Pensione Enzo ❷,** Gradinata d. Rose 3, has jovial owners and a fantastic view. (☎69 13 83. Breakfast included. Open Mar. to Sept. Doubles €40-60.) **Camping Del Mulino ❶,** on V. Castelli, has a restaurant and mini-market. Take the Calvisio bus from the station to the Boncardo Hotel, turn left at Piazza Oberdan, then right on V. Porro, and follow the signs up the hill. (☎60 16 69; www.campingmulino.it. Reception 8am-8pm. Open Apr.-Sept. Tent sites €9.50-14. MC/V.) Cheap restaurants lie along **Via Rossi, Via Roma,** and **Via Garibaldi.** Eat huge, two-person portions of delicious pasta at **Spaghetteria Il Posto ❷.** (☎60 00 95. Entrees around €7. Cover €1. Open Tu-Su 7-10:30pm. Closed 1st 2 weeks of Mar. Cash only.) **Di per Di Express** supermarket is at V. Alonzo 10. (Open M-Sa 8:30am-1pm and 3:45-7:45pm, Su 9am-1pm. MC/V.)

Trains leave P. V. Veneto for Genoa (1hr., every 30min., €10-16). SAR **buses** run from the station to Borgo Verezzi (10min., 4 per hr., €1). The city has three sections: **Finalpia** to the east, **Finalmarina** in the center, home to the station and most sights, and **Finalborgo.** The IAT **tourist office,** V. S. Pietro 14, gives out free maps. (☎68 10 19; www.inforiviera.it. Open M-Sa 9am-12:30pm and 3-6:30pm, Su 9am-noon; low season closed Su.) **Postal Code:** 17024.

RIVIERA DI LEVANTE ☎0185

CAMOGLI

Postcard-perfect Camogli shimmers with color: Sun-faded peach houses crowd the hilltop and red and turquoise boats bob in the water. Turn right out of the train station and keep walking until V. Repubblica turns into V. P. Schaffino to reach the handsomely furnished ■**Hotel Augusta ❸**, V. P. Schaffino 100. (☎77 05 92; www.htlaugusta.com. Buffet breakfast €10 per room. 15min. free Internet. Singles €35-65; doubles €68-98; triples €90-135. AmEx/MC/V.) The creamy gelato from ■**Gelato e Dintorni ❶**, V. Garibaldi 104/105, puts nationally ranked rivals to shame. (Open daily 10:30am-11pm. Cash only.) **Trains** run on the Genoa-La Spezia line to Genoa (40min., 38 per day, €1.60) and La Spezia (1½hr., 24 per day, €3.95). Golfo Paradiso **ferries**, V. Scalo 3 (☎77 20 91; www.golfoparadiso.it), near P. Colombo, go to Cinque Terre (round-trip €20) and Portofino (round-trip €12). Buy tickets on the dock; call for the schedule. Turn right from the station to find the **tourist office**, V. XX Settembre 33, which helps find rooms. (☎77 10 66. Open M-Sa 9am-12:30pm and 3:30-7pm, Su 9am-12:30pm; low season reduced hours.) **Postal Code:** 16032.

SANTA MARGHERITA LIGURE

Santa Margherita Ligure was a calm fishing village until the early 20th century, when it fell into favor with Hollywood stars. Today, glitz and glamor paint the shore, but the serenity of the town's early days still lingers. Cozy beds and private showers make ■ **Hotel Conte Verde ❸**, V. Zara 1, a great find. From the train station turn right on V. Trieste, which becomes V. Roma. (☎387 139; www.hotelconteverde.it. Breakfast included. Singles €40; doubles €80-130; triples €100-160; quads €120-200. AmEx/MC/V.) **Trattoria Da Pezzi ❷**, V. Cavour 21, is popular with the locals for its homestyle Genovese cuisine. (☎28 53 03. Open Su-F 10am-2:15pm and 5-9:15pm. MC/V.) **Trains** along the Pisa-Genoa line go from P. Federico Raoul Nobili, at the top of V. Roma, to Genoa (50min., 2-4 per hr., €2.10) and La Spezia (1½hr., 1-2 per hr., €3.95). Tigullio **buses** (☎28 88 34) go from P. V. Veneto to Camogli (30min., 1-2 per hr., €1.10) and Portofino (20min., 3 per hr., €1.50). Tigullio **ferries**, V. Palestro 8/1B (☎28 46 70), run tours to Cinque Terre (early May-late Sept. 9am, round-trip €22) and Portofino (Sa-Su 1 per hr., €4.50). Turn right out of the train station, go right on C. Rainusso, and take the first left on V. Gimelli to find the **tourist office**, V. XXV Aprile 2/B, which arranges lodging. (☎28 74 85; www.apt-tigullio.liguria.it. Open M-Sa 9:30am-12:30pm and 3-7:30pm, Su 9:30am-12:30pm and 4:30-7:30pm.) **Postal Code:** 16032.

CINQUE TERRE ☎0187

Cinque Terre is an outdoorsman's paradise. Strong hikers can cover all five villages—Corniglia, Manarola, Monterosso, Riomaggiore, and Vernazza—in about 5hr., and numerous opportunities for kayaking, cliff jumping, or horseback riding present themselves along the way. Rather than rushing, though, take the time to wander through the villages' tiny clusters of rainbow-colored houses amid hilly stretches of olive groves and vineyards. Though Cinque Terre was formerly a hidden treasure of the Ligurian coastline, increased publicity and word of mouth have made the towns fodder for a booming tourism industry.

⊞🗹 TRANSPORTATION AND PRACTICAL INFORMATION. Trains run along the Genoa-La Spezia (Pisa) line. A **Cinque Terre Card** (1-day €5.40, 3-day €13, 7-day €21) allows for unlimited train, bus, and path access among the five towns, La Spezia, and Levanto; buy it at the train stations and Cinque Terre National Park. Monterosso is the most accessible by train. From the station on V. Fegina, in the northern end of town, trains run to: Florence (3½hr., 1 per hr., €7.90); Genoa (1½hr., 1 per hr., €4.50); La Spezia (20min., 2 per hr., €1.60); Pisa (2½hr., 1 per hr., €4.65); Rome (7hr., every 2hr., €17-27). **Ferries** run from La Spezia to Monterosso (2hr., 4 per day, €18). The five villages stretch along the shore between Levanto and La Spezia, connected by trains (5-20min., 1 per hr., €1.10), roads (although cars are not allowed in the towns), and footpaths. **Monterosso** is the largest town, followed by higher-end **Vernazza,** cliffside **Corniglia,** swimming-cove-dotted **Manarola,** and affordable **Riomaggiore.** The Monterosso **park office** is at P. Garibaldi 20. (☎81 78 38. Open daily 8am-8pm.) The Pro Loco **tourist office,** V. Fegina 38, in Monterosso, below the train station, has info on hiking and rooms. (☎/fax 81 75 06. Open daily 9:30am-6:30pm.) **Postal Codes:** 19016 (Monterosso); 19017 (Manarola and Riomaggiore); 19018 (Corniglia and Vernazza).

ACCOMMODATIONS AND FOOD. Most of the hotels are in Monterosso, and they fill quickly in summer. For help finding the more plentiful *affittacamere* (private rooms), try the tourist office. For help in Riomaggiore, call **Edi,** V. Colombo 111. (☎92 03 25; edi-vesigna@iol.it.) Popular with students, **Hotel Souvenir ❷,** V. Gioberti 30, in Monterosso, has 47 beds, a friendly staff, and a garden. (☎/fax 81 75 95. Breakfast €5. Dorms €25; private rooms €40. Cash only.) **Ostello Cinque Terre ❷,** V. B. Riccobaldi 21, in Manarola, is modern with a sweeping roof terrace. Turn right from the train station and continue up the hill. (☎92 02 15; www.hostel5terre.com. Kayak, bike, and snorkeling equipment rental. Breakfast €4. Laundry wash €6. Curfew 1am, in winter midnight. Dorms €22. MC/V.) All 23 rooms at **Hotel Gianni Franzi ❹,** P. Marconi 1, in Vernazza, have lovely antiques; some have balconies. (☎82 10 03; www.giannifranzi.it. Singles €42; doubles €60, with bath €80; triples €100. AmEx/MC/V.) **Mar-Mar ❷,** V. Malborghetto 4, in Riomaggiore, rents dorms and rooms with bath. (☎92 09 32; www.5terre-marmar.com. Dorms €20; doubles €65-90. Cash only.)

Meals at **Il Ciliegio ❷,** Località Beo, in Monterosso, near P. Garibaldi, feature ingredients from the owner's garden. Take a 10min. shuttle there. (☎81 78 29. *Primi* €6-10. *Secondi* €7-13. Open Tu-Su 12:30-2:30pm and 7:30-10:30pm. AmEx/MC/V.) Famed for its pesto, Vernazza's oldest *trattoria,* **Trattoria Gianni Franzi ❷,** P. Marconi 1, has local specialties. (☎82 10 03. *Primi* €4-11. *Secondi* €5-16. Open M-Tu and Th-Su noon-3pm and 7:30-9:30pm. AmEx/MC/V.) Perched on a cliff, **Ripa del Sole ❸,** V. de Gasperi 282, in Riomaggiore, serves some of the area's most flavorful seafood. (☎92 07 43. *Primi* €7-10. *Secondi* €8-21. Open Tu-Su noon-2pm and 7-10pm. AmEx/MC/V.) Get groceries at **SuperCONAD Margherita,** P. Matteotti 9, in Monterosso. (Open June-Sept. M-Sa 8am-1pm and 5-8pm, Su 8am-1pm. MC/V.)

OUTDOOR ACTIVITIES AND NIGHTLIFE. The best sights in Cinque Terre are the five villages themselves, and the gorgeous paths that connect them. Monterosso has Cinque Terre's largest free

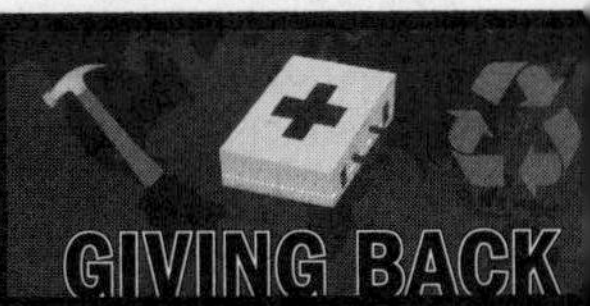

THE HILLS ARE ALIVE

While hiking in Cinque Terre you may have noticed that the paths feel a little more crumbly than perhaps they should. Over the past few years, the huge influx of tourists to the region has boosted the economy, but it has also begun to take its toll on the land. Increased foot traffic, combined with a dry climate and rugged terrain, has caused deterioration of the hillside, resulting in Cinque Terre's placement on the "World Monument Watch List of 100 Most Endangered Sites."

However, the devoted workers at the **Parco Nazionale delle Cinque Terre** refuse to let their beloved cliffs and vineyards be destroyed. The park has allied with local restaurants, accommodations, and businesses to ensure that they stay as friendly to the environment as they are to the tourists. Establishments which display the park's official "Eco-Quality" plaque have committed to using recycling bins, eco-friendly energy sources, or reusable products.

Visitors to the park can lend a helping hand by joining one of the park's service camps. Hikers who rebuild fallen walls, restore foot paths, and promote growth along the hillsides are essential to the continuing preservation of Cinque Terre's precious landscape.

(For more information, contact Parco Nazionale delle Cinque Terre, ☎0187 76 00 00; info@parconazionale5terre.it.)

beach, in front of the historic center, sheltered by a cliff cove. The hike between Monterosso and Vernazza (1½hr.) is the most difficult, with steep climbs winding past terraced vineyards and hillside cottages. From there, the trip to Corniglia (1½hr.) offers breathtaking views of the sea and olive groves, with scents of rosemary, lemon, and lavender. Near Corniglia, the secluded **Guvano Beach,** accessed through a tunnel, is popular with adventurous types willing to make the trek down. Take the stairs down to the station from V. della Stazione in Corniglia and turn left, following the path along the railroad tracks to the public beach; the hike to youthful Manarola (1hr.) begins just past the beach. The most famous Cinque Terre hike, the **Via dell'Amore,** from Manarola to Riomaggiore, the smallest of the five towns, is a 20min. slate-paved walk that features a stone tunnel of love.

At night, the most happening towns are Monterosso, Manarola, and Riomaggiore. In Monterosso, **Il Casello,** V. Lungo Fessario 70, lures backpackers with a beachy location. (Beer and mixed drinks from €2.50. Open daily noon-2am. Cash only.) **Bar Centrale,** V. C. Colombo 144, in Riomaggiore, caters to a young, international crowd. (Beer €2-4. Mixed drinks €4-6. Open daily 7:30am-1am. Cash only.)

EMILIA-ROMAGNA

Go to Florence, Venice, and Rome to sightsee; come to Emilia-Romagna to eat. Italy's wealthy wheat- and dairy-producing region covers the fertile plains of the Po River Valley whose harvest weighs tables with some of the finest culinary traditions on the peninsula—often freed from binds of the elsewhere omnipresent *menù turistico*. The Romans originally settled here, but the towns later fell under the rule of Renaissance families whose names still adorn *palazzi* and *piazze*.

BOLOGNA ☎051

Affectionately referred to as the *grassa* (fat) and *dotta* (learned) city, Bologna (pop. 369,955) has a legacy of excellent food, education, and art. Bologna's museums and churches house priceless artistic treasures, and its university is Europe's oldest. Academic liberalism drove political activism, and the city's involvement in 19th-century socialism earned it the nickname "Red Bologna." Be as cautious in Bologna as in a big city; guard your wallet, and don't travel solo at night.

TRANSPORTATION AND PRACTICAL INFORMATION. Trains leave the northern tip of Bologna's walled city for: Florence (1½hr., 53 per day, €6); Milan (3hr., 63 per day, €10); Rome (4hr., 39 per day, €20); Venice (2hr., 25 per day, €8). **Buses** #25 and 30 run between the train station and the center at **Piazza Maggiore** (€1). Alternatively, head through P. XX Settembre to V. dell'Indipendenza, which leads to P. del Nettuno, behind which lies P. Maggiore. The **tourist office,** P. Maggiore 1, is in Palazzo del Podestà. (☎24 65 41; www.iperbole.bologna.it/bolognaturismo. Open daily 9:30am-7:30pm.) **Postal Code:** 40100.

ACCOMMODATIONS AND FOOD. Reserve ahead at Bologna's hotels, especially during high season. Take V. Ugo Bassi from P. del Nettuno, then take the third left to reach **Albergo Panorama ❹,** V. Livraghi 1, 4th fl., where sunny rooms look out over V. Ugo Bassi or a cheery rooftop terrace. (☎22 18 02; www.hotelpanoramabologna.it. Curfew 3am. Singles €50-60; doubles €60-70; triples €75-85; quads €85-95; quints €100. AmEx/DC/MC/V.) Six kilometers northeast of the *centro*, **Ostello due Torre San Sisto (HI) ❷,** V. Viadagola 5, has a basketball court and a reading room with satellite TV. Take bus #93 (#301 on Su) from V. Marconi 69 (M-Sa every 30min.); ask the driver for the San Sisto stop. The hostel is the yellow building on the right. (☎/fax 50 18 10. Lockout 10am-3:30pm. No curfew. Dorms €18; doubles €36. €3 HI discount. AmEx/DC/MC/V.)

Scout **Via Augusto Righi, Via Piella,** and **Via Saragozza** for traditional *trattorie* with *spaghetti alla Bolognese.* **Nuova Pizzeria Gianna ❶**, V. S. Stefano 76A, has some of the freshest pizza in Italy. (☎22 25 16. Pizzas from €2.90. Open M-Sa 8:30am-11pm. Closed 2 weeks in Aug. Cash only.) **Osteria dell'Orsa ❶**, V. Mentana 1/F has communal tables where students eat before hitting nearby nightlife. (☎23 15 76. Open daily noon-1:30am. Cash only.) Some of the best gelato in Italy is churned at **Il Gelatauro,** V. S. Vitale 98B. (☎23 00 49. 2 scoops €1.90. Open daily 11am-11pm. Closed Aug. Cash only.) A **PAM** supermarket, V. Marconi 26, is by the intersection with V. Riva di Reno. (Open M 8am-7pm, Tu-Su 11am-midnight. AmEx/MC/V.)

SIGHTS AND NIGHTLIFE. The ancient *palazzi* and expensive boutiques in **Piazza Maggiore** are lorded over by the Romanesque **Palazzo del Podestà** and the nearby **Basilica di San Petronio,** P. Maggiore 3. The basilica hosted the Council of Trent (when not in Trent) and the 1530 ceremony in which Pope Clement VII gave Italy to Germany. (Open daily 7:30am-1pm and 2:30-6pm. Free.) The **Palazzo Archiginnasio,** behind S. Petronio, was the first home of Bologna's modern university. (V. Archiginnasio 1. Open daily 9am-6:45pm. Closed 1st 2 weeks of Aug. Free.) **Piazza del Nettuno** contains Giambologna's stone-and-bronze 16th-century fountain, **Neptune and Attendants.** Two towers rise from P. Porta Ravegana, at the end of V. Rizzoli; the **Torre degli Garisenda** cants violently to one side, but the nearly 98m **Torre degli Asinelli** is climbable. (Open daily 9am-6pm. €3.) From V. Rizzoli, follow V. S. Stefano to P. S. Stefano, where the Romanesque **Chiesa Santo Stefano** contains the basin where Pontius Pilate absolved himself of responsibility for Christ's death. (☎22 32 56. Modest dress required. Open M-Sa 9am-noon and 3:30-6pm, Su 9am-12:45pm and 3:30-6:30pm. Free.) The **Pinacoteca Nazionale,** V. delle Belle Arti 56, off V. Zamboni, traces the history of Bolognese artists. (☎420 94 11. Open Tu-Su 9am-7pm. €4, EU students €2.)

Bologna's hip students ensure raucous nighttime fun, especially around V. Zamboni. **Cluricaune,** V. Zamboni 18/B, a multi-level Irish pub, ropes in students with its beer selection. (☎26 34 19. Pints €3.10-4.20. Happy hour W 7-10:30pm; pints €2.50. Open Su-F noon-2am, Sa 4pm-3am.) **Cassero,** located in the Porta Saragozza, is popular with the gay community, but both men and women are welcome. (☎649 44 16.

FROM THE ROAD

A BIG, FAT ITALIAN WEDDING

As the remaining survivors broke out cases of *grappa* at 5am, it all came back to me in a frenzied, food-coma haze. The occasion—the wedding of a distant cousin in Bologna—began in a tiny hillside church overlooking the Emilia-Romagna landscape. Only a fraction of the 400 guests piled inside the church to escape the summer heat and listen to the priest's sermon about *l'amore.*

The real celebration began immediately afterward in a nearby villa. A caravan of vehicles spilled guests into a courtyard already filled with festive trays of *prosciutto* and *salame,* mozzarella wrapped in bacon, exquisite cheese plates, sparkling wine bottles branded with a picture of the couple, and the *tour de force:* 60kg of traditional tortellini, handmade by the bride's mother over the course of two months. After the Smart Car-sized gelato wedding cake had been rolled out, and *bambini* had mercilessly destroyed a piñata, the dancing began. Half-hearted swaying gave way to more impressive moves, then to a drunken mosh pit. Delicious food aside, the small cultural difference by the the end became simply that. What stood out was, just as anywhere else, the union of two people was taking place, and that—as it is the world wide, the nuptials provided yet another excuse to party.

– Felipe Tewes

Drinks €3-6. ARCI-GAY card, available at ARCI-GAY, V. Don Minzoni 18, required. Open M-F 10pm-2am, Sa-Su 10pm-3am.) Every year from mid-June to mid-September, the city commune sponsors a **festival** of dance, theater, music, cinema, and art. Many events are free, but few cost more than €5.

PARMA

☎0521

Though famous for its *parmigiano* cheese and *prosciutto*, Parma's (pop. 172,000) artistic excellence is not confined to the kitchen. Giuseppe Verdi composed some of his greatest works here, and native artists Parmigianino and Correggio cultivated Mannerist painting in the 16th century. The town centers around the 11th-century **duomo** where Correggio's *Virgin* ascends to a golden heaven. From P. Garibaldi, follow Str. Cavour and take the third right on Str. al Duomo. The pink-and-white marble **baptistry** displays early Medieval frescoes of enthroned saints and apostles. (Duomo open daily 9am-12:30pm and 3-6:30pm. Baptistry open daily 9am-12:30pm and 3-6:30pm. Duomo free. Baptistry €4, students €3.) Built in 1521 to house a miraculous picture of the Virgin Mary, the **Chiesa Magistrale di Santa Maria della Staccata,** up V. Garibaldi from P. Garibaldi, features frescoes by Parmigianino on the arch above the presbytery. Ask the priest to see the **Crypt of the Garnese Dukes.** (Open daily 7:30am-noon and 3-6:30pm. Free.) From P. del Duomo, follow Str. al Duomo across Str. Cavour, walk one block down Str. Piscane, and cross P. della Pace to reach the 17th-century **Palazzo della Pilotta,** with the **Galleria Nazionale** and the wooden **Teatro Farnese.** (Both open Tu-Su 8:30am-1:45pm. Ticket office closes 1pm. Theater €2, students €1. Gallery €6, students €4.)

From the train station, take bus #9 (€0.80) and get off when the bus turns left on Str. M. della Libertà for the **Ostello/Camping città della (HI) ❶,** Parco della Cittàdella, then turn right on V. Passo Bueole to enter the park with the campsite and hostel. (☎96 14 34; ostellocittadella@libero.it. HI members only. Open Apr.-Oct. 3-night max. stay. Lockout 9:30am-5pm. Curfew 11pm. Dorms €11. Camping tent sites €11, €7.50 per person. Cash only.) **Albergo Leon d'Oro ❸,** V. Fratti 4a, after intersection Str. Garibaldi, has clean, basic rooms near the train station. (☎77 31 82; www.leondoroparma.com. Singles €35-55; doubles €60-80. AmEx/MC/V.) To reach **Trattoria Sorelle Picchi ❸**, Str. Farini 27, walk down Str. Farini several blocks from P. Garibaldi; the restaurant is on your left behind the *salumeria*. Savvy locals lunch here on roast pheasant, lasagna, and sweet-and-sour onions. (☎23 35 28. *Primi* €8-8.50. *Secondi* €9-14. Cover €2. Open M-Sa noon-3pm. Cash only.) **K2,** Str. Cairoli 23, next to the Chiesa di San Giovanni Evangelista has the creamiest gelato. (From €1.50. Open M-Tu and Th-Su 11am-midnight.) An **open-air market** comes to P. Ghiaia, off V. Marcotti near the intersection with Str. Mazzini, every Wednesday and Saturday morning 8am-1pm. **Dimeglio** supermarket is at Str. Ventidue Luglio 27/c. (Open daily 8:30am-1:30pm and 4:30-8pm.) **Trains** go from P. Carlo Alberto della Chiesa to: Bologna (1hr., 3 per hr., €4.80); Florence (2hr., 3 per day, €8.95); Milan (1½hr., 3-5 per hr., €6.80). Walk left on V. Bottego from the station, turn right on Str. Garibaldi, then left on Str. Melloni to reach the **tourist office,** Str. Melloni 1/A. (☎21 88 89; www.turismo.comune.parma.it). Open M-Tu and Th-Sa 9am-7pm, W 9am-1pm and 3-7pm, Su 9am-1pm.) Walking 1 km on Str. Garibaldi then making a left on Str. Mazzini will take you to Piazza Garibaldi, the **town center. Postal Code:** 43100.

RAVENNA

☎0544

Ravenna (pop. 150,000) was made headquarters of the Byzantine Empire's 7th-century western campaign. The invaders, Justinian and Theodora, created an artistic culture whose legacy is evident in Ravenna's many beautiful mosaics. Take V. Argentario from V. Cavour to reach the **Basilica di San Vitale,** V. S. Vitale 17,

ITALY

whose apse is framed by mosaics depicting Empress Theodora and Emperor Justinian. More mosaics are in the tiny brick **Mausoleo di Galla Placidia,** across the courtyard and behind the church. (☎21 62 92. Open daily Apr.-Sept. 9am-7pm; Mar. and Oct. 9am-5:30pm; Nov.-Feb. 9am-4:30pm.) To see the pastoral mosaics in the **Basilica di Sant'Apollinare,** take bus #4 or 44 (€0.75) across from the train station to Classe. (Open M-Sa 8:30am-7:30pm, Su 9am-7pm. Last admission 30min. before close. €2. Su 9am-1pm free.) Much to Florence's dismay, Ravenna is also home to the **Tomb of Dante Alighieri** and the adjoining **Dante Museum.** From P. del Popolo, cut through P. Garibaldi to V. D. Alighieri. (☎33 667. Tomb open daily 9am-7pm. Free. Museum open Apr.-Sept. 9am-noon and 3:30-6pm; Oct.-Mar. Tu-Su 9am-noon. €2.)

Take bus #70 or 80 from the train station (3-6 per hr., €1) to reach **Ostello Dante (HI) ❷,** V. Nicolodi 12, a basic hostel with a well-stocked common room. (☎42 11 64. Wheelchair-accessible. Breakfast included. Laundry €2.50. Internet €5.16 per hr. Lockout 9:30am-5pm. Curfew 11:30pm. Dorms €16.50; family rooms €17 per person. €3 HI discount. MC/V.) **Piazza del Popolo** has a number of authentic restaurants and cafes. From P. Garibaldi, turn right on V. Gordini, then left on V. Ricci for **Cà de' Ve'n ❷,** V. Ricci 24, where the changing menu features fresh meats and pastas. (☎301 63. *Primi* and *secondi* from €6. Open in summer Tu-Su 11am-2:15pm and 6-10:30pm; in winter Tu-Su 11am-2:15pm and 5-10:30pm. AmEx/MC/V.) **Trains** run from P. Farini to Bologna (1hr., 19 per day, €5). Follow V. Farini from the station to V. Diaz, and the central P. del Popolo where the **tourist office,** V. Salara 8, is. (☎354 04; www.turismo.ravenna.it. Open Apr.-Sept. daily 8:30am-7:30pm; Oct.-Mar. M-Sa 8:30am-6pm.) **Postal Code:** 48100.

RIMINI ☎0541

The Ibiza of the Adriatic, Rimini is the party town of choice for young European fashionistas, a place where it is perfectly acceptable—and admirable—to collapse into bed and bid the rising sun good night. Rimini's most treasured attraction is its remarkable **beach** with fine sand and mild Adriatic waves. Hotels reserve strips of beach with chairs and umbrellas; non-guests can slip in for €3.50; there's also a public beach at the end of the shore. Rimini's nightlife heats up around the **lungomare** in southern Rimini, and near the port. At **Coconuts,** Lungomare Tintorin 5, a diverse crowd gathers to dance at two outdoor dance floors until the wee hours. (☎52 35; www.coconuts.it. Drinks €4-8. No cover. Open daily 6pm-5am.)

FELLINI'S RIMINI

One of the most ingenious, oft-imitated artists of the 20th century, Italian director Federico Fellini remains in a category all his own. Born in Rimini in 1920, Fellini spent much of his childhood at the local cinema, where he soaked up films by the Marx Bros. and Chaplin. Rimini, the carnevalesque, seaside town, was a haven for for Vaudevillians and circus performers–young Fellini became fascinated, even claiming that he ran away to join the circus for months. (He later confessed: "It was more like an afternoon.") These gaudy performers transformed into "Fellini-esque" characters, such as the extravagant Silvia in *La Dolce Vita.*

As Fellini became internationally renowned, he did not leave his childhood town in the dust. For example, Piazza Cavour, in the *centro,* provided Fellini with the fodder to create the square in his masterpiece, the film *Amarcord.* The Grand Hotel inspired the luxury hotel in the same movie. A stroll through nearby Borgo San Giuliano has houses adorned with movie scene murals.

Shortly after being awarded the Lifetime Achivement Oscar in 1993, Fellini passed away. Thousands of citizens packed the narrow streets of Rimini, applauding as the director's casket was carried to the cinema where Fellini had watched his first films. It was a fitting tribute to one of Italy's favorite sons and an internationally respected movie *maestro.*

From Coconuts, walk north along the *lungomare* to **Rock Island by Black Jack,** at the farthest point from shore, on a pier. Inside, guests sidle up to the bar for drinks (€3-6, after midnight €3) before dancing. (☎0541 50 178. Open Tu-Su. Dinner served 7:30-11:30pm; dancing until late. Reserve ahead for dinner.)

Hotel Jammin (HI) ❷, Vle. Derna 22, is at stop 13 of bus #11. Brand new and just seconds from the beach, the hostel is accommodating to the Rimini partying lifestyle. (Breakfast €4.50. Linens included. Lockout 1:30-5:30pm. Closed Jan. Dorms €19-21. €3 HI discount. AmEx/MC/V.) After overspending on drinks and clubs, pick up groceries at the **STANDA** supermarket, V. Vespucci 13. (Open daily 8am-9pm. AmEx/MC/V.) To reach the beach from the train station in **Piazzale Cesare Battisti,** turn right from the station, again into the tunnel at the yellow arrow indicating *"al mare,"* and follow Vle. Principe Amedeo. **Trains** (☎89 20 21) run to: Bologna (1½hr., 58 per day, €10), Milan (3hr., 25 per day, €20), and Ravenna (1hr., 21 per day, €3). The **IAT tourist office** is at P. Fellini 3, stop 10 on bus #11. (Open in summer M-Sa 8:30am-7pm, Su 9:30am-12:30pm and 4-7pm; winter M-Sa 9:30am-12:30pm and 3:30-6:30pm.) **Postal Code:** 47900.

FERRARA ☎0532

Rome has mopeds, Venice has gondolas, and Ferrara (pop. 135,000) has *biciclette* (bicycles). Energetic visitors can take the 9km bike ride along Ferrara's **medieval wall.** The 14th-century **Castello Estense,** a former fortress surrounded by a fairy-tale moat, has themed rooms, gardens, and dungeon tunnels inside. (☎29 92 33. Open Tu-Su 9:30am-5:30pm. €6, students €5. Audio tour €3.) From the *castello*, take C. Martiri della Libertà to P. Cattedrale and the rose-windowed **Duomo San Romano,** across V. S. Romano from the **Museo della Cattedrale.** (*Duomo* open M-Sa 7:30am-noon and 3-6:30pm, Su 7:30am-12:30pm and 3:30-7:30pm. Museum open Tu-Su 9am-1pm and 3-6pm. €5, students €3.) From the *castello*, cross Largo Castello to where C. Ercole I d'Este intersects C. Rossetti to reach the pyramid-studded **Palazzo Diamanti.** Within, the **Pinacoteca Nazionale** holds works from the Ferrarese school and panels by El Greco. (Open Tu-W and F-Sa 9am-2pm, Th 9am-7pm, Su 9am-1pm. €4, students €2.) Follow C. Ercole I d'Este behind the *castello* to find the **Palazzo Massari,** C. Porta Mare 9, home to three art museums, including one devoted to Giovanni Boldini. (All open Tu-Su 9am-1pm and 3-6pm. Filippo de Pisis €3, students €2. Ottocentro/Boldini €5/3. Combination ticket €8/3.)

Casa degli Artisti ❷, V. Vittoria 66, near P. Lampronti, lets its guests cook their own food. From C. Martiri d. Libertà, turn left at the cathedral, right on V. S. Romano, left on V. Ragno, then immediately left to reach the Casa. (☎76 10 38. Singles €25; doubles €43, with bath €60. Cash only.) Hearty regional fare graces plates in the 16th-century dining room at **Osteria Degli Angeli ❸,** V. delle Volte 4. From the basilica, take C. Pta. Reno and turn left under the arch. (*Primi* €7-8. *Secondi* €8-16. Open daily 6pm-11pm. MC/V.) **Osteria Al Brindisi ❸,** V. G. degli Adelardi 11, has wined and dined the likes of Titian and Pope John Paul II since 1435. (☎20 91 42. Cover €2. Open Tu-Su 9am-1am. MC/V.) For picnic supplies, stop by the **Supermercato Conad,** V. Garibaldi 53. (Open daily 8:30am-8pm. MC/V.)

Trains go to: Bologna (30min., 52 per day, €3); Padua (1hr., 39 per day, €6); Rome (3-4hr., 11 per day, €31); Venice (1½hr., 26 per day, €6.10). **Buses** (ACFT; ☎59 94 92) run from the train station to local beaches (1½hr., 12 per day, €4.30) and Bologna (1½hr., 15 per day, €3.40). Rent **bikes** at **Pirani e Bagni,** P. Stazione 2. (☎77 21 90. €2 per hr., €7 per day. Open M-F 7am-8pm, Sa 6:30am-noon. Cash only.) To get to the *centro*, turn left out of the station onto Vle. Costituzione, which becomes Vle. Cavour and runs to the Castello Estense (1km). Bus #2 runs to Castello (every 20min., €0.83). The **tourist office** is in Castello Estense. (☎20 93 70. Open M-Sa 9am-1pm and 2-6pm, Su 9:30am-1pm and 2-5:30pm.)

THE DOLOMITES (I DOLOMITI)

The Dolomites appeal to nearly all outdoor enthusiasts, with steep mountain trails to trendy lodges. The near-impenetrable dolomitic rock has slowed major industrialization, preserving the jagged pink-purple cliffs and evergreen forests that Le Corbusier once called "the most beautiful natural architecture in the world."

TRENT (TRENTO) ☎0461

Between the Dolomites and the Veneto, Trent (pop. 105,000) offers an affordable sampling of northern Italian life with festivals, delicious food, and spectacular scenery. The **Piazza del Duomo,** Trent's bustling epicenter, is anchored by the trident-wielding **Fontana del Nettuno** in the center of the *piazza*. Nearby is the **Cattedrale di San Vigilio,** where the Council of Trent regulated the Counter-Reformation. (Open daily 7am-noon and 2:30-6pm. Free.) Walk down V. Belenzani and head right on V. Roma to reach the historically rich **Castello del Buonconsiglio,** home to the famed **Ciclo dei Mesi,** a series of frescoes depicting an ideal feudal system. (www.buonconsiglio.it. Open Apr.-Sept. Tu-Su 10am-6pm; Oct.-Mar. Tu-Su 9am-noon and 2-5pm. €6, students €3.) From the station, turn right on V. Pozzo then right on V. Torre Vanga to get to the tidy rooms of **Ostello Giovane Europa (HI) ❶**, V. Torre Vanga 11. (☎26 34 84. Breakfast included. Reception 7:30am-11pm. Ask for door code if returning after 11:30pm. Dorms €14; singles €25; doubles €40. AmEx/MC/V.) **Hotel Venezia ❹**, P. Duomo 45, offers rooms right across from the *duomo*. (☎23 41 14. Singles €47; doubles €67. MC/V.) The area around **Piazza del Duomo** hosts a market Thursdays until 3:30pm; for a Trentino meal, try **Osteria Il Cappello ❸**, P. Lunelli 5. (☎23 58 50. *Primi* €8-9. *Secondi* €13-16. Cover €2. Open Tu-Sa noon-2pm and 7:30-10pm, Su noon-2pm. AmEx/MC/V.) Turn right from the train station and turn left on V. Roma, which becomes V. Manci, to reach the **tourist office,** V. Manci 2, which offers advice on local trails, festivals, and guided tours. (☎98 38 80; www.apt.trento.it. Open daily 9am-7pm.) **Postal Code:** 38100.

BOLZANO (BOZEN) ☎0471

German street names begin to appear alongside their Italian equivalents in Bolzano (pop. 100,000), signifying its Italian-Austrian cultural fusion. A spiny Gothic bell tower tops the Romanesque **duomo,** in P. Walther. (Open M-F 9:45am-noon and 2-5pm, Sa 9:45am-noon. Free.) The **South Tyrol Museum of Archaeology,** V. Museo 43, near Ponte Talvera, lets tourists file by the freezer holding **Ötzi,** a 5000-year-old frozen Neanderthal. (Open Tu-W and F-Su 10am-5pm, Th 10am-7pm. €8, students €6.) Take a right from the train station and walk 5min. to reach the **Youth Hostel Bolzano ❷**, V. Renon 22, where guests enjoy ultra-clean rooms and ultra-slick decor. (☎39 04 71. Breakfast included. Internet €2 per hr. Reception 8am-9pm. Dorms €21. €2 discount for longer stays. AmEx/MC/V.) Sample Bolzano's Austrian-influenced fare at the all-day markets of the **Piazza delle Erbe** and the **wurst stand** there, at the intersection of V. Museo and P. delle Erbe (open M-Sa 8am-7pm). The **tourist office,** P. Walther 8, is near the *duomo*. (☎30 70 00; www.bolzano-bozen.it. Open M-F 9am-1pm and 2-7pm, Sa 9am-2pm.) **Postal Code:** 39100.

THE VENETO

Once loosely united under the Venetian Empire, the towns of the Veneto have retained their cultural independence, and visitors are likely to hear regional dialects spoken. The tenacity of local culture and customs will come as a pleasant surprise for those who come expecting only mandolins and gondolas.

VENICE (VENEZIA) ☎041

From its hedonistic, devil-may-care *Carnevale*, to its penitent, God-may-care-too services of its marble cathedrals, Venice (pop. 60,000) is a mystical, water-logged city. Lavish palaces stand proudly on a steadily sinking network of wood, and the waters of age-old canals lap at the mossy steps of abandoned front doors. In the end, Venice's wealth of architectural and cultural treasures proves that it is not *la Serenissima* (the Most Serene One) who surrenders to tourists, but they who succumb to her entrancing spectacle.

TRANSPORTATION

The **train station** is on the northwest edge of the city; be sure to get off at **Santa Lucia,** not at Mestre on the mainland. Buses and boats arrive at **Piazzale Roma,** just across the Canal Grande from the train station. To get from either station to **Piazza San Marco,** take *vaporetto* (water bus) #82 or follow the signs for a 40min. walk. From the train station, exit left on Lista di Spagna.

Flights: Aeroporto Marco Polo (VCE; ☎260 92 60; www.veniceairport.it), 10km north of the city. Take the **ATVO shuttlebus** (☎042 138 36 71) from the airport to Ple. Roma on the main island (30min., 1 per hr. 8am-midnight, €3).

Trains: Stazione Santa Lucia. Open daily 3:45am-12:30am. **Information office** (☎89 20 21) to the left as you exit the platforms. Open daily 7am-9pm. Trains go to: **Bologna** (2hr., 27 per day, €10); **Florence** (3hr., 9 per day, €25); **Milan** (3hr., 24 per day, €24); **Rome** (4½hr., 7 per day, €37). **Luggage storage** by track #4.

Buses: Local **ACTV** buses (☎24 24; www.hellovenezia.it), in Ple. Roma. Open daily 7:30am-8pm. **ACTV long-distance carrier** runs buses to **Padua** (1½hr., 2 per hr., €4).

Public Transportation: The **Canal Grande** can be crossed on foot only at the Scalzi, Rialto, and Accademia *ponti* (bridges). **Traghetti** (gondola ferry boats) traverse the canals at 7 locations, including Ferrovia, San Marculola, Cà d'Oro, and Rialto (€0.50). **Vaporetti** (V; water buses) provide 24hr. service, with reduced service midnight-5am (single-ride €3.50, the Canal Grande €5; 24hr. *biglietto turistico* pass €12, 3-day €25). Buy tickets at *vaporetti* stops. Stock up on tickets by asking for an unvalidated pass *(non timbrato),* then validate before boarding by inserting tickets into one of the yellow boxes at each stop. Unvalidated tickets risk a fine. **Lines #1** (slow) and **82** (fast) run from the station down Canal Grande and Canale della Giudecca; **lines #41** and **51** circumnavigate Venice, from the station to Lido; **#42** and **52** do the reverse; **line LN** runs from Fond. Nuove to Burano, Murano, and Lido, and connects to Torcello.

ORIENTATION

Venice is composed of 118 islands in a lagoon, connected to the mainland by a thin causeway. The city is a veritable labyrinth and can confuse even its natives, most of whom simply set off in a general direction and then patiently weave their way. If you unglue your eyes from your map and go with the flow, you'll discover some of the unexpected surprises that make Venice spectacular. As landmarks, locate the following sites on a map; yellow signs all over the city point accurately toward them: **Ponte di Rialto** (in the center), **Piazza San Marco** (central south), **Ponte Accademia** (southwest), **Ferrovia** (or the train station, in the northwest), and **Piazzale Roma** (directly south of the station). The **Canal Grande** winds through the city, creating six nebulous *sestieri* (sections): **Cannaregio** is in the north and includes the train station, Jewish ghetto, and Cà d'Oro; **Castello** extends east toward the Arsenale; **Dorsoduro,** across the bridge from S. Marco, stretches the length of Canale della Giudecca and up to Campo S. Pantalon; **Santa Croce** lies west of S. Polo, across the Canal Grande from the train station; **San Marco** fills in the area between the Ponte di Rialto and Ponte Accademia; and **San Polo** runs north from Chiesa S. Maria dei Frari to the Ponte di Rialto. Within each *sestiere*, addresses are not specific to a particular street, and every building is given a number, and jumps between address numbers are completely unpredictable.

PRACTICAL INFORMATION

Tourist Office: APT, Cal. della Ascensione, S. Marco 71/F (☎529 87 40; www.doge.it), directly opposite the basilica. Open daily 9am-3:30pm. Avoid the mobbed branch at the train station. The **Rolling Venice Card** offers discounts on transportation and at over 200 restaurants, cafes, hotels, museums, and shops for those aged 14-29. Cards cost €3 and are valid for 1 year from date of purchase. The card can be purchased at APT, which provides a list of participating vendors, or at the **ACTV VeLa** office (☎274 76 50) in Ple. Roma. Open daily 7am-8pm. **VeneziaSi** (☎800 843 006), next to the tourist office in the train station, books rooms for a €2 fee. Open daily 8am-10pm. Branches in Ple. Roma (☎522 86 40) and the airport (☎541 51 33).

Budget Travel: CTS, Fond. Tagliapietra, Dorsoduro 3252 (☎520 56 60; www.cts.it). From Campo S. Barnaba, cross the bridge closest to church and follow the road through the *piazza.* Turn left at the foot of the large bridge. Sells discounted student plane tickets and issues ISICs. English spoken. Open M-F 9:30am-1:30pm and 2:30-6pm. MC.

Currency Exchange: Use **banks** whenever possible and inquire about fees beforehand. The streets around S. Marco and S. Polo are full of banks and **ATMs.**

Emergency: ☎113. **Police:** ☎112. **Ambulance:** ☎118. **Fire:** ☎115.

Pharmacy: Farmacia Italo-Inglese, Cal. della Mandola, S. Marco 3717 (☎522 48 37). Follow Cal. Cortesia out of Campo Manin. Open Apr.-Nov. M-F 9am-1:30pm and 2:30-7:30pm, Sa 9am-12:45pm; Dec.-Mar. M-F 9am-12:30pm and 3:45-7:30pm, Sa 9am-12:45pm. MC/V. Pharmacies rotate staying open late-night and weekends; check the list posted in the window of any pharmacy.

Hospital: Ospedale Civile, Campo S. S. Giovanni e Paolo, Castello (☎529 41 11).

Internet Access: ABColor, Lista di Spagna, Cannaregio 220 (☎524 43 80). Look for the "@" symbol on the yellow sign, a left off the *lista* heading from the train station. €6 per hr., students €4. Printing €0.15 per page. Open M-Sa 10am-8pm. **Internet Station,** Cannaregio 5640. Just over the bridge toward S. Marco from C. Apostoli. €4 per 30min., €7 per hr. 20% student discount with ID. Open M-Sa 10am-1pm and 3-8pm.

Post Office: Poste Venezia Centrale, Salizzada Fontego dei Tedeschi, S. Marco 5554 (☎271 71 11), off Campo S. Bartolomeo. Open M-Sa 8:30am-6:30pm. **Postal Codes:** 30121 (Cannaregio); 30122 (Castello); 30123 (Dorsoduro); 30135 (S. Croce); 30124 (S. Marco); 30125 (S. Polo).

ACCOMMODATIONS

Hotels in Venice are often more expensive than those elsewhere, but savvy travelers can find cheap alternatives if they sniff out options early in the summer. Agree on a price before booking, and try to reserve one month ahead. The **VeneziaSi** (see **Tourist Offices,** p. 631) finds rooms with same-day availability. Religious institutions often offer rooms in the summer for €25-110. Options include: **Casa Murialdo,** Fond. Madonna dell'Orto, Cannaregio 3512 (☎71 99 33); **Patronato Salesiano Leone XIII,** Cal. S. Domenico, Castello 1281 (☎240 36 11); **Domus Cavanis,** Dorsoduro 896 (☎528 73 74), near the Ponte Accademia. In addition to these campground listings, Litorale del Cavallino, on the Lido's Adriatic side, has several sites. Call **Questura,** Fta. S. Lorenzo, Castello 5056 (☎270 55 11), for complaints about your hotel.

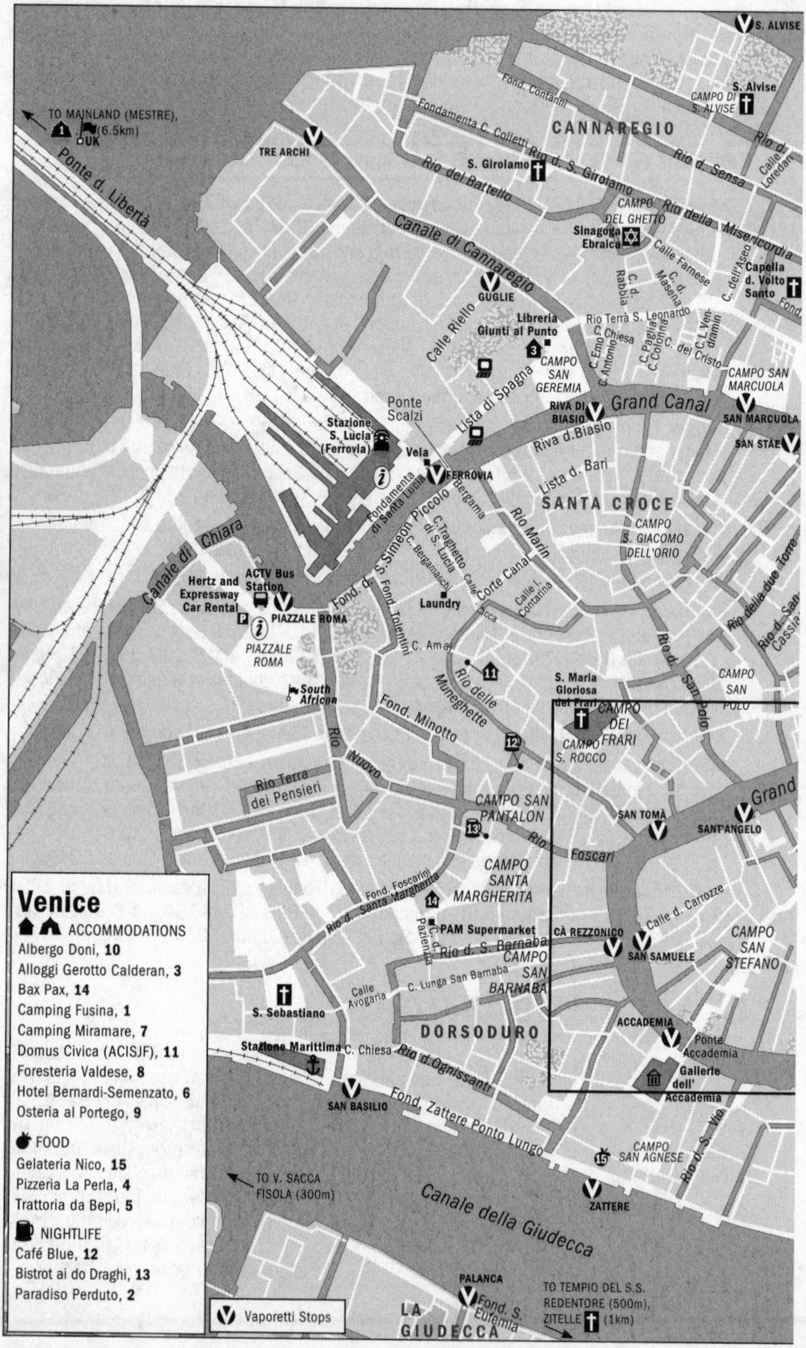
Venice
ACCOMMODATIONS
Albergo Doni, 10
Alloggi Gerotto Calderan, 3
Bax Pax, 14
Camping Fusina, 1
Camping Miramare, 7
Domus Civica (ACISJF), 11
Foresteria Valdese, 8
Hotel Bernardi-Semenzato, 6
Osteria al Portego, 9
FOOD
Gelateria Nico, 15
Pizzeria La Perla, 4
Trattoria da Bepi, 5
NIGHTLIFE
Café Blue, 12
Bistrot ai do Draghi, 13
Paradiso Perduto, 2
Vaporetti Stops
TO MAINLAND (MESTRE), (6.5km)
UK
Ponte d. Libertà
TRE ARCHI
S. ALVISE
S. Alvise
CAMPO DI S. ALVISE
CANNAREGIO
Fond. Contarini
Fondamenta C. Colletti
Rio d. S. Girolamo
Rio d. Sensa
S. Girolamo
Rio del Battello
Calle Loredan
CAMPO DEL GHETTO
Rio della Misericordia
Sinagoga Ebraica
Calle Farnese
Canale di Cannaregio
GUGLIE
C. d. Rabbia
C. d. Masena
C. dell'Aseo
Capella d. Volto Santo
Libreria Giunti al Punto
Calle Riello
Rio Terrà S. Leonardo
C. Chiesa
C. Emo
C. Antonio
C. Paglia
C. Colonna
C. dei Cristo
C. L. Vendramin
CAMPO SAN GEREMIA
CAMPO SAN MARCUOLA
Lista di Spagna
Ponte Scalzi
Stazione S. Lucia (Ferrovia)
RIVA DI BIASIO
Grand Canal
SAN MARCUOLA
SAN STAE
Riva d. Biasio
Vela
FERROVIA
Lista d. Bari
Fondamenta di Santa Lucia
Bergama
SANTA CROCE
Fond. d. S. Simeon Piccolo
C. Traghetto di S. Lucia
C. Bergamaschi
Rio Marin
CAMPO S. GIACOMO DELL'ORIO
Rio della due Torre
Canale di Chiara
ACTV Bus Station
Hertz and Expressway Car Rental
PIAZZALE ROMA
Corte Canal
Calle I. Contarina
Laundry
Rio d. San Cassian
Fond. Tolentini
C. Amai
Rio d. San Polo
CAMPO SAN POLO
Rio delle Muneghette
South African
S. Maria Gloriosa dei Frari
CAMPO DEI FRARI
CAMPO S. ROCCO
Fond. Minotto
Rio Nuovo
Rio Terra dei Pensieri
CAMPO SAN PANTALON
SAN TOMÀ
SANT'ANGELO
Rio Foscari
CAMPO SANTA MARGHERITA
Fond. Foscarini
Rio d. Santa Margherita
Calle d. Carrozze
C. d. Pazienza
PAM Supermarket
CÀ REZZONICO
SAN SAMUELE
CAMPO SAN STEFANO
Rio d. S. Barnaba
CAMPO SAN BARNABA
C. Lunga San Barnaba
Calle Avogaria
S. Sebastiano
DORSODURO
ACCADEMIA
Ponte Accademia
Stazione Marittima
C. Chiesa
Rio d. Ognissanti
Gallerie dell' Accademia
SAN BASILIO
Fond. Zattere Ponto Lungo
Rio d. S. Vio
CAMPO SAN AGNESE
TO V. SACCA FISOLA (300m)
ZATTERE
Canale della Giudecca
PALANCA
Fond. S. Eufemia
LA GIUDECCA
TO TEMPIO DEL S.S. REDENTORE (500m), ZITELLE (1km)

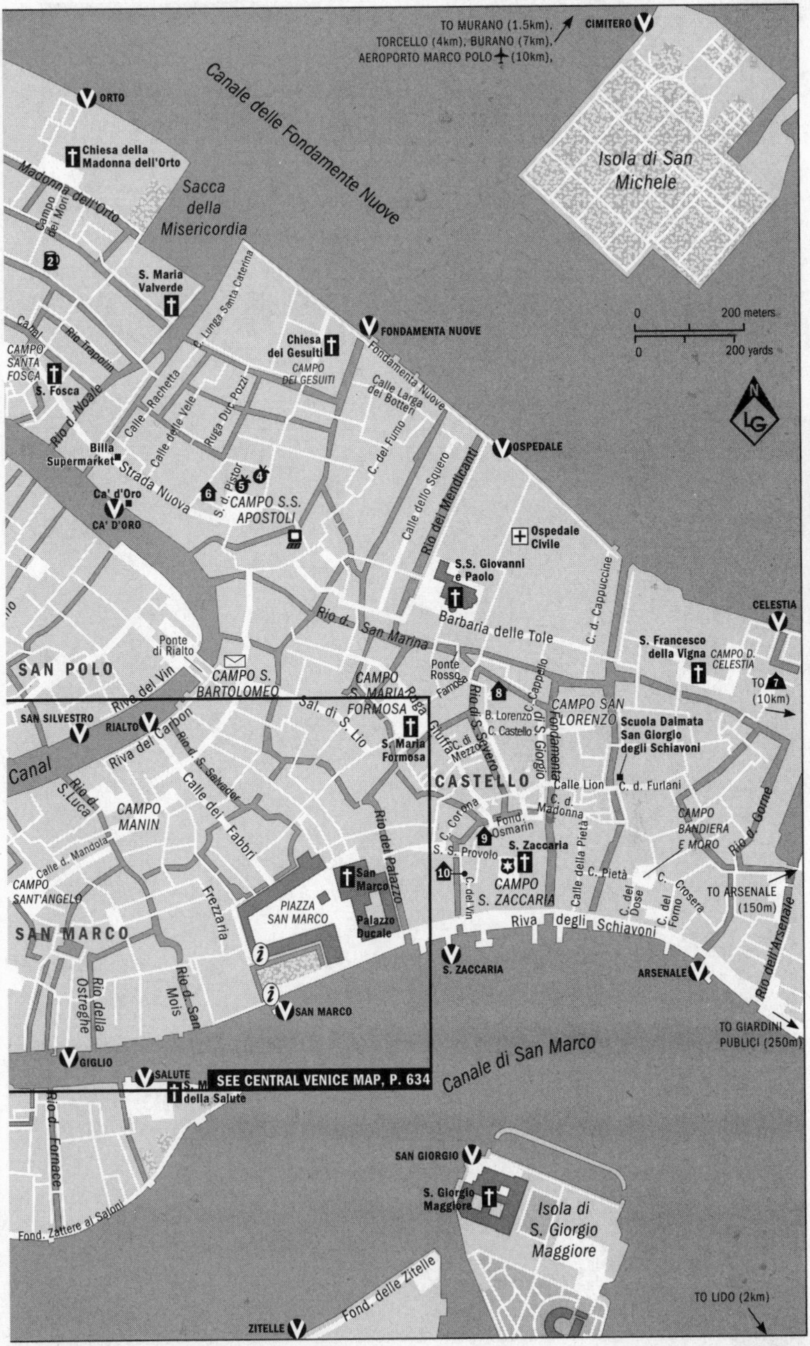
TO MURANO (1.5km), TORCELLO (4km), BURANO (7km), AEROPORTO MARCO POLO (10km),
CIMITERO
Isola di San Michele
Canale delle Fondamente Nuove
ORTO
Chiesa della Madonna dell'Orto
Madonna dell'Orto
Campo dei Mori
Sacca della Misericordia
S. Maria Valverde
Lunga Santa Caterina
FONDAMENTA NUOVE
Chiesa dei Gesuiti
CAMPO DEI GESUITI
Fondamenta Nuove
Calle Larga dei Botteri
200 meters
200 yards
CAMPO SANTA FOSCA
S. Fosca
Rio Trapolin
Rio d. Noale
Calle Rachetta
Calle delle Vele
Ruga Due Pozzi
C. del Fumo
OSPEDALE
Billa Supermarket
Strada Nuova
CAMPO S.S. APOSTOLI
Ca' d'Oro
CA' D'ORO
Calle dello Squero
Rio dei Mendicanti
Ospedale Civile
S.S. Giovanni e Paolo
C. d. Cappuccine
Rio d. San Marina
Barbaria delle Tole
CELESTIA
S. Francesco della Vigna
CAMPO D. CELESTIA
TO 7 (10km)
Ponte di Rialto
SAN POLO
Riva del Vin
CAMPO S. BARTOLOMEO
CAMPO S. MARIA FORMOSA
Ponte Rosso
Famosa
Rio di S. Severo
C. Cappello
CAMPO SAN LORENZO
B. Lorenzo
C. Castello
Fondamenta
Scuola Dalmata San Giorgio degli Schiavoni
SAN SILVESTRO
RIALTO
Riva del Carbon
Rio d. S. Salvader
Sal. di S. Lio
Ruga Giuffa
S. Maria Formosa
C. di Mezzo
CASTELLO
Calle Lion
C. d. Furlani
Canal
Rio d. S. Luca
CAMPO MANIN
Calle dei Fabbri
Rio del Palazzo
C. Corona
Fond. Osmarin
C. d. Madonna
CAMPO BANDIERA E MORO
Rio d. Gorne
Calle d. Mandola
CAMPO SANT'ANGELO
Frezzaria
PIAZZA SAN MARCO
San Marco
Palazzo Ducale
S. S. Provolo
S. Zaccaria
CAMPO S. ZACCARIA
C. del Vin
Calle della Pietà
C. Pietà
C. del Dose
C. del Forno
C. Crosera
TO ARSENALE (150m)
Rio dell'Arsenale
SAN MARCO
Riva degli Schiavoni
S. ZACCARIA
ARSENALE
Rio della Ostreghe
Rio d. San Mois
SAN MARCO
TO GIARDINI PUBLICI (250m)
GIGLIO
SALUTE
SEE CENTRAL VENICE MAP, P. 634
della Salute
Canale di San Marco
Rio d. Fornace
SAN GIORGIO
S. Giorgio Maggiore
Isola di S. Giorgio Maggiore
Fond. Zattere ai Saloni
Fond. delle Zitelle
ZITELLE
TO LIDO (2km)
ITALY

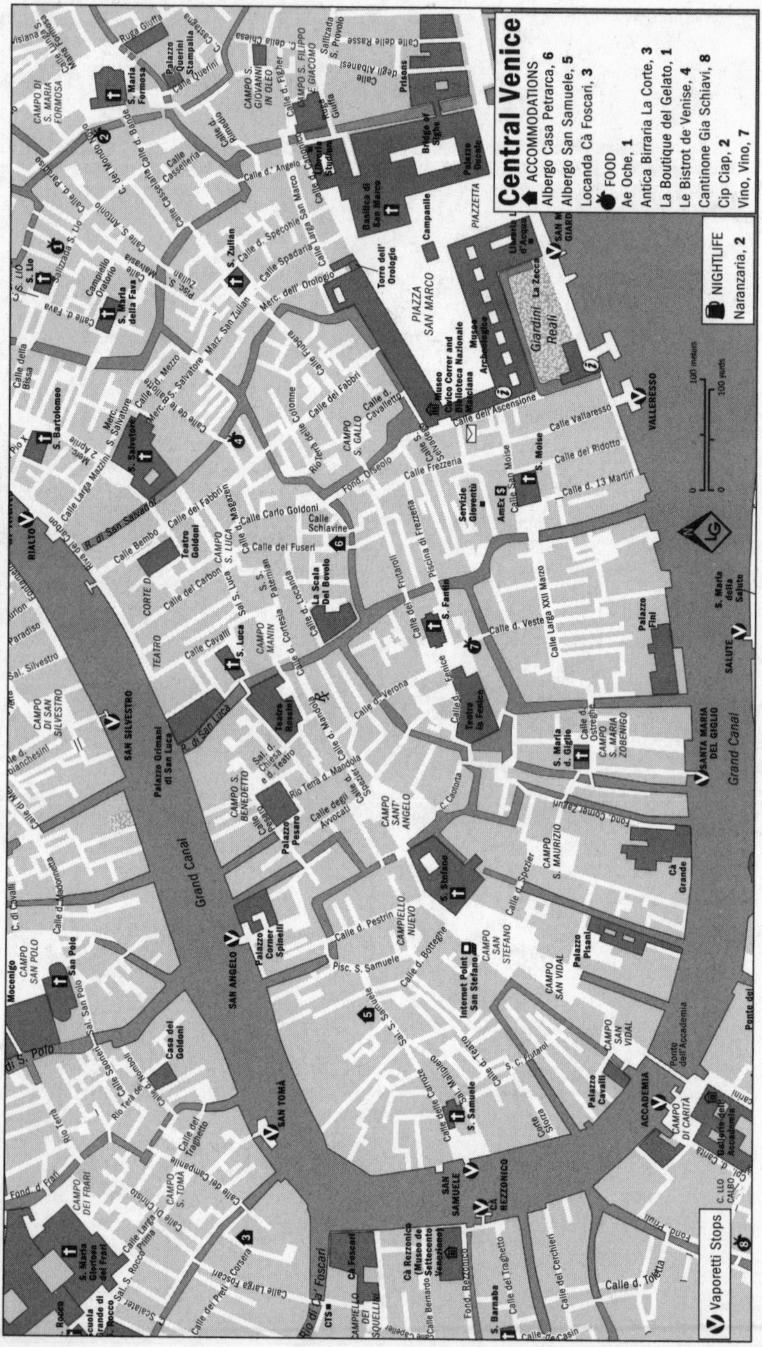
Central Venice
ACCOMMODATIONS
Albergo Casa Petrarca, 6
Albergo San Samuele, 5
Locanda Cà Foscari, 3
FOOD
Ae Oche, 1
Antica Birraria La Corte, 3
La Boutique del Gelato, 1
Le Bistrot de Venise, 4
Cantinone Gia Schiavi, 8
Cip Ciap, 2
Vino, Vino, 7
NIGHTLIFE
Naranzaria, 2
Vaporetti Stops
100 meters
100 yards
PIAZZA SAN MARCO
Grand Canal
Basilica di San Marco
Campanile
Torre dell' Orologio
Bridge of Sighs
Palazzo Ducale
RIALTO
SAN MARCO
VALLARESSO
SALUTE
SANTA MARIA DEL GIGLIO
ACCADEMIA
CÀ REZZONICO
SAN SAMUELE
SAN TOMÀ
SAN ANGELO
SAN SILVESTRO

ITALY

Alloggi Gerotto Calderan, Campo S. Geremia 283 (☎71 55 62; www.casagerottocalderan.com). Half hostel, half hotel, all good. Location makes it the best deal in Venice. Check-in 2pm. Check-out 10am. Curfew 12:30am. Reserve at least 15 days ahead. Dorms €25; singles €36, with bath €41; doubles €60/95; triples €84/93. 10% Rolling Venice discount; reduced prices for extended stays. Cash only. ❷

Hotel Bernardi-Semenzato, Cal. dell'Oca, Cannaregio 4366 (☎522 72 57; www.hotelbernardi.com). From V: Cà d'Oro, turn right on Str. Nuova, left on Cal. del Duca, and then right. Helpful staff, great views, and decor that manages to be both elegant and homey. Check-out 11am. Singles €30; doubles €45-60, with bath €60-90; triples €78-90; quads €85-118. 10% Rolling Venice discount on larger rooms. AmEx/MC/V. ❸

Albergo Casa Petrarca, Cal. Schiavine, San Marco 4386 (☎520 04 30). From Campo S. Luca, follow Cal. Fuseri, take the 2nd left, then a right. Tiny hotel, most rooms with bath and A/C. Breakfast included. Singles €65-85; doubles €100-110. Cash only. ❹

Bax Pax, C. S. Margherita 2931 (☎099 45 54; baxpaxvenice@yahoo.it). As its name would suggest, a backpacker's dream. Unbelievably located, large single-sex or co-ed dorm rooms are situated in a romantic *palazzo.* Kitchen available. Breakfast, linens, laundry, and Internet included. No curfew. Dorms €20-32. Cash only. ❷

Locanda Cà Foscari, Cal. della Frescada, Dorsoduro 3887/B (☎71 04 01; www.locandacafoscari.com), in a quiet neighborhood. From V: San Tomà, turn left at the dead end, cross the bridge, turn right, then left at the alley. *Carnevale* masks embellish this tidy hotel, run for over 40 years by the Scarpa family. Breakfast included. Reception 24hr. Reserve 2-3 months ahead. Closed July 28-1st week in Aug. Singles €57, with bath €62; doubles €72/93; triples €90/114; quads €112. MC/V. ❹

Albergo San Samuele, Salizzada S. Samuele, San Marco 3358 (☎522 80 45; www.albergosansamuele.it). Follow Cal. delle Botteghe from Campo S. Stefano and turn left on Salizzada S. Samuele. Reserve 1-2 months ahead. Singles €26-45; doubles €50-100, with bath €60-105; triples €135. Cash only. ❸

Domus Civica (ACISJF), Campiello Chiovere Frari, San Polo 3082 (☎72 11 03). From the station, cross Ponte Scalzi and turn right. Turn left on Fond. dei Tolentini and left through the courtyard onto Corte Amai. The hostel's rounded facade is after the bridge. Spartan white rooms with shared TV, piano, and bath. Free Internet. Reception 7am-12:30am. Strict curfew 11:30pm. Open June-Sept. 25. Singles €30; doubles and triples €27 per person. 15% Rolling Venice discount; 20% ISIC discount. AmEx/MC/V. ❸

Foresteria Valdese, Castello 5170 (☎528 67 97; www.diaconiavaldese.org/venezia). From Campo S. Maria Formosa, take Cal. Lunga S. Maria Formosa. A grand 18th-century guest house run by Venice's largest Protestant church, 2min. from sights. Breakfast included. Internet €5 per hr. Reception 9am-1pm and 6-8pm. Lockout 10am-1pm. Reservations required. Dorms €21-22; doubles €60-78; apartments (no breakfast) €104. Rooms larger than singles have 2 night min. stay. €1 Rolling Venice discount. MC/V. ❷

Albergo Doni, Calle del Vin, Castello 4656 (☎522 42 67; www.albergodoni.it). From P. San Marco, turn left immediately after the 2nd bridge on Cal. del Vin and take the left fork when the street splits. Cheery staff and proximity to P. San Marco make this hotel an amazing deal. Rooms with phone, TV, and either a fan or A/C. Breakfast included. Reception 24hr. Singles €40-65; doubles €60-95, with bath €80-120; triples €80-125/120-160; quads €140-200. €5 discount with cash payment. MC/V. ❸

Camping Miramare, Lungomare Dante Alighieri 29 (☎96 61 50; www.camping-miramare.it). A 1hr. ride on V #LN from P. S. Marco to Punta Sabbioni. Campground is 700m along the beach on the right. Min. 2-night stay in high season. Open Apr.-Oct. Tent sites €14-16; cabins €27-60 plus per-person charge. MC/V. ❶

Camping Fusina, V. Moranzani 93 (☎54 70 055; www.camping-fusina.com), in Malcontenta. From Mestre, take bus #11. Restaurant, laundromat, ATM, Internet, and TV onsite. Free hot showers. Call ahead to reserve cabins. €8.50 per tent, €8-9 per person. Cabin singles €22; doubles €30. AmEx/MC/V. ❷

FOOD

Beware the overpriced restaurants that line the canals around San Marco. With few exceptions, the best restaurants hide along less-traveled alleyways. *Sarde in saor* (sardines in vinegar and onions) is available only in Venice and can be sampled cheaply at most bars with *cicchetti* (tidbits of seafood, rice, meat, and the ever-famous Venetian sardines; €1-3). For informal meals, visit an *osteria* or *bacaro* for stuffed pastries, seafood, rice, or *tramezzini* (soft white bread with any imaginable filling). The BILLA **supermarket,** Str. Nuova, Cannaregio 3660, is near Campo S. Fosca. (Open M-Sa 8:30am-8:30pm, Su 9am-8:30pm. AmEx/MC/V.)

Le Bistrot de Venise, Cal. dei Fabbri, San Marco 4685 (☎52 36 651). From P. S. Marco, go through 2nd Sottoportego dei Dai under the awning. Follow road around and over a bridge and turn right. Scrumptious Venetian dishes, true to Medieval and Renaissance recipes. *Enoteca: primi* €8-12, *secondi* €12-18. Restaurant: *primi* €16-20, *secondi* €20-28. Wine €3-12 per glass. Service 12%. Open daily 10am-1am. MC/V. ❺

Cantinone Gia Schiavi, Fond. Meraviglie, Dorsoduro 992 (☎523 00 34). From the Frari, follow signs for Ponte Accademia. Just before Ponte Meraviglie, turn right toward the church of S. Trovaso and cross the 1st bridge. Friendly owner serves chilled wine, including a delicate strawberry variety (€8.50 per bottle). Enjoy a glass (€0.80-3) with flavorful *cicchetti* (from €1). Open M-Sa 8am-8pm. Cash only. ❶

Gelateria Nico, Fond. Zattere, Dorsoduro 922 (☎522 52 93). Near V: Zattere. Try the Venetian **gianduiotto de passeggio,** a brick of dense chocolate-hazelnut ice cream dropped into a cup of dense whipped cream (€2.50). Gelato €1, 2 scoops €1.50, 3 scoops €2. Prices increase at tables. Open M-W and F-Su 6:45am-10pm. Cash only. ❶

Antica Birraria La Corte, Campo S. Polo, San Polo 2168 (☎27 50 570). This former brewery features a large restaurant and bar, outside tables, and usually a wait. Pizza €5-9. *Primi* €7.20-8.20. *Secondi* €9.50-17. Cover €1. Open daily 12:30-3pm and 7-10:30pm; mid-July to mid-Aug. Sa-Su open 12:30-3pm only. AmEx/MC/V. ❸

Cip Ciap, Cal. del Mondo Novo 5799/A, Castello (☎523 66 21). From Campo S. Maria Formosa, follow Cal. del Mondo Novo. Tiny pizzeria uses fresh ingredients and sells by the gram (€2-2.50 per kg). Cheap, filling calzones (€2.40). There's no seating, but box it up and nab a bench in the nearby *campo.* Open M and W-Su 9am-9pm. Cash only. ❶

Trattoria da Bepi, Cannaregio 4550. From Campo S. S. Apostoli, turn left on Salizzada del Pistor. Traditional Venetian *trattoria* attracts tourists and locals who come for the expertly prepared cuisine. *Primi* €7-11. *Secondi* from €10. Cover €1.50. Reserve ahead for outdoor seating. Open M-W and F-Su noon-2:30pm and 7-10pm. MC/V. ❸

Osteria al Portego, Cal. Malvasia, Castello 6015. Heading south on Salizzada S. Lio, turn left onto Cal. Malvasia, and left again toward Cte. Perina. This hidden *osteria,* filled with barrels of wine, is a favorite of students and locals. Huge array of *cicchetti.* Open M-Sa 10:30am-3pm and 6-10pm; in summer also Su 6-10pm. Cash only. ❶

La Boutique del Gelato, Salizzada S. Lio, Castello 5727 (☎522 32 83). Popular stand doles out generous portions of rich gelato. 1 scoop €1, 2 scoops €1.50. Open daily July-Aug. 10am-11pm; Sept.-June 10am-8:30pm. Cash only. ❶

Ae Oche, Santa Croce 1552A/B (☎524 11 61). From Campo S. Giacomo, take Cal. del Trentor. 60s American advertisements and a cartoonish duck logo create a charming, if strange effect. *Pizza* €4.50-9. *Primi* €5.50-7. *Secondi* €7.50-12.50. Cover €1.50. Service 12%. Open daily noon-2pm and 6:30-10:30pm. MC/V. ❷

Pizzeria La Perla, Rio Terra dei Franceschi, Cannaregio 4615. From Str. Nuova, turn left on Salizzada del Pistor in Campo S. S. Apostoli. Follow to the end, then follow signs for the Fondamente Nuove. Pizza €4.65-9. Pasta €6.10-8.20. Cover €1.10. Service 10%. Open M-Tu and Th-Su noon-3pm and 7-9:45pm; daily in Aug. AmEx/MC/V. ❷

Vino, Vino, Ponte delle Veste, San Marco 2007/A. From Cal. Larga XXII Marzo, turn on Cal. delle Veste. No-frills wine bar serves over 350 kinds, plus traditional *sarde in saor* and pasta from a daily menu. *Primi* €6.50. *Secondi* €9-10.50. Cover €1. Open M and W-Su 11am-3pm and 6-11:30pm. 10% Rolling Venice discount. Cash only. ❸

SIGHTS

Venice's layout make sightseeing a disorienting affair. Most sights center around the **Piazza San Marco,** but getting lost can be better than being found in its tourist crowds. Museum passes (€18, students €12), sold at participating museums, grant one-time admission to each of 10 museums over the course of three months.

AROUND PIAZZA SAN MARCO

Venice's only official *piazza*, **Piazza San Marco,** is an un-Venetian expanse of light, space, and architectural harmony. The 96m brick **campanile** (bell tower; open daily 9am-9pm, €6), built on a Roman base, provides one of the best views of the city; on clear days, the panorama spans Croatia and Slovenia.

BASILICA DI SAN MARCO. The symmetrical arches and incomparable mosaics of Venice's crown jewel grace **Piazza San Marco.** The city's premier tourist attraction, the **Basilica di San Marco** also has the longest lines. Late afternoon visits profit from the best natural light but are most crowded. Built to house the remains of St. Mark, 13th-century Byzantine and 16th-century Renaissance mosaics now make the interior sparkle. Behind the altar, the **Pala d'Oro** relief frames a parade of saints in gem-encrusted gold. Steep stairs in the atrium lead to the **Galleria della Basilica,** whose view is of tiny golden tiles in the basilica's vast ceiling mosaics and the original bronze **Cavalli di San Marco** (Horses of St. Mark); a balcony overlooks the *piazza*. *(Basilica open M-Sa 9:45am-5pm, Su 2-4pm. Modest dress required. Pala d'Oro open M-Sa 9:45am-5:30pm, Su 2-4pm; €1.50. Treasury open M-Sa 9:45am-5:30pm; €2. Galleria open M-F 9:45am-4:15pm, Sa-Su 9:45am-4:45pm; €3.)*

PALAZZO DUCALE (DOGE'S PALACE). Once the home of Venice's *doge* (mayor), the Palazzo Ducale is now a museum. Veronese's *Rape of Europa* is among its spectacular artwork. In the courtyard, Sansovino's enormous sculptures, *Mars* and *Neptune*, flank the **Scala dei Giganti** (Stairs of the Giants), upon which new *doges* were crowned. The Council of Ten, the *doge*'s administrators, would drop the names of suspected criminals into the **Bocca di Leone** (Lion's Mouth), on the balcony. Climb the **Scala d'Oro** (Golden Staircase) to the **Sala delle Quattro Porte** (Room of the Four Doors), whose ceiling depicts biblical judgements, and the **Sala dell'Anticollegio** (Antechamber of the Senate), whose decorations are myths about Venice. Courtrooms of the Council of Ten and the Council of Three lead to the **Sala del Maggior Consiglio** (Great Council Room), dominated by Tintoretto's *Paradise*, the largest oil painting in the world. Near the end, thick stone lattices line the **Ponte dei Sospiri** (Bridge of Sighs), named after the mournful groans of prisoners who walked it on their way to the prison's damp cells. *(Wheelchair-accessible. Open daily Apr.-Oct. 9am-7pm; Nov.-Mar. 9am-5pm. €12, students €6.50.)*

AROUND THE PONTE RIALTO

THE GRAND CANAL. The Grand Canal is Venice's "main street." Over 3km long and nearly 50m wide, it loops through the city and passes under three bridges: the **Ponte Scalzi, Rialto,** and **Accademia.** The candy-cane posts used for mooring boats on the canal, called *bricole*, are painted with the colors of the family whose *palazzo* adjoins them. *(For great facade views, ride V. #1, 4, or 82 from the train station to P. S. Marco. The facades are lit at night and produce dazzling reflections.)*

ITALY

■**RIVOALTUS LEGATORIA.** Step into the book-lined Rivoaltus on any given day and hear Wanda Scarpa shouting greetings from the attic, where she has been sewing leatherbound, antique-style ■**journals** for an international cadre of customers and faithful locals for more than three decades. Though Venice is now littered with shops selling journals, Rivoaltus was the first, and remains the best. *(Ponte di Rialto 11. Notebooks €18-31. Photo albums €31-78. Open daily 10am-7:30pm.)*

SAN POLO

The second-largest *campo* in Venice, **Campo San Polo** once hosted bloody bull-baiting matches during *Carnevale*. Today, blood is no longer spilled—only gelato.

SCUOLA GRANDE DI SAN ROCCO. The most illustrious of Venice's *scuola* (schools) stands as a monument to Jacopo Tintoretto, who left Venice only once in his 76 years, and who sought to combine "the color of Titian with the drawing of Michelangelo." The school had Tintoretto complete all the paintings in the building, which took 23 years. The *Crucifixion* in the last room upstairs is the collection's crowning glory. Step outside to admire it to strains of classical music performed by street musicians. *(Behind Basilica dei Frari in Campo S. Rocco. Open daily Apr.-Oct. 9am-5:30pm; Nov.-Mar. 10am-4pm. €7, students and Rolling Venice €5.)*

DORSODURO

■**COLLEZIONE PEGGY GUGGENHEIM.** Guggenheim's Palazzo Venier dei Leoni displays works by Dalí, Duchamp, Ernst, Kandinsky, Klee, Magritte, Picasso, and Pollock. The Marini sculpture *Angel in the City*, in front of the *palazzo*, was designed with a detachable penis so that Ms. Guggenheim could avoid offending her more prudish guests. *(Fond. Venier dei Leoni, Dorsoduro 710. V: Accademia. Turn left and follow the yellow signs. Open M and W-Su 10am-6pm. €10; students, ISIC, Rolling Venice €5.)*

■**GALLERIE DELL'ACCADEMIA.** The Accademia houses the world's most extensive collection of Venetian art. Among the enormous altarpieces in **Room II**, Giovanni Bellini's *Madonna Enthroned with Child, Saints, and Angels* is a beacon of calm. **Rooms IV** and **V** have more Bellinis plus Giorgione's enigmatic *La Tempesta*. In **Room VI**, three paintings by Tintoretto, *The Creation of the Animals*, *The Temptation of Adam and Eve*, and *Cain and Abel*, grow progressively darker. **Room X** displays Titian's last painting, a *Pietà* intended for his tomb—to no avail. In **Room XX**, works by Bellini and Carpaccio depict Venetian processions and cityscapes so accurately that scholars use them as "photos" of Venice's past. *(V: Accademia. Open M 8:15am-2pm, Tu-Su 8:15am-7pm. €6.50. English tours Tu-Su 11am €7.)*

CASTELLO

SCUOLA DALMATA SAN GIORGIO DEGLI SCHIAVONI. Carpaccio's finest art, visual tales of St. George, Jerome, and Tryfon, hang in the early 16th-century building. *(Castello 3259/A. V: S. Zaccaria. Modest dress. Open Apr.-Oct. Tu-Sa 9:30am-12:30pm and 3:30-6:30pm, Su 9:30am-12:30pm; Nov.-Mar. reduced hours. €3, Rolling Venice €2.)*

CANNAREGIO

JEWISH GHETTO. In 1516 the *doge* forced Venice's Jewish population into the old cannon-foundry area, creating the first Jewish ghetto in Europe and coining the word ghetto, the Venetian word for "foundry." In the Campo del Ghetto Nuovo, the **Schola Grande Tedesca** (German Synagogue), the area's oldest synagogue, now shares a building with the **Museo Ebraica di Venezia** (Hebrew Museum of Venice). *(Cannaregio 2899/B. V: S. Marcuola. Museum open Su-F June-Sept. 10am-7pm; Oct.-May 10am-4:30pm. Enter synagogue by ■40min. tour. English tours every hr. daily June-Sept. 10:30am-5:30pm; Oct.-May 10:30am-4:30pm. Museum €3, students €2. Museum and tour €8.50/7.)*

CÀ D'ORO. Delicate spires and interlocking arches make the Cà d'Oro's facade the most spectacular on the Canal Grande. Built between 1425 and 1440, it now houses the **Galleria Giorgio Franchetti.** For the best view of the palace, take a *traghetto* (ferry) across the canal to the Rialto Markets. *(V: Cà d'Oro. Open M 8:15am-2pm, Tu-Su 8:15am-7:15pm. €5, EU students and under 35 €2.50. Audio tour €4.)*

CHURCHES

The Foundation for the Churches of Venice sells the **Chorus Pass** (☎275 0462; www.chorusvenezia.org), which provides admission to all of Venice's churches. A yearly pass (€8, students €5) is available at most participating churches.

CHIESA DI SAN ZACCARIA. Designed in the late 1400s by Coducci and others, and dedicated to John the Baptist's father, this Gothic-Renaissance church holds S. Zaccaria's corpse in an elevated sarcophagus along the nave's right wall. Nearby is Bellini's *Virgin and Child Enthroned with Four Saints*, a Venetian Renaissance masterpiece. *(S. Marco. V: S. Zaccaria. Open daily 10am-noon and 4-6pm. Free.)*

CHIESA DI SAN GIACOMO DI RIALTO. Between the Rialto and the surrounding markets stands Venice's first church, diminutively called "San Giacometto." Across the *piazza*, the statue *Il Gobbo* (The Hunchback) supports the steps, at whose foot convicted thieves would collapse after being forced to run naked from P. S. Marco. *(V: Rialto. Cross bridge and turn right. Church open daily 10am-5pm. Free.)*

BASILICA DI SANTA MARIA GLORIOSA DEI FRARI. Titian's corpse and two of his paintings reside within this Gothic church. **Assumption** (1516-18), on the high altar, marks the height of the Venetian Renaissance. The golden Florentine chapel, to the right of the high altar, frames Donatello's gaunt wooden sculpture, **St. John the Baptist.** Titian's tomb is an elaborate lion-topped triumphal arch with bas-relief scenes of Paradise. *(S. Polo. V: S. Tomà. Open M-Sa 9am-6pm, Su 1-6pm. €2.50.)*

CHIESA DI SANTA MARIA DELLA SALUTE. The *salute* (Italian for "health") is a hallmark of the Venetian skyline: perched on Dorsoduro's peninsula just southwest of San Marco, the church and its domes are visible from everywhere in the city. In 1631, the city had **Longhena** build the church for the Virgin, who they believed would end the current plague. Next to the *salute* stands the *dogana*, the customs house, where ships sailing into Venice were required to pay duties. *(Dorsoduro. V: Salute. ☎522 55 58. Open daily 9am-noon and 3-5:30pm. Free. Entrance to sacristy with donation. The inside of the dogana is closed to the public.)*

CHIESA DI SAN SEBASTIANO. The Renaissance painter **Veronese** took refuge in 16th-century church when he fled Verona after allegedly killing a man. In 10 years he filled the church with a cycle of paintings and frescoes. His *Stories of Queen Esther* covers the ceiling, while the artist's body is by the organ. *(Dorsoduro. V: S. Basilio. Continue straight. Open M-Sa 10am-5pm, Su 1-5pm. €2.50.)*

ISLANDS OF THE LAGOON

LIDO. The breezy resort island of Lido provided the tragic setting for Thomas Mann's haunting novella, *Death in Venice*. Visonti's film version was also shot here at the Hotel des Bains. Today, people flock to Lido to enjoy the surf at the popular public beach. A casino, horseback riding, and the Alberoni Golf Club complete the idyll. *(V #1 and 82: Lido. Beach open daily 9am-8pm. Free.)*

MURANO. Famous since 1292 for its glass, the six-island cluster of Murano affords visitors the opportunity to witness resident artisans blow and spin free of charge. For demonstrations, look for signs directing to the *fornace*. Quiet streets are lined with tiny shops and glass boutiques. The collection at the **Museo Vetrario**

(Glass Museum) ranges from first-century funereal urns to a cartoonish, sea green octopus. *(V #DM, LN, 5, 13, 41, 42: Faro from either S. Zaccaria or Fondamenta Nuove. Museo Vetrario, Fond. Giustian 8. Open M-Tu and Th-Su Apr.-Oct. 10am-5pm; Nov.-Mar. 10am-4pm. €4, students and Rolling Venice €2.50. Combined ticket with Burano Lace Museum €6/4. Basilica open daily 8am-7pm. Modest dress required. Free.)*

ENTERTAINMENT

Admire Venetian houses and *palazzi* via their original canal pathways, on **gondola** rides, most romantic about 50min. before sunset and most affordable if shared by six people. The most price-flexible gondoliers are those standing by themselves rather than those in groups at the "taxi-stands" throughout the city. The "official" price starts at €73 per 50min., with a maximum of six people; prices rise at night.

Teatro Goldoni, Cal. del Teatro, S. Marco 4650/B (☎240 20 11; teatrogoldini@libero.it), near the Ponte di Rialto, showcases various types of live productions, often with seasonal themes. The **Mostra Internazionale di Cinema** (Venice International Film Festival), held annually from late August to early September, draws established names and rising phenoms from around the world. Movies are shown in their original language. (☎521 88 78. Tickets sold throughout the city, €20. Some late-night outdoor showings are free.) The famed **Biennale di Venezia** (☎521 18 98; www.labiennale.org) is a contemporary exhibit of provocative art or architecture. The weekly publication *A Guest in Venice*, offered for free at hotels and tourist offices or online (www.unospitedivenezia.it), lists current festivals, concerts, and gallery exhibits.

ITALY

Long banned, Venice's famous **Carnevale** was reinstated in the early 1970s, and the 10 days before Ash Wednesday see masked figures in the streets and outdoor performances all over. For **Mardi Gras,** the population doubles; make arrangements well ahead. Venice's second-most colorful festival is the **Festa del Redentore** (3rd Su in July), originally held to celebrate the end of a 16th-century plague, which kicks off with fireworks at 11:30pm the Saturday before.

NIGHTLIFE

Most residents of Milan would much rather spend an evening sipping wine or beer in a *piazza* than bumping and grinding in a disco. Establishments come and go with some regularity, though student nightlife is consistently concentrated around **Campo Santa Margherita,** in Dorsoduro, while places frequented by tourists centers around the **Lista di Spagna.**

Café Blue, Dorsoduro 3778 (☎71 02 27). From S. Maria Frari, take Cal. Scalater and turn right at the end. Grab some absinthe (€6) and a stool to watch the daytime coffee crowd turn into a chill and laid-back set as night falls. Free Internet. F in winter live music, W DJ. Open in summer noon-2am; winter 8pm-2am. MC/V.

Naranzaria, Sottoportego del Banco, S. Polo 130 (☎72 41 035). At the canal-side corner of C. S. Giacomo. Up-close views of the Grand Canal and Rialto are secondary to the wine, arrays of *cicchetti,* and trendy vibe at this bistro. Open Tu-Su 11am-11pm. MC/V.

Bistrot ai Do Draghi, Campo S. Margherita 3665 (☎52 89 731). While not as fierce as the name (translated: dragon) implies, the crowd at this tiny bistro is more artsy than that at its C. S. Margherita counterparts. Wine €1.20 per glass. Open daily 7am-2am.

Paradiso Perduto, Fond. della Misericordia, Cannaregio 2540 (☎099 45 40). From Str. Nuova, cross Campo S. Fosca and the bridge, and continue in the same direction, traversing 2 more bridges. Students flood this unassuming bar, which also serves *cicchetti* (mixed plate; €19). F nights live jazz. Open M-Sa 9:30am-3pm and 7pm-2am.

PADUA (PADOVA) ☎049

Padua's oldest institutions are the ones that still draw visitors: San Antonio's tomb, the looping Prato della Valle, and the university, founded in 1222. It once hosted such luminaries as Copernicus, Donatello, Galileo, and Giotto, and now keeps a young and energetic population buzzing in the streets well past dusk. The starry blue ceiling of the **Cappella degli Scrovegni,** P. Eremitani 8, overlooks Giotto's epic 38-panel fresco cycle, depicting Mary, Jesus, St. Anne, and St. Joachim; in *Last Judgment*, Giotto appears himself among the blessed—fourth from the left, in a pink robe. Buy tickets at the attached **Musei Civici Eremitani,** whose art collection includes Giotto's beautiful crucifix, which once adorned the Scrovegni Chapel. (☎820 10 020; www.cappelladegliscrovegni.it. Entrance to the chapel only with museum. Open M-F 9am-7pm, Sa 9am-6pm. Reserve ahead. Museum €10, combined with chapel €12, students €5. AmEx/DC/MC/V.) Pilgrims flock to see St. Anthony's jawbone, tongue, and tomb displayed at the **Basilica di Sant'Antonio,** in P. del Santo. (☎824 28 11. Modest dress required. Open daily Apr.-Sept. 6:30am-7:45pm; Nov.-Mar. 6:30am-7pm. Free.) The university centers around the two interior courtyards of **Palazzo Bò,** as does the student-heavy nightlife. Across the street, **Caffè Pedrocchi** once served as the headquarters for 19th-century liberals who supported Risogimento leader Giuseppe Mazzini. Next to the **duomo,** in P. Duomo, sits the tiny **Battistero,** whose domed interior has New Testament frescoes. (*Duomo* open M-Sa 7:30am-noon and 3:45-7:45pm, Su 7:45am-1pm and 3:45-8:30pm. Free. *Battistero* open daily 10am-6pm. €2.50, students €1.50.)

The stonework in the lobby of **Hotel Al Santo ❹,** V. del Santo 147, near the basilica, leads to spacious rooms. (☎875 21 31. Breakfast included. Reception 24hr. Singles €55-60; doubles €80-100; triples €130. AmEx/MC/V.) Go to V. Aleardi and turn left; walk to the end of the block and **Ostello Città di Padova (HI) ❷,** V. Aleardi 30, will be on your left. (☎875 22 19; pdyhtl@tin.it. Wheelchair accessible. Internet €5 per hr. Lockout 9:30am-3:30pm. Curfew midnight. Reserve ahead. Dorms €18. €3 HI discount. MC/V.) The place to go for Paduan cuisine is **Antica Trattoria Paccagnella ❷,** V. del Santo 113. (☎/fax 875 05 49. *Primi* €6-10. *Secondi* €4.50-17. Cover €2. Open daily noon-2:30pm and 7-10pm. AmEx/MC/V.) **Trains** run from P. Stazione to: Bologna (1½hr., 34 per day, €6); Milan (2½hr., 25 per day, €12); Venice (30min., 82 per day, €2.50); Verona (1hr., 44 per day, €4.30). **SITA Buses** (☎820 68 34) leave from P. Boschetti for Venice (45min., 32 per day, €3.05). The **tourist office** is in the train station. (☎875 20 77. Open M-Sa 9am-7pm, Su 8:30am-12:30pm.) To reach the *centro* from the station, take the main street through town and turn right on V. Rogati. **Postal Code:** 35100.

VERONA ☎045

Bright gardens and realistic sculptures fill Verona (pop. 245,000) with enough majesty to overwhelm any romantics who wander into its walls seeking Romeo or Juliet, whose drama Shakespeare set here. But there's more to Verona: its rich wines, cuisine, and renowned opera are kept affordable by student prices.

TRANSPORTATION AND PRACTICAL INFORMATION. Trains (☎89 20 21) go from P. XXV Aprile to: Bologna (2hr., 27 per day, €6); Milan (2hr., 37 per day, €7); Trent (1hr., 25 per day, €5); Venice (1½hr., 41 per day, €8). From the station walk 20min. up **Corso Porta Nuova** or take bus #11, 12, 13, 51, 72, or 73 (Sa-Su take #91, 92, or 93) to Verona's center, the **Arena** in **Piazza Brà.** The **tourist office** is just off the *piazza* at V. d. Alpini 9. (☎806 86 80; iatverona@provincia.vr.it. Open M-Sa 9am-7pm, Su 9am-3pm.) Check email at **Internet Train,** V. Roma 17/A. (☎801 33 94. €2.50 per 30min. Open M-F 10am-10pm, Sa-Su 2-8pm. MC/V.) **Postal Code:** 37100.

ITALY

ACCOMMODATIONS AND FOOD. Reserve hotel rooms ahead, especially during opera season (June-Sept.). The **Ostello della Gioventù (HI) ❶**, Villa Francescatti, Salita Fontana del Ferro 15, is in a renovated 16th-century villa with gorgeous gardens and aging frescoes. From the station, take bus #73 or night bus #90 to P. Isolo, turn right, and follow the yellow signs uphill. (☎59 03 60. Breakfast and communal showers included. Lockout 9am-5pm. Curfew 11:30pm; flexible for opera-goers. Dorms €15; family rooms €19. HI members only. Cash only.) To get to the romantic, central **Bed and Breakfast Anfiteatro ❹**, V. Alberto Mario 5, follow V. Mazzini toward P. Brà until it branches to the right to become V. Alberto Mario. (☎347 24 88 462; www.anfiteatro-bedandbreakfast.com. Breakfast included. Doubles €65-130.) Verona is famous for wines like the dry white *soave* and red *valpolicella*. The **Enoteca dal Zovo ❶**, Vicolo S. Marco in Foro 7/5, near P. Brà, was once the chapel of Verona's archbishop. Now it plays the role of wine bar and resembles an apothecary's shop with bottles cluttered on every surface. (☎803 43 69. Open in summer daily 8am-8pm; winter Tu-Su 8am-8pm. Cash only.) A **Pam** supermarket is at V. dei Mutilati 3. (Open M-Sa 8am-8pm, Su 9am-8pm.)

SIGHTS AND ENTERTAINMENT. The physical and social heart of Verona is the tiered first-century **Arena** in P. Brà. (☎800 32 04. Open M 1:45-6:30pm, Tu-Su 8:30am-6:30pm. Closes 4:30pm on opera nights. Ticket office closes 45min. before Arena. €4, students €3. Cash only.) From late June to September, tourists and singers from around the world descend on the Arena for the annual **Opera Festival.** *Aida*, *La Bohème*, *Nabucco*, *La Traviata*, and *The Barber of Seville* are among the 2007 highlights. (☎800 51 51; www.arena.it. Box office open on performance days 10am-9pm, non-performance days 10am-5:45pm. General admission Su-Th €17-25, F-Sa €19-27. AmEx/DC/MC/V.) From P. Brà, V. Mazzini leads to the markets and stunning medieval architecture of **Piazza delle Erbe.** The 83m **Torre dei Lambertini,** in P. dei Signori, offers a perfect view of Verona. (Open M 1:30-7:30pm, Tu-Su 8:30am-7:30pm. Elevator €4, students €3; stairs €3. Cash only.) The **Giardino Giusti,** V. Giardino Giusti 2, is a 16th-century garden with a thigh-high floral labyrinth, whose cypress-lined avenue gradually winds up to porticoes and curving balconies with more views of Verona. (☎803 40 29. Open daily 9am-8pm. €4.50.) The della Scala family fortress, **Castelvecchio,** down V. Roma from P. Brà, now has an art collection that includes Pisanello's *Madonna della Quaglia*. (☎806 26 11. Open M 1:30-7:30pm, Tu-Su 8:30am-7:30pm. €4, students €3. Cash only.) The balcony at **Casa di Giulietta** (Juliet's House), V. Cappello 23, overlooks a courtyard of tourists waiting to rub the statue of Juliet and lovers adding their vows to graffitied walls. The Capulets never lived here, so skip entering. (☎803 43 03. Open M 1:30-7:30pm, Tu-Su 8:30am-7:30pm. €4, students €3. Courtyard free.)

ITALY

FRIULI-VENEZIA GIULIA

The potpourri of cuisines, styles, and architecture that is Friuli-Venezia Giulia apparently appeals to writers: James Joyce penned the bulk of *Ulysses* in Trieste coffeehouses; Ernest Hemingway envisioned the plot of *A Farewell to Arms* in the region's Carso cliffs; and Franz Liszt, Sigmund Freud, and Rainer Maria Rilke all worked in Friuli. While smaller towns retain their idyllic charm, its growing gothams make Friuli-Venezia Giulia one of Italy's most international provinces.

TRIESTE (TRIEST) ☎040

After being volleyed among Italian, Austrian, and Slavic powers for hundreds of years, Trieste (pop. 241,000) celebrated its 50th anniversary as an Italian city in 2004. Subtle reminders of Trieste's Eastern European past are manifest in its arches, cuisine, and portraits of smirking Hapsburg rulers. The Città Nuova, part tangled streets, part gridded, all lined with majestic Neoclassical palaces, centers around the Canale Grande. Facing the canal from the south is the blue-domed Serbian Orthodox **Chiesa di San Spiridione.** (Open Tu-Sa 9am-noon and 5-8pm, Su 9am-noon. Modest dress required.) The P. dell'Unità d'Italia is the largest waterfront *piazza* in Italy. P. della Cattedrale overlooks the town center. Archduke Maximilian of Austria commissioned the lavish **Castello Miramare** in the mid-19th century. Take bus #36 (15min.; €0.90) to Ostello Tergeste and walk along the water for 15min. (Open M-Sa 9am-7pm, Su 8:30am-7pm. €4.)

Centrally located **Nuovo Albergo Centro ❸**, V. Roma 13, has spacious rooms. (☎34 78 790; www.hotelcentrotrieste.it. Breakfast included. Internet €4 per hr. Singles €35, with bath €48; doubles €50/68; triples €68/116; quads €85/116. 10% discount with *Let's Go*. AmEx/MC/V.) On a shaded *piazza*, family-run **Buffet da Siora Rosa ❷**, P. Hortis 3, serves Triestini favorites. (☎30 14 60. *Primi* €4-7. *Secondi* €5-10. Cover €1. Reserve ahead. Open daily 8am-4pm and 6:30-9:30pm.) The covered market at V. Carducci 36/D has tables piled high with fruits and cheese for budget meals. (Open M and W 8am-2pm, Tu and Th-Su 8am-6:30pm.) Find groceries at the giant **PAM** supermarket, V. Miramare 1, across from the train station. (Open M-Sa 8:30am-7:30pm and Su 9am-7pm.) **Trains** leave P. della Libertà 8, down C. Cavour from the quay, for Budapest, HUN (12hr., 2 per day, €80-90) and Venice (2hr., 20 per day, €8). The APT **tourist office** is at P. dell'Unità d'Italia 4/E. (☎347 83 12. Open daily 9:30am-7pm.) **Postal Code:** 34100.

ITALY

PIEDMONT (PIEMONTE)

More than just the source of the Po River, Piedmont rose to prominence in 1861 when the Savoys briefly named Turin capital of a re-united Italy. Today, European tourists escape the whirlwind city pace on the banks of Lake Maggiore (p. 618), while hikers and skiers conquer Alpine mountaintops. Piedmont is renowned for its high standard of living and modern, well-organized infrastructure.

TURIN (TORINO) ☎011

A century and a half before Turin (pop. 910,000) was selected to host the 2006 Winter Olympics, it served as the first capital of a unified Italy. Renowned for its chocolate, Turin also lays claim to many parks and some of the country's best nightlife.

TRANSPORTATION AND PRACTICAL INFORMATION. Trains (☎66 53 098) run from **Porta Nuova,** in the center of the city, on C. V. Emanuele II to: Genoa (2hr., 1 per hr., €7.90); Milan (2hr., 1 per hr., €7.90); Rome (6-7hr., 26 per day, from €44); Venice (5hr., 20 per day, €31). A new **metro line** was recently installed and Turin's entire transportation system will continue to change post-Olympics. Eventually, Porta Susa will be the main station. Contact the **tourist office, Turismo Torino,** P. Solferino (☎53 51 81; www.turismotorino.org), for updates and maps. (☎53 51 81; www.turismotorino.org. Open M-Sa 9:30am-7pm, Su 9:30am-3pm.) V. Roma is the major north-south thoroughfare, with the principal sights and shops. It runs to P. Castello, from which V. Pietro Micca goes to the Olympic Atrium. **Postal Code:** 10100.

ACCOMMODATIONS AND FOOD. Turin's budget accommodations are scattered around the city. Family-run bed and breakfasts offer some of the city's best deals, though many close in July and August. To get to the clean, comfortable **Ostello Torino (HI) ❶**, V. Alby 1, take bus #52 (#64 on Su) from Pta. Nuova. After crossing the river, get off at the Lanza stop at V. Crimea and follow the "Ostello" signs to C. G. Lanza, before turning left at V. L. Gatti. (☎66 02 939; www.ostello-torino.it. Breakfast and linens included. Laundry €4. Reception M-Sa 7am-12:30pm and 3-11pm, Su 7-10am and 3-11pm. Lockout 10am-3pm. Curfew 11pm; ask for key if going out. Closed Dec. 21-Jan. 14. Single-sex and co-ed 3- to 10-bed dorms €14.50; doubles €31-38; triples €51; quads €68. MC/V.) The **Albergo Azalea ❸**, V. Mercanti 16, 3th floor, is cozy and clean Exit Porta Nuova on the right and take #58 or 72 to V. Garibaldi. Turn left on V. Garibaldi, then left on V. Mercanti. (☎53 81 15; albergo.azalea@virgilio.it. Singles €35, with bath €45; doubles €55-65. MC/V.)

Chocolate has been the city's glory, ever since Turin nobles began taking an evening cup of in 1678. **Tre Galli ❶**, V. S. Massimo 17, off V. Po near P. Carlo Emanuele II is in the *Quadrilatero Romano*, where people-watching happily mixes with Piemonte fare. (☎52 16 027. *Agnolotti* (lamb and cabbage ravioli) €7. *Primi* €7-10, *secondi* €8-18. Open M-Sa 12:30-2:30pm and 7:30pm-2am. Closed first 2 weeks in Jan. MC/V.) Sample *bicerin* (Turin's hot coffee-chocolate-cream drink; €4), craved by Nietzsche and Dumas, at **Caffè Cioccolateria al Bicerin ❶**, V. della Consolata, 5 (☎43 69 325. Open M-Tu and Th-F 8:30am-7:30pm, Sa-Su 8:30am-1pm and 3:30-7:30pm). Fresh food is at **Porta Palazzo,** P. della Repubblica, perhaps Europe's largest open-air market (M-F 7:30am-2pm, Sa 7:30am-sunset).

ITALY

SIGHTS AND NIGHTLIFE. Once the largest structure in the world built using traditional masonry, the **Mole Antonelliana,** V. Montebello 20, a few blocks east of P. Castello, was originally a synagogue. It's home to the eccentric **Museo Nazionale del Cinema,** which plays hundreds of movie clips. (Museum open Tu-F and Su 9am-8pm, Sa 9am-11pm. €5.20, students 4.20.) The city possesses one of the more famous relics of Christianity: the **Holy Shroud of Turin,** is housed in the **Cattedrale di San Giovanni,** behind the **Palazzo Reale.** With rare exception, a photo of the shroud is as close as most will get. (Open daily 8am-noon and 3-6pm. Free.) The **Museo Egizio,** in the **Palazzo dell'Accademia delle Scienze,** V. dell'Accademia delle Scienze 6, has world-class Egyptian artifacts. (Open Tu-Su 8:30am-7:30pm. €6.50, ages 18-25 €3.) The **Galleria Sabauda,** also in the *palazzo*, displays Renaissance paintings. (Open Nov.-May Tu and Tu and F-Su 8:30am-2pm, W 2-7:30pm, Th 10am-7:30pm; June-Oct. Tu and Tu and F-Su 8:30am-2pm, W 2-7:30pm, Th 2-7:30pm. €4, ages 18-25 €2.) The sleek venue, **Castello di Rivoli Museo D'Arte Contemporanea,** P. Mafalda di Savoia, has works from the 50s onward. (☎95 65 222. In Rivoli. Take bus #36 or 66. Open Tu-Th 10am-5pm, F-Su 1am-9pm. €6.50, students €3.50.)

I Murazzi is the center of Turin's social scene and consists of two stretches of boardwalk, one between Ponte V. Emanuele I and Ponte Umberto and another downstream from the Ponte V. Emanuele I. At **The Beach,** V. Murazzi del Po 18-22, the young and modern chill outside or dance to the best techno on the Po. (☎88 87 77. Drinks €5-6. Happy hour 7-10pm. No cover. Open Tu-W 10pm-2am and Th-Sa noon-4am.) **Quadrilatero Romano,** between P. della Repubblica and V. Garibaldi is an increasingly popular place to start and finish a night. **Shore,** P. E. Filiberto 10/G, serves large cocktails until the wee hours. (Open daily 6:30pm-2:30am.)

TUSCANY (TOSCANA)

Recently, popular culture has glorified Tuscany as a sun-soaked sanctuary of art, nature, and civilization, and for once pop culture has gotten it right. Every town claims a Renaissance master, every highway pauses at scenic vistas, every celebration climaxes in parades, festivals, and galas, and every year brings more tourists to the already beaten Tuscan path.

FLORENCE (FIRENZE) ☎055

Florence (pop. 400,000) is the city of the Renaissance: city of rebirth, of ingenuity, and of progress. By the 14th century, Florence had already become one of the most influential cities in Europe. In the 15th century, Florence received kudos for artistic excellence as the Medici family amassed a peerless collection, supporting masters like Botticelli, Brunelleschi, Donatello, and Michelangelo.

TRANSPORTATION

Flights: Amerigo Vespucci Airport (**FLR;** ☎306 1300), in Peretola. **SITA** runs buses connecting the airport to the train station (€4).

Trains: Stazione Santa Maria Novella, across from S. Maria Novella. Trains run every hr. to: **Bologna** (1hr., €4.65-6.80); **Milan** (3½hr., €29); **Rome** (3½hr., €30); **Siena** (1½hr., €5.70); **Venice** (3hr., €16). Check out www.trenitalia.it for schedules.

Buses: SITA, V. S. Caterina da Siena 15R (☎800 37 37 60; www.sita-on-line.it), runs buses to **San Gimignano** (1½hr., 14 per day, €5.90) and **Siena** (1½hr., 2 per day, €6.50). **LAZZI,** P. Adua 1-4R (☎35 10 61; www.lazzi.it), runs to **Pisa** (1 per hr., €6.10). Both offices are near S. Maria Novella.

Public Transportation: ATAF (☎800 42 45 00; www.ataf.net), outside the train station, runs orange city buses (6am-1am). 1hr. ticket €1; 3hr. €1.80; 24hr. €4.50; 3-day €7.20. Buy tickets at any newsstand, *tabaccherie,* or ticket dispenser before boarding. Validate your ticket using the orange machine onboard or risk a €50 fine.

Taxis: ☎43 90, 47 98, or 42 42. Outside the train station.

Bike/Moped Rental: Alinari Noleggi, V. Guelfa 85R (☎28 05 00; www.alinarirental.com). Bikes €12-16 per day. Scooters €28-55 per day. Open M-Sa 9:30am-1:30pm and 2:45-7:30pm, Su and holidays 10am-1pm and 3-6pm. MC/V.

ORIENTATION

From the train station, a short walk on V. Panzani and a left on V. dei Cerretani leads to the **duomo,** in the center of Florence. The bustling walkway **Via dei Calzaiuoli** runs south from the *duomo* to **Piazza della Signoria.** V. Roma leads from the *duomo* through **Piazza della Repubblica** to the **Ponte Vecchio** (Old Bridge), which crosses from central Florence to **Oltrarno,** the district south of the **Arno River.** Note that most streets change names unpredictably. Street numbers are either in red (commercial establishments) or black, and occasionally blue (residences.) If you reach an address and it's not what you expected, you may have the wrong color.

PRACTICAL INFORMATION

Tourist Office: Informazione Turistica, P. della Stazione 4 (☎21 22 45). Info on cultural events. Free maps with street index. Open M-Sa 8:30am-7pm, Su 8:30am-2pm.

Consulates: UK, Lungarno Corsini 2 (☎28 41 33). Open M-F 9am-1pm and 2-5pm. **US,** Lungarno Amerigo Vespucci 38 (☎26 69 51), right near the station. Open M-F 9am-12:30pm.

Currency Exchange: Local banks offer the best rates; beware of independent exchange services with high commissions. Most banks are open M-F 8:20am-1:20pm and 2:45-3:45pm. **24hr. ATMs** are common throughout the city.

American Express: V. Dante Alighieri 22R (☎50 98). From the *duomo,* walk down V. dei Calzaiuoli and turn left on V. dei Tavolini. Mail held free for AmEx customers, otherwise €1.55. Open M-F 9am-5:30pm.

Emergency: ☎113. **Police:** ☎112. **Ambulance:** ☎118. **Fire:** ☎115.

24hr. Pharmacies: Farmacia Comunale (☎28 94 35), at the train station by track #16. **Molteni,** V. dei Calzaiuoli 7R (☎28 94 90). AmEx/MC/V.

Internet Access: Walk down almost any busy street and you'll find an Internet cafe. **Internet Train,** V. Guelfa 54/56R, has 15 locations in the city listed on www.internettrain.it. €4.30 per hr., students €3.20. Most branches open M-F 9am-midnight, Sa 10am-8pm, Su noon-9pm. AmEx/MC/V.

Post Office: V. Pellicceria (☎273 64 80), off P. della Repubblica. Address mail to be held: First name LAST NAME, In Fermo Posta, L'Ufficio Postale, V. Pellicceria, Firenze, 50100 ITALY. Open M-Sa 8:15am-7pm. **Postal Code:** 50100.

ACCOMMODATIONS AND CAMPING

Lodging in Florence doesn't come cheap. **Consorzio ITA,** in the train station by track #16, can find rooms for a €3-8.50 fee. (☎066 99 10 00. Open M-Sa 8am-8pm, Su 10am-7pm.) It is best to make reservations *(prenotazioni)* ahead, especially if you plan to visit during Easter or summer.

ITALY

HOSTELS

Ostello Archi Rossi, V. Faenza 94r (☎29 08 04; www.hostelarchirossi.com), near S. Maria Novella station. Outdoor patio is packed after dark. Home-cooked breakfast included. Laundry €6. Free Internet. Dorm lockout 11am-2:30pm. Curfew 2am. Reserve online 1 week ahead, especially in summer. Dorms €22-26. MC/V. ❷

Istituto Gould, V. dei Serragli 49 (☎21 25 76; www.istitutogould.it), in the Oltrarno. Take bus #36 or 37 from the train station to the 2nd stop across the river. Spotless rooms. Reception M-F 8:45am-1pm and 3-7:30pm, Sa 9am-1:30pm. Dorms €21; singles €36, with bath €41; doubles €50/60. MC/V. ❷

Ostello Santa Monaca, V. S. Monaca 6 (☎26 83 38; www.ostello.it). Follow the directions to the Istituto Gould but turn left off V. dei Serragli on V. S. Monaca. Breakfast €2.70-3.80. Laundry €6.50 per 5kg. Internet €3 per hr. June-Sept. max. stay 7 nights. Curfew 1am. Reserve ahead. 10-bed dorms €18. AmEx/MC/V. ❷

Ostello della Gioventù Europa Villa Camerata (HI), V. Augusto Righi 2-4 (☎60 14 51), northeast of town. Take bus #17 from the train station (near track #5); ask for Salviatino. From the entrance, walk 10min. up a driveway past a vineyard. Tidy and crowded, in a beautiful villa. Breakfast included. Laundry €5.20. Max. stay 3 nights. Lockout 10am-2pm. Strict midnight curfew. Dorms €21. €3 HI discount. MC/V. ❷

HOTELS

OLD CITY (NEAR THE DUOMO)

Hotel Il Perseo, V. de Cerretani 1 (☎21 25 04; www.hotelperseo.com), en route to the *duomo* from the train station, opposite the Feltrinelli bookstore. 20 immaculate rooms with fans, satellite TV, and free Internet access. Breakfast included. Singles €95; doubles €125; triples €155; quads €180. AmEx/MC/V with min. stay 2 nights. ❺

Locanda Orchidea, Borgo degli Albizi 11 (☎248 03 46; hotelorchidea@yahoo.it). Turn left off V. Proconsolo from the *duomo*. Dante's wife was born in this 12th-century *palazzo,* built around a still-intact tower. Helpful, English-speaking staff. Carefully decorated rooms with marble floors; some open onto a garden. Singles €55; doubles €75; triples with shower €100; quads with shower €120. Cash only. ❹

Relais Cavalcanti, V. Pellicceria 2 (☎21 09 62). Unbeatable location just steps from P. della Repubblica. Ring bell to enter. Beautiful gold-trimmed rooms with antique wardrobes. Singles €100; doubles €125; triples €155. 10% *Let's Go* discount. MC/V. ❺

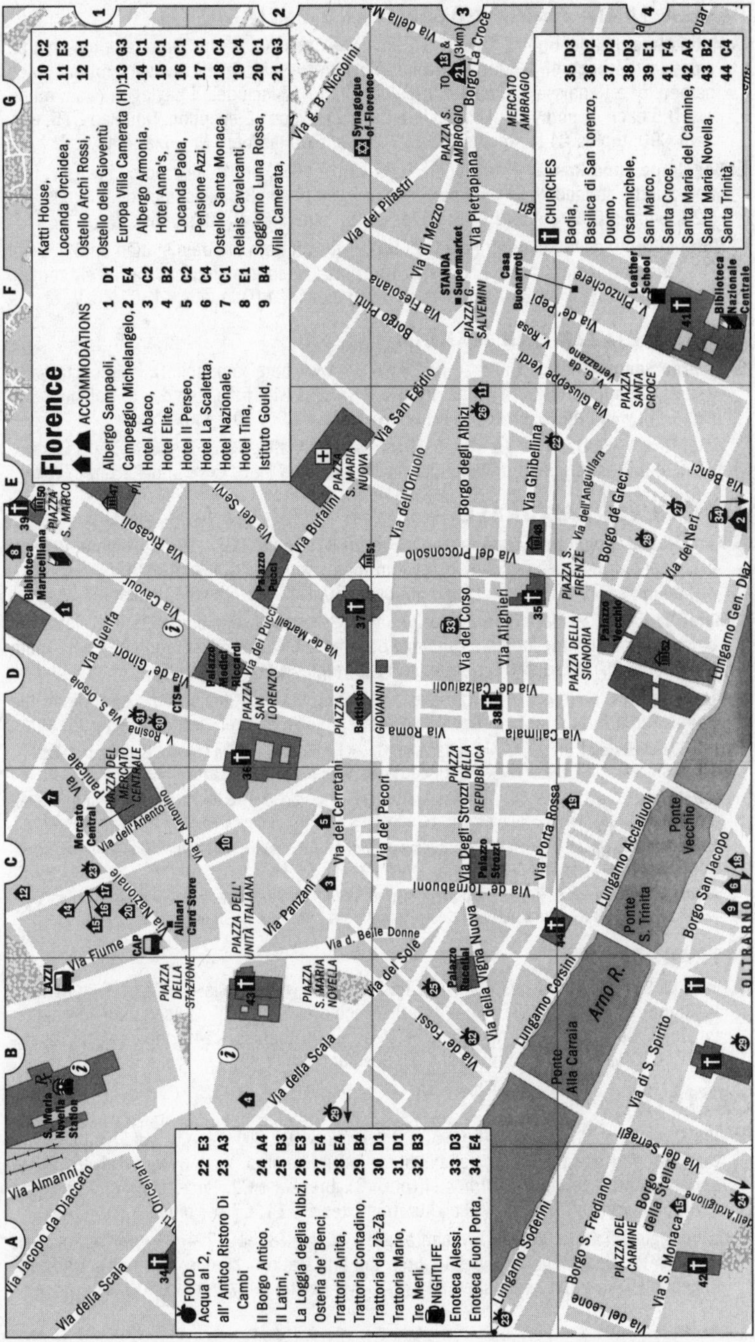
Florence
ACCOMMODATIONS
Albergo Sampaoli, 1 D1
Campeggio Michelangelo, 2 E4
Hotel Abaco, 3 C2
Hotel Elite, 4 B2
Hotel Il Perseo, 5 C2
Hotel La Scaletta, 6 C4
Hotel Nazionale, 7 C1
Hotel Tina, 8 E1
Istituto Gould, 9 B4
Katti House, 10 C2
Locanda Orchidea, 11 E3
Ostello Archi Rossi, 12 C1
Ostello della Gioventù
Europa Villa Camerata (HI), 13 G3
Albergo Armonia, 14 C1
Hotel Anna's, 15 C1
Locanda Paola, 16 C1
Pensione Azzi, 17 C1
Ostello Santa Monaca, 18 C4
Relais Cavalcanti, 19 C4
Soggiorno Luna Rossa, 20 C1
Villa Camerata, 21 G3
FOOD
Acqua al 2, 22 E3
all' Antico Ristoro Di Cambi 23 A3
Il Borgo Antico, 24 A4
Il Latini, 25 B3
La Loggia degli Albizi, 26 E3
Osteria de' Benci, 27 E4
Trattoria Anita, 28 E4
Trattoria Contadino, 29 B4
Trattoria da Zà-Zà, 30 D1
Trattoria Mario, 31 D1
Tre Merli, 32 B3
NIGHTLIFE
Enoteca Alessi, 33 D3
Enoteca Fuori Porta, 34 E4
CHURCHES
Badia, 35 D3
Basilica di San Lorenzo, 36 D2
Duomo, 37 D2
Orsanmichele, 38 D3
San Marco, 39 E1
Santa Croce, 41 F4
Santa Maria del Carmine, 42 A4
Santa Maria Novella, 43 B2
Santa Trinità, 44 C4

ITALY

PIAZZA SANTA MARIA NOVELLA AND ENVIRONS

Hotel Abaco, V. dei Banchi 1 (☎238 19 19; www.abaco-hotel.it). From the train station, cross to the back of S. Maria Novella and into the *piazza*. Extravagant rooms, each named for a Renaissance master. Breakfast and A/C included if paying in cash, otherwise €5 each. Laundry €7. Limited Internet access free at reception. Doubles €75, with bath €90; triples €110; quads €135. 10% *Let's Go* discount Nov.-Mar. MC/V. ❺

Soggiorno Luna Rossa, V. Nazionale 7 (☎23 02 185). 3rd fl. Airy rooms have TV, fan, and colorful stained-glass windows. Small shared baths. Breakfast included. Single bed €22. Singles €35; doubles €85; triples €100; quads €140. Cash only. ❷

Hotel Elite, V. della Scala 12 (☎21 53 95). Exit right from the train station onto V. degli Orti Oricellari; turn left on V. della Scala. Brass bedposts shine in the lovely rooms. Breakfast €6. Singles €80; doubles €75-90; triples €110; quads €130. MC/V. ❺

AROUND PIAZZA SAN MARCO

Albergo Sampaoli, V. S. Gallo 14 (☎28 48 34; www.hotelsampaoli.it). Helpful staff and a large common area with fridge access. All rooms with fans, some with balcony. Singles €42, with bath €50; doubles €65/85; triples €90/105. MC/V. ❹

Hotel Tina, V. S. Gallo 31 (☎48 35 19; www.hoteltina.it). *Pensione* with English magazines, new furniture, and amiable owners. Doubles €75-85; extra bed €25. MC/V. ❹

ITALY

AROUND VIA NAZIONALE

Katti House/Soggiorno Annamaria, V. Faenza 21, 24 (☎21 34 10). Lovingly kept, with 400-year-old antiques.Recently renovated rooms with A/C, TV, and bath. Singles €60-75; doubles €75-120; triples €90; quads €120. Nov.-Mar. reduced rates. MC/V. ❹

Hotel Nazionale, V. Nazionale 22 (☎238 22 03; www.nazionalehotel.it). Turn left from train station. 9 sunny rooms with comfy beds and A/C. Breakfast brought to your room 8-9:30am (€6). Singles €75; doubles €115; triples €160. MC/V. ❺

Via Faenza 56 houses 4 *pensioni* that are among the best deals in the area. From the train station, exit left onto V. Nazionale, walk 1 block, and turn left on V. Faenza.

Pensione Azzi (☎21 38 06; www.hotelazzi.com) has large rooms and a terrace. Styled as an artists' inn. Breakfast included. Singles €70; doubles €110. AmEx/MC/V. ❺

Hotel Anna's (☎230 27 14; www.hotelannas.com), on the 2nd fl. Rooms with TV, bath, phone, and A/C. Breakfast €5. Singles €40-60; doubles €60-90; triples €75-130. AmEx/MC/V. ❹

Locanda Paola (☎21 36 82) has doubles with views of the surrounding hills. Breakfast included. Internet access. Flexible 2am curfew. Dorms €25. MC/V. ❸

Albergo Armonia (☎21 11 46). Rooms have high ceilings. No curfew. Singles €42; doubles €50-60; triples €60-69. Extra bed €25. Low season reduced rates. Cash only. ❸

OLTRARNO

Hotel La Scaletta, V. Guicciardini 13B (☎28 30 28; www.hotellascaletta.it). Turn right on V. Roma from the *duomo,* cross Ponte Vecchio, and take V. Guicciardini. Breakfast included. Reception until midnight. Singles €100; doubles €140; triples €160; quads €180. €10 *Let's Go* discount with cash payment. MC/V. ❺

CAMPING

Villa Camerata, V. A. Righi 2-4 (☎60 03 15; fax 61 03 00). Take bus #17 outside the train station (near track #5); ask driver for Salviatino stop. Walk down driveway. Same entrance and reception as HI hostel (p. 646). Breakfast €2. Reception 7am-12:30pm and 1pm-midnight. Max. stay 6 nights. Tent sites €7-14; €7 per person. MC/V. ❶

Campeggio Michelangelo, V. Michelangelo 80 (☎681 19 77; www.ecvacanze.it), beneath P. Michelangelo. Bus #13 from the bus station (15min.; last bus 11:25pm). Reception 7am-11pm. Tent sites €16, €10 per person. MC/V; min €100. ❶

FOOD

Florentine specialties include *bruschetta* (grilled bread soaked in oil and garlic and topped with tomatoes, basil, and anchovy or liver paste) and *bistecca alla Fiorentina* (thick sirloin). The best local cheese is pecorino, made from sheep's milk. A liter of house wine costs €3.50-6 in a *trattoria*, but stores sell bottles of *chianti* for as little as €2.50. The local dessert is *cantuccini di prato* (almond cookies) dipped in *vinsanto* (a rich dessert wine). Florence's own Buontalenti family supposedly invented gelato; extensive sampling is a must. For lunch, peruse the city's pushcarts or pick up produce and meats at the **Mercato Centrale,** between V. Nazionale and S. Lorenzo. (Open June-Sept. M-Sa 7:30am-2pm; Oct.-May M-F 7am-2pm, Sa 7am-2pm and 4-8pm.) To get to **STANDA** supermarket, V. Pietrapiana 1R, go right on V. del Proconsolo, take the first left on Borgo degli Albizi, and go through P. G. Salvemini. (Open M-Sa 8am-9pm, Su 9am-9pm. MC/V.)

RESTAURANTS

OLD CITY (NEAR THE DUOMO)

Trattoria Anita, V. del Parlascio 2R (☎21 86 98), behind the Bargello. Dine by candlelight, surrounded by shelves of expensive wine. Traditional Tuscan fare, including pasta, roast chicken, and steak. *Primi* €5. *Secondi* from €6. Lunch *menù* €6. Cover €1. Open M-Sa noon-2:30pm and 7-10pm. AmEx/MC/V. ❷

Osteria de' Benci, V. de' Benci 13R (☎234 49 23), on the corner of V. dei Neri. Join the locals for classics like *carpaccio* (thinly sliced beef; €14). *Primi* €9. *Secondi* €9-14. Cover €3.30. Reserve ahead. Open M-Sa 1-2:45pm and 7:30-11:45pm. AmEx/MC/V. ❹

La Loggia degli Albizi, Borgo degli Albizi 39R (☎247 95 74). From behind the *duomo*, go right on V. del Proconsolo and take the 1st left onto Borgo degli Albizi. Head 2 blocks down and look right. A hidden treasure, this bakery/cafe offers an escape from the tourist hordes. Pastries and coffee from €0.80, more at tables. Open M-Sa 7am-8pm. ❶

Acqua al 2, V. Vigna Vecchia 40R (☎28 41 70), behind the Bargello. Popular with young Italians and tourists. Serves Florentine specialties, including an excellent *filetto al mirtillo* (steak in a blueberry sauce; €15). *Primi* €7. *Secondi* €8-19. Cover €1. Service 10%. Reserve ahead. Open daily 7pm-1am. AmEx/MC/V. ❸

PIAZZA SANTA MARIA NOVELLA AND ENVIRONS

Il Latini, V. dei Palchetti 6R (☎21 09 16). Crowds line up nightly; prepare to wait for your *arrosto misto* (platter of roast meats). Waiters keep the wine flowing. *Primi* €6-8. *Secondi* €10-18. Reserve ahead. Open Tu-Su 12:30-2:30pm and 7:30-10:30pm. AmEx/MC/V. ❸

Trattoria Contadino, V. Palazzuolo 71R (☎238 2673). Filling, homestyle, fixed-price *menù* (€10-11) includes *primo, secondo,* bread, water, and 0.25L of wine. Open daily 11am-2:30pm and 6-9:30pm. June-July closed Sa-Su. AmEx/MC/V. ❷

Tre Merli, entrances on V. del Moro 11R and V. dei Fossi 12R (☎28 70 62). In a dining room close to the river, soft red light accents sumptuous dishes like *spaghettino all'Imperiale* (with mussels, clams, and shrimp; €14). *Primi* €7.50-14. *Secondi* €12-19. Lunch *menù* €12. Cover €2. Open daily 11am-11pm. 10% discount and free glass of wine with *Let's Go.* AmEx/MC/V. ❹

THE STATION AND UNIVERSITY QUARTER

Trattoria Zà-Zà, P. del Mercato Centrale 26R (☎21 54 11). Wooden-beam ceilings and brick archways inside, lively patio outside. Try the *tris* (mixed bean and vegetable soup; €7) or the *tagliata di manzo* (cut of beef; €14-19). Cover €2. Reserve ahead. Open daily noon-3pm and 7-11pm. AmEx/MC/V. ❸

ITALY

AN EDIBLE DEGREE

Forget law school. Bypass the sleepless years of medical residency. Instead, learn how to dollop meringue, bake the perfect flaky pastry, and cook pasta *al dente* without setting the timer. If you've ever secretly wanted a culinary degree in Italian Baking with a minor in Wine Expertise, opportunities abound at **Apicius,** the Culinary Institue of Florence.

Established in 1996, Apicius provides professional classes for those wishing to create *una bella tavola.* Curious students from all over the world flock to these state-of-the-art facilities to study in courses like *Physiology of Taste and Flavor, Pairing Italian Food and Wine,* and *Dessert Styling.* Take part in the free-elective program, which gives students the flexibility to choose from varied coursework and then transfer credits to home institutions. Upon successful completion of the two-year program, which includes qualification in an Italian language class, 15-week internships are available at local restaurants. All programs, from monthly to yearly, are offered in English by an international faculty. So bypass the leather jackets, hold off on the soccer jerseys, and immerse yourself in Italian culture via *la cucina*–what Italians' life is truly all about anyway.

(For more information, contact Apicius, V. Guelfa 85, Florence 50129. ☎055 26 58 135; www.apicius.it.)

Trattoria Mario, V. Rosina 2R (☎21 85 50), around the corner from P. del Mercato Centrale. Informal lunch establishment with incredible pasta, a stellar rendition of *bistecca alla Fiorentina,* and a loyal local following. *Secondi* €3.10-11. Cover €0.50. Open M-Sa noon-3:30pm. Closed Aug. Cash only. ❷

OLTRARNO

all' Antico Ristoro Di' Cambi, V. S. Onofrio 1R (☎21 71 34). Near Ponte Vespucci. Prosciutto hangs from the 5th-century ceiling. 3rd-generation owner Stefano serves up *bistecca alla Fiorentina* (€4 per 100g). *Primi* €5-7. *Secondi* €7-17. Cover €1. Open M-Sa noon-2:30pm and 7:30-11:30pm. Closed 2 weeks in mid-Aug. AmEx/MC/V. ❹

Il Borgo Antico, P. S. Spirito 6R (☎21 04 37). Trendy spot with young staff and student-heavy clientele. Memorable pastas, pizzas, and salads (€7). *Primi* €7. *Secondi* €10-20. Cover €2. Reservation recommended. Open June-Sept. daily 1pm-12:30am; Oct.-May 12:45-2:30pm and 7:45pm-1am. AmEx/MC/V. ❸

GELATERIE

To avoid making gelato salespeople cranky, follow this protocol: first, pay at the register for the size you request, *then,* receipt in hand, choose a flavor.

Vivoli, V. Isole della Stinche 7 (☎29 23 34), behind the Bargello. A renowned *gelateria* and long-time contender for best ice cream in Florence. Cups from €1.60. Open Tu-Sa 7:30am-1am, Su 9:30am-1am.

Gelateria dei Neri, V. dei Neri 20-22R (☎210 034). Stand outside and watch through the window as dozens of delicious flavors are mixed right before your eyes. Try *crema giotto* (coconut, almond, and hazelnut). Cones and cups from €1.40.

Perchè No?, V. Tavolini 19R (☎239 89 69), off V. dei Calzaiuoli. This central, crowded parlor serves mouthwatering chocolate and chunky *nocciolosa.* Cones from €1.80. Open M and W-Su 11am-1am.

Carabè, V. Ricasoli 60R (☎28 94 76). Lemons shipped direct from Sicily. Cups from €2. Open daily May-Sept. 10am-midnight; Mar.-Apr. and Oct. noon-midnight.

ENOTECHE (WINE BARS)

Check out an *enoteca* to sample Italy's finest wines. Make a meal out of complementary side dishes (cheeses, olives, toast and spreads, and salami).

Enoteca Alessi, V. della Oche 27/29R (☎21 49 66), 1 block from the *duomo.* Among Florence's finest wine bars, with a cavernous interior that stocks over 1000 wines. Doubles as a candy store. Open M-F 9am-1pm and 3:30-7:30pm. AmEx/MC/V.

International Student Identity Card
Carte d'étudiant internationale / Carné internacional de estudiante
STUDENT
Studies at / Étudiant à / Est. de Enseñanza
University of Student Travel
Name / Nom / Nombre
PEREZ, J
Born / Né(e) le / Nacido/a el
23/06/1986
Validity / Validité / Validez
09/2005 - 12/2006
ISIC
S 000 123 456 789

Enoteca Fuori Porta, V. Monte alle Croci 10R (☎234 24 83), near S. Miniato. This casual *enoteca,* popular with young Italians, serves an extensive selection of *bruschetta* (€1-2.50) and *crostini* (€4.50-7.50). Cover €1.50. Open daily noon-4pm and 7-10pm. Closed Su in Aug. MC/V.

SIGHTS

For a full list of museum openings, check out www.firenzeturismo.it. For museum reservations, call **Firenze Musei** (☎294 883; www.firenzemusei.it). There are **no student discounts** at museums. Choose destinations carefully and plan to spend a few hours at each landmark; museum-hopping will seriously deplete your budget.

PIAZZA DEL DUOMO

DUOMO (CATTEDRALE DI SANTA MARIA DEL FIORE). In 1296, the city fathers commissioned Arnolfo di Cambio to erect a cathedral so magnificent that it would be "impossible to make it either better or more beautiful with the industry and power of man." Di Cambio succeeded, completing the massive but domeless nave by 1418. **Filippo Brunelleschi** was called in to add a dome: after studying long-neglected classical methods, he came up with his double-shelled, interlocking-brick construction. The *duomo* claims the world's third longest nave, trailing only St. Peter's in Rome and St. Paul's in London. *(Open M-W and F-Sa 10am-5pm, Th 10am-3:30pm, Su 1:30-4:45pm. Mass daily 7am, 12:30, 5-7pm. Free.)* Climb the 463 steps inside the dome to **Michelangelo's lantern,** which offers an expansive view of the city from the 100m high external gallery. *(Open M-F 8:30am-7pm, Sa 8:30am-5:40pm. €6.)* The climb up the 82m **campanile** next to the *duomo,* also called "Giotto's Tower," reveals views of the *duomo,* the city, and the **battistero** (baptistry), whose bronze doors, forged by Ghiberti, are known as the **Gates of Paradise.** Byzantine-style mosaics inside the baptistry inspired details of the *Inferno* by Dante, who was christened here. *(*Campanile *open daily 8:30am-6:30pm. €6. Baptistry open M-Sa noon-7pm, Su 8:30am-2pm. €3.)* Most of the *duomo*'s art resides behind the cathedral in the **Museo dell'Opera del Duomo.** Up the first flight of stairs is a late *Pietà* by Michelangelo; according to legend, he broke Christ's left arm in a fit of frustration. *(P. del Duomo 9, behind the* duomo. *☎23 02 885. Open M-Sa 9am-7:30pm, Su 9am-1:40pm. €6.)*

ORSANMICHELE. Built in 1337 as a granary, the Orsanmichele became a church after a fire convinced officials to move grain operations outside the city. The ancient grain chutes are still visible outside. Within, tenacious visitors will discover Ghiberti's *St. John the Baptist* and *St. Stephen,* Donatello's *St. Peter* and *St. Mark,* and Giambologna's *St. Luke.* *(V. Arte della Lana, between the* duomo *and P. della Signoria. Open Tu-Su 10am-5pm. Free.)*

PIAZZA DELLA SIGNORIA AND ENVIRONS

From P. del Duomo, **Via dei Calzaiuoli,** one of the city's oldest streets, runs south past crowds, street vendors, *gelaterie,* and chic shops to **Piazza della Signoria.** From P. del Duomo, **Via dei Calzaiuoli,** one of the city's oldest streets, runs south through crowds, street vendors, *gelaterie,* and chic shops to P. della Signoria, the 13th-century *piazza* bordered by the Palazzo Vecchio and the Uffizi. With the construction of the Palazzo Vecchio in 1299, the square became Florence's civic and political center, and, in 1497, its pyromaniacal one. Religious zealot Girolamo Savonarola lit the **Bonfire of the Vanities** here, barbecuing some of Florence's best art. Today P. della Signoria fills daily with photo-snapping tourists who later return for drinks and dessert in its upscale cafes. Monumental sculptures cluster in front of the palazzo and inside the 14th-century **Loggia dei Lanzi,** free to the public. From the Uffizi, follow V. Georgofili left and turn right along the river to reach the **Ponte Vec-**

ITALY

chio (old bridge), the oldest bridge in Florence. From the neighboring **Ponte alle Grazie,** th heart-melting **view** of the Ponte Vecchio is worth all its jewels.

THE UFFIZI. Giorgio Vasari designed this palace in 1554 for the offices *(uffizi)* of Duke Cosimo's administration; today, the gallery holds one of the world's finest art collections. Beautiful statues overlook the walkway from niches in the columns; play "spot the Renaissance man" and try to find da Vinci, Vespucci, Machiavelli, and Petrarch among them. Botticelli, Caravaggio, Cimabue, Fra Angelico, della Francesca, Giotto, Michelangelo, Raphael, del Sarto, Titian, da Vinci, even Dürer, Rembrandt, Rubens—you name it, it's here. Be sure to visit the **Cabinet of Drawings and Prints** on the first floor before confining yourself to the U-shaped corridor of the second, art-filled floor. A few rooms are usually closed each day, and some works are usually on loan. A sign at the ticket office lists the rooms that will be closed that day; ask when they will reopen. *(From P. B. S. Giovanni, take V. Roma past P. della Repubblica, where the street turns into V. Calimala. Continue until V. Vaccerecia and turn left. ☎238 86 51. Open Tu-Su 8:15am-6:50pm. Mar.-Jan. €9.50; Feb. €6.50. Reserve ahead for €3 fee. Audio tour €4.65.)*

PALAZZO VECCHIO. Arnolfo del Cambio designed this fortress-like *palazzo* in the late 13th century to be the seat of government. It included apartments which served as living quarters for members of the city council while they served two-month terms. After the *palazzo* became the Medicis' home in 1470, Michelozzo decorated the **courtyard.** The **Monumental Apartments,** which house the *palazzo*'s extensive art collections, are now an art and history museum. The worthwhile **Activities Tour** includes the "Secret Routes," which reveal hidden stairs and chambers tucked behind exquisite oil paintings. The ceiling of the **Salone del Cinquecento,** where the Grand Council of the Republic met, is so elaborately decorated that the walls can hardly support its weight. *(☎276 82 24. Open M-W and F-Sa 9am-7pm, Su 9am-1pm.* Palazzo *and Monumental Apartments each €6, ages 18-25 €4.50. Activities Tour €8/5.50. Courtyard free. Reserve ahead for tours.)*

ITALY

THE BARGELLO AND ENVIRONS

BARGELLO. The heart of medieval Florence is in this 13th-century fortress, which was once the residence of the chief magistrate and later a brutal prison. It now houses the sculpture-filled, largely untouristed **Museo Nazionale.** Donatello's bronze *David*, the first free-standing nude since antiquity, stands opposite the two bronze panels of the *Sacrifice of Isaac*, submitted by Ghiberti and Brunelleschi in the baptistry door competition (p. 651). Michelangelo's early works, including *Bacchus*, *Brutus*, and *Apollo*, are on the ground floor. *(V. del Proconsolo 4, between the duomo and P. della Signoria. ☎238 86 06. Open daily 8:15am-1:50pm. Closed 1st and 3rd Su and 2nd and 4th M of each month. Hours and additional closing days vary by month. €4.)*

BADIA. The site of medieval Florence's richest monastery, the Badia church is now buried in the interior of a residential block. Filippino Lippi's *Apparition of the Virgin to St. Bernard*, one of the most famous paintings of the 15th century, hangs in eerie gloom to the left of the church. Be sure to glance up at the intricately carved dark wood ceiling. Visitors are asked to walk silently among the prostrate, white-robed worshippers. *(Entrance on V. Dante Alighieri, off V. Proconsolo. Open to tourists M 3-6pm, but respectful visitors can walk through at any time.)*

MUSEO DI STORIA DELLA SCIENZA. The telescopes, astrological models, clock workings, and anatomical figures of this collection date from the Renaissance. **Room 4** displays Galileo's tools, including the lens through which he first saw Jupiter's satellites. *(P. dei Giudici 1, behind Palazzo Vecchio and the Uffizi. Open M and W-F 9:30am-5pm, Tu and Sa 9:30am-1pm; Oct.-May open 2nd Su of each month 10am-1pm. €6.50.)*

PIAZZA DELLA REPUBBLICA AND FARTHER WEST

The large P. della Repubblica teems with crowds, overpriced cafes, restaurants, and *gelaterie*. In 1890, it replaced the Mercato Vecchio as the site of the city market, but has since traded stalls for more fashionable vendors. The inscription *"antico centro della città, da secolare squalore, a vita nuova restituito"* ("Ancient center of the city, squalid for centuries, restored to new life") makes a derogatory reference to the *piazza*'s location in the old Jewish ghetto.

■ **CHIESA DI SANTA MARIA NOVELLA.** This church, near the train station, houses the chapels of the wealthiest 13th- and 14th-century merchants. Santa Maria Novella was home to an order of Dominicans, or *Domini canes* (Hounds of the Lord), who took a bite out of sin and corruption. The Romanesque-Gothic facade of the *chiesa* is made of Florentine marble and is considered one of the great masterpieces of early Renaissance architecture. The Medicis commissioned Vasari to paint new frescoes over the 13th-century ones on the walls, but the painter spared Masaccio's ■**Trinity,** the first painting to use geometric perspective. In the **Gondi Chapel** stands Brunelleschi's *Crucifix*, designed in response to Donatello's in Santa Croce, which Brunelleschi found too full of "vigorous naturalism." Donatello was supposedly so impressed with his rival's creation that he dropped the bag of eggs he was carrying. *(Open M-Th and Sa 9am-5pm, F and Su 1-5pm. €2.50.)*

CHIESA DI SANTA TRINITÀ. Hoping to spend eternity in elite company, the most fashionable *palazzo* owners commissioned family chapels in this church. The facade, designed by Bernardo Buontalenti in the 16th century, is almost Baroque in its elaborate ornamentation. Scenes from Ghirlandaio's *Life of St. Francis* decorate the **Sassetti Chapel** in the right arm of the transept. The famous altarpiece, Ghirlandaio's *Adoration of the Shepherds*, resides in the Uffizi—this one is a copy. *(In P. S. Trinità. Open M-Sa 8am-noon and 4-6pm, Su 4-6pm. Free.)*

MERCATO NUOVO. The *loggie* (guilds) of the New Market have housed gold and silk traders since 1547. Today, imitation designer gear dominates vendors' wares. Rubbing the snout of Pietro Tacca's plump statue, *Il Porcellino* (The Little Pig) is reputed to bring luck, but don't wait for that purse you covet to become real leather. *(Off V. Calimala, between P. della Repubblica and the Ponte Vecchio. Open dawn-dusk.)*

SAN LORENZO AND FARTHER NORTH

■ **ACCADEMIA.** It doesn't matter how many pictures of him you've seen—when you come around the corner and see Michelangelo's triumphant ■**David** towering in self-assured perfection under the rotunda designed just for him, you will be blown away. The statue's base was struck by lightning in 1512, the figure was damaged by anti-Medici riots in 1527, and David's left wrist was broken by a stone, after which he was finally moved here from P. della Signoria in 1873. In the hallway leading to *David* are Michelangelo's four ■**Slaves** and a *Pietà*. The master purposely left these statues unfinished, staying true to his ideas about "releasing" figures from the living stone. Botticelli's Madonna paintings and Uccello's works are worth seeing. *(V. Ricasoli 60, between the churches of S. Marco and S. S. Annunziata. ☎ 29 48 83. Open Tu-Su 8:15am-6:50pm. Reserve ahead. May-Sept. €9.50; Oct.-Apr. €6.50.)*

BASILICA DI SAN LORENZO. Because the Medicis lent the funds to build this church, they retained artistic control over its construction and decided to add Cosimo dei Medici's grave to Brunelleschi's spacious basilica. They cunningly placed it in front of the high altar and made the entire church his personal mausoleum. Michelangelo began the exterior but abandoned the project, which accounts for the plain facade. *(Open M-Sa 10am-5pm. €2.50.)* While the **Cappelle dei Medici** (Medici Chapels) offer a rare glimpse of the Baroque in Florence, the **Cappella dei**

Principi (Princes' Chapel) emulates the baptistry in P. del Duomo. Michelangelo sculpted the **Sacrestia Nuova** (New Sacristy) to hold two Medici tombs. *(Walk around to the back entrance in P. Madonna degli Aldobrandini. Open daily 8:15am-4:50pm. Closed 1st, 3rd, and 5th M and 2nd and 4th Su of each month. €6.)* The adjacent **Laurentian Library** shows Michelangelo at his most innovative: his *pietra serena* sandstone stairs, at the entry. *(Open daily 8:30am-1:30pm. Free with entrance to San Lorenzo.)*

MUSEO DELLA CHIESA DI SAN MARCO. Remarkable works by Fra Angelico adorn this museum, once part of a convent complex and one of the most peaceful and spiritual places in Florence. A large room to the right of the courtyard houses some of the painter's major works, including the church's altarpiece. The second floor displays Angelico's *Annunciation.* Every cell in the convent has its own Angelico fresco, simply executed to facilitate somber meditation. To the right of the stairwell, Michelozzo's library, modeled on Michelangelo's work in S. Lorenzo, is designed for reflection. In cells 17 and 22, underground artwork, excavated from the medieval period, peeks through a glass floor. Toward the exit, the two rooms of the **Museo di Firenze Antica** show the archaeology of Florence's ancient roots. Be sure to peek into the church itself, next to the museum, to admire the elaborate altar and vaulted ceiling. *(Enter at P. S. Marco 3. Open M-F 8:15am-1:50pm, Sa 8:15am-6:50pm, Su 8:15am-7pm. Closed 2nd and 4th M and 1st, 3rd, and 5th Su of each month. €4.)*

PALAZZO MEDICI RICCARDI. The palace's facade is the work of Michelozzo, and the chapel inside features Benozzo Gozzoli's wrap-around fresco of the **Three Magi.** Rotating exhibits range from Renaissance architectural sketches to Fellini memorabilia. *(V. Cavour 3. ☎276 03 40. Open M-Tu and Th-Su 9am-7pm. €4, children €2.50.)*

ITALY

PIAZZA SANTA CROCE AND ENVIRONS

CHIESA DI SANTA CROCE. The Franciscans built this church as far as possible from their Dominican rivals at S. Maria Novella. Ironically, the ascetic Franciscans produced what is arguably the most splendid church in the city. Luminaries buried here include Galileo, Machiavelli, Michelangelo (whose tomb was designed by Vasari), and Leonardo Bruni, shown holding his beloved *History of Florence*, all lie here. Check out Donatello's *Crucifix*, so irksome to Brunelleschi, in the Vernio Chapel, and his gilded *Annunciation*, by Bruni's tomb. *(Open M-Sa 9:30am-5:30pm, Su 1-5:30pm. €5.)* At the end of the cloister next to the church is the **Cappella Pazzi,** whose proportions are perfect and whose decorations include Luca della Robbia's *tondi* of the apostles and Brunelleschi's moldings of the evangelists.

SYNAGOGUE OF FLORENCE. This synagogue, also known as the **Museo del Tempio Israelitico,** is resplendent with Sephardic domes, arches, and patterns. David Levi, a wealthy Florentine Jewish businessman, donated his fortune in 1870 to build "a monumental temple worthy of Florence," in recognition of the Jews' new freedom to live and worship outside the old Jewish ghetto. *(V. Farini 4, at V. Pilastri. ☎24 52 52. Free tours every hr.; reserve ahead. Open Su-Th 10am-6pm, F 10am-2pm. €4.)*

THE OLTRARNO

Historically disdained by downtown Florentines, the far side of the Arno remains an animated and unpretentious quarter, filled with students and, thankfully, not too many tourists. Head back over Ponte S. Trinità after dallying in P. S. Spirito.

PALAZZO PITTI. Luca Pitti, a 15th-century banker, built his *palazzo* east of P. S. Spirito against the Boboli hill. The Medicis acquired the *palazzo* and the hill in 1550 and expanded it in every way possible. Today, it houses six museums, including the **Galleria Palatina,** one of only a few public galleries when it opened in 1833, which now contains Florence's most important art collection after the Uffizi, the gallery has works by Caravaggio, Raphael, Rubens, and Titian. Other museums display Medici family costumes, porcelain, carriages, and **Royal Apartments**—lavish reminders of the time when the *palazzo* was the living quarters of the royal House of Savoy. The **Galleria d'Arte Moderna** hides one of Italian art history's big surprises, the proto-Impressionist works of the Macchiaioli group. *(Open Tu-Su 8:15am-6:50pm. Ticket for Palatine Gallery, Royal Apartments, and Modern Art Gallery €8.50.)* An elaborately designed park, the **Boboli Gardens,** with geometrically sculpted hedges, contrasting groves of holly and cypress trees, and bubbling fountains, are an exquisite example of stylized Renaissance landscaping. A large oval lawn is just up the hill from the back of the *Palazzo Pitti*, with an Egyptian obelisk in the middle and marble statues in portals dotting the perimeter. *(Open daily June-Aug. 8:15am-7:30pm; Apr.-May and Sept.-Oct. 8:15am-6:30pm; Nov.-Feb. and Mar. reduced hours. €8.)*

SAN MINIATO AL MONTE AND ENVIRONS

SAN MINIATO AL MONTE. An inlaid marble facade and 13th-century mosaics provide a prelude to the floor inside, patterned with lions, doves, and astrological signs. Visit at 5:40pm to hear the monks chanting. *(Take bus #13 from the station or climb the stairs from Piazzale Michelangelo. ☎234 27 31. Open daily 8am-7:30pm. Free.)*

PIAZZALE MICHELANGELO. A visit to Piazzale Michelangelo is a must. At sunset, waning light casts a warm glow over the city; views from here are even better (and certainly cheaper) than those from the top of the *duomo*. Make the challenging uphill trek at around 8:30pm during the summer to arrive at the *piazza* in time for sunset. Unfortunately, the *piazza* doubles as a large parking lot, and is home to hordes of tour buses during summer days. *(Cross the Ponte Vecchio to the Oltrarno and turn left, walk through the piazza, and turn right up V. de Bardi. Follow it uphill as it becomes V. del Monte alle Croci, where a staircase to the left heads to the piazza.)*

ITALY

ENTERTAINMENT

May starts the summer music festival season with the classical **Maggio Musicale.** The **Festa del Grillo** (Festival of the Cricket) is held on the first Sunday after Ascension Day, when crickets in tiny wooden cages are sold in the Cascine park to be released into the grass—Florentines believe the song of a cricket is good luck. In June, the *quartieri* of Florence dress up to play a medieval version of soccer, known as **calcio storico.** Two teams face off over a wooden ball in one of the city's *piazze*, their games bordering on riots. Tickets (€10-40) are sold at the box office across from P. S. Croce. Check with the tourist office for times and locations of matches. The **Festival of San Giovanni Battista,** on June 24, features a tremendous fireworks display visible along the Arno, beginning around 10pm. The **Estate Fiesolana** (June-Aug.) fills the Roman theater in nearby Fiesole with concerts, opera, theater, ballet, and film events (☎800 41 42 40; www.estatefiesolana.com).

SHOPPING

For both the budget shopper and the big spender who's looking to make the splurge of a lifetime, Florence offers too many options and temptations. *Saldi* (sales) take over in January and July, even in V. Tornabuoni's swanky boutiques. The city's artisan traditions thrive at its open markets. **San Lorenzo,** the largest, cheapest, and most touristed, sprawls for several blocks around P. S. Lorenzo. In front of the leather-shops, vendors sell all kinds of goods—bags, clothes, food, toys, and flags. High prices are rare, but so are quality and honesty. (Open daily 9am-twilight.) Stands throughout the city stock the same selection of generic T-shirts; skip these and try **T-shirt Gallery,** V. Guicciardini 15R, with two stories of *Ita-*

lia- and *Firenze*-printed merchandise. (Open M-Sa 9:30am-7:30pm, Su 10am-7pm. MC/V.) For everything from pot-holders to parakeets, shop at the market in **Parco delle Cascine,** which begins four bridges west of the Ponte Vecchio at P. V. Veneto and stretches along the Arno River each Tuesday morning. For a flea market with furniture and postcards, visit **Piazza Ciompi,** off V. Pietrapiana from Borgo degli Albizi. (Open Tu-Sa.) *Carta fiorentina*, paper covered in intricate floral designs, adorns books and journals at **Alinari,** L. Alinari 15. (☎23 951. Open M 2:30-6:30pm, Tu-F 9am-1pm and 2:30-6:30pm, Sa 9am-1pm and 3-7pm. Closed 2 weeks in Aug. AmEx/MC/V.) Florentine **leatherwork** is affordable and known worldwide. Some of the best artisans work around P. S. Croce and V. Porta S. Maria. The **Santa Croce Leather School,** in Chiesa di Santa Croce, offers first-rate products at reasonable prices. (☎24 45 34; www.leatherschool.it. Open Mar. 15-Nov. 15 daily 9:30am-6pm; Nov. 16-Mar. 14 M-Sa 10am-12:30pm and 3-6pm. AmEx/MC/V.)

NIGHTLIFE

For reliable info, consult the city's entertainment monthly, *Firenze Spettacolo* (€2), or www.informacittafirenze.it. **Piazza Santo Spirito** in Oltrarno has live music in the summer. If you go to clubs or bars that run late and are far from the *centro*, keep in mind that the last bus may leave before the fun winds down, and taxis are hard to come by in the area with the most popular discos.

ITALY

Moyo, V. dei Banchi 23R (☎247 97 38), near P. Santa Croce. Thriving lunch spot by day, hip bar by night, always crowded with young Italians. Lunch options from €7. Evening cocktails include free, self-serve snacks. Open daily 8am-3am. AmEx/MC/V.

Capocaccia, Lungarno Corsini 12R (☎21 07 51). This bar mixes mojitos (€7) and other refreshing cocktails for locals. After paying, take your drink outside by the Arno. Cocktails €5-6.50. Beer from €3.50. Open 11am-1am. Closed 2 weeks in Aug. MC/V.

Central Park, in Parco della Cascinè (☎35 35 05). Open-air dance floor pulses with hip hop, reggae, and rock. Favored by Florentine and foreign teens and college students. Mixed drinks €8. Cover €20; no cover for foreign students before 12:30am. Open M-Tu and Th-Sa 11pm-late, W 9pm-late. AmEx/MC/V.

May Day Lounge, V. Dante Alighieri 16R. Aspiring artists display their work on the walls of this eclectic lounge that fills with offbeat Italians. Play Pong on the early 80s gaming system or sip mixed drinks (€4.50-6.50) to the beat of the background funk. Beer €4.50. Happy hour 8-10pm. Open daily 8pm-2am. Closed most of Aug. AmEx/MC/V.

Tabasco Gay Club, P. S. Cecilia 3R, near Palazzo Vecchio. Smoke machines and strobe lights on the dance floor. Florence's most popular and classy gay disco caters primarily to men. 18+. Cover €13, includes 1 drink. Open Tu-Su 10pm-4am. AmEx/MC/V.

SIENA ☎0577

Many travelers rush from Rome to Florence, ignoring medieval Siena (pop. 50,000) despite its rich artistic, political, and economic history. *Il Palio*, Siena's intoxicating bareback horse races, are a party and a spectacle.

TRANSPORTATION AND PRACTICAL INFORMATION. **Trains** run from P. Rosselli to Florence (1¾hr., 16 per day, €5.70) and Rome (3hr., 20 per day, €13) via Chiusi. TRA-IN/SITA **buses** (☎20 42 46) run from P. Gramsci and the train station to Florence (1 per hr., €6.50) and San Gimignano (31 per day, €5.20). Across from the train station, take TRA-IN buses #3, 4, 7-10, 17, or 77 (€0.90) to **Piazza del Sale** or **Piazza Gramsci,** then follow signs to **Piazza del Campo,** Siena's *centro storico*, also known as **Il Campo.** The **tourist office** is at P. del Campo 56. (☎28 05 www.terresiena.it. Open mid-Mar. to mid-Nov. daily 9:30am-1pm and 2:30-6pm; mid-Nov. to mid-Mar. M-Sa 8:30am-1pm and 3-7pm, Su 9am-1pm.) Check email at **Cafe Internet,** Galleria Cecco Angiolieri 16. (€1.80 per hr. Open M-Sa 8:30am-11pm, Su 9am-11pm.) **Postal Code:** 53100.

ACCOMMODATIONS AND FOOD. Finding a room is difficult from Easter to October. Reserve a month ahead for *Il Palio.* **Prenotazioni Alberghi e Ristoranti,** in P. S. Domenico, finds rooms for a €2 fee. (☎94 08 09. Open M-Sa 9am-7pm, Su 9am-noon.) **Piccolo Hotel Etruria ❹,** V. Donzelle 3, is right near Il Campo. (☎28 80 88; www.hoteletruria.com. Breakfast €5. Curfew 1am. Singles €48-53; doubles €86; triples €114. AmEx/MC/V.) Bus #10 and 15 from P. Gramsci stop at **Ostello della Gioventù "Guidoriccio" (HI) ❶,** V. Fiorentina 89, in Località Lo Stellino. (☎522 12. Curfew midnight. Dorms €14. Cash only.) **Casa Laura ❸,** V. Roma 3, is in the less touristy university area; ring the third doorbell, labeled "Bencini Valentini." (☎22 60 61; fax 0577 22 52 40. Kitchen. Doubles €65-67; triples €70; quads €75. MC/V.) To **camp** at **Colleverde ❶,** Str. di Scacciapensieri 47, take bus #3 or 8 from P. del Sale; confirm destination with driver. (☎28 00 44; www.terresiena.it. Open late Mar. to mid-Nov. Tent sites €3.50, €7.75 per person. MC/V.)

Sienese bakeries prepare *panforte,* a confection of honey, almonds, and citron, sold at **Bar/Pasticceria Nannini ❶,** V. Banchi di Sopra 22-24 (€2.10 per 100g). At **Il Cantiere del Gusto ❸,** V. Calzoleria 12, behind P. del Campo, off V. Banchi d. Sotto, classics like *tagliatelle al ragù di coniglio* (with rabbit sauce; €6.50) await. (☎28 90 10. Service 10%. *Primi* €5-6. *Secondi* €8-12. Cover €1. Open M 12:30-2:30pm, Tu-Sa 12:30-2:30pm and 7-10pm. MC/V.) A **CONAD** supermarket is in P. Matteoti. (Open M-Sa 8:30am-8:30pm, Su 9am-1pm and 4-8pm.)

SIGHTS AND ENTERTAINMENT. Siena radiates from **Piazza del Campo (Il Campo),** a shell-shaped brick square designed for civic events. At the top of the slope by Il Campo is the **Fonte Gaia,** a rectangular marble fountain that has refreshed Siena since the 1300s. At the bottom, the **Torre del Mangia** bell tower looms over the graceful **Palazzo Pubblico.** Inside the *palazzo* is the **Museo Civico.** (*Palazzo*, museum, and tower open daily Mar.-Oct. 10am-6:15pm; Nov.-Feb. 10am-5:30pm. Museum €7, students €4.50. Tower €6. Combo €10.) From the *palazzo* facing Il Campo, take the left stairs and cross V. di Città to get to Siena's hilltop **duomo.** To prevent the apse from being left hanging in mid-air, the lavish **baptistry** was constructed below. (Open June-Aug. M-Sa 10:30am-8pm, Su 1:30-6pm; Mar.-May and Sept.-Oct. M-Sa 10:30am-7:30pm, Su 1:30-6pm; Nov.-Feb. M-Sa 10:30am-6:30pm, Su 1:30-5:30pm. €3-5.50.) The decorated underground rooms of the **cripta** (crypt) were used by pilgrims about to enter the *duomo.* (Check hours at the *duomo.* €6, students €5.) The **Museo dell'Opera della Metropolitana,** to the right of the *duomo,* houses its overflow art. (Open mid-Mar. to Sept. daily 9am-7:30pm; Oct. to mid-Mar. reduced hours. €6.) Twice each year, **Il Palio** morphs the mellow Campo into a chaotic arena as horses speed around its edge. Arrive three days early to watch the trial runs and to pick a *contrada* (city district) to root for.

DAYTRIP FROM SIENA: SAN GIMIGNANO. The hilltop village of San Gimignano (pop. 7000) looks like an illustration from a medieval manuscript, with prototypical towers, churches, and palaces looming above the city's walls. San Gimignano's 14 famous towers, all that remain of the original 72, attract so many daytrippers that it's begun to feel like medieval Disneyland. The **Museo Civico,** on the second floor of **Palazzo Comunale,** has a collection of Sienese and Florentine artwork. Within the museum is the entrance to the **Torre Grossa,** the *palazzo's* tallest remaining tower; climb its 218 steps for a view of Tuscany. (Open daily Mar.-Oct. 9:30am-7pm; Nov.-Feb. 10am-5:30pm. €5, students €4.) **Piazza della Cisterna** is the center of life in San Gimignano and adjoins **Piazza del Duomo.** The famous

Vernaccia di San Gimignano, a light, sweet white wine, is sold at **La Buca,** V. S. Giovanni 16. (Open daily Apr.-Oct. 9am-8pm; Nov.-Mar. 10am-6pm. AmEx/MC/V.) TRA-IN **buses** leave P. Montemaggio for Florence (1½hr., 1 per hr., €6) via Poggibonsi and Siena (1½hr., every 1-2hr., €5.20). To reach the *centro*, pass through Pta. San Matteo and follow V. San Giovanni to P. della Cisterna, which merges with P. del Duomo on the left. **Postal Code:** 53037.

PISA ☎050

Millions of tourists arrive in Pisa (pop. 95,000) each year to marvel at the famous "Leaning Tower," forming a gelato-slurping, photo-snapping mire. Commanding a beautiful stretch of the Arno, Pisa also has an array of cultural diversions, as well as a top-notch university. The **Piazza del Duomo,** or the **Campo dei Miracoli** (Field of Miracles), is the grassy area around the tower, *duomo*, baptistry, Camposanto, Museo delle Sinopie, and Museo dell'Opera del Duomo. Begun in 1173, the **Leaning Tower** began to tilt when soil beneath it shifted. The tilt intensified after WWII, and thanks to the tourists climbing its steps, it slips 1-2m each year, though it's now considered stable. Tours of 30 visitors can ascend the 294 steps once every 30min. (Tours depart daily June-Aug. 8:30am-11pm; Sept.-May 8:30am-7:30pm. Gather next to info office 10min. before tour. €15.) Also on the Campo, the **duomo** has a collection of splendid art and is considered one of the finest Romanesque cathedrals in the world. (Open Apr.-Sept. M-Sa 10am-8pm; Mar. and Oct. M-Sa 10am-7pm, Su 1-5:45pm; Nov.-Feb. M-F 10am-1pm and 3-5pm. €2.) Next door is the **Battistero** (Baptistry), whose precise acoustics allow an unamplified choir to be heard 2km away. An acoustic demonstration occurs every 30min. (Open daily Apr.-Sept. 8am-7:30pm; Oct. and Mar. 9am-5:30pm; Nov.-Feb. 9am-4:30pm. €6, includes admission to one other monument.) Concerts take place in the *duomo;* call **Opera della Primaziale Pisana,** P. Duomo 17 (☎387 22 10; www.opapisa.it). The adjoining **Camposanto,** a cloistered cemetery, is filled with Roman sarcophagi. An **all-inclusive ticket** to the Campo's sights—excluding the tower—costs €10.50 and is available at the two *biglietterie* (ticket booths) on the Campo.

ITALY

Two minutes from the *duomo*, the **Albergo Helvetia ❸,** V. Don G. Boschi 31, off P. Archivescovado, has large, clean rooms, a multilingual staff, and a welcoming bar downstairs. (☎55 30 84. Reception 8am-midnight. Singles €35-50; doubles €45-60. Cash only.) **Centro Turistico Madonna dell'Acqua ❶,** V. Pietrasantina 15, is 2km from the tower, next to a creek that attracts mosquitoes. Take bus #1 from the station (4 per hr., last bus 9:45pm); ask the driver to stop at *ostello*. (☎89 06 22. Linens €1. Dorms €15. MC/V.) Steer clear of the touristy pizzerias near the tower and head for the river, where restaurants are authentic and of higher quality. Try the heavenly risotto at **Il Paiolo ❶,** V. Curtatone e Montanara 9. (*Menù* €4.90-8. Open M-F 12:30-3pm and 8pm-1am, Sa-Su 8pm-2am only. MC/V.) Get groceries at **Pam,** V. Pascoli 8, off C. Italia. (Open M-Sa 8am-8pm. Cash only.) **Trains** (☎89 20 21) run from P. della Stazione, in the south of town, to Florence (1hr., 1 per hr., €5.20), Genoa (2½hr., 1 per hr., €7.90), and Rome (3hr., 12 per day, €23-29). For the **tourist office,** walk out of the train station and go left in P. V. Emanuele. (☎422 91; www.turismo.toscana.it. Open M-F 9am-7pm, Sa 9am-1:30pm.) Take bus #3 (€0.85) from the station to the Campo. **Postal Code:** 56100.

UMBRIA

Umbria is known as the "green heart of Italy." This landlocked region is rich in wild woods and fertile plains, craggy gorges and gentle hills, cobblestoned villages and active international universities. The region holds Giotto's greatest masterpieces and produced medieval masters Perugino and Pinturicchio.

PERUGIA ☎075

Perugia (pop. 160,000) is very walkable; visitors quickly become familiar with the layout of the winding streets and hilltop monuments, all the better to experience the city's renowned jazz festival, digest its decadent chocolate, and meander through its two universities. The city's most popular sights frame **Piazza IV Novembre,** Perugia's social heart. In its center, the **Fontana Maggiore** is adorned with sculptures and bas-reliefs. At the end of the *piazza,* the imposing Gothic **Cattedrale di San Lorenzo,** also known the *duomo,* houses the purported wedding ring of the Virgin Mary. (Open M-Sa 8am-12:45pm and 4-5:15pm, Su 4-5:45pm.) The 13th-century **Palazzo dei Priori,** on the left when looking at the fountain, contains the impressive **Galleria Nazionale dell'Umbria,** C. Vannucci 19, which displays magnificent 13th- and 14th-century religious works. (Open Tu-Su 8:30am-7:30pm. €6.50.) **Ostello della Gioventù/Centro Internazionale di Accoglienza per la Gioventù ❶,** V. Bontempi 13, is homey, social, well-located, and clean. From P. IV Novembre, keep to the right past the *duomo* and P. Danti into P. Piccinino, and on V. Bontempi. (☎572 28 80; www.ostello.perugia.it. Linens €2. Lockout 9:30am-4pm. Curfew 1am, midnight in winter. Closed mid-Dec. to mid-Jan. Dorms €15. AmEx/MC/V.) Visit the famous Perugia **chocolate store,** C. Vannucci 101. (Open M 3-8pm, Tu-Sa 9:30am-7:45pm, Su 10:30am-1:30pm and 3-8pm.) Local favorite **Trattoria Dal Mi Cocco ❷,** C. Garibaldi 12, provides prompt service and an extensive and reasonable fixed menu. (*Menù* €13. Reserve ahead. Open Tu-Su 1-3pm and 8:30pm-midnight. MC/V.) **Pizzeria Mediterranea ❶,** P. Piccinino 11/12, appeals to both locals and visitors. (Pizza €3.70-12. Cover €1.10. Open daily 12:30-2:30pm and 7:30-11pm. MC/V.) **Coop,** P. Matteotti 15, has groceries. (Open M-Sa 9am-8pm. MC/V.) **Trains** leave Perugia FS in P. V. Veneto, Fontiveggio, for: Assisi (25min., 1 per hr., €1.65); Florence (2hr., 6 per day, from €8); Orvieto (€11); Rome (2½hr., 7 per day, €11) via Terontola or Foligno. From the station, take bus #6, 7, 9, 11, 13D, or 15 to the central P. Italia (€1), then walk down C. Vannucci, the main shopping street, to P. IV Novembre and the *duomo.* V. Baglioni is one block off P. IV Novembre and leads to P. Matteotti and the **tourist office,** P. Matteotti 18. (☎57 36 458. Open M-Sa 8:30am-1:30pm and 3:30-6:30pm, Su 9am-1pm.) **Postal Code:** 06100.

ITALY

ASSISI ☎075

Assisi's serene atmosphere and renowned spirituality are owed to the legacy of St. Francis, patron saint of Italy and the town's favorite son. The undeniable jewel of Assisi (pop. 25,000) is the 13th-century **Basilica di San Francesco.** The subdued art of the lower church celebrates St. Francis's modest lifestyle, while Giotto's renowned fresco cycle, the *Life of St. Francis,* adorns the walls of the upper church, paying tribute to the saint's consecration. (Lower basilica open daily 6am-6:45pm. Upper basilica open daily 8:30am-6:45pm. Modest dress required. Free.) The fortress **Rocca Maggiore** looms above the town, offering an incredible panoramic view of the countryside. From P. del Comune, follow V. S. Rufino to P. S. Rufino. Continue up V. Pta. Perlici and take the first left up a narrow staircase. (Open daily 9am-8pm. €3.50, students €2.50.) The pink-and-white **Basilica of Santa Chiara** houses the crucifix that is said to have spoken to St. Francis. (Open daily 6:30am-noon and 2-7pm.) The charming **Camere Martini ❷,** V. S. Gregorio 6, has sunny rooms and a familial atmosphere. (☎35 36; cameremartini@libero.it. Singles €25-27; doubles €40; triples €55; quads €65. Cash only.) **Ostello Fontemaggio ❷,** V. Eremo delle Carceri 24, has a hostel, hotel, bungalows, campground, and restaurant, all in one. Take V. Eremo delle Carceri from P. Matteotti about 1.5km. (☎36 36. Curfew 11pm. Camping €5.50; dorms €20; singles €35; doubles €52; triples €73; quads €96. MC/V.) Grab a personal pizza (€5-7) at **Pizzeria Otello ❶,** V. San Antonio 1. (Open daily noon-3pm and 7-10:30pm. AmEx/MC/V.) From the station near the Basilica Santa Maria degli Angeli, **trains** go to Florence (2½hr., 7 per day, €9) and Rome (2½hr., 7 per day, €9). **Buses** run from P. Unita d'Italia to Florence (2½hr., 1 per day, €11) and Perugia (1½hr., 12 per day, €3). From P. Matteotti, follow V. del Torrione to P. S. Rufino, where the downhill left leads to V. S. Rufino, **Piazza del Comune,** the town center, and the **tourist office.** (☎25 34. Open M-Sa 8am-2pm and 3-6pm, Su 9am-1pm.) **Postal Code:** 06081.

ORVIETO ☎0763

A city upon a city, Orvieto (pop. 21,000) was built in layers: medieval structures stand over ancient tunnels, which 7th-century BC Etruscans began digging into the hill. **Underground City Excursions** offers the most complete tour of the dark, twisted bowels of the city. (☎34 48 91. Tours leave the tourist office daily 11am, 12:15, 4, 5:15pm. €5.50, students €3.50.) It took 600 years, 152 sculptors, 68 painters, 90 mosaic artisans, and 33 architects to construct Orvieto's ■ **duomo.** The **Capella della Madonna di San Brizio,** off the right transept, houses the dramatic apocalypse frescoes of Luca Signorelli; opposite, the ■**Cappella Corporale** holds the gold-encrusted chalice-cloth, soaked with the blood of Christ. (Open M-Sa 7:30am-12:45pm and 2:30-7pm, Su 2:30-6:45pm. Modest dress required. *Duomo* free. *Capella* €3.) Two blocks down from the *duomo,* V. della Piazza del Popolo leads to **Grand Hotel Reale ❸,** P. del Popolo 25. The deal is unparalleled; the hotel luxurious. (Breakfast €8. Singles €35, with bath €76; doubles €80/160. V.) ■**Nonnamelia ❸,** V. del Duomo 25, cooks creatively. (☎34 24 02. *Primi* €5-7. *Secondi* €7-13. Open daily noon-3pm and 7-11pm. Cash only.) For a free tasting of *Orvieto Classico,* try **Cantina Freddano,** C. Cavour 5. (☎30 82 48. Bottles from €4. Open daily 9:30am-7:30pm.) **Trains** run every hr. to Florence (2½hr., €11) and Rome (1½hr., €11). The funicular travels up the hill from the station to **Piazza Cahen,** and a shuttle goes to the **tourist office,** P. del Duomo 24. (☎34 17 72. Open M-F 8:15am-1:50pm and 4-7pm, Sa-Su 10am-1pm and 3-6pm.) **Postal Code:** 05018.

THE MARCHES (LE MARCHE)

In the Marches, green foothills separate the gray shores of the Adriatic from Apennine peaks, and umbrella-dotted beaches from traditional hill towns. Inland villages, easily accessible by train, rely on agriculture and preserve the region's historical legacy in the architectural remains of the Gauls and Romans.

URBINO ☎0722

With stone dwellings scattered along its streets and a turreted palace accenting its skyline, Urbino (pop. 15,500) is the birth city of Raphael. Most remarkable is the Renaissance **Palazzo Ducale,** in P. Rinascimento. Stairs in the courtyard lead to the former apartments of the duke, now home to the **Galleria Nazionale delle Marche.** Watch for Raphael's *Portrait of a Lady.* (☎32 26 25. Open M 8:30am-2pm, Tu-Su 8:30am-7:15pm. €4.) Walk back across P. della Repubblica onto V. Raffaello to the site of Raphael's birth in 1483, the **Casa Natale di Raffaello,** V. Raffaello 57. It is now a museum of period furniture, works by local masters, and the *Madonna col Bambino,* attributed to Raphael himself. (☎32 01 05. Open Mar.-Oct. M-Sa 9am-1pm and 3-7pm, Su 10am-1pm; Nov.-Feb. M-Sa 9am-2pm, Su 10am-1pm. €3.) **Pensione Fosca ❷,** V. Raffaello 67, is just doors from Raphael's birthplace. (☎32 96 22. Singles €21; doubles €35; triples €45. Cash only.) At **Pizzeria Le Tre Piante ❷,** V. Voltaccia della Vecchia 1, large pizzas (€2.50-8) are served in view of the Apennines. (☎48 63. *Primi* from €5.50. *Secondi* from €8. Reserve ahead F-Sa. Open Tu-Su noon-3pm and 7-11pm. Cash only.) **Supermarket Margherita,** V. Raffaello 37, stocks everything but fruits and veggies. (Open M-Sa 7:30am-2pm and 4:30-8pm.

Cash only.) Bucci **buses** (☎0721 32 401) run from Borgo Mercatale to Rome (5hr., 1 per day, €25). V. Mazzini leads from Borgo Mercatale to P. della Repubblica, the city's hub. From there, V. V. Veneto leads to the *palazzo* and the **tourist office,** V. Puccinotti 35. (☎26 13. Open M and Sa 9am-1pm, Tu-F 9am-1pm and 3-6pm.)

ANCONA ☎071

Ancona (pop. 102,000) is a transport hub for those heading east. The P. del Duomo, atop Monte Guasco, offers a view of the town's red rooftops and port. Across the *piazza* is the **Cattedrale di San Ciriaco,** a Romanesque church with its namesake shrouded in velvet. (☎52 688. Open in summer M-Sa 8am-noon and 3-7pm; winter M-Sa 8am-noon and 3-6pm. Su hours vary.) From the train station, cross the *piazza*, turn left, turn right, and make a sharp right behind the newsstand to **Ostello della Gioventù (HI) ❶,** V. Lamaticci 7. (☎42 257. Lockout 11am-4:30pm. Dorms €16. HI members only. Cash only.) Decent hotels surround the station. **La Cantineta ❷,** V. Gramsci, has specialties like *stoccafisso* (stockfish) at reasonable prices. (☎20 11 07. *Primi* €2.60-7.50. *Secondi* €4.20-14. Cover €1.50. Open Tu-Su noon-2:45pm and 7:30-10:45pm. AmEx/MC/V.) **Di per Di** supermarket is at V. Matteotti 115. (Open M-W and F 8:15am-1:30pm and 5-7:35pm, Sa 8:15am-1pm and 5-7:40pm. Cash only.) **Ferries** leave Stazione Marittima for Croatia, Greece, and northern Italy. Adriatica (☎502 11 621; www.adriatica.it), Jadrolinija (☎20 43 05; www.jadrolinija.tel.hr), and SEM Maritime Co. (☎20 40 41; www.marittimamauro.it) run to Split, CRO (9hr., €37-47). ANEK (☎207 23 46; www.anekitalia.com) ferries go to Patras, GCE (20hr., €54-73). All these accept AmEx/MC/V. Get schedules and tickets at the Stazione Marittima or www.doricaportservices.it. **Trains** leave P. Rosselli for: Bologna (2½hr., 43 per day, €10); Milan (5hr., 24 per day, €25); Rome (3-4hr., 10 per day, €14); Venice (5hr., 4 per day, €23). The train station is a 25min. walk from Stazione Marittima. Buses #1, 1/3, and 1/4 (€0.90) head up C. Stamira to P. Cavour, the city center. The **tourist office** is across from Stazione Marittima. (☎207 90 29. Open in summer M 9am-7pm, Tu 11am-7pm, W-Su 10am-7pm.) **Postal Code:** 60100.

CAMPANIA

Sprung from the shadow of Mt. Vesuvius, Campania thrives in defiance of natural disasters. The submerged city at Baia, the relics at Pompeii, and the ruins at Cumae all attest to a land resigned to harsh natural outbursts. While the vibrant city of Naples and the emerald waters of the Amalfi Coast reel in tourists, Campania is one of Italy's poorest regions, often overshadowed by the prosperous North.

NAPLES (NAPOLI) ☎081

Italy's third-largest city, Naples (pop. 1,000,000), is also its most chaotic—Naples moves a million miles per minute. Neapolitans spend their waking moments out on the town, eating, drinking, shouting, laughing, and pausing in the middle of busy streets to finish conversations. The birthplace of pizza and the modern-day home of tantalizing seafood, Naples's cuisine is unbeatable. Once you submit to the rapid pulse of Naples, everywhere else will seem simply slow.

TRANSPORTATION

Flights: Aeroporto Capodichino, V. Umberto Maddalena (**NAP;** ☎789 6259; www.gesac.it), northeast of the city. Connects to major Italian and European cities. **Alibus** (☎531 1706) goes to P. Municipio and P. Garibaldi (20min., 6am-11:30pm, €3).

Trains: Trenitalia (www.trenitalia.it) goes from Stazione Centrale in P. Garibaldi to **Milan** (9hr., 13 per day, €50) and **Rome** (2hr., 40 per day, €11). **Circumvesuviana** (☎800 05 39 39) runs to **Herculaneum** (€1.70) and **Pompeii** (€2.30).

Ferries: Depart from **Stazione Marittima,** on Molo Angioino, and **Molo Beverello,** at the base of P. Municipio. From P. Garibaldi, take the R2, 152, 3S, or the Alibus to P. Municipio. **Caremar,** Molo Beverello (☎551 38 82), runs frequently to **Capri** and **Ischia** (both 1½hr., €4.80). **Tirrenia Lines,** Molo Angioino (☎199 12 31 199), goes to **Cagliari** (16hr.) and **Palermo** (11hr.). Hydrofoils are generally faster and more expensive. The daily newspaper *Il Mattino* (€0.90) lists up-to-date ferry schedules.

Public Transportation: One **UnicoNapoli** (www.napolipass.it) ticket is valid on buses, Metro, train, and funicular in Naples (€1 per 1½hr., full-day €3). Route information for the Metro and funiculars is at www.metro.na.it.

Taxis: Consortaxi (☎081 55 25 252). **Radio** (☎081 55 15 151). **Napoli** (☎556 4444). Only take metered taxis, and always ask about prices up front. Meter starts at €2.60 and goes up €0.05 every 70m. Add a €2.10 surcharge from 10pm-7am.

ORIENTATION AND PRACTICAL INFORMATION

ITALY

The main train and bus terminals are in the immense **Piazza Garibaldi** on the east side of Naples; explore various ethnic markets in the congested neighborhood around it. From P. Garibaldi, a left on **Corso Garibaldi** leads to the waterfront district; **Piazza Guglielmo Pepe** is at the end of C. Garibaldi. **Piazza Plebiscito,** home to upscale little restaurants and shops, is accessible by walking down **Via Nuova Marina** with the water on your left. **Via Toledo,** a chic pedestrian shopping street, links the waterfront to the **Plebiscito** district, where the well-to-do hang out, and the maze-like **Spanish Quarter.** Along V. Toledo, **Piazza Dante** lies on the western extreme of the **Spaccanapoli** *(centro storico)* neighborhood. Walking away from the waterfront, a right at any of the streets will lead to the historic district. While violent crime is rare in Naples, theft is fairly common, so exercise caution.

Tourist Offices: EPT (☎26 87 79; www.eptnapoli.info), at Stazione Centrale. Free maps. Grab **Qui Napoli,** a bimonthly publication full of listings and events. Open M-Sa 9am-7pm, Su 9am-1pm. **Branch** at P. Gesù Nuovo (☎551 27 01).

Consulates: Canada, V. Carducci 29 (☎40 13 38). **UK,** V. dei Mille 40 (☎42 38 911). **US,** P. della Repubblica (☎58 38 111, 24hr. emergency 033 79 45 083).

Currency Exchange: Thomas Cook, at the airport and in P. Municipio 70 (☎551 83 99). Open M-F 9:30am-1pm and 3-7pm. **Branch** at P. Municipio 70 (☎55 18 399).

Emergency: ☎113. **Police:** ☎112 or 794 11 11. **Ambulance:** ☎752 82 82.

Hospital: Cardarelli (☎74 72 859), on the R4 or OF line.

Post Office: P. Matteotti (☎552 42 33), at V. Diaz on the R2 line. Unreliable *fermo-posta.* Address mail to be held: First name LAST NAME, *In Fermo Posta,* P. Matteotti, Naples 80100, ITALY. Open M-F 8:15am-6pm, Sa 8:15am-noon. **Postal Code:** 80100.

ACCOMMODATIONS

Although Naples has some fantastic lodgings bargains, especially near **Piazza Garibaldi,** be cautious when choosing a room. Avoid hotels that solicit customers at the station, never give your passport until you've seen the room, agree on the price before unpacking, and be alert for hidden costs.

Hostel Pensione Mancini, V. P. S. Mancini 33, Stazione Centrale (☎081 55 36 731; www.hostelpensionemancini.com), off far end of P. Garibaldi from station, 2nd fl.; not to be confused with more distant V. Mancini. Owners share local knowledge. Bright,

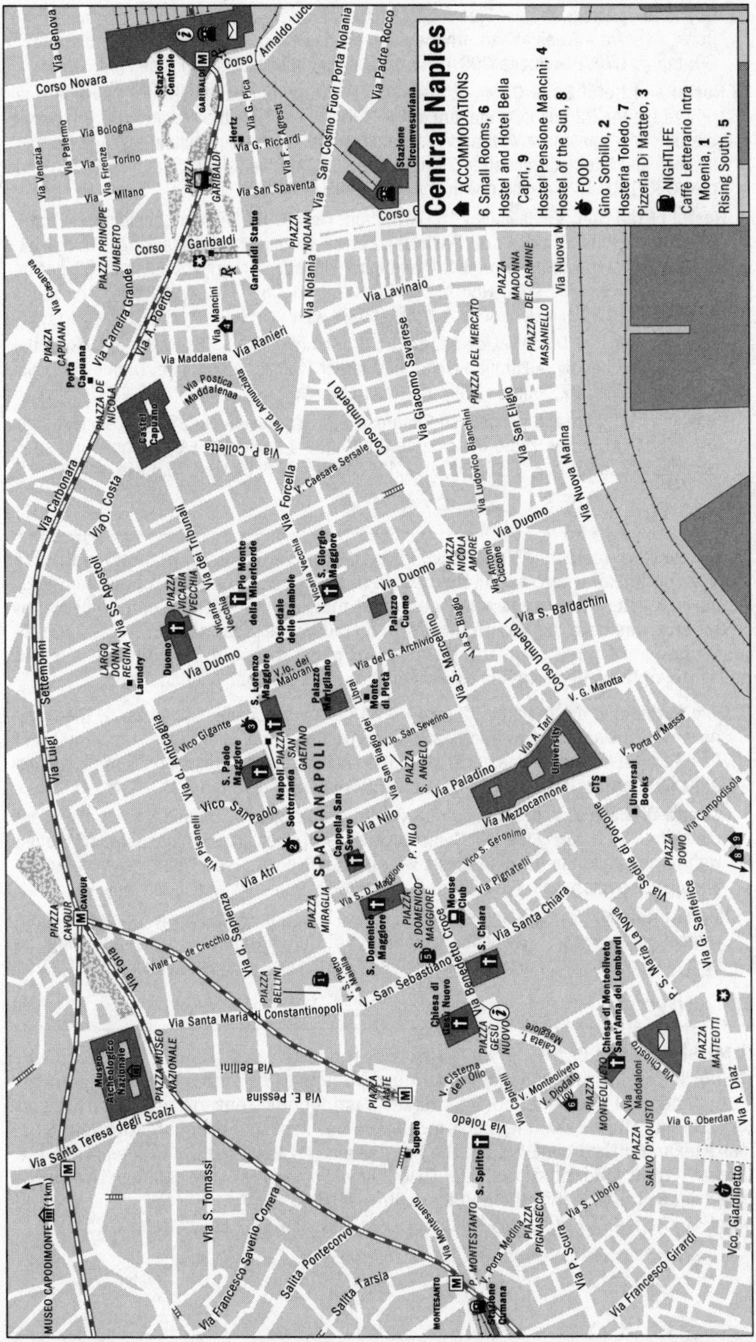
Central Naples
ACCOMMODATIONS
6 Small Rooms, 6
Hostel and Hotel Bella Capri, 9
Hostel Pensione Mancini, 4
Hostel of the Sun, 8
FOOD
Gino Sorbillo, 2
Hosteria Toledo, 7
Pizzeria Di Matteo, 3
NIGHTLIFE
Caffè Letterario Intra Moenia, 1
Rising South, 5
Stazione Centrale
GARIBALDI
PIAZZA GARIBALDI
Corso Garibaldi
Garibaldi Statue
Corso Novara
Via Genova
Corso Arnaldo Lucci
Corso Fuori Porta Nolania
Via Padre Rocco
Stazione Circumvesuviana
Via G. Pica
Hertz
Via G. Riccardi
Via F. Agresti
Via San Spaventa
Via San Cosmo Fuori Porta Nolania
PIAZZA NOLANA
Via Nolania
Via Lavinaio
Via Venezia
Via Palermo
Via Bologna
Via Torino
Via Firenze
Via Milano
PIAZZA PRINCIPE UMBERTO
Via Casanova
Via Carreira Grande
Via A. Poerio
Via Mancini
Via Maddalena
Via Ranieri
Via Postica Maddalenaa
Via d. Annunziata
PIAZZA CAPUANA
Porta Capuana
PIAZZA DE NICOLA
Castel Capuano
Via P. Colletta
Via Carbonara
Via O. Costa
Via SS Apostoli
Via dei Tribunali
Via Forcella
V. Caesare Sersale
Corso Umberto I
Via Giacomo Savarese
PIAZZA DEL MERCATO
PIAZZA MADONNA DEL CARMINE
PIAZZA MASANIELLO
Via Nuova Marina
Via Ludovico Bianchini
Via San Eligio
PIAZZA NICOLA AMORE
Via Duomo
Via Antonio Ciccone
Via S. Baldachini
Via S. Biagio
Via S. Marcellino
Via del G. Archivio
Palazzo Cuomo
PIAZZA VICARIA VECCHIA
Vicaria Vecchia
Pio Monte della Misericorde
S. Giorgio Maggiore
Ospedale delle Bambole
Duomo
LARGO DONNA REGINA
Laundry
Via Settembrini
Via Luigi Settembrini
S. Lorenzo Maggiore
V.lo. dei Maiorani
Palazzo Marigliano
Monte di Pietà
Librai
Via San Biagio dei Librai
V.lo. San Severino
PIAZZA S. ANGELO
Via d. Anticaglia
Vico Gigante
S. Paolo Maggiore
Napoli Sotterranea
PIAZZA SAN GAETANO
SPACCANAPOLI
Vico San Paolo
Via Pisanelli
Cappella San Severo
Via Nilo
P. NILO
Via Paladino
Via A. Tari
University
V. G. Marotta
V. Porta di Massa
CTS
Universal Books
Via Mezzocannone
Via Sedile di Porto
Via Campodisola
PIAZZA BOVIO
Via Atri
Via d. Sapienza
PIAZZA MIRAGLIA
Via S. D. Maggiore
PIAZZA S. DOMENICO MAGGIORE
S. Domenico Maggiore
Vico S. Geronimo
Via Pignatelli
Mouse Club
S. Chiara
Via Santa Chiara
Via Benedetto Croce
V. San Sebastiano
V. S. Pietro a Maiella
PIAZZA BELLINI
Viale L. de Crecchio
PIAZZA CAVOUR
CAVOUR
Via Foria
Via Santa Maria di Constantinopoli
Chiesa di Gesù Nuovo
PIAZZA GESÙ NUOVO
Calata T. Maggiore
Chiesa di Monteoliveto
Sant'Anna dei Lombardi
Via Chiostro
PIAZZA MATTEOTTI
P. S. Maria La Nova
Via G. Sanfelice
Museo Archeologico Nazionale
PIAZZA MUSEO NAZIONALE
Via Bellini
Via E. Pessina
PIAZZA DANTE
V. Cisterna dell'Olio
V. Capitelli
V. Monteoliveto
V. Diodato Lioy
PIAZZA MONTEOLIVETO
Via Maddaloni
PIAZZA SALVO D'AQUISTO
Via G. Oberdan
Via A. Diaz
Via Toledo
Via Santa Teresa degli Scalzi
Supero
S. Spirito
MUSEO CAPODIMONTE (1km)
Via S. Tomassi
Via Francesco Saverio Correra
Salita Pontecorvo
Salita Tarsia
Via Montesanto
MONTESANTO
P. MONTESTANTO
Stazione Cumana
V. Porta Medina
PIAZZA PIGNASECCA
Via P. Scura
Via S. Liborio
Via Francesco Girardi
Vco. Giardinetto

ITALY

tidy, and spacious rooms. Free luggage storage and lockers. Check-in and check-out noon. Reserve 1 week ahead. Dorms €20; singles €35, with bath €45; doubles €55/60; triples €75/80; quads €90/100. 10% discount with *Let's Go*. Cash only. ❷

Hostel and Hotel Bella Capri, V. Melisurgo 4, Waterfront (☎55 29 494; www.bellacapri.it).Take the R2 bus from station, exit at V. De Pretis. Take the elevator (€0.05) during the day. All rooms have A/C and TV. Breakfast included. Free kitchen, luggage storage, lockers, and Internet. Reception 24hr. Dorms €20; singles €45-70; doubles €55-70; triples €80-100. 10% discount with *Let's Go.* AmEx/MC/V. ❷

Hostel of the Sun, V. Melisurgo 15, Waterfront (☎420 63 93; www.hostelnapoli.com). Take the R2 bus, exit at V. de Pretis, and cross the street to V. Melisurgo. Buzz #51. First-rate hostel with large rooms. Breakfast included. Laundry €3. Internet €3 per hr. Dorms €20; singles €45, with bath €50; doubles €55/70; triples €80/90; quads €90/100. 10% *Let's Go* discount. AmEx/MC/V. ❷

6 Small Rooms, V. Diodato Lioy 18, Centro Storico (☎790 13 78). No sign; look for the call button. Friendly, Australian owner and larger rooms than implied. Dorms €18; singles with bath €35; doubles €55/65. Cash only. ❷

Pensione Margherita, V. Domenico Cimarosa 29, 5th fl. (☎578 2852; pensione.margherita@tiscali.it), in the same building as the Centrale Funicular. Large rooms and spotless baths. Closed Aug. 1-15. Singles €40; doubles €70; triples €95. Cash only. ❹

ITALY

FOOD

If you ever doubted that Neapolitans invented pizza, Naples's *pizzerie* will take that doubt, knead it into a ball, throw it in the air, spin it on their collective finger, punch it down, and bury it with sauce and mozzarella. Nothing can compare to Neapolitan **seafood;** the **waterfront** offers a traditional Neapolitan fare and a culinary change of pace from the plethora of pizza. Some of the cheapest, most authentic options lie along **Via dei Tribunali** in the heart of Spaccanapoli.

Gino Sorbillo, V. dei Tribunali 32 (☎44 66 43; www.accademiadellapizza.it). The pizzeria's owners claim links to a forbearer who invented the *ripieno al forno* (calzone) and has 21 pizza-makers in this generation. The kitchen has the original brick oven. *Margherita* €3. Service 10%. Open M-Sa noon-3:30pm and 7-11:30pm. MC/V. ❶

Pizzeria Di Matteo, V. dei Tribunali 94 (☎45 52 62), near V. Duomo. Former President Clinton ate here during the G-7 Conference in 1994. Pies, like the *marinara* (€2), burst with flavor, while the building bursts with pizza aficionados—put your name on the list and expect a short wait. Pies €2.50-6. Open M-Sa 9am-midnight. Cash only. ❶

Hosteria Toledo, Vicolo Giardinetto 78A (☎42 12 57), in the Spanish Quarter. Prepare yourself for courses of Neapolitan comfort food. The *gnocchi* (€6) is hearty enough to be a meal on its own. *Primi* €6-12. *Secondi* €5-10. Open daily 8pm-midnight. MC/V. ❷

SIGHTS

MUSEO ARCHEOLOGICO NAZIONALE. Situated in a 16th-century *palazzo* and former barracks, the archaeological museum houses treasures from Pompeii and Herculaneum. Unreliable labeling makes a guidebook, tour, or audio tour a good investment. The mezzanine has a mosaic room, with one design featuring a fearless Alexander the Great routing the Persian army. Check out the Farnese Bull, the largest extant ancient statue. The *Gabinetto Segreto* (secret cabinet) of Aphrodite grants glimpses into the goddess's life. *(M: P. Cavour. Turn right from the station and walk 2 blocks. ☎44 01 66. Open M and W-Su 9am-7:30pm. €6.50, EU students €3.25.)*

MUSEO AND GALLERIE DI CAPODIMONTE. Housed in another 16th century *palazzo*, the museum is inside a park filled with playful young Italians. A plush royal apartment and the Italian National Picture Gallery are within the palace. Among its impressive works are Bellini's *Transfiguration*, Masaccio's *Crucifixion*, and Titian's *Danae*. *(Take bus #24, 110, M4, or M5 from the Archaeological Museum and exit at the gate to the park, on the right. 2 entrances: Pta. Piccola and Pta. Grande. ☎74 99 111. Open M-Tu and Th-Su 8:30am-7:30pm. €7.50, after 2pm €3.75.)*

PALAZZO REALE AND MASCHIO ANGIONO. The 17th-century Palazzo Reale has opulent royal apartments, the **Museo di Palazzo Reale,** and a view from the terrace of the **Royal Chapel.** *(P. Plebescito 1. Take the R2 bus from P. Garibaldi to P. Trieste e Trento and walk around the palazzo to the entrance on P. Plebiscito. ☎40 05 47; www.pierreci.it. Open M-Tu and Th-Su 9am-7pm. €7.50, students €3.75.)* The **Biblioteca Nazionale** stores 1.5 million volumes, including the scrolls from the **Villa dei Papiri** in Herculaneum. *(☎78 19 231. Visits M-F 10am-1pm with reservation.)* The **Teatro San Carlo's** acoustics are reputed to top those of Milan's La Scala. *(Theater entrance on P. Trieste e Trento. ☎66 45 45; www.itineranapoli.com. Open daily 9am-6:30pm. Tours €5, students €3.)* **Maschio Angiono's** five turrets' shadow the bay. Built in 1286 by Charles II of Anjou as his royal residence, the fortress's most stunning feature is its entrance, with reliefs of Alphonse I of Aragon. *(P. Municipio. Take the R2 bus from P. Garibaldi or walk from anywhere in the historic center. ☎795 58 77. Open M-Sa 9am-7pm. €5.)*

VIRGIL'S TOMB. *Mirabile dictu!* The celebrated Latin poet's resting place is at V. Salita della Grotta. Below the tomb is the entrance to the closed Crypta Neapolitana, built under Augustus, connecting ancient Neapolis to Pozzuoli and Baia. Call ahead for a translator to explain the inscriptions, or come for the view. *(M: Mergellina. From the station, take 2 rights. Entrance between overpass and tunnel. ☎66 93 90. Guided tours upon request. Open daily 9am-1hr. before sunset. Free.)*

NAPOLI SOTTERRANEA. The catacombs of S. Gennaro, S. Gaudioso, and S. Severo date back to the early centuries AD. Tours of the subterranean alleys involve crawling through narrow underground passageways, spotting Mussolini-era graffiti, and exploring aqueducts. *(P. S. Gaetano 68. Take V. dei Tribunali and turn left before S. Paolo Maggiore. ☎29 69 44. Tours every 2hr. M-F noon-4pm, Sa-Su 10am-6pm. €9.30, students €8.)*

DUOMO. The *duomo's* main attraction is the **Capella del Tesoro di San Gennaro.** A bronze grille protects the altar, home to the saint's head and two vials of his blood. The **excavation site** is open for visits. *(Walk 3*

JUL 17

FROM THE ROAD

"RED" MEANS "GO"

Visitors accustomed to restraint and rules may at first view Naples's fast pace and chaos as intimidating. But those who stick around will soon begin to see the city as delightfully uninhibited, its inhabitants living for the moment and loving it. For me, this change in outlook occured on a scooter.

The brazen scooter drivers of Naples seem to follow a hard-to-discern code of conduct. Used to adhering to speed limits and driving rules back home in America, I was, to say the least, intimidated when a new Neapolitan friend with a scooter offered to help me get around Naples. At first, my hesitation seemed warranted: zipping through the twisted streets, I was convinced that I would soon take off a rear-view mirror as we veered dangerously close to careening Fiats. My driver remained chatty the entire time, apparently unconcerned by his or anyone else's wild driving patterns. And, as he assured me, "*Non c'è problemo,* no problem. Once you learn how to handle Napoli, you'll love this city like none other." After my speed adventures, I told him that I would consider getting a Vespa of my own once I returned to America.

He laughed loudly. "No, in America, Vespas are no fun!" he chided. "You can't swerve among the cars, speed against oncoming traffic, or criss-cross over sidewalks to weave through the terrified pedestrians!"

– Lindsay Crouse

blocks up V. Duomo from C. Umberto I or take bus #42 from P. Garibaldi. Open M-Sa 8:30am-noon and 4:30-6pm. Free. Excavation site €3.)

NIGHTLIFE

Piazza Vanvitelli in Vomero draws young people. Take the funicular from V. Toledo or bus C28 from P. Vittoria. **Via Santa Maria La Nova** is another hot spot. Outdoor bars and cafes are a popular choice in **Piazza Bellini,** near P. Dante. **Caffè Letterario Intra Moenia,** P. Bellini 70, appeals to intellectuals by keeping books amid the wicker furniture. (Open daily 10am-2am. Cash only.) **Rising South,** V.S. Sebastiano 19, nearby P. Gesu Nuovo, does it all: *enoteca*, bar, cultural association, cinema. (Drinks €3-6. Bar open daily Sept.-May 10pm-3am, with special events in the summer.) **ARCI-GAY/Lesbica** (☎552 88 15) has info on gay and lesbian club nights.

DAYTRIPS FROM NAPLES

HERCULANEUM. Herculaneum is less excavated than Pompeii because the city was buried much deeper; a modern city sits on top. One highlight is the House of Deer. *(Open daily 8:30am-7:30pm. €10.)* The House of the Mosaic of Neptune and Anfitrite is famous for its breathtaking mosaic. The city is 500m downhill from the Ercolano Scavi stop on the Circumvesuviana train from Naples (dir.: Sorrento; 20min.). The tourist office, V. IV Novembre 84 (☎081 788 12 43), has free maps.

POMPEII. On the morning of August 24, AD 79, a deadly cloud of volcanic ash from Mt. Vesuvius overtook the Roman city of Pompeii, catching the 12,000 residents by surprise. Mere hours after the eruption, stately buildings, works of art, and—ghastliest of all—human bodies, were sealed in casts of ash. These natural tombs would remain undisturbed until 1748, when excavations began to unearth a stunningly well-preserved picture of daily Roman life. Walk down V. della Marina to reach the colonnaded **Forum,** which was once the civic and religious center of the city. Exit the Forum through the upper end and head right on V. della Fortuna to reach the **House of the Faun,** where a bronze dancing faun and the Alexander Mosaic (today in the Museo Archeologico Nazionale) were found. Continue on V. della Fortuna and turn left on V. dei Vettii to reach the **House of the Vettii** and the most vivid frescoes in Pompeii. V. dei Teatri, across the street, leads to the oldest standing **amphitheater** in the world (80 BC), which once held up to 20,000 spectators. To get to the **Villa of the Mysteries,** the complex's best-preserved villa, head west on V. della Fortuna, right on V. Consolare, and all the way up Porta Ercolano and V. della Tombe. *(Archaeological site open daily Apr.-Oct. 8:30am-7:30pm; Nov.-Mar. 8:30am-5pm. €10.)* Take the Circumvesuviana **train** (☎772 24 44) from Naples to the Pompeii Scavi stop *(dir.: Sorrento; 40min., 2 per hr., round-trip €2.30).*

MOUNT VESUVIUS. You can peer into the only active volcano in mainland Europe at Mt. Vesuvius. Although it hasn't erupted since March 31, 1944 (scientists estimate the volcano becomes active, on average, every 30 years), experts deem the trip up the mountain relatively safe. *(Vesuvio Express buses (☎739 36 66) run from Herculaneum up to the crater of Vesuvius. Every 20min. or as soon as the van is filled. Round-trip €10.)*

BAY OF NAPLES

SORRENTO ☎807

Cliffside Sorrento makes a convenient base for daytrips around the Bay of Naples. **Ostello Le Sirene ❷,** V. degli Aranci 160, is located near the station. (☎807 29 25. 8-bed dorms €18; doubles €60.) Wooded seaside campground **Santa Fortunata Cam-**

pogaio, V. del Capo 39, has a private beach. (☎807 35 79. Tent sites €16-25. Dorms €17.) After dark, a crowd gathers on the rooftop above **The English Inn,** C. Italia 57. (Open daily 9am-1am.) Ferries and hydrofoils depart for the Bay of Naples islands. **Linee Marittime Partenopee** (☎80 71 812) runs **ferries** (40min., 5 per day, €7.50) and **hydrofoils** (20min., 19 per day, €11) to Capri. The **tourist office,** L. de Maio 35, is just off P. Tasso, in the C. dei Forestieri compound. (☎081 807 40 33. Open M-Sa Apr.-Sept. 8:30am-6:30pm; Oct.-Mar. 8:30am-2pm and 4-6:15pm.) **Postal Code:** 80067.

CAPRI ☎081

Gem-like in both size and sparkle, glittering Capri has been a hot spot for the rich and famous for thousands of years: Augustus fell in love with the island in 29 BC. There are two towns on the island—**Capri** proper, near the ports, and the quaint **Anacapri,** on the hills. Visitors flock to the **Blue Grotto,** a sea cave where the water glows neon blue. (Short boat ride from Marina Grande €8.50. Tickets at Grotta Azzurra Travel Office, V. Roma 53. Tours until 5pm.) Buses departing from V. Roma make the trip up the mountain to Anacapri every 15min. until 1:40am; buses leave Anacapri for most tourist attractions. Away from the throngs of pricey Capri, Anacapri is home to budget hotels, lovely vistas, and mountain paths. Upstairs from P. Vittoria in Anacapri, **Villa San Michele** has lush gardens, ancient sculpture, and summer concerts. (Open daily 9am-6pm. €6.) Take the chairlift up **Monte Solaro** from P. Vittoria to see the Apennines and the mountains of Calabria. (Chairlift open Mar.-Oct. daily 9:30am-4:45pm. Round-trip €6.) The **Faraglioni,** three massive rocks, are accessible by a 1hr. walk. A steep 1½hr. hike leads to the ruins of Emperor Tiberius's **Villa Jovis.** The view from the **Cappella di Santa Maria del Soccorso,** built onto the villa, is unrivaled. (Open daily 9am-6pm. €2.)

Bussola di Hermes ❸, V. Traversa La Vigna 14, in Anacapri, has a friendly proprietor and is one of the best deals on the island. Call from P. Vittoria in Anacapri for pickup. (☎838 20 10; www.bussolahermes.com. Dorms €27-30; doubles €70-110. MC/V.) For more convenient access to the beach and the center of Capri, stay at **Vuotto Antonio ❸,** V. Campo di Teste 2. Take V. V. Emanuele out of P. Umberto, a left onto V. Camerelle, right onto V. Cerio, and left onto V. Campo di Teste. Housed in "Villa Margherita," simple, elegant rooms are decorated in majolica tiles. (☎837 02 30. Doubles €55-95. Cash only.) **Ristorante Il Cucciolo ❷,** V. La Fabbrica 52, in Anacapri, has fresh food, with huge *Let's Go* discounts. (☎83 71 917. *Bruschette* €3.50. *Primi* and *secondi*

SOLE OF CAPRI

Every day, shoemaker Antonio Viva sits on a stool outside his shop in Anacapri. His hands are always moving as he makes shoes and talks to passersby. There are many shoemakers on Capri, but Signor Viva is the only one with a personality big enough to make him, and not just his shoes, a tourist destination. With his two sons, Giancarlo and Antonio, Signor Viva does the same thing day after day as the world around him changes.

On Capri: My family has been on Capri for four generations, and I've been making shoes here for 50 years. There are so many people here now, I don't know what will happen to Capri. It's hard in Italy now. Not many jobs. People are working very hard.

On himself: People come here for me. The shoes are good, but they come to talk to me. It's like a museum when I'm here. People come and look. I am here, there, everywhere. Posters, billboards, TV. People take pictures with me. Viva is like Julia Roberts.

On selling shoes: If a poor man comes to me, I try to give him shoes cheaper. I can see he is not rich. I can see he is not a bad man. I work for everyone. Workers, presidents, everyone in the middle. Everyone needs shoes. If you sit and talk, I'll help you and make a deal.

(To visit Signor Viva, go to L'Arte del Sandalo Caprese, V. Orlandi 75 (☎081 837 35 83).)

€6-9.) The **supermarket,** V. G. Orlandi 299, in Anacapri, is well stocked. (Open M-Sa 8:30am-1:30pm and 5-8:30pm, Su 8:30am-noon.) At night, Italians, dressed to kill, come out for Capri's bars near **Piazza Umberto,** open late; younger crowds go to Anacapri.

Caremar (☎837 07 00) **ferries** run from Marina Grande to Naples (1¼hr., 3 per day, €7). LineaJet (☎837 08 19) runs **hydrofoils** to Naples (40-50min., 11 per day, €12) and Sorrento (25min., 15 per day, €10). Boats to other destinations run much less frequently; check at Marina Grande for information. The Capri **tourist office** (☎837 06 34; www.capritourism.com) sits at the end of Marina Grande; in Anacapri, it's at V. Orlandi 59 (☎837 15 24); make a right from the bus stop. (Capri open June-Sept. daily 9am-1pm and 3:30-6:45pm; Anacapri open M-Sa 9am-3pm; both reduced hours Oct.-May.) **Postal Codes:** 80073 (Capri); 80021 (Anacapri).

ISCHIA ☎081

Travelers have sought out Ischia since ancient times (gaining it mention in both *The Iliad* and *The Aeneid*). The island (pop. 60,000) was once an active volcano, and hot springs, ruins, and lemon groves create an atmosphere that is downright idyllic. SEPSA **buses** CS, CD, and #1 (every 15-30min.) depart from V. Iasolino at V. B. Cossa, stopping at: **Ischia Porto,** the major port town and site of the island's most active nightlife, **Casamicciola Terme** and **Lacco Ameno,** homes of legendary thermal waters, and **Forio,** the largest town on the island. The **Ring Hostel ❷,** V. Gaetano Morgera 66, in Forio, is in a 19th-century convent. (☎98 75 46; www.ringhostel.com. 12-bed dorms €17; singles €30). **Pensione Di Lustro ❹,** V. Filippo di Lustro 9, is in a gorgeous old building near the beach. (☎99 71 63; www.pensionedilustro.com. €40-60 per person. AmEx/MC/V.) **Ristorante Emiddio ❸,** V. Porto 30, is a family-run restaurant that features locally caught fish. (*Primi* €6-8. *Secondi* €7-16. Cover €1. Open daily noon-3pm and 7pm-midnight. MC/V.) Caremar **ferries** (☎98 48 18; www.caremar.it) head to Naples (1½hr., 8 per day, €10.50). Alilauro (☎99 18 88) runs **hydrofoils** to Capri (1 per day, €13) and Sorrento (1 per day, €15). The **tourist office** is on V. Iasolino. (☎507 42 31. Open M-Sa 9am-2pm and 3-8pm.) **Postal Code:** 80077.

ITALY

AMALFI COAST ☎089

It happens almost imperceptibly: after the exhausting tumult of Naples and the compact grit of Sorrento, the highway narrows to a two-lane, coastal road, and the hazy horizon becomes brightened with lemon orchards and bright village pastels. Suddenly, the Amalfi Coast hits the bloodstream and the euphoria kicks in.

TRANSPORTATION. Trains run to Salerno from Naples (45min., 40 per day, €5-10) and Rome (2½-3hr., 22 per day, €21-33). SITA buses (☎26 66 04) connect Salerno to Amalfi (1¼hr., 20 per day, €1.80). From Amalfi, buses also go to Positano (40min., 25 per day, €1.30) and Sorrento (1¼hr., 29 per day, €2). Travelmar (☎87 29 50) runs **hydrofoils** from Amalfi to Positano (25min., 7 per day, €5) and Salerno (35min., 6 per day €4), and from Salerno to Positano (1¼hr., 6 per day €6).

AMALFI AND ATRANI. Jagged rocks of the Sorrentine Peninsula, azure waters of the Tyrrhenian, and lemon groves (and the plump lemons they produce) define Amalfi. P. del Duomo, at the center, has the elegant 9th-century **Duomo di Sant'Andrea** and the **Fontana di Sant'Andrea,** a marble nude fountain, nearby. The hostel **A'Scalinatella ❶,** P. Umberto 6, runs dorms, private rooms, and camping all over Amalfi as well as Atrani. (☎87 19 30; www.hostelscalinatella.com. Tent sites €5 per person. Dorms €21; doubles €50-60, with bath €73-83. Cash only.) Amalfi's *paninoteche* (sandwich shops) suit a tight budget. The **AAST Tourist Office** is at C.

Repubblica Marinara 27. The beach town Atrani is 750m down the coast. The 4hr. **Path of the Gods,** hike follows the coast from **Bomerano** to **Positano.** The hike from Atrani to **Ravello** (1½-2hr.) runs through lemon groves and green cliff valleys. **Postal Code:** 84011.

RAVELLO. Perched atop cliffs, Ravello has been claimed by artists and intellectuals. The Moorish cloister and gardens of **Villa Rufolo,** off P. del Duomo, inspired Boccaccio's masterwork *Decameron* as well as Wagner's opera *Parsifal.* (Open daily 9am-8pm. €5.) The villa puts on a summer concert series in the gardens; tickets are sold at the Ravello Festival box office, V. Roma 10-12 (☎85 84 22; www.ravellofestival.com). Ravello's **duomo** has bronze doors; follow V. S. Francesco out of P. Duomo to the impressive **Villa Cimbrone,** whose floral walkways hide temples, grottoes, and views. (Open daily 9am-sunset. €5.) A bit of a walk, **Hotel Villa Amore ❹,** V. dei Fusco 4, has 12 tidy rooms and a garden. Follow V. S. Francesco out of P. Duomo toward Villa Cimbrone, and take a left on V. dei Fusco. (☎/fax 85 71 35. Breakfast included. Singles €56; doubles €80-95. MC/V.) **Postal Code:** 84010.

POSITANO. Today, Positano's most frequent visitors are the wealthy few who can afford the pricey Positanese lifestyle, but the town still has its charms for the budget traveler. To see the large *pertusione* (hole) piercing the mountain **Montepertuso,** hike 45min. uphill or take the bus from P. dei Mulini. The three **Isole dei Galli,** islands peeking out of the waters off Positano's coast, were allegedly home to Homer's mythical Sirens. The beach at **Fornillo** is a serene, secluded alternative to **Spaggia Grande,** the area's main beach. **Ostello Brikette ❷,** V. Marconi 358, with two large terraces and free wireless Internet, is accessible by the orange Interno bus or SITA bus; exit at the Chiesa Nuova stop and walk 100m to the left of Bar Internazionale. (☎87 58 57. Dorms €22-25; doubles €65-100. MC/V.) Try a *granita* at the stand in P. dei Mulini. The simple *pasta alla norma* (€8) at **Da Gabrisa,** Vle. Pasitea 219, is a treat. (*Primi* and *secondi* €6-15.) The four small bars on the beach at Fornillo serve simple, fresh food. The **tourist office,** V. del Saraceno 4, is below the *duomo.* (☎87 50 67. Open M-Sa 8am-2pm and 3-8pm; low season reduced hours.) **Postal Code:** 84017.

WELL, THE WATER IS (ALMOST) FREE...

Though it was the Greeks who believed that Ischia's thermal springs had supernatural powers, it was the Romans who developed a penchant for their luxury. Historically used as a cure for weak spirits, a pre-antibiotic remedy for war wounds, and plumbing for Roman public baths, the thermal springs in Ischia have erupted into a major destination for the rich, famous, and ailing.

While their growing popularity has made the number of affordable spas scarce, there's still hope for those without VIP credentials. **'O Vagnitiello,** a hotel and spa, is one of the world's finest destinations for mud wallowing, seaweed wrapping, and hot-tub soaking, yet it's also accessible for budget travelers. The least expensive spa on the island, 'O Vagnitiello has six different pools of thermal water, saunas, and a swimming area filled with inner tubes. Along the beach, umbrellas line the gardened terraces overlooking the sea, while dense forests shade the grounds. A whole day of "therapy" costs only €10, and for those who wish to extend their stay, one night—including breakfast and access to the baths—costs only €50.

(To reach the spa, take the CD, CS, or #1 bus from the port toward Casamicciola. Ask driver for 'O Vagnitiello stop, and follow the narrow path uphill. ☎081 99 39 75; www.vagnitiello.it.)

SICILY (SICILIA)

An island of contradictions, Sicily has a culture that owes its complexity to Phoenicians, Greeks, Romans, Arabs, and Normans, all of whom invaded and left their mark. Ancient Greeks lauded the golden island as the second home of the gods; now, eager tourists seek it as the home of *The Godfather.* While the *Cosa Nostra* remains a presence in Sicily, it's decreasingly powerful.

TRANSPORTATION

From southern Italy, take a **train** to Reggio di Calabria, then a Trenitalia **hydrofoil** (25min., 7-14 per day, €2.80) to Messina, Sicily's transport hub. **Buses** (☎090 77 19 14) serve destinations on the island and the mainland. **Trains** head to Messina (via ferry) from Rome (9hr., 6 per day, €43), then to Palermo (3½hr., 22 per day, €11), Syracuse (3½hr., 16 per day, €8.75), and Taormina (40min., 27 per day, €15).

PALERMO ☎091

From twisting streets lined with ancient ruins to the shrinking shadow of organized crime, gritty Palermo (pop. 680,000) is a city whose recent history fills in the shade and texture of its rich cultural heritage. Operas and ballets are performed year-round at the Neoclassical **Teatro Massimo,** where the climactic opera scene of *The Godfather: Part III* was filmed. Walk up V. Maqueda from Quattro Canti; it's on P. Verdi. (Open for 20min. tours every 30min. Tu-Su 10am-3pm. €3.) From Quattro Canti, take a left on V. Vittorio Emanuele and another one just before P. Indipendenza to get to the **Cappella Palatina,** full of incredible golden mosaics, in **Palazzo dei Normanni.** (Open M-Sa 8:30am-noon and 2-5pm, Su 8:30am-12:30pm. Tu-Th €4; M and F-Su €6, with entrance to entire palace.) At the haunting **Cappuccini Catacombs,** P. Cappuccini 1, 8000 corpses line the underground tunnels. Take bus #109 from Stazione Centrale to P. Indipendenza, then transfer to bus #327. (Open daily 9am-noon and 3-5:30pm. €1.50.) For the sake of comfort and, more importantly, safety, plan to spend a bit more on accommodations in Palermo. Homey **Hotel Regina ❷,** C. Vittorio Emanuele 316, is near the intersection of V. Maqueda and C. V. Emanuele. Triple-check your reservation before arriving. (☎61 14 216;. Singles €25; doubles €44-54; triples €66-75. AmEx/MC/V.) The best restaurants are between Teatro Massimo and the Politeama. **Trains** leave Stazione Centrale in P. Giulio Cesare, at the southern terminus of V. Roma and V. Maqueda, for Rome (12hr.; 6 per day; €45, with bunk €70). All **bus** lines run from V. Balsamo, next to the train station. Pick up a metro and bus map from an **AMAT** or **metro** information booth. Buses #101 and 102 (€1 for 2hr.) circle the large downtown area. To reach the **tourist office,** P. Castelnuovo 34, at the west end of the *piazza,* take a bus from the station to P. Politeama, at the end of V. Maqueda. (☎60 58 351; www.palermotourism.com. Open M-F 8:30am-2pm and 2:30-6pm.) **Postal Code:** 90100.

SYRACUSE (SIRACUSA) ☎0931

With the glory of its Grecian golden days behind it, the modern city of Syracuse (pop. 121,000) takes pride in its ruins and the architectural beauty of its offshore island, Ortigia. Syracuse's one-time role as a Mediterranean superpower is still evident in the **Archaeological Park.** Aeschylus premiered his *Persians* before 15,000 spectators in the park's enormous **Greek theater.** (Open daily 9am-2hr. before sunset; low season 9am-3pm. €6.) Across from the tourist office on V. S. Giovanni are the **Catacomba di San Giovanni,** 20,000 now-empty tombs carved into the remains of a Greek aqueduct. (Open Tu-Su 9:30am-12:30pm and 2:30-5:30pm. Mandatory guided tour every 15-20min. €5.) More ruins lie over the Ponte Umbertino on **Orti-**

gia, the serene island on which the attacking Greeks first landed. The ruined **Temple of Apollo** has a few columns still standing, but those at the **Temple of Diana** are much more impressive. For those who prefer tans to temples, take bus #21 or 22 to **Fontane Bianche,** a glitzy beach with plenty of discos. **Pensione Bel Sit ❷,** V. Oglio 5, 5th fl., has centrally located rooms with airy windows. (☎60 245; fax 46 28 82. Singles €20; doubles €34. Cash only.) On the mainland, C. Umberto links Ponte Umbertino to the train station, passing through P. Marconi, from which C. Gelone extends through town to the Archaeological Park. **Trains** leave V. Francesco Crispi for Messina (3hr., 19 per day, €8.75) and Rome (10-13hr., 6 per day, €38). To get from the train station to the **tourist office,** V. S. Sebastiano 45, take V. F. Crispi to C. Gelone, turn right on V. Teocrito, then left on V. S. Sebastiano. (☎48 12 32. Open M-F 8:30am-1:30pm and 3:30-6:30pm, Sa 9am-1pm and 3:30-6:30pm, Su 9am-1pm; low season reduced hours.) **Postal Code:** 96100.

TAORMINA ☎0942

Legend has it that Neptune wrecked a Greek boat off the eastern coast of Sicily in the 8th century BC, and the sole survivor, inspired by the scenery on shore, founded Taormina. As historians tell it, the Carthaginians founded Tauromenium at the turn of the 4th century BC only to have it wrested away by the Greek tyrant Dionysius. Taormina's Greek roots are apparent in its best-preserved treasure, the **Greek theater.** (Open daily 9am until 1hr. before sunset. €6.) The 5000-seat theater offers unrivaled views of Mt. Etna and hosts the annual ☒**Taormina Arte** summer concert, theater, and dance series. (www.taormina-arte.com. Box office in P. V. Emanuele.) The 13th-century **duomo** was rebuilt during the Renaissance. (Hours vary; inquire at Museo Sacra next door.) From the intersection of C. Umberto and V. L. Pirandello, take V. C. Patrizio to V. Cappuccini; when it forks, veer right onto V. Fontana Vecchia and follow the signs to ☒**Taormina's Odyssey Youth Hostel ❷,** which offers clean rooms and a social atmosphere that make it worth the hike. (☎24 533. Breakfast included. Dorms €18; doubles €60. Cash only.) An **SMA** supermarket is at V. Apollo Arcageta 21, at the end of C. Umberto, near the post office. (Open July-Aug. M-Sa 8:30am-9:30pm; Sept.-June M-Sa 8:30am-1pm and 4:40-8:30pm.) **Trains** run to Messina (1hr., 25 per day, €3.05) and Syracuse (2hr., 11 per day, €10). The **tourist office** is in the courtyard of Palazzo Corvaja, off C. Umberto across from P. V. Emanuele. (☎23 243; www.gate2taormina.com. Open daily 9am-2pm and 4-7pm.) **Postal Code:** 98039.

AEOLIAN ISLANDS (ISOLE EOLIE) ☎090

Le Perle del Mare (Pearls of the Sea) are what inhabitants deem the Aeolian islands. Rugged shores, pristine landscapes, ruins, volcanoes, and mud baths pretty much confirm the residents' word choice. Prices rise steeply in the summer.

🄴 TRANSPORTATION. The archipelago is off the Sicilian coast, north of **Milazzo,** the principal and least expensive departure point. Trains run from Milazzo to Messina (30min., 21 per day, €2.75) and Palermo (3hr., 13 per day, €9.20). An orange AST **bus** runs from Milazzo's train station to the port (10min., 2 per hr., €0.90). Siremar (☎928 32 42) and Navigazione Generale Italiana (NGI; ☎928 40 91) **ferries** depart for Lipari (2hr., 3 per day, €6.60) and Vulcano (1½hr., 3 per day, €6.30). Ticket offices are on V. dei Mille in Milazzo.

🄿 LIPARI. Lipari, the largest and most developed of the islands, is renowned for its beaches. To reach the beaches of **Spiaggia Bianca** and **Porticello,** take the Lipari-Cavedi **bus** a few kilometers to **Canneto.** Lipari's best sights—aside from its beaches—are all in the *castello* on the hill, where a **fortress** with ancient Greek foundations dwarfs the surrounding town. In the vicinity is the **Museo Archeological Eoliano,** whose collection includes galleries of Greek and Sicilian pottery. (Open daily May-Oct. 9am-1pm and 3-7pm; Nov.-Apr. reduced hours. €6.) **Pensione Enzo il Negro ❹,** V. Garibaldi 29, 3rd fl., is 20m up V. Garibaldi from the hydrofoil dock and has harbor views. (☎98 13 163. Singles €60-70; doubles €90-130. AmEx/MC/V.) Camp at **Baia Unci ❶,** V. Marina Garibaldi 2, at the entrance to the hamlet of Canneto, 2km from Lipari. (☎981 19 09. Open mid-Mar. to mid-Oct. Tent sites €8-14. Cash only.) Get great sandwiches (€4) at **Da Gilberto e Vera ❶,** V. Marina Garibaldi 22-24. (Open daily Mar.-Oct. 7am-4am; Nov.-Feb. 7am-2am. AmEx/MC/V.) The **tourist office,** C. V. Emanuele 202, is near the dock. (☎988 00 95; www.aasteolie.191.it. Open July-Aug. M-F 8am-2pm and 4:30-9:30pm, Sa 8am-2pm and 4-9pm; Sept.-June M-F 8am-2pm and 4:30-9:30pm.) **Postal Code:** 98050.

VULCANO. Black beaches, bubbling seas, and sulfuric mud spas attract visitors from around the world. A steep 1hr. **hike** to the inactive **Gran Cratere** (Grand Crater), the summit of Fossa di Volcane, snakes among the volcano's *fumaroli* (noxious emissions). On a clear day, you can see all the other islands from the top. The allegedly therapeutic **Laghetto di Fanghi** (mud pool) is up V. Provinciale from the port. Step into the waters of the **acquacalda,** where volcanic outlets make the shoreline bubble, or tan on the black sands of **Sabbie Nere** (follow signs off V. Ponente). To get to Vulcano, take the **hydrofoil** from the port at Lipari (10min., 17 per day, €4.50). Ferries and hydrofoils dock at **Porto di Levante,** on the east side of **Vulcanello,** the youngest volcano. V. Provinciale heads to Fossa di Vulcane from the port. The **tourist office** is at V. Provinciale 41 (☎985 20 28. Open Aug. daily 8am-1:30pm and 3-5pm) or get info at the Lipari office. **Postal Code:** 98050.

ITALY

STROMBOLI. If you find luscious beaches and hot springs a bit tame, a visit to Stromboli's active **volcano,** which spews orange lava and molten rock every 10min., will quench your thirst for adventure. Hiking the volcano on your own is illegal and dangerous, but **Magmatrek,** on V. V. Emanuele, offers tours, which also should be taken at your own risk. Don't wear contact lenses, as the wind sweeps ash and dust everywhere. (☎/fax 986 57 68. Helmets provided. Reserve 2-3 days ahead. €25.) From the main road, walk uphill to P. S. Vincenzo and follow the side street next to the church to reach **Casa del Sole ❶,** on V. Cincotta, the best value in town. (☎/fax 98 60 17. Open Mar.-Oct. Dorms €13-27; doubles €30-70. Prices vary by season. Cash only.) From July to September, you won't find a room without a reservation; your best bet may be one of the non-reservable *affittacamere.* Siremar (☎98 60 16) runs **ferries** and **hydrofoils** between Stromboli and the other Aeolian Islands, Milazzo, and Reggio Calabria. **Postal Code:** 98050.

SARDINIA (SARDEGNA)

An old Sardinian legend says that when God finished making the world, He had a handful of dirt left over, which He took, threw into the Mediterranean, stepped on, and—behold—created the island of Sardinia. African, Spanish, and Italian influences have steeped its architecture, language, and cuisine.

TRANSPORTATION

Alitalia **flights** link Alghero, Cagliari, and Olbia to major Italian cities, and Ryanair and easyJet serve Sardinia's airports as well. Tirrenia **ferries** (☎081 317 29 99; www.tirrenia.it) run to Olbia from Civitavecchia, north of Rome (5-7hr., 1-2 per day, €20-91), and Genoa (10hr., 5 per week, from €24-50), and to Cagliari from Civitavecchia (14½hr., 1 per day, €29-44), Naples (16hr., 1-2 per week, €29-44), and Palermo (11½hr., 1 per week, €28-42). **Trains** run from Cagliari to Olbia (4hr., 1 per day, €13) and Oristano (1hr., 23 per day, €4.80) and to Sassari (4hr., 5 per day, €13). From Sassari, trains run to Alghero (1hr., 15 per day, €2.20). **Buses** connect Cagliari to Oristano (1½hr., 2 per day); buses run from Olbia (14 per day, €2.80) and Sassari (4 per day) to Palau, where ferries access La Maddalena.

CAGLIARI ☎070

Cagliari combines the bustle and energy of a modern city with the endearing rural atmosphere of the rest of the island. The **Roman amphitheater** comes alive for the **arts festival** in July and August. Take bus P, PF, or PQ to **Il Poetto** beach (20min., €0.77) whose sand is brown but whose crystal-clear waters are beautiful regardless. **Hotel aer Bundes Jack ❹,** is at **V.** Roma 75 and **B&B Vittoria ❸,** is on the other half of the floor. Cross V. Roma from the train or ARST station and turn right. The B&B's rooms are cheaper but as lovely as the hotel's. (☎/fax 66 79 70; hotel.aerbundesjack@libero.it. ☎640 4026; www.bbvittoria.com. Breakfast €6. Check-in on 3rd fl. Singles €45, with bath €52-55; doubles €72/84. Cash only.) The **tourist office** is in P. Matteotti. (☎66 92 55. Open M-Sa 8:30am-1:30pm.) **Postal Code:** 09100.

ALGHERO ☎079

Vineyards, ruins, and horseback rides are a short trip from Alghero's parks and palms. Between massive cliffs, 632 steps plunge down at **Grotte di Nettuno,** a 70-million-year-old, stalactite-filled cavern. Take the bus (50min., 3 per day, round-trip €2) or a boat (2½hr. round-trip; 3-8 per day; round-trip €13, includes tour but not €10 cave entrance). (Cave open daily Apr.-Sept. 9am-7pm; Oct. 10am-4pm; Nov.-Mar. 9am-1pm. €10.) Take bus AF from the port to Fertilia to reach the **Hotel San Francesco ❹,** V. Ambrogio Machin 2/4. (☎98 03 30. Breakfast included. Singles €58; doubles €90. MC/V.) Toward Fertilia, 2km from Alghero, **La Mariposa ❶** campground, V. Lido 22, has a restaurant, bar, bikes, diving excursions, and beach access. (☎95 03 60. Hot showers €0.50. Mar.-Oct. tent sites €4-13, €9-10.50 per person; 4-person bungalows €56-75. Apr.-June tents and cars free. AmEx/MC/V.) The **tourist office,** P. Porta Terra 9, is at the bus stop. (☎97 90 5. Open Apr.-Oct. M-Sa 8am-8pm, Su 10am-1pm; Nov.-Mar. M-Sa 8am-8pm.) **Postal Code:** 07041.

LA MADDALENA ARCHIPELAGO ☎078

La Maddalena, now a national park, was once part of a land bridge that connected Corsica and Sardinia. The nearby island of **Razzoli** has magnificent swimming holes and is the gateway to all of the other islands. **Marinella IV** (☎33 92 30 28 42; www.marinellagite.it) runs tour boats from the town of Palau on Sardinia. They make two or three 2hr. stops at beaches. (€30-35; boats leave at 10 or 11am and return between 5 and 6pm. Purchase tickets 1 day ahead.) **Panoramica Dei Comi** is a paved road circling the island with sea views and beaches for sunbathing. **Hotel Arcipelago ❹,** V. Indipendenza 2, is a 20min. walk from the *centro*. From P. Umberto, follow V. Mirabello along the water until the intersection with the stoplight, turn left, then take your first right on V. Indipendenza. Take the first left on a branch of the main road; the hotel is around the corner from the grocery store. (☎72 73 28. Breakfast included. Reservation required July-Aug. Singles €55; doubles €82; triples €110. V.) **Saremar ferries** run from Palau (15min., 3 per hr., round-trip €2.90). A **map** of La Maddelena is on the Palau map; pick it up before boarding the ferry in Palau. **Postal Code:** 07024.

LATVIA (LATVIJA)

At the Baltic crossroads, Latvia has been caught in international political struggles for hundreds of years. The country has been conquered and reconquered so many times that this year will only be Latvia's 16th year of independence. National pride, however, abounds—from patriotically renamed streets to a rediscovery of native holidays to the colors of the flag (Latvian red and white). Rīga, Latvia's largest city, lures international investors, while the rest of the country is a provincial expanse of green pastures, tall birches, and quiet towns.

DISCOVER LATVIA: SUGGESTED ITINERARIES

THREE DAYS. Settle into **Rīga** (p. 678) to enjoy stunning **Art Nouveau** architecture, cafe culture, and the Baltics's best music and performing arts scene. Daytrip to **Cēsis Castle** for great views.

ONE WEEK. After four days in **Rīga,** head to **Cēsis** (3 days; p. 682) to enjoy **Cēsis Castle** and the wilds of **Gaujas Valley National Park.**

ESSENTIALS

FACTS AND FIGURES

Official Name: Republic of Latvia.

Capital: Rīga.

Major Cities: Daugavpils, Liepaja.

Population: 2,307,000 (59% Latvian, 29% Russian, 4% Belarusian, 3% Polish, 3% Ukrainian, 2% other).

Land Area: 64,589 sq. km.

Time Zone: GMT +2.

Language: Latvian.

Religions: Lutheran (55%), Roman Catholic (19%), Russian Orthodox (9%), Jewish (0.5%), other (16.5%).

WHEN TO GO

Latvia is wet year-round, with cold, snowy winters, and short, rainy summers. Tourism peaks in July and August; if you'd rather not experience Rīga in the company of throngs of British stag parties (bachelor-party-type outings), late spring or early fall is the best time to visit. Much of the coast is untouristed even in summer.

DOCUMENTS AND FORMALITIES

EMBASSIES. Embassies of other countries are in **Rīga** (p. 678). Latvia's embassies abroad include: **Australia,** 2 Mackennel St., East Ivanhoe, Victoria, 3079; P.O. Box 23 Kew, VIC, 3101 (☎3 9499 6920); **Canada,** 280 Albert St., Ste. 300 Ottawa, ON, K1R 5G8 (☎613-238-6014); **Ireland,** Ballyedmonduff Rd., Kilternan, Co. Dublin (☎01 295 41 82); **UK,** 45 Nottingham Pl., London, W1M 3FE (☎7312 0040); **US,** 2306 Massachusetts Ave., NW, Washington, D.C., 20008 (☎202-328-2840; www.latvia-usa.org).

VISA AND ENTRY INFORMATION. Citizens of Australia, Canada, New Zealand, the UK, and the US do not need a visa for stays of up to 90 days. If you are staying longer, you will need a temporary residency permit. For special visas and residency permits, consult the Office of Citizenship and Migration Affairs, Alunāna Str. 1, Rīga, Latvia (☎721 9656; www.pmlp.gov.lv).

TOURIST SERVICES AND MONEY

ENTRANCE REQUIREMENTS

Passport: Required of all travelers.
Visa: Not required for stays of up to 90 days of citizens of Australia, Canada, Ireland, New Zealand, the UK, and the US.
Letter of Invitation: Not required of citizens of Australia, Canada, Ireland, New Zealand, the UK, and the US.
Inoculations: None required. Recommended up-to-date on DTaP (diphtheria, tetanus, and pertussis), hepatitis A, hepatitis B, MMR (measles, mumps, and rubella), polio booster, and typhoid.
Work Permit: Required of all foreigners planning to work in Latvia.
Driving Permit: Required of all those planning to drive in Latvia.

TOURIST OFFICES. Look for the green "i" marking official **tourist offices,** which are rather scarce. In Rīga, employees of such establishments will speak fluent English, but elsewhere, they may not. Private tourist offices such as **Patricia** (p. 679) are much more helpful.

MONEY. The Latvian currency unit is the **lats,** plural **lati** (1Ls=100 santîmi). **Inflation** averages around 2% per year. There are many MC/V **ATMs** in Rīga, and at least one or two in larger towns. Larger businesses, restaurants, and hotels catering to Westerners accept **MasterCard** and **Visa. Traveler's checks** are more difficult to use, but both AmEx and Thomas Cook checks can be converted in Rīga. It's often difficult to exchange non-Baltic currencies other than US dollars or euro.

HEALTH AND SAFETY

Water in Latvia is generally safe; however, as a precaution, drink bottled water or boil tap water for 10min. before drinking. **Medical facilities** do not meet Western standards. **Pharmacies** carry bandages, condoms, and tampons. **Restrooms** are marked with an upward-pointing triangle for women, downward for men.

LATI		
	AUS$1 = 0.41LS	1LS = AUS$2.40
	CDN$1 = 0.50LS	1LS = CDN$2.01
	EUR€1 = 0.70LS	1LS = EUR€1.42
	NZ$1 = 0.35LS	1LS = NZ$2.86
	UK£1 = 1.03LS	1LS = UK£0.97
	US$1 = 0.55LS	1LS = US$1.82

Foreigners in Rīga may be targets for petty crime. **Pickpocketing** is a problem, especially in crowded areas. At night, beware of drunken crowds around bars. Both men and women should avoid walking alone at night. *"Ej prom"* (EY prawm) means "go away"; *"Lasies prom"* (LAH-see-oos PRAWM) says it more offensively; and *"Lasies lapās"* (LAH-see-oos LAH-pahs; "go to the leaves") is even more rude. You are more likely to find help in English from your **consulate** than from the police. **Women** may be verbally hassled, especially if traveling alone, but there is generally no physical threat. **Minorities** in Latvia are rare; they receive stares but generally experience little discrimination. **Homosexuality** is legal, but public displays may result in violence. Women walk down the street holding hands, but this is strictly a sign of friendship. Expect less tolerance outside Rīga. The Latvian Gay and Lesbian Hotline offers help for anyone dealing with **GBLT** issues (☎959 2229).

EMERGENCY	**Police:** ☎02. **Ambulance:** ☎03. **Fire:** ☎01.

TRANSPORTATION

BY PLANE. Airlines flying to Latvia use the Rīga airport **(RIX). Air Baltic, SAS, Finnair, Lufthansa,** and others make the hop to Rīga from their hubs.

BY TRAIN, BUS, AND FERRY. Trains and long-distance buses link Latvia to the major Eastern European capitals. Trains are cheap and efficient, but stations aren't well marked, so make sure to have a map handy. The commuter rail system renders the entire country a suburb of Rīga. Domestic buses are quicker than trains, but beware of the standing-room-only long-distance jaunt. Ferries go to Kiel and Lübeck (GER), and Stockholm (SWE), but are slow and expensive.

BY CAR. Road conditions in Latvia are improving after years of deterioration. For more info, consult the **Latvian State Roads** (www.lad.lv). Taxi stands in front of hotels charge higher rates. Let's Go does not recommend hitchhiking, but it is common. Drivers may ask for a fee comparable to bus fares.

KEEPING IN TOUCH

PHONE CODES	**Country code:** 371. **International dialing prefix:** 00. For more information on how to place international calls, see inside back cover. Rīga's phone code is ☎2 for all 6-digit numbers; there is no phone code for 7-digit numbers. Info: ☎800 8008. Latvian operator: ☎116. International operator: ☎115. Directory services: ☎118 or 722 2222.

TELEPHONE AND INTERNET. Pay phones take **cards** (2, 3, or 5Ls denominations), sold at post offices, telephone offices, kiosks, and state stores. To call abroad from an analog phone, dial 1, then 00, then the country code. If it's digital, dial 00, then the country code. Phone offices and *Rīga in Your Pocket* have the latest updates on the phone system. International access codes include **AT&T Direct** (☎800 2288) and **MCI WorldPhone** (☎800 8888). Internet is readily available in Rīga but rarer elsewhere; it generally costs 0.5Ls per hour.

MAIL. Ask for *gaisa pastu* to send by **airmail.** The rate for a letter to Europe is 0.30Ls, for a postcard 0.20Ls; to anywhere else 0.40Ls/0.30Ls. Mail can be received general delivery through *Poste Restante.* Address envelopes: First name LAST NAME, *POSTE RESTANTE*, post office address, Postal Code, city, LATVIA.

LANGUAGE. Drawing from Estonian, German, Russian, and Swedish, **Latvian** is one of two languages in the Baltic language group. Life in Latvia, however, is bilingual. **Russian** is common in Rīga; though still spoken in the country, its popularity is waning. Some young Latvians know **English;** the older set knows some **German.**

ACCOMMODATIONS AND CAMPING

LATVIA	❶	❷	❸	❹	❺
ACCOMMODATIONS	under 8Ls	8-15Ls	15-20Ls	20-25Ls	over 25Ls

Beware the raucous European parties that invade hostels, especially on summer weekends. Contact the **Latvian Youth Hostel Association,** 17-2 Siguldas pr., Rīga, 1014 (☎921 8560; www.hostellinglatvia.com), for more info. In summer, **college dormitories** are often the cheapest option. Rīga's array of **hotels** satisfy any budget. Most small towns outside the capital have only one hotel (if any) in the budget range; expect to pay 3-15Ls per night. **Camping** isn't very popular. Campgrounds exist in the countryside; camping beyond marked areas is prohibited.

FOOD AND DRINK

LATVIA	❶	❷	❸	❹	❺
FOOD	under 2Ls	2-4Ls	4-6Ls	6-7Ls	over 7Ls

Latvian food is heavy, starchy, and—not coincidentally—delicious. Tasty specialties include *maizes zupa* (soup made from cornbread, currants, and cream), and the warming *Rīgas* (or *Melnais*) *balzams*, a black liquor. Dark rye bread is a staple. Try *speķa rauši*, a warm pastry, or *biezpienmaize*, bread with sweet curds. Regional Latvian beers are great, particularly *Porteris* from the Aldaris brewery.

HOLIDAYS AND FESTIVALS

Holidays: New Year's Day (Jan. 1); Good Friday (Apr. 6); Easter Holiday (Apr. 8); Labor Day (May 1); Ligo Day (June 23); St. John's Day (June 24); Independence Day (Nov. 18); Boxing Day (Dec. 26); New Year's Eve (Dec. 31).

Festivals: Gadatirgus is an annual festival of arts and crafts, held the first weekend in June. Mid-summer celebrations (June 21-22) involve strewing grass around the house and feasting in the countryside. In July, the Rīga Summer Festival presents chamber and classical music around the city. The Arsenals film festival hits Rīga in September.

BEYOND TOURISM

American Field Service (AFS), 17th fl., 71 W. 23rd St., New York, NY, 10010, US (☎212-807-8686; www.afs.org). Homestay exchange programs for high-school students in Eastern Europe, including Latvia. Community service programs for young adults 18+. Teaching programs for current and retired teachers. Financial aid available.

The Baltic Times (☎371 722 9978; www.baltictimes.com). English-language newspaper with classified ads for short and long-term employment.

RĪGA ☎7

Rīga (pop. 750,000) is the center of Latvia's cultural and economic life, and fuses a fascinating mix of Russian and Latvian influences. The recent boom in tourism has transformed large sections of the city, particularly the Old Town, but it's not hard to find unspoiled sections off the main drags. The city's calendar is filled with music, theater, and opera festivals, and visitors can enjoy its spectacular Art Nouveau architecture any time of year. Soviet Realist sculptures still dot the streets between museums and medieval churches.

TRANSPORTATION

Flights: Lidosta Rīga (**RIX;** ☎720 70 09; www.riga-airport.com), 8km southwest of Vecrīga. Take bus #22 from Janvara iela 13 (30min., every 10-30min., 0.20-0.25Ls). **Air Baltic** (☎720 77 77; www.airbaltic.com) flies cheaply to many European cities.

Trains: Centrālā Stacija (Central Station), Stacijas laukums (☎723 31 13; www.ldz.lv), next to the bus station south of the Old Town. International tickets are sold at counters 1-6 and 24; destinations include **Moscow, RUS** (17hr., 2 per day, 16Ls); **St. Petersburg, RUS** (14hr., 1 per day, 9Ls); and **Vilnius, LIT** (5hr., 1 per day, 10-17Ls).

Buses: Autoosta, Prāgas 1 (☎900 00 09; www.autoosta.lv), 100m from the train station, across the canal from the Central Market. To: **Kaunas, LIT** (4½-5½hr., 5-10 per day, 7-8.30Ls); **Minsk, BLR** (10-12hr., 1-5 per day, 14-15Ls); **Tallinn, EST** (4-6hr., 8 per day, 7-10Ls); **Vilnius, LIT** (5-6hr., 4-6 per day, 7-9Ls).

ORIENTATION AND PRACTICAL INFORMATION

The city is divided in half by **Brīvības bulvāris,** which leads from the outskirts of town to the **Freedom Monument** in the center, becomes **Kaļķu iela,** and passes through **Vecrīga** (Old Rīga). To reach Vecrīga from the train station, turn left on **Marijas iela** and then right on any of the small streets beyond the canal.

Tourist Office: Rātslaukums 6 (☎703 43 77; www.rigatourism.com), in the town square, next to the House of the Blackheads. Sells maps (up to 2Ls), arranges walking and bus tours (6-9Ls), books accommodation for 10% commission, and provides advice and brochures, including *Rīga in Your Pocket* (1.20Ls). Open daily in summer 9am-7pm; low season 10am-7pm. AmEx/MC/V.

Embassies and Consulates: Australia, Alberta iela 13 (☎733 63 83; acr@latnet.lv). Open Tu 10am-noon, Th 3-5pm. **Canada,** Baznīcas 20/22 (☎781 39 45; riga@dfait-maeci.gc.ca). Open M-F 9am-5:30pm. **Ireland,** Brīvības bul. 54 (☎702 52 22; fax 702 52 23). Entrance on Blaumana. Open M-Tu and Th-F 10am-noon. **UK,** Alunāna iela 5 (☎777 47 00; www.britain.lv). Open M-F 9am-5pm. **US,** Raiņa bul. 7 (☎703 62 00; www.usembassy.lv). Open M-Tu and Th 9-11:30am.

Currency Exchange: At any of the **Valutos Maiņa** kiosks. **Unibanka,** Pils iela 23, gives MC/V cash advances and cashes both **AmEx** and **Thomas Cook traveler's checks** without commission. Open M-F 9am-5pm.

24hr. Pharmacy: Vecpilsētas Aptieka, Audeju 20 (☎721 33 40).

Internet Access: Elik, Kaļķu iela 11 (☎722 70 79; www.elikkafe.lv), in the center of Vecrīga; branch at Merķeļa iela 1 (☎722 11 75). 3Ls per day. Open 24hr. Cash only.

Post Office: Stacijas laukumā 1 (☎701 88 04; www.pasts.lv/en), near the train station. *Poste Restante* at window #9. Open M-F 7am-8pm, Sa 8am-6pm, Su 8am-4pm. Another Branch at Brīvības bul. 19. Address mail to be held: First name LAST NAME, *POSTE RESTANTE,* Stacijas laukumā 1, Rīga, LV-1050 LATVIA. **Postal Code:** LV-1050.

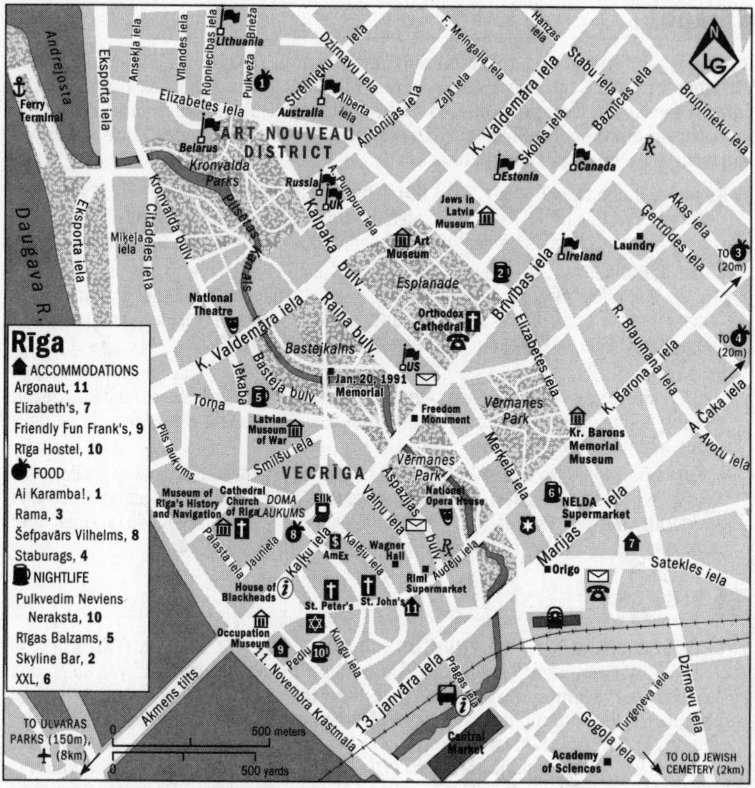

ACCOMMODATIONS

Make reservations well in advance during the high season. **Patricia,** Elizabetes iela 22 (☎728 48 68; room@findroom.net), arranges homestays from 22Ls and apartments for 40-60Ls. (Open M-F 8:30am-6pm, Sa-Su 11am-3pm. MC/V.)

Rīga Hostel, Mārstalu 12 (☎722 4520; www.riga-hostel.com). Well-decorated rooms with a prime Old Town location. Fabulous staff, free Internet and wireless, and a funky, sociable common area. Airport transport 4Ls. Dorms 5-18Ls; doubles 25Ls. Cash only. ❶

Friendly Fun Frank's, 11 Novembra krastmala 29 (☎599 0612; www.franks.lv). Walk toward the river and turn right on Novembra krastmala. Peach building with koala plaque beside buzzer. Spacious dorms and common room. Nightly outings (cover waived). Free Internet and wireless. Dorms 7-12Ls, online booking discount. MC/V. ❶

Elizabeth's, Elizabetes iela 101 (☎670 5476; www.youthhostel.lv). From the station, turn right and walk along Marijas; turn right on Elizabetes. Clean wooden bunks in a converted town house make for a quiet, comfy stay. Free Internet and wireless. 14-bed dorm 6Ls, 8- to 10-bed 7Ls, 3- to 4-bed 10Ls. Low season discount. Cash only. ❶

Argonaut, Kalēju 50 (☎614 7214; www.argonauthostel.com). Key-card door access to ensure security. Dorms are slightly crowded, with mosquitoes in the summer, but staff is friendly. Free Internet and wireless. 4- to 12-bed dorms 7-14Ls. MC/V. ❷

FOOD

For midnight snackers, 24hr. food and liquor stores are at Marijas 5 (Nelda) and Brīvības bul. 68. **Centrālais Tirgus** (Central Market), behind the bus station, is the largest market in Europe. (Open M and Su 8am-4pm, Tu-Sa 8am-5pm.) One fabulous Russian import that has stuck around are the tearooms sprinkling the city—perfect for an afternoon or evening snack.

Rama, K. Barona iela 56 (☎727 24 90). Between Gertrudes and Stabu iela. Eat well for about 2Ls at this Hare-Krishna-run cafeteria, which dishes out hearty Indian-style vegetarian fare and donates profits to feed the poor. Open M-Sa 10am-7pm. Cash only. ❶

Šefpavārs Vilhelms, Škuņu iela 6. Look for the large chef statue outside this pancake house that offers meat, vegetarian, sweet, and salty pancakes. Slather on jam or sour cream, grab a glass of milk or yogurt, and you'll be well-fed for under 2Ls. Open M-Th 9am-10pm, F-Sa 10am-11pm, Su 10am-10pm. Cash only. ❶

Staburags, A. Čaka iela 55 (☎729 97 87). Follow A. Čaka iela away from Vecrīga until it intersects with Stabu iela. Authentic Latvian cuisine served amid rustic decor. Try the unprocessed house beer (1.50Ls per 0.5L). Entrees 1.80-8.50Ls. Open daily noon-midnight. Cash only. ❷

Ai Karamba!, Pulkveza Brieza 2 (☎733 4672). American-themed diner with Baltic twists that offers all-day breakfast, including omelettes (1.59-2.29Ls), as well as lunch and dinner. Try the mint leaf tea (0.65Ls) after a night out. Entrees 1.90-3.45Ls. Open M-Th 8am-midnight, F-Sa 8am-1am, Su 10am-midnight. AmEx/MC/V. ❷

LATVIA

SIGHTS

FREEDOM MONUMENT AND ENVIRONS. In the center of Vecrīga (Old Rīga) is the Freedom Monument (Brīvības Piemineklis), known as "Milda." *(At Raiņa bul. and Brīvības bul.)* Continuing along Kaļķu iela to the river, you'll see one of the few remaining Soviet monuments: the **Latvian Riflemen Monument** (Latviešu Strēlnieku Laukums) in the town square, honoring Lenin's famous bodyguards. Rising behind the statues is the **Occupation Museum** (Okupācijas muzejs), Strēlnieku laukums 1, where displays vividly depict the Soviet and Nazi occupations. *(Open May-Sept. daily 11am-6pm; Oct.-Apr. Tu-Su 11am-5pm. Donations accepted.)* Next to the museum stands the **House of the Blackheads** (Melngalvju nams) Rātslaukums 7. Built in 1344 and destroyed by the Nazis and Soviets, the unusual but magnificent building was reconstructed in honor of Rīga's 800th birthday. The structure houses a museum and an assembly hall; it occasionally hosts concerts. *(Open Tu-Sa May-Sept. 10am-5pm, Tu-Su Oct.-Apr. 11am-5pm. 1.50Ls, students 0.70Ls. Cash only.)*

ELSEWHERE IN VECRĪGA. Follow Kaļķu iela from the Freedom Monument and turn right on Šķūņu iela to reach the **Dome Square** (Doma laukums), and the **Cathedral Church of Rīga** (Doma baznīca). The organ boasts over 6700 pipes. *(Open May-Sept. M-Tu, Th, Sa-Su 9am-6:30pm, W and F 9am-5:30pm; Oct.-May M-Th and Sa-Su 10am-6:30pm, F 10am-5:30pm. Concerts Oct.-Dec. Th-F 7pm (3-7Ls) and occasionally in summer (5-20Ls). Cathedral 1Ls, students 0.50Ls. Cash only.)* Next to the cathedral is the **Museum of Rīga's History and Navigation** (Rīgas Vēstures un Kugnie-cības Muzejs), Palasta iela 4. Established in 1773, this collection helped rekindle Latvia's cultural heritage after Soviet efforts to suppress it. *(Open May-Sept. daily 10am-5pm; Oct.-Apr. W-Su 11am-5pm. 2Ls, students 0.40Ls. Tours 3/2Ls. Cash only.)* From the top of the 123m spire of **St. Peter's Church** (Sv. Pētera baznīca), you can see the city and the Baltic Sea. *(On Skāmu iela, off Kaļķu iela. Open in summer Tu-Su 10am-6pm; low season 10am-5pm. Ticket office closes for lunch. Church 0.50Ls, students 0.10Ls. Tower 2Ls, under 18 1Ls. Cash only.)* The magnificent Neoclassical **State Museum of Art**

(Latvjas nacionalais), Kr. Valdemāra iela 10A, has 18th- to 20th-century Latvian art and occasional concerts. *(Near the corner of Elizabetes iela and Kr. Valdemāra iela. www.lnmm.lv. Open M, W, F-Su 11am-5pm, Th 11am-7pm. 1Ls, students 0.50Ls. Free last Su of each month. Cash only.)* The newer areas of Rīga host **Art Nouveau** *Jugendstil* architecture; most is on Alberta iela, Elizabetes iela, and Strēlnieku laukums.

BASTEJKALNS. Rīga's central park, surrounded by the old city moat (Pīlsētas kanāls), has ruins of the old city walls. Across and around the canal, five red slabs of stone stand as **memorials** to the events of January 20, 1991, when Soviet special forces stormed the Interior Ministry on Raiņa bul. At the northern end of Bastejkalns, on K. Valdemāra iela, sits the **National Theater,** where Latvia first declared its independence on November 18, 1918. *(Open daily 10am-7pm.)*

ENTERTAINMENT AND NIGHTLIFE

The night scene is centered in **Vecrīga**, but **Skyline Bar,** Elizabetes iela 55, on the 26th floor of the Reval Hotel Latvija, has the best view in the city. (Beer 1.50Ls. Mixed drinks 3-5Ls. F-Sa DJ from 9pm. 21+ after 11pm. Open Su-Th 3pm-2am, F-Sa 3pm-3am. AmEx/DC/MC/V.) If you prefer a more relaxed, alternative scene, spend the evening with great DJs at **Pulkvedim Neviens Neraksta,** Peldu 26/28. The dark upstairs bar and dance floor contrasts with the colorful basement lounge. (www.pulkvedis.lv. Beer 1.30Ls. 21+. Cover M-Th 2Ls, F-Sa 3Ls. Open M-Th 8pm-3am, F-Sa 8pm-5am. AmEx/MC/V.) Try *balzams*, Latvia's national liquor—a mysterious and heady herb and berry brew—in one of the dozen creative cocktails at **Rīgas Balzams,** Torņa iela 4, in Vecrīga, 100m east of Rīga Castle's Powder Tower. (*Balzam* drinks 3-4Ls. Open Su-Th 11am-midnight, F-Sa 11am-1am. AmEx/MC/V.) The gay bar, club, and sauna **XXL,** A. Kalniņa iela 4, is off K. Barona iela; buzz to be let in. (☎728 2276; www.xxl.lv. Mixed men and women F-Sa. Cover Tu-Sa 1-3Ls. Open daily 6pm-7am. Club open F-Sa 10pm-7am. MC/V.)

DAYTRIPS FROM RĪGA

JŪRMALA. Boardwalks and sun-bleached sand cover the narrow spit of Jūrmala. Visitors, including the Soviet elite, have been drawn to its warm waters since the 19th century. The coastal towns between **Bulduri** and **Dubulti** are popular for sunning and swimming, but Jūrmala's social center is **Majori,** where masses flock to the crowded beach or wander along **Jomas iela,** a pedestrian street lined with cafes and

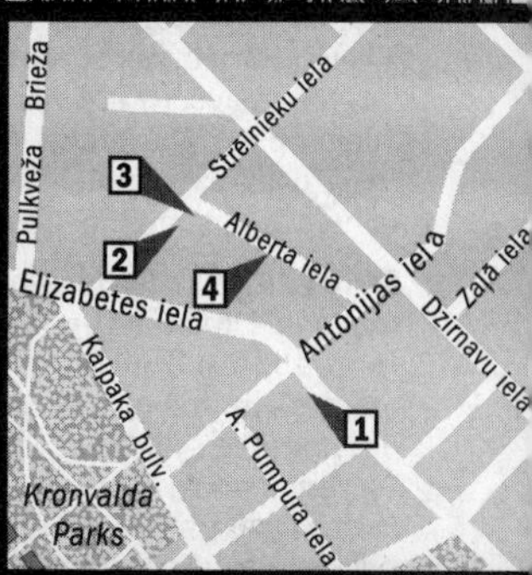

ART NOUVEAU RĪGA

Look up while you wander the streets of Rīga to appreciate the city's remarkable architecture. About 40% of the downtown area was built in the unique Art Nouveau style, with an international mix of influences. For a short tour of some of the most impressive buildings, take this walk:

1. From K. Valdemāra iela, turn left on Elizabetes iela to reach 10B, on your left.
2. Turn right on Strēlnieku to take in the blue-and-white masterpiece at 4b. The 1905 building is now the home of the Stockholm School of Economics.
3. Next door is the massive, cream-colored corner edifice at Alberta iela 13, the Belgian embassy. Recently repaired, it has pronounced details and pointed turrets.
4. Turn on Alberta iela. Numbers 8, 6, 4, 2, and 2A, in various states of repair, showcase a colorful and impressive catalogue of Art Nouveau balconies and brickwork.

shops. **Bicycles** are a popular mode of transport; rent one along the beach. (2Ls per hr.) **Sue's Asia ❸**, Jomas iela 74, offers Chinese, Indian, and Thai cuisine, serving the same fine fare that scored Rīga's branch a spot on *Conde Nast*'s list of the world's 100 best restaurants. (☎775 59 00. Entrees 4-10Ls. Open in summer daily noon-midnight; winter M-Th noon-11pm, F-Su noon-midnight. MC/V.) The **commuter rail** runs from Rīga to Jūrmala (30min., every 30min., 0.50Ls). **Public buses** (0.28Ls) and **microbuses** (0.35Ls) string together Jūrmala's towns, but you can follow the beach. There are two **tourist offices** in Majori. The first, Lienes iela 5, by the train station, has free maps. (☎714 7900; www.jurmala.lv. Open M-F 9am-7pm, Sa 10am-5pm, Su 10am-3pm.) The other, Jomas iela 42, arranges accommodations for a 1Ls fee. (☎77 642 76; jurmalainfo@bkc.lv. Open in summer M-F 9am-7pm, Sa-Su 1-7pm; winter M-F 9am-7pm. Cash only.) **Postal Code:** LV-2105.

SIGULDA. The Knights of the Sword, the Germanic crusaders who Christianized much of Latvia in the 13th century, staked their base at Segewald—now Sigulda (pop. 10,000). Now the Gauja National Park Administration has planted its headquarters in this charming town 50km from Rīga. The area offers biking, bobsledding, bungee-jumping, horseback riding, hot-air ballooning, and skiing. **Makars Tourism Agency,** Peldu 1, arranges excursions. (☎924 49 48; www.makars.lv.) The main sights of the area are along a 4km stretch of road. Farthest from town are the restored brick fortifications of the **Turaida Castle Complex** (Turaidas Muzejrezervats), Turaidas iela 10, visible throughout the Gauja Valley. Climb the staircase in the main tower for a view of the region. (Tower open daily 8am-9pm. Other exhibits open daily 10am-6pm. 2Ls, students 0.80Ls. Cash only.) Take Turaidas iela back down the hill to reach the famous **caves** of Sigulda. Inscriptions and coats of arms from as early as the 16th century cover the chiseled mouth of **Gutman's Cave** (Gūtmaņa ala), whose spring has any number of legends attached to it. On a ridge to the right of Gaujas iela, on the same side of the river as town, is the **Sigulda Dome** palace, behind which lie the ruins of **Sigulda Castle** (Siguldas pilsdrupas).

Pilsmuižas Restorāns ❸, Pils iela 16, in Pilseta Dome, serves generous portions of Latvian fare. (Entrees 4-15Ls. Open daily noon-2am. MC/V.) For a cheap bite, try **Trīs Draugi ❶,** Pils iela 9, a cafeteria with English-speaking staff. (Open daily 8am-10pm. MC/V.) **Trains** run from Rīga on the Rīga-Lugaži commuter rail line (1hr., 9 per day, 0.71Ls). From the station, walk up Raiņa iela, passing the bus station, to the town center. **Buses** run from Rīga every hour (1Ls). Continue on as Raiņa iela turns into Gaujas iela, which, after the Bridge, becomes the steep Turaidas iela and passes Turaida Castle. A bus labeled "Turaida" runs directly to Turaida Castle (7 per day, 0.20Ls). From the station 1km along Raiņa iela is the **Gauja National Park Visitor Centre,** Baznicas 3, which provides basic tourist information, books accommodation for free, and offers an essential map of the park for 1.80Ls. (☎7800 388; www.gnp.gov.lv. Open M 9am-5:30pm, Tu-Su 9am-7pm.) **Postal Code:** LV-2150.

CĒSIS. Sprawling medieval ruins and Cēsu, the local brew, make Cēsis (TSEY-sis; pop. 18,400) the classic Latvian town. Crusading Germans came in 1209 and built the famous **Cēsis Castle.** The new castle's **tower** offers stunning views of the Gauja Valley. Explore the old castle's **ruins** with a hard-hat and lantern, or check out the fallen Lenin statue, complete with wooden coffin, at the garden entrance. (☎412 1815. Open mid-May to Sept. Tu-Su 10am-6pm, ruins also open M 10am-6pm, tickets at the garden entrance; Nov. to mid-May W-Su 10am-5pm. 2Ls, students 1Ls. Cash only.) Cēsis is served by infrequent **trains** from Rīga via Sigulda (1½-2hr., 2 per day, about 1Ls). **Buses** are more convenient (2hr., 1-2 per hr., 1.70Ls). The **tourist office,** Pils laukums 1, across from the castle, offers free maps, has Internet access (1Ls per hr.), and arranges **private rooms** for 1Ls. (☎412 18 15; www.cesis.lv. Open mid-May to mid-Sept. M-F 9am-6pm, Sa 9am-5pm, Su 10am-3pm; mid-Sept. to mid-May M-F 9am-5pm. AmEx/MC/V.) **Postal Code:** LV-4101.

LIECHTENSTEIN

A tourist brochure once amusingly mislabeled this tiny 160 sq. km country of Liechtenstein an even tinier 160 sq. m. That's just about how much most tourists see of the world's only German-speaking monarchy, even though its cliffside roads are gateways to unspoiled mountains with great biking and hiking.

ESSENTIALS

FACTS AND FIGURES

Official Name: Principality of Liechtenstein.

Capital: Vaduz.

Major Villages: Schaan, Triesen.

Population: 34,000.

Form of Government: Hereditary constitutional monarchy.

Land Area: 160 sq. km.

Major Exports: Electronic equipment, dental products.

Language: German (see p. 1055).

Religions: Roman Catholic (76%), Protestant (7%).

DOCUMENTS AND FORMALITIES. Citizens of Australia, Canada, New Zealand, the UK, and the US do not need visas for stays of up to 90 days.

TRANSPORTATION. Catch a **bus** from Buchs or Sargans in Switzerland, or from Feldkirch, across the Austrian border (20-30min., 3.60SFr). Liechtenstein has no rail system. Its cheap, efficient **PostBus** system links all 11 villages. A **one-week bus ticket** (13SFr) covers all of Liechtenstein and buses to Swiss and Austrian border towns. You can buy all tickets (including the pass) on the bus. Swisspass is valid and discounted student rates are available.

EMERGENCY **Police:** ☎117. **Ambulance:** ☎144. **Fire:** ☎118.

MONEY. Liechtenstein uses the **Swiss Franc (SFr).** Go to Switzerland to exchange currency at reasonable rates. Conversion rates for the franc are listed on p. 993.

BEYOND TOURISM. Travelers wishing to volunteer in Liechtenstein should visit the local tourist office to see if there are any opportunities available in one of the country's many **forests.** Travelers may also consider contacting the **Special Olympics** (www.specialolympics.li) to see if there are volunteer positions available.

VADUZ AND LOWER LIECHTENSTEIN ☎00423

As the national capital, Vaduz (pop. 5000) attracts the most visitors of any village in Liechtenstein. The 12th-century **Schloß Vaduz** (Vaduz Castle) is home to the Prince of Liechtenstein. Its interior is off-limits, but visitors can hike up to the castle for a closer look. The 20min. trail begins down the street from the tourist office and heads away from the post office. Facing the tourist office is the big black marble box building that houses the art exhibits of **Kunstmuseum Liechtenstein.** (☎235 0300; www.kunstmuseum.li. Open Tu-W and F-Su 10am-5pm, Th 10am-8pm. 8SFr, students 5SFr.)

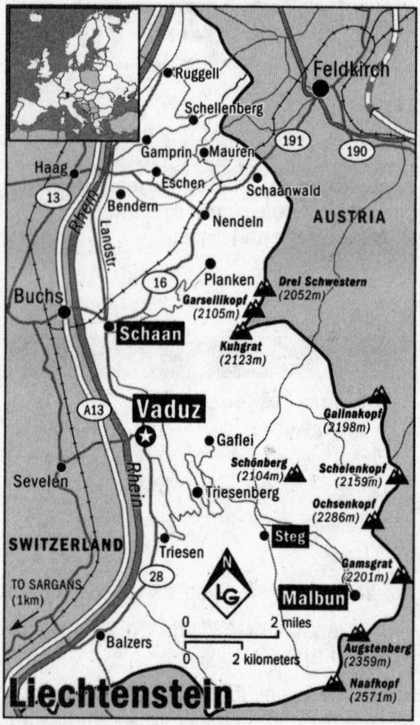

The village of **Schaan** houses Liechtenstein's sole **Jugendherberge (HI)** ❷, Untere Rüttig. 6. From Vaduz, take bus #1 to Mühleholz, walk to the intersection, turn left on Marianumstr., and then follow the signs. (☎232 5022; www.youthhostel.ch/schaan. Breakfast included. Laundry 6SFr. Internet 1SFr per 5min. Reception 7:30-10am and 5-10pm. Open Mar.-Oct. Dorms 37SFr; singles 62SFr; doubles 94SFr. 6SFr HI discount. AmEx/DC/MC/V.) In Vaduz, crowds pack the candlelit outdoor patio of **B'eat** ❷, Städtle 3. (☎232 8484. Lunch 18SFr, vegetarian 15SFr. Open M-Th 10:30am-1am, F-Sa until 3am, Su noon-1am. Cash only.)

There is a **Coop** supermarket at Aulestr. 20 in Vaduz. (Open M-F 8am-7pm, Sa-Su 8am-5pm. MC/V.) Pick up a **hiking map** (15.50SFr) and countless hiking route suggestions at Liechtenstein's **tourist office,** Städtle 37, located just up the hill from the Vaduz PostBus stop. (☎239 6300; www.tourismus.li. Open July-Sept. daily 9am-5pm at the bus stop welcome desk; Oct.-June M-F 9am-noon and 1:30-5pm.)

UPPER LIECHTENSTEIN ☎00423

Full of winding roads and hiking trails, the villages of Upper Liechtenstein are where the country's real beauty lies. **Malbun** sits in an Alpine valley in the southeastern corner of Liechtenstein, accessible by bus #10 (40min., 1 perhr.). Great hiking and affordable ski slopes (day pass 37SFr) make this the hippest place in the principality. The most popular hiking trail (4-5hr.) starts at the chairlift base at the Malbun Zentrum bus stop and follows Fürstin-Gina-Weg along two mountain crests. (Chairlift open July to mid-Oct. daily 8am-12:15pm and 1:15-4:50pm. 7.50SFr, students 5.90SFr; round-trip 11.70/9SFr.) **Hotel Steg** ❶, in the village of Steg, has the country's cheapest lodging, but the 10 dorm beds are barely separated. Take bus #10 to Hotel Steg. (☎263 2146. Breakfast included. Blanket and pillow provided in dorm, but no linens available. Linens included for private rooms. Dorms 25SFr; singles 45SFr; doubles 80SFr. MC/V.) **Alpenhotel Malbun** ❸, opposite the Malbun PostBus stop, has an indoor pool. (☎263 1181; www.alpenhotel.li. Reception 8am-10pm. Open mid-May to Oct. and mid-Dec. to Apr. Singles 45-65SFr, with bath 65-95SFr; doubles 80-130/120-170SFr. AmEx/MC/V.) The **Schädler-Shop,** between the chairlift and the tourist office, has groceries. (Open M-F 8am-12:30pm and 1:30-5pm, Sa-Su 8am-6pm.) The **tourist office** is down the street from the Malbun Zentrum bus stop. (☎263 6577. Open June-Oct. and mid-Dec. to mid-Apr. M-F 8am-6pm, Sa 9am-5pm, Su 8am-5pm.)

LITHUANIA (LIETUVA)

Once part of the largest country in Europe, Lithuania shrank significantly in the face of oppression from Tsarist Russia, Nazi Germany, and the Soviet Union. Since the fall of the USSR, Lithuania has become more Western with each passing year. This transformation was confirmed when it entered the European Union in 2004. Vilnius, the spectacular capital, welcomes visitors with the largest Old Town in Europe. In the other corner of the country, the mighty Baltic Sea washes up against Palanga and the towering dunes of the Curonian Spit.

DISCOVER LITHUANIA: SUGGESTED ITINERARIES

THREE DAYS. Head to the **Baltic Coast** to enjoy the stunning sands of the **Drifting Dunes of Parnidis** (p. 695), then leave the **Curonian Spit** and go inland to the flourishing capital of **Vilnius** (p. 689).

ONE WEEK. After 4 days on the **Baltic Coast,** visit **Vilnius** (3 days), where you can explore the **Old Town,** wander through offbeat **Užupis,** and take a daytrip to **Trakai Castle,** the ancient capital.

ESSENTIALS

FACTS AND FIGURES

Official Name: Republic of Lithuania.

Capital: Vilnius.

Major Cities: Kaunas, Klaipėda.

Population: 3,596,000.

Land Area: 65,200 sq. km.

Time Zone: GMT +2.

Language: Lithuanian.

Religion: Roman Catholic (79%).

WHEN TO GO

Lithuanian summers are brief but glorious, while winters are long and cold. Tourist season peaks in July and August, especially along the coast. June and September are pleasant times to visit. A winter visit also has its charms, especially in the major cities. Be aware that many coastal establishments close in low season.

DOCUMENTS AND FORMALITIES

EMBASSIES AND CONSULATES. All foreign embassies in Lithuania are in Vilnius (p. 689). Lithuanian embassies and consulates abroad, include: **Australia,** 40B Fiddens Wharf Rd., Killara, NSW, 2071 (☎2 9498 2571); **Canada,** 130 Albert St., Ste. 204, Ottawa, ON, K1P 5G4 (☎613-567-5458; www.lithuanianembassy.ca); **Ireland,** 90 Merrion Rd., Ballsbridge, Dublin, 4 (☎01 668 82 92); **New Zealand,** 28 Heather St., Parnell, Auckland (☎64 9 336 7711); **UK,** 84 Gloucester Pl., London, W1U 6AU (☎020 7486 6401, ext. 2; http://lithuania.embassyhomepage.com); **US,** 2622 16th St., NW, Washington, D.C., 20009 (☎202-234-5860; www.ltembassyus.org).

VISA AND ENTRY INFORMATION. Citizens of Australia, Canada, New Zealand, the UK, and the US do not need a visa for stays of up to 90 days. Special visas (€35-60) for temporary residence are valid for up to one year and can be purchased from the Migration Department of the Ministry of the Interior. Avoid crossing through Belarus to enter or exit Lithuania: not only will you need to obtain a visa (US$100) for Belarus in advance, but guards may hassle you at the border.

TOURIST SERVICES AND MONEY

ENTRANCE REQUIREMENTS

Passport: Required for all travelers.

Visa: Not required for stays under 90 days for citizens of Australia, Canada, Ireland, New Zealand, the UK, and the US.

Letter of Invitation: Not required for citizens of Australia, Canada, Ireland, New Zealand, the UK, and the US.

Inoculations: Not required. Recommended up-to-date on DTaP (diphtheria, tetanus, and pertussis), hepatitis A, hepatitis B, MMR (measles, mumps, and rubella), polio booster, and typhoid.

Work Permit: Required for all foreigners planning to work in Lithuania.

Driving Permit: Required for all those planning to drive in Lithuania; US driver's license valid up to 3 months.

TOURIST OFFICES. Major cities have official tourist offices. **Litinterp** reserves accommodations and rental cars in Kaunas, Klaipėda, and Vilnius, usually without a surcharge (www.litinterp.com). Kaunas, Klaipėda, Nida, Palanga, and Vilnius each have an edition of the *In Your Pocket* series, available at kiosks and some hotels. Employees at tourist offices will often, but not always, speak English.

MONEY. The unit of currency is the **lita (Lt),** plural litai. One lita is equal to 100 centas. The lita is fixed to the euro at €1 = 3.4528Lt. Prices are stable, with inflation hovering at 2.7%. **ATMs** are available in most cities, though few accept American Express. Exchange bureaus near the train station usually have poorer rates than banks. Most banks cash **traveler's checks** for 2-3% commission. Visa **cash advances** can usually be obtained with minimal hassle. **Vilniaus Bankas,** with outlets in major cities, accepts major credit cards and traveler's checks for a small commission. Outside Vilnius, most places catering to locals don't take credit cards. Some establishments that claim to take MasterCard and/or Visa may not actually do so.

LITAI (LT)		
	AUS$1 = 2.05LT	1LT = AUS$0.49
	CDN$1 = 2.43LT	1LT = CDN$0.41
	EUR€1 = 3.45LT	1LT = EUR€0.29
	NZ$1 = 1.71LT	1LT = NZ$0.60
	UK£1 = 5.03LT	1LT = UK£0.20
	US$1 = 2.69LT	1LT = US$0.37

HEALTH AND SAFETY

Well-stocked **pharmacies** are common and carry most medical supplies, tampons, condoms, and toiletries. Drink bottled mineral water, and **boil tap water** for 10min. before drinking. An upward-pointing triangle indicates women's **restrooms;** a triangle pointing downward indicates men's bathrooms. Many restrooms are nothing but a hole in the ground, so carry your own **toilet paper.** Lithuania's **crime rate** is generally low, though unscrupulous cab drivers will think nothing of ripping off a tourist. Lithuanian **police** are generally helpful but understaffed, so your best bet for assistance in English is still your **consulate.**

Women traveling alone will be noticed but shouldn't encounter too much difficulty. Skirts, blouses, and heels are more common than jeans, shorts, tank tops, or sneakers, though showing a little skin is more acceptable in clubs. **Minorities** traveling to Lithuania may encounter unwanted attention or discrimination, though most is directed toward Roma (gypsies). Lithuania has made little effort to provide for **disabled** travelers. **Homosexuality** is legal but not always tolerated. Vilnius has the most nightclubs, hotlines, and services for gays and lesbians in the Baltics.

EMERGENCY	**Police, Ambulance,** and **Fire:** ☎112.

TRANSPORTATION

BY PLANE AND TRAIN. Finnair, LOT, Lufthansa, SAS, and other airlines fly into Vilnius International Airport (**VNO;** www.vilnius-airport.lt). Trains are also popular for international and long-distance travel. **Lithuanian Railways** connects major cities and towns (☎5 233 00 87; www.litrail.lt).

BY BUS. Domestic buses are faster, more common, and only a bit more expensive than trains, which are often crowded. When possible, try to catch an express bus, typically marked with an asterisk or an "E" on the timetable. They are normally direct and can be up to twice as fast. Kaunas, Klaipėda, and Vilnius are easily reached by train or bus from Estonia, Latvia, Poland, and Russia.

BY FERRY. Ferries connect Klaipėda with and Aabenra, Århus, and Copenhagen, DEN; Kiel, Mukran, and Travemünde, GER; Åhus and Stockholm, SWE.

BY CAR. All travelers planning to drive in Lithuania must purchase a **liability insurance policy** at the Lithuanian border (79Lt for a min. 15-day). These policies may only be purchased with litai, so make sure to convert some cash before reaching the border. **US** citizens may drive with an American driver's license for up to three months; all others must have an **International Driving Permit.** Inexpensive taxis are available in most cities; agree on a price before getting in. Hitchhiking is common; many drivers charge a fee comparable to local bus or train fares. Locals line up along major roads leaving large cities. Let's Go does not recommend hitchhiking.

KEEPING IN TOUCH

PHONE CODES	**Country code:** 370. **International dialing prefix:** 810. For more information on how to place international calls, see inside back cover.

EMAIL AND THE INTERNET. Internet is widely available, though rarely free. Most well-located Internet cafes charge 3-6Lt per hour.

TELEPHONE. There are two kinds of pay phones: rectangular ones take magnetic strip cards and rounded ones take chip cards. Phone cards (8-30Lt) are sold at phone offices and kiosks. Calls to **Estonia** and **Latvia** cost 1.65Lt per minute; to the rest of **Europe** 5.80Lt; to the **US** 7.32Lt. International access numbers include: **AT&T Direct** (☎8 800 90028); **Canada Direct** (☎8 800 90004); **Sprint** (☎800 95877).

MAIL. Airmail *(oro pastu)* letters abroad cost 1.70Lt (postcards 1.20Lt) and take about one week to reach the US. **Poste Restante** is available in Vilnius but hard to find elsewhere. Address envelope as follows: First name LAST NAME, POSTE RESTANTE, post office address, Postal Code, city, LITHUANIA.

LANGUAGE. **Lithuanian** is one of only two Baltic languages (Latvian is the other). All "r"s are trilled. **Polish** is helpful in the south and **German** on the coast. **Russian** is understood in most places, and most Lithuanians understand basic English phrases. If someone seems to sneeze at you, he might be saying *ačiu* (ah-choo; thank you). For a few helpful phrases see **Phrasebook: Lithuanian,** p. 1059.

ACCOMMODATIONS AND CAMPING

LITHUANIA	❶	❷	❸	❹	❺
ACCOMMODATIONS	under 30Lt	30-80Lt	80-130Lt	130-180Lt	over 180Lt

Lithuania has several youth **hostels,** particularly in Klaipėda and Vilnius. HI membership is nominally required, but an LJNN guest card (10.50Lt at any hostel) will suffice. **Hotels** abound. **Litinterp,** with offices in Kaunas, Klaipėda, and Vilnius, assists in finding homestays or apartments for rent. **Camping** is gaining popularity, but it is restricted to marked campgrounds by a well-enforced law.

FOOD AND DRINK

LITHUANIA	❶	❷	❸	❹	❺
FOOD	under 11Lt	11-20Lt	20-30Lt	30-40Lt	over 40Lt

Lithuanian cuisine is heavy and sometimes greasy. Keeping a **vegetarian** or **kosher** diet is difficult but possible. Restaurants serve various types of *blynai* (pancakes) with *mėsa* (meat) or *varske* (cheese). *Cepelinai* are heavy, potato-dough missiles of meat, cheese, and mushrooms; *saltibarščiai* is a beet-and-cucumber soup prevalent in the east; *karbonadas* is breaded pork fillet; and *koldunai* are meat dumplings. Good Lithuanian **beer** flows freely. *Kalnapis* is popular in Vilnius and most of Lithuania, *Baltijos* reigns supreme around Klaipėda, and the award-winning *Utenos* is everywhere. Lithuanian **vodka** *(degtinė)* is also very popular.

HOLIDAYS AND FESTIVALS

Holidays: New Year's Day and Flag Day (Jan. 1); Independence Day (Feb. 16); Restoration of Independence (Mar. 11); Easter (Apr. 8); Labor Day (May 1); Statehood Day (July 6); Feast of the Assumption (Aug. 15); All Saints' Day (Nov. 1).

Festivals: Since the 19th century, craftsmen from around Eastern Europe have gathered to display their wares each March in Vilnius at the **Kaziukas Fair** (Mar. 2-4).

BEYOND TOURISM

The Baltic Times (☎370 5 212 15 45; www.baltictimes.com). English-language newspaper with classified ads for short-term and long-term employment.

Lithuanian Academy of Music, Gedimino pr. 42, 2600 Vilnius (☎370 5 261 26 91). Classes in music, art, and theater in Lithuania. Music classes in English offered.

VILNIUS ☎5

Founded in 1321 after a prophetic dream by Grand Duke Gediminas, Vilnius (pop. 542,000) has a unique design that reflects the city's rich heritage. Baroque church spires rise above the treetops, and the cobblestone streets display a melange of crumbling medieval brick alongside freshly painted modern architecture. Lithuania's capital has flourished through the centuries, surviving WWII and the iron grip of the Soviet Union. The proud residents look forward to a boost in tourism in 2009, when Vilnius will serve as one of the European Capitals of Culture.

TRANSPORTATION

Flights: Vilnius International Airport (Vilniaus oro uostas), Rodūnės Kelias 2 (☎230 6666; www.vilnius-airport.lt), 6km south of town. Take bus #1 to the Old Town.

Trains: Geležinkelio Stotis, Geležinkelio 16 (☎233 0086, reservations in English 269 3722). Domestic tickets are sold in the hall to the left of the main entrance; international ticketing is directly to the left of the main doors. Open daily 6-11am and noon-6pm. Most international trains pass through Belarus, requiring a Belarussian transit visa (US$30). Trains run to: **Moscow, RUS** (16hr., 1 per day, 112Lt); **Rīga, LAT** (7½hr., 1 every other day, 54Lt); **St. Petersburg, RUS** (14½hr., 1 every other day, 97Lt); **Warsaw, POL** (8hr., 2 per day, 80Lt).

Buses: Autobusų Stotis, Sodų 22 (☎290 1661, reservations 216 2977; www.toks.lt). **Eurolines** (☎215 1377; www.eurolines.lt) serves: **Rīga, LAT** via Truskavecas (5hr., 4 per day, 45Lt); **St. Petersburg, RUS** via Rīga (18hr., 1 per day, 59Lt); **Tallinn, EST** (9hr., 2 per day, 90Lt); **Warsaw, POL** (9-10hr., 2 per day, 87-97Lt). ISIC discount.

Public Transportation: Buses and **trolleys** run daily 4am-midnight. Buy tickets at any Lietuvos Spauda kiosk (1.10Lt) or from the driver (1.40Lt). Tickets are checked frequently; punch them onboard to avoid the 20Lt fine. Monthly student passes 5Lt.

Taxis: Martono (☎240 0004). Cabbies are notorious for overcharging foreigners; get a local to hail one for you if at all possible.

ORIENTATION AND PRACTICAL INFORMATION

Geležinkelio runs east from the train and bus stations to **Aušros Vartų,** which leads downhill through the **Gates of Dawn** (Aušros Vartai) and into the **Old Town** (Senamiestis). Heading north, Aušros Vartų becomes **Didžioji** and then **Pilies** before reaching the base of Gediminas Hill. On the hill, the **Gediminas Tower** of the Higher Castle presides over **Cathedral Square** (Katedros Aikštė) and the banks of the River Neris. **Gedimino,** the main commercial artery, runs west from Katedros Aikštė.

Tourist Office: Vilniaus 22 (☎262 9660; www.vilnius.lt). Open M-F 9am-6pm, Sa 10am-4pm. Branches in the train station (☎269 2091) and town hall (☎262 6470). Open M-F 9am-6pm, Sa-Su 10am-4pm. **Laisvalaikis** discount card (99Lt) offers good deals for long-term visitors; the card is available at Respublika offices (☎85 212 3344).

Embassies: Australia, Vilniaus 23 (☎212 3369; www.lithuania.embassy.gov.au/lt.html). Open Tu 10am-1pm, Th 2-5pm. **Canada,** Jogailos 4 (☎249 0950; www.canada.lt). Open daily 8:30am-5pm. **UK,** Antakalnio 2 (☎246 2900, emergency 869 83 7097; www.britain.lt). Open M-Th 8:30am-5:45pm, F 8:30am-3:30pm. **US,** Akmenų 6 (☎266 5600; www.usembassy.lt). Open M-F 8am-4pm. Closed last W of each month.

Currency Exchange: Vilniaus Bankas, Vokiečių 9, cashes traveler's checks. Open M-Th 9am-6pm, F 9am-5pm. **Parex Bankas,** Geležinkelio 6, to the left of the train station, accepts many currencies. Open 24hr.

24hr. Pharmacy: Gedimino Vaistinė, Gedimino pr. 27 (☎261 0135). Only essential items available at night.

Hospital: Baltic-American Medical and Surgical Clinic, Nemenčinės 54A (☎234 2020 or 698 526 55; www.bak.lt). Accepts major American, British, and international insurance plans. Doctors on call 24hr.

Internet Access: Collegium, Pilies 22 (☎ 261 8334). 6Lt per hr. Open 8am-midnight.

Post Office: Lietuvos Paštas, Gedimino 7 (☎261 6759; www.post.lt), west of Katedros Aikštė. *Poste Restante* at the window labeled "iki pareikalavimo"; 0.50Lt fee. Open M-F 7am-7pm, Sa 9am-4pm. **Postal Code:** 01001.

ACCOMMODATIONS AND FOOD

Young travelers flock to the clean, friendly **Filaretai Youth Hostel (HI) ❷,** Filaretų 17, in Užupis, 1km east of the Old Town. Walk east on Užupio across the Vilnia River. At the fork, bear left onto Krivių, then bear right onto Filaretų. (☎215 4627; www.filaretaihostel.lt. Laundry 10Lt. Free Internet. Reserve ahead June-Sept. and weekends. Dorms 31Lt first night, 28Lt every night thereafter; triples and quads 42Lt. HI discount 4Lt. MC/V.) **VDA Hostel ❶,** Latako 2, provides basic, centrally located rooms at unbeatable prices. Dorms are only available during the summer. (☎212 0102. Dorms 18Lt; singles 43Lt; doubles 52-60Lt; triples 66-78Lt. Cash only.) Tucked into a courtyard 100m south of the Gates of Dawn, the **Old Town Hostel (HI) ❷,** Aušros Vartų 20-15A, gets high marks from guests. (☎262 5357; www.lithuanianhostels.org. Reserve ahead. Dorms 34Lt, HI members 32Lt. MC/V.)

Keep company with Vilnius's counterculture at the peaceful **Balti Drambliai ❶,** Vilniaus 41, the only vegetarian restaurant in the city. (Entrees from 8Lt. Open M-F 11am-midnight, Sa-Su noon-midnight. MC/V.) **Čili Pica ❶,** Didžioji 5, dishes out pizza until 3am. **Iki** supermarkets stock local and Western brands. (Branch at Sodu 22. Open daily 8am-10pm.) For the cheapest eats, join women in babushka scarves at **Turgus Dirbu Market,** sandwiched between Pylimo and Bazilijonų near the Gates of Dawn. Choose from a wide selection of fresh produce, meats, and pastries. Large loaves of bread cost just 0.50-2Lt. (Open M-F 7am-7pm, Sa-Su 7am-3pm.).

THE REAL DEAL. If you ask locals where to try authentic Lithuanian food, they will likely suggest Čili Kaimas, Vokiečių 8, a branch of the popular Čili chain. Although the food is tasty and affordable, be forewarned: while many locals do eat there, so does every other remotely intrepid traveler in Lithuania.

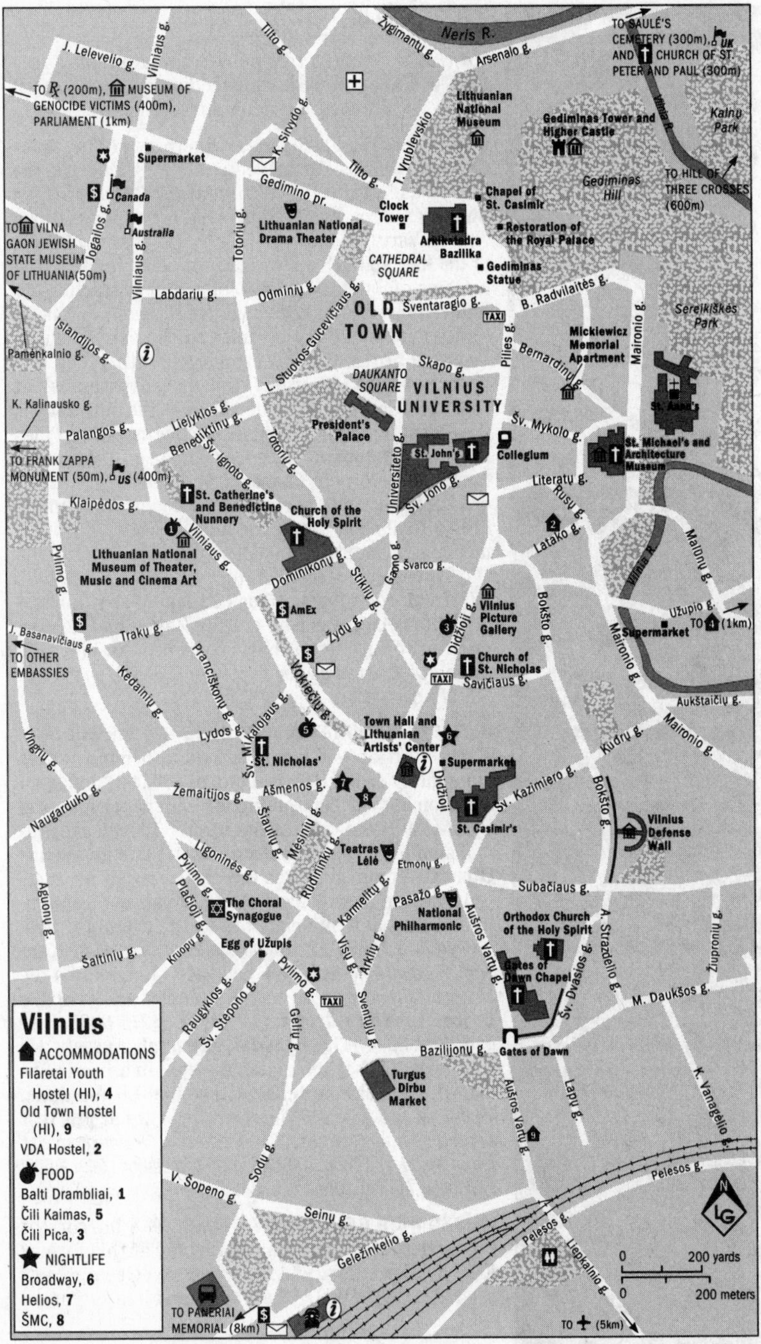
Vilnius
ACCOMMODATIONS
Filaretai Youth Hostel (HI), 4
Old Town Hostel (HI), 9
VDA Hostel, 2
FOOD
Balti Drambliai, 1
Čili Kaimas, 5
Čili Pica, 3
NIGHTLIFE
Broadway, 6
Helios, 7
ŠMC, 8
Neris R.
Žygimantų g.
Arsenalo g.
TO SAULĖ'S CEMETERY (300m), UK AND CHURCH OF ST. PETER AND PAUL (300m)
J. Lelevelio g.
Vilniaus g.
Tilto g.
TO (200m), MUSEUM OF GENOCIDE VICTIMS (400m), PARLIAMENT (1km)
Lithuanian National Museum
Gediminas Tower and Higher Castle
Vilnia R.
Kalnų Park
K. Sirvydo g.
T. Vrublevskio
Supermarket
Gedimino pr.
Tilto g.
Gediminas Hill
TO HILL OF THREE CROSSES (600m)
Canada
Australia
Chapel of St. Casimir
Clock Tower
Lithuanian National Drama Theater
Arkikatedra Bazilika
Restoration of the Royal Palace
TO VILNA GAON JEWISH STATE MUSEUM OF LITHUANIA(50m)
Jogailos g.
Totorių g.
CATHEDRAL SQUARE
Gediminas Statue
Labdarių g.
Odminių g.
Šventaragio g.
B. Radvilaitės g.
OLD TOWN
TAXI
Sereikiškės Park
L. Stuokos-Gucevičiaus g.
Maironio g.
Islandijos g.
Pamėnkalnio g.
Skapo g.
Bernardinų g.
Mickiewicz Memorial Apartment
Pilies g.
DAUKANTO SQUARE
VILNIUS UNIVERSITY
St. Anne's
K. Kalinausko g.
Liejyklos g.
Benediktinų g.
President's Palace
Šv. Mykolo g.
Palangos g.
Totorių g.
St. John's
Collegium
St. Michael's and Architecture Museum
TO FRANK ZAPPA MONUMENT (50m), US (400m)
Šv. Ignoto g.
Universiteto g.
Literatų g.
St. Catherine's and Benedictine Nunnery
Šv. Jono g.
Rusų g.
Klaipėdos g.
Church of the Holy Spirit
Vilniaus g.
Latako g.
Malūnų g.
Lithuanian National Museum of Theater, Music and Cinema Art
Dominikonų g.
Gaono g.
Švarco g.
Vilnia R.
Stiklių g.
Vilnius Picture Gallery
Pylimo g.
AmEx
Didžioji g.
Bokšto g.
Užupio g.
J. Basanavičiaus g.
Trakų g.
Žydų g.
TO (1km)
Supermarket
TO OTHER EMBASSIES
Pranciškonų g.
Vokiečių g.
Church of St. Nicholas
Maironio g.
Kėdainių g.
Savičiaus g.
Aukštaičių g.
Town Hall and Lithuanian Artists' Center
Vingrių g.
Lydos g.
Šv. Mikalojaus g.
Kudrų g.
Maironio g.
St. Nicholas'
Supermarket
Ašmenos g.
Žemaitijos g.
Naugarduko g.
Didžioji
Šv. Kazimiero g.
Šaulių g.
Mėsinių g.
St. Casimir's
Bokšto g.
Vilnius Defense Wall
Ligoninės g.
Rūdininkų g.
Teatras Lėlė
Etmonų g.
Aguonų g.
Pylimo g.
Karmelitų g.
Subačiaus g.
Plačioji g.
The Choral Synagogue
Pasažo g.
National Philharmonic
Aušros Vartų g.
Orthodox Church of the Holy Spirit
Žiupronių g.
Visų g.
Egg of Užupis
Šaltinių g.
Kruopų g.
Arklių g.
A. Strazdelio g.
Gates of Dawn Chapel
Šv. Dvasios g.
Pylimo g.
M. Daukšos g.
Raugyklos g.
Šv. Stepono g.
Gėlių g.
Šventųjų g.
TAXI
Bazilijonų g.
Gates of Dawn
Turgus Dirbu Market
Lapų g.
K. Vanagėlio g.
Aušros Vartų g.
Sodų g.
V. Šopeno g.
Pelesos g.
Seinų g.
Geležinkelio g.
Pelesos g.
Liepkalnio g.
0
200 yards
0
200 meters
TO PANERIAI MEMORIAL (8km)
TO (5km)

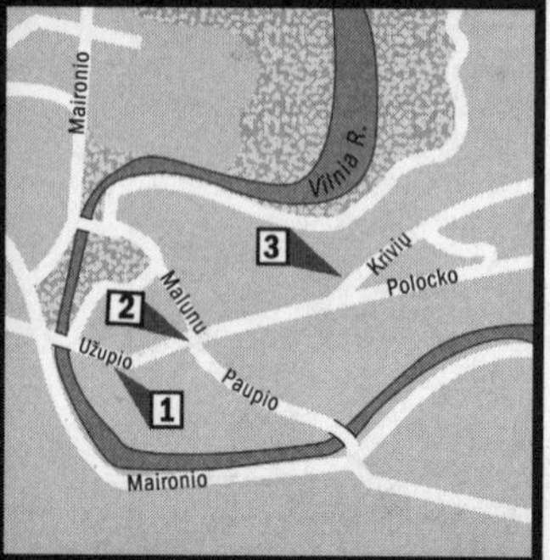

UŽUPIO RESPUBLIKA

Užupis, a zany artist's haven in the eastern part of Old Town, "seceded" from the capital a decade ago and declared itself a separate republic.

1 Cross the Vilnia River and soak in the bohemian vibe while sipping coffee outside on the deck at **Užupio Kavinė**, Užupio 2, opposite the bridge. (☎212 2138. Open daily 10am-11pm.) Peek into the **Alternatyvaus Menos Centras** gallery next door, Užupio 2 (☎262 0083).

2 In the main square, the **Angel of Užupis** statue celebrates the area's joking declaration of independence and very real sense of community. The angel took the place of Užupis's beloved giant **egg**, which now presides over the square on Raugyklos g. in the Old Jewish Quarter.

3 Visit the blacksmiths' gallery **Kalvystes Galerija**, Užupio 26 (☎215 3757), and the offbeat eatery **Tores**, Užupio 40, with the best view of Old Town. (☎262 9304. Open Su-Th 11am-midnight, F-Sa 11am-2am.)

SIGHTS

Vilnius on Foot, a free publication available at the tourist office, provides an excellent walking tour of the city's churches and other attractions.

SENAMIESTIS. Facing the northern side of the **Gates of Dawn** (Aušros Vartai), enter the first door on the left to ascend to the 17th-century **Gates of Dawn Chapel** (Aušros Vartai Koplyčia). A few steps down Aušros Vartų, a gateway leads to the **Orthodox Church of the Holy Spirit** (Šv. Dvasios bažnyčia), home to the remains of Saints Anthony, John, and Eustachio, the beloved martyrs of Lithuania. Bright paint and neon lights lend a cheeky vivacity to the saintly quiet. Heading north, the street merges with Pilies and leads to **Vilnius University** (Vilniaus Universitetas), at Pilies and Šv. Jono. Founded in 1579, the university is the oldest in Eastern Europe. Farther north on Pilies is **Cathedral Square** (Katedros Aikštė); its **cathedral** contains the ornate **Chapel of St. Casimir** (v. Kazimiero koplyčia) and the royal mausoleum. Walk up the hill to **Gediminas Tower** for a great view. Europe's most unexpected monument stands 50km west of the Old Town: a 4m steel shaft topped with a bust of the late freak-rock legend **Frank Zappa** against a backdrop of spectacular wall graffiti. Zappa had no connection to Lithuania, but apparently he had fans there. *(Off Pylimo, between Kalinausko 1 and 3, on the right side of a parking lot.)*

OLD JEWISH QUARTER AND PANERIAI MEMORIAL. At the start of WWII, Vilnius had a thriving Jewish community of 100,000 (in a city of 230,000). Nazi persecution left just 6000 survivors, and the **synagogue** at Pylimo 39 is the only of the former 105 synagogues still standing. The **Vilna Gaon Jewish State Museum of Lithuania** commemorates the city's Jewish heritage, providing an honest account of Lithuanians' persecution of their Jewish neighbors on the eve of the war. *(Pylimo 4. ☎212 7912; www.jmuseum.lt. Open M-Th 10am-5pm, F 10am-4pm. Donations requested.)* For info on the Jewish Quarter or on locating ancestors, visit the **Chabad Lubavitch Center.** *(Šaltiniv 12. ☎215 0387. Open daily 9am-6pm.)* The **Paneriai Memorial,** Agrastų 15, southwest of the city, marks the spot in an eerie forest where Nazis butchered 100,000 Lithuanians, 70,000 of them Jews. The memorials are at pits that served as mass graves. *(Take the train to Paneriai from Platforms 5 and 7. 10min., 0.90Lt. From the station, take a right and follow Agrastų. Open M and W-F 11am-5pm. Free.)*

MUSEUM OF GENOCIDE VICTIMS. The horrors of the Soviet regime are on full display at this former KGB headquarters, which served as a Gestapo outpost during WWII. The basement has isolation rooms, torture chambers, and an execution cell open to the public. *(Aukų 2A, at the intersection with Gedimino. ☎249 7427; www.genocid.lt/muziejus. Open Tu-Sa 10am-5pm, Su 10am-3pm. 4Lt, Sept.-June students 2Lt. Sept.-June W free. Guided tours in Lithuanian 15Lt, in English or Russian 30Lt.)*

TRAKAI CASTLE. Built in the 14th century, Trakai Castle lies on an island 28km west of Vilnius and once served as a residence for the Grand Dukes of Lithuania. Consisting of a wonderfully preserved palace, dungeon, and four defense towers, the castle currently displays priceless collections of porcelain, weaponry, and artifacts (including hundreds of smoking pipes). Highlights include the coin gallery and the fascinating ethnography exhibit about the Dzūkija, Tartar, and Karaimai minority groups. *(Buses leave for Trakai from Vilnius every 35min. from platforms 8 and 9. 3Lt; pay driver. From Trakai station, head toward the water and bear left on the lakeside path. Continue for approximately 3km to reach the castle. Open daily 10am-7pm. 10Lt, 5Lt ISIC discount.)*

ENTERTAINMENT AND NIGHTLIFE

The National Philharmonic's **Vilniaus Festivalis** starts in late May or early June (www.filharmonija.lt). Check *Vilnius in Your Pocket* and *Exploring Vilnius*, distributed at hotels, for info on festivals. Whimsy abounds at the outstanding puppet shows at **Vilniaus Teatras Lėlė,** Arklīų 5. (☎262 8678; www.teatraslele.lt. Open Tu-Su 10am-4pm. Tickets 6-8Lt.) Look for postcards announcing events and offering discounts to clubs. For info on **gay nightlife,** check www.gayline.lt.

Broadway (Brodvėjus), Mėsinių 4, is an enormously popular club. (Cover 10Lt, includes 2 drinks. Open M noon-3am, Tu noon-4am, W-Sa noon-5am, Su noon-2am. MC/V.) Ultra-modern style and an all-night sushi bar make **Helios,** Didžioji 28, the latest craze in Vilnius. (Dress code enforced. 21+. Cover 15Lt. Open Th 10pm-4am, F-Sa 10pm-5am.) The chrome-and-black outdoor patio at **ŠMC** (Contemporary Art Center), Vokiečių 2, fills with a matching young and hip clientele. (Beer 5Lt. Open Su-Th 11am-midnight, F 11am-3am, Sa noon-1am. Cash only.)

KAUNAS ☎37

Kaunas (pop. 381,300) marked the Russian border in the late 17th century and served as the capital of Lithuania between WWI and WWII; today it is the nation's second-largest city. At the eastern end of **Laisvės,** the main pedestrian boulevard, the blue domes of the **Church of St. Michael the Archangel** sparkle over the city. (Open M-F 8:30am-4pm, Sa-Su 8:30am-2pm. Free.) Nearby, the **Devil Museum,** V. Putvinskio 64, exhibits more than 2000 depictions of the devil, who was revered as a guardian in Lithuanian folklore until Christianity came to rain on the Satanic parade. (Open Tu-Su 11am-5pm. 5Lt, students 2.50Lt.) The western end of Laisvės merges with Vilniaus and leads to the well-preserved **Old Town.** Walk west from Old Town Square to reach the meeting of the Neris and Nemunas rivers and the beautiful **Santakos Parkas.** The Nazis killed 50,000 prisoners, including 30,000 Jews, at the **Ninth Fort,** which now holds an exhibit on Lithuanians sent to Siberia by Stalin's purges. Flag down microbus 21 or 38 (1.50Lt) from Kęstučio, request to be dropped off at the Mega Mall, and continue on foot to the museum. (Open M and W-Su 10am-6pm. 4Lt, students 2Lt.) The **Sugihara House,** Vaĺzganto 30, details the courage of Diplomat Sugihara, the "Japanese Schindler," who helped 6000 Jews escape the Nazis by issuing them travel visas to Japan. Go east on Laisvės, turn left on Vytauto, and walk through Vytauto park heading southeast to Vaĺzganto. (Open high season M-F 10am-5pm, Sa-Su 11am-4pm; low season M-F 11am-3pm. Free.)

Litinterp ❸, Gedimino 28, arranges private rooms. (☎22 87 18; www.litinterp.lt. Open M-F 8:30am-5:30pm, Sa 9:30am-3pm. Singles 80-120Lt; doubles 140-160Lt. MC/V.) Just off Laisvės, **Metropolis ❷,** S. Daukanto 21, is popular with backpackers. (☎20 59 92. Singles 70Lt; doubles 100Lt. MC/V). Tables quake and chairs levitate without warning at the wacky **Crazy House ❶**, Vilniaus 16, in the basement. It's one of only two restaurants in the world where diners have to contend with moving furniture. (☎22 11 82. Entrees 6-18Lt. Open Su-Th 11am-midnight, F-Sa 11am-2am. MC/V.) In the evenings, traditional music fills **Žalias Ratas ❷**, Laisvės 36B, through the alley to the left of the tourist office. (Entrees 5-28Lt. Open daily 11am-midnight. MC/V.) The brewery **Avilys**, Vilniaus 34, features a hops- and honey-tinged menu, as well as an award-winning house brew. (www.avilys.lt. 0.5L beer 7Lt. Open M-Th 11am-midnight, F-Sa noon-2am, Su noon-midnight.) **Exit**, A. Jakšto 4, and **Deep Light**, Laisvės 59, are nighttime hot spots. (Exit open F-Sa 10pm-6am. Deep Light open M-Th 9am-midnight, F-Sa 9am-2am, Su 10am-midnight.) On Thursday nights, students flock to the party at **Siena**, Laisvės 93. (Cover 15Lt. Open W-Th 9pm-2am, F-Sa 9pm-4am.) To reach Kaunas from Vilnius, take the **bus** (1½hr., 2-3 per hr., 11-16Lt). The **tourist office** is at Laisvės 36. (☎32 34 36; http://visit.kaunas.lt. Open M-F 9am-6pm, Sa-Su 9am-1pm and 2-6pm.) **Postal Code:** 3000.

KLAIPĖDA ☎46

Strategically located on the tip of the Neringa peninsula, Klaipėda (pop. 192,500) was briefly the Prussian capital in the 19th century. As the northernmost Baltic harbor that doesn't freeze, Klaipėda's port still serves as a major shipping hub, and the city has a growing reputation as a jazz center. The **Clock Museum** (Laikrodžių Muziejus), Liepų 12, displays everything from Egyptian sundials to Chinese candle clocks. Follow Liepų eastward from the intersection with H. Manto. (Open Tu-Sa noon-6pm, Su noon-5pm. Tickets 2-4Lt.) The top of the 46m **Mary Queen of Peace Church Tower**, Rumpiškės 6A, offers a panoramic view. (Tickets 1-2Lt, available from the tourist office.) **Smiltynė**, across the lagoon, has gorgeous beaches. Would-be pirates will enjoy roaming the decks of the three **Old Fishing Vessels** on the road leading toward the **Sea Museum** (Lietuvos Jūrų Muziejus) in Smiltynė. To reach the museum, purchase a ticket at the kiosk at the ferry terminal (2Lt) and ride a small yellow tram. (www.juru.muziejus.lt. Open June-Aug. Tu-Su 10:30am-6:30pm; May and Sept. W-Su 10:30am-6:30pm; Oct.-Apr. Sa-Su 10:30am-5pm. Tickets 4-8Lt.)

Klaipėda Traveller's Guesthouse (HI) ❷, Butkų Juzės 7-4, near the bus station, has spotless, large dorms. (☎21 18 79; guestplace@yahoo.com. Bike rental 30Lt per day. Free Internet, coffee, and tea. Dorms 34Lt. HI discount 2Lt.) **Memelis ❷**, Žvejų 4, a red-brick brewery on the canal, serves tasty regional dishes. Enjoy the house beer while looking at historic photos of Klaipėda's waterfront. (☎40 30 40. Entrees 6-18Lt. Beer from 3Lt. Open Su-M noon-midnight, Tu-Th noon-2am, F-Sa noon-3am. MC/V.) **Kebab stands** near the ferry terminal in Smiltynė sell cheap and satisfying fare (4Lt). The **central market** in Klaipėda is on Turgaus aikštė. (Open daily 8am-6pm.) The best bars line H. Manto on the mainland. **Kurpiai**, Kurpių 1A, is a popular restaurant and jazz club. (☎41 05 55; www.jazz.lt. Live jazz nightly 9:30pm. Cover F-Sa 5-10Lt. Open daily noon-last customer. MC/V.)

LITHUANIA

Buses (☎41 15 47, reservations 41 15 40) go from Butkų Juzės 9 to Kaunas (3hr., 14 per day, 38Lt), Palanga (30-40min., 23 per day, 4Lt), and Vilnius (4-5hr., 10-14 per day, 49Lt). **Ferries** (☎31 42 17, info 31 11 17) run from Old Port Ferry Terminal, Žvejų 8, to Smiltynė (7min., every 30min., 1.50Lt) and connect with buses to Nida (1½hr., 7Lt). From the International Ferry Terminal, take microbus 8A to the city center (2Lt). The **tourist office** is at Turgaus 7. (☎41 21 86; www.klaipedainfo.lt. Open June-Aug. M-F 9am-6pm, Sa-Su 10am-4pm; May and Sept. M-F 10am-6pm, Sa 10am-4pm; Oct.-Apr. M-F 9am-6pm.) **Internet** access is available at the Preybos Tinklas shopping center, Taikos 15 (2Lt per hr.). **Postal Code:** 91247.

NIDA ☎469

Windswept sand dunes have long drawn vacationers to the former fishing village of **Nida** (pop. 1,500). One of four municipalities that make up the town of Neringa, Nida is the largest settlement on the Curonian Spit, one of the longest sea spits in the world. From the center, turn onto Naglių and head to the **Drifting Dunes of Parnidis.** The remains of an immense sundial sit atop the tallest dune (52m), marking a spot where beachgoers have the unique opportunity to look down on both the Curonian Lagoon and the Baltic Sea at once. Along Naglių on the way to the dunes, the **Fisherman's Ethnography Museum** provides a snapshot of one local fisherman's life (☎52 372). Doubling back toward the center of town, follow the waterfront promenade away from the dunes and bear right on Skruzdynės to reach the **Thomas Mann Museum** (Thomo Manno Namelis), up a large staircase at #17. Mann, a Nobel Prize-winning German author, built the cottage in 1930 but left when Hitler invaded. (Open June-Aug. daily 10am-6pm; Sept.-May Tu-Sa 10am-5pm. 2Lt, students 0.50Lt.) Luxurious **camping ❶,** with toilets, showers, and a Chinese restaurant, is just past the top of the hill at Taikos 45A. (Gear rental available. Tent sites 10-20Lt. 15Lt per person.) On the way to the dunes, a breathtaking seascape makes **Ešerinė ❸,** Naglių 2, a scenic place to indulge in a frosty beer. (☎527 57. Entrees 16-40Lt. Beer 3-5Lt. Open daily 10am-midnight. MC/V.) From Naglių 18E, **buses** (☎52 472) run to Klaipėda/Smiltynė (1½hr., 1 per hr., 7Lt). The **tourist office,** Taikos 4, opposite the bus station, arranges private rooms for a 5Lt fee. (☎52 345; www.visitneringa.com. Rooms 30-50Lt. Open June-Aug. M-Sa 10am-6pm, Su 10am-3pm; Sept.-May M-F 10am-1pm and 2-6pm, Sa 10am-3pm.) **Postal Code:** 93121.

PALANGA ☎460

The country's largest botanical park, over 20km of shoreline, and an exuberant nightlife make Palanga (pop. 20,000) the hottest summer spot in Lithuania. The beach is the main attraction, but Palanga's pride and joy is the **Amber Museum** (Gintaro Muziejus), in a mansion in the tranquil **Botanical Gardens.** The collection includes 15,000 pieces of the fossilized resin—known as "Baltic Gold"—with primeval flora and fauna trapped inside. (☎51 319; www.pgm.lt. Open daily June-Aug. 10am-12:30pm and 1:30-7pm; Sept.-May 11am-4:30pm. 5Lt, students 2.50Lt.) **Palangos Žuvėdra ❷,** Melies 11, has a run-down exterior but offers beachfront rooms at bargain prices. (☎53 253; www.palangos-zuvedra.lt. Reception 24hr. Singles 30-80Lt; doubles 50-90Lt; suites 70-250Lt.) Cafes and restaurants line **Vytauto,** which runs parallel to the coastline and passes the bus station, as well as the lively pedestrian thoroughfare **J. Basanavičiaus,** perpendicular to Vytauto. Locals hit the dance floor at **Honolulu Night Club,** S. Nerės 39, north of J. Basanavičiaus. (☎35 641. Open 10pm-late.) **Buses** (☎53 333) or **microbuses** from Klaipėda (30min., 2 per hr., 4Lt) arrive at Kretinjos 1. The **tourist office** to the right of the station books private rooms by email. (☎48 811; palangaturinfo@is.lt. Open daily 9am-2pm and 3-6pm.)

LUXEMBOURG

The forgotten "lux" of the Benelux countries, tiny Luxembourg is often overlooked by travelers smitten with Dutch windmills or impatient to press east into Germany. Luxembourg's castles rival those of the Rhineland, and the charming villages of the Ardennes are less touristed than their Belgian cousins. White-collar financiers keep prices in Luxembourg City high, but the eminently walkable capital remains a promising alternative to Bruges or Ghent.

DISCOVER LUXEMBOURG

Budget two days for **Luxembourg City** (p. 698), where you can explore the capital's maze of well-fortified tunnels by day and its lively nightlife after hours. The towns of **Echternach** (p. 704) and **Vianden** (p. 704) are notable stops, the former for its historic basilica and the latter for its hilltop château. From there, you can proceed south to the flyspeck village of **Esch-sur-Sûre** (p. 704) for hiking through wooded river valleys.

ESSENTIALS

FACTS AND FIGURES

Official Name: Grand Duchy of Luxembourg.

Capital: Luxembourg City.

Population: 465,000.

Land Area: 2,600 sq. km.

Time Zone: GMT +1.

Languages: Lëtzebuergesch; French, German, and English are widely spoken.

Religions: Roman Catholic (87%).

WHEN TO GO

The sea winds that routinely douse Belgium with rain have usually shed their moisture by the time they reach Luxembourg; good weather prevails from May through October, although travelers leery of crowds may want to avoid July and August. Temperatures average 17°C (64°F) in summer, and 1°C (34°F) in winter.

DOCUMENTS AND FORMALITIES

EMBASSIES AND CONSULATES. All foreign embassies and consulates are in Luxembourg City. For Luxembourg's embassies and consulates at home: **Australia,** Level 4, Quay West, 111 Harrington St., Sydney, NSW, 2000 (☎02 9253 4708); **UK,** 27 Wilton Cres., London, SW1X 8SD (☎20 7235 6961); **US,** 2200 Massachusetts Ave., NW, Washington, D.C., 20008 (☎202-265-4171; www.luxembourg-usa.org). **Canadians** should visit the embassy in Washington, D.C., **Irish** citizens should go to the London embassy, and **New Zealanders** should contact the embassy in Brussels.

VISA AND ENTRY INFORMATION. EU citizens do not need a visa. Citizens of Australia, Canada, New Zealand, and the US do not need a visa for stays of up to 90 days, beginning upon entry into any of the EU freedom-of-movement zone countries.

TOURIST SERVICES AND MONEY

TOURIST OFFICES. For general info, contact the **Luxembourg National Tourist Office,** Gare Centrale, P.O. Box 1001, L-1010 Luxembourg (☎42 82 82 1; www.ont.lu), or check out www.visitluxembourg.lu.

EMERGENCY	**Police:** ☎113. **Ambulance:** ☎112. **Fire:** ☎112.

MONEY. On January 1, 2002, the **euro (€)** replaced the **Luxembourg franc** as the unit of currency in Luxembourg. For exchange rates and more info on the euro, see p. 18. The cost of living in Luxembourg City is quite high, although the surrounding countryside is more reasonable. All countries that are members of the European Union impose a **Value Added Tax (VAT)** on goods and services purchased within the EU. Prices in Luxembourg already include the country's 15% VAT rate, one of the lowest in Europe. Partial refunds are also available for visitors who are not EU citizens (p. 22). Restaurant bills usually include a service charge, although an extra 5-10% tip can be a classy gesture. Tip taxi drivers 10%.

TRANSPORTATION

BY PLANE. The Luxembourg City airport (LUX) is serviced by **Luxair** (☎2456 4242; www.luxair.lu) and a slew of other European airlines. Cheap last-minute flights on Luxair (from €129) are available online.

BY TRAIN AND BUS. A **Benelux Tourrail Pass** (US$176, under 26 US$132; see p. 99) allows five days of unlimited train travel in a one-month period in Belgium, Luxembourg, and the Netherlands. Within Luxembourg itself, the **Billet Réseau** (€5, book of 5 €120) is good for one day of unlimited bus and train travel. The **Luxembourg Card** (€9-22) includes one to three days of unlimited transportation along with free or discounted admission to 50+ sights around the country.

BY BIKE AND THUMB. A 575km network of **cycling paths** snakes its way through Luxembourg, and plans are in place to add another 325km. Bikes aren't permitted on buses, but domestic trains will transport them for a fee (€1.20). While *Let's Go* does not recommend hitchhiking as a safe means of transport, service areas in Luxembourg are popular places to hitch rides into Belgium, France, and the Netherlands.

KEEPING IN TOUCH

TELEPHONES. There are no city codes in Luxembourg; from outside the country, dial 352 plus the local number. Public phones can only be operated with a phone card, available at post offices, train stations, and newspaper stands. Internet cafes are not abundant. **Mobile phones** are an increasingly popular and economical alternative (p. 29). International direct dial numbers include: **AT&T** (☎8002 0111); **British Telecom** (☎0800 0044); **Canada Direct** (☎8002 0119); **MCI** (☎8002 0112); **Sprint** (☎8002 0115); **Telecom New Zealand** (☎800 20064); **Telstra Australia** (☎0800 0061).

PHONE CODES	Country code: 352. International dialing prefix: 00. Luxembourg has no city codes. For more information on how to place an international call, see inside back cover.

LANGUAGE. The three official languages of Luxembourg are *Lëtzebuergesch*, French, and German. While *Lëtzebuergesch*, a West Germanic language, is used primarily in everyday conversations, official and administrative documents are written in French. German is most commonly used by the press, and English is often spoken as a second, third, or fourth language.

ACCOMMODATIONS AND CAMPING

LUXEMBOURG	❶	❷	❸	❹	❺
ACCOMMODATIONS	under €18	€18-24	€24-34	€34-55	over €55

Luxembourg's nine **HI youth hostels** *(Auberges de Jeunesse)* are often booked solid with school groups during the summer, so it's wise to reserve ahead. Almost half of the hostels remain open year-round, while the rest close for several weeks in December. Beds are approximately €17-20. Contact **Centrale des Auberges de Jeunesse Luxembourgeoises** (☎26 27 66 40; www.youthhostels.lu) for more info. **Hotels** are typically expensive, costing upwards of €40 per night. Happily, Luxembourg is a camper's paradise, and most towns have campsites close by. One person with a tent will typically pay €8-12 per night. Contact **Camprilux** (www.camping.lu/gb/gbstart.htm) for more info.

FOOD AND DRINK

LUXEMBOURG	❶	❷	❸	❹	❺
FOOD	under €5	€5-9	€9-14	€14-22	over €22

Traditional Luxembourgish cuisine combines elements of French and German cooking. Some specialties include *Judd mat Gaardenbou'nen* (smoked neck of pork with beans), *Friture de la Moselle* (fried fish), *Gromperekichelcher* (potato fritters), and *Quetscheflued* (plum tart). Fruity Riesling wines are produced in the Moselle Valley and show up most Chardonnays.

HOLIDAYS AND FESTIVALS

Holidays: New Year's Day (Jan. 1); Easter Sunday and Monday (Apr. 8-9); Labor Day (May 1); Ascension (May 17); Whit Sunday and Monday (May 27-28); National Day (June 23); Assumption (Aug. 15); All Saints' Day (Nov. 1); Christmas (Dec. 25), St. Stephen's Day (Dec. 26).

Festivals: The weeks leading up to Lent bring parades and masked balls under the guise of Carnival. Echternach hosts the International Music Festival in May and June, while Riesling Open wine festivals kick off in Wormeldange, Ahn, and Ehnen on the 3rd weekend of Sept.

LUXEMBOURG CITY

Luxembourg City (pop. 84,000) is an international banking hotspot home to thousands of frenzied business executive and has long been of military significance. Despite this, the metropolis more or less shuts down at 2am.

TRANSPORTATION

Flights: Findel International Airport (LUX), 6km from the city. Bus #16 (€1.50; every 15-30min.) is the cheapest way to get to the train station. Taxis are €15-20 (more at night) to the city center.

Trains: Gare CFL, av. de la Gare (☎24 89 24 89; www.cfl.lu), a 15min. walk south of the city center. To: **Amsterdam, NTH** (6hr.; 1 per hr.; €49, under 26 €34.50); **Brussels, BEL** (2¾hr., 1 per hr., €28/16); **Ettelbrück** (25min., 3 per hr., €4.50); **Paris, FRA** (4hr., every 2hr., €46.50). Ticket booth open daily 5:00am-9:30pm.

Buses: For travel only within the city, buy a short-distance ticket (*billet courte distance;* €1.50, book of 10 €10), valid for 1hr. A network pass (*billet réseau;* €5, book of 5 €20), also accepted on trains, allows for unlimited travel throughout the country for 1 day and is the most economical option for intercity travel. Most buses run until midnight. The free night bus (☎4796 2975) runs F-Sa 10pm-330am.

Taxis: €2 per km. 10% more 10pm-6am. **Colux Taxis:** ☎48 22 33.

Bikes: Rent from **Vélo en Ville,** 8 r. Bisserwé (☎47 96 23 83), in the Grund. Open Apr.-Oct. M-Sa 10am-noon and 1-8pm. €5 per hr., €12.50 per half-day, €20 per day, €37.50 per weekend, €75 per week. Under 26 20% discount for full day and longer. V.

ORIENTATION AND PRACTICAL INFORMATION

Five minutes by bus and 15min. by foot from the train station, Luxembourg City's historical center revolves around the **Place d'Armes.** From the train station, follow av. de la Gare or av. de la Liberté, then watch for signs with directions to the city's main sights. Facing the tourist office in the pl. d'Armes, the Pétrusse Valley is to your right; take r. Chimay to reach **Place de la Constitution** and the **Pétrusse Casemates.** The city's lower areas, the **Grund** and the **Clausen,** are located diagonally to your right and left, 10min. and 15min. on foot, respectively. Halfway between these areas are the **Bock Casemates;** from the pl. d'Armes, walk straight down r. du Curé, which becomes r. Boucherie and then r. Sigefroi.

Tourist Offices: Grand Duchy National Tourist Office (☎42 82 82 20; www.ont.lu), in the train station. Open daily June-Sept. 8:30am-6:30pm; Oct.-May 9:15am-12:30pm and 1:45-6pm. **Luxembourg City Tourist Office,** pl. d'Armes (☎22 28 09; www.lcto.lu). Open Oct.-Mar. M-Sa 9am-6pm, Su 10am-6pm; Apr.-Sept. M-Sa 9am-7pm, Su 10am-6pm. Look for the helpful, yellow-shirted **"Ask Me"** representatives around the city—they give out free tourist info. **Centre Information Jeunes,** 26 pl. de la Gare (☎26 29 32 00), opposite the train station in Galerie Kons, provides everything from tourist information to help on finding jobs in the area. Open M-F 10am-6pm.

Embassies: Ireland, 28 rte. d'Arlon (☎45 06 10). Open M-F 9:30am-12:30pm. **UK,** 5 bd. Joseph II (☎22 98 64; www.britain.lu). Open M-F 9:30am-12:30pm. **US,** 22 bd. Emmanuel Servais (☎46 01 23). **Australians, Canadians,** and **New Zealanders** should contact their embassies in France or Belgium.

Currency Exchange: Banks are the only option for changing money or cashing traveler's checks. Most are open M-F 8:30am-4 or 4:30pm. All are closed on weekends. Expect to pay commissions of €5 for cash and €8 for traveler's checks.

Luggage Storage: (☎49 90 55 74). In the train station. €3 per bag. 1-day storage during opening hours. Open daily 6:30am-9:30pm.

Laundromat: Quick Wash, 31 r. de Strasbourg (☎26 19 65 42), near the station. Wash and dry €10. Open M-F 8:30am-6:30pm, Sa 8am-6pm.

Pharmacy: Pharmacie Goedert, 5 pl. d'Armes (☎22 23 99). Open M-F 8am-6:15pm, Sa 8am-12:30pm. Pharmacies are marked by green crosses and are fairly prevalent. Call ☎9007 12 34 32 for a schedule of 24hr. pharmacies.

Emergency: Police: ☎113. **Ambulance and Fire:** ☎112.

Hospital: Clinique St-Thérèse, 36 r. Ste-Zithe (☎49 77 61 or 49 77 65; www.zitha.lu). Call ☎9007 1234 32 for a schedule of 24hr. hospitals.

Internet Access: Centre Information Jeunes (see p. 699) has limited free Internet for students. **Cyberbeach,** 3 r. du Cure, by pl. d'Armes. (☎26 47 80 70; www.cyberbeach.lu) €3.60 per hr. Open M-F 10am-8pm, Sa-Su 2-8pm.

Post Office: 38 pl. de la Gare, across the street and to the left of the train station. Open M-F 6am-7pm, Sa 6am-noon. Address mail to be held in the following format: First name LAST NAME, *Poste Restante,* L-1009 Luxembourg G-I Gare, LUXEMBOURG. Another branch, 25 r. Aldringen, near pl. d'Armes. Open M-F 7am-7pm, Sa 7am-5pm.

ACCOMMODATIONS AND CAMPING

The city hostel is the only budget option in Luxembourg City. Hotels are cheaper near the train station than in the city center.

Auberge de Jeunesse (HI), 2 r. du Fort Olisy (☎22 68 89 20; www.youthhostels.lu). Take bus #9 (dir.: Neudorf) and ask to get off at the hostel. From bus stop, take steep pathway down alongside bridge. Call ahead to reserve shuttles straight from the airport (€3) or train station (€2), M-F 9am-5pm. New, with river views and a restaurant. Bike rentals €2.50 per hr., €15 per day. Breakfast and sheets included. Lockers in rooms; bring a lock or rent one. Laundry €7.50. Internet access €3 per 30min. Reception 24hr. Dorms €21; singles €33; doubles €52. €3 HI discount. AmEx/MC/V. ❷

Bella Napoli, 4 r. de Strasbourg (☎48 46 29). From the train station, go straight down r. de la Liberté and turn left onto r. de Strasbourg. Hostel located above a pizza joint. Simple rooms with hardwood floors and full bath. Breakfast included. Reception 8am-midnight. Singles €38; doubles €45; triples €60. AmEx/MC/V. ❹

Hotel Schintgen, 6 r. Notre Dame (☎22 28 44). Down r. Chimay from the pl. d'Armes, turn right onto r. Notre Dame. One of the best deals in the Old Center, though loud. Breakfast included and delivered to room. Private shower and bath. Reception 7am-11pm. Singles €55-70; doubles €80-87; triples €90; quads €95. AmEx/MC/V. ❺

Camping Kockelscheuer, 22 rte. de Bettembourg (☎47 18 15), 4km outside Luxembourg City. Take bus #5 from the city center to Kockelscheuer-Camping. Tennis courts, washing machines (€1.50), hot water. Showers included. Open Easter-Oct. Reception 7am-noon and 2-10:30pm. Tent sites €4.50, additional adult €3.75. Cash only. ❶

FOOD

The area near the pl. d'Armes teems with fast-food joints and upscale restaurants, but there are a few appealing options. Stock up on groceries at **Supermarché Boon,** across from the train station. (Open M-F 8am-8pm, Sa 8am-6pm, Su 8am-noon.)

Restaurant-Café Chiggeri, 15 r. du Nord (☎22 82 36). Serves traditional French food amid shimmering, night-sky decor. Wine list offers 2300 vintages. Dine more affordably at the cafe downstairs. Entrees €11-14. Open daily 11am-midnight. AmEx/MC/V. ❹

Mesa Verde, 11 r. du St-Esprit (☎46 41 26), down the street from the pl. de Clairefontaine. A local favorite, this bright vegetarian restaurant features an ever-changing array of hand-painted murals and billowing fabrics decorating the walls. Entrees €19-25. Open Tu-Sa 6:30-11:30pm. Open for lunch W-F noon-2pm. MC/V. ❹

Namur, 27 r. des Capucins (☎22 34 08), down the street from pl. d'Armes. Marble floors, outdoor seating, and elegant ambience make the selection of pastries, chocolates, and sundaes (€5-6) even sweeter. Open M 2-6pm, Tu-Sa 8:30am-6pm. MC/V. ❷

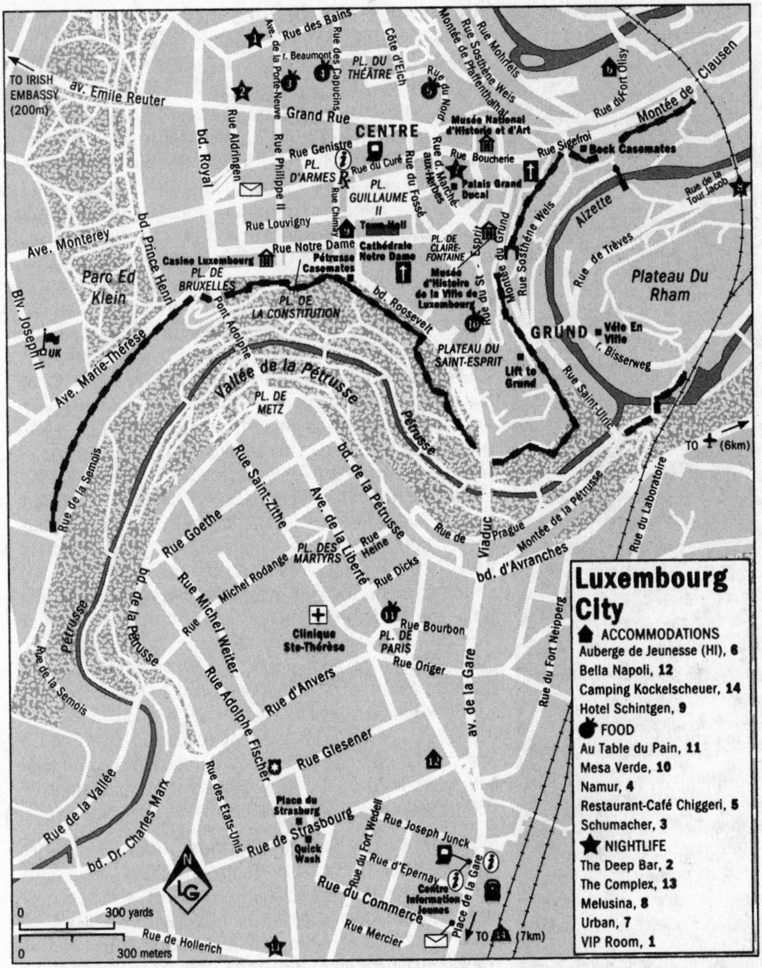

Au Table du Pain, 377 av. de la Liberté (☎29 56 63). Serves sandwiches (€5-7) salads (€8-13), and baked goods on wooden tables. Open M-F 7am-6pm. Cash only. ●

Schumacher, 18 av. de la Porte-Neuve (☎22 90 09). An elderly crowd frequents this sandwich spot; get takeout for picnics in the Pétrusse Valley. Sandwiches €3-4. Salads €6-7. Open M-Sa 7am-6pm. AmEx/DC/MC/V. ●

SIGHTS

The most spectacular views of the city can be seen from **Place de la Constitution** and from the bridge closest to the **Bock Casemates.** Signs indicate the **Wenzel Walk,** which leads visitors through 1000 years of history as it winds around the old city, from the **Chemin de la Corniche** down into the casemates.

MAKE A WISH, YOUR HIGHNESS

.uxembourg's diminutive size loesn't stop it from throwing one nell of a royal birthday party. The circumstances around the June 23 bash are a little puzzling, since Grand Duke Henri, the head of .uxembourg's constitutional monrchy, was born on April 16, 1955. Henri inherited the datechanging from his grandmother, Grand Duchess Charlotte, born on anuary 23, 1896. When her court realized that mid-winter loesn't lend itself to open-air bashes, they pushed celebrations back five months. Reluctant to urther confuse their subjects, both Henri and his father Jean ook June 23 as their own.

A procession through the old city starts things off on the evening of June 22. At 11pm, fireworks rip through the air, putting he city's bridges into sharp relief. n a flash, the narrow streets are ransformed into impromptu allages bars and dance floors; alcohol flows like water, spirits are nigh, and it takes the rising sun to inally break up the party. The disheveled revelers pour into the Place d'Armes for breakfast before staggering home to sleep. une 23 is a public holiday, so once the city wakes around noon, everyone heads downtown to see Henri strolling through the streets. With his aged parents in tow and oyal security out of sight, the duke restores calm and a sense of routine to a city unaccustomed o such glorious commotion.

FORTRESSES AND THE OLD CITY. The city's first fortress, built in AD 963, has has seen its network of fortifications expand so much over the years that the city has earned the nickname "Gibraltar of the North." The fortress contains the **casemates,** an intricate 23km network of tunnels through the fortress walls. First built to fortify the city's defenses, the casemates were almost dismantled when Luxembourg was declared a neutral state in 1867; during WWII the tunnels sheltered 35,000 people during bomb raids. The **Bock Casemates** fortress, part of Luxembourg's original castle, offers a fantastic view of the **Grund** and the **Clausen.** A brochure helps navigate. *(☎22 28 09 or 22 67 53. Entrance on r. Sigefroi, just past the bridge leading to the hostel. Open Mar.-Oct. daily 10am-5pm. €1.75, students €1.50.)* A visit to the **Pétrusse Casemates,** built by the Spanish in the 1600s, takes explorers down 250 steps into historic chambers while providing views of the Pétrusse Valley. A tour is required, but it's interesting, short (30min.), and cheap. *(Pl. de la Constitution. English-language tours every hr., July-Aug. 11am-4pm; intermittently in June. €1.75, students €1.50.)* The peaceful paths of the green **Pétrusse Valley** beckon for a stroll or an afternoon picnic in the shadow of the fortress walls. **Pétrusse Express tourist trains** depart from pl. de la Constitution and meander through the city and into the valley. *(Mid-Mar. to Oct. every 30min. 10am-6pm except 1pm. Trip lasts 50-60min. €8. Purchase tickets at pl. de la Constitution.)* Double decker, roofless **tourist buses** allow you to "hop on" and "hop off" as you please. *(Every 20min. 9:40am-5:20 or 6:20pm from several marked stops throughout the city. Info for train and buses ☎26 65 11; www.sightseeing.lu. €12, students €10. Ticket valid for 24hr. Wheelchair accessible.)*

MUSEUMS. The **Luxembourg Card** covers transport and entrance to 55 attractions throughout the country. *(Available at tourist offices, youth hostels, and most train stations. www.luxembourgcard.lu. 1-day card €9, 2-day €16, 3-day €22.)* The eclectic, well-organized collection at the **Musée National d'Histoire et d'Art** includes both modern and ancient art and a visual chronicle of the conquering powers' influences on Luxembourg's art. English translations are available on each floor. *(Marché-aux-Poissons, at r. Boucherie. ☎4793 30 214; www.mnha.lu. Open Tu-Su 10am-5pm. €5, students free.)* There's no gambling at **Casino Luxembourg,** only changing contemporary art exhibits. *(41 r. Notre Dame, near pl. de la Constitution. ☎22 50 45. Open M, W, F 11am-7pm, Th 11am-8pm, Sa-Su 11am-6pm. €4, under 26 €3, under 18 free.)* The **Musée d'Histoire de la Ville de Luxembourg** narrates the history of the city with artifacts and interactive displays. *(14 r. du St-Esprit, near pl. de Clairefontaine. ☎47 96 45 00. Open Tu-W and F-Su 10am-6pm, Th 10am-8pm. €5, students €3.70.)*

NIGHTLIFE

There is no central location for nightlife in Luxembourg City, so an evening of bar-hopping also involves hopping on and off of the city's night bus, until 2am, when bars usually close. In the summer, the **Place d'Armes** comes to life with free concerts (www.summerinthecity.lu) and stand-up comedy. Pick up a copy of *Nico* at the tourist office for a list of nightlife action and events.

Melusina, 145 r. de la Tour Jacob (☎43 59 22; www.melusina.lu). Cross the bridge from the Grund lift, then follow the left side of r. de Trèves and veer left as it becomes r. de la Tour Jacob. Eat at the classy restaurant or dance at the weekend spot. Restaurant open M-Sa 11:30am-2pm and 7-11pm. Club open F-Sa 11pm-4am. Cover €7.50-15. 1 free drink 11pm-midnight. Club is cash only.

Urban, at the corner of r. de la Boucherie and r. du Marché-aux-Herbes (☎26 47 85 78; www.urban.lu). A friendly, crowded bar in the heart of downtown. Food served until 6pm M-F, 7pm Sa-Su. Open daily noon-1am. Beer €2.20-3.60; cocktails €6. AmEx/MC/V.

The Complex, 42-44 r. de Hollerich. Take bus #1 or 22, or walk down av. de la Gare away from the city center. This cluster provides the most convenient bar-hopping. **Marx** caters to crowds over 25. DJs W and F-Sa inside. (☎48 84 26. Beer €2.20. Mixed drinks €6.50. Open daily 5pm-1am. MC/V.) **Chocolate Elvis** has party music and beer (€2.20), the **Bronx** high decibels. (Drinks €6-6.50. M-F 5pm-1am, Sa-Su 6pm-1am.)

VIP Room, 19 r. des Bains (☎26 18 78 67), near the pl. du Théatre. Glitzy and exclusive, this club has an atmosphere modeled after VIP clubs in Paris and St-Tropez. Open before 7pm for dinner. Club open Tu 7pm-midnight, W-Sa 7pm-late. AmEx/MC/V.

The Deep Bar, 11 r. Aldringen (☎26 20 04 23). Friendly gay bar; all welcome. DJ and dancing F-Sa. Open M 9am-9pm, Tu-Th 9am-1am, F 7am-3am, Sa 2pm-3am.

THE ARDENNES

In 1944, the Battle of the Bulge raged through the rolling hills of this region. Today, quiet towns, looming castles, and pleasant hiking trails are powerful attractions on which www.ardennes-lux.lu offers a wealth of info. Carry raingear; the humidity in the Ardennes often breaks into rain, which usually lasts only a short time. Check transportation schedules thoroughly; the system is geared towards locals, not tourists, who often rent cars: budget extra time for waiting.

ETTELBRÜCK. The main railway line linking Luxembourg City to Liège, BEL runs through Ettelbrück (pop. 7500), making the town the transportation hub for the Ardennes. Little else draws tourists to Ettelbrück, although history buffs might want to investigate the **General Patton Memorial Museum,** 5 r. Dr. Klein, which commemorates Luxembourg's WWII liberation. (☎81 03 22. Open June-Sept. 15 daily 10am-5pm; Sept. 16-May 30 Su 2-5pm. €2.50.) Stay at **Hotel Herckmans ❹,** 3 pl. de la Résistance. (☎81 74 28. Singles €35-40; doubles €45-60; triples €80. AmEx/MC/V.) Buy groceries at **Match,** near the train station. (Open M-Th 7:30am-7:30pm, F 7:30am-8pm, Sa 7:30am-6pm, Su 9am-12:30pm.) **Trains** go to Clervaux (30min., 1 per hr., €4.60) and Luxembourg City (25min., 3 per hr., €2.60). The **tourist office** is in the station. (☎81 20 68; www.sit-e.lu. Open M-F 9am-noon and 1:30-5pm, Sa 10am-noon and 2-4pm; Sept.-June closed Sa.)

ECHTERNACH. In the heart of the Little Switzerland region, Echternach (pop. 4500) is a charming tourist village and a paradise for **hikers** and **bikers** who venture out into the surrounding woodlands. In town, the turrets of the 15th-century **town hall** share the skyline with the towering **Basilica of St. Willibrord.** To get to the basilica, go down r. de la Gare in front of the station and take a left at pl. du Marché. St.

Willibrord draws more than 10,000 pilgrims every Whit Tuesday (Pentecost) for the **Dancing Procession.** The remains of a **Roman villa,** 47a r. des Romans, can be found near the lake, a 25min. walk from the station; take r. de la Gare and make a right from pl. du Marché onto rte. de Luxembourg, then a left on r. C.M. Spoo which will become r. des Romans, and follow signs. (☎26 72 09 74; www.villa-echternach.lu. Open Tu-Sa July-Aug. 11am-6pm; Su before Easter-June and Oct.-Nov. 1 11am-1pm and 2-5pm 11am-1pm and 2-5pm. €3.)

A new, lakeside **Auberge de Jeunesse (HI) ❷,** 1 chemin vert Roudenhaff, is a 30min. walk from the station. Walk past the Roman villa, passing a playground, to get there. (☎72 01 58; www.youthhostels.lu. Wheelchair-accessible. Breakfast and linens included. Reception 8am-10pm. Check-in 2-10pm. Bike rental €2.50 per hr., €8 per half day, €16 per day. Dorms €19.60; singles €31.60; doubles €24.60. €3 HI discount. MC/V.) Pick up groceries at **Match,** near pl. du Marché. (Open M-F 8am-7pm, Sa 8am-1pm, Su 8am-noon.) **Buses** run to Ettelbrück (50min., 1 per hr.) and Luxembourg City (#111 or 110; 45-60min., 2 per hr.). Rent **bikes** at Trisport, 31 rte. de Luxembourg. (☎72 00 86. Open Tu-Su 9am-noon and 2-6pm. €2.50 per hr., €15 per day.) The **tourist office,** 9 parvis de la Basilique, suggests hikes and bike routes in the area. (☎72 02 30; www.echternach-tourist.lu. Open daily July-Aug. 9:30am-12:30pm and 1:30-5:30pm; June and Sept. M-Sa 9am-noon and 2-5pm; Oct.-May M-F 9am-noon and 2-5pm.)

VIANDEN. The village of Vianden (pop. 2000) is home to one of the most impressive castles in Western Europe, the stoic **Château de Vianden.** It holds several displays of armor, furniture, and tapestries. Captions are mainly in French, but the view from the top of the hill is universally impressive. (☎84 92 91; www.castle-vianden.lu. Open daily Apr.-Sept. 10am-6pm; Oct. and Mar. 10am-5pm; Nov.-Feb. 10am-4pm. €5.50, students €4.50.) Take the **Chairlift** from 3 r. du Sanatorium up to the top of the mountain for more thrilling views. (☎83 43 23. €2.75, round-trip €4.25. Open Easter-Oct. 10am-5 or 6pm.) **Hikers** enjoy Vianden's trails; some also bike to Diekirch (22 km) and Echternach (30km). Rent **bikes** at the bus station in July and August (M-Sa 8am-noon and 3-5pm €10 for half day, €14 for full day.) Modern and clean rooms await at the **Auberge de Jeunesse (HI) ❷,** 3 Montée du Château, near the foot of the castle. To get there, climb Grande Rue up the hill and toward the castle; the hostel will be on your left when the road turns right. (☎83 41 77. Dorms €17.50; singles €19.50. €3 HI discount.) **Buses** head to Ettelbrück (#570; 30min., 2 per hr.) and to Clervaux (#663; 40min., 4 per day). Buying the €5 all-day pass for buses and trains is the best deal. The **tourist office,** 1 r. du Vieux Marché, is over the bridge on the right from the center of town. (☎83 42 571; www.tourist-info-vianden.lu. Internet €2 per hr. Open summer M-F 8am-6pm, Sa-Su 10am-2pm; winter 8am-noon and 1-5pm.)

ESCH-SUR-SÛRE. Cradled by the green Ardennes mountains and encircled by the ruins of Luxembourg's oldest castle, this tiny village (pop. 320) is an ideal base for those looking to explore the beautiful **Haute-Sûre nature reserve,** 15 rte. de Lultzhausen (☎899 3311), or the area's 700km of nature trails. (Open Mar.-Oct. M-Tu, Th-F 10am-noon and 2-6pm, Sa-Su 2-6pm; Nov.-Apr. closes 5pm.) **Hotel de la Sûre ❸,** 1 r. du Pont, is the village's unofficial tourist office and best bet for lodgings. From the bus stop, walk up r. de l'Église (the street on the left closest to the tunnel) past the church; the hotel is on the left. There are numerous activities, such as a free wine-tasting and canoe loans. (☎83 91 10; www.hotel-de-la-sure.lu. Pick up from Ettelbrück, €15-20; reserve 1 day ahead. Breakfast included. Free Internet. Reception 7am-midnight. Singles from €26, weekends €29. AmEx/MC/V.) The **bus** to Ettelbrück runs only on weekdays (#502; 25min., every 2-4hr.).

THE NETHERLANDS (NEDERLAND)

The Dutch are given to saying that although God created the rest of the world, *they* created the Netherlands. As most of their land area is below sea level, the task of keeping their iconic tulips and windmills on dry ground has become a national pastime. Early planners built dikes higher and higher in order to hold back the sea, but a new "flexible coast" policy depends on spillways and reservoirs to contain flood waters. For a people whose land constantly threatens to become ocean, the staunch Dutch have a deeply grounded culture and a down-to-earth friendliness. Time-tested art, ambitious architecture, and dynamic nightlife make the Netherlands one of the most popular destinations in Western Europe.

DISCOVER THE NETHERLANDS: SUGGESTED ITINERARIES

THREE DAYS. Go no farther than the canals and coffeeshops of **Amsterdam** (p. 709). **Museumplein** is home to some of the finest art collections in Europe, while the houses of ill repute in the **Red Light District** are delightfully lurid.

ONE WEEK. Begin in the capital, **Amsterdam** (2 days), then zip out to the beach parties in **Bloemendaal aan Zee** (1 day; p. 728). Recover in historic **Haarlem** (1 day, p. 727), then amble among the stately monuments of **The Hague** (1 day; p. 729). End in youthful, hypermodern **Rotterdam** (2 days; p. 731).

BEST OF THE NETHERLANDS, TWO WEEKS. You can't go wrong starting off in **Amsterdam** (4 days). **Bloemendaal aan Zee** (1 day) and **Haarlem** (1 day) are next, then on to **The Hague** (1 day) and **Rotterdam** (1 day). Take two days to explore the museums in the college town of **Utrecht** (p. 732). Spend the night in **Arnhem,** and the next day on the trails and galleries of **De Hoge Veluwe National Park** (1 day; p. 733). End in the trendy city of **Groningen** (2 days; p. 734).

ESSENTIALS

FACTS AND FIGURES

Official Name: Kingdom of the Netherlands.

Capital: Amsterdam; The Hague is the seat of government.

Major Cities: The Hague, Rotterdam, Utrecht.

Population: 16,492,000.

Land Area: 41,526 sq. km.

Time Zone: GMT +1.

Language: Dutch; English is spoken almost universally.

Religions: Catholic (31%), Protestant (20%), Muslim (6%).

WHEN TO GO

July and August are lovely for travel to the Netherlands, as the crowded hostels and lengthy lines during those months will confirm. If you fancy a bit more elbow room, you may prefer April, May, and early June, as tulips and fruit trees furiously bloom and temperatures hover around 12-20°C (53-68°F). The Netherlands is famously drizzly year-round, so travelers should bring raingear.

DOCUMENTS AND FORMALITIES

EMBASSIES AND CONSULATES. All foreign embassies and most consulates are in The Hague (p. 729). Both the UK and the US have consulates in Amsterdam (p. 709). Dutch embassies abroad include: **Australia,** 120 Empire Circuit, Yarralumla Canberra, ACT, 2600 (☎02 62 20 94 00; www.netherlands.org.au); **Canada,** 350 Albert St., Ste. 2020, Ottawa, ON, K1R 1A4 (☎613-237-5030; www.netherlandsembassy.ca); **Ireland,** 160 Merrion Rd., Dublin, 4 (☎012 69 34 44; www.netherlandsembassy.ie); **New Zealand,** P.O. Box 840, at Ballance and Featherston St., Wellington (☎044 71 63 90; www.netherlandsembassy.co.nz); **UK,** 38 Hyde Park Gate, London, SW7 5DP (☎020 75 90 32 00; www.netherlands-embassy.org.uk); **US,** 4200 Linnean Ave., NW, Washington, D.C., 20008 (☎202-244-5300; www.netherlands-embassy.org).

VISAS AND ENTRY INFORMATION. EU citizens do not need a visa. Citizens of Australia, Canada, New Zealand, and the US do not need a visa for stays of up to 90 days, beginning upon entry into any of the countries in the EU's freedom of movement zone. For more information, see p. 18.

TOURIST SERVICES AND MONEY

EMERGENCY	**Police, Ambulance,** and **Fire:** ☎112.

TOURIST OFFICES. VVV (vay-vay-vay) tourist offices are marked by triangular blue signs. The website www.visitholland.com is also a useful resource. The **Holland Pass** (www.hollandpass.com, €25), lets you choose the five museums or sites you get into free, plus grants discounts at restaurants and attractions.

MONEY. The **euro (€)** has replaced the guilder as the unit of currency in the Netherlands. For exchange rates and more info on the euro, see p. 18. As a general rule, it's cheaper to exchange money in the Netherlands than at home. A bare-bones day in the Netherlands will cost €35-40; a slightly more comfortable day will run €50-60. Hotels and restaurants include a service charge in the bill; additional tips are appreciated but not necessary. Taxi drivers are generally tipped 10% of the fare. Retail goods in the Netherlands bear a 19% **value-added tax (VAT),** included in the listed price. In the airport, upon departure, non-EU citizens who have stayed in the EU fewer than 180 days can claim a refund on the tax paid for purchases at participating stores for items more than approximately €130; ask at stores for forms.

TRANSPORTATION

BY PLANE. Many major airlines, including the Dutch **KLM,** fly into Amsterdam's **Schiphol Airport** (AMS). **Ryanair** flies from London Stansted into secondary airports in Aachen (AAH), Eindhoven (EIN), and Groningen (GRQ), all accessible by rail. For more info on flying to Europe, see p. 42.

BY TRAIN. The national rail company is the efficient **Nederlandse Spoorwegen** (NS; Netherlands Railways; www.ns.nl). Train service tends to be faster than bus service. *Sneltreinen* are the fastest, while *stoptreinen* make many local stops. One-way tickets are called *enkele reis;* same-day, round-trip tickets *(dagretour)* are valid only on the day of purchase, but are roughly 15% cheaper than normal round-trip tickets. *Weekendretour* tickets are not quite as cheap, but are valid from Friday at 7pm through Monday at 4am. A day pass *(dagkaart)* allows unlimited travel throughout the country for one day, for the price equivalent to the most expensive one-way fare across the country. **Eurail** and **InterRail** have passes that are valid in the Netherlands. The **Holland Railpass** is good for three or five travel

days in any one-month period. Although available in the US, the Holland Railpass is cheaper in the Netherlands at DER Travel Service or RailEurope offices. For more information on train travel in Europe, see p. 46.

TIP **WHERE'S THE RAIL?** Nederlandse Spoorwegen is the Dutch national rail company, operating the country's intercity train service. Their website, www.ns.nl, has an English-language section with train times, costs, and door-to-door directions for all stops in the Netherlands.

BY BUS. A nationalized fare system covers city buses, trams, and long-distance buses. The country is divided into zones: a trip between destinations in the same zone costs two strips on a *strippenkaart* (strip card); a trip in two zones will set you back three strips. On buses, tell the driver your destination and he or she will cancel the correct number of strips; on trams and subways, stamp your own *strippenkaart* in either a yellow box at the back of the tram or in the subway station. Tram and bus drivers sell cards with two, three, and eight strips, but it's cheaper to buy 15-strip or 45-strip cards at tourist offices, post offices, and some newsstands near a rail station. Day passes *(dagkaarten)* are valid for travel throughout the country and are discounted as special summer tickets *(zomerzwerfkaarten)* June through August. Riding without a ticket can result in a fine.

BY CAR. Normally, tourists with a driver's license valid in their home country can drive in the Netherlands for fewer than 185 days. The country has well-maintained roadways, although drivers may cringe at high fuel prices, traffic, and scarce parking near Amsterdam, The Hague, and Rotterdam. The yellow cars of the **Royal Dutch Touring Club** (ANWB) patrol many major roads, and will offer prompt roadside assistance. In the case of a breakdown, call the ANWB (☎08 00 08 88) toll-free from any yellow phone booth.

BY BIKE AND BY THUMB. Cycling is the way to go in the Netherlands—distances between cities are short, the countryside is absolutely flat, and most streets have separate bike lanes. Bike rentals run €6-7 per day and €25-40 per week. For a database of bike rental shops and other cycling tips and information, visit www.holland.com/global/discover/active/cycling. **Hitchhiking** is illegal on highways but common elsewhere; droves of hitchhikers can be found along roads leading out of Amsterdam. Those choosing this mode of transport often take public transportation to a nearby town before trying their luck. *Let's Go* does not recommend hitchhiking.

KEEPING IN TOUCH

PHONE CODES	**Country code:** 31. **International dialing prefix:** 00. For more information on how to place international calls, see inside back cover.

EMAIL AND THE INTERNET. Email is easily accessible within the Netherlands. In small towns, try the public library. Travelers with wireless-enabled computers may be able to take advantage of an increasing number of hot spots, which offer wireless Internet for free or for a small fee. Websites like www.jiwire.com, www.wi-fihotspotlist.com, and www.locfinder.net can help locate hot spots.

TELEPHONE. Some pay phones still accept coins, but phone cards are the rule. KPT and Telfort are the most widely accepted varieties, the former available at post offices and the latter at train stations (from €5). **Mobile phones** are an increasingly popular and economical alternative (p. 29). For directory assistance, dial ☎09 00 80 08, for collect calls 08 00 01 01. International direct dial numbers include: **AT&T Direct** (☎0800 022 91 11); **British Telecom** (☎0800 89 00 31); **Canada Direct** (☎0800 022 91 16); **MCI WorldPhone** (☎0800 023 5103); **Sprint** (☎0800 022 91 19); **Telecom New Zealand** (☎0800 022 44 64); **Telstra Australia** (☎0800 022 0061).

MAIL. Post offices are generally open Monday through Friday 9am-5pm, Thursday or Friday nights, and Saturday mornings in some larger towns. In Amsterdam and Rotterdam, there are 24hr. post offices. Mailing a postcard or letter (up to 20g) within the EU costs €0.69 and goes up to €0.85 outside of Europe.

LANGUAGE. Dutch is the official language. Most natives speak excellent English, thanks to mandatory English education and English-language media exports.

ACCOMMODATIONS AND CAMPING

THE NETHERLANDS	❶	❷	❸	❹	❺
ACCOMMODATIONS	under €25	€25-32	€32-45	€45-55	over €55

VVV offices supply accommodation listings and can almost always reserve rooms for a €2-5 fee. **Private rooms** cost about two-thirds as much as hotels, but they are harder to find; check with the VVV. During July and August, many cities add a tourist tax (€1-2) to the price of all rooms. The country's 30 **Hostelling International (HI) youth hostels,** run by **Stayokay** (www.stayokay.com), are dependably clean and modern. There is **camping** across the country, although sites tend to be crowded during the summer months; **CityCamps Holland** has a network of 17 well-maintained sites. Visit www.strandheem.nl for more information.

FOOD AND DRINK

THE NETHERLANDS	❶	❷	❸	❹	❺
FOOD	under €7	€7-11	€11-16	€16-21	over €21

Traditional Dutch cuisine is hearty, heavy, and meaty. Expect bread for breakfast and lunch, topped with melting *hagelslag* (flaked chocolate topping) in the morning and cheese later in the day. Generous portions of meat and fish make up dinner, traditionally the only hot meal of the day. Seafood, from various grilled fish and shellfish to fish stews and raw herring, is popular. For a truly authentic Dutch meal (most commonly available in May and June), ask for white asparagus, served with potatoes, ham, and eggs. Light snacks include *tostis* (hot grilled-cheese sandwiches, sometimes with ham) and *broodjes* (light, cold sandwiches). Colonialism's legacy has brought Surinamese and Indonesian cuisine to Holland, bestowing cheaper and lighter dining options. Falafel stands proliferate in cities. Wash down meals with foamy glasses of Heineken or Amstel.

HOLIDAYS AND FESTIVALS

Holidays: New Year's Day (Jan. 1); Good Friday (Apr. 6); Easter (Apr. 8-9); Queen's Day (Apr. 30); WWII Remembrance Day (May 4); Liberation Day (May 5); Ascension Day (May 17); Whit Sunday and Monday (May 27-28); Boxing Day (Dec. 26).

Festivals: Koninginnedag (Queen's Day; Apr. 30) turns the country into a huge carnival. The Holland Festival (June; www.hollandfestival.nl) has been celebrating the performing arts in Amsterdam since 1948. In the Bloemen Corso (Flower Parade; early September), flower-covered floats crawl from Aalsmeer to Amsterdam. Historic canal houses and windmills are open to the public for National Monument Day (2nd weekend in Sept.). The High Times Cannabis Cup (Late Nov.) simply celebrates pot.

BEYOND TOURISM

Volunteer and work opportunities often revolve around international politics or programs resulting from liberal social attitudes. Studying in the Netherlands can be mundane, but it can also entail in-depth looks at sex and drugs.

Het Vrouwenhuis (The Women's House), Nieuwe Herengracht 95, Amsterdam (☎625 20 66). A center for several organizations and magazines dedicated to supporting women. An array of classes and workshops are offered, most often in Dutch.

University of Amsterdam, Spui 21, Amsterdam (☎525 80 80 or 525 33 33; www.uva.nl/english). Amsterdam's largest university offers a full range of degree programs in Dutch. Open to college and graduate students. The Summer Institute on Sexuality, Culture, and Society (www.ishss.uva.nl/summerinstitute), set in the heart of one of the world's most tolerant cities, examines sexuality in various cultures. Tuition €1445-10,000 per year, depending on the program. Discounts offered for EU citizens.

AMSTERDAM ☎020

Amsterdam's reputation precedes it—and what a reputation it is. Born out of a murky bog and cobbled together over eight centuries, the "Dam on the River Amstel" (pop. 735,238) hooks visitors with an alluring blend of polish and decadence. Geometry-defying canals support palatial museums and narrow, gabled houses.

Thick clouds of marijuana smoke waft from subdued coffeeshops, and countless bicycles whoosh past blooming tulip markets. Yet there is much more to Amsterdam than debauchery and picture-perfect sights. Against the backdrop of van Gogh's thick swirls and Vermeer's luminous figures, less institutionalized artists graffiti the streets, and politicians push the boundaries of progressive reform. Gay and lesbian citizens blend seamlessly into a social landscape that defines tolerance, but one that today faces difficult questions. Muslim integration into Dutch secularism, the limits of liberalism in an interdependent world, and the endless fight to fend off encroaching seas show how this city has its work cut out for itself.

Amsterdam

ACCOMMODATIONS
Aivergo Youth Hostel, **6**
Bicycle Hotel, **35**
Bob's Youth Hostel, **8**
Euphemia Budget Hotel, **31**
Flying Pig Downtown, **7**
Flying Pig Palace, **30**
Frederic Rent a Bike, **2**
The Golden Bear, **4**
Hemp Hotel, **32**
Hotel Asterisk, **33**
Hotel Bema, **36**
Hotel Brouwer, **5**
Hotel Clemens, **11**
Fantasia Hotel, **26**
Hotel Pension Kitty, **27**
Hotel Royal Taste, **12**
Quentin Hotel, **24**
The Shelter Jordan, **10**
StayOkay Amsterdam Stadsdoelen, **17**
StayOkay Amsterdam Vondelpark, **29**
Weichmann Hotel, **16**
The Winston Hotel, **9**

BEST OF FOOD
Cinema Paradiso, **22**
Harlem: Drinks and Soulfood, **3**
In de Waag, **13**

BEST OF COFFEESHOPS
Abraxas, **14**
Barney's Coffeeshop, **1**

BEST OF NIGHTLIFE
Bourbon Street Jazz & Blues Club, **25**
Cafe de Jaren, **18**
Club NL, **15**
Escape, **21**
Melkweg, **23**
Paradiso, **28**
De Trut, **19**

TRANSPORTATION

Flights: Schiphol Airport (AMS; ☎0800 72 44 74 65, for flight info 0900 724 47 46.). **Sneltrains** connect the airport to Centraal Station (20min., €3.60).

Trains: Centraal Station, Stationspl. 1 (☎09 00 92 92, €0.30 per min.; www.ns.nl), at the northern end of the Damrak. To: **Brussels, BEL** (2½-3hr., 1-2 per hr., €40); **Groningen** (2¼hr., 2 per hr., €27); **Haarlem** (15 min., 6 per hr., €3.40); **The Hague** (50-55min., 2-3 per hr., €9.50); **Leiden** (45min., 3 per hr., €7.50); **Rotterdam** (1hr., 3 per hr., €13); **Utrecht** (30min., 3 per hr., €6.30).

Buses: Trains are quicker, but the **GVB** (see below) will direct you to a bus stop for domestic destinations not on a rail line. **Muiderpoort** (2 blocks east of Oosterpark) sends buses east; **Marnixstation** (at the corner of Marnixstr. and Kinkerstr.) west; and the **Stationsplein** depot north and south.

Public Transportation: GVB (☎0900 80 11, €0.10 per min.; www.gvb.nl), on Stationspl. in front of Centraal Station. Open M-F 7am-9pm, Sa-Su 10am-7pm. **Tram, metro,** and **bus** lines radiate from Centraal Station. Trams are most convenient for center-city travel; the metro leads to farther-out neighborhoods. Normal public transportation runs daily 6am-12:30am. **Night buses** traverse the city 12:30am-7am; pick up a schedule and map at the GVB (€3 per trip, night bus strip card available). *Strippenkaarten* (strip cards) are used on all public transportation in Amsterdam; 2 strips (€1.60) get you to almost all sights within the city center and include unlimited transfers for 1hr. *Strippenkaarten* are cheapest bought in bulk (up to bundles of 45; 15-strip card €6.70) and are available everywhere. The tourist office sells 24hr. (€6.30), 48hr. (€10), and 72hr. (€13) tickets good on all buses, trams, and the metro.

Bike Rental: Frédéric Rent a Bike, Brouwersgr. 78 (☎624 55 09; www.frederic.nl), in the Shipping Quarter. Bikes €10 per day, €40 per week. Lock, theft insurance, and map included. Credit card required. Open daily 9am-5:30pm. Cash only. **MacBike Rentals** (www.macbike.nl) has 3 locations: at Stationspl. 5, near Centraal (☎62 483 91); at Weteringsschans 2, near Museumpl. (☎528 76 88); and at Mr. Visserpl. 2. Bikes €6-9 per 3hr., €8.50-13 per day. €50 deposit or credit card required. Free city map, or buy maps with suggested routes. Open daily 9am-5:45pm. AmEx/MC/V.

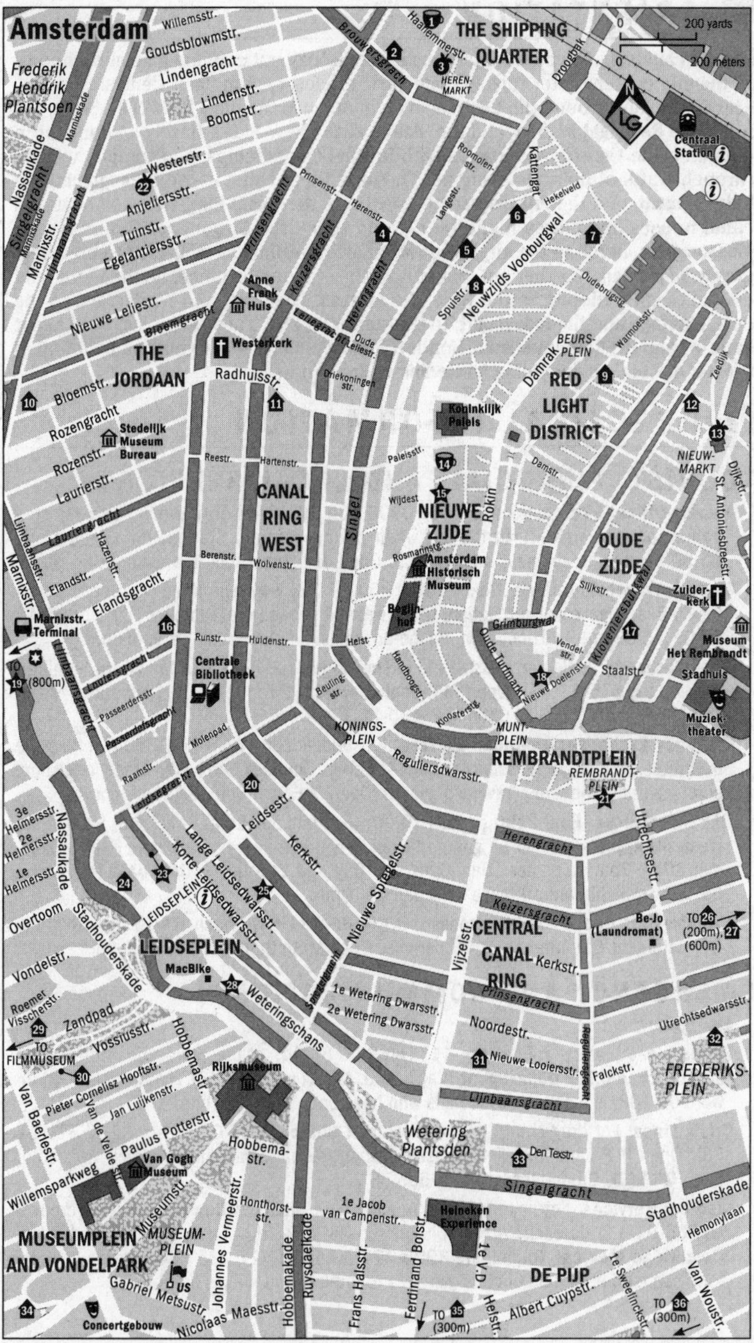
Amsterdam
THE SHIPPING QUARTER
THE JORDAAN
CANAL RING WEST
NIEUWE ZIJDE
RED LIGHT DISTRICT
OUDE ZIJDE
REMBRANDTPLEIN
CENTRAL CANAL RING
LEIDSEPLEIN
MUSEUMPLEIN AND VONDELPARK
DE PIJP
Centraal Station
Anne Frank Huis
Westerkerk
Koninklijk Paleis
Stedelijk Museum Bureau
Amsterdam Historisch Museum
Begijnhof
Centrale Bibliotheek
Marnixstr. Terminal
Zuiderkerk
Museum Het Rembrandt
Stadhuis
Muziektheater
Be-Jo (Laundromat)
MacBike
Rijksmuseum
Van Gogh Museum
Heineken Experience
Concertgebouw
US
Wetering Plantsden
FREDERIKSPLEIN
Frederik Hendrik Plantsoen
TO FILMMUSEUM
200 yards
200 meters

ORIENTATION

Let the canals guide you through Amsterdam's cozy but confusing neighborhoods. In the city center, water runs in concentric circles, beginning at Centraal Station. The **Singel** runs around the **Centrum,** which includes the **Oude Zijde** (Old Side), the infamous **Red Light District,** and the **Nieuwe Zijde** (New Side). Barely a kilometer in diameter, the Centrum overflows with brothels, bars, clubs, and tourists wading through wafts of marijuana smoke. The next three canals—the **Herengracht,** the **Keizersgracht,** and the **Prinsengracht**—constitute the **Canal Ring,** home to beautiful canal houses and classy nightlife. Beyond them, the **Singelgracht** courses past **Museumplein,** home to the city's renowned art museums as well as the sprawling, grassy **Vondelpark.** Farther out, but still within walking distance, lie the more residential neighborhoods: to the west, the **Jordaan, Oud-West,** and **Westerpark;** to the east, **Plantage** and the **Jodenbuurt;** to the south, **De Pijp.** These areas have excellent eateries and brilliant museums. South of Leidseplein, a few sights can be found in **Greater Amsterdam,** including **Amsterdamse Bos** (Forest).

PRACTICAL INFORMATION

TOURIST, FINANCIAL, AND LOCAL SERVICES

Tourist Office: VVV, Stationspl. 10 (☎0900 400 40 40 €0.55 per min.; www.iamsterdam.nl or www.atcb.nl), to the left when exiting Centraal Station. Books rooms for €3.50 per person and sells maps for €2. Open daily 9am-5pm. Branch at Leidsepl. 1.

Budget Travel: Eurolines, Rokin 10 (☎560 87 88; www.eurolines.nl). Books coach travel. Buses leave Amstel Station. Call if website shows no availability. Office open M-F 9:30am-5:30pm, Sa 10am-4pm. Phone bookings M-F 9am-7pm, Sa 9am-5pm.

Consulates: All foreign embassies are in **The Hague** (p. 729). **UK Consulate,** Koningslaan 44 (☎676 43 43). Open M-F 9am-noon and 2-5:30pm. **US Consulate,** Museumpl. 19 (☎575 53 09). Open M-F 8:30-11:30am.

Currency Exchange: American Express, Amsteldijk 166 (☎20 504 8504), offers the best rates, with no commission on AmEx Travelers' Cheques and a €4 flat fee for all non-euro cash and non-AmEx traveler's checks. Open M-F 9am-5pm, Sa 9am-noon.

GLBT Resources: Pink Point (☎428 10 70; www.pinkpoint.org), a kiosk in front of the Westerkerk, provides info on gay and lesbian nightlife and events. Open daily in summer 10am-8pm; in winter 10am-6pm. The **Gay and Lesbian Switchboard** (☎623 65 65; www.switchboard.nl) takes calls daily 2-10pm.

Laundromat: Happy Inn, Warmoesstr. 30 (☎624 84 64). Wash €3.20 per 13kg, dry €1, detergent €1. Internet €1.20 per min. Open M-Sa 8am-9pm, Su 9am-9pm.

EMERGENCY AND COMMUNICATIONS

Emergency: ☎112.

Police: Headquarters at Elandsgr. 117 (☎09 00 88 44), at the intersection with Marnixstr. The **Rape Crisis Department** is also here. **ATAS** (☎625 3246), Nieuwezijds Voorburwal 104-108, is a service for tourists who have been victims of crimes.

Crisis Lines: For drug counseling, call **Jellinek Clinic,** Jacob Obrechstr. 92 (☎570 23 78). Open M-F 9am-5pm. For counseling about sexually transmitted infections, call or go to **GG&GD,** Groenburgwal 44 (☎555 58 22).

Medical Services: For hospital care, **Academisch Medisch Centrum,** Meibergdreef 9 (☎566 91 11), is easily accessible on subway #54 (dir.: Gein; stop: Holendrecht). **Cambridge Medical,** Rapenburg 30 (☎427 50 11 or 627 235 380; www.touristdoctor.huisartsen.nl), offers doctors' services to tourists and makes hotel visits.

24hr. Pharmacy: A hotline (☎59 23 315) will direct you to the nearest 24hr. pharmacy.

Internet Access: Many coffeeshops and hostels offer Internet access for customers and guests, charging €1-2 per 30min. **easyInternetCafe,** Reguliersbreestr. 22 and Damrak 34, approx. €1 per 25min. Open 24hr. Free 30min. slots are also available at the **Centrale Bibliotheek** (library), Prinsengr. 587 (☎523 09 00; www.oba.nl). Open M 1-9pm, Tu-Th 10am-9pm, F-Sa 10am-5pm.

Post Office: Singel 250, at Radhuisstr. Address mail to be held in the following format: First name, LAST NAME, *Poste Restante,* Singel 250, 1016 AB, Amsterdam, THE NETHERLANDS. Open M-W and F 9am-6pm, Th 9am-8pm, Sa 10am-1:30pm.

ACCOMMODATIONS

The chaos of the Red Light District prompts accommodations near **Centraal Station** to enforce strong security measures, while hostels and hotels near **Museumplein** and out in the **Jordaan** are more laissez-faire. These locations are close to bars and coffeeshops and only 2min. by tram from the city's heart. Accommodations in the **Red Light District** are often bars with beds over them. Prices vary dramatically by season and amenities desired.

NIEUWE ZIJDE, OUDE ZIJDE, AND THE RED LIGHT DISTRICT

Flying Pig Downtown, Nieuwendijk 100 (☎420 68 22; www.flyingpig.nl). A great location and lounge ingratiate this hostel to backpackers unbothered by smoke clouds. Breakfast and linens included. Lockers available. Free Internet. Key deposit €1. Reception 24hr. Online reservations recommended, but walk in by 8:30am for a bed that night. Dorms €25-33; singles or doubles €86, F-Sa extra. AmEx/MC/V. ❶

Aivengo Youth Hostel, Spuistr. 6 (☎421 36 70; www.aivengoyouthhostel.com). Brightly painted and bejeweled walls endow this hostel with a uniformly cool vibe despite its lack of social area. €5 deposit for safe-deposit box. Linens included. Free Internet. In summer, 2-night min. stay on weekends. Reception 6am-4am. Internet or same-day phone reservations (at 8am), or walk in by 10am for a bed that night. Closed Dec. 20-27 and Jan. 15-Mar. 1. Dorms €20-25; 4-person "sky room" €30 per person. MC/V. ❶

The Winston Hotel, Warmoesstr. 129 (☎623 13 80; www.winston.nl). Most rooms painted by local artists. Breakfast included. Dorms €22-24; singles €60-75; doubles €90-105; triples €110-123; quads €124-156. AmEx/MC/V. ❷

Stayokay Amsterdam Stadsdoelen (HI), Kloveniersburgwal 97 (☎624 68 32; www.hihostel.com). Clean, drug-free canal-side lodgings in a quiet corner of Oude Zijde. Breakfast and linens included. Lockers available. Laundry €4.50. Internet €5 per hr. Reception 7am-midnight. Dorms €24. €2.50 HI discount. AmEx/MC/V. ❶

Hotel Royal Taste, Oudezijds Achterburgwal 47 (☎623 24 78; www.hotelroyaltaste.nl). Clean, almost-fancy accommodations at reasonable prices, right in the Red Light District. Rooms with bath, fridge, and TV; some with kitchen. Breakfast included. 24hr. bar. Singles €50-60; doubles €100-120; triples €150; quads €200. Cash only. ❹

Hotel Brouwer, Singelgr. 83 (☎624 63 58; www.hotelbrouwer.nl). 8 gorgeously restored rooms. Breakfast included. Reception 8am-6pm. Reserve 1 per hr. Singles €55; doubles €90; triples €155. Cash and traveler's checks only. ❹

Bob's Youth Hostel, Nieuwezijds Voorburgwal 92 (☎623 00 63; www.bobsyouthhostel.nl). Big, airy, no-frills dorms packed with friendly backpackers. Bar downstairs. Breakfast and linens included. Locker deposit €10. Internet €2 per hr. Key deposit €10. 2-night min. stay on weekends. Reception 8am-3am. Internet reservations only; walk in before 10am for a room. Dorms €20; doubles €70; triples €90. Cash only. ❶

SHIPPING QUARTER, CANAL RING WEST, AND THE JORDAAN

Wiechmann Hotel, Prinsengr. 328-332 (☎626 33 21; www.hotelwiechmann.nl). 3 charming, restored canal houses with living room details. Breakfast included. Singles €80-100; doubles €130-150; triples, quads, and suites €180-245. MC/V. ❺

Frédéric Rent a Bike, Brouwersgr. 78 (☎624 55 09; www.frederic.nl). In addition to bikes (see p. 710), Frédéric rents a range of beautiful rooms, apartments, and houseboats through connections with various locals. Frédéric also has 3 homey, cheerful rooms in the back of the rental shop; 1 has waterbed and private bathtub with sauna jets while the other 2 share a bath. Reception 9am-6pm. Check website for listing. Rooms €40-100. Cash only; AmEx/MC/V required for reservation. ❹

Hotel van Onna, Bloemgr. 104 (☎626 58 01; www.hotelvanonna.nl). Sleep peacefully in this restored historic building on the prettiest canal in the Jordaan. Small but very comfortable rooms with shiny white bathrooms. Breakfast included. Reception 8am-11pm. Singles €45; doubles €90; triples €135; quads €180. Cash only. ❸

Hotel Clemens, Raadhuisstr. 39 (☎624 60 89; www.clemenshotel.com). Each elegant suite has a safe, TV, phone, and fridge. Breakfast included. Key deposit €10. 3-night min. stay on weekends. Reception 24hr. Reserve ahead. Singles €60; doubles €75, with shower €120; triples with bath start at €150. AmEx/MC/V. ❺

The Shelter Jordan, Bloemstr. 179 (☎624 47 17; www.shelter.nl). Religious but not proselytizing, this Christian hostel lets visitors retreat to single-sex dorms. A branch, **Shelter City,** Barndesteeg 21 (☎62 53 230), has a 2am curfew. No smoking or alcohol. Breakfast included. Locker deposit €5. Linens €2. Internet €1.50 per hr. Reception 24hr. Dorms €16-19; quads €20-23. F-Sa €3 extra. MC/V; 2% surcharge. ❶

LEIDSEPLEIN AND MUSEUMPLEIN

Flying Pig Uptown, Vossiusstr. 46-47 (☎400 41 87; www.flyingpig.nl). From Centraal, take the #20 or 5 tram to Leidseplein to get to this laid-back, friendly hostel beside Vondelpark. Popular bar downstairs. Under 40 only. Kitchen available. Breakfast and linens included. Lockers available. Free Internet and Skype phones. 7-night max. stay. Reception 8am-10pm. Internet reservation only or arrive at 8:30am for that night. Dorms €23-28; doubles €64; triples €90. Low season reduced rates. AmEx/MC/V. ❶

Stayokay Amsterdam Vondelpark (HI), Zandpad 5 (☎589 89 96; www.stayokay.com/vondelpark). One of the most palatial hostels in the Stayokay empire, in a lovely parkside location, and drug-free. Breakfast and linens included. Lockers available. Laundry €4.50. Internet €5 per hr. Reception 7:30am-midnight. Reserve well ahead. Dorms €24; doubles €74. F-Sa €2 extra. €2.50 HI discount. AmEx/MC/V. ❶

Quentin Hotel, Leidsekade 89 (☎626 21 87; www.quentinhotels.com). A chic lobby leads to white, almost minimalist rooms with canal views and TVs. Breakfast €7. Reception 24hr. 3-night min. stay F-Sa. Singles €30-45, with bath €35-45; doubles €59-85/69-99; triples with bath €95-110. AmEx/MC/V; 5% surcharge. ❸

Hotel Bema, Concertgebouwpl. 19b (☎679 13 96; www.bemahotel.com). Charming and tiny, with skylights. Breakfast included. Reception 8am-midnight. Singles €35-45; doubles €55-85; triples €75-90; quads €90-105. AmEx/MC/V; 5% surcharge. ❸

CENTRAL CANAL RING AND REMBRANDTPLEIN

The Golden Bear, Kerkstr. 37 (☎624 47 85; www.goldenbear.nl). Opened in 1948, The Golden Bear may be the oldest openly gay hotel in the world. Mainly male couples frequent the bright rooms; lesbians are welcome but children aren't. TV and DVD players in all rooms. Breakfast included. Internet €4 per hr., free wireless. Singles €60, with bath €109; doubles €74/114. AmEx/MC/V required for reservations. ❺

Hemp Hotel, Frederikspl. 15 (☎625 44 25; www.hemp-hotel.com). Small hotel exalts all things hemp: towels, soap, beer breakfast are all made of the stuff. Reception 11am-1pm and 3pm-3am. Singles €50; doubles €65-70. MC/V; 5% surcharge. ❹

Euphemia Budget Hotel, Fokke Simonszstr. 1-9 (☎622 90 45; www.euphemiahotel.com). Quiet digs in a former monastery. Breakfast €5-7. Internet €1 per 20min. Reception 8am-11pm. Dorms €23-32; doubles €66-86; triples €72-120; quads €92-128. 10% off 1st night with online reservation. AmEx/MC/V; 5% surcharge. ❸

Hotel Asterisk, Den Texstr. 16 (☎626 23 96 or 624 17 68; www.asteriskhotel.nl). 40 quiet rooms have cable TV, phone, and safe. Free breakfast if you pay in cash (€8 otherwise). Internet €0.50 per 10min. Reception 24hr. Singles €44-62; doubles €59-125; triples €99-140; quads €115-160. MC/V; 4% surcharge. ❸

DE PIJP, JODENBUURT, AND THE PLANTAGE

Lucky Travellers Fantasia Hotel, Nieuwe Keizersgr. 16 (☎623 82 59; www.fantasia-hotel.com). Family-owned, in an 18th-century house on a quiet canal. Ask for a room on the top floor. Breakfast included. Free wireless Internet. Reception 8am-9pm. Singles €67; doubles €86-97; triples €124; quads €145. AmEx/MC/V; 10% surcharge. ❺

Bicycle Hotel, Van Ostadestr. 123 (☎679 34 52; www.bicyclehotel.com). Bicycle-friendly hotel rents bikes (€5 per day) and stores them. Breakfast included. Free Internet. Doubles €75-110; triples €95-140; quads €160. AmEx/MC/V; 4% surcharge. ❸

Hotel Adolesce, Nieuwe Keizersgrt. 26 (☎626 39 59; www.adolesce.nl). Clean, spacious rooms with TV in an old canal house steps away from the Magere Brug (Skinny Bridge). No drugs. All-day breakfast included. Free Internet. Reception 8:30am-1am. Singles €60-65; doubles €80-85; triples €120. MC/V; 3% surcharge. ❺

OUTSIDE AMSTERDAM

Flying Pig Beach Hostel, Paralellboulevard 108 (☎071 362 25 33. www.flyingpig.nl), in Noordwijk, 35km from the city, is a 2min. walk from the beach and offers a break from the Amsterdam frenzy. Free, crowded shuttles (45min., 11am and 8pm) run to Amsterdam locations. A train goes from Amsterdam Centraal to Leiden Centraal, where bus #40 or 42 to Noordwijk then runs to the Vuurtorenplein stop and the hostel. Kitchen. Breakfast and linens included. Free Internet. Reception 9am-midnight. Dorms €19.50-23; singles €31.50-37.50; quads €100. ❷

MUNCHIES

In most areas, the sheer number of options—from Shawarma to Argentinian barbecue to pan-Asian noodles—can be dizzying. Cheap restaurants cluster around **Leidseplein, Rembrandtplein,** and **De Pijp.** Cafes, especially in the **Jordaan,** serve inexpensive sandwiches (€2-5) and good meat-and-potatoes fare (€5.50-9). Bakeries line **Utrechtsestraat,** south of Prinsengr. Fruit, cheese, flowers, and even live chickens are sold at markets on **Albert Cuypstraat,** behind the Heineken brewery. (Open M-Sa 9am-6pm.) **Albert Heijn** supermarkets are plentiful in Amsterdam. Two of the most popular reside in Dam Sq. and underneath Museumplein. Check for more locations at www.ah.nl. Hours vary depending on location.

NIEUWE ZIJDE AND OUDE ZIJDE

In de Waag, Nieuwmarkt 4 (☎452 77 72; www.indewaag.nl). In the late 1400s, this castle served as the eastern entrance to the city. Today, it serves lunch sandwiches and salads (€3.50-6.50) and Italian, Spanish, and Dutch dinner entrees (€18-25). Open Su-Th 10am-midnight, F-Sa 10am-1am; often open until 3am. MC/V. ❹

Pannenkoekenhuis Upstairs, Grimburgwal 2 (☎626 56 03). Sweet, filling pancakes (up to €9) await up the staircase. Open M-F noon-7pm, Sa noon-8pm, Su noon-5pm. ❷

Cafe Latei, Zeedijk 143 (☎625 74 85). At this unique cafe nearly everything is for sale—even your plate. Hanging lamps, old-fashioned crockery, and wall hangings may come and go, but the affable atmosphere remains. Large sandwiches about €3. All-day continental breakfast €7. Couscous menu with meat and vegetarian options €6-10. Open M-W 8am-6pm, Th-F 8am-10pm, Sa 9am-10pm, Su 11am-6pm. Cash only. ❶

Ristorante Caprese, Spuistr. 259-261 (☎620 00 59). From Dam Sq., follow Spuistr. south a few blocks. Authentic Italian food is made atmospheric by jazz, peach walls, and comforting candlelight. All meat is organically raised. Pasta entrees €9-12. Open daily 5:15-11:15pm. AmEx/MC/V. ❷

Green Planet, Spuistr. 122 (☎625 82 80). Vegetarian restaurant with salads (€9-12) and creative veggie entrees (€11-18). Rest easy afterwards: takeout meals come in biodegradable packaging and ingredients are all natural. Daily special €10.90. Organic beers and wine from €2.50. Open Tu-Sa 5:30pm-midnight. ❷

Aneka Rasa, Warmoesstr. 25-29 (☎626 15 60). If gritty Warmoesstr. is taking its toll, this clean Indonesian joint will relax and satisfy you with dishes like chicken in coconut sauce (€11.60). 2-person entrees €17-29. Open daily 5-10:30pm. AmEx/MC/V. ❸

SHIPPING QUARTER, CANAL RING WEST, AND THE JORDAAN

Harlem: Drinks and Soulfood, Haarlemmerstr. 77 (☎330 14 98). When American-style soul food collides with Cajun and Caribbean flavors, the crowds arrive. Sandwiches €6.80-7.50. Dinner entrees (€12-17) served starting 6pm. Open M-Th 10am-1am, F-Sa 10am-3am, Su 11am-1am. Kitchen closes 10pm. Cash only. ❸

Cinema Paradiso, Westerstr. 186 (☎623 73 44). Fans of purist Italian food fill this cavernous, windowless former cinema. *Antipasti* €5-11. Pasta €9-15. Reservations recommended. Open Tu-Su 6-11pm. Kitchen closes around 11pm. AmEx/MC/V. ❷

Hein, Berenstr. 20 (☎623 10 48). Watch your own meals prepared fresh in the open kitchen. Menu changes daily. Snacks €4.50-6.50. Daily special €10. Reservations accepted. Open M-Sa 8:30am-4pm, Su 9am-4pm. Cash only. ❷

Winkel, 43 Noodermarket, at corner of Westerstr. and Princengr. Hailed for its apple pie (slices €2.50-3), supposedly the best in Amsterdam, there's also soup, salad, sandwiches (€3.75), and outdoor seating. Open M-F 8am-1 or 2am, Sa-Su 8am-3am. ❶

Broodje Bert, Singel 321 (☎623 03 82). Sandwiches (€4-5) and salads (€8.50-9.50) are prepared quickly; grab them to munch by the canal. Open daily 8am-8pm. ❷

De Vliegende Schotel, Nieuwe Leliestr. 162-168 (☎625 20 41). The name may be complicated, but the vegetarian food is simple, organic, and delicious. Entrees €9-13. Open M-Tu and Th-Su 4:30-11:30pm. Food served until 10:45pm. AmEx/MC/V. ❷

LEIDSEPLEIN AND MUSEUMPLEIN

Cafe Vertigo, Vondelpark 3 (☎612 30 21). Pop over to Vertigo's tree-lined terrace overlooking Vondelpark. The dinner menu's pricey (€7.50-19), but light sandwiches, soups (€4-5), and pastries (€2) hit the spot at lunch. Open daily 10am-1am. MC/V. ❷

Ristorante Il-Palio, Leidsekruisstr. 23. Great deal for Leidseplein; cheap pizza and pastas €5. Open daily noon-11pm. ❶

Het Blauwe Theehuis, Vondelpark 5 (☎662 02 54; www.blauwetheehuis.nl). Peeking through the trees in Vondelpark lies a strange looking blue circular structure—actually a restaurant with two-level terrace serving sandwiches (€4-5), tapas (€3-4), and dinner (entrees €8.50-17). DJs spin Su afternoon. Open Su-Th 9am-midnight, F-Sa 9am-2am. Lunch served 10am-4pm, tapas 4-6pm, dinner 6-10pm. ❶

CENTRAL CANAL RING AND REMBRANDTPLEIN

Lanskroon, Singel 385 (☎623 77 43). Pastries baked on site. Chocolate-, almond-, and honey-filled cookies around €1.50. Fresh fruit pie slices €2.20-2.65. Ice cream €1.25-2.25. Open Tu-F 8am-5:30pm, Sa 9am-5:30pm, Su 10am-6pm. Cash only. ❶

Maoz Falafel, has locations outside Centraal Station (☎624 92 90; www.maoz-falafel.nl), at Ferdinand Bolstr. 67, Leidsestr. 85, and Muntpl. 1. Flavorful falafel and all-you-can-stack-in-your-pita salad bar make these kiosks invaluable for a speedy bite. Falafel sandwich €3.90. Open daily 11am-1am or 3am, depending on location. ❶

Coffee and Jazz, Utrechtsestr. 113 (☎624 58 51). Dutch-Indonesian fusion turns colonialism on its ear; fresh mackerel shares the menu with beef satay (€10.50). Nurse a cup of dark coffee by the window, or talk a waiter into letting you take it outside. Reservations recommended. Open Tu-F 10:30am-11pm. ❷

Ristorante Pizzeria Firenze, Halvemaansteeg 9-11 (☎627 33 60; www.pizzeria-firenze.nl). A delightful Italian restaurant and pizzeria—one of the least expensive stops for a sit-down meal in the Rembrandtplein. 25 types of pizza (€3.50-5.90) and pasta (€3.30-7). Open daily noon-midnight. MC/V. ❶

DE PIJP, JODENBUURT, AND PLANTAGE

Soup En Zo, Jodenbreestr. 94a (☎422 22 43). Choose a soup and a size (€2.60-5.70), then add a roll and toppings. Open M-F 11am-8pm, Sa-Su noon-7pm. Takeout only at branch at Nieuwe Spiegelstr. 54. Open M-F 11am-7pm, Sa noon-6pm. Cash only. ❶

Abe Veneto, Plantage Kerklaan 2 (☎639 23 64). Eat in or take out fresh pizza (€5-9.50), pasta (€6.50-9.50), or salad (€3-5). Open daily noon-midnight. Cash only. ❷

Cafe De Pijp, Ferdinand Bolstr. 17-19 (☎670 41 61). Fusion fare in stylish yet low-key surroundings. Tapas €3.90-7.50. Entrees, like trout and grilled steak, €14-15. Open M-Th 3:30pm-1am, F-Sa noon-3am, Su noon-1am. Cash only. ❷

Eeetkunst Asmara, J.D. Meyer Pl. 8 (☎627 10 02). A crowd of friendly regulars frequents this small restaurant, operated by a group of Eritrean immigrants. Vegetarian options €7-8. East African entrees €8.50-10.50. Open Tu-Su 6-10pm. Cash only. ❷

SIGHTS

Amsterdam is fairly compact, so tourists can easily explore the area from the Rijksmuseum to the Red Light District on foot. For those not inclined toward pedestrian navigation, the tram system will get you to any of the city's major sights within minutes. You'll see great views of the city aboard **Museumboot Canal Cruises;** the company allows you to hop on and off at any stop. Tickets grant half-price entry at most museums. (☎530 10 90. Boats every 15-40min. 1-day ticket €14.25.) The **I Amsterdam** (www.iamsterdam.com) card, sold by the tourist office and some museums, includes one canal cruise, all public transportation, and entrance into many museums. (24hr. €33, 48hr. €43, 72hr. €53.)

NIEUWE ZIJDE, OUDE ZIJDE, AND THE RED LIGHT DISTRICT

THE RED LIGHT DISTRICT. No trip to Amsterdam would be complete without witnessing the notorious spectacle that is the Red Light District. After dark, the area actually glows red, and the main streets grow thick with people gawking at lingerie-clad prostitutes in windows. Wall-to-wall brothels crowd **Warmoesstraat**

> TIP **FLESH PHOTOGRAPHY.** As tempting as it may be, **do not** take pictures in the Red Light District. Taking pictures can land the photographer in trouble.

THE RED LIGHT SPECIAL

'rostitution has always been legal n the Netherlands, yet brothels vere illegal for most of the 20th entury. Since October 2000, it ıas been legal for a business to employ men or women as prositues as long as they are over the egal age of consent (16) and vork voluntarily. The owner of a orothel must have a license from he government and adhere to pecific regulations, set by local ıuthorities. These require the paynent of a tax by both prostitutes ınd employers, mandate the ıpkeep of a certain sized work space, and suggest that prositues get medical checkups four imes per year.

There are thought to be 25,000 men and women of the ight in the Netherlands; about 2,000 of them work at any given ime, in about 6000 locations. he Netherlands has 12 red-light listricts with window prostitution. he majority of prostitutes work in orothels and sex clubs; many also vork as escorts. While statistics vary, research has reported that a najority of the prostitutes are foreigners.

Windows are generally rented o prostitutes for 8hr. shifts which cost them €60-150; they make oack the payment by charging 40-50 for 15-20min. of sex. Negotiations occur between prositute and potential customer, hrough a propped-open door. 'rostitutes have the final say ıbout who gets admitted.

and **Oudezijds Achterburgwal.** The most famous **sex shows,** in which actors perform strictly choreographed fantasies on stage, is at **Casa Rosso,** Oudezijds Achterburgwal 106-108, where €30 will buy you admission to eight or nine consecutive acts in the evening. Some claim that the show is quite tame, and not worth the money. *(☎627 89 54; www.janot.com. Afternoon shows daily 1:30-7:30pm. 1hr. 15min. €25. Evening shows Su-Th 7:30pm-2am, F-Sa 7:30pm-3am. 1hr.)*

OUDE KERK. Amsterdam's Old Church may come as a welcome, wholesome shock, smack in the middle of the otherwise lurid District. The stunning structure in place today began as a narrow, crude basilica around 1300 and took on new architectural features, such as the magnificent stained-glass windows, well into the 16th century. Today, Oude Kerk's enormous interior plays host to photography and modern art exhibits and the massive Vater-Müller organ, built in 1724 and still played in public concerts every weekend in summer. *(Oudekerkspl. 23. ☎625 82 84; www.oudekerk.nl. Open M-Sa 11am-5pm, Su 1-5pm. €5, students €4. Exhibits usually €6-7. Concerts up to €6, students €5.)*

NIEUWMARKT. A square on the border between the Oude Zijde and the Jodenbuurt, Nieuwmarkt is worth a visit simply for a look at the **Waag,** Amsterdam's largest surviving medieval building. Dating from the 15th century, the Waag was one of Amsterdam's fortified city gates and later housed the Surgeons Guild's amphitheater. Public dissections and private anatomy lessons were once held there, as Rembrandt's *The Anatomy Lesson of Dr. Tulp* famously depicts. Now the only way to enter is to eat at **In de Waag Restaurant** (see p. 715).

SINT NICOLAASKERK. A burst of color emanates from the stained-glass of the otherwise foreboding, gray Sint Nicolaaskerk. Erected by A.C. Bleys and completed in 1887 to honor the patron saint of sailors, it replaced secret Catholic churches formed after Calvinists ordered the destruction of Catholic icons in the 1570s. *(Prins Henrikkade 73. ☎624 87 49. Open M and Sa noon-3pm, Tu-F 11am-4pm. Su mass 10:30am. Free.)*

DAM SQUARE AND KONINKLIJK PALEIS. The **Koninklijk Paleis** (Royal Palace) was completed in 1655 and functioned as the town hall until Louis Napoleon had it renovated in 1808 to better look the part of a royal residence. Queen Beatrix still uses the building for official receptions. The palace's highlight is the **Citizen's Hall,** a one-room replica of the universe. *(☎620 40 60; www.koninklijkhuis.nl. Royal Palace closed for renovations until 2008.)* Across the large Dam Sq. is the Dutch **Nationaal Monument,** unveiled on May 4, 1956, to honor Dutch victims of WWII.

BEGIJNHOF AND SPUI. Unlike the 14th-century Beguine sect of religiously devoted laywomen who lived here, you don't have to take vows to enter this secluded courtyard. Begijnhof's rose-lined gardens and manicured lawns afford a welcome respite from the Nieuwe Zijde's excesses. The oldest house in Amsterdam, **Het Houten Huys** (The Wooden House), is located on the premises. *(Entrance at gate at Gedempte Begijnensloot. Open daily July-Aug. 9-11am; Sept.-June 9am-5pm. Free.)* Just to the south, **Spui** ("spow") is a tree-lined square for lounging or browsing its many bookstores. A book market descends Fridays, an art market Sundays.

CANAL RING WEST AND THE JORDAAN

WESTERKERK. A Protestant church designed by Roman Catholic architect Hendrick de Keyser and completed in 1631, Westerkerk was one of the last structures built in the Dutch Renaissance style, typified by a mix of brick and stone. Vertical lines inside recall a Gothic tradition. Rembrandt is believed to be buried here, though his whereabouts are unknown. The **Westerkerkstoren tower,** currently closed for renovations, is scheduled to open for 30min. tours in April 2007. *(Prinsengr. 281. ☎624 77 66. Church open Apr.-Sept. M-F 11am-3pm; July-Aug. M-Sa 11am-3pm.)*

HOMOMONUMENT. Homomonument, built in 1987, stands in front of Westerkerk as a memorial to all who have been oppressed because of their homosexuality. Karin Daan's design, three pink granite triangles, alludes to the emblem that homosexuals were forced to wear in Nazi concentration camps. During Amsterdam Pride, held in the first week of August, the monument takes on a happier cast, drawing DJs and performers for a four-night "Summer Camp" party.

LEIDSEPLEIN AND MUSEUMPLEIN

LEIDSEPLEIN. Leidseplein proper is a din of cacophonous street musicians, blaring neon lights, and clanging trams. Daytime finds the square packed with shoppers, smokers, and drinkers. When night falls, locals retreat to the less populated surrounding streets to make way for tourists. **Max Euweplein,** a square along Weteringschans named for the famous Dutch chess master, houses an enormous chess board with people-sized pieces.

VONDELPARK. With meandering walkways, green meadows, several ponds, and a 1.5km paved path for bikers and skaters, this English-style park—the largest within the city center—is a lovely place to enjoy a picnic, some wine, or a smoke. Named after 17th-century poet and playwright Joost van den Vondel, Vondelpark is home to the open-air **Openluchttheater,** where visitors can enjoy free summer concerts from Wednesday through Sunday, listed on the schedule beside the theater. *(Openluchttheater ☎673 14 99; www.openluchttheater.nl. Park in the southwestern corner of the city, outside the Singelgr. a short walk across the canal and to the left from the Leidsepl.)*

CENTRAL CANAL RING AND REMBRANDTPLEIN

CENTRAL CANAL RING. You haven't seen Amsterdam until you've spent some time wandering in the Central Canal Ring, the city's highest rent district and arguably its most beautiful. **Prinsengracht** (Prince's canal), **Keizersgracht** (Emperor's canal), and **Herengracht** (Gentlemen's canal) are collectively known as the *grachtengordel* (literally "canal girdle"). The Ring, especially the stretch known as the **Golden Bend,** on Herengr. between Leidsegr. and Vijzelstr., sports some of Amsterdam's most lavish homes. *(Over the Singel and just south of Centrum.)*

REMBRANDTPLEIN. Rembrandtplein proper consists of a grass rectangle surrounded by scattered flowerbeds. A bronze sculpture of Rembrandt van Rijn and a large replica of his painting, *The Nightwatch,* peer at the hordes of out-of-towners who elbow their way into the bars and cafes in the surrounding area. South and west of the square you'll find **Reguliersdwarsstraat,** ground zero for Amsterdam's gay nightlife. *(In the northeastern corner of the Central Canal Ring, just south of the Amstel.)*

DE PIJP, JODENBUURT, AND THE PLANTAGE

HEINEKEN EXPERIENCE. Heineken stopped producing beer at this—the original brewery—in 1988, and the place is now a shamelessly self-promoting multimedia amusement park devoted to their green-bottled lager. A visit includes three beers and a free gift. *(Heinekenpl. ☎523 96 66; www.heinekenexperience.com. Open Tu-Su 10am-6pm; last entry 5pm. Guests under 18 must be accompanied by a parent. €10. MC/V.)*

PORTUGEES-ISRAELIETISCHE SYNAGOGUE. This beautifully maintained Portuguese synagogue dates to 1675, when it was founded by Jews fleeing the Spanish Inquisition. It has miraculously remained virtually unchanged since then and holds services each Saturday at 9am. *(Mr. Visserpl. 1-3. ☎624 53 51; www.esnoga.com. Open Apr.-Oct. Su-F 10am-4pm; Nov.-Mar. Su-Th 10am-4pm, F 10am-3pm. €6.50.)*

HOLLANDSCHE SCHOUWBURG. This historic building was founded as a Dutch theater on the edge of the old Jewish quarter. In 1941, Nazi occupiers converted it into the Jewish Theatre, in which only Jews could perform. Not long after, the building became an assembly point for Dutch Jews who were to be deported to concentration camps in the north. Today it houses a memorial to the 6700 Dutch Jews killed in the Holocaust. *(Plantage Middenlaan 24. ☎531 03 40; www.hollandscheschouwburg.nl. Open daily 11am-4pm. Closed on Yom Kippur and Rosh Hashanah. Free.)*

HORTUS BOTANICUS. Founded in 1638, these gardens were originally established in response to the plague epidemic as medicinal resources for the city's physicians. The garden and greenhouses nourish 6000 species, including the *Victoria amazonica*, the world's largest waterlily, pineapple-scented and strong enough to hold a baby on its blossoms. *(Plantage Middenlaan 2A. ☎90 21 625; www.dehortus.nl. Open July-Aug. M-F 9am-9pm, Sa-Su 10am-9pm; Feb.-June and Sept.-Nov. M-F 9am-5pm, Sa-Su 10am-5pm; Dec.-Jan. M-F 9am-4pm, Sa-Su 10am-4pm. Guided tours Su 2pm. €8. Tours €1.)*

DE PIJP. South of the tourist-filled canal rings, De Pijp (pronounced "pipe") is a mishmash of various immigrant ethnicities and cultures. The neighborhood was constructed in the 19th century to ease cramped housing in the Jordaan.The best place to start exploring is amid the crowded din of the **Albert Cuypmarkt,** a vibrant market and home to some of the best no-name eateries in the city. The market is along Albert Cuypstr., between **Ferdinand Bolstraat** (the district's largest thoroughfare) and Van Woustr.

MUSEUMS

Whether you crave Rembrandts and van Goghs, cutting-edge photography, WWII history, or sexual oddities, Amsterdam has a museum for you. The useful www.amsterdammuseums.nl has info for easy planning.

THE REAL DEAL. Amsterdam has more museums per square meter than any other city in the world. Visitors planning to see even a handful may want to invest in a Museumkaart. The pass (€30, under 25 €15) entitles the holder to admission at most major museums in Amsterdam and many museums all over the Netherlands. Cards are good for 1 year, but can be worth it even for those staying 1 week. To buy the pass, bring a passport photo to a participating museum. For more information, check www.museumjaarkaart.nl (in Dutch).

NIEUWE ZIJDE, OUDE ZIJDE, AND THE RED LIGHT DISTRICT

STEDELIJK MUSEUM OF MODERN ART. The Stedelijk has amassed a world-class collection on par with MoMA or the Tate Modern, which a distinguished jury decided was worthy of a new home, to open on Museumpl. in 2008. Meanwhile, temporary modern and contemporary art exhibits are shown on the second and third floors of the Post-CS Building, to the left upon exiting Centraal Station. *(Oosterdokskade 5. ☎573 29 11; www.stedelijk.nl. Open daily 10am-6pm. €9, students €4.50.)*

AMSTERDAM HISTORISCH MUSEUM. This museum uses its diverse collection of art, paintings, and archeological objects to illustrate Amsterdam's evolution from a settlement to an internationally renowned city. In the passageway to the Begijnhof, see the extensive collection of 17th-century paintings of Amsterdam's civic guards. *(Nieuwezijds Voorburgwal 357, entrances at Sint Luciensteeg 27, and Kalverstr. 92. ☎523 18 22; www.ahm.nl. Open M-F 10am-5pm, Sa-Su 11am-5pm. Closed Apr. 30. €6.)*

THE VICES. If it's weed that interests you, your best bet is the informative **Cannabis College.** The center for "higher" education informs on the uses of medicinal marijuana, the war on drugs, and creative applications of industrial hemp. To test your knowledge, the college has a vaporizer it lets visitors inhale from a couple times free of charge. Downstairs, artificial lighting in the Cannabis Garden ensure that "students" will always see a plant in bloom. *(Oudezijds Achterburgwal 124. ☎423 44 20. www.cannabiscollege.com. Open daily 11am-7pm. Free. €2.50 donation to see Cannabis Garden.)* For a curated, less crude version of the Red Light District, visit the **Amsterdam Sex Museum,** where walls are plastered with pictures of bestiality and S&M. *(Oudezijds Achterburgwal 124. Open daily 9:30am-11:30pm. 16+. €3.)*

CANAL RING WEST AND THE JORDAAN

ANNE FRANK HUIS. A visit to the Anne Frank House is a must, whether or not you've read the famous diary. The museum chronicles the two years the Frank family and four other Jews spent hiding in the annex of this warehouse on the Prinsengr. The rooms are no longer furnished, but personal objects in display cases and panels with excerpts from the diary bring the story of the eight inhabitants to life. Footage of interviews with Otto Frank, Miep Gies (who ran supplies to the refugees), and friends of

BICYCLE BUILT FOR YOU

Even if you've experienced the Red Light District or clouded yourself in smoke at all of Amsterdam's coffeeshops, you can't say you've truly done this city unless you've ridden a bike here. The red bike lanes and special bike lights, as well as the multitude of cheap and convenient rental companies, permit tourists to whiz around as if they were locals. If you're bent on remaining a tourist, you can pay for a guided bike tour or a map with one laid out, but if you're keen on blending in, you can simply pedal your way to destinations you'd planned on seeing anyway. A horseshoe-shaped path along any of the canals of the Central Canal Ring—Prinsengracht is prettiest—passes near the Anne Frank Huis, the Rijksmuseum, the van Gogh Museum, and the Heineken Brewery.

Of course you might as well take advantage of your increased mobility to explore places your tootsies wouldn't take you. Leave Amsterdam to ride along the Amstel River, glimpsing windmills, houseboats, and quintessentially Dutch rolling hills. Cycle east along green trails to the seaside town of Spaarndam (20-25km). Or, use the canals as racetracks, leaving mellow locals in the dust.

MacBike (p. 710), Weteringsschans 2 (☎528 76 88; www.macbike.nl), in Leidseplein, rents bikes and sells reliable bike-tour maps.

Anne complete the scene. Lines are long. *(Prinsengr. 267. ☎556 71 05; www.annefrank.org. Open daily mid-Mar. to mid-Sept. 9am-9pm; mid-Sept. to mid-Mar. 9am-7pm. Closed on Yom Kippur. Last admission 30min. before closing. €7.50.)*

ELECTRIC LADYLAND: THE FIRST MUSEUM OF FLUORESCENT ART. Endearingly eccentric owner Nick Padalino has collected an impressive, interactive assortment of fluorescent objects, including rocks that glow green in black light. *(2E Leliedwarsstr. 5. ☎420 37 76; www.electric-lady-land.com. Open Tu-Sa 1-6pm. €5.)*

STEDELIJK MUSEUM BUREAU AMSTERDAM. This adjunct of the Stedelijk (p. 721) devotes itself to exhibiting the newest in Amsterdam art. A pure-white space made light and breezy by a vaulted glass ceiling, the museum bureau is something of a testing ground for avant-garde artists and material designers. The temporary shows last for eight weeks and range from traditional forms of painting and sculpture to outrageous attempts at installation, as well as furniture and fashion design. The museum closes for one to two weeks between exhibits; check the website for a schedule. *(Rozenstr. 59. ☎422 04 71; www.smba.nl. Open Tu-Su 11am-5pm. Free.)*

MUSEUMPLEIN

VAN GOGH MUSEUM. The museum houses the largest collection of van Goghs in the world and a diverse group of 19th-century paintings by contemporaries admired by van Gogh, such as Gaugin and Emile Bernard. While the Rijksmuseum and the Stedelijk undergo renovations, this museum's collection of Impressionist, post-Impressionist, Realist, and Symbolist art has acquired a new luster. *(Paulus Potterstr. 7. ☎570 52 00; www.vangoghmuseum.nl. Open M-Th and Sa-Su 10am-6pm, F 10am-10pm; ticket office closes 30min. before closing time. €10. Audio tour €4.)*

RIJKSMUSEUM AMSTERDAM. Amsterdam's "state museum" has long been known as the continent's preeminent destination for Dutch Golden Age art. Though the museum's main building is closed, the smaller Philips Wing still shows 400 masterpieces, including works by Rembrandt and Vermeer. *(Jan Luijkenstr. 1. ☎674 70 00; www.rijksmuseum.nl. Open daily 10am-5pm. €10. Audio tour included.)*

FILMMUSEUM. Although the Filmmuseum is dedicated to the celebration and preservation of film, don't come here expecting mundane museum exhibits: most visitors come simply to see movies. Movies are generally chosen by theme, actor, or director and are always screened in their original language with Dutch subtitles. Filmmuseum maintains an information center at 69 Vondelstr. (across the path from the entrance), with the country's largest collection of books and periodicals on film, many of them in English. Movies are screened outdoors on Friday nights in August; a €3 ticket includes a drink, although penny-pinchers can watch for free from across the pond. *(Vondelpark 3, between the Roemer Visscherstr. and Vondelstr. entrances. ☎589 14 00; www.filmmuseum.nl. Film screenings €7.20-8.60, students €6-7.30.)*

CENTRAL CANAL RING

FOAM PHOTOGRAPHY MUSEUM. Inside a traditional canal house, Foam stages a fearless exploration of modern photography. Every genre of the photographed image is fair game, from the purely aesthetic to the explicitly political, in realms from fashion to history. *(Keizersgr. 609. ☎551 65 00; www.foam.nl. Open M-W and Sa-Su 10am-5pm, Th-F 10am-9pm. €6.50, students €5.)*

DE APPEL. This ultra-contemporary art museum has a small permanent collection. More importantly, it draws compelling, global-conscious exhibits, cutting-edge films, and installations that make even the Stedelijk look out-of-date. *(Nieuwe Spiegelstr. 10. ☎625 56 51; www.deappel.nl. Open Tu-Su 11am-6pm. €4.)*

MUSEUM WILLET-HOLTHUYSEN. In 1895, Sandrina Holthuysen donated the 17th-century canal house she shared with her collector husband Abraham Willet to the Amsterdam Historisch Museum. The mansion has been redone with gilt-edged walls, glittering chandeliers, family portraits, Rococo furnishings, and other signs of conspicuous consumption. The French Neoclassical garden out back remains as finely manicured as it was in the Golden Age. *(Herengr. 605. ☎523 18 22; www.willetholthuysen.nl. Open M-F 10am-5pm, Sa-Su 11am-5pm. €4.)*

JODENBUURT AND PLANTAGE

MUSEUM HET REMBRANDT. Dutch master Rembrandt van Rijn's house at Waterlooplein is home to 250 of his etchings, as well as a number of paintings by his pupils. See the claustrophobic box-bed in which Rembrandt slept and tour the studio in which he mentored promising painters. Etching demonstrations occur daily, and painting demonstrations take place on weekends. *(Jodenbreestr. 4. ☎520 04 00; www.rembrandthuis.nl. Open daily 10am-5pm. €7.50, students €5.)*

VERZETSMUSEUM (DUTCH RESISTANCE MUSEUM). Though the Nazis quickly overran Dutch armed forces in May 1940, the Netherlands maintained an active resistance throughout WWII. The Resistance Museum focuses on the members of this secret army, providing visitors with the details of their lives and struggles. Model streets, buildings, and tape-recorded radio reports recreate the rebels' experiences—from smuggling food to issuing counterpropaganda on an illicit printing press. *(Plantage Kerklaan 61. ☎620 25 35; www.verzetsmuseum.org. Open M and Sa-Su noon-5pm, Tu-F 10am-5pm, public holidays noon-5pm. €5.50.)*

NEMO (NEW METROPOLIS). By the Oosterdok, the half-submerged green structure shaped like a ship's hull is the home of NEMO, a hands-on science museum. Renzo Piano's whimsical architecture pays tribute to the Netherlands's seafaring past. Inside, four stories are littered with science exhibits that beg to be poked at, jumped on, and experimented with. NEMO targets children, but adult visitors soon find themselves shooting each other conspiratorial grins as they partake. *(Oosterdok 2, east of Centraal Station. ☎0900 919 11 00, €0.35 per min.; www.e-nemo.nl. Open Tu-Su 10am-5pm. €11.50, students €6.50.)* Afterward, don't miss the spectacular view of the shipyard and the historic city from the structure's slanted roof. *(Open Su-Th noon-10pm, F-Sa noon-11:30pm. €2.50 includes free drink, free with museum entrance.)*

TROPENMUSEUM (MUSEUM OF THE TROPICS). Visitors take an anthropological tour of equatorial civilizations through ancient artifacts, contemporary objects, and religious relics alongside video interviews. Sponsored by the Dutch Royal Institute of the Tropics, the museum is in one of Amsterdam's most awe-inspiring buildings. Most of the works on display were obtained through Dutch colonial expansion; others are contemporary ethnographic studies. *(Linnaeusstr. 2. ☎568 82 15; www.tropenmuseum.nl. Open daily 10am-5pm. €7.50, students €6. Audio tour included.)*

COFFEESHOPS AND SMART SHOPS

COFFEESHOPS

The coffee at Amsterdam's coffeeshops is beside the point if it's brewed at all. Establishments calling themselves coffeeshops usually sell pot or hash; most will let customers buy a drink and smoke their own stuff. Visit www.greenlightdistrict.nl for tons of coffeeshop information. Look for the **green-and-white sticker** signifying the shop's affiliation with the Bond voor Cannabisdetaillisten (BCD), an organized union of coffeeshops. While Amsterdam was once known as the **hashish** capital of the world, **marijuana** is more prominent. Technically, pot is illegal in the

Netherlands, but the country's tolerance policy means that you are unlikely to face legal action if you carry or buy no more than 5 grams at a time. Possession of harder drugs like cocaine and heroin will be severely punished. For more info on

> TIP **DRUG DICTION.** A Dutch slang term for marijuana is "blow," not to be confused with the American-English slang use of the same word to signify cocaine, a hard drug neither tolerated nor legal in the Netherlands.

pot's legality, call the **Jellinek clinic** (☎408 77 77) or visit the English-language website of the Dutch Ministry of Justice (www.justitie.nl/english); to learn about cannabis's progress from seed to spliff, ask the staff at **Cannabis College** (p. 721).

Let's Go does not recommend drug use in any form. Those who decide to partake should use common sense and remember that any experimentation with drugs can be dangerous. **Never buy drugs from street dealers,** because there is no way of knowing whether their products are laced with more harmful drugs or are simply expensive oregano. Coffeeshops are licensed to sell cannabis and hashish, and the good ones carefully regulate the quality of their smokeables. When cus-

> TIP **TALKING BEFORE TOKING.** Amsterdam may be a liberal city, but smoking marijuana outside of a coffeeshop is not acceptable. Although smoking cigarettes is permitted in most restaurants, smoking weed is not. If you are at all unsure and really want to toke up, ask first.

tomers walk into a coffeeshop, they should ask for a menu, because the shops are not allowed to leave menus out or otherwise advertise their wares. The legal age to enter a coffeeshop is 18, and it's not unusual for staff to ask for ID when you enter.

Marijuana is the dried, cured flower of the cannabis plant, and costs anywhere from €3 to €15 per gram. Different strains fall in and out of favor, but are divided into two main subspecies: Sativa strains (like "Kali Mist" or anything marked "Thai") get users high, giggly, and energized, while Indica strains (like "Northern Lights") get users really stoned and relaxed. Increasingly popular hybrid strains (like "White Widow" or "AK-47") combine both effects. Keep in mind that pot in the Netherlands is very potent; visitors report that they smoke noticeably less than they would at home and still achieve the same high. Pre-rolled joints are sometimes available, but smoking one (or a pipe) clearly identifies its user as a tourist—there's also no telling what else has been rolled into the joint. Staff at coffeeshops are not going to be enthusiastic about explaining how to roll a joint, but they will be happy to explain the different menu options. Vaporizers, which many coffeeshops have available for use, are becoming increasingly popular as an effective means of inhaling without too much damage to the lungs. Be careful: vaporizers tend to have a very strong effect, especially if combined with alcohol.

Hashish is made from the resin crystals extracted from the flowers of the cannabis plant, and it comes in three varieties: black (Indian, Afgan, Nepalese), blonde (Moroccan, Lebanese), and Dutch (also called ice-o-lator). The first two grades run €4-35 per gram, averaging somewhere around €7, while increasingly popular **ice-o-lator hash** tops out at €20-35 per gram. Typically, the cost of the hash is proportional to its quality and strength; black hash hits harder than blonde, and ice-o-lator can send even seasoned smokers sky-high. Hash can be smoked directly out of a glass hash pipe, or sprinkled into a joint containing either tobacco or marijuana.

Both hash and weed can be used to make **space cakes** and other food items; the effects are normally stronger than that of smoking, although they take longer to set in and longer to disappear. Because of the time delay, those who partake should do so slowly, rather than binging just because a high has not been reached.

SMART SHOPS

Smart shops peddle a variety of **"herbal enhancers"** and **hallucinogens** that walk the line between soft and hard drugs. Remember that drugs can be dangerous and can cause long-term damage. If you're interested in experimenting with **magic mushrooms** ('shrooms), it is crucial, as with all soft drugs, that you do thorough research beforehand. In general, magic mushrooms start to work 30min. to 1hr. after consumption and act on your system for 4-8hr., depending on how much you weigh and whether you've eaten beforehand. Different types give different highs: **Mexican** and **Thai** mushrooms are recommended for beginners; they are the least potent and give a colorful, playful high with some visual hallucination. **Philosophers' stones** (colors and lights interspersed with deep thoughts) and **Hawaiians** (visual trips similar to LSD) are much more intense and should be taken only by experienced users. Wandering the city tripping on mushrooms can be a majestic, mind-expanding experience, but it can also leave you lost and unable to find your way home. It's often more pleasant to trip in daylight and to stay in familiar surroundings, like a favorite coffeeshop or a corner of the Vondelpark. Never look for mushrooms in the wild and never buy from a street dealer; you don't want to end up with poisonous ones. It is generally advised not to eat before smoking, but talk to a smart shop worker for more detailed instructions. **Never mix hallucinogens with alcohol.** If you have a bad trip, call ☎ 122 to go to the hospital or ask someone for help; you won't be arrested (they've seen tourists like you before).

WHERE TO GO

Barney's Coffeeshop, Haarlemmerstr. 102 (☎ 625 97 61; www.barneys.biz). Some pairings are just meant to be; pot and all-day breakfast (€4.20-12) is one of them. Barney's, 4-time winner of the "best marijuana strain" at the Cannabis Club, serves them separately and together, in their space cakes (€6.50). Open daily 7am-1am.

Abraxas, J. Roelensteeg 12-14. Hot spots come and go, but pretty Abraxas is perennially one of Amsterdam's most popular coffeeshops. Open daily 10am-1am.

The Magic Mushroom, Spuistr. 249 (www.magicmushroom.com). In addition to offering 8 different types of 'shrooms (€8.50-17.50) and a chill lounge, this smart shop hawks herbal ecstasy, energizers, and other products obscure enough to baffle any alchemist. Free energizer with mention of *Let's Go.* Open daily 10am-10pm.

Dampkring, Handboogstr. 29 (www.dampkring.net). Several scenes from the 2004 film *Ocean's Twelve* were filmed in this subterranean space. Weed €70-150 per 15g. Carries hard-to-find Nepal hash. Open M-Th 10am-1am, F-Sa 10am-2am, Su 11am-1am.

Hill Street Blues, Warmoesstr. 52. Even if you're not smoking, you won't be able to resist the cheap beer (pint €2.80) in this endearingly grungy hot spot. Weed €3.50-13 per g. Pre-rolled joints €3. Space cakes €3.60. Cocktail Happy hour Tu-Th 9-10pm, drinks €3.20; beer Happy hour daily 6-9pm, beer €2.10. Open Su-Th 9am-1am, F-Sa 9am-3am.

Amnesia, Herengr. 133. Dark-red walls and cushioned benches make for a comfortable, newbie-friendly atmosphere in a city with many standoffish, veterans-only shops. Vaporizer available for use. Weed €6.80-11. Hash €6-17 per g. Open daily 9:30am-1am.

Paradox, 1E Bloemdwarsstr. 2. This nonchalant coffeeshop jives with the neighborhood's relaxed vibe, counting many of the area's artists among its clientele. Weed €2.50-6.90 per g. Hash €5.45-11 per g. Open daily 10am-8pm. Kitchen closes 3pm.

ENTERTAINMENT AND NIGHTLIFE

Leidseplein and **Rembrandtplein** remain the liveliest areas for nightlife, with coffeeshops, loud bars, and tacky clubs galore. Not far from Leidsepl., pricey discos abound on **Prinsengracht** near **Leidsestraat,** and on **Lange Leidsedwarsstraat.** Some clubs charge a membership fee in addition to normal cover. Amsterdam's most traditional joints are the old, dark, wood-paneled *bruin café* (brown cafes) mainly on the **Jordaan;** those lining **Prinsengracht** often have outdoor seating. The concept of a completely "straight" versus "gay" nightlife does not really apply; most establishments are gay-friendly and attract a mixed crowd. Around Rembrandtpl., gay bars almost exclusively for men line **Amstelstraat** and **Reguliersdwarsstraat** as well as **Kerkstraat,** north of Leidsepl. Pick up a *Clu* guide at cafes and coffeeshops for a club map of the city, or the free monthly *Gay and Night*.

The **Amsterdams Uit Buro (AUB),** Leidsepl. 26, is stuffed with flyers, pamphlets, and guides to help you sift through upcoming events; pick up the free monthly *Uitkrant* to see what's on. Copies of *Shark* have even more listings online (www.underwateramsterdam.com) and in print versions throughout the city. In summer, the **Vondelpark Openluchttheater** (☎673 14 99; www.openluchttheater.nl) hosts free rock and jazz concerts Wednesday through Sunday. The **Royal Concertgebouw Orchestra,** regarded as one of the world's finest, plays at Concertgebouwpl. 2-6. (Tram #316 to Museumpl. ☎671 83 45; www.concertegebouw.nl. Tickets from €12. Last-minute tickets €7. Ticket office open daily 10am-7pm.) The stately **Filmmuseum,** on Stadhouderskade, shows independent films. (☎589 14 00; www.filmmuseum.nl. Open M-F 10am-10pm. €7.20.)

BARS AND CAFES

Club NL, Nieuwezijds Voorburgwal 169 (www.clubnl.nl). This is the unmarked destination for Amsterdam's slickest, best-dressed, and most savvy insiders. Mixed drinks €8. F-Sa cover €5. Mandatory €1 coat check. Open Su-Th 10pm-3am, F-Sa 10pm-4am.

Café de Jaren, Nieuwe Doelenstr. 20-22. Spacious cafe on par with the best of Paris or Vienna. 2 sprawling floors offer indoor and outdoor seating options an arm's length away from the Klovenierburgswal canal. Beer and mixed drinks €1.90-3.80. Kitchen closes 11pm, F-Sa midnight. Open Su-Th 10am-1am, F-Sa 10am-2am.

Wijnand Fockink, 31 Pijlsteeg (☎639 26 95), on an alleyway just off Dam Sq. Over 300 years old, with unequivocally the best *fockink* (Dutch gin) in the city. It's made especially for this tiny bar and available in over 60 flavors, including apple tart, peppermint, and the famous half-and-half. Glass €2. Open daily 3-9pm. Cash only.

Café Brandon, Kiezersgracht 157. A visit to Café Brandon is like a voyage through time. An older, local crowd relaxes to Pink Floyd and late '70s English rock. Amstel on tap from €1.60. Open Su-Th noon-1am, F-Sa noon-3am. Cash only.

Absinthe, Nieuwezijds Voorburwal 171 (☎623 4413). Absinthe's environment is psychedelic, its briskest hour late, and its token drink the real deal. 15 different absinthe shots (€5-12). DJ F-Sa. Open M-Th and Su 9pm-3:30am, F-Sa 9pm-4:30am.

Cafe April, Reguliersdwarsstr. 37. Popular gay bar that's laid-back by day and increasingly active and cruisy as the night wears on. Beer €2. Mixed drinks €6.20. 2-for-1 Happy hour M-Sa 6-7pm, Su 6-8pm makes it a popular after-work stop. 4 additional brief Happy hour M-Sa between 7pm and closing. Open Su-Th 2pm-1am, F-Sa 2pm-2am. Kitchen closes 1am. Cash only.

NJOY, Korte Leidsedwarsstr. 93. Menu lists over 60 drinks (€5-10); bartenders make more. Dance floor and in-house DJ. Open Su-Th 8pm-3am, F-Sa 8pm-4am. Cash only.

CLUBS AND DISCOS

Escape, Rembrandtpl. 11. Well-dressed party animals pour into the 6 bars on 2 floors at this massive venue, one of the city's nightlife institutions. Beer €2.30. Mixed drinks €7.50. Cover €10-15. Open Th and Su 11pm-4:30am, F-Sa 11pm-5am. Cash only.

De Trut, Bilderdijkstr. 165. A low-ceilinged basement in an apartment building west of the city center hosts Su night-parties exclusively for gay and lesbian locals skipping the cruisy downtown scene. Don't be chased off by 2m pictures of genitalia on the doors; the emphasis inside is on dancing and mingling. Small beer €1. Cover €1.50. Doors open 11pm and close once the club fills, so join the line on the sidewalk by 10:30pm.

Dansen Bij Jansen, Handboogstr. 11-13. *The* student dance club in town, popular with University of Amsterdam students and backpackers. Dance floor grooves to hip-hop. Must have student ID or a friend who does. Beer €1.70-3.30. Mixed drinks from €3.30. Cover Su-W €2, Th-Sa €4. Open Su-Th 11pm-4am, F-Sa 11pm-5am.

Meander, Voetboogstr. 3b. Smoky atmosphere, constant clamor, and dense crowds make for a raucous, high-energy time. Beer €1.80. M student night, F-Sa disco with live music. Cover €4. Open Su-Th 10pm-3am, F-Sa 9pm-4am.

Exit, Reguliersdwarsst. 42 (☎625 87 88). Exit is one of the most popular gay discos in Amsterdam. Downstairs bar is laid-back; upstairs is a DJ-driven, high-energy, low-inhibition techno party. Darkroom reserved for men. Cover €4-9. Th night straight-friendly Everyone Party; women free until midnight. Open Su-Th 11pm-4am, F-Sa 11pm-5am.

LIVE MUSIC

Paradiso, Weteringschans 6-8 (☎626 45 21; www.paradiso.nl). Hosts a summertime line-up of big-name acts. Upstairs, a smaller stage showcases up-and-coming talent. Tickets €10-14 plus €3 monthly membership fee. M and Th-Su after the shows, the space becomes "Paradisco," a dance club. M-Th cover €6, F-Su €12.50. Open daily 10pm-4am. Hours vary depending on performances; check website for showtimes.

Melkweg, Lijnbaansgr. 234a (☎531 81 81; www.melkweg.nl). A legendary nightspot in an old milk factory, Melkweg's one-stop shopping for live music, films, and dance parties. Hosts live hip-hop, reggae, and metal concerts before midnight, then morphs into a happening club. Concert tickets €9.50-28 plus €3 monthly membership fee. Box office open M-F 1-5pm, Sa-Su 4-6pm; show days from 7:30pm to end of show.

Bourbon Street Jazz and Blues Club, Leidsekruisstr. 6-8 (☎623 34 40; www.bourbonstreet.nl). A slightly older crowd comes to listen to blues, soul, funk, and rock bands. Th-Sa pop; M Latin; Tu-W jam session. Postings in the window list events. Beer €2.50. Su-Th cover €3, F-Sa €5; free daily 10-10:30pm. Open Su-Th 10pm-4am, F-Sa 10pm-5am.

HAARLEM ☎023

Haarlem's (pop. 150,000) narrow cobblestone streets, rippling canals, and fields of tulips in spring make for a great escape from the urban frenzy of Amsterdam, but the city also bustles with a relaxed energy that befits its size. Coffeeshops and a slew of restaurants ensure that there's fun to be had even after the sun goes down.

TRANSPORTATION AND PRACTICAL INFORMATION. Trains run to Amsterdam's Centraal Station (15min., 4 per hr., €3.60) and Rotterdam (45min., 2 per hr., €11). The **tourist office,** Stationspl. 1, to your right as you exit the train station, sells maps of the city (€2) and books bed and breakfasts for €5 and hotels for €3 per person. (☎090 06 16 16 00; www.vvvzk.nl. Open Apr.-Sept. M-F 9:30am-5pm, Sa 10am-4pm; Oct.-Mar. M-F 9am-5:30pm, Sa 10am-2pm.)

ACCOMMODATIONS AND FOOD. To get to **Stayokay Haarlem (HI) ❶**, Jan Gijzenpad 3, take bus #2 (dir.: Haarlem-Noord; every 10-15min., 2 strips) to the Stayokay stop. (☎537 3793; www.stayokay.com/haarlem. Breakfast and linens included. Laundry €4.30. Reception 8am-1am. Dorms €26-27; doubles €65-74; triples €82-96; quads €74-65. €2.50 HI discount. AmEx/MC/V.) **Hotel Carillon ❸**, Grote Markt 27, is ideally located. Most rooms have a shower, phone, and TV. (☎531 05 91; www.hotelcarillon.com. Breakfast included. Reception in summer 7:30am-1am; in winter 7:30am-midnight. Singles €38, with bath €58; doubles €63/78; triples €99; quads €108. AmEx/MC/V.) Take the *Stoptrein* that goes between Haarlem and Amsterdam and get off at the Haarlem-Spaarnwoude stop to reach **De Liede Campground ❶,** Lie Oever 68, a 15min. walk from the station. Bus #2 connects Spaarnwoude to Haarlem Centraal. (☎535 86 66. Tent sites €3.50. €3.50 per person.) Cheap eateries line Bruisst./Bartejlorisst. between the station and Grote Markt. There are patioed cafes in the **Grote Markt** or **Botermarkt.**

SIGHTS AND ENTERTAINMENT. The action centers on the **Grote Markt,** Haarlem's bustling main square, which gets taken over by a textile market on Monday afternoons and by a general one on Saturdays. To get there from the train station, head south along Kruisweg, which becomes Kruisstr. and then Barteljorisstr. A 2min. walk down Barteljorisstr. from the Grote Markt is the poignant **Corrie Ten Boomhuis,** Barteljorisstr. 19. This museum in Corrie Ten Boom's former house, was a center of underground activities during WWII; Corrie offered asylum to Jews and members of the Dutch resistance, helping many to escape Hitler. Corrie was caught and sent to a concentration camp but survived to write *The Hiding Place.* (☎5310 823; www.corrietenboom.com. Open Tu-Sa Apr.-Oct. 10am-3:30pm; Nov.-Mar. 11am-2:30pm. Access by 1hr. guided tours only. Free.) The **Grote Kerk,** on the Grote Markt, houses the tomb of portraitist Frans Hals, a Haarlem-born artist, and a mammoth 1738 Müller organ once played by Handel and Mozart. (☎553 20 40; www.bavo.nl. Open Mar.-Oct. Tu-Sa 10am-4pm; Nov.-Feb. M-Sa 10am-4pm. €2.) **De Hallen,** Grote Markt 16, hosts various modern art exhibits of videos, photographs, and paintings that rotate three or four times per year. (☎511 5775. Open Tu-Sa 11am-5pm, Su noon-5pm. €5, under 19 free.) From the front of the church, take a right onto Warmoesstr. and walk three blocks to the **Frans Hals Museum,** Groot Heiligland 62, which houses 11 of Hals's canvases and work by other Golden Age Dutchmen in a 17th-century almshouse. (☎511 57 75; www.franshalsmuseum.nl. Open Tu-Sa 11am-5pm, Su noon-5pm. €7, under 19 free.) **Teylers Museum,** Spaarne 16, the oldest museum in the country, contains a hodgepodge of scientific tools, fossils, paintings, and drawings. Walk behind the church, turn left onto Damstr., and take a left at the river. (Open Tu-Sa 10am-5pm, Su noon-5pm. €5.50. Audio tour €3.40.) Nightlife clusters near Grote Markt. **Cafe Stiel's,** Smedestr. 21, features live jazz and R&B music. (☎531 69 40. Open Su-Th 6pm-2am, F-Sa 6pm-4am.)

DAYTRIP FROM HAARLEM: ZANDVOORT. A mere 11km from Haarlem, the seaside town of **Zandvoort** (pop. 16,000) draws the sun-starved to its sandy beaches. The patios of **beach clubs,** where revelers carouse on lounge chairs, line the shore. Clubs open in the morning and close at midnight, and they're only open in summer. Nearby **Bloemendaal aan Zee** does not even qualify as a town; it's simply five or six beach clubs open from mid-April to mid-September. To get there from Zandvoort, walk 30min. to your right when facing the water. The irresistible hippie-ish club **Woodstock 69,** Zeedijk 8 (☎573 21 52; open daily Mar.-Sept. 9am-midnight), hosts **Beach Bop** (www.beachbop.info) on the beach the last Sunday of every month. Patrons at local favorite **Bloomingdale** recline on elegant sofas, which hosts the **Sundale** party (€5), with a DJ every Sunday 4pm-midnight. (☎0900 606 06 66. Open daily Apr.-Sept. 11am-midnight.) **Trains** go from Zandvoort to Haarlem (7min.; 2 per hr.; €2.60, round-trip €3.70). You can also take **bus** #81 from Haarlem Centraal (20min., 2 per hr., 3 strips). The **tourist office,** Schoolpl. 1, is east of the town square, off Louis Davidstr. Head away from the beach on Engelberst. and take a left on Zeest., a right on Haltest., and a left on Schoolst. (☎571 79 47; www.vvvzk.nl. Open M-F 9am-5pm, Sa 10am-4pm; in winter M-F 9am-5pm, Sa 10am-2pm.) Most visitors sleep in Haarlem, but the tourist office books inexpensive B&Bs in Zandvoort (€3-per-person).

LEIDEN ☎071

Home to one of the oldest and most prestigious universities in Europe, Leiden (pop. 118,000) brims with bookstores, gated gardens, and hidden walkways. This endearing town is notable both for giving the world Rembrandt and for bringing tulips to the Netherlands. Leiden once had 19 windmills, but only one remains, **Molenmuseum "De Valk,"** 2E Binnenvestgr. 1, near the tourist office, which you can visit and climb up for views. (☎516 53 53. Open Tu-Sa 10am-5pm, Su 1-5pm. €3.) Near the canal, the **Museum De Lakenhal,** Oude Singel 28-32, displays Dutch art, old and new. (☎516 53 60. Open Tu-Su 10am-5pm. €10. Audio tour included.) In spring, visit the **Hortus Botanicus,** Rapenburg 73, for some tulip appreciation. (☎527 72 49; www.hortusleiden.nl. Open Apr.-Oct. daily 10am-6pm; Nov.-Apr. Su-F 10am-4pm. €5.) Head indoors at the **Rijksmuseum van Oudheden** (Museum of National Antiquities), Rapenburg 28, tracks the history of the Netherlands through the Middle Ages. (☎516 31 63; www.rmo.nl. Open Tu-F 10am-5pm, Sa-Su noon-5pm. €7.50.) Near the train station, the **Museum Naturalis** traces the formation of the earth and its inhabitants in interactive displays. (☎568 76 00. Open July-Aug. M-F 10am-5pm. Sa-Su 10am-6pm; Sept.-June Tu-Su 10am-6pm. €9.)

Pension Witte Singel ❷, Witte Singel 80, overlooks serene canals and gardens and offers newly remodeled rooms. (☎512 45 92; www.pension-ws.demon.nl. Breakfast included. Singles €41; doubles €76. Call ahead.) A budget traveler's dream, **Olive Garden ❶,** Lange Mare 71, is a small Italian shop known for its killer food and lip-smacking prices. (☎514 44 66; www.olivegarden.nl. 100g homemade pasta €1.65-3. Panini €3-4.25. Open Tu-Sa 10:30am-6:30pm, Su noon-6:30pm.) For up-to-date information on Leiden's entertainment scene, grab a copy of the free magazine *L.O.S.* **Trains** run to Amsterdam (35min., every 15min., €8), Rotterdam (30min., 4 per hr., €6.70), and The Hague (15min., every 15min., €3.50). To get to the **tourist office,** Stationsweg 2D, take the city center exit from the station; it's on the right before the canal. (☎090 02 22 23 33; www.vvvleiden.nl. Open Apr.-Aug. M 11am-5:20pm, Tu-F 10am-5:30pm, Sa 9:30am-5:30pm, Su 11am-3pm.)

THE HAGUE (DEN HAAG) ☎070

The Hague (pop. 470,000) is the political nucleus of the Netherlands. With its international lawyers, bureaucrats, and government buildings, one might expect The Hague to be a bit stiff in the collar. But world-class art museums, a lively city center, and a huge jazz festival make the Netherlands's political capital anything but boring.

TRANSPORTATION AND PRACTICAL INFORMATION. Trains run to Amsterdam (45min., every 10min., €9.50) and Rotterdam (30min., 8 per hr., €4.60) from both of The Hague's major stations, **Centraal Station,** closer to the city center, and **Holland Spoor,** nearer to the hostel. Trams #1, 9, 12, and 17 connect the two stations. The **tourist office,** Hofweg 1C, by Binnehof, has **Internet** (€1 per 30min.) and sells detailed city maps for €2. (☎090 03 40 35 05; www.denhaag.com. Open M-F 10am-6pm, Sa 10am-5pm, Su noon-5pm.)

ACCOMMODATIONS AND FOOD. The **Stayokay City Hostel Den Haag (HI) ❷,** Scheepmakerstr. 27, is near Holland Spoor. From Centraal Station, take tram #1 (dir.: Delft), 9 (dir.: Vrederust), or 12 (dir.: Duindorp) to Rijswijkseplein (2 strips), cross left in front of the tram, and cross the intersection; Scheepmakerstr. is straight ahead. (☎315 78 88; www.stayokay.com/denhaag. Breakfast and linens included. Reception daily 7:30am-10:30pm. Dorms €21-25; singles €41-45; doubles €58-66; triples €75-87; quads €92-108. €2.50 HI discount. MC/V.) Restaurants—not all budget—are plentiful on **Lange Poten, the Plein,** and **Korte Poten** near the Binnenhof. Tapas await at **Cafe de Oude Mol ❶**, Oude Molstr. 61, near from Grote Halstr. (☎345 16 23. Tapas €3.50-7.50. Open M-W 5pm-1am, Th-Sa 5pm-2am. Kitchen open W-Sa. Live music M. Cash only.)

SIGHTS AND ENTERTAINMENT. The **Peace Palace** (Het Vredespaleis), Carnegiepl. 2, was funded by American industrialist Andrew Carnegie in 1913 and today is the opulent home of the International Court of Justice. It contains impressive gifts from countries all over the world, which can be viewed on the 1hr. tour. From Centraal Station, take tram #17 to Knentersdijk and tram #1 to Vredespaleis. (☎302 42 42; www.vredespaleis.nl. Tours M-F 10, 11am, 2, 3pm. Reserve ahead and arrive 10min. early. €5.) Take a stroll through the courtyard of the **Binnenhof,** The Hague's Parliament complex. Tours of the complex visit the 13th-century Ridderzaal (Knights' Hall) and leave from inside the courtyard at Binnenhof 8A. (☎364 61 44; www.binnenhofbezoek.nl. Open M-F 9am-5pm. Tour €5.) Near the Binnenhof's entrance, the 17th-century **Mauritshuis Royal Picture Gallery,** Korte Vijverberg 8, features an impressive collection of paintings, including works by Rembrandt and the bawdy Jan Steen, and Vermeer's famous *Girl With a Pearl Earring.* (☎302 34 35; www.mauritshuis.nl. Open Apr.-Aug. M-Sa 10am-5pm, Su 11am-5pm; Sept.-Mar. Tu-Sa 10am-5pm, Su 11am-5pm. €9.50, under 18 free. Audio tour included.) The **Gemeentemuseum,** Stadhouderslaan 41, houses the world's largest collection of Piet Mondrian works (temporarily on loan to Cologne starting Dec. 2007), as well as temporary exhibits. Take tram #17 (dir.: Statenkwartier) to Gemeentemuseum. (☎338 11 11; www.gemeentemuseum.nl. Open Tu-Su 11am-5pm. €8.) Windsurfers and kite-flyers pack the beach in nearby **Scheveningen,** which also has a nightlife accented by a casino, restaurants, cafes, and pubs.

On the first Saturday of June, The Hague hosts what the Netherlands hails as the largest free public pop concert in Europe—**Parkpop.** Held on three big stages in the Zuiderpark, the concert has seen acts including the Dandy Warhols, Suzanne Vega, and the Bloodhound Gang (☎523 90 64; www.parkpop.nl). Experimental theater, opera, jazz, blues, classical ensembles, indie music, and dance all find a home at **Theater aan het Spui,** Spui 187, near Stadhuis. Pick up a free schedule of events at the box office or tourist office. Take tram #16 or 17 to Spui. (Box office ☎070 302 4070 or 880 03 00. Open Tu-Sa 11am-6pm.)

DAYTRIP FROM THE HAGUE: DELFT. The lilied canals and stone footbridges that line the streets of Delft (pop. 97,000) offer the same views that

IN RECENT NEWS

TRIALS AND TRIBULATIONS

Charles Taylor, warlord and former president of Liberia, is set to go on trial in The Hague. He is accused of supporting rebels who committed atrocities in neighboring Sierra Leone and of trafficking in guns and diamonds. The judges who will preside over Taylor's trial wished for the trial to occur in a more neutral place than Sierra Leone, where it could instigate instability; in The Hague, his supporters would be unable to disrupt decorum.

The Hague is the rational choice for the trial, since it has an established practice for hosting infamous war-crimes suspects, gaining visas for involved parties, and consolidating international agencies as it is in the former president's case: Taylor will be tried under the auspices of the Special Court of Sierra Leone, held in the Netherlands, and jailed, if found guilty, in Britain.

The International Court of Justice is housed in the neo-Baroque Peace Palace, which was endowed by Andrew Carnegie in the 1900s, mostly designed by French architect Louis Cordonnier, and completed in 1913. The city itself was put on the map in 1899, when the young Nicholas II, czar of Russia, planned a disarmament conference here. Since then, The Hague has held international courts and weapons conferences, and has ushered in a tradition of world leaders assembling in support of peace.

native Johannes Vermeer immortalized in paint over 300 years ago. It's best to visit on Thursdays and Saturdays, when townspeople flood the marketplace. The town is renowned for **Delftware,** blue-on-white earthenware developed in the 16th century. Watch it being made from scratch at homey **De Candelaer,** Kerkstr. 13a-14, in the center of town. (☎213 18 48; www.candelaer.nl. Open Apr.-Oct. M-F 9am-5:30pm, Sa 9am-5pm, Su 10am-6pm. Nov.-Mar. M-Sa 9am-5pm. Free.) Built in 1381, the **Nieuwe Kerk** holds the restored mausoleum of Dutch liberator William of Orange. Climb the 109m tower, which shelters a 36-bell carillon and offers a magnificent view of old Delft. (☎212 30 25; www.nieuwekerk-delft.nl. Church open Apr.-Oct. M-Sa 9am-6pm; Nov.-Mar. M-F 11am-4pm, Sa 11am-5pm. Tower closes 1hr. before church. Church €3. Tower €2.50.) Built in 1200, the brighter **Oude Kerk** lays claim to Vermeer's gravestone and a leaning 75m tower erected in 1325. (☎212 30 15; www.oudekerk-delft.nl. Open Apr.-Oct. M-Sa 9am-6pm; Nov.-Mar. M-F 11am-4pm, Sa 11am-5pm. Free with entrance to Nieuwe Kerk.) There are no budget accommodations in Delft; stay in The Hague. Restaurants line **Volderstraat** and **Oude Delft. Tram** #1 runs to The Hague (20min., 2 strips). **Trains** also run to Amsterdam (1hr., 2-5 per hr., €11) and Rotterdam (10min., 8 per hr., €2.90). The **tourist office** (Tourist Information Point; TIP), Hippolytusbuurt 4, near the Stadhuis, distributes a free map of the city and has free **Internet.** (☎215 40 51; www.delft.nl. Open Apr.-Sept. Su-M 10am-4pm, Tu-F 9am-6pm, Sa 9am-5pm; Oct.-Mar. M 11am-4pm, Tu-Sa 10am-4pm, Su 10am-3pm.)

ROTTERDAM ☎010

The second-largest city in the Netherlands and among the busiest port cities in the world, Rotterdam (pop. 660,000) lacks the quaint, gingerbread-house feel that characterizes neighboring areas. Its festivals, art galleries, and dynamic nightlife make Rotterdam the most up-and-coming city in the Netherlands. Dalí, Magritte, Monet, Rothko, Rubens, and van Gogh line the walls at the **Museum Boijmans van Beuningen,** Museumpark 18-20. (Subway to Eendractspl. or tram #5 to Witte de Withstr. ☎441 91 75; www.boijmans.nl. Open Tu-Su 11am-5pm. €8. Audio tour €3.) Walk through the Museumpark to reach the **Kunsthal,** Westzeedijk 341, which Rem Koolhaas designed to feature rotating exhibits of architecture, painting, and photography. (☎440 03 01; www.kunsthal.nl. Open Tu-Sa 10am-5pm, Su 11am-5pm. €8.50.) The 170m **Euromast,** built in 1958 is the best way to admire Rotterdam's skyline. (Parkhaven 20. Tram #8 to Euromast. ☎436 48 11; www.euromast.nl. Elevator to top open daily 9:30am-11pm; last ride up 9:45pm. €8. Zipline from top to bottom open May-Sept. Sa-Su. €40.) Down by the wharf, floodlights illuminate the **Erasmus Bridge** in a ghostly white haze each night.

For an escape from bland hostel accommodations without the price of a hotel, head to the new **Room Rotterdam ❶,** Van Vollenhovenst. 62. From Centraal Station, walk 20min. down Kruisplein/Westersingel to Van Vollenhovenst., or take tram #5 (dir.: Willemspein) to the fifth stop, in front of Cafe Loos, and backtrack for 1min. to the hostel. (☎282 72 77; www.roomrotterdam.nl. Kitchen. Breakfast €3-4.50. Linens €2. Internet €0.50 per 20min. Reception 24hr. Dorms €15-18; doubles €35; quads €88. AmEx/MC/V). **Bazar ❷,** Witte de Withstr. 16, in a hotel of the same name, serves Middle Eastern fusion cuisine. The service is definitively relaxed. (☎206 51 51. Sandwiches €4-6. Entrees €8-15. Open M-Th 8am-1am, F 8am-2am, Sa 10am-2am, Su 10am-midnight. AmEx/MC/V.) Groceries are at **Spar,** Witte de Withstr. 36. (Open M-F 8:30am-7pm, Sa 8:30am-5pm.) Coffeeshops line **Oude Binnenweg** and **Nieuwe Binnenweg.** For the scoop on Rotterdam nightlife and events, pick up *Zone 010* (free); for gay nightlife, *The Gaymap*, at Use-It.

Trains run to Amsterdam (1hr., 4 per hr., €13) and The Hague (25min., 8 per hr., €4.60). The **tourist office,** called the **Rotterdam Store,** Coolsingel 5, books rooms for free and provides free maps and info packets. (☎0900 40 340 85; www.rotterdam.info. Open M-Th 9:30am-6pm, F 9:30am-9pm, Sa 9:30am-5pm, Su 10am-5pm.) **Use-It Rotterdam,** Schaatsbaan 41-45, for young, budget-conscious backpackers, publishes the *Simply the Best* guide to the city. (☎240 91 58; www.use-it.nl. Open July-Aug. 24hr.; Sept.-June Tu-Sa 9am-6pm.)

UTRECHT

☎030

Utrecht is free of tourist hordes but chock-full of cultural events, museums, and a swinging nightlife supported by its robust student population. Even the canals are visitor-friendly; they lie below street level and are ideal for picnicking and strolling. Ground was broken in 1254 for construction of the oddly shaped **Domkerk,** Achter de Dom 1, and work continued for a good 250 years. Originally a Roman Catholic cathedral, the Domkerk was taken over by Protestants in 1581. (☎231 04 03; www.domkerk.nl. Open May-Sept. M-F 10am-5pm, Sa 10am-3:30pm, Su 2-4pm; Oct.-Apr. M-F 11am-4pm, Sa 11am-3:30pm, Su 2-4pm. Free.) The 112m tower, the **Domtoren,** was attached to the cathedral until a tornado blew away the nave in 1674. A tour, offered in English, is required for entrance. (Tickets for tours sold at RonDom desk in tourist office. 50min. tours July-Aug. daily 11am-5pm., every 30min.-1hr.; Oct.-Mar. M-F noon, 2, 4pm. €7.50.) The **Museumkwartier** is the nucleus of all Utrecht's museums, including the circuitous **Centraal Museum,** Nicolaaskerkhof 10, founded in 1838, whose galleries pay tribute to Utrecht's artistic past. (☎236 23 62; www.centraalmuseum.nl. Open Tu-Th and Sa-Su noon-5pm, F noon-9pm. €8.) The **Nationaal Museum Van Speelklok tot Pierement,** Steenwag 6, traces the history of mechanical musical instruments. (☎231 27 89; www.museumspeelklok.nl. Open Tu-Su 10am-5pm. €7.)

At **B&B Utrecht City Centre ❶,** Lucasbolwerk 4, European backpackers use their knees to feast on meals prepared from cook-it-yourself ingredients in the kitchen and cupboard. From the station, walk toward the city center down Vredenburg, which turns into Nobelstr. Turn left before the canal; the B&B is there on your left but is poorly marked. (☎0650 43 48 84; www.hostelutrecht.nl. Linens €2.50. Free Internet. Dorms €16; singles €55; doubles €65; triples €90; quads €120. MC/V.) **Strowis Hostel ❶,** Boothstr. 8, has colorful rooms and an outdoor terrace overlooking a garden. Walk toward the city center down Vredenburg, turn left on Janskerkhof and left on Boothstr. (☎238 02 80; www.strowis.nl. Bikes €5 per day, €50 deposit. Breakfast €5. Linens €1.25. Free Internet. Dorms €14-17; doubles €55-63; triples €66. AmEx/MC/V.) Cheap fare, in the form of pizzerias, pubs, and sandwich shops, can always be found along **Nobelstraat.** Sit at the canalside **Het Nachtrestaurant ❷,** Oudegrt. 158, which doles out great tapas (€3.40-6) and sangria (€3.90) by the glass. (☎230 30 36. Open daily 6-10 or 11pm. Sa nightclub upstairs after 11pm. MC.) Utrecht is the Netherlands's largest college town, and it has the social scene to prove it. Pick up *UitLoper* (in Dutch) at bars, restaurants, or the tourist office to scout out events. Big going-out nights are Wednesday through Friday; on Saturday many students leave town. **'t Oude Pothuys,** Oudegr. 279, is a converted cellar that hosts live music nightly. (Beer €2-3. Open daily 3pm-3am.) Once the rest of Utrecht has shut down, students party at fraternity-run **Woolloo Moollo** (the "Wo"), Janskerkhof 14. (Beer €1.10. Student ID required. Cover €3. Open M, W-Sa 11pm-late.) **De Winkel van Sinkel,** Oudegr. 158, is the city's most popular grand-cafe and doubles as a club. (☎230 30 30. Beer from €2.10. Sa DJs spin house and hip hop 11pm. Cover Sa €9-13. Open Su-F 11pm-2am, Sa 11pm-5am.)

Trains run from Hoog Catharijne station to Amsterdam (30min., every 15 min., €6.80) and Maastricht (2hr., 2 per hr., €23.10). To get to the **tourist office,** Dompl. 9, follow Vredenburg over the canal, make a right onto Neude, and find it on the right in the square. Pick up a map of the city and a complete listing of museums and sights for €1.50. (☎0900 128 87 32; www.12utrecht.nl. Open M noon-6pm, T-W and F 10am-6pm, Th 10am-8pm, Sa 9:30am-5pm, Su noon-5pm.)

DE HOGE VELUWE NATIONAL PARK ☎0318

The impressive **De Hoge Veluwe National Park** (HO-geh VEY-loo-wuh) is a 13,565-acre preserve of woods, heath, dunes, red deer, and wild boar; bikes, free for all visitors, let you best experience the park, and, if you're lucky, see its wildlife. (☎0900 464 3825; www.hogeveluwe.nl. Park open daily Apr. 8am-8pm; May and Aug. 8am-9pm; June-July 8am-10pm; Sept. 9am-8pm; Oct. 9am-7pm; Nov.-Mar. 9am-6pm. Last entrance 1hr. before closing. €6, includes bike use in park.) Deep within, the **Kröller-Müller Museum** has troves of van Goghs and key works by Giacometti, Gris, Mondrian, Picasso, and Seurat. The museum's striking **sculpture garden,** one of the largest in Europe, is home to exceptional works by Rodin and Serra in addition to Jean Dubuffet's delightfully wacky *Jardin d'email.* (☎59 12 41; www.kmm.nl. Open Tu-Su 10am-5pm. Sculpture garden closes 4:30pm. €6 in addition to park admission.) Explore over 40km of paths with a free **White Bicycle** and a map (€2.50) from the **visitors' center** (open daily Apr.-Oct. 9:30am-6pm, Nov.-Mar. 9:30am-5pm); signs marked *"Bezoekerscentrum"* lead to it.

Arnhem is a good base for exploring the park; bus #107 (20min., 1 per hr., 5 strips) traverses the 15km from Arnhem's Centraal Station to the park's northwestern entrance. From the Otterlo stop, you can walk to the park entrance and grab a bike or transfer to bus #110 (free), which stops in the park at the museum and the visitors center. The **tourist office** in Otterlo (open M-F 9:30am-4:30pm, Sa 9:30am-1:30pm) can provide information, as can the one at Arnhem, Willemspl. 8. (☎0900 202 40 75; www.vvvarnhem.nl. Open M 11am-5:30pm, Tu-F 9am-5:30pm, Sa 10am-4pm.) To get to the **Stayokay Hostel (HI)** ❶, Diepenbrocklaan 27, take bus #3 (2 strips) from the Arnhem train station to Rijnstate Hospital; facing the hospital, turn right, then left on Cattepoelseweg. About 150m ahead, turn right up the brick steps, and go right at the top. (☎442 01 14; www.stayokay.com/arnhem. Breakfast and linens included. Reception 8am-11pm. Dorms €27-29; singles €52-54; doubles €74-78. €2.50 HI discount. Low season reduced rates. MC/V.)

MAASTRICHT ☎043

Situated on a strategic strip of land between Belgium and Germany, Maastricht (pop. 125,000) was once descended upon by warring foreigners but is now inundated only by gallery visitors, antiques junkies, and highfalutin art theorists seeking out the prestigious **Jan van Eyck Academie** modern art institute. The futuristic rocketship design of the **Bonnefantenmuseum,** ave. Céramique 250, contrasts with the building's traditional Dutch brickwork; pieces by up-and-coming Dutch artists similarly clash with the works of the Old Master usual suspects. (☎329 01 90; www.bonnefanten.nl. Open Tu-Su 11am-5pm. €7.) Centuries of territorial conflicts around Maastricht prompted the city to invest in an innovative subterranean defense system; the 20,000 underground passages of the **Mount Saint Pieter Caves** were once the site of a Roman limestone quarry but became siege shelters used as late as WWII. Now they contain inscriptions and artwork by generations of inhabitants. They are accessible at two locations, but only with a tour guide. Visit either the **Zonneberg Caves,** Buitengoe Slavante, Slavante 1 (open frequently during high season) or the **Northern System,** Chalet Bergrust, Luikerweg 71 (open more frequently during low season); check the tourist office website for specific opening times. The caves get chilly; bring a jacket. An English tour is given in the Zonneberg Caves. (July 1-Sept. 3 daily 1:55pm. €3.95.) The caves are a long walk from the city center; the best option is to take the 20min. boat tour offered by Rederij Striphout, which will drop you off near the Zonneberg cave entrance. Buy combo boat/cave tickets at Maaspromenade 58, along the water. (☎351 53 00; www.striphout.nl. €10.) Above ground, the **Basilica of St. Servatius,** Keizer Karelpl., off the central Vrijthof Sq., rings one of the country's largest bells, affectionately known as Grameer, meaning "Grandmother." (☎350 62 62; www.sintservaas.nl. Open daily 10am-5pm, Su 12:30-5pm. May-Oct. tours M-F 1 and 5pm. €3.50.)

Maastricht's popularity with gourmands and art dealers means that budget lodgings can be difficult to find. Fortunately, a new **Stayokay hostel** is due to open in 2007; check status updates on the general website (www.stayokay.com). The tourist office website has a list of reasonable B&Bs, of which some are quite out of the way. The extraordinarily tiny cabins of the floating **Botel ❷**, Maasboulevard 95, are the cheapest options in town. Above-deck rooms are cheerier. (☎321 90 23. Breakfast €6. Reception 24hr. Singles €26-31; doubles €42-46. Cash only.) **'t Liewe ❸**, Grote Gracht 62, has French and Mediterranean cuisine. (☎321 04 59. Entrees €11-19. Open M and Th-Su 5pm-midnight. Cash only.) **Slagerij Franssen ❶**, St. Pietersstr. 42, makes an array of sandwiches (€1.25-4). (☎321 29 00. No tables. Open Tu-F 8am-6pm, Sa 8am-4pm. Cash only.) Try the bars like **De Uni**, Brusselsestr. 31, run by frat brothers and filled with local students (Beer €1. Open W-F 9:30pm-2am. Closed mid-July to mid-Aug.) After 2am, partiers go to **Allebonner (De Alla)**, Leliestr. 5-7, a dance club. (☎325 4724. Open daily 11pm-6am.)

Trains go from the east side to Amsterdam (2½hr., 2 per hr., €27). To get from the station to the **tourist office**, Kleine Str. 1, follow Stationstr. over the bridge, and take a right. They book beds for €3-5. (☎328 0808; www.vvvmaastricht.nl. Open May-Oct. M-Sa 9am-6pm, Su 11am-3pm; Nov.-Apr. M-Th 9am-6pm, Sa 9am-5pm.)

GRONINGEN ☎050

College-town Groningen pulses with youthful energy: more than half of the city's 180,000 inhabitants are under 35, perpetuating Groningen's reputation as a great party city. Heavily bombed in WWII, the city rebuilt itself completely, yet managed to keep the old-world appeal that Rotterdam consciously kicked to the curb.

TRANSPORTATION AND PRACTICAL INFORMATION. **Trains** run from Groningen to Amsterdam (2½hr., 2 per hr., €24), though passengers sometimes need to switch trains at Amersfoot; ask the conductor to be sure. The **tourist office**, Grote Markt 25, is in the far corner of the Markt next to the Martinitoren. (☎0900 202 3050, €1 per min.; www.vvvgroningen.nl. Open July-Aug. M-F 9am -6pm, Sa 10am-5pm, Su 11am-3pm; Sept.-June M-F 9am-6pm, Sa 10am-5pm.)

ACCOMMODATIONS AND FOOD. You'll find clean, imaginatively decorated rooms at **Simplon Jongerenhotel ❶**, Boterdiep 73-2, a 7min. walk from the Grote Markt. Take bus #1 from the station (dir.: Korrewegwijk) to Boterdiep; the hostel is through the yellow- and black-striped entrance. (☎313 52 21; www.simplon-jongerenhotel.nl. Breakfast €4, included with private rooms. Linens €2.80. Internet €1 per 10min. Reception 24hr. Lockout noon-3pm. All-female dorm available. Dorms €13-17; singles €33-39; doubles €47-55; quads €100. Cash only.) To get to unexciting **Hotel Friesland ❶**, Kleine Pelsterstr. 4, cross the canal at the Groninger Museum and walk up Ubbo Emmiusstr., turn right on Gedempte Zuiderdiep, left on Pelsterstr., and go right onto Kleine Pelsterstr. (☎312 13 07. Breakfast included. Singles €30; doubles €50. AmEx/MC/V.) Attune your palate to the spices of the East at **De Kleine Moghul ❷**, Nieuwe Boteringstr. 62, an Indian restaurant serving inventive, seasonal fare. (☎318 89 05. Entrees around €9. Takeout 2-10pm. Open daily 5-10pm. MC/V.) At **Ben'z ❷**, Peperstr. 17, dinner is served by lantern-light in a Bedouin tent. Take a puff on the *nargileh*, a traditional water pipe. (☎313 79 17. Student menu €7.60-9.10. Open M-Sa 5-9pm. Cash only.)

SIGHTS AND ENTERTAINMENT. The town's spectacular **Groninger Museum**, housed in three whimsical, angular pavilions, rotates exhibits of modern art, traditional paintings, and ancient artifacts. The multi-colored galleries create a futuristic laboratory atmosphere for daring exhibits. (☎366 65 55; www.groningermuseum.nl. Open July-Aug. M 1-5pm, Tu-Su 10am-5pm; Sept.-June Tu-Su 10am-5pm. €8. Audio tour €2.50.) Admire the city from atop the Grote Markt's **Martinitoren,** a 97m tower that weathered the German attacks during WWII. Midway up the tower, you can pull cords to simulate ringing the tower's bells. Buy tickets at the tourist office. (Open daily Apr.-Oct. 11am-5pm; Nov.-Mar. noon-4pm. €3.) Soak up the sunshine amid beautiful flowers blooming in summer in the serene **Prinsenhoftuin** (Princes' Court Gardens); the entrance is on the canal by the Maagden bridge. (Open Apr. to mid-Oct. daily 10am-dusk.) Inside the gardens, the tiny **Theeschenkerij Tea Hut** offers 37 kinds of tea (€1) under charming canopied underpasses. (Open M-F 10am-6pm, Sa-Su noon-6pm.) At day's end, cool off at **Noorderplantsoen,** a rolling, fountain-filled park that hosts late August's **Noorderzon Festival,** 10 days of outdoor theater and concerts, some of which are free.

Groningen parties like a city several times its size. Drink cheap pitchers of beer in crowded bars near the Grote Markt on Poelestr. and Peperstr. For outdoor nightlife, try the megabar overlooking the Grote Markt, known familiarly as the **Zuid Zijd** (South Side). The staff at **Vera,** Oosterstr. 44, proclaim it to be the "club for the international pop underground." Pick up a copy of the *VeraKrant* newsletter in the box outside for a schedule of events. (☎313 46 81; www.vera-groningen.nl. Some gigs start at 1am. Open daily 1pm-3 or 4am. Closed July 10-Aug. 14.) Candlelit **Jazzcafe de Spieghel,** Peperstr. 11, offers two floors of live jazz, funk, or blues nightly at 9 or 11pm. Pick up a free copy of *UITLoper* (in Dutch) from the tourist office to find out what's on. (☎321 63 00. Wine €2.20. Open daily 8pm-4am.) Groningen's coffeeshops are cheaper than their Amsterdam brethren. **Dee's Cafe,** Papengang 3, tucked unassumingly into a small alley, is a perfect spot for night owls. (☎31 32 410; www.cafedees.nl. Weed €5 and €12 sizes. Space cakes €2.50. Internet €2 per hr. Open M-Th 11am-midnight, F-Sa noon-3am, Su noon-midnight.)

WADDEN ISLANDS (WADDENEILANDEN) ☎0222

Wadden means "mudflat" in Dutch, but sand is the defining characteristic of this cluster of islands; gorgeous beaches hide behind dunes covered in swaying golden grass. Tulip-lined bike trails carve up vast, flat stretches of grazing land to the sea. Sleepy, isolated, and stunning in a simple way, the islands are the Netherlands's best-kept secret.

TRANSPORTATION. The islands arch clockwise around the northwestern coast of the Netherlands: Texel (closest to Amsterdam), Vlieland, Terschelling, Ameland, and Schiermonnikoog. To reach Texel, take the train from Amsterdam to Den Helder (1¼hr., €13), then grab bus #33 for the 5 min. trip to the ferry dock (5min., about 1 per hr., 2 strips). **Ferries** (☎369 600; www.teso.nl) head to 't Hoorntje, Texel's southernmost town (20min., 1 per hr. 6:30am-9:30pm, round-trip €3.) To reach the other islands from Amsterdam, catch a **train** from Centraal Station to Harlingen Haven (3hr., €28). From Harlingen, ferries (☎562 44 20 02; www.rederij-doeksen.nl) depart for Terschelling and Vlieland (both 45min.-2hr., 3-5 per day, €21-25). Ferries also run among Texel, Vlieland, and Terschelling (Terschelling to Vlieland 30min., 1 per day, €5.75, round-trip €11; Texel to Vlieland 30min., 2-4 per day, €12, round-trip €18.) Tickets must be purchased on Vlieland, optimally one day ahead. (Ticket office ☎316 451; www.waddenveer.nl.) Traveling between Texel and Terschelling is difficult. To best avoid transport-induced stress, pick only one island to visit, or budget extra days.

TEXEL. The largest and most populous of the Wadden Islands, Texel (pop. 14,000) is still home to more sheep than people. Spectacular **beaches** lie near De Koog, on the western side of the island. *Naakstranden* (nude beaches) beckon the uninhibited; you can bare it all near Paal 9 (2km southwest of Den Hoorn) or Paal 27 (5km west of De Cocksdorp). Watch frolicsome seals being fed at the **EcoMare Museum and Aquarium,** Ruijslaan 92, south of De Koog. (Take bus #28 from the ferry landing. ☎31 77 41; www.ecomare.nl. Open daily 9am-5pm. Seal feeding 11am, 3pm. €7.75.) On the other side of the island in the quaint town of **Oudeschild,** the **Maritime and Beachcomber's Museum** (Maritiem en Jutters Museum), Barentzstr. 21, invites visitors to life-sized replicas of smithy and fishermen's houses meant to depict Oudeschild at the turn of the 20th century. (☎31 49 56; www.texelsmaritiem.nl. Open June-Aug. daily 10am-5pm; Sept.-June Tu-Sa 10am-5pm. €4.75.)

The new **Stayokay Texel ❶,** at Haffelderweg in Den Burg, is slated to open in autumn 2006. To get there, take bus #28 and ask to get off at the Elemert bus station. (☎31 54 41. Bike rental. Dorms approximately €15-25. €2.50 HI discount. Call to check on hostel opening.) **Campgrounds** are abundant south of De Koog and near De Cocksdorp. **Buses** depart from Texel's ferry dock to various locales around the island, though the best way to travel is to rent a **bike** from **Fietsvervhuurbedrijf** (☎219 588), opposite the ferry dock. (Bikes €4.75-6.75 per day. Open daily 9am-8pm.) A **Texel Ticket** (€4.50), which you can buy on any bus, is good for one day of unlimited travel on the island's bus system. The **tourist office,** Emmaln 66, is located just outside Den Burg, about 300m south of the main bus stop. (☎31 47 41; www.texel.net. A 24hr., free Internet kiosk lets you arrange accommodations on Texel. Open M-F 9am-5:30pm, Sa 9am-5pm.)

TERSCHELLING. Terschelling's secluded beaches stretch around its western tip and across its northern coast; 90% of the island is protected as a nature reserve. To explore the island, rent a **bike** from Haantjes Fietsverhuur, W. Barentzskade 23. (☎05 62 44 29 29. Bikes €5-6.50 per day, €20 per week. Open M-Sa 9am-5:30pm, Su 9:30am-5:30pm.) The **Terschelling Stayokay Hostel (HI) ❶,** Burg van Heusdenweg 39, is a 15min. walk along the water with the dock behind you. (☎05 62 44 23 38; www.stayokay.com/terschelling. Breakfast and linens included. Laundry €3.50. Internet €5 per hr. Reception 9am-10pm. Dorms €20-25. €1.50 extra F-Sa. €2.50 HI discount. AmEx/MC/V.) It's worth the 14km trek out to the beach and the beachside restaurant, **Heartbreak Hotel ❶,** in Oosterend. This Elvis shrine serves great diner-style food in red pleather booths. (☎05 62 44 86 34. Burger with fries €10. Open daily 10am-midnight. Cash only.) The most convenient place to grab a bite is in the island's main village, West Terschelling. **Zeezicht ❸,** W. Barentszkade 20, features local specialties and a sweeping view of the sea. (☎05 62 44 22 68. Seafood and meat entrees €14-22. Daily special €12. Open daily 10am-midnight. AmEx/MC/V.) From mid-July to mid-August, it seems every partier in the Netherlands flocks to Terschelling. Head to **Braskoer,** Torenstr. 32, to join a young crowd on the dance floor (☎05 62 46 21 97. Beer €2-4. Cover €5 after 9pm. Open daily 10am-2am.), or to dimly lit **Cafe De Zeevaart,** Torenstr. 22, to join an older one. (☎05 62 44 26 77. Beer €1.40. Open daily 10am-2am. Cash only.) The **tourist office,** W. Barentzkade 19A, is opposite the ferry. (☎05 62 44 30 00; www.vvvterschelling.nl. Open M-F 9:30am-5:30pm, Sa 10am-3pm.)

NORWAY (NORGE)

The rugged fjords and remote mountain farms of Norway gave birth to one of the most feared seafaring civilizations of pre-medieval Europe, the Vikings. Modern-day Norwegians have inherited their ancestors' independent streak, voting against joining the EU in 1994 and drawing the ire of environmental groups for their refusal to ban commercial whaling. Because of high revenues from petroleum exports, Norway enjoys one of the highest standards of living in the world. Its stunning fjords and miles of undisturbed coastline make Norway a truly worthwhile destination—but sky-high prices and limited public transportation in rural areas make it a practical trip for only the most well-prepared budget traveler.

DISCOVER NORWAY: SUGGESTED ITINERARY

Oslo (p. 742) is the best jumping-off point for travels in Norway. Tear yourself away from the museums and ethnic restaurants long enough to visit seaside **Stavanger** (p. 750), then catch a westbound train for the long, scenic ride to **Bergen** (p. 752). Get sidetracked on a trip up the **Flåm Railway** (p. 758), or hike on the Hardangervidda plateau near **Eidfjord** (p. 758). Plan a few days to explore Bergen, then head north to postcard-perfect **Geirangerfjord** (p. 760) and less-trafficked **Sognefjord** (p. 758). Visit the Art Nouveau architecture in **Ålesund** (p. 761) and the magnificent Nidaros Cathedral in **Trondheim** (p. 762). Make time to see the fishing villages of the beautiful **Lofoten Islands** (p. 766).

ESSENTIALS

FACTS AND FIGURES

Official Name: Kingdom of Norway.

Capital: Oslo.

Major Cities: Bergen, Stavanger, Tromsø, Trondheim.

Population: 4,640,000.

Land Area: 385,000 sq. km.

Time Zone: GMT +1.

Languages: Bokmål and Nynorsk Norwegian; Sámi; Swedish and English are both widely spoken.

Religion: Evangelical Lutheran (86%).

WHEN TO GO

Oslo averages 18°C (63°F) in July and -4°C (24°F) in January. The north is the coldest and wettest region; Bergen and the surrounding mountains are rainy. For a few weeks around the summer solstice (June 21), the area north of Bodø basks in the midnight sun. The **Northern Lights,** spectacular nighttime displays formed when solar flares produce plasma clouds that run into atmospheric gases, peak from November to February above the Arctic Circle. Skiing is best just before Easter.

DOCUMENTS AND FORMALITIES

EMBASSIES. Foreign embassies for Norway are in Oslo. Norwegian embassies abroad include: **Australia,** Royal Norwegian Embassy, 17 Hunter St., Yarralumla, Canberra, ACT, 2600 (☎262 73 34 44; www.norway.org.au); **Canada,** 90 Sparks St., Ste. 532, Ottawa, ON, K1P 5B4 (☎613-238-6571; www.emb-norway.ca); **Ireland,**

34 Molesworth St., Dublin, 2 (☎16 62 18 00; www.norway.ie); **UK,** 25 Belgrave Sq., London, SW1X 8QD (☎20 75 91 55 00; www.norway.org.uk); **US,** 2720 34th St., NW, Washington, D.C., 20008 (☎202-333-6000; www.norway.org).

VISA AND ENTRY INFORMATION. EU citizens do not need a visa. Citizens of Australia, Canada, New Zealand, and the US do not need a visa for stays of up to 90 days, beginning upon entry into any of the countries within the EU's freedom of movement zone. For more information, see p. 16.

TOURIST SERVICES AND MONEY

EMERGENCY **Police:** ☎112. **Ambulance:** ☎113. **Fire:** ☎110.

TOURIST OFFICES. Virtually every town and village has a **Turistinformasjon** office; look for a white "i" on a square green sign. From the latter half of June through the first half of August, most tourist offices are open daily; expect reduced hours at other times. Check www.visitnorway.com for a directory of local offices.

MONEY. The unit of currency is the **krone (kr),** plural kroner. One kroner is equal to 100 øre. Banks and large post offices change money, usually for a small commission. It's usually cheaper to exchange money in Norway than at home. **Tipping** is not essential, but an extra 5-10% is always welcome for good restaurant service. It is customary to leave coins on the counter or table rather than putting the tip on a credit card. Hotel bills often include a 15% service charge. Refunds for the 24% **value added tax (VAT)** are available for single-item purchases of more than 310kr in a single store for customers who are not EU citizens. See p. 22 for more info.

NORWEGIAN KRONER (KR)

AUS$1 = 4.90KR	10KR = AUS$2.04
CDN$1 = 5.27KR	10KR = CDN$1.90
EUR€1 =7.90KR	10KR = EUR€1.27
NZ$1 = 4.97KR	10KR = NZ$2.24
UK£1 = 11.47KR	10KR = UK£0.87
US$1 = 6.33KR	10KR = US$1.58

TRANSPORTATION

BY PLANE. The main international airport is in Oslo (OSL), though a few international flights land at Bergen and Trondheim. **SAS** (Scandinavian Airlines; Norway ☎91 50 54 00, UK 08 70 60 72 77 27, US 800-221-2350) flies to Norway, as do Finnair and Icelandair. Students and travelers under 25 qualify for special youth fares when flying domestically on SAS. The new budget airline, **Norwegian** (www.norwegian.no), has introduced internal fares under €100, as well as cheap fares to destinations throughout Europe. Book early for the best fares on both SAS and Norwegian, or try your luck with SAS domestic standby tickets *(sjanse billetter)* that can be purchased at the airport on the day of travel for around 400kr.

BY TRAIN. Norway's train system includes a commuter network around Oslo and long-distance lines running from Oslo to Bergen and to Stavanger via Kristiansand. Contact **Norwegian State Railways (NSB)** for timetables and tickets (☎81 50 08 88; www.nsb.no). The unguided **Norway in a Nutshell** tour combines a ride along the **Flåm Railway,** a **cruise** through Aurlandsfjord and Nærøyfjord to the port of Gudvangen, and a **bus** ride over the mountains to Voss. Tickets can be purchased from tourist offices or train stations in Bergen and Oslo. (☎81 56 82 22; www.norwaynutshell.com. Round-trip from Voss 510kr, from Bergen 790kr, from Oslo

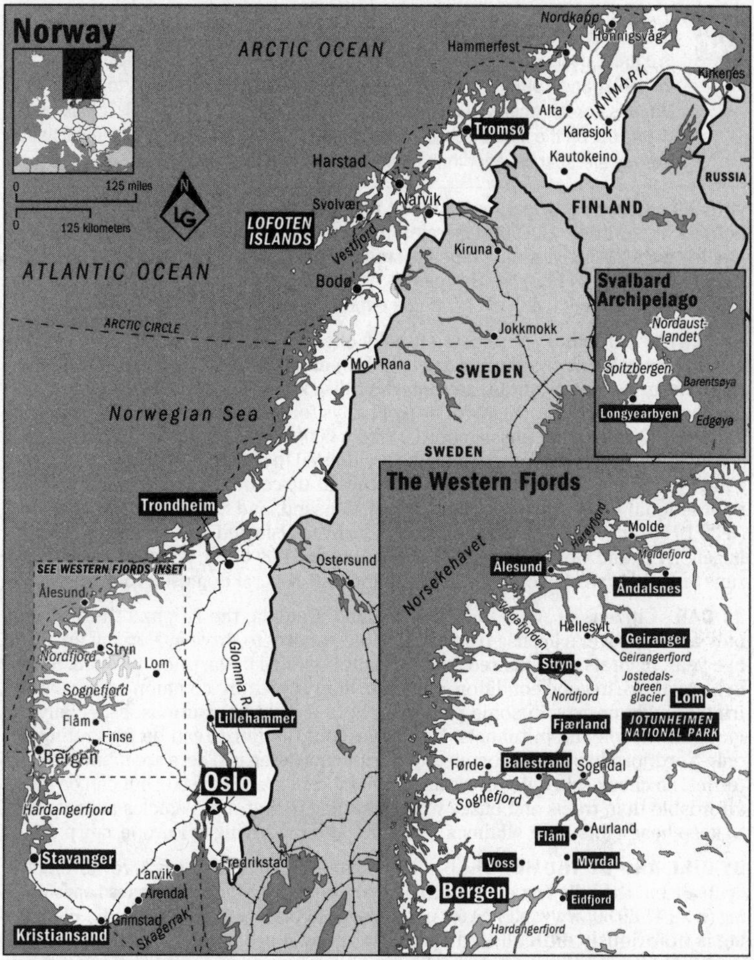

1585kr.) Overnight trains may be the best option for travel as far north as Bodø and Trondheim; from there, you'll need buses or ferries to get farther north. **Eurailpasses** are valid in Norway. The **Norway Railpass,** which cannot be purchased in Norway, allows three to five days of unlimited travel in a one-month period (from US$146). A **Scanrail pass** purchased in Norway allows five travel days in a 15-day period (1956kr, under 26 1360kr) or 21 consecutive travel days (3044/2117kr) of unlimited rail travel, as well as discounted fares on many ferries and buses. However, only three of those travel days can be used in the country of purchase, so a Scanrail pass purchased at home (p. 52) may be more economical. Neither pass includes trips on the Flåm Railway.

BY BUS. Buses can be quite expensive but are the only land travel option north of Bodø and in the fjords. **Nor-way Bussekspress** (☎81 54 44 44; www.nor-way.no) operates most of the domestic bus routes and publishes a timetable *(Rutehefte)*

> **TIP** **RAIL SAVINGS.** For rail travel within Norway, the **Minipris** offered by NSB is a great deal. A limited number of seats are made available on regional trains for 199kr and 299kr, even on expensive routes. Go to www.nsb.no to purchase Minipris tickets; when you are asked to choose the type of ticket, select Minipris. (If it is not on the menu, tickets are sold out.) Minipris tickets purchased outside Norway are 50kr cheaper than those purchased in the country.

with schedules and prices, available at bus stations and on buses. Scanrail pass holders are entitled to a 50% discount on most routes, and students with ISIC are eligible for a 25-50% discount—be insistent, and follow the rules listed in the *Norway Bussekspress* booklet. Bus passes, valid for 10 or 21 consecutive travel days (1300/2400kr), are good deals for those exploring the fjords or the north.

BY FERRY. **Car ferries** *(ferjer)* are usually cheaper (and slower) than the passenger **express boats** (*hurtigbat* or *ekspressbat*) cruising the coasts and fjords; both often have student, Scanrail, and InterRail discounts. The **Hurtigruten** (☎81 03 00 00; www.hurtigruten.com) takes six to 11 days for the incredible cruise from Bergen to Kirkenes on the Russian border (from 6000kr in high season, 3500kr in low season). Discounts for railpass holders are limited to 50% off the Bergen-Stavanger route, but some lines also offer a 50% student discount. The common ports for international ferries are Oslo, Bergen, Kristiansand, and Stavanger. **DFDS Seaways** (☎38 10 55 00; www.dfdsseaways.com) sails from Oslo and Kristiansand to Copenhagen, DEN and Gothenburg, SWE. **Color Line** (☎81 00 08 11; www.colorline.com) runs ferries between Norway and Denmark, plus several domestic routes.

BY CAR. Citizens of Australia, New Zealand, Canada, the EU, and the US need only a valid driver's license from their home country to drive in Norway for up to one year. Insurance is required and is usually included in the price of rental. Roads in Norway are in good condition, although blind curves are common and roads are frighteningly narrow in some places. Drivers should be cautious, especially on mountain roads and in tunnels. Driving around the fjords can be frustrating, as only Nordfjord has a road completely circumnavigating it. There are numerous car ferries, so check schedules in advance. Rental cars are expensive, but can be more affordable than trains and buses when traveling in a group. Vehicles are required to keep headlights on at all times. For more info on driving in Europe, see p. 54.

BY BIKE AND BY THUMB. The beautiful scenery around Norway is rewarding for cyclists, but the hilly terrain can be rough on bikes. Contact **Syklistenes Landsforening** (☎22 47 30 30; www.slf.no) for maps, suggested routes, and other info. **Hitchhiking** is notoriously difficult in mainland Norway, but easier on the Lofoten and Svalbard Islands. Some successfully hitchhike beyond the rail lines in northern Norway and the fjord areas of the west; many others try for hours and end up exactly where they started. Hitchhikers bring several layers of clothing, rain gear, and a warm sleeping bag. Let's Go does not recommend hitchhiking.

KEEPING IN TOUCH

PHONE CODES	**Country code:** 47. **International dialing prefix:** 095. There are no city codes in Norway. For more information on how to place international calls, see inside back cover.

EMAIL AND THE INTERNET. Oslo and Bergen have many Internet cafes. Expect to pay about 1kr per min. Smaller cities might have one or two Internet cafes, and most have a public library open on weekdays that offers 15-30min. of free Internet. Free wireless connections for travelers with laptops are also readily available.

TELEPHONE. There are three types of **public phones:** black and gray phones accept 1, 5, 10, and 20kr coins; green phones accept only phone cards; red phones accept coins, phone cards, and major credit cards. **Phone cards** (*telekort;* 40, 90, or 140kr at post offices and Narvesen kiosks) are the most economical option, especially when prices drop between 5pm and 8am. **Mobile phones** are increasingly popular and cheap; for more info, see p. 29. In Norway, **Netcom** offers the best prepaid deals for those traveling with a GSM mobile phone. A starter pack sells for 200kr, which includes 150kr of calling time. **Telenor,** which has the widest coverage, sells starter packs for 200kr, which includes 100kr of calling time. "Top-up" refills for both operators are widely available. For help with domestic calls, dial ☎117. International direct access numbers include: **AT&T Direct** (☎800 9011); **British Telecom** (☎80 01 99 44); **Canada Direct** (☎80 01 91 11); **MCI WorldPhone** (☎80 01 99 12); **Sprint** (☎80 01 98 77); **Telecom New Zealand** (☎80 01 99 64); **Telstra Australia** (☎80 01 99 61).

MAIL. Mailing a first-class postcard or letter (under 20g) within Norway costs 6kr; outside Norway costs 7.50-10.50kr. Address mail to be held *Poste Restante* as follows: First name LAST NAME, *Poste Restante*, Postal Code, city, NORWAY.

LANGUAGE. Norwegian is universally spoken, although many Norwegians also speak excellent English and Swedish. The indigenous people of northern Norway speak the Sámi languages. For basic Norwegian words and phrases, see **Phrasebook: Norwegian** (p. 1059).

ACCOMMODATIONS AND CAMPING

NORWAY	❶	❷	❸	❹	❺
ACCOMMODATIONS	under 160kr	160-260kr	260-400kr	400-550kr	over 550kr

HI youth hostels *(vandrerhjem)* are run by **Norske Vandrerhjem** (☎23 12 45 10; www.vandrerhjem.no). Beds run 175-250kr for nonmembers, though hostels in the Lofoten Islands are closer to 125kr. HI members receive a 25kr discount. Linens typically cost 45-60kr per stay. Few hostels have curfews. Most hostels open in mid- to late-June and close after the third week in August. Many tourist offices book **private rooms** and hotels for a fee (usually 30kr). Norwegian law allows free **camping** anywhere on public land for fewer than three nights, provided that you keep 150m from buildings and leave no trace. **Den Norske Turistforening** (DNT; Norwegian Mountain Touring Association) sells excellent maps (60-70kr), offers guided hiking trips, and maintains more than 350 **mountain huts** *(hytter)* throughout Norway. A one-year membership (445kr, under 26 260kr) entitles the holder to discounts on DNT lodgings (☎22 82 28 00; www.dntoslo.no). The 43 staffed huts are open in summer; most have showers and serve dinner. Unstaffed huts are open mid-February to mid-October; a sizable minority have basic provisions for sale on the honor system. Leave a 200-500kr deposit at any tourist office to borrow a key. Official campgrounds ask 60-130kr for tent sites, 300-700kr for cabins.

FOOD AND DRINK

NORWAY	❶	❷	❸	❹	❺
FOOD	under 60kr	60-100kr	100-150kr	150-250kr	over 250kr

Eating in Norway is a pricey affair. Many restaurants have inexpensive *dagens ret* (dish of the day; 70-80kr); otherwise, you'll rarely spend less than 150kr for a full meal. Fish—cod, herring, and salmon—is fresh and relatively inexpensive. Non-fish specialties include cheese *(ost);* pork-and-veal meatballs *(kjøttkaker)* with boiled potatoes; and, for more adventurous carnivores, reindeer, ptarmigan, and whale meat *(hval)*. Christmas brings a special meal of dried fish soaked in water and lye *(lutefisk)*. Beer is very expensive in bars (45-60kr for 0.5L), though 0.33L bottles hover around 10-13kr in supermarkets. Try the local favorite, *Frydenlund*, or go rock-bottom with Danish *Tuborg*. You must be 18 to buy beer, and 20 to buy wine and alcohol at the aptly named **Vinmonopolet** (wine monopoly) stores.

HOLIDAYS AND FESTIVALS

Holidays: New Year's Day (Jan. 1); Maundy Thursday (Apr. 5); Good Friday (Apr. 6); Easter (Apr. 8-9); Labor Day (May 1); Ascension Day (May 25); Whit (June 4-5); Constitution Day (May 17); Christmas (Dec. 24-25); Boxing Day (Dec. 26).

Festivals: Norway throws festivals virtually year-round, from the Tromsø International Film Festival (Jan. 16-21; www.tiff.no) to Bergen's operatic Festpillene (May 31-June 5; www.fib.no). The Norwegian Wood festival in Frognerbadet (mid-June; www.norwegianwood.no) features pop, folk, and classic rock. Heavy metal enthusiasts flock to Inferno, held in Oslo on Easter weekend. For more info, check www.norwayfestivals.com.

BEYOND TOURISM

Citizens of the 39 signatory countries of the Svalbard Treaty, including Australia, Canada, New Zealand, the UK, and the US, can work on the Svalbard archipelago (p. 768). See p. 61 for Beyond Tourism opportunities throughout Europe.

The American-Scandinavian Foundation (AMSCAN), 725 Park Ave., New York, NY, 10016, US (☎212-879-9779; www.amscan.org/jobs/index.html). Volunteer and job opportunities throughout Scandinavia. Limited number of study fellowships in Norway available to Americans.

Norsk Økologisk Landbrukslag (APØG), Langeveien 18, Bergen (☎47 55 32 04 80). The Norse Organic Farmers Union is sometimes willing to organize volunteer service on organic farms throughout Norway.

OSLO ☎21, 22, 23

Scandinavian capitals consent to being urban without renouncing the landscape around them, and Oslo (pop. 550,000) is no exception. The pine-covered hills to the north and Oslofjord to the south bracket the city's cultural institutions, busy cafes, and elegant boutiques. While most of Norway remains homogeneous, Oslo has a small, multiethnic immigrant community. The residents of the capital accept the changes that globalization has brought while maintaining their folk traditions.

TRANSPORTATION

Flights: Oslo Airport Gardermoen (OSL; ☎815 50 250; www.osl.no), 45km north of the center. The high-speed **FlyToget train** (☎815 0777; www.flytoget.no) runs between the airport and downtown (19-22min.; M-F every 10min., Sa-Su every 20min. 4:45am-midnight train station to airport, 5:36am-12:36am airport to downtown; 120-190kr, 50% student discount with ID). White SAS **Flybussen** drive a similar route. (☎2280 4971; www.flybussen.no. 40min.; every 20-30min. 4:05am-9:50pm bus terminal to airport, 5:20am-1am airport to downtown; 120kr, round-trip 220kr, 50% student discount.)

Trains: Oslo Sentralstasjon (Oslo S), Jernbanetorget 1 (☎8150 0888). To: **Bergen** (6-8hr., 4-5 per day, 716kr); **Copenhagen, DEN** via **Gothenburg, SWE** (7-8hr., 2 per day, from 717kr); **Stockholm, SWE** (4¾hr., 3 per day, from 650kr); **Trondheim** (6-8hr., 2-5 per day, 797kr). Mandatory seat reservations for long-distance domestic trains 41-71kr.

Buses: Nor-way Bussekspress, Schweigårds gt. 8 (☎8154 4444; www.nor-way.no). Follow the signs from the train station through the Oslo Galleri Mall to the Bussterminalen Galleriet. Schedules available at the info office. 25-50% student discount with ISIC.

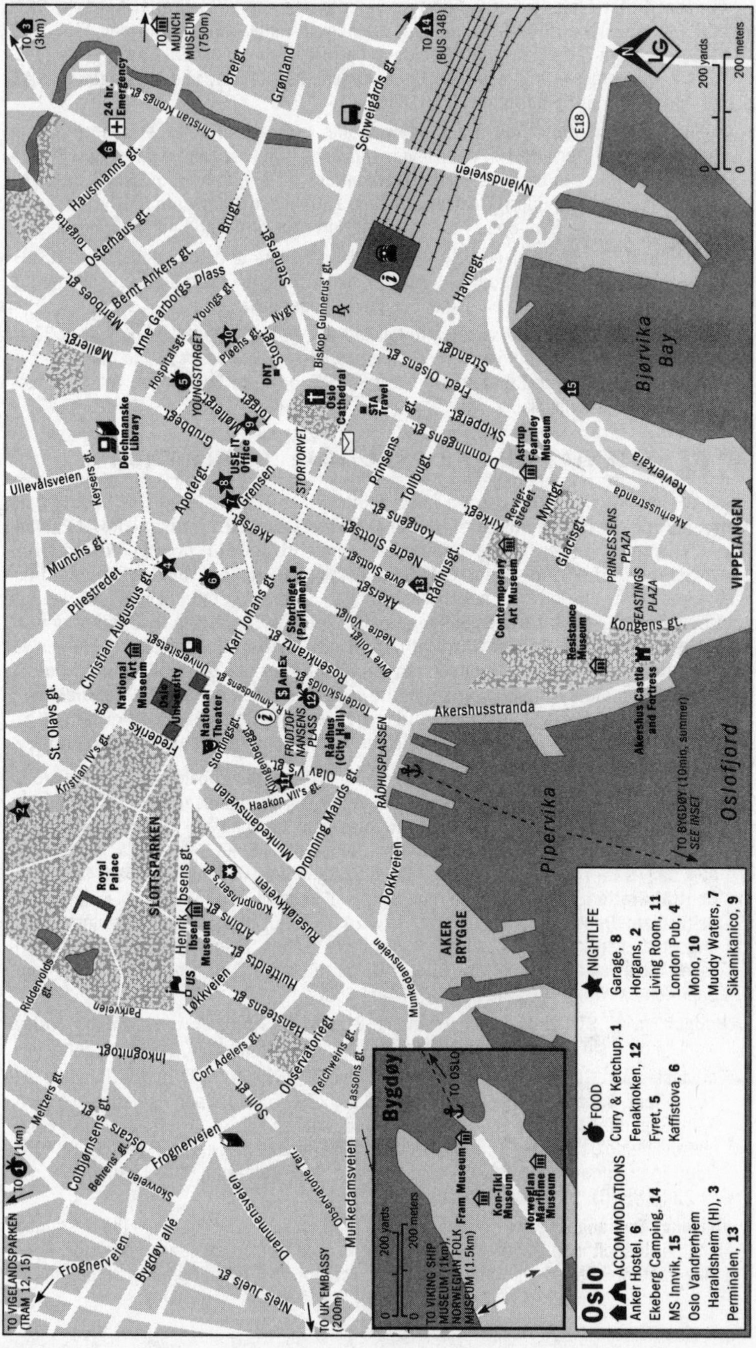
Oslo
ACCOMMODATIONS
Anker Hostel, 6
Ekeberg Camping, 14
MS Innvik, 15
Oslo Vandrerhjem
Haraldsheim (HI), 3
Perminalen, 13
FOOD
Curry & Ketchup, 1
Fenaknoken, 12
Fyret, 5
Kaffistova, 6
NIGHTLIFE
Garage, 8
Horgans, 2
Living Room, 11
London Pub, 4
Mono, 10
Muddy Waters, 7
Sikamikanico, 9
Bygdøy
TO OSLO
Fram Museum
Kon-Tiki Museum
Norwegian Maritime Museum
TO VIKING SHIP MUSEUM (1km), NORWEGIAN FOLK MUSEUM (1.5km)
TO VIGELANDSPARKEN (TRAM 12, 15)
TO UK EMBASSY (200m)
TO 1 (1km)
TO 3 (3km)
TO MUNCH MUSEUM (750m)
TO 14 (BUS 34B)
TO BYGDØY (10min, summer) SEE INSET
Royal Palace
SLOTTSPARKEN
Henrik Ibsens Museum
US
National Art Museum
Oslo University
National Theater
FRIDTJOF NANSENS PLASS
Rådhus (City Hall)
RÅDHUSPLASSEN
Stortinget (Parliament)
AmEx
USE IT Office
Deichmanske Library
YOUNGSTORGET
STORTORVET
Oslo Cathedral
STA Travel
DNT
24 hr. Emergency
Contemporary Art Museum
Astrup Fearnley Museum
Resistance Museum
Akershus Castle and Fortress
AKER BRYGGE
PRINSESSENS PLAZA
FEASTINGS PLAZA
VIPPETANGEN
Pipervika
Oslofjord
Bjørvika Bay
E18
Karl Johans gt.
Frederiks gt.
Akershusstranda
Dronning Mauds gt.
Munkedamsveien
Drammensveien
Bygdøy allé
Frognerveien
Schweigaards gt.
Nylandsveien
Ullevålsveien
Pilestredet
Grensen
Kongens gt.
Rådhusgt.
Prinsens gt.
Tollbugt.
Dronningens gt.
Skippergt.
Strandgt.
Havnegt.
Hausmanns gt.
Storgt.
Grønland
Brugt.
200 yards
200 meters

NORWAY

Ferries: Color Line (☎8100 0811; www.colorline.com). To **Frederikshavn, DEN** (12½hr.; 7:30pm; 250-490kr, student discount in winter 95kr-230kr) and **Kiel, GER** (19½hr.; 2pm; 780-3690kr, 50% student discount in winter). **DFDS Seaways** (☎2162 1340; www.dfdsseaways.com). To **Copenhagen, DEN** (16hr.) and **Helsingborg, SWE** (14½hr.) daily at 5pm (both 810-1010kr).

Public Transportation: Bus, tram, subway, and **ferries** cost 30kr per ride or 20kr in advance. Tickets include 1hr. of unlimited transfers. If you are caught traveling without a valid ticket, you can be fined 750kr. **Trafikanten** (☎177), in front of Oslo S, sells the **Dagskort** (day pass; 60kr), **Flexicard** (8 trips; 160kr), and **7-day Card** (210kr). Open M-F 7am-8pm, Sa-Su 8am-6pm. Tickets also at Narvesen kiosks and Automat machines.

Bike Rental: The city's bike-share system allows visitors to borrow one of the 1000+ bikes available at racks throughout the city center. Both the main tourist office and the Oslo S branch sell system enrollment cards (60kr per day).

Hitchhiking: Hitchers heading south to Kristiansand or Stavanger take bus #31 or 32 to Maritim and catch rides from there. Hitchers to Bergen take bus #161 to the last stop. Those bound east into Sweden ride bus #81, 83, or 85 to Bekkelaget. Let's Go does not recommend hitchhiking.

ORIENTATION AND PRACTICAL INFORMATION

In the center of Oslo, the garden plaza **Slottsparken (Castle Park)** lies beside **Oslo University** and the **Nationaltheatret (National Theater)** and surrounds the **Royal Palace.** The city's main street, **Karl Johans gate,** runs through the heart of town from Slottsparken to the train station **Oslo Sentralstasjon (Oslo S)** at the eastern end. Ferries depart from the harbor, southwest of Oslo S near Akershus Castle. Museums and beaches cluster on the **Bygdøy** peninsula southwest; ferries to Bygdøy depart from the dock behind **Rådhus (City Hall).** Parks are scattered throughout Oslo, especially north of the Nationaltheatret. An excellent network of public trams, buses, and subways makes transport through the outskirts quick and easy. **Grünerløkka** to the north and **Grønland** to the east tend to be less safe than Oslo's other neighborhoods, but their parks, cafes, and boutiques showcase the latest urban trends.

Tourist Offices: Fridtjof Nansenspl. 5 (☎2314 7700; www.visitoslo.com). From Oslo S, walk 15min. down Karl Johans gt. and turn left on Roald Amundsens gt.; the office is on the right before City Hall. Sells the **Oslo Pass,** offering unlimited public transport and admission to most museums. 1-day pass 195kr, 2-day 285kr, 3-day 375kr. Open June-Aug. daily 9am-7pm; Sept. and Apr.-May M-Sa 9am-5pm; Oct.-Mar. M-F 9am-4pm. **Oslo Central Station Tourist Info,** Jernbanetorget 1, outside Oslo S. Open M-F 7am-8pm, Sa-Su 8am-8pm. **Use-It,** Møllergt. 3 (☎2414 9820; http://unginfo.oslo.no/useit), targets students and backpackers. Books beds for free, offers free Internet, and publishes the invaluable *Streetwise Budget Guide to Oslo.* Open July-Aug. M-F 9am-6pm; Sept.-June M-W and F 11am-5pm, Th 11am-6pm.

Budget Travel: STA Travel, Karl Johans gt. 8 (☎8155 9905; www.statravel.no), a few blocks from Oslo S. Books student airfares. Open M-F 10am-5pm, Sa 11am-3pm.

Embassies and Consulates: Australia, Strandvn 20, Lysaker (☎6758 4848). Open M-F 10am-3pm. **Canada,** Wergelandsv. 7, 4th fl. (☎2299 5300). Open June-Aug. M-F 8am-4pm; Sept.-May M-F 8:30am-4:30pm. **Ireland,** Haakon VII's gt. 1 (☎2201 7200; hibernia@online.no). Open M-F 8:30am-4:30pm. **UK,** Thomas Heftyes gt. 8 (☎2313 2700). Open in summer M-F 8:30am-4pm; in winter M-F 9am-4pm. **US,** Drammensv. 48 (☎2244 8550). Open M-F 7:30am-5pm.

Currency Exchange: Forex, Fridtjof Nansens pl. 6 (☎2241 3060), offers the best rates. Another branch is in Oslo S. **Nordea Bank,** in Oslo S, also exchanges currency. Open May-Sept. M-F 7am-6pm, Sa-Su 9am-4pm; Oct.-Apr. M-F 10am-6pm, Sa 8am-5pm.

TIP **A HAPPENING PLACE.** Use-It organizes summer events and "happenings" for youth and foreign travelers in Oslo. Check at the office for details.

Luggage Storage: Lockers at Oslo S and at the Nationaltheatret station. 20-45kr per 24hr. Max. 7 days. Available 4:30am-1:10am. Office open M-F 9am-3pm. Bags can be left in the Use-It office (see above) for an afternoon or night.

Library and Internet Access: Free terminals at the stately **Deichmanske Library,** Arne Garborgs pl. 4. Sign up for 1hr. or use a terminal for 15min. Open June-Aug. M-F 10am-6pm, Sa 9am-2pm; Sept.-May M-F 10am-7pm, Sa 10am-4pm.

GLBT Resources: Landsforeningen for Lesbisk og Homofil fri gjøring (LLH), Kongensgt. 12 (☎23 10 39 39; www.llh.no).

Laundromat: Look for the word *"myntvaskeri."* **Selva AS,** Ullevålsveien 15 (☎4164 0833). Wash 40kr, dry 30kr. Open M-F 8am-9pm, Sa 10am-3pm.

Emergency: Police: ☎112. **Ambulance:** ☎113. **Fire:** ☎110.

24hr. Pharmacy: Jernbanetorvets Apotek (☎2335 8100), opposite Oslo S.

Hospital: Oslo Kommunale Legevakt, Storgt. 40 (☎2211 8080). Open 24hr.

Post Office: Main branch at Kirkegt. 20 (☎2335 8690). Address mail to be held in the following format: First name LAST NAME, *Poste Restante,* Oslo Central Post Office, N-0101 Oslo, NORWAY. Open M-F 9am-5pm, Sa 10am-3pm. The post office at Oslo S is open M-F 9am-8pm.

ACCOMMODATIONS AND CAMPING

Hostels in Oslo fill up quickly in the summer, so reservations are essential. The **private rooms** available through **Use-It** (at left) are good deals, starting from 140kr. **Pensions** *(pensjonater)* are centrally located but can often be more expensive than private rooms. Check with the tourist office for last-minute accommodation deals. Travelers can **camp** for free in the forest north of town (no open fires); try the end of the Sognsvann line #3. Although young Norwegians often drink at home before heading out on the town, most hostels, including HI, prohibit alcohol consumption on their premises.

Anker Hostel, Storgt. 55 (☎2299 7200, bookings 2299 7210; www.ankerhostel.no). Walk 10min. from the city center or take tram #11, 12, 13, or 17 to Hausmanns gt. Comfortable but often crowded rooms have kitchenettes and bathrooms. Buffet breakfast (65kr) served at the hotel next door is a great deal. Linens 45kr. Internet 10kr per 15min. Reception in summer 24hr. Dorms 160kr; doubles 460kr. AmEx/D/MC/V. ❷

Oslo Vandrerhjem Haraldsheim (HI), Haraldsheimvn. 4 (☎2222 2965; www.haraldsheim.oslo.no). Take tram #17 from Stortorvet for 15min. to Sinsenkrysset and walk up the hill through the park. Tidy dorms situated in a quiet residential neighborhood far from the city center. Breakfast included. Linens 50kr. Reception 24hr. Dorms 200kr, with bath 220kr; singles 320/390kr; doubles 435/515kr. 25kr HI discount. MC/V. ❷

Perminalen, Øvre Slottsgt. 2 (☎2309 3081; www.perminalen.no). Tram #12 to Christianian Torv. Backpackers looking to travel in style head to this central hotel/hostel. Enjoy the view from the spacious, air-conditioned rooms equipped with cable TV and phones. Breakfast included. Internet 15kr per 15min. Reception 24hr. Dorms 295kr; singles 495kr; doubles 670kr. AmEx/D/MC/V. ❸

MS Innvik, Langkaia 49 (☎2241 9500; www.msinnvik.no). From Oslo S, cross the overpass and head right along the harbor. The waters of Bjørvika Bay rock guests to sleep at this artsy, boat-borne B&B. Compact cabins come with bathrooms. Breakfast included. Reception 24hr. Check-out noon. Singles 400kr; doubles 700kr. AmEx/MC/V. ❹

Ekeberg Camping, Ekebergveien 65 (☎2219 8568; www.ekebergcamping.no), 3km from town. Bus #34A or 46. 24hr. security. Grocery store open daily 8am-10pm. Showers 10kr per 6min. Laundry 40kr. Reception 7:30am-11pm. Open late May-Aug. 2-person tent sites 150kr, 4-person 220kr; extra person 50kr. AmEx/D/MC/V. ❶

FOOD

Visitors can choose between Norwegian fare and a wide array of ethnic dishes, but either way they will usually feel robbed blind once the check arrives. Smart backpackers raid the city's **grocery stores;** look for the chains **Rema 1000** or **Kiwi,** or invest in fresh produce at the **open-air market** at Youngstorget (M-Sa 7am-2pm). In the **Grønland** district east of Oslo S, vendors hawk **kebabs** and **falafel** (around 40kr), and halal butchers can provide Muslim travelers with cooking meat.

Fyret, Youngstorget 6, 2nd fl. (☎2220 5182). Cozy restaurant and bar serves fresh meat, shellfish, and Oslo's largest selection of potent *akvavit* (a flavored liquor), best enjoyed on the terrace that offers stellar views of the square. Entrees 65-110kr. Live jazz M 8pm. Open M-W 11am-1am, Th-Sa 11am-2am. AmEx/D/MC/V. ❷

Kaffistova, Rosenkrantz gt. 8 (☎2321 4100). Cafeteria-style eatery with big portions of Norwegian meat, fish, and porridges. Vegetarian options. Daily dish (140kr) comes with dessert and coffee. Open M-F 9:30am-9pm, Sa-Su 10:30am-7pm. AmEx/D/MC/V. ❸

Krishna's Cuisine, Kirkeveien 59B (☎2260 6250), on the 2nd fl. Huge portions of inexpensive Indian food. Exclusively vegetarian fare prepared with fresh seasonal ingredients. Lunch served all day 65kr. Entrees 60-90kr. Open M-F noon-8pm. Cash only. ❷

Curry and Ketchup, Kirkeveien 51 (☎2269 0522). Generous helpings of Indian mainstays served to a young crowd. Entrees 79-99kr. Open daily 2-10:30pm. Cash only. ❷

Fenaknoken, Matkultur i Tordenskidsgt. 7 (☎2242 3457). Gourmet Norwegian food store offers free samples of delicacies such as smoked elk or reindeer sausage. Snack rolls prepared fresh daily, 25kr. Open M-F 10am-5pm, Sa 10am-2pm. AmEx/MC/V. ❷

SIGHTS

VIGELANDSPARKEN. Famous sculptor Gustav Vigeland (1869-1943) designed this meticulously landscaped 80-acre expanse west of the city center. The park is home to over 200 of Vigeland's mammoth works, each of which depicts a stage of the human life cycle. His art is controversial and puzzling, but it's worth deciphering. Each year the park draws more than a million visitors who gaze at works like the *Monolith*, a towering granite column of intertwining bodies. *(Entrance on Kirkeveien. Take bus #20 or tram #12 or 15 to Vigelandsparken. Open 24hr. Free.)* Next to the park, the **Vigelandmuseet** (Vigeland Museum) traces the artist's development from his smaller early works to the imposing and monumental pieces of his later years. The museum is housed in the building the artist used as his studio and apartment. *(Nobelsgt. 32. ☎2349 3700. Open June-Aug. Tu-Su 11am-5pm; Sept.-May Tu-Su noon-4pm.)*

ART MUSEUMS. The **Munchmuseet** reopened after security improvements following the 2004 theft of two valuable paintings, including a version of *The Scream (Shrik)*, Munch's most famous work. *(Tøyengt. 53. Take the subway to Tøyen or bus #20 to Munchmuseet. ☎2349 3500. Open June-Aug. daily 10am-6pm; Sept.-May Tu-F 10am-4pm, Sa-Su 11am-5pm. 65kr, students 35kr. Free with Oslo Pass. AmEx/D/MC/V.)* The definitive version of *The Scream* is at the **Nasjonalmuseet** (National Art Museum), which boasts an impressive collection of works by artists such as Cézanne, Gauguin, van Gogh, Matisse, Picasso, and Sohlberg. *(Universitetsgt. 13. ☎2198 2000; www.nasjonalmuseet.no. Open Tu-W and F 10am-6pm, Th 10am-8pm, Sa-Su 10am-5pm. Free.)* Next door at Oslo University's **Aulaen** (Assembly Hall), several of Munch's late, dreamy, and optimistic murals show his interest in bringing art to the masses. *(Enter through the door by the columns off Karl Johans gt. Open late June-July M-F 10am-2:45pm. Free.)*

The **Museet for Samtidskunst** (Contemporary Art Museum) displays works from the heavily Norwegian permanent collection, as well as avant-garde temporary exhibits. Ilya Kabakov's *Garbage Man* depicts the apartment of a man who refuses to throw anything away. *(Bankplassen 4. Take bus #60 or tram #10, 12, 13, or 19 to Kongens gt. ☎2286 2210. Open Tu-W and F 10am-6pm, Th 10am-8pm, Sa-Su 10am-5pm. Free.)* Nearby, the private **Astrup Fearnly Museum of Modern Art** has a more international collection, with many striking installation and video pieces. *(Dronningens gt. 4. ☎2293 6060; www.afmuseet.no. Open Tu-W and F 11am-5pm, Th 11am-7pm, Sa-Su noon-5pm. Free.)*

AKERSHUS CASTLE AND FORTRESS. Built in 1299, this waterfront complex was reconstructed as a Renaissance palace after Oslo burned to the ground in 1624. Norway's most famous traitor, Vidkun Quisling, was imprisoned here prior to his execution for collaborating with the Nazi invasion of 1940. *(Tram #10 or 12 to Rådhusplassen. ☎2309 3917. Fortress complex open daily 6am-9pm. Castle open May-Aug. M-Sa 10am-4pm, Su 12:30-4pm; Sept.-Oct. admission for guided tours only. Guided tours in English and Norwegian mid-June to early Aug. M-Sa 10am, noon, 2, 3, 4pm; Su 1, 3pm; winter in English 1pm. Fortress free. Castle 50kr, students 35kr. Free with Oslo Pass. Cash only.)* The castle grounds include the powerful **Resistance Museum,** which documents the country's efforts to subvert Nazi occupation. *(☎2309 3190. Open May-Aug. M-F 10am-5pm, Sa-Su 11am-5pm; Sept.-Apr. Tu-F 11am-4pm, Sa-Su 11am-5pm. 30kr, students 15kr.)*

BYGDØY. The Bygdøy peninsula, across the inlet from downtown Oslo, is mainly residential, but its beaches and museums are worth a visit. In the summer, a public **ferry** leaves from Pier 3 in front of City Hall. *(☎177; www.boatsightseeing.com. 10min.; runs Apr.-Sept. and late May to mid-Aug. every 15-30min. daily 8:45am-8:45pm; 20kr, 30kr if purchased onboard. Or take bus #30 from Oslo S to Folkemuseet or Bygdøynes.)* The open-air **Norsk Folkemuseum,** near the ferry's first stop at Dronningen, recreates the lifestyle of medieval Norway with actors in period costume and restored thatch huts. Summertime attractions include folk dances and songs. *(Walk uphill from the dock and follow signs to the right for 10min., or take bus #30 from Nationaltheatret. ☎2212 3700; www.norskfolkemuseum.no. Open mid-May to mid-Sept. daily 10am-6pm; mid-Sept. to mid-May M-F 11am-3pm, Sa-Su 11am-4pm. In summer 90kr, students 60kr; in winter 70/45kr.)* Nearby, the **Vikingskipshuset** (Viking Ship Museum) showcases three well-preserved burial vessels. *(☎2213 5280; www.khm.uio.no. Open daily May-*

ON THE MENU

VENTURING EAST

Norway's sky-high food prices can bring even trust-fund travelers to tears. Luckily, visitors to Oslo who want to grab a bite on the cheap can venture beyond Karl Johans gate for a taste of Norway's much spicier flavors.

Over the past two decades, immigrants from Pakistan and India have settled east of Oslo S in the Grønland neighborhood, bringing with them incredible home cooking. Sit with locals at the crowded **Tandoori Curry Corner,** Grønland 22, on the corner of Motzfieldgt. A curry dish with french fries will set you back a mere 46kr. (☎2217 9906. Open Su-Th 11am-4am, F-Sa 11am-6am. AmEx/MC/V.) Sample the lamb curry and delicious vegetarian dishes at **Tasty Grill and Tandoori,** Norbygt. 56. From Grønland, turn left onto Tøyengt. and continue to Norbygt., or take bus #60 to Norbygt. (☎2267 1615. Open daily noon-10pm. V.)

After dinner, walk down Grønland, which changes names to Grønlandsleiret, to appreciate the packed cafes and bazaars in this energetic neighborhood. Have a nightcap pint at **Grønlandshagen Bar and Restaurant,** Grønlandsleiret 61. This popular local bar features live music on Sunday nights and a big front patio for enjoying a beer under the stars. (☎4022 2786. Open daily noon-1am. Beer 43kr. D/MC/V.) By the time the band is done playing, you may just be ready for another round of curry.

Sept. 9am-6pm; Oct.-Apr. 11am-4pm. 50kr, students 25kr. Free with Oslo Pass. MC/V.) At the ferry's second stop at Bygdøynes, the **Kon-Tiki Museet** depicts Oscar-winning documentarian Thor Heyerdahl's globe-trotting adventures. *(Bygdøynesveien 36. ☎2308 6767; www.kon-tiki.no. Open daily June-Aug. 9am-5:30pm; Apr.-May and Sept. 10am-5pm; Oct.-Mar. 10:30am-4pm. 45kr, students 30kr. Free with Oslo Pass. D/MC/V.)* Next door, the **Norsk Sjøfartsmuseum** (Norwegian Maritime Museum) is home to Norway's oldest boat. Learn about the nation's seafaring history from log canoes to cruise ships, and enjoy the view of Oslofjord. *(Bygdøynesveien 37. ☎2411 4170. Open May 15-Aug. daily 10am-6pm; Sept.-May 14 M-W and Sa-Su 10:30am-4pm, Th 10:30am-6pm. 40kr, students 25kr. D/MC/V.)* The Arctic exploration vessel **FRAM,** adjacent to the museum, was used on three expeditions in the early 20th century and has advanced farther north and south than any other vessel in history. Visitors can roam through the preserved interior. *(Bygdøynesveien 36. ☎2328 2950. Open daily May to mid-June 10am-5:45pm; mid-June to Aug. 9am-6:45pm; Sept. 10am-4:45pm; Oct.-Apr. 10am-3:45pm. 40kr, students 20kr. MC/V.)* The southwestern side of Bygdøy is home to two popular beaches: **Huk** appeals to a younger crowd, while **Paradisbukta** is more family-oriented. A stretch of shore between them is a nude beach. *(Take bus #30 or walk south for 25min. from the Bygdøynes ferry stop.)*

OTHER SIGHTS. The **Royal Palace,** on a hill in Slottsparken, is open to the public for guided tours, although tickets sell out well in advance. You can watch the daily changing of the guard for free at 1:30pm in front of the palace. *(Tram #12, 15, 19, or bus #30-32 or 45 to Slottsparken. Open late June to mid-Aug. Tours in English M, Th, Sa noon, 2, 2:20pm; F and Su 2 and 2:20pm. Buy tickets at post offices. 80kr, students 70kr.)* Reopened after renovations, the nearby **Ibsenmuseet** (Henrik Ibsen Museum) provides insight into this notoriously private playwright's life. The museum presents photos and information in a dark, dramatic exhibition space and offers guided tours of Ibsen's restored apartment. *(Henrik Ibsens gt. 26. ☎2212 3550; www.ibsenmuseet.no. Open May 24-Sept. 15 Tu-Su 11am-6pm; Sept. 16-May 23 Tu-Su noon-3pm. Tours hourly in summer 11am-5pm, in winter noon-2pm. 70kr for exhibition and tour, 45kr students. 35kr for admission to exhibit only. AmEx/D/MC/V.)* The **Domkirke,** next to Stortorvet in the city center, is hard to miss. The classically simple Lutheran cathedral has a colorful ceiling covered with biblical motifs. *(Karl Johans gt. 11. ☎2331 4600; www.oslodomkirke.no. Open M-Th 10am-4pm, F 10am-4pm and 10pm-midnight, Sa 10am-4pm and 9-11pm. Free.)* Bound up the stairs of the Holmenkollen ski jump (after an elevator ride halfway up) and explore 4000 years of skiing history at the world's oldest **Ski Museum,** founded in 1923. A simulator recreates the rush of a leap off a ski jump and a blisteringly swift downhill run. *(Kongeveien 5. Take subway #1 on the Frognerseteren line to Holmenkollen, and walk 10min. uphill. ☎2292 3264; www.skiforeningen.no. Open daily June-Aug. 9am-8pm; Sept. and May 10am-5pm; Oct.-Apr. 10am-4pm. Museum 70kr, students 60kr. Free with Oslo Pass. Simulator 50kr, 40kr with Oslo Pass. AmEx/D/MC/V.)*

ENTERTAINMENT AND NIGHTLIFE

The monthly *What's On in Oslo,* free at tourist offices, follows the latest in opera, symphony, and theater. **Filmens Hus,** Dronningens gt. 16, is the center of Oslo's indie film scene. (☎2247 4500. Open Tu-W and F noon-5pm, Th noon-7pm, Sa noon-4pm. 70kr per movie, members 45kr, 100kr to join.) Jazz enthusiasts head to town for the **Oslo Jazz Festival** in mid-August (☎2242 9120; www.oslojazz.no).

Countless bars along **Karl Johans gate** and in the **Aker Brygge** harbor complex attract a hard-partying crowd, while a mellow mood prevails at the cafe-by-day, bar-by-night lounges along **Thorvald Meyers gate** in Grüner Løkka. Alcohol tends to be egregiously expensive out on the town, so young Norwegians have taken to the custom of the *Vorspiel*—gathering at private homes to sip comparatively cheap, store-bought liquor before wobbling out to paint the town red.

Mono, Pløens gt. 4 (☎2241 4166). Lines form out the door at this bar, which has a relaxed, funky atmosphere and frequent concerts and DJs. Beer 52kr. Su-Th 20+, F-Sa 22+. Cover for concerts 50-70kr. Open M-Sa 3pm-3:30am, Su 6pm-3:30am. MC/V.

Sikamikanico, Møllergt. 2 (☎2241 4409; www.sikamikanico.no). Oslo's young and trendy let loose as DJs spin drum and bass and experimental house. Beer 47kr. 20+. Cover F-Sa 50-100kr. Open Tu-W 9pm-3am, Th-Sa 9pm-3:30am, Su 10pm-3am. MC/V.

Garage, Grensen 9 (☎2242 3744; www.garageoslo.no). Caters to the metal scene but also draws international acts. Beer 52kr at night, 42kr during the day. Su-Th 20+, F-Sa 22+. Cover for concerts 50-180kr. Open M-Sa 2pm-3:30am, Su 6pm-3:30am. MC/V.

Muddy Waters, Grensen 13 (☎2240 3370; www.muddywaters.no). Lives up to its billing as one of Europe's top blues clubs. An older crowd comes for live music most nights. Beer from 56kr. 20+. Cover F-Sa around 90kr. Open daily 2pm-3am. AmEx/D/MC/V.

Living Room, Olav V's gt. 1 (☎4000 3360; www.living-room.no). Popular lounge morphs into dance floor on weekends. Owners keep things fresh by changing the decor frequently. Beer 61kr. 24+. Cover F-Sa 100kr. Open W-Su 11pm-3am. AmEx/D/MC/V.

Horgans, Hegdehaugsv. 24 (☎2260 8187). Boisterous sports bar with a club on weekends. Beer 54kr. Th student night. F-Sa club, cover Sa 50kr. 22+. Open M-Tu 5pm-midnight, W-Th and Su 5pm-1:30am, F-Sa 5pm-3am. AmEx/D/MC/V.

London Pub, C.J. Hambros pl. (☎2270 8700; www.londonpub.no). Entrance on Rosenkrantz gt. The "gay headquarters" of the city since 1979. Beer 48kr after 9pm, 33kr during the day. 21+. Cover F-Sa 40kr. Open daily 3pm-3:30am. AmEx/D/MC/V.

DAYTRIPS FROM OSLO

AROUND OSLO. Harbor cruises show off the nearby islands of inner **Oslofjord.** The ruins of a **Cistercian Abbey,** as well as a picnic-friendly southern shore, lie on the island of **Hovedøya,** while **Langøyene** has Oslo's best **beach** and a free campground. *(Take bus #60 (22kr) from City Hall to Vippetangen to catch ferry #92 or 93 to Hovedøya or ferry #94 to Langøyene.)* The fortress town of **Fredrikstad** is less than 2hr. south of Oslo. The 28km **Glommastien** bike path winds through abandoned brickyards and timber mills along the Glomma River, and ferries travel to seaside resorts on the **Hvaler Islands.** The **tourist office,** Toyhusgt. 98, has ferry schedules. *(☎6930 4600. Open M-F 9am-5pm, Sa-Su noon-5pm. Train to Fredrikstad 1hr.; every 2hr.; 161kr, 10% student discount.)*

LILLEHAMMER

Lillehammer (pop. 25,000) still cherishes the laurels it earned as host of the Winter Olympics in 1994. The **Norwegian Olympic Museum** in Olympic Park traces the history of the Games. From the train station, it's a 15-20min. walk; head two blocks uphill, turn left on Storgt., right on Tomtegt., go up the stairs, and follow the road uphill to the left. Or take bus #5 to Sigrid Undsetsveg (5min., 17kr). The museum is in the far dome. (☎6125 2100; www.ol.museum.no. Open June-Aug. daily 10am-6pm; Sept.-May Tu-Su 11am-4pm. 60kr, students 50kr. AmEx/D/MC/V.) Climb the steps of the **ski jump** in Olympic Park for a sweeping view of Lake Mjøsa, Norway's largest lake, and the surrounding forests. Give your spine a jolt on the **bobsled simulator** at the bottom of the hill. (☎6105 4200; www.olympiaparken.no. Open daily June 10-Aug. 20 9am-8pm; May 29-June 9 and Aug. 21-Sept. 9 9am-5pm. Ski jump tower 15kr. Chairlift 40kr. Simulator 45kr. Combination ticket including chairlift ride 65kr.) The open-air museum **Maihaugen** provides a glimpse into rural Norwegian life over the past 300 years. From the train station, head up Jernbanegt., turn right onto Gågt., and take the next left onto Bankgt.; continue until turning right on S. Undsets veg. (☎6128 8900; www.maihaugen.no. Open mid-May to Sept. daily 10am-5pm; Oct. to mid-May Tu-Su 11am-4pm. 100kr, students 80kr. AmEx/D/MC/V.) The basic accommodations at **Gjeste Bu ❶,** Gamleveien 110, come with a dose of mountainside charm. (☎6125 4321; gjestebu@lillehammer.online.no. Breakfast 45kr. Linens 50kr. Reception M-Sa 9am-11pm, Su 11am-11pm. Dorms 120kr; singles 250-275kr; doubles 350-375kr. Cash only.) Pizzerias and candy shops line Gågt., which runs north-south through the town center, changing names to Storgt. at both ends. Buy groceries at **Spar,** up the hill north of Storgt. on Lilletorget 1. (☎6122 1640. Open M-F 8am-9pm, Sa 8am-8pm.) **Trains** run to Oslo (2¼hr., 10-19 per day, 304kr) and Trondheim (4½-5½hr., 4 per day, 596kr). The **tourist office** is in the station. (☎6128 9800; www.lillehammerturist.no. Open mid-June to mid-Aug. M-Sa 9am-6pm, Su noon-5pm; mid-Aug. to mid-June M-F 9am-4pm, Sa 10am-2pm.)

SOUTHERN NORWAY

Norway's southern coastline has become a summer holiday destination, and its towns feature red-tiled bungalows and jetties full of powerboats. The rocky archipelagos *(skjærgarden)* can be explored on the cheap by hopping a local ferry.

KRISTIANSAND ☎38

Vacationers on their way from the Danish ferry to Oslo often tarry in Kristiansand (pop. 75,000). In the old town of **Posebyen,** the wooden houses quartered soldiers over the centuries and hid Jewish refugees during WWII. Take in the view of the **skerries,** a string of tiny islands and coves, on a boat trip with the **M/S Patricia.** (☎9076 1453; www.pollen.as. 2½hr; July 1-Aug. 20 daily 10:30am, 12:30, 3:30pm; 150kr.) Back on land, **Dyreparken,** 11km east of the city, includes an amusement park and zoo. Catch bus #1 (dir.: Sørlandsparken; 33kr) around the corner from the tourist office. (☎04 97 00; www.dyreparken.com. Open June-late Aug. daily 10am-7pm; late Aug.-May M-F 10am-3pm, Sa-Su 10am-5pm. 260kr, low season from 90kr.) Every July, music fans descend on Kristiansand for the **Quart Festival,** which features acts such as Tool, Kanye West, and Death Cab for Cutie. (☎3814 6969; www.quart.no. July 3-7, 2007.) The beachfront **Kristiansand Youth Hostel (HI)** ❷, Skansen 8, is a 25min. walk from the center. Head away from the water until you reach Elvegt., turn right, then turn left onto Skansen. Reserve far ahead during the festival. (☎02 83 10. Breakfast included. Linens 60kr. Internet 2kr per 15min. Reception mid-June to Aug. 3-11pm; Sept. to mid-June 5-9pm. Dorms 220kr; private rooms 490kr. 25kr HI discount. D/MC/V.) For cheap fare, head to the **harbor** between 11am and 4pm, when fishermen's families sell part of the morning's catch. **Rimi,** on the corner of Festningsgt. and Gyldenløvesgt, sells groceries. (☎02 95 16. Open M-F 8am-9pm, Sa 9am-6pm. Cash only.) **Trains** run to Oslo (4½-5½hr.; 4 per day; 569kr, students from 427kr) and Stavanger (3hr.; 6 per day; 383kr, students from 287kr). Color Line **ferries** (☎81 00 08 11; www.colorline.no) sail to Hirsthals, DEN (2½-4hr.; 1-5 per day; in summer M-F 440kr, Sa-Su 480kr, low season 280-320kr; students 50% discount in low season). The **tourist office,** Vestre Strandgt. 32, opposite the train station at the junction of Henrik Wegerlandsgt. and Vestre Strandgt., books rooms and arranges **elk safaris** for groups of six or more. (☎12 13 14. Open June 20-Aug. 14 M-F 8:30am-6pm, Sa 10am-6pm, Su noon-6pm; Aug. 15-June 19 M-F 8:30am-3:30pm. Internet 1kr per min. Safaris run July 17-Oct. 4; reserve ahead by 3pm. 250kr per person.) **Postal Code:** 4601.

STAVANGER ☎51

The port town of Stavanger (pop. 110,000) is the headquarters of Norway's oil industry, and it draws a delightfully contradictory mix of tree huggers and budding oil magnates. On the western side of the harbor is the old town, **Gamle Stavanger,** where lamp-lit lanes wind past well-preserved cottages. The 12th-century **Sta-**

vanger Domkirke is Norway's oldest cathedral, although time and overzealous renovations have not been kind to its Anglo-Norman towers. (Open June-Aug. daily 11am-7pm; Sept.-May Tu-Th and Sa 11am-4pm. Free.) The sleek **Norwegian Petroleum Museum** (Norsk Oljemuseum), down Kirkegt. from the church, explains drilling, refining, and life on oil platforms with high-tech, if somewhat romanticized, displays. (☎93 93 00; www.norskolje.museum.no. Open June-Aug. daily 10am-7pm; Sept.-May M-Sa 10am-4pm, Su 10am-6pm. 80kr, students 40kr. AmEx/D/MC/V.) In nearby Lysefjord, perennial postcard-pick **Pulpit Rock** (Preikestolen) affords travelers a magnificent view from an altitude of 600m. If the crowds and your sense of vertigo permit, lie flat and look into the abyss below. Take the ferry to Tau from the Fiskepiren dock, catch a waiting bus, and hike up the well-marked trail (1½-2hr.) to Pulpit Rock.

To reach the remote, homey **Jæren Vandrerhjem (HI)** ❷, Hårr Vigrestad, take the local train bound for Egersund and get off at Vigrestad. Exit the station, turn left, and walk 50m until you reach a small road. Turn left, walk through the tunnel, follow the road about 1km, and take the first right; the hostel is a 15min. walk ahead. (☎5143 5755. Linens 50kr. Dorms 200kr; doubles 350kr. 25kr HI discount. Cash only.) Sample native strawberries at the **market** opposite the cathedral (open M-F 8am-5pm). **Trains** run to Kristiansand (4hr., every 3hr., 383kr) and Oslo (8hr., 4 per day, 833kr). **Buses** to Bergen (5-6hr.; 400kr, students 300kr) leave from Stavanger Byterminal every 30min. For schedules and prices, check www.nor-way.no. The Flaggruten **express boat** (4hr., 200kr-620kr) sails past fjords to Bergen. (☎05505; www.hsd.no. M-F 4 per day, Sa-Su 1-2 per day. 50% Eurail and Scanrail discount. 40% student discount.) Fjordline **ferries** (☎81 53 35 00; www.fjordline.co.uk) go from Strandkaien, on the western side of the harbor, to Newcastle, BRI (19½hr.; 2-3 per week; from 760kr, 50% student discount). The **tourist office,** Domkirkeplassen 3, books rooms for a 30kr fee. (☎85 92 00; www.regionstavanger.com. Open June-Aug. daily 9am-8pm; Sept.-May M-F 9am-4pm, Sa 9am-2pm.) **Postal Code:** 4001.

NORWAY

THE FJORDS AND WEST NORWAY

Western Norway possesses a dramatic grandeur, from the vast depths of Sognefjord to the rugged peaks of Jotunheimen National Park. Crowds of tourists come to walk on the Jostedalsbreen glacier, the largest on the European continent at 487 sq. km, and explore the idyllic fjord towns. No trip to Norway is complete without a journey west to see some of the world's most breathtaking natural sights.

TRANSPORTATION

Transportation around the fjords can involve lengthy rides, but gazing at the scenery out the window is half the fun of visiting this region. Schedules vary from day to day; call ☎177 for transportation info. Tourist offices, boat terminals, and bus stations can also help plan itineraries. **Bergen** is the major port serving the region. From Strandkaiterminalen in Bergen, **HSD express boats** (☎55 23 87 80; www.hsd.no) run to Stavanger and points south of the city, while **Fylkesbaatane** (☎55 90 70 710; www.fylkesbaatane.no) sails north into Sognefjord, Nordfjord, and Sunnfjord. Almost all destinations connect via **bus** to Bergen; check www.nor-way.no for schedules and fares. **Fjord1** (www.fjord1.no), a consortium of bus, ferry, and boat companies, is an excellent resource for planning trips in the region. The Norway in a Nutshell tour (p. 738) offers a discounted combination trip to some of the top destinations.

BERGEN ☎55

Situated in a narrow valley between steep mountains and the waters of the Puddefjorden, Bergen (pop. 235,000) bills itself as the "Gateway to the Fjords." Norway's second-largest city has a pedestrian-friendly downtown, meticulously preserved medieval district, and thriving late-night music scene.

TRANSPORTATION

Trains: The **station** is on Strømgtn. (☎96 69 00), 10min. south of the harbor. Trains run to **Myrdal** (2¼hr., 6-8 per day, 226kr), **Oslo** (6½-7½hr., 4-5 per day, 716kr), and **Voss** (1¼hr., every 1-2hr., 148kr).

Buses: Busstasjon, Strømgtn. 8 (☎177, outside Bergen 55 90 70), in the Bergen Storsenter mall. Buses run to **Ålesund** (9-10hr., 2 per day, 560kr), **Oslo** (9-11hr., 4 per day, 450kr), and **Trondheim** (14½hr., 2 per day, 399kr). 25% student discount.

Domestic Ferries: The **Hurtigruten** steamer (☎81 03 00 00; www.hurtigruten.com) begins its coastal journey in **Bergen** and stops in **Ålesund,** the **Lofoten Islands, Tromsø,** and **Trondheim.** (Departs mid-Apr. to mid-Sept. daily 8pm, 612-5688kr; mid-Sept. to mid-Apr. 10:30pm, 30% discount except on Tu. 50% student discount.) **Flaggruten** express boats (☎05505; www.flaggruten.no) head south to **Stavanger** (4hr.; Su-F 4 per day, Sa 2 per day).

International Ferries: Depart from **Skoltegrunnskaien,** a 10-15min. walk past Bryggen along the right side of the harbor. **Fjord Line** (☎81 53 35 00; www.fjordline.co.uk) sends ships to **Hanstholm, DEN** (16hr.; 3-4 per week; mid-June to mid-Aug. from 500kr, low season from 300kr) and **Newcastle, BRI** (25hr.; 2-3 per week; mid-May to early Sept. from 800kr, low season from 500kr). **Smyril Line** (☎59 65 20; www.smyril-line.no) goes to the **Faroe Islands** (24hr.; 1240kr, students 560kr, low season from 875/400kr) and **Iceland** (41hr.; 2050kr, students 1430kr, low season 900/620kr), both departing June-Aug. Tu 3pm; check website for low season hours.

Public Transportation: Buses are 23kr within the city center, 31-38kr outside. The **Bergen Card** (1-day 170kr, 2-day 250kr), available at the train station, includes unlimited rides on city buses as well as free admission to most of the city's museums and discounts at select shops and restaurants.

ORIENTATION AND PRACTICAL INFORMATION

The **Torget** (fish market) by the harbor is a central landmark. North of the Torget, **Bryggen** curves around the harbor to the well-tended old city. **Torgalmenningen,** the city's main pedestrian thoroughfare, runs southwest from the Torget. Locals tend to stay farther down Torgalmenningen, near **Håkons gaten** and **Nygårds gaten.** South of the Torget is **Lille Lungegårdsvann,** a lake bordered by a park; the train and bus stations are just beyond the lake.

Tourist Office: Vågsalmenningen 1 (☎55 20 00; www.visitbergen.com), past the Torget in the Fresco Hall. Crowded in summer, but the friendly, dedicated staff make it worth the wait. Books private rooms for a 30kr fee and helps visitors plan travel through the fjords. Open June-Aug. daily 8:30am-10pm; May and Sept. daily 9am-8pm; Oct.-Apr. M-Sa 9am-4pm. **DNT,** Tverrgt. 4-6 (☎33 58 10), off Marken, sells maps (94-119kr) and provides hiking info. Open M-W and F 10am-4pm, Th 10am-6pm, Sa 10am-2pm.

Budget Travel: STA Travel, Vaskerelven 32 (☎55 99 05; bergen@statravel.no). Sells student airline tickets and books accommodations. Open M-F 10am-5pm. D/MC/V.

Currency Exchange: At banks near the harbor and at the post office. Usually open M-W and F 9am-3pm, Th 9am-4:30pm; low season reduced hours. Tourist office changes currency at a less favorable rate.

Luggage Storage: At train and bus stations. 20-40kr per day, depending on locker size.

Laundromat: Jarlens Vaskoteque, Lille Øvregt. 17 (☎32 55 04; www.jarlens.no). Wash and dry 70kr. Open M-Tu and F 10am-6pm, W-Th 10am-8pm, Sa 10am-3pm.

Emergency: Police: ☎112. **Ambulance:** ☎113. **Fire:** ☎110.

Pharmacy: Apoteket Nordstjernen (☎21 83 84), 2nd fl. of bus station. Open M-Sa 8am-11pm, Su 10am-11pm. AmEx/D/MC/V.

Hospital: 24-Hour Clinic, Vestre Strømkai 19 (☎56 87 00).

Internet Access: The public **library,** Strømgt. 6 (☎55 56 85), offers free 15-30min. slots. Open May-Aug. M-Th 10am-6pm, F 10am-4:30pm, Sa 10am-4pm; Sept.-Apr. M-Th 10am-8pm, F 10am-4:30pm, Sa 10am-4pm. **Bergen Internet C@fe,** Kong Oscars gt. 2B (☎96 08 36). Open M-F 9am-11pm, Sa-Su 10am-10pm. 1kr per min. Minimum 15kr. Students 25kr for 30min. Cash only.

Post Office: Småstrandgt. (☎81 00 07 10). Open M-F 9am-8pm, Sa 9am-6pm. *Poste Restante* office closes M-Sa 3pm. Address mail to be held in the following format: First name LAST NAME, *Poste Restante,* 5014 Bergen, NORWAY.

ACCOMMODATIONS

The tourist office books **private rooms** for a 30kr fee; travelers can sometimes nab doubles for as little as 300kr. You can **camp** for free on the far side of the hills above the city; walk 30min. up the slopes of Mount Fløyen or take the funicular.

Jacobs Dorm.no/Apartments and Cafe, Kong Oscars gt. 44 (☎9823 8600; www.dorm.no or www.apartments.no). Bright, tidy dorms with comfy beds. The outdoor patio stays busy until late as hostel guests get acquainted over beer. Breakfast 55kr. Linens 55kr. Free Internet. Lockout 11am-1pm. Dorms 165kr. AmEx/MC/V. ❷

Intermission, Kalfarveien 8 (☎30 04 00), near the train station. Students from a Christian college in the US staff this hostel and cultivate a chatty vibe. Waffle night M and Th. Breakfast 35kr. Linen deposit 30kr. Laundry included; detergent 5kr. Reception Su-Th 7-11am and 5pm-midnight, F-Sa until 1am. Lockout 11am-5pm. Curfew Su-Th midnight, F-Sa 1am. Open mid-June to mid-Aug. Dorms 120kr. Cash only. ❶

Marken Gjestehus, Kong Oscars gt. 45 (☎31 44 04; www.marken-gjestehus.com). Spotless, sunny rooms with great views. Breakfast 55kr. Linens 55kr. Reception May-Sept. 9am-11pm; Oct.-Apr. 11am-6pm. All dorms single-sex. Reserve ahead for dorms. 4- to 8-person dorms 155-195kr; singles 380kr; doubles 480kr. AmEx/D/MC/V. ❶

YMCA InterRail Center (HI), Nedre Korskirkealm. 4 (☎60 60 55; ymca@online.no), right near the Torget. Backpackers clamber to the rooftop balcony; the dormitory, with over 40 beds, is barracks-like. Linens 45kr. Reception 7-10:30am and 3:30pm-midnight. Dorms 150kr; 4- to 6-person rooms 185kr per person. 25kr HI discount. MC/V. ❶

Vandrerhjem Montana (HI), Johan Blyttsvei 30 (☎20 80 70; www.montana.no), at the base of Mt. Ulriken, 5km outside the city. Head down Kong Oscars gt. away from the center until you see a bus shelter next to a cemetery. From there, take bus #31 to Montana and follow the signs. Breakfast included. Linens 65kr. Dorms 185kr; singles 685kr; doubles 710kr. 25kr HI discount. MC/V. ❷

FOOD

Bergen's irresistible **Torget** panders to tourists with colorful tents, raucous fishmongers, and free samples of salmon, caviar, whale, reindeer, and wild shrimp. (Open June-Aug. Su-F 7am-5pm, Sa 7am-4pm; Sept.-May M-Sa 7am-4pm.)

Viva las Vegis, Steinkjellergt. 2 (☎92 66 99 11; www.vivalasvegis.com). This small, neon-colored vegetarian eatery celebrates Elvis's legacy with a large picture of the King outside. Veggie burgers 44-48kr. Pizza slices 20kr. 10% student discount. Open June-Aug. M-F 11am-11pm, Sa-Su 11am-3am; Sept.-May M-F 1pm-9pm. AmEx/D/MC/V. ❶

Kafe Kippers, Georgernes Verft. 12 (☎31 00 60). In USF Verftet, a large warehouse with studios, a theater, and a cinema. Dockside tables have views of the fjords. Specialties include Caribbean prawn curry (128kr) and Iranian beef stew (112kr). Open M-F 11am-midnight, Sa-Su noon-midnight. 10% discount with Bergen Card. AmEx/D/MC/V. ❸

Capello, Skosteredet 14 (☎96 12 11; www.capello.no). Take in the warped Americana at this tile-floored eatery. Pancakes stuffed with seasonal ingredients 44-62kr. Open M-W 1pm-midnight, Th-Sa 1pm-1am. Kitchen closes M-W 6pm, Th-Sa 10pm. D/MC/V. ❶

Vågen Fetevare, Kong Oscars gt. 10 (☎31 65 13). The sunny back porch and indoor used books and leather sofas create a relaxing environment. For lunch, locals love the open-faced sandwich (32kr) made with seasonal ingredients. Open M-Th 8am-11pm, F 8am-9pm, Sa 9am-7pm, Su 11am-11pm. Cash only. ❶

Pølsemannens Beste, Kong Oscars gt. 16 (☎31 73 33). This famous harborside hot dog stand offers a wide range of options, from basic pork hot dogs (12kr) to gourmet reindeer sausages infused with French cheeses and chili (40kr). A local favorite. Open Su-Th 11am-4am, F-Sa 11am-6am. Cash only. ❶

SIGHTS

BRYGGEN AND BERGENHUS. Gazing down the right side of the harbor from the Torget brings Bryggen's signature pointed gables into view. This row of medieval buildings, the most touristed area in Bergen for good reason, serves as a reminder of the city's past status as the major Nordic port of the Hanseatic trading league. The narrow alleys and crooked balconies have survived numerous fires and the explosion of a Nazi munitions ship; today Bryggen is home to galleries and shops specializing in traditional Norwegian crafts. The **Bryggens Museum** displays archaeological artifacts and a multimedia display on the city's history. *(Dreggsalm. 3, behind a small park at the end of the Bryggen houses. ☎58 80 10. Open May-Aug. daily 10am-5pm; Sept.-Apr. M-F 11am-3pm, Sa noon-3pm, Su noon-4pm. 40kr, students 20kr. AmEx/D/MC/V.)* History buffs can continue their education at the **Hanseatic Museum,** located in an old trading house near the Fløibanen funicular station. *(Finnegaardsgt. 1A. ☎5446 9031 4189; www.hanseatisk.museum.no. Open June-Aug. daily 9am-5pm; Sept.-May Tu-Su 11am-2pm. May to mid-Sept. 45kr, mid-Sept. to Apr. 25kr. MC/V.)* **Bergenhus,** the city's harborside fortress, is home to the 16th-century **Rosenkrantz Tower,** which has splendid views of the city. The **Håkonshallen** contains the restored grand hall where Norwegian kings held court in the Middle Ages. *(Walk down Bryggen away from the Torget. ☎55 31 43 80. Hall and tower open mid-May to mid-Sept. daily 10am-4pm; Sept. to mid-May hall open M-W and F-Su noon-3pm, Th 3-6pm, tower open Su noon-3pm only. In summer, guided tours every hr. on Su included in admission. 30kr, students 12kr. Cash only.)*

MUSEUMS. Three branches of the **Bergen Art Museum** line the western side of Lille Lungegårdsvann. The **Lysverket** holds 13th-century Russian icons and works of 15th-century Dutch Masters, while the **Rasmus Meyers Collection** displays the canvases of Munch, Dahl, and Norway's neo-Impressionists. The **Stenersen Collection** specializes in temporary exhibits as well as Northern Europe's most extensive collection of Paul Klee's work. *(Rasmus Meyers allé 3, 7, and 9. ☎56 80 00; www.bergenart-museum.no. Open mid-May to mid-Sept. daily 11am-5pm; mid-Sept. to mid-May Tu-Su 11am-5pm. 50kr for all 3 museums, students 35kr, temporary exhibits 15kr. AmEx/D/MC/V.)*

HIKING

Bergen is the only city in the world surrounded by **seven fjords** and **seven mountains.** Visits to the waterways require careful planning—and usually a private vessel—but the peaks are easily accessible from the city center and have well-kept **hiking trails.** Locals are keen to inform visitors that they have not seen Bergen until they have seen it from above. Free **maps** are available at the tourist and DNT offices, but if you plan to spend the night in the mountains, or if the weather seems less than perfect, invest in a more detailed map. The four eastern mountains are the most popular, largely due to their proximity. **Mount Fløyen** can be reached by the **Fløibanen funicular** or by hiking up a steep, paved road for 45min. Board the funicular 150m from the Torget; the road up the mountain begins next to it. (☎33 68 09. Funicular open May-Aug. M-F 7:30am-midnight, Sa 8am-midnight, Su 9am-midnight; Sept.-May closes 11pm. 35kr.) At the summit, several relatively easy trails lead away from the crowds into a forest with secluded ponds and stunning vistas. A bus and cable car combination also runs from the city center to the top of **Mount Ulriken,** the highest of the peaks. The mountain provides a panoramic view of the city, fjords, mountains, and islands. Take bus #31 to Haukeland Sykehus and walk up Haukelandsbakken until you reach the cable car. (☎20 20 20. Cable car daily May-Sept. 9am-9pm; Oct.-Apr. 10am-5pm. 50kr. Cash only.) Once on top, check the forecast at the restaurant before heading out onto the trails or hiking down.

> **!** Even though the mountains are close to Bergen, they can still be dangerous, especially if inclement weather hits or thick fog rolls in. Always check with the tourist office or the DNT for up-to-date weather and safety information before departing for a hike.

ENTERTAINMENT AND NIGHTLIFE

Bergen hosts two festivals in late May and early June: **Festspillene** (☎21 06 30; www.festspillene.no), a 12-day program of music and dance, and **Nattjazz,** a series of more than 60 jazz concerts. (☎30 72 50; www.nattjazz.no. Day pass 345kr.) October brings the up-and-coming **Bergen International Film Festival.** (☎30 08 40; www.biff.no.) Bergen has an excellent live music scene, but nightlife rarely picks up until around 11:30pm on weekends; many locals throw back a round or two at home to avoid costly drinks at bars and clubs. Steer clear of pricey harborside tourist traps and head to the cafes and pubs on **Nygårds gaten.**

Det Akademiske Kvarteret, Olav Kyrres gt. 49-53 (☎58 99 10). This half-salon, half-cultural center is run by student volunteers from the University of Bergen. The happening **Grøhndals** bar sells some of the cheapest beer in all of Bergen (Su-W 43kr, Th-Sa 39kr), while the **Teglverket** hosts a multitude of summer jazz and rock concerts (usually 10pm; tickets 30-100kr). 18+; low season 20+. Open Su-W 7pm-1am, Th 7pm-2am, F-Sa 7pm-3am.

Café Opera, Engen 18 (☎23 03 15). Draws a mixed clientele, with DJs spinning after 11pm. Beer 48-59kr. F-Sa club nights pound a mix of house, disco, and funk. No cover. Open M 11am-12:30am, Tu-Sa noon-3:30am, Su noon-12:30am. AmEx/D/MC/V.

Garage Bar, at the corner of Nygårdsgtn. and Christiesgt. (☎32 02 10). A friendly crowd queues up at Bergen's most popular alt-rock pub. 20+. Cover 30kr after 1am. Open M-Sa 1pm-3:30am, Su 3pm-3:30am. MC/V.

Metro, Ole Bulls pl. 4 (☎57 30 37). The young and trendy come for hip-hop beats. Beer 56kr. Su-Th 20+, F-Sa 24+. Cover 90kr. Open daily 10pm-3am. AmEx/D/MC/V.

ALONG THE OSLO-BERGEN RAIL LINE

The 7hr. journey by train from Oslo to Bergen is one of the world's most scenic rides. From Oslo, trains climb 1222m to remote Finse, stop in Myrdal for transfers to the Flåm railway, and then pass through Voss en route to Bergen.

FINSE. Outdoor enthusiasts hop off at Finse and hike several days north through the Aurlandsdalen valley into **Aurland,** 53km from Flåm. Before you set out, be sure to ask about trail conditions at Finse's train station or at the DNT offices in Oslo or Bergen; the trails are usually snow-free and accessible between early July and late September. You can sleep in DNT *hytte* (mountain huts), spaced one day's walk apart along the Aurland trails. **Bikers** can head down the rutted **Rallarvegen** trail, which parallels the Oslo-Bergen train and extends 81km west to Voss. Most of the ride is downhill; exercise extreme caution on the steep curves in the **Flåmdalen valley.** Break up the ride by staying in a *hytte* in Hallingskeid (21km from Finse) or forge on to Flåm (57km). Rent bikes at **Finsehytta.** (☎56 52 67 32. Open July-Aug. daily 8am-11pm. Bike rental M-F 390kr, Sa-Su 495kr for 2 days.)

FLÅM AND THE FLÅM RAILWAY. The historic railway connecting Myrdal, a stop on the Oslo-Bergen line, with the tiny fjord town of Flåm (pop. 450) is one of Norway's most celebrated attractions. An incredible feat of engineering, it has the steepest descent of any railway in the world and ducks through hand-excavated tunnels. The highlight of the 55min. ride is a view of the thunderous **Kjosfossen** waterfall. (☎57 63 14 00; www.flaamsbana.no. 55min.; 8-10 per day; 175kr, round-trip 275kr, 30% ScanRail or Eurail discount.) A 20km **hike** (4-5hr.) on the well-tended paths between Myrdal and Flåm more or less follows the train route and lets hikers tarry by smaller cascades before camping along the knolls. You can also take the train uphill from Flåm to Myrdal and cycle back down; check your brakes beforehand, and be ready to dismount on the steepest sections. The **Flåm Vandrerhjem (HI) ❶**, a half-hostel, half-campground, is the best bet for cheap overnight stays. (☎57 63 21 21. Shower 10kr per 5min. Linens 65kr. Laundry 50kr. Dorms 155kr; singles 225kr; doubles 400-450kr. Tent sites 140kr; cabins 450-750kr. 25kr HI discount for dorms. MC/V.) Flåm's **tourist office** is next to the train station. (☎57 63 21 06; www.visitflam.com. Open daily June-Aug. 8:30am-8pm; Sept. 8:45am-4pm; May 8:30am-4pm.) Between October and April, direct questions about Flåm to the tourist office in nearby Aurland, 9km to the north. (☎57 63 33 13; www.alr.no. Bike rental 30kr per hr., 175kr per day. Open June-Aug. M-F 8:30am-7pm, Sa-Su 10am-5pm; Sept.-May M-F 8:30am-3:30pm.) Fylkesbaatane **express boats** run daily to Aurland (10min.), Balestrand (1½hr.), and Bergen (5hr.); check www.fylkesbaatane.no for schedules. **Postal Code:** 5742.

VOSS. Located next to a glassy lake that reflects the snow-capped peaks above, Voss (pop. 14,000) is an adventurer's dream. Deep powder and 40km of marked trails attract skiers during the winter, while sports including kayaking, paragliding, and parabungeeing (jumping from a flying parasail) draw devotees in summer. The safety-conscious staff at **Nordic Ventures,** behind the Park Hotel in a mini-mall, runs adventure expeditions. The **kayaking** trips to nearby Nærøyfjord allow beginners to visit otherwise inaccessible areas of the fjord. (☎56 51 00 17; www.nordicventures.com. Open daily May to mid-Oct. 9am-9pm; mid-Oct. to Apr. 10am-5pm. Kayaking daytrips 895kr; 2 days 1895kr; 3 days including hiking 2595kr. All trips fully catered. MC/V.) **Voss Rafting Center,** Nedkvitnesvegen 25, based 3.5km from Voss in Skulestadmo, leads rafting trips (from 450kr). Pickup from Voss can be arranged. (☎56 51 05 25; www.vossrafting.no. Open in summer daily 9am-5pm, phone bookings until 10pm; winter M-F 9am-4pm. MC/V.) If you'd rather stick to *terra firma*, take the easy 30min. walk from Voss to **Bordal Gorge,** where water rushes through a narrow path lined by overhanging cliffs. Hikers should only make the trek in the months of July and August, when the path is safest. To reach Bordal, turn left from the train station, walk along the shore, and turn right onto the gravel path; after crossing the bridge, turn right and follow signs to Bordalgjelet.

Turn right as you exit the train station and walk along the lake to take in the views from **Voss Vandrerhjem (HI) ❷**. If money is short, sleep on a foam mattress in the attic for 150kr. (☎56 51 20 17. Bike, canoe, and kayak rental. Breakfast included. Linens 65kr. Internet 1kr per min. Reception 24hr. Dorms 240kr; singles 470kr; doubles 640kr. 25kr HI discount. MC/V.) To reach the lakeside **Voss Camping ❶,** head left from the station, stick to the lake shore, and turn right onto the gravel path at the church. (☎56 51 15 97; www.vosscamping.no. Showers 10kr per 6min. Reception May-Sept. 8am-10pm. Reserve ahead. Tent sites 90kr. 5-person cabin 450kr. MC/V.) Pick up groceries at **Kiwi,** on the main street past the post office. (☎56 51 27 35. Open M-F 9am-9pm, Sa 9am-8pm.) **Trains** leave for Bergen (1¼hr., every 1-2hr., 148kr) and Oslo (5½-6hr., 4-5 per day, 623kr). To get to the **tourist office,** Uttrågt. 9, turn left as you exit the train station and bear right at the fork by the church. (☎56 52 08 00; www.visitvoss.no. Open June-Aug. M-F 8am-7pm, Sa 9am-7pm, Su noon-7pm; Sept.-May M-F 8am-3:30pm. MC/V.) **Postal Code:** 5702.

EIDFJORD. Tucked into an eastern arm of the orchard-lined Hardangerfjord, the town of Eidfjord (pop. 950) draws hikers bound for the nearby **Hardangervidda** mountain plateau, the largest of its kind in Europe. Greenhorns stick to the plateau's eastern half, while more seasoned adventurers head to the **Hardangerjøkulen Glacier** in the north or to the virtually untouched southern tip. A 2hr. walk along a trail from the harbor leads to a **Viking burial ground** on top of a plateau in **Hereid.** Pick up a map of the trail from the tourist office and then head out along Simadalvegen. After passing the bridge, turn right and walk along the river; follow the path as it goes by the lake and winds uphill. A **mini-tour** whisks a mixed-age crowd to **Hardangervidda Nature Center.** (☎53 66 59 00; www.hardangervidda.org. Open daily June-Aug. 10am-8pm; Apr.-May and Sept.-Oct. 10am-6pm. 80kr. MC/V.) From there, the tour continues to the roaring **Vøringfossen Waterfall,** which plummets 182m into a serrated glacial valley. Be careful; the stones are slippery, and safety rails are few and far between. (Mini-tour daily mid-June to mid-Aug. Departs from the harbor after ferry arrival. 195kr.) **Sæbø Camping** ❶ (☎53 66 59 27), 7km from town near the Nature Center, has a spectacular lakeside location. Eidfjord is best reached from Voss via Ulvik. **Buses** leave Voss at 8:45am (1 per day; 69kr, students 57kr) and arrive in Ulvik at 11:10am. From there, the **ferry** travels the rest of the way to Eidfjord, returning at 2:40pm (runs June-Aug.). The **tourist office,** in the town center, finds accommodations for a 50kr fee. (☎53 67 34 00. Open mid-June to mid-Aug. M-F 9am-6pm, Sa-Su noon-6pm; May to mid-June and mid-Aug. to Sept. M-F 8:30am-4pm; low season M, W, and every other F 10am-4pm.)

SOGNEFJORD

The slender fingers of Sognefjord, the longest fjord in Europe, reach all the way to the foot of the Jotunheimen Mountains in central Norway. **Fylkesbaatane** boats (☎55 90 70 70; www.fylkesbaatane.no) leave from Bergen on tours of Sognefjord and the Flåm valley. Due to uncertain road conditions and the limited number of bus routes, overland transportation is often more confusing than it's worth.

BALESTRAND. Balestrand (pop. 1400) is a jumping-off point for travelers exploring Sognefjord. Adventure companies such as **Jostedalen Breførarlag** (☎57 68 31 11; www.bfl.no) run easy glacier walks (from 150kr) and offer courses in rock climbing and advanced glacier walking (from 2050kr, not including equipment). **Icetroll** (☎57 68 32 50; www.icetroll.com) runs kayaking trips on the glacial lakes of Jostedalsbreen (from 690kr); during the summer, kayakers watch agape as huge boulders of ice splinter off the glacier into the water. In front of Balestrand's ferry docks, **Sognefjord Akvarium** showcases the rarely seen marine life of the fjords. (☎57 69 13 03. Open daily late June to mid-Aug. 9am-11:30pm; May to late June and mid-Aug. to early Sept. 10am-6pm. 60kr. 50% discount for Kringsjå Hostel guests. AmEx/D/MC/V.) To reach the clear, color-coded **hiking trails** from the harbor, head uphill to the right, take the second left, and walk along the main road for 10min.; turn right on Sygna and follow the signs. Walk up the hill past the tourist office and take the second left to reach the **Kringsjå Hotel and Youth Hostel (HI)** ❷. The dorm rooms on the top floor have balconies overlooking the fjord. (☎57 69 13 03; www.kringsja.no. Breakfast included. Linens 50kr. Laundry 15kr. Open July to mid-Aug. Dorms 210kr; singles 450kr; doubles 620kr; triples 750kr. 20kr HI discount. MC/V.) **Sjøtun Camping** ❶ is past the brown church on the coastal road. (☎57 69 12 23; www.sjotun.com. Showers free. Reception 9-9:30am, 6-6:30pm, and 9-9:30pm; call for other arrival times. Open June-early Sept. Tent sites 50kr. 4- to 6-person cabins 225-310kr. Cash only.) Fylkesbaatane **express boats** connect Bergen and Balestrand (4hr.; M-Sa 2 per day; 425kr, students 200kr). The **tourist office** is near the quay. (☎57 69 12 55. Internet 15kr per 15min. Open mid-June to mid-Aug. M-F 7:30am-7pm, Sa-Su 8am-5:30pm; May to mid-June and mid-Aug. to Sept. M-F 10am-5pm, Sa-Su 10am-3pm; Oct.-Apr. M-F 8:30am-3:30pm.)

FJÆRLAND AND FJÆRLANDSFJORD. Fjærlandsfjord branches off Sognefjord in a thin northward line past Balestrand to the small town of **Fjærland** (pop. 300) at the base of the Jostedalsbreen glacier. The town's preserved houses have been converted into stores and cafes and sit against a glorious natural backdrop. **The Norwegian Book Town** attracts bookworms with a network of 12 secondhand shops that hold over 200,000 volumes. (☎57 69 22 10; www.bokbyen.no. Open May-Sept. daily 10am-6pm. MC/V.) The **Norsk Bremuseum** (Glacier Museum), 3km outside town on the only road, screens a beautiful panoramic film about the glacier. (☎57 69 32 88; www.bre.museum.no. Open daily June-Aug. 9am-7pm; Apr.-May and Sept.-Oct. 10am-4pm. 80kr, students 40kr. AmEx/D/MC/V.) To reach the 1000m level, hike 2-3hr. up **Flatbreen,** one of the arms of Jostedalsbreen, to the Flatbrehytta self-service **cabin.** (☎57 69 32 29. Limited availability June-Aug. Bring a sleeping bag.) While the hike is only moderately difficult, it can pass through areas covered with snow well into July; bring cold-weather gear. The hike begins 5km northeast from the Norsk Bremuseum at the Øygard parking lot. **Ferries** run from Fjærland to Balestrand (1¼hr.; 2 per day; 152kr, students 76kr). Local buses shuttle passengers from the ferry dock to the Norsk Bremuseum, whisk them to view two Jostedalsbreen outcroppings, then return them to the harbor (9:40am bus 135kr, 1:25pm bus 105kr). From the Norsk Bremuseum, **buses** run to Ålesund (6hr.; 4 per day; 349kr, students 277kr) and Sogndal (30min.; M-Sa 2-5 per day; 65kr, students 49kr). The **tourist office,** near the harbor, rents bikes (30kr per hr.) and solves transportation woes. (☎57 69 32 11; info@fjaerland.org. Open daily 10am-6pm.)

LOM AND JOTUNHEIMEN NATIONAL PARK

Between the last tributaries of the western fjords and the remote towns of the interior lies the pristine landscape of Jotunheimen National Park. Hunters chased wild reindeer here for thousands of years. Norwegian writers and painters discovered it anew in the 19th century, channeling its rugged beauty into a National Romantic artistic movement. In 1862, the poet Aasmund Olavsson Vinje christened the region "Jotunheimen," the name for the home of the giants in Norse mythology.

LOM. Lom (pop. 2500) is a major hub for excursions farther into the park. Travelers leave from here on the trek to the summit of 2469m **Galhøpiggen,** northern Europe's tallest mountain, or on the **Memurubu-Gjendsheim** trail mentioned in Henrik Ibsen's *Peer Gynt.* Ask at the tourist office for the best departure points, which vary according to skill level and weather conditions. The 6hr. trail from **Juvashytta** is the most popular route, but can only be completed with the help of paid guides who navigate the perilous soft spots of the Jostedalsbreen glacier. Before guides were made mandatory, several inexperienced tourists fell through the glacier and died. A bus leaves from Lom for Juvashytta (mid-June to mid-Aug. daily 8:45am, 60kr). From **Krossbu,** hikers can take a 4-6hr. glacier walk. Less experienced travelers looking to reach the summit without a guide should catch the bus to **Spiterstulen** (daily 8:45am, 60kr). From there, plan to hike 8-9hr., although not on the glacier. No extensive hiking should be done before early July; locals generally tackle the mountains between mid-July and mid-August. To get to the **Nordal Turistsenter ❷,** walk left as you exit the tourist office and cross the bridge to the main roundabout. Take a left and follow the road until you see the signs and cabins on your left. (☎6121 9300; www.nordalturistsenter.no. Showers free. Laundry 25kr. Reception 8am-11pm. Tent sites 140kr, 50kr per person.) Pick up groceries at **Kiwi,**

off the main roundabout. (Open M-F 9am-9pm, Sa 9am-6pm. Cash only.) **Buses** run to: Bergen (8½hr., 2 per day, 435kr); Oslo (6-6½hr., 5 per day, 460kr); Sogndal (3½hr., mid-June to mid-Sept. 2 per day, 220kr); Trondheim (5½hr., 2 per day, 425kr). The excellent **tourist office,** in the Fjellmuseum, provides park info, sells maps (99kr), and directs travelers to accommodations. From the bus station, turn left and cross the bridge. (☎61 21 29 90; www.visitlom.com. Open mid-June to mid-Aug. M-F 9am-7pm, Sa-Su 10am-7pm; low season reduced hours.)

NORDFJORD AND JOSTEDALSBREEN

Nordfjord is less popular than Geirangerfjord and Sognefjord, but the towering, ice-blue expanse of the nearby Jostedalsbreen glacier has drawn more tourists to the region in recent years. Although solo trips onto the glacier are tempting, it has dangerous soft spots and crevasses, so guided tours are essential.

STRYN. Stryn (pop. 6600) is a departure point for trips on Briksdalsbreen, one of the smaller glaciers that make up the giant Jostedalsbreen. The **Glacier Bus** (79kr) runs to the base of Briksdalsbreen from Stryn's bus terminal (daily June-Aug. 9:30am, returning 1:40pm). **Olden Aktiv** (☎57 87 38 88; www.oldenaktiv.no) runs a variety of glacier tours and ice climbs (300-550kr; reserve ahead). The tours depart from **Melkevoll Bretun ❶**, a campground 45min. from Stryn. In addition to huts and holiday cabins, Melkevoll Bretun also features an open-air **cave dorm,** where guests sleep on wooden slabs swaddled in reindeer skins with 800 tons of rock overhead. Bring an insulated sleeping bag. (☎57 87 38 64. Showers 10kr per 5min. Firewood 50kr. Huts from 290kr. Cabins 590-750kr. Cave dorm 110kr per person; min. 4 people to reserve. Call ahead to check availability. MC/V.) To reach the family-friendly **Stryn Vandrerhjem (HI) ❷** from the bus station, turn left on Setrevegen, head up the hill, and look for signs. If you arrive in the evening, call to ask about pickup. (☎57 87 11 06. Breakfast included. Linens 50kr. Laundry 30kr. Internet 15kr per 15min. Reception 4-11pm. Lockout 11am-4pm. Open June-Aug. Dorms 225kr; singles 375kr; doubles with bath 600kr. 25kr HI discount. D/MC/V.) **Bus** #440 leaves Stryn daily at 3pm for Trondheim (7½hr., 399kr) via Lom (2hr., 200kr). Buses also run to Ålesund (3½hr., 4-5 per day, 239kr) and Bergen (6hr., 4 per day, 399kr). All fares are discounted 25% for students. Check www.nor-way.no or www.fjord1.no for schedules. Stryn's **tourist office** is at Perhusveien 19, past the Esso station. (☎57 87 40 40; www.nordfjord.no. Internet 15kr per 15min. Open July daily 8:30am-8pm; June and Aug. daily 8:30am-6pm; Sept.-May M-F 8:30am-3:30pm.)

GEIRANGERFJORD

Only 16km long, Geirangerfjord is lined with cliffs and waterfalls that make it one of Norway's most spectacular—and most heavily touristed—destinations. While cruising through the iridescent water, watch for the Seven Sisters waterfalls and the Suitor geyser. Geirangerfjord can be reached from the north via the Trollstigen road from Åndalsnes or by the bus from Ålesund or Stryn that stops in Hellesylt.

GEIRANGER. Tiny Geiranger (pop. 210), at the eastern end of Geirangerfjord, marks the final point of the Trollstigen road. In the summer, tourists overrun the town, fighting to take in the stunning views of the fjord. The well-marked trails allow some escape from the crowds, although hikers are unlikely to be alone. Nearby natural attractions include peering down from **Flydalsjuvet Cliff** (2hr. round-trip), sidling behind the **Storseter Waterfall** (2½hr.), and catching a glimpse of the Seven Sisters waterfalls from **Skageflå Farm** (5hr.), which was abandoned in 1916. At **Lanfvaten,** hikers can climb into the cloud cover that shrouds the top of the **Dalsnibba Mountain Plateau.** To get there, take a bus from opposite the ferry docks (1hr., departs 9:30am and 2pm, 140kr). To explore the fjord on your own, call ahead to rent a motor boat from **Holenaustet.** (☎95 10 75 21. From 110kr per hr. AmEx/D/MC/V.) ☒**Geiranger Camping ❶,** 100m from the town center by the water, offers budget accommodations in a beautiful location at the mouth of the fjord. (☎70 26 31 20. Showers 10kr per 5min. Laundry 80kr. Reception 8am-10pm. Open mid-May to early Sept. Tent sites 86kr. MC/V.) **Buses** run to Ålesund (3hr., 2-4 per day, 176kr). There is no bus station; buy tickets onboard with cash. **Ferries** depart for Hellesylt (1¼hr.; June-Aug. 6 per day, Sept.-May 4 per day; 98kr). For info on hiking, kayaking, biking, and glacial trekking, visit the **tourist office,** up the path from the ferry landing. (☎70 26 30 99; www.visitgeirangerfjorden.com. Open daily mid-June to Aug. 9am-7pm; mid-May to mid-June 9am-5pm.)

ROMSDAL AND TRØNDELAG

Between the western fjords and the long, sparsely inhabited stretch of Norway that extends north past the Arctic Circle, a group of small coastal cities forms the third point of a triangle with Oslo and Bergen. Travelers are only now beginning to discover this Norwegian heartland, hemmed in by the spiny Trollstigen range and the fertile valleys along the Trondheimsfjord.

ÅLESUND ☎70

Often described as a scaled-down version of Bergen, seaside Ålesund (OH-less-oont; pop. 40,000) features splashy Art Nouveau architecture to welcome travelers emerging from fjord country. Climb up 418 steps to the **Aksla** viewpoint for the best glimpses of the city and the distant mountains. To get there, head through the park across from the youth hostel and walk 25min. to the top. The Time Machine exhibit at the ☒**Art Nouveau Center,** Apotekergt. 16, transports visitors back to Ålesund's devastating fire of 1904. This engaging museum, located in a historic pharmacy building, also traces the city's century-long rebirth. (☎10 49 70. Open June-Aug. M-F 10am-7pm, Sa-Su noon-5pm; Sept.-May Tu-Sa 11am-4pm, Su noon-4pm. 50kr, students 40kr. AmEx/MC/V.) To travel back farther in time, visit the **Sunnmøre Museum,** which has reconstructed farmhouses and the excavated remains of an 11th-century trading post. On Wednesday afternoons, locals demonstrate traditional handicrafts, and a replica Viking ship takes visitors for a short cruise. Take bus #13 or 18 (10min.) to Sunnmøre. (☎17 40 00; www.sunnmore.museum.no. Open late June-late Aug. M-Sa 11am-5pm, Su noon-5pm; late Aug.-late June M-Tu and F 11am-3pm, Su noon-3pm. Cruise 30kr. Museum 60kr, students 45kr. MC/V.)

At the **Ålesund Vandrerhjem (HI) ❷,** Parkgt. 14, tight bunks stacked three high bring travelers closer together. From the tourist office, walk up to Konensgt., take a right, and turn left on Løvenvoldgt., which becomes Parkgt. as you head away from the harbor; the hostel is on the right. (☎11 58 30. Breakfast, linens, and laundry included. Reception 8:30-11am and 3:30pm-midnight. Open May-Sept. Dorms 200kr; singles 415kr; doubles 550kr. 25kr HI discount. D/MC/V.) Folksy alternative music plays in the background at the popular organic restaurant **Let's Eat ❶,** Keiser Wilhelmsgt. 37, at the corner of Storgt. (☎13 13 07. Hearty sandwiches 55-68kr. Open M-F 10:30am-5pm, Sa 10:30am-4pm. V.) Across the street on Keiser Wilhelmsgt., **Rema 1000** stocks groceries. (☎12 42 57. Open M-F 9am-10pm. Cash only.) **Buses** go to Stryn (3½hr., 2-3 per day, 249kr) and Trondheim (8hr., 2 per day, 511kr). A shorter route involves a bus to Åndalsnes (2½hr., 3 per day, 176kr) and a seat on the waiting train to Trondheim (4-5hr., 525kr). **Hurtigruten express boats** to Trondheim are costly, but trips include one night of lodging on the boat; beware that "dormitory accommodations" can mean a space on the floor. (Departs daily 6:45pm, arrives 8:15am; 942kr, students 471kr.) The **tourist office,** at the Skateflukaia dock, arranges walking tours. (☎15 76 00; www.visitalesund.com. Tours depart daily June 20-Aug. 20 at noon, 75kr. Internet 10kr per 10min. Open June-Aug. M-F 8:30am-7pm, Sa 9am-5pm, Su 11am-5pm; Sept.-May M-F 8:30am-4pm.)

ÅNDALSNES ☎71

Åndalsnes (pop. 2700), on Romsdalsfjord, is a lightly industrialized port on the perimeter of fjord country. **Hikes** along the **Trollstigen** (Troll's Road) climb to 850m above sea level and make zigzag turns. The trail passes through mist as it goes by the 180m **Stigfossen** waterfall and approaches the sheer **Trollveggen** (Troll's Wall). The lip of the wall lured base jumpers for years, until the burden of making helicopter rescues drove the town into debt and the activity was outlawed. Thrill-seeking scofflaws continue to make jumps on the sly. Head back to Åndalsnes on the **Kløvstien path** (5hr.), which was recently smoothed over for walkers but is still steep enough to require a handrail in some places. In mid-July, the paths fill with outdoor enthusiasts who come for the **Norwegian Mountain Festival** (www.norskfjellfestival.no). During the first week of August, Åndalsnes hosts the **Rauma Rock Festival** (www.raumarock.com; 2-day pass 650kr). The outdoor theater in the nearby town of Klungnes is the site of the **Sinclairfestivalen,** an open-air re-enactment of a 1612 battle between Scottish mercenaries and Norwegian farmers. (www.sinclairfestivalen.com. Adults 250kr, students 150kr.) An annual rowboat **regatta** provides sporting thrills. Just 2km outside of town, **Åndalsnes Vandrerhjem (HI) ❷,** Setnes, is a good starting point for journeys along the Trollstigen. The Ålesund bus will stop at the hostel upon request. (☎22 13 82. Breakfast included. Linens 50kr. Internet 15kr per 15min. Reception 4pm-10am. Dorms 230kr; singles 395kr; doubles 600kr. 25kr HI discount. MC/V.) **Trains** run to Oslo (5½hr., 2-4 per day, 692kr). **Buses** depart outside the train station for Ålesund (2½hr., 1-2 per day, 176kr) and Geiranger (3hr., 1-2 per day, 197kr). The **tourist office,** in the same building as the train station, helps book rooms. (☎22 16 22; www.visitandalsnes.com. Open mid-May to mid-Sept. M-Sa 9am-6pm, Su noon-6pm.)

TRONDHEIM ☎73

A thousand years have come and gone since Viking kings turned Trondheim (pop. 150,000) into Norway's seat of power. Today, almost 30,000 university students lend Trondheim's well-kept canals and restored townhouses a youthful energy during term time. Though the city can feel a bit empty in the summer, this gateway to the north country still serves as a meeting point for travelers.

TRANSPORTATION AND PRACTICAL INFORMATION. Trains go to Bodø (11hr., 2 per day, 924kr) and Oslo (6½hr., 3-5 per day, 797kr). **Buses** leave the train station for Ålesund (8hr.; 4 per day; 500kr, students 375kr) and Bergen (14½hr.; 2 per day; 735kr, students 536kr). The **Hurtigruten** boat departs daily at noon for Stamsund, in the Lofoten Islands (31½hr.; 1873kr, 50% student discount). To get to the **tourist office,** Munkegt. 19, from the train station, cross the bridge, walk six blocks down Søndregt., turn right on Kongensgt., and look to your left as you approach the roundabout. (☎80 76 60; www.visit-trondheim.com. Open July-early Aug. M-F 8:30am-8pm, Sa-Su 10am-6pm; low season reduced hours.) **DNT** (Norwegian Mountain Touring Association), Sandgt. 30, has maps and hiking info. (☎92 42 00; www.turistforeningen.no. Open May-Sept. M-W and F 8am-4pm, Th 8am-6pm.)

ACCOMMODATIONS AND FOOD. The fun-loving atmosphere at **Trondheim InterRail Center ❶,** Elgesetergt. 1, in the Studentersamfundet (p. 763), more than makes up for the dark dorms. Cross the bridge from the train station, walk south along Søndregt., and go right on Kongensgt. Turn left on Prinsensgt.; the hostel is on the left after the bridge. (☎89 95 38; www.tirc.no. Breakfast included. Linens 60kr deposit. Free Internet. Open July 5-Aug. 19. Dorms 135kr. Cash only.) For a quiet, tidy budget option, take Lillegårdsbakken, off Øvre Bakklandet, uphill to **Singsaker Sommerhotell ❶**, Rogertsgt. 1. (☎89 31 00; http://sommerhotell.singsaker.no. Breakfast included. Linens 45kr. Open mid-June to mid-Aug. Dorms 155kr; singles 380-485kr; doubles 695kr; triples 795kr. MC/V.) Gluttony may be one of the seven deadly sins, but that doesn't detract from the appeal of the all-you-can-eat **cake buffet** (54kr) on Sundays 1-7pm at **Mormors Stue ❷,** Nedre Enkeltskillingsveita 2. (☎52 20 22. Open M-Sa 10am-11:30pm, Su 1-11:30pm. MC/V.) The early-bird dinner crowd snaps up fresh fish platters (125kr) prepared by some of Trondheim's finest chefs at the riverside **Den Gode Nabo ❸,** Øvre Bakklandet 66, just over the Old Town Bridge in a basement to the right. After dinner, students sample over 70 varieties of beer. (☎87 42 40; www.dengodenabo.com. Dinner special daily 4-7pm. Beer M 42kr, Tu-Su 52kr. Open daily 1pm-1:30am. D/MC/V.) Norway's future poets and artists dine at student-friendly **Ramp ❷,** Strandv. 25A. For a big meal on a budget, try the Cowboy Breakfast (75kr), served all day. (☎51 80 20; www.lamoramp.net. Entrees 67-100kr. Beer 43kr. Open M-W 10am-midnight, Th-F 10am-1am, Sa noon-1am, Su noon-midnight. MC/V.)

TIP **A ROOM OF ONE'S OWN.** If you fall in love with this funky neighborhood, check the ads at **Ramp** for cheap apartments (from 100kr per night).

SIGHTS. **Nidaros Cathedral,** in the southern end of the city, tops the list of churches for travelers to visit in Norway. Nidaros was built on King Olof's tomb in the 11th century and completed around 1300, and today it is still the site of royal coronations. The cathedral is home to one of five large organs built by Joachim Wagner, Bach's contemporary, and it hosts organ concerts throughout the year. (☎53 91 60; www.nidarosdomen.no. Open mid-June to mid-Aug. M-F 9am-6pm, Sa 9am-2pm, Su 1-4pm; low season reduced hours. Organ concerts mid-June to mid-Aug. M-Sa 1pm; low season Sa 1pm. Mid-June to mid-Aug. 50kr admission includes the nearby Museum at the Archbishop's Palace. Low season cathedral free, palace 50kr. AmEx/D/MC/V.) The same complex is also home to a museum for the **Crown Jewels and Regalia.** (☎53 91 60. Open June-Aug. M-F 10am-4pm, Sa 10am-2pm, Su noon-4pm; low season reduced hours. 70kr. AmEx/D/MC/V.) Across the scenic **Gamle Bybro** (Old Town Bridge) to the east, the former fishing houses of the **old district** have morphed into chic galleries and cafes, but they maintain their weather-worn maritime appearance. On the hill opposite Gamle Bybro is the world's first **bicycle elevator,** built in 1993 to encourage bike riding in hilly Trondheim. Test your balance as you are shoved up the steep hill by an automated mechanical pulley with a stirrup for your foot. The reward is a speedy ride down. (Access card available at the tourist office for 100kr deposit.) Perched on a promontory overlooking Trondheim and the fjords, **Kristiansten Festning** (Kristiansten Fortress) is one of the city's best picnic spots. Built in 1681 after a fire destroyed Trondheim, the fortress saved the city from Swedish invaders in 1781 and served as the Nazis' execution grounds for members of the Norwegian resistance. (Grounds open daily 8am-midnight. Interior open June-Aug. daily 11am-4pm.)

ENTERTAINMENT AND NIGHTLIFE. From the end of July through early August, the **Olavsfestdagene Medieval Festival** fills the city with everyone from pop bands to pilgrims (☎84 14 50; www.olavsfestdagene.no). The **Studentersamfundet,** the Trondheim student society's headquarters, houses a cafe with cheap food and beer next to the InterRail Center. Befriend the local students and you may discover one of the 18 private bars in the maze-like building. (☎89 95 00; www.samfundet.no. Beer 48kr; 38kr for guests of the InterRail Center. Tu and F 8-10pm beer 25kr. Open daily until 2am.) The **Solsiden** ("Sunny Side") district is home to popular restaurants and lounges. The standout **Club Blæst,** TMV kaia 17, has three bars and a black box theater that hosts rock acts and DJs most weekends and an improv comedy troupe on Saturdays. (☎60 01 06; www.blaest.no. Beer 58kr. Concerts from 50kr. 20+. Open daily noon-3:30am. AmEx/D/MC/V.) Just 50m away, **Cafe Bare Blåbær,** Innherredsveien 16, serves burgers and pizza (99-129kr) until midnight and then turns into a lounge and bar. (☎53 30 33. Beer 53kr. 20+ after 6pm. Open M-Th 11am-1:30am, F-Sa 11am-3:30am, Su 3pm-1:30am. AmEx/D/MC/V.) When school is in session, the clubs and bars along **Brattorgata** offer everything from tapas to fine malt whiskey. During the summer, a stroll along **Carl Johans gate** or **Nordre gate** is the best bet for nightlife beyond Solsiden.

FARTHER NORTH

TROMSØ ☎77

The self-proclaimed "Paris of the Arctic," Tromsø (pop. 60,000) exudes a worldly sensibility that belies its location 720km north of the Arctic Circle. The town serves as a base for exploring the pristine beauty of Norway's northern mountains and lakes. However, a few days wandering the pedestrian-friendly center by day or pub-crawling by night will do wonders for travelers who long for an urban scene.

TRANSPORTATION AND PRACTICAL INFORMATION. The **Hurtigruten express boat** arrives in Tromsø from Stamsund, in the Lofoten Islands (departs 7:30pm, arrives 2:30pm the next day; seats 1008kr, students 510kr; sleeping cabins 1578/1074kr). **Buses** go to Narvik (4½hr.; 2-4 per day; 360kr, students and Scanrail holders 180kr), a transportation hub for Finnish and Swedish destinations. The **tourist office,** Kirkegt. 2, books private rooms, as well as dogsled, snowmobile, and raft excursions. (☎61 00 00; www.destinasjontromso.no. Open May 22-Aug. M-F 8:30am-6pm, Sa-Su 10am-5pm; low season reduced hours.) For detailed hiking advice, check out **DNT** (Norwegian Mountain Touring Association), Grønnegt. 32., in the same building as the tourist office on the second floor. (☎68 51 75; www.turistforeningen.no/tromsturlag. Open June-Aug. 10am-4pm.) Down the street from the tourist office along the harbor, **Rica Ishavshotel,** Fredrik Langesgt. 2, offers free 6hr. **bike rental** with 200kr deposit. (☎66 64 00. Open 24hr.) **Postal Code:** 9253.

ACCOMMODATIONS AND FOOD. The **Fjellheim Sommerhotell ❶,** Mellomvegen 96, in a Bible school 10min. from the center, has the cheapest accommodations in town. The dorms are basic, with mattresses on the floor, but the hostel offers free Internet and 24hr. make-your-own waffles. Take bus #28 to Bjerkely or walk along Mellomvegen. (☎75 55 60; fjellheim@nlm.no. Breakfast and linens included. Laundry 25kr. Reception 24hr. Open mid-June to mid-Aug. Dorms 150kr; singles 400kr; doubles 600kr. AmEx/D/MC/V.) To reach the oceanside **Tromsø Vandrerhjem (HI) ❷,** Åsgårdv. 9, from the tourist office, turn right and walk two blocks down Storgt., take another right on Fr. Langes gt., and catch bus #26. The simple dorms have great views, and guests can take in the midnight sun from the balconies. (☎65 76 28. Linens 50kr. Reception 8-10:30am and 4-10pm. Open mid-June to mid-Aug. Dorms 195kr; singles 325kr; doubles 450kr. 25kr HI discount. MC/V.) To get to **Tromsø Camping ❶,** take bus #20 or 24 to Kraftforsyninga, walk back across the red bridge, turn left, and follow the road 400m. (☎63 80 37; www.tromsocamping.no. Reception 7am-11pm. Tent sites 150kr. 2- to 5-person cabins May-Sept. 300-950kr; Oct.-Apr. 400-700kr. MC/V.) For ham or seal sandwiches (49kr), head to

Skarven ❷, Strandtorget 1, by the harbor. (☎60 07 20; www.skarven.no. Beer 60kr. Open Su-Th 11am-12:30am, F-Sa 11am-1am. AmEx/D/MC/V.) Stock up on groceries at **Spar**, Storgt. 63. (☎68 21 40. Open M-F 9am-8pm, Sa 9am-7pm.)

SIGHTS. At the Tromsdalen end of the Tromsøbua bridge, the **Arctic Cathedral** resembles a glacier; metallic plates covering its surface reflect natural light in long, diaphanous streaks. Eleven tons of glass were used to fashion the triangular stained-glass window behind the altar. In the summer, the cathedral hosts daily organ recitals (50kr) at 7:30pm and performances of Norwegian folk songs (80kr) at 11:30pm. (Open June to mid-Aug. M-Sa 9am-7pm, Su 1-7pm; mid-Aug. to May daily 4-6pm. 22kr. Services Su 11am.) **Polaria,** Hjarlmar Johansens gt. 12, off Strandv., is a sleek, interactive museum and aquarium focused on Arctic ecosystems. (☎75 01 00; www.polaria.no. Open daily mid-May to mid-Aug. 10am-7pm; mid-Aug. to Apr. noon-5pm. Seal feedings 12:30 and 3:30pm. 90kr, students 65kr. AmEx/D/MC/V.) The **Tromsø University Museum** delves into geology, zoology, and the indigenous Sámi culture (see box at right), then dazzles visitors with a short video about the Northern Lights. Take bus #28 from the city center or walk along Mellomvegen for 25min. (☎64 50 00; www.tmu.uit.no. Open daily June-Aug. 9am-6pm; low season reduced hours. 40kr, students 20kr. MC/V.) The tour at the **Mack Microbrewery,** Storgt. 5-13, introduces visitors to the art of brewing and the economics of running a microbrewery. (☎62 45 80; www.mack.no. 1hr. English-language tours leave from Øllhallen at Storgt. 4 June-Aug. M-Th 1 and 3:30pm, F-Sa 3:30pm; Sept.-May M-Th 1pm. 110kr, including 1 beer.) To see the midnight sun hovering above Tromsø in June and early July, take the **Fjellheisen** cable car, Solliveien 12, up 420m to the top of Mt. Storsteinen. (☎63 87 37; www.utelivsbyen.no. Daily every 30min. 10am-1am. 85kr.) Students like to take the lift late at night for an introspective evening at the **Fjellstua** cafe. (☎63 86 55. Beer 58kr. Open daily mid-May to mid-Aug. 10am-1am; Apr. to mid-May and mid-Aug. to Sept. 10am-5pm. AmEx/D/MC/V.) Tromsø is nestled in a mountain valley, with several non-strenuous **hikes** nearby, including the climb up **Tromsdalstinden,** a peak of 1238m (6-8hr.).

ENTERTAINMENT AND NIGHTLIFE. The **Tromsø International Film Festival** is Norway's largest film festival, bringing over 40,000 visitors to town annually. (Jan. 16-21, 2007; ☎75 30 90; www.tiff.no.) Tromsø is a university town and famous for its nightlife, which centers on **Stortorget** and along **Sjøgata.**

IN RECENT NEWS

SUCCESS FOR THE SÁMI

For centuries, the Sámi people have herded reindeer, hunted and farmed in some of Norway's most remote and inhospitable regions. One of the largest indigenous groups in Europe, the Sámi live in northern Norway, Finland, Sweden, and part of Russia, and their current population is estimated to be around 85,000.

Because they occupied such rugged territory, the Sámi largely escaped outside influence until the 20th century, and they were poorly understood by their neighbors. Lappland, the European name for the Sámi homeland, was considered the mythical home of Santa Claus in many European cultures. In the early 20th century, the Norwegian government made aggressive attempts to wipe out Sámi culture, including banning the use of their languages in schools.

But now, with increasing awareness of the importance of indigenous cultures, Norwegians are taking steps to protect the livelihood of the Sámi. The Sámediggi, the representative assembly for the Sámi in Norway, held its first session in 1989. Among other responsibilities, the parliament is charged with ensuring that the rights of the Sámi are upheld. In Norway, Finland, and Sweden, festivals celebrate Sámi music, a newspaper is published in the Sámi language, and each year February 6 is observed as Sámi National Day.

Drop in for tapas or an afternoon cappuccino at **Åpen,** Grønnegt. 81, a relaxed lounge and bar where students unwind on plush sofas by candlelight. (☎68 49 06. Beer 56kr, 2-for-1 on summer weekends. Sept.-May F-Sa DJ. 20+. Cover F-Sa 50kr. Restaurant open Tu-F 3-10pm, Sa noon-10pm. Nightclub open F-Sa 10pm-3:30am. AmEx/D/MC/V.) Monday nights at **Kaos,** Strangt. 22, bring out the DJ in everyone with the **Free-Jay** promotion: spin your own tunes for 30min. on the club's stereo system and get two free beers. The pros take over on weekends, when a young crowd parties to avant-garde tunes spun by some of Norway's best DJs. (☎63 59 99. Beer 54kr, M all night and F-Sa 8pm-midnight 35kr. 18+. Cover 30kr. Concerts W-Th 30-80kr. Open Su-Th 6pm-2am, F-Sa 6pm-3:30am. Cash only.)

LOFOTEN ISLANDS

A jumble of emerald mountains, glassy waters, and colorful villages, the Lofoten Islands prove there is more to Norwegian beauty than the western fjords. As late as the 1950s, isolated fishermen lived in *rorbuer*, raised red wooden shacks along the coast. Today, the same shacks are rented out to tourists venturing above the Arctic Circle to visit fishing villages aglow with the pale rays of the midnight sun.

TRANSPORTATION. The **Hurtigruten express boat** runs from Trondheim to Stamsund (31hr.; departs daily at noon, arrives at 7pm the next day; 1873kr, 50% student discount). Another option is to take a **train** to Bodø (11hr., 2 per day, 924kr). From there you can catch a **ferry** to Moskenes (3-4hr.; 4-7 per day; 143kr, 50% student discount) or take the Hurtigruten to Svolvær (6hr.; 3pm; 398kr, 50% student discount) via Stamsund (4hr.; 9:30pm; 331kr, 50% student discount). **Flights** go from Bodø to Leknes (45min., 5-6 per day, 783kr). Check www.wideroe.no for more information and possible discounts. Bodø's **tourist office** is down Sjogt. from the train station. (☎75 54 80 00; www.visitbodo.com. Open June-Aug. M-F 9am-8pm, Sa 10am-6pm, Su noon-8pm; Sept.-May M-F 9am-4pm, Sa 10am-2pm.) Within the islands, **local buses** (☎7606 4040; additional route info 177) are the main form of transport; pick up schedules at tourist offices. Visitors occasionally hitchhike by boat and by car; Let's Go does not recommend hitchhiking.

MOSKENESØYA. At the southern tip of the Lofotens' scenic E10 highway, the tiny island of Moskenesøya (pop. 1300) accommodates both well-preserved 19th-century fishing communities and eco-adventure tourism organizations. Frequent ferries from Bodø make **Moskenes,** in the south of Moskenesøya, a crossroads for tourists, although the town itself is just a small collection of fishing lodges. At the **Moskenes Harbour Tourist Office,** 100m from the ferry landing, the knowledgeable staff provide info on the area's adventure boat tours (400-900kr), guided hikes (250kr), or fishing trips with locals (400kr). For 400kr, one notable 6hr. boat tour takes you through the **Maelstrom,** one of the most dangerous ocean currents in the world, past the abandoned fishing hamlet of **Hell,** and into the ancient **Refsvikhula caves** to view their mysterious 3000-year-old drawings. (☎7609 1599; www.lofoten-info.no. Internet 15kr per 15min. Open late June-early Aug. daily 10am-7pm; early May-late June and late Aug. M-F 10am-5pm.) Challenging mountainous **hikes** are the primary attraction in the Lofotens, although trails are often sparsely marked; pick up a map (105kr) at the tourist office. It's a 3hr. trek to the DNT's **Munkebu cabin,** where you can spend the night. DNT membership (p. 741) and a 300kr deposit are required for key rental, but non-members may accompany members. (200kr per night, under 25 100kr. Members 100/50kr.) Keys are available at the Sørvågen Handel (☎76 09 12 15) and KIN Trykk, Ramberg (☎76 09 34 20).

South of Moskenes, the lovely, well-preserved fishing village of **Å** (OH) is the poster child for the Lofotens' tourist industry. Experienced hikers can tackle the 8hr. **Stokkvikka hike** by heading down the southern bank of Lake Ågvatnet and up

400m to cross the Stokkvikskaret Pass; bring a map. A somewhat less difficult 3hr. hike from **Sørvågen** (between Å and Moskenes; 2.5km from each) leads up **Tinstinden** to its 490m peak, where you can take in the region's best views. The **Norsk Fiskeværsmuseum** uses reenactments to explain the island's maritime economy and offers visitors with strong stomachs a spoonful of homemade cod-liver oil. For a more conventional snack, try cinnamon rolls (10kr) from the 160-year-old bakery. (☎7609 1488. Open mid-June to mid-Aug. daily 10:30am-5:30pm; mid-Aug. to mid-June M-F 11am-3:30pm. 50kr, students 25kr. AmEx/D/MC/V.) Visitors can rent doubles at one of the private fishing lodges by the dock. **Å Hamna Rorbuer As** ❷ has tidy, functional dorms and rents comfortable *rorbuer* cabins to groups of four or more. (☎7609 1211. Reception June-Sept. 10am-10pm; call ahead at other times. Dorms 100kr. Cabins 400-1000kr. AmEx/D/MC/V.) **Å Lofoten Vandrerhjem (HI)** ❷ provides simple accommodations in an attic above the Fiskeværsmuseum bakery. (☎7609 1121; www.lofoten-rorbu.com. Linens 60kr. Reception daily 8:30am-10:30pm. Dorms 195kr; doubles 360kr. 30kr HI discount. MC/V.) **Å Dagligvarer A/S** sells groceries. (☎7609 1206. Open M-F 9am-7pm, Sa 9am-5pm, Su 4-7pm. Cash only.) **Buses** depart from behind the tourist office (15min., 2-4 times per day, 23kr).

VESTVÅGØY. North of Moskenesøya, the island of Vestvågøy (pop. 11,000) is home to some of the Lofotens' most striking scenery. Flights from Bodø and most buses arrive in **Leknes,** which has squat concrete buildings and less charm than Vestvågøy's coastal towns. Local favorite **Surprise Cafe** ❶, Idrettgaten 27, is probably the closest you will come to an American diner in Scandinavia. Surprise serves burgers (54kr) and beer (50kr), but the mainstay is a hot sandwich (37kr) stuffed with ham, cheese, and toppings. (☎7608 1510. Open June-Aug. M-W 10am-6pm, Th-F 10am-10pm, Sa 11am-4pm, Su 1-6pm; low season reduced hours. Cash only.) The sparsely populated town of **Stamsund** is a port of call for the Hurtigruten coastal steamer, making it an ideal stop for last-minute fishing and hiking. **Hikers** are serenaded by ptarmigans, a local bird species, on the way up to the peaks of **Stein Tinden** (500m) and **Justad Tinden** (732m). Both treks take roughly 6hr. round-trip and provide panoramic views. During June and early July, visitors can tan into the wee hours under the midnight sun, while clear nights in late autumn or early spring could mean seeing the **Northern Lights.** The knowledgeable proprietor and homey common rooms at **Stamsund Vandrerhjem (HI)** ❶ have kindled enough friendships between travelers to earn the

IN RECENT NEWS

HUNTING FOR CONTROVERSY

Since 1993, Norway has rejected the International Whaling Commission's ban on whale hunting, making it the only country in the world to sanction the activity for purposes other than scientific research. The Lofoten Islands, which serve as the base of Norway's whaling industry, have become a battleground in the conflict between whalers and environmental activists. Supporters of whaling argue that they are protecting an indigenous way of life. Opponents cite the need to sustain endangered species, and they disapprove of the method used to hunt whales, which involves grenade-tipped harpoons that explode in the whale's body.

Poor weather during the 2006 hunting season reinvigorated this debate. The Norwegian government set the whaling industry's quota at 1,052 Minke Whales, the highest quota since 1993. But as of mid-July 2006, only 444 whales had been caught, and parts of the fleet had temporarily ceased whaling. Industry leaders say that the reduction in whaling is due to bad fishing conditions and other expected factors. But activists credit the drop to a dwindling demand for whale meat and growing international opposition.

For now, adventurous visitors can still try a traditional Norwegian dish—red-meat whale steak. Just don't be surprised if your four-star dinner is disrupted by protestors outside.

hostel a reputation across Norway. (☎7608 9334. Wheelchair accessible. Fishing gear 100kr deposit. Free use of rowboats. Bike rental 100kr per day. Showers 5kr per 5min. Laundry 30kr. Open mid-Dec. to mid-Oct. Dorms 115kr; doubles 350kr. 25kr HI discount. Cabins 400-650kr. Cash only.) Given the sporadic bus schedules, a car may be the best way to get around. The 24hr. gas station uphill from the hostel rents **cars** (☎9091 2300; 300kr per day).

SVALBARD ARCHIPELAGO ☎79

Between the North Pole and the Arctic Circle, the Svalbard archipelago is home to some of the earth's most hostile territory; if bone-chilling temperatures don't frighten you, the thousands of polar bears should. Outside the mining and research community of Longyearbyen (pop. 1800) on the island of Spitsbergen, the bears are so prevalent that visitors are strongly encouraged to carry rifles. Still, tens of thousands of tourists arrive each year to experience the vast, windswept beauty.

TRANSPORTATION AND PRACTICAL INFORMATION. **Planes** arrive at Longyearbyen Airport from Oslo (3hr., 1-3 per day in summer, from 1465kr) and Tromsø (1½hr., 1-3 per day in summer, from 1310kr). The **Flybus** (40kr) will take you from the airport directly to your hotel or hostel. **SAS Braathens** (www.sasbraathens.no) offers the lowest fares, but the best deals require flexibility and advance planning. The tourist season peaks in the last week of July and first week of August, when temperatures climb as high as 6°C (43°F). Late spring (Apr.-May) is an ideal time to visit, since there is no snow on the ground. The remaining months make up the dark season, when minimal sunlight and ice-cold temperatures keep visitors away. Whenever you come to Svalbard, bring plenty of cold-weather gear. The exceptional **tourist office,** in the UNIS building complex 500m north of Longyearbyen center, is the first stop for navigating address-less Longyearbyen and the rest of Svalbard. (☎02 55 50; www.svalbard.net. Open M-F 8am-6pm, Sa 9am-4pm, Su noon-4pm.) The library at the Lompensenteret provides 30min. free **Internet.** (☎02 23 70. Open July to mid-Aug. M-Th 10am-5pm, F 10am-4pm.) Svalbard's weather makes **taxis** an attractive option (☎02 13 75 or 02 13 05), but **hitchhiking** around Longyearbyen is common. Let's Go does not recommend hitchhiking.

TIP **BEYOND TOURISM.** Svalbard is technically a part of Norway, but the archipelago is governed by a special treaty that allows many foreigners to **work** without a permit. Students with an interest in the hard sciences can study at the **University Center in Svalbard (UNIS).** (☎02 33 00; www.unis.no.)

ACCOMMODATIONS AND FOOD. Accommodations on Svalbard are limited; book well in advance. Budget lodgings cluster in Nybyen, a 25min. walk north of Longyearbyen center. **Gjestehuset 102** ❸ has no-frills dorms and a helpful owner. (☎02 57 16; 102@wildlife.no. Breakfast included. Dorms 290kr; singles Mar.-Sept. 475kr, Oct.-Feb. 350kr; doubles 790kr/550kr. AmEx/D/MC/V.) The neighboring **Spitsbergen Guesthouse** ❸ offers more space in its three cabins but is less social. (☎02 63 00; spitsbergen.guesthouse@spitsbergentravel.no. Breakfast included. Dorms 295-360kr; singles 480-660kr; doubles 780-990kr. D/MC/V.) The centrally located **Mary-Ann's Polarrigg** ❺ has a charming greenhouse-bar. (☎02 37 42; info@polarriggen.com. Breakfast 95kr. Beer 45kr. Singles Mar.-Sept. 595kr, Oct.-Feb. 495kr; doubles 850/750kr. AmEx/D/MC/V.) Since camping on public land is strictly prohibited, try **Longyearbyen Campground** ❶, 4.5km outside of town next to the airport. Late arrivals can pay the next morning. (☎02 14 44; info@longyearbyen-camping.no. Open late June-early Sept. Reception 8-10am and 8-10pm. Tent sites 80kr. Tent rental 100kr per night. Mattress rental 20kr per night. Cash only.) Food is very expensive in Svalbard, but other goods (including alcohol) are often cheaper due to the archipelago's tax-free status. **Kroa** ❷, centrally located in Basecamp Spitsbergen, serves hearty fare at long wooden tables. In the evenings it's a popular bar where patrons enjoy drinks beneath the gaze of a huge bust of Lenin. (☎02 13 00; post@kroa-svalbard.no. Beer 38kr. Open daily 11:30am-2am. AmEx/D/MC/V.) **Svalbard Butikken** stocks groceries and duty-free goods. (☎02 25 20; www.svalbardbutikken.no. Open M-F 10am-8pm, Sa 10am-6pm. AmEx/D/MC/V.)

SIGHTS AND NIGHTLIFE. Stop by the new and expanded **Svalbard Museum** at the University Center in Svalbard (UNIS) to learn about the flora and fauna of the islands as well as the history of their settlements. (☎02 13 84; www.svalbardmuseum.no. Open May-Sept. daily 10am-5pm; Oct.-Apr. M-W and F-Su noon-5pm. 50kr, students 30kr. AmEx/D/MC/V.) In July and August, a long-time resident leads **Historical Wanderings with Anne.** (Tours depart from the museum Tu and F 6pm. 100kr. Cash only.) Since twentysomethings arrive in Svalbard from around the world to work by day and party by night, Longyearbyen's social scene is surprisingly happening. The **Karls-Bergers Pub,** which stocks 1100 liquors, is a favorite haunt for miners. (☎02 25 11; www.karlsbergerpub.com. Beer 38kr. Cocktails 35kr. Open M-F 5pm-2am, Sa-Su 3pm-2am. MC/V.) The fancier **Barents Pub,** in the lobby of the Radisson, draws tourists and a few locals with its cheap beer. (☎02 34 66. Beer 39kr. Open daily 4pm-2am. AmEx/D/MC/V.) The legendary **Huset** nightclub has been the stomping grounds for generations of miners, naturalists, and geology students since the 1950s. Today it is still the premier nightlife destination for students at UNIS when they aren't hosting underground parties in abandoned mines. (☎02 25 00; huset@longyearbyen.net. Beer 39kr. Restaurant open daily 4-11pm. Nightclub open F-Sa 9pm-4am. AmEx/D/MC/V.)

OUTDOOR ACTIVITIES

No activity in Svalbard is perfectly safe; the widespread glacial cover and wandering polar bears make any trip outside Longyearbyen center dangerous. **Safety information** is on the Governor's Office website, www.sysselmannen.svalbard.no. Even the most experienced hikers often travel with guided tours. Those who decide to venture beyond Longyearbyen without a guide must first register with the Governor. Registration requires proof of insurance to cover potential rescue operations. Never leave Longyearbyen alone; always travel with at least one companion.

GUIDED TOURS. For most travelers, tours are by far the safest and most practical option; unfortunately, they are expensive. Winter activities include dogsledding, ice caving, skiing, and snowmobiling. In summer, travelers can take boat trips, cross glaciers, hunt for fossils, and hike. Tours of abandoned mines and visits to the Wilderness Center are possible year-round. For a complete listing of tours, visit www.svalbard.net. Tours can be booked online or at guesthouses and hotels. A boat trip to either the abandoned mining town of **Pyramiden** or the inhabited Russian mining settlement of **Barentsburg** should be included in every itinerary. The energetic guides at **Svalbard Wildlife Service,** in Longyearbyen center, lead trips to both destinations. (☎02 56 60; info@wildlife.no. Office open in summer M-F 8am-6pm, Sa 10am-1pm; winter M-F 10am-4pm. All trips

> **!** Svalbard is dangerous. We mean it. If you don't know what you are doing, do not venture outside of Longyearbyen without a well-trained guide. In recent years, several tourists have been killed by polar bears and glacier accidents.

include hot lunch. Pyramiden 930kr. Barentsburg 990kr.) Join the huskies of **Svalbard Villmarksenter** for a 6-7hr. tour of Foxfonna, a region outside Longyearbyen that is a "no-go" zone for snowmobiles. Hikers and skiers arrive year-round to spot Svalbard reindeer. (☎02 19 85; www.svalbard-adventure.com. All trips include lunch. Foxfonna hike 550kr.) **Spitsbergen Travel,** Svalbard's biggest tour provider, organizes trips up the **Trollsteinen** mountain, crossing a glacier on the way. (☎02 61 00; www.spitsbergentravel.no. Trip includes sandwiches and hot drinks. 540kr.) For **polar bear** spotting in a safe setting, book a multi-day boat tour with Spitsbergen Travel or Svalbard Wildlife Service.

INDEPENDENT TRAVEL. Only experienced hikers should venture into the Svalbardean wilderness without a guide. Quick-flaring foul weather makes even brief hikes from Longyearbyen surprisingly challenging; the polar bears that roam the islands ensure that overnight trips require the use of emergency beacons, trip-wire with flares, and a rifle. If you do not know how to use a rifle, do not travel on your own. Those experienced with rifles can rent equipment at the **Sportscenteret** in the Lompensenteret Mall. (☎02 15 35; sports.centeret@longyearbyen.net. Rifle rental 100kr per day, 500kr per week. 1000kr cash-only deposit for rifle plus 200kr for ammunition. AmEx/D/MC/V.) Permits are not required by law in Svalbard, but some stores may ask for one. Solo travelers should spend several days in Longyearbyen to plan routes and meet up with other travelers to form hiking groups. Bear in mind, however, that relatively few travelers arrive alone; most groups have planned their trips well in advance. One of the most popular routes is the three-day hike from Longyearbyen to Barentsburg. Several companies (p. 769) run boat trips between the two destinations; arrange to travel at least part of the way with them.

POLAND (POLSKA)

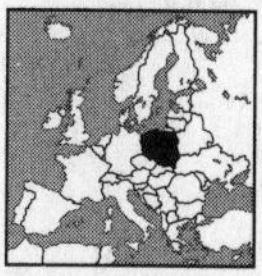

Poland's moments of independence have always been brief; the country did not exist on any map of Europe between 1795 and 1918. Ravaged in WWII, then trapped as a member of the Soviet bloc, Poland is now taking advantage of its breathing room, raising its economic output and having entered both NATO and the EU. Involvement with Western Europe has increased Poland's wealth, though its restrictive bureaucracy remains. This new growth is being used to restore Poland's architecture and culture to its former glory.

DISCOVER POLAND: SUGGESTED ITINERARIES

THREE DAYS. In **Kraków** (p. 784), enjoy the stunning **Wawel Castle,** medieval **Stare Miasto,** and the bohemian nightlife of **the Kazimierz area.** Take a daytrip to the sobering **Auschwitz-Birkenau** concentration camp.

ONE WEEK. After three days in **Kraków,** go to **Warsaw** (2 days; p. 776), where the **Uprising Museum** and **Russian Market** shouldn't be missed; then head north to **Gdańsk** (2 days; p. 796) and soak up the sun on the beach of **Sopot.**

BEST OF POLAND, THREE WEEKS. Begin with five days in **Kraków,** including a daytrip to **Auschwitz-Birkenau** or the **Wieliczka** salt mines. Spend two days in lovely **Wrocław** (p. 792), then enjoy the mountain air of **Zakopane** (1 day; p. 791). After a night at the edgy bars and clubs of **Poznań** (p. 794), head east to dynamic **Warsaw** (6 days), then take a break in scenic **Toruń** (2 days; p. 794). In **Gdańsk** (4 days), don't miss **Sopot** or **Malbork Castle.**

ESSENTIALS

FACTS AND FIGURES

Official Name: Republic of Poland.	**Land Area:** 313,000 sq. km.
Capital: Warsaw.	**Time Zone:** GMT +1.
Major Cities: Katowice, Kraków, Lódź.	**Language:** Polish.
Population: 39,000,000.	**Religion:** Roman Catholic (90%).

WHEN TO GO

Poland has warm summers and cold, snowy winters; summer weather can be capricious, and rain is frequent in July. Tourist season runs from late May to early September, except in mountain regions, which also have a winter high season (Dec.-Mar.). Late spring and early fall are pleasantly mild—though they, too, can be rainy. Late April, May, September, and early October are the best times to travel because the crowds will be sparser. Many attractions close for the winter.

DOCUMENTS AND FORMALITIES

EMBASSIES AND CONSULATES. Foreign embassies and consulates for Poland are in Warsaw and Kraków. Polish embassies and consulates abroad include **Australia,** 7 Turrana St., Yarralumla, Canberra, ACT, 2600 (☎2 6272 1000; www.poland.org.au); **Canada,** 443 Daly Ave., Ottawa, ON, K1N 6H3 (☎613-789-0468; www.polishembassy.ca); **Ireland,** 5 Ailesbury Rd., Ballsbridge, Dublin, 4 (☎1 283 0855; www.polishembassy.ie); **New Zealand,** 17 Upland Rd., Kelburn, Welling-

ton (☎4 475 9453; http://poland.org.nz); **UK,** 47 Portland Pl., London, W1B 1JH (☎0774 2700; www.polishembassy.org.uk); **US,** 2640 16th St., NW, Washington, D.C., 20009 (☎202-234-3800; www.polandembassy.org).

VISA AND ENTRY INFORMATION. Citizens of **Australia, Canada, Ireland, New Zealand, the UK,** and **the US** do not need a visa for stays of up to 90 days. Single-entry visas cost US$60, students US$45. Applications require a passport, two photos, and payment by money order, certified check, or cash. Regular service takes four days with a US$10 surcharge; 24hr. rush service costs an extra US$35. To extend your stay, apply in the city where you are staying to the regional government *(voi vodine)* or to the **Ministry of Internal Affairs,** ul. Stefana Batorego 5, Warsaw, 02-591 (☎22 621 20 20; fax 622 79 73). **Passports** must be valid for at least three months after the scheduled departure from Poland.

TOURIST SERVICES AND MONEY

TOURIST OFFICES. City-specific tourist offices are the most helpful. Almost all provide free English-language info and help arrange accommodations. Most have good free maps and sell more detailed ones. **Orbis,** the state-sponsored travel bureau, operates hotels in most cities and sells transportation tickets. **Almatur,** the student travel organization, offers ISICs, arranges dorm stays, and sells discounted transportation tickets (www.almatur.pl). The state-sponsored **PTTK** and **IT**

ENTRANCE REQUIREMENTS

Passport: Required for all travelers.

Visa: Not required for stays under 90 days for citizens of Australia, Canada, Ireland, New Zealand, the US, and the UK.

Letter of Invitation: Not required.

Inoculations: Not required. Recommended up-to-date on DTaP (diphtheria, tetanus, and pertussis), hepatitis A, hepatitis B, MMR (measles, mumps, and rubella), polio booster, and typhoid.

Work Permit: Required for all foreigners planning to work in Poland.

International Driving Permit: Required for all those planning to drive.

(Informacji Turystycznej) bureaus, located in nearly every city, are helpful for basic traveling needs (http://english.pttk.pl). Try the *Polish Pages*, a free guide available at hotels and travel agencies.

MONEY. The Polish currency is based on the **złoty,** plural złotych (1 złoty=100 groszy). **Inflation** is around 2%, so prices should be reasonably stable. **Kantory** (except those at the airport and train stations, which often attempt to scam tourists) offer better exchange rates than banks. **Bank PKO SA** and **Bank Pekao** have decent exchange rates; they cash traveler's checks and give **cash advances.** All **ATMs** *(bankomat)* are in English; MasterCard and Visa are widely accepted at ATMs. Budget accommodations rarely accept **credit cards,** but some restaurants and upscale hotels do. **Normal business** hours in Poland are 8am-4pm.

ZŁOTYCH (ZŁ)		
	AUS$1 = 2.29ZŁ	1ZŁ = AUS$0.44
	CDN$1 = 2.77ZŁ	1ZŁ = CDN$0.36
	EUR€1 = 3.96ZŁ	1ZŁ = EUR€0.25
	NZ$1 = 1.94ZŁ	1ZŁ = NZ$0.52
	UK£1 = 5.74ZŁ	1ZŁ = UK£0.17
	US$1 = 3.09ZŁ	1ZŁ = US$0.32

HEALTH AND SAFETY

Private **medical clinics** in major cities have English-speaking doctors, but they may not be up to Western standards. Expect to pay 50zł per visit. Avoid state hospitals. In an emergency, go to your embassy. **Pharmacies** are well stocked, and some stay open 24hr. **Public restrooms** are marked with a triangle for men and a circle for women. They range from squalid to pristine and cost up to 0.70zł; soap, towels, and toilet paper may cost extra. **Tap water** is drinkable in theory, but **bottled water** will spare you unpleasant metals and chemicals.

Crime rates are low, but tourists are sometimes targeted. Watch for muggers and **pickpockets,** especially on trains and in lower-priced hostels. Cab drivers will attempt to cheat those who do not speak Polish, and "friendly locals" looking to assist tourists are sometimes merely setting them up for scams. **Minorities** may receive unwanted attention. Darker-skinned people may be mistaken for Roma (gypsies) and discriminated against. There also may be lingering prejudice against Jews. **Homosexuality** is legal and a frequent topic of media debate, although it remains fairly underground.

TRANSPORTATION

BY PLANE. Warsaw's modern **Okęcie Airport (WAW)** is the hub for international flights. **LOT,** the national airline, flies to major cities in Poland.

BY TRAIN. Trains (☎22 94 36) are faster and more comfortable than buses. For a **timetable,** see **www.pkp.pl.** *Odjazdy* (departures) are in yellow, *przyjazdy* (arrivals) in white. *InterCity* and *ekspresowy* (express) trains are listed in red with an "IC" or "Ex" before the train number. *Pośpieszny* (direct; in red) are almost as fast and cheaper. Low-priced *osobowy* (slow; in black) are the slowest and have no restrooms. If you see a boxed "R" on the schedule, ask the clerk for a *miejscówka* (reservation). Students and seniors buy *ulgowy* (half-price) tickets instead of *normalny,* but **foreign travelers are not eligible for discounts** on domestic buses and trains. **Eurail** is not valid in Poland. **Wasteels** tickets and **Eurotrain** passes, sold at Almatur and Orbis, get 40% off international train fares for those under 26. Buy tickets in advance or wait in long lines. Stations are not announced and can be poorly marked. **Do not take night trains,** as theft and crime are very common.

BY BUS. **PKS** buses are cheapest and fastest for short trips. There are *pośpieszny* (direct; in red) and *osobowy* (slow; in black). In the countryside, PKS markers (yellow steering wheels that look like upside-down Mercedes-Benz symbols) indicate stops. Buses have no luggage compartments. **Polski Express,** a private company, offers more luxuries, but does not run to all cities.

POLAND

BY CAR. For **taxis,** arrange the price before getting in (in Polish, if possible) or make sure the driver turns on the meter. The going rate is 1.50-3zł per kilometer. Try to arrange cabs by phone. **Rental cars** are available in Warsaw and Kraków. Though legal, **hitchhiking** is rare and can be dangerous for foreigners. Hand-waving is the accepted sign. Let's Go does not recommend hitchhiking.

KEEPING IN TOUCH

PHONE CODES	**Country code:** 48. **International dialing prefix:** 00. For more information on how to place international calls, see inside back cover.

EMAIL AND THE INTERNET. Some **Telekomunikacja Polska** offices offer Internet. Most mid-sized towns have at least one Internet cafe and larger cities have several. Prices range 2-5zł per hour.

TELEPHONE. Pay phones take phone cards, sold at post offices, Telekomunikacja Polska offices, and kiosks. Before using a card, break off its perforated corner. To make a **collect call,** hand the clerk the name of the city or country and the number plus "*Rozmowa 'R'.*" International access codes include: **AT&T Direct** (☎800 111 11 11); **Canada Direct** (☎800 111 41 18); **MCI WorldPhone** (☎800 111 21 22).

MAIL. The Polish take pride in their postal system, *Poczta Polska.* In many cities, the main post office has its own marching band. Airmail *(lotnicza)* takes two to five days to Western Europe and seven to 10 days to Australia, New Zealand, and the US. Mail can be received via **Poste Restante.** Address the envelope thus: First Name LAST NAME, POSTE RESTANTE, post office address, Postal Code city, POLAND. Letters cost about 2.20zł. Bring your passport to pick up *Poste Restante* or pay a 1.10zł fee.

LANGUAGE. Polish is a West Slavic language written in the Latin alphabet, and is closely related to Czech and Slovak. The language varies little across the country (see **Phrasebook: Polish,** p. 1060). The two exceptions are in the Kaszuby region, whose Germanized dialect is sometimes classified as another language, and in Karpaty, where the highlander accent is thick. In western Poland, German is the most common foreign language, though many Poles in big cities speak English. Most can understand other Slavic languages if they're spoken slowly. The older generation may speak Russian. Note: the English word "no" means "yes" in Polish.

ACCOMMODATIONS AND CAMPING

POLAND	❶	❷	❸	❹	❺
ACCOMMODATIONS	under 45zł	45-65zł	65-80zł	80-120zł	over 120zł

Hostels *(schroniska młodzieżowe)* abound and cost 15-40zł. They are often booked solid by tour groups; call ahead. **PTSM** is the national hostel organization. **Dom Wycieczkowy** and **Dom Turystyczny** hostels, both geared toward adults, cost around 50zł. **University dorms** open to travelers in July and August, and are an especially good option in Kraków. The **Almatur** office in Warsaw arranges stays throughout Poland. PTTK runs several **hotels** called **Dom Turysty**, which have multi-bed rooms and budget singles and doubles. Hotels generally cost 80-180zł. **Pensions** are often the best deal; the owner's service more than makes up for the small sacrifice in privacy. **Private rooms** *(wolne pokoje)* are common; be sure to establish the terms beforehand. Find rooms at the tourist office. Private rooms should cost 20-60zł. **Campsites** average 10-15zł per person, 20zł with a car. Campgrounds may rent **bungalows;** a bed costs 20-30zł. *Polska Mapa Campingów*, available at tourist offices, lists campsites. Almatur runs a number of sites in summer; ask them for a list. Camp only in designated campsites or risk a night in jail.

POLAND

FOOD AND DRINK

POLAND	❶	❷	❸	❹	❺
FOOD	under 8zł	8-18zł	18-30zł	30-45zł	over 45zł

Polish cuisine blends French, Italian, and Slavic traditions. Meals begin with soup, usually *barszcz* (beet or rye), *chłodnik* (cold beets with buttermilk and eggs), *ogórkowa* (sour cucumbers with yogurt), *kapuśniak* (cabbage), or *rosól* (chicken). Main courses include *gołąbki* (cabbage rolls with meat and rice), *kotlet schabowy* (pork cutlet), *naleśniki* (crepes filled with cheese or jam), and *pierogi* (dumplings). Finding vegetarian food is feasible if you stick to dumplings and crepes, but kosher eating is very difficult; you'll eat lots of pizza. Poland bathes in beer, vodka, and spiced liquor. *Żywiec* is the most popular beer. Even those who dislike beer will enjoy sweet **piwo z sokiem,** beer with raspberry syrup. *Wyborowa*, *Żytnia*, and *Polonez* are popular vodka *(wódka)* brands while *Belweder* (Belvedere) is Poland's main alcoholic export. *Żubrówka* vodka comes with a blade of grass from Woliński, where bison roam. It's often mixed with apple juice *(z sokem jabłkowym)*. *Miód* and *krupnik* (mead) are beloved by the gentry; grandmas make *nalewka na porzeczce* (black currant vodka).

HOLIDAYS AND FESTIVALS

Holidays: New Year's Day (Jan. 1); Easter (Apr. 8); May Day (May 1); Constitution Day (May 3); Corpus Christi (June 15); Assumption Day (Aug. 15); All Saints' Day (Nov. 1); Independence Day (Nov. 11); Christmas (Dec. 25-26).

Festivals: Festivals are tied to Catholic holidays, though folk tradition adds variety. Businesses close on Corpus Christi (June 15) and Assumption Day (Aug. 15), which are not as widely observed elsewhere in Europe.

BEYOND TOURISM

Auschwitz Jewish Center, 36 West 44th St., Ste. 310, New York, NY, 10036, USA (☎212-575-1050; www.ajcf.org). Offers fully paid 2- or 8-week programs for college students and recent graduates, focusing on cultural exchange and pre-war Jewish life in Poland, with visits to the Auschwitz-Birkenau State Museum and other sites.

Jagiellonian University, Centre for European Studies, ul. Garbarska 7a, 31-131 Kraków, POL (☎12 431 1575; www.ces.uj.edu.pl). University founded in 1364 offers undergraduates summer and semester programs in Central European studies and Polish language. Semester tuition €3500. Scholarships available.

WorldTeach, 79 JFK St., Cambridge, MA, 02138, USA (☎800-483-2240; www.worldteach.org). Arranges work teaching English in high schools, and homestays with families in Poland. US$3990.

WARSAW (WARSZAWA) ☎022

After rebuilding itself from the near-total destruction of WWII and weathering a half-century of Communist rule, Warsaw (pop. 1.7 million) has sprung to life as a dynamic center of business, politics, and culture. With Poland's recent entrance into the EU, the pace is even faster in this youthful, underrated capital city. At first glance, Warsaw offers two varieties of architecture: impeccably restored historical facades and Soviet-era concrete blocks. However, from cutting-edge art installations in a rebuilt castle to the sobering stillness of the Jewish Cemetery, the city holds out its most compelling sights for those who get to know it better.

TRANSPORTATION

Flights: Port Lotniczy Warszawa-Okęcie (Terminal 1), ul. Żwirki i Wigury (☎650 17 50). Take bus #175 (after 10:40pm bus #611) for a 20min. ride to the city center (35zł). Tickets are sold at the Ruch kiosk in the departure hall. Open M-F 5:30am-10:30pm.

Trains: Warszawa Centralna, al. Jerozolimskie 54 (☎94 36; www.intercity.pkp.pl), is the most convenient of Warsaw's 3 major train stations. The **IT office** provides schedules. Yellow signs list departures *(odjazdy);* white signs list arrivals *(przyjazdy).* English is rarely understood; write down when and where you want to go, then ask *"Który peron?"* ("Which platform?"). Prices listed are for IC (intercity) trains and *normale* (2nd class) fares. To: **Berlin, GER** (6hr., 7 per day, 159zł); **Budapest, HUN** (10-13hr., 1 per day, 298zł); **Gdańsk** (3hr., 12 per day, 82-90zł); **Kraków** (2½-5hr., 29 per day, 81-90zł); **Łódź** (1½-2hr., 17 per day, 25-45zł); **Lublin** (2½hr., 17 per day, 32-48zł); **Poznań** (2½-3hr., 21 per day, 81-89zł); **Prague, CZR** (9-12hr., 2 per day, 238zł); **St. Petersburg, RUS** (25-30hr., 1 per day, 280zł); **Toruń** (2½-5hr., 5 per day, 38zł); **Wrocław** (4½-6hr., 12 per day, 47-96zł).

Buses: Many buses arrive at **Warszawa Zachodnia,** west of the city center.

Polski Express, al. Jana Pawła II (☎844 55 55; www.polskiexpress.pl), next to Warszawa Centralna. To: **Gdańsk** (6hr., 2 per day, 47zł); **Kraków** (8hr., 1 per day, 62zł); **Łódź** (2½hr., 7 per day, 28zł); **Lublin** (3hr., 7 per day, 27zł); **Toruń** (4hr., 15 per day, 41zł). Open daily 6:30am-9pm.

PKS Warszawa Zachodnia, al. Jerozolimskie 144 (☎822 48 11, international info 823 55 70; www.pks.warszawa.pl), Zachodnia station. Take bus #127, 130, 508, 517, 523, 605, or E5 to the center. To: **Gdańsk** (7hr., 14 per day, 50zł); **Kraków** (6hr., 12 per day, 38zł); **Kyiv, UKR** (14½hr., 1 per day, 155zł); **Lublin** (3hr., 5 per day, 22zł); **Toruń** (4½hr., 17 per day, 39zł); **Vilnius, LIT** (9½hr., 2 per day, 135zł); **Wrocław** (9½hr., 17 per day, 32zł). Open daily 6am-9:30pm.

Centrum Podróży AURA, al. Jerozolimskie 144 (☎659 47 85; www.aura.pl), Zachodnia station. To: **Amsterdam, NTH** (23hr., 2 per day, 250-270zł); **Geneva, SWI** (27hr., 2 per day, 270-350zł); **London, BRI** (27hr., 3 per day, 250-340zł); **Minsk, BLR** (service can be irregular; 13hr., 2 per week, 80-86zł); **Paris, FRA** (25hr., 2 per day, 220-240zł); **Prague, CZR** (11½hr.; 3 per wk., M, W, F; 115zł); **Rome, ITA** (28hr., 1 per day, 332-350zł). Open M-F 9am-5pm, Sa 9am-2pm.

Public Transportation: (Info ☎0300 300 130, mobiles 720 83 83; www.ztm.waw.pl.) **Trams, buses,** and the **metro** run 4:30am-midnight. Fare 2.40zł; day pass 7.20zł; 1-week pass 24zł. Punch the ticket in the machines onboard or face a 120zł fine. Tickets purchased from drivers cost 0.60zł extra. Warsaw's 1 metro line runs north-south through the center. There are 2 **sightseeing bus** routes: #180 (M-F) and 100 (Sa-Su).

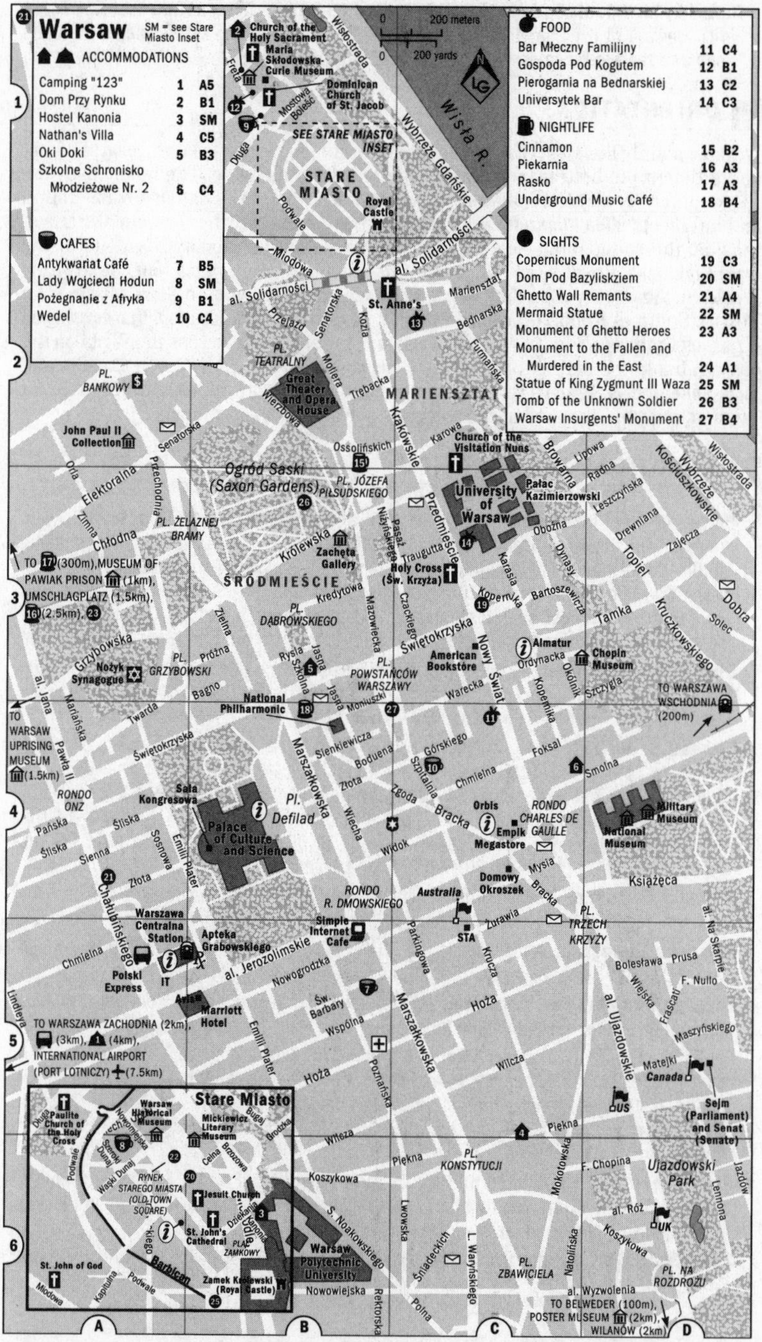
Warsaw
SM = see Stare Miasto Inset
ACCOMMODATIONS
Camping "123" 1 A5
Dom Przy Rynku 2 B1
Hostel Kanonia 3 SM
Nathan's Villa 4 C5
Oki Doki 5 B3
Szkolne Schronisko Młodzieżowe Nr. 2 6 C4
CAFES
Antykwariat Café 7 B5
Lady Wojciech Hodun 8 SM
Pożegnanie z Afryka 9 B1
Wedel 10 C4
FOOD
Bar Mleczny Familijny 11 C4
Gospoda Pod Kogutem 12 B1
Pierogarnia na Bednarskiej 13 C2
Universytek Bar 14 C3
NIGHTLIFE
Cinnamon 15 B2
Piekarnia 16 A3
Rasko 17 A3
Underground Music Café 18 B4
SIGHTS
Copernicus Monument 19 C3
Dom Pod Bazyliszkiem 20 SM
Ghetto Wall Remants 21 A4
Mermaid Statue 22 SM
Monument of Ghetto Heroes 23 A3
Monument to the Fallen and Murdered in the East 24 A1
Statue of King Zygmunt III Waza 25 SM
Tomb of the Unknown Soldier 26 B3
Warsaw Insurgents' Monument 27 B4
0 200 meters
0 200 yards
Church of the Holy Sacrament
Maria Skłodowska-Curie Museum
Dominican Church of St. Jacob
SEE STARE MIASTO INSET
STARE MIASTO
Royal Castle
Wisła R.
Wybrzeże Gdańskie
al. Solidarności
St. Anne's
MARIENSZTAT
PL. TEATRALNY
Great Theater and Opera House
PL. BANKOWY
John Paul II Collection
Church of the Visitation Nuns
University of Warsaw
Pałac Kazimierzowski
Ogród Saski (Saxon Gardens)
PL. JÓZEFA PIŁSUDSKIEGO
PL. ŻELAZNEJ BRAMY
Zachęta Gallery
Holy Cross (Św. Krzyża)
ŚRÓDMIEŚCIE
TO 17 (300m), MUSEUM OF PAWIAK PRISON (1km), UMSCHLAGPLATZ (1.5km), 16 (2.5km), 23
PL. DĄBROWSKIEGO
Almatur
Chopin Museum
American Bookstore
Nożyk Synagogue
PL. GRZYBOWSKI
PL. POWSTAŃCÓW WARSZAWY
National Philharmonic
TO WARSZAWA WSCHODNIA (200m)
TO WARSAW UPRISING MUSEUM (1.5km)
RONDO ONZ
Sala Kongresowa
Palace of Culture and Science
Pl. Defilad
Orbis
Empik Megastore
RONDO CHARLES DE GAULLE
Military Museum
National Museum
Domowy Okroszek
RONDO R. DMOWSKIEGO
Australia
STA
PL. TRZECH KRZYŻY
Warszawa Centralna Station
Apteka Grabowskiego
Simple Internet Cafe
Polski Express
IT
Avis
Marriott Hotel
TO WARSZAWA ZACHODNIA (2km), (3km), (4km), INTERNATIONAL AIRPORT (PORT LOTNICZY) (7.5km)
Canada
Sejm (Parliament) and Senat (Senate)
US
PL. KONSTYTUCJI
Ujazdowski Park
UK
PL. ZBAWICIELA
PL. NA ROZDROŻU
Warsaw Polytechnic University
TO BELWEDER (100m), POSTER MUSEUM (2km), WILANÓW (2km)
Stare Miasto
Paulite Church of the Holy Cross
Warsaw Historical Museum
Mickiewicz Literary Museum
RYNEK STAREGO MIASTA (OLD TOWN SQUARE)
Jesuit Church
St. John's Cathedral
PLAC ZAMKOWY
St. John of God
Barbican
Zamek Królewski (Royal Castle)
1 2 3 4 5 6
A B C D

Taxis: Try **MPT Radio Taxi** (☎91 91), **Merc Taxi** (☎677 77 77), or **Sawa Taxi** (☎644 44 44). Beware of overcharging. State-run cabs, such as those listed, display a mermaid logo and tend to be safer. 5-6zł base fare, 1.80-3zł per km.

ORIENTATION

Warsaw mainly lies west of the **Wisła River.** Although the city is large, its grid layout and efficient public transportation make it easy to navigate. The main east-west thoroughfare is **aleja Jerozolimskie,** which passes **Warszawa Centralna** train station and intersects **ulica Marszałkowska,** a major tram route. Farther east on al. Jerozolimskie, the roundabout **Rondo Charles de Gaulle** marks the southern end of the **Trakt Królewski** (Royal Way), which runs north and becomes **ulica Nowy Świat** (New World St.) and then **ulica Krakówskie Przedmieście** as it leads to **Stare Miasto** (Old Town). South of Rondo Charles de Gaulle, the street becomes **aleja Ujazdowskie** as it passes Embassy Row, several palaces, and **Łazienki Park.** Across the Wisła on the eastern bank, the district of **Praga** is accessible by tram via al. Jerozolimskie and **aleja Solidarności.** Praga's two most trafficked north-south thoroughfares are **ulica Targowa,** near the zoo, and **ulica Francuska,** south of al. Jerozolimskie.

PRACTICAL INFORMATION

Tourist Offices: Informacji Turystyczna (IT), al. Jerozolimskie 54 (☎94 31; www.warsawtour.pl), inside Warszawa Centralna train station. Informative, English-speaking staff. Arranges accommodations for no charge and provides maps (free-4zł). The free *Warsaw In Short* lists restaurants and events. Open daily May-Sept. 8am-8pm; Oct.-Apr. 8am-6pm. **Branches:** al. Jerozolimskie 144, at Zachodnia station. Open daily 9am-6pm. In the airport, open daily May-Sept. 8am-8pm; Oct.-Apr. 8am-6pm.

Budget Travel: Almatur, ul. Kopernika 23 (☎826 26 39). ISIC discount. Open M-F 9am-7pm, Sa 10am-3pm. AmEx/MC/V. **Orbis,** ul. Bracka 16 (☎827 71 40), entrance on al. Jerozolimskie. Open M-F 8am-6pm, Sa 9am-3pm. MC/V.

Embassies: Australia, ul. Nowogrodzka 11 (☎521 34 44; ambasada@australia.pl). Open M-F 9am-1pm and 2-5pm. **Canada,** al. Matejki 1/5 (☎584 31 00; wsaw@international.gc.ca). Open M-F 8:30am-4:30pm. **Ireland,** ul. Mysia 5 (☎849 66 33; ambasada@irlandia.pl). Open M-F 9am-1pm and 2-5pm. **UK,** al. Róż (☎311 00 00; www.britishembassy.pl). Open M-F 8:30am-12:30pm and 1:30-4:30pm. **US,** al. Ujazdowskie 29/31 (☎504 20 00; http://poland.usembassy.gov). Open M-F 8:30am-5pm.

Currency Exchange: Except at tourist sights, *kantory* have the best rates. Rates may be higher at night. 24hr. currency exchange at Warszawa Centralna and al. Jerozolimskie 61.

American Express: al. Jerozolimskie 65/79 (☎ 630 69 52). Offers **Western Union** services. Open M-F 9am-8pm, Sa 10am-6pm.

Luggage Storage (Kasa Bagażowa): At Warszawa Centralna. 5zł per item per day, plus 2.25zł per 50zł of declared value for optional insurance. Lockers available. Open 24hr.

English-Language Bookstore: American Bookstore (Księgarnia Amerykańska), ul. Nowy Świat 61 (☎827 48 52; american@americanbookstore.pl). Good but pricey selection of fiction, history, and maps. Open M-Sa 10am-7pm, Su 10am-6pm. AmEx/MC/V. **Empik Megastore,** ul. Nowy Świat 15-17 (☎627 06 50). Great selection of maps. Open M-Sa 9am-10pm, Su 11am-7pm.

GLBT Resources: Lambda (☎628 52 22; www.lambda.org.pl), in English and Polish. Open M-Sa 9am-6pm. Also try http://warsaw.gayguide.net. The GLBT scene in Warsaw is generally discreet and lacks widespread political support.

24hr. Pharmacy: Apteka Grabowskiego "21" (☎825 69 86), 3rd level of Warszawa Centralna. AmEx/MC/V.

Hospitals: Centrum Medyczyne LIM, al. Jerozolimskie 65/79, 9th fl. (24hr. emergency line ☎458 70 00, 24hr. ambulance 430 30 30; www.cm-lim.pl), in the Marriott. English-speaking doctors. Open M-F 7am-9pm, Sa 8am-8pm, Su 9am-1pm. **Branch** at ul. Domaniewski 41 (☎458 70 00). Open M-F 7am-9pm, Sa 8am-8pm. **Central Emergency Station,** ul. Hoża 56 (☎999), also has a 24hr. ambulance.

Telephones: Phones are at the post office and train station and are scattered throughout the city. All require cards, available at the post office and at many kiosks. Ask for a *karta telefoniczna.* Directory assistance ☎118 913.

Internet Access: Simple Internet Cafe, ul. Marszałkowska 99/101 (☎628 31 90), at the corner of al. Jerozolimskie and ul. Marszałkowska, is the largest and most orange Internet cafe in Warsaw, with low rates and an English-speaking staff. Rates vary from 1zł per hr. late at night to 4zł per hr. midday. Open 24hr. Several 24hr. Internet cafes also line Warszawa Centralna.

Post Office: Main branch, ul. Świętokrzyska 31/33 (☎827 00 52). Take a number at the entrance. For stamps and letters push "D"; for packages push "F." For *Poste Restante,* inquire at window #41. Open 24hr. *Kantor* open daily 7am-10pm. Most other branches open 8am-8pm. **Postal Code:** 00 001.

POLAND

ACCOMMODATIONS

Although accommodation options are rapidly improving, demand still outpaces supply, so reserve ahead, especially in the summer. **Informacji Turystyczna** (IT; p. 778) maintains a list of accommodations in the city, including private rooms, and also arranges stays in **university dorms** (25-30zł) from July through September.

Oki Doki, pl. Dąbrowskiego 3 (☎826 51 12; www.okidoki.pl). From the city center, take any tram north on Marszałkowska to Świętokrzyska. Walk 1 block north and turn right on Rysia. In the heart of town bordering a quiet park, this hostel gets high marks for its spirited atmosphere, themed rooms, and enthusiastic English-speaking staff. Bike rental 26zł per day, 6zł per hr. Breakfast 10zł. Laundry 10zł. Free Internet. Reception 24hr. Check-in 3pm. Check-out 11am. Dorms 45-60zł; singles 120zł; doubles 140zł, with bath 185zł. Reduced rates Sept.-Apr. MC/V. ❷

Nathan's Villa, ul. Piękna 24/26 (☎622 29 46; www.nathansvilla.com). From Płac Konstytucji, south of the city center, go east on ul. Piękna. Bright dorms, restrooms that could pass for Ikea showcases, and a party-friendly crowd. English-speaking staff eagerly dispenses advice. Breakfast and laundry included. Free Internet 30min. per day. Reception 24hr. Reserve ahead. Cots rented to the truly desperate when beds fill up. Dorms 45-60zł; private rooms 130-170zł. MC/V. ❷

Szkolne Schronisko Młodzieżowe Nr 2, ul. Smolna 30 (☎827 89 52). From the center, take any tram east on al. Jerozolimskie and get off at Rondo Charles de Gaulle. Smolna is off ul. Nowy Świat; the hostel is 2 blocks up. Just off one of Warsaw's busiest streets, this quiet, air-conditioned hostel has clean dorms and small, well-kept rooms. Lockout is not conducive to partying. Linens 5zł. Reception 24hr. Lockout 10am-4pm and midnight-6am. Dorms 36zł; singles 65zł. HI discount 3.60zł. Cash only. ❶

Dom Przy Rynku, Rynek Nowego Miasta 4 (☎/fax 831 50 33; www.cityhostel.net). Take bus #175 from the center to Franciszkańska. Turn right, then right again into the Rynek; the hostel is downhill on the left. In summer, this school for disadvantaged children offers budget accommodations. Reception 24hr. Open July-Aug. daily; Sept.-June F-Su. Dorms 55zł. Cash only. ❷

Hostel Kanonia, ul. Jezuicka 2 (☎635 06 76; www.kanonia.pl). Tucked into an alley right in the thick of Stare Miasto, this hostel's cheery yellow paint softens the no-frills, spartan rooms. Free Internet. Check-in noon. Check-out 10am. Dorms 40-50zł; doubles 120-140zł. ISIC discount. ❶

MILKING IT FOR ALL IT'S WORTH

t's been nearly 20 years since he fall of the Iron Curtain, and Poland has embraced capitalism vhole-heartedly, trading in can-eens for Chinese take-out and neal rations for McDonalds. Still, even though fast-food chains and street-side kebab stands maintain brisk business, truly budget-avvy Poles searching for a meal-on-the-go make their way to the ocal Bar Mleczny, or milk bar, for a quick and nutritious bite.

One of the only vestiges of Communism still looked upon ondly in Poland, the bare, cafete-ia-style milk bars sell heaping plates of traditional Polish fare for a pittance. Milk bars were estab-ished in the 60s by Polish Com-nunist officials seeking to provide a cheap dining option for workers n offices without government-run canteens. They earned their name because of the prevalence of dairy products during the era of neat rations.

Milk bars have since become government-subsidized entities, allowing them to continue serving satisfying and tasty food at bar-gain prices. Soups, *pierogi*, cut-ets, and omelettes cost just a raction of the price that restau-ants charge, offering students, amilies, and budget travelers the chance to get a square meal for as little as 3-7zł.

With this combination of value and convenience, milk bars truly do a body good.

Camping 123, ul. Bitwy Warszawskiej 15/17 (☎/fax 822 91 21). By Warszawa Zachodnia station. Take bus #508, 127, 130, or 517 to Zachodnia, cross al. Jerozolimskie, walk right to the roundabout, and turn left on Bitwy Warszawskiej. Open May-Sept. Singles 80zł; doubles 130zł; triples 135zł; quads 171zł. Tent sites 10zł, plus 10zł per person and per vehicle. Cash only. ❷

FOOD

At roadside stands across the city, the food of choice is the *kebab turecki*, a pita with spicy meat, cabbage, and pickles (5-10zł). The stand **Kebab Bar,** ul. Nowy Świat 31, serves up an excellent version. **MarcPol,** on ul. Marszałkowska, is a 24hr. grocery store.

RESTAURANTS

Bar Mleczny Familijny, ul. Nowy Świat 39. Dine along swanky ul. Nowy Świat without breaking the piggy bank at this popular milk bar. Polish dishes 2-10zł. Open M-F 7am-8pm, Sa-Su 9am-5pm. ❶

Pierogarnia na Bednarskie, ul. Bednarska 28/30 (☎828 03 92), on a side street west of ul. Krakówskie Przedmieście. Locals get their pierogi fix at this tiny, pleasant, and deliciously fragrant shop. Pierogi 6-12zł. Open daily 11am-9pm. ❶

Gospoda Pod Kogutem, ul. Freta 48 (☎635 82 82). Authentic local food. Beer 6zł. Entrees 15-40zł. Open M noon-midnight, Tu-Su 11am-midnight. MC/V. ❸

Bar Vega, ul. Jana Pawła II 36C (☎654 41 11). Branch at ul. Nowy Świat 52. Tasty vegetarian and vegan Indian dishes, including *pakora* (deep-fried vegetables) and *kofta* (cabbage patty). Proceeds go to feed the hungry children of Warsaw. Small plate 8zł; large 11zł. Open daily 11am-8pm. Cash only. ❷

Universytecki Bar, ul. Krakówskie Przedmiescie 20/22 (☎826 07 93), near the university, is a favorite among students. The simple interior and long lines set the tone for traditional dishes such as soups, pierogi, and cutlets for as little as 5zł. Open M-F 7am-8pm, Sa-Su 9am-5pm. Cash only. ❶

CAFES

Pożegnanie z Afryka, ul. Freta 4/6 (☎602 356 287), ul. Ostrobranmska 75C, and ul. Dobra 56/66. Coffee and iced coffee (11-15zł), with a wide selection of exotic blends. The decor evokes an African safari. Open M-Th 10am-9pm, F-Su 10am-10pm.

Lody Wojciech Hoduń, ul. Nowomiejka 7/9 (☎635 73 46). This ice cream shop in Stare Miasto serves up 24 heavenly flavors in crisped-to-perfection waffle cones. Worth the inevitable wait. Ice cream 1.50zł per scoop. Open daily 10am-9pm.

Wedel, ul. Szpitalnia 17 (☎827 29 16). Enjoy extraordinary hot chocolate (8zł), stained glass, rich mahogany, doilies, and the suspicion that you've traveled back in time to pre-war Warsaw. Open M-Sa 8am-10pm, Su 11am-8pm. AmEx/MC/V.

Antykwariat Cafe, ul. Źurawia 45 (☎629 99 29). Head south on ul. Marszałkowska and turn right on ul. Źurawia. Lounge in plush chairs amid the book-lined walls of this old-fashioned cafe. Coffee 5-17zł. Open M-F 1-11pm, Sa-Su 4-11pm. Cash only.

SIGHTS

The **sightseeing bus** routes #100 and 180 conveniently hit most major attractions. They begin at pl. Zamkowy in Stare Miasto and run along pl. Teatralny, ul. Marszałkowska, al. Ujazdowskie, Łazienki Park, back up the Trakt Królewski, and then loop through Praga before returning to pl. Zamkowy.

STARE MIASTO. Warsaw's postwar reconstruction shows its finest face in Stare Miasto (Old Town), which features narrow cobblestoned streets and colorful facades. *(Take bus #175 or E3 from the city center to Miodowa.)* The landmark **Statue of King Zygmunt III Waza,** constructed in 1644 to honor the king who moved the capital from Kraków to Warsaw, towers over the entrance to Stare Miasto. To the right stands the impressive **Royal Castle** (Zamek Królewski), the royal residence from the 17th through 19th centuries. When the Nazis plundered and burned the castle in September 1939, many Varsovians risked their lives hiding priceless works, hoping they might one day be returned. Today, these rescued treasures are housed in the **Royal Castle Museum,** which has paintings, artifacts, and the stunning Royal Apartments. *(pl. Zamkowy 4. ☎657 21 70. Tickets and guides inside the courtyard. Open Su-M 11am-6pm, Tu-Sa 10am-6pm. 18zł, students 10zł. Free highlights tour Su 11am-6pm. English-language tour M-Sa, 70zł per group. MC/V.)* Across ul. Świętojańska sits Warsaw's oldest church, **St. John's Cathedral** (Katedra św. Jana), which was destroyed in the 1944 uprising but rebuilt after the war. *(Open daily 10am-1pm and 3-5:30pm. Entrance to crypts 1zł.)*

Ul. Świętojańska leads to the restored Renaissance and Baroque **Rynek Starego Miasta** (Old Town Sq.); the statue of the **Warsaw Mermaid** (Warszawa Syrenka) marks the center. According to legend, a greedy merchant kidnapped the mermaid from the Wisła River, but local fishermen rescued her. In return, she swore to defend the city, and now protects it with a shield and raised sword. Ul. Krzywe Koło runs from the northeast corner of the Rynek to the restored **Barbican** *(barbakan)*, a rare example of 16th-century Polish fortification and a popular spot to relax. The Barbican opens onto ul. Freta, the edge of **Nowe Miasto** (New Town). Nobel Prize-winning physicist and chemist **Marie Curie** was born at ul. Freta 16, and the house is now a museum. *(Open Tu-Sa 10am-4pm, Su 10am-2pm. 6zł, students 3zł. Th free.)*

TRAKT KRÓLEWSKI. The Trakt Królewski begins at the entrance to Stare Miasto on pl. Zamkowy and stretches 4km south in the direction of Kraków, the former capital. On the left after pl. Zamkowy, the 15th-century **St. Anne's Church** (Kościół św. Anny) features a striking gilded altar. *(Open daily 7:30-8am and 3:30-7pm.)* Frederick Chopin grew up near ul. Krakówskie Przedmieście and gave his first public concert in **Pałac Radziwiłłów,** ul. Krakówskie Przedmieście 46/48. Guarded by four stone lions, the building is now **Pałac Namiestnikowski,** the Polish presidential mansion. A block down the road and set back from the street behind a grove of trees, the **Church of the Visitation Nuns** (Kościół Wizytówek) once resounded with Chopin's Romantic chords. *(Open daily dawn-1pm and 3pm-dusk.)* The composer died abroad at the age of 39 and was buried in Paris, but his heart belongs to Poland; it now rests in an urn in **Holy Cross Church.** *(Kościół św. Krzyża. ul. Krakówskie Przedmiescie 3. Open daily 9:30am-4:30pm.)* More Chopin relics are displayed at the **Frederick Chopin Museum** (Muzeum Fryderyka Chopina), which has a collection of original letters, scores, paintings, and keepsakes, including the composer's last piano and a section of his first *polonaise*, penned when he was seven years old. *(ul. Okólnik 1, in Ostrogski Castle. Enter from ul. Tamka. ☎826 59 35; www.chopin.pl. Open Tu-Su 10am-6pm. 10zł, students 5zł. Audio tour 4zł. Concerts 30zł, students 15zł. Cash only.)*

The Royal Way continues down fashionable **ulica Nowy Świat.** Turn left at Rondo Charles de Gaulle to reach Poland's largest museum, the **National Museum** (Muzeum Narodowe), which holds 16th- to 20th-century paintings and ancient statues. *(al. Jerozolimskie 3. ☎629 30 93, English-language tours 629 50 60; www.mnw.art.pl. Open M-W and F-Su 10am-4pm, Th 10am-4pm. Permanent exhibits 12zł, students 7zł. Special exhibits 17zł/10zł. Free Sa. AmEx/MC/V.)* Farther down, the Royal Way turns into al. Ujazdowskie and runs alongside **Łazienki Park.** The park houses the striking Neoclassical **Palace on Water** (Pałac na Wodzie or Pałac na Wyspie); the grounds are a popular place for family picnics. Buildings in the park feature rotating art exhibits. *(Take bus #116, 180, or 195 from ul. Nowy Świat or #119 from the city center to Bagatela. Park open daily dawn-dusk. Palace open Tu-Su 9am-3:30pm. 12zł, students 9zł.)* Just north of the park, off ul. Agrykola, the **Center for Contemporary Art** (Centrum Sztuki Współczesnej), al. Ujazdowskie 6, hosts installations in the reconstructed 17th-century Ujazdowskie Castle. *(Open Tu-Th and Sa-Su 11am-5pm, F 11am-9pm. 10zł, students 5zł. Cash only.)*

POLAND

FORMER GHETTO AND SYNAGOGUE. Muranów, the former ghetto, is the walled neighborhood north of the city center. It holds few traces of the nearly 400,000 Jews who made up one-third of Warsaw's population before WWII. The **Umschlagplatz,** at the corner of ul. Dzika and ul. Stawki, was the railway platform where the Nazis gathered 300,000 Jews for transport to death camps. *(Take tram #35 from ul. Marszałkowska to Dzika.)* With the Umschlagpl. monument to your left, continue down ul. Stawki and turn right on ul. DuBois, which becomes ul. Zamenhofa. Along the road, a stone monument marks the location of the command bunker of the Warsaw Ghetto Uprising, the Jewish armed resistance to the Nazis in 1943. In the park to the right, the **Monument of the Ghetto Heroes** (Pomnik Bohaterów) honors the uprising's leaders. Continue along ul. Zamenhofa for two blocks and take a right on ul. Dzielna. On the corner of ul. Dzielna and al. Jana Pawła II, the **Museum of Pawiak Prison** (Muzeum Więzienia Pawiaka) exhibits the artwork and poetry of former prisoners. Over 100,000 Polish Jews were imprisoned here from 1939 to 1944; 37,000 were executed and 60,000 were moved to concentration camps. *(ul. Dzielna 24/26. ☎831 92 89. Open Su-Tu, Th, and Sa 10am-4pm, W and F 9am-5pm. Donation requested.)* Follow al. Jana Pawła II, take a left on ul. Anielewicza, and continue five blocks to reach the **Jewish Cemetery** (Cmentarz Żydowski), in the western corner of Muranów. The thickly wooded cemetery is the resting place of 250,000 Polish Jews. *(Tram #22 from the center to Cm. Żydowski. ☎827 83 72; www.jewishcem.waw.pl. Open Apr.-Oct. M-Th 10am-5pm, F 9am-1pm, Su 9am-4pm; Nov.-Mar. closes at dusk. Closed Jewish holidays. 4zł.)* The beautifully reconstructed **Nożyk Synagogue** (Synagoga Nożyka) is the only synagogue in Warsaw to survive the war, and now serves as the spiritual home for the few hundred observant Jews remaining in the city. *(ul. Twarda 6. From the center, take any tram along al. Jana Pawła II to Rondo Onz. Turn right on ul. Twarda and left at the Teatr Żydowski, the Jewish Theater. ☎320 70 25. Open Su-F Apr.-Oct. 10am-5pm, Nov.-Feb. 10am-3pm. Closed Jewish holidays. Morning and evening prayer daily. 5zł.)*

ELSEWHERE IN WARSAW. Warsaw's commercial district, southwest of Stare Miasto, is dominated by the 70-story Stalinist **Palace of Culture and Science** (Pałac Kultury i Nauki) on ul. Marszałkowska, which contains shops and offices. Locals claim the view from the top is the best in Warsaw—partly because you can't see the building itself. *(☎656 76 00. Open daily 9am-6pm. Observation deck on 33rd fl. 20zł, students15zł.)* Farther north, adjacent to the **Saxon Garden** (Ogród Saski), the **John Paul II Collection** has works by Dalí, van Gogh, Goya, Rembrandt, and Renoir. *(pl. Bankowy 1. ☎620 27 25. Open Tu-Su 10am-1pm. 11zł, students 5.50zł. Polish tour 1zł.)*

Though a bit far from the city center, the recently opened **Warsaw Uprising Museum** is a must-see attraction. Educational without being pedantic and somber without being heavy-handed, the museum recounts the tragic 1944 Uprising with full-scale replica bunkers and ruins haunted by the sound of approaching bombs. The excellent multimedia presentations have English-language subtitles. *(ul. Grzybowska 79, enter on ul. Przyokopowa. From the center, take tram #12, 20, or 22 to ul. Grzybowska; the museum is on the left. ☎626 95 06; www.1944.pl. Open M, W, F 8am-6pm, Th 8am-10pm, Sa-Su 10am-6pm. 4zł, students 2zł. Su free. Cash only.)*

PRAGA. Across the Wisła River from central Warsaw, the formerly run-down district of Praga is undergoing a renaissance, though visitors should still exercise caution, especially after dark. In the Stadion Dziesięciolecia, the **Russian Market** offers great deals on anything from sunglasses and baked goods to t-shirts with subversive Polish phrases. Keep a low profile and beware of pickpockets. *(Take any train from al. Jerozolimskie going east, and get off at the 1st stop over the river. The market is across the street on the left. Open daily dawn-dusk.)* The onion domes of the **St. Mary Magdalene Cathedral** hint at the pre-Soviet Russian presence in Warsaw. *(al. Solidarnosci 52. From the Russian Market, take tram #2, 8, 12, or 25 to the intersection of Targowa and al. Solidarnosci; the church is across the street on the left. ☎619 84 67. Open Su-M 1-4pm, Tu-Sa 11am-3pm. Donation requested.)* **Skaryszewski Park,** the most serene of Praga's attractions, contains sculptures by early 20th-century Polish artists and a lovely network of willow-lined ponds and streams. *(East of al. Zieleniecka. Free.)*

POLAND

WILANÓW. In 1677, King Jan III Sobieski bought the sleepy village of Milanowo, rebuilt the existing mansion into a Baroque palace, and named the new residence Villa Nova (Wilanów). Since 1805, **Pałac Wilanowski,** south of the city center, has served as a public museum and a residence for the highest-ranking guests of the Polish state. Surrounded by elegant gardens, the palace is filled with frescoed rooms, portraits, and extravagant royal apartments. *(Take bus #180 from ul. Krakówskie Przedmiesce, #516 or 519 from ul. Marszałkowska south to Wilanów, or #116 or 180 south along the Trakt Królewski. From the bus stop, cross the highway and follow signs for the Pałac. ☎842 07 95; www.wilanow-palac.art.pl. Open mid-May to mid-Sept. M-F 9am-4pm; mid-Sept. to mid-May M and W 9am-6pm, Tu and Th 9am-4pm, Sa 10am-4pm, Su 9am-7pm. Last entrance 1½hr. before closing. Call ahead for English-language tour. Gardens open M and W-F 9:30am-dusk. Orangery open Su-M and W-F 9:30am-3:30pm. Wilanów 20zł, students 10zł; Th free. Gardens 4.50/2.50zł; Th free. Cash only.)*

ENTERTAINMENT AND NIGHTLIFE

Warsaw offers a variety of live music options, and free outdoor concerts abound in the summer. Classical music performances rarely sell out; standby tickets cost as little as 10zł. Inquire at the **Warsaw Music Society** (Warszawskie Towarzystwo Muzyczne), ul. Morskie Oko 2 (☎849 56 51). Take tram #4, 18, 19, 35, or 36 to Morskie Oko from ul. Marszałkowska. Nearby Łazienki Park has free Sunday performances at the **Chopin Monument** (Pomnik Chopina; concerts mid-May to Sept. Su noon, 4pm). **Jazz Klub Tygmont** (☎828 34 09; www.tygmont.com.pl), ul. Mazowiecka 6/8, hosts free concerts on weekday evenings. From July through September, the Old Market Sq. of Stare Miasto swings with free jazz nightly at 7pm.

Teatr Dramatyczny, in the Pałac Kultury, has a stage for big productions and a studio theater playing more avant-garde works. (☎656 68 65; www.teatrdramatyczny.pl. Tickets 18-40zł; standby tickets 11-17zł.) **Teatr Żydowski,** pl. Grzybowski 12/16 (☎620 62 81), is a Jewish theater with primarily Yiddish-language shows. **Kinoteka** (☎826 19 61), in the Pałac Kultury, shows Hollywood blockbusters in a Stalinist setting. **Kino Lab,** ul. Ujazdowskie 6 (☎628 12 71), features independent films. See **Center for Contemporary Art,** p. 781.

Warsaw is full of energy in the evenings. *Kawiarnie* (cafes) around Stare Miasto and ul. Nowy Świat are open late, and pubs attract crowds with live music. In the summer, outdoor beer gardens complement the pub scene. Several publications, including *Gazeta Wyborcza*, list gay nightlife.

Piekarnia, ul. Mlocinska 11 (☎636 49 79). The center of Warsaw's club scene has a packed dance floor and expert DJs. Cover 20-35zł. Open F-Sa 10pm-last customer.

Underground Music Cafe, ul. Marszałkowska 126/134 (☎826 70 48; www.under.pl), across from Oki Doki hostel. Popular 2-level dance club. Beer 5-9zł. Cover W and F 10zł, students 5zł; Sa 20/10zł; Th 10zł. Open M-Sa 1pm-5am, Su 4pm-5am.

Rasko, ul. Krochmalna 32A (☎890 02 99; www.rasko.pl). A staple of the underground GLBT scene, this secluded, bohemian club attracts a varied clientele. Daily drag shows. Friendly staff will direct you to other GLBT nightlife. Beer 7zł. Open daily 5pm-3am. DC/MC/V.

The Cinnamon, pl. Piłsudskiego 1 (☎323 76 00), is a bar with attitude, favored by the hottest locals and expats. Open daily 9am-last customer, sometimes until dawn. MC/V.

KRAKÓW ☎012

The regal architecture, rich cafe culture, and palpable sense of history in Kraków (KRAHK-oof; pop 758,000) have drawn kings, artists, and scholars for centuries, and now foreign visitors are beginning to discover the city as well. Unlike most areas of Poland, Kraków emerged from WWII and years of socialism relatively unscathed. The maze-like Old Town and the old Jewish quarter of Kazimierz contain scores of museums, galleries, cellar pubs, and clubs, with 130,000 students adding spirit to the nightlife. Still, the city's glamor can't completely hide the scars of the 20th century; the Auschwitz-Birkenau Nazi death camps that lie 70km away are a sobering reminder of the atrocities committed in the not-so-distant past.

TRANSPORTATION

Flights: Balice Airport (☎411 19 55; www.lotnisko-balice.pl), 10km west of the city center. Take northbound bus #192 (40min.) to Kraków Główny. Radtur (www.radtur.com) also runs a shuttle to the station (7zł). Taxis to downtown Kraków cost 50-60zł.

Trains: Kraków Główny, pl. Kolejowy 1 (☎624 54 39, info 624 15 35). Trains to: **Bratislava, SLK** (8hr., 1 per day, 269zł); **Budapest, HUN** (11hr., 1 per day, 218zł); **Gdańsk** (7-10hr., 12 per day, 66zł); **Kyiv, UKR** (22hr., 2 per day, 210zł); **Poznań** (6-8hr., 8 per day, 48zł); **Prague, CZR** (9hr., 1 per day, 173zł); **Vienna, AUT** (8½hr., 2 per day, 200zł); **Warsaw** (4½-5hr., 30 per day, 44zł); **Zakopane** (3-5hr., 17 per day, 18zł).

Buses: ul. Bosacka 18 (☎411 73 90), adjacent to the train station. Open 5am-11pm. Buses to: **Łódź** (6½hr., 2 per day, 40zł); **Warsaw** (6hr., 1 per day, 50zł); **Wrocław** (6½hr., 2 per day, 43zł); **Zakopane** (2hr., 78 per day, 13zł). The travel agency kiosk in the main hall (☎333 52 55) sells international tickets. Open M-F 8am-5:30pm, Sa 9am-2pm. To: **Vienna, AUT** (9hr.; 3 per week; 76-102zł, under 26 10% discount).

Public Transportation: Buy **bus** and **tram** tickets at *Ruch* kiosks (2.50zł) or from drivers (3zł) and punch them onboard. Large backpacks need their own tickets. Buses run 5am-11pm. Night buses from 11pm 5zł. Day pass 10.40zł.

Taxis: Reliable taxi companies include: **Barbakan Taxi** (☎96 61 or 0800 400 400); **Euro Taxi** (☎96 64); **Radio Taxi** (☎919 or 0800 500 919); **Wawel Taxi** (☎96 66). Base fare about 5zł, plus 2zł per km. It is cheaper to call a taxi than to hail one.

ORIENTATION AND PRACTICAL INFORMATION

The heart of the city is the huge **Rynek Główny** (Main Marketplace) in the center of **Stare Miasto** (Old Town). Stare Miasto is encircled by the **Planty Gardens** and, a bit

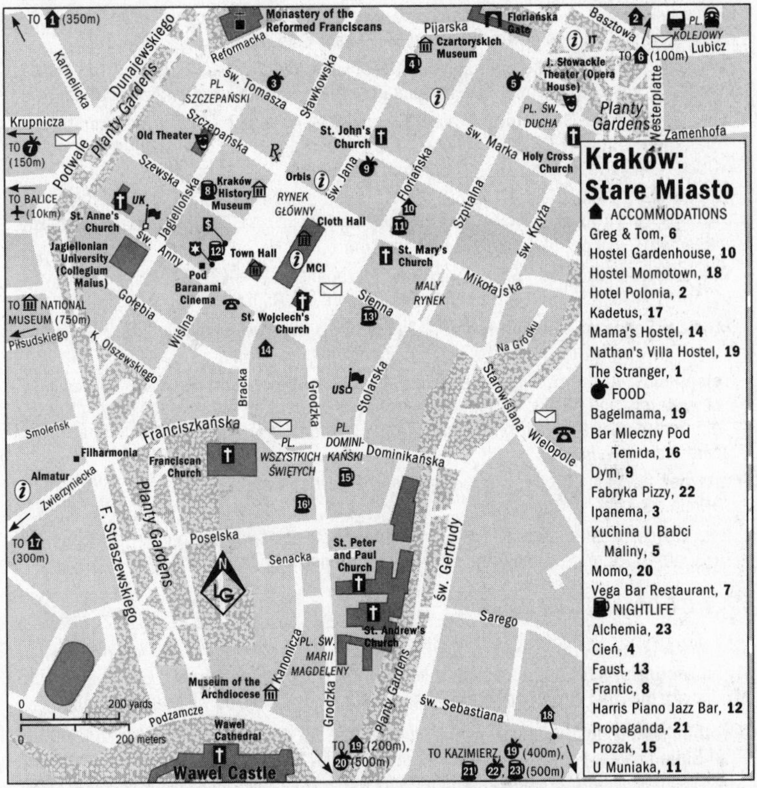

farther out, by a broad ring road, which is confusingly divided into sections with different names: **Basztowa, Dunajewskiego, Podwale, F. Straszewskiego, św. Gertrudy,** and **Westerplatte.** The celebrated **Wawel Castle** looms south of Rynek Główny. Snaking past the castle, the **Wisła River** (VEE-swah) borders the old Jewish district of **Kazimierz.** The city's main bus and train stations are just northeast of Stare Miasto. Turn left from the train station exit to Stare Miasto or right from the bus station exit to reach a large, well-marked underpass, which cuts directly beneath the ring road and into the Planty gardens. A number of paths lead from there into the Rynek (5min.).

Tourist Offices: City Tourist Information, Szpitalna 25 (☎432 01 10; www.krakow.pl). Arranges accommodations and tours, and sells maps (7-12zł). English spoken. **MCI,** Rynek Główny 1/3 (☎421 77 06; www.mcit.pl), in the main square, sells maps, *Kraków in Your Pocket* (5zł, English 10zł), and the cultural guide *Karnet* (4zł). Open May-Sept. M-F 8am-8pm, Sa 10am-4pm; Oct.-Apr. M-F 9am-6pm, Sa 10am-2pm.

Budget Travel: Orbis, ul. Kremerowska 5 (☎422 18 05; www.orbis.krakow.pl).

Consulates: UK, św. Anny 9, 4th fl. (☎421 70 30). Open M-F 9am-3pm. **US,** Stolarska 9 (☎424 51 00; http://krakow.usconsulate.gov). Open M-F 8:30am-5pm.

Currency Exchange: ATMs, found all over the city, offer the best rates. *Kantory* (exchange kiosks) have widely varying rates. Avoid those around the train station and near Floriańska Gate. Check rates carefully around Rynek Główny. **Bank PKO SA,** Rynek

Główny 31 (☎420 37 00), cashes traveler's checks for 1-2% commission (min. 10zł) and gives MC/V cash advances. Open M-F 11am-6pm.

Luggage Storage: At the train station. 1% of value per day plus 3.90zł for the 1st day and 2zł for each additional day. Lockers near the exit. Small 4zł. Large 8zł. Open 24hr.

English-Language Bookstore: Massolit, Felicjanek 4 (☎432 41 50). An intimate nook crammed with over 25,000 popular, classic, and academic English-language books. Open Su-Th 10am-8pm, F-Sa 10am-9pm.

Laundromat: Piastowska 47 (☎622 31 81), in the basement of Hotel Piast. Take tram #4, 13, or 14 to WKS Wawel and turn left on Piastowska. Complete load (wash, dry, detergent) 36zł per 5kg. Open M-F 10am-7pm.

Pharmacy: Apteka Pod Zółtym Tygrysem, Szczepańska 1 (☎422 92 93), just off Rynek Główny. Posts a list of 24hr. pharmacies. Open M-Sa 8am-8pm. MC/V.

Medical Services: Medicover, Krótka 1 (☎616 10 00; www.medicover.pl). 24hr. ambulance services available (☎96 77). English spoken.

Telephones: At the post office and throughout the city. Phone cards are sold at most newsstands and kiosks. To make international calls using public phones, you need 2 different cards: a public phone card *(karty telefoniczne)* and an international phone card *(karta telegrosik).*

Internet Access: The imaginatively named **Internet Cafe,** Rynek Główny 23. 2zł per 30min., 3zł per hr. Open 24hr.

Post Office: Westerplatte 20 (☎422 48 11). *Poste Restante* at counter #1. Open M-F 7:30am-8:30pm, Sa 8am-2pm, Su 9am-2pm. **Postal Code:** 31075.

POLAND

ACCOMMODATIONS

New hostels frequently open in Kraków to meet the growing demand, but budget accommodations fill up quickly in the summer, so travelers should call ahead. University dorms open up in July and August; *Kraków in Your Pocket* has a list.

Nathan's Villa Hostel, ul. św. Agnieszki 1 (☎422 35 45; www.nathansvilla.com), south of Stare Miasto. Famous for its social atmosphere, the hostel has spacious rooms and a lively cellar pub. Breakfast, laundry and wireless Internet included. Reception 24hr. Dorms 50-65zł. MC/V; 3% surcharge. ❷

The Stranger, ul. Kochanowskiego 1 (☎634 25 16; www.thestrangerhostel.com), northwest of Stare Miasto. A laid-back hostel with mellow, retro-lit dorms. Common room has a mammoth couch, a fantastic entertainment system, and free Internet. Breakfast included. Reception 24hr. Dorms 55-60zł. Cash only. ❷

Mama's Hostel, ul. Bracka 4 (☎429 59 40; www.mamashostel.com.pl), off Rynek Główny. A popular hostel with bright, clean facilities, though the central, party-friendly location means it can get noisy. Breakfast and laundry included. Reception 24hr. Flexible check-in and check-out. Dorms 40-55zł. MC/V; 3% surcharge. ❶

Hostel Momotown, ul. Miodowa 28 (☎429 69 29; www.momotownhostel.com), in the Kazimierz district. Artsy murals and magazine clippings cover the walls of this vibrant, brand-new hostel. Breakfast and Internet included. Reception 24hr. Flexible check-in and check-out. Dorms 42-55zł, every 5th night free. MC/V. ❷

Hostel Gardenhouse, ul. Floriańska 5 (☎431 28 24; www.gardenhousehostel.com), in a courtyard off Rynek Główny. Spotless, quiet dorms with floral motif. Breakfast, laundry, and Internet included. Reception 24hr. Dorms 55-60zł; doubles 150zł. MC/V. ❷

Hotel Polonia, Basztowa 25 (☎422 12 33; www.hotel-polonia.com.pl), across from the train station. Neoclassical exterior, modern rooms, and see-through bathtubs in suites. Breakfast 18zł, included for rooms with bath. Reception 24hr. Check-out noon. Singles

109zł, with bath 295zł; doubles 109/360zł; triples 139/429zł. MC/V. ❹

Greg and Tom, ul. Pawia 12/15 (☎422 41 00; www.gregtomhostel.com). Look past the climb to the 4th fl. of a weary Soviet-era building: this small hostel is clean, attractive, and next to the train and bus stations. Breakfast, laundry, and Internet included. Reception 5:30am-10pm. Dorms 45zł-50zł. Cash only. ❷

Kadetus, ul. Zwierzyniecka 25 (☎422 36 17; www.kadetus.com), southwest of Rynek Główny. Simple, colorful dorms with modern furnishings. Laundry and Internet included. Reception 24hr. Dorms 55zł; doubles 60zł. Cash only. ❷

FOOD

Many restaurants, cafes, and grocery stores are located on and around Rynek Główny. More grocery stores surround the bus and train stations.

Bagelmama, ul. Podbrzezie 2 (☎431 19 42), in Kazimierz, facing the Tempel Synagogue. Poland is the mother of the bagel (see right); here the blessed food returns home in triumph (2.50zł, with cream cheese or hummus 5-8.50zł). Also has Kraków's best burritos (12-14zł). Open Tu-Th and Su 10am-9pm, F-Sa 10am-10pm. Cash only. ❶

Kuchina U Babci Maliny, ul. Szpitalna 38 (☎421 48 18). Hearty Polish food served in quarters resembling a wooden stable upstairs and, incongruously, a Victorian drawing room below. Soup 3zł. Pierogi 6-12zł. Open daily 11am-10pm. Cash only. ❶

Ipanema, św. Tomasza 28 (☎422 53 23). Toucan figurines, bright paint, and hanging plants create a rainforest aura to go along with the superb Brazilian cuisine. Entrees 17-40zł. Open Su-Th noon-11pm, F-Sa noon-midnight. MC/V. ❸

Dym, św. Tomasza 13 (☎429 66 61). A hub for sophisticated locals, Dym (meaning "smoke") earns high praise for its coffee (4.50zł), though many prefer to enjoy the relaxed atmosphere over beer (5.50zł). Open daily 10am-midnight. Cash only. ❶

Fabryka Pizzy, Józefa 34 (☎433 80 80). This wildly popular Kazimierz pizza place lives up to the hype, preparing unusual pizzas that go by even more unusual monikers. Pizzas 17.50-25zł. Open Su-Th 11am-11pm, F-Sa noon-midnight. MC/V. ❷

Vega Bar Restaurant, Krupnicza 22 (☎430 08 46), also at św. Gertrudy 7 (☎422 34 94). Fresh flowers set the mood for delightful veggie cuisine (3-10zł). 32 varieties of tea (2.50zł). Open daily 9am-9pm. MC/V. ❶

THE HOLE STORY

According to legend, a Jewish baker in Vienna concocted the first bagel in 1683 as a gift to Polish king Jan Sobieski, to thank the king for turning back Turkish invaders. The bread was shaped like a *beugal* (stirrup) in honor of Sobieski's heroic horsemanship.

The historical record, however, traces the bagel back as far as 1610 in Kraków, when community regulations decreed that bagels be served to pregnant women to promote easier childbirth. Whatever the bagel's origins, it thrived in Poland, especially around Kraków. According to a 1915 account, the smell of freshly baked bagels often wafted through the streets of the Jewish neighborhood of Kazimierz, especially near the Tempel Synagogue, where a tiny shop called Pan Bejgul (Mr. Bagel) stood at the end of ul. Podbrzezie.

In Kraków today, street vendors hawk the Polish descendant of the original bagel, a crisp ring of bread known as *obwarzanki*. The smell of baking bagels, meanwhile, has returned to ul. Podbrzezie, where **Bagelmama** opened in a spot facing the Tempel Synagogue in 2001. Run by an American expat chef, Bagelmama sells fresh bagels as they have evolved in Polish Jewish immigrants' kitchens and shops in North America: soft and chewy, with cream cheese spreads. Since the day that Sobieski tasted his first bagel, Polish bakers have made the world go 'round.

Momo, Dietla 49 (☎609 68 5775), in Kazimierz. Serves fresh, mostly vegan dishes, with sparse but funky decor. Entrees 4-12zł. Open daily 11am-8pm. Cash only. ❶

Bar Mleczny Pod Temida, ul. Grodzka 43. Conveniently located between Rynek Główny and Wawel Castle, this milk bar is a crowd-pleasing lunch spot. Entrees 2.50-10zł. Open daily 9am-8pm. ❶

SIGHTS

STARE MIASTO. In the center of Stare Miasto, Rynek Główny is a sea of cafes and bars surrounded by multicolored row houses. The yellow **Cloth Hall** (Sukiennice) in the Rynek houses souvenir hawkers and a gallery of Polish art. *(Open Tu, Th, and Sa-Su 10am-3:30pm, W and F 10am-6pm. 8zł, students 5zł. Th free.)* A trumpet call blares every hour from Wieża Mariacka, the taller tower of **St. Mary's Church** (Kościół Mariacki), and cuts off abruptly to recall the near-destruction of Kraków in 1241, when invading Tartars shot down the trumpeter as he attempted to warn the city. A stunning blue-and-gold interior encases the world's oldest **Gothic altarpiece,** a 500-year-old treasure dismantled, but not destroyed, by the Nazis. *(At the corner of the Rynek closest to the train station. Cover shoulders and knees. Church open daily 11:30am-6pm. Tower open Tu, Th, and Sa 9-11:30am and 1-5:30pm. Tower 5zł, students 3zł. Altar 4/2zł.)* **Collegium Maius** of Kraków's **Jagiellonian University** (Uniwersytet Jagielloński) is the third-oldest university in Europe, founded in 1364. Alumni include astronomer Mikołaj Kopernik, or Copernicus, and painter Jan Matejko. Once a lecture hall and professors' quarters, the Collegium became a museum in 1964 and boasts an extensive collection of historical scientific instruments. *(ul. Jagiellońska 15. From the corner of the Rynek near the Town Hall, walk down św. Anny and turn left onto Jagiellońska. ☎633 15 21; www.uj.edu.pl/muzeum. Open M-W and F 10am-2:20pm, Th 10am-5:20pm, Sa 10am-1:20pm. Guided visits only; tours begin every 20min. English-language tour daily 1pm. 12zł, students 6zł. Sa free.)* **Ulica Floriańska** runs from the Rynek to the **Barbakan** and the **Floriańska Gate,** which formed the entrance to the old city and are now the only remnants of the medieval fortifications. The **Czartoryskich Museum** has letters by Copernicus and paintings by Matejko, da Vinci, and Rembrandt. *(św. Jana 19, parallel to ul. Floriańska. Open Tu and Th 10am-4pm, W and F-Sa 11am-7pm, Su 10am-3pm. 9zł, students 6zł. Th free.)* From the Rynek, walk down Grodzka and turn right to reach the brightly colored **Franciscan Church,** which displays Stanisław Wyspiański's stained-glass window, *God the Father*. *(Open daily 6am-7:45pm. Free English-language tours.)*

WAWEL CASTLE AND SURROUNDINGS. **Wawel Castle** (Zamek Wawelski), one of Poland's top attractions, is an architectural masterpiece. Begun in the 10th century and remodeled in the 16th, the castle contains 71 chambers, including the **Komnaty** (state rooms) and the **Apartamenty** (royal chambers). Among the treasures are a magnificent sequence of 16th-century tapestries commissioned by the royal family and a cache of armor, swords, spears, and ancient guns. *(☎422 51 55; www.wawel.krakow.pl. Open Apr.-Oct. M 9:30am-noon, Tu and F 9:30am-4pm, W-Th and Sa 9:30am-3pm, Su 10am-3pm; Nov.-Mar. Tu-Sa 9:30am-3pm, Su 10am-3pm. Royal Chambers, Lost Wawel, and Oriental Collection closed M. Castle 35zł, students 23zł. M free. Lost Wawel and Oriental Collection 7/4zł each. Royal Apartments, Treasury, and Armory 15/8zł each.)* Next door is **Wawel Cathedral** (Katedra Wawelska), which once hosted the coronations and funerals of Polish monarchs. Famed poet Adam Mikiewicz lies entombed here, and Kraków native Karol Wojtyła served as archbishop at the cathedral before becoming Pope John Paul II. Steep wooden stairs from the church lead to **Sigismund's Bell** (Dwon Zygmunta); the view of the city is worth the climb. *(Open M-F 9am-5:15pm, Sa 9am-4:45pm, Su 12:15-5:15pm. 10zł, students 5zł.)* In the complex's southwest corner is the entrance to the **Dragon's Den** (Smocza Jama), a small underground cavern. Legend has it that a shepherd left a poisoned sheep outside the cave as bait; the dragon ate it and became so thirsty that it drank itself to death at the Wisła River. *(Open Apr.-Oct. daily 10am-5pm. 3zł.)*

KAZIMIERZ. South of Stare Miasto lies Kazimierz, Kraków's 600-year-old **Jewish quarter.** On the eve of WWII, 68,000 Jews lived in the Kraków area, many of them in Kazimierz. The Nazis deported all of them by March 1943, many to the nearby Płaszów and Auschwitz-Birkenau concentration camps. Only about 100 practicing Jews now live here, but Kazimierz is a favorite haunt of Kraków's artists and intellectuals and the center of a resurgence of Central European Jewish culture. *(From the Rynek, go down ul. Sienna, which turns into Starowiślana. After 1km, turn right onto Miodowa, then left onto Szeroka.)* The **Galicia Jewish Museum** documents the past and present of Galicia, a region in southern Poland that was once the heart of Ashkenazi Jewish culture, and poses difficult questions about the future of Judaism in Poland. *(Dajwór 18. ☎421 68 42; www.galiciajewishmuseum.org. Open daily 9am-8pm. 7zł, students 5zł.)* The tiny **Remuh Synagogue** is surrounded by **Remuh's Cemetery,** which has graves dating to the plague of 1551-1552 and a wall constructed from tombstones recovered after WWII. For centuries, the cemetery was covered with sand, protecting it from 19th-century Austrian invaders and from the Nazis, who used the area as a garbage dump. *(ul. Szeroka 40. Open M-F 9am-4pm. Services F at sundown and Sa morning. 5zł, students 3zł.)* Also on Szeroka, the **Old Synagogue** is Poland's earliest example of Jewish religious architecture and now houses a museum. *(ul. Szeroka 24. Open M 10am-2pm, W-Th and Sa-Su 9am-4pm, F 10am-5pm. 7zł, students 5zł. M free.)* The **Center for Jewish Culture** organizes cultural events and arranges heritage tours. *(Rabina Meiselsa 17, off pl. Nowy. ☎430 64 49; www.judaica.pl. Open daily 10am-6pm. Closed Jewish holidays.)*

ENTERTAINMENT

The **Cultural Information Center,** ul. św. Jana 2, sells the comprehensive monthly guide *Karnet.* (4zł; www.karnet.krakow.pl. Center ☎421 77 87. Open M-F 10am-6pm, Sa 10am-4pm.) Notable summer festivals include the **International Short Film Festival** (late May), the **Floating of Wreaths on the Wisła** (Wianki; June), the **Festival of Jewish Culture** (early July), the **Street Theater Festival** (early July), and the **Jazz Festival** (late July). Kraków jumps with jazz; check out **U Muniaka,** Floriańska 3 (☎423 12 05; live jazz nightly 9:30pm; open daily 6:30pm-2am), and **Harris Piano Jazz Bar,** Rynek Główny 28 (☎421 57 41; shows 9pm-midnight; open daily 9am-3am). Kraków's opera performs at **J. Słowacki Theater,** pl. św. Ducha 1. (☎422 40 22; www.opera.krakow.pl. Tickets 30-50zł, students 25-30zł.) **Stary Teatr** hosts movies, plays, and other exhibits. (☎422 40 40. Open Tu-Sa 10am-1pm and 5-7pm, Su 5-7pm. Tickets 22-40zł, student discount available.) European and American films roll at **Kino Pod Baranami,** Rynek Glówny 27. (☎423 07 68. 12-14zł.)

NIGHTLIFE

Kraków in Your Pocket has up-to-date info on the hottest club and pub scenes, while the free monthly English-language *KrakOut* magazine has day-by-day listings. Most dance clubs are in **Stare Miasto,** while bohemian pubs and cafes cluster in **Kazimierz.** For more info, see www.puby.krakow.pl. Nightlife here has a high turnover rate. For tips on Kraków's **gay nightlife,** see http://gayeuro.com/krakow.

Alchemia, Estery 5 (☎292 09 70). Dripping candelabras and discarded armoires accent this quintessential Kazimierz bar, which masquerades by day as a smoky cafe. Occasional live music and film screenings. Open daily 9am-4am.

Prozak, Dominikańska 6 (☎429 11 28; www.prozak.pl), in Stare Miasto. This über-popular, maze-like club has more dance floors, bars, and intimate nooks than you'll be able to count. Beer 7zł. Mixed drinks 12-22zł. Cover F-Sa 10zł. Open daily 4pm-2am.

Frantic, ul. Szewska 5 (☎423 04 83), in Stare Miasto. When it's time to give Prozak a break, the fashionable crowd flocks to the smaller Frantic for boozing and schmoozing. Beer 6zł. Mixed drinks 8-23zł. Open daily 7pm-4am.

Propaganda, Miodowa 20. Despite the candles and wobbly tables, Propaganda's take on Kazimierz bohemia has a punk-rock feel. Decor mixes posters of Stalin with guitars of Polish rockers. Beer 3-10zł. Open daily 1pm-midnight. Cash only.

Cień, św. Jana 15 (☎422 21 77). Modernist underground vaults filled with Kraków's beautiful people and house techno. Open W-Sa 7pm-7am. Cash only.

Faust, Rynek Główny 6 (☎423 83 00). Sell your soul in this cavernous club with long wooden tables and techno-pop hits. Beer 4-6zł. Occasional klezmer or metal nights. Cover F-Sa 5zł. Open Su-Th noon-1am, F-Sa noon-4am. Cash only.

DAYTRIPS FROM KRAKÓW

AUSCHWITZ-BIRKENAU. An estimated 1.5 million people, mostly Jews, were murdered—and thousands more suffered unthinkable horrors—in the Nazi concentration camps at **Auschwitz** (in Oświęcim) and **Birkenau** (in Brzezinka). The gates over the smaller **Konzentrationslager Auschwitz I** are inscribed with the ironic dictum *"Arbeit Macht Frei"* (Work Will Set You Free). Tours begin at the **museum** at Auschwitz. As you walk past the remainders of thousands of lives—suitcases, shoes, glasses, kilos upon kilos of women's hair—the sheer enormity of the atrocity begins to come into focus. A 15min. English-language film, with footage shot by the Soviet Army that liberated the camp on January 27, 1945, is shown at 11am and 1pm. Children under 14 are strongly advised not to visit the museum. *(☎843 20 22. Open daily June-Aug. 8am-7pm; Sept. and May 8am-6pm; Oct. and Apr. 8am-5pm; Nov. and Mar. 8am-4pm; Dec.-Feb. 8am-3pm. English-language tour daily 11:30am. Museum free. Film 3.50zł. 3½hr. tour 26zł; film and bus included.)*

The larger, starker **Konzentrationslager Auschwitz II-Birkenau** is in the countryside 3km from the original camp, a 30min. walk along a well-marked route or a quick **shuttle** ride from the parking lot of the Auschwitz museum (1 per hr. 11:30am-5:30pm, free). Birkenau was built later in the war, when the Nazis developed a more brutally efficient means of killing. Little is left of the camp today; most was destroyed by retreating Nazis to conceal the genocide. The reconstructed train tracks lead to the ruins of the crematoria and gas chambers. Near the monument lies a pond still gray from the ashes deposited there over 60 years ago. *(Open mid-Apr. to Oct. 8am-dusk. Free.)* **Auschwitz Jewish Center and Synagogue** features exhibits on pre-war Jewish life in the town of Oświęcim, films based on survivors' testimonies, genealogy resources, and a reading room. Guides offer tours of the compound. Take a taxi for about 17zł, or take bus #1, 3-6, or 8 from the train station in the town center, get off at the first stop after the bridge, and backtrack. *(Pl. Ks. Jana Skarbka 5. ☎844 70 032; www.ajcf.pl. Open Apr.-Sept. Su-F 8:30am-8pm; Oct.-Mar. Su-F 8:30am-6pm.)*

Buses from Kraków's central station go to Oświęcim (1½-2hr., 5 per day, 7-10zł). Return buses and minibuses leave frequently from the stop on the other side of the parking lot; turn right out of the museum. PKS buses also depart from the stop outside the premises. Less convenient **trains** leave from Kraków Płaszów, south of the town center (10zł). Buses #2-5, 8-9, and 24-29 connect the Oświęcim train station to the Muzeum Oświęcim stop; alternatively, walk a block to the right out of the station, turn left onto ul. Więźniów Oświęcimia, and continue 1.6km to Auschwitz.

WIELICZKA. The tiny town of Wieliczka, 13km southeast of Kraków, is home to a 700-year-old **salt mine.** Pious Poles carved the immense underground complex of chambers out of salt; in 1978, UNESCO declared the mine one of the 12 most priceless monuments in the world. The most spectacular cavern is **St. Kinga's Chapel,**

complete with salt chandeliers, an altar, and relief works. Most travel companies, including **Orbis** (p. 785), organize trips to the mines, but it's cheapest to take a private **minibus,** like "Lux-Bus," that departs near the train and bus stations (30min., every 15min., 2.50zł). Look for "Wieliczka" marked on the door. In Wieliczka, head along the path of the former tracks, then follow signs marked *"do kopalni."* The only way to see the mines is by taking a lengthy guided tour, so allot at least 3½hr. for the daytrip. *(ul. Daniłowicza 10. ☎278 73 02; www.kopalnia.pl. Open daily Apr.-Oct. 7:30am-7:30pm; Nov.-Mar. 8am-5pm. English-language tours available July-Aug. 2 per hr.; June and Sept. 8 per day; Oct.-May 2 per day. 2hr. 60zł, students under 25 50zł. MC/V.)*

LUBLIN ☎081

Unlike most Polish cities, Lublin (LOO-bleen; pop. 400,000) survived WWII with cobblestones and medieval buildings intact. The **Rynek** (main square) of the **Stare Miasto** (Old Town) contains many of the city's historic sights. The 14th-century **Lublin Castle** (Zamek Lubelski) was used as a Gestapo jail during the Nazi occupation. The adjacent **Holy Trinity Chapel** has stunning Russo-Byzantine frescoes from 1418. (☎532 50 01, ext. 35; www.zamek-lublin.pl. Museum and chapel open M 10am-2pm, Tu-Sa 9am-6pm. Tours 45zł each, 55zł for both. Entrance to each 6.50zł, students 4.50zł.) Take eastbound bus #28 from the train station or trolley #153 or 156 from al. Racławickie to reach **Majdanek,** the second-largest Nazi concentration camp. The Nazis did not have time to destroy the camp, so the original structures are still standing. Visitors can also get there from Lublin by walking along Droga Męczenników Majdanka (Road of the Martyrs of Majdanek; 30min.) to Zamość. (☎744 26 48; www.majdanek.pl. Open May-Sept. Tu-Su 8am-6pm; Oct.-Apr. Tu-Su 8am-3pm. Children under 14 not permitted. Free.)

From the bus station, bear left around pl. Zamkowy and head past the castle to reach **Domu Rekolekcyjnym ❶**, ul. Podwale 15, a rectory with simple rooms, friendly nuns, and an unbeatable location. (☎532 41 38; j.halasa@kuria.lublin.pl. Dorms 35-40zł.) **Szkolne Schronisko Młodziezowe ❶**, ul. Długowsza 6, is a quiet youth hostel located in a residential area. (☎53 30 628. Open 6-10am and 5-10pm. Dorms 20-25zł.) Lublin's eateries cluster near **ulica Krakówskie Przedmieście;** a dozen beer gardens can be found in Stare Miasto. The pleasantly snug **Zadora ❷**, ul. Rynek 8, tucked in an alley on the northeast side of the square, adds a creative touch to its savory buckwheat and dessert crepes. (☎534 55 34; www.zadora.com.pl. Polish crepes 8-12zł. AmEx/MC/V.) **Café Szeroka 28 ❹**, ul. Grodzka 21, serves traditional Polish food with a view of the castle. (Entrees 30zł. Sa live klezmer. Open Su-Th 11am-11pm, F-Sa 11am-midnight. AmEx/MC/V.) **Trains** (☎94 36) run from pl. Dworcowy 1 to Kraków (5hr., 2 per day, 45zł), Warsaw (3hr., 13 per day, 32zł), and Wrocław (9½hr., 2 per day, 51zł). From the train station, take bus #1 to Stare Miasto and the bus station. The **tourist office,** ul. Jezuica 1/3, is near the Kraków Gate. (☎532 44 12; itlublin@onet.pl. Open M-F 9am-5pm, Sa 10am-4pm, Su 10am-3pm.)

ZAKOPANE ☎018

The year-round resort of Zakopane (zah-ko-PAH-neh; pop. 28,000) lies in a valley surrounded by jagged Tatran peaks and alpine meadows. During prime vacation seasons (Jan.-Feb. and June-Sept.), the town fills with skiers or hikers headed for the magnificent **Tatra National Park** (Tatrzański Park Narodowy; 5zł, students 2.50zł). To find accommodations, look for signs marked *"pokój"* and *"noclegi"* that indicate private rooms; owners may greet you at the station. **Schronisko PISM "Szarotka" ❶**, ul. Notowarska 45G, has small but clean rooms with private bathrooms. (☎201 36 18; schroniskoptsm@pn.onet.pl. Linens 6zł. Lockout 11pm. Reserve ahead. Dorms 35-50zł, low season 26-30zł. Cash only.) **Schronisko Morskie Oko ❶**, by the Morskie Oko lake, is in an ideal hiking location. Take a bus (45min.,

11 per day, 4zł) to Palenice Białczańska or a direct minibus (20min., 5zł) from opposite the bus station, and then hike (1-2hr., 9km) up the paved road. (☎207 76 09. Linens 7zł. Reserve ahead. June-Oct. space on floor 34zł; 3- to 6-bed dorms 44zł. Nov.-June 24/34zł. Cash only.) Most restaurants and shops can be found along ul. Krupówki. The live music and regional fare at the kitschy **Gazdowo Kuznia ❸**, ul. Krupówki 1, always draw a crowd. (☎206 41 11; www.gazdowokuznia.pl. Entrees 15-25zł. Open daily 2pm-10pm.) Next door, **Bar Mleczny Bozena Majoch ❷** serves the cheapest eats around. (Entrees 6-12zł. Open daily 8am-8pm. Cash only.) A Super Sam **grocery store** is at ul. Kościuszki 3. (Open 24hr. AmEx/MC/V.)

The bus station (☎201 46 03) is located on the corner of ul. Kościuszki and ul. Jagiellońska, facing the train station (☎201 45 04). **Buses** run to Kraków (2-2½hr., 2 per day, 10zł) and Warsaw (8½hr., 4 per day, 55zł). A private express line runs between Zakopane and Kraków (2hr., 15 per day, 13zł), leaving from a stop on ul. Kościuszki 50m toward the center from the station. **Trains** go to Kraków (3-4hr., 18 per day, 19zł) and Warsaw (8hr., 9 per day, 50zł). To reach the center from the station, walk down ul. Kościuszki, which intersects ul. Krupówki (15min.). The **tourist office,** ul. Kościuszki 17, provides info on hiking, sells maps (5-9zł), helps locate rooms, and books English-language rafting trips (70-80zł) on the Dunajec. (☎201 22 11. Open daily July-Sept. 8am-8pm; Oct.-June 9am-6pm.) **Postal Code:** 34-500.

POLAND

HIKING NEAR ZAKOPANE. Kuźnice, south of Zakopane, is a popular place to begin hikes. To get there, head uphill on ul. Krupówki to ul. Zamoyskiego; follow this road as it becomes ul. Chałubińskiego, which turns into ul. Przewodników Tatrzańskich and continues to the trailheads (1hr. from Zakopane center). You can also take a "mikro-bus" (2zł) from the stop in front of the bus station. From Kuźnice, the Kasprowy Wierch **cable car** takes passengers to the top of **Kasprowy Mountain,** 1987m above sea level, where Poland borders the Slovak Republic.

Trails from Kuźnice are well marked. The Tatrzański Park Narodowy map (7zł), available at kiosks or bookstores, is a useful guide. The **Valley of the Five Polish Tarns** (Dolina Pięciu Stawów Polskich; 1 day) is an intense, beautiful hike. It starts at Kuźnice and follows the yellow trail through **Dolina Jaworzynka** (Jaworzynka Valley) to the steep blue trail, which leads to **Hala Gasienicowa** (2½hr.). Crowds tend to gather on the steep final ascent to the peak of **Mount Giewont** (1894m; 6½hr.). The mountain's silhouette resembles a man lying down; you'll envy him after the climb. From Kuźnice, the moderately difficult blue trail (7km) to the peak has a view of Zakopane, the Tatras, and the Slovak Republic.

Morskie Oko ("Sea Eye"; 1406m) is a dazzling glacial lake. Take a bus from Zakopane (45min., 11 per day, 5zł) or a private minibus from opposite the station (30min., 6zł) to **Palenice Białczańska** or **Polona Palenica.** Hike the popular paved 18km loop (5-6hr.) or take the green trail to the blue trail (4hr.) for a majestic view. Donkey carts also take passengers to the lake (30min.; 30zł up, 20zł down).

WROCŁAW

☎071

Wrocław (pop. 657,000), the capital of Lower Silesia, is a city of spires, islands, gardens, and stone bridges. Passed among competing powers for centuries, the city became Festung Breslau (Fortress Wrocław) during WWII, one of the last Nazi holdouts en route to Berlin. Today, Wrocław's Gothic beauty and energetic nightlife win over unsuspecting visitors and entice them to stay longer.

TRANSPORTATION AND PRACTICAL INFORMATION. Trains, ul. Piłsudskiego 105 (☎367 58 82), run from Wrocław Główny to: Berlin, GER (6¼hr., 1 per day, 181zł); Bratislava, SLK (7½hr., 10:30pm, 161zł); Kraków (4½hr., 19 per day, 24-62zł); Poznań (3¼hr., 25 per day, 19-32zł); Prague, CZR (5¼hr., 1 per day, 127zł);

Warsaw (4¼hr., 10 per day, 27-70zł). **Buses** leave from behind the train station. From the station, turn left on ul. Piłsudskiego, take a right on ul. Świdnicka, and go past Kościuszki pl. over the Fosa River to reach the **Rynek** (main square). The **tourist office,** Rynek 14, books student dorms. (☎344 31 11; fax 344 29 62; www.itwroclaw.pl. Dorms 20-50zł. Free Internet. Bike rental 10zł for the 1st hr., 5zł every hr. thereafter, 50zł per day; 400zł deposit required. Open daily 9am-9pm.) Surf the Internet at **Cafe W Sera Miasta,** ul. Przejscie Zelaznicze 4, located in the Rynek in an alley just behind the Ratusz. (4zł per hr. Open 24hr.) **Postal Code:** 50-900.

ACCOMMODATIONS AND FOOD. **The Stranger Hostel ❷,** ul. Kołłątaja 16/3, is opposite the train station on a road perpendicular to ul. Piłsudskiego, on the third floor behind an unmarked wooden doorway (ring buzzer #3). Filled with quirky touches like decorated glass toilet seats, the hostel features a home theater and large, comfortable dorms. (☎344 12 06. Laundry and Internet included. Reception 24hr. Dorms 50-60zł. AmEx/MC/V.) Across the street, the **Youth Hostel Mlodziezowy Dom Kultury im. Kopernika (HI) ❶,** ul. Kołłątaja 20, has basic dorms. (☎343 88 56. Lockout 10am-5pm. Curfew 10pm. Reserve ahead. Dorms 22zł; doubles 28zł. Discount after 2 nights.) Though past its prime, the stately **Hotel Monopol ❺,** ul. Modrzejewskiej 2, is a Wrocław legend; former guests include Picasso, Hitler, and Marlene Dietrich. (☎343 70 41. Check-in and check-out 2pm. Singles 122zł, with bath 182zł; doubles 164/264zł; triples with bath 326zł. AmEx/MC/V.)

With its sleek, modern decor, **Bazylia ❶,** ul. Kuźnicza 42, is more posh than traditional milk bars, but still serves reliably inexpensive fare. (Open M-F 7am-8pm, Sa-Su 7:30am-8pm. Cash only.) Order one of the myriad Polish options off the burlap menuboard at **Kurna Chata ❶,** ul. Odrzańska 7, and soak in the peasant-chic atmosphere. (☎341 06 68; www.kurnachata.pl. Entrees 5.50-18zł. Open M-F 10am-midnight, Sa-Su noon-midnight. Cash only.) Mosaics and frescoes spruce up **Żacek ❶,** ul. Kuźnicza 47, a popular student restaurant. (Beer 5zł. Entrees 6-13zł. Open daily 7am-7pm.) An **Albert's** supermarket is located in the basement of the Mercure shopping center at the intersection of Czesław Katarzyny and Oławska Traugutta. From the train station, follow ul. Kołłątaja as it becomes ks. Skargl and then Czesław Katarzyny; the shopping center is on the right. (Open daily 8am-8pm.)

SIGHTS AND NIGHTLIFE. The Gothic **Ratusz** (Town Hall) towers over the **Rynek** in the heart of the city. The beautiful central street **ulica Świdnicka** runs past the Rynek. The rotunda containing the 120m-by-5m **Racławice Panorama,** ul. Purkyniego 11, transports visitors to the 18th-century peasant insurrection against the Russian occupation. To reach it, face away from the Ratusz, bear left onto ul. Kuźnicza, then turn right onto ul. Kotlarska, which becomes ul. Purkyniego. (☎344 23 44; www.panoramaraclawicka.pl. Shows every 30min. Open Tu-Su 9am-4pm. 20zł, students 15zł.) Across the street, the **Muzeum Narodowe** (National Museum), pl. Powstańców Warszawy 5, displays exhibits ranging from medieval sculpture to modern art. (Open W, F, and Su 10am-4pm, Th 9am-4pm, Sa 10am-6pm. 15zł, students 10zł. Sa free.) The impressive Gothic buildings and winding roads of **Uniwersytet Wrocławski** (Wrocław University) form the cultural center of the city. The **Mathematical Tower,** pl. Uniwersytecka 1, has a sweeping view of Wrocław. (Open M-Tu and Th-Su 10am-3:30pm. 4.50zł, students 2.50zł.) Across the Oder River lies the serene **Plac Katedralny** (Cathedral Square) and the 13th-century **Katedra św. Jana Chrzciciela** (Cathedral of St. John the Baptist) with its impressive spires. (Open M-Sa 10am-5:30pm, Su 2-4pm. 4zł, students 3zł.)

Renowned for producing some of the best beer in Poland, **Spiż,** Rynek 2, always has long lines and at least three excellent homemade brews on tap. (www.spiz.pl. Beer 4-8zł. Open Su-M 10am-midnight, Tu-Th 10am-2am, F-Sa 10am-3am. MC/V.) Get your groove on with the locals in the alley on ul. Ruska, near the corner with Nowy Św., where clubs and bars overflow with merry-makers every night of the week. Stop by **Niebo Cafe,** ul. Ruska 51, a boisterous alt-rock hideout, for a few down-and-dirty Polish beers. (☎342 98 67. Beer 6zł. Open 1pm-last customer.) Next door, **Ibiza** is a popular disco. (Beer 5zł. Open daily 6pm-5am.) For a more laid-back crowd, the bar and cafe **Kawiarnia "Pod Kalamburem,"** ul. Kuźnicza 29A, founded by an experimental theater group, now hosts readings and film screenings. (Beer 6zł. Open M-Th 10am-midnight, F-Su 11am-2am.)

POZNAŃ ☎061

International trade fairs throughout the year bring business travelers to industrial Poznań (pop. 600,000), the capital of Wielkopolska (Greater Poland). The sprawling city has inefficient public transportation and few tourist attractions outside of the cobblestoned **Stary Rynek** (Old Square). Opulent 15th-century merchants' residences surround the Renaissance **Ratusz** (Town Hall), now home to a history museum. (Open M-Tu 10am-4pm, W noon-6pm, F 10am-6pm, Su 10am-3pm. 5.50zł, students 3.50zł.) The **Museum of Musical Instruments** (Muzeum Instrumentów Muzycznych), Stary Rynek 45, exhibits an eclectic assortment of antique music-makers, including one of Chopin's pianos. (Open Tu-Sa 11am-5pm, Su 11am-4pm. 5.50zł, students 3.50zł. Sa free.) Sculpted ceilings and columns spiral heavenward in the **Parish Church of the City of Poznań of St. Stanislaus,** at the end of ul. Świętosławska off Stary Rynek. (Concerts Sa 12:15pm. Free.) The first Polish cathedral, the **Cathedral of St. Peter and St. Paul** (Katedra Piotra i Pawła), is on the outskirts of town. Its **Golden Chapel** (Kaplica Złota) contains the tombs of Prince Mieszko I and his son Bolesław Chrobry, the first king of Poland. (Cathedral open M-Sa 9am-6pm, Su 1:15-6:30pm. Crypt 1.85-2.85zł.)

Reasonably priced beds near the center are extremely elusive; book in advance. **Przemysław ❶,** ul. Głogowska 16, books private rooms near the main square. (☎866 35 60; reservacja@przemyslaw.com.pl. Singles 43zł; doubles 65zł. Open M-F 8am-6pm, Sa 10am-2pm.) **Bar Mleczny Apetyt ❶,** ul. Szkolna 4, is a budget-friendly alternative to Stary Rynek's ritzier options. (Entrees 2.50-6.50zł. Open M-Sa 8am-10pm, Su 10am-10pm. Cash only.) **Tapas Bar,** Stary Rynek 60, draws both a lunchtime and late-night crowd for bite-sized *tapas* and a hopping downstairs club. (☎832 25 32. Beer 6zł. Entrees 9-25zł. Open daily 9am-4am. MC/V.) **Trains** run from Poznań Główny, ul. Dworcowa 1 (☎866 12 12), to Berlin, GER (3½hr., 7 per day, 138zł); Kraków (5hr., 11 per day, 45-79zł); and Warsaw (3hr., 25 per day, 57-87zł). To reach Stary Rynek from the train station, go straight, take any tram from ul. Dworcowa heading to the right on św. Marcin, and get off at ul. Marcinkowskiego. The **tourist office,** Stary Rynek 59/60, has free maps and books rooms. (☎852 61 56. Open June-Aug. M-F 9am-6pm, Sa 10am-3pm.) **Postal Code:** 61-890.

TORUŃ ☎056

During the summer, lakeside breezes drift through the red brick streets of Toruń (pop. 210,000), a college town with character. Proud of its legacy as the birthplace of famed astronomer Mikołaj Kopernik (Copernicus), Toruń also boasts Poland's best gingerbread and most impressive Gothic brick architecture.

TRANSPORTATION AND PRACTICAL INFORMATION. Across the Wisła River from the city center, the **train station,** ul. Kujawska 1, serves: Gdynia via Gdańsk (3¼hr., 9 per day, 36zł); Łódz (2¾hr., 8 per day, 32zł); Poznań (2¼hr., 6 per day, 30zł); Warsaw (2¾hr., 7 per day, 38zł). Dworzec PKS **buses,** ul. Dąbrowskiego 26, leave for Berlin, GER (9½hr., 1 per day, 120zł) and Kołobrzeg (7hr., 2 per day, 40zł). Polski Express buses leave from Ruch Kiosk just north of pl. Teatralny for many of the same destinations, with student discounts. The IT **tourist office,** Rynek Staromiejski 25, offers free maps and helps find lodgings. From the train station, take bus #22 or 27 (2zł) across the river to pl. Rapackiego and head through the park. (☎621 09 31; www.it.torun.pl. Open May-Dec. M and Sa 9am-4pm, Tu-F 9am-6pm, Su 9am-1pm; Sept.-Apr. closed Su.) **Postal Code:** 87-100.

ACCOMMODATIONS AND FOOD. Inexpensive hotels are frequently the best value and are centrally located. **Hotel Kopernik ❸**, ul. Wola Zamkowa 16, decks out its rooms with satellite TV and fluffy towels, offering excellent amenities for a low price. (☎652 25 73. Breakfast 11zł. Reception 24hr. Check-in and check-out 2pm. Dorms 25zł; singles 105zł, with bath 125zł; doubles 130/185zł. 30% discount F 2pm-M noon. MC/V.) Wood furnishings and floral bed-spreads are among the appealing comforts at **Hotelik w Centrum ❸**, ul. Szumana 2. From Rynek Staromiejski, follow ul. Szeroka, veer left on ul. Królowej Jadwigi through Rynek Nowomiejski, and cross ul. Szumana; the hotel is on the left. (☎652 22 46. Breakfast 10zł. Internet 2zł per hr. Check-in 2pm. Check-out noon. Singles 70zł, with bath 90zł; doubles 140zł.) To reach the student-filled **PTTK Dom Turystyczny ❶**, ul. Legionów 24, follow ul. Chełmińska past pl. Teatralny; take the second right after the park and turn left on ul. Legionów. The rooms are spotless but run-down. (☎/fax 622 38 55. Dorms 28-38zł; singles 60zł; doubles 76zł.)

The popular **Manekin ❶**, Rynek Staromiejski 16, serves massive yet artful *naleśniki* (filled pancakes; 6.50-19.50zł), made to order. (☎652 28 85. Open M-Th 10am-10pm, F-Sa 10am-midnight, Su 10am-11pm.) **Kopernik Factory Store ❷**, Rynek Staromiejski 6, sells the most collectible dessert in town: gingerbread effigies of Polish kings, saints, and astronomers for 1.60-26zł. (Open M-F 9am-7pm, Sa-Su 10am-6pm. MC/V.) A 24hr. grocery store, **Supersam,** is at ul. Chełmińska 22.

SIGHTS AND NIGHTLIFE. **Stare Miasto** (Old Town), on the right bank of the Wisła River, was constructed by the Teutonic Knights in the 13th century. The 14th-century **Town Hall** (Ratusz) that dominates **Rynek Staromiejski** (Old Town Sq.) is a fine example of monumental burgher architecture. (Museum open daily 10am-7pm. 10zł, students 6zł; Su free. Medieval tower open May-Sept. Tu-Su. 10/6zł.) Copernicus was born at ul. Kopernika 15/17; the restored **Dom Kopernika** features a comprehensive museum, complete with historical artifacts and a sound and light show. (Open Tu-Su 10am-6pm. 10zł, students 6zł. Sound and light show 12/7zł.) A revolt in 1454 led to the destruction of the **Teutonic Knights' Castle,** but its ruins, on ul. Przedzamcze, are still impressive. The 15m **Leaning Tower** (Krzywą Wieżą), ul. Krzywą Wieżą 17, was built in 1271 by a Teutonic Knight as punishment for infringing on his order's rule of celibacy. The **Cathedral of St. John the Baptist and St. John the Evangelist** (Bazylika Katedralna pw. św. Janów), at the corner of ul. Żeglarska and św. Jana, is the most impressive of the many Gothic churches in the area. (Open Apr.-Oct. M-Sa 8:30am-5:30pm, Su 2-5:30pm. 2zł, students 1zł.) Just across the Rynek Staromiejski are the stained-glass windows and intricate altar pieces of the **Church of the Virgin Mary** (Kosciól sw. Marii), on ul. Panny Marii. (Open M-Sa 8am-5pm.)

The improbable Victorian aura and crowded top-floor bar at **Kredens Pub,** ul. Łazienna 3 (☎ 373 24 34), ensure a night of bacchanalian revelry. Toruń's beautiful people flaunt it under careening laser lights and lascivious music videos at **Hypnoza,** ul. Wysoka 2 (☎662 59 00; www.hipnoza.torun.pl). The more laid-back head to **Jazzgod,** ul. Rabiańska 17 (☎652 13 08), for an evening of chill music.

ŁÓDŹ ☎042

Poland's second-largest city, Łódź (WOODGE; pop. 1,055,000) has few postcard-worthy attractions, but it holds a treasure trove of undiscovered sights and tastes. Łódź once housed the largest Jewish ghetto in Europe; today, residents are putting this plucky working-class city back on the map by hosting extraordinary art festivals and Jewish heritage exhibits. The eerily beautiful **Jewish Cemetery** (Cmentarz Żydowski), on ul. Zmienna, has over 200,000 time-worn graves. Near the entrance is a memorial to the Jews killed in the ghetto; signs lead to the **Ghetto Fields** (Pole Ghettowe), which are lined with faintly marked graves. Take tram #1 from ul. Kilinskiego or #6 from ul. Kościuszki or Zachodnia north to the end of the line (20min.); continue up the street, turn left on ul. Zmienna, and enter through the small gate on the right. (☎656 70 19. Open Apr.-Sept. Su-F 9am-5pm; Oct.-Mar. Su-Th 9am-5pm, F 9am-3pm. Closed Jewish holidays. 4zł, free for those visiting relatives' graves.) The **Jewish Community Center** (Gmina Wyznaniowa Żydowska), ul. Pomorska 18, in the town center, has information on those buried in the cemetery. (☎633 51 56. Open M-F 10am-2pm. English spoken.)

The convenient **PTSM Youth Hostel (HI) ❶**, ul. Legionów 27, has quiet rooms and spacious baths. Take tram #4 toward Helenówek from Fabryczna station to pl. Wolnosci; walk on Legionów past Zachodnia. (☎630 66 80; www.yhlodz.pl. Curfew 10pm. Dorms 30-40zł; singles 45-69zł; doubles 70-80zł. MC/V.) **Anatewka ❸**, ul. 6 Sierpnia 2-4, serves phenomenal Jewish cuisine with flair. A live fiddler perched atop a curio cabinet and extraordinarily attentive waitstaff complete the dining experience. (Entrees 20-50zł. Open daily 11am-11pm.) **Green Way Bar Wegetarianski ❶**, ul. Zielona 1, off ul. Piotrkowska, serves healthy vegetarian meals with an emphasis on the fresh and seasonal. (☎632 62 42. Entrees 3-6zł. Open M-F 9am-8pm, Sa 9am-6pm.) Łódź's main thoroughfare, **ulica Piotrkowska,** is a bustling pedestrian shopping drag by day and a lively pub strip by night. Designed by an arts collective, the legendary bar and club **Łódź Kaliska,** ul. Piotrkowska 102, draws famous Polish actors and artists to its quirky dance floor. (www.klub.lodz-kaliska.pl. Beer 6zł. Disco F-Sa. Open M-Sa noon-3am, Su 4pm-3am.)

Trains run from **Łódź Fabryczna** station, pl. B. Salacinskiego 1 (☎205 59 39), to Kraków (3¼hr., 3 per day, 41zł) and Warsaw (2hr., 17 per day, 28zł). Trains also go from **Łódź Kaliska** station, al. Unii 1 (☎205 44 08), to Gdańsk (7½hr., 3 per day, 46zł), Poznań (3½hr., 2 per day, 24zł), and Wrocław (3¾hr., 3 per day, 35zł). Tram #12 serves both stations. Polski Express (☎205 56 30) **buses** depart from Łódź Fabryczna to Kraków (5hr., 2 per day, 41zł) and Warsaw (2½hr., 7 per day, 28zł). The IT **tourist office,** ul. Piotrkowska 87, can help book lodgings, including university dorms in summer. (☎/fax 638 59 56; cit@cit.uml.lodz.pl. Open M-F 9am-7pm, Sa-Su 10am-3pm.) **Postal Code:** 90-001.

GDAŃSK ☎058

With its strategic location at the mouth of the Wisła River on the Baltic coast, Gdańsk (pop. 481,000) has been at the forefront of Polish history. As the free city of Danzig, it was the gateway to the sea during occupation in the 18th and 19th centuries. During WWII, it was the site of the first casualties and of the German army's last stand. Recent reconstruction and renovations have restored the charm of the quayside town. Efficient transport makes it a good starting point for Sopot and Gdynia, which join with Gdańsk to form the Trójmiasto (Tri-City Area).

TRANSPORTATION

Planes: Gdańsk Lech Wałesa Airport, 8km west of the city center. Take Bus B from Gdańsk Główny train station (30-40min., 4.20zł). **Ryanair** (www.ryanair.com) flies direct to Frankfurt, GER, London's Stansted airport, and Stockholm, SWE.

Trains: Gdańsk Główny, ul. Podwale Grodzkie 1 (☎94 36; www.pkp.pl). To: **Kołobrzeg** (2¾hr., 12 per day, 41zł); **Kraków** (7hr., 11 per day, 58zł); **Łódź** (8hr., 15 per day, 50zł); **Lublin** (8hr., 3 per day, 52zł); **Malbork** (50min., 40 per day, 9.30zł); **Poznań**

(4½hr., 6 per day, 43zł); **Toruń** (3¼hr., 7 per day, 36zł); **Warsaw** (4hr., 12 per day, 82zł); **Wrocław** (6-7hr., 3 per day, 50zł). **SKM** (Fast City Trains; ☎628 57 78) run to **Gdynia** (35min.; 4zł, students 2.50zł) and **Sopot** (20min., 5/3zł) every 10min. during the day. Punch your ticket in a *kasownik* (ticket machine) before boarding.

Buses: PKS, ul. 3-go Maja 12 (☎302 15 32; www.pks.pl), behind the train station. To: **Kołobrzeg** (6hr., 1 per day, 41zł); **Kraków** (10¾hr., 1 per day, 65zł); **Łódź** (8hr., 3 per day, 56zł); **Malbork** (1hr., 4 per day, 10zł); **Toruń** (2½hr., 2 per day, 30zł); **Warsaw** (5¾hr., 9 per day, 50zł). **Polski Express** buses run to **Warsaw** (4½hr., 2 per day, 50zł).

Local Transportation: Gdańsk has an extensive **bus** and **tram** system. 10min. 1.40zł; 30min. 2.80zł; 1hr. 4.30zł; day pass 9.10zł. Buses run 6am-10pm. Bags over 60cm long need their own tickets.

Taxis: MPT (☎96 33; www.artusmpt.gda.pl) is a state-run taxi service.

ORIENTATION AND PRACTICAL INFORMATION

While Gdańsk technically sits on the Baltic coast, its center is 5km inland. Southeast of the **Gdańsk Główny** train and bus stations, the city center is bordered by the major street **Wały Jagiellońskie** on the west and the **Motława River** on the east. To get to the center, take the underpass next to the KFC in front of the train station, go right, and turn left on **ulica Heweliusza.** Turn right on **ulica Rajska** and follow the signs to **Główne Miasto** (Main Town), turning left on **ulica Długa.** Długa becomes the square **Długi Targ** as it widens near the Motława River.

Tourist Office: PTTK Gdańsk, ul. Długa 45 (☎301 91 51; www.pttk-gdansk.pl), in Główne Miasto. Tour guides (☎301 60 96) May-Sept. for groups of 3-10, 80zł per person. Open May-Sept. M-F 9am-5pm, Sa-Su 9am-3pm; Oct.-Apr. M-F 9am-6pm.

Budget Travel: Almatur, Długi Targ 11, 2nd fl. (☎301 24 03). Sells ISICs (75zł) and books international air and ferry tickets. Open M-F 10am-6pm, Sa 10am-2pm. MC/V.

Currency Exchange: Bank Pekao SA, ul. Grunwaldeka 92/98 (☎801 365 365), cashes travelers checks for 1% commission and gives MC/V cash advances for no commission. Open M-F 8am-6pm. For other offices that offer these services, look for *"Kantor"* signs.

English-Language Bookstore: Empik, ul. Podwale Grodzkie 8 (☎301 62 88, ext. 115). Sells maps and *Gdańsk in Your Pocket* (5zł). Open M-Sa 9am-9pm, Su 11am-8pm.

24hr. Pharmacy: Apteka Drowcow (☎301 28 41), at the train station, upstairs. Ring bell for service at night.

Medical Services: Emergency care available at **Szpital Specjalistyczny im. M. Kopernika,** ul. Nowe Ogrody 5 (☎302 30 31).

Internet Access: Jazz'n'Java, ul. Tkacka 17/18 (☎305 36 16), in the Old Town. 3zł per 30min., 5zł per hr. Free coffee and tea. Open daily 10am-10pm.

Post Office: Ul. Długa 23/28 (☎301 80 49). For *Poste Restante,* enter on ul. Pocztowa. Currency exchange and fax. Open M-F 8am-8pm, Sa 9am-3pm. **Postal Code:** 80-801.

ACCOMMODATIONS

With Gdańsk's limited tourist infrastructure and increasing popularity among travelers, it's best to make accommodations arrangements ahead, especially in summer. **University dorms** are open to travelers in July and August; for further info consult the **PTTK** tourist office. Private rooms (20-80zł) can be arranged through either PTTK or **Grand-Tourist** (Biuro Podróży i Zakwaterowania), ul. Podwale Grodzkie 8, across from Empik. (☎301 26 34; www.grand-tourist.pl. Singles from 90zł; 2- to 4-person apartments from 180zł. Open July-Aug. daily 8am-8pm; Sept.-June M-Sa 10am-6pm, Su 10am-2pm.)

Hostel Przy Targu Rybnym, ul. Grodzka 21 (☎301 56 27; www.gdanskhostel.com), off Targ Rybny, across from the *baszta* (tower). The service is uneven, but guests enjoy the chummy common room, Internet access, free soup, and delicious complimentary breakfast. Reception 24hr. Dorms 40zł; doubles 150zł; quads 250zł. ❶

Baltic Hostel, ul. 3-go Maja 25 (☎721 96 57; www.baltichostel.com). From the train station, take the KFC underpass to the bus station, turn right on ul. 3-go Maja, and take the path on your right. In an aging brick building, Baltic offers rooms with hardwood floors and eclectic furnishings. Bike and kayak rental available. Breakfast included. Free Internet. Reception 24hr. Dorms 35-40zł; doubles 100zł. ❶

Skolne Schronisko Młodzieżowe (HI), ul. Wałowa 21 (☎301 23 13). From the train station, follow ul. Karmelicka, turn left on ul. Rajska, and then right on ul. Wałowa. Unusually large rooms are clean and well lit. No smoking or drinking. Check-in 3pm. Check-out 10am. Curfew midnight. Reserve ahead. Dorms 20zł; singles 35zł; doubles 55zł. ❶

FOOD

Gdańsk has a wealth of excellent traditional food options. During warm weather, stalls selling fresh produce line ul. Podwale Staromiejskie at the intersection with ul. Grobla IV. For dairy, fish, and smoked meats, try **Hala Targowa** on ul. Panska, off Podwale Staromiejskie. (Open M-F 9am-6pm, Sa-Su 9am-3pm.) **Green Way,** ul. Długa 11, is a vegetarian milk bar chain with branches throughout Poland.

Cafe Kamienica, ul. Mariacka 37/39, in the shadow of St. Mary's Church, masters casual elegance. Superb *szarlotka* (apple pie; 5zł). Tea 4zł. Coffee 5zł. Light entrees 14-22zł. Open daily 10am-midnight. AmEx/MC/V. ❸

Pierogarnia u Dzika, ul. Piwna 59/60. Locals swear by these pierogi (10 pieces 12-18zł), stuffed with everything from fruit to caviar. Open daily 10am-10pm. MC/V. ❷

Bar Pod Ryba, Długi Targ 35/38/1. This eatery has a limited menu; the specialty is stuffed baked potatoes overflowing with cheese and meat. Entrees 6-20zł. Open daily July-Aug. 11am-10pm; Sept.-June 11am-7pm. AmEx/MC/V. ❶

Restauracja Gdańska, ul. Sw. Ducha. 16/24. Clocks, oil paintings, and figurines add a sense of Baroque topsy-turvy to cut-crystal elegance. A favorite of local celebrities, including former president Lech Wałęsa. Entrees 18-60zł. Open daily 11am-midnight. ❸

Bar Mleczny Turystyczny, ul. Szeroka 8/10. Battle tray-wielding locals for seat space at this cafeteria-style milk bar. Polish specialties include *gołąbki* (stuffed cabbage; 4.10zł). Entrees 3-6zł. Open M-F 7:30am-6pm, Sa-Su 9am-4pm. Cash only. ❶

SIGHTS

DŁUGI TARG. Długi Targ (Long Market) is the handsome square at the heart of **Główne Miasto** (Main Town). The stone Upland Gate and the elegant blue-gray Golden Gate, emblazoned with gold leaf moldings and the shields of Poland, Prussia, and Germany, mark the western entrance to ul. Długa. In the square, **Neptune's Fountain** (Fontanna Neptuna) faces the 16th-century facade of **Arthur's Court** (Dwór Artusa), a palace with a Renaissance interior and wood-carved spiral staircase that was restored in 1997. At the intersection of ul. Długa and Długi Targ, the 14th-century **Ratusz** (Town Hall) houses a branch of the **Gdańsk History Museum** (Muzeum Historii Gdańska), which covers the city's past from its first historical mention to the rubble left behind by WWII. *(Court and museum open June-Sept. M 10am-3pm, Tu-Sa 10am-6pm, Su 11am-6pm; Oct.-May Tu-Sa 10am-4pm, Su 11am-4pm. Each branch 8zł, students 4zł; free June-Sept. M, Oct.-May Su.)* A block north, the brick **St. Mary's Church** (Kościół Najświętszej Marii Panny) has an intricate 15th-century astronomical clock and a panoramic view of the city. *(Open June-Aug. M-Sa 9am-5:30pm, Su 1-5:30pm; low season reduced hours. 3zł, students 1.50zł.)*

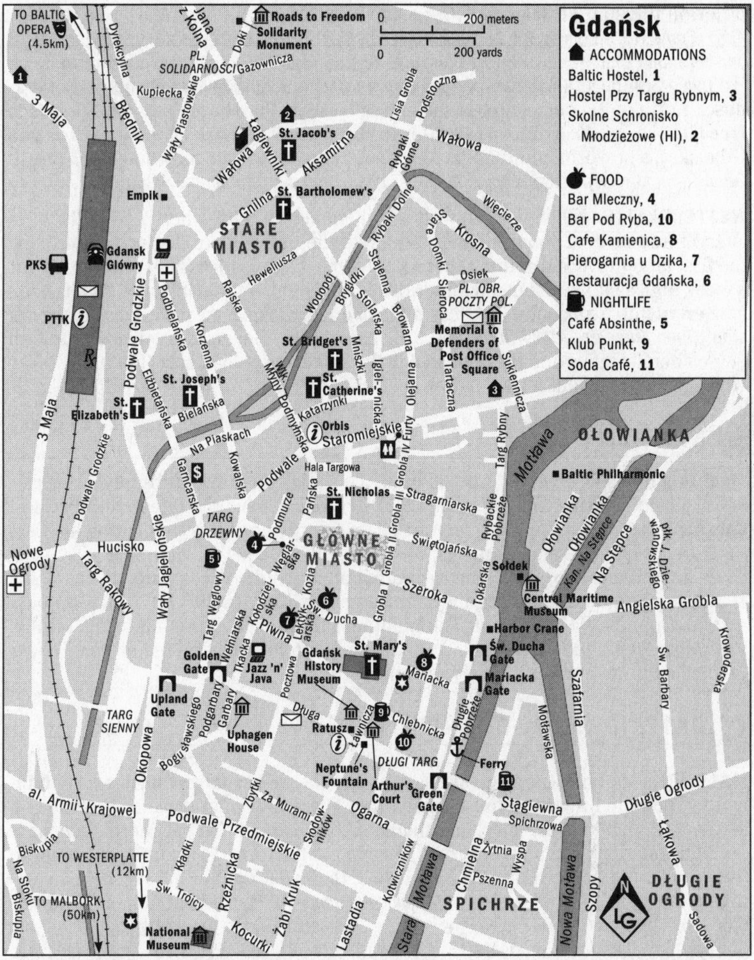

ELSEWHERE IN GŁÓWNE MIASTO. In the vaults of a former Franciscan monastery, the **National Museum** (Muzeum Narodowe Gdańsku) has a large collection of 16th- to 20th-century art and furniture, including Hans Memling's *Last Judgment. (ul. Toruńska 1, off Podwale Przedmiejskie. Open June to mid-Sept. Tu-F 9am-4pm, Sa-Su 10am-4pm; mid-Sept. to May Tu-Su 9am-4pm. 10zł, students 6zł. Sa free.)* The **Memorial to the Defenders of the Post Office Square** (Obrońców Poczty) honors the postal workers' courageous stand on September 1, 1939, at the start of WWII. *(From Podwale Staromiejskie, go north on Olejarna and right at the sign for Urzad Poctowy Gdańsk 1. Open Tu-F noon-6pm, Sa-Su 10:30am-4pm. 3zł, students 2zł; Tu free.)* Row houses line the cobblestoned ul. św. Ducha, ul. Mariacka, and ul. Chlebnicka, north of Długi Targ. Ul. Mariacka, with its stone porches and gaping dragon-head gutter spouts, leads to riverside ul. Długie Pobrzeże. To the left is the huge Gothic **Harbor Crane** (Żuraw) from the 13th century, part of the **Central Maritime Museum** (Centralne Muzeum Morskie). Two more branches of the museum lie across the river: one on land, the other on the ship **Sołdek.** *(Open June-Aug. daily 10am-6pm; Sept.-May Tu-Su 9:30am-4pm. Crane 6zł, students 4zł. Museum 6/4zł. Sołdek 6/4zł. Shuttle boat round-trip 2/1zł. All museums and shuttle boat 14/8zł.)* The flags of the Soviet bloc's first trade union, Lech Wałęsa's Solidarity (Solidarność), fly again at the **Solidarity Monument,** pl. Solidarności, north of the city center at the end of ul. Wały Piastowskie. At the **Roads to Freedom** (Drogi do wolnisci) exhibit in the nearby Gdańsk Shipyard (Stocznia Gdańska), a powerful multimedia epic depicts the rise of the movement. *(ul. Doki 1. Open Tu-Su May-Sept. 10am-5pm; Oct.-Apr. 10am-4pm. 5zł, students 3zł; W free.)*

WESTERPLATTE. When Germany attacked Poland on September 1, 1939, the little island fort guarding Gdańsk's harbor gained the unfortunate distinction of being the first target of WWII. Outnumbered 20 to one, its defenders held out bravely for a week until a lack of food and munitions forced them out. **Guardhouse #1** has been converted into a museum. *(Take bus #106 or 606 south from the train station to the last stop. Open May-Sept. daily 9am-7pm. 3zł, students 2zł.)* Beyond the museum, a path passes bunker ruins and the **Memorial to the Defenders of the Coast** (Pomnik Obrońców Wybrzeża). Giant letters below spell "Nigdy Więcej Wojny" ("No More War").

POLAND

NIGHTLIFE

Długi Targ hums at night as crowds of all ages pack its pubs, clubs, and beer gardens. *City* magazine and *Gdańsk in Your Pocket* have the latest club listings. **Cafe Absinthe,** ul. św. Ducha 2, next to Teatr Wybreże, attracts ruminating intellectuals by day and a rambunctious, absinthe-imbibing set by night. (☎320 37 84. Open daily 10am-4am.) The chic restaurant and nightclub **Soda Cafe,** ul. Chmielna 103/104, pulsates with neon energy and enthusiasm. (☎305 12 56; www.sodacafe.pl. Open Su-W 11am-2am, Th-Sa noon-5am. Kitchen closes midnight.) Bohemian **Klub Punkt,** ul. Chlebnicka 2, stands apart from Gdańsk's tamer bars. (Beer 7zł. Open Su-Th 4pm-1am, F-Sa 7pm-5am.)

DAYTRIP FROM GDAŃSK

MALBORK. Malbork (pop. 40,000) is home to the **world's largest brick castle,** built by the Teutonic Knights in the 14th century. The spectacular grounds include collections of amber, weaponry, and medieval tombstones. To get there, turn right out of the station onto ul. Dworcowa, then left at the fork. Go around the corner to the roundabout and cross to ul. Kościuszki, then veer right on ul. Piasłowska and follow the signs for the castle. *(SKM trains run frequently from Gdańsk to Malbork. 40min., 6.60-14zł. Castle ☎055 647 09 78; www.zamek.malbork.pl. Open Tu-Su May-Sept. 9am-7pm; Oct.-Apr. 9am-3pm. 30zł, students 17.50zł. Polish tour included. Kiosks sell English-language booklets, 7zł. Call ahead for English-language tours, 150zł. Courtyards, terraces, and moats open Tu-Su May-Sept. 9am-8pm; Oct.-Apr. 9am-4pm. 6/4zł.)*

SOPOT ☎058

Poland's premier resort town, magnetic Sopot (pop. 50,000) draws visitors to its sandy beaches and renowned nightlife. Restaurants, shops, and street musicians dot the graceful pedestrian promenade, **ulica Bohaterów Monte Cassino.** The wooden **pier** *(molo)*, the longest in Europe at 512m, provides sweeping views of the Baltic. (Pier M-F 2.50zł, Sa-Su 3.50zł.) **Remanent,** al. Niepodległości 786/2, at the base of ul. Monte Cassino, is a time warp furnished entirely with Soviet-era cast-offs, including dusty TVs, motorbikes, and cardboard boxes. Beer (5zł) is served in mustard jars. (☎888 33 44. Open daily 4pm-2am.) **Soho clubogaleria,** ul. Monte Cassino 61, spins lounge, house, and electropop while brandishing art and attitude. (☎551 65 27. Beer 7zł. Open daily noon-5am.) **Mandarynka,** ul. Bema 6, off ul. Monte Cassino, offers three tangerine-splashed floors of partying; each floor has faster music and even faster drinking than the one below. (☎550 45 63. Beer 7zł. Open M 1pm-last customer, Tu-Su noon-last customer.)

Affordable university **dorms,** which can be arranged through the tourist office, are available throughout the summer. Local institution **Bar Przystań ❶,** al. Wojska Polskiego 11, along the beach, serves fresh seafood under fishing nets and hanging dried blowfish. (☎550 02 41; www.barprzystan.pl. Fresh fish 4.20-7zł per 100g. Hevelius vodka 5zł. Open daily 11am-11pm. Cash only.) *Naleśniki* (filled pancakes) are serious business at **Parasolka ❷,** ul. Monte Cassino 31, where you can choose from 50 different fillings and sit in a garden with an avant-garde fountain. (☎550 46 44. Entrees 7-18zł. Open daily 10am-10pm. Cash only.)

The **SKM commuter rail** connects Sopot to Gdańsk (20min.; 1-6 per hr.; 2.80zł, students 1.40zł). Ul. Dworcowa begins at the station and leads to ul. Monte Cassino, which runs along the sea to the pier. **Ferries** (☎604 837 793) head from the end of the pier to Gdynia (35min.; 2 per day; 24zł, students 14zł) and Hel (30min, 7 per day, 45/29zł). The IT **tourist office,** ul. Dworcowa 4, by the train station, sells maps (4-5zł) and arranges rooms. (☎550 37 83. Open daily June to mid-Sept. 10am-8pm; mid-Sept. to May M-F 10am-6pm.)

PORTUGAL

Today's Portugal wears the ornaments of new trends and thriving cities while still showing the scars and raw elements of its past. Portugal's history has been turbulent, reaching highs during the Golden Age of Vasco da Gama's maritime discoveries and plummeting to lows in the dark years of vassal status under the Moors, Spanish, and French. These extremes of fortune have contributed to the uniquely Portuguese concept of *saudade*, a yearning for the glories of the past and a dignified resignation to the fact that the future can never compete. To experience *saudade* through a *fado* singer's tender song or over a glass of port is to know Portugal.

DISCOVER PORTUGAL: SUGGESTED ITINERARIES

THREE DAYS. Make your way through **Lisbon** (1 day; p. 806); venture through its famous Moorish district, the Alfama, Castelo de São Jorge, and the Parque das Nações. By night, listen to *fado* and hit the clubs in Barrio Alto. Daytrip to **Sintra's** fairy-tale castles (1 day; p. 816), then sip wine in **Porto** (1 day; p. 821).

ONE WEEK. After wandering the streets of **Lisbon** (2 days) and **Sintra** (1 day), lounge on the beaches of **Lagos** (1 day; p. 819) and admire the windswept cliffs of **Sagres** (1 day; p. 821). From there, move to vibrant **Coimbra** (1 day; p. 817) before ending your week in **Porto** (1 day).

BEST OF PORTUGAL, TWO WEEKS. After the sights, sounds, and cafes of **Lisbon** (4 days), daytrip to enchanting **Sintra** (1 day). Head down to the infamous beach-and-bar town of **Lagos** (2 days), where hordes of visitors dance the night away. Head over to **Sagres** (1 day), once considered the edge of the world, then check out the macabre bone chapel in **Évora** (1 day; p. 818). Head north to the university town of **Coimbra** (2 days) and **Porto** (2 days), then finish your tour in the impressive squares of **Viana do Castelo** (1 day; p. 823).

ESSENTIALS

WHEN TO GO

Summer is high season, but the southern coast draws tourists between March and November. In the low season, many hostels slash their prices and reservations are seldom necessary. While Lisbon and some of the larger towns (especially the university town of Coimbra) burst with vitality year-round, many smaller towns virtually shut down in winter, and sights reduce their hours nearly everywhere.

DOCUMENTS AND FORMALITIES

EMBASSIES AND CONSULATES. Foreign embassies in Portugal are in Lisbon. Portuguese embassies abroad include: **Australia,** 23 Culgoa Circuit, O'Malley, Canberra, ACT 2606; mailing address: P.O. Box 9092, Deakin, ACT 2600 (☎612 6290 1733); **Canada,** 645 Island Park Dr., Ottawa, ON K1Y 0B8 (☎613-729-2270); **Ireland,** Knocksinna Mews, 7 Willow Park, Foxrock, Dublin 18 (☎353 289 4416); **UK,** 3 Portland Pl., London W1B 1HR (☎020 7291 3770); **US,** 2012 Massachusetts Ave., NW, Washington, D.C. 20036 (☎202-332-3007). **New Zealand** citizens should contact the embassy in Australia.

FACTS AND FIGURES

Official Name: Portuguese Republic.
Capital: Lisbon.
Major Cities: Coimbra, Porto.
Population: 10,606,000.
Land Area: 92,000 sq. km.
Time Zone: GMT.
Language: Portuguese.
Religion: Roman Catholic (94%).
Number of Grape Varieties Authorized for Making Port: 48.

VISA AND ENTRY INFORMATION. EU citizens do not need a visa. Citizens of Australia, Canada, New Zealand, the UK, and the US do not need a visa for stays up to 90 days, beginning upon entry into any of the countries within the EU's freedom-of-movement zone. Portugal does not allow entrance if the holder's passport expires in fewer than three months following the expected departure date.

TOURIST SERVICES AND MONEY

EMERGENCY	**Police, Ambulance,** and **Fire:** ☎ 112.

TOURIST OFFICES. The official tourism website is www.portugalinsite.com. When in Portugal, stop by municipal and provincial tourist offices, listed in the **Practical Information** section of each city and town, for maps and advice.

MONEY. The **euro (€)** has replaced the escudo as the unit of currency in Portugal. As a general rule, it's cheaper to exchange money in Portugal than it is to exchange it at home. **ATMs** offer the best exchange rates once in Portugal. Credit cards also offer decent exchange rates and may even sometimes be required to reserve hotel rooms or rental cars. **MasterCard** (known in Portugal as **Eurocard**) and **Visa** are the most frequently accepted. **Tips** of 5-10% are customary only in fancy restaurants or hotels. Some cheaper restaurants include a 10% service charge; if they don't and you'd like to leave a tip, round up and leave the change. Taxi drivers do not expect a tip unless the trip was especially long. Retail goods in Portugal bear a 16% **value added tax (VAT),** usually included in the listed price. In the airport, upon departure, non-EU citizens who have stayed in the EU fewer than 180 days can claim a refund on the tax paid for purchases at participating stores. Ask the shop where you have made the purchase to supply you with a tax return form, but note that stores will often provide them only for purchases of more than €50-100. **Bargaining** is not customary in shops, but you can give it a shot at the local market *(mercado)* or when looking for a private room *(quarto)*.

TRANSPORTATION

BY PLANE. Most major international airlines serve Lisbon (LIS; ☎218 413 500); some also serve Faro (FAO; ☎289 800 800) and Porto (OPO; 229 432 400). **TAP Air Portugal** (Canada and the US ☎800-221-7370, Portugal 707 20 57 00, UK 845 601 09 32; www.tap.pt) is Portugal's national airline, serving domestic locations and many major international cities. **Portugália** (☎351 218 93 80 70; www.flypga.pt) is a smaller Portuguese airline that flies between Faro, Lisbon, Porto, major Spanish cities, and other Western European destinations. For more information on European air travel, see p. 46.

BY TRAIN. Caminhos de Ferro Portugueses (☎213 21 57 00; www.cp.pt) is Portugal's national railway. Lines run to domestic destinations, Madrid, and Paris. For travel outside of the Braga-Porto-Coimbra-Lisbon line, the bus is better. Lisbon, where local trains are fast and efficient, is the exception. Trains often leave at irregular hours, and posted schedules *(horários)* aren't always accurate; check ticket booths upon arrival. Fines for riding without a ticket *(sem bilhete)* are exorbitant. Those under 12 or over 65 get half-price tickets. **Youth discounts** are only available to Portuguese citizens. The Portugal Flexipass is not worth buying, as train tickets are inexpensive. For more information on getting to Portugal, see p. 46.

BY BUS. Buses are cheap, frequent, and connect to just about every town in Portugal. **Rodoviária** (☎212 94 71 00), the national bus company, has recently been privatized. Each company name corresponds to a particular region of the country, such as Rodoviária Alentejo or Minho e Douro, with a few exceptions such as EVA in the Algarve. Private regional companies also operate, including **AVIC, Cabanelas,** and **Mafrense.** Beware of non-express buses in small regions like Estremadura and Alentejo, which stop every few minutes. Express service *(expressos)* between major cities is good, and inexpensive city buses often run to nearby villages. Portugal's main **Euroline** (p. 54) affiliates are Internorte, Intercentro, and Intersul. **Busabout** coaches stop in Portugal at Lisbon, Lagos, and Porto. Every coach has a guide onboard to answer questions and to make travel arrangements en route.

BY CAR. A **driver's license** from one's home country is all that is required to rent a car. Portugal has the highest automobile accident rate per capita in Western Europe. The highway system *(itinerarios principais)* is good, but off the main arteries, the narrow roads are difficult to negotiate. Speed limits are ignored, recklessness is common, and lighting and road surfaces are often inadequate. Parking space in cities is nonexistent. The national automobile association, the **Automóvel Clube de Portugal (ACP),** Shopping Center Amoreiras, Loja 1122 Lisbon (☎213 71 47 20; www.acp.pt), has breakdown and towing service and first aid.

BY THUMB. In Portugal, **hitchhiking** is rare. Beach-bound locals occasionally hitchhike in summer, but more commonly stick to the inexpensive bus system. Rides are easiest to come by between smaller towns and at gas stations near highways and rest stops. Let's Go does not recommend hitchhiking.

KEEPING IN TOUCH

PHONE CODES	**Country code:** 351. **International dialing prefix:** 00. Within Portugal, dial city code + local number. For more info on placing international calls, see the inside back cover.

EMAIL AND THE INTERNET. Cybercafes in cities and most towns charge around €1.20-4 per hr. for Internet access. When in doubt, try the library, where there is often at least one computer equipped for (occasionally free) Internet access.

TELEPHONE. The national company is **Portugal Telecom.** Pay phones are coin- or phone card-operated. Portugal uses the **Credifone** and Portugal Telecom systems. For both, the basic call unit is €0.10. Telecom cards using "patch" chips are common in Lisbon and Porto and increasingly elsewhere. Credifone cards with magnetic strips are most useful outside these two big cities. Find them at drugstores, post offices, and locations posted on phone booths. City codes all begin with a 2; local calls do not require dialing the city code. For directory assistance, dial ☎118. **Calling cards** are normally the best method of making international calls.

MAIL. Mail in Portugal is somewhat inefficient. **Airmail** *(via aerea)* takes one to two weeks to reach Canada or the US, and more to get to Australia and New Zealand. **Surface mail** *(superficie)*, for packages only, takes up to two months. **Registered** or **blue mail** takes five to eight business days for roughly three times the price of airmail. **EMS** or **Express Mail** will probably arrive overseas in three to four days, though it costs more than double the blue mail price. Address mail to be held as follows: LAST NAME, First Name; Posta Restante; post office street address; city, Postal Code, PORTUGAL; PAR AVION.

ACCOMMODATIONS AND CAMPING

PORTUGAL	❶	❷	❸	❹	❺
ACCOMMODATIONS	under €16	€16-20	€20-30	€30-40	over €40

Movijovem, R. Lúcio de Azevedo 27, 1600-146 Lisbon (☎707 20 30 30; www.pousadasjuventude.pt), the Portuguese Hostelling International affiliate, oversees the country's HI hostels. All bookings can be made through them. A bed in a *pousada da juventude* costs €9-15 per night, slightly less in the low season, and includes breakfast and linens. Though often the cheapest option, hostels may lie far from the town center. To reserve in high season, get an **International Booking Voucher** from Movijovem (or your country's HI affiliate) and send it to the desired hostel four to eight weeks in advance. In the low season (Oct.-Apr.), double-check to see if the hostel is open. **Hotels** in Portugal tend to be pricey. Prices typically include breakfast and showers, and most rooms without bath or shower have a sink. **Pensões,** also called **residencias,** are a budget traveler's mainstay, cheaper than hotels and only slightly more expensive (and much more common) than crowded youth hostels. Like hostels, *pensões* generally provide sheets and towels. Many do not take reservations in high season, but for those that do, book a week ahead. **Quartos** are rooms in private residences, similar to Spain's *casas particulares*. These may be the only option in smaller towns or the cheapest one in cities; tourist offices can help find one. Prices are flexible and bargaining expected. Portugal has 150 **official campgrounds** *(parques de campismo)*, often beach-accessible and equipped with grocery stores. Police are cracking down on illegal camping, so don't try it. Tourist offices stock *Portugal: Camping and Caravan Sites*, a free guide to official campgrounds. For more info, contact the **Federação de Campismo e Montanhismo de Portugal,** Av. Coronel Eduardo Galhardo 24D, 1199-007 Lisbon (☎218 12 68 90; www.fcmportugal.com).

FOOD AND DRINK

PORTUGAL	❶	❷	❸	❹	❺
FOOD	under €6	€6-10	€10-15	€15-20	over €20

Portuguese dishes are seasoned with olive oil, garlic, herbs, and sea salt, but few spices. The fish selection includes *choco grelhado* (grilled cuttlefish), *linguado grelhado* (grilled sole), and *peixe espada* (swordfish). Portugal's renowned *queijos* (cheeses) are made from the milk of cows, goats, and sheep. For dessert, try *pudim*, or *flan* (caramel custard). A hearty *almoço* (lunch) is eaten between noon and 2pm; *jantar* (dinner) is served between 8pm and midnight. *Meia dose* (half-portions) cost more than half-price but are often more than adequate; full portions may satisfy two. The *prato do dia* (special of the day) and the set *menú* of appetizer, bread, entree, and dessert, are also filling choices. The cheap, high-quality Portuguese *vinho* (wine) is astounding. Its delicious relative, *vinho do porto* (port), is a dessert in itself. Coffees include *bica* (black espresso), *galão* (with milk, in a glass), and *café com leite* (with milk, in a cup).

> TIP **NO SUCH THING AS A FREE LUNCH.** Waiters in Portugal will put an assortment of snacks, ranging from simple bread and butter to sardine paste, cured ham, or herbed olives, on your table before the appetizer is served. But check the menu for the prices before you dig in: you nibble it, you bought it.

HOLIDAYS AND FESTIVALS

Holidays: New Year's Day (Jan. 1); Good Friday (Apr. 6); Easter (Apr. 8); Liberation Day (Apr. 25); Labor Day (May 1); Corpus Christi (May 29); Portugal Day (June 10); Feast of the Assumption (Aug. 15); Republic Day (Oct. 5); All Saints' Day (Nov. 1); Restoration of Independence Day (Dec. 1); Feast of the Immaculate Conception (Dec. 8); Christmas (Dec. 25); New Year's Eve (Dec. 31).

Festivals: All of Portugal celebrates *Carnaval* (Feb. 20) and Holy Week (Apr. 1-8). Coimbra holds the *Queima das Fitas* (Burning of the Ribbons) festival in early May, celebrating the end of the school year. In June, Batalha holds a *Feira International* celebrating the food, wine, and traditional handicrafts of the region, and Lisbon hosts the *Festas da Cidade*, honoring the birth of St. Anthony with music, games, and parades. For more information on Portuguese festivals, see www.portugal.org.

BEYOND TOURISM

As a **volunteer** in Portugal, you can contribute to efforts concerning environmental protection, social welfare, or political activism. While not many students think of **studying** abroad in Portugal, most Portuguese universities accept foreign students. Being an au pair and teaching English are popular options for long-term **work**.

Grupo de Acção e Intervenção Ambiental (GAIA), Faculdade de Ciências e Tecnologia, 2829-516 Caparica, POR (☎212 94 96 50; www.gaia.org.pt). Works to educate the Portuguese public about environmental issues and campaigns against the production and sale of genetically modified food.

Teach Abroad (www.teachabroad.com). Brings you to listings around the world for paid or stipend positions teaching English.

Universidade de Lisboa, Rectorate Al. da Universidade, Cidade Universitária, 1649-004 Lisbon, POR (☎217 96 76 24; www.ul.pt). Allows foreign students to enroll directly.

LISBON (LISBOA) ☎21

A rare combination of glorious history and bittersweet memory awaits in Lisbon (pop. 2,500,000), where a sense of *saudade* (nostalgia) permeates everyday life. Travelers hear it in the traditional *fado* music, drink it in the celebrated wines, and, above all, see it in local faces. Such is the glory of Lisbon—it can fill you with wonder and break your heart all at once.

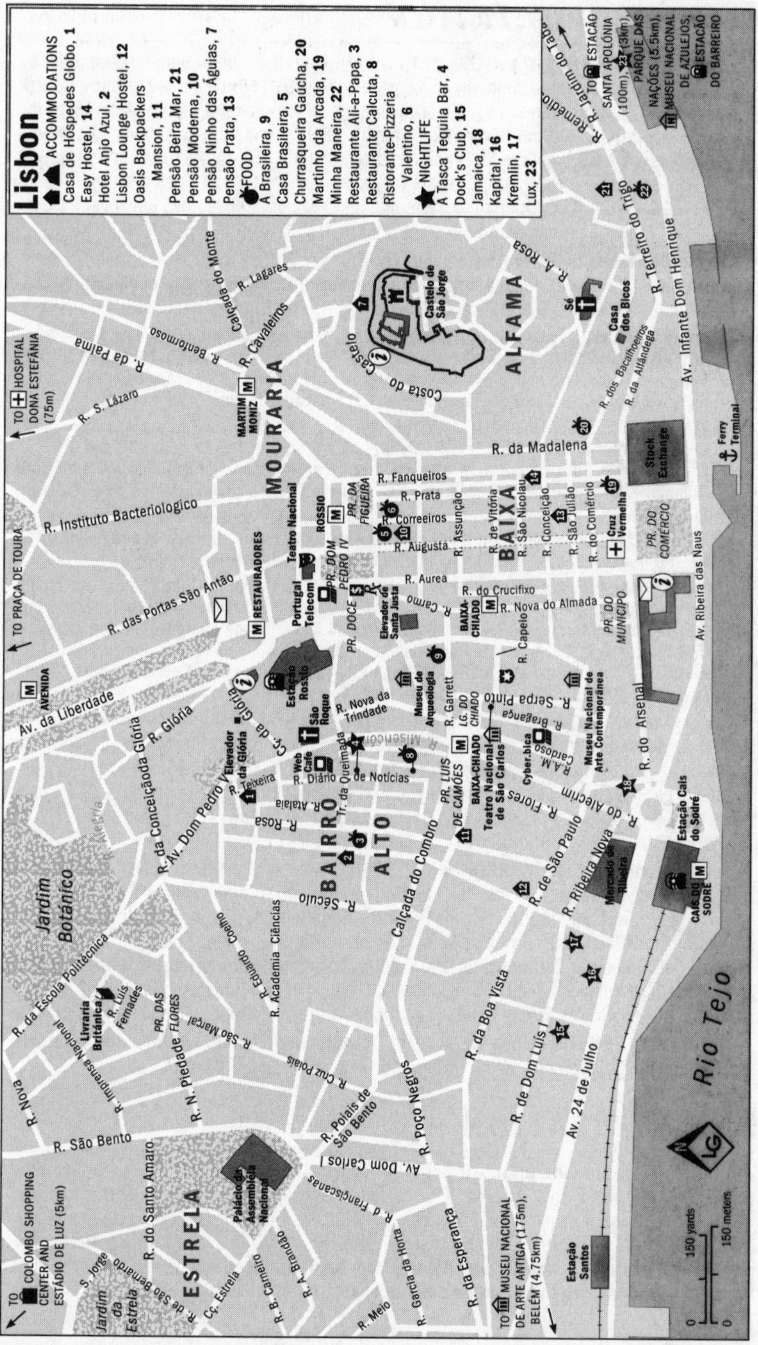
Lisbon
ACCOMMODATIONS
Casa de Hóspedes Globo, 1
Easy Hostel, 14
Hotel Anjo Azul, 2
Lisbon Lounge Hostel, 12
Oasis Backpackers Mansion, 11
Pensão Beira Mar, 21
Pensão Moderna, 10
Pensão Ninho das Águias, 7
Pensão Prata, 13
FOOD
A Brasileira, 9
Casa Brasileira, 5
Churrasqueira Gaúcha, 20
Martinho da Arcada, 19
Minha Maneira, 22
Restaurante Ali-a-Papa, 3
Restaurante Calcuta, 8
Ristorante-Pizzeria Valentino, 6
NIGHTLIFE
A Tasca Tequila Bar, 4
Dock's Club, 15
Jamaica, 18
Kapital, 16
Kremlin, 17
Lux, 23
TO HOSPITAL DONA ESTEFÂNIA (75m)
TO PRAÇA DE TOURA
TO COLOMBO SHOPPING CENTER AND ESTÁDIO DE LUZ (5km)
TO MUSEU NACIONAL DE ARTE ANTIGA (175m), BELÉM (4.75km)
TO ESTAÇÃO SANTA APOLÓNIA (100m), 23 (3km), PARQUE DAS NAÇÕES (5.5km), MUSEU NACIONAL DE AZULEJOS, ESTAÇÃO DO BARREIRO
MOURARIA
ALFAMA
BAIXA
BAIRRO ALTO
ESTRELA
Castelo de São Jorge
Sé
Casa dos Bicos
Stock Exchange
Ferry Terminal
PR. DO COMÉRCIO
PR. DO MUNICÍPIO
ROSSIO
RESTAURADORES
AVENIDA
MARTIM MONIZ
BAIXA-CHIADO
CAIS DO SODRÉ
Estação Rossio
Estação Cais do Sodré
Estação Santos
Teatro Nacional
Portugal Telecom
Elevador de Santa Justa
Elevador da Glória
São Roque
Museu de Arqueologia
Web Cafe
Cyber.bica
Teatro Nacional de São Carlos
Museu Nacional de Arte Contemporânea
Mercado da Ribeira
Cruz Vermelha
Livraria Britânica
Jardim Botânico
Jardim da Estrela
Palácio da Assembleia Nacional
PR. DOM PEDRO IV
PR. DA FIGUEIRA
PR. LUIS DE CAMÕES
LG. DO CHIADO
PR. DAS FLORES
Av. da Liberdade
Av. Infante Dom Henrique
Av. Ribeira das Naus
Av. 24 de Julho
Av. Dom Carlos I
R. da Madalena
R. Fanqueiros
R. Prata
R. Correeiros
R. Augusta
R. Aurea
R. Assunção
R. de Vitória
R. São Nicolau
R. Conceição
R. São Julião
R. do Comércio
R. do Crucifixo
R. Nova do Almada
R. Carmo
R. Capelo
R. Garrett
R. Serpa Pinto
R. do Arsenal
R. do Alecrim
R. Flores
R. de São Paulo
R. Ribeira Nova
R. da Boa Vista
R. de Dom Luís I
R. Instituto Bacteriologico
R. das Portas São Antão
R. da Palma
R. S. Lázaro
R. Benformoso
R. Cavaleiros
Calçada do Monte
R. Lagares
Costa do Castelo
R. dos Bacalhoeiros
R. da Alfândega
R. Terreiro do Trigo
R. A. Rosa
R. Remédios
R. Jardim do Tabaco
R. Glória
Cç. da Glória
R. da Conceição da Glória
R. Av. Dom Pedro V
R. Teixeira
R. Diário de Notícias
Tr. da Queimada
R. Atalaia
R. Rosa
R. Nova da Trindade
R. Século
Calçada do Combro
R. Misericórdia
R. Bragança
R.A.M. Cardoso
R. da Escola Politécnica
R. Luis Fernandes
R. Imprensa Nacional
R. Nova
R. N. Piedade
R. São Marçal
R. Eduardo Coelho
R. Academia Ciências
R. Cruz Polais
R. Polais de São Bento
R. Poço Negros
R. São Bento
R. do Santo Amaro
R. de São Bernardo
S. Jorge
Cç. Estrela
R. B. Carneiro
R. A. Brandão
R. Garcia da Horta
R. d Franciscanas
R. da Esperança
R. Meio
Rio Tejo
150 yards
150 meters
N
LG

TRANSPORTATION

Flights: Aeroporto de Lisboa (**LIS;** ☎841 3500). From the terminal, turn right and follow the path to the bus stop. Take the express AeroBus #91 (15min., every 20min., €1.20) to Pr. dos Restauradores, in front of the tourist office, or take bus #44 or 45 to the same location (15-20min., every 12-15min., €1.20). A taxi from downtown costs about €10 plus a €1.50 baggage fee. Trips are billed by time. Ask at the tourist office (☎845 0660) inside the airport about buying prepaid vouchers for taxi rides from the airport. (M-F €14, Sa-Su €17. Open daily 7am-midnight.) Major airlines have offices at Pr. Marquês do Pombal and along Av. da Liberdade.

Trains: Caminhos de Ferro Portugueses (☎808 20 82 08; www.cp.pt). 5 main stations, each serving different destinations. Trains are slow, inconsistent, and confusing; buses, though more expensive and without toilets, are faster and more comfortable.

Estação do Barreiro (☎347 2930), across Rio Tejo. Serves southern destinations. Ferries leave from the Terreiro do Paço dock off Pr. do Comércio. (Ferry ride 30min., every 30min., €1.90.) To: **Évora** and **Lagos,** take train to **Pinhal Novo** (25min., every 25min., €1.20) and transfer. From Pinhal Novo, trains go to **Évora** (1½hr., 2 per day, €7) and **Lagos** (3½hr., 5 per day, €12-17).

Estação Cais do Sodré (☎347 0181), just beyond R. do Alecrim, near Baixa. M: Cais do Sodré. Take the metro or bus #36, 45, or 91 from Pr. dos Restauradores or tram #28 from Estação Santa Apolónia. To: the monastery in **Belém** (10min., every 15min., €1.05), **Cascais** and **Estoril** (30min., every 30min., €1.55), and the youth hostel in **Oeiras** (20min., every 30min., €1.20).

Estação Rossio (☎346 5022). M: Rossio or Restauradores. Serves western destinations. Estação Rossio is closed until the end of 2006 due to tunnel construction. To reach its destinations, **Sintra** and **Queluz,** take the metro to another train station or travel directly by bus.

Estação Santa Apolónia (☎888 4025), Av. Infante Dom Henrique, runs the international, northern, and eastern lines. All trains to Santa Apolónia also stop at **Estação Oriente** (M: Oriente) by the Parque das Nações. The international terminal has currency exchange and an info desk (English spoken). To reach downtown, take bus #9, 46, or 59 to Pr. dos Restauradores. To: **Aveiro** (3-3½hr., 20 per day, €16-24); **Braga** (5hr., 3 per day, €28); **Coimbra** (2½hr., 24 per day, €21); **Madrid, SPA** (10hr., 10:05pm, €56); **Porto** (3-4½hr., 20 per day, €24-29).

Buses: The bus station is at M: Jardim Zoológico. In the metro station, follow exit signs to Av. C. Bordalo Pinheiro, cross the street, and follow the path up the stairs. Look for signs saying *"autocarros."* **Rede Expressos** buses (☎707 22 33 44; www.rede-expressos.pt) go to: **Braga** (5hr., 13 per day, €17); **Coimbra** (2½hr., 25 per day, €11); **Évora** (2hr., 20 per day, €11); **Faro** (4hr., 16 per day, €16); **Lagos** (4-5hr., 16 per day, €16); **Porto** (3½-4hr., 19 per day, €14) via **Leiria** (2hr., €9).

Public Transportation: CARRIS (☎361 3000; www.carris.pt) runs **buses, trams,** and **funiculars.** If you plan to stay in Lisbon for any length of time, consider a *passe turístico,* good for unlimited travel on all CARRIS transports. 1-, 5-, and 30-day passes are sold in CARRIS booths in most train stations and busier metro stations. (€3.20/13/27.) The 4 lines of the **metro** (☎350 0100; www.metrolisboa.pt) cover downtown and the modern business district. Single ride €0.70; unlimited daily use ticket €3.20; book of 10 tickets €6.50. Trains run daily 6:30am-1am; some stations close earlier.

Taxis: Rádio Táxis de Lisboa (☎811 9000), **Autocoope** (☎793 2756), and **Teletáxis** (☎811 1100). Along Av. da Liberdade and Rossio. Luggage €1.50.

ORIENTATION

The city center is made up of three neighborhoods: **Baixa** (low district), **Bairro Alto** (high district), and hilly **Alfama.** The suburbs extending in both directions along the river represent some of the fastest-growing sections of the city and are interesting for their contrast with the historic districts. Other areas include **Belém** (p. 813), a walk into Portugal's past, **Alcântara,** whose docks are home to much of Lisbon's party scene, and the **Parque das Nações,** site of the 1998 World Expo. Baixa's grid of pedestrian streets is bordered to the north by **Rossio** (a.k.a. Praça Dom Pedro IV) and to the south by **Praça do Comércio,** on the Rio Tejo (River Tagus). East of Baixa is Alfama, Lisbon's oldest, labyrinthine district, and west of Baixa is Bairro Alto with its upscale shopping district, the **Chiado,** crossed by R. do Carmo and R. Garrett. **Avenida da Liberdade** runs north, uphill from Pr. dos Restauradores.

PRACTICAL INFORMATION

Tourist Office: Palácio da Foz, Pr. dos Restauradores (☎346 3314). M: Restauradores. Open daily 9am-8pm. The **Welcome Center,** Pr. do Comércio (☎031 2810), is the city's main office. It sells the Lisbon Card, which includes transportation and entrance to most sights (1-day €14, 2-day €23, 3-day €28). English spoken. Open daily 9am-8pm. Kiosks at Santa Apolónia, Belém, and other locations provide tourist info.

Currency Exchange: Banks are open M-F 8:30am-3pm. **Cota Câmbios,** Pr. Dom Pedro IV 41 (☎322 0480), exchanges currency. Open daily 9am-8pm. The main post office, most banks, and travel agencies also change money.

Emergency: ☎112.

Police: R. Capelo 13 (☎346 6141 or 342 1634). English spoken.

Late-Night Pharmacy: ☎118 (directory assistance). Look for the green cross at intersections, or try **Farmácia Azevedos,** Pr. Dom Pedro IV 31 (☎343 0482), at the base of Rossio in front of the metro.

Hospital: Hospital de Saint Louis, R. Luz Soriano 182 (☎321 6500), Bairro Alto. Open daily 9am-6pm.

Internet Access: Web C@fé, R. Diário de Notícias 126 (☎342 1181). €0.75 per 15min. Open daily 4pm-2am. **Cyber.bica,** R. Duques de Bragança 7 (☎322 5004), in Bairro Alto. €0.75 per 15min. Open M-Sa 11am-midnight.

Post Office: Main office, Ctt Correios, Pr. dos Restauradores (☎323 8700). Open M-F 8am-10pm, Sa-Su 9am-7pm. Often crowded. Branch at Pr. do Comércio (☎322 0920). Open M-F 8:30am-6:30pm. Cash only. Central Lisbon **Postal Code:** 1100.

ACCOMMODATIONS AND CAMPING

Hotels cluster in the center of town on **Avenida da Liberdade,** while many convenient budget hostels are in **Baixa** along the **Rossio** and on **Rua da Prata, Rua dos Correiros,** and **Rua do Ouro.** You'll find some great youth hostels in Bairro Alto and around Santa Catarina, perfect areas for hitting the bars and clubs at night. Lodgings near the **Castelo de São Jorge** are quieter and closer to the sights. At night, be careful in Baixa, Bairro Alto, and Graça; many streets are isolated and poorly lit.

BAIRRO ALTO

Oasis Backpackers Mansion, R. de Santa Catarina 24 (☎347 8044; www.oasislisboa.com). M: Baixa-Chiado, exit Largo do Chiado. The Oasis is a backpacker's dream: gorgeous building, spacious living room, and extremely clean. Enjoy an incredible dinner M-Sa for only €5 and take advantage of the complimentary F Portuguese lessons. Breakfast included. Laundry €6. Free Internet. Co-ed dorms €18. Cash only. ❷

Lisbon Lounge Hostel, R. de São Paulo 11 (☎346 2061; www.lisbonloungehostel.com). M: Cais do Sodré. Co-ed dorms with 4-6 people and great common room. Breakfast €3. Free Internet. Dorms €20; low season €18. AmEx/MC/V. ❷

Hotel Anjo Azul, R. Luz Soriano 75 (☎/fax 347 8069; www.anjoazul.com). Caters to gay travelers, but accepts all sexual preferences. Helpful and friendly staff; rooms complete with minifridges and Internet access. Laundry €10 per 6kg. Check-out 11:30am. Doubles €50-75; triples €75. 10% *Let's Go* discount. ❹

BAIXA

Easy Hostel, R. de São Nicolau 13, 4th fl. (☎886 4280). This recently opened hostel in the middle of Baixa offers spacious rooms, free breakfast, and Internet. Laundry is cheap (€3) and there is a great living room area for hanging out with fellow travelers. It's a not-so-easy hike to the top floor, but well worth it. Dorms €18. Cash only. ❷

Pensão Prata, R. da Prata 71, 3rd fl. (☎346 8908). M: Baixa-Chiado. Basic rooms, decently sized, some with baths. Friendly owner; good value for the area. Quiet at night with a nice view of the streets below. Singles €15-20; doubles €20-35. ❷

Pensão Moderna, R. dos Correeiros 205, 4th fl. (☎346 0818). M: Rossio. This centrally located family-run hostel has big rooms with sinks. Shared baths. May-Aug. singles €15; doubles €25; triples €35; quads €45. Reduced prices Sept.-Apr. Cash only. ❶

ALFAMA

Pensão Ninho das Águias, Costa do Castelo 74 (☎885 4070). Climb the spiral staircase and ring the bell to get to the reception desk. English and French spoken. Reserve ahead in summer. May-Aug. singles €30; doubles €45, with bath €50; triples (some with bath) €60. Sept.-Apr. prices drop by €5. Cash only. ❸

Pensão Beira Mar, Largo do Terreiro do Trigo 16 (☎886 9933; beira@iol.pt), near Sta. Apolónia train station. Situated by the water, this is a calm getaway for travelers on a budget. Reservations by email. June-Aug. singles €20-35; doubles €30-40; triples €45; quads €60. Oct.-May prices drop by €5. Cash only. ❷

Casa de Hóspedes, R. da Padaria 38 (☎886 7710). Clean floors and bathrooms. Near many of the district's sights. June-Aug. doubles €30; triples €45. Cash only. ❶

OTHER AREAS

Pousada de Juventude de Lisboa (HI), R. Andrade Corvo 46 (☎353 2696). M: Picoas. Spacious, recently renovated rooms with a bar and reading room. HI card required. Breakfast included. Reserve ahead. Dorms €16; doubles with bath €43. MC/V. ❶

Parque de Campismo Municipal de Lisboa (☎62 31 00), on the road to Benfica. Take bus #14 to Parque Florestal Monsanto; campsite is at entrance to park. Pool and supermarket nearby. High-season tent sites €4.80, €4.80 per person, €3.10 per car. Low-season prices are slightly lower. ❶

FOOD

Lisbon has some of the best wine and cheapest restaurants of any European capital. Dinner costs €7-12 per person; the *prato do dia* (daily special) is often only €5. Head to **Rua dos Bacalhoeiros** and **Rua dos Correeiros** to find smaller and usually less expensive restaurants. Snack on filling and incredibly cheap Portuguese pastries; *pastelarias* are everywhere. For cheap groceries, look for any **Mini-Preço** or **Pingo Doce** supermarket. (Most open M-Sa 8:30am-9pm.)

BAIRRO ALTO

A Brasileira, R. Garrett 120-122 (☎346 9541). M: Baixa-Chiado. A former stomping ground of early 20th-century poets and intellectuals, this cafe is a great place to people-watch after traipsing through Lisbon. Sandwiches and croissants €2-5. Mixed drinks €5. Open daily 8am-2am. AmEx/MC/V. ❷

Restaurante Calcuta, R. do Norte 17 (☎342 8295), near Lg. Camões. Listen to soothing music while you enjoy Indian favorites like prawn masala (€9.50). In addition to several curry-based dishes, the restaurant has many veggie options (€6.50-7.50). Open M-F noon-3pm and 6-11pm, Sa-Su 6-11pm. AmEx/MC/V. ❷

Restaurante Ali-a-Papa, R. da Atalaia 95 (☎347 4143), serves generous helpings of traditional Moroccan food in a quiet atmosphere; many vegetarian options are available. Entrees €9-15. Open M and W-Sa 7pm-12:30am. AmEx/MC/V. ❸

BAIXA AND ALFAMA

A Minha Maneira, Largo do Terreiro do Trigo 1 (☎886 1112; www.a-minha-maneira.pt). This quaint restaurant is situated beside the 13th-century St. John's fountain. Try the codfish "homestyle" or the champagne chicken (both €14) while enjoying the artwork. Free Internet and printing for customers. Entrees €8-15. Open daily 12:30-11pm. ❷

Churrasqueira Gaúcha, R. dos Bacalhoeiros 26C-D (☎887 0609). Affordable Portuguese food cooked to perfection in a comfortable, cavern-like setting. The best restaurant on a street already packed with great deals and incredibly fresh meat, poultry, and fish. Entrees €5-12. Open M-Sa 10am-midnight. AmEx/DC/MC/V. ❷

Ristorante-Pizzeria Valentino, R. Jardim do Regedor 37-45 (☎346 1727), in the Pr. do Restauradores. Watch the chefs prepare a variety of pizzas and pastas in an open kitchen. Try the popular Pizza Hawaii (€8) or the pasta dish *Tagliatelle Mare e Monti* (€8). Pizzas €3-10. Entrees €7-19. Open daily noon-midnight. AmEx/MC/V. ❷

Martinho da Arcada, Pr. do Comércio 3 (☎887 9259). Founded in 1782, this is the oldest restaurant in Lisbon and a famed haunt of poet Fernando Pessoa. The entree prices (€15-32) are somewhat high for what you get, but the ambience is one of a kind. Outdoor seating available. Open M-Sa noon-3pm and 7-10:30pm. AmEx/MC/V. ❸

Casa-Brasileira, R. Augusta 267-269 (☎346 9713). A great place to grab a quick bite while sightseeing in Baixa, Casa-Brasileira offers cheap sandwiches (€3), pizza (€2-4), and a variety of milkshakes (€2.30). Open 10am-midnight. ❶

PORTUGAL

SIGHTS

BAIXA

Though Baixa has few historic sights, the lively atmosphere and dramatic history of the neighborhood make it a monument in its own right.

AROUND THE ROSSIO. Begin in the heart of Lisbon, the Rossio (also known as Pr. Dom Pedro IV). Once a cattle market, the site of public executions, a bullring, and carnival ground, the *praça* is now the domain of tourists and ruthless local motorists who circle a statue of Dom Pedro IV. A statue of Gil Vicente, Portugal's first great dramatist, peers from the top of the **Teatro Nacional de Dona Maria II** (easily recognized by its large columns) at one end of the *praça*. Adjoining the Rossio is the elegant **Praça da Figueira,** on the border of Alfama.

AROUND PRAÇA DOS RESTAURADORES. Just past the Rossio train station, an obelisk and a bronze sculpture of the "Spirit of Independence" commemorate Portugal's independence from Spain in 1640. Numerous shops line the *praça* and C. da Glória, the hill that leads to Bairro Alto. Pr. dos Restauradores also begins **Avenida da Liberdade,** Lisbon's most elegant promenade. Modeled after the wide boulevards of 19th-century Paris, this shady thoroughfare ends at **Praça do Marquês de Pombal,** where an 18th-century statue of the Marquês overlooks the city.

BAIRRO ALTO

In the Bairro Alto, pretentious intellectuals mix with idealistic university students. At the center of the neighborhood is **Praça Luís de Camões,** adjoining **Largo do Chiado** at the top of R. Garrett and a good place to rest and orient yourself.

MUSEU ARQUEOLÓGICO DO CARMO. Located under the skeletal arches of an old church destroyed in the 1755 earthquake, this partially outdoor museum allows visitors to get very close to historical relics like a 16th-century coat of arms. Check out the two Peruvian mummies inside. *(Largo do Carmo. Open M-Sa 10am-8pm. €2.50, students €1.50, under 14 free.)*

BASÍLICA DA ESTRELA. Directly across from the Jardim da Estrela, the Basílica da Estrela dates back to 1796 and casts an imposing presence over the *Praça.* Its dome, poised behind a pair of tall belfries, towers over surrounding buildings to take its place in the Lisbon skyline. Half-mad Dona Maria I promised God anything and everything if she were granted a son. When she finally gave birth to a baby boy, she built this church, and today, architecture aficionados are grateful. *(Pr. da Estrela. ☎396 0915. Open daily 7:45am-8pm. Free.)*

ALFAMA

Alfama, Lisbon's medieval quarter, was the only neighborhood to survive the infamous 1755 earthquake. The area descends in tiers from the **Castelo de São Jorge** facing the Rio Tejo. Between Alfama and Baixa is the **Mouraria** (Moorish quarter), ironically established after Dom Afonso Henriques and the Crusaders expelled the Moors in 1147. Visitors can hop on tram #28 (€1.20) from Pr. do Comércio, which winds past most of the neighborhood's sights.

PORTUGAL

CASTELO DE SÃO JORGE. Built in the 5th century by the Visigoths and enlarged 400 years later by the Moors, this castle was again improved and converted into a playground for the royal family between the 14th and 16th centuries. Today the Castelo consists of little more than stone ramparts, but the towers allow for spectacular views of Lisbon. Wander around the ruins, explore the ponds, or gawk at exotic birds in the gardens. *(☎880 0620; www.egeac.pt. Open daily Mar.-Oct. 9am-9pm; Nov.-Feb. 9am-6pm. €3, students €1.50, under 10 and over 65 free.)*

LOWER ALFAMA. The small **Igreja de Santo António** was built in 1812 over the beloved saint's alleged birthplace. The construction was funded with money collected by the city's children, who fashioned miniature altars bearing saintly images to place on doorsteps. *(☎886 9145. Open daily 8am-7pm. Mass daily 11am, 5, 7pm.)* In the square beyond the church is the 12th-century **Sé de Lisboa.** Although the cathedral's interior lacks the ornamentation of the city's other churches, its age and treasury make for an intriguing visit. The cloister includes an archaeological dig with ruins from the Iron Age, the Roman Empire, and the Muslim and Medieval Ages in Lisbon. *(☎886 6752. Open daily 9am-7pm except during Mass, held Tu-Sa 6:30pm and Su 11:30am and 7pm. Free. Treasury open M-Sa 10am-5pm. €2.50, students €1.50. Cloister open May-Sept. daily 2-7pm; Oct.-Apr. M-Sa 10am-6pm, Su 2-6pm. €2.50, students €1.25.)*

GRAÇA

PANTEÃO NACIONAL. The massive building that is now the Panteão Nacional (National Pantheon) was originally meant to be the Igreja da Santa Engrácia. The citizens of Graça started building the church in 1680 to honor their patron saint, but their ambitions soon outstripped their finances and the building project was abandoned. Salazar's military regime eventually took over construction, completing the project and dedicating it in 1966 as the Panteão Nacional, a burial ground for important statesmen. Ironically, when democracy was restored in 1975, the new government relocated the remains of prominent anti-fascist opponents to this building and prohibited those who had worked with Salazar from entering. Today, the building houses the honorary tombs of explorers like Vasco da Gama and Pedro Cabral, the man who discovered Brazil in 1500, as well as the remains of Portuguese artists, including Amália Rodrigues, the queen of *fado.* *(Take the #28 tram from R. do Loreto or R. Garrett. ☎885 4820. Open Tu-Su 10am-5pm. €2, seniors €1.)*

IGREJA DE SÃO VICENTE DE FORA. The *igreja*, built between 1582 and 1692, is dedicated to Lisbon's patron saint. Especially noteworthy are the *sacristia* with inlaid walls of Sintra marble and the geometrically confused walls at the base of the dome. *(Open daily 10am-6pm except for Mass, held Tu and Th-F 6:30am, Sa 9:30am, Su 11:30am. Free. Chapel open Tu-Su 10am-5pm. €2.)*

SÃO SEBASTIÃO

Located north of Baixa, this area features busy avenues, department stores, and scores of strip malls. São Sebastião, however, also houses two of the finest art museums in Portugal; both are legacies of oil tycoon Calouste Gulbenkian.

MUSEU CALOUSTE GULBENKIAN. When Calouste Gulbenkian died in 1955, he left his extensive art collection to his beloved Portugal. Though the philanthropist was a British citizen of Armenian descent, it was Portugal he chose to call home. The formidable collection is divided into sections of ancient art—Egyptian, Greek, Roman, Mesopotamian, Islamic, and Oriental—and European pieces from the 15th to 20th centuries. Highlights include works by Dégas, Manet, Monet, Rembrandt, Renoir, and Rodin. *(Av. Berna 45. M: São Sebastião. ☎ 782 3000; www.museu.gulbenkian.pt. Open Tu-Su 10am-5:45pm. €3. Free for students, teachers, and seniors every day; Su free for everyone.)*

CENTRO DE ARTE MODERNO. Though not as famous as its neighbor, the Museu Calouste Gulbenkian, this museum, also funded by Gulbenkian's foundation, houses a large modern collection dedicated to promoting Portuguese talent. *(R. Dr. Nicolau Bettencourt. M: São Sebastião. ☎ 782 3474. Open Tu-Su 10am-5:45pm. €3. Free Tu-F and Su for students, teachers, and seniors.)*

BELÉM

Belém is more of a suburb than a neighborhood of Lisbon, but its concentration of monuments and museums makes it a crucial stop on any tour of the capital. To reach Belém, take tram #15 from Pr. do Comércio (15min.) and get off at the Mosteiro dos Jerónimos stop, one stop beyond the regular Belém stop.

MOSTEIRO DOS JERÓNIMOS. Established in 1502 to give thanks for the success of Vasco da Gama's expedition to India, the Mosteiro dos Jerónimos was granted UN World Heritage status in the 1980s. The country's most refined celebration of the Age of Discovery, the monastery showcases Portugal's native Manueline style, combining Gothic forms with minute Renaissance detail. On the main door of the church, to the right of the monastery entrance, Prince Henry the Navigator anachronistically mingles with the Twelve Apostles. The symbolic tombs of Luís de Camões and Vasco da Gama lie in two opposing transepts. *(☎ 362 0034. Open Tu-Su May-Sept. 10am-6:30pm; Oct.-Apr. 10am-5pm. Church free, cloister €4.50.)*

TORRE DE BELÉM. The best-known tower in all of Portugal and a UN World Heritage site, the Torre de Belém rises from the north bank of the Rio Tejo and is surrounded by the ocean on three sides. This icon of Portuguese grandeur offers panoramic views of Belém, the Rio Tejo, and the Atlantic. Built under Manuel I in 1515-1520 as a harbor fortress, it originally sat directly on the shoreline. Today, due to the receding beach, it is only accessible by a small bridge. *(A 10min. walk from the monastery, with the water on your left. Take the overpass by the gardens to cross the highway. Open Tu-Su May-Sept. 10am-6:30pm; Oct.-Apr. 10am-5:30pm. €3, under 25 and seniors €1.50.)*

PARQUE DAS NAÇÕES

The Parque das Nações (Park of Nations) inhabits the former Expo '98 grounds. Until the mid-1990s, the area was a muddy wasteland with a few run-down factories and warehouses along the banks of the Tejo. However, the government transformed it to prepare for the 1998 World Exposition and afterward spent millions converting the grounds into a park. The entrance leads through the Centro Vasco da Gama **shopping mall** (open daily 10am-midnight) to the center of the grounds, where information kiosks provide maps. *(To reach the park from Lisbon, take the metro to Oriente at the end of the red line. City buses #5, 10, 19, 21, 25, 28, 44, 50, 68, 114, 208, and 210 all stop at the Oriente station; €1.20. Park ☎891 9393; www.parquedasnacoes.pt.)* The park's biggest attraction, the **Oceanário** has interactive exhibits that explore the four major oceans, complete with sounds and smells; every section connects to the main tank, which houses fish, sharks, and other sea creatures. *(☎891 7002; www.oceanario.pt. Open daily Apr.-Oct. 10am-7pm; Nov.-Mar. 10am-6pm. €10.50, over 65 €5.75, under 12 €5.25, families €25.)* Pavilions scattered around the park appeal to a variety of interests. The **Pavilhão do Conhecimento** (Pavilion of Knowledge) hosts an interactive science museum. *(☎891 7100; www.pavconhecimento.pt. Open Tu-F 10am-6pm, Sa-Su 11am-7pm. €6, under 17 and over 65 €3.)* The **Virtual Reality Pavilion** holds a ride that challenges the senses. The **Atlantic Pavilion** hosts many of Lisbon's concerts, and the **International Fairgrounds** accommodate rotating exhibits.

PORTUGAL

ENTERTAINMENT

Agenda Cultural and *Follow Me Lisboa*, free at the tourist office and at kiosks in the Rossio on R. Portas de Santo Antão, have information on concerts, *fado*, movies, plays, and bullfights. They also have lists of museums, gardens, and libraries.

FADO

Lisbon's trademark is **fado,** combining singing and narrative poetry that expresses *saudade* (nostalgia). Numerous *fado* houses lie in the small streets of **Bairro Alto** and near R. de São João da Praça in **Alfama.** Some have both *fado* and folk-dancing performances. All of the popular houses have high minimum consumption requirements (normally €15-20). To avoid these, explore nearby streets where various bars and small venues offer free shows with less notable performers.

Café Luso, Tv. da Queimada 10 (☎213 42 22 81; www.cafeluso.pt). Pass below the club's giant yellow sign to reach *fado* nirvana. Lisbon's premier *fado* club combines the best of Portuguese music, cuisine, and atmosphere. *Fado* and folk dance, 5 singers each night. Set menu €25. Entrees €22-29. Min. consumption €20, for late-night show €15. *Fado* 9-10:30pm and 11pm-2am. Open M-Sa 8pm-2am. AmEx/MC/V. ❹

O Faia, R. Barroca 56 (☎342 6742). Performances by famous *fadistas* like Anita Guerreiro and Lenita Gentil and some of the finest Portuguese cuisine available make O Faia worth your time and money. 4 singers. Entrees €23-30. Min. consumption €17.50, includes 2 drinks. *Fado* at 9:30 and 11:30pm. Open M-Sa 8pm-2am. AmEx/MC/V. ❹

BULLFIGHTING

The drama that is Portuguese bullfighting differs from the Spanish variety in that the bull is not killed in the ring, a tradition that dates back to the 18th century. These spectacles take place most Thursdays from late June to late September at **Praça de Touros de Lisboa,** Campo Pequeno. (☎793 2143. Open daily 10pm-2am.) The newly renovated *praça* is a shopping center during the day and a venue for the distinctly Portuguese *toureio equestre* (horseback bullfighting) at night.

FESTIVALS

In June, the people of Lisbon spill into the city for a summer's worth of revelry. Open-air *feiras* (fairs)—smorgasbords of food, drink, live music, and dance—fill the streets. On the night of June 12, the streets explode in song and dance during the **Festa de Santo António.** From late May to early June, bookworms burrow for three weeks in the outdoor **Feira do Livro** in the Parque Eduardo VII behind Pr. Marquês do Pombal. The **Feira Internacional de Lisboa** occurs every few months in the Parque das Nações, while in July and August the **Feira de Mar de Cascais** and the **Feira de Artesania de Estoril** (celebrating famous Portuguese pottery) take place near the casino. Year-round *feiras* include the **Feira de Oeiras** (antiques) on the fourth Sunday of every month and the **Feira de Carcanelos,** for clothes (Th 8am-2pm) in Rato. Packrats will enjoy the **Feira da Ladra** (flea market, but literally translated "thieves' fair"), held behind the Igreja de São Vicente de Fora in Graça (Tu 7am-1pm, Sa 7am-3pm). To get there, take tram #28 (€1.20).

NIGHTLIFE

Bairro Alto, where innumerable small bars and clubs fill the side streets, is the first place to go for nightlife. **Rua do Norte, Rua do Diário Notícias,** and **Rua da Atalaia** have many small clubs packed into three short blocks. Several gay and lesbian clubs are between **Praça de Camões** and **Travesa da Queimada,** as well as in the **Rato** area near the edge of Bairro Alto. The **Docas de Santo Amaro** host waterfront clubs and bars, while **Avenida 24 de Julho** and **Rua das Janelas Verdes** in the Santos area have the most popular clubs and discos. Jeans, sandals, and sneakers are generally not allowed. At clubs, beer runs €3-5. Crowds flow in around 2am and stay until dawn.

PORTUGAL

A Tasca Tequila Bar, Tv. da Queimada 13-15 (☎919 40 79 14). This rollicking Mexican bar serves up some potent mixed drinks; despite its name, the house specialty is the mojito. Mixed drinks €5. Open M-Sa 6pm-2am.

Dock's Club, R. da Cintura do Porto de Lisboa 226 (☎395 0856). Arguably the best place in the area, Dock's is a huge club that plays great hip-hop, latino, and house music. Tu ladies' night; women get in free and receive 4 complimentary mixed drinks. Cover men €12, includes 2 drinks. Open Tu-Sa 11pm-6am.

Jamaica, R. Nova do Carvalho 6 (☎342 1859). M: Cais do Sodré. Small club famous for playing great 80s music. Packed until the early morning, Jamaica is guaranteed to keep your feet moving all night. Be careful when leaving the club; it's not the safest neighborhood late at night. Cover men €6, includes 3 beers. Open Tu-Sa 10:30pm-6am.

Lux, Av. Infante Dom Henrique A, Cais da Pedra a Sta. Apolónia (☎882 0890). Take a taxi (€6) to the area opposite Sta. Apolónia train station. One of Europe's hottest clubs since opening in 1998. Amazing rooftop view. Arrive after 2am. Beer €1.50-2.50. Min. consumption depends on the night, usually €12. Open Tu-Sa 10pm-6am. AmEx/MC/V.

Kapital, Av. 24 de Julho 68 (☎395 7101). The classiest club in Lisbon has a ruthless door policy that makes admission a competitive sport. 3 floors, with a terrace on top level. Mixed drinks €5-8. Cover €10-20. Open M-Sa 11pm-6am. AmEx/MC/V.

Kremlin, Escandinhas da Praia 5 (☎395 7101; www.kremlin-k.com), off Av. 24 de Julho. Run by the same management as Kapital, but a more mixed crowd, including Kapital rejects. Door policy is harsh but not impossible; come nicely dressed. The club has 3 rooms throbbing with house music. Mixed drinks €4-6. Cover for men €12, for women €7. Open W-Th midnight-7am, F-Sa midnight-9am.

DAYTRIPS FROM LISBON

CASCAIS

Trains from Lisboa's Estação Cais do Sodré (☎213 42 48 93; M: Cais do Sodré) head to Cascais (30min., every 20min., €1.50). ScottURB has a bus terminal in downtown Cascais, underground next to the blue glass tower of the shopping center by the train sta-

tion. Buses #417 (40min., every 50min.) and the more scenic #403 (60-80min., every 75min.) go from Cascais to Sintra for €3.10. To visit Praia de Guincho, take the circular route bus #405/415 to the Guincho stop (22min., every 1-2hr., €2.25).

Cascais is a beautiful beach town, serene during the low season but brimming with vacationers in the summer. To reach **Praia da Ribeira,** take a right upon leaving the tourist office and walk down Av. dos Combatantes de Grande Guerra until you see the water. Facing the water, **Praia da Rainha** and **Praia da Conceição** are to your left. Those in search of less crowded beaches should take advantage of the **free bike rentals** offered at two kiosks in Cascais (one is in front of the train station; the other is in the parking lot of the Cidadela fortress, up Av. dos Carlos I). Bring your passport or driver's license and hotel information to use the bikes from 8am to 6:30pm. Ride along the coast (to your right if facing the water) and check out the **Boca de Inferno** (Mouth of Hell), so named because the cleft carved in the rock by the Atlantic surf creates a haunting sound as waves pummel the cliffs. When the sun sets, nightlife picks up on **Largo Luís de Camões,** the main pedestrian square.

There are several good restaurants on Av. dos Combatantes de Grande Guerra, between the tourist office and the ocean. The best among them is **Restaurante Dom Manolo ❷,** which serves big portions of mussels, salmon, and chicken. (☎214 83 11 26. Open daily 10am-midnight.) The **tourist office,** Av. dos Combatantes de Grande Guerra 25, is near the McDonalds arches next to the train station. The staff speaks English, French, and Spanish. (☎214 86 82 04. Open in summer M-Sa 9am-8pm, Su 10am-6pm; winter M-Sa 9am-7pm, Su 10am-6pm.)

PORTUGAL

SINTRA ☎21

Trains (☎923 2605) arrive at Av. Dr. Miguel Bombarda from Lisbon's Estação Sete Rios (35min., every 10min., €1.50). ScottURB buses (☎469 9100; www.scotturb.com) leave from Av. Dr. Miguel Bombarda for Cascais (#417 or 403; 40min., 1 per hr., €3) and Estoril (#418; 40min., 1 per hr., €3.10).

With its fairy-tale castles, enchanting gardens, and spectacular mountain vistas, Sintra (pop. 20,000) is Portugal's crowning jewel. A must-see when in Sintra is the UNESCO World Heritage Site, **Quinta da Regaleira,** a stunning palace whose backyard was turned into a fantasy land by its eccentric millionaire owner. Statues, fountains, and ponds blanket the small park, which is surrounded by lush green trees and beautiful gardens. To get to the palace, turn right out of the tourist office and follow R. Consiglieri Pedroso out of town as it turns into R.M.E.F. Navarro. (☎910 6650. Open daily May-Sept. 10am-8pm; Oct. and Feb.-Apr. 10am-6:30pm; Nov.-Jan. 10am-5:30pm. Tours 10:30, 11am, noon, 2:30, 3:30pm. €5, students €4. Guided tours €10/8.) Equally embellished is the **Palácio de Pena,** a colorful Bavarian palace featuring a lavish ballroom, the elaborate fresco-covered Arab Room, and a fantastic terrace view. ScottURB bus #434 (€3.85) goes to the palace. (☎910 5340; www.parquesdesintra.pt. Open Tu-Su June-Sept. 10am-5:30pm; Oct.-May 10am-4pm. €6, students €4. Guided tours €3.50.) Other Sintra highlights include the **Palácio Nacional de Sintra** in the center of town and the 8th-century **Castelo dos Mouros,** down the hill from the Palácio de Pena. Restaurants crowd the end of **Rua João de Deus** and **Avenida Heliodoro Salgado.** Sintra's **tourist offices** are located in Pr. da República 23 (☎923 1157) and in the train station (☎924 1623). Both have multilingual staff. (Both open daily June-Sept. 9am-8pm; Oct.-May 9am-7pm.)

CENTRAL PORTUGAL

Jagged cliffs and whitewashed fishing villages line the Costa de Prata of Estremadura, with beaches that rival even those in the Algarve. In the fertile region of the Ribatejo (banks of the Rio Tejo), lush greenery surrounds historical sights.

COIMBRA ☎239

Coimbra (pop. 200,000) possesses the urban sophistication of a metropolis many times its size. Local university students and backpackers make Coimbra a youthful city unlike any other in Portugal.

TRANSPORTATION AND PRACTICAL INFORMATION. Regional **trains** (☎808 20 82 08; www.cp.pt) stop at both at both Estação Coimbra-B (Velha) and Estação Coimbra-A (Nova), just two short blocks from the lower town center of Coimbra, while long-distance trains stop only at Coimbra-B station. A local train connects the two stations, departing after regional trains arrive (4min.; €1.08, free if transferring from another train). Trains run to Lisbon (2-3hr., 17 per day, €20-30) and Porto (1-2hr., 28 per day, €5.60-6.40). **Buses** (☎23 87 69) go from the end of Av. Fernão de Magalhães, 15min. past Coimbra-A, to Lisbon (2½hr., 18 per day, €9.40) and Porto (1-2hr., 14 per day, €14-20). From the bus station, turn right, follow the avenue to Coimbra-A, then walk to Largo da Portagem to reach the **tourist office.** The multilingual staff distributes maps. (☎85 59 30; www.turismo-centro.pt. Open June-Sept. M-F 9am-7pm, Sa-Su 10am-1pm and 2:30-5:30pm; Oct.-May M-F 9am-6pm, Sa-Su 10am-1pm and 2:30-5:30pm.) **Espaço Internet,** Pr. 8 de Maio, offers free **Internet,** but you may have to wait 15-30min. (Passport or driver's license required. Open M-Sa 10am-midnight, Su 2pm-midnight.) **Postal Code:** 3000.

ACCOMMODATIONS AND FOOD. The **Pousada da Juventude de Coimbra ❶,** R. Henrique Seco 14, is an uphill hike, but has a kitchen and a TV room with foosball and a pool table, as well as impeccably clean bathrooms. (☎82 59 55. Dorms €11; doubles €24, with bath €30. Low season €9/22/25. AmEx/MC/V.) **Restaurante Adega Paço do Conde ❶,** R. do Paço do Conde, is a local favorite, offering a variety of fish and meat options for only €5. (☎82 56 05. Open M-Sa 11:30am-3pm and 7-10:30pm.) Amazingly, even cheaper fare can be found at the **UC Cantinas ❶,** the university student cafeterias, where full meals run under €2. One is on the right side of R. Oliveiro Matos and the other is up the stairs in Lg. Dom Dinis, but you'll need an ISIC. (Open for lunch at noon, dinner at 7pm.) Supermarket **Pingo Doce,** R. João de Ruão 14, is up R. da Sofia. (☎85 29 30. Open daily 8:30am-9pm.)

SIGHTS AND ENTERTAINMENT. Take in the sights in the **old town** by following the narrow stone steps from the river up to the university. Begin your ascent at the **Arco de Almedina,** a remnant of the Moorish town wall, one block uphill from Largo da Portagem. The looming 12th-century Romanesque **Sé Velha** (Old Cathedral) is at the top. (Open M-Th and Sa 10am-6pm, F 10am-1pm. Cloister €1, students €0.75.) Just a few blocks uphill is the 16th-century **Universidade de Coimbra.** Enter through the **Porta Férrea** (Iron Gate), off R. São Pedro, to the **Pátio das Escolas,** which has an excellent view of the rural outskirts of Coimbra, stretching out to the horizon. The stairs to the right lead to the **Sala dos Capelos** (Graduates' Hall), which houses portraits of Portugal's kings, six of whom were born in Coimbra. The **Capela de São Miguel,** the university chapel, is adorned with magnificent *talha dourada* (gilded wood) carvings. The mind-boggling 18th-century **Biblioteca Joanina** (university library) lies past the Baroque clock tower. Tickets to all university sights can be purchased outside the Porta Férrea, in the Biblioteca General. (☎85 98 00. Open daily Mar. 13-Oct. 9am-7:20pm; Nov.-Mar. 12 10am-5:30pm. Each costs €3.50, students and seniors €2.45; combined ticket €6/4.20.)

Coimbra's nightlife is best experienced from October to July, when students are in town. **A Capella,** R. Corpo de Deus, a former chapel converted into a small late night cafe, is the best place to hear Coimbra-style *fado,* which is performed by both students and professionals from the chapel's altar. (☎83 39 85. Mixed drinks

€4-5. *Fado* at 9:30, 10:30, 11:30pm. Cover €5. Open daily 1pm-3am.) **Quebra Club,** Parque Verde do Mondego, blasts jazz and funk. (☎83 60 36. Beer €1-3. Mixed drinks €4-5. Open Su-Th noon-2am, F-Sa noon-4am. AmEx/MC/V.) Students run wild during the **Queima das Fitas** (Burning of the Ribbons), Coimbra's infamous festival in the second week of May. Festivities commence when graduates burn the narrow ribbons they got as first-years and receive wide ribbons in return.

ÉVORA ☎266

Évora (pop. 55,000) is the capital and largest city of the Alentejo region. Moorish arches line the streets of this historic center, which boasts a Roman temple, an imposing cathedral, and a 16th-century university. Attached to the pleasant **Igreja Real de São Francisco** in Pr. 1 de Mayo, the bizarre **Capela dos Ossos** (Chapel of Bones) was built by three Franciscan monks out of the bones of 5000 people as a hallowed space to reflect on the profundity of life and death. The walls are covered in neatly piled bones and anonymous skulls. From Pr. do Giraldo, follow R. República; the church is on the right and the chapel is to the right of the main entrance. (☎70 45 21. Open daily May-Sept. 9am-12:50pm and 2:30-5:45pm; Oct.-Apr. 9am-1pm and 2:30-5:15pm. €1; photographs €0.25.) According to legend, the 2nd-century **Templo Romano,** on Largo Conde do Vila Flor, was built for the goddess Diana. Its large and well-preserved columns look spectacular when lit at night. Facing the temple is the **Convento dos Loíos,** whose chapel interior is covered with dazzling *azulejos.* The actual monastery is now a luxury hotel. (Open Tu-Su 10am-12:30pm and 2-6pm. €3.)

Pensões cluster around **Praça do Giraldo.** Take a right out of the tourist office and turn right onto R. Bernardo Matos to get to cozy **Casa Palma ❷,** R. Bernardo Matos 29A, which has reasonable prices for the petite rooms on the top floor. (☎70 35 60. Singles €15-25; doubles €30-35. Cash only.) Budget restaurants are hard to find, but check out **Rua Mercadores.** Intimate **Restaurante Burgo Velho ❷,** R. de Burgos 10, serves large portions of *alentejano* cuisine. (☎22 58 58. Entrees €5-9. Open M-Sa noon-3pm and 7-10pm. AmEx/MC/V.) After sunset, head to **Praxis,** R. Valdevinos, the only real disco in town. From Pr. do Giraldo, take R. 5 de Outubro; the club will be on the right. (☎933 35 57 82. Beer €1.50. Mixed drinks €4-6. Min. consumption for men €7, women €5. Open daily 11pm-4am.) **Trains** (☎70 21 25 or 808 20 82 08; www.cp.pt) run from Av. dos Combatentes de Grande Guerra to Faro (5hr., 2 per day, €13) and Lisbon (2½hr., 4-6 per day, €6.50-8). **Buses** (☎76 94 10;

LOCAL LEGEND

THE REAL CORPSE BRIDE

)ne of the most tragic and bizarre narriages in Portuguese history ook place in the 14th century between King Dom Pedro and his not-so-lively bride, Inês de Castro.

When Prince Dom Pedro took one look at Inês, his first wife's ady-in-waiting, it was forbidden ove at first sight. Upon discovering this illicit *amor,* Dom Pedro's ather, King Alfonso, condemned he affair and had Inês exiled to a convent in Coimbra. Relentless, he young Dom Pedro sent Inês notes down a water duct connected to the convent, and the overs frequently met for midnight endezvous in the nearby woods.

Upon the death of his wife in childbirth, Dom Pedro became available for Inês, who had eturned from the convent. She and Pedro openly continued their affair for the next decade. Dom Pedro arranged a wedding in 354, but his father would have none of it; the king sent three assassins to kill his son's bride-to-be for fear that Inês and Pedro's children would eventually claim he throne.

The love-stricken prince eturned from a hunting trip to ind that Inês had been murdered. That devastation became rage upon his discovery of the murderer's identity, and Pedro waged war against his father for retribuion. It took the vengeful prince's mother to convince him to put the civil strife to an end. But the

www.rede-expressos.pt) go from Av. São Sebastião to: Braga (8-10hr., 8 per day, €19) via Porto (6-8½hr., 10 per day, €18); Faro (4hr., 3 per day, €14); Lisbon (2hr., 20 per day, €11). The **tourist office** is at Pr. do Giraldo 73. (☎73 00 30. Open daily May-Oct. 9am-7pm; Nov.-Apr. 9am-6pm.) **Postal Code:** 7999.

ALGARVE

Nearly 3000 hours of sunshine per year have transformed the Algarve, a desert on the sea, into a popular vacation spot. In July and August, sun-seeking tourists mob the resorts, packing bars and discos from sunset until long after sunrise. In the low season, the resorts become pleasantly de-populated.

LAGOS ☎282

As the town's countless international expats will attest, Lagos (pop. 17,500) is a black hole: come for two days and you'll stay two months. Lagos keeps you soaking in the ocean views, the sun on the beach, and the drinks at the bars.

TRANSPORTATION AND PRACTICAL INFORMATION. Trains (☎76 29 87) run from behind the marina to Évora (5-5½hr., 3 per day, €16) and Lisbon (3½-4½hr., 5-6 per day, €16). The bus station (☎76 29 44), off **Avenida dos Descobrimentos,** is across the channel from the train station and marina. **Buses** run to Faro (2½hr., 6 per day, €4), Lisbon (5hr., 6 per day, €15), and Sagres (1hr., 16 per day, €3). Running along the channel, Av. dos Descobrimentos is the main road carrying traffic to and from Lagos. From the train station, walk through the marina and cross the pedestrian suspension bridge, then turn left onto Av. dos Descobrimentos. From the bus station, walk straight until you reach Av. dos Descobrimentos and turn right; after 15m, take another right onto R. Porta de Portugal to reach **Praça Gil Eanes,** the center of the old town. The **tourist office** is on Lg. Marquês de Pombal, up R. Lima Leitão, which extends from Pr. Gil Eanes. (☎76 41 11. Open M-Sa 10am-6pm.) Check email and the inferior weather back home at **Inter-Net,** Av. dos Descobrimentos 19. (☎08 95 86. €2 per 30min., €3.50 per hr. Open M-Sa 10am-10pm, Su 10am-6pm.) **Postal Code:** 8600.

ACCOMMODATIONS AND FOOD. In the summer, budget accommodations fill up quickly, so reserve ahead. If full, the youth hostel will happily refer you to a *quarto* nearby for about the same price. Locals trying to rent rooms in their homes will probably greet you at the station or in

desire for revenge would return: upon taking the throne two years later, he had the assassins tracked down and brought to the public courtyard. There, he watched as their hearts were torn from their living bodies.

Dom Pedro then set about making his and Inês's children rightful heirs to the throne. In a shocking announcement, he declared that he had been secretly married to Inês. Legend has it that Dom Pedro subsequently ordered Inês's body exhumed so a posthumous marriage ceremony could take place. Five years after her death, Inês was removed from her grave, dressed like a queen, and carried over 80km to the Alcobaça Monastery in the greatest Royal Procession the people of Portugal had ever witnessed. Dom Pedro had her crowned as Queen and forced the court to kneel before her corpse and kiss her rotting hand. He had his own tomb built opposite hers, and on it reads, *"Até ao fim do mundo"* (until the end of the world).

Whether factually accurate or not, one thing is incontrovertible: the story of the king and his doomed "queen" transcends time. Their romance lives on in the imagination of their countrymen, and their thwarted love continues to be a recurring theme theme in Portuguese and Spanish literature.

NAUGHTY, NAUGHTY NUN

In a time when women were forbidden to leave the home without their husbands and were intentionally kept illiterate, Beja's most famous nun, Mariana Alcoforado, transgressed all boundaries. Having vowed to live a life of piety, she proceeded to have a scandalous affair with a dashing army officer—and then to write about it, in the process establishing a new genre of literature.

While living in the Convento de Nossa Senhora da Conceição, Mariana engaged in an illicit romance with the French Marquis of Chamilly who was fighting in the War of Portuguese Restoration (1640-1668). When he was called back to France, Mariana wrote the Marquis a series of five love letters, collected in 1669 as *Les Lettres Portugaises*. Since then, the letters have been translated into more than thirty languages and are considered a landmark work of literature.

Mariana's self-reflection and earnestness in expressing her undying love set a precedent for sentimentalism in literature, later reflected in works such as Samuel Richardson's epistolary novel, *Pamela* (1740). Although there has always been the question of the letters' authenticity, today Mariana's story continues to capture readers' imaginations. Recently, novelist Katherine Vaz wrote *Mariana* (2004), another of the numerous attempts to imagine the life of one of the most passionate women of all time.

the streets. Though these rooms are often inconveniently located, they are frequently the best deals (€10-15 per person). A short walk from most of Lagos's bars, the recently renovated **Rising Cock ❷**, Tv. do Forno 14, keeps up Lagos's famous party-town reputation with two patios, a beer garden, the "Hard Cock Cafe," and a DVD library. (☎969 41 11 31; www.risingcock.com. Free Internet. High season dorms €20, low season €15; prices may vary. Cash only.) Peruse multilingual menus around **Praça Gil Eanes** and **Rua 25 de Abril.** A dedicated following gets stuffed at **Casa Rosa ❶**, R. do Ferrador 22. On Monday nights, €6 buys all the spaghetti you can eat. (☎18 02 38. Vegetarian options. Free Internet for diners. Open daily 5-11pm.) The indoor **market,** just outside Pr. Gil Eanes on Av. dos Descobrimentos, has cheap, fresh food (open Sa). **Supermercado São Roque** is on R. das Portas de Portugal 61. (☎282 76 28 55. Open July-Sept. M-F 9am-8pm, Sa 9am-7pm; Oct.-June M-F 9am-7:30pm, Sa 9am-7pm. AmEx/MC/V.)

SIGHTS AND BEACHES. Though sunbathing and non-stop debauchery have long erased memories of Lagos's rugged, seafaring past, it's worth taking some time to visit the city's centuries-old fortifications and other historical sights. The **Fortaleza da Ponta da Bandeira,** a 17th-century fortress, overlooks the marina. (☎76 14 10. Open Tu-Sa 10am-1pm and 2-6pm, Su 10am-1pm. €2, students €1, under 13 free.) Also on the waterfront is the old **Mercado dos Escravos,** the site of the first sale of African slaves in Portugal in 1441. EVA **buses** (☎76 29 44) run to nearby **Sagres** (1hr., 14 per day, €3), site of the **Fortaleza de Sagres,** where Prince Henry stroked his beard, decided to map the world, and founded his famous school of navigation. The pentagonal 15th-century fortress and surrounding paths yield striking views of the cliffs and sea. (Open daily May-Sept. 9:30am-8pm; Oct.-Apr. 9:30am-5:30pm. €3, under 25 €1.50.)

The waterfront and marina offer jet ski rentals, scuba diving lessons, sailboat trips, and motorboat tours of the **coastal rocks and grottoes.** Flat, smooth sands line the 4km **Meia Praia,** across the river from town. For less crowded beaches, caves, and beautiful cliffs that plunge into the sea, follow Av. dos Descobrimentos toward Sagres to **Praia de Pinhão** (20min.). A bit farther down the coast, **Praia Dona Ana** has sculpted cliffs and grottoes that grace many Algarve postcards. Lagos also offers a wide variety of outdoor sports, from scuba diving to surfing to (booze) cruising. Companies that offer tours of the grottoes line Av. dos Descobrimentos. Most tours last 45min. and begin at €25 per two people.

NIGHTLIFE. As the sun sets on Lagos, beachgoers head en masse to bars and cafes between **Praça Gil Eanes** and **Praça Luis de Camões.** For late-night bars and clubs, try **Rua Cândido dos Reis** and **Rua do Ferrador,** as well as the intersection of **Rua 25 de Abril, Rua Silva Lopes,** and **Rua Soeiro da Costa.** At **Metro Bar,** R. Lançarote de Freitas 30, find an eclectic crowd, laid-back vibe, and friendly staff. (Beer €2. Mixed drinks €3-6. Happy hour 9-11:30pm. Open daily 2pm-2am.) Around midnight, Brits and Aussies flood **The Red Eye,** R. Cândido dos Reis 63, for classic rock, cheap liquor, and pool. (Beer €1.50-3. Mixed drinks €3-4. Free shot with first drink. Happy hour 8-10pm. Open daily 8pm-2am.)

FARO ☎289

The Algarve's capital, largest city, and transportation hub, Faro (pop. 55,000) is largely untouristed despite being perfectly charming. The **Vila Adentro** (Old Walled City) is a medley of museums, handicraft shops, and churches. On Lg. do Carmo stands the **Igreja de Nossa Senhora do Carmo** and its **Capela dos Ossos** (Chapel of Bones), built from the remains of monks buried in the church's cemetery. More than 1245 skulls and countless other bones are arrayed in geometric designs on the walls and ceiling. (☎82 44 90. Open May-Sept. M-F 10am-1pm and 3-6pm; Oct.-Apr. M-F 10am-1pm and 3-5pm, Sa 10am-1pm. Su Mass 8:30am. Church free. Chapel €1.) To get to the sunny beach **Praia de Faro,** take bus #16 from the bus station or from in front of the tourist office (5-10min.; 5 per day, return 9 per day; €1).

The price is right at **Pousada da Juventude (HI)** ❶, R. Polícia de Segurança Pública. (☎82 65 21; faro@movijovem.pt. Breakfast included. Check-out noon. July-Aug. dorms €13; doubles €28, with bath €36. Sept.-June €9/22/25. AmEx/MC/V.) Try marzipan at cafes on **Rua Conselheiro Bívar** and **Praça Dom Francisco Gomes.** The **Alisuper** grocery store is on Lg. de Carmo, next to the church. (☎82 49 20. Open daily 8:30am-8pm. AmEx/MC/V.) **Trains** (☎82 64 72) run from Lg. da Estação to Évora (4½-6hr., 3-4 per day, €13) and Lagos (1½hr., 8 per day, €17). EVA **buses** (☎89 97 00) go from Av. da República to Lagos (2hr., 8 per day, €4.30). Renex (☎81 29 80), across the street, sends buses to Porto (7½hr., 6-13 per day, €22) via Lisbon (4hr., 9 per day, €15). Turn left past the garden on Av. República to reach the **tourist office,** R. da Misericórdia 8. (☎80 36 04. Open daily May-Sept. 9:30am-12:30pm and 2-7pm; Oct.-April 9:30am-12:30pm and 2-5:30pm.) **Postal Code:** 8000.

PORTUGAL

NORTHERN PORTUGAL

The unspoiled Costa da Prata (Silver Coast), the plush greenery of the interior, and the rugged peaks of the Serra Estrela compose the Three Beiras region. Beyond trellised vineyards, *azulejo*-lined houses grace charming streets.

PORTO (OPORTO) ☎22

Porto (pop. 263,000) is famous for its namesake product—a strong, sugary wine developed by English merchants in the early 18th century. The port industry is at the root of the city's successful economy, but Porto has more to offer than fine wine. The city retains traditional charm with granite church towers, orange-tiled houses, and graceful bridges alongside a sophisticated modern lifestyle.

TRANSPORTATION AND PRACTICAL INFORMATION. Most **trains** (☎808 20 82 08; www.cp.pt) pass through Porto's main station, **Estação de Campanhã,** on R. da Estação. Trains run to: Aveiro (1hr., 47 per day, €2-13); Braga (1hr., 26 per day, €2-13); Coimbra (1½-2hr., 24 per day, €8-13); Lisbon (3½-4½hr., 18 per day, €18-24); Madrid, SPA (11-12hr., daily 10pm, €64; transfer at Entroncamento);

Viana do Castelo (1½-2hr., 11 per day, €4-6.80). **Estação São Bento,** Pr. Almeida Garrett, serves local and regional trains. Internorte (☎605 24 20), Pr. Galiza 96, sends **buses** to Madrid, SPA (10hr.; Su-F 10am and 8:30pm, Sa 10am; €43) and other international cities. Rede Expressos buses (☎200 69 54; www.redeexpresso.pt), R. Alexandre Herculano 366, travel to: Braga (1¼hr., 10 per day, €5); Coimbra (1½hr., 11 per day, €10); Lisbon (4hr., 11 per day, €16); Viana do Castelo (1¾hr., 4 per day, €6.20). Renex (☎200 33 95), Campo Mártires da Pátria, has express service to Lagos (8½hr., 6 per day, €23) via Lisbon (3½hr., 12 per day, €16). Buy tickets for local buses and **trams** at kiosks or at the **STCP** office, Pr. Almeida Garrett 27, across from Estação São Bento (€0.85, day-pass €4).

The city's main **tourist office,** R. Clube dos Fenianos 25, is off Pr. da Liberdade. (☎339 34 70; www.portoturismo.pt. Open July-Sept. daily 9am-7pm; Oct.-June M-F 9am-5:30pm, Sa-Su 9:30am-4:30pm.) **OnWeb,** Pr. Gen. Humberto Delgado 291, has **Internet** access. (€1.20 per hr., wireless €0.60 per hr. Open M-Sa 10am-2am, Su 3pm-2am.) The **post office** is in Pr. Gen. Humberto Delgado. (☎340 02 00. Open M-F 8:30am-7:30pm, Sa 9:30am-3pm.) **Postal Code:** 4000.

ACCOMMODATIONS AND FOOD. For good lodging deals, look on **Praça Filipa de Lancastre** or near the *mercado* on **Rua Fernandes Tomás** and **Rua Formosa.** The **Pensão Duas Nações ❶,** Pr. Guilherme Gomes Fernandes 59, has low prices and high comfort level. (☎208 16 16. Reserve ahead or arrive before noon. Laundry €7. Internet €1 per 30min. Dorms €11; singles €14, with bath €23-25; doubles €23-25; triples €36; quads €46. Cash only.) Find quality budget meals near Pr. da Batalha on **Rua Cimo de Vila** and **Rua do Cativo.** Places selling *bifanas* (small pork sandwiches) line R. Bomjardim. **Ribeira** is the place for a high-quality, affordable dinner. The **Café Majestic ❷,** R. de Santa Catarina 112, is one of the best snapshots of 19th-century bourgeois opulence, the oldest and most famous in the city. (☎200 38 87. Entrees €9-16. Open M-Sa 9:30am-midnight. AmEx/MC/V.) The sprawling **Mercado de Bolhão** has a range of fresh bread, cheese, meat, and produce. (Open M-F 8:30am-5pm, Sa 8:30am-1pm.)

SIGHTS AND ENTERTAINMENT. Your first brush with Porto's rich stock of fine artwork may be the celebrated collection of *azulejos* in the **São Bento train station.** From the station, follow signs downhill on R. Mouzinho da Silveira to R. Ferreira Borges and the **Palácio da Bolsa** (Stock Exchange), the epitome of 19th-century Portuguese elegance. The most striking room is the **Sala Árabe** (Arabian Hall). Its gold and silver walls are covered with the oddly juxtaposed inscriptions "Glory to Allah" and "Glory to Dona Maria II." (☎339 90 00. Multilingual tours every 30min. Open daily Apr.-Oct. 9am-7pm; Nov.-Mar. 9am-1pm and 2-6pm. €5, students €3.) Nearby on R. Infante Dom Henrique, the Gothic **Igreja de São Francisco** glitters with an elaborately gilded wood interior. The museum has religious art and artifacts; in the basement is the *Ossário*, a labyrinth of catacombs with mass graves. (☎206 21 00. Open daily in summer 9am-8pm; winter 9am-5pm. €3, students €2.50.) On R. dos Clérigos rises the **Torre dos Clérigos** (Tower of Clerics), adjacent to the 18th-century **Igreja dos Clérigos,** adorned with Baroque carvings. (☎200 17 29. Tower open daily Apr.-Oct. 9:30am-1pm and 2:30-7pm; Nov.-Mar. 10am-noon and 2-5pm. Church open M-Sa 9am-12:30pm and 3:30-7:30pm, Su 10am-1pm and 9-10:30pm. Tower €1.50, church free.) After hours, most people congregate around the bar-restaurants of **Ribeira,** where Brazilian music plays until 2am.

BRAGA

☎253

The beautiful gardens, plazas, museums, and markets of Braga (pop. 166,000) have earned it the nickname "Portuguese Rome." In the **Sé,** Portugal's oldest cathedral, the treasury showcases the archdiocese's most precious paintings and relics, including a collection of *cofres cranianos* (brain boxes), one of which contains the 6th-century cortex of Braga's first bishop. (☎26 33 17. Open Tu-Su 9am-noon and 2-6:30pm. Mass daily 5:30pm. Cathedral free. Treasury and chapels €2.) Braga's most famous landmark, **Igreja do Bom Jesús,** is actually 5km outside of town. This 18th-century church was built in an effort to recreate Jerusalem in Braga, providing Iberian Christians with a pilgrimage site closer to home. Take the bus labeled "#02 Bom Jesús" at 10 and 40min. past the hour from in front of Farmácia Cristal, Av. da Liberdade 571 (€1.20). At the site, either take the 285m ride on the funicular (8am-8pm, every 30min., €1) or walk 20-25min. up the granite pathway that leads to a 326-step zig-zagging staircase.

Take a taxi (€5) from the train station to **Pousada da Juventude de Braga (HI) ❶,** R. Santa Margarida 6, which has a friendly atmosphere and a convenient location. (☎61 61 63. Reception 8am-noon and 6pm-midnight. Lockout noon-6pm. Dorms €7; doubles with bath €19.) When in Braga, be sure to try the *pudim do Abade de Priscos*, a pudding flavored with caramel and port wine. The **market** is in Pr. do Comércio. (Open M-Sa 7am-3pm.) The supermarket, **Pingo Doce,** is in the basement of the Braga shopping mall. (Open daily 10am-11pm.) **Trains** (☎808 20 82 08) pull into Estação da Braga, 1km from Pr. da República. Trains run to Lisbon (4-5½hr., 3 per day, €24-36) via Porto (45-60min., 26 per day, €2-13). **Buses** leave Central de Camionagem (☎20 94 00) for: Coimbra (3hr., 6 per day, €12); Faro (12-15hr., 3-6 per day, €24); Lisbon (5¼hr., 10-11 per day, €17); Porto (1¼hr., 25 per day, €5). The **tourist office** is at Av. da Liberdade 1. (☎26 25 50. Open June-Sept. M-F 9am-7pm, Sa-Su 9am-12:30pm and 2-5:30pm; Oct.-May M-Sa 9am-12:30pm and 2-5:30pm.) **Postal Code:** 4700.

VIANA DO CASTELO ☎258

Situated in the northwest corner of the country, Viana do Castelo (pop. 37,000) is one of the loveliest coastal cities in all of Portugal. Though visited mainly as a beach resort, Viana also has a historical district centered around the stately **Praça da República.** Here, the **Museu de Traje** provides a glimpse into the region's distinctive attire. (☎80 01 71. Open Tu-Su 10am-1pm and 3-7pm. €2, students €1.) Across the plaza, granite columns support the flowery facade of the **Igreja da Misericórdia,** known for its *azulejo* interior. (Open daily 9:30am-12:30pm and 2-5:30pm. Free.) The **Monte de Santa Luzia** is guarded by the **Templo de Santa Luzia.** This early 20th-century church isn't much to look at, but the view from the hill is fantastic. Either brave the hundreds of stairs (45min.) or take a taxi (€5) to the top. (Open daily in summer 8am-7pm; winter 8am-5pm. Mass daily 4pm. Free.)

For accommodations, try the side streets off Av. dos Combatentes da Grande Guerra. The **Pousada de Juventude de Viana do Castelo (HI) ❶,** R. de Límia, right on the marina off R. da Argaçosa and Pr. da Galiza, has a bar, ping-pong tables, and rooms with balconies. (☎80 02 60. Breakfast included. Laundry €2.50. Internet €1 per 20min. Reception 8am-midnight. Check-out noon. Mid-June to mid-Sept. dorms €12.50; doubles with bath €35. Mid-Sept. to mid-June €10/28.) Try the warm *bolos de berlim* (cream-filled pastries; €0.75) at **Pastelaria Zé Natário ❶,** R. Manuel Espregueira 37. (☎82 23 76. Open M and W-Su 9am-10pm.) Buy groceries at **Estação Supermercado** on the second floor of the mall next to the train station. (☎288 10 08 10. Open daily 9am-11pm.) A weekly **market** is held Fridays off Av. Campo do Castelo. **Trains** (☎82 13 15) run from the station at the top of Av. dos Combatentes da Grande Guerra to Porto (2hr., 13 per day, €5.50-6.10). **Buses** (☎82 50 47) run from the basement of the mall next to the train station to Braga (1½hr., 4-9 per day, €3.20), Lisbon (5½hr., 2-3 per day, €14), and Porto (2hr., 9-11 per day, €5). The **tourist office** is at Tv. do Hospital Velho 8. (☎82 26 20; www.cm-viana-castelo.pt. Open M-F 9am-12:30pm and 2:30-6pm, Sa 9:30am-1pm and 2:30-6pm, Su 9:30am-1pm.) **Postal Code:** 4900.

ROMANIA (ROMÂNIA)

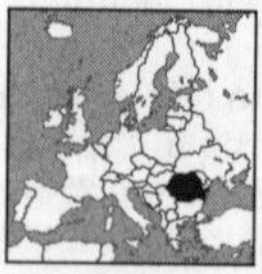

As it emerges from decades of dictatorship under Nicolae Ceaușescu, modern Romania is in a state of transition. Some citizens are eager to Westernize, while others prefer to follow the rural lifestyles of their ancestors. The resulting state of confusion, combined with a largely undeserved reputation for poverty and crime, discourages foreign visitors. But travelers who dismiss Romania do themselves an injustice—it is a country rich in history, rustic beauty, and hospitality. Romania's fascinating legacy draws visitors to Dracula's dark castle and to the Bucovina monasteries, famous for their colorful frescoes. Meanwhile, new Romania is burgeoning in the heavily touristed resort towns along the Black Sea Coast.

DISCOVER ROMANIA: SUGGESTED ITINERARIES

THREE DAYS. Head for **Transylvania** (3 days; p. 834), a budget traveler's haven, to relax in the Gothic towns of **Sighișoara** (1 day; p. 835), **Sinaia** (1 day; p. 834), and **Brașov** (1 day; p. 836).

ONE WEEK. After three days in **Transylvania** (p. 834), head to medieval **Bran** (1 day; p. 836) and stylish **Brașov** (1 day; p. 836), before ending in **Bucharest** (2 days; p. 829), the enigmatic capital.

ESSENTIALS

FACTS AND FIGURES

Official Name: Romania.
Capital: Bucharest.
Major Cities: Constanța, Iași, Oradea.
Population: 22,304,000.
Land Area: 237,500 sq. km.
Time Zone: GMT +2.
Language: Romanian.
Religions: Eastern Orthodox (87%), Protestant (7%), Roman Catholic (5%).

WHEN TO GO

Romania's varied climate makes it a year-round destination. The south has hot summers and mild winters, while winters are harsh and summers are cooler in the north, especially in the mountains. Summer tourist season reaches a fever pitch in July and August only along the Black Sea Coast; elsewhere, travelers will find a refreshing lack of crowds even mid-summer. They should, however, remember that summer can be brutally hot in much of Romania.

DOCUMENTS AND FORMALITIES

EMBASSIES AND CONSULATES. Foreign embassies for Romania are in Bucharest (p. 829). Romanian embassies and consulates abroad include: **Australia,** 4 Dalman Cres., O'Malley, ACT, 2606 (☎02 6286 2343); **Canada,** 655 Rideau St., Ottawa, ON, K1N 6A3 (☎613-789-3709; www.cyberus.ca/~romania); **Ireland,** 26 Waterloo Rd., Dublin, 4 (☎01 668 1085); **UK,** Arundel House, 4 Palace Green, London, W8 4QD (☎020 7937 9666; www.roemb.co.uk); **US,** 1607 23rd St., NW, Washington, D.C., 20008 (☎202-332-4846; www.roembus.org).

VISA AND ENTRY INFORMATION. Romanian visa rules change frequently; check with your embassy or consulate for the most accurate information. Citizens of

Canada, Ireland, the UK, and the US can visit Romania for up to 90 days without a visa. Citizens of Australia and New Zealand need visas for any length of stay. In all cases, passports are required and must be valid six months after the date of return from Romania. Consult the Romanian embassy in your home country to apply for a visa. A visa application requires a passport, an application form, two recent photographs, tickets for return or onward travel, and the application fee. For Americans, a single-entry visa costs US$40, and a multiple-entry visa US$75. Visas are not available at the border. Romanian embassies estimate a 30-day processing time for some visas. Apply early to allow the bureaucratic process to run its slow-course. **Visa extensions** and related services are available at police headquarters in large cities or at Bucharest's Visas for Foreigners Office (☎01 650 3050), Str. Luigi Cazzavillan 11. Long lines are common at the border.

ENTRANCE REQUIREMENTS

Passport: Required for all travelers.

Visa: Not required for stays under 90 days for citizens of Canada, Ireland, the UK, and the US. Citizens of Australia and New Zealand require a visa for any length of stay.

Letter of Invitation: Not required for citizens of Australia, Canada, Ireland, New Zealand, the UK, and the US.

Inoculations: Not required. Recommended up-to-date on DTaP (diphtheria, tetanus, and pertussis), hepatitis A, hepatitis B, MMR (measles, mumps, and rubella), polio booster, and typhoid.

Work Permit: Required for all foreigners planning to work in Romania.

Driving Permit: Required for all those planning to drive in Romania.

TOURIST SERVICES AND MONEY

TOURIST OFFICES. Although Romania has limited tourist resources, the National Tourist Office (☎021 314 9957; www.romaniatourism.com) can be useful.

MONEY. The Romanian currency is the **leu,** plural lei (abbreviated L), which was revalued in 2005. The recently revalued leu is called the RON (Romanian New

Leu), whereas the old leu is called the ROL (Romanian Leu); 1RON=10,000ROL. Bank notes are issued in amounts of L1, L5, L10, L50, L100, and L500; coins come in amounts of 1, 5, 10, and 50 bani (singular ban; L1=100 bani). **Inflation** rates have dropped dramatically and now hover around 9%. Romania has a **value added tax (VAT)** of 19%. **ATMs** generally accept MasterCard, sometimes accept Visa, and are the best way to get money. However, as identity theft rings sometimes target ATMs, travelers should use machines located inside banks and check for evidence of tampering before they use the machines. **Private exchange bureaus** often offer better exchange rates than banks and deal in common foreign currencies. Few, however, take credit cards or traveler's checks. Although most **banks** will cash traveler's checks, they generally charge exorbitant fees. Changing money on the street is both illegal and a surefire way to get cheated.

LEI (L)		
	AUS$1 = L2.05	1L = AUS$0.49
	CDN$1 = L2.48	1L = CDN$0.40
	EUR€1 = L3.53	1L = EUR€0.28
	NZ$1 = L1.72	1L = NZ$0.58
	UK£1 = L5.14	1L = UK£0.19
	US$1 = L2.73	1L = US$0.37

HEALTH AND SAFETY

If possible, avoid Romanian **hospitals,** as most are not up to Western standards. Pack a **first-aid kit.** Go to a private doctor for medical emergencies; your embassy can recommend a good one. Some **American medical clinics** in Bucharest have English-speaking doctors; pay in cash. *Farmacies* (pharmacies) stock basic medical supplies. *Antinevralgic* is for headaches, *aspirină* or *piramidon* for colds and the flu, and *saprosan* for diarrhea. *Prezervatives* (condoms), *tampoane* (tampons), and *şervețele igienice* (sanitary napkins) are available at drugstores and kiosks. Most **public restrooms** lack soap, towels, and toilet paper. Attendants may charge L1-1.50 for a single square of toilet paper, so pick up a roll at a drugstore and carry it with you. Beware of **stray dogs,** as they often carry **rabies.** Water in Romania is less contaminated than it once was. Still, avoid untreated **tap water** and do not use **ice cubes;** boil water before drinking it or drink imported **bottled water.** Beware of water-contaminated vendor food.

Violent **crime** is not a major concern, but petty crime against tourists is common. Be especially careful on public transport and night trains. Beware of distracting children and con artists dressed as policemen who ask for your passport or wallet. If someone shows a badge and claims to be a plainclothes policeman, he is probably trying to scam you; ask to be escorted to the nearest police station. Money exchange and taxi scams abound. While the **drinking age** of 18 is not enforced, **drug laws** are strictly enforced. Single **female travelers** should say they are traveling with a male and shouldn't go out alone after dark; tank tops and shorts may attract unwanted attention. **Minorities,** especially those with darker skin, may encounter discrimination, as they may be mistaken for Roma (Gypsies). In Moldavia, persons of **religions** other than Orthodox Christianity may feel uncomfortable. **Homosexuality** is now legal in Romania, but public displays are ill-advised. Most Romanians hold conservative attitudes toward sexuality, which may translate into harassment of GLBT travelers and sometimes manifests itself in the form of anti-gay propaganda in major cities. Still, women who walk arm-in-arm will not draw attention.

EMERGENCY	**Police:** ☎955. **Ambulance:** ☎961. **Fire:** ☎981.

TRANSPORTATION

BY PLANE. Airlines fly into the **Bucharest Henri Coanda International Airport** (☎021 204 1200) which, though recently renovated, is not completely modern. **TAROM** (Romanian Airlines; ☎21 201 4000; www.tarom.ro) recently updated its fleet; it flies from Bucharest to New York and major European and Middle Eastern cities.

BY TRAIN. Trains are better than buses for international travel. To buy tickets for the national railway, go to the **CFR** (Che-Fe-Re) office in larger towns. You must buy international tickets in advance. Train stations sell tickets up to 1hr. before departure times. The English-language timetable *Mersul Trenurilor* (www.cfr.ro/calatori) is very useful. There are four types of trains: *InterCity* (indicated by an "IC" on timetables and at train stations; grey-and-red livery); *rapid* (red livery with horizontal white stripe); *accelerat* (blue livery, solid or with horizontal white stripe); and *personal* (blue livery). *InterCity* trains stop only at major cities. *Rapid* trains are the next fastest; *accelerat* trains are slower and dirtier. The sluggish and decrepit *personal* trains stop at every station. The difference between **first class** (*clasa întâi;* CLAH-sa UHN-tuy; 6 people per compartment) and **second class** (*clasa doua;* CLAH-sa DOUGH-wuh; 8 people) is small, except on *personal* trains. In an **overnight train,** shell out for a *vagon de dormit* (sleeping carriage); buy tickets for both compartments if you don't want to share.

BY BUS. Traveling to Romania by bus is often cheaper than entering by plane or train. Travel agencies may sell timetables and tickets, but buying tickets from the carrier is often cheaper. Use the slow **local bus system** only when trains are unavailable. Local buses are slightly cheaper but are packed, poorly ventilated, and make perfect locations for pickpocketing and other forms of petty theft. Cheap, fast, and clean, **minibuses** are a good option for short distances. Rates are posted inside.

BY FERRY, CAR, AND BIKE. In the Danube delta, boats are the best mode of transport. Passenger boats run down the new European riverway from Rotterdam, NTH, to Constanța. Be wary of **taxis;** only use cars that post a company name, phone number, and rate per kilometer. Be sure the driver uses the meter. Your ride should cost about L1.1 per kilometer plus a L1 flat fee. US driver's licenses are valid for 90 days; after that time, you must obtain either an international driving permit or a Romanian driver's license. Make sure you are insured and have your registration papers. MyBike (www.mybike.ro) provides info on biking in Romania.

BY THUMB. Let's Go does not recommend **hitchhiking.** Hitchhikers stand on the side of the road and put out their palm, as if waving. Drivers generally expect a **payment** similar to the price of a train or bus ticket for the distance traveled.

KEEPING IN TOUCH

PHONE CODES	**Country code:** 40. **International dialing prefix:** 00. For more information on how to place international calls, see inside back cover.

TELEPHONE AND INTERNET. Many pay phones are orange and accept **phone cards,** sold at metro stops, convenience stores, gas stations, and post offices. Only buy cards sealed in plastic wrap. Rates are around L1.60 per minute to most of Europe and L2 per minute to the US. At an analog phone, dial ☎971 for international calls. You may need to make a phone call *prin comandă* (with the help of the operator) at the telephone office; this takes longer and costs more. There are **no toll-free calls** in Romania—you even need a phone card to call the police, an ambulance, or the operator. People with European mobile phones can avoid roaming charges by buying a **SIM card** at **Connex, Dialog,** or **RomTelecom.** When calling from a mobile phone, always use the city code. For directory inquiries, dial ☎931; for general inquiries 930; for information 951. International access codes include: **AT&T Direct** (☎800 42 88); **Canada Direct** (☎800 50 00); **MCI WorldPhone** (☎800 18 00); **Sprint** (☎800 08 77). **Internet** cafes are common in cities and cost L1.50-3 per hour.

MAIL. At the post office, request *par avion* for **airmail,** which takes about two weeks for delivery to the US. Postcards or letters cost around L2.10 to Europe and L3.10 for the rest of the world. **Mail** can be received through **Poste Restante,** but you may run into problems picking up your package. Address envelopes as follows: First name LAST NAME, Oficiul Postal, post office address, city, POSTE RESTANTE, Romania, Postal Code. Major cities have **UPS** and **Federal Express.**

LANGUAGE. Romanian is a Romance language with a Slavic-influenced vocabulary. Those familiar with Italian, Portuguese, or Spanish should be able to decipher many words. **Hungarian** is widely spoken in Transylvania. Throughout the country, **French** is a common second language for the older generation; **English** is prevalent with the younger. For useful expressions see **Phrasebook: Romanian,** p. 1062.

ACCOMMODATIONS AND CAMPING

ROMANIA	❶	❷	❸	❹	❺
ACCOMMODATIONS	under L40	L40-70	L70-100	L100-200	over L200

Hostels are often fairly pleasant, but few are accredited. Some have perks like free beer and breakfast. While some **hotels** charge foreigners more than Romanians, moderately priced lodgings can be found. In July and August, reservations are helpful, but not vital. **Guesthouses** and **pensions** are simple and comfortable but rare. During the summer, many towns rent low-priced rooms in **university dorms;** consult local tourist offices for help locating these. **Private rooms** and **homestays** are a good option, but hosts rarely speak English. Renting a room "together" means sharing a bed. Rooms cost L19-33 in the countryside and L40-55 in cities. Look at the room and fix a price before accepting. **Campgrounds** can be crowded and have frighteningly dirty bathrooms. **Bungalows** are often full in summer; reserve far in advance. Hotels and hostels often provide useful information for tourists.

FOOD AND DRINK

ROMANIA	❶	❷	❸	❹	❺
FOOD	under L7	L7-11	L11-15	L15-20	over L20

A complete **Romanian meal** includes an appetizer, soup, fish, entree, and dessert. Lunch includes **soup,** called *supă* or *ciorbă* (the former has noodles or dumplings, whereas the latter is saltier and has vegetables), an entree (typically grilled meat), and dessert. Soups can be very tasty; try *ciorbă de perişoare* (with vegetables and meatballs) or *supă cu găluşte* (with fluffy dumplings). **Pork** comes in several varieties; *muşchi* and *cotlet* are of the highest quality. Common entrees include *mici* (rolls of fried meat), *sarmale* (stuffed cabbage), and *mămăligă* (polenta). **Beef** and **lamb** are other common meats. *Clătite* (crepes), *papanaşi* (doughnuts with jam and sour cream), and *torts* (creamy cakes), *mere în aluat* (doughnuts with apples) and sugary *gogoşi* (fried doughnuts) are delectable. In the west, you'll find lots of **Hungarian food.** Some restaurants charge by weight rather than by portion; it's difficult to predict how many grams you will receive. *Garnituri*, or extras, are usually charged separately. Pork rules in Romania, so keeping **kosher** is difficult, though possible. **Vegetarian** eating is also feasible, if you are willing to eat foods that are not traditionally Romanian. Local **drinks** include *ţuică*, a brandy distilled from plums and apples, and *pălincă*, a stronger version of *ţuică* that approaches 70% alcohol. *Vişnată* is a delicious liqueur made from wild cherries.

HOLIDAYS AND FESTIVALS

Holidays: New Year's (Jan. 1-2); Epiphany (Jan. 6); Mărţişor (Mar. 1); Easter (Apr. 8-9); Labor Day (May 1); National Day/Union Day (Dec. 1); Christmas (Dec. 25-26).

Festivals: On March 1, locals celebrate the beginning of spring by wearing Mărţişoare, good-luck charms that consist of small jewels or decorations and red-and-white string,. National Day commemorates the day in 1918 that Transylvania, Bessarabia, and Bucovina were united with the Kingdom of Romania.

BEYOND TOURISM

Projects Abroad, 347 W. 36th St., Ste. 901, New York, NY 10018, US (☎888-839-3535; http://www.teachabroad.com/listingsp3.cfm/listing/20334). Places English teachers in primary or secondary schools in Romania for a fee (US$1695).

University of Bucharest, B-dul. M. Kogălniceanu 36-46, Sector 5, 70709 Bucharest, ROM (☎40 21 307 73 00; www.unibuc.ro). Accepts international students.

BUCHAREST (BUCUREŞTI) ☎021

Although Bucharest (pop. 1,922,000) is sometimes passed over by backpackers, the city once dubbed the "Paris of the East" is now experiencing a rebirth of sorts. While wide highways and harsh concrete buildings are tangible reminders of the city's Communist past, contemporary Bucharest, with its stunning architecture and thriving nightlife, serves as a window for exploring the new Eastern Europe.

TRANSPORTATION

Flights: Bucharest Henri Coanda International Airport/Otopeni Airport (☎204 10 00), 16km from the city. Bus #783 to Otopeni runs from Pţa. Unirii with stops throughout the center. Buy **tickets** at the **TAROM office,** Spl. Independenţei 17 (☎303 44 37, 303 44 21, or 303 44 14; www.tarom.ro.). Open M-F 9am-7pm. MC/V.

Trains: Gara de Nord (☎95 21) is the main station. M1: Gara de Nord. Check out www.infofer.ro for updated schedule information. To: **Braşov** (2-4hr., over 20 per day, L22-30); **Budapest, HUN** (13-15hr., 4 per day, L159); **Cluj-Napoca** (7½-11hr., 7 per day, L37-55); **Kraków, POL** (24hr., 1 per day, L301); **Prague, CZR** (24hr., 1 per day, L342); **Sighişoara** (4-5 hr., 10 per day, L28-42); **Sofia, BUL** (11hr., 2 per day, L95). **CFR,** Str. Domniţa Anastasia 10-14 (☎314 55 28; www.cfr.ro), books train tickets. Open M-F 7:30am-7:30pm, Sa 9am-1:30pm. Inside Gara de Nord, **Wasteels** (☎317 03 70; www.wasteelstravel.ro) books international tickets. Open M-F 8am-7pm, Sa 8am-2pm. MC/V.

Buses: Filaret, Cuţitul de Argint 2 (☎335 11 40). M2: Tineretului. To **Athens, GCE,** buy tickets from **Ager Agency** (☎336 67 83). To **İstanbul, TUR,** try **Toros** (☎223 18 98; 2 per day, L125) or **Murat** (☎224 92 93) from outside Gara de Nord. **Double T,** Calea Victoriei 2 (☎313 36 42), a Eurail affiliate, and **Eurolines Touring,** Str. Ankara 6 (☎230 03 70), travel to Western Europe.

Public Transportation: Buses, trams, and **trolleys** run daily 5:30am-11:30pm. Tickets (L1.10) sold at kiosks only; validate in one of the boxes on the poles on board or face fines. **Express buses** take only magnetic cards (L6 for 2 trips; sold at kiosks). Pickpocketing is a problem during peak hours. The **metro** offers reliable and less-crowded service to major destinations. Be careful when counting stops; signs are unreliable. Open daily 5am-11:30pm. Magnetic cards L2 for 2 trips, L6 for 10 trips.

Taxis: Taxi drivers will cheerfully rip off foreigners. Drivers rarely speak English. More reliable companies include **ChrisTaxi** (☎94 61), **Leone** (☎94 25), and **Taxi2000** (☎94 94). **Flight Taxi** (☎94 40) is recommended to or from the airport.

ORIENTATION AND PRACTICAL INFORMATION

The main street changes from **Bulevardul Lascăr Catargiu** to **Bulevardul General Magheru** to **Bulevardul Nicolae Bălcescu** to **Bulevardul I.C. Brătianu** as it runs north-south through Bucharest's four main squares: **Piaţa Victoriei, Piaţa Romană, Piaţa Universităţii,** and **Piaţa Unirii. Gara de Nord,** the train station, lies along the M1 metro line. From there, to reach the city center take the M1 (dir.: Dristor) one stop to Pţa. Victoriei, then change to the M2 (dir.: Depotul IMGB). One stop reaches Piaţa Romană, two stops Pţa. Universităţii, and three stops Pţa. Unirii. The helpful *Bucharest In Your Pocket* is free at museums, bookstores, and hotels.

Tourist Information: Gara de Nord has a booth, but hotels tend to be better resources.

Embassies and Consulates: Australia, World Trade Center Entrance F, at Regus Centre 10, Montreal Sq. (☎316 75 53, consular section 316 75 58). Open M-Th 9am-5:30pm, F 9am-2:30pm. **Canada,** Str. Nicolae Iorga 36 (☎307 50 00). M2: Pţa. Romană. Open M-Th 8:30am-5pm, F 8:30am-2pm. **Ireland,** Str. V. Lascăr 42-44, 6th fl. (☎212 20 88). M2: Pţa. Romană. Open M-F 9am-noon. **UK,** Str. Jules Michelet 24 (☎201 72 00, visas 201 73 00). M2: Pţa. Romană. Open M-Th 8:30am-1pm and 2-5pm, F 8:30am-1:30pm. **US,** Str. Nicolae Filipescu 26 (☎200 33 00). M2: Pţa. Universităţii, behind Hotel Intercontinental. Open M-F 9am-5:30pm. **New Zealand** citizens should use the UK embassy.

Currency Exchange: Exchange agencies and **ATMs** are everywhere. **Banca Comercială Română,** in Pţa. Victoriei and Pţa. Universităţii (☎312 61 85; www.bcr.com), has good rates and exchanges **AmEx Traveler's Cheques** for a 1.5% commission. Open M-F 8:30am-5:30pm, Sa 8:30am-12:30pm. It is illegal to change money on the street. **AmEx Travel Services** available upstairs at **Marshal Tourism**, 43 B-dul. Magheru. (☎319 44 55. Open M-F 9am-6pm.)

ROMANIA

Luggage Storage: Gara de Nord. Small bags L3, large bags L6. Open 24hr.

GLBT Resources: Accept Romania, Str. Lirei 10 (☎252 16 37; www.accept-romania.ro). News on gay rights in Romania, events, and useful links. Open M-F 10am-6pm.

Emergency: Police: ☎955. **Ambulance:** ☎961. **Fire:** ☎981.

Pharmacies: Sensiblu pharmacies (☎0800 080 234) are ubiquitous. Some open 24hr.

Medical Services: American Medical Center, Str. Dragoş Voda 70 (☎210 27 06).

Telephones: Phone cards (L10 or L15) are necessary for all calls.

Internet Access: Club Jazz Cafe, Calea Victoriei 120 (☎312 48 41). M2: Pţa. Romană. 9am-11pm L3 per hr., 11pm-9am L2 per hr. Open 24hr.

Post Office: Str. Matei Millo 10 (☎316 24 94). M2: Pţa. Universităţii. *Poste Restante* available. Open M-F 7:30am-8pm, Sa 8am-2pm. **Postal Code:** 014700.

ACCOMMODATIONS

Renting private rooms is uncommon. Travelers won't go wrong with established hostels, but should avoid "representatives" that greet them at Gara de Nord.

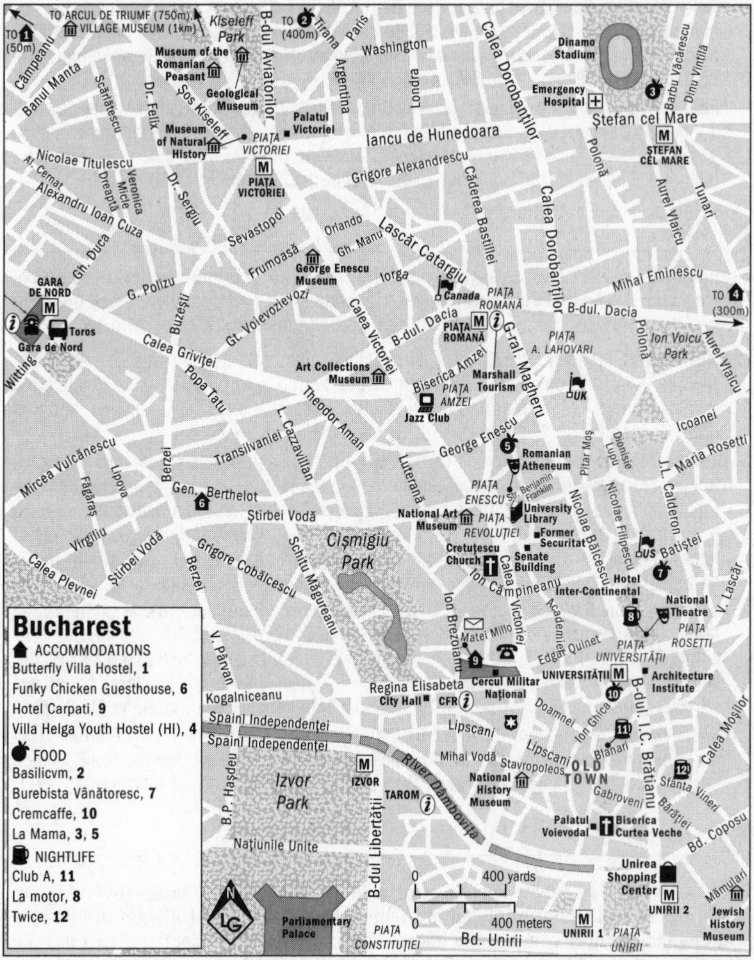

Butterfly Villa Hostel, Dometru Zosima 82 (☎224 19 18, mobile 0 747 032 644; www.villa-butterfly.com). From Piaţa Domeni, cross and turn left on the main street, then go right on Dometru Zosima. Includes free laundry, Internet, and WiFi access, as well as cheap international phone calls (US L0.11 per min., EU L0.12 per min.). Security lockers, DVD/PS2, and satellite TV also available. Reception 24hr. Helpful English-speaking staff. Reserve ahead in summer. Dorms €10; doubles €28. Cash only. ❶

Villa Helga Youth Hostel (HI), Str. Salcâcmilor 2 (☎610 22 14; villa_helga@yahoo.com). M2: Pţa. Romană. Take bus #86, 79, or 135 and travel 2 stops from Pţa. Romană. 28 comfortable beds and helpful staff. Breakfast and laundry included. Kitchen and common room with TV. Reserve ahead in summer. Check-out noon. Dorms €12; singles €16; doubles €28. 5% HI discount. Cash only. ❶

Funky Chicken Guesthouse, Str. Gen. Berthelot 63 (☎312 14 25; www.funkychicken-hostel.com). From Gara de Nord, go right on Calea Griviţei, right on Str. Berzei, and left on Str. Gen. Berthelot. Bucharest's cheapest and best-located hostel. Kitchen and laundry facilities available. Dorms €8. Cash only. ❶

Hotel Carpati, Str. Matei Millo 16 (☎315 01 40). M2: Pţa. Universităţii. Walk down B-dul. Regina Elisabeta to Str. I. Brezoianu and turn right. Central location, new furnishings, TV in every room, and a professional staff. Most doubles have balconies. Breakfast included. Singles L90-95; doubles L140, with bath L220; suites L250. MC/V. ❷

FOOD

The **open-air market** at Pţa. Amzei, near Pţa. Romană has meat, cheese, and produce. A large **La Fourmi Supermarket** is in the basement of the Unirea Shopping Center on Pţa. Unirii. (Open M-F 8am-9:30pm, Sa 8:30am-9pm, Su 9am-4pm.)

Burebista Vânătoresc, Str. Batistei 14 (☎211 89 29). M2: Pţa. Universităţii. Off B-dul. Nicolae Bălcescu. Complete with a stuffed bear, hunting trophies, and a live folk band (M-Sa evenings). Menu features several tasty wild game dishes, including bear and wild boar. Entrees L6-58. Full bar. Open daily noon-midnight. MC/V. ❸

Cremcaffe, Str. Toma Caragiu 3 (☎313 97 40). M2: Pţa. Universităţii. Just off B-dul. Regina Elisabeta, find Str. Toma Caragiu behind the statues, 1 block from Pţa. Universităţii. Established in 1950, this elegant Italian coffeehouse features delicious foccaccia and ciabatta sandwiches (L11-19), along with a good vegetarian selection. Variety of specialty coffees L6-18. English menu and English-speaking staff. Live piano music daily 8-10pm. Open M-F 7:30am-midnight, Sa-Su 9am-midnight. Cash only. ❷

La Mama, Str. Barbu Văcărescu 3 (☎212 40 86; www.lamama.ro). M1: Ştefan cel Mare. Other branches: Str. Delea Veche 51 (☎320 52 13), M1: Pţa. Muncii; Str. Episcopiei 9 (☎312 97 97), M2: Pţa. Romană. Lives up to its motto "like at mom's house," with traditional Romanian dishes, low prices, and a relaxed atmosphere. Appetizers L3.60-9. Entrees L10-17. Open Tu-Th and Su 10am-2am, F-Sa 10am-4am. MC/V. ❷

Basilicvm, Str. Popa Savu 7 (☎222 67 79). M2: Aviatorilor. Praiseworthy food and Italian menu are complemented by a refined setting and attentive service. Sa-Su lunch special puts everything at half-price. Entrees L14-65. Open daily 11am-1am. MC. ❹

SIGHTS

CIVIC CENTER. To create his ideal Socialist capital, Ceauşescu destroyed five sq. km of Bucharest's historical center, demolishing over 9000 19th-century houses and displacing more than 40,000 people. The Civic Center (Centru Civic) that he built lies at the end of the 6km B-dul. Unirii, built 1m wider than its inspiration, the Champs-Elysées. Its centerpiece, the 1000-room **Parliamentary Palace** (Palatul Parlamentului), is the world's second-largest building after the Pentagon. In the last years of the Ceauşescu regime, over 20,000 workers assembled it from Romanian wood, crystal, and marble. *(☎402 14 26. M1 or 3: Izvor, M2: Unirii. Open daily 10am-4pm. Mandatory English tours L20, students L5; photography L30. 1-2 tours per hr.)*

SIGHTS OF THE REVOLUTION. The first shots of the Revolution were fired at **Piaţa Revoluţiei** on December 21, 1989. The square contains the **University Library,** the **National Art Museum,** and the former **Senate Building**, on whose balcony Ceauşescu delivered his final speech. A white marble triangle in the square with the inscription *"Glorie martirilor nostri"* (Glory to our martyrs) commemorates the rioters who overthrew the dictator. The former **Security Building** was partially destroyed and now has a modern glass facade surrounding the ruins. The **Roma-**

nian Atheneum (Ateneul Roman) is one of Bucharest's architectural gems, featuring a Neoclassical dome and columns. It is now home to Bucharest's renowned **Filharmonica** orchestra. *(☎315 68 75. M2: Pţa. Universităţii. With Hotel Intercontinental on your left, turn right on B-dul. Regina Elisabeta and right again on Calea Victoriei.)* Nearby, at Calea Victoriei 47 stands **Creţulescu Church,** Bucharest's most famous church. **Piaţa Universităţii** features memorials to victims of the 1989 revolution and the protests of 1990. Along the center of B-dul. Nicolae Bălcescu there are crosses, including a black one marking the spot where the first victim of the revolution died. In June of 1990, the *piaţa* was again gripped by student riots. Ceauşescu's replacement, Ion Iliescu, bused in 10,000 miners to put down the protest, killing 21 students. He was later democratically elected, but anti-Iliescu graffiti persists on the walls of **Bucharest University** and the **Architecture Institute.** *(M2: Pţa. Universităţii.)*

MUSEUMS. The **Village Museum** (Muzeul Satului), Şos. Kiseleff 28-30, is an excellently designed open-air replica of traditional rural village life in different Romanian regions. *(M2: Aviatorilor. ☎222 90 68. Open daily 9am-7pm. L5, students L2.50; photography L20. Audio tour L7.)* The massive **National Art Museum** (Muzeul Naţional de Artă al României) has works by famous Westerners, but the highlights are paintings by Nicolae Grigorescu and sculptures by Constantin Brâncuşi. *(Calea Victoriei 49-53, in Pţa. Revoluţiei. M2: Pţa. Universităţii. ☎314 81 19; http://art.museum.ro. Open W-Su May-Sept. 1-7pm; Oct.-Apr. 10am-6pm. L12, students L6.)* The **Museum of the Romanian Peasant** (Muzeul Ţăranului Român) captures Romanian rural life and has a small anti-Communist display in the basement. Exhibits are mostly translated into English. *(Şos. Kiseleff 3. ☎212 96 61; www.muzeultaranului.ro. M2 or 3: Pţa. Victoriei. Open Tu-Su 10am-6pm. L6, students L2; photography L50.)* The **National History Museum** (Muzeul Naţional de Istorie al României), has extensive jewel collections. *(Calea Victoriei 12. M2: Pţa. Universităţii. ☎315 70 56. Open Tu-Su 10am-6pm. L3, students L1.50.)*

OTHER SIGHTS. Several of modern Bucharest's most fashionable streets, including **Calea Victoriei, Şoseauna Kiseleff, Bulevardul Aviatorilor,** and **Bulevardul Magheru,** are sights in themselves. Side streets just off Pţa. Victoriei and Pţa. Dorobanţilor are lined with villas and houses typical of beautiful 19th-century Bucharest. **Herăstrău Park,** bordering Şos. Kiseleff, is a popular place for people of all ages to stroll; it also contains rides for people of all ages. At the head of Şos. Kiseleff is Romania's **Arcul de Triumf,** commemorating Romania's WWI casualties. The **old center** lies west of B-dul. Brătianu and south of B-dul. Regina Elisabeta. On Str. Lipscani, cafes, art galleries, and quaint cobblestone streets abound. The ruins of one of Dracula's actual palaces, **Curtea Veche** (Old Court), can be seen on Str. Franceza.

ENTERTAINMENT AND NIGHTLIFE

Theater, symphony, and **opera** performances are cheap; for the best deals, stop by the box office about a week before a show. No performances are staged during the summer. (Opera at B-dul. Mihail Kogălniceanu 70-72; ☎313 18 57.) At night, pack a map and cab fare—many streets are poorly lit and public transportation stops at 11:30pm. Nightclub **Twice,** Str. Sfânta Vineri 4, has bars and dance floors on multiple levels. (☎313 55 92. M2: Pţa. Universităţii. Cover for men W L5, F-Sa L10. 18+. Open W-Su 9pm-5am.) **Club A,** Str. Blănari 14, is Bucharest's most famous nightspot, with absurdly cheap drinks at the bar and loud music on the dance floor. (☎315 55 92; www.cluba.ro. M2: Pţa. Universităţii. Beer L2.50-8. Gin and tonic L3. Cover F-Sa men L5, women L2. Open daily 11am-8pm as a student hangout, 9pm-5am as a club.) **La motor,** B-dul. Bălcescu 1-3, atop the National Theater, is a student bar with cheap drinks and a huge terrace. (M2: Pţa. Universităţii. Beer L3-4.50. Food L3-7.50. Open Su-Th 2pm-late, F-Sa 4pm-late. Cash only.)

SINAIA ☎0244

Sinaia (sih-NYE-uh; pop. 15,000) first made its mark in the late 1880s as an Alpine getaway for Romania's royal family. Carol I, king of the newly independent country, oversaw construction of the fantastically opulent **Peleş Castle** (Castelul Peleş), completed in 1914. The more modest **Pelişor Castle,** built in 1902, was furnished in the Art Nouveau style. (Both castles open Tu 11am-5pm, W-Su 9am-5pm; low season closed Tu. Compulsory tours at Peleş L12, students L5; Pelişor L9/3.) The nearby **Bucegi Mountains** are good for hiking in the summer and skiing in the winter. A cable car *(telecabină)* to the mountains leaves from B-dul. Carol I 26; to reach it, turn up the hill across from the tourist office on Str. Cuza Vodă. There are two stops, one at 1400m and the other at 2000m. (☎311 939. Cars run M-F 8:30am-4pm, Sa-Su 8:30am-5pm. L10 to 1400m, L19 to 2000m; round-trip L18/L36.)

The **Cabana Mioriţa ❶,** at the Cota 2000 station, with a bar and restaurant, is the queen of the mountain cabin system. (Dorms L30; private rooms L50.) For traditional fare in a small-town cafe atmosphere, head to **Restaurant Bucegi ❶,** near the station. (Entrees L5.50-29. Open daily 9am-10pm. Cash only.) After a long day of hiking, grab a beer and some pizza with the locals at **Old Nick's Pub,** B-dul. Carol I 8, by Hotel Sinaia. (☎31 24 91; www.oldnickpub.ro. Beer L5-12. Entrees L9-14. Open Su-Th 9am-1am, F-Sa 9am-2am. Cash only.) **Trains** (☎31 00 40) run to Braşov (1hr., over 20 per day, L7.30), Bucharest (2-3hr., over 20 per day, L19-27), and Cluj-Napoca (6-7hr., 7 per day, L29). To get to the center of town from the train station, climb the set of stone steps across from the station. The friendly, English-speaking staff at the **tourist office,** B-dul. Carol I 47, has an official list of **private rooms,** as well as information about hiking and skiing. (☎315 656; www.infosinaia.ro. Rooms €7-12. Open M-F 8:30am-4:30pm, some Sa-Su 10am-12:30pm.) The Bancpost **ATM, telephone office,** and **post office** are in the same building at B-dul. Carol I 33. (Post office open M-F 7am-8pm, Sa 8am-1pm.) **Postal Code:** 106100.

ROMANIA

TRANSYLVANIA (TRANSILVANIA)

In Western imagination, Transylvania evokes a dark land of black magic and vampires, and those seeking the Transylvania of legend will not be disappointed by the region's Gothic buildings. Architecture aside, Transylvania is a relatively Westernized region with beautiful hills descending from the Carpathian Mountains.

CLUJ-NAPOCA ☎0264

Cluj-Napoca (KLOOZH nah-POH-kah; pop. 318,000) is Transylvania's student center and unofficial capital. The city is a friendly destination for young people. The 80m Gothic steeple of the 14th-century Catholic **Church of St. Michael** (Biserica Sf. Mihail) rises from **Piaţa Unirii.** Take Str. Regele Ferdinand across the river, turn left on Str. Dragalina, and climb the stairs to your right for a dazzling city view from atop **Cetătuie Hill.** Over 12,000 plant species grow in the **Botanical Garden** (Grădina Botanica), Str. Republicii 42, off Str. Napoca. (Gardens open daily 9am-7pm, greenhouses daily 9am-6pm, museum Tu-Th 10am-1pm. L4, students L2.) Hotels distribute the free *Zile si Nopţi? (Days and Nights?)*, which lists the latest nightlife. The **National History Museum of Transylvania,** on the corner of Str. Constantin Daicoviciu and Str. Roosevelt, has over 400,000 pieces on display. (☎595 677. Open Tu-Su 10am-4pm. L2, students L1; photography L5.) **Opera Naţională Romană,** located in the **National Theater** at Ştefan cel Mare 24, has shows many evenings at 7pm. (Theater ☎597 175; www.operanationalacluj.ro. Ticket office Ştefan cel Mare 14; ☎595 363; open daily 11am-5pm and 30min. before shows.) The **Transylvanian International Film Festival** takes place in early

June; most films are subtitled or in English. There is live music in town every night during the festival. (Films about L5-10; student discounts available.)

Retro Youth Hostel ❷, Str. Potaissa 13, has clean dorm rooms and arranges excursions for groups to nearby ice caves and salt mines. (☎450 452; http://retro.ro. Second location at Avram Iancu 9. Breakfast L10. Laundry facilities available. Dorms L40. HI and ISIC discount 5%. MC/V.) **Roata ❷,** Str. Alexandru Ciura 6A, off Str. Emil Isac, is a traditional Romanian restaurant that serves up excellent food in big portions. (☎592 022. Appetizers L4-10. Entrees L13-28. Open Su-M 1pm-midnight, Tu-Sa noon-midnight. MC/V.) **Diesel,** Piaţa Unirii 17, is a busy cafe; the club and lounge in the cellar attract beautiful people on weekends. (☎439 043. Dress code at club and lounge. Cafe open daily 8am-late. Club open daily 7pm-late. Parties with live music or DJs Th-Sa. Cover varies, sometimes up to L100 with open bar. Lounge open Th-Sa. Beer L5-15. Mixed drinks L7-15. Cash only.)

Trains go to: Bucharest (8-11hr., 7 per day, L37-55) via Braşov (5-7hr., L30-45); Budapest, HUN (6½-7hr., 2 per day, L140); Sibiu (4hr., 1 per day, L32); Timişoara (6-7hr., 6 per day, L30-45). Local **buses** and **trams** run 5am-10pm; tickets (L1.20) are sold at **RATUC** kiosks (open 5:30am). Validate your ticket on board. **ATMs** line B-dul. Ferdinand. **Tomis Club Internet,** Str. Oberth 3, is just off B-dul. Erialor. (L1.40 per hr.; midnight-8am L0.70 per hr. Open 8am-midnight.) **Postal Code:** 400110.

SIGHIŞOARA ☎0265

Vlad Ţepeş, the inspiration for Bram Stoker's *Dracula* (see **Bran,** p. 836), was born in this enchanting hillside town (pop. 32,000). Its gilded steeples and old clock tower have survived centuries of attacks, fires, and floods. The **Cetatea** (Citadel), built by the Saxons in 1191, is now a tiny medieval city within a city. Enter through the **turnul cu ceas** (clock tower), off Str. O. Goga; the **History Museum** is scattered through rooms on the way up. To the left as you leave the clock tower, the **Colecţia de Arme Medievale** (Museum of Medieval Armory) offers a modest, English-captioned exhibit on Vlad Ţepeş and international weaponry. The **torture room** houses a very small collection of pain-inflicting instruments. (Open M 10am-4:30pm, Tu-F 9am-6:30pm, Sa-Su 9am-4:30pm. Clock tower L4, students L3; museum L3/L2; torture room L2. Combined ticket L7.) Central **Piaţa Cetăţii** was historically used for markets, executions, and impalings. The nearby church, **Biserica Mănăstirii,** sometimes holds concerts. (Open daily 10am-6pm. L2.) Turn right from the station to reach

SON OF A...

Yes, Dracula did exist—sort of. H
was not the ruler of Transylvania
but of Wallachia; he was not
count, but a *voivod* (a local gove
nor or "prince"); and he was not
vampire. Still, the truth abou
Vlad Ţepeş (1431-1476), fondl
known as Dracula, is enough t
make anyone lock the lid to his o
her coffin at night.

Dracula's story begins with hi
father, the ruthless Vlad Basarab
who became known as Vla
Dracul (Dragon) for his member
ship in the Order of the Dragon
"Drac" in Romanian can be trans
lated as either dragon or, fittingly
devil. In a diplomatic move
Dracul sent his 10-year-old son
Dracula (Son of the Dragon), t
the Ottoman Empire as a hostag
in 1442. There, young Vla
learned his preferred method o
torture: impalement. Victims o
impalement—which involved th
insertion of a large wooden stak
into the victim's body, avoidin
piercing the vital organs—begge
for a swift death throughout th
slow, agonizing process.

Known as Vlad the Impaler du
ing his reign as *voivod,* Dracul
impaled murderers, thieves, an
political rivals; he also targete
the destitute and the crippled in
bid to rid his territory of poverty
His crowning achievement was i
turning the Turks' gruesome pra
tice against them. In 1462, th
invading Turks turned tail a
Wallachia's border, which ha
been decorated with 20,000 o
their impaled countrymen.

Nathan's Villa Hostel ❶, Str. Libertății 8. The friendly, multilingual staff organizes daytrips. (☎772 546; www.nathansvilla.com. Breakfast included. Free laundry. Kitchen available. Reception 24hr. Dorms L30; private rooms L76. Cash only.) The fare at **Casa Vlad Dracul ❷** is not cheap; however, the opportunity to eat in the house where Vlad Țepeș was born is undeniably unique. (Beer L6.50-7.50. Appetizers L4.50-11. Entrees L11-47. Vegetarian options available. Open daily 10am-midnight. Cash only.) **International Cafe ❶** has tasty snacks. **Internet** access is available downstairs at **Catacombs-Net.** (Open M-Sa 10am-6pm. Internet available M-F 1-7pm. Pastries L1-3.50. Sandwiches L5-6. Cash only.) **Trains** go to Bucharest (5hr., 4 per day, L28-42) via Brașov (1¾-3hr., 6 per day, L19-23), and Cluj-Napoca (3-4hr., 3 per day, L26-35). To reach the city center from the train station, turn right on Str. Libertății and left on Str. Gării, veer left at the Russian cemetery, turn right on the footbridge over Târana Mare, and walk down Str. Morii. There is currently no tourist office, but one is slowly being built on Str. O. Goga; info is available at the train station. **Postal Code:** 545400.

BRAȘOV ☎0268

Brașov (pop. 284,000) is an ideal departure point for trips into the mountains. A cable car *(telecabină)* goes up **Muntele Tâmpa;** to reach it from the main square, **Piața Sfatului,** walk down Apollonia Hirscher, make a left on Str. Castelui, a right on Suișul Castelui, and head up the stairs to the beige building on the right. (Cable car runs Tu-Su 9:30am-4:45pm. L4, round-trip L6.) Alternatively, follow the red triangle markings to hike to the top (1-1½hr.). Brașov is a picturesque town with a lively German heritage. **Str. Republicii** is the city's main pedestrian avenue, while beyond the square and along Str. Gh. Barițiu is Romania's most celebrated Gothic edifice, the Lutheran **Black Church** (Biserica Neagră). Built in 1383, it received its name after being charred by fire in 1689. (Open M-Sa 10am-5pm. Organ concerts Tu 6pm. L4, students L2.) Tickets to the **opera** (Str. Bisericii Române 51; ☎415 990; www.opera-brasov.ro) and **orchestra** (Str. Apollonia Hirscher 10; ☎473 058; www.filarmonica-brasov.ro) may be purchased at the Agencia Teatrală de Bilete, Str. Republicii 4. (☎471 889. Open Tu-F 10am-5pm, Sa 10am-2pm. Opera tickets L8-10, students L3. Orchestra L10/5. Cash only.) Each summer (Aug.-Sept.), Pța. Sfatului hosts the **Golden Stag Festival** (Cerbul de Aur), which attracts international musicians. The **International Chamber Music Festival** is held in September.

ROMANIA

Locals offer **private rooms** at the train station; expect to pay €10-15 per night. **Kismet Dao Villa Hostel ❷**, located at Str. Democrației 2B, has a big common room and an on-site bar. From Pța. Unirii, walk up Str. Bâlea and turn right on Str. Democrației. (☎514 296. Breakfast, laundry, and daily drink included. Dorms €10; doubles €26. MC/V for 4% extra.) Romantic, candlelit **Bella Muzica ❷**, downstairs at Str. G. Barițiu 2, has an eclectic Mexican-Romanian menu, as well as free tortilla chips and free shots of *pălincă*. (☎476 946. English menu. Beer L4-7. Appetizers L5-24. Entrees L8-44. Open daily noon-midnight. MC/V.) **Trains** run to: Bucharest (2-4hr., over 20 per day, L22-30); Cluj-Napoca (7hr., 8 per day, L30-45); Iași (9hr., 1 per day, L31); Sibiu (2½-4hr., 8 per day, L23). Buy tickets at **CFR**, B-dul. 15 Noiembrie 43. (☎470 696. Open M-F 8am-7:30pm.) From the station, take bus #4 (dir.: Pța. Unirii) to Pța. Sfatului (10min.); get off in front of Black Church. The **tourist office,** located inside the museum in Pța. Sfatului, has an English-speaking staff. (☎419 078; www.brasovcity.ro. Open daily 9am-5pm.) **TibNet Internet Cafe,** G. Baritsiu 8, is cheap (L2 per hr.) and open 24hr. (☎410 185.) **Postal Code:** 500001.

BRAN ☎0268

Vlad Țepeș, the model for the hero-villain of Bram Stoker's novel *Dracula*, may have once lived in Bran. Dracula's fictional exploits pale in comparison with Țepeș's actual ones: as a local prince of the Wallachia region, he protected the

Bran pass from the encroaching Turks of the Ottoman Empire, garnering infamy for impaling his enemies. While Țepeș may have been a guest at **Bran Castle,** built under Hungarian rule in 1377-1382, there is little evidence that he lived there. Nor, in fact, did Stoker, an Irishman, ever visit Romania. The ticket to the castle also includes a visit to the small **Bran Village Museum,** which re-creates a traditional Romanian village. (Castle open M noon-6pm, Tu-Su 9am-6pm. L12, students L6; photography L10.) To reach Bran from Brașov, take a taxi or city **bus** #12 to Autogară 2 (45min., 2 per hr. 7am-11:30pm, L3). Get off at the souvenir market or at the sign marked "Cabana Bran Castle—500m." Backtrack along the road toward Brașov; the castle is on the right. **Postal Code:** 507025.

TIMIȘOARA ☎0256

Though an important place in Romania's past and present, Timișoara (pop. 318,000) may offer less for travelers than other Romanian cities. In 1989, an anti-Ceaușescu rally in **Piața Victoriei** ignited the revolution that overthrew the Communists. At one end of the square stands the imposing **Metropolitan Cathedral,** with a brightly tiled roof in the Byzantine and Moldavian folk style. (Open daily 6am-8pm.) In nearby historic **Huniade Castle,** the **Banat Museum** (Muzeul Banatului) traces Timișoara's history. (Open Tu-Su 10am-4:30pm. L2, students L1.) Across the square is the grandiose **National Theater and Opera.** (Box office Str. Mărășești 2. Open daily Sept.-June 10am-1pm and 5-7pm. Theater up to L15, opera up to L20.) **Hotel Nord ❷,** Str. Gen. Ion Dragalina 47, by the train station, has comfy rooms with TV and fridge. (☎497 504. Breakfast included. Singles L70-105; doubles L105-125. MC/V.) **Restaurant Club XXI ❶,** Pța Victoriei 2, serves authentic Romanian food. (Appetizers L2-9; salads under L4; entrees L4-16. Live music every night. Open daily 10am-11pm. Cash only.) **Trains** run from Timișoara Nord to Brașov (9hr., 2 per day, L40), Bucharest (8hr., 7-8 per day, L57), and Cluj-Napoca (7hr., 5 per day, L35). From the station, take city bus #11 or 14 to the center of town (L1.20; buy tickets at **RATT** kiosks). **Librăria Mihai Eminescu,** Str. Maceșilor 2, in Pța. Victoriei, sells maps. (Open M-F 9am-8pm, Sa 9am-1pm. MC/V.) **Postal Code:** 300005.

ROMANIA

MOLDAVIA AND BUCOVINA

Northeastern Romania, known as Moldavia, extends from the Carpathian Mountains to the Prut River. Starker than Transylvania but more developed than Maramureș, Moldavia is home to the painted monasteries of Bucovina, which combine Moldavian and Byzantine architecture with Romanian Orthodox Christian images. Dress modestly; avoid wearing shorts or sleeveless tops.

GURA HUMORULUI ☎0230

Gura Humorului can serve as an ideal base for monastery tours. Ștefan cel Mare built **Voroneț** in 1488, and in 1524 his illegitimate son, Petru Rareș, added its famous frescoes. Walk left from the train station, turn left on Cartierul Voroneț, and follow the signs for a scenic 5km. (Open in summer daily 8am-7pm;

> **MOLDAVIA MADNESS.** Moldavia and Moldova are not the same place! While Moldavia is the northeastern part of Romania, Moldova is a separate country between Russia and Romania. The distinction is further confused because the region of Moldavia is known as "Moldova" in Romanian. You need a visa to go to the country of Moldova, so make sure you don't accidentally book a bus that passes through Moldova unless you have proper documentation.

winter 8am-5pm. L4, students L2.) Bucovina's renowned indoor frescoes, which depict the life of the Virgin Mary, are at **Humor.** Walk right on Str. Ştefan cel Mare from the train or bus station to the town center. Take Str. Manasteria Humorului at the fork and continue 6km to the monastery. (Open in summer daily 8am-7pm; winter 8am-5pm. L4, students L2.) A half-day trip from Gura Humorului leads to the frescoes of **Moldoviţa.** (Open in summer daily 8am-7pm; winter 8am-5pm. L4, students L2.) Take a **train** from Gura Humorului to Vama (20min., 9 per day, L3.90) and continue to Vatra Moldoviţei (45min., 3 per day, L2.40).

Pensiune Casa Ella ❷, Str. Cetaţii 7, off B-dul. Bucovina, has soft beds and a central location. The owner speaks French and some English. (☎23 29 61. Kitchen facilities available; TV in rooms. Singles L50; doubles L60. Cash only.) On B-dul. Bucovina, **Restaurant Lions ❷** has an international menu in a royalty-themed setting. (Beer L2.50-4.50. Pizza L7-10. Entrees L9-20. Open daily 9am-11:30pm. MC/V.) **Trains** go to Bucharest (6hr., 1 per day, L45), Cluj-Napoca (5hr., 4 per day, L26), and Suceava (1hr., 10 per day, L3.50-6.20). From the station, turn right on Str. Ştefan cel Mare to reach the city center. **Postal Code:** 725300.

SUCEAVA ☎0230

Once Moldavia's capital and 34km from Gura Humorului, Suceava is home to the grand 1388 **Citadel of the Throne** (Cetatea de Scaun). Climb up and walk along the ramparts for a spectacular view. Taxis (5min., L4) can be arranged from the main square, Pţa. 22 Decembrie, but the 10min. hike uphill following the forest path is pleasant. (Open daily 8am-8pm; low season 10am-6pm. L4, students L2. Photography L5.) The nearby **Village Museum of Bucovina** immortalizes traditional life. (Open Tu-F 10am-6pm, Sa-Su 10am-8pm. L2.) On Str. Ana Ipătescu, walk past the bus shelter and turn left to find the **Biserica St. Dumitru,** built in 1535 and decorated inside with frescoes. It is a functioning church, so visiting hours vary.

The delightful **High Class Hostel ❷,** Str. Aurel Vlaicu 195, is 7km from town (bus #1, L1), but the exceptional service is worth the travel time. (Mobile ☎0 723 782 328, landline 515 213; www.classhostel.ro. 2-4 beds per room. Breakfast included, dinner L25. Laundry L10 per 3kg. Free Internet. Dorms L50. MC/V.) **Pub Chagall ❷,** in a courtyard off Str. Ştefan cel Mare, serves thin-crust pizzas and filling pub food in a cozy cellar. (☎530 261. Entrees L8-19. Open M-Sa 10am-midnight, Su 11am-midnight. Cash only.) **Trains** run to: Braşov (6hr., 1 per day, L23-42); Bucharest

THE LOCAL STORY

ROMANIAN HOLIDAY

Let's Go got the scoop on the "Romanina spirit" from Monica Cavoianu, who has run Class Hostel in Moldavia for four years.

On local food and EU regulations: In the EU they use a lot of chemicals. We don't use any sprays, only vegetable [compost] and cow manure. West Europeans know that the taste of their food is so damaged by the chemicals, when they come here they go crazy for it. If I ever have to move I will have to buy my own cow. When I was in Australia, I wrote a postcard to the [Australian] lady I buy milk from and said, "Please take care of your cows, because the milk here is garbage!"

On hospitality: Many people when they've stayed here have said, "I want to help you with the dishes." But when you are a visitor as a guest in a Romanian house, you are not allowed to help in the kitchen. You have your nails painted, and you just sit and eat. I've been in Sweden...and my friend said "We have to cook now." At my house I would have had the food ready! And then, when we finished, she said, "We have to do the dishes now." I asked, "We do the dishes?" And she handed them to me! There is a lot of concern about hospitality [in Romania], which is lost in other European countries.

On the locus of the Romanian spirit: [It exists] in the countryside. In Bucharest, don't expect anything.

(8hr., 7-8 per day, L23-37); Cluj-Napoca (6hr., 4 per day, L18-28); Gura Humorului (1hr., 10 per day, L3.50-6.20). Buy tickets at **CFR,** Str. N. Bălcescu 4. (☎21 43 35. Open M-F 7:30am-7pm.) Turn right off Str. N. Bălcescu for **buses** (☎52 43 40) that run from the station on Str. V. Alecsandri (open 5am-9pm) to Bucharest (8hr., 5-6 per day, L32), Cluj-Napoca (7hr., 2 per day, L31), and Gura Humorului (1hr., 11-13 per day, L4.50). **Taxis** around town charge L1.20-1.50 per km. **Librăria Alexandria,** Str. N. Bălcescu 8, sells **maps** and **English books.** (☎53 03 37. Open M-F 8am-7:30pm, Sa 8am-5pm. MC/V.) **Postal Code:** 720290.

THE BLACK SEA COAST

CONSTANȚA ☎0241

Constanța (pop. 311,000) straddles the line between industrial port city and beach resort, while neighboring Mamaia and other resort towns have a more singular purpose—the beach. The **Museum of Art,** B-dul. Tomis 84, highlights 19th- and 20th-century Romanian art. (☎61 80 19. Open in high season daily 9am-8pm; low season W-Su 9am-5pm. L8, students L4; photography L10.) In Piața Ovidiu lies the **Museum of National History and Archaeology,** which celebrates Constanța's Roman heritage. This was also the site of the Forum from the 4th to the 6th centuries. (Pța. Ovidiu 12; ☎61 87 63. Open in high season daily 8am-8pm; low season W-Su 9am-5pm. L10, students L5; photography L10.) The impressive **Great Mosque** stands at Str. Arhiepiscopiei 5; climb the 50m minaret for the best view of the city. (L4, students L2.) However, as Constanța isn't known primarily for its museums, make sure to head for the beaches. **Modern Beach** is located in town, while **Mamaia** and other resort areas have extensive beachfronts. Another way to cool down is to careen down the waterslides at **Aqua Magic,** the waterpark near the entrance to Mamaia resort. (☎83 31 73; www.aquamagic.ro. L30-40.) Get an overview of the resort by taking the **Telegondola** next to Aqua Magic. (Open 9am-midnight. L5.)

Hotel Tineretului ❸, B-dul. Tomis 20-26, is a two-star hotel. (☎613 590. English speaking reception. TVs in all rooms and disco downstairs. Breakfast included. Free Internet. Singles L82; doubles L92. Cash only.) **Restaurant Nur ❸,** B-dul. Tomis 48, offers good quality Turkish food with music and decor to match. (☎61 50 25. Hookahs available. Appetizers L5. Beer L6. Entrees L10-22. Open daily 8am-midnight. Cash only.) Nightclubs to check out include **Oscar,** Str. Sarmisegetusa 15, for older tunes, or **Club "No Problem,"** Complex Dacia on B-dul. Tomis, for dance music. (☎51 33 77. Cover L10 when live music. Open Th-Sa 10pm-5am.) The **tourist office,** Alexander Lăpuşneanu 185A (☎555 000; www.infolitoral.ro), has an English-speaking staff that books accommodations for a commission. (Open M-F 8am-4pm.) The **post office** is at B-dul. Tomis 79-81. (☎55 22 22. Open M-F 7am-7pm, Sa 7am-1pm.) **Taxis** (☎555 555) are easily waved down. **Public transit** consists of buses, trolleys, and trams, and runs 5am-11:30pm. **Trains** run to Bucharest (3-4hr., 6 per day). Buy tickets at **CFR,** Vasile Canarache 4. (☎61 49 50. Open M-F 7:30am-8pm, Sa 8am-2pm. International booth open M-F 9am-4pm. MC/V.) Mozlem, Condor, and Niş-Tur (☎63 83 43), run **buses** to İstanbul, TUR (L125) via Varna, BUL (L80). The bus station is open 5am-11pm.

RUSSIA (РОССИЯ)

More than a decade after the collapse of the Soviet Union, vast Russia stumbles along with no real clear direction; former Communists run the state, while impoverished pensioners long for a rose-tinted Soviet past. Heedless of surrounding provinces, urbane Moscow gorges on hyper-capitalism, while majestic St. Petersburg struggles to remain one of Europe's major cultural centers. Although traveling here can be a bureaucratic nightmare, Russia is in many ways the ideal destination for a budget traveler—historical, inexpensive, and well served by public transportation.

ESSENTIALS

FACTS AND FIGURES

Official Name: Russian Federation.

Capital: Moscow.

Population: 142,894,000.

Land Area: 16,995,800 sq. km.

Time Zone: Moscow and St. Petersburg are GMT +3.

Language: Russian.

Religion: Russian Orthodox (15-20%), Muslim (10-15%).

WHEN TO GO

It may be wise to plan around the high season (June-Aug.). The fall and spring (Sept.-Oct. and Apr.-May) are better times to visit; the weather is moderate and flights are cheaper. If you intend to visit the large cities and linger indoors at museums and theaters, the bitter winter (Nov.-Mar.) is most economical. Keep in mind, however, that sights and accommodations often close or reduce their hours, especially in rural areas. Another factor to consider is hours of daylight—in St. Petersburg, summer light lasts almost to midnight, but in winter the sun may set as early as 3:45pm. Whenever you go, it will rain; have warm, waterproof clothing on hand.

DOCUMENTS AND FORMALITIES

EMBASSIES. Foreign embassies for Russia are in Moscow (p. 846). Russian embassies abroad include: **Australia,** 78 Canberra Ave., Griffith, ACT, 2603 (☎6 6295 9033; www.australia.mid.ru); **Canada,** 285 Charlotte St., Ottawa, ON, K1N 8L5 (☎613-235-4341; www.rusembcanada.mid.ru); **Ireland,** 184-186 Orwell Rd., Rathgar, Dublin, 14 (☎492 34 92; http://ireland.ru/embassy); **New Zealand,** 57 Messines Rd., Karori, Wellington, 6005 (☎4 476 6113; www.rus.co.nz); **UK,** 5 Kensington Palace Gardens, London, W8 4QS (0207 229 80 27; www.rusemblon.org); **US,** 2650 Wisconsin Ave., NW, Washington, D.C., 20007 (☎202-298-5700; www.russianembassy.org).

VISA AND ENTRY INFORMATION. Almost every visitor to Russia needs a visa. Several types exist; the standard tourist visa is valid for 30 days, a business visa up to three months, and both come in single- and double-entry varieties. Applications for Russian visas require an **invitation** stating the traveler's itinerary. Hostels and hotels can often provide invitations for tourist visas. **Visa services** and **travel agencies** (see p. 841) can provide you with invitations (US$30-80), and/or get you an actual visa (from US$160). Students may be able to obtain student visas from their school or host organization. Upon arrival, travelers are required to fill out an immigration card, part of which must be kept until departure from Russia, and to **register** their visa within three working days (see **Entering Russia,** below).

GETTING A VISA ON YOUR OWN. If you have an invitation from a travel agency or Russian organization and want to get a visa on your own, apply for the visa in person or by mail at the nearest Russian embassy or consulate. (You can download an application form directly from the website www.ruscon.org.) Bring your original invitation; your passport; a completed application; three passport-size photographs; a cover letter stating your name, dates of arrival and departure, cities you plan to visit in Russia, date of birth, and passport number; and a money order or certified check. (Single-entry, 30-day visas US$100-300; double-entry US$100-350; multiple-entry US$100-$450.) If you have even tentative plans to visit a city, add it to your visa.

VISA AGENCIES. Travel agencies that advertise discounted tickets to Russia often are also able to provide invitations and visas. Listed below are other organizations you may consider using.

ENTRANCE REQUIREMENTS

Passport: Required for all travelers.
Visa: Required for all travelers.
Letter of Invitation: Required for all travelers.
Inoculations: Recommended up-to-date on DTaP (diphtheria, tetanus, and pertussis), hepatitis A, hepatitis B, MMR (measles, mumps, and rubella), polio booster, and typhoid.
Work Permit: Required for all foreigners planning to work in Russia.
Driving Permit: Required for all those planning to drive in Russia.

Host Families Association (HOFA), 3 Linia, 6, V.O., St. Petersburg, 199053, RUS (☎812 275 19 92; www.hofa.us). Arranges homestays in 40 Russian cities. Single rooms with breakfast start at US$20. Discounts for stays over 1 week with the same family. Visa invitations available (US$30, non-guests US$40).

VISAtoRUSSIA.com, Leninsky Prospekt 29, Offices 401-408, Moscow, 117912, RUS (☎7 495 956 44 22; www.visatorussia.com). Russian visa invitations start at US$30.

Russia-visa.com, 2005 Massachusetts Ave., NW, Washington, D.C., 20036, USA (☎800-567-4175; www.russia-visa.com). Cheap, reliable visa service starts at US$160. US$20 discount if you provide the invitation.

STAR Travel, Metro station Sokol, 9 Baltiyskaya, 3rd fl., Moscow, 9, RUS (☎095 797 95 55; www.startravel.ru). Catering to those on a budget, this Russian travel agency arranges train and air travel around the region.

ENTERING RUSSIA. The best way to cross the **border** is to fly directly into Moscow or St. Petersburg. Another option is to take a train or bus into one of the major cities. Expect long delays and red tape. Russian law dictates that all visitors must **register** their visas within three days of arrival. Many travelers skip this purgatory, but it is the law, and taking care of it will leave one less thing over which bribe-seeking authorities can hassle you—typical fines for visa non-registration run about US$150. While in Russia, carry your passport on your person at all times.

TOURIST SERVICES AND MONEY

TOURIST OFFICES. There are two types of Russian tourist offices—those that only arrange tours and those that offer general travel assistance. Offices of the former type are often unhelpful or even rude, but those of the latter are usually eager to assist, particularly with visa registration. While Western-style tourist offices are not common, big hotels often contain travel agencies with English-speaking staffs (see also **Visa Agencies,** above). Buy maps at kiosks on the street.

PAYING IN RUSSIA. Due to the fluctuating value of the Russian ruble, some establishments list their prices in US dollars. For this reason, some prices in this book may also appear in US dollars, but be prepared to pay in rubles.

MONEY. The Russian unit of currency is the **ruble,** which comes in 1, 2, and 5R coins and 10, 50, 100, 500, and 1000R bills. One hundred kopecks make a ruble. Government regulations require that you show your passport when exchanging money. Most *obmen valyuti* (обмен валюты; currency exchanges) will only exchange US dollars and euros. With **inflation** around 15%, expect prices quoted in rubles and **exchange rates** to undergo frequent changes. **Do not exchange money on the street.** Banks offer the best combination of good rates and security. You'll have no problem changing rubles back at the end of your trip. **ATMs** *(bankomat)*, linked to major networks and credit cards, can be found in most cities. Banks, ATMs, and

RUBLES		
	AUS$1 = 20.32R	10R = AUS$0.49
	CDN$1 = 24.49R	10R = CDN$0.41
	EUR€1 = 34.64R	10R = EUR€0.29
	NZ$1 = 17.21R	10R = NZ$0.58
	UK£1 = 50.56R	10R = UK£0.20
	US$1 = 26.99R	10R = US$0.37

currency exchanges often accept major **credit cards,** especially Visa. Main branches of banks will usually accept **traveler's checks** and give cash advances on credit cards. It's wise to keep a small amount (around US$20) of dollars on hand. Be aware that most establishments don't accept crumpled, torn, or written-on bills of any denomination. Russians are also wary of old US dollars; bring new bills.

HEALTH AND SAFETY

In a **medical emergency,** either leave the country or go to the American Medical Centers in Moscow or St. Petersburg. Russian **bottled water** is often mineral water; you may prefer to boil or filter your own, or buy imported bottled water at a supermarket. Water is drinkable in much of Russia, but not in Moscow or St. Petersburg. Men's **toilets** are marked with an "M," women's with a "Жю" The 0.5-5R charge for public toilets generally gets you a hole in the ground and a single square of toilet paper; it is prudent to carry your own. **Pharmacies** abound and offer a range of Western medicine and hygiene products; look for the "Аптека" (Apteka) signs.

Crime against foreigners is a problem, particularly in Moscow and St. Petersburg. Although it is often tough to blend in, try not to flaunt your nationality. It is extremely unwise to take pictures of anything **military** or to do anything that might attract the attention of a man in uniform. Generally, avoid interaction with the police unless an emergency necessitates it; officers will attempt to cheat foreigners and locals alike. Do not let officials go through your possessions, and if they try to detain you unreasonably, threaten to call your embassy *("ya pozvonyu svoyu posolstvu.")* The concept of **sexual harassment** has yet to reach Russia. While traveling alone as a **woman** is generally safe, local men will try to pick up women and will get away with offensive language and actions. The routine usually starts with an innocent-sounding *"Devushka..."* (young lady); just say *"Nyet"* (No) or walk away. Those who do not speak Russian will often be subject to price hikes. Authorities on the metro may stop and question people with **dark skin;** minorities may also receive rude treatment in shops and restaurants. Outside of Moscow and St. Petersburg, where a gay scene thrives and people are generally accepting, **homosexuality** is still largely taboo; discretion is best.

EMERGENCY	**Police:** ☎02. **Ambulance:** ☎03. **Fire/General:** ☎01.

TRANSPORTATION

BY PLANE. Most major international airlines fly into either **Sheremetyevo-2 (SVO)** in Moscow or **Pulkovo (LED)** in St. Petersburg. **Aeroflot,** Leningradsky Prospekt 37, Building 9, Moscow, 125167 (☎495 223 55 55; www.aeroflot.org), is the most popular domestic carrier. Aeroflot has recently upgraded its fleet of airplanes, replacing the notoriously unsafe Soviet-era planes with more modern Airbuses and Boeings. While flying to Russia from Asia, Europe, and the US can be expensive, indirect routes offer a relatively cheaper entrance. A number of European budget airlines fly into Tallinn, EST, Rīga, LAT, or Helsinki, FIN; from there, a bus or train can carry you into Russia.

BY TRAIN. Avoid entering Russia through Belarus; you need a visa and the border crossing is unpleasant. Trains are the best option for **domestic** travel. Weekend or holiday trains between St. Petersburg and Moscow sometimes sell out a week in advance. If you plan ahead, you'll choose from four **classes.** The best is *lyuks*, with two beds, while the second-class *kupeyny* has four bunks. The next class down is *platskartny*, an open car with 52 shorter, harder bunks. Aim for places #1-33. Places #34-37 abut the bathroom, while places #38-52 are on the side; in summer they can get incredibly hot. **Women traveling alone** can try to buy out a *lyuks* compartment for security, or can travel *platskartny* and depend on the crowds to shame would-be harassers. *Platskartny* is also a good idea on the theft-ridden St. Petersburg-Moscow line, as you are less likely to be targeted there. Board your train on time, as changing your ticket can carry a fee of up to 25% of the ticket cost.

BY BUS. Buses, only slightly less expensive than trains, are better for shorter distances. However, they are often crowded and overbooked; don't be shy about ejecting people who try to sit in your seat.

BY BOAT. Cruise ships stop in the main Russian ports: Murmansk, St. Petersburg, and Vladivostok. However, they usually only allow travelers less than 48hr. in the city. Ferries run from Kaliningrad to St. Petersburg one to two times per week. Kaliningrad ferries also go to Germany and Poland. Additionally, ferries traverse the Khabarovsk-China, Novorossiysk-Georgia, Sochi-Georgia, Sochi-Turkey, Vladivostok-Japan, and Vladivostok-Korea routes.

BY CAR AND BY BIKE. Russia's highly variable road conditions and weather create an interesting driving experience. Gasoline can be difficult to find, and police officers may pull you over seemingly without provocation. Biking is relatively rare, but motorists are generally polite to bikers.

BY TAXI AND BY THUMB. Hailing a taxi is indistinguishable from **hitchhiking,** and should be treated with equal caution. Most drivers who stop will be private citizens trying to make a little extra cash. Those seeking a ride stand off the curb and hold out a hand into the street, palm down; when a car stops, riders tell the driver the destination before getting in; he will either refuse altogether or ask "*Skolko?*" (How much?), leading to protracted negotiations. Non-Russian speakers will get ripped off unless they manage a firm agreement on the price—if the driver agrees without asking for a price, you must ask "*Skolko?*" yourself. **Never get into a car that has more than one person in it.** Let's Go does not recommend hitchhiking.

KEEPING IN TOUCH

PHONE CODES	**Country code:** 7. **International dialing prefix:** 8, await a second tone, then 10. For more information on placing international calls, see inside back cover.

EMAIL AND THE INTERNET. Email is your best bet for keeping in touch in Russia. Internet cafes are readily available in Moscow and St. Petersburg. Rates vary 35-70R per hour depending on the time of day. Many Internet cafes are open 24hr.

TELEPHONE. Most pay phones take phonecards, good for both local and intercity calls and sold at central telephone offices, metro stations, and newspaper kiosks. When you are purchasing phonecards from a telephone office or metro station, the attendant will often ask, "Na ulitsu?" ("На улицу?"; On the street?) to find out whether you want a card for the phones in the office or for outdoor public phones. Be careful; phonecards in Russia are very specific, and it is easy to purchase the wrong kind. Often, hostels, Internet cafes, and similar locations will try to sell you phonecards that work only in their establishments.

For five-digit numbers, insert a "2" between the dialing code and the phone number. Make direct **international** calls from telephone offices in St. Petersburg and Moscow: prices run US$1-1.50 per minute to Europe; US$1.50-2 to Australia and the US. International access codes include: **AT&T Direct** from Moscow ☎755 5042, from St. Petersburg 325 5042; **Canada Direct** ☎800 110 1012; **MCI WorldPhone** using Sovintel from Moscow ☎960 2222, from St. Petersburg 346 8022; **Sprint** ☎747 3324.

Mobile phones have become a popular accessory among Russians and a comforting safety blanket for visitors. Most new phones bought in Russia are compatible with Russian networks and mobile phone shops are common, but service can be costly. The average cost is US$0.20 per min., and users are charged for incoming calls. Major providers MegaFon, Bee Line GSM, and MTS have stores throughout the cities, as do rental chains like Euroset and Svyaznoy.

MAIL. Mail service is more reliable leaving the country than coming in. Letters to the US will arrive a week after mailing; letters to other destinations take two to three weeks. Domestic mail will usually reach its destination; from abroad, it's best to send letters to Russia via friends who are traveling there. Airmail is *avia* (авиа). Send your mail "заказное" (certified; 40R) to reduce the chance of it being lost. Letters to the US cost 16R; postcards 11R. **Poste Restante** is "Pismo Do Vostrebovania." Address envelopes as follows: LAST NAME First name, Postal Code, city, Письмо До Востребования, RUSSIA.

LANGUAGE. Russian is an East Slavic language written in the Cyrillic (p. 1052) alphabet. **English** is increasingly common, but come equipped with a few helpful Russian phrases. For a glossary, see **Phrasebook: Russian,** p. 1062.

ACCOMMODATIONS AND CAMPING

RUSSIA	❶	❷	❸	❹	❺
ACCOMMODATIONS	under 400R	400-700R	700-1200R	1200-2000R	over 2000R

The **hostel** scene in Moscow and St. Petersburg often involves less-than-stellar service and facilities and isn't particularly cheap: US$18-25 per night is average. Hostels often have an English-speaking staff. Reserve in advance. **Hotels** offer several classes of rooms. *Lux*, usually two-room doubles with TV, phone, fridge, and bath, are the most expensive. *Polu-lux* rooms are singles or doubles with TV, phone, and bath. The lowest-priced rooms are *bez udobstv*, one room with a sink. Expect to pay about 500R for a single in a budget hotel. Usually, only cash is accepted as payment. In many hotels, **hot water**—sometimes all water—is only turned on for a few hours each day. **University dorms** offer cheap rooms; some accept foreign students for around US$10 per night. The rooms are livable, but don't expect sparkling bathrooms or reliable hot water. Make arrangements from home through an educational institution. In the cities, **private rooms** and **apartments** can often be found for very low prices (about US$6-10 per night). Outside major train stations, there are usually *babushki* offering private rooms to rent—be sure to bargain.

FOOD AND DRINK

RUSSIA	❶	❷	❸	❹	❺
FOOD	under 70R	70-150R	150-300R	300-500R	over 500R

Russian cuisine is a medley of dishes both delectable and unpleasant; tasty *borscht* (beet soup) can come in the same meal as *salo* (pig fat). The main meal of the day, *obed* (lunch), is eaten at midday and includes: *salat* (salad), usually cucumbers and tomatoes or beets and potatoes with mayonnaise or sour cream; *sup* (soup); and *kuritsa* (chicken) or *myaso* (meat), often called *kotlyety* (cutlets) or *bifshteks* (beefsteaks). Other common foods include *shchi* (cabbage soup) and *blini* (pancakes). Ordering a number of *zakuski* (small appetizers) instead of a main dish can save money. **Desserts** include *morozhenoye* (ice cream) or *tort* (cake) with *cofe* (coffee) or *chai* (tea), which Russians drink at the slightest provocation. **Vegetarian** and **kosher** travelers in Russia will probably find it easiest to eat in foreign restaurants and pizzerias. On the streets, you'll see a lot of *shashlyki* (barbecued meat on a stick) and *kvas*, a (usually) nonalcoholic dark-brown drink. Beware of meat from sidewalk vendors; it may be several days old. Kiosks often carry **alcohol;** imported cans of beer are safe, but be wary of Russian labels—you have no way of knowing what's inside. *Russky Standart* and *Flagman* are the best **vodkas;** *Stolichnaya* is primarily made for export. Among **beers,** *Baltika* (numbered 2 through 9 according to brew and alcohol content) is the most popular. *Baltika* 2 is the weakest (4.7%), while *Baltika* 9 the strongest (8%).

HOLIDAYS AND FESTIVALS

Holidays: New Year's (Jan. 1-5); Orthodox Christmas (Jan. 7); Defenders of the Motherland Day (Feb. 23); Women's Day (Mar. 8); Orthodox Easter (Mar. 26); Labor Day (May 1); Victory Day (May 9); Independence Day (June 12); Day of National Unity (Nov. 4).

Festivals: Midnight services, gift-giving, and candlelit folk celebrations mark Easter, Christmas, and the secular New Year, while national holidays are occasions for large parades. In June and early July, St. Petersburg stays up late to celebrate the sunlight of **White Nights** *(Beliye Nochi)* with concerts and fireworks. *Maslyanitsa* (Butter Festival) takes place in Feb. just before Lent and is a farewell to winter in which people eat delectable *blini* covered in caviar, cream, honey, and butter.

BEYOND TOURISM

Kitezh Children's Community (http://atschool.eduweb.co.uk/ecoliza/files/kitezh.html). Teach English to Russian orphans in a rural setting. Young people taking a "gap year" between high school and college are especially welcome as volunteers.

The School of Russian and Asian Studies (☎800-557-8774; www.sras.org). Provides study-abroad opportunities and arranges internships and homestays in Russia.

The Russia Journal (www.russiajournal.com). English newspaper with classified job ads.

MOSCOW (МОСКВА) ☎8495

Moscow (pop. 10,400,000) has long regulated the pulse of Russia. When Communism swept through Moscow, it leveled most of the capital's golden domes and left behind massive buildings, crumbling outskirts, and countless statues of Lenin. But things change quickly in this audacious city, and Moscow is now recreating itself using the same resourcefulness that helped it engineer, and then survive, perhaps the most ambitious social experiment in its history.

TRANSPORTATION

Flights: International flights arrive at **Sheremetyevo-2** (Шереметьево-2; ☎578 91 01; www.sheremetyevo-airport.ru). Take **minivan** #49 under the "автолайн" sign in front of the station to M2: Rechnoy Vokzal (Речной Вокзал). **Taxis** to the center of town tend to be overpriced; bargain down to at most US$30. **City Taxi** (☎560 05 00) and other operators have fixed prices, about US$25. Taxis outside the departure level charge approximately US$20; agree on a price before getting in.

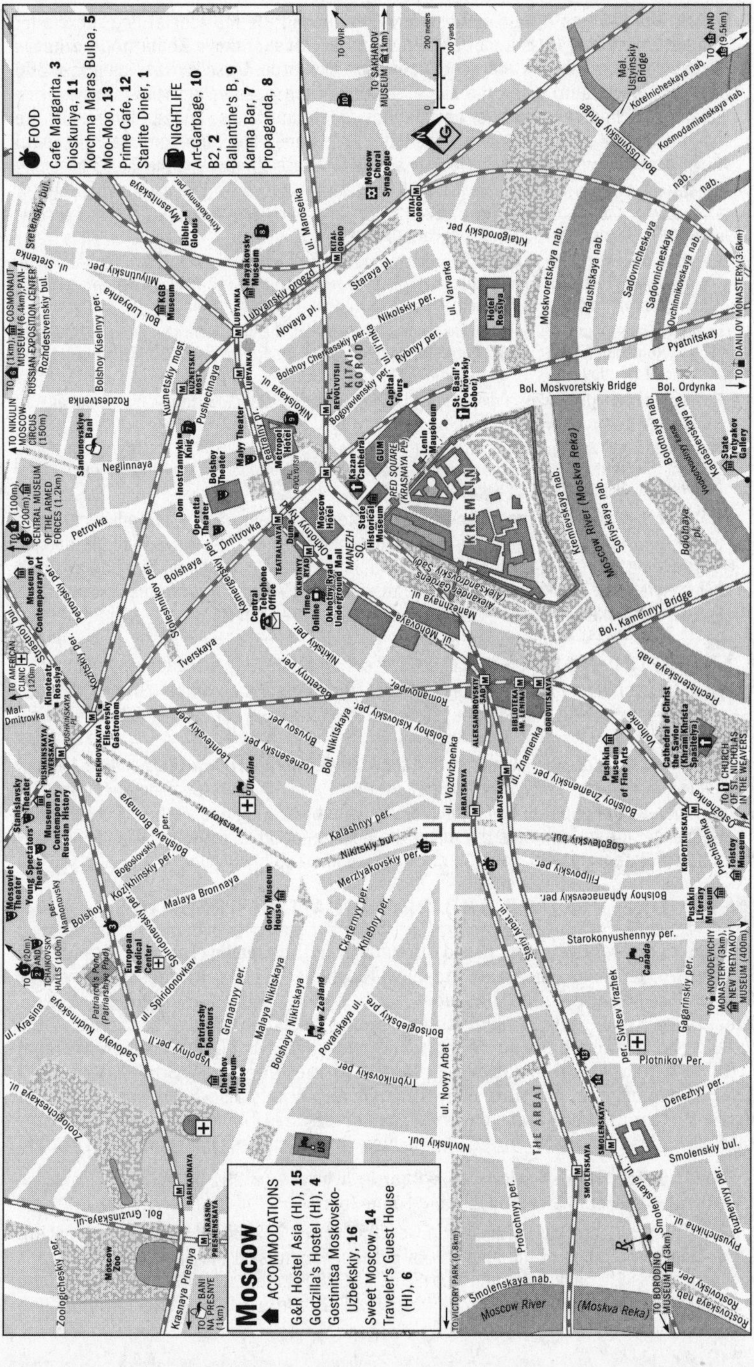
Moscow
ACCOMMODATIONS
G&R Hostel Asia (HI), 15
Godzilla's Hostel (HI), 4
Gostinitsa Moskovsko-Uzbekskiy, 16
Sweet Moscow, 14
Traveler's Guest House (HI), 6
FOOD
Cafe Margarita, 3
Dioskuriya, 11
Korchma Maras Bulba, 5
Moo-Moo, 13
Prime Cafe, 12
Starlite Diner, 1
NIGHTLIFE
Art-Garbage, 10
B2, 2
Ballantine's B, 9
Karma Bar, 7
Propaganda, 8
KREMLIN
RED SQUARE (KRASNAYA PL.)
KITAI-GOROD
Moscow River (Moskva Reka)
THE ARBAT
Bol. Moskvoretskiy Bridge
Bol. Kamennyy Bridge
Bol. Ustyinskiy Bridge
Hotel Rossiya
St. Basil's (Pokrovskiy Sobor)
Lenin Mausoleum
GUM
State Historical Museum
Bolshoy Theater
Malyy Theater
Cathedral of Christ the Savior (Khram Khrista Spasitelya)
Pushkin Museum of Fine Arts
State Tretyakov Gallery
Patriarch's Pond (Patriarshiye Prud)
Moscow Zoo

Trains: Moscow has 8 train stations arranged around the M5 (circle) line. Tickets for longer trips within Russia can be bought at the **Moskovskoye Zheleznodorozhnoye Agenstvo** (Московскоые Железнодорожноые Агенство; Moscow Train Agency; ☎266 93 33; www.mza.ru). From the Metro, go behind the glass-walled Yaroslavskiy Voksal terminal. Schedules of trains, destinations, departure times, and station names are posted in Cyrillic on both sides of the hall. (*Kassa* open M-F 8am-7pm, Sa 8am-6pm.) Buying more expensive tickets through a hotel or hostel spares you the *kassa* hassle.

Belorusskiy Vokzal (Белорусский), pl. Tverskoi Zastavy 7 (☎266 03 00). To: **Berlin, GER** (28hr., 1 per day except F, 4700R); **Prague, CZE** (32hr., 1 per day, 3700R); **Vilnius, LIT** (15hr., 1 per day, 1950R); **Warsaw, POL** (21hr., 1 per day, 2520R).

Kievskiy Vokzal (Киевский), pl. Kievskovo Vokzala 2 (Киевского; ☎240 70 71). M3 or 5: Kievskaya (Киевская). To destinations in Ukraine, including: **Kyiv** (10-13hr., 5 per day, 1300R), **Lviv** (24hr., 1 per day, 1300R), and **Odessa** (23-27hr., 4 per day, 1500R).

Leningradskiy Vokzal (Ленинградский), Komsomolskaya pl. 3 (Комсомолская; ☎262 91 43). M1 or 5: Komsomolskaya. To: **St. Petersburg** (5-8hr., 15-18 per day, 500-1500R); **Helsinki, FIN** (14hr., 1 per day, 3100R); and **Tallinn, EST** (15hr., 1 per day, 1550R).

Rizhskiy Vokzal (Рижский), Prospekt Mira 79/3 (☎631 15 88). M6: Rizhskaya (Рижская). To **Rīga, LAT** (16hr., 2 per day, 2500R).

Yaroslavskiy Vokzal (Ярославский), Komsomolskaya pl. 5A (☎266 63 00). M1 or 5: Komsomolskaya. The starting point for the legendary **Trans-Siberian Railroad.** To: **Novosibirsk** (48hr., 1 per day, 1900-5000R); **Siberia** and the **Far East.**

Public Transportation: The **Moscow Metro** (Метро) is fast, clean, and efficient. Metro trains run daily 6am-1am. A station serving multiple lines may have multiple names. Buy token-cards (15R, 10 trips for 125R) from the *kassy* in stations. Buy **bus** and **trolley** tickets from kiosks labeled "проездные билеты" (13R) or from the driver (15R). Punch your ticket when you get on, or risk a fine. Buses run 24hr.

METRO MADNESS. *Let's Go* has tried to simplify navigation by numbering each Metro line; for a key, see this guide's color map of the Moscow Metro. When speaking with Russians, use the color or name, not our given number.

Taxis: Most taxis do not use meters and tend to overcharge. **Yellow Taxis** charge 10R per km (after midnight 15R). **City Taxi** (☎560 05 00) has English-speaking operators. It is common and cheaper to hail a private car, done by holding one's arm out horizontally. Before getting in, one tells the driver the destination and agrees on a price (usually 100-200R across town). Let's Go does not recommend hitchhiking.

ORIENTATION AND PRACTICAL INFORMATION

A series of concentric rings spread outward from the **Kremlin** (Кремль; Kreml) and **Red Square** (Красная Плошадь; Krasnaya Ploshchad). The outermost **Moscow Ring Road** marks the city limits, but most sights lie within the **Garden Ring** (Садовое Кольцо; Sadovoe Koltso). Main streets include **Tverskaya Ulitsa** (Тверская), which extends north along the Metro's green line, as well as **Arbat** (Арбат) and **Novyy Arbat** (Новый Арбат), which run west parallel to the blue lines. Some kiosks sell English-language and Cyrillic maps; hostels and hotels also have English tourist maps. Be careful when crossing streets, as drivers are oblivious to pedestrians; for safety's sake, most major intersections have an underpass (переход; perekhod).

Tourist Office: Tourist Information Centre, Ilyinka 4 (☎232 56 57; www.moscow-city.ru). M: Gostiny Dvor. Open daily 10am-7pm.

Tours: Capital Tours, ul. Ilyinka 4, in Gostiny Dvor (☎232 2442; www.capitaltours.ru). Specializes in tours of the Kremlin. An efficient way to skip the lines, but the price is high. 3hr. tour daily 10:30am and 3pm. 1400R, students 1200R. **Patriarshy Dom Tours,** Vspolny per. 6 (Всполний; ☎795 09 27; http://russiatravel-pdtours.netfirms.com). M5 or 7: Barrikadnaya. Wide range of English-language tours including a behind-the-scenes tour of the former KGB headquarters (US$18). Open M-F 9am-6pm.

Budget Travel: Student Travel Agency Russia (STAR), Baltiyskaya ul. 9, 3rd fl. (Балтийская; ☎797 95 55; www.startravel.ru). M2: Sokol (Сокол). Discount plane tickets, ISICs, and worldwide hostel booking. Open M-F 10am-9pm, Sa 11am-4pm.

Embassies: Australia, Podkolokolny per. 10A/2 (☎656 60 70). M6: Kitai-Gorod (Китаи Город). Open M-F 9am-5pm. **Canada,** Starokonyushennyy per. 23 (Староконюшенный; ☎105 60 00). M1: Kropotkinskaya or M4: Arbatskaya (Арбатская). Open M-F 9am-3pm. **Ireland,** Grokholskiy per. 5 (Грохольский; ☎937 59 11). M5 or 6: Prospekt Mira. Open M-F 9:30am-1pm and 2:30-5:30pm. **New Zealand,** Povarskaya ul. 44 (Поварская; ☎956 35 79). M7: Barikadnaya (Барикадная). Open M-F 9am-12:30pm and 1:30-5:30pm. **UK,** Smolenskaya nab. 10 (Смоленская; ☎956 72 00; www.britemb.msk.ru). M3: Smolenskaya. Open M-F 9am-5pm. **US,** Novinskiy 19/23 (Новинский; ☎728 50 00; www.usembassy.ru). M5: Krasnopresnenskaya (Краснопресненская). Open M-F 9am-6pm. **American Citizen Services** (☎728 55 77 or 728 50 00) lists English-speaking establishments. Open M-F 9am-noon and 2-4pm.

Currency Exchange: Banks are everywhere. Typically only main branches cash **traveler's checks** or issue **cash advances.** Many banks and hotels have **ATMs.** Avoid withdrawing cash from machines on busy streets, as they make you a target for muggers.

American Express: ul. Usacheva 33, bldg. 1 (☎933 84 00). M1: Sportivnaya. Exit at the front of the train, turn right, and then right again on Usacheva. Open M-F 9am-5pm.

English-Language Bookstore: Anglia British Bookshop, Vorotnikovskiy per. 6 (Воротниковский; ☎299 77 66). Open M-F 10am-7pm, Sa 10am-6pm, Su 10am-5pm. AmEx/MC/V.

Emergency: Police: ☎02. **Ambulance:** ☎03. **Fire:** ☎01.

24hr. Pharmacies: Tverskaya ul. 25 (☎299 24 59), M2: Tverskaya/Mayakovskaya; ul. Zemlyanoi Val 25 (☎917 12 85), M5: Kurskaya; Kutuzovskiy Prospekt 24 (Кутузовский; ☎249 19 37), M4: Kutuzovskaya (Кутузовская).

Medical Services: American Clinic, Grokholskiy per. 31 (☎937 57 57; www.americanclinic.ru). M5 or 6: Prospekt Mira. American board-certified doctors that practice family medicine and dentistry. Consultations 3540R. Open 24hr., including house calls. MC/V. **European Medical Center**, Spiridonievsky per. 5 (☎933 66 55; www.emcmos.ru). Medical services and 24hr. house calls.

Telephones: Local calls require phone cards, sold at kiosks and some Metro stops.

Internet Access: Timeonline (☎223 96 87), on the bottom level of the Okhotnyy Ryad underground mall. M1: Okhotnyy Ryad. In the center of the city, with over 100 computers, copying, and photo services. 35-80R per hr. depending on time of day. Open 24hr. **Cafemax** (☎787 68 58; www.cafemax.ru) has 3 locations: ul. Pyatnitskaya 25/1M (M2: Novokuznetskaya), Akademika Khokhlova 3 (M1: Universitet), and ul. Novoslobodskaya 3 (M9: Novoslobodskaya). Well-lit, modern, with many terminals. WiFi, copying, and other services available. 50-200R per hr. depending on demand. Open 24hr.

Post Offices: Moscow Central Telegraph, Tverskaya ul. 7, uphill from the Kremlin. M1: Okhotnyy Ryad. International calls; buy phone cards at the counter, 0.9R per min. to North America, 0.9-6R per min. to Europe. International mail at window #23; faxes at #11-12. Bring packages unwrapped. DHL office inside. Open M-F 8am-1pm and 2-9pm, Sa 9am-1pm and 2-7pm, Su 10am-1pm and 2-6pm. **Postal Code:** 125 009.

ACCOMMODATIONS

Older women standing outside major rail stations often rent private rooms (сдаю комнату) or apartments (сдаю квартиру) to travelers emerging from the gates—be sure to haggle.

Godzilla's Hostel (HI), Bolshoy Karetniy 6/5 (Большой Каретний; ☎299 42 23; www.godzillashostel.com). M9: Tsvetnoy Bulvar. Helpful, English-speaking staff. 52 dorm beds; co-ed unless arranged otherwise in advance. Reserve ahead in summer. Reception 24hr. Check-out noon. Dorms US$25; doubles US$60. Cash only. ❷

Sweet Moscow, Stariy Arbat ul. 51, 8th fl. #31 (☎241 14 46; www.sweetmoscow.com). M4: Smolenskaya. Turn right on Smolenskaya pl. out of Metro, then left at the McDonald's onto Stariy Arbat. The hostel is located across from Hard Rock Cafe; no signs are displayed, so ring the buzzer. Sweet Moscow offers the best location among Moscow hostels—right in the middle of the city's most famous pedestrian street. Contains only 20 beds, so reserve ahead. Small space, with only 1 shower at press time, but management plans to add another. Free laundry. Free Internet. Extremely helpful English-speaking reception 9am-11pm. Dorms US$25. Cash only. ❷

G&R Hostel Asia (HI), Zelenodolskaya ul. 3/2 (Зеленодольская; ☎378 00 01; www.hostels.ru). M7: Ryazanskiy Prospekt (Рязанский). On the 5th fl. of the Gostinitsa Moskovsko-Uzbekskiy. Clean rooms and helpful staff. Breakfast included. Visa invitation €30. Free visa registration. Reception 10am-10pm. Singles €30-60; doubles €50-60. 5% HI discount. ❸

Traveler's Guest House (HI), Bolshaya Pereslavskaya ul. 50, 10th fl. (Болшая Переславская; ☎631 40 59; www.tgh.ru). M5 or 6: Prospekt Mira. Turn right across from Prospekt Mira 61, then left on B. Pereslavskaya. This hostel remains busy despite its dim atmosphere and sometimes slow service. English-speaking staff. Visa invitations US$30. Laundry 130R per 3kg. 1 Internet terminal, 2R per min. Check-out 11am. Reception 8am-midnight. Reservations require prepayment. Dorms US$25; singles US$50; doubles US$60, with bath US$65. HI discount. MC/V. ❷

Gostinitsa Moskovsko-Uzbekskiy, Zelenodolskaya ul. 3/2 (Зеленодольская; ☎378 21 77; hotel@caravan.ru). M7: Ryazanskiy Prospekt (Рязанский). A "Гостиница" sign marks the hotel. Wide range of rooms. Singles 750-1200R; doubles 1000-2000R. ❷

FOOD

Many restaurants offer "business lunch" specials (бизнес ланч; typically noon-3pm; US$4-8). **Eliseevskiy Gastronom** (Елисеевский), ul. Tverskaya 14, is Moscow's most famous supermarket. (☎209 07 60. Open M-Sa 8am-9pm, Su 10am-8pm.) For fresh produce, try the **markets** by the Turgenevskaya and Smolenskaya Metro stops. Grocery stores are marked by "продукти" (produkti) signs.

Korchma Maras Bulba (Корчма Марас Бульба), Sadovaya-Samotechnaya ul. 13 (☎778 34 30; www.tarasbulba.ru). M9: Tsvetnoy Bulvar (Цветной Бульвар). 12 locations around the city. Delicious Ukrainian specialities amidst authentic decor and costumes. English menu available. Appetizers 60-185R. Entrees available in 2 sizes, 70-185R. Draft beer from 50R. Vodka 90-110R. Open 24hr. MC/V. ❸

Starlite Diner, Bolshaya Sadovaya 16 (☎290 96 38; starlite@starlite.ru). M2: Mayakovskaya. Restaurant is in the gardens of Mossoviet Theater. American diner packed with expats on weekends. Serves all-day breakfast and claims "more sales per square foot than any other diner in the world." Cheeseburger with fries 230R. Milkshakes 200R. Draft beer 90-200R. WiFi 300R per hr. Entrees 210-575R. Open 24hr. AmEx/MC/V. ❸

Prime Cafe, ul. Arbat 9 (☎739 00 14; www.primeshop.ru). M3 or 4: Arbatskaya. 3 locations in the city (also Kamergerskiy per. 5/7 and ul. Pyatnitskaya 5). Grab a tasty sandwich (69-155R) or salad (59-145R), or choose from a wide range of baked goods and snacks, all displayed with English translations. Open 8am-11pm. Cash only. ❷

Cafe Margarita (Кафе Маргарита), Malaya Bronnaya ul. 28 (Малая Вронная; ☎299 65 34), at the intersection with Malyy Kozikhinskiy per. (Малый Козихинский). M2: Mayakovskaya. Turn left on Bolshaya Sadovaya, then again left on Malaya Bronaya. Locals love this Russian cafe and restaurant. Entrees 250-450R. Open daily 1pm-midnight. ❸

Dioskuriya (Диоскурия), Merzlyakovskiy per. 2 (Мерзляковский; ☎290 69 08; www.dioskuriya.narod.ru). M4: Arbatskaya. Head west down ul. Novyy Arbat and turn right up the first narrow street. Good Georgian eats and English-language menu. Entrees 100-280R. Live Georgian music M-Sa 7-11pm. Open daily 11am-midnight. ❷

Moo-Moo (My-My), Koroviy Val 1 (☎237 29 00) M5: Dobryninskaya; 2nd location at ul. Arbat 45/42 (☎241 13 64) M4: Smolenskaya. Excellent value and cheap, tasty European and Russian home cooking, served cafeteria-style. Appetizers 30-85R. Entrees 30-100R. Draft beer 73-120R. Open daily 10am-11pm. Cash only. ❶

SIGHTS

Moscow's sights reflect the city's interrupted history: because St. Petersburg was the tsar's seat for 200 years, there are 16th-century churches and Soviet-era museums, but little in between. Though Moscow has no grand palaces and 80% of its pre-revolutionary splendor was demolished by the Soviet regime, the city's museums house the very best of Russian art and history.

THE KREMLIN

The Kremlin (Кремль; Kreml) is the geographical and historical center of Moscow, its origins dating back to the 12th century. In the Kremlin's Armory and in its magnificent churches, the glory and the riches of the Russian Empire are on display. Besides the sights listed below, the only other place in the triangular complex visitors may enter is the **Kremlin Palace of Congresses,** the white marble behemoth built by Khrushchev in 1961 for the Communist Party, and since converted into a theater. Tourists were banned from entering the Kremlin until the 1960s; now English-speaking guides offer **tours** of the complex at steep prices. Haggle away or consider a prearranged tour through Capital Tours (see **Tours,** p. 848). *(☎202 37 76; www.kremlin.museum.ru. M1, 3, 4, or 9: Aleksandrovskiy Sad. Open M-W and F-Su 10am-5pm. Buy tickets at the kassa in the Alexander Gardens 9:30am-4:30pm. Large bags not allowed. 300R, students 150R. Audio tour 200R. MC/V.)*

ARMORY MUSEUM AND DIAMOND FUND. At the southwest corner of the Kremlin, the Armory Museum (Оружейная Палата; Oruzheynaya Palata) shows the opulence of the Russian court and includes coronation gowns, crowns, and the best collection of carriages in the world. Each of the Fabergé Eggs in Room 2 reveals an intricate jeweled miniature. The Diamond Fund (Выставка Алмазного Фонда; Vystavka Almaznovo Fonda) has even more glitter, including the world's largest chunks of platinum. Consider hiring a guide, as most exhibits are in Russian. *(Armory ☎202 37 76, Diamond Fund 229 20 36. Both open M-W and F-Su. The Armory lets in groups for 1½hr. at 10am, noon, 2:30, and 4:30pm. Diamond Fund open 10am-1pm and 2-6pm. Armory 350R, students 175R; Diamond Fund 350/250R.)*

CATHEDRAL SQUARE. Russia's famous golden domes can be seen in Cathedral Square. Nine cathedrals in all were constructed to display the might of the tsars. The church closest to the Armory is the **Annunciation Cathedral** (Благовещенский Собор; Blagoveshchenskiy Sobor), the former private church of the tsars, which guards luminous icons by Andrei Rublev and Theophanes the Greek. The square **Archangel Michael Cathedral** (Архангельский Собор; Arkhangelskiy Sobor), which gleams with metallic coffins, is the final resting place for many tsars who ruled before Peter the Great, including Ivans III (the Great) and IV (the Terrible), and Mikhail Romanov. The colorful 15th-century **Assumption Cathedral** (Успенский Собор; Uspenskiy Sobor), located in the center of the square, was used to host tsars' coronations and weddings and housed Napoleon's cavalry in 1812. To the right lies the **Ivan the Great Bell Tower** (Колокольная Ивана Великого; Kolokolnaya Ivana Velikovo), once the highest point in Moscow; the tower is currently under renovation. Directly behind it is the 200-ton **Tsar Bell** (Царь-колокол; Tsar-kolokol), the world's largest bell. It has never rung and probably never will—a 1737 fire caused an 11½-ton piece to break off. *(All cathedrals included in Kremlin entrance fee except Assumption Cathedral Exhibition Hall, which is 100R, students 50R, and is open 10am-4:30pm. No photos inside cathedrals.)*

AROUND RED SQUARE

The 700m-long Red Square (Красная Площадь; Krasnaya Ploshchad) has hosted everything from farmer's markets to public hangings, from Communist parades to renegade Cessna landings. Across Red Square, northeast of the Kremlin, is **GUM,** once the world's largest purveyor of Soviet "consumer goods," now an upscale shopping mall. Also flanking the square are the **Lenin Mausoleum, St. Basil's Cathedral,** the **State Historical Museum,** and the pink-and-green **Kazan Cathedral.**

LENIN'S MAUSOLEUM. Lenin's likeness can be seen in bronze all over the city, but he appears in the eerily luminescent flesh in Lenin's Mausoleum (Мавзолей В. И. Ленина; Mavzoley V.I. Lenina). In the Soviet era, this squat red structure was guarded fiercely, and the wait to get in took three hours. Today's line is still long, and the guards remain stone-faced, but the atmosphere is more curious than reverent. Exit along the Kremlin wall, where Stalin, Brezhnev, and John Reed, founder of the American Communist Party, are buried. *(Line up between State Historical Museum and wall of Kremlin. Open Tu-Th and Sa-Su 10am-1pm. Free. No cameras, phones, or large bags.)*

ST. BASIL'S CATHEDRAL. Moscow has no more familiar symbol than the colorful onion-shaped domes of St. Basil's Cathedral (Собор Василия Блаженного; Sobor Vasiliya Blazhennovo). Ivan the Terrible commissioned it to celebrate his victory over the Tatars in Kazan in 1552, and it was completed in 1561. "Basil" is the English equivalent of Vasily, the name of a holy fool who correctly predicted that Ivan would murder his own son. St. Basil's labyrinthine interior is filled with decorative and religious frescoes. *(M3: Ploshchad Revolyutsii (Площадь Революции). ☎298 33 04. Open daily 11am-5:30pm. 100R, students 50R. Photography 100R.)*

NORTH OF RED SQUARE

Just outside the main gate to Red Square is an elaborate gold circle marking **Kilometer 0,** the spot from which all distances from Moscow are measured. Don't be fooled by this tourist attraction—the real Kilometer 0 lies underneath the Lenin Mausoleum. Just a few steps away, the **Alexander Gardens** (Александровский Сад; Aleksandrovskiy Sad) are a green respite from the pollution of central Moscow. At the northern end of the gardens is the **Tomb of the Unknown Soldier** (Могила Неизвестного Солдата; Mogila Neizvestnovo Soldata), where an **eternal flame** burns in memory of the losses suffered in the Great Patriotic War (WWII). Soldiers still regularly perform ceremonies here. To the west is **Manezh Square** (Манежная Площадь; Manezhnaya Ploshchad), recently converted into a pedestrian area; nearby lies the smaller **Revolution Square** (Площадь Революции; Ploshchad Revolyutsii). Both squares are connected in the north by **Okhotnyy Ryad** (Охотный Ряд; Hunters' Row), an underground mall. *(Enter directly from the square or through the underpass. Open daily 11am-10pm.)* Across Okhotnyy Ryad is the **Duma,** the lower house of Parliament. Opposite Revolution Square is **Theater Square** (Театральная Площадь; Teatralnaya Ploshchad), home of the **Bolshoi Theatre** (see **Entertainment,** p. 855). More posh hotels, chic stores, and government buildings line **Tverskaya Ulitsa,** Moscow's main thoroughfare.

CHURCHES, MONASTERIES, AND SYNAGOGUES

CATHEDRAL OF CHRIST THE SAVIOR. Moscow's most controversial landmark is the enormous gold-domed Cathedral of Christ the Savior (Храм Христа

Спасителя; Khram Khrista Spasitelya). Stalin demolished Nicholas I's original cathedral on this site to make way for a gigantic Palace of the Soviets, but Khrushchev abandoned the project and built a heated outdoor pool instead. In 1995, after the pool's water vapors damaged paintings in the nearby Pushkin Museum, Mayor Yury Luzhkov and the Orthodox Church won a renewed battle for the site and built the US$250 million cathedral in only five years. *(Volkhonka 15, between ul. Volkhonka* (Волхонка) *and the Moscow River. M1: Kropotkinskaya. Cathedral open daily 10am-5pm; museum open daily 10am-6pm. Cathedral free. No cameras, hats, shorts, or bare arms.)*

NOVODEVICHY MONASTERY AND CEMETERY. Moscow's most famous monastery (Новодевичий Монастырь; Novodevichiy Monastyr) is hard to miss thanks to its high brick walls, golden domes, and tourist buses. In the center, the **Smolensk Cathedral** (Смоленский Собор; Smolenskiy Sobor) displays icons and frescoes. The cemetery (кладбище; kladbishche) is a pilgrimage site that holds the graves of such famous figures as Khrushchev, Chekhov, and Shostakovich. *(M1: Sportivnaya. ☎246 56 07. Open M and W-Su 10am-5:15pm; kassa closes at 4:45pm. Closed 1st M of each month. Cathedral closed on humid days. Cemetery open daily 9am-7pm; low season 9am-6pm. Grounds 40R, students 20R. Cathedral and special exhibits 150R/75R.)*

MOSCOW CHORAL SYNAGOGUE. Over 100 years old, the synagogue provides a break from the city's ubiquitous onion domes. Though the synagogue remained open during Soviet rule, all but the bravest Jews were deterred by KGB agents who photographed anyone who entered. More than 200,000 Jews now live in Moscow, and services are increasingly well attended, but the occasional graffiti is a sad reminder that anti-Semitism in Russia is not dead. *(M6 or 7: Kitai-Gorod. Go north on Solyanskiy Proyezd* (Солянский Проезд) *and take the 1st left. Open daily 8am-10pm. Services M-F 8:30am and 7:30pm, Sa-Su 9am and 9pm. Evening services earlier in the winter.)*

OTHER SIGHTS

MOSCOW METRO. All the beautiful Moscow Metro (Московское Метро) stations are unique. See the Baroque elegance of **Komsomolskaya** (Косомолская), the stained glass of **Novoslobodskaya** (Новослободская), and the bronze statues of revolutionary archetypes from farmer to factory worker of **Ploshchad Revolyutsii** (Площадь Революции).

THE ARBAT. Now a pedestrian shopping arcade, the Arbat (Арбат) was once a showpiece of *glasnost* and a haven for political radicals, Hare Krishnas, street poets, and *metallisty* (heavy metal rockers). Some of that eccentric flavor remains thanks to street performers and guitar-playing teenagers. Nearby runs the bigger, newer, and uglier **Novyy Arbat,** lined with gray high-rises and massive modern stores. *(M3 or 4: Arbatskaya or Smolenskaya.)*

VICTORY PARK. On the left past the **Triumphal Arch,** which celebrates the 1812 defeat of Napoleon, lies Victory Park (Парк Победы; Park Pobedy), a monument to WWII. It includes the **Museum of the Great Patriotic War** (Музей Отечественной Войны; Muzey Otechestvennoy Voyny; open Tu-Su 10am-7pm, closed last Th of each month), the **Victory Monument**, and the gold-domed **Church of St. George the Victorious** (Храм Георгия Победаносного; Khram Georgiya Pobedonosnovo), which honors the 27 million Russians who died in battle during WWII. *(M4: Park Poebedi.)*

MUSEUMS

Moscow's museum scene is by far the most patriotic part of the city. Government museums and small galleries alike proudly display Russian art, and dozens of historical and literary museums are devoted to the nation's past.

RUSSIA

NEW TRETYAKOV GALLERY. Where the first Tretyakov chronologically leaves off, this new gallery (Новая Третьяковская Галерея; Novaya Tretyakovskaya Galereya) begins. The collection starts on the third floor with early 20th-century art and moves through the neo-Primitivist, Futurist, Suprematist, Cubist, and Social Realist schools. The second floor holds temporary exhibits; go on weekday mornings. Leaving the front door, turn left to find a statue gallery; it is a real gem. The main dumping ground for decapitated Lenins and Stalins and other former Soviet-era statues, it now also contains captioned sculptures of Gandhi, Einstein, Niels Bohr, and Dzerzhinsky, the founder of the Soviet secret police. *(Ul. Krymskiy Val 10* (Крымский Вал), *☎230 77 88. M5: Oktyabraskaya. Open Tu-Su 10am-7:30pm;* kassa *closes at 6:30pm. 240R, students 140R. Statue gallery open daily 9am-9pm; 100R.)*

STATE TRETYAKOV GALLERY. A treasury of 11th- to early 20th-century Russian art, the Tretyakov Gallery (Государственная Третьяковская Галерея; Gosudarstvennaya Tretyakovskaya Galereya) also has a superb collection of icons, including works by Andrei Rublev and Theophanes the Greek. *(Lavrushinskiy per. 10. www.tretyakovgallery.ru. M8: Tretyakovskaya* (Третьяковская). *Turn left out of the Metro, left again, then take an immediate right on Bolshoy Tolmachevskiy per.; turn right after 2 blocks on Lavrushinskiy per. Open Tu-Su 10am-7:30pm.* Kassa *closes at 6:30pm. 225R, students 130R.)*

PUSHKIN MUSEUM OF FINE ARTS. Moscow's most important collection of non-Russian art, the Pushkin Museum (Музей Изобразительных Искусств им. А.С. Пушкина; Muzey Izobrazitelnykh Iskusstv im. A.S. Pushkina) contains major Classical, Egyptian, and Renaissance works, as well as superb pieces by Chagall, Picasso, and van Gogh. *(Ul. Volkhonka 12* (Волхонка), *☎203 79 98. M1: Kropotkinskaya. Open Tu-Su 10am-7pm;* kassa *closes 6pm. 300R, students 100R.)* The building to the right of the entrance houses the Pushkin **Museum of Private Collections** (Музей Личныч Коллеций; Muzey Lichnych Kolletsiy), with artwork by Kandinsky, Rodchenko, and Stepanov. *(☎203 15 46. Open W-Su noon-7pm;* kassa *closes 6pm. 100R, students 50R.)*

STATE HISTORICAL MUSEUM. This English-language exhibit (Государственный Исторический Музей; Gosudarstvennyy Istoricheskiy Muzey) on Russian history runs from the Neanderthals through Kyivan Rus to modern Russia. *(Krasnaya pl. 1/2. M1: Okhotnyy Ryad. Open M and W-Sa 10am-6pm, Su 11am-8pm. Closed 1st M of each month. 150R, students 75R. Combination ticket with St. Basil's Cathedral 230/115R.)*

KGB MUSEUM. Documenting the history and strategies of Russian secret intelligence from Ivan the Terrible to Putin, the KGB Museum (Музей КГБ; Muzey KGB) gives a chance to quiz a current FSB agent. *(Ul. Bul. Lubyanka 12. M1: Lubyanka. Prearranged tours only. Patriarshy Dom Tours,* *p. 848**, leads 2hr. group tours. US$18 per person.)*

HOMES OF THE LITERARY AND FAMOUS. The **Mayakovsky Museum** (Музей им. В. В. Маяковского; Muzey im. V. V. Mayakovskovo) is a walk-through work of Futurist art, created as a biography of the Revolution's greatest poet. Mayakovsky lived and died in a communal apartment on the fourth floor of this building. *(Lubyanskiy pr. 3/6;* Лубянский. *☎628 25 69. M1: Lubyanka. Behind a bust of Mayakovsky on ul. Myasnitskaya;* Мясницкая. *Open M-Tu and F-Su 10am-5pm, Th 1-8pm. Closed last F of each month. 80R, students 40R.)* If you've never seen Pushkin-worship first-hand, the **Pushkin Literary Museum** (Литературный Музей Пушкина; Literaturnyy Muzey Pushkina) with its large collection of Pushkin memorabilia, will either convert or frighten you. *(Ul. Prechistenka 12/2;* Пречистенка. *☎201 56 74. Entrance on Khrushchevskiy per. M1: Kropotkinskaya. Open Tu-Su 10am-6pm. Closed last F of each month. 40R.)* The **Tolstoy Museum** (Музей Толстого; Muzey Tolstovo), in the neighborhood of the author's first Moscow residence, displays original texts, paintings, and letters related to his masterpieces. *(Ul. Prechistenka 11, ☎202 21 90. M1: Kropotkinskaya. Open Tu-Su 11am-6pm. 100R, students 30R.)*

ENTERTAINMENT

From September through June, Moscow boasts some of the world's best ballet, opera, and theater performances. Tickets can be purchased from the theater *kassa* or from kiosks in town; advance tickets are often cheap (from US$5).

Bolshoi Theater (Большой Театр), Teatralnaya pl. 1 (Театральная; ☎250 73 17; www.bolshoi.ru). M2: Teatralnaya. Home to the opera and world-renowned ballet company. Main stage under renovation until at least 2008. Performances continue on the secondary stage. *Kassa* on Petrovska ul. open daily 11am-3pm and 4-8pm. Performances Sept.-June daily 7pm, occasional matinees. Tickets 250-1000R. MC/V.

Moscow Operetta Theater, Bolshaya Dmitrovka 6 (Большая Дмитровка; ☎692 12 37; www.mosoperetta.ru), left of the Bolshoi. Famous operettas staged year-round. *Kassa* open daily 11am-2pm and 3-7:30pm. Performances daily 6 or 7pm. Tickets 80-1000R.

NIGHTLIFE

Moscow's nightlife is the most varied, expensive, and debaucherous in Eastern Europe. Many clubs flaunt their exclusivity. Check the weekend editions of *The Moscow Times* or *The Moscow Tribune* for club reviews and music listings.

Art-Garbage, Starosadskiy per. 5 (☎928 87 45; www.art-garbage.ru). M6 or 7: Kitai-Gorod. This laid-back cafe, gallery, and bar is better for relaxing than for hardcore clubbing. Draft beer 70-170R; vodka 50R; rum 100R. Appetizers 80-230R. Entrees 180-400R. Cover 150R-300R for live music, most days at 8 or 9pm. Open daily noon-6am.

Propaganda (Пропаганда), Bolshoy Zlatoustinskiy per. 7 (Большой Златоустинский; ☎924 57 32). M6 or 7: Kitai-Gorod. Exiting the Metro, walk down Maroseyka and turn left on Bolshoy Zlatoustinsky per. Get down to house music without feeling like you're in a meat market. Beer 70R. Sangria 120R per 0.5L. Dancing after midnight. Th night is the most popular. Sa cover 100R. Open daily noon-6am.

Karma Bar, Pushechnaya ul. 3 (☎624 56 33; www.karma-bar.ru). M1 or 7: Kuznetzky Most. Crowd-pleasing dance music emanates from this hip club. Mixed drinks 180R. Th-Sa 9pm-midnight Latin parties with free salsa lessons; midnight-6am Th R&B, F-Sa Euro. F-Sa 2am dancing on bar. Cover F-Sa 200R for women, 300R for men. Open Th-Sa 7pm-6am, Su 8pm-6am.

B2, Bolshaya Sadovaya 8 (☎209 99 09; www.b2club.ru). M5: Mayakovskaya. This multi-story complex truly has it all: a quiet beer garden (1st fl.), restaurant (2nd fl.), sushi bar, jazz club, billiard room (3rd fl.), several dance floors, and ballroom dancing (4th fl., cover charge). Draft beer 110-170R. Nightclub Th-Su 6pm-6am. Live music F-Sa, cover 200-500R. Open noon-6am. MC/V.

Ballantine's Bar, Nikolskaya ul. 17 (Николская; ☎928 46 92; www.ballantines-bar.ru). M3: Ploshchad Revolyutsii. Great dance music and a lively student crowd. Selective admission based on appearance. Pint of beer 75-180R; vodka 70-95R. Appetizers 85-210R. Sandwiches 90R. Entrees 115-295R. Live DJ Th-Sa 10pm. Cover F-Sa 120R. Open daily 11am-6am. AmEx/MC/V.

DAYTRIP FROM MOSCOW

SERGIYEV POSAD. Russia's most famous pilgrimage site, Sergiyev Posad (Сергиев Посад; pop. 200,000) attracts believers to several churches huddled around its centerpiece: the fully operational **St. Sergius's Trinity Monastery** (Свято-Троицкая Сергиева Лавра; Svyato-Troitskaya Sergiyeva Lavra). After decades of state-propagated atheism, the stunning monastery, founded in about 1340, is once again a thriving religious center. The splendid **Assumption Cathedral** (Успенский Собор; Uspenskiy Sobor) was modeled after its namesake cathedral in Moscow's Kremlin. The frescoes of the **Refectory** (Трапезная; Trapeznaya) and the gilded icons by Andrei Rublev at **Trinity Cathedral** (Троицкий Собор; Troitskiy Sobor) are equally colorful and captivating. *(Monastery open daily 9am-6pm.)* **Commuter trains** *(elektrichki)* run to Sergiyev Posad from Moscow's Yaroslavskiy Vokzal (1½-2hr., 2-3 per hr., round-trip 128R). From the station, turn right, cross the street, and walk down the road until you see the city. *(☎254 453 42; www.musobl.divo.ru. Open daily 10am-5pm. 160R, students 60R.)*

ST. PETERSBURG (САНКТ-ПЕТЕРБУРГ) ☎8812

St. Petersburg's wide boulevards and bright facades are exactly what Peter the Great envisioned when he founded his "window on the West" in 1703. The curtain closed, however, after the 1917 February Revolution in St. Petersburg (pop. 4,700,000) turned Russia into a Communist state. Known as Petrograd from 1914 to 1924 and renamed Leningrad after Lenin's death, the city reverted back to its original name in 1991. Having recently undergone massive renovations, St. Petersburg has unearthed the artistic genius of its former residents Dostoevsky, Gogol, Tchaikovsky, and Stravinsky, reawakening its latent majesty and sophistication.

TRANSPORTATION

Flights: The main airport, **Pulkovo** (Пулково; www.pulkovo.ru), has 2 terminals: Pulkovo-1 (☎723 38 22) for domestic flights, and Pulkovo-2 (☎704 34 44) for international flights. From M2: Moskovskaya (Московская), take bus #39 to Pulkovo-1 (25min.) or bus #13 to Pulkovo-2 (20min.). Hostels can arrange taxis (usually US$30-35).

Trains: Central Ticket Offices (Центральные Железнодорожные Кассы; Tsentralnye Zheleznodorozhnye Kassy), Canal Griboyedovo 24 (Грибоедого). Tickets to most destinations are sold at *kassy* on the left. Tickets to Helsinki sold upstairs. **Intourist** offices in train stations also sell tickets. Open M-Sa 8am-8pm, Su 8am-4pm.

Ladozhsky Station, Zhanevsky pr. 73 (Ладожский Вокзал; Ladozhsky Vokzal). M4: Ladozhskaya. To **Helsinki, FIN** (6hr., 2 per day).

Moscow Station, Nevsky pr. 85 (Московский Вокзал; Moskovskiy Vokzal; ☎768 45 97). M1: Pl. Vosstaniya (Восстания). To: **Moscow** (5-8hr., 10-15 per day, 500-1700R); **Novgorod** (3-5hr., 3 per day, 250R); and **Sevastopol, UKR** (33-36hr., 3 per day, 2000R).

Vitebskiy Station, Zagorodny pr. 52 (Витебский Вокзал; Vitebskiy Vokzal; ☎768 58 07). M1: Pushkinskaya (Пушкинская). To: **Kaliningrad** (27hr., 1 per day, 2000R); **Kyiv, UKR** (24hr., 1 per day, 1500R); **Odessa, UKR** (36hr., 3 per week, 1500R); **Rīga, LAT** (13hr., 1 per day, 2100R); **Vilnius, LIT** (14hr., every 2 days, 1600R).

Buses: Nab. Obvodnovo Kanala 36 (Обводного Канала; ☎766 57 77). M4: Ligovskiy pr. Take tram #19, 25, 44, or 49 or trolley #42 to the stop just across the canal. Facing the canal, turn right and walk 2 long blocks. The station will be on your right, behind the abandoned building. Surcharge for advance tickets. Open daily 6am-8pm.

Local Transportation: St. Petersburg's **Metro** (Метро) runs daily 5:45am-12:15am. Tokens (жетон; *zheton*) cost 12R. Passes available for 7, 15, or 30 days. 4 lines cover much of the city. Trains usually run every 1-2min. **Buses** (normal 12R, "commercial" 17R), **trams** (12R), and **trolleys** (12R) run fairly frequently 6am-midnight. Licensed private **minibuses** (маршрутки; *marshrutki;* 7-30R) move more quickly through traffic and stop on request (routes and prices are displayed on windows in Cyrillic).

Taxis: Both marked and private cabs operate in St. Petersburg. **Taxi Blues** (☎321 88 88 or 271 88 88) works 24hr., but little English is spoken, so get someone to call on your behalf. Marked cabs have a metered rate of 15-20R per km but most cabs want to set prices without the meter. Because taxis are notorious for overcharging tourists, always confirm the price before your trip. Instead of taking a taxi, many locals hail private cars, which is usually cheaper but unsafe for travelers new to the area. Never get in a car with more than 1 person in it. Let's Go does not recommend hitchhiking.

ORIENTATION AND PRACTICAL INFORMATION

St. Petersburg sits at the mouth of the **Neva River** (Нева) on 44 islands among 50 canals. The heart of the city lies on the mainland, between the south bank of the Neva and the **Fontanka River.** Many of St. Petersburg's major sights—including the Hermitage—are on or near **Nevskiy Prospekt** (Невский Проспект), the city's main street, which extends from the **Admiralty** to the **Alexander Nevskiy Monastery; Moscow Train Station** is near the midpoint. Trolleys #1, 5, 7, 10, 17, and 22 run along Nevskiy pr. Northwest of the center and across the Neva lies **Vasilevskiy Island** (Василевский Остров; Vasilevskiy Ostrov), the city's largest island. On the north side of the Neva is the **Petrograd Side** archipelago, where the **Peter and Paul Fortress** stands.

Tourist Office: City Tourist Information Center, ul. Sadovaya 14 (☎310 82 62 or 310 28 22; www.saintpetersburgvisit.ru). M: Gostinly Dvor. English-language advice, brochures, and guidebooks. Open M-Sa 10am-7pm. Another location in Palace Square beside the Winter Palace, open daily. *Where* and *St. Petersburg Times* (www.sptimes.ru), free in tourist offices, hotels, and hostels, provide culture, entertainment, and nightlife listings.

Tours: Peter's Walking Tours (www.peterswalk.com). Specialty tours (4-6hr.) focusing on topics like WWII and "Communist Legacy" available on certain days. Leaves Apr.-Sept. daily 10:30am from International Youth Hostel at 3-ya Sovetskaya 28. 400R.

Budget Travel: Sindbad Travel (FIYTO), 2-ya Sovetskaya 12 (☎332 20 20; www.sindbad.ru). Books plane, train, and bus tickets. Student discounts on flights, partnered with STA Travel. English spoken. Open M-F 10am-10pm, Sa-Su 10am-6pm.

Consulates: Australia: Italyanskaya 1 (☎/fax 325 73 33; www.australianembassy.ru). M2: Nevskiy pr. Open M-F 9am-6pm. **Canada:** Malodetskoselskiy pr. 32/B (Малодетскосельский; ☎325 84 48; www.dfait-maeci.gc.ca/canadaeuropa/russia). M2: Frunzenskaya. Open M-F 9am-1pm and 2-5pm. **UK:** Pl. Proletarskoy Diktatury 5 (Пролетарской Диктатуры; ☎320 32 00; www.britain.spb.ru). M1: Chernyshevskaya. Open M-F 9am-5pm. **US:** Furshtatskaya 15 (Фурштатская; ☎331 26 00, after-hours emergency 331 28 88; www.stpetersburg-usconsulate.ru). M1: Chernyshevskaya. Open M-F 9am-5:30pm. In case of an emergency, citizens of **Ireland** and **New Zealand** may call the UK consulate or the embassy in Moscow.

Currency Exchange: ATMs are ubiquitous downtown and occasionally dispense dollars or euros. As most establishments prefer rubles, withdraw rubles in order to avoid having to change cash later. "Обмен валюты" *(obmen valyuty)* means "currency exchange."

English-Language Bookstore: Anglia Bookstore, nab. Reki Fontanka 38, 2nd fl. (☎579 82 84). Biggest English bookstore in town. Knigi Books, Nevsky pr. 66, has English maps and a room of English novels. Open M-F 11am-9pm, Sa-Su 11am-8pm. MC/V.

Emergency: Police: ☎02. **Ambulance:** ☎03. **Fire:** ☎01.

Tourist Police: ☎278 30 14.

24hr. Pharmacy: PetroFarm, Nevskiy pr. 22 (☎314 54 01), stocks Western medicines and toiletries. Pharmacist daily 9am-10pm. MC/V. The **36-6** chain of pharmacies also offers Western products and often has English-speaking staff.

Medical Services: American Medical Center, nab. Reki Moyki 78 (Реки Мойки; ☎740 20 90; www.amclinic.com). M2/4: Sennaya Pl./Sadovaya. English-speaking doctors provide comprehensive services, including house calls. Insurance billing available. Consultation €50. Open 24hr. AmEx/MC/V.

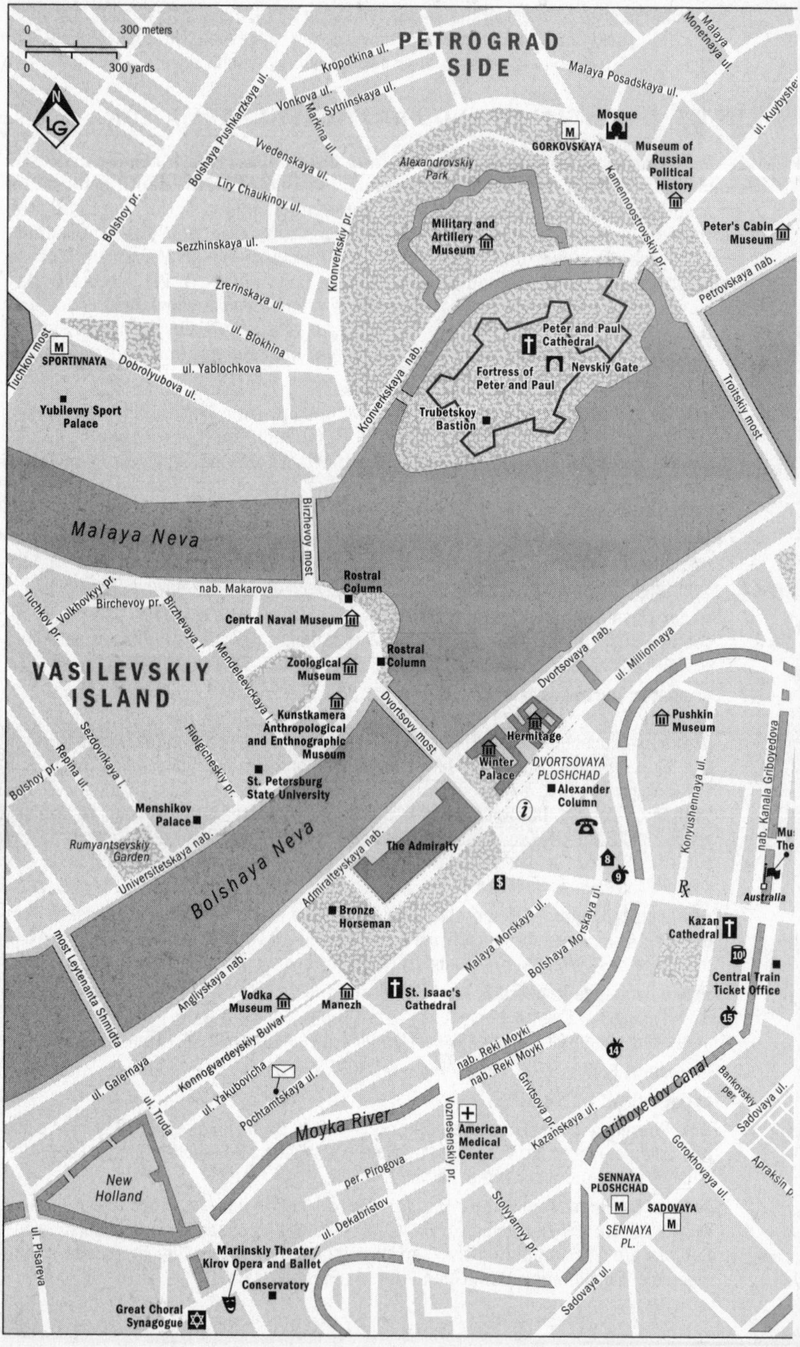
0 300 meters
0 300 yards
PETROGRAD SIDE
VASILEVSKIY ISLAND
Kropotkina ul.
Malaya Monetnaya ul.
Malaya Posadskaya ul.
ul. Kuybysheva
Vonkova ul.
Sytninskaya ul.
Markina ul.
Bolshaya Pushkarzkaya ul.
Vvedenskaya ul.
Liry Chaukinoy ul.
Bolshoy pr.
Sezzhinskaya ul.
Kronverkskiy pr.
Zrerinskaya ul.
ul. Blokhina
ul. Yablochkova
Dobrolyubova ul.
Tuchkov most
SPORTIVNAYA
Yubilevny Sport Palace
Alexandrovskiy Park
GORKOVSKAYA
Mosque
Museum of Russian Political History
Kamennoostrovskiy pr.
Peter's Cabin Museum
Petrovskaya nab.
Military and Artillery Museum
Peter and Paul Cathedral
Nevskiy Gate
Fortress of Peter and Paul
Trubetskoy Bastion
Kronverkskaya nab.
Troitskiy most
Malaya Neva
Birzhevoy most
Rostral Column
nab. Makarova
Volkhovkyy pr.
Birchevoy pr.
Tuchkov pr.
Birzhevaya l.
Central Naval Museum
Mendeleevckaya l.
Zoological Museum
Rostral Column
Dvortsovaya nab.
ul. Millionnaya
Kunstkamera Anthropological and Enthnographic Museum
Dvortsovy most
Hermitage
Pushkin Museum
Sezdovnkaya l.
Filologicheskiy pr.
Repina ul.
Bolshoy pr.
St. Petersburg State University
Winter Palace
DVORTSOVAYA PLOSHCHAD
Alexander Column
Konyushennaya ul.
nab. Kanala Griboyedova
Menshikov Palace
Rumyantsevskiy Garden
Universitetskaya nab.
Bolshaya Neva
Admiralteyskaya nab.
The Admiralty
Australia
Bronze Horseman
Malaya Morskaya ul.
Bolshaya Morskaya ul.
Kazan Cathedral
most Leytenanta Shmidta
Angliyskaya nab.
Vodka Museum
Manezh
St. Isaac's Cathedral
Central Train Ticket Office
Konnogvardeyskiy Bulvar
ul. Galernaya
nab. Reki Moyki
nab. Reki Moyki
Grivtsova pr.
ul. Yakubovicha
Pochtamtskaya ul.
ul. Truda
Moyka River
Voznesenskiy pr.
American Medical Center
Kazanskaya ul.
Griboyedov Canal
Bankovskiy per.
Sadovaya ul.
Gorokhovaya ul.
Apraksin pr.
New Holland
per. Pirogova
ul. Dekabristov
Stolyarnyy pr.
SENNAYA PLOSHCHAD
SADOVAYA
SENNAYA PL.
ul. Pisareva
Mariinskiy Theater/ Kirov Opera and Ballet
Conservatory
Great Choral Synagogue
Sadovaya ul.

RUSSIA

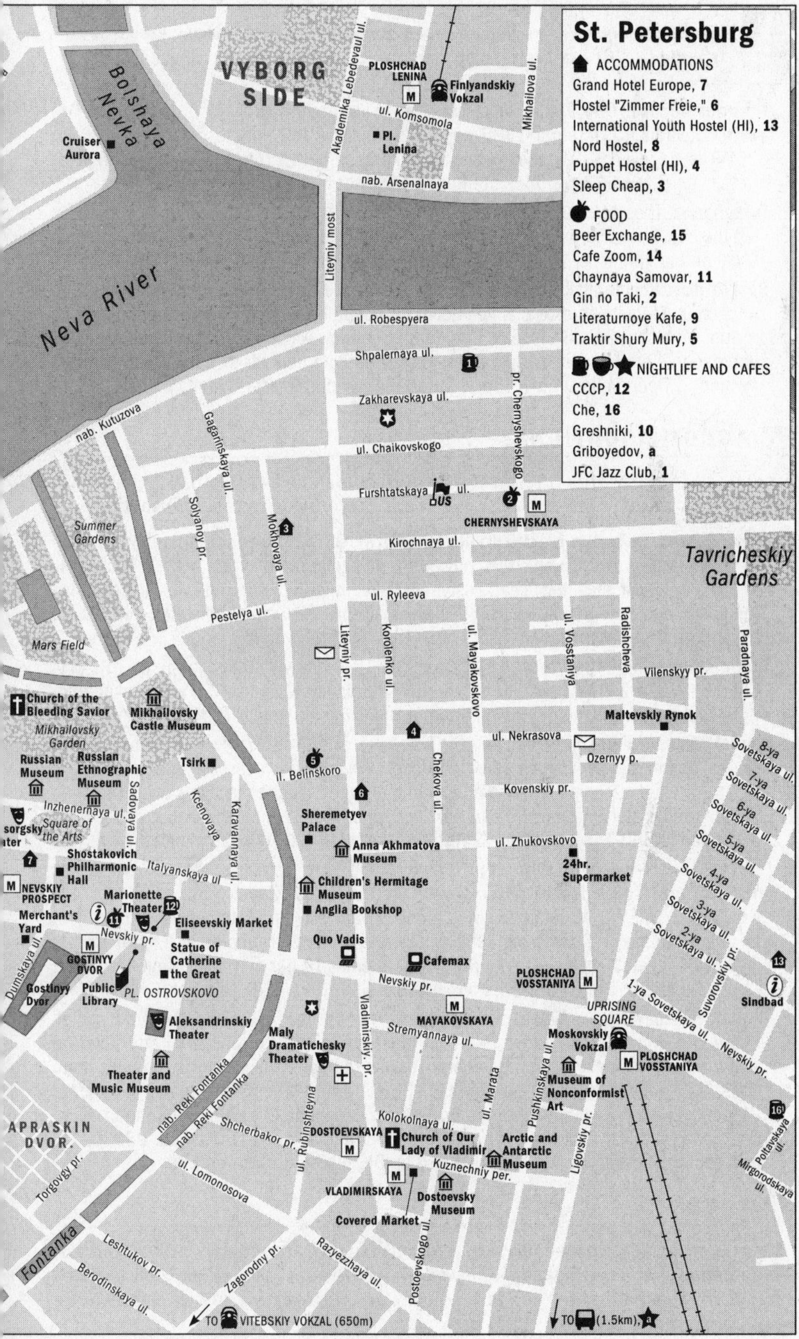
St. Petersburg
ACCOMMODATIONS
Grand Hotel Europe, 7
Hostel "Zimmer Freie," 6
International Youth Hostel (HI), 13
Nord Hostel, 8
Puppet Hostel (HI), 4
Sleep Cheap, 3
FOOD
Beer Exchange, 15
Cafe Zoom, 14
Chaynaya Samovar, 11
Gin no Taki, 2
Literaturnoye Kafe, 9
Traktir Shury Mury, 5
NIGHTLIFE AND CAFES
CCCP, 12
Che, 16
Greshniki, 10
Griboyedov, a
JFC Jazz Club, 1
VYBORG SIDE
PLOSHCHAD LENINA
Finlyandskiy Vokzal
Akademika Lebedevaul ul.
Mikhailova ul.
ul. Komsomola
Pl. Lenina
Bolshaya Nevka
Cruiser Aurora
nab. Arsenalnaya
Liteyniy most
Neva River
ul. Robespyera
Shpalernaya ul.
Zakharevskaya ul.
pr. Chernyshevskogo
nab. Kutuzova
Gagarinskaya ul.
ul. Chaikovskogo
Furshtatskaya ul.
US
CHERNYSHEVSKAYA
Solyanoy pr.
Mokhovaya ul.
Summer Gardens
Kirochnaya ul.
Tavricheskiy Gardens
ul. Ryleeva
Pestelya ul.
Mars Field
Liteyniy pr.
Korolenko ul.
ul. Mayakovskovo
ul. Vosstaniya
Radishcheva
Paradnaya ul.
Vilenskyy pr.
Church of the Bleeding Savior
Mikhailovsky Castle Museum
Mikhailovsky Garden
Maltevskiy Rynok
ul. Nekrasova
Russian Museum
Russian Ethnographic Museum
Tsirk
Il. Belinskoro
Chekova ul.
Ozernyy p.
8-ya Sovetskaya ul.
7-ya Sovetskaya ul.
6-ya Sovetskaya ul.
5-ya Sovetskaya ul.
4-ya Sovetskaya ul.
3-ya Sovetskaya ul.
2-ya Sovetskaya ul.
Inzhenernaya ul.
Sadovaya ul.
Kcenovaya
Karavannaya ul.
Kovenskiy pr.
Square of the Arts
Sheremetyev Palace
Anna Akhmatova Museum
ul. Zhukovskovo
Shostakovich Philharmonic Hall
Italyanskaya ul
Children's Hermitage Museum
24hr. Supermarket
NEVSKIY PROSPECT
Marionette Theater
Anglia Bookshop
Merchant's Yard
Eliseevskiy Market
Nevskiy pr.
Quo Vadis
Cafemax
Statue of Catherine the Great
GOSTINYY DVOR
PLOSHCHAD VOSSTANIYA
Suvorovskiy pr.
Sindbad
Dumskaya ul.
Gostinyy Dvor
Public Library
PL. OSTROVSKOVO
Nevskiy pr.
MAYAKOVSKAYA
UPRISING SQUARE
1-ya Sovetskaya ul.
Aleksandrinskiy Theater
Maly Dramatichesky Theater
Vladimirskiy. pr.
Stremyannaya ul.
Moskovskiy Vokzal
PLOSHCHAD VOSSTANIYA
Theater and Music Museum
nab. Reki Fontanka
ul. Rubinshteyna
ul. Marata
Pushkinskaya ul.
Museum of Nonconformist Art
Kolokolnaya ul.
Ligovskiy pr.
APRASKIN DVOR.
Shcherbakor pr.
DOSTOEVSKAYA
Church of Our Lady of Vladimir
Arctic and Antarctic Museum
Poltavskaya ul.
Mirgorodskaya ul.
Torgovgy pr.
ul. Lomonosova
Kuznechniy per.
VLADIMIRSKAYA
Dostoevsky Museum
Covered Market
Fontanka
Leshtukov pr.
Zagorodny pr.
Razyezzhaya ul.
Postoevskogo ul.
Berodinskaya ul.
TO VITEBSKIY VOKZAL (650m)
TO (1.5km), a
RUSSIA

St. Petersburg lacks an effective water purification system, making exposure to **giardia** (p. 26) very likely, so boil tap water, buy bottled water, or use iodine.

Internet Access: Quo Vadis, Nevskiy pr. 76, entrance off Liteyny pr. (☎333 07 08; www.quovadis.ru). Internet 130R per hr., 9am-noon 90R. Wireless access 115R for 25MB of bandwidth. DJs spin W and F 8pm. Open 9am-11pm. Cash only. **CafeMax,** Nevsky pr. 92 (☎273 66 55). Internet 50-90R per hr. Open 24hr.

Telephones: The easiest way to make phone calls is to use pay phones located throughout the city. Phone cards can be purchased at many locations, including Metro stations. Local and international calling are also available at the central post office.

Post Office: Pochtamtskaya ul. 9 (Почтамтская; ☎312 83 02). From Nevskiy pr., go west on ul. Malaya Morskaya, which becomes Pochtamtskaya ul. The central post office is about 2 blocks past St. Isaac's Cathedral. Currency exchange and telephone service. International mail at windows #24-30. *Poste Restante* held up to 1 month at windows #1 and 2. Open M-Sa 9am-7:45pm, Su 10am-5:45pm. **Postal Code:** 190 000.

ACCOMMODATIONS

Hostels geared towards international tourists may be pricier than Soviet-style hotels, but staff generally speaks English and can provide tourist information.

Nord Hostel, Bolshaya Morskaya ul. 10 (☎571 03 42; www.nordhostel.com). M2: Nevskiy Prospekt. No sign on street; ring buzzer and go to reception on 3rd fl. A 5min. walk from many tourist sites, this clean hostel offers free drinking water, free washing machine (no dryer), and free Internet. Kitchen facilities available. 36 beds. Dorms are co-ed, except by request. Breakfast included. Check-out 11am. Dorms €18. ❸

Sleep Cheap, Mokhovaya ul. 18/32 (☎715 13 04; www.sleepcheap.spb.ru). M1: Chernyshevskaya. Light pine floors, modern furnishings, and A/C. Pickup available. Breakfast included. Laundry US$5. Internet US$2 per hr. Dorms 700R. Cash only. ❸

Hostel "Zimmer Freie," Liteyniy pr. 46 (Литейный; ☎273 08 67; www.zimmer.ru). Don't let the lack of signs dissuade you—go through the archway, bear left, and enter at the "Fast Link" sign. Rooms are clean and location is good. Kitchen facilities available. Free laundry and water. Internet 50R per hr. Reception 8am-11pm. Check-out noon. May-Sept. dorms 550-740R, singles 1240R; Oct.-Apr. dorms 340-455R, singles 740R. 5% HI or ISIC discount. Cash only. 2nd location at Pestelya ul. 7, 4th fl. ❶

International Youth Hostel (HI), 3-ya Sovetskaya 28 (Советская; ☎329 80 18; www.ryh.ru). M1: Pl. Vosstaniya. Walk along Suvorovskiy pr. (Суворовский), then right on 3-ya Sovetskaya. Rooms with large windows in a quiet neighborhood. English-speaking staff. Breakfast included. Laundry US$4. Internet 1R per min. Reception 7am-1am. Check-out 11am. Dorms US$23; doubles $56. US$2 HI or ISIC discount. Cash only. ❷

Puppet Hostel (HI), ul. Nekrasova 12, 4th fl. (Некрасова; ☎272 54 01; www.hostel-puppet.ru). M3: Mayakovskaya. Walk up Mayakovskovo (Маяковского) and take the 2nd left on ul. Nekrasova. Complimentary tickets to Puppet Theater for guests. 32 dorm beds, 3-5 per room, single-sex unless special arrangements are made. Breakfast included. Laundry available. Internet 80R per hr. Reception 24hr. Check-out noon. Mar.-Oct. dorms US$23, doubles US$58; Nov. to mid-Dec. and mid-Jan. to Feb. US$15/38; mid-Dec. to mid-Jan. US$16/42. US$1 HI or ISIC discount. Cash only. ❷

FOOD

The **covered market,** Kuznechniy per. 3 (Кузнечьный), around the corner from M1: Vladimirskaya, and the **Maltsevskiy Rynok** (Мальцевский Рынок), ul. Nekrasova 52 (M1: pl. Vosstaniya), at the top of Ligovskiy pr. (Лиговский), are the largest outdoor markets, offering extensive selections of fruits, vegetables, meat, and fish. (Open 9am-10pm.) **Eliseevskiy Market,** Nevskiy pr. 56, has offered high-quality food for over 100 years in a beautiful store built by a pre-Revolution merchant. (☎312 18 65. Open M-F 10am-10pm, Sa-Su 11am-10pm.) There are **24-hour supermarkets** on side streets off Nevskiy Prospekt; look for "24 Часа" (24hr.) signs.

Cafe Zoom, Gorokhovaya 22 (Гороховая; ☎448 50 01; www.cafezoom.ru). With vaulted ceilings, a subterranean feel, and eclectic music, it's no wonder artists and intellectuals swarm to this hip European and Russian eatery. Menu includes vegetarian options. Appetizers 70-160R. Entrees 90-210R. Some English spoken. Open daily 11am-midnight, kitchen closes 11pm. 20% discount M-F before 4pm. Cash only. ❸

Literaturnoye Kafe (Литературное Кафе), Nevskiy pr. 18 (☎312 60 57; www.litcafe.restoran.ru). M2: Gostiniy Dvor. Pushkin came here the night before his fatal duel. An extensive English-language menu of Russian and European cuisine. Live pianist most evenings. Fairly slow service by Western standards. Appetizers 90-420R, caviar menu sampler 1050R. Entrees 150-450R. 10% service automatically added to bill, plus extra 5% for music. Open daily 11am-11pm. Cash only. ❸

Traktir Shury Mury (Трактир Шуры Муры), Belinskovo 8 (Белинского; ☎579 85 50). M1: Vladimirskaya. Authentic Russian cuisine served in a rustic setting. English-language menu. Appetizers 90-160R. Entrees 100-290R. Open daily 11am-6am. MC/V. ❷

Chaynaya Samovar (Чайная Самовар), Nevskiy pr. 44 (☎449 65 67; www.teaspoon.ru). Perhaps the best place in St. Petersburg for *blini;* branches throughout the city. English-language menu available. *Blini* 14-76R. This location open 24hr. ❶

Gin no Taki (Гин но Таки), Chernyshevskogo pr. 17 (Чернышевского; ☎272 09 58). M: Chernyshevskaya. Japanese restaurant combines an upscale atmosphere with moderate sushi prices and excellent service. English-language menu. 1 pc. sushi 40-65R. Maki 90-235R. Fried dishes 120-235R. Open daily 11am-6am. MC/V. ❸

Beer Exchange, nab. Kanala Griboyedova 25 (☎571 56 59). 3-course fixed business lunch menu, including a drink (111R). Entrees from 130R. Large selection of beers on tap. Some English spoken. Live music F-Sa 9pm. Open daily noon-1am. Cash only. ❷

SIGHTS

Museums and sights often charge foreigners several times more than Russians. Avoid paying the higher price by handing the cashier the exact amount for a Russian ticket and saying "adeen" (one). Walk as if you know where you are going, and do not keep your map, camera, or *Let's Go* in plain sight.

THE HERMITAGE. Originally a collection of 255 paintings bought by Catherine the Great in 1764, the State Hermitage Museum (Эрмитаж; Ermitazh) houses the world's largest art collection; it rivals the Louvre and the Prado in architectural, historical, and artistic significance. The collection is housed in the **Winter Palace** (Зимний Дворец; Zimniy Dvorets), commissioned in 1762. Tsars lived in the complex until 1917, when the museum was nationalized. Only 5% of the three million-piece collection is on display at a time. English-language floor plans are available at the info desk. *(Nab. Dvortsovaya 34* (Дворцовая). *☎710 96 25; www.hermitagemuseum.org. M2: Nevskiy pr. Open Tu-Sa 10:30am-6pm, Su 10:30am-5pm. Long lines; arrive early. 350R, Russian citizens 150R, students free. Audio tour 280R. Photography 100R. Free entrance 1st Th of every month.)*

ST. ISAAC'S CATHEDRAL. Intricately carved masterpieces of iconography are housed under the awesome 19th-century dome of St. Isaac's Cathedral (Исаакиевский Собор; Isaakievskiy Sobor). On a sunny day, the 100kg of gold that coats the dome is visible for miles. The 360° view of the city from atop the **colonnade** is worth the 260-step climb. *(M2: Nevskiy pr. Turn left on Nevskiy pr., then left on ul. Malaya Morskaya.*

RUSSIA

THE LOCAL STORY

THE CATS THAT SAVED ART HISTORY

While cats have historically served as popular pets for Russians, during the 900-day siege of Leningrad in World War II, they served as something else as well. As food supplies dwindled and growing numbers of citizens died of starvation, cats suffered the brutal indignity of being added to the menus of the desperate.

The obliteration of cats led to a revitalization of the city's rodent population. Any naturalist will tell you that such an upset of balance can only have disastrous results. Having no plans to starve, the colossal vermin population infiltrated the Hermitage and began to nosh on the paintings that had been stored in its basement as protection from the relentless German bombing. When the siege finally ended, hundreds of furry felines were purchased by the state and set free in the Hermitage to help eliminate their filthy arch-enemies. The program was successful, and it is said that today there are still 150 cats on staff at the Hermitage patrolling the storage areas.

This accounts in part for cats' ubiquitous presence in the city. In fact, the pedestrian stretch of Mikhailovskaya ul. beside Eliseevskiy is lined with small cat statues paying tribute to the rodent-hunters. For good luck, throw a coin up on these figurines, many of which are located on platforms one story above street-level.

☎315 97 32. Cathedral open M-Tu and Th-Su in summer 10am-8pm; in winter 11am-7pm. Colonnade open in summer M-Tu and Th-Su 10am-7pm; winter Tu-Th 11am-3pm. Cathedral 270R, students 150R; colonnade 120R/70R. Photography: 50R museum, 25R colonnade.)

CHURCH OF THE BLEEDING SAVIOR. (Спас На Крови; Spas Na Krovi) Also known as the Church of the Resurrection, this brilliantly colored edifice lies along Canal Griboyedova on the site of the 1881 assassination of Tsar Aleksandr II. It is equally impressive on the inside, housing the largest display of tile mosaic in the world. The church took 24 years to build and 27 years to restore after WWII; it was used as a vegetable warehouse and morgue during the Communist crackdown on religion. *(☎315 16 36. Open M-Tu and Th-Su in summer 10am-8pm; in winter 11am-7pm. Kassa closes 1hr. before closing. 300R, students 170R. Photography 50R.)*

PALACE SQUARE. (Дворцовая Площадь; Dvortsovaya Ploshchad) This huge, windswept expanse in front of the Winter Palace has witnessed many turning points in Russia's history. Catherine took the crown here after overthrowing her husband, Tsar Peter III. Much later, Nicholas II's guards fired into a crowd of protestors on "Bloody Sunday," which precipitated the 1905 revolution. Finally, Lenin's Bolsheviks seized power from the provisional government during the storming of the Winter Palace in October 1917. The 700-ton **Alexander Column,** held in place by its weight alone, commemorates Russia's defeat of Napoleon in 1812.

PETER AND PAUL FORTRESS. Across the river from the Hermitage stand the walls and golden spire of the Peter and Paul Fortress (Петропавловская Крепость; Petropavlovskaya Krepost). Originally built as a defense against the Swedes in 1703, the fortress was later used as a prison for political dissidents. Inside, the **Peter and Paul Cathedral** (Петропавловский Собор; Petropavlovskiy Sobor) glows with rosy marble walls and a Baroque partition covered with intricate iconography. The cathedral holds the remains of Peter the Great and his successors. Turn right upon entering to view the **Chapel of St. Catherine the Martyr.** The remains of the last Romanovs—Tsar Nicholas II and his family—were moved here from the Artists' Necropolis on July 17, 1998, the 80th anniversary of their murder at the hands of the Bolsheviks. Condemned prisoners awaited their fate at **Trubetskoy Bastion** (Трубецкой Бастон), where Peter the Great tortured his son, Aleksei. Dostoevsky and Trotsky served time here. *(M2: Gorkovskaya. ☎498 05 05. Open M and W-Su 11am-5pm, Tu 11am-4pm; closed last*

Tu of each month. A single ticket covers most sights. Purchase at the central kassa *or in the smaller one inside the main entrance. 120R, students 60R.)*

ALEXANDER NEVSKIY MONASTERY. Alexander Nevskiy Monastery (Александро-Невская Лавра; Aleksandro-Nevskaya Lavra) is a major pilgrimage site and peaceful strolling ground. The **Artists' Necropolis** (Некрапол Мастеров Искусств; Nekropol Masterov Iskusstv) is the resting place of Fyodor Dostoevsky and composers Mussorgsky, Rimsky-Korsakov, and Tchaikovsky. The **Church of the Annunciation** (Благовещенская Церков; Blagoveshchenskaya Tserkov), along the stone path on the left, holds the remains of war heroes. At the end of the path is the **Holy Trinity Cathedral** (Свято-Тройтский Собор; Svyato-Troytskiy Sobor), teeming with devout *babushki* kissing Orthodox icons. This is an active monastery, so there is a strict dress code in the Cathedral: no shorts, and women must cover their shoulders and heads. *(M3/4: Pl. Aleksandra Nevskovo. ☎274 16 12. Grounds open daily 6am-10pm. Artists' Necropolis open daily 9:30am-6pm. Cathedral open daily 6am-8pm.* Kassa *open Tu-W and F-Su 11am-4:30pm. Cemetery 120R, students 60R; cathedral grounds 100/50R.)*

ALONG NEVSKIY PROSPEKT. Many sights are clustered around the western end of bustling Nevskiy pr., the city's 4.5km main thoroughfare. Unfortunately, there is no metro station immediately nearby; one was built, but after the station was completed, construction of an entrance or exit connecting it to the surface was not approved due to concerns about crime and vagrancy. The **Admiralty** (Адмиралтейство; Admiralteystvo), across the street from the Winter Palace, towers over the surrounding gardens and most of Nevskiy pr. Originally intended for shipbuilding by Peter the Great, it was a naval headquarters until recently, when it became a naval college. In the park to the left of the Admiralty stands the **Bronze Horseman** statue of Peter the Great, one of the most widely recognized symbols of the city. *(M2: Nevskiy pr.)* Walking east on Nevskiy pr., the enormous, Roman-style **Kazan Cathedral** (Казанский Собор; Kazanskiy Sobor) looms to the right. It houses the remains of General Kutuzov, commander of the Russian army in the war against Napoleon. *(☎570 45 28. M2: Nevskiy pr. Open daily 8:30am-7:30pm. Free.)* The 220-year-old **Merchants' Yard** (Гостиный Двор; Gostiniy Dvor), one of the world's oldest indoor shopping malls, is to the right. *(M3: Gostiniy Dvor. Open M-Sa 10am-10pm, Su 10am-9pm.)* Continuing down the street, the **Marionette Theater** on the left is the oldest in Russia. *(Nevsky pr. 52, ☎310 58 79; www.demmeni.org. Open 10:30am-6pm.)* Nearby **Ostrovskovo Square** (Островского) houses the Aleksandrinskiy Theater (see **Festivals and Entertainment,** below), a massive statue of Catherine the Great, and the **public library,** which contains Voltaire's private library, purchased in its entirety by Catherine the Great. *(Foreigners can obtain a library card for free; bring passport, visa, and two photographs. Library open M-F 9am-9pm, Sa-Su 11am-7pm.)* Turn left before the Fontanka canal on nab. Reki Fontanka and look down before crossing the bridge at ul. Pestelya to find the **Smallest Monument in the World**. According to lore, landing a coin on the platform of the tiny bird statue brings good luck. The **Museum of Nonconformist Art,** on John Lennon St., is housed in apartments where rebellious artists displayed their work illegally during Communist times. *(☎764 53 71; www.pushkinskaja-10.spb.ru. Open W-Su 3-7:30pm.)*

SUMMER GARDENS AND PALACE. The long, shady paths of the Summer Gardens and Palace (Летний Сад и Дворец; Letniy Sad i Dvorets) are a lovely place to rest and cool off. Peter's modest **Summer Palace,** in the northeast corner, reflects his diverse taste in everything from Spanish and Portuguese chairs to Dutch tile and German clocks. **Mars Field** (Марсово Поле; Marsovo Pole), a memorial to the victims of the Revolution and Civil War (1917-1919), extends out from the Summer Gardens. *(M2: Nevskiy pr. Turn right on nab. Kanala Griboyedova* (Канала Грибоедова)*, cross the Moyka, and turn right on ul. Pestelya* (Пестеля)*. ☎314 03 74. Garden open daily May-Oct.*

BLAST IN THE BANYA

The *banya* is the real Russian bathing experience—it has been a part of Slavic culture since long before there was a Russia to claim it as Russian. Traditionally a way for villagers to cleanse their bodies, *banyas* have recently been shown to improve health by increasing metabolism and enhancing circulation.

A modern *banya* is usually single-sex and involves several stages. During the first, you enter the *parilka* (парилка), a steam room that reaches temperatures upward of 70°C. The idea is to stay in the *parilka* as long as you can stand it, then cool down under a shower before going out into the open air. This is repeated several times in order to acclimate the body to cardiac workout, before a plunge into the icy cold pool (холодный бассейн) is added to the cycle. At this point, it is customary to offer and receive a beating with a wet birch-tree switch—which apparently feels like a pleasant massage. Bring sandals and a sheet, or rent them upon arrival. Also bring shampoo and soap for a Western-style shower to wrap things up. Birch switches can be purchased on-site.

There is a public banya *at Bolshoy Kazachiy per 11. (☎315 07 34). M1: Pushkinskaya. Open daily 8am-8pm. 35R. Private* banya *holds up to 10 people. 700R per hr.*

10am-10pm; Nov.-Apr. 10am-8pm. Palace open Tu-Su 10am-6pm; closed on the last Tu of each month. Kassa closes 4pm. Gardens free. Palace 300R, students 150R. 3rd Th of each month free.)

OTHER MUSEUMS. The **State Russian Museum** (Русский Музей; Russkiy Muzey) boasts the world's second-largest collection of Russian art. Exhibits are displayed in three other locations throughout the city. *(M3: Gostiniy Dvor. ☎595 42 48. Open M 10am-5pm, W-Su 10am-6pm. 300R, students 150R. Tickets to all museum sites 600R/300R. Photography 100R.)* **Dostoevsky's House** (Дом Достоевского; Dom Dostoevskovo) is where the author penned *The Brothers Karamazov*. *(M1: Vladimirskaya. On the corner of ul. Dostoevskovo. ☎571 40 31. Open Tu-Su 11am-6pm; closed last W of each month. 100R, students 50R.)* The **Museum of Russian Political History** (Музей Политической Истории России; Muzey Politicheskoy Istorii Rossii) showcases WWII artifacts and Soviet propaganda portraying the "ideal reality" of the Communist ethos. *(M2: Gorkovskaya. Go down Kamennoostrovskiy (Каменноостровский) and turn left on Kuybysheva. ☎233 70 52. Open M-W and F-Su 10am-6pm. 150R, students 70R.)*

FESTIVALS AND ENTERTAINMENT

From mid-May to mid-July, the city holds a series of outdoor concerts as part of the **White Nights Festival.** Bridges over the Neva River go up at 1:30am, and most don't come back down until 4:30 or 5:30am.

The home of Tchaikovsky, Prokofiev, and Stravinsky still lives up to its reputation as a mecca for the performing arts. *Yarus* (ярус), the cheapest (standing room) seats, cost as little as 100R. The **Mariinskiy Teatr** (Марийнский; a.k.a. Kirov), Teatralnaya pl. 1 (Театральная), M4: Sadovaya, is perhaps the world's most famous ballet hall. Tchaikovsky's *Nutcracker* and *The Sleeping Beauty*, Baryshnikov, and Nijinsky all premiered here. Tickets can be purchased in Gostiniy Dvor. (☎326 41 41. Tickets 320-4800R. *Kassa* open Tu-Su 10am-7pm.) **Aleksandrinskiy Teatr** (Александринский Театр), pl. Ostrovskovo 2, M3: Gostiniy Dvor, attracts famous Russian actors and companies. (☎312 15 45. Tickets 200-800R.) **Mussorgsky Opera and Ballet Theater** (Театр Имени Муссоргского; Teatr Imeni Mussorgskovo), pl. Iskusstv, is open all summer, when the Mariynskiy is closed for several weeks. (☎595 43 05. Bring your passport. Tickets 300-1500R. *Kassa* open 11am-3pm, 4-6pm, and until 7pm for same-day tickets.) **Shostakovich Philharmonic Hall,** ul. Mikhailovskaya 2, opposite the Russian Museum, has classical and modern concerts. (☎710 42 57; www.philharmonia.spb.ru. M3:

Gostiniy Dvor. Tickets 720-1080R. *Kassa* open daily 11am-3pm and 4-7:30pm.) The Mussorgsky and Shostakovich Theaters both lie around the **Square of the Arts.** The Friday issue of the *St. Petersburg Times* has comprehensive listings of entertainment and nightlife. Use website **www.kassir.ru** to book tickets to various performances online in English.

NIGHTLIFE

JFC Jazz Club, Shpalernaya ul. 33 (Шпалерная; ☎272 98 50; www.jfc.sp.ru). M1: Chernyshevskaya. Go right on pr. Chernyshevskovo (Чернышевского) and left on Shpalernaya. Quality jazz in a relaxed atmosphere. Different band nightly. Come early or call ahead to score a table; otherwise stand at the bar area. Beer 70-120R. Shots 40-150R. Live music 8-10pm. Cover 150R for bar, 300R for table seating. Open daily 7-10:45pm.

Che, Poltavskaya ul. 3 (Полтавская; ☎717 76 00). M1: Vosstaniya. Walk east on Nevskiy pr. and turn right on Poltavskaya. Relax with trendy bourgeoisie largely oblivious to the irony. Breakfast 70-130R, dinner 270R and up. Drinks 110-400R; extensive wine list. Live latin/jazz music 10pm-midnight. Open 24hr. Cash only.

Griboyedov, Voronezhskaya ul. 2a (☎764 43 55; www.griboedovclub.ru). M4: Ligovsky pr. Break it down in an historical WWII underground bunker. Live music nightly 10pm-midnight, followed by popular DJs. Cover 250R. Open Su-Th 6pm-6am, F-Sa 6pm-7am.

CCCP, Nevskiy pr. 54 (☎310 49 29). M2: Nevskiy Prospekt. With funky red lighting reminiscent of the Soviet era, the lounge is popular and centrally located, with an interesting menu. The 2 cafes next door, Ili and Cafe Jili-Bili, are also heavily frequented spots. Appetizers 135-270R, entrees 260-320R, desserts 120-185R, healthy "fitness menu" 135R. Drinks from 100R. Dancing Sa after 4am. Open daily 1pm-6am. AmEx/MC/V.

Greshniki (Грешники; Sinners), nab. Kanala Griboyedova 28 (☎318 42 91; www.greshniki.ru). M2: Nevskiy pr. Look for "Sinners" sign. Rocker-dungeon-themed 4-floor gay club, primarily for men. Drinks 40-250R. Male strip shows daily. 18+. Cover for men 40-80R, women 200-350R, free for men in drag. Open daily 10pm-6am.

DAYTRIP FROM ST. PETERSBURG

PETERHOF (Петергоф). Now the largest and the best-restored of the Russian palaces, Peterhof was burned to the ground during the Nazi retreat. Today, the gates open onto the **Lower Gardens,** a perfect place for a picnic along the shores of the Gulf of Finland. (Open daily 10:30am-5pm.) Bent on creating his own Versailles, Peter started building the **Grand Palace** (Большой Дворец; Bolshoy Dvorets) in 1714; Catherine the Great later expanded and remodeled it. (☎420 00 73. Open Tu-Su 10:30am-5pm; closed last Tu of each month. 430R, students 215R.) The 64 fountains of the **Grand Cascade** shoot into the Grand Canal. (Fountains operate May-Oct. M-F 10:30am-5pm, Sa-Su 10:30am-6pm. 300R, students 150R.) There are 17 museums on the grounds, and the **Upper Gardens** can be roamed for free. Take the **train** from Baltiyskiy station (Балтийский; M1: Baltiyskaya; 35min., 1-6 per hr., 36R). Tickets are sold at the courtyard office (пригородная касса; *prigorodnaya kassa*). Get off at Novyy Peterhof (Новый Петергоф). From the station, take any minivan (5min.; 10R) or bus (10min.; 7R) to Petrodvorets (Петродворец; Peter's Palace). On the way back, take a minivan to the Metro (30R). Alternatively, in summer, take the **hydrofoil** from the quay on nab. Dvortsovaya (Дворцовая) in front of the Hermitage (40min.; 1-2 per hr. 9:30am-6pm; 450R, round-trip 800R).

SLOVAK REPUBLIC (SLOVENSKÁ REPUBLIKA)

After centuries of nomadic invasions and Hungarian rule, as well as 40 years of Soviet domination, the Slovak Republic has finally emerged as an independent nation. While the country was still part of Czechoslovakia, Slovaks rejected Communism in the 1989 Velvet Revolution, then split from the Czechs in the peaceable 1993 Velvet Divorce. Slovakia gained entrance to the European Union in 2004 and has seen its economy skyrocket. With the country now in flux between industry and agriculture, many older, rural Slovaks still embrace their peasant traditions, while the younger generation is drawn to the cities. While all this is happening, in Bratislava and the surrounding countryside, budget travelers are treated to impressive castle ruins and stunning terrain.

ESSENTIALS

FACTS AND FIGURES	
Official Name: Slovak Republic.	**Land Area:** 49,035 sq. km.
Capital: Bratislava.	**Time Zone:** GMT +1.
Major City: Košice.	**Language:** Slovak.
Population: 5,400,000.	**Religions:** Roman Catholic (69%), Protestant (11%), Greek Catholic (4%).

WHEN TO GO

High season occurs in the Tatras in July and August, when it is advisable to book rooms in advance. The lower elevations tend to be warmer; summers in the mountains are cool and good for hiking, and winter brings excellent skiing conditions.

DOCUMENTS AND FORMALITIES

EMBASSIES. Foreign embassies in the Slovak Republic are in Bratislava. Slovak embassies abroad include: **Australia,** 47 Culgoa Circuit, O'Malley, Canberra, ACT, 2606 (☎2 6290 1516; www.slovakemb-aust.org); **Canada,** 50 Rideau Terr., Ottawa, ON, K1M 2A1 (☎613-749-4442; www.ottawa.mfa.sk); **Ireland,** 20 Clyde Rd., Ballsbridge, Dublin, 4 (☎1 660 0012); **UK,** 25 Kensington Palace Gardens, London, W8 4QY (☎090 6550 8956; www.slovakembassy.co.uk); **US,** 3523 International Ct., NW, Washington, D.C., 20008 (☎202-237-1054; www.slovakembassy-us.org).

VISA AND ENTRY INFORMATION. Citizens of Australia, Canada, Ireland, New Zealand, the UK, and the US can visit without a visa for up to 90 days. Those traveling to the Slovak Republic for employment, study, or other longer-term purposes must obtain a temporary residence permit. Contact your embassy for info.

TOURIST SERVICES AND MONEY

TOURIST OFFICES. The **Slovak Tourist Board** (☎48 413 61 46; www.sacr.sk) provides useful information for finding accommodations, enjoying the country's natural resources, and learning about its culture. Public tourist offices are marked with a green square containing a white "i." English is often spoken at tourist offices, which usually provide maps and information about transportation.

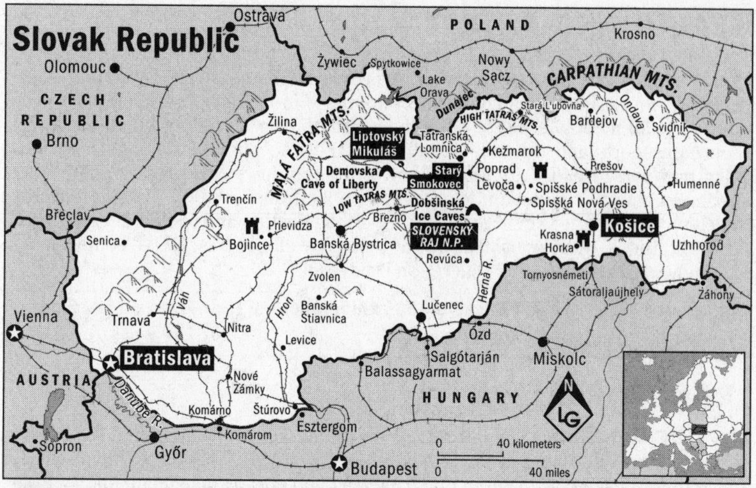

ENTRANCE REQUIREMENTS

Passport: Required for all travelers.

Visa: Not required for stays under 90 days for citizens of Australia, Canada, New Zealand, the UK, and the US.

Letter of Invitation: Not required for citizens of Australia, Canada, Ireland, New Zealand, the UK, and the US.

Inoculations: Not required. Recommended up-to-date on DTaP (diphtheria, tetanus, and pertussis), hepatitis A, hepatitis B, MMR (measles, mumps, and rubella), polio booster, and typhoid.

Work Permit: Required for all foreigners planning to work.

Driving Permit: Required for all those planning to drive.

MONEY. The Slovak Republic is a member of the EU and hopes to switch to the euro in 2009. Currently, the unit of currency is the Slovak koruna (Sk), plural koruny. One koruna is equal to 100 haliers. Credit cards are not accepted in many Slovak establishments, but MasterCard and Visa are the most useful, followed by American Express. Inflation is currently around 3%. ATMs are plentiful and give the best exchange rates, but also tend to charge a flat service fee, so it is most economical to withdraw large amounts at a time. Banks Slovenská-Sporitelňa and Unibank handle Master Card and Visa cash advances. Banks require a passport for most transactions. Slovakia imposes a **value added tax (VAT)** of 19% on most goods. A partial refund may be available for non-EU citizens; however, the paperwork must be completed before leaving the country.

KORUNY (SK)		
	AUS$1 = 22.26SK	10SK = AUS$0.45
	CDN$1 = 27.00SK	10SK = CDN$0.37
	EUR€1 = 38.07SK	10SK = EUR€0.26
	NZ$1 = 18.73SK	10SK = NZ$0.53
	UK£1 = 55.77SK	10SK = UK£0.18
	US$1 = 30.15SK	10SK = US$0.33

HEALTH AND SAFETY

Tap **water** varies in quality and appearance—water bubbles may make it appear cloudy—but is generally safe. Drugstores *(drogerii)* stock Western brands. Aspirin *(aspirena)*, bandages *(obväz)*, condoms *(kondómy)*, and tampons *(tampony)* are all available. Petty crime is common; be wary in crowded areas and secure passports and valuables at all times. Few accommodations exist for **disabled** travelers. **Women** traveling alone will likely have few problems but may encounter stares. Avoid walking or riding public transportation at night. **Minority** travelers with darker skin may encounter discrimination and should exercise caution at all times. **Homosexuality** is not accepted by all Slovaks; GLBT couples may experience stares or insults. Discretion is advised.

EMERGENCY	**Police:** ☎150. **Ambulance:** ☎155. **Fire:** ☎158. **Emergency:** ☎112.

TRANSPORTATION

BY PLANE AND TRAIN. Flying to Bratislava may be inconvenient and expensive because many international carriers have no direct flights. Flying to Vienna, AUT, and taking a bus or train is often much cheaper and doesn't take much longer. **EastPass** is valid in the Slovak Republic, but Eurail is not. **ŽSR** is the national rail company. InterCity or EuroCity trains are faster but more expensive. Master schedules (*cestovný poriadok;* 58Sk) are available for sale at info desks and are posted on boards in most stations. A boxed "R" on the timetable means a reservation (*miestenka;* 7Sk) is required. There is a fine for boarding an international train without a reservation. Reservations are advisable and often required for express *(expresný)* trains and first-class seats, but are not necessary for *rychlík* (fast), *spešný* (semi-fast), or *osobný* (local) trains. Both first and second class are relatively comfortable and considered safe. Buy tickets before boarding the train, except in very tiny towns. For train info, check www.zsr.sk.

BY BUS. In hilly regions, **ČSAD** or **SAD buses** are the best and sometimes the only option. Except for very long trips, buy tickets onboard. You can probably ignore most footnotes on schedules, but the following are important: "X" (crossed hammers) means weekdays only; "a" is Saturday and Sunday; "b" is Monday through Saturday; "n" is Sunday; and "r" and "k" mean excluding holidays. *Premava* means including; *nepremava* is except; following those words are often lists of dates (day is listed before month). Check www.eurolines.sk for bus schedules.

BY BIKE AND BY THUMB. Rambling wilds and castle ruins inspire ever-popular bike tours, especially in the Tatras, the western foothills, and Šariš. **VKÚ** publishes color bike maps (70-80Sk). Let's Go does not recommend hitchhiking.

KEEPING IN TOUCH

PHONE CODES	**Country code:** 421. **International dialing prefix:** 00. For more information on placing international calls, see inside back cover.

EMAIL AND THE INTERNET. Internet access is common in Slovakia, even in smaller towns. Internet cafes usually have fast access for around 1Sk per hour.

TELEPHONE. Recent modernization of the Slovak phone system has required many businesses and individuals to switch phone numbers. The phone system is still somewhat unreliable, however, so try multiple times if you don't get through.

Some pay phones allow international calls, while others do not; both types of phones exist in each city, but there is no good way to distinguish between them. Card phones are common and are usually more reliable than the coin-operated variety. Purchase cards (100-500Sk) at the post office. Be sure to buy the "Global Phone" card if you plan to make an international call.

MAIL. The Slovak Republic has an efficient mail service. Letters sent abroad take two to three weeks to arrive. Letters to Europe cost 11-14Sk; letters to the US cost 21Sk. Most post offices *(pošta)* provide express mail. To send a package abroad, go to a customs office *(colnice)*. Those without permanent addresses can receive mail through **Poste Restante.** Address envelopes as follows: First Name LAST NAME, POSTE RESTANTE, post office address, Postal Code, city, SLOVAK REPUBLIC.

LANGUAGE. Slovak is a West Slavic language written in the Latin alphabet. It is similar enough to **Czech** and **Polish** that speakers of one will understand the others. A traveler's attempts to speak Slovak itself, though, will be appreciated. Older Slovaks usually speak a little Polish. **English** is common among Bratislava's youth, but **German** is more useful outside the capital. **Russian** is occasionally understood but is sometimes unwelcome. The golden rules of speaking Slovak are to pronounce every letter and stress the first syllable. Accents over vowels lengthen them.

ACCOMMODATIONS AND CAMPING

SLOVAK REPUBLIC	❶	❷	❸	❹	❺
ACCOMMODATIONS	under 250Sk	250-500Sk	500-800Sk	800-1000Sk	over 1000Sk

Beware of scams and overpricing. Foreigners are often charged up to twice as much as Slovaks for the same room. Finding cheap accommodations in Bratislava before student dorms open in July is difficult. Those without reservations may also have trouble in Slovenský Raj and the Tatras. In other regions, finding a bed is relatively easy if you call ahead. The tourist office, **SlovakoTourist,** and other travel agencies can usually help. The Slovak Republic has few hostels; most are in and around Bratislava. These usually provide towels and a bar of soap. **Hotel** prices are dramatically lower outside Bratislava and the Tatras, with budget hotels running 300-600Sk. **Pensions** *(penzióny)* are smaller and less expensive than hotels. **Campgrounds** are common and are located on the outskirts of most towns; they usually rent bungalows to travelers without tents. Camping in national parks is illegal. In the mountains, mountain huts *(chaty)* range from bunks with outhouses (about 200Sk) per night to plush quarters (around 600Sk).

FOOD AND DRINK

SLOVAK REPUBLIC	❶	❷	❸	❹	❺
FOOD	under 120Sk	120-190Sk	190-270Sk	270-330Sk	over 330Sk

The national dish, *bryndzové halušky* (small dumplings in sauce), is a godsend for **vegetarians** and those keeping **kosher.** Pork products, however, are central to many meals in the Slovak Republic. *Knedliky* (dumplings) often accompany entrees, but it's often possible to opt for *zemiaky* (potatoes) instead. Enjoy *kolačky* (pastry), baked with cheese, honey, and jam or poppyseeds, for dessert. Most white **wines** are made northeast of Bratislava, though *Tokaj* wines (distinct from the Hungarian wine) are produced near Košice. Enjoy them both at a *vináreň* (wine hall). *Pivo* (beer) is served at a *pivnica* or *piváreň* (tavern). The favorite Slovak beer is the slightly bitter *Spis*.

HOLIDAYS AND FESTIVALS

Holidays: Origin of the Slovak Republic (Jan. 1); Epiphany (Jan. 6); Good Friday (Apr. 6); Easter (Apr. 8); May Day (May 1); St. Cyril and Methodius Day (July 5); Anniversary of Slovak National Uprising (Aug. 29); Constitution Day (Sept. 1); Our Lady of the 7 Sorrows (Sept. 15); All Saints' Day (Nov. 1); Day of Freedom and Democracy (Nov. 17).

Festivals: Banská Bystrica's Festival of Ghosts and Spirits, in late spring, is a celebration for the dead. Folk dancers gather in Poprad for the mid-summer Vychodna Folk Festival.

BEYOND TOURISM

Brethren Volunteer Service, 1451 Dundee Ave., Elgin, IL 60120, USA (☎800-323-8039; www.brethrenvolunteerservice.org). Places volunteers with environmental and civic groups in the Slovak Republic.

BTVC, 163 Balby Rd., Balby, Doncaster, DN4 0RH, UK (☎01302 57 22 44; www.btcv.org). Week-long wildlife-and-wilderness preservation projects throughout Central and Eastern Europe. Book early for one of the Slovak Republic trips, which monitor bear and wolf predator populations in the Tatras Mountains.

The Slovak Spectator (www.slovakspectator.sk). An English-language newspaper with classified job ads.

BRATISLAVA ☎02

Often eclipsed by its famous neighboring capitals, sophisticated Bratislava (pop. 450,000) is finally stepping into the limelight. Every night of the week, the city's artfully lit streets buzz with activity. During the day, both locals and visitors can be found sipping coffee at the hundreds of chic cafes dotting the cobblestoned Staré Mesto (Old Town), sauntering along the Danube River, or exploring the well-kept castle that shines over the city.

TRANSPORTATION

Trains: Bratislava Hlavná Stanica, north of the city center. To get downtown, take tram #2 to the 6th stop. International tickets are sold at counters #5-13. To **Prague, CZR** (4½-5½hr., 3 per day, 663Sk) and **Warsaw, POL** (8hr., 1 per day, 1089Sk).

Buses: Mlynské nivy 31 (☎55 42 16 67), east of the city center. From the bus station, take trolley #202, or turn right on Mlynské nivy and continue to Dunajská, which leads to Kamenné nám. and the center of town. **Eurolines** runs buses to **Budapest, HUN** (4hr., 1 per day, 570Sk), **Prague, CZR** (4¾hr., 5 per day, 245Sk), and **Vienna, AUT** (1½hr., every 1-2hr., 210Sk). Check ticket for bus number *(č. aut.),* as several different buses may depart from the same stand.

Public Transportation: Tram and **bus** tickets (10min., 14Sk; 30min., 18Sk; 1hr. 22Sk) are sold at kiosks or the orange *automats* in bus stations. Use an *automat* only if its light is on. Stamp your ticket when you board (1400Sk fine for riding without a stamp). Trams and buses run 4am-11pm. **Night buses,** marked with numbers in the 500s, run midnight-4am; 2 tickets required. Some kiosks and ticket machines sell **passes** (1-day 90Sk, 2-day 170Sk, 3-day 210Sk). For schedules and routes, check www.imhd.sk.

Taxis: FunTaxi (☎167 77); **Taxi Bratislava Profi** (☎162 22), 24hr.

ORIENTATION AND PRACTICAL INFORMATION

Bratislava's city center is bordered by the **Danube River** (Dunaj) on the south and **Námestie Slovenského Národného Povstania** (Nám. SNP; Slovak National Uprising

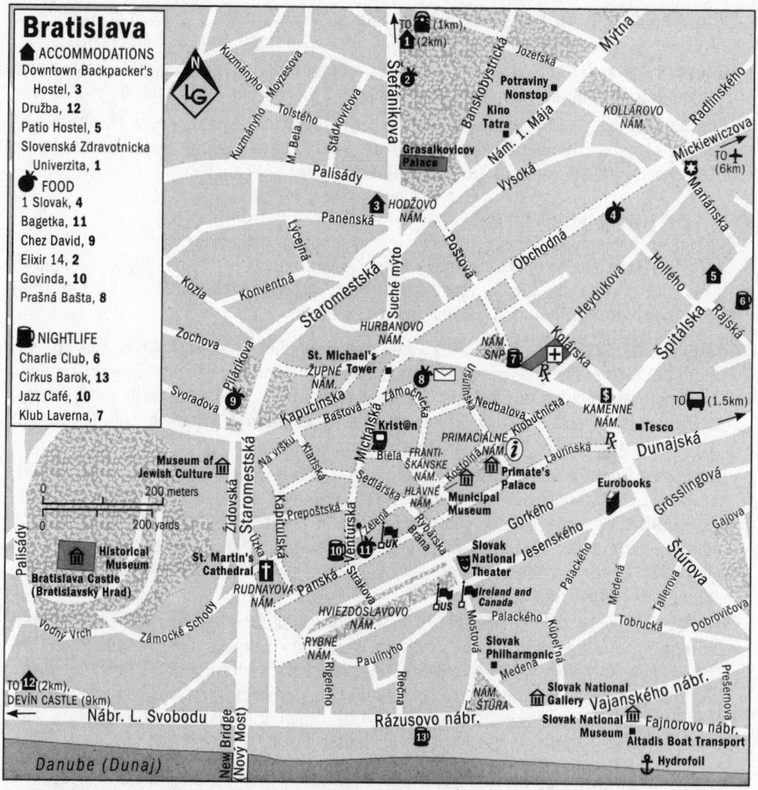

Square) on the north. The castle **Bratislavský Hrad** sits on a hill to the west of the center. **Nový Most** (New Bridge), the largest of four bridges spanning the Danube, connects the major thoroughfare **Staromestská** to the commercial and entertainment district on the southern bank.

Tourist Office: Bratislavská Kultúrna a Informačná Stredisko (BKIS), Klobučnícka 2 (☎161 86; www.bkis.sk). Books private and hotel rooms (800-3000Sk; 50Sk fee). Sells maps (free-80Sk) and the **City Card** (1-day 200Sk, 2-day 300Sk, 3-day 370Sk), which offers unlimited transportation and discounts at museums and restaurants. Open M-F 8:30am-7pm, Sa 9am-7pm, Su 9:30am-7pm.

Embassies: Canada, Mostová 2 (☎59 20 40 31). Open M-F 8:30am-noon and 1:30-4:30pm. **Ireland,** Mostová 2 (☎59 30 96 11; bratislava@iveagh.irlgov.ie). Open M-F 9am-12:30pm and 2:30-4:30pm. **UK,** Panská 16 (☎59 98 20 00; www.britishembassy.sk). Open M-Th 8:30am-5pm, F 8:30am-2pm. **US,** Hviezdoslavovo nám. 5 (☎54 43 08 61, emergency 09 03 70 36 66; www.usis.sk). Open M-F 8-11:45am and 2:30-4:30pm. Visa office open M-F 8-11:30am. In an emergency, citizens of **Australia** and **New Zealand** should contact the UK embassy.

Currency Exchange: Ľudová Banka, Nám. SNP 15 (☎54 41 89 84; www.luba.sk) cashes AmEx/V traveler's checks for 1% commission and offers MC/V cash advances. Open M-F 8am-7pm. **ATMs** are at the train station and throughout the city center.

Emergency: Police: ☎158. **Ambulance:** ☎155. **Fire:** ☎150.

Pharmacy: Lekáreň Pod Manderlom, Nám. SNP 20 (☎54 43 29 52). Open M-F 7:30am-8pm, Sa 8am-7pm, Su 9am-7pm. Ring bell after hours in an emergency.

Internet Access: There are Internet cafes all over, especially along Michalská and Obchodná. **Megainet,** Klariska 4, has wireless. 1Sk per min. Open daily 9am-10pm.

Post Office: Nám. SNP 35 (☎59 39 33 30). Offers fax service. *Poste Restante* and phone cards at counters #2-4. Open M-F 7am-8pm, Sa 7am-6pm, Su 9am-2pm. *Poste Restante* M-F 7am-8pm, Sa 7am-2pm. **Postal Code:** 81000.

ACCOMMODATIONS

In July and August, several **university dorms** open as hostels (from 150Sk). Pensions and private rooms are inexpensive and comfy alternatives. **BKIS** (see **Orientation and Practical Information,** p. 870) has more info.

Patio Hostel, Špitálska 35 (☎529 257 97; www.patiohostel.com), near the bus station. From the train station, take tram #13 to the arch. The entrance is tucked behind a dimly lit, run-down archway, but the hostel itself is clean and comfortable, with sunny rooms, a friendly staff, and a colorful common area. Free Internet. Check-in 1pm. Check-out 10pm. 2- to 12-person dorms 500-900Sk. MC/V. ❷

Downtown Backpacker's Hostel, Panenská 31 (☎546 411 91; www.backpackers.sk). From the train station, turn left on Stefánikova and right on Panenská, or take bus #81, 91, or 93 for 2 stops. Swank, centrally located 19th-century building, with backpackers relaxing under a bust of Lenin and enjoying beers from the bar. Laundry 100Sk. Reception 24hr. Check-out noon. Reserve ahead. Dorms 500-600Sk; doubles 1000Sk. HI discount 60/100Sk. Tourist tax 30Sk. MC/V. ❷

Družba, Botanická 25 (☎654 200 65; www.hotel-druzba.sk). Take bus #32 (dir.: Pri Kríži) or tram #1 to Botanická Záhrada. Cross the pedestrian overpass and go to the 2nd of the 2 red, blue, and green concrete blocks. The combination university dorm/hotel is far from the Old Town, but its dorms are brightly painted and remarkably cheap. Dorms open early July to late Aug. Reception 24hr. Dorms 190Sk. Hotel open year-round. Reception M-Th 7am-3:30pm, F 7am-1pm. Singles 790Sk; doubles 1400Sk. MC/V. ❶

Slovenská Zdravotnicka Univerzita, Limbová 12 (☎593 701 00; www.szu.sk). From the train station, take bus #32 or tram #204 for 5 stops to Nemocnica Kramárel. Clean, comfortable rooms in a green concrete tower located far from the city center. Reception 24hr. Check-out 11am. 790Sk per person. Tourist tax 30Sk. Cash only. ❸

FOOD

Buy groceries at **Tesco Potraviny,** Kamenné nám. 1. (Open M-F 7am-9pm, Sa 8am-8pm, Su 9am-8pm.) Or try the nearby indoor **fruit market** at Stará Trzníćá, Kamenné nám. (Open M-F 7am-6pm, Sa 7am-1pm.)

1 Slovak, Obchodná 62 (☎253 963 67; www.slovakpub.sk). Join the student crowd at one of Bratislava's largest and cheapest traditional Slovak restaurants. Each of the rooms has a theme, including the country cottage and the Room of Poets. Lunch (served until 5pm) 35-89Sk. Dinner entrees 79-179Sk. 10% discount for Patio Hostel guests. Open M-Th 10am-midnight, F-Sa 10am-2pm, Su noon-midnight. MC/V. ❷

Govinda, Obchodná 30 (☎529 623 66). The veggie fare is heavenly. Combination plate 95/150Sk. Open M-F 11am-8pm, Sa 11:30am-7:30pm. Cash only. ❶

Elixir 14, Stefánikova 14 (☎524 998 49; www.elixir.sk). The menu is a treasure trove of creative vegetarian dishes. Vegan and meat options available. Daily lunch special 99Sk. Entrees 115-235Sk. Open M-W 10am-10pm, Th 10am-11pm, F-Sa 10am-midnight, Su 11am-10pm. MC/V. ❷

Prašná Bašta, Zámočnícka 11 (☎544 349 57; www.prasnabasta.sk). Hidden away from the Old Town bustle, this eatery's counter-culture atmosphere draws 20-somethings for generous portions of Slovak cuisine. Sit outside on the leafy terrace or downstairs amid sculptures and artful decor. Entrees 95-325Sk. Open daily 11am-11pm. MC/V. ❸

Bagetka, Zelená 8 (☎544 194 36). This relaxed sandwich bar is a fast, cheap, and satisfying option. Entrees 40-90Sk. Open M-Sa 9:30am-9pm, Su 1:30-9pm. Cash only. ❶

Chez David, Zámocká 13 (☎544 138 24). The only kosher restaurant in Bratislava. Elegant decor and excellent dishes (90-397Sk). Open daily 7am-10pm. AmEx/MC/V. ❸

SIGHTS

NÁMESTIE SNP AND ENVIRONS. Most of the city's major attractions are in the **Staré Mesto** (Old Town). From Nám. SNP, which commemorates the bloody 1944 Slovak National Uprising, walk down Uršulínska to the pink-and-gold **Primate's Palace** (Primaciálný Palác), built in the 1700s for Hungary's religious leaders and now home to Bratislava's mayor. In the **Hall of Mirrors** (Zrkadlová Sieň), Napoleon and Austrian Emperor Franz I signed the 1805 Peace of Pressburg. *(Primaciálné nám. 1. Open Tu-Su 10am-5pm. 40Sk, students free.)* Turn left down Kostolná out of the palace to reach **Hlavné námestie,** home to the **Municipal Museum** (Muzeum Mesta) and its 1:500 scale model of mid-1900s Bratislava. *(Hlavné nám. 1. ☎592 051 30. Open Tu-F 10am-5pm, Sa-Su 11am-6pm. 30Sk, students 20Sk.)* Continue to the opposite end of the square and go left onto Rybárska Brána to reach **Hviezdoslavovo námestie,** home to the gorgeous 1886 **Slovak National Theater** (Slovenské Národné Divadlo). Go through the square, head down Mostová, and turn left at the river to reach the **Slovak National Gallery** (Slovenská Národná Galéria), which displays Gothic and Baroque art and some modern sculptures. *(Rázusovo nábr. 2. ☎544 345 87; www.sng.sk. Open Tu-Su 10am-6pm. 80Sk, students 40Sk.)* With the Danube on your left, walk along the waterfront to the gaudy, neon-lit **Nový Most** (New Bridge), designed by the Communist government in the 70s. Backtrack from the bridge, turn left on Rigeleho, go straight onto Strakova (which becomes Ventúrska, then Michalská), and pass through **St. Michael's Tower** (Michalská Brána), the city's last remaining medieval gateway. Turn left onto Kapucínska and cross the pedestrian bridge over the highway to reach the **Museum of Jewish Culture,** which preserves artifacts from Slovak Jews. *(Múzeum Židovskej Kultúry; Židovská 17. ☎54 41 85 07; www.slovak-jewish-heritage.org. Open Su-F 11am-5pm. Last admission 4:30pm. 200Sk, students 60Sk.)*

CASTLES. The four-towered **Bratislava Castle** (Bratislavský hrad) is the city's defining landmark. After an 1811 fire and WWII bombing, the castle was restored in the Communist era. A museum displays art and artifacts, and the towers provide fantastic views of the Danube. From Nový Most, climb the stairs to Židovská; turn left and climb another set of stairs to the castle. *(Museum ☎544 114 44. Castle open daily Apr.-Sept. 9am-8pm; Oct.-Mar. 9am-6pm. Museum open Tu-Su 9am-5pm. Last admission 4:15pm. Castle free. Museum 80Sk, students 40Sk.)* The ruins of **Devín Castle** (Devínsky hrad) lie on an imposing cliff above the Danube and Morava, a stone's throw from Austria. Originally a Celtic fortification, the castle was owned by the Romans, Slavs, and Hungarians before Napoleon destroyed it in 1809. A museum highlights its history. *(Bus #29 from below Nový Most to the last stop, 9km west of Bratislava. ☎657 301 05. Open May-Sept. daily 9am-6pm. Last admission 5:30pm. Museum 80Sk, students 40Sk.)*

ENTERTAINMENT AND NIGHTLIFE

The theater season runs September through June. BKIS (p. 870) carries the monthly *Kam v Bratislave,* with film, concert, and theater schedules. Ballets and operas at the **Slovak National Theater** (Slovenské Národné Divadlo), Hviezdoslavovo nám. 1, draw crowds from Austria. (☎544 337 94; www.snd.sk. Box office open Sept.-June M-F noon-8pm. Tickets 100-200Sk.) The **Slovak Philharmonic** (Slovenská Filharmónia), Medená 3, has two to three performances per week in fall and winter. The box office, Palackého 2, is around the corner. (☎544 333 51; www.filharm.sk. Open M-Tu and Th-F 1-7pm, W 8am-2pm. Tickets 100-200Sk.)

By day, **Hlavné námestie** has souvenir stands and free outdoor concerts; by night, it fills with couples and teens. Join the menagerie onboard Bratislava's wildest floating disco, **Cirkus Barok,** Rázusovo nábrezie, on a boat in the Danube. (www.cirkusbarok.sk. Beer 45Sk. Open Su-Th 11am-4am, F-Sa 11am-6am.) **Klub Laverna,** Nám. SNP 25, has a packed dance floor and a slide between its levels. (Cover 100Sk. Open daily 9pm-6am.) DJs spin hot tunes at **Charlie Club,** Špitálska 4. (Open W-Sa 6pm-6am.) The slick **Jazz Café,** Ventúrska 5, has a reputation for excellent live jazz. (Drinks 90-170Sk. Jazz Th-Sa 9pm-2am. Cafe open daily 10am-2am. Club open M-F 2pm-2am, Sa-Su 11am-2am.)

THE TATRA MOUNTAINS (TATRY)

> **!** The Tatras are a great place to hike, but many of the hikes require experience and are extremely demanding, even in summer. In winter, a guide is almost always necessary. For current conditions, check **www.tanap.sk.**

The mesmerizing Tatras, spanning the border between the Slovak Republic and Poland, form the highest part of the Carpathian mountain range. The High Tatras feature sky-scraping hikes, glacial lakes, and deep snows. Sadly, many of the lower slopes on the Slovak side of the High Tatras were devastated by freak storms and mudslides in the fall of 2004, and vast swaths of the formerly lush pine forest are now brown fields of broken trees. Recent forest fires further scarred the landscape, though the upper regions escaped largely unscathed. To the south, the separate Low Tatras have ski resorts and tree-covered mountains.

LIPTOVSKÝ MIKULÁŠ

Liptovský Mikuláš (pop. 33,000) is a springboard for hikes in the **Low Tatras** (Nízke Tatry). To scale **Mt. Ďumbier** (2043m), the region's tallest peak, catch an early bus to Liptovský Ján (25-30min., every 1-2hr., 16-20Sk), then follow the blue trail up the Štiavnica River toward the **Svidovské Sedlo.** Go right at the red trail (2hr.), then begin the 1½hr. climb up Sedlo Javorie. Head left on the yellow trail to the summit of Mt. Ďumbier (2½hr.). Descend the ridge and follow the red sign to **Chopok** (2024m), the second-highest peak in the range. From Chopok, it's a winding walk down the blue trail to the bus stop behind the Hotel Grand at Otupné (1¾hr.).

Hotel Kriváň ❷, Štúrova 5, opposite the tourist office, has basic, centrally located rooms. (☎044 552 24 14. Singles 350Sk, with bath 450Sk; doubles 570/770Sk. Cash only.) The local favorite **Liptovská Izba Reštaurácia ❶,** nám. Osloboditeľov 22, serves delicious Slovak dishes. (☎044 551 48 53. Entrees 65-188Sk. Open M-Sa 10am-10pm, Su noon-10pm. Cash only.) Buy supplies at **Coop Supermarket,** ul. 1 Maja 54, in the Prior Building. (Open M-F 7am-8pm, Sa 7am-7pm, Su 8am-5pm. MC/V.) **Trains** from Liptovský Mikuláš to Bratislava (4hr., 12 per day, 364Sk) are cheaper than buses. To reach the town center from the station, follow Štefánikova toward the gas station at the far end of the lot, go right on Hodžu, and take a left on Štúrova. The **tourist office,** nám. Mieru 1, in the Dom Služieb complex, books private rooms (245-400Sk) and sells hiking maps. (☎044 552 24 18; www.mikulas.sk. Open mid-June to mid-Sept. M-F 8am-6pm, Sa 8am-noon, Su 11am-4pm; low season reduced hours.)

DEMÄNOVSKÁ JASKYŇA SLOBODY (DEMÄNOV CAVE OF LIBERTY). Named for its role in WWII, this two-million-year-old cave stored Slovak National Uprising supplies. Tours are mandatory, with two lengths offered. The short tour covers 1.5km and passes through breathtaking underground chambers, lakes, and a magnificent waterfall, all carved out of rock by water falling at a rate of one drop per day. The longer tour includes 2km of additional corridors. Bring a sweater. (☎559 16 73; www.ssj.sk. Open June-Aug. Tu-Su 9:30am-4pm, entrance every hr.; Sept. to mid-Nov. and mid-Dec. to May 9:30am-2pm, entrance every 1½hr. 45min. tour 150Sk, with ISIC 130Sk. 2hr. tour 300/200Sk.) To get to the cave, take the **bus** from platform #2 in Liptovský Mikuláš to Demänovská Dolina, get off at Demänovská jaskyňa slobody (20-35min., 1 per hr. 6:25am-10pm, 18Sk), and walk to the cave on the blue trail toward Pusté Sedlo Machnate (1½hr.).

STARÝ SMOKOVEC ☎052

Spectacular trails begin at Starý Smokovec, the central resort in the **High Tatras.** A funicular picks up passengers behind the train station and takes them to **Hrebienok** (1285m), the starting point for many hikes. (Open daily 7:30am-5pm. Ascent July-Aug. 120Sk, Sept.-June 90Sk; descent 40/30Sk; round-trip 150/100Sk.) Alternatively, from the funicular station, hike 35min. up the green trail to Hrebienok. The green trail then continues 20min. north to the foaming **Cold Stream Waterfalls** (Volopáday studeného potoka). From the falls, take the red trail, which connects with the eastward blue trail to **Tatranská Lomnica** (1¾hr.). The hike to **Little Cold Valley** (Malá studená dolina) is fairly relaxed.

Several chalets along the trails provide lodging for travelers. **Zamkovského chata** ❷ (☎442 26 36) is on the red trail (40min.) from Hrebienok. The green trail (2hr.) climbs above the treeline to a high lake and another chalet, **Téryho chata ❷.** (☎442 52 45. Dorms 360Sk.) Inexpensive accommodations in the town of Starý Smokovec are scarce; inquire at the tourist office. *Penzión* runners greeting backpackers at the station often offer the cheapest beds (500-600Sk per person). The conveniently located, newly refurbished **Penzión Tatra** ❸ offers tidy rooms and comfortable amenities. Turn right out of the train station; the pension is on the right just before the bus station. (☎903 650 802; www.tatraski.sk. Rooms 650-750Sk.) More budget options are located two TEŽ stops away in **Horný Smokovec.** Worthwhile restaurants cluster above the bus and train stations in Starý Smokovec. Buy supplies at **Supermarket Sintra** in the shopping complex opposite the bus station. (Open M-F 8am-8pm, Sa 8am-8:45pm, Su noon-8:45pm. MC/V.)

TEŽ trains run to Poprad (30min., 1 per hr., 20Sk). **Buses** run to Bratislava (6hr., 2 per day, 440Sk) and Levoča (20-50min., 2-4 per day, 60Sk). The **Tatranská Informačná Kanceléria (TIK),** in Dom Služieb, provides weather forecasts, sells the essential VKÚ map #113 (90Sk) and other hiking maps, and books private rooms. (☎442 34 40; www.zcrvt.szm.sk. Rooms 250-300Sk; pensions 500Sk; hotels 650Sk. Open daily June-Sept. 8am-5pm; Oct.-May. 9am-noon and 12:30-4pm.)

HIKING NEAR STARÝ SMOKOVEC. The town of **Štrbské Pleso** is the base for many beautiful hikes. From the tourist office, pass the souvenir lot and go left at the junction. Head uphill to reach the lift that carries visitors 1840m up to **Chata pod Soliskom,** a chalet overlooking the lakes and valleys. (☎905 652 036. Dorms 230Sk. Lift open daily late May-Sept. and Dec.-Mar. 8:30am-4pm. Last lift up 3:30pm. 130Sk, children 90Sk; round-trip 190/130Sk.) Alternatively, continue on the challenging yellow trail and along **Mlynická dolina** past several enchanting mountain lakes and the dramatic **Vodopády Skok** waterfalls. The path (6-7hr.) involves strenuous ascents on **Bystré Sedlo** (2314m) and **Veľké Solisko** (2412m). At the end of the yellow trail, turn left onto the red trail to complete the loop and return to Štrbské Pleso (30min.). Stock up on trail snacks at the **grocery store** opposite the train station (open 7am-10pm). A **TEŽ train** runs to Štrbské Pleso from Starý Smokovec (30min., 1-2 per hr., 30Sk). The **tourist office** is across from the train station. (Open M-F 8:30am-4pm, Sa-Su 8:30am-3:30pm; low season reduced hours.)

SLOVENSKÝ RAJ. Southeast of the Low Tatras, the less-touristed Slovenský Raj (Slovak Paradise) National Park is filled with forested hills, deep ravines, and fast-flowing streams. The excellent **trail guide,** VKÚ map #4, is available at many hotels. The **Dobšinská Ice Caves** (Dobšinská ľadová jaskyňa) are composed of 110,000 cubic meters of water still frozen from the last Ice Age. Tours cover 475m, passing halls of frozen columns, gigantic ice wells, and waterfalls that don't fall. Dress warmly. (☎788 14 70; www.ssj.sk. Open daily July-Aug. 9am-4pm, entrance every hr.; mid-May to June and early to mid-Sept. 9:30am-2pm, entrance every 1½hr. Guided tour only; min. 40 people for English-language. 150Sk, with ISIC 20Sk.) **Buses** run directly to the caves from Poprad (2hr., 8 per day, 34Sk) and Spišská Nová Ves (3-3½hr., 6 per day, 73-146Sk). To get to the caves from **Dedinky** (pop. 400), on the park's southern border, take the train two stops toward Červana Skala (15min., 3 per day, 36Sk). Head 100m to the main road, turn left, and continue to the parking lot, where the steep blue trail (20min.) leads up to the caves.

KOŠICE ☎055

Established nearly 900 years ago, Košice (KO-shih-tseh; pop. 236,000) is the Slovak Republic's second-largest city. Every October, athletes from around the world converge at the Košice Peace Marathon, the oldest in Europe. The city's enchanting Staré Mešto (Old Town) is home to peaceful fountains, shady parks, and the largest church in the Slovak Republic, the magnificent Cathedral of St. Elizabeth. Outside the center, towering concrete housing blocks surround the city for miles, providing a stark reminder of Košice's Communist past.

TRANSPORTATION AND PRACTICAL INFORMATION. Trains (☎613 20 68) run from the station on Predstaničné nám. to: Bratislava (6hr., 13 per day, 518Sk); Budapest, HUN (5hr., 3 per day, 741Sk); Kraków, POL (6-7hr., 3 per day, 855Sk); Poprad (1¼hr., 15 per day, 154Sk); Prešov (50min., 10 per day, 42Sk). **Buses** (☎625 16 19), slightly cheaper and slower, depart from the terminal to the left of the train station. To reach the city center, exit the train station and follow the "Centrum" signs across the park. Walk down **Mlynská** to reach the main square, **Hlavná námestie,** or take tram #6 to nám. Osloboditeľov and turn right to find the **tourist office,** Hlavná nám. 58. (☎625 88 88; www.kosice.sk. Open M-F 9am-6pm, Sa 9am-1pm.) Check email at **Internet Cafe,** Hlavná nám. 24. (40Sk per hr. Open daily 9am-11pm.) Košice's **post office,** Poštová 20, has *Poste Restante* at window #16. (☎617 14 01. Open M-F 7am-7pm, Sa 8am-noon.) **Postal Code:** 04001.

ACCOMMODATIONS AND FOOD. Hotels and pensions add a tax of 20Sk per person per night. **K2 Tourist Hotel ❷,** Štúrova 32, is a bargain near Staré Mešto and provides lots of info for travelers. From Hlavná nám., turn right on Štúrova. (☎625 59 48. Reception 24hr. Check-in and check-out noon. 3- to 4-bed dorms 375Sk. AmEx.) Farther away from the city center, **Hotel Kohal ❸,** Trieda SNP 61, includes a hostel with bare-bones singles and doubles. Hotel rooms have TV and apartments have private bath. To get there, take tram #6 from the train/bus station to the fifth stop, "Ferrocentrum" or "Spoločenský Pavilón." (☎/fax 642 55 72; www.hotelkohal.sk. Breakfast 80Sk. Laundry 10-70Sk per item. Reception 24hr. Check-out 11am. Hostel singles 375Sk; doubles 600Sk. Hotel singles 600Sk; doubles 990Sk. Apartments 1400Sk. AmEx/MC/V.)

The popular **Reštaurácia Veverička** ❷ (Squirrel Restaurant), Hlavná nám. 97, serves local dishes on its sun-drenched patio. (☎622 33 60. English menu. Entrees 85-290Sk. Open daily 9am-2am. Cash only.) **Reštaurácia Ajvega** ❶, Orlia 10, offers organic Slovak and Mexican food, including vegetarian options. (☎622 04 52. Soups 40-50Sk. Entrees 89-155Sk. Open Su-Th 11am-11pm, F-Sa 11am-midnight. Cash only.) A **Tesco** supermarket is located at Hlavná nám. 109. (☎670 48 10. Open M-Th 8am-10pm, F 8am-midnight, Sa-Su 11am-10pm. MC/V.)

SIGHTS AND NIGHTLIFE. The **Cathedral of St. Elizabeth** (Dom sv. Alžbety), in Hlavná nám., was begun in the high Gothic style in 1378 and has been renovated repeatedly since then. It houses the grave of local revolutionary hero Ferenc Rakóczi II. Climb the north tower for a view of Staré Mešto and the intricate cathedral roof. (Crypt and tower open M 1-5pm, Tu-F 9am-5pm, Sa 9am-1pm. Crypt 20Sk, students 15Sk; tower 35/20Sk; interior 30/15Sk; combination ticket 70/35Sk.) The **East Slovak Museum** (Východnoslovenské Múzeum), Hrnčiarska 7, includes Rakóczi's House, an exhibit on the rebellion leader, and Mikluš's Prison, an exposé of life behind bars from the 17th to 19th centuries. From Hlavná nám., take a right at the State Theatre onto Univerzitná. (Open Tu-Sa 9am-5pm, Su 9am-1pm. Mandatory Slovak-language tours every hr. 40Sk, students 20Sk. Prison exhibit 30/15Sk.) The **archaeological branch** of the museum, Hviezdoslavova nám. 2, chronicles the Sariš region with tools, bones, and photos. (☎622 05 71. Open Tu-Sa 9am-5pm, Su 9am-1pm. 50Sk, students 20Sk. English guidebook 30Sk.)

The stylish **Jazz Club,** Kováčska 39, houses a disco and pub. (☎622 42 37. Beer 25-35Sk. M and W jazz and funk. Tu and Th-Sa disco nights, cover 30-50Sk. Open daily 4pm-2am, disco nights until 3am.) Party-goers are off to the races at the Formula 1-themed **Monopost,** Hlavná nám. 54. (Tu and F-Sa disco nights. Open M and W-Th 11am-midnight, Tu 11am-3am, F 11am-4am, Sa 2pm-4am.)

SLOVENIA (SLOVENIJA)

Slovenia, the most prosperous of Yugoslavia's breakaway republics, has reveled in independence and quickly distinguished itself from its neighbors. With an eye westward, Slovenia has used its liberal politics and economic output to enter NATO and the EU, and it is poised to become the first Eastern European country to adopt the euro. Modernization, however, has not affected the tiny country's natural beauty and diversity. It is still possible to eat breakfast on an Alpine peak, lunch under the Adriatic sun, and dinner in a Pannonian vineyard, all in one day.

DISCOVER SLOVENIA: SUGGESTED ITINERARIES

THREE DAYS. In **Ljubljana** (p. 882), the charming cafe culture and nightlife, especially in eclectic, Soviet-chic Metelkova, is worth at least two days. Then relax in tranquil, fairy-tale **Bled** (1 day; p. 886).

ONE WEEK. After 3 days in the capital city **Ljubljana,** enjoy **Bled** (1 day) and its cousin **Bohinj** (1 day; p. 887). Head down the coast to the mini-Venice of **Piran** (2 days; p. 885).

ESSENTIALS

FACTS AND FIGURES

Official Name: Republic of Slovenia.
Capital: Ljubljana.
Major Cities: Celje, Kranj, Maribor.
Population: 2,010,000.
Land Area: 20,151 sq. km.
Time Zone: GMT +1.
Language: Slovenian.
Religions: Roman Catholic (58%), Orthodox (2%), Muslim (2%).

WHEN TO GO

During the hot months of July and August, tourists flood the coast and accommodation prices rise with the temperature. The early autumn and spring offer sparse crowds and great weather for hiking and exploring the countryside. Skiing is popular from December to March.

DOCUMENTS AND FORMALITIES

EMBASSIES AND CONSULATES. Embassies of other countries in Slovenia are all in Ljubljana (p. 882). Slovenia's embassies and consulates abroad include: **Australia,** Level 6, St. George's Building, 60 Marcus Clarke St., Canberra, ACT, 2601 (☎2 6243 4830); **Canada,** 150 Metcalfe St., Ste. 2101, Ottawa, ON, K2P 1P1 (☎613-565-5781); **Ireland,** Morrison Chambers, 2nd fl., 32 Nassau St., Dublin, 2 (☎1 670 5240); **New Zealand,** P.O. Box 30247, Eastern Hutt Rd., Pomare, Lower Hutt, Wellington (☎4 567 0027); **UK,** 10 Little College St., London, SW1P 3SH (☎7222 5400); **US,** 1525 New Hampshire Ave., NW, Washington, D.C., 20036 (☎202-667-5363).

VISA AND ENTRY INFORMATION. A **visa** is not required for EU citizens. Citizens of Australia, Canada, New Zealand, and the US do not need visas for stays of up to 90 days. Visas cost US$45 and require an application, a letter of guarantee, and a personal interview at your home embassy or consulate. Visas are not available at the border, and there is no fee for crossing.

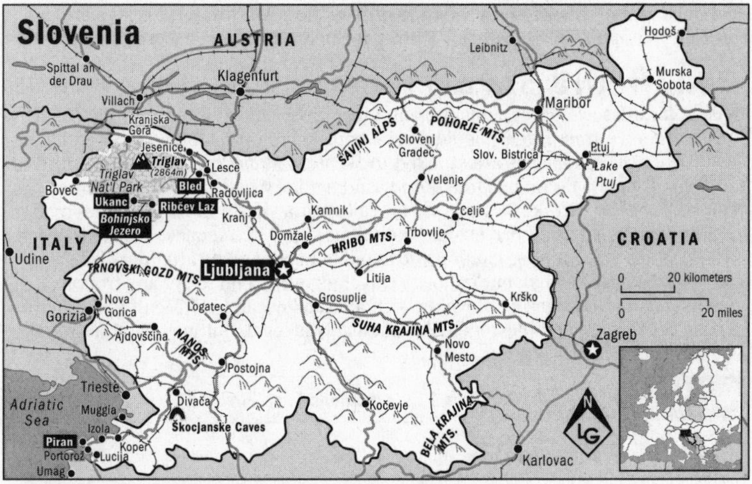

TOURIST SERVICES AND MONEY

ENTRANCE REQUIREMENTS

Passport: Required for all travelers.
Visa: Not required for EU citizens. Not required for stays of under 90 days for citizens of Australia, Canada, New Zealand, and the US.
Letter of Invitation: Not required.
Inoculations: Not required. Recommended up-to-date on DTaP (diphtheria, tetanus, and pertussis), hepatitis A, hepatitis B, MMR (measles, mumps, and rubella), polio booster, and typhoid.
Work Permit: Required for all foreigners planning to work.
Driving Permit: Required for all those planning to drive.

TOURIST OFFICES. There are tourist offices in most major cities and tourist destinations. Staffs generally speak English or German and, on the coast, perfect Italian. They can usually find accommodations for a small fee and generally give advice and maps for free. **Kompas** is the main private tourist organization.

MONEY. The Slovenian unit of currency is the tolar (1Sit=100 stotins), plural tolarjev, which comes in denominations of 10, 20, 50, 100, 200, 500, 1000, 5000, and 10,000. Although inflation is currently around 2%, prices may rise when Slovenia adopts the euro on January 1, 2007. **SKB Banka, Nova Ljubljanska Banka,** and **Gorenjska Banka** are common banks. American Express Travelers Cheques are accepted almost everywhere, but major **credit cards** are not consistently accepted. MasterCard and Visa **ATMs** are everywhere. Normal business hours are Monday through

TOLAR (SIT)		
	AUS$1 = 139.57SIT	100SIT = AUS$0.72
	CDN$1 = 168.52SIT	100SIT = CDN$0.60
	EUR€1 = 239.76SIT	100SIT = EUR€0.42
	NZ$1 = 117.04SIT	100SIT = NZ$0.86
	UK£1 = 349.23SIT	100SIT = UK£0.29
	US$1 = 185.51SIT	100SIT = US$0.54

Friday 8am-4pm; banks and exchange offices Monday through Friday 7am-7pm, Saturday 7am-noon; shops Monday through Friday 9am-7pm, Saturday 9am-4pm.

HEALTH AND SAFETY

Medical facilities are of high quality, and most have English-speaking doctors. UK citizens receive free urgent medical care with a valid passport; other foreigners must pay cash. **Pharmacies** are stocked to Western standards; there you will find bandages *(obliž)*, tampons *(tamponi)*, and sanitary pads *(vložki)*. **Tap water** is generally safe to drink. **Crime** is rare in Slovenia. Even in large cities, overly friendly drunks and bad drivers are the greatest public menace. **Female travelers** should, as always, exercise caution and avoid being out alone after dark. There are few **minorities** in Slovenia, but minority travelers don't tend to get any trouble, just curious glances. Navigating Slovenia with a **disability** can be difficult and requires caution on slippery cobblestones. **Homosexuality** is legal, but may elicit unfriendly reactions outside urban areas.

EMERGENCY	**Police:** ☎113. **Ambulance** and **Fire:** ☎112.

TRANSPORTATION

BY PLANE AND BOAT. Commercial flights all arrive at **Ljubljana Airport (LJU).** Most major European airlines offer connections to the national carrier **Adria Airways.** To enter the country cheaply, consider flying to Vienna, AUT, and taking a train to Ljubljana. Regular **ferry** services connect Piran and Portorož to Venice, ITA, during the summer.

BY TRAIN AND BUS. First and second class do not differ much; save your money and take the latter. Travelers under 26 can get a 20% discount on most international rail fares. ISIC holders get 30% off domestic tickets; ask for a discount *(popust)*. Some useful transportation terms are arrivals *(prihodi vlakov)*, departures *(odhodi vlakov)*, and daily *(dnevno)*. Though usually more expensive than trains, buses are often the only option in mountainous regions. The bus is also a better choice than the train to Bled, as the train station is far from town. Buy bus tickets at the station or on board. Large backpacks cost 220Sit extra.

BY CAR AND BIKE. Car rental agencies in Ljubljana offer reasonable rates, and Slovenia's roads are in good condition. Nearly every town has a bike rental office; renting one will generally cost 2000-3000Sit per day. While those who partake in it insist upon its safety, **hitchhiking** is not recommended by Let's Go.

KEEPING IN TOUCH

PHONE CODES	**Country code:** 386. **International dialing prefix:** 00. For more information on placing international calls, see inside back cover.

EMAIL AND THE INTERNET. Internet connections are very fast and common. Though free Internet access is rare, there are Internet cafes in most major tourist destinations. Expect to pay 1000-1500Sit per hour.

TELEPHONE. All phones take **phonecards,** sold at post offices, kiosks, and gas stations. Fifty units (1½min. to the US) cost 750Sit. Dial ☎115 for collect calls, and 1180 for the international operator. Calling abroad without a phonecard is expensive (over US$6 per min. to the US). Use phones at the post office and pay when you're finished.

MAIL. Airmail *(letalsko)* takes one to two weeks to reach North America, Australia, and New Zealand. Letters to Australia and New Zealand cost 110Sit and postcards cost 100Sit; to the UK 100/90Sit; to the US 105/100Sit. Mail can be received through **Poste Restante.** Address envelopes as follows: First name LAST NAME, *Poste Restante,* post office address, Postal Code, city, SLOVENIA.

LANGUAGE. **Slovenian** is a South Slavic language written in the Latin alphabet. Most young Slovenes speak at least some **English,** but the older generations are more likely to understand **German** or **Italian.** The tourist industry is generally geared toward Germans, but most tourist office employees speak some English.

ACCOMMODATIONS AND CAMPING

SLOVENIA	❶	❷	❸	❹	❺
ACCOMMODATIONS	under 3500Sit	3500-5000Sit	5000-6500Sit	6500-8000Sit	over 8000Sit

A nightly **tourist tax** is charged at all accommodations. **Youth hostels** and **student dormitories** are cheap (2500-3500Sit) and fun, but generally open only in summer (approximately June 25-Aug. 25). **Hotels** fall into five categories—L (deluxe), A, B, C, and D—and are expensive. **Pensions** are the most common form of accommodation; usually they have private singles as well as inexpensive dorms. **Private rooms** are the only cheap option on the coast and at Lake Bohinj. Prices vary, but they rarely exceed US$30. Inquire at the tourist office or look for *Zimmer frei* or *Sobe* signs. **Campgrounds** can be crowded, but are in excellent condition. Camp in designated areas to avoid fines.

FOOD AND DRINK

SLOVENIA	❶	❷	❸	❹	❺
FOOD	under 800Sit	800-1200Sit	1200-1800Sit	1800-2400Sit	over 2400Sit

For homestyle cooking, try a *gostilna* or *gostišče* (country-style inn or restaurant). Traditional meals begin with *jota*, a soup with potatoes, beans, and sauerkraut. Pork is the basis for many dishes, such as *vinjska pečenka* (roast pork) and the uniquely Slovenian *Karst* ham. **Kosher** eating thus becomes very difficult, as does finding a **vegetarian** meal. Slovenia's **wine-making** tradition dates from antiquity. *Renski Rizling* and *Šipon* are popular whites and *Cviček* and *Teran* are favorite reds. Brewing is centuries old as well; good beers include *Laško* and *Union*. For something stronger, try *žganje*, a fruit brandy, or *Viljamovka*, a *raki* distilled by monks who know the secret of getting a whole pear inside the bottle.

HOLIDAYS AND FESTIVALS

Holidays: New Year's Day (Jan. 1); Prešeren Day (Feb. 8); Easter (Apr. 8); Day of Uprising against Occupation (WWII; Apr. 27); Labor Day (May 1); Reformation Day (Oct. 31).

Festivals: In July and August, Ljubljana's International Summer Festival is the nation's most famous, featuring ballet, music, and theater. The Peasant Wedding *(Kmečka Ohcet)*, held in Bohinj at the end of July or in early August, and the Cows' Ball *(Kravji Bal)* in mid-September, which celebrates the return of the cows to the valleys from higher pastures, are a couple of the country's many summertime folk exhibitions.

BEYOND TOURISM

Central Bureau for Educational Visits and Exchanges, 10 Spring Gardens, London, SW1A 2BN, UK (www.britishcouncil.org/learnenglish). Places qualified British undergraduates and teachers in teaching positions in Hungary, Russia, and Slovenia.

World-Wide Opportunities on Organic Farms (WWOOF), Main Office, P.O. Box 2675, Lewes, East Sussex, BN7 1RB, UK (www.wwoof.org). Arranges volunteer work on organic and eco-conscious farms in Slovenia and around the world. Membership €10.

LJUBLJANA ☎01

The average traveler only stops in Ljubljana (loob-lee-AH-na; pop. 280,000) for an hour en route from Venice to Zagreb, but those who stay longer become enchanted by this lively town full of folklore. Dragons protect one of the many bridges, street performances liven up summer nights, and Baroque monuments, Art Nouveau facades, and modern high-rises tell of the city's richly layered history.

TRANSPORTATION

Trains: Trg O.F. 6 (☎291 33 32; www.slo-zeleznice.si). To: **Bled** (1hr., 14 per day, 890Sit); **Budapest, HUN** (9hr.; 3 per day; 14,836Sit); **Munich, GER** (7hr.; 3 per day; 15,200Sit); **Trieste, ITA** (3¾hr., 3 per day, 4110Sit); **Vienna, AUT** (5-6hr.; 3 per day; 12,800Sit); **Zagreb, CRO** (2hr., 9 per day, 2700Sit).

Buses: Trg O.F. 4 (☎090 42 30; www.ap-ljubljana.si). To **Bled** (1½hr., 14 her day, 1400Sit) and **Zagreb, CRO** (3hr., 2 per day, 3310Sit).

Public Transportation: Buses run until 10:30pm. Drop 300Sit in the box by the driver or buy 190Sit tokens *(žetoni)* at the tourist office, post offices, or kiosks. Day passes (900Sit) sold at **Ljubljanski Potniški Promet,** Celovška c. 160. Open M-F 6:45am-7pm, Sa 6:45am-1pm.

ORIENTATION AND PRACTICAL INFORMATION

The train and bus stations are on **Trg Osvobodilne Fronte** (Trg O.F. or O.F. Sq.). Turn right as you exit the train station, then left on **Miklošičeva cesta** and follow it to **Prešernov trg,** the main square. Cross the **Tromostovje** (Triple Bridge) over the **Ljubljanica River** to **Stare Miasto** (Old Town) at the base of the castle hill.

Tourist Office: Tourist Information Center, Stritarjeva 1 (☎306 12 15, 24hr. English-language info 090 939 881; www.ljubljana-tourism.si). Pick up **free maps** and the useful, free *Ljubljana from A to Z.* Open daily June-Sept. 8am-9pm; Oct.-May 8am-7pm.

Embassies: Australia, Trg Republike 3 (☎425 42 52). Open M-F 9am-1pm. **Canada,** Miklošičeva c. 19 (☎430 35 70). Open M-F 9am-1pm. **Ireland,** Poljanski nasip 6 (☎300 89 70). Open M-F 9am-noon. **UK,** Trg Republike 3 (☎200 39 10). Open M-F 9am-noon. **US,** Prešernova 31 (☎200 55 00). Open M-F 9am-noon and 2-4pm.

Currency Exchange: Menjalnice booths abound. **Ljubljanska banka** branches throughout town exchange currency for no commission and cash **traveler's checks** for a 1.5% commission. Open M-F 9am-noon and 2-5pm.

Luggage Storage: Lockers *(garderoba)* at train station. 500Sit per 24hr.

24hr. Pharmacy: Lekarna Ljubljana, Prisojna 7 (☎230 62 30).

Internet: Most hostels in Ljubljana offer free Internet. **Cyber Cafe Xplorer,** Petkovško nab. 23 (☎430 19 91; www.sisky.com), has fast connections. 530Sit per 30min., students 477Sit. 20% discount 10am-noon. Open M-F 10am-10pm, Sa-Su 2-10pm.

Post Office: Slovenska 32 (☎426 46 68). *Poste Restante* at *izročitev pošiljk* (outgoing mail) counter. Open M-F 8am-7pm, Sa 8am-1pm. **Postal Code:** 1000.

ACCOMMODATIONS

Finding cheap accommodations in Ljubljana is easier in July and August. The **Slovene National Hostel Association** (**PZS;** ☎231 21 56) provides info on youth hostels in

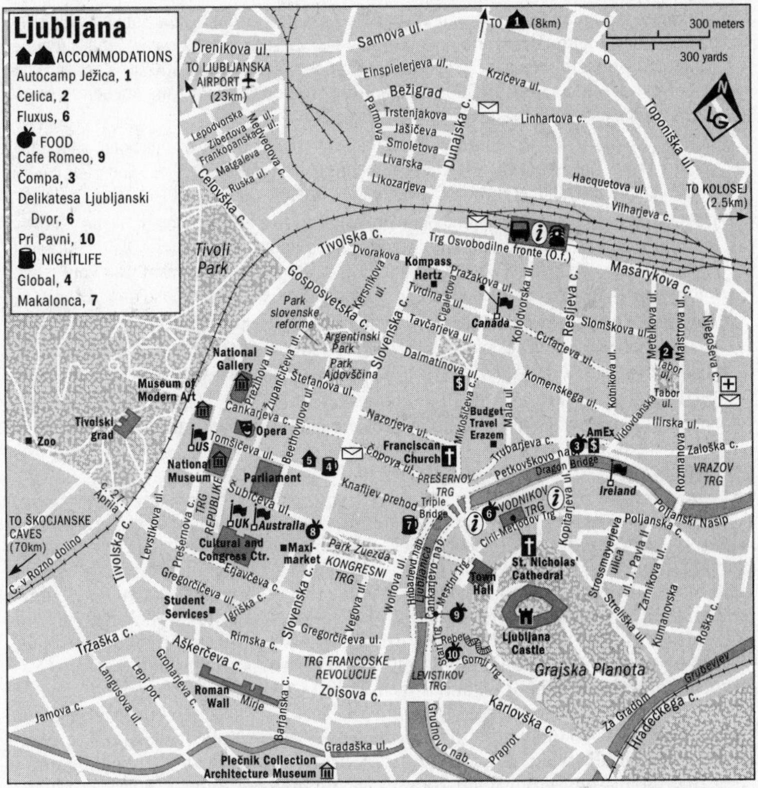

Slovenia. The **Tourist Info Center** finds private rooms (singles 4000-10,000Sit; doubles 7000-15,000Sit). There is a daily **tourist tax** (240Sit) at all establishments.

Celica, Metelkova 8 (☎430 18 90; www.hostelcelica.com). With your back to the train station, walk left down Masarykova, then right on Metelkova. Blue signs will lead the way. Local and foreign artists have transformed this former prison into a modern work of art. Bar, cafe, free Internet, and cultural arts programs. Breakfast included. Reception 24hr. Reserve ahead July-Aug. Dorms 3750-5250Sit. ❷

Fluxus, Tomšičeva 4 (☎251 57 60; www.fluxus-hostel.com). High ceilings, long curtains, and winding staircase in the lobby make Fluxus seem fancier than it is. Free Internet. Check-in 3-8pm. Reserve ahead. Dorms 4900Sit; 1 double 13,000Sit. Cash only. ❷

Autocamp Ježica, Dunajska 270 (☎568 39 13; ac.jezica@gpl.si). Take bus #6 or 8 to Ježica's wooded campgrounds. Bungalows have spacious, impeccably clean rooms with TV and private shower. Reception 24hr. Reserve ahead. Camping 1680-2160Sit per person. Bungalow singles 11,000Sit; doubles 15,000Sit. MC/V. ❶

FOOD

Maximarket, on Trg Republike, has a basement **Mercator** grocery store. (Open M-F 7am-7pm, Sa 7am-5pm.) Buy fruits and vegetables at the **open-air market** by St. Nicholas's Cathedral. (Open M-Sa June-Aug. 6am-6pm; Sept.-May 6am-4pm.)

Cafe Romeo, Stari trg 6. A bakery in the Middle Ages, this haunt is now popular with local hipsters for its retro decor, and is one of few places serving food on Su. Toast grande sandwich with ham, peppers, cucumbers, tomatoes, and cheese 600Sit. Nachos 800-1000Sit. Dessert crepes 650-890Sit. Open for drinks daily 10am-1am; kitchen open M-Sa 11am-midnight, Su 11am-11pm. Cash only. ❷

Čompa, Trubarjeva ul. 40. This cozy little family-run restaurant serves delicious, light Slovenian cuisine. Baked potato with cheese, meat goulash, mixed veggies, and sour cream 1600Sit. Free after-dinner drink with every meal. Open M-Sa 11am-11pm. Cash only. ❹

Pri Pavni, Stari trg 21. Serving traditional Slovenian cuisine and recognized by the "Society for the Recognition of Sauteed Potato and Onions as an Independent Dish," Pri Pavni offers generous portions of flavorful, filling dishes. Try the smoked meat with corn mush with a side of roasted potatoes (1850Sit). Open M-Sa 8am-11pm. Cash only. ❸

Delikatesa Ljubljanski Dvor, Dvorni trg 1, the delicatessen at the back of the riverside pizzeria, serves filling slices of pizza (350Sit). Open M-Sa 9am-midnight. Cash only. ❶

Tomato, Šubičeva ul. 1 (☎252 75 55; www.tomato-si.com). Fast hot or cold sandwiches (380-820Sit). Salads 950-1150Sit. Entrees 1150-1500Sit. Vegetarian and takeout options. Open May-Oct. M-F 7am-10pm; Nov.-Apr. M-F 7am-9pm. AmEx/DC/MC/V. ❷

SIGHTS

A good way to see the sights is a 2hr. walking tour, in English and Slovenian, that departs from the city hall *(rotovž)*, Mestni trg 1. (May-Sept. daily 10am; July-Aug. also M-F 1pm, Su 11am; Oct.-Apr. F-Su 11am. 1500Sit, students 800Sit. Buy tickets right before the tour or at tourist office.) A short walk from city hall, down Stritarjeva and across the Tromostovje (Triple Bridge), leads to Prešernov trg with its pink 17th-century **Franciscan Church** (Frančiškanska cerkev). Cross back to Old Town and take a left to reach the dazzling **St. Nicholas's Cathedral.** (Stolnica Sv. Nikolaia; open daily 6am-noon and 3-7pm. Free.) Continue along the river to Vodnikov trg, where **Zmajski Most** (Dragon Bridge) stretches across the Ljubljanica. On the far side of Vodnikov trg, the narrow path Studentovska leads uphill to **Ljubljana Castle** (Ljubljanski Grad), which has a breathtaking view. (Open daily May-Oct. 10am-9pm; Nov.-Apr. 10am-7pm. English-language tours 1100Sit, students 790Sit.) Cross the Dragon Bridge to Resljeva c., turn left on Tubarjeva c., continue to Prešernov trg, take a left on Wolfova (which becomes Gosposka), then take a right on Zoisova c., and a left onto Emonska ul. Across the bridge is the **Plečnik Collection** (Plečnikova Zbrika), Karunova 5, which exhibits the works of Ljubljana's best-known architect. (Open Tu-Th 10am-2pm. 1000Sit, students 500Sit.) Walking back from the museum, take a left on Zoisova c. and a right onto Slovenska c.; after the Ursuline Church, take a left to find **Trg Republike,** home to the National Parliament and Cankarjev Dom, the city's cultural center. Two blocks past the square, the **National Museum** (Narodni Musei) contains the world's oldest musical instrument and an impressive taxidermy collection. (Open Tu-W, F, and Su 10am-6pm. 1000Sit, students 700Sit. 1st Su of each month free.)

ENTERTAINMENT AND NIGHTLIFE

Ljubljana International Summer Festival hosts music, opera, and theater from mid-June to mid-September. The neighborhood surrounding the former military compound in **Metelkova Mesto,** behind the Celica hostel from Trg Osvobodilne Fronte to the Ethnographic Museum, is now a graffiti-covered artists' colony with plenty of bars and clubs. You might find Sierra Leonean cuisine, an art-house movie screening, or an impromptu sing-along. On a terrace below the waterfront, the cavernous bar **Makalonca,** Hribarjevo nab., just past the Triple Bridge, has gorgeous views of the river, fewer crowds, and more attitude than its neighbors. (Sangria 350Sit. Mixed drinks 500-900Sit. Open M-Sa 10am-1am, Su 10am-3pm.) With castle views, eclectic music, and a disco-era ambience, rooftop **Global,** Tomšičeva 2, is the city's top dance club. (Mixed drinks 900-1400Sit. Sept.-June 1000Sit cover after 9pm; July-Aug. no cover. Bar open M-Sa 8am-9pm. Disco open Th-Sa 9pm-5am.)

PIRAN ☎05

Unlike more modern towns on the Istrian Peninsula, Piran has retained its Venetian charm, with beautiful churches, winding cobblestone streets, and dilapidated medieval architecture. A short walk uphill from behind the red building at Tartinijev trg, the town's central square, leads to the Gothic **Church of St. George** (Cerkev sv. Jurija) and the 17th-century **St. George's Tower,** with a view of Piran and the Adriatic. (Church and tower open daily mid-June to Sept. 10am-1pm and 4-7pm; Oct. to mid-June 11am-5pm. Church free. Tower 150Sit.) From the tower, head away from the church and continue uphill to the medieval **city walls** for the best view of the surrounding area. (Open Apr.-Oct. 8am-8pm; Nov.-Mar. 9am-5pm. Free.) Piran's real attraction, however, is the sea. While the closest sand beach is the neighboring town of Portorož, it's possible to go swimming off the rocky shores, and excellent **scuba diving** can be arranged through **Sub-net,** Prešemovo nab. 24, which runs certification classes and guided dives. (☎673 22 18; www.sub-net.si. 1-3hr. dives 6000-8400Sit for certified divers; 1hr. dives 9600Sit for beginners. Equipment 3000Sit. Open M-F 10am-4pm, Sa 9am-7pm. Cash only.) The **Maritime Museum** (Pomorski Muzej), off Tartinijev trg on Cankarjevo nab., has three stories of exhibits on marine archaeology and seamanship, and an impressive collection of ship replicas. (Open Tu-Su July-Aug. 9am-noon and 6-9pm; Sept.-June 9am-noon and 3-6pm. 800Sit, students 500Sit. Cash only.) July welcomes the **Primorska Summer Festival,** featuring outdoor plays, ballets, and concerts; inquire at the tourist office for schedules.

Maona Travel Agency, Cankarjevo nab. 7, on the waterfront before Tartinijev trg, books private rooms. (☎673 45 20; www.maona.si. Open May-Sept. M-Sa 9am-7pm, Su 9am-1pm and 5-7pm; Oct.-Apr. M-F 9am-4pm, Sa 10am-1pm. Singles 4100-4800Sit; doubles 5800-8400Sit.) **Youth Hostel Val (HI) ❸,** Gregorčičeva 38A, has spotless two- to four-bed suites. From the bus station, follow the coast past Tartinijev trg as it curves away from the harbor; the hostel is three blocks up. (☎673 25 55; www.hostel-val.com. Breakfast included. Reception 8am-10pm. Dorms mid-May to mid-Sept. 5760Sit; mid-Sept. to mid-May

IN RECENT NEWS

BEAR NECESSITIES

Home to one of the largest bea populations in Europe, Sloveni has been helping maintain bea populations in other parts o Europe through its program o bear exports. While the dens woods that cover over half of Slo venia are home to up to 70(black bears, the population in th Pyrenees, for example, has dwi dled to less than 20. As the cl mate and vegetation of th Pyrenees and the Slovenia mountains are quite similar, th French turned to Slovenia fo help. France and Slovenia hav thus signed yet another agree ment for the relocation of five Slo venian bears to the mountainou region in 2006.

The indigenous Slovenian bea population had itself been unde threat of extinction in 1848, bu since black bears were declared protected species after WWII their numbers have increase steadily. The Balkan conflict con tributed to population increase even further, as refugee bear abandoned their disturbed habi tat and fled into Slovenia.

These efforts to safeguard th bears were perhaps a bit to effective, though, and by th 1980s the Slovenian bear popu lation was already considered to high. This resulted in a lift of th bearhunting ban, and in 2006 laws allowed up to 100 bears t be hunted. Thus, all things co sidered, forced migration may no be the worst of the bears' possi ble fates.

4800Sit.) Waterfront cafes line Prešemovo nab., but **Tri Vdove ❷** stands out for its tasty seafood dishes. (☎673 02 90. Entrees 1300-5200Sit. Open daily 10am-midnight.) A **Mercator** supermarket is behind the tourist office, at Levstikova 5. (Open M-F 7am-8pm, Sa 7am-1pm, Su 8am-noon. AmEx/MC/V.) **Buses** arrive from Ljubljana (2¾hr.; M-F 8 per day, Sa 4 per day, Su 6 per day; 2800Sit). The **tourist office** at the central square, Tartinijev trg 2, has bus schedules and free maps. (☎673 02 20. Open daily mid-June to mid-Sept. 8am-1pm and 3-9pm, mid-Sept. to mid-June daily 10am-5pm.) **Postal Code:** 6330.

BLED

☎04

Alpine hills, snow-covered peaks, a turquoise lake, and a stately castle make Bled (pop. 11,000) one of Slovenia's most striking and popular destinations. The **Church of the Assumption** (Cerkev Marijinega Vnebovzetja) rises from the only Slovenian island in the center of the lake. To get there, either rent a boat (1st hr. 2400-2500Sit, each additional hr. 1500Sit), hop on a gondola (round-trip 2400Sit), or just swim (500m from the west side of the lake, next to the campground). At the edge of a rock face rising above the lake's shores is **Bled Castle** (Blejski grad), built in 1004. It contains a museum detailing the archaeological history of the region and an amazing view of Bled and the mountains surrounding it. (Open daily May-Oct. 8am-8pm; Nov.-Apr. 8am-5pm. 1450Sit, students 1200Sit. AmEx/DC/MC.) **Soteska Vintgar,** a 1.6km gorge carved by the waterfalls and rapids of the Radovna River, winds through the rocks of the **Triglav National Park** (Triglavski Narodni Park) and culminates with the 16m **Šum Waterfall** (go down the stairs behind the second ticket booth). To reach the trailhead (4km from Bled), follow the signs for Blejski Grad. Once at the bottom of the castle hill, follow the signs for Vintgar. (Tourist bus from Bled mid-June to Sept. 10am, 700Sit. Trail open daily 8am-7pm. 700Sit, students 600Sit. Cash only.)

Agency Kompas, Ljubljanska c. 4, on the top floor of the shopping center, books private rooms and rents outdoor equipment. (☎572 75 00; www.kompas-bled.si. Singles 2400-5000Sit. Bikes 700Sit per hr., 1800Sit per ½-day, 2400Sit per day. Open mid-May to Sept. M-Sa 8am-8pm, Su 8am-noon and 4-7pm; Oct. to mid-May 8am-7pm, Su 8am-noon and 4-7pm. AmEx/MC/V.) The comfortable dorm beds, spotless private baths, and filling breakfast at **Bledec Youth Hostel (HI) ❸,** Grajska c. 17, make it more like a pension. Turn left from the bus station and follow the street to the top, bearing left at the fork. (☎574 52 50; www.mlino.si. Breakfast included. Laundry 2000Sit. Internet 500Sit per 30min. Reception 24hr. Book ahead in July-Aug. Dorms 4200-4560Sit; doubles 9000Sit. 480Sit HI discount.) To reach lakeside **Camping Bled ❶,** Kidričeva 10C, from the Bled Jezero train station, walk down the steep footpath across from the station and then bear right along the lake for 5min. From the bus station, walk downhill on c. Svobode, turn right, and walk along the lake for about 3km. (☎575 20 00; www.camping.bled.si. Electricity 745Sit. Laundry 1100Sit. Reception 24hr. Check-out at noon. Open Apr. to mid-Oct. Tent sites 1560-2650Sit. AmEx/DC/MC/V.) Big portions and excellent service distinguish **Gostilna pri Planincu ❸,** Grajska c. 8, near the bus station. (☎574 16 13. Pizza 1100-2500Sit. Crepes 600-800Sit. Entrees 900-1700Sit. Open daily 9am-11pm.) **Trains** leave from the Lesce-Bled station, about 4km from Bled, for Ljubljana (1hr., 11 per day, 1150Sit). **Buses** from Bled go to: Bohinjsko Jezero (35min., 1 per hr. 7:20am-8:20pm, 790Sit); Lesce (10min., 4 per hr. 5am-10pm, 300Sit); Ljubljana (1½hr., 1 per hr. 5am-9:30pm, 1400Sit); Vintgar (June-Sept. 1 per day 10am, returns 12:30pm; 600Sit, round-trip 1080Sit.) The lakeside **tourist office,** on the corner of the c. Svobode 10 building, sells fishing licenses (5400Sit and up) and detailed maps (1800Sit) of Bled and nearby hiking trails. (☎574 11 22; www.bled.si. Open July-Aug. M-Sa 8am-9pm, Su 10am-6pm; Sept.-Oct. M-Sa 8am-7pm, Su 11am-5pm; Nov.-

Apr. M-Sa 9am-6pm, Su noon-4pm; May M-Sa 8am-7pm, Su noon-5pm; June M-Sa 8am-8pm, Su 11am-6pm.) **Postal Code:** 4260.

LAKE BOHINJ (BOHINJSKO JEZERO) ☎04

Although it is only 26km southwest of Bled, Bohinjsko Jezero (BOH-heen-sko YEH-zeh-roh) is worlds away from Bled's five-star hotels. The three farming villages that border the glacial lake, Ribčev Laz, Stara Fužina, and Ukanc, retain a traditional Slovenian atmosphere. Surrounded by **Triglav National Park,** Lake Bohinj is Slovenia's center for alpine tourism. Hikes range from casual to nearly impossible. Trails are marked with a white circle inside a red circle; trail maps are available at the **tourist office** in Bohinjska Bistrica, a bigger town 6km east of the lake. The most popular hike, **Savica Waterfall** (Slap Savica), at the Ukanc end of the lake, is often crowded; strike out on your own. Off the beaten path, just beyond Stara Fužina, the impressive 2km **Mostnica Canyon** (Korita Mostice) ends at a mountain hut with lodging and hot meals. To get to the trailhead, ignore the sign at the bridge in Stara Fužina and cross the bridge, following the road up to the church; turn left at the church and keep right on the road past farmhouses and fields.

The cheapest accommodation options around the lake are private rooms (2200-3600Sit), mountain huts (2400-3600Sit), and campgrounds. In Bohinjska Bistrica, to reach **Camping Danica ❶,** Triglavska 60, head downhill from both the train and bus stations. (☎572 10 55; www.bohinj.si/camping-danica. Electricity 480Sit. Wash and dry each 1000Sit. Reception 24hr. in high season. Check-out 1pm. Open May-Sept., 1370-1920Sit per person. AmEx/MC/V.) Take the bus to Hotel Zlatorog and backtrack 300m to reach the lakeside **AvtoCamp Zlatorog ❶,** Ukanc 2. (☎572 34 82. Electricity 550Sit. Tent rental 1200Sit. Wash and dry each 1000Sit. Reception mid-June to Sept. 7am-10pm, May to mid-June 8am-noon and 4-8pm. Check-out noon. July-Aug. 2020-2520Sit; May-June and Sept. 1520-1920Sit. AmEx/DC/MC/V.) A **Mercator** supermarket neighbors the tourist office. (Open M-Sa 7am-8pm.) **Trains** go from there to Ljubljana via Jesenice (2½hr., 8 per day, 1250Sit). More conveniently, **buses** from Ljubljana (2hr., 1 per hr., 1950Sit) go to Bled (35min., 790Sit) and Bohinjska Bistrica (15min., 1 per hr., 380Sit) en route to the lake; they stop at Hotel Jezero in Ribčev Laz or at Hotel Zlatorog in Ukanc, across the lake. There are many private tourist bureaus in the town of Ribčev Laz, on the eastern edge of Lake Bohinj that book private rooms. In Bohinjska Bistrica, the friendly and helpful **tourist office,** Triglavska c. 35, sells maps, books rooms, and plans guided outings. (☎574 75 90; www.bohinj.si. Open daily June-Aug. and Dec.-Feb. 7am-5pm, Sept.-Nov. and Mar.-May 7am-3pm.) **Postal Code:** 4265.

SPAIN (ESPAÑA)

The fiery spirit of flamenco; the inspirational energy of artistic genius; the explosive merging of urban style and archaic tradition—this is Spain. Here, dry, golden plains give way to rugged coastline, and modern architectural feats rise from ancient plazas. Lose yourself in winding medieval alleyways that lead to bustling city centers, or watch from a sidewalk cafe as curiously hair-styled youth pass by. In Spain, there is always a reason to stay up late, and there is always time for an afternoon *siesta*. Take in the beauty and prepare to be spellbound by the country's contagious passion for life.

DISCOVER SPAIN: SUGGESTED ITINERARIES

THREE DAYS. Soak in **Madrid's** (p. 893) blend of art and culture as you walk through the **Retiro's** gardens and peruse the famed halls of the **Prado, Thyssen-Bornemisza,** and **Nacional Centro de Arte Reina Sofía.** By night, move from the tapas bars of Santa Ana to Malasaña and Chueca. Daytrip to **Segovia** (p. 908) or **El Escorial** (p. 905).

ONE WEEK. Begin in southern Spain, exploring the Alhambra's Moorish palaces in **Granada** (1 day; p. 923) and the mosque in **Córdoba** (1 day; p. 911). After two days in **Madrid,** travel northeast to **Barcelona** (2 days) and the beaches of **Costa Brava** (1 day; p. 944).

BEST OF SPAIN, THREE WEEKS. Begin in **Madrid** (3 days), with a daytrip to **El Escorial** (1 day). Take the high-speed train to **Córdoba** (2 days), and on to **Sevilla** (2 days; p. 914). Catch the bus to to partake in the old-world majesty of **Ronda** (1 day; p. 921) before heading south to charming **Málaga,** on the **Costa del Sol** (1 day, p. 922). Head inland to **Granada** (2 days), then seaward again to **Valencia** (1 day; p. 928) before traveling up the coast to **Barcelona** (3 days). Daytrip to the **Costa Brava** (1 day), taking care not to miss the Teatre-Museu Dalí or the Casa-Museu Salvador Dalí. From Barcelona, head to the beaches and tapas bars of **San Sebastián** (1 day; p. 949) and **Bilbao** (2 days; p. 952), home of the world-famous Guggenheim Museum.

ESSENTIALS

FACTS AND FIGURES

Official Name: Kingdom of Spain.

Capital: Madrid.

Government: Parliamentary monarchy.

Major Cities: Barcelona, Granada, Sevilla, Valencia.

Population: 40,398,000

Time Zone: GMT +1.

Languages: Spanish (Castilian), Basque, Catalán, Galician.

Religions: Roman Catholic (94%).

Largest Paella Ever Made: 20m in diameter; fed 100,000 people (1992).

WHEN TO GO

Summer is high season in Spain. In many parts of the country, *Semana Santa* and other festival days are particularly busy. Tourism peaks in August, when the coastal regions overflow while inland cities empty out. Low season travel has the advantage of lighter crowds and lower prices, but sights reduce their hours.

DOCUMENTS AND FORMALITIES

EMBASSIES. Foreign embassies in Spain are in Madrid. Countries below have consulates in Barcelona. Australia, the UK, and the US have consulates in Sevilla. Spanish embassies abroad include: **Australia,** 15 Arkana St., Yarralumla, ACT 2600; mailing address: P.O. Box 9076, Deakin, ACT 2600 (☎02 62 73 35 55; www.embaspain.com); **Canada,** 74 Stanley Ave., Ottawa, ON K1M 1P4 (☎613-747-2252; www.embaspain.ca); **Ireland,** 17 Merlyn Park, Ballsbridge, Dublin 4 (☎353 269 1640; www.mae.es/embajadas/dublin); **UK,** 39 Chesham Pl., London SW1X 8SB (☎020 7235 5555); **US,** 2375 Pennsylvania Ave., NW, Washington, D.C. 20037 (☎202-728-2330; www.spainemb.org). **New Zealand** citizens should contact the embassy in Australia.

VISA AND ENTRY INFORMATION. EU citizens do not need a visa. Citizens of Australia, Canada, New Zealand, the UK, and the US do not need a visa for stays of up to 90 days, beginning upon entry into any of the countries in the EU's freedom-of-movement zone. For more information, see p. 15.

TOURIST SERVICES AND MONEY

EMERGENCY	**Local Police:** ☎092. **National Police:** ☎091. **Ambulance:** ☎061. **Fire:** ☎080. **Emergency:** ☎112.

TOURIST OFFICES. Spain's official tourist board operates an extensive website at www.tourspain.es. Tourist offices within Spain usually have free maps and region-specific advice for travelers.

MONEY. The **euro (€)** has replaced the peseta as the unit of currency in Spain. For more information, see p. 18. As a general rule it's cheaper to exchange money in Spain than at home. In restaurants, all prices include a service charge. Satisfied customers occasionally toss in some spare change—usually no more than 5%—and while it is purely optional, **tipping** is becoming increasingly widespread in restaurants and other places that cater to tourists. Many people give train, airport, and hotel porters €1 per bag, while taxi drivers sometimes get 5-10%. **Bargaining** is only common at flea markets and with street vendors. Spain has a 7% **value added tax (VAT;** in Spain, **IVA)** on all restaurant meals and accommodations. The prices listed in *Let's Go* include VAT. Retail goods bear a 16% VAT, usually included in the listed price. Non-EU citizens who have stayed in the EU fewer than 180 days can claim a refund on the tax paid. Ask the shop to supply you with a tax return form; most will often provide them only for purchases of more than €50-100.

TRANSPORTATION

BY PLANE. Flights land mainly at Madrid's Barajas Airport (MAD; ☎913 93 60 00) and the Barcelona International Airport (BCN; ☎932 98 38 38). Contact AENA (☎902 40 47 04; www.aena.es) for more info. See p. 42 for info on flying to Spain.

BY TRAIN. Direct trains are available to Madrid and Barcelona from several European cities, including Geneva, Lisbon, and Paris. Spanish trains are clean, relatively punctual, and reasonably priced. However, most train routes do tend to bypass small towns. Spain's national railway is **RENFE** (☎902 24 02 02; www.renfe.es). Avoid *transvía, semidirecto,* or *correo* trains, as they are very slow. *Estrellas* are slow night trains with bunks and showers. *Cercanías* (commuter trains) go from cities to suburbs and nearby towns. There is no reason to buy a Eurailpass if you plan to travel only within Spain. Trains are cheap, so a pass saves little money; moreover, buses are an easier and more efficient means of traveling around Spain. Several Rail Europe passes cover travel within Spain. See www.raileurope.com for more information on the following passes. The **Spain Flexipass** offers three days of unlimited travel in a two-month period. The **Spain Rail 'n' Drive Pass** is good for three days of unlimited first-class train travel and two days of unlimited mileage in a rental car. The **Spain 'n' Portugal Pass** is good for unlimited first-class travel in Spain and Portugal. For more info, see p. 46.

TIP **JUST SAY NO.** If you are planning on traveling only within Spain (and Portugal), do not buy a Eurailpass. Train travel in these countries is less expensive than in the rest of Europe. A Eurailpass makes sense only for those planning to travel in other European countries as well.

BY BUS. In Spain, buses are cheaper and have far more comprehensive routes than trains. Buses provide the only public transportation to many isolated areas. For those traveling primarily within one region, **buses are the best method of transportation.** Spain has numerous private companies; the lack of a centralized bus company may make itinerary planning difficult. Companies' routes rarely overlap, so it is unlikely that more than one will serve your intended destination. **Alsa/Enatcar** (☎913 27 05 40; www.alsa.es) serves Asturias, Castilla and León, Galicia, and Madrid, as well as international destinations including France, Germany, Italy, and Portugal. **Auto-Res/Cunisa, S.A.** (☎902 02 00 52; www.auto-res.net) serves Castilla and León, Extremadura, Galicia, Valencia, and Portugal.

BY CAR. Spain's highway system connects major cities by four-lane *autopistas.* **Speeders beware:** police can "photograph" the speed and license plate of your car and issue a ticket without pulling you over. If you are pulled over, fines must be paid on the spot. **Gas** prices are €0.80-1.10 per liter. **Renting** a car is cheaper than elsewhere in Europe. Spain accepts Canadian, EU, and US driver's licenses; otherwise, an International Driving Permit (IDP) is required. Try **Atesa** (Spain ☎902 10 01 01, elsewhere 10 05 15; www.atesa.es), Spain's largest rental agency. The automobile association is **Real Automóvil Club de España** (**RACE;** ☎902 40 45 45; www.race.es.) For more on renting and driving a car, see p. 54.

BY FERRY. Spain's islands are accessible by ferry. For specifics on island travel, see the **Balearic Islands** (p. 954). Ferries are also the least expensive way of traveling between Spain and **Tangier** or the Spanish enclave of **Ceuta** in Morocco.

BY THUMB. Hitchhikers report that Castilla and Andalucía are long waits, and hitchhiking out of Madrid is virtually impossible. The Mediterranean coast and the islands are more promising; areas in the Balearics, Catalonia, or Galicia may be best accessible by hitchhiking. While approaching people for rides at gas stations and rest stops purportedly gets results, Let's Go does not recommend hitchhiking.

KEEPING IN TOUCH

PHONE CODES	**Country code:** 34. **International dialing prefix:** 00. Within Spain, dial city code + local number, even when dialing inside the city. For more information on how to place international calls, see inside back cover.

EMAIL AND THE INTERNET. Email is easily accessible within Spain. An increasing number of bars offer Internet access for fees of €1-4 per hr. Cybercafes are listed in most towns and all cities. If Internet is not listed, check the library or the tourist office. For a list of cybercafes in Spain, see www.cybercafes.com.

TELEPHONE. The central phone company is Telefónica. Make local calls with a phone card, issued in denominations of €6 and €12, and sold at kiosks, tobacconists (*estancos* or *tabacos;* look for brown signs with yellow lettering and tobacco leaf icons), and most post offices. Calling internationally with a Spanish phone card is easy and inexpensive. For info on mobile phones in Spain, see p. 28.

MAIL. Airmail *(por avión)* takes five to eight business days to reach Canada or the US; service is faster to the UK and Ireland and slower to Australia and New Zealand. Standard postage is €0.80 to North America. Surface mail *(por barco)* can take over a month, and packages take two to three months. Certified mail *(certificado)* is the most reliable way to send a letter or parcel and takes four to seven business days. Spain's overnight mail is not actually overnight, and is thus not worth the expense. Address mail to be held **Poste Restante** as follows: LAST NAME, First Name; *Lista de Correos;* City; Postal Code; SPAIN; AIRMAIL.

LANGUAGE. *Castellano* (Castilian) Spanish is the official language of the Kingdom of Spain, but each region has its own specific language which, in addition to Castilian, is official in that region. Under Franco's dictatorship, local languages were repressed, but today, protected under the Spanish constitution, local languages are again a source of great regional pride and identity. Most Spaniards are at least bilingual, speaking Castilian in addition to their regional language. The languages with the highest number of speakers are Catalán (spoken in Catalonia), Euskera (spoken in the Basque Country), and Galician (spoken in Galicia). However, there are many other region-specific languages, all of which are protected. It would be incorrect to label these languages "dialects"; while many sound similar to Castilian, they are still linguistically distinct. For a Castilian Spanish phrasebook and pronunciation guide, see the **Phrasebook: Spanish,** p. 1063.

ACCOMMODATIONS AND CAMPING

SPAIN	❶	❷	❸	❹	❺
ACCOMMODATIONS	under €15	€15-25	€25-35	€35-40	over €40

The cheapest and most basic options are *casas de huéspedes* and *hospedajes*, while *pensiones* and *fondas* tend to be a bit nicer. All are essentially boarding houses with basic rooms, shared bath, and no A/C. Higher up the ladder, *hostales* generally have sinks in bedrooms and provide sheets and lockers, while *hostal-residencias* are similar to hotels in overall quality. The government rates *hostales* on a two-star system; even establishments receiving one star are typically quite comfortable. Prices invariably dip below the official rates in the low season (Sept.-May), so bargain away. **Red Española de Albergues Juveniles** (REAJ), the Spanish Hostelling International (HI) affiliate (Sevilla ☎954 21 62 03; www.reaj.com), runs 165 hostels year-round. Prices depend on season, location, and services offered, but are generally €9-15 for guests under 26 and higher for those 26 and over. Breakfast is usually included; lunch and dinner are occasionally offered at an additional charge. Hostels usually have lockouts around 11am and have curfews between midnight and 3am. Don't expect much privacy—rooms typically have 4-20 beds in them. To reserve a bed in the high season (July-Aug. and during festivals), call at least a few weeks in advance. A national **Youth Hostel Card** is usually required. **Campgrounds** are generally the cheapest choice for two or more people. Most charge separate fees per person, per tent, and per car; others charge for a *parcela* (a small plot of land), plus per-person fees. Tourist offices can provide more info, including the *Guía de Campings*.

FOOD AND DRINK

SPAIN	❶	❷	❸	❹	❺
FOOD	under €6	€6-10	€10-15	€15-20	over €20

Fresh, local ingredients are still an integral part of Spanish cuisine, varying according to each region's climate, geography, and history. The old Spanish saying clearly holds true: "*Que comer es muy importante, porque de la panza, ¡nace la danza!*" (Eating is very important, because from the belly, dance is born!)

Spaniards start the day with a light breakfast *(desayuno)* of coffee or thick, liquid chocolate, and a pastry. The main meal of the day *(la comida)* consists of several courses and is typically eaten around 2 or 3pm. Dinner at home *(la cena)* tends to be light. Dining out begins anywhere between 8pm and midnight. Barhopping for tapas is an integral part of the Spanish lifestyle. Some restaurants are "open" from 8am until 1 or 2am, but most serve meals only from 1 or 2 to 4pm and 8pm to midnight. Many restaurants offer a *plato combinado* (main course, side dish, bread, and sometimes a beverage) or a *menú del día* (two or three set dishes, bread, beverage, and dessert) for roughly €5-9. If you ask for a *menú*, this is what you may receive; *carta* is the word for menu.

Tapas (small dishes of savory meats and vegetables cooked according to local recipes) are quite tasty, and in some regions they are complimentary with beer or wine. *Raciones* are large tapas served as entrees; *bocadillos* are sandwiches. Spanish specialties include *tortilla de patata* (potato omelet), *jamón serrano* (smoked ham), *calamares fritos* (fried squid), *arroz* (rice), *chorizo* (spicy sausage), *gambas* (shrimp), *lomo de cerdo* (pork loin), *paella* (steamed saffron rice with seafood, chicken, and vegetables), and *gazpacho* (cold tomato-based soup). Vegetarians should learn the phrase *"yo soy vegetariano"* (I am a vegetarian) and specify this means no *jamón* (ham) or *atún* (tuna). A normal-sized draft beer is a *caña de cerveza;* a *tubo* is a little bigger. A *calimocho* is a mix of Coca-Cola and red wine, while sangria is a drink of red wine, sugar, brandy, and fruit. *Café solo* means black coffee; add a touch of milk for a *nube;* a little more and it's a *café cortado;* half milk and half coffee makes a *café con leche.*

HOLIDAYS AND FESTIVALS

Holidays: New Year's Day (Jan. 1); Epiphany (Jan. 6); Maundy Thursday (Apr. 5); Good Friday (Apr. 6); Easter (Apr. 8); Easter Monday (Apr. 9); Labor Day (May 1); Assumption Day (Aug. 15); National Day (Oct. 12); All Saints' Day (Nov. 1); Constitution Day (Dec. 6); Feast of the Immaculate Conception (Dec. 8); Christmas (Dec. 25); New Year's Eve (Dec. 31).

Festivals: Almost every town in Spain has several festivals. In total, there are more than 3000. Nearly everything closes during festivals. All of Spain celebrates *Carnaval* the week before Ash Wednesday (Feb. 21); the biggest parties are in Catalonia and Cádiz. During the annual festival of *Las Fallas* in mid-March, Valencia honors St. Joseph with parades, fireworks, and the burning of effigies. April 1-8, the entire country honors the Holy Week, or *Semana Santa.* During the same week, Sevilla's *Feria de Abril* has events showcasing many different Andalusian traditions, including bullfighting and flamenco. *San Fermín* (The Running of the Bulls) takes over Pamplona July 5-13. For more information, see www.tourspain.es or www.gospain.org/fiestas.

BEYOND TOURISM

As a volunteer in Spain, you can participate in projects from protecting dolphins to fighting for immigrants' rights. Universities host thousands of foreign students yearly; language schools are a good option for those seeking a lighter courseload.

Don Quijote, Placentinos 2, 37008 Salamanca, SPA (☎923 26 88 60; www.donquijote.org). A nationwide language school offering Spanish courses in Barcelona, Granada, Madrid, Málaga, Salamanca, Sevilla, Tenerife, and Valencia. Very social atmosphere. 2-week intensive courses start at €375. €33 enrollment fee.

Ecoforest, Apdo. Correos 29, 29100 Coin, Málaga, SPA (☎661 07 99 50; www.ecoforest.org). Fruit farm and vegan community in southern Spain that uses ecoforest education to develop a sustainable lifestyle.

Escuela de Cocina Luis Irizar, C. Mari 5, 20003 San Sebastián, SPA (☎943 43 15 40; www.escuelairizar.com). Learn how to cook Basque cuisine at this culinary institute. Programs range from week-long summer courses to the comprehensive 2-year apprenticeship. Some of the summer courses may be taught in English.

MADRID ☎91

After Franco's death in 1975, young *madrileños* celebrated their liberation from totalitarian repression with raging, all-night parties in bars and on streets across the city. This revelry became so widespread that it defined an era, and *la Movida* (the Movement) is now recognized as a world-famous nightlife renaissance. While the newest generation is too young to recall the Franco years, it has kept the spirit of *la Movida* alive. Today, Madrid continues to be Spain's political, intellectual, and cultural center. It is neither as funky as Barcelona nor as charming as Sevilla, but it is undeniably the capital—the wild, pulsing heart of Spain. Students, families, artists, and immigrants flock here in pursuit of their dreams, and Madrid con-

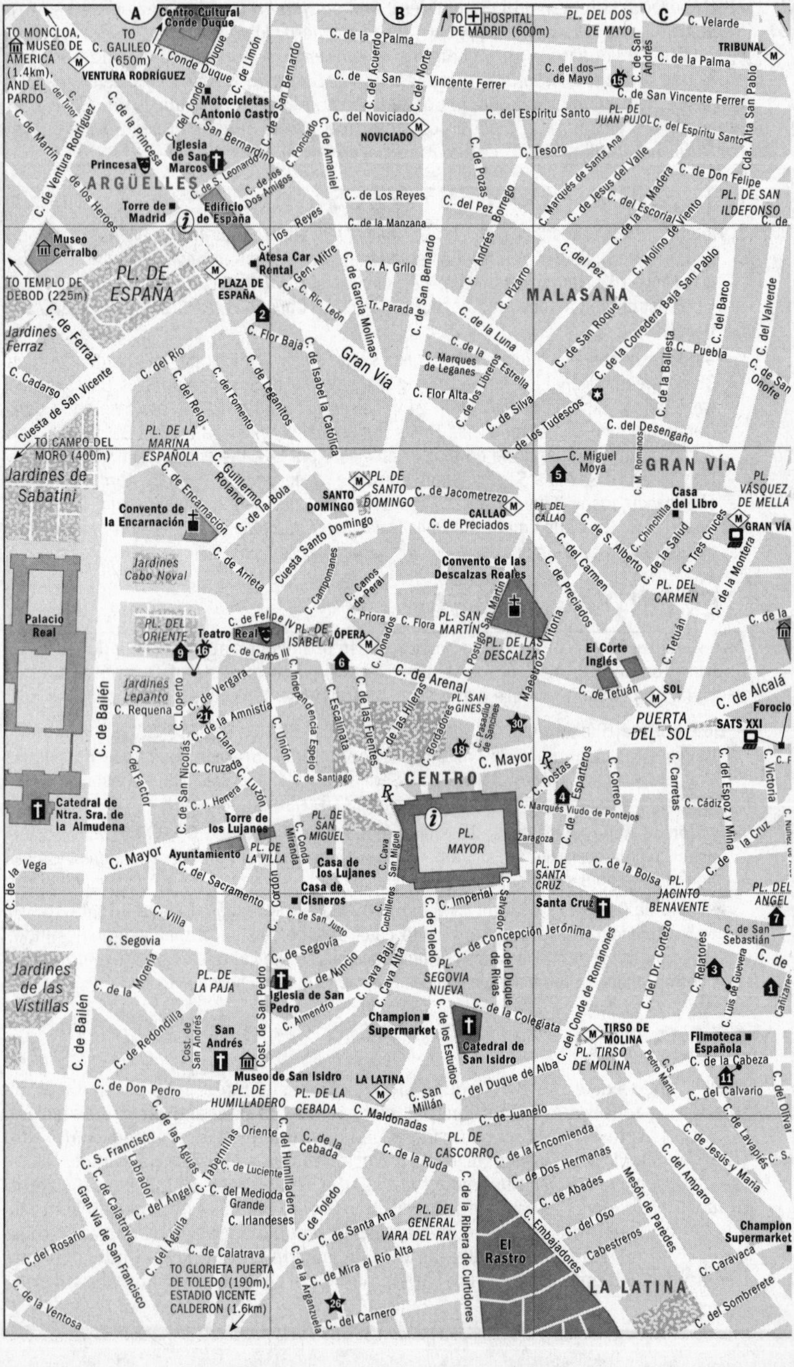
A
B
C
Centro Cultural Conde Duque
TO MONCLOA, MUSEO DE AMERICA (1.4km), AND EL PARDO
TO C. GALILEO (650m)
VENTURA RODRÍGUEZ
TO HOSPITAL DE MADRID (600m)
PL. DEL DOS DE MAYO
C. Velarde
TRIBUNAL
C. de la Palma
C. de San Vicente Ferrer
Vincente Ferrer
C. del dos de Mayo
C. de San Andrés
Motocicletas Antonio Castro
C. del Noviciado
NOVICIADO
C. del Espíritu Santo
PL. DE JUAN PUJOL
Princesa
ARGÜELLES
Iglesia de San Marcos
C. San Bernardino
C. de Los Reyes
C. del Pez
C. del Escorial
C. de Don Felipe
PL. DE SAN ILDEFONSO
Torre de Madrid
Edificio de España
C. de la Manzana
Museo Cerralbo
TO TEMPLO DE DEBOD (225m)
PL. DE ESPAÑA
PLAZA DE ESPAÑA
Atesa Car Rental
C. A. Grilo
MALASAÑA
Jardines Ferraz
C. de Ferraz
C. Flor Baja
Gran Vía
C. de la Luna
C. Puebla
C. Cadarso
Cuesta de San Vicente
C. del Río
C. del Reloj
C. de Leganitos
C. de Isabel la Católica
C. Flor Alta
C. de Silva
C. de los Tudescos
C. del Desengaño
TO CAMPO DEL MORO (400m)
PL. DE LA MARINA ESPAÑOLA
Jardines de Sabatini
C. Miguel Moya
GRAN VÍA
PL. DE SANTO DOMINGO
SANTO DOMINGO
C. de Jacometrezo
CALLAO
PL. DEL CALLAO
Casa del Libro
PL. VÁSQUEZ DE MELLA
GRAN VÍA
Convento de la Encarnación
C. de Preciados
Cuesta Santo Domingo
C. de Arrieta
Jardines Cabo Noval
Convento de las Descalzas Reales
C. del Carmen
PL. DEL CARMEN
C. de la Montera
Palacio Real
PL. DEL ORIENTE
Teatro Real
PL. DE ISABEL II
ÓPERA
PL. SAN MARTÍN
PL. DE LAS DESCALZAS
El Corte Inglés
C. de Arenal
C. de Tetuán
SOL
C. de Alcalá
Forocio
SATS XXI
PUERTA DEL SOL
Jardines Lepanto
C. de Bailén
C. Requena
C. de la Amnistía
PL. SAN GINES
C. Mayor
CENTRO
C. Cruzada
C. de Santiago
C. Marqués Viudo de Pontejos
C. Cádiz
Catedral de Ntra. Sra. de la Almudena
Torre de los Lujanes
PL. DE SAN MIGUEL
PL. MAYOR
Zaragoza
Ayuntamiento
PL. DE LA VILLA
Casa de los Lujanes
PL. DE SANTA CRUZ
C. de la Bolsa
PL. JACINTO BENAVENTE
PL. DEL ANGEL
C. de la Vega
C. del Sacramento
Casa de Cisneros
C. Imperial
Santa Cruz
C. Villa
C. Segovia
C. de Concepción Jerónima
C. de San Sebastián
Jardines de las Vistillas
PL. DE LA PAJA
Iglesia de San Pedro
PL. SEGOVIA NUEVA
C. de Toledo
C. de la Colegiata
Champion Supermarket
Catedral de San Isidro
TIRSO DE MOLINA
PL. TIRSO DE MOLINA
Filmoteca Española
C. de la Cabeza
San Andrés
Museo de San Isidro
LA LATINA
C. del Duque de Alba
C. de Don Pedro
PL. DE HUMILLADERO
PL. DE LA CEBADA
C. Maldonadas
C. de Juanelo
C. del Calvario
PL. DE CASCORRO
C. de la Ruda
C. de la Encomienda
C. de Dos Hermanas
C. de Abades
C. del Oso
Cabestreros
Mesón de Paredes
C. de Jesús y María
C. de Lavapiés
C. del Amparo
Gran Vía de San Francisco
C. de Calatrava
C. Irlandeses
PL. DEL GENERAL VARA DEL RAY
C. de la Ribera de Curtidores
C. de Embajadores
El Rastro
Champion Supermarket
C. Caravaca
TO GLORIETA PUERTA DE TOLEDO (190m), ESTADIO VICENTE CALDERON (1.6km)
C. de Mira el Río Alta
C. del Carnero
LA LATINA
C. del Sombrerete
C. de la Ventosa
C. del Rosario

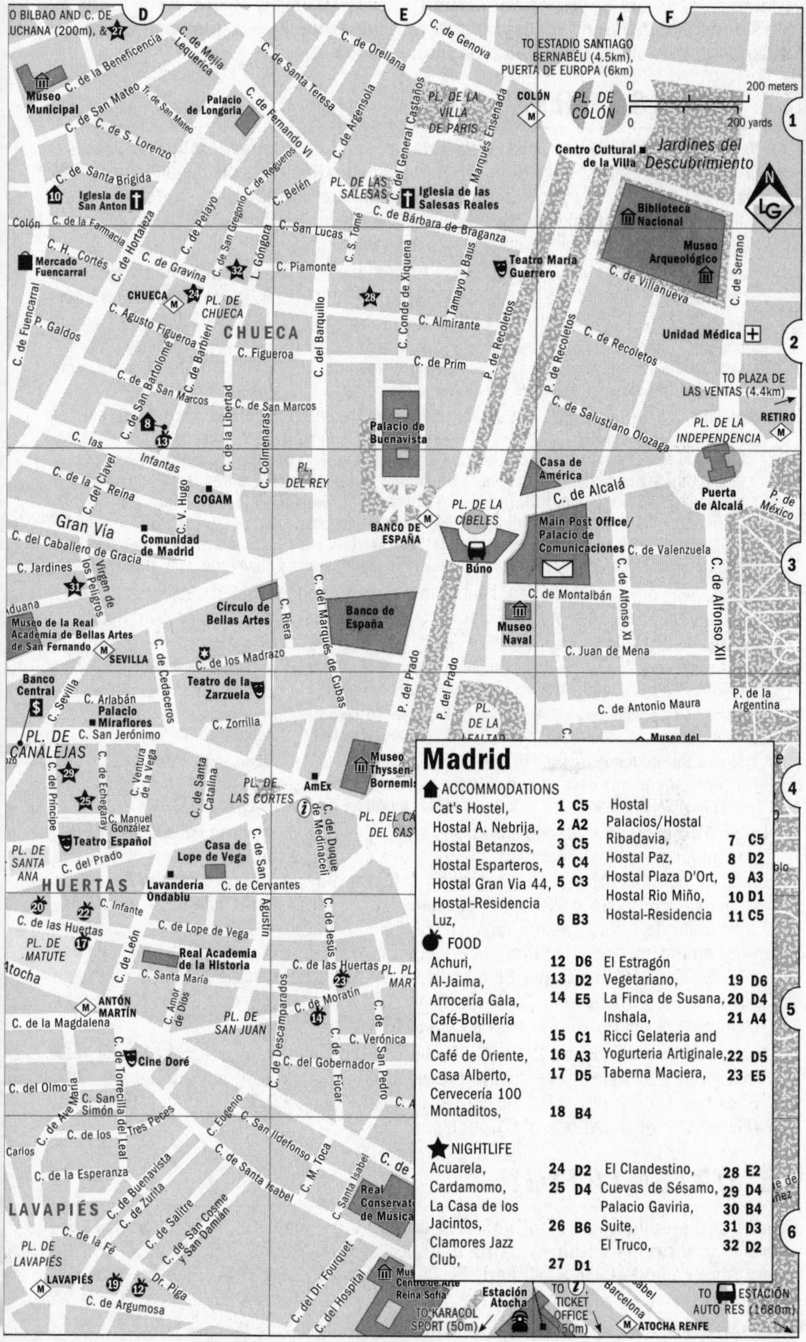

Madrid

ACCOMMODATIONS

Cat's Hostel,	1	C5
Hostal A. Nebrija,	2	A2
Hostal Betanzos,	3	C5
Hostal Esparteros,	4	C4
Hostal Gran Via 44,	5	C3
Hostal-Residencia Luz,	6	B3
Hostal Palacios/Hostal Ribadavia,	7	C5
Hostal Paz,	8	D2
Hostal Plaza D'Ort,	9	A3
Hostal Rio Miño,	10	D1
Hostal-Residencia	11	C5

FOOD

Achuri,	12	D6
Al-Jaima,	13	D2
Arrocería Gala,	14	E5
Café-Botillería Manuela,	15	C1
Café de Oriente,	16	A3
Casa Alberto,	17	D5
Cervecería 100 Montaditos,	18	B4
El Estragón Vegetariano,	19	D6
La Finca de Susana,	20	D4
Inshala,	21	A4
Ricci Gelateria and Yogurteria Artiginale,	22	D5
Taberna Maciera,	23	E5

NIGHTLIFE

Acuarela,	24	D2
Cardamomo,	25	D4
La Casa de los Jacintos,	26	B6
Clamores Jazz Club,	27	D1
El Clandestino,	28	E2
Cuevas de Sésamo,	29	D4
Palacio Gaviria,	30	B4
Suite,	31	D3
El Truco,	32	D2

tinues to grow as a city of opportunity. Its very architecture, with modern skyscrapers and shining industrial spaces rising from ancient plazas, epitomizes the mix of galvanizing history and passion for life that defines Spain.

TRANSPORTATION

Flights: All flights land at **Aeropuerto Internacional de Barajas** (**MAD;** ☎902 40 47 04), 20min. northeast of Madrid. The **Barajas metro line** connects the airport to all of Madrid (€1). Another option is the blue **Bus-Aeropuerto** #200 (look for "EMT" signs), which runs to the city center. (☎902 50 78 50. Every 10-15min., €1.) The bus stops beneath the Jardines del Descubrimiento in Plaza de Colón (M: Colón).

Trains: 2 *largo recorrido* (long distance) **RENFE** stations, **Atocha** and **Chamartín,** connect Madrid to the rest of Europe. Call RENFE (☎902 24 02 02; www.renfe.es) for info.

Estación de Atocha (☎506 6137). M: Atocha Renfe. Domestic service only. AVE (☎506 6329) offers high-speed service to the south of Spain, including **Málaga** (4½hr., 7 per day, €52-58) and **Sevilla** (2½hr., 22 per day, €63-70) via **Córdoba** (1¾hr., €40-52), and Grandes Líneas leave for **Barcelona** (4½-5hr., 9 per day, €36-63).

Estación Chamartín (☎300 6969). M: Chamartín. Bus #5 runs to and from Puerta del Sol (45min.). Alternatively, take a red Cercanías train (15min., every 5-10min., €1.05) from M: Atocha Renfe. Chamartín services both international and domestic destinations in the northeast and south. Major destinations include: **Barcelona** (9hr., 2 per day, €35-42); **Bilbao** (6½hr., 3 per day, €32-81); **Lisbon, POR** (9¼hr., 10:45pm, €54); **Paris, FRA** (13½hr., 7pm, €112-129). Chamartín offers services, including a **tourist office,** Vestíbulo, Puerta 14 (☎315 9976; open M-Sa 8am-8pm, Su 8am-2pm), **accommodations service, car rental, currency exchange, luggage storage** (*consignas;* €2.40-4.50; open daily 7am-11pm), **police,** and **post office.**

Buses: Many private companies, each with its own station and set of destinations, serve Madrid; most pass through the Estación Sur de Autobuses and Estación Auto-Res.

Estación Auto-Res: C. Fernández Shaw 1 (☎902 02 09 99; www.auto-res.net). M: Conde de Casal. Info open daily 6:30am-1am. To **Cuenca** (2½hr., 5-10 per day, €10-14), **Salamanca** (3hr., 9-16 per day, €11-16), and **Valencia** (5hr., 10-11 per day, €22-27).

Estación La Sepulvedana: C. Palos de la Frontera 16 (☎559 5955; www.lasepulvedana.es). M: Príncipe Pío (via extension from M: Ópera). To **Segovia** (1½hr., 2 per hr., €5.84).

Estación Sur de Autobuses: C. Méndez Álvaro (☎468 4200; www.estaciondeautobuses.com). M: Méndez Álvaro. Info desk open daily 6am-1am. **ATMs** and **luggage storage** (€1.25 per bag per day) available. Destinations include **Alicante, Santiago de Compostela,** and **Toledo.**

Local Transportation: Madrid's **metro** is safe, speedy, and spotless (☎902 44 44 03; www.metromadrid.es). Individual metro tickets cost €1; a *metrobus* (ticket of 10 rides valid for both the metro and bus system) is €5.80. Buy both at machines in any metro stop, *estanco* (tobacco shop), or newsstand. Also available are 1-, 2-, 3-, 5-, and 7-day unlimited ride tickets (*abono turístico;* €3.50-37). Travelers found without tickets are fined exorbitantly; hold onto your ticket until you leave the metro. Spanish-language **bus** info ☎406 8810. Buses run 6am-11pm. Bus fares are the same as metro fares and tickets are interchangeable. *Búho* (owl), the **night bus** service, runs every 20min. midnight-3am, 1 per hr. 3-6am. Look for buses N1-N24.

Taxis: Call **Radio Taxi** (☎405 5500), **Radio-Taxi Independiente** (☎405 1213), or **Teletaxi** (☎371 3711). A *libre* sign in the window or a green light indicates availability. Base fare €1.65, plus €0.75-0.90 per km 6am-10pm; €0.90-1 per km 10pm-6am. Teletaxi charges a flat rate of €1 per km.

ORIENTATION

Marking the epicenter of both Madrid and Spain, **"Kilómetro 0"** in **Puerta del Sol** ("Sol" for short) is within walking distance of most sights. To the west are the **Plaza Mayor,** the **Palacio Real,** and the **Ópera** district. East of Sol lies **Huertas,** the heart of cafe, theater, and museum life. The area north of Sol is bordered by **Gran Vía,** which runs northwest to **Plaza de España.** North of Gran Vía are three club- and bar-hopping districts, linked by Calle de Fuencarral: **Malasaña, Bilbao,** and **Chueca.** Modern Madrid is beyond Gran Vía and east of Malasaña and Chueca. East of Sol, the tree-lined thoroughfares **Paseo de la Castellana, Paseo de Recoletos,** and **Paseo del Prado** split Madrid in two, running from **Atocha** in the south to **Plaza Castilla** in the north, passing the Prado, the fountains of **Plaza de Cibeles,** and **Plaza de Colón.** Refer to the color map of Madrid's metro at the beginning of this book. Madrid is safer than many European cities, but some plazas are still intimidating at night.

SPAIN

TIP **READ THIS.** The *Guía del Ocio* (€1; www.guiadelocio.com), available at any news kiosk, should be your first purchase in Madrid. It has concert, theater, sports, cinema, and TV schedules. It also lists exhibits, restaurants, bars, and clubs. Although they are in Spanish, the alphabetical listings are decipherable even to non-speakers. For an English magazine with articles on finds in the city, pick up *In Madrid,* distributed free at tourist offices and restaurants.

PRACTICAL INFORMATION

Tourist Offices: Madrid Tourism Centre, Pl. Mayor 27 (☎588 1636; www.esmadrid.com). M: Sol. **Branches** at Estación Chamartín, Estación de Atocha, and the airport. All open daily 9:30am-8pm. Regional Office of the **Comunidad de Madrid,** C. del Duque de Medinaceli 2 (☎429 4951; www.madrid.org). M: Banco de España. Open M-Sa 8am-8pm, Su 9am-2pm.

General Information Line: ☎901 30 06 00 or 010. Info on anything about Madrid, from police locations to zoo hours. Ask for *inglés* for an English-speaking operator.

Embassies: Australia, Pl. del Descubridor Diego de Ordás 3, 2nd fl. (☎353 6600; www.spain.embassy.gov.au). **Canada,** Núñez de Balboa 35 (☎423 3250; www.canada-es.org). **Ireland,** Po. Castellana 46, 4th fl. (☎436 4093; www.foreignaffairs.gov.ie/irishembassy/Spain.htm). **New Zealand,** Pl. de la Lealtad 2, 3rd fl. (☎523 0226; www.nzembassy.com). **UK,** Po. de Recoletos 7-9 (☎524 9700; www.ukinspain.com). **US,** C. Serrano 75 (☎587 2200; www.embusa.es).

Currency Exchange: In general, credit and ATM cards offer the best exchange rates. Avoid changing money at airport and train station counters; they tend to charge exorbitant commissions. **Banco Santander Central Hispano** charges no commission on AmEx **Travelers Cheques** up to €300. Main branch, Po. Castellana 7 (☎558 1111). M: Sol. Follow C. San Jerónimo to Pl. Canalejas. Open Apr.-Sept. M-F 8:30am-2pm; Oct.-Mar. M-F 8:30am-2pm, Sa 8:30am-1pm. **American Express,** Pl. de las Cortés 2 (☎393 8222). M: Banco de España. Currency exchange open M-F 9am-7:30pm, Sa 9am-2pm.

Luggage Storage: At the airport and bus and train stations (€1.25-2.75 per bag per day).

GLBT Resources: Most establishments in Chueca carry a free guide to gay nightlife in Spain called **Shanguide.** The **Colectivo de Gais y Lesbianas de Madrid (COGAM),** C. de las Infantas 40, 1st fl. (☎522 4517; www.cogam.org), M: Gran Vía, provides a wide range of services and activities. Reception M-Sa 5-10pm.

Laundromat: Lavandería Ondablu, C. León 3 (☎369 5071). M: Antón Martín, Sevilla, or Sol. Wash €2, dry €1. Internet access. Open M-F 9:30am-10pm, Sa 10:30am-7pm.

Police: C. de los Madrazos 9 (☎322 1160). M: Sevilla. From C. de Alcalá take a right onto C. Cedacneros and a left onto C. de los Madrazos. Open daily 9am-2pm. To report crimes committed in the **metro,** go to the office in the Sol station.

Medical Services: In a medical emergency, dial ☎061 or 112. **Hospital de Madrid,** Pl. del Conde del Valle Suchil 16 (☎447 6600; www.hospitaldemadrid.com). **Hospital**

Ramón y Cajal, Ctra. Colmenar Viejo, km 9100 (☎336 8000). Bus #135 from Pl. de Castilla. For non-emergencies, got to **Unidad Médica,** C. del Conde de Aranda 1, 1st fl. (☎914 35 18 23; www.unidadmedica.com). M: Serrano or Retiro. Regular personnel on duty M-F 9am-8pm, Sa 10am-1pm. Initial visit €110, students €75. AmEx/MC/V. Embassies and consulates keep lists of English-speaking doctors.

Internet Access: New Internet cafes are surfacing everywhere in Madrid. While the average rate for access is around €2 per hr., small shops in apartments charge even less; keep a lookout. **SATS XXI,** C. San Jerónimo (☎/fax 532 0970), shares a floor with Asatej travel agency. Fast connections, printing, fax, disks, and CDs. €1.60 per hr. Open daily 10am-midnight.

Post Office: Palacio de Comunicaciones, C. Alcalá 51, on Pl. de Cibeles (☎902 19 71 97). M: Banco de España. Windows open M-Sa 8:30am-9:30pm, Su 8:30am-2pm for stamp purchases. **Postal Code:** 28080.

ACCOMMODATIONS

Make reservations for summer visits. Expect to pay €17-50 per person, depending on location, amenities, and season. Tourist offices provide info about the 22 **campgrounds** within 50km of Madrid. The prices and location in **El Centro,** the triangle between Puerta del Sol, Ópera, and Pl. Mayor, are as good as they get. The cultural hotbed of **Huertas,** framed by Ctra. de San Jerónimo, C. de las Huertas, and C. de Atocha, is almost as central and more fun. Trendy and eclectic **Malasaña** and **Chueca,** bisected by C. Fuencarral, boast cheap rooms in the heart of the action, but the sleep-deprived should beware; the party never stops. *Hostales*, like temptations, are everywhere among **Gran Vía's** sex shops and scam artists.

EL CENTRO: SOL, ÓPERA, AND PLAZA MAYOR

Hostal-Residencia Luz, C. Fuentes 10, 3rd fl. (☎542 0759; www.hostalluz.com), off C. Arenal. M: Ópera. Bright, modern, inexpensive, and friendly. Elegant rooms have hardwood floors, tasselled curtains, marble fireplaces, and satiny sheets. Dorms €18. Singles, doubles, and triples available. MC/V. Paypal accepted. ❷

Hostal Paz, C. Flora 4, 1st and 4th fl. (☎547 3047). M: Ópera. On a quiet street, parallel to C. Arenal, off C. Donados or C. Hileras. Unbeatable hospitality. Peaceful rooms with large windows, satellite TV, and A/C are sheltered from street noise. Reservations recommended. Laundry €10. Singles €30; doubles €36-42; triples €54. MC/V. ❸

Hostal Esparteros, C. Esparteros 12, 4th fl. (☎/fax 521 0903). M: Sol. The 4-flight hike to this hostel is worth it for excellent location and large rooms, some with private baths. Singles €25; doubles €35; triples €45. Cash only. ❷

HUERTAS

Cat's Hostel, C. Cañizares 6 (☎ 902 88 91 92; www.catshostel.com). M: Antón Martín. Join over 200 other travelers at this high-tech hostel in a renovated 18th-century palace. Small, clean 2- to 16-bed dorms, and small rooms with private baths, a fantastic Mudéjar patio area, a bar, and an underground cafe. Cheapest beer around (€2-3). English spoken. Breakfast included. Laundry €2.50. Free Internet. Reception 24hr. Key deposit €10; cash only. Reserve ahead by phone or email. Dorms €19; singles €21. MC/V. ❷

Hostal Plaza D'Ort, Pl. del Angel 13 (☎429 9041; www.plazadort.com). Beautifully decorated rooms exude comfort. All with TV, phone, and A/C; Internet available for a fee. Reception 24hr. Singles €30, with bath €37; doubles €50/55; triples €75. MC/V. ❸

Hostal Betanzos, C. Luis de Guevera 8, 3rd fl. (☎369 1440). M: Antón Martín. This old-fashioned pension has rooms with balconies, wooden furniture, and French windows. Singles €15; doubles €25. Cash only. ❶

GRAN VÍA

Hostal Gran Vía 44, Gran Vía 44, 8th fl. (☎915 21 00 51; www.hostalgranvia44.com). M: Callao. Well-lit, spacious rooms with great views, high ceilings, and brightly colored bedspreads. Private bath, TV, fan, and balcony. Lounge area with free wireless Internet access. Breakfast included. Singles with bath €50; doubles €55; triples €70. MC/V. ❺

Hostal A. Nebrija, Gran Vía 67, 8th fl., elevator A (☎915 47 73 19). M: Pl. de España. Pleasant, spacious rooms with TV and fan offer magnificent views of the city. All rooms with shared baths. Singles €27; doubles €39; triples €54. AmEx/MC/V. ❸

MALASAÑA AND CHUECA

Hostal-Residencia Domínguez, C. de Santa Brígida 1, 1st fl. (☎/fax 915 32 15 47). M: Tribunal. A modern look and low prices. The doubles on the 2nd and 3rd fl. are immaculate and brand new. Hospitable young owner provides tips on local nightlife. Singles €30; doubles with bath and A/C €43; triples €43. Cash only. ❸

Hostal Rio Miño, C. de Babieri 3, 1st fl. (☎915 22 14 17). M: Chueca. Clean, simple rooms at an unbeatable price. Rooms have A/C; common baths are immaculate. Reserve 2 weeks ahead. Singles €17; doubles €25, with bath €36. Cash only. ❷

Hostal Palacios/Hostal Ribadavia, C. de Fuencarral 25, 1st-3rd fl. (☎915 22 71 35; www.hostal-palacios.com). M: Gran Vía. Both are run by the same cheerful family. Palacios's tiled rooms have bath, TV, and A/C; Ribadavia's have TVs and fans. Singles €20, with bath €30; doubles with shower €32, with bath €38; triples €54. MC/V. ❷

FOOD

Small eateries line **Calles Echegaray, Bentura de la Vega,** and **Manuel Fernández González** in Huertas; **Calle Agurrosa** at Lavapiés has outdoor cafes; **Calle Fuencarral** in Gran Vía is lined with cheap eats. **Bilbao** boasts ethnically diverse culinary choices. Bars along **Calle Hartzenbusch** and **Calle Cardenal Cisneros** offer cheap tapas. The *Guía del Ocio* has a complete listing of Madrid's vegetarian options. **%Día** and **Champion** are the cheapest supermarket chains.

La Finca de Susana, C. Arlabán, 4 (☎913 69 35 57). M: Sevilla. Student chefs make this one of the most popular lunch eateries in all of Madrid, where delicious fine dining and swanky surroundings come at an extremely low price. Arrive early to avoid the line. *Menú* M-F €7.75. Open daily 1-3:45pm and 8:30-11:45pm. AmEx/MC/V. ❷

Ricci Gelateria and Yogurteria Artiginale, C. de las Huertas 9 (☎687 98 96 12). M: Antón Martín. Forget tapas and *jamón;* this ice cream is euphoric. Most patrons request 2 flavors, which counts as one scoop. Vegan-soy ice cream available Sa-Su. Small €2, large €3. Open Su-Th 9am-12:30am, F-Sa 9am-1:30am. Cash only. ❶

Al-Jaima, Cocina del Desierto, C. de Barbieri 1 (☎915 23 11 42). M: Gran Vía or Chueca. Lebanese, Moroccan, and Egyptian food served to patrons seated on pillows on the floor. Specialties include kebabs and tajine (1st courses €4, main courses €8). Try *pollo con higos y miel* (chicken with figs and honey; €6.10). Open daily 1:30-4pm and 9pm-midnight. Reserve ahead. MC/V. ❷

Taberna Maceira, C. de Jesús 7 (☎914 29 15 84). M: Antón Martín. Branch at C. Huertas 66 (☎914 29 58 18). Galician seafood served in a lively Irish atmosphere at very reasonable prices. Try the *pulpo gallego* (octopus; €9) or the *mejillones con tomate* (mussels in tomato broth; €4.50). Open M 8pm-12:45am, Tu-F 1-4:15pm and 8:30pm-12:45am, Sa-Su 1-4:45pm and 8:30pm-1:30am. ❸

Inshala, C. de la Amnistía 10 (☎915 48 26 32). M: Ópera. Eclectic menu filled with delicious Italian, Japanese, Mexican, Moroccan, and Spanish dishes. Weekday lunch *menú* €9. Dinner €10-26. Reserve ahead. Open in summer M-Th noon-5pm and 8pm-1am, F-Sa noon-5pm and 8pm-2am; in winter M-Sa noon-2am. ❸

TAPAS A TO Z

Food on toothpicks and in small bowls? No, the restaurant isn't being stingy, and your food isn't shrinking; you're merely experiencing an integral part of the Spanish lifestyle. The tapas tradition is one of the oldest in Spain. These tasty little dishes are Spain's answer to hors d'oeuvres, but have more taste, less pretension, and are eaten instead of meals. To the untrained tourist, tapas menus are often indecipherable—if the bar has even bothered to print any. In order to avoid awkward encounters with tentacles or the parts of the ox you rode in on, keep the following things in mind before *tapeando*.

Servings come in three sizes: *pinchos* (eaten with toothpicks), tapas (small plate), or *ración* (meal portion). *Aceitunas* (olives), *albóndigas* (meatballs), *callos* (tripe), *chorizo* (sausage), *gambas* (shrimp), *jamón* (ham), *patatas bravas* (fried potatoes with spicy sauce), *pimientos* (peppers), *pulpo* (octopus), and *tortilla española* (onion and potato omelette), will be on most basic menus. The more adventurous should try *morcilla* (blood sausage), or *sesos* (cow's brains). Often, bartenders will offer tastes of tapas with your drink and strike up a conversation. Ask for a *caña* of the house *cerveza* to attain the full respect of the establishment.

Arrocería Gala, C. de Moratín 22 (☎914 29 25 62; www.paellas-gala.com). M: Antón Martín. The decor is as colorful as the specialty, paella. *Menú* (€13) includes paella, salad, bread, wine, and dessert. Excellent sangria. Lush, vine-covered interior garden. Reserve ahead F-Sa. Open daily 1-5pm and 9pm-1:30am. Cash only. ❸

El Estragón Vegetariano, Pl. de la Paja 10 (☎913 65 89 82). M: La Latina. Vegetarian offerings so good they'd tempt a puma. Treat yourself to *crêpes à la Museliño* (€13), or try the delicious *menús* (M-F €9.50, Sa-Su and evenings €25). Open daily 1:30-4pm and 8pm-midnight. AmEx/MC/V. ❸

Achuri, C. Argumosa 21 (☎914 68 78 56). M: Lavapiés. A young crowd gathers on the patio for great music and cheap food. Mainly vegetarian dishes. *Bocadillos* €3. Entrees €5. Wine €0.80-2.20. Open Su-Th 1:30pm-2am, F-Sa 1:30pm-2:30am. Cash only. ❶

TAPAS

Not long ago, bartenders in Madrid used to cover *(tapar)* drinks with saucers to keep the flies out. Later, servers began putting little sandwiches on top of the saucers. These became known as *"tapas."* Many tapas bars *(tascas or tabernas)* cluster around **Plaza Santa Ana** and **Plaza Mayor.**

Casa Alberto, C. de las Huertas 18 (☎429 9356; www.casaalberto.es). M: Antón Martín. Tapas don't get more authentic than this. Patrons spill out into the night air to wait for a spot at the bar. Open Tu-Sa noon-5:30pm and 8pm-1:30am. AmEx/MC/V. ❷

Cerveceria 100 Montaditos, C. Mayor 22 (☎902 19 74 94. www.cerveceria100montaditos.es.) M: Sol. One of several locations in the city, this quick little cafe offers up 100 varieties of delicious *bocadillos* for €1 per piece. 4 are enough for a full meal. Open M-Th 10am-12:30am, F-Sa 10am-2am. MC/V. ❶

CAFES

Linger for an hour or two in these cafes for an economical way to soak up a little of Madrid's culture. You won't be bothered with the check until you ask.

Café-Botillería Manuela, C. de San Vicente Ferrer 29 (☎531 7037; www.manuelacafe.com). M: Tribunal. Occasional impromptu piano music adds to Manuela's old-world charm. Coffee €3.50-4.50. Mixed drinks €3-5. Tapas €2-8. Open June-Aug. M-Th 6pm-2am, F-Su 4pm-3am; Sept.-May daily 4pm-2am. MC/V.

Café de Oriente, Pl. del Oriente 2 (☎547 1564). M: Ópera. An old-fashioned cafe catering to a ritzy older crowd. Spectacular view of the Palacio Real from the *terraza*. Coffee €2.50-6.50. Open Su-Th 8:30am-1:30am, F-Sa 8:30am-12:30am. AmEx/D/MC/V.

SIGHTS

Madrid, large as it may seem, is a walker's city. Its fantastic public transportation system should only be used for longer distances or between the day's starting and ending points; you don't want to miss the beauty above ground. While Madrid is perfect for walking, it also offers some of the world's best places to relax.

EL CENTRO

The area known as El Centro, spreading out from Puerta del Sol (Gate of the Sun), is the gateway to the history of Madrid. Although several rulers carved the winding streets, the Hapsburgs and the Bourbons built El Centro's most celebrated monuments. As a result, the easily navigable area is divided into two major sections: Hapsburg Madrid and Bourbon Madrid. Unless otherwise specified, Hapsburg directions are given from Puerta del Sol and Bourbon directions from Ópera.

PUERTA DEL SOL

Kilómetro 0, the origin of six national highways, marks the center of the city in the most chaotic of Madrid's plazas. Puerta del Sol bustles day and night with taxis, performers, and countless locals trying to evade the luggage-laden tourists. *Madrileños* and tourists alike converge upon **El oso y el madroño,** a bronze statue of the bear and berry tree that graces the city's heraldic coat of arms *(M: Sol).*

HAPSBURG MADRID

PLAZA MAYOR. Juan de Herrera, the architect of El Escorial (p. 905), also designed this plaza. Its elegant arcades, spindly towers, and open verandas, erected for Felipe III in 1620, are defining elements of the "Madrid-style," which inspired architects nationwide. Toward evening, Pl. Mayor awakens as *madrileños* resurface, tourists multiply, and cafes fill with lively patrons. Live flamenco performances are a common treat. While the cafes are a nice spot for a drink, food is overpriced; have dinner elsewhere. *(M: Sol. Walk down C. Mayor. The plaza is on the left.)*

CATEDRAL DE SAN ISIDRO. Though Isidro, patron saint of crops, farmers, and Madrid, was humble, his final resting place is anything but. Designed in the Jesuit Baroque style at the beginning of the 17th century, the cathedral received San Isidro's remains in 1769. During the Civil War, rioters burned the exterior and damaged much of the cathedral—all that survived were the main *Capilla*, a 17th-century banner, and the mummified remains of San Isidro and his wife. *(M: Latina. Open daily in summer 7:30am-1:30pm and 5:30-9pm; in winter 7:30am-1pm and 5:30-8:30pm. Free.)*

PLAZA DE LA VILLA. Plaza de la Villa marks the heart of what was once old Madrid. Though only a few medieval buildings remain, the plaza still features a stunning courtyard around the statue of Don Alvara de Bazón, beautiful tile-work, and eclectic architecture. Across the plaza is the 17th-century **Ayuntamiento (Casa de la Villa),** designed in 1640 by Juan Gomez de Mora as both the mayor's home and the city jail. *(M: Sol. Go down C. Mayor and past Pl. Mayor.)*

BOURBON MADRID

PALACIO REAL. Palacio Real sits at the western tip of central Madrid, overlooking the Río Manzanares. Felipe V commissioned Giovanni Sachetti to replace the Alcázar, which burned down in 1734, with a palace that would dwarf all others. Today, the palace is used by King Juan Carlos and Queen Sofía only on special occasions. The **Salón del Trono** (Throne Room) contains a ceiling fresco outlining the qualities of the ideal ruler, and the **Salón de Gasparini** houses Goya's portrait of Carlos IV. Perhaps the most beautiful is the **Chinese Room,** whose walls swirl with green tendrils. The **Biblioteca** shelves first editions of *Don Quixote*. *(M: Ópera. ☎914*

54 87 00. Open Apr.-Sept. M-Sa 9am-6pm, Su 9am-3pm; Oct.-Mar. M-Sa 9:30am-5pm, Su 9am-2pm. Arrive early. €8, with tour €9; students €3.50/8. Under 5 free.W EU citizens free.)

PLAZA DE ORIENTE. Royal paranoia was responsible for this sculpture park. Most of the statues here were designed for the palace roof, but because the queen had a nightmare about the roof collapsing under their weight, they were placed in this shady plaza instead. Treat yourself to a pricey coffee on one of the elegant *terrazas* that ring the plaza. The **Jardines de Sabatini,** to the right as you face the palace, is the romantic's park of choice. *(M: Ópera.)*

ARGÜELLES

Argüelles and the zone surrounding C. de San Bernardo form a mix of elegant homes, student apartments, and bohemian hangouts. Unlike most of Madrid, it is easily navigable due to its gridlike orientation. By day, families and joggers roam the city's largest park, **Casa del Campo.** Night tends to bring unsafe activity. The **Parque de la Montaña** is home to the **Templo de Debod,** built by King Adijalamani of Meröe in the 2nd century BC; it is the only Egyptian temple in Spain. *(M: Pl. de España or Ventura Rodríguez. ☎913 66 74 15; www.munimadrid.es/templodebod. Guided tours available. Open Apr.-Sept. Tu-F 10am-2pm and 6-8pm, Sa-Su 10am-2pm; Oct.-Mar. Tu-F 9:45am-1:45pm and 4:15-6:15pm, Sa-Su 10am-2pm. Closed M. Free. Park open daily year-round. Free.)*

OTHER SIGHTS

PARQUE DEL BUEN RETIRO. Join vendors, palm-readers, soccer players, and sunbathers in the area Felipe IV converted from a hunting ground into a *buen retiro* (nice retreat). The finely landscaped 300-acre park is centered around a monument to King Alfonso XII and a rectangular lake, the **Estanque Grande.** Rowboats for four people can be rented for €4.25 per 45min. Sundays from 5pm to midnight, over 100 percussionists gather for an intense **drum circle** by the colonnaded monument on the Estanque; hypnotic rhythms and hash smoke fill the air.

MUSEUMS

Considered individually to be among the world's best art galleries, the Museo del Prado, Museo de Thyssen-Bornemisza, and the Museo Nacional Centro de Arte Reina Sofía together form the impressive "Avenida del Arte." You won't be able to visit museums of such renown within such easy walking distance anywhere else.

MUSEO DEL PRADO. The Prado is one of Europe's finest museums. It provides a free and indispensable guide for each room. On the first floor, watch for the realism of **Diego Velázquez** (1599-1660). His technique of "illusionism" climaxed in the opus **Las Meninas.** Court portraitist **Francisco de Goya y Lucientes** (1746-1828) created the *Pinturas Negras (Black Paintings)*, named for the darkness of both their color and their subject matter. The Prado also displays many of **El Greco's** religious paintings along with a formidable collection of Italian works, including pieces by **Botticelli, Raphael, Rubens, Tintoretto,** and **Titian.** As a result of the Spanish Hapsburgs' control of the Netherlands, Flemish holdings are top-notch. Works by **van Dyck** and **Albrecht Durer** are here, as well as **Peter Bruegel the Elder's** delightful *The Triumph of Death*,. **Hieronymus Bosch's** moralistic *The Garden of Earthly Delights* depicts hedonists and the destiny that awaits them. *(Po. del Prado at Pl. Cánovas del Castillo. M: Banco de España or Atocha. ☎330 2800; www.museoprado.es. Open Tu-Su 9am-8pm. €6, students €3, under 18, seniors, and Su free.)*

MUSEO NACIONAL CENTRO DE ARTE REINA SOFÍA. Since Juan Carlos I decreed this renovated hospital a national museum in 1988, the Reina Sofía's collection of **20th-century art** has grown steadily. The building itself is a work of art, and is much easier to navigate than the Prado. Rooms dedicated to Dalí, Gris, and Miró display Spain's contributions to Surrealism. Picasso's masterpiece, **Guernica** (p. 953), is the permanent collection's highlight. *(Pl. Santa Isabel 52. ☎917 74 10 00; www.museoreinasofia.es. M: Atocha. Open M and W-Sa 10am-9pm, Su 10am-2:30pm. €3, students €1.50. Sa after 2:30pm, Su, holidays, under 18, and over 65 free.)*

MUSEO THYSSEN-BORNEMISZA. The Thyssen-Bornemisza exhibits works ranging from 14th-century paintings to 20th-century sculptures. The museum's 775 pieces constitute the world's most extensive private showcase. To view the evolution of styles and themes, begin on the top floor. The top floor is dedicated to the **Old Masters** collection, which includes El Greco's *Annunciation*. The highlight of the museum is the **20th-century** collection on the first floor. *(On the corner of Po. del Prado and C. Manuel González. M: Banco de España or Atocha. ☎913 69 01 51; www.museothyssen.org. Open Tu-Su 10am-7pm. €6, students with ISIC and seniors €4, under 12 free. Audio tour €3.)*

ENTERTAINMENT

EL RASTRO (FLEA MARKET)

The market begins in La Latina at Pl. Cascorro off C. de Toledo and ends at the bottom of C. Ribera de Curtidores. As crazy as the market seems, it is actually thematically organized. The main street is a labyrinth of clothing, cheap jewelry, leather goods, incense, and sunglasses. The flea market is a pickpocket's paradise. Fortunately, police are ubiquitous. *(Open Su and holidays 9am-2pm.)*

MUSIC AND FLAMENCO

Anyone interested in live entertainment should stop by the **Círculo de Bellas Artes.** *(C. de Alcalá 2. ☎360 5400. Open Tu-F 5-9pm, Sa 11am-2pm and 5-9pm, Su 11am-2pm.)* Their free magazine, *Minerva*, is indispensable. Check the *Guía del Ocio* for information on city-sponsored movies, plays, and concerts. Flamenco in Madrid is tourist-oriented and expensive. A few nightlife spots are authentic, but pricey. **Las Tablas,** Pl. de España, 9 on the corner of C. Bailén and Cuesta San Vicente, has lower prices than most other flamenco clubs (€15). Shows start nightly at 10:30pm. *(M: Pl. de España. ☎915 42 05 20; www.lastablasmadrid.com.)* Though not cheap, **Casa Patas,** C. Cañizares 10, is well priced for the quality. *(M: Antón Martín. ☎369 0496; www.casapatas.com. €25-30. Shows M-Th 10:30pm, F-Sa 8pm and midnight.)*

FÚTBOL

Spanish sports fans go ballistic for *fútbol* (soccer). Every Sunday and some Saturdays from September to June, one of the two local teams plays at home. **Real Madrid** plays at Estadio Santiago Bernabéu. *(Av. Cochina Espina 1. M: Santiago Bernabéu. ☎457 1112.)* **Atlético de Madrid** plays at Estadio Vicente Calderón. *(Po. de la Virgen del Puerto 67. M: Pirámides or Marqués de Vadillos. ☎364 2234.)*

BULLFIGHTS

Bullfights are a Spanish tradition, and locals joke that they are the only events in Spain to start on time. Hemingway-toting Americans and true fans of this struggle between man and beast clog Pl. de las Ventas for the heart-pounding, gruesome, events. From May to June, the **Fiestas de San Isidro** has a daily *corrida* (bullfight) with the top *matadores* and the fiercest bulls. There are bullfights every Sunday from March to October and less often during the rest of the year. Look for posters in bars and cafes (especially on C. Victoria). **Plaza de las Ventas,** C. de Alcalá 237, is the biggest ring in Spain. *(M: Ventas. ☎356 2200; www.las-ventas.com. Seats €2-115, more expensive in the shade,* sombra, *than in the sun,* sol. *Tickets available in person F-Sa.)* **Plaza de Toros Palacio de Vistalegre** also hosts bullfights and cultural events. *(M: Vista*

IN RECENT NEWS

SAME SEX, SAME RIGHTS

In July 2005, Spain passed a same-sex civil union law to become the third country in the world to legalize same-sex marriage nationwide. At the same time, the Convergència i Unió party submitted a proposal to permit transgendered individuals to legally change their names and sex designation without surgery. For a Catholic country that has been notably conservative for hundreds of years, these steps provide hope to the growing GLBT population in cities beyond Madrid and Barcelona.

Only eight days after the law was passed, the first legal same-sex marriage took place in Madrid. According to government officials, more than 1000 same-sex marriages had taken place as of March 2006, making same-sex marriages 10% of all civil marriage ceremonies in Spain. Although the ruling came with heavy opposition led by the Catholic church, a national poll in July 2005 revealed that 66% of Spaniards were in favor of the law. These sentiments were shared by Prime Minister Zapatero, when in the face of criticism he affirmed, "Spain is a democracy whose sovereignty resides in the Parliament...we must make the difference between civil space and the intimate space of personal conviction. The worst occurs when the two are confused."

Alegre. ☎422 0780. Call for schedule and prices.) To watch amateurs, head to the **bullfighting school,** which has its own *corridas. (M: Batán. ☎470 1990. Tickets €7, children €3.50. Open M-F 10am-2pm.)*

NIGHTLIFE

Madrileños start the night in the tapas bars of **Huertas,** move to the youthful scene in **Malasaña,** and end at the wild parties of **Chueca** or late-night clubs of **Gran Vía.** Students fill the streets of **Bilbao** and **Moncloa.** Madrid's superb gay scene centers on **Plaza Chueca.** Chueca establishments carry *Shanguide*, a free guide to gay nightlife. Most clubs don't heat up until 2am; don't be surprised to see lines at 5am. Dress to impress, as bouncers love to make examples.

Palacio Gaviria, C. Arenal 9 (☎526 6069). M: Sol or Ópera. Party like royalty in 3 ballrooms of a palace-turned-disco. Sweeping marble staircase and blazing light shows. Mixed drinks €9. Cover Su-Th €9, F-Sa €15; includes 1 drink. Open Tu-W and Su 11pm-3:30am, Th 10:30pm-4:30am, F-Sa 11pm-6am.

Cuevas de Sésamo, C. del Príncipe 7 (☎914 29 65 24). M: Antón Martín. "Descend into these caves like Dante!" (Antonio Machado) is one of many literary tidbits that welcome you to this underground gem. Cheap sangria pitchers (small €5.50, large €9) and live jazz piano make a chill atmosphere. Open daily 7pm-2am.

Acuarela, C. de Gravina 10 (☎915 22 21 43). M: Chueca. A welcome alternative to the club scene. Naked angels and candles surround cushy antique furniture, inspiring good conversation. Coffees and teas €1.80-4.50. Liquor €3.20-5. Open daily 11pm-3am.

Suite, C. Virgen de los Peligros 4 (☎915 21 40 31; www.suitecafeclub.com). M: Sevilla. Retro-chic restaurant, bar, and club boasts a *menú* (€10) by day and sleek drinks (€7) by night. Upstairs dance floor rolls with house and downstairs crowd at the bar makes its own music. Open daily 2-4pm and 9pm-3:30am.

Cardamomo, C. de Echegaray 15 (☎913 69 07 57; www.cardamomo.net). M: Sevilla. Flamenco and Latin music spin all night. Beer €4. Live music W midnight brings out the crowd for intoxicating dancing. Open daily 9pm-3:30am.

Clamores Jazz Club, C. Albuquerque 14 (☎914 45 79 38; www.salaclamores.com), off C. Cardenal Cisneros. M: Bilbao. Swanky, neon setting and interesting jazz. The cover (€5-12) is added to the bill if you're there for the music (daily starting around 10pm). See website for schedule; arrive early for a seat. Open in summer Su-Th 6:30pm-3am, F-Sa 6pm-4am; in winter Su-Th 7:30pm-1:30am, F-Sa 7:30pm-3am.

El Clandestino, C. del Barquillo 34 (☎915 21 55 63). M: Chueca. A chill twenty-something crowd drinks and debates at the bar upstairs, then heads down to the caves to nod and dance to the DJ's acid jazz, fusion, and funk selections. Beer €3. Mixed drinks €6. Live music most Th-Sa 11:30pm. Open M-Sa 6:30pm-3am.

La Casa de los Jacintos, C. Arganzuela 11 (www.lacasadelosjacintos.net). M: La Latina or Puerta de Toledo. A cross between an art gallery and cafe, this intimate venue hosts improv on Th (10:30pm-midnight) and one of the cheapest flamenco performances in town on F (9:30pm-midnight). Performances, movies, and mojitos (€3). Open W-Su.

El Truco, C. de Gravina 10 (☎915 32 89 21). M: Chueca. Watch the smoky windows from Pl. Chueca for shadows of people dancing inside. This gay- and lesbian-friendly bar features local artists' works and pop artists' hits. Same owners also run the popular **Escape,** also on the plaza. Open Th 10pm-late, F-Sa midnight-late.

DAYTRIP FROM MADRID

EL ESCORIAL. Though "El Escorial" loosely translates to "The Slag Heap," the enormous complex was better described by Felipe II as "majesty without ostentation." The **Monasterio de San Lorenzo del Escorial** was a gift from Felipe II to God, the people, and himself, commemorating his victory over the French at the battle of San Quintín in 1557. Near the town of San Lorenzo, El Escorial is filled with artistic treasures, two palaces, two pantheons, a church, and a magnificent library. The adjacent **Museo de Arquitectura y Pintura** has an exhibit comparing El Escorial's construction to that of similar structures. The **Palacio Real,** lined with azulejo tiles, includes the majestic **Salón del Trono** (Throne Room), Felipe II's spartan 16th-century apartments, and the luxurious 18th-century rooms of Carlos III and Carlos IV. *(Autocares Herranz buses run between El Escorial and Madrid's Moncloa metro station (50min., every 10-30min., €3.20). Complex ☎918 90 59 03. Open Tu-Su Apr.-Sept. 10am-7pm; Oct.-Mar. 10am-6pm. Last entrance 1hr. before closing. Monastery €7, with guide €9; seniors and students €3.50.)*

CENTRAL SPAIN

Medieval cities and olive groves fill Castilla La Mancha, the land south and east of Madrid. Castilla y León's dramatic cathedrals are testaments to its glorious history. Farther west, bordering Portugal, stark Extremadura was the birthplace of world-famous explorers such as Hernán Cortés and Francisco Pizarro.

CASTILLA LA MANCHA

Castilla La Mancha, a battered, wind-swept plateau, is one of Spain's least developed regions. Its austere beauty shines through its tumultuous history, gloomy medieval fortresses, and awe-inspiring crags.

TOLEDO ☎925

Miguel de Cervantes called Toledo (pop. 66,000) "the glory of Spain and light of her cities." The city may now be marred by hordes of tourists, but this former capital of the Holy Roman, Visigoth, and Muslim empires maintains a wealth of Spanish culture. Toledo's numerous churches, synagogues, and mosques share twisting alleyways, emblematic of a time when Spain's three religions coexisted peacefully.

TRANSPORTATION AND PRACTICAL INFORMATION. From the station on Po. de la Rosa, just over Puente de Azarquiel, **trains** (RENFE info ☎902 24 02 02) run to Madrid (1¼-1½hr., 10 per day, €8.30). **Buses** run from Av. Castilla La Man-

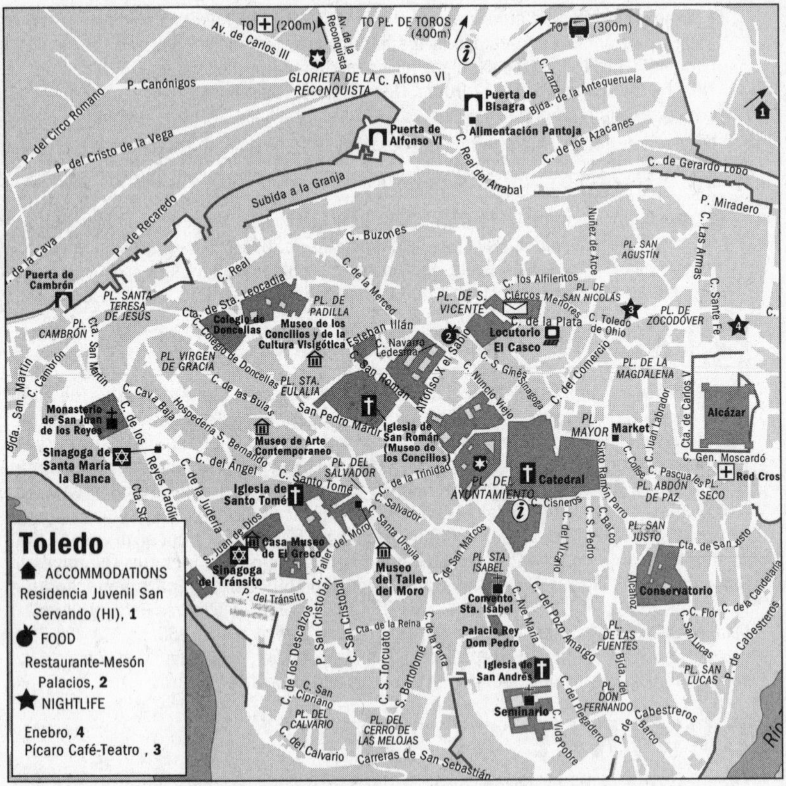

cha (☎21 58 50), 5min. from Pta. de Bisagra (the city gate) to Madrid (1½hr., 2 per hr., €4.25) and Valencia (5½hr., M-F 3pm, €22). Within the city, buses #5 and 6 serve the bus and train stations and the central **Plaza de Zocodóver.** Buses (€0.85; at night €1.10) stop to the right of the train station, underneath and across the street from the bus station. Toledo is an almost unconquerable maze of narrow streets. Though they are well labeled, it's easy to get lost; pick up a map at the **tourist office,** at Pta. de Bisagra. (☎22 08 43. English spoken. Open daily July-Sept. 9am-7pm; Oct.-June M-F 9am-6pm.) **Postal Code:** 45070.

ACCOMMODATIONS AND FOOD. Toledo is full of accommodations, but finding a bed during the summer can be a hassle, especially on weekends. Reservations are recommended, particularly during the summer. Last-minute planners should try the tourist office. Spacious rooms among suits of armor await at the **Residencia Juvenil San Servando (HI) ❶**, Castillo San Servando, uphill on Subida del Hospital from the train station, an amazing 14th-century castle with a pool, TV room, and Internet. (☎22 45 54. Dorms €11, with breakfast €15; under 30 €9.20/11. MC/V.) Toledo is famous for its marzipan; *pastelerías* beckon on every corner. The **market** is in Pl. Mayor, behind the cathedral. (Open M-Sa 9am-8pm.) Homey **Restaurante-Mesón Palacios ❷**, C. Alfonso X El Sabio 3, has two *menús* (€7.50-12.90), one including Toledo's famous partridge dish. (☎21 59 72. Entrees €5-12. Open M-Sa 1-4pm and 7-10:30pm, Su 1-4pm. Closed Su in Aug. AmEx/D/DC/MC/V.)

SIGHTS AND NIGHTLIFE. Toledo's vast collection of museums, churches, synagogues, and mosques make the city impossible to see in one day. Within the fortified walls, Toledo's attractions form a belt around its middle. Most sights are closed Mondays. At Arco de Palacio, up C. del Comercio from Pl. de Zocodóver, Toledo's **cathedral** boasts five naves, delicate stained glass, and unapologetic ostentation. Beneath the dome is the **Capilla Mozárabe,** the only place where the ancient Visigoth Mass (in Mozarabic) is still held. The **Sacristía** is home to 18 El Grecos, two van Dycks, a Caravaggio, and several Goyas, Riberas, and other works from Spanish and European masters. (☎22 22 41. Cathedral open daily 10am-noon and 4-6pm. Capilla and Sacristía open M-Sa 10am-6:30pm, Su 2-6:30pm. €8, students €6. Audio tour €3. Dress modestly.) Greek painter Doménikos Theotokópoulos, commonly known as El Greco, spent most of his life in Toledo. Though the majority of his masterpieces have been carted off to the Prado, many are still displayed throughout town. The best place to start is the **Casa Museo de El Greco,** on C. Samuel Leví 2, which contains 19 of his works. (☎22 44 05. Open in summer Tu-Sa 10am-2pm and 4-9pm, Su 10am-2pm; in winter Tu-Sa 10am-2pm and 4-6pm, Su 10am-2pm. €2.40; students, under 18, Sa afternoon, and Su free.) On the same street as the Museo El Greco is the ornate **Sinagoga del Tránsito,** one of two remaining synagogues in Toledo's *judería* (Jewish quarter).

For nightlife, head through the arch and to the left from Pl. de Zocodóver to **Calle Santa Fé,** where beer and local youth can be found in abundance. **Enebro,** on Pl. Santiago de los Caballeros 4, off C. Cervantes, serves free tapas with every drink in the evenings. (Beer €1.30. Open M-F 9am-1am.) For more upscale bars and clubs, try **Calle de la Sillería** and **Calle los Alfileritos,** west of Pl. de Zocodóver. Relax in the funky lighting of artsy **Pícaro Café-Teatro,** C. Cadenas 6, to escape the rowdiness and noise. (☎22 13 01; www.picarocafeteatro.com. Pints €1.50-2.50. Mixed drinks €4. Open M-F 4pm-3am, Sa-Su 4pm-5am.)

CUENCA ☎969

Cuenca's (pop. 50,000) urban planners were either totally insane or total geniuses; perched atop a hill, the city is flanked by two rivers and the stunning rock formations they have carved. The enchanting **old city** safeguards most of Cuenca's unique charm, including the famed **casas colgadas** (hanging houses) that perch precariously on the cliffs above the Río Huécar. Walk across the San Pablo Bridge for a spectacular view of the *casas* and cliffs. The **Museo de Arte Abstracto Español,** in Pl. Ciudad de Ronda, is housed in the only *casa* open to the public. (☎21 29 83. Open July-Sept. Tu-F 11am-2pm and 5-7pm, Sa 11am-2pm and 4-9pm, Su 11am-2:30pm; Oct.-June reduced hours. €3, students €1.50.)

It's worth spending a little extra to stay in the quaint old city with its stunning views of the gorge. **Posada de San José ❷,** C. Julián Romero 4, a block up from the left side of the cathedral, has bright, comfortable rooms with gorgeous views. (☎21 13 00. Breakfast €8. Singles €25, with bath €50; doubles €38/75; triples with bath €83; quads with bath €128. *Semana Santa* increased prices; Su-Th and low season reduced prices. AmEx/MC/V.) Enjoy delicious *bocadillos* and omelettes (€2-4) on the terrace of Posada de San José's **restaurant ❷.** (☎21 13 00. Entrees €3.50-9. Open Tu-Su 8-11am and 6-10:30pm. AmEx/MC/V.) Budget eateries line **Calle Cervantes** and **Avenida de la República Argentina;** the cafes off **Calle Fray Luis de León** are even cheaper. Get groceries at **%Día,** on Av. Castilla La Mancha. (Open M-Th 9:30am-2pm and 5:30-8:30pm, F-Sa 9am-2:30pm and 5:30-9pm.)

Trains (☎902 24 02 02) run from C. Mariano Catalina 10 to Madrid (2½-3hr., 5-6 per day, €9.40) and Valencia (3-4hr., 3-4 per day, €11). **Buses** (☎22 70 87) depart from C. Fermín Caballero 20 to Barcelona (9hr.; M-Sa 9:30am, Su 2pm; €32), Madrid (2½hr., 8-9 per day, €9-11), and Toledo (2¼hr., 1-2 per day, €9.45-13). To get to Pl. Mayor from either station, turn left onto C. Fermín Caballero, following it as it becomes C. Cervantes and C. José Cobo, and then bearing left through Pl. Hispanidad as the street becomes C. Carretería. The **tourist office** is at Pl. Mayor 1 or C. Alfonso VII 2. (☎24 10 51; www.cuenca.org. Open daily July-Sept. 9am-9pm; Oct.-June M-Sa 9am-2pm and 4-6:30pm, Su 9am-2pm.) **Postal Code:** 16002.

CASTILLA Y LEÓN

Castilla y León's cities rise like green oases from a desert of burnt sienna. The aqueduct of Segovia, the Gothic cathedrals of León, and the sandstone of Salamanca stand out as regional and national images.

SEGOVIA ☎921

Legend has it that the devil built Segovia's (pop. 56,000) famed aqueduct in an effort to win the soul of a Segovian water-seller named Juanilla. With or without the help of the devil, Segovia's attractions draw their share of eager tourists.

TRANSPORTATION AND PRACTICAL INFORMATION. Trains (RENFE info ☎902 24 02 02) run from Po. Obispo Quesada, rather far from town, to Madrid (2hr., 7-9 per day, €5.20). La Sepulvedana **buses** (☎42 77 07) run from Estación Municipal de Autobuses, Po. Ezequiel González 12, to Madrid (1½hr., every 30min., €6) and Salamanca (3hr., 2 per day, €9). From the train station, take any bus (€0.73) to the **Plaza Mayor,** the city's historical center and site of the regional **tourist office.** Segovia is impossible to navigate without a map, so pick one up here. (☎46 03 34. Open July-Sept. 15 Su-Th 9am-8pm, F-Sa 9am-9pm; daily Sept. 16-June 9am-2pm and 5-8pm.) To access the **Internet,** try the **public library,** C. Juan Bravo 11, where you can use a fast connection for free. (☎46 35 33. Passport required. Limit 30min. Open July-Aug. M-F 9am-3pm, Sa 9am-2pm; Sept.-June M-F 9am-9pm, Sa 9am-2pm.) **Postal Code:** 40001.

ACCOMMODATIONS AND FOOD. Reservations are a must for any of Segovia's hotels, especially those near major plazas. Arrive early to ensure space and expect to pay €21 or more for a single. *Pensiones* are significantly cheaper, with basic rooms and shared bathrooms. To reach **Hospedaje El Gato ❷**, Pl. del Salvador 10, which has modern rooms with comfortable beds, satellite TV, A/C, and private baths, follow the aqueduct up the hill, turning left on C. Ochoa Ondategui; it meets San Alfonso Rodríguez, which leads into Pl. del Salvador. (☎42 32 44. Singles €23; doubles €38; triples €52. MC/V.) Sample Segovia's famed lamb, *cochinillo asado* (roast suckling pig), or *sopa castellana* (soup with bread, eggs, and garlic), but steer clear of pricey Pl. Mayor and Pl. del Azoguejo. For tasty vegetarian and meat dishes (€4-11), try **Restaurante La Almuzara ❷**, C. Marqués del Arco 3, past the cathedral. (☎46 06 22. Open Tu 8-11:30pm, W-Su 12:45-4pm and 8-11:30pm. MC/V.) Buy groceries at **%Día,** C. Gobernador Fernández Giménez 3, off Av. Fernández Ladreda. (Open M-Th 9:30am-2pm and 5:30-8:30pm, F-Sa 9am-9pm.)

SIGHTS AND ENTERTAINMENT. Segovia's picturesque museums, palaces, churches, and streets reward the wanderer. The serpentine **Roman aqueduct,** built in 50 BC and spanning 813m, commands the entrance to the old city. Some 20,000 blocks of granite were used in the construction—without a drop of mortar. This spectacular feat of engineering, restored by the monarchy in the 15th century, can transport 30L of water per second and was used until the late 1940s. The 23 chapels of the **cathedral,** towering over Pl. Mayor, earned it the nickname "The Lady of all Cathedrals." The interior may look less impressive than the facade, but its enormity will make you feel truly small. (☎46 22 05. Open daily Apr.-

Oct. 9am-6:30pm; Nov.-Mar. 9:30am-5:30pm. Mass M-Sa 10am, Su 11am and 12:30pm. €2, under 14 free.) Segovia's **Alcázar,** a late-medieval castle and site of Isabel's coronation in 1474, resembles a fairy-tale castle. In the **Sala de Solio** (throne room), an inscription reads: *Tanto monta, monta tanto* ("she mounts, as does he"). Get your mind out of the gutter—this means Fernando and Isabel had equal authority as sovereigns. The **Torre de Juan II** (80m high), 140 steps up a nausea-inducing spiral staircase, affords a marvelous view of Segovia and the surrounding plains. (Pl. de la Reina Victoria Eugenia. ☎46 07 59. Alcázar open daily Apr.-Sept. 10am-7pm; Oct.-Mar. 10am-6pm. Tower closed Tu. Palace €3.50, seniors and students €2.30. Tower €1.50. English-language audio tour €3.)

Segovianos know how to party. Packed with bars and cafes, the **Plaza Mayor** is the center of it all; head for **Calle Infanta Isabel,** appropriately nicknamed *calle de los bares* (street of the bars). Clubs abound on **Calle Ruíz de Alda,** off Pl. del Azoguejo. You can count on a party at **La Luna,** C. Puerta de la Luna 8, where a young crowd downs cheap shots (€2.50) and Heineken (€1.30) every night. (☎46 26 51. Open daily 5pm-4am.) From June 23 to 29, Segovia holds a **fiesta** in honor of San Juan and San Pedro, featuring free concerts, dances, and fireworks.

SALAMANCA ☎923

Salamanca la blanca, city of scholars, saints, royals, and rogues, glows with the finest examples of Spanish Plateresque stonework by day and a vivacious club scene by night. The prestigious Universidad de Salamanca, grouped in medieval times with Bologna, Oxford, and Paris as one of the "four leading lights of the world," continues to add the energy of its thousands of students.

TRANSPORTATION AND PRACTICAL INFORMATION. **Trains** go from Po. de la Estación (☎12 02 02) to Lisbon, POR (6hr., daily 4:51am, €46) and Madrid (2½hr., 5-6 per day, €15). **Buses** leave from the station (☎23 67 17) on Av. Filiberto Villalobos 71-85 for: Barcelona (11hr., 2 per day, €42); León (2½hr., 4-6 per day, €12); Madrid (2½hr., 16 per day, €11-15); Segovia (2¾hr., 2 per day, €8.85). Gorgeous **Plaza Mayor** is the center of Salamanca. From the train station, catch bus #1 (€1) to Gran Vía and ask to be let off at Pl. San Julián, a block from Pl. Mayor. It's a 20min. walk from the train station and a 15min. walk from the bus station. The **tourist office** is at Pl. Mayor 32. (☎27 24 08. Open June-Sept. M-F 9am-2pm and 4:30-8pm, Sa 10am-8pm, Su 10am-2pm; Oct.-May M-F 9am-2pm and 4:30-6:30pm, Sa 10am-2pm and 4:30-6:30pm, Su 10am-2pm.) *DGratis*, a free weekly newspaper about events in Salamanca, is available from newsstands, tourist offices, and locations in Pl. Mayor. For free **Internet,** try the **public library,** C. Compañía 2 in Casa de las Conchas. (☎26 93 17. Limit 30min. Open July to mid-Sept. M-F 10am-noon, Sa 11am-2pm; mid-Sept. to June M-F 9am-9pm, Sa 9am-2pm.) **Postal Code:** 37080.

ACCOMMODATIONS AND FOOD. Reasonably priced *hostales* and *pensiones* cater to the floods of student visitors, especially off Pl. Mayor and C. Meléndez. **Hostal Las Vegas ❷,** C. Meléndez 13, 1st fl., has a friendly staff and spotless rooms with terraces and TVs. (☎21 87 49; www.lasvegascentro.com. Singles €20, with bath €24; doubles €30/36. MC/V.) Cafes and restaurants surround **Plaza Mayor,** where three-course meals run about €9. *Salamantinos* crowd **El Patio Chico ❷,** C. Meléndez 13, but their hefty portions are worth the wait. (☎26 51 03. Entrees €4-8. *Menú* €11. Open daily 1-4pm and 8pm-midnight. MC/V.) Near Plaza Mayor, busy **Restaurante Isidro ❷,** C. Pozo Amarillo 19, has prompt service and large portions. (☎26 28 48. Entrees €3-15. *Menú* €9. Open M-Sa 1-3:30pm and 8-11:30pm. MC/V.) The closest supermarket is **Champion,** C. Toro 82. (☎21 22 08. Open M-Sa 9am-9:30pm.)

SPAIN

SIGHTS AND NIGHTLIFE. From Pl. Mayor, follow R. Mayor, veer right onto T. Antigua, and left onto C. Libreros to reach **La Universidad de Salamanca** (est. 1218), the city's focal point. The 15th-century classroom **Aula Fray Luis de León** has been left in its original state. On the second floor is the **Antigua Biblioteca,** one of Europe's oldest libraries. Don't miss the 800-year-old scrawlings ub the **Capilla del Estudiante.** Across the street and through the hall on the left corner of the patio is the **University Museum.** (University ☎29 44 00, museum 29 12 25. Open M-F 9:30am-1:30pm and 4-7:30pm, Sa 9:30am-1:30pm and 4-7pm, Su 10am-1:30pm. University and museum €4, students and seniors €2.) It took 220 years to build the stunning **Catedral Nueva,** in Pl. de Anaya. The church is best viewed from the ground first, but be sure to climb the tower for a spectacular **view.** (Open daily Apr.-Sept. 9am-8pm; Oct.-Mar. 9am-1pm and 4-6pm. Tower open daily 10am-7pm, last entrance 30min. before closing. Cathedral free. Tower €2.50.)

According to *salmantinos*, Salamanca is the best place in Spain to party; it is said that there is one bar for every 100 people living in the city. Nightlife centers on **Plaza Mayor** and spreads out to **Gran Vía, Calle Bordadores,** and side streets. **Calle Prior** and **Rúa Mayor** are also full of bars, while intense partying occurs off **Calle Varillas.** After a few candy-colored shots (€1) at **Bar La Chupitería,** Pl. Monterrey, wander from club to club on C. Prior and C. Compañía, where young Americans mingle with tireless *salmantinos.* Once you get past the picky bouncers, **Niebla,** C. Bordadores 14 (☎26 86 04), **Gatsby,** C. Bordadores 16 (☎21 73 62), **Camelot,** C. Bordadores 3 (☎21 21 82), and **Cum Laude,** C. Prior 5-7 (☎26 75 77) all offer an ambience of tight pants and loose morals. The party doesn't peak until 2:30-3:30am and stays strong for another 2hrs. (Beer €3-4. Mixed drinks €5.50-6.50. Dress to impress. All clubs have no cover and are cash only.)

DAYTRIP FROM SALAMANCA: ZAMORA

Perched atop a rocky cliff over the Río Duero, Zamora (pop. 70,000) owes much of its character to the medieval churches dotting its streets. The **Museo de Semana Santa,** Pl. Santa María la Nueva 9, is a welcome diversion. Hooded mannequins guard elaborate floats, used during the *romería* processions of *Semana Santa.* The crypt-like setting and impressive collection make this museum an eerie yet worthwhile stop. (☎980 53 22 95. Open M-Sa 10am-2pm and 5-8pm, Su 10am-2pm. €3, under 12 €1.) Twelve striking **Romanesque churches** remain within the old city's walls. A self-guided tour of all of the churches is available from the tourist office, though they tend to blend together. (All churches open Mar.-Sept. Tu-Sa 10am-1pm and 5-8pm. Free.) Zamora's chief monument is its **Romanesque cathedral.** Inside the cloister, the **Museo de la Catedral** features the 15th-century Black Tapestries, which tell the story of Achilles's defeat during the Trojan War. (Currently under renovation. Call ahead for information. ☎980 53 06 44. Cathedral and museum open Tu-Su 10am-2pm and 5-8pm. Mass M-F 10am, Sa 10am and 6pm, Su 10am and 1pm. Cathedral free. Museum €3, students €1.50.) The best way to reach Zamora is by bus. Buses run from Salamanca to the station on Av. Alfonso Peña (☎980 52 12 81. 1hr., 6-15 per day, €4). The **tourist office** is at C. Santa Clara 20. (☎980 53 18 45; www.ayto-zamora.org. Open July to mid-Sept. Su-Th 9am-8pm, F-Sa 9am-9pm; mid-Sept. to June daily 9am-2pm and 5-8pm.)

EXTREMADURA

Arid plains bake under the intense summer sun, relieved only by scattered patches of golden sunflowers. This land of harsh beauty and cruel extremes hardened New World conquistadors such as Hernán Cortés and Francisco Pizarro.

TRUJILLO ☎927

The gem of Extremadura, hilltop Trujillo (pop. 10,000) is an enchanting old-world town. It's often called the "Cradle of Conquistadors" because the city produced over 600 explorers of the New World. Scattered with medieval palaces, Roman ruins, Arabic fortresses, and churches of all eras, Trujillo is a glorious hodgepodge of histories and cultures. Crowning the hill are the ruins of a 10th-century **Moorish castle.** Pacing the battlements and ramparts is like playing in your best Lego creation. (Open daily June-Sept. 10am-2pm and 5-8:30pm; Oct.-May 9:30am-2pm and 4:30-8:30pm. €1.40.) Trujillo's **Plaza Mayor** was the inspiration for the Plaza de Armas in Cuzco, Perú, constructed after Francisco Pizarro defeated the Incas. To reach the Gothic **Iglesia de Santa María la Mayor,** take C. de las Cambroneras from the plaza in front of the Iglesia de San Martín and turn right on C. de Sta. María. The tiny steps leading to the top of the Romanesque church tower are exhausting, but the **360° view** is worth the effort. (Open daily May-Oct. 10am-2pm and 4:30-8:30pm; Nov.-Apr. 10am-2pm and 4-6:30pm. Su Mass 11am. €1.25.) At the bottom of the hill lies the **Museo del Queso y el Vino,** which offers historical information and advice enjoying wine and cheese. (☎32 30 31. Open daily May-Sept. 11am-3pm and 6-8pm; Oct.-Apr. 11am-3pm and 5:30-7:30pm. Tickets €1.30, with tasting €2.40.)

Find the pleasant rooms of **Pensión Boni** ❶ on C. Mingos Ramos 11, off Pl. Mayor on the street to the right when facing Iglesia de San Martín. (☎32 16 04. Laundry €5. Singles €15; doubles €25, with bath €30-35. Cash only.) Exit Pl. Mayor by the church, and walk four blocks down the street to reach **La Tahona** ❶, C. Afueras 2, which dishes up homemade pizza (€3.50-9), pasta (€4-5.20), and other tasty, wallet-friendly meals. (☎32 18 49. Open M 7:30pm-midnight, Tu-Su 1-4pm and 7:30pm-midnight.) **Buses** (☎32 12 02) run from the corner of C. de las Cruces and C. del M. de Albayada to Madrid (2½hr., 5-8 per day, €14-18). The **tourist office** is in Pl. Mayor, on the left when facing Pizarro's statue. Info is posted in the windows when it's closed. Guided tours (€6.75) leave from the front of the office at 11am and 5pm. (☎32 26 77. English spoken. Open daily June-Sept. 10am-2pm and 4:30-7:30pm; Oct.-May 9:30am-2pm and 4-7pm.) **Postal Code:** 10200.

SOUTHERN SPAIN

Southern Spain (Andalucía) is all that you expect of Spanish culture—flamenco shows, bullfighting, pitchers of sangria, whitewashed villages, and streets lined with orange trees. Andalusians have always maintained a passionate, unshakable dedication to living the good life. The extravagance of their never-ending *festivales*, *ferias*, and *carnavales* is world-famous.

CÓRDOBA ☎957

Captivating Córdoba (pop. 321,000), perched on the south bank of the Río Guadalquivir, was once the largest city in Western Europe. The city remembers its heyday with amazingly well-preserved Roman, Jewish, Islamic, and Catholic monuments. Today, lively festivals, balconies dripping with flowers, and nonstop nightlife make Córdoba one of Spain's most beloved cities.

TRANSPORTATION. RENFE **trains** (☎902 24 02 02; www.renfe.es) run from Pl. de las Tres Culturas, off Av. de América, to: Barcelona (10-11hr., 4 per day, €50-76); Cádiz (2½hr., 5 per day, €17-33); Madrid (2-4hr., 21-31 per day, €27-50); Málaga (2-3hr., 8-11 per day, €12-22); Sevilla (45min., 20-30 per day, €8-25). **Buses** (☎40 40 40) leave from Estación de Autobuses, on Glorieta de las Tres Culturas across from the train station. Alsina Graells Sur (☎27 81 00) sends buses to: Cádiz

(4-5hr., 1-2 per day, €20) via Sevilla (2hr., 9-10 per day, €10); Granada (3-4hr., 8 per day, €12); Málaga (3-3½hr., 5 per day, €12). Bacoma (☎902 42 22 42) runs to Barcelona (10hr., 3 per day, €59-69). Secorbus (☎902 22 92 92) buses go to Madrid (4½hr., 3-6 per day, €14). Autocares Priego (☎40 44 79) and Empresa Rafael Ramírez (☎42 21 77) run buses to nearby towns and campgrounds.

ORIENTATION AND PRACTICAL INFORMATION. Córdoba is split into the old city and new city. The modern and commercial northern half extends from the train station on Av. de América to **Plaza de las Tendillas,** the city center. The old section in the south includes the medieval of the **Judería** (Jewish quarter). The easiest way to reach the old city from the train station is to walk (20min.). Exit left from the station, cross the plaza, and take a right onto Av. de los Mozárabes.

To get to the **tourist office,** C. Torrijos 10, from the train station, take bus #3 along the river to the Puente Romano. Walk under the stone arch and the office will be on your left. (☎47 12 35. English spoken. Open May-Sept. M-F 9am-8pm, Sa 10am-7pm, Su 10am-2pm; Oct.-Apr. M-Sa 9am-7:30pm, Su 10am-2pm.) **Banks** and **ATMs** can be found on the streets around the Mezquita and Pl. de las Tendillas. **Tele-Click,** C. Eduardo Dato 9, has **Internet.** (☎29 05 87. €1.80 per hr. Open M-F 10am-3pm and 5:30-10:30pm, Sa-Su noon-11pm.) The **post office** is located at C. José Cruz Conde 15. (☎47 97 96. Open M-F 8:30am-8:30pm, Sa-Su 9:30am-2pm.) **Postal Code:** 14070.

ACCOMMODATIONS AND FOOD. Most accommodations cluster around the whitewashed walls of the Judería and in old Córdoba between the Mezquita and C. de San Fernando, a more residential area. Reserve well in advance during *Semana Santa* and May through June. Popular **Instalación Juvenil Córdoba (HI)** ❷, Pl. Judá Leví, is a former mental asylum converted into a backpacker's paradise. The large rooms all have A/C and bath. (☎29 01 66. Wheelchair-accessible. Breakfast included, dinner €5.50. Linens €1.10. Laundry €4. Reception 24hr. Private rooms available. Mar.-Oct. dorms €19, under 26 €18; Nov.-Feb. €7/5. €3.50 HI discount. MC/V.) **Hostal el Portillo** ❷, C. Cabezas 2, is a quirkily decorated Andalusian house in the quieter part of the neighborhood. Rooms are spacious and equipped with baths and A/C. (☎47 20 91. Singles €18-20; doubles €30-35. MC/V.)

Córdobeses converge on the outdoor *terrazas* between **Calle Dr. Severo Ochoa** and **Calle Dr. Jiménez Díaz** for drinks and tapas before dinner. Cheap eateries cluster farther away from the Judería in **Barrio Cruz Conde** and around **Avenida Menéndez Pidal** and **Plaza de las Tendillas.** Regional specialties include *salmorejo* (a gazpacho-like cream soup) and *rabo de toro* (bull's tail simmered in tomato sauce). **Mundano** ❶, C. Conde de Cárdenas 3, combines delicious home-style food—including many vegetarian options—with a funky style and art shows. (☎47 37 85. Entrees €3-5. Tapas €1-2.50. Open M-F 10am-5pm and 10pm-2am, Sa noon-6pm and 10pm-2am. Cash only.) For a taste of the old Moorish Córdoba, head to **Salon de Té** ❶, C. Buen Pastor 13, a recreated 12th-century teahouse with a huge variety of teas, juices, and Arab pastries. (☎48 79 84. Beverages €2-4. Pastries €1.50-3. Open daily 11am-10:30pm. Cash only.) **El Corte Inglés,** Av. Ronda de los Tejares 30, has a grocery store. (Open M-Sa 10am-10pm. AmEx/MC/V.)

SIGHTS. Built in AD 784, Córdoba's famous **La Mezquita** is considered the most important Islamic monument in the Western Hemisphere. Visitors enter through the **Patio de los Naranjos,** an arcaded courtyard featuring carefully spaced orange trees and fountains. Inside the mosque, 850 granite and marble columns support hundreds of striped arches. In the center lies the **Mihrab** (prayer niche), which is covered in Kufic inscriptions of the 99 names of Allah. Although the town rallied violently against the proposed erection of a **cathedral** in the center of the mosque, after the Crusaders conquered Córdoba in 1236, the towering *crucero* (transept) and *coro* (choir dome) were built. (☎47 05 12. Strict silence enforced.

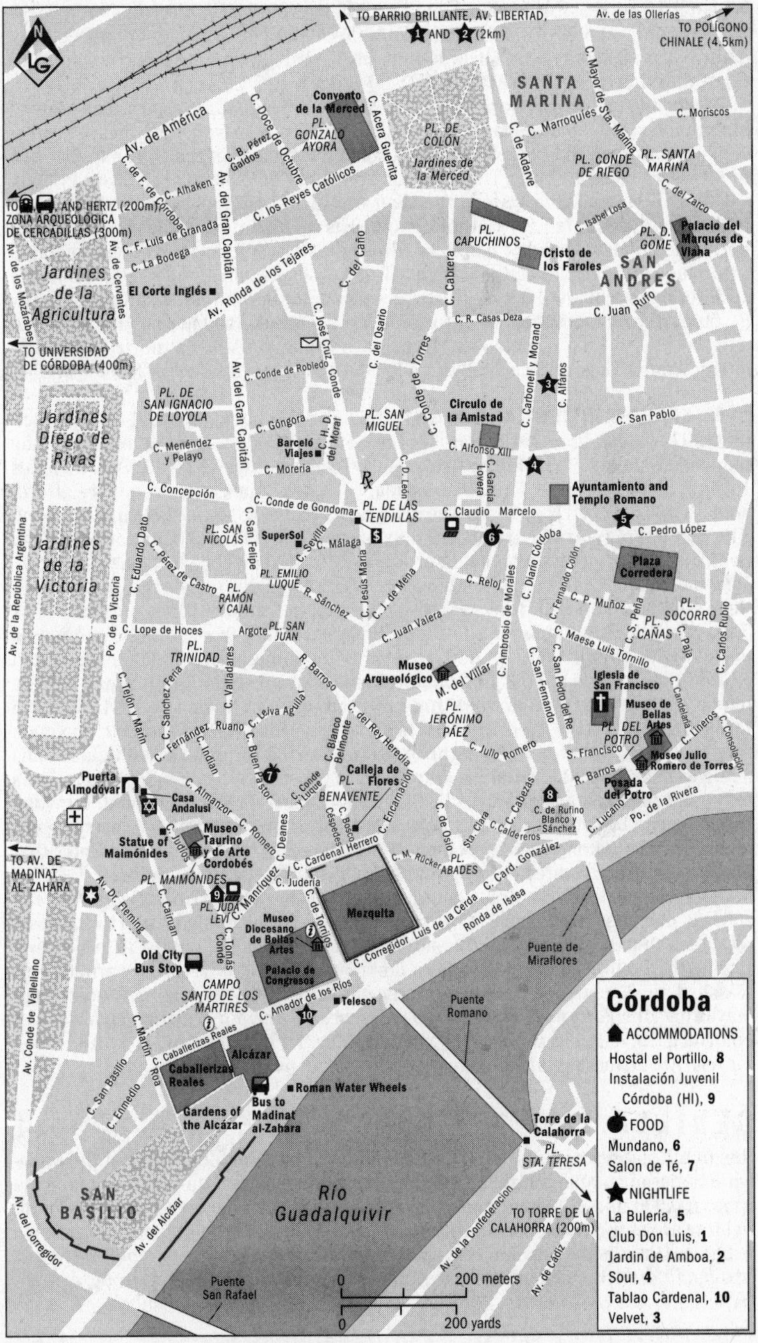
Córdoba
ACCOMMODATIONS
Hostal el Portillo, 8
Instalación Juvenil Córdoba (HI), 9
FOOD
Mundano, 6
Salon de Té, 7
NIGHTLIFE
La Bulería, 5
Club Don Luis, 1
Jardin de Amboa, 2
Soul, 4
Tablao Cardenal, 10
Velvet, 3
TO BARRIO BRILLANTE, AV. LIBERTAD, 1 AND 2 (2km)
Av. de las Ollerías
TO POLÍGONO CHINALE (4.5km)
SANTA MARINA
C. Mayor de Sta. Marina
C. Moriscos
C. Marroquíes
C. de Adarve
PL. CONDE DE RIEGO
PL. SANTA MARINA
C. del Zarco
C. Isabel Losa
PL. D. GOME
Palacio del Marqués de Viana
SAN ANDRES
Cristo de los Faroles
PL. CAPUCHINOS
C. Juan Rufo
Convento de la Merced
PL. GONZALO AYORA
C. Acera Guerrita
PL. DE COLÓN
Jardines de la Merced
C. Doce de Octubre
C. B. Pérez Galdós
Av. de América
C. de F. de Córdoba
C. Alhaken
C. los Reyes Católicos
TO AND HERTZ (200m)
ZONA ARQUEOLÓGICA DE CERCADILLAS (300m)
C. F. Luis de Granada
C. La Bodega
Av. de Cervantes
Av. de los Mozárabes
Jardines de la Agricultura
El Corte Inglés
Av. del Gran Capitán
Av. Ronda de los Tejares
C. del Caño
C. Cabrera
C. R. Casas Deza
TO UNIVERSIDAD DE CÓRDOBA (400m)
C. José Cruz Conde
C. del Osario
C. Conde de Torres
C. Carbonell y Morand
C. Alfaros
C. Conde de Robledo
PL. DE SAN IGNACIO DE LOYOLA
Jardines Diego de Rivas
C. Góngora
C. H. D. del Moral
PL. SAN MIGUEL
Circulo de la Amistad
C. San Pablo
C. Menéndez y Pelayo
Barceló Viajes
C. Morería
C. D. León
C. Alfonso XIII
C. García Lovera
Ayuntamiento and Templo Romano
C. Concepción
C. Conde de Gondomar
PL. DE LAS TENDILLAS
C. Claudio Marcelo
C. Pedro López
PL. SAN NICOLÁS
SuperSol
C. Sevilla
C. Málaga
C. San Felipe
C. Eduardo Dato
C. Diario Córdoba
Plaza Corredera
Jardines de la Victoria
Av. de la República Argentina
C. Pérez de Castro
PL. EMILIO LUQUE
PL. RAMÓN Y CAJAL
R. Sánchez
C. Jesús María
C. J. de Mena
C. Reloj
C. Ambrosio de Morales
C. Fernando Colón
C. P. Muñoz
PL. SOCORRO
PL. CAÑAS
C. S. Peña
C. Paja
C. Carlos Rubio
Po. de la Victoria
C. Lope de Hoces
Argote
PL. SAN JUAN
C. Juan Valera
C. Maese Luis Tornillo
PL. TRINIDAD
C. Valladares
R. Barroso
Museo Arqueológico
M. del Villar
C. San Fernando
C. San Pedro del Re
Iglesia de San Francisco
C. Candelaria
C. Tejón y Marín
C. Sanchez Feria
C. Fernández Ruano
C. Leiva Aguilar
C. del Rey Heredia
PL. JERÓNIMO PÁEZ
Museo de Bellas Artes
PL. DEL POTRO
C. Lineros
C. Consolación
C. Indian
C. Buen Pastor
C. Blanco Belmonte
C. Julio Romero
S. Francisco
Museo Julio Romero de Torres
Puerta Almodóvar
C. Conde y Luque
Calleja de Flores
PL. BENAVENTE
C. Encarnación
C. Cabezas
R. Barros
Posada del Potro
Casa Andalusí
C. Almanzor
C. de Rufino Blanco y Sánchez
C. Lucano
Po. de la Rivera
TO AV. DE MADINAT AL-ZAHARA
Statue of Maimónides
Museo Taurino y de Arte Cordobés
C. Judíos
C. Romero
C. Deanes
C. Céspedes
C. Bosco
C. de Osio
Sta. Clara
C. Calderereros
C. Cardenal Herrero
C. M. Rücker
PL. ABADES
C. Card. González
PL. MAIMÓNIDES
C. Manríquez
C. Judería
Av. Dr. Fleming
PL. JUDÁ LEVÍ
C. Cairuan
C. Tomás Conde
C. de Torrijos
Mezquita
Ronda de Isasa
C. Corregidor Luis de la Cerda
Museo Diocesano de Bellas Artes
Palacio de Congresos
Puente de Miraflores
Old City Bus Stop
CAMPO SANTO DE LOS MÁRTIRES
C. Amador de los Ríos
Telesco
Puente Romano
Av. Conde de Vallellano
C. Martín Roa
C. Caballerizas Reales
Alcázar
Caballerizas Reales
Roman Water Wheels
C. San Basilio
C. Enmedio
Gardens of the Alcázar
Bus to Madinat al-Zahara
Torre de la Calahorra
PL. STA. TERESA
SAN BASILIO
Río Guadalquivir
Av. del Corregidor
Av. del Alcázar
TO TORRE DE LA CALAHORRA (200m)
Av. de la Confederacion
Av. de Cádiz
Puente San Rafael
0
200 meters
200 yards

Wheelchair-accessible. Open Mar.-June daily 8:30am-7:30pm; July-Oct. M-Sa 8:30am-7pm, Su 8:30-10:15am and 2-7pm; Feb. and Nov. 8:30am-6pm; Dec.-Jan. daily 8:30am-5:30pm. M-Sa Mass 9:30am. Su Mass 11am, noon, 1pm. €8, under 10 €4. Admission free during Mass M-Sa 8:30-10am.)

The **Judería** is the historic area northwest of the Mezquita. Just past the statue of Maimonides, the small **Sinagoga,** C. Judíos 20, is one of very few Spanish synagogues to survive the Inquisition; it is a solemn reminder of the 1492 expulsion of the Jews. (☎20 29 28. Open Tu-Sa 9:30am-2pm and 3:30-5:30pm, Su 9:30am-1:30pm. €0.30, EU citizens free.) Along the river on the left side of the Mezquita, is the **Alcázar,** constructed for Catholic monarchs in 1328 during the *Reconquista.* Fernando and Isabel bade Columbus *adiós* here; the building later served as Inquisition headquarters. (☎42 01 51. Open Tu-Sa 8:30am-2:30pm and 4:30-6:30pm, Su and holidays 9:30am-2:30pm. Gardens open June-Sept. 8pm-midnight. Alcázar €2.50. F free.) A **combined ticket** for the Alcázar, **Museo Taurino y de Arte Cordobés,** and the **Museo Julio Romero,** which displays Romero's sensual portraits of Cordoban women, is available at all three locations. (€7.10, students €3.60. F free.)

ENTERTAINMENT AND NIGHTLIFE. For the latest cultural events, pick up the *Guía del Ocio* at the tourist office. Hordes flock to see the prize-winning flamenco dancers at the **Tablao Cardenal,** C. Torrijos 10. (☎48 33 20. €18, includes 1 drink. Shows M-Sa 10:30pm.) **La Bulería,** C. Pedro López 3, is even more affordable. (☎48 38 39. €11, includes 1 drink. Shows daily 10:30pm.) **Soul,** C. Alfonso XIII 3, is a hip, relaxed bar with friendly bartenders; it is also open for breakfast. (☎49 15 80; www.bar-soul.com. Beer €1.50-2.10. Mixed drinks €4.50. Open Sept.-June daily 9am-4am.) **Velvet,** C. Alfaros 29, is a popular retro-style pub. (☎48 60 92. Beer €1.50-2.40. Mixed drinks €3.60-4.80. Open in summer 10pm-4am; in winter 5pm-4am.) Starting in June, the **Barrio Brillante,** uphill from Av. de América, is packed with young, well-dressed *cordobeses* hopping between dance clubs and outdoor bars. Bus #10 goes to Brillante from the train station until 11pm, but the bars don't wake up until around 1am (most are open until 4am); a lift from **Radio Taxi** (☎76 44 44) costs €4-6. To walk, head up Av. Brillante; be prepared, however, for the 30min. uphill hike from the Judería. A string of popular nightclubs runs along **Avenida Brillante,** including **Club Don Luis** (open Th-Sa midnight-4:30am; cash only) and **Jardín de Amboa** (open Th-Sa 11pm-4:30am). Trendy pubs with crowded *terrazas* can be found on nearby **Avenida Libertad.** An alternative to partying is a nighttime stroll along the **walk-through fountains** and falling sheets of water that line Av. de América directly between Pl. de Colón and the train station.

Of Córdoba's festivals, floats, and parades, **Semana Santa** (Holy Week; Apr. 1-8, 2007) is the most extravagant. The first few days of May are dedicated to the **Festival de las Cruces,** during which residents make crosses decorated with flowers. During the **Festival de los Patios** in the first two weeks of May, the city erupts with classical music concerts, flamenco, and a city-wide patio-decorating contest. Late May brings the **Feria de Nuestra Señora de Salud** *(La Feria de Córdoba)*, a week of colorful garb, dancing, music, and wine-drinking. Every July, Córdoba hosts a guitar festival, attracting talented strummers from all over the world.

SEVILLA ☎954

Site of a Roman acropolis, capital of the Moorish empire, focal point of the Spanish Renaissance, and guardian of traditional Andalusian culture, romantic Sevilla (pop. 700,000) is a conglomeration of varied influences. Flamenco, tapas, and bullfighting are at their best here, and Sevilla's cathedral is among the most impressive in Spain. But it is the city's infectious spirit that defines it, and its *Semana Santa* and *Feria de Abril* celebrations are among the most elaborate in Europe.

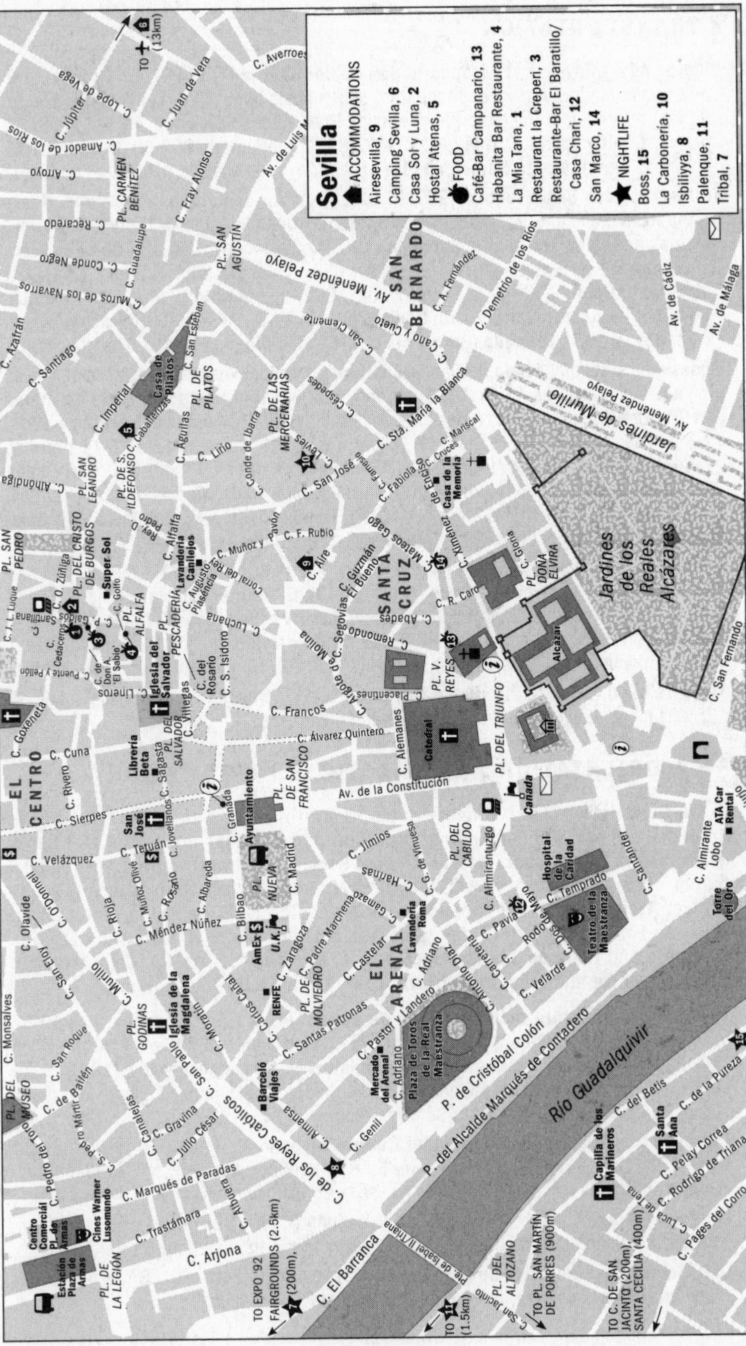
Sevilla
ACCOMMODATIONS
Airesevilla, 9
Camping Sevilla, 6
Casa Sol y Luna, 2
Hostal Atenas, 5
FOOD
Café-Bar Campanario, 13
Habanita Bar Restaurante, 4
La Mia Tana, 1
Restaurant la Creperi, 3
Restaurante-Bar El Baratillo/
Casa Chari, 12
San Marco, 14
NIGHTLIFE
Boss, 15
La Carbonería, 10
Isbiliyya, 8
Palenque, 11
Tribal, 7
EL CENTRO
SANTA CRUZ
SAN BERNARDO
EL ARENAL
Jardines de los Reales Alcázares
Jardines de Murillo
Alcázar
Catedral
Ayuntamiento
Casa de Pilatos
Plaza de Toros de la Real Maestranza
Río Guadalquivir
Torre del Oro
Hospital de la Caridad
Teatro de la Maestranza
Iglesia del Salvador
Iglesia de la Magdalena
Av. de la Constitución
Av. Menéndez Pelayo
P. de Cristóbal Colón
P. del Alcalde Marqués de Contadero
C. de los Reyes Católicos
TO EXPO '92 FAIRGROUNDS (2.5km)
TO PL. SAN MARTÍN DE PORRES (900m)
TO C. DE SAN JACINTO (200m), SANTA CECILIA (400m)

TRANSPORTATION

Flights: All flights arrive at **Aeropuerto San Pablo** (**SVQ;** ☎44 90 00), 12km out of town on Ctra. de Madrid. A taxi ride to the town center costs about €20. **Los Amarillos** (☎98 91 84) buses run to the airport from outside Hotel Alfonso XIII at the Pta. de Jerez (1-2 per hr., €2.40). **Iberia,** C. Guadaira 8 (☎22 89 01, nationwide 902 40 05 00; open M-F 9am-1:30pm), flies to **Barcelona** (1hr., 6 per day) and **Madrid** (45min., 6 per day).

Trains: Estación Santa Justa (☎902 24 02 02), on Av. de Kansas City. Near Pl. Nueva is the **RENFE** office, C. Zaragoza 29. (☎54 02 02. Open M-F 9am-1:15pm and 4-7pm.) Altaria and Talgo trains run to: **Barcelona** (9-13hr., 3 per day, €54-88); **Córdoba** (1hr., 6 per day, €13); **Madrid** (3½hr., 2 per day, €53); **Valencia** (9hr., 8:20am, €44). AVE trains go to **Córdoba** (45min., 15-20 per day, €22) and **Madrid** (2½hr., 15-21 per day, €64-70). Regionales trains run to: **Cádiz** (2hr., 7-12 per day, €9.10); **Córdoba** (1½hr., 6 per day, €7.55); **Granada** (3hr., 4 per day, €21); **Málaga** (2½hr., 5-6 per day, €17).

Buses: The station at **Prado de San Sebastián,** C. Manuel Vázquez Sagastizabal, serves most of Andalucía. (☎41 71 11. Open daily 5:30am-1am.) **Estación Plaza de Armas** (☎90 80 40) mainly serves areas outside of Andalucía. To: **Arcos de la Frontera** (2hr., 2-3 per day, €7); **Cádiz** (1½hr., 12-16 per day, €11); **Córdoba** (2hr., 8-11 per day, €9.43); **Granada** (3½hr., 9 per day, €18); **Lagos, POR** (7hr., 2 per day, €18); **León** (11hr., 3 per day, €38); **Lisbon, POR** (6¼hr., 9:30am, €29); **Madrid** (6hr., 14 per day, €18); **Málaga** (2½hr., 10-12 per day, €14); **Ronda** (2½hr., 3-6 per day, €10); **Salamanca** (8hr., 5-6 per day, €27); **Valencia** (9-11hr., 3 per day, €44-51).

Public Transportation: TUSSAM (☎900 71 01 71; www.tussam.es) is the city bus network. Lines run daily every 10min. (6am-11:15pm) from Pl. Nueva, Pl. de la Encarnación, and the cathedral. C-3 and C-4 circle the city center, and #34 serves the youth hostel, university, cathedral, and Pl. Nueva. **Night service** departs Pl. Nueva (Su-Th 1 per hr. midnight-2am, F-Sa 1 per hr. all night). Fare €1, 10-ride *(bonobús)* ticket €4.50.

Taxis: TeleTaxi (☎62 22 22). **Radio Taxi** (☎58 00 00). Base rate €1, €0.40 per km, Su 25% surcharge. Extra charge for luggage and night taxis.

ORIENTATION AND PRACTICAL INFORMATION

The **Río Guadalquivir** flows roughly north to south through the city. Most of the touristed areas of Sevilla, including **Santa Cruz** and **El Arenal,** are on the east bank. The *barrios* of **Triana, Santa Cecilia,** and **Los Remedios,** as well as the Expo '92 fairgrounds, occupy the west bank. The cathedral, next to Santa Cruz, is Sevilla's centerpiece. **Avenida de la Constitución** runs alongside it. **El Centro,** a commercial pedestrian zone, lies north of the cathedral, starting where Av. Constitución hits **Plaza Nueva** and **Plaza de San Francisco,** site of the *Ayuntamiento*. **Calle Tetuán,** a popular street for shopping, runs north from Pl. Nueva through El Centro.

Tourist Offices: Centro de Información de Sevilla, Pl. de San Francisco 19 (☎59 52 88; www.turismo.sevilla.org). Free Internet M-F 10am-2pm and 5-8pm; limit 1hr. Open M-F 8am-8pm, Sa-Su 8am-3pm. **Turismo Andaluz,** Av. de la Constitución 21B (☎22 14 04; fax 22 97 53). Info on Andalucía and free maps. English spoken. Open M-F 9am-7pm, Sa 10am-2pm and 3-7pm, Su 10am-2pm.

Currency Exchange: Banco Santander Central Hispano, C. Tetuán 10 (☎902 24 24 24). Open Sept.-Apr. M-F 8:30am-2pm, Sa 8:30am-1pm; May-Aug. M-F 8:30am-2pm. **Banks** and **ATMs** can be found along Av. de la Constitución and near Pl. Nueva.

Luggage Storage: Estación Prado de San Sebastián (€1 per bag per day; open 6:30am-10pm), Estación Plaza de Armas (€3 per day), and the train station (€3 per day).

GLBT Resources: Colectiva de Lesbianas y Gays de Andalucía (COLEGA; ☎56 33 66; www.arrakis.es/~colega), C. Gerona 41. Open M-F 10am-2pm.

Laundromat: Lavandería Roma, C. Castelar 2 (☎21 05 35). Wash and dry €6 per load. Open M-F 9:30am-1:30pm and 5-8:30pm, Sa 9am-2pm.

24hr. Pharmacy: Check list posted at any pharmacy for those open 24hr.

Medical Services: Red Cross (☎913 35 45 45). **Ambulatorio Esperanza Macarena** (☎42 01 05). **Hospital Universitario Virgen Macarena,** Av. Dr. Fedriani 56 (☎00 80 00).

Internet Access: Sevilla Internet Center, C. Almirantazgo 2, 2nd fl. (☎50 02 75), in a building overlooking Av. de la Constitución. €3 per hr., €2 per hr. with prepaid card *(bono)*. Open M-F 9am-10pm, Sa-Su 10am-10pm. **Distelco,** C. Ortiz Zuñiga 3 (☎22 99 66). €2 per hr., €1.10 per hr. with *bono*. Open M-F 11am-11pm, Sa-Su 6-11pm.

Post Office: Av. de la Constitución 32 (☎21 64 76), opposite the cathedral. *Lista de Correos* and fax. Open M-F 8:30am-8:30pm, Sa 9:30am-2pm. **Postal Code:** 41080.

ACCOMMODATIONS

Prices soar during *Semana Santa* and the *Feria de Abril;* reserve several months ahead. In Santa Cruz, the streets around **Calle Santa María la Blanca** are full of cheap, centrally located hostels.

Casa Sol y Luna, C. Pérez Galdós 1A (☎21 06 82). A friendly Spanish and British couple keep the most beautiful hostel in town. Homey rooms make you feel like you're staying at a friend's amazing house. Laundry €10. Min. 2-night stay. Singles €22; doubles €38, with bath €45; triples €60; quads €80. Cash only. ❷

Oasis Sevilla, C. Alonso el Sabio 1A (☎29 37 77; www.hostelsoasis.com). Takes the amenities of a four-star hotel and converts them into hostel form. Multi-level roof terrace, spacious dorms and bathrooms, and a chic central lounge area. Includes tapas tours, breakfast, and free Internet. Reserve ahead. Dorms €18; doubles €40. MC/V. ❷

Hostal Atenas, C. Caballerizas 1 (☎21 80 47; fax 22 76 90; atenas@hostal-atenas.com), near Pl. Pilatos. Slightly pricier than other options but with good reason—everything about this hostel is appealing, from the ivy arches leading to the old-fashioned indoor patio to the modern, spotless rooms. All rooms with A/C and bath. Singles €35; doubles €58; triples €70. MC/V. ❸

Airesevilla, C. Aire 13 (☎50 09 05; www.airesevilla-gay.com). This gorgeous guesthouse tastefully merges Andalusian styles with modern art for gay guests. Singles €35-45; doubles €55-75. Prices vary with season. MC/V. ❹

Camping Sevilla, Ctra. Madrid-Cádiz km 534 (☎51 43 79), near the airport. From Pr. San Sebastián, take bus #70 (stops 800m away at Parque Alcosa). Hot showers, supermarket, and pool. 1-person tent €3.75, car €3.25. MC/V. ❶

FOOD

Sevilla, the birthplace of tapas, keeps its cuisine light. Tapas bars cluster around **Plaza San Martín** and along **Calle San Jacinto.** Popular venues for *"el tapeo"* (tapas barhopping) are **Barrio de Santa Cruz** and **El Arenal.** Find fresh meat and produce at **Mercado de la Encarnación,** near the bullring in Pl. de la Encarnación. (Open M-Sa 9am-2pm.) There is an enormous supermarket in the basement of **El Corte Inglés,** in Pl. del Duque de la Victoria. (☎27 93 97. Open M-Sa 9am-10pm. AmEx/MC/V.)

Restaurante-Bar El Baratillo/Casa Chari, C. Pavía 12 (☎22 96 51), off C. Dos de Mayo. Excellent Spanish cuisine and hospitality. Order at least 1hr. in advance for the tour-de-force: homemade paella (vegetarian options available) with a pitcher of wine, beer, or sangria (€20; serves 2). Afterward, leave a note in Chari's "paella book," filled with signatures, notes, and coins from all over the world. *Menú* €5. Entrees €5-9. Open M-F 10am-10pm, Sa 10am-5pm; open later when busy. Cash only. ❷

La Mia Tana, C. Pérez Galdós 24 (☎22 68 97). The smell of pizza and pasta wafts out to the streets, drawing locals to the intimate setting. Pizza €4.70-6.20. Pastas €4-4.60. Open daily 1-5pm and 8pm-midnight. DC/MC/V. ❶

Habanita Bar Restaurant, C. Golfo 3 (☎606 71 64 56; www.andalunet.com/habanita), on a tiny street off C. Pérez Galdós, next to Pl. Alfalfa. Exquisite Cuban fare, including *yuca* and *ropa vieja* ("old clothes"; shredded beef and rice). Entrees €5-14. Open M-Sa 12:30-4:30pm and 8pm-12:30am, Su 12:30-4:30pm. MC/V. ❷

Restaurant La Creperi, C. Pérez Galdós 22 (☎22 28 02). Black-and-white pictures of Paris abound in this little French-owned creperie. The salty crepes (€2.50-6) are reason enough to frequent the restaurant, but the scrumptious dessert crepes (€2-5) will keep you coming back. Open M-Sa 1:30-4:30pm and 9pm-midnight. MC/V. ❶

San Marco, C. Mesón del Moro 6 (☎21 43 90), in Santa Cruz's *casco antiguo.* Pizza, pasta, and dessert in an 18th-century house with 17th-century Arab baths. Other San Marco locations around town are in equally impressive settings. Entrees €5-10. Open daily 1:15-4:30pm and 8:15pm-12:30am. AmEx/DC/MC/V. ❷

Café-Bar Campanario, C. Mateos Gago 8 (☎56 41 89). This clean-cut, modern cafe-bar is more vegetarian-friendly than most tapas bars. Sit outside and gaze at the cathedral as you sip some of the strongest sangria in town (0.5L €10, 1L €12). Tapas €2-3. *Raciones* €8-11. Open daily noon-midnight. AmEx/DC/MC/V. ❷

SIGHTS

CATEDRAL. Legend has it that the *reconquistadores* wished to demonstrate their religious fervor by constructing a church so great that "those who come after us will take us for madmen." With 44 individual chapels, the Cathedral of Sevilla is the third largest in the world (after St. Peter's Basilica in Rome and St. Paul's Cathedral in London) and the biggest Gothic edifice ever constructed. In the center of the cathedral, the **Capilla Real** stands opposite **choir stalls** made of mahogany recycled from a 19th-century Austrian railway. The **retablo mayor** is a golden wall of intricately wrought saints and disciples. Nearby is the **Sepulcro de Cristóbal Colón** (Columbus's tomb), which supposedly holds the explorer's remains. The black-and-gold pallbearers represent the eternally grateful monarchs of Castilla, León, Aragón, and Navarra. Farther on and to the right stands the **Sacristía Mayor** (treasury), which holds Juan de Arefe's gilded panels of Alfonso X el Sabio, works by Ribera and Murillo, and a glittering Corpus Christi icon, **La Custodia Processional.** In the northwest corner of the cathedral lies the architecturally stunning **Sala de Las Columnas.** In 1401, a 12th-century Almohad mosque was destroyed to clear space for the massive cathedral. All that remains of it is the **Patio de Los Naranjos,** where the faithful would wash before prayer, the **Puerta del Perdón** entryway on C. Alemanes, and **La Giralda,** a minaret with 35 ramps leading to the top. *(☎21 49 71. Entrance by the Pl. de la Virgen de los Reyes. Open M-Sa 9:30am-4pm, Su 2:30-7pm. Cathedral €7.50, seniors and students €2, under 12 and Su free. Audio tour €3. Mass in the Capilla Real M-Sa 8:30, 10am, noon, 5pm; Su 8:30, 10, 11am, noon, 1, 5, 6pm. Free.)*

ALCÁZAR. The oldest European palace still used as a private residence for royals, Sevilla's Alcázar oozes extravagance. Built by the Moors in the 7th century, the palace was embellished greatly during the 15th century. It now displays an interesting mix of Moorish, Gothic, Renaissance, and Baroque architecture, most prominently on display in the *mudéjar* style of many of the arches, tiles, and ceilings. Catholic monarchs Fernando and Isabel are the palace's best-known former residents. Visitors enter through the **Patio de la Montería,** directly across from the intricate Almohad facade of the Moorish palace. Through the archway lie the Arabic residences, including the **Patio del Yeso** and the exquisitely carved **Patio de las**

Muñecas (Patio of the Dolls), so named because of the miniature faces carved into the bottom of one of the room's pillars. Of the Christian additions, the most notable is the **Patio de las Doncellas** (Patio of the Maids). The golden-domed **Salón de los Embajadores** (Ambassadors' Room) is allegedly the site where Fernando and Isabel welcomed Columbus back from the New World. The upstairs **private residences,** the official home of the king and queen of Spain and their accommodations when they visit Sevilla, have been renovated and redecorated throughout the centuries.*(Pl. del Triunfo 7. ☎50 23 23. Open Tu-Sa 9:30am-7pm, Su 9:30am-6pm. Mandatory tours of the upper palace living quarters every 30min. Aug.-May 10am-1:30pm and 3:30-5:30pm; June-July 10am-1:30pm; max. 15 people per tour, so buy tickets in advance. Alcázar €7; disabled, students, under 16 and over 65 free. Tour and audio tour €3.)*

CASA DE PILATOS. Inhabited continuously by Spanish aristocrats since the 15th century, this large private residence combines all the virtues of Andalusian architecture and art and has only recently been opened to the public. On the ground floor, Roman artifacts and tropical gardens coexist in *mudéjar* patios. The second floor features rooms decorated over the centuries with oil portraits, sculptures, and tapestries. *(Pl. de Pilatos 1. ☎22 52 98. Open daily 9am-7pm. Guided tours every 30min. Ground level and upper chambers €8; ground level only €5. EU citizens free Tu 1-5pm.)*

MUSEO PROVINCIAL DE BELLAS ARTES. This museum contains Spain's finest collection of works by painters of the *Sevillana* School, notably Murillo, Valdés Leal, and Zurbarán, as well as El Greco and Dutch master Jan Brueghel. While the art is biased toward religious themes, later works include landscape paintings and portraits depicting Sevilla, its environs, and its residents. *(Pl. del Museo 9. ☎22 07 90. Open Tu 2-8:30pm, W-Sa 9am-8:30pm, Su 9am-2:30pm. €1.50, EU citizens and students free.)*

PLAZA DE TOROS DE LA REAL MAESTRANZA. Home to one of the two great bullfighting schools (the other is in Ronda, p. 921), Plaza de Toros de la Real Maestranza fills to capacity (13,800) for weekly fights and the 13 *corridas* of the *Feria de Abril.* Visitors must follow the multilingual tours through the small but informative **Museo Taurino de la Real Maestranza.** *(☎22 45 77. Open non-bullfight days 9:30am-8pm, bullfight days 9:30am-3pm. Tours every 20min.; €4.)*

ENTERTAINMENT

The tourist office distributes *El Giraldillo*, a free monthly magazine with complete listings of the arts. It can also be found online at www.elgiraldillo.es.

FLAMENCO. Flamenco, traditionally consisting of dance, guitar, and song and originally brought to Spain by gypsies, is at its best in Sevilla. It can be seen either in highly touristed *tablaos*, where skilled professional dancers perform, or in *tabernas*, bars where locals merrily dance *sevillanas.* Both have merit, but the *tabernas* tend to be free. The tourist office provides a complete list of both *tablaos* and *tabernas*. **Los Gallos,** Pl. de Santa Cruz 11, is arguably the best tourist show in Sevilla. Buy tickets in advance and arrive early. (☎954 21 69 81; www.tablaolosgallos.com. Shows nightly 8 and 10:30pm. €27, includes 1 drink.) A less expensive alternative is the impressive 1hr. show at the cultural center **Casa de la Memoria Al-Andalus,** C. Ximénez de Enciso 28, in the middle of Santa Cruz. (☎/fax 954 56 06 70. Shows daily in summer 9 and 10:30pm; low season 9pm. Very limited seating; buy tickets in advance. €12, students €10, under 10 €6.)

BULLFIGHTING. Sevilla's bullring, one of the most beautiful in Spain, hosts bullfights from *Semana Santa* through October. The cheapest place to buy tickets is at the ring on Po. Alcalde Marqués de Contadero. When there's a good *cartel* (lineup), the booths on C. Sierpes, C. Velázquez, and Pl. de Toros might be the only source of advance tickets. Tickets range from €20 for a *grada de sol* (nosebleed seat in the sun) to €75 for a *barrera de sombra* (front-row seat in the shade); scalpers usually add 20%. *Corridas de toros* (bullfights) and *novilladas* (fights with apprentice bullfighters and younger bulls) are held on the 13 days around the *Feria de Abril* and into May, on Sundays April-June and September-October, more often during Corpus Cristi in June and early July, and during the *Feria de San Miguel* at the end of September. During July and August, *corridas* occasionally occur on Thursday at 9pm. For info and **ticket sales,** call the Plaza de Toros ticket office at ☎954 50 13 82.

FESTIVALS

If you're in Spain during any of the major festivals, head to Sevilla. Reserve a room a few months in advance, and expect to pay two or three times the normal rate.

SEMANA SANTA. Sevilla's world-famous *Semana Santa* lasts from Palm Sunday to Easter Sunday. In each neighborhood of the city, thousands of robed penitents guide *pasos* (extravagantly decorated floats) through the streets, illuminated by hundreds of candles. The climax is Good Friday, when the entire city turns out for the procession along the bridges and through the oldest neighborhoods.

FERIA DE ABRIL. From April 24-29, 2007, the city rewards itself for its Lenten piety with the *Feria de Abril.* Circuses, bullfights, and flamenco shows roar into the night in a showcase of local customs and camaraderie. At the fairgrounds on the southern end of Los Remedios, a spectacular array of flowers and lanterns decorates over 1000 kiosks, tents, and pavilions, collectively called *casetas.* The city holds bullfights daily during the festival; buy tickets in advance.

NIGHTLIFE

Sevilla's reputation for gaiety is tried and true—most clubs in town don't get going until after midnight, and the real fun often doesn't start until after 3am. Popular bars are lined up along **Calle Mateos Gago**, **Calle Adriano** by the bullring, and **Calle del Betis** in Triana.

La Carbonería, C. Levies 18 (☎21 44 60), off C. Santa María La Blanca. Guitar-strumming Romeos abound on the massive outdoor patio. Tapas €1.50-2. Beer €1.50. Mixed drinks €5. Sangria pitchers €8. Th free live flamenco. Open July-Aug. M-Sa 8pm-4am, Su 8pm-2:30am; Sept.-May M-Sa 8pm-4am, Su 7pm-3am. Cash only.

Boss, C. del Betis, will show you who knows how to get a crowd fired up. Irresistible beats and a hip atmosphere make this a wildly popular destination. Beer €3.50. Mixed drinks €6. Open fall-spring daily 9pm-5am. MC/V.

Palenque, Av. Blas Pascal (☎46 74 08). Cross Pte. de la Barqueta, turn left, and follow C. Materático Rey Pastor to the first big intersection. Turn left again and look for the entrance on the right. Gigantic dance club, complete with 2 dance floors and a small ice skating rink (€3; includes skate rental; closes at 4am). During the summer, the crowd consists largely of scandalous teenagers. Beer €3. Mixed drinks €5. Cover Th free, F-Sa €7. Dress to impress. Open June-Sept. Th-Sa midnight-7am. MC/V.

Isbiliyya, Po. de Cristóbal Colón 2 (☎21 04 60). Popular riverfront gay and lesbian bar with outdoor seating. Beer €2-2.50. Tu, Th, Su drag performances after midnight. Open daily 8pm-5am. AmEx/MC/V.

Tribal, Av. de los Descubrimientos, next to Pte. de la Barqueta. Popular *discoteca* plays hip-hop, Latin favorites, and reggaetón. Outdoor patio overlooks the river. Pitchers €5-10. W hip-hop draws an international crowd. Open W-Sa midnight-6am. MC/V.

DAYTRIP FROM SEVILLA: RONDA

Trains (☎952 87 16 73 or 902 24 02 02) depart from Av. Alferez Provisional for Granada (3hr., 3 per day, €11), Madrid (4½hr., 2 per day, €40-49), and Málaga (2hr., 1 per day, €8). Buses (☎952 18 70 61) go from Pl. Concepción García Redondo 2 to Cádiz (4hr., 2-3 per day, €12), Málaga (2½hr., 4-10 per day, €8), and Sevilla (2½hr., 3-5 per day, €10).

Ancient bridges, majestic scenery, old dungeons, and a famed bullring attract visitors to picturesque Ronda (pop. 350,000), which has all the charm of a small, medieval town with the amenities and cultural opportunities of a thriving city. A precipitous 100m gorge, carved by the Río Guadalevín, drops below the **Puente Nuevo,** opposite Pl. España. The **views** from the Puente Nuevo, **Puente Viejo,** and **Puente San Miguel** are unparalleled. Take the first left after crossing the Puente Nuevo to Cuesta de Santo Domingo 17, and descend the steep stairs of the **Casa Del Rey Moro** into the 14th-century water mine for an otherworldly view of the ravine. (☎952 18 72 00. Open daily 10am-7pm. €4, children €2.) Bullfighting aficionados charge over to Ronda's **Plaza de Toros,** Spain's oldest bullring (est. 1785) and currently the cradle of the modern *corrida.* In early September, the Pl. de Toros hosts *corridas goyescas* (bullfights in traditional costumes) as part of the **Feria de Ronda.** The town fills to capacity during the festival; reserve rooms months in advance. The **Museo Taurino** traces the history of bullfighting. (☎952 87 15 39; www.rmcr.org. Bullring and museum open daily mid-Apr. to Oct. 10am-8pm; Nov.-Feb. 10am-6pm; Mar. to mid-Apr. 10am-7pm. €5. Museum audio tour €3.) The **tourist office** is at Po. Blas Infante, across from the bullring. (☎952 18 71 19. English spoken. Open June-Aug. M-F 9:30am-7:30pm, Sa-Su 10am-2pm and 3:30-6:30pm; Sept.-May M-F 9:30am-6:30pm, Sa-Su 10am-2pm and 3:30-6:30pm.)

GIBRALTAR

The craggy face of the Rock of Gibraltar emerges from the morning mist just off the southern shore of Spain. Ancient seafarers called "Gib" one of the Pillars of Hercules, believing that it marked the end of the world. Among history's most contested plots of land, Gibraltar today is officially a self-governing British colony, though Spain continues to campaign for its sovereignty. Gibraltar has a culture all its own—a curious mixture of not-quite-British, definitely-not-Spanish culture that makes it a sight worth visiting, despite being something of a tourist trap.

PHONE CODES	☎350 from the UK or the US. ☎9567 from Spain.

TRANSPORTATION AND PRACTICAL INFORMATION. **Buses** arrive in the Spanish border town of La Línea from: Algeciras (40min., every 30min., €1.78); Cádiz (3hr., 4 per day, €12); Granada (5hr., 2 per day, €19); Madrid (7hr., 2 per day, €25); Sevilla (6hr., 4 per day, €19). Turner & Co., 65/67 Irish Town St. (☎783 05; fax 720 06), runs **ferries** to Tangier, Morocco (1¼hr.; 1 per day; £18/€32, under 12 £9/€17). British Airways (☎793 00) flights leave from Gibraltar's **airport** (GIB; ☎730 26) for London, BRI (2½hr., 2 per day, £168/€233). Before you head to Gibraltar, make sure you have a valid passport. From the bus station, walk toward the Rock; the border is 5min. away. Catch bus #9 or 10 (£0.60/€1) or walk across the airport tarmac into town (20min.). Stay left on Av. Winston Churchill when the road forks with Corral Ln. The **tourist office** is at Duke of Kent House, Cathedral Sq. (☎450 00. Open M-F 9am-5:30pm, Sa 10am-3pm, Su 10am-1pm.)

ACCOMMODATIONS AND FOOD. Gibraltar is best done as a daytrip. The accommodations in the area are relatively pricey and often full, especially in the summer, and camping is illegal. **Emile Youth Hostel Gibraltar ❷,** Montague Bastian,

THE REAL DEAL. Although euros are accepted almost everywhere (except in pay phones and post offices), the **pound sterling (£)** is the preferred method of payment in Gibraltar. ATMs dispense money in pounds. Merchants and sights sometimes charge a higher price in euros than in the pound's exchange equivalent. However, unless stated otherwise, assume an establishment will accept euros, although change is often given in British currency. The exchange rate fluctuates around £1 to €1.50. As of press date, **£1 = €1.47.**

behind Casemates Sq., has bunk beds and clean communal bathrooms. (☎/fax 511 06; www.emilehostel.com. Breakfast included. Luggage storage available. Towels £1. Lockout 10:30am-4:30pm. Dorms £15/€25; doubles £34/€51. Cash only.) Spending the night at La Línea across the border is a cheaper option. International restaurants in Gibraltar have steep prices. **Marks & Spencer** on Main St. has a small grocery with pre-packaged foods, baked goods, and a good exchange rate. (Open M-F 8:30am-8pm, Sa 10am-6pm, Su 10am-3pm. AmEx/MC/V.)

SIGHTS. No trip to Gibraltar is complete without a visit to the legendary **Rock of Gibraltar.** About halfway up is the infamous **Apes' Den,** where Barbary Macaques cavort on the sides of rocks, the tops of taxis, and the heads of tourists. At the northern tip of the Rock, facing Spain, are the **Great Siege Tunnels.** Originally used to fend off a Franco-Spanish siege in the 18th century, the underground tunnels were expanded during WWII to span 53km. The eerie chambers of **St. Michael's Cave,** 500m from the siege tunnels, were cut into the rock by thousands of years of water erosion. At the southern tip of Gibraltar, **Europa Point** commands a view of the straits; its signature lighthouse can be seen from 27km away at sea. (Cable car up the Rock daily every 10min. 9:30am-5:15pm. £8/€13.50. Combined ticket to all sights, including one-way cable car ride, £16/€21.50.)

COSTA DEL SOL

The Costa del Sol combines rocky beaches with chic promenades and swank hotels. While some spots are over-developed and expensive, elsewhere the coast's stunning landscape remains untouched.

MÁLAGA ☎952

Málaga (pop. 550,000) is the busiest city on the coast, and while its beaches are known more for bars than for natural beauty, the city has much to offer. Guarding the east end of Po. del Parque, the **Alcazaba** was originally a military fortress and royal palace for Moorish kings. (Open June-Aug. Tu-Su 9:30am-8pm; Sept.-May Tu-Sa 8:30am-7pm. €2, students €0.60. Free Su after 2pm.) Málaga's **cathedral,** C. Molina Lario 4, has been nicknamed *La Manquita* (One-Armed Lady) because one of its two towers was never completed. (☎22 03 45. Open M-F 10am-6pm, Sa 10am-5pm. Mass daily 9am. €3.50, includes audio tour.) Picasso's birthplace at Pl. de la Merced 15 is now home to the **Casa Natal y Fundación Picasso,** which organizes exhibits, concerts, and lectures. Upstairs is a permanent collection of Picasso's photographs, drawings, and correspondence. (☎06 02 15; www.fundacionpicasso.es. Open M-Sa 10am-8pm, Su 10am-2pm. €1, students and under 17 free.)

One of the few spots in Málaga just for backpackers, friendly **Picasso's Corner ❷,** C. San Juan de Letrán 9, off Pl. de la Merced, has free Internet and top-notch bathrooms. (☎21 22 87; www.picassoscorner.com. Dorms €18-19; doubles €45. MC/V.) Sit amid stacks of books and magazines at **Café Con Libros ❶,** Pl. de la Merced 19, as you enjoy wholesome breakfasts for €1.50-3. (Open daily 11am-1am. Cash only.) RENFE (☎902 24 02 02) **trains** leave from Explanada de la Estación for: Barcelona (13hr., 7:20am and 8:20pm, €55); Córdoba (2hr., 9 per day, €16); Madrid (5hr., 7 per day, €35); Sevilla (3hr., 5-6 per day, €17). **Buses** run from Po. de los Tilos (☎35 00 61), one block from the RENFE station along C. Roger de Flor, to: Cádiz (5hr., 3-6 per day, €21); Córdoba (3hr., 3-5 per day, €12); Granada (2hr., 17-18 per day, €9); Madrid (7hr., 8-11 per day, €20); Marbella (1½hr., 1 per hr., €4.70); Ronda (3hr., 8-17 per day, €9.36); Sevilla (3hr., 11-12 per day, €14). To get to the city center from the bus station, exit right onto Callejones del Perchel, walk straight through the intersection with Av. de la Aurora, turn right on Av. de Andalucía, and cross Puente de Tetuán. From here, Alameda Principal leads into Pl. de la Marina, where the **tourist office** is located. (☎12 20 20. Open M-F 9am-7pm.) **Postal Code:** 29080.

GRANADA ☎958

Legend has it that in 1492, when Moorish ruler Boabdil fled Granada (pop. 237,000), Spain's last Muslim stronghold, his mother berated him for casting a longing look back at the Alhambra. "You do well to weep as a woman," she told him, "for what you could not defend as a man." The Alhambra continues to inspire melancholy in those leaving its timeless beauty. The Albaicín, a maze of Moorish houses, is Spain's best-preserved Arab quarter and the only part of the Muslim city to survive the *Reconquista.* Granada has grown into a university city infused with the energy of international students, backpackers, and Andalusian youth.

TRANSPORTATION

Trains: RENFE Station, Av. Andaluces (☎902 24 02 02; www.renfe.es). To **Barcelona** (12-13hr., 1-2 per day, €54), **Madrid** (5-6hr., 2 per day, €32-36), and **Sevilla** (4-5hr., 4 per day, €21).

Buses: The bus station (☎18 54 80) is on the outskirts of Granada on Ctra. de Madrid, near C. Arzobispo Pedro de Castro. **BACOMA** (☎902 42 22 42) goes to **Alicante** (6hr., 6-7 per day, €26), **Barcelona** (14hr., 6 per day, €62), and **Valencia** (10hr., 6 per day, €36.50). **Alsina Graells** (☎18 54 80) runs to: **Cádiz** (5½hr., 4 per day, €26); **Córdoba** (3hr., 7-8 per day, €11); **Madrid** (5-6hr., 12-15 per day, €15); **Málaga** (2hr., 17-19 per day, €8.30); **Marbella** (2hr., 8 per day, €14); **Sevilla** (3hr., 10 per day, €17).

Public Transportation: Pick up a free bus map at the tourist office. Important buses include: Alhambra bus #30 from Gran Vía de Colón or Pl. Nueva to the Alhambra; #31 from Gran Vía or Pl. Nueva to the Albaicín; #10 from the bus station to C. de Ronda, C. Recogidas, and C. Acera de Darro; #3 from the bus station to Av. de la Constitución, Gran Vía, and Pl. Isabel la Católica. Rides €0.95, *bonobus* (10 rides) €5.20.

ORIENTATION AND PRACTICAL INFORMATION

The geographic center of Granada is the small **Plaza Isabel la Católica,** at the intersection of the city's two main arteries, **Calle de los Reyes Católicos** and **Gran Vía de Colón.** The **cathedral** is on Gran Vía. Two blocks uphill on C. de los Reyes Católicos sits **Plaza Nueva.** Downhill on C. de los Reyes Católicos lies Pl. Carmen, site of the **Ayuntamiento** and **Puerta Real.** The **Alhambra** commands the hill above Pl. Nueva.

Tourist Office: Junta de Andalucía, C. Santa Ana 2 (☎22 59 90). Open M-Sa 9am-7pm, Su 10am-2pm. **Oficina Provincial,** Pl. Mariana Pineda 10 (☎24 71 28; www.turismodegranada.org). Open M-F 9am-8pm, Sa 10am-7pm, Su 10am-4pm.

American Express: C. de los Reyes Católicos 31 (☎22 45 12), between Pl. Isabel la Católica and Pta. Real. Open M-F 9:30am-1:30pm and 4:30-7:30pm, Sa 10am-1pm.

Luggage Storage: 24hr. storage at the train station (€3).

Laundromat: C. de la Paz 19. Wash €5; dry €1 per 15min. Detergent (€1), softener (€0.50), and bleach (€0.50) available. Open M-F 10am-2pm and 5-8pm.

Police: C. Duquesa 21 (☎092). English spoken.

Medical Services: Clínica de San Cecilio, C. Dr. Olóriz 16 (☎28 02 00), toward Jaén.

Internet Access: NavegaWeb, C. de los Reyes Católicos 55 (navegagranada@terra.es). English spoken. €1.40 per hr., students €1.10 per hr. *Bono* cards available for 5hr. (€6/5) and 10hr. (€10/9). Open daily 10am-11pm.

Post Office: Pta. Real (☎22 48 35). *Lista de Correos* and fax service. Open M-F 8:30am-8:30pm, Sa 9:30am-2pm. **Postal Code:** 18009.

ACCOMMODATIONS

Hostels line **Cuesta de Gomérez, Plaza Trinidad,** and **Gran Vía.**

Oasis Granada, Placeta Correo Viejo 3 (☎21 58 48; free from inside Spain 900 162 747; www.hostelsoasis.com). Modern facilities include free wireless, satellite TV, bath, and en-suite fridges. Parties and activities like tapas tours and pub crawls. Breakfast included. 3-course dinner €3.50. Reserve ahead. Dorms €15; doubles €36. MC/V. ❶

Hospedaje Almohada, C. Postigo de Zarate 4 (☎20 74 46 or 627 47 25 53). A communal atmosphere will make you feel at home. Laundry €3. Dorms €14; singles €16; doubles €30; triples €40. Cash only. ❶

Funky Backpackers', Cuesta de Rodrigo del Campo 13 (☎22 14 62). The young, friendly staff at this welcoming hostel hangs out with travelers in the living room or on the roof terrace. Breakfast included. Free Internet. Dorms €16; doubles €38. MC/V. ❶

Hostal Venecia, Cuesta de Gomérez 2, 3rd fl. (☎22 39 87). Sergio and María del Carmen offer cozy rooms, attentive service, and morning coffee or tea. Dorms €15; singles €18; doubles €30; triples €45; quads €60. MC/V. ❷

Hostal Antares, C. Cetti Meriém 10 (☎22 83 13; www.hostalantares.com). TV and A/C. Singles Su-Th €18; doubles €28, with bath €38; F-Sa €20/30/40. Cash only. ❷

FOOD

The best way to eat on a budget is to order a few beers and then take advantage of the free tapas. *Menús* await in Pl. Nueva and Pl. Trinidad. Picnickers can gather produce at the indoor **market** on Pl. San Agustín. (Open M-Sa 9am-3pm.)

Hicuri, C. Santa Escolástica 12 (☎22 12 82), on the corner of Pl. de los Girones. Healthful, affordable, and frequented by young locals. Its selection of vegetarian and vegan dishes will satisfy any tofu craving. Entrees €5-6. *Menú* €10. Open daily 1:30-4:30pm. ❷

Bocadillería Baraka, C. Elvira 20 (☎22 97 60). The cheapest and tastiest among Middle Eastern eateries, Bakara serves delicious pitas (€2.50-4) and homemade lemonade infused with *hierbabuena* (€1). Open daily 1pm-2am. Cash only. ❶

Botánico Café, C. Málaga 3 (☎27 15 98), 2 blocks from Pl. Trinidad. This trendy restaurant draws in fashionable students for fusion cuisine. Appetizers €5-10. Entrees €6-14. Open Su-Th noon-1am, F-Sa noon-2am. MC/V. ❸

Los Italianos, Gran Vía 4 (☎22 40 34). Very tasty ice cream at extremely affordable prices. Cups and cones from €0.50. Open daily 9am-3am. Cash only. ❶

Samarcanda, C. Calderería Vieja 3 (☎21 00 04). Delicious Lebanese food. Entrees €6-10. Open M-Tu and Th-Su 1-4:30pm and 7:30pm-midnight. MC/V. ❷

SIGHTS

THE ALHAMBRA. From the streets of Granada, the Alhambra appears blocky and practical. Up close, you will discover elaborate and detailed architecture that

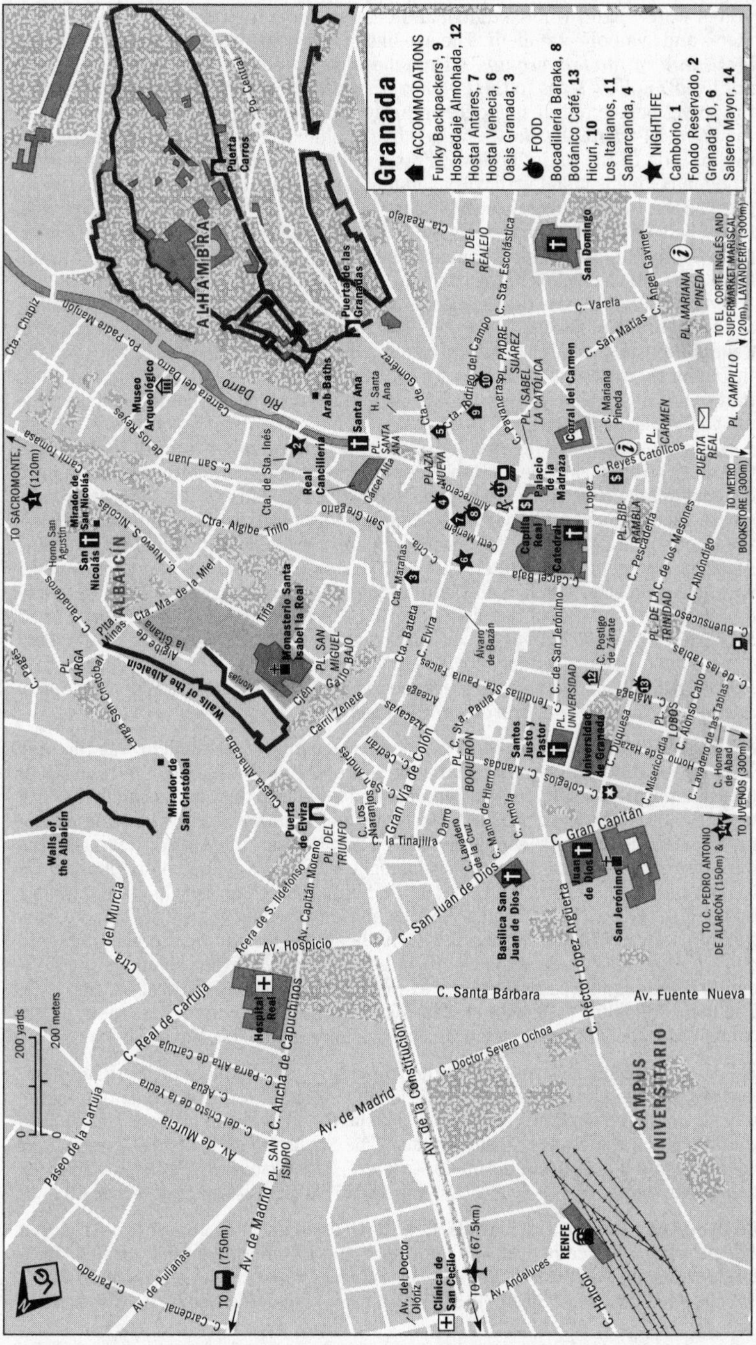
Granada
ACCOMMODATIONS
Funky Backpackers', 9
Hospedaje Almohada, 12
Hostal Antares, 7
Hostal Venecia, 6
Oasis Granada, 3
FOOD
Bocadillería Baraka, 8
Botánico Café, 13
Hicuri, 10
Los Italianos, 11
Samarcanda, 4
NIGHTLIFE
Camborio, 1
Fondo Reservado, 2
Granada 10, 6
Salsero Mayor, 14
ALHAMBRA
ALBAICÍN
Puerta Carros
Puerta de las Granadas
Arab Baths
Santa Ana
Real Cancillería
Museo Arqueológico
Mirador de San Nicolás
San Nicolás
Monasterio Santa Isabel la Real
Walls of the Albaicín
Mirador de San Cristóbal
Puerta de Elvira
Hospital Real
Basílica San Juan de Dios
Juan de Dios
San Jerónimo
Santos Justo y Pastor
Universidad de Granada
Capilla Real
Catedral
Palacio de la Madraza
Corral del Carmen
San Domingo
PLAZA NUEVA
PL. ISABEL LA CATÓLICA
PL. BIB-RAMBLA
PL. DE LA TRINIDAD
PL. UNIVERSIDAD
PL. DEL TRIUNFO
PL. SAN ISIDRO
PL. MARIANA PINEDA
PL. DEL REALEJO
PL. CAMPILLO
Gran Vía de Colón
C. Reyes Católicos
C. San Juan de Dios
Av. de la Constitución
Av. de Madrid
C. Gran Capitán
Av. Fuente Nueva
C. Santa Bárbara
Av. Hospicio
Río Darro
Carrera del Darro
CAMPUS UNIVERSITARIO
RENFE
Clínica de San Cecilio
TO SACROMONTE (120m)
TO METRO BOOKSTORE (300m)
TO JUVENOS (300m)
TO EL CORTE INGLÉS AND SUPERMARKET MARISCAL (20m), LAVANDERÍA (300m)
TO C. PEDRO ANTONIO DE ALARCÓN (150m) &
200 yards
200 meters

unites water, light, wood, stucco, and ceramics in a fortress-palace of rich aesthetic and symbolic grandeur. The age-old saying holds true: *"Si mueres sin ver la Alhambra, no has vivido."* (If you die without seeing the Alhambra, you have not lived.) Follow signs to the *Palacio Nazaries* to see the **Alcázar,** a 14th-century royal palace full of stalactite archways and sculpted fountains. The walls of the **Patio del Cuarto Dorado** are topped by the shielded windows of the harem. Off the far side of the patio, archways open onto the **Cuarto Dorado,** whose carved wooden ceiling is inlaid with ivory and mother-of-pearl. From the top of the patio, glimpse the 14th-century **Fachada de Serallo,** the palace's intricately carved facade. In the **Sala de los Abencerrajes,** Boabdil had the throats of 37 sons of the Abencerrajes family slit after one of them allegedly had amorous encounters with the sultana. Rust-colored stains in the basin are said to be traces of the massacre.

Over a bridge, across the **Callejón de los Cipreses** and the **Callejón de las Adelfas,** are the vibrant blossoms, towering cypresses, and meandering waterways of **El Generalife,** the sultan's vacation retreat. Over the centuries, the estate passed through private hands until it was finally repatriated in 1931. The two buildings that make up El Generalife, the **Palacio** and the **Sala Regia,** connect across the placid **Patio de la Acequia.**

When the Christians drove the first Nasrid King Alhamar from the Albaicín to this more strategic hill, he built the series of rust-colored brick towers which form the **Alcazaba** (fortress). A dark, spiraling staircase leads to the **Torre de la Vela,** where visitors have a 360° view of Granada and the surrounding mountains. After the Reconquista drove the Moors from Spain, Fernando and Isabel restored the Alcázar. Two generations later, Emperor Carlos V demolished part of it to make way for his **Palacio,** which, while incongruous with the surrounding Moorish splendor, is considered one of the most beautiful Renaissance buildings in Spain. *(☎57 51 26, reservations 902 22 44 60; www.alhambratickets.com. Open Apr.-Sept. daily 8:30am-8pm; Oct.-Mar. M-Sa 8:30am-6pm. Nighttime visits June-Sept. Tu-Sa 10-11:30pm; Oct.-May Sa 8-9:30pm. €10. Worthwhile English-language audio tour €3. Admission is limited, so arrive early or reserve tickets in advance at local banks (reservation fee €0.88) or online.)*

THE ALBAICÍN. A labyrinth of steep, narrow alleys, the Albaicín was the only Moorish neighborhood to escape the torches of the *Reconquista.* After the fall of the Alhambra, a Muslim population remained here until their expulsion in the 17th century. Today, with its North African cuisine, outdoor bazaars blasting Arabic music, tea houses, and the mosque near Pl. San Nicolás, the Albaicín attests to the persistence of Islamic influence in Andalucía. The best way to explore this maze is to proceed along Carrera del Darro off Pl. Santa Ana, climb the Cuesta del Chapiz on the left, then wander through the Muslim ramparts and gates. On Pl. Santa Ana, the 16th-century **Real Cancillería,** with its beautiful arcaded patio and stalactite ceiling, was the Christians' *Ayuntamiento* (city hall). Farther uphill are the 11th-century **Arab baths.** *(Carrera del Darro 31. ☎02 78 00. Open Tu-Sa 10am-2pm. Free.)* The **mirador** adjacent to **Iglesia de San Nicolás** affords the city's best view of the Alhambra, especially in winter when snow adorns the Sierra Nevada behind it.

CAPILLA REAL. Downhill from the Alhambra's Arab splendor, Fernando and Isabel's private chapel exemplifies Christian Granada. Gothic masonry and meticulously rendered figurines, as well as **La Reja,** the gilded iron grille of Master Bartolomé, grace the couple's resting place. The **Sacristía** houses Isabel's private **art collection** and the **royal jewels.** *(The Capilla is on C. Oficios through the Pta. Real. ☎22 92 39. Capilla and Sacristía open M-Sa 10:30am-1pm and 4-7pm, Su 11am-1pm and 4-7pm. €3.)*

CATHEDRAL. Behind the Capilla Real is Granada's 1704 cathedral. After the *Reconquista,* the cathedral was built upon the smoldering embers of Granada's largest mosque. *(☎22 29 59. Open Apr.-Sept. M-Sa 10:45am-1:30pm and 4-8pm, Su 4-8pm; Oct.-Mar. M-Sa 10:30am-1:30pm and 3:30-6:30pm, Su 11am-1:30pm and 3:30-6:30pm. €3.)*

NIGHTLIFE

Granada's "free tapas with a drink" tradition lures students and tourists to its pubs and bars. Great tapas bars can be found off the side streets near Pl. Nueva. The most boisterous nightspots are on **Calle Pedro Antonio de Alarcón,** while hip new bars and clubs line **Calle Elvira**. Gay bars cluster around Carrera del Darro. The *Guía del Ocio,* sold at newsstands (€1), lists clubs, pubs, and cafes.

Camborio, Camino del Sacromonte 48 (☎22 12 15), a 20min. walk uphill from Pl. Nueva. Night bus #31 runs there until 2am. Pop music spun by live DJs echoes through dance floors to the rooftop patio above. Striking view of the Alhambra. Beer €1.80-3. Mixed drinks €5-6. Cover F-Sa €5. Open Tu-Sa 11pm-dawn. Cash only.

Salsero Mayor, C. la Paz 20 (www.salseromayorgranada.com). The name says it all—locals and tourists alike flock here for crowded nights of salsa, *bachata,* and merengue. Beer €2-3. Mixed drinks €5. Open W-Sa 10pm-4:30am. Cash only.

Granada 10, C. Cárcel Baja 3 (☎22 40 01). Movie theater by evening (shows at 8 and 10pm), raging dance club by night. Flashy and opulent. No sneakers or sportswear. Open Su-Th 12:30am-4am, F-Sa 12:30am-5am. MC/V.

Fondo Reservado, Cuesta de Sta. Inés, off Carrera del Darro. Gay-friendly bar with a trendy crowd. Beer €2.60-3. Mixed drinks €4-5. Open Tu-Th 11pm-3am, F-Sa 11pm-4am. Cash only.

EASTERN SPAIN

Its rich soil and famous orange groves, fed by Moorish irrigation systems, have earned Eastern Spain the nickname *Huerta de España* (Spain's Orchard).

ALICANTE (ALICANT) ☎965

While undoubtedly a traditional Spanish city, there is an extra sparkle and unique energy to Alicante (pop. 328,000). The residents are friendlier, the nightlife is livelier, and even the beaches seem sunnier. Alicante is an unforgettable stop along the Mediterranean frequented by Spaniards and foreigners alike.

TRANSPORTATION AND PRACTICAL INFORMATION. RENFE **trains** (☎902 24 02 02) run from Estación Término on Av. Salamanca to: Barcelona (4½-6hr., 5-6 per day, €65), Madrid (4hr., 4-9 per day, €42-73), and Valencia (1½hr., 10 per day, €12-24). **Buses** (☎13 07 00) leave C. Portugal 17 for: Barcelona (7hr., 15 per day, €37-44); Granada (6hr., 10 per day, €24-30); Madrid (5hr., 15 per day, €24-32); Málaga (8hr., 5 per day, €33-40); Sevilla (10hr., 11:45pm, €44); Valencia (2½hr., 14-21 per day, €16-18). The **tourist office** is at C. Portugal 17. (☎92 98 02; www.alicanteturismo.com. Open M-F 9am-2pm and 5-8pm, Sa 10am-2pm.) Use the **Internet** at **Fundación BanCaja,** Rbla. Méndez Nuñez 4, 2nd fl. (1hr. free for students. Open M-F 9am-2pm and 4-9pm, Sa 9am-2pm.) **Postal Code:** 03002.

ACCOMMODATIONS AND FOOD. Cheap hostels are everywhere and easy to find. For simple, sunny rooms with A/C and great views, try **Residencia La Milagrosa ❶,** C. Villa Vieja, which has a rooftop terrace for socializing and admiring the incredible castle view. (☎21 69 18. Laundry €2. Internet €1 per hr. Dorms €15. MC/V.) **Kebap ❶,** Av. Dr. Gadea 5, has the best Middle Eastern food in Alicante. (☎22 92 35. Entrees €5.70-7. Open Su-Th 1-4pm and 8pm-midnight, F-Sa 1pm-midnight. MC/V.) For a more local taste, try the family-run restaurants in the *casco antiguo.* Buy groceries at **Supermarket Mercadona,** C. Alvarez Sereix 5, off Av. Federico Soto. (☎21 58 94. Open M-Sa 9am-9pm.)

NO WORK, ALL PLAY

LAS FALLAS NEVER FAILS

It's not just any region in the world that can combine the burning of artistic political effigies, the election of a societal beauty queen, and a religious ceremony all into one festival celebrating the coming of spring. But every March (12-19, 2007), the *valenciano* community revels in the massive carnival that is Las Fallas, during which visitors from all over the globe come to experience first hand what most say can only be believed if seen.

Originating as a pagan ritual celebrating the coming of warm weather, the "apotheosis of fire" has now been adopted by the Catholic Church as a tribute to the city's patron saint, Our Lady of the Forsaken. Specialized artists work all year to design and build giant, caricatured papier-mâché puppets called *ninots*, which depict anything and everything from pop-culture icons to overtly satirical political references. Originally, the *ninots* were faceless wooden structures created in the winter and dressed in old clothing. They were then used to feed the fires that celebrated the coming of spring. This tradition turned into a form of political expression for the townspeople, and the once faceless *ninots* began to closely resemble government officials, clergy, and aristocrats. Thus, in the 18th century, the puppets were often banned and the designers heavily fined.

SIGHTS AND NIGHTLIFE. With its drawbridges, dark passageways, and hidden tunnels, the ancient and highly touristed **Castell de Santa Bárbara** keeps guard over Alicante's beach. (☎26 31 31. Open daily Apr.-Sept. 10am-7:30pm; Oct.-Mar. 9am-6:30pm. Elevator €2.40 on C. Jovellanos near the beach.) The **Museu Arqueológico Provincial de Alicante,** Pl. Dr. Gomez Ulls, imaginatively showcases artifacts from a variety of periods, including an entire hall dedicated to historical Alicante. (☎14 90 00; www.marqalicante.com. Open Tu-Sa 10am-7pm, Su 10am-2pm. €3, students €1.50.) Alicante's **Playa del Postiguet** attracts beach-lovers, as do nearby **Playa de San Juan** (TAM bus #21, 22, or 31) and **Playa del Mutxavista** (TAM bus #21). Buses (€0.95) depart every 15-25min.

Nightlife in Alicante is fantastic. Most begin their night bar-hopping in the *casco antiguo*, locally referred to as "el barrio." The complex of bars that overlooks the water in Alicante's **main port** and the discos on **Puerto Nuevo** tend to fill up after 2:30am. Don't miss **El Coscorrón,** C. Tarifa 3, named for the bump on the head you might receive from the 4 ft. doorframe. Open since 1936, it claims to be the oldest bar in Alicante. (Beer €2.50. Mojito €2.50. Mixed drinks €4-6. Open Su-W 10:30pm-2:30am, Th-Sa 7pm-4am.) The hedonistic **Festival de Sant Joan** (June 20-29) is a celebration of the summer solstice. *Fogueras* (giant papier mâché structures) are erected and then burned in the streets during *la Cremà*. Afterward, firefighters soak everyone during *la Banyà* and the party continues until dawn.

VALENCIA ☎963

Valencia's white beaches and palm-tree-lined avenues are less touristed than those of Spain's other major cities. And yet, it seems to possess all the best aspects of its sister cities: the energy of Madrid, the vibrant spirit of Alicante, the off-beat sophistication of Barcelona, and the warmth of Sevilla.

TRANSPORTATION AND PRACTICAL INFORMATION. Trains arrive at Estació del Nord, C. Xàtiva 24 (☎52 02 02). RENFE (☎902 24 02 02) runs to: Alicante (2-3hr., 12 per day, €9.40-24); Barcelona (3hr., 8-16 per day, €29-37); Madrid (3½hr.; 12 per day; €20-39, Su prices vary); Sevilla (8½hr., 11:20am, €44). **Buses** (☎46 62 66) go from Av. Menéndez Pidal 13 to: Alicante via the Costa Blanca (4½hr., 10-30 per day, €16-18); Barcelona (4½hr., 19 per day, €21); Granada (8hr., 9 per day, €36-43); Madrid (4hr., 13 per day, €21-26); Málaga (11hr., 9 per day, €44-53); Sevilla (11hr., 3-4 per day, €43-50). Trasmediterránea **ferries,** Muelle de

Poniente (☎902 45 46 45; www.trasmediterranea.es), sail to the Balearic Islands (p. 954). Take bus #1 or 2 from the bus station. The main **tourist office,** C. de la Paz 48, has branches at the train station and at Pl. de la Reina. (☎98 64 22; www.valencia.es. Open M-F 9am-2:30pm and 4:30-8pm.) **Ono,** C. San Vicente Mártir 22, has **Internet.** (☎28 19 02. €1-4 per hr. Open M-F 9am-1am, Sa-Su 10am-1am.) The **post office** is at Pl. del Ajuntament 24. (☎51 23 70. Open M-F 8:30am-8:30pm, Sa 9:30am-2pm.) **Postal Code:** divided into zones, center 46005.

ACCOMMODATIONS AND FOOD. The best lodging deals are around **Plaça del Ajuntament** and **Plaça del Mercat.** The **Home Youth Hostel ❶,** C. Lonja 4, is across from the Mercado Central, on a side street off Pl. Dr. Collado. A lounge and laid-back environment make this the most social hostel in town. (☎91 62 29; www.likeathome.net. Fully equipped kitchen. Linens included. Internet €0.50 per 15min. Dorms €17; singles €21. MC/V.) Paella is the most famous of Valencia's 200 rice dishes; try as many of them as you can. **Sugar Cafe ❶,** C. de la Paz 1, one block from Pl. de la Reina, is a classy little cafe serving coffee and tea (€1-3.45), sandwiches (€1.30-4), and salads (€3.50-4) to the sound of Frank Sinatra. (☎15 38 47. Open M-F 8am-9pm. Cash only.) Try some exquisite Paella Valenciana at cute **El Rall ❸,** by the old silk exchange on C. Tundidores 2. The portions are huge and the paella is delicious. (☎92 20 90. Paella €10-21 per person, min. 2 people. Reserve ahead. Open daily 1:30-4pm and 9-11:30pm. MC/V.) The **Mercado Central** sells fresh meat and fruit (including Valencia's famous oranges) from an Art Nouveau building on Pl. del Mercat. (Open M-Sa 7am-2:30pm. Cash only.) For groceries, try the basement of **El Corte Inglés,** C. Colón. (Open M-Sa 10am-10pm.)

SIGHTS. Most sights line Río Turia or cluster near Pl. de la Reina. EMT bus #5 is the only public bus that passes by most of the historical sites; for a guided tour try the **Bus Turistic,** which goes to the old town sights. (☎15 85 15. €12.) Take bus #35 from Pl. del Ajuntament to reach the ultra-modern and fascinating **Ciutat de les Arts i de les Ciències.** The complex is divided into five large spaces including **L'Hemisfèric,** with an IMAX theater and planetarium, the **Museu de les Ciències Príncipe Felipe,** an interactive playground for science and technology fiends, and **L'Oceanogràfic,** an aquarium that recreates different aquatic environments. The **Palau de les Arts** hosts performances, while **L'Umbracle** is an enormous garden terrace and sculpture garden above the parking lot. (☎902 10 00 31; www.cac.es. Shows at L'Hemis-

Today, las Fallas commissions decide a year in advance which artists will participate in the festival and what sort of budget they will receive (often it reaches the millions); once selected, it is the artists who have creative reign. During Fallas week, the 10 ft. *ninots* are paraded down the street in a colorful display of artistic mastery and fireworks, gunpowder, and music announcing the coming of spring. With a religious tradition added in 1945, a stunning 14m floral Virgin is stationed outside the basilica as an offering to the saint and in recognition of *valenciana* women. On the last day, a Fallas Queen is chosen from among the village girls, who dance and revel in their traditional garb until 10pm. The festival culminates in a massive bonfire, the eerie *crema,* in which the *ninots* are stuffed with fireworks, streetlights are extinguished, the crowd begins to chant, and the *ninots* are set ablaze at precisely midnight. While their European neighbors may disapprove of such massive destruction of artistry, the *valencianos* see the tradition as a fitting display of the fleetingness and ephemerality of life.

For more information and history on the festival, visit the Museo Fallero, Pl. de Monteolivete, where many salvaged puppets–one from each year of the festival–are on display.

fèric IMAX and planetarium every hr. M-Th 11am-7pm, F-Sa 11am-9pm. Museum open mid-June to mid-Sept. daily 10am-8pm; Mar. to mid-June and mid-Sept. to Jan. Su-F 10am-6pm, Sa 10am-8pm. L'Oceanogràfic open Aug. daily 10am-midnight; mid-June to Aug. daily 10am-8pm; Sept. to mid-June Su-F 10am-6pm, Sa 10am-8pm. Combination tickets for the entire complex €29.) Across the river, the **Museu Provincial de Belles Artes,** C. Sant Pío V, displays superb 14th- to 16th-century Valencian art and is home to El Greco's *San Juan Bautista*, Velázquez's self-portrait, and a number of works by Goya. (☎60 57 93. Open Tu-Sa 10am-8pm. Free.) Next door, check out the bizarre **Jardines del Real** (free).

ENTERTAINMENT AND NIGHTLIFE. The most popular beaches are **Las Arenas** and **Malvarrosa,** accessible by bus #20, 21, 22, or 23. To get to the more attractive **Salér,** 14km from the city, take an Autocares Herca **bus** from Gran Vía de Germanias at C. Sueca. (☎49 12 50. 30min., 1 per hr. 7am-9pm, €1-1.10.) Bars and pubs abound in El Carme, while discos dominate the university area. The gay and lesbian scene centers on **Calle Quart** and around **Plaza Vicente Iborra.** Follow C. Bolsería out of Pl. del Mercat to guzzle *agua de Valencia* (orange juice, champagne, and vodka) at outdoor terraces in Pl. Tossal. In El Carme, **Bolsería Café,** C. Bolsería 41, is packed nightly with the very beautiful and the very chic. (☎91 89 03. Beer €3. Mixed drinks €6. W funk, Sa-Su house music. Open daily 7:30pm-3:30am. Cash only.) **Radio City,** C. Sta. Teresa 19, is a great after-hours salsa club with no cover charge and a huge dance floor. (☎91 41 51; www.radiocityvalencia.com. Beer €3.50. Mixed drinks from €6. Tu flamenco 11pm. Open daily 7:30pm-3:30am. Cash only.) Consult the weekly *Qué y Dónde* (€0.50), the weekly entertainment supplement *La Cartelera* (€0.50), or the free *24/7 Valencia*. The most famous festival in Valencia, **Las Fallas** (p. 928), takes place in March.

NORTHEASTERN SPAIN

Northeastern Spain encompasses the country's most fiercely regionalistic areas. From Costa Brava to Barcelona, Cataluña is graced with the nation's richest resources. The area is also home to the jaw-dropping slopes of the Pyrenees, the running bulls of Navarra, the industrious cities of Aragón, the beautiful coasts of the Basque Country, and the unrestrained revelry of the Balearic Islands.

BARCELONA ☎93

From the urban carnival of Las Ramblas to buildings with no straight lines, from wild festivals to even wilder nightlife, Barcelona pushes the limits in everything it does—with amazing results. The center of the whimsical and daring *Modernisme* architectural movement and once home to Pablo Picasso and Joan Miró, the city is grounded in an alternate reality through its art. Yet the draw of the city extends beyond its artistic merits. Its residents exhibit the same energy when it comes to fashion, food, and above all, hospitality. Since the end of Franco's oppressive regime, Barcelona has led the autonomous region of Cataluña in a cultural resurgence. The result is a city of striking colors and shapes. Don't worry if you don't speak Spanish—neither does Barcelona.

INTERCITY TRANSPORTATION

Flights: Aeroport El Prat de Llobregat (**BCN;** ☎902 40 47 04; www.aena.es), 13km southwest of Barcelona. To get to Pl. Catalunya, take **RENFE** train L10 (20-25min., every 30min., €2.40) or the **Aerobus** (☎415 6020; 30min., every 8-13min.; €3.75).

Trains: Barcelona has 2 main train stations. **Estació Barcelona-Sants,** in Pl. Països Catalans (M: Sants-Estació), is the main terminal for domestic and international traffic. **Estació de França,** on Av. Marquès de l'Argentera (M: Barceloneta), serves regional destinations and some international arrivals. **RENFE** (Spain ☎902 24 02 02, international 902 24 34 02; www.renfe.es) trains go to: **Bilbao** (9-10hr., 12:30 and 10pm, €38-49); **Madrid** (5-9hr., 10 per day, €37-63); **Sevilla** (10-12hr., 3 per day, €54-88); **Valencia** (3-5hr., 15 per day, €21-37). 20% discount on round-trip tickets.

Buses: Most buses arrive at the **Barcelona Nord Estació d'Autobusos,** C. Alí Bei 80 (☎902 26 06 06; www.barcelonanord.com.) M: Arc de Triomf. Buses also depart from Estació Barcelona-Sants and the airport. **Sarfa** (☎902 30 20 25; www.sarfa.es) goes to **Cadaqués** (2½hr., 2 per day, €18). **Eurolines** (☎932 32 10 92; www.eurolines.es) travels to **Naples, ITA** (24hr; M, W, F 5:30pm; €120) and **Paris, FRA** (15hr., M-Sa 8:30pm, €84) via Lyon. **ALSA/Enatcar** (☎902 42 22 42; www.alsa.es) goes to: **Alicante** (8-9hr., 11 per day, €37-42); **Madrid** (8hr., 20 per day, €25-34); **Sevilla** (14-16hr., 2 per day, €70-82); **Valencia** (4-5hr., 14 per day, €23-28).

Ferries: Trasmediterránea (☎902 45 46 45; www.trasmediterranea.com), in Terminal Drassanes, Moll Sant Bertran. Ferries go to **Ibiza** (5-9hr., 1 per day, €50), **Mahón** (3½-9hr., 1 per day, €50), and **Palma** (3½-7hr., 2-3 per day, €70).

ORIENTATION

Imagine yourself perched on Columbus's head at the **Monument a Colom** (on Passeig de Colom, along the shore), viewing the city with the sea at your back. From the harbor, the city slopes upward to the mountains. From the Monument a Colom, **La Rambla,** the main thoroughfare, runs from the harbor to **Plaça de Catalunya** (M: Catalunya), the city center. *Let's Go* uses "Las Ramblas" to refer to the general area and "La Rambla" in address listings. The touristed **Ciutat Vella** (Old City) centers around Las Ramblas and includes the Barri Gòtic, La Ribera, and El Raval. The **Barri Gòtic** is east of La Rambla, enclosed on the other side by **Vía Laietana.** East of V. Laietana lies the maze-like neighborhood of **La Ribera,** bordered by Parc de la Ciutadella and Estació de França. Beyond La Ribera—farther east, outside the Ciutat Vella—are **Poble Nou** and **Port Olímpic.** To the west of Las Ramblas is **El Raval.** Farther west rises **Montjuïc,** with sprawling gardens, museums, the 1992 Olympic grounds, and a fortress. Directly behind the Monument a Colom is the **Port Vell** (old port) development, where a wavy bridge leads across to the ultra-modern shopping and entertainment complexes **Moll d'Espanya** and **Maremàgnum.** North of the Ciutat Vella is **l'Eixample,** a gridded neighborhood created during the expansion of the 1860s, which sprawls from Pl. Catalunya toward the mountains. **Gran Via de les Corts Catalanes** defines its lower edge, and the **Passeig de Gràcia,** l'Eixample's main avenue, bisects the neighborhood. **Avinguda Diagonal** marks the border between l'Eixample and the **Zona Alta** (uptown), which includes **Pedralbes, Gràcia,** and other older neighborhoods in the foothills. The peak of **Tibidabo,** the northwest border of the city, offers the most comprehensive view of Barcelona.

LOCAL TRANSPORTATION

Public Transportation: ☎010. Passes *(abonos)* work for the Metro, bus, urban lines of FGC commuter trains, RENFE *cercanías,* Trams, and Nitbus. One ride *(sencillo)* costs €1.20. A **T-10 pass** (€6.65) is valid for 10 rides; a **T-Día pass** entitles you to unlimited bus and Metro travel for 1 (€5), 2 (€9.20), 3 (€12.40), 4 (€16), or 5 days (€20).

Metro: ☎298 70 00; www.tmb.net. Vending machines and ticket windows sell passes. Hold on to your ticket until you exit or risk a €40 fine. Trains run M-Th 5am-midnight, F-Sa 5am-2am, Su and holidays 6am-midnight.

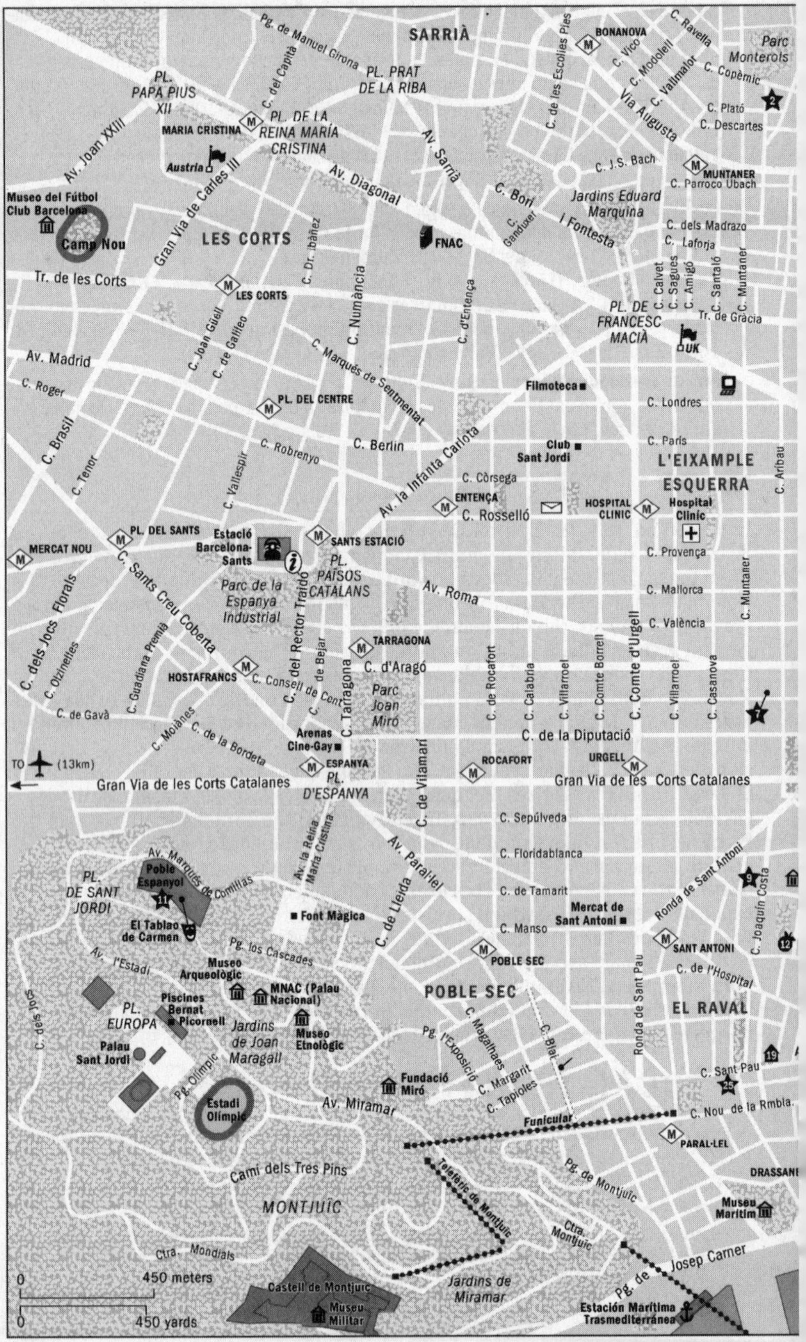

SARRIÀ
Pg. de Manuel Girona
PL. PAPA PIUS XII
PL. PRAT DE LA RIBA
PL. DE LA REINA MARÍA CRISTINA
MARIA CRISTINA
Austria
Av. Joan XXIII
C. del Capità
Av. Diagonal
Av. Sarrià
BONANOVA
C. de les Escoles Pies
C. Vico
C. Modolell
C. Vallmajor
C. Ravella
Parc Monterols
C. Copèrnic
C. Plató
C. Descartes
Via Augusta
C. J.S. Bach
MUNTANER
C. Parroco Ubach
C. Bori
Jardins Eduard Marquina
I Fontesta
C. Ganduxer
C. dels Madrazo
C. Laforja
Museo del Fútbol Club Barcelona
Camp Nou
Gran Via de Carles III
LES CORTS
C. Dr. Ibañez
FNAC
Tr. de les Corts
LES CORTS
C. Numància
C. d'Entença
C. Calvet
C. Sagues
C. Amigó
C. Santaló
C. Muntaner
Tr. de Gràcia
PL. DE FRANCESC MACIÀ
UK
C. Joan Güell
C. de Galileo
Av. Madrid
C. Marqués de Sentmenat
C. Roger
Filmoteca
C. Londres
PL. DEL CENTRE
C. Brasil
C. Robrenyo
C. Berlin
Club Sant Jordi
C. París
L'EIXAMPLE ESQUERRA
C. Aribau
C. Tenor
C. Vallespir
Av. la Infanta Carlota
C. Còrsega
ENTENÇA
C. Rosselló
HOSPITAL CLINIC
Hospital Clínic
PL. DEL SANTS
Estació Barcelona-Sants
SANTS ESTACIÓ
MERCAT NOU
PL. PAÏSOS CATALANS
C. Provença
C. Sants Creu Coberta
Parc de la Espanya Industrial
C. del Rector Triadó
Av. Roma
C. Mallorca
C. dels Jocs Florals
C. València
C. Muntaner
C. Olzinelles
C. Guadiana Premià
TARRAGONA
C. d'Aragó
HOSTAFRANCS
C. Consell de Cent
C. de Bejar
C. Tarragona
Parc Joan Miró
C. de Rocafort
C. Calabria
C. Villarroel
C. Comte Borrell
C. Comte d'Urgell
C. Villarroel
C. Casanova
C. de Gavà
C. Moianes
C. de la Bordeta
Arenas Cine-Gay
C. de la Diputació
TO (13km)
ESPANYA
PL. D'ESPANYA
ROCAFORT
URGELL
Gran Via de les Corts Catalanes
Gran Via de les Corts Catalanes
C. de Vilamarí
C. Sepúlveda
Av. la Reina Maria Cristina
Av. Marquès de Comillas
Av. Paral·lel
C. Floridablanca
PL. DE SANT JORDI
Poble Espanyol
C. de Tamarit
Ronda de Sant Antoni
C. Joaquín Costa
El Tablao de Carmen
Font Màgica
C. de Lleida
Mercat de Sant Antoni
C. Manso
SANT ANTONI
Av. l'Estadi
Pg. los Cascades
POBLE SEC
C. de l'Hospital
Museo Arqueològic
MNAC (Palau Nacional)
POBLE SEC
Ronda de Sant Pau
EL RAVAL
PL. EUROPA
Piscines Bernat Picornell
C. Magalhaes
Jardins de Joan Maragall
Museo Etnològic
Pg. l'Exposició
C. Blai
C. dels Jocs
Palau Sant Jordi
C. Margarit
C. Sant Pau
Pg. Olímpic
Fundació Miró
C. Tapioles
Estadi Olímpic
Av. Miramar
Funicular
C. Nou de la Rmbla.
PARAL·LEL
DRASSANES
Camí dels Tres Pins
Telefèric de Montjuïc
Pg. de Montjuïc
MONTJUÏC
Museu Marítim
Ctra. Montjuïc
Ctra. Mondials
Pg. de Josep Carner
0
450 meters
Jardins de Miramar
Castell de Montjuïc
Museu Militar
Estación Marítima Trasmediterránea
0
450 yards

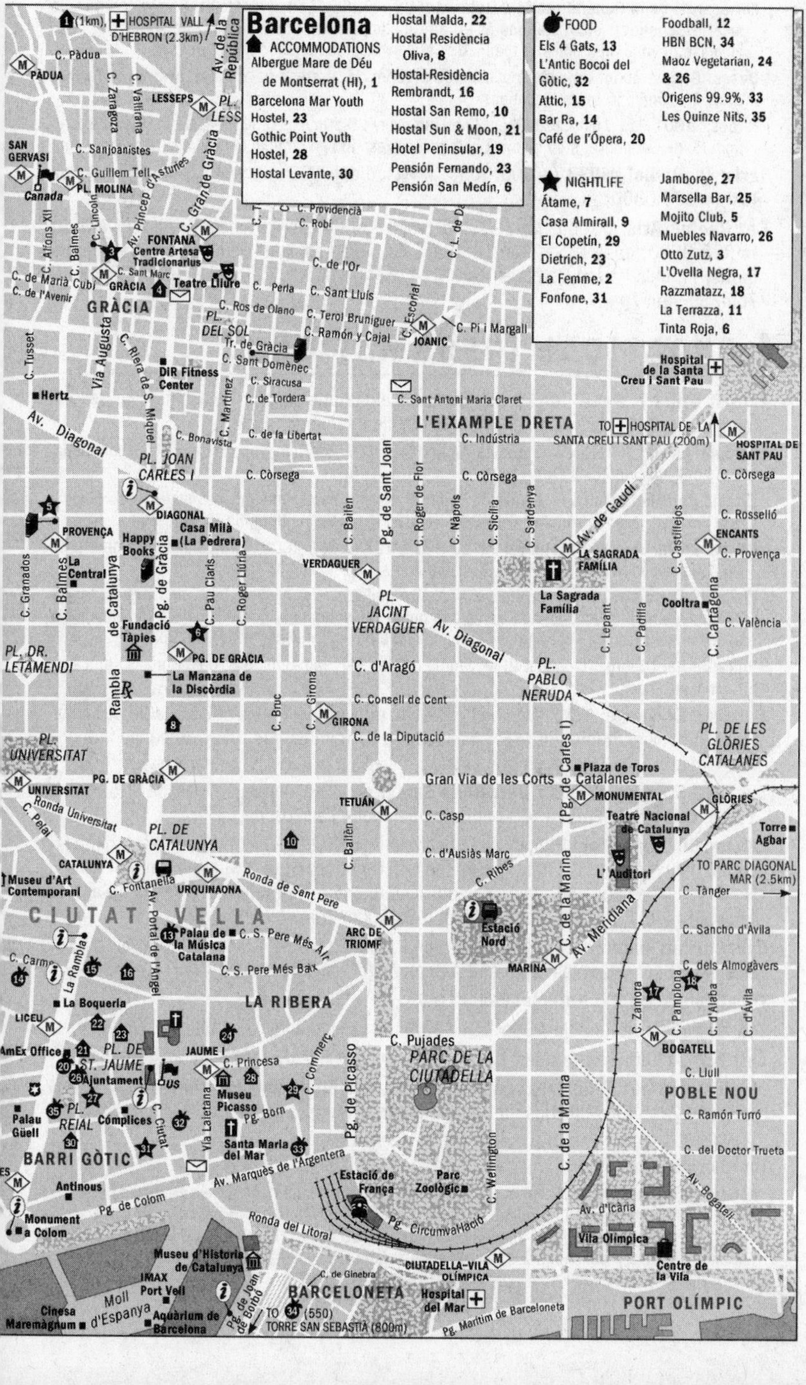
Barcelona
ACCOMMODATIONS
Albergue Mare de Déu de Montserrat (HI), 1
Barcelona Mar Youth Hostel, 23
Gothic Point Youth Hostel, 28
Hostal Levante, 30
Hostal Malda, 22
Hostal Residència Oliva, 8
Hostal-Residència Rembrandt, 16
Hostal San Remo, 10
Hostal Sun & Moon, 21
Hotel Peninsular, 19
Pensión Fernando, 23
Pensión San Medín, 6
FOOD
Els 4 Gats, 13
L'Antic Bocoi del Gòtic, 32
Attic, 15
Bar Ra, 14
Café de l'Ópera, 20
Foodball, 12
HBN BCN, 34
Maoz Vegetarian, 24 & 26
Origens 99.9%, 33
Les Quinze Nits, 35
NIGHTLIFE
Átame, 7
Casa Almirall, 9
El Copetín, 29
Dietrich, 23
La Femme, 2
Fonfone, 31
Jamboree, 27
Marsella Bar, 25
Mojito Club, 5
Muebles Navarro, 26
Otto Zutz, 3
L'Ovella Negra, 17
Razzmatazz, 18
La Terrazza, 11
Tinta Roja, 6
(1km), HOSPITAL VALL D'HEBRON (2.3km)
Av. de la República
PÀDUA
LESSEPS
SAN GERVASI
PL. MOLINA
Canada
FONTANA
Centre Artesa Tradicionarius
GRÀCIA
Teatre Lliure
DIR Fitness Center
Hertz
L'EIXAMPLE DRETA
JOANIC
Av. Diagonal
PL. JOAN CARLES I
DIAGONAL
Casa Milà (La Pedrera)
PROVENÇA
Happy Books
La Central
Fundació Tàpies
PG. DE GRÀCIA
La Manzana de la Discòrdia
VERDAGUER
PL. JACINT VERDAGUER
LA SAGRADA FAMÍLIA
La Sagrada Família
Hospital de la Santa Creu i Sant Pau
TO HOSPITAL DE LA SANTA CREU I SANT PAU (200m)
HOSPITAL DE SANT PAU
ENCANTS
Cooltra
PL. PABLO NERUDA
GIRONA
PL. DR. LETAMENDI
PL. UNIVERSITAT
UNIVERSITAT
Gran Via de les Corts Catalanes
Plaza de Toros
MONUMENTAL
PL. DE LES GLÒRIES CATALANES
GLÒRIES
Teatre Nacional de Catalunya
L' Auditori
Torre Agbar
TO PARC DIAGONAL MAR (2.5km)
TETUÁN
PL. DE CATALUNYA
CATALUNYA
Museu d'Art Contemporani
URQUINAONA
Ronda de Sant Pere
CIUTAT VELLA
Palau de la Música Catalana
ARC DE TRIOMF
Estació Nord
MARINA
Av. Meridiana
La Boqueria
LICEU
LA RIBERA
AmEx Office
PL. DE ST. JAUME
Ajuntament
US
JAUME I
Museu Picasso
PARC DE LA CIUTADELLA
BOGATELL
POBLE NOU
Palau Güell
PL. REIAL
Còmplices
BARRI GÒTIC
Santa Maria del Mar
Antinous
Monument a Colom
Av. Marquès de l'Argentera
Estació de França
Parc Zoològic
Vila Olímpica
Centre de la Vila
Museu d'Historia de Catalunya
IMAX Port Vell
Moll d'Espanya
Cinesa Maremàgnum
Aquàrium de Barcelona
BARCELONETA
CIUTADELLA-VILA OLÍMPICA
Hospital del Mar
TO (550) TORRE SAN SEBASTIÀ (800m)
PORT OLÍMPIC
Pg. Marítim de Barceloneta
Ronda del Litoral

Ferrocarrils de la Generalitat de Catalunya (FGC): ☎205 1515; www.fgc.es. Commuter trains to local destinations; main stations at Pl. de Catalunya and Pl. d'Espanya. After Tibidabo, rates increase by zone. Info office at the Pl. de Catalunya station open M-F 7am-9pm.

Buses: Go just about anywhere, usually 5am-10pm. Most stops have maps posted. Buses run every 10-15min. in central locations.

Nitbus: ☎901 511 151. 16 different lines run every 20-30min. 10:30pm-4:30am. Buses depart from Pl. de Catalunya, stop by most club complexes, and go through Ciutat Vella and Zona Alta.

Taxis: Try **RadioTaxi033** (☎303 3033; www.radiotaxi033.com; AmEx/MC/V) or **Servi-Taxi** (☎330 0300).

Car Rental: Avis, C. Corcega 293-295 (☎237 5680; www.avis.com). Also at **airport** (☎298 3600; open M-Sa 7am-12:30am, Su 7am-midnight) and **Estació Barcelona-Sants,** Pl. dels Països Catalans. (☎330 4193. Open M-F 7:30am-10:30pm, Sa 8am-7pm, Su 9am-7pm.)

PRACTICAL INFORMATION

Tourist Offices: ☎907 30 12 82; www.barcelonaturisme.com. In addition to several tourist offices, Barcelona has numerous mobile information kiosks.

Aeroport El Prat de Llobregat, terminals A and B (☎478 0565). Info and last-minute accommodation booking. Open daily 9am-9pm.

Estació Barcelona-Sants, Pl. Països Catalans. M: Sants-Estació. Info and last-minute accommodation booking. Open in summer daily 8am-8pm; winter M-F 8am-8pm, Sa-Su 8am-2pm.

Oficina de Turisme de Catalunya, Pg. de Gràcia 107 (☎238 4000; www.gencat.es/probert). M: Diagonal. Open M-Sa 10am-7pm, Su 10am-2pm.

Plaça de Catalunya, Pl. de Catalunya 17S. M: Catalunya. The biggest, best, and busiest tourist office. Free maps, brochures on sights and public transportation, booking service for last-minute accommodations, gift shop, money exchange, and box office. Open daily 9am-9pm.

Plaça de Sant Jaume, C. Ciutat 2. M: Jaume I. Open M-F 9am-8pm, Sa 10am-8pm, Su and holidays 10am-2pm.

Currency Exchange: ATMs give the best rates; the next best rates are available at banks. General banking hours are M-F 8:30am-2pm. La Rambla has many exchange stations open late, but the rates are not as good.

Luggage Storage: Estació Barcelona-Sants. €3-4.50 per day. Open daily 5:30am-11pm. **Estació de França.** €3 per day. Open daily 7am-10pm.

Library: Biblioteca Sant Pau, C. de l'Hospital 56 (☎302 0797). M: Liceu. Walk to the far end of the courtyard; the library is on the left. Do not confuse it with the Catalán library, which you'll see first and requires permission to enter. Free Internet. Open mid-Sept. to June M-Tu and F 3:30-8:30pm, W-Th and Sa 10am-2pm.

Laundromat: Tintorería San Pablo, C. San Pau 105 (☎329 4249). M: Paral·lel. €7.25. Open M-F Sept.-June 9am-2pm and 4-8pm; Aug. 8am-2pm; July 9:30am-1:30pm.

Local Police: ☎092. **National Police:** ☎091.

Tourist Police: La Rambla 43 (☎344 1300). M: Liceu. Multilingual officers. Open 24hr.

Late-Night Pharmacy: Rotates; check any pharmacy window for the nearest on duty.

Medical Services: Medical Emergency: ☎061. **Hospital Clìnic i Provincal,** C. Villarroel 170 (☎227 5400). M: Hospital Clìnic. Enter at the intersection of C. Roselló and C. Casanova.

Internet Access:

Easy Internet Café, La Rambla 31 (www.easyinternetcafe.com). M: Liceu. Reasonable prices and over 200 terminals in a bright, modern center make this Internet heaven. Digital camera, CD burning, faxing, copying, and scanning services. €1.80 per hr., 1-day pass €7, 1-week €15, 1-month €30. Open daily 8am-2:30am. **Branch** at Ronda Universitat 35. M: Catalunya. €2 per hr., 1-day pass €3, 1-week €7, 1-month €15. Open daily 8am-2am.

Navegaweb, La Rambla 88-94 (☎317 9026; navegabarcelona@terra.es). M: Liceu. Good rates on international calls. Internet €1.80 per hr. Open Su-Th 9am-midnight, F 9am-1am, Sa 9am-2am.

World Telecom Network, C. Unió 16. (☎238 4449). 30 fast, fully equipped new computers. €1 per hr., €1.90 per 2hr. Open daily 11am-10pm.

Contacta, Gran Vía 600. M: Universitat. €1 per hr. Open M-F 9am-11pm, Sa-Su noon-11pm.

Post Office: Pl. d'Antoni López (☎902 19 71 97). M: Jaume I or Barceloneta. Fax and *Lista de Correos.* Open M-F 8:30am-10pm, Su noon-10pm. **Postal Code:** 08003.

SPAIN

ACCOMMODATIONS

Finding an affordable room in Barcelona can be difficult. To crash in touristy **Barri Gòtic** or **Las Ramblas** during the busier months (June-Sept. and Dec.), make reservations weeks or months in advance. Consider staying outside of touristy Ciutat Vella; many nice hostels in **l'Eixample** and **Gràcia** tend to have more vacancies. For camping info, contact the **Associació de Càmpings i C.V. de Barcelona,** Gran Via de les Corts Catalanes 608 (☎412 5955; www.campingsbcn.com).

BARRI GÒTIC

Backpackers flock to these hostels to be close to happening Las Ramblas.

Hostal Levante, Baixada de San Miquel 2 (☎933 17 95 65; www.hostallevante.com). M: Liceu. 50 large rooms with light wood furnishings and fans; some have balconies. TV lounge. 4- to 8-person apartments have kitchen, living room, and laundry machine. Singles €30; doubles €50, with bath €60; apartments €30 per person. MC/V. ❸

Pensión Fernando, C. Ferran 31 (☎933 01 79 93; www.hfernando.com). M: Liceu. This clean hostel is conveniently located and has dorms with A/C and lockers. Common kitchen with dining room and TV on 3rd fl. Lockers €1.50. Dorms €16-21; singles €30-36, with bath €40-45; doubles with bath €52-64; triples with bath €58-70. MC/V. ❷

Hostal-Residència Rembrandt, C. de la Portaferrissa 23 (☎933 18 10 11; www.hostrembrandt.com). M: Liceu. This fantastic hostel has 28 rooms, some with bath, patio, sitting area, and TV. Restaurant-quality breakfast (€5) and fans. Reception 9am-11pm. Reservations require credit card. Singles €28; doubles €45-55; triples €70. MC/V. ❸

Hostal Maldà, C. Pi 5 (☎933 17 30 02). M: Liceu. The friendly owner keeps the hostel occupied year-round. 26 quality rooms with shared baths at unbeatable prices. Check-in 9-11am. No reservations. Doubles €30; triples with shower €45. Cash only. ❸

Hostel Sun & Moon, C. Ferran 17 (☎932 70 20 60; www.smhostel.net). M: Liceu. Low prices in an ideal location. Communal kitchen. Includes breakfast, sheets, blanket. Towels €2. Free Internet. 6- and 8-bed dorms €20. AmEx/MC/V. ❷

LA RIBERA AND EL RAVAL

Be careful in the areas near the port and farther from Las Ramblas at night.

Gothic Point Youth Hostel, C. Vigatans 5 (☎932 68 78 08; www.gothicpoint.com). M: Jaume I. Lobby with free Internet and TV is usually filled with backpackers. 150 beds in jungle-gym rooms with A/C. Biweekly Gaudí and city walking tours (€5) and weekly crafts fair. Refrigerator access. Breakfast included. Lockers €1.50 per day. Linens €2, towels €2. High-season dorms €23; mid-season €19; low season €17. AmEx/MC/V. ❷

Barcelona Mar Youth Hostel, C. de Sant Pau 80 (☎933 24 85 30; www.barcelonamar.es). M: Paral·lel. 6-16 per room, with curtains for privacy. Breakfast included. A/C and free Internet. All beds come with lockers. Linens €2.50, towels €2.50, both €3.50. Laundry €4.50. Dorms in summer €22-23; winter €15-19. AmEx/MC/V. ❷

Hotel Peninsular, C. de Sant Pau 34 (☎933 02 31 38). M: Liceu. Lovely rooms with phone and A/C and a 4-story interior courtyard festooned with plants. Breakfast included. Singles €30, with bath €50; doubles with bath €75. MC/V. ❸

L'EIXAMPLE

Accommodations in this area tend to be nicer than those in Ciutat Vella.

Hostal Residència Oliva, Pg. de Gràcia 32, 4th fl. (☎934 88 01 62; www.lasguias.com/hostaloliva). M: Pg. de Gràcia. Elegant bureaus, mirrors, ceilings, and a light marble floor give this hostel a classy ambience. Rooms have high ceilings, TVs, and fans. Singles €35; doubles €58, with bath €70; triples with bath €99. Cash only. ❸

Hostal San Remo, Ausiàs Marc 19 (☎933 02 19 89; www.hostalsanremo.com). M: Urquinaona. TV and A/C. Free Internet. Reserve ahead. Singles €20, with bath €36; doubles €50/60; triples €60/72. Nov. and Jan.-Feb. reduced rates. MC/V. ❸

ZONA ALTA: GRÀCIA AND OUTER BARRIS

Gràcia is Barcelona's "undiscovered" quarter, so last-minute arrivals may find vacancies here, even though options are few.

Pensión San Medín, C. Gran de Gràcia 125 (☎932 17 30 68; www.sanmedin.com). M: Fontana. Ornate tiling adorns this family-run pension's rooms. Small common room with TV. Reception 8am-midnight. Singles €32, with bath €42; doubles €54/65. MC/V. ❸

Albergue Mare de Déu de Montserrat (HI), Pg. Mare de Déu del Coll 41-45 (☎932 10 51 51; www.xanascat.net). M: Vallcarca. This 220-bed hostel, though far from the city center, is a great place to meet other backpackers. Breakfast included. Flexible max. stay 5 days. Dorms €19-23, under 25 €16-19. DC/MC/V. ❷

FOOD

The eateries on **Carrer Aragó** by Pg. de Gràcia have lunchtime *menús*, and the **Passeig de Gràcia** has outdoor dining. Gràcia's **Plaça Sol** and La Ribera's **Santa Maria del Mar** are the best tapas spots. For fruit, cheese, and wine, head to **La Boqueria (Mercat de Sant Josep),** off La Rambla outside M: Liceu. (Open M-Sa 6am-8pm.) Buy groceries at **Champion,** La Rambla 13. (M: Liceu. Open M-Sa 9am-10pm.)

BARRI GÒTIC

Les Quinze Nits, Pl. Reial 6 (☎933 17 30 75). M: Liceu. One of the most popular restaurants in Barcelona, with nightly lines halfway through the plaza. Satisfying Catalán entrees at shockingly low prices. Try the "Catalán dessert," made with nougat ice cream, melted chocolate, and *crema catalana.* Pasta and rice €4-6. Fish €7-9. Meat €6-9. Open daily 1-3:45pm and 8:30-11:30pm. MC/V. ❶

L'Antic Bocoi del Gòtic, Baixada de Viladecols 3 (☎933 10 50 67). M: Jaume I. This rustic and romantic restaurant is formed in part by a 1st-century Roman wall. Excellent salads (€6.50-7.50) and exquisite *pâtés* (€9-12) contain *jamón iberico* and local produce. Reserve ahead. Open M-Sa 8:30pm-midnight. AmEx/DC/V. ❷

Attic, La Rambla 120 (☎933 02 48 66). M: Liceu. Hard to believe that this chic restaurant has reasonable prices right on La Rambla. Mediterranean fusion, including fish (€9-13), meat (€6-14), and rice (€6-9). Open daily 1pm-1am. AmEx/DC/MC/V. ❸

Els 4 Gats, C. Montsió 3 (☎933 02 41 40; www.4gats.com). M: Catalunya. Picasso's old *Modernista* hangout, with lots of bohemian character. High-quality cuisine includes Mediterranean salad (€9.50) and Iberian pork with apples (€18). Lunch *menú* (€12) is the best deal and comes with epic desserts; try the *crema catalana.* Entrees €12-26. Live piano 9pm-1am. Open daily 1pm-1am. AmEx/MC/V. ❹

Maoz Vegetarian, 3 locations: C. Ferran 13, La Rambla 95, and C. Jaume I 7. Vegetarian chain with 1 menu option—falafel, with or without hummus—and fresh vegetable toppings. Don't expect to sit down; it's barely big enough to contain the stream of customers. Falafel €3-4. Open Su-Th 11am-2:30am, F-Sa 11am-3am. ❶

Café de l'Ópera, La Rambla 74 (☎933 17 75 85; www.cafeoperabcn.com). M: Liceu. A drink in this antique cafe used to be a post-opera bourgeois tradition; now it's a hidden favorite amid tourist traps. The hot chocolate (€1.80) is thick as a melted candy bar. *Churros* €1.30. Tapas €3-6. Salads €3-8. Open daily 8am-2:30am. Cash only. ❶

ELSEWHERE IN BARCELONA

Orígens 99'9%, C. Enric Granados 9 (☎934 53 11 20; www.origen99.com); C. Vidrieria, 6-8 (☎933 10 75 31); Pg. de Born 4 (☎932 95 66 90); and C. Ramón y Cajal 12 (☎932 13 60 31). Rustic shelves and free samples in the storefront belie a hip crowd packed into the adjoining restaurant. Entrees such as beef-stuffed onion (€4.85) and rabbit with almonds (€4.95) are made with 99.9% local ingredients. Small soups and vegetarian and meat dishes €3-6. Open 12:30pm-1am. AmEx/MC/V. ❶

Bar Ra, Pl. de la Garduña (☎933 01 41 63; www.ratown.com). M: Liceu. Behind the Boqueria market. Creative fusion cuisine includes vegetarian options. Entrees €9-15. Obligatory lunch *menú* €11. Dinner *menú* €13; reserve ahead. Open daily 9:30am-1:30am. Kitchen open 1:30-4pm and 9:30pm-midnight. AmEx/DC/MC/V. ❷

HBN BCN, C. Escar 1 (☎932 25 02 63). M: Barceloneta. The name stands for Habana Barcelona, the perfect place for Latin American cuisine. Try the plate of Cuban tapas (€8). Lunch *menú* €8.50. Reserve ahead. Kitchen open 1-4pm and 7:30pm-midnight. Salsa lessons Tu 9:30 and 11pm. MC/V. ❸

Foodball, C. Elisabets 9 (☎932 70 13 63). M: Catalunya. Offers just what the name implies, combining organic ingredients with artistic flair. Some foodballs are savory, others sweet; all are eaten with fingers while sitting on cushioned steps. Foodballs each €2-3. Combos with soup or drink €5-9. Open Su-Th 1-10pm, F-Sa 1-11pm. MC/V. ❶

SIGHTS

The **Ruta del Modernisme** pass is the cheapest and most flexible option for those with an interest in seeing Barcelona's major sights. Passes (€5) are good for a month and give holders a 25-30% discount on attractions including Palau de la Música Catalana, the Museu de Zoología, tours of Hospital de la Santa Creu i Sant Pau, and the facades of La Manzana de la Discòrdia. Purchase passes at the Pl. Catalunya tourist office or at the Modernisme Centre at Hospital Santa Creu i Sant Pau, C. Sant Antoni Maria Claret 167. (☎902 07 66 21; www.rutadelmodernisme.com.)

BORN AND BREAD IN CATALUÑA

Once you hit Cataluña, it is inescapable: at each meal, expect to spend some quality time with your new best friend, *pa amb tomàquet*, known to the rest of Spain as *pan con tomate.* A step up from the ubiquitous dry bread basket, this Catalán specialty is an interactive experience. The premise is simple (and frankly, locals like to make it out to be more elaborate than it really is): slice the tomato in half, rub it on the bread to saturate the slice with juice, then do the same with a clove of garlic and add some olive oil. Then eat.

Of course, there are variables at play. Some establishments present the bread pre-rubbed. Usually the bread is toasted, but sometimes it is not. Furthermore, you will find an extensive range of breads being used; the crusty *pan de pagès* (farmer's bread) is most common, but baguettes and smaller rolls have been known to make appearances on the table. Whatever the case, learn it and love it. Waiters delight in instructing travelers on the proper method of dressing the bread, supplementing tradition with their own lively opinions on just how high to pour the oil from and how much garlic to use.

Fundamentally a simple appetizer, *pa amb tomàquet* takes on a new life at the Catalán table. Plus, it's fun to say.

LAS RAMBLAS

This pedestrian-only strip (roughly 1km long) is a cornucopia of street performers, fortune-tellers, human statues, pet and flower stands, and artists. The wide, tree-lined street, known in Catalán as Les Rambles, is actually six *ramblas* (promenades) that form one boulevard from the Pl. de Catalunya and the **Font de Canaletes.** Visitors who wish to return to Barcelona are supposed to sample the water.

LA BOQUERIA (MERCAT DE SANT JOSEP). Besides being one of the cheapest places to get food in the city, La Boqueria is a sight in itself. It is a traditional Catalán market located in a giant, all-steel Modernist structure. Inside, vendors sell delicious produce, fish, and meat. *(La Rambla 89. M: Liceu. Open M-Sa 6am-8pm.)*

GRAN TEATRE DEL LICEU. Ravaged by anarchists, bombs, and fires during its 150-year history, this is one of Europe's top stages, featuring Catalán opera, and is adorned with gold facades and sculptures. Don't miss the Hall of Mirrors. *(La Rambla 51-59, by C. Sant Pau. M: Liceu. ☎934 85 99 13, tours 85 99 14; www.liceubarcelona.com. Box office open M-F 2-8:30pm, Sa 1hr. before show or by ServiCaixa. Short 20min. semi-guided visits daily 10am-1pm; €4. 1¼hr. tours 10am by reservation only, call 9am-2pm; €8.50.)*

MONUMENT A COLOM. Ruis i Taulet's Monument a Colom towers at the port end of Las Ramblas. Nineteenth-century *Renaixença* enthusiasts convinced themselves that Columbus was Catalán, but historians agree that he was Italian. Oddly enough, the explorer proudly points toward Libya, not the Americas. Take the elevator to the top for a stunning view. *(Portal de la Pau. M: Drassanes. Elevator runs daily June-Sept. 9am-8:30pm; Oct.-May 10am-6:30pm. €2.20, children and seniors €1.40.)*

BARRI GÒTIC

Brimming with cathedrals, palaces, and tourism, Barcelona's oldest zone and political center masks its old age with unflagging energy.

ESGLÉSIA CATEDRAL DE LA SANTA CREU. This cathedral is one of Barcelona's most popular monuments. Beyond the choir are an altar designed by Frederic Marès in 1976 and the sunken Crypt of Santa Eulàlia, one of Barcelona's patron saints. The cathedral museum holds Bartolomé Bermejo's *Pietà.* See a performance of the *sardana* in front of the cathedral on Sundays after Mass; services begin at noon and 6:30pm. *(In Pl. Seu, up C. Bisbe from Pl. Sant Jaume. M: Jaume I. Cathedral open daily 8am-12:45pm and 5:15-7:30pm. Cloister open daily 9am-12:30pm and 5:15-7pm. Elevator to the roof open M-Sa 10:30am-6pm. Choir area open M-F 9am-12:30pm and 5:15-7pm, Sa-Su 9am-12:30pm. Elevator €2. Choir €1. Tours 1-5pm include all sights, €4.)*

MUSEU D'HISTÒRIA DE LA CIUTAT. There are two components to the Museu d'Història de la Ciutat (Museum of the History of Barcelona). Built on top of the 4th-century city walls, the **Palau Reial Major** served as the residence of the Catalán-Aragonese monarchs. Underground is a 4000 sq. m **archaeological exhibit** that was excavated between 1930 and 1960 and displays incredibly intact first- to 6th-century remains of the Roman city of Barcino. *(Pl. del Rei. M: Jaume I. ☎315 1111; www.museuhistoria.bcn.es. Wheelchair-accessible. Open June-Sept. Tu-Sa 10am-8pm, Su 10am-3pm; Oct.-May Tu-Sa 10am-2pm and 4-8pm, Su 10am-3pm. Pamphlets available in English. Palace €4, students €2.50. Archaeological exhibit €1.50/1. Combination ticket €4.50/3.50.)*

LA RIBERA

This neighborhood has recently evolved into a bohemian nucleus, with art galleries, chic eateries, and exclusive bars.

PALAU DE LA MÚSICA CATALANA. Modernist Luis Domènech i Montaner was commissioned to design this must-see concert venue, which glows with stained-glass, marble reliefs, intricate woodwork, and ceramic mosaics. *(C. Sant Francese de Paula 2. M: Jaume I. ☎295 7200; www.palaumusica.org. Mandatory 50min. English-language tours almost every hr. Open daily July-Sept. 10am-7pm; Oct.-June 10am-3:30pm. €8, students €7. Check the* Guía del Ocio *for concerts. Concert tickets €6-330. MC/V.)*

MUSEU PICASSO. The most-visited museum in Barcelona traces Picasso's artistic development with the world's most comprehensive collection of work from his formative Barcelona period. Picasso donated over 1700 of his works to the museum; it now boasts 3600. *(C. Montcada 15-23. M: Jaume I. Open Tu-Su 10am-8pm. €6, students €4, under 16 and 1st Su of the month free. Temporary exhibit €2.50/1.)*

PARC DE LA CIUTADELLA. Host of the 1888 World's Fair, the park harbors several museums, well-labeled horticulture, the Cascada fountains, a pond, and a zoo. Buildings of note include Domènech i Montaner's Modernist **Castell dels Tres Dracs** (now the **Museu de Zoología**), the geological museum, and Josep Amergós's **Hivernacle.** The **Parc Zoològic** is home to several threatened and endangered species. *(M: Ciutadella or Marina. Park open daily 8am-9pm. Zoo open daily in summer 10am-7pm; winter 10am-5pm. Park €14.50, children 3-12 €8.75, over 65 €7.70.)*

MUSEU DE LA XOCOLATA (CHOCOLATE MUSEUM). Arguably the most delectable museum in Spain. The museum presents gobs of information about the history, production, and ingestion of this sensuous sweet. Perhaps more interesting are the exquisite chocolate sculptures, particularly the edible La Sagrada Família. Others include soccer star Ronaldo and Dalí-inspired pieces. The cafe offers chocolate-tasting and baking workshops. *(Pl. Pons i Clerch, by C. Comerç. M: Jaume I. ☎268 7878; www.museudelaxocolata.com. Open M and W-Sa 10am-7pm, Su 10am-3pm. €3.80, students €3.30, with Barcelona Card €2.70, under 7 free. Workshops from €6.30; reservations required.)*

EL RAVAL

Where over-crowding once led to crime, prostitution, and drug use, revitalization efforts, especially since the '92 Olympic Games, have worked wonders. New museums and cultural centers in Raval have paved the way for hip restaurants and bars.

PALAU GÜELL. Gaudí's 1886 Palau Güell, the Modernist residence built for patron Eusebi Güell (of Park Güell fame), has one of Barcelona's most spectacular interiors. Güell spared no expense on this house, considered to be the first example of Gaudí's revolutionary style. The *palau* is closed for renovations until January 2007. *(C. Nou de La Rambla 3-5. M: Liceu. ☎317 3974. Mandatory tour every 15min. Open Mar.-Oct. M-Sa 10am-8pm, Su 10am-2pm; Nov.-Dec. M-Sa 10am-6pm. €3, students €1.50.)*

CENTRE DE CULTURA CONTEMPORÀNIA DE BARCELONA (CCCB). The center stands out for its mixture of architectural styles, consisting of an early 20th-century theater and its 1994 addition, a sleek wing of black glass. The institute shows a variety of temporary exhibits, film screenings, and music performances; check the *Guía del Ocio* for scheduled events. *(Casa de Caritat. C. Montalegre 5. M: Catalunya or Universitat. ☎306 4100; www.cccb.org. Open June 21-Sept. 21 Tu-Sa 11am-7:30pm, Su 11am-2:30pm. Sept. 22-June 20 Tu and Th-F 11am-1:30pm and 4-7:30pm, W and Sa 11am-7:30pm, Su and holidays 11am-6:30pm. Tours Tu and F 6pm, Sa-Su and holidays 11:30am. €6.60, students €4.40, under 16 free. First W of each month €1 off.)*

L'EIXAMPLE

The Catalán Renaissance during the 19th century pushed the city into modernity. Though Ildefons Cerdà drew up a plan for a new neighborhood where people of all classes could live side by side, l'Eixample (luh-SHOMP-luh) did not thrive as a utopian community; it emerged instead as a playground for the bourgeoisie. Today, L'Eixample remains a pretty neighborhood full of idealistic Modernist oddities.

LA SAGRADA FAMÍLIA. Although Antoni Gaudí's unfinished masterpiece is barely a shell of the intended product, La Sagrada Família is without a doubt the world's most visited construction site. Despite the fact that only eight of the 18 planned towers have been completed and the church still doesn't have an interior, millions make the touristic pilgrimage to witness this work-in-progress. Of the three proposed facades, only the Nativity Facade was finished under Gaudí; there is controversy over recent additions being inconsistent with the Modernist's original plans. *(C. Mallorca 401. M: Sagrada Família. ☎207 3031; www.sagradafamilia.org. Open daily Apr.-Sept. 9am-8pm; Oct.-Mar. 9:30am-5:45pm. Great English-language tour in summer 11am, 1, 3, 5:30pm; low season 11am and 1pm. €8, with ISIC €5. Combined ticket with Casa-Museu Dalí €9. Tour €3. Elevator €2. Cash only.)*

CASA MILÀ (LA PEDRERA). Gaudí's most refined work is worth the walk, the wait, and the climb. From the outside, it looks like the sea—the undulating walls are the waves and the iron balconies are seaweed. From the roof sprout chimneys resembling armored soldiers; one of them is decorated with broken champagne bottles. The entrance fee entitles visitors to tour one well-equipped apartment, the roof, and the winding brick attic, now functioning as the **Espai Gaudí,** a multimedia presentation of Gaudí's life and works. *(Pg. de Gràcia 92. ☎902 40 09 73. Open daily 10am-8pm. Free audio tour. Reopens for concerts F-Sa in July 9:30pm-midnight. €12, drink included. Tickets only through Telentrada.)*

LA MANZANA DE LA DISCÒRDIA. The odd-numbered side of Pg. de Gràcia between C. Aragó and Consell de Cent is popularly known as *la manzana de la discòrdia* (block of discord), referring to the stylistic clashing of three buildings. Regrettably, the bottom two floors of **Casa Lleó i Morera,** by Domènech i Montaner, were destroyed to make room for a store, but with the **Ruta del Modernisme** pass (sold on the ground floor), you can take a short tour of the upper floors with their sprouting flowers, stained glass, and legendary doorway sculptures. Puig i Cadafalch opted for a geometric, Moorish-influenced pattern on the facade of **Casa Amatller** at #41. Gaudí's balconies ripple like water in an idyllic lake and purple-blue tiles sparkle enticingly on **Casa Batlló,** #43. The most popular interpretation of Casa Batlló is that the building represents Cataluña's patron Sant Jordi slaying a dragon; the chimney plays the lance, the scaly roof is the dragon's back, and the bony balconies are the remains of its victims. *(☎488 0666; www.casabatllo.es. Open daily 9am-8pm. €16.50, students €13.20. Free audio tour.)*

HOSPITAL DE LA SANTA CREU I SANT PAU. The Modernist Hospital was Domènech i Montaner's lifetime masterpiece. The entire complex covers nine full l'Eixample blocks; its whimsically decorated pavilions resemble gingerbread houses and little Taj Mahals. The outdoor spaces once included a small forest; today, they still have more than 300 different types of plants. *(Sant Antoni M. Claret 167. M: Hospital de Sant Pau. ☎291 9000. Open 24hr. Free. Tours 10:15am-1:15pm; €5.)*

MONTJUÏC

Historically, whoever controlled Montjuïc (mon-joo-EEK; Hill of the Jews) controlled the city. Franco made **Castell de Montjuïc** one of his "interrogation" headquarters, and the fort was not given back to the city until 1960. Since then, Barcelona has given Montjuïc a new identity, transforming it from a military stronghold into a peaceful park by day and a debaucherous playground by night.

FUNDACIÓ MIRÓ. Designed by Miró's friend Josep Lluis Sert and tucked into the side of Montjuïc, the Fundació links modern spaces with massive windows and patios. Skylights illuminate an extensive collection of Miró's sculptures, drawings, and paintings. The gallery downstairs displays experimental works by young artists. Garden paths run to the Palau Nacional. The Fundació also sponsors music and film festivals. *(Av. Miramar 71-75. Funicular from M: Paral·lel. ☎443 9470; www.bcn.fjmiro.es. Open July-Sept. Tu-W and F-Su 10am-8pm, Th 10am-9:30pm, Su and holidays 10am-2:30pm; Oct.-June Tu-W and F-Sa 10am-7pm, Th 10am-9:30pm, Su and holidays 10am-2:30pm. €7.50, students and seniors €5, under 14 free. Temporary exhibits €4/3.)*

MUSEU NACIONAL D'ART DE CATALUNYA (PALAU NACIONAL). Designed by Enric Catá and Pedro Cendoya, the Palau Nacional has housed the Museu Nacional d'Art de Catalunya (MNAC) since 1934. Its main hall is an event space, while the wings house the world's finest collection of Catalán Romanesque art and a variety of Gothic pieces. *(M: Espanya. ☎622 0376; www.mnac.es. Open Tu-Sa 10am-7pm, Su 10am-2:30pm. Temporary exhibits €3-5; both temporary exhibits €6; all exhibits €8.50. students 30% discount, seniors free. First Su of each month free. Audio tour included.)*

CASTELL DE MONTJUÏC. A visit to this historic fortress and its **Museu Militar** is a great way to get an overview of the city's layout and history. The castle's external *mirador* offers spectacular views of the city. Though it's now closed for renovations, taking the **funicular** to and from the castle is half the fun. *(From M: Paral·lel, walk up the steep hill on C. Foc, next to the funicular station. Or, take the funicular to Av. Miramar and then the Teleféric de Montjuïc to the castle. ☎329 8613. After renovations, Teleféric de Montjuïc open in high season M-Sa 11:15am-9pm, low season 11am-7:15pm. Fortress and* mirador *open daily 9am-10pm. Museum open Tu-Sa Mar.-Nov. 9:30am-8pm; Dec.-Feb. 9:30am-5pm. Funicular €3.60, round-trip €5. Fortress and* mirador *€1. Including museum €2.50.)*

WATERFRONT

TORRE SAN SEBASTIÀ. One of the easiest and best ways to view the city is from the cable cars, which span the Port Vell, connecting beachy Barceloneta with mountainous Montjuïc. *(Pg. Joan de Borbó. M: Barceloneta. Open daily 11am-8pm. Elevator to the cable cars €4. To Montjuïc €9, round-trip €12.50.)*

MUSEU D'HISTÒRIA DE CATALUNYA. The Museu provides an exhaustive and patriotic introduction to Catalán history, politics, and culture. Touring the exhibit is a full sensory experience—you will touch, hear, and even smell the region's dynamic and often tragic history. *(Pl. Pau Vila 3. ☎225 4700. Open Tu and Th-Sa 10am-7pm, W 10am-8pm, Su 10am-2:30pm. €3, students €2.10, under 7 and over 65 free.)*

L'AQUÀRIUM DE BARCELONA. The largest aquarium in Europe is a wonder, with countless octopi and penguins. The highlight is a 75m glass tunnel through a tank of sharks, sting rays, and seahorses. *(Moll d'Espanya, next to Maremàgnum. M: Drassanes or Barceloneta. ☎221 7474; www.aquariumbcn.com. Open daily July-Aug. 9:30am-10pm; June and Sept. 9:30am-9pm; Oct.-May 9:30am-8pm. €15, students with ISIC €13.50, under 12 and seniors €9.50. Short tour available in English. AmEx/DC/MC/V.)*

ZONA ALTA

The most visited part of Zona Alta is Gràcia, which was incorporated into Barcelona in 1897 despite the protests of its residents. The area has always had a political streak, and calls for Gràcian independence crop up sporadically. Today, Gràcia packs a multitude of Modernist buildings, restaurants, and shops.

PARK GÜELL. This fantastic park was designed entirely by Gaudí but, in typical Gaudí fashion, was not completed until after his death. Gaudí intended Park Güell to be a garden city; its dwarfish buildings and sparkling ceramic-mosaic stairways were designed to house the city's elite. Only one house was actually built, which is now the **Casa-Museu Gaudí.** The longest park bench in the world, a multicolored serpentine wonder made of tile shards, decorates the top of the pavilion. *(Bus #24 from Pl. Catalunya stops at the upper entrance. Park open daily 10am-dusk. Museum open daily Apr.-Sept. 10am-8pm; Oct.-Mar. 10am-6pm. Park free. Museum €4, with ISIC €3.)*

MUSEU DEL FÚTBOL CLUB BARCELONA. The FCB is a close second to the Picasso as Barcelona's most-visited museum. The high point is the chance to enter the stadium and take in the enormity of 120,000-seat Camp Nou. It costs extra to see the facilities, such as the field and dressing rooms. *(C. Arístides Maillol. Enter through access gates 7 or 9. M: Collblanc. ☎496 3608. Open M-Sa 10am-6:15pm, Su and holidays 10am-2pm. €7, students and seniors €4.50. Facilities and museum €11/7.50.)*

ENTERTAINMENT AND FESTIVALS

For tips on entertainment, nightlife, and food, pick up the *Guía del Ocio* (www.guiadelociobcn.es; €1) at any newsstand. The best shopping in the city is in the **Barri Gòtic,** but if you feel like dropping some extra cash, check out the posh **Passeig de Gràcia** in l'Eixample. Grab face paint to join fans of **F.C. Barcelona (Barça)** at the Camp Nou stadium for **fútbol.** (Box office C. Arístedes Maillol 12-18. ☎902 18 99 00. Tickets €30-60.) **Barceloneta** and **Poble Nou** feature sand for topless tanning and many places to rent sailboats and water-sports equipment. Head up to Montjuïc to take advantage of the **Olympic Facilities,** which are now open for public use, including **Piscines Bernat Picornell,** a gorgeous pool complex. (Av. de l'Estadi 30-40. ☎423 4041. Open M-F 6:45am-midnight, Sa 7am-9pm, Su 6am-4pm.)

Festivals in Barcelona, as in the rest of Spain, occur often. Double-check sight and museum hours during festival times, as well as during the Christmas season and *Semana Santa.* The **Festa de Sant Jordi** (St. George; Apr. 23) celebrates Cataluña's patron saint with a feast. In the last two weeks of August, city folk jam at Gràcia's **Festa Mayor;** lights blaze in *plaças* and music plays all night. The three-day **Sónar** music festival comes to town in mid-June, attracting renowned DJs and electronica enthusiasts from all over the world. In July and August, the **Grec Festival** hosts dance performances, concerts, and film screenings. On September 11, the **Festa Nacional de Catalunya** brings traditional costumes, dancing, and Catalán flags. The **Festa de Sant Joan** is celebrated on the night of June 23 with ceaseless fireworks. The largest Barcelona celebration, is the **Festa de Mercè,** the week around September 24. To honor their city's patron saint, *Barceloneses* revel with fireworks, *sardana* dancing, and concerts.

NIGHTLIFE

Barcelona's wild nightlife treads a precarious line between slick and kitschy. In many ways, the city is a tourist's clubbing heaven—things don't get going until late (don't bother showing up at a club before 1am), and they continue until dawn. Yet for every full-blown dance club, there are 100 more relaxed bars. Check the *Guía del Ocio* for up-to-date listings of nighttime fun, as the hot spots change often.

CIUTAT VELLA

Main streets such as C. Ferran have cookie-cutter *cervecerías* and *bar-restaurantes* every five steps. C. Escudellers is the location for post-bar dancing, while Pl. Reial remains packed until the early morning. Las Ramblas, while lively, becomes a bit questionable late at night. In recent years, La Ribera has evolved into a hip, artsy district, attracting a young crowd of tourists and locals. The streets of El Raval are densely packed with a place for every variety of bar-hopper.

Jamboree, Pl. Reial 17 (☎933 19 17 89; www.masimas.com). M: Liceu. A disorienting maze of stone arches and swirling lights thumps with "FunkyR&BSwingBeatHip-Hop"; 2nd fl. plays 80s and 90s music. Drinks €8-10. Jazz 9-11pm (€3-10). Open daily 8pm-1am; nightclub 2-5am. Upstairs, **Tarantos** hosts flamenco shows (€5). Cover M €3, Tu-Su €9; look for flyers with discounts in the city. Open M-Sa 8-11pm.

El Copetín, Pg. del Born 19. M: Jaume I. Cuban rhythm invades everything in this casual, dimly lit nightspot with clientele of all ages. Awe-inspiring mojitos €6.50. Open Su-Th 7pm-2:30am, F-Sa 7pm-3am. Cash only.

Marsella Bar, C. de Sant Pau 65. M: Liceu. Religious figurines grace the walls of Barcelona's oldest bar, open since 1820; perhaps they're praying for the *absenta* (absinthe; €3.30) drinkers. Mixed drinks €4-6. Open M-Th 10pm-2:30am, F-Sa 10pm-3:30am.

Fonfone, C. Escudellers 24 (www.fonfone.com). M: Liceu or Drassanes. Funky music and trippy orange and red bubbles protruding from the wall draw crowds 1-3am. International DJs nightly. Beer €3. Mixed drinks €6-8. Open daily 10pm-2:30 or 3am.

Casa Almirall, C. Joaquín Costa 33. M: Universitat. Cavernous space with laid-back clientele. Staff walks you through your 1st glass of absinthe and cuts you off after your 3rd. Beer €2-4. Mixed drinks €5-7. Open Su-Th 7pm-2:30am, F-Sa 7pm-3am. Cash only.

L'EIXAMPLE

L'Eixample has upscale bars and some of the best gay nightlife in Europe.

Mojito Club, C. Rosselló 217 (☎932 37 65 28; www.mojitobcn.com). M: Diagonal. This over-the-top club lures a fun-loving crowd with Latin beats. Free samba lessons W 11pm; salsa F-Sa 11pm-1:30am. W Brazilian party with live salsa all night. Cover F-Sa after 2:30am €10, includes 1 drink. Open daily 11pm-4:30am. V.

Dietrich, C. Consell de Cent 255 (☎934 51 77 07; www.dietrichcafe.com). M: Pg. de Gràcia. A caricature of a semi-nude Marlene Dietrich greets patrons at this inclusive gay bar. Beer €4. Nightly trapeze show 1:30am. Open M-Sa 11pm-2:30am. MC/V.

Átame, C. Consell de Cent 257 (☎934 54 92 73). M: Pg. de Gràcia. Next door to Dietrich, with an industrial gray interior, this relaxed bar is frequented mainly by gay men. It's not as scandalous as its name ("tie me up") might imply. Beer €3. Mixed drinks €4-6. Happy hour Tu 7-10pm; free tapas. Open daily 7pm-2:30am. Cash only.

MONTJUÏC

Lower Montjuïc is home to **Poble Espanyol,** Av. Marqués de Comillas, a re-creation of famous buildings and sights from all regions of Spain. At night the complex becomes a disco theme park that offers the craziest clubbing experience in all of Barcelona. (☎508 6300; www.poble-espanyol.com. M: Espanya.)

Tinta Roja, C. Creus dels Molers 17 (☎443 3243; www.tintaroja.net), near Poble Espanyol. Live tango. Open Th 8pm-1:30am, F-Sa 8pm-2:30am, Su 7pm-midnight. Cash only.

La Terrazza, Poble Espanyol (☎423 1285). Fantastic outdoor dance floor. The winter counterpart is **Discothèque.** Dress to impress at Discothèque or risk a blunt denial at the door. La Terrazza cover €15 (includes 1 drink), Discothèque €18. La Terrazza open June-Oct. Th-Sa midnight-6am, Discothèque open Oct.-May F-Sa midnight-6am.

WATERFRONT

Poble Nou and **Port Olímpic** are home to a long strip of nightclubs. The entire waterfront area, which stretches from **Maremàgnum** to **Port Vell,** may be as hedonistic and touristy as Barcelona gets. At night, Maremàgnum, the city's biggest mall, turns into a three-level maze of clubs packed with crowds even on weeknights. There is no cover; clubs make their money by charging exorbitant drink prices (beer €5; mixed drinks €8-10). Catching a cab home can be difficult. A night by the waterfront isn't over until a drunk tourist falls into the harbor.

L'Ovella Negra (Megataverna del Poble Nou), C. Zamora 78 (☎933 09 59 38; www.ovellanegra.net). M: Bogatell or Marina. What was once a warehouse is now the place to go for the first few beers of the night. Large beers €2, 2L pitchers €8.50. Mixed drinks €4-5. Open Th 10pm-2:30am, F-Sa 5pm-3am, Su 5-10pm. Cash only.

Razzmatazz, C. Pamplona 88, and Almogàvers 122, around the corner (☎932 72 09 10; www.salarazzmatazz.com). M: Marina. A huge warehouse-turned-entertainment complex now houses 5 clubs: Pop, The Loft, Razz Club, Lo*Li*Ta, and Rex Room. The overall feel is decidedly rock and techno, with strobe-lit dance floors and concert space for indie rock. Concert prices vary; check website. Beer €3.50. Mixed drinks €7. Cover €12-15, includes access to all 5 clubs. Open F-Sa and holidays 1-5am. AmEx/MC/V.

ZONA ALTA

The area around C. de Marià Cubí has great nightlife undiscovered by tourists, but you'll have to take a taxi. For more accessible fun in Gràcia, head to Pl. del Sol.

■ **Otto Zutz,** C. Lincoln 15 (☎932 38 07 22). FGC: Pl. Molina or M: Fontana. Groove to house, hip-hop, and funk while Japanimation lights up the top fl. in one of Barcelona's most famous clubs. Beer €6. Mixed drinks €9. Cover €10-15, includes 1 drink; look for flyers in the city to get in free before 3:30am. Open Tu-Sa midnight-5am. AmEx/MC/V.

La Femme, C. Plató 13 (☎932 01 62 07), on the corner with Muntaner. FCG: Muntaner. A welcoming haven for lesbians of all ages. A touch of class, a dash of whimsy, and a ton of fun in this small club. Beer €5. Mixed drinks €7. Open Th-F 11pm-3am, Sa 11:30pm-late. Cash only.

▶ DAYTRIPS FROM BARCELONA

THE COSTA BRAVA: FIGUERES AND CADAQUÉS

From Figueres, trains (☎902 24 02 02) leave Pl. de l'Estació for Barcelona (2hr., 14-22 per day, €8-10) and Girona (30min., 13-23 per day, €3). Buses (☎972 67 33 54) run from Pl. de l'Estació to Barcelona (2¼hr., 2-5 per day, €14), Cadaqués (1hr., 6-7 per day, €4), and Girona (1hr., 2-5 per day, €4). Buses from Cadaqués go to Barcelona (2½hr., 3-5 per day, €19), Figueres (1hr., 3-7 per day, €4), and Girona (2hr., 1-2 per day, €8).

The Costa Brava's jagged cliffs cut into the Mediterranean Sea from Barcelona to the French border. Despite its name, the Brave Coast cowers under the plane-loads of Europeans dumped onto its once-tranquil beaches in July and August. In 1974, Salvador Dalí chose his native, beachless **Figueres** (pop. 35,000) as the site to build a museum to house his works, catapulting the city to international fame. His personal tribute is a Surrealist masterpiece, the second most popular museum in Spain, and a prime example of ego run delightfully amok. The ■**Teatre-Museu Dalí** is at Pl. Gala i Salvador Dalí 5. From La Rambla, take C. Girona, which becomes C. Jonquera, and climb the steps to your left. The museum contains the artist's nightmarish landscapes and his tomb. (☎972 67 75 00; www.salvador-dali.org. Open July-Sept. daily 9am-7:45pm; Oct.-June Tu-Su 10:30am-5:45pm. €10, students and seniors €7. Aug. also 10pm-12:30am, €11.) The **tourist office** is in Pl. Sol. (☎972 50 31 55; www.figueresciutat.com. Open July-Aug. M-Sa 9am-8pm, Su 10am-3pm; Sept. M-Sa 9am-8pm; Apr.-June and Oct. M-F 8:30am-3pm and 4:30-8pm, Sa 9:30am-1:30pm and 3:30-6:30pm; Nov.-Mar. M-F 8:30am-3pm.) **Postal Code:** 17600.

The whitewashed houses and small bay of **Cadaqués** (pop. 2000) have attracted artists, writers, and musicians ever since Dalí built his summer home in nearby Port Lligat. Facing uphill with your back to the bus station, take the right fork and follow the signs to Port Lligat and then to the Casa de Dalí (30min.). Alternatively, take a trolley to Port Lligat (1hr., 6 per day, €7) from Pl. Frederic Rahola. ■**Casa-Museu Salvador Dalí** was the home of Dalí and his wife until her death in 1982. Though two of Dalí's unfinished original paintings remain in the house, the real artwork is the decorations, including a lip-shaped sofa and a Pop-Art miniature Alhambra. (☎972 25 10 15. Open mid-June to mid-Sept. daily 10:30am-9pm; mid-Sept. to Jan. and mid-Mar. to mid-June Tu-Su 10:30am-6pm. Tours are the only way to see the house; make reservations 4-5 days in advance. €8, students, seniors, and children €6.) With your back to the bus station, walk right along Av. Caritat Serinyana to get to Plaça Frederic Rahola; the **tourist office,** C. Cotxe 2, is to the right of the *plaça*, opposite the beach. (☎972 25 83 15. Open July-Aug. M-Sa 9am-2pm and 3-9pm, Su 10:30am-1pm; Sept.-June M-Sa 9am-2pm and 4-7pm.) **Postal Code:** 17488.

GIRONA

RENFE trains (☎902 24 02 02) run from Pl. de Espanya to Barcelona (1½hr., 25 per day, €6-7), Figueres (30-40min., 13 per day, €2.40-2.70), and Madrid (10½hr., 1 per day, €36). Barcelona Bus (☎902 36 15 50; www.barcelonabus.com) sends express buses to Barcelona (1¼hr., 3-5 per day, €9.50-12) and Figueres (1hr., 3-6 per day, €4-5).

A world-class city patiently waiting to be noticed, Girona (pop. 92,000) is really two cities in one: a hushed medieval masterpiece on one riverbank and a thriving, modern metropolis on the other. The **Riu Onyar** separates the new city from the old. Nine bridges connect the two banks, including **Pont de Pedra.** This bridge leads to the old quarter by way of C. dels Ciutadans, which becomes C. Bonaventura Carreras i Peralta and then C. Força. This street leads to the cathedral and **El Call,** a thriving Jewish community in the Middle Ages that was virtually wiped out by the 1492 Inquisition. Uphill and around the corner to the right on C. Força, the imposing Gothic **Cathedral de Girona** rises 90 steps from the plaza below. Within, the **Tresor Capitular** contains some of Girona's most precious art. (☎972 21 44 26; www.lacatedraldegirona.com. Open daily Apr.-Oct 10am-8pm; Nov.-Mar. 10am-6pm. Cathedral free. *Tresor* and cloister €3, students and over 65 €2, ages 7-16 €0.90, under 7 free.) Girona's renowned **Passeig de la Muralla,** a trail along the fortified walls of the old city, is a nice way to stretch your legs. Join the path at the Jardins de la Francesa (behind the cathedral), the Jardins d'Alemanys (behind the Museu d'Art), or the main entrance at the bottom of La Rambla in Pl. de la Marvà. (Open daily 8am-10pm.)

Carrer Cort-Reial is the best place to find good, cheap food, while cafes on **Plaza de la Independencia** offer outside seating on the beautiful square. Pick up groceries at **Caprabo,** C. Sèquia 10, a block off Gran Via de Jaume I. (☎902 11 60 60. Open July-Aug. M-Sa 9am-9pm; Sept.-June 9am-2pm and 5-9pm. MC/V.) The **tourist office,** Rbla. de la Libertat 1, is by Pont de Pedra on the old bank. (☎972 22 65 75; www.ajuntament.gi. Open M-Sa 8am-8pm, Su 9am-2pm.) **Postal Code:** 17007.

THE PYRENEES

The jagged green mountains, Romanesque churches, and tranquil towns of the Pyrenees draw hikers and skiers in search of outdoor adventure.

VAL D'ARAN ☎973

Some of the most dazzling peaks of the Catalán Pyrenees cluster around the Val d'Aran, in the northwest corner of Cataluña, best known for its chic ski resorts. The Spanish royal family's favorite slopes are those of **Baqueira-Beret.** Salardú's 13th-century **Església de Sant Andreu** houses beautifully restored 16th-century murals. For skiing info and reservations, contact the **Oficeria de Baqueira-Beret.** (☎63 90 00; www.baqueira.es. €39 per day for 5000 acres of impressive mountain terrain.) The palatial **Auberja Era Garona (HI) ❶,** on Ctra. de Vielha, is in the more economical town of Salardú. (☎64 52 71; www.eragarona.com. Breakfast included. Linens €3. Laundry €3.70. Internet €3 per hr. Reception 8am-11pm. Rooms €16-22, with bath €18-25; under 25 €15-19/18-22.)

The biggest town in the valley, **Vielha** (pop. 1000) welcomes hikers and skiers to its streets and offers many services for the eager wilderness adventurer. Several inexpensive *pensiones* cluster at the end of C. Reiau, off Pg. Libertat. **Ostau d'Óc ❷,** C. Castéth 13, across the traffic rotary on the main road and up the hill to the left, has clean, spacious rooms with full bath. (☎64 15 97. Singles €22-33; doubles €32-45; quads €55-78.) **Era Plaça ❶,** Pl. de Glèisa, serves up big pizzas for €6-8 and even bigger sandwiches for €3.50-4. (☎973 64 02 49. Open daily 9am-midnight.) Alsina Graells (Lleida office ☎27 14 70) runs **buses** from Vielha to Barcelona (5hr., 5:30am and 1:30pm, €28-33), Lleida (2hr., 5:30am and 1:30pm), and Salardú (20min., 7-13 per day, €0.85). The **tourist office,** C. Sarriulèra 10, is one block from Pl. de Glèisa. (☎64 01 10; www.torismearan.org. Open daily 9am-9pm.)

PARQUE NACIONAL DE ORDESA ☎974

The beauty of Ordesa's Aragonese Pyrenees will enchant even the most seasoned traveler. Well-maintained trails cut across idyllic forests, escarpments, and snow-covered peaks. The main **trail** that runs up the Río Arazas to the foot of Monte Perdido and Refugio Góriz, with three spectacular waterfalls within 1hr. of the trailhead, is the most practical and rewarding hike. Several local companies offer expeditions and adventure sports. For more information, visit www.ordesa.net.

In the park, many *refugios* (mountain huts) are open for overnight stays. In the center of Torla, diagonally across from the tourist office, is **La Casa de Laly ❷,** C. Fatas, a comfortable place to spend the night after a day of hiking. (☎48 61 68. Doubles with hall bath €25-28.) Pick up food at **Supermercado Torla,** C. Francia near L'Atalaya. (☎48 63 88. Open daily May-Oct. 9am-2pm and 5-9pm; Nov.-Apr. 10am-2pm and 5-9pm. MC/V.) La Oscense (☎48 00 45) runs a **bus** from Jaca to Sabiñánigo (20min., 4-6 per day, €1.31), and all **trains** on the Zaragoza-Huesca-Jaca line stop at Sabiñánigo. From there, Compañía Hudebus (☎21 32 77) runs to Torla (55min., 1-2 per day, €2.78). From July to October, a bus shuttles between Torla and Ordesa (15min.; about every 15min.; €2.20, round-trip €3.20). In the low season, you'll have to hike the beautiful 8km to the park entrance or catch a Jorge Soler **taxi** (☎48 62 43; €12). The same company also offers van tours for up to eight people. The **tourist office** is 1.8km past the park entrance. (Open Mar.-Dec. daily 9am-2pm and 4-7pm.) The park **info center** in Torla, across the street from the bus stop, takes over in the low season. Here you can pick up free maps and the *Senderos Sector Ordesa* trail guide. (☎48 64 72. Open July-Sept. M-F 8am-3pm, Sa-Su 9am-2pm and 4:30-7pm; Oct.-June M-F 8am-3pm.) **Postal Code:** 22376.

NAVARRA

Bordered by the Basque Country to the west and Aragón to the east, Navarra's villages—from rustic Pyrenean *pueblos* to energetic Pamplona—are seldom visited except during the festival of *San Fermín.* However, at any other time of year these mellow towns welcome non-bull-running tourists with open arms.

PAMPLONA (IRUÑA) ☎948

El encierro, la Fiesta de San Fermín, the Running of the Bulls, utter debauchery; call it what you will, the outrageous festival is the reason tourists come to Pamplona (pop. 200,000). Since its immortalization in Ernest Hemingway's *The Sun Also Rises,* hordes of travelers flock to the city for a week in July to witness the eight-minute event and ensuing chaos. The city's grand parks, museums, and monuments all merit exploration as well.

> **!** Although Pamplona is usually very safe, crime skyrockets during *San Fermín.* Beware of assaults and muggings, do not walk alone at night, and take care in the *casco antiguo.*

TRANSPORTATION AND PRACTICAL INFORMATION. **Trains** (☎902 24 02 02) run from Estación RENFE, Av. de San Jorge, to Barcelona (6-8hr., 3 per day, from €33), Madrid (3¾hr., 4 per day, €49), and San Sebastián (2-3 per day, €18). **Buses** leave from the corner of C. Conde Oliveto and C. Yangüas y Miranda for Barcelona (6-8hr., 4 per day, €24), Bilbao (2hr., 4-7 per day, €12), and Madrid (5hr., 6-10 per day, €23). From Pl. del Castillo, take C. San Nicolás, turn right on C. San Miguel, and walk through Pl. San Francisco to get to the **tourist office,** C. Hilarión Eslava 1. (☎42 04 20; www.turismo.navarra.es. Open during *San Fermín* daily 8am-8pm; July-Aug. M-Sa 9am-8pm, Su 10am-2pm; Sept.-June M-Sa 10am-2pm and 4-7pm, Su 10am-2pm.) During *San Fermín,* **luggage storage** is available at the Escuelas de San Francisco, in Pl. San Francisco. (€2 per day. Open from July 5 at 8pm to July 15 at 2pm.) Check email at **Kuria.Net,** C. Curia 15. (€2.50 per hr. Open July-Aug. daily 10am-10pm; Sept.-June M-Sa 10am-10pm.) **Postal Code:** 31001.

ACCOMMODATIONS AND FOOD. Book at least five months ahead to avoid paying rates up to four times higher than those listed below. Check the newspaper *Diario de Navarra* for *casas particulares* (private homes that rent rooms); be aware, though, that many owners prefer Spanish guests. Roomless backpackers are forced to fluff up their sweatshirts and sleep outside. Stay in large groups, and if you can't store your backpack, sleep on top of it. During the rest of the year, finding a room in Pamplona is no problem. Budget accommodations line **Calle San Gregorio** and **Calle San Nicolás** off Pl. del Castillo. Deep within the *casco antiguo,* **Pensión Eslava ❶,** C. Hilarión Eslava 13, 2nd fl., is quieter and less crowded than other *pensiones.* These older rooms have a balcony and shared bath. (☎22 15 58. Singles €10-15; doubles €20-30, during *San Fermín* €100. Cash only.) Thoroughfares **Calle Navarrería** and **Paseo de Sarasate** are home to good *bocadillo* bars. **Café-Bar Iruña ❸,** Pl. del Castillo, is the former casino made famous in Hemingway's *The Sun Also Rises.* The *menú* (€12) is required eating at a table, but you can have drinks at the bar or terrace. (☎22 20 64. Open M-Th 8am-11pm, F 8am-2am, Sa 9am-2am, Su 9am-11pm. MC/V.) Get groceries at **Vendi Supermarket,** C. Hilarión Eslava and C. Mayor. (☎948 22 15 55. Open M-F 9am-2pm and 5:30-7:30pm, Sa 9am-2pm; *San Fermín* M-Sa 9am-2pm. MC/V.)

SIGHTS AND NIGHTLIFE. The city's architectural legacy is reason enough to visit during the 51 other weeks of the year. The restored 14th-cen-

IT'S NOT WHAT YOU DRINK, IT'S HOW

Partygoers at festivals like the *San Fermines* tend to be on the move, and it's not always convenient to carry an open glass while following a *peña* through crowded cobblestone streets. Clever Pamplonans have reverted to a pastoral solution for carrying their drinks: the *bota.*

A *bota* is a 1-3L bag, traditionally handmade, constructed by inverting a piece of goat hide (covered in pitch to seal in the contents), and triple-stitching the leather. A spout at one end is used to spray the contents in a stream into the user's mouth. Technique is key: the *bota* must be held above your mouth, and pressure maintained at all times by continually squeezing the bag with one hand and steering the stream with the other. Nobody will be impressed unless you can extend the *bota* a full arm's length away from your mouth—practice with water first.

Finally, *botas* are social instruments: don't be surprised if passersby reach for it or expect you to offer them a mouthful of its contents. You can pick one up for €20-35 at any of the various liquor shops that display them in their windows, or go straight to the source: Las Tres Z.Z.Z., Carretera Puente Miluce nº 6, bajo (☎48 25 26 29; www.lastreszzz.com).

TIP **RUNNING SCARED.** So, you're going to run, and nobody's going to stop you. Because nobody—except the angry, angry bulls—wants to see you get seriously injured, here are a few words of *San Fermín* wisdom:

1. Research the *encierro* before you run; the tourist office has a pamphlet that outlines the route and offers tips for inexperienced runners. Running the entire 850m course is highly inadvisable. (This would mean 3min. of evading 6 bulls running at 24kph.) Instead, pick a 50m stretch.
2. Don't stay up all night drinking and carousing. Experienced runners get lots of sleep the night before and arrive at the course around 6:30am.
3. Take a fashion tip from the locals: wear the white-and-red outfit with closed-toe shoes. Ditch the baggy clothes, backpacks, and cameras.
4. Give up on getting near the bulls and concentrate on getting to the bullring in one piece. Though some whack the bulls with rolled newspapers, runners should never distract or touch the animals; this will annoy the bulls and the runners.
5. Never stop in doorways, alleys, or corners; you can be trapped and killed.
6. Run in a straight line; if you cut someone off, they can easily fall.
7. Be particularly wary of isolated bulls—they seek company in the crowds.
8. If you fall, stay down. Curl up into a fetal position, lock your hands behind your head, and do not get up until the clatter of hooves has passed.

tury Gothic **Catedral de Santa María,** at the end of C. Navarrería, has a kitchen with five chimneys and is one of only four cathedrals of its kind in Europe. (☎21 08 27. Open M-F 10am-1:30pm and 4-7pm, Sa 10am-2:30pm. Tours €4.) The walls of the pentagonal **Ciudadela** enclose free art exhibits, summer concerts, and an amazing *San Fermín* fireworks display every year. To get there, follow Po. de Sarasate to its end and take a right on C. Navas de Tolosa; take the next left onto C. Chinchilla and follow it to its very end. (☎22 82 37. Open M-Sa 7:30am-9:30pm, Su 9am-9:30pm. Closed for *San Fermín*. Free.) At night, a young crowd boozes up in the *casco antiguo*, particularly along **Calle San Nicolás, Calle Jarauta,** and **Calle San Gregorio,** before hitting the **Travesía de Bayona,** a plaza of bars and *discotecas*.

■ **FIESTA DE SAN FERMÍN (JULY 5-13, 2007).** Visitors overcrowd the city as Pamplona delivers an eight-day frenzy of bullfights, concerts, dancing, fireworks, parades, parties, and wine. Pamplonese, clad in white with red sashes and bandanas, literally throw themselves into the merry-making, displaying obscene levels of both physical stamina and alcohol tolerance. The "Running of the Bulls," called *el encierro*, is the highlight of *San Fermines;* the first *encierro* takes place on July 6 at 8am and is repeated at 8am every day for the next seven days. Hundreds of bleary-eyed, hungover, hyper-adrenalized runners flee from large bulls as bystanders cheer from barricades, windows, balconies, and doorways. Both the bulls and the mob are dangerous; terrified runners react without any concern for any of those around them.

To participate in the bullring excitement without the risk of the *encierro*, don't run. Instead, arrive at the bullring around 6:45am to watch. Tickets for the *grada* section of the ring are available at 7am in the bullring box office (M-F €3.80, Sa-Su €4.40). You can watch for free, but the free section is overcrowded, making it hard to see and breathe. To watch a **bullfight,** wait in the line that forms at the bullring around 7:30pm. As one fight ends, the next day's tickets go on sale. (Tickets €6-992; check www.feriadeltoro.com for details.) Once the running ends, insanity spills into the streets and gathers steam until nightfall, when it explodes with singing in bars, dancing in alleyways, spontaneous parades, and a no-holds-barred party in Pl. del Castillo, Europe's biggest open-air dance floor.

BASQUE COUNTRY (PAÍS VASCO)

Basque Country's varied landscape resembles a nation in itself, combining energetic cities, verdant hills, industrial wastelands, and quaint fishing villages. Many believe that the strongly nationalistic Basques are the native people of Iberia.

SAN SEBASTIÁN (DONOSTIA) ☎943

Glittering on the shores of the Cantabrian Sea, coolly elegant San Sebastián (pop. 185,000) is known for its world-famous beaches, bars, and scenery. Locals and travelers down *pintxos* (tapas) and drinks in the *parte vieja* (old city), which claims the most bars per square meter in the world.

TRANSPORTATION. RENFE **trains** (☎902 24 02 02) run from Estación del Norte, Po. de Francia, to Barcelona (9hr., 1-2 per day, €37-47), Madrid (8hr., 2-3 per day, €33-54), and Salamanca (6½hr., 2 per day, €29). Estación de Amara runs *cercanías* to local destinations and to Bilbao (3hr., 1 per hr., €6). San Sebastián has no actual bus station, only a platform and a series of ticket windows at Av. de Sancho el Sabio 31-33 and Po. de Vizcaya 16. Buses run to: Barcelona (7hr., 3 per day, €26); Bilbao (1¼hr., 1-2 per hr., €8.30); Madrid (6hr., 7-9 per day, €29); Pamplona (1hr., 6-10 per day, €6); Paris, FRA (12hr., 1 per day, €68).

ORIENTATION AND PRACTICAL INFORMATION. The **Río Urumea** splits San Sebastián down the middle, with the **parte vieja** and **El Centro** (the new downtown) to the west, separated by the wide walkway **Alameda del Boulevard.** The city center, most monuments, and the two most popular beaches, Playa de la Concha and Playa de Ondarreta, also line the peninsula on the western side of the river. At the tip of the peninsula rises **Monte Urgull.** The **bus platform** is south of the city center on Pl. Pío XII. To get to the *parte vieja* from the train station, cross the Puente María Cristina and turn right at the fountain. Continue four blocks north to Av. de la Libertad, then turn left and follow it to the port; the *parte vieja* fans out to the right and Playa de la Concha sits to the left.

The **tourist office** is at C. Reina Regente 3, in front of Puente de la Zurriola. (☎48 11 66; www.sansebastianturismo.com. English spoken. Open July-Aug. M-Sa 9am-8pm, Su 10am-2pm and 3:30-7pm; Sept.-May M-Sa 9am-1:30pm and 3:30-7pm, Su 10am-2pm; June M-Sa 9am-8pm, Su 10am-2pm.) **Luggage storage** is available at Estación del Norte. (€3 per day. Open daily 7am-11pm.) Check email at **Zarr@net,** C. San Lorenzo 6. (☎43 33 81. €2 per hr. Open M-Sa 10am-2:30pm and 3:15-10pm, Su 4-10pm.) The **post office** is behind the cathedral, on C. Urdaneta. (☎44 68 26. Open M-F 8:30am-8:30pm, Sa 9:30am-2pm.) **Postal Code:** 20006.

ACCOMMODATIONS AND FOOD. *Pensiones* are scattered throughout the streets of the noisy *parte vieja*. For a more restful night's sleep, look for hostels and *pensiones* on the outskirts of El Centro. **Pensión Amaiur ❷**, C. 31 de Agosto 44, 2nd fl., has a friendly, English-speaking owner who offers lovely rooms in an historic house. (☎42 96 54; www.pensionamaiur.com. Internet €1 per 18min. Singles €20-35, with balcony €24-40; doubles €33-48/38-55; triples €51-75; quads €63-90. MC/V.) **Pensión San Lorenzo ❷**, C. San Lorenzo 2, off C. San Juani, has sunny doubles with TV, fridge, and spotless private baths. (☎42 55 16; www.pensionsanlorenzo.com. Internet €1.50 per hr.; wireless free. July-Aug. doubles €48. June and Sept. €36. Oct.-May €25.) The **Albergue Juvenil la Sirena (HI) ❶**, Po. Igueldo 25, is 3min. from the beach and has clean 2- to 4-person rooms. (☎31 02 68. Breakfast included. Linens €2.65. Max. stay 3 nights if full. May-Sept. dorms €18, under 26 €15. Oct.-Apr. reduced rates. HI members and ISIC holders only. MC/V.)

Pintxos (tapas; €1.50 each), chased down with the fizzy regional white wine *txakoli*, are a religion here. At **Juantxo ❶**, C. Esterlines, choose from a selection of *bocadillos* (€3-3.50) and *pintxos* (€1.20-2); *raciones* range €3-5. (☎42 74 05. Open M-Th 9am-11:30pm, F-Su 9am-1:45am. Cash only.) **La Cueva ❸**, Pl. Trinidad, off C. 31 de Agosto, is a cavernous restaurant that serves traditional seafood dishes. (☎42 54 37. Entrees €8-15. Tu-F *menú* €15. Open Tu-Su 1-3:30pm and 8-11pm. MC/V.) At Pl. del Buen Pastor 1, chic and artsy **Caravanseraí Café ❶** has vegetarian options. (☎47 54 18. Entrees €6-10. Open M-Th 8am-midnight, Sa-Su 10:30am-11:30pm. MC/V.) The clean and modern **Mercado de la Bretxa**, in an underground shopping center, sells everything from fresh produce and meat to *pintxos*. The huge supermarket inside offers a choice of groceries. (Open M-Sa 9am-9pm.)

SIGHTS. The **Museo Chillida-Leku** features a beautiful permanent exhibit of Eduardo Chillida's work that extends throughout the garden of a 16th-century farmhouse restored by the sculptor himself. The farmhouse, a spectacular construction of interlaced wood and arching stone, houses some of the artist's earliest works. (Bo. Jauregui 66. ☎33 60 06; www.museochillidaleku.com. Open July-Aug. M-Sa 10:30am-8pm, Su 10:30am-3pm; Sept.-June daily 10:30am-3pm. Daily tours and 45min. audio tours in 5 languages included in admission. €8, under 12 and seniors €6.) Though the views from both of San Sebastián's mountains are spectacular, those from **Monte Igueldo** are superior. The sidewalk toward the mountain ends just before the base of Monte Igueldo with Eduardo Chillida's sculpture *El Peine de los Vientos* (Comb of the Winds). The road leading to the top is bordered by a low cliffside stone wall, a local favorite for picnics at sunset. A **funicular** (€1.90) runs every 15min. to the summit. (☎21 02 11. Open June-Sept. daily 10am-10pm; Oct.-Feb. Sa-Su 11am-8pm; Mar.-May Sa 11am-8pm, Su 11am-9pm.)

When Queen Isabel II started vacationing in San Sebastián in the mid-19th century, fancy buildings began to spring up in the area like wildflowers. The **Palacio de Miramar** has passed through the hands of the Spanish court, Napoleon III, and Bismarck; it now serves as the País Vasco University. The adjacent **Parque de Miramar** has beautiful views of the bay. (Between Playa de la Concha and Playa de Ondarreta. Open daily June-Aug. 8am-9pm; Sept.-May 8am-7pm. Free.) The other royal residence, **Palacio de Aiete,** is closed to the public, but surrounding trails are open. (Head up Cta. de Aldapeta or take bus #19 or 31. Grounds open daily 8am-9pm. Free.)

Gorgeous **Playa de la Concha** curves from the port to the **Pico del Loro,** the promontory home of the Palacio de Miramar. The virtually flat beach disappears during high tide. Sunbathers crowd onto the smaller and steeper **Playa de Ondarreta,** beyond the Palacio de Miramar, and surfers flock to **Playa de la Zurriola,** across the river from Monte Urgull. Picnickers head for the **Isla de Santa Clara.** (Motorboat ferry 5min., June-Sept. every 30min., round-trip €3.25.) Check the portside kiosk for info. **Surfers** should check out the **Pukas Surf Club,** Av. de la Zurriola 24, for lessons and rentals. (☎32 00 68. Open M-Sa 9:30am-9pm. MC/V.)

ENTERTAINMENT AND NIGHTLIFE. The *parte vieja* pulls out all the stops in the months of July and August, particularly on **Calle Fermín Calbetón,** which is just three blocks away from Alameda del Boulevard. During the year, when students outnumber backpackers, nightlife moves beyond the *parte vieja*. **Ostadar,** C. Fermín Calbetón 13, attracts locals and tourists alike with its dance mix. (☎42 62 78. Beer €2. Mixed drinks €5. Open Su-Th 5pm-3am, F-Sa 5pm-4am. Cash only.) **Zibbibo,** Pl. de Sarriegi 8, is a popular dance club for young tourists. (☎42 53 34. 2-pint Heineken €5. Happy hour daily 7-9pm and 10-11:30pm. Open M-W 4pm-2:30am, Th-Sa 4pm-3:30am. MC/V.)

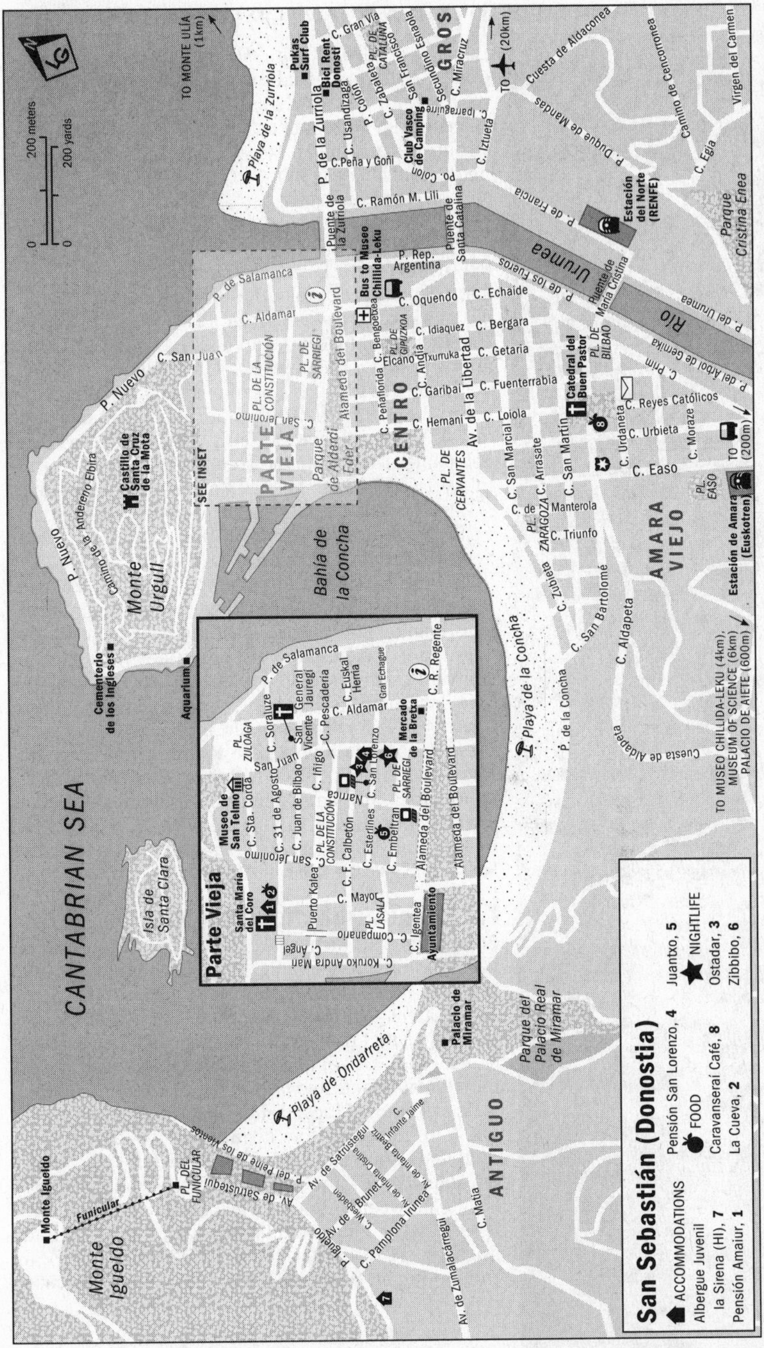
San Sebastián (Donostia)
ACCOMMODATIONS
Albergue Juvenil la Sirena (HI), 7
Pensión Amaiur, 1
Pensión San Lorenzo, 4
FOOD
Caravanserai Café, 8
La Cueva, 2
Juantxo, 5
NIGHTLIFE
Ostadar, 3
Zibbibo, 6
Parte Vieja
SEE INSET
CANTABRIAN SEA
Isla de Santa Clara
Monte Urgull
Castillo de Santa Cruz de la Mota
Cementerio de los Ingleses
Aquarium
Bahía de la Concha
Playa de la Concha
Playa de Ondarreta
Playa de la Zurriola
Monte Igueldo
Funicular
PL. DEL FUNICULAR
Palacio de Miramar
Parque del Palacio Real de Miramar
ANTIGUO
CENTRO
PARTE VIEJA
GROS
AMARA VIEJO
Río Urumea
Estación del Norte (RENFE)
Estación de Amara (Euskotren)
Catedral del Buen Pastor
Bus to Museo Chillida-Leku
Club Vasco de Camping
Bici Rent Donosti
Pukas Surf Club
Museo de San Telmo
Santa María del Coro
Mercado de la Bretxa
Ayuntamiento
Parque Cristina Enea
Parque de Alderdi Eder
Alameda del Boulevard
TO MONTE ULÍA (1km)
TO (20km)
TO (200m)
TO MUSEO CHILLIDA-LEKU (4km), MUSEUM OF SCIENCE (6km), PALACIO DE AIETE (600m)
0 200 meters
0 200 yards

THE TRAGEDY OF GUERNICA

Founded on April 28, 1366, Guernica was virtually erased from the map on April 26, 1937. It was a Monday market day when the church bell rang three times to warn the small town of an aerial attack. The German Condor Legion began to bomb at 4:30pm and didn't stop until 7:45pm. Heavy bombs and hand grenades were dropped first, causing mass panic and a general stampede, which created perfect targets for low-flying fighter planes. These planes forced the townspeople into buildings, where they were trapped while 12 bombers wrecked and burned the structures around them. The entire city center was quickly and efficiently gutted, leaving only a smoldering shell of what had once been a thriving community. Only the old Iglesia de Santa María, the Casa de Juntas, and the oak tree were spared the devastation. Not surprisingly, Franco's war-material factory a few kilometers down the road also survived.

As it turned out, Franco had given the Nazis the go-ahead for the bombing raid, which was to be a test-run of the effectiveness of their bombers. Guernica was far behind the war's front lines, but Franco was perfectly ready to make an example of the innocent villagers in order to quell the rising Basque resistance.

Many pictures, sketches, and paintings have attempted to cap-

BILBAO (BILBO) ☎944

Bilbao (pop. 385,000) is a city transformed; what was once a gritty industrial town is now a graceful city with wide boulevards and expansive parks. The Guggenheim Museum has been the most visible contribution to Bilbao's rise to international prominence, but there is more to the city than its oddly shaped claim to fame.

TRANSPORTATION AND PRACTICAL INFORMATION. To reach the **airport** (☎86 96 64), 25km from Bilbao, take the Bizkai bus (☎902 22 22 65) marked *Aeropuerto* from Pl. Moyúa, in front of the Hacienda building (line A-3247; 25min., 2 per hr., €1.10). RENFE **trains** (☎902 24 02 02) leave from Estación de Abando, Pl. Circular 2, for Barcelona (9-10hr., 2 per day, €38-49), Madrid (6hr., 2 per day, €37-42), and Salamanca (5hr., 2pm, €27). Most **bus** companies leave from the Termibús terminal, C. Gurtubay 1 (☎27 42 00; M: San Mamés), for: Barcelona (7¼hr., 4 per day, €39); Madrid (4-5hr., 10-18 per day, €25); Pamplona (2hr., 4-6 per day, €12); San Sebastián (1¼hr., 1-2 per hr., €8.65).

The city's major thoroughfare, **Gran Vía de Don Diego López de Haro,** or just **Gran Vía,** connects three of Bilbao's main plazas. Heading east from Pl. de Sagrado Corazón, Gran Vía continues through the central Pl. Moyúa and ends at Pl. Circular. Past Pl. Circular, cross the Río de Bilbao on **Puente del Arenal** to arrive in **Plaza de Arriaga,** the entrance to the *casco viejo* and **Plaza Nueva.** The **tourist office** is at Pl. Ensanche 11. (☎79 57 60; www.bilbao.net/bilbaoturismo. Open M-F 9am-2pm and 4-7:30pm.) Surf the **Internet** at **Net House,** C. Villariás 6. (☎23 71 53. €1.50 per 30min., €0.05 per min. thereafter. Open daily 9am-11pm.) **Postal Code:** 48008.

ACCOMMODATIONS AND FOOD. The **Plaza Arriaga** and **Calle Arenal** have budget accommodations galore, while upscale hotels pepper the new city off **Gran Vía.** Rates climb during *Semana Grande* (Aug. 12-19, 2007). **Pensión Méndez ❷,** C. Sta. María 13, 4th fl., offers sunlit rooms with spacious balconies. (☎16 03 64. Singles €25; doubles €35; triples €50. Cash only.) Restaurants and bars in the *casco viejo* offer a wide selection of local dishes, *pintxos,* and *bocadillos.* The new city has even more variety. As its English-Basque name suggests, **New Inn Urrestarazu ❶,** Alameda de Urquijo 9, is perfect if you just can't decide between authentic local cuisine and comfort food. Try the Idiazábal cheese (€5.55) or €5 onion rings. (☎944 15 40 53. Open M-Th 7:30am-10pm, F-Sa 7am-midnight, Su 10am-10pm. Cash only.) **Mercado**

de la Ribera is the biggest indoor **market** in Spain; it's worth a trip even if you're not eating. (Open M-Th and Sa 8am-2:30pm, F 8am-2:30pm and 4:30-7:30pm.) Pick up groceries at **Champion,** Pl. Santos Juanes, past Mercado de la Ribera. (Open M-Sa 9am-9:30pm. AmEx/MC/V.)

SIGHTS. Although the **Museo de Bellas Artes,** Pl. del Museo 2, can't boast the name recognition of the Guggenheim, it still wins the favor of locals. Behind an unassuming facade, the museum holds an impressive collection including 15th- to 17th-century Flemish paintings, canvases by Basque artists, and works by Mary Cassatt, El Greco, Gauguin, Goya, and Velázquez. Take C. Elcano to Pl. del Museo or bus #10 from Pte. del Arenal. (☎39 60 60, guided tours 39 61 37. Open Tu-Sa 10am-8pm, Su 10am-2pm. €5, students and seniors €3.50, under 12 and W free.) As every tourist pamphlet points out, Frank Gehry's **Museo Guggenheim Bilbao,** Av. Abandoibarra 2, is breathtaking. The €95 million titanium, limestone, and glass building, said to resemble either an iridescent fish or a blossoming flower, has catapulted Bilbao into cultural stardom. (☎35 90 80; www.guggenheim-bilbao.es. Open July-Aug. daily 10am-8pm; Sept.-June Tu-Su 10am-8pm. Admission includes English-language guided tours Tu-Su 11am, 12:30, 4:30, 6:30pm. Sign up 30min. before tour at the info desk. Wheelchair-accessible. €12.50, students €7.50, under 12 free.)

ENTERTAINMENT AND NIGHTLIFE. In the *casco viejo*, revelers spill out into the streets to sip their *txikitos* (chee-KEE-tos; small glasses of wine), especially on **Calle Barrenkale.** Teenagers and twenty-somethings fill **Calle Licenciado Poza** on the west side of town, especially between C. General Concha and Alameda de Recalde. **The Cotton Club,** C. Gregorio de la Revilla 25, (entrance on C. Simón Bolívar), is decorated with over 30,000 beer bottle caps. (☎944 10 49 51. Beer €3. Over 100 choices of whiskey €6. Rum €6. DJ spins Th 11pm, F-Sa 1am; live music some Th during the college term. Open M-Th 5pm-3:30am, F-Sa 5pm-6am, Su 6:30pm-3:30am.) The huge fiesta in honor of *Nuestra Señora de Begoña* occurs during **Semana Grande,** a nine-day party with fireworks, concerts, and theater (Aug. 12-19, 2007). Pick up a *Bilbao Guide* from the tourist office for listings.

DAYTRIP FROM BILBAO: GUERNICA (GERNIKA). Founded in 1366, Guernica (pop. 15,600) long served as the ceremonial seat of the Basque Country. On April 26, 1937, at the behest of General Francisco Franco, the Nazi "Condor Legion"

ture this nightmarish day. In a painting now at the Guernica Peace Museum (p. 954), Sofía Gandarias depicts clocks stopped at 4:30, women holding dead children, and the words *"y del cielo llovía sangre"* (blood rained from the sky). But it was Picasso who brought international recognition to the town's tragedy. The Republican government had commissioned him to paint a mural for the Universal Exhibition in Paris in 1937, and he used the bombing for inspiration. In 10 days, he had 25 sketches; he finished the painting—his largest work—in only one month. After much controversy, *Guernica*, Picasso's masterpiece, now resides in Madrid's Reina Sofía (p. 902). When asked the meaning of the painting as a whole, he replied "Let them interpret as they wish." Picasso was even approached by a German ambassador who asked him, "Did you do this?" Picasso answered simply, "No, you did."

Today, Guernica's town motto is *"Renunciar a olvidar, renunciar a la venganza"* (refusing to forget but without seeking vengeance). It took five years to rebuild the town and many more of enduring cultural and political repression under Franco. Finally, though, in 1989, the president of Germany publicly admitted the German role in the massacre and officially apologized to the citizens of Guernica. Today, this reconciliation is the hallmark of the town's rebirth and its message of peace.

dropped 29,000kg of explosives on Guernica, obliterating 70% of the city in three hours. The atrocity, which killed nearly 2000 people, is immortalized in Pablo Picasso's masterpiece, **Guernica** (p. 902). The thought-provoking **Gernika Peace Museum,** Pl. Foru 1, features a variety of multimedia exhibits. From the train station, walk two blocks up C. Adolfo Urioste and turn right on C. Artekalea. (☎946 27 02 13. Open July-Aug. M-Sa 10am-7pm, Su 10am-2pm; Sept.-June Tu-Sa 10am-2pm and 4-7pm, Su 10am-2pm. Guided English-language tours noon and 5pm, or call for an appointment. €4, students €2.) A replica of Picasso's *Guernica* is displayed on C. Pedro de Elejalde, two blocks up San Juan. **Trains** (☎902 54 32 10; www.euskotren.es) head to Bilbao (45min.; 1-2 per hr.; €2.25, round-trip €3.80). Bizkai Bus (☎902 22 22 65) sends more frequent **buses** between Guernica and Bilbao's Estación Abando; buses leave from Hdo. Amezaga in front of the Bilbao RENFE station. (Lines A-3514 and A-3515; 45min., every 15-30min., €2.15.) To reach the **tourist office,** C. Artekale 8, from the train station, walk three blocks up C. Adolfo Urioste, turn right on C. Barrenkale, go left at the alleyway, and look for the signs. (☎946 25 58 92; www.gernika-lumo.net. Open July-Aug. M-Sa 10am-7pm, Su 10am-2pm; Sept.-June M-Sa 10am-2pm and 4-7pm, Su 10am-2pm.)

BALEARIC ISLANDS ☎971

While all of the *Islas Baleares* are famous for their gorgeous beaches and landscapes, each island has its own character. Mallorca absorbs the bulk of high-class, package-tour invaders, Ibiza affords the best nightlife in Europe, and quieter Menorca offers empty white beaches, hidden coves, and Bronze Age megaliths.

TRANSPORTATION

Flying is the easiest way to reach the islands. Students with an ISIC can often get discounts from **Iberia** (☎902 40 05 00; www.iberia.com), which flies to Ibiza and Palma de Mallorca from Barcelona (40min., €15-300) and Madrid (1hr., €15-250). **Air Europa** (☎902 40 15 01; www.air-europa.com), **Spanair** (☎902 92 91 91; www.spanair.com), and **Vueling** (☎902 33 39 33; www.vueling.com) offer budget flights to and between the islands. Another option is a **charter flight,** which may include a week's stay in a hotel; some companies, called *mayoristas,* sell leftover spots on package-tour flights as "seat-only" (find them through travel agencies). Prices during the summer are higher than in low season.

Ferries to the islands are less popular and take longer. Trasmediterránea (☎902 45 46 45; www.trasmediterranea.com) departs from Barcelona's Estació Marítima Moll and Valencia's Estació Marítima for Ibiza, Mallorca, and Menorca (€68-100). Fares between the islands run €28-75. Buquebus (☎902 41 42 42) has fast catamaran service between Barcelona and Palma de Mallorca (4hr., 2 per day, €11-150). The three major islands have extensive **bus** systems with fares ranging €1.20-7, though transportation comes to a halt on Sundays in most locations; check schedules. **Car** rental costs about €40 per day, **mopeds** €30, and **bikes** €6-15.

MALLORCA

A favorite of Spain's royal family, Mallorca has long attracted the rich and famous. The capital of the Balearics, **Palma** (pop. 323,000) is a resort haven for Germans and Brits, but still retains genuine local flavor. In many of its cafes, the native dialect of *mallorquí* is the only language heard. The tourist office distributes a list of over 40 nearby **beaches.** One popular choice is **El Arenal** (S'Arenal; Platja de Palma; bus #15), 11km southeast of town toward the airport. The *casco viejo* is the place to be for your first drink of the evening. For fantastic cookies during the day and a chill scene at night, try **Costa Galana,** Av. Argentina 45. (Cookies €1.20. Beer €2. Mixed drinks €3-5. Open daily 8am-3am. MC/V.) Palma's clubbers start their night in the *bares-musicales* lining the **Passeig Marítim** strip. When the bar scene fades at 3am, partiers move to the *discotecas.* **Tito's,** in a gorgeous Art Deco palace on Pg. Marítim, sports fountains, a glass elevator, and a rockin' view of the water. (Beer €3. Mixed drinks €5. Cover €15-18, includes 1 drink. Open daily 11pm-6:30am. MC/V.)

Hostal Ritzi ❷, C. Apuntadors 6, is a block away from Pl. de la Reina. Cheap meals are served in a Victorian dining room, which doubles as a TV lounge. (☎71 46 10. Breakfast included. Laundry €7. Singles €30; doubles €45, with shower €48, with bath €52. Cash only.) Travelers on a budget head to the side streets off **Passeig del Born,** the cafes along **Avinguda Joan Miró,** or the carbon-copy pizzerias along **Passeig Marítim.** Near Pl. Obispo at Berenguer de Palou 8, **Sa Premsa ❶** is a huge eatery with an endless selection of local food. (☎72 35 29; www.cellersapremsa.com. Entrees €3.75-8.50. Open M-Sa noon-4pm and 7:30-11:30pm. MC/V.) **Eurosky,** on C. Felip Bauzá, sells groceries. (☎900 70 30 70. Open M-F 8:30am-8:30pm, Sa 9am-2pm.) From the airport, take bus #1 to **Plaza d'Espanya** (15min., every 20min., €1.30). To reach the **tourist office,** Pg. del Born 27, in the bookshop of Casa Solleric, walk up Pg. del Born from Pl. de la Reina. (☎22 59 00; www.a-palma.es. Open daily 9am-8pm.) **Postal Code:** 07003.

IBIZA

Nowhere else on Earth are decadence, opulence, and hedonism celebrated as religiously as on the beautiful island of Ibiza (pop. 84,000). A hippie enclave in the 1960s, Ibiza has entered a new age of debauchery and extravangance. Only one of Ibiza's beaches **(Figueretes)** is within walking distance of **Eivissa** (Ibiza City), but most, including bar-lined **Platja d'en Bossa,** are a 20min. bike ride away; bus #14 also leaves from Av. d'Isidor Macabich 20 for Platja d'en Bossa (every 30min., €1.30). The best beach closest to the city is **Playa de Las Salinas.** (Bus #11 runs every 30min. to Salinas from Av. d'Isidor Macabich.)

The crowds return from the beaches by nightfall. The bar scene centers around **Carrer de Barcelona,** while **Carrer de la Verge** is the nexus of gay nightlife. The island's giant **discos** are world-famous and virtually all gay-friendly. The best sources of information on parties and DJs are posters plastered around town and the daily newspaper **Diario Ibiza** (€1). The **Discobus** runs to major hot spots (leaves Eivissa from Av. d'Isidor Macabich every hr. 12:30-6:30am, €1.75). World-famous **Pachá,** on Pg. Perimitral, is a 15min. walk or a 2min. cab ride from the port. (☎31 36 00; www.pacha.com. M "Release Yourself" with DJ Roger Sanchez or F "Fuck Me, I'm Famous" party. Cover €50-60. Open daily midnight-7:30am.) At **Amnesia,** a cave-like club on the road to San Antonio, you can forget who you are and who you came with. (☎19 80 41. M "Cocoon" draws huge crowds. W drag performances and foam party. Cover €30-50. Open daily midnight-8am. MC/V at bar, cash only for tickets.)

Cheap *hostales* in town are rare, especially in the summer; reserve ahead. The letters "CH" *(casa de huéspedes)* mark many doorways and are a much better deal. **CH La Peña ❷,** C. La Virgen 76, offers clean rooms at low prices. (☎19 02 40. Open June-Sept. Singles €23; doubles €32; triples €48. MC/V.) Eat hearty Spanish fare for the lowest prices on the island at **Bon Profit ❶,** Pl. del Parc. (Entrees €3-9. Open M-Sa 1-3pm and 8-10pm. MC/V.) The **Mercat Vell,** at the end of the bridge leading to *D'alt Villa,* sells meat and produce. (Open M-Sa 7am-7pm.) The **tourist office,** Pl. d'Antoni Riquer 2, is across from the Estació Marítima, with booths on Pg. Vara del Rey and at the airport. (☎30 19 00. Open June-Nov. M-F 9am-9pm, Sa 9:30am-7:30pm; Dec.-May M-F 8:30am-3pm, Sa 10:30am-1pm.) **Postal Code:** 07800.

☒ MENORCA

Menorca's (pop. 75,000) fantastic 200km of coastline, rustic landscapes, and picturesque towns draw sun-worshippers, photographers, and ecologists alike. Atop a steep bluff, **Mahón** (Maó; pop. 21,180) is the gateway to the island. The popular **beaches** outside Mahón are accessible by **bus.** Transportes Menorca buses leave from the bus station, up C. Vasallo at the far end of Pl. de s'Esplanada, for **Platges de Son Bou** (30min., 7 per day, €1.85), the island's largest beach, which spreads out into 4km of gorgeous but crowded sand on the southern shore. Autobuses Fornells buses leave Mahón for the breathtaking **Arenal d'en Castell** (30min., 2-5 per day, €1.85), while TMSA buses go to the heavily touristed **Cala'n Porter** (7 per day, €1.20). While there, don't miss the ☒**Covas d'en Xoroi,** an amazing network of natural caves nestled in the cliffs high above the sea. The naturally air-conditioned caves house several bars during the day (cover €3.50-9, includes 1 drink; open Apr.-Oct. daily 11am-11pm) and a crowded, popular ambient disco at night. (☎37 72 36. Beer €3. Mixed drinks €5-8. Th foam parties. Cover €17-21. Open Apr.-Oct. daily 11pm-late.)

To get to the exquisitely decorated rooms of ☒**Posada Orsi ❷**, C. de la Infanta 19, from Pl. de s'Esplanada, take C. Moreres, which becomes C. Hannover; turn right at Pl. Constitució and follow C. Nou through Pl. Reial. (☎36 47 51. Fans available on request. Singles €20-25; doubles €30-40, with shower €40-50. Cash only.) Mahón takes its restaurants very seriously. ☒**Elefant ❷**, Moll. de Llevant 106, is a vegetarian's dream. This hip, French-run cafe serves deliciously creative and affordable lunches. (☎676 89 24 23. Tapas €3.80-5. Entrees €8-14. Open M and W-Su noon-4pm and 7pm-midnight. Cash only.) The Mahón **tourist office,** Moll. de Llevant 2, at the port, has a branch at the airport that is open 24hr. (☎35 59 52; www.e-menorca.org. Open M-F 8am-8:30pm, Sa 8am-1pm.) **Postal Code:** 07700.

NORTHWESTERN SPAIN

Northwestern Spain is the country's best-kept secret; its seclusion is half its charm. Rainy Galicia hides mysterious Celtic ruins, and on the northern coast tiny Asturias allows access to the dramatic Picos de Europa mountain range.

GALICIA (GALIZA)

If, as the Galician saying goes, "rain is art," then there is no gallery more beautiful than the Northwest's misty skies. Locals speak *gallego,* a linguistic hybrid of Castilian and Portuguese.

SANTIAGO DE COMPOSTELA ☎981

Santiago (pop. 94,000) is a city of song. From magnificent outdoor operas to roving bands of *guita* players to the thumping of all-night discos, every street and plaza is filled with musical celebration. Each of the four facades of Santiago's **cathedral** is a masterpiece of a different era, with entrances opening to four different plazas: Inmaculada, Obradoiro, Praterías, and Quintana. (☎58 35 48. Open daily 7am-9pm. Free.) Entrance to the cathedral **museums** includes a visit to the treasury and relics, the cloister, the tapestry room, the archaeology rooms, the chapter house, the library, and the archives. (☎58 11 55. Open June-Sept. M-Sa 10am-2pm and 4-8pm, Su and holidays 10am-2pm; Oct.-May M-Sa 10am-1:30pm and 4-6:30pm, Su and holidays 10am-1:30pm. €5, students €3.)

Nearly every street in the *ciudad vieja* has at least one *pensión.* In the center of the *ciudad vieja,* ☒**Hospedaje Ramos ❷**, R. da Raíña 18, 2nd fl., has well-lit rooms and private baths. (☎58 18 59. Singles €18; doubles €30. Cash only.) Most restaurants are on R. do Vilar, R. do Franco, R. Nova, and R. da Raíña. A hole in the wall, **A Tulla ❷,** R. de Entrerúas 1, is a family restaurant accessible only through an obscure alley between R. do Vilar and R. Nova. The *menús* (€9-12) are a superb value. (☎58 08 89. Entrees €6.50-8.50. Open M-Sa noon-midnight. MC/V.) Santiago's **mercado** is located between Pl. San Felix and Convento de Santo Agustín. (Open M-Sa 7:30am-2pm.) At night, take R. Montero Ríos to the bars and clubs off **Praza Roxa.** **Casa das Crechas,** Vía Sacra 3, is a cavernous, witchcraft-themed drinking hole renowned for live jazz and Galician folk concerts. (☎56 07 51. Beer €2. Open daily in summer noon-4am; winter 4pm-3am.)

Trains (☎902 24 02 02) run from R. do Hórreo to Bilbao (10¾hr., 9am, €34) via León (6½hr., €26), and Madrid (8hr., 2 per day, €39). To reach the city, take bus #6 to Pr. de Galicia. **Buses** (☎54 24 16) run from R. de Rodríguez to Madrid (8-9hr.; 4-6 per day; €36, round-trip €58) and San Sebastián (13½hr., 3 per day, €36/58) via Bilbao (11¼hr., 3 per day, €44-59). To get to the old city from the bus station, take bus #5 or 10 to Pr. de Galicia. The **tourist office** is at R. do Vilar 63. (☎55 51 29; www.santiagoturismo.com. Multilingual staff. Open daily June-Sept. 9am-9pm; Oct.-May 10am-3pm and 5-8pm.) Use the **Internet** at **CyberNova 50,** R. Nova 50. (☎57 51 88. €1-1.20 per hr. Open M-Sa 9am-1am, Su 10am-1am.) **Postal Code:** 15701.

ASTURIAS

Spaniards call Asturias a *"paraíso natural"* (natural paradise). Thanks to its insurmountable peaks and dense alpine forests, Asturias remained untouched for centuries, but a sort of invasion is now at hand, as visitors rush to take part in the booming adventure tourism industry.

PICOS DE EUROPA

The Picos de Europa mountain range is home to **Picos de Europa National Park,** one of the largest national parks in Europe. The most popular trails and peaks lie near **Garganta del Cares** (Cares Gorge) in the Macizo Central (Central Massif). For a list of *refugios* (cabins with bunks but no blankets), hiking advice, and general info, contact the **Picos de Europa National Park Visitors' Center** in Cangas de Onís.

CANGAS DE ONÍS ☎985

The accessibility of Cangas (pop. 6370) makes it an ideal base for exploring the Picos de Europa National Park. Cangas itself is, if not particularly thrilling, a relaxing, history-rich town. Founded in AD 718, it was for 70 years the first capital of what would become present-day Spain. The town's sights show the impact of Paleolithic, Celtic, and Roman inhabitants. There are many mid-range hotels in Cangas, and moderately priced pensions abound along Av. Covadonga. **Pensión Principado ❶,** Av. Covadonga 6, 4th fl., has comfortable rooms with TV and hall bath. (☎84 83 50 or 667 983 185. Dorms €20; doubles €25. Cash only.) Pick up groceries at **Alimerka Supermercado,** Av. Covadonga 13. (☎84 94 13. Open Su-M 9am-2pm, Tu-Sa 9am-9:30pm.) **Alsa,** Av. Covadonga 18 (☎84 81 33), across from the tourist office, sends **buses** to Madrid (7hr., 3:20pm, €27). Find information on accommodations, adventure tourism, and town history at the **tourist office,** Jardines del Ayuntamiento 2, located in the Pl. del Ayuntamiento, across from the bus stop. (☎/fax 84 80 05. Open *Semana Santa*-Oct. daily 9am-10pm; Nov.-*Semana Santa* M-Sa 10am-2pm and 4-7pm, Su 10am-3pm.)

SWEDEN (SVERIGE)

With the design world cooing over bright, blocky Swedish furniture and college students donning faux-designer wear from H&M, Scandinavia's largest nation has earned a reputation abroad for its chic yet mass-marketable style. At home, Sweden's struggle to balance a market economy with its generous social welfare system stems from its belief that all citizens should have access to education and affordable health care. Cradle-to-grave programs like these come at a price, and top wage-earners pay out as much as 60% of their annual incomes in taxes. This neutral nation's zest for spending money on butter instead of guns has also shored up a strong sense of national unity, from Sámi reindeer herders above the Arctic Circle to bankers in bustling Stockholm.

DISCOVER SWEDEN: SUGGESTED ITINERARY

Plan for three days in the capital city of **Stockholm** (p. 963), including one sunny afternoon out on the rocky **Skärgård archipelago** (p. 973). Daytrip north to the university town of **Uppsala** (p. 978), or take an eastbound ferry out to the island of **Gotland** (p. 974), where serene bike paths and medieval towns overlook the Baltic Sea. Neither **Malmö** (p. 977) nor **Lund** (p. 978) are known for their serenity, with clamorous ethnic markets in the former and booming student nightlife in the latter. Soak up some high culture in the museums of elegant **Gothenburg** (p. 980), then get ready to rough it on hikes out of **Åre** (p. 987) and **Örnsköldsvik** (p. 988). **Kiruna** (p. 990) is the end of the line up in mountainous Lappland, where ore miners and the indigenous Sami share vast stretches of Arctic wilderness.

ESSENTIALS

FACTS AND FIGURES

Official Name: Kingdom of Sweden.
Capital: Stockholm.
Major Cities: Gothenburg, Malmö.
Population: 9,067,000.
Land Area: 449,000 sq. km.
Time Zone: GMT +1.
Language: Swedish.
Religion: Lutheran (87%).

WHEN TO GO

The most popular months to visit Sweden are July and August, when temperatures average 20°C (68°F) in the south and 16°C (61°F) in the north. Travelers who arrive in May and early June can take advantage of low season prices and enjoy the late-spring wildflowers, but some attractions don't open until late June. The 24 hours of daylight known as the **midnight sun** are best experienced between early June and mid-July. During the winter, keep an eye out for the **Northern Lights** (p. 737) and bring heavy cold-weather gear; temperatures hover around -5°C (23°F).

DOCUMENTS AND FORMALITIES

EMBASSIES AND CONSULATES. All foreign embassies are in Stockholm (p. 964). Swedish embassies and consulates abroad include: **Australia,** 5 Turrana St., Yarralumla, Canberra, ACT, 2600 (☎2 62 70 27 00; www.swedenabroad.com/canberra); **Canada,** 377 Dalhousie St., Ottawa, ON, K1N 9N8 (☎613-241-8553; www.swedenabroad.ca); **Ireland,** 13-17 Dawson St., Dublin 2 (☎1 474 44 00;

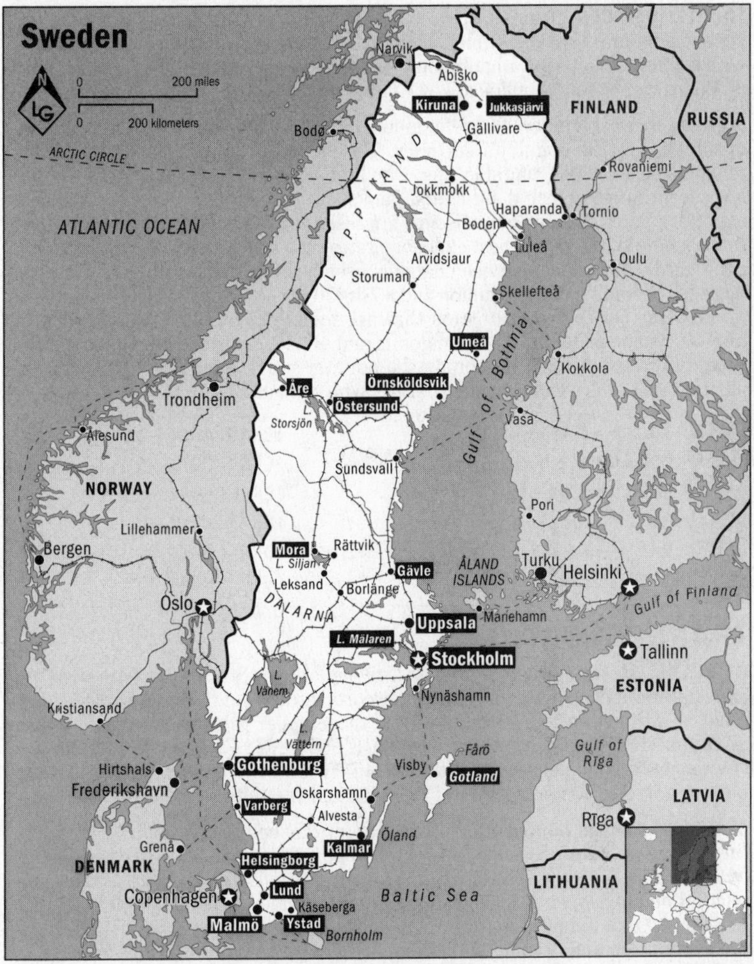

www.swedenabroad.com/dublin); **New Zealand,** Vogel Building, Level 13, Aitken St., Wellington (☎4 499 9895; sweden@extra.co.nz); **UK,** 11 Montagu Pl., London, W1H 2AL (☎020 79 17 64 00; www.swedenabroad.com/london); **US,** 1501 M St., NW, Washington, D.C., 20005 (☎202-467-2600; www.swedishemb.org).

VISA AND ENTRY INFORMATION. EU citizens do not need a visa to enter Sweden. Citizens of Australia, Canada, New Zealand, and the US do not need a visa for stays of up to 90 days, beginning upon entry into any of the countries that belong to the European Union's specially-designated freedom-of-movement zone. For more information, see p. 16.

TOURIST SERVICES AND MONEY

EMERGENCY	**Police, Ambulance,** and **Fire:** ☎112.

TOURIST OFFICES. There are two types of tourist offices: those marked with a yellow and blue "I" have both local and national information, while those marked with a green "I" have information only on the town they serve. The Swedish Tourist Board can be found online at www.visit-sweden.com.

MONEY. In a September 2003 referendum, Sweden's voters rejected the adoption of the euro as the country's currency. The Swedish unit of currency therefore remains the **krona (kr),** plural kronor. One krona is equal to 100 öre. Many **ATMs** do not accept non-Swedish debit cards. Banks and post offices exchange currency; expect to pay a 20-35kr commission for cash, and 5-15kr for traveler's checks. **Forex** generally offers the best exchange rates, and has ATMs that accept foreign debit cards. Although a service charge is usually added to the bill at restaurants, **tipping** is becoming more common and a 7-10% tip is now considered standard. Tip taxi drivers 5-10%. All countries that are members of the European Union impose a **value added tax (VAT)** on goods and services purchased within the EU. Prices in Sweden already include the country's whopping 25% VAT, although partial refunds are available for visitors who are not EU citizens (p. 22).

SWEDISH KRONOR (KR)		
	AUS$1 = 5.45KR	10KR = AUS$1.83
	CDN$1 = 6.63KR	10KR = CDN$1.51
	EUR€1 = 9.30KR	10KR = EUR€1.08
	NZ$1 = 4.58KR	10KR = NZ$2.18
	UK£1= 13.54KR	10KR = UK£0.78
	US$1 = 7.39KR	10KR = US$1.35

TRANSPORTATION

BY PLANE. Most international flights arrive in or near Stockholm, with domestic and charter flights connecting to other airports throughout the country. **SAS** (Scandinavian Airlines) offers youth fares (for those under 26) on some flights within Scandinavia (Sweden ☎08 797 4000, UK 0870 6072 7727, US 800-221-2350; www.scandinavian.net). **Ryanair** (☎353 1249 7700; www.ryanair.com) flies at rock-bottom prices to Västerås Airport (VST), located 1hr. outside of Stockholm.

BY TRAIN. **Statens Järnväger (SJ),** the state railway company, runs reliable trains throughout southern Sweden, and offers a 30% discount for travelers under 26 (☎0771 75 75 75; www.sj.se/english). Seat reservations (28-55kr) are required on **InterCity** and high-speed **X2000** trains; they are included in the ticket price but not in railpasses. On other routes, check to see how full the train is; don't bother with reservations on empty trains. In northern Sweden, **Connex** runs trains from Stockholm through Umeå and Kiruna to Narvik, NOR (☎0771 26 00 00; https://bokning.connex.se/connexp/index_en.html). The 35min. trip over the **Øresund bridge** connecting Malmö to Copenhagen, DEN (70kr) is the fastest way to travel from continental Europe; reserve ahead. Timetables for all SJ and Connex trains can be found at www.resplus.se. **Eurailpasses** are valid on all of these trains. In the south, purple **pågatågen** trains service local traffic between Helsingborg, Lund, Malmö, and Ystad; **Scanrail** and **Eurailpasses** are valid, or purchase tickets from special vending machines. The **Scanrailpass,** purchased outside Scandinavia, is good for rail travel through Denmark, Finland, Norway, and Sweden, as well as many discounted ferry and bus rides. Passes can also be purchased within Scandinavia, but passholders can only use three travel days in the country of purchase.

BY BUS. In the north, buses may be a better option than trains. **Swebus** (Sweden ☎02 0021 8218, international 46 36 290 80 00; www.swebusexpress.se) is the main carrier nationwide; **Swebus Express** only serves the region around Stockholm and

TIP **RAIL SAVINGS.** Scanrail passes purchased outside Scandinavia are much more flexible than Scanrail passes purchased once you arrive, and may be less expensive depending on the exchange rate. Check www.scanrail.com for more information on where to purchase passes at home.

Gothenburg. **Biljettservice** (p. 963), inside Stockholm's Cityterminalen, will reserve tickets for longer routes. Students and travelers under 26 get a 20% discount on express buses. Bicycles are not allowed on board.

BY FERRY. Ferries run from Stockholm (p. 963) to the Åland Islands, Gotland, Finland, and the Baltic states. Ystad (p. 979) sends several ferries a day to Bornholm, DEN. Ferries from Gothenburg (p. 981) serve Frederikshavn, DEN; Kiel, GER; and Newcastle, BRI. Popular lines include the **Silja Line,** Kungsg. 2 (US ☎800-533-3755 ext. 114; www.silja.com), and the **Viking Line** (US ☎800-843-0602; www.vikingline.fi). On Silja, both Scan- and Eurailers ride for free or at reduced rates. On Viking ferries, Scanrail holders get 50% off, and a Eurailpass plus a train ticket entitles holders to a free passenger fare. (Mention this discount when booking.) Additionally, Viking offers "early bird" discounts of 15-50% for those who book at least 30 days in advance within Finland or Sweden.

BY CAR. Sweden honors foreign drivers' licenses for up to one year, although drivers under 18 cannot take the wheel. **Speed limits** are 110kph on expressways, 50kph in densely populated areas, and 70-90kph elsewhere. Headlights must be used at all times. Swedish roads are uncrowded and in good condition, but take extra care in winter weather and be wary of reindeer or elk in the road. Many gas stations are open until 10pm; after hours, look for cash-operated pumps marked *sedel automat*. For more info on car rental and driving in Europe, see p. 54.

BY BIKE AND THUMB. Bicycling is easy; bike paths are common, and both the **Sverigeleden** (National Route) and **Cykelspåret** (Bike Path) traverse the entire country. **Hitchhiking** is uncommon. Let's Go does not recommend hitchhiking.

KEEPING IN TOUCH

EMAIL AND THE INTERNET. There are a limited number of cybercafes in Stockholm and other big cities. Expect to pay about 20kr per hr. In smaller towns, Internet is available for free at most tourist offices marked with the yellow and blue "I" (p. 960), as well as for a small fee at most public libraries.

TELEPHONE. Pay phones often accept phone cards *(Telefonkort)*; buy them at newsstands or other shops (60kr and 100kr). **Mobile phones** are an increasingly popular and economical alternative; for more info, see p. 29. International direct dial numbers include: **AT&T Direct** (☎020 79 91 11); **British Telecom** (☎0800 89 0046); **Canada Direct** (☎020 79 90 15); **MCI WorldPhone** (☎0200 895 438); **Sprint** (☎020 799 011); **Telecom New Zealand** (☎020 79 90 64).

PHONE CODES	**Country code:** 46. **International dialing prefix:** 00. For more information on how to place international calls, see inside back cover.

MAIL. Postcards and letters under 50g can be sent for 10kr.

LANGUAGE. Sweden has no official language, although Swedish is universally spoken. The region around Kiruna is home to a small minority of Finnish speakers, as well as 7000 speakers of the Sámi languages. Almost all Swedes speak English fluently. For basic Swedish words and phrases, see **Phrasebook: Swedish,** p. 1064.

ACCOMMODATIONS AND CAMPING

SWEDEN	❶	❷	❸	❹	❺
ACCOMMODATIONS	under 160kr	160-230kr	230-350kr	350-500kr	over 500kr

Youth hostels *(vandrarhem)* cost 120-200kr per night. The hostels run by the **Svenska Turistföreningen (STF)** and affiliated with HI are uniformly top-notch. Non-members should expect to pay 200-240kr per night; HI members receive a 45kr discount (☎08 463 21 00; www.svenskaturistforeningen.se). STF also manages **mountain huts** in the northern wilds (150-350kr). Many **campgrounds** (tent sites 80-110kr; www.camping.se) offer **cottages** *(stugor)* for 100-300kr per person. International Camping Cards aren't valid in Sweden; **Swedish Camping Cards,** available at all SCR campgrounds, are mandatory (one-year pass 90kr). The Swedish **right of public access** *(allemansrätten)* means travelers can camp for free in the countryside, as long as they are a reasonable distance from private homes (www.allemansratten.se).

FOOD AND DRINK

SWEDEN	❶	❷	❸	❹	❺
FOOD	under 50kr	50-75kr	75-100kr	100-160kr	over 160kr

Restaurant fare is usually expensive in Sweden, but **food halls** *(saluhallen)*, open-air markets, and **hot dog stands** *(varmkorv)* make budget eating easy enough. Many restaurants offer affordable **dagens rätt,** daily lunch specials, for 60-75kr. The Swedish palate has long been attuned to simple, hearty meat-and-potatoes fare, but immigrant communities in Malmö and Stockholm have spiced things up for budget travelers. A league of five-star chefs in Gothenburg are tossing off increasingly imaginative riffs on herring and salmon. The Swedish love **drip coffee** (as opposed to espresso) and have institutionalized coffee breaks as a near-sacred rite of the workday. Aside from light beer containing less than 3.5% alcohol, alcohol can be purchased only at **Systembolaget** liquor stores and in licensed bars and restaurants. You can buy light beer at 18, but it's 20+ otherwise and you will be carded. Some classier bars and clubs have age restrictions as high as 25.

HOLIDAYS AND FESTIVALS

Holidays: New Year's Day (Jan. 1); Epiphany (Jan. 6); Good Friday (Apr. 6); Easter (Apr. 8-9); May Day (May 1); Ascension Day (May 25); Whit (June 4-5); National Day (June 6); All Saints' Day (Nov. 1); Christmas (Dec. 24-25); Boxing Day (Dec. 26).

Festivals: Valborgsmässoafton (Walpurgis Eve; Apr. 30) celebrates the arrival of spring with roaring bonfires in Dalarna and choral singing in Lund and Uppsala. Dalarna erects flowery maypoles in time for Midsummer (June 23-24), as young people flock to the islands of Gotland, Öland, and the Skärgård archipelago for all-night parties. July welcomes the Stockholm Jazz Festival to the capital, while crayfish parties in August and eel parties in September leave the timid swimming for sanctuary.

BEYOND TOURISM

Summer employment is often easier to find than long-term work, since Sweden has fairly strict regulations governing the employment of foreigners. See p. 61 for Beyond Tourism opportunities throughout Europe.

The American-Scandinavian Foundation (AMSCAN), 58 Park Ave., New York, NY 10016, USA (☎212 8799 779; www.amscan.org/jobs/index.html). Volunteer and job opportunities throughout Scandinavia. Fellowships for study in Sweden for Americans.

Council of International Fellowship (CIF), Karlbergsvägen 80 nb. ög, 113 35 Stockholm, SWE (☎04 68 32 31 21; www.cif-sweden.org). Funds exchange programs for service professionals, including homestays in various Swedish cities. Must have 3 years professional experience.

Internationella Arbetslag, Tegelviksgatan 40, 116 41 Stockholm, SWE (☎08 643 08 89; www.ial.nu). The Swedish branch of Service Civil International (SCI; www.sciint.org) organizes a broad range of workcamps throughout Sweden. 700-900kr camp fee plus 150kr SCI membership fee.

STOCKHOLM ☎08

Surrounded by water, elegant Stockholm (pop. 1,250,000) exists by virtue of a delicate latticework of bridges that connects its islands and peninsulas and brings together individual neighborhoods that have developed characters of their own. Sophistication reigns supreme in the self-styled "capital of Scandinavia," and visitors can't help but get swept into the current.

TRANSPORTATION

Flights: Arlanda Airport (ARN; ☎797 60 00), 45km north of the city. **Flygbussarna** shuttles (☎600 10 00; www.flygbussarna.se) run between Arlanda and the bus station (40min.; every 15min. 4am-10pm station to airport, 4am-11:45pm airport to station; 95kr; students, children, and seniors 65kr; MC/V), as do **Arlanda Express** trains (☎020 22 22 24; www.arlandaexpress.com; 20min.; every 15min. 5am-midnight; 200kr, students 100kr). **Bus** #583 runs to the T-bana stop Märsta (10min., 20kr); then take the T-bana to T-Centralen in downtown Stockholm (40min., 20kr). Flygbussarna also operates shuttles to **Västerås Airport** (VST; ☎021 80 56 10) timed to line up with Ryanair departures (1½hr., 100kr).

Trains: Centralstationen (☎762 25 80). T-bana: T-Centralen. To: **Copenhagen, DEN** (6hr.; 5-8 per day; 1099kr, under 26 948kr); **Gothenburg** (3-5hr.; every 1-2hr.; 512-1110kr, under 26 437-955kr); and **Oslo, NOR** (6-8hr.; 2 per day; 672kr, under 26 572kr).

Buses: Cityterminalen, upstairs on the north end of Centralstationen. **Terminal Service** (☎762 59 97) goes to the airport (80kr) and Gotland ferries (70kr). **Biljettservice** (☎762 59 79) makes reservations with Sweden's bus companies for longer routes. **Swebus,** one of the largest, runs to **Copenhagen, DEN** (9hr., 3 per day, 400-500kr); **Gothenburg** (7hr., 7 per day, 250-300kr); and **Malmö** (8½hr., 3 per day, 400-500kr).

Ferries: Silja Line, Kungsg. 2 (☎22 21 40; www.silja.com), sails to Finland: **Helsinki** (17hr., 1 per day, from 75kr) and **Turku** (12hr., 2 per day, from 92kr). T-bana: Gärdet and follow signs to Värtahamnen, or take the Silja bus (20kr) from Cityterminalen. 50% Scanrail discount on selected fares. **Viking Line** (☎452 40 00; www.vikingline.fi) sails to **Helsinki, FIN** (17hr.; 1 per day; mid-June to mid-Aug. 430kr, low season from 300kr) and **Turku, FIN** (12hr.; 2 per day; mid-June to mid-Aug. 230kr, low season from 130kr). Office in Cityterminalen. **Tallink** (☎666 60 01; www.tallink.ee) sails to **Tallinn, EST** (16hr.; 1 per day; from 470kr, low season from 260kr). Shuttle buses (20kr) run from Cityterminalen to the Tallink port. Office in Cityterminalen.

Public Transportation: T-bana (Tunnelbana; subway) runs Su-Th 5am-12:30am, F-Sa 5am-3am. **Night buses** run 12:30am-5:30am. Tickets 20kr; 10 rides 180kr, sold at Pressbyrån news agents; 1hr. unlimited transfer. The **SL Tourist Card** (Turistkort) is valid on all public transportation. 1-day 60kr; 3-day 180kr. Office in Centralstationen (☎600 10 00). T-bana: T-Centralen. Open M-Sa 6:30am-11:15pm, Su 7am-11:15pm. MC/V.

Taxis: Many cabs have fixed prices to certain destinations; ask when you enter the cab. Expect to pay 450kr from Arlanda to Centralstationen. Major companies include **Taxi 020** (☎33 66 99), **Taxi Kurir** (☎30 00 00), and **Taxi Stockholm** (☎15 00 00).

Bike Rental: Rent-a-Bike, Strandvägen, Kajplats 24 (☎660 79 59). From 200kr per day. Open May-Sept. daily 10am-6pm. MC/V. **Djurgårdsbrons Sjöcafé,** Galärvarvsvägen 2 (☎660 57 57). Bikes 250kr per day. In-line skates 200kr per day. Canoes 300kr per day; kayaks 500kr per day. Open June-Aug. daily 9am-9pm. MC/V.

ORIENTATION AND PRACTICAL INFORMATION

Stockholm spans a number of small islands (linked by bridges and the T-bana) at the junction of **Lake Mälaren** to the west and the **Baltic Sea** to the east. The large northern island is divided into two sections: **Norrmalm,** home to Centralstationen and the crowded shopping district around Drottningg., and **Östermalm,** which boasts the **Strandvägen** waterfront and upscale nightlife fanning out from **Stureplan.** The mainly residential western island, **Kungsholmen,** holds beaches, waterside promenades, and the Stadhuset (city hall) on its eastern tip. The southern island of **Södermalm** retains a traditional feel in the midst of a budding cafe culture and club scene. Nearby **Långholmen** houses a nature preserve and a prison-turned-hotel/museum, while the similarly woodsy eastern island **Djurgården** exhibits several museums on its western side. At the center of these five islands is **Gamla Stan** (Old Town). Gamla Stan's less-trafficked neighbor (via Norrmalm) is **Skeppsholmen,** home to many of the city's art museums. Each of Stockholm's streets begins with number "1" at the end closest to the Kungliga Slottet (p. 970) in Gamla Stan; the lower the numbers, the closer you are to the Old Town. Street signs also contain the address numbers for that block.

TIP **PEDESTRIAN TACTICS 101.** Stockholm lends itself to exploration on foot, but the network of elevated streets and footbridges can be confusing. To get from Centralstationen to Sergels Torg, turn left out of the station onto Vasag., take the stairs up to Klarag., and head straight. To get to the Stadhuset, turn right out of the station and walk to Vasabron, then walk down the steps to the water just before the bridge and follow the quay under Centralbron. There are different ways to navigate the cloverleaf bridge from Gamla Stan to Södermalm, depending on your destination; to reach Södermalmstorg or the cliffs, stay on the bridge to the left. To reach Södermalärstrand, stay as far to the right as possible and then take the ramp down to the water.

Tourist Offices: Sweden House, Hamng. 27 (☎508 28 508; www.stockholmtown.com), entrance off Kungsträdsgården. From Centralstationen, walk up Klarabergsg. to Sergels Torg (look for the glass obelisk), bear right on Hamng., and turn right at the park. Agents sell the **SL card** and **Stockholm Card** (Stockholmskortet), which includes public transportation and admission to 75 museums and attractions. 1-day 270kr; 2-day 420kr; 3-day 540kr. Internet 1kr per min. Open M-F 9am-7pm, Sa 10am-5pm, Su 10am-4pm. AmEx/DC/MC/V. The **HotellCentralen** branch, in Centralstationen (☎789 24 56), also sells the SL and Stockholm Cards and books rooms for a 25-60kr fee. Open June-Aug. daily 8am-8pm; Sept.-May M-F 9am-6pm, Sa 9am-4pm, Su 10am-4pm. AmEx/DC/MC/V. The **Typical Swedish** design shop, Slussplan 7 (☎31 11 80, www.typicalswedish.com), on the south shore of Gamla Stan, sells the Stockholm Card. Open June-Aug. M-F 10am-6pm, Sa 10am-4pm, Su noon-4pm; Sept.-May call for hours. MC/V.

Budget Travel: Kilroy Travels, Kungsg. 4 (☎0771 54 57 69; www.kilroytravels.com). Open M-F 10am-6pm. **STA Travel,** Kungsg. 30 (☎0771 61 10 10; www.statravel.se). Open July-Aug. M-F 10am-6pm; Sept.-June M-F 10am-6pm, Sa 11am-2pm.

Embassies: Australia, Sergels Torg 12, 11th fl. (☎613 29 00; www.sweden.embassy.gov.au). Open M-F 8:30am-4:50pm. **Canada,** Tegelbacken 4, 7th fl. (☎453 30 00; www.canadaemb.se). Open 8:30am-noon and 1-5pm. **Ireland,** Oster-

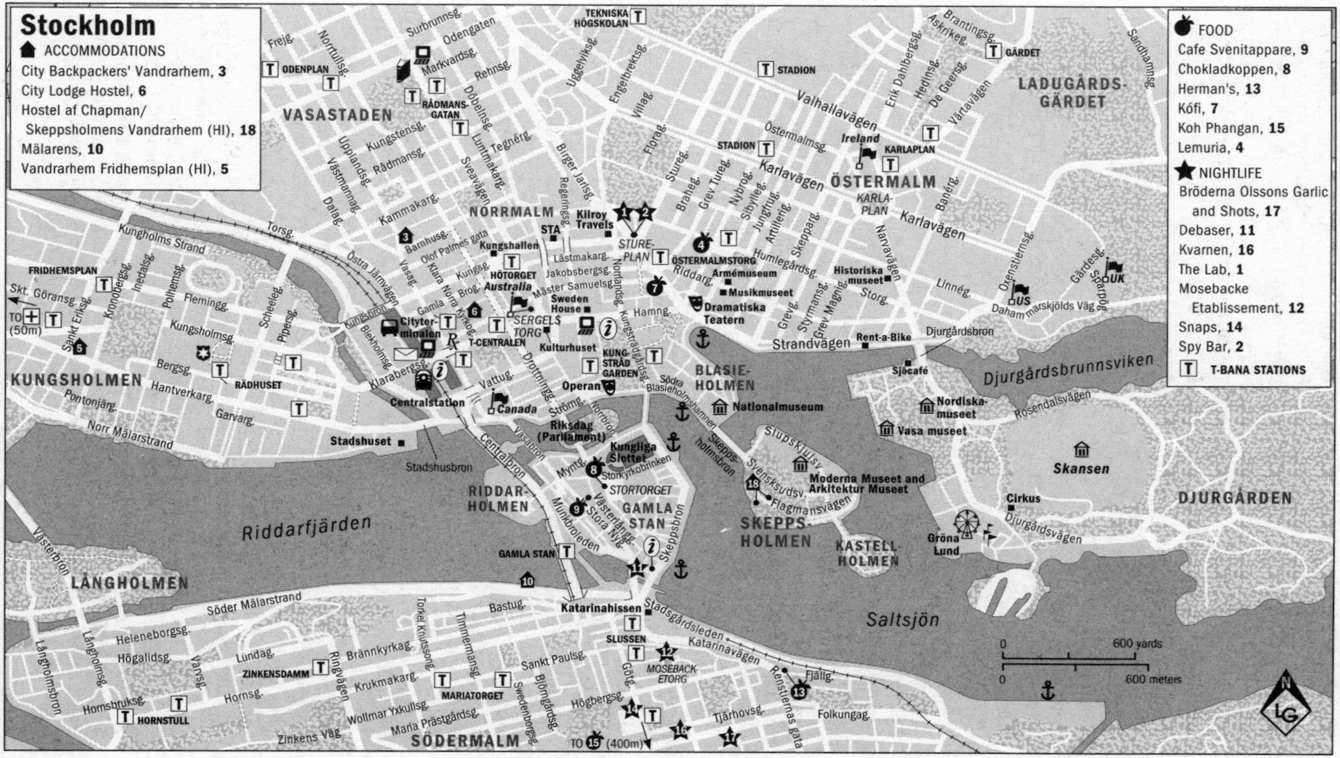
Stockholm
ACCOMMODATIONS
City Backpackers' Vandrarhem, 3
City Lodge Hostel, 6
Hostel af Chapman/
Skeppsholmens Vandrarhem (HI), 18
Mälarens, 10
Vandrarhem Fridhemsplan (HI), 5
FOOD
Cafe Svenitappare, 9
Chokladkoppen, 8
Herman's, 13
Kófi, 7
Koh Phangan, 15
Lemuria, 4
NIGHTLIFE
Bröderna Olssons Garlic and Shots, 17
Debaser, 11
Kvarnen, 16
The Lab, 1
Mosebacke Etablissement, 12
Snaps, 14
Spy Bar, 2
T-BANA STATIONS
VASASTADEN
NORRMALM
ÖSTERMALM
LADUGÅRDS-GÄRDET
KUNGSHOLMEN
RIDDAR-HOLMEN
GAMLA STAN
BLASIE-HOLMEN
SKEPPS-HOLMEN
KASTELL-HOLMEN
DJURGÅRDEN
LÅNGHOLMEN
SÖDERMALM
Riddarfjärden
Saltsjön
Djurgårdsbrunnsviken
Skansen
Centralstation
Stadshuset
Riksdag (Parliament)
Kungliga Slottet
Nationalmuseum
Moderna Museet and Arkitektur Museet
Nordiska-museet
Vasa museet
Historiska museet
Armémuseum
Musikmuseet
Dramatiska Teatern
Operan
Kulturhuset
Sweden House
Kilroy Travels
Rent-a-Bike
Sjöcafé
Cirkus
Gröna Lund
Katarinahissen
Cityter-minalen
Kungshallen
Australia
Canada
Ireland
US
UK
ODENPLAN
RÅDMANS-GATAN
TEKNISKA HÖGSKOLAN
STADION
GÄRDET
KARLAPLAN
ÖSTERMALMSTORG
STURE-PLAN
HÖTORGET
T-CENTRALEN
KUNG-STRÄD GARDEN
FRIDHEMSPLAN
RÅDHUSET
GAMLA STAN
SLUSSEN
MOSEBACK ETORG
MARIATORGET
ZINKENSDAMM
HORNSTULL
STORTORGET
SERGELS TORG
KARLA-PLAN
TO (50m)
TO 15 (400m)
0 600 yards
0 600 meters

malmsg. 97 (☎661 80 05). Open M-F 10am-noon and 2:30-4pm. **UK,** Skarpög. 6-8 (☎671 30 00; www.britishembassy.se). Open M-F 9am-5pm. **US,** Daghammarskjölds väg 31 (☎783 53 00; www.usemb.se). Open M-Th 9-11am and 1-3pm, F 9-11am.

Currency Exchange: Forex, Centralstationen (☎411 67 34; open daily 7am-9pm) and Cityterminalen (☎21 42 80; open M-F 7am-8pm, Sa 8am-5pm). 15-20kr commission.

Luggage Storage: Lockers are available at Centralstationen and Cityterminalen (30-80kr per day). Cash only.

GLBT Resources: Queer Extra (QX) and the QueerMap, available at Sweden House, give info about Stockholm's gay hot spots, as does www.qx.se/english, updated daily.

Emergencies: ☎112.

24hr. Pharmacy: Look for green-and-white Apoteket signs. **Apoteket C. W. Scheele,** Klarabergsg. 64 (☎454 81 30), at the overpass over Vasag. T-bana: T-Centralen.

Hospitals: Karolinska (☎517 740 93), north of Norrmalm near Solnavägen. T-Bana: Skt. Eriksplan. **Sankt Göran** (☎587 010 00), on Kungsholmen. T-Bana: Fridhemsplan.

Medical Services: ☎32 01 00.

Telephones: Almost all public phones require Telia phone cards; buy them at Pressbyrån newsstands in increments of 60 (50kr) or 120 (100kr) units.

Internet Access: Stadsbiblioteket (library), Odeng. 53, in the annex. T-bana: Odenplan. Sign up for 2 free 30min. slots daily or drop in for 15min., but bring your passport. Open M-Th 9am-9pm, F 9am-7pm, Sa-Su noon-4pm. **Dome House,** Sveavg. 108, has almost 80 terminals. 19kr per hr. Open 24hr. **Sidewalk Express** Internet stations are located inside malls and 7-Elevens throughout the city. 19kr per hr. Open 24hr. MC/V.

Post Office: 84 Klarabergsg. (☎23 22 20). Open M-F 7am-7pm. Address mail to be held as follows: First name LAST NAME, *Poste Restante,* Postal Code, city, SWEDEN.

ACCOMMODATIONS AND CAMPING

Reservations are indispensable in summer, and many HI hostels limit stays to five nights. If you haven't booked ahead, arrive around 8am. Some non-HI hostels are hotel/hostels; specify that you want to stay in a dorm-style hostel, or risk paying hotel rates. Stockholm's several **botels** (boat-hotels) are a novel solution to space issues. While they often make for camaraderie and a unique experience, they can be cramped—request a room on the water side of the boat. There are also various **B&B booking services,** including the **Bed and Breakfast Agency.** (☎643 80 28; www.bba.nu. Open M 10am-1pm and 2-5pm, Tu-W 9am-1pm and 2-5pm.) An SL or Stockholm Card is the cheapest way for **campers** to reach some of the more remote campgrounds. The right of public access (p. 962) does not apply within the city limits, although camping is allowed on most of the Skärgård archipelago (p. 973).

Hostel af Chapman/Skeppsholmens Vandrarhem (HI), Flaggmansväg. 8 (☎463 22 66; www.stfchapman.com). T-bana: Kungsträdgården. Modern on-shore hostel and a 19th-century schooner pinch-hitting as an unusually roomy botel. Breakfast 70kr. Linens 65kr. Laundry 35kr. Internet 1kr per min. Reception 24hr. Lockout 11am-3pm. Dorms 200-245kr; doubles 550kr. 45kr HI discount. MC/V. ❷

City Backpackers' Vandrarhem, Upplandsg. 2A (☎20 69 20; www.citybackpackers.se). T-bana: T-centralen. Dorms are a bit crowded, but the free pasta, coffee, and tea make up for it. Free morning sauna, 20kr other times. Linens 50kr. Laundry 50kr. Free Internet and wireless. Reception 8am-10pm. Dorms from 190kr; doubles 520kr. MC/V. ❷

City Lodge Hostel, Klara Norra Kyrkog. 15 (☎22 66 30; www.citylodge.se). T-bana: T-centralen. Newly renovated rooms and a can't-beat location make this a great place to rest. Linens 50kr. Laundry 50kr. Free Internet. Reception 7:30am-10pm. 16-person dorms 175kr, 6-person 230kr; doubles from 550kr. MC/V. ❷

Mälarens, Södermälarstrand, Kajplats 6 (☎644 43 85; www.theredboat.com). T-bana: Gamla Stan. The steamer has a great location. Breakfast 60kr. Reception 7:30am-1am. Dorms 210kr; singles 430kr; doubles 530kr; triples 720kr; quads 960kr. MC/V. ❷

Vandrarhem Fridhemsplan (HI), S:t Eriksg. 20 (☎653 88 00; www.fridhemsplan.se). T-bana: Fridhemsplan. The city's largest hostel has large rooms. Wheelchair-accessible. Breakfast 60kr. Storage 20kr. Linens 50kr. Laundry 50kr. Free Internet. Reception 24hr. Dorms 240kr; singles 435kr; doubles 585kr. 45kr HI discount. AmEx/MC/V. ❸

Ängby Camping, Blackebergsv. 24 (☎37 04 20; www.angbycamping.se), on Lake Mälaren. T-bana: Ängbyplan. Wooded campsite with swimming area. Electricity from 35kr. Cable TV 10kr. Reception daily June-Aug. 8am-10pm, Sept.-May 5-8pm. 2-person tent sites 135kr, extra person 80kr; cabins 400-725kr. AmEx/MC/V. ❶

FOOD

Götgatan and **Folkunggatan** in Södermalm offer affordable cuisine from around the world, while pizza and kebabs are plentiful on Vasastaden's **Odengatan.** Grocery stores are easy to find around any T-bana station. Head to the outdoor fruit market at **Hötorget** for your Vitamin C fix (open M-Sa 7am-6pm), or to the **Kungshallen** food hall, Kungsg. 44, for a meal from one of the international food stands. (www.kungshallen.com. Open M-F 9am-11pm, Sa 11am-11pm, Su noon-11pm.) The **Östermalms Saluhall,** Nybrog. 31 (T-bana: Östermalmstorg), is a more traditional indoor market with fish and meat stands, as well as more expensive restaurants serving Swedish dishes. (www.ostermalmshallen.se. Open M-Th 9:30am-6pm, F 9:30am-6:30pm, Sa 9:30am-4pm.) Prices in Stockholm are lowest at lunch time; track down lunch specials (*dagens rätt;* 50-80kr) to save money.

Herman's, Fjällg. 23A (☎643 94 80). T-bana: Slussen. Hearty, well-seasoned vegetarian fare, served buffet-style. Lunch (78-118kr) and dinner (118-168kr) include dessert and drink combos. Open daily June-Aug.11am-11pm; Sept.-May 11am-9pm. MC/V. ❹

Koh Phangan, Skåneg. 57 (☎642 50 40). T-Bana: Skanstull. Splurge on Thai food in this stellar restaurant done up like a South Asian jungle treehouse. Vegetarian entrees 135-155kr. Meat entrees 150-180kr. Seafood 180-265kr. Open M-Th 11am-1am, F-Su 2pm-1am. Kitchen closes 11pm. AmEx/DC/MC/V. ❺

Chokladkoppen, Stortorg. 18 (☎20 31 70). T-bana: Gamla Stan. Chokladkoppen caters to a younger set and serves light meals (36-75kr) and generous desserts (34kr). One of the best people-watching spots on Stortorget. Open in summer Su-Th 9am-11pm, F-Sa 9am-midnight; low season Su-Th 9am-10pm, F 9am-midnight. Cash only. ❷

Lemuria, Nybrog. 26 (☎660 02 21). T-bana: Östermalmstorg. Across from the Östermalms Saluhall. Serves carefully balanced, gluten- and lactose-free vegetarian and vegan lunches (55kr). Open M-F 11am-3pm. AmEx/MC/V. ❶

Cafe Svenitappare, Sven Vintappares grand 3 (22 26 40). T-bana: Gamla Stan. This tiny cafe is meant to resemble a 17th-century shop. It serves up savory pastries (15kr) and a limited selection of sandwiches (20-30kr). Open daily 8am-5pm. MC/V. ❶

Kófi, Birger Jarlsg. 11 (☎611 33 35). T-bana: Östermalmstorg. A haven of stylish affordability in an upscale neighborhood, this cafe serves sandwiches (36-49kr) ideal for a light lunch. Open M-F 7am-last customer (usually around midnight), Sa 8am-1am, Su 9am-last customer (usually around midnight). MC/V. Branch at Dottningg. 42. ❶

SIGHTS

Break up your walking tour (p. 968) of Stockholm's inner neighborhoods with T-bana rides to more remote locations in order to get a sense of the capital's sweeping scope. The T-bana has been called the world's longest art exhibit, since over

> *A leisurely saunter through the city center and selected adjoining islands.*
>
> **TIME:** 4hr., 5-6hr. with visits to the Stadhuset, Moderna Museet, or Kungliga Slottet.
>
> **DISTANCE:** About 6km.
>
> **SEASON:** Mid-April to late October.

A walking tour of a city spread out over a dozen islands sounds unlikely, but both goods and people have streamed across Stockholm's bridges since it emerged as a 13th-century trading port. These bridges string their way across the city's waterways like strands of pearls, and are at least half the reason why Stockholm is such a walkable city. Factor in a network of parks and thoroughly continental boulevards, and it's not hard to see why residents of Stockholm happily hoof it during the summer months—even though comfortable mass transit options are never very far away when in Stockholm.

This tour starts at **Sweden House** (p. 964), Stockholm's main tourist office, and ends in the old town of **Gamla Stan.**

1 SERGELS TORG. Begin by walking west on Hamngatan past the exclusive **NK** department store. Make for the 37m glass obelisk at the center of Sergels Torg, the plaza that was carved out of Lower Norrmalm after WWII in what the Swedes called "the great demolition wave." Modernist city planners were convinced that they could arbitrarily designate a new city center and have civic life revolve around it, but they got more than they bargained for with the covey of drug dealers who flocked to the western side of Sergels Torg. Known as the **Plattan,** this sunken plaza should be avoided at night. The glassy **Kulturhuset** (p. 971), on the southern side of the square, is a more savory point of interest; check the schedule of events posted inside **Lava,** a hangout popular with Stockholm's university students.

2 STADHUSET. Turn left onto Drottninggatan, Norrmalm's main pedestrian thoroughfare, and then turn right just before the bridge onto Strömgatan. Take the steps down to the quay just before the Centralbron overpass and go under two bridges and over one to the majestic Stadshuset (p. 970). Guided tours leave on the hour, last around 45min., and cost 50kr. If time or money is short, make a point of walking around the manicured waterside grounds before continuing on your way.

3 RIDDARHOLMEN. Head back to Centralbron by crossing back over the bridge, take the steps up, and then turn right on the second bridge, Vasabron, onto Gamla Stan. Turn to your right onto Riddarhuskajen and hug the waterfront. Peek into the manicured lawns of Riddarhuset on your left, built in the 17th century for parliament and now occasionally used by Swedish nobility. Take a right on the first bridge you come to, Riddarhbron, into the plaza on Riddarholmen (The Knight's Island). Stockholm's 17th-century elite built private palaces around the **Riddarholmskyrkan** church. Parts of the church date back to the 13th century, when it was used as a Franciscan monastery, although Lutherans booted out the Franciscans after the Protestant Reformation and then set aside the church as the burial place for Swedish monarchs in 1807. Almost every Swedish king from 1290 to 1950 has been buried there.

4 SKEPPSHOLMEN. Head straight out of the plaza, cross Centralbron, and make a right onto charming Stora Nygatan. Turn left down any of the side streets and then left onto Västerlånggatan, lined with shops and confectionaries. Cross two bridges, cutting through the back of the Riksdag (Parliament), then turn right onto Strömgatan and right again back across the water, this time past the Riksdag's long east-facing facade. Turn left onto Slottskajen alongside the royal palace of Kungliga Slottet (p. 970), and left onto the bridge toward the Grand Hotel. Bear right onto Södra Blasieholmshamnen and then cross the scenic Skeppsholmbron bridge onto the island of Skeppsholmen. The main attraction here is the Moderna Museet (p. 970), home to the works of many celebrated artists from the 20th century. Admission is deliciously free.

5 KUNGLIGA SLOTTET. Retrace your steps and turn right back onto Gamla Stan, flanking the palace on Skappsbron this time. You could spend a full day wandering through the pal-

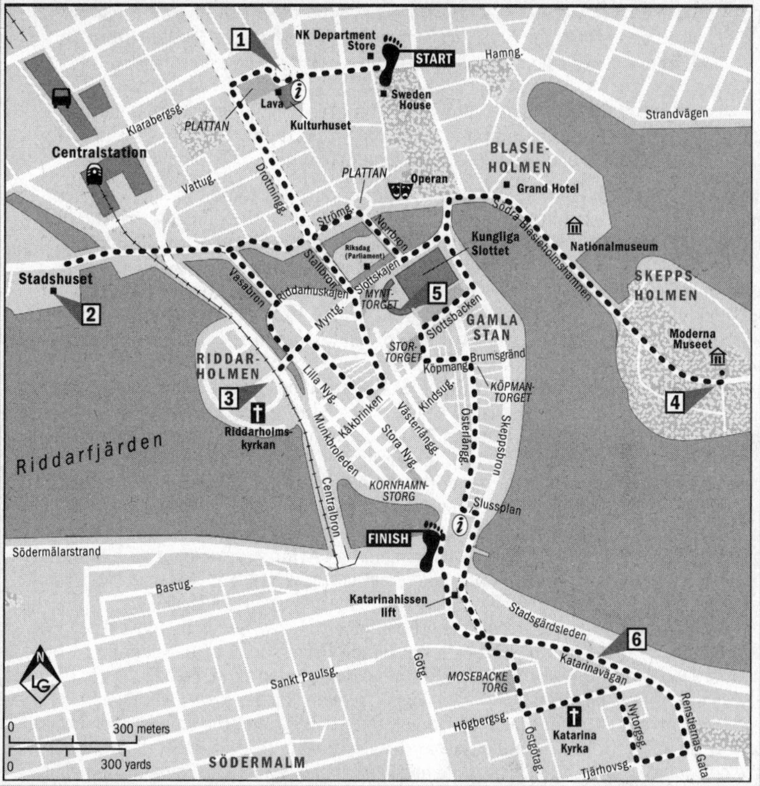

ace's museums and courtyards, but for the sake of time confine your visit to the **Royal Apartments.** Turn into the plaza leading up to Storkyrkan; the ticket office is directly on the right.

6 SÖDERMALM. From the palace, walk straight into Stortorget, the main square of the island. Take a left and walk along its east end, and then another left onto Köpmangatan, with its pleasant array of antique shops. At the St. George and Dragon statue, make a right along Österlånggatan. When it ends, take a left on Slussplan, then a right on the bridge connecting Gamla Stan to the southern island of Södermalm. Keep to the left as you cross the bridge, hop the **Katarinahissen lift** (10kr), and cross the bridge to the north-facing cliffs for one of the best views of the city. You can also get the view for free by walking up the steps on the opposite side of Katarinavägen. Head straight to intimate Mosebacke Torg and continue south down Östgötagatan. Take your first left onto Högbergsgatan, passing by the octagonal tower of the **Katarina kyrka,** devastated by fire in 1990 but rebuilt to its former Baroque splendor. At the end of Högbergsgatan, turn right onto Nytorgsgatan, left onto Tjärhovsgatan, and then left onto Renstiernas gata. As the street begins its languid arch to the west, a beautiful view of Stockholm's spires spreads out before you. Finish by heading down to Slussen and crossing back onto Gamla Stan to rest your weary legs.

TIP **SOMETHING FOR NOTHING.** It may be expensive to get by in Stockholm, but many of the city's excellent museums are free. The **Sweden House** (p. 964) provides a complete listing for all your wallet-saving cultural needs.

the past 50 years the city has commissioned more than 140 artists to decorate its stations—but keep your eyes open or you may miss them. The murals and sculptures of T-Centralen remain the best-recognized example of T-bana artistry.

GAMLA STAN (OLD TOWN). The Baltic trading port of Stockholm was once confined to the small island of Staden. Today, the island is the epicenter of the city. The main pedestrian street is **Västerlånggatan,** but it's the maze of small side streets that preserves the area's feel. *(Tours of the island are available June-Aug. M and W-Th 7:30pm. Meet at the obelisk in front of Storkyrkan. 60kr. Cash only.)* Gamla Stan is dominated by the magnificent 1754 **Kungliga Slottet** (Royal Palace), one of the largest palaces in Europe and the winter home of the Swedish royal family. The **Royal Apartments** and the adjacent **Rikssalen** (State Hall) and **Slottskyrkan** (Royal Chapel, open W-F) are all dizzyingly lavish. The **Skattkammaren** (Royal Treasury) houses a small collection of jewel-encrusted objects. The statues in the **Gustav III Antikmuseum** are forgettable, but the **Museum Tre Konor** includes the foundation of the 13th-century castle that once stood on the same site. Expect lines in summer. *(Main ticket office and info area at the rear of the complex, near the Storkyrkan. ☎402 61 30; www.royalcourt.se. Open mid-May to June daily 10am-4pm; July to mid-Aug. daily 10am-5pm; mid-Aug. to mid-May Tu-Su noon-3pm. Each attraction 90kr, students 35kr. Combination ticket 130/65kr. MC/V.)* The **Livrustkammaren** (Armory) presents an extensive collection of royal accoutrements. *(Slottsbacken 3. ☎519 555 44; www.livrustkammaren.se. Open June-Aug. daily 10am-5pm; Sept.-May Tu-W and F-Su 11am-5pm, Th 11am-8pm. Free.)* Just across the street from the palace ticket office is the gilded **Storkyrkan** church, where winners of the Nobel Peace Prize speak after accepting their awards. Don't miss the statue of St. George slaying the dragon. *(☎723 30 16. Open M-Sa June-Aug. 9am-6pm; Sept.-May 9am-4pm. In summer 3 tower tours daily. Church 20kr. Cash only.)* Around the corner on **Stortorget,** the main square, the small **Nobelmuseet** traces the story of the Nobel Prize and its winners. *(☎534 818 00; www.nobelprize.org/nobelmuseum. Open mid-May to mid-Sept. M and W-Su 10am-5pm, Tu 10am-8pm; mid-Sept. to mid-May Tu 11am-8pm, W-Su 11am-5pm. 60kr, students 40kr. MC/V.)*

KUNGSHOLMEN. The exterior of **Stadshuset** (City Hall) is a study of contrasts. The required tour of the interior takes you through the council room and then into the enormous Blue Hall, where a 10,000-pipe organ greets Nobel Prize banquet attendees. In the breathtaking **Gold Room,** millions of shimmering tiles make up an Art Deco mosaic. The **tower** provides the best panoramic view of the city center. *(Hantverkarg. 1. T-bana: T-Centralen. ☎508 29 058; www.stockholm.se/stadshuset. Tower open daily May-Sept. 9am-5pm. 20kr. Tours daily June-Aug. 10, 11am, noon, 2, 3pm; Sept. 10am, noon, 2pm; Oct.-May 10am, noon. 60kr, students 50kr. MC/V.)*

SKEPPSHOLMEN AND BLASIEHOLMEN. The stunning building that houses the eclectic collection of the **Moderna Museet,** on the island of Skeppsholmen (SHEPS-hole-men), contains canvases by Matisse, Picasso, Pollack, and Warhol. In the same building, the **Arkitekturmuseet** uses 3-D models to display the history of Swedish design. *(Moderna Museet ☎519 552 00; www.modernamuseet.se. Arkitekturmuseet ☎587 270.)* Across the bridge on the Blasieholmen peninsula, the **Nationalmuseum** features a series of focused displays of Swedish and European art. *(T-bana: Kungsträdgården. ☎51 95 44 10; www.nationalmuseum.se. Open Sept.-May Tu and Th 11am-8pm, W and F-Su 11am-5pm; June-Aug. Tu 11am-8pm, W-Su 11am-5pm. Permanent collection free, temporary exhibits 60-80kr, students 40-60. AmEx/MC/V.)*

OSTERMALM. Among the houses of this quiet area are a number of small and quirky museums—the **Musikmuseet** (Music Museum) is both. Try dozens of instruments in the collection of 6000, or visit the room dedicated completely to ABBA. *(Sibylleg. 2. T-bana: Östermalmstorg, exit Sibylleg. ☎519 554 90; http://stockholm.music.museum. Open Tu-Su July-Aug. 10am-5pm; Sept.-June noon-5pm. Free.)* Less than a block away, the **Armémuseum** chronicles Swedish military history. *(Riddarg. 13. T-bana: Östermalmstorg, exit Sibylleg. ☎51 956 300; www.armemuseum.se. Open Tu 11am-8pm, W-Su 11am-4pm. Free.)* For a more complete account of Sweden's history, head to the **Historiska Museet,** which plays host to famous collections of both Viking and ecclesiastical memorabilia. *(Narvav. 13-17. T-bana: Karlaplan. ☎519 556 00; www.historiska.se. Open May-Sept. daily 10am-5pm; Oct.-Apr. M-W and F-Su 11am-5pm, Th 11am-8pm. Free.)*

SWEDEN

DJURGÅRDEN. Djurgården, a national park, is a perfect spot for a summer picnic. The main attraction is the haunting **Vasamuseet,** which contains a massive warship that sank in the middle of Stockholm's harbor on its maiden voyage in 1628 and was salvaged, fantastically preserved, three centuries later. *(☎519 548 00; www.vasamuseet.se. Galärvarvet. Take bus #44, 47, or 69. Open June-Aug. daily 8:30am-6pm; Sept.-May M-Tu and Th-Su 10am-5pm, W 10am-8pm. 80kr, students 40kr. AmEx/DC/MC/V.)* Next door, the **Nordiska museet** sheds light on Swedish cultural history. *(☎519 546 00; www.nordiskamuseet.se. Open June-Aug. daily 10am-5pm; Sept.-Aug. M-F 10am-4pm, Sa-Su 11am-5pm. Free, special exhibitions 60kr. MC/V.)* The **Gröna Lund** amusement park features a handful of exciting rides. *(Open daily mid-May to late Aug., usually 11am-11pm; check www.gronalund.se/program for detailed schedule. Admission 60kr. Rides 20-60kr each.)* Djurgården is also home to **Skansen,** an open-air museum the size of Gamla Stan that features 150 historical buildings, handicrafts, and a small zoo. Costumed actors inhabit the homes, and their attention to period authenticity somehow redeems the project from kitschiness. *(☎442 8000; www.skansen.se. Take bus #44 or 47. Park and zoo open daily June-Aug. 10am-10pm; Sept.-May 10am-5pm. Most homes open daily June-Aug. 11am-7pm; Sept.-May 11am-5pm. 80kr, Sa-Su 60 kr., low season 50kr. AmEx/MC/V.*

ENTERTAINMENT AND FESTIVALS

Stockholm's smaller performance venues are showcased in *What's On*, available at the tourist office. There are also a number of larger, more widely known performance spots. The stages of the national theater, **Dramatiska Teatern,** Nybroplan (☎667 06 80), feature performances of works by August Strindberg and others (60-300kr). Backstage highlights more experimental material. The **Kulturhuset at Sergels Torg** (☎508 15 08) houses art galleries, performance spaces, and a variety of cultural venues that are often free to the public. It also plays host to **Lava** (☎508 31 508; closed in July), a popular hangout with a stage, library, and cafe that lend themselves to poetry readings and other student events. Check www.kulturhuset.se for details. The **Operan,** Jakobs Torg 2 (☎24 82 40), stages operas and ballets from late August through mid-June. (Tickets 150-460kr. Student rush tickets available. MC/V.) The imposing **Konserthuset,** Hötorg. 8 (☎10 21 10), hosts the Stockholm Philharmonic. (100-270kr. AmEx/MC/V.) Culture buffs on a budget should sample the sights and sounds of the **Parkteatern** (☎506 20 299; www.stadsteatern.stockholm.se), a summer-long program of free theater, dance, and music staged in parks around the city. Call **BiljettDirect** (☎07 7170 7070; www.ticnet.se) for tickets. The world-class **Stockholm Jazz Festival** arrives in mid- to late July. (☎556 924 40; www.stockholmjazz.com.) Other festivals include the gay blowout **Stockholm Pride** (late July or early Aug.; ☎33 59 55; www.stockholmpride.org) and late August's **Strindberg Festival,** a celebration of Sweden's most famous morose playwright for the turtlenecked, furrowed-brow literati.

NIGHTLIFE

For a city where "night" barely exists in summer, Stockholm knows a thing or two about nightlife. The scene varies by neighborhood, with particular social codes prevailing in different areas. The posh **Stureplan** area in Östermalm (T-bana: Östermalmtorg), along with **Kungsgatan** (T-bana: Hötorget), is where beautiful people party until 5am. Expect long lines and note that many clubs honor strict guest lists. On the cliffs across the river, **Södermalm's** (T-bana: Mariatorget) nightlife is less glitzy but just as popular, with a diverse mix of bars and clubs along Götg. and around Medborgarpl. In the northern part of town, nightlife options line **Sveavägen** and the **Vasastaden** area (T-bana: Odenplan or Rådmansg.). Many bars and clubs set age limits as high as 25 to avoid crowds of drunk teenagers, but showing up early may get you in. Stockholm is compact enough to walk among all the islands, although night buses cover most of the city. The T-bana is generally safe until closing. Pick up *Queer Extra (QX)* and the *QueerMap* for gay nightlife tips.

Mosebacke Etablissement, Mosebacke Torg 3 (☎55 60 98 90). T-bana: Slussen. Take the Katarina lift (10kr) to Söder Heights. Enjoy the view from one of the terrace's themed bars. Beer 43kr. Mixed drinks 74kr. 20+. Cover 50-150kr. Terrace open in summer daily 11am-1am. Indoors open Su-Th 5pm-1am, F-Sa 5pm-2am. AmEx/DC/MC/V.

Kvarnen, Tjärhovsg. 4 (☎643 03 80). T-bana: Medborgarpl. Look for the red windmill. The mod cocktail lounge **H2O,** the energetic **Eld** dance club, and a 200-year-old beer hall somehow coexist under the same roof. Beer 29kr, 42kr after 7pm. Su-Th 21+, F-Sa 23+. Beer hall open late June-Aug. 5pm-3am; Sept. to mid-June M-F 11am-3am, Sa-Su 5pm-3am. Lounge open late June-Aug. M-Th 8pm-3am, F 7pm-3am, Su 9pm-3am; Sept. to mid-June M-F 5pm-3am, Sa 7pm-3am, Su 9pm-3am. Club open late June-Aug. F-Sa 9pm-3am; Sept. to mid-June W-Sa 9pm-3am. AmEx/DC/MC/V.

Connection, Storkyrkobrinken 9 (☎20 18 18; www.clubconnection.nu). T-bana: Gamla Stan, or bus #3 or 53. This gay bar fills up quickly with a diverse clientele that drinks and dances to disco and Madonna. Beer 44kr, mixed drinks 78-108kr. Mixed crowd W and Sa, mostly men F. W 18+, F-Sa 23+. Open W and F-Sa 10pm-3am.

Debaser, Karl Johans Torg 1 (☎462 98 60; www.debaser.nu). T-bana: Slussen. The city's most popular rock club draws crowds with live music. 18+. Cover 60-100kr. Bar open daily 5pm-3am. Club open daily June-Aug. 10pm-3am, Sept.-May 8pm-3am.

The Lab, Birjer Jarlsg. 20 (☎545 03 700). T-bana: Östermalmtorg. Stureplan's most down-to-earth venue. Beer 46kr. Mixed drinks 72-118kr. Age limits vary. Cover F-Sa 1-4:30am 80kr. Open daily 10pm-5am, closed Su in winter. AmEx/D/DC/MC/V.

Snaps, Götg. 48 (☎640 28 68). T-bana: Medborgarpl. On the corner of Medborgarpl. Dark wood rooms on top and an intimate basement dance floor that starts to get surreal around midnight. Beer 48kr. Wine 55kr. Mixed drinks from 60kr. W-Th 21+, F-Sa 23+. Cover F-Sa 60kr. Open M-W 5pm-1am, Th-Sa 5pm-3am. AmEx/DC/MC/V.

Bröderna Olssons Garlic and Shots, Folkungag. 84 (☎640 84 46; www.garlicandshots.com). T-bana: Medborgarpl. Follow your nose 3 blocks up Folkungag. Tattooed bartenders serve garlic beer (35-50kr) and a repertoire of 101 shots (35kr) to a crowd sporting both leather and sport coats. 20+. Open daily 5pm-1am.

Spy Bar, Birjer Jarlsg. 20 (☎545 03 701). T-bana: Östermalmtorg. Moulin Rouge meets office chic in one of Stockholm's hottest nightspots. Beer 54kr. Mixed drinks 92-142kr. 23+. Cover 100-120kr. Open W-Sa 10pm-5am. AmEx/DC/MC/V.

DAYTRIPS FROM STOCKHOLM

Stockholm is situated in the center of an archipelago, where the mainland gradually crumbles into the Baltic. The islands in either direction—east toward the Baltic or west toward Lake Mälaren—are a lovely escape from the city. **Ferries** to the archipelago leave from in front of the Grand Hotel on the **Stromkajen** docks between Gamla Stan and Skeppsholmen or the **Nybrohamnen** docks (T-bana: Kungsträdgården). Visit the **Excursion Shop** in Sweden House (p. 964) for more info.

STOCKHOLM ARCHIPELAGO (SKÄRGÅRD). The wooded islands of the Stockholm archipelago become less developed as the chain coils its way out into the Baltic Sea. **Vaxholm** (tourist office ☎08 541 314 80; www.vaxholm.se) is the archipelago's most popular island to visit. Its pristine beaches and 16th-century fortress have spawned pricey waterside cafes, but the rest of the streets still maintain their charm. Take a quick walk through before heading to the other islands. Vaxholm is accessible by ferry (1hr., late June-late Aug. 2 per hr., 65kr) or bus #670 from T-bana: Tekniska Hogskolan (45min., 1-4 per hr., 20kr). Three hours from Stockholm, **Sandhamn** is a bit quieter, although the white sands of Trouville Beach have plenty of devotees. Hikers can escape the crowds by exploring the coastal trails on the **Finnhamn** group and **Tjockö** to the north. Ask at Sweden House about **hostels;** they tend to be booked up months in advance, but the islands are a promising place to exercise the right of public access. Waxholmsbolaget runs **ferries** to even the tiniest islands year-round. (☎08 679 58 30; www.waxholmsbolaget.se.) Sweden House sells the **Båtluffarkort,** good for unlimited Waxholmsbolaget rides; the pass pays for itself in a few long trips. (5-day 300kr; 30-day 700kr, under 20 420kr.)

LAKE MÄLAREN. **Drottningholms Slott** was built for the queens of Sweden in the late 17th century and has served as the royal family's residence since 1981, when they left Kungliga Slottet (p. 970). The Rococo interior and sprawling formal gardens are impressive, but the highlight is the 1766 **Court Theater,** where artistic director Per-Erik Öhrn uses 18th-century sets and stage equipment to mount provocative modern productions. Tickets start at 165kr; guided tours are also available. (Open May-Aug. daily 10am-4:30pm; Sept. daily noon-3:30pm; Oct.-Apr. Sa-Su noon-3:30pm. 11kr, students 50kr. English-language tours mid-June to Aug. daily 1 per hr. 11am-3pm; May to mid-June Sa-Su 1 per hr. 11am-3pm.) **Ferries** depart May through October from the Stadshusbron docks next to the Stadhusent. (Return ticket 125kr, return ticket and admission 205kr.) The island of **Björkö** on Lake Mälaren is home to **Birka,** Sweden's largest Viking-era settlement. All that remains are some burial mounds and hill fort, but in July and August, amateur excavations and modern Vikings bring the island to life. Strömma Kanalbolaget **ferries** depart Stockholm May to early Sept. from the Stadshusbron docks next to the Stadshuset. (☎587 140 00; www.strommakanalbolaget.com. July-Aug. 9:30am and 1:15pm, return 3 and 6:45pm; May and Sept. 9:30am, return 3pm. Guided tour, museum admission, and round-trip ferry 255kr.)

UPPSALA ☎018

Archbishop Jakob Ulvsson founded **Uppsala University** in 1477, but the Reformation wrested control away from the Catholic Church and set the stage for the secular inquiry that today dominates the college town. The footbridges and side streets of Uppsala (pop. 127,000) teem with almost 40,000 undergraduates. **Domkyrka,** Domkyrkoplan 5-7, is the largest cathedral in Sweden; its red-brick facade houses a bright interior, with artwork spanning eight centuries. Many famous Swedes, ranging from spiritualist Emanuel Swedenborg to scientist Carolus Linnaeus, are buried within. (☎18 72 01; www.uppsaladomkyrka.se. Open daily 8am-6pm. Free.) Just across Akademig. from the church, the **Gustavianum,** Akademig. 3, takes you through the university's scientific past with scientic tools and a reconstructed Anatomical Theater, where public dissections were conducted in the late 17th century. (☎471 75 71. Open Tu-Su late June-late Aug. 10am-4pm; Jan.-late June 11am-

4pm. Tours Sa-Su 1pm. 40kr, students 30kr. AmEx/MC/V.) A walk through the center of town along the Fyrisån River is an excellent way to get a taste of the city's flourishing gardens and cafes. Up the hill on Övre Slottsgatan lies the light pink castle/fortress **Uppsala Slott**. Inside is the **Uppsala Konstmuseum,** with art exhibits from the university's collection. (☎727 24 82; www.uppsala.se/konstmuseum. Museum open Tu-F noon-4pm, Sa-Su 11am-5pm. Guided tours of the castle June-Aug. 1 and 3pm. Museum 30kr, museum and tour 60kr. MC/V.) On the other side of the river, the **Linnéträdgården,** Svartbäcksg. 27, reconstructs the botanical gardens tended by Carolus Linnaeus using his 1745 sketch. The grounds include a small museum in Linnaeus's former home. (☎471 25 76; www.linnaeus.uu.se. Gardens open daily May-Aug. 9am-9pm; Sept. 9am-7pm. 30kr. Museum open June to mid-Sept. Tu-Su noon-4pm. 25kr. Cash only.) The M/S Kung Carl Justaf sails 2hr. south of Uppsala to **Skoklosters Slott,** a 17th-century castle with an impressive armory. (☎38 60 77; www.lsh.se/skokloster. Boat departs mid-May to mid-Aug. daily 11am from Islandsbron on Östra Åg. and Munkg.; returns 4:15pm. Castle 40kr. Boat round-trip 200kr. Purchase tickets upon departure. Cash only.)

Bars cluster around **Stortorget,** especially on **Sysslomansgatan, Västra Ågatan,** and the pedestrian areas of **Svartbäcksgatan** and **Kungsgatan.** During the academic year, nightlife in Uppsala revolves around the university's **"nations,"** organizations that every student joins upon enrollment in the university. Each nation owns a house, most with their own restaurants or bars, which have lower prices than other establishments in town. However, only students are allowed in; non-Uppsalans can pick up a guest pass at **Ubbo,** Övre Slottsg. 7. (☎480 31 47; www.kuratorskonventet.se. Open Tu-F 5-7pm. 1-week pass 50kr; 2-week 70kr; 4-week 90kr. Valid student ID and another form of ID required. MC/V.) One nation restaurant does serve non-students June to August: **Västamanlands-Dale's Taken ❶,** S:t Larsgatan 13 (enter on Sysslomangs.), offers a sizable 45kr lunch, with salad, drink, and coffee or tea included. (☎13 48 59; www.taket06.se. AmEx/MC/V.) **Hugo's ❶,** Svartbacksg. 21, is a retro cafe with popular lunch deals. (☎181 300 83. Entrees 20-45kr. Open daily 9am-8pm. AmEx/Mc/V.) Pick up groceries at **Hemköp,** Kungsg. 95 (Open daily 8am-10pm.) The dorms at **Hotel Uppsala ❷,** Kungsg. 27, are luxurious, with in-room shower, kitchen, and TV. (☎480 50 00. Breakfast 60kr. Linens 60kr. Laundry 10kr. Dorms 225kr; singles 410kr; doubles 540kr. 45kr HI discount. AmEx/DC/MC/V.)

Trains run to Stockholm (40min., 1-4 per hr., 64kr). To get from the station to the **tourist office,** Fyristorg 8, walk right on Kungsg., left on St. Persg., and across the bridge. The office books rooms for free and sells the **Uppsalakortet,** which offers up to 50% off admission to sights. 100kr covers one adult and two children. (☎727 48 00; www.uppland.nu. Open in summer M-F 10am-6pm, Sa-Su 10am-3pm; in winter closed Su.) The **library,** Stadbiblioteket, Svartbäcksg. 17, offers 1hr. slots of free **Internet,** as well as 15min. drop-in times. (☎727 1700. Open M-Tu 10am-8pm, W-Th 10am-7pm, F 10am-6pm, Sa 11am-3pm.) **Postal Code:** 75320.

GOTLAND ☎0498

Along the shores of Gotland, Sweden's largest island, families flock to sandy beaches in the east before making their way back to Visby, which recalls the Middle Ages with its winding alleyways and historic city wall. Each May, the entire island is transformed when 30 species of orchids simultaneously come into bloom. The summer months are busy, but even then, visitors can leave the crowds behind to stroll along the cliffs and the coast.

TRANSPORTATION. Destination Gotland **ferries** (☎0771 22 33 00; www.destinationgotland.se) sail from Visby to Nynäshamn (3¼hr.) and Oskarshamn (2¾hr.). (June-Aug. 2-6 per day; Oct.-May 1-3 per day. 228-511kr, students 174-238kr; 40%

Scanrail discount. AmEx/DC/MC/V.) To get to Nynäshamn from **Stockholm,** take the Båtbussen bus from Cityterminalen (1hr.; leaves 1¾hr. before ferry departures; 80kr, 110kr on bus) or the Pendeltåg train from Centralstationen (1hr.; 90kr, SL passes valid). To get to Oskarshamn from **Kalmar,** hop on a KLT bus (1½hr., every 1-2hr., 73kr). If you're planning your trip from Stockholm, **Gotland City,** Kungsg. 57A, books ferries. (☎08 406 15 00. Open June-Aug. M-F 9:30am-6pm, Sa 10am-2pm; Sept.-May M-F 9:30am-5pm. AmEx/DC/MC/V.) On Gotland, it's worth picking up a bus timetable at the ferry terminal or at the Visby **bus station,** Kung Magnusväg 1, outside the wall east of the city. (☎21 41 12; www.gotland.se/kollektivtrafiken. Cash only on buses; AmEx/DC/MC/V at station.) Buses are fairly expensive (59kr) and only three or four buses cover the routes each day, making it almost impossible to daytrip. **Cycling** is a far better way to explore Gotland's terrain; extensive paths and bike-friendly motorways can be supplemented by strategic bus rides, as buses will carry bikes for an extra 40kr. Bike rental shops are plentiful in Visby and in most towns across the island.

SWEDEN

VISBY. Passing through the medieval **Ringmuren** (Ring Wall) of Visby (pop. 22,500) is like stepping into a fairy tale. The wall encloses the ruins of churches, the most intricate of which, **S:ta Karin** (or S:ta Katarina), can be fully explored. (Open in summer Su-F 8am-9pm, Sa 8am-7pm.) Stairs behind the **Domkyrka** lead to a scenic terrace; follow the path along the cliff for a view of the town and sea, then walk left along the northern perimeter of the wall to end up in the botanical gardens *(botanika trädgarden)*. Thousands flock to Visby in the first week of August for **Medieval Week** (☎29 10 70; www.medeltidsveckan.se.), with a jousting tournament, a seminar on runes, and wandering minstrels strumming their lutes.

The dorms at **Vandrarhem Visby (HI) ❷,** Fältg. 30, are 2km from the docks at the Alléskolan but within walking distance of the wall. (☎26 98 42. Linens 55kr. Laundry 30kr. Reception 8-10am and 4-7:30pm. Open late June to mid-Aug. Dorms 165kr; doubles 470kr. 45kr HI discount. Cash only.) You'll recognize **Visby Fängelse Vandrarhem ❷,** Skeppsbron 1, by the barbed wire atop its walls, remnants of the prison that preceded this whimsical hostel. (☎20 60 50. Breakfast 50kr for dorms. Laundry 30kr. Reception in summer 11am-noon and 5-9pm; low season 11am-2pm. Call ahead at other times. Dorms 210kr; doubles 460-620kr; quads 920-1240kr. AmEx/DC/MC/V.) Outdoor bars and cafes are everywhere, especially on **Stora Torget** and by the harbor, as well as on Adelsg. Take advantage of lunch specials (70-90kr), or stock up on groceries at the **ICA** on Stora Torg. (Open daily 8am-10pm.)

From the ferry terminal, walk left to the **tourist office,** Skeppsbron 4-6. (☎20 17 00; www.gotland.info. Internet 2kr per min. Open mid-June to mid-Aug. daily 8am-7pm; low season reduced hours.) **Gotlandsresor,** Färjeleden 3, right of the ferry terminal, books ferries, finds private rooms, and rents bikes. (☎20 12 60; www.gotlandsresor.se. Open daily June-Aug. 6am-10pm; Sept.-May 8am-6pm.) Dozens of other **bike rental** shops surround the terminal; prices start at 70kr per day. Internet is available at the Gotlands Bibliotek (library), Cramerg. 5, in 1hr. slots. (☎29 90 00. Sept.-June free, July-Aug. 20kr. Open Sept.-June M-F 10am-7pm, Sa-Su noon-4pm; July-Aug. M-F 10am-7pm, Sa noon-4pm. Cash only.) **Postal Code:** 62101.

ELSEWHERE ON GOTLAND. Use Visby as a launchpad to **Tofta** beach at the village of **Klintehamn** (bus #10, 40min.), or the cliffs of **Hoburgen,** at the island's southernmost tip (bus #11, 2hr.). Bus #20 runs from Visby to Fårösund (1½hr.), taking passengers to a free 15min. ferry ride past **Fårö,** a small island off Gotland's northern tip. Take the earliest bus to Hoburgen and Fårösund unless you plan to stay overnight. **Gotlandsresor** (see above) can book accommodations at more than 30 hostels and campgrounds outside of Visby, but many take advantage of the right of public access (p. 962) and **camp** by the brackish waters of the Baltic Sea.

SOUTHERN SWEDEN (SKÅNE)

Once a fiercely contested no-man's-land during 17th-century wars between Sweden and Denmark, this region bears witness to its martial past with well-preserved castles and forts. Today, the only invaders are the cranes and cormorants that nest alongside marshes and lakes, and the flocks of vacationers who savor the region's immaculate beaches and supremely polished cities of Malmö and Gothenburg.

KALMAR ☎0480

An important border city when southern Sweden was part of Denmark, Kalmar (pop. 60,000) is no longer at the center of Scandinavian politics, but retains much of the dignity of its glory days. Across from downtown, the medieval **Kalmar Slott** is the town's greatest attraction. In 1397, the castle witnessed the birth of the Union of Kalmar, a short-lived arrangement that united Denmark, Norway, and Sweden under the rule of Queen Margaret I. King Johann III gave the castle a Renaissance makeover in the 1580s, and today it houses lavish furnishings and exhibits. (☎45 14 90. Open daily July 10am-6pm; Aug. 10am-5pm; May-June and Sept. 10am-4pm; low season reduced hours. Free tours mid-June to mid-Aug. 75kr, students 50kr. AmEx/V.) Adjoining the castle's moat are the majority of the town's other sights: the cobblestoned **Gamla Stan** (Old Town), the tree-lined **Kyrkogarden** cemetery with a Jewish section in the far right corner, the lush **Stadspark,** and a handful of small museums. In the center of town, Kalmar's luminous **Domkyrkan** is a beautiful example of a 17th-century Baroque church. If you have an extra day, duck across the Kalmar Sound to the long, thin island of **Öland;** laze about on the white-sand beaches of Böda in the northeast or bike through the orchid-dotted steppe of Stora Alvaret in the south. The Träffpunkt Öland **tourist office** has a list of shops that rent bikes; follow signs from the first bus stop after the bridge to the mainland. (☎04 85 56 06 00; www.olandsturist.se. Open May-June M-F 9am-6pm, Sa 9am-4pm, Su 10am-4pm; July M-F 9am-7pm, Sa 9am-6pm, Su 10am-5pm; Aug. 1-20 M-F 9am-6pm, Sa 9am-4pm, Su 10am-4pm; low season reduced hours.) Bus #106 goes from Kalmar's train station to Borgholm, on the island (50min., 46kr).

To reach **Vandrarhem Svanen (SVIF) and Hotel ❷,** Rappeg. 1, 2km from the tourist office, on the island of Ängö. Take bus #402 from the train station (13kr), or, walking, turn left onto Larmg., right on Södra Kanalg., continue to the end, and turn left across the bridge onto Ängöleden. (☎129 28. Breakfast 60kr. Linens 50kr. Laundry 30kr. Internet 1kr per min. Reception late June to mid-Aug. 7:30am-10pm; low season 7:30am-9pm. Dorms 195kr; doubles 390kr; triples 600kr.) **Söderportshotellet ❹,** Slottsväg. 1, across from Kalmar Slott, rents centrally located student housing during the summer. (☎125 01. Breakfast included. Open mid-June to mid-Aug. Reception 7:30am-1am in the cafe. Singles 495kr; doubles from 550kr. MC/V.) Seaside **Stensö Camping ❶** is 3km south of Kalmar; take bus #121 to Lanssjukhuset, turn right onto Stensbergsv., and right onto Stensöv. (☎888 03. Water included. Electricity 35kr. Open Apr.-Sept. Tent sites 120-165kr; cabins from 400kr. MC/V.) Hunt for cheap eats along **Larmtorget, Larmgata,** and **Storgata,** or pick up groceries at **ICA** in Baronen pl. near the station. (Open M-F 8am-8pm, Sa 8am-6pm, Su 11am-6pm.)

Trains and **buses** arrive in Kalmar south of the center. Trains go to Gothenburg (4hr.; every 2hr.; 400kr, under 26 300kr), Malmö (3hr., every 2hr., 341/245kr), and Stockholm (4½hr., every 2hr., 1055/895kr). Buses run directly to Stockholm (6hr.; 3 per day; 250kr, students 200kr. AmEx/DC/MC/V.) The **tourist office,** Ölandskajen 9, offers **Internet** (10kr per 15min.). From the train station, turn right onto Stationsg., and then right onto Ölandskajen. (☎41 77 00; www.kalmar.se. Open July to mid-Aug. M-F 9am-9pm, Sa-Su 10am-5pm; June and late Aug. M-F 9am-7pm, Sa-Su 10am-4pm; Sept.-May M-F 9am-5pm. AmEx/DC/MC/V.) **Postal Code:** 39120.

MALMÖ ☎040

A (vigorous) stone's throw from Copenhagen, Sweden's third-largest city boasts a cultural diversity unmatched elsewhere in the country. Malmö's (pop. 300,000) proximity to the rest of Europe makes it a major gateway for the thousands of immigrants who flock to the country each year. Intimate and full of outdoor cafes, Lilla Torg is a mecca for people-watching, especially as outdoor patios light up under the glow of evening lamps. Möllevångstorget, south of the city center, has a spirted open-air market, folksy local bars, and affordable ethnic eateries.

TRANSPORTATION AND PRACTICAL INFORMATION. The train station and harbor lie just north of the old town. **Trains** go to Copenhagen (35min., every 20min., 96kr), Gothenburg (3hr., 1 per hr., 500kr), and Stockholm (4½hr.; 1 per hr.; 1065kr, under 26 300kr). Malmö has an efficient **bus** system; rides within most of the city are 15kr with 1hr. transfer, and many buses pass by the train station. The **tourist office** is located in the station and offers the **Malmö Card,** which provides free public transportation, parking, sightseeing bus tours, and admission to various museums. (1-day 130kr, 2-day 160kr, 3-day 190kr.) The office also books rooms for a 50-70kr fee. (☎34 12 00; www.malmo.se/tourist. Open June-Aug. M-F 9am-7pm, Sa-Su 10am-5pm; low season reduced hours. AmEx/MC/V.) **Internet** can be found in the train station (19kr per hr.; MC/V), or at the atmospheric **Cafe ZeZe,** Engelbrektsg. 13, between Lilla Torg and Gustav Adolfs Torg. (☎23 81 28. 30kr per hr. Open M-Th 11am-11pm, F 11am-midnight, Sa 1pm-midnight, Su 1-11pm. 10% student discount. Cash only.) **Postal Code:** 20110.

ACCOMMODATIONS AND FOOD. The 30 beds in **Vandrarhemmet Villa Hilleröd ❷,** Ängdalav. 38, fill up quickly, but the stay is worth the extra planning. Take bus #3 from the train station to Mellanheden, turn left on Piläkersv., and left on Ängdalav. (☎26 56 26; www.villahillerod.se. Breakfast 50kr. Linens 50kr, towels 25kr. Reception 8-10am and 4-8pm. 6-person dorms 190kr; doubles and quads 230-245kr. DC/MC/V.) **Vandrarhem Malmö (HI) ❶,** Backav. 18, is the cheapest option. Take bus #2 from the train station to the Vandrarhemmet stop. Brace yourself for the communal showers. (☎822 20; www.malmohostel.com. Breakfast 50kr. Linens 50kr. Reception May-Aug. 8-10am and 4-10pm; Sept.-Apr. 8-10am and 4-8pm. Dorms 175kr; singles 340kr; doubles 460kr; triples 615kr. 45kr HI discount. MC/V.)

For food, you can't really go wrong with any of Malmö's international offerings. Restaurants with affordable lunches (50-75kr) line Lilla Torg and Södra Förstadsg. The moorish **Gök Boet ❶,** Lilla Torg 3, is an intimate restaurant by day and a popular bar at night. (Open M-Th 11am-midnight, F-Sa 11am-2am, Su noon-11pm. AmEx/MC/V.) Next door, the **Saluhallen** is a massive food court with inexpensive restaurants ranging from Greek to Japanese. (Open M-F 10am-6pm, Sa 10am-3pm.) Ten minutes down Stora Nyg. is **Vegegården ❷,** Rörsjög. 23, which features all-vegetarian Chinese dishes (65-85kr) and a buffet (M-F 58kr, Sa-Su 98kr) for the thrifty herbivore. (☎611 38 88. Open M-W 11am-5pm, Th 11am-9pm, F 11am-11pm, Sa noon-11pm, Su noon-9pm. Buffet M-F 11am-3pm, Sa-Su 4-8pm. AmEx/MC/V.)

SIGHTS AND ENTERTAINMENT. Malmö's most famous sight is the **Malmöhus Castle** complex, which holds five museums. Within the castle walls, the **Stadsmuseet** documents the city's history. The **Konstmuseum** offers thought-provoking modern exhibits and a small **Aquarium** and **Tropicarium**. Across the moat, the **Kommendanthuset** hosts rotating exhibits on pop culture. The **Teknikens och Sjöfartens Hus** (Technology and Maritime Museum) down the road lets you ogle ships and airplane mock-ups. Squeeze inside the **U3 Submarine**; on Sunday and Tuesday afternoons, veterans gather by the vessel to swap war stories. (All 5 museums

☎040 34 44 37; www.malmo.se/museer. Open daily June-Aug. 10am-4pm; Sept.-May noon-4pm. Combination ticket 40kr, students 20kr. MC/V.) The **Form/Design Center,** Lilla Torg 9, shows off the cutting edge of Swedish design for the Ikea generation. (☎664 51 50; www.formdesigncenter.com. Open Tu-W and F 11am-5pm, Th 11am-6pm, Sa-Su 11am-4pm. Free.) The stark **Malmö Konsthall,** St. Johannesg. 7, hosts exhibits covering a wide range of modern art, and has a playground that resembles a chrome-and-rubber Dr. Seuss world. (☎34 12 93; www.konsthall.malmo.se. Open M-Tu and Th-Su 11am-5pm, W 11am-9pm. Tours daily 2pm. Free.) After strolling through the museums, kick back at the **bars** on Lilla Torg and Möllevångstorget, or case the **club** scene around Stortorg.

LUND ☎046

What Oxford and Cambridge are to England, Lund (pop. 100,400) and Uppsala are to Sweden. **Lund University's** antagonism toward its scholarly northern neighbor in Uppsala has inspired countless pranks, in addition to the drag shows and drinkfests that grace Lund's busy streets. With its vibrant student life and proximity to Malmö and Copenhagen, Lund makes an excellent base for exploring Skåne. The Romanesque **Lunds Domkyrka** is a massive 900-year-old reminder of the time when Lund was the religious center of Scandinavia. Its floor-to-ceiling astronomical clock rings at noon and 3pm, and its 7074-pipe organ is Sweden's largest. (☎35 88 80; www.lundsdomkyrka.org. Open M-F 8am-6pm, Sa 9:30am-5pm, Su 9:30am-6pm. Free tours mid-June to mid-Aug. daily 2:50pm.) The **university campus** is just across the park from the cathedral; get briefed on upcoming events at **Student Info,** Sang. 2, in the Akademiska Föreningen building. (☎38 49 49; http://af.lu.se. Open late Aug. to May M-F 10am-4pm, June M-F 10am-5pm.) **Kulturen,** an open-air museum behind the Student Union at the end of Sankt Anneg. on Tegnerplastén, weaves visitors into the daily lives of Lund residents from the Middle Ages on through a series of reconstructed houses. The center also hosts temporary exhibitions with a more modern flavor. (☎35 04 00; www.kulturen.com. Open mid-Apr. to Sept. daily 11am-5pm; Oct. to mid-Apr. Tu-Su noon-4pm. 50kr, free with student ID. MC/V.) Continuing north on Sandg. will bring you to the one-of-a-kind **Skissernas Museum** (Sketch Museum), whose rooms are flooded from floor to ceiling with paper and sculpture studies of art from around the world. (☎222 7283; www.adk.lu.se. Open Tu-Su noon-5pm, W during term noon-9pm. 30kr, free for students with ID. MC/V.) As in Uppsala (p. 974), Lund's nightlife revolves around the "nations," student clubs that throw parties and serve as social centers. Stop by Student Info for tips on snagging a guest pass. Another popular option is **Kulturmejeriet,** Stora Söderg. 64, an arthouse cinema, concert venue, and bar. (☎211 00 23; www.kulturmejeriet.se. Films Th 7pm, free. Concerts 25-100kr. MC/V.) **Stortorget/Herkules Bar,** Stortorg. 1, started off as a bank and morphed into a low-key restaurant, bar, and club with theme nights. (☎13 92 90. Beer 49kr. Mixed drinks from 82kr. Wine 56kr. 22+. Club cover 70kr. Bar open M-Tu 11am-11pm, W 11am-1am, Th-Sa 11am-3am. Club open Th-Sa 11pm-3am. AmEx/MC/V.)

The cramped **Vandrarhem Tåget (HI) ❷,** Vävareg. 22, is housed in the sleeping compartments of a 1940s train. Take the overpass to the park side of the train station. (☎14 28 20; www.trainhostel.com. Located in a potentially unsafe area. Breakfast 50kr. Linens 60kr. Hot water 1kr per 2min. Reception Apr.-Oct. 8-10am and 5-8pm; Nov.-Mar. 8-10am and 5-7pm. Dorms 175kr. 45kr HI discount. Cash only.) To get to **Källby Camping ❶,** next to the Källby Bad outdoor swimming pool, take bus #1 (dir.: Klostergården; 18kr) 2km south of the city center. A free swim is included with your stay. (☎35 51 88. Water included. Electricity 10kr. Laundry 40kr. Reception 7am to 9pm. Open mid-June to Aug. Tent sites 5kr per person. MC/V.) The **open-air market** at Mårtenstorg. (open daily 7am-2pm) and the adjoining turn-of-the-century **Saluhallen** (open M-F 9:30am-6pm, Sa 9am-3pm) are the best bet for budget food; cafes around Stortorg. and the cathedral are pricier. Decorated with caricatures of professors, **Conditori Lundagård ❶**, Kyrkog. 17, serves tasty salads (68kr), sandwiches (30-45kr), and pastries. (☎211 13 58. Open mid-June to mid-Aug. daily 10am-6pm; Sept. to mid-June M-F 7:30am-8pm, Sa 8:30am-6pm, Su 10am-6pm. MC/V.)

Lund is accessible from Malmö on SJ **trains** (43kr) and by local **pågatågen** trains (10-20min., 1-5 per hr., 36kr). Trains also run to Gothenburg (3½hr., 1 per hr., 580kr), Kalmar (3hr., every 2hr., 335kr), and Stockholm (4-5hr.; every 1-2hr.; 1040kr, under 26 879kr). The **tourist office,** Kyrkog. 11, across from the cathedral, sells maps (50-120kr) of the nearby **Skåneleden trail**. (☎35 50 40; www.lund.se. Open June-Aug. M-F 10am-6pm, Sa-Su 10am-2pm; May and Sept. M-F 10am-5pm, Sa 10am-2pm; Oct.-Apr. M-F 10am-5pm. MC/V.) **Internet** is available 24hr. in the 7-Eleven across from the station. (19kr per hr. MC/V.) **Postal Code:** 22100.

TIP **AUGUST AND EVERYTHING AFTER.** Many establishments in Lund, from restaurants to museums to the otherwise invaluable Student Info office, are **closed** from June through August. Consult www.lund.se before planning a trip.

KÅSEBERGA ☎0411

Most travelers would drive by the quiet valley in which Kåseberga (pop. 150) is nestled without giving it much notice, were it not for what lies on the coast beside it. The riddle of **Ales Stenar** is Sweden's answer to Stonehenge; its 59 stones are set in the shape of a ship, with the bow and stern aligned to the position of the sun at the solstices. The stones are a popular picnic spot as well as the starting point of several trails along the surrounding windswept hills. The closest hostels are in Ystad, but there are a number of B&B's in Kåseberga. **Ales Smedja ❸**, Kasevag. 13, also offers cabins that could be worth the extra money for families. (☎52 74 87. Breakfast 65kr. Linens 50kr. Reception open 7am-6pm. Singles 350kr, doubles 600kr; cabins 800kr. MC/V.) Cafe Solständet, in the village's small marina, is home to **Kåseberga Fisk Ab ❶**, a well-known fish smokery. Resist the temptation to buy a raw flounder filet (239kr) and sample the *sillamacka* (fried herring served on bread with tartar sauce, 35kr) instead. (☎52 71 80; www.kaseberga-fisk.se. Fresh fish available June-Aug. Open daily 9am-6pm. MC/V.) Bus #322 from Ystad (30min., 3 per day, 24kr) is the only public transportation that serves Kåseberga, but it is also possible to bike the 18km between the towns.

YSTAD ☎0411

Best known as a ferry port for those heading on to Bornholm, DEN (p. 275), Ystad (EE-stad, pop. 27,000) is better known by Swedes as the home of fictional detective Kurt Wallander. It has one of Sweden's best-preserved downtowns, a tight network of streets just inland of the terminal. A few of the town's half-timbered houses date back to the 15th century; you'll find the oldest one in Scandinavia at the corner of Pilgr. and Stora Österg. The **Klostret** (Monastery), on Klosterg., showcases church and town history. From the tourist office, turn left onto Lingsg., left onto Stora Österg., and right out of Stortorg. onto Klosterg. (Open June-Aug. Tu-F 10am-5pm, Sa-Su noon-4pm; low season reduced hours. 40kr. MC/V.) Next to the tourist office, the **Konstmuseum** features work by Swedish and Danish artists. (☎57 72 85. Open Tu-F noon-5pm, Sa-Su noon-4pm. 20kr. MC/V.)

The train station houses the **Vandrarhemmet Stationen ❷**, a small hostel conveniently located for those passing through. (☎07 08 57 79 95. Breakfast 50kr. Linens 60kr. Reception June-Aug. 9-10am and 5-7pm; Oct.-May call ahead. Dorms 195kr; doubles 390kr. Cash only.) **Stora Österg.,** or **Gågatan** (a pedestrian street), passes through the main square and teems with cafes and shops. The **Saluhallen** market is just off Stortorg. (Open daily 8am-9pm. MC/V.) Bornholms Trafikken (☎55 87 00) **ferries** sail to Bornholm, DEN (1¼hr., up to 4 per day, 216kr; AmEx/MC/V). **Trains** run to Malmö (45min., 1 per hr., 72kr; MC/V). The **tourist office** across from the station offers 30min. of free Internet. (☎57 76 81. Open mid-June to mid-Aug. M-F 9am-7pm, Sa-Su 10am-2pm; low season reduced hours.) **Postal Code:** 27101.

HELSINGBORG ☎042

Warring armies of Swedes and Danes passed Helsingborg (pop. 122,000) back and forth 12 times in the 17th century. By the time Magnus Stenbock gained the town for the Swedes once and for all in 1710, most of it lay in shambles. It wasn't until the industrial era that Helsingborg was restored to affluence; more recently, it has transformed into an elegant cultural center with a coastline full of wealthy summer homes. The city's showpiece, **Knutpunkten,** houses train, bus, and ferry terminals, restaurants, and shops under one glass roof. Exit Knutpunkten and make a left on Järnvägsg. to reach **Stortorget,** the long, wide main square that branches out into shopping streets like swanky **Kullagatan.** Stortorget ends at the **Terrassen,** a series of steps leading up to **Kärnan,** a remnant of the fortress that once loomed over the city. The tower offers a view all the way to Copenhagen for those who ascend its 146 steps on a clear day. (☎10 59 91. Open June-Aug. daily 11am-7pm; low season reduced hours. 20kr. Cash only.) Closer to sea level, the harborside **Dunkers Kulturhus,** Kungsg. 11, is the city's newest venue, with a concert hall and theater, modern art exhibits, and a multimedia installation on the city's history. From the tourist office, turn right onto Drottningg. and left into Sundstorg. (☎10 74 00; www.dunkerskulturhus.com. Open Tu-W and F-Su 10am-5pm, Th 10am-8pm. 80kr, students 40kr. MC/V.) North of Helsingborg, the former royal retreat of **Sofiero Slott** sits on a hillside overlooking the sound. The castle itself is a glorified manor. Take bus #219 (18kr) from Knutpunkten to Sofiero Huvudentréen. (☎13 74 00; www.sofiero.helsingborg.se. Open daily May-Aug. 10am-6pm; Sept.-Apr. 11am-5pm. Grounds 70kr, with castle 90kr. 10kr student discount. MC/V.).

To reach the well-kept **Helsingborgs Vandrarhem ❷,** Järnvägsg. 39, from Knutpunkten, cross Järnvägsg., turn right, and walk three blocks. (☎14 58 50; www.hbgturist.com. Linens 40kr. Laundry 25kr. Reception 4-7pm. Dorms 185kr; singles 275kr; doubles 395kr. MC/V.) Inexpensive cafes line S. Storg., the last right off of Stortorg. before Terrassen. The Knutpunkten's upstairs food court is surprisingly varied. Pick up groceries at the **ICA,** Drottningg. 48, past the Rådhuset. (☎13 15 70. Open M-Sa 8am-8pm, Su 10am-8pm. MC/V.) The harbor area has a handful of late-night bars and clubs, although the rowdy Helsingør ferries (see below) can be more fun than terrestrial options during the summer.

Trains depart for Gothenburg (2½hr.; every 2hr.; 292kr, under 26 250kr), Malmö (50min., 1 per hr., 84kr), and Stockholm (4-6hr.; 2-4 per day; 1066kr, under 26 912kr). MC/V. **Ferries** leave almost continuously for Helsingør, DEN (p. 273), near Copenhagen; popular **Scandlines boats** depart every 20min. (☎18 61 00. 20min.; 26kr, round-trip 48kr. AmEx/MC/V.) Most **city buses** (15-20kr) pass Knutpunkten and include 1hr. of free transfers. To reach the **tourist office,** which books rooms for free, exit the station in the direction of the towering Rådhuset; the office is through the doors next to the closest turret. (☎10 43 50; www.helsingborg.se. Open mid-June to mid-Aug. M-F 9am-8pm, Sa 9am-5pm, Su 10am-3pm; mid-Aug. to mid-June M-F 10am-6pm, Sa 10am-2pm.) **Internet** is available in the 7-Eleven across from the train station. (29kr for 90min. MC/V.) **Postal Code:** 25189.

GOTHENBURG (GÖTEBORG) ☎031

Occasionally dismissed as Sweden's industrial center, Gothenburg (YO-teh-bor-ee; pop. 600,000) is a sprawling, active metropolis threaded with parks, strewn with museums and theaters, and intersected by the glitzy Avenyn thoroughfare that slashes through the heart of the city. While Gothenburg is often overlooked on whirlwind tours of northern Europe, it has the cultural attractions of any of the Scandinavian capitals, but with an unapologetically youthful twist.

TRANSPORTATION

Trains run from Central Station to Malmö (2¾-3¾hr.; every 1-2hr.; 329kr, under 26 280kr); Oslo, NOR (5¾-8hr., 3 per day, 392/274kr); and Stockholm (3-5hr., every 1-2hr., 489/418kr). Stena Line **ferries** (☎704 00 00; www.stenaline.com) sail to Frederikshavn, DEN (2-3¼hr.; 6-10 per day; 160-200kr, 50% Scanrail or Eurail discount) and Kiel, GER (13½hr., daily 7:30pm, 340-810kr). DFDS Seaways (☎65 06 50; www.dfdsseaways.co.uk) sails to Newcastle, BRI (24hr., Th and Su 10am, 695-1195kr). Gothenburg has an extensive **tram** and **bus** system; rides are 20kr, and most trams and buses pass by the train station or through Brunnsparken, south of the Nordstan mall. A **day pass,** valid on both trams and buses, is available at kiosks throughout the city for just 50kr (MC/V).

SWEDEN

ORIENTATION AND PRACTICAL INFORMATION

Central Gothenburg is on the southern bank of the Göta River. The city's transportation hub is located in **Nordstaden,** the northernmost part of the center. Across the Stora Hamn canal lies the busy central district of **Inom Vallgraven.** The main street, **Kungsportsavenyn** ("Avenyn"), begins just north of the Vallgraven canal at Kungsportsplatsen and continues south 1km to **Götaplatsen,** the main square in the Lorensberg district, where theaters and museums cluster. Vasagatan leads west through Vasastaden to the city's newly trendy but oldest suburb, the **Haga** district.

The **tourist office** has a branch in the Nordstan mall near the train and bus stations. (Open M-Sa 10am-6pm, Su noon-5pm.) The crowded main branch, Kungsportspl. 2, books rooms for a 60kr fee and sells the **Göteborg pass** (1-day 210kr, 2-day 295kr), which includes unlimited public transit and admission to many attractions; the pass, however, is probably only worthwhile for those planning to either take a city tour or see at least four sights. (☎61 25 00; www.goteborg.com. Open late June-early Aug. daily 9:30am-8:15pm; low season M-F 9:30am-5pm, Sa 10am-2pm. AmEx/MC/V.) The **Stadsbibliotek** (public library), off Götapl., provides free **Internet** in 15min. slots. Book at the desk and be prepared to wait in line. (Open M-F 10am-8pm, Sa 11am-5pm.) There are Sidewalk Express Internet stations in the train and bus stations. **Postal Code:** 40401.

ACCOMMODATIONS AND CAMPING

Most of Gothenburg's hostels are found in the west end of the city, in and around Masthugget; trams and buses make it an easy ride to the city center. It's wise to reserve ahead, especially in July.

Slottsskogens Vandrarhem (HI), Vegag. 21 (☎42 65 20; www.sov.nu). Bus #60 (dir.: Masthugget) to Vegag. Spacious dorms and common areas combine with amenities like a sauna and pool table in this quality hostel. Bike rental 90kr per day. Sauna 40kr. Breakfast 50kr. Linens 50kr. Laundry 40kr. Free Internet. Reception 8am-noon and 2pm-6am. 12- to 14-bed dorms 165kr; 3- to 6-bed dorms 185kr; singles 305kr; doubles 420kr. 45kr HI discount. MC/V. ❷

Masthuggsterrassens Vandrarhem, Masthuggsterr. 10H (☎42 48 20; www.mastenvandrarhem.com). Tram #3, 9, or 11 to Masthuggstorget. Cross the square diagonally, walk up the stairs, then follow the signs. Classic movie posters and long hallways give this hostel a college-dorm feel. Breakfast 55kr. Linens 55kr. Laundry 45kr. Reception 8-10am and 5-7pm. Dorms 155kr; doubles 440kr; triples 520kr; quads 620kr. MC/V. ❷

Vandrarhem Stigbergsliden (HI), Stigbergsl. 10 (☎24 16 20). Tram #3, 9, or 11 to Masthuggstorget. Walk uphill in the direction of the tram. Cozy rooms organized around a lovely courtyard, though common areas are lacking. Bike rental 50kr per day. Breakfast 45kr. Linens 50kr. Internet 1kr per min. Reception 8am-noon and 4-10pm. Dorms 180kr; singles 310kr; doubles 400kr. 45kr HI discount. AmEx/MC/V. ❷

Linné Vandrarhem, Vegag. 22 (☎12 10 60; www.vandrarhemmet-linne.com). Take bus #60 (dir.: Masthugget) to Vegag. Bright private rooms turn into dorms when space is available. Breakfast 45kr, summer only. Linens 45kr. Reception 9am-noon and 3-7pm. Dorms 180kr; doubles 380kr; triples 540kr; quads 720kr. AmEx/DC/MC/V. ❷

Camping Kärralund, Olbersg. 9 (☎84 02 00; www.liseberg.se). Take tram #5 to Welanderg. and turn right onto Olbersg. Conveniently located in Liseberg Park, but pricey. Breakfast 55kr. Laundry 20-30kr. Reception May-Aug. 7am-11pm; low season reduced hours. July-Aug. tent sites 235kr, electricity and water included; Sept.-June 100-165kr, electricity 45kr. AmEx/DC/MC/V. ❷

SWEDEN

FOOD

The Avenyn is a great place for a stroll, but steer clear of its pricey eats in favor of the affordable restaurants and cafes on **Vasagatan, Linnégatan,** and anywhere near the **Haga** neighborhood. Cheap food is also elegantly housed at food halls; the **Saluhallen,** in Kungstorg., has the iron arches and the glass ceiling of a huge train station. (Open M-F 9am-6pm, Sa 9am-3pm.) **Saluhallen Briggen,** Nordhemsg. 28, is housed in an old fire station. (Open M-F 9am-6pm, Sa 9am-2pm.)

Caféva, Haga Nyg. 5E (☎711 63 64). Locals flock here to sample traditional fare with some quirky twists. You can't go wrong with fresh-baked bread, hearty soups (48kr), and filling sandwiches (18-50kr). Open June-Aug. M-F 10am-6pm; Sept.-May M-F 9am-6pm, Sa 11am-4pm. MC/V. ❶

Solrosen, Kaponjärg. 4 (☎711 66 97). Even carnivores come to chow down at this cozy, flower-themed vegetarian haven in Haga. Entrees 70kr including salad bar. Soup 50kr. Open M-F 11:30am-1am, Sa 2pm-1am. Kitchen closes 9pm. AmEx/MC/V. ❷

Thai Garden, Andra Långg. 18 (☎12 76 60). Fill up on the delicious buffet (F 11am-2pm, 65kr) at this stand-out on a street lined with Thai eateries. Open M-F 11am-10pm, Sa noon-midnight, Su noon-10pm. AmEx/DC/MC/V. ❷

Tabla Cafe, Södra Vägen 54 (☎63 27 20). Upstairs in the Världskulturmuseet. The renowned Dahlbom brothers craft lavish creations for reasonable prices in this cafe. Try the bread (35-40kr) or exquisite salads (75-80kr). Open Tu and Sa-Su noon-5pm, W-F noon-9pm. AmEx/DC/MC/V. ❸

Egg & Milk, Ovre Husarg. 23 (☎70 10 350). This hip 50s-style diner has an English menu for effect and serves generous portions of all things breakfast (pancakes 50-54kr, omelettes 54-58kr, bagel platters 43-45kr). Open daily 7am-3pm. MC/V. ❷

Eva's Paley, Avenyn 39 (☎16 30 70), at the Götapl. end. Tasty food at quality location without an astronomical tab. Sandwiches 59kr. Salad platters 75-85kr. Open M-Th 8am-11pm, F 8am-midnight, Sa-Su 10am-11pm. AmEx/MC/V. ❷

SIGHTS

CITY CENTER. Nordstan, Scandinavia's largest indoor shopping center is across from the train station. *(Open M-F 10am-7pm, Sa 10am-6pm, Su 11am-5pm.)* The **Stadsmuseum,** Norra Hamng. 12, uses large-scale re-creations to recall the city's history. *(☎61 27 70; www.stadsmuseum.goteborg.se. Open May-Aug. daily 10am-5pm; Sept.-Apr. Tu-Su*

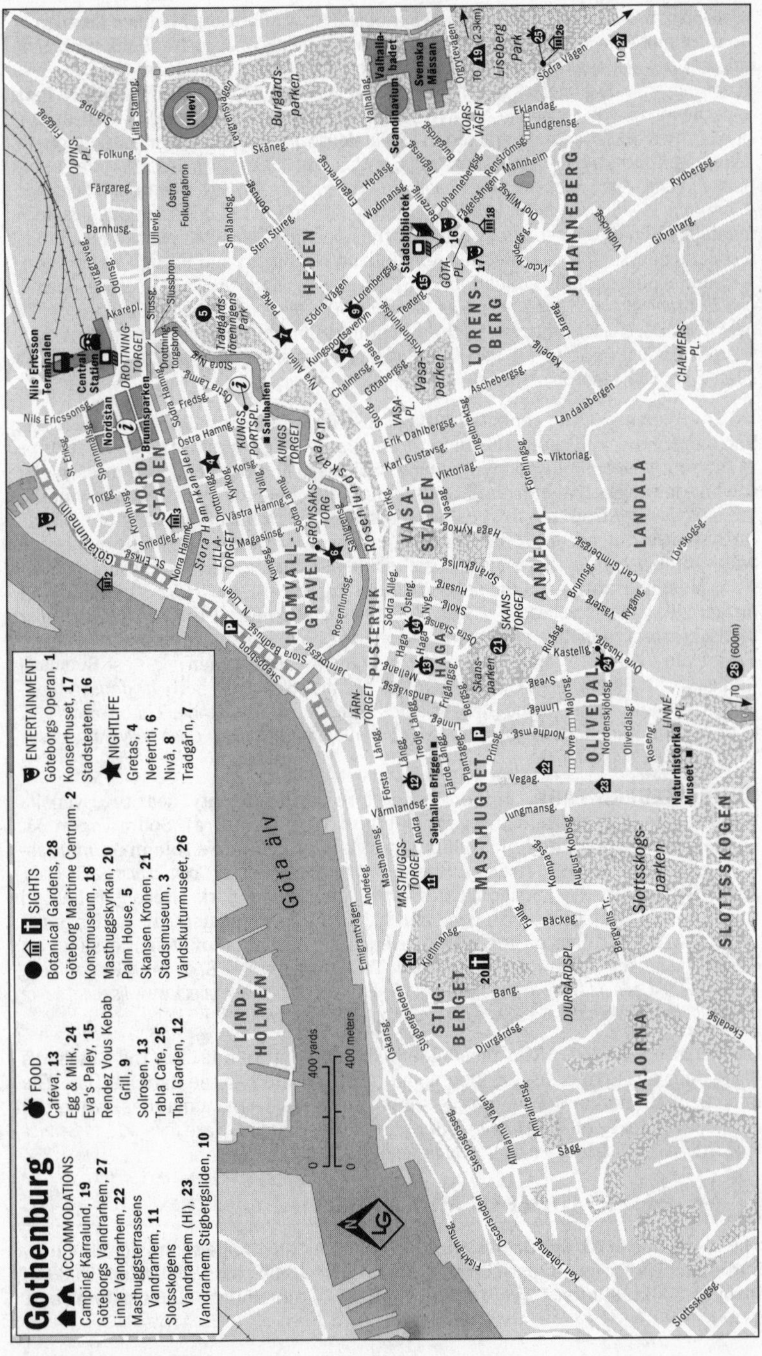
Gothenburg
ACCOMMODATIONS
Camping Kärralund, 19
Göteborgs Vandrarhem, 27
Linné Vandrarhem, 22
Masthuggsterrassens Vandrarhem, 11
Slotsskogens Vandrarhem (HI), 23
Vandrarhem Stigbergsliden, 10
FOOD
Caféva, 13
Egg & Milk, 24
Eva's Paley, 15
Rendez Vous Kebab Grill, 9
Solrosen, 13
Tabla Cafe, 25
Thai Garden, 12
SIGHTS
Botanical Gardens, 28
Göteborg Maritime Centrum, 2
Konstmuseum, 18
Masthuggskyrkan, 20
Palm House, 5
Skansen Kronen, 21
Stadsmuseum, 3
Världskulturmuseet, 26
ENTERTAINMENT
Göteborgs Operan, 1
Konserthuset, 17
Stadsteatern, 16
NIGHTLIFE
Gretas, 4
Nefertiti, 6
Nivå, 8
Trädgår'n, 7
0 400 yards
0 400 meters
Göta älv
LIND-HOLMEN
NORD-STADEN
INOMVALL-GRAVEN
VASA-STADEN
HEDEN
LORENS-BERG
JOHANNEBERG
PUSTERVIK
HAGA
ANNEDAL
LANDALA
OLIVEDAL
MASTHUGGET
STIG-BERGET
MAJORNA
SLOTTSSKOGEN
Slottsskogs-parken
Vasa-parken
Burgårds-parken
Liseberg Park
Ullevi
Scandinavium
Valhalla-badet
Svenska Mässan
Stadsbibliotek
Central Station
Nils Ericsson Terminalen
Nordstan
Brunnsparken
Saluhallen
Saluhallen Briggen
Naturhistorika Museet
Trädgårds-föreningens Park
DROTTNING-TORGET
KUNGSTORGET
KUNGS-PORTSPL.
GRÖNSAKS-TORG
LILLA-TORGET
JÄRN-TORGET
MASTHUGGS-TORGET
SKANS-TORGET
GÖTA-PL.
VASA-PL.
LINNÉ-PL.
CHALMERS-PL.
DJURGÅRDSPL.
KORS-VÄGEN
Götatunneln
Stora Hamnkanalen
Rosenlundskanalen
Kungsportsavenyn
TO 19 (2.3km)
TO 27
TO 28 (600m)

10am-5pm, W 10am-8pm. 40kr, under 20 free. AmEx/MC/V.) **Göteborg Maritime Centrum,** a floating museum of 19 ships, includes a WWII destroyer. *(☎10 59 60; www.maritima.se. Open May-Aug. daily 10am-6pm; Sept.-Oct. and Mar.-Apr. daily 10am-4pm; Nov. F-Su 10am-4pm. 75kr. English tours in summer noon and 2pm. MC/V.)* **Trädgårdsföreningens Park** is to the left as you cross the Avenyn bridge. Wend your way through the rosarium, one of the world's most diverse, to the **Palm House.** *(☎365 58 58; www.tradgardsforeningen.se. Park open daily Apr.-Sept. 7am-9pm; Oct.-Mar. 7am-7:30pm. Apr.-Sept. 15kr, free before 9am and after 8pm; Sept.-Apr. free. Palm House open daily May-Aug. 10am-5pm; Sept.-Apr. 10am-4pm. 20kr.)* Avenyn ends at Götapl., the site of Carl Milles's famous **Poseidon fountain.** Even the sea god is dwarfed by the imposing **Konstmuseum,** which holds a spectacular sculpture collection, exhibits on Nordic art and French Impressionism, and a photography collection. *(☎61 29 80; www.konstmuseum.goteborg.se. Open Tu and Th 11am-6pm, W 11am-9pm, F-Su 11am-5pm. 40kr, temporary exhibits 20-40kr, under 20 free. AmEx/DC/MC/V.)* Adjacent to the Konstmuseum, the **Konsthall** showcases contemporary art. *(☎61 50 40; www.konsthallen.goteborg.se. Open Tu and Th 11am-6pm, W 11am-8pm, F-Su 11am-5pm. Free.)*

SWEDEN

HAGA. Westward, the gentrifying Haga district offers art galleries, bookstores, and cafes, especially along the main thoroughfare, **Haga Nygata.** The flight of steps at the southern end of Kaponjärg. leads to **Skansen Kronen,** the most impressive of the hilltop towers that surround Gothenburg; the climb may be strenuous, but the view of the city from the tower's base is stellar. For a bird's-eye view of Gothenburg's harbor, head out to the **Masthuggskyrkan,** Storebackeg. 1, a brick church with a timber ceiling that suggests the inside of a Viking ship. Take tram #3, 9, or 11 to Masthuggstorg—it's the second church up the hill. *(☎731 92 30. Open in summer daily 9am-6pm; low season usually M-F 11am-4pm.)* South of the church, the vast **Slottsskogsparken** invites you to wander among its ponds, meadows, and aviaries. Take tram #1 or 6 to Linnépl. Across the highway lies Sweden's largest **Botanical Gardens,** Carl Skottsbergs G. 22A, home to orchid hothouses, herb gardens, a bamboo grove, and some 12,000 plant species from across the globe. Take tram #1, 7, 8, or 13 to Botaniska Trädgården. *(☎741 11 00; www.gotbot.se. Open daily 9am-sunset. 20kr. Hothouses 20kr. MC/V.)*

NEAR LISEBERG PARK. In the southeastern part of the city, near the Svenska Mässan, the **Världskulturmuseet** (Museum of World Culture), Södra Vägen 54, challenges visitors with bold exhibits that address culture's role in an increasingly globalized society. *(☎63 27 00; www.varldskulturmuseet.se. Open Tu and Sa-Su noon-5pm, Th-F noon-9pm. Free.)* Scandinavia's largest amusement park, **Liseberg,** is behind the museum. Strap yourself in good and tight for a ride on **Balder,** the park's bone-rattling wooden rollercoaster, or experience the sensation of weightlessness on the park's newest rollercoaster, **Kanonen.** Take tram #4, 5, 6, 8, or 14 to Korsvägen. *(☎40 01 00. Open mid-May to late Aug. daily; Sept. Th-Su. Hours vary; check www.liseberg.se for schedule. Entry 60kr; rides 15-60kr each, 1-day ride pass 265kr. MC/V.)*

GÖTEBORGS SKÄRGÅRD. Beachgoers should venture out onto the **Göteborgs Skärgård,** a string of islands dribbling out into the waters of the Kattegat Bay. The islands of Brännö and Styrsö have shops and other resort amenities, while the cliffs and beaches of Vargö are wilder and more secluded. *(Take tram #11 to Saltholmen, 30min., and make a free transfer to the ferry, 30-50min.)*

ENTERTAINMENT AND NIGHTLIFE

The enormous **Göteborgs Operan,** at Lilla Bommen, hosts opera, musical theater, and concerts from August through May. (☎13 13 00; www.opera.se. Tickets from 95-530kr, students 25% off Su-Th. MC/V.) Gothenburg's **Stadsteatern** (☎61

50 50) and **Konserthuset** (☎726 53 00) round out its highbrow theater and music scene; swing by the tourist office for the latest issue of *What's On in Göteborg* for details. Gothenburg's annual **film festival** (www.filmfestival.org), the largest in Scandinavia, will draw more than 100,000 film lovers to the city for 10 days, starting January 26, 2007. Mid-August brings the **Göteborgskalaset,** an annual party that transforms the city with music, entertainment, and culinary masterpieces.

The chic and affordable bars that line Linnégatan are a good place to start or end an evening. Gothenburg's club scene is one of the most exclusive in Scandinavia. Many posh restaurants on Avenyn morph into equally posh clubs after nightfall, so expect lines, steep covers, and strict dress codes. **Nivå,** Kungsportsavenyn 9, is the scene's standard-bearer. (☎701 80 90. W "Soul Train" night. 27+. Cover F 70kr, Sa 100kr. Open Tu 11:30am-midnight, W-Th 11:30am-3am, F 11:30am-4am, Sa 6pm-4am. AmEx/DC/MC/V.) For a little less attitude, head for **Trädgår'n,** on Nya Allén, an ivy-clad concert venue, club, and patio bar. (☎10 20 80. 21+. Cover from 100kr. Club open F-Sa 10pm-5am.) The biggest gay club in Sweden, **Gretas,** Drottningg. 35, has plenty of room to party in its upstairs bar as well as its dance floor. (☎13 69 49; www.gretas.nu. Happy hour W-Th all day, F-Sa 6-11pm. 20+. Club cover 50-80kr. Open W-Th 6pm-2am, F-Sa 6pm-4am.) On a more down-tempo evening, head to **Nefertiti,** Hvitfeldtspl. 6, an intimate jazz bar that reinvents itself as a dance club after 1am. (☎711 15 33; www.nefertiti.se. 20+. Club cover 80kr. Tickets 80-280kr. Concerts in summer Tu-W and F-Sa 8:30 or 9pm.)

SWEDEN

DAYTRIP FROM GOTHENBURG: VARBERG

This summer paradise, a classic seaside town replete with beaches and bath houses, beckons from between Gothenburg and Helsingborg. Varberg's spectacular **fortress** is home to a number of attractions. The **Länsmuseet Varberg** features the **Bocksten Man,** a bog corpse from 1360 found with his clothing intact. To reach the fortress, turn right out of the station and right onto S. Hamnv. (☎03 40 828 30; www.lansmuseet.varberg.se. Museum open June to mid-Aug. daily 10am-5pm; mid-Aug. to May M-F 10am-4pm, Sa-Su noon-4pm. June-Aug. 50kr; low season 30kr. AmEx/MC/V.) Follow the boardwalk 2km south of town to reach the shallow **Apelviken Bay,** which offers some of the best surfing and windsurfing in Northern Europe. **Surfers Paradise,** Söderg. 22 (☎03 40 67 70 55), rents gear and gives both formal lessons and informal tips. The boardwalk also passes several **nude beaches:** Kärringhålan for women and Goda Hopp for men. North 5km is the Getterön peninsula, a popular spot for camping and raucous parties. The peninsula can also be reached by taking the 15min. **Getteröbåtarna** boat taxi from the harbor. (☎070 310 13 24; www.getterobatarna.se. 1 per hr.; 30kr, bikes 10kr. Runs late June-Aug. 10am-midnight. Cash only.) **Trains** leave for Gothenburg (45min.; 83kr, under 26 59kr) and Helsingborg (1½hr., 188/161kr). To reach the **tourist office,** in Brunnsparken, turn right out of the train station and walk two blocks. (☎03 40 868 00. Open July M-Sa 9:30am-7pm, Su 1-6pm; May-June and Aug. M-F 10am-5pm, Sa 10am-3pm; Sept.-Apr. M-F 10am-5pm.) **Postal Code:** 43201.

CENTRAL SWEDEN

Central Sweden extends from the swampy foothills along the Norwegian border through sleepy lakeside villages in the center of the country. When farming could no longer support the population, the county of Dalarna turned to handicrafts to bolster its economy; by the 19th century, its stylized religious paintings and colorful wooden horses filled the homes of the eastern urban bourgeoisie. Neighboring Jämtland is home to some of the country's premier cross-country and downhill skiing in the winter and popular hiking trails in the summer

MORA. The quiet town of Mora (pop. 22,000) sits in the crater hollowed out by a meteorite more than 360 million years ago, bordered to the north by Lake Orsa and to the south and east by the shimmering Lake Siljan. On the first Sunday in March, Mora marks the finish of the **Vasaloppet,** the world's oldest and longest cross-country ski race; it hosts a week-long **festival** (www.vasaloppet.se; Feb. 23-Mar. 4, 2007) in conjunction with the race. The **Vasaloppet Museum** chases the hero worship of past winners down with the same warm blueberry soup that greets skiers at the 23km mark. (☎0250 392 25. Open mid-June to mid-Aug. daily 10am-5pm; mid-Aug. to mid-June M-F 10am-5pm; Th closes at 3pm year-round. 30kr, including guided tour and soup. MC/V.) Tucked away behind the city's church, **Zorngården,** Vasag. 37, is the 19th-century home of Anders Zorn, a Swedish painter best remembered for his nude portraits. The estate can only be seen by tour. The **Zornmuseet** showcases a collection of Zorn's work as well as canvases by his contemporaries. (☎0250 59 23 10; www.zorn.se. 50kr, students 45kr. Museum open mid-May to mid-Sept. M-Sa 9am-5pm, Su 11am-5pm; mid-Sept. to mid-May M-Sa noon-5pm, Su 1-5pm. AmEx/MC/V.) Hikers can tackle the **Siljansleden** network of trails that circles the two lakes, including a well-marked 310km **bike trail** skirting the shore. In the winter, a ploughed track across Lake Orsa draws long-distance **skaters.** (☎0250 17 230; www.frilufts.se/mora/is.)

Vandrarhem Mora (HI) ❷, Fredsg. 6, has comfy dorm rooms; turn left on the main road and right on Fredsg. (☎0250 381 96; www.maalkullann.se. Breakfast 60kr. Linens 80kr. Reception M-F 5-7pm, Sa-Su 6-7pm. Dorms 230kr; singles 320kr; doubles 440kr. 45kr HI discount on dorms. AmEx/MC/V.) **Mora Parken Camping ❶** sits on the last stretch of the Vasaloppet track. (☎0250 27 600; www.moraparken.se. Free showers. Breakfast 60kr. Linens 75kr. Laundry 20kr. Reception in the Mora Parken Hotel. Late June to mid-Aug. tent sites 85kr, with electricity 140kr; 2-person cabins 320kr, 4-person 460kr; low season reduced rates. AmEx/DC/MC/V.) Restaurants in Mora tend to come in two varieties: overpriced and pizzeria-kebaberies. A departure from both is **Coffee Shop ❶,** across from the tourist office on the water, which serves light meals for 45-55kr. (☎0250 380 40. www.kajen-glassbar.com. Open June-Aug daily 10am-9pm. AmEx/MC/V.) Pick up **groceries** at ICA on Kyrkog. (☎0250 103 28. Open M-Sa 9am-8pm, Su 10am-8pm. MC/V.)

Trains run to Östersund (6hr., mid-June to early Aug. 2 per day, 847kr) and Stockholm (4hr., 7 per day, 368kr). **Buses** also head to Östersund year-round (5¼hr., 2 per day, 175kr). The **tourist office** is on Strandg.; turn left out of the station and follow Vasag. for about 15min. It books rooms for a 25kr fee and exchanges currency and traveler's checks for 70kr. (☎0250 592 020; www.siljan.se. Open mid-June to mid-Aug. and during the ski race M-F 10am-7pm, Sa-Su 10am-5pm; mid-Aug. to mid-June M-F 10am-5pm. AmEx/MC/V.) **Internet** is available at the library, Köpmang. 4, off Kyrkog., 1 block from the bus station. (☎0250 267 79. Open June-Aug. M-F 10am-7pm, Sa 10am-2pm. 10kr per 30min. Cash only.) **Postal Code:** 79200.

ÖSTERSUND. Travelers heading north into Lappland often tarry for a few days in Östersund (pop. 58,000). Deep, reedy Lake Storsjön laps against the town's western shores, and many residents sincerely believe that the lake is home to the **Storsjöodjuret monster;** there continue to be sightings each year. In 1894, the town called in a harpooner to flush out the creature, but appeals by local Quakers and then the tourist office resulted in a 1986 ban (revoked in 2005) on any harrassment of the monster. The steamer *S/S Thomée* runs cruises and monster-spotting tours. (2-3 per day; 80-110kr.) Rent a **bike** at the Badhusparken, next to where the *S/S Thomée* docks, and pedal over the footbridge to **Frösön Island,** a getaway aptly named for the Norse god of crops and fertility. (☎07 30 62 99 72. Open June-Aug. M-F 8am-5pm. 50kr per ½-day. Cash only.) Swedish couples have taken the hint by making the island's 12th-century **church** one of the country's most popular wedding chapels. Take bus #3 (18kr) from the center, or make the 8km trek by bike. (☎063 161 150. Open daily 8am-8pm.) On the edge of the island closer to town, at the top of Frösön's highest point, stands the **Frösötornet** (Frösö Tower) and the Frösötornets Vandrarhem (see below). From the top, the Norwegian mountains can be seen on a clear day. (☎063 128169. Open daily late June to mid-Aug. 9am-9pm, mid-Aug. to Sept. and mid-May to late June 11am-5pm. 10kr. Cash only.)

Hostels in tend to fill up in high season—reserve ahead. Wild strawberries grow on the roof of the 255-year-old cabin at **Frösötornets Vandrarhem ❶**, Utsiktv. 10, Frösön. Bus #5 runs from the city center (11am-10:20pm), and stops at the bottom of a steep hill. The fairy-tale setting is worth the difficult climb. (☎063 51 57 67; vandrarhem@froson.com. No lockers. Linens 50kr. Call for reception. Dorms 140kr; singles 180kr. Cash only.) Travelers chatter at the more centrally located **Hostel Rallaren ❶**, Bangårdsg. 6. (☎063 13 22 32; sventa_rallaren@hotmail.com. No lockers available. Linens 40kr. Reception 9:30am-2:30pm, Sa-Su reduced hours. Dorms 150kr; singles 200kr; doubles 340kr. Cash only.) Pick up **groceries** at Hemköp, Kyrkg. 56. (Open M-Sa 8am-10pm, Su 10am-10pm.)

Trains run to Stockholm (6hr.; 6 per day; 554kr, under 26 461kr) and Trondheim, NOR (4hr., 2 per day, 268/187kr). From mid-June to early August, an Inlandsbanan train (☎0771 53 53 53; www.inlandsbanan.se) runs to Gällivare (14hr., 1 per day, from 571kr) and Mora (6hr., 2 per day, 347kr). The **tourist office,** Rådhusg. 44, books rooms for free. (☎063 144 001; www.turist.ostersund.se. Open July M-Sa 9am-9pm, Su 10am-7pm; June and Aug. M-F 9am-5pm, Sa-Su 10am-3pm; Sept.-May M-F 9am-5pm. MC/V.) **Internet** (19kr per hr.) is available in the train station. Open M-F 5:30am-9:15pm, Sa 7:30am-5pm, Su 7:30am-9:15pm. **Postal Code:** 83100.

ÅRE. The **Åre Ski Resort** (☎0647 177 00; www.skistar.com/english/are) is the largest in Sweden, with a rich variety of beginner and intermediate trails as well as an excellent ski school. After the snow melts, the town of Åre (pop. 10,000) is a promising base for outdoor activities on and around **Åreskutan,** the highest peak in the region. Serious cyclists can take their chances at downhill mountain biking, a sport extreme enough to justify sky-high bike rental prices (300-800kr per day). Rental shops abound around the base of the mountain, and the World Cup chairlift brings you halfway up the mountain to a number of trailheads. (Lift runs daily July-Aug. 10am-4pm. Round-trip 60kr.) Ambitious hikers make their way up the difficult 7km Åreskutan trail from the town square to a 1420m peak, while the Kabinbanan cable car shortens the trip to under 1km. (Cable car runs July-Aug. 10am-4pm. Round-trip 100kr.) The **Åre Ski Lodge ❶**, Trondheimsleden 44, has well-equipped rooms. (☎0647 510 29. Linens 90kr. Laundry available. Reserve ahead during ski season. Dorms 110kr; doubles 290kr. Cash only.) **Trains** run from Åre to Östersund (1¼hr.; 2 per day; 130kr, students 65kr) and Trondheim, NOR (2¾hr., 2 per day, 180kr). The Nabotåget website (www.nabotaget.nu) has the best fares. The **tourist office,** in the station, sells essential hiking maps (99kr), organizes outdoor activities, and provides free **Internet.** (☎0647 177 20; www.visitare.se. Open late June-Aug. and mid-Dec. to Apr. daily 9am-6pm; Sept. to mid-Dec. and May-late June M-F 9am-5pm, Sa-Su 10am-3pm. AmEx/DC/MC/V.) **Postal Code:** 83013.

GULF OF BOTHNIA

The Gulf of Bothnia region of Sweden is deservedly well-known for its untouched landscape of deep pine forests, stark ravines, and stretches of pristine coastline. Its quiet, friendly cities contrast with Sweden's glittery metropolitan centers to the south, but a visit to the region is most worthwhile due to its potential for short wilderness excursions.

GÄVLE. Two hours north of Stockholm, Gävle (YEV-leh; pop. 90,000) is the first stop on the way to northern Sweden. **Gamle Gefle** (old town), the only part of Gävle that survived a 19th-century fire, lie just across the canal. At the **Länsmuseet Gävleborg,** Södra Strandg. 20, contemporary art is placed side-by-side with its traditional counterpart. (☎026 65 56 35; www.lansmuseetgavleborg.se. Open June-Aug. M-F 11am-5pm, Sa-Su noon-4pm; Sept.-May M-F 10am-4pm, Sa-Su noon-4pm. 40kr, students free. W free. MC/V.) Farther inland, the **Gävle Konstcentrum,** Kungsbäcksv. 32, displays changing exhibits of international contemporary art. (☎026 17 94 24; www.galve.se/konstcentrum. Open June to mid-Aug. Tu-Su noon-4pm; mid-Aug. to May Tu-F noon-5pm, Th noon-7pm, Sa-Su noon-4pm. Free.) On the opposite bank, stroll through the city park's **sculpture garden.**

■**Vandrarhem Gävle (HI) ❶,** Södra Rådmansg. 1, has well-lit rooms and a flower-filled courtyard in the middle of the old town. From the train station, turn left, cross the canal, and make your first right on Södra Strandg. After the library, make a left, go through the square, then up the stairs and past the parking lot. (☎026 62 17 45. Breakfast 55kr. Linens 70kr. Laundry 30kr. Reception 8-10am and 4:30-7pm. Dorms 190-220kr; singles 320kr; doubles 375kr. 45kr HI discount. MC/V.) For a delectable lunch (35-50kr, daily special 55kr) in a traditional Swedish setting, head to ■**Mamsell ❷,** Kyrkog. 14, in the Berggrenska Gårdens. From the market square, walk one block on N. Stottsg. toward the canal. (☎026 12 34 10. Open M-F 11am-5pm, Sa 11am-3pm. MC/V.) Pick up **groceries** at the ICA across the street from the train station. (Open M-Sa 9am-8pm, Su 11am-8pm. MC/V.) **Trains** run from Gävle to Östersund (4-6hr., 2-4 per day, 345kr) and Stockholm (1½hr., 1 per hr., 177kr). To get to the **tourist office,** Drottningg. 9, which books rooms all over Sweden for 50kr, head straight out of the train station, down Drottningg. to the market square; it is in the center of the Gallerian Nian shopping center. (☎026 14 74 30; www.gastrikland.com. Open M-F 10am-7pm, Sa 10am-4pm, Su noon-4pm. AmEx/DC/MC/V.) **Internet** is available at the library (Stadsbiblioteket), Slottstorget 1, for 15min. slots, generally with a short wait. (☎026 17 99 56. Open M-Th 10am-7pm, F 10am-5pm, Sa-Su 10am-2pm.) **Postal Code:** 80250.

ÖRNSKÖLDSVIK. Although shapeless concrete dominate the center of drab Örnsköldsvik (urn-SHULDS-vik; "Ö-vik" to locals; pop. 27,000), the town is a popular base for **hiking** excursions. The 127km **High Coast Trail** (Höga Kusten Leden) winds south through Skuleskogen National Park as far as Veda, just north of Sundsvall. Flanked by cliffs that drop dizzyingly into the Gulf of Bothnia, the trail is divided into 13 segments with free mountain huts at the end of each leg; bring an insulated sleeping bag or arrive early enough to cut firewood. Day hikes include the 6km **Yellow Trail** loop; although the hike is easy, steep drop-offs along the path may frighten some travelers. You'll find the trailhead on Hantverkareg.; from the tourist office, walk up Centralespl., turn left on Storg., and then left again. **Örnsköldsviks Vandrerhem ❷,** Viktoriaespl. 32, lets you stay in a converted family manor. From the bus station, turn left onto Lasarettsg., follow it four blocks, make a right onto Bergsg. for three blocks, then a left onto Viktoriaespl. (☎0660 296 111. Breakfast 40kr. Linens 40kr. Call for reception. Dorms 180kr; doubles 360kr. MC/V.) ■**Lundberg Bröd o Cafe ❷,** Nygatan 35, serves large meals for 50kr. (☎0660 125 125. Open M-F 7am-5pm, Sa 10am-2pm. AmEx/MC/V.) Pick up **groceries** at Hemköp, Stora Torg. 3. (Open daily 8am-8pm. MC/V.) **Buses** run to Östersund (4½hr.; M-F 3 per day, Sa-Su 1 per day; 262kr) and Umeå (2hr., 7 per day, 111kr). The **tourist office,** Strandg. 24, next to the station, books rooms for a 40kr fee. (☎06 60 881 00; www.ornskoldsvik.se. Free Internet, limited to 30min. if there's a line. Open late June to mid-Aug. M-F 9am-6pm, Sa-Su 10am-2pm; mid-Aug. to late June M-F 10am-6pm, Sa 10am-2pm. AmEx/DC/MC/V.) **Postal Code:** 89188.

UMEÅ. In the 1970s, leftist students in Umeå (OOM-eh-oh; pop. 110,000) earned their alma mater the nickname "the red university." Times change, though, and today northern Sweden's largest city is better known for its birch-lined boulevards than its Marxist leanings, although echoes of its egalitarian past live on in a slew of free attractions. At the **Gammlia** open-air museum, a 20min. walk east of the city center and up a small hill, period actors give visitors a crack at 19th-century crafts like churning butter, as well as the opportunity to sample freshly baked *tunnbröd* (20kr), traditional flatbread from northern Sweden. In the same complex, the **Västerbottens Museum** houses not only the world's oldest ski but also the modern **forUm** exhibit about the town, where visitors can relax while listening to recordings by local artists. The **BildMuseet** displays Swedish and international contemporary art. (Open in summer W-Su noon-5pm; low season Tu-Sa noon-4pm, Su noon-5pm. Free.) Umeå is also en route to the celebrated Umedalen Sculpture Park 5km away. Take bus #1 or 61 from Vasaplan (20kr, 1hr. transfer) to Umedalen. (☎090 903 64; www.gsa.se. Free.) West of the city, the 30km **Umeleden** bike and car trail snakes past 5000-year-old rock carvings, an arboretum, one of Europe's largest hydropower stations, and **Baggböle Herrgård,** a cafe nestled into a 19th-century manor house. (☎090 321 51. Open June-Aug. Tu-Su 11am-6pm. MC/V.) Pick up the trail at the **Gamla Bron** (Old Bridge) and veer across the Norvarpsbron to cut the route in half. Hikers can follow the **Tavelsjöleden** trail (30km) along a boulder ridge, or brave the **Isälvsleden** trail (60km), carved out of the stone by melting pack ice.

YMCA Hostel (SVIF) ❷, Järvägsallen 22, offers spacious common areas. (☎090 903 28; www.hostel.kfum.nu. Breakfast 45kr. Linens 60kr, towel 20kr. Laundry 6kr. Internet 30kr per hr. or 200kr per stay with your own laptop. Reception M-F 8am-noon and 1-7pm, Sa-Su 8-10am and 4-7pm. Dorms 160kr; singles from 330kr; doubles from 380kr. MC/V.) The city center has engaging cafes and patisseries (32-48kr), and **Taj Mahal ❸,** Vasag. 10, offers a vegetarian-friendly lunch buffet for 75kr. (☎090 12 12 52; www.tajmahalumea.com. Open M-Th 11am-2pm and 4-9pm, F 11am-2pm and 4-10pm, Sa noon-10pm, Su 2-8pm. MC/V.) **Groceries** are available at ICA, across from the bus station (Open M-Sa 8am-10pm, Su 8am-8pm. MC/V.) Mingle with students at the **bars** along Rådhusg. and Kungsg. **Trains** run to Gothenburg (14½hr.; 1 per day; 490kr, with sleeping berth 670kr). Ybuss **buses** (☎090 70 65 00) run to Stockholm (10hr.; 3 per day; 370kr, students 280kr). The bus terminal is across from the train station on the right. The **tourist office,** Renmarkstorg. 15, runs free English-language tours of the city in summer. From the stations, walk straight down Rådhusespl. and turn right on Skolg. (☎090 16 16 16; www.visitumea.se. Free Internet. Tours W 4pm, Sa 2pm. Open mid-June to mid-Aug. M-F 8:30am-7pm, Sa 10am-4pm, Su noon-4pm; low season M-F 10am-5pm.) **Cykel och Mopedhandlaren,** Kungsg. 101, rents **bikes.** (☎090 14 01 70. Open M-F 9:30am-5:30pm, Sa 10am-1pm. 70kr per day, 25kr thereafter, 195kr per week. MC/V.) **Postal Code:** 90326.

LAPPLAND (SÁPMI)

Lappland, known as "Europe's last wilderness," is filled with mountains and alpine dales that sprawl across northern Sweden, as well as Norway, Finland, and Russia, and are touristed only by the most mosquito-proof hikers. Today, the region's indigenous Sámi people use technology like helicopters and snowmobiles to tend their herds of reindeer while they continue to wrangle with Stockholm over the hunting and grazing rights their ancestors enjoyed for centuries.

TIP **BUG CONTROL.** While locals swear by a concoction of diluted vinegar—imbibed every morning—to keep mosquitoes at bay, most travelers will want to carry a large supply of old-fashioned bug spray when heading into forests up north.

THE BIG SPLURGE

COLD COMFORT

Rising out of the Torne River in tiny Jukkasjärvi, the remarkable **Icehotel** melts away each May and then crystallizes anew in November. Take the name at face value—the entire building is made out of ice. Production starts even before the previous year's hotel has entirely melted away. A team of artists from around the world spray tall metal frames with snow cannons to form walls, while ice pillars support the cavernous ceiling from which ice chandeliers dangle. The masterminds behind the Icehotel also allow for innovation and use a new set of blueprints every year, so each version is unique.

However, innovation has yet to reveal how to pipe hot water into an ice hotel. Washroom facilities are outside, but the hotel gives its guests thermal suits for the wintry dash to the showers. Reindeer skins line the ledges that serve as beds, and thermal sleeping bags keep guests toasty until the staff arrives mid-morning with cups of hot lingonberry juice. More potent drinkables are on tap at the Absolut Icebar.

The Icehotel's counterpart, the Ice Church, has become a popular wedding spot for over 150 couples each year. Ensembles range from fur parkas to snowmobile overalls—but the choice for the chilly wedding night is practically universal: matching flannel.

For more info see **Icehotel,** at right.

TRANSPORTATION

Connex runs **trains** along the coastal route from Stockholm through Umeå, Boden, and Kiruna to Narvik, NOR, along the ore railway. From late June to early August, the private **Inlandsbanan** runs north from Mora (p. 986) through the country. (☎063 19 44 12; www.inlandsbanan.se.) **Buses** are the only way to reach smaller towns; call ☎020 47 00 47 or stop by Kiruna's tourist office for schedules.

KIRUNA ☎0980

The only large settlement in Lappland, Kiruna (pop. 23,000) retains the rough edges of a mining town, despite its proximity to chic **Riksgänsen,** the world's northernmost ski resort. Kiruna's main appeal is its proximity for exploring other sights, but the town does have some surprisingly innovative architecture: **Kiruna Church,** Kyrkog. 8, resembles a Sámi *goahti* dwelling. (☎678 12. Open daily 9am-6pm. Free.) **City Hall,** designed by architect Arthur von Schmalensee, houses a modern art collection. (☎700 00. Open June-Aug. M-F 7am-5pm; Sept.-May M-F 8am-5pm. Free.) The state-owned mining company, **LKAB,** hauls an astonishing 20 million tons of iron ore out of the ground each year and offers 3hr. **InfoMine** tours, which descend 540m to an informative museum. (2-3 per day. Tickets available at the tourist office. 220kr, students 140kr. AmEx/MC/V.) **Esrange,** 40km outside Kiruna, is Europe's only non-military space station. Scientists launch short-range sounding rockets to conduct research on the ozone layer using high-altitude weather balloons. (☎04 02 70. 4hr. tours leave Kiruna late June to mid-Aug. Tu and Th 9:15am. Reserve at the tourist office at least 24hr. ahead. 390kr. AmEx/MC/V.) Hikers take bus #92 from Kiruna to Nikkaluokta (1¼hr., 1-3 per day, 67kr) and pick up the well-marked **Kungsleden** trail at Kebnekaise Fjällstation. A week's trek north brings travelers into Abisko National Park; the STF runs cabins 10-20km apart on the trail. (☎084 63 22 00; www.stfturist.se. Cabins mid-July to mid-Sept. 255-355kr; late Feb. to mid-July 190-235kr. 100kr HI discount. MC/V.) Those looking for a day hike can journey directly from Kiruna to Abisko on bus #91 (1¼hr., 1-3 per day, 67kr), and pick from any number of trails there.

The **Yellow House Hostel ❶,** Hantverkareg. 25, resembles an old farmhouse and has bright, spacious rooms. From the tourist office, walk uphill and turn left onto Vänortsg., which turns into Hantverkareg. (☎1 37 50; www.yellowhouse.nu. Breakfast 50kr. Linens 50kr. Reception 2-11pm. Book far ahead. Dorms 150-160kr; singles 300kr; doubles 400kr. Cash only.) **STF Vandrarhem (HI) ❷,** Bergmästareg 7, offers standard rooms in the town center. From the tourist office, walk across the plaza, along the path next to the supermarket, past the fountain and pharmacy, then make a left onto Bergmästareg. (☎171 95; www.kirunahostel.com. Sauna 50kr. Luggage storage 50kr. Breakfast 60kr. Linens 50kr, towel 15kr. Free wireless Internet. Reception M-F 7-10am and 4-9pm, Sa-Su 8-10am and 4-8pm. Dorms 205kr; singles 345kr; doubles 470kr. 45kr HI discount. MC/V.) For a two-course lunch special (9am-2pm; 65kr), a sandwich (30-50kr), or a good selection of other dishes (50-120kr), head to the cafeteria-style **Svarta Björn ❷,** Hj. Lundbohmsv. 42, across the street from the Stadshus and the clock tower. (☎157 90. Open July-Aug. M-F 8am-9pm, Sa-Su 11am-7pm; Sept.-June M-F 6:30am-7pm, Sa-Su 11am-3pm. Cash only.) **Kaffekoppen ❶,** Föreningsg. 13B, serves up light meals and various permutations of wraps *(souvas)* from 37kr, along with mugs of hot chocolate (25kr) the size of small mixing bowls. (☎180 61. Open M 9am-6pm, Tu-Sa 9am-10pm, Su 10am-10pm. MC/V.) Get groceries at **ICA** in the central square. (Open M-F 9am-7pm, Sa 10am-4pm, Su 11am-4pm. MC/V.)

Connex **trains** run to Narvik, NOR (3hr., 3-4 per day, 221kr) and Stockholm (18hr., 3-4 per day, from 430kr). **Flights** to Stockholm depart from Kiruna Flygplats. (KRN; ☎680 00. 3-4 per day; from 500kr, students from 350kr.) The **tourist office,** L. Janssonsgat. 17, is in the Folkets Hus. Walk from the train station, follow the footpath through the tunnel, and go up the stairs through the park to the top of the hill. The office arranges dogsled excursions and moose safaris year-round. (☎188 80; www.lappland.se. Luggage storage 20kr per bag. Internet 25kr per 20min. Open mid-June to Aug. M-F 8:30am-8pm, Sa-Su 8:30am-6pm; Sept. to mid-June M-F 8:30am-5pm, Sa 8:30am-2pm. AmEx/MC/V.) The town library, Biblioteksg. 4, offers free **Internet.** Expect lines in winter. (☎707 50. Open June-Aug. M-Th 1-6pm, F 1-5pm; Sept.-May M-Th 10am-7pm, F 2:30-6pm, Sa-Su 11am-3pm.) **Postal Code:** 98122.

DAYTRIP FROM KIRUNA: JUKKASJÄRVI. Nestled on the shores of the Torne River, Jukkasjärvi (pop. 800) has left much of its peacefulness behind as it transforms into one of the country's hottest tourist spots—particularly when it gets below freezing. The main reason for the sudden acclaim is the **Icehotel,** which crystallizes anew each November only to melt back into the river in May. The hotel is open for tours in winter, while summertime visitors get a taste of the cold by sipping drinks (45-105kr) from ice glasses inside the hotel's ice storage center, which is kept at the same temperature as the wintertime interior. (☎668 00; www.icehotel.com. Open mid-June to Aug. daily 10am-6pm; Dec.-Apr. M-F 10am-5pm. 130kr, students 120kr. AmEx/DC/MC/V.) The hotel's affiliated museum, **The Homestead,** is a short boat ride or 10min. walk away. The tour takes you into a 19th-century family home and a small Sámi exhibit. (☎668 00. Open daily 10am-6pm. Tours daily 10am-5pm, on the hour. 40kr. MC/V.) Across the street lies the fascinating open-air **Sámi Siida Kulturcenter,** where guides intermingle discussions of their struggle to preserve the Sámi cultural identity with reindeer lassoing lessons. Several reindeer are kept on site and can be petted and fed. (Open daily early June to mid-Aug. 10am-6pm. Tours daily 11am, 12:30, 2, 3:30, 5pm. 90kr. Cash only.)

Budget lodgings do not exist in Jukkasjärvi, unless you find a good spot to pitch your tent. The only restaurants are in the Icehotel and museums. In the summer, **Sámi Siida ❷** has traditional Sámi dishes like char and reindeer meat platters (70-75kr) and sandwiches (25-35kr) inside a cozy tent lined with reindeer skins. The **Homestead Restaurant ❸** serves sandwiches (55-95kr), and has a 75kr lunch buffet 11:30am-2:30pm. (Open daily 10am-10pm. MC/V.) Just up the main road, **Konsum** is a well-equipped supermarket. (Open M-F 9am-noon and 1-7pm, Sa 9am-2pm, Su 2-5pm. MC/V.) **Bus** #501 goes to the Kiruna bus station (40min., 2-3 per day, 27kr, 51kr return.) Wireless **Internet** is available for those with their own laptops at the Icehotel reception. **Postal Code:** 98191.

SWITZERLAND
(SCHWEIZ, SUISSE, SVIZZERA)

Switzerland's gorgeous lakes and formidable peaks entice outdoor enthusiasts from around the globe. Three-fifths of the country is dominated by mountains: the Jura cover the northwest bordering France, and the Alps stretch gracefully across the lower half, with the eastern Rhaetian Alps bordering Austria. While stereotypes of Switzerland as a country of bankers and watchmakers are to some extent true, an energetic youth culture belies its staid reputation. Although the country is not known for being cheap, the best things—warm hospitality and Europe's most impressive Alpine playland—remain priceless.

DISCOVER SWITZERLAND: SUGGESTED ITINERARIES

THREE DAYS. Experience the great outdoors at **Interlaken** (1 day; p. 999), and then head to **Luzern** (1 day; p. 1007) for the perfect combination of city culture and natural splendor before jetting to international **Geneva** (1 day; p. 1014).

ONE WEEK. Begin in **Luzern** (1 day), where your vision of a typical Swiss city will, strangely, be all too true. Then head to the capital, **Bern** (1 day; p. 996), before getting your adventure thrills in **Interlaken** (1 day). Get a taste of Italian Switzerland in **Locarno** (1 day; p. 1022), then traverse northern Italy to reach **Zermatt** (1 day; p. 1013). End your trip in the cosmopolitan city of **Geneva** (2 days).

TWO WEEKS. Start in **Geneva** (2 days), then check out **Lausanne** (1 day; p. 1019) and **Montreux** (1 day; p. 1020). Tackle the Matterhorn in **Zermatt** (1 day) and keep hiking above **Interlaken** (1 day). Bask in **Locarno's** Mediterranean climate (1 day) then explore the **Swiss National Park** (1 day; p. 1013). Head to **Zürich** (2 days; p. 1002) and **Luzern** (1 day). Unwind in tiny, romantic **Stein am Rhein** (2 day; p. 1008) and then return to civilization via the capital, **Bern** (1 day).

ESSENTIALS

FACTS AND FIGURES

Official Name: Swiss Confederation.

Capital: Bern.

Major Cities: Basel, Geneva, Zürich.

Population: 7,489,000 (65% German, 18% French, 10% Italian).

Time Zone: GMT +1.

Languages: German, French, Italian, Romansch.

Religions: Roman Catholic (46%), Protestant (40%), other or unaffiliated (14%).

WHEN TO GO

During ski season—from November to March—prices double in eastern Switzerland and travelers need reservations months ahead. The situation reverses in the summer, especially July and August, when the flatter, western half of Switzerland fills with vacationers and hikers. A good budget option is to travel during the shoulder season: sights and accommodations are cheaper and less crowded May-June and September-October. Many mountain towns throughout Switzerland shut down completely in May and June, though, so call ahead to make sure that the attractions you want to visit will be open.

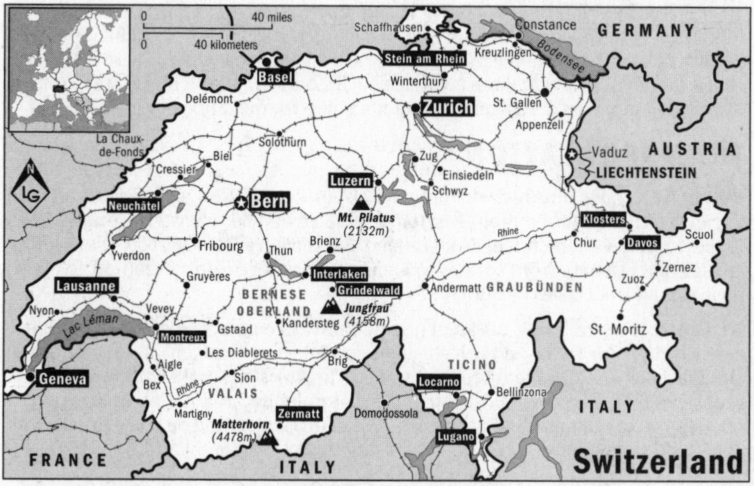

DOCUMENTS AND FORMALITIES

EMBASSIES. Most foreign embassies are in **Bern** (p. 996). Swiss embassies abroad include: **Australia,** 7 Melbourne Ave., Forrest, Canberra, ACT 2603 (☎02 6162 8400); **Canada,** 5 Marlborough Ave., Ottawa, ON K1N 8E6 (☎613-235-1837); **Ireland,** 6 Ailesbury Rd., Ballsbridge, Dublin 4 (☎353 12 18 63 82); **New Zealand,** 22 Panama St., Wellington 6001 (☎04 472 15 93); **UK,** 16-18 Montagu Pl., London W1H 2BQ (☎020 76 16 60 00); **US,** 2900 Cathedral Ave., NW, Washington, D.C. 20008-3499 (☎202-745-7900).

VISA AND ENTRY INFORMATION. EU citizens do not need a visa. Citizens of Australia, Canada, New Zealand, and the US do not need a visa for stays of up to 90 days. Switzerland is not a member of the EU.

TOURIST SERVICES AND MONEY

EMERGENCY	**Police:** ☎117. **Ambulance:** ☎144. **Fire:** ☎118.

TOURIST OFFICES. Branches of the **Swiss National Tourist Office,** designated by a blue "i" sign, exist in nearly every town in Switzerland; most agents speak English. The official tourism website for Switzerland is www.myswitzerland.com.

MONEY. The Swiss monetary unit is the **Swiss Franc (SFr/CHF),** which is divided into 100 *centimes* (called *Rappen* in German Switzerland). Coins come in 5, 10, 20, and 50 *centimes* and 1, 2, and 5SFr; bills come in 10, 20, 50, 100, 500, and

SWISS FRANC (SFR)		
	AUS$1 = 0.96SFR	1SFR = AUS$1.05
	CDN$1 = 1.06SFR	1SFR = CDN$0.94
	EUR€1 = 1.55SFR	1SFR = EUR€0.65
	NZ$1 = 0.88SFR	1SFR = NZ$1.14
	UK£1 = 2.27SFR	1SFR = UK£0.44
	US$1 = 1.26SFR	1SFR = US$0.80

1000SFr. Switzerland is not cheap; if you stay in hostels and prepare your own food, expect to spend 55-80SFr per day. Generally, it's cheaper to exchange money in Switzerland than at home. ATMs offer the best exchange rates. There is no **value added tax (VAT),** although there is often a small tourist tax for a hostel stay. **Gratuity** is included in prices at restaurants, but it's polite to round up your bill 1-2SFr.

TRANSPORTATION

BY PLANE. Major international airports are in Bern (BRN), Geneva (GVA), and Zürich (ZRH). From London, **easyJet** (☎0871 244 23 66; www.easyjet.com) has flights to Geneva and Zürich. From Ireland, **Aer Lingus** (☎0818 365 000; www.aerlingus.ie) sells tickets from Dublin to Geneva. For more information on flying to Switzerland from other locations, see p. 42.

BY TRAIN. Federal **(SBB, CFF)** and private railways connect most towns, with frequent trains. For times and prices, check online (www.sbb.ch). **Eurail, Europass,** and **Inter Rail** are all valid on federal trains. The **SwissPass,** sold worldwide, offers four, eight, 15, 21, or 30 consecutive days of unlimited rail travel. In addition, it entitles you to unlimited public transportation in 36 cities and on some private railways and lake steamers. (2nd class 4-day pass US$185, 8-day US$264, 15-day US$322, 21-day US$374, 1-month US$415.)

BY BUS. PTT PostBuses, a barrage of government-run yellow coaches, connect rural villages and towns that trains don't service. **SwissPasses** are valid on many buses; **Eurail** passes are not. Even with the SwissPass, you might have to pay 5-10SFr extra if you're riding certain buses.

BY CAR. With armies of mechanized road crews ready to remove snow at a moment's notice, roads at altitudes of up to 1500m generally remain open throughout winter. The speed limit is 50kph in cities, 80kph on open roads, and 120kph on highways. Many small towns forbid cars to enter; some require special permits or restrict driving hours. Call ☎140 for roadside assistance.

BY BIKE. Cycling, though strenuous, is a splendid way to see the country; most train stations rent bikes and let you return them at another station. The **Touring Club Suisse,** Chemin de Blandonnet 4, Case Postale 820, 1214 Vernier (☎022 417 27 27; www.tcs.ch), is a good source for maps and route descriptions.

KEEPING IN TOUCH

PHONE CODES	**Country code:** 41. **International dialing prefix:** 00. For more information on how to place international calls, see inside back cover.

EMAIL AND THE INTERNET. Most Swiss cities, as well as a number of smaller towns, have at least one Internet cafe with web access available for about 5-12SFr per hour. Hostels and restaurants frequently offer Internet access as well, but it seldom comes for free: rates can climb as high as 15SFr per hour.

TELEPHONE. Whenever possible, use a calling card for international phone calls, as long-distance rates are often exorbitant for national phone services. For info about using mobile phones abroad, see p. 29. Most pay phones in Switzerland accept only prepaid phone cards, available at kiosks, post offices, and train stations. Direct access numbers include: **AT&T** (☎0800 89 00 11); **British Telecom** (☎0800 55 25 44); **Canada Direct** (☎0800 55 83 30); **MCI WorldPhone** (☎0800 89 02 22); **Sprint** (☎0800 899 777); **Telecom New Zealand** (☎0800 55 64 11).

MAIL. Airmail from Switzerland averages four to seven days to North America, although times are unpredictable from smaller towns. Domestic letters take one to three days. Address mail to be held according to the following example: First name LAST NAME, *Postlagernde Briefe*, CH-8021 Zürich, SWITZERLAND.

ACCOMMODATIONS AND CAMPING

SWITZERLAND	❶	❷	❸	❹	❺
ACCOMMODATIONS	under 26SFr	26-42SFr	42-65SFr	65-125SFr	over 125SFr

There are **hostels** (*Jugendherbergen* in German, *Auberges de Jeunesse* in French, *Ostelli* in Italian) in all big cities in Switzerland as well as in most small towns. **Schweizer Jugendherbergen** (SJH; www.youthhostel.ch) runs HI hostels throughout Switzerland. Non-HI members can stay in any HI hostel, where beds are usually 30-44SFr; members typically receive a 6SFr discount. The more informal **Swiss Backpackers (SB)** organization (www.backpacker.ch) has 31 hostels aimed at the young, foreign traveler interested in socializing. Most Swiss **campgrounds** are not idyllic refuges but large plots glutted with RVs. Prices average 12-20SFr per tent site and 6-9SFr per extra person. **Hotels** and **pensions** tend to charge at least 65-80SFr for a single room and 80-120SFr for a double. The cheapest have *Gasthof*, *Gästehaus*, or *Hotel-Garni* in the name. **Privatzimmer** (rooms in a family home) run about 30-60SFr per person. Breakfast is included at most hotels, pensions, and *Privatzimmer*.

HIKING AND SKIING. Nearly every town has **hiking trails;** consult the local tourist office. Luzern (p. 1007), Interlaken (p. 999), Grindelwald (p. 1001), and Zermatt (p. 1013) offer particularly good hiking opportunities. Trails are usually marked with either red-white-red markers (only sturdy boots and hiking poles needed) or blue-white-blue markers (mountaineering equipment needed). **Skiing** in Switzerland is often less expensive than in North America—if you avoid pricey resorts. **Ski passes** run 40-70SFr per day, 100-300SFr per week; a week of lift tickets, equipment rental, lessons, lodging, and *demi-pension* (breakfast plus one other meal) averages 475SFr. **Summer skiing** is less common than it once was but is still available in a few towns such as Zermatt and Saas Fee.

FOOD AND DRINK

SWITZERLAND	❶	❷	❸	❹	❺
FOOD	under 9SFr	9-23SFr	23-32SFr	32-52SFr	over 52SFr

Switzerland is not for the lactose intolerant. The Swiss are serious about dairy products of all kinds, from rich and varied **cheeses** to decadent **milk chocolate**—even the major Swiss soft drink, **Rivella,** contains dairy. Swiss dishes vary from region to region. Bernese *Rösti*, a plateful of hash-brown potatoes, is prevalent in the German regions; cheese or meat **fondue** is popular in the French regions. Try Valaisian *raclette*, made by melting cheese over a fire, scraping it onto a baked potato, and garnishing it with meat or vegetables. Supermarkets **Migros** and **Co-op** double as cafeterias; stop in for a cheap meal and groceries. Each canton has its own local beer, which is often cheaper than Coca-Cola.

HOLIDAYS AND FESTIVALS

Holidays: New Year's Day (Jan. 1); Good Friday (Apr. 6); Easter Monday (Apr. 9); Labor Day (May 1); Swiss National Day (Aug. 1).

Festivals: Two raucous festivals are the *Fasnacht* (Carnival; late Feb. to early Mar.) in Basel and the *Escalade* (early Dec.) in Geneva. Music festivals occur throughout the summer, including Open-Air St. Gallen (late June) and the Montreux Jazz Festival (July).

BEYOND TOURISM

Although Switzerland's volunteer opportunities are limited, a number of ecotourism and rural development organizations allow you to give back to the country. Your best bet is to go through a placement service. Look for opportunities for short-term work on websites like www.emploi.ch.

Bergwald Projekt/Mountain Forest Project, Hauptstr. 24, 7014 Trin, Switzerland (☎41 81 630 4145; www.bergwaldprojekt.ch). Organizes week-long conservation projects in Austria, Germany, and Switzerland.

Workcamp Switzerland, Bastionweg 15, 4500 Solothurn, Switzerland (☎41 32 621 50 37; www.workcamp.ch). Offers 2-week-long sessions in which volunteers live in a group environment and work on a common community service project.

GERMAN SWITZERLAND

BERNESE OBERLAND

The peaks of the Bernese Oberland shelter a pristine wilderness that lends itself to discovery through scenic hikes up the mountains and around the twin lakes, the Thunersee and Brienzersee. Not surprisingly, the area's opportunities for paragliding, mountaineering, and whitewater rafting are unparalleled. North of the mountains lies tranquil Bern, Switzerland's capital and the heartbeat of the region.

BERN ☎031

Bern (pop. 127,000) has been Switzerland's capital since 1848, but don't expect fast tracks, power politics, or men in suits—the Bernese prefer to focus on the more leisurely things in life, nibbling the local Toblerone chocolate and lolling along the banks of the serpentine Aare.

TRANSPORTATION AND PRACTICAL INFORMATION. Bern's **airport** (**BRN;** ☎960 21 11) is 20min. from the city. A **bus** runs from the train station 50min. before each flight (10min., 14SFr). **Trains** run from the station at Bahnhofpl. to: Geneva (2hr., 3 per hr., 45SFr); Luzern (1½hr., every 30min., 30SFr); Munich, GER (6hr., 1 per hr., 124SFr); Paris, FRA (6hr., approx. 1 per hr., 115SFr); Salzburg, AUT (7¼hr., 2 per day, 142SFr); Zürich (1¼hr., every 30min., 45SFr). Local Bernmobil **buses** run 5:45am-midnight. (☎321 86 41. Single ride 3.20SFr, day pass 12SFr.) **Free bikes** are available from **Bern Rollt** at two locations, one at Bahnhofpl., in front of the station, and another on Zeugausg., near Waisenhauspl. (☎079 277 28 57; www.bernrollt.ch. Deposit of passport and 20SFr required. Open May-Oct. daily 7:30am-9:30pm.)

Most of medieval Bern lies in front of the train station and along the Aare River. Take extra caution in the parks around the Parliament (Bundeshaus), especially at night. The friendly staff at the **tourist office,** on the street level of the station, book hotel rooms and provide maps, both for free. (☎328 1212; www.berninfo.ch. Open June-Sept. daily 9am-8:30pm; Oct.-May M-Sa 9am-6:30pm, Su 10am-5pm.) The **post office** is at Schanzenpost 1, one block from the train station. (Open M-F 7:30am-9pm, Sa 8am-4pm, Su 4-9pm.) **Postal Codes:** CH-3000 to CH-3030.

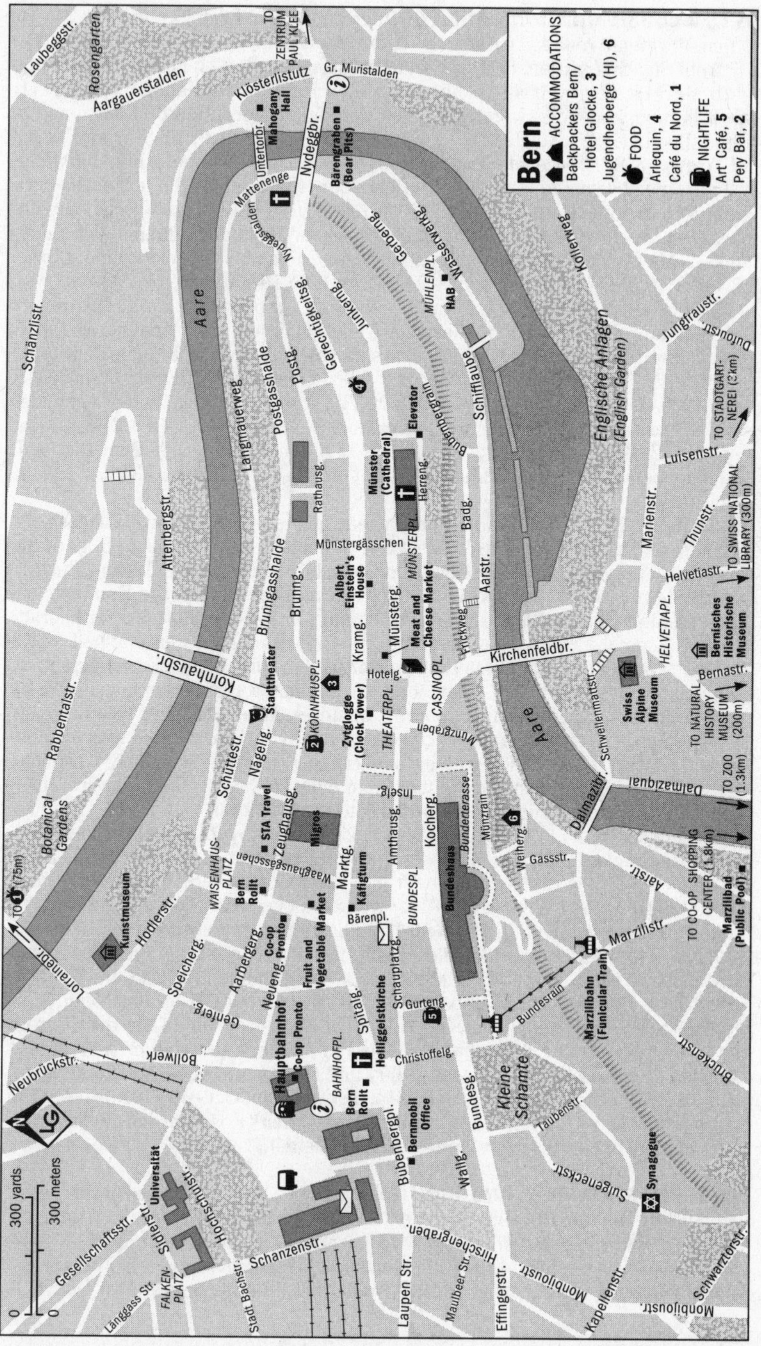

SWITZERLAND

ACCOMMODATIONS AND FOOD. In addition to hostels, check the tourist office for private rooms. To reach the **Backpackers Bern/Hotel Glocke ❷,** Rathausg. 75, from the train station, cross the tram lines and turn left on Spitalg., continuing onto Marktg. Turn left at Kornhauspl., then right on Rathausg. (☎311 3771; www.bernbackpackers.ch. Internet 2SFr per 15min. Reception 8-11:30am and 3-10pm. Dorms 31SFr; singles 75SFr; doubles 80SFr, with bath 160SFr. AmEx/DC/MC/V; min. 35SFr.) **Jugendherberge (HI) ❷,** boasts a free swimming pool. Weiherg. 4. From the station, go down Christoffelg.; take the stairs to the left of the park gates, go down the slope, and turn left on Weiherg. (☎311 6316; www.jugibern.ch. Breakfast included. Reception June to mid-Sept. 7-10am and 3pm-midnight; mid-Sept. to May 7-10am and 5pm-midnight. Closed 2nd and 3rd weeks of Jan. Dorms 38-43SFr; singles 56-61SFr; doubles 92-102SFr. 6SFr HI discount. MC/V.)

Markets sell produce daily from May through October at Bärenpl. and every Tuesday and Saturday on Bundespl. A friendly couple owns **Arlequin ❶,** Gerechtigkeitsg. 51, which serves Swiss dishes like meat fondue (35SFr) in addition to sandwiches. (☎311 3946. Sandwiches 4-9SFr. Open Tu-W 10am-11:30pm, Th-F 10am-1:30am, Sa 11:30am-11pm. AmEx/MC/V.) A diverse crowd socializes under stained glass and on the terrace at **Café du Nord ❷,** Lorrainestr. 2. (☎332 2328. Meat entrees 22-32SFr. Pasta 18-25SFr. Open M-F 8am-12:30am, Sa 9am-12:30am. Kitchen open M-Sa 11:30am-2pm and 6:30-10pm, Su 4:30-11:30pm. MC/V.)

SIGHTS. The Swiss national parliament meets in the massive **Bundeshaus,** which rises high over the Aare while water tumbles from fountains in front of the entrance. (www.parlament.ch. 45min. tour every hr. M-Sa 9-11am and 2-4pm. English-language tour usually 2pm; arrive 30min. before. Free.) From the Bundeshaus, Kocherg. and Herreng. lead to the 15th-century Protestant **Münster** (Cathedral); above the main entrance, a golden sculpture depicts the torments of hell. For a fantastic view of the city, climb the Münster's 100m spire. (Open Easter-Oct. Tu-Sa 10am-5pm; Nov.-Easter Tu-F 10am-noon and 2-4pm, Sa 10am-noon and 2-5pm, Su 11am-2pm. Tower 4SFr.) Hidden in a row of stores, **Albert Einstein's house,** Kramg. 49, where he conceived the theory of general relativity, is now filled with his photos and letters. (☎312 0091; www.einstein-bern.ch. Open Mar.-Sept. daily 10am-5pm; Oct. to mid-Dec. Tu-F 10am-5pm, Sa 10am-4pm. 6SFr, students 4.50SFr.) Several steep walkways lead down from the Bundeshaus to the **Aare River.**

A recent addition to Bern's plethora of museums is the **Zentrum Paul Klee,** Monument im Fruchtland 3, which houses the world's largest Klee collection in a ripple-shaped building that's fluidly built into the encompassing hillside. Take bus #12 to Zentrum Paul Klee. (☎359 0101; www.zpk.org. Open Tu-Su 10am-5pm, Th 10am-9pm. 14Fr, students 12Fr.) Near Lorrainebrücke, the **Kunstmuseum,** Hodlerstr. 8-12, has paintings from the Middle Ages to the contemporary era and features a smattering of big 20th-century names: Giacometti, Kirchner, Picasso, and Pollock. (☎328 0944; www.kunstmuseumbern.ch. Open Tu 10am-9pm, W-Su 10am-5pm. 7SFr, students 5SFr. Special exhibitions up to 18SFr.) At the east side of the river, across the Nydeggbr., lie the **Bärengraben** (Bear Pits), where gawking crowds amuse themselves by tossing fruit pieces (3SFr) into the cement abodes of three European brown bears. (Open daily June-Sept. 9:30am-5pm; Oct.-May 10am-4pm.) The path up the hill to the left leads to the **Rosengarten** (Rose Garden), which provides visitors one of the best views of Bern's Altstadt.

ENTERTAINMENT AND NIGHTLIFE. Check out *Bewegungsmelder*, available at the tourist office, for events. July's **Gurten Festival** (www.gurtenfestival.ch) draws young and energetic crowds and has attracted such luminaries as Bob Dylan, Elvis Costello, and Björk, while jazz-lovers arrive in early May for the **International Jazz Festival** (www.jazzfestivalbern.ch). Bern's best-known festival is probably the off-the-wall **Onion Market,** on the fourth Monday in November. The orange grove at **Stadtgärtnerei Elfenau** (take tram #19, dir.: Elfenau, to Luternauweg) has free Sunday concerts in summer. From mid-July to mid-August, **Orange-Cinema** (☎0800 078 078; www.orangecinema.ch) screens recent films outdoors; tickets are available from the tourist office in the train station.

At night, the fashionable folk linger in the Altstadt's bars and cafes while a leftist crowd gathers under the gargoyles of the Lorrainebrücke, behind the station down Bollwerk. When new DJs come to town, they can invariably be found spinning for the fashionable crowd at **Art' Café,** Gurteng. 6, a cafe by day and club by night with huge windows overlooking the street. (☎318 20 70; www.artcafe.ch. Open M-W 7am-8pm, Th-Sa 7am-2:30am, Su 7am-12:30pm. Cash only.) The candlelit, all-wood interior at **Pery Bar,** Schmiedenpl. 3, provides a romantic setting for early-evening drinks before the DJs begin spinning later in the night. (☎311 59 08. Beer 5.50SFr. Wine 7SFr. DJs W-Sa. Open M-W 5pm-1:30am, Th 5pm-2:30am, F 5pm-3:30am, Sa 4pm-3:30am. AmEx/MC/V.)

JUNGFRAU REGION

The most famous (and most visited) region of the Bernese Oberland, Jungfrau draws tourists with glorious hiking trails, turquoise glacier lakes, and permanently snow-capped peaks. From Interlaken, the valley splits at the foot of the Jungfrau Mountain: the eastern valley contains Grindelwald, with easy access to two glaciers, while the western valley harbors many smaller towns, each with unique hiking opportunities. The two valleys are divided by an easily hikeable ridge.

INTERLAKEN ☎033

Interlaken (pop. 21,000) lies between the Thunersee and the Brienzersee at the foot of the largest mountains in Switzerland. The countless hiking trails, raging rivers, peaceful lakes, and skyward-reaching peaks have turned the town into one of Switzerland's prime tourist attractions and its top adventure-sport destination.

TRANSPORTATION AND PRACTICAL INFORMATION. Westbahnhof (☎826 47 50) and Ostbahnhof (☎828 73 19) have **trains** to: Basel (2-3hr., 1-2 per hr., 53SFr); Bern (1hr., 1-2 per hr., 25SFr); Geneva (61SFr); Luzern (2hr., 1 per hr., 30SFr); Lugano/Locarno (74SFr); Zürich (2hr., every 2hr., 61SFr). Ostbahnhof also sends trains to Grindelwald (June-Sept. 2 per hr., Sept.-May 1 per hr.; 9.80SFr).

The **tourist office,** Höheweg 37, in Hotel Metropole, gives out maps and books hotel rooms, both for free. (☎826 53 00; www.interlakentourism.ch. Open July to mid-Sept. M-F 8am-7pm, Sa 8am-5pm, Su 10am-noon and 5-7pm; May-June M-F 8am-6pm, Sa 8am-4pm; mid-Sept. to Oct. M-F 8am-6pm, Sa 8am-1pm; Nov.-Apr. M-F 8am-noon and 1:30-6pm, Sa 9am-noon.) Both train stations rent **bikes.** (31SFr per day. Open daily 7am-7:30pm.) For **weather info,** call ☎828 79 31. In an **emergency,** call the **police** (☎117) or the **hospital** (☎826 26 26). The **post office** is at Marktg. 1. (Open M-F 8am-noon and 1:45-6pm, Sa 8:30-11am.) **Postal Code:** CH-3800.

ACCOMMODATIONS AND FOOD. Interlaken is a backpacking hot spot, especially in the summer months, so hostels tend to fill up quickly; reserve more than a month ahead. Diagonally across the Höhenmatte from the tourist office, the friendly and low-key **Backpackers Villa Sonnenhof ❷,** Alpenstr. 16, includes free admission to a nearby spa for the duration of your stay. (☎826 7171. Mountain bike rental 28SFr per day. Breakfast included. Laundry 10SFr. Internet 1SFr per 5min., free wireless. Reception 7:30-11am and 4-10pm. May to mid-Sept. and mid-Dec. to mid-Jan. dorms 33-40SFr; doubles 96-108SFr; triples 129-144SFr. Mid-Sept. to mid.-Dec. and mid-Jan. to Apr. 29-37/88-105/117-137SFr. AmEx/MC/V.) By contrast, the lively **Balmer's Herberge ❶,** Hauptstr. 23, Switzerland's oldest private hostel (est. 1945), is a place to party, not to relax. Services include mountain bike rental (35SFr per day), nightly movies, free sleds, and an extremely popular bar. (☎822 1961. Breakfast included. Internet 12SFr per hr. Reception in summer 24hr., in winter 6:30-10am and 4:30-10pm. Dorms 25-29SFr; doubles 64-77SFr; triples 81-104SFr; quads 124-132SFr. AmEx/MC/V.) At the friendly **Walter's Bed and Breakfast Guest House ❶,** Oelestr. 35, enormous rooms with hardwood floors and views of the Alps await. From the Ostbahnhof, follow Allmendstr. until it becomes Oelestr. (☎822 7688; walter.rooms@gmx.ch. Breakfast 7SFr. Laundry 6SFr. Internet 3SFr per 15min. Reception noon-8pm. Doubles 46SFr; quads 80SFr. Cash only.) **Funny Farm ❶,** just off Hauptstr., attracts partiers with outdoor bonfires, a climbing wall temptingly situated above a swimming pool, and a crazy Saturday night beach volleyball competition. (☎079 652 6127; www.funny-farm.ch. Laundry 10SFr. Internet 5SFr per 25min. Reception 24hr. Dorms 20-29SFr, with bath 30-39SFr. MC/V.)

My Little Thai ❷, Hauptstr. 19, fills with hungry backpackers in the evening. (☎821 1017. Pad thai 15-21SFr. Vegetarian options available. Internet 8SFr per hr. Open daily 11:30am-10pm. Cash only.) Anything but local food is also to be found at **El Azteca ❸,** Jungfraustr. 30, which serves cactus salad (16SFr), fajitas (24-35SFr), and other Mexican fare. (☎822 7131. Open daily noon-3pm and 6-11pm. AmEx/MC/V.) There are **Migros** and **Coop** supermarkets by both train stations. (Open M-Th 8am-6:30pm, F 8am-9pm, Sa 7:30am-5pm.)

SWITZERLAND

OUTDOOR ACTIVITIES. **Alpin Raft,** Hauptstr. 7, the most established company in Interlaken, has qualified and entertaining guides and offers a wide range of activities, including paragliding (150SFr), river rafting (95-110SFr), skydiving (380SFr), and hang gliding (185SFr). They also offer two different types of **bungee jumping:** at the 85m Glacier Bungee Jump (125SFr), thrill-seekers leap off a ledge above the Lutschine River. At the Alpin Rush Jump (165SFr), jumpers attached to one of the longest bungee cords in the world leap out of a gondola 134m above a lake, surrounded by the green peaks of the Simmental Valley and herds of grazing cattle. There are daily trips to Glacier Bungee, and the bus to Alpin Rush departs Monday, Wednesday, Friday, and Saturday at 4:30pm. One of the most popular adventure activities at Alpin Raft is **canyoning** (110-170SFr), which involves rappelling down a series of gorge faces, jumping off cliffs into pools of churning water, and swinging, Tarzan-style, from ropes and zip cords through the canyon. All prices include transportation to and from any hostel in Interlaken, and usually a beer upon completion. **Outdoor Interlaken,** Hauptstr. 15 (☎826 7719; www.outdoor-interlaken.ch), offers many of the same activities as Alpin Raft at similar prices, as well as **rock-climbing** lessons (½-day 89SFr) and whitewater **kayaking** tours (½-day 155SFr). **Swissraft,** Jungfraustr. 72 (☎821 6650; www.swissraft.ch), offers the cheapest river rafting in Interlaken (½-day 95-110SFr), as well as **hydro-speeding** (aided body-surfing down the river; 120SFr). At **Skydive Xdream,** you can skydive with one of the best in the world; the owner, Stefan Heuser, was on the Swiss skydiving team for 12 years and won three world championship medals. Skydivers can make their ascent in a glass-walled helicopter, then jump from a standing position—an exhilarating option that's very different from the usual sitting take-off that skydivers make from planes. (☎079 759 34 83; www.justjump.ch. 380SFr per tandem plane jump; 430SFr per tandem helicopter jump. Open Apr.-Oct. Pick-ups 9am and 1pm, Sa-Su also 4pm. Call for winter availability.) **Swiss Alpine Guides** offers **ice climbing,** running full-day trips to a glacier and providing all the equipment needed to scale walls and rappel into icy crevasses. (☎822 6000; www.swissalpineguides.ch. Trips May-Nov. daily, weather permitting. 160SFr.)

Interlaken's most traversed trail climbs to the **Harder Kulm** (1310m). From the Ostbahnhof, head toward town, take the first road bridge right across the river, and follow the yellow signs that later give way to white-red-white rock markings. From the top, signs lead back down to the Westbahnhof. The hike should be about 2½hr. up and 1½hr. down. In summer, a funicular runs from the trailhead near the Ostbahnhof to the top. (Runs May to mid-Oct. daily; 15SFr, round-trip 24SFr. 25% Eurail and 50% SwissPass discount.) For flatter trails, turn left from the train station and left before the bridge, then follow the canal over to the nature reserve on the shore of the Thunersee. The trail winds along the Lombach River, through pastures at the base of the Harder Kulm, and back toward town (3hr.).

> **!** Interlaken's adventure sports industry is thrilling, but accidents do happen. On July 27, 1999, 21 tourists were killed by a sudden flash flood while canyoning. Be aware that you participate in all adventure sports at your own risk.

GRINDELWALD ☎033

Crouching beneath the north face of the Eiger and peering up at the Jungfraujoch, Grindelwald (pop. 4500) is the launching point to the only glaciers accessible by foot in the Bernese Oberland. The **Bergführerbüro** (Mountain Guide's Office), in the sports center near the tourist office, sells hiking maps and coordinates glacier walks, ice climbing, and mountaineering. (☎853 1200. Open June-Oct. M-F 9am-noon and 2-5pm.) The **Untere Grindelwaldgletscher** (Lower Glacier) hike is moderately steep (5hr.). For the trailhead, walk away from the train station on the main street and follow the signs downhill to Pfinstegg. Hikers can either walk the first forested section of the trail (1hr.), following signs up to Pfinstegg., or take a funicular (July to mid-Sept. 8am-7pm; mid-Sept. to June 9am-5:30pm; 12SFr, SwissPass 9SFr). From the hut, signs lead to Stieregg., a hut that sells food. Pet goats greet you at the **Jugendherberge (HI) ❷**, where terraces offer spectacular views of the Jungfraujoch. To reach the lodge, head left out of the train station for 400m, then cut uphill to the right and follow the steep trail all the way up the hill. (☎853 1009; www.youthhostel.ch/grindelwald. Breakfast included. Reception 7:30-10am and 3-11pm. Dorms 38SFr; doubles 90-120SFr. 6SFr HI discount. AmEx/MC/V.) **Grindelwald Downtown Lodge ❶** is conveniently located 200m past the tourist office, to the right of the train station. It offers great views of the mountains, as well as free entrance to the public swimming pool. (☎853 0825; www.downtown-lodge.ch. Breakfast 6SFr. Dorms 25-35SFr; doubles 70-90SFr. AmEx/MC/V.) Hotel Eiger, on Hauptstr. near the tourist office, houses a bar and two restaurants, **Memory** and **Barry's.** (☎854 3131. Memory open daily 8:30am-midnight, Barry's open daily 6pm-midnight, bar open daily 5pm-1:30am. AmEx/MC/V.) The Jungfraubahn **train** runs to Grindelwald from Interlaken's Ostbahnhof (35min., 1 per hr., 9.80SFr). The **tourist office,** in the Sport-Zentrum 200m to the right of the station, provides various services, including chairlift information and a list of free guided excursions. (☎854 1212. Open July-Aug. M-F 8am-noon and 1:30-6pm, Sa 8am-noon and 1:30-5pm, Su 9am-noon and 1:30-5pm; Sept.-June M-F 9am-noon and 2-5pm, Sa-Su 2-5pm.) **Postal Code:** CH-3818.

CENTRAL SWITZERLAND

Considerably more populous than the mountainous cantons to the south, the central parts of Switzerland overflow with all manner of culture. Innovative museums, enchanting castles, and lovely old towns in Zürich and Luzern add richness to life along the lake shore.

ZÜRICH ☎044

Battalions of briefcase-toting executives charge daily through the world's largest gold exchange and fourth-largest stock exchange, bringing with them enough money to keep Zürich's upper-crust boutiques thriving. A walk through Zürich's student quarter immerses you in the energetic counter-culture that encouraged Switzerland's great philosophers and artists of the past, only footsteps away from the showy capitalism of the Bahnhofstr. shopping district.

TRANSPORTATION

Flights: Unique Airport (**ZRH;** ☎816 22 11; www.zurich-airport.com) is a major stop for Swiss International Airlines (☎084 885 20 00; www.swiss.com). Daily connections to **Frankfurt, London, New York,** and **Paris.** Trains connect the airport to the Hauptbahnhof in the city center. (Every 10-20min., 5.80SFr. Eurail and SwissPass valid.)

Trains: To: **Basel** (1¼hr., 1-2 per hr., 30SFr); **Bern** (1¼hr., 1-2 per hr., 45SFr); **Geneva** (3hr., 1 per hr., 77SFr); **Luzern** (1hr., 2 per hr., 22SFr); **Milan, ITA** (4hr., 1 per hr., 72-87SFr); **Munich, GER** (5hr., 1 per hr., 90SFr); **Paris, FRA** (5hr.; 1 per hr.; 112-140SFr, under 26 86SFr); **Salzburg, AUT** (5hr., 1 per hr., 115SFr); **Vienna, AUT** (9hr., 1 per hr., 134SFr).

Public Transportation: Trams criss-cross the city, originating at the Hauptbahnhof. Tickets valid for 1hr. cost 3.80SFr (press the blue button on automatic ticket machines); tickets for short rides (valid for 30min.) cost 2.40SFr (yellow button). Police will fine you 60SFr if you ride without a ticket. If you plan to ride several times, buy a 24hr. **Tageskarte** (7.60SFr), valid on trams, buses, and ferries. **Night buses** (5SFr ticket valid the whole night) run from the city center to outlying areas (F-Su).

Car Rental: The tourist office offers a 20% discount and free upgrade deal with **Europcar** (☎804 46 46; www.europcar.ch). Prices start at 152SFr per day for 1-2 days with unlimited mileage. 20+. Branches at the airport (☎043 255 56 56); Josefstr. 53 (☎271 56 56); Lindenstr. 33 (☎383 17 47). Try to rent in the city; a 40% tax is added at the airport.

Bike Rental: Bike loans from **Züri Rollt** (☎043 288 34 00; www.zuerirollt.ch) are free for 6hr. at a time during business hours, otherwise 5Sfr per day and 20Sfr per night. Pick up a bike from these locations: Globus City, the green hut on the edge of the garden between Bahnhofstr. and Löwenstr.; Opernhaus, by the opera house past Bellevuepl.; Velogate, across from Hauptbahnhof's tracks next to the Landesmuseum castle. Passport and 20SFr deposit. Open May-Oct. 7:30am-9:30pm. **Zürich by Bike** runs bike day tours (2½hr.) of the city departing from Opernhaus F-Su 10am, and departing from Velogate F-Sa evenings. (☎308 70 16; www.zurichbybike.ch. 25SFr, students 17SFr. Cash only.)

TIP **LOOSE CHANGE.** Travelers should keep change on them for local transportation on buses in Switzerland. You have to buy your tickets from machines before you get on the bus, and the machines don't give change.

ORIENTATION AND PRACTICAL INFORMATION

Zürich is in north-central Switzerland, close to the German border and on some of the lowest land in the entire country. The **Limmat River** splits the city down the middle on its way to the **Zürichsee.** The **Hauptbahnhof** (train station) lies on the western bank and marks the beginning of **Bahnhofstraße,** the city's main shopping street. Two-thirds of the way down Bahnhofstr. lies **Paradeplatz,** the banking center of Zürich, marking the beginning of the last stretch of the shopping street reserved only for those with trust funds. The eastern side of the river is dominated by the university district, which stretches above the narrow **Niederdorfstraße** and pulses with bars, restaurants, and hostels.

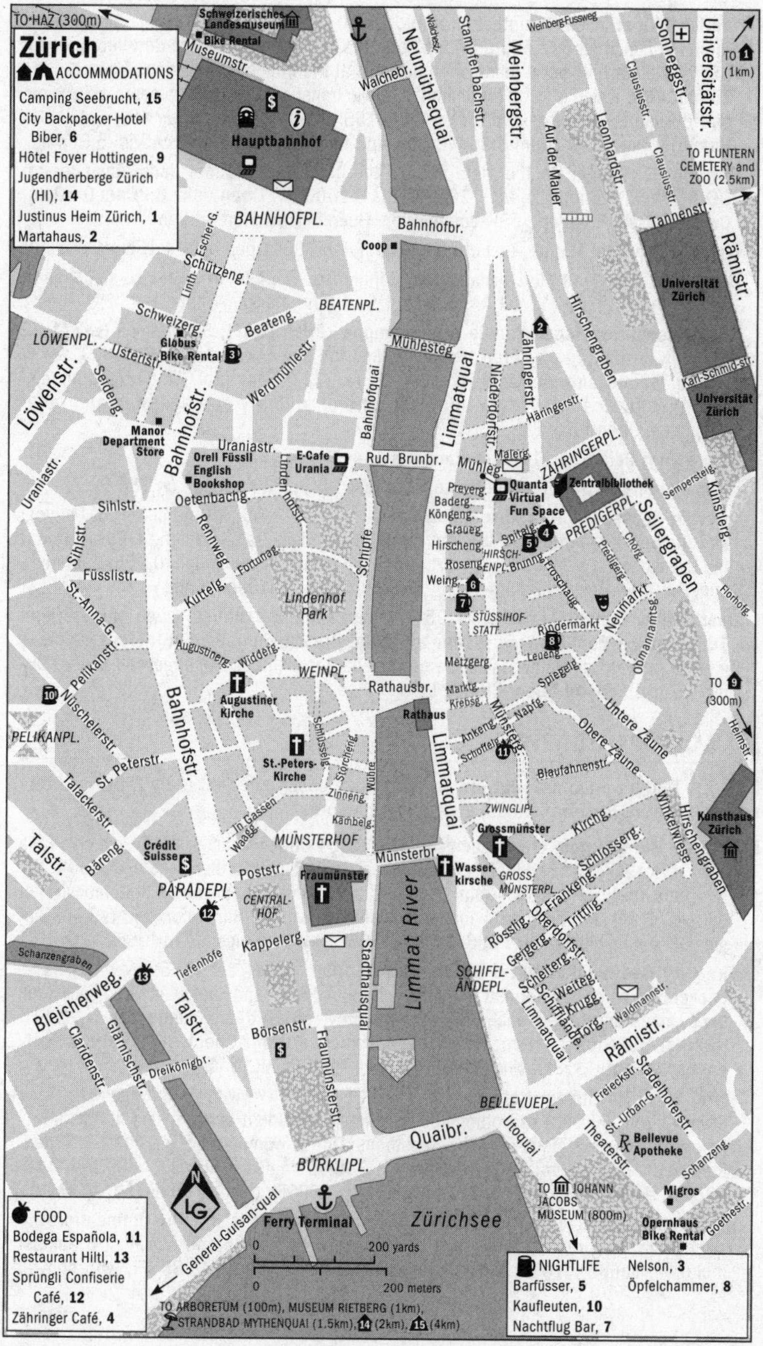
Zürich
ACCOMMODATIONS
Camping Seebrucht, 15
City Backpacker-Hotel Biber, 6
Hôtel Foyer Hottingen, 9
Jugendherberge Zürich (HI), 14
Justinus Heim Zürich, 1
Martahaus, 2
FOOD
Bodega Española, 11
Restaurant Hiltl, 13
Sprüngli Confiserie Café, 12
Zähringer Café, 4
NIGHTLIFE
Barfüsser, 5
Kaufleuten, 10
Nachtflug Bar, 7
Nelson, 3
Öpfelchammer, 8
TO HAZ (300m)
Schweizerisches Landesmuseum
Bike Rental
Museumstr.
Hauptbahnhof
BAHNHOFPL.
Bahnhofbr.
Coop
Walchebr.
Neumühlequai
Stampfenbachstr.
Weinbergstr.
Weinberg-Fussweg
Sonneggstr.
Universitätstr.
TO 1 (1km)
TO FLUNTERN CEMETERY and ZOO (2.5km)
Tannenstr.
Rämistr.
Universität Zürich
Karl-Schmid-str.
Leonhardstr.
Clausiusstr.
Auf der Mauer
Hirschengraben
Schützeng.
Linth-Escher-G.
BEATENPL.
Beateng.
Schweizerg.
LÖWENPL.
Globus Bike Rental
Usteristr.
Löwenstr.
Seideng.
Werdmühlestr.
Mühlesteg
Bahnhofquai
Limmatquai
Niederdorfstr.
Zähringerstr.
Häringerstr.
ZÄHRINGERPL.
Zentralbibliothek
Manor Department Store
Bahnhofstr.
Uraniastr.
Orell Füssli English Bookshop
E-Cafe Urania
Rud. Brunbr.
Mühleg.
Malerg.
Quanta Virtual Fun Space
Preyerg.
Baderg.
Köngeng.
Graueg.
Hirscheng.
Roseng.
Weing.
HIRSCH-ENPL.
Spitalg.
Brunng.
PREDIGERPL.
Seilergraben
Sempersteig
Künstlerg.
Predigerg.
Chorg.
Froschaug.
Neumarkt
Florhofg.
Oetenbachg.
Sihlstr.
Lindenhofstr.
Rennweg
Fortunag.
Schipfe
Lindenhof Park
Füsslistr.
Kuttelg.
St-Anna-G.
STÜSSIHOF-STATT
Rindermarkt
Obmannamtsg.
Augustinerg.
Widderg.
Pelikanstr.
WEINPL.
Metzgerg.
Leueng.
Spiegelg.
Augustiner Kirche
Rathausbr.
Marktg.
Krebsg.
Rathaus
TO 9 (300m)
Heimstr.
Nüschelerstr.
PELIKANPL.
Schlüsselg.
St.-Peters-Kirche
Storcheng.
Wühre
Münsterg.
Napfg.
Ankeng.
Schoffelg.
Untere Zäune
Obere Zäune
St. Peterstr.
Talackerstr.
Zinneng.
Kämbelg.
Blaufahnenstr.
ZWINGLIPL.
In Gassen
Waag.
MÜNSTERHOF
Grossmünster
Kirchg.
Winkelwiese
Kunsthaus Zürich
Talstr.
Bäreng.
Crédit Suisse
Münsterbr.
Wasserkirche
GROSS-MÜNSTERPL.
Schlosserg.
Poststr.
Fraumünster
PARADEPL.
CENTRAL-HOF
Frankeng.
Trittlig.
Oberdorfstr.
Rösslig.
Geigerg.
Schanzengraben
Tiefenhöfe
Kappelerg.
Stadthausquai
Limmat River
SCHIFFL-ÄNDEPL.
Scheiterg.
Weiteg.
Krugg.
Torg.
Schifflände
Limmatquai
Waldmannstr.
Bleicherweg.
Talstr.
Claridenstr.
Glärnischstr.
Dreikönigbr.
Börsenstr.
Fraumünsterstr.
BELLEVUEPL.
Freieckstr.
Stadelhoferstr.
St.-Urban-G.
Quaibr.
Utoquai
Theaterstr.
Bellevue Apotheke
Schanzeng.
BÜRKLIPL.
TO JOHANN JACOBS MUSEUM (800m)
Migros
General-Guisan-quai
Ferry Terminal
Zürichsee
Opernhaus Bike Rental
Goethestr.
0 200 yards
0 200 meters
TO ARBORETUM (100m), MUSEUM RIETBERG (1km), STRANDBAD MYTHENQUAI (1.5km), 14 (2km), 15 (4km)

Tourist Office: In the Hauptbahnhof (☎215 40 00; www.zuerich.com). Books hotel rooms in Zürich for free and provides both free city maps and more detailed ones for 3SFr. An electronic hotel reservation board is at the front of the station. Also sells the **ZürichCARD,** which is good for unlimited public transportation, free museum admission, and discounts on sights and tours; 1-day 15SFr, 3-day 30SFr. Open May-Oct. M-Sa 8am-8:30pm, Su 8:30am-6:30pm; Nov.-Apr. M-Sa 8:30am-7pm, Su 9am-6:30pm.

Currency Exchange: On the main floor of the main train station. Cash advances for DC/MC/V with photo ID; min. 200SFr, max. 1000SFr. Open daily 6:30am-9:30pm. **Crédit Suisse,** Paradepl. 5SFr commission. Open M-F 8:15am-4:30pm.

Luggage Storage: Middle level of Hauptbahnhof. 5-8SFr. Open daily 4:15am-1:30am.

Bookstore: The Orell Füssli Bookshop, Bahnhofstr. 70, has an extensive selection of books in English. (☎211 04 44. Open M-F 9am-8pm, Sa 9am-5pm).

GLBT Resources: Homosexuelle Arbeitsgruppe Zürich (HAZ), Sihlquai 67 (☎271 22 50; www.haz.ch), has a library, meetings, and the free newsletter *InfoSchwül.* Open W 2-6pm. **Frauenzentrum Zürich,** Matteng. 27 (☎272 05 04; http://frauenzentrum.fem-bit.ch), provides information for lesbians and a library of magazines and other resources. Open Tu and Th 6-8pm.

SWITZERLAND

Emergency: Police: ☎117. **Ambulance:** ☎144. **Fire:** ☎118.

24hr. Pharmacy: Bellevue Apotheke, Theaterstr. 14, on Bellevuepl. (☎266 62 22).

Internet Access: Quanta Virtual Fun Space (☎260 72 66), at the corner of Mühleg. and the busy Niederdorfstr. 3SFr per 15min. Open daily 9am-midnight. **E-Cafe Urania,** the Uraniastr. 3 (☎210 33 11), next to parking garage at the bridge. 0.25SFr per min., min. 2.50SFr. Open M-F 7am-11pm, Sa 8am-11pm, Su 10am-10pm.

Post Office: Sihlpost, Kasernestr. 95-97, just behind the station. Open M-F 7:30am-10:30pm, Sa 8am-8pm, Su 11am-10:30pm. Branches throughout the city. Address mail to be held as follows: First name Last name, Sihlpost, *Postlagernde Briefe,* CH-8021 Zürich. **Postal Code:** CH-8021.

ACCOMMODATIONS

The few budget accommodations in Zürich are easily accessible by foot or public transportation. Reserve ahead, especially in summer.

Justinus Heim Zürich, Freudenbergstr. 146 (☎361 3806; justinuszh@bluewin.ch). Take tram #9 or 10 (dir.: Bahnhof Oerlikon) to Seilbahn Rigiblick, then take funicular to the top (runs daily 5:20am-12:40am). Features quiet, private rooms and a beautiful view of the city. Breakfast included. Laundry available. Reception 8am-noon and 5-9pm. Singles 35-50SFr, with shower 60SFr; doubles 85/100SFr; triples 120-140SFr. V. ❷

The City Backpacker-Hotel Biber, Niederdorfstr. 5 (☎251 9015; www.city-backpacker.ch). With Niederdorfstr. nightlife right outside, you may not even need your bunk bed. Linens and towels each 3SFr, blanket provided. Next-day laundry service 10SFr. Internet 6SFr per hr. Reception 8-11am and 3-10pm. Check-out 10am, strictly enforced. Dorms 31SFr; singles 66SFr; doubles 92SFr. MC/V. ❷

Hôtel Foyer Hottingen, Hottingenstr. 31 (☎256 1919; www.foyer-hottingen.ch). Take tram #3 (dir.: Kluspl.) to Hottingerpl. Families and student backpackers fill this newly renovated house a block from the Kunsthaus. Dorms women only. Breakfast included. Reception 7am-11pm. Partitioned dorms 38SFr; singles 75-85SFr, with bath 110-125SFr; doubles 115/155-165SFr; triples 145/190SFr; quads 180SFr. MC/V. ❷

Martahaus, Zähringerstr. 36 (☎251 4550; www.martahaus.ch). The dorms are oversized "changing rooms" with beds separated by thin walls and curtains. Breakfast included. Laundry 10SFr. Free Internet. Dorms 38SFr; singles 85SFr, with shower

115SFr; doubles 98-114/150-160SFr; triples 135SFr; quads 200SFr; studio with kitchen for 1-2 people 150SFr. ❷

Jugendherberge Zürich (HI), Mutschellenstr. 114 (☎399 7800; www.youthhostel.ch/zuerich). Take tram #7 (dir.: Wollishofen) to Morgental. 24hr. snack bar; beer on tap. Breakfast included. Internet 1SFr per 4min. Reception 24hr. Dorms 44SFr; singles with shower 105SFr; doubles 128SFr; triples 153SFr, with shower 168SFr; quads 174-196SFr; quints 246SFr. Rates higher July-August. 6SFr HI discount. MC/V. ❸

Camping Seebrucht, Seestr. 559 (☎482 1612), on the edge of the lake. Take tram #11 to Bürklipl., then bus #161 or 165 to Stadtgrenze. Showers 2SFr. Reception 8am-noon and 3-9pm. Check-out 11:30am. Tent sites 20SFr, extra person 8SFr. MC/V. ❶

FOOD

Zürich's 1300+ restaurants offer a bit of everything. The cheapest meals are available at *Würstli* stands for about 5SFr. The **farmer's markets** at Bürklipl. (Tu and F 6-11am) and Rosenhof (Th 10am-8pm, Sa 10am-5pm) sell produce and flowers.

Zähringer Café, Zähringerpl. 11 (☎252 0500; www.cafe-zaehringer.ch). Enjoy mainly vegetarian and vegan fare in this colorful cafe. Try their *kefirwasser,* a purple, fizzy drink made from dates and mushrooms fed with sugar (4SFr). Order at the front. Stir-fries 16-27SFr. Open M 6pm-midnight, Tu-Su 8am-midnight. ❷

Bodega Española, Münsterg. 15. Catalán delights served by charismatic waiters since 1874. Egg-and-potato tortilla dishes 18SFr. Tapas 4.80SFr. Open daily 10am-midnight. Kitchen open noon-2pm and 6-10pm. AmEx/DC/MC/V. ❷

Sprüngli Confiserie Café, Paradepl. (☎224 4711), a Zürich landmark, was founded by one of the original Lindt chocolate makers. Pick up a handful of the bite-size *luxemburgerli* (8.40SFr per 100g) or eat a full meal (19-28SFr). Confectionary open M-F 7:30am-6:30pm, Sa 8am-4pm. Cafe open M-F 7:30am-6:30pm, Sa 8am-6pm, Su 9:30am-5:30pm. AmEx/DC/MC/V. ❷

Restaurant Hiltl, Bleicherweg 5 (☎227 7000; www.hiltl.ch). A popular lunch destination for employees of the surrounding banks. Serves delicious vegetarian fare in a chic atmosphere. All-day salad buffet and nightly Indian buffet both 3.90SFr per 100g, all-you-can-eat 44SFr. Open M-Sa 7am-11pm, Su 11am-11pm. AmEx/DC/MC/V. ❷

SIGHTS

Most visitors start a tour of Zürich with the stately **Bahnhofstraße,** which leads into the city from the train station and bustles with shoppers during the day but falls dead quiet after 6pm and on weekends. At the Zürichsee end of Bahnhofstr., **Bürkliplatz** is a good place to start a walk along the lake. The *platz* itself hosts a colorful Saturday **flea market** (May-Oct. 6am-3pm). On the other side of the Limmat River, the pedestrian zone continues on Niederdorfstr. and Münsterg., where shops run from the ritzy to the erotic. Off Niederdorfstr., **Spiegelgasse** was once home to Goethe and Lenin. **Fraumünster, Grossmünster,** and **St. Peters Kirche** straddle the Limmat. For a view of Zürich from the water, **boat tours** leave every 30min. from the ferry terminal at Bürklipl. A Kleine Rundfahrten, the shortest tour, lasts 1½hr. (May-Sept. daily 11am-7pm. 7.60SFr.)

FRAUMÜNSTER. This 13th-century cathedral's Gothic style is juxtaposed with **Marc Chagall's** stained-glass windows, which depict Biblical scenes. In the courtyard, a mural decorating an archway pictures Felix and Regula (the decapitated patron saints of Zürich) with their heads in their hands. *(Off Paradepl. Open May-Nov. M-Sa 10am-6pm, Su 11:30am-6pm; Dec.-Apr. M-Sa 11am-4pm, Su 11:30am-4pm. Free.)*

GROSSMÜNSTER. The twin towers of this church can be best viewed from the bridge near the Fraumünster. The mother church of the Swiss-German Reformation, it is a symbol of Zürich. A Zwingli Bible lies in a protected case near his pulpit. Downstairs in the cavernous 12th-century crypt is a statue of Charlemagne and his 2m sword. *(Church open daily mid-Mar. to Oct. 9am-6pm; Nov. to mid-Mar. 10am-5pm. Tower open Mar.-Oct. M-Sa 9:15am-5pm, Su 12:30-5pm; Nov.-Feb. M-Sa 10:15am-4:30pm, Su 12:30-4:30pm. Church and steeple free. Tower 2SFr.)*

BEACHES. The convenient and popular **Arboretum** is about 100m down from the Quaibrücke. Take tram #5 to Rentenanstalt and head to the water. **Strandbad Mythenquai** lies along the western shore and offers diving towers and a water trampoline. *(Take tram #7 to Brunaustr. and walk 2min. in the same direction until you see a set of stairs. Signs lead the way. Free map at tourist office. ☎201 00 00. www.badi-info.ch. Open daily May-early Sept. 9am-8pm. 6SFr, ages 16-20 4.50SFr.)*

MUSEUMS

KUNSTHAUS ZÜRICH. The Kunsthaus, the largest privately funded museum in Europe, houses a collection ranging from religious works by the Old Masters to 21st-century American Pop Art. Works by Chagall, Dalí, Gauguin, Picasso, Rembrandt, Renoir, Rubens, and van Gogh stretch from wall to wall in a patchwork of color. The Kunsthaus also houses the largest Munch collection outside of Norway. *(Heimpl. 1. Take tram #3, 5, 8, or 9 to Kunsthaus. ☎253 84 84; www.kunsthaus.ch. English audio tour and brochures. Open Tu-Th 10am-9pm, F-Su 10am-5pm. 12SFr, students 6SFr.)*

MUSEUM RIETBERG. Rietberg presents an exquisite collection of Asian, African, and other non-European art, housed in two spectacular mansions in the Rieter-Park. **Park-Villa Rieter** features internationally acclaimed exhibits of Chinese, Japanese, and Indian paintings. **Villa Wesendonck** houses a sculpture collection. *(Gablerstr. 15. Take tram #7 to Museum Rietberg. ☎206 31 31; www.rietberg.ch. Both buildings open Apr.-Sept. Tu and Th-Su 10am-5pm, W 10am-8pm; Oct.-Mar. Tu-Su 10am-5pm. 6SFr, students 3SFr, under 16 free. MC/V; only at Wesendonck.)*

ENTERTAINMENT AND NIGHTLIFE

For information on after-dark happenings, check ZüriTipp (www.zueritipp.ch) or pick up a free copy of *ZürichGuide* or *ZürichEvents* from the tourist office. On **Niederdorfstraße,** the epicenter of Zürich's Altstadt nightlife, bars are packed almost every night. **Kreis 5,** once the industrial area of Zürich, has developed into party central, with clubs, bars, and lounges taking over former factories; this is the spot where the city's young, hip, and in-the-know come to play when the sun goes down. Kreis 5 lies northwest of the Hauptbahnhof, with Hardstr. as its axis. To get there, take tram #4 (dir.: Bahnhof Tiefenbrumen) or tram #13 (dir.: Albisgütli) to Escher-Wyss-Pl. and follow the crowds. Closer to the old town, the **Langstraße,** donning a red-light district reputation, has a number of cheap bars and clubs that walk the line of being strip clubs. Beer in Zürich is pricey (from 6SFr), but a number of cheap bars have established themselves on Niederdorfstr. near Mühleg.

Most movies are screened in English with French and German subtitles (marked "E/D/F"). Films cost 15SFr and up, less on Mondays. From July to August, the **OrangeCinema,** an open-air cinema at Zürichhorn (take tram #2 or 4 to Fröhlichstr.), attracts crowds to its lakefront screenings. Every August, the **Street Parade** (mid-Aug.) brings together ravers from all over the world for a giant techno party.

TIP **THAT EXPLAINS THE TASSELS.** Beware the deceptive and common "night club"—it's really just a euphemism for "strip club."

Kaufleuten, Pelikanstr. 18 (☎225 3322; www.kaufleuten.ch). A former theater, this trendy club still decked out in red velvet attracts the who's-who of Zürich with nightly themed parties; check website to see what's going on any given evening. Cover 10-30SFr. Hours vary, but generally open Su-Th 11pm-2am, F-Sa 11pm-4am. MC/V.

Nelson, Beateng. 11 (☎212 6016). Locals, backpackers, and businessmen chug exotic beer (pints 8.50SFr) at this large Irish pub. 20+. Open M-W 11:30am-2am, Th 11:30am-3am, F 11:30am-4:30am, Sa 3pm-4:30am, Su 3pm-2am. AmEx/MC/V.

Barfüsser, Spitalg. 14 (☎251 4064), off Zähringerpl. Switzerland's oldest gay bar. Delicious sushi is accompanied by freely flowing mixed drinks (14-17SFr) and wine (6-9SFr). Open M-Th noon-1am, F-Sa noon-2am, Su 5pm-1am. AmEx/DC/MC/V.

Nachtflug Bar, Café, and Lounge, Stüssihofstatt 4 (☎261 9966). Sleek bar with outdoor seating. Wine from 6SFr. Beer from 4.90SFr. Open Su-Th 11am-midnight, F-Sa 11am-1:30am. Outdoor bar open Th-Su 10pm-midnight. AmEx/MC/V.

Öpfelchammer, Rindermarkt 12 (☎251 2336). This popular Swiss wine chamber (8-10SFr per glass) has low ceilings and wooden crossbeams covered with initials and messages from 200 years of merry-making. Those who climb the rafters and drink a free glass of wine while hanging upside down from the beams get to engrave their names on the walls or ceiling. Open mid-Aug. to mid-July Tu-Sa 11am-12:30am. AmEx/DC/MC/V.

SWITZERLAND

LUZERN (LUCERNE) ☎041

Luzern (pop. 60,000) welcomes busloads of tourists each day in the summer, and with good reason. The streets of the engaging old city lead down to a placid lake, the covered bridges over the river are among the most photographed sights in Switzerland, and the sunrise over the famous Mt. Pilatus has hypnotized hikers and artists—including Goethe, Twain, and Wagner—for centuries.

TRANSPORTATION AND PRACTICAL INFORMATION. **Trains** leave Bahnhofpl. for Basel (1hr., 1-2 per hr., 30SFr), Geneva (3½hr., every 2-3hr., 70SFr), and Zürich (1hr., 2 per hr., 22SFr). VBL **buses** depart in front of the train station and provide extensive coverage of Luzern; route maps are available at the **tourist office** in the station, which sells the **Museum Pass** (30SFr, valid for one month all over Switzerland), and reserves rooms. (☎227 1717; www.luzern.org. Open May-Oct. M-F 8:30am-6:30pm, Sa-Su 9am-6:30pm; Nov.-Apr. M-F 8:30am-5:30pm, Sa-Su 9am-1pm.) The **post office** is by the train station. Address mail to be held as follows: First name LAST NAME, *Postlagernde Briefe*, Hauptpost, CH-6000 Luzern 1, SWITZERLAND. (Open M-F 7:30am-6:30pm, Sa 8am-noon.) **Postal Code:** CH-6000.

ACCOMMODATIONS AND FOOD. Inexpensive beds are limited, so call ahead. To reach **Backpackers ❷,** Alpenquai 42, turn right from the station on Inseliquai and follow it for 20min. until it turns into Alpenquai; the hostel is on the right. Balconies in the rooms look out on the lake. (☎360 0420; www.backpackerslucerne.ch. Bike rental 18SFr per day. Laundry 6SFr. Internet 10SFr per hr. Reception 7:30-10am and 4-11pm. Dorms 30SFr; singles 45SFr; doubles 68SFr. Cash only.) Overlooking the river from the Altstadt is the **Tourist Hotel ❷,** St. Karliquai 12, which offers plain rooms and a prime location. From the station, walk along Bahnhofstr., cross the river at the second covered bridge, and make a left onto St. Karliquai. (☎410 2474; www.touristhotel.ch. Breakfast included. Dorms 35SFr; singles 75SFr; doubles 98SFr. AmEx/MC/V; dorms cash only.) **Markets** along the river sell cheap, fresh food on Tuesday and Saturday mornings. There's also a **Migros** supermarket at the train station. (Open M-Sa 6:30am-9pm, Su 8am-9pm.)

SIGHTS AND ENTERTAINMENT. The Altstadt, across the river over the Spreuerbrücke from the station, is famous for its frescoed houses; the best examples are those on Hirschenpl. and Weinmarkt. The 14th-century **Kapellbrücke,** a wooden-roofed bridge, runs from left of the train station to the Altstadt and is decorated with Swiss historical scenes; farther down the river, the **Spreuerbrücke** is decorated by Kaspar Meglinger's eerie *Totentanz* (Dance of Death) paintings. On the hills above the river, the **Museggmauer** and its towers are all that remain of the medieval city's ramparts. Three of the towers are accessible to visitors and provide panoramic views of the city; from Mühlenpl., walk up Brugglig., then head uphill to the right on Museggstr. and follow the brown castle signs. (Open in summer daily 8am-7pm.) To the east is the **Löwendenkmal,** the dying lion of Luzern, carved into a cliff on Denkmalstr.

Europe's largest transportation museum, the **Verkehrshaus der Schweiz** (Swiss Transport Museum), Lidostr. 5, has interactive displays on all kinds of vehicles, but the real highlight is the warehouse of trains. Take bus #6, 8, or 24 to Verkehrshaus. (☎375 7575; www.verkehrshaus.ch. Open daily Apr.-Oct. 10am-6pm; Nov.-Mar. 10am-5pm. 24SFr, students 22SFr, with Eurailpass 14SFr.) The **Picasso Museum,** Am Rhyn Haus, Furreng. 21, displays a large collection of Picasso's lesser-known works. From Schwanenpl., take Rathausquai to Furreng. (☎410 3533. Open daily Apr.-Oct. 10am-6pm; Nov.-Mar. 11am-5pm. 8SFr, students 5SFr.)

Although Luzern's nightlife is more about chilling than club-hopping, **The Loft,** Haldenstr. 21, hosts special DJs and theme nights. (Beer 9-11SFr. Open W 9pm-2am, Th-Su 10am-4am.) The mellow **Jazzkantine,** Grabenstr. 8, is a product of the Jazz School of Luzern. (Sandwiches 6-8SFr. Open mid-Aug. to mid-July M-Sa 7am-12:30am, Su 4pm-12:30am; mid-July to mid-Aug. Su-F 4pm-12:30am, Sa 10am-12:30am. MC/V.) Gay nightlife centers around the industrial area intersected by Tribschenstr., in the south end of the city. Luzern attracts big names for its two jazz festivals: **Blue Balls Festival** (end of July) and **Blues Festival** (2nd week of Nov.).

STEIN AM RHEIN ☎052

The tiny medieval Altstadt of Stein am Rhein (pop. 3000) is postcard-perfect, with traditional Swiss architecture framed by hills and the Rhine River. The houses on the square date back to the 15th century and have paintings on their facades depicting the animal or scene for which each house is named. Stein am Rhein first became prominent in the 12th century through the establishment **Kloster St. Georgen.** You can reach the tucked-away entrance to the Benedictine monastery by going through the arch across from the tourist office. Inside the monastery's gor-

FONDUES AND DON'TS

Although known worldwide as a Swiss tradition, fondue is a complex cultural artifact. Here are a few things to keep in mind the next time you dive into a bowl of boiling cheese.

First, fondue is no monolith. The most common form is a mix of two cheeses, the French-Swiss Gruyère and Fribourger cheeses, but there are substantial regional variations. Likewise, *Kirsch,* the clear schnapps that farmers still make in their backyards, is added in quantities that vary by canton, ensuring that each brew retains its own unique bite.

The eating of fondue is likewise a playground of cultural variety. In some circles, if you lose your bread somewhere in the pot, you have to kiss your neighbor; in others, you buy him a bottle of wine or sing a song. As the meal winds to a close, a ring of cheese is inevitably found stuck to the bottom of the pot, burned to a crisp. In Basel, this is called the *Oma* (Grandmother), while in Wallis, it's simply know as the *gut* part. No matter what its name, though, all Swiss cut up and eat the burnt cheese, sometimes with an egg or two on top.

Be sure to only drink white wine or hot tea with fondue: if you're quaffing a cold beverage, the cheese forms a hard ball in your stomach and leads to indigestion. Most importantly, as any Swiss will tell you, fondue is best when shared.

geous **Festsaal,** the red-and-green tiled floor is off-limits to feet, and the sun is the only source of lighting. Try to go on a sunny day for the best view of the paintings and prints. (☎741 2142. Open Apr.-Oct. Tu-Su 10am-5pm. 4SFr, students 2SFr.) The stately **Rathaus** is to the right in the main square, the Rathauspl. Heading away from the Rathaus, the Understadt, the main road running through the village, leads to the **Museum Lindwurm,** where visitors are greeted by roosters that wander along through the house, which depicts 19th-century bourgeois life and culture. (Open Mar.-Oct. M and W-Su 10am-5pm. 5SFr.) **Burg Hohenklingen** sits atop a hill overlooking Stein am Rhein; although the castle will be closed until mid- to late summer 2007, the view of the Rhine and the villages below is worth the hike. From the Rathauspl., take Brodlauberg. 30min. away from the river and follow the signs.

The family-oriented **Jugendherberge (HI) ❷,** Hemishoferstr. 87, is a 15min. walk from the train station; cross the Rhine and walk left out of the old town along the main road. Bus #7349 (dir.: Singen) runs once per hour; take it to Strandbad and walk 5min. farther in the same direction. (☎741 1255; www.youthhostel.ch/stein. Breakfast included. Internet 1SFr per 5min. Reception 8-10am and 5-9pm. Open Mar.-Oct. Dorms 32-36SFr; singles 46SFr; doubles 80SFr. 6SFr HI discount. AmEx/MC/V.) In a neighboring town, right on the Rhine, **Campingplatz Wagenhausen ❶,** Hauptstr. 82, can most easily be reached from the train station by walking left down Wagenhauserstr. from Bahnhofstr. for about 15min. For a much more scenic route, walk toward the old town, turn left before the bridge, and follow the *Wanderweg* signs along the river. (☎741 4271; www.campingwagenhausen.ch. Showers 1SFr. Check-out noon. Tent sites 14SFr, extra person 7SFr. Cash only.) The **Weinstube Rother Ochsen ❷,** Rathauspl. 9, built in 1466, is the oldest public house in the town. Though full meals are not available, their regional soups (8.50SFr), appetizers (9-18SFr), and wines (4-14SFr) are sustenance enough. (☎741 2328. Open Tu-Sa 10am-11pm, Su 10am-6pm. Kitchen open 11:30am-2pm and 6-10pm) A Vogl **supermarket** is located at Rathauspl. 17. (Open M-F 8:15am-6:30pm.)

Trains connect Stein to Constance (40min., 1 per hr., 10SFr) via Kreuzlingen, and to Zürich (1hr., 1-2 per hr., 21SFr) via Winterthur or Schaffhausen. **Boats** (☎634 08 88; www.urh.ch) depart for Bodensee towns and Schaffhausen (1¼hr., 21SFr), which is an hour's walk of the Rhine Falls, Europe's biggest waterfall. Those who want to explore the area by land can rent **bikes** from **River Bike,** Rathauspl. 15. (☎741 55 41; www.riverbike.ch. 15-20SFr per 2hr.; 29-35SFr per day. Open M 1:30-6:30pm, Tu-F 9am-6:30pm, Sa 9am-4pm, Su 11am-5pm.) The **tourist office,** Oberstadt. 3, lies on the other side of the Rathaus, has free maps for visitors, and books rooms for free. From the station, walk down Bahnhofstr., turn right onto Wagenhauserstr., and then head downhill and over the bridge. (☎742 20 90; www.steinamrhein.ch. Open July-Aug. M-F 9:30am-noon and 1:30-5pm, Sa 9:30am-noon and 1:30-4pm; Sept.-June M-F 9:30am-noon and 1:30-5pm.) **Postal Code:** CH-8260.

NORTHWESTERN SWITZERLAND

The cantons of Basel-Stadt, Basel-Land, Solothurn, and Aargau inspire peaceful contentment in visitors and locals alike. No matter what time of year you visit, stellar landscapes await.

BASEL (BÂLE) ☎061

Situated on the Rhine near France and Germany, Basel is home to a large medieval quarter as well as one of the oldest universities in Switzerland—graduates include Erasmus and Nietzsche. Though Basel is primarily known as a transportation hub and the center of the chemical industry, the city and its surrounding area also have excellent museums, bright houses, and relaxing riverside promenades.

TRANSPORTATION AND PRACTICAL INFORMATION. Basel has three train stations: the French (SNCF) and Swiss (SBB) stations on Centralbahnpl., near the Altstadt, and the German (DB) station across the Rhine (take tram #2 from the other train stations). **Trains** leave from the SBB to: Bern (1¼hr., 1 per hr., 36SFr); Geneva (3hr., 1 per hr., 67SFr); Lausanne (2½hr., 1 per hr., 57SFr); Zürich (1hr., every 15-30min., 30SFr). Make international connections at the French (SNCF) or German (DB) stations. The **tourist office** on Steinenbergstr. is in the Stadt Casino building on Barfüsserpl. From the SBB station, take tram #6, 8, 14, 16, or 17 to Barfüsserpl. (☎268 68 68; www.baseltourismus.ch. Open M-F 8:30am-6:30pm, Sa 10am-5pm, Su 10am-4pm.) To reach the **post office,** Rüdeng. 1, take tram #1 or 8 to Marktpl. and backtrack one block away from the river. (Open M-W 7:30am-6:30pm, Th-F 7:30am-7pm, Sa 8am-5pm.) Address mail to be held as follows: *Postlagernde Briefe für* First name LAST NAME, Rüdeng., CH-4001 Basel, Switzerland. **Postal Codes:** CH-4000 to CH-4059.

SWITZERLAND

ACCOMMODATIONS AND FOOD. The **Jugendherberge (HI) ❷,** St. Alban-Kirchrain 10, has a convenient location close to the Rhine and just down the hill from the Altstadt. To get there, take tram #2 to Kunstmuseum; turn right on St. Alban-Vorstadt, then follow the signs. (☎272 0572; www.youthhostel.ch/basel. Breakfast included. Laundry 7SFr. Internet 5SFr per 25min. Reception Mar.-Oct. 7-10am and 2-11:30pm; Nov.-Feb. 7-10am and 2-11pm. Dorms 37-41SFr; singles 86SFr; doubles 96, with shower 112SFr. 6SFr HI discount. MC/V.) **Basel Back Pack ❷,** Dornacherstr. 192, is a good distance from the old town, but provides free tickets for all trams and buses. Take the south exit from the station, turn left at Tellpl., and follow the signs. (☎333 0037. Breakfast 7SFr. Laundry 6SFr. Internet 1SFr per 5min. Reception 8-11:30am, 2-5:30pm, and 8-11:30pm. Dorms 31SFr; singles 80SFr; doubles 96SFr; triples 123SFr; quads 144SFr. AmEx/MC/V; min. 60SFr.)

In the old town, **Barfüsserplatz, Marktplatz,** and the streets connecting them are full of satisfying restaurants. On the other bank of the Rhine in Klein-Basel, **Restaurant Hirscheneck ❷,** Lindenberg 23, is popular with students, vegetarians, and Basel's small alternative crowd. (☎692 7333. Daily menu 12-23SFr, smaller portions 9-14SFr. Su brunch 10am-4pm. Open M 2pm-midnight, Tu-Th 11am-midnight, F-Sa 11am-1am, Su 10am-midnight. Cash only.) **Brauerei Fischerstube ❹,** Rheing. 45, serves literally intoxicating dishes like beer soup. (☎692 66 35. Beer 4.30SFr. Full dinner menu 42SFr, served from 6pm. Open M-Th 10am-12:30am, F-Sa 10am-1:30am, Su 5pm-midnight. AmEx/MC/V.) Groceries are available at the **Migros** in the SBB station. (Open M-F 6am-10pm, Sa-Su 7:30am-10pm.)

SIGHTS AND ENTERTAINMENT. Greater Basel (Groß-Basel) and the train station are separated from Lesser Basel (Klein-Basel) by the Rhine. Behind the Marktpl. is the 775-year-old **Middle Rhine Bridge** (Mittlere Rheinbrücke), which connects the two halves of the city. To get to the old town from the train station, take tram #16. The very red **Rathaus** brightens the lively **Marktplatz** with its blinding facade and striking gold-and-green statues. Behind Marktpl. stands the red sandstone **Münster** (Cathedral), where you can visit the tomb of Erasmus or climb the tower for a spectacular view of the city. (Church open Easter to mid-Oct. M-F 10am-5pm, Sa 10am-4pm, Su 1-5pm; mid-Oct. to Easter M-Sa 11am-4pm, Su 2-4pm. Church free. Tower 3SFr.) Get off at the Theater stop to see the spectacular **Jean Tinguely Fountain,** also known as the **Fasnachtsbrunnen.** The fountain's various moving metal parts spray water in all directions. Basel has over 30 museums; pick up a comprehensive guide at the tourist office. **Museum Tinguely,** Paul-Sacher-Anlage 1, is an homage to the Swiss sculptor's vision of metal and movement. Take tram #2 or 15 to Wettsteinpl., then bus #31 or 36 to Museum Tinguely. (☎681 93 20. Open Tu-Su 11am-7pm. 10SFr, students 7SFr.) The **Kunstmuseum** (Museum of Fine Arts),

St. Alban-Graben 16, houses collections of new and old masters; admission also gives access to the **Museum für Gegenwartskunst** (Museum of Modern Art), St. Alban-Rheinweg 60. (Kunstmuseum open Tu and Th-Su 10am-5pm, W 10am-7pm. Gegenwartskunst open Tu-Su 11am-5pm. Each museum 10SFr, students 5SFr. Free daily 4-5pm and 1st Su of every month.)

Basel's carnival, the **Fasnacht,** commences the Monday before Lent with the *Morgestraich*, a three-day parade with a 600-year-old tradition. The parade begins at 4am; its cheerfully impossible goal is to scare away winter. During the rest of the year, head to **Barfüsserplatz** for an evening of bar-hopping. **Atlantis,** Klosterberg 13, is a multi-level, sophisticated bar with reggae, jazz, and funk. (☎228 96 96. Cover 10-15SFr, July-Sept. no cover F; year-round 5SFr student discount. Open M 11:30am-2pm, Tu-Th 11:30am-2pm and 6pm-midnight, F 11:30am-2pm and 6pm-4am, Sa 6pm-4am. AmEx/MC/V.)

GRAUBÜNDEN

Graubünden's rugged gorges, fir forests, and eddying rivers give the region a wildness seldom found in comfortably settled Switzerland. Visitors should plan their trips carefully, especially in ski season when reservations are absolutely required, and in May and June, when nearly everything shuts down.

DAVOS ☎081

Davos (pop. 13,000) sprawls along the valley floor under seven mountains criss-crossed with chairlifts and cable cars. Originally a health resort, the city catered to such *fin-de-siècle* giants as Robert Louis Stevenson and Thomas Mann. The influx of tourists and international political conferences in recent decades has given the city an impersonal feel, but the thrill of carving down the famed, wickedly steep ski slopes or exploring some of the 700km of hiking paths may make up for it. Davos provides direct access to two mountains—**Parsenn** and **Jakobshorn**—and four skiing areas. Parsenn, with long runs and fearsome vertical drops, is the mountain around which Davos built its reputation. (www.fun-mountain.ch. Day pass 60SFr.) Jakobshorn has found a niche with the younger crowd since it opened a snowboarding park with two half-pipes (day pass 55SFr). Cross-country trails cover 75km as they run through the valley, and one is even lit at night. In the summer, the ski lifts (½ price after 3pm) connect to **hikes,** such as the 2hr. **Panoramaweg.** In winter, Europe's largest natural **ice rink** (18,000 sq. m),

IN RECENT NEWS

BUNA SAIRA!

Switzerland's oft-forgotten fourth national language, Romansch, is spoken only in the province of Graubünden. A Romance language like French and Italian, Romansch is descended from Latin. Romansch was first written down in the 16th century, when Biblical texts and historical ballads were translated from Latin. Now, Romansch has a small literature of its own, and its speakers support five different Romansch newspapers, TV news broadcasts, and 100hr. of radio time per week. Today, many schools in Lower Engandine teach strictly in Romansch until students are 10 years old. At this time, students elect to continue their education in either German or Romansch with continued study of the other language.

Until about 1850, it was the most spoken language in the canton. By 1880, Romansch speakers dropped to 39.8% of the population, a percentage that kept sinking through the 20th century, finally leveling out around 22%. Today, in some small villages like S-chanf Romansch speakers remain in the majority. Even in larger towns like Chur they make up as much as a quarter of the population. The language is supported by the Swiss government, but differences in local dialects and pressures to speak more well-known languages means only time will tell the fate of Romansch.

between Platz and Dorf, allows curling, figure skating, hockey, ice dancing, and speed skating. (☎415 36 004. Open July-Aug. and Dec. 15-Feb. 15 M-W and F-Su 10am-4pm, Th 8-10pm. 5SFr. Skate rental 6.50SFr.) For joggers, birdwatchers, and aspiring windsurfers, the **Davosersee** is the place to be. At the **Davosersee Surfcenter,** Obere Str. 18, board rentals are 30SFr per hr., 60SFr per day. (Take bus #1 to Flueelastr. and follow the yellow signs to the lake. ☎076 589 38 46; www.davos-surf.ch. Open mid-June to mid-Sept. daily 11am-6:30pm.) To experience the full-on adrenaline high that only art history can provide, visit the **Kirchner Museum,** on the Promenade. It houses an extensive collection of Ernst Kirchner's artwork, in which harsh colors and long figures defined 20th-century German Expressionism. Take the bus or walk down the street from the tourist office toward Davos-Dorf. (☎413 2202; www.kirchnermuseum.ch. Open Tu-Su July-Aug. and Dec. 25-Easter 10am-6pm; Sept.-Dec. 24 and Easter-June 2-6pm. 10SFr, students 8SFr.)

Overlooking Davos-Dorf, **Youthpalace Davos (HI) ❸,** Horlaubenstr. 27, has spacious rooms with bath. Go left out of the Dorf train station, take the first right, and turn left at the major street, Promenade. Take a right onto Horlaubenstr. and walk up the hill for 15min. (☎410 1920; www.youthhostel.ch/davos. Breakfast, dinner, and towel included. Wireless Internet available. Reception 8-10am and 3-10pm. Mid-Dec. to mid-Mar. dorms 61-101SFr; singles 145SFr; doubles 230SFr. Early June to mid.-Oct. 51-71/81/162SFr. Mid-Mar. to early June and mid-Oct. to mid-Dec. reduced rates. 6SFr HI discount. AmEx/MC/V.) At Jakobshorn Ski Mountain's **Snowboardhotel Bolgenschanze ❸,** Skistr. 1, dorm rooms are sold as a package with ski passes. (☎414 9020; www.davosklosters.ch. 18+. Open mid-Dec. to mid-Mar. 1-night, 2-day ski pass 195-405SFr; 6-night, 7-day pass 650-865SFr. AmEx/MC/V.)

Davos is accessible by **train** from Chur (1½hr., 7 per day, 27SFr) via Landquart or from Klosters (25min., 2 per hr., 9.20SFr). The town is divided into two areas, Davos-Platz and Davos-Dorf, each with a train station. **Buses** (2.70SFr) run between the two stations. The main **tourist office,** Promenade 67, is up the hill and to the right on Promenade from the Platz station. (☎415 21 21; www.davos.ch. Open Dec. to mid-Apr. and mid-June to mid-Oct. M-F 8:30am-6:30pm, Sa 9am-5pm, Su 10am-noon and 3-5:30pm; mid-Oct. to Nov. and mid-Apr. to mid-June M-F 9am-6pm, Sa 9am-noon.) **Postal Code:** CH-7270.

KLOSTERS ☎081

Though Klosters (pop. 3000) is only 25min. from Davos by train, it feels a world away. Davos makes every effort to be hip and urbane, while Klosters capitalizes on its natural serenity and cozy chalets. Most ski packages include mountains from both towns, and Klosters's main lift leads to a mountain pass where one can ski down to either. In summer, Klosters has better access to fantastic biking trails. On the lush, green valley floor, **hikers** can make a large loop, from Klosters's Protestant church on Monbielstr. to Monbiel. The route continues to an elevation of 1488m and turns left, passing through Bödmerwald, Fraschmardintobel, and Monbieler Wald before climbing to its highest elevation of 1634m and returning to Klosters via Pardels. Several adventure companies offer a variety of activities, including **river rafting, canoeing, horseback riding, paragliding,** and **glacier trekking.** The Klosters-Davos region also issues **ski passes** that run 121SFr for two days and 282SFr for six days, including public transportation. The **Madrisabahn** leaves from Klosters-Dorf (1-day pass; 47SFr). The **Grotschnabahn** gives access to Parsenn and Strela in Davos and Madrisa in Klosters. (1-day pass 60SFr; 6-day pass 324SFr.) Summer cable car passes (valid on Grotschnabahn and Madrisabahn) are also available (4-day pass; 80SFr). **Bananas,** operated out of Duty Boardsport, Bahnhofstr. 16, gives snowboard lessons. (☎422 6660. Lessons 70SFr per 4hr. Board rental 38SFr per day. MC/V.) **Ski rental** is also available at **Sport Gotschna,** Alte Bahnhofstr. 5. (☎422 1197. Skis and snowboards 28-50SFr per day plus 10% insurance.

Open M-F 8am-6:30pm, Sa-Su 8am-6pm. AmEx/MC/V.) **Andrist Sport,** Gotschnastr. 8, rents **bikes.** (☎410 2080. About 38SFr per day, 130SFr per 6 days. Open M-F 8am-noon and 2-6:30pm, Sa 8am-noon and 2-4pm. AmEx/MC/V.)

To get to **Jugendherberge Soldanella (HI) ❷,** Talstr. 73, from the station, go left uphill past Hotel Alpina to the church, then cross the street and head up the alleyway to the right of the Kirchpl. bus station sign. Walk 10min. along the gravel path. This massive, renovated chalet has a comfortable reading room, a flagstone terrace, and friendly, English-speaking owners. (☎422 1316; www.youthhostel.ch/klosters. Breakfast included. Reception 7-10am and 5-10:30pm. Open mid-Dec. to mid-Apr. and late June to mid-Oct. Dorms 35SFr; singles 46SFr; doubles 88SFr; family rooms 44SFr per person. 6SFr HI discount. AmEx/DC/MC/V.) Turn right from the train station to reach the **Coop** supermarket, Bahnhofstr. 10. (Open M-F 8am-12:30pm and 2-6:30pm; Sa 8am-5pm.)

The main **tourist office,** in Platz by the station, has Internet (5SFr per 30min.) and sells hiking (18SFr) and biking (7.50SFr) maps of the area. (☎410 20 20; www.klosters.ch. Open May-Nov. M-F 8:30am-6pm, Sa 8:30am-noon and 2-4pm; July to mid-Aug. also Su 9-11am; Dec.-Apr. M-Sa 8:30am-noon and 2-6pm, Su 9-11:30am and 4-6pm.)

SWITZERLAND

THE SWISS NATIONAL PARK ☎081

No other area can match the Swiss National Park's isolation from man-made structures or its unspoiled natural terrain. A network of 20 hiking trails runs throughout the park and is mostly concentrated in the center. Few of the trails are level; most involve a lot of climbing, often into snow-covered areas. All trails are clearly marked, and it is against park rules to wander off the designated trails. Trails that require no mountaineering gear are marked with white-red-white blazes. Keep in mind, though, that even some of the no-gear routes can be tricky.

Zernez is the main gateway to the park and home to its headquarters, the **National Parkhouse.** The staff provides helpful trail maps as well as up-to-date information on which trails are navigable. (☎856 1378; www.nationalpark.ch. Headquarters open June-Oct. daily 8:30am-6pm.) From Zernez, **trains** and **post buses** run to other towns in the area, including Scuol, Samedan, and S-chanf. The park is closed November through May. The Swiss National Park is one of the most strictly regulated nature reserves in the world. Camping and campfires are prohibited in the park, as is collecting flowers and plants. A team of wardens patrols the park at all times, so it's better not to test the rules. The nearby towns Zernez, Scuol, and S-chanf have campgrounds right outside the park boundaries.

VALAIS

The Valais occupies the deep glacial gorge traced by the Rhône River. The clefts of the valley divide the land linguistically: in the west, French predominates, and in the east, Swiss German is used. Though its mountain resorts can be over-touristed, the region's spectacular peaks make fighting the traffic worthwhile.

ZERMATT AND THE MATTERHORN ☎027

Year-round, tourists pack the trains to Zermatt (pop. 3500) where the monolithic **Matterhorn** (4478m) rises above the seemingly endless hotels and lodges in town. The area has attained mecca status with Europe's longest **ski** run, the 13km trail from Klein Matterhorn to Zermatt, and more **summer ski trails** than any other Alpine resort. The **Zermatt Alpin Center,** Bahnhofstr. 58, just past the post office houses both the **Bergführerbüro** (Mountain Guide's Office; ☎966 2460) and the **Skischulbüro** (Ski School Office; ☎966 2466). The center provides ski passes (½-day

52SFr, 1-day 68SFr), four-day weather forecasts, and info on guided climbing. (Open daily July-Sept. 8:30am-noon and 3-7pm; late Dec. to mid-May 4-7pm.) The Bergführerbüro is the only company to lead formal expeditions above Zermatt. Groups scale Breithorn (4164m, 2hr., 155SFr), Castor (4228m, 5-6hr., 314SFr), and Pollux (4091m, 5-6hr., 297SFr) daily in summer. Prices do not include equipment, insurance, hut accommodations, or lifts to departure points. **Rental prices** for skis and snowboards are standardized throughout Zermatt (28-50SFr per day). For a new perspective on the Matterhorn and something to brag about when you get home, try a tandem flight with **Paraglide Zermatt.** (☎967 67 44. 150-190SFr.)

Hotel Bahnhof ❷, Bahnhofpl. 54, to the left of the station, provides hotel housing at hostel rates. The central location, mountain views, and clean rooms make up for the slightly cramped space. (☎967 2406; www.hotelbahnhof.com. Reception 8am-8pm. Dorms 35SFr; singles 65SFr, with shower 76SFr; doubles 90/104SFr. MC/V.) Get groceries at the **Coop Center,** opposite the station. (Open M-Sa 8:15am-7pm, Su 4-7pm.) Get traditional Swiss food at **Walliserkanne ❷,** Bahnhofstr. 32, by the post office. (☎966 4610. *Raclette* 8SFr. Pasta 17-25SFr. Cheese fondues 23-25SFr. Open daily 8am-midnight. Kitchen closes 11pm. AmEx/MC/V.) **The Pipe Surfer's Cantina,** on Kirchstr., specializes in Mexican-Thai-Indian cuisine, and by night throws the craziest "beach parties" in the Alps. (☎079 213 3807; www.gozermatt.com/thepipe. Salads 23-27SFr. Entrees 28-32SFr. Happy hour daily 6-7pm, in winter 4-5pm. Open daily 4pm-midnight. MC/V.)

To preserve the Alpine air, cars and buses are banned in Zermatt; the only way in is the hourly **BVZ** (Brig-Visp-Zermatt) rail line, which connects to Lausanne (71SFr) and Bern (78SFr). The **tourist office,** in the station, sells hiking maps (26SFr) and gives out free town maps. (☎966 81 00; www.zermatt.ch. Open mid-June to mid-Oct. M-Sa 8:30am-6pm, Su 8:30am-noon and 1:30-6pm; mid-Oct. to mid-Dec. and May to mid-June M-F 8:30am-noon and 2-6pm, Sa 9:30am-noon, Su 9:30am-noon and 4-6pm; mid-Dec. to Apr. M-F 8:30am-noon and 2-6pm, Sa 8:30am-6:30pm, Su 9:30am-noon and 4-6pm.) **Postal Code:** CH-3920.

FRENCH SWITZERLAND

Around Lac Léman and Lac Neuchâtel, hills blanketed by patchwork vineyards seem tame and settled—until the haze clears. Mountain peaks surge from behind the hills, and trees descend from the wilderness to each shore. Some travelers suffer financial anxiety when they consider venturing to the expensive cities of refined French Switzerland. However, visitors are often relieved to find that tranquility lies in a simple stroll along a tree-lined avenue, and that the best entertainment is not always the kind money can buy.

GENEVA (GENÈVE) ☎022

Birthplace of the League of Nations and current home to dozens of multinational organizations (including the Red Cross and the United Nations), Geneva exudes worldliness. But this does not fully overshadow the city's storied history, evident in the Roman ruins and Calvinist cathedral of the *vieille ville*.

TRANSPORTATION

Flights: Cointrin Airport (**GVA;** ☎717 71 11, flight info 799 31 11 or 717 71 05) is a hub for **Swiss International Airlines** (☎0848 85 20 00) and also serves **Air France** (☎827 87 87) and **British Airways** (☎0848 80 10 10). Several flights per day to **Amsterdam, NTH; London, BRI; Paris, FRA;** and **Rome, ITA.** Bus #10 runs to the Gare Cornavin (15min., every 5-10min., 3SFr); the train is faster (6min., every 10min., 3SFr).

Trains: Trains run 4:30am-1am. **Gare Cornavin,** pl. Cornavin, is the main station. To: **Basel** (2¾hr., 1 per hr., 67SFr); **Bern** (2hr., 1 per hr., 45SFr); **Interlaken** (3hr., 1 per hr., 63SFr); **Lausanne** (40min., every 15-30min., 20SFr); **Montreux** (1hr., 2 per hr., 27SFr); **Zürich** (3½hr., every 30min., 77SFr). Ticket counter open M-F 5:15am-9:30pm, Sa-Su 5:30am-9:30pm. **Gare des Eaux-Vives** (☎736 16 20), on av. de la Gare des Eaux-Vives (tram #12 to Amandoliers SNCF), connects to France's regional rail through **Annecy, FRA** (1½hr., 6 per day, 15SFr) or **Chamonix, FRA** (2½hr., 4 per day, 25SFr).

Public Transportation: Geneva has an efficient bus and tram network (www.tpg.ch). Single tickets valid for 1hr. within the "orange" city zone, which includes the airport, are 3SFr, rides of 3 stops or less 2SFr. **Day passes** (10SFr) and a **9hr. pass** (7SFr) are available for the canton of Geneva. Day passes for the whole region 18SFr. Stamp multi-use tickets before boarding at machines in the station. Buses run 5am-12:30am; **Noctambus** (F-Sa 12:30-3:45am, 3SFr) runs after the other buses have stopped.

Taxis: Taxi-Phone (☎331 41 33). 6.80SFr plus 2.90SFr per km. Taxi from airport 30SFr.

Bike Rental: Geneva has bike paths and special traffic lights. Behind the station, **Genève Roule,** pl. Montbrillant 17 (☎740 1343), has **free bikes** available (passport and 50SFr deposit; heavy fines if bike is lost or stolen). Slightly nicer bikes from 10SFr per day. Other locations at Bains des Pâquis and pl. du Rhône. Arrive before 9am, as bikes go quickly. Open daily May-Oct. 7:30am-9:30pm; Nov.-Apr. 8am-6pm. Cash only.

Hitchhiking: *Let's Go* does not recommend hitchhiking. Those headed to Germany or northern Switzerland take bus #4 to Jardin Botanique. Those headed to France take bus #4 to Palettes, then line D to St-Julien.

SWITZERLAND

ORIENTATION AND PRACTICAL INFORMATION

The cobbled streets and quiet squares of Geneva's historic *vieille ville* (old town), centered around **Cathédrale de St-Pierre,** make up the heart of Geneva. Across the **River Rhône** to the north, five-star hotels give way to lakeside promenades, **International Hill,** and rolling parks. Across the **River Arve** to the south lies the village of **Carouge,** home to bars and clubs (take tram #12 or 13 to pl. du Marché).

Tourist Office: r. du Mont-Blanc 18 (☎909 70 00), in the Central Post Office Building. From Cornavin, walk 5min. toward the Pont du Mont-Blanc. Staff books hotel rooms for 5SFr, leads English-language walking tours, and offers free city maps. Open mid-June to Aug. M 10am-6pm, Tu-Su 9am-6pm; Sept. to mid-June M 10am-6pm, Tu-Sa 9am-6pm.

Consulates: Australia, chemin des Fins 2 (☎799 91 00). **Canada,** av. de l'Ariana 5 (☎919 92 00). **New Zealand,** chemin des Fins 2 (☎929 03 50). **UK,** r. de Vermont 37 (☎918 24 26). **US,** r. Versonnex 7 (☎840 51 60, recorded info 840 51 61).

Currency Exchange: ATMs have the best rates. The currency exchange inside the **Gare Cornavin** has good rates with no commission on traveler's checks, makes cash advances on credit cards (min. 200SFr), and arranges **Western Union** transfers. Open M-Sa 7am-7:40pm, Su 9:15am-6pm.

GLBT Resources: Dialogai, r. de la Navigation 11-13 (☎906 4040). From Gare Cornavin, turn left, walk 5min. down r. de Lausanne, and turn right onto r. de la Navigation. Offers brochures and maps on GBLT nightlife; doubles as a cafe and nighttime hot spot. Mostly male, but women welcome. Open M 9:30am-1pm and 2-8pm, Tu 9:30am-6pm, W-F 9:30am-1am and 2-6pm.

Laundromat: Lavseul, r. de Monthoux 29 (☎735 9051). Wash 5SFr, dry 1SFr per 9min. Open daily 7am-midnight.

Emergency: Ambulance: ☎144. **Fire:** ☎118.

Police Station: ☎117. R. de Berne 6. Open M-F 9am-noon and 3-6:30pm, Sa 9am-noon.

Hospital: Hôpital Cantonal, r. Micheli-du-Crest 24 (☎372 3311; www.hug-ge.ch). Bus #1 or 5 or tram #12. Door #2 is for emergency care; door #3 is for consultations. For info on walk-in clinics, contact the **Association des Médecins** (☎320 8420).

Internet Access: Charly's Multimedia Check Point, r. de Fribourg 7 (☎901 1313; www.charlys.com). 1SFr per 10min., 5SFr per hr. Open M-Sa 9am-midnight, Su 2pm-midnight. **12Mix,** r. de-Monthoux 58 (☎731 6747; www.12mix.com). 3SFr per 30min., 5SFr per hr. Open daily 10am-midnight.

Post Office: Poste Centrale, r. du Mont-Blanc 18, 1 block from Gare Cornavin. Open M-F 7:30am-6pm, Sa 9am-4pm. *Poste Restante.* **Postal Code:** CH-1200.

ACCOMMODATIONS

The indispensable *Info Jeunes* lists about 50 budget options, and the tourist office publishes *Budget Hotels*, which stretches the definition of budget to 120SFr per person. Cheap beds are relatively scarce, so be sure to reserve ahead.

Auberge de Jeunesse (HI), r. Rothschild 30 (☎732 6260; www.yh-geneva.ch). Standard rooms, some with a beautiful lake views. Breakfast included. Laundry 8SFr. Internet. Max. stay 6 nights. Reception 6:30-10am and 2pm-midnight. Dorms 33SFr; doubles 92SFr, with shower 102SFr; triples 139SFr. 6SFr HI discount. AmEx/MC/V. ❷

City Hostel Geneva, r. Ferrier 2 (☎901 1500; www.cityhostel.ch). From the train station, head down r. de Lausanne for 5min. Take the 1st left onto r. du Prieuré, which becomes r. Ferrier. Spotless, cozy rooms. Delicious smells wafting out of the kitchens on each floor will make you want to take a break from restaurant fare. Lockers 10SFr deposit. Linens 3.50SFr. Internet 8SFr per hr. Reception 7:30am-noon and 1pm-midnight. Check-out 10am. Single-sex dorms 28SFr; singles 58SFr; doubles 85SFr. MC/V. ❷

Hôme St-Pierre, Cour St-Pierre 4 (☎310 3707; info@homestpierre.ch). Take bus #5 to pl. Neuve or walk from the station. Tourist groups flock to this 150-year-old "home," which has comfortable beds and a great location in the middle of old town, beside the cathedral. Church bells ring every 15min. Breakfast M-Sa 7SFr. Reception M-Sa 9am-noon and 4-8pm, Su 9am-noon. Dorms 27SFr; singles 40SFr; doubles 60SFr. MC/V. ❶

Cité Bleu Universitaire, av. Miremont 46 (☎839 2222). Take bus #3 (dir.: Crets-de-Champel) from the station to the last stop. University housing during the academic year; from July to Sept. dorm rooms, singles, and doubles are available. TV rooms, restaurant, disco (Th and Sa, free to guests), and small grocery. Reception M-F 8am-noon and 2-10pm, Sa 8am-noon and 6-10pm, Su 9-11am and 6-10pm. Check-out 10am. Dorm lockout 11am-6pm. Dorm curfew 11pm. Dorms 22SFr; singles 55SFr, students 46SFr; doubles 84/65SFr; studios with kitchenette and bath 84SFr. AmEx/MC/V. ❶

Camping Pointe-à-la-Bise, chemin de la Bise (☎752 1296). Take bus #8 or tram #16 to Rive, then bus E north to Bise and walk 10min. to lake. Reception July-Aug. 8am-noon and 2-9pm; Apr.-June and Sept. 8am-noon and 4-8pm. Open Apr.-Sept. Reserve ahead. Tent sites 18SFr, extra person 7SFr. 4-person bungalows 98SFr. AmEx/MC/V. ❶

FOOD

The frugal can pick up basics at *boulangeries*, *pâtisseries*, or at supermarkets. Many supermarkets have attached cafeterias; try the **Coop** on the corner of r. du Commerce and r. du Rhône, in the Centre Rhône Fusterie. Relatively cheap restaurants center in the **Les Pâquis** area, bordered by r. de Lausanne and Gare Cornavin on one side and quais Mont-Blanc and Wilson on the other. To the south, **Carouge** is known for its cozy pizzerias and funky *brasseries*.

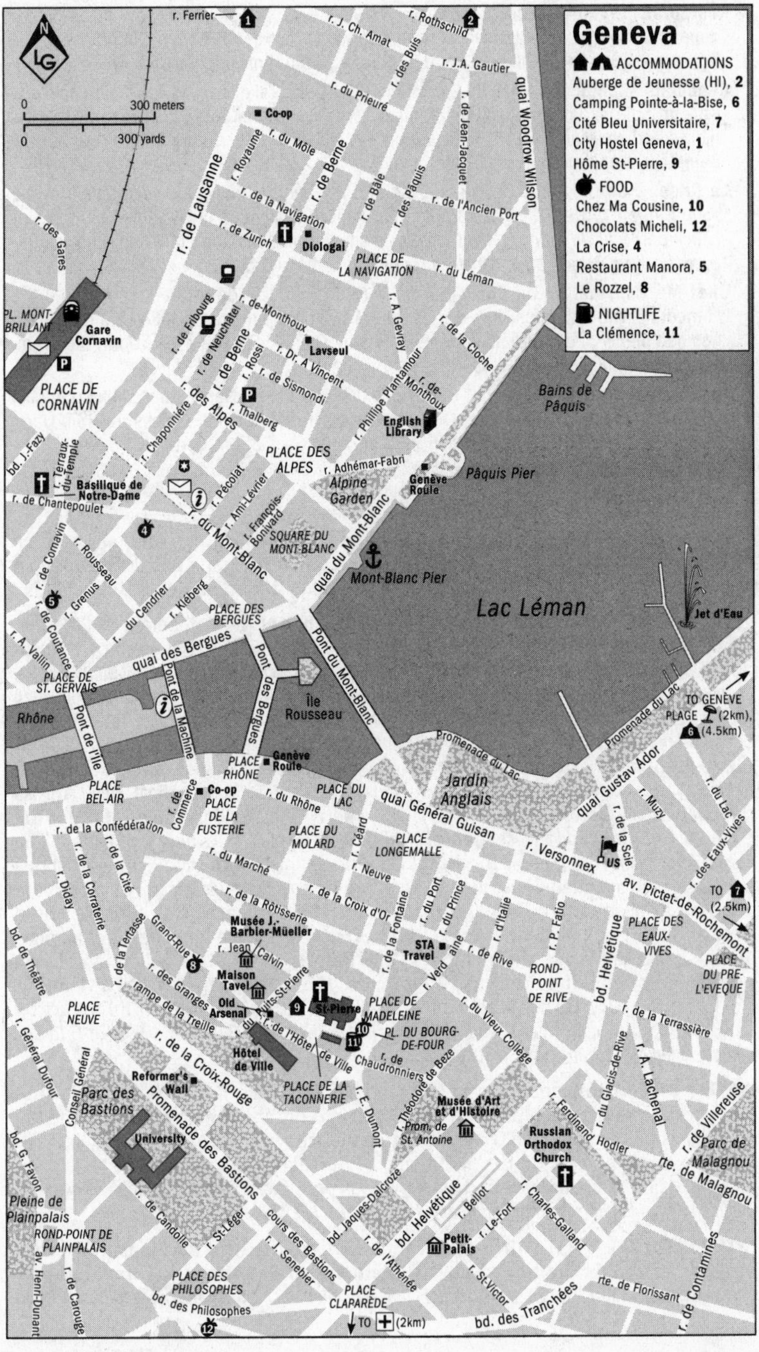

SWITZERLAND

Restaurant Manora, r. de Cornavin 4 (☎909 490), right of the station in the Manor department store. Varied selection and free water. Entrees 5-12SFr. Open M-W and F 7:30am-9:30pm, Th 7:30am-10pm, Su 9am-9:30pm. AmEx/DC/MC/V. ❶

Chocolats Micheli, r. Micheli-du-Crest 1 (☎329 9006). Take tram #13 to Plainpalais and walk up bd. des Philosophes until it intersects r. Micheli-du-Crest. Confectionary masterpieces and croissants (1-3SFr) abound in this Victorian cafe. Coffee 3.40SFr. Open Tu-F 8am-7pm, Sa 8am-5pm. MC/V. ❶

La Crise, r. de Chantepoulet 13 (☎738 0264). Every morning, the vegetables for the soup of the day (3.50SFr) are prepared in front of customers at this small but popular snack bar. *Plat du jour* 15SFr; 11SFr for a smaller portion. Open M-F 6am-3pm and 5-8pm, Sa 6am-3pm. Lunch served after noon. Cash only. ❶

Chez Ma Cousine, pl. du Bourg-de-Four 6 (☎310 9696), down the stairs behind the cathedral. With only 3 chicken dishes (all 14SFr) on the menu, this cheerful restaurant has had plenty of opportunities to perfect them. Open M-Sa 11am-11:30pm, Su 11am-10:30pm. AmEx/DC/MC/V. ❷

Le Rozzel, Grand-Rue 18 (☎311 89 29). Take bus #5 to pl. Neuve, then walk up the hill on r. Jean-Calvin to Grand-Rue. Outdoor seating in the Altstadt. Crepes 4-18SF. Open M, W, F 7:30am-8:30pm, Tu and Th 7:30am-7pm, Sa 7:30am-6pm. MC/V. ❶

SIGHTS

The most interesting sites are in a dense, easily walkable area. The tourist office offers 2hr. English-language walking tours. (Mid-June to Sept. M, W, F-Sa 10am, Tu and Th at 6:30pm; Oct. to mid-June only Sa at 10am. 15SFr, students 10SFr.)

VIEILLE VILLE. From 1536 to 1564, Calvin preached at the **Cathédrale de St-Pierre.** Climb the **north tower** if the stairs around the cathedral aren't enough of a workout. *(Open June-Sept. M-Sa 9:30am-6:30pm, Su noon-6:30pm; Oct.-May M-Sa 10am-5:30pm, Su noon-5:30pm. Tower 4SFr.)* Ruins, including a Roman sanctuary and a 4th-century basilica, rest in an **archaeological site** below the cathedral. *(Open June-Sept. Tu 11am-5pm, Sa-Su 11am-5:30pm; Oct.-May Tu-F 2-5pm, Sa-Su 1:30-5:30pm. 8SFr, students 4SFr.)* At the western end of the *vieille ville* sits the 14th-century **Maison Tavel,** which now houses a museum showcasing Geneva's history. *(Open Tu-Su 10am-5pm. Free.)* Across the street is the **Hôtel de Ville** (Town Hall), where world leaders met in 1864 for the Geneva Convention, the results of which still govern war conduct today. The **Grand-Rue,** which begins at the Hôtel de Ville, is lined with medieval workshops and 18th-century mansions; plaques commemorate famous residents like Jean-Jacques Rousseau, who was born at #40. Below the cathedral, along r. de la Croix-Rouge, the **Parc des Bastions** stretches from pl. Neuve to pl. des Philosophes and includes **Le Mur des Réformateurs** (The Reformers' Wall), a collection of bas-relief figures depicting Protestant Reformers. The park's center walkway leads to the **Petit-Palais,** Terrasse St-Victor 2, a beautiful mansion containing art by Chagall, Gauguin, Picasso, and Renoir. *(Bus #36 to Petit-Palais or #1, 3, or 5 to Claparède. Open M-F 10am-6pm, Sa-Su 10am-5pm. 10SFr, students 5SFr.)*

WATERFRONT. Down quai Gustave Ardor, the **Jet d'Eau,** Europe's highest fountain, spews a seven-ton plume of water 134m into the air. The **floral clock** in the **Jardin Anglais** pays homage to Geneva's watch industry. For a day at the beach, head down to **Genève Plage,** on the south side of the lake about halfway to the campground, where a water slide and an enormous pool await. *(☎736 24 82; www.geneve-plage.ch. Open mid-May to mid-Sept. daily 10am-8pm. 7SFr, students 4.50SFr.)*

INTERNATIONAL HILL. North of the train station, the International Red Cross building contains the impressive **International Red Cross and Red Crescent Museum,** av. de la Paix 17. *(Bus #8 or F to Appia or bus V or Z to Ariana. www.micr.org. Open*

M and W-Su 10am-5pm. 10SFr, students 5SFr. English-language audio tour 3SFr.) The nearby European headquarters of the **United Nations** is in the same building that once sheltered the League of Nations. The constant traffic of international diplomats provides enough entertainment in itself. *(Open July-Aug. daily 10am-5pm; Apr.-June and Sept.-Oct. daily 10am-noon and 2-4pm; Nov.-Mar. M-F 10am-noon and 2-4pm. 10SFr, students 8SFr.)*

ENTERTAINMENT AND NIGHTLIFE

Genève Agenda features event listings from festivals to movies. Be warned, however—a movie runs about 17SFr. From July to August, the **Cinelac** turns Genève Plage into an open-air cinema for American films, and free **jazz concerts** take place in Parc de la Grange. Geneva hosts the biggest celebration of **American Independence Day** outside the US (July 4), and the **Fêtes de Genève** in August fill the city with music and fireworks. The best party is **L'Escalade** in December, which lasts a full weekend and commemorates the repulsion of invading Savoyard troops.

Diverse nightlife offerings in Geneva are grouped in each of its distinct neighborhoods. **Place Bourg-de-Four,** below the cathedral in the *vieille ville*, attracts students and professionals to its charming terraces. **Place du Molard,** on the right bank by the pont du Mont-Blanc, has loud bars and clubs. **Les Pâquis,** near Gare Cornavin and pl. de la Navigation, is the city's red-light district, but it also has a wide array of rowdy, low-lit bars. This neighborhood is also home to many gay bars. **Carouge,** across the Arve, is a student-friendly locus of activity. In the *vieille ville*, generations of students have had their share of drinks at the intimate bar of **La Clémence,** pl. du Bourg-de-Four 20. You can count on it to be open, even when the rest of the city has shut down. (Open M-Th 7am-12:30am, F-Sa 7am-1:30am.)

LAUSANNE ☎021

The unique museums, distinctive neighborhoods, and lazy Lac Léman waterfront of Lausanne (pop. 125,000) make it well worth a stay. In the *vieille ville*, two flights of medieval stairs lead to the Gothic **Cathédrale.** (Open July to mid-Sept. M-F 7am-7pm, Sa-Su 8am-7pm; mid-Sept. to June daily 8am-5:30pm.) Below the cathedral is the **Hôtel de Ville,** on pl. de la Palud, the meeting point for **guided tours** of the town. (☎321 7766; www.lausanne.ch/visites. Tours May-Sept. M-Sa 10am and 3pm. 10SFr, students free.) The **Musée Olympique,** quai d'Ouchy 1, is a high-tech shrine to modern Olympians. Take bus #2 to Ouchy and follow the signs. (☎621 6511; www.olympic.org. Open May-Sept. daily 9am-6pm; Oct.-Apr. Tu-Su 9am-6pm. 15SFr, students 10SFr.) The **Collection de l'Art Brut,** av. Bergières 11, is filled with unusual sculptures, drawings, and paintings by fringe artists—schizophrenics, peasants, and criminals. Take bus #2 to Jomini or 3 to Beaulieu. (Open July-Aug. daily 11am-6pm; Sept.-June Tu-Su 11am-10pm. 8SFr, students 5SFr.) In Ouchy, several booths along quai de Belgique offer **water skiing** or **wake boarding** (35SFr per 15min.). **Lausanne Roule,** Haldimand 15, loans **free bikes** beside pl. de l'Europe. (☎076 441 8378. Open mid-Apr. to late Oct. daily 7:30am-9:30pm.)

Lausanne Guesthouse and Backpacker ❷, chemin des Epinettes 4, at the train tracks, manages to keep the noise out; it has a cozy living room. Head left and downhill out of the station on W. Fraisse; take the first right on chemin des Epinettes. (☎601 8000; www.lausanne-guesthouse.ch. Bike rental 20SFr per day. Linens 4SFr. Laundry 5SFr. Internet 8SFr per hr. Key deposit 20SFr. Reception 7:30am-noon and 3-10:30pm. Dorms 33SFr; singles 85SFr, with bath 94SFr; doubles 90/110SFr. 5% ISIC discount. MC/V; min. 300SFr.) Restaurants, cafes, and bars cluster around **Place St-François** and the *vieille ville*, while *boulangeries* sell cheap sandwiches on every street. Stop by **Le Barbare ❶,** Escaliers du Marché 27, near the cathedral and halfway down the covered staircase, for a sandwich (5.50SFr) or an omelette. (☎312 2132. Open M-Sa 8:30am-midnight. AmEx/MC/V.)

Trains leave from Lausanne for: Basel (2½hr., 1 per hr., 57SFr); Geneva (50min., every 20min., 20SFr); Montreux (20min., 2 per hr., 10SFr); Zürich (2½hr., 3 per hr., 65SFr). The **tourist office** in the train station reserves rooms for 4SFr and provides free city maps. (☎613 7373. Open daily 9am-7pm.) **Postal Code:** CH-1000.

MONTREUX

☎021

Palm trees line the Montreux shore, while tree-covered mountains frame **Lac Léman** and rise to snow-capped peaks. A resort town past its Jazz Age heyday, Montreux continues to draw travelers with its sublime scenery and the music that still swings during the annual **Montreux Jazz Festival,** which erupts for 15 days starting the first Friday in July. Famous for discovering and drawing exceptional talent, the festival has hosted icons like Bob Dylan, Paul Simon, and Miles Davis. (www.montreuxjazz.com. Tickets 59-179SFr.) If you can't get tickets, come anyway for **Montreux Jazz Under the Sky,** 500 hours of free, open-air concerts on three stages. The **Château de Chillon,** a medieval fortress on a nearby island, features all the comforts of home: prison cells, a torture chamber, and a weapons room. Take the CGN ferry (15SFr) or bus #1 (3SFr) to Chillon. (☎966 8910; www.chillon.ch. Open daily Apr.-Sept. 9am-6pm; Mar. and Oct. 9:30am-6pm; Nov.-Feb. 10am-5pm. 10SFr, students 8SFr. In summer, tours daily 11:30am and 3:30pm. 6SFr.)

SWITZERLAND

Cheap rooms in Montreux are scarce year-round and almost nonexistent during the Jazz Festival. **Riviera Lodge ❷**, pl. du Marché 5, in the town of Vevey, is worth the commute for its friendly staff, water views, and unbeatable prices. Guests also get a pass that includes free bus transportation and discounts on museums and attractions. Take the train or bus #1 to Vevey (20min., 6 per hr., 2.80SFr). From the bus stop, head to the left away from the train station on the main road and follow the brown signs to the lodge, located in the main square on the water. (☎923 8040; www.rivieralodge.ch. Breakfast 8SFr. Linens 5SFr. Laundry 6SFr. Internet 7SFr per hr. Reception 8am-noon and 4-8pm. Call ahead if arriving late. Dorms 27SFr; doubles 88SFr. MC/V.) **Babette's ❷,** Grand-Rue 60, downstairs from the station and to the left, serves affordable crepes for lunch and dessert. (☎963 7796. Crepes 7-14SFr. Sandwiches 7-15SFr. Open daily 7am-7pm. MC/V.) Grand-Rue and av. de Casino have inexpensive markets. There is a **Coop Pronto** supermarket to the right of the train station. (Open daily 6am-10pm.) **Trains** leave for: Bern (1½hr., 2 per hr., 37SFr), Geneva (1hr., 2 per hr., 27SFr), and Lausanne (20min., 3-5 per hr., 9.80SFr). Descend the stairs opposite the station and head left on Grand-Rue for 5-10min. to reach the **tourist office,** on pl. du Débarcadère, which provides free maps. (☎962 8484; www.montreux-vevey.com. Open mid-June to mid-Sept. M-F 9am-6pm, Sa-Su 10am-5pm; mid-Sept. to mid-June M-F 9am-noon and 1-5:30pm, Sa-Su 10am-2pm.) **Postal Code:** CH-1820.

NEUCHÂTEL

☎032

Alexandre Dumas once said that Neuchâtel (pop. 164,000) appeared to be carved out of butter; visitors gazing down street after street filled with yellow stone architecture will immediately see why. The old town centers around **place des Halles,** a block from **place Pury,** the hub of every bus line. From pl. des Halles, turn left onto r. de Château and climb the stairs on the right to reach **Collégiale Church** and the **château** that gives the town its name. (Church open daily Apr.-Sept. 9am-8pm; Oct.-Mar. 9am-6:30pm.) Entrance to the château is available only through a free tour. (1 per hr., every hr. Apr.-Sept. M-F 10am-noon and 2-4pm, Sa 10-11am and 2-4pm, Su 2-4pm.) The nearby **Tour des Prisons** (Prison Tower), on r. Jeanne-Hochberg, has a prime view of the entire city and the lake. (Open Apr.-Sept. daily 8am-6pm. 1SFr.) The **Musée d'Histoire Naturelle,** off r. de l'Hôpital, has a great collection of just about every stuffed creature that you could imagine. Turn right from pl. des Halles onto Croix du Marché, which becomes r. de l'Hôpital. (☎717 79 60. Open

Tu-Su 10am-6pm. 6SFr, students 3SFr. W free.) The **Musée d'Arts et d'Histoire,** esplanade Léopold-Robert 1, houses an eclectic collection of paintings, weapons, textiles, and teacups. Exit the tram station and head to the right along the lake promenade about 100m. (Open Tu-Su 10am-6pm. 8SFr, students 4SFr. W free.) Beside the water and at the edge of the square by the tourist office, **Neuchâtel Roule** lends free bikes. (☎717 7675; www.newride.ch. Passport and 20SFr deposit. Open Apr.-Sept. daily 7:30am-9:30pm.) For the best views of the area, ride your bike or take bus #7 to La Coudre, where you can hop on the **funicular** that rises up through the forest to the little village of Chaumont (1 per hr. 9am-7pm. 4.60SFr).

The **Hôtel des Arts ❹,** r. Pourtalès 3, is the closest it comes to budget accommodation in Neuchâtel. From the underground tram exit, walk a block toward the city center on av. du Premier-Mars and turn left onto r. Pourtalès. Ask for a room on the "quiet side" of the building. (☎727 6161. Breakfast included. Reception 24hr. Check-out noon. Singles 87SFr, with bath 98-136SFr; doubles 112/155-180SFr. AmEx/DC/MC/V.) In the heart of the old town at **A.R. Knecht Boulangerie et Pâtisserie ❶,** on the corner of pl. des Halles and r. du Coq d'Inde, locals munch on croissants stuffed with spiced ham (3SFr) and *pain noix* (bread with nuts; 3SFr) while enjoying the busy come-and-go of passersby. (☎725 1321. Open Tu-Sa 6am-6:30pm. Cash only.) **Migros,** r. de l'Hôpital 12, sells groceries. (Open M-W 8am-6:30pm, Th 8am-10pm, F 7:30am-6:30pm, Sa 7:30am-7pm.)

Trains run to Basel (1¾hr., 1 per hr., 34SFr), Bern (45min., 1 per hr., 18SFr), and Geneva (1½hr., 1 per hr., 37SFr). A underground **tram** (1SFr) runs from the station to the shore area. Head to the right after disembarking and walk 5min. along the lake to the **tourist office,** in the same building as the post office, which provides free city maps and book rooms for free. (☎889 6890; www.neuchateltourisme.ch. Open July-Aug. M-F 9am-6:30pm, Sa 9am-4pm, Su 10am-2pm; Sept.-June M-F 9am-noon and 1:30-5:30pm, Sa 9am-noon.) **Postal Code:** CH-2001.

ITALIAN SWITZERLAND

Ever since Switzerland won Ticino, the only Italian-speaking Swiss canton, from Italy in 1512, the region has been renowned for its mix of Swiss efficiency and Italian *dolce vita.* It's no wonder the rest of Switzerland vacations here among jasmine-laced villas painted in the muted pastels of Italian gelato.

LUGANO ☎091

Set in a valley between sloping mountains, Lugano (pop. 52,000) draws plenty of visitors with its seamless blend of artistic flair and historical religious sites. The frescoes of the 16th-century **Cattedrale San Lorenzo,** just south of the train station, are still vivid despite their age. The most spectacular fresco in town is the gargantuan crucifix in the **Chiesa Santa Maria degli Angiuli,** 200m to the right of the tourist office. Armed with topographic maps and trail guides (sold at the tourist office), **hikers** can tackle the rewarding 5hr. hike to the top of Monte Boglia (1516m), while tamer souls can reach the peaks of Monte Bré (923m), which is also accessible by **funicular.** The **Asbest Adventure's Best,** V. Basilea 28 (☎966 1114), provides information on various adventure sports in the area, from snowshoeing and skiing (90SFr per day) to paragliding (165SFr) and canyoning (from 90SFr).

The pink 19th-century villa of **Hotel and Hostel Montarina ❶,** V. Montarina 1, has a swimming pool and terrace. (☎966 7272; www.montarina.ch. Breakfast 12SFr. Linens 4SFr. Laundry 5SFr. Reception 8am-10:30pm. Open Mar.-Oct. Dorms 25SFr; singles 70SFr, with bath 80SFr; doubles 100/120SFr. AmEx/MC/V.) Groceries are at **Piccobello** at the train station. (Open daily 6am-10pm.) The **Coop City** supermarket, V. Nassa 22, also has a food court on the top floor. (Open M-W and F

8am-6:30pm, Th 8am-9pm, Sa 8am-5pm.) **Trains** leave P. della Stazione on the hill above the city for Locarno (1hr., 2 per hr., 17SFr), Milan, ITA (1½hr., 1 per hr., 21SFr), and Zürich (3hr., 8 per day, 57SFr). The **tourist office,** across from the ferry station at the corner of P. Rezzonico, provides free maps, makes hotel reservations for 4SFr, and has free guided walks of the city on Monday at 9am. (☎913 3232; www.lugano-tourism.ch. Open Apr.-Oct. M-F 9am-7pm, Sa 9am-6pm, Su 10am-6pm; Nov.-Mar. M-F 9am-noon and 2-5pm.) **Postal Code:** CH-6900.

LOCARNO ☎091

A Swiss vacation spot on the shores of Lago Maggiore, Locarno (pop. 30,000) gets over 2200 hours of sunlight per year—more than anywhere else in Switzerland. For centuries, visitors have journeyed here solely to see the orange-yellow church of **Madonna del Sasso** (Madonna of the Rock), founded in 1487. A 20min. walk up V. al Sasso leads to the top and passes life-sized wooden niche statues along the way. Hundreds of heart-shaped medallions on the church walls commemorate acts of Mary's intervention in the lives of worshippers who have journeyed here. (Grounds open daily 6:30am-6:45pm.) For 10 days at the beginning of each August, Locarno swells with pilgrims of a different sort and prices shoot through the roof when its world-famous **film festival** draws over 150,000 cinephiles.

To reach **Pensione Città Vecchia ❷,** V. Toretta 15, turn right onto V. Toretta from P. Grande. (☎751 4554. Breakfast included. Dorms 40SFr; doubles 120SFr; triples 150SFr. Cash only.) **Ristorante Manora ❶,** V. della Stazione 1, offers cheap, self-service dining. (Salad bar 4.50-10SFr. Pasta buffet 8-13SFr. Entrees 11-17SFr. Open Nov.-Feb. M-Sa 7:30am-9pm, Su 8am-9pm; Mar.-Oct. M-Sa 7:30am-10pm, Su 8am-9pm. V.) Get groceries at the **Aperto** in the station. (Open daily 6am-10pm.) **Trains** run from P. Stazione to Lugano (1hr., 2 per hr., 16.20SFr), Luzern (2½hr., 2 per hr., 51SFr), and Milan, ITA (2hr., 1 per hr., 37SFr). The **tourist office,** on P. Grande in the casino, makes hotel reservations and has free maps. From the station, go left down V. della Stazione until you reach P. Grande. (☎791 00 91; www.maggiore.ch. Open Apr.-Oct. M-F 9am-6pm, Sa 10am-6pm, Su 10am-1:30pm and 2:30-5pm; Nov.-Mar. M-F 9am-6pm, Sa 10am-6pm.) **Postal Code:** CH-6600.

ST. MORITZ ☎081

The tourism pioneers of St. Moritz (pop. 5600) were the first to bring their British summer guests to the "top of the world" in winter, giving birth to Alpine winter tourism. It is thus no surprise that St. Moritz, having hosted the only Olympic Games in Switzerland, is still a major destination for year-round sports. But the average 322 days of sunshine per year fall mostly upon the skin of the rich, as the luxury tourism sector dominates St. Moritz. But one doesn't have to stay at the world-famous Kulm Hotel to enjoy the slopes that have hosted the Alpine skiing world championships four times; ski and snowboard rentals (38SFr per day, 139SFr per 6 days), and the ski lifts are no more expensive than at other resorts in the region. In summer, **St. Moritz Experience** (☎833 77 14) organizes adventures like canyoning and hiking. The cheapest beds in town are at **Central Lodge ❸,** V. Dal Bagn 17. (☎833 15 50; www.central-lodge.ch. Breakfast included. Reception 5-8pm. Dorms 35SFr; doubles 110SFr; triples 135SFr.) To reach **Camping Olympiaschanze ❶,** take bus #1 or 4 from the station. (☎833 40 90. Tent sites 18SFr, 5.60SFr per person. MC/V.) The **Coop** supermarket also has a restaurant (open M-Th 8am-6:30pm, F 8am-8pm, Sa 8am-5pm). **Trains** run to Davos (1½hr., 1 per hr., 26SFr) and Zürich (3½hr., 1 per hr., 67SFr) via Chur. The **tourist office,** V. Maista 12, is uphill from the station. (☎837 33 33. Open mid-June to mid-Sept. and mid-Dec. to mid-Apr. M-F 9am-6:30pm, Sa 9am-6pm, Su 4-6pm; mid-Apr. to mid-June and mid-Sept. to mid-Dec. M-F 9am-noon and 4-6pm, Sa 9am-noon.) **Postal Code:** CH-7500.

TURKEY (TÜRKİYE)

Since the first human settlements in Asia minor, Turkey has hosted some of the world's greatest civilizations, each waxing with exuberance and then fading with despair. Hellenes, Hittites, Macedonians, Romans, Byzantines, and Ottomans each left their mark. Though resolutely secular by government degree, every facet of Turkish life is graced by the religious traditions of a 99% Muslim population. Tourists cram İstanbul and the glittering western coast, while Anatolia (the Asian portion of Turkey) remains a purist backpacker's paradise: pristine alpine meadows, cliffside monasteries, and a truly hospitable people.

ESSENTIALS

FACTS AND FIGURES

Official Name: Republic of Turkey.

Form of Government: Republican parliamentary democracy.

Capital: Ankara.

Major Cities: Adana, Bursa, Gaziantep, İstanbul, İzmir.

Population: 70,414,000.

Land Area: 770,760 sq. km.

Time Zone: GMT +2 or +3.

Language: Turkish (official). Also Kurdish and Arabic.

Religions: Muslim (99.8%).

Largest Skewer of Kebap Meat: Created by the Melike Döner Co. in Osmangazi-Bursa, Turkey on November 6, 2005. Weighed in at 2698kg (5948 lb.).

WHEN TO GO

With mild winters and hot summers, there is no bad time to travel to Turkey. While most tourists go in July and August, it's best to visit between April and June or September and October, when days are temperate, crowds are smaller, and prices are lower. November to February is the rainy season, so bring appropriate gear.

DOCUMENTS AND FORMALITIES

VISA AND ENTRY INFORMATION. Turkish visa requirements vary from country to country; most visas are multiple-entry and last up to 90 days (see below). If arriving by ferry, expect to pay a €10 port tax.

ENTRANCE REQUIREMENTS

Passport: Required for all travelers.

Visa: Required for citizens of Australia, Canada, some EU countries, the UK, and the US. Citizens of New Zealand do not need a visa to enter. Single-entry visas (US$20) are available at the border and are valid for up to 90 days.

Letter of Invitation: Not required.

Inoculations: Not required. Recommended up-to-date on DTaP (diphtheria, tetanus, and pertussis), hepatitis A, hepatitis B, MMR (measles, mumps, and rubella), polio booster, and typhoid.

Work Permit: Required for all foreigners planning to work in Turkey.

Driving Permit: Required for all those planning to drive.

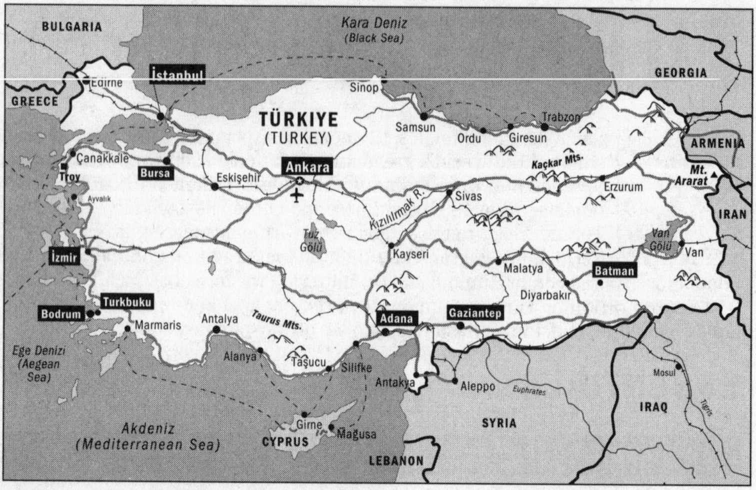

EMBASSIES AND CONSULATES. Foreign embassies for Turkey are in Ankara. Turkish embassies and consulates abroad include: **Australia,** 60 Mugga Way, Red Hill, Canberra, ACT 2603 (☎02 6295 0227; www.turkishembassy.org.au); **Canada,** 197 Wurtemburg St., Ottawa, ON K1N 8L9 (☎613-789-4044; www.turkishembassy.com); **Ireland,** 11 Clyde Rd., Ballsbridge, Dublin 4 (☎668 52 40; www.mzv.cz/dublin); **New Zealand,** 15-17 Murphy St., Level 8, Wellington (☎04 472 1290; TURKEM@xtra.co.nz); **UK,** 43 Belgrave Sq., London SW1X 8PA (☎20 7393 0202; www.turkishembassylondon.org); **US,** 2525 Massachusetts Ave., NW, Washington, D.C. 20008 (☎202-612-6700; www.turkishembassy.org).

PRICES

TURKEY	❶	❷	❸	❹	❺
ACCOMMODATIONS	under 15YTL	15-30YTL	30-50YTL	50-70YTL	over 70YTL
FOOD	under 5YTL	6-10YTL	11-15YTL	15-20YTL	over 20YTL

TOURIST SERVICES AND MONEY

TOURIST OFFICES. In big cities like İstanbul, many places that claim to be tourist offices are actually travel agencies. That said, **travel agencies** can often be more helpful for finding accommodations or booking transportation than the official Turkish **tourist offices.** Though it's best to shop around from agency to agency for a deal on tickets, be wary of exceptionally low prices—they may tack on exorbitant hidden charges. The official tourism website (www.tourismturkey.org) has a list of all offices, visa information, and helpful links.

NEW TURKISH LIRA (YTL)		
	AUS$1 = 1.11YTL	1YTL = AUS$0.90
	CDN$1 = 1.30YTL	1YTL = CDN$0.77
	EUR€1 = 1.87YTL	1YTL = EUR€0.54
	NZ$1 = 0.91YTL	1YTL = NZ$1.09
	UK£1 = 2.76YTL	1YTL = UK£0.36
	US$1 = 1.45YTL	1YTL = US$0.69

MONEY. In response to rampant inflation and ever-confusing prices, Turkey revalued its currency in 2005, dropping 6 zeroes. One million Turkish Lira became 1 **Yeni Türk Lirası** (New Turkish Lira; YTL). One New Turkish Lira equals 100 **New Kuruş.** While Old Turkish Lira are no longer accepted as currency, Turkish Lira banknotes (bills) can be redeemed until 2016 and coins can be redeemed until January 1, 2007 by the **Central Bank of the Republic of Turkey (CBRT)** and **T.C. Ziraat Bank** branches. Banks are generally open 8:30am-noon and 1:30-5:30pm. **Inflation** has decreased dramatically in recent years, going from 45% in 2003 to just 8.2% in 2006. The best **currency exchange** rates can be found at state-run **post and telephone offices (PTT).** Many places in İstanbul and other major cities accept **euros. Tipping** isn't required in Turkey: at bathhouses, hairdressers, hotels, and restaurants, a tip of 5-15% is common, but taxis and *dolmuş* drivers do not expect tips.

If **bargaining** is a fine art, then İstanbul has lots and lots of that art. In most places, bargaining is expected. Never pay full price at the Grand Bazaar; start out by offering less than 50% of the asking price. If you're not asked to pay a service charge when paying by credit card, you're probably paying too much for your purchase. The **value added tax (VAT)** is 18% on general purchases and 8% on food and is included in most prices. Spending more than 118YTL in one day entitles travelers to a tax refund upon leaving Turkey; look for "Tax-Free Shopping" stickers in shop windows or ask for a form inside.

SAFETY AND OTHER CONCERNS

WOMEN TRAVELERS. Foreign women, especially those traveling alone, attract significant attention in Turkey. Unwanted catcalls and other forms of verbal harassment are common; physical harassment is rare. Regardless of the signals a foreign woman intends to send, her foreignness alone may suggest a liberal openness to friendly or amorous advances. Turks often stare at one another more than visitors are used to, and women in particular may feel uncomfortable about the stares. Smiling, regarded in the West as a sign of confidence and friendliness, is sometimes associated in Turkey with a lack of sincerity or deception. However, as long as women expect plenty of attention and take certain common-sense precautions, there is no need for anxiety.

GLBT TRAVELERS. Although homosexuality is legal in Turkey, religious and social dictates keep most homosexual activity discreet. Homophobia can be a problem, especially in remote areas; expect authorities to be unsympathetic. Gay and lesbian travelers will benefit from the close contact that Turks maintain with same-sex friends, but public displays of affection should be avoided. Turkey's urban centers have bars and informal cruising areas for men only, though they may not be very overt. **Lambda İstanbul,** a GBLT support group, lists resources and guides to gay-friendly establishments on its website (www.qrd.org/www/world/europe/turkey).

ETIQUETTE. Turks value **hospitality** and will frequently go out of their way to welcome travelers, commonly offering to buy visitors a meal or a cup of *çay* (tea). Do not refuse tea unless you have very strong objections; accepting the offer provides a friendly, easy way to converse with locals. If you are invited to a Turkish house as a guest, it is customary to bring a small gift such as flowers or chocolates and to remove your shoes before entering. A pair of slippers will usually be provided. When chatting with Turks, do not speak with any disrespect or skepticism about **Atatürk,** founder of modern Turkey, and avoid other sensitive subjects. In particular, do not discuss the Kurdish issue, the PKK, Northern Cyprus, or Turkey's human rights record.

BODY VIBES. In Turkey, **body language** often matters as much as the spoken word. When a Turk raises his chin and clicks his tongue, he means *hayır* (no); this gesture is sometimes accompanied by a shutting of the eyes or the raising of eyebrows. A sideways shake of the head means *anlamadım* (I don't understand), and *evet* (yes) may be signalled by a sharp downward nod. If a Turk waves a hand up and down at you, palm toward the ground, she is signaling you to come, not bidding you farewell. In Turkey the idle habit of snapping the fingers of one hand and then slapping the top of the other fist is considered obscene. It is also considered rude to point your finger or the sole of your shoe toward someone. Though public displays of affection by couples are considered inappropriate, Turks of both sexes greet each other with a kiss on both cheeks, and often touch or hug one another during conversation. They also tend to stand close to one another when talking.

DRESS. Wearing shorts will single you out as a tourist, as most Turks, particularly women, do not wear them. Women will probably find a head scarf or a bandana handy, perhaps essential, in more conservative regions. Even in İstanbul and the resort towns of the Aegean and Mediterranean coasts where casual, "beachy" dress is more widely accepted, scant clothing sends an audacious or flirtatious signal. Long skirts and lightweight pants are most acceptable, and they are also comfortable and practical, especially in summer. T-shirts are generally acceptable, though you should cover your arms in the more religious parts of the country. Topless bathing is common in some areas along the Aegean and Mediterranean coasts, but unacceptable in other regions.

RELIGION

About 99% of the Turkish population is **Muslim.** Jews and Orthodox Christians of Greek, Armenian, and Syrian backgrounds compose the remainder. While Turkey does not have an official state religion, every Turkish citizen's national identification card states his or her creed. Although Atatürk's reforms aimed to secularize the nation, Islam continues to play a key role in the country's politics and culture.

Many of Turkey's greatest architectural monuments, including **tombs** and **mosques,** have religious significance. Visitors are welcome, but they ought to show respect for the holiness of these places by dressing and acting appropriately. Shorts and skimpy clothing are forbidden inside mosques. Women must cover their arms, heads, and legs, and both sexes should take off their shoes and carry them inside. There are usually shoe racks in the back of the mosques; otherwise, caretakers will provide plastic bags for carrying shoes. Do not take flash photos, never photograph people in prayer, and avoid visits on Fridays (Islam's holy day). Also forgo visiting during prayer times, which are announced by the *müezzin*'s call to prayer from the mosque's minarets. Donations are sometimes expected.

LANGUAGE

Turkish (Türkçe), the official language of Turkey, is spoken by approximately 55 million people domestically and about one million abroad. It is the most prominent member of the Turkic language family, which also includes Azerbaijani, Kazakh, Kirgiz, Uyghur, and Uzbek. Turkish is also related to other languages spoken in central Asia, such as Mongolian and Manchu. Korean is sometimes included in this group as well.

Originally written in Arabic script with strong Arabic and Persian influences, Atatürk reformed the language in 1928 using a Romanized alphabet and attempted to purge foreign influences so as to minimize Islam's sway on secular life. This linguistic cleansing was not absolute, and common Arabic and Persian words such as *merhaba* (hello) remain.

Visitors with little or no experience with Turkish should not be intimidated. Any attempt at speaking Turkish will be much appreciated. English is widely spoken wherever tourism is big business—mainly in the major coastal towns. A small phrasebook will help greatly during your travels. For more in-depth study, consult *Teach Yourself Turkish* by Pollard and Pollard (New York, 1996; $12).

BEYOND TOURISM

Finding work in Turkey is difficult, as the government tries to restrict employment to Turkish citizens. Foreigners wishing to work must obtain a **work visa,** which in turn requires a **permit** issued by the Ministry of the Interior. An excellent prospect for working in Turkey is **teaching English.** Because English is the language of instruction at many Turkish universities, it is possible to enroll directly as a special student. Doing so might be less expensive than enrolling in an American university program.

Buğday Ekolojik Yaşam Kapısı İletişim Bilgileri, Lüleci Hendek Cad. 120/1-2, Kuledibi, İstanbul (☎212 252 52 55; www.bugday.org/eng). Support sustainable agriculture by living or working on an *Ekolojik TaTuTa* (organic farm), or volunteer at the national organic farm association.

Gençtur Turizm ve Seyahat Ac. Ltd., İstiklal Cad. 212, Aznavur Pasajı, Kat: 5, Galatasaray, İstanbul 80080 (☎212 244 62 30; http://genctur.com). A tourism and travel agency that sets up various workshops, nannying jobs, volunteer camps, and year-round study tours in Turkey.

Volunteers for Peace, 1034 Tiffany Rd., Belmont, VT 05730, USA (☎802-259-2759; www.vfp.org). Arranges placement in volunteer camps in Turkey. Registration fee $250.

TURKEY

İSTANBUL

In Turkey, the "East meets West" refrain of fusion restaurants, trendy boutiques, and yoga studios returns to its semantic roots. On two intercontinental bridges over the Bosphorus, Europe and Asia meet. İstanbul, Turkey's largest city, is the site of this encounter. The city's Asian side sprawls with Western-style suburbs, while the mosques and bazaars of Old İstanbul sit on the European half.

PHONE CODES: The code is **212** on the European side, **216** on the Asian side. All numbers listed here begin with 212 unless otherwise specified.

INTERCITY TRANSPORTATION

Flights: İstanbul's airport, **Atatürk Havaalanı (IST;** ☎663 6400), is 30km from the city. Buses (3 per hr. 6am-11pm) connect domestic and international terminals. To get to Sultanahmet from the airport, catch the HAVAS bus or the metro to the Aksaray stop at the end of the line. From there catch a tram to Sultanahmet. A direct taxi to Sultanahmet costs 25YTL. Most hostels and hotels in Sultanahmet arrange convenient airport shuttles several times a day.

Trains: Haydarpaşa Garı (☎216 336 04 75 or 336 20 63), on the Asian side, sends trains to Anatolia. To get to the station, take the ferry from Karaköy pier #7 (every 20min. 6am-midnight), halfway between Galata Bridge and the Karaköy tourist office. Rail tickets for Anatolia can be bought in advance at the TCDD office upstairs or at any of the travel agencies in Sultanahmet. Trains go to **Ankara** (6½-9½hr., 6 per day, from 22YTL) and **Kars** (11-13½hr., 1 per day, from 35YTL). Sirkeci Garı (☎527 00 50 or 527

Tram and Cable Car
Metro and Tünel
BALAT
FENER
HALİÇ (GOLDEN HORN)
Arda Cad.
Ibadullah Cad.
Hasköy Yolu
St. Stephen of the Bulgars
Orthodox Patriarchate
Fethiye Museum
Kariye Camii (Chora Church)
Old City Walls
Savaklar Cad.
Topkapı-Edirnekapı Cad.
Demirhisar Cad.
Mürselpaşa Cad.
Kirkanber Sok.
Malla Şakir So
Çınçınlı Çeşme Sok.
Mumhanesi Cad.
Egrikapı
Ulubat I Hasan Sok.
Paşa Hamam Sok.
Küküçeşme Sok.
Kamış Sok.
Rifat Ef. Sok.
Çilinger Sok.
Hacı Isa Bostan Sok.
Neşter Sok.
Kaya Cad.
Miraç Sok.
Draman Cad.
Kalpakçıçeşme Sok.
Kiremit Cad.
Pr. Naci Şensoy Cad.
Salma Tomruk Cad.
Fethiye Cad.
Niyazi Mısrı Sok.
KARAGÜMRÜK
Kefevi Sok.
Allşah Sok.
Dılmaç Sok.
Dolaplı Bostan Sok.
Ismailaga Cad.
Selimiye Camii
Sarmaşik Sok.
Prof. Naci Sensoy Cad.
Kelebek S.
Nurettin Tekkesi Sok.
Manyasa Zade Cad.
Sultan Selim Sok.
Tabak Yunus Sok.
Uzunyol Sok.
Fevzipaşa Cad.
Karakol Sok.
Beycegiz Fırın Sok.
ÇARŞAMBA
Haliç Cad.
Kara Sankli Sok.
Boston Sok.
Sofalı Çeşme Sok.
Hasan Fehmi Paşa Cad.
Saray Ağası Sok.
Hüseyin Remzi Bay Sok.
Ispanakcı Sok.
Çirakcı Çeş. Sok.
Abdülezel Paşa Cad.
Nalıncı Cemal Cad.
Bostan Hamam Sok.
Melekhoca Cad.
Eski Alipaşa Cad.
Altay Sok.
Darüşşafaka Cad.
Kadı Çeşmesi Sok.
Müftü Hamam Sok.
Karadeniz Cad.
Cibali Cad.
Salihpaşa Cad.
Kabakulak Sok.
Ahşanminare Sok.
Yavuz Selim Cad.
Yusuf Ziyapaşa Sok.
Başhoca Sok.
Sinancamii Sok.
Ali Tekin Sok.
Keçeciler Cad.
Tetimmeler Cad.
Yeşarizade Sok.
ZEYREK
Unkapanı
Adnan Menderes Bul.
Akbilek Sok.
Zembilci Sok.
Sarıgüzel Cad.
Karkut Ata Sok.
Hoca Effendi Sok.
Başmüezzin S Sok.
Baş Imam Sok.
Zeyrek Mehmet P. Sok.
Şemsettin Sami Sok.
Zülali Çeşme Sok.
Fatih Camii
Hattat Nazif Sok.
KÜÇÜKPAZAR
Akşemsettin Cad.
Balipaşa Cad.
Hüsrevpaşa Sok.
Sar Nusuh Sok.
Kocasinan Cad.
FATİH
Fatih Türbesi Sok.
Mıhcılar Cad.
Haydar Cad.
Hacıkadın Cad.
ÇAPA
Akdeniz Cad.
Mutemet Sok.
Ocaklı Sok.
Okmuşadam Sok.
Zeyrek Sok.
Itfaiye Sok.
SÜLEYMANİYE
Guraba Hastanesi Cad.
EMNİYET
Karaman Sok.
Çamsokağı
Niyza Sok.
Atatürk Bul.
Halıcılar Cad.
Macar Kardeşler Cad.
Açiklar Sok.
Vatanperver Sok.
Dolap Cad.
Himmet Sok
Kirazcimescit Sok.
ÇAPA
Oğuzhan Cad.
Havlucu Sok.
Yeşil Tekke Sok.
SARAÇHANE
Cemal Yener Tosyal Cad.
S. Baş -Vezneciler Cad.
Belediye (City Hall)
Millet Cad.
Adnan Menderes Bul.
Horhor Cad.
Molla Husrev Toprak Sok.
Rogip Bey Sok.
Dedeefendi
Besim Ömer Paşa Cad.
Ahmet Vekif Paşa Cad.
FINDIKZADE
Atatürk Bul.
Fevzibey Cad.
Mart Şeh. Cad.
Süleymaniye Cad.
Gökalp Ziya Sok.
HASEKİ
AKSARAY
Yeşiltulumba Sok.
Fethibey Cad.
H. Zedeler Sok.
Reşitpaşa Cad.
Kimyager Dervis Sok.
Kızılelma Cad.
Tevfik Fikaret Sok.
Özbek Süleyman Efendi Sok.
YUSUFPAŞA
AKSARAY
LALELİ
ÜNİVERSİTE
Ordu Cad.
Yeniçeriler
Haseki Cad.
Inkilap Cad.
Aksaray Cad.
Lalell Cad.
Koska Cad.
Mesih Paşa Cad.
Pehlivan
Tatlıkuyu
Cerrahpaşa Cad.
Tir. Hasan P.Sok.
Azimkar Sok.
Koca Ragıp Sok.
Sümbül Sinan Sok.
Kurban Sok.
Yokuşu
Nişancabostanı
Hekimoğlu Alipaşa Cad.
Küçük Langa Cad.
Hayriye Tüccar Cad.
Türkeli Cad.
Esekkapı Sok.
Koca Mustafa Paşa Cad.
Langabastoni Sok.
Mustafa Kemal Cad.
Güvenlik Cad.
Hadımodalar Sok.
Hemşeri Sok.
Sepetçi Selim Sok.
Mollataşi Cad.
Kenanbey Sok.
Daltaban
Mithatpaşa Cad.
Çifte
Küçük Langa Cad.
Namık Kemal Cad.
Bostani Sok.
YENİKAPI
Telliodalar Cad.
Sarapnel Sok.
Kennedy Cad.
Arapzede
A. Nafiz Gürman Cad.
Yenikapı Seabus Pier
K. Mustafa Paşa Tren. İst.

TURKEY

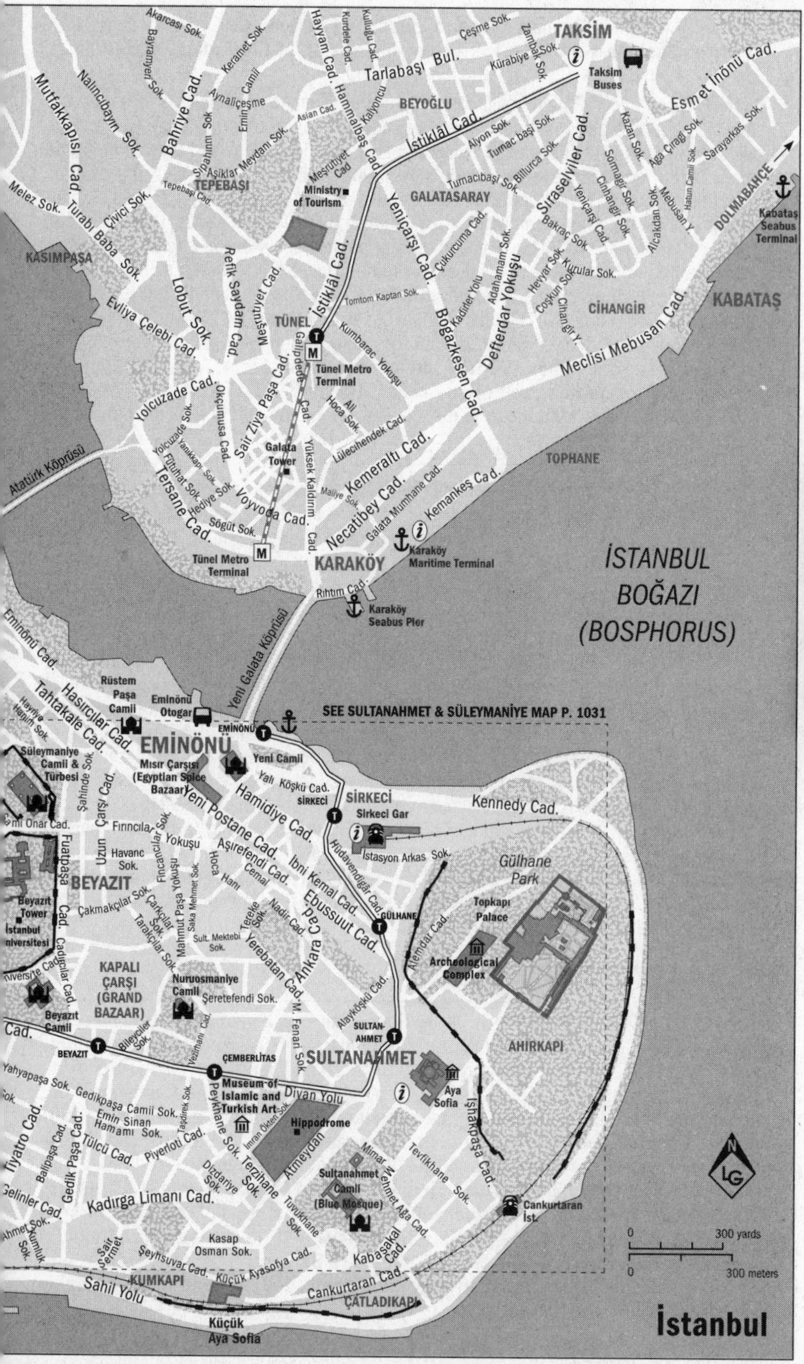

TAKSİM
Taksim Buses
Tarlabaşı Bul.
BEYOĞLU
İstiklâl Cad.
Esmet İnönü Cad.
DOLMABAHÇE
Kabataş Seabus Terminal
TEPEBAŞI
Ministry of Tourism
GALATASARAY
KASIMPAŞA
Sıraselviler Cad.
Yeniçarşı Cad.
CİHANGİR
KABATAŞ
TÜNEL
Tünel Metro Terminal
Meclisi Mebusan Cad.
Boğazkesen Cad.
Defterdar Yokuşu
Galata Tower
Kemeraltı Cad.
Necatibey Cad.
Kemankeş Cad.
TOPHANE
Atatürk Köprüsü
Tersane Cad.
Voyvoda Cad.
KARAKÖY
Karaköy Maritime Terminal
Karaköy Seabus Pier
Rıhtım Cad.
İSTANBUL BOĞAZI (BOSPHORUS)
Yeni Galata Köprüsü
Rüstem Paşa Camii
Eminönü Otogar
SEE SULTANAHMET & SÜLEYMANİYE MAP P. 1031
EMİNÖNÜ
Yeni Camii
Mısır Çarşısı (Egyptian Spice Bazaar)
Süleymaniye Camii & Türbesi
SİRKECİ
Sirkeci Gar
Kennedy Cad.
Hamidiye Cad.
Yeni Postane Cad.
Gülhane Park
Topkapı Palace
Archeological Complex
GÜLHANE
BEYAZIT
Beyazıt Tower
İstanbul Üniversitesi
KAPALI ÇARŞI (GRAND BAZAAR)
Nuruosmaniye Camii
Beyazıt Camii
Ebussuut Cad.
Yerebatan Cad.
Ankara Cad.
AHIRKAPI
SULTANAHMET
ÇEMBERLİTAŞ
Museum of Islamic and Turkish Art
Divan Yolu
Aya Sofia
Hippodrome
Sultanahmet Camii (Blue Mosque)
Kadırga Limanı Cad.
Cankurtaran İst.
Kabasakal Cad.
KUMKAPI
Sahil Yolu
Cankurtaran Cad.
ÇATLADIKAPI
Küçük Aya Sofia
0 300 yards
0 300 meters
İstanbul

TURKEY

00 51), in Eminönü, sends trains to Europe via **Athens, GCE** (24hr., 1 per day, 102YTL), **Bucharest, ROM** (17½hr., 1 per day, 80YTL), and **Budapest, HUN** (40hr., 1 per day, 200YTL).

Buses: Modern, comfortable buses run frequently to all major destinations in Turkey and are the cheapest and most convenient way to get around. If you arrange your tickets with any of the travel agencies in Sultanahmet, a free ride is included from there to the bus station. To reach **Esenler Otobüs Terminal** (☎658 00 36), take the tram to Yusufpaşa (1.30YTL), walk to the Aksaray Metro, and take it to the *otogar* (bus station; 15min., 1.30YTL). Most companies have courtesy buses, called *servis,* that run to the *otogar* from Eminönü, Taksim, and other city points (free with bus ticket purchase). From İstanbul, buses travel to every city in Turkey. Buses run to: **Ankara** (8hr., 6-8 per day, 30YTL); **Bodrum** (15hr., 2 per day, 45YTL); **İzmir** (10hr., 4 per day, 38YTL); **Kappadokia** (8hr., 2 per day, 30YTL). International buses to: **Athens, GCE** (19hr., daily 10am, 108YTL, students 135YTL); **Sofia, BUL** (15hr., daily 10am and 9pm, 40YTL); **Amman, Jordan** (28hr., daily noon, 100YTL); **Damascus, Syria** (25hr., daily 1:30pm and 7:30pm, 65YTL); **Tehran, Iran** (40hr., M-Sa 1:30pm, 65YTL). To get to Sultanahmet from the *otogar,* catch the metro to the Aksaray stop at the end of the line. From there catch a tram to Sultanahmet.

TURKEY

> **!** Be wary of bus companies offering ridiculously low prices. Unlicensed companies have been known to offer discounts to Western European destinations and then ditch passengers somewhere en route to Eastern Europe. To make sure you're going on a legit bus, reserve your tickets with a travel agency in advance.

Ferries: Turkish Maritime Lines (reservations ☎252 1700 info 212 249 9222), near pier #7 at Karaköy, to the left of the Haydarpaşa ferry terminal (blue awning marked Denizcilik İşletmeleri). To İzmir (16hr., every 2 days, 65YTL) and other destinations on the coast. Many travel agencies don't know too much about ferry connections, so you're better off going to the pier by the Galata Bridge, where you can pick up a free schedule. For more info, call ☎444 44 36 or visit www.ido.com.tr. **To and from Greece:** One of the most popular routes into Turkey is from the Greek Dodecanese and Northern Aegean islands, whose proximity to the Turkish coast makes for an easy and inexpensive way into Asia for backpackers tired of island-hopping. There are 5 main crossing points from Greece to Turkey: Rhodes to Marmaris, Kos to Bodrum, Samos to Kusadasi, Chios to Çeşme, and Lesvos to Ayvalik. Ferries run 1-2 times per day in summer, the ride takes under 2hr., and the tickets are usually €25-34, plus €10 port tax when entering Turkey and a €10-20 visa (see p. 1023). If you are visiting a Greek island as a daytrip from Turkey, port taxes are usually waived.

ORIENTATION

Waterways divide İstanbul into three sections. The **Bosphorus Strait** (Boğaz) separates **Asya** (Asia) from **Avrupa** (Europe). The **Golden Horn,** a sizeable river originating just outside the city, splits Avrupa into northern and southern parts. Directions in İstanbul are usually further specified by neighborhood. On the European side, **Sultanahmet,** home to the major sights, is packed with tourists and has plenty of parks and benches and many monuments, shops, and cafes. In Sultanahmet, backpackers congregate in **Akbıyık Cad.,** while **Divan Yolu** is the main street. Walk away from **Aya Sofya** and the **Blue Mosque** to reach the **Grand Bazaar.** As you walk out the covered Bazaar on the northern side, you'll reach more streets of outdoor markets that lead uphill to the massive **Suleymaniye Mosque** and the gardens of İstanbul's **University.** To the right, descend through the **Spice Bazaar** to reach the well-lit **Galata Bridge,** which is livened with street vendors and seafood restaurants at night.

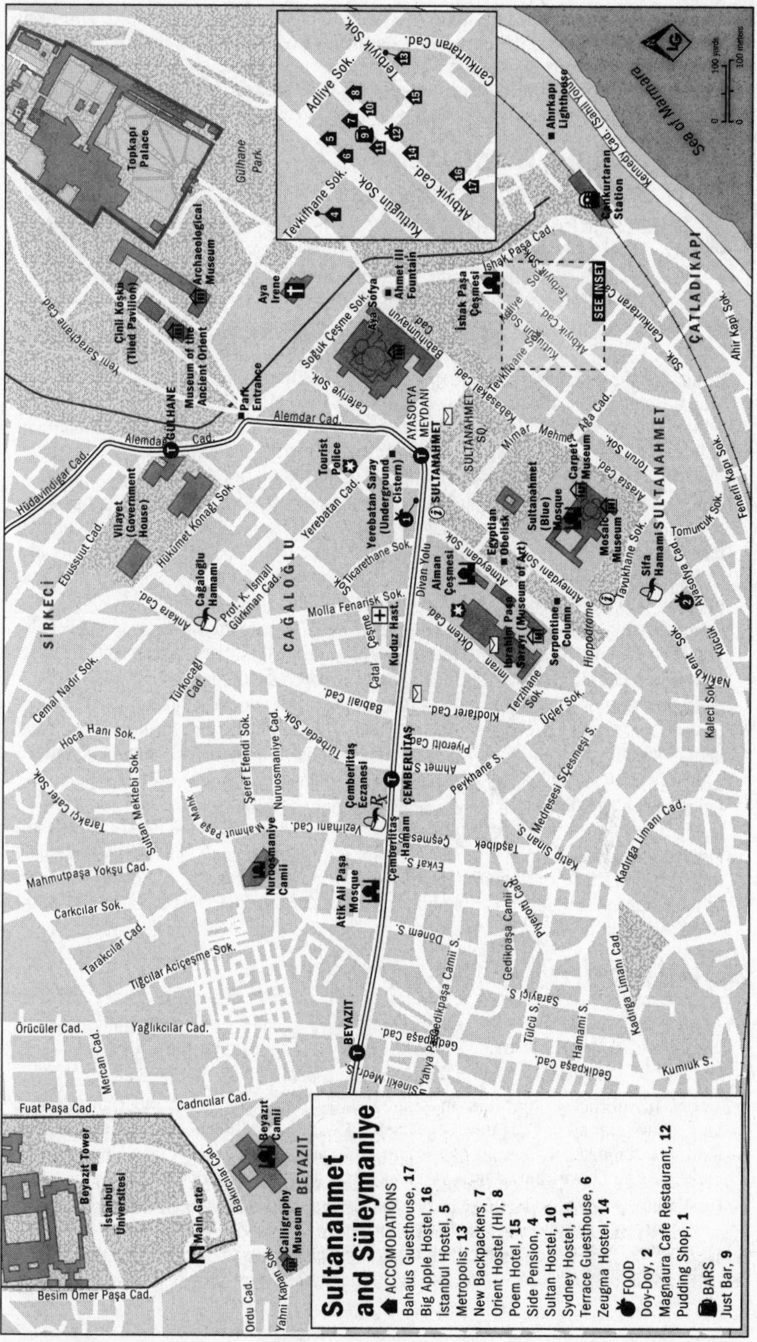
Sultanahmet and Süleymaniye
ACCOMODATIONS
Bahaus Guesthouse, 17
Big Apple Hostel, 16
İstanbul Hostel, 5
Metropolis, 13
New Backpackers, 7
Orient Hostel (HI), 8
Poem Hotel, 15
Side Pension, 4
Sultan Hostel, 10
Sydney Hostel, 11
Terrace Guesthouse, 6
Zeugma Hostel, 14
FOOD
Doy-Doy, 2
Magnaura Cafe Restaurant, 12
Pudding Shop, 1
BARS
Just Bar, 9
Topkapı Palace
Gülhane Park
Archaeological Museum
Çinili Köşkü (Tiled Pavilion)
Museum of the Ancient Orient
Aya Irene
Aya Sofya
Ahmet III Fountain
İshak Paşa Çeşmesi
SEE INSET
Ahırkapı Lighthouse
Cankurtaran Station
Sea of Marmara
Kennedy Cad. (Sahil Yolu)
ÇATLADIKAPI
SULTANAHMET
Sultanahmet (Blue) Mosque
Carpet Museum
Mosaic Museum
Egyptian Obelisk
Serpentine Column
Hippodrome
İbrahim Paşa Sarayı (Museum of Art)
Alman Çeşmesi
Yerebatan Saray (Underground Cistern)
Tourist Police
AYASOFYA MEYDANI
SULTANAHMET SQ.
GÜLHANE
Park Entrance
Vilayet (Government House)
Cağaloğlu Hamamı
CAĞALOĞLU
SİRKECİ
Kuduz Hast.
Sifa Hamamı
ÇEMBERLİTAŞ
Çemberlitaş Eczanesi
Çemberlitaş Hamam
Atik Ali Paşa Mosque
Nuruosmaniye Camii
BEYAZIT
Beyazıt Camii
Calligraphy Museum
Beyazıt Tower
İstanbul Üniversitesi
Main Gate
Alemdar Cad.
Divan Yolu
Yerebatan Cad.
Babıali Cad.
Ankara Cad.
Hüdavendigar Cad.
Ordu Cad.
Kadırga Limanı Cad.
Gedikpaşa Cad.
Adliye Sok.
Terbıyık Sok.
Cankurtaran Cad.
Akbıyık Cad.
Kutlugün Sok.
Tevkifhane Sok.
Torun Sok.
Arasta Cad.
Mimar Mehmet Ağa Cad.
Küçük Ayasofya Cad.
Nakilbent Sok.
Kaleci Sok.
Fenerli Kapı Sok.
Ahır Kapı Sok.
Tomurcuk Sok.
Peykhane S.
Piyerloti Cad.
Klodfarer Cad.
Üçler Sok.
Türbedar Sok.
Nuruosmaniye Cad.
Vezirhanı Cad.
Mahmutpaşa Yokuşu Cad.
Yağlıkcılar Cad.
Örücüler Cad.
Mercan Cad.
Fuat Paşa Cad.
Cadırcılar Cad.
Bakırcılar Cad.
Besim Ömer Paşa Cad.
Yahni Kapan Sok.
100 yards
100 meters

TURKEY

Across the two-level bridge, narrow warehouse-filled streets lead to the panoramic **Galata Tower.** Past the tower is the broad main shopping drag **İstiklâl Cad.,** that will take you right to **Taksim Square,** modern İstanbul's pulsing center. Sultanahmet and Taksim (on the European side), and **Kadıköy** (on the Asian side) are the most relevant for sightseers. Asya is primarily residential.

TRANSPORTATION

PUBLIC TRANSPORTATION. AKBİL is an electronic ticket system that saves you 15-50% on fares for municipal ferries, buses, trams, water taxis, and subway (but not *dolmuş*). Cards (6YTL) are sold at tram stations or ticket offices, and can be recharged it in 1YTL increments at the white IETT public bus booths, marked **AKBİL satılır.**

Buses: Run 6am-midnight, less frequently after 10:30pm, arriving every 10min. to most stops. Hubs are Eminönü, Aksaray (Yusuf Paşa tram stop), Beyazıt, Taksim, Beşiktaş, and Üsküdar. Signs on the front of buses indicate destination, and signs on the right side list major stops. **Dolmuş** (shared taxi vans) are more comfortable but less frequent than buses. Most *dolmuş* gather on the side streets north of Taksim Sq.

Tram: The *Tramvay* runs from Eminönü to Zeytinburnu every 5min. Make sure to be on the right side of the street, as the carriage follows the traffic. Get tokens at any station and toss them in at the turnstile to board (1.30YTL). The old-fashioned carriages of the **historical tram** run 1km uphill from Tunel (by the Galata Bridge) through İstiklâl Cad. and up to Taksim Sq. They're the same ones that made the trip in the early 20th century.

Metro: İstanbul operates two metro lines (☎568 9970): one from Aksaray to the Esenler Bus Terminal and the other from Taksim Sq. to 4th Levent. A funicular connects the tram stop Cabatas to Taksim Sq. The metro runs daily every 5min. 5:40am-11:15pm.

Commuter Rail: A slow commuter rail (known locally as *tren*) runs 6am-11pm between Sirkeci Gar and the far western suburbs, as well as the Asian side. The stop in Bostanci is near the ferry to the Princes Islands. Keep your ticket until the end of the journey.

Taxis: Taxi drivers are even more reckless and speed-crazed than other İstanbul drivers, but the over 20,000 taxis in the city offer an undoubtedly quick way to get around, even in the city's most stalled traffic. Don't ask the driver to fix a price before getting on; instead make sure he starts the meter from zero. Night fares are double. Always check that 1 light or the word *Gunduz* is on 6am-midnight; after midnight, it should be 2 lights or the word *Gece*. Rides from Sultanahmet to Taksim Sq. should be around 15YTL, and to the airport around 25YTL.

PRACTICAL INFORMATION

Tourist Office: 3 Divan Yolu (☎/fax 518 87 54), at the north end of the Hippodrome in Sultanahmet. Open daily 9am-5pm. Branches in Taksim's Hilton Hotel Arcade on Cumhuriyet Cad., Sirkeci train station, Atatürk Airport, and Karaköy Maritime Station.

Budget Travel: Every other door in İstanbul is a travel agency, and most hostels and hotels have started running travel agency services as well. Though most are trustworthy, there are some scams. Always check that the agency is licensed. If anything happens, make sure you have your agent's info and report it to the tourist police.

Fez Travel, 15 Akbıyık Cad. (☎516 9024; www.feztravel.com). İstanbul's most efficient and well informed, Fez's English-speaking staff organizes anything from accommodations to ferries, flights, and buses, as well as their own backpacker-tailored tours of Turkey and Greece. STA-affiliated. Open daily 9am-7pm. MC/V.

Hassle Free, 10 Akbıyık Cad. (☎458 95 00; www.anzacgouse.com), right next to New Backpackers. The name is self-explanatory and the young, friendly staff provides the best deals and tips. Books local buses or boat cruises of southern Turkey. Open daily 9am-11pm.

Barefoot Travel, 1 Cetinkaya Sok. (☎517 02 69; www.barefoot-travel.com), just off Akbıyık Cad. The English-speaking staff is helpful and offers good deals on airfares, as well as free Turkey and İstanbul maps. Open daily in summer 8am-8pm; in winter 8am-6pm. AmEx/MC/V.

Indigo Tourism and Travel Agency, 24 Akbıyık Cad. (☎517 72 66; www.indigo-tour.com), in Sultanahmet's hotel cluster. Sells bus, plane, and ferry tickets. Arranges airport shuttle service and tours, car rentals, and accommodations for all budgets. Open daily 9am-7pm.

Consulates: Australia, 15 Asker Ocaği Cad., Elmadag Sisli (☎243 13 33; fax 243 13 32). **Canada,** 373/5 İstiklâl Cad. (☎251 98 38; fax 251 98 88). **Ireland,** 26 Cumhuriyet Cad., Mobil Altı, Elmadağ (☎246 60 25). **UK,** 34 Meşrutiyet Cad., Beyoğlu/Tepebaşı (☎252 6436). **US,** 2 Kaplicalar Mevkii Sok., Istinye (☎335 90 00).

Currency Exchange: *Bureaux de change* around the city are open M-F 8:30am-noon and 1:30-5pm. Most don't charge commission. **ATMs** generally accept all international cards. Most banks exchange **traveler's checks.** Exchanges in Sultanahmet have poor rates, but are open late and weekends. There is a yellow **PTT** kiosk between the Aya Sofya and the Blue Mosque that changes currency for no commission.

English-Language Bookstores: In Sultanahmet, *köşk* (kiosks) at the Blue Mosque, on Aya Sofya Meydanı, and on Divan Yolu sell international papers. **Galeri Kayseri,** 58 Divan Yolu (☎512 04 56), caters to thinking tourists with books on Turkish and Islamic history and literature, as well as a host of guidebooks. Open daily 9am-9pm. D/MC/V.

Laundromat: Star Laundry, 18 Akbıyık Cad., between New Backpackers and Hassle Free. Wash and dry 4YTL per kg. Min. 2kg. Ready in 3hr. Open daily 9am-8pm.

Emergency: ☎112. **Police:** ☎155. **Fire:** ☎110.

Tourist Police: In Sultanahmet, at the beginning of Yerebatan Cad. (24hr. hotline ☎527 45 03 or 528 53 69). Police speak excellent English, and their mere presence causes hawkers and postcard-selling kids to scatter. In an **emergency,** call from any phone.

Hospitals: American Hospital, Admiral Bristol Hastanesi, 20 Güzelbahçe Sok., Nişantaşı (☎231 40 50), is applauded by locals and tourists. Has many English-speaking doctors. **German Hospital,** 119 Sıraselviler Cad., Taksim (☎293 21 50), also has a multilingual staff and is conveniently located for Sultanahmet hostelers. **International Hospital,** 82 İstanbul Cad., Yesilköy (☎663 30 00).

Internet Access: Internet in İstanbul is everywhere from hotels to barber shops, and connections are usually cheap and decently fast—except for the frequent power cuts. Most hostels have free Internet, though most impose a 15min. limit. Rates at travel agencies are usually 1YTL per 15min., 3YTL per hr.

Post and Telephone Offices: Known as **PTTs.** All accept packages. **Main branch** in Sirkeci, 25 Büyük Postane Sok. Stamp and currency exchange services open daily 8:30am-midnight. 24hr. phones. Phone cards available for 5-10YTL. There is a yellow PTT kiosk in Sultanahmet between the Aya Sofya and the Blue Mosque, which changes currency and sells stamps. Open daily 9am-5pm.

ACCOMMODATIONS

Budget accommodations are concentrated in **Sultanahmet** (a.k.a. Türist Şeğntral). In the past couple of years, as Turkey has become a backpacker's must, there has been an explosion of cheap places to stay, turning Akbıyık Cad. into a virtually uninterrupted line of hostels. All offer similar quality and prices. The side streets around **Sirkeci** railway station and **Aksaray** have dozens of dirt-cheap, rundown hotels, while fancy and expensive options abound in the more touristy districts. All accommodations listed below are in Sultanahmet, but it's hard to keep track of

IN RECENT NEWS

GOİN' COLD TURKEY

Forget hookahs, cigars, and puffs of white smoke swirling around İstanbul's mosques and bazaars. Turkey's prospective entrance to the EU demands more than reestablishing ties with southern Cyprus and solving the Kurdish issue: it asked Turkey to hang up "No Smoking" signs on its doors. Ankara's Parliament conceded, and since March 2006, no smoking has been allowed in public spaces.

How did Turkey take the news? Not too well, apparently. In this case, the cost of becoming European is seeming a bit too high. For once, Islamists and secularists stand together in opposing this regulation. Smoking has always been one of Turkey's unifying elements. Turks light up incessantly—in hospitals, schools, cabs, bars, and mosques. Even in nicotine-addicted Europe, to say someone "smokes like a Turk" means something.

So Turkey has begun to quit smoking, but at the mention of the new law many Turks smile ironically, for this isn't the first time smoking has been outlawed in the country. In 1633, Sultan Murat IV sanctioned the death penalty for the consumption of alcohol and tobacco throughout the Ottoman Empire, but he himself died at age 27 of cirrhosis.

the hostels that continue to open up, so make sure you look around for what's new. Also, despite their number, hostels in Sultanahmet fill up quickly in high season. Though you will always find a bed somewhere, you need to reserve ahead if you want to get the hostel of your choice. Hotels in **Lâleli** are in İstanbul's center of prostitution and should be avoided. Rates can rise by up to 20% in July and August.

Sultan Hostel, 21 Akbıyık Cad. (☎516 92 60; www.sultanhostel.com). Right in the middle of backpackers' land, this happening hostel is İstanbul's most famous. With streetside, rooftop restaurant and comfortable, clean dorms, Sultan's is a great place to meet fellow travelers. Breakfast included. Free safes. Free Internet. Reserve ahead—it is seriously popular. 20-bed dorms 16YTL; 4-bed 18YTL; singles 35YTL, with bath 40YTL; doubles 40/50YTL. ❷

New Backpackers, 14/1 Akbıyık Cad. (☎638 5586; www.newbackpackers.com). In the best people-watching spot on the street, New Backpackers has the most popular bar and is quite the hangout place. Though there is only one bathroom for 14 beds, the atmosphere here is unparalleled; the staff, guests, and other travelers spend their afternoons playing backgammon at the cozy tables outside. Free beach daytrips. Free Internet at nearby Aussie Travel Agency. Dorms 18YTL; doubles 80YTL. ❷

İstanbul Hostel, 35 Kutlugün Sok. (]516 93 80; www.istanbulhostel.net). In business well before Sultanahmet was invaded by backpackers, this hostel has all the usual amenities, as well as a welcoming family feel, all-day Turkish food and an extremely helpful staff. Bar, travel agency, rooftop, and board games also available. The canteen's fireplace makes this the best place for a cozy winter visit. Breakfast included. Free Internet. Dorms 20YTL; doubles 50YTL. ❷

Terrace Guesthouse, 39 Kutlugün Sok. (☎638 97 33; www.terracehotelistanbul.com), behind Akbıyık Cad. Housed in a narrow carpet shop, this elegant hotel has beautifully decorated rooms and luxury for affordable prices. A stay here will truly make you feel you are in the city of sultans. Breakfast included. Dec. 23-Jan. 5 and mid-Mar. to Oct. singles 100YTL; doubles 120YTL; triples 140YTL. Low season 90/100/120YTL. ❺

Sydney Hostel, 42 Akbıyık Cad. (☎518 6671; fax 518 66 72), in the middle of Akbıyık. This brand-new hostel is surprisingly very quiet and also has a very kind staff. The cheerful walls are painted sky-blue, the rooms are modern and spotless, and the bathrooms look like they belong in a 4-star hotel. Dorms 20YTL; doubles 60-70YTL. ❷

Orient Hostel (HI), 13 Akbıyık Cad. (☎518 07 89; www.orienthostel.com), across the street from New Backpackers and next-door to Sultan, this is another excellent hostel that offers similar services, along with movies, *nargila* (hookahs), BBQ nights, and a helpful budget travel agency. M, W, F belly dancing. Breakfast included. Free Internet. 16-bed dorms 15YTL; smaller dorms 18YTL; doubles 45YTL; quads 80YTL. ❷

Metropolis, 24 Terbıyık Sok. (☎212 518 18 22; www.metropolishostel.com), removed from the hustle of Akbıyık, in a quieter yet still central back street. This beautifully kept hostel has comfortable, stylish rooms, friendly staff, and a perfect location. Guests get a 10-15% discount at the Metropolis Restaurant and Downunder bar around the corner. Breakfast included. Single-sex dorms 20-22YTL; doubles 45YTL; quads 90YTL. ❷

Big Apple Hostel, 12 Bayram Fırını Sok. (☎517 7931; www.hostelbigapple.com), down the road from Akbıyık Cad., next to Barefoot Travel. This funky hostel is recognizable by the many international flags outside. Great rooftop terrace with swing. Linens included. Dorms 10YTL; singles 22YTL; doubles 25YTL. MC/V. ❶

Zeugma Hostel, 35 Akbıyık Cad. (☎517 40 40; www.zeugmahostel.com). The cheapest in Sultanahmet, this clean hostel has a huge basement dorm with comfortable wooden bunks separated by colorful curtains, giving it a bedouin camp feel. Airport pick-up available. Linens included. Free Internet. Reception 24hr. Dorms 10YTL. ❶

Bahaus Guesthouse, 11-13 Akbıyık Cad. (☎638 65 34; www.travelinistanbul.com), across the street from Big Apple. Travelers rave about this place; the elegant rooms are inevitably full. Airport pickup available. Free Internet. Dorms 18YTL; doubles 48YTL. ❷

Poem Hotel, Akbıyık Cad. and 12 Terbıyık Sok. (☎638 97 44; www.hotelpoem.com), next to Metropolis on a quiet side street of Akbıyık. Surrounded by an incredibly lush forest, this hotel has tastefully furnished rooms named after famous Turkish poems like "Bazaar" or "Listening To İstanbul." Rooms have safes, TV, A/C, and bath, but these amenities come with price tags to match. Reserve online. Singles 100YTL; doubles 150YTL; triples 170YTL. Winter discount 25%. MC/V. ❶

Side Pension/Hotel, 20 Utangaç Sok. (☎517 65 90; www.sidehotel.com). This 2-building complex near the entrance of the Four Seasons Hotel has comfortable pension rooms and slightly more luxurious hotel ones. Some have balconies. Pension singles 50YTL, with bath 70YTL, hotel 90YTL; doubles 70/90/120YTL. MC/V. ❹

FOOD

İstanbul's restaurants, like its clubs and bars, often demonstrate the golden rule: if it's well advertised or easy to find, it's not worth a visit. Sultanahmet's "Turkish" restaurants are convenient, but much better meals can be found across the **Galata Bridge** and around **Taksim Square.** Small Bosphorus suburbs such as **Arnavutköy** and **Sariyer** (on the European side) and **Çengelköy** (on the Asian side) are the best places for fresh fish. For a cheaper meal, **İstiklâl Cad.** has all the major Western chains, as well as quick and tasty Turkish fast food. Vendors in Ottoman dress wearing big steel teapots on their backs sell *Vişne suyu* (sour cherry juice), and on any street you'll find plenty of dried fruit and nuts for sale, as well as the omnipresent stalls of sesame bagels (1YTL). The best open-air **market** is the daily one in **Beşiktaş,** near Barbaros Cad., while at the Egyptian Spice Bazaar *(Mısır Çarşısı)* you can find almonds, fruit, and—of course—**kebaps.**

Doy-Doy, 13 Şifa Hammamı Sok. (☎517 15 88). From the south end of the Hippodrome, walk down the hill around the edge of the Blue Mosque and look for the blue sign. The best in Sultanahmet, 3-story Doy-Doy keeps locals and backpackers coming back for more. The rooftop tables are right under the Blue Mosque, and on the lower levels you'll find cushioned floors and plenty of *nargilas* (hookahs). Tasty *kebap* (5-8YTL) and refreshing shepherd salads with *cacik* (yogurt and cucumber; 4YTL). No alcohol served. Open daily 8am-11pm. MC/V. ❶

Hacı Abdullah, 17 Sakizağacı Cad. (☎293 85 61; www.haciabdullah.com.tr), down the street from Ağa Camii, in Taksim Sq. Find out what comes out of a real Turkish kitchen (hint: it's not *kebap*). This family-style restaurant has been going strong since 1888 and features huge vases of preserved fruit and high-tech bathrooms. Their homemade grapefruit juice is fantastic. Soups and salads 3-4YTL. Entrees 11-15YTL. No alcohol served. Open daily noon-11pm. Kitchen closes 10:30pm. MC/V. ❸

Magnaura Cafe Restaurant, 27 Akbıyık Cad. (☎518 76 22; www.magnauracaferestaurant.com). Fancier and more expensive than most of the surrounding broke-traveler eateries, Magnaura is somewhat out of place, but it's quite a good value. Extensive menu and plenty of vegetarian options make it a favorite (with foreigners). Pastas and salads 10-13YTL. Entrees 15-22YTL. Open daily 9am-11pm. ❹

Koska Helvacısı, 12 Ali Rıza Gürcan Cad. (]481 54 62; www.koskahelvacisi.com.tr), in Tozkoparan. This supermarket is any sugar-lover's dream. Fantastic take-out baklava trays (3YTL) and boxed assortments of sweets (6-20YTL) in all colors and flavors. Open daily 9am-11:30pm. ❷

Pudding Shop, 6 Divan Yolu Cad. (☎522 29 70). A major pit stop on the Hippie Trail to the Far and Middle East during the 70s. Young travelers en route to Goa and Kathmandu left messages on a board that's still here. The setting for the drug deal scene in *Midnight Express* is now a clean and tasty fast-food joint, more nostalgic than exciting. A/C upstairs. *Kebaps* 5-8YTL. Open daily 7am-11pm. ❷

SIGHTS

İstanbul's incomparable array of churches, mosques, palaces, and museums can keep an ardent tourist busy for weeks. Most budget travelers spend a lot of time in Sultanahmet, the area around the Aya Sofya, south of and uphill from Sirkeci. Merchants crowd the district between the enormous Grand Bazaar, east of the university, and the less touristy Egyptian Spice Bazaar, just southeast of Eminönü. To soak in the city's sights the easy way, hop on one of the small boats on either side of the Galata Bridge and go for a relaxing and panoramic **Bosphorus tour.** Most tours last about 2hr. and return to their starting point.

BARGAINING FOR BEGINNERS. Though the Grand Bazaar is haggling at its finest, bargaining doesn't end at carpets. It's acceptable to bargain for almost anything in İstanbul, including tours. For the best deals on boat trips, bargain with boat owners at the port. Trips shouldn't be more than 20YTL per person for a few hours of floating down the Bosphorus.

AYA SOFYA (HAGIA SOPHIA). When Aya Sofya (Divine Wisdom) was built in AD 537, it was the biggest building in the world. Built as a church, it fell to the Ottomans in 1453 and was converted into a mosque; it remained as such until 1932, when Atatürk declared it a museum. Though named for one of the three adjectives describing God, finding words to describe Aya Sofya proves much more difficult. Its austere interior amplifies its awesome size. The nave is overshadowed by the gold-leaf mosaic dome lined with hundreds of circular windows that make it seem as though the dome is floating on a bed of luminescent pearls. Throughout the building, Qur'anic inscriptions and mosaics of Mary and the angels intertwine in a fascinating symmetry. The gallery contains Byzantine mosaics uncovered from beneath a thick layer of Ottoman plaster, as well as the famed sweating pillar, sheathed in bronze. The pillar has a hole big enough to stick a finger in and collect the odd drop of water, believed to possess healing powers, but the column is disappointingly dry. *(Open daily 9am-7:30pm. Upper gallery open 9:30am-6:45pm. 10YTL.)*

BLUE MOSQUE (SULTANAHMET CAMİİ). Named for the beautiful blue İznik tiles that cover the interior, the Blue Mosque was Sultan Ahmet's 1617 "size doesn't matter" response to Justinian's Aya Sofya. The mosque's 16 balconies and six **minarets** are the primary source of its fame; at the time of construction, only the mosque at Mecca had that many minarets, and the thought of rivaling that sacred edifice was considered heretical. The crafty Sultan circumvented this difficulty by financing the construction of a seventh minaret at Mecca. The interior was originally lit with candles, the chandelier structure intended to create the illusion that tiny starlights floated freely in the air. The small, square, single-domed structure in front of the Blue Mosque is **Sultanahmet'in Türbesi,** or Sultan Ahmet's Tomb, which contains the sultan and his family's remains. The reliquary in the back contains strands of the Prophet Muhammad's beard. *(Open Su-Th and Sa 9am-12:30pm, 1:45-4:40pm, and 5:40-6:30pm, F noon-2:20pm. The Blue Mosque is a working religious facility, and closes to the public for prayer 5 times a day. Scarves are provided at the entrance. Inside the mosque, behave respectfully and don't cross on to the sections limited to prayer. Donations are welcome on the way out. See p. 1026 for more on mosque etiquette.)*

TOPKAPI PALACE (TOPKAPI SARAYI). Towering from the high ground at the tip of the old city and hidden behind walls up to 12m high, Topkapı was the nerve center of the Ottoman Empire. Built by Mehmet the Conqueror in 1458-1465, the palace became an imperial residence during the reign of Süleyman the Magnificent. The palace is divided into a series of courtyards. The **first courtyard** was the popular center of the palace, where the general public could enter to watch executions and view the nexus of the empire's glory. The **second courtyard** leads to displays of wealth, including collections of porcelain, silver, gold, and torture instruments. The Gate of Felicity leads to the **third courtyard,** which houses a collection of imperial clothing, as well as the awesome **Palace Treasury.** The **fourth courtyard** is the pleasure center of the palace—it was among these pavilions, gardens, and fountains that the Ottomans really got their mojo working. The most interesting part of Topkapı is the 400-plus-room **harem.** Tours of the harem begin at the Black Eunuchs' Dormitory and continue into the chambers of the Valide Sultan, the sultan's mother and the most powerful woman in the harem. Surrounding the room of the queen mum are the chambers of the concubines. If a particular woman attracted the sultan's affections or if the sultan spent a night with her, she would be promoted to "odalisque" status, which meant that she had to stay in İstanbul forever, but got nicer quarters in exchange for her undying ministrations. *(Palace open M and W-Su 9am-7pm. Harem open 10am-5pm. Palace 10YTL. Harem 10YTL. Audio tour of palace 5YTL. Harem can only be visited on guided tours, which leave every 30min. Lines for tours can be long; arrive early.)*

ARCHAEOLOGICAL MUSEUM COMPLEX. The Archaeological Museum Complex is made of four distinct museums. The **Tiled Pavilion** explains more than you ever wanted to know about the omnipresent İznik tiles. The once fully tiled pavilion was built in 1472 by Mehmet to view the athletic competitions below. The smaller, adjacent building is the **Ancient Orient Museum.** It houses an excellent collection of 3000-year-old stone artifacts from the ancient Middle East and a the Treaty of Kadesh, the world's oldest known written treaty, drafted after a battle between Ramses II of Egypt and the Hittite King Muvatellish. The immense **Archaeology Museum** has one of the world's greatest collections of Classical and Hellenistic art, but is surprisingly bereft of visitors. The highlight is the famous Alexander Sarcophagus, covered with intricate carvings depicting the king in battle. The superb **Museum of Turkish and Islamic Art** features a large collection of Islamic art, organized by period. The Selçuk displays and the Ottoman calligraphy with the seals of sultans are particularly impressive. *(150m downhill from the Topkapı Palace's 1st courtyard. All museums open Tu-Su 8:30am-5pm. 5YTL.)*

UNDERGROUND CISTERN (YEREBATAN SARAYI). This underground "palace" is actually a vast cavern whose shallow water eerily reflects the images of its 336 supporting columns. The columns are all illuminated by colored ambient lighting, making the cistern slightly resemble a horror-movie set. Underground walkways originally linked the cistern to Topkapı Palace, but were blocked to curb rampant trafficking in stolen goods and abducted women. At the far end of the cistern, two huge Medusa heads lay upside-down in the water. Legend has it that looking at them directly can turn people to stone. The cistern's **cafe,** in a dark corner, is a cross between creepy and romantic. *(The entrance lies 175m from the mosque in the small stone kiosk on the left side of Yerebatan Cad. Open daily 9am-6:30pm. 10YTL.)*

HIPPODROME (AT MEYDANI). Though all of the major Sultanahmet sights provide insight into pre-Ottoman and Ottoman history, few conjure images of the glory of Byzantine Constantinople like the **Hippodrome,** behind the Blue Mosque. Built by the Roman Emperor Septimus Severus in AD 200, it served as the stage for chariot races and public executions. The tall, northernmost column with hieroglyphics is the **Dikili Taş,** an Egyptian obelisk erected by the Pharaoh Thutmose III in 1500 BC and brought to Constantinople in the 4th century. Farther south, the subterranean bronze stump is all that remains of the **Serpentine Column,** originally placed at the Oracle of Delphi (p. 496). The southernmost column is the **Column of Constantine,** whose original gold-plated bronze tiling was looted by Crusaders during the sack of Constantinople.

GRAND BAZAAR. Through banter, barter, and haggle, a day spent at the **Kapalı Çarşısı** (Grand Bazaar) is bound to tempt and tantalize on a scale unmatched by even the most frenetic of markets elsewhere in the Europe. The largest and oldest covered bazaar in the world, the Grand Bazaar began in 1461 as a modest affair during the reign of Mehmet the Conqueror. Today, the enormous Kapalı Çarşısı combines the best and worst of shopping in Turkey to form the massive mercantile sprawl that starts at Çemberlitaş and covers the hill down to Eminönü, ending at the more authentic and less claustrophobic **Mısır Çarşısı** (Egyptian Spice Bazaar) and the Golden Horn waterfront. Rule number one in bargaining: never settle for more than half the first price you are asked; the place is touristy and shop owners know their tricks. Don't stress out, but don't pay what you are asked—bazaar-shopping is a game. And don't bother keeping your bearings, there are directional arrows from virtually any spot, and you'll surely get lost, so enjoy the ride. *(From Sultanahmet, follow the tram tracks toward Aksaray until you see the Nuruosmanıye Camii on the right. Walk down Vezirhanı Cad. for one block, keeping the mosque on your left. Otherwise, follow the crowds. www.grandbazaar.com. Open M-Sa 9am-7pm.)*

RUSTEM PASA MOSQUE. Hidden between the dry-fruit stalls and warehouse shops of the Spice Bazaar, this tiny mosque is a hidden jewel. Walk up the stairs to enter this small blue mosque, its interior covered in light-blue tiles as fine and beautiful as those of its better-known sister. The mosque is a working religious facility and all the same rules for visiting apply as for the other mosques.

SÜLEYMANİYE COMPLEX. To the north of İstanbul University stands the elegant **Süleymaniye Camii,** one of Ottoman architect Sinan's great masterpieces. This mosque is part of a larger **külliye** (complex), which includes **tombs,** an **imaret** (soup kitchen), and several **madrasas** (Islamic schools). After walking through the cemetery to see the **royal tombs** of Süleyman I and his wife, proceed inside the vast and perfectly proportioned mosque—the height of the dome (53m) is exactly twice the measurement of each side of the square base. The **stained-glass windows** are the sobering work of the master Sarhoş İbrahim (İbrahim the Drunkard). The İznik tile İnzanity all started here: the area around the **mihrab** showcases Sinan's first experiment in blue tiles. *(From Sultanahmet, take the* tramvay *to the Üniversite stop, walk across the square, and take Besim Ömer Paşa Cad. past the walls of the university to Süleymaniye Cad. Open daily except during prayer. Leave your shoes at the entrance. Women need to cover their shoulders, men and women should cover their heads. Scarves are available at the entrance.)*

HAMMAMS (TURKISH BATHS)

In the past a man found in a women's bath was sentenced to death, but today customs have relaxed and it's not rare to find co-ed baths where both genders strip beyond their skivvies. Most baths have separate women's sections or hours, but only some have designated female attendants. If you'd rather have a masseuse of your same gender, make sure to ask at the entrance.

Cağaloğlu Hamami, on Yerebatan Cad. at Babiali Cad. (☎522 2424; www.cagaloglu-hamami.com.tr), near Cağaloğlu Sq. in Sultanahmet. Donated to İstanbul in 1741 by Sultan Mehmet I, this luxurious white-marble bath is one of the city's most illustrious. Self-service bath 20YTL, bath with scrub 30YTL, complete bath and massage 40YTL, luxury treatment with hand-knit Oriental wash cloth 60YTL. Slippers, soap, and towels included. Open daily for women 8am-8pm, for men 7am-10pm.

Çemberlitaş Hammamı, 8 Verzirhan Cad. (☎522 79 74; www.cemberlitashamami.com.tr). Just a soap-slide away from the Çemberlitaş tram stop. Built by Sinan in 1584, with marble interiors. Vigorous "towel service" after the bath; guests are welcome to hang around the hot marble rooms afterward. Open daily 6am-midnight.

TURKEY

NIGHTLIFE

After the hot afternoons, İstanbul lights up its mosques. Locals and travelers alike pour into the streets to savor intense nightlife, which falls into three categories. The first includes male-only *çay* (tea) houses, backgammon parlors, and dancing shows. Women are not prohibited but are unwelcome and should avoid these places, which are often unsafe for male travelers as well. Let's Go does not endorse patronage of these establishments. The second category includes the local youth **cafe-bars, rock bars,** and many **backpacker bars.** In **Sultanahmet,** pubs are crammed within 10m of one another, usually on the rooftop or front tables of the hostels. They have standardized beer prices (5YTL) and are usually Australian-dominated; the most popular hostel bars, **New Backpackers** and **Orient,** are open to all. **Clubs** and **discos** comprise the third nightlife category. Even taxi drivers can't keep up with the ever-fluctuating club scene. The Beşiktaş end of **Ortaköy** is a maze of upscale hangouts. The cheerful **Nevizade** is a virtually uninterrupted row of wine shops and tapas bars, parallel to İstiklâl Cad. İstanbul's local specialty is *balyoz* (sledgehammer/wrecking ball). Getting wrecked won't be difficult: *balyoz* consists of *rakı*, whiskey, vodka, and gin with orange juice. Bottoms up.

Just Bar, 18 Akbıyık Cad. (☎012 345 6789). This bar has become almost as much of as must-see as the Aya Sofya. Outdoor wooden pub tables, rock/funk/R&B music, and free-flowing beer make for a typical backpacker's night, every night. Beer 5YTL. Mixed drinks 7-10YTL. Open daily 11am-4am. It's hard to tell where Just Bar stops and **Cheers,** next door, begins. Cheers is equally popular, friendly, and laid-back. Beer 4-5YTL. Mixed drinks and shots 7YTL. Open daily noon-late.

Jazz Stop, at the end of Büyük Parmakkapı Sok., in Taksim. A mixed group of music lovers sit in this large underground tavern while live bands lay the funk, blues, and jazz on thick. The owner, a talented drummer from one of Turkey's oldest and most respected rock groups, occasionally takes part in the jams. Beer 5YTL. Mixed drinks 7-20YTL. Live music daily midnight. Cover F-Sa 10YTL; includes 1 drink. Open daily 7pm- 6am.

Araf, İstiklâl Cad. and 32 Balo Sok. (☎244 8301), across from the entrance to Nevizade. Take the elevator to the 4th fl., then walk upstairs to reach this funky rooftop veranda with international music and freestyle dancing in a birthday-party atmosphere. Beer 4YTL. Mixed drinks 7YTL. Open daily 5pm-2am.

Pangea, 6 Büyük Parmakkapı Sok., in Taksim, formerly the popular Riddim. If you are looking for Jah, he is here in the first bar in Taksim dedicated to spinning reggae all night long. Unaccompanied men turned away F-Sa. Beer 5YTL. Mixed drinks 10YTL. Cover 10YTL for men on busy nights; includes 1 drink. Open daily 9pm-4am.

Sinerji Bar, İpek Sok. (☎249 84 26), off Küçük Parmakkapı Sok. Fascinated with Spanish surrealist paintings and Turkish indie rock, the understated Sinerji is popular with Turkish students and young foreigners looking for one of the cheapest pints in Taksim. Beer 4YTL. Mixed drinks 5-10YTL. Open daily 2pm-2am.

Nayah Music Club, 14/1 Balo Sok. (☎244 1183; www.nayah.org), in Beyoğlu. This relaxed reggae bar is a smaller version of Pangea, with rasta bartenders. Customers don't really dance, but instead sit and accompany the music with subtle head bobs. Beer 4YTL. Mixed drinks 7YTL. Open M-Th 6pm-2am, F-Sa 6pm-4am.

UKRAINE (УКРАЇНА)

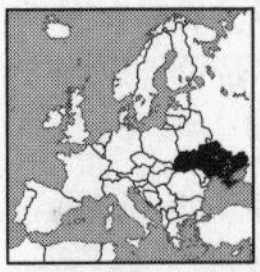

"Ukraine" literally means "borderland," and the country has occupied this precarious position for most of its history. Today it shares frontiers with both its former Soviet comrades and members of the European Union. With the recent Orange Revolution and the beginnings of an effort to join the EU, Ukraine is more than ever aligning itself with the West. This makes it a fascinating time to visit; with no beaten path from which to stray, travelers to Ukraine are rewarded with uncrowded museums, ancient castles, and the relaxing Black Sea Coast.

DISCOVER UKRAINE: SUGGESTED ITINERARIES

THREE DAYS. Stick to **Kyiv,** the epicenter of the Orange Revolution. Check out **Independence Square,** stop by **Shevchenko Park** to enjoy real Ukrainian fare at **O'Panas,** and ponder your mortality among the mummified monks of the **Kyiv-Cave Monastery** (p. 1047).

ONE WEEK. After three days in **Kyiv,** take a train to **Lviv** (2 days; p. 1049), the cultural capital of Ukraine. Spend your last two days in **Odessa** (p. 1050) soaking up the sun on the beach and experiencing high culture for cheap at the **Theater of Opera and Ballet.**

ESSENTIALS

FACTS AND FIGURES

Official Name: Ukraine.
Capital: Kyiv.
Major Cities: Lviv, Odessa.
Population: 46,711,000.
Time Zone: GMT +2.
Language: Ukrainian.
Religions: Ukrainian Orthodox (35%), Eastern Orthodox (9%), Ukrainian Greek Catholic (6%).

WHEN TO GO

Ukraine has a diverse climate; generally speaking, aim to visit in spring or summer. Reserve in advance from June to August in Odessa and Crimea, which have a climate similar to the Mediterranean Coast and are the prime destinations for Ukrainian vacationers. Kyiv enjoys moderate weather, while the more mountainous west remains cool even in summer. Winter tourism is popular in the Carpathians. Reserve accommodations early around the May 1 holiday.

DOCUMENTS AND FORMALITIES

EMBASSIES AND CONSULATES. Foreign embassies for Ukraine are in Kyiv (p. 1046). Ukrainian embassies abroad include: **Australia,** Level 12, St. George Centre, 60 Marcus Clarke St., Canberra, ACT, 2601 (☎02 6230 5789; www.ukremb.info); **Canada,** 310 Somerset St., Ottawa, ON, K2P 0J9 (☎613-230-2961; www.ukremb.ca); **UK,** 60 Holland Park, London, W11 3SJ (☎020 7727 6312, consular/visas 7243 8923; www.ukremb.org.uk); **US,** 3350 M St., NW, Washington, D.C., 20007 (☎202-333-0606; www.ukraineinfo.us).

VISA AND ENTRY INFORMATION. Ukraine's visa requirements have been changing a great deal recently as the government works to encourage tourism. **Visas** are no longer required of Canadian, EU, or US citizens staying in Ukraine for fewer than 90 days. Citizens of Australia and New Zealand must obtain a visa (AUS$65) and letter of introduction from a tour agency or Ukrainian hotel. Proceeding through **customs** requires that you declare all cash, traveler's checks, and jewelry. Check with your country's Ukrainian embassy for more restrictions.

ENTRANCE REQUIREMENTS

Passport: Required for all travelers.

Visa: Not required for Canadian, EU, or US citizens. Required of citizens of Australia and New Zealand.

Letter of Invitation: Required for citizens of Australia and New Zealand.

Inoculations: Not required. Recommended up-to-date on DTaP (diphtheria, tetanus, and pertussis), hepatitis A, hepatitis B, MMR (measles, mumps, and rubella), polio booster, and typhoid.

Work Permit: Required for all foreigners planning to work in Ukraine.

Driving Permit: Required for all those planning to drive in Ukraine.

TOURIST SERVICES AND MONEY

TOURIST OFFICES. Lviv's tourist office is extremely helpful; it is also the only official one in Ukraine. The remains of the Soviet giant **Intourist** have offices in hotels, though they rarely speak English. Local travel agencies can be helpful, but they rarely speak English and are delighted to lighten your wallet.

HRYVNIA (HV)

AUS$1 = 3.85HV	1HV = AUS$0.26
CDN$1 = 4.58HV	1HV = CDN$0.22
EUR€1 = 6.47HV	1HV = EUR€0.15
NZ$1 = 3.23HV	1HV = NZ$0.31
UK£1 = 9.45HV	1HV = UK£0.11
US$1 = 5.05HV	1HV = US$0.20

MONEY. The Ukrainian unit of currency is the **hryvnia** (hv), and **inflation** is around 10%. The best places to **exchange currency** are the Obmin Valyut (Обмшн Валют) kiosks in the centers of most cities. **Traveler's checks** can be changed for small commissions in many cities. **Western Union** franchises and **ATMs** are everywhere. Most banks give MasterCard and Visa cash advances for a high commission. The lobbies of fancier hotels usually exchange US dollars at lousy rates. **Do not exchange money with private money changers;** it's illegal and a good way to get ripped off. Banks are open Monday through Friday approximately 9am-1pm.

HEALTH AND SAFETY

EMERGENCY **Police:** ☎02. **Ambulance:** ☎03. **Fire:** ☎01.

Hospital facilities in Ukraine are limited and do not meet Western standards. Very few staff members speak English. Basic supplies are often missing and patients may be required to supply their own medical items (e.g., bandages). Foreigners are required to have medical insurance to receive health care, but be prepared to front the bill yourself and get reimbursed by your insurer later. When in doubt, go to your embassy; they will find you adequate care or fly you out of the country. Medical evacuations to Western Europe cost US$25,000-50,000 and those to the United States can run US$70,000. Most areas of Ukraine now have safe drinking water, but there are frequent shortages, and tap water may only be turned on for a few hours per day. Embassy officials declare that Chernobyl-related **radiation** poses

negligible risk to short-term travelers; however, they do not recommend buying berries, mushrooms, or game from street markets. Meat purchased at open markets should be checked carefully and cooked thoroughly; refrigeration is infrequent and insects run rampant. **Public restrooms** are horrifying. Pay toilets (платні; platni) are cleaner and may provide toilet paper, but bring your own anyway. **Pharmacies** (Аптеки; Apteky) are common and carry basic Western products. Anything more complicated should be brought from home. **Sanitary napkins** (гігієнчні пакети; hihienchni pakety), **condoms** (презервативи; prezervativy), and **tampons** (прокладки; prokladky) are sometimes sold at kiosks.

While Ukraine is relatively politically stable, it is poor. **Pickpocketing** and wallet scams are the most common crimes, although armed robbery and assault have been reported. Don't exchange money on the street and don't accept drinks from strangers. Credit card and ATM fraud are endemic; do not to use credit or ATM cards. Be careful when crossing the street—drivers do not stop for pedestrians. **Register** with your embassy once you get to Ukraine. **Women** traveling alone will be addressed by men anywhere they go, but usually will be safe beyond that. Women may request to ride in female-only train compartments, though most travel co-ed. **Minorities,** especially those of African or Asian descent, may experience harassment from both civilians and law enforcement. **Disabled** travelers will encounter difficulties, as few places are accessible. **Homosexuality** was decriminalized in 1991, but is not yet accepted in most of Ukraine; caution is advised, especially outside of Kyiv.

TRANSPORTATION

BY PLANE. Ukraine is expensive to reach by plane. Ground transportation is safer and more pleasant, but can take a long time. **Air Ukraine** flies to Kyiv, Lviv, and Odessa from many European capitals; **Aerosvit, Air France, British Airways, ČSA, Delta, LOT, Lufthansa, Malév,** and **SAS** fly to Kyiv.

BY TRAIN. The national rail system, *Ukrainski Zaliznitsi*, runs frequently from all of Ukraine's neighbors and is the best way to travel. Ukraine's night transit system is relatively, though not completely, safe. When coming from a non-ex-Soviet country, expect a 2hr. stop at the border. You must present a passport when purchasing train tickets. Once onboard, present your ticket and passport to the *konduktor*. On most Ukrainian trains, there are three classes: плацкарт *(platskart)*, crammed with *babushki* and baskets of strawberries; купе *(kupe)*, a clean, more private, four-person compartment; and first class, referred to as "CB" in Cyrillic (or *SV* in the Latin alphabet), which is twice as roomy, but twice as expensive, as *kupe*. The *kasa* will sell you a *kupe* seat unless you say otherwise. Except in larger cities, where platform numbers are posted on an electronic board, the only way to figure out from which platform your train leaves is by showing your ticket to cashiers and asking цplaht-FORM-ah?"

BY BUS. Buses cost about the same as trains, but are often shabbier. One exception is **AutoLux** (АвтоЛюкс; www.autolux.ua), which runs buses with A/C, snacks, and movies. Bus schedules are generally reliable, but low demand sometimes causes cancellations. Buy tickets at the *kasa* (ticket office); if they're sold out, try going directly to the driver. The bus system can be tricky for those who do not speak Ukrainian or Russian, so memorize departure times and prices in advance.

BY CAR AND BY THUMB. Taxi drivers love to rip off tourists, so negotiate prices beforehand. In urban areas, road conditions are fair; in rural areas, they are not. Let's Go does not recommend hitchhiking. Few Ukrainians hitchhike; those who do hold a sign with their desired destination or just wave an outstretched hand.

KEEPING IN TOUCH

PHONE CODES	**Country code:** 380. **International dialing prefix:** 8, await a second tone, then 10. For more information on placing international calls, see inside back cover.

TELEPHONE AND INTERNET. Telephones in Ukraine are stumbling toward modernity. The easiest way to make an international call is with **Utel.** Buy a phonecard (sold at most Utel phone locations) and dial the number of your international operator (considered a local call). International access codes include: **AT&T Direct** (☎8 100 11); **Canada Direct** (☎8 100 17); **MCI WorldPhone** (☎8 100 13). Or call at the central telephone office—estimate how long your call will take, pay at the counter, and they'll direct you to a booth. Local calls from gray pay phones cost 10-30hv. For an English-speaking operator, dial ☎8192. Internet cafes in major cities typically charge 3-7hv per hour.

MAIL. Mail is cheap and reliable, and takes about eight to 10 days to reach North America. Sending a letter internationally costs 3.34hv. Mail can be received through **Poste Restante** (до запитання; do zapytannya). Address envelopes as follows: First name LAST NAME, "до запитання" post office address, Postal Code, city, UKRAINE.

LANGUAGE. Traveling in Ukraine is much easier if you know **Ukrainian** or **Russian.** Ukrainian is an East Slavic language written in the Cyrillic alphabet. In Kyiv, Odessa, and Crimea, Russian is more commonly spoken than Ukrainian. If you're trying to get by with Russian in Western Ukraine, note that while everyone understands Russian, some people will answer in Ukrainian out of habit or nationalist sentiment. Try to preface Russian statements with "I'm sorry, I don't speak Ukrainian." Practically no English is spoken outside of Kyiv, and very little is spoken there. *Let's Go* provides all city names in Ukrainian; Ukrainian street names are given for Kyiv and Western Ukraine; Russian street names are used for Crimea and Odessa.

ACCOMMODATIONS AND CAMPING

UKRAINE	❶	❷	❸	❹	❺
ACCOMMODATIONS	under 55hv	55-105hv	105-265hv	265-480hv	over 480hv

Not all **hotels** accept foreigners, and those that do often charge them more than they do locals. Room prices in Kyiv are astronomical, but singles run 50-90hv elsewhere. A few **youth hostels** can be found in Lviv, Kyiv, and Yalta; budget accommodations are usually in unrenovated Soviet-era buildings. In some hotels, solo women may be mistaken for prostitutes. You will be given a *vizitka* (hotel card) to show to the *dezhurnaya* (hall monitor) to get a key. **Hot water** is rare—ask before checking in. **Private rooms** in locals' houses are the best bargain at 20-50hv and can be arranged at the train station. Most cities have a **camping** facility. Camping outside designated areas is illegal, and enforcement is merciless.

FOOD AND DRINK

UKRAINE	❶	❷	❸	❹	❺
FOOD	under 11hv	11-27hv	27-54hv	54-105hv	over 105hv

New, fancy restaurants accommodate tourists and the few Ukrainians who can afford them, while *stolovayas* (cafeterias) serve cheap, hot food. *Vavenyky* (pierogi-like dumplings) are delicious. **Vegetarians** beware: meat has a tendency to show up even in so-called "vegetarian" dishes. Finding **kosher** foods can be a daunting task, but it helps to eat non-meat items or to dine in primarily Jewish areas. **State food stores** are classified by content: *hastronom* (packaged goods); *moloko* (milk products); *ovochi-frukty* (fruits and vegetables); *myaso* (meat); *khlib* (bread); *kolbasy* (sausage); and *ryba* (fish). *Kvas* is a popular, nonalcoholic fermented-bread drink. Grocery stores are often simply labeled *mahazyn* (store).

UKRAINE

HOLIDAYS AND FESTIVALS

Holidays: Orthodox Christmas (Jan. 7); Old New Year's Day (Jan. 13); International Women's Day (Mar. 8); Orthodox Easter (about 2 weeks after Catholic Easter); Labor Day (May 1); Victory Day (May 9); Holy Trinity Day (50 days after Orthodox Easter); Constitution Day (June 28); Independence Day (Aug. 24).

Festivals: One of the most widely celebrated festivals is the **Donetsk Jazz Festival,** usually held in April. The **Chervona Ruta Festival,** which occurs each year from April to May in different Ukrainian cities, celebrates modern Ukrainian pop as well as more traditional music. The **Molodist Kyiv International Film Festival,** held in the last week of October, screens student films and film debuts.

BEYOND TOURISM

The Kyiv Post (www.kyivpost.com). English-language newspaper with classified job ads.

Odessa Language Center (☎380 482 345 058; www.studyrus.com). Spend a year or a summer in Ukraine learning Russian and taking courses on history and culture.

KYIV (КИЇВ) ☎8044

Birthplace of the Kyivan Rus empire and no stranger to foreign control, Kyiv (pop. 2,700,000) weathered the Nazis only to be rebuilt with Stalinist pomp by the Soviets. Kyiv has reemerged as a proud capital since Ukraine gained its independence from the USSR, and it recently earned international acclaim as the epicenter of the Orange Revolution. Today, the streets buzz with optimistic energy, even as the cost of living rises and the government struggles to institute promised reforms.

TRANSPORTATION

Flights: Boryspil International Airport (Бориспіль; ☎490 47 77; www.boryspilairport.kiev.ua), 30km southeast of the capital. **Polit** (Політ; ☎296 73 67), just to the right when exiting the main entrance, sends buses to Ploscha Peremohi and the metro/train station. Buy tickets at the bus stop (2 per hr., 20hv). When you arrive at the train station, walk through to the end of the train terminal; the metro is located behind and to the left. A taxi to the center costs about 100hv, but try to negotiate.

Trains: Kyiv-Pasazhyrskyy (Київ-Пасажирський), Vokzalna pl. (☎005). MR: Vokzalna (Вокзальна). Ticket counters in the main hall require passports. For international tickets, go to window #40 or 41 in the newest section, across the tracks. An **Advance Ticket Office** is next to Hotel Express, blv. Shevchenka 38. Trains run to: **Bratislava, SLK** (18hr., 1 per day, 478hv); **Budapest, HUN** (24hr., 1 per day, 592hv); **Lviv** (10hr., 6-7 per day, 60hv); **Moscow, RUS** (15-17hr., 13-16 per day, 260hv); **Odessa** (11hr., 5-6 per day, 70hv); **Prague, CZR** (35hr., 1 per day, 584hv); **Warsaw, POL** (17hr., 2 per day, 332hv).

Buses: Tsentralny Avtovokzal (Центральний Автовокзал), Moskovska pl. 3 (Московська; ☎525 57 74). Take bus #1 or trolley #4 from the Libidska metro station. Open 9am-9pm. Buses to: **Lviv** (10-12hr., 4 per day, 70hv); **Moscow, RUS** (18hr., 1 per day, 150hv); **Odessa** (8-10hr., 9 per day, 66-88hv); **Prague, CZR** (28hr.; 1 per day Tu, Th-F, and Su; 372hv); **Simferopol** (15-16hr., 2 per day, 143hv).

Public Transportation: The 3 **metro** lines—blue (MB), green (MG), and red (MR)—cover the city center. Purchase tokens (житон; zhyton; 0.50hv) at the *kasa* (каса). "Вхід" *(vkhid)* indicates an entrance, "перехід" *(perekhid)* a walkway to another station, and "вихід у місто" *(vykhid u misto)* an exit onto the street. **Trolleys, buses,** and **marshrutki** (private vans) go where the metro doesn't. Bus tickets are sold at kiosks or can be purchased from the driver; punch your ticket using the manual lever onboard or face a fine. Marshrutki tickets (0.60-1hv) are sold onboard; pay attention and request stops from the driver. Public transport runs approximately 5:45am-12:15am. The *elektrychka* (електричка) commuter rail, leaves from Prymiskyy Vokzal (Приміський Вокзал).

Taxis: Taxis to the center of town should cost about 10-20hv.

ORIENTATION AND PRACTICAL INFORMATION

Most attractions and services lie on the west bank of the Dniper River. Three metro stops from the train station lies the main avenue, **vulitsa Khreshchatyk** (Хрещатик; MR line). The center of Kyiv is vul. Khreshchatyk's fountained **Independence Square** (Майдан Незалежності; Maidan Nezalezhnosti; MB line).

Tourist Offices: Kyiv lacks official tourist services. Representatives of various agencies at the airport offer excursions, hotel arrangements, and other services. Try **Carlson Wagonlit Travel,** Ivana Franka 33/34, 2nd fl. (☎238 61 56). Open daily 9am-9pm. **STI Ukraine,** Priorizna 18/1 (Пріорізна) #6, 2nd fl., represents the STA travel network (☎490 5960; www.sti.com.ua). Open M-F 9am-9pm, Sa 10am-4pm.

Embassies: Australia, Kominternu 18/137 (Комінтерну; ☎235 75 86). Open M-Th 10am-1pm. **Canada,** Yaroslaviv Val 31 (Ярославів Вал; ☎590 31 00; www.dfait-maeci.gc.ca/canada-europa/ukraine). Open M-F 8:30am-1pm and 2-5pm. **UK,** Desyatynna 9 (Десятинна; ☎490 36 60). Consular section at Glybochytska 4 (Глибочицька; ☎494 34 00). Open M-Th 9am-1pm and 2-5:30pm, F 9am-1pm and 2-4pm. **US,** Yu. Kotsyubynskoho 10 (Ю. Коцюбинського; ☎490 40 00; www.usembassy.kiev.ua). Consulate at Mukolu Pymonenka 6 (Пимоненка; ☎490 44 22). Open M-F 8:30am-12:30pm or by appointment.

Emergency: ☎03.

Medical Services: American Medical Center, Berdycherska 1 (Бердичерска; ☎490 76 00; www.amcenters.com), has English-speaking doctors, and takes patients without documents or insurance. Open 24hr. MC/V.

Telephones: Telephone-Telegraph (Телефон-Телеграф; telefon-telehraf) at the post office (enter on Khreshchatyk). Open daily 8am-10:30pm. Buy cards for **public telephones** (таксофон; taksofon) at any post office. **English-language operator** ☎81 92. **Utel phones** are in the post office, train station, hotels, and nice restaurants.

Internet Access: C-Club, Besarabskaye pl. 1 (Бесарабскае; ☎247 56 47), in the underground mall between the market and the Lenin statue. 3hv per hr. Open 24hr.

Post Office: vul. Khreshchatyk 22 (☎230 08 38; www.poshta.kiev.ua). *Poste Restante* at counters #28 and 30. Internet, copy, fax, and photo services available. Open M-Sa 8am-9pm, Su 9am-7pm. **Postal Code:** 01 001.

ACCOMMODATIONS AND FOOD

Hotels in Kyiv tend to be expensive; the *Kyiv Post* (www.kyivpost.com) lists short-term apartment rentals. People at train stations offer even cheaper rooms (from US$5). Another way to find lodging is through the commission-free telephone service **Okean-9.** (☎443 6167. Open M-F 9am-5pm, Sa 9am-3pm.) Backpackers flock to **International Youth Hostel Yaroslav ❸** (Ярослав), vul. Yaroslavska 10 (Ярославська), in the historic Podil district. This 12-bed hostel with an English-speaking staff fills up quickly. (☎417 31 89. MB: Kontraktova Plosha. Internet next door 5hv per hr. Dorms US$25. $1 HI discount.) Down vul. Kominternu from the train station, **Hotel Express ❸** (Експрес), bul. Shevchenka 38/40, has rooms with TV, A/C, and balconies. (☎239 8995; www.expresskiev.com.ua. Internet 4hv for 30min. Singles with showers 484hv; doubles 390hv, with shower 708hv.)

Antresol ❸ (Антресоль), bul. Shevchenka 2, has a hip bookstore-cafe downstairs and a restaurant upstairs. (☎235 8347. English-language menu. Entrees 41-68hv. Beer 10-21hv. Tu and Th live piano 8-10pm. Open daily 9am-late. Cash only.) Located in the Taras Shevchenko Park, **O'Panas ❸** (О'Панас), Tereshchenkivska vul. 10 (Терещенківська), serves local dishes amid traditional Ukrainian decor. (☎235 2132. Entrees 28-98hv. Open daily 10am-2am. MC/V.) **King David's ❹,** Esplanadna 24 (Еспланадна), is a kosher restaurant. (☎235 74 36. MG: Palats Sportu; Палац Спорту. Entrees 40-110hv. Open Su-Th 10am-11pm, F 10am-8:30pm. Cash only.) Hit Besarabsky Market at Besarabska ploscha for fresh produce. (MR: Teatralna. Open until about 6pm.)

SIGHTS

KYIV-CAVE MONASTERY. The Kyiv-Cave Monastery (Київо-Печерська Лавра; Kyivo-Pecherska Lavra), Kyiv's oldest holy site, houses the **Refectory Church,** the 12th-century **Holy Trinity Gate Church,** and caves where monks lie mummified. The **Great Lavra Bell Tower** offers views of the domes. *(MR: Arsenalna;* Арсенальна. *Turn left*

ily Chronicle

N RECENT NEWS

CHERNOBYL REMEMBERED?

\pril 2006 marked the 20th anni-
'ersary of what is generally con-
;idered to be the world's worst
ıuclear accident, the explosion of
ı nuclear facility at Chernobyl.
;aused by a flagrant violation of
)rocedures during the testing of
)ne of the facility's four reactors
ınd by the breakdown of commu-
ıication among personnel, the
ıccident immediately killed more
han 30 people and exposed
housands to high levels of radia-
ion. Controversy still exists about
he overall effect of the disaster: a
ecent Greenpeace study contests
he UN's estimate of 4000-9000
;ancer deaths, suggesting
nstead a startling figure of
)3,000 casualties.

As memorial vigils took place
n Ukraine in April, protestors
ined the streets of nearby
3elarus, challenging the ongoing
levelopment in regions contami-
ıated by the explosion. Neverthe-
ess, Ukraine continues to sing
he praises of nuclear energy.
'God gave us uranium," Prime
Minister Yuri Yekhanurov has said,
'and today we should use it."

The utilization of God's
esources seems to be on
Jkraine's horizon. Though there
ıre plans to complete a new
'massive containment arch" over
he disaster site by 2010, several
eactors have already come on-
ine in recent years, and at least
11 more are planned by 2030.

out of the metro and walk down vul. Sichnevoho Povstaniya. Open daily May-Aug. 9am-7pm; Sept.-Apr. 9:30am-6pm. Monastery 10hv, students 5hv. Photography 12hv.)

ST. SOPHIA CATHEDRAL. Once the religious center of Kyivan Rus, the St. Sophia Cathedral, with its ornamented facades and Byzantine mosaics has long been a spiritual and political center of Ukraine. *(vul. Volodymyrska. MG: Zoloti Vorota or trolley #16 from Maidan Nezalezhnosti. Grounds open daily 9am-7pm. Museums open M-Tu and F-Su 10am-6pm, W 10am-5pm. Grounds 1hv. Museums 16hv, students 5hv. Bell tower 5/3hv.)*

VULITSA KHRESHCHATYK AND ENVIRONS. Kyiv's spinal cord, vul. Khreshchatyk (Хрещатик), begins at bul. Shevchenka and extends to **Independence Square** (Майдан Незалежності; Maidan Nezalezhnosti). This square hosted a massive tent city that persevered through the Orange Revolution. **Khreshchaty Park,** past the **Friendship of the Peoples Arch,** contains a monument to Prince Volodymyr, who converted the Kyivan Rus to Christianity. *(MR: Khreshchatyk; Хрещатик.)*

ANDRIYIVSKYY RISE AND THE PODIL DISTRICT. Full of cafes and galleries, the cobblestone Andriyivskyy Rise (Андріївский Узвіз; Andriyivskyy uzviz) can be reached by walking down Desyatynna from Mikhaylivska Sq. *(MB: Poshtova; Поштова.)* The **Museum of One Street,** Andriyivskyy uzviz 2B, recounts the street's colorful history. *(Open Tu-Su noon-6pm. 5hv. 45min. English-language tour 50hv.)* At the corner of Desyatinna and Andriyivskyy uzviz is **St. Andrew's Church.** *(Open 10am-6pm. Kasa closes 30min. before closing.)* One block down Andriyivskyy uzviz, steep wooden stairs lead to a great view of **Podil,** Kyiv's oldest district. The **Chernobyl Museum,** Provulok Khoryva 1, details the nuclear disaster's aftermath. *(Open M-F 10am-6pm, Sa 10am-5pm. Closed last M of each month. 5hv, with ISIC 1hv.)*

ENTERTAINMENT AND NIGHTLIFE

The last weekend in May brings **Kyiv Days,** with performances all over the city. During the rest of the year, the **National Philharmonic,** Volodymyrsky uzviz 2, holds concerts most nights at 7pm. (☎278 16 97; www.filharmonia.com.ua. *Kasa* open Tu-Su noon-2pm and 3-7pm. 5-30hv.) **Shevchenko Opera and Ballet Theater,** vul. Volodymyrska 50, has several performances each week. (MR: Teatralna; Театральна. ☎279 1169. *Kasa* open M 3-7pm, Tu-Su 11am-3pm and 4-7:30pm. 5-100hv.) If you're in town in the summer, don't miss **Dynamo Kyiv,** one of Europe's top soccer teams. (Ticket office in front of stadium. 10-

50hv.) On hot days, head to **Hydropark** (Гідропарк), an **amusement park, sports complex,** and **nightclub.** (MR: Hydropark.)

Check out *What's On* magazine and the *Kyiv Post* (www.kyivpost.com) for nightlife listings. Kyiv's popular jazz club, **Artclub 44,** vul. Khreshchatyk 44, has live music nightly starting at 10pm. (☎279 4137. Cover Th-Sa 20hv. Open daily 11am-last customer.) **Eric's Bierstube,** vul. Chervonoarmiyiska 20 (Червоноармійська) draws a large crowd to its underground bar. From MB: pl. Lva Tolstoho, walk 10m toward Khreshchatyk on vul. Chervonoarmiyiska. At #20, follow the "КАФЕ ЂАР" (Cafe Bar) sign. (☎235 9472. Beer 8-20hv. Appetizers 8-28hv. Entrees 19-48hv. M live music. Open daily 8am-2am. Cash only.) **Androhin** (Андрогин), vul. Harmatna 26/2, is a gay-friendly club. (MR: Shulyavska. ☎496 19 83. Transvestite and striptease show every F-Sa 11pm. Cover men 40hv, women 50hv. Open Tu-Su 7pm-6am.)

LVIV (ЛЬВІВ) ☎80322

Teeming with energy and more affordable than Kyiv, Lviv (pop. 734,000) offers an open invitation to tourists. Those who visit can meander down picturesque cobblestone streets, marvel at medieval churches untouched by WWII, sip coffee in quaint cafes, and watch Ukraine's cultural and patriotic center come into its own.

TRANSPORTATION AND PRACTICAL INFORMATION. **Trains** go from pl. Vokzalna (Вокзальна) to: Budapest, HUN (13hr., 1 per day, 405hv); Kraków, POL (7½hr., 1 per day, 220hv); Kyiv (9hr., over 10 per day, 52hv); Moscow, RUS (25hr., 4 per day, 235hv); Odessa (12hr., 2 per day, 51hv); Prague, CZR (24hr., 1 per day, 400hv); Warsaw, POL (13½hr., every other day, 200hv). Tickets can be bought at the railway *kasa* at Hnatyuka 20. (Гнатюка; ☎226 52 76. Open M-Sa 8am-2pm and 3-8pm, Su 8am-2pm and 3-6pm.) **Taxis** from the train station into town cost about 20hv. **Buses** run from the main station, vul. Stryyska 189 (Стрийська; ☎294 98 17) to **Kraków, POL** (8-9hr., 1 per day, 98hv) and **Warsaw, POL** (10hr., 3 per day, 109hv). **Trolleys** in town cost 0.50hv. The **Lviv Tourist Info Center,** vul. Pidvalna 3, has an English-speaking staff. (☎297 57 51; www.tourism.lviv.ua. Open M-F 10am-6pm.) **Internet Club,** vul. Dudaeva 12, offers Internet and international calling. (☎72 27 38; www.ic.lviv.ua. Open 24hr. Internet 4hv per hr.) For local phone calls from a landline, dial "2" before numbers that begin with "9." **Postal Code:** 79 000.

ACCOMMODATIONS AND FOOD. **Hotel George ❸** (Готель Жорж), pl. Mitskevycha 1, retains some of its 100-year-old charm. (☎72 59 52; www.georgehotel.com.ua. English-speaking reception. Breakfast included. Singles 153hv, with bath 319-508; doubles 187/388-541hv. MC/V.) Many backpackers stay at clean **Hotel Lviv ❶,** vul. Chornovola 7 (Чорновола), behind the opera house. (☎792 22 70 or 72 75 82. Tram #6 or bus #66 from the train station. Some English spoken. Singles 65hv, with bath 110-170hv; doubles 110-130/160-280hv; triples 135-180hv without bath; quads 180/280hv. Cash only.) **Veronika ❶** (Вероніка), pr. Shevchenko 21, serves pastries (3-9hv), pizza (16-74hv), and coffee. (☎297 81 28. Open daily 10am-11pm. MC/V.) With local food at local prices, **Noah's Ark ❶** (Ноув Ковчет), ul. Stavropihiyska 9, also offers *gorilka*, the local firewater. (☎72 65 21. English menu. Appetizers 3-14hv. Entrees 6-20hv. Open 11am-11pm. Cash only.)

SIGHTS AND ENTERTAINMENT. Climb up the **High Castle Hill** (Високий Замок; Vysokyy Zamok), the former site of the Galician King's Palace, for a stunning panoramic view of Lviv. **Ploschad Rynok,** the historic market square, is surrounded by richly decorated homes and numerous Baroque churches. The **History Museum** (Історичний Музей; Istorichnyy Muzey) complex is at Pl. Rynok #2,

4, 6, and 24. Exhibits on the upper floors recount the history of Ukraine's struggle for liberation during WWI and WWII; some are accompanied by English translations. (☎72 06 71. Open M-Tu and Th-Su 10am-5pm. Each museum 2-4hv, some student discounts.) Walk up to the end of vul. Staroyevreiska (Old Jewish St.), and on your left at Arsenalna Square find the ruins of the 16th-century **Golden Rose Synagogue,** a center of Jewish culture before its destruction by the Nazis. **Ivano-Franko Opera and Ballet Theater,** Prospekt Svobody 28, holds performances at fantastic prices in a turn-of-the-century hall. (☎72 85 62. Performances several times per week at noon and 6pm. 10-75hv.) **Cafe Karyarnya** ("Dyerza"), vul. Virmenska 35, is a cafe-bar inside a funky art gallery. There is an English menu with a huge range of drinks and desserts, including "Lard in chocolate: It's not a joke!" for 5hv. (☎297 56 12. Coffee and tea 4-7hv. Beer 5-7hv. Snacks 6-15hv. Desserts 5-10hv. Open daily 10am-10pm. Cash only.) The party at **Millennium,** vul. Chornovola 2, revolves around its three levels of dance floors. (☎40 35 91; www.favorite-club.com. Beer 5hv. Cover free-20hv for women, 30-40hv for men. Open Tu-Su 9pm-3 or 4am.)

ODESSA (ОДЕСА) ☎80482

Odessa (pop. 1,000,000) has been blessed with prosperity and cursed with corruption since its founding by Catherine the Great in 1794. With a full set of European influences, this port town has been kept lively by *mafiosi* and intellectuals, and it has inspired writers from Alexander Pushkin to Isaac Babel. The **Odessa Art Museum** (Художний Музей; Khudozhniy Muzey), ul. Sofiyevskaya 5A, houses a collection of 19th-century art. (☎23 84 62. Open M and W-Su 10:30am-5pm. 3hv.) Odessa's loveliest street is **ulitsa Pushkinskaya.** The **Pushkin Museum and Memorial** (Литературно-мемориальний Музей Пушкина; Literaturno-memorialniy Muzey Pushkina) at #13 was the hotel where Pushkin lived during his 1823-1824 exile from St. Petersburg. (Open Tu-Su 10am-5pm. 5hv, students 2hv.) Beneath the city lies the world's longest series of **catacombs;** the tunnels were the base of partisan resistance during the Nazi occupation. Odessa has established a subterranean museum in its honor. The city's crowded **beaches** are easily accessible. To reach nearby **Lanzheron** (Ланжерон) beach, walk through Shevchenko park or take *marshrutki* 253, 233, or 2MT. Tram #5 goes to **Arkadiya** (Аркадия), the city's most popular beach. At the end of ul. Rishelyevskaya, the **Opera and Ballet Theater** (Театр Оперы и Балета; Teatr Opery i Baleta) has been under renovation but is expected to reopen in 2007 or 2008. (*Kasa* ul. Preobrazhenskaya 28. ☎22 02 45. Open daily 10am-5pm.)

Private rooms (from 30hv) are the cheapest option for accommodation; hosts solicit customers at the train station. **Hotel Passage** ❷ (Пассаж), ul. Preobrazhenskaya 34, is a basic budget hotel with an Internet cafe in the same building. (Reservations ☎726 95 37; reception 728 55 01; www.passage.odessa.ua. Singles 65hv, with bath 105-325hv; doubles 100/140-325hv. Cash only.) The cafeteria **Zharu Paru** ❶ (Жару Пару), ul. Grechevskaya 45 (Гречевская), serves Ukrainian fare. (☎22 44 30. Full meal 5-10hv. Open daily 8am-10pm. Cash only.) At **Kumanets** ❸, bul. Havanna 7, English-speaking waiters dressed in Ukrainian garb dish out high-quality authentic local meals. (☎37 69 46. Menu in English. Draft beer 7-15hv. Big salads 17-39hv. Entrees 29hv and up. Cash only.) In the summer, the best nightlife option is to traipse **ulitsa Deribasovskaya** (Дерибасовская), where many restaurants, cafes, and bars stay open late and play music that ranges from techno to Slavic folk.

Trains run from pl. Privokzalnaya 2 (Привокзальная; tickets ☎005), at the northern end of ul. Pushkinskaya, to: Kyiv (10hr., 3 per day, 35-52hv); Lviv (12hr., 2 per day, 35-52hv); Moscow, RUS (23-27hr., 2-4 per day, 173-287hv); Simferopol (route to Yalta, 12hr., 29-40hv); Warsaw, POL (29hr., even-numbered days, 400hv). To reach the bus station, take tram #5 to the last stop. **Buses** run from ul. Kolontayevskaya 58 (Колонтаевская) to Kyiv (8-10hr., 8 per day, 66-88hv). **FGT Travel,** ul.

Deribasovskaya 13, in Hotel Frapolli, provides info. (☎37 52 01; www.odessapassage.com. Open daily 8:30am-8pm.) **Eugenia Travel**, ul. Rishelievskaya 23, runs tours including the catacombs and can help with hotel bookings in Odessa and Yalta. (☎22 03 31; www.eugeniatours.com.ua.) For Internet access, go to **Internet Kiev,** ul. Deribasovskaya 8. (☎37 70 44. 6hv per hr. Open 24hr.) **Postal Code:** 65 001.

YALTA (ЯЛТА) ☎80654

A former vacation spot for the Russian elite, Yalta (pop. 81,000) is the city that inspired Chekhov and Tolstoy. Some of Yalta's best sights are located outside town. The **Great Livadiya Palace,** which hosted the Yalta Conference in WWII (☎31 55 79; open M-Tu and Th-Su 10am-5pm; 12hv; photography 2hv), and **Swallow's Nest,** a picturesque castle that hangs precariously over a cliff face (take a taxi or a ferry from Embankment dock #7, 30min., 4 per day, 15hv; open Tu-Su 9am-8pm; 3hv), are worthwhile daytrips. At ul. Kirova 12, explore the **white dacha** that Anton Chekhov built in 1899. Take *marshrutka* #8 from Kinoteatr Spartak on ul. Pushkinskaya. (☎39 49 47. Open June-Sept. Tu-Su 10am-5:15pm; Oct.-May W-Su 10am-4pm. 15hv.) Catch a gondola up the mountain for the view of the city. (Open daily 10am-8pm. 14hv.) Follow the shore away from the harbor to reach Yalta's **beaches** (2-5hv).

The weather is pleasant and accommodations are easy to book in May and June; reserve at least two months ahead for July and August. If you arrive in the summer and don't have prior arrangements, negotiate with locals at the bus station offering private rooms (20-100hv). A good mid-range place if traveling in pairs is **Hotel Otdizh ❶,** vul. Drazhynskoho 14. (☎35 30 79. Breakfast included. Doubles with bathroom 270hv, suites 350hv. Cash only.) **Pension T.M.M. ❸,** ul. Lesi Ukrayinki 16, has views of the sea and rooms with balconies, TVs, and baths. (☎23 09 50. Little English spoken. 3 meals included. Singles 160hv; doubles 300-415hv.) Several **cafeterias** (столовая; *stolovaya*) in the center of town serve cheap fare (10-20hv); **Stolovaya Rabotaet ❶,** on vul. Ihnatenko, is one of the better ones. (Full meal 10hv. Open daily 8am-8pm.) **Cafe Voschod ❷,** ul. Ignatenko 2, near pl. Sovetskaya, serves Turkish and Russian cuisine and has an English menu. (☎23 39 43. Open daily May-Sept. 24hr.; Oct.-Apr. 8am-midnight.) At night, walk the strip, nab. Lenina 11, or try one of its many cafes. Overlooking the waterfront is the nightclub **Tornado,** nab. Lenina 11. (☎32 20 36. Beer 8hv. Cover 50-100hv. Open July-Sept. daily 10pm-5am; Oct.-Nov. Th-Sa 10pm-5am; Dec.-May F-Sa 10pm-5am.)

Yalta is not accessible directly by train. **Buses** run from ul. Moskovskaya to Kyiv (17½hr., 2 per day, 110-150hv) and Odessa (14hr., 2 per day, 70-100hv). Most buses to Yalta terminate in Simferopol; make your way to Yalta via trolley (2½ hrs.) or *marshrutka* (2hr.) from the main bus/train terminal. Once in Yalta, take a trolley or taxi (10-15hv) into the center of town. Although **Eugenia Travel** has closed its office in Yalta, its representative can be reached at ☎34 77 40 or 067 652 6828, or through the Odessa office (p. 1050). **Postal Code:** 98 600.

APPENDIX

LANGUAGE PHRASEBOOK

CYRILLIC ALPHABET

Bulgaria and **Ukraine** use variations of the Russian Cyrillic alphabet.

CYRILLIC	ENGLISH	PRONOUNCE	CYRILLIC	ENGLISH	PRONOUNCE
А а	a	*ah* as in Pr**a**gue	Р р	r	*r* as in **r**evolution
Б б	b	*b* as in **B**osnia	С с	s	*s* as in **S**erbia
В в	v	*v* as in **V**olga	Т т	t	*t* as in **t**ank
Г г	g	*g* as in **G**lasnost	У у	u	*oo* as in B**u**dapest
Д д	d	*d* as in **d**ictatorship	Ф ф	f	*f* as in **f**ormer USSR
Е е	e	*yeh* as in **Ye**ltsin	Х х	kh	*kh* as in Ba**ch**
Ё ё	yo	*yo* as in **yo!**	Ц ц	ts	*ts* as in **ts**ar
Ж ж	zh	*zh* as in mira**ge**	Ч ч	ch	*ch* as in Gorba**ch**ev
З з	z	*z* as in communi**s**m	Ш ш	sh	*sh* as in Bol**sh**evik
И и	i	*ee* as in Gr**ee**k	Щ щ	shch	*shch* in Khru**shch**ev
Й й	y	*y* as in bo**y** or ke**y**	Ъ ъ	(hard sign)	(not pronounced)
К к	k	*k* as in **K**remlin	Ы ы	y	*y* as in s**i**lver
Л л	l	*l* as in **L**enin	Ь ь	(soft sign)	(not pronounced)
М м	m	*m* as in **M**oscow	Э э	e	*eh* as in **E**stonia
Н н	n	*n* as in **n**uclear	Ю ю	yu	*yoo* as in **U**kraine
О о	o	*o* as in Cr**o**atia	Я я	ya	*yah* as in **Ya**lta
П п	p	*p* as in **P**oland			

GREEK ALPHABET

SYMBOL	NAME	PRONOUNCE	SYMBOL	NAME	PRONOUNCE
α Α	alpha	*a* as in f**a**ther	ν Ν	nu	*n* as in **n**et
β Β	beta	*v* as in **v**elvet	ξ Ξ	xi	*x* as in mi**x**
γ Γ	gamma	*y* as in **y**o or *g* as in **g**o	ο Ο	omicron	*o* as in r**o**w
δ Δ	delta	*th* as in **th**ere	π Π	pi	*p* as in **p**eace
ε Ε	epsilon	*e* as in j**e**t	ρ Ρ	rho	*r* as in **r**oll
ζ Ζ	zeta	*z* as in **z**ebra	σ Σ	sigma	*s* as in **s**ense
η Η	eta	*ee* as in qu**ee**n	τ Τ	tau	*t* as in **t**ent
θ Θ	theta	*th* as in **th**ree	υ Υ	upsilon	*ee* as in gr**ee**n
ι Ι	iota	*ee* as in tr**ee**	φ Φ	phi	*f* as in **f**og
κ Κ	kappa	*k* as in **k**ite	χ Χ	chi	*h* as in **h**orse
λ Λ	lambda	*l* as in **l**and	ψ Ψ	psi	*ps* as in oo**ps**
μ Μ	mu	*m* as in **m**oose	ω Ω	omega	*o* as in Let's G**o**

CROATIAN

ENGLISH	CROATIAN	PRONOUNCE	ENGLISH	CROATIAN	PRONOUNCE
Yes/No	Da/Ne	da/neh	**Train/Bus**	Vlak/Autobus	vlahk/aw-TOH-bus
Please	Molim	MO-leem	**Station**	Kolodvor	KOH-loh-dvor
Thank you	Hvala lijepa	HVAH-la lye-pa	**Airport**	Zračna Luka	ZRA-chna LU-kah
Good day	Dobar dan	do-bar DAHN	**Ticket**	Karta	KAHR-tah
Goodbye	Zbogom	ZBO-gohm	**Taxi**	Taksi	TAH-ksee
Sorry/Excuse me	Oprostite	o-PRO-stee-teh	**Hotel**	Hotel	HOH-tel
Help!	U pomoć!	OO po-moch	**Bathroom**	WC	VAY-tsay
I'm lost. (m/f)	Izgubljen(a) sam.	eez-GUB-lye-n(a) sahm	**Open/Closed**	Otvoreno/ Zatvoreno	OHT-voh-reh-noh/ZAHT-voh-reh-noh
Police	Policija	po-LEE-tsee-ya	**Left/Right**	Lijevo/Desno	lee-YEH-voh/ DEHS-noh
Embassy	Ambasada	ahm-bah-SAH-da	**Bank**	Banka	BAHN-kah
Passport	Putovnica	POO-toh-vnee-tsah	**Exchange**	Mjenjačnica	myehn-YAHCH-nee-tsah
Doctor/Hospital	Liječnik/Bolnica	lee-YECH-nik/ bol-NI-tsa	**Grocery/Market**	Trgovina	TER-goh-vee-nah
Pharmacy	Ljekarna	lye-KHAR-na	**Post Office**	Pošta	POSH-tah

ENGLISH	CROATIAN	PRONOUNCE
Where is...?	Gdje je...?	GDYE yeh
How much does this cost?	Koliko to košta?	KO-lee-koh toh KOH-shta
When is the next...?	Kada polazi sljedeći...?	ka-DA po-LA-zee SLYE-de-tchee
Do you have (a vacant room)?	Imate li (slobodne sobe)?	ee-MAH-teh lee (SLOH-boh-dneh SOH-beh)
I would like...	Želim...	ZHE-leem
I don't eat...	Ne jedem...	ne YEH-dem
Do you speak English?	Govorite li engleski?	GO-vor-ee-teh lee eng-LEH-skee
I don't speak Croatian.	Ne govorim hrvatski.	neh goh-VOH-reem KHR-va-tskee

CZECH

ENGLISH	CZECH	PRONOUNCE	ENGLISH	CZECH	PRONOUNCE
Yes/No	Ano/Ne	AH-no/neh	**Train/Bus**	Vlak/Autobus	vlahk/OUT-oh-boos
Please	Prosím	PROH-seem	**Station**	Nádraží	NA-drah-zhee
Thank you	Děkuji	DYEH-koo-yih	**Airport**	Letiště	LEH-teesh-tyeh
Hello	Dobrý den	DO-bree den	**Ticket**	Lístek	LIS-tek
Goodbye	Nashledanou	NAH-sleh-dah-noh-oo	**Taxi**	Taxi	TEHK-see
Sorry/Excuse me	Promiňte	PROH-mihn-teh	**Hotel**	Hotel	HOH-tel
Help!	Pomoc!	POH-mots	**Bathroom**	WC	VEE-TSEE
I'm lost. (m/f)	Zabloudil(a) jsem.	ZAH-bloh-dyeel-(ah) sem.	**Open/Closed**	Otevřeno/ Zavřeno	O-te-zheno/ZAV-rzhen-o
Police	Policie	PO-leets-iye	**Left/Right**	Vlevo/Vpravo	VLE-voh/VPRAH-voh
Embassy	Velvyslanectví	VEHL-vee-slah-nehts-vee	**Bank**	Banka	BAN-ka

APPENDIX

ENGLISH	CZECH	PRONOUNCE	ENGLISH	CZECH	PRONOUNCE
Passport	Cestovní pas	TSEH-stohv-nee pahs	**Exchange**	Směnárna	smyeh-NAR-na
Doctor	Lékař	LEK-arzh	**Grocery**	Potraviny	PO-tra-vee-nee
Pharmacy	Lékárna	LEE-khaar-nah	**Post Office**	Pošta	POSH-tah

ENGLISH	CZECH	PRONOUNCE
Where is...?	Kde je...?	k-DEH
How much does this cost?	Kolik to stojí?	KOH-lihk STOH-yee
When is the next...?	Kdy jede příští...?	gdi YEH-deh przh-EESH-tyee
Do you have (a vacant room)?	Máte (volný pokoj)?	MAA-teh (VOHL-nee POH-koy)
I would like...	Prosím...	PROH-seem
I do not eat...	Nejím...	NEH-yeem
Do you speak English?	Mluvíte anglicky?	MLOO-vit-eh ahng-GLIT-skee
I don't speak Czech.	Nemluvim Česky.	NEH-mloo-veem CHESS-kee

FINNISH

ENGLISH	FINNISH	PRONOUNCE	ENGLISH	FINNISH	PRONOUNCE
Yes/No	Kyllä/Ei	KEW-la/ay	**Ticket**	Lipun	LIP-ooh
Please	Olka hyvä	OHL-ka HEW-va	**Train/Bus**	Juna/Bussi	YU-nuh/BUS-see
Thank you	Kiitos	KEE-tohss	**Boat**	Vene	VEH-nay
Hello	Hei	hay	**Departures**	Lähtevät	lah-teh-VAHT
Goodbye	Näkemiin	NA-keh-meen	**Market**	Tori	TOH-ree
Sorry/Excuse me	Anteeksi	ON-take-see	**Hotel**	Hotelli	HO-tehl-lee
Help!	Apua!	AH-poo-ah	**Hostel**	Retkeilymaja	reht-kayl-oo-MAH-yuh
Police	Poliisi	POH-lee-see	**Bathroom**	Vessa	VEHS-sah
Embassy	Suurlähetystö	SOOHR-la-heh-toos-ter	**Telephone**	Puhelin	POO-heh-leen
I'm lost!	Olen kadok-sissa!	OH-lehn cou-doc-sissa	**Open/Closed**	Auki/Kiinni	OUH-kee/KEEN-ne
Railway station	Rautatieasema	ROW-tah-tiah-ah-seh-ma	**Hospital**	Sairaala	SAIH-raah-lah
Bank	Pankki	PAHNK-kih	**Left/Right**	Vasen/Oikea	VAH-sen/OY-kay-uh
Currency exchange	Rahanvaihto-piste	RAA-han-vyeh-tow-pees-teh	**Post Office**	Posti	PAUS-teeh
Airport	lentokenttä	LEH-toh-kehnt-tah	**Pharmacy**	Apteekki	UHP-take-kee

ENGLISH	FINNISH	PRONOUNCE
Where is...?	Missä on...?	MEE-sah ohn
How do I get to...?	Miten pääsen...?	MEE-ten PA-sen
How much does this cost?	Paljonko se maksaa?	PAHL-yon-ko seh MOCK-sah
I'd like to buy...	Haluaisin ostaa...	HUH-loo-ay-sihn OS-tuh
Do you speak English?	Puhutteko englantia?	POO-hoot-teh-kaw ENG-lan-tee-ah
When is the next...?	Milloin on seuraava...?	MEEHL-loyhn OHN SEUH-raah-vah
I don't speak Finnish.	En puhu suomea.	ehn POO-hoo SUA-meh-ah
I'm allergic to/I cannot eat...	En voi syödä...	ehn voy SEW-dah

APPENDIX

FRENCH

ENGLISH	FRENCH	PRONOUNCE	ENGLISH	FRENCH	PRONOUNCE
Hello	Bonjour	bohn-ZHOOR	**Exchange**	L'échange	lay-SHANZH
Please	S'il vous plaît	see voo PLAY	**Grocery**	L'épicerie	lay-PEES-ree
Thank you	Merci	mehr-SEE	**Market**	Le marché	leuh MARZH-chay
Excuse me	Excusez-moi	ex-KU-zay MWAH	**Police**	La police	la poh-LEES
Yes/No	Oui/Non	wee/nohn	**Embassy**	L'ambassade	lahm-ba-SAHD
Goodbye	Au revoir	oh ruh-VWAHR	**Passport**	Le passeport	leuh pass-POR
Help!	Au secours!	oh seh-COOR	**Post Office**	La poste	la POHST
I'm lost.	Je suis perdu.	zhe SWEE pehr-doo	**One-way**	Le billet simple	leuh bee-AY samp
Train/Bus	Le train/Le bus	leuh tran/leuh boos	**Round-trip**	Le billet aller-retour	leuh bee-AY a-LAY-re-TOOR
Station	La gare	la gahr	**Ticket**	Le billet	leuh bee-AY
Airport	L'aéroport	la-ehr-o-POR	**Single room**	Une chambre simple	oon SHAM-br samp
Hotel	L'hôtel	lo-TEL	**Double room**	Une chambre pour deux	oon SHAM-br poor duh
Hostel	L'auberge	lo-BERZHE	**With shower**	Avec la douche	a-VEK la doosh
Bathroom	La salle de bain	la SAL de BAHN	**Taxi**	Le taxi	leuh tax-EE
Open/Closed	Ouvert/Fermé	oo-VEHR/fer-MAY	**Ferry**	Le bac	leuh bak
Doctor	Le médecin	leuh mehd-SEN	**Tourist office**	Le bureau de tourisme	leuh byur-OH de toor-EESM
Hospital	L'hôpital	loh-pee-TAL	**Town hall**	L'hôtel de ville	lo-TEL de VEEL
Pharmacy	La pharmacie	la far-ma-SEE	**Vegetarian**	Végétarien	vay-jay-ta-ree-EHN
Left/Right	À gauche/À droite	a GOSH/a DWAT	**Kosher/Halal**	Kascher/Halal	ka-SHAY/ha-LAL
Straight	Tout droit	too DWA	**Newsstand**	Le tabac	leuh ta-BAC
Turn	Tournez	toor-NAY	**Cigarette**	La cigarette	la see-ga-RET

ENGLISH	FRENCH	PRONOUNCE
Do you speak English?	Parlez-vous anglais?	PAR-lay VOO ahn-GLAY
Where is...?	Où se trouve...?	OO seh-TRHOOV
When is the next...?	À quelle heure part le prochain...?	ah KEL ur par leuh PRO-chan
How much does this cost?	Ça fait combien?	SAH fay com-bee-EN
Do you have rooms available?	Avez-vous des chambres disponibles?	AV-ay voo day SHAM-br DEES-pon-EEB-bl
I would like ...	Je voudrais...	zhe voo-DRAY
I don't speak French.	Je ne parle pas Français.	zhe neuh PARL pah FRAWN-say
I'm allergic to...	Je suis allergique à...	zhe swee al-ehr-ZHEEK a
I love you.	Je t'aime.	zhe tem

GERMAN

Every letter is pronounced. Consonants are as in English with the following exceptions: "g" is always hard (as in "bug"), "j" is pronounced as "y," "qu" is "kv," a single "s" is "z," "v" is "f," "w" is "v," and "z" is "ts." "Sch" is "sh," "st" is "sht," and "sp" is "shp." The "ch" sound, as in "ich" ("I") and "nicht" ("not"), is tricky; you can substitute a "sh." The letter ß (ess-tset) spells a double "s"; pronounce it "ss."

ENGLISH	GERMAN	PRONOUNCE	ENGLISH	GERMAN	PRONOUNCE
Yes/No	Ja/Nein	yah/nein	**Train/Bus**	Zug/Bus	tsoog/boos
Please	Bitte	BIH-tuh	**Station**	Bahnhof	BAHN-hohf
Thank you	Danke	DAHNG-kuh	**Airport**	Flughafen	FLOOG-hah-fen
Hello	Hallo	HAH-lo	**Taxi**	Taxi	TAHK-see
Goodbye	Auf Wiedersehen	owf VEE-der-zayn	**Ticket**	Fahrkarte	FAR-kar-tuh
Excuse me	Entschuldigung	ent-SHOOL-dih-gung	**Departure**	Abfahrt	AHB-fart
Help!	Hilfe!	HIL-fuh	**One-way**	Einfache	AYHN-fah-kuh
I'm lost.	Ich habe mich verlaufen.	eesh HAH-buh meesh fer-LAU-fun	**Round-trip**	Rundreise	RUND-RYE-seh
Police	Polizei	poh-leet-ZAI	**Reservation**	Reservierung	reh-zer-VEER-ung
Embassy	Botschaft	BOAT-shahft	**Ferry**	Fährschiff	FAYHR-shiff
Passport	Reisepass	RYE-zeh-pahss	**Bank**	Bank	bahnk
Doctor/Hospital	Arzt/Krankenhaus	ahrtzt/KRANK-en-house	**Exchange**	Wechseln	VEHK-zeln
Pharmacy	Apotheke	AH-po-TAY-kuh	**Grocery**	Lebensmittelgeschäft	LAY-bens-miht-tel-guh-SHEFT
Hotel/Hostel	Hotel/ Jugendherberge	ho-TEL/YOO-gend-air-BAIR-guh	**Tourist office**	Touristbüro	TU-reest-byur-oh
Single room	Einzellzimmer	EIN-tsel-tsihm-muh	**Post Office**	Postamt	POST-ahmt
Double room	Doppelzimmer	DOP-pel-tsihm-muh	**Old town/City center**	Altstadt	AHLT-shtat
Dorm	Schlafsaal	SHLAF-zahl	**Vegetarian**	Vegetarier	veh-geh-TAYR-ee-er
With shower	Mit dusche	mitt DOO-shuh	**Vegan**	Veganer	VAY-gan-er
Bathroom	Badezimmer	BAH-deh-tsihm-muh	**Kosher/Halal**	Koscher/Halaal	KOH-shayr/ hah-LAAL
Open/Closed	Geöffnet/ Geschlossen	geh-UHF-net/ geh-SHLOS-sen	**Nuts/Milk**	Nüsse/Milch	NYOO-seh/ mihlsh
Left/Right	Links/Rechts	lihnks/rekhts	**Bridge**	Brücke	BRUKE-eh
Straight	Geradeaus	geh-RAH-de-OWS	**Castle**	Schloß	shloss
(To) Turn	Drehen	DRAY-ehn	**Square**	Platz	plahtz

ENGLISH	GERMAN	PRONOUNCE
Where is...?	Wo ist...?	vo ihst
How do I get to...?	Wie komme ich nach...?	vee KOM-muh eesh NAHKH
How much does that cost?	Wieviel kostet das?	VEE-feel KOS-tet das
Do you have...?	Haben Sie...?	HOB-en zee
I would like...	Ich möchte...	eesh MERSH-teh
I'm allergic to...	Ich bin zu...allergisch.	eesh bihn tsoo...ah-LEHR-gish
Do you speak English?	Sprechen sie Englisch?	SHPREK-en zee EHNG-lish
I do not speak German.	Ich spreche kein Deutsch.	eesh-SHPREK-eh kyne DOYCH
Leave me alone or I'll call the police!	Lassen sie mich in ruhe oder ich rufe die polizei!	LAH-sen see meesh in ROO-eh OH-dur eesh ROO-fuh dee poh-leet-ZAI
I'm waiting for my boyfriend/husband.	Ich warte auf meinen Freund/ Mann.	eesh VAHR-tuh owf MYN-en froynd/mahn

APPENDIX

GREEK

ENGLISH	GREEK	PRONOUNCE	ENGLISH	GREEK	PRONOUNCE
Yes/No	Ναι/Όχι	neh/OH-hee	**Train/Bus**	Τραίνο/ Λεωφορείο	TREH-no/leh-o-fo-REE-o
Please	Παρακαλώ	pah-rah-kah-LO	**Ferry**	Πλοίο	PLEE-o
Thank you	Ευχαριστώ	ef-hah-ree-STO	**Station**	Σταθμός	stath-MOS
Hello/ Goodbye	Γειά σας	YAH-sas	**Airport**	Αεροδρόμιο	ah-e-ro-DHRO-mee-o
Sorry/ Excuse me	Συγνόμη	sig-NO-mee	**Taxi**	Ταξί	tah-XEE
Help!	Βοηθειά!	vo-EE-thee-ah	**Hotel/Hostel**	Ξενοδοχείο	kse-no-dho-HEE-o
I'm lost.	Έχω χαθεί.	EH-o ha-THEE	**Room to let**	Δωμάτια	do-MA-tee-ah
Police	Αστυνομία	as-tee-no-MEE-a	**Bathroom**	Τουαλέττα	tou-ah-LET-ta
Embassy	Πρεσβεία	prez-VEE-ah	**Open/closed**	Ανοικτό/ Κλειστό	ah-nee-KTO/ klee-STO
Passport	Διαβατήριο	dhee-ah-vah-TEE-ree-o	**Left/Right**	Αριστερά/ Δεξία	aris-te-RA/ de-XIA
Doctor	Γιατρός	yah-TROSE	**Bank**	Τράπεζα	TRAH-peh-zah
Pharmacy	Φαρμακείο	fahr-mah-KEE-o	**Exchange**	Ανταλλάσσω	an-da-LAS-so
Post Office	Ταχυδρομείο	ta-hi-dhro-MEE-o	**Market**	Αγορά	ah-go-RAH

ENGLISH	GREEK	PRONOUNCE
Where is...?	Που είναι...?	poo-EE-neh
How much does this cost?	Πόσο κάνει?	PO-so KAH-nee
Do you have (a vacant room)?	Μηπώς έχετε (ελέυθερα δωμάτια)?	mee-POSE EK-he-teh (e-LEF-the-ra dho-MA-tee-a)
I would like...	Θα ήθελα...	thah EE-the-lah
Do you speak English?	Μιλάς αγγλικά?	mee-LAHS ahn-glee-KAH
I don't speak Greek.	Δεν μιλαώ ελληνικά.	dthen mee-LOW el-lee-nee-KAH

HUNGARIAN

ENGLISH	HUNGARIAN	PRONOUNCE	ENGLISH	HUNGARIAN	PRONOUNCE
Yes/No	Igen/Nem	EE-ghen/nehm	**Train/Bus**	Vonat/Autóbusz	VAW-noht/OW-toh-boos
Please	Kérem	KAY-rehm	**Station**	Pályaudvar	pah-yoh-OOT-vahr
Thank you	Köszönöm	KUH-suh-nuhm	**Airport**	Repülőtér	rehp-ewlu-TAYR
Hello	Szervusz	SAYHR-voose	**Ticket**	Jegyet	YEHD-eht
Goodbye	Viszontlátásra	VEE-sohnt-lah-tah-shraw	**Tram**	Villamos	vil-LAH-mosh
Excuse me	Elnézést	EHL-nay-zaysht	**Hotel**	Szálloda	SAH-law-dah
Help!	Segítség!	she-GHEET-sheg	**Toilet**	WC	VAY-tsay
I'm lost.	Eltévedtem.	el-TEH-ved-tem	**Open/Closed**	Nyitva/Zárva	NYEET-vah/ ZAHR-vuh
Police	Rendőrség	REN-dur-shayg	**Left/Right**	Bal/Jobb	bol/yowb
Embassy	Követséget	ker-vet-SHE-get	**Bank**	Bank	bohnk
Passport	Az útlevelemet	ahz OOT-leh-veh-leh-meht	**Exchange**	Pénzaváltó	pehn-zah-VAHL-toh
Doctor/ Hospital	Orvos/Kórház	OR-vosh/kohr-HAAZ	**Grocery**	Élelmiszerbolt	AY-lel-meser-balt
Pharmacy	Gyógyszertár	DYAW-dyser-tar	**Post Office**	Posta	PAWSH-tuh

ENGLISH	HUNGARIAN	PRONOUNCE
Where is...?	Hol van...?	hawl von
How much does this cost?	Mennyibe kerül?	MEHN-ye-behe KEH-rewl
When is the next...?	Mikor indul a következő...?	mee-KOR in-DUL ah ker-VET-ke-zoer
Do you have (a vacant room)?	Van üres (szoba)?	vahn ew-REHSH (SAH-bah)
Can I have...?	Kaphatok...?	KAH-foht-tohk
I do not eat...	Nem eszem...	nem EH-sem
Do you speak English?	Beszél angolul?	BESS-ayl ON-goal-ool
I don't speak Hungarian.	Nem tudok magyarul.	Nehm TOO-dawk MAH-dyah-rool

ITALIAN

ENGLISH	ITALIAN	PRONOUNCE	ENGLISH	ITALIAN	PRONOUNCE
Hello (informal/formal)	Ciao/Buongiorno	chow/bwohn-JOHR-noh	**Bank**	La banca	lah bahn-KAH
Please	Per favore/Per piacere	pehr fah-VOH-reh/pehr pyah-CHE-reh	**Exchange**	Il cambio	eel CAHM-bee-oh
Thank you	Grazie	GRAHT-see-yeh	**Grocery**	Gli alimentari	lee ah-lee-mehn-TA-ree
Sorry/Excuse me	Mi dispiace/Scusi	mee dees-PYAH-cheh/SKOO-zee	**Police**	La Polizia	lah po-LEET-ZEE-ah
Yes/No	Sì/No	see/no	**Embassy**	L'Ambasciata	lahm-bah-SHAH-tah
Goodbye	Arrivederci/Arrivederla	ah-ree-veh-DAIR-chee/ah-ree-veh-DAIR-lah	**Passport**	Il passaporto	eel pahs-sah-POHR-toh
Help!	Aiuto!	ah-YOO-toh	**Post Office**	L'ufficio postale	loof-FEETCH-io pohs-TAL-e
I'm lost.	Sono perso.	SO-noh PERH-so	**One-way**	Solo andata	SO-lo ahn-DAH-tah
Train/Bus	Il treno/l'autobus	eel TRAY-no/aow-toh-BOOS	**Round-trip**	Andata e ritorno	ahn-DAH-tah ay ree-TOHR-noh
Station	La stazione	lah staht-see-YOH-neh	**Ticket**	Il biglietto	eel beel-YEHT-toh
Airport	L'aeroporto	LAYR-o-PORT-o	**Single room**	Una camera singola	OO-nah CAH-meh-rah SEEN-goh-lah
Hotel/Hostel	L'albergo	lal-BEHR-go	**Double room**	Una camera doppia	OO-nah CAH-meh-rah DOH-pee-yah
Bathroom	Un gabinetto/Un bagno	oon gah-bee-NEHT-toh/oon BAHN-yoh	**With shower**	Con doccia	kohn DOH-cha
Open/Closed	Aperto/Chiuso	ah-PAIR-toh/KYOO-zoh	**Taxi**	Il tassì	eel tahs-SEE
Doctor	Il medico	eel MEH-dee-koh	**Ferry**	Il traghetto	eel tra-GHEHT-toh
Hospital	L'ospedale	lohs-sped-DAL-e	**Tourist office**	L'Azienda Promozione Turistica	lah-tzee-EHN-da pro-mo-tzee-O-nay tur-EES-tee-kah
Pharmacy	La farmacia	lah far-mah-CHEE-ah	**Vegetarian**	Vegetariano	ve-ge-tar-ee-AN-o

ENGLISH	ITALIAN	PRONOUNCE	ENGLISH	ITALIAN	PRONOUNCE
Left/Right	La sinistra/ destra	lah see-NEE-strah/DEH-strah	**Kosher/Halal**	Kasher/Halal	KA-sher/HA-lal
Straight	Sempre diritto	SEHM-pray DREET-toh	**Cover charge**	Il coperto	eel koh-PEHR-toh
Turn	Gira a	JEE-rah ah	**Bill**	Il conto	eel COHN-toh
Stop	Ferma/ Smetta	FEHR-mah/ SMEHT-tah	**Tip**	La mancia	lah MAHN-chee-yah

ENGLISH	ITALIAN	PRONOUNCE
Do you speak English?	Parla inglese?	PAHR-lah een-GLAY-zeh
Where is...?	Dov'è...?	doh-VEH
When is the next...?	A che ora è il prossimo...?	AH keh OH-rah eh eel pross-SIM-oh
How much does this cost?	Quanto costa?	KWAN-toh CO-stah
Do you have rooms available?	Hai camere libere?	i CAH-mer-reh LEE-ber-eh
I would like...	Vorrei...	VOH-ray
I don't speak Italian.	Non parlo italiano.	nohn PARL-loh ee-tahl-YAH-noh
I'm allergic to...	Ho delle allergie...	oh DEHL-leh ahl-lair-JEE-eh

LITHUANIAN

ENGLISH	LITHUANIAN	PRONOUNCE	ENGLISH	LITHUANIAN	PRONOUNCE
Yes/no	Taip/ne	TAYE-p/neh	**Train/Bus**	Traukinys/autobusas	TROW-kihn-ees/ ow-to-BOO-sahs
Please	Prašau	prah-SHAU	**Station**	Stotis	STOH-tees
Thank you	Ačiū	AH-chyoo	**Airport**	Oro uostas	OH-roh oo-OH-stahs
Hello	Labas	LAH-bahss	**Ticket**	Bilietas	BEE-lee-tahs
Goodbye	Viso gero	VEE-soh GEH-roh	**Hotel**	Viešbutis	vee-esh-BOO-tihs
Sorry/excuse me	Atsiprašau	AHT-sih-prh-SHAU	**Bathroom**	Tualetas	too-ah-LEH-tas
Help!	Gelbėkite!	GYEL-behk-ite	**Open/Closed**	Atidarytas/ uždarytas	ah-tee-DAH-ree-tas/ oozh-DAH-ree-tas
Police	Policija	po-LEET-siya	**Exchange**	Valiutos keitimas	va-lee-OOT-os kay-TEE-mahs
Market	Turgus	TOORG-us	**Post Office**	Paštas	PAHSH-tahs

ENGLISH	LITHUANIAN	PRONOUNCE
Where is...?	Kur yra...?	koor ee-RAH
How much does this cost?	Kiek kainuoja?	KEE-yek KYE-new-oh-yah
Do you speak English?	Ar kalbate angliškai?	ahr KULL-buh-teh AHN-gleesh-kye
I do not speak Lithuanian.	Aš nekalbu lietuviškai	ash ne-KAL-boo lut-VEESH-kee

NORWEGIAN

ENGLISH	NORWEGIAN	PRONOUNCE	ENGLISH	NORWEGIAN	PRONOUNCE
Yes/No	Ja/Nei	yah/nay	**Ticket**	Billett	bee-LEHT
Please	Vær så snill	vay sho SNEEL	**Train/Bus**	Toget/Buss	TOR-guh/buhrs (büs)
Thank you	Takk	tuhk	**Airport**	Lufthavn	LUFT-hahn

APPENDIX

ENGLISH	NORWEGIAN	PRONOUNCE	ENGLISH	NORWEGIAN	PRONOUNCE
Hello	Goddag	gud-DAHG	**Departures**	Avgang	AHV-gahng
Goodbye	Ha det bra	HUH deh brah	**Market**	Torget	TOHR-geh
Sorry/Excuse me	Unnskyld	UHRN-shuhrl (ÜN-shül)	**Hotel/Hostel**	Hotell/Vandrerhjem	hoo-TEHL/VAN-drair-yaim
Help!	Hjelp!	yehlp	**Pharmacy**	Apotek	ah-pu-TAYK
Police	Politit	po-lee-TEE-uh	**Toilets**	Toalettene	tuah-LEHT-tuh-nuh
Embassy	Ambassade	uhm-bah-SAH-duh	**City center**	Sentrum	SEHN-trum
I'm lost.	Jeg har gätt meg bort.	yeh haar got meh boo't	**Open/Closed**	Åpen/Stengt	AW-pen/Stengt
Railway station	Jernbanestasjon	YEH'N-baa-ner-stah-shuh-nern	**Hospital**	Sykehus	SHUCK-hoos
Bank	Bank	banhk	**Left/Right**	Venstre/Høyre	VEHN-stre/HUHR-uh
Currency exchange	Vekslingskontor	VEHK-shlings-koon-toohr	**Post Office**	Postkontor	POST-koon-toohr

ENGLISH	NORWEGIAN	PRONOUNCE
Where is...?	Hvor er...?	VORR ayr
How do I get to...?	Hvordan kommer jeg til...?	VORR-duhn KOM-morr yay teel
How much is...?	Hvor mye koster det...?	vorr MOO-yuh KOS-tor deh
Do you speak English?	Snakker du engelsk?	SNA-koh du EHNG-olsk
When is the...?	När gär...?	nor gawr
I don't speak Norwegian.	Jeg snakker ikke norsk.	yeh SNAH-kerr IK-ker noshk
Do you have any vacancies?	Har dere noen ledige rom?	haar DAY-rer NUH-ern LAY-dee-yer room

POLISH

ENGLISH	POLISH	PRONOUNCE	ENGLISH	POLISH	PRONOUNCE
Yes/No	Tak/Nie	tahk/nyeh	**Train/Bus**	Pociąg/Autobus	POH-chawnk/ow-TOH-booss
Please	Proszę	PROH-sheh	**Station**	Dworzec	DVOH-zhets
Thank you	Dziękuję	jen-KOO-yeh	**Airport**	Lotnisko	loht-NEE-skoh
Hello	Dzień dobre	djen DOH-bray	**Ticket**	Bilet	BEE-leht
Goodbye	Do widzenia	doh veedz-EN-yah	**Hostel**	Schronisko młodzieżowe	sroh-NEE-skoh mwo-jeh-ZHO-veh
Sorry/Excuse me	Przepraszam	psheh-PRAH-shahm	**Bathroom**	Toaleta	toh-ah-LEH-tah
Help!	Na pomoc!	nah POH-mots	**Open/Closed**	Otwarty/Zamknięty	ot-FAHR-tih/zahmk-NYENT-ih
I'm lost. (m/f)	Zgubiłem/am się.	zgoo-BEE-wem/wam sheh	**Left/Right**	Lewo/Prawo	LEH-voh/PRAH-voh
Police	Policja	poh-LEETS-yah	**Bank**	Bank	bahnk
Embassy	Ambasada	am-ba-SA-da	**Exchange**	Kantor	KAHN-tor
Doctor/Hospital	Lekarz/Szpital	LEH-kazh/SHPEE-tal	**Grocery/Market**	Sklep spożywczy	sklehp spoh-ZHIV-chih
Pharmacy	Apteka	ahp-TEH-ka	**Post Office**	Poczta	POHCH-tah

ENGLISH	POLISH	PRONOUNCE
Where is...?	Gdzie jest...?	g-JEH yest
How much does this cost?	Ile to kosztuje?	EE-leh toh kohsh-TOO-yeh
When is the next...?	O której jest następny...?	o KTOO-rey yest nas-TEMP-nee
Do you have (a vacant room)?	Czy są (jakieś wolne pokoje)?	chih SAWM (YAH-kyesh VOHL-neh poh-KOY-eh)
I'd like to order...	Chciałbym zamówić...	kh-CHOW-bihm za-MOOV-eech
I do not eat...	Nie jadam...	nye YA-dam
Do you (male/female) speak English?	Czy pan(i) mówi po angielsku?	chih PAHN(-ee) MOO-vee poh ahn-GYEL-skoo
I don't speak Polish.	Nie mowię po polsku.	nyeh MOO-vyeh poh POHL-skoo

PORTUGUESE

All vowels with a *til* (ã, õ, etc.) or those that come before *m* or *n* are pronounced with a nasal twang. At the end of a word, *o* is pronounced "oo" as in "room," and *e* is sometimes silent. *S* is pronounced "sh" or "zh" when it occurs before another consonant. *Ch* and *x* are pronounced "sh." *J* and *g* (before *e* or *i*) are pronounced "zh." The combinations *nh* and *lh* are pronounced "ny" and "ly," respectively.

ENGLISH	PORTUGUESE	PRONOUNCE	ENGLISH	PORTUGUESE	PRONOUNCE
Hello	Olá/Oi	oh-LAH/oy	**Hotel**	Pousada	poh-ZAH-dah
Please	Por favor	pohr fah-VOHR	**Bathroom**	Banheiro	bahn-YAY-roo
Thank you (m/f)	Obrigado/ Obrigada	oh-bree-GAH-doo/dah	**Open/Closed**	Aberto/ Fechado	ah-BEHR-toh/ feh-CHAH-do
Sorry/ Excuse me	Desculpe	dish-KOOLP-eh	**Doctor**	Médico	MEH-dee-koo
Yes/No	Sim/Não	seem/now	**Pharmacy**	Farmácia	far-MAH-see-ah
Goodbye	Adeus	ah-DAY-oosh	**Left/Right**	Esquerda/ Direita	esh-KER-dah/ dee-RAY-tah
Help!	Socorro!	soh-KOO-roh	**Bank**	Banco	BAHN-koh
I'm lost. (m/f)	Estou perdido/ perdida.	ish-TOW per-DEE-doo/dah	**Exchange**	Câmbio	CAHM-bee-yoo
Ticket	Bilhete	beel-YEHT	**Market**	Mercado	mer-KAH-doo
Train/Bus	Comboio/ Autocarro	kom-BOY-yoo/ OW-to-KAH-roo	**Police**	Polícia	po-LEE-see-ah
Station	Estação	eh-stah-SAO	**Embassy**	Embaixada	ehm-bai-SHAH-dah
Airport	Aeroporto	aye-ro-POR-too	**Post Office**	Correio	coh-RAY-yoh

ENGLISH	PORTUGUESE	PRONOUNCE
Do you speak English?	Fala inglês?	FAH-lah een-GLAYSH
Where is...?	Onde é...?	OHN-deh eh
How much does this cost?	Quanto custa?	KWAHN-too KOOSH-tah
Do you have rooms available?	Tem quartos disponíveis?	teng KWAHR-toosh dish-po-NEE-veysh
I want/would like...	Eu quero/gostaria de...	eh-oo KER-oh/gost-ar-EE-uh day
I don't speak Portuguese.	Não falo Português	now FAH-loo por-too-GEZH
I cannot eat...	Não posso comer...	now POH-soh coh-MEHR
Another round, please.	Mais uma rodada, por favor.	mighsh OO-mah roh-DAH-dah pohr fah-VOHR

ROMANIAN

ENGLISH	ROMANIAN	PRONOUNCE	ENGLISH	ROMANIAN	PRONOUNCE
Yes/No	Da/Nu	dah/noo	**Train/Bus**	Trenul/Autobuz	TRAY-nool/aw-toh-BOOS
Please/ Thank you	Vă rog/ Mulţumesc	vuh rohg/ mool-tsoo-MESK	**Station**	Gară	GAH-ruh
Hello	Bună ziua	BOO-nuh ZEE-wah	**Airport**	Aeroportul	air-oh-POR-tool
Goodbye	La revedere	lah reh-veh-DEH-reh	**Ticket**	Bilet	bee-LEHT
Sorry	Îmi pare rău	im PA-reh rau	**Taxi**	Taxi	tak-SEE
Excuse me	Scuzaţi-mă	skoo-ZAH-ts muh	**Hotel**	Hotel	ho-TEHL
Help!	Ajutor!	AH-zhoot-or	**Bathroom**	Toaletă	toh-ahl-EH-tah
I'm lost.	Sînt pierdut.	sunt PYER-dut	**Open/Closed**	Deschis/închis	DESS-kees/un-KEES
Police	Poliţie	poh-LEE-tsee-eh	**Left/Right**	Stânga/ Dreapta	STYN-gah/ drahp-TAH
Embassy	Ambasada	ahm-bah-SAH-da	**Bank**	Banca	BAHN-cah
Passport	Paşaport	pah-shah-PORT	**Exchange**	Birou de schimb	bee-ROH deh skeemb
Doctor/ Hospital	Doctorul/ spitalul	DOK-to-rul/ SPEE-ta-lul	**Grocery**	Alimentară	a-lee-men-TA-ra
Pharmacy	Farmacie	fahr-ma-CHEE-ah	**Post Office**	Poşta	POH-shta

ENGLISH	ROMANIAN	PRONOUNCE
Where is...?	Unde e...?	OON-deh yeh
How much does this cost?	Cât costă?	kyht KOH-stuh
When is the next...?	Cînd este următorul...?	kuhnd es-te ur-muh-TOH-rul
Do you have (a vacant room)?	Aveţi (camere libere)?	a-VETS (KUH-mer-eh LEE-ber-e)
I would like...	Aş vrea...	ahsh VREH-ah
I do not eat...	Eu nu mănînc...	eu nu MUH-nink
Do you speak English?	Vorbiţi englezeşte?	vor-BEETS ehng-leh-ZESH-te
I don't speak Romanian.	Nu vorbesc Româneşte.	noo vohr-BEHSK roh-myn-EHS-HTE

RUSSIAN

ENGLISH	RUSSIAN	PRONOUNCE	ENGLISH	RUSSIAN	PRONOUNCE
Yes/No	Да/нет	dah/nyet	**Train/Bus**	Поезд/автобус	POH-yihzt/av-TOH-boos
Please	Пожалуйста	pa-ZHAL-sta	**Station**	вокзал	vak-ZAL
Thank you	Спасибо	spa-SEE-bah	**Airport**	аэропорт	ai-roh-PORT
Hello	Добрый день/ Привет	DOH-breh DYEHN/pree-VYET	**Ticket**	билет	bil-YET
Goodbye	До свидания/ Пока	da svee-DAHN-ya/ pah-KAH	**Hotel**	гостиница	gahs-TEE-nee-tsah
Sorry/ Excuse me	Извините	eez-vee-NEET-yeh	**Dorm/Hostel**	общежитие	ob-sheh-ZHEE-tee-yeh
Help!	Помогите!	pah-mah-GIT-yeh	**Bathroom**	туалет	twah-LYET
I'm lost. (m/f)	Я потерен(а).	ya po-TYE-ren-(ah)	**Open/Closed**	открыт/ закрыт	ot-KRIHT/ za-KRIHT

APPENDIX

ENGLISH	RUSSIAN	PRONOUNCE	ENGLISH	RUSSIAN	PRONOUNCE
Police	милиция	mee-LEE-tsee-ya	**Left/Right**	налево/направо	nah-LYEH-vah/ nah-PRAH-vah
Embassy	посольство	pah-SOHL'-stva	**Bank**	банк	bahnk
Passport	паспорт	PAS-pahrt	**Exchange**	обмен валюты	ab-MYEHN val-ee-YU-tee
Doctor/Hospital	Врач/больница	vrach/bol-NEE-tsa	**Grocery/Market**	гастроном/ рынок	gah-stroh-NOM/ REE-nohk
Pharmacy	аптека	ahp-TYE-kah	**Post Office**	Почта	POCH-ta

ENGLISH	RUSSIAN	PRONOUNCE
Where is...?	Где находится...?	gdyeh nah-KHOH-dee-tsah
How much does this cost?	Сколько это стоит?	SKOHL-ka EH-ta STOY-iht
When is the next...?	Когда будет следуший...?	kog-DAH BOOD-yet SLYED-ooshee
Do you have (a vacant room)?	У вас есть (свободный номер)?	oo vahs yehst (svah-BOHD-neey NOH-mehr)
I'd like (m/f)...	Я хотел(а) бы...	ya khah-TYEL(a) bwee
I do not eat...	Я не ем...	ya nye yem
Do you speak English?	Вы говорите по-английски?	vy gah-vah-REE-tyeh pa-an-GLEE-ski
I don't speak Russian.	Я не говорю по-русски.	yah neh gah-vah-RYOO pah ROO-skee

SPANISH

ENGLISH	SPANISH	PRONOUNCE	ENGLISH	SPANISH	PRONOUNCE
Hello	Hola	OH-lah	**Hotel/Hostel**	Hotel/Hostal	oh-TEL/oh-STAHL
Please	Por favor	pohr fah-VOHR	**Bathroom**	Baño	BAHN-yoh
Thank you	Gracias	GRAH-see-ahs	**Open/Closed**	Abierto(a)/Cerrado(a)	ah-bee-AYR-toh/ sehr-RAH-doh
Sorry/ Excuse me	Perdón	pehr-DOHN	**Doctor**	Médico	MEH-dee-koh
Yes/No	Sí/No	see/no	**Pharmacy**	Farmacia	far-MAH-see-ah
Goodbye	Adiós	ah-dee-OHS	**Left/Right**	Izquierda/ Derecha	ihz-kee-EHR-da/ deh-REH-chah
Help!	¡Ayuda!	ay-YOOH-duh	**Bank**	Banco	BAHN-koh
I'm lost.	Estoy perdido (a).	ess-TOY pehr-DEE-doh (dah)	**Exchange**	Cambio	CAHM-bee-oh
Ticket	Boleto	boh-LEH-toh	**Grocery**	Supermercado	soo-pehr-mer-KAH-doh
Train/Bus	Tren/ Autobús	trehn/ ow-toh-BOOS	**Police**	Policía	poh-lee-SEE-ah
Station	Estación	es-tah-see-OHN	**Embassy**	Embajada	em-bah-HA-dah
Airport	Aeropuerto	ay-roh-PWER-toh	**Post Office**	Oficina de correos	oh-fee-SEE-nah day coh-REH-ohs

ENGLISH	SPANISH	PRONOUNCE
Do you speak English?	¿Habla inglés?	AH-blah een-GLEHS
Where is...?	¿Dónde está...?	DOHN-day eh-STA
How much does this cost?	¿Cuánto cuesta...?	KWAN-toh KWEHS-tah
Do you have rooms available?	¿Tiene habitaciones libres?	tee-YEH-neh ah-bee-tah-see-YOH-nehs LEE-brehs

APPENDIX

ENGLISH	SPANISH	PRONOUNCE
I want/ would like...	Quiero/Me gustaría...	kee-YEH-roh/may goos-tah-REE-ah
I don't speak Spanish.	No hablo español.	no AH-bloh ehs-pahn-YOHL
I cannot eat...	No puedo comer...	no PWAY-doh coh-MEHR...

SWEDISH

ENGLISH	SWEDISH	PRONOUNCE	ENGLISH	SWEDISH	PRONOUNCE
Yes/No	Ja/Nej	yah/nay	**Ticket**	Biljett	bihl-YEHT
Please	Va så snäll	VAH sahw snel	**Train/Bus**	Tåget/Buss	TOH-get/boos
Thank you	Tack	tahk	**Ferry**	Färjan	FAR-yuhn
Hello	Hej	hay	**Departure**	Avgångar	uhv-GONG-er
Goodbye	Hejdå	HAY-doh	**Market**	Torget	TOHR-yet
Excuse me	Ursäkta mig	oor-SHEHK-tuh MAY	**Hotel/Hostel**	Hotell/Vandrar-hem	hoo-TEHL/vun-DRAR-huhm
Help!	Hjälp!	yehlp	**Pharmacy**	Apotek	uh-poo-TEEK
Police	Polisen	poo-LEE-sehn	**Toilets**	Toaletten	too-uh-LEHT-en
Embassy	Ambassad	uhm-bah-SAHD	**Post Office**	Posten	POHS-tehn
I'm lost.	Jag har kommit bort.	yuh hahr KUM-met borht	**Open/Closed**	Öppen/Stängd	UH-pen/staingd
Railway station	Järnvägsstationen	yairn-vas-guess-stah-SHO-nen	**Hospital**	Sjukhus	SHUHK-huhs
Currency exchange	Växel kontor	vai-xil KOON-toohr	**Left/Right**	Vänster/Höger	VAIN-ster/HUH-ger

ENGLISH	SWEDISH	PRONOUNCE
Where is...?	Var finns...?	vahr FIHNS
How much does this cost?	Hur mycket kostar det?	hurr MUEK-keh KOS-tuhr deh
I'd like to buy...	Jag skulle vilja köpa...	yuh SKOO-leh vihl-yuh CHEU-pah
Do you speak English?	Talar du engelska?	TAH-luhr du EHNG-ehl-skuh
I don't speak Swedish.	Jag talar inte svenska.	yuh tahlahr ihntuh svenskah
I'm allergic to/I cannot eat...	Jag är allergisk mot/Jag kan inte ata...	yuh air ALLEHR-ghihsk moot/ yuh kahn intuh aitah
Do you have rooms available?	Har Ni fria rum?	harh nih freeah ruhm

WEATHER

City	JANUARY High (F/C)	JANUARY Low (F/C)	JANUARY Rain (in.)	APRIL High (F/C)	APRIL Low (F/C)	APRIL Rain (in.)	JULY High (F/C)	JULY Low (F/C)	JULY Rain (in.)	OCTOBER High (F/C)	OCTOBER Low (F/C)	OCTOBER Rain (in.)
Amsterdam	41/5	34/1	3.1	53/11	40/4	1.5	69/20	55/12	2.9	57/13	46/7	4.1
Athens	55/12	44/6	1.9	66/18	52/11	0.9	89/31	73/22	0.2	73/22	60/15	2.1
Berlin	35/1	26/-3	1.7	54/12	37/2	1.7	73/22	56/13	2.1	56/13	42/5	1.4
Copenhagen	37/2	30/-1	1.7	49/9	36/2	1.6	69/20	55/12	2.6	53/11	44/6	2.1
Dublin	46/7	37/2	2.5	52/11	41/5	1.9	66/18	54/12	2.6	55/12	46/7	2.9
London	44/6	34/1	3.1	54/12	38/3	2.1	71/21	53/11	1.8	58/14	44/6	2.9
Madrid	51/10	32/0	1.8	63/17	42/5	1.8	90/32	61/16	0.4	68/20	47/8	1.8
Paris	43/6	34/1	2.2	57/13	42/5	1.7	75/23	58/14	2.3	59/15	46/7	2.0
Rome	55/12	39/3	3.2	63/17	47/8	2.6	83/28	66/18	0.6	71/21	56/13	4.5
Vienna	36/2	27/-2	1.5	57/13	41/5	2.0	77/25	59/15	2.5	57/13	43/6	1.6

INDEX

C

INDEX

INDEX

H

I

M

N

O

P

Q

R

T

U

V

W

Y

Z

MAP INDEX

MAP LEGEND

Point of Interest
Accommodation
Camping
Food
Café
Museum
Sight
Bar/Pub
Nightlife
Airport
Arch/Gate
Bank
Beach
Bus Station/Stop
Capital City
Castle
Church
Consulate/Embassy
Convent/Monastery
Ferry Landing
347 Highway Sign
Hospital
Internet Cafe
Library/Bookstore
M M Metro Station
Mountain
Mosque
Pharmacy
Police
Post Office
Skiing
Synagogue
Telephone Office
Theater
Tourist Office
Train Station
Park
Water
Beach
Building
Pedestrian Zone
Stairs
The Let's Go compass always points NORTH.